영어는 반드시 1등급을 받아야 합니다.

수능 출제 원칙이 킬러 문항을 배제한다고 했지만,
낯설고 긴 지문이 많아지고, 선택지가 까다로워서
수험생들은 여전히 독해 문제가 많이 어렵다고 느낍니다.

자이스토리는 수능 영어 독해 문제를
단순히 유형별로 분류한 것이 아니라
각 문제 유형에 맞는 이해 순서와 논리적 풀이법을 제공하여
빠르고 정확하게 정답을 찾는 방법을 습득하도록 하였습니다.

각 유형마다 따라가기만 하면
저절로 독해 유형 공부가 되는
'자이 쌤's Follow Me!'가 영어 1등급으로 가는
가장 똑똑한 독해 공부법입니다.
꼭 따라서 공부해 보세요.

문제를 풀고 난 이후에는
정답의 근거와 오답 함정까지 알려주는 입체 첨삭 해설을 통해
모든 문제를 완전히 이해하면서 공부할 수 있습니다.

이 책의 마지막 페이지를 넘길 때쯤
여러분은 이미 영어 1등급에 도달해 있을 것입니다.

– 대한민국 No.1 수능 문제집 자이스토리 –

🍀 내신＋수능 **1등급** 완성 학습 계획표 [26일]

Day	문항 번호	틀린 문제 / 헷갈리는 문제 번호 적기	날짜		복습 날짜	
1	**A** 01~20		월	일	월	일
2	**B** 01~22		월	일	월	일
3	**C** 01~23		월	일	월	일
4	**D** 01~28		월	일	월	일
5	**E** 01~22		월	일	월	일
6	**F** 01~23		월	일	월	일
7	**G** 01~26		월	일	월	일
8	**H** 01~22		월	일	월	일
9	**I** 01~22		월	일	월	일
10	**J** 01~43		월	일	월	일
11	**K** 01~30		월	일	월	일
12	31~60		월	일	월	일
13	61~93		월	일	월	일
14	**L** 01~24		월	일	월	일
15	**M** 01~23		월	일	월	일
16	24~46		월	일	월	일
17	**N** 01~22		월	일	월	일
18	23~44		월	일	월	일
19	**O** 01~25		월	일	월	일
20	**P** 01~23		월	일	월	일
21	24~48		월	일	월	일
22	**Q** 01~27		월	일	월	일
23	28~63		월	일	월	일
24	**모의 1회** 01~12		월	일	월	일
25	**모의 2회** 01~12		월	일	월	일
26	**모의 3회** 01~12		월	일	월	일

- 나는 _____ 대학교 _____ 학과 _____ 학번이 된다.

- **磨斧作針** (마부작침) – 도끼를 갈아 바늘을 만든다. (아무리 어려운 일이라도 끈기 있게 노력하면 이룰 수 있음을 비유하는 말)

🍀 자이스토리 영어 독해 실전 활용법+α

❶ 유형별 출제 경향 파악과 중요 어휘 예습으로 워밍업!

• 최근 수능이 어떻게 출제되어 왔는지 경향을 파악하고 앞으로의 수능을 예측하세요.
• 각 유형의 특징을 파악하고, 단계별 유형 풀이 비법을 익히세요.

❷ 자이 쌤's Follow Me!를 통해 유형 풀이법을 익히자!

• 술술 읽히는 강의식 설명으로 효과적인 문제 풀이 접근법을 터득하세요.

❸ 유형별 기출 문제 풀이로 실력 향상!

• 각 문제를 풀 때 자이 쌤's Follow Me!에서 학습한 문제 해결 스킬을 적용해보세요.
• 모르는 단어나 구문이 나와도 찾아보지 말고 제한시간 내에 푸는 연습을 하세요.

❹ 1등급, 2등급 대비로 어려운 문제까지 완벽 대비!

• 1등급, 2등급 대비 문제 특별 해설을 통해 어려운 문제를 어떻게 해결해야 하는지 터득하세요.

❺ 고난도 유형 독해 모의고사는 더욱 확실한 1등급을 위해 풀자!

• 난이도가 높은 최신 경찰대, 삼사 기출 문제들을 통해 1등급에 더 확실하게 가까워지는 훈련을 할 수 있습니다.

> 보다 강화된
> 단계별
> 입체 첨삭 해설

❻ 쉽게 이해되는 입체 첨삭 해설로 다시는 틀리지 말자!

• 정답만 맞는지, 틀렸는지 보지 말고, 틀린 문제나 찍어서 맞힌 문제 등은 꼭 다시 푸세요.
• 해설에 제시된 정답의 단서를 파악하고, 매력적인 오답에 대한 설명도 놓치지 마세요.
• 직독직해를 통해 해석이 되지 않던 부분이나 잘 이해가 가지 않았던 문장을 이해하세요.
• 첨삭 설명된 구문풀이로 문장 해석력을 키우고, 몰랐던 어휘나 표현을 익히세요.

❼ 특별부록 – 단어장을 100% 활용하자!

• 문제에 제시된 수능 필수 어휘를 총정리한 단어장을 매일 꾸준히 익히세요.
• 각 단원마다 제공되는 단어장 QR코드를 통해 언제 어디서나 단어를 공부할 수 있어요.

▶ 단원별 핵심 문제 + 최신·중요 문제
동영상 강의 QR코드

1 해설의 줄글보다 동영상을 선호하는 경우 빠르게 이해할 수 있어요!
2 해설과 다른 풀이를 알고 싶을 때 확인해 보세요!
3 긴 시간 혼자서 공부하느라 집중력이 떨어질 때 사용해 보세요!
4 어법, 문법을 혼자서 이해하기에 아직 조금 부족한 실력을 강의를 통해 보충할 수 있어요!

🍀 차 례

[★ 1등급 대비 유형]

＊실제 시험 독해 문제 출제 순서대로 배열하였고,
최신 문제를 우선 배치하였습니다.

🍀 완벽한 기출 분석, 유형별 풀이법 훈련으로 내신 + 수능 **1등급** 완성

❶ 기출 독해 문제 유형 분석 및 풀이 비법

수능을 철저히 분석하여 독해 유형별로 기출 문제를 정리했으며 유형에 대한 기본 개념을 잡을 수 있도록 하였습니다. 또, 문제 분석 단계별로 유형 풀이 비법을 익힐 수 있습니다.

● **유형 풀이 비법** : 좀 더 빠르고 정확하게 문제에 접근하는 풀이법 정리

● **중요 어휘+표현 Preview** : 유형별로 시험에 자주 나오는 어휘와 표현 수록

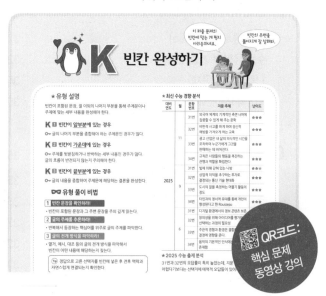

❷ 자이 쌤's Follow Me!

유형을 가장 잘 나타내는 대표 유형 문제를 강의식으로 설명하여 읽기만 해도 독해 학습이 저절로 이해되도록 구성하였습니다.

● **1st, 2nd, 3rd** : 유형별 효과적인 문제 접근법 제시
● **빈칸 문제** : 직접 빈칸을 채우면서 문제를 해결하는 스킬 연습
● **수능 Tip** : 해당 유형을 심화학습 할 수 있도록 수록

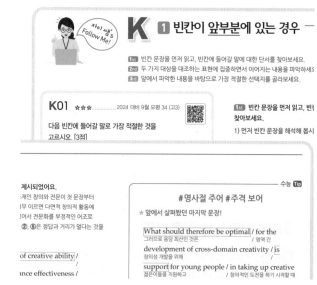

❸ 수능 유형별 기출 문제

독해 유형별 풀이법을 쉽게 이해하고 훈련할 수 있도록 꼼꼼히 유형을 분류하고 난이도별로 문항을 배열하였습니다. 이를 통해 독해 공부가 한층 쉬워질 것입니다.

● **난이도** : ✿✿✿ – 상, ✿✿❀ – 중, ✿❀❀ – 하, 1등급, 2등급

● **출처표시** : 수능, 평가원 – 대비연도, 학력평가 – 실시연도
  • 2024 실시 3월 학평 20(고3): 2024년 3월에 실시한 학력평가 20번
  • 2025 대비 9월 모평 20(고3): 2024년 9월에 실시한 모의고사 20번
  • 2025 대비 수능 20(고3): 2024년 11월에 실시한 수능 홀수형 20번

❹ 1등급, 2등급 대비 문제 **선별 수록**

1등급, 2등급을 가르는 고난이도 문제들을 별도로 표시하여 수록하였습니다. 한 문제씩 꼼꼼히 풀어가면 반드시 1등급에 도달할 수 있습니다.

● ✪ **1등급 대비** : 어려운 지문 또는 정답을 쉽게 찾기 힘든, 1등급을 가르는 최고난도 문제
● ✪ **2등급 대비** : 헷갈리기 쉬운 매력적 오답이 있어 정답률이 낮은, 2등급을 가르는 고난도 문제

❺ 고난도 유형 독해 모의고사 3회

2025~2024 대비 경찰대, 삼사 기출 문제 중 고난도 독해
유형에 해당하는 문항을 포함시켜 12문항으로 구성하여
어려워지는 시험에 대비할 수 있습니다.

> **HIGH LEVEL** **1**회 고난도 유형 독해 **모의고사** 경찰대, 삼사, 수능 대비 문
>
> **📱01** .... 2025 대비 육해공사관 7 (고3)
> 다음 글에서 밑줄 친 부분이 의미하는 바로 가장 적절한 것은?
> [4점]
>
> Compared to other primates, we are freakishly social
> and cooperative; not only do we sit obediently on
> airplanes, we labor collectively to build houses,
> specialize in different skills, and live lives that are
> driven by our specific role in the group. This is quite
> a trick for a primate to pull off, considering our most
> recent evolutionary history. Hive life is (literally)
> a no-brainer for ants: They share the same genes,
>
> **📱02**
> 다음 글의 주제로 가장 적절한
>
> By the start of the 16
> movement had giv
> Reformation and an
> change. The art of
> disruption caused b
> named the Baroqu
> distorted, European
> largely focused on

❻ 1등급 대비 · 2등급 대비 문제 **단계별 해설**

> **D 21** 정답 ② ◆ 1등급 대비 [정답률 61%]
>
> 1등급 1등급? '아침 통근을 위해 준비할지 말지가 신뢰해야 하는 전문가의 지식을
> 가리킨다는 의미를 글을 읽으면서 파악해야 한다. 과학자나 물리학자를 언급하며
> 설명하는 내용을 제대로 파악하지 못하면 풀기 힘든 문제이다.
>
> **| 문제 풀이 순서 |**
>
> **1번** 첫 문장과 밑줄 친 부분이 포함된 문장을 읽고, 글의 내용을 예상한다.
> ▸ 첫 문장: 과학자는 자신의 전문 분야에 대해서만 전문 지식을 갖고 있음
> ▸ 밑줄 친 부분이 포함된 문장: 우리가 사는 자연 세계에 관한 어려운 질문들을
> 처리하는 데 생애를 바친 남녀들 = 전문가를 어느 정도 신뢰해야 함
> ▸ 전문가는 신뢰할 때는 매우 주의해야 한다. 하지만 전문가를 어느 정도 신뢰하지
> 않으면 우리는 마비된다.'라는 내용임을 예상할 수 있다.
>
> **2번** 글이 나머지 부분을 읽고, 예상한 내용이 맞는지 확인한다.
> ▸ 전문가에 대한 신뢰는 매우 한정되고 특정해야 한다. 하지만 전문가를 어느 정도
> 신뢰하지 않으면 마비된다. ▸ 1번 에서 예상한 흐름과 맞음
>
> **3번** 파악한 글의 내용을 종합하여 밑줄 친 부분의 의미를 파악한다.
> '아침 통근을 위해 준비할지 말지는 우리가 마비되지 않기 위해 어느 정도 신뢰해야
> 하는 전문가의 지식을 가리킨다. 따라서 정답은 ② '전문화된 전문가들에 의해 제공된
> 쉽게 적용할 수 있는 정보'이다.
>
> **| 선택지 분석 |**
>
> ① questionable facts that have been popularized by non-experts
> 비전문가에 의해 보급된 의심스러운 사실
> 밑줄 친 부분이 포함된 문장은 우리가 어느 정도 전문가를 신뢰해야 한다는
> 내용인데, 의심스러운 사실을 믿어야 한다는 것은 어색하다.
>
> ② readily applicable information offered by specialized experts
> 전문화된 전문가들에 의해 제공된 쉽게 적용할 수 있는 정보
> 1번 문장을 통해 전문화된 영역에서의 전문 지식은 신뢰할 만하다는 것을 알 수
> 있다. '전문화된 영역에서의 전문 지식'이 곧 '전문화된 전문가들에 의해 제공되는
> 정보'이다.
>
> ③ common knowledge that hardly influences crucial decisions
> 중대한 결정에 거의 영향을 주지 않는 일반 지식

문제 분석
왜 이 문제가 등급을 가르는
대비 문제인지를 설명하고
정답을 찾는 데 가장 핵심이
되는 단서를 설명했습니다.

문제 풀이 순서
단순히 정답만 설명하는 것이
아니라 정답을 찾아가는 과정을
단계별로 자세히 설명함으로써
앞으로 만날 고난도 문제를
스스로 풀 수 있도록
훈련시킵니다.

선택지 분석
오답 선택지까지 다시 한번
완벽히 분석하여 더이상 오답의
함정에 빠지지 않도록 합니다.

❼ 더욱 강화된 단계별 입체 첨삭 해설!

글의 주제
지문의 내용을 한 눈에 파악할 수
있도록 주제를 제시하였습니다.

> **자이 쌤's Follow Me!** - 홈페이지에서 제공
> **자이 쌤 제공** 문제편에 실리지 않은 자이 쌤을 홈페이지에 제공해드립니다.

직독직해
의미 중심의 문장별 끊어 읽기
표시와 해석을 달아주어 바로바로
해석할 수 있도록 돕습니다.

왜 정답
정답이 되는 핵심 이유와
문제풀이를 알기 쉽고 자세하게
수록하였습니다.

핵심 문장
글의 핵심문장을 표시하였습니다.

구문 풀이
해석과 지문 이해에 기본이
되는 구문 설명을 직접 첨삭하여
문법과 독해 실력 모두를 키울 수
있습니다.

어휘 풀이
필수 어휘와 어려운 어휘의 뜻을
정리하여 독해를 하면서 어휘의
뜻도 자연스럽게 익히고 어휘 실력
또한 키울 수 있게 하였습니다.

단서
문제를 푸는 데 핵심이 되는
어구나 문장을 표시했습니다.

글의 흐름
고난도 지문의 경우, 글의 전개
방식을 한눈에 파악할 수 있도록
도표로 정리하여 수록하였습니다.

선택지 첨삭 해설
정확한 정답을 확인할 수 있도록
선택지를 꼼꼼하게 분석해
설명했습니다.

배경 지식
지문과 관련 있는 알아두면 유용한
배경 지식을 수록하였습니다.

> **F 08** 정답 ① ＊체력을 길러야 하는 필요성
>
> The word sin itself / is an interesting concept. //
> sin(죄)이라는 말 자체는 / 흥미로운 개념이다 //
> It's actually a term from archery, / and it means "to miss the
> mark." /
> 그것은 실제로 궁술에서 온 용어인데 / 그것은 '과녁을 빗나가다'를 의미한다 //
> When we commit the "sin" / of failing to take care of our bodies /
> through proper nutrition, exercise, and rest, / we're missing the
> mark / of what life is all about. //
> 우리가 '죄'를 저지를 때 / 우리의 몸을 돌보는 데 실패하는 것은 인생의
> 중요한 것을 놓치는 것
> 서 / 우리는 과녁에서 빗나가고 있는 셈이다 / 인생의 중요한 것의 //
> Businesspeople will tell you / that the individual / who is in the
> best physical shape / often wins in negotiations, /
> 사업가들은 여러분에게 말할 것이다 / 사람은 / 최상의 신체적 건강 상태에 있는 / 흔히 협상
> 에서 이긴다고 /
> because he has the physical stamina / to see the deal through. //
> 그가 체력을 지니고 있으므로 / 계약을 끝까지 성사시킬 수 있는 //
> One of the reasons / world-class golfers are head and shoulders
> above the other golfers / of their era / is that they are in so much
> better shape / than the others are. //
> 이유들 중 하나는 / 세계 수준의 골프 선수들이 / 그들의 시대의 다른 골프 선수들보다 훨씬 더
> 나은 상태에 있는 / 다른 선수들이다 //
>
> · concept ⓝ 개념   · term ⓝ 용어   · archery ⓝ 궁술, 양궁
> · miss ⓥ 빗나가다   · mark ⓝ 과녁   · commit ⓥ 저지르다
> · proper @ 적절한   · nutrition ⓝ 영양
>
> sin(죄)이라는 말 자체는 흥미로운 개념이다. 그것은 실제로 궁술에서 온
> 용어인데, 그것은 '과녁을 빗나가다'를 의미한다. 우리가 적절한 영양, 운
> 동, 휴식을 통해서 우리의 몸을 관리하는 데 실패하는 '죄'를 저지를 때, 우
> 리는 인생의 중요한 것의 과녁에서 빗나가고 있는 셈이다. 최상의 신체적
> 건강 상태에 있는 사람은 계약을 끝까지 성사시킬 수 있는 체력을 지니고
> 있으므로, 그런 사람이 흔히 협상에서 이긴다고 사업가든 여러분에게 말
> 할 것이다. 세계 수준의 골프 선수들이 자기 시대의 다른 골프 선수들보다
> 훨씬 더 나은 상태에 있는 이유들 중 하나는 그들이 다른 선수들보다 몸 상태가 훨씬
> 더 낫다는 것이다. 그들은 골프 연습장에서뿐만 아니라 체력단련실에서도
> 운동을 하는데, 이것은 그들이 중요한 토너먼트에서 상대편 선수를 물리치
> 기 위해서 육체적인 경기에서뿐만 아니라 정신적인 경기에서도 이길 수 있
> 는 힘과 체력을 지니고 있다는 것을 의미한다.
>
> 다음 글의 주제로 가장 적절한 것은?
> ① the necessity to build up physical strength
>   체력을 길러야 하는 필요성
> ② the importance of setting specific goals
>   목표 설정의 중요성
> ③ various ways to overcome obstacles
>   장애를 극복하는 다양한 방법들
> ④ differences between business and sports
>   사업과 스포츠의 차이들
> ⑤ things to consider for successful negotiations
>   성공적인 협상을 위해 고려해야 할 것들
>
> ＊ **맥락 효과**(context effect)
> 처음 주어진 정보나 조건이 이후의 정보들을 받아들이고 해석하는 데 영향을
> 미치는 현상을 말한다. 다시 말해, 새로운 정보를 받아들이거나 해석할 때
> 활용되는 기존 지식이나 태도, 감정 상태 등이 새로운 정보를 수용하기 위한 '맥락'
> 으로 작용한다는 것이다.
> 이는 수많은 정보들을 짧은 시간 안에 효율적으로 해석하고 받아들이기 위한 인지적
> 노력으로 볼 수도 있고, 기존 생각이나 태도로 인지적 일관성을 유지하고자 하는 시도로도
> 해석할 수 있다.

> **꿀팁** 문제를 쉽고 빠르게 풀 수 있는
> 특별한 꿀팁입니다.
>
> **왜 정답?** [정답률 89%]
> 첫인상에 가려져 사람들이 나의 재능을 알아차리지 못하는 경우가 있으므로 다른
> 사람들에게 나 자신에 대해 보여줄 기술을 적극적으로 개발해야 한다고 했다. 즉 내
> 가 타인에게 매력적으로 보이도록 나의 첫인상을 훌륭하게 재단하는 방법을 배우
> 는 것이 중요하며 / 라고 했으므로 정답은 ⑤ '당신이 스스로를 보여주는 방식을 발전시
> 킬 필요성'이다.
>
> **왜 오답?**
> ① 책임질 것이 너무 많을 때는 타인에게 도움을 요청하여 스스로에게 책임감을 피
>   할 기회를 수록해야 한다는 것이다.
> ④ 우선순위 정하는 등의 방법으로 업무 효율성을 높이라는 것과 반대의 주
>   장을 하는 것이다. (▶ 이유: 옳음 일부라고 표현한다면, 답이 될 수 있다.)
> ⑤ 타인에게 자신의 이한 상태를 이야기하라는 것이지, 그들의 의견을 경청하여 갈
>   등을 해결하라는 것이 아니다.
>
> **| 글의 흐름 |**
>
> | 도입 | 입찻을 취하는 것은 당신의 위치를 알리는 집합 지점이 되기 때문에 중요하다 |
> |---|---|
> | 전개 | 최고의 마케팅은 당신의 관점을 보여줌으로써 고객이 그것에 동의하게나 반대하게 만드는 것임 |
> | 부연 | 상품은 바꾸거나 고칠 수 있지만 당신의 입장이 집한 지점은 그 이면의 가치와 의미를 나타냄 |

> ＊ **「동사 vs. 준동사」** 해결하기
> · 모든 문장에는 원칙적으로 주어와 동사가 있어야 한다.
> · to부정사, 동명사, 분사 따위의 준동사는 문장에서 동사의 역할을 할 수 없다.

정답률
교육청 자료, 기타 기관 공지
자료와 내부 검토 과정을 거쳐
제시됩니다.

주의
풀이 과정에서 지문의 단서를
잘못 이용할 가능성이 있을 때,
적절한 주의를 주어서 올바른
풀이로 나아갈 수 있도록 한
코너입니다.

함정
지문을 정확히 이해하지
못한다면 반드시 빠지게
되어 있는 함정을 체크해
주고 해결할 수 있는 방법을
제시하였습니다.

KEY: 문제 속 어법 설명
해당 어법 사항이 문제로
출제됐을 때 정답을 찾는 가장
핵심적인 방법을 설명했습니다.

> **| 어법 특강 |**
>
> ＊ 목적격 보어로 원형부정사를 취하는 동사
> − 지각동사: feel, hear, listen to, see, watch 등
> − 사역동사: let, make, have
> · He heard the bell strike thirteen times at midnight.
>   지각동사   목적어   목적격 보어(원형부정사)
>   (그는 자정에 종이 열세 번 치는 것을 들었다.)
> · Inserting seeds and watching them grow is not difficult.
>   지각동사   목적어   목적격 보어(원형부정사)
>   (씨앗을 심고 그것들이 자라는 것을 보는 것은 어렵지 않다.)
> · Many presents made her eyes shine.
>   사역동사   목적어   목적격 보어(원형부정사)
> · Sean had the plumber repair the leak.
>   사역동사   목적어   목적격 보어(원형부정사)
>   (Sean은 배관공이 물이 새는 곳을 수리하도록 시켰다.)

어법 특강
핵심 어법 사항을 한 번 더 짚어
주어 심화학습을 돕습니다.

매력적 오답 이유
매력적 오답이 되는 이유를
자세히 설명합니다.

왜 오답
오답 선택지와 매력적 오답을
상세히 분석하여 오답의 함정에
빠지지 않도록 하였습니다.

매력적 오답
오답을 정답이라고 착각하게
되는 이유에 대해 철저히
분석하고 대책까지 제시합니다.

특별 부록 – 휴대용 단어장

이 책에 나오는 모든
핵심 어휘를 정리해
놓은 단어장 부록을
휴대하기 편리하게
구성하였습니다.

집필진 · 감수진 선생님들

자이스토리는 수능 준비를 가장 효과적으로 할 수 있도록
수능, 평가원, 학력평가 기출문제를 개념별, 유형별, 난이도별로
수록하였으며, 명강의로 소문난 학교 · 학원 선생님들께서
명쾌한 해설을 입체 첨삭으로 집필하셨습니다.

[집필진]

김도원 군포 수리고등학교	신수진 서울 한영외국어고등학교	차덕원 서울 신일고등학교
김범우 메가스터디 온라인 강사	윤혜경 부천 소사고등학교	한규리 안산 성안고등학교
김현아 서울 가락고등학교	이아영 오산 매홀고등학교	수경 English Lab.
박상규 광주 대동고등학교	이탁균 서울 대일외국어고등학교	
박새별 광주 광주과학고등학교	이혜은 서울 잠실고등학교	
박형우 안산 경안고등학교	장정근 서울 대성고등학교	

중요 · 핵심 문제 동영상 강의
자이스토리 유튜브 채널
황영희

[특별 감수진]

박유나 광주 서석고등학교	배세진 일산 이영신EST학원	Jennifer Kim 김해 일타수학원
양희준 대구 협성고등학교	한기윤 서울 수능영어의 神– Iris	

[감수진]

William 인천 JLS청라정상어학원	라승희 통영 아이작잉글리쉬	이연선 인천 MD학원
고미경 고양 일산탑그래머잉글리쉬	박민호 고양 일산이영신EST학원	이예원 서울 대치엠학원
고우리 수원 광교절대영어학원	박병노 대전 제이워크학원,	이위동 서울 강서에듀라인학원
구은서 인천 별별아카데미	크러쉬온영어학원	이진환 파주 코치스에듀
권세지 서울 목동이맥영어	박선우 서울 이바인진어학원	이태희 서울 플랜에이영어학원
김가영 김천 탑클래스영어	박수진 서울 송파이은재어학원	이현재 서울 가나안아카데미
김경훈 서울 신도림케이투학원	박일진 김해 루체테어학원율하캠퍼스	정시은 포항 SE잉글리시어학원
김고은 서울 강남마가학원	박정선 평창 잉글리쉬클럽	정재식 수원 마스터제이학원
김다래 부산 김다래영어전문	서지안 광주 ALCC고등영어학원	정형권 목포 워너비영어전문교습소
김문희 서울 브랜뉴영어	송봉규 서울 창동JS영어수학학원	정활상 서울 관악공잘학원
김민희 군포 에임영어학원	송석준 부산 대치명인학원	조미혜 양주 옥정KU영어학원
김선경 용인 수지엘앤케이영어학원	신인철 부산 오아시스영어학원	조형철 춘천 엠베스트SE남춘천점
김소라 서울 씨앤씨학원	양정숙 울산 길버트어학원	주미현 대구 범어주샘영어
김솔비 세종 폴리어학원	엄여은 울산 준쌤영어	주성훈 인천 청담바름학원
김수연 서울 잠실두림학원	오유림 서울 헬리오 오쌤영어	최미진 양주 옥정홍은비학원
김아영 서울 신용화수리논술연구	유우석 고령 단비영수학원	최진영 전주 오스카영어학원
김예리 서울 목동탑앤탑학원	윤용배 대전 이룸학원	최형석 부천 에이펙스영어학원
김정원 부산 영어의정원	윤정원 남양주 다산윤앤강학원	하해준 대구 일라영어학원
김정훈 제주 터닝포인트영수학원	이가희 인천 S&U영어	한동수 제주 위드유학원
김종순 대구 체리시영어교습소	이계훈 서울 이지영어학원	한수연 세종 리딩테이블
김주연 순천 JY제이와이영어	이권철 안양 평촌종로학원/군포 생각	한지현 용인 유캔영어학원
김창옥 전주 더베스트영어학원	하는방법학원	홍미의 평택 홍샘영어
김치훈 김해 에센셜영어학원	이다니엘 울산 반석성균관학원	홍석균 인천 STN학원
김현경 대전 해달영어	이민정 광주 롱맨어학원	황보훈 제주 이루다잉글리쉬학원
김혜진 서울 목동데몬스영어	이수영 서울 목동리젠영어	황주현 세종 위너서클영어
니콜 서울 SAT학원	이승혜 서울 스텔라영어	황혜진 서울 송파이루다영어

수능 선배들의 **비법** 전수 – 수험장 생생 체험 소개

긴장되고 떨리는 수험장에서 선배들이
문제를 풀면서 겪은 생생한 체험과 나만의 풀이 비법을
자이스토리 해설편에 수록했습니다.

2025 응시

강다은
대구 계성고 졸업
– 문학 실전

김강민
광주 국제고 졸업
– 세계지리

김덕우
부산 해운대고 졸업
– 지구과학Ⅱ

김연우
대구 정화여고 졸업
– 화학Ⅰ

김효원
제주 제일고 졸업
– 고3 미적분

박서영
부산 금곡고 졸업
– 사회·문화

박정빈
대구 남산고 졸업
– 생활과 윤리

배지오
성남 낙생고 졸업
– 독해 실전, 어법·어휘 실전

백승준
광주 광주숭일고 졸업
– 독해 실전, 어법·어휘 실전

서정후
광주 숭덕고 졸업
– 지구과학Ⅰ

성예현
대전 대전전민고 졸업
– 언어와 매체 실전

안한민
익산 남성고 졸업
– 화법과 작문 실전

오현준
서울 한영고 졸업
– 생명과학Ⅱ

윤혁준
서울 강서고 졸업
– 생명과학Ⅰ

이예슬
서울 독산고 졸업
– 동아시아사

이정근
안양 평촌고 졸업
– 기하

이지원
대구 성화여고 졸업
– 고3 수학Ⅰ, 고3 수학Ⅱ

임지호
부산 동아고 졸업
– 물리학Ⅰ

장윤서
부산 사직여고 졸업
– 독서 실전

정규원
부산 남성여고 졸업
– 고3 확률과 통계

최승우
광주 광주서석고 졸업
– 화학Ⅱ

최아람
서울 광영고 졸업
– 윤리와 사상

최여진
광주 국제고 졸업
– 한국지리

한규진
대구 계성고 졸업
– 독해 실전, 어법·어휘 실전

한상효
성남 낙생고 졸업
– 수능 한국사

한성은
익산 남성여고 졸업
– 고3 수학Ⅰ, 고3 수학Ⅱ

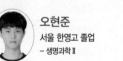

• 2024년

곽지훈 서울 한영외고 졸 (서울대 자유전공학부)
권민재 서울 광영여고 졸 (강릉원주대 치의예과)
김동현 안성 안법고 졸 (연세대 실내건축학과)
김서현 대전한빛고 졸 (카이스트 새내기과정학부)
김신유 익산 남성고 졸 (순천향대 의예과)
김아린 대전한빛고 졸 (충남대 의예과)
김용희 화성 화성고 졸 (단국대 의예과)
김지희 광주 국제고 졸 (고려대 한국사학과)
김태현 부산 대연고 졸 (서울대 수리과학부)
류이레 광주대동고 졸 (연세대 의예과)
문지민 대구 정화여고 졸 (고려대 중어중문학과)
변준서 화성 화성고 졸 (연세대 실내건축학과)
심기현 대구 계성고 졸 (경북대 의예과)
오서윤 서울 광문고 졸 (충남대 의예과)
진성연 부산국제고 졸 (서울대 사회학과)
조수근 성남 태원고 졸 (순천향대 의예과)

• 2023년

강 한 서울 배재고 졸 (고려대 융합에너지공학과)
권주원 서울 배재고 졸 (서울대 정치외교학부)
김보겸 광주서석고 졸 (연세대 지구시스템과학과)
김수정 부산국제고 졸 (고려대 서어서문학과)
김준서 부산 대연고 졸 (부산대 의예과)
김태산 광주서석고 졸 (고려대 정치외교학과)
김현서 경기 평택고 졸 (서강대 정치외교학과)
나인규 광주 국제고 졸 (한양대 경영학과)
명준하 광주서석고 졸 (연세대 사회환경시스템공학부)
박서영 부산 해운대고 졸 (서울대 심리학과)
박세민 광주 광덕고 졸 (서울대 의예과)
장경은 서울 세화여고 졸 (고려대 통계학과)
장성욱 부산 대연고 졸 (동아대학교 의예과)
정서린 서울 세화여고 졸 (서울대 약학과)
조현준 익산 이리고 졸 (전북대 의예과)
최윤성 서울 양정고 졸 (서울대 공과대학 광역)
홍채연 서울 한영고 졸 (고려대 불어불문학과)

🍀 문항 배열 및 구성 [630제+어휘 리뷰 505제]

❶ 최신 5개년 수능, 모의평가 전 문항 수록 [390문항]

• 최신 5개년 수능과 평가원 모의평가의 모든 문제를
  수록하여 해설했습니다.

❷ 2024년 실시 고3 학력평가 전 문항 수록 [104문항]

• 2024년에 시행된 학력평가의 모든 문항을 수록하여 최신
  경향을 완벽히 파악할 수 있습니다.

❸ 최신 4개년 고3 학력평가 우수 문항 수록 [100문항]

• 수능 및 모의평가 문제만으로는 부족한 유형 학습을 채울
  수 있도록 난이도와 유형을 고려하여 학력평가 문항 중에서
  우수 문항을 선별, 수록하였습니다.

**❹ 최신 경찰대, 삼사 기출 문제, 고3 수능 대비 선별
  문항 – 고난도 유형 모의고사 수록 [36문항]**

• 회차별 문제 구성(12문항)

01번 – 밑줄 친 부분의 의미 찾기	07번 – 글의 순서 정하기
02번 – 주제 찾기	08번 – 글의 순서 정하기 or 주어진 문장 넣기
03번 – 제목 찾기	09번 – 주어진 문장 넣기
04번 05번 06번 } 빈칸 완성하기	10번 – 요약문 완성하기
	11번 12번 } 장문의 이해

❺ 독해 유형별 핵심 어휘 Review [505문항]

• 각 유형이 끝날 때마다 출제된 핵심 어휘를 다시 한 번
  확인하고 완전히 암기할 수 있도록 다양한 유형의 어휘
  테스트 문제를 수록하였습니다.

[독해 실전 수록 문항 구성표]

대비연도	3월	4월	6월	7월	9월	10월	수능	경찰대·삼사	수록
2025	26	26	26	26	26	26	26	15	197
2024	16	17	26	26	26	26	26	3	166
2023	4	7	26	8	26	8	26		105
2022	2		26	1	26	3	26		84
2021			26		26		26		78
총 문항 수									630

2025학년도 6월, 9월 모의+수능
영어 독해+어법·어휘 문항 배치표 (홀수형 기준)

문항 번호	수록 교재	6월	수록 교재	9월	수록 교재	수능
18		A01		A04		A03
19		B02		B04		B03
20		C01		C04		C03
21		D06		D04		D03
22		E01		E04		E03
23	독해 실전	F07	독해 실전	F04	독해 실전	F03
24		G01		G04		G03
25		H07		H04		H03
26		I05		I04		I03
27		J07		J05		J03
28		J08		J06		J04
29	어법·어휘 실전	O02	어법·어휘 실전	L01	어법·어휘 실전	J02
30		U09		U04		U03
31		K26		K04		K02
32		K65		K24		K22
33		K21		K64		K23
34		K93		K25		K03
35		L05		L04		L03
36		M01		M05		M03
37		M07		M06		M04
38	독해 실전	N06	독해 실전	N02	독해 실전	N03
39		N07		N05		N04
40		O01		O04		O03
41		P07		P05		P03
42		P08		P06		P04
43		Q10		Q07		Q04
44		Q11		Q08		Q05
45		Q12		Q09		Q06

* 독해 실전 : 자이스토리 영어 독해 실전

* 어법·어휘 실전 : 자이스토리 영어 어법·어휘 실전

A 목적 찾기

목적은 중요하니까 마지막에도 한 번 더 써야지!

★ 유형 설명

다음 글의 목적으로 가장 적절한 것은?

Dear Hylean Miller,
    Hello, I'm Nelson Perkins, a teacher and

주로 편지글이 지문으로 출제되며, 필자가 편지를 쓴 목적이 무엇인지 찾아야 한다.

☞ 편지를 쓴 사람은 누구이고, 편지를 받는 사람은 누구인지 먼저 파악한다. 편지를 쓴 목적을 직접적으로 나타내는 문장이 글에 등장하는 경우가 많으므로 조동사 (would, will 등)나 연결어, 특정 어구 (please, request)에 주의하며 단서를 찾는다.

🎭 유형 풀이 비법

1 글의 종류를 파악하라!
- 광고문, 기사문, 소설, 편지 등 글의 종류를 먼저 파악한다.

2 필자와 받는 사람을 확인하라!
- 필자가 글을 누구에게 쓰는지, 관계가 공적인지 사적인지, 어느 집단이나 회사 소속인지를 파악한다.

3 글을 쓴 의도를 찾아라!
- 필자가 글을 통해 전달하고자 하는 최종적인 의도에 집중한다.

Tip 글에서 언급된 내용의 일부분을 근거로 정답을 고르지 않도록 주의한다.

★ 최신 수능 경향 분석

대비 연도	월	문항 번호	지문 주제	난이도
	11	18번	Rosydale City 마라톤 대회 취소 공지	✿❀❀
2025	9	18번	Royal Ocean Cruises 독점 판촉 상품 안내	✿❀❀
	6	18번	부적절한 댓글 자제 요청	✿✿❀
	11	18번	웹툰 제작 온라인 강좌 홍보	✿❀❀
2024	9	18번	교통안전 봉사 참여 요청	✿❀❀
	6	18번	공원 재개장 행사 초대	✿❀❀
	11	18번	조류 관찰 클럽 가입 방법 문의	✿✿❀
2023	9	18번	Millstown 출신인 Natalie Talley 응원	✿❀❀
	6	18번	수영장 추가 대여 요청	✿❀❀

★ 2025 수능 출제 분석

2025 수능에서는 편지를 받는 사람이 누구인지를 밝히는 문장으로 시작하며, As a result, we have decided to cancel the race.라는 문장을 통해 글의 목적을 직접적으로 드러내어 난이도가 높지 않았다.

★ 2026 수능 예측

최근 수년 간 한 해도 빠짐없이 18번 문항으로 출제되었으므로 2026 수능에서도 출제될 것이다.
난이도가 높지 않은 유형이므로 긴장하지 말고 차분히 글을 읽기만 하면 정답을 찾을 수 있다.

📌 자주 출제되는 표현

☐ **Dear Residents** 주민들께
☐ **on behalf of** ~을 대신하여
☐ **in regard to** ~와 관련하여
☐ **Please ensure** ~을 확실히 하십시오
☐ **To whom it may concern** 관계자분께
☐ **I would like to-v** 저는 ~하고 싶습니다
☐ **Thank you in advance** 미리 감사드립니다
☐ **I look forward to v-ing** 저는 ~을 고대합니다
☐ **I'm the manager of** ~ 저는 ~의 관리인입니다
☐ **Please join us for** ~에 우리와 함께해 주세요
☐ **We kindly ask that** 우리는 ~을 정중히 요청합니다
☐ **I'm asking you to-v** 저는 당신이 ~할 것을 요청합니다
☐ **We hope to see you at** ~에서 당신을 뵙기를 바랍니다

📖 어휘 및 표현 Preview

☐ **offer** 제공하다
☐ **recently** 최근
☐ **welcome** 환영하다
☐ **appreciate** 감사하다
☐ **favorite** 가장 좋아하는
☐ **loyalty** 충심
☐ **promotion** 판촉, 홍보
☐ **reservation** 예약
☐ **discount** 할인
☐ **enjoy** 즐기다
☐ **unacceptable** 받아들일 수 없는
☐ **comment** 댓글
☐ **specialty** 특별 (사항)

자이 쌤's Follow Me!

A 목적 찾기 (첫 번째)

1st 각 선택지의 핵심 어구에 표시한 후 글을 읽기 시작하세요.
2nd 연결어나 명령문, 특정 어구를 찾아 필자가 하고 싶은 말을 추론하세요.
3rd 나머지 문장들의 내용을 종합하여 글의 목적을 찾으세요.

A01 ✿✿✿ .... 2025 대비 6월 모평 18 (고3)

다음 글의 목적으로 가장 적절한 것은?

 Ethan 2 days ago

Hello, everyone! Welcome back to your favorite online channel, *With Ethan*. As always, I'm trying to make this channel a place that my followers of all ages can enjoy. Recently, in the comments section, there have been some examples of language that is inappropriate for younger viewers. Also, there have been some comments that are not relevant to this channel. These kinds of comments are unacceptable for a channel like this. I would really like to ask that all of my followers keep these things in mind so that we can all enjoy this channel. I always appreciate your time and support.
Please keep watching.

👍 178   👎 0   ↪ ⊙

① 새로 개설한 온라인 채널을 홍보하려고
② 온라인 생방송 날짜 변경을 공지하려고
③ 부적절한 댓글을 쓰지 않도록 요청하려고
④ 온라인 채널 구독 연령 제한을 고지하려고
⑤ 온라인 구독자들의 요청 사항을 공유하려고

1st 각 선택지의 핵심 어구에 표시한 후 글을 읽기 시작하세요.

① 새로 개설한 온라인 채널을 홍보하려고
② 온라인 생방송 날짜 변경을 공지하려고
③ 부적절한 댓글을 쓰지 않도록 요청하려고
④ 온라인 채널 구독 연령 제한을 고지하려고
⑤ 온라인 구독자들의 요청 사항을 공유하려고

● 선택지를 통해 글의 소재가 무엇인지 추론할 수 있어요.
거의 모든 선택지에 ❶(   )이 있는 것으로 보아 (단서)
그것과 관련하여 무언가를 홍보하거나 안내하는 글일 것이라고 예상할 수 있어요. (발상)
이 소재에 대해서 구체적으로 어떤 내용이 나오는지 파악해서 정답을 찾아야 하는데, 각 선택지의 핵심 내용에 표시를 하면서 읽으면 좀 더 빠르게 정답을 찾을 수 있어요.
온라인 채널을 홍보하는 것인지, 온라인 생방송 날짜를 변경하려는 것인지, 부적절한 댓글을 쓰지 말라고 하는 것인지, 온라인 채널 구독 연령 제한을 얘기하려는 것인지, 온라인 구독자들의 요청 사항을 공유하려는 것인지 글을 읽으면서 확인해 봅시다.

● 선택지를 확인하고 난 후에는 글을 빠르게 훑어보세요.
선택지를 먼저 확인하고 나서 글을 훑어보니까 your favorite online channel, inappropriate for younger viewers처럼 선택지의 내용을 담은 어구들이 눈에 띄어요. 이제 본격적으로 글을 읽으면서 필자가 편지를 쓴 목적이 무엇인지 찾아봅시다.

2nd 연결어나 명령문, 특정 어구를 찾아 필자가 하고 싶은 말을 추론하세요.

I would really like to ask / that all of my followers
간절히 부탁드립니다   / 모든 팔로워가 이러한
keep these things in mind / so that we can all enjoy
점을 염두에 두시길   / 우리 모두 이 채널을
this channel. //
즐길 수 있도록   //

● would like to-v는 '~을 하고 싶다'라는 뜻이에요.
I would really like to ask는 '간절히 부탁드립니다'라는 의미예요. 이는 편지를 쓰고 있는 필자의 행위가 요청하는 것이고, 뒤에 '모든 팔로워가 이러한 점을 염두에 두시길' 바란다고 했으므로, 이 편지의 목적은 어떤 것을 요청하는 것이에요.

● 선택지 중에 정답으로 예상되는 것이 있나요?
편지의 목적이 요청이라는 것을 알았으니, 선택지 중 유일하게 요청하는 ③이 정답이라고 예상할 수 있어요.

● **구체적으로 무엇을 요청하는지 확인해야 해요.**
　필자가 온라인 채널과 관련해서 무엇을 요청하는 것일까요? 글의 다른 부분을 통해 확인해야 해요.

3rd 나머지 문장들의 내용을 종합하여 글의 목적을 찾으세요.

1) 앞부분에 편지의 수신자를 언급했어요.

Welcome back / to your favorite online channel,
다시 오신 것을 환영합니다 / 여러분이 가장
With Ethan. //
좋아하는 온라인 채널인 *With Ethan*에 //

● **이 편지의 수신자는 누구인가요?**
　online channel, *With Ethan* 즉 온라인 채널인 *With Ethan*의 구독자들에게 편지를 보낸 것을 알 수 있어요.

2) 다음에 이어지는 내용을 더 살펴봅시다.

Recently, in the comments section, / there have
최근 댓글난에　　　　　　　　　　　　／ 언어 사례가
been some examples of language / that is
몇 가지 있었습니다　　　　　　　　　／ 어린
inappropriate for younger viewers. //
시청자에게 부적절한　　　　　　　　　//
Also, there have been some comments / that are
또한, 댓글도 일부 있었습니다　　　　　／ 이 채널과
not relevant to this channel. //
관련이 없는　　　　　　　　　//

● **온라인 채널의 댓글과 관련된 내용을 말했어요.**
　어린 시청자에게 부적절한 **2**(　　　　　)이 있었다고 했고, 채널과 관계없는 댓글도 있었다고 언급했어요.

3) 온라인 채널의 구독자들에게 무엇을 요청하는지 다시 확인합시다.

I would really like to ask / that all of my followers
간절히 부탁드립니다　　　　　　　／ 모든 팔로워가 이러한
keep these things in mind / so that we can all enjoy
점을 염두에 두시길　　　　　／ 우리 모두 이 채널을
this channel. //
즐길 수 있도록　　 //

모든 팔로워가 부적절하거나 관계없는 댓글이 있었다는 점을 염두에 두기를 부탁했어요.

4) 이제 우리가 예상한 정답이 맞는지 확인해 봅시다.
　필자가 운영하는 온라인 채널의 댓글에 어린 시청자에게 부적절한 언어 사례가 있었고, 앞으로 이러한 일이 발생하지 않기를 부탁하는 내용이이에요.
　따라서 우리가 예상한 대로 이 글의 목적은 **3**(　　　　　)이에요.

이 박물관에 온 '목적'은 바로 이 도자기지!

A 목적 찾기 (두 번째)

1st 각 선택지의 핵심 어구에 표시한 후 글을 읽기 시작하세요.
2nd 연결어나 명령문, 특정 어구를 찾아 필자가 하고 싶은 말을 추론하세요.
3rd 나머지 문장들의 내용을 종합하여 글의 목적을 찾으세요.

A02 ✿❀❀ .... 2024 대비 6월 모평 18 (고3)

다음 글의 목적으로 가장 적절한 것은?

Dear Custard Valley Park members,
Custard Valley Park's grand reopening event will be held on June 1st. For this exciting occasion, we are offering free admission to all visitors on the reopening day. There will be a food stand selling ice cream and snacks. We would like to invite you, our valued members, to celebrate this event. Please come and explore the park's new features such as tennis courts and a flower garden. Just relax and enjoy the beautiful scenery. We are confident that you will love the new changes, and we are looking forward to seeing you soon.
Sincerely,
Katherine Carter
Park Management Team

① 공원 재개장 행사에 초대하려고
② 공원 운영 시간 변경을 공지하려고
③ 공원 이용 규칙 준수를 당부하려고
④ 공원 입장 시 유의 사항을 안내하려고
⑤ 공원 리모델링 사업 계획을 설명하려고

1st 각 선택지의 핵심 어구에 표시한 후 글을 읽기 시작하세요.

① 공원 재개장 행사에 초대하려고
② 공원 운영 시간 변경을 공지하려고
③ 공원 이용 규칙 준수를 당부하려고
④ 공원 입장 시 유의 사항을 안내하려고
⑤ 공원 리모델링 사업 계획을 설명하려고

● **선택지를 통해 글의 소재가 무엇인지 추론할 수 있어요.**
모든 선택지에 ❶( )이 있는 것으로 보아 [단서] 공원과 관련하여 무언가를 안내하거나 요구하는 글일 것이라고 예상할 수 있어요. [발상]
정답을 찾으려면 공원과 관련하여 구체적으로 무엇을 안내하거나 요구하는지 파악해야 해요. 이때 각 선택지의 핵심 내용에 표시를 하면 좀 더 빠르게 정답을 찾을 수 있어요.
재개장 행사에 초대하는 것인지, 공원 운영 시간이 변경된다는 것인지, 공원 이용 규칙 준수를 당부하는 것인지, 입장 시 유의 사항을 안내하는 것인지, 리모델링 사업 계획을 설명하는 것인지 글을 읽으면서 확인해 봅시다.

● **선택지를 확인하고 난 후에는 글을 빠르게 훑어보세요.**
선택지를 먼저 확인하고 나서 글을 훑어보니까 reopening event, free admission처럼 선택지의 내용을 담은 어구들이 눈에 띄어요. 이제 본격적으로 글을 읽으면서 Katherine Carter가 편지를 쓴 목적이 무엇인지 찾아봅시다.

2nd 연결어나 명령문, 특정 어구를 찾아 필자가 하고 싶은 말을 추론하세요.

We would like to invite you, our valued members, /
저희는 저희의 소중한 회원인 여러분을 초대하고 싶습니다 /
to celebrate this event. //
이 행사를 축하하기 위해 //

● **would like to-v는 '~을 하고 싶다'라는 뜻이에요.**
We would like to invite you는 '저희는 귀하를 초대하고 싶습니다'라는 의미예요. 이는 편지를 쓰고 있는 We의 행위가 초대하는 것이고, 이 편지의 목적은 행사에 초대하는 것이에요.

Please come and explore the park's new features /
공원의 새로운 특별시설을 오셔서 둘러보세요 /
such as tennis courts and a flower garden. //
테니스 코트와 꽃 정원과 같은 //

● 「Please + 동사원형」은 '~ 해주세요'라는 부탁의 뜻이에요.
Please come and explore는 '오셔서 둘러보세요'라는 의미예요. 바로
이전 문장을 통해 편지의 수신자들을 공원의 행사에 초대하는 것에
이어서, 수신자들에게 공원에 와서 둘러보는 행위를 부탁하는 의미예요.

We are confident / that you will love the new
저희는 확신하며   / 새로운 변화를 매우 좋아하실 것으로
changes, / and we are looking forward to seeing
         / 여러분을 곧 다시 뵙기를 고대하고 있습니다 //
you soon. //

● look forward to-ing는 '~할 것을 고대하다'라는 뜻이에요.
we are looking forward to seeing you soon은 '귀하를 곧 다시
뵙기를 고대하고 있습니다'라는 의미예요. 초대와 부탁에 이어서, 행사에
올 것을 기대한다는 문장으로 편지를 마무리하는 것이죠.

● 선택지 중에 정답으로 예상되는 것이 있나요?
편지의 목적이 초대라는 것을 알았으니, 선택지 중 유일하게 초대를
언급하는 ①이 정답이라고 예상할 수 있어요.

● 구체적으로 '누구를' '어떤' 행사에 초대하는 것인지 확인해야 해요.
필자인 Katherine Carter가 초대하는 대상은 '소중한 회원'이라고 하는데
어디의 회원일까요? 또한 '이 행사'라고 하는데 어떤 행사일까요? 글의
다른 부분을 통해 확인해야 해요.

3rd 나머지 문장들의 내용을 종합하여 글의 목적을 찾으세요.

1) Dear로 시작하는 첫 줄에 편지의 수신자가 적혀 있네요.

Dear Custard Valley Park members, /
Custard Valley 공원 회원께   /

● 이 편지의 수신자는 누구인가요?
Custard Valley Park members, 즉 공원 회원들에게 이 편지를 보낸
것을 알 수 있어요.

2) 회원들을 어떤 행사에 초대하는 것인지 확인합시다.

Custard Valley Park's grand reopening event / will
Custard Valley 공원의 성대한 재개장 행사가   / 열릴
be held / on June 1st. //
것입니다 / 6월 1일에   //

● 공원 재개장 행사의 개최와 그 날짜를 안내했어요.
편지 본문의 첫 문장에 reopening event가 6월 1일에 열릴 것이라는
정보가 있어요. 공원의 ❷(   )를 공원 회원들에게 알리려고
하나 봐요.

3) 이제 우리가 예상한 정답이 맞는지 확인해 봅시다.
Katherine Carter는 Custard Valley 공원 회원들에게 6월 1일에 있을
공원 재개장 행사를 알리며 이들을 초대하기 위해 이 편지를 썼어요.
따라서 우리가 예상한 대로 이 글의 목적은 ❸(   )이에요.

먼저 선택지의
핵심 어구에
표시하자!

A03 ~ 07 ▶ 제한시간 10분

A03 ✱❅❅ ·················· 2025 대비 수능 18 (고3)

다음 글의 목적으로 가장 적절한 것은?

Dear Rosydale City Marathon Racers,

We are really grateful to all of you who have signed up for the 10th Rosydale City Marathon that was scheduled for this coming Saturday at 10 a.m. Unfortunately, as you may already know, the weather forecast says that there is going to be a downpour throughout the race day. We truly hoped that the race would go smoothly. However, it is likely that the heavy rain will make the roads too slippery and dangerous for the racers to run safely. As a result, we have decided to cancel the race. We hope you understand and we promise to hold another race in the near future.

Sincerely,
Martha Kingsley
Race Manager

① 마라톤 경기 취소 사실을 공지하려고
② 마라톤 경기 사전 행사 참여를 독려하려고
③ 마라톤 경기 참가비 환불 절차를 설명하려고
④ 마라톤 경기 참여 시 규칙 준수를 당부하려고
⑤ 마라톤 경기 진행에 따른 도로 통제를 안내하려고

A04 ✱❅❅ ·················· 2025 대비 9월 모평 18 (고3)

다음 글의 목적으로 가장 적절한 것은?

Dear Valued Members,

We have exciting news here at Royal Ocean Cruises! To thank you for your loyalty, we are thrilled to offer you an exclusive promotion! Make a reservation for any cruise departing within the next six months and enjoy a 15% discount. Additionally, we are offering a free specialty dining package and a $20 coupon to use at the onboard gift shop. To take advantage of this offer, simply go to our website and enter the promotion code 'ROC25'. We look forward to welcoming you back aboard for another unforgettable journey. Thank you for your continued loyalty and support.

Sincerely,
Cindy Robins
Customer Relations Manager

① 식사 메뉴 변경 사유를 설명하려고
② 여행 후기 작성 참여를 독려하려고
③ 여행 일정 변경 사항을 공지하려고
④ 여행 상품 판촉 행사를 안내하려고
⑤ 고객 감사 행사 아이디어를 공모하려고

A05 ❀❋❋ .... 2024 실시 10월 학평 18 (고3)

다음 글의 목적으로 가장 적절한 것은?

I hope this email finds you well. Thank you for considering me as a speaker for the upcoming Digital Marketing Workshop. I appreciate the invitation and your thoughtfulness. The workshop sounds like an amazing event, and I would have loved to participate. However, I regret to inform you that I will be overseas on a business trip during the workshop. It is unfortunate that the timing does not work out. Although I cannot attend as a speaker this time, I remain hopeful for future opportunities where our schedules might coincide. I hope the workshop goes well.

① 디지털 마케팅 워크숍에 참여를 독려하려고
② 연설자로 참석해 달라는 제안을 거절하려고
③ 워크숍의 변경된 장소를 안내하려고
④ 행사가 취소되었음을 공지하려고
⑤ 해외 출장 일정을 조정하려고

A06 ❀❋❋ .... 2024 실시 7월 학평 18 (고3)

다음 글의 목적으로 가장 적절한 것은?

Dear Staff,

My name is Laura Miller, the Human Resources Manager. As part of our efforts to reduce traffic on newly built area roadways, we are starting to offer flextime working hours to eligible employees. Under the plan, staffers could begin work 60 to 90 minutes before or after ordinary business hours, adjusting their scheduled departure time accordingly. All requests for flextime must be submitted to departmental supervisors and will be approved if they do not conflict with the staffing needs of the company. In addition, flextime schedules will be reviewed every four months to assure that they do not adversely affect company goals.

Best regards,
Laura Miller

① 유연 근무제 실시 계획을 안내하려고
② 직장 내 갈등 조정 기구 신설을 홍보하려고
③ 유연 근무제의 만족도 조사 참여를 독려하려고
④ 부서별 유연 근무 신청 승인 결과를 통보하려고
⑤ 교통량 감소를 위한 대중교통 이용을 장려하려고

A07 ❀❋❋ .... 2024 실시 5월 학평 18 (고3)

다음 글의 목적으로 가장 적절한 것은?

My name is Rohan Kaul, the producer of the upcoming film 'Upagrah.' I am reaching out to you regarding a matter of importance concerning the shooting of some scenes for our film. We have identified Gulab Park, Mumbai, as an ideal location for these scenes. We are hoping to conduct this shoot on 3rd June 2024, from 1 p.m. to 6 p.m. We have chosen Monday for the shooting day to minimize traffic issues and disruption to the public. During the shoot, our team promises to follow all rules and regulations, ensuring no inconvenience is caused to the public. We would be so grateful if you granted permission for the shoot so that we can put the beautiful scenery of the park in our film. We look forward to your response.

① 주말 영화 시사회에 초대하려고
② 공원 이용 시간의 연장을 건의하려고
③ 촬영을 위한 장비 대여 방법을 문의하려고
④ 행사 운영을 위한 교통 통제를 요청하려고
⑤ 영화 촬영을 위해 장소 사용 허가를 얻으려고

A08 ✽✽✽.................2024 실시 3월 학평 18 (고3)

다음 글의 목적으로 가장 적절한 것은?

It has been a privilege to serve in this company for the past four years. The experiences and insights I have gained as a safety manager have been invaluable. However, after careful consideration, I have accepted a position at another company and will be leaving Lewis Ltd. This was not an easy decision to make, but I am confident that my new role will help me with my future goals. My last day of work will be on April 30th. I will do all I can to assist in a smooth transfer of duties. I wish both you and Lewis Ltd. every good fortune.

① 업무에 대한 조언을 구하려고
② 다른 부서로의 이동을 요청하려고
③ 신규 채용 조건에 대해 안내하려고
④ 구직자를 위한 프로그램을 홍보하려고
⑤ 다른 회사로 이직하게 되었음을 알리려고

A09 ✽✽✽.................2022 대비 6월 모평 18 (고3)

다음 글의 목적으로 가장 적절한 것은?

Dear Ms. Larson,
  I am writing to you with new information about your current membership. Last year, you signed up for our museum membership that provides special discounts. As stated in the last newsletter, this year we are happy to be celebrating our 50th anniversary. So we would like to offer you further benefits. These include free admission for up to ten people and 20% off museum merchandise on your next visit. You will also be invited to all new exhibition openings this year at discounted prices. We hope you enjoy these offers. For any questions, please feel free to contact us.
Best regards,
Stella Harrison

① 박물관 개관 50주년 기념행사 취소를 공지하려고
② 작년에 가입한 박물관 멤버십의 갱신을 요청하려고
③ 박물관 멤버십 회원을 위한 추가 혜택을 알려 주려고
④ 박물관 기념품점에서 새로 판매할 상품을 홍보하려고
⑤ 박물관 전시 프로그램에서 변경된 내용을 안내하려고

A10 ✽✽✽.................2023 대비 6월 모평 18 (고3)

다음 글의 목적으로 가장 적절한 것은?

Dear Hylean Miller,
  Hello, I'm Nelson Perkins, a teacher and swimming coach at Broomstone High School. Last week, I made a reservation for one of your company's swimming pools for our summer swim camp. However, due to its popularity, thirty more students are coming to the camp than we expected, so we need one more swimming pool for them. The rental section on your website says that there are two other swimming pools during the summer season: the Splash Pool and the Rainbow Pool. Please let me know if an additional rental would be possible. Thank you in advance.
Best Wishes,
Nelson Perkins

① 수영 캠프 참가 날짜를 변경하려고
② 수영장 수용 가능 인원을 확인하려고
③ 수영 캠프 등록 방법에 대해 알아보려고
④ 수영장 추가 대여 가능 여부를 문의하려고
⑤ 수영장 대여 취소에 따른 환불을 요청하려고

다음 글의 목적으로 가장 적절한 것은?

Dear Mr. Bernstein,

My name is Thomas Cobb, the marketing director of Calbary Hospital. Our hospital is planning to hold a charity concert on September 18th in the Main Hall of our hospital. We expect it to be helpful in raising money to cover the medical costs of those in need. To make the concert more special, we want to invite you for the opening of the concert. Your reputation as a pianist is well known, and everyone will be very happy to see your performance. Beautiful piano melodies will help create an enjoyable experience for the audience. We look forward to your positive reply.

Sincerely,

Thomas A. Cobb

① 의료비 지원이 필요한 이들을 위한 기부를 독려하려고
② 자선 음악회 연주자로 참여해 줄 것을 요청하려고
③ 피아노 독주회 관람 신청 방법을 문의하려고
④ 병원 개관 기념행사 참가 방법을 안내하려고
⑤ 병원 진료 시간이 변경된 것을 알려 주려고

다음 글의 목적으로 가장 적절한 것은?

Dear Mr. Anderson:

My name is Sophia Willis, Events Manager of the 2020 Caroline County Art Contest. I am currently looking for a place for this year's contest exhibition. The Caroline County Art Contest has had over one hundred artworks submitted to us by local artists. For the theme, we wanted artists to explore the natural world of Caroline County. I believe the Garden Café Gallery would be a perfect place to host the event, as your gallery is well-known for its beautiful garden. The exhibition is usually held throughout October, and we very much hope that we can rent a space for the exhibition at the Garden Café Gallery during this time. I look forward to your response.

Yours sincerely,

Sophia Willis

① 출품 작품 전시회에 초대하려고
② 작품 제출 방법의 변경을 안내하려고
③ 출품 작품 전시 장소 대여를 문의하려고
④ 정원 박람회의 변경된 일정을 공지하려고
⑤ 지역 예술가들에게 작품 제출을 독려하려고

A13 ✿❀❀ .... 2022 대비 수능 18 (고3)

다음 글의 목적으로 가장 적절한 것은?

Dear Ms. Green,

My name is Donna Williams, a science teacher at Rogan High School. I am planning a special workshop for our science teachers. We are interested in learning how to teach online science classes. I have been impressed with your ideas about using internet platforms for science classes. Since you are an expert in online education, I would like to ask you to deliver a special lecture at the workshop scheduled for next month. I am sure the lecture will help our teachers manage successful online science classes, and I hope we can learn from your insights. I am looking forward to hearing from you.

Sincerely,

Donna Williams

① 과학 교육 정책 협의회 참여를 독려하려고
② 과학 교사 워크숍의 특강을 부탁하려고
③ 과학 교사 채용 계획을 공지하려고
④ 과학 교육 프로그램 개발을 요청하려고
⑤ 과학 교육 워크숍 일정의 변경을 안내하려고

A14 ✿❀❀ .... 2023 대비 9월 모평 18 (고3)

다음 글의 목적으로 가장 적절한 것은?

Dear Natalie Talley,

My name is Olivia Spikes, the mayor of Millstown. Before you attend the world championships next month, on behalf of everyone in Millstown, I wish to let you know that we are supporting you all the way. As you are the first famous figure skater from Millstown, we are all big fans of yours. Our community was so proud of you for winning the national championships last year. Your amazing performance really moved us all. We all believe that you are going to impress the entire nation again. Your hometown supporters will cheer for you whenever you perform on the ice. Good luck!

Best wishes,

Olivia Spikes

① 지역 사회 홍보 대사로 활동해 줄 것을 제안하려고
② 이웃 도시와 예정된 친선 경기 취소를 통보하려고
③ 지역 사회 출신 피겨 스케이팅 선수를 응원하려고
④ 시청에서 주관하는 연례 자선 행사를 홍보하려고
⑤ 피겨 스케이팅 경기장 건립을 위한 기부를 요청하려고

A15 ✱❀❀ .... 2021 대비 6월 모평 18 (고3)

다음 글의 목적으로 가장 적절한 것은?

To whom it may concern,

My name is Daniel. Since I joined your youth sports program several years ago, I have really enjoyed swimming. Thanks to your program, I have become a good swimmer. Now I want to go one step further. I like helping people and hope to get a job as a lifeguard later. So I tried to sign up for your lifeguard training course this summer. But the course was so popular that the registration closed almost as soon as it opened. I couldn't register and was really disappointed. I heard some of my friends couldn't, either. I'm kindly asking you to open an additional course. I appreciate your consideration.

Sincerely,
Daniel Smith

① 구조원 양성 과정의 추가 개설을 요청하려고
② 구조원 양성 과정의 우수성을 홍보하려고
③ 동계 수영 강습 프로그램 수강을 신청하려고
④ 수영 강사 일자리가 있는지 문의하려고
⑤ 구조원 양성 과정의 등록 방법을 안내하려고

A16 ✱❀❀ .... 2024 대비 수능 18 (고3)

다음 글의 목적으로 가장 적절한 것은?

I'm Charlie Reeves, manager of Toon Skills Company. If you're interested in new webtoon-making skills and techniques, this post is for you. This year, we've launched special online courses, which contain a variety of contents about webtoon production. Each course consists of ten units that help improve your drawing and story-telling skills. Moreover, these courses are designed to suit any level, from beginner to advanced. It costs $45 for one course, and you can watch your course as many times as you want for six months. Our courses with talented and experienced instructors will open up a new world of creativity for you. It's time to start creating your webtoon world at https://webtoonskills.com.

① 웹툰 제작 온라인 강좌를 홍보하려고
② 웹툰 작가 채용 정보를 제공하려고
③ 신작 웹툰 공개 일정을 공지하려고
④ 웹툰 창작 대회에 출품을 권유하려고
⑤ 기초적인 웹툰 제작 방법을 설명하려고

A17 ✽❀❀ .... 2021 대비 수능 18 (고3)

다음 글의 목적으로 가장 적절한 것은?

Dear Friends,

Season's greetings. As some of you already know, we are starting the campus food drive. This is how you participate. You can bring your items for donation to our booths. Our donation booths are located in the lobbies of the campus libraries. Just drop off the items there during usual library hours from December 4 to 23. The donated food should be non-perishable like canned meats and canned fruits. Packaged goods such as jam and peanut butter are also good. We will distribute the food to our neighbors on Christmas Eve. We truly appreciate your help.

Many blessings,

Joanna at Campus Food Bank

① 음식 기부에 참여하는 방법을 안내하려고
② 음식 배달 자원봉사 참여에 감사하려고
③ 도서관 이용 시간 변경을 공지하려고
④ 음식물 낭비의 심각성을 알려 주려고
⑤ 크리스마스 행사 일정을 문의하려고

A18 ✽❀❀ .... 2023 대비 수능 18 (고3)

다음 글의 목적으로 가장 적절한 것은?

To whom it may concern,

My name is Michael Brown. I have been a bird-watcher since childhood. I have always enjoyed watching birds in my yard and identifying them by sight and sound. Yesterday, I happened to read an article about your club. I was surprised and excited to find out about a community of passionate bird-watchers who travel annually to go birding. I would love to join your club, but your website appears to be under construction. I could not find any information except for this contact email address. I would like to know how to sign up for the club. I look forward to your reply.

Sincerely,

Michael Brown

① 조류 관찰 클럽에 가입하는 방법을 문의하려고
② 조류 관찰 시 주의해야 할 사항을 전달하려고
③ 조류 관찰 협회의 새로운 규정을 확인하려고
④ 조류 관찰과 관련된 웹 사이트를 소개하려고
⑤ 조류 관찰 시 필요한 장비를 알아보려고

2등급 대비 문제

A19 ~ 20 ▶ 제한시간 5분

A19 ✪ 2등급 대비 .... 2024 대비 9월 모평 18 (고3)

다음 글의 목적으로 가장 적절한 것은?

Dear Parents,

My name is Danielle Hamilton, and I am the principal of Techville High School. As you may know, there is major road construction scheduled to take place in front of our school next month. This raises safety concerns. Therefore, we are asking for parent volunteers to help with directing traffic. The volunteer hours are from 8:00 to 8:30 a.m. and from 4:30 to 5:00 p.m. on school days. If you are willing to take part in the traffic safety volunteer group, please email us with your preferred schedule at info@techville.edu. Your participation will be helpful in building a safer school environment for our students. Thank you in advance for your contributions.

Sincerely,
Danielle Hamilton

① 교통안전 봉사 참여를 요청하려고
② 자원봉사 교육 일정을 공지하려고
③ 학교 시설 공사에 대한 양해를 구하려고
④ 학교 앞 도로 공사의 필요성을 설명하려고
⑤ 등·하교 차량 안전 수칙 준수를 당부하려고

A20 ✪ 2등급 대비 .... 2023 실시 10월 학평 18 (고3)

다음 글의 목적으로 가장 적절한 것은?

We hope this notice finds you in good health and high spirits. We are writing to inform you that a package was delivered to the Rosehill Apartment Complex on October 9th, specifically addressed to your home. However, despite multiple attempts to deliver the package to you, it has remained unclaimed at our front desk for an extended period. As the management office, it is our responsibility to ensure the safekeeping of all delivered items and help deliver them quickly to the right residents. Therefore, we kindly request that you visit the management office during our office hours to claim your package. We genuinely appreciate your cooperation in this matter.

① 관리 사무실 공사 일정을 알리려고
② 배달된 물품을 찾아갈 것을 요청하려고
③ 잘못 찾아간 물품의 반납을 부탁하려고
④ 배달 물품의 도난 방지 조치를 설명하려고
⑤ 관리 사무실 운영 시간 변경을 공지하려고

※ 다음 영어는 우리말 뜻을, 우리말은 영어 단어를 〈보기〉에서
 찾아 쓰시오.

〈보기〉

rental	further	대표하다	unclaimed
부적절한	현재, 지금	aboard	참여하다
occasion	인기	passenger	특색

01 feature _____

02 inappropriate _____

03 represent _____

04 currently _____

05 popularity _____

06 찾아가지 않은 _____

07 대여, 임대 _____

08 탑승하여 _____

09 더 멀리에[로] _____

10 행사, 때 _____

※ 다음 우리말에 알맞은 영어 표현을 찾아 연결하시오.

11 ~을 대표[대신]하여 • • drop off

12 미리, 사전에 • • on behalf of

13 ~에 관해서 • • in regard to

14 ~을 가져다주다 • • in advance

15 참여하다 • • take part in

※ 다음 우리말 표현에 맞는 단어를 고르시오.

16 귀하의 긍정적인 답변 ➡ your (positive / negative)
 reply

17 전시를 위한 공간을 빌리다 ➡ (land / rent) a space for
 the exhibition

18 Millstown의 시장 ➡ the (mayor / major) of
 Millstown

19 이 제의를 이용하기 위해 ➡ to take (advantage /
 advancement) of this offer

20 무료입장 ➡ free (administration / admission)

※ 다음 문장의 빈칸에 알맞은 단어를 〈보기〉에서 찾아 쓰시오.

〈보기〉

relevant	national	reservation	charity
interpersonal	genuinely	exhausted	moved
explore	impress	confident	stare

21 우리 지역 사회는 당신이 지난해에 전국 선수권 대회에서
 우승한 것을 자랑스럽게 생각했다.
 ➡ Our community was proud of you for
 winning the _____ championships
 last year.

22 우리 병원은 9월 18일에 자선 음악회 개최를 계획하고 있다.
 ➡ Our hospital is planning to hold a(n)
 _____ concert on September 18th.

23 당신의 놀라운 연기는 우리 모두를 진정 감동하게 했다.
 ➡ Your amazing performance really
 _____ us all.

24 향후 6개월 이내에 출발하는 어느 유람선 여행이든 예약하세요.
 ➡ Make a(n) _____ for any cruise
 departing within the next six months.

25 그녀는 또한 놀라운 대인관계 능력을 지니고 있다.
 ➡ She also has remarkable _____ skills.

26 저희는 여러분이 새로운 변화를 매우 좋아하실 것으로
 확신합니다.
 ➡ We are _____ that you will love the
 new changes.

27 우리는 예술가들이 캐롤라인 카운티의 자연 세계를 탐색하기를
 원했습니다.
 ➡ We wanted artists to _____ the
 natural world of Caroline County.

28 이 채널과 관련이 없는 댓글도 일부 있었습니다.
 ➡ There have been some comments that are
 not _____ to this channel.

29 이 문제와 관련하여 귀하의 협조에 진심으로 감사드립니다.
 ➡ We _____ appreciate your
 cooperation in this matter.

30 우리 모두 당신이 다시 온 나라를 감동하게 할 것이라고
 믿는다.
 ➡ We all believe that you are going to
 _____ the entire nation again.

B 심경의 이해
└→ 마음의 상태

사람들 앞에서 발표를 하려니까 심장이 터질 것 같았어.

★ 유형 설명

다음 글에 드러난 David의 심경 변화로 가장 적절한 것은?

As he stepped onto the basketball court, David suddenly thought of the day he had

등장인물이나 상황에 대한 직접적·간접적인 묘사를 읽고 등장인물의 심리 상태, 묘사된 상황의 분위기를 파악해야 한다.

☞ 심경이나 분위기를 나타내는 형용사에 특히 주의를 기울인다. 글에서 묘사되는 상황이 어떤 상황인지, 등장인물이 어떤 상황에 처해 있는지를 파악한다.

🎀 유형 풀이 비법

1 글의 상황을 파악하라!
• 필자나 등장인물이 어떤 상황에 처해 있는지 정확히 이해해야 한다.

2 특정 표현들을 찾아라!
• 글에서 다뤄지는 중심 사건이나 심경을 나타내는 단어나 표현을 파악한다.

3 심경과 분위기를 파악하라!
• 글을 읽으면서 찾은 단서들을 바탕으로 심리 상태와 분위기를 파악한다.

> (Tip) 심경 변화를 묻는 문제는 글에서 상황이 바뀌는 부분을 찾는다. 주로 부사(suddenly 등)나 접속사(but, however)로 상황이 전환된다.

★ 최신 수능 경향 분석

대비 연도	월	문항 번호	지문 주제	난이도
2025	11	19번	Valentine's Day 기념 식당 예약에 실패한 Peter	✿❀❀
	9	19번	항공기 탑승 시간에 늦을 뻔한 Sophie	✿❀❀
	6	19번	과학 프로젝트 아이디어에 도움을 준 누나	✿❀❀
2024	11	19번	지각할까 봐 걱정하다 안도한 David	✿❀❀
	9	19번	Midtown 대신 Pland Zoo에 가게 됨	✿❀❀
	6	19번	안심한 Jennifer	✿❀❀
2023	11	19번	Jamie의 기운을 북돋운 Ken	✿❀❀
	9	19번	Jenny가 그린 아빠 얼굴	✿❀❀
	6	19번	일몰을 보게 된 Jessica	✿❀❀

★ 2025 수능 출제 분석

Peter의 심경 변화를 묻는 문제였다. he was absolutely sure ~ the new, five-star restaurant downtown을 통해 전반부의 심경을 직접적으로 드러냈고, 후반부에는 Unfortunately, his smile quickly disappeared를 통해 심경의 변화를 알 수 있었다.

★ 2026 수능 예측

전반부와 후반부, 두 가지 심경을 추론해야 하는 심경 변화 문제나 하나의 심경을 추론해야 하는 문제, 또는 제시된 상황의 분위기를 추론하는 문제가 출제될 수 있다.

🔑 자주 출제되는 감정 및 분위기를 나타내는 형용사

□ **content** 만족한
□ **grateful** 감사하는
□ **cheerful** 유쾌한
□ **relieved** 안도하는
□ **confident** 자신감 있는
□ **lively** 활기찬
□ **delighted** 기쁜
□ **thrilled** 흥분한
□ **mysterious** 신비한
□ **curious** 호기심에 찬
□ **startling** 놀라운
□ **monotonous** 단조로운

□ **desperate** 필사적인
□ **urgent** 긴급한
□ **horrified** 공포에 질린
□ **frightened** 두려운
□ **ashamed** 부끄러운
□ **embarrassed** 당황한
□ **irritated** 짜증이 난
□ **furious** 화가 난
□ **disappointed** 실망한
□ **anxious** 염려스러운
□ **frustrated** 좌절하는
□ **regretful** 후회하는

🍔 어휘 및 표현 Preview

□ **glance** 힐끗 보다
□ **endless** 끝없는
□ **chaotic** 혼란 상태의
□ **traffic** 교통(량)
□ **worried** 걱정하는
□ **crowd** 사람들, 군중
□ **announcement** 발표
□ **shout** 소리[고함]치다
□ **intense** 격심한
□ **desperately** 필사적으로
□ **unexpected** 예기치 않은
□ **due** 마감일이 된

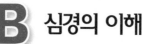

B 심경의 이해 첫 번째

1st 글의 앞부분을 통해 주인공이 처한 상황을 파악하세요.
2nd 전반부를 읽으면서 주인공의 심경을 나타내는 어구들을 찾으세요.
3rd 심경이 전환되는 부분에 주의하며 후반부의 내용을 파악하세요.

B01 ✽❀❀............ 2023 대비 6월 모평 19 (고3)

다음 글에 드러난 Jessica의 심경 변화로 가장 적절한 것은?

The island tour bus Jessica was riding on was moving slowly toward the ocean cliffs. Outside, the sky was getting dark. Jessica sighed with concern, "I'm going to miss the sunset because of the traffic." The bus arrived at the cliffs' parking lot. While the other passengers were gathering their bags, Jessica quickly got off the bus and she ran up the cliff that was famous for its ocean views. She was about to give up when she got to the top. Just then she saw the setting sun and it still shone brightly in the sky. Jessica said to herself, "The glow of the sun is so beautiful. It's even better than I expected."

① worried → delighted
② bored → confident
③ relieved → annoyed
④ joyful → indifferent
⑤ regretful → depressed

1st 글의 앞부분을 통해 주인공이 처한 상황을 파악하세요.

The island tour bus / Jessica was riding on / was
섬 관광버스는   / Jessica가 타고 있는   / 천천히
moving slowly / toward the ocean cliffs. //
움직이고 있었다   / 바다에 면한 절벽 쪽으로   //
Outside, / the sky was getting dark. //
바깥에서는 / 하늘이 점점 어두워지고 있었다   //

● **관광버스를 타고 바닷가 절벽 쪽으로 가고 있는 상황이에요.**
섬 관광버스를 탄 것으로 보아 Jessica는 섬을 여행하는 중인 것 같은데,
단서 그렇다면 신이 나거나 뭔가를 기대하는 심경일까요?
하늘이 점점 어두워지고 있었다고 하니까 해가 지거나 먹구름이
몰려와서 실망하는 것일 수도 있겠네요! 발상 좀 더 읽으면서 단서를
찾아야겠어요.

2nd 전반부를 읽으면서 주인공의 심경을 나타내는 어구들을 찾으세요.

Jessica sighed with concern, / "I'm going to miss the
Jessica는 걱정스럽게 한숨지었다   / "나는 일몰을 놓칠 거야
sunset / because of the traffic." //
/ 교통 때문에"   //

● **이제 상황을 완전히 파악할 수 있어요.**
하늘이 점점 어두워진 건 먹구름 때문이 아니라 해질녘이라서 그런
거였어요! 그리고 앞에서 관광버스가 천천히 움직였다고 했는데, 그건
차가 밀려서 그런 거였고요!

● **Jessica는 걱정스럽게 한숨을 지었어요.**
차가 밀려서 일몰을 못 보게 될까 봐 걱정스럽게 한숨지었다고
했으니까 전반부에 묘사된 Jessica의 심경은 '걱정스러운'이라는 뜻의
❶( )예요.

3rd 심경이 전환되는 부분에 주의하며 후반부의 내용을 파악하세요.

1) Jessica가 정말 일몰을 놓쳤나요?

Just then / she saw the setting sun / and it still
바로 그때   / 그녀는 지는 해를 보았는데   / 그것은 여전히
shone brightly in the sky. //
하늘에서 밝게 빛나고 있었다   //

● **절벽의 꼭대기에 도착했을 때 지는 해를 봤어요.**
Jessica는 해가 지는 광경을 놓칠까 봐 걱정했던 건데, 다행히 여전히
하늘에서 밝게 빛나고 있는 지는 해를 봤어요!
그렇다면 후반부의 Jessica의 심경은 '매우 기쁜'을 의미하는
❷( )가 적절하겠군요.

2) 심경이 좀 더 확실히 드러나는 문장도 있어요.

Jessica said to herself, / "The glow of the sun is so
Jessica는 혼잣말을 했다   / "노을이 너무 아름다워
beautiful. // It's even better / than I expected." //
// 그건 훨씬 더 좋아   / 내가 기대했던 것보다"라고 //

● **노을이 어떻다고 혼잣말을 했나요?**
노을을 보면서 Jessica는 너무 아름답다며 감탄했고, 자신이 기대했던
것보다 훨씬 더 좋다고 혼잣말을 했어요. 보고자 했던 노을을 보게
되었고, 그 광경이 기대했던 것보다 훨씬 더 좋았으니까 정답은
❸( )!

빈칸 정답 ① worried ❷ delighted ❸ delighted

B 심경의 이해 (두 번째)

1st 글의 앞부분을 통해 주인공이 처한 상황을 파악하세요.
2nd 전반부를 읽으면서 주인공의 심경을 나타내는 어구들을 찾으세요.
3rd 심경이 전환되는 부분에 주의하며 후반부의 내용을 파악하세요.

B02 ✽✻✻ .... 2025 대비 6월 모평 19 (고3)

다음 글에 드러난 Timothy의 심경 변화로 가장 적절한 것은?

Timothy sat at his desk, desperately turning the pages of his science book. His science project was due in a few days and he had no idea where to start. Finally, he closed his book, hit the table, and shouted, "This is impossible!" His sister, Amelia, drawn by the noise, came into his room. "Hey, little brother, can I help?" Timothy explained his situation and Amelia immediately had a solution. She knew that Timothy enjoyed learning about environmental issues and suggested he do a project about climate change. Timothy thought about the idea and agreed that his sister was right. "Oh, Amelia, your idea is fantastic! Thank you. You are the best sister ever!"

① frustrated → grateful
② disappointed → envious
③ hopeful → thrilled
④ encouraged → ashamed
⑤ fearful → indifferent

1st 글의 앞부분을 통해 주인공이 처한 상황을 파악하세요.

Timothy sat at his desk, / desperately turning the
Timothy는 책상에 앉아 / 필사적으로 자신의 과학책

pages of his science book. //
페이지를 넘겼다 //

His science project was due in a few days / and he
그의 과학 프로젝트 마감일이 며칠 남지 않았는데 / 그는

had no idea where to start. //
어디서부터 시작해야 할지 막막했다 //

● Timothy가 과학 프로젝트 준비를 하고 있는 상황이에요.
과학 프로젝트를 위해서 과학책 페이지를 넘기고는 있는데, 마감일이 며칠 남지 않아서 어디서부터 시작해야 할지 막막한 상황이에요. (단서) 확신할 수는 없지만 전반부에는 과학 프로젝트 때문에 '좌절하는' 심경인 것 같군요!

2nd 전반부를 읽으면서 주인공의 심경을 나타내는 어구들을 찾으세요.

Finally, he closed his book, hit the table, and
마침내 그는 책을 덮고 테이블을 치며

shouted, / "This is impossible!" //
외쳤다 / "이건 불가능해!"라고 //

● impossible은 '불가능한'이라는 뜻이에요.
"This is impossible!"이라고 했으니까 과학 프로젝트를 며칠 안에 끝내는 게 불가능하다는 의미겠죠?

● **1st** 에서 예상한 전반부의 심경이 정답이군요.
과학 프로젝트를 며칠 안에 끝내야 하는데 막막했다고 했으니까 전반부의 심경은 '좌절한'이라는 뜻의 **❶**( )예요.

3rd 심경이 전환되는 부분에 주의하며 후반부의 내용을 파악하세요.

1) 누나가 들어오기 전과 후의 심경이 달라져요.

His sister, Amelia, / drawn by the noise, / came into
그의 누나 Amelia가 / 그 소리에 이끌려 / 그의 방으로

his room. //
들어왔다 //

"Hey, little brother, can I help?" //
"이봐, 동생, 누나가 도와줄까" //

● 누나의 말 can I help에 표시했나요?
누나가 방에 들어오기 전까지는 과연 며칠 안에 과학 프로젝트를 끝낼 수 있을지 의심을 품고 좌절했어요. 그런데 누나가 '도와줄까?'라고 물으며 방으로 들어왔으니 '감사하는' 마음을 가지게 되겠죠?

2) 정답을 확실히 하기 위해 한 문장만 더 봅시다.

"Oh, Amelia, your idea is fantastic! // Thank you. //
"오, Amelia 누나, 누나의 아이디어는 정말 환상적이야 // 고마워 //

You are the best sister ever!" //
누나는 정말 최고의 누나야" //

● 누나의 말에 Timothy가 어떻게 대답했죠?
누나가 자신의 과학 프로젝트를 도와주겠다는 아이디어는 환상적이라고 하면서 누나가 최고라고 했어요. 따라서 정답은 **❷**( )!

빈칸 정답 ① ❷ grateful ❶ frustrated

B03 ~ 07 ▶ 제한시간 10분

B03 ✿❀❀ .... 2025 대비 수능 19 (고3)

다음 글에 드러난 Peter의 심경 변화로 가장 적절한 것은?

It was Valentine's Day on Friday and Peter was certain that his wife, Amy, was going to love his surprise. Peter had spent a long time searching online for an event that would be a new way to spend time with Amy. He had finally found the perfect thing for her. She often told him that she liked to go to places she had never visited before, and he was absolutely sure that she would love going to the new, five-star restaurant downtown. He smiled as he called the restaurant and asked for a reservation for Friday. Unfortunately, his smile quickly disappeared when he was told that the restaurant was fully reserved. "That's too bad," he said quietly. "I thought that I had found the right place."

① relaxed → indifferent
② confident → disappointed
③ confused → satisfied
④ jealous → discouraged
⑤ embarrassed → joyful

B04 ✿❀❀ .... 2025 대비 9월 모평 19 (고3)

다음 글에 드러난 Sophie의 심경 변화로 가장 적절한 것은?

The whole morning had been chaotic. Sophie's day began with her alarm clock failing to ring, which had thrown her into an intense rush. After terrible traffic, her taxi finally arrived at the airport, where she was met with endless security lines. Sophie kept glancing at her watch with each second feeling like an hour. Worried that she could not get to the boarding gate in time, she rushed through the crowds of people. Just then, she heard an announcement saying that her flight had been "delayed." Letting out a deep sigh, she finally felt at ease. With an unexpected hour to spare, she would have time to relax and browse the airport shops before her journey.

① calm → delighted
② pleased → indifferent
③ anxious → relieved
④ joyful → disappointed
⑤ bored → satisfied

B05 ✽❀❀ .... 2024 실시 10월 학평 19 (고3)

다음 글에 드러난 Sarah의 심경 변화로 가장 적절한 것은?

Setting out to find some wood for the campfire, Sarah moved through the forest. Just then, she noticed an approaching danger — a large, threatening bear. Panic spread through her body. Frozen and unable to shout, she watched in horror. Her heart beat louder with each step the bear took. But then, as if by a miracle, the bear paused, looked around, and, uninterested, turned away, retreating into the shadows of the woods. When the bear had disappeared completely out of her sight, her knees nearly gave way. Sarah could finally let out the breath she had been holding. A wave of immense relief washed over her.

① envious → regretful   ② frightened → relieved
③ eager → indifferent   ④ bored → satisfied
⑤ excited → furious

B06 ✽❀❀ .... 2024 실시 7월 학평 19 (고3)

다음 글에 드러난 Joshua의 심경 변화로 가장 적절한 것은?

Joshua had spent ten weeks crafting a presentation for an upcoming meeting. He had worked very hard on analyzing data, making beautiful plots and projections, and he had often stayed in the office past midnight polishing his presentation. He was delighted with the outcome and happily e-mailed the presentation to his boss, who was going to make the presentation at the all-important meeting. His boss e-mailed him back a few hours later: "Sorry, Joshua, but just yesterday we learned that the deal is off. I did look at your presentation, and it is an impressive and fine piece of work. Well done." Joshua realized that his presentation would never see the light of day. The fact that all his effort had served no ultimate purpose created a deep rift between him and his job. He'd quickly gone from feeling useful and happy in his work to feeling dissatisfied and that his efforts were in vain.

① isolated → optimistic
② curious → bored
③ anxious → thrilled
④ terrified → relieved
⑤ pleased → discouraged

B07 ✽❀❀ .... 2024 실시 5월 학평 19 (고3)

다음 글에 드러난 Charles의 심경 변화로 가장 적절한 것은?

Charles was taking a quiz in his math class. He stared at the questions, but they looked completely unfamiliar. Charles flipped through the pages of the quiz for a while. His palms grew sweaty as he realized that he didn't know a single answer. A moment later, a few other students began raising their hands. One said, "I don't think we ever learned about the stuff on this quiz, Mrs. Smith." The teacher quickly looked over a copy of the quiz and announced, "I'm sorry, class. It appears that I have given you the wrong quiz by mistake. We'll take the right quiz next class." As Charles heard what the teacher said, the tension in his shoulders began to melt away.

① nervous → relieved
② relaxed → regretful
③ amazed → annoyed
④ indifferent → satisfied
⑤ shocked → sympathetic

B08 ✿ ❀ ❀ .... 2024 실시 3월 학평 19 (고3)

다음 글에 드러난 Anna의 심경 변화로 가장 적절한 것은?

The piece of wreckage Anna held on to that served as a life preserver had a window. Now that there was light, she looked through it and down into the water. She wished she hadn't. She spied dark shapes moving beneath her. What could they be? Fish? Sharks? Anna shook with fear, her blood running cold. The last bits of strength were draining away from her arms and upper body. She did not know how much longer she could hang on, but then Anna glanced up and couldn't believe what she saw. A fishing boat was approaching over the big waves. After being in the water for 3 hours, she was finally rescued. When she got on the boat, she felt a sense of relief spread through her body.

① eager → sorrowful
② terrified → relieved
③ excited → confused
④ indifferent → irritated
⑤ confident → ashamed

B09 ✿ ❀ ❀ .... 2022 대비 6월 모평 19 (고3)

다음 글에 드러난 Natalie의 심경 변화로 가장 적절한 것은?

As Natalie was logging in to her first online counseling session, she wondered, "How can I open my heart to the counselor through a computer screen?" Since the counseling center was a long drive away, she knew that this would save her a lot of time. Natalie just wasn't sure if it would be as helpful as meeting her counselor in person. Once the session began, however, her concerns went away. She actually started thinking that it was much more convenient than expected. She felt as if the counselor were in the room with her. As the session closed, she told him with a smile, "I'll definitely see you online again!"

① doubtful → satisfied
② regretful → confused
③ confident → ashamed
④ bored → excited
⑤ thrilled → disappointed

B10 ✿ ❀ ❀ .... 2024 대비 6월 모평 19 (고3)

다음 글에 드러난 Jennifer의 심경 변화로 가장 적절한 것은?

While the mechanic worked on her car, Jennifer walked back and forth in the waiting room. She was deeply concerned about how much it was going to cost to get her car fixed. Her car's engine had started making noises and kept losing power that morning, and she had heard that replacing an engine could be very expensive. After a few minutes, the mechanic came back into the waiting room. "I've got some good news. It was just a dirty spark plug. I already wiped it clean and your car is as good as new." He handed her the bill and when she checked it, the overall cost of repairs came to less than ten dollars. That was far less than she had expected and she felt at ease, knowing she could easily afford it.

① worried → relieved
② calm → terrified
③ bored → thrilled
④ excited → scared
⑤ disappointed → indifferent

다음 글에 드러난 David의 심경 변화로 가장 적절한 것은?

As he stepped onto the basketball court, David suddenly thought of the day he had gotten injured last season and froze. He was not sure if he could play as well as before the injury. A serious wrist injury had caused him to miss the rest of the season. Remembering the surgery, he said to himself, "I thought my basketball career was completely over." However, upon hearing his fans' wild cheers, he felt his body coming alive and thought, "For sure, my fans, friends, and family are looking forward to watching me play today." As soon as the game started, he was filled with energy. The first five shots he attempted went in the basket. "I'm back! I got this," he shouted.

① disappointed → unhappy
② excited → indifferent
③ anxious → confident
④ impatient → calm
⑤ eager → ashamed

다음 글에 나타난 Evelyn의 심경 변화로 가장 적절한 것은?

It was Evelyn's first time to explore the Badlands of Alberta, famous across Canada for its numerous dinosaur fossils. As a young amateur bone-hunter, she was overflowing with anticipation. She had not travelled this far for the bones of common dinosaur species. Her life-long dream to find rare fossils of dinosaurs was about to come true. She began eagerly searching for them. After many hours of wandering throughout the deserted lands, however, she was unsuccessful. Now, the sun was beginning to set, and her goal was still far beyond her reach. Looking at the slowly darkening ground before her, she sighed to herself, "I can't believe I came all this way for nothing. What a waste of time!"

① confused → scared
② discouraged → confident
③ relaxed → annoyed
④ indifferent → depressed
⑤ hopeful → disappointed

B13 ✽✽✾.......................... 2023 실시 3월 학평 19 (고3)

다음 글에 드러난 Mark의 심경 변화로 가장 적절한 것은?

Mark was participating in freestyle swimming competitions in this Olympics. He had a firm belief that he could get a medal in the 200m. Swimming was dominated by Americans at the time, so Mark was dreaming of becoming a national hero for his country, Britain. That day, Mark was competing in his very last race — the final round of the 200m. He had done his training and was ready. One minute and fifty seconds later, it was all over. He had tried hard and, at his best, was ranked number four. He fell short of a bronze medal by 0.49 of a second. And that was the end of Mark's swimming career. He was heartbroken. He had nothing left.

① worried → hopeful

② grateful → fearful

③ pleased → jealous

④ indifferent → upset

⑤ confident → disappointed

B14 ✽✾✾.......................... 2023 실시 7월 학평 19 (고3)

다음 글에 드러난 Susan의 심경 변화로 가장 적절한 것은?

Susan's daughter Carrie is a special needs kid. She goes to a special school, special camp, special therapists. One day, out of the blue, she asked Susan if she could go get a slice of pizza on her own, not far from their apartment. Anxious, Susan said, "Well... why not get the pizza and bring it home to eat?" "No!" said Carrie, sixteen at the time. "Other people eat at the pizza place, and I want to, too!" Susan was concerned, but said okay, and Carrie went off by herself a block or two away. After a while, Carrie came back, grinning. "You made it! What made you want to do this?" Susan asked. Carrie had seen her friend Izzy on TV talking about his subway ride. "I thought if he could do it, I could do it too." Susan's heart swelled, realizing her daughter was braver and much more grown-up than she thought.

① indifferent → thrilled

② worried → proud

③ hopeful → regretful

④ ashamed → satisfied

⑤ surprised → disappointed

B15 ✱❀❀ — 2021 대비 6월 모평 19 (고3)

다음 글에 드러난 Sharon의 심경 변화로 가장 적절한 것은?

Sharon received a ticket to an upcoming tango concert from her friend. While surfing the Internet, she came across a review for the concert. The reviewer was harsh, calling it "an awful performance." That raised in Sharon's mind the question of whether it was worthwhile to go, but in the end, she reluctantly decided to attend the concert. The hall located in the old town was ancient and run-down. Looking around, Sharon again wondered what kind of show she could expect. But as soon as the tango started, everything changed. The piano, guitar, flute, and violin magically flew out in harmony. The audience cheered. "Oh my goodness! What fantastic music!" Sharon shouted. The rhythm and tempo were so energetic and sensational that they shook her body and soul. The concert was far beyond her expectations.

① excited → bored
② doubtful → amazed
③ calm → upset
④ ashamed → grateful
⑤ envious → indifferent

B16 ✱❀❀ — 2024 대비 수능 19 (고3)

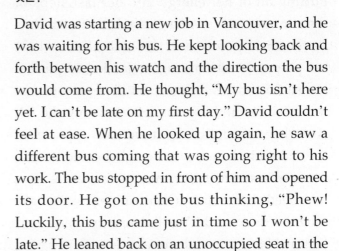

다음 글에 드러난 'David'의 심경 변화로 가장 적절한 것은?

David was starting a new job in Vancouver, and he was waiting for his bus. He kept looking back and forth between his watch and the direction the bus would come from. He thought, "My bus isn't here yet. I can't be late on my first day." David couldn't feel at ease. When he looked up again, he saw a different bus coming that was going right to his work. The bus stopped in front of him and opened its door. He got on the bus thinking, "Phew! Luckily, this bus came just in time so I won't be late." He leaned back on an unoccupied seat in the bus and took a deep breath, finally able to relax.

① nervous → relieved
② lonely → hopeful
③ pleased → confused
④ indifferent → delighted
⑤ bored → thrilled

❖ 정답 및 해설 20 ~ 23p

B17 ✽❀❀ .... 2023 대비 수능 19 (고3)

다음 글에 드러난 Jamie의 심경 변화로 가장 적절한 것은?

Putting all of her energy into her last steps of the running race, Jamie crossed the finish line. To her disappointment, she had failed to beat her personal best time, again. Jamie had pushed herself for months to finally break her record, but it was all for nothing. Recognizing how she felt about her failure, Ken, her teammate, approached her and said, "Jamie, even though you didn't set a personal best time today, your performances have improved dramatically. Your running skills have progressed so much! You'll definitely break your personal best time in the next race!" After hearing his comments, she felt confident about herself. Jamie, now motivated to keep pushing for her goal, replied with a smile. "You're right! Next race, I'll beat my best time for sure!"

① indifferent → regretful
② pleased → bored
③ frustrated → encouraged
④ nervous → fearful
⑤ calm → excited

B18 ✽❀❀ .... 2023 실시 10월 학평 19 (고3)

다음 글에 드러난 'I'의 심경 변화로 가장 적절한 것은?

I hurried to the bus terminal to return home for Christmas. As soon as I arrived at the terminal, I saw my bus pulling away. I called out and ran after the bus, but it was too late. I felt a wave of disappointment wash over me as I realized that I would have to wait three hours for the next bus. I must have been visibly upset because a woman came over, took my arm, and led me to the street. She called a taxi and gave the driver a five-dollar bill. She told him to take me to the ferry terminal, because the bus made a stop there before heading out onto the highway. She also wished me a Merry Christmas, and all I could do was smile. I couldn't believe what she had done for me, a complete stranger!

① frustrated → touched
② jealous → proud
③ thrilled → doubtful
④ calm → regretful
⑤ indifferent → sympathetic

B19 ✽❀❀ .... 2023 대비 9월 모평 19 (고3)

다음 글에 드러난 Nathan의 심경 변화로 가장 적절한 것은?

"Daddy!" Jenny called, waving a yellow crayon in her little hand. Nathan approached her, wondering why she was calling him. Jenny, his three-year-old toddler, was drawing a big circle on a piece of paper. "What are you doing, Sweetie?" Nathan asked with interest. She just kept drawing without reply. He continued watching her, wondering what she was working on. She was drawing something that looked like a face. When she finished it, Jenny shouted, "Look, Daddy!" She held her artwork up proudly. Taking a closer look, Nathan recognized that it was his face. The face had two big eyes and a beard just like his. He loved Jenny's work. Filled with joy and happiness, Nathan gave her a big hug.

*toddler: 아장아장 걷는 아이

① sorrowful → relieved
② frustrated → satisfied
③ worried → scared
④ curious → delighted
⑤ hopeful → disappointed

B20 ✱✱❋ .... 2021 대비 수능 19 (고3)

다음 글에 드러난 'I'의 심경 변화로 가장 적절한 것은?

Once again, I had lost the piano contest to my friend. When I learned that Linda had won, I was deeply troubled and unhappy. My body was shaking with uneasiness. My heart beat quickly and my face became reddish. I had to run out of the concert hall to settle down. Sitting on the stairs alone, I recalled what my teacher had said. "Life is about winning, not necessarily about winning against others but winning at being you. And the way to win is to figure out who you are and do your best." He was absolutely right. I had no reason to oppose my friend. Instead, I should focus on myself and my own improvement. I breathed out slowly. My hands were steady now. At last, my mind was at peace.

① grateful → sorrowful
② upset → calm
③ envious → doubtful
④ surprised → disappointed
⑤ bored → relieved

B21 ✱❋❋ .... 2024 대비 9월 모평 19 (고3)

다음 글에 드러난 Nancy의 심경 변화로 가장 적절한 것은?

The day trip to Midtown scheduled for today was canceled because the road leading there was blocked by heavy snow. "Luck just didn't run my way. Sightseeing in Midtown was why I signed up for this trip ..." Nancy said to herself, with a long sigh. She was thinking of all the interesting sights she wouldn't be able to enjoy. All of a sudden, there was a knock at the door. "News! We are going to the Pland Zoo near the hotel. We will meet in the lobby soon." It was the voice of her tour guide. She sprung off the couch and started putting on her coat in a hurry. "The Pland Zoo! That's on my bucket list! What a turn of fortune!" shouted Nancy.

① disappointed → excited
② relieved → anxious
③ surprised → annoyed
④ ashamed → grateful
⑤ indifferent → amazed

B22 ✱✱❋ .... 2021 대비 9월 모평 19 (고3)

다음 글에 드러난 Annette의 심경 변화로 가장 적절한 것은?

The day of the Five Mile Fun Walk had arrived. Annette had been waiting for Reiner at the registration point for over an hour. There was still no sign of him. She started thinking that something bad might have happened to him. Getting concerned, she tried calling Reiner's phone again, but there was no response. At that moment, she heard a voice calling her name. She found Reiner coming toward her. "Thank goodness! What happened?" she asked. He explained that the traffic had been terrible. What was worse, he had left his phone at home. "I'm so sorry," he said. She started to relax. "I'm fine now. As long as you're here and safe. Why don't we go and register?" They headed into the event together.

① worried → relieved   ② confident → nervous
③ calm → upset   ④ regretful → grateful
⑤ bored → amazed

❖ 정답 및 해설 23 ~ 27p

B 어휘 Review

※ 다음 영어는 우리말 뜻을, 우리말은 영어 단어를 〈보기〉에서 찾아 쓰시오.

〈보기〉

턱수염	passenger	황폐한	typical
장악하다	disappointment	격심한	doubtful
traffic	무관심한	calm	천성

01 beard   _____

02 run-down   _____

03 intense   _____

04 indifferent   _____

05 dominate   _____

06 승객   _____

07 실망감   _____

08 의심스러운   _____

09 차분한   _____

10 차량들, 교통(량)   _____

※ 다음 우리말에 알맞은 영어 표현을 찾아 연결하시오.

11 ~이 부족하다 •   • in time

12 시간 맞춰[늦지 않게] •   • at ease

13 ~하기로 되어 있다 •   • fall short of

14 직접 •   • be supposed to-v

15 걱정없이, 편안한 •   • in person

※ 다음 우리말 표현에 맞는 단어를 고르시오.

16 전체 수리 비용 ➡ the (overactive / overall) cost of repairs

17 확고한 믿음을 가지다 ➡ have a (firm / fair) belief

18 즉시 해결책을 내놓다 ➡ (immediately / reluctantly) had a solution

19 완전히 모르는 사람 ➡ a (consistent / complete) stranger

20 엔진 교체 ➡ (replacing / reimbursing) an engine

※ 다음 문장의 빈칸에 알맞은 단어를 〈보기〉에서 찾아 쓰시오.

〈보기〉

glow	sighed	headed	violation
toddler	attempted	arrived	reluctantly
grown-up	upcoming	interrupt	scheduled

21 오늘 예정된 Midtown으로 가는 당일치기 여행은 취소되었다.
➡ The day trip to Midtown _____ for today was canceled.

22 5마일 걷기 대회의 날이 도래했다.
➡ The day of the Five Mile Fun Walk had _____.

23 결국 그녀는 마지못해 콘서트에 참석하기로 마음먹었다.
➡ In the end, she _____ decided to attend the concert.

24 그녀의 딸은 그녀가 생각했던 것보다 더 용감하고 훨씬 더 성장했다.
➡ Her daughter was braver and much more _____ than she thought.

25 그의 걸음마를 하는 세 살배기 Jenny는 종이 한 장에 큰 원을 그리고 있었다.
➡ Jenny, his three-year-old _____, was drawing a big circle on a piece of paper.

26 Jessica는 걱정스럽게 한숨을 쉬었다.
➡ Jessica _____ with concern.

27 노을이 너무 아름답다. 그건 내가 기대했던 것보다 훨씬 더 좋다.
➡ The _____ of the sun is so beautiful. It's even better than I expected.

28 그가 시도한 첫 다섯 차례의 슛이 바스켓으로 들어갔다.
➡ The first five shots he _____ went in the basket.

29 그들은 함께 그 행사로 향했다.
➡ They _____ into the event together.

30 Sharon은 자신의 친구로부터 다가오는 탱고 콘서트 표를 받았다.
➡ Sharon received a ticket to a(n) _____ tango concert from her friend.

C 주장 찾기

★ 유형 설명

다음 글에서 필자가 주장하는 바로 가장 적절한 것은?

Learning a certain concept such as "molecules" requires more than just a single

어떤 논점에 대해 필자(글쓴이)가 갖는 주장(의견)이 무엇인지 파악해야 한다.

🔑 '~해야 한다.'라고 끝맺는 우리말 선택지가 등장하는 경우가 많다. 필자의 어조가 명확하게 드러나는 문장, 즉 명령문이나 must, have to, should 등의 조동사, important, necessary, in my opinion 등의 표현이 포함된 문장에 주의를 기울인다.

∞ 유형 풀이 비법

1 반복되는 부분에 주목하라!
• 반복되는 부분을 중심으로 필자가 전달하고자 하는 내용을 파악한다.

2 처음과 끝을 확인하라!
• 주로 글의 첫 부분과 끝부분에 필자의 주장이 나타난다는 점을 기억한다.

3 반전이 있는지 잘 보자!
• 글의 중간이나 마지막에 필자가 태도를 바꾸는 곳이 있는지 꼭 확인한다.

> Tip 보통 명령문이나 의무의 조동사가 포함된 문장에 필자의 주장을 드러내는 경우가 많다.

★ 최신 수능 경향 분석

대비 연도	월	문항 번호	지문 주제	난이도
2025	11	20번	학습 효과 증진에 도움이 되는 게임 개발의 필요성	★★★
	9	20번	소셜 미디어 사용자의 정보의 정확성과 신뢰성 확보	★☆☆
	6	20번	인간의 오류 극복 능력을 활용하여 AI를 감독할 수 있다.	★★☆
2024	11	20번	조직의 문화 형성을 위해 필요한 플레이 북	★★☆
	9	20번	자신감을 키우는 방법	★☆☆
	6	20번	창의성의 영역 간 활용	★★☆
2023	11	20번	성공 가능성에 대한 확률적 분석	★★☆
	9	20번	타 문화의 이면을 보는 것의 중요성	★★★
	6	20번	정신적 추진력의 중요성	★★☆

★ 2025 수능 출제 분석
교육자들이 게임의 가치를 인정하고 오히려 학습에 활용할 수 있는 게임을 개발하는 것이 바람직하다는 내용의 글이다. 중심 내용을 파악했더라도, 모든 선택지에 '게임'과 '학습'이라는 단어가 들어가 있어 쉽게 정답을 고르기 힘든 문제였다.

★ 2026 수능 예측
비유적 표현이 의미하는 바를 파악하며 전략적으로 읽어야 한다.

👤 주장을 명확하게 드러내는 표현

☐ **You must ~** 당신은 ~해야 한다
☐ **You should ~** 당신은 ~해야 한다
☐ **You have to-v** 당신은 ~해야 한다
☐ **You ought to-v** 당신은 ~해야 한다
☐ **You need to-v** 당신은 ~할 필요가 있다
☐ **You can ~** 당신은 ~할 수 있다
☐ **Don't** + 동사원형 ~을 하지 마라
☐ **Never** + 동사원형 절대 ~을 하지 마라
☐ **Avoid -ing** ~하는 것을 피하라
☐ **Start from -ing** ~하는 것으로부터 시작하라
☐ **Keep in mind that** ~한다는 것을 명심하라
☐ **No one can ~** 아무도 ~할 수 없다

☐ **It is crucial to-v** ~하는 것은 중요하다
☐ **It is important to-v** ~하는 것은 중요하다
☐ **It is vital to-v** ~하는 것은 필수적이다
☐ **It is essential to-v** ~하는 것은 필수적이다
☐ **It is necessary to-v** ~하는 것은 필수적이다

🍰 어휘 및 표현 Preview

☐ **essential** 필수적인
☐ **influence** 영향력
☐ **document** 입증하다
☐ **knowledge** 지식
☐ **development** 발전
☐ **serve as** ~의 역할을 하다
☐ **foundation** 토대
☐ **imagine** 상상하다
☐ **anticipation** 기대
☐ **decline** 감소
☐ **threat** 위협
☐ **primary** 주된

C 주장 찾기 첫 번째

1st 선택지를 통해 '무엇'에 관한 주장인지 글의 소재를 예측해 보세요.

2nd 명령문이나 should, must, have to, important 등의 표현이 쓰인 문장이 있는지 확인하세요.

3rd 필자의 주장을 드러내는 문장과 같은 의미를 지닌 선택지를 찾으세요.

C01 ✿❀❀ .... 2025 대비 6월 모평 20 (고3)

다음 글에서 필자가 주장하는 바로 가장 적절한 것은?

As the world seems to be increasingly affected by the ever-expanding influence of machines in general and artificial intelligence (AI) specifically, many begin to imagine, with either fear or anticipation, a future with a diminished role for human decision making. Whether it be due to the growing presence of AI assistants or the emergence of self-driving cars, the necessity of the role of humans as the decision makers would appear to be in decline. After all, our capacity for making mistakes is well documented. However, perhaps the saving grace of human determination is to be found here as well. Little evidence exists that suggests modern AI's infallibility or predicts it in the future. It is crucial that, in light of humanity's acceptance of our own fallibility, we utilize our capacity to overcome such failures to position ourselves as the overseers of AI's own growth and applications for the foreseeable future.

① 인간은 AI의 발전 가능성과 불안정성을 동시에 고려해야 한다.

② 인간은 창의력을 향상시키기 위해 AI에 의존하지 말아야 한다.

③ 실수를 보완하기 위해 인간은 AI의 활용 방안을 모색해야 한다.

④ AI에 대한 학습을 통해 인간은 미래 사회 변화에 대비해야 한다.

⑤ AI의 영향력 확산에 대비하여 인간은 오류 극복 능력을 활용해야 한다.

1st 선택지를 통해 '무엇'에 관한 주장인지 글의 소재를 예측해 보세요.

① 인간은 AI의 발전 가능성과 불안정성을 동시에 고려해야 한다.

② 인간은 창의력을 향상시키기 위해 AI에 의존하지 말아야 한다.

③ 실수를 보완하기 위해 인간은 AI의 활용 방안을 모색해야 한다.

④ AI에 대한 학습을 통해 인간은 미래 사회 변화에 대비해야 한다.

⑤ AI의 영향력 확산에 대비하여 인간은 오류 극복 능력을 활용해야 한다.

● **반복되어 등장하는 어구를 찾았나요?**

다섯 개 선택지 모두가 **❶**( )은, AI가 들어가 있는 내용이에요.

글을 읽지 않고 선택지만으로도 이 글이 인간과 AI와 관련된 내용이라는 것을 알 수 있죠. 단서

이렇게 글의 소재에 대해 어느 정도 예상을 한 후에 글을 읽기 시작하면 훨씬 수월하게 글의 핵심을 파악할 수 있어요. 그래서 선택지를 먼저 확인하는 게 중요하죠.

● **각 선택지를 보면서 글의 내용을 예상해 보세요.**

①이 정답이라면 인간이 AI의 발전 가능성과 불안전성을 함께 고려해야 한다는 내용일 거예요.

②은 창의력을 향상시키기 위해 주의해야 한다는 내용이 제시될 것이고,

③은 AI를 활용해서 실수를 보완하기 위한 방안을 찾아야 한다고 하겠죠.

④은 미래의 변화에 대비해서 AI에 대해 학습해야 한다는 내용일 것이고,

⑤은 오류 극복 능력을 활용해서 AI의 영향력 확산에 대비하라는 내용일 거예요.

과연 글이 어떤 내용일지 차근차근 확인해 봅시다.

2nd 명령문이나 should, must, have to, important 등의 표현이 쓰인 문장이 있는지 확인하세요.

It is crucial that, / in light of humanity's acceptance
매우 중요하다 / 인류가 스스로 오류성을 인정한다는

of our own fallibility, / we utilize our capacity to
점으로 미루어 볼 때 / 우리가 이러한 실패를 극복할 수

overcome such failures / to position ourselves / as
있는 능력을 활용하여 / 자리 잡는 것이 /

the overseers of AI's own growth and applications /
AI 자체의 성장과 적용의 감독관으로서 /

for the foreseeable future. //
가까운 미래에 //

● **crucial이 들어간 문장이 보이네요.**

crucial은 **❷**( )'이라는 뜻의 형용사예요. 인간이 오류를 인정하고 실패를 극복할 수 있는 능력을 활용해서 AI를 감독하는 역할을 할 수 있다고 하는 이 문장이 이 글의 주장을 나타내는 핵심 문장이라고 할 수 있어요.

- **이 문장에서 선택지와 겹치는 단어들이 있어요!**

  여기서 '인류'와 '오류성', 'AI'라는 단어들에 주목해 볼까요? 이 단어들이 모두 포함된 선택지가 하나 있는데, 바로 ❸(　　　　　)이에요. 하지만 다른 선택지들에도 '인간'이나 'AI' 같은 키워드가 있으니 나머지 부분을 더 살펴보면서 확실한 근거를 찾아봅시다.

3rd 필자의 주장을 드러내는 문장과 같은 의미를 지닌 선택지를 찾으세요.

1) 필자의 주장을 뒷받침하는 문장을 찾아봅시다.

As the world seems to be increasingly affected / by
전 세계가 점점 더 영향을 받는 듯 보이면서　　　　　　　　/

the ever-expanding influence of machines in
전반적으로 기계의 계속 확대되는 영향력에 의해

general / and artificial intelligence (AI) specifically,
　　　　/ 구체적으로 말하면 인공지능(AI)

/ many begin to imagine, with either fear or
/ 많은 사람은 두려움 속에 또는 기대를 품고 상상하기 시작한다

anticipation, / a future with a diminished role for
　　　　　　/ 인간의 의사 결정 역할이 줄어드는 미래를 //

human decision making. //

- **영향력이 커지고 있는 AI가 언급되었어요.**

  선택지를 구성하는 두 가지 주요 소재인 '인간'과 'AI'가 첫 문장부터 나타났네요. 세계가 전반적으로 AI의 영향을 점점 더 받고 있고, 인간은 의사 결정 역할이 줄어드는 미래를 생각하면서 두려움이나 기대를 품고 있다고 했어요.

However, perhaps the saving grace of human
하지만, 아마도 인간 결단력의

determination / is to be found here as well. //
장점은　　　　　/ 또한 여기에서 발견될 것이다　　//

- **반대 내용을 연결하는 However가 나왔네요!**

  앞 문장에서 말한 것처럼 AI의 영향력이 확대되고 있지만, 인간 결단력의 장점도 발견될 것이라고 했어요. 앞에서 살펴봤던 문장이 생각나지 않나요?

  crucial이 포함된 문장에서 나온 내용, 인간의 능력을 활용해 AI를 ❹(　　　　　) 수 있다는 것과 연결되고 있죠.

2) 필자의 주장이 직접적으로 드러나는 문장을 자세히 살펴봅시다.

It is crucial that, / in light of humanity's acceptance
매우 중요하다　　　/ 인류가 스스로 오류성을 인정한다는

of our own fallibility, / we utilize our capacity to
점으로 미루어 볼 때　　/ 우리가 이러한 실패를 극복할 수

overcome such failures / to position ourselves / as
있는 능력을 활용하여　　/ 자리 잡는 것이　　/

the overseers of AI's own growth and applications /
AI 자체의 성장과 적용의 감독관으로서　　　　　/

for the foreseeable future. //
가까운 미래에　　　//

- **crucial이 들어간 문장을 다시 살펴봅시다.**

  인간은 오류를 범하면서도 극복하는 능력이 있으므로, 이 능력을 통해서 AI를 감독하는 역할을 해야 한다는 내용이에요.

  AI의 영향력이 점차 확대되고 미래에 인간의 의사 결정 능력이 감소하겠지만, 인간의 이런 능력으로 충분히 극복할 수 있다는 것이죠!

선택지로 글의 소재를 예측해 보자!

❖ 정답 및 해설 27 ~ 28p

C 주장 찾기 （두 번째）

1st 선택지를 통해 '무엇'에 관한 주장인지, 글의 소재를 예측해 보세요.
2nd 명령문이나 should, must, have to, important 등의 표현이 쓰인 문장이 있는지 확인하세요.
3rd 필자의 주장을 드러내는 문장과 같은 의미를 지닌 선택지를 찾으세요.

C02 ★★❀................ 2024 대비 6월 모평 20 (고3)

다음 글에서 필자가 주장하는 바로 가장 적절한 것은?

Certain hindrances to multifaceted creative activity may lie in premature specialization, i.e., having to choose the direction of education or to focus on developing one ability too early in life. However, development of creative ability in one domain may enhance effectiveness in other domains that require similar skills, and flexible switching between generality and specificity is helpful to productivity in many domains. Excessive specificity may result in information from outside the domain being underestimated and unavailable, which leads to fixedness of thinking, whereas excessive generality causes chaos, vagueness, and shallowness. Both tendencies pose a threat to the transfer of knowledge and skills between domains. What should therefore be optimal for the development of cross-domain creativity is support for young people in taking up creative challenges in a specific domain and coupling it with encouragement to apply knowledge and skills in, as well as from, other domains, disciplines, and tasks.

① 창의성을 개발하기 위해서는 도전과 실패를 두려워하지 말아야 한다.
② 전문 지식과 기술을 전수하려면 집중적인 투자가 선행되어야 한다.
③ 창의적인 인재를 육성하기 위해 다양한 교육과정을 준비해야 한다.
④ 특정 영역에서 개발된 창의성이 영역 간 활용되도록 장려해야 한다.
⑤ 조기 교육을 통해 특정 분야의 전문가를 지속적으로 양성해야 한다.

1st 선택지를 통해 '무엇'에 관한 주장인지, 글의 소재를 예측해 보세요.

① 창의성을 개발하기 위해서는 도전과 실패를 두려워하지 말아야 한다.
② 전문 지식과 기술을 전수하려면 집중적인 투자가 선행되어야 한다.
③ 창의적인 인재를 육성하기 위해 다양한 교육과정을 준비해야 한다.
④ 특정 영역에서 개발된 창의성이 영역 간 활용되도록 장려해야 한다.
⑤ 조기 교육을 통해 특정 분야의 전문가를 지속적으로 양성해야 한다.

● 선택지에서 반복되고 있는 어구를 찾았나요?
다섯 개의 선택지가 '창의'와 '전문'이라는 두 가지 소재로 나뉘네요. 단서 창의성과 전문화에 관한 내용이 이어질 것으로 보여지는데, 발상 글의 나머지 부분을 통해 필자의 주장이 무엇인지 확인해 봅시다.

2nd 명령문이나 should, must, have to, important 등의 표현이 쓰인 문장이 있는지 확인하세요.

What should therefore be optimal / for the
그러므로 응당 최선인 것은   /
development of cross-domain creativity /
영역 간 창의성 개발을 위해   /

● should가 쓰인 문장이 보이네요.
should는 의무, 당위의 의미를 더하는 조동사예요. 영역 간 창의성 개발을 위해 최선인 것이 무엇인지 설명하고 있는 이 문장이 이 글의 주장을 나타내는 핵심 문장이라고 할 수 있어요.

● 이 문장에서 선택지와 겹치는 단어들이 있어요!
여기서 '영역 간'과 '창의성'이라는 두 가지 단어에 주목해 볼까요? 이 두 가지가 동시에 포함된 선택지가 하나 있는데, 바로 ❶( )이에요. ⑤에도 마찬가지로 '특정 분야'라는 키워드가 있으니 글의 나머지 부분을 더 살펴보면서 확실한 근거를 찾아봅시다.

3rd 필자의 주장을 드러내는 문장과 같은 의미를 지닌 선택지를 찾으세요.

1) 필자의 주장을 뒷받침하는 문장을 찾아봅시다.

Certain hindrances / to multifaceted creative
어떤 방해 요인은   / 다면적인 창의적 활동에 대한
activity / may lie / in premature specialization, /
    / 있을 수 있다 / 너무 이른 전문화에   /

● **창의적 활동과 전문화의 관계가 제시되었어요.**

선택지를 구성하는 두 가지 주요 소재인 창의와 전문이 첫 문장부터 나타났네요. ❷( )가 너무 이르면 다면적 창의적 활동에 방해가 된다고 했어요. 창의성에 있어서 전문화를 부정적인 어조로 표현하고 있으므로 '전문'이 포함된 ②, ⑤은 정답과 거리가 멀다는 것을 알 수 있어요.

> However, / development of creative ability /
> 그러나　　 / 창의적 능력 개발은　　　/
> in one domain / may enhance effectiveness /
> 한 영역에서의 / 효과를 높일 수 있다　　　 /
> in other domains /
> 다른 영역에서　 /

● **한 영역에서의 창의적 능력 개발이 어떤 결과를 낳는지 설명하고 있어요.**

한 영역에서의 창의적 능력 개발이 다른 영역에서 효과를 높인다고 했어요. 한 영역이 다른 영역에 영향을 끼치는 것인데 뭔가 익숙한 키워드가 생각나지 않나요? 맞아요, should가 포함된 문장에서 '영역 간 창의성 개발'이 언급되었고 '영역 간'이라는 키워드가 이 부분과 연결되죠.

2) 필자의 주장이 직접적으로 드러나는 문장을 자세히 살펴봅시다.

> ... is support for young people / in taking up
> … 젊은이들을 지원하는 것이다　　　　　　　 /
> creative challenges / in a specific domain / and
> 창의적인 도전을 하기 시작할 때 / 특정한 영역에서 /
> coupling it with encouragement / to apply
> 그것을 장려하는 것과 결합하는 것이다　　 /
> knowledge and skills / in, as well as from, other
> 지식과 기술을 적용하도록　 / 다른 영역, 분야, 과업으로부터 나온
> domains, disciplines, and tasks. //
> 것뿐만 아니라, 다른 영역, 분야, 과업에　 //

● **should가 포함된 문장의 뒷부분을 마저 살펴봅시다.**

이제 영역 간 창의성 개발을 위해 무엇이 필요한지 파악해야겠죠? 특정 영역에서 창의적인 도전을 하기 시작할 때 젊은이들을 ❸( )해야 한다고 하며, 그것을 다른 영역과 관련된 지식과 기술을 적용하도록 ❹( )하는 것과 결합해야 한다고 했어요.
즉, 특정 영역의 창의성 개발이 다른 영역에도 적용되도록 지원하고 장려하는 것이라고 요약할 수 있어요.
이를 가장 잘 나타내는 선택지는 ❶( )이에요.

#명사절 주어 #주격 보어

★ 앞에서 살펴봤던 마지막 문장!

> What should therefore be optimal / for the
> 그러므로 응당 최선인 것은　　　　/ 영역 간
> development of cross-domain creativity / is
> 창의성 개발을 위해　　　　　　　　　　/
> support for young people / in taking up creative
> 젊은이들을 지원하고　　　　/ 창의적인 도전을 하기 시작할 때
> challenges / in a specific domain / and coupling
> / 특정한 영역에서　　 / 그것을 장려하는 것과
> it with encouragement / to apply knowledge
> 결합하는 것이다　　　　 / 지식과 기술을 적용하도록
> and skills / in, as well as from, other domains,
> / 다른 영역, 분야, 과업으로부터 나온 지식과 기술을
> disciplines, and tasks. //
> 적용할 뿐만 아니라, 다른 영역, 분야, 과업에 //

1 명사절 주어는 단수 취급해요.

What should therefore be optimal은 명사절 주어이고, 명사절 주어는 단수 취급하므로 동사도 단수형인 is가 왔어요.

2 주격 보어는 두 개가 있어요.

주격 보어는 support와 coupling이에요. support는 앞에 to가 생략된 to부정사이고, coupling은 동명사예요.

주장을 나타내는 should, must, have, to와 같은 주요 표현을 익혀두자!

C03 ~ 06 ▶ 제한시간 8분

C03 ★★❀ .... 2025 대비 수능 20 (고3)

다음 글에서 필자가 주장하는 바로 가장 적절한 것은?

We almost universally accept that playing video games is at best a pleasant break from a student's learning and more often what prevents a student from accomplishing their goals. Games catch and hold attention in a way that few things can. And yet once they have our focus, they rarely seem to offer anything meaningful to help students grow in their lives outside the games. While this may be true for many games, we are too easily ignoring a valuable tool that could be used to enhance productivity instead of derailing it. Rather, it is desirable that we develop games that connect to the learning outcomes we want for our students. This will enable educators to take advantage of games' attention commanding capacities and allow our students to enjoy their games while learning.

① 학습 효과 증진에 활용될 수 있는 게임을 개발해야 한다.
② 교육 현장에서 학습과 게임 활동을 적절하게 분배해야 한다.
③ 학습 활동에 게임이 초래하는 집중력 저하를 경계해야 한다.
④ 여가 시간에 게임을 활용함으로써 학습 효율을 향상해야 한다.
⑤ 게임의 부정적 영향을 줄이기 위해 학습 공동체가 노력해야 한다.

C04 ★❀❀ .... 2025 대비 9월 모평 20 (고3)

다음 글에서 필자가 주장하는 바로 가장 적절한 것은?

Truth is essential for progress and the development of knowledge, as it serves as the foundation upon which reliable and accurate understanding is built. However, one of the greatest threats to the accumulation of knowledge can now be found on social media platforms. As social media becomes a primary source of information for millions, its unregulated nature allows misinformation to spread rapidly. Social media users may unknowingly participate in creating and circulating misinformation, which can influence elections, cause violence, and create widespread panic, as seen in various global incidents. As creators and consumers, it is our responsibility to take on a greater role in the enhancement of fact-checking protocols in order to ensure accuracy. It is critical that participants safeguard the reliability of information, supporting a more informed and rational public community.

① 소셜 미디어 플랫폼을 운영할 때 사용자의 의견을 반영해야 한다.
② 디지털 창작물의 저작권 보호에 관한 사회적 합의를 도출해야 한다.
③ 소셜 미디어 사용자는 정보의 정확성과 신뢰성 확보를 위해 힘써야 한다.
④ 광범위한 지식을 축적하기 위해 다양한 정보의 유통을 촉진해야 한다.
⑤ 소셜 미디어 기업은 개인 정보 보호를 위한 대책을 세워야 한다.

C05 ✿✿✿ .... 2024 실시 10월 학평 20 (고3)

다음 글에서 필자가 주장하는 바로 가장 적절한 것은?

There are few universals in this world, but among them are our love for our children and our love of music. When we hold a baby in our arms, comforting her with song, we are channelling the emotional power of music. We do so instinctively, just as our ancestors did. Music can be a powerful parental ally during the challenging child-rearing years. To successfully prepare our children for life in the twenty-first century, we will need to nurture qualities such as curiosity, imagination, empathy, creative entrepreneurship, and most of all resilience. Musical practice in early childhood develops all of the above and more. Research has shown that musical practice in early childhood is beneficial not only for mental acuity but for social and emotional development as well. Music is not just a hobby, a pleasant pastime; it is an integral part of what makes us happy, healthy, and whole. Indeed, if we want to do one thing to help our children develop into emotionally, socially, intellectually, and creatively competent human beings, we should start the musical conversation — the earlier the better.

*resilience: 회복력 **acuity: 예리함

① 아이의 전인적 성장을 위해 어릴 때부터 음악을 접하게 해줘야 한다.
② 음악이 단순한 취미 이상이 되려면 악기를 꾸준히 연습해야 한다.
③ 질 높은 음악 교육을 위해 이론과 실습을 병행해야 한다.
④ 음악을 아이 양육에 활용하려면 음악적 전문성이 있어야 한다.
⑤ 어린 연주자들에게도 재능을 발휘할 수 있는 기회가 주어져야 한다.

C06 ✿✿✿ .... 2024 실시 7월 학평 20 (고3)

다음 글에서 필자가 주장하는 바로 가장 적절한 것은?

Walk into a bookstore and you'll see some authors have a whole shelf. Authors with just one book are hard to find and it's the same for digital shelf-space. Look at the most loved and top-selling authors and they all have a lot of books. One book is not enough to build a career as a fiction author if that is a goal of yours. So, don't obsess over that one book, consider it just the beginning, and get writing on the next one. Of course, first-time authors don't want to hear this! I certainly didn't when I put my first book out. I've tried every single marketing tool possible and I still continue to experiment with new forms. But after 27 books, writing more books is what I personally keep coming back to as the best marketing tool and the best way to increase my income as a writer. Because every time a new book comes out, more readers discover the backlist. You also have another chance to 'break out'.

① 작가로 성공하려면 계속해서 출간해야 한다.
② 좋은 글을 쓰려면 먼저 글을 많이 읽어야 한다.
③ 자신의 경험을 글쓰기 소재로 적극 활용해야 한다.
④ 책을 홍보하기 위해 다양한 마케팅 수단을 마련해야 한다.
⑤ 작가별 전시에서 벗어나 새로운 도서 전시 방식을 시도해야 한다.

C07 ★★❀ .... 2024 실시 5월 학평 20 (고3)

다음 글에서 필자가 주장하는 바로 가장 적절한 것은?

When you are middle-aged, the risk of connective tissue injuries peaks as decreased load tolerance combines with continued high activity levels. The path of least resistance is to stop doing the things that hurt — avoid uncomfortable movements and find easier forms of exercise. However, that's the exact opposite of what you should do. There is a path forward. But it doesn't involve following the typical pain management advice of rest, ice, and medicine, which multiple reviews have shown is not effective for treating age-related joint pain and dysfunction. These methods do nothing more than treat superficial symptoms. The only practical solution is to strengthen your body with muscle training. Whether you've been training for a few years or a few decades, or haven't ever stepped foot in the weight room, it's not too late to restore your body, build real strength, and achieve your physical potential.

① 관절의 노화를 늦추기 위해 적절한 체중을 유지해야 한다.
② 근육을 강화하기 위해 다양한 강도의 운동을 병행해야 한다.
③ 중년층은 근 손실 예방을 위해 식단을 철저히 관리해야 한다.
④ 노화와 관련된 관절 질환에는 치료보다 예방이 우선되어야 한다.
⑤ 중년에는 통증이 따르더라도 근력 운동으로 신체를 강화해야 한다.

C08 ★❀❀ .... 2024 실시 3월 학평 20 (고3)

다음 글에서 필자가 주장하는 바로 가장 적절한 것은?

By definition, adult learners have a self-concept of being in charge of their own lives and have a need to be seen and treated as being capable of taking responsibility for their own learning. As such, learners need to be given the freedom and autonomy to assume responsibility for their own choices and to be proactive in making decisions that contribute to their educational experiences. Rather than perform the role of the "sage on the stage," in working with adult learners, the instructor's role should be the "guide on the side" — a facilitator of learning, and a coach or mentor who works alongside their learners to promote achievement and academic success. The facilitator role extends beyond course delivery, and includes the broader pedagogical tasks that will support learners on their growth such as helping them effectively manage their time; fostering engagement; assigning meaningful and relevant learning activities; and so on.

*autonomy: 자율성, 자주성 **sage: 현자 ***pedagogical: 교육적인

① 학생들의 성취도를 측정할 수 있는 객관적인 평가 도구를 개발해야 한다.
② 성인 학습자를 가르치는 교사는 촉진자의 역할을 수행해야 한다.
③ 교사는 지식 전달을 최우선으로 하여 수업을 진행해야 한다.
④ 교사는 학생들의 연령에 상관없이 시각 자료를 활용해야 한다.
⑤ 성인 학습자는 새로운 것을 배울 때 더 많은 시간을 투자해야 한다.

C09 ✹✹❋

다음 글에서 필자가 주장하는 바로 가장 적절한 것은?

New ideas, such as those inspired by scientific developments, are often aired and critiqued in our popular culture as part of a healthy process of public debate, and scientists sometimes deserve the criticism they get. But the popularization of science would be greatly enhanced by improving the widespread images of the scientist. Part of the problem may be that the majority of the people who are most likely to write novels, plays, and film scripts were educated in the humanities, not in the sciences. Furthermore, the few scientists-turned-writers have used their scientific training as the source material for thrillers that further damage the image of science and scientists. We need more screenplays and novels that present scientists in a positive light. In our contemporary world, television and film are particularly influential media, and it is likely that the introduction of more scientist-heroes would help to make science more attractive.

① 과학의 대중화를 위해 여러 매체에서 과학자를 긍정적으로 묘사해야 한다.
② 작가로 전업한 과학자는 전공 지식을 작품에 사실적으로 반영해야 한다.
③ 공상 과학 작가로 성공하려면 과학과 인문학을 깊이 이해해야 한다.
④ 과학의 저변 확대를 위해 영화 주인공으로 과학자가 등장해야 한다.
⑤ 과학 정책 논의에 과학자뿐만 아니라 인문학자도 참여해야 한다.

C10 ✹✹✹

다음 글에서 필자가 주장하는 바로 가장 적절한 것은?

We live in a time when everyone seems to be looking for quick and sure solutions. Computer companies have even begun to advertise ways in which computers can replace parents. They are too late — television has already done that. Seriously, however, in every branch of education, including moral education, we make a mistake when we suppose that a particular batch of content or a particular teaching method or a particular configuration of students and space will accomplish our ends. The answer is both harder and simpler. We, parents and teachers, have to live with our children, talk to them, listen to them, enjoy their company, and show them by what we do and how we talk that it is possible to live appreciatively or, at least, nonviolently with most other people.

① 교육은 일상에서 아이들과의 상호 작용을 통해 이루어져야 한다.
② 도덕 교육을 강화하여 타인을 배려하는 공동체 의식을 높여야 한다.
③ 텔레비전의 부정적 영향을 줄이려는 사회적 노력이 있어야 한다.
④ 다양한 매체를 활용하여 학교와 가정 교육의 한계를 보완해야 한다.
⑤ 아이들의 온라인 예절 교육을 위해 적절한 콘텐츠를 개발해야 한다.

C11 ★★☀ .... 2022 대비 수능 20 (고3)

다음 글에서 필자가 주장하는 바로 가장 적절한 것은?

One of the most common mistakes made by organizations when they first consider experimenting with social media is that they focus too much on social media tools and platforms and not enough on their business objectives. The reality of success in the social web for businesses is that creating a social media program begins not with insight into the latest social media tools and channels but with a thorough understanding of the organization's own goals and objectives. A social media program is not merely the fulfillment of a vague need to manage a "presence" on popular social networks because "everyone else is doing it." "Being in social media" serves no purpose in and of itself. In order to serve any purpose at all, a social media presence must either solve a problem for the organization and its customers or result in an improvement of some sort (preferably a measurable one). In all things, purpose drives success. The world of social media is no different.

① 기업 이미지에 부합하는 소셜 미디어를 직접 개발하여 운영해야 한다.
② 기업은 사회적 가치와 요구를 반영하여 사업 목표를 수립해야 한다.
③ 기업은 소셜 미디어를 활용할 때 사업 목표를 토대로 해야 한다.
④ 소셜 미디어로 제품을 홍보할 때는 구체적인 정보를 제공해야 한다.
⑤ 소비자의 의견을 수렴하기 위해 소셜 미디어를 적극 활용해야 한다.

C12 ★★☀ .... 2021 대비 수능 20 (고3)

다음 글에서 필자가 주장하는 바로 가장 적절한 것은?

Developing expertise carries costs of its own. We can become experts in some areas, like speaking a language or knowing our favorite foods, simply by living our lives, but in many other domains expertise requires considerable training and effort. What's more, expertise is domain specific. The expertise that we work hard to acquire in one domain will carry over only imperfectly to related ones, and not at all to unrelated ones. In the end, as much as we may want to become experts on everything in our lives, there simply isn't enough time to do so. Even in areas where we could, it won't necessarily be worth the effort. It's clear that we should concentrate our own expertise on those domains of choice that are most common and/or important to our lives, and those we actively enjoy learning about and choosing from.

① 자신에게 의미 있는 영역을 정해서 전문성을 키워야 한다.
② 전문성 함양에는 타고난 재능보다 노력과 훈련이 중요하다.
③ 전문가가 되기 위해서는 다양한 분야에 관심을 가져야 한다.
④ 전문성을 기르기 위해서는 구체적인 계획과 실천이 필수적이다.
⑤ 전문가는 일의 우선순위를 결정해서 업무를 수행해야 한다.

C13 ★☀☀ .... 2023 실시 3월 학평 20 (고3)

다음 글에서 필자가 주장하는 바로 가장 적절한 것은?

There is no denying that engaging in argument carries certain significant risks. When we argue, we exchange and examine reasons with a view toward believing what our best reasons say we should believe; sometimes we discover that our current reasons fall short, and that our beliefs are not well supported after all. Or sometimes we discover that a belief that we had dismissed as silly or obviously false in fact enjoys the support of highly compelling reasons. On other occasions, we discover that the reasons offered by those with whom we disagree measure up toe-to-toe with our own reasons. In any of these situations, an adjustment in our belief is called for; we must change what we believe, or revise it, or replace it, or suspend belief altogether.

① 논쟁 중에 알게 된 바에 따라 자신의 믿음을 조정해야 한다.
② 논쟁을 하기 전에 상대방의 주장을 면밀히 검토해야 한다.
③ 논쟁에서 불리해지더라도 감정적으로 반응해서는 안 된다.
④ 의사 결정 시에는 충분한 시간을 갖고 신중하게 해야 한다.
⑤ 반대 의견을 제시할 때 상대의 논리적 허점을 공략해야 한다.

다음 글에서 필자가 주장하는 바로 가장 적절한 것은?

Leaving behind technology during intentional time alone is essential for the cognitive benefits, neurological repair, and spiritual clarity that are the gifts of solitude. Multiple studies show that anxiety is markedly reduced, and we gain benefits similar to solitude, not by simply turning our phones off but by having them *not physically with us*. If a phone is essential for safety during time alone, then turn off alerts, cover the screen — just tape paper right over it — and keep it somewhere that is terribly inconvenient to access. I am always surprised by how long it takes me to give up the impulse to reach for my phone, often for no reason at all, other than to "just check." Check what? Always it is something that can do without me for the moment. It is important that we allow ourselves time to free our minds from even the possibility of constant connectivity, to "normalize deactivation," as herbalist Sophia Rose puts it, allowing our overstimulated neuronal connections to rest and reassemble.

① 개인정보 유출을 막기 위해 휴대전화 보안을 강화해야 한다.
② 물리적 고립 상황에 대응하기 위한 통신 기술을 개발해야 한다.
③ 업무에 집중하기 위해 근무 시간에 휴대전화 사용을 자제해야 한다.
④ 혼자 있는 시간의 이점을 얻으려면 휴대전화와 떨어져 있어야 한다.
⑤ 고독감을 느끼지 않기 위해 사람들과 정서적인 연결을 지속해야 한다.

다음 글에서 필자가 주장하는 바로 가장 적절한 것은?

Given the right conditions, entrepreneurship can be fully woven into the fabric of campus life, greatly expanding its educational reach. One study showed that, within the workplace, peers influence each other to spot opportunities and act on them: the more entrepreneurs you have working together in an office, the more likely their colleagues will catch the bug. A study of Stanford University alumni found that those "who have varied work and educational backgrounds are much more likely to start their own businesses than those who have focused on one role at work or concentrated in one subject at school." To cultivate an entrepreneurial culture, colleges and universities need to offer students a broad choice of experiences and wide exposure to different ideas. They are uniquely positioned to do this by combining the resources of academic programming, residential life, student groups, and alumni networks.   *entrepreneur: 기업가 **alumni: 졸업생

① 훌륭한 기업가가 되기 위해서 관심 있는 한 분야에 집중해야 한다.
② 대학은 학생들이 기업가 정신을 함양하도록 환경을 조성해야 한다.
③ 좋은 직장을 얻기 위해서 학업과 대외 활동에 충실해야 한다.
④ 기업은 대학생들의 다양한 소모임 활동을 적극 지원해야 한다.
⑤ 대학생은 학업 성취를 위하여 경험과 생각의 폭을 넓혀야 한다.

C16 ✹✹✦ .... 2023 실시 4월 학평 20 (고3)

다음 글에서 필자가 주장하는 바로 가장 적절한 것은?

Anthropology has become relevant for addressing global issues. This is not to deny the vital role of 'hard' sciences in addressing these problems. However, if we are to solve global problems we need a new way of thinking based in humanities and social sciences. It is impossible to resolve global issues merely by looking at numbers and statistics. Anthropology thus becomes crucial, as a discipline and a profession enabling the collection and interpretation of 'thick data' — in addition to 'big data' — and helps us to understand the world we live in more comprehensively. Why is a brand new and expensive 'smart' building a disaster? What will happen in the future with passenger cars? In answering such questions, we should stop relying only on quantitative data analytics; instead, the most important decisions should also be informed by anthropological qualitative approaches which provide a more complete and nuanced picture of people's lives.

① 광범위한 규모의 문제를 다룰 때는 처리 단계를 세분화해야 한다.
② 실증적 자료를 토대로 해결할 수 있는 문제를 먼저 처리해야 한다.
③ 글로벌 문제 해결을 위해 인류학의 질적 접근법을 활용해야 한다.
④ 전 인류적 문제에 대한 질적 연구는 정량화된 수치에 기반해야 한다.
⑤ 사회 문제의 포괄적 이해를 위해 자료를 반복적으로 검증해야 한다.

C17 ✹✹✦ .... 2023 대비 6월 모평 20 (고3)

다음 글에서 필자가 주장하는 바로 가장 적절한 것은?

Consider two athletes who both want to play in college. One says she has to work very hard and the other uses goal setting to create a plan to stay on track and work on specific skills where she is lacking. Both are working hard but only the latter is working smart. It can be frustrating for athletes to work extremely hard but not make the progress they wanted. What can make the difference is drive — utilizing the mental gear to maximize gains made in the technical and physical areas. Drive provides direction (goals), sustains effort (motivation), and creates a training mindset that goes beyond simply working hard. Drive applies direct force on your physical and technical gears, strengthening and polishing them so they can spin with vigor and purpose. While desire might make you spin those gears faster and harder as you work out or practice, drive is what built them in the first place.

* vigor: 활력, 활기

① 선수들의 훈련 방식은 장점을 극대화하는 방향으로 이루어져야 한다.
② 선수들은 최고의 성과를 얻기 위해 정신적 추진력을 잘 활용해야 한다.
③ 선수들은 단기적 훈련 성과보다 장기적 목표 달성에 힘써야 한다.
④ 선수들은 육체적 훈련과 정신적 훈련을 균형 있게 병행해야 한다.
⑤ 선수들은 수립한 계획을 실행하면서 꾸준히 수정하여야 한다.

다음 글에서 필자가 주장하는 바로 가장 적절한 것은?

Occasionally individuals do not merely come out as well as clearly state what is troubling them and instead select more indirect means of expressing their annoyance. One companion might talk to the various other in a way that is condescending and also indicates underlying hostility. Numerous other times, partners may mope and even frown without genuinely dealing with an issue. Companions may likewise merely prevent discussing an issue by swiftly switching over topics when the subject turns up or by being incredibly vague. Such indirect ways of expressing temper are not useful since they don't provide the individual that is the target of the behaviors, an idea of exactly how to react. They understand their companion is irritated, but the absence of directness leaves them without advice regarding what they can do to solve the issue.

*condescend: 거들먹거리다 **mope: 울적해하다

① 이성보다 감정에 호소하여 상대방을 설득해야 한다.
② 상대방의 기분을 상하게 하는 행동을 자제해야 한다.
③ 문제 해결을 위해서는 문제를 직접적으로 언급해야 한다.
④ 타인의 입장을 이해하려면 경청하는 자세를 가져야 한다.
⑤ 목표 달성을 방해하는 문제점을 지속적으로 파악해야 한다.

다음 글에서 필자가 주장하는 바로 가장 적절한 것은?

Values alone do not create and build culture. Living your values only some of the time does not contribute to the creation and maintenance of culture. Changing values into behaviors is only half the battle. Certainly, this is a step in the right direction, but those behaviors must then be shared and distributed widely throughout the organization, along with a clear and concise description of what is expected. It is not enough to simply talk about it. It is critical to have a visual representation of the specific behaviors that leaders and all people managers can use to coach their people. Just like a sports team has a playbook with specific plays designed to help them perform well and win, your company should have a playbook with the key shifts needed to transform your culture into action and turn your values into winning behaviors.

① 조직 문화 혁신을 위해서 모든 구성원이 공유할 핵심 가치를 정립해야 한다.
② 조직 구성원의 행동을 변화시키려면 지도자는 명확한 가치관을 가져야 한다.
③ 조직 내 문화가 공유되기 위해서 구성원의 자발적 행동이 뒷받침되어야 한다.
④ 조직의 핵심 가치 실현을 위해 구성원 간의 지속적인 의사소통이 필수적이다.
⑤ 조직의 문화 형성에는 가치를 반영한 행동의 공유를 위한 명시적 지침이 필요하다.

C20 ★★❀ .... 2023 대비 9월 모평 20 (고3)

다음 글에서 필자가 주장하는 바로 가장 적절한 것은?

Becoming competent in another culture means looking beyond behavior to see if we can understand the attitudes, beliefs, and values that motivate what we observe. By looking only at the visible aspects of culture — customs, clothing, food, and language — we develop a short-sighted view of intercultural understanding — just the tip of the iceberg, really. If we are to be successful in our business interactions with people who have different values and beliefs about how the world is ordered, then we must go below the surface of what it means to understand culture and attempt to see what Edward Hall calls the "hidden dimensions." Those hidden aspects are the very foundation of culture and are the reason why culture is actually more than meets the eye. We tend not to notice those cultural norms until they violate what we consider to be common sense, good judgment, or the nature of things.

① 타 문화 사람들과 교류를 잘하려면 그 문화의 이면을 알아야 한다.
② 문화 배경이 다른 직원과 협업할 때 공정하게 업무를 나눠야 한다.
③ 여러 문화에 대한 이해를 통해 공동체 의식을 길러야 한다.
④ 원만한 대인 관계를 위해서는 서로의 공통점을 우선 파악해야 한다.
⑤ 문화적 갈등을 줄이려면 구성원 간의 소통을 활성화해야 한다.

C21 ★★❀ .... 2023 대비 수능 20 (고3)

다음 글에서 필자가 주장하는 바로 가장 적절한 것은?

At every step in our journey through life we encounter junctions with many different pathways leading into the distance. Each choice involves uncertainty about which path will get you to your destination. Trusting our intuition to make the choice often ends up with us making a suboptimal choice. Turning the uncertainty into numbers has proved a potent way of analyzing the paths and finding the shortcut to your destination. The mathematical theory of probability hasn't eliminated risk, but it allows us to manage that risk more effectively. The strategy is to analyze all the possible scenarios that the future holds and then to see what proportion of them lead to success or failure. This gives you a much better map of the future on which to base your decisions about which path to choose.

*junction: 분기점 **suboptimal: 차선의

① 성공적인 삶을 위해 미래에 대한 구체적인 계획을 세워야 한다.
② 중요한 결정을 내릴 때에는 자신의 직관에 따라 판단해야 한다.
③ 더 나은 선택을 위해 성공 가능성을 확률적으로 분석해야 한다.
④ 빠른 목표 달성을 위해 지름길로 가고자 할 때 신중해야 한다.
⑤ 인생의 여정에서 선택에 따른 결과를 스스로 책임져야 한다.

2등급 대비 문제

C22 ~ 23 ▶ 제한시간 5분

C22 ✪ 2등급 대비 .... 2024 대비 9월 모평 20 (고3)

다음 글에서 필자가 주장하는 바로 가장 적절한 것은?

Confident is not the same as comfortable. One of the biggest misconceptions about becoming self-confident is that it means living fearlessly. The key to building confidence is quite the opposite. It means we are willing to let fear be present as we do the things that matter to us. When we establish some self-confidence in something, it feels good. We want to stay there and hold on to it. But if we only go where we feel confident, then confidence never expands beyond that. If we only do the things we know we can do well, fear of the new and unknown tends to grow. Building confidence inevitably demands that we make friends with vulnerability because it is the only way to be without confidence for a while. But the only way confidence can grow is when we are willing to be without it. When we can step into fear and sit with the unknown, it is the courage of doing so that builds confidence from the ground up.

*vulnerability: 취약성

① 적성을 파악하기 위해서는 자신 있는 일을 다양하게 시도해야 한다.

② 자신감을 키우기 위해 낯설고 두려운 일에 도전하는 용기를 가져야 한다.

③ 어려운 일을 자신 있게 수행하기 위해 사전에 계획을 철저히 세워야 한다.

④ 과도한 자신감을 갖기보다는 자신의 약점을 객관적으로 분석해야 한다.

⑤ 자신의 경험과 지식을 바탕으로 당면한 문제에 자신 있게 대처해야 한다.

C23 ✪ 2등급 대비 .... 2023 실시 10월 학평 20 (고3)

다음 글에서 필자가 주장하는 바로 가장 적절한 것은?

The chemists Hans Ebel, Claus Bliefert, and William Russey note: "It goes without saying that scientists need to be skillful *readers*. Extensive reading is the principal key to expanding one's knowledge and keeping up with developments in a discipline. However, what is often overlooked here is that scientists are also obliged to be skillful *writers*. Only the researcher who is competent in the art of *written* communication can play an active and effective role in *contributing* to science." From the perspective of readability, moreover, scientists should always write with a reader-centered mentality; even in the act of writing they must be mindful of the act of reading. It would be beneficial for them to understand how readers read in order to improve their writing.

① 과학자는 독자와 만나는 기회를 자주 가져야 한다.

② 과학자는 독자의 관점에서 글을 쓸 줄 알아야 한다.

③ 과학자는 다양한 의견에 개방적인 태도를 가져야 한다.

④ 과학자는 자기 연구 분야 이외의 책도 많이 읽어야 한다.

⑤ 과학자는 연구 결과가 사회에 미치는 영향을 인식해야 한다.

※ 다음 영어는 우리말 뜻을, 우리말은 영어 단어를 〈보기〉에서 찾아 쓰시오.

〈보기〉

좌절감을 주는	strengthen	concentrate	spot
철학	영감을 주다	circulate	진전, 진행
필수적인	perspective	배치	execute

01 frustrating _____

02 progress _____

03 inspire _____

04 configuration _____

05 essential _____

06 강화하다 _____

07 발견하다, 찾다 _____

08 집중하다 _____

09 관점 _____

10 유포하다 _____

※ 다음 우리말에 알맞은 영어 표현을 찾아 연결하시오.

11 ~을 요구하다 •   • matter to

12 ~에게 중요하다 •   • call for

13 제대로 진행되고 있는 •   • hold on to

14 ~을 고수하다 •   • contribute to

15 ~에 기여하다 •   • on track

※ 다음 우리말 표현에 맞는 단어를 고르시오.

16 커지는 AI 비서의 존재감 때문이든 ⇒ Whether it be due to the growing presence of AI (assurances / assistants)

17 교육의 모든 분야에서 ⇒ in every (branch / batch) of education

18 이점을 극대화하다 ⇒ (maximize / minimize) gains

19 신뢰할 수 있고 정확한 이해 ⇒ (Reliable / Doubtful) and accurate understanding

20 빙산의 일각 ⇒ the tip of the (island / iceberg)

※ 다음 문장의 빈칸에 알맞은 단어를 〈보기〉에서 찾아 쓰시오.

〈보기〉

argument	competent	excessive	athletes
fearlessly	addressing	deserve	multiple
extensive	obliged	expanding	morale

21 논쟁에 참여하는 것은 어떤 중대한 위험을 수반한다.
⇒ Engaging in _____ carries certain significant risks.

22 인류학은 글로벌 문제를 다루는 데 있어 적절해졌다.
⇒ Anthropology has become relevant for _____ global issues.

23 과학자들은 때로 그들이 받는 비판을 받는 것이 마땅하다.
⇒ Scientists sometimes _____ the criticism they get.

24 과학자는 숙련된 필자가 되어야 한다.
⇒ Scientists are _____ to be skillful writers.

25 타 문화에 유능해진다는 것은 행동 그 이상의 것을 살펴보는 것을 의미한다.
⇒ Becoming _____ in another culture means looking beyond behavior.

26 둘 다 대학에서 뛰고 싶어 하는 두 명의 운동선수를 생각해 보라.
⇒ Consider two _____ who both want to play in college.

27 그것은 두려움 없이 사는 것을 의미한다.
⇒ It means living _____.

28 그 사람은 그것을 여러 번 경험해야 한다.
⇒ He or she should experience it _____ times.

29 다독은 자신의 지식을 확장하는 주요한 비결이다.
⇒ Extensive reading is the principal key to _____ one's knowledge.

30 지나친 일반성은 혼돈, 모호함, 얕음을 초래한다.
⇒ _____ generality causes chaos, vagueness, and shallowness.

D 밑줄 친 부분의 의미 찾기

말풍선: 이 수학 문제를 푸는 것은 정말 식은 죽 먹기네요!

말풍선: 어려움 없이 쉽게 풀었다는 뜻이구나?

★ 유형 설명

밑줄 친 we have "confusion at the frontier"가 다음 글에서 의미하는 바로 가장 적절한 것은? [3점]

Two independent research groups have discovered that we have "confusion at the

밑줄 친 부분은 비유적인 표현인 경우가 많다. 글의 내용과 문맥에 맞게 그 직접적인 의미가 무엇인지 추론해야 한다.

☛ 똑같은 비유적인 표현도 어떤 글에서 쓰였는지에 따라 그 의미가 달라지므로 글의 내용을 정확히 파악한 후에 그에 맞게 비유적 표현의 의미를 찾아야 한다.

🕶 유형 풀이 비법

1 밑줄 친 부분을 파악하라!

• 밑줄 친 부분이 어디 있는지 확인한 후, 어떤 부분에 집중해서 전체 글을 읽어야 하는지 파악한다.

2 핵심 내용을 종합하라!

• 처음부터 글을 읽으면서 전체 내용을 이해하고 핵심어와 요지를 찾는다.

3 선택지를 해석해 넣어 보라!

• 밑줄 친 부분에 정답으로 고른 선택지를 넣어 보고 자연스러운지 확인한다.

Tip 밑줄 친 부분의 앞뒤 내용뿐만 아니라 전체 글의 흐름에 매끄럽게 들어맞는지 확인한다.

★ 최신 수능 경향 분석

대비 연도	월	문항 번호	지문 주제	난이도
2025	11	21번	실용적, 이론적 지식을 모두 필요로 하는 건축가	★★★
	9	21번	인류학자들의 문화 집단 연구 방식	★★★
	6	21번	번아웃은 '상태가 아닌 '범위'로 간주해야 한다.	★★★
2024	11	21번	주의의 초점이 넓으면 스트레스 수준이 낮아짐	★★★
	9	21번	최고는 좋음의 적	★★★
	6	21번	막대 다발로 묘사되는 소유권	★★★
2023	11	21번	자신을 되돌아보는 수단으로서의 일기	★★☆
	9	21번	보석을 찾아주는 알고리즘	★★☆
	6	21번	세계를 있는 그대로 볼 수는 없는 우리	★★☆

★ 2025 수능 출제 분석

건축가에게는 실용적 지식과 이론적 지식 모두 필요하다는 글의 핵심을 파악하기는 어렵지 않을 수 있지만, 이것을 통해 '실체가 아닌 그림자를 쫓고 있었다'는 비유적 표현이 의미하는 바를 파악하기가 상당히 어려웠다.

★ 2026 수능 예측

추상적인 소재와 어구를 사용하여 난이도를 높일 가능성이 크므로 대비해야 한다.

🔑 어휘 및 표현 Preview

- □ symptom 증상
- □ train 훈련하다
- □ all-or-nothing 양자택일의
- □ humanity 인류학
- □ ought to ~해야 하다
- □ insist 주장하다
- □ significant 상당한, 중요한
- □ actually 실제로
- □ observe 관찰하다
- □ exist 존재하다
- □ remote 외딴
- □ location 지역
- □ degree 정도

- □ businessman 사업가
- □ missionary 선교사
- □ overcome 극복하다
- □ community 주민, 지역 사회
- □ generally 일반적으로
- □ spend (시간을) 보내다
- □ primarily 주로
- □ conduct (특정한 활동을) 하다
- □ relationship 관계
- □ native 원주민
- □ collaborative 공동의
- □ criteria 기준
- □ exhaustion 탈진

- □ severity 심각성
- □ individual 개인, 개인의
- □ cooperate 협력하다
- □ a bit 약간
- □ culture 문화적인
- □ examine 조사[검토]하다
- □ research 연구
- □ seek to ~하려고 애쓰다
- □ balance 균형을 맞추다
- □ breadth 폭
- □ depth 깊이
- □ state 상태
- □ spectrum 범위

- □ public 대중적인
- □ discussion 논의
- □ clear 명확한
- □ categorize 분류하다
- □ manage to 용케도 ~을 해내다
- □ competently 유능하게
- □ solve 해결하다
- □ claim 주장하다
- □ deal with 다루다
- □ partial 부분적인
- □ experience 경험하다
- □ applicable 해당되는

D 밑줄 친 부분의 의미 찾기 (첫 번째)

1st 첫 문장과 밑줄 친 부분이 포함된 문장을 읽고, 글의 내용을 예상하세요.
2nd 글의 나머지 부분을 읽고, 예상한 내용이 맞는지 확인하세요.
3rd 파악한 글의 내용을 종합하여 밑줄 친 부분의 의미를 파악하세요.

D01 ★★❀ ·············· 2023 대비 9월 모평 21 (고3)

밑줄 친 send us off into different far corners of the library가 다음 글에서 의미하는 바로 가장 적절한 것은? [3점]

You may feel there is something scary about an algorithm deciding what you might like. Could it mean that, if computers conclude you won't like something, you will never get the chance to see it? Personally, I really enjoy being directed toward new music that I might not have found by myself. I can quickly get stuck in a rut where I put on the same songs over and over. That's why I've always enjoyed the radio. But the algorithms that are now pushing and pulling me through the music library are perfectly suited to finding gems that I'll like. My worry originally about such algorithms was that they might drive everyone into certain parts of the library, leaving others lacking listeners. Would they cause a convergence of tastes? But thanks to the nonlinear and chaotic mathematics usually behind them, this doesn't happen. A small divergence in my likes compared to yours can send us off into different far corners of the library.

*rut: 관습, 틀 **gem: 보석 ***divergence: 갈라짐

① lead us to music selected to suit our respective tastes
② enable us to build connections with other listeners
③ encourage us to request frequent updates for algorithms
④ motivate us to search for talented but unknown musicians
⑤ make us ignore our preferences for particular music genres

1st 첫 문장과 밑줄 친 부분이 포함된 문장을 읽고, 글의 내용을 예상하세요.

1) 첫 문장부터 읽어 봅시다.

You may feel / there is something scary / about an
여러분은 느낄 수 있다 / 뭔가 무서운 것이 있다고 /
algorithm / deciding / what you might like. //
알고리즘에 대해 / 결정하는   / 여러분이 좋아할지도 모르는 것을 //

● 첫 문장에서 알고리즘에 대해 언급했어요.
여러분이 좋아할지도 모르는 것을 결정하는 알고리즘이 뭔가 무서운 부분이 있다고 느낄 수 있다고 했어요. (단서)
앞으로 이 알고리즘, 혹은 내가 좋아하는 것과 관련된 내용이 이어질 것 같아요. (발상)

2) 밑줄 친 부분이 포함된 문장을 살펴볼까요?

A small divergence / in my likes / compared to
작은 갈라짐이   / 내가 좋아하는 것의 / 여러분의 것과
yours / can send us off / into different far corners of
비교되어 / 우리를 보낼 수 있다   / 라이브러리의 서로 다른 저 멀리 떨어진
the library. //
구석들로   //

● 주어가 있는 부분부터 직독직해로 해석한 것을 곰곰이 생각해 봅시다.
내가 좋아하는 것이 여러분이 좋아하는 것과 비교되어 갈라진다는 것은, 내가 좋아하는 것과 여러분이 좋아하는 것이 서로 다르다는 의미예요.

● 이제 밑줄 친 부분이 포함된 부분을 봅시다.
우리를 라이브러리의 저 멀리 떨어진 서로 다른 구석들로 보낸다는 게 무슨 의미일까요?
일단 library는 우리가 흔히 아는 ❶'(   )'이라는 뜻은 아니지만, 책을 모아 놓는 ❷(   )처럼 컴퓨터에서 프로그램이나 데이터 등을 한데 모아놓은 곳을 library라고 해요.
소재가 '음악'이라는 것을 생각하면, 이 글의 library는 우리가 듣는 음악 파일들을 모아놓은 곳을 가리킬 거예요.
그렇다면 우리를 라이브러리의 서로 다른 멀리 떨어진 구석들로 보낸다는 것은, 우리 각각으로 하여금 (라이브러리에 저장된) 서로 다른 음악들을 듣게 한다는 의미이겠군요!

● 이제 글의 내용을 확실히 예상할 수 있겠죠?
사람들이 좋아하는 음악이 각각 다르다는 점이 사람들을 각각의 취향에 맞게 라이브러리에 저장된 다양한 음악으로 안내한다는 내용일 거예요.

2nd 글의 나머지 부분을 읽고, 예상한 내용이 맞는지 확인하세요.

1) 앞부분부터 확인해 볼까요?

> My worry originally / about such algorithms / was /
> 원래 나의 걱정은   / 그런 알고리즘에 대한   / ~이었다 /
>
> that they might drive everyone / into certain parts
> 그것이 모든 사람을 몰아넣을 수 있다는 것   / 라이브러리의 특정 부분으로
>
> of the library, / leaving others lacking listeners. //
>   / 나머지는 듣는 이들이 부족하게 하면서   //
>
> Would they cause / a convergence of tastes? //
> 그것은 일으킬 것인가 / 취향의 수렴을   //

● **필자가 걱정한 바는 무엇인가요?**

필자는 **②**(   )이 모든 사람들을 라이브러리의 특정
음악으로만 안내해서 그 음악만 청취자가 많고, 다른 음악들은 청취자가
부족하게 만들까 걱정했어요.
'수렴(convergence)'은 의견이나 사상 등이 여럿으로 나뉘어 있는 것을
하나로 모으는 것을 의미하는데, 이 글에 대입해서 이해하면, 사람들의
서로 다른 음악 취향이 알고리즘 때문에 하나로 모인다는 의미겠군요!

2) 필자가 걱정하는 일은 일어나지 않는다고 했어요.

> But thanks to the nonlinear and chaotic mathematics
> 그러나 비선형적이고 불규칙적인 수학 덕분에
>
> / usually behind them, / this doesn't happen. //
> / 일반적으로 그 배후에 있는 / 이런 일은 발생하지는 않는다 //

● **필자가 걱정하는 일이 일어나지 않는다네요.**

비선형적이고 불규칙적인 수학으로 인해 사람들의 **③**(   )은 하나로
수렴하지 않고, 오히려 알고리즘은 각각 다른 **③**(   )에 따라 다양한
음악으로 사람들을 안내한다고 해요.

3rd 파악한 글의 내용을 종합하여 밑줄 친 부분의 의미를
파악하세요.

1) 글의 내용을 종합해봅시다.

나를 내가 좋아할 음악으로 안내하는 알고리즘에 대해, 원래는 그것이
모든 사람을 특정 음악으로 몰아넣고 다른 음악은 듣는 사람이 부족하게
만들까 봐 걱정했지만, 그런 일은 일어나지 않는다고 했어요.
그러므로 글의 내용을 종합해 밑줄 친 부분의 의미를 파악할 수 있어요.
내가 좋아하는 것과 다른 사람이 좋아하는 것이 갈라진다는 사실이 우리
각각을 뮤직 라이브러리의 다양한 부분으로 보낸다는 것은, 우리가
각자의 취향에 의해 우리가 좋아할 음악으로 안내받는다는 의미죠.

2) 마지막으로 선택지 해석을 확인해보세요.

① lead us to music selected to suit our respective
tastes
우리를 우리 각각의 취향에 맞도록 선택된 음악으로 이끌다

② enable us to build connections with other listeners
우리가 다른 청취자들과 관계를 맺을 수 있게 하다

③ encourage us to request frequent updates for
algorithms
우리에게 알고리즘을 위한 잦은 업데이트를 요구하라고 권하다

④ motivate us to search for talented but unknown
musicians
재능이 있지만 알려지지 않은 음악가들을 찾도록 우리에게 동기를 주다

⑤ make us ignore our preferences for particular
music genres
우리가 특정 음악 장르에 대한 우리의 선호를 무시하도록 만들다

따라서 정답은 **④**(   )이 되겠죠!

반복되는 어구를 찾아
글의 소재를 파악하자!

D 밑줄 친 부분의 의미 찾기 (두 번째)

1st 첫 문장과 밑줄 친 부분이 포함된 문장을 읽고, 글의 내용을 예상하세요.
2nd 글의 나머지 부분을 읽고, 예상한 내용이 맞는지 확인하세요.
3rd 파악한 글의 내용을 종합하여 밑줄 친 부분의 의미를 파악하세요.

D02 ★★☆ .... 2023 대비 6월 모평 21 (고3)

밑줄 친 "view from nowhere"가 다음 글에서 의미하는 바로 가장 적절한 것은? [3점]

Our view of the world is not given to us from the outside in a pure, objective form; it is shaped by our mental abilities, our shared cultural perspectives and our unique values and beliefs. This is not to say that there is no reality outside our minds or that the world is just an illusion. It is to say that our version of reality is precisely that: *our* version, not *the* version. There is no single, universal or authoritative version that makes sense, other than as a theoretical construct. We can see the world only as it appears to us, not "as it truly is," because there is no "as it truly is" without a perspective to give it form. Philosopher Thomas Nagel argued that there is no "view from nowhere," since we cannot see the world except from a particular perspective, and that perspective influences what we see. We can experience the world only through the human lenses that make it intelligible to us.

*illusion: 환영

① perception of reality affected by subjective views
② valuable perspective most people have in mind
③ particular view adopted by very few people
④ critical insight that defeats our prejudices
⑤ unbiased and objective view of the world

1st 첫 문장과 밑줄 친 부분이 포함된 문장을 읽고, 글의 내용을 예상하세요.

1) 첫 문장부터 읽어 봅시다.

Our view of the world / is not given to us / from the
세계에 대한 우리의 관점은   / 우리에게 주어지지 않는다 / 외부에서
outside / in a pure, objective form; / it is shaped /
         / 순수하고 객관적인 형태로   / 그것은 형성된다 /
by our mental abilities, our shared cultural
우리의 정신 능력, 우리의 공유된 문화적 관점,
perspectives and our unique values and beliefs. //
그리고 우리의 독특한 가치관과 신념에 의해   //

● 첫 문장에 우리의 세계관에 대한 내용이 나오네요.
우리의 세계관은 우리의 정신력, 문화적 관점, 가치관 등에 의해
형성된다고 했어요. (단서)
앞으로 이런 방식에 의해 형성된 세계관과 관련된 내용이 이어질 것
같아요. (발상)

2) 밑줄 친 부분이 포함된 문장을 살펴볼까요?

Philosopher Thomas Nagel argued / that there is no
철학자 Thomas Nagel은 주장했다   / '입장이 없는 관점'은
"view from nowhere," / since we cannot see the
없다고   / 우리는 세계를 볼 수 없기 때문에
world / except from a particular perspective, / and
      / 특정한 관점에서를 제외하고는   / 그리고
that perspective influences / what we see. //
그 관점이 영향을 미치기 (때문에)   / 우리가 보는 것에 //

● 주절과 〈이유〉의 부사절로 이루어진 문장이에요.
주절과 since가 이끄는 부사절로 이루어진 문장인데, since는 '~한
이래로'라는 의미로 〈시간〉의 부사절을 이끌기도 하지만, '~ 때문에'라는
의미로 〈이유〉의 부사절을 이끌기도 해요.
이 문장에서는 문맥상 '~ 때문에'라는 의미로, 주절과 연결해서 생각해
보면, 철학자 Thomas Nagel이 '입장이 없는 관점'은 없다고 주장한
이유를 since가 이끄는 부사절에서 설명하는 것이죠.

● Thomas Nagel은 왜 '입장이 없는 관점'은 없다고 주장했나요?
부사절을 해석해 보면, 우리는 특정 관점에서만 세계를 볼 수 있고,
그 관점은 우리가 보는 것에 영향을 미친다는 의미예요.
다시 말해, 우리는 그 관점으로만 세계를 본다는 거예요. 이것을 앞서
살펴본 선택지와 연결해서 생각하면, 우리는 객관적으로 세계를 보는
것이 아니라 우리가 가진 ❶(   ) 관점을 통해 세계를
본다는 의미라는 것을 추론할 수 있어요.

- 밑줄 친 부분 앞에 부정어 **②**(　　　　　)가 있다는 점에 주의해야 돼요.

  since가 이끄는 부사절을 통해서 이 글은 핵심 내용이 '우리는 주관적인 관점을 통해 세계를 본다'인 글임을 예상했어요. 이러한 글의 핵심 내용을 뒷받침하는 사람의 주장을 인용했을 테니까 Thomas Nagel의 주장도 같은 내용이겠죠.

2nd 글의 나머지 부분을 읽고, 예상한 내용이 맞는지 확인하세요.

1) 앞부분부터 확인해 볼까요?

Our view of the world / is not given to us / from the
세계에 대한 우리의 관점은　　/ 우리에게 주어지지 않는다 / 외부에서

outside / in a pure, objective form; / it is shaped /
　　　 / 순수하고 객관적인 형태로　　 / 그것은 형성된다 /

by our mental abilities, our shared cultural
우리의 정신 능력, 우리의 공유된 문화적 관점,

perspectives and our unique values and beliefs. //
그리고 우리의 독특한 가치관과 신념에 의해　　　 //

- 우리의 세계관이 객관적이라는 건가요, 주관적이라는 건가요?

  세계에 대한 우리의 관점이 우리에게 외부에서 객관적인 형태로 주어지지 않는다는 건 우리의 세계관이 객관적이지 않으며, 우리의 내부로부터의 영향, 즉 주관적인 영향을 받는다는 의미예요.

2) 한 문장만 더 볼까요?

We can see the world / only as it appears to us, / not
우리는 세계를 볼 수 있다　　 / 그것이 우리에게 보이는 대로만　　 /

"as it truly is," / because there is no "as it truly is" /
'정말로 있는 그대로'가 아니라 / '정말로 있는 그대로'란 없기 때문에　　 /

without a perspective / to give it form. //
관점 없이　　　 / 그것에 형태를 부여하는 //

- 우리는 세계를 정말 있는 그대로 볼 수 없대요.

  세계를 있는 그대로, 객관적으로 보는 게 아니라 우리가 가진 관점에 따라 우리에게 보이는 대로만 본다는 거니까 이 글은 확실히 '우리는 주관적인 관점을 통해 세계를 본다'는 내용이고, 이 내용을 뒷받침하기 위해 제시한 Thomas Nagel의 주장 역시 같은 맥락이어야 해요.

3rd 파악한 글의 내용을 종합하여 밑줄 친 부분의 의미를 파악하세요.

1) 글의 내용을 종합해봅시다.

세계를 보는 우리의 관점은 외부에서 객관적인 형태로 주어지는 것이 아니라 우리의 정신, 문화, 가치관 등에 의해 형성된다면서 우리는 우리에게 보이는 대로만 세계를 볼 수 있고, 인간의 렌즈를 통해서만 세계를 경험할 수 있다고 했어요.

그러므로 글의 내용을 종합해 밑줄 친 부분의 의미를 파악할 수 있는데, 이러한 글의 내용을 뒷받침하기 위해 Thomas Nagel의 말을 인용한 것이죠.

Thomas Nagel이 없다고 주장한 '입장이 없는 관점'은 '편견이 없으면서 객관적인 세계관'이에요.

따라서 정답은 **③**(　　　　　)이 되겠죠!

2) 마지막으로 선택지 해석을 확인해보세요.

① perception of reality affected by subjective views
　 주관적인 관점에 영향을 받는 현실 인식

② valuable perspective most people have in mind
　 대부분의 사람이 염두에 두고 있는 가치 있는 관점

③ particular view adopted by very few people
　 극소수의 사람에게 채택된 특정한 관점

④ critical insight that defeats our prejudices
　 우리의 편견을 물리치는 비판적 통찰

⑤ unbiased and objective view of the world
　 편견이 없으면서 객관적인 세계관

밑줄이 포함된 문장을 유심히 읽자!

PATTERN PRACTICE

D03 ~ 06 ▶ 제한시간 8분

D03 ★★★ .... 2025 대비 수능 21 (고3)

밑줄 친 hunting the shadow, not the substance가 다음 글에서 의미하는 바로 가장 적절한 것은? [3점]

The position of the architect rose during the Roman Empire, as architecture symbolically became a particularly important political statement. Cicero classed the architect with the physician and the teacher and Vitruvius spoke of "so great a profession as this." Marcus Vitruvius Pollio, a practicing architect during the rule of Augustus Caesar, recognized that architecture requires both practical and theoretical knowledge, and he listed the disciplines he felt the aspiring architect should master: literature and writing, draftsmanship, mathematics, history, philosophy, music, medicine, law, and astronomy — a curriculum that still has much to recommend it. All of this study was necessary, he argued, because architects who have aimed at acquiring manual skill without scholarship have never been able to reach a position of authority to correspond to their plans, while those who have relied only upon theories and scholarship were obviously "hunting the shadow, not the substance."

① seeking abstract knowledge emphasized by architectural tradition

② discounting the subjects necessary to achieve architectural goals

③ pursuing the ideals of architecture without the practical skills

④ prioritizing architecture's material aspects over its artistic ones

⑤ following historical precedents without regard to current standards

D04 ★★★ .... 2025 대비 9월 모평 21 (고3)

밑줄 친 from their *verandas*가 다음 글에서 의미하는 바로 가장 적절한 것은?

Around the turn of the twentieth century, anthropologists trained in the natural sciences began to reimagine what a science of humanity should look like and how social scientists ought to go about studying cultural groups. Some of those anthropologists insisted that one should at least spend significant time actually observing and talking to the people studied. Early ethnographers such as Franz Boas and Alfred Cort Haddon typically traveled to the remote locations where the people in question lived and spent a few weeks to a few months there. They sought out a local Western host who was familiar with the people and the area (such as a colonial official, missionary, or businessman) and found accommodations through them. Although they did at times venture into the community without a guide, they generally did not spend significant time with the local people. Thus, their observations were primarily conducted from their *verandas*.

*anthropologist: 인류학자 **ethnographer: 민족지학자

① seeking to build long-lasting relationships with the natives

② participating in collaborative research with natural scientists

③ engaging in little direct contact with the people being studied

④ cooperating actively with Western hosts in the local community

⑤ struggling to take a wider view of the native culture examined

D05 ✽✽❀ .... 2024 실시 7월 학평 21 (고3)

밑줄 친 the breadcrumbs of the conversation이 다음 글에서 의미하는 바로 가장 적절한 것은? [3점]

In improv, the actors have no control of the conversation or the direction it takes. They can only react to the other actors' words or nonverbal communication. Because of this, the actors become experts at reading body language and reading between the lines of what is said. If they are unable to do this, they are left in the dark and the performance crumbles. This applies to our daily conversations, but we're usually too self-centered to notice. Just like the improv actors become adept at picking up on the breadcrumbs of the conversation, we need to do the same. When people want to talk about something specific, rarely will they come out and just say it. 99 percent of people won't say, "Hey, let's talk about my dog now. So...." Instead, they will hint at it. When they bring up a topic unprompted, or ask questions about it, they want to talk about it. Sometimes, when the other person seems to not pick up on these signals, they will keep redirecting the conversation to that specific topic. If they seem excited whenever the topic comes up, they want to talk about it.

*improv: 즉흥 연극 **crumble: 무너지다 ***adept: 능숙한

① roundabout hints revealing the speaker's intention
② opening words to make the topic more interesting
③ part of the conversation that distracts the listeners
④ characteristics that are unique to the actors themselves
⑤ unexpected reactions of the audience to the performance

D06 ✽❀❀ .... 2025 대비 6월 모평 21 (고3)

밑줄 친 Burnout hasn't had the last word.가 다음 글에서 의미하는 바로 가장 적절한 것은?

To balance the need for breadth (everyone feels a bit burned out) and depth (some are so burned out, they can no longer do their jobs), we ought to think of burnout not as a *state* but as a *spectrum*. In most public discussion of burnout, we talk about workers who "are burned out," as if that status were black and white. A black-and-white view cannot account for the variety of burnout experience, though. If there is a clear line between burned out and not, as there is with a lightbulb, then we have no good way to categorize people who say they are burned out but still manage to do their work competently. Thinking about burnout as a spectrum solves this problem; those who claim burnout but are not debilitated by it are simply dealing with a partial or less-severe form of it. They are experiencing burnout without *being* burned out. Burnout hasn't had the last word.

*debilitate: 쇠약하게 하다

① Public discussion of burnout has not reached an end.
② There still exists room for a greater degree of exhaustion.
③ All-or-nothing criteria are applicable to burnout symptoms.
④ Exhaustion is overcome in different ways based on its severity.
⑤ Degrees of exhaustion are shaped by individuals' perceptions.

D07 ★★★ .... 2024 실시 5월 학평 21 (고3)

밑줄 친 Approximate perfection is better than perfect perfection이 다음 글에서 의미하는 바로 가장 적절한 것은? [3점]

Turn the lights out and point the beam of a small flashlight up into one of your eyes. Shake the beam around while moving your gaze up and down. You should catch glimpses of what look like delicate branches. These branches are shadows of the blood vessels that lie on top of your retina. The vessels constantly cast shadows as light streams into the eye, but because these shadows never move, the brain ceases responding to them. Moving the flashlight beam around shifts the shadows just enough to make them momentarily visible. Now you might wonder if you could cause an image to fade just by staring at something unmoving. But that is not possible because the visual system constantly jiggles the eye muscles, which prevents the perfect stabilization of images of the world. These muscle movements are unbelievably small, but their effect is huge. Without them, we would go blind by tuning out what we see shortly after fixating our gaze! It's an interesting notion: Approximate perfection is better than perfect perfection.

*retina: 망막 **jiggle: 가볍게 흔들다

① What makes your vision blurry actually protects your eyes.
② The more quickly an object moves, the more sensitively eyes react.
③ Eyes exposed to intense light are subject to distortion of images.
④ Constant adjustment of focusing makes your eye muscles tired.
⑤ Shaky eye-muscle movements let us see what the brain might ignore.

D08 ★★★ .... 2024 실시 3월 학평 21 (고3)

다음 밑줄 친 you taste its price가 의미하는 바로 가장 적절한 것은?

That perception is a construction is not true just of one's perception of sensory input, such as visual and auditory information. It is true of your social perceptions as well — your perceptions of the people you meet, the food you eat, and even of the products you buy. For example, in a study of wine, when wines were tasted blind, there was little or no correlation between the ratings of a wine's taste and its cost, but there *was* a significant correlation when the wines were labeled by price. That wasn't because the subjects consciously believed that the higher-priced wines should be the better ones and thus revised whatever opinion they had accordingly. Or rather, it wasn't true *just* at the conscious level. We know because as the subjects were tasting the wine, the researchers were imaging their brain activity, and the imaging showed that drinking what they believed was an expensive glass of wine really did activate their centers of taste for pleasure more than drinking a glass of the same wine that had been labeled as cheaper. That's related to the placebo effect. Like pain, taste is not just the product of sensory signals; it depends also on psychological factors: you don't just taste the wine; you taste its price.

① Customer ratings determine the price of a product.
② We fool ourselves into thinking our unplanned buying was reasonable.
③ We immediately dismiss opposing opinions without any consideration.
④ The brain shows consistent response regardless of personal preference.
⑤ The perceived value of a product influences one's subjective experience of it.

밑줄 친 a stick in the bundle이 다음 글에서 의미하는 바로 가장 적절한 것은? [3점]

Lawyers sometimes describe ownership as a *bundle of sticks*. This metaphor was introduced about a century ago, and it has dramatically transformed the teaching and practice of law. The metaphor is useful because it helps us see ownership as a grouping of interpersonal rights that can be separated and put back together. When you say *It's mine* in reference to a resource, often that means you own a lot of the sticks that make up the full bundle: the sell stick, the rent stick, the right to mortgage, license, give away, even destroy the thing. Often, though, we split the sticks up, as for a piece of land: there may be a landowner, a bank with a mortgage, a tenant with a lease, a plumber with a license to enter the land, an oil company with mineral rights. Each of these parties owns a stick in the bundle.

*mortgage: 저당잡히다 **tenant: 임차인

① a legal obligation to develop the resource
② a priority to legally claim the real estate
③ a right to use one aspect of the property
④ a building to be shared equally by tenants
⑤ a piece of land nobody can claim as their own

밑줄 친 live in the shadow of the future가 다음 글에서 의미하는 바로 가장 적절한 것은?

Thanks to the power of reputation, we help others without expecting an immediate return. If, thanks to endless chat and intrigue, the world knows that you are a good, charitable guy, then you boost your chance of being helped by someone else at some future date. The converse is also the case. I am less likely to get my back scratched, in the form of a favor, if it becomes known that I never scratch anybody else's. Indirect reciprocity now means something like "If I scratch your back, my good example will encourage others to do the same and, with luck, someone will scratch mine." By the same token, our behavior is endlessly shaped by the possibility that somebody else might be watching us or might find out what we have done. We are often troubled by the thought of what others may think of our deeds. In this way, our actions have consequences that go far beyond any individual act of charity, or indeed any act of mean-spirited malice. We all behave differently when we know we live in the shadow of the future. That shadow is cast by our actions because there is always the possibility that others will find out what we have done.

*malice: 악의

① are distracted by inner conflict
② fall short of our own expectations
③ seriously compete regardless of the results
④ are under the influence of uncertainty
⑤ ultimately reap what we have sown

D11 ✽✽✽ .... 2022 대비 6월 모평 21 (고3)

밑줄 친 an empty inbox가 다음 글에서 의미하는 바로 가장 적절한 것은? [3점]

The single most important change you can make in your working habits is to switch to creative work first, reactive work second. This means blocking off a large chunk of time every day for creative work on your own priorities, with the phone and e-mail off. I used to be a frustrated writer. Making this switch turned me into a productive writer. Yet there wasn't a single day when I sat down to write an article, blog post, or book chapter without a string of people waiting for me to get back to them. It wasn't easy, and it still isn't, particularly when I get phone messages beginning "I sent you an e-mail *two hours ago...!*" By definition, this approach goes against the grain of others' expectations and the pressures they put on you. It takes willpower to switch off the world, even for an hour. It feels uncomfortable, and sometimes people get upset. But it's better to disappoint a few people over small things, than to abandon your dreams for an empty inbox. Otherwise, you're sacrificing your potential for the illusion of professionalism.

① following an innovative course of action
② attempting to satisfy other people's demands
③ completing challenging work without mistakes
④ removing social ties to maintain a mental balance
⑤ securing enough opportunities for social networking

D12 ✽✽✽❀ .... 2023 실시 10월 학평 21 (고3)

밑줄 친 squeeze economies into a test tube가 다음 글에서 의미하는 바로 가장 적절한 것은?

Physicians and other natural scientists test their theories using controlled experiments. Macroeconomists, however, have no laboratories and little ability to run economy-wide experiments of any kind. Granted, they can study different economies around the world, but each economy is unique, so comparisons are tricky. Controlled experiments also provide the natural sciences with something seldom available to economists — the chance, or serendipitous, discovery (such as penicillin). Macroeconomists studying the U.S. economy have only one patient, so they can't introduce particular policies in a variety of alternative settings. You can't squeeze economies into a test tube. Cries of "Eureka!" are seldom heard from macroeconomists. An economy consisting of hundreds of millions of individual actors is a complicated thing. As Nobel Prize-winning physicist Murray Gell-Mann once observed, "Think how hard physics would be if particles could think."

*serendipitous: 우연히 발견하는

① admit economists' contributions to the natural sciences
② conduct controlled experiments on the economy
③ employ complex economic theories
④ share test results with other scientists
⑤ collect economic data over a long period of time

D13 ★★★ .... 2024 대비 9월 모평 21 (고3)

밑줄 친 "The best is the enemy of the good."이 다음 글에서 의미하는 바로 가장 적절한 것은? [3점]

Gold plating in the project means needlessly enhancing the expected results, namely, adding characteristics that are costly, not required, and that have low added value with respect to the targets — in other words, giving more with no real justification other than to demonstrate one's own talent. Gold plating is especially interesting for project team members, as it is typical of projects with a marked professional component — in other words, projects that involve specialists with proven experience and extensive professional autonomy. In these environments specialists often see the project as an opportunity to test and enrich their skill sets. There is therefore a strong temptation, in all good faith, to engage in gold plating, namely, to achieve more or higher-quality work that gratifies the professional but does not add value to the client's requests, and at the same time removes valuable resources from the project. As the saying goes, "The best is the enemy of the good."

*autonomy: 자율성 **gratify: 만족시키다

① Pursuing perfection at work causes conflicts among team members.
② Raising work quality only to prove oneself is not desirable.
③ Inviting overqualified specialists to a project leads to bad ends.
④ Responding to the changing needs of clients is unnecessary.
⑤ Acquiring a range of skills for a project does not ensure success.

D14 ★★★ .... 2024 대비 수능 21 (고3)

밑줄 친 a nonstick frying pan이 다음 글에서 의미하는 바로 가장 적절한 것은? [3점]

How you focus your attention plays a critical role in how you deal with stress. Scattered attention harms your ability to let go of stress, because even though your attention is scattered, it is narrowly focused, for you are able to fixate only on the stressful parts of your experience. When your attentional spotlight is widened, you can more easily let go of stress. You can put in perspective many more aspects of any situation and not get locked into one part that ties you down to superficial and anxiety-provoking levels of attention. A narrow focus heightens the stress level of each experience, but a widened focus turns down the stress level because you're better able to put each situation into a broader perspective. One anxiety-provoking detail is less important than the bigger picture. It's like transforming yourself into a nonstick frying pan. You can still fry an egg, but the egg won't stick to the pan.

*provoke: 유발시키다

① never being confronted with any stressful experiences in daily life
② broadening one's perspective to identify the cause of stress
③ rarely confining one's attention to positive aspects of an experience
④ having a larger view of an experience beyond its stressful aspects
⑤ taking stress into account as the source of developing a wide view

D15 ✱✱✱ .... 2021 실시 3월 학평 21 (고3)

밑줄 친 last in, first out이 다음 글에서 의미하는 바로
가장 적절한 것은? [3점]

While user habits are a boon to companies fortunate enough to generate them, their existence inherently makes success less likely for new innovations and startups trying to disrupt the *status quo*. The fact is, successfully changing long-term user habits is exceptionally rare. Altering behavior requires not only an understanding of how to persuade people to act but also necessitates getting them to repeat behaviors for long periods, ideally for the rest of their lives. Companies that succeed in building a habit-forming business are often associated with game-changing, wildly successful innovation. But like any discipline, habit design has rules that define and explain why some products change lives while others do not. For one, new behaviors have a short half-life, as our minds tend to return to our old ways of thinking and doing. Experiments show that lab animals habituated to new behaviors tend to regress to their first learned behaviors over time. To borrow a term from accounting, behaviors are LIFO — "last in, first out."

*boon: 요긴한 것 **regress: 되돌아가다

① The behavior witnessed first is forgotten first.
② Almost any behavior tends to change over time.
③ After an old habit breaks, a new one is formed.
④ The habit formed last is the hardest to get rid of.
⑤ The habit most recently acquired disappears soonest.

D16 ✱✱✲ .... 2023 실시 4월 학평 21 (고3)

밑줄 친 it's an angry protest from the brain's reward system이 다음 글에서 의미하는 바로 가장 적절한 것은?
[3점]

Our brains light up when our predicted reality and actual reality match. Our brains love to be right. We also don't like to be wrong, and we feel threatened when our stereotyped predictions don't come true. Psychologist Wendy Mendes asked White and Asian college students to interact with Latino students who had been hired as actors by the researchers. Some of the Latino students portrayed themselves as socioeconomically "high status," with lawyer fathers, professor mothers, and summers spent volunteering in Europe. Others portrayed themselves as "low status," with unemployed parents and part-time summer jobs. The researchers found that when participants interacted with the Latino students who appeared to come from wealth and thus challenged American stereotypes, they responded physiologically as if to a threat: their blood vessels constricted and their heart activity changed. In these interactions, participants also saw the students who violated stereotypes as less likable. In this way, stereotypes that are *descriptive* can easily become *prescriptive*. The phenomenon, it turns out, may have a neuroscientific explanation: it's an angry protest from the brain's reward system.

① Our brain prefers actual reality to predicted reality.
② Humans have a tendency to deny that they are stereotyped.
③ Humans are conditioned to avoid people who resemble them.
④ Our brain dislikes when something goes against its prediction.
⑤ When dissatisfied, the brain operates to make itself feel better.

D17 ★★★ .... 2022 실시 3월 학평 21 (고3)

밑줄 친 carries the stamp of this age가 다음 글에서 의미하는 바로 가장 적절한 것은? [3점]

Thomas Edison's name is synonymous with invention, and his most famous invention, the electric light bulb, is a familiar symbol for that flash of inspired genius traditionally associated with the inventive act. Besides being the exemplar of the "bright idea," however, Edison's electric light is worthy of study for other reasons. The technical and economic importance of the light and of the electrical system that surrounded it matches that of any other invention we could name, at least from the last two hundred years. The introduction and spread of electric light and power was one of the key steps in the transformation of the world from an industrial age, characterized by iron and coal and steam, to a post-industrial one, in which electricity was joined by petroleum, light metals and alloys, and internal combustion engines to give the twentieth century its distinctive form and character. Our own time still largely carries the stamp of this age, however dazzled we may be by the electronic, computerized, and media wonders of the twenty-first century.

*alloy: 합금

① combines creative ideas from various disciplines

② strives to overcome limitations of the industrial age

③ is a theoretical background for academic exploration

④ is under the influence of earlier electrical innovations

⑤ is dependent on resources reserved for future generations

D18 ★★★ .... 2021 대비 수능 21 (고3)

밑줄 친 the role of the 'lion's historians'가 다음 글에서 의미하는 바로 가장 적절한 것은?

There is an African proverb that says, 'Till the lions have their historians, tales of hunting will always glorify the hunter'. The proverb is about power, control and law making. Environmental journalists have to play the role of the 'lion's historians'. They have to put across the point of view of the environment to people who make the laws. They have to be the voice of wild India. The present rate of human consumption is completely unsustainable. Forest, wetlands, wastelands, coastal zones, eco-sensitive zones, they are all seen as disposable for the accelerating demands of human population. But to ask for any change in human behaviour — whether it be to cut down on consumption, alter lifestyles or decrease population growth — is seen as a violation of human rights. But at some point human rights become 'wrongs'. It's time we changed our thinking so that there is no difference between the rights of humans and the rights of the rest of the environment.

① uncovering the history of a species' biological evolution

② urging a shift to sustainable human behaviour for nature

③ fighting against widespread violations of human rights

④ rewriting history for more underrepresented people

⑤ restricting the power of environmental lawmakers

D19 ★★★ .... 2022 실시 10월 학평 21 (고3)

밑줄 친 do not have the ears to hear it이 다음 글에서 의미하는 바로 가장 적절한 것은? [3점]

Far from a synonym for capitalism, consumerism makes capitalism impossible over the long term, since it makes capital formation all but impossible. A consumer culture isn't a saving culture, isn't a thrift culture. It's too fixated on buying the next toy to ever delay gratification, to ever save and invest for the future. The point is elementary: you can't have sustainable capitalism without capital; you can't have capital without savings; and you can't save if you're running around spending everything you've just earned. But the confusion has grown so deep that many people today do not have the ears to hear it. Indeed, the policies of our nation's central bank seem to reinforce this habit by driving down interest rates to near zero and thereby denying people a material reward — in the form of interest on their banked savings — for foregoing consumption.

*fixated: 집착하는 **gratification: 욕구 충족 ***forego: 단념하다

① disagree with the national policy of lowering interest rates
② ignore the fact that consumerism is a synonym for capitalism
③ believe that consumerism doesn't really do much for well-being
④ form a false assumption that savings can make nations prosper
⑤ fail to understand that consumption alone can't sustain capitalism

D20 ★★★ .... 2021 대비 9월 모평 21 (고3)

밑줄 친 don't knock the box가 다음 글에서 의미하는 바로 가장 적절한 것은?

By expecting what's likely to happen next, you prepare for the few most likely scenarios so that you don't have to figure things out while they're happening. It's therefore not a surprise when a restaurant server offers you a menu. When she brings you a glass with a clear fluid in it, you don't have to ask if it's water. After you eat, you don't have to figure out why you aren't hungry anymore. All these things are expected and are therefore not problems to solve. Furthermore, imagine how demanding it would be to always consider all the possible uses for all the familiar objects with which you interact. *Should I use my hammer or my telephone to pound in that nail?* On a daily basis, functional fixedness is a relief, not a curse. That's why you shouldn't even attempt to consider all your options and possibilities. You can't. If you tried to, then you'd never get anything done. So don't knock the box. Ironically, although it limits your thinking, it also makes you smart. It helps you to stay one step ahead of reality.

① Deal with a matter based on your habitual expectations.
② Question what you expect from a familiar object.
③ Replace predetermined routines with fresh ones.
④ Think over all possible outcomes of a given situation.
⑤ Extend all the boundaries that guide your thinking to insight.

D21 ★★✿ .... 2022 실시 4월 학평 21 (고3)

밑줄 친 news 'happens'가 다음 글에서 의미하는 바로 가장 적절한 것은? [3점]

Journalists love to report studies that are at the "initial findings" stages — research that claims to be the first time anyone has discovered a thing — because there is newsworthiness in their novelty. But "first ever" discoveries are extremely vulnerable to becoming undermined by subsequent research. When that happens, the news media often don't go back and inform their audiences about the change — assuming they even hear about it. Kelly Crowe, a CBC News reporter writes, quoting one epidemiologist, "There is increasing concern that in modern research, false findings may be the majority or even the vast majority of published research claims." She goes on to suggest that journalists, though blameworthy for this tendency, are aided and abetted by the scientists whose studies they cite. She writes that the "conclusions" sections in scientific abstracts can sometimes be overstated in an attempt to draw attention from prestigious academic journals and media who uncritically take their bait. Even so, Crowe ends her piece by stressing that there is still an incompatibility between the purposes and processes of news and science: Science 'evolves,' but news 'happens.'

*epidemiologist: 전염병학자 **aid and abet: 방조하다

① News follows the process of research more than the outcome.

② News focuses not on how research changes but on the novelty of it.

③ News attracts attention by criticizing false scientific discoveries.

④ Reporters give instant feedback to their viewers, unlike scientists.

⑤ Reporters create and strengthen trust in the importance of science.

D22 ★★✿ .... 2023 실시 7월 학평 21 (고3)

밑줄 친 production and marketing이 다음 글에서 의미하는 바로 가장 적절한 것은?

Humans already have a longer period of protected immaturity — a longer childhood — than any other species. Across species, a long childhood is correlated with an evolutionary strategy that depends on flexibility, intelligence, and learning. There is a developmental division of labor. Children get to learn freely about their particular environment without worrying about their own survival — caregivers look after that. Adults use what they learned as children to mate, hunt, and generally succeed as grown-ups in that environment. Children are the R&D (research and development) department of the human species. We grown-ups are production and marketing. We start out as brilliantly flexible but helpless and dependent babies, great at learning everything but terrible at doing just about anything. We end up as much less flexible but much more efficient and effective adults, not so good at learning but terrific at planning and acting.

① agents who conduct the tasks of living with what they learned

② executives who assign roles according to one's characteristics

③ actors who realize their dreams by building better relations

④ traders who contribute to economic development

⑤ leaders who express their thoughts to others

D23 ★★※.................... 2022 실시 7월 학평 21 (고3)

밑줄 친 this civilization of leisure was, in reality, a Trojan horse가 다음 글에서 의미하는 바로 가장 적절한 것은? [3점]

It seemed like a fair deal: we would accept new technologies, which would modify our habits and oblige us to adjust to certain changes, but in exchange we would be granted relief from the burden of work, more security, and above all, the freedom to pursue our desires. The sacrifice was worth the gain; there would be no regrets. Yet it has become apparent that this civilization of leisure was, in reality, a Trojan horse. Its swelling flanks hid the impositions of a new type of enslavement. The automatons are not as autonomous as advertised. They need us. Those computers that were supposed to do our calculations for us instead demand our attention: for ten hours a day, we are glued to their screens. Our communications monopolize our time. Time itself is accelerating. The complexity of the system overwhelms us. And leisure is often a costly distraction.

*flank: 측면, 옆구리 **automaton: 자동 장치

① Doing leisure activities increased communication between colleagues.
② Labor was easily incorporated with leisure by the media.
③ People's privacy was attacked because of low security.
④ Technology's promise for leisure actually made people less free.
⑤ Technological innovations did not improve hierarchical working culture.

D24 ★★★.................... 2021 대비 6월 모평 21 (고3)

밑줄 친 journey edges가 다음 글에서 의미하는 바로 가장 적절한 것은? [3점]

Many ancillary businesses that today seem almost core at one time started out as journey edges. For example, retailers often boost sales with accompanying support such as assembly or installation services. Think of a home goods retailer selling an unassembled outdoor grill as a box of parts and leaving its customer's mission incomplete. When that retailer also sells assembly and delivery, it takes another step in the journey to the customer's true mission of cooking in his backyard. Another example is the business-to-business service contracts that are layered on top of software sales. Maintenance, installation, training, delivery, anything at all that turns do-it-yourself into a do-it-for-me solution originally resulted from exploring the edge of where core products intersect with customer journeys.

* ancillary: 보조의, 부차적인 ** intersect: 교차하다

① requiring customers to purchase unnecessary goods
② decreasing customers' dependence on business services
③ focusing more on selling end products than components
④ adding a technological breakthrough to their core products
⑤ providing extra services beyond customers' primary purchase

D25 ✪ 2등급 대비 .... 2023 대비 수능 21 (고3)

밑줄 친 make oneself public to oneself가 다음
글에서 의미하는 바로 가장 적절한 것은? [3점]

Coming of age in the 18th and 19th centuries, the personal diary became a centerpiece in the construction of a modern subjectivity, at the heart of which is the application of reason and critique to the understanding of world and self, which allowed the creation of a new kind of knowledge. Diaries were central media through which enlightened and free subjects could be constructed. They provided a space where one could write daily about her whereabouts, feelings, and thoughts. Over time and with rereading, disparate entries, events, and happenstances could be rendered into insights and narratives about the self, and allowed for the formation of subjectivity. It is in that context that the idea of "the self [as] both made and explored with words" emerges. Diaries were personal and private; one would write for oneself, or, in Habermas's formulation, one would make oneself public to oneself. By making the self public in a private sphere, the self also became an object for self-inspection and self-critique.

*disparate: 이질적인 **render: 만들다

① use writing as a means of reflecting on oneself
② build one's identity by reading others' diaries
③ exchange feedback in the process of writing
④ create an alternate ego to present to others
⑤ develop topics for writing about selfhood

D26 ✪ 2등급 대비 .... 2022 대비 9월 모평 21 (고3)

밑줄 친 Flicking the collaboration light switch가
다음 글에서 의미하는 바로 가장 적절한 것은? [3점]

Flicking the collaboration light switch is something that leaders are uniquely positioned to do, because several obstacles stand in the way of people voluntarily working alone. For one thing, the fear of being left out of the loop can keep them glued to their enterprise social media. Individuals don't want to be — or appear to be — isolated. For another, knowing what their teammates are doing provides a sense of comfort and security, because people can adjust their own behavior to be in harmony with the group. It's risky to go off on their own to try something new that will probably not be successful right from the start. But even though it feels reassuring for individuals to be hyperconnected, it's better for the organization if they periodically go off and think for themselves and generate diverse — if not quite mature — ideas. Thus, it becomes the leader's job to create conditions that are good for the whole by enforcing intermittent interaction even when people wouldn't choose it for themselves, without making it seem like a punishment.

*intermittent: 간헐적인

① breaking physical barriers and group norms that prohibit cooperation
② having people stop working together and start working individually
③ encouraging people to devote more time to online collaboration
④ shaping environments where higher productivity is required
⑤ requiring workers to focus their attention on group projects

D27 ⊙ **1등급 대비** .... 2022 대비 수능 21 (고3)

밑줄 친 whether to make ready for the morning commute or not이 다음 글에서 의미하는 바로 가장 적절한 것은? [3점]

Scientists have no special purchase on moral or ethical decisions; a climate scientist is no more qualified to comment on health care reform than a physicist is to judge the causes of bee colony collapse. The very features that create expertise in a specialized domain lead to ignorance in many others. In some cases lay people — farmers, fishermen, patients, native peoples — may have relevant experiences that scientists can learn from. Indeed, in recent years, scientists have begun to recognize this: the Arctic Climate Impact Assessment includes observations gathered from local native groups. So our trust needs to be limited, and focused. It needs to be very *particular*. Blind trust will get us into at least as much trouble as no trust at all. But without some degree of trust in our designated experts — the men and women who have devoted their lives to sorting out tough questions about the natural world we live in — we are paralyzed, in effect not knowing whether to make ready for the morning commute or not.

*lay: 전문가가 아닌 **paralyze: 마비시키다 ***commute: 통근

① questionable facts that have been popularized by non-experts
② readily applicable information offered by specialized experts
③ common knowledge that hardly influences crucial decisions
④ practical information produced by both specialists and lay people
⑤ biased knowledge that is widespread in the local community

D28 ⊙ **1등급 대비** .... 2024 실시 10월 학평 21 (고3)

밑줄 친 Now I zip along the surface like a guy on a Jet Ski가 다음 글에서 의미하는 바로 가장 적절한 것은? [3점]

In 1890, William James described attention as "the taking possession by the mind, in clear and vivid form, of one out of what seem several simultaneously possible objects or trains of thought." Attention is a choice we make to stay on one task, one line of thinking, one mental road, even as attractive off-ramps signal. When we fail to make that choice and allow ourselves to be frequently sidetracked, we end up in "the confused, dazed, scatterbrained state" that James said is the opposite of attention. Staying on one road got much harder when the internet arrived and moved much of our reading online. Every hyperlink is an off-ramp, calling us to abandon the choice we made moments earlier. Nicholas Carr, in his 2010 book, grieved his lost ability to stay on one path. Life on the internet changed how his brain sought out information, even when he was off-line trying to read a book. It reduced his ability to focus and reflect because he now craved a constant stream of stimulation: "Once I was a scuba diver in the sea of words. Now I zip along the surface like a guy on a Jet Ski."

*off-ramp: 빠져나가는 길 ** dazed: 멍한 *** crave: 갈망하다

① Ironically, the convenience of downloading digital creations restrains people's creativity.
② By uncritically accepting information, we get trapped in a cycle of misunderstanding.
③ People's attention is naturally drawn to carefully analyzed and well-presented data.
④ We now deal with the information in a skin-deep manner, constantly being distracted.
⑤ With the help of the internet, we comprehend the information quickly and thoroughly.

D 어휘 Review

※ 다음 영어는 우리말 뜻을, 우리말은 영어 단어를 〈보기〉에서 찾아 쓰시오.

〈보기〉

수축하다	reality	외부의	complicated
의무	particle	평판	conclude
전략	tricky	효율적인	attach

01 reputation _____

02 constrict _____

03 obligation _____

04 efficient _____

05 strategy _____

06 현실 _____

07 복잡한 _____

08 입자 _____

09 까다로운 _____

10 결론을 내리다 _____

※ 다음 우리말에 알맞은 영어 표현을 찾아 연결하시오.

11 분리하다   •   • in exchange

12 ~와 상호 관련이 있다 •   • a string of

13 ~와 비교하여   •   • be correlated with

14 그 대신   •   • split up

15 여러 개의, 일련의   •   • compared to

※ 다음 우리말 표현에 맞는 단어를 고르시오.

16 틀에 갇힌 ⇒ (stuck / struck) in a rut

17 순수하고 객관적인 형태로 ⇒ in a (pure / sure), objective form

18 취향의 수렴 ⇒ a (converse / convergence) of tastes

19 실업자인 부모님 ⇒ (unemployed / unemotional) parents

20 비선형적인 수학 ⇒ the (linear / nonlinear) mathematics

※ 다음 문장의 빈칸에 알맞은 단어를 〈보기〉에서 찾아 쓰시오.

〈보기〉

intelligible	theoretical	reassuring	peer
temptation	transformed	immaturity	alternative
immediate	violated	external	discipline

21 우리는 즉각적인 보답을 기대하지 않고 남들을 돕는다.
   ⇒ We help others without expecting a(n) _____ return.

22 그것은 법학교육을 극적으로 변화시켰다.
   ⇒ It has dramatically _____ the teaching of law.

23 인간은 이미 더 긴 기간의 보호받는 미성숙 상태를 갖는다.
   ⇒ Humans already have a longer period of protected _____.

24 여느 분야와 마찬가지로 습관 설계에도 규칙이 있다.
   ⇒ Like any _____, habit design has rules.

25 사람들은 과잉 연결되는 것이 안도감이 든다고 느낀다.
   ⇒ It feels _____ for individuals to be hyperconnected.

26 금도금에 참여하려는 강한 유혹이 있다.
   ⇒ There is a strong _____ to engage in gold plating.

27 그들은 다양한 다른 상황에서 특정 정책을 도입할 수 없다.
   ⇒ They can't introduce particular policies in a variety of _____ settings.

28 이론적 구성물로서가 아닌 보편적이거나 권위 있는 버전은 없다.
   ⇒ There is no universal or authoritative version, other than as a(n) _____ construct.

29 참가자들은 고정 관념을 깨뜨린 학생들을 덜 호감이 가는 것으로 간주했다.
   ⇒ Participants saw the students who _____ stereotypes as less likable.

30 우리는 세계를 우리가 이해할 수 있게 만드는 인간의 렌즈를 통해서 세계를 경험한다.
   ⇒ We experience the world through the human lenses that make it _____ to us.

연세문학회

연세대학교 문예 창작 동아리

윤동주가 동아리 선배라고?!

〈연세문학회〉는 윤동주, 정현종, 기형도, 나희덕, 마광수, 성석제, 원재길, 황경신, 우상호 등 유명한 문인들을 배출한 문예 창작 동아리입니다.

1941년 윤동주 시인이 만든 〈문우〉에서 출발하여
1958년 정현종 시인에 의해 〈연세문학회〉라는 현재의 이름을 얻었습니다.

매주 문학에 열정을 가진 학우들이 모여
시, 소설, 독서, 합평 분야별로 창작 활동을 합니다.
학우들이 직접 쓴 작품을 함께 읽으며 창조적 비평을 진행하고,
학기 말에는 학우들의 작품을 수합하여 정기 문집 《연세문학》을 발간합니다.
또한 합동 합평회를 통해 다른 학교의 문학 동아리와 교류하기도 합니다.

〈연세문학회〉는 연세 대학교의 문학청년들이
마음껏 창작의 나래를 펼치는 드넓은 '광장'입니다.

전공과 관계없이, 문학을 사랑하는 학우라면 〈연세문학회〉의 문을 두드리세요!

E 요지 찾기

> 매월 캠핑 오니까 너무 좋다. 공기도 맑고, 마음도 편안해지네. 한 달에 한 번씩 캠핑 오는 것은 내 삶의 활력이 될 것 같아.

> 네 말의 요지는 한 달에 한 번씩 캠핑을 가자는 거구나!

★ 유형 설명

> 다음 글의 요지로 가장 적절한 것은?
>
> The twenty-first century is the age of information and knowledge. It is a century

글의 주제에 대해 어떠한 견해를 갖고 있는 글인지를 우리말로 표현한 선택지를 찾는 유형이다.

O━ 명확히 드러나는 주제문이나 반복되는 부분, 같은 의미를 다른 말로 바꾸어 표현한 부분을 중심으로 글의 주제를 파악하고, 그 주제에 부합하는 요지를 선택지에서 고른다.

유형 풀이 비법

1 주제문을 찾아라!
• 반복되는 부분에 주목하면서 필자가 전달하려는 중심 내용을 파악한다.

2 특정 부분을 잘 보자!
• 요지는 주로 글의 첫 부분과 끝부분에 잘 나온다.

3 요지의 범위를 확인하라!
• 요지의 범위가 너무 넓거나 좁지 않은지, 중간에 필자의 태도가 바뀌는 곳은 없는지도 확인한다.

> Tip 주로 명령문이나 의무의 조동사가 포함된 문장과 특정 어구(rather, however, while 등) 앞뒤에 글의 요지가 담겨 있다.

★ 최신 수능 경향 분석

대비 연도	월	문항 번호	지문 주제	난이도
2025	11	22번	집단에서 협력하는 사람들의 특성	★★★
	9	22번	인간 사회에서만 나타나는 '도덕성'	★★☆
	6	22번	인간 의사소통의 평등성이 형성한 공유와 공조 가치	★★★
2024	11	22번	고객의 브랜드 칭찬에 응답하는 것의 중요성	★★☆
	9	22번	이민자의 권리에 대한 인식 변화 필요성	★★☆
	6	22번	가상 세계에서는 덜 방어적인 우리	★★☆
2023	11	22번	효율적인 배송 수단으로서의 자전거	★★☆
	9	22번	도덕적 목표 설정의 중요성	★★☆
	6	22번	수동적 방관자에서 능동적 참여자로	★★☆

★ 2025 수능 출제 분석

먼저 선택지를 읽고 글을 읽으면, '감정과 소통'이 핵심 소재임을 미리 파악할 수 있고, 감정과 소통과 관련해 어떤 내용인지 글의 첫 문장부터 확실히 드러나서 정답을 빠르게 찾을 수 있었을 것이다.

★ 2026 수능 예측

간혹 선택지가 영어로 제시되기도 하지만 최근에는 모두 한글이었으며, 이는 2026 수능에서도 마찬가지일 것이다.

요지를 뒷받침하는 주요 표현

☐ Well begun is half done. 시작이 반이다.

☐ Every cloud has a silver lining. 새옹지마

☐ Habit is a second nature. 습관은 제2의 천성이다.

☐ No pains, no gains. 노력이 있어야 얻는 것이 있다.

☐ Honesty is the best policy. 정직이 최상의 방책이다.

☐ Look before you leap. 돌다리도 두들겨 보고 건너라.

☐ Blood is thicker than water. 피는 물보다 더 진하다.

☐ Two heads are better than one. 백지장도 맞들면 낫다.

☐ Better late than never. 늦더라도 하지 않는 것보다 낫다.

☐ All that glitters is not gold. 번쩍인다고 다 금은 아니다.

☐ Actions speak louder than words. 행동은 말보다 미덥다.

☐ A good turn deserves another. 좋은 일은 보답을 받는다.

☐ The end justifies the means. 목적이 수단을 정당화시킨다.

어휘 및 표현 Preview

☐ reason 이유

☐ consider 간주하다

☐ rough 개략적인

☐ sentient 지각력 있는

☐ suppose 추정하다

☐ immoral 부도덕적인

☐ attack 공격하다

☐ universal 보편적인

☐ concept 개념

☐ equally 똑같이, 공평하게

☐ measure 측정하다

☐ specifically 특별히

☐ language 언어

 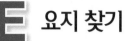 

E 요지 찾기 (첫 번째)

1st 선택지를 통해 글의 소재를 파악하세요.
2nd 글을 읽으며 특정 어구(연결어, 의미가 연관된 어휘들, 명령문 등)를 찾아 글의 요지를 생각해 보세요.
3rd 글의 내용이 한눈에 들어오도록 정리하여 생각한 글의 요지가 맞는지 확인하세요.

E01 ✿❈❈ .... 2025 대비 6월 모평 22 (고3)

다음 글의 요지로 가장 적절한 것은?

In both the ancient hunter-gatherer band and our intimate speech communities today, the diffusion of speech shaped values. The fact that everyone was going to be able to speak and listen had to be accommodated ethically, and it was via a rough egalitarianism. In terms of communications, people were equal and therefore it was believed they *should be* equal, or at least relatively so. By this code, ancient Big Men were not allowed to act controllingly and modern office managers are not allowed to silence anyone at will. Moreover, equal access to speech and hearing promoted the notion that property should be held in common, that goods and food in particular should be shared, and that everyone had a duty to take care of everyone else. This was probably more true among hunter-gatherers than it is in the modern family, circle of friends, or workplace. But even in these cases we believe that sharing and mutual aid are right and proper. Remember, if you bring something, you should bring enough for everyone.

*diffusion: 확산 **egalitarianism: 인류 평등주의

① 수렵인과 현대인은 언어에 대한 유사한 가치를 가지고 있다.
② 인간은 언어를 사용하여 자원을 보다 효율적으로 배분해 왔다.
③ 현대 사회는 고대 수렵 사회보다 평등한 체계에 의해 운영된다.
④ 인간 의사소통의 평등성은 공유와 공조 가치 기반을 형성했다.
⑤ 인간은 의사소통을 통해 자원을 공유하는 평등한 사회를 건설했다.

1st 선택지를 통해 글의 소재를 파악하세요.

① 수렵인과 현대인은 언어에 대한 유사한 가치를 가지고 있다.
② 인간은 언어를 사용하여 자원을 보다 효율적으로 배분해왔다.
③ 현대 사회는 고대 수렵 사회보다 평등한 체계에 의해 운영된다.
④ 인간 의사소통의 평등성은 공유와 공조 가치 기반을 형성했다.
⑤ 인간은 의사소통을 통해 자원을 공유하는 평등한 사회를 건설했다.

● **반복되어 등장하는 어구를 찾았나요?**

인간, 의사소통, 평등성, 공유, 공조 등의 핵심 어구가 다섯 개 선택지에 등장하고 있어요. **단서** ①은 수렵인과 현대인이 언어에 대해 가지는 가치가 비슷하다는 의미이고, ②은 언어를 사용한 자원의 효율적인 배분, ④은 의사소통의 평등성을 통한 공유와 공조 가치 기반, ⑤은 의사소통을 통한 자원 공유에 대해 이야기하고 있어요.

● **③을 제외한 선택지에 공통점이 있어요.**

인간의 언어나 의사소통에 대해 말한다는 점에서 ③을 제외한 나머지 선택지들이 공통점을 가져요.
이 글에서 설명하는 것이 '언어와 관련해서 수렵인과 현대인의 비교'인지, '인간 의사소통의 평등성'인지, '의사소통을 통한 평등한 사회'인지 글을 읽으면서 확인해 봅시다. **발상**

2nd 글을 읽으며 특정 어구(연결어, 의미가 연관된 어휘들, 명령문 등)를 찾아 글의 요지를 생각해 보세요.

1) 눈에 띄는 문장이 중반 이후에 등장하네요!

Moreover, equal access to speech and hearing /
게다가, 말하기와 듣기에 대한 평등한 접근은   /
promoted the notion / that property should be held
생각을 촉진했다   / 재산은 공동으로 소유되어야
in common, / that goods and food in particular
하고   / 특히 물자와 식량은 공유되어야 하며
should be shared, / and that everyone had a duty /
                  / 모든 사람은 의무가 있다는   /
to take care of everyone else. //
다른 사람을 돌볼   //

● **should be를 통해 필자의 주장이 나타났어요.**

should be는 '~이어야 한다'라는 뜻으로서, 필자의 생각이나 주장을 담은 말을 할 때 쓸 가능성이 높은 표현이에요.

- Moreover를 쓰며 필자가 말하고자 하는 바가 이어지는 것도 알 수 있어요.

  Moreover는 **❶**( )'라는 뜻으로, 필자는 의사소통의 평등이, 재산은 공동으로 소유되어야 하고 물자와 식량은 공유되어야 하며 다른 사람을 돌볼 의무가 있다는 생각을 촉진시켰다고 했어요.

  즉 의사소통의 **❷**( )이 공유, 상호 협력의 가치를 촉진시켰다는 내용이죠.

2) Moreover를 쓰며 필자의 생각을 덧붙이는 문장이 왔으니 앞으로 거슬러 올라가 봅시다.

  In both the ancient hunter-gatherer band / and our
  고대의 수렵·채집인 무리와   / 오늘날

  intimate speech communities today, / the diffusion
  우리의 친밀한 언어 공동체 둘 다에서   / 언어의 확산은

  of speech shaped values. //
  가치를 형성했다   //

- 첫 문장을 살펴봅시다.

  수렵인과 현대인 모두 언어의 확산은 어떠한 가치를 형성했다고 했어요.
  언어와 관련해서 수렵인과 현대인의 공통점을 이야기하고 있네요.

3) 이제 중반부의 다음 문장을 살펴봅시다.

  In terms of communications, / people were equal
  의사소통의 측면에서   / 사람들은 평등했고

  and therefore / it was believed / they *should* be
  그리고 그러므로 / 여겨졌다   / 그들은 평등'해야

  equal, / or at least relatively so. //
  평등 / 하거나, 적어도 비교적 그렇다(평등하다)고 //

- In terms of는 '~의 측면에서'라는 뜻이에요.

  In terms of를 써서 '의사소통의 측면에서'라고 하며 사람들은 평등했고,
  그래서 평등해야 한다고 여겨졌다고 했어요. 한 마디로, **❸**( )의
  측면에서 인간은 평등하다는 것이죠.

- 첫 문장부터 연결된 내용이 나온 거네요.

  인간의 언어의 확산은 어떤 가치를 형성했고, 의사소통의 측면에서
  인간은 평등하다고 여겨졌다는 내용으로 연결되고 있어요.

- 앞서 파악한 내용을 종합하여 정답을 골라봅시다.

  필자는 인간이 의사소통 측면에서 평등하고, 이런 특징이 가져온 생각이
  공유와 공조 가치를 촉진했다는 주장을 펼쳤어요.
  이 내용과 가장 일치하는 선택지는 **❹**( )이에요.

3rd 글의 내용이 한눈에 들어오도록 정리하여 생각한 글의 요지가 맞는지 확인하세요.

| 도입 | 언어의 확산은 가치를 형성했다. |

↓

| 부연 | 의사소통 측면에서 사람들은 평등하게 여겨졌다. |

↓

| 결론 | 의사소통의 평등은 공유, 상호 협력의 가치를 촉진했다. |

⑤은 의사소통과 평등이라는 소재를 다 포함하고 있긴 해요. 하지만
의사소통 평등성이 공유와 상호 협력의 가치를 촉진했다는 것이지,
의사소통을 통해 평등한 사회를 건설했다는 것은 확대하여 해석한 것이므로
정답이 될 수 없어요.

글의 내용을 요약해서
정답이 맞는지 확인하자!

E 요지 찾기 (두 번째)

1st 선택지를 통해 글의 소재를 파악하세요.
2nd 글을 읽으며 특정 어구(연결어, 의미가 연관된 어휘들, 명령문 등)를 찾아 글의 요지를 생각해 보세요.
3rd 글의 내용이 한눈에 들어오도록 정리하여 생각한 글의 요지가 맞는지 확인하세요.

E02 ★★❀ ············· 2024 대비 6월 모평 22 (고3)

다음 글의 요지로 가장 적절한 것은?

When it comes to the Internet, it just pays to be a little paranoid (but not a lot). Given the level of anonymity with all that resides on the Internet, it's sensible to question the validity of any data that you may receive. Typically it's to our natural instinct when we meet someone coming down a sidewalk to place yourself in some manner of protective position, especially when they introduce themselves as having known you, much to your surprise. By design, we set up challenges in which the individual must validate how they know us by presenting scenarios, names or acquaintances, or evidence by which to validate (that is, photographs). Once we have received that information and it has gone through a cognitive validation, we accept that person as more trustworthy. All this happens in a matter of minutes but is a natural defense mechanism that we perform in the real world. However, in the virtual world, we have a tendency to be less defensive, as there appears to be no physical threat to our well-being.

*paranoid: 편집성의 **anonymity: 익명

① 가상 세계 특유의 익명성 때문에 표현의 자유가 남용되기도 한다.
② 인터넷 정보의 신뢰도를 검증하는 기술은 점진적으로 향상되고 있다.
③ 가상 세계에서는 현실 세계와 달리 자유로운 정보 공유가 가능하다.
④ 안전한 인터넷 환경 구축을 위해 보안 프로그램을 설치하는 것이 좋다.
⑤ 방어 기제가 덜 작동하는 가상 세계에서는 신중한 정보 검증이 중요하다.

1st 선택지를 통해 글의 소재를 파악하세요.

① 가상 세계 특유의 익명성 때문에 표현의 자유가 남용되기도 한다.
② 인터넷 정보의 신뢰도를 검증하는 기술은 점진적으로 향상되고 있다.
③ 가상 세계에서는 현실 세계와 달리 자유로운 정보 공유가 가능하다.
④ 안전한 인터넷 환경 구축을 위해 보안 프로그램을 설치하는 것이 좋다.
⑤ 방어 기제가 덜 작동하는 가상 세계에서는 신중한 정보 검증이 중요하다.

● **선택지에서 반복되고 있는 어구를 찾았나요?**
가상 세계, 인터넷, 정보 검증, 정보 공유 등의 핵심 어구가 여러 선택지에 고르게 분포되어 있어요. (단서) 아무래도 가상 세계나 인터넷에서 정보를 무분별하게 받아들일 수 있기 때문에 정보를 검증할 필요가 있다거나, 정보량이 많기 때문에 정보를 자유롭게 공유할 수 있다는 맥락일 것 같네요! (발상)

● **정답에 가까운 선택지를 찾아 볼까요?**
우선 핵심 어구가 두 개씩 포함된 선택지로는 ②, ③, ⑤이 보여요.
· 그렇다면 가상 세계나 인터넷과 관련하여 (정보 검증 / 정보 공유)라는 두 갈래로 답이 나뉘게 되는데, 나머지 글을 읽어보면서 확실한 단서를 찾아 봅시다.

2nd 글을 읽으며 특정 어구(연결어, 의미가 연관된 어휘들, 명령문 등)를 찾아 글의 요지를 생각해 보세요.

1) 앞부분부터 확인해 볼까요?

Given the level of anonymity / with all that resides
익명성 수준을 고려할 때 / 인터넷에 있는 모든 것의
on the Internet, / it's sensible / to question the
/ ~이 합리적이다 / 어떤 자료든 그것의
validity of any data / that you may receive. //
타당성에 대해 의문을 제기하는 것이 / 여러분이 받을지도 모르는 //

● **sensible을 통해 필자의 주장이 나타났어요.**
sensible은 ❶'(   )'이라는 뜻으로서, it's sensible to question은 '의문을 제기하는 것이 합리적이다'라고 해석되어요. 필자가 보기엔 무언가에 의문을 제기하는 것이 필요하다는 것이죠.

● **필자가 합리적이라고 생각하는 바는 무엇인가요?**
필자는 여러분이 받을 어떤 자료든 그 타당성에 의문을 제기하는 것이 합리적이라고 했어요. 첫 마디에 '익명성 수준'을 고려한다고 했는데, 익명성이 높은 인터넷 공간에서 그러한 자료들이 타당한지 의심해봐야 한다는 맥락으로 보여요.

2) 필자의 주장을 확인했으니, 이를 부연하는 문장을 살펴봅시다.

> All this happens / in a matter of minutes / but is a
> 이 모든 것이 일어나지만 / 몇 분 안에 /
> natural defense mechanism / that we perform / in
> 자연스러운 방어 기제이다 / 우리가 수행하는 /
> the real world. //
> 현실 세계에서 //

● 첫 문장 이후로는 새로운 누군가를 만날 때 우리의 방어 본능에 대해 쭉 이야기하고 있어요.

  현실 세계에서 우리는 (새로운 누군가를 대할 때) 자연스러운
  ❷(   )를 갖추고 있다고 했어요. 앞부분에서 우리는 가상
  세계에 대해 이야기했는데 현실 세계의 방어 기제가 어떻게 연관되는지는
  뒷부분에서 더 알아봐야겠어요.

3) 이제 마지막 문장을 살펴봅시다.

> However, in the virtual world, / we have a
> 하지만 가상 세계에서는 / 우리는 경향이 있다
> tendency / to be less defensive, / as there appears to
> / 덜 방어적인 / 물리적인 위협이 없는 것처럼
> be no physical threat / to our well-being. //
> 보이기 때문에 / 우리의 행복에 //

● However는 '하지만'이라는 뜻이에요.

  However는 역접의 연결어로서 앞의 내용과 반대되는 내용을 언급할 때
  쓰여요. 앞 문장에서 우리가 현실 세계에서 방어 기제를 갖추고 있다고
  했지만 가상 세계에서는 '덜 방어적인 경향'이 있다고 하네요.

● '의문을 제기하는 것'과 '덜 방어적인 경향'은 어떤 관계인가요?

  정보를 받아들이기에 앞서, 그 정보의 타당성에 의문을 제기하는 것은
  우리가 무분별하게 정보를 받아들이지 않도록 '막는' 역할을 하죠?
  그렇기에 의문을 제기하는 것은 곧 ❸(   )이라고 볼 수 있어요.
  따라서, 덜 방어적인 경향은 (새로운 정보를 발견했을 때) 검증 없이
  정보를 받아들이는 것과 같죠.

● 앞서 파악한 내용을 종합하여 정답을 골라봅시다.

  필자는 우리가 익명성이 강한 가상 세계에서 정보를 검증 없이
  받아들이는, 다시 말해, 덜 방어적인 경향이 있으니 그 타당성에 의문을
  제기하는 것(정보 검증)이 합리적이라는 주장을 펼쳤어요. 이 내용과 가장
  일치하는 선택지는 ❹(   )이에요.

3rd 글의 내용이 한눈에 들어오도록 정리하여 생각한 글의 요지가 맞는지 확인하세요.

> **도입** 익명성이 높은 인터넷의 어떤 자료든 그 타당성에 의문을 제기하는 것이 합리적이다.
>
> ↓
>
> **부연** 우리는 현실 세계에서 새로운 누군가를 만날 때 그 사람을 검증하는 방어 기제를 수행한다.
>
> ↓
>
> **결론** 우리는 가상 세계에서 덜 방어적인 경향이 있다.

도입의 '타당성에 의문을 제기하는 것'을 정보 검증으로 바꾸고 부연의 '방어 기제'와 결론의 '가상 세계'를 활용하여 선택지를 구성했어요.
②은 인터넷과 정보 검증이라는 소재를 둘 다 포함하지만, 이 글에서 정보 검증 기술의 발전이 나타나지는 않았으며 방어 기제에 더 초점을 맞추고 있기 때문에 정답이 될 수 없어요.

정답의 단서가 되는 특정 어구를 찾자!

E03 ~ 06 ▶ 제한시간 8분

E03 ✽❀❀ .... 2025 대비 수능 22 (고3)

다음 글의 요지로 가장 적절한 것은?

The ability to understand emotions — to have a diverse emotion vocabulary and to understand the causes and consequences of emotio — is particularly relevant in group settings. Individuals who are skilled in this domain are able to express emotions, feelings and moods accurately and thus, may facilitate clear communication between co-workers. Furthermore, they may be more likely to act in ways that accommodate their own needs as well as the needs of others (i.e. cooperate). In a group conflict situation, for example, a member with a strong ability to understand emotion will be able to express how he feels about the problem and why he feels this way. He also should be able to take the perspective of the other group members and understand why they are reacting in a certain manner. Appreciation of differences creates an arena for open communication and promotes constructive conflict resolution and improved group functioning.

① 집단 구성원 간 갈등 해소를 위해 감정 조절이 중요하다.
② 감정 이해 능력은 집단 내 원활한 소통과 협력을 촉진한다.
③ 타인에 대한 공감 능력은 자신의 감정 표현 능력을 향상한다.
④ 감정 관련 어휘에 대한 지식은 공감 능력 발달의 기반이 된다.
⑤ 자신의 감정 상태에 대한 이해는 사회성 함양에 필수적 요소이다.

E04 ✽✽❀ .... 2025 대비 9월 모평 22 (고3)

다음 글의 요지로 가장 적절한 것은?

Even though there is good reason to consider a dog a sentient being capable of making choices and plans — so that we might suppose 'it could have conceived of acting otherwise' — we're unlikely to think it is wicked and immoral for attacking a child. Moral responsibility is not some universal concept like entropy or temperature — something that applies equally, and can be measured similarly, everywhere in the cosmos. It is a notion developed specifically for human use, no more or less than languages are. While sentience and volition are aspects of mind and agency, morals are cultural tools developed to influence social behaviour: to cultivate the desirable and discourage the harmful. They are learnt, not given at birth. It's possible, indeed likely, that we are born with a predisposition to cooperate with others — but only within human society do we come to understand this as *moral behaviour*. *sentient: 지각력이 있는 **volition: 의지

① 도덕성은 자신의 선택에 대해 책임을 진다는 개념이다.
② 동물과 인간을 구별하는 중요한 특징은 분별력과 언어이다.
③ 도덕성은 학습되는 문화적 도구로서 인간 사회에만 나타난다.
④ 동물과 인간은 공통적으로 다른 개체와 협력하는 경향이 있다.
⑤ 문화적 도구로서의 도덕성은 개체의 의사 결정에 영향을 미친다.

다음 글의 요지로 가장 적절한 것은?

Technical, book knowledge consists of "formulated rules which are, or may be, deliberately learned." Practical knowledge, on the other hand, cannot be taught or learned but only transmitted and acquired. It exists only in practice. When we talk about practical knowledge, we tend to use bodily metaphors. We say that somebody has a *touch* for doing some activity — an ability to hit the right piano key with just enough force and pace. We say that somebody has a *feel* for the game, an intuition for how events are going to unfold, an awareness of when you should plow ahead with a problem and when you should put it aside before coming back to it. When the expert is using her practical knowledge, she isn't thinking more; she is thinking less. She has built up a repertoire of skills through habit and has thereby extended the number of tasks she can perform without conscious awareness. This sort of knowledge is built up through experience, and it is passed along through shared experience.

*intuition: 직감, 직관 **plow ahead: 밀고 나가다

① 실용적 지식은 실행과 경험을 통해 체득되고 전수된다.
② 직감에 의한 판단이 옳아 보여도 심사숙고의 과정은
　필요하다.
③ 기술적 지식을 완전히 이해해야만 이를 실제로 적용할 수
　있다.
④ 상황에 맞게 행동하게 하는 실용적 지식은 타고나는
　능력이다.
⑤ 실용적 지식과 기술적 지식의 균형 있는 학습이 중요하다.

다음 글의 요지로 가장 적절한 것은?

The relevance of science in understanding organizational behavior can start with asking this question: Why do good managers make bad decisions? Too often managers make mistakes when it comes to fostering conditions that inspire positive outcomes in the workplace, such as performance, satisfaction, team cohesion, and ethical behavior. Why does this happen? Part of the reason is that rather than relying on a clearly validated set of scientific discoveries, managers use less reliable sources of insight such as gut feel, intuition, the latest trend, what a highly paid consultant might say, or what is being done in another company. Like most of us, managers tend to rely on their own strengths and experiences when making choices about how to get the best from others. But what works for one manager may not work for another. In the absence of a scientific approach, managers tend to make mistakes, offer ill-conceived incentives, misinterpret employee behavior, and fail to account for the many possible explanations for why employees might perform poorly.

① 직원들의 성과에 대한 다양한 평가 기준이 필요하다.
② 성공적인 관리자는 실패로부터 교훈을 이끌어 낸다.
③ 직원 간의 목표 공유가 조직을 결속하는 데 효과적이다.
④ 조직 문화의 혁신적 변화를 위해서는 관리자의 경험에 의한
　직관이 중요하다.
⑤ 조직 행동 이해에서 관리자가 과학적 접근법을 활용하지
　않으면 잘못된 판단을 할 수 있다.

E07 ★★✿............2024 실시 5월 학평 22 (고3)

다음 글의 요지로 가장 적절한 것은?

Most opposition to wilderness preservation doesn't come from environmentalists but from corporate interests and developers. When wild places are designated as wilderness, they are closed to most commercial activities and residential or infrastructure development. There is thus frequently an economic cost to wilderness preservation. Some critics claim that when wilderness and economic interests clash, economic interests should normally prevail. This argument, even if it is sound, won't exclude all wilderness preservation efforts, because some wilderness areas have little economic value. But a deeper problem with the argument is that it views nature from a human-focused and excessively economic point of view. Allowing economic considerations to outweigh all other forms of value is inconsistent with the biocentric reasons that support wilderness preservation. Thus, while it certainly makes sense to weigh the economic costs of wilderness protection, especially when such costs are high, the biocentric values underlying wilderness preservation exclude viewing economic considerations as the most important.

① 야생 보호 구역 보존의 생명 중심적 가치는 경제적 고려에 우선한다.
② 자연과의 공존을 고려한 상업 활동이 기업에 경제적 이익을 가져다준다.
③ 야생 보호에 있어 우선적으로 고려하는 가치는 문화에 따라 다양하다.
④ 야생 보호는 경제적 가치와 상관없이 모든 생물에 똑같이 적용된다.
⑤ 야생의 보호와 회복을 위한 비용 부담은 공동체 모두의 몫이다.

E08 ★★✿............2024 실시 3월 학평 22 (고3)

다음 글의 요지로 가장 적절한 것은?

Though it may seem extreme, a multilingual can quite literally feel differently about people, events or things when using one language versus another. The likelihood of being rattled by curse words or taboo words changes across native and second languages. Speakers of multiple languages not only report feeling different, but their bodies have different physiological reactions and their minds make different emotionally driven decisions across languages. The exact relationship between positive and negative emotions and language varies across people. For some, the second language carries more positive connotations because it is associated with freedom, opportunity, financial well-being and escape from persecution, whereas the native language is associated with poverty and hardship. For others, the opposite is true — the second language is associated with post-immigration challenges, discrimination and lack of close relationships, whereas the native language is associated with family, friends and parental love. And many are somewhere in between, having a mix of positive and negative experiences associated with each language.

*rattle: 당황하게[겁먹게] 하다 **connotation: 함축(된 의미)
***persecution: 박해

① 다중 언어 환경은 모국어 학습 발달을 지연시킨다.
② 모국어 실력이 뛰어날수록 외국어를 습득하는 속도가 빠르다.
③ 다중 언어 사용자는 사용하는 언어에 따라 다르게 느끼고 반응한다.
④ 부정적인 어휘가 긍정적인 어휘보다 감정에 미치는 영향이 크다.
⑤ 긍정적인 감정을 나타내는 어휘량이 문화권마다 다르다.

다음 글의 요지로 가장 적절한 것은?

Contractors that will construct a project may place more weight on the planning process. Proper planning forces detailed thinking about the project. It allows the project manager (or team) to "build the project in his or her head." The project manager (or team) can consider different methodologies thereby deciding what works best or what does not work at all. This detailed thinking may be the only way to discover restrictions or risks that were not addressed in the estimating process. It would be far better to discover in the planning phase that a particular technology or material will not work than in the execution process. The goal of the planning process for the contractor is to produce a workable scheme that uses the resources efficiently within the allowable time and given budget. A well-developed plan does not guarantee that the executing process will proceed flawlessly or that the project will even succeed in meeting its objectives. It does, however, greatly improve its chances.

*execute: 실행하다

① 계획 수립 절차를 간소화하면 일의 진행 속도가 빨라진다.
② 안정적인 예산 확보는 일의 원활한 진행을 위해 필수적이다.
③ 사업 계획은 급변하는 상황에 따라 유연하게 변경될 수 있다.
④ 면밀한 계획 수립은 일의 효율성을 증대시키고 성공 가능성을 높인다.
⑤ 대규모 사업에서는 지속적인 성장을 목표로 하는 세부 계획이 중요하다.

다음 글의 요지로 가장 적절한 것은?

Historically, the professions and society have engaged in a negotiating process intended to define the terms of their relationship. At the heart of this process is the tension between the professions' pursuit of autonomy and the public's demand for accountability. Society's granting of power and privilege to the professions is premised on their willingness and ability to contribute to social well-being and to conduct their affairs in a manner consistent with broader social values. It has long been recognized that the expertise and privileged position of professionals confer authority and power that could readily be used to advance their own interests at the expense of those they serve. As Edmund Burke observed two centuries ago, "Men are qualified for civil liberty in exact proportion to their disposition to put moral chains upon their own appetites." Autonomy has never been a one-way street and is never granted absolutely and irreversibly.

*autonomy: 자율성 **privilege: 특권 ***premise: 전제로 말하다

① 전문직에 부여되는 자율성은 그에 상응하는 사회적 책임을 수반한다.
② 전문직의 권위는 해당 집단의 이익을 추구하는 데 이용되어 왔다.
③ 전문직의 사회적 책임을 규정할 수 있는 제도 정비가 필요하다.
④ 전문직이 되기 위한 자격 요건은 사회 경제적 요구에 따라 변화해 왔다.
⑤ 전문직의 업무 성과는 일정 수준의 자율성과 특권이 부여될 때 높아진다.

E11 ★★❀ .... 2022 대비 수능 22 (고3)

다음 글의 요지로 가장 적절한 것은?

Environmental hazards include biological, physical, and chemical ones, along with the human behaviors that promote or allow exposure. Some environmental contaminants are difficult to avoid (the breathing of polluted air, the drinking of chemically contaminated public drinking water, noise in open public spaces); in these circumstances, exposure is largely involuntary. Reduction or elimination of these factors may require societal action, such as public awareness and public health measures. In many countries, the fact that some environmental hazards are difficult to avoid at the individual level is felt to be more morally egregious than those hazards that can be avoided. Having no choice but to drink water contaminated with very high levels of arsenic, or being forced to passively breathe in tobacco smoke in restaurants, outrages people more than the personal choice of whether an individual smokes tobacco. These factors are important when one considers how change (risk reduction) happens.

*contaminate: 오염시키다 **egregious: 매우 나쁜

① 개인이 피하기 어려운 유해 환경 요인에 대해서는 사회적 대응이 필요하다.
② 환경오염으로 인한 피해자들에게 적절한 보상을 하는 것이 바람직하다.
③ 다수의 건강을 해치는 행위에 대해 도덕적 비난 이상의 조치가 요구된다.
④ 환경오염 문제를 해결하기 위해서는 사후 대응보다 예방이 중요하다.
⑤ 대기오염 문제는 인접 국가들과의 긴밀한 협력을 통해 해결할 수 있다.

E12 ★★❀ .... 2021 대비 6월 모평 22 (고3)

다음 글의 요지로 가장 적절한 것은?

Official definitions of sport have important implications. When a definition emphasizes rules, competition, and high performance, many people will be excluded from participation or avoid other physical activities that are defined as "second class." For example, when a 12-year-old is cut from an exclusive club soccer team, she may not want to play in the local league because she sees it as "recreational activity" rather than a real sport. This can create a situation in which most people are physically inactive at the same time that a small number of people perform at relatively high levels for large numbers of fans — a situation that negatively impacts health and increases health-care costs in a society or community. When sport is defined to include a wide range of physical activities that are played for pleasure and integrated into local expressions of social life, physical activity rates will be high and overall health benefits are likely.

① 운동선수의 기량은 경기 자체를 즐길 때 향상된다.
② 공정한 승부를 위해 합리적인 경기 규칙이 필요하다.
③ 스포츠의 대중화는 스포츠 산업의 정의를 바꾸고 있다.
④ 스포츠의 정의는 신체 활동 참여와 건강에 영향을 미친다.
⑤ 활발한 여가 활동은 원만한 대인 관계 유지에 도움이 된다.

다음 글의 요지로 가장 적절한 것은?

Music is a human art form, an inseparable part of the human experience everywhere in the world. Music is social, and tightly woven into the tapestry of life, and young children are very much a part of this multifaceted fabric. The musical experiences they have provide opportunities for them to know language, behaviors, customs, traditions, beliefs, values, stories, and other cultural nuances. As they become musically skilled through experiences in song and instrumental music, young children can also grow cultural knowledge and sensitivity. Music is an extremely important aspect of culture, shaping and transmitting the above-mentioned aspects that characterize groups of people. Exposing young children to the world's musical cultures brings them into the cultural conversation, allowing them to learn about self and others in an artistically meaningful and engaging way. Prior to the development of social biases and cultural preferences that all too easily turn into prejudices, the opportunity to know people through song, dance, and instrument play is a gift to all who work for the well-balanced development of young children into the responsible citizens they will one day become.

*tapestry: 색색의 실로 수놓은 장식 걸개 ** multifaceted: 다면의

① 아이들의 균형 잡힌 성장을 위해서는 다양한 경험이 중요하다.
② 사회적 편견과 문화적 선호도는 서로 밀접하게 관련되어 있다.
③ 어린 나이에 다양한 음악에 노출되면 예술적 감각이 향상된다.
④ 음악을 포함한 예술은 특정 문화에 대한 당대의 사회적 시각을 반영한다.
⑤ 음악은 아이들을 사회·문화적으로 균형 잡힌 시민으로 성장하게 해 준다.

다음 글의 요지로 가장 적절한 것은?

Historically, drafters of tax legislation are attentive to questions of economics and history, and less attentive to moral questions. Questions of morality are often pushed to the side in legislative debate, labeled too controversial, too difficult to answer, or, worst of all, irrelevant to the project. But, in fact, the moral questions of taxation are at the very heart of the creation of tax laws. Rather than irrelevant, moral questions are fundamental to the imposition of tax. Tax is the application of a society's theories of distributive justice. Economics can go a long way towards helping a legislature determine whether or not a particular tax law will help achieve a particular goal, but economics cannot, in a vacuum, identify the goal. Creating tax policy requires identifying a moral goal, which is a task that must involve ethics and moral analysis.

*legislation: 입법 **imposition: 부과

① 분배 정의를 실현하려면 시민 단체의 역할이 필요하다.
② 사회적 합의는 민주적인 정책 수립의 선행 조건이다.
③ 성실한 납세는 안정적인 정부 예산 확보의 기반이 된다.
④ 경제학은 세법을 개정할 때 이론적 근거를 제공한다.
⑤ 세법을 만들 때 도덕적 목표를 설정하는 것이 중요하다.

E15 ✱✱✱ .... 2023 실시 7월 학평 22 (고3)

다음 글의 요지로 가장 적절한 것은?

In order to be successful and equitable, ecosystem management must be linked to poverty reduction. Urban infrastructure projects need to address the trade-offs between conservation, livelihoods, and equitable distribution of resources. Historically there has been tension when conservation models that create protected areas are perceived as inaccessible to communities. Often, these models are implemented at the expense of poor and marginalized residents and users of resources from the areas. Social, economic, and environmental development programs have become obstacles to sustainable development because there is no balance between the need to protect ecosystem services and the desire to use resources to address community needs. Communities need to be allowed to identify and negotiate their own options and to increase their flexibility to cope with unexpected change.   *equitable: 공평한

① 무분별한 도시 개발은 사회적 양극화를 심화한다.
② 도시 기반 시설 확충 시 안정적인 재정 지원이 중요하다.
③ 인근 지역 간의 긴밀한 협력은 생태계 보존의 기반이 된다.
④ 자원의 순환과 공정한 배분은 지속가능한 발전의 필수조건이다.
⑤ 생태계 관리 시 빈곤층을 포함한 지역사회의 요구를 고려할 필요가 있다.

E16 ✱✱❋ .... 2023 대비 6월 모평 22 (고3)

다음 글의 요지로 가장 적절한 것은?

Often overlooked, but just as important a stakeholder, is the consumer who plays a large role in the notion of the privacy paradox. Consumer engagement levels in all manner of digital experiences and communities have simply exploded — and they show little or no signs of slowing. There is an awareness among consumers, not only that their personal data helps to drive the rich experiences that these companies provide, but also that sharing this data is the price you pay for these experiences, in whole or in part. Without a better understanding of the what, when, and why of data collection and use, the consumer is often left feeling vulnerable and conflicted. "I love this restaurant-finder app on my phone, but what happens to my data if I press 'ok' when asked if that app can use my current location?" Armed with tools that can provide them options, the consumer moves from passive bystander to active participant.

*stakeholder: 이해관계자 **vulnerable: 상처를 입기 쉬운

① 개인정보 제공의 속성을 심층적으로 이해하면 주체적 소비자가 된다.
② 소비자는 디지털 시대에 유용한 앱을 적극 활용하는 자세가 필요하다.
③ 현명한 소비자가 되려면 다양한 디지털 데이터를 활용해야 한다.
④ 기업의 디지털 서비스를 이용하면 상응하는 대가가 뒤따른다.
⑤ 타인과의 정보 공유로 인해 개인정보가 유출되기도 한다.

다음 글의 요지로 가장 적절한 것은?

To overcome death as the obstacle that was hindering the evolution of human intelligence, our ancestors developed the killer app that propelled our species forward, ahead of all others: namely, spoken and written language in words and maths. I believe communication was, and still is, our most valuable invention. It has helped us preserve the knowledge, learning, discoveries and intelligence we have gained and pass them on from person to person and from generation to generation. Imagine if Einstein had had no way of telling the rest of us about his remarkable understanding of the theory of relativity. In the absence of our incredible abilities to communicate, each and every one of us would need to discover relativity on his or her own. Leaps of human intelligence have happened, then, as a response to the way human society and culture developed. A lot of our intelligence resulted from our interaction with each other, and not just in response to our environments.

① 인간의 언어는 환경과의 상호 작용을 통해 발달한다.
② 인간의 지능 발달은 상호 간 의사소통의 결과물이다.
③ 과학의 발전은 인간 사회의 문화 보존에 필수적이다.
④ 언어의 변화가 세대 간 의사소통의 단절을 초래한다.
⑤ 기술에 대한 의존이 인간의 학습 능력 발달을 저해한다.

다음 글의 요지로 가장 적절한 것은?

Urban delivery vehicles can be adapted to better suit the density of urban distribution, which often involves smaller vehicles such as vans, including bicycles. The latter have the potential to become a preferred 'last-mile' vehicle, particularly in high-density and congested areas. In locations where bicycle use is high, such as the Netherlands, delivery bicycles are also used to carry personal cargo (e.g. groceries). Due to their low acquisition and maintenance costs, cargo bicycles convey much potential in developed and developing countries alike, such as the *becak* (a three-wheeled bicycle) in Indonesia. Services using electrically assisted delivery tricycles have been successfully implemented in France and are gradually being adopted across Europe for services as varied as parcel and catering deliveries. Using bicycles as cargo vehicles is particularly encouraged when combined with policies that restrict motor vehicle access to specific areas of a city, such as downtown or commercial districts, or with the extension of dedicated bike lanes.

① 도시에서 자전거는 효율적인 배송 수단으로 사용될 수 있다.
② 자전거는 출퇴근 시간을 줄이기 위한 대안으로 선호되고 있다.
③ 자전거는 배송 수단으로의 경제적 장단점을 모두 가질 수 있다.
④ 수요자의 요구에 부합하는 다양한 용도의 자전거가 개발되고 있다.
⑤ 세계 각국에서는 전기 자전거 사용을 장려하는 정책을 추진하고 있다.

E19 ✹✹✧ .... 2021 대비 수능 22 (고3)

다음 글의 요지로 가장 적절한 것은?

Prior to file-sharing services, music albums landed exclusively in the hands of music critics before their release. These critics would listen to them well before the general public could and preview them for the rest of the world in their reviews. Once the internet made music easily accessible and allowed even advanced releases to spread through online social networks, availability of new music became democratized, which meant critics no longer had unique access. That is, critics and laypeople alike could obtain new music simultaneously. Social media services also enabled people to publicize their views on new songs, list their new favorite bands in their social media bios, and argue over new music endlessly on message boards. The result was that critics now could access the opinions of the masses on a particular album before writing their reviews. Thus, instead of music reviews guiding popular opinion toward art (as they did in preinternet times), music reviews began to reflect — consciously or subconsciously — public opinion.

* laypeople: 비전문가

① 미디어 환경의 변화로 음악 비평이 대중의 영향을 받게 되었다.
② 인터넷의 발달로 다양한 장르의 음악을 접하는 것이 가능해졌다.
③ 비평가의 음악 비평은 자신의 주관적인 경험을 기반으로 한다.
④ 오늘날 새로운 음악은 대중의 기호를 확인한 후에 공개된다.
⑤ 온라인 환경의 대두로 음악 비평의 질이 전반적으로 상승하였다.

E20 ✹✹✧ .... 2024 대비 수능 22 (고3)

다음 글의 요지로 가장 적절한 것은?

Being able to prioritize your responses allows you to connect more deeply with individual customers, be it a one-off interaction around a particularly delightful or upsetting experience, or the development of a longer-term relationship with a significantly influential individual within your customer base. If you've ever posted a favorable comment — or any comment, for that matter — about a brand, product or service, think about what it would feel like if you were personally acknowledged by the brand manager, for example, as a result. In general, people post because they have something to say — and because they want to be recognized for having said it. In particular, when people post positive comments they are expressions of appreciation for the experience that led to the post. While a compliment to the person standing next to you is typically answered with a response like "Thank You," the sad fact is that most brand compliments go unanswered. These are lost opportunities to understand what drove the compliments and create a solid fan based on them.

* compliment: 칭찬

① 고객과의 관계 증진을 위해 고객의 브랜드 칭찬에 응답하는 것은 중요하다.
② 고객의 피드백을 면밀히 분석함으로써 브랜드의 성공 가능성을 높일 수 있다.
③ 신속한 고객 응대를 통해서 고객의 긍정적인 반응을 이끌어 낼 수 있다.
④ 브랜드 매니저에게는 고객의 부정적인 의견을 수용하는 태도가 요구된다.
⑤ 고객의 의견을 경청하는 것은 브랜드의 새로운 이미지 창출에 도움이 된다.

E21 ⚙ 2등급 대비 ············· 2024 대비 9월 모평 22 (고3)

다음 글의 요지로 가장 적절한 것은?

The need to assimilate values and lifestyle of the host culture has become a growing conflict. Multiculturalists suggest that there should be a model of partial assimilation in which immigrants retain some of their customs, beliefs, and language. There is pressure to conform rather than to maintain their cultural identities, however, and these conflicts are greatly determined by the community to which one migrates. These experiences are not new; many Europeans experienced exclusion and poverty during the first two waves of immigration in the 19th and 20th centuries. Eventually, these immigrants transformed this country with significant changes that included enlightenment and acceptance of diversity. People of color, however, continue to struggle for acceptance. Once again, the challenge is to recognize that other cultures think and act differently and that they have the right to do so. Perhaps, in the not too distant future, immigrants will no longer be strangers among us.

① 이민자 고유의 정체성을 유지할 권리에 대한 공동체의 인식이 필요하다.

② 이민자의 적응을 돕기 위해 그들의 요구를 반영한 정책 수립이 중요하다.

③ 이민자는 미래 사회의 긍정적 변화에 핵심적 역할을 수행할 수 있다.

④ 다문화 사회의 안정을 위해서는 국제적 차원의 지속적인 협력이 요구된다.

⑤ 문화적 동화는 장기적이고 체계적인 과정을 통해 점진적으로 이루어진다.

E22 ⚙ 2등급 대비 ············ 2023 실시 10월 학평 22 (고3)

다음 글의 요지로 가장 적절한 것은?

Imagine a movie where nothing but terrible things happen. But, in the end, everything works out. Everything is resolved. A sufficiently happy ending can change the meaning of all the previous events. They can all be viewed as worthwhile, given that ending. Now imagine another movie. A lot of things are happening. They're all exciting and interesting. But there are a lot of them. Ninety minutes in, you start to worry. "This is a great movie," you think, "but there are a lot of things going on. I sure hope the filmmaker can pull it all together." But that doesn't happen. Instead, the story ends, suddenly, unresolved, or something facile and clichéd occurs. You leave deeply annoyed and unsatisfied — failing to notice that you were fully engaged and enjoying the movie almost the whole time you were in the theatre. The present can change the past, and the future can change the present.

*facile: 지나치게 단순한 **clichéd: 상투적인

① 결말에 따라 이전 상황에 대한 인식이 달라진다.

② 익숙하지 않은 이야기는 대중의 사랑을 받기 어렵다.

③ 흥행에 성공한 영화가 항상 작품성이 뛰어난 것은 아니다.

④ 상황에 대한 집단의 평가는 개인의 평가에 영향을 끼친다.

⑤ 같은 영화를 반복적으로 보는 것이 영화에 대한 이해를 높인다.

※ 다음 영어는 우리말 뜻, 우리말은 영어 단어를 〈보기〉에서 찾아 쓰시오.

〈보기〉

broad	해결하다	본능	worthwhile
ethics	bystander	부분적인	흠 없이
notion	짜증나게 하다	innovation	보완하다

01 irritate　　　　＿＿＿＿＿＿＿＿

02 instinct　　　　＿＿＿＿＿＿＿＿

03 flawlessly　　　＿＿＿＿＿＿＿＿

04 partial　　　　＿＿＿＿＿＿＿＿

05 resolve　　　　＿＿＿＿＿＿＿＿

06 광대한, 폭넓은　＿＿＿＿＿＿＿＿

07 윤리학　　　　　＿＿＿＿＿＿＿＿

08 가치있는　　　　＿＿＿＿＿＿＿＿

09 개념　　　　　　＿＿＿＿＿＿＿＿

10 구경꾼, 행인　　＿＿＿＿＿＿＿＿

※ 다음 우리말에 알맞은 영어 표현을 찾아 연결하시오.

11 ~하는 경향이 있는 •　　• prone to

12 ~할 수 있다 •　　• be capable of

13 ~의 희생으로 •　　• engage in

14 ~에 관여하다 •　　• at the expense of

15 ~와 관계없는 •　　• irrelevant to

※ 다음 우리말 표현에 맞는 단어를 고르시오.

16 도덕적 질문들 ➡ (moral / cultural) questions

17 감정을 경험하다 ➡ experience (effect / affect)

18 인지적 검증을 통해 ➡ through a (congested / cognitive) validation

19 모든 방식의 디지털 경험에서 ➡ in all (inner / manner) of digital experiences

20 세금 부과에 근본적인 ➡ (fundamental / environmental) to the imposition of tax

※ 다음 문장의 빈칸에 알맞은 단어를 〈보기〉에서 찾아 쓰시오.

〈보기〉

conceived	granted	legislature	own
explicitly	exclusion	grasping	forces
property	identify	inseparable	armed

21 경제학은 입법부가 특정 세법이 특정 목표를 달성하는 데 도움이 될지를 결정하는 것을 도울 수 있다.
➡ Economics can help a(n) ＿＿＿＿＿＿ determine whether a particular tax law will help achieve a particular goal.

22 그들은 명시적으로 날씨에 대해 질문받지 않는다.
➡ They are not ＿＿＿＿＿＿ asked about the weather.

23 우리는 개념을 이해하는 데 어려움을 겪는 경향이 있다.
➡ We tend to have trouble ＿＿＿＿＿＿ the concept.

24 재산은 공동으로 소유되어야 한다.
➡ ＿＿＿＿＿＿ should be held in common.

25 지역사회는 자신이 선택할 수 있는 것들을 파악하여 협상하도록 허락되어야 한다.
➡ Communities need to be allowed to ＿＿＿＿＿＿ and negotiate their own options.

26 도구로 무장하여, 소비자는 수동적 방관자에서 능동적 참여자로 이동한다.
➡ ＿＿＿＿＿＿ with tools, the consumer moves from passive bystander to active participant.

27 많은 유럽인이 배제와 빈곤을 경험했다.
➡ Many Europeans experienced ＿＿＿＿＿＿ and poverty.

28 그것은 다른 방식으로 행동하는 것을 상상할 수 있었을 것이다.
➡ It could have ＿＿＿＿＿＿ of acting otherwise.

29 적절한 계획은 면밀한 사고를 하게 한다.
➡ Proper planning ＿＿＿＿＿＿ detailed thinking.

30 자율성은 결코 절대적이고 뒤집을 수 없게 주어지지 않는다.
➡ Autonomy is never ＿＿＿＿＿＿ absolutely and irreversibly.

F 주제 찾기

말풍선: 이 영화의 주제는 뭐라고 생각해?

말풍선: 영화를 끝까지 봐야 알 수 있을 것 같아.

★ 유형 설명

다음 글의 주제로 가장 적절한 것은? [3점]

In Kant's view, geometrical shapes are too perfect to induce an aesthetic experience.

'무엇'에 관해 이야기하는 글인지를 찾는 문제로, 주제를 찾는 것이 요지, 주장, 제목을 찾는 밑바탕이 된다.

☞ 주제는 글에서 중심이 되는 이슈로, 주장 찾기 유형이 글의 주제에 대한 필자의 주장을 묻는 문제라면 주제 찾기 유형은 주제 그 자체를 찾는 문제이다. "무엇에 관한 글인가?"라는 질문에 대답한다는 생각으로 정답을 찾는다.

🎭 유형 풀이 비법

1 핵심어를 찾아라!
• 글 전체적으로 반복해서 나오는 핵심어를 찾는 것이 가장 중요하다.

2 글의 처음과 끝에 집중하라!
• 글의 처음이나 끝에 주제가 나오는 경우가 많으므로 특히 주의해서 본다.

3 태도가 바뀌는 부분에 유의하라!
• 반대 내용을 나타내는 접속사 뒤에 주제문이 나올 가능성이 높으므로 태도가 바뀌는지 확인한다.

> (Tip) 범위가 넓거나 좁은 내용이 들어간 선택지를 고르지 않도록 주의한다.

★ 최신 수능 경향 분석

대비 연도	월	문항 번호	지문 주제	난이도
2025	11	23번	산업화가 가져온 노동과 시간의 변화	✹✹✺
	9	23번	특이한 것을 이해하기 위해 일상적인 것에 대해 질문 제기하기	✹✹✺
	6	23번	식품 광고와 관련된 단어 의미의 변화	✹✹✹
2024	11	23번	산림 자원의 비시장적 가치를 따져 보는 것의 의의	✹✹✹
	9	23번	청취자를 끌어들이려는 시도의 결과	✹✹✺
	6	23번	박물관의 이윤 지향 경영의 결과	✹✹✹
2023	11	23번	정보 공개의 이점	✹✹✺
	9	23번	농업에서 경험적 관찰 사용의 한계	✹✹✺
	6	23번	문화적으로 구성되는 감정	✹✹✺

★ 2025 수능 출제 분석

공장의 기계화로 인간의 작업일은 8시간 근무 교대로 나뉘게 되었다는 것을 언급하면서, 산업화로 인해 어떻게 일과 시간의 패러다임이 변화했는지에 대해 말하는 내용이었다. 글 전체적으로 계속해서 반복되는 산업화에 대한 내용을 잘 이해하면 주제를 찾을 수 있는 문제였다.

★ 2026 수능 예측

언제든지, 얼마든지 어렵게 출제될 수 있으니 항상 글의 주제를 찾는 훈련을 기본적으로 해야 한다.

🔑 어휘 및 표현 Preview

- [ ] natural 자연스러운
- [ ] physicist 물리학자
- [ ] shocked 충격을 받은
- [ ] frightened 겁먹은
- [ ] ultimately 궁극적으로
- [ ] accustomed 익숙한
- [ ] base on ~에 기초를 두다
- [ ] habitual 습관적인
- [ ] frequent 빈번한
- [ ] account for 설명하다
- [ ] singular 기묘한
- [ ] necessary 필요한

- [ ] response 대답
- [ ] a broad range of 폭넓은
- [ ] bizarre 기이한
- [ ] occur 일어나다
- [ ] universe 우주
- [ ] sociologist 사회학자
- [ ] preference 선호
- [ ] mythical 신화적인
- [ ] explanation 설명
- [ ] scientific 과학적인
- [ ] limitation 한계
- [ ] interpretation 해석

- [ ] perception 인식
- [ ] reality 현실
- [ ] pose 제기하다
- [ ] usual 일상적인
- [ ] difficulty 어려움
- [ ] conclusion 결론
- [ ] widespread 광범위한
- [ ] law 법(칙)
- [ ] phenomena 현상
- [ ] fall 낙하하다
- [ ] surprise 놀라게 하다
- [ ] notion 개념

- [ ] create 만들어내다
- [ ] product 제품
- [ ] attachment 부속물
- [ ] separate 분리된
- [ ] meaningful 의미 있는
- [ ] association 연관
- [ ] increasingly 점차
- [ ] fresh 신선한
- [ ] opposite 반대
- [ ] traditional 기존의, 전통적인
- [ ] supply 공급하다
- [ ] match 부응하다, 어울리다

F 주제 찾기 첫 번째

1st 첫 문장을 통해 핵심 소재를 확인하고 글의 내용을 예상하세요.
2nd **1st** 에서 발상한 것을 토대로 글을 읽고, 내용을 파악하세요.
3rd 선택지에서 글의 주제를 고르세요.

F01 ★★❀ ·············· 2023 대비 6월 모평 23 (고3)

다음 글의 주제로 가장 적절한 것은? [3점]

Considerable work by cultural psychologists and anthropologists has shown that there are indeed large and sometimes surprising differences in the words and concepts that different cultures have for describing emotions, as well as in the social circumstances that draw out the expression of particular emotions. However, those data do not actually show that different cultures have different emotions, if we think of emotions as central, neurally implemented states. As for, say, color vision, they just say that, despite the same internal processing architecture, how we interpret, categorize, and name emotions varies according to culture and that we learn in a particular culture the social context in which it is appropriate to express emotions. However, the emotional states themselves are likely to be quite invariant across cultures. In a sense, we can think of a basic, culturally universal emotion set that is shaped by evolution and implemented in the brain, but the links between such emotional states and stimuli, behavior, and other cognitive states are plastic and can be modified by learning in a specific cultural context.

*anthropologist: 인류학자 **stimuli: 자극
***cognitive: 인지적인

① essential links between emotions and behaviors
② culturally constructed representation of emotions
③ falsely described emotions through global languages
④ universally defined emotions across academic disciplines
⑤ wider influence of cognition on learning cultural contexts

1st 첫 문장을 통해 핵심 소재를 확인하고 글의 내용을 예상하세요.

1) 첫 문장부터 읽어 봅시다.

Considerable work / by cultural psychologists and
주목할 만한 연구는   / 문화 심리학자들과 인류학자들에 의한
anthropologists / has shown / that there are indeed
               / 보였다   / 정말로 크고, 때로는 놀랄 만한
large and sometimes surprising differences / in the
차이가 있다는 것을   / 어휘와
words and concepts / that different cultures have /
개념에   / 서로 다른 문화가 가진   /
for describing emotions, / as well as in the social
감정을 묘사하기 위해   / 사회적 상황에서만이 아니라
circumstances / that draw out the expression of
              / 특정한 감정의 표현을 끌어내는 //
particular emotions. //

has shown의 목적어절에서 어떤 데이터인지 구체적으로 나오는데,
서로 다른 ❶(   )가 감정을 묘사하기 위해 가진 어휘와 개념에
정말 크고 놀랄 만한 차이가 있다는 것을 보여주는 데이터군요. (단서)
연구 결과는 문화마다 감정을 묘사하는 ❷(   )와 개념에 큰
차이가 있음을 보여주는데, 이러한 데이터가 서로 다른 문화가 서로 다른
감정을 갖고 있다는 것을 보여주는 것은 아니라는 내용이에요.
그러니까 감정 그 자체는 다르지 않지만, 문화마다 그것을 묘사하는
어휘와 개념은 서로 다르다는 거죠. (발상)
이제 우리는 이 글의 내용을 예상했어요!

2nd **1st** 에서 발상한 것을 토대로 글을 읽고, 내용을 파악하세요.

1) 역접의 연결어 However가 눈에 띄네요.

However, / those data do not actually show / that
하지만   / 그런 데이터가 실제로 보이지는 않는다   / 서로
different cultures have different emotions, /
다른 문화가 서로 다른 감정을 가지고 있다는 것을   /
if we think of emotions / as central, neurally
만약 우리가 감정을 생각한다면 / 중추 신경의, 즉 신경계에서
implemented states. //
실행되는 상태라고   //

● however가 무조건 정답의 단서가 되는 건 아니에요.
역접의 연결어가 중요하다고 하면서 however가 포함된 문장만 읽으면
정답을 찾을 수 있는 것처럼 말하는 건 아주 잘못된 접근 방법이에요.
however가 포함된 문장을 읽으면서 그게 의미하는 것이 무엇인지,
정답을 찾기 위해 그 문장을 어떻게 활용해야 할지를 스스로 곰곰이
생각해야 돼요.

● 먼저 이 문장을 해석해 봅시다.

주절을 단순히 해석해 보면, '그런' 데이터가 서로 다른 문화가 서로 다른 감정을 갖는다는 것을 보여주는 것은 아니라는 내용이에요.
뒤집어 생각하면, 문화가 다르다고 해서 감정도 다른 것은 아니라는 거니까 문화가 다르더라도 느끼는 감정은 똑같다는 말인데, if가 이끄는 조건절과 함께 해석해봅시다. 감정이 신경계의 작용이라면, 똑같은 신경계를 가진 인간은 문화가 다르더라도 느끼는 ❸(   )은 똑같다는 거예요. 문화가 다르다고 해서 인간의 신경계가 다르지는 않으니까요.

2) 다음 문장을 살펴봅시다.

As for, say, color vision, / they just say / that,
예를 들어 색 식별에 대해   / 데이터들은 단지 말할 뿐이다 /

despite the same internal processing architecture, /
체내에서 일어나는 동일한 처리 구조에도 불구하고   /

how we interpret, categorize, and name emotions
우리가 감정을 해석하고 범주화하며 명명하는 방식은 다르고

varies / according to culture / and that we learn in a
        / 문화에 따라   / 우리는 사회적 상황을 특정

particular culture the social context / in which it is
문화에서 배운다는 것을   / 감정을 표현하는

appropriate to express emotions. //
것이 적절한   //

● 여기까지만 읽어도 글의 내용을 파악할 수 있겠죠?

앞의 내용에 As for, say라고 하며 앞의 문장에 대한 예를 들고 있어요.
인간의 감정은 다르지 않다고 한 앞 문장에 이어서, 감정을 표현하는 것이 적절한 상황이 문화에 따라 다르다고 했어요.
즉 서로 다른 문화가 감정을 묘사하기 위해 가진 어휘와 개념에는 큰 차이가 있다는 첫 문장부터 시작해서 이 글은 감정 표현이 문화적으로 구성된다는 내용임을 알 수 있어요.

① essential links between emotions and behaviors
  감정과 행동 간의 근본적 연관성
② culturally constructed representation of emotions
  문화적으로 구성되는 감정 표현
③ falsely described emotions through global languages
  세계 공용어를 통해 잘못 묘사되는 감정
④ universally defined emotions across academic disciplines
  학문 분야 전반에 걸쳐 보편적으로 정의되는 감정
⑤ wider influence of cognition on learning cultural contexts
  문화적 상황을 학습하는 데 미치는 인식의 더 광범위한 영향

글에서는 '감정을 묘사하는 어휘와 개념이 문화마다 다르다'는 설명으로 글의 주제를 나타냈어요.
이 주제를 선택지에서는 '문화적으로 구성되는 감정 표현'이라는 어구를 사용해서 글에서 쓰인 것과는 다르게 표현한 것이죠. 따라서 정답은 ❹(   )!
이렇게 글에서 주제를 파악한 다음 그것을 어떻게 다르게 표현할 수 있을지 생각하는 훈련을 평소에 꾸준히 해야 돼요.

연결어나 예시의 내용에 주목하자!

F 주제 찾기 (두 번째)

1st 첫 문장을 통해 핵심 소재를 확인하고 글의 내용을 예상해 보세요.
2nd 예상한 내용을 토대로 글을 읽고, 전체적인 내용을 파악해 보세요.
3rd 파악한 내용을 바탕으로 선택지 중에서 글의 주제를 골라보세요.

F02 ★★★............. 2024 대비 6월 모평 23 (고3)

다음 글의 주제로 가장 적절한 것은? [3점]

There are pressures *within* the museum that cause it to emphasise what happens in the galleries over the activities that take place in its unseen zones. In an era when museums are forced to increase their earnings, they often focus their energies on modernising their galleries or mounting temporary exhibitions to bring more and more audiences through the door. In other words, as museums struggle to survive in a competitive economy, their budgets often prioritise those parts of themselves that are consumable: infotainment in the galleries, goods and services in the cafes and the shops. The unlit, unglamorous storerooms, if they are ever discussed, are at best presented as service areas that process objects for the exhibition halls. And at worst, as museums pour more and more resources into their publicly visible faces, the spaces of storage may even suffer, their modernisation being kept on hold or being given less and less space to house the expanding collections and serve their complex conservation needs.

① importance of prioritising museums' exhibition spaces
② benefits of diverse activities in museums for audiences
③ necessity of expanding storerooms for displaying objects
④ consequences of profit-oriented management of museums
⑤ ways to increase museums' commitment to the public good

1st 첫 문장을 통해 핵심 소재를 확인하고 글의 내용을 예상해 보세요.

There are pressures within the museum / that cause
박물관 '내부의' 압력이 있다   / 그것이
it to emphasise / what happens in the galleries /
강조하게 만드는   / 갤러리에서 발생하는 것을   /
over the activities / that take place in its unseen
활동보다   / 그것의 보이지 않는 구역에서 일어나는 //
zones. //

● 첫 문장에 나타난 핵심 소재가 나왔어요!
❶(   ) '내부의' 압력이 있다고 하며 글의 중심 소재를 제시했어요. 단서 보이지 않는 구역의 활동보다 갤러리에서 발생하는 것을 강조하게 한다는 이 압력에 대해 이야기할 것으로 보여져요. 발상

2nd 예상한 내용을 토대로 글을 읽고, 전체적인 내용을 파악해 보세요.

1) 글의 전반부를 확인해 봅시다.

In an era / when museums are forced / to increase
시대에   / 박물관이 강요당하는   / 그것의 수입을
their earnings, / they often focus their energies / ...
늘리도록   / 그것은 흔히 자기 에너지를 집중시킨다 / ...
to bring more and more audiences through the
점점 더 많은 관객을 문으로 데려오기 위해 //
door. //

● 박물관이 강요를 받는다고요?
박물관이 수입을 늘리도록 강요를 받는다고 했어요. 그리고 이러한 시대에는 박물관이 관객 수를 늘리는 것에 에너지를 집중한다고 했어요. 박물관은 역사적 자료를 보존하는 데 의미가 있을 텐데 수입을 늘리는 것에 집중한다니, 왠지 예감이 좋지 않네요. 나머지 글을 읽으며 박물관의 이러한 경향이 어떤 결과를 낳을지 더 알아볼까요?

2) 박물관의 그러한 경향이 어떤 결과를 낳는지 살펴봅시다.

The unlit, unglamorous storerooms, / if they are
불이 켜져 있지 않은 매력 없는 저장실은   / 그것들이

ever discussed, / are at best presented as service
논의가 된다고 해도   / 기껏해야 서비스 공간으로 제시된다

areas / that process objects / for the exhibition
      / 물건을 처리하는   / 전시 홀에 둘 //

halls. //

● 역시나 문제가 발생하고 있었어요.
   매력 없는 저장실이 물건을 처리하는 서비스 공간으로 제시된다는 문제가
   발생했어요. 수익성에 집중하는 박물관의 입장에서 매력이 없다는 것은
   수익을 내지 못한다는 것과 같죠. 그런 공간은 결국 소홀하게 관리된다는
   내용이에요.

● 이 문장으로 구성한 선택지가 바로 **②**(   )이에요.
   이 문장의 storerooms와 object가 선택지 **②**(   )과 겹치고
   있어요. 물건을 전시하는 저장실을 늘릴 필요성이라고 했는데, 과연 이
   글의 주제가 저장실을 늘릴 필요성일까요? 글의 뒷부분도 마저 읽으며
   답을 찾아봅시다.

3) 이제 마지막 문장을 살펴봅시다.

And at worst, / as museums pour more and more
그리고 최악의 경우   / 박물관이 점점 더 많은 자원을 쏟아붓기 때문에

resources / into their publicly visible faces, / the
        / 공개적으로 보이는 겉면에   /

spaces of storage may even suffer, / ...
저장 공간은 더 나빠질지도 모른다   / …

● at worst는 **③**'(   )'라는 뜻이에요.
   at worst를 통해 박물관이 수익성을 지향하면 끝내 최악의 결과를
   낳는다는 점을 암시하고 있어요. 과연 어떤 결과일지 이어서 살펴봅시다.

● 왜 겉면에만 집중했으며, 이는 어떤 결과를 맞이했나요?
   박물관이 겉면에 더 많은 자원을 쏟아붓는 것은 이목을 끌어 수익을
   낼 만한 것에 집중하기 위함이겠죠. 그리고 이것 때문에 저장 공간이
   더 나빠질지도 모른다고 하네요! 이것이 바로 박물관의 수익 지향성이
   마주할 최악의 결과라고 볼 수 있어요. 뒤에 남은 내용은 구체적으로
   어떻게 나빠지는지에 대한 부연 설명이니 이쯤에서 글의 주제를 짚어
   봅시다.

3rd 파악한 내용을 바탕으로 선택지 중에서 글의 주제를 골라보세요.

① importance of prioritising museums' exhibition
   spaces
   박물관 전시 공간을 우선시하는 것의 중요성
② benefits of diverse activities in museums for
   audiences
   관객을 위한 박물관에서의 다양한 활동의 이점
③ necessity of expanding storerooms for displaying
   objects
   물건 전시를 위해 저장실을 확장할 필요성
④ consequences of profit-oriented management of
   museums
   박물관의 이윤 지향 경영의 결과
⑤ ways to increase museums' commitment to the
   public good
   공공의 이익에 대한 박물관의 헌신을 늘리는 방법

이 글의 주제는 박물관이 수익을 내도록 강요를 받기 때문에, 겉면에
자원을 쏟아부으면서 저장 공간이 나빠지는 결과를 낳는다는 것이에요.
박물관이 수익성에 집중하며 운영하는 것은 이윤 지향 경영(profit-
oriented management)이라고 표현될 수 있어요. 그러한 경영의
결과(consequence)를 언급했기 때문에 **④**(   )이 가장 적절한
선택지임을 알 수 있죠.
글의 주제를 파악하더라도 선택지에서는 다른 단어로 표현될 수 있기
때문에, 같은 말이더라도 다른 표현으로 바꾸어 생각해보는 훈련이
필요해요.

먼저 글의 소재를
파악하자!

F03 ~ 06 ▶ 제한시간 8분

F03 ✱✱❈ .... 2025 대비 수능 23 (고3)

다음 글의 주제로 가장 적절한 것은?

The arrival of the Industrial Age changed the relationship among time, labor, and capital. Factories could produce around the clock, and they could do so with greater speed and volume than ever before. A machine that runs twelve hours a day will produce more widgets than one that runs for only eight hours per day — and a machine that runs twenty-four hours per day will produce the most widgets of all. As such, at many factories, the workday is divided into eight-hour shifts, so that there will always be people on hand to keep the widget machines humming. Industrialization raised the potential value of every single work hour — the more hours you worked, the more widgets you produced, and the more money you made — and thus wages became tied to effort and production. Labor, previously guided by harvest cycles, became clock-oriented, and society started to reorganize around new principles of productivity.

*widget: 제품

① shift in the work-time paradigm brought about by industrialization
② effects of standardizing production procedures on labor markets
③ influence of industrialization on the machine-human relationship
④ efficient ways to increase the value of time in the Industrial Age
⑤ problems that excessive work hours have caused for laborers

F04 ✱✱❈ .... 2025 대비 9월 모평 23 (고3)

다음 글의 주제로 가장 적절한 것은? [3점]

It is much more natural to be surprised by unusual phenomena like eclipses than ordinary phenomena like falling bodies or the succession of night into day and day into night. Many cultures invented gods to explain these eclipses that shocked, frightened, or surprised them; but very few imagined a god of falling bodies — to which they were so accustomed that they did not even notice them. But the reason for eclipses is ultimately the same as that of the succession of night and day: the movement of celestial bodies, which itself is based on the Newtonian law of attraction and how it explains why things fall when we let them go. For the physicist, understanding the ordinary, the habitual, and the frequent thus allows us to account for the frightening and the singular. As such, it was thus necessary to ask "Why do things fall?" and to have Newton's response to understand a broad range of much more bizarre phenomena occurring at every level of the universe.

*eclipse: 일식, 월식 **celestial: 천체의 ***bizarre: 이상한

① widespread preference for mythical explanations over scientific ones
② limitations of Newtonian law in explaining eclipse phenomena
③ influence of scientific interpretations on perceptions of reality
④ need to pose questions about the usual to understand the unusual
⑤ difficulty of drawing general conclusions from unusual phenomena

다음 글의 주제로 가장 적절한 것은?

The human desire to make pictures is deeply rooted. At least 64,000 years ago, Neanderthals used colored oxide and charcoal to make paintings of large wild animals, tracings of human hands, and abstract patterns on cave and rock walls. Today, people create images with a multitude of mediums, including photography. What drives this picturemaking impulse? Some make pictures for commercial reasons. Others create informational systems or employ scientific imaging tools to visualize the unseen. Artists use images expressionistically, to conceptualize and articulate who they are and how they view the world. However, the fundamental motive for making the vast majority of pictures is a desire to preserve: to document, and therefore honor, specific people, events, and possessions of importance. Regardless of purpose, the making of images persists because words alone cannot always provide a satisfactory way to describe and express our relationship to the world. Pictures are an essential component of how humans observe, communicate, celebrate, comment, and, most of all, remember. What and how we remember shapes our worldview, and pictures can provide a stimulus to jog one's memory.

*oxide: 산화물 **impulse: 충동 ***articulate: 분명히 표현하다

① factors that influence the art evaluation process
② difference between commercial images and informative pictures
③ explanation for the human desire of creating images to remember
④ benefits of written records in understanding our ancestors
⑤ change in the value of the same painting across history

다음 글의 주제로 가장 적절한 것은? [3점]

Natural disasters and aging are two problems that societies have been dealing with for all of human history. Governments must respond to both, but their dynamics are entirely different and this has profound consequences for the nature of the response. Simply by plotting the aging slope, policy makers go a long way toward understanding the problem: People get older at a constant and reliable rate. There can be disagreements over how to solve the aging problem (this is political complexity), but the nature of the problem is never in dispute. Plotting the number of people killed in natural disasters does very little to advance understanding of this problem other than emphasizing the randomness of natural disasters. Preparing a policy response is, therefore, much easier in some areas than in others. When inputs are reliable and easy to predict, it greatly facilitates information processing and allows for anticipatory problem-solving. When problems are causally complex and multivariate, determining the appropriate response is a reactionary endeavor.

① risks of hasty decision-making during natural disasters
② reasons for governmental concern about aging populations
③ significance of studying the comprehensive history of policy making
④ different approaches of governments depending on the nature of the problem
⑤ advantages of anticipatory problem-solving in dealing with social problems

F07 ✿❀❀ .... 2025 대비 6월 모평 23 (고3)

다음 글의 주제로 가장 적절한 것은?

While many city shoppers were clearly drawn to the notion of buying and eating foods associated with nature, the nature claimed by the ads was no longer the nature that created the foods. Indeed, the nature claimed by many ads was associated with food products *only* by the ads' attachment. This is clearly a case of what French sociologist Henri Lefebvre has called "the decline of the referentials," or the tendency of words under the influence of capitalism to become separated from meaningful associations. Increasingly, food ads helped shoppers become accustomed to new definitions of words such as "fresh" and "natural," definitions that could well be considered opposite of their traditional meanings. The new definitions better served the needs of the emerging industrial food system, which could not supply foods that matched customary meanings and expectations. And they better met shoppers' desires, although with pretense.

① decline of reliability in the ads of natural foods
② changes in the senses of words linked to food ads
③ influence of capitalism on the industrial food system
④ various ways to attract customers in the food industry
⑤ necessity of meaningful word associations in commercials

F08 ✿✿❀ .... 2024 실시 5월 학평 23 (고3)

다음 글의 주제로 가장 적절한 것은?

During the day, a molecule called adenosine builds up in your brain. Adenosine binds with receptors on nerve cells, or neurons, slowing down their activity and making you feel drowsy. But caffeine is also able to bind with these receptors, and by doing so it blocks adenosine's effect, making your neurons fire more and keeping you alert. Caffeine also activates a gland at the base of your brain. This releases hormones that tell the adrenal glands on your kidneys to produce adrenaline, causing your heart to beat faster and your blood pressure to rise. If, however, your daily caffeine intake is consistent, your brain will adapt to it. Your brain is like, 'Okay, every morning I'm getting this caffeine that's binding to these receptors and blocking adenosine from binding to them.' So your brain creates extra receptors to give adenosine more of an opportunity to bind with them and have its usual effect. And more adenosine is also produced to counteract the caffeine. That's why it takes more and more caffeine to have the same effect.

*drowsy: 나른한 **gland: (분비)선

① what your brain does for regular hormone production
② consequences of sleep deprivation caused by caffeine
③ connection between brain health and hormone balance
④ efforts to overcome the constant temptation of caffeine
⑤ how your brain adapts to a steady caffeine consumption

다음 글의 주제로 가장 적절한 것은? [3점]

Sociologist Brooke Harrington said if there was an $E=mc^2$ of social science, it would be SD>PD, "social death is more frightening than physical death." This is why we feel deeply threatened when a new idea challenges the ones that have become part of our identity. For some ideas, the ones that identify us as members of a group, we don't reason as individuals; we reason as a member of a tribe. We want to seem trustworthy, and reputation management as a trustworthy individual often overrides most other concerns, even our own mortality. This is not entirely irrational. A human alone in this world faces a lot of difficulty, but being alone in the world before modern times was almost certainly a death sentence. So we carry with us an innate drive to form groups, join groups, remain in those groups, and oppose other groups. But once you can identify *them*, you start favoring *us*; so much so that given a choice between an outcome that favors both groups a lot or one that favors both much less but still favors yours more than theirs, that's the one you will pick.

*innate: 타고난

① tendency to prefer the group that one identifies with
② necessity of social isolation to build a reputation
③ ways to ease one's irrational fear of crowds
④ importance of forming groups with different interests
⑤ tips for staying objective during heated group discussions

다음 글의 주제로 가장 적절한 것은? [3점]

In Kant's view, geometrical shapes are too perfect to induce an aesthetic experience. Insofar as they agree with the underlying concept or idea — thus possessing the *precision* that the ancient Greeks sought and celebrated — geometrical shapes can be grasped, but they do not give rise to emotion, and, most importantly, they do not move the imagination to free and new (mental) lengths. Forms or phenomena, on the contrary, that possess a degree of immeasurability, or that do not appear constrained, stimulate the human imagination — hence their ability to induce a sublime aesthetic experience. The pleasure associated with experiencing immeasurable objects — indefinable or formless objects — can be defined as enjoying one's own emotional and mental activity. Namely, the pleasure consists of being challenged and struggling to understand and decode the phenomenon present to view. Furthermore, part of the pleasure comes from having one's comfort zone (momentarily) violated.

*geometrical: 기하학의 **aesthetic: 심미적인 ***sublime: 숭고한

① diversity of aesthetic experiences in different eras
② inherent beauty in geometrically perfect shapes
③ concepts of imperfection in modern aesthetics
④ natural inclination towards aesthetic precision
⑤ aesthetic pleasure from things unconstrained

F11 ★★★❋.................. 2023 실시 3월 학평 23 (고3)

다음 글의 주제로 가장 적절한 것은? [3점]

Whenever possible, we should take measures to *re-socialize* the information we think about. The continual patter we carry on in our heads is in fact a kind of internalized conversation. Likewise, many of the written forms we encounter at school and at work — from exams and evaluations, to profiles and case studies, to essays and proposals — are really social exchanges (questions, stories, arguments) put on paper and addressed to some imagined listener or interlocutor. There are significant advantages to turning such interactions at a remove back into actual social encounters. Research demonstrates that the brain processes the "same" information differently, and often more effectively, when other human beings are involved — whether we're imitating them, debating them, exchanging stories with them, synchronizing and cooperating with them, teaching or being taught by them. We are inherently social creatures, and our thinking benefits from bringing other people into our train of thought.

*patter: 재잘거림 **interlocutor: 대화자
***at a remove: 조금 거리를 둔

① importance of processing information via social interactions
② ways of improving social skills through physical activities
③ necessity of regular evaluations of cognitive functions
④ influence of personality traits on social interactions
⑤ socialization as a form of internalized social control

F12 ★★★❋.................. 2021 대비 9월 모평 23 (고3)

다음 글의 주제로 가장 적절한 것은? [3점]

Conventional wisdom in the West, influenced by philosophers from Plato to Descartes, credits individuals and especially geniuses with creativity and originality. Social and cultural influences and causes are minimized, ignored, or eliminated from consideration at all. Thoughts, original and conventional, are identified with individuals, and the special things that individuals are and do are traced to their genes and their brains. The "trick" here is to recognize that individual humans are social constructions themselves, embodying and reflecting the variety of social and cultural influences they have been exposed to during their lives. Our individuality is not denied, but it is viewed as a product of specific social and cultural experiences. The brain itself is a social thing, influenced structurally and at the level of its connectivities by social environments. The "individual" is a legal, religious, and political fiction just as the "I" is a grammatical illusion.

① recognition of the social nature inherent in individuality
② ways of filling the gap between individuality and collectivity
③ issues with separating original thoughts from conventional ones
④ acknowledgment of the true individuality embodied in human genes
⑤ necessity of shifting from individualism to interdependence

F13 ✹✹✷ ·························· 2022 대비 6월 모평 23 (고3)

다음 글의 주제로 가장 적절한 것은? [3점]

Children can move effortlessly between play and absorption in a story, as if both are forms of the same activity. The taking of roles in a narratively structured game of pirates is not very different than the taking of roles in identifying with characters as one watches a movie. It might be thought that, as they grow towards adolescence, people give up childhood play, but this is not so. Instead, the bases and interests of this activity change and develop to playing and watching sports, to the fiction of plays, novels, and movies, and nowadays to video games. In fiction, one can enter possible worlds. When we experience emotions in such worlds, this is not a sign that we are being incoherent or regressed. It derives from trying out metaphorical transformations of our selves in new ways, in new worlds, in ways that can be moving and important to us.

*pirate: 해적 **incoherent: 일관되지 않은

① relationship between play types and emotional stability
② reasons for identifying with imaginary characters in childhood
③ ways of helping adolescents develop good reading habits
④ continued engagement in altered forms of play after childhood
⑤ effects of narrative structures on readers' imaginations

F14 ✹✹✷ ·························· 2023 대비 수능 23 (고3)

다음 글의 주제로 가장 적절한 것은? [3점]

An important advantage of disclosure, as opposed to more aggressive forms of regulation, is its flexibility and respect for the operation of free markets. Regulatory mandates are blunt swords; they tend to neglect diversity and may have serious unintended adverse effects. For example, energy efficiency requirements for appliances may produce goods that work less well or that have characteristics that consumers do not want. Information provision, by contrast, respects freedom of choice. If automobile manufacturers are required to measure and publicize the safety characteristics of cars, potential car purchasers can trade safety concerns against other attributes, such as price and styling. If restaurant customers are informed of the calories in their meals, those who want to lose weight can make use of the information, leaving those who are unconcerned about calories unaffected. Disclosure does not interfere with, and should even promote, the autonomy (and quality) of individual decision-making.

*mandate: 명령 **adverse: 거스르는 ***autonomy: 자율성

① steps to make public information accessible to customers
② benefits of publicizing information to ensure free choices
③ strategies for companies to increase profits in a free market
④ necessities of identifying and analyzing current industry trends
⑤ effects of diversified markets on reasonable customer choices

F15 ❋❋❋ .... 2022 대비 수능 23 (고3)

다음 글의 주제로 가장 적절한 것은? [3점]

Scientists *use* paradigms rather than believing them. The use of a paradigm in research typically addresses related problems by employing shared concepts, symbolic expressions, experimental and mathematical tools and procedures, and even some of the same theoretical statements. Scientists need only understand *how* to use these various elements in ways that others would accept. These elements of shared practice thus need not presuppose any comparable unity in scientists' beliefs about what they are doing when they use them. Indeed, one role of a paradigm is to enable scientists to work successfully without having to provide a detailed account of what they are doing or what they believe about it. Thomas Kuhn noted that scientists "can agree in their *identification* of a paradigm without agreeing on, or even attempting to produce, a full *interpretation* or *rationalization* of it. Lack of a standard interpretation or of an agreed reduction to rules will not prevent a paradigm from guiding research."

① difficulty in drawing novel theories from existing paradigms
② significant influence of personal beliefs in scientific fields
③ key factors that promote the rise of innovative paradigms
④ roles of a paradigm in grouping like-minded researchers
⑤ functional aspects of a paradigm in scientific research

F16 ❋❋❋ .... 2023 실시 4월 학평 23 (고3)

다음 글의 주제로 가장 적절한 것은?

Facing large-scale, long-term change can seem overwhelming. Problems like global contagion or economic inequality are so complex that it can be hard to believe any intervention might make a difference. Working through fears of what could be depends on connecting with the abstract. Linking issues like climate change, for example, with the realities of our own neighborhoods, jobs, and relationships, translates conceptual ideas into concrete emotions. Thinking of how the beaches we love might disappear, how more frequent floods might destroy our homes, or how we might have to move to flee mounting wildfire risk, evokes feelings like anger, sadness, or guilt — feelings that inspire us to act. A recent study found that when people feel personally affected by potential climatic change, they are more likely to support carbon reduction efforts and push for proactive policies. Forming emotional connections to potential futures helps us move from denial and despair to action.

① effectiveness of making remote problems personal
② impacts of negative tone in news on problem solving
③ contribution of experts to solving large-scale problems
④ limits of personal intervention in minimizing climate change
⑤ risks of attempting to predict events with limited information

F17 ✹✹✹❀ .... 2023 대비 9월 모평 23 (고3)

다음 글의 주제로 가장 적절한 것은? [3점]

Environmental learning occurs when farmers base decisions on observations of "payoff" information. They may observe their own or neighbors' farms, but it is the empirical results they are using as a guide, not the neighbors themselves. They are looking at farming activities as experiments and assessing such factors as relative advantage, compatibility with existing resources, difficulty of use, and "trialability" — how well can it be experimented with. But that criterion of "trialability" turns out to be a real problem; it's true that farmers are always experimenting, but working farms are very flawed laboratories. Farmers cannot set up the controlled conditions of professional test plots in research facilities. Farmers also often confront complex and difficult-to-observe phenomena that would be hard to manage even if they could run controlled experiments. Moreover farmers can rarely acquire payoff information on more than a few of the production methods they might use, which makes the criterion of "relative advantage" hard to measure.

<small>*empirical: 경험적인 **compatibility: 양립성 ***criterion: 기준</small>

① limitations of using empirical observations in farming
② challenges in modernizing traditional farming equipment
③ necessity of prioritizing trialability in agricultural innovation
④ importance of making instinctive decisions in agriculture
⑤ ways to control unpredictable agricultural phenomena

F18 ✹✹✹ .... 2021 대비 수능 23 (고3)

다음 글의 주제로 가장 적절한 것은? [3점]

Difficulties arise when we do not think of people and machines as collaborative systems, but assign whatever tasks can be automated to the machines and leave the rest to people. This ends up requiring people to behave in machine-like fashion, in ways that differ from human capabilities. We expect people to monitor machines, which means keeping alert for long periods, something we are bad at. We require people to do repeated operations with the extreme precision and accuracy required by machines, again something we are not good at. When we divide up the machine and human components of a task in this way, we fail to take advantage of human strengths and capabilities but instead rely upon areas where we are genetically, biologically unsuited. Yet, when people fail, they are blamed.

① difficulties of overcoming human weaknesses to avoid failure
② benefits of allowing machines and humans to work together
③ issues of allocating unfit tasks to humans in automated systems
④ reasons why humans continue to pursue machine automation
⑤ influences of human actions on a machine's performance

F

F19 ★★★ .... 2024 대비 수능 23 (고3)

다음 글의 주제로 가장 적절한 것은?

Managers of natural resources typically face market incentives that provide financial rewards for exploitation. For example, owners of forest lands have a market incentive to cut down trees rather than manage the forest for carbon capture, wildlife habitat, flood protection, and other ecosystem services. These services provide the owner with no financial benefits, and thus are unlikely to influence management decisions. But the economic benefits provided by these services, based on their non-market values, may exceed the economic value of the timber. For example, a United Nations initiative has estimated that the economic benefits of ecosystem services provided by tropical forests, including climate regulation, water purification, and erosion prevention, are over three times greater per hectare than the market benefits. Thus cutting down the trees is economically inefficient, and markets are not sending the correct "signal" to favor ecosystem services over extractive uses.

*exploitation: 이용　**timber: 목재

① necessity of calculating the market values of ecosystem services
② significance of weighing forest resources' non-market values
③ impact of using forest resources to maximize financial benefits
④ merits of balancing forests' market and non-market values
⑤ ways of increasing the efficiency of managing natural resources

1등급 대비 문제

F20 ～ 23 ▶ 제한시간 11분

F20 ⭐ 2등급 대비 .... 2023 실시 10월 학평 23 (고3)

다음 글의 주제로 가장 적절한 것은? [3점]

Just as today some jobs are better than others, so would they have been in early societies with their blossoming towns and eventually cities, with some roles more dangerous and some having more plentiful access to food or other resources. The archeological record shows that soon after the appearance of towns, agriculture, and surpluses, some burials start to look different from others. Some individuals are buried with more precious goods (metals, weapons, and maybe even art), some are in group graves and some by themselves, and still others don't even seem to be buried at all. The bones from the burials start to show us differences as well — chemical and isotope analyses of teeth and long bones reveal that some members of groups were getting more protein or minerals than others; some have more evidence of diseases and greater physical injuries from their labors. Early on these differences are small, but by 5,000 to 7,000 years ago they are becoming quite pronounced.

*archeological: 고고학의　**surplus: 잉여물　***isotope: 동위 원소

① the evidence of social inequality found in ancient burials
② scientific efforts to preserve ancient remains
③ attempts to overcome inequality in history
④ cultural differences in the concept of better jobs
⑤ ancient agricultural methods passed down to the present

다음 글의 주제로 가장 적절한 것은? [3점]

For those of any age with an existing network of friendships built up in the three-dimensional world, social networking sites can be a happy extension of communication, along with email, video calls, or phone calls, when face-to-face time together just isn't possible. The danger comes when a fake identity is both tempting and possible through relationships that are *not* based on real, three-dimensional interaction, and / or when the most important things in your life are the secondhand lives of others rather than personal experiences. Living in the context of the screen might suggest false norms of desirable lifestyles full of friends and parties. As ordinary human beings follow the activities of these golden individuals, self-esteem will inevitably drop; yet the constant narcissistic obsession with the self and its inadequacies will dominate. We can imagine a vicious circle where the more your identity is harmed as a result of social networking and the more inadequate you feel, the greater the appeal of a medium where you don't need to communicate with people face-to-face.

*narcissistic: 자아도취적인

① negative effects of social networking services on self-perception
② unknown risks to personal well-being from internet addiction
③ software features to make virtual lives more realistic
④ efforts to increase face-to-face interaction for social bonds
⑤ difficulties of filtering out fake information on social media

다음 글의 주제로 가장 적절한 것은?

Problem framing amounts to defining *what* problem you are proposing to solve. This is a critical activity because the frame you choose strongly influences your understanding of the problem, thereby conditioning your approach to solving it. For an illustration, consider Thibodeau and Broditsky's series of experiments in which they asked people for ways to reduce crime in a community. They found that the respondents' suggestions changed significantly depending on whether the metaphor used to describe crime was as a virus or as a beast. People presented with a metaphor comparing crime to a virus invading their city emphasized prevention and addressing the root causes of the problem, such as eliminating poverty and improving education. On the other hand, people presented with the beast metaphor focused on remediations: increasing the size of the police force and prisons.

① importance of asking the right questions for better solutions
② difficulty of using a metaphor to find solutions to a problem
③ reasons why problem framing prevents solutions from appearing
④ usefulness of preventive measures in reducing community crime
⑤ effect of problem framing on approaching and solving problems

다음 글의 주제로 가장 적절한 것은?

The primary purpose of commercial music radio broadcasting is to deliver an audience to a group of advertisers and sponsors. To achieve commercial success, that audience must be as large as possible. More than any other characteristics (such as demographic or psychographic profile, purchasing power, level of interest, degree of satisfaction, quality of attention or emotional state), the quantity of an audience aggregated as a mass is the most significant metric for broadcasters seeking to make music radio for profitable ends. As a result, broadcasters attempt to maximise their audience size by playing music that is popular, or — at the very least — music that can be relied upon not to cause audiences to switch off their radio or change the station. Audience retention is a key value (if not the key value) for many music programmers and for radio station management. In consequence, a high degree of risk aversion frequently marks out the 'successful' radio music programmer. Playlists are restricted, and often very small.

*aggregate: 모으다 **aversion: 싫어함

① features of music playlists appealing to international audiences
② influence of advertisers on radio audiences' musical preferences
③ difficulties of increasing audience size in radio music programmes
④ necessity of satisfying listeners' diverse needs in the radio business
⑤ outcome of music radio businesses' attempts to attract large audiences

반복되는 핵심어를 찾자!

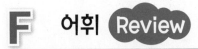

F 어휘 Review

※ 다음 영어는 우리말 뜻, 우리말은 영어 단어를 〈보기〉에서 찾아 쓰시오.

〈보기〉

notice	평범한	overcome	개입
underlying	경향	evolution	퇴행하다
critical	연속	resource	잔인한

01 ordinary   _____

02 tendency   _____

03 succession   _____

04 regress   _____

05 intervention   _____

06 근본적인   _____

07 진화, 발전   _____

08 알아차리다   _____

09 대단히 중요한   _____

10 자원   _____

※ 다음 우리말에 알맞은 영어 표현을 찾아 연결하시오.

11 설명하다   •   • be forced to

12 계속하다   •   • carry on

13 ~에 초점을 맞춘   •   • account for

14 ~와 관련된   •   • be associated with

15 ~하도록 강요당하다   •   • addressed to

※ 다음 우리말 표현에 맞는 단어를 고르시오.

16 그들의 갤러리를 현대화하다 ➡ (modernise / realize) their galleries

17 소통의 행복한 연장선 ➡ a happy (excursion / extension) of communication

18 그들의 번창하는 마을과 ➡ with their (blossoming / breathing) towns

19 고고학적 기록 ➡ the (archeological / ecological) record

20 농업의 출현 ➡ the appearance of (agreement / agriculture)

※ 다음 문장의 빈칸에 알맞은 단어를 〈보기〉에서 찾아 쓰시오.

〈보기〉

accustomed	confront	emerging	incoherent
retention	inevitably	justice	illustration
principle	grasped	frequent	implemented

21 식품 광고는 구매자가 단어의 새로운 개념에 익숙해지도록 도왔다.
➡ Food ads helped shoppers become _____ to new definitions of words.

22 하나의 예로, Thibodeau와 Broditsky의 일련의 실험에 대해 생각해 보라.
➡ For a(n) _____, consider Thibodeau and Broditsky's series of experiments.

23 더 빈번한 홍수가 우리의 집을 파괴할지도 모른다.
➡ More _____ floods might destroy our homes.

24 그 새로운 정의는 신흥 식품 산업 시스템의 요구에 더 잘 부합했다.
➡ The new definitions better served the needs of the _____ industrial food system.

25 이는 우리가 일관되지 않다는 신호가 아니다.
➡ This is not a sign that we are being _____.

26 기하학적 모양은 이해될 수는 있지만 감정을 불러일으키지 않는다.
➡ Geometrical shapes can be _____, but they do not give rise to emotion.

27 우리는 감정을 중추 신경의, 즉 신경계에서 실행되는 상태라고 생각한다.
➡ We think of emotions as central, neurally _____ states.

28 농부는 복잡하고 관찰하기 어려운 현상에 자주 직면한다.
➡ Farmers often _____ complex and difficult-to-observe phenomena.

29 자존감은 필연적으로 떨어질 것이다.
➡ Self-esteem will _____ drop.

30 청취자 보유가 하나의 핵심 가치이다.
➡ Audience _____ is a key value.

KUAAA

고려대학교 천문 동아리

우리 같이 별 보러 가지 않을래?

매달 정기 관측회를 떠나고 싶은 사람!
망원경이 없지만 별을 보고 싶은 사람!
사진기가 없지만 사진 찍고 싶은 사람!
이 중 하나라도 해당되는 사람, **KUAAA**로 초대합니다!

KUAAA(Korea University Amateur Astronomical Association)는 별 보기를 좋아하는 아마추어들을 위한 동아리입니다. 학술연구분과 소속인 **KUAAA**에서는 천문과 관련된 배경지식이 없더라도 세미나를 통해 기초 지식부터 알려드리니 부담 없이 오세요!

KUAAA에 오신다면 맨눈으로 별자리를 찾는 법, 별이나 성운 사진을 멋지게 찍는 법을 배우게 될 것이고, 매달 도시 밖으로 떠나는 1박 2일 정기 관측회, 당일치기로 떠나는 비정기 관측회 등 즐거운 친목 도모 활동까지 모두 경험하실 수 있습니다!

G 제목 찾기

〈소설가 구보 씨의 일일〉? 제목을 보니까 이 글이 무슨 내용일지 대충 알겠단 말이지!

★ 유형 설명

다음 글의 제목으로 가장 적절한 것은?

There is a story about F. Yates, a prominent UK statistician. During his student years at

글의 중심 내용을 간결하고 명료하게, 그리고 비유적으로 나타낸 제목을 찾아야 한다.

☞ 글의 주제에 대해 필자가 갖고 있는 생각을 파악한 다음 그것을 압축해서 나타낸 선택지를 찾는다.
글의 주제와 제목이 동일한 경우도 있지만, 비유적으로 나타낸 표현이 제목이 되는 경우가 더 많다.

🎭 유형 풀이 비법

1 중심 문장을 찾아라!
• 필자가 전달하려는 중심 생각이나 요지가 드러나 있는 문장을 찾는다.

2 세부 사항을 종합하라!
• 글의 세부 사항들을 종합해서 주제를 파악한다.

3 글의 내용을 적절히 압축하라!
• 글의 내용을 너무 넓거나 좁게 나타내지 않은 제목을 고른다.

> (Tip) 글의 일부분에만 해당하는 선택지를 정답으로 선택하지 않도록 한다.

★ 최신 수능 경향 분석

★ 2025 수능 출제 분석

첫 문장에서 셀피가 자화상의 오랜 역사를 발전시키고 확장해 간다고 언급한 것부터 이 글의 제목에 대한 단서를 제공했다. 이후에 글을 읽으면서 우리 자신을 표현하는 최신 혁신으로서의 셀피에 대한 내용임을 파악하면 적절한 제목을 고를 수 있었다.

★ 2026 수능 예측

난이도가 높은 유형으로, 언제든지 어렵게 출제될 수 있으므로, 독해 문제를 풀면서 글에 비유적인 제목을 붙이는 훈련을 통해 실력을 향상시켜야 한다.

🔵 제목에 자주 쓰이는 표현

□ A Secret to ~의 비결
□ A Way to-v ~하는 방법
□ Don't ~ ~하지 마라
□ Factors for ~에 대한 요소들
□ Functions of ~의 기능들
□ How to ~하는 방법
□ The History of ~의 역사
□ The Kinds of ~의 종류
□ Why ~? 왜 ~하는가
□ Increase of ~의 증가
□ Effects of ~의 영향
□ Needs of ~의 필요성

🍪 어휘 및 표현 Preview

□ gain 얻다
□ currency 유행
□ overly 지나치게
□ compare 비교하다
□ choice 선택
□ instead 대신에
□ convention 관습
□ threaten 위협하다
□ innovation 혁신
□ take-away 핵심
□ analyze 분석하다
□ straight 일직선의

□ progress 발전
□ myth 근거 없는 믿음
□ survey 조사하다
□ space 공간
□ cycle 주기
□ repeat 반복[되풀이]하다
□ productivity 생산성
□ manage 관리하다
□ prehistoric 선사시대의
□ skillfully 능숙하게
□ shadow 그림자
□ Western 서양의

□ representation 표현
□ transition 전환
□ consistent 일관된
□ fixed 고정된
□ geometric 기하학적인
□ artistic 예술적인
□ root 뿌리, 근원
□ practice 방식, 관행
□ debate 논쟁, 토론
□ challenge 도전, 과제
□ unique 독특한
□ theoretician 이론가

1st 첫 문장을 통해 핵심 소재를 확인하고 글의 내용을 예상하세요.
2nd **1st** 에서 발상한 것을 토대로 글을 읽고, 내용을 파악하세요.
3rd 글의 주제에 알맞은 제목을 고르세요.

G01 ✷❋❋.............. 2025 대비 6월 모평 24 (고3)

다음 글의 제목으로 가장 적절한 것은? [3점]

As far back as 32,000 years ago, prehistoric cave artists skillfully used modeling shadows to give their horses and bison volume. A few thousand years ago ancient Egyptian and then ancient Greek art presented human forms in shadow-style silhouette. But cast shadows do not appear in Western art until about 400 BCE in Athens. It was only after shadows had become an established, if controversial, part of representation that classical writers claimed that art itself had begun with the tracing of a human shadow. Greeks and Romans were the first to make the transition from modeling shadows to cast shadows, a practice that implied a consistent light source, a fixed point of view, and an understanding of geometric projection. In fact, what we might now call "shadow studies" — the exploration of shadows in their various artistic representations — has its roots in ancient Athens. Ever since, the practice of portraying shadows has evolved along with critical analysis of them, as artists and theoreticians have engaged in an ongoing debate about the significance of shadow representation.

*geometric: 기하학의

① The Journey of Shadows in Art from Prehistoric Caves Onward
② Portrayals of Human Shadows from the Artistic Perspective
③ Representing Shadows as a Key Part of Contemporary Art
④ What Are the Primary Challenges for Shadow Painters?
⑤ Unique Views on Shadows: From Cave Artists to Romans

1st 첫 문장을 통해 핵심 소재를 확인하고 글의 내용을 예상하세요.

1) 첫 문장부터 읽어 봅시다.

As far back as 32,000 years ago, / prehistoric cave
무려 3만 2천 년 전으로 거슬러 올라가   / 선사시대 동굴

artists skillfully used modeling shadows / to give
예술가들은 모형화한 그림자를 능숙하게 사용했다   /

their horses and bison volume. //
자신의 말과 들소 그림에 입체감을 주기 위해   //

● **첫 문장에 바로 핵심 소재가 나왔어요!**
아주 오래전으로 거슬러 올라가면 선사시대 동굴 벽화 예술가들은 그림자를 능숙하게 사용했다고 했어요. 예술에서 과거부터 **❶**(   )를 어떻게 사용했는지 언급했어요. (단서)

2) 글의 내용을 예상할 수 있겠죠?
선사시대 동굴 예술가들이 그림자를 사용해 벽화에 입체감을 줬다고 했으므로 그림자의 역사적 변화에 대해 설명할 것이라고 예상할 수 있어요. (발상)

2nd **1st** 에서 발상한 것을 토대로 글을 읽고, 내용을 파악하세요.

1) A few thousand years ago가 눈에 들어와요.

A few thousand years ago / ancient Egyptian and
수천 년 전   / 고대 이집트와 그 이후

then ancient Greek art / presented human forms in
고대 그리스 예술은   / 그림자 스타일의 실루엣으로

shadow-style silhouette. //
인간 형태를 나타냈다   //

● **앞에서 말한 선사시대에 이어지는 내용이에요.**
앞에서 As far back as 32,000 years ago라고 하면서 선사시대의 동굴 예술가들에 대해 말했었죠?
여기서는 그보다 더 시간이 지나서 고대 이집트와 고대 그리스 예술에 대해 언급하고 있어요. 그 당시에는 인간 형태를 그림자 스타일의 **❷**(   )으로 나타냈다고 했어요.

2) 그 뒤에는 그리스와 로마인들에 대한 내용이 나와요.

Greeks and Romans were the first / to make the
그리스인과 로마인은 최초였다   / 그림자를 모형화하는

transition from modeling shadows to cast shadows, /
방식에서 그림자를 드리우는 방식으로 전환한   /

a practice that implied / a consistent light source, /
이는 함축하는 관행이었다   / 일관된 광원   /

a fixed point of view, / and an understanding of
고정된 시점   / 기하학적 투영에 대한 이해를 //

geometric projection. //

● **시대가 과거부터 현재로 계속 가까워지고 있죠?**

그리스와 로마인들은 그림자 표현 방식을 전환시켰다고 했어요. 그림자를
모형화하는 방식에서 그림자를 드리우는 방식으로 바꾼 것이죠.

3) 이제 마지막 문장을 살펴봅시다.

Ever since, / the practice of portraying shadows /
그 이후로   / 그림자를 묘사하는 방식은   /

has evolved along with critical analysis of them, / as
그림자에 대한 비판적 분석과 더불어 발전해왔다   /

artists and theoreticians have engaged in an
예술가와 이론가가 지속적인 논쟁을 벌임에 따라

ongoing debate / about the significance of shadow
              / 그림자 표현의 중요성에 대한 //

representation. //

● **마지막 문장까지도 그림자의 묘사 방식에 대한 설명이 이어졌어요.**

그리스와 로마인들이 그림자 표현 방식을 ❸(   )시킨
이후에도 그림자의 묘사 방식은 계속 발전해왔다고 했어요. 그림자를
묘사하는 방식은 그림자에 대한 비판적 분석과 함께 발전해왔다는
거예요.

3rd 글의 주제에 알맞은 제목을 고르세요.

1) 글의 주제부터 생각해 봅시다.

예술에서 그림자를 표현하는 방식은 선사시대 동굴 벽화에서 시작하여,
고대 이집트와 고대 그리스를 거쳐 아테네와 로마에 이르러 모형화하는
방식에서 그림자를 드리우는 방식으로 변화했다고 했어요.
그리고 그 이후 계속 발전해왔다는 내용이므로 '예술에서 그림자의
역사적 발전'이 이 글의 주제예요.

2) 이제 선택지를 살펴봅시다.

① The Journey of Shadows in Art from Prehistoric
Caves Onward
선사시대 동굴에서 이어져 온 예술 속 그림자의 여정

② Portrayals of Human Shadows from the Artistic
Perspective
예술적 관점에서 본 사람 그림자의 묘사

③ Representing Shadows as a Key Part of
Contemporary Art
현대 예술의 핵심 요소로 그림자 표현하기

④ What Are the Primary Challenges for Shadow
Painters?
그림자 화가에게 주요 과제란 무엇인가?

⑤ Unique Views on Shadows: From Cave Artists to
Romans
그림자에 대한 독특한 관점: 동굴 예술가부터 로마인까지

예술에서 그림자가 역사적으로 어떻게 발전해왔는지를 서술한
글이었으므로 제목은 ❹(   )이 적절해요.

글의 주제부터
파악하자!

 첫 문장을 통해 핵심 소재를 확인하고 글의 내용을 예상해 보세요.

 예상한 내용을 토대로 글을 읽고, 전체적인 내용을 파악해 보세요.

 내용을 종합하여 글의 주제에 알맞은 제목을 골라 보세요.

G02 ★★ ☀ .... 2024 대비 6월 모평 24 (고3)

다음 글의 제목으로 가장 적절한 것은?

Hyper-mobility — the notion that more travel at faster speeds covering longer distances generates greater economic success — seems to be a distinguishing feature of urban areas, where more than half of the world's population currently reside. By 2005, approximately 7.5 billion trips were made each day in cities worldwide. In 2050, there may be three to four times as many passenger-kilometres travelled as in the year 2000, infrastructure and energy prices permitting. Freight movement could also rise more than threefold during the same period. Mobility flows have become a key dynamic of urbanization, with the associated infrastructure invariably constituting the backbone of urban form. Yet, despite the increasing level of urban mobility worldwide, access to places, activities and services has become increasingly difficult. Not only is it less convenient — in terms of time, cost and comfort — to access locations in cities, but the very process of moving around in cities generates a number of negative externalities. Accordingly, many of the world's cities face an unprecedented accessibility crisis, and are characterized by unsustainable mobility systems.

*freight: 화물

① Is Hyper-mobility Always Good for Cities?
② Accessibility: A Guide to a Web of Urban Areas
③ A Long and Winding Road to Economic Success
④ Inevitable Regional Conflicts from Hyper-mobility
⑤ Infrastructure: An Essential Element of Hyper-mobility

1st 첫 문장을 통해 핵심 소재를 확인하고 글의 내용을 예상해 보세요.

Hyper-mobility / — the notion / that more travel at
하이퍼 모빌리티는 / 개념 / 더 많은 여행

faster speeds / covering longer distances / generates
더 빠른 속도의 / 더 먼 거리를 이동하는 /

greater economic success — / seems to be a
더 큰 경제적 성공을 만든다는 / ~인 것으로 보인다

distinguishing feature of urban areas, / where more
도시 지역의 두드러진 특징 /

than half of the world's population / currently
세계 인구의 절반보다 더 많은 사람이 / 현재 거주하는 //

reside. //

● **첫 줄에 핵심 소재가 등장했어요!**
하이퍼 모빌리티를 소개하며 그 개념을 설명했어요. 요약하자면, 더 많은 여행이 더 큰 경제적 성공을 만든다는 것인데, 이것이 도시 지역의 특징이라고 하네요. 단서 하이퍼 모빌리티가 무엇인지 알았으니, 이제 이것이 도시에 미치는 영향에 대한 내용이 이어질 것이라고 예상할 수 있어요. 발상

2nd 예상한 내용을 토대로 글을 읽고, 전체적인 내용을 파악해 보세요.

1) 역접의 연결어 Yet이 눈에 띄네요.

Yet, / despite the increasing level of urban mobility /
그러나 / 증가하는 도시 이동성 수준에도 불구하고 /

worldwide, / access to places, activities and services
전 세계적으로 / 장소, 활동 및 서비스에 대한 접근은

/ has become increasingly difficult. //
/ 점점 더 어려워졌다 //

● **글의 흐름은 역접의 연결어로 전환돼요.**
Yet이 나오기 전까지는 하이퍼 모빌리티와 도시 이동성의 흐름이 도시의 핵심인 것처럼 보였는데, Yet 뒷부분은 ❶( )이 증가해도 장소, 활동 및 서비스에 대한 접근이 어려워졌다는 내용이에요.

2) 흐름이 전환된 이후의 내용에 주목해 봅시다.

Not only is it less convenient / — in terms of time,
~이 덜 편리할 뿐만 아니라 / 시간, 비용 및 편안함의

cost and comfort — / to access locations in cities, /
측면에서 보면 / 도시에서 장소에 접근하는 것이 /

but the very process of moving around in cities /
도시에서 돌아다니는 바로 그 과정이 /

generates a number of negative externalities. //
많은 부정적인 외부 효과를 발생시킨다 //

● **하이퍼 모빌리티의 부정적인 영향에 대해 부연하는 문장이
이어졌어요.**

도시에서 장소에 접근하는 것이 덜 편리하고, 도시를 돌아다니는 과정이
부정적 외부 효과를 발생시킨다는 내용이에요. 하이퍼 모빌리티로 도시의
이동성이 증가했으나 장소로 접근하는 것이 어려워졌으므로 불편하다는
맥락으로 보여지네요.

3) 이제 마지막 문장을 살펴봅시다.

Accordingly, / many of the world's cities face / an
그에 따라 / 세계의 많은 도시는 직면하고 /

unprecedented accessibility crisis, / and are
전례 없는 접근성 위기를 /

characterized / by unsustainable mobility systems. //
특징지어진다 / 지속 불가능한 이동성 시스템으로 //

● **하이퍼 모빌리티에 대해 마지막 문장까지도 부정적인 설명이
이어졌어요.**

crisis, ❷(   )처럼 부정적인 단어로 글이 마무리되네요.
Yet 이후로 하이퍼 모빌리티에 대한 평가가 다시 뒤집히지 않았으니,
이제 글의 주제를 확정지어 봅시다.

3rd 내용을 종합하여 글의 주제에 알맞은 제목을 골라 보세요.

1) 글의 주제부터 생각해 봅시다.

첫 문장에서 하이퍼 모빌리티가 도시 지역의 두드러진 특징이라고 하며
도시의 핵심인 듯한 느낌을 줬지만, Yet 이후로는 하이퍼 모빌리티가
도시 이동성에 부정적인 영향을 끼쳤다고 했어요. 이 두 가지를 통해
하이퍼 모빌리티가 도시 이동성에 핵심인 것처럼 보였지만 결국 도시
이동성에 부정적인 영향을 끼쳤다는 것이 주제임을 알 수 있어요.

2) 이 주제에 맞는 선택지가 있는지 확인해 볼까요?

① Is Hyper-mobility Always Good for Cities?
하이퍼 모빌리티는 도시에 항상 이로운가?

② Accessibility: A Guide to a Web of Urban Areas
접근성: 도시 지역망 가이드

③ A Long and Winding Road to Economic Success
경제적 성공으로 가는 길고 구불구불한 길

④ Inevitable Regional Conflicts from Hyper-mobility
하이퍼 모빌리티로 인한 불가피한 지역 갈등

⑤ Infrastructure: An Essential Element of Hyper-
mobility
사회 기반 시설: 하이퍼 모빌리티의 필수 요소

● **핵심 소재가 담긴 선택지부터 찾아볼까요?**
❸(   )가 언급되는 선택지는 총 세 개, ①, ④, ⑤이네요.
그 중 하이퍼 모빌리티에 대해 부정적인 ①, ④에 집중해 봅시다.

● **이제 두 선택지 중에서 하나의 정답을 골라봅시다.**
①, ④ 각각 '도시에 항상 이로운가?'라는 의문과 지역 갈등을 언급했는데,
이 글에서 지역 갈등이라는 단어는 등장하지 않았어요.
그렇기 때문에 정답은 ❹(   )이에요. 하이퍼 모빌리티가
이로운지 묻는 질문에 대해, 이는 도시의 핵심이지만 도시에 부정적인
영향을 끼쳤다는 대답이 가능한 것이죠.

이 글의
주제는 뭘까?

G03 ～06 ▶ 제한시간 8분

G03 ★★★ .... 2025 대비 수능 24 (고3)

다음 글의 제목으로 가장 적절한 것은?

The selfie resonates not because it is new, but because it expresses, develops, expands, and intensifies the long history of the self-portrait. The self-portrait showed to others the status of the person depicted. In this sense, what we have come to call our own "image" — the interface of the way we think we look and the way others see us — is the first and fundamental object of global visual culture. The selfie depicts the drama of our own daily performance of ourselves in tension with our inner emotions that may or may not be expressed as we wish. At each stage of the self-portrait's expansion, more and more people have been able to depict themselves. Today's young, urban, networked majority has reworked the history of the self-portrait to make the selfie into the first visual signature of the new era.

*resonate: 공명(共鳴)하다 **depict: 그리다

① Are Selfies Just a Temporary Trend in Art History?
② Fantasy or Reality: Your Selfie Is Not the Real You
③ The Selfie: A Symbol of Self-oriented Global Culture
④ The End of Self-portraits: How Selfies Are Taking Over
⑤ Selfies, the Latest Innovation in Representing Ourselves

G04 ★★❀ .... 2025 대비 9월 모평 24 (고3)

다음 글의 제목으로 가장 적절한 것은?

There are good reasons why open-office plans have gained currency, but open offices may not be the plan of choice for *all* times. Instead, the right plan seems to be building a culture of change. Overly rigid habits and conventions, no matter how well-considered or well-intentioned, threaten innovation. The crucial take-away from analyzing office plans over time is that the answers keep changing. It might seem that there is a straight line of progress, but it's a myth. Surveying office spaces from the past eighty years, one can see a cycle that repeats. Comparing the offices of the 1940s with contemporary office spaces shows that they have circled back around to essentially the same style, via a period in the 1980s when partitions and cubicles were more the norm. The technologies and colors may differ, but the 1940s and 2000s plans are alike, right down to the pillars running down the middle.

*rigid: 굳은 **pillar: 기둥

① Why Are Open-office Plans So Cost-efficient?
② How to Incorporate Retro Styles into Office Spaces
③ An Office Divided: Why Partitions Limit Productivity
④ Office Designs: What Goes Around Comes Around
⑤ Tips for Managing Contemporary Office Spaces

다음 글의 제목으로 가장 적절한 것은? [3점]

We naturally gravitate toward people whose views and beliefs are similar to our own, seeking what the eighteenth-century moral philosopher Adam Smith called "a certain harmony of minds." Spending time with people who share our opinions reinforces our group identity, strengthening trust, cooperation, equality, and productivity. Our shared reality grounds us not just in our common perceptions but in similar feelings and worldviews. This helps to preserve our core values and beliefs about ourselves. It also provides us with meaning and a feeling of self-worth. And with each decision or interaction that confirms our tribe's common experience, we get rewarded with the hormonal happiness we crave. Our perception of ourselves is a mixture of our own unique characteristics and our sense of belonging to our in-groups. In fact, our personal identity is so closely interwoven with our social identity that our brains can't tell them apart. If I put you in a scanner and ask you to talk about yourself and then about the groups to which you feel the closest affinity, it will activate the same neural networks in your brain.

*gravitate toward: ~에 자연히 끌리다 **affinity: 유사성

① The Secret to Becoming a Unique Individual
② Societal Conflict: Shared Reality Breeding Mutual Distrust
③ Our Identity Shaped by Shared Views: Comfort of Like Minds
④ Sympathy: Key to Resolving Disharmony in the Workplace
⑤ How We Balance Personal Identity with Social Identity

다음 글의 제목으로 가장 적절한 것은?

A scholar Eve Tuck urges researchers to move away from what she calls "damage-based research," or "research that operates, even benevolently, from a theory of change that establishes harm or injury in order to achieve reparation." Citing studies in education that sought to increase resources for marginalized youths by documenting the "illiteracies" of indigenous youths and youths of color, Tuck explains that damage-based research is a popular mechanism by which "pain and loss are documented in order to obtain particular political or material gains." While damagebased studies have proven successful in attaining political or material gains in the form of funding, attention, and increased awareness related to the struggles of marginalized communities, Tuck points researchers to the ongoing violence damage-based research inflicts on marginalized communities, even under benevolent or perceivably beneficial circumstances. Among the many issues associated with damage-based research are the underlying assumptions this type of work makes and sustains about marginalized people; namely, that marginalized communities lack communication, civility, intellect, desires, assets, innovation, and ethics.

*reparation: 보상 **marginalized: 소외된 ***indigenous: 토착의

① Marginalized Yesterday, Privileged Today
② How Damage-Based Research Can Backfire
③ Research: An Endless Journey to the Truth
④ Different Era, Different Education for Minority Youth
⑤ The Growth of Diversity Among Younger Generations

G07 ★★❀·····················2024 실시 5월 학평 24 (고3)

다음 글의 제목으로 가장 적절한 것은?

When viewed from space, one of the Earth's most commanding features is the blueness of its vast oceans. Small amounts of water do not indicate the color of these large bodies of water; when pure drinking water is examined in a glass, it appears clear and colorless. Apparently a relatively large volume of water is required to reveal the blue color. Why is this so? When light penetrates water, it experiences both absorption and scattering. Water molecules strongly absorb infrared and, to a lesser degree, red light. At the same time, water molecules are small enough to scatter shorter wavelengths, giving water its blue-green color. The amount of long-wavelength absorption is a function of depth; the deeper the water, the more red light is absorbed. At a depth of 15m, the intensity of red light drops to 25% of its original value and falls to zero beyond a depth of 30m. Any object viewed at this depth is seen in a blue-green light. For this reason, red inhabitants of the sea, such as lobsters and crabs, appear black to divers not carrying a lamp.

*penetrate: 관통하다 **infrared: 적외선

① We Should Go Green with the Ocean Exploration
② Various Tones of Water Our Deceptive Eyes Show Us
③ How Deep-Sea Microorganisms Affect the Ocean's Color
④ Why So Blue: The Science Behind the Color of Earth's Oceans
⑤ The Bigger Volume Water Has, the Lower Temperature It Gets

G08 ★★❀·····················2024 실시 3월 학평 24 (고3)

다음 글의 제목으로 가장 적절한 것은?

Distance in time is like distance in space. People matter even if they live thousands of miles away. Likewise, they matter even if they live thousands of years hence. In both cases, it's easy to mistake distance for unreality, to treat the limits of what we can see as the limits of the world. But just as the world does not stop at our doorstep or our country's borders, neither does it stop with our generation, or the next. These ideas are common sense. A popular proverb says, "A society grows great when old men plant trees under whose shade they will never sit." When we dispose of radioactive waste, we don't say, "Who cares if this poisons people centuries from now?" Similarly, few of us who care about climate change or pollution do so solely for the sake of people alive today. We build museums and parks and bridges that we hope will last for generations; we invest in schools and longterm scientific projects; we preserve paintings, traditions, languages; we protect beautiful places. In many cases, we don't draw clear lines between our concerns for the present and the future — both are in play.

*radioactive: 방사선의

① How to Be Present: Discover the Benefits of Here and Now
② The Power of Time Management: The Key to Success
③ Why Is Green Infrastructure Eventually Cost-Effective?
④ Solving Present-Day Problems from Past Experiences
⑤ How We Act Beyond the Bounds of Time

다음 글의 제목으로 가장 적절한 것은?

The approach, *joint cognitive systems*, treats a robot as part of a human-machine team where the intelligence is synergistic, arising from the contributions of each agent. The team consists of at least one robot and one human and is often called a *mixed team* because it is a mixture of human and robot agents. Self-driving cars, where a person turns on and off the driving, is an example of a joint cognitive system. Entertainment robots are examples of mixed teams as are robots for telecommuting. The design process concentrates on how the agents will cooperate and coordinate with each other to accomplish the team goals. Rather than treating robots as peer agents with their own completely independent agenda, joint cognitive systems approaches treat robots as helpers such as service animals or sheep dogs. In joint cognitive system designs, artificial intelligence is used along with human-robot interaction principles to create robots that can be intelligent enough to be good team members.

① Better Together: Human and Machine Collaboration
② Can Robots Join Forces to Outperform Human Teams?
③ Loss of Humanity in the Human and Machine Conflict
④ Power Off: When and How to Say No to Robot Partners
⑤ Shifting from Service Animals to Robot Assistants of Humans

다음 글의 제목으로 가장 적절한 것은?

The most innovative teams are those that can restructure themselves in response to unexpected shifts in the environment; they don't need a strong leader to tell them what to do. Moreover, they tend to form spontaneously; when like-minded people find each other, a group emerges. The improvisational collaboration of the entire group translates moments of individual creativity into group innovation. Allowing the space for this self-organizing emergence to occur is difficult for many managers because the outcome isn't controlled by the management team's agenda and is therefore less predictable. Most business executives like to start with the big picture and then work out the details. That's why so many of the best examples of improvised innovation take place outside of formal organizations. In improvisational innovation, teams start with the details and then work up to the big picture. It's riskier and less efficient, but when a successful innovation emerges, it's often very surprising and imaginative.

① The Start of Innovation: A Leader's Big Picture
② Unpredictable Changes: Challenges to Innovation
③ Conflicting Ideas Lead to the Ultimate Innovation
④ Weakness of Improvisational Teams in Emergencies
⑤ Improvised Innovation Emerges from the Bottom Up

G11 ❀❀❀ .... 2023 실시 3월 학평 24 (고3)

다음 글의 제목으로 가장 적절한 것은?

Every day an enormous amount of energy is created by the movement of people and animals, and by interactions of people with their immediate surroundings. This is usually in very small amounts or in very dispersed environments. Virtually all of that energy is lost to the local environment, and historically there have been no efforts to gather it. It may seem odd to consider finding ways to "collect" energy that is given off all around us — by people simply walking or by walking upstairs and downstairs or by riding stationary/exercise bicycles, for example — but that is the general idea and nature of energy harvesting. The broad idea of energy harvesting is that there are many places at which small amounts of energy are generated — and often wasted — and when collected, this can be put to some practical use. Current efforts have begun, aimed at collecting such energy in smaller devices which can store it, such as portable batteries.

① Energy Harvesting: Every Little Helps
② Burning Waste for Energy Is Harmful
③ Is Renewable Energy Really Green?
④ Pros and Cons of Energy Harvesting
⑤ Can Natural Energy Sources Fulfill the Demand?

G12 ❀❀❀ .... 2023 실시 10월 학평 24 (고3)

다음 글의 제목으로 가장 적절한 것은?

When you break up with a partner or close friend, the natural response (after having a good cry, obviously) is to blame yourself. You wonder what you did wrong and what you might have done differently. Bonds can help us reach a more balanced perspective; there are some bonds that were simply never meant to last, even if they played an essential role in your evolution to this point. Perhaps the most valuable thing is to know that seeing bonds break doesn't have to break us. In chemistry, by definition, a change in the atomic bonding is not just the end of one state, but the beginning of another: creating the space for new bonding potential. The same is true for us as humans. It might take a cup of warm milk to reset us and give us comfort after a relationship has broken down. But however many bonds we see come apart, we will always retain one of our most human abilities: to connect afresh, find new friends and love again.

① Relationships: The Older, The Better
② A Break in a Bond: A New Beginning
③ Shared Experiences Make Strong Bonds
④ A Friend in Need, A Friend Indeed
⑤ Two Heads Are Better Than One

다음 글의 제목으로 가장 적절한 것은? [3점]

Before the web, newspaper archives were largely the musty domain of professional researchers and journalism students. Journalism was, by definition, current. The general accessibility of archives has greatly extended the shelf life of journalism, with older stories now regularly cited to provide context for more current ones. With regard to how meaning is made of complex issues encountered in the news, this departure can be understood as a readiness by online news consumers to engage with the underlying issues and contexts of the news that was not apparent in, or even possible for, print consumers. One of the emergent qualities of online news, determined in part by the depth of readily accessible online archives, seems to be the possibility of understanding news stories as the manifest outcomes of larger economic, social and cultural issues rather than short-lived and unconnected media spectacles.

*archive: 기록 보관소 **musty: 곰팡내 나는 ***manifest: 분명한

① Web-based Journalism: Lasting Longer and Contextually Wider
② With the Latest Content, Online News Beats Daily Newspapers!
③ How Online Media Journalists Reveal Hidden Stories Behind News
④ Let's Begin a Journey to the Past with Printed Newspapers!
⑤ Present and Future of Journalism in the Web World

다음 글의 제목으로 가장 적절한 것은?

As much as we like to think of ourselves as being different and special, humans are a part of Earth's biosphere, created within and by it. Ultimately, it is the living, breathing elements of this world that we need more than inanimate supplies, such as coal, gas, or bauxite ore. We can live without cars or beer cans, but we cannot without food and oxygen. As nations around the globe try to band together to attack the problems of greenhouse gas emissions and the shrinking availability of fresh drinking water, in all corners of the world thousands of species quietly go extinct. E. O. Wilson, the renowned Harvard biologist, recently presented the problem our species faces in a succinct law: "If you save the living environment, the biodiversity that we have left, you will also automatically save the physical environment, too. But if you only save the physical environment, you will ultimately lose both."

*biosphere: 생물권 **ore: 광석 ***succinct: 간결한

① Save Biodiversity to Save the Earth
② Invasive Alien Species Threaten Biodiversity
③ Potentiality and Utilization of Renewable Energy
④ Tackling Climate Change Has a Long Way to Go
⑤ Worldwide Efforts to Protect Endangered Species

G15 ✱✱❀ .... 2021 대비 6월 모평 24 (고3)

다음 글의 제목으로 가장 적절한 것은?

A common error in current Darwinian thinking is the assumption that "selfish genes" are the prime mover in evolution. In strict Darwinism the prime mover is environmental threat. In the absence of threat, natural selection tends to *resist* change. It is un-biological to "explain" behavioural change as *resulting from* genetic change or the *ex vacuo* emergence of domain-specific brain modules. Evolutionary psychologists surely know why brains evolved: as Cosmides and Tooby point out, brains are found only in animals that move. Brains are behavioural organs, and behavioural adaptation, being immediate and non-random, is vastly more efficient than genetic adaptation. So, in animals with brains, behavioural change is the usual first response to environmental threat. If the change is successful, genetic adaptation to the new behaviour will follow more gradually. Animals do not evolve carnivore teeth and then decide it might be a good idea to eat meat.

ex vacuo: 무(無)에서의   **carnivore: 육식 동물

① Which Adapts First, Behaviour or Genes?
② The Brain Under Control of Selfish Genes
③ Why Animals Eat Meat: A Story of Survival
④ Genes Always Win the Battle Against Nature!
⑤ The Superior Efficiency of Genetic Adaptation

G16 ✱✱❀ .... 2022 실시 10월 학평 24 (고3)

다음 글의 제목으로 가장 적절한 것은?

In making sense of cave art, anthropologists have turned to surviving hunter-gatherer societies that continue to paint inside caves, particularly the San peoples, who live in communities across a wide region of southern Africa. What began to fascinate anthropologists who studied the San was their detailed imitations of the animals they hunt. The hunters, in some sense, become animals in order to make inferences about how their prey might behave. This spills over into ritual. The San use hyperventilation and rhythmic movement to create states of altered consciousness as part of a shamanistic culture. In the final stage of a trance, Lewis-Williams writes, 'people sometimes feel themselves to be turning into animals and undergoing other frightening or exalting transformations'. For anthropologist Kim Hill, identifying and observing animals to eat and those to escape might merge into 'a single process' that sees animals as having humanlike intentions that 'can influence and be influenced'.

*hyperventilation: 과호흡 **trance: 무아지경
***exalt: 의기양양하게 하다

① Cave Paintings: The Dawn of Human Creativity
② Early Humans' Communication Through Cave Art
③ Hardships of Early Humans Depicted in Cave Art
④ Shamanistic Culture for Paying Honor to Ancestors
⑤ Animal Imitation Rituals and Understanding Cave Art

다음 글의 제목으로 가장 적절한 것은?

Melody is one of the primary ways that our expectations are controlled by composers. Music theorists have identified a principle called gap fill; in a sequence of tones, if a melody makes a large leap, either up or down, the next note should change direction. A typical melody includes a lot of stepwise motion, that is, adjacent tones in the scale. If the melody makes a big leap, theorists describe a tendency for the melody to "want" to return to the jumping-off point; this is another way to say that our brains expect that the leap was only temporary, and tones that follow need to bring us closer and closer to our starting point, or harmonic "home." In "Over the Rainbow," the melody begins with one of the largest leaps we've ever experienced in a lifetime of music listening: an octave. This is a strong schematic violation, and so the composer rewards and soothes us by bringing the melody back toward home again, but not by too much because he wants to continue to build tension. The third note of this melody fills the gap.

*adjacent: 인접한

① How Awesome Repetition in Melody Can Be!
② Why a Big Leap Melody Tends to Go Back Home
③ Lyrics of Songs: Key Controller of Our Emotions
④ Should Composers Consider Their Potential Audience?
⑤ Misunderstanding of Composers' Intention with Melody

다음 글의 제목으로 가장 적절한 것은?

Chimpanzees are known to hunt and eat red colobus monkeys. Although a solo male typically initiates a hunt, others often join in, and hunting success is much higher when chimps hunt as a group rather than individually. During the hunt, chimpanzees adopt different roles: one male might flush the monkeys from their refuge, while another blocks the escape route. Somewhere else, an ambusher hides, ready to make his deadly move. Although this sounds a lot like teamwork, recent work offers a simpler interpretation. Chimps are more likely to join others for hunts because larger hunting groups increase each *individual's* chance of catching a monkey — they aren't interested in collective goals. The appearance of specialised roles in the hunt may also be an illusion: a simpler explanation is that each chimp places himself where his own chance of catching a monkey is highest, relative to the positions the others have already taken. Collaboration in chimps seems to emerge from an 'every chimp for himself' mentality.

*refuge: 은신처 **ambusher: 복병

① Chimps' Group Hunt: It's All about Myself, Not Ourselves
② Obstacles to Chimps in Assigning Roles for Group Hunting
③ How One Selfish Chimp Can Ruin a Cooperative Group Hunt
④ Hunting in Concert with Other Chimps Determines Social Status!
⑤ Which Are Better Hunters, Cooperative or Competitive Chimps?

G19 ★★❀.................... 2024 대비 수능 24 (고3)

다음 글의 제목으로 가장 적절한 것은? [3점]

The concept of overtourism rests on a particular assumption about people and places common in tourism studies and the social sciences in general. Both are seen as clearly defined and demarcated. People are framed as bounded social actors either playing the role of hosts or guests. Places, in a similar way, are treated as stable containers with clear boundaries. Hence, places can be full of tourists and thus suffer from overtourism. But what does it mean for a place to be full of people? Indeed, there are examples of particular attractions that have limited capacity and where there is actually no room for more visitors. This is not least the case with some man-made constructions such as the Eiffel Tower. However, with places such as cities, regions or even whole countries being promoted as destinations and described as victims of overtourism, things become more complex. What is excessive or out of proportion is highly relative and might be more related to other aspects than physical capacity, such as natural degradation and economic leakages (not to mention politics and local power dynamics).

*demarcate: 경계를 정하다

① The Solutions to Overtourism: From Complex to Simple
② What Makes Popular Destinations Attractive to Visitors?
③ Are Tourist Attractions Winners or Losers of Overtourism?
④ The Severity of Overtourism: Much Worse than Imagined
⑤ Overtourism: Not Simply a Matter of People and Places

G20 ★★★.................... 2021 대비 9월 모평 24 (고3)

다음 글의 제목으로 가장 적절한 것은?

The discovery that man's knowledge is not, *and never has been*, perfectly accurate has had a humbling and perhaps a calming effect upon the soul of modern man. The nineteenth century, as we have observed, was the last to believe that the world, as a whole as well as in its parts, could ever be perfectly known. We realize now that this is, and always was, impossible. We know within limits, not absolutely, even if the limits can usually be adjusted to satisfy our needs. Curiously, from this new level of uncertainty even greater goals emerge and appear to be attainable. Even if we cannot know the world with absolute precision, we can still control it. Even our inherently incomplete knowledge seems to work as powerfully as ever. In short, we may never know precisely how high is the highest mountain, but we continue to be certain that we can get to the top nevertheless.

① Summits Yet to Be Reached: An Onward Journey to Knowledge
② Over the Mountain: A Single But Giant Step to Success
③ Integrating Parts into a Whole: The Road to Perfection
④ How to Live Together in an Age of Uncertainty
⑤ The Two Faces of a Knowledge-Based Society

다음 글의 제목으로 가장 적절한 것은?

Although cognitive and neuropsychological approaches emphasize the losses with age that might impair social perception, motivational theories indicate that there may be some gains or qualitative changes. Charles and Carstensen review a considerable body of evidence indicating that, as people get older, they tend to prioritize close social relationships, focus more on achieving emotional well-being, and attend more to positive emotional information while ignoring negative information. These changing motivational goals in old age have implications for attention to and processing of social cues from the environment. Of particular importance in considering emotional changes in old age is the presence of a positivity bias: that is, a tendency to notice, attend to, and remember more positive compared to negative information. The role of life experience in social skills also indicates that older adults might show gains in some aspects of social perception.

*cognitive: 인식의 **impair: 해치다

① Social Perception in Old Age: It's Not All Bad News!
② Blocking Out the Negative Sharpens Social Skills
③ Lessons on Life-long Goals from Senior Achievers
④ Getting Old: A Road to Maturity and Objectivity
⑤ Positive Mind and Behavior: Tips for Reversing Aging

다음 글의 제목으로 가장 적절한 것은?

There was once a certain difficulty with the moons of Jupiter that is worth remarking on. These satellites were studied very carefully by Roemer, who noticed that the moons sometimes seemed to be ahead of schedule, and sometimes behind. They were *ahead* when Jupiter was particularly *close* to the earth and they were *behind* when Jupiter was *farther* from the earth. This would have been a very difficult thing to explain according to the law of gravitation. If a law does not work even in *one place* where it ought to, it is just wrong. But the reason for this discrepancy was very simple and beautiful: it takes a little while to *see* the moons of Jupiter because of the time it takes light to travel from Jupiter to the earth. When Jupiter is closer to the earth the time is a little less, and when it is farther from the earth, the time is more. This is why moons appear to be, on the average, a little ahead or a little behind, depending on whether they are closer to or farther from the earth.

*discrepancy: 불일치

① The Difficulty of Proving the Gravitational Law
② An Illusion Created by the Shadow of the Moon
③ Why Aren't Jupiter's Moons Observed Where They Should Be?
④ Obstacles in Measuring Light's Speed: Limits of Past Technology
⑤ Ahead and Behind: Moons Change Their Position by Themselves

G23 ~ 26 ▶ 제한시간 11분

G23 ★ 2등급 대비 .... 2023 대비 수능 24 (고3)

다음 글의 제목으로 가장 적절한 것은?

Different parts of the brain's visual system get information on a need-to-know basis. Cells that help your hand muscles reach out to an object need to know the size and location of the object, but they don't need to know about color. They need to know a little about shape, but not in great detail. Cells that help you recognize people's faces need to be extremely sensitive to details of shape, but they can pay less attention to location. It is natural to assume that anyone who sees an object sees everything about it — the shape, color, location, and movement. However, one part of your brain sees its shape, another sees color, another detects location, and another perceives movement. Consequently, after localized brain damage, it is possible to see certain aspects of an object and not others. Centuries ago, people found it difficult to imagine how someone could see an object without seeing what color it is. Even today, you might find it surprising to learn about people who see an object without seeing where it is, or see it without seeing whether it is moving.

① Visual Systems Never Betray Our Trust!

② Secret Missions of Color-Sensitive Brain Cells

③ Blind Spots: What Is Still Unknown About the Brain

④ Why Brain Cells Exemplify Nature's Recovery Process

⑤ Separate and Independent: Brain Cells' Visual Perceptions

G24 ✪ 2등급 대비 .... 2022 대비 수능 24 (고3)

다음 글의 제목으로 가장 적절한 것은?

Mending and restoring objects often require even more creativity than original production. The preindustrial blacksmith made things to order for people in his immediate community; customizing the product, modifying or transforming it according to the user, was routine. Customers would bring things back if something went wrong; repair was thus an extension of fabrication. With industrialization and eventually with mass production, making things became the province of machine tenders with limited knowledge. But repair continued to require a larger grasp of design and materials, an understanding of the whole and a comprehension of the designer's intentions. "Manufacturers all work by machinery or by vast subdivision of labour and not, so to speak, by hand," an 1896 *Manual of Mending and Repairing* explained. "But all repairing *must* be done by hand. We can make every detail of a watch or of a gun by machinery, but the machine cannot mend it when broken, much less a clock or a pistol!"

① Still Left to the Modern Blacksmith: The Art of Repair

② A Historical Survey of How Repairing Skills Evolved

③ How to Be a Creative Repairperson: Tips and Ideas

④ A Process of Repair: Create, Modify, Transform!

⑤ Can Industrialization Mend Our Broken Past?

다음 글의 제목으로 가장 적절한 것은?

The world has become a nation of laws and governance that has introduced a system of public administration and management to keep order. With this administrative management system, urban institutions of government have evolved to offer increasing levels of services to their citizenry, provided through a taxation process and/or fee for services (e.g., police and fire, street maintenance, utilities, waste management, etc.). Frequently this has displaced citizen involvement. Money for services is not a replacement for citizen responsibility and public participation. Responsibility of the citizen is slowly being supplanted by government being the substitute provider. Consequentially, there is a philosophical and social change in attitude and sense of responsibility of our urban-based society to become involved. The sense of community and associated responsibility of all citizens to be active participants is therefore diminishing. Governmental substitution for citizen duty and involvement can have serious implications. This impedes the nations of the world to be responsive to natural and man-made disasters as part of global preparedness.

*supplant: 대신하다 **impede: 방해하다

① A Sound Citizen Responsibility in a Sound Government
② Always Better than Nothing: The Roles of Modern Government
③ Decreased Citizen Involvement: A Cost of Governmental Services
④ Why Does Global Citizenship Matter in Contemporary Society?
⑤ How to Maximize Public Benefits of Urban-Based Society

다음 글의 제목으로 가장 적절한 것은?

Not only musicians and psychologists, but also committed music enthusiasts and experts often voice the opinion that the beauty of music lies in an expressive deviation from the exactly defined score. Concert performances become interesting and gain in attraction from the fact that they go far beyond the information printed in the score. In his early studies on musical performance, Carl Seashore discovered that musicians only rarely play two equal notes in exactly the same way. Within the same metric structure, there is a wide potential of variations in tempo, volume, tonal quality and intonation. Such variation is based on the composition but diverges from it individually. We generally call this 'expressivity'. This explains why we do not lose interest when we hear different artists perform the same piece of music. It also explains why it is worthwhile for following generations to repeat the same repertoire. New, inspiring interpretations help us to expand our understanding, which serves to enrich and animate the music scene.

*deviation: 벗어남

① How to Build a Successful Career in Music Criticism
② Never the Same: The Value of Variation in Music Performance
③ The Importance of Personal Expression in Music Therapy
④ Keep Your Cool: Overcoming Stage Fright When Playing Music
⑤ What's New in the Classical Music Industry?

※ 다음 영어는 우리말 뜻을, 우리말은 영어 단어를 〈보기〉에서 찾아 쓰시오.

〈보기〉

굳은	implication	획기적 발견	apparent
improvised	volume	보유하다	substitution
저장하다	악보, 점수	논란의 여지가 있는	abandon

01 score   _____

02 store   _____

03 retain   _____

04 controversial   _____

05 rigid   _____

06 영향, 결과, 함축   _____

07 부피, 양   _____

08 분명한   _____

09 대체   _____

10 즉흥의   _____

※ 다음 우리말에 알맞은 영어 표현을 찾아 연결하시오.

11 ~에서 쫓아내다 •   • flush from

12 ~의 면에서 •   • spill over into

13 ~로 번지다 •   • in terms of

14 ~에 주력하다 •   • back around

15 돌아 오다 •   • focus on

※ 다음 우리말 표현에 맞는 단어를 고르시오.

16 막대한 양의 에너지 → a(n) (famous / enormous) amount of energy

17 우리의 본질적으로 불완전한 지식 → our (inhabitant / inherently) incomplete knowledge

18 보통의 첫 번째 대응 → the usual first (response / responsibility)

19 그들의 다양한 예술적 표현에서 → in their (various / similar) artistic representations

20 인간 행위자와 로봇 행위자가 혼합된 것 → a mixture of human and robot (agendas / agents)

※ 다음 문장의 빈칸에 알맞은 단어를 〈보기〉에서 찾아 쓰시오.

〈보기〉

diverges	artificial	domain	substantial
established	significance	absence	currency
tension	accurate	pioneer	analyzing

21 그림자가 표현의 확고한 한 부분으로 자리 잡게 되고 난 이후였다.
→ It was only after shadows had become a(n) _____ part of representation.

22 개방형 사무실 계획이 유행하는 데는 그럴 만한 이유가 있다.
→ There are good reasons why open-office plans have gained _____.

23 그는 긴장감을 조성하는 것을 계속하기를 원한다.
→ He wants to continue to build _____.

24 인간의 지식은 완벽하게 정확하지 않고 결코 완벽하게 정확했던 적이 없다.
→ Man's knowledge is not, and never has been, perfectly _____.

25 위협이 없을 때, 자연 선택은 변화에 저항하는 경향이 있다.
→ In the _____ of threat, natural selection tends to resist change.

26 예술가와 이론가가 그림자 표현의 중요성에 대한 지속적인 논쟁을 벌여왔다.
→ Artists and theoreticians have engaged in an ongoing debate about the _____ of shadow representation.

27 신문 기록 보관소는 주로 곰팡내 나는 영역이었다.
→ Newspaper archives were largely the musty _____.

28 시간이 지남에 따른 사무실 계획을 분석할 때 매우 중요한 핵심은 답이 계속 바뀐다는 것이다.
→ The crucial take-away from _____ office plans over time is that the answers keep changing.

29 이러한 변화는 작품에 기초하지만 개별적으로 그것으로부터 갈라진다.
→ Such variation is based on the composition but _____ from it individually.

30 인간-로봇 상호작용 원리와 함께 인공 지능이 사용된다.
→ _____ intelligence is used along with human-robot interaction principles.

도표의 이해

> 도표를 잘못 보셨어요. 물냉면 막대의 길이가 더 길어요.

> 역시 사람들은 비빔냉면을 더 선호하는군요.

★ 유형 설명

다음 도표의 내용과 일치하지 <u>않는</u> 것은?

Americans' Preferred Type of Place to Live (surveyed in 2020)

Age Group

18-34 Year-Olds 33% 27% 39%

다양한 분야의 통계 자료를 이해하고 그것을 제대로 설명했는지를 판단해야 한다.

☞ 비교 표현, 증가나 감소를 나타내는 표현, 배수 표현 등이 많이 쓰이는 점에 주의한다.

🥸 유형 풀이 비법

1 정보를 파악하라!

- (도)표와 (도)표의 제목, 글의 시작 부분을 보고 어떤 것에 대한 내용인지 이해한다.

2 한 문장씩 정확히 해석하라!

- (도)표와 글, 글과 선택지가 일치하는지 확인하려면 각 문장을 정확히 해석해야 한다.

3 일치하는지 판단하라!

- 선택지와 자료를 하나씩 빠르게 대조해서 일치하는지 판단해야 한다.

> (Tip) 두 개의 절로 이루어진 한 문장에서 하나의 절은 (도)표와 일치하지만, 다른 한 절은 일치하지 않는 경우가 많다.

★ 최신 수능 경향 분석

대비 연도	월	문항 번호	지문 주제	난이도
2025	11	25번	미국 영화 제작 현장에 고용된 역할별 여성 비율	★☆☆
	9	25번	4개국의 가상 현실과 증강 현실에 친숙한 응답자 비율	★☆☆
	6	25번	독서가 개인 취미 중 하나라고 응답한 각국의 남녀 비율	★☆☆
2024	11	25번	뉴스를 회피한 다섯 개 국가의 응답자 비율	★★☆
	9	25번	미국의 인종 / 민족별 대학 등록률	★★☆
	6	25번	관광에 참여한 EU-28 인구의 점유율	★★☆
2023	11	25번	미국인의 연령대별 선호 주거지 유형	★★☆
	9	25번	유럽 상위 4개국의 재생에너지 발전 용량	★★☆
	6	25번	거주민 특허 출원 통계	★★☆

★ 2025 수능 출제 분석

미국 상위 100개 영화의 세 연도에 어떤 역할로 제작 현장에 여성이 고용되었는지 비율을 보여주는 그래프로 출제된 문제였다. 도표 지문에서 보통 출제되는 길이로 구성된 문장들이어서 크게 어렵지 않았다.

★ 2026 수능 예측

도표의 형식이 어떻게 출제되든 두 형식 모두 정답을 찾는 해법은 똑같으므로, 지금까지 훈련한 대로 꾸준히 학습해야 한다.

🔑 도표의 자료를 설명할 때 자주 쓰이는 표현

① 분수
- half (1/2), one third, a third (1/3), two thirds (2/3), a quarter, one fourth (1/4)

② 배수
- double, twice (2배), three times (3배), four times (4배), ten times (10배)

③ 증가 (오르다, 늘어나다)
- grow, increase, rise, go up, soar, climb, add to, raise, multiply

④ 감소 (줄다, 떨어지다)
- drop, decrease, fall, go down, decline, reduce, diminish

⑤ 비교
- more than ~ (~보다 더 많은), less than ~ (~보다 더 적은), higher than ~ (~보다 더 높은), lower than ~ (~보다 더 낮은), largest, most, greatest (가장 큰/많은), smallest, least (가장 작은/적은)

🍱 어휘 및 표현 Preview

- □ survey 설문조사
- □ conduct 수행하다
- □ respondent 응답자
- □ reading 독서
- □ share 비율
- □ gender 성
- □ female 여성
- □ gap 차이
- □ select 선택하다
- □ among ~중에
- □ respectively 각각
- □ show 보여주다

H 도표의 이해 (첫 번째)

1st 무엇을 다룬 도표인지 분석하고, 어떤 변수에 주의해야 하는지 확인하세요.
2nd 각각의 문장을 읽고, 도표에서 확인해야 하는 부분에 □ 표시를 하세요.
3rd 정답 문장을 도표와 일치하도록 수정해 보세요.

H01 ★★✦............... 2023 대비 9월 모평 25 (고3)

다음 도표의 내용과 일치하지 <u>않는</u> 것은?

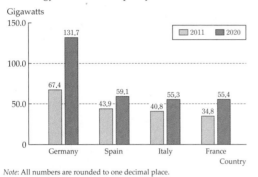

Top Four European Countries with the Most Renewable Energy Generation Capacity in 2011 and in 2020

Note: All numbers are rounded to one decimal place.

The graph above shows the top four European countries with the most renewable energy generation capacity in 2011 and in 2020. ① Each of the four countries in the graph had a higher capacity to generate renewable energy in 2020 than its respective capacity in 2011. ② Germany's capacity to generate renewable energy in 2011 reached more than 50.0 gigawatts, which was also the case in 2020. ③ Among the countries above, Spain ranked in second place in terms of renewable energy generation capacity in 2011 and remained in second place in 2020. ④ The renewable energy generation capacity of Italy in 2020 was lower than that of Spain in the same year. ⑤ The renewable energy generation capacity of France was higher than that of Italy in both 2011 and 2020.

* decimal: 소수의

1st **무엇을 다룬 도표인지 분석하고, 어떤 변수에 주의해야 하는지 확인하세요.**

Top Four European Countries with the Most Renewable Energy Generation Capacity in 2011 and in 2020
2011년과 2020년에 가장 많은 재생에너지 발전 용량을 가진 유럽의 상위 4개국

● **유럽의 상위 4개국의 재생에너지 발전 용량을 보여주는 도표예요.** (단서)
재생에너지의 발전 용량을 측정하는 단위는 기가와트이고, 4개국은 각각 독일, 스페인, 이탈리아, 프랑스예요. 그리고 2011년과 2020년의 재생에너지 발전 용량을 비교해야 하죠. (발상)
각각의 문장이 어느 나라의 어느 해의 재생에너지 발전 용량을 설명하는지를 정확히 파악하고, 해당 변수를 도표에서 찾아 문장의 설명과 대조해야 해요.

2nd **각각의 문장을 읽고, 도표에서 확인해야 하는 부분에 □ 표시를 하세요.**

1) ① 문장부터 차근차근 살펴봅시다.

① <u>Each / of the four countries</u> in the graph / had a
각각은 / 그래프에 있는 4개국의   / 더 높은
higher capacity / to generate renewable energy /
용량을 가졌다   / 재생에너지를 발전하는   /
<u>in 2020</u> / than its respective capacity / <u>in 2011</u>. //
2020년에 / 그것의 각각의 용량보다   / 2011년에 //

● **4개국 각각의 2011년과 2020년 용량을 확인해야 돼요.**

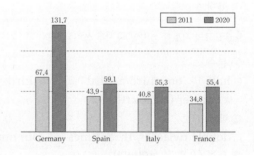

진한 막대그래프가 2020년의 발전 용량이고, 옅은 그래프가 2011년의 발전 용량이에요. 4개국 모두 진한 막대그래프가 더 기니까,
① 문장에서 설명한 것처럼, 4개국 모두 ❶(   )년의 발전 용량이 ❷(   )년의 발전 용량보다 더 큰 거예요!

2) ② 문장은 독일에 대해 이야기하고 있어요.

② Germany 's capacity to generate renewable
독일의 재생에너지 발전 용량은
energy / in 2011 / reached more than 50.0 gigawatts,
/ 2011년에 / 50.0기가와트가 넘는 수준에 달했으며
/ which was also the case / in 2020. //
/ 이는 마찬가지였다 / 2020년에도 //

● 표에서 독일 부분만 확인해 봅시다.

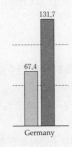

독일에 대해서만 이야기하는 문장이니까 다른 나라는 볼 필요가
없어요. 표에서 독일은 2011년에 67.4기가와트, 2020년에는
131.7기가와트로,
두 해 모두 ❸(   )기가와트가 넘는 수준이군요!

3) ③ 문장은 스페인에 대한 내용이에요.

③ Among the countries above, / Spain ranked in
상기 국가 중 / 스페인은 2위에 있었고
second place / in terms of renewable energy
/ 재생에너지 발전 용량 면에서
generation capacity / in 2011 / and remained in
/ 2011년에 / 2위를 유지했다
second place / in 2020. //
/ 2020년에도 //

● ① 문장을 확인했을 때처럼 전체 도표를 살펴봐야 해요.
스페인에 대해서만 설명하는 문장인 것은 맞지만, 스페인이 2위가 맞는지
확인해야 하니까 4개국 전부를 확인해야 돼요.
2011년에는 독일이 1위이고, ❹(   )이 2위, 2020년에도
1위는 독일, 2위는 ❹(   )이군요!

4) ④ 문장도 도표와 일치할까요?

④ The renewable energy generation capacity of
이탈리아의 재생에너지 발전 용량은
Italy / in 2020 / was lower / than that of Spain /
/ 2020년에 / 더 낮았다 / 스페인의 그것보다 /
in the same year. //
같은 해에 //

● 이탈리아와 스페인의 2020년 발전 용량을 비교해야 돼요.

2020년에 이탈리아의 재생에너지 발전 용량은 55.3기가와트이고,
스페인은 59.1기가와트이므로, ❺(   )의 발전 용량이
❹(   )보다 더 낮았어요!

5) 마지막으로 ⑤ 문장을 확인합시다.

⑤ The renewable energy generation capacity of
프랑스의 재생에너지 발전 용량은
France / was higher / than that of Italy / in both 2011
/ 더 높았다 / 이탈리아의 그것보다 / 2011년과 2020년
and 2020. //
모두 //

● 이번엔 프랑스와 이탈리아의 그래프를 봅시다.

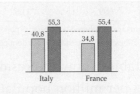

2011년과 2020년을 모두 비교해야 하는데, 2020년에는
❻(   )의 발전 용량이 이탈리아의 발전 용량보다 더
높았지만, 2011년에는 이탈리아의 발전 용량이 ❻(   )의
발전 용량보다 더 높았어요.
그러니까 ⑤ 문장은 도표와 일치하지 않아요!

3rd 정답 문장을 도표와 일치하도록 수정해 보세요.

⑤ The renewable energy generation capacity of
프랑스의 재생에너지 발전 용량은
France / was higher / than that of Italy / in both 2011
/ 더 높았다 / 이탈리아의 그것보다 / 2011년과 2020년
and 2020. //
모두 //

● in both 2011 and 2020가 문제예요.
프랑스의 재생에너지 발전 용량이 이탈리아의 재생에너지 발전 용량보다
더 높았던 해는 ❶(   )년이니까 in both 2011 and
2020를 in 2020로 바꿔야 해요.

빈칸 정답   ❶ 2020 ❷ 20-11 ❸ 50.0 ❹ 스페인 ❺ 이탈리아 ❻ 프랑스

❖ 정답 및 해설 124 ~ 125p

H 도표의 이해 (두 번째)

1st 무엇을 다룬 표인지 분석하고, 어떤 변수에 주의해야 하는지 확인하세요.
2nd 각각의 문장을 읽고, 표에서 확인해야 하는 부분에 □ 표시를 하세요.
3rd 정답 문장을 표와 일치하도록 수정해 보세요.

H02 ★★※ .... 2023 대비 6월 모평 25 (고3)

다음 표의 내용과 일치하지 <u>않는</u> 것은?

Resident Patent Applications per Million Population for the Top 6 Origins, in 2009 and in 2019

2009			2019		
Rank	Origin	Resident patent applications per million population	Rank	Origin	Resident patent applications per million population
1	Republic of Korea	2,582	1	Republic of Korea	3,319
2	Japan	2,306	2	Japan	1,943
3	Switzerland	975	3	Switzerland	1,122
4	Germany	891	4	China	890
5	U.S.	733	5	Germany	884
6	Finland	609	6	U.S.	869

Note: The top 6 origins were included if they had a population greater than 5 million and if they had more than 100 resident patent applications.

The above tables show the resident patent applications per million population for the top 6 origins in 2009 and in 2019. ① The Republic of Korea, Japan, and Switzerland, the top three origins in 2009, maintained their rankings in 2019. ② Germany, which sat fourth on the 2009 list with 891 resident patent applications per million population, fell to fifth place on the 2019 list with 884 resident patent applications per million population. ③ The U.S. fell from fifth place on the 2009 list to sixth place on the 2019 list, showing a decrease in the number of resident patent applications per million population. ④ Among the top 6 origins which made the list in 2009, Finland was the only origin which did not make it again in 2019. ⑤ On the other hand, China, which did not make the list of the top 6 origins in 2009, sat fourth on the 2019 list with 890 resident patent applications per million population.

1st 무엇을 다룬 표인지 분석하고, 어떤 변수에 주의해야 하는지 확인하세요.

Resident Patent Applications / per Million
거주민 특허 출원   / 인구 100만 명당
Population / for the Top 6 Origins, / in 2009 and in
/ 상위 6개 출처에 대한   / 2009년과 2019년에
2019

● **인구 100만 명당 거주민 특허 출원 건수를 나타낸 표예요.**

변수는 네 가지로, 연도(2009년과 2019년), 국가(대한민국, 일본, 스위스, 독일, 미국, 핀란드, 중국), 그리고 특허 출원 건수와 특허 출원 건수에 따른 순위예요.
각각의 문장이 이 네 가지 변수 중에서 어떤 것을 설명하는지를 정확히 파악하고, 그 변수를 표에서 찾아 설명과 대조해야 해요.

2nd 각각의 문장을 읽고, 표에서 확인해야 하는 부분에 □ 표시를 하세요.

1) ① 문장부터 차근차근 살펴봅시다.

① The Republic of Korea, Japan, and Switzerland, /
대한민국과 일본, 스위스는   /
the top three origins in 2009, / maintained their
2009년에 상위 3개 출처였던   / 2019년에도 자신들의
rankings in 2019. //
순위를 유지했다   //

● **표에서 대한민국, 일본, 스위스의 2009년과 2019년 순위를 확인해야 돼요.**

2009			2019		
Rank	Origin	Resident patent applications per million population	Rank	Origin	Resident patent applications per million population
1	Republic of Korea	2,582	1	Republic of Korea	3,319
2	Japan	2,306	2	Japan	1,943
3	Switzerland	975	3	Switzerland	1,122

표를 보니까 2009년과 2019년 모두 1위는 ❶(   ), 2위는 ❷(   ), 3위는 ❸(   )네요.
① 문장은 표를 정확하게 설명했군요.

2) ② 문장은 독일에 대해 이야기하고 있어요.

② Germany, / which sat fourth on the 2009 list /
독일은 / 2009년 목록에서 4위를 차지했던 /

with 891 resident patent applications per million
인구 100만 명당 891건의 거주민 특허 출원으로

population, / fell to fifth place on the 2019 list / with
/ 2019년 명단에서 5위로 떨어졌다 / 인구

884 resident patent applications per million
100만 명당 884건의 거주민 특허 출원으로 //

population. //

● 표에서 독일 부분만 확인해 봅시다.

2009			2019		
Rank	Origin	Resident patent applications per million population	Rank	Origin	Resident patent applications per million population
4	Germany	891	5	Germany	884

독일에 대해서만 이야기하는 문장이니까 다른 나라는 볼 필요가 없어요.
표에서 독일은 정말 2009년에 891건으로 ❹(   )위였는데,
2019년에는 884건으로 ❺(   )위로 떨어진 것을 확인할 수
있어요.

3) ③ 문장은 미국에 대한 내용이군요.

③ The U.S. fell / from fifth place on the 2009 list /
미국은 떨어졌는데 / 2009년 목록에서 5위였다가 /

to sixth place on the 2019 list, / showing a decrease /
2019년 목록에서 6위로 / 감소를 보여 주었다 /

in the number of resident patent applications per
인구 100만 명당 거주민 특허 출원 건수에서 //

million population. //

● 이번엔 표에서 미국 부분만 확인하면 돼요.

2009			2019		
Rank	Origin	Resident patent applications per million population	Rank	Origin	Resident patent applications per million population
5	U.S.	733	6	U.S.	869

표를 보니까, 미국이 2009년에 5위에서 2019년에 6위로 떨어진 건
맞아요. 그런데 특허 출원 건수는 2009년에는 ❻(   )건이고,
2019년에는 ❼(   )건이네요?
그렇다면 인구 100만 명당 거주민 특허 출원 건수에서 감소를 보였다는
설명은 표와 일치하지 않아요!

4) 정답을 찾았지만, 확실히 하기 위해 나머지 문장들도 봐야 돼요.

④ Among the top 6 origins / which made the list in
상위 6개 출처들 중에서 / 2009년에 목록에 들었던

2009, / Finland was the only origin / which did not
/ 핀란드가 유일한 출처였다 / 2019년에 다시 순위에

make it again in 2019. //
들지 못한 //

● 이번엔 핀란드에 대해 이야기하는 문장이에요.

2009			2019		
1	Republic of Korea	2,582	1	Republic of Korea	3,319
2	Japan	2,306	2	Japan	1,943
3	Switzerland	975	3	Switzerland	1,122
4	Germany	891	4	China	890
5	U.S.	733	5	Germany	884
6	Finland	609	6	U.S.	869

2009년에 핀란드가 6위를 차지했는데, 2019년에는 정말 목록에
없네요!

5) 마지막으로 ⑤ 문장을 확인합시다.

⑤ On the other hand, / China, / which did not make
반면에 / 중국은 / 2009년에 상위 6개 출처

the list of the top 6 origins / in 2009, / sat fourth on
목록에 오르지 못한 / 2009년에 / 2019년 목록에서

the 2019 list / with 890 resident patent applications
4위를 차지했다 / 인구 100만 명당 890건의 거주민 특허 출원 건수로 //

per million population. //

● 핀란드를 확인했을 때처럼 전체 표를 살펴봐야 해요.
위의 표를 보니까, 중국은 2009년에는 목록에 없었는데, 2019년에는
890건으로 4위를 차지했어요.

3rd 정답 문장을 표와 일치하도록 수정해 보세요.

③ The U.S. fell / from fifth place on the 2009 list /
미국은 떨어졌는데 / 2009년 목록에서 5위였다가 /

to sixth place on the 2019 list, /
2019년 목록에서 6위로 /

showing a decrease / in the number of resident
감소를 보여 주었다 / 인구 100만 명당 거주민 특허 출원

patent applications per million population. //
건수에서 //

● a decrease가 문제예요.
2009년에는 ❻(   )건이고, 2019년에는 ❼(   )건이니까
a decrease를 반의어인 an increase로 바꿔야 표와 일치해요.

단어장

PATTERN PRACTICE

H03 ~ 06 ▶ 제한시간 8분

H03 ✱❀❀ .... 2025 대비 수능 25 (고3)

다음 도표의 내용과 일치하지 <u>않는</u> 것은?

Percentages of Women Employed Behind the Scenes on Top 100 U.S. Films by Role in 2020, 2021, and 2022

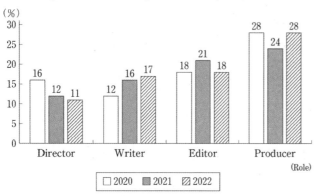

The graph above shows the percentages of women employed behind the scenes on the top 100 U.S. films by role in 2020, 2021, and 2022. ① For each of the three years, the percentage of women employed as producers on the top 100 U.S. films was the highest as compared with the percentages of each of the other three roles. ② The percentage of women employed as directors on the top 100 U.S. films in 2021 was lower than in 2020 but higher than in 2022. ③ The percentage of women employed as writers on the top 100 U.S. films increased by 4 percentage points from 2020 to 2021 and by 1 percentage point from 2021 to 2022. ④ The percentage of women employed as editors on the top 100 U.S. films was less than 20% in each of the three years. ⑤ In 2022, the percentage of women employed as producers on the top 100 U.S. films was the same as that in 2020.

H04 ✱❀❀ .... 2025 대비 9월 모평 25 (고3)

다음 도표의 내용과 일치하지 <u>않는</u> 것은?

Percentages of Respondents Familiar with the Concepts of Virtual Reality and Augmented Reality in Four Countries in 2022

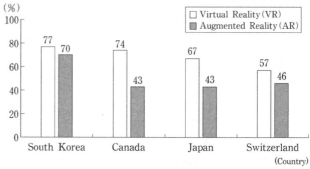

Note: The responses of "very familiar" and "somewhat familiar" are combined as "faniliar" in the given data.

The graph above shows the percentages of respondents who were familiar with the concept of virtual reality (VR) and those who were familiar with the concept of augmented reality (AR) in four countries in 2022. ① For each country, the percentage of respondents familiar with VR was greater than the percentage of respondents familiar with AR. ② The country with the highest percentage of respondents familiar with AR was South Korea. ③ The country with the largest gap between the percentage of respondents familiar with VR and that of respondents familiar with AR was Canada. ④ In Japan, the percentage of respondents familiar with VR was greater than 60%. ⑤ The percentage of respondents familiar with VR and that of respondents familiar with AR were lower in Switzerland than in Japan, respectively.

*augmented reality: 증강 현실

다음 도표의 내용과 일치하지 <u>않는</u> 것은?

Awareness and Usage of Smartphone Applications Featuring Machine Learning in 2017

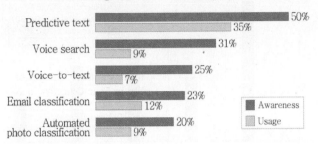

The above graph shows awareness and usage of smartphone applications featuring machine learning in 2017. ① In each of the five surveyed applications, the percentage of respondents demonstrating awareness was higher than that of respondents demonstrating usage. ② Predictive text had the highest percentages of respondents in both awareness and usage, among the five applications. ③ The percentage of respondents displaying awareness of voice search was more than four times that of respondents using it. ④ Voice-to-text showed a higher percentage of the respondents reporting awareness of it than email classification, while this was not the case in their usage. ⑤ The percentage of respondents showing usage of automated photo classification was less than half of the percentage of those showing awareness of it.

다음 도표의 내용과 일치하지 <u>않는</u> 것은?

Environmental Footprints of Dairy and Plant-Based Milks in 2018
(Impacts are measured per liter of milk.)

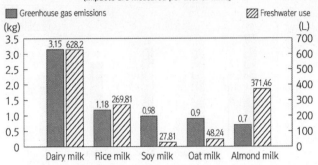

The above graph shows the environmental footprints in terms of greenhouse gas emissions (measured per kilogram) and freshwater use (measured per liter) of dairy and the four plant-based milks in 2018. ① Dairy milk had the largest environmental footprint of both greenhouse gas emissions and freshwater use. ② Rice milk used more than ten times the amount of fresh water that soy milk did. ③ Oat milk ranked fourth in both environmental footprint categories. ④ In the category of greenhouse gas emissions, the gap between soy milk and oat milk was less than the gap between oat milk and almond milk. ⑤ Among plant-based milks, almond milk consumed the largest amount of freshwater, yet emitted the least amount of greenhouse gas.

H07 ❀❀❀ .... 2025 대비 6월 모평 25 (고3)

다음 도표의 내용과 일치하지 <u>않는</u> 것은?

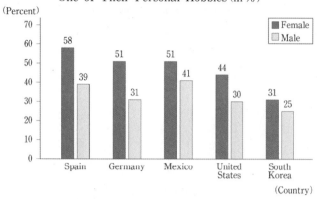

Share of Respondents Who Say Reading Is One of Their Personal Hobbies (in %)

Note: 12,000 - 60,000 respondents (18 - 64 years old) surveyed per selected country Jan. - Dec. 2023.

The above graph, based on a survey conducted in 2023, shows the share of respondents who say reading is one of their personal hobbies according to their gender group in five countries. ① Among the countries shown in the graph, Spain had the largest share of females who said reading was one of their hobbies, which was 58%. ② The gap between the share of females and that of males who selected reading as one of their hobbies was larger in Germany than in Mexico. ③ The share of males who selected reading as one of their hobbies in Mexico was 41%, which was smaller than that in the United States. ④ The share of females who selected reading as one of their hobbies in the United States was larger than that in South Korea. ⑤ As for South Korea, the share of respondents who selected reading as one of their hobbies was the smallest among the countries shown in the graph for each gender, respectively.

H08 ★★❀ .... 2024 실시 5월 학평 25 (고3)

다음 도표의 내용과 일치하지 <u>않는</u> 것은?

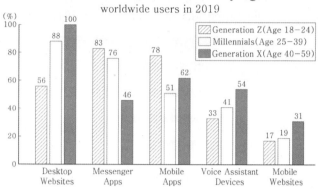

Preferable Chatbot Platforms by Age
worldwide users in 2019

※ Respondents were allowed to choose multiple platforms.

The above graph shows the percentage of preferable chatbot platforms by age categorized by Generation Z, Millennials, and Generation X. ① Millennials and Generation X had the highest percentage of respondents who preferred Desktop Websites while Generation Z had the highest percentage for Messenger Apps. ② In Generation Z, the percentage of respondents who preferred Mobile Apps was more than twice that of those who preferred Voice Assistant Devices. ③ Messenger Apps was the only platform where the percentage of respondents' preference for it sank lower and lower from Generation Z, to Millennials, to Generation X. ④ The percentage point gap between Millennial and Generation X respondents who preferred Mobile Apps was larger than the percentage point gap between the same two groups for Voice Assistant Devices. ⑤ The percentage of respondents who preferred Mobile Websites was the lowest in all the age groups.

다음 도표의 내용과 일치하지 <u>않는</u> 것은?

Changes in Pet Population

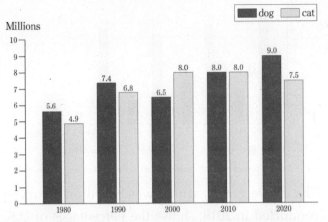

The above graph shows the pet population changes from 1980 to 2020. ① The population of pet dogs was higher than or equal to that of pet cats except for the year 2000. ② In 1990, the difference between the population of pet dogs and pet cats was less than 1 million. ③ In 2020, the population of pet dogs reached its highest point, yet it was still less than double the number of pet dogs in 1980. ④ The population of pet cats reached its highest population of 8 million in 2000, and it was the same in 2010. ⑤ Although the population of pet cats decreased from 2010 to 2020, the population of pet cats in 2020 still exceeded that of pet dogs in 2020.

다음 도표의 내용과 일치하지 <u>않는</u> 것은?

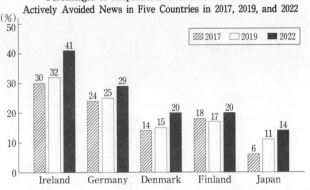

Percentages of Respondents Who Sometimes or Often Actively Avoided News in Five Countries in 2017, 2019, and 2022

The above graph shows the percentages of the respondents in five countries who sometimes or often actively avoided news in 2017, 2019, and 2022. ① For each of the three years, Ireland showed the highest percentage of the respondents who sometimes or often actively avoided news, among the countries in the graph. ② In Germany, the percentage of the respondents who sometimes or often actively avoided news was less than 30% in each of the three years. ③ In Denmark, the percentage of the respondents who sometimes or often actively avoided news in 2019 was higher than that in 2017 but lower than that in 2022. ④ In Finland, the percentage of the respondents who sometimes or often actively avoided news in 2019 was lower than that in 2017, which was also true for Japan. ⑤ In Japan, the percentage of the respondents who sometimes or often actively avoided news did not exceed 15% in each of the three years.

H11 ✿❀❀ .... 2021 대비 9월 모평 25 (고3)

다음 표의 내용과 일치하지 <u>않는</u> 것은?

Top 7 Asia-Pacific Destinations (2018)

Rank	Destination	International Overnight Arrivals (million)	Average Spend per Day (USD)
1	Bangkok	22.8	$184
2	Singapore	14.7	$272
3	Kuala Lumpur	13.8	$142
4	Tokyo	12.9	$196
5	Seoul	11.3	$155
6	Osaka	10.1	$223
7	Phuket	9.9	$247

The table above shows the top seven destination cities in the Asia-Pacific region in 2018 by international overnight arrivals, with additional information on the average spend per day in those cities. ① Bangkok was the top destination in the Asia-Pacific region with 22.8 million international overnight arrivals, immediately followed by Singapore with 14.7 million international overnight arrivals. ② Kuala Lumpur was ranked in third place based on the number of international overnight arrivals, and the average spend per day in this city was more than $150. ③ Tokyo was ranked in fourth place for the number of international overnight arrivals, and the average spend per day in this city was $196. ④ The number of international overnight arrivals in Seoul was larger than that of Osaka. ⑤ Phuket was the only city where the number of international overnight arrivals was less than 10 million, and the average spend per day in this city was $247.

H12 ✿✿❀ .... 2022 대비 6월 모평 25 (고3)

다음 도표의 내용과 일치하지 <u>않는</u> 것은?

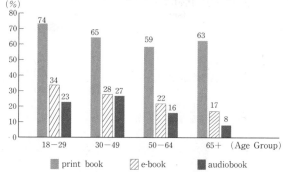

U.S. Adults' Book Consumption by Age Group and Format

Note: Those who gave other answers or no answer are not shown.

The above graph, which was based on a survey conducted in 2019, shows the percentages of U.S. adults by age group who said they had read (or listened to) a book in one or more of the formats — print books, e-books, and audiobooks — in the previous 12 months. ① The percentage of people in the 18–29 group who said they had read a print book was 74%, which was the highest among the four groups. ② The percentage of people who said they had read a print book in the 50–64 group was higher than that in the 65 and up group. ③ While 34% of people in the 18–29 group said they had read an e-book, the percentage of people who said so was below 20% in the 65 and up group. ④ In all age groups, the percentage of people who said they had read an e-book was higher than that of people who said they had listened to an audiobook. ⑤ Among the four age groups, the 30–49 group had the highest percentage of people who said they had listened to an audiobook.

다음 도표의 내용과 일치하지 <u>않는</u> 것은?

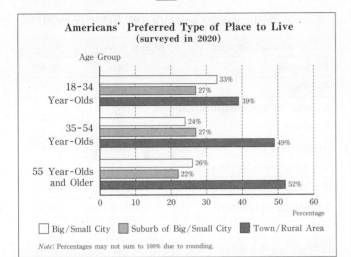

Americans' Preferred Type of Place to Live
(surveyed in 2020)

Age Group

18-34 Year-Olds: 33%, 27%, 39%
35-54 Year-Olds: 24%, 27%, 49%
55 Year-Olds and Older: 26%, 22%, 52%

Percentage

☐ Big/Small City ▨ Suburb of Big/Small City ■ Town/Rural Area

Note: Percentages may not sum to 100% due to rounding.

The above graph shows the percentages of Americans' preferred type of place to live by age group, based on a 2020 survey. ① In each of the three age groups, Town/Rural Area was the most preferred type of place to live. ② In the 18–34 year-olds group, the percentage of those who preferred Big/Small City was higher than that of those who preferred Suburb of Big/Small City. ③ In the 35–54 year-olds group, the percentage of those who preferred Suburb of Big/Small City exceeded that of those who preferred Big/Small City. ④ In the 55 year-olds and older group, the percentage of those who chose Big/Small City among the three preferred types of place to live was the lowest. ⑤ Each percentage of the three preferred types of place to live was higher than 20% across the three age groups.

다음 표의 내용과 일치하지 <u>않는</u> 것은?

U.S. States That Added the Most Solar Industry Workers Between 2015 and 2020

Rank	State	Number of Workers Added	Growth Percentage (%)
1	Florida	4,659	71
2	Utah	4,246	158
3	Texas	3,058	44
4	Virginia	2,352	120
5	Minnesota	2,003	101
6	New York	1,964	24
7	Pennsylvania	1,810	72

The table above shows seven U.S. states ranked by the number of workers added in the solar industry between 2015 and 2020, and provides information on the corresponding growth percentage in each state. ① During this period, Florida, which ranked first with regard to the number of workers added, exhibited 71% growth. ② The number of workers added in Utah was more than twice the number of workers added in Minnesota. ③ Regarding Texas and Virginia, each state showed less than 50% growth. ④ New York added more than 1,900 workers, displaying 24% growth. ⑤ Among these seven states, Pennsylvania added the lowest number of workers during this period.

H

H15 ★★❀.................. 2022 대비 수능 25 (고3)

다음 도표의 내용과 일치하지 <u>않는</u> 것은?

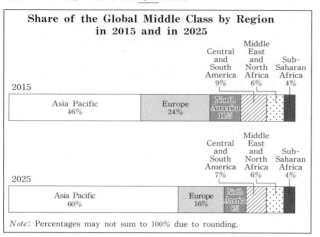

Share of the Global Middle Class by Region in 2015 and in 2025

Note: Percentages may not sum to 100% due to rounding.

The above graphs show the percentage share of the global middle class by region in 2015 and its projected share in 2025. ① It is projected that the share of the global middle class in Asia Pacific will increase from 46 percent in 2015 to 60 percent in 2025. ② The projected share of Asia Pacific in 2025, the largest among the six regions, is more than three times that of Europe in the same year. ③ The shares of Europe and North America are both projected to decrease, from 24 percent in 2015 to 16 percent in 2025 for Europe, and from 11 percent in 2015 to 8 percent in 2025 for North America. ④ Central and South America is not expected to change from 2015 to 2025 in its share of the global middle class. ⑤ In 2025, the share of the Middle East and North Africa will be larger than that of sub-Saharan Africa, as it was in 2015.

H16 ★★❀.................. 2021 대비 6월 모평 25 (고3)

다음 표의 내용과 일치하지 <u>않는</u> 것은?

Global Plastic Waste Generation by Industry in 2015

Market Sectors	Million Tons	%
Packaging	141	46.69
Textiles	38	12.58
Consumer and Institutional Products	37	12.25
Transportation	17	5.63
Electrical and Electronic	13	4.30
Building and Construction	13	4.30
Industrial Machinery	1	0.33
Others	42	13.91
Total	302	100

Note: Due to rounding, the percentages may not sum to 100%.

The above table shows global plastic waste generation by industry in 2015. ① The sector that generated plastic waste most was packaging, accounting for 46.69% of all plastic waste generated. ② The textiles sector generated 38 million tons of plastic waste, or 12.58% of the total plastic waste generated. ③ The consumer and institutional products sector generated 37 million tons of plastic waste, and the amount was more than twice that of plastic waste the transportation sector generated. ④ The electrical and electronic sector generated just as much plastic waste as the building and construction sector did, each sector accounting for 8.60% of the total plastic waste generation. ⑤ Only one million tons of plastic waste were generated in the industrial machinery sector, representing less than 0.50% of the total plastic waste generated.

H17 ✿✿✿

다음 도표의 내용과 일치하지 <u>않는</u> 것은?

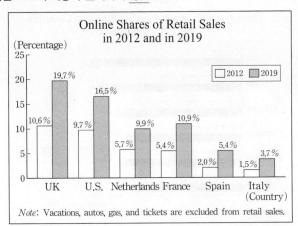

The graph above shows the online shares of retail sales for each of six countries in 2012 and in 2019. The online share of retail sales refers to the percentage of retail sales conducted online in a given country. ① For each country, its online share of retail sales in 2019 was larger than that in 2012. ② Among the six countries, the UK owned the largest online share of retail sales with 19.7% in 2019. ③ In 2019, the U.S. had the second largest online share of retail sales with 16.5%. ④ In 2012, the online share of retail sales in the Netherlands was larger than that in France, whereas the reverse was true in 2019. ⑤ In the case of Spain and Italy, the online share of retail sales in each country was less than 5.0% both in 2012 and in 2019.

H18 ✿✿✿

다음 도표의 내용과 일치하지 <u>않는</u> 것은?

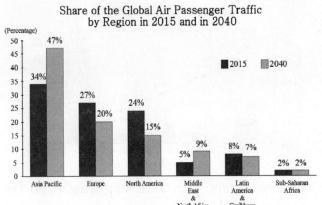

The graph above shows the share of the global air passenger traffic by region in 2015 and its projected share in 2040. ① Asia Pacific had the highest share of 34 percent among the six regions in 2015 and is expected to have the highest share in 2040. ② Europe is projected to rank second in 2040, with its share less than half of that of Asia Pacific that year. ③ The shares of Europe and North America are both expected to decrease from 2015 to 2040, the decrease of the latter being greater than that of the former. ④ The share of Middle East and North Africa in 2040 is projected to be more than double that of 2015, while in Latin America and Caribbean, the share will decline slightly from 2015 to 2040. ⑤ Sub-Saharan Africa, which had the lowest share in 2015 among the regions, with 2 percent, will be the only region to keep the same share in 2040.

H19 ✿❀❀ ·········· 2023 실시 10월 학평 25 (고3)

다음 도표의 내용과 일치하지 <u>않는</u> 것은?

How Naps Change As We Age

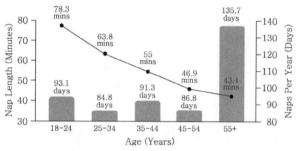

The above graph shows the nap length and the number of nap days per year by age group. ① As people get older, the nap length consistently decreases, but that is not the case with the number of nap days per year. ② The 18 to 24 age group, which has the longest nap length, naps over 30 minutes longer than the 55 and older age group, which has the shortest nap length. ③ As for the number of nap days per year, the 55 and older age group has the most days, 135.7 days, whereas the 25 to 34 age group has the fewest days, 84.8 days. ④ The 35 to 44 age group is ranked third in the nap length, and second in the number of nap days per year. ⑤ The nap length and the number of nap days per year of the 45 to 54 age group are lower than those of the 35 to 44 age group.

H20 ✿❀❀ ·········· 2023 실시 4월 학평 25 (고3)

다음 도표의 내용과 일치하지 <u>않는</u> 것은?

Population with Dementia in Six European Countries per 1,000 Inhabitants

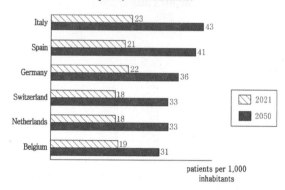

The graph above shows the number of dementia patients per 1,000 inhabitants in six European countries in 2021 and in 2050 (The number in 2050 is estimated). ① By 2050, the number of dementia patients per 1,000 people is expected to increase by more than 10 in all given countries compared to 2021. ② In 2021, Italy recorded the highest proportion of dementia patients out of the six countries and it is expected to do so in 2050 as well. ③ The proportion of dementia patients in Spain was lower than that of Germany in 2021, but is expected to exceed that of Germany in 2050. ④ Switzerland and the Netherlands had the same proportion of dementia patients in 2021, and by 2050 those proportions are both projected to more than double. ⑤ Among the six countries, Belgium shows the smallest gap between the number of dementia patients per 1,000 inhabitants in 2021 and in 2050.

＊dementia: 치매

H21 ~ 22 ▶ 제한시간 5분

H21 ⭐ 2등급 대비 .... 2024 대비 9월 모평 25 (고3)

다음 표의 내용과 일치하지 <u>않는</u> 것은?

College Enrollment Rates of 18- to 24-year-olds
by Race/Ethnicity in the U.S. in 2011, 2016, and 2021

Race/Ethnicity Year	2011	2016	2021
White	45%	42%	38%
Black	37%	36%	37%
Hispanic	35%	39%	33%
Asian	60%	58%	61%
American Indian/ Alaska Native	24%	19%	28%

Note: Rounded figures are displayed.

The table above shows the college enrollment rates of 18- to 24-year-olds from five racial/ethnic groups in the U.S. in 2011, 2016, and 2021. ① Among the five groups, Asians exhibited the highest college enrollment rate with more than 50% in each year listed in the table. ② Whites were the second highest in terms of the college enrollment rate among all the groups in all three years, while the rate dropped below 40% in 2021. ③ The college enrollment rates of both Blacks and Hispanics were higher than 35% but lower than 40% in 2011 and in 2021. ④ Among the years displayed in the table, 2016 was the only year when the college enrollment rate of Hispanics was higher than that of Blacks. ⑤ In each year, American Indians/Alaska Natives showed the lowest college enrollment rate.

H22 ⭐ 2등급 대비 .... 2024 대비 6월 모평 25 (고3)

다음 도표의 내용과 일치하지 <u>않는</u> 것은?

Share of the EU-28 Population Participating in Tourism,
by Age Group and Destination Category, 2017

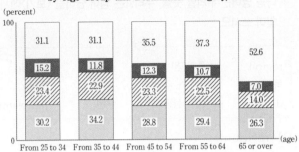

Domestic Trips Only   Domestic & Outbound Trips
Outbound Trips Only   No Trips

Note: Percentages may not sum to 100% due to rounding.

The above graph shows the share of the EU-28 population participating in tourism in 2017 by age group and destination category. ① The share of people in the No Trips category was over 30% in each of the five age groups. ② The percentage of people in the Outbound Trips Only category was higher in the 25 — 34 age group than in the 35 — 44 age group. ③ In the 35 — 44 age group, the percentage of people in the Domestic Trips Only category was 34.2%. ④ The percentage of people in the Domestic & Outbound Trips category was lower in the 45 — 54 age group than in the 55 — 64 age group. ⑤ In the 65 or over age group, the percentage of people in the No Trips category was more than 50%.

※ 다음 영어는 우리말 뜻을, 우리말은 영어 단어를 〈보기〉에서 찾아 쓰시오.

〈 보기 〉
region	특허(권)	select	ethnic
목적지	거주자, 주민	친숙한	table
decline	능력, 용량	부문	represent

01 resident _____

02 familiar _____

03 patent _____

04 destination _____

05 capacity _____

06 감소하다 _____

07 표, 목록 _____

08 지역, 지방 _____

09 인종의 _____

10 고르다 _____

※ 다음 우리말에 알맞은 영어 표현을 찾아 연결하시오.

11 ~을 차지하다 •   • as for

12 ~에 관해서는 •   • account for

13 ~을 제외하고 •   • except for

14 목록에 오르다 •   • in terms of

15 ~ 면에서 •   • make the list

※ 다음 우리말 표현에 맞는 단어를 고르시오.

16 인구 백만 명당 ⇒ per million (popularity / population)

17 웹사이트에서 미디어 광고에 무관심한 ⇒ (indifferent / different) to media ads in websites

18 두 배가 넘지 않을 것으로 예상되는 ⇒ (projected / presented) to less than double

19 재생에너지를 발생시키다 ⇒ generate (renewable / disposable) energy

20 태양 에너지 산업 ⇒ the (lunar / solar) industry

※ 다음 문장의 빈칸에 알맞은 단어를 〈보기〉에서 찾아 쓰시오.

〈 보기 〉
corresponding	enrollment	males	exceeded
whereas	industry	maintained	share
respectively	quarter	emissions	round

21 캐나다는 실제 음식물 쓰레기에서 20퍼센트를 초과했다.
⇒ Canada _____ twenty percent in actual food waste.

22 이 표는 그에 상응하는 증가율에 관한 정보를 제공한다.
⇒ The table provides information on the _____ growth percentage.

23 위 도표는 차량 대 선박의 이산화탄소 배출량을 보여 준다.
⇒ The graph above shows the CO_2 _____ from cars versus ships.

24 대한민국과 스위스는 2019년에 자신들의 순위를 유지했다.
⇒ The Republic of Korea and Switzerland _____ their rankings in 2019.

25 '공포'와 '공상 과학'은 각각 39퍼센트와 35퍼센트를 차지했다.
⇒ "Horror" and "Science Fiction" accounted for 39% and 35% _____.

26 위의 표는 유럽 연합에서의 신차 점유율을 보여 준다.
⇒ The table above shows the _____ of new cars in the EU.

27 스웨덴이 가장 적은 이산화탄소 배출량을 가진 반면에 네덜란드는 가장 많은 이산화탄소 배출량을 가졌다.
⇒ The Netherlands had the largest CO_2 emissions, _____ Sweden had the smallest CO_2 emissions.

28 멕시코에서 독서를 취미 중 하나로 고른 남성의 비율은 41퍼센트였다.
⇒ The share of _____ who selected reading as one of their hobbies in Mexico was 41%.

29 아시아인은 가장 높은 대학 등록률을 보였다.
⇒ Asians exhibited the highest college _____ rate.

30 디젤 차량은 신차의 4분의 1보다 더 많이 차지했다.
⇒ Diesel vehicles made up more than a(n) _____ of new cars.

I 내용 불일치

1992년도에 지어진 이 건물에 대해 아시나요? 초록색 지붕에 큰 창문을 가지고 있으며...

★ 유형 설명

Josef Sudek에 관한 다음 글의 내용과 '일치하지 않는 것은?

Josef Sudek was born in the Czech Republic. Originally a bookbinder, Sudek was badly

특정 인물이나 동식물 등에 대해 설명하는 글을 정확하게 해석해 선택지와 대조해야 한다.

☞ 글에서 언급된 내용과 똑같은 순서로 선택지가 제시된다. 선택지를 먼저 읽은 후에 글에서 해당 내용을 찾아 그 선택지의 일치 여부를 확인한다. 일치하는 것을 찾는 문제인지, 일치하지 않는 문제인지 꼭 다시 한 번 확인한다.

유형 풀이 비법

1 지시문을 확인하라!

• 문제를 읽고 무엇에 관한 글인지, 일치를 묻는지, 불일치를 묻는지 확인한다.

2 선택지를 살펴보라!

• 선택지를 빠르게 훑어보면서 글에서 어떤 세부 정보를 확인해야 하는지 알아본다.

3 선택지와 글을 대조하라!

• 선택지에 해당하는 글의 부분을 정확하게 대조하며 정답을 찾는다.

Tip 글에 나온 내용에만 근거해서 답을 골라야지, 상식이나 배경지식으로 판단하면 안 된다.

★ 최신 수능 경향 분석

대비 연도	월	문항 번호	지문 주제	난이도
2025	11	26번	스포츠 방송인 Dick Enberg의 일생	✹✺✺
	9	26번	예술가이자 교육자였던 György Kepes	✹✹✺
	6	26번	미국의 유명한 공인 Will Rogers의 일생	✹✺✺
2024	11	26번	Charles H. Townes의 일생	✹✺✺
	9	26번	Charles Rosen의 일생	✹✺✺
	6	26번	프랑스 영화감독 Jean Renoir	✹✺✺
2023	11	26번	20세기의 사회학자 Niklas Luhmann	✹✹✺
	9	26번	Leon Festinger의 생애	✹✺✺
	6	26번	위대한 지질학자 William Buckland	✹✺✺

★ 2025 수능 출제 분석

글에서 died the following year라고 해서 '그 다음 해에 사망했다'고 했는데, 이 부분을 '3년 뒤에'라고 바꿔서 일치하지 않는 선택지를 만들었으므로, 정신만 똑바로 차리고 푼다면 정답을 못 찾을 수 없는 문제였다.

★ 2026 수능 예측

매해 출제되어 온 유형으로 2026 수능에서도 출제될 것이다.

🔑 어휘 및 표현 Preview

□ artist 예술가
□ educator 교육자
□ film 영화
□ decade 10년
□ visual 시각의
□ found 설립하다
□ form 만들다, 형성하다
□ composed of ~로 구성된
□ scientist 과학자
□ exhibition 전시회
□ basis 기반
□ publish 출판하다

□ several 몇몇의
□ later 후에
□ present 선보이다
□ previously 이전에
□ available 사용 가능한
□ capture 포착하다
□ latest 최신의
□ scientific 과학적인
□ device 기기
□ museum 박물관
□ house 소장하다
□ work 작품

□ pioneer 선구자
□ connect 연결하다
□ establish 설립하다
□ famous 유명한
□ figure 인물
□ child 아이
□ clever 영리한
□ mature 어른스러운
□ grade 학년
□ talent 재능
□ learn 배우다
□ trick 묘기

□ return 돌아오다
□ appear 출현하다
□ entertainer 연예인, 엔터테이너
□ outstanding 뛰어난
□ humor 유머
□ unfortunately 안타깝게도
□ at the height of ~이 한창일 때에
□ career 경력
□ popular 인기가 많은
□ death 죽음
□ statue 동상
□ install 설치하다

I 내용 불일치 (첫 번째)

1st 각 선택지의 내용을 다룬 부분을 글에서 쉽게 찾을 수 있도록 선택지의 핵심 어구에 □ 표시하세요.
2nd 글에서 해당 부분을 확인하여 선택지의 일치/불일치 여부를 판단하세요.
3rd 선택지가 글의 내용과 일치하면 ○, 일치하지 않으면 × 표시를 하고, 글의 지시문을 다시 한번 확인하세요.

I01 ✸❈❈ ·········· 2023 대비 6월 모평 26 (고3)

William Buckland에 관한 다음 글의 내용과 일치하지 <u>않는</u> 것은?

William Buckland (1784–1856) was well known as one of the greatest geologists in his time. His birthplace, Axminster in Britain, was rich with fossils, and as a child, he naturally became interested in fossils while collecting them. In 1801, Buckland won a scholarship and was admitted to Corpus Christi College, Oxford. He developed his scientific knowledge there while attending John Kidd's lectures on mineralogy and chemistry. After Kidd resigned his position, Buckland was appointed his successor at the college. Buckland used representative samples and large-scale geological maps in his lectures, which made his lectures more lively. In 1824, he announced the discovery of the bones of a giant creature, and he named it *Megalosaurus*, or 'great lizard'. He won the prize from the Geological Society due to his achievements in geology.

① 태어난 곳은 화석이 풍부하였다.
② John Kidd의 강의를 들으며 자신의 과학 지식을 발전시켰다.
③ John Kidd의 사임 전에 그의 후임자로 임명되었다.
④ 자신의 강의에서 대축척 지질학 지도를 사용하였다.
⑤ 1824년에 거대 생물 뼈의 발견을 발표하였다.

1st 각 선택지의 내용을 다룬 부분을 글에서 쉽게 찾을 수 있도록 선택지의 핵심 어구에 □ 표시하세요.

① 태어난 곳은 화석이 풍부하였다.
② John Kidd의 강의를 들으며 자신의 과학 지식을 발전시켰다.
③ John Kidd의 사임 전에 그의 후임자로 임명되었다.
④ 자신의 강의에서 대축척 지질학 지도를 사용하였다.
⑤ 1824년에 거대 생물 뼈의 발견을 발표하였다.

● □ 표시한 부분을 글에서 어떻게 찾을 수 있을까요?
　① 태어난 곳에 화석이 풍부했는지 안 풍부했는지를 설명하려면 일단 문장에 '화석'이라는 단어가 포함되어야 해요. '화석'은 영어로 fossil이라고 하니 글에서 fossil이 포함된 문장을 찾으면 ①이 글과 일치하는지 여부를 확인할 수 있는 것이죠.
　'태어난 곳'에 □ 표시할 수도 있는데, '태어난 곳'은 영어로 the place where he was born이라고 할 수도 있고, birthplace, 또는 hometown이라고도 할 수 있죠. 그러니까 '태어난 곳'으로 단서 문장을 찾는 건 fossil보다는 좀 더 시간이 걸릴 거라는 말이에요.

● 나머지 선택지도 핵심 어구를 확인해 봅시다.
　②과 ③은 John Kidd와 관련된 내용이에요. ②은 John Kidd의 '강의'를, ③은 John Kidd의 '사임'을 다룬 문장을 찾으면 되는데, '강의'는 영어로 보통 lecture라고 하고, '사임'은 동사 resign(사임하다)의 명사형인 resignation을 써요.
　④은 '대축척 지질학 지도'가 핵심 어구라고 할 만한데, '대축척'이나 '지질학'은 영어로 잘 모르겠지만 '지도'가 map인 것은 알고 있죠? 글에서 map이 포함된 문장을 찾으면 될 거예요.
　마지막으로 ⑤은 '1824년에' 무슨 일이 일어났는지 확인하면 되니까 in 1824 같은 어구를 찾아서 확인하면 돼요.

2nd 글에서 해당 부분을 확인하여 선택지의 일치/불일치 여부를 판단하세요.

1) '화석'을 의미하는 fossil을 찾았나요?

His birthplace, Axminster in Britain, was rich with
그의 출생지인 영국의 Axminster에는 화석이 풍부했고
fossils, / and as a child, / he naturally became
　　　　/ 어릴 때 　　　/ 그는 자연스럽게 화석에 관심을 갖게
interested in fossils / while collecting them. //
되었다 　　　　　　 / 그것들을 수집하면서 　　//

● **두 번째 문장에 등장하는군요, fossils!**
William Buckland의 출생지인 영국의 Axminster에는 화석이
풍부했고, William은 어릴 때 화석을 수집하면서 자연스럽게 그것에
관심을 가졌대요. 선택지와 글이 일치하는군요!
참고로 '태어난 곳'은 **❶**(   )라는 표현을 썼네요.

2) ②은 John Kidd의 '강의'를 다룬 문장을 찾아야 해요.

He developed his scientific knowledge there / while
그는 거기서 자신의 과학 지식을 발전시켰다   / John
attending John Kidd's lectures / on mineralogy and
Kidd의 강의를 들으면서   / 광물학과 화학에 관한 //
chemistry. //

● **John Kidd's lectures, 찾았나요?**
there가 어디인지는 모르겠지만, 아무튼 William Buckland는 John
Kidd의 강의를 들으면서 광물학과 화학에 관한 자신의 과학 지식을
발전시켰다고 했어요!

3) 이번에는 John Kidd의 '사임'에 관한 문장을 찾아봅시다.

After Kidd resigned his position, / Buckland was
Kidd가 자신의 직위에서 사임한 후에   / Buckland가 그의
appointed his successor / at the college. //
후임자로 임명되었다   / 대학에서   //

● **명사 resignation이 아니라 동사 resign이 쓰였군요.**
Kidd가 사임한 후에 William Buckland가 Kidd의 후임자로
임명되었다는 내용인데, 중요한 건 접속사로 **❷**(   )가
쓰였다는 거예요!
아까 선택지는 분명히 Kidd의 사임 '전에' 후임자로 임명되었다는
내용이었는데, 글에서는 Kidd의 사임 '후에' 임명되었다고 했으니
❸(   )이 글과 일치하지 않는 선택지군요!
여기서 알 수 있듯이, 선택지의 핵심 어구로 글에서 단서 문장을 찾은
이후에는 그 문장을 정확히 해석해서 선택지와 꼼꼼히 대조해야 돼요.

4) 정답은 찾았지만 혹시 모르니 끝까지 확인해 봅시다.

Buckland used / representative samples and large-
Buckland는 사용했는데 / 대표 표본과 대축척 지질학 지도를
scale geological maps / in his lectures, / which made
                 / 자신의 강의에서   / 그것이 그의 강의를
his lectures more lively. //
더 활기차게 만들었다   //

● **maps가 등장한 문장이 과연 있군요.**
Buckland가 자신의 강의에서 대표 표본과 대축척 지질학 지도를
사용했고, 이는 그의 강의를 더 활기차게 만들었다는 내용이에요.
사실 representative samples나 계속적 용법의 관계대명사인 which가
이끄는 절은 정답을 찾는 데 별로 필요가 없어요. 우리는 Buckland가
자신의 강의에서 대축척 지질학 지도를 사용했는지 아닌지만 확인하면
되니까요.

5) 1824년에 무슨 일이 있었는지까지 마저 확인합시다.

In 1824, / he announced the discovery / of the bones
1824년에   / 그는 발견을 발표했으며   / 거대한 생물의 뼈의
of a giant creature, / and he named it *Megalosaurus*,
                     / 그는 그것을 Megalosaurus 즉 '거대한
or 'great lizard'. //
도마뱀'이라고 이름 붙였다 //

● **연도나 세기 등의 비교적 긴 기간을 나타낼 때는 전치사 in을 써요.**
1824년에 William Buckland는 거대한 생물 뼈의 발견을 발표했고,
그것을 Megalosaurus라고 이름 붙였다는 내용이에요.
이 문장을 통해 ⑤ 역시 글과 일치한다는 것을 확인할 수 있죠.

3rd **선택지가 글의 내용과 일치하면 ○, 일치하지 않으면 × 표시를**
하고, 글의 지시문을 다시 한번 확인하세요.

1) 각 선택지의 일치/불일치 여부를 표시해 봅시다.

① 태어난 곳은 화석이 풍부하였다. **❹**(   )
② John Kidd의 강의를 들으며 자신의 과학 지식을 발전시켰다.
                                       ❺(   )
③ John Kidd의 사임 전에 그의 후임자로 임명되었다. **❻**(   )
④ 자신의 강의에서 대축척 지질학 지도를 사용하였다. **❼**(   )
⑤ 1824년에 거대 생물 뼈의 발견을 발표하였다. **❽**(   )

2) 지시문을 다시 한번 꼭 확인하세요!

William Buckland에 관한 다음 글의 내용과 일치하지 않는 것은?

● **일치하지 '않는' 선택지를 찾는 문제예요.**
William Buckland가 John Kidd의 후임으로 임명된 것은 맞지만,
John Kidd가 사임한 이후에 임명되었다고 했어요!
그러니까 일치하지 않는 선택지는 **❸**(   )!

I

I 내용 불일치 (두 번째)

1st 각 선택지의 내용을 다룬 부분을 글에서 쉽게 찾을 수 있도록 선택지의 핵심 어구에 □ 표시하세요.
2nd 글에서 해당 부분을 확인하여 선택지의 일치/불일치 여부를 판단하세요.
3rd 선택지가 글의 내용과 일치하면 ○, 일치하지 않으면 × 표시를 하고, 글의 지시문을 다시 한 번 확인하세요.

I02 ✿✿✿ .... 2023 대비 9월 모평 26 (고3)

Henry Moore에 관한 다음 글의 내용과 일치하지 <u>않는</u> 것은?

Henry Moore (1898–1986), one of the most significant British artists of the 20th century, was the seventh child of a coal miner. Henry Moore showed a talent for art from early on in school. After World War I, during which he volunteered for army service, Moore began to study sculpture at the Leeds School of Art. Then, he entered the Royal College of Art in London and earned his degree there. His sculptures, known around the world, present the forms of the body in a unique way. One of his artistic themes was mother-and-child as shown in *Madonna and Child* at St. Matthew's Church in Northampton. He achieved financial success from his hard work and established the Henry Moore Foundation to support education and promotion of the arts.

① 석탄 광부의 일곱 번째 자녀였다.
② 학창 시절에 일찍이 예술에 재능을 보였다.
③ 런던에 있는 Royal College of Art에서 학위를 취득했다.
④ 그의 조각은 신체 형태를 독특한 방식으로 나타낸다.
⑤ 경제적으로 성공을 거두지 못했다.

1st 각 선택지의 내용을 다룬 부분을 글에서 쉽게 찾을 수 있도록 선택지의 핵심 어구에 □ 표시하세요.

① 석탄 광부의 [일곱 번째 자녀]였다.
② 학창 시절에 일찍이 [예술에 재능]을 보였다.
③ 런던에 있는 Royal College of Art에서 [학위를 취득]했다.
④ [그의 조각]은 신체 형태를 독특한 방식으로 나타낸다.
⑤ [경제적으로 성공]을 거두지 못했다.

● **글에 등장하는 순서대로 선택지를 구성한다는 건 알고 있죠?**
출제자의 입장에서 생각하면 글을 처음부터 읽어 나가면서 ①부터 ⑤까지 순서대로 선택지를 만들어내는 거예요. 영어로 된 글에서 한글로 된 선택지를 만드는 거니까 각 문장을 우리말로 해석한 다음에 그 해석과 일치하게, 또는 일치하지 않게 선택지를 만드는 거죠.

● **□ 표시한 어구가 언급된 부분을 글에서 찾아봅시다.**
순서를 나타낼 땐 서수를 써요. 그러니까 ①의 '일곱 번째'는 seventh가 쓰였을 거예요. ② '재능'은 영어로 보통 talent라고 해요. 예술적 재능에 대한 내용이니까 art도 언급되겠군요. ③ '학위'에 대해서는 아무래도 degree를 써서 설명하겠죠? 아니면 Royal College of Art를 찾아도 될 것 같아요. 학교 이름은 그대로 언급될 테니까요. ④ '조각'은 영어로 sculpture인 거, 알고 있죠? ⑤ '성공'은 영어로 success인데, 경제적 성공이니까 financial 또는 economic이라는 형용사와 함께 쓰였을 거예요.

2nd 글에서 해당 부분을 확인하여 선택지의 일치/불일치 여부를 판단하세요.

1) 서수인 seventh, 찾았나요?

Henry Moore (1898-1986), / one of the most
Henry Moore(1898~1986)는 / 가장 중요한 영국 예술가 중
significant British artists / of the 20th century, / was
한 명인 / 20세기의 / 일곱
the [seventh] child / of a coal miner. //
번째 자녀였다 / 석탄 광부의 //

● **첫 문장에 바로 등장하네요!**
20세기 영국의 가장 중요한 예술가들 중 한 명인 Henry Moore는 석탄 광부의 일곱 번째 자녀였대요. 선택지와 일치하는군요!

2) 두 번째 문장에 a talent for art가 등장하네요.

Henry Moore showed a talent for art / from early
Henry Moore는 예술에 재능을 보였다   / 일찍이
on / in school. //
/ 학창 시절에 //

● **an artistic talent라고 할 수도 있었을 거예요.**
우리말에서도 '예술적 재능' 또는 '예술에 대한 재능'처럼 여러 가지로
표현할 수 있는 것처럼 영어에서도 다양하게 표현할 수 있어요.
선택지만으로 정확히 어떻게 표현했는지를 예상할 수는 없으니까 핵심
단어인 art, talent 정도만 생각하고 관련된 어구를 글에서 찾는 거죠.

● **예술에 대한 재능을 언제 보였다고요?**
'학교에서 일찍부터' 보였대요. 그러니까 학창 시절에 일찍이 예술에
재능을 보인 것이 맞죠!

3) degree가 등장하는 문장, 찾았나요?

Then, he entered the Royal College of Art / in
그 후 그는 Royal College of Art에 들어갔고   /
London / and earned his degree there. //
런던에 있는 / 거기서 자신의 학위를 취득했다 //

● **같은 문장에 Royal College of Art도 등장했어요.**
런던에 있는 Royal College of Art에 들어갔고 '거기서' 자신의 학위를
취득했다고 했어요. there가 가리키는 것이 Royal College of Art인
것이죠.

4) 바로 다음 문장에서 그의 조각에 대해 이야기하고 있어요.

His sculptures, / known around the world, / present
그의 조각은   / 전 세계적으로 알려진   / 신체 형태를
the forms of the body / in a unique way. //
나타낸다   / 독특한 방식으로 //

● **문장을 그대로 해석해서 선택지로 만들었어요.**
His sculptures를 수식하는 삽입구인 known around the world를
제외하고, '그의 조각은 독특한 방식으로 신체 형태를 나타낸다'는 해석
그대로 선택지를 만들었어요.

5) 경제적 성공을 거두었나요, 못 거두었나요?

He achieved financial success / from his hard work /
그는 경제적인 성공을 거두었고   / 각고의 노력으로   /
and established the Henry Moore Foundation / to
Henry Moore 재단을 세웠다   /
support / education and promotion of the arts. //
후원하기 위해 / 예술 교육과 증진을   //

● **마지막 문장에 financial success가 등장해요.**
financial 아니면 economic을 예상했는데, financial이 쓰였네요!
이제 Henry Moore가 경제적인 성공을 거두었는지 아닌지를 판단해야
하는데, achieved financial success라고 했지, 부정어인 not이나
never는 문장에 쓰이지 않았어요!
글과 일치하지 않는 건 ❶(   )이군요.

3rd 선택지가 글의 내용과 일치하면 ○, 일치하지 않으면 × 표시를
하고, 글의 지시문을 다시 한 번 확인하세요.

1) 각 선택지의 일치/불일치 여부를 표시해 봅시다.

① 석탄 광부의 일곱 번째 자녀였다. ❷(   )
② 학창 시절에 일찍이 예술에 재능을 보였다. ❸(   )
③ 런던에 있는 Royal College of Art에서 학위를 취득했다.
❹(   )
④ 그의 조각은 신체 형태를 독특한 방식으로 나타낸다. ❺(   )
⑤ 경제적으로 성공을 거두지 못했다. ❻(   )

2) 지시문을 다시 한번 꼭 확인하세요!

Henry Moore에 관한 다음 글의 내용과 일치하지 <u>않는</u> 것은?

● **일치하지 않는 선택지가 정답이군요!**
Henry Moore는 열심히 노력해서 경제적인 성공을 거두었고, 그를
바탕으로 예술 교육과 증진을 후원하기 위해 Henry Moore 재단을
설립했어요!

선택지의
핵심 어구에 □
표시하자!

I03 ~ 06 ▶ 제한시간 8분

I03 ✿❀❀ .... 2025 대비 수능 26 (고3)

Dick Enberg에 관한 다음 글의 내용과 일치하지 <u>않는</u> 것은?

Dick Enberg was one of America's most beloved sports broadcasters. He was born in Michigan in 1935. In the early 1960s, he became an assistant professor at San Fernando Valley State College, where he also served as a coach of its baseball team. Afterwards, he began a full-time sportscasting career in Los Angeles. In 1973, he became the first U.S. sportscaster ever to visit China. He joined NBC Sports in 1975 and remained with the network for about 25 years, covering such big events as the Olympics. He later worked for other major sports broadcasting stations. He made his last live broadcast in 2016 and died the following year at the age of 82. He served as Chairman of the American Sportscaster Association for more than three decades. Enberg was also a best-selling writer and won Emmy Awards as a sportscaster, a writer, and a producer.

① Michigan에서 태어났다.
② 대학 야구팀 코치였다.
③ 중국을 방문한 첫 미국인 스포츠 캐스터였다.
④ 마지막 생방송 후 3년 뒤에 사망하였다.
⑤ Emmy Awards를 수상하였다.

I04 ✿✿✿ .... 2025 대비 9월 모평 26 (고3)

György Kepes에 관한 다음 글의 내용과 일치하지 <u>않는</u> 것은?

György Kepes was an artist and educator born in Selyp, Hungary in 1906. He studied painting at the Royal Academy of Fine Arts in Budapest, Hungary. Then, he studied design and film in Berlin, Germany. He went to the United States in 1937, and about a decade later, he started teaching visual design at the Massachusetts Institute of Technology (MIT). He founded the Center for Advanced Visual Studies at MIT to form a community composed of artists and scientists. His exhibition in 1951 titled *The New Landscape* became the basis of his book *The New Landscape in Art and Science*, which was published several years later. In the book, he presented images that were not previously available, captured by the latest scientific devices. In 1995, a museum to house his works was established in Eger, Hungary. He was a great pioneer in connecting art and technology.

① 헝가리에서 그림을 공부했다.
② 1937년에 MIT에서 시각 디자인을 가르치기 시작했다.
③ 그의 전시회를 기반으로 책이 출판되었다.
④ 그의 작품을 소장하기 위한 박물관이 설립되었다.
⑤ 예술과 기술을 연결하는 데 있어서 위대한 개척자였다.

I05

Will Rogers에 관한 다음 글의 내용과 일치하지 않는 것은?

Will Rogers (1879~1935) was a famous American public figure. He was born as the eighth child. When he was young, he was clever and mature but he dropped out of school after the 10th grade. He was very interested in cowboys and horses, and he even learned how to do rope tricks. He left the U.S. in 1902 and worked as a cowboy and roping artist in South Africa and Australia. After returning to the U.S., he appeared in more than 50 movies and was often heard on the radio as an entertainer. He was also an outstanding newspaper columnist with his wit and humor, writing more than 4,000 columns. He unfortunately died at the height of his career in 1935. Rogers was so popular that after his death his statue was installed in the U.S. Capitol. He will be remembered as a great American of many talents.

① 여덟 번째 아이로 태어났다.
② 카우보이와 말에 매우 관심이 있었다.
③ 미국에 돌아온 후 50편이 넘는 영화에 출연했다.
④ 뛰어난 신문 칼럼니스트였다.
⑤ 생전에 그의 동상이 U.S. Capitol에 설치되었다.

I06

Mary Douglas Leakey에 관한 다음 글의 내용과 일치하지 않는 것은?

Mary Douglas Leakey was born in 1913 in London, England in a family of scholars and researchers. Her father, who was an artist, took her to see the stone tools being studied by French prehistorians. This sparked her interest in archaeology. When she was just 17 years old, she served as an illustrator at a dig in England. Shortly after marrying Louis Leakey, she left for East Africa with her husband. Together, they made important fossil discoveries. In 1948, Mary found a partial skull fossil of *Proconsul africanus* on Rusinga Island in Lake Victoria. In 1959 in Tanzania, she discovered the skull of an early hominin that her husband named *Zinjanthropus boisei*, which is now known as *Paranthropus boisei*. Even after her husband's death in 1972, Mary continued her work in Africa. Mary died in 1996, in Nairobi, Kenya.

*archaeology: 고고학 **fossil: 화석 ***skull: 두개골

① 1913년에 영국 런던에서 태어났다.
② 17세의 나이에 영국에 있는 발굴지에서 삽화가로 일했다.
③ 그녀의 남편과 함께 동아프리카로 떠났다.
④ 1948년에 *Proconsul africanus*의 두개골 화석의 일부를 찾았다.
⑤ 1972년에 케냐 나이로비에서 사망했다.

I

I07 ❀❀❀ .... 2024 실시 7월 학평 26 (고3)

John Carew Eccles에 관한 다음 글의 내용과 일치하지 않는 것은?

John Carew Eccles was born on 27 January 1903 in Melbourne, Australia. Both his parents were school teachers, who home-schooled him until he was 12. In 1915, Eccles began his secondary schooling and after four years, prior to entering the University of Melbourne, he studied science and mathematics for another year at Melbourne High School. He completed his medical course in February 1925, and left Melbourne for Oxford the same year. From 1928 to 1931 he was a research assistant to Sir Charles Sherrington, and published eight papers conjointly. Returning to Australia with his family in 1937, he gave lectures to third-year medical students at the University of Sydney from 1938 to 1940. Eccles was the co-winner of the Nobel Prize in Physiology or Medicine along with A.L. Hodgkin and A.F. Huxley in 1963. In 1975, he voluntarily retired and moved to Switzerland to dedicate himself to work on the mind-brain problem.

① 12세까지 홈스쿨링을 받았다.
② Melbourne High School에서 과학과 수학을 공부했다.
③ Sir Charles Sherrington의 연구 조교였다.
④ 1963년에 노벨 생리 · 의학상을 단독으로 수상했다.
⑤ 은퇴하고 Switzerland로 이주했다.

I08 ❀❀❀ .... 2024 실시 5월 학평 26 (고3)

José Saramago에 관한 다음 글의 내용과 일치하지 않는 것은?

José Saramago was born in 1922 to a family of farmers in a little village north of Lisbon. For financial reasons he abandoned his high-school studies and worked as a mechanic. At this time, he acquired a taste for reading and started to frequent a public library in Lisbon in his free time. After trying different jobs in the civil service, he worked for a publishing company for twelve years and then as an editor of the newspaper 'Diário de Notícias.' Between 1975 and 1980 Saramago supported himself as a translator, but after his literary successes in the 1980s he devoted himself to his own writing. He achieved worldwide recognition in 1982 with the humorous love story *Baltasar and Blimunda*, a novel set in 18thcentury Portugal. Saramago's oeuvre totals 30 works, and comprises not only novels but also poetry, essays and drama.

*oeuvre: 전체 작품

① 재정적인 이유로 고등학교 공부를 그만두었다.
② 독서에 흥미가 생겨 공립 도서관을 자주 방문하기 시작했다.
③ 신문사의 편집자로 일한 후 출판사에서 12년간 일했다.
④ 포르투갈이 배경인 소설로 세계적인 인정을 받았다.
⑤ 소설뿐 아니라 시, 수필, 희곡 또한 집필하였다.

Ilya Prigogine에 관한 다음 글의 내용과 일치하지 <u>않는</u> 것은?

Ilya Prigogine was born into a Jewish family in Moscow. In 1921, he and his family left Russia, eventually settling in Belgium. His parents encouraged him to become a lawyer, and he first studied law at the Free University of Brussels. It was then that he became interested in psychology and behavioral research. In turn, reading about these subjects sparked his interest in chemistry since chemical processes affect the mind and body. He eventually dropped out of law school. Prigogine then studied chemistry and physics at the same time at the Free University of Brussels. He obtained the equivalent of a master's degree in both fields in 1939, and he obtained a PhD in chemistry in 1941 at the Free University of Brussels, where he accepted the position of professor in 1947. Considered one of the founders of complexity science, Ilya Prigogine was awarded the Nobel Prize in Chemistry in 1977.

*equivalent: 상응하는 것

① 1921년에 그와 그의 가족은 러시아를 떠났다.
② 부모님은 그가 변호사가 되기를 권했다.
③ Free University of Brussels에서 화학과 물리학을 동시에 공부했다.
④ 1941년에 Free University of Brussels의 교수직을 수락했다.
⑤ 1977년에 노벨 화학상을 수상했다.

Jean Renoir에 관한 다음 글의 내용과 일치하지 <u>않는</u> 것은?

Jean Renoir (1894 – 1979), a French film director, was born in Paris, France. He was the son of the famous painter Pierre-Auguste Renoir. He and the rest of the Renoir family were the models of many of his father's paintings. At the outbreak of World War I, Jean Renoir was serving in the French army but was wounded in the leg. In 1937, he made *La Grande Illusion*, one of his better-known films. It was enormously successful but was not allowed to show in Germany. During World War II, when the Nazis invaded France in 1940, he went to Hollywood in the United States and continued his career there. He was awarded numerous honors and awards throughout his career, including the Academy Honorary Award in 1975 for his lifetime achievements in the film industry. Overall, Jean Renoir's influence as a film-maker and artist endures.

① 유명 화가의 아들이었다.
② 제1차 세계대전이 발발했을 때 프랑스 군에 복무 중이었다.
③ *La Grande Illusion*을 1937년에 만들었다.
④ 제2차 세계대전 내내 프랑스에 머물렀다.
⑤ Academy Honorary Award를 수상하였다.

I11 ✿✿❀.................................2022 대비 6월 모평 26 (고3)

Emil Zátopek에 관한 다음 글의 내용과 일치하지 <u>않는</u> 것은?

Emil Zátopek, a former Czech athlete, is considered one of the greatest long-distance runners ever. He was also famous for his distinctive running style. While working in a shoe factory, he participated in a 1,500-meter race and won second place. After that event, he took a more serious interest in running and devoted himself to it. At the 1952 Olympic Games in Helsinki, he won three gold medals in the 5,000-meter and 10,000-meter races and in the marathon, breaking Olympic records in each. He was married to Dana Zátopková, who was an Olympic gold medalist, too. Zátopek was also noted for his friendly personality. In 1966, Zátopek invited Ron Clarke, a great Australian runner who had never won an Olympic gold medal, to an athletic meeting in Prague. After the meeting, he gave Clarke one of his gold medals as a gift.

① 독특한 달리기 스타일로 유명했다.
② 신발 공장에서 일한 적이 있다.
③ 1952년 Helsinki 올림픽에서 올림픽 기록을 깨지 못했다.
④ 올림픽 금메달리스트인 Dana Zátopková와 결혼했다.
⑤ 자신의 금메달 중 하나를 Ron Clarke에게 주었다.

I12 ✿❀❀.................................2022 대비 수능 26 (고3)

Donato Bramante에 관한 다음 글의 내용과 일치하지 <u>않는</u> 것은?

Donato Bramante, born in Fermignano, Italy, began to paint early in his life. His father encouraged him to study painting. Later, he worked as an assistant of Piero della Francesca in Urbino. Around 1480, he built several churches in a new style in Milan. He had a close relationship with Leonardo da Vinci, and they worked together in that city. Architecture became his main interest, but he did not give up painting. Bramante moved to Rome in 1499 and participated in Pope Julius II's plan for the renewal of Rome. He planned the new Basilica of St. Peter in Rome — one of the most ambitious building projects in the history of humankind. Bramante died on April 11, 1514 and was buried in Rome. His buildings influenced other architects for centuries.

① Piero della Francesca의 조수로 일했다.
② Milan에서 새로운 양식의 교회들을 건축했다.
③ 건축에 주된 관심을 갖게 되면서 그림 그리기를 포기했다.
④ Pope Julius II의 Rome 재개발 계획에 참여했다.
⑤ 그의 건축물들은 다른 건축가들에게 영향을 끼쳤다.

Marc Isambard Brunel에 관한 다음 글의 내용과 일치하지 않는 것은?

Marc Isambard Brunel (1769–1849) is best known for the design and construction of the Thames Tunnel. Originally born in France, Brunel escaped to the United States during the French Revolution. He later moved to London. When the Napoleonic Wars were at their height, he invented machines for making boots. During the Napoleonic Wars, Brunel's factory supplied British troops with boots. After the Wars ended, however, the government stopped buying his boots and he went out of business. A few years later, Brunel was imprisoned for several months because of his debt. At that time, London was very much divided by the River Thames and needed more ways for people and goods to move across it. In 1825, Brunel designed a tunnel under the river. The Thames Tunnel officially opened on 25 March 1843, and Brunel, despite being in ill health, attended the opening ceremony.

① 프랑스 혁명 중에 미국으로 달아났다.
② 부츠를 만드는 기계를 발명하였다.
③ 그의 공장은 영국 군대에 부츠를 공급한 적이 있다.
④ 빚 때문에 감옥에 수감되었다.
⑤ Thames Tunnel 개통식에 아파서 참석하지 못했다.

Ann Bancroft에 관한 다음 글의 내용과 일치하지 않는 것은?

Ann Bancroft was born in Minnesota, U.S. Bancroft grew up in rural Minnesota in what she described as a family of risk-takers. Although she struggled with a learning disability, she graduated from St. Paul Academy and became a physical education teacher. Bancroft resigned her teaching position in 1986 in order to participate in the Will Steger International Polar Expedition. The group departed from Ellesmere Island on March 6, and after 56 days, she and five other team members arrived at the North Pole by dogsled. She thus became the first woman to reach the North Pole by sled and on foot. In November 1992, she led three other women on the American Women's Expedition to Antarctica. It took them 67 days to reach the South Pole on skis and Bancroft became the first woman to have stood at both poles.

① Minnesota의 시골에서 자랐다.
② St. Paul Academy를 졸업하고 체육 교사가 되었다.
③ 1986년에 교직을 그만두었다.
④ Ellesmere섬에서 출발한 지 56일 후에 북극에 도달했다.
⑤ 세 명의 남자 대원과 남극까지 스키를 타고 갔다.

I

I15 ✽❀❀.....................2024 대비 9월 모평 26 (고3)

Charles Rosen에 관한 다음 글의 내용과 일치하지
않는 것은?

Charles Rosen, a virtuoso pianist and distinguished writer, was born in New York in 1927. Rosen displayed a remarkable talent for the piano from his early childhood. In 1951, the year he earned his doctoral degree in French literature at Princeton University, Rosen made both his New York piano debut and his first recordings. To glowing praise, he appeared in numerous recitals and orchestral concerts around the world. Rosen's performances impressed some of the 20th century's most well-known composers, who invited him to play their music. Rosen was also the author of many widely admired books about music. His most famous book, *The Classical Style*, was first published in 1971 and won the U.S. National Book Award the next year. This work, which was reprinted in an expanded edition in 1997, remains a landmark in the field. While writing extensively, Rosen continued to perform as a pianist for the rest of his life until he died in 2012.

① 어려서부터 피아노에 재능을 보였다.
② 프랑스 문학으로 박사 학위를 받았다.
③ 유명 작곡가들로부터 그들의 작품 연주를 요청받았다.
④ *The Classical Style*이 처음으로 출판되고 다음 해에 상을 받았다.
⑤ 피아니스트 활동을 중단하고 글쓰기에 매진하였다.

I16 ✽❀❀.....................2023 대비 9월 모평 26 (고3)

Leon Festinger에 관한 다음 글의 내용과 일치하지
않는 것은?

Leon Festinger was an American social psychologist. He was born in New York City in 1919 to a Russian immigrant family. As a graduate student at the University of Iowa, Festinger was influenced by Kurt Lewin, a leading social psychologist. After graduating from there, he became a professor at the Massachusetts Institute of Technology in 1945. He later moved to Stanford University, where he continued his work in social psychology. His theory of social comparison earned him a good reputation. Festinger actively participated in international scholarly cooperation. In the late 1970s, he turned his interest to the field of history. He was one of the most cited psychologists of the twentieth century. Festinger's theories still play an important role in psychology today.

① 러시아인 이민자 가정에서 태어났다.
② 사회 심리학자 Kurt Lewin에게 영향을 받았다.
③ Stanford University에서 사회 심리학 연구를 중단했다.
④ 국제 학술 협력에 활발하게 참여했다.
⑤ 1970년대 후반에 역사 분야로 관심을 돌렸다.

Anna May Wong에 관한 다음 글의 내용과 일치하지 않는 것은?

Anna May Wong is considered the first Chinese-American movie star in Hollywood. She dropped out of high school to pursue a full-time acting career and, at 17, she played her first leading role in *The Toll of the Sea*. Reviewers praised her extraordinary acting but her ethnicity prevented U.S. filmmakers from casting her as a leading lady. Frustrated, Wong left for Europe in 1928, where she had main roles in many notable films. When American studios wanted fresh European talent in the 1930s, Wong's new prestige immediately led to a main role on Broadway. She returned to America and used her influence to advocate for better film opportunities for Chinese-Americans. In 1938, she sold her movie costumes and donated the money from the sale to organizations supporting Chinese refugees. During World War II, she gave political speeches against the anti-Asian attitudes in the U.S. In 2022, she became the first Asian American to appear on U.S. currency — a century after she landed her first leading role.

① 전업 배우가 되기 위해 고등학교를 중퇴했다.
② 유럽에서는 영화에 출연하지 못했다.
③ 자신의 영화 의상 판매 수입금을 기부했다.
④ 반아시아적 태도에 대항하는 연설을 했다.
⑤ 미국 화폐에 등장한 최초의 아시아계 미국인이 되었다.

Charles H. Townes에 관한 다음 글의 내용과 일치하지 않는 것은?

Charles H. Townes, one of the most influential American physicists, was born in South Carolina. In his childhood, he grew up on a farm, studying the stars in the sky. He earned his doctoral degree from the California Institute of Technology in 1939, and then he took a job at Bell Labs in New York City. After World War II, he became an associate professor of physics at Columbia University. In 1958, Townes and his co-researcher proposed the concept of the laser. Laser technology won quick acceptance in industry and research. He received the Nobel Prize in Physics in 1964. He was also involved in Project Apollo, the moon landing project. His contribution is priceless because the Internet and all digital media would be unimaginable without the laser.

① 어린 시절에 농장에서 성장하였다.
② 박사 학위를 받기 전에 Bell Labs에서 일했다.
③ 1958년에 레이저의 개념을 제안하였다.
④ 1964년에 노벨 물리학상을 수상하였다.
⑤ 달 착륙 프로젝트에 관여하였다.

I19 ✽✽❀.................................2023 대비 수능 26 (고3)

Niklas Luhmann에 관한 다음 글의 내용과 일치하지 않는 것은?

Niklas Luhmann, a renowned sociologist of the twentieth century, was born in Lüneburg, Germany in 1927. After World War II, he studied law at the University of Freiburg until 1949. Early in his career, he worked for the State of Lower Saxony, where he was in charge of educational reform. In 1960–1961, Luhmann had the chance to study sociology at Harvard University, where he was influenced by Talcott Parsons, one of the most famous social system theorists. Later, Luhmann developed his own social system theory. In 1968, he became a professor of sociology at the University of Bielefeld. He researched a variety of subjects, including mass media and law. Although his books are known to be difficult to translate, they have in fact been widely translated into other languages.

① 제2차 세계 대전 이후에 법을 공부했다.
② State of Lower Saxony에서 교육 개혁을 담당했다.
③ Harvard University에 있을 때 Talcott Parsons의 영향을 받았다.
④ 다양한 주제에 관해 연구했다.
⑤ 그의 책은 번역하기가 쉽다고 알려져 있다.

I20 ✽✽❀.................................2021 대비 수능 26 (고3)

Frank Hyneman Knight에 관한 다음 글의 내용과 일치하지 않는 것은?

Frank Hyneman Knight was one of the most influential economists of the twentieth century. After obtaining his Ph.D. in 1916 at Cornell University, Knight taught at Cornell, the University of Iowa, and the University of Chicago. Knight spent most of his career at the University of Chicago. Some of his students at Chicago later received the Nobel Prize. Knight is known as the author of the book *Risk, Uncertainty and Profit*, a study of the role of the entrepreneur in economic life. He also wrote a brief introduction to economics entitled *The Economic Organization*, which became a classic of microeconomic theory. But Knight was much more than an economist; he was also a social philosopher. Later in his career, Knight developed his theories of freedom, democracy, and ethics. After retiring in 1952, Knight remained active in teaching and writing.

＊entrepreneur: 기업가

① 20세기의 가장 영향력 있는 경제학자들 중 한 명이었다.
② 경력의 대부분을 University of Chicago에서 보냈다.
③ 그의 학생들 중 몇 명은 나중에 노벨상을 받았다.
④ *Risk, Uncertainty and Profit*의 저자로 알려져 있다.
⑤ 은퇴 후에는 가르치는 일은 하지 않고 글 쓰는 일에 전념했다.

Josef Frank에 관한 다음 글의 내용과 일치하지 않는 것은?

Josef Frank, born in Austria of Jewish heritage, studied architecture at the Vienna University of Technology. He then taught at the Vienna School of Arts and Crafts from 1919 to 1925. He founded an interior design firm together with some architect colleagues in 1925. He was one of early Vienna modernism's most important figures, but already in the beginning of the 1920s he started to question modernism's growing pragmatism. He had little appreciation for the French architect Le Corbusier's belief that a house should be "a machine for living in." He was against the standardized interior design trend of the time, fearing that it would make people all too uniform. He moved to Sweden with his Swedish wife in 1933 to escape growing Nazi discrimination and gained citizenship in 1939. He was the most prestigious designer at his Stockholm design company. In addition to his architectural work he created numerous designs for furniture, fabric, wallpaper and carpet. *pragmatism: 실용주의

① Vienna University of Technology에서 건축학을 공부했다.
② 건축가 동료들과 함께 인테리어 디자인 회사를 설립했다.
③ 초기 비엔나 모더니즘의 가장 중요한 인물 중 한 명이었다.
④ 당시의 표준화된 인테리어 디자인 경향을 옹호했다.
⑤ 나치의 차별을 피해 스웨덴으로 가서 시민권을 얻었다.

William McDougall에 관한 다음 글의 내용과 일치하지 않는 것은?

Born in Lancashire, England, in 1871, William McDougall left his mark on experimental and physiological psychology. After receiving a degree in natural sciences in Cambridge University, he became interested in human behavior. He believed human behavior to be based on three abilities — intellect, emotion, and will. Being a hardworking scholar, he held academic positions in several universities in England. He also wrote many books on psychology including the well-known *Introduction to Social Psychology*. In 1920, he published *The Group Mind* opposing mechanistic interpretations of human behavior. However, *The Group Mind* was poorly received when published. Somewhat disappointed, he moved to the United States in the same year to be a professor at Harvard University. Seven years later, he moved to Duke University, where he developed a psychology department and continued various research. Today many people read his books, and psychologists celebrate his intellectual achievements.

① Cambridge University에서 학위를 받았다.
② 인간 행동이 세 가지 능력에 근거한다고 믿었다.
③ *The Group Mind*는 출판되었을 때 매우 인정받았다.
④ Duke University에서 다양한 연구를 계속하였다.
⑤ 오늘날 심리학자들은 그의 지적 업적을 기린다.

※ 다음 영어는 우리말 뜻을, 우리말은 영어 단어를 〈보기〉에서 찾아 쓰시오.

〈보기〉

geologist	설립하다	descend	폭넓게
promotion	조각(품)	원정	debt
prestige	협력, 협조	devote	수정하다

01 extensively _____

02 expedition _____

03 sculpture _____

04 cooperation _____

05 found _____

06 명성 _____

07 지질학자 _____

08 (노력·시간 등을) 바치다 _____

09 증진, 촉진 _____

10 빚, 부채 _____

※ 다음 우리말에 알맞은 영어 표현을 찾아 연결하시오.

11 ~가 한창일 때 •   • be rich with

12 ~이 풍부하다 •   • drop out

13 ~로 유명한 •   • at one's height

14 탈퇴하다, 중퇴하다 •   • noted for

15 ~에 발자취를 남기다 •   • leave one's mark on

※ 다음 우리말 표현에 맞는 단어를 고르시오.

16 화석에 관심을 갖게 되다 ⇒ become interested in (fossils / fuels)

17 약 10년 후 ⇒ about a (century / decade) later

18 John Kidd의 강의를 듣는 동안 ⇒ while attending John Kidd's (creatures / lectures)

19 표준화된 인테리어 디자인 경향 ⇒ the (strengthened / standardized) interior design trend

20 제1차 세계대전이 발발했을 때 ⇒ at the (outbreak / outburst) of World War I

※ 다음 문장의 빈칸에 알맞은 단어를 〈보기〉에서 찾아 쓰시오.

〈보기〉

struggled	offered	uniform	appointed
notable	resigned	leading	actively
wounded	will	cooperation	

21 Festinger는 국제 학술 협력에 적극적으로 참여했다.
⇒ Festinger _____ participated in international scholarly cooperation.

22 그는 인간 행동이 지력, 감정, 그리고 의지라는 세 가지 능력에 근거한다고 믿었다.
⇒ He believed human behavior to be based on three abilities — intellect, emotion, and _____.

23 Kidd가 자신의 직위에서 사임한 후에 Buckland가 그의 후임자로 임명되었다.
⇒ After Kidd _____ his position, Buckland was appointed his success.

24 그것은 사람들을 너무 획일적으로 만들 것이다.
⇒ It would make people all too _____.

25 Jean Renoir는 프랑스 군에 복무 중이었지만 다리에 부상을 입었다.
⇒ Jean Renoir was serving in the French army but was _____ in the leg.

26 그는 Seychelles 공화국에 미국 대사로 임명되었다.
⇒ He was _____ the U.S. Ambassador to the Republic of Seychelles.

27 Festinger는 대표적인 사회 심리학자 Kurt Lewin의 영향을 받았다.
⇒ Festinger was influenced by Kurt Lewin, a(n) _____ social psychologist.

28 그녀는 많은 저명한 영화에서 주요한 역할을 맡았다.
⇒ She had main roles in many _____ films.

29 그녀는 학습 장애로 어려움을 겪었다.
⇒ She _____ with a learning disability.

J 실용문의 이해

행사의 내용, 날짜, 준비물 등을 빠짐없이 확인하세요!

★유형 설명

Singing Tommy 사용에 관한 다음 안내문의 내용과 일치하지 않는 것은?

Singing Tommy

Congratulations! Tommy is now your singing

광고문이나 안내문, 제품의 설명서 등에 담긴 정보를 제대로 선택지와 대조해야 한다.

○┯ 날짜나 금액, 할인 대상 등이 정답이 되는 경우가 많다.

🎭 유형 풀이 비법

1 선택지를 먼저 읽어라!

• 안내문보다 선택지를 먼저 읽고, 안내문에서 확인해야 하는 부분이 무엇인지 각 선택지에 표시한다.

2 한 문장씩 정확하게 해석하라!

• 안내문과 선택지가 일치하는지 혹은 일치하지 않는지를 확인하려면 각 문장을 정확하게 해석해야 한다.

3 일치 여부를 판단하라!

• 안내문과 선택지를 일대일로 꼼꼼하게 비교하여 일치 여부를 각 선택지에 ○, ×로 표시하여 정답을 결정한다.

> (Tip) 각 선택지에 ○, ×로 표시한 후에는 반드시 지시문을 다시 확인하여 일치하는 선택지를 찾는 문제인지, 일치하지 않는 선택지를 찾는 문제인지를 확실히 한다.

★최신 수능 경향 분석

대비 연도	월	문항 번호	지문 주제	난이도
2025	11	27번	Adenville 시티 패스 카드 안내	✿❀❀
		28번	Luckwood 눈 축제 안내문	✿❀❀
	9	27번	Teverley 대학교 캠퍼스 방문의 날	✿❀❀
		28번	2024 녹색 미래 웹툰 공모전	✿❀❀
	6	27번	야생 동물 구조 센터 여름 일자리	✿❀❀
		28번	LCU 지리 현장 학습	✿❀❀
2024	11	27번	Turtle Island 보트 투어	✿❀❀
		28번	2023 Eastland 고등학교 비디오 클립 경연대회	✿❀❀
	9	27번	Brushwood 국립 공원 투어 프로그램	✿❀❀
		28번	WGHS 지리 사진 대회	✿❀❀
	6	27번	2023 Cierra 농구 주간 캠프	✿❀❀
		28번	아이들을 위한 창의적인 미술 강좌	✿❀❀

★2025 수능 출제 분석

2025 수능에서도 예년과 마찬가지로 두 개의 실용문의 이해 문제가 출제되었고, 하나는 일치하지 않는 것을 찾는 문제였고, 다른 하나는 일치하는 것을 찾는 문제였다.

★2026 수능 예측

내용 불일치 유형과 다른 점은 제시되는 글이 안내문 등의 실용문이라는 것뿐이므로, 같은 풀이법을 적용하면 된다.

🔑 실용문에 자주 쓰이는 표현

- Price 가격, Cost 비용
- Categories 부문, Theme 주제
- How to Enter 참가 방법
- registration 등록
- Other Information 기타 정보
- Register at ~에서 등록하세요
- Join us for ~에 참여하세요
- Winner Announcement Date 수상자 발표일
- Prize 시상, 1st place 1등, 2nd place 2등
- Participation Fee & Qualification 참가비 & 자격
- How to submit your entry 출품작 제출 방법
- Notices 공지, Guidelines 지침, Details 세부 사항
- Location 위치, Place 장소
- Opening Times 운영 시간
- Cancellation Policy 취소 방침
- refreshment 다과
- Submission Deadline 제출 마감 기한
- Participate in ~에 참가하세요
- Join us on ~에 참여하세요

📖 어휘 및 표현 Preview

- wildlife 야생 동물
- rescue 구조
- look for 찾다, 모집하다
- apply 지원하다
- take care of 돌보다
- age 나이
- previous 이전의
- experience 경험
- prepare 준비하다
- feed 먹이를 주다
- report 보고서
- training 교육, 훈련

1st 선택지를 보고 안내문에서 찾아야 할 핵심 사항에 □ 표시하세요.
2nd 각 선택지의 내용을 다룬 부분을 안내문에서 찾아 확인하세요.
3rd 지시문을 다시 한번 확인하고, 일치하거나 일치하지 않는 선택지를 고르세요.

J01 ✿❀❀ .... 2023 대비 6월 모평 28 (고3)

Shooting Star Viewing Event에 관한 다음 안내문의 내용과 일치하는 것은?

Shooting Star Viewing Event

Would you like to watch the rare shooting star, coming on Sunday, July 24? The Downtown Central Science Museum is the perfect spot to catch the vivid view!

Registration

- Online only — www.dcsm.org
- From July 1 to July 14
- The number of participants will be limited to 50.

Schedule on July 24

- 8:00 p.m.: Participants will gather at the hall and then move to the rooftop.
- 8:30 p.m.: Guides will explain how to observe the shooting star.
- 9:00 p.m.–11:00 p.m.: We will share the experience of the shooting star.

Notes

- If the event is cancelled due to the weather conditions, notice will be given via text message.
- Outside food and drinks are not allowed.

① 현장 등록이 가능하다.
② 참가 인원에 제한이 없다.
③ 참가자들은 오후 9시에 홀에서 모여 옥상으로 이동할 것이다.
④ 기상 상황으로 인한 행사 취소 시 문자 메시지로 공지될 것이다.
⑤ 외부 음식과 음료는 허용된다.

1st 선택지를 보고 안내문에서 찾아야 할 핵심 사항에 □ 표시하세요.

① 현장 등록이 가능하다.
② 참가 인원에 제한이 없다.
③ 참가자들은 오후 9시에 홀에서 모여 옥상으로 이동할 것이다.
④ 기상 상황으로 인한 행사 취소 시 문자 메시지로 공지될 것이다.
⑤ 외부 음식과 음료는 허용된다.

● 안내문에서 다섯 가지 사항을 찾아서 확인하면 돼요.
① 현장 등록이 가능한지 여부, ② 참가 인원에 제한이 있는지 여부, ③ 참가자들이 오후 9시에 무엇을 하는지, ④ 행사가 취소되면 어떻게 안내되는지, ⑤ 외부 음식과 음료가 허용되는지 여부를 안내문에서 찾아 확인해 봅시다.

2nd 각 선택지의 내용을 다룬 부분을 안내문에서 찾아 확인하세요.

1) 현장 등록의 가능 여부는 '등록'에 대한 안내를 보면 되겠죠?

Registration /
등록   /
- Online only — www.dcsm.org /
온라인으로만 가능 — www.dcsm.org   /

● '현장 등록'이라는 말이 등장하지는 않아요.
현장 등록이 가능한지 불가능한지를 직접적으로 안내하는 것은 아니지만, 등록이 온라인으로만 가능하다는 안내를 통해 현장 등록이 ❶(가능 / 불가능)하다는 것을 알 수 있어요.

2) '참가자'는 영어로 participant라고 해요.

- The number of participants / will be limited to 50. //
참가자 수는   / 50명으로 제한될 것입니다   //

● 참가자의 수에 제한이 없다는 건가요?
will be limited to 50라고 했으므로 참가자의 수는 50명으로 제한될 거예요. 그러므로 참가 인원에 제한이 없다는 것은 안내문과 일치하지 않는 선택지이죠.

3) 참가자들이 오후 9시에 무엇을 하는지 살펴봅시다.

• 8:00 p.m.: / Participants will gather at the hall /
오후 8시:　　　　　　/ 참가자들은 홀에서 모이고　　　　　/
and then move to the rooftop. //
그다음 옥상으로 이동할 것입니다 　　//
9:00 p.m. — 11:00 p.m.: / We will share / the
오후 9시~오후 11시:　　　　　　　　　/ 우리는 공유할 것입니다 /
experience of the shooting star. //
유성을 본 경험을 　　　　　//

● 오후 9시에는 유성을 본 경험을 공유할 거라고 했어요.
　참가자들이 홀에서 모인 후 옥상으로 이동하는 것은
　오후 ❷(　　　　　　　)가 아니라 오후 ❸(　　　　　　)에
　일어날 일이에요. ❸ 역시 안내문과 일치하지 않네요.

4) ④은 행사 취소에 대한 내용이에요.

• If the event is cancelled / due to the weather
행사가 취소되면　　　　　　　/ 기상 상황으로 인해
conditions, / notice will be given / via text message. //
　　　　　/ 공지가 주어질 것입니다 　/ 문자 메시지를 통해 　//

● 행사 취소 시 어떻게 할 건지 설명한 부분에는 cancel이 있겠죠?
　기상 상황 때문에 행사가 취소되면 문자 메시지를 통해 공지될 것이라는
　안내예요. 선택지에서 말한 내용과 일치하는군요!

5) 정답은 찾았지만 그래도 끝까지 확인해 봅시다.

• Outside food and drinks / are not allowed. //
외부 음식과 음료는　　　　　　 / 허용되지 않습니다 　//

● '허용하다'라는 뜻을 가진 동사인 allow가 쓰였어요.
　외부 음식과 음료가 허용된다는 건가요? 부정어인 ❹(　　　　　)이
　쓰였으니까 허용되지 않는다는 거예요!

3rd 지시문을 다시 한번 확인하고, 일치하거나 일치하지 않는 선택지를 고르세요.

1) 지시문을 다시 한번 꼭 확인하세요!

　Shooting Star Viewing Event에 관한 다음 안내문의 내용과 일치하는 것은?

● 일치하는 선택지를 골라야 하는 문제예요.
　지시문을 제대로 확인하지 않으면 일치하는 선택지를 골라야 하는데
　반대로 일치하지 않은 선택지를 골라서 정답으로 표시하는 경우가
　있어요. 그렇게 문제를 틀리면 정말 너무 슬프겠죠?

2) 각 선택지의 일치/불일치 여부를 ○, ×로 표시해 봅시다.

① 현장 등록이 가능하다. ❺(　　　　　)
② 참가 인원에 제한이 없다. ❻(　　　　　)
③ 참가자들은 오후 9시에 홀에서 모여 옥상으로 이동할 것이다.
　　　　　　　　　　　　　　　❼(　　　　　)
④ 기상 상황으로 인한 행사 취소 시 문자 메시지로 공지될 것이다.
　　　　　　　　　　　　　　　❽(　　　　　)
⑤ 외부 음식과 음료는 허용된다. ❾(　　　　　)

● 일치하는 것을 찾는 문제니까 ○로 표시한 선택지가 정답!
　등록은 온라인으로만 가능하고, 참가 인원은 50명으로 제한되며,
　참가자들은 오후 8시에 홀에 모인 후 옥상으로 이동했다가 오후 9시에는
　유성을 본 경험을 공유할 거예요. 그리고 외부 음식과 음료는 허용되지
　않는다고 했어요.
　안내문과 일치하는 건 기상 상황 때문에 행사가 취소되면 문자 메시지로
　공지될 것이라는 ❿(　　　　　)뿐이에요!

선택지부터
확인하자!

1st 선택지를 보고 안내문에서 찾아야 할 핵심 사항에 □ 표시하세요.
2nd 각 선택지의 내용을 다룬 부분을 안내문에서 찾아 확인하세요.
3rd 지시문을 다시 한번 확인하고, 일치하거나 일치하지 않는 선택지를 고르세요.

J02 ✹❀❀ ················· 2022 대비 9월 모평 28 (고3)

Mary High School Foreign Language Program에 관한 다음 안내문의 내용과 일치하는 것은?

Mary High School Foreign Language Program

Would you like to learn about another culture? Learning a new language is the best way to do it. Please come and enjoy our new foreign language classes.

Languages: Arabic, French, Spanish
          (A student can choose only one.)

Dates and Times: September 13, 2021
          – October 29, 2021
          Monday to Friday,
          4:00 p.m. – 6:00 p.m.

Registration: Available from September 1 to
          September 5 on our website
          (www.maryhighs.edu)

Tuition Fee: $50 (Full payment is required
          when registering.)

Refund Policy: If you cancel on or before
          September 5, your payment
          will be refunded.

For more information about the classes, feel free to contact us at (215) 8393-6047 or email us at info@maryhighs.edu.

① 학생은 두 개의 언어를 선택할 수 있다.
② 수업은 주말에 진행된다.
③ 수업료는 등록 시 전액 납부하지 않아도 된다.
④ 9월 5일까지 취소하면 환불받을 수 있다.
⑤ 수업 관련 문의는 이메일을 통해서만 할 수 있다.

1st 선택지를 보고 안내문에서 찾아야 할 핵심 사항에 □ 표시하세요.

① 학생은 두 개의 언어를 선택할 수 있다.
② 수업은 주말에 진행된다.
③ 수업료는 등록 시 전액 납부하지 않아도 된다.
④ 9월 5일까지 취소하면 환불받을 수 있다.
⑤ 수업 관련 문의는 이메일을 통해서만 할 수 있다.

● 우리는 안내문에서 다섯 가지 정보만 찾아서 읽으면 돼요.
① 학생이 선택할 수 있는 언어의 수가 두 개가 맞는지, ② 수업은 주중이 아니라 주말에 진행되는지, ③ 수업료는 등록할 때 전액을 납부하지 않아도 되는지, ④ 9월 5일까지 취소해야 환불을 받을 수 있는지, ⑤ 수업 관련 문의는 전화나 다른 방법은 불가능하고 이메일로만 가능한지를 안내문에서 찾아 확인해 봅시다.

2nd 각 선택지의 내용을 다룬 부분을 안내문에서 찾아 확인하세요.

1) 학생이 몇 개의 언어를 선택할 수 있나요?

Languages: Arabic, French, Spanish / (A student can
언어: 아랍어, 프랑스어, 스페인어   / (한 학생은 선택할 수
choose / only one.) //
있습니다 / 하나만)   //

● 일단 제공되는 언어는 세 가지예요.
아랍어와 프랑스어, 스페인어 중에서 한 학생은 ❶(한 개 / 두 개)의 언어만 선택할 수 있다고 했어요.

2) 수업은 언제 진행되나요?

Monday to Friday, 4:00 p.m. — 6:00 p.m. /
월요일부터 금요일까지, 오후 4시 ~ 오후 6시   /

● 월요일부터 금요일까지 진행된대요.
월요일부터 금요일은 주말이 아니라 주중이에요. 주중 오후 4시부터 오후 6시까지 진행되는 수업이네요.

3) 수업료에 대한 설명을 찾아봅시다.

Tuition Fee: $50 / (Full payment is required / when
수업료: 50달러   / (전액 납부가 요구됩니다   / 등록 시 //
registering.) //

● 일단 수업료는 50달러래요.
근데 우린 지금 수업료가 얼마인지가 중요한 게 아니에요. 등록할 때 50달러 수업료를 전액 납부해야 하는지가 중요한데, 등록 시 전액 납부가 요구된다고 했어요.

4) 환불 정책은 어떤가요?

> Refund Policy: / If you cancel on or before
> 환불 방침: / 여러분이 9월 5일이나 그 이전에 취소하시면
> September 5, / your payment will be refunded. //
>   / 여러분의 대금이 환불될 것입니다   //

● **안내문의 다른 부분은 볼 필요 없어요.**
  9월 5일까지 취소하면 환불이 되는지 안 되는지 확인하려면 Refund
  Policy(환불 정책) 항목만 보면 돼요.
  안내문에서 9월 5일까지 취소하면 대금이 환불될 거라고 했으니까
  선택지와 일치하는군요.

5) 정답은 나왔지만 나머지 선택지도 꼭 확인해야 돼요.

> For more information about the classes, /
> 수업에 대한 더 많은 정보를 원하시면   /
> feel free to contact us at (215) 8393-6047 / or email
> 자유롭게 저희에게 (215) 8393-6047로 연락하시거나   /
> us at info@maryhighs.edu. //
> info@maryhighs.edu로 저희에게 이메일을 보내세요 //

● **이메일 말고도 문의할 수 있는 방법이 있어요.**
  수업에 대한 정보가 더 필요하면 전화번호로 연락하거나 이메일을
  보내라고 했으니까 이메일을 통해서만 수업에 관련된 문의를 할 수 있는
  것은 아니에요.

3rd 지시문을 다시 한번 확인하고, 일치하거나 일치하지 않는
선택지를 고르세요.

Mary High School Foreign Language Program에 관한 다음
안내문의 내용과 일치하는 것은?

● **일치하는 선택지를 고르는 문제예요.**
  한 학생은 한 개의 언어만 선택할 수 있으니까 ①은 일치하지 않고,
  수업은 주중에 진행되니까 ②도 일치하지 않고, 등록할 때 수업료
  50달러를 전액 납부해야 하니까 ③도 일치하지 않아요. 수업과 관련된
  문의는 전화나 이메일을 통해서 하라고 했으니까 ⑤도 안내문과
  일치하지 않죠.
  일치하는 선택지는 9월 5일까지 취소하면 환불이 가능하다는 환불
  정책에 대해 설명한 ④예요.

⤷ 안내문의 나머지 부분들도 정확히 이해했는지 다음 문제들을 풀면
서 내용을 정리해 봅시다.

▶ 안내문의 내용과 일치하면 ○, 일치하지 않으면 ×로 표시하세요.
• 수업은 2021년 11월까지 진행된다. **2** (   )
• 등록은 웹사이트에서 가능하다. **3** (   )

⤷ 추가 문제에 대한 정답을 확인해 볼까요?

> Dates and Times: September 13, 2021 — October
> 날짜 및 시간: 2021년 9월 13일 ~ 2021년 10월 29일 /
> 29, 2021 /

● **Dates and Times 항목을 봅시다.**
  수업은 2021년 9월 13일부터 2021년 10월 29일까지라고 했어요.
  그러니까 11월까지 진행된다는 건 안내문과 일치하지 않죠.

> Registration: / Available / from September 1 to
> 등록: / 가능함   / 9월 1일부터 9월 5일까지
> September 5 / on our website (www.maryhighs.edu) /
>   / 저희 웹사이트(www.maryhighs.edu)에서   /

● **Registration 항목에 단서가 있어요.**
  등록은 9월 1일부터 9월 5일까지 웹사이트에서 가능하다고 했으니까
  안내문과 일치해요!

정답을 마킹하기
전에 지시문을 다시
확인하자!

J03 ∼ 06 ▶ 제한시간 8분

J03 ✽✿✿ .... 2025 대비 수능 27 (고3)

Adenville City Pass Card에 관한 다음 안내문의 내용과 일치하지 않는 것은?

Adenville City Pass Card

The Adenville City Pass Card is a public transportation card for tourists visiting Adenville.

Service Range
- Adenville-based subway lines
- Adenville-licensed buses
※ This card cannot be used for city tour buses.

Card Type

	Price	Additional Benefit
1-Day	$10	10% off admission for major tourist attractions
3-Day	$25	
5-Day	$40	

※ Unused cards are refundable within 30 days of the purchase date.

Purchase Information
- Physical cards can be purchased at subway stations.
- Mobile cards can be purchased on the A-Transit app.

① 관광객을 위한 대중교통 카드이다.
② 시티 투어 버스에는 사용할 수 없다.
③ 5일 패스 카드에만 주요 관광지 입장료 할인 혜택이 제공된다.
④ 미사용 카드는 구입일로부터 30일 이내에 환불이 가능하다.
⑤ 모바일 카드는 A-Transit 앱에서 구입할 수 있다.

J04 ✽✿✿ .... 2025 대비 수능 28 (고3)

Luckwood Snow Festival에 관한 다음 안내문의 내용과 일치하는 것은?

Luckwood Snow Festival

We're happy to announce the 15th annual Luckwood Snow Festival. Come to the festival to enjoy winter activities.

When & Where
- January 24th – 30th (7 days), from 9 a.m. to 8 p.m.
- Luckwood Park

Special Activities
- Snow Sculpture Contest: 11 teams will participate.
- Fun in the Snow: Kids can enjoy snow tunnels and snow slides.

Transportation
- Parking is not available (Use public transportation and/or shuttle bus service).
- The shuttle bus runs between Luckwood Subway Station and Luckwood Park (One-way fare: $1, cash only).

※ For more information, please visit www.lwsnow.org.

① 2년에 한 번 열린다.
② 열흘 동안 진행된다.
③ 눈 조각 경연에는 11개 팀이 참가할 것이다.
④ 주차가 가능하다.
⑤ 셔틀버스 이용은 무료이다.

University of Teverley Campus Visit Day에 관한 다음 안내문의 내용과 일치하지 <u>않는</u> 것은?

University of Teverley Campus Visit Day

Do you want to see if the University of Teverley is the right fit for you? Come to our annual campus visit event for prospective students on Thursday, September 26th.

Participants
- 3rd-year high school students only

Meeting Time & Place
- The auditorium at the Student Center at 9:30 a.m.

Schedule
- 10:00 a.m.: Presentation on the admissions process
- 10:30 a.m.: Campus tour
- 12:00 p.m.: Free lunch provided at the students' cafeteria
- 1:00 p.m.: Q&A with the student tour staff

※ After the event, a T-shirt with our university logo will be given out as a gift.

Registration
- Register by 6 p.m., September 17th, on our website, www.teverley.edu.

① 고등학교 3학년 학생만 참여할 수 있다.
② 입학 절차에 관한 소개가 예정되어 있다.
③ 점심은 무료로 제공되지 않는다.
④ 티셔츠가 선물로 주어질 것이다.
⑤ 등록은 학교 웹사이트에서 한다.

2024 Green Future Webtoon Contest에 관한 다음 안내문의 내용과 일치하는 것은?

2024 Green Future Webtoon Contest

Showcase your creativity and artistic talents by creating a webtoon that captures your vision of a cleaner environment.

Theme: Renewable energy for a green future

Submission Details
- Submissions will be accepted from October 1st to November 30th.
- Submissions should be uploaded to our website.
- Each participant is allowed to submit only one webtoon.

Prizes

	Number of winners	Prize money (per winner)
1st prize	1	$3,000
2nd prize	2	$2,000
3rd prize	3	$1,000

- The winners will be decided by the selection committee and will be announced on December 30th.

※ For more information, visit our website, www.grnftr.org.

① 주제는 농업 기술의 미래이다.
② 출품은 11월 30일부터이다.
③ 각 참가자는 두 개의 웹툰을 제출할 수 있다.
④ 2등상은 세 명에게 주어진다.
⑤ 수상자는 선정 위원회에서 결정될 것이다.

J07 ✿❀❀.........................2025 대비 6월 모평 27 (고3)

Summer Job at Wildlife Rescue Center에 관한 다음 안내문의 내용과 일치하지 <u>않는</u> 것은?

Summer Job at Wildlife Rescue Center

We are looking for summer workers who will take care of the animals rescued from Mount Donovahn.

Schedule
• Dates: August 1st to 31st
• Hours: 10 a.m. – 4 p.m.

※ On rainy days, working hours may change.

Requirements
• Only those aged 18 and over can apply.
• Previous experience with animals

Tasks
• Preparing food for animals and feeding them
• Writing reports about animals

– Summer workers will get training from our caretakers.
– Free shuttle bus service will be provided twice a day.

To learn more about the summer job, please visit our website, www.dwildliferescue.org.

① Mount Donovahn으로부터 구조된 동물을 돌본다.
② 우천 시 업무 시간이 변경될 수 있다.
③ 18세 이상만 지원할 수 있다.
④ 동물에 관한 보고서를 작성한다.
⑤ 무료 셔틀 버스 서비스가 하루에 세 번 제공된다.

J08 ✿❀❀.........................2025 대비 6월 모평 28 (고3)

LCU Geography Field Trip에 관한 다음 안내문의 내용과 일치하는 것은?

LCU Geography Field Trip

Lionsford City University is offering a one-day geography field trip on June 17th. We believe it is one of the finest field trips in the country.

Participants: First-year students majoring in geography

Course Options

A	B
Exploring the landscape while hiking Mount Belena	Examining coastal features along Lionsford Beach

Participation Fee: $70 per person (lunch included)

How to Apply
• Email the application to geography@lcu.edu or drop it off at the department office.
• Deadline: June 4th

※ For further information, please contact us at 607-223-2127.

① 2일 동안 진행된다.
② 모든 전공의 학생들이 참여할 수 있다.
③ A코스에서는 Lionsford Beach 해안의 특징을 조사한다.
④ 참가비에 점심이 포함되어 있다.
⑤ 지원서는 이메일로만 제출이 가능하다.

J09 ✿❀❀ .... 2024 실시 10월 학평 27 (고3)

2024 "Be Active" Community Challenge에 관한 다음 안내문의 내용과 일치하지 <u>않는</u> 것은?

2024 "Be Active" Community Challenge

The "Be Active" Community Challenge invites all of you.
Let's get moving this fall!

- **When**: October 1 – October 31

- **How It Works**:
- Keep track of the number of minutes you were active every day.
- Every kind of exercise counts: jogging, dancing, football, etc.

- **Tracking Your Progress**:
- Log your active minutes daily on the "Be Active" app.
- Deadline for submitting your total time is November 1, 10:00 a.m.

- **Entry Fees**: $10 (12 years and under are FREE.)

- **Rewards and Recognition**:
- The three participants who recorded the highest total time will win a prize.
- Winners will be announced online.

① 기간은 10월 1일부터 10월 31일까지이다.
② 모든 종류의 운동이 인정된다.
③ 총합 시간의 제출 기한은 11월 1일 오후 10시이다.
④ 12세 이하는 참가비가 무료이다.
⑤ 우승자는 온라인으로 발표될 것이다.

J10 ★★❀ .... 2024 실시 10월 학평 28 (고3)

Heritage Hotel Stay Information에 관한 다음 안내문의 내용과 일치하는 것은?

Heritage Hotel Stay Information

Dear guests, please read the following to ensure your safety and comfort during your stay.

- **Check in & Check out**
- Room check in is from 2 p.m.
- Room check out is until 12 p.m.

- **During the Stay**
- Used towels are changed every other day.
- Free Wi-Fi is available ONLY in the lobby.
- Two bottles of water are provided for FREE.

- **Facilities**
- The gym and business center are open 24 hours.
- The parking lot is in front of the hotel.

① 객실 체크아웃은 오후 2시까지이다.
② 사용한 수건은 매일 교체된다.
③ 무료 와이파이는 호텔 전체에서 이용 가능하다.
④ 물 두 병이 무료로 제공된다.
⑤ 주차장은 호텔 뒤편에 있다.

J11 ✿❀❀ .... 2024 실시 7월 학평 27 (고3)

Dolphin Tours에 관한 다음 안내문의 내용과 일치하지 <u>않는</u> 것은?

Dolphin Tours

Come join Dolphin Tours sailing from Golden Bay and dive into the enchanting world of marine life.

Daily Tour Times
- 11 a.m., 2 p.m., & Sunset
※ Each tour lasts two hours.

Tickets & Booking
- Adult (ages 12 and over): $20
- Child (ages 11 and under): Free
- Reserve your tickets on our website at www.dolphintourgb.com.

Activities
- Dolphin watching guided by a marine biologist
- Swimming with dolphins (Optional)

Notices
- Reservations are required for all activities.
- Children must be accompanied by a parent or guardian.
- In the case of cancellation due to bad weather, a full refund will be provided.

① 각 투어는 2시간이 소요된다.
② 11세 이하의 어린이는 무료로 참가할 수 있다.
③ 해양 생물학자가 돌고래 관찰을 안내한다.
④ 일부 활동은 예약 없이 참여할 수 있다.
⑤ 어린이는 부모나 보호자를 동반해야 한다.

J12 ✿❀❀ .... 2024 실시 7월 학평 28 (고3)

2024 Celton Math Night에 관한 다음 안내문의 내용과 일치하는 것은?

2024 Celton Math Night

Celton High School invites students to experience how math connects to the real world! Students will search supermarket aisles for answers to math questions on their activity sheets.

Who: Teams of 10th and 11th Grade Students

Where: Jay Supermarket

When: July 26th, 5 p.m. – 7 p.m.

Event Information
- Each team should consist of 3 students.
- Bringing a calculator is allowed.
- A prize will not be given to the first team to finish the activity sheet. It's not a race.
- Sign up for the event at www.celtonmath.com no later than July 24th.

※ For more information, please contact us at (512)1654−9783 or visit our website.

① 오후 5시에 종료된다.
② 각 팀은 3명의 학생으로 구성되어야 한다.
③ 계산기 반입이 허용되지 않는다.
④ 가장 먼저 활동지를 완성하는 팀이 상을 받는다.
⑤ 7월 26일까지 등록해야 한다.

Scottish Day Trip Package에 관한 다음 안내문의 내용과 일치하지 <u>않는</u> 것은?

Scottish Day Trip Package

Don't miss the chance to soak up the spirit of Scotland! A full-day trip through the Highlands is waiting for you.

Schedule
- Departs at 7 a.m. from the Highland Tours office
- Returns around 9 p.m. to the original departure point

Details
- Max of 40 people per group
- Minimum age: 5 years old
- Price: $150 per person

Booking
- Only online booking is available.
- You will receive an email once your booking is confirmed.
- For a refund, cancel at least two days before the tour departs.

Note
- The tour will not hold back for tourists who arrive at the departure point late.

① 출발하는 장소와 돌아오는 장소가 같다.
② 한 그룹당 40명까지 참여할 수 있다.
③ 예약이 확정되면 이메일을 받을 것이다.
④ 환불을 위해서는 출발 하루 전까지 취소해야 한다.
⑤ 출발지에 늦게 도착하는 여행자를 기다려 주지 않는다.

Jr. Chef Class에 관한 다음 안내문의 내용과 일치하는 것은?

JR. CHEF CLASS *with Chef Scott Gomez*

Professional Chef Scott Gomez offers cooking classes to provide your children with hands-on experience and happy memories. He has picked pizza for the menu this week.

Details
- Date: Tuesday, May 14th, 2024
- Place: Rosehill Community Center Cafeteria
- Available for children ages 6–12

Cost
- $20 per child includes all ingredients, chef hat and apron.

Schedule

Time	Contents
5:00 – 5:20 p.m.	rolling pizza dough
5:20 – 6:00 p.m.	topping and baking
6:00 – 6:30 p.m.	plating and serving

Note
- Call 876−725−7501 to register.
- A parent or guardian must stay on site during class.
- Since parking space is limited, using public transportation is recommended.

① 이번 주의 메뉴는 아이들이 택한다.
② 비용에는 앞치마가 포함되지 않는다.
③ 피자 반죽 밀기는 30분간 진행된다.
④ 부모 혹은 보호자는 수업 동안 현장에 머물러야 한다.
⑤ 충분한 주차 공간이 확보되어 있다.

J15 ✽❀❀.......................... 2024 실시 3월 학평 27 (고3)

Electronic Safe User Manual에 관한 다음 안내문의
내용과 일치하지 <u>않는</u> 것은?

Electronic Safe User Manual

OPENING THE SAFE FOR THE FIRST TIME
Upon first use, users should open the safe
with the emergency key.

INSERTING THE BATTERIES
• Insert four AA batteries, and the green light
will flash.
• If both the green light and the red light are
on, replace the batteries.

SETTING A PASSWORD
• With the door open, press the reset button.
Then, input a four-digit password and press
the **"enter"** button.
• When the new password is set, the green
light will flash twice.

OPENING THE DOOR WITH A PASSWORD
Input your password and press the **"enter"**
button.

CAUTION: A wrong password input will set
off an alarm.

*digit: (숫자의) 자리

---

① 처음으로 금고를 열 때는 비상 열쇠를 사용해야 한다.
② AA 건전지 네 개를 넣으면, 녹색 불이 깜빡일 것이다.
③ 녹색과 빨간색 불이 둘 다 켜져 있으면, 건전지를 교체해야
한다.
④ 새로운 비밀번호가 설정되면, 녹색 불이 세 번 깜빡일
것이다.
⑤ 잘못된 비밀번호의 입력은 경보음을 울릴 것이다.

J16 ✽❀❀.......................... 2024 실시 3월 학평 28 (고3)

World Poetry Day Competition에 관한 다음
안내문의 내용과 일치하는 것은?

World Poetry Day Competition

In honor of World Poetry Day, let's experience
the power of words with our poetry competition!

Competition Details
• Theme: Unexpected Moments
• Deadline: March 21, 2024 (World Poetry
Day)
• Age: Only those who are under age 18 can
participate.

Special Opportunities
• Poetry Workshop: All participants can join
our poetry workshop led by well-known
poets.

How to Participate
• Compose your poem inspired by the theme.
• You can submit your piece only through
E-mail at administer@worldpoetry.org.

---

① 주제는 예상했던 순간들이다.
② 마감일은 2024년 3월 21일이다.
③ 18세 이상도 대회에 참가할 수 있다.
④ 대회에서 수상한 사람들만 워크숍에 참석할 수 있다.
⑤ 작품은 직접 또는 이메일로 제출할 수 있다.

Singing Tommy 사용에 관한 다음 안내문의 내용과 일치하지 <u>않는</u> 것은?

Singing Tommy

Congratulations! Tommy is now your singing friend. Read these instructions to learn how to play with and care for him. Tommy sings to you anytime, anywhere. An Internet connection is not required to play the songs!

Before Use

1. Remove the protective film covering Tommy's eyes.
2. Insert two AA batteries into the battery box and press the power button.
3. Choose your volume setting: LOW volume or HIGH volume.

Operation

1. Play
   – Touch Tommy's right ear to start a song.
2. Stop
   – Press Tommy's hat to stop the song.

3. Control
   – Choose from five songs.
   – Push Tommy's badge to skip to the next song.

Caution

Tommy is not waterproof. Be careful not to get Tommy wet!

① 인터넷에 연결되지 않아도 노래를 재생할 수 있다.
② 사용 전에 두 개의 AA 건전지를 넣어야 한다.
③ 모자를 누르면 노래가 시작된다.
④ 다섯 곡의 노래 중에 선택할 수 있다.
⑤ 방수가 되지 않는다.

Wing Cheese Factory Tour에 관한 다음 안내문의 내용과 일치하지 <u>않는</u> 것은?

Wing Cheese Factory Tour

Attention, all cheese lovers!
Come and experience our historic cheese-making process at the Wing Cheese Factory. Look around, taste, and make!

Participation

• Adults: $30,
  Children: $10 (Ages 3 and under: Free)
• The fee includes cheese tasting and making.
• Sign up for the tour at www.cheesewcf.com by June 30.

Tour Schedule

• 10:00 a.m.: Watch a video about the factory's history
• 10:30 a.m.: Factory tour and cheese tasting
• 11:30 a.m.: Cheese making

Note

• Participants can buy a cheese-shaped key chain for $15.
• No photography is allowed inside the factory.
• We are closed on Saturdays, Sundays, and holidays.

① 참가비에는 치즈 만들기 비용이 포함된다.
② 참가 신청은 6월 30일까지 해야 한다.
③ 공장의 역사에 대한 비디오를 보는 일정이 있다.
④ 참가자는 치즈 모양의 열쇠고리를 15달러에 살 수 있다.
⑤ 공장 안에서 사진 촬영이 허용된다.

J19 ✿❀❀ .... 2023 대비 9월 모평 27 (고3)

2022 K-Tea Culture Program에 관한 다음 안내문의 내용과 일치하지 <u>않는</u> 것은?

2022 K-Tea Culture Program

Evergreen Tea Society invites you to the second annual K-Tea Culture Program! Come and enjoy a refreshing cup of tea and learn about traditional Korean tea culture.

Program Includes:

1) Watching a short video about the history of Korean tea culture
2) Observing a demonstration of a traditional Korean tea-ceremony (*dado*)
3) Participating in the ceremony yourself
4) Tasting a selection of teas along with cookies

When: Saturday, September 24,
　　　　3:00 p.m. – 5:00 p.m.

Where: Evergreen Culture Center

Participation Fee: $20 per person (traditional teacup included)

Reservations should be made online (www. egtsociety.or.kr) at least one day before your visit.

① 한국의 차 문화 역사에 관한 영상을 시청한다.
② 한국 전통 다도 시연을 본다.
③ 쿠키와 함께 차를 맛본다.
④ 참가비에는 전통 찻잔이 포함되어 있다.
⑤ 예약은 방문 일주일 전까지 해야 한다.

J20 ✿❀❀ .... 2021 대비 9월 모평 27 (고3)

Springfield Science Invention Contest에 관한 다음 안내문의 내용과 일치하지 <u>않는</u> 것은?

Springfield Science Invention Contest

Springfield High School invites all students to participate in the Springfield Science Invention Contest. In this annual contest, you have the opportunity to invent a useful object and show your creativity!

Details

• Judging criteria are creativity and usefulness of the invention.
• Participants must enter in teams of four and can only join one team.
• Submission is limited to one invention per team.

Prizes

• 1st Place — $50 gift certificate
• 2nd Place — $30 gift certificate
• 3rd Place — $10 gift certificate

Note

• Inventions must be submitted to the science lab by October 1, 2020.

For more information,
visit www.hsspringfield.edu.

① 매년 개최되는 대회이다.
② 심사 기준은 발명품의 창의성과 유용성이다.
③ 발명품은 한 팀당 두 개까지 제출할 수 있다.
④ 1등은 50달러 상품권을 받는다.
⑤ 발명품은 과학 실험실로 제출해야 한다.

Treehouse Drive-in Movie Night에 관한 다음 안내문의 내용과 일치하는 것은?

Treehouse Drive-in Movie Night

Looking for a fun night out with the family? Come with your loved ones and enjoy our first drive-in movie night of 2021! All money from ticket sales will be donated to the local children's hospital.

Featured Film: *Dream Story*

Date: June 13, 2021

Place: Treehouse Parking Lot

Showtimes
- First Screening: 7:30 p.m.
- Second Screening: 10:00 p.m.

Tickets: $30 per car

Additional Information
- 50 parking spots are available (The gate opens at 6 p.m.).
- Ice cream and hot dogs are sold on site.
- Make your reservation online at www.tdimn.com.

① 2021년에 두 번째로 열리는 행사이다.
② 티켓 판매 수입금 전액은 어린이 도서관에 기부될 것이다.
③ 첫 번째 상영 시작 시간은 오후 10시이다.
④ 티켓 가격은 자동차 한 대당 50달러이다.
⑤ 아이스크림과 핫도그가 현장에서 판매된다.

2021 Whir Car Drawing Contest for Kids에 관한 다음 안내문의 내용과 일치하지 <u>않는</u> 것은?

2021 Whir Car Drawing Contest for Kids
Theme: Family

Does your child love cars? Take this opportunity for your child to think about what they love and draw it. They will definitely enjoy and learn from this contest!

Details
- Ten entries are chosen, and each is awarded a $50 gift certificate.
- Drawing skills are not considered in judging.

Submission
- Take a photo of your child's drawing.
- Visit our website (www.whircar4kids.com) and upload the photo by October 3.

Note
- The drawing should contain your family and a car.
- Participants must be 3 to 7 years old.
Please visit our website to learn more.

① 출품작 중 10개를 선정해서 시상한다.
② 그림 기술이 심사에서 고려된다.
③ 그림을 찍은 사진을 웹사이트에 업로드해야 한다.
④ 그림은 가족과 차를 포함해야 한다.
⑤ 참가자의 나이는 3세에서 7세까지로 제한된다.

J23 ✽❀❀ .... 2022 대비 수능 28 (고3)

Goldbeach SeaWorld Sleepovers에 관한 다음 안내문의 내용과 일치하는 것은?

Goldbeach SeaWorld Sleepovers

Do your children love marine animals? A sleepover at Goldbeach SeaWorld will surely be an exciting overnight experience for them. Join us for a magical underwater sleepover.

Participants
- Children ages 8 to 12
- Children must be accompanied by a guardian.

When: Saturdays 5 p.m. to Sundays 10 a.m. in May, 2022

Activities: guided tour, underwater show, and photo session with a mermaid

Participation Fee
- $50 per person
 (dinner and breakfast included)

Note
- Sleeping bags and other personal items will not be provided.
- All activities take place indoors.
- Taking photos is not allowed from 10 p.m. to 7 a.m.

For more information, you can visit our website at www.goldbeachseaworld.com.

① 7세 이하의 어린이가 참가할 수 있다.
② 평일에 진행된다.
③ 참가비에 아침 식사가 포함된다.
④ 모든 활동은 야외에서 진행된다.
⑤ 사진 촬영은 언제든지 할 수 있다.

J24 ✽❀❀ .... 2024 대비 6월 모평 27 (고3)

2023 Cierra Basketball Day Camp에 관한 다음 안내문의 내용과 일치하지 <u>않는</u> 것은?

2023 Cierra Basketball Day Camp

Cierra Basketball Day Camp provides opportunities for teens to get healthy and have fun. Come and learn a variety of skills from the experts!

Site & Dates
- Cierra Sports Center
- July 17th – July 21st

Ages & Level: 13 – 18 years, for beginners only

Camp Activities
- Skill Drills: 1:00 p.m. – 2:00 p.m.
- Team Games: 2:30 p.m. – 3:30 p.m.
- Free Throw Shooting Contests: 4:00 p.m. – 5:00 p.m.

Registration & Cost
- Register online at www.crrbbcamp.com.
- $40 (Full payment is required when registering.)

 ※ A towel will be provided for free.

① 전문가들로부터 다양한 기술을 배울 수 있다.
② 초급자만을 대상으로 한다.
③ 팀 경기는 오후 1시에 시작한다.
④ 온라인으로 등록할 수 있다.
⑤ 수건이 무료로 제공될 것이다.

2020 Crime & Spy Science Workshop에 관한 다음 안내문의 내용과 일치하는 것은?

2020 Crime & Spy Science Workshop

Come learn to be a top detective! In this workshop, you will investigate crime scenes and learn skills necessary to become a detective and solve mysteries!

When & Where
• 9 a.m. to 3 p.m. on Tuesday, August 18, 2020
• Conference Room #103, ZBU Student Union

Who : Ages 14 and up

Participation Fee : $20
                    (insurance not included)

Registration
• Call 555–540–0421, or email spyscience@zbu.edu by Wednesday, July 29, 2020.

Preparations
• Bring comfortable shoes and a bag to carry detective tools.
• Lunch and snacks are provided.

You will learn
• how to find traces of suspects.
• how to manage the scene of a crime.
• how to choose the right tools.

① 이틀 동안 진행된다.
② 참가비에 보험이 포함되어 있다.
③ 등록은 이메일로만 할 수 있다.
④ 점심과 간식은 제공되지 않는다.
⑤ 적절한 도구를 선택하는 방법을 배울 것이다.

Cornhill No Paper Cup Challenge에 관한 다음 안내문의 내용과 일치하지 <u>않는</u> 것은?

Cornhill No Paper Cup Challenge

Cornhill High School invites you to join the "No Paper Cup Challenge." This encourages you to reduce your use of paper cups. Let's save the earth together!

How to Participate
1) After being chosen, record a video showing you are using a tumbler.
2) Choose the next participant by saying his or her name in the video.
3) Upload the video to our school website within 24 hours.
※ The student council president will start the challenge on December 1st, 2021.

Additional Information
• The challenge will last for two weeks.
• All participants will receive T-shirts.

If you have questions about the challenge, contact us at cornhillsc@chs.edu.

① 참가자는 텀블러를 사용하는 자신의 동영상을 찍는다.
② 참가자가 동영상을 업로드할 곳은 학교 웹사이트이다.
③ 학생회장이 시작할 것이다.
④ 두 달 동안 진행될 예정이다.
⑤ 참가자 전원이 티셔츠를 받을 것이다.

J27 ✻❀❀ .... 2023 실시 10월 학평 27 (고3)

2023 Greenfield City Run에 관한 다음 안내문의 내용과 일치하지 <u>않는</u> 것은?

2023 Greenfield City Run

Are you eager for the race that can awaken the running spirit within you? Maybe the Greenfield City Run is best for you.

- **When**: Sunday, November 5
  - Assembly time is 9:00 a.m.
  - Start time is 9:30 a.m.
- **Where**: Riverside Park
- **Races**: 2km, 5km, 10km (The 2km race is only for kids.)
- **Registration**
  - Registration starts on October 16.
  - The registration fees depend on the date you sign up.
    $30: October 16 – November 4 /
    $40: November 5
  - Register online at www.finishrace.com.
- **Activities**
  - Coffee and Cookie Fair & Outdoor Charity Bazaar

  For more information, call (516) 703–1737.

① 집합 시간은 오전 9시이다.
② 2km 종목은 아이들만 참가할 수 있다.
③ 등록은 10월 16일부터 시작된다.
④ 날짜와 상관없이 등록비는 동일하다.
⑤ 야외 자선 바자회가 있다.

J28 ✻❀❀ .... 2023 대비 수능 27 (고3)

다음 Renovation Notice의 내용과 일치하지 <u>않는</u> 것은?

Renovation Notice

At the Natural Jade Resort, we are continually improving our facilities to better serve our guests. Therefore, we will be renovating some areas of the resort, according to the schedule below.

Renovation Period: November 21 to December 18, 2022
- Renovations will take place every day from 9:00 a.m. to 5:00 p.m.

Areas to be Closed: Gym and indoor swimming pool

Further Information
- All outdoor leisure activities will be available as usual.
- Guests will receive a 15% discount for all meals in the restaurant.
- Guests may use the tennis courts for free.

We will take all possible measures to minimize noise and any other inconvenience. We sincerely appreciate your understanding.

① 보수 공사는 2022년 11월 21일에 시작된다.
② 보수 공사는 주말에만 진행될 것이다.
③ 체육관과 실내 수영장은 폐쇄될 것이다.
④ 모든 야외 레저 활동은 평소와 같이 가능할 것이다.
⑤ 손님은 무료로 테니스장을 이용할 수 있다.

Poetry Writing Basics Workshop에 관한 다음 안내문의 내용과 일치하는 것은?

Poetry Writing Basics Workshop

Join our Poetry Writing Basics Workshop and meet the poet, Ms. Grace Larson!

All students of George Clarkson University are invited.

When: Thursday, September 24, 2020
       (1:00 p.m. – 4:00 p.m.)
Where: Main Seminar Room, 1st Floor, Student Union

After an introduction to the basic techniques of poetry writing, you will:

1. Write your own poem.
2. Read it aloud to the other participants.
3. Receive expert feedback from Ms. Larson.

Registration Fee: $10
※ Register on or before September 18 and pay only $7.

Any related inquiries should be sent via email to studentun@georgeclarkson.edu.

① 목요일 오전에 진행된다.
② 학생회관 3층에서 열린다.
③ 참가자는 자신이 창작한 시를 낭독할 것이다.
④ 9월 18일까지는 등록비가 10달러이다.
⑤ 관련 문의는 이메일로 할 수 없다.

2022 Sunbay High School Benefit Concert에 관한 다음 안내문의 내용과 일치하지 <u>않는</u> 것은?

2022 Sunbay High School Benefit Concert

Sunbay High School students will be holding their benefit concert for charity. All profits will be donated to the local children's hospital. Come and enjoy your family and friends' performances.

Date & Time: Thursday, June 30, 2022
       at 6 p.m.

Place: Sunbay High School's Vision Hall

Events
• singing, dancing, drumming, and other musical performances
• special performance by singer Jonas Collins, who graduated from Sunbay High School

Tickets
• $3 per person
• available to buy from 5 p.m. at the front desk of Vision Hall

Other Attractions
• club students' artwork on display, but not for purchase
• free face-painting

For more information about the concert, feel free to contact us at concert@sunbayhighs.edu.

① 수익금 전액은 지역 아동 병원에 기부될 것이다.
② Sunbay 고등학교의 Vision Hall에서 열린다.
③ Sunbay 고등학교를 졸업한 가수의 특별 공연이 있다.
④ 티켓은 오후 5시부터 살 수 있다.
⑤ 동아리 학생들의 전시 작품은 구입이 가능하다.

J31 ❋❋❋............................ 2024 대비 9월 모평 27 (고3)

Brushwood National Park Tour Program에 관한 다음 안내문의 내용과 일치하지 <u>않는</u> 것은?

Brushwood National Park Tour Program

Walking in nature is a great way to stay fit and healthy. Enjoy free park walks with our volunteer guides, while appreciating the beautiful sights and sounds of the forest.

Details

- Open on weekdays from March to November
- Easy walk along the path for one hour (3 km)
- Groups of 15 to 20 per guide

Registration

- Scan the QR code to sign up for the tour.

Note

- A bottle of water will be provided to each participant.
- Children under 12 must be accompanied by an adult.
- Tours may be canceled due to weather conditions.

※ If you have any questions, please email us at brushwoodtour@parks.org.

① 자원봉사 안내자가 동행한다.
② 주말에 진행된다.
③ QR 코드를 스캔하여 신청한다.
④ 각 참가자에게 물이 한 병씩 제공될 것이다.
⑤ 날씨에 따라 취소될 수 있다.

J32 ❋❋❋.............................. 2024 대비 수능 27 (고3)

Turtle Island Boat Tour에 관한 다음 안내문의 내용과 일치하지 <u>않는</u> 것은?

Turtle Island Boat Tour

The fantastic Turtle Island Boat Tour invites you to the beautiful sea world.

Dates: From June 1 to August 31, 2024

Tour Times

Weekdays	1 p.m. – 5 p.m.
Weekends	9 a.m. – 1 p.m.
	1 p.m. – 5 p.m.

※ Each tour lasts four hours.

Tickets & Booking

- $50 per person for each tour (Only those aged 17 and over can participate.)
- Bookings must be completed no later than 2 days before the day of the tour.
- No refunds after the departure time
- Each tour group size is limited to 10 participants.

Activities

- Snorkeling with a professional diver
- Feeding tropical fish

※ Feel free to explore our website, www.snorkelingti.com.

① 주말에는 하루에 두 번 운영된다.
② 17세 이상만 참가할 수 있다.
③ 당일 예약이 가능하다.
④ 출발 시간 이후에는 환불이 불가능하다.
⑤ 전문 다이버와 함께 하는 스노클링 활동이 있다.

2023 Oyster Bay Town Toddler Sports Program에 관한 다음 안내문의 내용과 일치하는 것은?

2023 Oyster Bay Town Toddler Sports Program

The Town's Toddler Sports Program will return this spring on April 7th. This 6-week program offers sports classes at the Youth Center for children aged 3 and 4.

- Parents who sign their toddler up for the program must choose one class per week, per child. Classes will take place on:
  Wednesdays 10 a.m. or 11 a.m. & Fridays 10 a.m. or 11 a.m.
- Registration will take place ONLINE at www.obtown.org starting Friday, March 24th, at 9 a.m.

Fee
− $75 per resident child
− $90 for any non-resident child

For more information, call (516) 797−1234.

① 7주간 진행되는 프로그램이다.
② 참가 아동마다 매주 두 개의 수업을 선택해야 한다.
③ 수업은 수요일과 금요일 오후에 있다.
④ 등록은 3월 24일 오전 9시에 시작될 것이다.
⑤ 지역 거주 아동의 참가비는 90달러이다.

Creative Art Class for Kids에 관한 다음 안내문의 내용과 일치하는 것은?

Creative Art Class for Kids

Want to encourage your child's artistic talent? Color World Art Center is going to have art classes for kids from June 1st to August 31st.

Class Programs & Schedule
- Clay Arts: Ages 4 − 6, Every Monday
- Cartoon Drawing: Ages 7 − 9, Every Thursday
- Watercolors: Ages 10 − 12, Every Friday

Class Time: 4 p.m. − 6 p.m.

Monthly Fee
- $30 per child (snacks included)
- Family discounts are available (10% discount for each child).

Notes
- Only 10 kids are allowed per class.
- Kids should wear clothes that they don't mind getting dirty.

  ※ Sign up at Color World Art Center.

① 6월부터 9월까지 진행된다.
② 만화 그리기 강좌가 월요일마다 있다.
③ 모든 강좌는 오전에 열린다.
④ 월 수강료에 간식이 포함되어 있다.
⑤ 강좌당 수강 아동 수에 제한이 없다.

J35 ✿❀❀ .... 2024 대비 9월 모평 28 (고3)

WGHS Geography Photo Contest에 관한 다음 안내문의 내용과 일치하는 것은?

WGHS Geography Photo Contest

The event you've been waiting for all this year is finally here! Please join Wood Gate High School's 10th annual Geography Photo Contest.

Guidelines
- Participants should use the theme of the "Beauty of Rivers Crossing Our City."
- Submissions are limited to one photo per person.
- Files should not be larger than 50 MB.

Schedule

	When	Where
Submission	October 2 – October 8	Email: geography@woodgate.edu
Voting	October 11 – October 13	School Website: https://www.woodgate.edu
Exhibition	October 16 – October 20	Main Lobby

Note
- The top 10 photos selected by students will be exhibited.

※ For more information, visit the geography teacher's room.

---

① 처음으로 개최되는 대회이다.
② 출품 사진 주제에 제한이 없다.
③ 100 MB 크기의 파일을 제출할 수 있다.
④ 투표는 일주일간 실시된다.
⑤ 학생들이 선정한 사진들이 전시될 것이다.

J36 ✿❀❀ .... 2021 대비 수능 27 (고3)

City of Sittka Public Bike Sharing Service에 관한 다음 안내문의 내용과 일치하지 <u>않는</u> 것은?

City of Sittka Public Bike Sharing Service

Are you planning to explore the city?
This is the eco-friendly way to do it!

Rent
- Register anywhere via our easy app.
- Payment can be made only by credit card.

Fee
- Free for the first 30 minutes
- One dollar per additional 30 minutes

Use
- Choose a bike and scan the QR code on the bike.
- Helmets are not provided.

Return
- Return the bike to the Green Zone shown on the app.
- Complete the return by pressing the OK button on the bike.

---

① 신용 카드 결제만 가능하다.
② 처음 30분은 무료이다.
③ 자전거의 QR 코드를 스캔해서 이용한다.
④ 헬멧이 제공된다.
⑤ 자전거의 OK 버튼을 눌러서 반납을 완료한다.

Bluehill Apple Picking에 관한 다음 안내문의 내용과 일치하는 것은?

Bluehill Apple Picking

Take home a bag full of apples fresh from the orchard. This year, unfortunately, apple pie eating contests will not be held due to time constraints.

- **Date**: Saturday, October 21, 2023
- **Time**
  - Departure: 8:15 a.m. for pre-trip meeting
    Buses leave at 8:30 a.m.
    SHARP!
  - Return: Approximately 7:00 p.m.
- **Price**: $20 per person
  (transportation included, meals not included)
- Pre-registration is required at www.blueapple.com.
  - 12 years and under must be accompanied by adults.

① 애플파이 먹기 대회가 열릴 예정이다.
② 버스는 오전 8시 15분에 출발한다.
③ 참가비에 식사가 포함되어 있다.
④ 사전 등록은 필요 없다.
⑤ 12세 이하는 성인이 동반해야 한다.

Career Day with a Big Data Expert에 관한 다음 안내문의 내용과 일치하는 것은?

Career Day with a Big Data Expert

Meet a Big Data expert from a leading IT company! Jill Johnson, famous data analyst and bestselling author, will be visiting Sovenhill High School to give a lecture on careers related to Big Data.

Participation:
- Sovenhill High School students only
- Limited to 50 students

When & Where:
- October 15, 10:00 a.m. to 11:30 a.m.
- Library

Registration: Scan the QR code to fill in the application form.

Note:
- Drinking beverages is not permitted during the lecture.
- The lecture will be followed by a Q&A session.
- All participants will receive a free copy of the lecturer's book.

① 학부모도 참여할 수 있다.
② 참석 인원에 제한이 없다.
③ QR 코드를 스캔하여 신청서를 작성한다.
④ 강연 중에 음료수를 마실 수 있다.
⑤ 참석자 중 일부만 강연자의 책을 무료로 받는다.

J39 ✿❀✿ .... 2023 실시 4월 학평 28 (고3)

International Mask Festival에 관한 다음 안내문의 내용과 일치하는 것은?

International Mask Festival

Would you like to appreciate masks from all over the world? Visit Maywood Hills Museum and enjoy their beauty!

When: Every Tuesday to
Sunday in April
(10:00 a.m. – 8:00 p.m.)

Admission Price: $10 per person

Event Information
- Booth A: Exhibition of masks from 25 countries
- Booth B: Mask making activity (reservation required)

Details
- Audio guides are available in Booth A and are included in the admission price.
- After making a mask in Booth B, you can take it home as a souvenir.

Any related inquiries are welcome via email (maskfestival@maywood.org) or phone call (234-567-7363).

① 화요일에는 축제가 운영되지 않는다.
② 가면 만들기 활동은 예약 없이 참여할 수 있다.
③ 오디오 가이드는 입장료에 포함되지 않는다.
④ 만든 가면은 기념품으로 집에 가져갈 수 있다.
⑤ 관련 문의는 전화로만 가능하다.

J40 ✿✿✿ .... 2021 대비 수능 28 (고3)

Jason's Photography Class에 관한 다음 안내문의 내용과 일치하는 것은?

Jason's Photography Class

Are you tired of taking pictures with your camera set to "Auto"? Do you want to create more professional-looking photos? You won't want to miss this opportunity.

- Date: Saturday, December 19
- Time: 1:30 p.m. – 5:30 p.m.
- Place: Thrombon Building, Room 2 on the first floor
- Tuition Fee: $50 (snacks provided)
- Level: Beginner
- Topics to Be Covered:
  – Equipment Selection
  – Lighting Techniques
  – Color Selection
  – Special Effects
- Class size is limited to eight, so don't delay!

Visit our web site at www.eypcap.com to register.

① 오전에 시작된다.
② 3층에서 진행된다.
③ 중급자 수준이다.
④ 다루는 주제 중 하나는 특수 효과이다.
⑤ 수강 학생 수에는 제한이 없다.

J41 ❈❈❈ ⋯⋯⋯⋯⋯⋯⋯⋯ 2023 실시 7월 학평 28 (고3)

2023 Oakfield Mini Marathon에 관한 다음 안내문의 내용과 일치하는 것은?

2023 Oakfield Mini Marathon

Join the 2023 Oakfield Mini Marathon to celebrate the opening of Central Park in our town! Runners, joggers, and walkers are all welcome.

When: Saturday, October 21, starting at 8:30 a.m.

Where: Start at Gate 1 of Central Park and finish in the parking lot

Who: Ages 13 and above

Distance: 10 km

Participation Fee: $5 per person

Registration
- Online only (www.oakfieldminimarathon.com)
- September 1 to 30

※ If you finish the race, you will receive a T-shirt and an e-certificate.

For more information, visit our website.

① Central Park 주차장에서 출발한다.
② 13세 이상 참여할 수 있다.
③ 참가비는 무료이다.
④ 9월 1일까지 등록해야 한다.
⑤ 등록을 하면 티셔츠를 받는다.

J42 ❈❈❈ ⋯⋯⋯⋯⋯⋯⋯⋯ 2023 대비 수능 28 (고3)

2022 Valestown Recycles Poster Contest에 관한 다음 안내문의 내용과 일치하는 것은?

2022 Valestown Recycles Poster Contest

Join this year's Valestown Recycles Poster Contest and show off your artistic talent!

Guidelines
- Participation is only for high school students in Valestown.
- Participants should use the theme of "Recycling for the Future."

Submission Format
- File type: PDF only
- Maximum file size: 40MB

Judging Criteria
- Use of theme   - Creativity   - Artistic skill

Details
- Submissions are limited to one poster per person.
- Submissions should be uploaded to the website by 6 p.m., December 19.
- Winners will be announced on the website on December 28.

For more information, please visit www.vtco.org.

① Valestown의 모든 학생들이 참여할 수 있다.
② 참가자는 포스터의 주제 선정에 제약을 받지 않는다.
③ 출품할 파일 양식은 자유롭게 선택 가능하다.
④ 심사 기준에 창의성이 포함된다.
⑤ 1인당 출품할 수 있는 포스터의 수에는 제한이 없다.

2023 Eastland High School Video Clip Contest
에 관한 다음 안내문의 내용과 일치하는 것은?

2023 Eastland High School Video Clip Contest

Shoot and share your most memorable moments with your teachers and friends!

Guidelines

- Theme: "Joyful Moments" in Our Growing Community
- Submissions will be accepted from December 1 to December 14.
- Submissions should be uploaded to our school website.
  − Video length cannot exceed three minutes.
  − Entries are limited to one per student.

Prizes

- 1st place: $100 gift card, 2nd place: $50 gift card
- Winning videos will be posted to our school's app.
- The prize winners will be chosen by the school art teachers.

※ For more information, visit the school website.

① 출품작의 주제가 정해져 있지 않다.
② 한 달 동안 동영상을 접수할 예정이다.
③ 출품할 동영상의 길이는 3분을 초과할 수 없다.
④ 출품작은 학생 1인당 두 개로 제한된다.
⑤ 학생회가 수상자를 선정할 것이다.

선택지 순서대로 안내문을 확인하자!

J 어휘 Review

※ 다음 영어는 우리말 뜻을, 우리말은 영어 단어를 〈보기〉에서 찾아 쓰시오.

〈보기〉

observe	추가의	tuition	refreshing
분석가	구입, 구매	선명한, 생생한	rare
benefit	동반하다	support	이전의

01 purchase _____

02 vivid _____

03 previous _____

04 analyst _____

05 accompany _____

06 (모금을 위한) 자선 행사 _____

07 드문, 희귀한 _____

08 관측[관찰]하다 _____

09 신선한, 상쾌하게 하는 _____

10 수업(료) _____

※ 다음 우리말에 알맞은 영어 표현을 찾아 연결하시오.

11 ~을 돌보다 •   • sign up for

12 ~을 신청하다 •   • care for

13 현장에(서) •   • on site

14 ~로 제한되다 •   • due to

15 ~ 때문에 •   • be limited to

※ 다음 우리말 표현에 맞는 단어를 고르시오.

16 특집 영화 ➡ (featured / figured) film

17 전시 중인 예술 작품 ➡ artwork on (display / play)

18 그 광경을 포착하는 최적의 장소 ➡ the perfect (spot / stop) to catch the view

19 치즈 제조 과정 ➡ cheese-making (process / possess)

20 우리 대학 로고가 새겨진 티셔츠 ➡ a T-shirt with our (universe / university) logo

※ 다음 문장의 빈칸에 알맞은 단어를 〈보기〉에서 찾아 쓰시오.

〈보기〉

profits	submission	participants	rooftop
poetry	beverages	announced	mind
via	limited	at least	introduction

21 참가자들은 홀에서 모이고 그다음 옥상으로 이동할 것입니다.
➡ Participants will gather at the hall and then move to the _____.

22 수익금 전액은 지역 아동 병원에 기부될 것입니다.
➡ All _____ will be donated to the local children's hospital.

23 강의 중에 음료수를 마시는 것은 허용되지 않습니다.
➡ Drinking _____ is not permitted during the lecture.

24 수상팀은 4월 21일에 안내될 것입니다.
➡ Winning teams will be _____ on April 21.

25 기상 상황으로 인해 행사가 취소되면, 문자 메시지를 통해 공지가 주어질 것입니다.
➡ If the event is cancelled due to the weather conditions, notice will be given _____ text message.

26 그들은 더러워져도 신경쓰지 않는다.
➡ They don't _____ getting dirty.

27 예약은 적어도 여러분의 방문 하루 전에 온라인으로 이루어져야 합니다.
➡ Reservations should be made online _____ one day before your visit.

28 모든 참석자는 강연자의 무료 책 한 부를 받을 것입니다.
➡ All _____ will receive a free copy of the lecturer's book.

29 제출은 한 팀당 하나의 발명품으로 제한됩니다.
➡ _____ is limited to one invention per team.

30 참가자 수는 50명으로 제한될 것입니다.
➡ The number of participants will be _____ to 50.

JDA

성균관대학교 댄스 동아리

춤을 좋아하는 사람들이 모여 함께 즐기는 JDA(제이다)는 제일 좋아서 제이다!

JDA는 성균관대학교 인문사회과학캠퍼스 중앙 댄스 동아리입니다.

JDA는 Jazz Dance Association의 약자이며, 재즈 댄스를 중심으로 시작했지만
지금은 얼반(Urban), 코리오(Choreo), 방송 댄스 등 다양한 댄스 커버를 진행하고 있습니다.

JDA에서는 정기 공연, 입학식, 새내기 배움터, 드림 클래스, 대학생 거리축제 등
다양한 공연들을 진행하고 있습니다.

춤에 대한 관심과 열정이 있으신 분이라면,
춤을 춰본 적이 없더라도 춤을 좋아하기만 한다면
모두 환영입니다!

K 빈칸 완성하기

> 이 퍼즐 문제의 빈칸에 맞는 게 뭔지 아리송하네요.

> 빈칸의 주변을 뚫어지게 잘 살펴봐.

★ 유형 설명

빈칸이 포함된 문장, 절 이외의 나머지 부분을 통해 주제문이나 주제에 맞는 세부 내용을 완성해야 한다.

K 1 빈칸이 앞부분에 있는 경우

⚷ 글의 나머지 부분을 종합해야 하는 주제문인 경우가 많다.

K 2 빈칸이 가운데에 있는 경우

⚷ 주제를 뒷받침하거나 반박하는 세부 내용인 경우가 많다. 글의 흐름이 반전되지 않는지 주의해야 한다.

K 3 빈칸이 끝부분에 있는 경우

⚷ 글의 내용을 종합하여 주제문에 해당하는 결론을 완성한다.

🕶 유형 풀이 비법

1 빈칸 문장을 확인하라!
- 빈칸이 포함된 문장과 그 주변 문장을 주의 깊게 읽는다.

2 글의 주제를 추론하라!
- 반복해서 등장하는 핵심어를 위주로 글의 주제를 파악한다.

3 글의 전개 방식을 파악하라!
- 열거, 예시, 대조 등의 글의 전개 방식을 파악해서 빈칸이 어떤 내용에 해당하는지 찾는다.

> Tip 정답으로 고른 선택지를 빈칸에 넣은 후 전후 맥락과 자연스럽게 연결되는지 확인한다.

★ 최신 수능 경향 분석

대비 연도	월	문항 번호	지문 주제	난이도
2025	11	31번	외국어 체계의 기계적인 측면 너머에 집중할 수 있게 해 주는 문학	★★★
		32번	비판적 사고를 하게 하여 정신적 해방을 가져오게 하는 교육	★★★
		33번	광고 산업은 내 삶의 의식적인 시간을 포착하여 누군가에게 그것을 판매하는 데 바쳐진다.	★★★
		34번	규칙은 사람들의 행동을 촉진하는 관행과 역할을 확립한다.	★★★
	9	31번	빛에 의해 갇혀 있는 나방	★★★※
		32번	상업적 이익을 추구하는 투자로 결정되는 통신 기술 현대화	★★★
		33번	도시의 질을 측정하는 머물기 활동의 정도	★★★
		34번	타인과의 정서적 유대를 통해 개인이 형성된다고 한 Rousseau	★★★
	6	31번	디지털 환경에서의 정보 콘텐츠 보존	★★★
		32번	창의성을 위해 아이디어를 평가하고 선택하는 과정의 필요성	★★★
		33번	주관적 경험과 환경은 결합하여 결정에 영향을 준다.	★★★
		34번	음악의 기본적인 인식에는 일관성이 존재함	★★★

★ 2025 수능 출제 분석

31번과 32번의 오답률이 특히 높았는데, 지문 자체의 내용이 어렵다기보다는 선택지에 매력적 오답들이 있어서 정답을 고르기가 꽤 까다로웠다. 내용이 어렵지 않더라도 빈칸 앞뒤의 문맥을 정확히 파악하지 못하면 틀리기 쉬운 문제였다.

★ 2026 수능 예측

가장 문항 수가 많고, 배점도 높은 유형으로, 평균적인 난이도 역시 매우 높다. 1등급 대비, 2등급 대비 문항들을 집중 분석하고 훈련한다.

🔑 어휘 및 표현 Preview

- ☐ **involved in** ~에 관여된
- ☐ **preservation** 보존
- ☐ **operational** 운영의
- ☐ **address** 다루다
- ☐ **preserve** 보존하다
- ☐ **environment** 환경
- ☐ **information** 정보
- ☐ **inextricably** 불가분하게
- ☐ **physical** 물리적인
- ☐ **medium** 매체
- ☐ **regardless of** ~에 관계없이

- ☐ **employ** 사용하다
- ☐ **as long as** ~하는 한
- ☐ **copy** 복사본
- ☐ **cheaply** 싸게
- ☐ **original** 원본의
- ☐ **delicate** 취약한
- ☐ **relative to** ~에 비해
- ☐ **expect** 예상하다
- ☐ **migrate** 이동하다
- ☐ **ongoing** 계속되는
- ☐ **storage** 저장

- ☐ **transformation** 변환
- ☐ **discussion** 논의
- ☐ **moth** 나방
- ☐ **consensus** 합의, 의견 일치
- ☐ **trap** 가두다
- ☐ **sensory** 감각
- ☐ **overload** 과부하
- ☐ **minimal** 최소한의
- ☐ **hypothesis** 가설
- ☐ **subjective** 주관적인
- ☐ **architectural** 건축의

- ☐ **escape** 탈출하다
- ☐ **perceive** 인지하다
- ☐ **attempt** 시도하다, 애쓰다
- ☐ **structure** 구조
- ☐ **profitability** 수익성
- ☐ **advanced** 진보된
- ☐ **hopelessly** 어쩔 도리 없이
- ☐ **purpose** 목적
- ☐ **opportunity** 기회
- ☐ **target** 대상으로 삼다
- ☐ **reject** 거절하다

K ① 빈칸이 앞부분에 있는 경우

1st 빈칸 문장을 먼저 읽고, 빈칸에 들어갈 말에 대한 단서를 찾아보세요.
2nd 두 가지 대상을 대조하는 표현에 집중하면서 이어지는 내용을 파악하세요.
3rd 앞에서 파악한 내용을 바탕으로 가장 적절한 선택지를 골라보세요.

K01 ★★★ ·············· 2024 대비 9월 모평 34 (고3)

다음 빈칸에 들어갈 말로 가장 적절한 것을 고르시오. [3점]

Prior to photography, _____. While painters have always lifted particular places out of their 'dwelling' and transported them elsewhere, paintings were time-consuming to produce, relatively difficult to transport and one of-a-kind. The multiplication of photographs especially took place with the introduction of the half-tone plate in the 1880s that made possible the mechanical reproduction of photographs in newspapers, periodicals, books and advertisements. Photography became coupled to consumer capitalism and the globe was now offered 'in limitless quantities, figures, landscapes, events which had not previously been utilised either at all, or only as pictures for one customer'. With capitalism's arrangement of the world as a 'department store', 'the proliferation and circulation of representations ... achieved a spectacular and virtually inescapable global magnitude'. Gradually photographs became cheap mass-produced objects that made the world visible, aesthetic and desirable. Experiences were 'democratised' by translating them into cheap images. Light, small and mass-produced photographs became dynamic vehicles for the spatiotemporal circulation of places.

*proliferation: 확산 **magnitude: (큰) 규모
***aesthetic: 미적인

① paintings alone connected with nature
② painting was the major form of art
③ art held up a mirror to the world
④ desire for travel was not strong
⑤ places did not travel well

1st 빈칸 문장을 먼저 읽고, 빈칸에 들어갈 말에 대한 단서를 찾아보세요.

1) 먼저 빈칸 문장을 해석해 봅시다.

Prior to photography, / _____. //
사진이 나오기 전에는 / _____ //

● 빈칸에 필요한 단서는 무엇인가요?

사진이 나오기 전에는 무엇이 어떠했는지 파악해야 해요. 빈칸 바로 뒤 문장에 관련된 내용이 나올 것으로 예상할 수 있어요.

2nd 두 가지 대상을 대조하는 표현에 집중하면서 이어지는 내용을 파악하세요.

1) 빈칸 문장 바로 뒤에 While이 등장하는군요.

While painters have always lifted particular places /
화가들이 항상 특정한 장소를 들어 올려 /
out of their 'dwelling' / and transported them
그것의 '거주지' 밖으로 / 그것을 다른 곳으로 이동시켜 왔지만
elsewhere, / paintings were time-consuming to
/ 그림은 제작에 시간이 많이 걸렸고
produce, / relatively difficult to transport / and one-
/ 상대적으로 운반이 어려웠고 /
of-a-kind. //
단품 수주 생산이었다 //

● While은 문장에서 어떤 역할을 하나요?

역접의 연결어인 While은 ❶(_____)라는 의미로 뒤의 내용과 반대되는 내용을 언급할 때 쓰여요.

● 그림과 사진은 어떤 관계인가요?

특정 장소를 다른 곳으로 이동시키는 방법으로서 그림이 제시되었어요. 화가가 특정 장소를 그림에 담아 다른 곳에서도 볼 수 있게 옮기는 것을 의미하죠. 하지만 그림은 여러 면에서 불편했고, 그러한 불편을 해소하기 위해 사진이 발명되었을 것으로 예상할 수 있죠.
사진을 사용하면서 그림을 사용할 때보다 나아진 상황이 무엇인지 파악해야 빈칸을 채울 수 있어요.

2) 사진이 상황을 어떻게 바꿨는지 나타내는 문장이 후반부에 있네요.

With capitalism's arrangement of the world / as a
자본주의가 세계를 정리함에 따라 /
'department store', / 'the proliferation and
'백화점'으로 / '표현물의 확산과 유통은
circulation of representations ... achieved / a
… 달성했다 /
spectacular and virtually inescapable global
극적이고 사실상 피할 수 없는 세계적 규모를' //
magnitude'. //

● **표현물의 확산과 유통은 무엇을 의미하나요?**
우리는 앞에서 특정 장소를 다른 곳으로 이동시키는 방법으로서 그림에
대해 살펴봤어요.
그림은 하나를 만드는 데에도 시간이 오래 걸려서 확산이 어려웠겠지만,
그에 비해 사진은 사실상 무제한으로 찍어낼 수 있죠? 표현물의 확산과
유통이 세계적 규모를 달성했다는 것은 사진이 그만큼 쉽게 유통될 수
있다는 의미임을 알 수 있어요.

3) 마지막 문장에서 사진과 그림을 명확하게 대조했어요.

Light, small and mass-produced photographs /
가볍고 작고 대량으로 제작된 사진은 /
became dynamic vehicles / for the spatiotemporal
역동적인 수단이 되었다 / 장소의 시공간적 순환을 위한 //
circulation of places. //

● **앞서 확인한 그림의 단점들과 대비되는 사진의 장점이
제시되었어요.**
그림과 반대로, 사진은 가볍고 작고 대량으로 제작이 가능하다고 하네요.
그림의 모든 단점들을 개선한 이러한 장점들 덕분에 사진은 당연히
그림을 대체했을 것이라고 예상할 수 있어요.

● **사진이 어떤 수단이 되었다고 했나요?**
❷( )을 위한 역동적인 수단이
되었다고 했어요. 어려운 말처럼 보이지만 쉽게 말해, 특정 장소를
그림이나 사진으로 담으면 나중에 어느 때나, 어디서나 볼 수 있게 될
테고, 그렇게 장소가 순환된다는 것이에요.

3rd 앞에서 파악한 내용을 정리하여 적절한 선택지를 골라보세요.

1) 먼저 글의 내용을 보기 쉽게 정리해 봅시다.

사진이 나오기 이전	장소들이 잘 이동하지 않았다.
사진의 도입	그림과 다르게 복제가 가능해진 덕분에 표현물의 확산과 유통이 세계적인 규모를 달성했다.
사진의 역할	장소의 시공간적 순환을 위한 역동적인 수단이 되었다.

사진이 나오기 이전에는 장소들을 담고 이동시키는 것이 원활하지
않았지만, 쉽게 복제가 가능한 사진이 도입되면서 역동적으로 장소의
시공간적 순환이 가능해졌다는 내용이에요.

2) 이제 각 선택지의 해석을 보며 정답을 골라 봅시다.

① paintings alone connected with nature
그림만이 자연과 연관되었다
② painting was the major form of art
그림은 예술의 주요한 형식이었다
③ art held up a mirror to the world
예술은 세상을 비추는 거울을 떠받쳤다
④ desire for travel was not strong
여행을 위한 욕구가 강하지 않았다
⑤ places did not travel well
장소들이 잘 이동하지 않았다

● **위 선택지 중에서 빈칸에 알맞은 표현을 찾아봅시다.**
우리는 앞서 그림과 사진의 관계를 살펴볼 때, 특정 장소를 다른 곳으로
이동시키는 방법으로서 그 둘의 관계를 살펴봤죠? 마지막 문장에서 알
수 있듯이, 사진은 장소를 이동시키는 역동적인 수단이에요. 그렇다면
그림은 사진에 비해 덜 역동적인 수단이죠.
장소의 이동과 관련된 선택지는 딱 하나, 바로 **❸**( )이에요.

빈칸 앞뒤 문장에서
단서를 찾아내자!

K. 빈칸 완성하기   **187**

K02 ~ 05 ▶ 제한시간 8분

K02 ★★★ .... 2025 대비 수능 31 (고3)

다음 빈칸에 들어갈 말로 가장 적절한 것을 고르시오.

Literature can be helpful in the language learning process because of the _____ it fosters in readers. Core language teaching materials must concentrate on how a language operates both as a rule-based system and as a sociosemantic system. Very often, the process of learning is essentially analytic, piecemeal, and, at the level of the personality, fairly superficial. Engaging imaginatively with literature enables learners to shift the focus of their attention beyond the more mechanical aspects of the foreign language system. When a novel, play or short story is explored over a period of time, the result is that the reader begins to 'inhabit' the text. He or she is drawn into the book. Pinpointing what individual words or phrases may mean becomes less important than pursuing the development of the story. The reader is eager to find out what happens as events unfold; he or she feels close to certain characters and shares their emotional responses. The language becomes 'transparent' — the fiction draws the whole person into its own world.   *sociosemantic: 사회의미론적인 **transparent: 투명한

① linguistic insight
② artistic imagination
③ literary sensibility
④ alternative perspective
⑤ personal involvement

K03 ★★★ .... 2025 대비 수능 34 (고3)

다음 빈칸에 들어갈 말로 가장 적절한 것을 고르시오. [3점]

Centralized, formal rules can _____. The rules of baseball don't just regulate the behavior of the players; they determine the behavior that constitutes playing the game. Rules do not prevent people from playing baseball; they create the very practice that allows people to play baseball. A score of music imposes rules, but it also creates a pattern of conduct that enables people to produce music. Legal rules that enable the formation of corporations, that enable the use of wills and trusts, that create negotiable instruments, and that establish the practice of contracting all make practices that create new opportunities for individuals. And we have legal rules that establish roles individuals play within the legal system, such as judges, trustees, partners, and guardians. True, the legal rules that establish these roles constrain the behavior of individuals who occupy them, but rules also create the roles themselves. Without them an individual would not have the opportunity to occupy the role.   *constrain: 속박하다

① categorize one's patterns of conduct in legal and productive ways
② lead people to reevaluate their roles and practices in a society
③ encourage new ways of thinking which promote creative ideas
④ reinforce one's behavior within legal and established contexts
⑤ facilitate productive activity by establishing roles and practices

다음 빈칸에 들어갈 말로 가장 적절한 것을 고르시오.

There has been a lot of discussion on why moths are attracted to light. The consensus seems to hold that moths are not so much attracted to lights as they are _____ by them. The light becomes a sensory overload that disorients the insects and sends them into a holding pattern. A hypothesis called the Mach band theory suggests that moths see a dark area around a light source and head for it to escape the light. Another theory suggests that moths perceive the light coming from a source as a diffuse halo with a dark spot in the center. The moths, attempting to escape the light, fly toward that imagined "portal," bringing them closer to the source. As they approach the light, their reference point changes and they circle the light hopelessly trying to reach the portal. Everyone is familiar with moths circling their porch lights. Their flight appears to have no purpose, but they are, it is believed, trying to escape the pull of the light.

*moth: 나방 **consensus: 합의 ***diffuse: 널리 퍼진

① warmed   ② trapped
③ targeted   ④ protected
⑤ rejected

다음 빈칸에 들어갈 말로 가장 적절한 것을 고르시오.

We are _____ than we are of visual ones. We notice and dislike breaks in audio, defects in audio, and static in audio. A bit less so for things on the visual side. For example, if a video has some scan lines in it, within a short period, you will start to ignore them. If the visual signal streams in 1080 instead of 4k, eventually you'll get used to it. However, if there is static in the audio, you will want to shut it off rather than endure the whole program. Or if the audio continues to drop out, you also will barely be able to tolerate it. In fact, probably more than any other aspect of filmmaking, it is via the audio that people determine silently to themselves, "Good, professional quality" or "low-budget student production" as soon as the film begins. These reactions are not just from seasoned filmmakers and educators, but the instinctual, natural reaction of all audiences.

① less aware of the sound techniques in film
② less forgiving of technical sound mistakes
③ more forgetful of auditory experiences
④ less desirous of sound effects
⑤ more in need of hearing aids

K06 ✱✱✱ ·························· 2024 실시 5월 학평 31 (고3)

다음 빈칸에 들어갈 말로 가장 적절한 것을 고르시오.

As colors came to take on meanings and cultural significance within societies, attempts were made to _____ their use. The most extreme example of this phenomenon was the sumptuary laws. While these were passed in ancient Greece and Rome, and examples can be found in ancient China and Japan, they found their fullest expressions in Europe from the mid-twelfth century, before slowly disappearing in the early modern period. Such laws could touch on anything from diet to dress and furnishings, and sought to enforce social boundaries by encoding the social classes into a clear visual system: the peasants, in other words, should eat and dress like peasants; craftsmen should eat and dress like craftsmen. Color was a vital signifier in this social language — dull, earthy colors like russet were explicitly confined to the poorest rural peasants, while bright ones like scarlet were the preserve of a select few.

① export
② restrict
③ conceal
④ liberate
⑤ tolerate

K07 ✱✱✱ ·························· 2023 실시 4월 학평 33 (고3)

다음 빈칸에 들어갈 말로 가장 적절한 것을 고르시오. [3점]

Running a business that sells goods and services to consumers requires getting to know the products they like. More than that, however, you want to _____. In traditional or online sales, people are bound to favorably regard the vendor and product that they could easily inquire about and quickly acquire in good order. Using the product can increase or decrease their satisfaction, and they will remember to repurchase products that meet and exceed their expectations. Traditional stores make the shopping experience pleasant by their displays and personal service. Internet retailers lead buyers to products they want through speedy searches and clicks. A new online selling method that can generate millions of dollars in purchases within a few minutes is livestream selling. That's when hosts streaming their shows live demonstrate a product and even interactively receive comments and answer questions from their viewers through the power of social media. If they like the product, they buy it immediately through an e-commerce feature on the platform. Buyers say that the experience is so convenient, it is like talking to a friend.

① provide rare items that can draw others' eyes
② maximize the profit through competitive incentives
③ link positive experiences to the products they purchase
④ examine the current state of digital marketing technologies
⑤ convince yourself the product is a must-have in their lives

K08 ★★★ .... 2021 대비 9월 모평 31 (고3)

다음 빈칸에 들어갈 말로 가장 적절한 것을 고르시오.

"What's in a name? That which we call a rose, by any other name would smell as sweet." This thought of Shakespeare's points up a difference between roses and, say, paintings. Natural objects, such as roses, are not _____. They are not taken as vehicles of meanings and messages. They belong to no tradition, strictly speaking have no style, and are not understood within a framework of culture and convention. Rather, they are sensed and savored relatively directly, without intellectual mediation, and so what they are called, either individually or collectively, has little bearing on our experience of them. What a work of art is titled, on the other hand, has a significant effect on the aesthetic face it presents and on the qualities we correctly perceive in it. A painting of a rose, by a name other than the one it has, might very well smell different, aesthetically speaking. The painting titled *Rose of Summer* and an indiscernible painting titled *Vermillion Womanhood* are physically, but also semantically and aesthetically, distinct objects of art.

*savor: 음미하다 **indiscernible: 식별하기 어려운
***semantically: 의미적으로

① changed   ② classified
③ preserved   ④ controlled
⑤ interpreted

K09 ★★★ .... 2022 실시 10월 학평 34 (고3)

다음 빈칸에 들어갈 말로 가장 적절한 것을 고르시오. [3점]

If you are unconvinced that _____ _____, consider the example of the "flying horse." Depictions of galloping horses from prehistoric times up until the mid-1800s typically showed horses' legs splayed while galloping, that is, the front legs reaching far ahead as the hind legs stretched far behind. People just "knew" that's how horses galloped, and that is how they "saw" them galloping. Cavemen *saw* them this way, Aristotle *saw* them this way, and so did Victorian gentry. But all of that ended when, in 1878, Eadweard Muybridge published a set of twelve pictures he had taken of a galloping horse in the space of less than half a second using twelve cameras hooked to wire triggers. Muybridge's photos showed clearly that a horse goes completely airborne in the third step of the gallop with its legs *collected* beneath it, not splayed. It is called the moment of suspension. Now even kids draw horses galloping this way.

*gallop: 질주(하다) **splay: 벌리다 ***gentry: 상류층

① our beliefs influence how we interpret facts
② what we see is an illusion of our past memories
③ even photographs can lead to a wrong visual perception
④ there is no standard by which we can judge good or bad
⑤ we adhere to our intuition in spite of irresistible evidence

K10 ★★★ .... 2023 실시 7월 학평 31 (고3)

다음 빈칸에 들어갈 말로 가장 적절한 것을 고르시오.

Learning is *constructive*, not *destructive*. This means we don't _____ mental models — we simply expand upon them. To understand what I mean, think back to your childhood. There was likely a time when you believed in Santa Claus; your mental model accepted him and your predictions accounted for his existence. At some point, however, you came to recognize he was fictitious and you updated your mental model accordingly. At that moment, you didn't suddenly forget everything about Santa Claus. To this day, you can still recognize him, speak of him and embrace young children's belief in him. In other words, you didn't destroy your old mental model, you simply added new information to it. By building upon old mental models we are able to maintain ties to the past, foster a deeper understanding of concepts and develop an ever-expanding pool of information to draw upon in order to continually adapt to an ever-evolving world.

*fictitious: 가상의

① replace   ② imagine   ③ predict
④ analyze   ⑤ imitate

K11 ✽✽✽ .... 2021 대비 6월 모평 31 (고3)

다음 빈칸에 들어갈 말로 가장 적절한 것을 고르시오. [3점]

Research with human runners challenged conventional wisdom and found that the ground-reaction forces at the foot and the shock transmitted up the leg and through the body after impact with the ground _____ as runners moved from extremely compliant to extremely hard running surfaces. As a result, researchers gradually began to believe that runners are subconsciously able to adjust leg stiffness prior to foot strike based on their perceptions of the hardness or stiffness of the surface on which they are running. This view suggests that runners create soft legs that soak up impact forces when they are running on very hard surfaces and stiff legs when they are moving along on yielding terrain. As a result, impact forces passing through the legs are strikingly similar over a wide range of running surface types. Contrary to popular belief, running on concrete is not more damaging to the legs than running on soft sand.

*compliant: 말랑말랑한 **terrain: 지형

① varied little
② decreased a lot
③ suddenly peaked
④ gradually appeared
⑤ were hardly generated

K12 ✽✽✽ .... 2021 대비 6월 모평 33 (고3)

다음 빈칸에 들어갈 말로 가장 적절한 것을 고르시오. [3점]

Even when we do something as apparently simple as picking up a screwdriver, our brain automatically _____. We can literally feel things with the end of the screwdriver. When we extend a hand, holding the screwdriver, we automatically take the length of the latter into account. We can probe difficult-to-reach places with its extended end, and comprehend what we are exploring. Furthermore, we instantly regard the screwdriver we are holding as "our" screwdriver, and get possessive about it. We do the same with the much more complex tools we use, in much more complex situations. The cars we pilot instantaneously and automatically become ourselves. Because of this, when someone bangs his fist on our car's hood after we have irritated him at a crosswalk, we take it personally. This is not always reasonable. Nonetheless, without the extension of self into machine, it would be impossible to drive.

*probe: 탐색하다

① recalls past experiences of utilizing the tool
② recognizes what it can do best without the tool
③ judges which part of our body can best be used
④ perceives what limits the tool's functional utility
⑤ adjusts what it considers body to include the tool

K13 ✽✽✽ .... 2023 실시 7월 학평 32 (고3)

다음 빈칸에 들어갈 말로 가장 적절한 것을 고르시오. [3점]

A commonality between conceptual and computer art was _____. Conceptual artists decoupled the relationship between the art object and artist by mitigating all personal signs of invention. The artist became detached from the idea of personalized draftsmanship by installing a predetermined system — a type of instruction for another to follow. That way there was, as Sol LeWitt states, no "dependence on the skill of the artist as a craftsman." Effectively any person could carry out the instructions. The same process was at work in computer art, where artists devised a predetermined drawing algorithm for the computer automaton to carry out the instruction. The human agent initiated the conceptual form, and a machine actuated it. Likewise, the computer artwork lacked any autographic mark, trace of spontaneity, or artistic authenticity. The plotter arm would replace the human arm in the production process.

*mitigate: 완화하다 **actuate: 작동시키다
***plotter: 플로터(데이터를 도면화하는 출력 장치)

① the suppression of authorial presence
② the rejection of meaningless repetition
③ the elevation of ordinary objects to art
④ the preference of simplicity to elaboration
⑤ the tendency of artists to work in collaboration

다음 빈칸에 들어갈 말로 가장 적절한 것을 고르시오. [3점]

Everyone who drives, walks, or swipes a transit card in a city views herself as a transportation expert from the moment she walks out the front door. And how she views the street _____. That's why we find so many well-intentioned and civic-minded citizens arguing past one another. At neighborhood meetings in school auditoriums, and in back rooms at libraries and churches, local residents across the nation gather for often-contentious discussions about transportation proposals that would change a city's streets. And like all politics, all transportation is local and intensely personal. A transit project that could speed travel for tens of thousands of people can be stopped by objections to the loss of a few parking spaces or by the simple fear that the project won't work. It's not a challenge of the data or the traffic engineering or the planning. Public debates about streets are typically rooted in emotional assumptions about how a change will affect a person's commute, ability to park, belief about what is safe and what isn't, or the bottom line of a local business.

*swipe: 판독기에 통과시키다 **contentious: 논쟁적인
***commute: 통근

① relies heavily on how others see her city's streets
② updates itself with each new public transit policy
③ arises independently of the streets she travels on
④ tracks pretty closely with how she gets around
⑤ ties firmly in with how her city operates

다음 빈칸에 들어갈 말로 가장 적절한 것을 고르시오.

Even as mundane a behavior as watching TV may be a way for some people to _____. To test this idea, Sophia Moskalenko and Steven Heine gave participants false feedback about their test performance, and then seated each one in front of a TV set to watch a video as the next part of the study. When the video came on, showing nature scenes with a musical soundtrack, the experimenter exclaimed that this was the wrong video and went supposedly to get the correct one, leaving the participant alone as the video played. The participants who had received failure feedback watched the video much longer than those who thought they had succeeded. The researchers concluded that distraction through television viewing can effectively relieve the discomfort associated with painful failures or mismatches between the self and self-guides. In contrast, successful participants had little wish to be distracted from their self-related thoughts!

*mundane: 보통의

① ignore uncomfortable comments from their close peers
② escape painful self-awareness through distraction
③ receive constructive feedback from the media
④ refocus their divided attention to a given task
⑤ engage themselves in intense self-reflection

K16 ★★★ .... 2022 대비 9월 모평 34 (고3)

다음 빈칸에 들어갈 말로 가장 적절한 것을 고르시오. [3점]

Enabling animals to _____ is an almost universal function of learning. Most animals innately avoid objects they have not previously encountered. Unfamiliar objects may be dangerous; treating them with caution has survival value. If persisted in, however, such careful behavior could interfere with feeding and other necessary activities to the extent that the benefit of caution would be lost. A turtle that withdraws into its shell at every puff of wind or whenever a cloud casts a shadow would never win races, not even with a lazy rabbit. To overcome this problem, almost all animals habituate to safe stimuli that occur frequently. Confronted by a strange object, an inexperienced animal may freeze or attempt to hide, but if nothing unpleasant happens, sooner or later it will continue its activity. The possibility also exists that an unfamiliar object may be useful, so if it poses no immediate threat, a closer inspection may be worthwhile. *innately: 선천적으로

① weigh the benefits of treating familiar things with care
② plan escape routes after predicting possible attacks
③ overcome repeated feeding failures for survival
④ operate in the presence of harmless stimuli
⑤ monitor the surrounding area regularly

K17 ★★★ .... 2023 실시 4월 학평 34 (고3)

다음 빈칸에 들어갈 말로 가장 적절한 것을 고르시오. [3점]

In Hegel's philosophy, even though there is interaction and interrelation between the universal and the individual, _____. For Hegel, individuals are not distinguished in terms of Reason. In *Philosophy of Right* Hegel stresses particularity and universality as follows: "A man, who acts perversely, exhibits particularity. The rational is the highway on which everyone travels, and no one is specially marked." Here, Hegel maintains that individuals can be differentiated from each other in terms of their acts but they are not differentiated with respect to reason. There are specific thoughts, but they are finally resolved into the universal. One might say that Hegel seems to focus on the individual like Aristotle but in reality, he subtly treats the universal as fundamental whereas Aristotle considers the individual as primary substance and universal as secondary substance; in so doing Aristotle emphasizes the universal to be subordinate to the individual in contrast to Hegel. *perversely: 별나게

① an individual stands alone apart from the universe
② the universal still has more priority than the individual
③ universal truth cannot be the key to individual problems
④ individuals can't deduce universal principles from reality itself
⑤ every individual should have his or her own particular universe

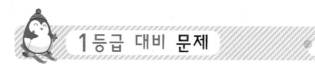

1등급 대비 문제

K18 ✪ 2등급 대비 .... 2022 대비 수능 32 (고3)

다음 빈칸에 들어갈 말로 가장 적절한 것을 고르시오.

News, especially in its televised form, is constituted not only by its choice of topics and stories but by its _____. Presentational styles have been subject to a tension between an informational-educational purpose and the need to engage us entertainingly. While current affairs programmes are often 'serious' in tone sticking to the 'rules' of balance, more popular programmes adopt a friendly, lighter, idiom in which we are invited to consider the impact of particular news items from the perspective of the 'average person in the street'.

Indeed, contemporary news construction has come to rely on an increased use of faster editing tempos and 'flashier' presentational styles including the use of logos, sound-bites, rapid visual cuts and the 'star quality' of news readers. Popular formats can be said to enhance understanding by engaging an audience unwilling to endure the longer verbal orientation of older news formats. However, they arguably work to reduce understanding by failing to provide the structural contexts for news events.

① coordination with traditional display techniques
② prompt and full coverage of the latest issues
③ educational media contents favoured by producers
④ commitment to long-lasting news standards
⑤ verbal and visual idioms or modes of address

K19 ⭐ 2등급 대비 .... 2022 대비 9월 모평 31 (고3)

다음 빈칸에 들어갈 말로 가장 적절한 것을 고르시오.

When examining the archaeological record of human culture, one has to consider that it is vastly _____. Many aspects of human culture have what archaeologists describe as low archaeological visibility, meaning they are difficult to identify archaeologically. Archaeologists tend to focus on tangible (or material) aspects of culture: things that can be handled and photographed, such as tools, food, and structures. Reconstructing intangible aspects of culture is more difficult, requiring that one draw more inferences from the tangible. It is relatively easy, for example, for archaeologists to identify and draw inferences about technology and diet from stone tools and food remains. Using the same kinds of physical remains to draw inferences about social systems and what people were thinking about is more difficult. Archaeologists do it, but there are necessarily more inferences involved in getting from physical remains recognized as trash to making interpretations about belief systems.   *archaeological: 고고학의

① outdated   ② factual
③ incomplete   ④ organized
⑤ detailed

K20 ⭐ 1등급 대비 .... 2021 대비 6월 모평 32 (고3)

다음 빈칸에 들어갈 말로 가장 적절한 것을 고르시오.

One of the great risks of writing is that even the simplest of choices regarding wording or punctuation can sometimes _____ in ways that may seem unfair. For example, look again at the old grammar rule forbidding the splitting of infinitives. After decades of telling students to never split an infinitive (something just done in this sentence), most composition experts now acknowledge that a split infinitive is *not* a grammar crime. Suppose you have written a position paper trying to convince your city council of the need to hire security personnel for the library, and half of the council members — the people you wish to convince — remember their eighth-grade grammar teacher's warning about splitting infinitives. How will they respond when you tell them, in your introduction, that librarians are compelled "to always accompany" visitors to the rare book room because of the threat of damage? How much of their attention have you suddenly lost because of their automatic recollection of what is now a nonrule? It is possible, in other words, to write correctly and still offend your readers' notions of your language competence.   *punctuation: 구두점   **infinitive: 부정사(不定詞)

① reveal your hidden intention
② distort the meaning of the sentence
③ prejudice your audience against you
④ test your audience's reading comprehension
⑤ create fierce debates about your writing topic

1st 빈칸이 포함된 문장을 읽고, 빈칸에 들어갈 말에 대한 단서를 얻으세요.
2nd 글의 나머지 부분을 읽고, 글의 내용을 이해하세요.
3rd 2nd 에서 이해한 내용을 선택지에서 고르세요.

K21 ★★❀·············· 2025 대비 6월 모평 33 (고3)

다음 빈칸에 들어갈 말로 가장 적절한 것을 고르시오. [3점]

Because the environment plays a significant role in aiding meaningful internal processes, subjective experience and the environment act as a 'coupled system.' This coupled system can be seen as a complete cognitive system of its own. In this manner, subjective experience is extended into the external environment and vice versa; the external environment with its disciplinary objects such as institutional laws and equipment becomes mental institutions that _____. A subjectively held belief attains the status of objectivity when the belief is socially shared. That is, even if we are trained as hard-nosed health care rationalists, or no-nonsense bureaucrats, or data-driven scientists, research has shown that our decisions are influenced by various institutional practices. They include bureaucratic structures and procedures, the architectural design of health care institutions, the rules of evidence and the structure of allowable questions in a courtroom trial, the spatial arrangement of kindergartens and supermarkets, and a variety of conventions and practices designed to manipulate our emotions.   *vice versa: 역으로 **bureaucrat: 관료

① affect our subjective experience and solutions
② serve as advocates for independent decision-making
③ position social experience within the cognitive system
④ comprise subjective interpretations of the environment
⑤ facilitate the construction of our concept of subjectivity

1st 빈칸이 포함된 문장을 읽고, 빈칸에 들어갈 말에 대한 단서를 얻으세요.

In this manner, / subjective experience is extended
이런 방식으로 / 주관적 경험은 외부 환경으로 확장되고
into the external environment / and vice versa; / the
/ 그 반대의 경우도 마찬가지여서 /
external environment with its disciplinary objects /
규율 객체를 지닌 외부 환경은 /
such as institutional laws and equipment / becomes
제도적 법률과 장비와 같은 / 정신적
mental institutions / that _____. //
제도가 된다 / _____ //

● 문장이 엄청 길어요. 차근차근 분석해 봅시다.
제도적 법률과 장비와 같은 규율을 갖춘 외부의 환경은 '어떤' 정신적 제도가 되는지를 말하는 부분에 빈칸이 있어요.
좀 더 문법적으로 설명하면, 이 문장의 핵심 주어는 the external environment이고 단수이므로 동사도 단수 동사 becomes가 왔어요. 그리고 뒤에 나온 mental institutions가 선행사이고, that은 주격 관계대명사 역할을 해요. 주어가 너무 길어서 해석이 어려울 수 있는 문장이에요.

● In this manner가 눈에 띄네요!
In this manner는 ❶ '(   )'라는 뜻으로 정답을 찾는 큰 단서가 될 수 있어요.
빈칸 문장은 외부의 환경이 '어떤' 정신적 제도가 되는지를 말하는 내용인데, 그렇다면 앞에서 말한 this manner가 무엇인지 파악하는 것이 빈칸 문장을 완성하는 데 있어 가장 먼저 할 일이겠죠?

2nd 글의 나머지 부분을 읽고, 글의 내용을 이해하세요.

1) 일단 앞부분을 살펴봅시다.

Because the environment plays a significant role /
환경이 중요한 역할을 하기 때문에

in aiding meaningful internal processes, / subjective
의미 있는 내적 과정을 돕는 데

experience and the environment / act as a 'coupled
주관적 경험과 환경은   / '결합된 시스템'으로

system.' //
작용한다 //

This coupled system can be seen / as a complete
이 결합된 시스템은 여겨질 수 있다   / 그 자체로 하나의

cognitive system of its own. //
완전한 인지 시스템으로   //

● **외부 환경과 주관적 경험에 대해 설명하고 있어요.**
　외부 환경이 내적 과정을 돕는 데에 중요한 역할을 해서, 외부 환경과
　개인의 주관적 경험은 결합된 시스템으로 작용한다고 했어요.
　그래서 이 결합 시스템은 완전한 인지 시스템으로 여겨질 수 있다고 했죠.

2) 이제 빈칸 뒤에 나오는 내용을 살펴봅시다.

A subjectively held belief / attains the status of
주관적으로 가지고 있는 믿음은   / 객관성의 지위를

objectivity / when the belief is socially shared. //
얻는다   / 그 믿음이 사회적으로 공유될 때   //

That is, even if we are trained / as hard-nosed
즉, 우리가 훈련되어 있다고 해도   / 엄격한 의료

health care rationalists, or no-nonsense bureaucrats,
합리주의자, 혹은 현실적인 관료, 혹은 데이터 기반의 과학자로서

or data-driven scientists, / research has shown / that
　　　　　　　　　　　 / 연구는 증명해왔다   /

our decisions are influenced by various
우리의 결정은 다양한 제도적 관행의 영향을 받는다고 //

institutional practices. //

● **앞에서 언급했던 주관적 믿음으로 문장을 시작하고 있어요.**
　주관적 믿음은 사회적으로 공유되면 **❷**(　　　　　)을 얻을 수 있다는
　것이죠. 다양한 제도적 관행은 우리의 결정에 영향을 끼친다는 것을
　연구는 증명해왔다는 설명이에요.

3rd **2nd** 에서 이해한 내용을 선택지에서 고르세요.

① affect our subjective experience and solutions
　우리의 주관적 경험과 해결책에 영향을 미치는

② serve as advocates for independent decision-making
　독립적인 의사 결정에 대한 옹호자의 역할을 하는

③ position social experience within the cognitive system
　인지 시스템 내에 사회적 경험을 배치하는

④ comprise subjective interpretations of the environment
　환경에 대한 주관적 해석을 구성하는

⑤ facilitate the construction of our concept of subjectivity
　주관성 개념의 형성을 촉진하는

지금까지 살펴본 내용에 따르면, 외부 환경과 주관적 경험은 영향을
주고받는 결합된 시스템으로 작용해요. 그리고 주관적 경험은 외부
환경으로 확장되고, 외부 환경은 주관적 경험에 영향을 미친다고 했어요.
제도적 법률과 장비 같은 외부의 환경은 '어떤' 정신적 제도가
된다고 했으므로 이것을 적절하게 표현한 선택지를 찾아야 하는데,
❸(　　　　　)이 바로 그런 선택지죠!

빈칸 문장을
먼저 읽자!

K22 ~ 25 ▶ 제한시간 8분

K22 ★★★ .... 2025 대비 수능 32 (고3)

다음 빈칸에 들어갈 말로 가장 적절한 것을 고르시오.

Education, at its best, teaches more than just knowledge. It teaches critical thinking: the ability to stop and think before acting, to avoid succumbing to emotional pressures. This is not thought control. It is the very reverse: mental liberation. Even the most advanced intellectual will be imperfect at this skill. But even imperfect possession of it _____ of being 'stimulus-driven', constantly reacting to the immediate environment, the brightest colours or loudest sounds. Being driven by heuristic responses, living by instinct and emotion all the time, is a very easy way to live, in many ways: thought is effortful, especially for the inexperienced. But emotions are also exhausting, and short-term reactions may not, in the long term, be the most beneficial for health and survival. Just as we reach for burgers for the sake of convenience, storing up the arterial fat which may one day kill us, so our reliance on feelings can do us great harm. *succumb: 굴복하다 **arterial: 동맥의

① intensifies people's danger
② enhances our understanding
③ frees a person from the burden
④ allows us to accept the inevitability
⑤ requires one to have the experience

K23 ★★★ .... 2025 대비 수능 33 (고3)

다음 빈칸에 들어갈 말로 가장 적절한 것을 고르시오. [3점]

We are famously living in the era of the attention economy, where the largest and most profitable businesses in the world are those that *consume* my attention. The advertising industry is literally dedicated to capturing the conscious hours of my life and selling them to someone else. It might seem magical that so many exciting and useful software systems are available to use for free, but it is now conventional wisdom that if you can't see who is paying for something that appears to be free, then _____.
Our creative engagement with other people is mediated by AI-based recommendation systems that are designed to trap our attention through the process that Nick Seaver calls *captology*, keeping us attending to work sold by one company rather than another, replacing the freedom of personal exploration with algorithm-generated playlists or even algorithm-generated art.

① all of your attention has already been spent
② the real product being sold is you
③ your privacy is being violated
④ the public may be sponsoring you
⑤ you owe the benefits to your friend AI

다음 빈칸에 들어갈 말로 가장 적절한 것을 고르시오. [3점]

One of the factors determining the use of technologies of communication will be the kinds of investments made in equipment and personnel; who makes them, and what they expect in return. There is no guarantee that the investment will necessarily be in forms of communication that _____. Because the ownership of investment funds tends to be in the hands of commercial organisations, the modernisation of communications infrastructure only takes place on the basis of potential profitability. Take, for example, the installation of fibre-optic communications cable across the African continent. A number of African nations are involved in the development but its operational structures will be oriented to those who can pay for access. Many states that might wish to use it for education and information may not only find it too expensive but also simply unavailable to them. There can be no doubt that the development has been led by investment opportunity rather than community demand. *fibre-optic: 광섬유의

① require minimal cost and effort to maintain
② are most appropriate for the majority of people
③ are in line with current standards and global norms
④ employ some of the most advanced technologies
⑤ promote the commercial interests of companies

다음 빈칸에 들어갈 말로 가장 적절한 것을 고르시오. [3점]

That people need other people is hardly news, but for Rousseau this dependence extended far beyond companionship or even love, into the very process of becoming human. Rousseau believed that people are not born but made, every individual a bundle of potentials whose realization requires the active involvement of other people. Self-development is a social process. Self-sufficiency is an impossible fantasy. Much of the time Rousseau wished passionately that it were not: *Robinson Crusoe* was a favorite book, and he yearned to be free from the pains and uncertainties of social life. But his writings document with extraordinary clarity _____. "Our sweetest existence is relative and collective, and our true *self* is not entirely within us." And it is kindness — which Rousseau analyzed under the rubric of *pitié*, which translates as "pity" but is much closer to "sympathy" as Hume and Smith defined it — that is the key to this collective existence. *yearn: 갈망하다 **rubric: 항목

① the necessity of philosophical study to understand human nature
② the development of self-sufficiency through literary works
③ the shaping of the individual by his emotional attachments
④ the making of the self-reliant man through his struggles
⑤ the difficulty of trusting other people wholeheartedly

K26 ✹✹✿..................... 2025 대비 6월 모평 31 (고3)

다음 빈칸에 들어갈 말로 가장 적절한 것을 고르시오.

When trying to establish what is meant by digital preservation, the first question that must be addressed is: what are you actually trying to preserve? This is clear in the analog environment where the information content is inextricably fixed to the physical medium. In the digital environment, the medium is not part of the _____. A bit stream looks the same to a computer regardless of the media it is read from. A physical carrier is necessary, but as long as the source media can be read, bit-perfect copies can be made cheaply and easily on other devices, making the preservation of the original carrier of diminishing importance. As the physical media that carry digital information are quite delicate relative to most analog media, it is expected that digital information will necessarily need to be migrated from one physical carrier to another as part of the ongoing preservation process. It is not the media itself but the information on the media that needs to be preserved.

*inextricably: 풀 수 없게

① platform   ② storage
③ message   ④ challenge
⑤ transformation

K27 ✹✹✿..................... 2024 실시 10월 학평 31 (고3)

다음 빈칸에 들어갈 말로 가장 적절한 것을 고르시오.

After we make some amount of scientific and technological progress, does further progress get easier or harder? Intuitively, it seems like it could go either way because there are two competing effects. On the one hand, we "stand on the shoulders of giants": previous discoveries can make future progress easier. On the other hand, we "pick the low-hanging fruit": we make the easy discoveries first, so those that remain are more difficult. You can only invent the wheel once, and once you have, it's harder to find a similarly important invention. Though both of these effects are important, when we look at the data it's the latter effect that _____. Overall, past progress makes future progress harder. It's easy to see this qualitatively by looking at the history of innovation. Consider physics. In 1905, his "miracle year," Albert Einstein revolutionized physics, describing the photoelectric effect, Brownian motion, the theory of special relativity, and his famous equation, $E=mc^2$. He was twenty-six at the time and did all this while working as a patent clerk. Compared to Einstein's day, progress in physics is now much harder to achieve.

① predominates   ② scatters
③ varies   ④ vanishes
⑤ fades

다음 빈칸에 들어갈 말로 가장 적절한 것을 고르시오. [3점]

Insect-eating plants' unique strategies for catching live prey have long captured the public imagination. But even within this strange group, in which food-trapping mechanisms have evolved multiple times independently, some unusual ones stand out. According to Ulrike Bauer, an evolutionary biologist, the visually striking pitcher plant *Nepenthes gracilis*, for example, can _____. This species' pitcher has a rigid, horizontal lid with an exposed underside that produces nectar, luring insects to land on it. When a raindrop strikes the lid's top, the lid jolts downward and throws any unsuspecting visitor into digestive juices below. Researchers used x-ray scans to analyze cross sections of the pitchers when the lid is raised, lowered, and in a neutral position. Their results revealed a structural weak point in the pitcher's neck: when a raindrop hits the lid, the weak spot folds in and forces the lid to quickly move downward, similar to a diving board. The weak point makes the pitcher's body bend and bounce back in a specific, consistent way, so the lid rises back up without bouncing too far — unlike a typical leaf's chaotic vibration when struck by rain.

*pitcher: 주머니 모양의 잎 **nectar: (식물의) 꿀
***jolt: 덜컹거리다, 흔들리다

① exploit external energy for a purpose
② hide itself with help of the environment
③ coordinate with other plants to trap insects
④ change its shape to absorb more rain water
⑤ modify its hunting strategy on a regular basis

다음 빈칸에 들어갈 말로 가장 적절한 것을 고르시오.

From about ages eight through sixteen, our manual dexterity has strengthened through continually improving eye-hand coordination. There is considerable improvement in handwriting skills. We gain mastery over the mechanics of language. We also gradually eliminate the logical gaps in our stories — characteristic of our earlier stage of perception — as intense preoccupation with the whole vision gives way to preoccupation with correctness. As a result, our writing and oral storying become increasingly conventional and literal, with an accompanying _____ of the spontaneity and originality that characterized our earlier efforts. At this stage our vocabulary is firmly grounded. We use words everyone else uses. We have little need to invent metaphors to communicate. By now we know that a star is "a hot gaseous mass floating in space" in contrast to our innocent stage, when we noticed, "Look that star is like a flower without a stem!"

*dexterity: (손이나 머리를 쓰는) 재주 **spontaneity: 즉흥성

① loss
② sense
③ increase
④ recovery
⑤ demonstration

K30 ✦✦✦.........................2024 실시 3월 학평 32 (고3)

다음 빈칸에 들어갈 말로 가장 적절한 것을 고르시오.

The commonsense understanding of the moral status of altruistic acts conforms to how most of us think about our responsibilities toward others. We tend to get offended when someone else or society determines for us how much of what we have should be given away; we are adults and should have the right to make such decisions for ourselves. Yet, when interviewed, altruists known for making the largest sacrifices — and bringing about the greatest benefits to their recipients — assert just the opposite. They insist that they _____. Organ donors, and everyday citizens who risk their own lives to save others in mortal danger are remarkably consistent in their explicit denials that they have done anything deserving of high praise as well as in their assurance that anyone in their shoes should have done exactly the same thing. To be sure, it seems that the *more* altruistic someone is, the more they are likely to insist that they have done no more than all of us would be expected to do, lest we shirk our basic moral obligation to humanity.

*altruistic: 이타적인   **lest: ～하지 않도록   ***shirk: (책임을) 회피하다

① had absolutely no choice but to act as they did
② should have been rewarded financially
③ regretted making such decisions
④ deserved others' appreciation in return
⑤ found the moral obligations inapplicable in risky situations

K31 ✦✦✦.........................2024 실시 3월 학평 33 (고3)

다음 빈칸에 들어갈 말로 가장 적절한 것을 고르시오. [3점]

Epictetus wrote, "A man's master is he who is able to confirm or remove whatever that man seeks or shuns." If you depend on no one except yourself to satisfy your desires, you will have no master other than yourself and you will be free. Stoic philosophy was about that — taking charge of your life, learning to work on those things that are within your power to accomplish or change and not to waste energy on things you cannot. In particular, the Stoics warned against _____. Often, Epictetus argued, it's not our circumstances that get us down but rather the judgments we make about them. Consider anger. We don't get angry at the rain if it spoils our picnic. That would be silly because we can't do anything about the rain. But we often do get angry if someone mistreats us. We usually can't control or change that person any more than we can stop the rain, so that is equally silly. More generally, it is just as pointless to tie our feelings of well-being to altering another individual's behavior as it is to tie them to the weather. Epictetus wrote, "If it concerns anything not in our control, be prepared to say that it is nothing to you."

*shun: 피하다   **the Stoics: 스토아학파

① making an argument without enough evidence
② listening to others' opinions without judgment
③ reacting emotionally to what is outside your control
④ pretending to have comprehended when you have not
⑤ rationalizing to yourself that the situation is out of control

다음 빈칸에 들어갈 말로 가장 적절한 것을 고르시오.

Some of the most insightful work on information seeking emphasizes "strategic self-ignorance," understood as "the use of ignorance as an excuse to engage excessively in pleasurable activities that may be harmful to one's future self." The idea here is that if people are present-biased, they might avoid information that would _____ — perhaps because it would produce guilt or shame, perhaps because it would suggest an aggregate trade-off that would counsel against engaging in such activities. St. Augustine famously said, "God give me chastity — tomorrow." Present-biased agents think: "Please let me know the risks — tomorrow." Whenever people are thinking about engaging in an activity with short-term benefits but long-term costs, they might prefer to delay receipt of important information. The same point might hold about information that could make people sad or mad: "Please tell me what I need to know — tomorrow."

*aggregate: 합계의 **chastity: 정결

① highlight the value of preferred activities
② make current activities less attractive
③ cut their attachment to past activities
④ enable them to enjoy more activities
⑤ potentially become known to others

다음 빈칸에 들어갈 말로 가장 적절한 것을 고르시오.

People have always needed to eat, and they always will. Rising emphasis on self-expression values does not put an end to material desires. But prevailing economic orientations are gradually being reshaped. People who work in the knowledge sector continue to seek high salaries, but they place equal or greater emphasis on doing stimulating work and being able to follow their own time schedules. Consumption is becoming progressively less determined by the need for sustenance and the practical use of the goods consumed. People still eat, but a growing component of food's value is determined by its _____ aspects. People pay a premium to eat exotic cuisines that provide an interesting experience or that symbolize a distinctive life-style. The publics of postindustrial societies place growing emphasis on "political consumerism," such as boycotting goods whose production violates ecological or ethical standards. Consumption is less and less a matter of sustenance and more and more a question of life-style — and choice.

*prevail: 우세하다 **cuisine: 요리

① quantitative
② nonmaterial
③ nutritional
④ invariable
⑤ economic

K34 ✽✽✽ .... 2022 실시 7월 학평 31 (고3)

다음 빈칸에 들어갈 말로 가장 적절한 것을 고르시오.

There is a difference between a newsworthy event and news. A newsworthy event will not necessarily become news, just as news is often about an event that is not, in itself, newsworthy. We can define news as an event that is recorded in the news media, regardless of whether it is about a newsworthy event. The very fact of its transmission means that it is regarded as news, even if we struggle to understand why that particular story has been selected from all the other events happening at the same time that have been ignored. News selection is _____ so not all events seen as newsworthy by some people will make it to the news. All journalists are familiar with the scenario where they are approached by someone with the words 'I've got a great story for you'. For them, it is a major news event, but for the journalist it might be something to ignore.

① subjective ② passive
③ straightforward ④ consistent
⑤ crucial

K35 ✽✽✽ .... 2024 대비 6월 모평 32 (고3)

다음 빈칸에 들어갈 말로 가장 적절한 것을 고르시오.

In labor-sharing groups, people contribute labor to other people on a regular basis (for seasonal agricultural work such as harvesting) or on an irregular basis (in the event of a crisis such as the need to rebuild a barn damaged by fire). Labor sharing groups are part of what has been called a "moral economy" since no one keeps formal records on how much any family puts in or takes out. Instead, accounting is _____. The group has a sense of moral community based on years of trust and sharing. In a certain community of North America, labor sharing is a major economic factor of social cohesion. When a family needs a new barn or faces repair work that requires group labor, a barn-raising party is called.

Many families show up to help. Adult men provide manual labor, and adult women provide food for the event. Later, when another family needs help, they call on the same people.

*cohesion: 응집성

① legally established
② regularly reported
③ socially regulated
④ manually calculated
⑤ carefully documented

K36 ✽✽❉ .... 2023 실시 4월 학평 32 (고3)

다음 빈칸에 들어갈 말로 가장 적절한 것을 고르시오.

Animals arguably make art. The male bowerbirds of New Guinea and Australia dedicate huge fractions of their time and energy to creating elaborate structures from twigs, flowers, berries, beetle wings, and even colorful trash. These are the backdrops to their complex mating dances, which include acrobatic moves and even imitations of other species. What's most amazing about the towers and "bowers" they construct is that they aren't stereotyped like a beehive or hummingbird nest. Each one is different. Artistic skill, along with fine craftsbirdship, is rewarded by the females. Many researchers suggest these displays are used by the females to gauge the cognitive abilities of her potential mates, but Darwin thought that she was actually attracted to their *beauty*. In other words, the bowers _____; they are appreciated by the females for their own sake, much as we appreciate a painting or a bouquet of spring flowers. A 2013 study looked at whether bowerbirds that did better on cognitive tests were more successful at attracting mates. They were not, suggesting whatever the females are looking for, it isn't a straightforward indicator of cognitive ability.

① block any possibility of reproduction
② aren't simply signals of mate quality
③ hardly sustain their forms long enough
④ don't let the mating competition overheat
⑤ can be a direct indicator of aggressiveness

다음 빈칸에 들어갈 말로 가장 적절한 것을 고르시오. [3점]

Innate behaviors used for finding food, such as grazing, scavenging, or hunting, are more dependent on learning than behaviors used to consume food. Mating, nesting, eating, and prey-killing behaviors tend to be governed more by instinct. The greater dependence on learning to find food makes animals in the wild _____. Behaviors used to kill or consume food can be the same in any environment. Ernst Mayr, an evolutionary biologist, called these different behavioral systems "open" or "closed" to the effects of experience. A lion hunting her prey is an example of an open system. The hunting female lion recognizes her prey from a distance and approaches it carefully. Charles Herrick, a neurobiologist, wrote, "the details of the hunt vary every time she hunts. Therefore no combination of simple reflex arcs laid down in the nervous system will be adequate to meet the infinite variations of the requirements for obtaining food."

*scavenge: 동물의 사체를 찾아 다니다
**reflex arc: 반사궁(충격이 통과하여 반사를 형성하는 신경 경로)

① less cooperative with others in their community
② less focused on monitoring predators' approaches
③ more intelligent to build their natural surroundings
④ more sensitive to visual information than any other stimuli
⑤ more flexible and able to adapt to a variety of environments

다음 빈칸에 들어갈 말로 가장 적절한 것을 고르시오.

In the classic model of the Sumerian economy, the temple functioned as an administrative authority governing commodity production, collection, and redistribution. The discovery of administrative tablets from the temple complexes at Uruk suggests that token use and consequently writing evolved as a tool of centralized economic governance. Given the lack of archaeological evidence from Uruk-period domestic sites, it is not clear whether individuals also used the system for _____. For that matter, it is not clear how widespread literacy was at its beginnings. The use of identifiable symbols and pictograms on the early tablets is consistent with administrators needing a lexicon that was mutually intelligible by literate and nonliterate parties. As cuneiform script became more abstract, literacy must have become increasingly important to ensure one understood what he or she had agreed to.

*archaeological: 고고학적인 **lexicon: 어휘 목록
***cuneiform script: 쐐기 문자

① religious events
② personal agreements
③ communal responsibilities
④ historical records
⑤ power shifts

K39 ✳✳✳ .... 2023 실시 7월 학평 34 (고3)

다음 빈칸에 들어갈 말로 가장 적절한 것을 고르시오. [3점]

The revolution's victorious party can claim to have resolved the fundamental anomalies of the old paradigm and to have renewed the prospects for successful research governed by shared assumptions. Indeed, the new community typically rewrites the textbooks, and retells its own history, to reflect this point of view. But from the standpoint of the losers, or even of those who look on impartially, such rewritings might seem to mark change without any genuine claim to progress, because there is no neutral standard by which to assess the merits of the change. The resulting body of knowledge is in any case not cumulative, since much of what was previously known (or merely believed) had to be excluded without ever having been conclusively refuted. One likewise cannot plausibly talk about revolutionary reconstitutions of science as aiming toward truth, for similarly, there can be no _____. The available justification of scientific knowledge after revolutions, couched in new terms according to newly instituted standards, may well be sufficient, but perhaps only because these standards and terms are now inevitably our own.

*anomaly: 변칙, 이례 **refute: 반박하다
***plausibly: 그럴듯하게

① official connection between scientists and policy makers
② impartial formulation of standards for its assessment
③ incomplete terms to describe the reconstitutions
④ easy process to learn about new scientific theories
⑤ strong belief that scientific progress benefits everyone

K40 ✳✳✳ .... 2024 대비 9월 모평 31 (고3)

다음 빈칸에 들어갈 말로 가장 적절한 것을 고르시오.

In the post-World War II years after 1945, unparalleled economic growth fueled a building boom and a massive migration from the central cities to the new suburban areas. The suburbs were far more dependent on the automobile, signaling the shift from primary dependence on public transportation to private cars. Soon this led to the construction of better highways and freeways and the decline and even loss of public transportation. With all of these changes came a _____ of leisure. As more people owned their own homes, with more space inside and lovely yards outside, their recreation and leisure time was increasingly centered around the home or, at most, the neighborhood. One major activity of this home-based leisure was watching television. No longer did one have to ride the trolly to the theater to watch a movie; similar entertainment was available for free and more conveniently from television.

*unparalleled: 유례없는

① downfall
② uniformity
③ restoration
④ privatization
⑤ customization

다음 빈칸에 들어갈 말로 가장 적절한 것을 고르시오. [3점]

Protopia is a state of becoming, rather than a destination. It is a process. In the protopian mode, things are better today than they were yesterday, although only a little better. It is incremental improvement or mild progress. The "pro" in protopian stems from the notions of process and progress. This subtle progress is not dramatic, not exciting. It is easy to miss because a protopia generates almost as many new problems as new benefits. The problems of today were caused by yesterday's technological successes, and the technological solutions to today's problems will cause the problems of tomorrow. This circular expansion of both problems and solutions _____. Ever since the Enlightenment and the invention of science, we've managed to create a tiny bit more than we've destroyed each year. But that few percent positive difference is compounded over decades into what we might call civilization. Its benefits never star in movies.

*incremental: 증가의 **compound: 조합하다

① conceals the limits of innovations at the present time
② makes it difficult to predict the future with confidence
③ motivates us to quickly achieve a protopian civilization
④ hides a steady accumulation of small net benefits over time
⑤ produces a considerable change in technological successes

다음 빈칸에 들어갈 말로 가장 적절한 것을 고르시오. [3점]

It is important to recognise the interdependence between individual, culturally formed actions and the state of cultural integration. People work within the forms provided by the cultural patterns that they have internalised, however contradictory these may be. Ideas are worked out as logical implications or consequences of other accepted ideas, and it is in this way that cultural innovations and discoveries are possible. New ideas are discovered through logical reasoning, but such discoveries are inherent in and integral to the conceptual system and are made possible only because of the acceptance of its premises. For example, the discoveries of new prime numbers are 'real' consequences of the particular number system employed. Thus, cultural ideas show 'advances' and 'developments' because they _____. The cumulative work of many individuals produces a corpus of knowledge within which certain 'discoveries' become possible or more likely. Such discoveries are 'ripe' and could not have occurred earlier and are also likely to be made simultaneously by numbers of individuals.

*corpus: 집적(集積) **simultaneously: 동시에

① are outgrowths of previous ideas
② stem from abstract reasoning ability
③ form the basis of cultural universalism
④ emerge between people of the same age
⑤ promote individuals' innovative thinking

K43 ★★★ .... 2024 대비 9월 모평 32 (고3)

다음 빈칸에 들어갈 말로 가장 적절한 것을 고르시오.

Many people create and share pictures and videos on the Internet. The difficulty is finding what you want. Typically, people want to search using words (rather than, say, example sketches). Because most pictures don't come with words attached, it is natural to try and build tagging systems that tag images with relevant words. The underlying machinery is straightforward — we apply image classification and object detection methods and tag the image with the output words. But tags aren't _____. It matters who is doing what, and tags don't capture this. For example, tagging a picture of a cat in the street with the object categories "cat", "street", "trash can" and "fish bones" leaves out the information that the cat is pulling the fish bones out of an open trash can on the street.

① a set of words that allow users to identify an individual object

② a comprehensive description of what is happening in an image

③ a reliable resource for categorizing information by pictures

④ a primary means of organizing a sequential order of words

⑤ a useful filter for sorting similar but not identical images

K44 ★★✵ .... 2023 실시 10월 학평 31 (고3)

다음 빈칸에 들어갈 말로 가장 적절한 것을 고르시오.

There's reason to worry that an eyes-on-the-prize mentality could be a mistake. Lots of research shows that we tend to be over-confident about how easy it is to be self-disciplined. This is why so many of us optimistically buy expensive gym memberships when paying per-visit fees would be cheaper, register for online classes we'll never complete, and purchase family-size chips on discount to trim our monthly snack budget, only to consume every last crumb in a single sitting. We think "future me" will be able to make good choices, but too often "present me" gives in to temptation. People have a remarkable ability to _____ their own failures. Even when we flounder again and again, many of us manage to maintain a rosy optimism about our ability to do better next time rather than learning from our past mistakes. We cling to fresh starts and other reasons to stay upbeat, which may help us get out of bed in the morning but can prevent us from approaching change in the smartest possible way.

*crumb: 부스러기 **flounder: 실패하다 ***upbeat: 낙관적인

① criticize
② remind
③ ignore
④ detect
⑤ overestimate

다음 빈칸에 들어갈 말로 가장 적절한 것을 고르시오.

Ecological health depends on keeping the surface of the earth rich in humus and minerals so that it can provide a foundation for healthy plant and animal life. The situation is disrupted if the soil loses these raw materials or if _____ _____. When man goes beneath the surface of the earth and drags out minerals or other compounds that did not evolve as part of this system, then problems follow. The mining of lead and cadmium are examples of this. Petroleum is also a substance that has been dug out of the bowels of the earth and introduced into the surface ecology by man. Though it is formed from plant matter, the highly reduced carbon compounds that result are often toxic to living protoplasm. In some cases this is true of even very tiny amounts, as in the case of "polychlorinated biphenyls," a petroleum product which can cause cancer.

*humus: 부식토, 부엽토 **protoplasm: 원형질

① the number of plants on it increases too rapidly
② it stops providing enough nourishment for humans
③ climate change transforms its chemical components
④ alien species prevail and deplete resources around it
⑤ great quantities of contaminants are introduced into it

다음 빈칸에 들어갈 말로 가장 적절한 것을 고르시오.

People have always wanted to be around other people and to learn from them. Cities have long been dynamos of social possibility, foundries of art, music, and fashion. Slang, or, if you prefer, "lexical innovation," has always started in cities — an outgrowth of all those different people so frequently exposed to one another. It spreads outward, in a manner not unlike transmissible disease, which itself typically "takes off" in cities. If, as the noted linguist Leonard Bloomfield argued, the way a person talks is a "composite result of what he has heard before," then language innovation would happen where the most people heard and talked to the most other people. Cities drive taste change because they _____ _____, who not surprisingly are often the creative people cities seem to attract. Media, ever more global, ever more far-reaching, spread language faster to more people.

*foundry: 주물 공장 **lexical: 어휘의

① provide rich source materials for artists
② offer the greatest exposure to other people
③ cause cultural conflicts among users of slang
④ present ideal research environments to linguists
⑤ reduce the social mobility of ambitious outsiders

K47 ✱✱✱.......................... 2023 실시 10월 학평 33 (고3)

다음 빈칸에 들어갈 말로 가장 적절한 것을 고르시오.

A connection with ancestors, especially remote ones, is useful for getting a wide-angled, philosophical view of life. Whereas our immediate ancestors are notably skilled at helping us with the "little pictures," namely the particular, the trees — say, a problem with a boss — our remote ones are best for seeing the "Big Picture," namely the general, the forest — say, the meaning of our job. As modern people rush around blowing small problems out of proportion, thus contributing to a global anxiety epidemic, ancestral spirits have a broader perspective that can _____. When it comes to a trivial problem, for example, they'll just tell us, "This too will pass." They appreciate how rapidly and often things change. According to American anthropologist Richard Katz, for instance, Fijians say that from the ancestral viewpoint whatever looks unfortunate may turn out to be fortunate after all: "What may seem to be a horrible outcome … is seen in another light by the ancestors." The ancestors, it might be said, keep their heads when everyone around them is losing theirs.

*epidemic: 확산 **anthropologist: 인류학자

① calm the disquieted soul
② boost cooperation in the community
③ make us stick to the specific details
④ result in a waste of time
⑤ complicate situations

K48 ✱✱✿.......................... 2021 대비 9월 모평 33 (고3)

다음 빈칸에 들어갈 말로 가장 적절한 것을 고르시오. [3점]

Since human beings are at once both similar and different, they should be treated equally because of both. Such a view, which grounds equality not in human uniformity but in the interplay of uniformity and difference, builds difference into the very concept of equality, breaks the traditional equation of equality with similarity, and is immune to monist distortion. Once the basis of equality changes so does its content. Equality involves equal freedom or opportunity to be different, and treating human beings equally requires us to take into account both their similarities and differences. When the latter are not relevant, equality entails uniform or identical treatment; when they are, it requires differential treatment. Equal rights do not mean identical rights, for individuals with different cultural backgrounds and needs might _____ in respect of whatever happens to be the content of their rights. Equality involves not just rejection of irrelevant differences as is commonly argued, but also full recognition of legitimate and relevant ones.

*monist: 일원론의 **entail: 내포하다

① require different rights to enjoy equality
② abandon their own freedom for equality
③ welcome the identical perception of inequality
④ accept their place in the social structure more easily
⑤ reject relevant differences to gain full understanding

다음 빈칸에 들어갈 말로 가장 적절한 것을 고르시오.

More than just *having* territories, animals also *partition* them. And this insight turned out to be particularly useful for zoo husbandry. An animal's territory has an internal arrangement that Heini Hediger compared to the inside of a person's house. Most of us assign separate functions to separate rooms, but even if you look at a one-room house you will find the same internal specialization. In a cabin or a mud hut, or even a Mesolithic cave from 30,000 years ago, this part is for cooking, that part is for sleeping; this part is for making tools and weaving, that part is for waste. We keep _____. To a varying extent, other animals do the same. A part of an animal's territory is for eating, a part for sleeping, a part for swimming or wallowing, a part may be set aside for waste, depending on the species of animal.

*husbandry: 관리

① an interest in close neighbors
② a neat functional organization
③ a stock of emergency supplies
④ a distance from potential rivals
⑤ a strictly observed daily routine

다음 빈칸에 들어갈 말로 가장 적절한 것을 고르시오.

Fans feel for feeling's own sake. They make meanings beyond what seems to be on offer. They build identities and experiences, and make artistic creations of their own to share with others. A person can be an individual fan, feeling an "idealized connection with a star, strong feelings of memory and nostalgia," and engaging in activities like "collecting to develop a sense of self." But, more often, individual experiences are embedded in social contexts where other people with shared attachments socialize around the object of their affections. Much of the pleasure of fandom _____. In their diaries, Bostonians of the 1800s described being part of the crowds at concerts as part of the pleasure of attendance. A compelling argument can be made that what fans love is less the object of their fandom than the attachments to (and differentiations from) one another that those affections afford.

*embed: 끼워 넣다 **compelling: 강력한

① is enhanced by collaborations between global stars
② results from frequent personal contact with a star
③ deepens as fans age together with their idols
④ comes from being connected to other fans
⑤ is heightened by stars' media appearances

K51 ✲✲✲ .... 2023 대비 6월 모평 32 (고3)

다음 빈칸에 들어갈 말로 가장 적절한 것을 고르시오.

The critic who wants to write about literature from a formalist perspective must first be a close and careful reader who examines all the elements of a text individually and questions how they come together to create a work of art. Such a reader, who respects the autonomy of a work, achieves an understanding of it by _____. Instead of examining historical periods, author biographies, or literary styles, for example, he or she will approach a text with the assumption that it is a self-contained entity and that he or she is looking for the governing principles that allow the text to reveal itself. For example, the correspondences between the characters in James Joyce's short story "Araby" and the people he knew personally may be interesting, but for the formalist they are less relevant to understanding how the story creates meaning than are other kinds of information that the story contains within itself.

*entity: 실체

① putting himself or herself both inside and outside it
② finding a middle ground between it and the world
③ searching for historical realities revealed within it
④ looking inside it, not outside it or beyond it
⑤ exploring its characters' cultural relevance

K52 ✲✲✲ .... 2022 실시 4월 학평 32 (고3)

다음 빈칸에 들어갈 말로 가장 적절한 것을 고르시오.

When you are born, your neocortex knows almost nothing. It doesn't know any words, what buildings are like, how to use a computer, or what a door is and how it moves on hinges. It has to learn countless things. The overall structure of the neocortex is not random. Its size, the number of regions it has, and how they are connected together is largely determined by our genes. For example, genes determine what parts of the neocortex are connected to the eyes, what other parts are connected to the ears, and how those parts connect to each other. Therefore, we can say that the neocortex is structured at birth to see, hear, and even learn language. But it is also true that the neocortex doesn't know what it will see, what it will hear, and what specific languages it might learn. We can think of the neocortex as starting life _____ but knowing nothing in particular. Through experience, it learns a rich and complicated model of the world.

*neocortex: (대뇌의) 신피질

① having some built-in assumptions about the world
② causing conflicts between genes and environments
③ being able to efficiently reprocess prior knowledge
④ controlling the structure and processing power of the brain
⑤ fighting persistently against the determined world of genes

다음 빈칸에 들어갈 말로 가장 적절한 것을 고르시오. [3점]

While early clocks marked only the hour or quarter-hour, by 1700 most clocks had acquired minute hands, and by 1800 second hands were standard. This unprecedented ability to measure time precisely _____, which became a prime weapon of the Industrial Revolution. As the historian of technology Lewis Mumford argued, "the clock, not the steam engine, is the key-machine of the modern industrial age." Soon factory workers were clocking in, filling out timesheets, and being punished for lateness. With time sliced into smaller and smaller periods, business owners could measure the speed of their workers down to the second, and gradually increase the pace of the production line. Workers who tried to reject this strict control by "going slow" were swiftly fired. The cruel power of the clock fed the growing culture of utilitarian efficiency, so brilliantly depicted by Charles Dickens in his 1854 novel *Hard Times*, where the office of Mr. Gradgrind contained "a deadly statistical clock in it, which measured every second with a beat like a rap upon a coffin-lid."

*rap: 두드림   **coffin-lid: 관 뚜껑

① allowed workers to climb up the ladder of social class
② liberated workers but imprisoned employers in a time trap
③ found its most authoritarian expression in the factory clock
④ veiled the violent nature and the discipline of measured time
⑤ paved the way for workers to control manufacturing machines

다음 빈칸에 들어갈 말로 가장 적절한 것을 고르시오. [3점]

Gordon Allport argued that history records many individuals who were not content with an existence that offered them little variety, a lack of psychic tension, and minimal challenge. Allport considers it normal to be pulled forward by a vision of the future that awakened within persons their drive to _____. He suggests that people possess a need to invent motives and purposes that would consume their inner energies. Similarly, Erich Fromm proposed a need on the part of humans to rise above the roles of passive creatures in an accidental if not random world. To him, humans are driven to transcend the state of merely having been created; instead, humans seek to become the creators, the active shapers of their own destiny. Rising above the passive and accidental nature of existence, humans generate their own purposes and thereby provide themselves with a true basis of freedom.

*transcend: 초월하다

① alter the course of their lives
② possess more than other people
③ suppress their negative emotions
④ sacrifice themselves for noble causes
⑤ show admiration for supernatural power

K55 ★★★.................................. 2021 대비 수능 32 (고3)

다음 빈칸에 들어갈 말로 가장 적절한 것을 고르시오.

Choosing similar friends can have a rationale. Assessing the survivability of an environment can be risky (if an environment turns out to be deadly, for instance, it might be too late by the time you found out), so humans have evolved the desire to associate with similar individuals as a way to perform this function efficiently. This is especially useful to a species that lives in so many different sorts of environments. However, the carrying capacity of a given environment _____. If resources are very limited, the individuals who live in a particular place cannot all do the exact same thing (for example, if there are few trees, people cannot all live in tree houses, or if mangoes are in short supply, people cannot all live solely on a diet of mangoes). A rational strategy would therefore sometimes be to *avoid* similar members of one's species.

① exceeds the expected demands of a community
② is decreased by diverse means of survival
③ places a limit on this strategy
④ makes the world suitable for individuals
⑤ prevents social ties to dissimilar members

K56 ★★★.................................. 2024 대비 수능 32 (고3)

다음 빈칸에 들어갈 말로 가장 적절한 것을 고르시오.

A musical score within any film can add an additional layer to the film text, which goes beyond simply imitating the action viewed. In films that tell of futuristic worlds, composers, much like sound designers, have added freedom to create a world that is unknown and new to the viewer. However, unlike sound designers, composers often shy away from creating unique pieces that reflect these new worlds and often present musical scores that possess familiar structures and cadences. While it is possible that this may interfere with creativity and a sense of space and time, it in fact _____. Through recognizable scores, visions of the future or a galaxy far, far away can be placed within a recognizable context. Such familiarity allows the viewer to be placed in a comfortable space so that the film may then lead the viewer to what is an unfamiliar, but acceptable vision of a world different from their own.

*score: 악보　**cadence: (율동적인) 박자

① frees the plot of its familiarity
② aids in viewer access to the film
③ adds to an exotic musical experience
④ orients audiences to the film's theme
⑤ inspires viewers to think more deeply

K57 ★★★ .... 2024 대비 수능 33 (고3)

다음 빈칸에 들어갈 말로 가장 적절한 것을 고르시오. [3점]

There have been psychological studies in which subjects were shown photographs of people's faces and asked to identify the expression or state of mind evinced. The results are invariably very mixed. In the 17th century the French painter and theorist Charles Le Brun drew a series of faces illustrating the various emotions that painters could be called upon to represent. What is striking about them is that _____. What is missing in all this is any setting or context to make the emotion determinate. We must know who this person is, who these other people are, what their relationship is, what is at stake in the scene, and the like. In real life as well as in painting we do not come across just faces; we encounter people in particular situations and our understanding of people cannot somehow be precipitated and held isolated from the social and human circumstances in which they, and we, live and breathe and have our being.

*evince: (감정 따위를) 분명히 나타내다 **precipitate: 촉발하다

① all of them could be matched consistently with their intended emotions

② every one of them was illustrated with photographic precision

③ each of them definitively displayed its own social narrative

④ most of them would be seen as representing unique characteristics

⑤ any number of them could be substituted for one another without loss

---

1등급 대비 문제

K58 ～ 62 ▶ 제한시간 13.5분

K58 ⊘ 2등급 대비 .... 2023 대비 수능 34 (고3)

다음 빈칸에 들어갈 말로 가장 적절한 것을 고르시오. [3점]

We understand that the segregation of our consciousness into present, past, and future is both a fiction and an oddly self-referential framework; your present was part of your mother's future, and your children's past will be in part your present. Nothing is generally wrong with structuring our consciousness of time in this conventional manner, and it often works well enough. In the case of climate change, however, the sharp division of time into past, present, and future has been desperately misleading and has, most importantly, hidden from view the extent of the responsibility of those of us alive now. The narrowing of our consciousness of time smooths the way to divorcing ourselves from responsibility for developments in the past and the future with which our lives are in fact deeply intertwined. In the climate case, it is not that _____ _____. It is that the realities are obscured from view by the partitioning of time, and so questions of responsibility toward the past and future do not arise naturally.

*segregation: 분리 **intertwine: 뒤얽히게 하다
***obscure: 흐릿하게 하다

① all our efforts prove to be effective and are thus encouraged

② sufficient scientific evidence has been provided to us

③ future concerns are more urgent than present needs

④ our ancestors maintained a different frame of time

⑤ we face the facts but then deny our responsibility

다음 빈칸에 들어갈 말로 가장 적절한 것을 고르시오. [3점]

Elinor Ostrom found that there are several factors critical to bringing about stable institutional solutions to the problem of the commons. She pointed out, for instance, that the actors affected by the rules for the use and care of resources must have the right to _____.
For that reason, the people who monitor and control the behavior of users should also be users and/or have been given a mandate by all users. This is a significant insight, as it shows that prospects are poor for a centrally directed solution to the problem of the commons coming from a state power in comparison with a local solution for which users assume personal responsibility. Ostrom also emphasizes the importance of democratic decision processes and that all users must be given access to local forums for solving problems and conflicts among themselves. Political institutions at central, regional, and local levels must allow users to devise their own regulations and independently ensure observance.

*commons: 공유지 **mandate: 위임

① participate in decisions to change the rules
② claim individual ownership of the resources
③ use those resources to maximize their profits
④ demand free access to the communal resources
⑤ request proper distribution based on their merits

다음 빈칸에 들어갈 말로 가장 적절한 것을 고르시오. [3점]

Development can get very complicated and fanciful. A fugue by Johann Sebastian Bach illustrates how far this process could go, when a single melodic line, sometimes just a handful of notes, was all that the composer needed to create a brilliant work containing lots of intricate development within a coherent structure. Ludwig van Beethoven's famous Fifth Symphony provides an exceptional example of how much mileage a classical composer can get out of a few notes and a simple rhythmic tapping. The opening da-da-da-DUM that everyone has heard somewhere or another _____ throughout not only the opening movement, but the remaining three movements, like a kind of motto or a connective thread. Just as we don't always see the intricate brushwork that goes into the creation of a painting, we may not always notice how Beethoven keeps finding fresh uses for his motto or how he develops his material into a large, cohesive statement. But a lot of the enjoyment we get from that mighty symphony stems from the inventiveness behind it, the impressive development of musical ideas.

*intricate: 복잡한 **coherent: 통일성 있는

① makes the composer's musical ideas contradictory
② appears in an incredible variety of ways
③ provides extensive musical knowledge creatively
④ remains fairly calm within the structure
⑤ becomes deeply associated with one's own enjoyment

다음 빈칸에 들어갈 말로 가장 적절한 것을 고르시오. [3점]

Manufacturers design their innovation processes around the way they think the process works. The vast majority of manufacturers still think that product development and service development are always done by manufacturers, and that their job is always to find a need and fill it rather than to sometimes find and commercialize an innovation that _____. Accordingly, manufacturers have set up market-research departments to explore the needs of users in the target market, product-development groups to think up suitable products to address those needs, and so forth. The needs and prototype solutions of lead users — if encountered at all — are typically rejected as outliers of no interest. Indeed, when lead users' innovations do enter a firm's product line — and they have been shown to be the actual source of many major innovations for many firms — they typically arrive with a lag and by an unusual and unsystematic route.

*lag: 지연

① lead users tended to overlook
② lead users have already developed
③ lead users encountered in the market
④ other firms frequently put into use
⑤ both users and firms have valued

다음 빈칸에 들어갈 말로 가장 적절한 것을 고르시오. [3점]

The entrance to a honeybee colony, often referred to as the dancefloor, is a market place for information about the state of the colony and the environment outside the hive. Studying interactions on the dancefloor provides us with a number of illustrative examples of how individuals changing their own behavior in response to local information _____ _____. For example, upon returning to their hive honeybees that have collected water search out a receiver bee to unload their water to within the hive. If this search time is short then the returning bee is more likely to perform a waggle dance to recruit others to the water source. Conversely, if this search time is long then the bee is more likely to give up collecting water. Since receiver bees will only accept water if they require it, either for themselves or to pass on to other bees and brood, this unloading time is correlated with the colony's overall need of water. Thus the individual water forager's response to unloading time (up or down) regulates water collection in response to the colony's need.

*brood: 애벌레 **forager: 조달자

① allow the colony to regulate its workforce
② search for water sources by measuring distance
③ decrease the colony's workload when necessary
④ divide tasks according to their respective talents
⑤ train workers to acquire basic communication patterns

❖ 정답 및 해설 229 ~ 233p

1st 먼저 빈칸이 포함된 문장을 읽고, 빈칸에 들어갈 말에 대한 단서와 발상을 찾으세요.
2nd **1st** 에서 발상한 것들을 토대로 글을 읽으며 핵심 내용을 파악하세요.
3rd 이해한 내용을 바탕으로 선택지를 골라 빈칸 문장을 완성하세요.

K63 ★★❋............. 2023 대비 9월 모평 33 (고3)

다음 빈칸에 들어갈 말로 가장 적절한 것을 고르시오. [3점]

There was nothing modern about the idea of men making women's clothes — we saw them doing it for centuries in the past. In the old days, however, the client was always primary and her tailor was an obscure craftsman, perhaps talented but perhaps not. She had her own ideas like any patron, there were no fashion plates, and the tailor was simply at her service, perhaps with helpful suggestions about what others were wearing. Beginning in the late nineteenth century, with the hugely successful rise of the artistic male couturier, it was the designer who became celebrated, and the client elevated by his inspired attention. In a climate of admiration for male artists and their female creations, the dress-designer first flourished as the same sort of creator. Instead of the old rule that dressmaking is a craft, _____ was invented that had not been there before.

*obscure: 무명의 **patron: 후원자
***couturier: 고급 여성복 디자이너

① a profitable industry driving fast fashion
② a widespread respect for marketing skills
③ a public institution preserving traditional designs
④ a modern connection between dress-design and art
⑤ an efficient system for producing affordable clothing

1st 먼저 빈칸이 포함된 문장을 읽고, 빈칸에 들어갈 말에 대한 단서와 발상을 찾으세요.

Instead of the old rule / that dressmaking is a craft, /
옛 규칙 대신에   / 의상 제작은 공예라는   /
_____ was invented / that had not been there
_____이 만들어졌다   / 예전에는 없던 //
before. //

● **빈칸 문장은 어떤 내용인가요?**
의상 제작은 공예라는 것이 규칙이었던 예전에는 존재하지 않았던 '무엇'이 만들어졌다는 내용이에요. (단서)
이 빈칸 문장을 곰곰이 곱씹어보면, 빈칸에 필요한 게 무엇인지 알 수 있는데, 의상 제작을 공예로 여겼던 예전의 생각이 없어지고 새롭게 만들어진 현대의 의상 제작에 대한 생각이 빈칸에 들어갈 거예요.
즉, 글을 통해 현대에는 의상 제작을 '무엇'으로 생각하는지를 파악하면 빈칸에 들어갈 말을 알 수 있다는 말이죠.

● **그렇다면 우리는 글의 흐름도 예상할 수 있어요!**
예전과 달라진 현대의 무언가를 설명하는 글이라면, 글의 일부는 예전에 대해 이야기하고, 나머지는 현대에 대해 이야기할 것이라고 쉽게 예상할 수 있어요.
'의상 제작에 대한 생각'이 글의 소재이니까, 어떤 시기를 기준으로 그 이전에는 의상 제작을 공예로 생각했다는 내용이 나오고, 그 이후에는 의상 제작을 '무엇'으로 생각하게 되었다는 내용이 나오겠죠. (발상)
아마도 시간의 흐름대로 과거를 먼저 이야기하고 나서 오늘날을 이야기할 거예요.

2nd **1st** 에서 발상한 것들을 토대로 글을 읽으며 핵심 내용을 파악하세요.

1) 전반부는 정말 옛 시절에 대해 이야기하고 있어요.

In the old days, however, / the client was always
하지만 옛 시절에는   / 고객이 항상 주됐고
primary / and her tailor was an obscure craftsman, /
                / 그녀의 재단사는 무명의 장인이었다   /
perhaps talented but perhaps not. //
재능이 있었을 수도 있고 그렇지 않았을 수도 있는 //
She had her own ideas / like any patron, / there
그녀는 자기 자신의 생각이 있었고 / 여느 후원자처럼 / 유행하는
were no fashion plates, / and the tailor was simply
옷의 본이 없었으며   / 재단사는 그저 그녀의 생각에 따랐다
at her service, / perhaps with helpful suggestions /
                / 아마도 도움이 되는 제안을 가지고   /
about what others were wearing. //
다른 사람들이 입고 있는 것에 관한   //

- **In the old days에 □ 표시했나요?**

  빈칸 문장만 보고도 우리는 이 글이 전반부에는 예전에 대한 이야기,
  후반부에는 현대에 대한 이야기를 할 거라고 예상했는데, 정확하게
  들어맞았어요!

- **옛 시절에는 어땠다고요?**

  긴 문장이지만, 요약하면, 옛날에는 ❶(   ), 그러니까 의상
  제작자는 그저 고객의 생각에 따르는 장인이었다는 내용이에요.
  바로 이 내용을 빈칸 문장에서 '의상 제작은 공예라는 옛 규칙'이라고
  표현한 거죠.
  '공예(craft)'는 '물건을 만드는 기술에 관한 재주'라는 뜻으로, 의상을
  제작함에 있어 재단사는 창의성 등을 발휘하기보다는 고객이 생각한
  의상을 제작하기만 한다는 것을 나타내는 단어라고 볼 수 있어요.

- **중요한 건 현대의 생각이에요.**

  사실 옛날에 의상 제작을 어떻게 생각했는지는 굳이 글의 전반부를 전부
  해석하지 않아도 알 수 있어요. 빈칸 문장에서 동격절을 이용한 the old
  rule that dressmaking is a craft가 이 글의 전반부 내용의 핵심을
  요약해서 나타낸 거죠.
  빈칸은 현대의 생각이 무엇인지를 파악해야 채울 수 있지, 옛 시절의
  생각으로는 채울 수가 없어요.

2) 이제 후반부, 즉 현대에 대한 내용을 살펴봅시다.

  Beginning in the late nineteenth century, / with the
  19세기 후반에 시작하여   / 매우 성공적인
  hugely successful rise / of the artistic male
  부상과 함께   / 예술적인 남성 고급 여성복
  couturier, / it was the designer / who became
  디자이너의   / 바로 디자이너가   / 유명해졌고
  celebrated, / and the client / elevated by his inspired
  / 고객은   / 그의 영감 어린 관심에
  attention. //
  의해 치켜세워졌다 //

- **19세기 후반부터 생각이 바뀌기 시작했군요.**

  19세기 후반에 고급 여성복을 디자인하는 '예술적인' 남성 디자이너가
  매우 성공적으로 부상했고, 디자이너의 '영감'이 중요해졌다는
  내용이에요. '장인', '공예'라는 단어에서 '예술', ❷(   )'이라는
  단어로 흐름이 달라졌다는 것이 느껴지죠.

3) 의상 제작에 대한 현대의 생각에 쐐기를 박는 문장이 등장해요.

  In a climate of admiration / for male artists and
  찬탄의 분위기 속에서   / 남성 예술가와 여성을 위한 그들의
  their female creations, / the dress-designer first
  창작물에 대한   / 의상 디자이너는 처음으로 번영했다
  flourished / as the same sort of creator. //
  / 같은 종류의 창작자로서

- **의상 디자이너가 어떻게 번영했다고요?**

  남성 예술가와 여성을 위한 그들의 창작물이 찬탄 받는 분위기 속에서
  의상 디자이너도 같은 종류의 ❸(   )로서 번영했대요.
  여성복을 만드는 남성 디자이너도 앞서 말한 남성 예술가와 같은 종류의
  ❸(   )로 번영했다는 거니까, 의상 디자인도 예술로
  생각되었다는 말이고, 이러한 현대의 생각이 과거의 생각과 대조되는
  거예요!

3rd 이해한 내용을 바탕으로 선택지를 골라 빈칸 문장을 완성하세요.

  ① a profitable industry driving fast fashion
  패스트 패션을 주도하는 수익성 있는 산업
  ② a widespread respect for marketing skills
  마케팅 기술에 대한 광범위한 존중
  ③ a public institution preserving traditional designs
  전통 디자인을 보존하는 공공 기관
  ④ a modern connection between dress-design and art
  의상 디자인과 예술 사이의 현대적 ❹(   )
  ⑤ an efficient system for producing affordable clothing
  적정 가격의 의류를 생산하기 위한 효율적인 체계

- **의상 디자인이 예술이라는 현대의 생각을 반영한 선택지가 뭔가요?**

  '현대에는 의상 디자인을 예술로 본다'라는 글의 핵심 내용을 선택지에서
  '의상 디자인과 예술 사이의 현대적 ❹(   )'이라고 표현했네요!

> 빈칸에 선택지를 넣어보며
> 어울리는 정답을 찾아내자!

K64 ～ 67 ▶ 제한시간 8분

K64 ✱✱✱ .... 2025 대비 9월 모평 33 (고3)

다음 빈칸에 들어갈 말로 가장 적절한 것을 고르시오.

City quality is so crucial for optional activities that the extent of staying activities can often be used as a measuring stick for the quality of the city as well as of its space. Many pedestrians in a city are not necessarily an indication of good city quality — many people walking around can often be a sign of insufficient transit options or long distances between the various functions in the city. Conversely, it can be claimed that a city in which many people are not walking often indicates good city quality. In a city like Rome, it is the large number of people standing or sitting in squares rather than walking that is conspicuous. And it's not due to necessity but rather that

_____. It is hard to keep moving in city space with so many temptations to stay. In contrast are many new quarters and complexes that many people walk through but rarely stop or stay in.

*pedestrian: 보행자 **conspicuous: 눈에 띄는

① the city quality is so inviting
② public spaces are already occupied
③ public transportation is not available
④ major tourist spots are within walking distance
⑤ the city's administrative buildings are concentrated

K65 ✱✱※ .... 2025 대비 6월 모평 32 (고3)

다음 빈칸에 들어갈 말로 가장 적절한 것을 고르시오.

Creativity is commonly defined as the production of ideas that are both novel (original, new) and useful (appropriate, feasible). Ideas that are original but not useful are irrelevant, and ideas that are useful but not original are unremarkable. While this definition is widely used in research, an important aspect of creativity is often ignored: Generating creative ideas rarely is the final goal. Rather, to successfully solve problems or innovate requires one or a few good ideas that really work, and work better than previous approaches. This requires that people evaluate the products of their own or each other's imagination, and choose those ideas that seem promising enough to develop further, and abandon those that are unlikely to be successful. Thus, being creative _____.
In fact, the ability to generate creative ideas is essentially useless if these ideas subsequently die a silent death.

① does not stop with idea generation
② rarely originates from practical ideas
③ is often regarded as a shortcut to innovation
④ frequently gives way to unanticipated success
⑤ brings out tension between novelty and relevancy

K66 ✱✱✿ ⋯⋯⋯ 2024 실시 10월 학평 32 (고3)

다음 빈칸에 들어갈 말로 가장 적절한 것을 고르시오.

Behavior is, for the most part, a product of genes and brain neuropathways. Consider the elegant chemistry at work when living organisms move, think, behave, and act. Certainly, the environment is a factor here because it can influence *how* we act. An analogy would illustrate this adequately. Think of the environment as gasoline, and our body as the engine. Truly, the engine does not run without the gasoline, but all the intricate parts of the engine are the product of *physical architecture*, designed and assembled for a reactive purpose long before the gasoline is injected. Inject more gas and the engine accelerates, less, and it slows. The same is true for an organism. Behavior is a *response* to the environment. We have 'free will,' but the ultimate characteristic of that response can only act with respect to the architecture of our genes and our brain. In other words, the environment can, effectively, accelerate or slow down a potential behavior, but the engine for that behavior _____; therefore, the environment is but a catalyst.

*analogy: 유사점 **intricate: 복잡한 ***catalyst: 촉매, 기폭제

① malfunctions even with correct input
② is already built and functional
③ tends to shut down periodically
④ runs in an unpredictable manner
⑤ is subject to change without notice

K67 ✱✱✱ ⋯⋯⋯ 2024 실시 10월 학평 33 (고3)

다음 빈칸에 들어갈 말로 가장 적절한 것을 고르시오. [3점]

The social-cognitive revolution at 1 year of age sets the stage for infants' second year of life, in which they begin to imitatively learn the use of all kinds of tools, artifacts, and symbols. For example, in a study by Meltzoff (1988), 14-month-old children observed an adult bend at the waist and touch its head to a panel, thus turning on a light. They followed suit. Infants engaged in this somewhat unusual and awkward behavior, even though it would have been easier and more natural for them simply to push the panel with their hand. One interpretation of this behavior is that infants understood that the adult had the goal of illuminating the light and then chose one means for doing so, from among other possible means, and if they had the same goal, they could choose the same means. Similarly, Carpenter et al. (1998) found that 16-month-old infants will imitatively learn from a complex behavioral sequence only those behaviors that appear intentional, ignoring those that appear accidental. Young children do not just imitate the limb movements of other persons, they attempt to _____.

*social-cognitive: 사회 인지의 ** artifact: 인공물 *** limb: 팔다리

① avoid looking awkward in the eyes of family members
② reproduce other persons' intended actions in the world
③ accept the value of chance incidents that turn out helpful
④ behave in an unprecedented way that others have missed
⑤ undermine any goal that does not coincide with their own

K68 ★★★ .... 2024 실시 10월 학평 34 (고3)

다음 빈칸에 들어갈 말로 가장 적절한 것을 고르시오.

As an ideal of intellectual inquiry and a strategy for the advancement of knowledge, the scientific method is essentially a monument to the utility of error. Most of us gravitate toward trying to prove our beliefs, to the extent that we bother investigating their validity at all. But scientists gravitate toward falsification; as a community if not as individuals, they seek to disprove their beliefs. Thus, the defining feature of a hypothesis is that it has the potential to be proven wrong (which is why it must be both testable and tested), and the defining feature of a theory is that it hasn't been proven wrong yet. But the important part is that it can be — no matter how much evidence appears to confirm it, no matter how many experts endorse it, no matter how much popular support it enjoys. In fact, not only *can* any given theory be proven wrong; sooner or later, it probably will be. And when it is, the occasion will mark the success of science, not its failure. This was the crucial insight of the Scientific Revolution: that the advancement of knowledge depends on current theories _____.

*endorse: 지지하다

① holding true regardless of temporal and spatial constraints

② collapsing in the face of new insights and discoveries

③ shifting according to scientists' pursuit of reputation

④ being exposed to the public and enjoying popularity

⑤ leaving no chance of error and failure

K69 ★★⊗ .... 2024 실시 7월 학평 31 (고3)

다음 빈칸에 들어갈 말로 가장 적절한 것을 고르시오.

Motivation doesn't have to be accidental. For example, you don't have to wait for hours until a certain song that picks up your spirits comes on the radio. You can control what songs you hear. If there are certain songs that always lift you up, make a mix of those songs and have it ready to play in your car. Go through all of your music and create a "greatest motivational hits" playlist for yourself. Use the movies, too. How many times do you leave a movie feeling inspired and ready to take on the world? Whenever that happens, put the name of the movie in a special notebook that you might label "the right buttons." Six months to a year later, you can watch the movie and get the same inspired feeling. Most movies that inspire us are even better the second time around. You have much more control over your environment than you realize. You can begin _____ yourself consciously to be more and more focused and motivated.

① isolating ② denying

③ programming ④ silencing

⑤ questioning

다음 빈칸에 들어갈 말로 가장 적절한 것을 고르시오.

Businesses are realizing that the way they operate and the impact they have on the environment greatly impacts their ability to maintain customers. Transitioning from a linear way of producing products to a circular one won't be necessary only from an environmental perspective, but from a social and economic perspective as well. To minimize the negative impact on the environment, businesses will need to adjust the relationship they have with customers to maximize the value of the products they create. Rather than businesses viewing success as the number of products made per year, they will instead base their bottom line on the number of products *kept in use* per year. Though waste certainly creates a demand for companies to continue selling new products, eliminating waste doesn't have to eliminate demand. By prolonging the ownership of a product rather than selling it, new business opportunities emerge in the world of maintenance and repair. Though eliminating waste minimizes the need for new products, it certainly increases the need to service existing products. The circular economy will demand that new business models focus on _____.

① returning much of their profits back to society
② producing user-friendly items to meet customers' needs
③ maintaining products rather than on making new products
④ creating a new demand at the expense of the environment
⑤ encouraging consumers to express their opinions frequently

다음 빈칸에 들어갈 말로 가장 적절한 것을 고르시오. [3점]

The term *Mother Tree* comes from forestry. It has been clear for centuries that tree parents play such an important role in raising their offspring that they can be compared to human parents. A mother tree identifies which neighboring seedlings are hers using her roots. She then, via delicate connections, supports the seedlings with a solution of sugar, a process similar to a human mother nursing her child. Shade provided by parents is another form of care, as it curbs the growth of youngsters living under their crowns. Without the shade and exposed to full sunlight, the young trees would shoot up and expand the width of their trunks so quickly they'd be exhausted after just a century or two. If, however, the young trees stand strong in the shadows for decades — or even centuries — they can live to a great age. Shade means less sunlight and therefore considerably less sugar. _____, as generations of foresters have observed. To this day, they talk of what is known in German as *erzieherischer Schatten* or "instructive shade."

* crown: 수관(나무의 가지와 잎이 있는 부분)

① One can pleasantly cool down under the shade of large trees
② The trees manage to extend their roots towards the water source
③ The attempts to outgrow neighboring seedlings are likely to succeed
④ Mother trees provide shade to accelerate the growth of their offspring
⑤ The slow pace of life gently imposed by the mother tree is no accident

K72 ✿✿※ ⋯⋯⋯⋯⋯⋯⋯ 2024 실시 5월 학평 32 (고3)

다음 빈칸에 들어갈 말로 가장 적절한 것을 고르시오.

John Douglas Pettigrew, a professor of psychology at the University of Queensland, found that the brain manages the external world by dividing it into separate regions, the *peripersonal* and the *extrapersonal* — basically, near and far. Peripersonal space includes whatever is in arm's reach; things you can control right now by using your hands. This is the world of what's real, right now. Extrapersonal space refers to everything else — whatever you can't touch unless you move beyond your arm's reach, whether it's three feet or three million miles away. This is the realm of possibility. With those definitions in place, another fact follows, obvious but useful: any interaction in the extrapersonal space must occur in the future. Or, to put it another way, _____. For instance, if you're in the mood for a peach, but the closest one is sitting in a bin at the corner market, you can't enjoy it now. You can only enjoy it in the future, after you go get it.

① distance is linked to time
② the past is out of your reach
③ what is going to happen happens
④ time doesn't flow in one direction
⑤ our brain is attracted to near objects

K73 ✿✿✿ ⋯⋯⋯⋯⋯⋯⋯ 2024 실시 5월 학평 34 (고3)

다음 빈칸에 들어갈 말로 가장 적절한 것을 고르시오. [3점]

Many fish generate their own light in a biological firework display called bioluminescence. The lanternfish creates beams that sweep the sea like headlamps. The dragonfish produces wavelengths that only it can see, leaving its victims unaware of the approaching threat. In contrast, the anglerfish hopes its prey will notice and be lured toward its rod-like bioluminescent barbel; its fierce jaws stay hidden in the shadows. Bioluminescence is also used to frustrate predators. A species from the spookfish family relies on a bellyful of symbiotic, glowing bacteria to save it from becoming a meal. It uses the same concept developed by the US Navy during World War II to make bomber aircraft difficult to see. Just as Project Yehudi designed planes with under-wing spotlights, the fish's glowing belly conceals its silhouette against sunlight to hide it from watching eyes below. In this fish-eat-fish world, survival is

_____.

*barbel: (물고기의) 수염 **symbiotic: 공생의

① dependent upon communication within the same species
② a game of hide-and-seek that prioritizes the sense of sight
③ up to the ability to detect the subtle dance of sound waves
④ a competition to imitate the illumination of different species
⑤ a war where wider vision means better chances to catch prey

다음 빈칸에 들어갈 말로 가장 적절한 것을 고르시오. [3점]

Japanese used to have a color word, *ao*, that spanned both green and blue. In the modern language, however, *ao* has come to be restricted mostly to blue shades, and green is usually expressed by the word *midori*. When the first traffic lights were imported from the United States and installed in Japan in the 1930s, they were just as green as anywhere else. Nevertheless, in common parlance the go light was called *ao shingoo*, perhaps because the three primary colors on Japanese artists' palettes are traditionally *aka*(red), *kiiro*(yellow), and *ao*. The label *ao* for a green light did not appear so out of the ordinary at first, because of the remaining associations of the word *ao* with greenness. But over time, the difference between the green color and the dominant meaning of the word *ao* began to feel awkward. Nations that are less assertive might have opted for the solution of simply changing the official name of the go light to *midori*. Not so the Japanese. Rather than alter the name to fit reality, the Japanese government announced in 1973 that _____: henceforth, go lights would be a color that better corresponded to the dominant meaning of *ao*.

*parlance: 용어

① reality should be altered to fit the name
② language reflected what people had in mind
③ the go light should follow the global standard
④ the use of the word *ao* for go light would be banned
⑤ they would not change the color of go light in any way

다음 빈칸에 들어갈 말로 가장 적절한 것을 고르시오.

The growth of academic disciplines and sub-disciplines, such as art history or palaeontology, and of particular figures such as the art critic, helped produce principles and practices for selecting and organizing what was worthy of keeping, though it remained a struggle. Moreover, as museums and universities drew further apart toward the end of the nineteenth century, and as the idea of objects as a highly valued route to knowing the world went into decline, collecting began to lose its status as a worthy intellectual pursuit, especially in the sciences. The really interesting and important aspects of science were increasingly those invisible to the naked eye, and the classification of things collected no longer promised to produce cutting-edge knowledge. The term "butterfly collecting" could come to be used with the adjective "mere" to indicate a pursuit of _____ academic status.

*palaeontology: 고생물학 **adjective: 형용사

① competitive   ② novel
③ secondary   ④ reliable
⑤ unconditional

K76 ✱✱✱ .... 2024 대비 6월 모평 33 (고3)

다음 빈칸에 들어갈 말로 가장 적절한 것을 고르시오. [3점]

Whatever their differences, scientists and artists begin with the same question: *can you and I see the same thing the same way? If so, how?* The scientific thinker looks for features of the thing that can be stripped of subjectivity — ideally, those aspects that can be quantified and whose values will thus never change from one observer to the next. In this way, he arrives at a reality independent of all observers. The artist, on the other hand, relies on the strength of her artistry to effect a marriage between her own subjectivity and that of her readers. To a scientific thinker, this must sound like magical thinking: *you're saying you will imagine something so hard it'll pop into someone else's head exactly the way you envision it?* The artist has sought the opposite of the scientist's observer-independent reality. She creates a reality dependent upon observers, indeed a reality in which _____ in order for it to exist at all.

① human beings must participate
② objectivity should be maintained
③ science and art need to harmonize
④ readers remain distanced from the arts
⑤ she is disengaged from her own subjectivity

K77 ✱✱✱ .... 2024 대비 6월 모평 34 (고3)

다음 빈칸에 들어갈 말로 가장 적절한 것을 고르시오. [3점]

One of the common themes of the Western philosophical tradition is the distinction between sensual perceptions and rational knowledge. Since Plato, the supremacy of rational reason is based on the assertion that it is able to extract true knowledge from experience. As the discussion in the *Republic* helps to explain, perceptions are inherently unreliable and misleading because the senses are subject to errors and illusions. Only the rational discourse has the tools to overcome illusions and to point towards true knowledge. For instance, perception suggests that a figure in the distance is smaller than it really is. Yet, the application of logical reasoning will reveal that the figure only appears small because it obeys the laws of geometrical perspective. Nevertheless, even after the perspectival correction is applied and reason concludes that perception is misleading, the figure still *appears* small, and the truth of the matter is revealed _____.

＊discourse: 담화 ＊＊geometrical: 기하학의

① as the outcome of blindly following sensual experience
② by moving away from the idea of perfect representation
③ beyond the limit of where rational knowledge can approach
④ through a variety of experiences rather than logical reasoning
⑤ not in the perception of the figure but in its rational representation

다음 빈칸에 들어갈 말로 가장 적절한 것을 고르시오.

Humour involves not just practical disengagement but cognitive disengagement. As long as something is funny, we are for the moment not concerned with whether it is real or fictional, true or false. This is why we give considerable leeway to people telling funny stories. If they are getting extra laughs by exaggerating the silliness of a situation or even by making up a few details, we are happy to grant them comic licence, a kind of poetic licence. Indeed, someone listening to a funny story who tries to correct the teller — 'No, he didn't spill the spaghetti on the keyboard and the monitor, just on the keyboard' — will probably be told by the other listeners to stop interrupting. The creator of humour is putting ideas into people's heads for the pleasure those ideas will bring, not to provide _____ information.

*cognitive: 인식의 **leeway: 여지

① accurate   ② detailed
③ useful   ④ additional
⑤ alternative

다음 빈칸에 들어갈 말로 가장 적절한 것을 고르시오.

Genetic engineering followed by cloning to distribute many identical animals or plants is sometimes seen as a threat to the diversity of nature. However, humans have been replacing diverse natural habitats with artificial monoculture for millennia. Most natural habitats in the advanced nations have already been replaced with some form of artificial environment based on mass production or repetition. The real threat to biodiversity is surely the need to convert ever more of our planet into production zones to feed the ever-increasing human population. The cloning and transgenic alteration of domestic animals makes little difference to the overall situation. Conversely, the renewed interest in genetics has led to a growing awareness that there are many wild plants and animals with interesting or useful genetic properties that could be used for a variety of as-yet-unknown purposes. This has led in turn to a realization that _____ because they may harbor tomorrow's drugs against cancer, malaria, or obesity.   *monoculture: 단일 경작

① ecological systems are genetically programmed
② we should avoid destroying natural ecosystems
③ we need to stop creating genetically modified organisms
④ artificial organisms can survive in natural environments
⑤ living things adapt themselves to their physical environments

K80 ✱✱❋ .... 2021 대비 수능 33 (고3)

다음 빈칸에 들어갈 말로 가장 적절한 것을 고르시오. [3점]

Thanks to newly developed neuroimaging technology, we now have access to the specific brain changes that occur during learning. Even though all of our brains contain the same basic structures, our neural networks are as unique as our fingerprints. The latest developmental neuroscience research has shown that the brain is much more malleable throughout life than previously assumed; it develops in response to its own processes, to its immediate and distant "environments," and to its past and current situations. The brain seeks to create meaning through establishing or refining existing neural networks. When we learn a new fact or skill, our neurons communicate to form networks of connected information. Using this knowledge or skill results in structural changes to allow similar future impulses to travel more quickly and efficiently than others. High-activity synaptic connections are stabilized and strengthened, while connections with relatively low use are weakened and eventually pruned. In this way, our brains are _____ .

*malleable: 순응성이 있는 **prune: 잘라 내다

① sculpted by our own history of experiences
② designed to maintain their initial structures
③ geared toward strengthening recent memories
④ twinned with the development of other organs
⑤ portrayed as the seat of logical and creative thinking

K81 ✱✱✱ .... 2024 대비 9월 모평 33 (고3)

다음 빈칸에 들어갈 말로 가장 적절한 것을 고르시오. [3점]

An invention or discovery that is too far ahead of its time is worthless; no one can follow. Ideally, an innovation opens up only the next step from what is known and invites the culture to move forward one hop. An overly futuristic, unconventional, or visionary invention can fail initially (it may lack essential not-yet-invented materials or a critical market or proper understanding) yet succeed later, when the ecology of supporting ideas catches up. Gregor Mendel's 1865 theories of genetic heredity were correct but ignored for 35 years. His sharp insights were not accepted because they did not explain the problems biologists had at the time, nor did his explanation operate by known mechanisms, so his discoveries were out of reach even for the early adopters. Decades later science faced the urgent questions that Mendel's discoveries could answer. Now his insights _____ . Within a few years of one another, three different scientists each independently rediscovered Mendel's forgotten work, which of course had been there all along.

*ecology: 생태 환경 **heredity: 유전

① caught up to modern problems
② raised even more questions
③ addressed past and current topics alike
④ were only one step away
⑤ regained acceptance of the public

다음 빈칸에 들어갈 말로 가장 적절한 것을 고르시오.

Over the last decade the attention given to how children learn to read has foregrounded the nature of *textuality*, and of the different, interrelated ways in which readers of all ages make texts mean. 'Reading' now applies to a greater number of representational forms than at any time in the past: pictures, maps, screens, design graphics and photographs are all regarded as text. In addition to the innovations made possible in picture books by new printing processes, design features also predominate in other kinds, such as books of poetry and information texts. Thus, reading becomes a more complicated kind of interpretation than it was when children's attention was focused on the printed text, with sketches or pictures as an adjunct. Children now learn from a picture book that words and illustrations complement and enhance each other. Reading is not simply _____. Even in the easiest texts, what a sentence 'says' is often not what it means.

*adjunct: 부속물

① knowledge acquisition
② word recognition
③ imaginative play
④ subjective interpretation
⑤ image mapping

다음 빈칸에 들어갈 말로 가장 적절한 것을 고르시오. [3점]

One of the criticisms of Stoicism by modern translators and teachers is the amount of repetition. Marcus Aurelius, for example, has been dismissed by academics as not being original because his writing resembles that of other, earlier Stoics. This criticism misses the point. Even before Marcus's time, Seneca was well aware that there was a lot of borrowing and overlap among the philosophers. That's because real philosophers weren't concerned with authorship, but only what worked. More important, they believed that what was said mattered less than what was done. And this is true now as it was then. You're welcome to take all of the words of the great philosophers and use them to your own liking (they're dead; they don't mind). Feel free to make adjustments and improvements as you like. Adapt them to the real conditions of the real world. The way to prove that you truly understand what you speak and write, that you truly are original, is to _____.

*Stoicism: 스토아 철학

① put them into practice
② keep your writings to yourself
③ combine oral and written traditions
④ compare philosophical theories
⑤ avoid borrowing them

K84 ✱✱❀·····················2023 실시 10월 학평 32 (고3)

다음 빈칸에 들어갈 말로 가장 적절한 것을 고르시오. [3점]

The way we perceive the colors of the rainbow, and the universe in general, is influenced by the words we use to describe them. This is not limited to visual perception but also applies to smell, taste, touch, our perception of time and countless other human experiences. A wine or Scotch connoisseur, for example, has a much richer vocabulary at their disposal to describe the fullness, finish, flavors and aroma of the drink, which in turn improves their ability to recognize and remember subtle differences of which a non-expert may be unaware. Similarly, a chef or perfumer has at their disposal labels for flavors and smells that allow them to perceive, differentiate among, prepare and remember subtle variations. The labels that we have at our disposal influence how we see the world around us. Regardless of where you place the limits of linguistic effects on cognition, there is evidence that at least some of the things that we perceive and remember differ depending on _____.

*connoisseur: (예술품 · 음식 · 음악의) 감정가   **cognition: 인식

① where we purchase them
② how expensive they are
③ what labels we use
④ how persuasive ads are
⑤ who makes the products

K85 ✱✱❀·····················2021 대비 6월 모평 34 (고3)

다음 빈칸에 들어갈 말로 가장 적절한 것을 고르시오. [3점]

A large part of what we see is what we expect to see. This explains why we "see" faces and figures in a flickering campfire, or in moving clouds. This is why Leonardo da Vinci advised artists to discover their motifs by staring at patches on a blank wall. A fire provides a constant flickering change in visual information that never integrates into anything solid and thereby allows the brain to engage in a play of hypotheses. On the other hand, the wall does not present us with very much in the way of visual clues, and so the brain begins to make more and more hypotheses and desperately searches for confirmation. A crack in the wall looks a little like the profile of a nose and suddenly a whole face appears, or a leaping horse, or a dancing figure. In cases like these the brain's visual strategies are _____.

*flicker: 흔들리다

① ignoring distracting information unrelated to visual clues
② projecting images from within the mind out onto the world
③ categorizing objects into groups either real or imagined
④ strengthening connections between objects in the real world
⑤ removing the broken or missing parts of an original image

K86 ★★★ .... 2021 대비 수능 34 (고3)

다음 빈칸에 들어갈 말로 가장 적절한 것을 고르시오. [3점]

Successful integration of an educational technology is marked by that technology being regarded by users as an unobtrusive facilitator of learning, instruction, or performance. When the focus shifts from the technology being used to the educational purpose that technology serves, then that technology is becoming a comfortable and trusted element, and can be regarded as being successfully integrated. Few people give a second thought to the use of a ball-point pen although the mechanisms involved vary — some use a twist mechanism and some use a push button on top, and there are other variations as well. Personal computers have reached a similar level of familiarity for a great many users, but certainly not for all. New and emerging technologies often introduce both fascination and frustration with users. As long as _____ _____ in promoting learning, instruction, or performance, then one ought not to conclude that the technology has been successfully integrated — at least for that user.

* unobtrusive: 눈에 띄지 않는

① the user successfully achieves familiarity with the technology

② the user's focus is on the technology itself rather than its use

③ the user continues to employ outdated educational techniques

④ the user involuntarily gets used to the misuse of the technology

⑤ the user's preference for interaction with other users persists

K87 ★★★ .... 2023 대비 6월 모평 31 (고3)

다음 빈칸에 들어갈 말로 가장 적절한 것을 고르시오.

Young contemporary artists who employ digital technologies in their practice rarely make reference to computers. For example, Wade Guyton, an abstractionist who uses a word processing program and inkjet printers, does not call himself a computer artist. Moreover, some critics, who admire his work, are little concerned about his extensive use of computers in the art-making process. This is a marked contrast from three decades ago when artists who utilized computers were labeled by critics — often disapprovingly — as computer artists. For the present generation of artists, the computer, or more appropriately, the laptop, is one in a collection of integrated, portable digital technologies that link their social and working life. With tablets and cell phones surpassing personal computers in Internet usage, and as slim digital devices resemble nothing like the room-sized mainframes and bulky desktop computers of previous decades, it now appears that the computer artist is finally _____.

① awake   ② influential

③ distinct   ④ troublesome

⑤ extinct

K88 ★★★ .... 2022 대비 6월 모평 33 (고3)

다음 빈칸에 들어갈 말로 가장 적절한 것을 고르시오. [3점]

Concepts of nature are always cultural statements. This may not strike Europeans as much of an insight, for Europe's landscape is so much of a blend. But in the new worlds — 'new' at least to Europeans — the distinction appeared much clearer not only to European settlers and visitors but also to their descendants. For that reason, they had the fond conceit of primeval nature uncontrolled by human associations which could later find expression in an admiration for wilderness. Ecological relationships certainly have their own logic and in this sense 'nature' can be seen to have a self-regulating but not necessarily stable dynamic independent of human intervention. But the context for ecological interactions _____. We may not determine how or what a lion eats but we certainly can regulate where the lion feeds.

*conceit: 생각 **primeval: 원시(시대)의 ***ecological: 생태학의

① has supported new environment-friendly policies

② has increasingly been set by humanity

③ inspires creative cultural practices

④ changes too frequently to be regulated

⑤ has been affected by various natural conditions

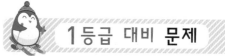

1등급 대비 문제

K89 ~ 91 ▶ 제한시간 7.5분

K89 ◎ 2등급 대비 .... 2022 대비 6월 모평 34 (고3)

다음 빈칸에 들어갈 말로 가장 적절한 것을 고르시오. [3점]

Emma Brindley has investigated the responses of European robins to the songs of neighbors and strangers. Despite the large and complex song repertoire of European robins, they were able to discriminate between the songs of neighbors and strangers. When they heard a tape recording of a stranger, they began to sing sooner, sang more songs, and overlapped their songs with the playback more often than they did on hearing a neighbor's song. As Brindley suggests, the overlapping of song may be an aggressive response. However, this difference in responding to neighbor versus stranger occurred only when the neighbor's song was played by a loudspeaker placed at the boundary between that neighbor's territory and the territory of the bird being tested. If the same neighbor's song was played at another boundary, one separating the territory of the test subject from another neighbor, it was treated as the call of a stranger. Not only does this result demonstrate that _____, but it also shows that the choice of songs used in playback experiments is highly important.

*robin: 울새 **territory: 영역

① variety and complexity characterize the robins' songs

② song volume affects the robins' aggressive behavior

③ the robins' poor territorial sense is a key to survival

④ the robins associate locality with familiar songs

⑤ the robins are less responsive to recorded songs

다음 빈칸에 들어갈 말로 가장 적절한 것을 고르시오. [3점]

In trying to explain how different disciplines attempt to understand autobiographical memory the literary critic Daniel Albright said, "Psychology is a garden, literature is a wilderness." He meant, I believe, that psychology seeks to make patterns, find regularity, and ultimately impose order on human experience and behavior. Writers, by contrast, dive into the unruly, untamed depths of human experiences. What he said about understanding memory can be extended to our questions about young children's minds. If we psychologists are too bent on identifying the orderly pattern, the regularities of children's minds, we may miss an essential and pervasive characteristic of our topic: the child's more unruly and imaginative ways of talking and thinking. It is not only the developed writer or literary scholar who seems drawn toward a somewhat wild and idiosyncratic way of thinking; young children are as well. The psychologist interested in young children may have to _____ in order to get a good picture of how children think.

*unruly: 제멋대로 구는 **pervasive: 널리 퍼져 있는
***idiosyncratic: 색다른

① venture a little more often into the wilderness
② help them recall their most precious memories
③ better understand the challenges of parental duty
④ disregard the key characteristics of children's fiction
⑤ standardize the paths of their psychological development

다음 빈칸에 들어갈 말로 가장 적절한 것을 고르시오.

There is something deeply paradoxical about the professional status of sports journalism, especially in the medium of print. In discharging their usual responsibilities of description and commentary, reporters' accounts of sports events are eagerly consulted by sports fans, while in their broader journalistic role of covering sport in its many forms, sports journalists are among the most visible of all contemporary writers. The ruminations of the elite class of 'celebrity' sports journalists are much sought after by the major newspapers, their lucrative contracts being the envy of colleagues in other 'disciplines' of journalism. Yet sports journalists do not have a standing in their profession that corresponds to the size of their readerships or of their pay packets, with the old saying (now reaching the status of cliché) that sport is the 'toy department of the news media' still readily to hand as a dismissal of the worth of what sports journalists do. This reluctance to take sports journalism seriously produces the paradoxical outcome that sports newspaper writers are much read but little _____.

*discharge: 이행하다 **rumination: 생각
***lucrative: 돈을 많이 버는

① paid   ② admired
③ censored   ④ challenged
⑤ discussed

K92 ⭐ 1등급 대비 .... 2022 대비 수능 34 (고3)

다음 빈칸에 들어갈 말로 가장 적절한 것을 고르시오. [3점]

Precision and determinacy are a necessary requirement for all meaningful scientific debate, and progress in the sciences is, to a large extent, the ongoing process of achieving ever greater precision. But historical representation puts a premium on a proliferation of representations, hence not on the refinement of one representation but on the production of an ever more varied set of representations. Historical insight is not a matter of a continuous "narrowing down" of previous options, not of an approximation of the truth, but, on the contrary, is an "explosion" of possible points of view. It therefore aims at the unmasking of previous illusions of determinacy and precision by the production of new and alternative representations, rather than at achieving truth by a careful analysis of what was right and wrong in those previous representations. And from this perspective, the development of historical insight may indeed be regarded by the outsider as a process of creating ever more confusion, a continuous questioning of _____, rather than, as in the sciences, an ever greater approximation to the truth.   *proliferation: 증식

① criteria for evaluating historical representations
② certainty and precision seemingly achieved already
③ possibilities of alternative interpretations of an event
④ coexistence of multiple viewpoints in historical writing
⑤ correctness and reliability of historical evidence collected

K93 ⭐ 1등급 대비 .... 2025 대비 6월 모평 34 (고3)

다음 빈칸에 들어갈 말로 가장 적절한 것을 고르시오. [3점]

Any attempt to model musical behavior or perception in a general way is filled with difficulties. With regard to models of perception, the question arises of whose perception we are trying to model — even if we confine ourselves to a particular culture and historical environment. Surely the perception of music varies greatly between listeners of different levels of training; indeed, a large part of music education is devoted to developing and enriching (and therefore likely changing) these listening processes. While this may be true, I am concerned here with fairly basic aspects of perception — particularly meter and key — which I believe are relatively consistent across listeners. Anecdotal evidence suggests, for example, that most people are able to ''find the beat'' in a typical folk song or classical piece. This is not to say that there is complete uniformity in this regard — there may be occasional disagreements, even among experts, as to how we hear the tonality or meter of a piece. But I believe _____.

*anecdotal: 일화의

① our devotion to narrowing these differences will emerge
② fundamental musical behaviors evolve within communities
③ these varied perceptions enrich shared musical experiences
④ the commonalities between us far outweigh the differences
⑤ diversity rather than uniformity in musical processes counts

K 어휘 Review

※ 다음 영어는 우리말 뜻을, 우리말은 영어 단어를 〈보기〉에서 찾아 쓰시오.

〈보기〉

commercialize	이해하다	precisely	추론하다
적절한	procedure	conceal	사소한
biography	언급, 참조	우려, 걱정	integrate

01 comprehend _____

02 deduce _____

03 adequate _____

04 reference _____

05 trivial _____

06 상업화하다 _____

07 통합하다 _____

08 정확히 _____

09 감추다, 숨기다 _____

10 전기(傳記) _____

※ 다음 우리말에 알맞은 영어 표현을 찾아 연결하시오.

11 ~와 관계없이 • • regardless of

12 ~ 등등 • • contrary to

13 ~에 반해서 • • and so forth

14 ~의 관점에서 • • in terms of

15 ~으로 향하다 • • head for

※ 다음 우리말 표현에 맞는 단어를 고르시오.

16 이례적인 경로 ➡ an unusual (route / root)

17 합리적 이성의 우월성 ➡ the (supremacy / surgery) of rational reason

18 참석의 즐거움 ➡ the pleasure of (abundance / attendance)

19 매우 일정한 몸무게를 유지하다 ➡ maintain a very (constant / contrast) body weight

20 부정사를 분리하는 것을 금지하다 ➡ (permit / forbid) the splitting of infinitives

※ 다음 문장의 빈칸에 알맞은 단어를 〈보기〉에서 찾아 쓰시오.

〈보기〉

untamed	perplexing	delicate	tangible
dramatic	flourished	wilderness	urgent
cumulative	discriminate	obese	exceptional

21 디지털 정보를 전달하는 물리적 매체는 상당히 취약하다.
➡ The physical media that carry digital information are quite _____.

22 같은 종류의 창작자로서 의상 디자이너는 처음으로 번영했다.
➡ The dress-designer first _____ as the same sort of creator.

23 심리학은 정원이고 문학은 황무지이다.
➡ Psychology is a garden, literature is a(n) _____.

24 이 미묘한 진보는 극적이지도 않고 자극적이지도 않다.
➡ This subtle progress is not _____, not exciting.

25 그들은 이웃 새와 낯선 새의 노래를 구별할 수 있었다.
➡ They were able to _____ between the songs of neighbors and strangers.

26 Ludwig van Beethoven의 유명한 5번 교향곡은 이례적일 정도로 우수한 예를 제공한다.
➡ Ludwig van Beethoven's famous Fifth Symphony provides a(n) _____ example.

27 고고학자들은 문화의 유형적인 측면에 초점을 맞추는 경향이 있다.
➡ Archaeologists tend to focus on _____ aspects of culture.

28 반면에 작가는 인간 경험의 제멋대로 굴고, 길들지 않은 깊이를 파고든다.
➡ Writers, by contrast, dive into the unruly, _____ depths of human experiences.

29 많은 개인의 축적된 작업은 집적된 지식을 생산한다.
➡ The _____ work of many individuals produces a corpus of knowledge.

30 과학은 Mendel의 발견이 답할 수 있는 긴급한 질문에 직면했다.
➡ Science faced the _____ questions that Mendel's discoveries could answer.

연세 국궁부

연세대학교 스포츠 동아리

전통 활쏘기의 매력 속으로!

우리나라의 전통 활쏘기를 이르는 말인 국궁은 생활체육 중 하나이며, 국궁을 통해 스트레스 해소와 심신단련, 전통의 매력을 동시에 느낄 수 있습니다.

연세 국궁부는 국궁의 기초부터 심화 과정까지 차근차근 가르쳐줌은 물론, 동아리의 공용 장비를 자유롭게 이용할 수도 있습니다. 현재 70여 명의 부원이 매주 자율적으로 활쏘기 연습에 참여해 국궁을 연마하고, 동아리 국궁대회를 개최하고 있습니다.

그 밖에도 매 홀수 달마다 자체 대회인 '사회'를 개최하여 부원들이 쌓아온 실력을 서로 겨룰 수 있는 기회를 마련합니다. 또한 국궁 연고전을 개최해 양교 궁사들 간의 화합을 도모하기도 하고, 14개의 서울 국궁 동아리가 모여 연합 교류전을 개최하는 등 외부 대회에도 적극적으로 참여하고 있습니다.

매년 다양한 궁도대회에서 대학부 1위를 차지하는 등 꾸준히 좋은 성적을 내고 있는 연세 국궁부의 일원이 되고 싶다면 매년 5월과 11월에 실시되는 신입부원 모집에 관심을 가져보세요.

L 흐름에 맞지 않는 문장 찾기

잠깐!
나는 여기에 속하지
않는 것 같아.

★ 유형 설명

다음 글에서 전체 흐름과 관계 없는 문장은?
Since their introduction, information systems have substantially changed the way

첫 문장 이후로 이어지는 글의 논리적인 흐름을 방해하거나 주제와 동떨어진 진술을 하는 문장을 골라내야 한다.

O━ 첫 문장을 읽고, 글의 핵심 소재와 주제를 파악한다. 이어지는 각각의 문장이 앞 문장과 자연스럽게, 적절한 연결어 등으로 연결되는지 확인한다. 전체 글이나 앞 문장에 등장한 소재를 다루긴 하지만 전혀 동떨어진 이야기를 하는 문장이 정답인 경우가 많다.

유형 풀이 비법

1 글의 흐름을 확인하라!
• 문장 간의 논리적 흐름을 위해 지시어와 연결어를 본다.

2 글의 주제를 파악하라!
• 주제나 요지를 파악하고, 이에 어긋나는 문장을 찾는다.

3 반전을 찾아라!
• 갑작스러운 비약이나 반전이 나타나는 곳이 있는지 살핀다.

Tip 정답으로 고른 문장을 빼고 읽어 보면서 앞뒤 연결이 자연스러운지 확인한다.

★ 최신 수능 경향 분석

대비 연도	월	문항 번호	지문 주제	난이도
2025	11	35번	스포츠와 관광의 발전에서 자동차의 중요한 역할	★★☆
	9	35번	판매업자의 물품 확보를 위한 조직망	★★★
	6	35번	새가 노래를 학습하는 단계	★★☆
2024	11	35번	빨리 말하는 것이 가져올 수 있는 언어적 위험 부담	★★☆
	9	35번	재택근무의 발전	★★☆
	6	35번	전문가와 초보자의 차이	★★☆
2023	11	35번	경력 초기의 교사에게 필요한 기술	★★☆
	9	35번	재해로부터 회복하는 식물의 특별한 능력	★★☆
	6	35번	동물의 의사 결정	★★☆

★ 2025 수능 출제 분석

선택지가 아닌 두 문장을 통해 글의 주제를 파악했다면, '가격이 합리적이고 질이 좋은 숙박 시설의 확대가 현지에 기반을 둔 식당의 성장을 촉진했다'고 한 문장이 글의 주제에서 벗어난다는 것을 어렵지 않게 알 수 있었다.

★ 2026 수능 예측

글을 읽고 글의 내용이 한눈에 들어오도록 정리하는 연습을 통해 글의 전개 방식을 이해하는 훈련을 하면 도움이 된다.

어휘 및 표현 Preview

□ memorize 암기하다
□ species 종(種)
□ overlap 겹치다
□ several 몇몇의
□ impressive 인상적인
□ storage 저장
□ initial 초기의
□ effort 노력
□ reproduce 재현하다
□ successful 성공적인
□ uneven 고르지 않은
□ pitch 음정
□ reveal 보여주다

□ period 기간
□ accurate 정확한
□ template 본보기
□ important 중요한
□ shape 형성하다
□ limitation 한계
□ deafen 귀를 먹게 만들다
□ emerge 드러나다, 판명되다
□ dealer 판매업자
□ offer 제공하다
□ merely 단지
□ on display 전시[진열]된
□ stock 재고

□ particular 특정한
□ actively 적극적으로
□ seek 찾다
□ specific 특정한
□ collection 소장품
□ business 사업
□ devote 전념하다
□ inevitably 필연적으로
□ professional 전문적인
□ subject 대상
□ enquire 문의하다
□ availability 구할[이용할] 수 있는

□ crucially 결정적으로
□ overseas 해외[외국/국외]의
□ category 범주
□ routinely 정례적으로
□ inform 알리다[통지하다]
□ auction 경매
□ private 개인의
□ enough 충분히
□ occasionally 가끔
□ on sale 판매되는[구입할 수 있는]

L 흐름에 맞지 않는 문장 찾기 (첫 번째)

1st 선택지가 아닌 문장을 통해 글의 소재를 확인하고, 전개 방향을 예측해 보세요.
2nd 글의 흐름이 전환되는 부분이 있는지에 특히 주의하면서 각 문장과 그 앞 문장의 연관성을 살피세요.
3rd 정답으로 추론한 문장을 제외하면 그 앞뒤 문장이 적절한 흐름이 되는지 확인하세요.

L01 ★★❀ .... 2023 대비 6월 모평 35 (고3)

다음 글에서 전체 흐름과 관계 없는 문장은?

The animal in a conflict between attacking a rival and fleeing may initially not have sufficient information to enable it to make a decision straight away. ① If the rival is likely to win the fight, then the optimal decision would be to give up immediately and not risk getting injured. ② But if the rival is weak and easily defeatable, then there could be considerable benefit in going ahead and obtaining the territory, females, food or whatever is at stake. ③ Animals under normal circumstances maintain a very constant body weight and they eat and drink enough for their needs at regular intervals. ④ By taking a little extra time to collect information about the opponent, the animal is more likely to reach a decision that maximizes its chances of winning than if it takes a decision without such information. ⑤ Many signals are now seen as having this information gathering or 'assessment' function, directly contributing to the mechanism of the decision-making process by supplying vital information about the likely outcomes of the various options.

1st 선택지가 아닌 문장을 통해 글의 소재를 확인하고, 전개 방향을 예측해 보세요.

The animal / in a conflict / between attacking a rival
동물은 / 갈등하는 / 상대를 공격하는 것과 도피하는 것
and fleeing / may initially not have sufficient
사이에서 / 처음에는 충분한 정보를 갖지 못할 수도 있다
information / to enable it to make a decision
/ 그것이 즉시 결정을 내릴 수 있게 할 //
straight away. //

● 어떤 상황에 처한 동물에 대해 이야기하는 글인가요?

상대를 공격할지 아니면 도망칠지 사이에서 ❶(　　　)하는 상황에 있는 동물에 대한 글이네요! [단서]

동사구까지 해석해 보면, 그런 갈등에 처한 동물이 처음에는 어떻게 할지 즉시 결정을 내릴 수 있는 충분한 정보를 갖지 못할 수도 있다는 내용으로, 앞으로는 동물이 그 상황에서 어떻게, 어떤 결정을 내리는지, 충분한 정보를 어떻게 수집하는지 등에 대해 이야기할 것이라고 예상할 수 있어요. [발상]

2nd 글의 흐름이 전환되는 부분이 있는지에 특히 주의하면서 각 문장과 그 앞 문장의 연관성을 살피세요.

1) ① 문장부터 살펴볼까요?

① If the rival is likely to win the fight, / then the
상대가 싸움에서 이길 것 같다면 / 최적의 결정은
optimal decision / would be to give up immediately
/ 즉시 포기하고 부상당할 위험을 무릅쓰지 않는 것일
and not risk getting injured. //
것이다 //

● 앞 문장과 자연스럽게 연결되나요?

상대를 공격할지 아니면 도망칠지 사이에서 갈등하는 동물을 설명한 앞 문장에 이어 ①에서는 동물이 도망치기로 결정하는 상황을 설명했어요. 상대가 싸움에서 이길 것 같은 상황에서는 즉시 포기하고 부상의 위험을 무릅쓰지 않는 것이 최적의 결정이라는 내용이죠.

● 앞으로는 어떤 내용이 전개될까요?

내릴 수 있는 두 가지 결정(도망치거나 혹은 공격하거나) 중에서 ① 문장이 도망치기로 결정하는 것을 다뤘으니까, ② 문장에서는 동물이 상대를 공격하기로 결정하는 상황을 이야기할 것이라고 예상할 수 있어요.

2) 예상이 맞는지 ② 문장을 확인해 봅시다.

② But if the rival is weak and easily defeatable, /
하지만 상대가 약하고 쉽게 이길 만하다면　　　　　　　　　　/
then there could be considerable benefit / in going
상당한 이익이 있을 수 있다　　　　　　　　　　　　　/ 싸워서 얻는
ahead and obtaining / the territory, females, food or
것에　　　　　　　　　/ 영역, 암컷, 먹이 또는 성패가 달린 것은
whatever is at stake. //
무엇이든　　　　　　　//

● 역접의 연결어로 문장이 시작되네요.
　앞 문장의 if절은 상대가 싸움에서 이길 것 같은 상황을 가정했고,
　이 문장에서는 상대가 약하고 쉽게 이길 만한 상황을 가정했기 때문에
　역접의 연결어 ❷(　　　　　　)이 쓰였어요.

● 우리의 예상에 들어맞는 내용이군요.
　①에서 가정한 상황과 달리, 상대가 약하고 쉽게 이길 만한 상황에서는
　싸우는 것에 상당한 이익이 있을 수 있다는 내용이에요.
　첫 문장에서 제시한 두 가지 상황에 대한 구체적인 설명이 ①과 ②에
　등장했고, 그렇다면 앞으로는 어떤 내용이 등장할까요?
　첫 문장에서 이야기한 '충분한 정보'에 관한 내용이 등장하지 않을까요?

3) 이번에도 예상이 맞는지 ③ 문장도 살펴봅시다.

③ Animals / under normal circumstances / maintain
동물은　　　/ 보통의 상황에서　　　　　　　/ 매우 일정한
a very constant body weight / and they eat and
체중을 유지하며　　　　　　　/ 그들은 충분히 먹고 마신다
drink enough / for their needs / at regular intervals. //
　　　　　　　/ 자신들에게 필요한 만큼 / 규칙적인 간격으로　//

● 음, 충분한 정보에 관한 내용이 전혀 아니네요.
　보통 상황에서 동물은 일정한 체중을 유지하고, 규칙적으로 필요한 음식을
　충분히 먹고 마신다는 내용이에요.
　우리가 지금까지 확인한 바로는 이 글은 보통 상황에서의 동물이 아니라
　적을 만나 도망칠지 싸울지 ❶(　　　　)하는 상황에서의 동물을
　설명하는 글이었으니까 전체 글의 흐름과 관계없는 문장은 ❸(　　　)인
　것 같아요.

4) 나머지 문장들이 무슨 이야기를 하는지 확인해서 정답을 확정합시다.

④ By taking a little extra time / to collect
약간의 추가 시간을 들임으로써　　　　　/ 상대에 대한
information about the opponent, / the animal is
정보를 수집하는 데　　　　　　　　/ 그 동물은 결정에
more likely to reach a decision / that maximizes its
도달할 가능성이 더 크다　　　　/ 이길 가능성을 최대화하는
chances of winning / than if it takes a decision /
　　　　　　　　　/ 결정을 내리는 경우보다　　　　　/
without such information. //
그러한 정보 없이　　　　　//

● 다시 적과 맞닥뜨린 동물에 대한 내용으로 돌아왔어요!
　②을 읽고 나서 앞으로는 '정보'에 대해 이야기하지 않을까 하는 예상을
　했는데, 그 예상이 그대로 들어맞았어요.
　첫 문장에서는 동물이 적을 맞닥뜨린 즉시에는 결정을 내리기에 충분한
　정보가 없을 수 있다고 했는데, 여기서는 상대에 대한 정보를 수집하는 데
　약간의 시간을 들이면 이길 가능성을 최대화하는 결정을 내릴 수 있다고
　했으니까 앞뒤 내용이 자연스럽게 연결되는 것이죠.

5) ⑤ 문장도 아마 정보 수집에 관한 이야기를 할 거예요.

⑤ Many signals are now seen / as having this
오늘날 많은 신호들이 간주되어　　　　/ 이러한 정보 수집 또는
information gathering or 'assessment' function, /
'평가' 기능을 갖는 것으로　　　　　　　　　　　　/
directly contributing / to the mechanism of the
직접적으로 기여한다　　　/ 의사 결정 과정의 메커니즘에
decision-making process / by supplying vital
　　　　　　　　　　　/ 매우 중요한 정보를 제공함으로써
information / about the likely outcomes / of the
　　　　　　/ 가능한 결과에 관한　　　　　/ 다양한
various options. //
선택의　　　　//

● 지시형용사 this가 쓰인 것에 주목하세요.
　앞 문장에서 약간의 추가 시간을 들여 상대에 대한 정보를 수집하면 이길
　가능성을 최대화하는 결정에 도달할 가능성이 더 크다고 했는데, 이러한
　정보 수집을 지시형용사를 이용해서 this information gathering or
　'assessment' function이라고 표현한 거예요.
　앞뒤 문장이 아주 자연스럽게 흘러가는 것이죠.

3rd 정답으로 추론한 문장을 제외하면 그 앞뒤 문장이 적절한 흐름이
되는지 확인하세요.

첫 문장에서 적을 만나 도망칠지, 싸울지 사이에서 갈등하는 상황에 처한
동물에게 처음에는 결정을 내릴 수 있게 하는 충분한 정보가 없을 수 있다고
한 후, ①에서는 도망치는 것이 최적의 결정인 상황, ②에서는 싸우는 것이
이득인 상황을 설명했고, 마지막 두 문장인 ④과 ⑤에서는 결정에 필요한
정보 수집에 대해 설명했어요.
그러므로 보통의 상황에서 동물이 일정한 체중을 유지하고, 규칙적으로
필요한 만큼 충분히 먹고 마신다는 ❸(　　　)은 나머지 문장들과 전혀
어울리지 않죠.

글의 앞부분에서
소재를 파악하자!

L 흐름에 맞지 않는 문장 찾기 (두 번째)

1st 선택지가 아닌 문장을 통해 글의 소재를 확인하고, 전개 방향을 예측해 보세요.
2nd 문장 하나하나를 살펴보면서 앞뒤 문장의 관계를 파악하세요.
3rd 정답으로 추론한 문장을 제외하면 그 앞뒤 문장이 적절한 흐름이 되는지 확인하세요.

L02 ★★☆ ·············· 2022 대비 6월 모평 35 (고3)

다음 글에서 전체 흐름과 관계 <u>없는</u> 문장은?

Kinship ties continue to be important today. In modern societies such as the United States people frequently have family get-togethers, they telephone their relatives regularly, and they provide their kin with a wide variety of services. ① Eugene Litwak has referred to this pattern of behaviour as the 'modified extended family'. ② It is an extended family structure because multigenerational ties are maintained, but it is modified because it does not usually rest on co-residence between the generations and most extended families do not act as corporate groups. ③ Although modified extended family members often live close by, the modified extended family does not require geographical proximity and ties are maintained even when kin are separated by considerable distances. ④ The oldest member of the family makes the decisions on important issues, no matter how far away family members live from each other. ⑤ In contrast to the traditional extended family where kin always live in close proximity, the members of modified extended families may freely move away from kin to seek opportunities for occupational advancement.

*kin: 친족 **proximity: 근접

1st 선택지가 아닌 문장을 통해 글의 소재를 확인하고, 전개 방향을 예측해 보세요.

1) 첫 문장부터 해석하고 살펴봅시다.

Kinship ties continue to be important / today. //
친족 유대 관계는 계속 중요하다   / 오늘날에도 //

● **오늘날의 친족 유대 관계에 대해서 설명하는 글이겠네요.**
현대 사회로 발전하면서 친족 사이의 유대감이 과거보다 약해졌다고 생각하기 쉽지만 사실은 오늘날에도 여전히 중요하다는 내용이에요. 일단 첫 문장을 통해 글의 핵심 소재를 파악했어요. 무작정 글을 읽기 시작하는 것보다 이렇게 미리 생각한 후에 읽으면 더 쉽고 빠르게 글의 내용을 파악할 수 있어요.

2) 두 번째 문장도 선택지가 아니네요!

In modern societies / such as the United States /
현대 사회에서   / 미국과 같은   /
people frequently have family get-togethers, / they
사람들이 자주 가족 모임을 갖는   /
telephone their relatives regularly, / and they
그들은 자신의 친척에게 자주 전화하고   / 그들은 자신의
provide their kin / with a wide variety of services. //
친척에게 제공한다 / 아주 다양한 도움을   //

● **첫 문장을 뒷받침하는 내용이에요.**
미국과 같은 현대 사회에서 사람들은 자주 가족 모임을 갖고, 친척에게 자주 전화하며, 아주 다양한 도움을 제공한다는 내용으로, 오늘날에도 친족 사이의 유대 관계가 계속 중요하다는 첫 번째 문장을 뒷받침하고 있어요. 이 글이 현대 사회에도 여전히 중요한 친족 사이의 유대 관계에 대한 내용임을 확신할 수 있죠.

2nd 문장 하나하나를 살펴보면서 앞뒤 문장의 관계를 파악하세요.

1) ① 문장부터 살펴볼까요?

① Eugene Litwak has referred to this pattern of
Eugene Litwak은 이 행동 양식을 언급했다
behaviour / as the 'modified extended family'. //
          / '수정 확대가족'이라고   //

● **지시형용사인 this가 쓰였어요.**
앞부분에 등장한 행동 양식, 즉 현대 사회에서 자주 가족 모임을 갖고, 친척에게 자주 전화하며 다양한 도움을 제공하는 행동 양식을 Eugene Litwak이 **❶**'(　　　　　　)'이라고 일컫는다는 내용이에요.
앞부분에 등장한 내용을 가리키는 지시형용사 this의 쓰임과 앞 문장에 이어지는 문맥상의 의미도 자연스러워요.

● **앞으로는 어떤 내용이 전개될까요?**
오늘날의 행동 양식을 설명하고 나서 이를 가리키는 용어가 '수정 확대가족'이라고 했으므로 앞으로는 수정 확대가족에 대한 추가적인 설명이 이어질 거라고 충분히 예상할 수 있어요.

2) ② 문장은 어떤 내용인가요?

② It is an extended family structure / because
그것은 확대가족 구조이지만　　　　　　　　　　/ 다세대의
multigenerational ties are maintained, / but it is
유대 관계가 유지되기 때문에　　　　　　　　/ 그것은
modified / because it does not usually rest on
수정된다 / 그것이 일반적으로 공동 거주에 기초를 두지 않고
co-residence / between the generations / and most
/ 세대 간　　　　　　　　　/ 대부분의
extended families do not act / as corporate groups. //
확대가족이 기능하지는 않기 때문에 / 공동 집단으로서 //

● **'수정 확대가족'이라는 용어에 대해 설명하는 문장이에요.**
여러 세대 사이의 유대 관계가 유지되지만, 전통적인 확대가족 구조와 달리 여러 세대가 공동으로 거주하지 않고, 대부분의 확대가족이 공동 집단으로 기능하지는 않기 때문에 '수정'이라는 용어가 붙은 것이군요! 앞 문장에 등장한 용어에 대한 구체적인 설명으로, 앞뒤 문장이 긴밀히 연결되고 있어요.

3) ③ 문장도 살펴봅시다.

③ Although modified extended family members
비록 수정 확대가족의 구성원들이 흔히 살기는 하지만
often live / close by, / the modified extended family
/ 가까이 / 수정 확대가족은 필요로 하지 않으며
does not require / geographical proximity / and ties
/ 지리적 근접을　　　　　　　/ 유대 관계는
are maintained / even when kin are separated / by
유지된다 / 친척이 떨어져 있더라도 /
considerable distances. //
상당한 거리에 의해 //

● **이 문장도 수정 확대가족에 대한 설명이군요.**
수정 확대가족의 구성원은 흔히 가까이 살긴 하지만 상당한 거리로 떨어져 살아도 유대 관계가 유지된다는 내용이에요. 공동 거주에 대해 언급한 앞 문장과 연결되는 내용이죠.

4) 정답은 ④ 아니면 ⑤ 문장이겠네요.

④ The oldest member of the family / makes the
그 가족의 최고 연장자가　　　　　　　　/ 결정을 내린다
decisions / on important issues, / no matter how far
/ 중요한 문제에 관해서는 / 가족 구성원들이 아무리 멀리
away family members live / from each other. //
떨어져 살지라도　　　　　/ 서로에게서 //

● **'멀리 떨어져 산다'라는 건 앞 문장과 연결돼요.**
③ 문장뿐 아니라 전체 글이 '현대 사회에서 멀리 떨어져 살더라도 친족 간의 유대 관계가 유지된다'는 내용이에요.
그런데 이 문장은 멀리 떨어져 살더라도 가족의 최고 연장자가 중요한 문제에 관해 결정을 내린다는 내용으로, 친족 사이의 유대 관계에 대한 설명이 아니죠!

5) 정답은 나왔지만 나머지 문장도 살펴봅시다.

⑤ In contrast to the traditional extended family /
전통적인 확대가족과는 대조적으로　　　　　　/
where kin always live / in close proximity, / the
친척이 항상 사는 / 아주 가까이에서 /
members of modified extended families / may
수정 확대가족의 구성원들은　　　　　/
freely move away from kin / to seek opportunities /
친척에게서 자유로이 멀리 이주해 가서 / 기회를 추구할 수도 있다 /
for occupational advancement. //
직업상의 발전을 위한 //

● **전통적인 확대가족과 수정 확대가족을 대조하는 문장이에요.**
전통적인 확대가족은 친척이 가까이 살았지만, 수정 확대가족은 직업 등의 이유로 멀리 떨어져 살 수도 있다는 내용으로, 멀리 떨어져 살더라도 유대 관계는 여전하다는 내용의 글에 잘 어울리는 문장이에요.

3rd **정답으로 추론한 문장을 제외하면 그 앞뒤 문장이 적절한 흐름이 되는지 확인하세요.**
수정 확대가족의 구성원들은 멀리 떨어져 살더라도 유대 관계가 유지된다는 ③ 문장과 수정 확대가족의 구성원들이 직업 등을 이유로 멀리 떨어져 살 수도 있다는 ⑤ 문장이 자연스럽게 연결돼요! **❷**(　　　) 문장은 빠지는 게 좋겠어요!

L03 ~ 07 ▶ 제한시간 10분

L03 ✶✶✽ ·································· 2025 대비 수능 35 (고3)

다음 글에서 전체 흐름과 관계 <u>없는</u> 문장은?

The expansion of sports tourism in the twentieth century has been influenced by further developments in transportation. Just as the railways revolutionized travel in the nineteenth century, so the automobile produced even more dramatic changes in the twentieth. ① The significance of the car in the development of sport and tourism generally has attracted considerable coverage and it has had no less an impact on sports tourism specifically. ② Although originally invented towards the end of the nineteenth century, it started to become a mass form of transport in the 1920s in the USA and rather later in Britain. ③ Apart from its convenience and flexibility, the car has the additional advantages of affording access to many areas not served by public transport, as well as allowing the easy transport of luggage and equipment. ④ The expansion of reasonably priced, good quality accommodation associated with tourism growth has also facilitated the growth of locally based restaurants. ⑤ As a result, it was invaluable for the development of many forms of sports tourism but especially those which require the transportation of people and equipment to relatively remote locations.

L04 ✶✶✽ ·························· 2025 대비 9월 모평 35 (고3)

다음 글에서 전체 흐름과 관계 <u>없는</u> 문장은?

The best dealers offer a much broader service than merely having their goods on display and 'selling from stock'. Once they know the needs of a particular collector they can actively seek specific items to fill gaps in the collection. ① Because it is their business, to which they devote themselves full-time, they will inevitably have a much wider network than any non-professional collector can ever develop. ② As a matter of course they can enquire about the availability of pieces from dealers in other cities and, most crucially in some categories, from overseas. ③ They will be routinely informed of news of all auctions and important private sales, and should be well-enough connected to hear occasionally of items which are not yet quite on sale but might be available for a certain price. ④ The main advantage of buying from a dealer is getting personalised service on your purchases. ⑤ In turn, they can circulate their own contacts with 'want-lists' of desired items or subjects, multiplying their client collectors' chances of expanding their collections.

L05 ✸✸❈ ········· 2025 대비 6월 모평 35 (고3)

다음 글에서 전체 흐름과 관계 <u>없는</u> 문장은?

Avian song learning occurs in two stages: first, songs must be memorized and, second, they must be practiced. In some species these two events overlap, but in others memorization can occur before practice by several months, providing an impressive example of long-term memory storage. ① The young bird's initial efforts to reproduce the memorized song are usually not successful. ② These early songs may have uneven pitch, irregular tempo, and notes that are out of order or poorly reproduced. ③ However, sound graphs of songs recorded over several weeks or months reveal that during this practice period the bird fine-tunes his efforts until he produces an accurate copy of the memorized template. ④ An important idea to emerge from the study of birdsong is that song learning is shaped by preferences and limitations. ⑤ This process requires hearing oneself sing; birds are unable to reproduce memorized songs if they are deafened after memorization but before the practice period.

＊avian: 조류의

L06 ✸✸✸❈ ········· 2024 실시 10월 학평 35 (고3)

다음 글에서 전체 흐름과 관계 <u>없는</u> 문장은?

It is important to remember that to achieve acceptance and use of new technologies/systems, the personal importance to the users has to be valued more highly than the degree of innovation. However, policies and political goals are often confused with the driver's personal goals. ① Societal goals and individual goals do not necessarily coincide. ② For example, the policy goal behind ISA (Intelligent Speed Adaptation; a system which warns the drivers when they exceed the speed limit, and may even prevent them from doing so) could be to increase traffic safety or to increase speed limit compliance. ③ Some drivers have a goal to collect many classic cars, although it has little impact on their use of new speed adaptation systems. ④ These goals might not be relevant to some drivers, for example, due to their feeling that safety measures are redundant because of their own personal driving skills or because speeding is not seen as a 'real crime.' ⑤ Nevertheless, they might find that the system helps them to avoid speeding tickets or they want to use the system simply because they have a general interest in innovative systems.

＊compliance: 준수 ＊＊redundant: 불필요한

L07 ✸✸✸ ········· 2024 실시 7월 학평 35 (고3)

다음 글에서 전체 흐름과 관계 <u>없는</u> 문장은? [3점]

In a context in which the cultural obligation to produce the self as a distinctive, authentic individual is difficult to fulfill, the burdensome work of individualizing the self is turned over increasingly to algorithms. ① The "personalization" that is promised on every front — in the domains of search, shopping, health, news, advertising, learning, music, and entertainment — depends on ever more refined algorithmic constructions of individuality. ② As it becomes more difficult to produce our digital selves as unique individuals, we are increasingly being produced as unique individuals from the outside. ③ When AI algorithms learn more about our identities, it becomes essential to safeguard this information and ensure that individuals have control and consent over the data collected about them. ④ Individuality is redefined from a cultural practice and reflexive project to an algorithmic process. ⑤ Our unique selfhood is no longer something for which we are wholly responsible; it is algorithmically guaranteed.

L08 ✖✖✖ .... 2024 실시 5월 학평 35 (고3)

다음 글에서 전체 흐름과 관계 <u>없는</u> 문장은?

The human race traces back to a surprisingly small number of common ancestors. It has been documented that the entire human race can be traced back to only seven different mothers, and one of these women is a common ancestor to roughly 40% of the human species. Why is this? The simple answer is that humans are extremely good at dying and at wiping each other out. ① History has had many successful rulers and conquerors who have got rid of entire populations, and even beyond that, our species has wiped out plenty of similar humanoid lines that existed on this earth. ② Scientific finds have so far discovered a number of other humanoid species that once shared the earth with us, some of which include Neanderthals and Denisovans. ③ There are still no clear examples of Neanderthals attempting to expressively symbolize real-life elements such as animals or people in creative works. ④ Yet of these lines, only homo sapiens have survived, only the modern humans. ⑤ That itself shows how difficult it is for a species to survive and thrive long-term on this planet. *humanoid: 인간에 가까운

L09 ✖✖✖ .... 2024 실시 3월 학평 35 (고3)

다음 글에서 전체 흐름과 관계 <u>없는</u> 문장은?

No doubt students collaborating with other speakers of English might encounter language variances, which may interfere with intentionality. ① To address such disparities, Horner, Lu, Royster, and Trimbur (2011) call for a "translingual approach" in which language varieties are not perceived as barriers, but as avenues for meaning making. ② Similarly, Galloway and Rose (2015) study of Global Englishes found that exposure to other Englishes helps normalize language differences. ③ Educators have to work with students to examine phrases, expressions, and other ranges of English language use for their rhetorical and communicative possibilities and not their perceived errors or inferior status. ④ Committing an error means unintentionally saying what isn't true, so any linguistic or perspective error should be avoided at all cost. ⑤ After all, students are constantly reading texts and listening to speakers whose Englishes do not necessarily conform to what is considered standard in their own communities.

*disparity: 차이 **rhetorical: 수사적인 ***inferior: 열등한

L10 ✖✖✖ .... 2023 실시 3월 학평 35 (고3)

다음 글에서 전체 흐름과 관계 <u>없는</u> 문장은?

According to the principle of social proof, one way individuals determine appropriate behavior for themselves in a situation is to examine the behavior of others there — especially similar others. ① It is through social comparison with these referent others that people validate the correctness of their opinions and decisions. ② Consequently, people tend to behave as their friends and peers have behaved. ③ Because the critical source of information within the principle of social proof is the responses of referent others, compliance tactics that employ this information should be especially effective in collectivistically oriented nations and persons. ④ That is, where the individualized self is both the focus and the standard, one's own behavioral history should be heavily weighted in subsequent behavior. ⑤ Some evidence in this regard comes from a study showing that advertisements that promoted group benefits were more persuasive in Korea (a collectivistic society) than in the United States (an individualistic society).

*tactic: 전술

L11 ✱✱※ 2022 대비 9월 모평 35 (고3)

다음 글에서 전체 흐름과 관계 <u>없는</u> 문장은?

A variety of theoretical perspectives provide insight into immigration. Economics, which assumes that actors engage in utility maximization, represents one framework. ① From this perspective, it is assumed that individuals are rational actors, i.e., that they make migration decisions based on their assessment of the costs as well as benefits of remaining in a given area versus the costs and benefits of leaving. ② Benefits may include but are not limited to short-term and long-term monetary gains, safety, and greater freedom of cultural expression. ③ People with greater financial benefits tend to use their money to show off their social status by purchasing luxurious items. ④ Individual costs include but are not limited to the expense of travel, uncertainty of living in a foreign land, difficulty of adapting to a different language, uncertainty about a different culture, and the great concern about living in a new land. ⑤ Psychic costs associated with separation from family, friends, and the fear of the unknown also should be taken into account in cost-benefit assessments.

＊psychic: 심적인

L12 ✱✱※ 2022 대비 수능 35 (고3)

다음 글에서 전체 흐름과 관계 <u>없는</u> 문장은?

Since their introduction, information systems have substantially changed the way business is conducted. ① This is particularly true for business in the shape and form of cooperation between firms that involves an integration of value chains across multiple units. ② The resulting networks do not only cover the business units of a single firm but typically also include multiple units from different firms. ③ As a consequence, firms do not only need to consider their internal organization in order to ensure sustainable business performance; they also need to take into account the entire ecosystem of units surrounding them. ④ Many major companies are fundamentally changing their business models by focusing on profitable units and cutting off less profitable ones. ⑤ In order to allow these different units to cooperate successfully, the existence of a common platform is crucial.

L13 ✱✱※ 2023 실시 4월 학평 35 (고3)

다음 글에서 전체 흐름과 관계 <u>없는</u> 문장은?

One of the branches of postmodernism examines the structure of language and how it is used. It challenges the assumption that language can be precisely used to represent reality. ① Meanings of words are ambiguous, as words are only signs or labels given to concepts (what is signified) and therefore there is no necessary correspondence between the word and the meaning, the signifier and the signified. ② The use of signs (words) and their meaning can vary depending on the flow of the text in which they are used, leading to the possibility of 'deconstructing' text to reveal its underlying inconsistencies. ③ Reality exists outside of our thoughts, and it is only through language that we are able to perceive the natural world as it really is. ④ This approach can be applied to all forms of representation — pictures, films, etc. that gain added or alternative meanings by the overlaying of references to previous uses. ⑤ This can be seen particularly in the media, where it is difficult to distinguish the real from the unreal — everything is representation, there is no reality.

L14 ✹✹❋ .... 2022 실시 10월 학평 35 (고3)

다음 글에서 전체 흐름과 관계 <u>없는</u> 문장은?

Except for grains and sugars, most foods humans eat are perishable. They deteriorate in palatability, spoil, or become unhealthy when stored for long periods. ① Surplus animal and crop harvests, however, can be saved for future use if appropriate methods of preservation are used. ② The major ways of preserving foods are canning, freezing, drying, salting, and smoking. ③ With all methods the aim is to kill or restrict the growth of harmful microbes or their toxins and to slow or inactivate enzymes that cause undesirable changes in food palatability. ④ Palatability is not static: it is always changing, based on the state of the individual, especially in regard to the time of food consumption. ⑤ For further protection during long periods of storage, preserved food is placed either in sterile metal cans or glass jars or frozen in airtight paper or plastic containers.

*palatability: (좋은) 맛 **enzyme: 효소 ***sterile: 멸균한

L15 ✹✹✹❋ .... 2023 실시 7월 학평 35 (고3)

다음 글에서 전체 흐름과 관계 <u>없는</u> 문장은?

The written word is the obvious, and easiest, place to start when exploring local history, if only to see what has already been written on the subject. Local history books have been written for centuries and are very variable in quality. ① These books will certainly not mention your ancestor by name unless they played a particularly prominent part in the development of the locality in question. ② However, they do provide information about how a place changed over time, who the major personalities were and the significant events that occurred there; or at least those selected by the author for inclusion. ③ If the author is writing from his personal experiences, he must be allowed to spend more energy on adding creative twists to a story that already exists. ④ Unless a book is extremely large or the district chosen is very small, then the author must choose very carefully what he is to include and their priorities may not be the same as all their readers. ⑤ It is well worth reading some or preferably all of the books written about a locality that your ancestors lived in.

L16 ✹✹❋ .... 2021 대비 9월 모평 35 (고3)

다음 글에서 전체 흐름과 관계 <u>없는</u> 문장은?

In a highly commercialized setting such as the United States, it is not surprising that many landscapes are seen as commodities. In other words, they are valued because of their market potential. Residents develop an identity in part based on how the landscape can generate income for the community. ① This process involves more than the conversion of the natural elements into commodities. ② The landscape itself, including the people and their sense of self, takes on the form of a commodity. ③ Landscape protection in the US traditionally focuses on protecting areas of wilderness, typically in mountainous regions. ④ Over time, the landscape identity can evolve into a sort of "logo" that can be used to sell the stories of the landscape. ⑤ Thus, California's "Wine Country," Florida's "Sun Coast," or South Dakota's "Badlands" shape how both outsiders and residents perceive a place, and these labels build a set of expectations associated with the culture of those who live there.

L17 ★★❀ .... 2023 실시 10월 학평 35 (고3)

다음 글에서 전체 흐름과 관계 <u>없는</u> 문장은?

Several common themes were found in the highly creative individuals regarding their early experiences and education. In early childhood their families accorded them a great deal of respect and allowed them to explore on their own and develop a strong sense of personal autonomy. ① There was also a lack of extreme emotional closeness with parents. ② There was little evidence of intensely negative experiences; for example there was, relative to the times in which they lived, very little physical punishment for transgressions. ③ Nor, on the positive side, was there evidence of extremely intense bonds of the sort that can smother independence. ④ There was more competition among brothers and sisters for parental love in nuclear families than in extended families. ⑤ On balance, for those who would grow up to be highly creative, relationships with parents were relatively easy and, in later life, pleasant and friendly rather than intensely intimate.

*autonomy: 자율성 **transgression: 일탈 ***smother: 억누르다

L18 ★★❀ .... 2024 대비 수능 35 (고3)

다음 글에서 전체 흐름과 관계 <u>없는</u> 문장은?

Speaking fast is a high-risk proposition. It's nearly impossible to maintain the ideal conditions to be persuasive, well-spoken, and effective when the mouth is traveling well over the speed limit. ① Although we'd like to think that our minds are sharp enough to always make good decisions with the greatest efficiency, they just aren't. ② In reality, the brain arrives at an intersection of four or five possible things to say and sits idling for a couple of seconds, considering the options. ③ Making a good decision helps you speak faster because it provides you with more time to come up with your responses. ④ When the brain stops sending navigational instructions back to the mouth and the mouth is moving too fast to pause, that's when you get a verbal fender bender, otherwise known as filler. ⑤ *Um, ah, you know*, and *like* are what your mouth does when it has nowhere to go.

L19 ★★★❀ .... 2021 대비 6월 모평 35 (고3)

다음 글에서 전체 흐름과 관계 <u>없는</u> 문장은?

One of the most widespread, and sadly mistaken, environmental myths is that living "close to nature" out in the country or in a leafy suburb is the best "green" lifestyle. Cities, on the other hand, are often blamed as a major cause of ecological destruction — artificial, crowded places that suck up precious resources. Yet, when you look at the facts, nothing could be farther from the truth. ① The pattern of life in the country and most suburbs involves long hours in the automobile each week, burning fuel and pumping out exhaust to get to work, buy groceries, and take kids to school and activities. ② City dwellers, on the other hand, have the option of walking or taking transit to work, shops, and school. ③ The larger yards and houses found outside cities also create an environmental cost in terms of energy use, water use, and land use. ④ This illustrates the tendency that most city dwellers get tired of urban lives and decide to settle in the countryside. ⑤ It's clear that the future of the Earth depends on more people gathering together in compact communities. *compact: 밀집한

L20 ✱✱❀ .... 2023 대비 9월 모평 35 (고3)

다음 글에서 전체 흐름과 관계 <u>없는</u> 문장은?

Because plants tend to recover from disasters more quickly than animals, they are essential to the revitalization of damaged environments. Why do plants have this preferential ability to recover from disaster? It is largely because, unlike animals, they can generate new organs and tissues throughout their life cycle. ① This ability is due to the activity of plant meristems — regions of undifferentiated tissue in roots and shoots that can, in response to specific cues, differentiate into new tissues and organs. ② If meristems are not damaged during disasters, plants can recover and ultimately transform the destroyed or barren environment. ③ You can see this phenomenon on a smaller scale when a tree struck by lightning forms new branches that grow from the old scar. ④ In the form of forests and grasslands, plants regulate the cycling of water and adjust the chemical composition of the atmosphere. ⑤ In addition to regeneration or resprouting of plants, disturbed areas can also recover through reseeding.

*revitalization: 소생

L21 ✱✱✱ .... 2021 대비 수능 35 (고3)

다음 글에서 전체 흐름과 관계 <u>없는</u> 문장은?

Workers are united by laughing at shared events, even ones that may initially spark anger or conflict. Humor reframes potentially divisive events into merely "laughable" ones which are put in perspective as subservient to unifying values held by organization members. Repeatedly recounting humorous incidents reinforces unity based on key organizational values. ① One team told repeated stories about a dumpster fire, something that does not seem funny on its face, but the reactions of workers motivated to preserve safety sparked laughter as the stories were shared multiple times by multiple parties in the workplace. ② Shared events that cause laughter can indicate a sense of belonging since "you had to be there" to see the humor in them, and non-members were not and do not. ③ Since humor can easily capture people's attention, commercials tend to contain humorous elements, such as funny faces and gestures. ④ Instances of humor serve to enact bonds among organization members. ⑤ Understanding the humor may even be required as an informal badge of membership in the organization.

*subservient: 도움이 되는

L22 ✱✱✱ ········· 2023 대비 수능 35 (고3)

다음 글에서 전체 흐름과 관계 <u>없는</u> 문장은?

Actors, singers, politicians and countless others recognise the power of the human voice as a means of communication beyond the simple decoding of the words that are used. Learning to control your voice and use it for different purposes is, therefore, one of the most important skills to develop as an early career teacher. ① The more confidently you give instructions, the higher the chance of a positive class response. ② There are times when being able to project your voice loudly will be very useful when working in school, and knowing that you can cut through a noisy classroom, dinner hall or playground is a great skill to have. ③ In order to address serious noise issues in school, students, parents and teachers should search for a solution together. ④ However, I would always advise that you use your loudest voice incredibly sparingly and avoid shouting as much as possible. ⑤ A quiet, authoritative and measured tone has so much more impact than slightly panicked shouting.

2등급 대비 문제

L23 ~ 24 ▶ 제한시간 5분

L23 ✪ 2등급 대비 ········· 2024 대비 6월 모평 35 (고3)

다음 글에서 전체 흐름과 관계 <u>없는</u> 문장은?

Interestingly, experts do not suffer as much as beginners when performing complex tasks or combining multiple tasks. Because experts have extensive practice within a limited domain, the key component skills in their domain tend to be highly practiced and more automated. ① Each of these highly practiced skills then demands relatively few cognitive resources, effectively lowering the total cognitive load that experts experience. ② Thus, experts can perform complex tasks and combine multiple tasks relatively easily. ③ Furthermore, beginners are excellent at processing the tasks when the tasks are divided and isolated. ④ This is not because they necessarily have more cognitive resources than beginners; rather, because of the high level of fluency they have achieved in performing key skills, they can do more with what they have. ⑤ Beginners, on the other hand, have not achieved the same degree of fluency and automaticity in each of the component skills, and thus they struggle to combine skills that experts combine with relative ease and efficiency.

L24 ✪ 2등급 대비 ········· 2024 대비 9월 모평 35 (고3)

다음 글에서 전체 흐름과 관계 <u>없는</u> 문장은?

Although organizations are offering telecommuting programs in greater numbers than ever before, acceptance and use of these programs are still limited by a number of factors. ① These factors include manager reliance on face-to-face management practices, lack of telecommuting training within an organization, misperceptions of and discomfort with flexible workplace programs, and a lack of information about the effects of telecommuting on an organization's bottom line. ② Despite these limitations, at the beginning of the 21st century, a new "anytime, anywhere" work culture is emerging. ③ Care must be taken to select employees whose personal and working characteristics are best suited for telecommuting. ④ Continuing advances in information technology, the expansion of a global workforce, and increased desire to balance work and family are only three of the many factors that will gradually reduce the current barriers to telecommuting as a dominant workforce development. ⑤ With implications for organizational cost savings, especially with regard to lower facility costs, increased employee flexibility, and productivity, telecommuting is increasingly of interest to many organizations.

*telecommute: (컴퓨터로) 집에서 근무하다

L 어휘 Review

※ 다음 영어는 우리말 뜻을, 우리말은 영어 단어를 〈보기〉에서 찾아 쓰시오.

〈보기〉

scar	처음에	expense	길들이다
prominent	자율성	essential	심하게
independence	수정된	요소, 부품	necessity

01 component _____

02 autonomy _____

03 modified _____

04 initially _____

05 intensely _____

06 흉터, 상처 _____

07 필수적인, 근본적인 _____

08 중요한, 눈에 띄는 _____

09 독립성 _____

10 비용 _____

※ 다음 우리말에 알맞은 영어 표현을 찾아 연결하시오.

11 연구 중인 · · on one's own

12 ~에 관련하여 · · with regard to

13 즉시, 곧바로 · · in question

14 위태로운, 성패가 달린 · · at stake

15 스스로 · · straight away

※ 다음 우리말 표현에 맞는 단어를 고르시오.

16 정보의 중요한 원천 ⇒ the (critical / trivial) source of information

17 대단히 상업화된 환경에서 ⇒ in a (highly / high) commercialized setting

18 동일한 수준의 능숙함과 자동성 ⇒ the same degree of (fluency / patience) and automaticity

19 그 특정 지역의 발달에서 ⇒ in the development of the (vocality / locality)

20 정보 기술의 지속적인 발전 ⇒ continuing (advances / observances) in information technology

※ 다음 문장의 빈칸에 알맞은 단어를 〈보기〉에서 찾아 쓰시오.

〈보기〉

sufficient	migration	assessment	referred
validate	fragile	ambiguous	experts
barren	organs	demand	

21 그 동물은 처음에는 충분한 정보를 갖지 못할 수도 있다.
⇒ The animal may initially not have _____ information.

22 그것은 그들이 그들의 생애 주기 내내 새로운 장기와 조직을 생성할 수 있기 때문이다.
⇒ It is because they can generate new _____ and tissues throughout their life cycle.

23 단어의 의미는 모호하다.
⇒ Meanings of words are _____.

24 사람들이 자신의 의견과 결정의 올바름을 확인한다.
⇒ People _____ the correctness of their opinions and decisions.

25 Eugene Litwak은 이 행동 양식을 '수정 확대가족'이라고 표현했다.
⇒ Eugene Litwak has _____ to this pattern of behaviour as the 'modified extended family'.

26 그들은 비용 및 편익에 대한 자신의 평가에 근거하여 이주 결정을 내린다.
⇒ They make _____ decisions based on their assessment of the costs and benefits.

27 많은 신호들이 이러한 정보 수집 또는 평가 기능을 갖는 것으로 간주된다.
⇒ Many signals are seen as having this information gathering or _____ function.

28 식물은 회복해서 파괴되거나 척박한 환경을 변화시킬 수 있다.
⇒ Plants can recover and transform the destroyed or _____ environment.

29 전문가는 제한된 영역 내에서 광범위한 연습을 한다.
⇒ _____ have extensive practice within a limited domain.

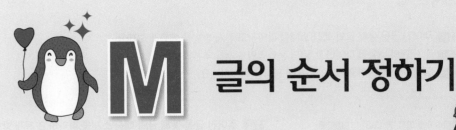

M 글의 순서 정하기

흠... 이 발자국들을 단서로 글의 순서를 파악하면 되겠군.

★유형 설명

주어진 글 다음에 이어질 글의 순서로 가장 적절한 것을 고르시오.

> Green products involve, in many cases, higher ingredient costs than those of

주어진 한 문단에 이어지는 나머지 세 문단의 논리적 순서를 연결어 등의 단서를 통해 추론해야 한다.

☞ ① this, that, these, it 등의 지시어가 가리키는 것이 무엇인지, on the other hand, similarly, however 등의 연결어로 서로 연결되어야 하는 내용이 무엇인지를 생각하면서 앞뒤에 올 내용을 확인한다.
② 처음 등장하는 것인지(a 또는 one), 앞에 이미 나온 것인지(the) 관사를 통해 파악한다.

유형 풀이 비법

1 글의 소재를 파악하라!
• 주어진 글을 통해 무엇에 관한 글인지를 알아낸다.

2 단서를 찾아라!
• 연결사, 대명사, 지시어 등 문장 간의 연결 고리 역할을 하는 단서들을 찾는다.

3 부사구를 확인하라!
• 시간적, 공간적 순서가 드러나는 글의 경우에 관련 부사구를 단서로 활용한다.

> Tip 순서를 맞추고 전체 글을 다시 읽으며 흐름이 맞는지 확인한다.

★최신 수능 경향 분석

대비연도	월	문항번호	지문 주제	난이도
2025	11	36번	평판 자본과 시장 규제 집행 가능성 간 관계	★★★
		37번	일렬로 선 새들의 관찰 조정력과 감정 전염	★★★
	9	36번	새로운 정보가 추가될 때 기존 패턴을 조정하는 정도	★★★
		37번	동물의 건강을 지키는 능력	★★※
	6	36번	호주에서 경관 관리를 위한 의도적인 불 지르기	★★★
		37번	조직의 학습을 지원하는 인적 자원 관리	★★★
2024	11	36번	협상의 목적과 이점, 기능	★★★
		37번	규범이 발생하고 순응하게 되는 과정	★★★
	9	36번	고정 관념의 효율성	★★★
		37번	똑똑한 식물	★★★
	6	36번	복잡해지는 컴퓨터 소프트웨어	★★★
		37번	얼굴이 붉어지는 것의 역할	★★★

★2025 수능 출제 분석

37번의 오답률이 특히 높았다. 36번은 (A)의 Similarly와 같은 단서들이 있었지만, 37번은 직접적인 연결어보다는 내용에 의해 순서를 유추해야 해서 어려웠다.

★2026 수능 예측

수능에서 반드시 출제되는 유형으로, 2026 수능에서도 두 문항이 출제될 것이다.

🔑 어휘 및 표현 Preview

□ **intentional** 의도적인
□ **landscape** 경관
□ **introduce** 도입하다
□ **condition** 여건
□ **function** 역할을 하다, 기능하다
□ **woody** 우거진
□ **vegetation** 초목
□ **stimulate** 촉진하다, 자극하다
□ **shrub** 관목
□ **strategy** 전략

□ **prevent** 막다
□ **consequence** 결과
□ **source** 자원
□ **reinforce** 강화하다
□ **accumulate** 축적하다
□ **difference** 차이
□ **beyond** ~너머
□ **totally** 완전히
□ **adjustment** 조정
□ **unit** 단위
□ **strength** 힘

□ **accommodate** 수용하다
□ **separately** 개별적으로
□ **organize** 조직하다
□ **activity** 활동
□ **material** 자료
□ **obtain** 얻다
□ **avoid** 피하다
□ **major** 주요한
□ **happen** 발생하다
□ **survival** 생존
□ **damage** 손상을 주다

□ **wound** 상처
□ **injured** 부상을 입은
□ **immune system** 면역 체계
□ **infection** 감염
□ **ward off** 피하다, 물리치다
□ **disease** 질병
□ **complex** 복잡한
□ **mechanism** 방법, 메커니즘
□ **aboriginal** 호주 원주민의
□ **consult** 상담하다
□ **advise** 조언하다

M 글의 순서 정하기 (첫 번째)

1st 주어진 글을 통해 글의 핵심 소재를 파악하고 전개 방향을 예측해 보세요.
2nd 각 문단의 내용을 파악하고, 글의 논리적인 순서를 추론하세요.
3rd 글이 한눈에 들어오도록 정리하여 정답을 확인하세요.

M01 ★★❀·············· 2025 대비 6월 모평 36 (고3)

주어진 글 다음에 이어질 글의 순서로 가장 적절한 것을 고르시오.

> Wildfire is a natural phenomenon in many Australian environments. The intentional setting of fire to manage the landscape was practised by Aboriginal people for millennia.

(A) However, the pattern of burning that stockmen introduced was unlike previous regimes. When conditions allowed, they would set fire to the landscape as they moved their animals out for the winter. This functioned to clear woody vegetation and also stimulated new plant growth in the following spring.

(B) Although grasses were the first kinds of plants to recolonize the burnt areas they were soon succeeded by further woody plants and shrubs. About the only strategy to prevent such regrowth was further burning — essentially using fire to control the consequences of using fire.

(C) The young shoots were a ready food source for their animals when they returned. However, the practice also tended to reinforce the scrubby growth it was intended to control.

*regime: 양식 **scrubby: 관목이 우거진

① (A)—(C)—(B) ② (B)—(A)—(C)
③ (B)—(C)—(A) ④ (C)—(A)—(B)
⑤ (C)—(B)—(A)

1st 주어진 글을 통해 글의 핵심 소재를 파악하고 전개 방향을 예측해 보세요.

Wildfire is a natural phenomenon / in many
산불은 자연스러운 현상이다   / 호주의 많은
Australian environments. //
환경에서   //
The intentional setting of fire / to manage the
의도적으로 불을 지르는 일은   / 경관을 관리하기 위해
landscape / was practised by Aboriginal people for
경관   / 수천 년 동안 호주 원주민들에 의해 행해졌다 //
millennia. //

● '의도적인 불 지르기'라는 것이 등장하는군요.
호주의 환경에서 산불은 자연스러운 현상으로, 경관 관리를 위해서 호주 원주민이 의도적으로 불을 지르는 것이 오랜 기간 행해졌다고 말했어요.

● 앞으로 나올 글의 나머지 내용을 예상해 봅시다.
경관을 관리하기 위한 의도적 불 지르기는 이미 호주 원주민들이 오랜 기간 해왔던 것이었다고 했으므로, 단서 원주민들이 오랫동안 해왔던 이 방식을 설명하는 내용이 나오거나, 이 방식과는 다르게 새로운 방식을 소개할 것이라는 예상이 가능하죠? 발상

2nd 각 문단의 내용을 파악하고, 글의 논리적인 순서를 추론하세요.

1) (A) 문단부터 확인해 봅시다.

(A) However, the pattern of burning that stockmen
하지만 목축업자들이 도입한 불 지르기 방식은
introduced / was unlike previous regimes. //
          / 이전 양식과는 달랐다   //
When conditions allowed, / they would set fire to
여건이 허락되면   / 그들은 경관에 불을 지르곤
the landscape / as they moved their animals out for
했다   / 그들은 겨울에 자신들의 가축을 외부로
the winter. //
이동시켜   //
This functioned to clear woody vegetation / and
이는 숲이 우거진 초목을 없애는 역할을 했고   /
also stimulated new plant growth in the following
또한 이듬해 봄에 새로운 식물의 성장을 촉진했다 //
spring. //

● **(A) 앞에는 어떤 내용이 있어야 할까요?**

However(하지만)는 반대 내용을 연결하는 연결어이므로 일단 앞에는 (A)와 반대되는 내용이 나와야 할 것임을 알 수 있어요.
목축업자들의 불 지르기 방식은 이전 양식과는 달랐는데, 겨울에 가축을 외부로 이동시켜서 경관에 불을 지르곤 했다고 했어요.
이것은 주어진 글에서 말한, 목축업자들의 방식과 다른 호주 원주민들의 방식에 이어질 수 있는 내용이죠.
▶ 주어진 글이 (A) 앞에 올 수 있음 (순서: 주어진 글 → (A))

● **(A) 뒤에 이어질 내용을 예상해 볼까요?**

가축을 외부로 이동시켰다고 했으므로 이동한 동물들은 어떻게 되었으며, 우거진 나무가 없어진 자리에 어떤 새로운 식물이 자랐는지 등에 대한 내용이 이어질 것이라는 예상을 할 수 있죠.
과연 우리의 예상이 맞는지 남은 두 문단도 읽어봅시다.

2) (B)는 접속사 Although로 시작하는군요!

> (B) Although grasses were the first kinds of plants /
> 첫 번째 식물류는 풀이었지만　　　　　　　　　　 /
> to recolonize the burnt areas / they were soon
> 불에 탄 지역에 다시 대량 서식한　　　 / 목본성 식물과
> succeeded by further woody plants and shrubs. //
> 관목이 곧 그것들의 뒤를 이었다　　　　　　　　 /
> About the only strategy to prevent such regrowth /
> 그러한 재성장을 막기 위한 거의 유일한 전략은　　 , 　 /
> was further burning / — essentially using fire to
> 불을 더 지르는 것이었는데　　 / 본질적으로는 불을
> control the consequences of using fire. //
> 사용하여 불을 사용한 결과를 통제하는 것이었다　　 //

● **(B) 앞에는 어떤 내용이 있어야 할까요?**

Although(~었지만, ~하더라도)는 양보·대조를 나타내는 접속사이므로 앞에는 이런 관계로 연결될 수 있는 내용이 나와야 해요.
풀이 자란 이후 다시 나무가 자라게 되었다는 내용이므로, 없애고자 했던 나무의 성장을 언급했던 내용이 앞에 와야겠죠?
이런 내용이 주어진 글이나 (A)에 없으므로 (C)가 올 것이라는 예상이 가능해요.
▶ (B) 앞에 (C)가 와야 함 (순서: (C) → (B))

● **(B) 뒤에 이어질 내용을 예상해 볼까요?**

목본성 식물과 관목이 다시 자라게 되어 ❶(　　　　)을 막기 위해서 불을 지른 자리에 다시 불을 지르게 된다고 했어요. 맥락상 마무리 내용이라는 생각이 강하게 드네요.
▶ (B)가 마지막에 올 확률이 큼

3) (C) 문단의 내용을 살펴볼까요?

> (C) The young shoots were a ready food source / for
> 어린 새싹은 준비된 먹을 수 있는 식량원이었다　　　　 /
> their animals when they returned. //
> 그들의 동물들이 돌아왔을 때　　　　　　 //
> However, the practice also tended to reinforce the
> 하지만, 그 관행은 우거진 관목의 성장을 강화하는 경향도 있었다
> scrubby growth / it was intended to control. //
> 　　　　　 / 그것(그 관행)이 통제하고자 했던　　　 //

● **(C) 앞에는 어떤 내용이 있어야 할까요?**

'그들의 동물들(their animals)'이 가리키는 것이 앞에 있어야 하는데, (A)에서 말한 ❷(　　　　)의 동물들이 바로 이 동물들을 가리켜요.
▶ 순서: (A) → (C)

● **(C) 뒤에 이어질 내용을 예상해 볼까요?**

원래 없애고자 했던 나무들의 성장이 다시 강화되는 경향이 있었다고 했으므로, (B) 문단에서 살펴봤던 것처럼 이와 관련된 내용인 (B)가 이어질 거예요.
▶ 순서: 주어진 글 → (A) → (C) → (B)

3rd 글이 한눈에 들어오도록 정리하여 정답을 확인하세요.

주어진 글: 호주에서 경관을 관리하기 위한 의도적 불 지르기는 이미 원주민들이 오랜 기간 해왔던 것이었다.

→ **(A)**: 목축업자들이 도입한 불 지르기 방식은 이전 양식(원주민)과는 달랐다. 겨울에 동물을 이동시킨 후 불을 질렀다.

→ **(C)**: 동물이 돌아왔을 때 새로 자란 어린 새싹은 동물의 식량원이 되었다. 그러나 원래 없애고자 했던 나무의 성장이 다시 강화되는 경향이 있었다.

→ **(B)**: 풀이 자란 이후 뒤이어 다시 나무가 자라게 되었고, 불을 더 질러야 했다.

▶ 주어진 글 다음에 이어질 글의 순서는 (A) → (C) → (B)이므로 정답은
❸(　　　　)

1st 주어진 글을 통해 글의 핵심 소재를 파악하고 전개 방향을 예측해 보세요.
2nd 각 문단의 내용을 파악하고, 글의 논리적인 순서를 추론하세요.
3rd 글이 한눈에 들어오도록 정리하여 정답을 확인하세요.

M02 ★★★ .... 2024 대비 6월 모평 36 (고3)

주어진 글 다음에 이어질 글의 순서로 가장 적절한 것을 고르시오.

> The growing complexity of computer software has direct implications for our global safety and security, particularly as the physical objects upon which we depend — things like cars, airplanes, bridges, tunnels, and implantable medical devices — transform themselves into computer code.

(A) As all this code grows in size and complexity, so too do the number of errors and software bugs. According to a study by Carnegie Mellon University, commercial software typically has twenty to thirty bugs for every thousand lines of code — 50 million lines of code means 1 million to 1.5 million potential errors to be exploited.

(B) This is the basis for all malware attacks that take advantage of these computer bugs to get the code to do something it was not originally intended to do. As computer code grows more elaborate, software bugs flourish and security suffers, with increasing consequences for society at large.

(C) Physical things are increasingly becoming information technologies. Cars are "computers we ride in," and airplanes are nothing more than "flying Solaris boxes attached to bucketfuls of industrial control systems."

*exploit: 활용하다

① (A) ― (C) ― (B)　　② (B) ― (A) ― (C)
③ (B) ― (C) ― (A)　　④ (C) ― (A) ― (B)
⑤ (C) ― (B) ― (A)

1st 주어진 글을 통해 글의 핵심 소재를 파악하고 전개 방향을 예측해 보세요.

The growing complexity of computer software / has
컴퓨터 소프트웨어의 증가하는 복잡성은　　　　/
direct implications / for our global safety and
직접적인 영향을 준다　　　/ 우리의 전 세계적인 안전과 보안에
security, / particularly as the physical objects / upon
　　　/ 특히 물리적 대상이 ~함에 따라　　　　/
which we depend / — things like cars, airplanes,
우리가 의존하는　　　/ 자동차, 비행기
bridges, tunnels, and implantable medical devices
교량, 터널, 이식형 의료 기기와 같은 것들
— / transform themselves / into computer code. //
　/ 그 자신을 변화시킴에 (따라)　/ 컴퓨터 코드로　　　//

● 주어진 글만으로 글의 주제를 알 수 있어요.
'컴퓨터 소프트웨어의 증가하는 복잡성'이라는 소재로 글이 시작되었어요. 물리적 대상이 컴퓨터 코드로 변화하게 되면서 소프트웨어가 많이 쓰이는데, 그 소프트웨어가 더 복잡해지니 세계적인 안전과 보안에 직접 영향을 줬다는 내용이 글의 주제로 보여요.

2nd 각 문단의 내용을 파악하고, 글의 논리적인 순서를 추론하세요.
1) (A) 문단부터 확인해 봅시다.

As all this code grows / in size and complexity, / so
이 모든 코드가 증가함에 따라　/ 크기와 복잡성에서　　　/ 또한
too do / the number of errors and software bugs. //
그렇다　/ 오류와 소프트웨어 버그 수　　　　//
... / — 50 million lines of code means / 1 million to
…　/ 5천만 줄의 코드는 의미한다　　　　/ 1백만에서
1.5 million potential errors / to be exploited. //
150만 개의 잠재적 오류를　　　/ 악의적으로 이용되는　//

● (A) 앞에는 어떤 내용이 있어야 할까요?
주어진 글 뒷부분의 ❶(　　　　　　　　　　)가 (A)에서
this code로 다시 등장했어요. 이것만 보면 (A) 앞에 주어진 글이 나올 것 같지만, (B)나 (C)에서 더 확실한 단서가 나올 수도 있으니 다른 문단을 더 읽어야 해요.

● (A) 뒤에 이어질 내용을 예상해 볼까요?
(A)의 뒷부분은 코드의 크기와 복잡성이 증가하면서 악의적으로 이용되는 잠재적 오류도 증가했다는 내용이므로, (A) 뒤에 이어질 문단은 잠재적 오류가 악의적으로 이용되는 것에 대해 이야기할 것으로 보여져요.

2) (B)는 지시대명사 This로 시작하는군요!

<u>This</u> is the basis / for all malware attacks / that take
이것이 근간이다   / 모든 악성 소프트웨어 공격의   /

advantage of <u>these computer bugs</u> / ... // As
이 컴퓨터 버그를 이용하는   / ... //

computer code grows more elaborate, / software
컴퓨터 코드가 더 정교해짐에 따라   / 소프트웨어

bugs flourish / and security suffers, / with
버그는 창궐하고   / 보안은 악화된다   /

increasing consequences for society at large. //
사회 전반에 미치는 증가하는 영향으로   //

● **(B) 앞에는 어떤 내용이 있어야 할까요?**
This가 악성 소프트웨어 공격의 근간이라고 했는데, (A) 뒷부분을 보면
(코드의 복잡성이 증가함에 따라) 잠재적 오류가 악의적으로 이용될 수
있다고 했어요. 즉, This는 '코드의 복잡성 증가'라고 볼 수 있죠. 또한
❷(   )는 (A)의 software bugs를
다시 언급한 것으로 보여요. 이처럼 (A)의 내용 및 단어를 곧바로 다시
언급하기 때문에 (A)가 (B) 앞에 나와야 함을 알 수 있어요.
▶ 순서: (A) → (B)

● **(B) 뒤에 이어질 내용을 예상해 볼까요?**
코드의 복잡성이 증가하여 결국 사회 전반에 악영향을 미친다는
내용이기에 (B)는 글의 결론에 해당할 가능성이 커요.

3) (C) 문단의 내용을 살펴볼까요?

Physical things are increasingly becoming /
물리적 사물은 점점 더 되어가고 있다   /

information technologies. // Cars are "computers /
정보 기술이   // 자동차는 '컴퓨터'이고   /

we ride in," / and airplanes are nothing more than
우리가 타는   / 비행기는 '비행 솔라리스 박스'에 불과하다

"flying Solaris boxes / attached to bucketfuls of
                    / 수많은 산업 제어 시스템에 부착된 //

industrial control systems." //
산업 제어 시스템의   //

● **(C) 앞에는 어떤 내용이 있어야 할까요?**
주어진 글의 Physical objects와 (C)의 Physical things가 동일 개념으로
연결되고 있어요. 또, 주어진 글의 예시로 나온 cars와 airplanes를
(C)에서 다시 설명하고 있죠.
주어진 글에 물리적 대상이 코드로 변환된다는 내용이 있었기 때문에 그
예시를 언급하는 (C) 앞에는 주어진 글이 나와야 해요.
▶ 순서: 주어진 글 → (C)

● **(C) 뒤에 이어질 내용을 예상해 볼까요?**
우선 ❸(   )이 코드로 변환되었고, 그렇게 변화된 코드의
크기와 복잡성이 증가했다는 맥락으로 이어지는 것이 자연스러워 보여요.
즉, (C) 뒤에 (A)가 이어지는 것이죠.
▶ 순서: 주어진 글 → (C) → (A) → (B)

3rd 글이 한눈에 들어오도록 정리하여 정답을 확인하세요.

주어진 글: 컴퓨터 소프트웨어의 증가하는 복잡성은 전 세계의 안전과
보안에 직접적인 영향을 주는데, 특히 물리적 대상이 컴퓨터 코드로 변함에
따라 그렇다.

→ **(C)**: 자동차, 비행기와 같은 물리적 사물은 점점 더 정보 기술이 되어 가고
있다.

→ **(A)**: 이러한 코드가 크고 복잡해짐에 따라 오류와 소프트웨어 버그의 수도
증가한다.

→ **(B)**: 컴퓨터 코드가 더 정교해짐에 따라 소프트웨어 버그는 창궐하고
보안은 악화되며 사회 전반에 더 큰 영향을 미친다.

▶ 주어진 글 다음에 이어질 글의 순서는 (C) → (A) → (B)이므로 정답은
❹(   )

말풍선: 지시어나 연결어를 통해
문장의 순서를 알아내자!

빈칸 정답 ④ ❹ 유바 ᄒ리치롬 ❸ 롬리치 대상 ❷ these computer bugs ❶ computer code

M03~06 ▶ 제한시간 8분

M03 ★★★ .... 2025 대비 수능 36 (고3)

주어진 글 다음에 이어질 글의 순서로 가장 적절한 것을 고르시오.

> The potential for market enforcement is greater when contracting parties have developed reputational capital that can be devalued when contracts are violated.

(A) Similarly, a landowner can undermaintain fences, ditches, and irrigation systems. Accurate assessments of farmer and landowner behavior will be made over time, and those farmers and landowners who attempt to gain at each other's expense will find that others may refuse to deal with them in the future.

(B) Over time landowners indirectly monitor farmers by observing the reported output, the general quality of the soil, and any unusual or extreme behavior. Farmer and landowner reputations act as a bond. In any growing season a farmer can reduce effort, overuse soil, or underreport the crop.

(C) Farmers and landowners develop reputations for honesty, fairness, producing high yields, and consistently demonstrating that they are good at what they do. In small, close-knit farming communities, reputations are well known. *ditch: 개천 **irrigation: 물을 댐

① (A)—(C)—(B) ② (B)—(A)—(C)
③ (B)—(C)—(A) ④ (C)—(A)—(B)
⑤ (C)—(B)—(A)

M04 ★★★ .... 2025 대비 수능 37 (고3)

주어진 글 다음에 이어질 글의 순서로 가장 적절한 것을 고르시오. [3점]

> Watch the birds in your backyard. If one bird startles and flies off, others will follow, not waiting around to assess whether the threat is real. They have been infected by emotional contagion.

(A) Marc wondered whether the birds in line were more fearful because they didn't know what their flockmates were doing. Emotional contagion would have been impossible for individual grosbeaks in the linear array except with their nearest neighbors.

(B) In a long-term research project that Marc did with some of his students on patterns of antipredatory scanning by western evening grosbeaks, they found that birds in a circle showed more coordination in scanning than did birds who were feeding in a line.

(C) The birds in a line, who could only see their nearest neighbor, not only were less coordinated when scanning, but also were more nervous, changing their body and head positions significantly more than grosbeaks in a circle, where it was possible for each grosbeak to see every other grosbeak. *grosbeak: 콩새류(類) **array: 정렬

① (A)—(C)—(B) ② (B)—(A)—(C)
③ (B)—(C)—(A) ④ (C)—(A)—(B)
⑤ (C)—(B)—(A)

주어진 글 다음에 이어질 글의 순서로 가장 적절한 것을 고르시오. [3점]

> If learning were simply a matter of accumulating lists of facts, then it shouldn't make any difference if we are presented with information that is just a little bit beyond what we already know or totally new information.

(A) If we are trying to understand something totally new, however, we need to make larger adjustments to the units of the patterns we already have, which requires changing the strengths of large numbers of connections in our brain, and this is a difficult, tiring process.

(B) The adjustments are clearly smallest when the new information is only slightly new — when it is compatible with what we already know, so that the old patterns need only a little bit of adjustment to accommodate the new knowledge.

(C) Each fact would simply be stored separately. According to connectionist theory, however, our knowledge is organized into patterns of activity, and each time we learn something new we have to modify the old patterns so as to keep the old material while adding the new information.   *compatible: 양립하는

① (A)—(C)—(B) ② (B)—(A)—(C)
③ (B)—(C)—(A) ④ (C)—(A)—(B)
⑤ (C)—(B)—(A)

주어진 글 다음에 이어질 글의 순서로 가장 적절한 것을 고르시오.

> The generally close connection between health and what animals want exists because wanting to obtain the right things and wanting to avoid the wrong ones are major ways in which animals keep themselves healthy.

(A) They can take pre-emptive action so that the worst never happens. They start to want things that will be necessary for their health and survival not for now but for some time in the future.

(B) Animals have evolved many different ways of maintaining their health and then regaining it again once it has been damaged, such as an ability to heal wounds when they are injured and an amazingly complex immune system for warding off infection.

(C) Animals are equally good, however, at dealing with injury and disease before they even happen. They have evolved a complex set of mechanisms for anticipating and avoiding danger altogether.

*pre-emptive: 선제의 **ward off: 막다

① (A)—(C)—(B) ② (B)—(A)—(C)
③ (B)—(C)—(A) ④ (C)—(A)—(B)
⑤ (C)—(B)—(A)

M07 ★★❄ .... 2025 대비 6월 모평 37 (고3)

주어진 글 다음에 이어질 글의 순서로 가장 적절한 것을 고르시오. [3점]

> There are a number of human resource management practices that are necessary to support organizational learning.

(A) Their role should be to assist, consult, and advise teams on how best to approach learning. They must be able to develop new mechanisms for cross-training peers — team members — and new systems for capturing and sharing information. To do this, human resource development professionals must be able to think systematically and understand how to promote learning within groups and across the organization.

(B) For example, performance evaluation and reward systems that reinforce long-term performance and the development and sharing of new skills and knowledge are particularly important. In addition, the human resource development function may be dramatically changed to keep the emphasis on continuous learning.

(C) In a learning organization, every employee must take the responsibility for acquiring and transferring knowledge. Formal training programs, developed in advance and delivered according to a preset schedule, are insufficient to address shifting training needs and encourage timely information sharing. Rather, human resource development professionals must become learning facilitators.

① (A)—(C)—(B)　　　② (B)—(A)—(C)
③ (B)—(C)—(A)　　　④ (C)—(A)—(B)
⑤ (C)—(B)—(A)

M08 ★★★ .... 2024 실시 10월 학평 36 (고3)

주어진 글 다음에 이어질 글의 순서로 가장 적절한 것을 고르시오.

> From infancy, even before we learn to speak, we absorb how to infer people's emotions from their behaviors.

(A) Some people, however, have a talent for detecting emotions, even when they're unspoken. We all know people like this: Friends who seem to intuit when we're feeling down, even if we haven't said anything; managers who sense when a kind word is needed to help us get over the hump at work.

(B) As we grow older, however, this capacity can atrophy. We start to pay increasing attention to what people say rather than what they do, to the point where we can fail to notice nonlinguistic clues. Spoken language is so information rich that it lulls us into ignoring hints that someone might be, say, upset and instead focus on their words when they say, *It's nothing. I feel fine.*

(C) It's natural to assume these people are unusually observant, or uncommonly sensitive. Sometimes they are. But years of research indicates this is a skill anyone can develop. We can learn to identify the nonverbal clues that indicate someone's true emotions and use these hints to understand what they are feeling.

*over the hump: 고비를 넘겨　**atrophy: 쇠퇴하다
***lull ~ into: ~을 (속이어) …하게 하다

① (A)—(C)—(B)　　　② (B)—(A)—(C)
③ (B)—(C)—(A)　　　④ (C)—(A)—(B)
⑤ (C)—(B)—(A)

주어진 글 다음에 이어질 글의 순서로 가장 적절한 것을 고르시오. [3점]

> Some epistemic feelings let us know that we know. These include the feeling of knowing, the feeling of certainty, and the feeling of correctness.

(A) Other epistemic feelings alert our attention to what we do not yet know. Curiosity, awe, and wonder fall into this category. As with the feelings of knowing, we can ask whether feelings of not-yet-knowing are necessarily right. It does seem that if you wonder at something, there is something that prompted you to wonder.

(B) This feeling alerts you to the fact that your current body of knowledge — the schemas, heuristics, and other information you use — did not prepare you for the thing you wonder at. As such, wonder is a useful emotion, because it points to gaps in what you thought you knew.

(C) For example, you feel sure that "1666" is the answer to the question, "When did the Great Fire of London occur?" Feeling that you know, even that you are sure, is not unfailing. We can be mistaken in those feelings.

*epistemic: 인식론적 **heuristics: 휴리스틱(특정 상황에서 사람들이 신속하게 사용하는 어림짐작의 기술)

① (A) ― (C) ― (B)　　② (B) ― (A) ― (C)
③ (B) ― (C) ― (A)　　④ (C) ― (A) ― (B)
⑤ (C) ― (B) ― (A)

주어진 글 다음에 이어질 글의 순서로 가장 적절한 것을 고르시오. [3점]

> Technocracy can be thought to influence technological decision-making in one of two ways.

(A) This is because policy-makers work within the constraints set by the experts and *choose from the options those experts provide*. The technocratic element is clear: experts set the agenda and political judgements are parasitic on the judgements of experts.

(B) An idealized science and technology replaces politics and technical experts become the decision-makers, planning and organizing societies according to whatever scientific principles the evidence supports. This form of technocracy is rarely found in practice.

(C) In contrast, a more moderate form in which experts advise and politicians decide is found in many democratic societies. Also called the 'decisionist model', this form of technocracy institutionalizes a division of labour based on the distinction between facts and values and allows specialist experts to wield significant power.

*parasitic: 기생하는

① (A) ― (C) ― (B)　　② (B) ― (A) ― (C)
③ (B) ― (C) ― (A)　　④ (C) ― (A) ― (B)
⑤ (C) ― (B) ― (A)

M11 ✱✱✱ ·························· 2024 실시 7월 학평 37 (고3)

주어진 글 다음에 이어질 글의 순서로 가장 적절한 것을 고르시오.

Land use change can be good or bad for the climate. Plants use photosynthesis to convert carbon dioxide from the air and water to carbohydrates.

(A) In those conditions microorganisms consume carbon that has been stored in the soil and in plants and animals, and respire that stored carbon back to atmosphere as CO_2. If the original ecosystem was a forest, much of the carbon stored in the trees may also be converted to CO_2 through burning.

(B) That extra carbon is stored in living biomass like tree trunks and soil bacteria and fungi, and as carbon compounds in the soil. But when actions like deforestation or plowing severely disturb a plant community, the remaining plants cannot photosynthesize enough to feed themselves, plus all the animals and microorganisms that depend on them.

(C) Those carbohydrates provide the energy plants need to live, and the building blocks for plant growth, as well as food for animals and microorganisms. In healthy ecosystems the plants pull more carbon out of the atmosphere than they, and the animals and microorganisms that consume them, need.

① (A)—(C)—(B) ② (B)—(A)—(C)
③ (B)—(C)—(A) ④ (C)—(A)—(B)
⑤ (C)—(B)—(A)

M12 ✱✱✱ ·························· 2024 실시 5월 학평 36 (고3)

주어진 글 다음에 이어질 글의 순서로 가장 적절한 것을 고르시오.

Philosophers who seek to understand the nature of time might consider the possibility of time travel. But there are no real-life cases of time travel.

(A) It seems that something must happen to prevent you from doing this, because if you were to succeed, you would not exist and so you would not have been able to go back in time. As a result of thinking through these sorts of cases, some philosophers claim that the very notion of time travel makes no sense.

(B) In situations such as this, philosophers often construct thought experiments — imagined scenarios that bring out the thoughts and presuppositions underlying people's judgments. Sometimes these scenarios are drawn from books, movies, and television. Other times, philosophers just make up their own scenarios.

(C) Either way, the point is to put such concepts to the test. In the case of time travel, for example, a common thought experiment is to imagine what would happen if you went back in time and found yourself in a position to interfere in such a way that you were never born.

① (A)—(C)—(B) ② (B)—(A)—(C)
③ (B)—(C)—(A) ④ (C)—(A)—(B)
⑤ (C)—(B)—(A)

A universal indicator of sleep is the loss of external awareness. You are no longer conscious of all that surrounds you, at least not explicitly. In actual fact, your ears are still 'hearing'; your eyes, though closed, are still capable of 'seeing.'

(A) Should they be granted its permission to pass, they are sent to the cortex at the top of your brain, where they are consciously perceived. By locking its gates shut, the thalamus imposes a sensory blackout in the brain, preventing onward travel of those signals to the cortex.

(B) As a result, you are no longer consciously aware of the information broadcasts being transmitted from your outer sense organs. At this moment, your brain has lost waking contact with the outside world. Said another way, you are now asleep.

(C) All these signals still flood into the center of your brain while you sleep, but they are blocked by a perceptual barricade set up in a structure called the thalamus. The thalamus decides which sensory signals are allowed through its gate, and which are not.

*cortex: 대뇌피질 **thalamus: 시상(視床)

① (A)—(C)—(B) 　　② (B)—(A)—(C)
③ (B)—(C)—(A) 　　④ (C)—(A)—(B)
⑤ (C)—(B)—(A)

Different creative pursuits require varying degrees of unconscious flexible thinking, in combination with varying degrees of the conscious ability to adjust it and shape it through analytical thinking. In music, for example, at one end of the creative spectrum are improvisational artists, such as jazz musicians.

(A) On the other end of the spectrum are those who compose complex forms, such as a symphony or concerto, that require not just imagination but also careful planning and exacting editing. We know, for example, through his letters and the reports of others, that even Mozart's creations did not appear spontaneously, wholly formed in his consciousness, as the myths about him portray.

(B) They have to be particularly talented at lowering their inhibitions and letting in their unconsciously generated ideas. And although the process of learning the fundamentals of jazz would require a high degree of analytical thought, that thinking style is not as big a factor during the performance.

(C) Instead, he spent long, hard hours analyzing and reworking the ideas that arose in his unconscious, much as a scientist does when producing a theory from a germ of insight. In Mozart's own words: "I immerse myself in music... I think about it all day long — I like experimenting — studying — reflecting..."

*improvisational: 즉흥적인 **immerse: ~에 몰두하다

① (A)—(C)—(B) 　　② (B)—(A)—(C)
③ (B)—(C)—(A) 　　④ (C)—(A)—(B)
⑤ (C)—(B)—(A)

M15 ★★★.......................... 2024 실시 3월 학평 37 (고3)

주어진 글 다음에 이어질 글의 순서로 가장 적절한 것을 고르시오.

> Today, historic ideas about integrating nature and urban/suburban space find expression in various interpretations of sustainable urban planning.

(A) But Landscape Urbanists find that these designs do not prioritize the natural environment and often involve diverting streams and disrupting natural wetlands. Still others, such as those advocating for "just sustainabilities" or "complete streets," find that both approaches are overly idealistic and neither pays enough attention to the realities of social dynamics and systemic inequality.

(B) However, critics claim that Landscape Urbanists prioritize aesthetic and ecological concerns over human needs. In contrast, New Urbanism is an approach that was popularized in the 1980s and promotes walkable streets, compact design, and mixed-use developments.

(C) However, the role of social justice in these approaches remains highly controversial. For example, Landscape Urbanism is a relatively recent planning approach that advocates for native habitat designs that include diverse species and landscapes that require very low resource use.

*compact: 고밀도, 촘촘한 **divert: 우회시키다, 방향을 바꾸게 하다

① (A) ─ (C) ─ (B)   ② (B) ─ (A) ─ (C)
③ (B) ─ (C) ─ (A)   ④ (C) ─ (A) ─ (B)
⑤ (C) ─ (B) ─ (A)

M16 ★★✿.......................... 2022 대비 6월 모평 36 (고3)

주어진 글 다음에 이어질 글의 순서로 가장 적절한 것을 고르시오.

> Spatial reference points are larger than themselves. This isn't really a paradox: landmarks are themselves, but they also define neighborhoods around themselves.

(A) In a paradigm that has been repeated on many campuses, researchers first collect a list of campus landmarks from students. Then they ask another group of students to estimate the distances between pairs of locations, some to landmarks, some to ordinary buildings on campus.

(B) This asymmetry of distance estimates violates the most elementary principles of Euclidean distance, that the distance from A to B must be the same as the distance from B to A. Judgments of distance, then, are not necessarily coherent.

(C) The remarkable finding is that distances from an ordinary location to a landmark are judged shorter than distances from a landmark to an ordinary location. So, people would judge the distance from Pierre's house to the Eiffel Tower to be shorter than the distance from the Eiffel Tower to Pierre's house. Like black holes, landmarks seem to pull ordinary locations toward themselves, but ordinary places do not.

*asymmetry: 비대칭

① (A) ─ (C) ─ (B)   ② (B) ─ (A) ─ (C)
③ (B) ─ (C) ─ (A)   ④ (C) ─ (A) ─ (B)
⑤ (C) ─ (B) ─ (A)

주어진 글 다음에 이어질 글의 순서로 가장 적절한 것을 고르시오. [3점]

A firm is deciding whether to invest in shipbuilding. If it can produce at sufficiently large scale, it knows the venture will be profitable.

(A) There is a "good" outcome, in which both types of investments are made, and both the shipyard and the steelmakers end up profitable and happy. Equilibrium is reached. Then there is a "bad" outcome, in which neither type of investment is made. This second outcome also is an equilibrium because the decisions not to invest reinforce each other.

(B) Assume that shipyards are the only potential customers of steel. Steel producers figure they'll make money if there's a shipyard to buy their steel, but not otherwise. Now we have two possible outcomes — what economists call "multiple equilibria."

(C) But one key input is low-cost steel, and it must be produced nearby. The company's decision boils down to this: if there is a steel factory close by, invest in shipbuilding; otherwise, don't invest. Now consider the thinking of potential steel investors in the region.

*equilibrium: 균형

① (A)—(C)—(B)　　② (B)—(A)—(C)
③ (B)—(C)—(A)　　④ (C)—(A)—(B)
⑤ (C)—(B)—(A)

주어진 글 다음에 이어질 글의 순서로 가장 적절한 것을 고르시오.

Green products involve, in many cases, higher ingredient costs than those of mainstream products.

(A) They'd rather put money and time into known, profitable, high-volume products that serve populous customer segments than into risky, less-profitable, low-volume products that may serve current noncustomers. Given that choice, these companies may choose to leave the green segment of the market to small niche competitors.

(B) Even if the green product succeeds, it may cannibalize the company's higher-profit mainstream offerings. Given such downsides, companies serving mainstream consumers with successful mainstream products face what seems like an obvious investment decision.

(C) Furthermore, the restrictive ingredient lists and design criteria that are typical of such products may make green products inferior to mainstream products on core performance dimensions (e.g., less effective cleansers). In turn, the higher costs and lower performance of some products attract only a small portion of the customer base, leading to lower economies of scale in procurement, manufacturing, and distribution.

*segment: 조각　**cannibalize: 잡아먹다　***procurement: 조달

① (A)—(C)—(B)　　② (B)—(A)—(C)
③ (B)—(C)—(A)　　④ (C)—(A)—(B)
⑤ (C)—(B)—(A)

M19 ✿✿❀.......................... 2023 대비 6월 모평 36 (고3)

주어진 글 다음에 이어질 글의 순서로 가장 적절한 것을 고르시오.

> The fossil record provides evidence of evolution. The story the fossils tell is one of change. Creatures existed in the past that are no longer with us. Sequential changes are found in many fossils showing the change of certain features over time from a common ancestor, as in the case of the horse.

(A) If multicelled organisms were indeed found to have evolved before single-celled organisms, then the theory of evolution would be rejected. A good scientific theory always allows for the possibility of rejection. The fact that we have not found such a case in countless examinations of the fossil record strengthens the case for evolutionary theory.

(B) The fossil record supports this prediction — multicelled organisms are found in layers of earth millions of years after the first appearance of single-celled organisms. Note that the possibility always remains that the opposite could be found.

(C) Apart from demonstrating that evolution did occur, the fossil record also provides tests of the predictions made from evolutionary theory. For example, the theory predicts that single-celled organisms evolved before multicelled organisms.

① (A)—(C)—(B) ② (B)—(A)—(C)
③ (B)—(C)—(A) ④ (C)—(A)—(B)
⑤ (C)—(B)—(A)

M20 ✿✿✿.......................... 2022 대비 9월 모평 37 (고3)

주어진 글 다음에 이어질 글의 순서로 가장 적절한 것을 고르시오. [3점]

> Recently, a number of commercial ventures have been launched that offer social robots as personal home assistants, perhaps eventually to rival existing smart-home assistants.

(A) They might be motorized and can track the user around the room, giving the impression of being aware of the people in the environment. Although personal robotic assistants provide services similar to those of smart-home assistants, their social presence offers an opportunity that is unique to social robots.

(B) Personal robotic assistants are devices that have no physical manipulation or locomotion capabilities. Instead, they have a distinct social presence and have visual features suggestive of their ability to interact socially, such as eyes, ears, or a mouth.

(C) For instance, in addition to playing music, a social personal assistant robot would express its engagement with the music so that users would feel like they are listening to the music together with the robot. These robots can be used as surveillance devices, act as communicative intermediates, engage in richer games, tell stories, or be used to provide encouragement or incentives.

*locomotion: 이동 **surveillance: 감시

① (A)—(C)—(B) ② (B)—(A)—(C)
③ (B)—(C)—(A) ④ (C)—(A)—(B)
⑤ (C)—(B)—(A)

M21 ✱✱❋ .... 2022 대비 수능 36 (고3)

주어진 글 다음에 이어질 글의 순서로 가장 적절한 것을 고르시오.

> According to the market response model, it is increasing prices that drive providers to search for new sources, innovators to substitute, consumers to conserve, and alternatives to emerge.

(A) Many examples of such "green taxes" exist. Facing landfill costs, labor expenses, and related costs in the provision of garbage disposal, for example, some cities have required households to dispose of all waste in special trash bags, purchased by consumers themselves, and often costing a dollar or more each.

(B) Taxing certain goods or services, and so increasing prices, should result in either decreased use of these resources or creative innovation of new sources or options. The money raised through the tax can be used directly by the government either to supply services or to search for alternatives.

(C) The results have been greatly increased recycling and more careful attention by consumers to packaging and waste. By internalizing the costs of trash to consumers, there has been an observed decrease in the flow of garbage from households.

① (A)—(C)—(B)   ② (B)—(A)—(C)
③ (B)—(C)—(A)   ④ (C)—(A)—(B)
⑤ (C)—(B)—(A)

M22 ✱✱✱ .... 2023 실시 3월 학평 36 (고3)

주어진 글 다음에 이어질 글의 순서로 가장 적절한 것을 고르시오.

> Aristotle explains that the Good for human beings consists in *eudaimoniā* (a Greek word combining *eu* meaning "good" with *daimon* meaning "spirit," and most often translated as "happiness").

(A) It depends only on knowledge of human nature and other worldly and social realities. For him it is the study of human nature and worldly existence that will disclose the relevant meaning of the notion of *eudaimoniā*.

(B) Some people say it is worldly enjoyment while others say it is eternal salvation. Aristotle's theory will turn out to be "naturalistic" in that it does not depend on any theological or metaphysical knowledge. It does not depend on knowledge of God or of metaphysical and universal moral norms.

(C) Whereas he had argued in a purely formal way that the Good was that to which we all aim, he now gives a more substantive answer: that this universal human goal is happiness. However, he is quick to point out that this conclusion is still somewhat formal since different people have different views about what happiness is.

*salvation: 구원 **theological: 신학의 ***substantive: 실질적인

① (A)—(C)—(B)   ② (B)—(A)—(C)
③ (B)—(C)—(A)   ④ (C)—(A)—(B)
⑤ (C)—(B)—(A)

M23 ✶✶❀ .... 2022 대비 수능 37 (고3)

주어진 글 다음에 이어질 글의 순서로 가장 적절한 것을 고르시오. [3점]

> In spite of the likeness between the fictional and real world, the fictional world deviates from the real one in one important respect.

(A) The author has selected the content according to his own worldview and his own conception of relevance, in an attempt to be neutral and objective or convey a subjective view on the world. Whatever the motives, the author's subjective conception of the world stands between the reader and the original, untouched world on which the story is based.

(B) Because of the inner qualities with which the individual is endowed through heritage and environment, the mind functions as a filter; every outside impression that passes through it is filtered and interpreted. However, the world the reader encounters in literature is already processed and filtered by another consciousness.

(C) The existing world faced by the individual is in principle an infinite chaos of events and details before it is organized by a human mind. This chaos only gets processed and modified when perceived by a human mind.

*deviate: 벗어나다 **endow: 부여하다 ***heritage: 유산

① (A)—(C)—(B)   ② (B)—(A)—(C)
③ (B)—(C)—(A)   ④ (C)—(A)—(B)
⑤ (C)—(B)—(A)

M24 ✶✶✶ .... 2024 대비 9월 모평 36 (고3)

주어진 글 다음에 이어질 글의 순서로 가장 적절한 것을 고르시오.

> The intuitive ability to classify and generalize is undoubtedly a useful feature of life and research, but it carries a high cost, such as in our tendency to stereotype generalizations about people and situations.

(A) Intuitively and quickly, we mentally sort things into groups based on what we perceive the differences between them to be, and that is the basis for stereotyping. Only afterwards do we examine (or not examine) more evidence of how things are differentiated, and the degree and significance of the variations.

(B) Our brain performs these tasks efficiently and automatically, usually without our awareness. The real danger of stereotypes is not their inaccuracy, but their lack of flexibility and their tendency to be preserved, even when we have enough time to stop and consider.

(C) For most people, the word stereotype arouses negative connotations: it implies a negative bias. But, in fact, stereotypes do not differ in principle from all other generalizations; generalizations about groups of people are not necessarily always negative.

*intuitive: 직관적인 **connotation: 함축

① (A)—(C)—(B)   ② (B)—(A)—(C)
③ (B)—(C)—(A)   ④ (C)—(A)—(B)
⑤ (C)—(B)—(A)

주어진 글 다음에 이어질 글의 순서로 가장 적절한 것을 고르시오.

> Shakespeare wrote, "What's in a name? That which we call a rose by any other name would smell as sweet."

(A) Take the word *bridge*. In German, *bridge* (die brücke) is a feminine noun; in Spanish, *bridge* (el puente) is a masculine noun. Boroditsky found that when asked to describe a bridge, native German speakers used words like *beautiful, elegant, slender*. When native Spanish speakers were asked the same question, they used words like *strong, sturdy, towering*.

(B) According to Stanford University psychology professor Lera Boroditsky, that's not necessarily so. Focusing on the grammatical gender differences between German and Spanish, Boroditsky's work indicates that the gender our language assigns to a given noun influences us to subconsciously give that noun characteristics of the grammatical gender.

(C) This worked the other way around as well. The word *key* is masculine in German and feminine in Spanish. When asked to describe a key, native German speakers used words like *jagged, heavy, hard, metal*. Spanish speakers used words like *intricate, golden, lovely*.

*jagged: 뾰족뾰족한 **intricate: 정교한

① (A)—(C)—(B)   ② (B)—(A)—(C)
③ (B)—(C)—(A)   ④ (C)—(A)—(B)
⑤ (C)—(B)—(A)

주어진 글 다음에 이어질 글의 순서로 가장 적절한 것을 고르시오. [3점]

> Darwin saw blushing as uniquely human, representing an involuntary physical reaction caused by embarrassment and self-consciousness in a social environment.

(A) Maybe our brief loss of face benefits the long-term cohesion of the group. Interestingly, if someone blushes after making a social mistake, they are viewed in a more favourable light than those who don't blush.

(B) If we feel awkward, embarrassed or ashamed when we are alone, we don't blush; it seems to be caused by our concern about what others are thinking of us. Studies have confirmed that simply being told you are blushing brings it on. We feel as though others can see through our skin and into our mind.

(C) However, while we sometimes want to disappear when we involuntarily go bright red, psychologists argue that blushing actually serves a positive social purpose. When we blush, it's a signal to others that we recognize that a social norm has been broken; it is an apology for a faux pas.

*faux pas: 실수

① (A)—(C)—(B)   ② (B)—(A)—(C)
③ (B)—(C)—(A)   ④ (C)—(A)—(B)
⑤ (C)—(B)—(A)

M27 ★★❂ .... 2021 대비 9월 모평 37 (고3)

주어진 글 다음에 이어질 글의 순서로 가장 적절한 것을 고르시오. [3점]

> It can be difficult to decide the place of fine art, such as oil paintings, watercolours, sketches or sculptures, in an archival institution.

(A) The best archival decisions about art do not focus on territoriality (this object belongs in my institution even though I do not have the resources to care for it) or on questions of monetary value or prestige (this object raises the cultural standing of my institution). The best decisions focus on what evidential value exists and what is best for the item.

(B) But art can also carry aesthetic value, which elevates the job of evaluation into another realm. Aesthetic value and the notion of artistic beauty are important considerations, but they are not what motivates archival preservation in the first instance.

(C) Art can serve as documentary evidence, especially when the items were produced before photography became common. Sketches of soldiers on a battlefield, paintings of English country villages or portraits of Dutch townspeople can provide the only visual evidence of a long-ago place, person or time.

*archival: 기록(보관소)의 **prestige: 명성, 위신 ***realm: 영역

① (A)─(C)─(B)   ② (B) ─(A)─(C)
③ (B) ─(C)─(A)   ④ (C)─(A)─(B)
⑤ (C) ─(B) ─(A)

M28 ★★❂ .... 2023 실시 10월 학평 37 (고3)

주어진 글 다음에 이어질 글의 순서로 가장 적절한 것을 고르시오. [3점]

> Our perception always involves some imagination. It is more similar to painting than to photography. And, according to the confirmation effect, we blindly trust the reality we construct.

(A) You will see that the majority of us are quite ignorant about what lies around us. This is not so puzzling. The most extraordinary fact is that we completely disregard this ignorance.

(B) This is best witnessed in visual illusions, which we perceive with full confidence, as if there were no doubt that we are portraying reality faithfully. One interesting way of discovering this — in a simple game that can be played at any moment — is the following.

(C) Whenever you are with another person, ask him or her to close their eyes, and start asking questions about what is nearby — not very particular details but the most striking elements of the scene. What is the color of the wall? Is there a table in the room? Does that man have a beard?

① (A)─(C)─(B)   ② (B) ─(A)─(C)
③ (B) ─(C)─(A)   ④ (C)─(A)─(B)
⑤ (C) ─(B) ─(A)

M29 ★★★ .... 2024 대비 9월 모평 37 (고3)

주어진 글 다음에 이어질 글의 순서로 가장 적절한 것을 고르시오. [3점]

> Plants show finely tuned adaptive responses when nutrients are limiting. Gardeners may recognize yellow leaves as a sign of poor nutrition and the need for fertilizer.

(A) In contrast, plants with a history of nutrient abundance are risk averse and save energy. At all developmental stages, plants respond to environmental changes or unevenness so as to be able to use their energy for growth, survival, and reproduction, while limiting damage and nonproductive uses of their valuable energy.

(B) Research in this area has shown that plants are constantly aware of their position in the environment, in terms of both space and time. Plants that have experienced variable nutrient availability in the past tend to exhibit risk-taking behaviors, such as spending energy on root lengthening instead of leaf production.

(C) But if a plant does not have a caretaker to provide supplemental minerals, it can proliferate or lengthen its roots and develop root hairs to allow foraging in more distant soil patches. Plants can also use their memory to respond to histories of temporal or spatial variation in nutrient or resource availability.

*nutrient: 영양소 **fertilizer: 비료 ***forage: 구하러 다니다

① (A)—(C)—(B) ② (B)—(A)—(C)
③ (B)—(C)—(A) ④ (C)—(A)—(B)
⑤ (C)—(B)—(A)

M30 ★★★ .... 2021 대비 수능 37 (고3)

주어진 글 다음에 이어질 글의 순서로 가장 적절한 것을 고르시오. [3점]

> Experts have identified a large number of measures that promote energy efficiency. Unfortunately many of them are not cost effective. This is a fundamental requirement for energy efficiency investment from an economic perspective.

(A) And this has direct repercussions at the individual level: households can reduce the cost of electricity and gas bills, and improve their health and comfort, while companies can increase their competitiveness and their productivity. Finally, the market for energy efficiency could contribute to the economy through job and firms creation.

(B) There are significant externalities to take into account and there are also macroeconomic effects. For instance, at the aggregate level, improving the level of national energy efficiency has positive effects on macroeconomic issues such as energy dependence, climate change, health, national competitiveness and reducing fuel poverty.

(C) However, the calculation of such cost effectiveness is not easy: it is not simply a case of looking at private costs and comparing them to the reductions achieved.

*repercussion: 반향, 영향 **aggregate: 집합의

① (A)—(C)—(B) ② (B)—(A)—(C)
③ (B)—(C)—(A) ④ (C)—(A)—(B)
⑤ (C)—(B)—(A)

M31 ✱✱✱ .... 2023 실시 4월 학평 37 (고3)

주어진 글 다음에 이어질 글의 순서로 가장 적절한 것을 고르시오. [3점]

Representation is control. The power to represent the world is the power to represent us in it or it in us, for the final stage of representing merges the representor and the represented into one. Imperializing cultures produce great works of art (great representations) which can be put to work intellectually as armies and trading houses work militarily and economically.

(A) That is because unless we can control the world intellectually by maps we cannot control it militarily or economically. Mercator, Molière, Columbus and Captain Cook imperialized in different ways, but they all imperialized, and ultimately the effectiveness of one depended upon and supported the effectiveness of all the others.

(B) Similarly the US form of contemporary colonization, which involves occupying economies and political parties rather than physical territories, is accompanied by the power of both Hollywood and the satellite to represent the world to and for the US.

(C) Shakespeare, Jane Austen and maps were as important to English Imperial power as was the East India Company, the British army and the churches of England. It is no coincidence that modern Europe, the Europe of colonization, was also the Europe of "great art," and no coincidence either that it was the Europe of great map makers.

① (A)—(C)—(B)　　② (B)—(A)—(C)
③ (B)—(C)—(A)　　④ (C)—(A)—(B)
⑤ (C)—(B)—(A)

M32 ✱✱✱ .... 2024 대비 수능 36 (고3)

주어진 글 다음에 이어질 글의 순서로 가장 적절한 것을 고르시오.

Negotiation can be defined as an attempt to explore and reconcile conflicting positions in order to reach an acceptable outcome.

(A) Areas of difference can and do frequently remain, and will perhaps be the subject of future negotiations, or indeed remain irreconcilable. In those instances in which the parties have highly antagonistic or polarised relations, the process is likely to be dominated by the exposition, very often in public, of the areas of conflict.

(B) In these and sometimes other forms of negotiation, negotiation serves functions other than reconciling conflicting interests. These will include delay, publicity, diverting attention or seeking intelligence about the other party and its negotiating position.

(C) Whatever the nature of the outcome, which may actually favour one party more than another, the purpose of negotiation is the identification of areas of common interest and conflict. In this sense, depending on the intentions of the parties, the areas of common interest may be clarified, refined and given negotiated form and substance.

*reconcile: 화해시키다　**antagonistic: 적대적인
***exposition: 설명

① (A)—(C)—(B)　　② (B)—(A)—(C)
③ (B)—(C)—(A)　　④ (C)—(A)—(B)
⑤ (C)—(B)—(A)

주어진 글 다음에 이어질 글의 순서로 가장 적절한 것을 고르시오.

> The objective of battle, to "throw" the enemy and to make him defenseless, may temporarily blind commanders and even strategists to the larger purpose of war. War is never an isolated act, nor is it ever only one decision.

(A) To be political, a political entity or a representative of a political entity, whatever its constitutional form, has to have an intention, a will. That intention has to be clearly expressed.

(B) In the real world, war's larger purpose is always a political purpose. It transcends the use of force. This insight was famously captured by Clausewitz's most famous phrase, "War is a mere continuation of politics by other means."

(C) And one side's will has to be transmitted to the enemy at some point during the confrontation (it does not have to be publicly communicated). A violent act and its larger political intention must also be attributed to one side at some point during the confrontation. History does not know of acts of war without eventual attribution.

*entity: 실체 **transcend: 초월하다

① (A)—(C)—(B)   ② (B)—(A)—(C)
③ (B)—(C)—(A)   ④ (C)—(A)—(B)
⑤ (C)—(B)—(A)

주어진 글 다음에 이어질 글의 순서로 가장 적절한 것을 고르시오. [3점]

> It raises much less reactance to tell people what to do than to tell them what not to do. Therefore, advocating action should lead to higher compliance than prohibiting action.

(A) This is a prescription that is rife with danger, failing to provide an implementation rule and raising reactance. Much better is to say, "To help make sure that other people provide answers as useful as yours have been, when people ask you about this study, please tell them that you and another person answered some questions about each other."

(B) For example, researchers have a choice of how to debrief research participants in an experiment involving some deception or omission of information. Often researchers attempt to commit the participant to silence, saying "Please don't tell other potential participants that feedback from the other person was false."

(C) Similarly, I once saw a delightful and unusual example of this principle at work in an art gallery. A fragile acrylic sculpture had a sign at the base saying, "Please touch with your eyes." The command was clear, yet created much less reactance in me than "Don't touch!" would have.

*reactance: 저항 **rife: 가득한
***debrief: 비밀[기밀] 준수 의무를 지우다[부여하다]

① (A)—(C)—(B)   ② (B)—(A)—(C)
③ (B)—(C)—(A)   ④ (C)—(A)—(B)
⑤ (C)—(B)—(A)

M35 ✽✽✽.........................2022 실시 7월 학평 37 (고3)

주어진 글 다음에 이어질 글의 순서로 가장 적절한 것을 고르시오.

> One common strategy and use of passive misdirection in the digital world comes through the use of repetition.

(A) This action is repeated over and over to navigate their web browsers to the desired web page or action until it becomes an almost immediate, reflexive action. Malicious online actors take advantage of this behavior to distract the user from carefully examining the details of the web page that might tip off the user that there is something amiss about the website.

(B) The website is designed to focus the user's attention on the action the malicious actor wants them to take (e.g., click a link) and to draw their attention away from any details that might suggest to the user that the website is not what it appears to be on the surface.

(C) This digital misdirection strategy relies on the fact that online users utilizing web browsers to visit websites have quickly learned that the most basic ubiquitous navigational action is to click on a link or button presented to them on a website.

① (A)—(C)—(B) ② (B)—(A)—(C)
③ (B)—(C)—(A) ④ (C)—(A)—(B)
⑤ (C)—(B)—(A)

M36 ✽✽✽.........................2022 실시 10월 학평 36 (고3)

주어진 글 다음에 이어질 글의 순서로 가장 적절한 것을 고르시오.

> Humans are unique in the realm of living beings in knowing there is a future. If people experience worry and hope, it is because they realize the future exists, that it can be better or worse, and that the outcome depends to some extent on them.

(A) That is why we so often have a poor relationship with the future and are either more fearful than we need to be or allow ourselves to hope against all evidence; we worry excessively or not enough; we fail to predict the future or to shape it as much as we are able.

(B) The future, on the other hand, must be imagined in advance and, for that very reason, is always uncertain. Getting along with the future is not an easy task, nor is it one in which instinct prevents us from blunders.

(C) But having this knowledge does not imply that they know what to do with it. People often repress their awareness of the future because thinking about it distorts the comfort of the now, which tends to be more powerful than the future because it is present and because it is certain.

＊blunder: 큰 실수

① (A)—(C)—(B) ② (B)—(A)—(C)
③ (B)—(C)—(A) ④ (C)—(A)—(B)
⑤ (C)—(B)—(A)

주어진 글 다음에 이어질 글의 순서로 가장 적절한 것을 고르시오.

> In the fifth century *B.C.E.*, the Greek philosopher Protagoras pronounced, "Man is the measure of all things." In other words, we feel entitled to ask the world, "What good are you?"

(A) Abilities said to "make us human" — empathy, communication, grief, toolmaking, and so on — all exist to varying degrees among other minds sharing the world with us. Animals with backbones (fishes, amphibians, reptiles, birds, and mammals) all share the same basic skeleton, organs, nervous systems, hormones, and behaviors.

(B) We assume that we are the world's standard, that all things should be compared to us. Such an assumption makes us overlook a lot.

(C) Just as different models of automobiles each have an engine, drive train, four wheels, doors, and seats, we differ mainly in terms of our outside contours and a few internal tweaks. But like naive car buyers, most people see only animals' varied exteriors.

* contour: 윤곽, 외형 ** tweak: 조정, 개조

① (A)—(C)—(B)　　② (B)—(A)—(C)
③ (B)—(C)—(A)　　④ (C)—(A)—(B)
⑤ (C)—(B)—(A)

주어진 글 다음에 이어질 글의 순서로 가장 적절한 것을 고르시오. [3점]

> The fruit ripening process brings about the softening of cell walls, sweetening and the production of chemicals that give colour and flavour. The process is induced by the production of a plant hormone called ethylene.

(A) If ripening could be slowed down by interfering with ethylene production or with the processes that respond to ethylene, fruit could be left on the plant until it was ripe and full of flavour but would still be in good condition when it arrived at the supermarket shelf.

(B) In some countries they are then sprayed with ethylene before sale to the consumer to induce ripening. However, fruit picked before it is ripe has less flavour than fruit picked ripe from the plant. Biotechnologists therefore saw an opportunity in delaying the ripening and softening process in fruit.

(C) The problem for growers and retailers is that ripening is followed sometimes quite rapidly by deterioration and decay and the product becomes worthless. Tomatoes and other fruits are, therefore, usually picked and transported when they are unripe.

* deterioration: (품질의) 저하

① (A)—(C)—(B)　　② (B)—(A)—(C)
③ (B)—(C)—(A)　　④ (C)—(A)—(B)
⑤ (C)—(B)—(A)

M39 ★★✿ .... 2023 대비 9월 모평 36 (고3)

주어진 글 다음에 이어질 글의 순서로 가장 적절한 것을 고르시오.

> When two natural bodies of water stand at different levels, building a canal between them presents a complicated engineering problem.

(A) Then the upper gates open and the ship passes through. For downstream passage, the process works the opposite way. The ship enters the lock from the upper level, and water is pumped from the lock until the ship is in line with the lower level.

(B) When a vessel is going upstream, the upper gates stay closed as the ship enters the lock at the lower water level. The downstream gates are then closed and more water is pumped into the basin. The rising water lifts the vessel to the level of the upper body of water.

(C) To make up for the difference in level, engineers build one or more water "steps," called locks, that carry ships or boats up or down between the two levels. A lock is an artificial water basin. It has a long rectangular shape with concrete walls and a pair of gates at each end.

*rectangular: 직사각형의

① (A)—(C)—(B) ② (B)—(A)—(C)
③ (B)—(C)—(A) ④ (C)—(A)—(B)
⑤ (C)—(B)—(A)

M40 ★★★✿ .... 2021 대비 6월 모평 36 (고3)

주어진 글 다음에 이어질 글의 순서로 가장 적절한 것을 고르시오.

> Studies of people struggling with major health problems show that the majority of respondents report they derived benefits from their adversity. Stressful events sometimes force people to develop new skills, reevaluate priorities, learn new insights, and acquire new strengths.

(A) High levels of adversity predicted poor mental health, as expected, but people who had faced intermediate levels of adversity were healthier than those who experienced little adversity, suggesting that moderate amounts of stress can foster resilience. A follow-up study found a similar link between the amount of lifetime adversity and subjects' responses to laboratory stressors.

(B) Intermediate levels of adversity were predictive of the greatest resilience. Thus, having to deal with a moderate amount of stress may build resilience in the face of future stress.

(C) In other words, the adaptation process initiated by stress can lead to personal changes for the better. One study that measured participants' exposure to thirty-seven major negative events found a curvilinear relationship between lifetime adversity and mental health.

*resilience: 회복력

① (A)—(C)—(B) ② (B)—(A)—(C)
③ (B)—(C)—(A) ④ (C)—(A)—(B)
⑤ (C)—(B)—(A)

M41 ★★★ .... 2024 대비 수능 37 (고3)

주어진 글 다음에 이어질 글의 순서로 가장 적절한 것을 고르시오. [3점]

> Norms emerge in groups as a result of people conforming to the behavior of others. Thus, the start of a norm occurs when one person acts in a particular manner in a particular situation because she thinks she ought to.

(A) Thus, she may prescribe the behavior to them by uttering the norm statement in a prescriptive manner. Alternately, she may communicate that conformity is desired in other ways, such as by gesturing. In addition, she may threaten to sanction them for not behaving as she wishes. This will cause some to conform to her wishes and act as she acts.

(B) But some others will not need to have the behavior prescribed to them. They will observe the regularity of behavior and decide on their own that they ought to conform. They may do so for either rational or moral reasons.

(C) Others may then conform to this behavior for a number of reasons. The person who performed the initial action may think that others ought to behave as she behaves in situations of this sort.

*sanction: 제재를 가하다

① (A)—(C)—(B)　　② (B)—(A)—(C)
③ (B)—(C)—(A)　　④ (C)—(A)—(B)
⑤ (C)—(B)—(A)

M42~46 ▶ 제한시간 13.5분

M42 ✪ 2등급 대비 .... 2023 대비 6월 모평 37 (고3)

주어진 글 다음에 이어질 글의 순서로 가장 적절한 것을 고르시오. [3점]

> In economics, there is a principle known as the *sunk cost fallacy*. The idea is that when you are invested and have ownership in something, you overvalue that thing.

(A) Sometimes, the smartest thing a person can do is quit. Although this is true, it has also become a tired and played-out argument. Sunk cost doesn't always have to be a bad thing.

(B) This leads people to continue on paths or pursuits that should clearly be abandoned. For example, people often remain in terrible relationships simply because they've invested a great deal of themselves into them. Or someone may continue pouring money into a business that is clearly a bad idea in the market.

(C) Actually, you can leverage this human tendency to your benefit. Like someone invests a great deal of money in a personal trainer to ensure they follow through on their commitment, you, too, can invest a great deal up front to ensure you stay on the path you want to be on.

*leverage: 이용하다

① (A)—(C)—(B)　　② (B)—(A)—(C)
③ (B)—(C)—(A)　　④ (C)—(A)—(B)
⑤ (C)—(B)—(A)

M

주어진 글 다음에 이어질 글의 순서로 가장 적절한 것을 고르시오.

> A fascinating species of water flea exhibits a kind of flexibility that evolutionary biologists call *adaptive plasticity*.

(A) That's a clever trick, because producing spines and a helmet is costly, in terms of energy, and conserving energy is essential for an organism's ability to survive and reproduce. The water flea only expends the energy needed to produce spines and a helmet when it needs to.

(B) If the baby water flea is developing into an adult in water that includes the chemical signatures of creatures that prey on water fleas, it develops a helmet and spines to defend itself against predators. If the water around it doesn't include the chemical signatures of predators, the water flea doesn't develop these protective devices.

(C) So it may well be that this plasticity is an adaptation: a trait that came to exist in a species because it contributed to reproductive fitness. There are many cases, across many species, of adaptive plasticity. Plasticity is conducive to fitness if there is sufficient variation in the environment.

*spine: 가시 돌기 **conducive: 도움되는

① (A)—(C)—(B)   ② (B)—(A)—(C)
③ (B)—(C)—(A)   ④ (C)—(A)—(B)
⑤ (C)—(B)—(A)

 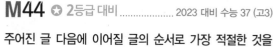

주어진 글 다음에 이어질 글의 순서로 가장 적절한 것을 고르시오. [3점]

> The most commonly known form of results-based pricing is a practice called *contingency pricing*, used by lawyers.

(A) Therefore, only an outcome in the client's favor is compensated. From the client's point of view, the pricing makes sense in part because most clients in these cases are unfamiliar with and possibly intimidated by law firms. Their biggest fears are high fees for a case that may take years to settle.

(B) By using contingency pricing, clients are ensured that they pay no fees until they receive a settlement. In these and other instances of contingency pricing, the economic value of the service is hard to determine before the service, and providers develop a price that allows them to share the risks and rewards of delivering value to the buyer.

(C) Contingency pricing is the major way that personal injury and certain consumer cases are billed. In this approach, lawyers do not receive fees or payment until the case is settled, when they are paid a percentage of the money that the client receives.

*intimidate: 위협하다

① (A)—(C)—(B)   ② (B)—(A)—(C)
③ (B)—(C)—(A)   ④ (C)—(A)—(B)
⑤ (C)—(B)—(A)

주어진 글 다음에 이어질 글의 순서로 가장 적절한 것을 고르시오. [3점]

> Culture operates in ways we can consciously consider and discuss but also in ways of which we are far less cognizant.

(A) In some cases, however, we are far less aware of why we believe a certain claim to be true, or how we are to explain why certain social realities exist. Ideas about the social world become part of our worldview without our necessarily being aware of the source of the particular idea or that we even hold the idea at all.

(B) When we have to offer an account of our actions, we consciously understand which excuses might prove acceptable, given the particular circumstances we find ourselves in. In such situations, we use cultural ideas as we would use a particular tool.

(C) We select the cultural notion as we would select a screwdriver: certain jobs call for a Phillips head while others require an Allen wrench. Whichever idea we insert into the conversation to justify our actions, the point is that our motives are discursively available to us. They are not hidden.

*cognizant: 인식하는 **discursively: 만연하게

① (A) — (C) — (B) 　② (B) — (A) — (C)
③ (B) — (C) — (A) 　④ (C) — (A) — (B)
⑤ (C) — (B) — (A)

주어진 글 다음에 이어질 글의 순서로 가장 적절한 것을 고르시오. [3점]

> There was a moment in research history when scientists wondered if the measure of choice — total minutes of sleep — was the wrong way of looking at the question of why sleep varies so considerably across species. Instead, they suspected that assessing sleep *quality*, rather than *quantity* (time), would shed some light on the mystery.

(A) When we can, our understanding of the relationship between sleep quantity and quality across the animal kingdom will likely explain what currently appears to be an incomprehensible map of sleep-time differences.

(B) In truth, the way quality is commonly assessed in these investigations (degree of unresponsiveness to the outside world and the continuity of sleep) is probably a poor index of the real biological measure of sleep quality: one that we cannot yet obtain in all these species.

(C) That is, species with superior quality of sleep should be able to accomplish all they need in a shorter time, and vice versa. It was a great idea, with the exception that, if anything, we've discovered the opposite relationship: those that sleep more have deeper, "higher"-quality sleep.

① (A) — (C) — (B) 　② (B) — (A) — (C)
③ (B) — (C) — (A) 　④ (C) — (A) — (B)
⑤ (C) — (B) — (A)

※ 다음 영어는 우리말 뜻, 우리말은 영어 단어를 〈보기〉에서 찾아 쓰시오.

〈보기〉

prediction	faithfully	economics	거부[거절]하다
기본적인	축적하다	unfortunately	payment
(~보다) 열등한	부여하다	값을 매기다	skeleton

01 reject _____

02 accumulate _____

03 elementary _____

04 inferior _____

05 assign _____

06 충실하게 _____

07 골격 _____

08 예측, 예견 _____

09 불행하게도 _____

10 경제학 _____

※ 다음 우리말에 알맞은 영어 표현을 찾아 연결하시오.

11 ~와 일직선을 이루는 •   • tend to

12 ~하는 경향이 있다 •   • in (a) line with

13 ~을 요구하다 •   • in one's tracks

14 즉시 •   • call for

15 ~을 야기하다 •   • bring on

※ 다음 우리말 표현에 맞는 단어를 고르시오.

16 기존 패턴을 수정하다 ⇒ (preserve / modify) the old patterns

17 그러한 상태에서 ⇒ under such (editions / conditions)

18 신체 조작 능력 ⇒ physical (intervention / manipulation) capability

19 진화의 증거 ⇒ (confidence / evidence) of evolution

20 매몰 비용 오류 ⇒ the sunk cost (fallacy / fellow)

※ 다음 문장의 빈칸에 알맞은 단어를 〈보기〉에서 찾아 쓰시오.

〈보기〉

naive	inaccuracy	ownership	spatial
dispersal	elaborate	suspected	evidential
imperializing	justify	evaporate	ultimately

21 여러분이 어떤 것에 투자하고 소유권을 가지면 여러분은 그것을 지나치게 중시한다.
→ When you are invested and have _____ in something, you overvalue that thing.

22 제국주의화하는 문화는 훌륭한 예술 작품을 생산한다.
→ _____ cultures produce great works of art.

23 컴퓨터 코드가 더 정교해진다.
→ Computer code grows more _____.

24 그들은 수면의 질을 평가하는 것이 그 비밀을 밝힐 것이라고 생각했다.
→ They _____ that assessing sleep quality would shed some light on the mystery.

25 흩어져 사는 것은 공적 생활로부터 놀라울 정도로 멀어지는 것과 관련이 있다.
→ Living in _____ correlates with a shocking retreat from public life.

26 공간적 상황이 중요하다는 점을 증거가 말해 준다.
→ Evidence suggests that the _____ landscape matters.

27 순진한 자동차 구매자들처럼, 대부분의 사람들은 오직 동물들의 다양한 겉모습만을 본다.
→ Like _____ car buyers, most people see only animals' varied exteriors.

28 고정 관념이 진정 위험한 것은 그것들의 부정확성이 아니라, 그것들의 유연성 부족이다.
→ The real danger of stereotypes is not their _____, but their lack of flexibility.

29 우리의 행동을 정당화하기 위해 대화에 어떤 생각을 넣든, 우리의 동기는 우리에게 만연하게 이용 가능하다.
→ Whichever idea we insert into the conversation to _____ our actions, our motives are discursively available to us.

30 최선의 결정은 어떤 증거 가치가 존재하는지에 초점을 맞춘다.
→ The best decisions focus on what _____ value exists.

N 주어진 문장 넣기

> 사고 장면이 묘사되고 있었는데 왜 갑자기 수술을 마친 내용이 나오지?

> 빠진 이 문장을 넣으면 말이 될 거예요!

★ 유형 설명

글의 흐름으로 보아, 주어진 문장이 들어가기에 가장 적절한 곳을 고르시오.

> Retraining current employees for new positions within the company will also

연결어 등의 단서를 이용하여 주어진 한 문장을 논리적인 흐름에 맞게 글의 중간에 끼워 넣어야 한다.

☞ 글을 읽으면서 앞뒤 연결이 어색한 문장들 사이에 주어진 문장을 넣어 보고 흐름이 매끄러워지는지 확인한다.
앞 문장에는 전혀 등장하지 않았던 어구가 갑자기 등장하거나 글의 흐름이 아무 연결어 없이 완전히 전환되는 부분이 정답이다.

🎭 유형 풀이 비법

1 주어진 글을 파악하라!
- 주어진 문장을 읽고, 문제 풀이에 활용할 만한 단서가 있는지 살펴본다.

2 문장 관계를 추론하라!
- 정관사, 대명사, 대동사, 지시어, 연결어 등에 유의하여 문장 간의 관계를 추론한다.

3 글의 주제를 파악하라!
- 통일성과 일관성을 유지하는 주제를 파악하여 주어진 문장의 위치를 찾는다.

> (Tip) 정답을 고른 후에는 주어진 문장을 알맞은 위치에 넣고 문맥이 자연스러운지 확인한다.

★ 최신 수능 경향 분석

대비 연도	월	문항 번호	지문 주제	난이도
2025	11	38번	영업 상의 비밀 보호법이 필요한 이유	✱✱✱
		39번	물건의 다양하고 역동적인 생애(수명) 주기	✱✱✱
	9	38번	로봇의 자신과 주변의 다른 실재물을 구별하는 능력	✱✱✱
		39번	생태계 관리를 위한 미래 생태계 모습 예측하기	✱✱✸
	6	38번	측정된 배출물에 기반한 환경세	✱✱✱
		39번	예술에서 주제(형상)와 스타일(배경) 간의 균형	✱✱✱
2024	11	38번	과학이 승자독식 대회라는 오해	✱✱✱
		39번	책의 오류와 돌연변이 간 유사점과 차이점	✱✱✱
	9	38번	음악 제작 방식의 변화	✱✱✱
		39번	예술 작품의 제작을 인정하는 데 필요한 것	✱✱✱
	6	38번	과학자가 도덕적 가치를 배우는 방법	✱✱✱
		39번	개별 나무를 돕는 것이 미치는 영향	✱✱✱

★ 2025 수능 출제 분석

38번은 정답률이 낮은 편이었지만 주어진 문장이 However를 포함하고 있다는 것을 생각하면, 앞에 반대 내용이 와야 한다는 것을 쉽게 알 수 있었다. 39번은 Additionally라는 연결어 덕분에 단서는 얻을 수 있었지만, Krebs와 Weber의 지적에 대한 언급 내용을 잘 파악해야 답을 찾을 수 있었다.

★ 2026 수능 예측

높은 난이도로 출제되는 경우에 대비하여 연결어나 지시어 등의 단서를 활용하는 방법뿐 아니라 내용 이해를 통해 정답을 찾는 훈련을 철저히 해야 한다.

🔑 자주 쓰이는 연결어

- □ in fact 사실상
- □ moreover 게다가
- □ in addition 게다가
- □ despite ~에도 불구하고
- □ in spite of ~에도 불구하고
- □ although ~에도 불구하고
- □ but 하지만, 그러나
- □ however 하지만, 그러나
- □ in contrast 대조적으로
- □ in comparison with ~와 비교해보면

- □ in summary 요약하면
- □ in a word 한마디로 말해서
- □ at the same time 동시에
- □ furthermore 더욱이, 더구나
- □ that is 즉
- □ namely 즉, 다시 말해
- □ thus 따라서, 그러므로
- □ therefore 따라서
- □ accordingly 따라서
- □ hence 그러므로, 따라서
- □ in other words 바꾸어 말하면

🎨 어휘 및 표현 Preview

- □ conception 구상
- □ discriminate 구별하다
- □ conventional 전통적인
- □ search for 찾다
- □ abatement 감소
- □ originate from 발생하다
- □ aesthetic 미학적인
- □ detect 감지하다
- □ external 외부의
- □ emission 배출
- □ atmosphere 분위기

N 주어진 문장 넣기 (첫 번째)

1st 주어진 문장을 해석하고, 연결어, 지시어 등을 확인하세요.
2nd 각 선택지의 앞뒤 흐름이 매끄러운지 확인하세요.
3rd 글이 한눈에 들어오도록 정리하여 정답을 확인하세요.

N01 ★★❀ .... 2023 대비 6월 모평 38 (고3)

글의 흐름으로 보아, 주어진 문장이 들어가기에 가장 적절한 곳을 고르시오.

> Also, it has become difficult for companies to develop new pesticides, even those that can have major beneficial effects and few negative effects.

Simply maintaining yields at current levels often requires new cultivars and management methods, since pests and diseases continue to evolve, and aspects of the chemical, physical, and social environment can change over several decades. (①) In the 1960s, many people considered pesticides to be mainly beneficial to mankind. (②) Developing new, broadly effective, and persistent pesticides often was considered to be the best way to control pests on crop plants. (③) Since that time, it has become apparent that broadly effective pesticides can have harmful effects on beneficial insects, which can negate their effects in controlling pests, and that persistent pesticides can damage non-target organisms in the ecosystem, such as birds and people. (④) Very high costs are involved in following all of the procedures needed to gain government approval for new pesticides. (⑤) Consequently, more consideration is being given to other ways to manage pests, such as incorporating greater resistance to pests into cultivars by breeding and using other biological control methods.

*pesticide: 살충제 **cultivar: 품종 ***breed: 개량하다

1st 주어진 문장을 해석하고, 연결어, 지시어 등을 확인하세요.

Also, / it has become difficult / for companies to
또한 / ~이 어려워졌다 / 기업들이 새로운 살충제를
develop new pesticides, / even those / that can have
개발하는 것이 / (~한) 것들조차 / 주요한 이로운 효과는
major beneficial effects and few negative effects. //
있지만 부정적인 효과는 거의 없을 수 있는 //

● **Also로 시작한 이 문장은 어떤 내용인가요?**

기업들이 새로운 살충제를, 주요한 이로운 효과는 있지만 부정적인 효과는 거의 없을 수 있는 살충제들조차도 개발하는 것이 어려워졌다는 내용이에요. 〔단서〕

이게 대체 무슨 내용일까, 왜 이런 내용이 등장했을까를 잠깐 고민해 보면, 이건 살충제가 광범위하게 사용되지 않는 이유일 거라고 어렵지 않게 짐작할 수 있어요.

이 점을 앞서 살펴본 also가 의미하는 바와 종합하면, 주어진 문장 앞에는 살충제가 널리 사용되지 않는 또다른 이유가 등장해 있어야 하겠군요! 〔발상〕

이제 정답을 찾는 단서를 얻었으니 글을 읽어봅시다.

2nd 각 선택지의 앞뒤 흐름이 매끄러운지 확인하세요.

1) ①의 앞 문장과 뒤 문장을 확인해 봅시다.

앞 문장: Simply maintaining yields / at current levels
단지 수확량을 유지하는 것만도 / 현재의 수준으로
/ often requires / new cultivars and management
/ 보통 필요로 한다 / 새로운 품종과 관리 기법을
methods, / since pests and diseases continue to
/ 해충과 질병이 계속 진화하고 있으므로
evolve, / and aspects / of the chemical, physical, and
/ 그리고 양상이 / 화학적, 물리적, 사회적 환경의
social environment / can change / over several
/ 변할 수 있으므로 / 수십 년에 걸쳐 //
decades. //

뒤 문장: In the 1960s, / many people considered
1960년대에 / 많은 사람은 살충제를 여겼다
pesticides / to be mainly beneficial / to mankind. //
/ 대체로 유익한 것으로 / 사람들에게 //

① ( )가 글의 소재라는 점을 생각하면서 필요한 부분만 요약하면, 이 문장은 한 마디로 해충과 질병이 계속 진화하고 여러 환경이 변하기 때문에 새로운 관리 기법이 필요하다고 말하는 거예요.

1960년대에는 많은 사람들이 살충제가 사람들에게 대체로 유익한 것으로 여겼다는 설명이 등장해요. 유익하다고 여겼으니까 많이 사용했겠죠? 그럼 기업들이 살충제를 많이 만들었겠죠?

▶ 주어진 문장이 ①에 들어갈 수 없음

2) ②의 앞 문장과 뒤 문장을 확인해 봅시다.

앞 문장: ①의 뒤 문장과 같음

뒤 문장: Developing / new, broadly effective, and
개발하는 것은 / 새롭고 널리 효과를 거두고 지속하는 살충제를

persistent pesticides / often was considered / to be
/ 흔히 여겨졌다 /

the best way / to control pests on crop plants. //
최고의 방법으로 / 농작물에의 해충을 통제하는 //

앞 문장에 이어 새롭고 널리 효과를 거두고 지속하는 살충제를 개발하는
것은 흔히 농작물 해충을 통제하는 최고의 방법으로 여겨졌다는 내용이
자연스럽게 이어진다.

▶ 주어진 문장이 ②에 들어갈 수 없음

3) ③의 앞 문장과 뒤 문장을 확인해 봅시다.

앞 문장: ②의 뒤 문장과 같음

뒤 문장: Since that time, / it has become apparent /
그때 이래로 / ~이 분명해졌다 /

that broadly effective pesticides / can have harmful
널리 효과를 거두는 살충제가 / 해로운 영향을 미칠 수

effects / on beneficial insects, / which can negate
있어서 / 유익한 곤충에 / 그것이 살충제의 효과를

their effects / in controlling pests, / and that
무효화할 수 있으며 / 해충을 통제하는 것에서 / 지속하는

persistent pesticides can damage / non-target
살충제는 해를 끼칠 수 있다는 것이 / 생태계의 목표 외

organisms in the ecosystem, / such as birds and
생물에게 / 새와 사람 같은 /

people. //

'그때'는 아마 아까 확인한 1960년대일 거예요. 그게 중요한 건 아니고,
아무튼 널리 효과를 거두는 살충제가 유익한 곤충, 새와 사람 등에 해로운
영향을 미칠 수 있다는 것이 분명해졌다는 내용이 정말 등장해요.

▶ 주어진 문장이 ③에 들어갈 수 없음

4) ④의 앞 문장과 뒤 문장을 확인해 봅시다.

앞 문장: ③의 뒤 문장과 같음

뒤 문장: Very high costs are involved / in following
매우 높은 비용이 수반된다 / 모든 절차를 따르는

all of the procedures / needed to gain government
것에 / 정부의 승인을 얻는 데 필요한

approval / for new pesticides. //
/ 새로운 살충제에 대한 //

살충제가 목표 외 생물에게 해를 끼친다는 것이 분명해졌다는 문장에
갑자기 새로운 살충제에 대한 정부의 승인을 얻는 절차에 높은 비용이
든다는 설명이 이어지는 건 한눈에 봐도 이상한 흐름이에요.

새로운 살충제에 대한 정부의 승인을 얻는 절차에 높은 비용이 든다는
건 살충제 개발이 어려운 이유이지, 살충제의 부작용과 관련 있는 것은
아니니까요.
정답이 ❷( )이 맞는 것 같죠?

▶ 주어진 문장이 ④에 들어가야 함

5) ⑤의 앞 문장과 뒤 문장을 확인해 봅시다.

앞 문장: ④의 뒤 문장과 같음

뒤 문장: Consequently, / more consideration is being
결과적으로 / 더 많은 고려가 주어지고 있다

given / to other ways / to manage pests, / such as
/ 다른 방법들에 / 해충을 관리하는 / 더 강한

incorporating greater resistance to pests / into
해충 저항력을 포함하는 것 같은 / 품종에

cultivars / by breeding and using / other biological
/ 개량하여 사용함으로써 / 다른 생물학적

control methods. //
통제 기법을 //

살충제 외의 방법이 고려되는 또 다른 이유를 설명하는 주어진 문장
다음에 주어진 문장에서 설명한 현상의 이유를 부연하는 흐름이
적절해요.

▶ 주어진 문장이 ⑤에 들어갈 수 없음

3rd 글이 한눈에 들어오도록 정리하여 정답을 확인하세요.

현재의 수준으로 수확량을 유지하는 것만도 해충과 질병이 계속 진화하고
화학적, 물리적, 사회적 환경의 양상이 수십 년에 걸쳐 변할 수 있으므로,
새로운 품종과 관리 기법이 필요하다.
(①) 1960년대에 많은 사람은 살충제가 사람들에게 유익한 것으로 여겼다.
(②) 새롭고 널리 효과를 거두고 지속하는 살충제를 개발하는 것은 농작물
해충을 통제하는 최고의 방법으로 여겨졌다.
(③) 널리 효과를 거두는 살충제가 유익한 곤충에 해로운 영향을 미칠 수
있어서 그것이 해충 통제 효과를 무효화할 수 있으며, 지속하는 살충제는
생태계의 목표 외 생물에게 해를 끼칠 수 있다는 것이 분명해졌다.
(④ 또한, 기업들이 새로운 살충제를, 주요한 이로운 효과는 있지만 부정적인
효과는 거의 없을 수 있는 것들조차, 개발하는 것이 어려워졌다.)
매우 높은 비용이 새로운 살충제에 대한 정부의 승인을 얻는 데 필요한 모든
절차를 따르는 것에 수반된다.
(⑤) 결과적으로, 다른 생물학적 통제 기법을 개량하여 사용함으로써
해충을 관리하는 다른 방법들이 더 많이 고려되고 있다.

자이 쌤's Follow Me!

N 주어진 문장 넣기 (두 번째)

- **1st** 주어진 문장을 해석하고, 연결어, 지시어 등을 확인하세요.
- **2nd** 각 선택지의 앞뒤 흐름이 매끄러운지 확인하세요.
- **3rd** 글이 한눈에 들어오도록 정리하여 정답을 확인하세요.

N02 ★★★ .... 2025 대비 9월 모평 38 (고3)

글의 흐름으로 보아, 주어진 문장이 들어가기에 가장 적절한 곳을 고르시오.

> If not, the robot might endlessly chase itself rather than the blocks.

People involved in the conception and engineering of robots designed to perceive and act know how fundamental is the ability to discriminate oneself from other entities in the environment. Without such an ability, no goal-oriented action would be possible. (①) Imagine that you have to build a robot able to search for blocks scattered in a room in order to pile them. (②) Even this simple task would require that your machine be able to discriminate between stimulation that originates from its own machinery and stimulation that originates from the blocks in the environment. (③) Suppose that you equip your robot with an artificial eye and an artificial arm to detect, grab, and pile the blocks. (④) To be successful, your machine will have to have some built-in system enabling it to discriminate between the detection of a block and the detection of its own arm. (⑤) Your robot would engage in circular, self-centered acts that would drive it away from the target or external goal.

*entity: 실재물(物)

1st 주어진 문장을 해석하고, 연결어, 지시어 등을 확인하세요.

If not, / the robot might endlessly chase itself /
그렇지 않으면 / 로봇이 자기 자신을 끝없이 쫓아갈 수도 있다 /
rather than the blocks. //
블록이 아닌 //

● **If not으로 문장이 시작했네요.**

'그렇지 않으면'이라는 뜻의 If not으로 시작했으므로, [단서] 앞의 내용과 반대로 하면 로봇이 블록이 아닌 자기 자신을 쫓아가게 될 수도 있다는 내용으로 연결되는 거죠.

이 문장 뒤에는 아마도 로봇이 원래의 목표와 달리 자기중심적인 행동을 하게 될 것이라는 내용이 이어질 거예요. [발상]

우리의 예상이 맞는지 이제 글을 처음부터 읽으면서 확인해 봅시다.

2nd 각 선택지의 앞뒤 흐름이 매끄러운지 확인하세요.

1) ①의 앞 문장과 뒤 문장을 확인해 봅시다.

앞 문장: People involved in the conception and
로봇의 구상과 엔지니어링에 관여하는 사람들은
engineering of robots / designed to perceive and act /
/ 인지하고 행동하도록 설계된 /
know how fundamental is / the ability to
얼마나 핵심적인지 알고 있다 / 자신을 구별하는
discriminate oneself / from other entities in the
능력이 / 주위의 다른 실재물과 //
environment. //
Without such an ability, / no goal-oriented action
그러한 능력이 없으면 / 목표 지향적인 행동은 불가능할
would be possible. //
것이다 //

뒤 문장: Imagine / that you have to build a robot /
상상해 보라 / 여러분이 로봇을 만들어야 한다고 /
able to search for blocks / scattered in a room / in
블록을 찾을 수 있는 / 방에 흩어져 있는 /
order to pile them. //
블록을 쌓기 위해 //

앞에서는 로봇을 설계할 때 주위의 다른 **❶**( )과 자신을 구별하는 능력이 핵심이라고 했어요. 그리고 이러한 능력이 없으면 목표 지향적 행동이 불가능하다고 했죠.

뒤에서는 이에 대한 예시가 나오는데, 블록을 쌓기 위해 방에 흩어진 블록을 찾는 로봇을 만드는 것을 상상해 보라고 했어요. 뒤에 예시가 나오면서 두 문장은 자연스럽게 연결되고 있는 걸 알 수 있죠?

▶ 주어진 문장이 **①**에 들어갈 수 없음

2) ②의 앞 문장과 뒤 문장을 확인해 봅시다.

앞 문장: ①의 뒤 문장과 같음

뒤 문장: Even this simple task would require / that
이 간단한 작업조차 요구할 것이다 / 기계는

your machine be able to discriminate / between
구별할 수 있어야 한다고 /

stimulation that originates from its own machinery /
자신의 시스템에서 발생하는 자극과 /

and stimulation that originates from the blocks in
주위의 블록에서 발생하는 자극을 //

the environment. //

앞 문장에서 블록을 쌓기 위해 방에 흩어진 블록을 쌓는 로봇을
상상해보라는 예시를 들었어요.
뒤 문장에서는 블록 찾기라는 이 간단한 작업을 하기 위해 기계(로봇)가
자신의 시스템에서 발생하는 자극과 블록에서 발생하는 자극을
❷(   )할 수 있어야 한다는 내용이 나와요. 역시 자연스러운
흐름으로 진행되고 있어요.
▶ 주어진 문장이 ②에 들어갈 수 없음

3) ③의 앞 문장과 뒤 문장을 확인해 봅시다.

앞 문장: ②의 뒤 문장과 같음

뒤 문장: Suppose / that you equip your robot with an
가정해 보라 / 로봇에 인공 눈과 인공 팔을 갖추게

artificial eye and an artificial arm / to detect, grab,
하는 것을 / 블록을 감지하고,

and pile the blocks. //
잡고, 쌓도록 하기 위해 //

블록 찾기를 위해 로봇이 자신의 자극과 블록을 구별할 수 있어야 한다고
한 다음에, 뒤에서 로봇에 인공 눈과 팔을 갖추게 해서 블록을 감지하고
쌓을 수 있게 하는 상황을 가정하라고 했어요.
앞에 말한 내용에 이어서 로봇의 블록 찾기를 위한 설계에 대한 설명이
연결되고 있네요.
▶ 주어진 문장이 ③에 들어갈 수 없음

4) ④의 앞 문장과 뒤 문장을 확인해 봅시다.

앞 문장: ③의 뒤 문장과 같음

뒤 문장: To be successful, / your machine will have to
(이 작업을) 성공적으로 수행하려면 / 여러분의 기계에는 있어야

have / some built-in system / enabling it to
할 것이다 / 어떤 내장된 시스템이 / 구별할 수 있게 해주는

discriminate / between the detection of a block /
/ 블록 감지와 /

and the detection of its own arm. //
자신의 팔 감지를 //

앞에서는 로봇이 인공 팔과 눈을 가지고 블록을 감지할 수 있게 한다고
했고, 뒤에서는 성공적으로 수행하기 위해 로봇 안에 블록 감지와 팔
감지를 구별할 수 있게 해주는 시스템이 내장되어야 한다고 설명하고
있죠?
두 문장은 인공 팔을 사용한 블록 쌓기에 대한 내용이 서술되고 있는
것이므로 역시 자연스럽게 이어져요.
▶ 주어진 문장이 ④에 들어갈 수 없음

5) ⑤의 앞 문장과 뒤 문장을 확인해 봅시다.

앞 문장: ④의 뒤 문장과 같음

뒤 문장: Your robot would engage in / circular,
로봇은 하게 될 것이다 / 순환적이고

self-centered acts / that would drive it away / from
자기중심적인 행동을 / 자신을 멀어지게 하는 /

the target or external goal. //
목표물이나 외부 목표에서 //

앞 문장에서 로봇이 인공 팔로 블록을 감지할 수 있게 하려면 로봇 안에
블록 감지와 팔 감지를 구별하게 해주는 시스템이 내장되어 있어야 할
것이라고 했어요.
뒤 문장에서는 로봇이 자신의 목표물이나 외부 목표에서 멀어지는
자기중심적인 행동을 하게 될 것이라고 했죠.
주어진 문장은 '그렇지 않으면' 로봇이 블록이 아니라 자신을 끊임없이
쫓아갈 수도 있다고 했으므로, 주어진 문장을 이 문장 전에 넣어야겠죠?
그래야 로봇이 블록 감지와 팔 감지를 구분하지 못하면 블록이 아니라
자기 자신을 쫓아감으로써 목표물에서 멀어지는 자기중심적인 행동을
한다는 내용으로 글이 흘러갈 수 있어요.
▶ 주어진 문장이 ⑤에 들어가야 함

3rd 글이 한눈에 들어오도록 정리하여 정답을 확인하세요.

인지하고 행동하도록 설계된 로봇의 구상에서 주위의 다른 실재물과 자신을
구별하는 능력은 핵심이다. 그러한 능력이 없으면 목표 지향적인 행동은
불가능할 것이다.
(①) 블록을 쌓기 위해 방에 흩어져 있는 블록을 찾을 수 있는 로봇을
만드는 것을 상상해라.
(②) 이 간단한 작업을 하기 위해서도 기계는 자신의 자극과 주위 블록에서
발생하는 자극을 구별할 수 있어야 한다.
(③) 로봇에 인공 눈과 인공 팔을 갖추게 하여 블록을 감지하고, 잡고,
쌓도록 한다고 가정하자.
(④) 성공적으로 수행하려면 로봇은 블록 감지와 자신의 팔 감지를
구별하는 시스템이 있어야 한다.
(⑤ 그렇지 않으면 로봇이 블록이 아닌 자기 자신을 끝없이 쫓아갈 수도
있다.)
로봇은 자신의 목표에서 멀어지는 자기중심적인 행동을 하게 될 것이다.

N. 주어진 문장 넣기   **283**

단어장

PATTERN PRACTICE

N03 ★★★ .... 2025 대비 수능 38 (고3)

글의 흐름으로 보아, 주어진 문장이 들어가기에 가장 적절한 곳을 고르시오. [3점]

> Without any special legal protection for trade secrets, however, the secretive inventor risks that an employee or contractor will disclose the proprietary information.

Trade secret law aims to promote innovation, although it accomplishes this objective in a very different manner than patent protection. (①) Notwithstanding the advantages of obtaining a patent, many innovators prefer to protect their innovation through secrecy. (②) They may believe that the cost and delay of seeking a patent are too great or that secrecy better protects their investment and increases their profit. (③) They might also believe that the invention can best be utilized over a longer period of time than a patent would allow. (④) Once the idea is released, it will be "free as the air" under the background norms of a free market economy. (⑤) Such a predicament would lead any inventor seeking to rely upon secrecy to spend an inordinate amount of resources building high and impassable fences around their research facilities and greatly limiting the number of people with access to the proprietary information.

*patent: 특허 **predicament: 곤경

N04 ★★★ .... 2025 대비 수능 39 (고3)

글의 흐름으로 보아, 주어진 문장이 들어가기에 가장 적절한 곳을 고르시오.

> In reality, objects do not conform to a linear lifecycle model; instead, they undergo breakdowns, await repairs, are stored away, or find themselves relegated to the basement, only to be rediscovered and repurposed later.

By their very nature, the concepts of maintenance and repair are predominantly examined from a process-oriented perspective. (①) The focus in related scholarly discourse often revolves around the lifespan or lifecycle of objects and technologies. (②) In this context, maintenance and repair are considered practices that have the potential to prolong the existence of objects, ensuring their sustained utilization over an extended period. (③) Krebs and Weber critically engage with anthropomorphic metaphors that imply a biography of things, appropriately highlighting that conventional understanding of the lifecycle of a technology, from its acquisition to its disposal from the household, provides an incomplete definition. (④) Additionally, objects may enter recycling or second-hand cycles, leading to a dynamic afterlife marked by diverse applications. (⑤) As such, the life of an object exhibits a far more complicated and adaptive path than a simplistic linear progression.

*relegate: 추방하다 **anthropomorphic: 의인화된

글의 흐름으로 보아, 주어진 문장이 들어가기에 가장 적절한 곳을 고르시오. [3점]

> Unfortunately, at the scales, accuracy, and precision most useful to protected area management, the future not only promises to be unprecedented, but it also promises to be unpredictable.

To decide whether and how to intervene in ecosystems, protected area managers normally need a reasonably clear idea of what future ecosystems would be like if they did not intervene. (①) Management practices usually involve defining a more desirable future condition and implementing management actions designed to push or guide ecosystems toward that condition. (②) Managers need confidence in the likely outcomes of their interventions. (③) This traditional and inherently logical approach requires a high degree of predictive ability, and predictions must be developed at appropriate spatial and temporal scales, often localized and near-term. (④) To illustrate this, consider the uncertainties involved in predicting climatic changes, how ecosystems are likely to respond to climatic changes, and the likely efficacy of actions that might be taken to counter adverse effects of climatic changes. (⑤) Comparable uncertainties surround the nature and magnitude of future changes in other ecosystem stressors.

*adverse: 해로운 **magnitude: 크기

글의 흐름으로 보아, 주어진 문장이 들어가기에 가장 적절한 곳을 고르시오.

> Continuous emissions measurement can be costly, particularly where there are many separate sources of emissions, and for many pollution problems this may be a major disincentive to direct taxation of emissions.

Environmental taxes based directly on measured emissions can, in principle, be very precisely targeted to the policy's environmental objectives. (①) If a firm pollutes more, it pays additional tax directly in proportion to the rise in emissions. (②) The polluter thus has an incentive to reduce emissions in any manner that is less costly per unit of abatement than the tax on each unit of residual emissions. (③) The great attraction of basing the tax directly on measured emissions is that the actions the polluter can take to reduce tax liability are actions that also reduce emissions. (④) Nevertheless, the technologies available for monitoring the concentrations and flows of particular substances in waste discharges have been developing rapidly. (⑤) In the future, it may be possible to think of taxing measured emissions in a wider range of applications.

*abatement: 감소 **liability: 부담액

N07 ✷✷❋ .... 2025 대비 6월 모평 39 (고3)

글의 흐름으로 보아, 주어진 문장이 들어가기에 가장 적절한 곳을 고르시오. [3점]

> This active involvement provides a basis for depth of aesthetic processing and reflection on the meaning of the work.

There are interesting trade-offs in the relative importance of subject matter (i.e., figure) and style (i.e., background). (①) In highly representational paintings, plays, or stories, the focus is on subject matter that resembles everyday life and the role of background style is to facilitate the construction of mental models. (②) Feelings of pleasure and uncertainty carry the viewer along to the conclusion of the piece. (③) In highly expressionist works, novel stylistic devices work in an inharmonious manner against the subject matter thereby creating a disquieting atmosphere. (④) Thus, when the work is less "readable" (or easily interpreted), its departure from conventional forms reminds the viewer or reader that an "aesthetic attitude" is needed to appreciate the whole episode. (⑤) An ability to switch between the "pragmatic attitude" of everyday life and an "aesthetic attitude" is fundamental to a balanced life.

*aesthetic: 미학의　**pragmatic: 실용주의의

N08 ✷✷✷ .... 2024 실시 10월 학평 39 (고3)

글의 흐름으로 보아, 주어진 문장이 들어가기에 가장 적절한 곳을 고르시오.

> We are also able to use the cerebellum to anticipate what our actions would be even if we don't actually take them.

One way to catch a fly ball is to solve all the differential equations governing the ball's trajectory as well as your own movements and at the same time reposition your body based on those solutions. (①) Unfortunately, you don't have a differential equation-solving device in your brain, so instead you solve a simpler problem: how to place the glove most effectively between the ball an your body. (②) The cerebellum assumes that your hand and the ball should appear in similar relative positions for each catch. (③) So, if the ball is dropping too fast and your hand appears to be going too slowly, it will direct your hand to move more quickly to match the familiar relative position. (④) These simple actions by the cerebellum to map sensory inputs onto muscle movements enable us to catch the ball without solving any differential equations. (⑤)Your cerebellum might tell you that you could catch the ball but you're likely to crash into another player, so maybe you should not take this action.

*cerebellum: 소뇌　**differential equation: 미분 방정식

***trajectory: 궤적

글의 흐름으로 보아, 주어진 문장이 들어가기에 가장 적절한 곳을 고르시오.

> Following this pathway, we act altruistically when we feel empathy for a person and can truly imagine a situation from their perspective.

Prosocial behavior — that is, behavior that is intended to help another person — can be motivated by two different pathways, according to Daniel Batson at the University of Kansas. (①) One pathway, the egoistic pathway, is largely self-focused: we provide help if the rewards to us outweigh the costs. (②) This pathway is the one that is operating if we hand a homeless person a dollar to make ourselves feel better. (③) Doing so costs us very little — only a dollar — and the reward of doing so — avoiding the guilt we'd feel from simply walking by — is greater. (④) But according to Batson's hypothesis, there is another pathway, which is other-focused — it's motivated by a genuine desire to help the other person, even if we incur a cost for doing so. (⑤) This ability to see the world from someone else's perspective can lead us to help, even if there are considerable costs.

글의 흐름으로 보아, 주어진 문장이 들어가기에 가장 적절한 곳을 고르시오.

> Without the anchor of intrinsic motivation however, even a small bump in the road may reset you back; we may go back to eating meat in February when the social support has disappeared.

Our behaviour can be modified externally without there being strong personal motivation. Everything from our supermarket shopping and online browsing choices are examples of how our actions are shaped without our conscious choice or motivation. (①) However, when processes police us but fail to truly influence us, we do not continue with the behaviours after the processes are removed. (②) This is passive engagement rather than ownership. (③) A better way in which we can be externally supported to take action is by having friends who encourage us. (④) You may not be sold on going vegan, but yet give veganism a try at the start of the year because some of your friends suggest you do it together. (⑤) Resonance helps us connect to our internal motivation to change rather than being 'pushed' from the outside, and in turn helps us form a habit, where our self-concept makes a shift from 'someone who does not like cycling' to 'someone who cycles'.

* resonance: 울림, 의의

N11 ★★★ .... 2024 실시 5월 학평 38 (고3)

글의 흐름으로 보아, 주어진 문장이 들어가기에 가장 적절한 곳을 고르시오.

> The norms of objectivity were constructed not because their creators thought most humans could be 'empty' of bias.

Emotional response to the world is an inherent part of ethics. In ethics, appeals to compassion and empathy can and should be part of rational arguments about ethical decisions. Moreover, the best practices of objectivity often combine partiality and impartiality. (①) In a trial, the partiality of the prosecutor and the defense attorney (and the parties they represent) occurs within a larger impartial context. (②) A judge or jury puts partial arguments to the test of objective evidence and to the impartial rules of law. (③) Ideally, what is fair and objective emerges during a trial where partialities make their case and are judged by objective norms. (④) The reverse is true: the norms were constructed because of an acute awareness of human bias, because it is evident. (⑤) Rather than conclude that objectivity is impossible because bias is universal, scientists, journalists, and others concluded the opposite: we biased humans need the discipline of objectivity to reduce the ineliminable presence of bias.

*prosecutor: 검사(檢事), 검찰관

N12 ★★★ .... 2024 실시 5월 학평 39 (고3)

글의 흐름으로 보아, 주어진 문장이 들어가기에 가장 적절한 곳을 고르시오. [3점]

> Cats 'pay' for this nighttime accuracy with less accurate daytime vision and an inability to focus on close objects.

The fact that cats' eyes glow in the dark is part of their enhanced light-gathering efficiency; there is a reflective layer behind the retina, so light can hit the retina when it enters the eye, or when it is reflected from behind the retina. (①) Light that manages to miss the retina exits the eye and creates that ghostly glow. (②) When cats' light-gathering ability is combined with the very large population of rods in their eyes, the result is a predator that can see exceptionally well in the dark. (③) This may seem counterproductive; what is the point of seeing a mouse in the dark if, in that final, close moment, the cat can't focus on it? (④) Tactile information comes into play at this time; cats can move their whiskers forward and use them to get information about objects within the grasp of their jaws. (⑤) So the next time you see a cat seeming to nap in the bright sunlight, eyes half-closed, remember that it may simply be shielding its retina from a surplus of light.

*rod: (시신경의) 간상체(杆狀體) **tactile: 촉각의
***whisker: (고양이의) 수염

글의 흐름으로 보아, 주어진 문장이 들어가기에 가장 적절한 곳을 고르시오.

> But in the future, real-time data collection will enable insurance companies to charge pay-as-you-drive rates depending on people's actual behavior on the road, as opposed to generalized stereotypes of certain "at-risk" groups.

Insurance companies are expected to err on the safe side. They calculate risks thoroughly, carefully picking and choosing the customers they insure. They are boring because their role in the economy is to shield everyone and everything from disastrous loss. (①) Unlike manufacturing, nothing truly revolutionary ever happens in the insurance industry. (②) For centuries, insurers have charged higher premiums to people in "high-risk categories" such as smokers, male drivers under the age of thirty, and extreme-sports enthusiasts. (③) This type of classification frequently results in biases and outright discrimination against disadvantaged groups. (④) Bad or high-risk individual drivers will end up paying more for insurance, regardless of whether they are men or women, young or old. (⑤) The Big Brother connotations are threatening, but many people might agree to the real-time monitoring of their driving behavior if it means lower rates.

*err on the safe side: 너무 만전(萬全)을 기하다

글의 흐름으로 보아, 주어진 문장이 들어가기에 가장 적절한 곳을 고르시오. [3점]

> This stands in contrast to earlier figurative art, which had been as focused on representing what the artist *knew* about the objects and the space he or she was painting as on how they *looked*.

Almost all the figurative paintings we are familiar with now are in perspective. They present foreshortened figures and objects that diminish as they move away from the focal point of the painting. (①) A painting in perspective represents how the world *looks* to a person seeing the scene from a particular position in space. (②) These pictures are beautiful in their own right, but they do not represent scenes as we might see them if we were looking at them. (③) They are also less informative as to the layout of the space they represent. (④) The fact that perspective and information about spatial layout go together reveals something important about *seeing*. (⑤) Not only do we see the world through an egocentric frame but we also see it in a way that allows us to extract information about distances to, and sizes of, objects relative to us, and relative to one another.

*perspective: 원근법, 시점
**foreshorten: (회화·사진에서 대상을) 축소하다

N15 ✹✹✳ .... 2022 대비 6월 모평 38 (고3)

글의 흐름으로 보아, 주어진 문장이 들어가기에 가장 적절한 곳을 고르시오.

> A problem, however, is that supervisors often work in locations apart from their employees and therefore are not able to observe their subordinates' performance.

In most organizations, the employee's immediate supervisor evaluates the employee's performance. (①) This is because the supervisor is responsible for the employee's performance, providing supervision, handing out assignments, and developing the employee. (②) Should supervisors rate employees on performance dimensions they cannot observe? (③) To eliminate this dilemma, more and more organizations are implementing assessments referred to as *360-degree evaluations*. (④) Employees are rated not only by their supervisors but by coworkers, clients or citizens, professionals in other agencies with whom they work, and subordinates. (⑤) The reason for this approach is that often coworkers and clients or citizens have a greater opportunity to observe an employee's performance and are in a better position to evaluate many performance dimensions.

*subordinate: 부하 직원

N16 ✹✹✹ .... 2024 대비 6월 모평 38 (고3)

글의 흐름으로 보아, 주어진 문장이 들어가기에 가장 적절한 곳을 고르시오.

> Instead, much like the young child learning how to play 'nicely', the apprentice scientist gains his or her understanding of the moral values inherent in the role by absorption from their colleagues — socialization.

As particular practices are repeated over time and become more widely shared, the values that they embody are reinforced and reproduced and we speak of them as becoming 'institutionalized'. (①) In some cases, this institutionalization has a formal face to it, with rules and protocols written down, and specialized roles created to ensure that procedures are followed correctly. (②) The main institutions of state — parliament, courts, police and so on — along with certain of the professions, exhibit this formal character. (③) Other social institutions, perhaps the majority, are not like this; science is an example. (④) Although scientists are trained in the substantive content of their discipline, they are not formally instructed in 'how to be a good scientist'. (⑤) We think that these values, along with the values that inform many of the professions, are under threat, just as the value of the professions themselves is under threat.

*apprentice: 도제, 견습 **inherent: 내재된

글의 흐름으로 보아, 주어진 문장이 들어가기에 가장 적절한
곳을 고르시오.

> I have still not exactly pinpointed Maddy's character since wickedness takes many forms.

Imagine I tell you that Maddy is bad. Perhaps you infer from my intonation, or the context in which we are talking, that I mean morally bad. Additionally, you will probably infer that I am disapproving of Maddy, or saying that I think you should disapprove of her, or similar, given typical linguistic conventions and assuming I am sincere. (①) However, you might not get a more detailed sense of the particular sorts of way in which Maddy is bad, her typical character traits, and the like, since people can be bad in many ways. (②) In contrast, if I say that Maddy is wicked, then you get more of a sense of her typical actions and attitudes to others. (③) The word 'wicked' is more specific than 'bad'. (④) But there is more detail nevertheless, perhaps a stronger connotation of the sort of person Maddy is. (⑤) In addition, and again assuming typical linguistic conventions, you should also get a sense that I am disapproving of Maddy, or saying that you should disapprove of her, or similar, assuming that we are still discussing her moral character.

*connotation: 함축

글의 흐름으로 보아, 주어진 문장이 들어가기에 가장 적절한
곳을 고르시오.

> When the team painted fireflies' light organs dark, a new set of bats took twice as long to learn to avoid them.

Fireflies don't just light up their behinds to attract mates, they also glow to tell bats not to eat them. This twist in the tale of the trait that gives fireflies their name was discovered by Jesse Barber and his colleagues. The glow's warning role benefits both fireflies and bats, because these insects taste disgusting to the mammals. (①) When swallowed, chemicals released by fireflies cause bats to throw them back up. (②) The team placed eight bats in a dark room with three or four fireflies plus three times as many tasty insects, including beetles and moths, for four days. (③) During the first night, all the bats captured at least one firefly. (④) But by the fourth night, most bats had learned to avoid fireflies and catch all the other prey instead. (⑤) It had long been thought that firefly bioluminescence mainly acted as a mating signal, but the new finding explains why firefly larvae also glow despite being immature for mating.

*bioluminescence: 생물 발광(發光) **larvae: larva(애벌레)의 복수형

N19 ✱✱✱.......................... 2022 대비 9월 모평 39 (고3)

글의 흐름으로 보아, 주어진 문장이 들어가기에 가장 적절한 곳을 고르시오. [3점]

> Personal stories connect with larger narratives to generate new identities.

The growing complexity of the social dynamics determining food choices makes the job of marketers and advertisers increasingly more difficult. (①) In the past, mass production allowed for accessibility and affordability of products, as well as their wide distribution, and was accepted as a sign of progress. (②) Nowadays it is increasingly replaced by the fragmentation of consumers among smaller and smaller segments that are supposed to reflect personal preferences. (③) Everybody feels different and special and expects products serving his or her inclinations. (④) In reality, these supposedly individual preferences end up overlapping with emerging, temporary, always changing, almost tribal formations solidifying around cultural sensibilities, social identifications, political sensibilities, and dietary and health concerns. (⑤) These consumer communities go beyond national boundaries, feeding on global and widely shared repositories of ideas, images, and practices.　　*fragmentation: 파편화　**repository: 저장소

N20 ✱✱✱❋................................. 2022 대비 수능 38 (고3)

글의 흐름으로 보아, 주어진 문장이 들어가기에 가장 적절한 곳을 고르시오.

> Retraining current employees for new positions within the company will also greatly reduce their fear of being laid off.

Introduction of robots into factories, while employment of human workers is being reduced, creates worry and fear. (①) It is the responsibility of management to prevent or, at least, to ease these fears. (②) For example, robots could be introduced only in new plants rather than replacing humans in existing assembly lines. (③) Workers should be included in the planning for new factories or the introduction of robots into existing plants, so they can participate in the process. (④) It may be that robots are needed to reduce manufacturing costs so that the company remains competitive, but planning for such cost reductions should be done jointly by labor and management. (⑤) Since robots are particularly good at highly repetitive simple motions, the replaced human workers should be moved to positions where judgment and decisions beyond the abilities of robots are required.

N21 ✱✱❋................................. 2021 대비 수능 39 (고3)

글의 흐름으로 보아, 주어진 문장이 들어가기에 가장 적절한 곳을 고르시오. [3점]

> Note that copyright covers the expression of an idea and not the idea itself.

Designers draw on their experience of design when approaching a new project. This includes the use of previous designs that they know work — both designs that they have created themselves and those that others have created. (①) Others' creations often spark inspiration that also leads to new ideas and innovation. (②) This is well known and understood. (③) However, the expression of an idea is protected by copyright, and people who infringe on that copyright can be taken to court and prosecuted. (④) This means, for example, that while there are numerous smartphones all with similar functionality, this does not represent an infringement of copyright as the idea has been expressed in different ways and it is the expression that has been copyrighted. (⑤) Copyright is free and is automatically invested in the author, for instance, the writer of a book or a programmer who develops a program, unless they sign the copyright over to someone else.　　*infringe: 침해하다　**prosecute: 기소하다

글의 흐름으로 보아, 주어진 문장이 들어가기에 가장 적절한 곳을 고르시오. [3점]

> As a result, they are fit and grow better, but they aren't particularly long-lived.

When trees grow together, nutrients and water can be optimally divided among them all so that each tree can grow into the best tree it can be. If you "help" individual trees by getting rid of their supposed competition, the remaining trees are bereft. They send messages out to their neighbors unsuccessfully, because nothing remains but stumps. Every tree now grows on its own, giving rise to great differences in productivity. (①) Some individuals photosynthesize like mad until sugar positively bubbles along their trunk. (②) This is because a tree can be only as strong as the forest that surrounds it. (③) And there are now a lot of losers in the forest. (④) Weaker members, who would once have been supported by the stronger ones, suddenly fall behind. (⑤) Whether the reason for their decline is their location and lack of nutrients, a passing sickness, or genetic makeup, they now fall prey to insects and fungi.

*bereft: 잃은 **stump: 그루터기 ***photosynthesize: 광합성하다

글의 흐름으로 보아, 주어진 문장이 들어가기에 가장 적절한 곳을 고르시오.

> In particular, they define a group as two or more people who interact with, and exert mutual influences on, each other.

In everyday life, we tend to see any collection of people as a group. (①) However, social psychologists use this term more precisely. (②) It is this sense of mutual interaction or inter-dependence for a common purpose which distinguishes the members of a group from a mere aggregation of individuals. (③) For example, as Kenneth Hodge observed, a collection of people who happen to go for a swim after work on the same day each week does not, strictly speaking, constitute a group because these swimmers do not interact with each other in a structured manner. (④) By contrast, a squad of young competitive swimmers who train every morning before going to school *is* a group because they not only share a common objective (training for competition) but also interact with each other in formal ways (e.g., by warming up together beforehand). (⑤) It is this sense of people coming together to achieve a common objective that defines a "team".

*exert: 발휘하다 **aggregation: 집합

N24 ✱✱✱ .... 2023 실시 3월 학평 39 (고3)

글의 흐름으로 보아, 주어진 문장이 들어가기에 가장 적절한 곳을 고르시오. [3점]

> However, human reasoning is still notoriously prone to confusion and error when causal questions become sufficiently complex, such as when it comes to assessing the impact of policy interventions across society.

Going beyond very simple algorithms, some AI-based tools hold out the promise of supporting better causal and probabilistic reasoning in complex domains. (①) Humans have a natural ability to build causal models of the world — that is, to explain *why* things happen — that AI systems still largely lack. (②) For example, while a doctor can explain to a patient why a treatment works, referring to the changes it causes in the body, a modern machine-learning system could only tell you that patients who are given this treatment tend, on average, to get better. (③) In these cases, supporting human reasoning with more structured AI-based tools may be helpful. (④) Researchers have been exploring the use of Bayesian Networks — an AI technology that can be used to map out the causal relationships between events, and to represent degrees of uncertainty around different areas — for decision support, such as to enable more accurate risk assessment. (⑤) These may be particularly useful for assessing the threat of novel or rare threats, where little historical data is available, such as the risk of terrorist attacks and new ecological disasters.

*notoriously: 악명 높게도

N25 ✱✱❋ .... 2023 대비 수능 38 (고3)

글의 흐름으로 보아, 주어진 문장이 들어가기에 가장 적절한 곳을 고르시오.

> There's a reason for that: traditionally, park designers attempted to create such a feeling by planting tall trees at park boundaries, building stone walls, and constructing other means of partition.

Parks take the shape demanded by the cultural concerns of their time. Once parks are in place, they are no inert stage — their purposes and meanings are made and remade by planners and by park users. Moments of park creation are particularly telling, however, for they reveal and actualize ideas about nature and its relationship to urban society. (①) Indeed, what distinguishes a park from the broader category of public space is the representation of nature that parks are meant to embody. (②) Public spaces include parks, concrete plazas, sidewalks, even indoor atriums. (③) Parks typically have trees, grass, and other plants as their central features. (④) When entering a city park, people often imagine a sharp separation from streets, cars, and buildings. (⑤) What's behind this idea is not only landscape architects' desire to design aesthetically suggestive park spaces, but a much longer history of Western thought that envisions cities and nature as antithetical spaces and oppositional forces.

*aesthetically: 미적으로 **antithetical: 대조적인

N26 ✱✱✱❋ .... 2021 대비 9월 모평 39 (고3)

글의 흐름으로 보아, 주어진 문장이 들어가기에 가장 적절한 곳을 고르시오. [3점]

> Rather, it evolved naturally as certain devices were found in practice to be both workable and useful.

Film has no grammar. (①) There are, however, some vaguely defined rules of usage in cinematic language, and the syntax of film — its systematic arrangement — orders these rules and indicates relationships among them. (②) As with written and spoken languages, it is important to remember that the syntax of film is a result of its usage, not a determinant of it. (③) There is nothing preordained about film syntax. (④) Like the syntax of written and spoken language, the syntax of film is an organic development, descriptive rather than prescriptive, and it has changed considerably over the years. (⑤) "Hollywood Grammar" may sound laughable now, but during the thirties, forties, and early fifties it was an accurate model of the way Hollywood films were constructed.

* preordained: 미리 정해진

N27 ✱✱✱❋ .... 2021 대비 9월 모평 38 (고3)

글의 흐름으로 보아, 주어진 문장이 들어가기에 가장 적절한 곳을 고르시오.

> As long as you do not run out of copies before completing this process, you will know that you have a sufficient number to go around.

We sometimes solve number problems almost without realizing it. (①) For example, suppose you are conducting a meeting and you want to ensure that everyone there has a copy of the agenda. (②) You can deal with this by labelling each copy of the handout in turn with the initials of each of those present. (③) You have then solved this problem without resorting to arithmetic and without explicit counting. (④) There are numbers at work for us here all the same and they allow precise comparison of one collection with another, even though the members that make up the collections could have entirely different characters, as is the case here, where one set is a collection of people, while the other consists of pieces of paper. (⑤) What numbers allow us to do is to compare the relative size of one set with another.

* arithmetic: 산수

N28 ✱✱✱ .... 2023 실시 4월 학평 39 (고3)

글의 흐름으로 보아, 주어진 문장이 들어가기에 가장 적절한 곳을 고르시오. [3점]

> Indeed, in the Middle Ages in Europe, calculating by hand and eye was sometimes seen as producing a rather shabby sort of knowledge, inferior to that of abstract thought.

Babylonian astronomers created detailed records of celestial movements in the heavens, using the resulting tables to sieve out irregularities and, with them, the favour of the gods. (①) This was the seed of what we now call the scientific method — a demonstration that accurate observations of the world could be used to forecast its future. (②) The importance of measurement in this sort of cosmic comprehension did not develop smoothly over the centuries. (③) The suspicion was due to the influence of ancient Greeks in the era's scholasticism, particularly Plato and Aristotle, who stressed that the material world was one of unceasing change and instability. (④) They emphasized that reality was best understood by reference to immaterial qualities, be they Platonic forms or Aristotelian causes. (⑤) It would take the revelations of the scientific revolution to fully displace these instincts, with observations of the night sky once again proving decisive.

* celestial: 천체의 ** sieve: 거르다

N29 ✿✿✾ .... 2023 실시 7월 학평 38 (고3)

글의 흐름으로 보아, 주어진 문장이 들어가기에 가장 적절한 곳을 고르시오.

> The result was that we don't always buy what we like best, but when things have to happen quickly, we tend to go for the product that catches our eye the most.

Often time, or lack of time, plays an important role in the purchase of everyday products. Milica Milosavljevic and his coworkers conducted an experiment looking at the relationship between visual salience and the decision to purchase. (①) They showed subjects 15 different food items on fMRI, such as those we find in a candy vending machine at the train station, that is, bars, chips, fruity items, etc. (②) These were rated by the subjects on a scale of 1–15 according to "favorite snack" to "don't like at all." (③) They were then presented in varying brightness and time, with subjects always having to make a choice between two products. (④) If we are also distracted because we are talking to someone, on the phone, or our thoughts are elsewhere at the moment, our actual preference for a product falls further into the background and visual conspicuousness comes to the fore. (⑤) Colors play an important role in this.

*salience: 두드러짐 **fMRI: 기능적 자기 공명 영상
***conspicuousness: 눈에 잘 띔

N30 ✿✿✾ .... 2023 실시 7월 학평 39 (고3)

글의 흐름으로 보아, 주어진 문장이 들어가기에 가장 적절한 곳을 고르시오.

> However, within British society not everybody would see football as 'their' game.

If we look at contemporary British 'culture' we will probably quickly conclude that sport is an important part of the culture. In other words, it is something that many people in the society share and value. (①) In addition, we would also probably conclude that the most 'important' sport within British culture is football. (②) We would 'know' this from the evidence that on a daily basis there is a significant amount of 'cultural' activity all focused on football in terms of the amount of people who play it, watch it, read about it and talk about it. (③) It could be argued from looking at their 'cultural' activities and habits, that people from a middle-class background seem to prefer rugby over football, or that more women play netball than football. (④) Equally, if you went to the USA and were talking about 'football', most people would assume you were talking about American football rather than soccer. (⑤) From this we can conclude that different cultures produce different ways of understanding, or evaluating, human activities such as sport.

N31 ★★★ ⋯⋯⋯⋯⋯⋯ 2024 대비 9월 모평 38 (고3)

글의 흐름으로 보아, 주어진 문장이 들어가기에 가장 적절한 곳을 고르시오.

> Because the manipulation of digitally converted sounds meant the reprogramming of binary information, editing operations could be performed with millisecond precision.

The shift from analog to digital technology significantly influenced how music was produced. First and foremost, the digitization of sounds — that is, their conversion into numbers — enabled music makers to undo what was done. (①) One could, in other words, twist and bend sounds toward something new without sacrificing the original version. (②) This "undo" ability made mistakes considerably less momentous, sparking the creative process and encouraging a generally more experimental mindset. (③) In addition, digitally converted sounds could be manipulated simply by programming digital messages rather than using physical tools, simplifying the editing process significantly. (④) For example, while editing once involved razor blades to physically cut and splice audiotapes, it now involved the cursor and mouse-click of the computer-based sequencer program, which was obviously less time consuming. (⑤) This microlevel access at once made it easier to conceal any traces of manipulations (such as joining tracks in silent spots) and introduced new possibilities for manipulating sounds in audible and experimental ways.

*binary: 2진법의 **splice: 합쳐 잇다

N32 ★★※ ⋯⋯⋯⋯⋯⋯ 2023 실시 10월 학평 39 (고3)

글의 흐름으로 보아, 주어진 문장이 들어가기에 가장 적절한 곳을 고르시오.

> In contrast, the other major advocate of utilitarianism, John Stuart Mill, argued for a more qualitative approach, assuming that there can be different subjective levels of pleasure.

Utilitarian ethics argues that all action should be directed toward achieving the greatest total amount of happiness for the largest number of people. (①) Utilitarian ethics assumes that all actions can be evaluated in terms of their moral worth, and so the desirability of an action is determined by its resulting hedonistic consequences. (②) This is a consequentialist creed, assuming that the moral value and desirability of an action can be determined from its likely outcomes. (③) Jeremy Bentham suggested that the value of hedonistic outcomes can be quantitatively assessed, so that the value of consequent pleasure can be derived by multiplying its intensity and its duration. (④) Higherquality pleasures are more desirable than lower-quality pleasures. (⑤) Less sophisticated creatures (like pigs!) have an easier access to the simpler pleasures, but more sophisticated creatures like humans have the capacity to access higher pleasures and should be motivated to seek those.

*utilitarianism: 공리주의 **hedonistic: 쾌락적인 ***creed: 신조

N33 ★★★ .... 2024 대비 9월 모평 39 (고3)

글의 흐름으로 보아, 주어진 문장이 들어가기에 가장 적절한 곳을 고르시오. [3점]

> In the case of specialists such as art critics, a deeper familiarity with materials and techniques is often useful in reaching an informed judgement about a work.

Acknowledging the making of artworks does not require a detailed, technical knowledge of, say, how painters mix different kinds of paint, or how an image editing tool works. (①) All that is required is a general sense of a significant difference between working with paints and working with an imaging application. (②) This sense might involve a basic familiarity with paints and paintbrushes as well as a basic familiarity with how we use computers, perhaps including how we use consumer imaging apps. (③) This is because every kind of artistic material or tool comes with its own challenges and affordances for artistic creation. (④) Critics are often interested in the ways artists exploit different kinds of materials and tools for particular artistic effect. (⑤) They are also interested in the success of an artist's attempt — embodied in the artwork itself — to push the limits of what can be achieved with certain materials and tools.

*affordance: 행위유발성 **exploit: 활용하다

N34 ★★★ .... 2023 실시 10월 학평 38 (고3)

글의 흐름으로 보아, 주어진 문장이 들어가기에 가장 적절한 곳을 고르시오. [3점]

> But when students were given "worked-examples" (such as pre-solved problems) placed between problems to solve, studying the worked-examples freed up cognitive resources that allowed students to see the key features of the problem and to analyze the steps and reasons behind problem-solving moves.

How can we help students manage cognitive load as they learn to perform complex tasks? One method that has proved effective in research studies is to support some aspects of a complex task while students perform the entire task. (①) For example, Swelter and Cooper demonstrated this with students learning to solve problems in a variety of quantitative fields from statistics to physics. (②) They found that when students were given typical word problems, it was possible for them to solve the problems without actually learning much. (③) This is because the problems themselves were sufficiently demanding that students had no cognitive resources available to learn from what they did. (④) The researchers found this improved students' performance on subsequent problem solving. (⑤) This result, called the *worked-example effect*, is one example of a process called *scaffolding*, by which instructors temporarily relieve some of the cognitive load so that students can focus on particular dimensions of learning.

*word problem: 문장제(이야기 형식으로 제시된 문제)
**scaffolding: 발판 놓기

글의 흐름으로 보아, 주어진 문장이 들어가기에 가장 적절한 곳을 고르시오. [3점]

> On top of the hurdles introduced in accessing his or her money, if a suspected fraud is detected, the account holder has to deal with the phone call asking if he or she made the suspicious transactions.

Each new wave of technology is intended to enhance user convenience, as well as improve security, but sometimes these do not necessarily go hand-in-hand. For example, the transition from magnetic stripe to embedded chip slightly slowed down transactions, sometimes frustrating customers in a hurry. (①) Make a service too burdensome, and the potential customer will go elsewhere. (②) This obstacle applies at several levels. (③) Passwords, double-key identification, and biometrics such as fingerprint-, iris-, and voice recognition are all ways of keeping the account details hidden from potential fraudsters, of keeping your data dark. (④) But they all inevitably add a burden to the use of the account. (⑤) This is all useful at some level — indeed, it can be reassuring knowing that your bank is keeping alert to protect you — but it becomes tiresome if too many such calls are received.

*fraud: 사기

글의 흐름으로 보아, 주어진 문장이 들어가기에 가장 적절한 곳을 고르시오.

> Yes, some contests are seen as world class, such as identification of the Higgs particle or the development of high temperature superconductors.

Science is sometimes described as a winner-take-all contest, meaning that there are no rewards for being second or third. This is an extreme view of the nature of scientific contests. (①) Even those who describe scientific contests in such a way note that it is a somewhat inaccurate description, given that replication and verification have social value and are common in science. (②) It is also inaccurate to the extent that it suggests that only a handful of contests exist. (③) But many other contests have multiple parts, and the number of such contests may be increasing. (④) By way of example, for many years it was thought that there would be "one" cure for cancer, but it is now realized that cancer takes multiple forms and that multiple approaches are needed to provide a cure. (⑤) There won't be one winner — there will be many.

*replication: 반복 **verification: 입증

N37 ✱✱✱ .... 2021 대비 6월 모평 38 (고3)

글의 흐름으로 보아, 주어진 문장이 들어가기에 가장 적절한 곳을 고르시오. [3점]

> Compounding the difficulty, now more than ever, is what ergonomists call information overload, where a leader is overrun with inputs — via e-mails, meetings, and phone calls — that only distract and confuse her thinking.

Clarity is often a difficult thing for a leader to obtain. Concerns of the present tend to seem larger than potentially greater concerns that lie farther away. (①) Some decisions by their nature present great complexity, whose many variables must come together a certain way for the leader to succeed. (②) Alternatively, the leader's information might be only fragmentary, which might cause her to fill in the gaps with assumptions — sometimes without recognizing them as such. (③) And the merits of a leader's most important decisions, by their nature, typically are not clear-cut. (④) Instead those decisions involve a process of assigning weights to competing interests, and then determining, based upon some criterion, which one predominates. (⑤) The result is one of judgment, of shades of gray; like saying that Beethoven is a better composer than Brahms.

＊ergonomist: 인간 공학자 ＊＊fragmentary: 단편적인

N38 ✱✱✱ .... 2024 대비 수능 39 (고3)

글의 흐름으로 보아, 주어진 문장이 들어가기에 가장 적절한 곳을 고르시오. [3점]

> At the next step in the argument, however, the analogy breaks down.

Misprints in a book or in any written message usually have a negative impact on the content, sometimes (literally) fatally. (①) The displacement of a comma, for instance, may be a matter of life and death. (②) Similarly most mutations have harmful consequences for the organism in which they occur, meaning that they reduce its reproductive fitness. (③) Occasionally, however, a mutation may occur that increases the fitness of the organism, just as an accidental failure to reproduce the text of the first edition might provide more accurate or updated information. (④) A favorable mutation is going to be more heavily represented in the next generation, since the organism in which it occurred will have more offspring and mutations are transmitted to the offspring. (⑤) By contrast, there is no mechanism by which a book that accidentally corrects the mistakes of the first edition will tend to sell better.

＊analogy: 유사 ＊＊mutation: 돌연변이

N39 ★★★ .... 2022 대비 6월 모평 39 (고3)

글의 흐름으로 보아, 주어진 문장이 들어가기에 가장 적절한 곳을 고르시오. [3점]

> This is particularly true since one aspect of sleep is decreased responsiveness to the environment.

The role that sleep plays in evolution is still under study. (①) One possibility is that it is an advantageous adaptive state of decreased metabolism for an animal when there are no more pressing activities. (②) This seems true for deeper states of inactivity such as hibernation during the winter when there are few food supplies, and a high metabolic cost to maintaining adequate temperature. (③) It may be true in daily situations as well, for instance for a prey species to avoid predators after dark. (④) On the other hand, the apparent universality of sleep, and the observation that mammals such as cetaceans have developed such highly complex mechanisms to preserve sleep on at least one side of the brain at a time, suggests that sleep additionally provides some vital service(s) for the organism. (⑤) If sleep is universal even when this potential price must be paid, the implication may be that it has important functions that cannot be obtained just by quiet, wakeful resting.

*metabolism: 신진대사 **mammal: 포유동물

N40~44 ▶ 제한시간 13.5분

N40 ✪ 2등급 대비 .... 2023 대비 6월 모평 39 (고3)

글의 흐름으로 보아, 주어진 문장이 들어가기에 가장 적절한 곳을 고르시오. [3점]

> This makes sense from the perspective of information reliability.

The dynamics of collective detection have an interesting feature. Which cue(s) do individuals use as evidence of predator attack? In some cases, when an individual detects a predator, its best response is to seek shelter. (①) Departure from the group may signal danger to nonvigilant animals and cause what appears to be a coordinated flushing of prey from the area. (②) Studies on dark-eyed juncos (a type of bird) support the view that nonvigilant animals attend to departures of individual group mates but that the departure of multiple individuals causes a greater escape response in the nonvigilant individuals. (③) If one group member departs, it might have done so for a number of reasons that have little to do with predation threat. (④) If nonvigilant animals escaped each time a single member left the group, they would frequently respond when there was no predator (a false alarm). (⑤) On the other hand, when several individuals depart the group at the same time, a true threat is much more likely to be present.

*predator: 포식자 **vigilant: 경계하는 ***flushing: 날아오름

글의 흐름으로 보아, 주어진 문장이 들어가기에 가장 적절한 곳을 고르시오. [3점]

> As long as the irrealism of the silent black and white film predominated, one could not take filmic fantasies for representations of reality.

Cinema is valuable not for its ability to make visible the hidden outlines of our reality, but for its ability to reveal what reality itself veils — the dimension of fantasy. (①) This is why, to a person, the first great theorists of film decried the introduction of sound and other technical innovations (such as color) that pushed film in the direction of realism. (②) Since cinema was an entirely fantasmatic art, these innovations were completely unnecessary. (③) And what's worse, they could do nothing but turn filmmakers and audiences away from the fantasmatic dimension of cinema, potentially transforming film into a mere delivery device for representations of reality. (④) But sound and color threatened to create just such an illusion, thereby destroying the very essence of film art. (⑤) As Rudolf Arnheim puts it, "The creative power of the artist can only come into play where reality and the medium of representation do not coincide."

*decry: 공공연히 비난하다   **fantasmatic: 환상의

글의 흐름으로 보아, 주어진 문장이 들어가기에 가장 적절한 곳을 고르시오.

> It was not until relatively recent times that scientists came to understand the relationships between the structural elements of materials and their properties.

The earliest humans had access to only a very limited number of materials, those that occur naturally: stone, wood, clay, skins, and so on. (①) With time, they discovered techniques for producing materials that had properties superior to those of the natural ones; these new materials included pottery and various metals. (②) Furthermore, it was discovered that the properties of a material could be altered by heat treatments and by the addition of other substances. (③) At this point, materials utilization was totally a selection process that involved deciding from a given, rather limited set of materials, the one best suited for an application based on its characteristics. (④) This knowledge, acquired over approximately the past 100 years, has empowered them to fashion, to a large degree, the characteristics of materials. (⑤) Thus, tens of thousands of different materials have evolved with rather specialized characteristics that meet the needs of our modern and complex society, including metals, plastics, glasses, and fibers.

글의 흐름으로 보아, 주어진 문장이 들어가기에 가장 적절한 곳을 고르시오. [3점]

> But what if memories about news stories are faulty and distort, forget, or invent what was actually reported?

Memory often plays tricks. (①) According to Mlodinow, we give "unwarranted importance to memories that are the most vivid and hence most available for retrieval — our memory makes it easy to remember the events that are unusual and striking not the many events that are normal and dull." (②) The self-serving bias works because, as Trivers observes, "There are also many processes of memory that can be biased to produce welcome results. Memories are continually distorting in self-serving ways." (③) A recent study argues that several forms of cognitive bias cause distortions in storing and retrieving memories. (④) This, in turn, has a bearing on theories of agenda setting, priming, and framing, which argue that how people respond to the news is strongly influenced by what is most easily and readily accessible from their memories. (⑤) In such cases, it may be the manipulation of memories in individual minds that primes, frames, and sets the agenda, not the original news stories.

*retrieval: 불러오기 **have a bearing on: ~에 영향을 미치다

글의 흐름으로 보아, 주어진 문장이 들어가기에 가장 적절한 곳을 고르시오. [3점]

> It may be easier to reach an agreement when settlement terms don't have to be implemented until months in the future.

Negotiators should try to find ways to slice a large issue into smaller pieces, known as using *salami tactics*. (①) Issues that can be expressed in quantitative, measurable units are easy to slice. (②) For example, compensation demands can be divided into cents-per-hour increments or lease rates can be quoted as dollars per square foot. (③) When working to fractionate issues of principle or precedent, parties may use the time horizon (when the principle goes into effect or how long it will last) as a way to fractionate the issue. (④) Another approach is to vary the number of ways that the principle may be applied. (⑤) For example, a company may devise a family emergency leave plan that allows employees the opportunity to be away from the company for a period of no longer than three hours, and no more than once a month, for illness in the employee's immediate family.

*increment: 증가 **fractionate: 세분하다

※ 다음 영어는 우리말 뜻을, 우리말은 영어 단어를 〈보기〉에서 찾아 쓰시오.

〈보기〉

demonstrate	상대적인	compound	함축, 암시
현대의	approval	경외심	정량적인
pest	inclination	옹호자	prison

01 advocate _____

02 quantitative _____

03 contemporary _____

04 implication _____

05 relative _____

06 보여주다 _____

07 가중시키다 _____

08 해충 _____

09 승인, 찬성 _____

10 기호, 성향 _____

※ 다음 우리말에 알맞은 영어 표현을 찾아 연결하시오.

11 결국 • • run out of

12 ~의 기반 • • in turn

13 ~을 다 써버리다[바닥내다] • • a basis for

14 다시 말해서 • • in other words

15 원칙적으로 • • in principle

※ 다음 우리말 표현에 맞는 단어를 고르시오.

16 자발적 통제 아래에 → under (voluntary / involuntary) control

17 정보 신뢰성의 관점 → the perspective of information (reliability / possibility)

18 이러한 종류의 우주의 이해 → this sort of cosmic (apprehension / comprehension)

19 생물학적 통제 기법들 → (geological / biological) control methods

20 사전에 함께 준비운동을 하다 → warm up together (second-hand / beforehand)

※ 다음 문장의 빈칸에 알맞은 단어를 〈보기〉에서 찾아 쓰시오.

〈보기〉

optimally	flee	immature	implementing
suspicious	empowered	constitute	inevitably
shelter	pad	embarrassed	

21 나무가 함께 자랄 때는 영양분과 물이 그것들 모두 사이에서 최적으로 분배된다.

→ When trees grow together, nutrients and water can be _____ divided among them all.

22 점점 더 많은 조직이 '다면 평가'라고 불리는 평가를 시행하고 있다.

→ More and more organizations are _____ assessments referred to as 360-degree evaluations.

23 그것들은 모두 불가피하게 계좌 사용에 부담을 가중한다.

→ They all _____ add a burden to the use of the account.

24 그것의 최선의 반응은 피난처를 찾는 것이다.

→ Its best response is to seek _____.

25 예금주는 본인이 그 의심스러운 거래를 했는지를 묻는 전화 통화를 응대해야만 한다.

→ The account holder has to deal with the phone call asking if he or she made the _____ transactions.

26 연구 결과는 짝짓기를 하기에 미숙함에도 불구하고 반딧불이 애벌레가 빛을 내는 이유를 설명한다.

→ The finding explains why firefly larvae glow despite being _____ for mating.

27 우연히 같은 날에 수영을 하러 가는 사람들의 무리는 집단을 구성하지 않는다.

→ A collection of people who happen to go for a swim on the same day does not _____ a group.

28 그것은 물질적인 즐거움으로 우리의 삶을 채워 넣는 우리의 능력에 달려 있다.

→ It depends on our capacity to _____ our lives with material pleasures.

29 이 지식은 그들이 물질의 특성을 형성할 수 있게 했다.

→ This knowledge has _____ them to fashion the characteristics of materials.

요약문 완성하기

★ 유형 설명

다음 글의 내용을 한 문장으로 요약하고자 한다. 빈칸 (A), (B)에 들어갈 말로 가장 적절한 것은?

> The computer has, to a considerable extent, solved the problem of acquiring,

글의 내용을 한 문장으로 요약하여 주제문을 완성한다는 생각으로 접근해야 한다.

☞ 요약문을 먼저 읽음으로써 글이 무슨 내용인지를 대강 파악한 다음 글을 읽기 시작한다. 주제를 담은 문장을 글에서 찾거나 (주제문이 없다면) 스스로 만들어 보고 그것과 똑같은 내용을 다르게 표현하는 문장이 되도록 요약문을 완성한다.

유형 풀이 비법

1 요약문을 확인하라!

· 제시된 요약문을 먼저 읽고, 글에서 찾아야 할 내용을 파악한다.

2 글의 주제를 파악하라!

· 글 전체를 읽으며 주제문을 찾고, 무엇에 관한 내용인지 파악한다.

3 직접 요약문을 완성하라!

· 글의 내용을 대표할 수 있는 핵심어를 찾아 요약문을 스스로 만들어 본다.

> (Tip) 핵심어나 주요 내용을 다르게 표현한 어구를 선택지에서 찾는다.

★ 최신 수능 경향 분석

대비 연도	월	문항 번호	지문 주제	난이도
2025	11	40번	합성 식품 성분 및 천연 식품 성분	★★☆
	9	40번	인간 언어가 다른 동물의 울음소리와 다르게 갖고 있는 특성	★★★
	6	40번	기근 예방을 위한 공적 개입의 역할과 필요성	★★★
2024	11	40번	여러 과학 주제를 탐구하는 것의 이점	★★★
	9	40번	역사 소설의 역할	★★★
	6	40번	생존 특성의 두 가지 측면	★★★
2023	11	40번	장인정신이 마주치는 장애물	★★☆
	9	40번	관리자로서 기능하는 디자이너	★★☆
	6	40번	신체적 움직임과 사회적 불평등	★★★

★ 2025 수능 출제 분석

문장을 이해하는 데 필요한 어휘의 난이도가 높지 않았으며, 두 번째 문장, 네 번째 문장의 표현들을 적절히 바꾼다면 쉽게 요약문을 채울 수 있었다.

★ 2026 수능 예측

글에 사용된 단어나 어구가 그대로 요약문의 빈칸에 들어가는 경우는 거의 없으므로 글의 내용을 다른 표현을 사용하여 요약하는 훈련을 평소에 꾸준히 해야 한다.

어휘 및 표현 Preview

- comprehensive 포괄적인
- desirable 바람직한
- distinction 차이
- general 일반적인
- principle 원칙
- communication 의사소통
- restrict 제한하다
- include 포함하다
- invent 만들어 내다, 발명하다
- remember 기억하다
- build on ~을 기반으로 하다
- revival 회복

- combine 결합하다
- unlimited 무제한의
- typical 전형적인, 일반적인
- literally 말 그대로
- infinitely 엄청, 무한히
- superior to 뛰어난, 우월한
- utilize 활용하다
- complicated 복잡한
- cost-effective 비용 효율이 높은
- symbolize 상징하다
- risk 위험

- distort 왜곡하다
- express 표현하다
- record 기록하다
- universal 보편적인
- novel 새로운
- tendency 경향
- emergency 비상
- dominant 우세한
- reduction 감소
- famine 기근
- vulnerability 취약성
- enhance 강화하다

- potential 잠재적인
- contribution 기여
- deny 부인하다
- population 인구
- specialized 특화된
- intervention 개입
- rapid 급속한
- explain 설명하다
- recurrent 되풀이되는, 반복되는
- crisis 위기
- fruitful 효과적인
- diminish 줄이다

O 요약문 완성하기 (첫 번째)

1st 요약문을 통해 글에서 무엇을 찾아야 하는지 확인하세요.
2nd 첫 문장을 통해 글의 전개 방향을 확인하고, 빈칸을 채우는 데 필요한 '무엇'을 글에서 찾으세요.
3rd 전체 글의 내용을 정리하여 요약문이 적절한지 확인하세요.

001 ★★❀ .... 2025 대비 6월 모평 40 (고3)

다음 글의 내용을 한 문장으로 요약하고자 한다.
빈칸 (A), (B)에 들어갈 말로 가장 적절한 것은?

There is a tendency, once the dust of an emergency has settled down, to seek the reduction of famine vulnerability primarily in enhanced economic growth, or the revival of the rural economy, or the diversification of economic activities. The potential contribution of greater economic success, if it involves vulnerable groups, cannot be denied. At the same time, it is important to recognize that, no matter how fast they grow, countries where a large part of the population derive their livelihood from uncertain sources cannot hope to prevent famines without specialized entitlement protection mechanisms involving direct public intervention. Rapid growth of the economy in Botswana, or of the agricultural sector in Kenya, or of food production in Zimbabwe, explains at best only a small part of their success in preventing recurrent threats of famine. The real achievements of these countries lie in having provided direct public support to their populations in times of crisis.

*famine: 기아 **vulnerability: 취약

⬇

Although economic growth can be somewhat _____(A)_____ in diminishing a country's risk of famine, direct approaches to helping the affected people play a(n) _____(B)_____ role in this process.

(A)	(B)
① productive	— complicated
② fruitful	— critical
③ dominant	— comprehensive
④ restrictive	— appropriate
⑤ desirable	— cost-effective

1st 요약문을 통해 글에서 무엇을 찾아야 하는지 확인하세요.

Although economic growth can be somewhat
비록 경제 성장이 어느 정도 ___(A)___ 수 있지만

___(A)___ / in diminishing a country's risk of famine, /
/ 한 국가의 기근 위험을 줄이는 데 /

direct approaches to helping the affected people /
피해를 입은 사람들을 돕는 것에 대한 직접적인 접근이 /

play a(n) ___(B)___ role in this process. //
이 과정에서 ___(B)___ 역할을 한다 //

● 요약문의 문장을 살펴봅시다.

경제 성장이 국가의 기근 위험을 줄이는 데 어느 정도 (A)할 수 있지만, 사람들을 돕는 것에 대한 직접적인 접근이 (B)한 역할을 한다는 내용이에요. (단서)

● (A)와 (B) 각각에 선택지를 넣어서 해석해 봅시다.

먼저 (A)는 경제 성장이 국가의 기근 위험을 줄이는 데 '생산적'인지, '효과적'인지, '우세한'지, '제한적인'지, '바람직한'지 판단해야 하고, (B)는 피해를 입은 사람들을 돕는 것에 대한 직접적인 접근이 '복잡한' 역할을 하는지, '중요한' 역할을 하는지, '포괄적인' 역할을 하는지, '적절한' 역할을 하는지, '비용 효율이 높은' 역할을 하는지 판단해야 해요. (발상)

2nd 첫 문장을 통해 글의 전개 방향을 확인하고, 빈칸을 채우는 데 필요한 '무엇'을 글에서 찾으세요.

1) 먼저 첫 문장을 확인해 봅시다.

There is a tendency, / once the dust of an
~하는 경향이 있다 / 일단 비상사태의 소요가

emergency has settled down, / to seek the reduction
진정되고 나면 / 기근 취약성 감소를

of famine vulnerability / primarily in enhanced
모색하는 / 주로 강화된 경제 성장이나

economic growth, / or the revival of the rural
/ 지방 경제의 회복

economy, / or the diversification of economic
/ 혹은 경제 활동의 다각화에서 //

activities. //

● 역시 요약문에 언급한 '기근'이 등장하네요.

첫 문장은 비상사태가 진정되면, 주로 경제 성장의 관점에서 기근 문제를 해결하고자 하는 경향이 있다는 통념을 말하는 내용이에요.
이제 우리는 나머지 글을 읽으면서 이 기근과 관련해 구체적인 국가의 역할을 확인해서 요약문을 완성하면 돼요.

2) 두 번째 문장에서 또 단서가 등장해요.

The potential contribution of greater economic
더 큰 경제적 성공의 잠재적 기여는

success, / if it involves vulnerable groups, / cannot
/ 만약 그것이 취약 계층에 영향을 미친다면 /

be denied. //
부인할 수 없다 //

- **기근과 관련해서 취약 계층이 언급되고 있어요.**
  더 큰 경제 성장이 취약 계층에게도 도움을 줄 수 있다면 기근 위험을
  줄이는 데 경제적 성공의 효과도 부인할 수 없다고 했죠.

- **요약문의 첫 번째 절과 이 문장을 비교해 봅시다.**
  경제 성장이 국가의 기근 위험을 줄이는 데 어느 정도 (A)할 수 있다는
  것이 요약문의 첫 번째 절의 내용이에요.
  위에서 살펴본 문장에서는 경제적 성공의 효과도 부인할 수 없다고
  했어요. 바로 이것을 요약문에서는 **❶**'(   )'일 수 있다고
  했어요.

3) 그 다음 문장의 의미도 알아봅시다.

At the same time, / it is important to recognize that, /
그와 동시에   / 인식하는 것이 중요하다   /

no matter how fast they grow, / countries where a
아무리 빠르게 성장하더라도   / 인구의 상당수가

large part of the population derive their livelihood
그들의 생계를 불확실한 원천으로부터 마련하는 국가는

from uncertain sources / cannot hope to prevent
/ 기근 예방을 기대할 수 없다는 점을

famines / without specialized entitlement
/ 특화된 재정 지원 혜택의 보호 방법 없이는

mechanisms / involving direct public intervention. //
/ 직접적인 공적 개입을 포함하는   //

- **At the same time으로 문장이 시작했어요.**
  '그와 동시에'라는 뜻의 At the same time이라고 했으므로 앞 문장과
  같은 맥락으로 내용이 이어짐을 알 수 있어요.
  아무리 경제가 빨리 성장하더라도, 기근 예방을 위해서는 직접적인 공적
  개입을 포함하는 기근에 특화된 재정 지원 혜택이 있어야 한다고 했어요.

4) 마지막 문장을 확인하고 (B)에 들어갈 말을 찾아볼까요?

The real achievements of these countries / lie in
이들 국가의 진정한 성과는   /

having provided direct public support / to their
직접적인 공적 지원을 제공했었다는 것에 있다   /

populations in times of crisis. //
위기 상황에서 국민들에게   //

- **기근과 관련된 국가의 성과를 언급했어요.**
  기근의 위기 상황에서 국민들에게 직접적인 공적 지원을 제공했던 것이
  진정한 성과임을 보여준 국가들이 있다는 예시를 들어 부연 설명하고
  있어요.
  따라서 이것을 요약문에서 피해를 입은 사람들을 돕는 것에 대한 직접적인
  접근이 **❷**'(   )' 역할을 한다고 표현한 거죠.

3rd 전체 글의 내용을 정리하여 요약문이 적절한지 확인하세요.

1) 글의 내용은 이렇게 정리할 수 있어요.

| 통념 | 일단 비상사태가 진정되면, 주로 경제 성장의 관점에서 기근 문제를 해결하고자 하는 경향이 있고, 물론 경제적 성공의 효과도 부인할 수는 없음 |

↓

| 주제 | 아무리 경제가 빨리 성장하더라도, 기근 예방을 위해서는 직접적인 공적 개입을 포함하는 기근에 특화된 재정 지원 혜택이 있어야 함 |

↓

| 예시 | 기근의 위기 상황에서 예시로 든 국가들이 국민들에게 직접적인 공적 지원을 제공했던 것이 진정한 성과임 |

2) 이제 선택지를 확인해 봅시다.

① productive — complicated
  생산적인   복잡한
② fruitful — critical
  효과적인   중요한
③ dominant — comprehensive
  우세한   포괄적인
④ restrictive — appropriate
  제한적인   적절한
⑤ desirable — cost-effective
  바람직한   비용 효율이 높은

경제 성장의 관점에서 기근 문제를 해결하는 것은 **❶**'(   )'
일 수 있고, 국가가 직접적인 개입으로 기근 피해자에 특화된 지원을
하는 것은 예시로 든 국가들에서 알 수 있듯이, **❷**'(   )' 역할을
한다는 것이죠.
따라서 정답은 **❸**(   )이에요.

1st 요약문을 통해 글에서 무엇을 찾아야 하는지 확인하세요.
2nd 첫 문장을 통해 글의 전개 방향을 확인하고, 빈칸을 채우는 데 필요한 '무엇'을 글에서 찾으세요.
3rd 전체 글의 내용을 정리하여 요약문이 적절한지 확인하세요.

002 ★★★ .... 2024 대비 6월 모평 40 (고3)

다음 글의 내용을 한 문장으로 요약하고자 한다. 빈칸 (A), (B)에 들어갈 말로 가장 적절한 것은?

The evolutionary process works on the genetic variation that is available. It follows that natural selection is unlikely to lead to the evolution of perfect, 'maximally fit' individuals. Rather, organisms come to match their environments by being 'the fittest available' or 'the fittest yet': they are not 'the best imaginable'. Part of the lack of fit arises because the present properties of an organism have not all originated in an environment similar in every respect to the one in which it now lives. Over the course of its evolutionary history, an organism's remote ancestors may have evolved a set of characteristics — evolutionary 'baggage' — that subsequently constrain future evolution. For many millions of years, the evolution of vertebrates has been limited to what can be achieved by organisms with a vertebral column. Moreover, much of what we now see as precise matches between an organism and its environment may equally be seen as constraints: koala bears live successfully on *Eucalyptus* foliage, but, from another perspective, koala bears cannot live without *Eucalyptus* foliage.   * vertebrate: 척추동물

↓

The survival characteristics that an organism currently carries may act as a(n) _____(A)_____ to its adaptability when the organism finds itself coping with changes that arise in its _____(B)_____.

	(A)		(B)
①	improvement	—	diet
②	obstacle	—	surroundings
③	advantage	—	genes
④	regulator	—	mechanisms
⑤	guide	—	traits

1st 요약문을 통해 글에서 무엇을 찾아야 하는지 확인하세요.

The survival characteristics / that an organism
생존 특성은   / 한 생물체가
currently carries / may act as a(n) __(A)__ / to its
현재 가지고 있는   /   __(A)__ 이/가 될 수 있다   / 그것의
adaptability / when the organism finds itself /
적응성에   / 그 생물체가 스스로를 발견할 때   /
coping with changes / that arise in its __(B)__ . //
변화에 대처하는   / 그것의 __(B)__ 에서 발생하는   //

● 요약문의 구조를 파악하고 해석해 볼까요?
　주절(결과): 한 생물체의 현재 생존 특성은 적응성에 '무엇'이 될 수 있다.
　부사절(조건): 그 생물체가 그것의 '무엇'에서 발생하는 변화에 대처하는
　스스로를 발견할 때 단서

● 글에서 무엇을 찾아야 할까요?
　현재 생존 특성이 ❶(　　　　　)에 '무엇'이 되는지, 생물체의
　'무엇'에서 변화가 발생하는지 확인해야 해요. 발상

2nd 첫 문장을 통해 글의 전개 방향을 확인하고, 빈칸을 채우는 데 필요한 '무엇'을 글에서 찾으세요.

1) 첫 문장과 그 다음 문장을 확인해 봅시다.

The evolutionary process works / on the genetic
진화 과정은 작용한다   / 유전적 변이에
variation / that is available. // It follows / that
variation / 이용 가능한   // ~이 이어진다   /
natural selection is unlikely to lead / to the
자연 선택이 이어질 가능성은 작다는 것이   / 진화로
evolution / of perfect, 'maximally fit' individuals. //
            / 완벽하고 '최대로 적합한' 개체의   /

● 아직은 빈칸의 단서가 뚜렷하지 않아요.
　진화 과정이 이용 가능한 유전적 변이에 작용하기 때문에 자연 선택이
　최대로 적합한 개체의 진화로 이어질 가능성은 작다는 내용이에요. 자연
　선택은 완벽한 진화가 아닌 이용 가능한 진화로 이어진다고 이해할 수
　있겠어요.
　생존 특성과 적응의 관계, 그리고 생물체의 무엇이 변화하는지에 대한
　확실한 단서가 나올 때까지 다른 부분도 더 읽어봅시다.

2) 요약문의 부사절은 생물체가 변화에 대처하는 것을 다루고 있어요.

> Part of the lack of fit arises / because the present
> 적합성 결여의 일부는 발생한다 / 현재의 생물체가 가진 특성이
> properties of an organism / have not all originated /
> / 모두 유래한 것이 아니기 때문에 /
> in an environment / similar in every respect / to the
> 환경에서 / 모든 면에서 유사한 / 환경과
> one / in which it now lives. //
> / 그 생물체가 현재 살고 있는 //

● 이 문장의 내용을 파악해 봅시다.
　생물체가 가진 현재의 특성 모두가 현재 살고 있는 환경과 같은
　환경에서 나온 것이 아니기 때문에 ❷(　　　　　　)가 발생한다는
　내용이에요. 다시 말해, 어떤 생물이 과거에 적응했던 환경과 현재
　적응해야 하는 환경이 다르기 때문에 적합하지 않을 수도 있다는 것이죠.

● 빈칸 (B)에 필요한 단서를 찾아봅시다.
　요약문에 있었던 '한 생물체가 현재 가지고 있는 특성'이 여기서는
　'생물체가 가진 현재의 특성'으로 표현되었네요. 단서
　요약문에서 조건에 해당하는 부분인 '무엇'에서 발생하는 변화가 생물체의
　'환경'에서 발생하는 변화임을 알 수 있어요. 발상

3) 요약문의 주절은 현재 생존 특성과 적응성의 관계를 다루고 있어요.

> Over the course of its evolutionary history, / an
> 진화 역사의 과정에서 /
> organism's remote ancestors / may have evolved a
> 생물체의 먼 조상들은 / 일련의 특성들을
> set of characteristics / — evolutionary 'baggage' —
> 진화시켰을 수도 있다 / 진화적 '짐'
> / that subsequently constrain future evolution. //
> / 후속적으로 미래의 진화를 제약하는 //

● 문장의 내용을 파악해 볼까요?
　진화 과정에서 생물체의 조상들이 진화적 '짐'을 진화시켰을 수도 있다는
　내용이에요. 방금 우리는 생물체가 과거에 적응한 환경과 현재 적응해야
　하는 환경이 다르다는 내용을 확인했어요. 과거 환경에 적응하며 얻은
　특성이 현재 환경에 적용되기 어려울 수 있기 때문에 단서 미래의 진화를
　제약하는 '짐'이 되는 것이라고 유추할 수 있죠. 발상

● 빈칸 (A)에 필요한 단서가 나왔군요!
　조상들이 얻은 과거의 생존 특성이 후손들의 미래의 진화를 제약하는
　짐이 된다고 했으므로, 현재 생존 특성은 적응성에 방해가 된다고 말할 수
　있어요.

3rd 전체 글의 내용을 정리하여 요약문이 적절한지 확인하세요.

1) 글의 내용은 이렇게 정리할 수 있어요.

> 도입　진화 과정은 이용 가능한 유전적 변이에 작용함
>
> ↓
>
> 설명　적합성 결여의 일부는 생물체가 가진 현재의 특성이 현재 살고
> 있는 환경과 모든 면에서 유사한 환경에서 유래한 것이 아니기
> 때문에 발생함
>
> ↓
>
> 부연　생물체의 먼 조상들은 후속적으로 미래의 진화를 제약하는
> 일련의 특성들, 즉 진화적 '짐'을 진화시켰을 수도 있음
>
> ↓
>
> 예시　코알라는 유칼립투스 잎으로 성공적으로 생활하지만, 다른
> 관점에서는 코알라는 유칼립투스 잎 없이는 살 수 없음

2) 이제 각 선택지의 내용을 확인해 봅시다.

	(A)		(B)
①	improvement 개선	—	diet 먹거리
②	obstacle 장애물	—	surroundings 환경
③	advantage 이점	—	genes 유전자
④	regulator 조절 장치	—	mechanisms 매커니즘
⑤	guide 길잡이	—	traits 특성

● 글과 요약문의 내용을 정리하고, 선택지를 해석하니 정답이
보이죠?
　생물체의 조상들이 진화시켰던 진화적 '짐'이 요약문에서는
　❸'(　　　　)'이라 표현되었어요. 또한 현재에 비해 과거와 달라져서
　적합성 결여의 원인이 되었던 것은 요약문 빈칸 (B)에서 ❹'(　　　　)'
　라 표현되었죠. 정답은 바로 ❺(　　　　)이에요.

글의 앞부분을 통해
앞으로의 전개 방향을
예상하자!

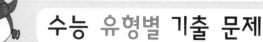
003~06 ▶ 제한시간 8분

003 ★★❀ ················· 2025 대비 수능 40 (고3)

다음 글의 내용을 한 문장으로 요약하고자 한다. 빈칸 (A), (B)에 들어갈 말로 가장 적절한 것은?

People often assume that synthetic food ingredients are more harmful than natural ones, but this is not always the case. Typically, synthetic ingredients can be made in a precisely controlled fashion and have well-defined compositions and properties, allowing careful evaluation of their potential toxicity. On the other hand, natural ingredients often vary appreciably in their composition and properties depending on their origin, the time of year they were harvested, the climate they experienced throughout their lifetime, the soil quality, and how they were isolated and stored. These variations can make testing their safety extremely difficult — one is never sure about the potential toxicity of minor components that may vary from time to time. In some cases, a natural food component has been consumed for hundreds or thousands of years without causing any obvious health problems and can, therefore, be assumed to be safe. However, one must still be very careful.

*synthetic: 합성의

⬇

The ___(A)___ of the production process for synthetic food ingredients and the variability of natural food ingredients may ___(B)___ people's commonly held assumption that the natural ingredients are more secure.

	(A)		(B)
①	controllability	—	challenge
②	predictability	—	support
③	manageability	—	intensify
④	affordability	—	reverse
⑤	accessibility	—	question

004 ★★★ ················· 2025 대비 9월 모평 40 (고3)

다음 글의 내용을 한 문장으로 요약하고자 한다. 빈칸 (A), (B)에 들어갈 말로 가장 적절한 것은?

Human speech differs from the cries of other species in many ways. One very important distinction is that all other animals use one call for one message as the general principle of communication. This means that the number of possible messages is very restricted. If a new message is to be included in the system, a new sound has to be introduced, too. After the first few tens of sounds it becomes difficult to invent new distinctive sounds, and also to remember them for the next time they are needed. Human speech builds on the principle of combining a restricted number of sounds into an unlimited number of messages. In a typical human language there are something like thirty or forty distinctive speech sounds. These sounds can be combined into chains to form a literally unlimited number of words. Even a small child, who can communicate by only one word at a time, uses a system for communication that is infinitely superior to any system utilized by any other animal.

⬇

In animal cries, each call ___(A)___ a different message, which limits the number of possible messages, whereas human language creates an unlimited number of messages using a ___(B)___ set of distinctive sounds.

	(A)		(B)
①	represents	—	finite
②	symbolizes	—	universal
③	distorts	—	fixed
④	expresses	—	novel
⑤	records	—	complex

005 ★★★ 2024 실시 10월 학평 40 (고3)

다음 글의 내용을 한 문장으로 요약하고자 한다. 빈칸 (A), (B)에 들어갈 말로 가장 적절한 것은?

Philosophical interest in poetry has been dominated by the question of whether poetry can aid philosophical thought and promote philosophical inquiry. This focus reflects a tradition of philosophers like Pope and Rumi presenting their philosophical work in verse. In addition, poets like William Wordsworth and T. S. Eliot have been celebrated as poet-philosophers, with their work valued as the product of philosophy through poetry. However, arguments against poetry having a role to play in philosophical inquiry have tended to focus on poetry's (negative) relationship to truth (or, as John Koethe puts it, poetry's indifference to truth). Although we may accept works of poetry as having philosophical themes, this does not amount to doing philosophy through poetry. One such argument hinges on the non-paraphrasability of poetry and form-content unity. The thought goes, if poetry is to play a role in philosophy, then it needs to be paraphrasable (that is, its content must be separable from its form). The assumption is that paraphrase is a mark of understanding and indicates that some proposition has a fixed meaning and that only a proposition with a fixed meaning can be evaluated in terms of truth or falsity. Poetry resists paraphrase: to change the words is to change the poem.

*hinge on: ~의 여하에 달려 있다 **proposition: 명제

↓

Some believe in the ability of poetry to ___(A)___ philosophy, but for others, its resistance to paraphrasing ___(B)___ its philosophical role.

	(A)		(B)
①	misinterpret	—	limits
②	deliver	—	expands
③	convey	—	restricts
④	reexamine	—	reinforces
⑤	seek	—	broadens

006 ★★★❀ 2024 실시 7월 학평 40 (고3)

다음 글의 내용을 한 문장으로 요약하고자 한다. 빈칸 (A), (B)에 들어갈 말로 가장 적절한 것은? [3점]

Communication is decisively influenced by how the partners define their relationship with each other at every moment of the communication process. If the communication is *symmetrical*, this means that both communication partners strive for equality and interact accordingly. They behave as mirror images of each other, so to speak. Strength is mirrored with strength, weakness is mirrored with weakness, or hardness is mirrored with hardness, etc. *Complementary communication* shows a matching difference in behaviour. It is not a matter of up and down, strong and weak, or good and bad, but of matching and expected difference. Such complementary relationships occur between teachers and students, mother and child, or managers and employees, etc. What the expectations are in such relationships depends, among other things, on the cultural background. If the expectations of complementarity are not met, communication breakdowns occur. For example, if an older person in Japan is not treated with a certain respect by a younger person, this circumstance can significantly impair communication or even make it impossible.

↓

The way the communication partners ___(A)___ their relationship determines the types of communication; symmetrical communication revolves around the pursuit of equality and the ___(B)___ interaction between them, whereas complementary communication involves aligning with matching and expected differences based on cultural background.

	(A)		(B)
①	perceive	—	corresponding
②	describe	—	postponed
③	manipulate	—	transactional
④	regulate	—	intimate
⑤	develop	—	lasting

007 ★★★ 2024 실시 5월 학평 40 (고3)

다음 글의 내용을 한 문장으로 요약하고자 한다.
빈칸 (A), (B)에 들어갈 말로 가장 적절한 것은?

In one study, researchers gave more than five hundred visitors to an art museum a special glove that reported their movement patterns along with physiological data such as their heart rates. The data showed that when people were not distracted by chatting with companions, they actually had a stronger emotional response to the art. Of course, there's nothing wrong with chatting and letting the art slide past, but think of the inspiration those museum visitors missed out on. Then apply that to life in general. When we surround ourselves with other people, we're not just missing out on the finer details of an art exhibition. We're missing out on the chance to reflect and understand ourselves better. In fact, studies show that if we never allow ourselves to be alone, it's just plain harder for us to learn. Other research found that young people who cannot stand being alone were less likely to develop creative skills like playing an instrument or writing because the most effective practice of these abilities is often done while alone.

*physiological: 생리적인

↓

The study above shows ____(A)____ conversation with companions while exploring an art museum intensifies emotional response to art, suggesting that absence of alone time may ____(B)____ personal growth and learning.

	(A)		(B)
①	avoiding	—	inhibit
②	recalling	—	restrain
③	preventing	—	enhance
④	facilitating	—	nurture
⑤	dominating	—	minimize

008 ★★☆ 2024 실시 3월 학평 40 (고3)

다음 글의 내용을 한 문장으로 요약하고자 한다. 빈칸 (A), (B)에 들어갈 말로 가장 적절한 것은?

"Brain plasticity" is a term we use in neuroscience. Whether intentionally or not, "plasticity" suggests that the key idea is to mold something once and keep it that way forever: to shape the plastic toy and never change it again. But that's not what the brain does. It carries on remolding itself throughout your life. Think of a developing city, and note the way it grows, improves, and responds to the world around it. Observe where the city builds its truck stops, how it crafts its immigration policies, and how it modifies its education and legal systems. A city is always changing. A city is not designed by urban planners and then immobilized like a plastic object. It continually develops. Just like cities, brains never reach an end point. We spend our lives blossoming toward something, even as the target moves. Consider the feeling of encountering a diary that you wrote many years ago. It represents the thinking, opinions, and viewpoint of someone who was a bit different from who you are now, and that previous person can sometimes border on the unrecognizable. Despite having the same name and the same early history, in the years between inscription and interpretation the narrator has altered. The word "plastic" can be stretched to fit this notion of ongoing change.

*mold: 성형(成形)하다   **inscription: 새겨진 글, 명문(銘文)

↓

While some understand "brain plasticity" to mean ____(A)____ upon molding, the brain is actually capable of ____(B)____.

	(A)		(B)
①	permanence	—	transformation
②	flexibility	—	sympathizing
③	adaptability	—	restoration
④	firmness	—	sympathizing
⑤	mobility	—	transformation

다음 글의 내용을 한 문장으로 요약하고자 한다. 빈칸 (A), (B)에 들어갈 말로 가장 적절한 것은?

The idea that *planting* trees could have a social or political significance appears to have been invented by the English, though it has since spread widely. According to Keith Thomas's history *Man and the Natural World*, seventeenth- and eighteenth-century aristocrats began planting hardwood trees, usually in lines, to declare the extent of their property and the permanence of their claim to it. "What can be more pleasant," the editor of a magazine for gentlemen asked his readers, "than to have the bounds and limits of your own property preserved and continued from age to age by the testimony of such living and growing witnesses?" Planting trees had the additional advantage of being regarded as a patriotic act, for the Crown had declared a severe shortage of the hardwood on which the Royal Navy depended.

*aristocrat: 귀족 **patriotic: 애국적인

⬇

For English aristocrats, planting trees served as statements to mark the ____(A)____ ownership of their land, and it was also considered to be a(n) ____(B)____ of their loyalty to the nation.

	(A)		(B)
①	unstable	—	confirmation
②	unstable	—	exaggeration
③	lasting	—	exhibition
④	lasting	—	manipulation
⑤	official	—	justification

다음 글의 내용을 한 문장으로 요약하고자 한다. 빈칸 (A), (B)에 들어갈 말로 가장 적절한 것은?

The computer has, to a considerable extent, solved the problem of acquiring, preserving, and retrieving information. Data can be stored in effectively unlimited quantities and in manageable form. The computer makes available a range of data unattainable in the age of books. It packages it effectively; style is no longer needed to make it accessible, nor is memorization. In dealing with a single decision separated from its context, the computer supplies tools unimaginable even a decade ago. But it also diminishes perspective. Because information is so accessible and communication instantaneous, there is a diminution of focus on its significance, or even on the definition of what is significant. This dynamic may encourage policymakers to wait for an issue to arise rather than anticipate it, and to regard moments of decision as a series of isolated events rather than part of a historical continuum. When this happens, manipulation of information replaces reflection as the principal policy tool.

*retrieve: (정보를) 추출하다 **diminution: 감소

⬇

Although the computer is clearly ____(A)____ at handling information in a decontextualized way, it interferes with our making ____(B)____ judgments related to the broader context, as can be seen in policymaking processes.

	(A)		(B)
①	competent	—	comprehensive
②	dominant	—	biased
③	imperfect	—	informed
④	impressive	—	legal
⑤	inefficient	—	timely

011 ✿✿❀.................. 2023 실시 3월 학평 40 (고3)

다음 글의 내용을 한 문장으로 요약하고자 한다. 빈칸 (A), (B)에 들어갈 말로 가장 적절한 것은?

The rise of large, industrial cities has had social consequences that are often known as urbanism. The city dissolves the informal controls of the village or small town. Most urban residents are unknown to one another, and most social interactions in cities occur between people who know each other only in specific roles, such as parking attendant, store clerk, or customer. Individuals became more free to live as they wished, and in ways that break away from social norms. In response, and because the high density of city living requires the pliant coordination of many thousands of people, urban societies have developed a wide range of methods to control urban behavior. These include regulations that control private land use, building construction and maintenance (to minimize fire risk), and the production of pollution and noise.

*pliant: 유순한

↓

The social conditions in large, industrial cities made urban societies ____(A)____ the informal controls of the village or small town, introducing ____(B)____ measures to effectively induce coordinated urban behaviors.

	(A)		(B)
①	limit	—	permissive
②	maintain	—	restrictive
③	evaluate	—	indirect
④	remove	—	restrictive
⑤	reinforce	—	permissive

012 ✿✿❀.................. 2022 실시 10월 학평 40 (고3)

다음 글의 내용을 한 문장으로 요약하고자 한다. 빈칸 (A), (B)에 들어갈 말로 가장 적절한 것은?

Put a hamster on a wheel, and it will start running. Give the hamster a treat, and it will run even longer. Stop dispensing the treats, and the hamster will stop running — completely. The original motivation has thereby become extinguished. The school system has been taking advantage of this psychological feature by replacing young children's natural curiosity and joy of discovery with praise, grades, and other short-term performance boosters. As the story goes, there once was an old man who enjoyed watching sunsets from his porch. One day, a bunch of kids came over and started playing loudly in front of his house. The man asked the kids to move over, but they ignored him. Next day, the children came again. The man called them over, gave each one a nickel, and asked them to make as much noise as they possibly could — to which they happily obliged. The man kept regularly handing out coins, until one day he told the kids that he was no longer paying them. "Then we aren't going to make noise for you," the children announced — and left.

↓

It is possible to ____(A)____ an individual's willingness to do something by consistently providing ____(B)____ for the action for some time and then withholding them.

	(A)		(B)
①	remove	—	rewards
②	remove	—	punishments
③	boost	—	explanations
④	evaluate	—	punishments
⑤	boost	—	rewards

다음 글의 내용을 한 문장으로 요약하고자 한다. 빈칸 (A), (B)에 들어갈 말로 가장 적절한 것은?

As a social species, should we not all be synchronized and therefore awake at the same time to promote maximal human interactions? Perhaps not. Humans likely evolved to co-sleep as families or even whole tribes, not alone or as couples. Appreciating this evolutionary context, the benefits of such genetically programmed variation in sleep/wake timing preferences can be understood. The night people in the group would not be going to sleep until one or two a.m., and not waking until nine or ten a.m. The morning people, on the other hand, would have retired for the night at nine p.m. and woken at five a.m. Consequently, the group as a whole is only collectively vulnerable (i.e., every person asleep) for just four rather than eight hours, despite everyone still getting the chance for eight hours of sleep. That's potentially a 50 percent increase in survival fitness. Mother Nature would never pass on a biological trait — here, the useful variability in when individuals within a collective tribe go to sleep and wake up — that could enhance the survival safety and thus fitness of a species by this amount. And so she hasn't.

*synchronize: 동시성을 갖게 하다 **vulnerable: 취약한

↓

Individuals have ____(A)____ in the time of the day when they prefer to sleep and wake up, which could promote their ____(B)____ as a group.

	(A)		(B)
①	differences	—	originality
②	differences	—	survivability
③	similarities	—	cooperation
④	similarities	—	adaptation
⑤	regularities	—	mobility

다음 글의 내용을 한 문장으로 요약하고자 한다. 빈칸 (A), (B)에 들어갈 말로 가장 적절한 것은? [3점]

Experiments suggest that animals, just like humans, tend to prefer exaggerated, supernormal stimuli, and that a preference can rapidly propel itself to extreme levels (*peak shift effect*). In one experiment, through food rewards rats were conditioned to prefer squares to other geometric forms. In the next step, a non-square rectangle was introduced and associated with an even larger reward than the square. As expected, the rats learned to reliably prefer the rectangle. Less predictable was the third part of the experiment. The rats were offered the opportunity to choose between the rectangle they already knew and associated with large rewards and another rectangle, the proportions of which were even more different from those of a square. Interestingly, rats picked this novel variant, without undergoing any reward-based conditioning in favor of it. A possible explanation is thus that they chose the larger difference from the original square (i.e., the exaggeration of *non-squareness*).

↓

In an experiment, after first establishing an ____(A)____ to squares, and then to non-square rectangles, rats were seen to pursue ____(B)____ rectangularity even without any additional reward.

	(A)		(B)
①	inclination	—	severe
②	opposition	—	familiar
③	inclination	—	vague
④	opposition	—	unexpected
⑤	attachment	—	subtle

015 ✹✹✣ .... 2021 대비 9월 모평 40 (고3)

다음 글의 내용을 한 문장으로 요약하고자 한다. 빈칸 (A), (B)에 들어갈 말로 가장 적절한 것은?

Research from the Harwood Institute for Public Innovation in the USA shows that people feel that 'materialism' somehow comes between them and the satisfaction of their social needs. A report entitled *Yearning for Balance*, based on a nationwide survey of Americans, concluded that they were 'deeply ambivalent about wealth and material gain'. A large majority of people wanted society to 'move away from greed and excess toward a way of life more centred on values, community, and family'. But they also felt that these priorities were not shared by most of their fellow Americans, who, they believed, had become 'increasingly atomized, selfish, and irresponsible'. As a result they often felt isolated. However, the report says, that when brought together in focus groups to discuss these issues, people were 'surprised and excited to find that others share[d] their views'. Rather than uniting us with others in a common cause, the unease we feel about the loss of social values and the way we are drawn into the pursuit of material gain is often experienced as if it were a purely private ambivalence which cuts us off from others.

*ambivalent: 양면 가치의

⬇

Many Americans, believing that materialism keeps them from _____(A)_____ social values, feel detached from most others, but this is actually a fairly _____(B)_____ concern.

	(A)		(B)
①	pursuing	—	unnecessary
②	pursuing	—	common
③	holding	—	personal
④	denying	—	ethical
⑤	denying	—	primary

016 ✹✹✣ .... 2023 대비 9월 모평 40 (고3)

다음 글의 내용을 한 문장으로 요약하고자 한다. 빈칸 (A), (B)에 들어갈 말로 가장 적절한 것은?

A striving to demonstrate individual personality through designs should not be surprising. Most designers are educated to work as individuals, and design literature contains countless references to 'the designer'. Personal flair is without doubt an absolute necessity in some product categories, particularly relatively small objects, with a low degree of technological complexity, such as furniture, lighting, small appliances, and housewares. In larger-scale projects, however, even where a strong personality exercises powerful influence, the fact that substantial numbers of designers are employed in implementing a concept can easily be overlooked. The emphasis on individuality is therefore problematic — rather than actually designing, many successful designer 'personalities' function more as creative managers. A distinction needs to be made between designers working truly alone and those working in a group. In the latter case, management organization and processes can be equally as relevant as designers' creativity.

*strive: 애쓰다 **flair: 재능

⬇

Depending on the _____(A)_____ of a project, the capacity of designers to _____(B)_____ team-based working environments can be just as important as their personal qualities.

	(A)		(B)
①	size	—	coordinate
②	cost	—	systematize
③	size	—	identify
④	cost	—	innovate
⑤	goal	—	investigate

O17 ★★★ .... 2024 대비 9월 모평 40 (고3)

다음 글의 내용을 한 문장으로 요약하고자 한다. 빈칸 (A), (B)에 들어갈 말로 가장 적절한 것은?

Research for historical fiction may focus on under-documented ordinary people, events, or sites. Fiction helps portray everyday situations, feelings, and atmosphere that recreate the historical context. Historical fiction adds "flesh to the bare bones that historians are able to uncover and by doing so provides an account that while not necessarily true provides a clearer indication of past events, circumstances and cultures." Fiction adds color, sound, drama to the past, as much as it invents parts of the past. And Robert Rosenstone argues that invention is not the weakness of films, it is their strength. Fiction can allow users to see parts of the past that have never — for lack of archives — been represented. In fact, Gilden Seavey explains that if producers of historical fiction had strongly held the strict academic standards, many historical subjects would remain unexplored for lack of appropriate evidence. Historical fiction should, therefore, not be seen as the opposite of professional history, but rather as a challenging representation of the past from which both public historians and popular audiences may learn.

↓

While historical fiction reconstructs the past using ____(A)____ evidence, it provides an inviting description, which may ____(B)____ people's understanding of historical events.

	(A)		(B)
①	insignificant	—	delay
②	insufficient	—	enrich
③	concrete	—	enhance
④	outdated	—	improve
⑤	limited	—	disturb

O18 ★★※ .... 2021 실시 10월 학평 40 (고3)

다음 글의 내용을 한 문장으로 요약하고자 한다. 빈칸 (A), (B)에 들어갈 말로 가장 적절한 것은?

Perhaps not surprisingly, given how long magicians have been developing their craft, a lot of creativity in magic is of the tweaking variety — some of the most skilled and inventive magicians gained fame by refining the execution of tricks that have been known for decades, or sometimes centuries. Nevil Maskelyne, one of magic's old masters, claimed that "the difficulty of producing a new magical effect is about equivalent to that of inventing a new proposition in Euclid." Whether it's because there's little that's completely new, or for some other reason, magicians seem to worry less about imitation. They do, however, worry a lot about *traitors* — those magicians who expose the secrets behind a trick to the public. Once a trick is exposed in this way, its value as "magic" is destroyed, and this harms everyone in the industry. For this reason, magicians' norms are focused mostly on punishing magicians who expose tricks to the public — even if the trick is the exposer's own invention.

*tweak: 살짝 변화를 주다 **traitor: 배신자

↓

Magicians, having long refined existing tricks, are not much worried about ____(A)____ tricks, but they are very strict about ____(B)____ the methods of tricks as it damages their industry.

	(A)		(B)
①	copying	—	blending
②	copying	—	disclosing
③	criticizing	—	distorting
④	modifying	—	evaluating
⑤	modifying	—	underestimating

019 ✱✱✱ .... 2024 대비 수능 40 (고3)

다음 글의 내용을 한 문장으로 요약하고자 한다. 빈칸 (A), (B)에 들어갈 말로 가장 적절한 것은?

Even those with average talent can produce notable work in the various sciences, so long as they do not try to embrace all of them at once. Instead, they should concentrate attention on one subject after another (that is, in different periods of time), although later work will weaken earlier attainments in the other spheres. This amounts to saying that the brain adapts to universal science in *time* but not in *space*. In fact, even those with great abilities proceed in this way. Thus, when we are astonished by someone with publications in different scientific fields, realize that each topic was explored during a specific period of time. Knowledge gained earlier certainly will not have disappeared from the mind of the author, but it will have become simplified by condensing into formulas or greatly abbreviated symbols. Thus, sufficient space remains for the perception and learning of new images on the cerebral blackboard.

*condense: 응축하다 **cerebral: 대뇌의

↓

Exploring one scientific subject after another _____(A)_____ remarkable work across the sciences, as the previously gained knowledge is retained in simplified forms within the brain, which _____(B)_____ room for new learning.

	(A)		(B)
①	enables	—	leaves
②	challenges	—	spares
③	delays	—	creates
④	requires	—	removes
⑤	invites	—	diminishes

020 ✱✱✱✱ .... 2023 실시 10월 학평 40 (고3)

다음 글의 내용을 한 문장으로 요약하고자 한다. 빈칸 (A), (B)에 들어갈 말로 가장 적절한 것은?

Music has no past; it exists only at the moment when it happens, and no two performances are identical. This is music's greatest asset because it brings out the essential 'now' without implications of a past and a potential future. Thus, Stravinsky pointed out that only through music are we able to 'realize the present.' Musical 'meaning' cannot be separated from the act of presentation. However, the necessity of *present*-ing music — making it present here and now, without which it will not be music at all — does not sit easily with a concept of education that rests mainly upon received factual knowledge and which, by tradition, uses the past to make sense of the present. If we want music to have a role in general education, it would seem logical to acknowledge this difference and give prominence to activities that will involve all pupils working directly with music. Yet, in spite of numerous attempts to develop a more *musical* music curriculum for the majority of school pupils, the emphasis is still on pupils absorbing factual information about music.

↓

Music's quality of being in the present is _____(A)_____ in formal music education, where delivering factual knowledge is _____(B)_____.

	(A)		(B)
①	overlooked	—	prioritized
②	overlooked	—	restricted
③	dismissed	—	disregarded
④	achieved	—	treasured
⑤	achieved	—	challenged

다음 글의 내용을 한 문장으로 요약하고자 한다. 빈칸 (A), (B)에 들어갈 말로 가장 적절한 것은?

Some environments are more likely to lead to fossilization and subsequent discovery than others. Thus, we cannot assume that more fossil evidence from a particular period or place means that more individuals were present at that time, or in that place. It may just be that the circumstances at one period of time, or at one location, were more favourable for fossilization than they were at other times, or in other places. Likewise, the absence of hominin fossil evidence at a particular time or place does not have the same implication as its presence. As the saying goes, 'absence of evidence is not evidence of absence'. Similar logic suggests that taxa are likely to have arisen before they first appear in the fossil record, and they are likely to have survived beyond the time of their most recent appearance in the fossil record. Thus, the first appearance datum, and the last appearance datum of taxa in the hominin fossil record are likely to be conservative statements about the times of origin and extinction of a taxon.

*subsequent: 다음의 **hominin fossil: 인류 화석
***taxa: taxon(분류군)의 복수형

⬇

Since fossilization and fossil discovery are affected by ____(A)____ conditions, the fossil evidence of a taxon cannot definitely ____(B)____ its population size or the times of its appearance and extinction.

	(A)		(B)
①	experimental	—	confirm
②	experimental	—	reveal
③	environmental	—	clarify
④	environmental	—	conceal
⑤	accidental	—	mask

1등급 대비 문제

022~25 ▶ 제한시간 11분

022 ✪ 2등급 대비 .... 2023 대비 수능 40 (고3)

다음 글의 내용을 한 문장으로 요약하고자 한다. 빈칸 (A), (B)에 들어갈 말로 가장 적절한 것은?

"Craftsmanship" may suggest a way of life that declined with the arrival of industrial society — but this is misleading. Craftsmanship names an enduring, basic human impulse, the desire to do a job well for its own sake. Craftsmanship cuts a far wider swath than skilled manual labor; it serves the computer programmer, the doctor, and the artist; parenting improves when it is practiced as a skilled craft, as does citizenship. In all these domains, craftsmanship focuses on objective standards, on the thing in itself. Social and economic conditions, however, often stand in the way of the craftsman's discipline and commitment: schools may fail to provide the tools to do good work, and workplaces may not truly value the aspiration for quality. And though craftsmanship can reward an individual with a sense of pride in work, this reward is not simple. The craftsman often faces conflicting objective standards of excellence; the desire to do something well for its own sake can be weakened by competitive pressure, by frustration, or by obsession.

*swath: 구획

⬇

Craftsmanship, a human desire that has ____(A)____ over time in diverse contexts, often encounters factors that ____(B)____ its full development.

	(A)		(B)
①	persisted	—	limit
②	persisted	—	cultivate
③	evolved	—	accelerate
④	diminished	—	shape
⑤	diminished	—	restrict

다음 글의 내용을 한 문장으로 요약하고자 한다. 빈칸 (A), (B)에 들어갈 말로 가장 적절한 것은?

Mobilities in transit offer a broad field to be explored by different disciplines in all faculties, in addition to the humanities. In spite of increasing acceleration, for example in travelling through geographical or virtual space, our body becomes more and more a passive non-moving container, which is transported by artefacts or loaded up with inner feelings of being mobile in the so-called information society. Technical mobilities turn human beings into some kind of terminal creatures, who spend most of their time at rest and who need to participate in sports in order to balance their daily disproportion of motion and rest. Have we come closer to Aristotle's image of God as the immobile mover, when elites exercise their power to move money, things and people, while they themselves do not need to move at all? Others, at the bottom of this power, are victims of mobility-structured social exclusion. They cannot decide how and where to move, but are just moved around or locked out or even locked in without either the right to move or the right to stay.

↓

In a technology and information society, human beings, whose bodily movement is less ___(A)___, appear to have gained increased mobility and power, and such a mobility-related human condition raises the issue of social ___(B)___.

    (A)   (B)
① necessary — inequality
② necessary — growth
③ limited — consciousness
④ desirable — service
⑤ desirable — divide

다음 글의 내용을 한 문장으로 요약하고자 한다. 빈칸 (A), (B)에 들어갈 말로 가장 적절한 것은?

Philip Kitcher and Wesley Salmon have suggested that there are two possible alternatives among philosophical theories of explanation. One is the view that scientific explanation consists in the *unification* of broad bodies of phenomena under a minimal number of generalizations. According to this view, the (or perhaps, a) goal of science is to construct an economical framework of laws or generalizations that are capable of subsuming all observable phenomena. Scientific explanations organize and systematize our knowledge of the empirical world; the more economical the systematization, the deeper our understanding of what is explained. The other view is the *causal/mechanical* approach. According to it, a scientific explanation of a phenomenon consists of uncovering the mechanisms that produced the phenomenon of interest. This view sees the explanation of individual events as primary, with the explanation of generalizations flowing from them. That is, the explanation of scientific generalizations comes from the causal mechanisms that produce the regularities.

*subsume: 포섭(포함)하다 **empirical: 경험적인

↓

Scientific explanations can be made either by seeking the ___(A)___ number of principles covering all observations or by finding general ___(B)___ drawn from individual phenomena.

    (A)   (B)
① least — patterns
② fixed — features
③ limited — functions
④ fixed — rules
⑤ least — assumptions

다음 글의 내용을 한 문장으로 요약하고자 한다. 빈칸 (A), (B)에 들어갈 말로 가장 적절한 것은?

From a cross-cultural perspective the equation between public leadership and dominance is questionable. What does one mean by 'dominance'? Does it indicate coercion? Or control over 'the most valued'? 'Political' systems may be about both, either, or conceivably neither. The idea of 'control' would be a bothersome one for many peoples, as for instance among many native peoples of Amazonia where all members of a community are fond of their personal autonomy and notably allergic to any obvious expression of control or coercion. The conception of political power as a *coercive* force, while it may be a Western fixation, is not a universal. It is very unusual for an Amazonian leader to give an order. If many peoples do not view political power as a coercive force, *nor as the most valued domain*, then the leap from 'the political' to 'domination' (as coercion), *and from there* to 'domination of women', is a shaky one. As Marilyn Strathern has remarked, the notions of 'the political' and 'political personhood' are cultural obsessions of our own, a bias long reflected in anthropological constructs.

*coercion: 강제 **autonomy: 자율
***anthropological: 인류학의

↓

It is ____(A)____ to understand political power in other cultures through our own notion of it because ideas of political power are not ____(B)____ across cultures.

	(A)		(B)
①	rational	—	flexible
②	appropriate	—	commonplace
③	misguided	—	uniform
④	unreasonable	—	varied
⑤	effective	—	objective

먼저 요약문을 읽고 빈칸에 필요한 것이 무엇인지 확인하자!

O 어휘 Review

※ 다음 영어는 우리말 뜻을, 우리말은 영어 단어를 〈보기〉에서 찾아 쓰시오.

〈보기〉

fellow	조정	passive	기르다
지나침, 과잉	testimony	이해하다, 감상하다	설명
disclose	prioritize	tremble	기호, 성향

01 excess _____

02 appreciate _____

03 account _____

04 coordination _____

05 inclination _____

06 우선시하다 _____

07 증언 _____

08 동료 _____

09 공개하다, 드러내다 _____

10 수동적인, 소극적인 _____

※ 다음 우리말에 알맞은 영어 표현을 찾아 연결하시오.

11 대조적으로 •   • settle down

12 진정되다 •   • in contrast

13 기껏해야 •   • at best

14 의존하다 •   • rest (up)on

15 ~와 다르다 •   • differ from

※ 다음 우리말 표현에 맞는 단어를 고르시오.

16 마술사들의 규범 ➡ magicians' (norms / terms)

17 큰 보상과 연관된 ➡ (associated / allocated) with large rewards

18 생물체가 가진 현재의 특성 ➡ the present (properties / proposal) of an organism

19 의심할 여지 없이 ➡ without (doubt / debt)

20 더 자신 없는 목소리를 잠재우다 ➡ silence the more (secure / insecure) voices

※ 다음 문장의 빈칸에 알맞은 단어를 〈보기〉에서 찾아 쓰시오.

〈보기〉

instantaneous	portray	isolated	broad
substantial	acknowledge	key	dissolves
restricted	distributed	industries	verbal

21 그 결과 그들은 종종 소외된 기분이 들었다.
➡ As a result they often felt _____.

22 도시는 마을이나 작은 소도시의 비공식적인 통제를 해체한다.
➡ The city _____ the informal controls of the village or small town.

23 의사소통이 순간적이기 때문에 그것의 중요성에 관한 관심 집중이 감소한다.
➡ Because communication is so _____, there is a diminution of focus on its significance.

24 소설은 일상적인 상황, 감정, 분위기를 묘사하는 데 도움이 된다.
➡ Fiction helps _____ everyday situations, feelings, and atmosphere.

25 일부 정부, 산업, 그리고 조직이 그 용어를 사용하기를 시작했다.
➡ Some governments, _____, and organizations started to use the term.

26 상당한 수의 디자이너가 계획을 실행하는 데 참여한다.
➡ _____ numbers of designers are employed in implementing a concept.

27 통행의 이동성은 탐구될 광범위한 분야를 제공한다.
➡ Mobilities in transit offer a(n) _____ field to be explored.

28 가능한 메시지의 수가 매우 제한적이다.
➡ The number of possible messages is very _____.

29 이러한 차이를 인정하는 것이 타당해 보일 것이다.
➡ It would seem logical to _____ this difference.

P 장문의 이해

내용이 길고 많네.
내가 여기서 알아야 하는
정보는 무엇이지?

★ **유형 설명:** 2가지 유형의 문제가 출제된다.

대의 파악 문제

● 윗글의 제목으로 가장 적절한 것은?

① Plant Growth Is Up to Soil Content
② Plants Do Behave and Have Intelligence

☞ 세부 정보 문제 풀이 후, 그 풀이 과정을 통해 확인한 글의 주제를 함축적이고 비유적으로 나타내는 제목을 고른다.

세부 정보 문제

● 밑줄 친 (a)~(e) 중에서 문맥상 낱말의 쓰임이 적절하지 <u>않은</u> 것은?

① (a)　② (b)　③ (c)　④ (d)　⑤ (e)

☞ 밑줄 친 낱말의 적절성을 판단하는 문제를 풀기 위해서는 그것이 포함된 문장과 그 앞뒤 내용을 살펴야 한다.

🎭 유형 풀이 비법

1 문제를 먼저 읽어라!

• 제시된 문제를 먼저 읽고, 어떤 유형의 문제인지 파악한다.

2 세부 정보를 묻는 문제를 풀어라!

• 처음부터 꼼꼼히 글을 읽으면서 흐름에 맞게 문장 간의 관계를 확인하고, 세부 정보를 묻는 문제를 푼다.

3 대의 파악 문제를 풀어라!

• 세부 정보를 파악하는 문제의 풀이 과정에서 확인한 글의 주제를 정리하고, 이를 반영하는 제목을 찾는다.

> (Tip) 적절하지 않은 낱말을 글의 흐름에 맞는 낱말로 직접 바꿔 보면서 정답을 다시 확인한다.

★ 최신 수능 경향 분석

대비 연도	월	문항 번호	지문 주제	난이도
2025	11	41~42번	인간의 손: 진화 경로의 결정적 도약	★★☆
	9	41~42번	일상 언어를 새롭게 만들어 주는 시	★★★
	6	41~42번	의사결정에서 윤리적 사고의 중요성	★★★
2024	11	41~42번	과학자가 언론과 소통하는 것의 장단점	★★★
	9	41~42번	학교에서 배운 것을 기억하지 못하는 이유	★★★
	6	41~42번	고정된 파이가 협상에 미치는 영향	★★★
2023	11	41~42번	전문가를 능가하는 간단한 공식	★★☆
	9	41~42번	상상력이 따라잡기 어려운 기후 변화	★★☆
	6	41~42번	주변 사람들의 반응으로 판단하는 것	★★☆

★ 2025 수능 출제 분석

글의 제목을 찾는 문제는 거의 모든 선택지에 '인간'과 '손'이 포함되어 있어서 헷갈릴 수 있었다. 문맥에 맞는 낱말을 찾는 문제는 돌로 창 촉이나 화살촉을 만들기 위해서는 손을 사용한 강한 쥐기 등이 요구된다는 맥락을 잘 파악해야 하는 문제였다.

★ 2026 수능 예측

42번 문제를 풀기 위해 각 선택지가 포함된 문장과 그 앞뒤 문장을 확인하고, 그 과정에서 알게 된 전체 글의 주제를 적절한 제목으로 바꾸어 41번 문제의 정답을 찾는 것이 시간을 절약하고 정답을 찾는 보다 효율적인 방법이다.

🔑 어휘 및 표현 Preview

□ **understand** 이해하다
□ **identification** 검증
□ **evaluation** 평가
□ **evidence** 증거
□ **guide** 안내하다
□ **decision-making** 의사결정
□ **ethical** 윤리적인
□ **perspective** 관점
□ **respond** 대응하다

□ **theory** 이론
□ **inspiration** 영감
□ **follow** 따르다
□ **prescribed** 규정된
□ **code** 규범
□ **encourage** 장려하다
□ **recognition** 인식
□ **define** 정의하다
□ **in accordance with** ~에 따라서

□ **individual** 개인
□ **religious** 종교적인
□ **formal** 공식적인
□ **civic** 시민의
□ **belief** 신념
□ **context** 상황
□ **inspiration** 영감
□ **circumstance** 사정, 상황
□ **factor** 요인
□ **coincide** 일치하다

□ **alongside** ~옆에, 나란히
□ **accept** 수용하다
□ **reasoning** 추론
□ **explore** 탐구하다
□ **priority** 우선, 우선권
□ **depict** 묘사하다
□ **literate** 글을 읽고 쓸 줄 아는
□ **manipulate** 조작하다
□ **considerably** 상당히
□ **vary** 다르다

P 장문의 이해

1st 어떤 문제들이 출제되었는지 확인하고, 각 유형의 풀이 방법을 떠올려 보세요.
2nd 글의 세부 사항을 묻는 문제를 먼저 풀면서 글의 내용을 파악하세요.
3rd 세부 사항을 묻는 문제를 풀면서 얻은 글의 내용을 바탕으로 글의 제목을 묻는 문제의 정답을 찾으세요.

[P01~P02] 다음 글을 읽고, 물음에 답하시오.

Many negotiators assume that all negotiations involve a fixed pie. Negotiators often approach integrative negotiation opportunities as zero-sum situations or win-lose exchanges. Those who believe in the mythical fixed pie assume that parties' interests stand in opposition, with no possibility for integrative settlements and mutually beneficial trade-offs, so they (a) suppress efforts to search for them. In a hiring negotiation, a job applicant who assumes that salary is the only issue may insist on $75,000 when the employer is offering $70,000. Only when the two parties discuss the possibilities further do they discover that moving expenses and starting date can also be negotiated, which may (b) block resolution of the salary issue.

The tendency to see negotiation in fixed-pie terms (c) varies depending on how people view the nature of a given conflict situation. This was shown in a clever experiment by Harinck, de Dreu, and Van Vianen involving a simulated negotiation between prosecutors and defense lawyers over jail sentences. Some participants were told to view their goals in terms of personal gain (e.g., arranging a particular jail sentence will help your career), others were told to view their goals in terms of effectiveness (a particular sentence is most likely to prevent recidivism), and still others were told to focus on values (a particular jail sentence is fair and just). Negotiators focusing on personal gain were most likely to come under the influence of fixed-pie beliefs and approach the situation (d) competitively. Negotiators focusing on values were least likely to see the problem in fixed-pie terms and more inclined to approach the situation cooperatively. Stressful conditions such as time constraints contribute to this common misperception, which in turn may lead to (e) less integrative agreements.

*prosecutor: 검사 **recidivism: 상습적 범행

P01 ★★★ .... 2024 대비 6월 모평 41 (고3)

윗글의 제목으로 가장 적절한 것은?

① Fixed Pie: A Key to Success in a Zero-sum Game
② Fixed Pie Tells You How to Get the Biggest Salary
③ Negotiators, Wake Up from the Myth of the Fixed Pie!
④ Want a Fairer Jail Sentence? Stick to the Fixed Pie
⑤ What Alternatives Maximize Fixed-pie Effects?

P02 ★★★ .... 2024 대비 6월 모평 42 (고3)

밑줄 친 (a)~(e) 중에서 문맥상 낱말의 쓰임이 적절하지 않은 것은?

① (a) ② (b) ③ (c) ④ (d) ⑤ (e)

1st 어떤 문제들이 출제되었는지 확인하고, 각 유형의 풀이 방법을 떠올려 보세요.

P01 윗글의 제목으로 가장 적절한 것은?

① Fixed Pie: A Key to Success in a Zero-sum Game
고정된 파이: 제로섬 게임에서 성공의 열쇠

② Fixed Pie Tells You How to Get the Biggest Salary
고정된 파이는 여러분에게 가장 큰 급여를 받는 방법을 알려 준다

③ Negotiators, Wake Up from the Myth of the Fixed Pie!
협상가들이여, 고정된 파이라는 미몽(근거없는 믿음)에서 깨어나라!

④ Want a Fairer Jail Sentence? Stick to the Fixed Pie
더 공정한 징역형을 원하는가? 고정된 파이를 고수하라

⑤ What Alternatives Maximize Fixed-pie Effects?
어떤 대안이 고정된 파이 효과를 극대화하는가?

● 제목 찾기 유형은 일단 선택지를 통해 핵심 소재를 파악해야 해요.
모든 선택지에서 고정된 파이를 언급하고 있어요. **단서** 글의 핵심 소재가 확실하므로 고정된 파이에 관하여 무엇을 구체적으로 설명하는 글인지 살펴봐야 해요. **발상**

● 각 선택지가 제목이라면 어떤 내용의 글이 될까요?
①은 제로섬 게임에서 성공의 열쇠로서 고정된 파이, ②은 가장 큰 급여를 받는 방법으로서 고정된 파이, ③은 협상가들에게 있어서 미몽(근거없는 믿음)인 고정된 파이, ④은 공정한 징역형을 위한 고정된 파이, ⑤은 고정된 파이 효과를 극대화하는 대안에 대해 이야기하는 글이 되겠죠?

P02 밑줄 친 (a)~(e) 중에서 문맥상 낱말의 쓰임이 적절하지 않은 것은?
① (a)　② (b)　③ (c)　④ (d)　⑤ (e)

● 적절한지, 그렇지 않은지를 파악하려면 어휘의 뜻부터 알아야겠죠?
글을 본격적으로 읽기 전에 각 어휘의 뜻을 적어 놓으세요.
(a) suppress는 ❶(　　　　　)'라는 뜻이에요.
(b) block은 '방해하다, 막다', vary의 단수 현재형인 (c) varies는 ❷(　　　　　)', (d) competitively는 '경쟁적으로', (e) less는 '덜'이라는 뜻이에요.

P02
2nd 글의 세부 사항을 묻는 문제를 먼저 풀면서 글의 내용을 파악하세요.

1) (a)부터 살펴봅시다.

Those / who believe in the mythical fixed pie /
사람들은 / 허구의 고정된 파이를 믿는 /
assume / that parties' interests / stand in
가정한다 / 당사자들의 이해관계가 / 반대 입장에
opposition, / with no possibility / for integrative
있다고 / 가능성이 없는 / 통합적인 합의와
settlements and mutually beneficial trade-offs, / so
상호 이익이 되는 절충안의 /
they (a) suppress efforts / to search for them. //
그래서 그들은 노력을 억누른다 / 그것들을 찾으려는 //

● 허구의 고정된 파이를 믿으면 어떻게 행동할까요?
허구의 고정된 파이를 믿는 사람들은 당사자들의 이해관계가 합의와 절충안의 가능성이 없는 반대 입장에 있다고 했어요.
합의의 가능성이 없다고 생각하면 당연히 합의를 하려는 노력도 하지 않겠죠? 그렇게 그들은 합의와 절충안을 찾으려는 노력을 '억누르게' 될 거에요.
▶ 따라서 (a) suppress는 문맥상 적절해요.

2) (b)가 포함된 문장을 살펴봅시다.

Only when the two parties discuss the possibilities
두 당사자가 가능성에 대해 논의할 때만 더 자세히
further / do they discover / that moving expenses
/ 그들은 사실을 발견하는데 / 이사 비용과
and starting date / can also be negotiated, / which
시작 날짜가 / 또한 협상될 수 있다는 / 이는
may (b) block / resolution of the salary issue. //
방해할 수 있을 것이다 / 급여 문제의 해결을 //

● 협상이 가능한데 문제 해결을 방해한다고요?
두 당사자가 이사 비용과 시작 날짜를 협상하는 예시를 들고 있어요.
가능성에 대해 자세히 논의해 봤더니 이사 비용과 시작 날짜에 협상의 여지가 있다고 가정해 봅시다. 분명 두 당사자 모두 만족할 협상안을 낼 수 있는데 급여 문제 해결에 방해가 될까요? 아니죠. 오히려 수월하게 급여 문제를 해결할 수 있겠죠.
▶ 따라서 (b) block은 facilitate(촉진하다)처럼 문제 해결을 돕는다는 뜻의 단어로 바꿔야 해요.

3) (c)가 포함된 문장을 살펴봅시다.

The tendency / to see negotiation / in fixed-pie
경향은 / 협상을 보는 / 고정된 파이
terms / (c) varies / depending on how people view /
관점에서 / 달라진다 / 사람들이 어떻게 보느냐에 따라 /
the nature of a given conflict situation. //
주어진 갈등 상황의 본질을 //

● 관점이 달라지면 무언가를 보는 경향도 달라지기 마련이죠.
❸(　　　　　)에서 협상을 보는 경향은 갈등의 본질을 어떻게 보느냐에 따라 달라진다는 내용이에요. 관점이 달라지면 경향도 달라지는 것이 당연한 듯하지만, 더 확실히 하기 위해 뒤의 예시도 마저 읽어 볼까요?

4) 예시 문장에 (d)가 있으니 이어서 살펴봅시다.

Negotiators / focusing on personal gain / were most
협상가들은 / 개인적 이득에 초점을 맞춘 / 영향을 받을

likely to come under the influence / of fixed-pie
가능성이 가장 컸다 / 고정된 파이에 대한

beliefs / and approach the situation (d) competitively.
믿음의 / 그리고 상황에 경쟁적으로 접근할 (가능성이 가장 컸다)

// Negotiators / focusing on values / were least likely
// 협상가들은 / 가치에 초점을 맞춘 / 문제를 볼

to see the problem / in fixed-pie terms / and more
가능성이 가장 낮았고 / 고정된 파이 관점에서 / 그리고 더

inclined / to approach the situation cooperatively. //
경향이 있었다 / 상황에 접근하려는 협력적으로 //

● **무엇에 초점을 맞추느냐에 따라 결과가 달라진 것이 확실하네요.**

개인적 이득에 초점을 맞추면 고정된 파이 관점의 영향을 받아
경쟁적으로, 가치에 초점을 맞추면 고정된 파이 관점과 상관없이
협력적으로 상황에 접근한다고 했어요. 앞서 관점이 달라지면 협상을
보는 경향이 '달라진다'는 내용과 일치함을 알 수 있어요.

▶ 따라서 (c) varies는 문맥상 적절해요.

● **개인적 이득에 초점을 맞추면 상황에 어떻게 접근할까요?**

가치에 초점을 맞춘 협상가들이 협력적으로 상황에 접근했다면, 개인적
이득에 초점을 맞춘 협상가들은 그 반대의 접근 방식을 취하겠죠. 즉,
협력적이 아니라 '경쟁적으로' 상황에 접근할 것임을 알 수 있어요.

▶ 따라서 (d) competitively는 문맥상 적절해요.

5) 마지막으로 (e)도 살펴봅시다.

Stressful conditions / such as time constraints /
스트레스가 많은 조건은 / 시간 제약과 같은 /

contribute to this common misperception, / which
이러한 흔한 오해의 원인이 되며 / 이는

in turn may lead / to (e) less integrative agreements. //
결국 이어질 수 있다 / 덜 통합적인 합의로 //

● **시간에 쫓기면 잘 풀릴 일도 안 풀리고는 하죠.**

스트레스가 많은 조건으로서 **4**( )을 예로 들었어요.
시간에 쫓겨서 조별 과제를 하다 보면 서로 소통이 부족해서 오해가
많아질 수밖에 없죠? 이런 조건에서 합의를 하면 역시나 '덜' 통합적으로
이어질 것이라고 예상할 수 있어요.

▶ 따라서 (e) less는 문맥상 적절해요.

P01

3rd 세부 사항을 묻는 문제를 풀면서 얻은 글의 내용을 바탕으로
글의 제목을 묻는 문제의 정답을 찾으세요.

1) 글의 첫 문장을 통해 핵심 소재를 다시 확인해 봅시다.

Many [negotiators] assume / that all negotiations
많은 협상가는 가정한다 / 모든 협상이

involve a [fixed pie]. //
고정된 파이를 수반한다고 //

● **여러 문장에서 나타났던 소재들이 역시나 글의 중심 소재였어요.**

많은 협상가들이 모든 협상에 고정된 파이가 있다고 가정한다는 내용으로
글이 시작되네요. 문맥 문제의 선택지들을 보면서 협상가, 협상, 합의,
고정된 파이 등의 단어들을 봐왔죠? 그러면 우리가 확인했던 문장들을
종합하여 글의 주제를 확정지어 봅시다.

2) 지금껏 파악한 내용을 종합하여 주제를 확정해 봅시다.

• (a): 고정된 파이를 믿는 사람들은 합의할 노력을 하지 않는다.
• (b): 두 당사자가 자세히 논의하면 합의점이 있고 이는 문제 해결을
촉진할 수 있다.
• (c): 고정된 파이 관점에서 협상을 보는 경향은 갈등에 대한 관점에
따라 달라진다.
• (d): 협상가들이 개인적 이득에 초점을 맞추면 고정된 파이의 영향을
받아 경쟁적으로, 가치에 초점을 맞추면 그와 상관없이 협력적으로
상황에 접근한다.
• (e): 스트레스가 많은 조건은 오해를 낳고, 덜 통합적인 합의로
이어지게 할 수 있다.

고정된 파이를 믿는 사람들은 합의할 노력을 하지 않지만 자세히
논의하면 분명히 합의점이 있어서 문제를 해결할 수 있다고 했어요.
또한 고정된 파이를 믿는 협상가들이 많다고 해도 갈등에 대한 관점이
바뀌면 얼마든지 협력적으로 상황에 접근할 수 있다고 했죠.
덜 통합적인 합의로 이어지는 것은 스트레스가 많은 조건이라는 요인도
있다는 내용으로 글이 마무리되네요.
이를 종합해보면, 협상가들이 고정된 파이 관점에서 얼마든지 벗어날 수
있고 가치에 초점을 두어 협력적인 상황 접근이 가능하다는 것이 글의
주제예요.
선택지 중 **5**( )이 협상가와 고정된 파이라는 핵심 소재를
모두 담고 있으며 고정된 파이 관점에서 벗어나라고 당부하고 있으므로
가장 적절한 제목이라고 볼 수 있어요.

[P03～04] ▶ 제한시간 5분

[P03~P04] 다음 글을 읽고, 물음에 답하시오.

Imagine grabbing a piece of paper between your thumb and index finger. Maybe you already are, as you turn this page. We use this type of forceful, pad-to-pad precision gripping without thinking about it, and literally in a snap. Yet it was a breakthrough in human evolution. Other primates exhibit some kinds of precision grips in the handling and use of objects, but not with the kind of (a) efficient opposition that our hand anatomy allows. In a single hand, humans can easily hold and manipulate objects, even small and delicate ones, while adjusting our fingers to their shape and reorienting them with (b) displacements of our fingertip pads. Our relatively long, powerful thumb and other anatomical attributes, including our flat nails (which nearly all primates possess), make this (c) possible. Just picture trying — and failing — to dog-ear this page with pointy, curved claws.

With a unique combination of traits, the human hand shaped our history. No question, stone tools couldn't have become a keystone of human technology and subsistence (d) without hands that could do the job, along with a nervous system that could regulate and coordinate the necessary signals. Anybody who's ever attempted to make a spear tip or arrowhead from a rock knows that it (e) excludes strong grips, constant rotation and repositioning, and forceful, careful strikes with another hard object. And even with a fair amount of know-how, it can be a bloody business.

*primate: 영장류 **anatomy: 해부학 ***subsistence: 생계

P03 ★★✲ ································· 2025 대비 수능 41 (고3)

윗글의 제목으로 가장 적절한 것은?

① Anatomical Distance Between Humans and Other Primates
② Human Hands: A Decisive Leap in the Evolutionary Path
③ Our Hands: An Unexpected Outcome of Evolution
④ Human Grip: The Dilemma of Human Survival
⑤ Hidden Power of the Daily Use of Tools

P04 ★★★✲ ··························· 2025 대비 수능 42 (고3)

밑줄 친 (a)~(e) 중에서 문맥상 낱말의 쓰임이 적절하지 않은 것은? [3점]

① (a)   ② (b)   ③ (c)   ④ (d)   ⑤ (e)

[P05~ P06] 다음 글을 읽고, 물음에 답하시오.

People are correct when they feel that the written poetry of literate societies and the oral poetry of non-literate ones differ considerably from the everyday language spoken in the community. Listeners not only accept the (a) strange use of words, rearrangement of word order, assonance, alliteration, rhythm, rhyme, compression of thought, and so on — they actually expect to find these things in poetry and they are disappointed when poetry does not sound "poetic." But those who regard poetry as a (b) different category of language altogether are deaf to the true achievements of the poet. Rather, the poet artfully manipulates the same raw materials of his language as are used in everyday speech; his skill is to find new possibilities in the resources already in the language. In much the same way that people living at the seashore become so accustomed to the sound of waves that they no longer hear it, most of us have become (c) sensitive to the flood tide of words, millions of them every day, that hit our eardrums. One function of poetry is to depict the world with a (d) fresh perception — to make it strange — so that we will listen to language once again. But the successful poet never departs so far into the strange world of language that none of his listeners can (e) follow him. He still remains the communicator, the man of speech.

*assonance: 유운(類韻) **alliteration: 두운(頭韻)
***depict: 묘사하다

P05 ✱✱❋ .... 2025 대비 9월 모평 41 (고3)

윗글의 제목으로 가장 적절한 것은?

① Make It New: How Poetry Refreshes Everyday Language
② Why Do Poets No Longer Seek Inspiration from Nature?
③ The Influence of Natural Sounds on Poetic Expression
④ Ways to Cite Poetic Expressions in Everyday Speech
⑤ Beauty Rediscovered: The Return of Oral Poetry

P06 ✱✱✱ .... 2025 대비 9월 모평 42 (고3)

밑줄 친 (a)~(e) 중에서 문맥상 낱말의 쓰임이 적절하지 않은 것은? [3점]

① (a)   ② (b)   ③ (c)   ④ (d)   ⑤ (e)

[P07~P08] 다음 글을 읽고, 물음에 답하시오.

If we understand critical thinking as: 'the identification and evaluation of evidence to guide decision-making', then ethical thinking is about identifying ethical issues and evaluating these issues from different perspectives to guide how to respond. This form of ethics is distinct from higher levels of conceptual ethics or theory. The nature of an ethical issue or problem from this perspective is that there is no clear right or wrong response. It is therefore (a) essential that students learn to think through ethical issues rather than follow a prescribed set of ethical codes or rules. There is a need to (b) encourage recognition that, although being ethical is defined as acting 'in accordance with the principles of conduct that are considered correct', these principles vary both between and within individuals. What a person (c) values relates to their social, religious, or civic beliefs influenced by their formal and informal learning experiences. Individual perspectives may also be context (d) dependent, meaning that under different circumstances, at a different time, when they are feeling a different way, the same individual may make different choices. Therefore, in order to analyse ethical issues and think ethically it is necessary to understand the personal factors that influence your own 'code of behaviour' and how these may (e) coincide, alongside recognizing and accepting that the factors that drive other people's codes and decision making may be different.

P07 ★★❋ ················· 2025 대비 6월 모평 41 (고3)

윗글의 제목으로 가장 적절한 것은?

① Critical Reasoning: A Road to Ethical Decision-making
② Far-reaching Impacts of Ethics on Behavioural Codes
③ Ethical Thinking: A Walk Through Individual Minds
④ Exploring Ethical Theory in the Eyes of the Others
⑤ Do Ethical Choices Always Take Priority?

P08 ★★★❋ ················· 2025 대비 6월 모평 42 (고3)

밑줄 친 (a)~(e) 중에서 문맥상 낱말의 쓰임이 적절하지 않은 것은? [3점]

① (a)   ② (b)   ③ (c)   ④ (d)   ⑤ (e)

[P09~P10] 다음 글을 읽고, 물음에 답하시오.

Vocal sounds produced by parrots, regardless of the fact that they may be audibly indistinguishable from spoken words and regardless of the fact that someone or some group of people may take them to be words, are not words. They are not given a semantic dimension by physical (a) <u>similitude</u> to spoken words. Nor can the "talk" of a parrot be given a semantic dimension by being taken to be a set of (b) <u>linguistic</u> acts. In like manner, weather etchings on a stone or shapes in the clouds, regardless of how physically similar they may be to written words or drawings of objects and regardless of what they are taken to be by observers, are not words or pictures. They do not have the appropriate etiology and they have no inherent semantic content or object. They are simply (c) <u>physical</u> objects that resemble certain other things. For observers, they may call to mind the things they (d) <u>resemble</u>. In this regard, they may function as natural signs by virtue of the physical resemblance, but they have no semantic content about which one could be right or wrong. If people take *A* to be a sign of *B* by virtue of some nonsemantic relation that holds, or is believed to hold, between *A* and *B*, *A* is a sign of *B*. But words, pictures, and images are not that way. They (e) <u>exclude</u> a semantic content to be understood.

*semantic: 의미론적, 의미의 **weather etching: 날씨 식각(蝕刻)

***etiology: 원인의 추구

P09 ✽✽❋ .... 2024 실시 10월 학평 41 (고3)

윗글의 제목으로 가장 적절한 것은?

① Why Not All Physical Resemblances Are Semantically Meaningful
② Uncovering Similarities in Human and Animal Vocal Sounds
③ Physical Objects: An Effective Medium to Deliver Subtext
④ Using Semantic Relation Makes Language Learning Easy
⑤ How Vocally Produced Words Shape Our Perception

P10 ✽✽✽ .... 2024 실시 10월 학평 42 (고3)

밑줄 친 (a)~(e) 중에서 문맥상 낱말의 쓰임이 적절하지 않은 것은? [3점]

① (a)   ② (b)   ③ (c)   ④ (d)   ⑤ (e)

[P11~P12] 다음 글을 읽고, 물음에 답하시오.

We have seen a clear rise in something called 'shrinkflation'. A basket of products is measured for inflation by price, not by volume or weight. If the products shrink in size but the price stays the same, technically no price (a) increase has occurred. But people aren't stupid, they know what that means. You can see this in everything from the reduced amount of cereal in a box to smaller-sized chocolate bars. You can see it in the form of ever-larger apertures in toothpaste tubes and powders of various sorts. The purpose of these changes is to make the consumer use up the product (b) faster and to pay more per weight. Toilet paper and paper towel rolls have ever-larger tube centres and ever-fewer sheets, while the price remains the same. There are (c) fewer potato crisps in the bag and cookies in the box. Bottles of liquids such as perfumes have ever-larger dimples on the bottom that displace the product and (d) prevent the illusion of more inside than there is. Shrinkflation is not restricted to retail products. Apartments are shrinking, too. Micro apartments are smaller than anything we lived in before but cost more per square foot. Shrinkflation is a signal that tells us that companies are facing higher costs. It is a signal that price pressures are starting to (e) build.

*aperture: 입구 **dimple: 움푹 들어간 곳

P11 ★★❀ 2024 실시 7월 학평 41 (고3)

윗글의 제목으로 가장 적절한 것은?

① Small Sizes Win Consumers Over in the Era of Shrinkflation
② Hidden Inflation: Paying the Same for Shrunken Goods
③ Business Marketing Strategy: Stand Out, Don't Shrink
④ Innovative Changes in Smaller-Sized Daily Products
⑤ Buy One, Get One Free: How Companies Attract You

P12 ★★❀ 2024 실시 7월 학평 42 (고3)

밑줄 친 (a)~(e) 중에서 문맥상 낱말의 쓰임이 적절하지 않은 것은?

① (a)   ② (b)   ③ (c)   ④ (d)   ⑤ (e)

❖ 정답 및 해설 429 ~ 432p

[P13~P14] 다음 글을 읽고, 물음에 답하시오.

There are a number of human characteristics that would seem to be disadvantageous yet continue to survive, generation after generation. One example is color blindness. Most color blindness is associated with genes on the X chromosome. Women have two X chromosomes, so if this problem occurs on one of them, the other can (a) compensate. But men have only one X chromosome. If the mutation occurs there, that male is color blind. We might ask why such a (b) deficiency would survive and not die out. To understand this, we can consider ancient hunter-gatherers, with the men doing most of the hunting for meat and the women doing most of the gathering of fruits and nuts. Gathering fruits, especially berries, and nuts is much more productive if it is easy to distinguish the red or purple fruit from the green leaves of the plant. If red-green color blindness were common among women, the resulting (c) lack of productivity would likely cause this trait to die out relatively quickly. On the other hand, the men out hunting don't much rely on being able to contrast red from green. Most of the animals they are hunting have fur or feathers that help them hide. Rather than relying on color, the hunter relies on an acute ability to detect motion. It is conceivable that a (d) reduction in color contrast in these circumstances might actually enhance one's ability to detect subtle motions. Given that a hunted animal blends into its surroundings, less background color variation would be (e) more of a visual distraction.

*chromosome: 염색체 **mutation: 돌연변이

P13 ✭✭✭ .... 2024 실시 5월 학평 41 (고3)

윗글의 제목으로 가장 적절한 것은?

① Genetic Code: The Key to Conquering Disorders
② Ancient People's Challenges from Genetic Weaknesses
③ What Makes a Great Hunter: An Ability to Move Quickly
④ In Evolution, Disadvantageous Doesn't Mean Destined to Vanish
⑤ Various Biological Factors Causing Red-Green Color Blindness

P14 ✭✭✭✤ .... 2024 실시 5월 학평 42 (고3)

밑줄 친 (a)~(e) 중에서 문맥상 낱말의 쓰임이 적절하지 않은 것은? [3점]

① (a)   ② (b)   ③ (c)   ④ (d)   ⑤ (e)

You are the narrator of your own life. The tone and perspective with which you describe each experience generates feelings associated with that narration. For example, if you find yourself constantly assuming, "This is hard," "I wonder whether I'm going to survive," or "It looks like this is going to turn out badly," you'll generate (a) anxious feelings. It's time to restructure the way you think. Underlying this narration are the beliefs that (b) frame your experience and give it meaning. Think of your beliefs as having many layers.

On the surface are your *automatic thoughts*. These are like short tapes that momentarily flash through your mind. Call these automatic thoughts a form of "self-talk" that you use as you navigate through the day. You (c) produce a wide variety of these automatic thoughts, some consciously and some unconsciously. For example, automatic thoughts that (d) relieve anxiety go something like this: You walk into a room, see a few new people, and say to yourself, "Oh no, I don't like this. This is not good." Or, "These people will soon find out that I am full of anxiety and will reject me." Automatic thoughts are bad habits that (e) cloud fresh and positive experiences. They can turn a potentially good experience into one fraught with anxiety. If you tell yourself that you are always stressed or full of anxiety before doing something new, that new experience will be tainted by that anxiety.

*fraught: 가득찬 **taint: 오염시키다, 더럽히다

P15 ★★✿ .... 2024 실시 3월 학평 41 (고3)

윗글의 제목으로 가장 적절한 것은?

① The Role of Automatic Thoughts in Language Learning
② Self-talk: The Best Way to Improve Your Speech
③ Reshaping Thoughts: Manage Your Self-talk
④ Heightened Anxiety Leads to Productivity
⑤ Ways to Read Others' Inner Thoughts

P16 ★★★ .... 2024 실시 3월 학평 42 (고3)

밑줄 친 (a)~(e) 중에서 문맥상 낱말의 쓰임이 적절하지 않은 것은? [3점]

① (a) ② (b) ③ (c) ④ (d) ⑤ (e)

[P17~P18] 다음 글을 읽고, 물음에 답하시오.

Douglas Hofstadter is a scholar who writes about stereotypical thinking. He discusses what he calls *default assumptions*. Default assumptions are (a) preconceived notions about the likely state of affairs — what we assume to be true in the absence of specific information. Given no other information, when I mention "secretary," you are likely to assume the secretary is a woman, because "woman" and "secretary" are associated stereotypically. In the absence of specific details, people rely on the stereotype as a default assumption for filling in the (b) blanks. Default assumptions have a tendency, in Hofstadter's words, to "permeate our mental representations and channel our thoughts." For instance, given the words "cat," "dog," and "chases," you are likely to think first of a dog chasing a cat. This line of thought (c) reflects a default assumption that, all else being equal, the dog is more likely to chase the cat than the other way around.

Default assumptions are rooted in our socially learned associative clusters and linguistic categories. They are (d) useless in that people cannot always afford the time it would take to consider every theoretical possibility that confronts them. Nonetheless, default assumptions are often wrong. Default assumptions are only one type of language-based categorization. Hofstadter is particularly interested in race-based and gender-based categorization and default assumptions. For instance, if you hear that your school basketball team is playing tonight, do you assume it's the men's team? Most people would assume so unless a *qualifier* is (e) added to provide specific information. In this case, the qualifier would be "the *women*'s basketball team is playing tonight."

*permeate: 스며들다 **cluster: 무리 ***qualifier: 수식어

P17 ✹✹✵ .... 2023 실시 3월 학평 41 (고3)

윗글의 제목으로 가장 적절한 것은?

① Quest for Novelty: Our Survival Instinct
② Gossip as a Source of Social Information
③ The Bias Behind Stereotypical Assumptions
④ The More Information, The More Confusion
⑤ Creativity: Free from the Prison of Our Assumptions

P18 ✹✹✵ .... 2023 실시 3월 학평 42 (고3)

밑줄 친 (a)~(e) 중에서 문맥상 낱말의 쓰임이 적절하지 않은 것은?

① (a)　　② (b)　　③ (c)　　④ (d)　　⑤ (e)

In studies examining the effectiveness of vitamin C, researchers typically divide the subjects into two groups. One group (the experimental group) receives a vitamin C supplement, and the other (the control group) does not. Researchers observe both groups to determine whether one group has fewer or shorter colds than the other. The following discussion describes some of the pitfalls inherent in an experiment of this kind and ways to (a) avoid them. In sorting subjects into two groups, researchers must ensure that each person has an (b) equal chance of being assigned to either the experimental group or the control group. This is accomplished by randomization; that is, the subjects are chosen randomly from the same population by flipping a coin or some other method involving chance. Randomization helps to ensure that results reflect the treatment and not factors that might influence the grouping of subjects. Importantly, the two groups of people must be similar and must have the same track record with respect to colds to (c) rule out the possibility that observed differences in the rate, severity, or duration of colds might have occurred anyway. If, for example, the control group would normally catch twice as many colds as the experimental group, then the findings prove (d) nothing. In experiments involving a nutrient, the diets of both groups must also be (e) different, especially with respect to the nutrient being studied. If those in the experimental group were receiving less vitamin C from their usual diet, then any effects of the supplement may not be apparent.

*pitfall: 함정

P19 ★★❀ .... 2022 대비 9월 모평 41 (고3)

윗글의 제목으로 가장 적절한 것은?

① Perfect Planning and Faulty Results: A Sad Reality in Research
② Don't Let Irrelevant Factors Influence the Results!
③ Protect Human Subjects Involved in Experimental Research!
④ What Nutrients Could Better Defend Against Colds?
⑤ In-depth Analysis of Nutrition: A Key Player for Human Health

P20 ★★★ .... 2022 대비 9월 모평 42 (고3)

밑줄 친 (a)~(e) 중에서 문맥상 쓰임이 적절하지 않은 것은?

① (a)　　② (b)　　③ (c)　　④ (d)　　⑤ (e)

[P21~P22] 다음 글을 읽고, 물음에 답하시오.

Generalization promotes cognitive economy, so that we don't focus on particulars that don't matter. The great Russian neuropsychologist Alexander Luria studied a patient, Solomon Shereshevsky, with a memory impairment that was the (a) opposite of what we usually hear about — Solomon didn't have amnesia, the loss of memories; he had what Luria called hypermnesia (we might say that his superpower was superior memory). His supercharged memory allowed him to perform amazing feats, such as repeating speeches word for word that he had heard only once, or complex mathematical formulas, long sequences of numbers, and poems in foreign languages he didn't even speak. Before you think that having such a fantastic memory would be great, it came with a (b) cost: Solomon wasn't able to form abstractions because he remembered every detail as distinct. He had particular trouble identifying people. From a neurocognitive standpoint, every time you see a face, it is (c) unlikely that it looks at least slightly different from the last time — you're viewing it at a different angle and distance than before, and you might be encountering a different expression. While you're interacting with a person, their face goes through a parade of expressions. Because your brain can (d) generalize, you see all of these different manifestations of the face as belonging to the same person. Solomon couldn't do that. As he explained to Luria, (e) recognizing his friends and colleagues was nearly impossible because "everyone has so many faces."

*impairment: 장애

P21 ✲✲✲ .... 2023 실시 7월 학평 41 (고3)

윗글의 제목으로 가장 적절한 것은?

① Face Recognition Technologies: Blessing or Not?
② The Faster You Memorize, the Faster You Forget
③ Generalization Can Be Both a Shortcut and a Trap!
④ The Flaw in Cognition Caused by Flawless Memory
⑤ Why It Gets Difficult to Remember Details As You Age

P22 ✲✲❀ .... 2023 실시 7월 학평 42 (고3)

밑줄 친 (a)~(e) 중에서 문맥상 낱말의 쓰임이 적절하지 않은 것은? [3점]

① (a)　　② (b)　　③ (c)　　④ (d)　　⑤ (e)

Although we humans are equipped with reflexive responses for survival, at birth we are (a) helpless. We spend about a year unable to walk, about two more before we can articulate full thoughts, and many more years unable to provide for ourselves. We are totally dependent on those around us for our survival. Now compare this to many other mammals. Dolphins, for instance, are born swimming; giraffes learn to stand within hours; a baby zebra can run within forty-five minutes of birth. Across the animal kingdom, our cousins are strikingly (b) independent soon after they're born.

On the face of it, that seems like a great advantage for other species — but in fact it signifies a limitation. Baby animals develop quickly because their brains are wiring up according to a largely preprogrammed routine. But that (c) preparedness trades off with flexibility. Imagine if some unfortunate rhinoceros found itself on the Arctic tundra, or on top of a mountain in the Himalayas, or in the middle of a metropolis. It would have no capacity to adapt (which is why we don't find rhinos in those areas). This strategy of arriving with a pre-arranged brain works inside a particular niche in the ecosystem — but put an animal outside of that niche, and its chances of thriving are (d) low.

In contrast, humans are able to thrive in many different environments, from the frozen tundra to the high mountains to crowded urban centers. This is possible because the human brain is born remarkably incomplete. Instead of arriving with everything wired up — let's call it "hardwired" — a human brain (e) forbids itself to be shaped by the details of life experience. This leads to long periods of helplessness as the young brain slowly molds to its environment. It's "livewired."

*niche: 적합한 장소

P23 ★★❀ ·························· 2023 실시 4월 학평 41 (고3)

윗글의 제목으로 가장 적절한 것은?

① Rewire Your Brain to Enhance Your Courage!
② Born Unfinished: A Gift of Adaptability to Humans
③ Evolutionary Rivalry Between Humans and Animals
④ How Does Human-Centered Thinking Bring Tragedy?
⑤ Human Brains Develop Through Interaction with Other Species

P24 ★★★ ························ 2023 실시 4월 학평 42 (고3)

밑줄 친 (a)~(e) 중에서 문맥상 낱말의 쓰임이 적절하지 않은 것은?

① (a)　② (b)　③ (c)　④ (d)　⑤ (e)

[P25~P26] 다음 글을 읽고, 물음에 답하시오.

One reason we think we forget most of what we learned in school is that we underestimate what we actually remember. Other times, we know we remember something, but we don't recognize that we learned it in school. Knowing where and when you learned something is usually called *context information*, and context is handled by (a) different memory processes than memory for the content. Thus, it's quite possible to retain content without remembering the context.

For example, if someone mentions a movie and you think to yourself that you heard it was terrible but can't remember (b) where you heard that, you're recalling the content, but you've lost the context. Context information is frequently (c) easier to forget than content, and it's the source of a variety of memory illusions. For instance, people are (d) unconvinced by a persuasive argument if it's written by someone who is not very credible (e.g., someone with a clear financial interest in the topic). But in time, readers' attitudes, on average, change in the direction of the persuasive argument. Why? Because readers are likely to remember the content of the argument but forget the source — someone who is not credible. If remembering the source of knowledge is difficult, you can see how it would be (e) challenging to conclude you don't remember much from school.

*illusion: 착각

P25 ★★★ .... 2024 대비 9월 모평 41 (고3)

윗글의 제목으로 가장 적절한 것은?

① Learned Nothing in School?: How Memory Tricks You
② Why We Forget Selectively: Credibility of Content
③ The Constant Battle Between Content and Context
④ How Students Can Learn More and Better in School
⑤ Shift Your Focus from Who to What for Memory Building

P26 ★★★ .... 2024 대비 9월 모평 42 (고3)

밑줄 친 (a)~(e) 중에서 문맥상 낱말의 쓰임이 적절하지 않은 것은?

① (a) ② (b) ③ (c) ④ (d) ⑤ (e)

Posts that hold up signs, street lights, and utility lines need to be strong and durable enough to withstand winds, storms, tsunamis, and earthquakes. Every so often, though, these same posts are called upon to do something crucial but fundamentally at odds with their everyday function: they need to break (a) easily on impact. If hit by a fast-moving vehicle, posts need to come apart in just the right way in order to reduce damage and save lives. Engineers have spent a lot of time attempting to resolve this apparent paradox.

One of the ways to get robust posts to break properly is called a "slip base" system. Instead of using a single continuous post, a slip base approach (b) joins two separate posts close to ground level using a connector plate. This joint allows the pair to break apart at an (c) intended juncture. It works basically like this: a lower post is put in the ground, then an upper post is attached to it using breakaway bolts. These bolts are made to fracture or dislodge when the post gets hit hard enough, so the upper post gets knocked over while the lower post passes safely under the moving vehicle. When everything works as designed, such posts can also help slow down a vehicle and (d) minimize damage. Subsequent infrastructure repair becomes easier as well — in many cases, a new upper post can simply be bolted onto the (e) damaged base post below it, which requires less material and work. The critical plate-to-plate connections underpinning slip systems can be obvious to the naked eye or tucked away under plate covers.

*juncture: 접합점 **dislodge: 이탈시키다

P27 ★★✿
2022 실시 7월 학평 41 (고3)

윗글의 제목으로 가장 적절한 것은?

① How Street Posts Ruin the City View
② Breakaway Posts Save Lives and Cost
③ Fewer Road Signs, Fewer Traffic Accidents
④ Recycled Materials Lead to Sustainable Cities
⑤ Dilemma Between Safety and Cost-efficiency

P28 ★★✿
2022 실시 7월 학평 42 (고3)

밑줄 친 (a)~(e) 중에서 문맥상 낱말의 쓰임이 적절하지 않은 것은?
[3점]

① (a)　② (b)　③ (c)　④ (d)　⑤ (e)

[P29~P30] 다음 글을 읽고, 물음에 답하시오.

To the extent that sufficient context has been provided, the reader can come to a well-crafted text with no expert knowledge and come away with a good approximation of what has been intended by the author. The text has become a public document and the reader can read it with a (a) minimum of effort and struggle; his experience comes close to what Freud has described as the deployment of "evenly-hovering attention." He puts himself in the author's hands (some have had this experience with great novelists such as Dickens or Tolstoy) and he (b) follows where the author leads. The real world has vanished and the fictive world has taken its place. Now consider the other extreme. When we come to a badly crafted text in which context and content are not happily joined, we must struggle to understand, and our sense of what the author intended probably bears (c) close correspondence to his original intention. An out-of-date translation will give us this experience; as we read, we must bring the language up to date, and understanding comes only at the price of a fairly intense struggle with the text. Badly presented content with no frame of reference can provide (d) the same experience; we see the words but have no sense of how they are to be taken. The author who fails to provide the context has (e) mistakenly assumed that his picture of the world is shared by all his readers and fails to realize that supplying the right frame of reference is a critical part of the task of writing.

*deployment: (전략적) 배치
**evenly-hovering attention: 고르게 주의를 기울이는 것

P29 ★★★❀ .... 2021 대비 9월 모평 41 (고3)

윗글의 제목으로 가장 적절한 것은?

① Building a Wall Between Reality and the Fictive World
② Creative Reading: Going Beyond the Writer's Intentions
③ Usefulness of Readers' Experiences for Effective Writing
④ Context in Writing: A Lighthouse for Understanding Texts
⑤ Trapped in Their Own Words: The Narrow Outlook of Authors

P30 ★★★ .... 2021 대비 9월 모평 42 (고3)

밑줄 친 (a)~(e) 중에서 문맥상 낱말의 쓰임이 적절하지 않은 것은?
[3점]

① (a)   ② (b)   ③ (c)   ④ (d)   ⑤ (e)

The domination of nature is a familiar trope in environmental ethics and environmental political theory. Its history is tied more broadly to the rise of modern science, philosophy, and politics. The effort to understand the causal relations that govern the physical world so as to intervene in these relations in ways that could, as Francis Bacon put it, "ameliorate the human condition," marked the beginning of modernity in the West. For a long time, the "domination of nature" referred to this effort to understand and (a) <u>control</u> the nonhuman environment, and it was seen as a clearly good thing. This effort made (b) <u>possible</u> new technologies and rising economic prosperity, promised an end to many forms of human suffering, and demonstrated the triumph of reason over ignorance and superstition. Its costs began to be (c) <u>invisible</u> with industrialization in the nineteenth century, which generated obvious environmental damage and caused among many people a sense of alienation from the land and the more-than-human communities composing it. One sees a growing (d) <u>unease</u> about these costs in novels of the era such as Mary Shelley's *Frankenstein* (1818), in poems like Wordsworth's "Michael" (1800) and later Whitman's *Leaves of Grass* (1855), and in the early nature writing of Thoreau's *Walden* (1854). Yet systematic, critical analysis of the domination of nature as a problem came into its own only with the environmental studies movement in the 1970s. Since then, the trope has come to have a broadly (e) <u>negative</u> meaning, with the domination of nature being viewed as harmful and illegitimate, as well as dangerous to human interests.

*trope: 수사적 표현 **ameliorate: 개선하다

P31 ★★❀ .... 2023 실시 10월 학평 41 (고3)

윗글의 제목으로 가장 적절한 것은?

① Changing Perspectives on the Domination of Nature
② Science Starts from a Desire for Knowledge
③ Ethics Is Central to Every Discipline
④ Nature in Literature Is Not Real
⑤ Is Going Green Really Green?

P32 ★★★❀ .... 2023 실시 10월 학평 42 (고3)

밑줄 친 (a)~(e) 중에서 문맥상 낱말의 쓰임이 적절하지 않은 것은?

① (a) ② (b) ③ (c) ④ (d) ⑤ (e)

[P33~ P34] 다음 글을 읽고, 물음에 답하시오.

In many mountain regions, rights of access to water are associated with the possession of land — until recently in the Andes, for example, land and water rights were (a) combined so water rights were transferred with the land. However, through state land reforms and the development of additional sources of supply, water rights have become separated from land, and may be sold at auction. This therefore (b) favours those who can pay, rather than ensuring access to all in the community. The situation arises, therefore, where individuals may hold land with no water. In Peru, the government grants water to communities separately from land, and it is up to the community to allocate it. Likewise in Yemen, the traditional allocation was one measure (*tasah*) of water to one hundred '*libnah*' of land. This applied only to traditional irrigation supplies — from runoff, wells, etc., where a supply was (c) guaranteed. Water derived from the capture of flash floods is not subject to Islamic law as this constitutes an uncertain source, and is therefore free for those able to collect and use it. However, this traditional allocation per unit of land has been bypassed, partly by the development of new supplies, but also by the (d) decrease in cultivation of a crop of substantial economic importance. This crop is harvested throughout the year and thus requires more than its fair share of water. The economic status of the crop (e) ensures that water rights can be bought or bribed away from subsistence crops.

* irrigation: 관개(灌漑) ** bribe: 매수하다

*** subsistence crop: 생계용 작물

P33 ❋❋❀.......................... 2021 대비 6월 모평 41 (고3)

윗글의 제목으로 가장 적절한 것은?

① Water Rights No Longer Tied to Land
② Strategies for Trading Water Rights
③ Water Storage Methods: Mountain vs. Desert
④ Water Supplies Not Stable in Mountain Regions
⑤ Unending Debates: Which Crop We Should Grow

P34 ❋❋❀.......................... 2021 대비 6월 모평 42 (고3)

밑줄 친 (a)~(e) 중에서 문맥상 낱말의 쓰임이 적절하지 <u>않은</u> 것은? [3점]

① (a)　　② (b)　　③ (c)　　④ (d)　　⑤ (e)

One way to avoid contributing to overhyping a story would be to say nothing. However, that is not a realistic option for scientists who feel a strong sense of responsibility to inform the public and policymakers and/or to offer suggestions. Speaking with members of the media has (a) <u>advantages</u> in getting a message out and perhaps receiving favorable recognition, but it runs the risk of misinterpretations, the need for repeated clarifications, and entanglement in never-ending controversy. Hence, the decision of whether to speak with the media tends to be highly individualized. Decades ago, it was (b) <u>unusual</u> for Earth scientists to have results that were of interest to the media, and consequently few media contacts were expected or encouraged. In the 1970s, the few scientists who spoke frequently with the media were often (c) <u>criticized</u> by their fellow scientists for having done so. The situation now is quite different, as many scientists feel a responsibility to speak out because of the importance of global warming and related issues, and many reporters share these feelings. In addition, many scientists are finding that they (d) <u>enjoy</u> the media attention and the public recognition that comes with it. At the same time, other scientists continue to resist speaking with reporters, thereby preserving more time for their science and (e) <u>running</u> the risk of being misquoted and the other unpleasantries associated with media coverage.

*overhype: 과대광고하다 **entanglement: 얽힘

P35 ★★★ .... 2024 대비 수능 41 (고3)

윗글의 제목으로 가장 적절한 것은?

① The Troubling Relationship Between Scientists and the Media
② A Scientist's Choice: To Be Exposed to the Media or Not?
③ Scientists! Be Cautious When Talking to the Media
④ The Dilemma over Scientific Truth and Media Attention
⑤ Who Are Responsible for Climate Issues, Scientists or the Media?

P36 ★★★ .... 2024 대비 수능 42 (고3)

밑줄 친 (a)~(e) 중에서 문맥상 낱말의 쓰임이 적절하지 않은 것은?

① (a)　　② (b)　　③ (c)　　④ (d)　　⑤ (e)

[P37 ~ P38] 다음 글을 읽고, 물음에 답하시오.

Our irresistible tendency to see things in human terms — that we are often mistaken in attributing complex human motives and processing abilities to other species — does not mean that an animal's behavior is not, in fact, complex. Rather, it means that the complexity of the animal's behavior is not purely a (a) product of its internal complexity. Herbert Simon's "parable of the ant" makes this point very clearly. Imagine an ant walking along a beach, and (b) visualize tracking the trajectory of the ant as it moves. The trajectory would show a lot of twists and turns, and would be very irregular and complicated. One could then suppose that the ant had equally complicated (c) internal navigational abilities, and work out what these were likely to be by analyzing the trajectory to infer the rules and mechanisms that could produce such a complex navigational path. The complexity of the trajectory, however, "is really a complexity in the surface of the beach, not a complexity in the ant." In reality, the ant may be using a set of very (d) complex rules: it is the interaction of these rules with the environment that actually produces the complex trajectory, not the ant alone. Put more generally, the parable of the ant illustrates that there is no necessary correlation between the complexity of an (e) observed behavior and the complexity of the mechanism that produces it.

* parable: 우화 ** trajectory: 이동 경로

P37 ✮✮✯ .... 2021 대비 수능 41 (고3)

윗글의 제목으로 가장 적절한 것은?

① Open the Mysterious Door to Environmental Complexity!
② Peaceful Coexistence of Human Beings and Animals
③ What Makes the Complexity of Animal Behavior?
④ Animals' Dilemma: Finding Their Way in a Human World
⑤ Environmental Influences on Human Behavior Complexity

P38 ✮✮✮ .... 2021 대비 수능 42 (고3)

밑줄 친 (a)~(e) 중에서 문맥상 낱말의 쓰임이 적절하지 <u>않은</u> 것은?
[3점]

① (a)　　② (b)　　③ (c)　　④ (d)　　⑤ (e)

Once an event is noticed, an onlooker must decide if it is truly an emergency. Emergencies are not always clearly (a) <u>labeled</u> as such; "smoke" pouring into a waiting room may be caused by fire, or it may merely indicate a leak in a steam pipe. Screams in the street may signal an attack or a family quarrel. A man lying in a doorway may be having a coronary — or he may simply be sleeping off a drunk.

A person trying to interpret a situation often looks at those around him to see how he should react. If everyone else is calm and indifferent, he will tend to remain so; if everyone else is reacting strongly, he is likely to become alert. This tendency is not merely blind conformity; ordinarily we derive much valuable information about new situations from how others around us behave. It's a (b) <u>rare</u> traveler who, in picking a roadside restaurant, chooses to stop at one where no other cars appear in the parking lot.

But occasionally the reactions of others provide (c) <u>accurate</u> information. The studied nonchalance of patients in a dentist's waiting room is a poor indication of their inner anxiety. It is considered embarrassing to "lose your cool" in public. In a potentially acute situation, then, everyone present will appear more (d) <u>unconcerned</u> than he is in fact. A crowd can thus force (e) <u>inaction</u> on its members by implying, through its passivity, that an event is not an emergency. Any individual in such a crowd fears that he may appear a fool if he behaves as though it were.

*coronary: 관상 동맥증 **nonchalance: 무관심, 냉담

P39 ★★※ .... 2023 대비 6월 모평 41 (고3)

윗글의 제목으로 가장 적절한 것은?

① Do We Judge Independently? The Effect of Crowds
② Winning Strategy: How Not to Be Fooled by Others
③ Do Emergencies Affect the Way of Our Thinking?
④ Stepping Towards Harmony with Your Neighbors
⑤ Ways of Helping Others in Emergent Situations

P40 ★★★※ .... 2023 대비 6월 모평 42 (고3)

밑줄 친 (a)~(e) 중에서 문맥상 낱말의 쓰임이 적절하지 <u>않은</u> 것은?

① (a)　　② (b)　　③ (c)　　④ (d)　　⑤ (e)

P41 ~ 44 ▶ 제한시간 12분

[P41 ~ P42] 다음 글을 읽고, 물음에 답하시오.

The right to privacy may extend only to the point where it does not restrict someone else's right to freedom of expression or right to information. The scope of the right to privacy is (a) <u>similarly</u> restricted by the general interest in preventing crime or in promoting public health. However, when we move away from the property-based notion of a right (where the right to privacy would protect, for example, images and personality), to modern notions of private and family life, we find it (b) <u>easier</u> to establish the limits of the right. This is, of course, the strength of the notion of privacy, in that it can adapt to meet changing expectations and technological advances.

In sum, *what* is privacy today? The concept includes a claim that we should be unobserved, and that certain information and images about us should not be (c) <u>circulated</u> without our permission. *Why* did these privacy claims arise? They arose because powerful people took offence at such observation. Furthermore, privacy incorporated the need to protect the family, home, and correspondence from arbitrary (d) <u>interference</u> and, in addition, there has been a determination to protect honour and reputation. *How* is privacy protected? Historically, privacy was protected by restricting circulation of the damaging material. But if the concept of privacy first became interesting legally as a response to reproductions of images through photography and newspapers, more recent technological advances, such as data storage, digital images, and the Internet, (e) <u>pose</u> new threats to privacy. The right to privacy is now being reinterpreted to meet those challenges.

* arbitrary: 임의의

P41 ✪ 2등급 대비 .... 2022 대비 6월 모평 41 (고3)

윗글의 제목으로 가장 적절한 것은?

① Side Effects of Privacy Protection Technologies
② The Legal Domain of Privacy Claims and Conflicts
③ The Right to Privacy: Evolving Concepts and Practices
④ Who Really Benefits from Looser Privacy Regulations?
⑤ Less Is More: Reduce State Intervention in Privacy!

P42 ✪ 2등급 대비 .... 2022 대비 6월 모평 42 (고3)

밑줄 친 (a)~(e) 중에서 문맥상 낱말의 쓰임이 적절하지 <u>않은</u> 것은? [3점]

① (a)   ② (b)   ③ (c)   ④ (d)   ⑤ (e)

There is evidence that even very simple algorithms can outperform expert judgement on simple prediction problems. For example, algorithms have proved more (a) <u>accurate</u> than humans in predicting whether a prisoner released on parole will go on to commit another crime, or in predicting whether a potential candidate will perform well in a job in future. In over 100 studies across many different domains, half of all cases show simple formulas make (b) <u>better</u> significant predictions than human experts, and the remainder (except a very small handful), show a tie between the two. When there are a lot of different factors involved and a situation is very uncertain, simple formulas can win out by focusing on the most important factors and being consistent, while human judgement is too easily influenced by particularly salient and perhaps (c) <u>irrelevant</u> considerations. A similar idea is supported by further evidence that 'checklists' can improve the quality of expert decisions in a range of domains by ensuring that important steps or considerations aren't missed when people are feeling (d) <u>relaxed</u>. For example, treating patients in intensive care can require hundreds of small actions per day, and one small error could cost a life. Using checklists to ensure that no crucial steps are missed has proved to be remarkably (e) <u>effective</u> in a range of medical contexts, from preventing live infections to reducing pneumonia.

*parole: 가석방 **salient: 두드러진 ***pneumonia: 폐렴

P43 ✪ 2등급 대비 .... 2023 대비 수능 41 (고3)

윗글의 제목으로 가장 적절한 것은?

① The Power of Simple Formulas in Decision Making
② Always Prioritise: Tips for Managing Big Data
③ Algorithms' Mistakes: The Myth of Simplicity
④ Be Prepared! Make a Checklist Just in Case
⑤ How Human Judgement Beats Algorithms

P44 ✪ 2등급 대비 .... 2023 대비 수능 42 (고3)

밑줄 친 (a)~(e) 중에서 문맥상 낱말의 쓰임이 적절하지 <u>않은</u> 것은?

① (a)　　② (b)　　③ (c)　　④ (d)　　⑤ (e)

[P45~P46] 다음 글을 읽고, 물음에 답하시오.

Climate change experts and environmental humanists alike agree that the climate crisis is, at its core, a crisis of the imagination and much of the popular imagination is shaped by fiction. In his 2016 book *The Great Derangement*, anthropologist and novelist Amitav Ghosh takes on this relationship between imagination and environmental management, arguing that humans have failed to respond to climate change at least in part because fiction (a) <u>fails</u> to believably represent it. Ghosh explains that climate change is largely absent from contemporary fiction because the cyclones, floods, and other catastrophes it brings to mind simply seem too "improbable" to belong in stories about everyday life. But climate change does not only reveal itself as a series of (b) <u>extraordinary</u> events. In fact, as environmentalists and ecocritics from Rachel Carson to Rob Nixon have pointed out, environmental change can be "imperceptible"; it proceeds (c) <u>rapidly</u>, only occasionally producing "explosive and spectacular" events. Most climate change impacts cannot be observed day-to-day, but they become (d) <u>visible</u> when we are confronted with their accumulated impacts.

Climate change evades our imagination because it poses significant representational challenges. It cannot be observed in "human time," which is why documentary filmmaker Jeff Orlowski, who tracks climate change effects on glaciers and coral reefs, uses "before and after" photographs taken several months apart in the same place to (e) <u>highlight</u> changes that occurred gradually.

*anthropologist: 인류학자 **catastrophe: 큰 재해 ***evade: 피하다

P45 ✪ 1등급 대비 .... 2023 대비 9월 모평 41 (고3)

윗글의 제목으로 가장 적절한 것은?

① Differing Attitudes Towards Current Climate Issues
② Slow but Significant: The History of Ecological Movements
③ The Silence of Imagination in Representing Climate Change
④ Vivid Threats: Climate Disasters Spreading in Local Areas
⑤ The Rise and Fall of Environmentalism and Ecocriticism

P46 ✪ 1등급 대비 .... 2023 대비 9월 모평 42 (고3)

밑줄 친 (a)~(e) 중에서 문맥상 낱말의 쓰임이 적절하지 않은 것은? [3점]

① (a)　　② (b)　　③ (c)　　④ (d)　　⑤ (e)

Classifying things together into groups is something we do all the time, and it isn't hard to see why. Imagine trying to shop in a supermarket where the food was arranged in random order on the shelves: tomato soup next to the white bread in one aisle, chicken soup in the back next to the 60-watt light bulbs, one brand of cream cheese in front and another in aisle 8 near the cookies. The task of finding what you want would be (a) time-consuming and extremely difficult, if not impossible.

In the case of a supermarket, someone had to (b) design the system of classification. But there is also a ready-made system of classification embodied in our language. The word "dog," for example, groups together a certain class of animals and distinguishes them from other animals. Such a grouping may seem too (c) abstract to be called a classification, but this is only because you have already mastered the word. As a child learning to speak, you had to work hard to (d) learn the system of classification your parents were trying to teach you. Before you got the hang of it, you probably made mistakes, like calling the cat a dog. If you hadn't learned to speak, the whole world would seem like the (e) unorganized supermarket; you would be in the position of an infant, for whom every object is new and unfamiliar. In learning the principles of classification, therefore, we'll be learning about the structure that lies at the core of our language.

P47 ✪ 1등급 대비 ·············· 2022 대비 수능 41 (고3)

윗글의 제목으로 가장 적절한 것은?

① Similarities of Strategies in Sales and Language Learning
② Classification: An Inherent Characteristic of Language
③ Exploring Linguistic Issues Through Categorization
④ Is a Ready-Made Classification System Truly Better?
⑤ Dilemmas of Using Classification in Language Education

P48 ✪ 1등급 대비 ·············· 2022 대비 수능 42 (고3)

밑줄 친 (a)~(e) 중에서 문맥상 쓰임이 적절하지 않은 것은?

① (a) ② (b) ③ (c) ④ (d) ⑤ (e)

P 어휘 Review

※ 다음 영어는 우리말 뜻을, 우리말은 영어 단어를 〈보기〉에서 찾아 쓰시오.

〈보기〉

경향, 성향	prescribed	신뢰할 수 있는	era
superstition	서서히	틈새	fearlessly
underestimate	interference	새기다	투쟁, 분투

01 tendency _____

02 niche _____

03 struggle _____

04 gradually _____

05 credible _____

06 규정된 _____

07 과소평가하다 _____

08 미신 _____

09 간섭 _____

10 시대 _____

※ 다음 우리말에 알맞은 영어 표현을 찾아 연결하시오.

11 ~에 관여하다 •   • belong to

12 ~에 속하다 •   • engage in

13 ~을 배제하다 •   • rule out

14 ~을 가지고 떠나다 •   • be inclined to

15 ~하는 경향이 있다 •   • come away with

※ 다음 우리말 표현에 맞는 단어를 고르시오.

16 명예와 평판을 보호하다 ⇒ protect honour and (reputation / repetition)

17 꽤 격렬한 분투의 대가로 ⇒ at the price of a fairly (intense / tension) struggle

18 감기의 지속 기간 ⇒ (durability / duration) of colds

19 구체적인 정보의 부재 속에서 ⇒ in a(n) (absence / presence) of specific information

20 실험 대상자들을 나누다 ⇒ divide the (objects / subjects)

※ 다음 문장의 빈칸에 알맞은 단어를 〈보기〉에서 찾아 쓰시오.

〈보기〉

perspectives	distinct	revive	improbable
dependent	artfully	mistakenly	negotiations
coordinate	circulated	ends	dedication

21 정치는 어떤 공동의 목표와 목적을 향한 독특한 집단 활동이다.
⇒ Politics is a unique collective activity that is directed at certain common goals and _____.

22 우리는 우리의 생존을 위해 우리 주변의 사람들에게 완전히 의존적이다.
⇒ We are totally _____ on those around us for our survival.

23 개인의 관점은 또한 상황에 따라 달라질 수도 있다.
⇒ Individual _____ may also be context dependent.

24 모든 협상은 고정된 파이를 수반한다.
⇒ All _____ involve a fixed pie.

25 사이클론, 홍수, 그리고 다른 큰 재해들은 그야말로 너무 '있을 것 같지 않아' 보인다.
⇒ The cyclones, floods, and other catastrophes simply seem too "_____".

26 시인은 동일한 언어의 원료를 교묘히 조작한다.
⇒ The poet _____ manipulates the same raw materials of his language.

27 그는 모든 세부 사항을 별개의 것으로 기억했다.
⇒ He remembered every detail as _____.

28 우리에 관한 특정 정보가 우리의 허락 없이 유포되어서는 안 된다.
⇒ Certain information about us should not be _____ without our permission.

29 그 작가는 세상에 대한 자신의 그림을 모든 독자가 공유한다고 잘못 가정한다.
⇒ The author has _____ assumed that his picture of the world is shared by all his readers.

Q 복합 문단의 이해

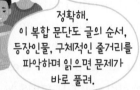

소설 읽을 때 무엇을 파악하며 읽니?

음... 등장인물과 줄거리요!

정확해. 이 복합 문단도 글의 순서, 등장인물, 구체적인 줄거리를 파악하며 읽으면 문제가 바로 풀려.

★유형 설명 ▷◁ 유형 풀이 비법

1 순서 배열 문제

● 주어진 글 (A)에 이어질 내용을 순서에 맞게 배열한 것으로 가장 적절한 것은?

　① (B) ─ (D) ─ (C)　② (C) ─ (B) ─ (D)

• 시간의 흐름 순 배열이 원칙이다.
• 단, 과거 회상 글의 경우, 중간에 과거 내용이 나올 수 있다. (예외)

2 지칭 추론 문제

● 밑줄 친 (a)~(e) 중에서 가리키는 대상이 나머지 넷과 다른 것은?

　① (a)　② (b)　③ (c)　④ (d)　⑤ (e)

• 각 선지 앞부분에 특히 유의한다.

3 내용 불일치 문제

● 윗글에 관한 내용으로 적절하지 않은 것은?

① Sally는 사진 수업 후 집으로 돌아왔다.

• 문단들의 흐름과 무관하게 (A)~(D)의 순서대로 선택지가 구성된다.

> Tip 새로운 유형의 문제들이 출제되는 것이 아니므로 그동안의 유형 풀이 비법들을 적용시켜 정답을 찾는다.

★최신 수능 경향 분석

대비연도	월	문항번호	지문 주제	난이도
2025	11	43~45번	아빠 Ethan과 아들 Sean의 하이킹	✮✮✮
	9	43~45번	중고 쇼핑 앱에서 Anna에게 식물을 구매하게 된 Helen	✮✮✮
	6	43~45번	긴장을 극복한 성공적인 공연	✮✮✮
2024	11	43~45번	비극을 극복한 Clara와 함께 자전거를 탄 Emma	✮✮✮
	9	43~45번	산에서의 하룻밤	✮✮✮
	6	43~45번	선물을 되찾은 Ellen	✮✮✮
2023	11	43~45번	아빠의 생신 선물	✮✮✮
	9	43~45번	Emilia와 Layla의 영국 여행	✮✮✮
	6	43~45번	기숙사 방 꾸미기	✮✮✮

★2025 수능 출제 분석

43번~45번 문제 모두 오답률이 아주 낮은 쉬운 문제였다. 아들 Sean이 중학교에 다니기 시작한 이후로 아빠 Ethan과 관계가 소원해진 것을 알아차리게 된 엄마 Grace가 아빠와 아들이 하이킹 가보기를 권하는 내용의 흐름만 파악하면 쉽게 풀 수 있었다.

★2026 수능 예측

필자나 제3자의 개인적인 경험을 다룬 긴 지문을 제시하고, 단락 순서 정하기 한 문제, 가리키는 대상이 다른 것을 찾는 한 문제, 그리고 내용 일치 또는 불일치를 묻는 한 문제로 구성되는 것은 변함없을 것이다.

🔑 어휘 및 표현 Preview

☐ **thrilled** 기쁜
☐ **receive** 받다
☐ **notification** 알림
☐ **second-hand** 중고의
☐ **velvety** 부드러운
☐ **almost** 거의
☐ **give up** 포기하다
☐ **for sale** 팔려고 내놓은
☐ **abroad** 해외로
☐ **current** 현재의

☐ **half** 절반
☐ **market rate** 시장 시세
☐ **arrive** 도착하다
☐ **identify** 알아보다
☐ **stick out of** ~밖으로 삐져나오다
☐ **glossy** 윤기가 나는
☐ **immediately** 바로, 즉시
☐ **purchase** 구매하다
☐ **expert** 전문가

☐ **condition** 상태
☐ **advice** 조언
☐ **hand over** 건네주다
☐ **cash** 현금
☐ **lively** 활기 넘치는
☐ **exclaim** 외치다, 소리치다
☐ **perform** 공연하다
☐ **pick out** 선택하다
☐ **traffic** 교통
☐ **apologize** 사과하다

☐ **enter** 들어가다
☐ **silent** 고요한
☐ **fascinate** 매혹[매료]하다
☐ **flawless** 나무랄 데 없는
☐ **audience** 관객
☐ **praise** 칭찬
☐ **clothes** 옷
☐ **quickly** 빠르게
☐ **beam** 활짝 웃다
☐ **rehearsal** 예행연습

Q 복합 문단의 이해

1st 글의 세부 사항을 묻는 일치/불일치 문제를 먼저 풀면서 글의 내용을 대략적으로 확인하세요.
2nd 마찬가지로 글의 세부 사항을 파악해야 하는 지칭 추론 문제를 통해 다시 한번 글의 내용을 확인하세요.
3rd 파악한 세부 사항을 활용하여 각 문단의 내용을 요약하고, 순서를 맞춰 보세요.

[Q01~Q03] 다음 글을 읽고, 물음에 답하시오.

(A)

Fighting against the force of the water was a thrilling challenge. Sophia tried to keep herself planted firmly in the boat, paying attention to the waves crashing against the rocks. As the water got rougher, she was forced to paddle harder to keep the waves from tossing her into the water. Her friends Mia and Rebecca were paddling eagerly behind her to balance the boat. They were soaked from all of the spray. Mia shouted to Sophia, "Are you OK? Aren't (a) you scared?"

*paddle: 노를 젓다

(B)

"You've got a good point. It's a real advantage to graduate from college with the mindset of a daring adventurer," Mia said. Rebecca quickly added, "That's why I went to Mongolia before I started my first job out of college. Teaching English there for two months was a big challenge for me. But (b) I learned a lot from the experience. It really gave me the courage to try anything in life." Listening to her friends, Sophia looked at (c) her own reflection in the water and saw a confident young woman smiling back at her.

(C)

"I'm great!" Sophia shouted back excitedly. Even though the boat was getting thrown around, the girls managed to avoid hitting any rocks. Suddenly, almost as quickly as the water had got rougher, the river seemed to calm down, and they all felt relaxed. With a sigh of relief, Sophia looked around. "Wow! What a wonderful view!" (d) she shouted. The scenery around them was breathtaking. Everyone was speechless. As they enjoyed the emerald green Rocky Mountains, Mia said, "No wonder rafting is the best thing to do in Colorado!"

(D)

Agreeing with her friend, Rebecca gave a thumbs-up. "Sophia, your choice was excellent!" she said with a delighted smile. "I thought you were afraid of water, though, Sophia," Mia said. Sophia explained, "Well, I was before I started rafting. But I graduate from college in a few months. And, before I do, I wanted to do something really adventurous to test my bravery. I thought that if I did something completely crazy, it might give (e) me more confidence when I'm interviewing for jobs." Now they could see why she had suggested going rafting.

Q01 ✽✽✽ ⋯⋯⋯⋯⋯⋯⋯⋯⋯⋯ 2022 대비 6월 모평 43 (고3)

주어진 글 (A)에 이어질 내용을 순서에 맞게 배열한 것으로 가장 적절한 것은?

① (B)—(D)—(C)   ② (C)—(B)—(D)
③ (C)—(D)—(B)   ④ (D)—(B)—(C)
⑤ (D)—(C)—(B)

Q02 ✽✽✽ ⋯⋯⋯⋯⋯⋯⋯⋯⋯⋯ 2022 대비 6월 모평 44 (고3)

밑줄 친 (a)~(e) 중에서 가리키는 대상이 나머지 넷과 다른 것은?

① (a)   ② (b)   ③ (c)   ④ (d)   ⑤ (e)

Q03 ✽✽✽ ⋯⋯⋯⋯⋯⋯⋯⋯⋯⋯ 2022 대비 6월 모평 45 (고3)

윗글에 관한 내용으로 적절하지 <u>않은</u> 것은?

① Mia와 Rebecca는 보트의 균형을 유지하려고 애썼다.
② Rebecca는 몽골에서 영어를 가르친 경험이 있다.
③ Sophia와 친구들이 함께 탄 보트는 바위에 부딪치지 않았다.
④ Sophia는 래프팅을 하기 전에는 물을 두려워했다.
⑤ Sophia는 용기를 시험할 모험을 대학 졸업 후에 하길 원했다.

Q03

1st 글의 세부 사항을 묻는 일치/불일치 문제를 먼저 풀면서 글의 내용을 대략적으로 확인하세요.

1) 먼저 선택지의 핵심 어구에 □ 표시를 하고, 글에서 찾아야 할 정보가 무엇인지 확인합시다.

① Mia와 Rebecca는 보트의 균형을 유지하려고 애썼다.
② Rebecca는 몽골에서 영어를 가르친 경험이 있다.
③ Sophia와 친구들이 함께 탄 보트는 바위에 부딪치지 않았다.
④ Sophia는 래프팅을 하기 전에는 물을 두려워했다.
⑤ Sophia는 용기를 시험할 모험을 대학 졸업 후에 하길 원했죠.

● 우리가 찾아야 하는 다섯 가지 정보를 찾았어요.
① Mia와 Rebecca가 보트의 균형을 유지하려고 애썼는지 아닌지, ② Rebecca가 몽골에서 영어를 가르쳤었는지 아닌지, ③ 세 사람이 탄 보트가 바위에 부딪쳤는지 안 부딪쳤는지, ④ Sophia가 원래는 물을 두려워했었는지, ⑤ Sophia가 모험을 대학을 졸업한 후에 하길 원했는지 아니면 대학 졸업 전에 하길 원했는지를 글을 읽으면서 확인하면 정답을 찾을 수 있어요.

2) 선택지의 일치 여부를 확인할 수 있는 단서는 (A), (B), (C), (D) 문단에 순서대로 제시돼요. ①과 (A) 문단부터 확인해 봅시다.

Her friends Mia and Rebecca / were paddling
그녀의 친구들인 Mia와 Rebecca는 / 열심히 노를 젓고 있었다
eagerly / behind her / to balance the boat. //
/ 그녀의 뒤에서 / 보트의 균형을 유지하려고 //

● to balance the boat가 언급된 문장을 찾았나요?
Her/her는 앞에 등장한 Sophia를 가리키는 대명사예요. 즉, 이 글에는 Sophia와 Mia, 그리고 Rebecca, 이렇게 세 사람이 등장하는 것이죠. Sophia의 친구인 Mia와 Rebecca가 보트의 균형을 유지하려고 열심히 노를 저었다고 했어요.

3) ②의 핵심 단어는 '몽골'이에요.

Rebecca quickly added, / "That's why I went to
Rebecca가 재빨리 덧붙였다 / "그게 내가 몽골에 간 이유야
Mongolia / before I started my first job / out of
/ 내가 내 첫 직장 생활을 시작하기 전에 / 대학을
college. //
나와서 //
Teaching English there / for two months / was a big.
그곳에서 영어를 가르친 것은 / 두 달 동안 / 큰 도전이었어
challenge / for me. //
/ 내게 //

● 몽골은 영어로 Mongolia라고 해요.
Mongolia가 등장한 문장을 찾아서 Rebecca가 몽골에서 영어를 가르친 경험이 있는지 없는지를 확인하면 돼요.
Rebecca가 "그게 내가 ❶(   )에 간 이유이고, 그곳에서 영어를 가르친 것은 내게 큰 도전이었어."라고 말했다는 내용이군요.

4) 세 사람의 보트가 바위에 부딪쳤는지 확인합시다.

Even though the boat was getting thrown around, /
보트가 이리저리 내던져지고 있었지만 /
the girls managed to avoid / hitting any rocks. //
그 여자들은 피했다 / 어느 바위에도 부딪치는 것을 //

● 이번에는 hitting any rocks가 포함된 문장을 찾았어요.
hitting any rocks는 '바위에 부딪치는 것'을 의미하는데, 앞에 '피하다'라는 뜻의 동사인 avoid에서 파생한 to avoid가 있으니까 바위에 부딪치지 않았다는 의미가 되죠.

5) Sophia는 물을 두려워했었나요?

"I thought you were afraid of water, though,
"근데, Sophia, 나는 네가 물을 무서워 한다고 생각했어"라고
Sophia," / Mia said. // Sophia explained, / "Well, I
/ Mia가 말했다 // Sophia가 설명했다 / "음, 나는
was / before I started rafting. //
그랬지 / 내가 래프팅을 시작하기 전에는 //

● afraid of는 '~을 두려워하는'이라는 의미예요.
Mia가 Sophia에게 "난 네가 물을 무서워 한다고 생각했어."라고 말했고, Sophia가 "래프팅을 시작하기 전에는 그랬지."라고 대답한 거예요.

6) 마지막으로 ⑤의 일치 여부를 확인해 봅시다.

But I graduate from college / in a few months. //
하지만 나는 대학을 졸업해 / 몇 달 후에 //
And, before I do, / I wanted to do something really
그리고 내가 그러기 전에 / 나는 진짜 모험적인 것을 해보고 싶었어
adventurous / to test my bravery. //
/ 내 용기를 시험할 //

● '~을 졸업하다'는 영어로 graduate from으로 표현해요.
Sophia가 "난 몇 달 후에 대학을 졸업하는데, 그러기 전에 내 용기를 시험할 모험적인 것을 해보고 싶었어."라고 말했어요. before에 밑줄을 그으면 ❷(   )이 글의 내용과 일치하지 않는다는 것을 알 수 있죠!

Q02

2nd 마찬가지로 글의 세부 사항을 파악해야 하는 지칭 추론 문제를 통해 다시 한번 글의 내용을 확인하세요.

1) 지칭 추론 문제는 선택지의 앞부분을 확인해야 돼요. (a)가 가리키는 대상부터 파악해 봅시다.

Mia shouted to Sophia, / "Are you OK? // Aren't
Mia는 Sophia에게 소리쳤다 / "너 괜찮니 // 너 무섭지
(a) you scared?" //
않니"라고 //

● **누가 누구에게 하는 말인가요?**

Mia가 Sophia에게 말하는 것이니까 Mia의 말에서 you는 Sophia를 가리켜요.

● **(A) 문단의 마지막 문장을 봤으니 이어질 내용을 생각해 볼까요?**

(A)는 Mia가 Sophia에게 괜찮은지 물어보는 내용으로 끝났어요.
그럼 당연히 이어지는 문장에는 Sophia가 괜찮다거나 괜찮지 않다고 대답하는 내용이 포함되어 있어야겠죠.
이 점을 기억했다가 이어지는 순서 문제를 해결해 봅시다.

2) (b)가 포함된 문장은 누가 하는 말인가요?

Rebecca quickly added, / "That's why I went to
Rebecca가 재빨리 덧붙였다   / "그게 내가 몽골에 간 이유야

Mongolia / before I started my first job / out of
Mongolia   / 내가 내 첫 직장 생활을 시작하기 전에   / 대학을

college. //   (…)
나와서 //   (중략)

But (b) I learned a lot / from the experience. //
그런데 나는 많은 것을 배웠어 / 그 경험에서   //

● **Rebecca quickly added라고 했어요.**

Rebecca가 하는 말에 등장하는 I는 당연히 Rebecca겠죠.

3) (c)는 물에 비친 자신의 모습을 보는 사람이에요.

Listening to her friends, / Sophia looked / at (c) her
자기 친구들의 말을 들으면서   / Sophia는 보았고   / 물에 비친 그녀

own reflection in the water / and saw a confident
자신의 모습을   / 자신만만한 젊은 여자를 보았다

young woman / smiling back at her. //
             / 자신에게 미소를 되돌려주는 //

● **'자신의' 모습을 보는 것이니까 문장의 주어를 파악해야 해요.**

주어 Sophia에 두 개의 동사, looked와 saw가 연결되는 구조예요. Sophia가 물에 비친 자신의 모습을 보는 것이니까 her는 **❸**(   )를 가리키죠.

(a), (b), (c) 중에 나머지와 다른 사람을 가리키는 대명사가 있어요. 정답은 나왔지만, 확실히 하기 위해 나머지 문장도 빠르게 확인해 봅시다.

4) 누가 멋진 풍경이라고 소리친 건가요?

With a sigh of relief, / Sophia looked around. //
안도의 한숨을 쉬면서   / Sophia는 주변을 둘러보았다 //

"Wow! // What a wonderful view!" / (d) she
"우아   // 정말 멋진 풍경이다"라고   / 그녀는

shouted. //
소리쳤다 //

● **she 복 가리키는 대상을 파악하려면 앞 문장을 봐야 돼요.**

안도의 한숨을 쉬면서 주변을 둘러본 Sophia가 "정말 멋진 풍경이네!"라고 소리친 것이군요.

5) 이제 (e)만 확인하면 돼요.

Sophia explained, / "Well, I was / before I started
Sophia가 설명했다   / "음, 나는 그랬지   / 내가 래프팅을 시작하기

rafting. //   (…)
전에는 //   (중략)

I thought / that if I did something completely crazy,
나는 생각했어 / 내가 완전히 미친 짓을 하면

/ it might give (e) me / more confidence / when I'm
/ 그것이 나에게 줄 거라고   / 더 많은 자신감을   / 취업 면접할 때" //

interviewing for jobs." //

● **Sophia가 하는 말이에요.**

Sophia가 하는 말에서 1인칭 대명사인 me가 가리키는 것은 Sophia죠!

Q01

3rd 파악한 세부 사항을 활용하여 각 문단의 내용을 요약하고, 순서를 맞춰 보세요.

1) 두 문제를 풀면서 많은 세부 사항을 파악했어요. 이를 토대로 각 문단을 요약해 봅시다.

(A) Sophia, Mia, Rebecca는 거친 물살에 맞서 보트의 균형을 유지하며 열심히 노를 저음
(B) Rebecca가 첫 직장 생활을 시작하기 전에 몽골에서 영어를 가르쳤던 자신의 경험을 이야기하며 Mia의 말에 동의함
(C) 거칠었던 물살이 빠르게 잔잔해졌고, 세 사람은 주변을 둘러보며 경치를 즐김
(D) Sophia는 대학을 졸업하기 전에 모험적인 것을 해보고 싶었다고 이야기함

2) 이제 논리적인 순서로 각 문단을 배열해 볼까요?

지칭 추론 문제를 풀면서 우리가 생각했던 것처럼, Mia가 Sophia에게 괜찮은지 묻는 내용으로 끝난 (A)에는 Sophia가 "나는 아주 좋아!"라고 대답하는 문장으로 시작한 (C)가 이어지는 것이 적절해요.
(C)의 마지막 문장에서는 Mia가 래프팅이 Colorado에서 할 수 있는 최고의 활동이라고 했는데, (D)에서 Rebecca가 Mia의 말에 동의하며 엄지손가락을 들어 올렸죠. (D)의 후반부에서는 Sophia가 래프팅을 제안한 이유가 등장하는데, 대학을 졸업하기 전에 모험적인 것을 해보는 것이 취업 면접에서 더 많은 **❹**(   )을 줄 거라고 생각했다는 게 그 이유예요.
Sophia의 이 말에 Mia가 동의하고, Rebecca가 자신의 비슷한 경험을 이야기하는 (B)가 (D) 뒤에, 맨 마지막 문단으로 이어지는 것이 자연스럽죠.

단어장

PATTERN PRACTICE

Q04 ~ 06 ▶ 제한시간 7.5분

[Q04 ~ Q06] 다음 글을 읽고, 물음에 답하시오.

(A)

"Do you remember when Sean used to tell me that I was the best dad in the world?" Ethan asked his wife, Grace. "Yes, I do. I always envied your relationship with Sean," she replied. Ethan then shared how things had changed since (a) his son started middle school. Grace had noticed Ethan often pushing Sean to study harder. "Maybe he isn't that into school right now. How about going hiking, just the two of you?" she suggested. He agreed, and realizing that both his and Sean's hiking jackets were still at the laundry, he asked his wife to go and pick them up with him.

(B)

Ethan and Grace came back home with the jackets and checked if Sean had everything else he needed for hiking. Luckily, in his drawers they found his hat, shoes, sunglasses, and hiking sticks. When Sean returned from school, Ethan softly said, "Sean, let's go hiking this Saturday, just the two of us." Though Sean thanked (b) him for the suggestion, he said he had to go to the library. Grace stepped in, "You know, the weather this weekend will be the best of the year. Why not enjoy it?" After a moment's hesitation, (c) he agreed.

(C)

"When did you bring the jackets in?" the clerk at the laundry asked. "Maybe two weeks ago," Ethan replied. Then, Grace quickly reminded (d) him, "Honey, we actually left them here a month ago." The clerk went into the storage area to look for the clothes. Finally, he returned with the jackets and handed them to Ethan. The clerk politely said, "I am sorry, but please collect your items earlier next time. Our storage is too full." Ethan felt embarrassed for the late collection and apologized.

(D)

The weather was perfect. Ethan and Sean set off hiking along the valley by Aicken Mountain. They walked in silence until Sean fell over a rock and twisted his ankle. Realizing he couldn't walk, Ethan carried his son down on his back. He felt Sean's heartbeat, something he hadn't felt since Sean was a baby. Suddenly, Sean said, "Dad, I'm sorry. At some point, I started to become afraid of disappointing (e) you. But you are still the best dad." Energized, he felt no weight on his back and replied, "You are the best son, no matter what."

Q04 ✿❋❋.. 2025 대비 수능 43 (고3)

주어진 글 (A)에 이어질 내용을 순서에 맞게 배열한 것으로 가장 적절한 것은?

① (B) — (D) — (C)   ② (C) — (B) — (D)
③ (C) — (D) — (B)   ④ (D) — (B) — (C)
⑤ (D) — (C) — (B)

Q05 ✿❋❋.. 2025 대비 수능 44 (고3)

밑줄 친 (a)~(e) 중에서 가리키는 대상이 나머지 넷과 다른 것은?

① (a)   ② (b)   ③ (c)   ④ (d)   ⑤ (e)

Q06 ✿❋❋.. 2025 대비 수능 45 (고3)

윗글에 관한 내용으로 적절하지 않은 것은?

① Grace는 Ethan과 Sean의 관계를 부러워했다고 말했다.
② Grace는 Ethan에게 Sean과 둘이서 하이킹할 것을 권했다.
③ Sean의 선글라스가 서랍장 안에 있었다.
④ Ethan은 혼자서 세탁소에 하이킹 재킷을 찾으러 갔다.
⑤ Sean은 하이킹하는 도중 돌에 걸려 넘어졌다.

[Q07 ~ Q09] 다음 글을 읽고, 물음에 답하시오.

(A)

Helen was thrilled when she received a notification on a second-hand shopping app from a seller named Anna. For months, she had been looking for a *Philodendron gloriosum*, a Colombian plant with dark, velvety leaves shaped like hearts. She had almost given up on getting one. Anna, though, had put one up for sale. The posting read, "(a) I'm selling my favorite plant, because I'm moving abroad. If you pick it up today from Edincester Heights, you can have it for the current price, which is half the market rate."

(B)

Arriving at the building, Helen could identify Julia by the large paper bag she was holding. The bag had leaves sticking out of the top. (b) She said, "You must be Julia!" Laughing, the woman said, "Yes! Please take good care of this plant. Anna had it for six years, so she considers it family." From the bag, she pulled out another plant, a tiny one with thick, glossy leaves. "Are you familiar with this? It's called a Dragon's Tail. (c) My housemate said you could take it too, if you'd like."

(C)

Helen immediately messaged the seller. "Hello! I'm interested in purchasing (d) your plant. If it works for your schedule, I can be there in 10 minutes!" Anna replied, "Hi, there! I am at work right now, but my housemate, Julia, can meet you in front of the building." Unable to believe her good luck, Helen typed back in excitement, "Great! I can leave now. I'll wear a black baseball cap."

(D)

Helen exclaimed, "Yes, I'd love to! Please thank Anna for me. Both are in such wonderful condition. Do you have any tips for keeping them in good shape?" Handing over the bag, Julia replied, "I'm not a plant expert, but I know that Anna kept them away from windows to avoid direct sunlight. Why don't you message (e) her? She would be happy to offer advice." "I'll be sure to do that," Helen said, as she handed over the cash.

Q07 ✽❀❀ .... 2025 대비 9월 모평 43 (고3)

주어진 글 (A)에 이어질 내용을 순서에 맞게 배열한 것으로 가장 적절한 것은?

① (B) — (D) — (C) ② (C) — (B) — (D)

③ (C) — (D) — (B) ④ (D) — (B) — (C)

⑤ (D) — (C) — (B)

Q08 ✽❀❀ .... 2025 대비 9월 모평 44 (고3)

밑줄 친 (a)~(e) 중에서 가리키는 대상이 나머지 넷과 다른 것은?

① (a) ② (b) ③ (c) ④ (d) ⑤ (e)

Q09 ✽❀❀ .... 2025 대비 9월 모평 45 (고3)

윗글에 관한 내용으로 적절하지 않은 것은?

① Helen은 중고 거래 앱에서 알림을 받았다.

② Julia는 큰 종이 가방을 들고 있었다.

③ Helen은 판매자와 메시지를 주고받았다.

④ Helen은 야구 모자를 쓰겠다고 답했다.

⑤ Julia는 자신이 식물 전문가라고 말했다.

(A)

Garcia stood outside Frontcountry Mall, waiting for his brother, Jeff. Garcia's band had been chosen to perform at the welcoming ceremony for a large group of students from their sister university in Singapore. Garcia was hoping to find the perfect clothing for the performance. That was why (a) he had asked Jeff to help him pick out new clothes. "I'm sorry. I'm late because traffic was terrible," Jeff apologized as he arrived. "Don't worry. I haven't waited long," Garcia replied as they entered the lively shopping center.

(B)

The band performance was the first event of the ceremony. The host introduced the band, and each member took their place on stage. Garcia stood at the center of the stage. As he started playing, everyone fell silent, fascinated by the music. Garcia's trumpet playing was flawless. When the band was finished, the audience loudly cheered. After the show, Jeff approached Garcia. "It was fantastic. I think that was the best performance I've ever seen," (b) he said. Garcia beamed with joy at his brother's praise.

(C)

Garcia felt good as he arrived at the concert hall for the rehearsal wearing his new clothes. His confidence was, however, quickly changed to nervousness when he thought of how many people would be there. As the rehearsal began, (c) he struggled with the rhythm, making several mistakes. Tom, Garcia's band mate, came over and put a hand on Garcia's back, saying, "Don't worry, I'll be right behind (d) you." He looked at his friend, took a deep breath and started to feel much better.

(D)

"Aren't these cool?" Garcia asked, pointing at a patterned red shirt and yellow pants he had found in the store. "Um, I think they're a bit too colorful," Jeff objected. Instead, Jeff picked out a white shirt and black jeans. He asked the store clerk, "Don't you think these would look great on (e) my brother?" The clerk stopped her work and looked at the clothes, quickly agreeing with Jeff's choice. Garcia bought the recommended clothes, saying, "Maybe I'll wear these for tonight's rehearsal, too."

Q10 ✶✶✶ ································· 2025 대비 6월 모평 43 (고3)

주어진 글 (A)에 이어질 내용을 순서에 맞게 배열한 것으로 가장 적절한 것은?

① (B) — (D) — (C) ② (C) — (B) — (D)
③ (C) — (D) — (B) ④ (D) — (B) — (C)
⑤ (D) — (C) — (B)

Q11 ✶✶✶ ································· 2025 대비 6월 모평 44 (고3)

밑줄 친 (a)~(e) 중에서 가리키는 대상이 나머지 넷과 다른 것은?

① (a) ② (b) ③ (c) ④ (d) ⑤ (e)

Q12 ✶✶✶ ································· 2025 대비 6월 모평 45 (고3)

윗글에 관한 내용으로 적절하지 않은 것은?

① Jeff는 교통 체증 때문에 늦었다.
② Garcia는 환영식 공연 무대의 중앙에 섰다.
③ 밴드가 환영식 공연에서 연주를 마치자 관객은 환호했다.
④ Garcia는 리허설을 앞두고 긴장감을 느꼈다.
⑤ Garcia는 본인이 가리킨 색상의 옷을 구매했다.

[Q13~Q15] 다음 글을 읽고, 물음에 답하시오.

(A)

One frosty morning, a rabbit was jumping about on a hill. There stood a snowman which had been made by some children. He had a broom in his hand and a carrot nose. The rabbit saw the carrot and swallowed hard. "I will have a delicious breakfast," (a) he thought and jumped up, reaching out for the snowman's nose. But before the rabbit even touched him, something hit him hard.

*broom: 빗자루

(B)

Excited by the offer, the rabbit told the snowman to wait and disappeared. (b) He returned shortly, dragging a sled and said to the snowman, "Let's go!" The sled ran smoothly over the snow. The snowman with joy waved his broom. After a while, they arrived in the middle of the village. "Here we are," said the rabbit. "Thank you. Here's the carrot," said the snowman, giving (c) him his carrot.

*sled: 썰매

(C)

The rabbit hesitated for a moment. "Come on, take it. I have a feeling that I'll get a new one," urged the snowman. (d) He finally accepted the carrot and leapt back into the woods. Not long after, the children gathered maround the snowman. Noticing that he had no nose, they gave him a fresh carrot. From that time on, the snowman stood in the middle of the village, with a broom in his hand and a marvelous new carrot nose.

(D)

"Go Away!" the snowman threatened him with his great broom. "Sorry, Mr. Snowman, I just..." murmured the rabbit. "You wanted to eat my nose!," (e) he shouted. "I was so hungry and it looked so tasty," apologized the rabbit. The snowman thought for a moment. "Hmm... Here, I am bored by myself. I would like to go to the village where the children are. If you take me there, I'll give you my carrot," said the snowman.

*murmur: 웅얼거리다

Q13 ✿❀❀ .... 2024 실시 10월 학평 43 (고3)

주어진 글 (A)에 이어질 내용을 순서에 맞게 배열한 것으로 가장 적절한 것은?

① (B) ─ (D) ─ (C)
② (C) ─ (B) ─ (D)
③ (C) ─ (D) ─ (B)
④ (D) ─ (B) ─ (C)
⑤ (D) ─ (C) ─ (B)

Q14 ✿❀❀ .... 2024 실시 10월 학평 44 (고3)

밑줄 친 (a)~(e) 중에서 가리키는 대상이 나머지 넷과 <u>다른</u> 것은?

① (a)   ② (b)   ③ (c)   ④ (d)   ⑤ (e)

Q15 ✿❀❀ .... 2024 실시 10월 학평 45 (고3)

윗글에 관한 내용으로 적절하지 <u>않은</u> 것은?

① 토끼는 당근을 보고 침을 삼켰다.
② 토끼는 눈사람에게 기다리라고 말하고 사라졌다.
③ 눈사람은 기쁨에 빗자루를 흔들었다.
④ 아이들은 눈사람에게 싱싱한 당근을 주었다.
⑤ 토끼가 빗자루로 눈사람을 위협했다.

(A)

On the northwestern coastline of Lake Superior is the city of Duluth, the westernmost port for transatlantic cargo ships. A lot of cargo comes into Duluth: coal, iron ore, grain, clothing and, in November 1962, a mongoose from India. The merchant seamen had enjoyed his company on the long journey and had sat drinking tea with him, but they decided he deserved a life on dry land so they presented (a) him as a gift to the city's Lake Superior Zoo. Lloyd Hackl, the director of the zoo, was delighted and named (b) his new mongoose Mr. Magoo. His fate took an unexpected turn when, labeled an invasive species, federal agents sentenced him to death.

(B)

Living out his days in the zoo, Mr. Magoo became a beloved figure. His daily routine included enjoying an egg, sipping tea, and charming zoo workers with his friendly nature. Popular among visitors, especially children, he received numerous letters and Christmas cards. When Mr. Magoo died peacefully in January 1968, his obituary in the *Duluth Herald* read: "OUR MR. MAGOO OF ZOO IS DEAD." The new zoo director, Basil Norton, vowed not to replace (c) him: "Another mongoose could never take his place in the hearts and affections of Duluth people," he said.

(C)

The citizens of Duluth were not taking the death sentence lying down. It was pointed out that, as the only mongoose in the country, Mr. Magoo was never going to be able to reproduce, so the country was unlikely to be overrun by the species. They demanded he be allowed to live out his days in peace. Petitions were signed and sent to powerful figures like the U.S. Secretary of the Interior Stewart Udall, U.S. Senator Hubert Humphrey, and Duluth Mayor George Johnson. A campaign, brilliantly nicknamed *No Noose for the Mongoose*, was backed by more than 10,000 citizens. There were even suggestions that the zoo director should take (d) him into hiding.   *noose: 올가미

(D)

Thanks to the efforts of the citizens of Duluth, Mr. Magoo was pardoned. A statement from Udall read, "Acting on the authority that permits importation of prohibited mammals — including mongooses — for zoological, education, medical and scientific purposes, I recommend that Mr. Magoo be granted non-political asylum in the United States." He added that it was dependent upon Mr. Magoo maintaining (e) his "bachelor existence." The *News Tribune* joyfully proclaimed, "MAGOO TO STAY. U.S. Asylum Granted." President Kennedy declared: "Let the story of the saving of Magoo stand as a classic example of government by the people."   *asylum: 망명

Q16 ✦✦✦✦ ··· 2024 실시 7월 학평 43 (고3)

주어진 글 (A)에 이어질 내용을 순서에 맞게 배열한 것으로 가장 적절한 것은?

① (B)—(D)—(C)   ② (C)—(B)—(D)
③ (C)—(D)—(B)   ④ (D)—(B)—(C)
⑤ (D)—(C)—(B)

Q17 ✦✦✦✦ ··· 2024 실시 7월 학평 44 (고3)

밑줄 친 (a)~(e) 중에서 가리키는 대상이 나머지 넷과 <u>다른</u> 것은?

① (a)   ② (b)   ③ (c)   ④ (d)   ⑤ (e)

Q18 ✦✦✦✦ ··· 2024 실시 7월 학평 45 (고3)

윗글에 관한 내용으로 적절하지 <u>않은</u> 것은?

① 몽구스 한 마리가 배를 타고 Duluth로 왔다.
② Mr. Magoo는 사형을 선고받았다.
③ Mr. Magoo는 수많은 편지와 카드를 받았다.
④ 10,000명이 넘는 시민들이 *No Noose for the Mongoose* 캠페인을 지지했다.
⑤ Mr. Magoo의 미국 망명이 허가되지 않았다.

[Q19~Q21] 다음 글을 읽고, 물음에 답하시오.

(A)

Pamela and Maggie were identical twins. Even their parents found it hard to tell them apart. But although they looked identical, they were different in every other way. They didn't have anything in common, so they fought all the time. Pamela thought that (a) her sister was weird and incomprehensible, and of course Maggie felt the same way.

(B)

Tired of the endless arguments, their mother Rachel decided to put an end to them. She would make them understand that each of their points of view could be correct. One day, the twins were brought to the dining table where a big board stood in the middle. Pamela sat on one side of the board and (b) her twin on the other. Rachel asked Pamela what the color of the board was. "Black," she said.

(C)

For example, Pamela was always upset at her sister waking up early in the morning. (c) She didn't understand why her sister couldn't finish what she needed to do at night and sleep peacefully the next morning. To Maggie, staying up past the time (d) she began to feel sleepy was exhausting. Besides, she loved the fresh morning air. They had fights about simple things like this every day.

(D)

After hearing Pamela's answer, Rachel asked the same question to (e) the other daughter. She replied it was white. Predictably, they began arguing. Rachel then asked them to switch seats. Each sitting on a new chair, they were surprised to realize the board was black on one side and white on the other. Understanding what their mother wanted to say, they promised they would never insist the other was wrong again.

Q19 ✽❀❀ .... 2024 실시 5월 학평 43 (고3)

주어진 글 (A)에 이어질 내용을 순서에 맞게 배열한 것으로 가장 적절한 것은?

① (B) — (D) — (C)   ② (C) — (B) — (D)
③ (C) — (D) — (B)   ④ (D) — (B) — (C)
⑤ (D) — (C) — (B)

Q20 ✽✽❀ .... 2024 실시 5월 학평 44 (고3)

밑줄 친 (a)~(e) 중에서 가리키는 대상이 나머지 넷과 다른 것은?

① (a)   ② (b)   ③ (c)   ④ (d)   ⑤ (e)

Q21 ✽❀❀ .... 2024 실시 5월 학평 45 (고3)

윗글에 관한 내용으로 적절하지 않은 것은?

① 자매는 외모를 제외한 모든 면에서 서로 달랐다.
② Rachel은 두 딸의 언쟁을 끝내기로 결심했다.
③ Pamela는 판자가 흰색이라고 대답했다.
④ Maggie는 상쾌한 아침 공기를 좋아했다.
⑤ Rachel은 두 딸이 자리를 바꾸도록 요청했다.

(A)

Once upon a time in the small town of Meadowville, there lived a curious boy named Tommy. Tommy's grandfather, affectionately known as Grandpa Joe, had always been a mysterious figure to (a) him. Grandpa Joe was a man of few words, but his eyes lit up from stories untold. One lazy summer afternoon, while searching the garage, Tommy found an old, forgotten box. As (b) he opened it, the treasure of memories spilled out, including an old baseball card featuring a young Grandpa Joe.

(B)

A spark of nostalgia lit up Grandpa Joe's eyes as he took the card. Memories flooded back, and he told stories of his youthful days on the baseball field. Grandpa Joe spoke of the thrill of the game and the joy of hitting a home run. Tommy, fascinated by these stories, felt more connected to his grandfather. Eager to learn more, (c) he asked Grandpa Joe to teach him about baseball.

(C)

They spent afternoons in the backyard as (d) he shared the wisdom of the game with his grandson. Together, they practiced hitting, catching, and even laughed over the mistakes. As they bonded over baseball, the gap between generations closed. Grandpa Joe's eyes no longer held just the twinkle of untold stories; they now radiated warmth and shared memories.

*twinkle: 반짝임

(D)

Tommy's eyes widened with excitement as he examined the card. In the card, Grandpa Joe stood proudly in a baseball uniform. He was not the quiet person Tommy knew. Intrigued by this discovery, Tommy rushed inside the house to find Grandpa Joe. "Hey, Grandpa! I found this cool baseball card of you. Were you a baseball player?" (e) he asked, eyes filled with curiosity.

Q22 ★★★ ❋ ·· 2024 실시 3월 학평 43 (고3)

주어진 글 (A)에 이어질 내용을 순서에 맞게 배열한 것으로 가장 적절한 것은?

① (B)－(D)－(C)　　② (C)－(B)－(D)
③ (C)－(D)－(B)　　④ (D)－(B)－(C)
⑤ (D)－(C)－(B)

Q23 ★★★ ❋ ·· 2024 실시 3월 학평 44 (고3)

밑줄 친 (a)~(e) 중에서 가리키는 대상이 나머지 넷과 다른 것은?

① (a)　② (b)　③ (c)　④ (d)　⑤ (e)

Q24 ★❋❋ ·· 2024 실시 3월 학평 45 (고3)

윗글에 관한 내용으로 적절하지 않은 것은?

① Tommy는 차고에서 오래되고 잊혀진 상자를 발견했다.
② Grandpa Joe는 야구장에서 보낸 그의 젊은 시절 이야기를 했다.
③ 그들은 함께 공 치기, 잡기를 연습했다.
④ 야구 카드 속에서 Grandpa Joe는 야구 유니폼을 입고 있었다.
⑤ Tommy는 Grandpa Joe를 찾기 위해 집 밖으로 서둘러 나왔다.

[Q25~Q27] 다음 글을 읽고, 물음에 답하시오.

(A)

"Congratulations!" That was the first word that Steven saw when he opened the envelope that his dad handed to him. He knew that he would win the essay contest. Overly excited, he shouted, "Hooray!" At that moment, two tickets to Ace Amusement Park, the prize, slipped out of the envelope. He picked them up and read the letter thoroughly while sitting on the stairs in front of his house. "Wait a minute! That's not my name!" (a) he said, puzzled. The letter was addressed to his classmate Stephanie, who had also participated in the contest.

(B)

Once Steven had heard his dad's words, tears started to fill up in his eyes. "I was foolish," Steven said regretfully. He took the letter and the prize to school and handed them to Stephanie. He congratulated her wholeheartedly and she was thrilled. On the way home after school, his steps were light and full of joy. That night, his dad was very pleased to hear what he had done at school. "(b) I am so proud of you, Steven," he said. Then, without a word, he handed Steven two Ace Amusement Park tickets and winked.

(C)

"If I don't tell Stephanie, perhaps she will never know," Steven thought for a moment. He remembered that the winner would only be notified by mail. As long as he kept quiet, nobody would know. So he decided to sleep on it. The next morning, he felt miserable and his dad recognized it right away. "What's wrong, (c) Son?" asked his dad. Steven was hesitant at first but soon disclosed his secret. After listening attentively to the end, his dad advised him to do the right thing.

(D)

Reading on, Steven realized the letter had been delivered mistakenly. "Unfortunately," it should have gone to Stephanie, who was the real winner. (d) He looked at the tickets and then the letter. He had really wanted those tickets. He had planned to go there with his younger sister. Steven was his sister's hero, and he had bragged to her that he would win the contest. However, if she found out that her hero hadn't won, she would be terribly disappointed, and (e) he would feel ashamed.

*brag: 허풍 떨다

Q25 ★★★✿ .... 2021 대비 6월 모평 43 (고3)

주어진 글 (A)에 이어질 내용을 순서에 맞게 배열한 것으로 가장 적절한 것은?

① (B) — (D) — (C)   ② (C) — (B) — (D)
③ (C) — (D) — (B)   ④ (D) — (B) — (C)
⑤ (D) — (C) — (B)

Q26 ★★✿ .... 2021 대비 6월 모평 44 (고3)

밑줄 친 (a)~(e) 중에서 가리키는 대상이 나머지 넷과 다른 것은?

① (a)   ② (b)   ③ (c)   ④ (d)   ⑤ (e)

Q27 ★✿✿ .... 2021 대비 6월 모평 45 (고3)

윗글에 관한 내용으로 적절하지 않은 것은?

① Steven은 집 앞 계단에 앉아 편지를 자세히 읽었다.
② 방과 후에 집으로 돌아오는 Steven의 발걸음은 무거웠다.
③ 아버지는 Steven에게 옳은 일을 하라고 조언했다.
④ 에세이 대회에서 우승한 사람은 Stephanie였다.
⑤ Steven은 여동생과 놀이공원에 갈 계획이었다.

(A)

When Sally came back home from her photography class, she could hear Katie moving around, chopping things on a wooden cutting board. Wondering what her roommate was doing, (a) she ran to the kitchen. Sally watched Katie cooking something that looked delicious. But Katie didn't notice her because she was too focused on preparing for her cooking test the next day. She was trying to remember what her professor had said in class that day.

(B)

Katie, surprised by her roommate's words, turned her head to Sally and sighed, "I don't know. This is really hard." Stirring her sauce for pasta, Katie continued, "Professor Brown said that visual aspects make up a key part of a meal. My recipe seems good, but I can't think of any ways to alter the feeling of the final dish." Visibly frustrated, (b) she was just about to throw away all of her hard work and start again, when Sally suddenly stopped her.

(C)

"Wait! You don't have to start over. You just need to add some color to the plate." Being curious, Katie asked, "How can (c) I do that?" Sally took out a container of vegetables from the refrigerator and replied, "How about making colored pasta to go with (d) your sauce?" Smiling, she added, "It's not that hard, and all you need are brightly colored vegetables to make your pasta green, orange, or even purple." Katie smiled, knowing that now she could make her pasta with beautiful colors like a photographer.

(D)

In that class, Professor Brown said, "You have to present your food properly, considering every stage of the dining experience. Imagine you are a photographer." Recalling what the professor had mentioned, Katie said to herself, "We need to see our ingredients as colors that make up a picture." Sally could clearly see that Katie was having a hard time preparing for her cooking test. Trying to make (e) her feel better, Sally kindly asked, "Is there anything I can do to help?"

Q28 ✳✿✿ .... 2022 대비 9월 모평 43 (고3)

주어진 글 (A)에 이어질 내용을 순서에 맞게 배열한 것으로 가장 적절한 것은?

① (B)—(D)—(C) ② (C)—(B)—(D)
③ (C)—(D)—(B) ④ (D)—(B)—(C)
⑤ (D)—(C)—(B)

Q29 ✳✳✿ .... 2022 대비 9월 모평 44 (고3)

밑줄 친 (a)~(e) 중에서 가리키는 대상이 나머지 넷과 다른 것은?

① (a)   ② (b)   ③ (c)   ④ (d)   ⑤ (e)

Q30 ✳✿✿ .... 2022 대비 9월 모평 45 (고3)

윗글에 관한 내용으로 적절하지 않은 것은?

① Sally는 사진 수업 후 집으로 돌아왔다.
② Brown 교수님은 음식에서 시각적인 면이 중요하다고 말했다.
③ Sally는 냉장고에서 채소가 든 그릇을 꺼냈다.
④ Sally는 색깔 있는 파스타를 만드는 것이 어렵다고 말했다.
⑤ Katie는 요리 시험 준비에 어려움을 겪고 있었다.

[Q31 ~ Q33] 다음 글을 읽고, 물음에 답하시오.

(A)

Walking out of Charing Cross Station in London, Emilia and her traveling companion, Layla, already felt their hearts pounding. It was the second day of their European summer trip. They were about to visit one of the world's most famous art galleries. The two of them started hurrying with excitement. Suddenly, Emilia shouted, "Look! There it is! We're finally at the National Gallery!" Layla laughed and responded, "(a) Your dream's finally come true!"

(B)

"Don't lose hope yet! Which gallery is the special exhibition at?" Layla asked. Emilia responded, "Well, his *Sunflowers* is still in England, but it's at a gallery in Liverpool. That's a long way, isn't it?" After a quick search on her phone, Layla stated, "No! It's only two hours to Liverpool by train. The next train leaves in an hour. Why don't we take it?" After considering the idea, Emilia, now relieved, responded, "Yeah, but (b) you always wanted to see Rembrandt's paintings. Let's do that first, Layla! Then, after lunch, we can catch the next train." Layla smiled brightly.

(C)

However, after searching all the exhibition rooms, Emilia and Layla couldn't find van Gogh's masterpiece anywhere. "That's weird. Van Gogh's *Sunflowers* should be here. Where is it?" Emilia looked upset, but Layla kept calm and said, "Maybe (c) you've missed a notice about it. Check the National Gallery app." Emilia checked it quickly. Then, she sighed, "*Sunflowers* isn't here! It's been lent to a different gallery for a special exhibition. (d) I can't believe I didn't check!"

(D)

Upon entering the National Gallery, Emilia knew exactly where to go first. (e) She grabbed Layla's hand and dragged her hurriedly to find van Gogh's *Sunflowers*. It was Emilia's favorite painting and had inspired her to become a painter. Emilia loved his use of bright colors and light. She couldn't wait to finally see his masterpiece in person. "It'll be amazing to see how he communicated the feelings of isolation and loneliness in his work," she said eagerly.

Q31 ✽❆❆ .... 2023 대비 9월 모평 43 (고3)

주어진 글 (A)에 이어질 내용을 순서에 맞게 배열한 것으로 가장 적절한 것은?

① (B) ─ (D) ─ (C) ② (C) ─ (B) ─ (D)
③ (C) ─ (D) ─ (B) ④ (D) ─ (B) ─ (C)
⑤ (D) ─ (C) ─ (B)

Q32 ✽❆❆ .... 2023 대비 9월 모평 44 (고3)

밑줄 친 (a)~(e) 중에서 가리키는 대상이 나머지 넷과 다른 것은?

① (a) ② (b) ③ (c) ④ (d) ⑤ (e)

Q33 ✽❆❆ .... 2023 대비 9월 모평 45 (고3)

윗글에 관한 내용으로 적절하지 않은 것은?

① Emilia와 Layla는 유럽 여행 중이었다.
② Layla는 Emilia에게 Liverpool로 가자고 제안했다.
③ Emilia는 기차를 점심 식사 전에 타자고 말했다.
④ National Gallery에는 van Gogh의 *Sunflowers*가 없었다.
⑤ Emilia는 van Gogh의 *Sunflowers*를 좋아했다.

[Q34~Q36] 다음 글을 읽고, 물음에 답하시오.

(A)

In the gym, members of the taekwondo club were busy practicing. Some were trying to kick as high as they could, and some were striking the sparring pad. Anna, the head of the club, was teaching the new members basic moves. Close by, her friend Jane was assisting Anna. Jane noticed that Anna was glancing at the entrance door of the gym. She seemed to be expecting someone. At last, when Anna took a break, Jane came over to (a) her and asked, "Hey, are you waiting for Cora?"

(B)

Cora walked in like a wounded soldier with bandages on her face and arms. Surprised, Anna and Jane simply looked at her with their eyes wide open. Cora explained, "I'm sorry I've been absent. I got into a bicycle accident, and I was in the hospital for two days. Finally, the doctor gave me the okay to practice." Anna said excitedly, "No problem! We're thrilled to have you back!" Then, Jane gave Anna an apologetic look, and (b) she responded with a friendly pat on Jane's shoulder.

(C)

Anna answered the question by nodding uneasily. In fact, Jane knew what her friend was thinking. Cora was a new member, whom Anna had personally invited to join the club. Anna really liked (c) her. Although her budget was tight, Anna bought Cora a taekwondo uniform. When she received it, Cora thanked her and promised, "I'll come to practice and work hard every day." However, unexpectedly, she came to practice only once and then never showed up again.

(D)

Since Cora had missed several practices, Anna wondered what could have happened. Jane, on the other hand, was disappointed and said judgingly, "Still waiting for her, huh? I can't believe (d) you don't feel disappointed or angry. Why don't you forget about her?" Anna replied, "Well, I know most newcomers don't keep their commitment to the club, but I thought that Cora would be

different. She said she would come every day and practice." Just as Jane was about to respond to (e) her, the door swung open. There she was!

Q34 ★★❀ .... 2022 대비 수능 43 (고3)

주어진 글 (A)에 이어질 내용을 순서에 맞게 배열한 것으로 가장 적절한 것은?

① (B) ─ (D) ─ (C) 　 ② (C) ─ (B) ─ (D)

③ (C) ─ (D) ─ (B) 　 ④ (D) ─ (B) ─ (C)

⑤ (D) ─ (C) ─ (B)

Q35 ★★❀ .... 2022 대비 수능 44 (고3)

밑줄 친 (a)~(e) 중에서 가리키는 대상이 나머지 넷과 다른 것은?

① (a) 　② (b) 　③ (c) 　④ (d) 　⑤ (e)

Q36 ★★★❀ .... 2022 대비 수능 45 (고3)

윗글에 관한 내용으로 적절하지 않은 것은?

① Anna는 신입 회원에게 태권도를 가르쳤다.

② Anna와 Jane은 Cora를 보고 놀라지 않았다.

③ Anna는 Cora에게 태권도 도복을 사 주었다.

④ Cora는 여러 차례 연습에 참여하지 않았다.

⑤ Anna는 Cora를 대다수의 신입 회원과 다를 것이라 생각했다.

[Q37~Q39] 다음 글을 읽고, 물음에 답하시오.

(A)

It was the first day of the semester. Looking around his shared dorm room, Noah thought that it looked exactly like every other dorm room at the university, and he became disappointed. His roommate Steve noticed it and asked what was wrong. Noah answered quietly that he thought their room was totally boring. (a) He wished the space felt a bit more like *their* space. Steve agreed and suggested that they could start personalizing the room like Noah wanted, the next day.

(B)

As they walked through a furniture store, Steve found a pretty yellow table. Since he knew that yellow was Noah's favorite color, Steve asked (b) him what he thought about buying that table. Noah was happy about the yellow table and said it would make their room more unique. Delighted, Noah added, "Well, yesterday our room was just like any other place at this school. But after today, (c) I really feel like it'll be *our* place." Now, they both knew that the place would provide them with energy and refreshment.

(C)

Noah hardly slept that night making plans for the room. After Steve woke up, they started to rearrange the furniture. All of the chairs and the sofa in their room were facing the TV. Noah mentioned to Steve that most of their visitors usually just sat and watched TV instead of chatting. In response to (d) his idea, Steve suggested, "How about we put the sofa over there by the wall so it will be easier to have conversations?" Noah agreed, and they moved it by the wall.

(D)

After changing the place of the sofa, they could see that they now had a lot of space in the middle of their room. Then, Noah remembered that his brother Sammy had a big table in his living room for playing board games and told Steve about it. Steve and Noah both really enjoyed playing board

games. So, Steve replied to Noah, "(e) I think putting a table in the middle of our room would be great for drinking tea as well as playing board games!" Both Noah and Steve agreed and decided to go shopping for a table.

Q37 ✽❄❄ .... 2023 대비 6월 모평 43 (고3)

주어진 글 (A)에 이어질 내용을 순서에 맞게 배열한 것으로 가장 적절한 것은?

① (B) ─ (D) ─ (C) ② (C) ─ (B) ─ (D)
③ (C) ─ (D) ─ (B) ④ (D) ─ (B) ─ (C)
⑤ (D) ─ (C) ─ (B)

Q38 ✽❄❄ .... 2023 대비 6월 모평 44 (고3)

밑줄 친 (a)~(e) 중에서 가리키는 대상이 나머지 넷과 다른 것은?

① (a) ② (b) ③ (c) ④ (d) ⑤ (e)

Q39 ✽❄❄ .... 2023 대비 6월 모평 45 (고3)

윗글에 관한 내용으로 적절하지 <u>않은</u> 것은?

① Noah는 학기 첫날 자신의 기숙사 방을 둘러보고 실망했다.
② Noah는 노란색 탁자가 자신들의 방을 더 독특하게 만들 것이라고 말했다.
③ Noah는 Steve가 잠든 사이에 가구를 다시 배치했다.
④ Noah는 Sammy의 거실에 커다란 탁자가 있던 것을 떠올렸다.
⑤ Noah와 Steve 둘 다 보드게임 하는 것을 즐겼다.

[Q40~Q42] 다음 글을 읽고, 물음에 답하시오.

(A)

"Hailey, be careful!" Camila yelled uneasily, watching her sister carrying a huge cake to the table. "Don't worry, Camila," Hailey responded, smiling. Camila relaxed only when Hailey had safely placed the cake on the party table. "Dad will be here shortly. What gift did (a) you buy for his birthday?" Camila asked out of interest. "Dad will be surprised to find out what it is!" Hailey answered with a wink.

(B)

"Dad, these glasses can help correct your red-green color blindness," said Hailey. He slowly put them on, and stared at the birthday presents on the table. Seeing vivid red and green colors for the first time ever, he started to cry. "Incredible! Look at those wonderful colors!" He shouted in amazement. Hailey told him in tears, "Dad, I'm glad you can now finally enjoy the true beauty of rainbows and roses. Red represents love and green represents health. You deserve both." Camila nodded, seeing how happy (b) her gift of the glasses had made their dad.

(C)

"Happy birthday! You're fifty today, Dad. We love you!" Camila said before (c) her sister handed him a small parcel. When he opened it, he discovered a pair of glasses inside. "Hailey, Dad doesn't have eyesight problems," Camila said, puzzled. "Actually Camila, I recently found out he has long been suffering from color blindness. He's kept it a secret so as not to worry us," Hailey explained.

(D)

"I bet (d) you bought a wallet or a watch for him," Camila said. In reply, Hailey answered, "No. I bought something much more personal. By the way, there's something (e) you should know about Dad..." They were suddenly interrupted by the doorbell ringing. It was their dad and they were overjoyed to see him. "My lovely ladies, thank you for inviting me to your place for my birthday." He walked in joyfully, hugging his daughters. They all walked into the dining room, where he was greeted with a rainbow-colored birthday cake and fifty red roses.

Q40 ★★★❀ .... 2023 대비 수능 43 (고3)

주어진 글 (A)에 이어질 내용을 순서에 맞게 배열한 것으로 가장 적절한 것은?

① (B)—(D)—(C) ② (C)—(B)—(D)
③ (C)—(D)—(B) ④ (D)—(B)—(C)
⑤ (D)—(C)—(B)

Q41 ★★★❀ .... 2023 대비 수능 44 (고3)

밑줄 친 (a)~(e) 중에서 가리키는 대상이 나머지 넷과 다른 것은?

① (a) ② (b) ③ (c) ④ (d) ⑤ (e)

Q42 ★★★❀ .... 2023 대비 수능 45 (고3)

윗글에 관한 내용으로 적절하지 않은 것은?

① Hailey는 생일 케이크를 테이블로 무사히 옮겨 놓았다.
② 아버지는 생일 선물로 받은 안경을 직접 써 보았다.
③ Hailey는 아버지가 색맹이라는 사실을 최근에 알게 되었다.
④ Hailey와 Camila는 아버지의 집을 방문하였다.
⑤ 아버지는 자신의 나이와 똑같은 수의 장미를 받았다.

[Q43~Q45] 다음 글을 읽고, 물음에 답하시오.

(A)

Ignace Jan Paderewski, the famous composer-pianist, was scheduled to perform at a great concert hall in America. It was an evening to remember — black tuxedos and long evening dresses, a high-society event. Present in the audience that evening was a mother with her nine-year-old son. Tired of waiting, (a) he squirmed constantly in his seat. His mother was in hopes that her son would be encouraged to practice the piano if he could just hear the great Paderewski at the keyboard. So, against his wishes, he had come.

*squirm: 꼼지락대다

(B)

The roar of the crowd became quiet as hundreds of frowning faces pointed in (b) his direction. Irritated and embarrassed, they began to shout: "Get that boy away from there!" "Who'd bring a kid that young in here?" "Where's his mother?" "Stop (c) him!" Backstage, Paderewski overheard the sounds out front and quickly put together in his mind what was happening. Hurriedly, he grabbed his coat and rushed toward the stage.

(C)

As she turned to talk with friends, her son could stay seated no longer. (d) He slipped away from her side, strangely drawn to the black concert grand piano and its leather stool on the huge stage flooded with blinding lights. Without much notice from the sophisticated audience, the boy sat down at the piano stool, staring wide-eyed at the black and white keys. He placed his small, shaky fingers in the right location and began to play "Chopsticks."

(D)

Without one word of announcement Paderewski bent over behind the boy, reached around both sides, began to improvise a countermelody to harmonize with and enhance "Chopsticks." As the two of them played together, (e) he kept whispering in the boy's ear: "Keep going. Don't quit. Keep on playing... don't stop... don't quit." Together, the old master and the little boy transformed an embarrassing situation into a wonderfully creative experience. The audience was mesmerized.

*improvise: 즉흥 연주하다 **mesmerize: 매혹하다

Q43 ★★★❀ .... 2023 실시 7월 학평 43 (고3)

주어진 글 (A)에 이어질 내용을 순서에 맞게 배열한 것으로 가장 적절한 것은?

① (B) — (D) — (C)   ② (C) — (B) — (D)
③ (C) — (D) — (B)   ④ (D) — (B) — (C)
⑤ (D) — (C) — (B)

Q44 ★★★❀ .... 2023 실시 7월 학평 44 (고3)

밑줄 친 (a)~(e) 중에서 가리키는 대상이 나머지 넷과 다른 것은?

① (a)   ② (b)   ③ (c)   ④ (d)   ⑤ (e)

Q45 ★★★❀ .... 2023 실시 7월 학평 45 (고3)

윗글에 관한 내용으로 적절하지 않은 것은?

① 소년은 연주회에 오고 싶지 않았으나 오게 되었다.
② 짜증이 나고 당황한 관중은 크게 소리치기 시작했다.
③ Paderewski는 서둘러 무대로 달려갔다.
④ 소년은 무대 위 피아노 의자에 앉아 건반을 응시했다.
⑤ Paderewski는 짧은 공지 후 소년과 함께 연주했다.

(A)

In a peaceful town surrounded by rolling hills, there lived a kind-hearted young woman named Emily. She had a strong desire to make a difference in the world, yet often felt that her efforts were insignificant. One day, Emily crossed paths with Martha, an elderly lady known for (a) her sour mood and tendency to keep to herself. Curiosity sparked within Emily, prompting her to initiate a conversation with Martha.

(B)

The event showcased the great works of many local artists, with a special surprise awaiting Martha. Emily had carefully prepared a section dedicated to Martha's paintings, hoping to unveil it to her and the community. The day of the exhibition arrived, and the townspeople eagerly gathered, excited to witness the artistic wonders of their community. Emily anxiously awaited Martha's arrival, wondering how Martha would react to the surprise (b) she had planned. Martha finally entered the exhibition hall, and her eyes filled with tears as she stood in front of her own artworks.

(C)

Martha slowly made her way through the section dedicated to (c) her paintings, examining each piece with a mix of nostalgia and longing. The crowd watched in silence, their hearts touched by Martha's emotional response. As Martha reached the last painting, she turned to Emily with a bright smile, tears still shining in her eyes. "Emily, you've given me back a part of myself that I thought was lost forever," Martha whispered, (d) her voice shaking with gratitude. "I had forgotten the joy that art once brought me, but you've reminded me of its power."

(D)

Despite Martha's initial resistance, Emily persistently reached out to her, sharing stories and expressing genuine interest in (e) her life. Through their conversations, Emily discovered that Martha had once been a famous painter. However, she had lost her passion for art due to personal hardships. Deeply moved by her sorrow, Emily resolved to help revive Martha's creative spirit. So, she organized an art exhibition in the town's community center.

Q46 ✱※※ .... 2023 실시 10월 학평 43 (고3)

주어진 글 (A)에 이어질 내용을 순서에 맞게 배열한 것으로 가장 적절한 것은?

① (B) — (D) — (C)   ② (C) — (B) — (D)
③ (C) — (D) — (B)   ④ (D) — (B) — (C)
⑤ (D) — (C) — (B)

Q47 ✱✱※ .... 2023 실시 10월 학평 44 (고3)

밑줄 친 (a)~(e) 중에서 가리키는 대상이 나머지 넷과 다른 것은?

① (a)   ② (b)   ③ (c)   ④ (d)   ⑤ (e)

Q48 ✱※※ .... 2023 실시 10월 학평 45 (고3)

윗글에 관한 내용으로 적절하지 않은 것은?

① Emily는 호기심이 생겨 Martha와 대화를 시작하게 되었다.
② 미술 전시회에서는 Martha의 작품만 전시했다.
③ 마을 사람들은 Martha의 반응을 보고 마음이 뭉클했다.
④ Martha는 마지막 그림에 이르러 Emily를 향해 미소를 지었다.
⑤ Martha는 개인적인 역경 때문에 미술에 대한 열정을 잃었다.

[Q49~Q51] 다음 글을 읽고, 물음에 답하시오.

(A)

The children arrived at sunrise at their grandmother's house. They always gathered at this time of year to assist with her corn harvest. In return, their grandmother would reward them with a present and by cooking a delicious feast. The children were all in great spirits. But not Sally. She disliked working in the corn field as she hated the heat and the dust. (a) She sat silently as the others took a sack each and then sang their way to the field.

(B)

Sally just wanted to get her present and leave the field because she was starting to get hot and feel irritated. (b) She had only filled her sack twice, but the others were now taking their third sacks to the granary. Sally sighed heavily. Then an idea struck her. To make the sack lighter and speed things up, she quickly filled her last sack with corn stalks. Sally reached the granary first, and her grandmother asked (c) her to put aside the final load and write her name on it.

*granary: 곡물창고 **stalk: 줄기

(C)

They reached the field and started to work happily. Soon after, Sally joined them with her sack. Around mid-morning, their grandmother came with ice-cold lemonade and peach pie. After finishing, the children continued working until the sun was high and their sacks were bursting. Each child had to make three trips to the granary. Grandmother was impressed by their efforts and (d) she wanted to give them presents accordingly.

(D)

Grandmother asked the other children to do the same thing. Then, all of the children enjoyed their grandmother's delicious lunch. "I am so pleased with your work," she told them after lunch. "This year, you can all take home your final load as a present!" The children cheered for joy, gladly thanked her, and lifted their sacks to take home.

Sally was terribly disappointed. There was nothing but useless corn stalks in (e) her sack. She then made the long walk home, pretending that she was carrying a heavy load.

Q49 ★★★ .... 2021 대비 9월 모평 43 (고3)

주어진 글 (A)에 이어질 내용을 순서에 맞게 배열한 것으로 가장 적절한 것은?

① (B) — (D) — (C) ② (C) — (B) — (D)
③ (C) — (D) — (B) ④ (D) — (B) — (C)
⑤ (D) — (C) — (B)

Q50 ★★★ .... 2021 대비 9월 모평 44 (고3)

밑줄 친 (a)~(e) 중에서 가리키는 대상이 나머지 넷과 다른 것은?

① (a)　② (b)　③ (c)　④ (d)　⑤ (e)

Q51 ★★★ .... 2021 대비 9월 모평 45 (고3)

윗글에 관한 내용으로 적절하지 않은 것은?

① 아이들은 할머니의 옥수수 수확을 돕기 위해 모였다.
② Sally는 덥고 짜증나서 옥수수 밭을 떠나고 싶었다.
③ 아이들은 각자 세 번씩 옥수수가 담긴 자루를 곡물창고로 날라야 했다.
④ 할머니는 아이들에게 맛있는 점심을 제공했다.
⑤ Sally는 옥수수가 담긴 무거운 자루를 가지고 집으로 갔다.

(A)

In this area, heavy snow in winter was not uncommon. Sometimes it poured down for hours and hours and piled up very high. Then, no one could go out. Today too, because of the heavy snow, Mom was doing her office work at the kitchen table. Felix, the high schooler, had to take online classes in his room. Five-year-old Sean, who normally went to kindergarten, was sneaking around in the house playing home policeman. (a) The kindergartener wanted to know what his family members were up to, and was checking up on everyone.

*sneak: 몰래 움직이다

(B)

"All right. I'm sure you're doing your work." Mom replied, and then sharply added a question. "Sean, what are *you* doing?" Sean's face immediately became blank, and he said, "Nothing." "Come here, Honey, and you can help me." Sean ran to the kitchen right away. "What can I do for you, Mom?" His voice was high, and Felix could sense that his brother was excited. Felix was pleased to get rid of (b) the policeman, and now he could concentrate on the lesson, at least till Sean came back.

(C)

While checking on his family, Sean interfered in their business as if it was his own. This time, (c) the playful and curious boy was interested in his brother Felix, who committed himself to studying no matter where he was. Sean secretly looked inside his brother's room from the door, and shouted toward the kitchen where Mom was working, "Mom, Felix isn't studying. He's just watching a funny video." Sean was naughtily smiling at his brother.

*naughtily: 짓궂게

(D)

Felix was mad because (d) his little brother was bothering him. Felix was studying science using a video posted on the school web site. He made an angry face at the naughty boy. Right then, Mom asked loudly from the kitchen, "What are you doing, Felix?" Felix's room was located next to the kitchen, and he could hear Mom clearly. "I'm watching a lecture video for my science class." Felix argued against Sean's accusation and mischievously stuck (e) his tongue out at his little brother.

*mischievously: 장난기 있게

Q52 ★★✾

주어진 글 (A)에 이어질 내용을 순서에 맞게 배열한 것으로 가장 적절한 것은?

① (B) ― (D) ― (C)　　② (C) ― (B) ― (D)
③ (C) ― (D) ― (B)　　④ (D) ― (B) ― (C)
⑤ (D) ― (C) ― (B)

Q53 ★★✾

밑줄 친 (a)~(e) 중에서 가리키는 대상이 나머지 넷과 다른 것은?

① (a)　　② (b)　　③ (c)　　④ (d)　　⑤ (e)

Q54 ★★★✾

윗글에 관한 내용으로 적절하지 않은 것은?

① 엄마는 폭설로 인해 집에서 업무를 보고 있었다.
② Sean은 엄마가 불러서 주방으로 달려갔다.
③ Sean은 몰래 형의 방을 들여다보았다.
④ Felix는 자신의 방에서 게임을 하고 있었다.
⑤ Felix의 방은 주방 옆에 있었다.

[Q55~Q57] 다음 글을 읽고, 물음에 답하시오.

(A)

Emma and Clara stood side by side on the beach road, with their eyes fixed on the boundless ocean. The breathtaking scene that surrounded them was beyond description. Just after sunrise, they finished their preparations for the bicycle ride along the beach road. Emma turned to Clara with a question, "Do you think this will be your favorite ride ever?" Clara's face lit up with a bright smile as she nodded. "Definitely! (a) I can't wait to ride while watching those beautiful waves!"

(B)

When they reached their destination, Emma and Clara stopped their bikes. Emma approached Clara, saying "Bicycle riding is unlike swimming, isn't it?" Clara answered with a smile, "Quite similar, actually. Just like swimming, riding makes me feel truly alive." She added, "It shows (b) me what it means to live while facing life's tough challenges." Emma nodded in agreement and suggested, "Your first beach bike ride was a great success. How about coming back next summer?" Clara replied with delight, "With (c) you, absolutely!"

(C)

Clara used to be a talented swimmer, but she had to give up her dream of becoming an Olympic medalist in swimming because of shoulder injuries. Yet she responded to the hardship in a constructive way. After years of hard training, she made an incredible recovery and found a new passion for bike riding. Emma saw how the painful past made her maturer and how it made (d) her stronger in the end. One hour later, Clara, riding ahead of Emma, turned back and shouted, "Look at the white cliff!"

(D)

Emma and Clara jumped on their bikes and started to pedal toward the white cliff where the beach road ended. Speeding up and enjoying the wide blue sea, Emma couldn't hide her excitement and exclaimed, "Clara, the view is amazing!" Clara's silence, however, seemed to say that she was lost in her thoughts. Emma understood the meaning of her silence. Watching Clara riding beside her, Emma thought about Clara's past tragedy, which (e) she now seemed to have overcome.

Q55 ✱✱✲ .... 2024 대비 수능 43 (고3)

주어진 글 (A)에 이어질 내용을 순서에 맞게 배열한 것으로 가장 적절한 것은?

① (B) ─ (D) ─ (C)   ② (C) ─ (B) ─ (D)
③ (C) ─ (D) ─ (B)   ④ (D) ─ (B) ─ (C)
⑤ (D) ─ (C) ─ (B)

Q56 ✱✱✱ .... 2024 대비 수능 44 (고3)

밑줄 친 (a)~(e) 중에서 가리키는 대상이 나머지 넷과 다른 것은?

① (a)   ② (b)   ③ (c)   ④ (d)   ⑤ (e)

Q57 ✱✱✱ .... 2024 대비 수능 45 (고3)

윗글에 관한 내용으로 적절하지 않은 것은?

① Emma와 Clara는 자전거 탈 준비를 일출 직후에 마쳤다.
② Clara는 자전거 타기와 수영이 꽤 비슷하다고 말했다.
③ Clara는 올림픽 수영 경기에서 메달을 땄다.
④ Emma와 Clara는 자전거를 타고 하얀 절벽 쪽으로 갔다.
⑤ Emma는 Clara의 침묵의 의미를 이해했다.

Q58~60 ▶ 제한시간 9분

[Q58~Q60] 다음 글을 읽고, 물음에 답하시오.

(A)

When invited by her mother to go shopping after lunch, Ellen hesitantly replied, "Sorry, Mom. I have an English essay assignment I need to finish." Her mother persisted, "Come on! Your father's birthday is just around the corner, and you wanted to buy his birthday present by yourself." Ellen suddenly realized that her father's birthday was just two days away. So (a) she altered her original plan to do the assignment in the library and decided to go to the shopping mall with her mother.

(B)

Ellen wanted to get a strawberry smoothie in the cafe, but it was sold out. So she bought a yogurt smoothie instead. The cafe was not very busy for a Saturday afternoon, and Ellen settled at a large table to work on her assignment. However, after a while, a group of students came in, and there weren't any large tables left. One of them came over to Ellen's table and politely asked, "Could (b) you possibly move to that smaller table?" Ellen replied, "It's okay. I was just leaving anyway." She hurriedly gathered her assignment leaving the shoe bag behind under the table.

(C)

Upon arrival at the shopping center, her mother inquired, "Ellen, have you decided what to buy for his birthday present?" She quickly replied, "(c) I would like to buy him a pair of soccer shoes." Ellen knew that her father had joined the morning soccer club recently and needed some new soccer shoes. She entered a shoe store and selected a pair of red soccer shoes. After buying the present, she told her mother, "Mom, now, I'm going to do my assignment in the cafe while you are shopping."

(D)

"It must be in the cafe," Ellen suddenly exclaimed when (d) she realized the gift for her father was missing upon returning home. She felt so disheartened, worrying it would be impossible to find it. "Why don't you call the cafe?" suggested her mother. When she phoned the cafe and asked about the shoe bag, the manager said that she would check and let her know. After a few minutes, she called back and told Ellen that (e) she had just discovered it. Ellen was so pleased that the birthday gift had been found.

Q58 ⭐ 2등급 대비 .... 2024 대비 6월 모평 43 (고3)

주어진 글 (A)에 이어질 내용을 순서에 맞게 배열한 것으로 가장 적절한 것은?

① (B)—(D)—(C)　　② (C)—(B)—(D)
③ (C)—(D)—(B)　　④ (D)—(B)—(C)
⑤ (D)—(C)—(B)

Q59 ⭐ 2등급 대비 .... 2024 대비 6월 모평 44 (고3)

밑줄 친 (a)~(e) 중에서 가리키는 대상이 나머지 넷과 다른 것은?

① (a)　　② (b)　　③ (c)　　④ (d)　　⑤ (e)

Q60 ⭐ 2등급 대비 .... 2024 대비 6월 모평 45 (고3)

윗글에 관한 내용으로 적절하지 않은 것은?

① Ellen은 끝내야 할 영어 과제가 있었다.
② 카페에서는 요거트 스무디를 팔지 않았다.
③ 한 무리의 학생들이 카페에 들어왔다.
④ Ellen의 아버지는 최근에 아침 축구 클럽에 가입했다.
⑤ Ellen은 카페에 전화를 걸었다.

[Q61 ~ Q63] 다음 글을 읽고, 물음에 답하시오.

(A)

In July, people in the city often escaped to relax in the mountains. Sean didn't yet know it, but he was about to have the experience of a lifetime. "When I look around, all I see is the work I haven't finished and the bills I haven't paid," he complained over the phone to his friend and doctor, Alex. Concerned about Sean, he said, "(a) You've been stressed for weeks. Come see me for medical treatment if things don't improve."

(B)

Having hiked for several hours, Sean was thrilled to reach the top of Vincent Mountain. As Toby started to bark, Sean turned around and found him running toward a large pond. "What a nice, quiet place," Sean whispered to himself. Among the trees, he could ease the stress of recent weeks. As night approached, however, the wind blew fiercely. Sean became nervous. Unable to sleep, (b) he called to his companion, "Come here, Boy!" He held the dog close in an effort to ignore the fear rushing in.

(C)

After what felt like the longest night of Sean's life, the sky finally turned a beautiful shade of pink, and the warm sun shone around him. He packed up his equipment, enjoying his last moments in the mountain air. Finding Toby energetically running next to the campsite, Sean said, "(c) You must be as excited as I am after surviving a night like that!" Sean went down the mountain with a renewed sense of joy, and he exclaimed, "My treatment worked like a charm!"

(D)

Upon hearing this offer, Sean replied, "Thanks, but (d) I know just the treatment I need." He told his friend about the Vincent Mountain hike he had read about. Alex anxiously warned, "Even in the summer, hiking can be dangerous. Don't forget your safety checklist." Following his friend's words, (e) he added protective gear to his camping equipment. Sean put on his hiking clothes and tied up his boots. He almost forgot his new hiking

sticks as he walked out the door with his dog, Toby.

Q61 ⭐ **2등급 대비** .... 2024 대비 9월 모평 43 (고3)

주어진 글 (A)에 이어질 내용을 순서에 맞게 배열한 것으로 가장 적절한 것은?

① (B) — (D) — (C) ② (C) — (B) — (D)
③ (C) — (D) — (B) ④ (D) — (B) — (C)
⑤ (D) — (C) — (B)

Q62 ⭐ **2등급 대비** .... 2024 대비 9월 모평 44 (고3)

밑줄 친 (a)~(e) 중에서 가리키는 대상이 나머지 넷과 다른 것은?

① (a) ② (b) ③ (c) ④ (d) ⑤ (e)

Q63 ⭐ **2등급 대비** .... 2024 대비 9월 모평 45 (고3)

윗글에 관한 내용으로 적절하지 않은 것은?

① Sean은 친구 Alex에게 어려움을 토로했다.
② Toby가 큰 연못으로 달려갔다.
③ 밤이 되자 바람이 잦아들었다.
④ Sean은 산을 내려오며 기쁨을 느꼈다.
⑤ Sean은 Vincent Mountain 하이킹에 대해 읽은 적이 있다.

※ 다음 영어는 우리말 뜻을, 우리말은 영어 단어를 〈보기〉에서 찾아 쓰시오.

┌─────〈 보기 〉─────┐

prompt	침착한, 잔잔한	급히, 서둘러	puzzled
수확	stir	전체의	initiate
비참한	친구, 동행	attribute	dorm

01 harvest _____

02 miserable _____

03 companion _____

04 hurriedly _____

05 calm _____

06 기숙사, 공동 침실 _____

07 시작하다 _____

08 젓다 _____

09 어리둥절해 하는 _____

10 ~하게 하다 _____

※ 다음 우리말에 알맞은 영어 표현을 찾아 연결하시오.

11 ~을 고르다 ・ ・ pick out

12 용케 ~을 해내다 ・ ・ put aside

13 ~을 한쪽에 두다 ・ ・ manage to-v

14 (~에 대한) 보답으로 ・ ・ in return

15 ~할 예정이다 ・ ・ be scheduled to

※ 다음 우리말 표현에 맞는 단어를 고르시오.

16 학기의 첫날 ➡ the first day of the (semester / disaster)

17 위험을 마다하지 않는 모험가 ➡ a (decisive / daring) adventurer

18 Layla의 손을 꼭 잡다 ➡ (crab / grab) Layla's hand

19 느낌을 바꿀 방법 ➡ ways to (alter / retain) the feeling

20 중고 쇼핑 앱에서의 알림 ➡ a(n) (notification / specification) on a second-hand shopping app

※ 다음 문장의 빈칸에 알맞은 단어를 〈보기〉에서 찾아 쓰시오.

┌─────〈 보기 〉─────┐

spray	correct	aspects	terribly
pounding	disclosed	rearrange	accordingly
ease	isolation	uneasily	gathered

21 Emilia와 그녀의 여행 동반자인 Layla는 벌써 가슴이 두근거리는 것을 느꼈다.
➡ Emilia and her traveling companion, Layla, already felt their hearts _____.

22 그들은 모든 물보라로 흠뻑 젖었다.
➡ They were soaked from all of the _____.

23 Sally는 몹시 실망했다.
➡ Sally was _____ disappointed.

24 그녀는 서둘러 과제를 챙겼다.
➡ She hurriedly _____ her assignment.

25 그가 자기 작품에서 고립과 고독의 느낌을 전달한 방식을 보면 놀라울 것이다.
➡ It'll be amazing to see how he communicated the feelings of _____ and loneliness in his work.

26 시각적인 면이 음식의 핵심 부분을 구성한다.
➡ Visual _____ make up a key part of a meal.

27 Steve가 일어난 후 그들은 가구를 다시 배치하기 시작했다.
➡ After Steve woke up, they started to _____ the furniture.

28 나무 사이에서, 그는 최근 몇 주간의 스트레스를 덜 수 있었다.
➡ Among the trees, he could _____ the stress of recent weeks.

29 Steven은 처음에 주저했지만, 곧 자신의 비밀을 털어놓았다.
➡ Steven was hesitant at first but soon _____ his secret.

30 할머니는 그들의 노력에 감동하였고, 그녀는 그에 맞춰 그들에게 선물을 주고 싶어 했다.
➡ Grandmother was impressed by their efforts and she wanted to give them presents _____.

방그사 (방과 후 그린 사업)

서울대학교 에너지환경 동아리

지속가능한 미래를 위한 '방그사'

방그사는 '방과 후 그린 사업'이란 뜻을 지닌 동아리로, 2020년에 신설된 젊은 동아리입니다. 2019년에 에너지자원공학과 학생 11명이 환경 NGO 대자연과 함께하는 #MakeZero #MakeGreenCampus 에너지 절약 실천 사업에 참여하면서 방그사가 시작되었습니다.

기후 변화 문제에 대처하는 하나의 주제(텀블러 사용, 분리수거 등)를 선정하여 한 달에 4번 이상 실천한 사진을 자신의 SNS에 인증하는 활동을 합니다.
또 초등학교 3, 4학년을 대상으로 한 환경 교육 수업 동영상을 제작하고, '기업의 환경 활동'을 주제로 한 기고문을 작성하여 Climate Times에 기고도 합니다.

그린캠퍼스 교육을 연수하고, 타 대학 그린캠퍼스 환경 동아리 및 환경 단체와 교류도 하는데, 이러한 활동의 노고를 인정받아 에코리그에서 서울시장상을 수상하기도 하였습니다.

기후 변화에 대처하고, 건강한 지구를 만드는 데 관심이 있는 신입 부원을 기다립니다.

★ 고난도 유형 독해 모의고사

[회별 12문항, 제한시간 30분]

1회 **모의고사** — 경찰대, 삼사, 수능 대비 문항 선별

2회 **모의고사** — 경찰대, 삼사, 수능 대비 문항 선별

3회 **모의고사** — 경찰대, 삼사, 수능 대비 문항 선별

*수록 유형

번호	유형
01번	밑줄 친 부분의 의미 찾기
02번	주제 찾기
03번	제목 찾기
04번	빈칸 완성하기
05번	
06번	
07번	글의 순서 정하기
08번	글의 순서 정하기 or 주어진 문장 넣기
09번	주어진 문장 넣기
10번	요약문 완성하기
11번	장문의 이해
12번	

1회 01 ·········· 2025 대비 육해공사관 7 (고3)

다음 글에서 밑줄 친 부분이 의미하는 바로 가장 적절한 것은?
[4점]

Compared to other primates, we are freakishly social and cooperative; not only do we sit obediently on airplanes, we labor collectively to build houses, specialize in different skills, and live lives that are driven by our specific role in the group. This is quite a trick for a primate to pull off, considering our most recent evolutionary history. Hive life is (literally) a no-brainer for ants: They share the same genes, so sacrificing for the common good is not really a sacrifice — if I'm an ant, the common good simply is my good. Humans, though, are apes, evolved to cooperate only in a limited way with close relatives and perhaps fellow tribe members, acutely alert to the dangers of being manipulated, misled, or exploited by others. And yet we march in parades, sit in obedient rows reciting lessons, conform to social norms, and sometimes sacrifice our lives for the common good with an enthusiasm that would put a soldier ant to shame. Trying to <u>hammer a square primate peg into a circular social insect hole</u> is bound to be difficult.

* freakishly: 이상할 정도로 ** no-brainer: 쉽게 할 수 있는 일

① downgrade humans' superiority over apes and ants

② enforce the collaboration between apes and social insects

③ manipulate hive insects into adopting ape-like characteristics

④ suppress our traits as apes in order to pursue communal benefits

⑤ maximize apes' physical capabilities in contributing to the common good

1회 02 ·········· 2022 실시 4월 학평 23 (고3)

다음 글의 주제로 가장 적절한 것은?

By the start of the 16th century, the Renaissance movement had given birth to the Protestant Reformation and an era of profound religious change. The art of this period reflected the disruption caused by this shift. Appropriately named the Baroque, meaning irregular or distorted, European painting in the 16th century largely focused on capturing motion, drama, action, and powerful emotion. Painters employed the strong visual tools of dramatic composition, intense contrast of light and dark, and emotionally provocative subject matter to stir up feelings of disruption. Religious subjects were often portrayed in this era through new dramatic visual language, a contrast to the reverential portrayal of religious figures in earlier traditions. In order to capture the social disruption surrounding Christianity and the Roman Catholic Church, many artists abandoned old standards of visual perfection from the Classical and Renaissance periods in their portrayal of religious figures.

*Protestant Reformation: 종교 개혁 **reverential: 경건한

① characteristics of Baroque paintings caused by religious disruption

② impacts of the Baroque on the development of visual perfectionism

③ efforts of Baroque painters to imitate the Renaissance style

④ roles of Baroque artists in stabilizing the disrupted society

⑤ reasons of idealizing religious figures in Baroque paintings

03
2025 대비 육해공사관 9 (고3)

다음 글의 제목으로 가장 적절한 것을 고르시오. [3점]

Business ethics was born in scandal. It seems to regenerate itself with each succeeding wave of scandal. And, there are two problems here. The first is that our world is so interconnected that we can no longer afford to see business as a separate institution in society, subject to its own moral code. Business must be thoroughly situated in society. This means that we can no longer accept the now rather commonplace narrative about businesspeople being economic profit-maximizers and little else. Business is a deeply human institution set in our societies and interconnected all over the world. The second problem is that business ethics, by being reborn in scandal, never escapes the presumption that business starts off by being morally questionable. It never seems to get any credit for the good it brings into the world, only questions about the bad. In fact, capitalism may well be the greatest system of social cooperation that we have ever invented. But, if it is, then it must stand the critical test of our best thinkers, if for no other reason than to make it better. Simply assuming that capitalism is either unquestionably morally good or unquestionably morally problematic violates both scholarly and practical norms.

① Forget Scandals, Let's Innovate!
② Innate Challenges of Business Ethics
③ Unavoidable Obstacles of Human Institutions
④ Business Ethics: An Emerging Scholarly Norm
⑤ Business Ethics as A Magic Bullet for Success

04
2022 실시 7월 학평 32 (고3)

다음 빈칸에 들어갈 말로 가장 적절한 것을 고르시오.

Infants' preference for looking at new things is so strong that psychologists began to realize that they could use it as a test of infants' visual discrimination, and even their *memory*. Could an infant tell the difference between two similar images? Between two similar shades of the same color? Could an infant recall having seen something an hour, a day, a week ago? _____ held the answer. If the infant's gaze lingered, it suggested that the infant could tell that a similar image was nonetheless different in some way. If the infant, after a week without seeing an image, didn't look at it much when it was shown again, the infant must be able at some level to *remember* having seen it the week before. In most cases, the results revealed that infants were more cognitively capable earlier than had been previously assumed. The visual novelty drive became, indeed, one of the most powerful tools in psychologists' toolkit, unlocking a host of deeper insights into the capacities of the infant mind.

① Memory distortion in infancy
② Undeveloped vision of newborns
③ The preference for social interaction
④ The inbuilt attraction to novel images
⑤ Infants' communication skills with parents

❖ 정답 및 해설 499 ~ 502p

다음 빈칸에 들어갈 말로 가장 적절한 것을 고르시오.

The quest for knowledge in the material world is a never-ending pursuit, but the quest does not mean that a thoroughly schooled person is an educated person or that an educated person is a wise person. We are too often blinded by our ignorance of our ignorance, and our pursuit of knowledge is no guarantee of wisdom. Hence, we are prone to becoming the blind leading the blind because our overemphasis on competition in nearly everything makes looking good more important than being good. The resultant fear of being thought a fool and criticized therefore is one of greatest enemies of true learning. Although our ignorance is undeniably vast, it is from the vastness of this selfsame ignorance that our sense of wonder grows. But, when we do not know we are ignorant, we do not know enough to even question, let alone investigate, our ignorance. No one can teach another person anything. All one can do with and for someone else is to facilitate learning by helping the person to _____.

* prone to: ~하기 쉬운 **selfsame: 똑같은

① find their role in teamwork
② learn from others' successes and failures
③ make the most of technology for learning
④ obtain knowledge from wonderful experts
⑤ discover the wonder of their ignorance

다음 빈칸에 들어갈 말로 가장 적절한 것을 고르시오.

Although a balance or harmony between partners clearly develops over time in a relationship, it is also a factor in initial attraction and interest in a partner. That is, to the extent that two people share similar verbal and nonverbal habits in a first meeting, they will be more comfortable with one another. For example, fast-paced individuals talk and move quickly and are more expressive, whereas slow-paced individuals have a different tempo and are less expressive. Initial interactions between people at opposite ends of such a continuum may be more difficult than those between similar types. In the case of contrasting styles, individuals may be less interested in pursuing a relationship than if they were similar in interaction styles. Individuals with similar styles, however, are more comfortable and find that they just seem to "click" with one another. Thus, _____ may provide a selection filter for the initiation of a relationship.

① information deficit
② cultural adaptability
③ meaning negotiation
④ behavioral coordination
⑤ unconditional acceptance

주어진 글 다음에 이어질 글의 순서로 가장 적절한 것을 고르시오. [3점]

"National forests need more roads like farmers need more drought." We heard somebody say this who was trying to persuade an audience that more roads would be bad for our national forests.

(A) An argument attempts to prove or support a conclusion. When you attempt to persuade someone, you attempt to win him or her to your point of view; trying to persuade and trying to argue are logically distinct enterprises. True, when you want to persuade somebody of something, you might use an argument.

(B) But not all arguments attempt to persuade, and many attempts to persuade do not involve arguments. In fact, giving an argument is often one of the least effective methods of persuading people — which, of course, is why so few advertisers bother with arguments. People notoriously are persuaded by the weakest of arguments and sometimes are undisturbed by even quite good arguments.

(C) The remark, however, is not an argument; it's just a statement that portrays road building in the forests in a bad light. Now, some writers define an argument as an attempt to persuade somebody of something. This is not correct.

① (A) — (C) — (B)　　② (B) — (A) — (C)
③ (B) — (C) — (A)　　④ (C) — (A) — (B)
⑤ (C) — (B) — (A)

주어진 글 다음에 이어질 글의 순서로 가장 적절한 것을 고르시오.

The desire to see and interact with animals, shaped as it is by popular culture, can be a motivating factor for travel, but negative perceptions of certain animals can perform an entirely opposite role in discouraging people from visiting some destinations.

(A) For example, there are a variety of t-shirt and tea towel designs which celebrate the dangerous animals that can be encountered in Australia. This is a whimsical reconfiguration of the perceived threat that these animals pose to some tourists considering travel to this country.

(B) The harmful effects of animals on tourism experiences has been the subject of analysis in a small number of studies, but deaths or injuries caused by animals to tourists are tiny in comparison to other causes such as drowning and vehicular accidents.

(C) Nevertheless, the possibility that they might encounter a dangerous animal such as shark or snake or catch a disease such as malaria is sufficient to stop at least some tourists from visiting destinations where such threats exist. Sometimes this fear is turned into a marketing opportunity.

*whimsical: 기발한 **reconfiguration: 재구성

① (A) — (C) — (B)　　② (B) — (A) — (C)
③ (B) — (C) — (A)　　④ (C) — (A) — (B)
⑤ (C) — (B) — (A)

모의고사 1회

글의 흐름으로 보아, 주어진 문장이 들어가기에 가장 적절한 곳을 고르시오. [3점]

> A principal vehicle of this enterprise was educational reform and specifically the building of a university system dedicated to the ideals of science, reason, and humanism.

Writing just after the end of World War I, an acute observer of the French philosophical scene judged that "philosophical research had never been more abundant, more serious, and more intense among us than in the last thirty years." (①) This flowering was due to the place of philosophy in the new educational system set up by the Third Republic in the wake of the demoralizing defeat in the Franco-Prussian War. (②) The French had been humiliated by the capture of Napoleon III at Sedan and wasted by the long siege of Paris. (③) They had also been terrified by what most of the bourgeoisie saw as seventy-three days of anarchy under the radical socialism of the Commune. (④) Much of the new Republic's effort at spiritual restoration was driven by a rejection of the traditional values of institutional religion, which it aimed to replace with an enlightened worldview. (⑤) Albert Thibaudet highlighted the importance of this reform when he labeled the Third Republic "the republic of professors."

*siege: 포위 **anarchy: 무정부

다음 글의 내용을 한 문장으로 요약하고자 한다. 빈칸 (A), (B)에 들어갈 말로 가장 적절한 것은?

> There is no question that losing weight is hard. According to one calculation, you must walk 35 miles or jog for seven hours to lose just one pound. One big problem with exercise is that we don't track it very scrupulously. A study in America found that people overestimated the number of calories they burned in a workout by a factor of four. They also then consumed, on average, about twice as many calories as they had just burned off. As Daniel Lieberman noted in *The Story of the Human Body*, a worker on a factory floor will in a year expend about 175,000 more calories than a desk worker — equivalent to more than sixty marathons. That's pretty impressive, but here's a reasonable question: how many factory workers look as if they run a marathon every six days? To be cruelly blunt, not many. That's because most of them, like most of the rest of us, replace all those burnt calories, and then some, when they are not working.
>
> *scrupulously: 용의주도하게

⬇

> Losing weight is hard because people usually think they burned a ___(A)___ number of calories than they actually did and ___(B)___ exercise by eating a lot of food.

	(A)		(B)
①	larger	—	undo
②	larger	—	intensify
③	higher	—	supplement
④	smaller	—	continue
⑤	smaller	—	delay

Cultural heritage can be understood in the narrow sense as the reservoir of cultural elements that are recognized as being significant and worthy of preservation and transfer to succeeding generations. Cultural heritage in the wide sense, however, is understood as a dynamic discursive area within which the cultural resources of the past, and their significance, are constructed through social interaction. Once (a) extracted from this discursive area, the reservoir becomes just an empty and meaningless collection of artefacts and ideas embedded in various forms. Such an understanding of cultural heritage is rooted in the idea of (b) collective memory introduced by Maurice Halbwachs. He argues that our memory about the past is socially constructed. To some extent, social conditions determine what and how we remember. The phenomenon of tradition and cultural heritage being socially determined is emphasized by Eric Hobsbawn and Terence Ranger, who consider that tradition is not reproduced but rather (c) invented.

Belief in the discursive nature of cultural heritage is based on the conviction that the criteria for determining which artefacts and behavioural patterns should be transmitted to posterity are (d) stable. On the one hand, a reservoir of cultural heritage is subject to selection and is determined by global flows, new technology, economics, cultural policy, or the sentiments of decision-makers. On the other hand, such a reservoir is the object of continual reinterpretation, which is influenced by the social position, background, biography, and cultural competences of the individuals who participate in a culture. Social interaction is the (e) essence of transition in cultural heritage.

*posterity: 후대

1회 11 .... 2025 대비 육해공사관 27 (고3)

윗글의 주제로 가장 적절한 것은? [3점]

① the significance of cultural heritage preservation
② procedures to build a reservoir for cultural heritage artefacts
③ cultural heritage's discursive characteristic as a social construct
④ discursive efforts by social organizations to designate world heritages
⑤ established criteria for categorizing artefacts based on historical values

1회 12 .... 2025 대비 육해공사관 28 (고3)

밑줄 친 (a)~(e) 중에서 문맥상 낱말의 쓰임이 적절하지 않은 것은? [3점]

① (a)　② (b)　③ (c)　④ (d)　⑤ (e)

2회 01 .... 2024 대비 육해공사관 7 (고3)

밑줄 친 stand before the long green table이 다음 글에서 의미하는 바로 가장 적절한 것은? [4점]

Serving in the military, I relied heavily on this saying to guide my actions. Whenever I had a difficult decision to make, I would ask myself, "Can you stand before the long green table?" Since WWII, the conference tables used in military boardrooms had been constructed of long, narrow pieces of furniture covered in green felt. Whenever a formal proceeding took place that required multiple officers to adjudicate an issue, the officers would gather around the table. The point of the saying was simple. If you *couldn't* make a good case to the officers sitting around the long green table, then you should reconsider your actions. Every time I was about to make an important decision, I asked myself, "Can I stand before the long green table and be satisfied that I took all the right actions?" It is one of the most fundamental questions a leader must ask themselves — and the old saying helped me remember what steps to take.

*felt: 펠트(모직이나 털을 압축해서 만든 천) **adjudicate: 판결하다

① adapt your strategy to constantly changing field conditions

② request assistance in your task from those more knowledgeable

③ courageously carry out your plan without the approval of peers

④ convincingly justify your actions to a group of authority figures

⑤ persuade your peers that their campaign strategy is not realistic

2회 02 .... 2025 대비 경찰대 28 (고3)

다음 글의 주제로 가장 적절한 것은?

No clear-cut category can encompass all jazz. Each performer's idiom is a style unto itself; if it were not so, the music would hardly be jazz. Jazz, like almost all other music, comprises three artistic activities: creating, performing, and listening. In traditional Western European music, these three activities are not always performed by the same individual, although they quite often are. In jazz, however, it is necessary for the performer to combine all three at the same time. Musical creation is an active part of any jazz performance and depends on the performers' understanding of the developing creation, an understanding gained only by their ability to listen well. They must react instantaneously to what they hear from their fellow performers, and their own contribution must be consistent with the unfolding themes and moods. Every act of musical creation in jazz is, therefore, as individual as the performer creating it.

① traits of jazz reflecting performers' individuality

② how to compose jazz for a great performance

③ similarities between jazz and Western music

④ celebrated figures in the modern jazz scene

⑤ influences of traditional music on jazz

다음 글의 제목으로 가장 적절한 것은?

There is a story about F. Yates, a prominent UK statistician. During his student years at St. John's College, Cambridge, Yates had been keen on a form of sport. It consisted of climbing about the roofs and towers of the college buildings at night. In particular, the chapel of St. John's College has a massive neo-Gothic tower adorned with statues of saints, and to Yates it appeared obvious that it would be more decorous if these saints were properly attired in surplices. One night he climbed up and did the job; next morning the result was generally much admired. But the College authorities were unappreciative and began to consider means of divesting the saints of their newly acquired garments. This was not easy, since they were well out of reach of any ordinary ladder. An attempt to lift the surplices off from above, using ropes with hooks attached, was unsuccessful. No progress was being made and eventually Yates came forward and volunteered to climb up in the daylight and bring them down. This he did to the admiration of the crowd that assembled.

*decorous: 품위 있는 **surplice: 흰 가운 ***divest: 벗기다

① A Scary Legend About the Statues at St. John's College
② A Student Who Solved a Problem of His Own Making
③ Standards of Beauty Varying from Person to Person
④ A Smart Professor Who Identified a Criminal
⑤ A Success Story of a Mysterious Architect

다음 글의 빈칸에 들어갈 말로 가장 적절한 것을 고르시오.

In terms of education, history has not always received a good press. Advising his son in 1656, Francis Osborne was far from enthusiastic about the subject. His experience of hearing contradictory reports about the Civil Wars of his own time (contemporary history), led him to be doubtful about the _____ of records of less recent events. Such historical records, he concluded, were likely to present a 'false, or at best but a contingent beliefe'; and as such they hardly warranted serious study. Osborne's anxiety about his son potentially wasting his time by studying history that is unreliable, implies an understanding of history as being ideally of a certain kind — the kind that yields certain, 'factual' knowledge about the past. Now, although that model was already under challenge in Osborne's day, it has persisted to some extent up to our own time.

*contingent: 부수적인

① continuity
② reliability
③ rediscovery
④ conciseness
⑤ predictability

다음 글의 빈칸에 들어갈 말로 가장 적절한 것을 고르시오.

Every intelligence has to _____. A human brain, which is genetically primed to categorize things, still needs to see a dozen examples as a child before it can distinguish between cats and dogs. That's even more true for artificial minds. Even the best-programmed computer has to play at least a thousand games of chess before it gets good. Part of the AI breakthrough lies in the incredible amount of collected data about our world, which provides the schooling that AIs need. Massive databases, self-tracking, web cookies, online footprints, terabytes of storage, decades of search results, and the entire digital universe became the teachers making AI smart. Andrew Ng explains it this way: "AI is akin to building a rocket ship. You need a huge engine and a lot of fuel. The rocket engine is the learning algorithms but the fuel is the huge amounts of data we can feed to these algorithms."

① be taught
② exceed itself
③ think by itself
④ be governed by rules
⑤ calculate all possibilities

다음 빈칸에 들어갈 말로 가장 적절한 것을 고르시오. [3점]

Lewis-Williams believes that the religious view of hunter groups was a contract between the hunter and the hunted. 'The powers of the underworld allowed people to kill animals, provided people responded in certain ritual ways, such as taking fragments of animals into the caves and inserting them into the "membrane".' This is borne out in the San. Like other shamanistic societies, they have admiring practices between human hunters and their prey, suffused with taboos derived from extensive natural knowledge. These practices suggest that honouring may be one method of softening the disquiet of killing. It should be said that this disquiet needn't arise because there is something fundamentally wrong with a human killing another animal, but simply because we are aware of doing the killing. And perhaps, too, because in some sense we 'know' what we are killing. We make sound guesses that the pain and desire for life we feel — our worlds of experience — have a counterpart in the animal we kill. As predators, this can create problems for us. One way to smooth those edges, then, is to _____.

*membrane: 지하 세계로 통하는 바위 표면 **suffused with: ~로 가득 찬

① view that prey with respect
② domesticate those animals
③ develop tools for hunting
④ avoid supernatural beliefs
⑤ worship our ancestors' spirits

주어진 글 다음에 이어질 글의 순서로 가장 적절한 것을 고르시오. [3점]

A large body of research in decision science has indicated that one attribute that is regularly substituted for an explicit assessment of decision costs and benefits is an affective valuation of the prospect at hand.

(A) People were willing to pay almost as much to avoid a 1 percent probability of receiving a shock as they were to pay to avoid a 99 percent probability of receiving a shock. Clearly the affective reaction to the thought of receiving a shock was overwhelming the subjects' ability to evaluate the probabilities associated.

(B) This is often a very rational attribute to substitute — affect does convey useful signals as to the costs and benefits of outcomes. A problem sometimes arises, however, when affective valuation is not supplemented by any analytic processing and adjustment at all.

(C) For example, sole reliance on affective valuation can make people insensitive to probabilities and to quantitative features of the outcome that should effect decisions. One study demonstrated that people's evaluation of a situation where they might receive a shock is insensitive to the probability of receiving the shock because their thinking is swamped by affective evaluation of the situation.

*swamp: 압도하다

① (A)—(C)—(B) ② (B)—(A)—(C)
③ (B)—(C)—(A) ④ (C)—(A)—(B)
⑤ (C)—(B)—(A)

주어진 글 다음에 이어질 글의 순서로 가장 적절한 것을 고르시오. [3점]

In the course of acquiring a language, children are exposed to only a finite set of utterances. Yet they come to use and understand an infinite set of sentences.

(A) Yet, they all arrive at pretty much the same grammar. The input that children get is haphazard in the sense that caretakers do not talk to their children to illustrate a particular point of grammar. Yet, all children develop systematic knowledge of a language.

(B) Thus, despite the severe limitations and variation in the input children receive, and also in their personal circumstances, they all develop a rich and uniform system of linguistic knowledge. The knowledge attained goes beyond the input in various ways.

(C) This has been referred to as the creative aspect of language use. This 'creativity' does not refer to the ability to write poetry or novels but rather the ability to produce and understand an unlimited set of new sentences never spoken or heard previously. The precise linguistic input children receive differs from child to child; no two children are exposed to exactly the same set of utterances.

*haphazard: 무작위적인, 되는 대로의

① (A)—(C)—(B) ② (B)—(A)—(C)
③ (B)—(C)—(A) ④ (C)—(A)—(B)
⑤ (C)—(B)—(A)

모의고사 2회

글의 흐름으로 보아, 주어진 문장이 들어가기에 가장 적절한 곳을 고르시오.

> But many signals, as they are passed from generation to generation by whatever means, go through changes that make them either more elaborate or simply different.

Many of the ritualized displays performed by animals look so bizarre to us that we wonder how they came about. (①) Most of the various forms of signaling that are used by different species of animals have not arisen afresh in each separate species. (②) As one species evolves into another, particular forms of signaling may be passed on, owing to the effects of both genes and learning or experience. (③) Some signals have significance across many species, and so remain much the same over generations and in a number of species. (④) If we examine closely related species, we can often see slight variations in a particular display and we can piece together an explanation for the spread of the display across species. (⑤) Some very elaborate displays may have begun as simpler versions of the same behavioral pattern that became more elaborate as they developed and were passed on from generation to generation.

*bizarre: 기이한

다음 글의 내용을 한 문장으로 요약하고자 한다. 빈칸 (A), (B)에 들어갈 말로 가장 적절한 것은?

> Martin Grunwald, leader of the Haptic Research Laboratory at the University of Leipzig, feels psychologists do not pay nearly enough attention to our sense of touch. With this in mind, he researched the way people spontaneously touch their faces. We all do it. You might be doing it right now while reading this. These movements are not for communication and, in most cases, we are not even aware of them. But that does not mean they serve no purpose, as Grunwald discovered. He measured the brain activity of test subjects while they tried to remember a sequence of haptic stimuli for five minutes. When he disturbed them with unpleasant noises, the subjects dramatically increased the rate at which they touched their faces. When the noises upset the rhythm of their brains and threatened to disrupt the subjects' concentration, self-touch helped them get their concentration back on track. To put it another way: self-touch grounded their minds.
>
> *haptic: 촉각의

⬇

> Even though touching our own faces seems to serve no special purpose, the research showed that the rate of subjects' self-touch ___(A)___ in accordance with the exposure to unpleasant noises, and this behavior helped their minds stay ___(B)___ .

	(A)		(B)
①	escalated	—	focused
②	escalated	—	creative
③	varied	—	hopeful
④	normalized	—	keen
⑤	normalized	—	calm

Pompeii was destroyed by the catastrophic eruption of Mount Vesuvius in 79 A.D., entombing residents under layers of volcanic ash. But there is more to this story of an ancient Roman city's doom. Research published in the journal *Frontiers in Earth Science* offers proof that Pompeii was simultaneously wrecked by a massive earthquake. The discovery establishes a new timeline for the city's collapse and shows that fresh approaches to research can (a) reveal additional secrets from well-studied archaeological sites. Researchers have always had an idea that seismic activity contributed to the city's destruction. The ancient writer Pliny the Younger reported that the eruption of Vesuvius had been accompanied by violent shaking. But, until now, no evidence had been discovered to (b) support this historical account. A team of researchers led by Domenico Sparice from Italy decided to investigate this (c) gap in the record. Dr. Sparice said that excavations of Pompeii to date had not included experts in the field of archaeoseismology, which deals with the effects of earthquakes on ancient buildings. Contributions from (d) specialists in this area were key to the discovery, he said. "The effects of seismicity have been speculated by past scholars, but no factual evidence has been reported before our study," Dr. Sparice said, adding that the finding was "very exciting." The team focused on the Insula of the Chaste Lovers. This area encompasses several buildings, including a bakery and a house where painters were evidently interrupted by the eruption, leaving their paintings (e) colored. After excavation and careful analysis, the researchers concluded that walls in the insula had collapsed because of an earthquake.

*seismic: 지진의 **excavation: 발굴

11

윗글의 제목으로 가장 적절한 것은?

① Who Found Pompeii Covered with Volcanic Ashes
② Mt. Vesuvius's Influence on the Scenery of Pompeii
③ The Eruption of Mt. Vesuvius Triggered by Earthquake
④ Seismic Timeline by Archaeological Discovery in Pompeii
⑤ The Eruption of Mt. Vesuvius Wasn't Pompeii's Only Killer

12

밑줄 친 (a)~(e) 중에서 문맥상 낱말의 쓰임이 적절하지 않은 것은? [3점]

① (a)　② (b)　③ (c)　④ (d)　⑤ (e)

3회01 .... 2021 실시 10월 학평 21 (고3)

밑줄 친 <u>we have "confusion at the frontier"</u>가 다음 글에서 의미하는 바로 가장 적절한 것은? [3점]

Two independent research groups have discovered that <u>we have "confusion at the frontier"</u> when we search the Internet. Adrian Ward, a psychologist at the University of Texas, found that engaging in Internet searches increased people's cognitive self-esteem, their sense of their own ability to remember and process information. Moreover, people who searched the Internet for facts they didn't know and were later asked where they found the information often misremembered and reported that they had known it all along. Many of them completely forgot ever having conducted the search. They gave themselves the credit instead of the Internet. In a different set of studies, researchers found that those who had searched the Internet to answer specific questions rated their ability to answer unrelated questions as higher than those who had not. The act of searching the Internet and finding answers to one set of questions caused the participants to increase their sense that they knew the answers to all questions, including those whose answers they had not researched.

① we tend to overestimate our knowledge and ability
② we are prone to putting off making final decisions
③ we often forget how easily we lose our self-esteem
④ we are overwhelmed by a vast amount of information
⑤ we strive to distinguish false information from the truth

3회02 .... 2022 실시 10월 학평 23 (고3)

다음 글의 주제로 가장 적절한 것은?

Most of us make our career choices when we are about eighteen. At eighteen, you have limited experience, very limited skills and most of what you know comes from your parents, your environment and the structured school system you have gone through. You are usually slightly better at some skills because you have spent a bit more time on them. Maybe someone in your environment was good at something and passionate enough to get you interested in spending more time in that area. It is also possible that you might have a specific physical feature — such as being tall — that might make you better at certain activities, such as playing basketball. In any case, most people make a decision regarding their career and direction in life based on their limited experiences and biases in their childhood and teenage years. This decision will come to dominate their life for many years to come. No wonder so many get it wrong! It is easier to get it wrong than to get it right, because statistically, there are more wrong ways than right ways.

① social factors that make employment unstable
② useful statistics for making a right career choice
③ reasons that an early career choice can go wrong
④ necessity to find one's aptitude as early as possible
⑤ how to overcome biases in making one's career choices

다음 글의 제목으로 가장 적절한 것은?

People don't usually think of touch as a temporal phenomenon, but it is every bit as time-based as it is spatial. You can carry out an experiment to see for yourself. Ask a friend to cup his hand, palm face up, and close his eyes. Place a small ordinary object in his palm — a ring, an eraser, anything will do — and ask him to identify it without moving any part of his hand. He won't have a clue other than weight and maybe overall size. Then tell him to keep his eyes closed and move his fingers over the object. He'll most likely identify it at once. By allowing the fingers to move, you've added time to the sensory perception of touch. There's a direct analogy between the fovea at the center of your retina and your fingertips, both of which have high acuity. Your ability to make complex use of touch, such as buttoning your shirt or unlocking your front door in the dark, depends on continuous time-varying patterns of touch sensation.

* analogy: 유사 ** fovea: (망막의) 중심와(窩) *** retina: 망막

① Touch and Movement: Two Major Elements of Humanity
② Time Does Matter: A Hidden Essence of Touch
③ How to Use the Five Senses in a Timely Manner
④ The Role of Touch in Forming the Concept of Time
⑤ The Surprising Function of Touch as a Booster of Knowledge

다음 빈칸에 들어갈 말로 가장 적절한 것을 고르시오. [4점]

In several ways, uncertainty can be understood as pervasive and written into the very script of life. Due to this, the craving for certainty has only become a means of stemming a perceived tide of phenomena that cannot yet be grasped and, to an even lesser extent, controlled. Consequently, the interplay between the desire to overcome uncertainty and instead strive towards certainty became inscribed into humans and society as a way of influencing the present and the future. This interplay is as old as the hills and is rooted in the human hope for security and the material, technological and social protection regarded as necessary for survival, comfort, and wellbeing. Mokyr shows how Western capitalist societies are indebted to all the systematic attempts to _____. According to Mokyr, the strong belief in technical progress and the continuous improvement of various aspects of life are rooted in the reasoning that emerged and developed in the philosophical movement of the Enlightenment and which created a "space" for humans' "desire to know" and practically experiment with a wide range of activities.

* stem: 저지하다

① reduce insecurity in terms of uncertainty
② outdo their forerunners in scientific areas
③ negate errors in interpretation of certainty
④ minimize the potential of human reasoning
⑤ survive the overloaded world of information

모의고사
3회

다음 빈칸에 들어갈 말로 가장 적절한 것을 고르시오. [4점]

So many accounts of democracy emphasize legislative processes or policy outcomes, but these often miss the depth of connection between communication and political culture. When culture is discussed, it's often in the context of liberal-democratic values. But the question we're asking is: What determines the valence of those values? If a democracy stands or falls on the quality of the culture propping it up, then we ought to know under what conditions those values are affirmed and rejected. We believe those conditions are determined by a society's tools of communication, facilitated through media, to persuade. Indeed, _____. If a democracy consists of citizens deciding, collectively, what ought to be done, then the manner through which they persuade one another determines nearly everything else that follows. And that privileges media ecology as the master political science. Some of its foremost practitioners, like Marshall McLuhan and Neil Postman, sensed, far better than political scientists or sociologists, that our media environment decides not just what we pay attention to but also how we think and orient ourselves in the world. *valence: 결합가

① media will soon solve communication issues in democracy
② democracies are defined by their cultures of communication
③ conflicts between individuality and collectivity are inevitable
④ democracy thrives on order rather than endless public discourse
⑤ democracies can be sustained by valuing socioeconomic dynamics

다음 빈칸에 들어갈 말로 가장 적절한 것을 고르시오. [3점]

The empiricist philosopher John Locke argued that when the human being was first born, the mind was simply a blank slate — a *tabula rasa* — waiting to be written on by experience. Locke believed that our experience shapes who we are and who we become — and therefore he also believed that, given different experiences, human beings would have different characters. The influence of these ideas was profound, particularly for the new colonies in America, for example, because these were conscious attempts to make a new start and to form a new society. The new society was to operate on a different basis from that of European culture, which was based on the feudal system in which people's place in society was almost entirely determined by birth, and which therefore tended to emphasize innate characteristics. Locke's emphasis on the importance of experience in forming the human being provided _____.

*empiricist: 경험주의자 **slate: 석판 ***feudal: 봉건 제도의

① foundations for reinforcing ties between European and colonial societies
② new opportunities for European societies to value their tradition
③ an optimistic framework for those trying to form a different society
④ an example of the role that nature plays in building character
⑤ an access to expertise in the areas of philosophy and science

주어진 글 다음에 이어질 글의 순서로 가장 적절한 것을 고르시오. [3점]

> On January 26, 2013, a band of al-Qaeda militants entered the ancient city of Timbuktu on the southern edge of the Sahara Desert.

(A) The mayor of Bamako, who witnessed the event, called the burning of the manuscripts "a crime against world cultural heritage." And he was right — or he would have been, if it weren't for the fact that he was also lying.

(B) There, they set fire to a medieval library of 30,000 manuscripts written in Arabic and several African languages and ranging in subject from astronomy to geography, history to medicine. Unknown in the West, this was the collected wisdom of an entire continent, the voice of Africa at a time when Africa was thought not to have a voice at all.

(C) In fact, just before, African scholars had collected a random assortment of old books and left them out for the terrorists to burn. Today, the collection lies hidden in Bamako, the capital of Mali, moldering in the high humidity. What was rescued by ruse is now once again in jeopardy, this time by climate.

*ruse: 책략

① (A) ─ (C) ─ (B) ② (B) ─ (A) ─ (C)
③ (B) ─ (C) ─ (A) ④ (C) ─ (A) ─ (B)
⑤ (C) ─ (B) ─ (A)

글의 흐름으로 보아, 주어진 문장이 들어가기에 가장 적절한 곳을 고르시오.

> However, while our resources come with histories of meanings, *how they come to mean* at a particular communicative moment is always open to negotiation.

The linguistic resources we choose to use do not come to us as empty forms ready to be filled with our personal intentions; rather, they come to us with meanings already embedded within them. (①) These meanings, however, are not derived from some universal, logical set of principles; rather, as with their shapes, they are built up over time from their past uses in particular contexts by particular groups of participants in the accomplishment of particular goals that, in turn, are shaped by myriad cultural, historical and institutional forces. (②) The linguistic resources we choose to use at particular communicative moments come to these moments with their conventionalized histories of meaning. (③) It is their conventionality that binds us to some degree to particular ways of realizing our collective history. (④) Thus, in our individual uses of our linguistic resources we accomplish two actions simultaneously. (⑤) We create their typical — historical — contexts of use and at the same time we position ourselves in relation to these contexts.

*myriad: 무수히 많은

모의고사 3회

글의 흐름으로 보아, 주어진 문장이 들어가기에 가장 적절한 곳을 고르시오.

> Jacques Derrida argues that instead of one line between Man on the one side and Animal on the other, there is a multiple and heterogeneous border; beyond the edge of the "so-called human," we find a heterogeneous plurality of the living.

Language, and the word "animal," deceives us. The word "animal" categorizes all non-human animals and distances humans from other animals. (①) Seeing all other animals as one group in contrast to humans reinforces anthropocentrism, which contributes to the legitimization of practices in which other animals are used for human benefit. (②) To account for this multitude, using the word "animot" has been proposed. (③) In speech it refers to the plural, the multiplicity of animals, which is necessary because there is no one "animal." (④) The "mot" in "animot" refers to the act of naming and the risks involved in drawing a distinction between human and animal by the human. (⑤) It reminds us of the fact that it is a word for animals, not a reference to an existing group of animals.

다음 글의 내용을 한 문장으로 요약하고자 한다. 빈칸 (A), (B)에 들어갈 말로 가장 적절한 것은?

> To be really smart, an online group needs to obey one final rule — and a rather counterintuitive one. The members can't have too much contact with one another. To work best, the members of a collective group ought to be able to think and work independently. This rule came to light in 1958, when social scientists tested different techniques of brainstorming. They posed a thought-provoking question: If humans had an extra thumb on each hand, what benefits and problems would emerge? Then they had two different types of groups brainstorm answers. In one group, the members worked face-to-face; in the other group, the members each worked independently, then pooled their answers at the end. You might expect the people working face-to-face to be more productive, but that wasn't the case. The team with independently working members produced almost twice as many ideas. Traditional brainstorming simply doesn't work as well as thinking alone, then pooling results.

⬇

> In brainstorming, group members who have direct contact produce ___(A)___ ideas than those who work physically separately from one another, which is against our ___(B)___.

	(A)		(B)
①	fewer	—	intuition
②	fewer	—	benefit
③	more	—	conclusion
④	more	—	intuition
⑤	smarter	—	benefit

[11~12] 다음 글을 읽고, 물음에 답하시오.

Morality is changeable and culture-dependent and expresses socially desirable behavior. But even if morality is changeable, it is by no means arbitrary, especially since the change process itself takes a relatively (a) long time (measured in years rather than weeks). This is also because a social value framework — and thus morality — provides an important orientation function: Since time immemorial, people have been thinking about moral issues and dealing with them. This makes it clear that (b) consistent values, norms, and moral concepts always play a major role when people organize themselves in social communities. Ultimately, this also results in answers to questions of justice, solidarity, and care as well as the distribution of goods and resources.

Morality acts here as the (c) common lowest denominator for a given society. The (d) advantage is based on the fact that the values underlying morality convey a socially accepted basic understanding and provide orientation in concrete decision-making situations. This makes morality functional and efficient for social groups: In order to be accepted in a community, the individual will strive not to act against this community. Conversely, this means that the behavior of the individual and the social group is ultimately (e) unpredictable. As a result, uncertainty about behavior is reduced and trust is built up.

*arbitrary: 임의적인 **denominator: 분모

11 .... 2024 대비 육해공사관 27 (고3)

윗글의 주제로 가장 적절한 것은? [4점]

① disregard of morality found in extreme conditions
② justice and solidarity as basic elements of morality
③ fundamental role of morality in human communities
④ development of morality through cultural exchanges
⑤ punishment of moral code violations across societies

12 .... 2024 대비 육해공사관 28 (고3)

밑줄 친 (a)~(e) 중에서 문맥상 낱말의 쓰임이 적절하지 않은 것은? [3점]

① (a) ② (b) ③ (c) ④ (d) ⑤ (e)

A 목적 찾기
01③ 02① 03① 04④ 05② 06① 07⑤ 08⑤ 09③ 10④
11② 12③ 13② 14③ 15① 16① 17① 18① 19① 20②

B 심경의 이해
01① 02① 03② 04③ 05② 06⑤ 07① 08② 09① 10①
11③ 12⑤ 13⑤ 14② 15② 16① 17③ 18① 19④ 20②
21① 22①

C 주장 찾기
01⑤ 02④ 03① 04③ 05① 06① 07⑤ 08② 09① 10①
11③ 12① 13① 14④ 15② 16③ 17② 18① 19⑤ 20①
21③ 22② 23②

D 밑줄 친 부분의 의미 찾기
01① 02⑤ 03③ 04③ 05① 06② 07⑤ 08⑤ 09③ 10⑤
11② 12② 13② 14④ 15⑤ 16④ 17④ 18② 19⑤ 20①
21② 22① 23④ 24⑤ 25① 26② 27② 28④

E 요지 찾기
01④ 02⑤ 03② 04③ 05① 06⑤ 07① 08③ 09④ 10①
11① 12④ 13⑤ 14⑤ 15⑤ 16① 17② 18① 19① 20①
21① 22①

F 주제 찾기
01② 02④ 03① 04④ 05③ 06④ 07② 08⑤ 09① 10⑤
11① 12① 13④ 14② 15⑤ 16① 17① 18③ 19② 20①
21① 22⑤ 23⑤

G 제목 찾기
01① 02① 03⑤ 04③ 05③ 06② 07④ 08⑤ 09① 10⑤
11① 12② 13① 14① 15① 16⑤ 17② 18① 19⑤ 20①
21① 22③ 23⑤ 24① 25③ 26②

H 도표의 이해
01⑤ 02③ 03④ 04⑤ 05③ 06② 07③ 08④ 09⑤ 10④
11② 12② 13④ 14③ 15④ 16④ 17⑤ 18④ 19④ 20④
21③ 22④

I 내용 불일치
01③ 02⑤ 03④ 04② 05⑤ 06⑤ 07④ 08③ 09④ 10④
11③ 12③ 13⑤ 14⑤ 15⑤ 16③ 17② 18④ 19⑤ 20⑤
21④ 22③

J 실용문의 이해
01④ 02④ 03③ 04③ 05③ 06⑤ 07⑤ 08④ 09③ 10④
11④ 12② 13④ 14④ 15④ 16② 17③ 18⑤ 19⑤ 20③
21⑤ 22② 23③ 24③ 25⑤ 26② 27④ 28② 29③ 30⑤
31② 32④ 33④ 34④ 35⑤ 36④ 37⑤ 38③ 39④ 40④
41② 42④ 43③

K 빈칸 완성하기
01⑤ 02⑤ 03⑤ 04② 05② 06② 07③ 08⑤ 09① 10①
11① 12⑤ 13① 14① 15② 16④ 17② 18⑤ 19③ 20③
21① 22③ 23② 24② 25③ 26③ 27① 28① 29① 30①
31③ 32④ 33② 34① 35③ 36② 37⑤ 38② 39② 40④
41④ 42① 43② 44③ 45⑤ 46② 47① 48① 49② 50④
51④ 52① 53③ 54① 55③ 56② 57⑤ 58⑤ 59① 60⑤
61② 62① 63④ 64① 65① 66② 67② 68② 69③ 70③
71⑤ 72① 73② 74① 75③ 76① 77⑤ 78① 79② 80①
81④ 82② 83① 84③ 85② 86② 87⑤ 88② 89④ 90①
91② 92② 93④

L 흐름에 맞지 않는 문장 찾기
01③ 02④ 03④ 04④ 05④ 06③ 07③ 08③ 09④ 10④
11③ 12④ 13③ 14④ 15③ 16③ 17④ 18③ 19④ 20④
21③ 22③ 23③ 24③

M 글의 순서 정하기
01① 02④ 03⑤ 04③ 05⑤ 06③ 07③ 08② 09④ 10③
11⑤ 12③ 13④ 14② 15⑤ 16① 17⑤ 18④ 19⑤ 20②
21② 22⑤ 23⑤ 24④ 25② 26③ 27⑤ 28③ 29⑤ 30⑤
31④ 32④ 33② 34④ 35④ 36⑤ 37② 38⑤ 39④ 40④
41④ 42② 43② 44④ 45③ 46⑤

N 주어진 문장 넣기
01④ 02⑤ 03④ 04④ 05④ 06④ 07⑤ 08⑤ 09⑤ 10⑤
11④ 12③ 13④ 14② 15② 16⑤ 17④ 18⑤ 19⑤ 20⑤
21④ 22② 23② 24③ 25⑤ 26④ 27③ 28③ 29④ 30③
31⑤ 32④ 33④ 34④ 35⑤ 36④ 37② 38④ 39⑤ 40④
41④ 42④ 43⑤ 44④

O 요약문 완성하기
01② 02② 03① 04① 05③ 06① 07① 08① 09③ 10①
11④ 12① 13② 14① 15② 16① 17② 18② 19① 20①
21③ 22① 23① 24① 25③

P 장문의 이해

01 ③ 02 ② 03 ② 04 ⑤ 05 ① 06 ③ 07 ③ 08 ⑤ 09 ① 10 ⑤
11 ② 12 ④ 13 ④ 14 ⑤ 15 ③ 16 ④ 17 ③ 18 ④ 19 ② 20 ⑤
21 ④ 22 ③ 23 ② 24 ⑤ 25 ① 26 ⑤ 27 ② 28 ⑤ 29 ④ 30 ③
31 ① 32 ③ 33 ① 34 ④ 35 ② 36 ⑤ 37 ③ 38 ④ 39 ① 40 ③
41 ③ 42 ② 43 ① 44 ④ 45 ③ 46 ③ 47 ② 48 ③

Q 복합 문단의 이해

01 ③ 02 ② 03 ⑤ 04 ② 05 ③ 06 ④ 07 ② 08 ② 09 ⑤ 10 ⑤
11 ② 12 ⑤ 13 ④ 14 ⑤ 15 ⑤ 16 ③ 17 ② 18 ⑤ 19 ② 20 ③
21 ③ 22 ④ 23 ④ 24 ⑤ 25 ⑤ 26 ② 27 ② 28 ④ 29 ① 30 ④
31 ⑤ 32 ③ 33 ③ 34 ③ 35 ③ 36 ② 37 ③ 38 ⑤ 39 ③ 40 ⑤
41 ⑤ 42 ④ 43 ② 44 ⑤ 45 ⑤ 46 ④ 47 ② 48 ② 49 ② 50 ②
51 ⑤ 52 ③ 53 ⑤ 54 ④ 55 ⑤ 56 ③ 57 ③ 58 ② 59 ⑤ 60 ②
61 ④ 62 ③ 63 ③

〈고난도 유형 독해 모의고사〉

1회

01 ④ 02 ① 03 ② 04 ④ 05 ⑤ 06 ④ 07 ④ 08 ③ 09 ⑤ 10 ①
11 ③ 12 ④

2회

01 ④ 02 ① 03 ② 04 ② 05 ① 06 ① 07 ③ 08 ④ 09 ④ 10 ①
11 ⑤ 12 ⑤

3회

01 ① 02 ③ 03 ② 04 ① 05 ② 06 ③ 07 ② 08 ④ 09 ② 10 ①
11 ③ 12 ⑤

A DREAM written down with a date becomes a GOAL.

A goal broken down becomes a PLAN.

A plan backed by ACTION makes your dream come true.

- Greg S. Reid

🍀 차 례

Special 고난도 유형 독해 모의고사

> **자이 쌤's Follow Me!** – 홈페이지에서 파일 제공
>
> 수경출판사 홈페이지 로그인 ➡ 상단 [학습자료실]
>
> ➡ [교재관련자료] ➡ [독해 실전] 검색
>
> ➡ [자이쌤 특별자료] 다운로드

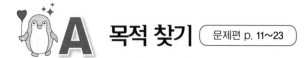

A 01 정답 ③ ＊부적절한 댓글 자제 요청

Hello, everyone! // Welcome back / to your favorite online channel, *With Ethan*. //

안녕하세요,여러분 // 다시 오신 것을 환영합니다 / 여러분이 가장 좋아하는 온라인 채널인 *With Ethan*에 //

as: ~처럼, ~듯이
목적격 관계대명사
As always, / I'm trying to make this channel a place / that my followers of all ages can enjoy. //

항상 그렇듯이 / 저는 이 채널을 공간으로 만들기 위해 노력하고 있습니다 / 모든 연령대의 팔로워가 즐길 수 있는 //

동사
Recently, in the comments section, / there have been
주어 주격 관계대명사(선행사 language)
some examples of language / that is inappropriate for younger viewers. // 단서 1 어린 시청자에게 부적절한 댓글이 있었음

최근 댓글난에 / 언어 사례가 몇 가지 있었습니다 / 어린 시청자에게 부적절한 //

주격 관계대명사
Also, there have been some comments / that are not relevant to this channel. // 단서 2 채널과 관계없는 댓글도 있었음

또한, 댓글도 일부 있었습니다 / 이 채널과 관련이 없는 //

These kinds of comments / are unacceptable for a channel like this. //

이런 종류의 댓글은 / 이런 채널에서 허용되지 않습니다 / 단서 3 부적절하거나 관련 없는 댓글은 이 채널에 달지 말 것을 요청함
목적어절 접속사
I would really like to ask / that all of my followers keep these
so that+주어+동사: ~가 …할 수 있도록
things in mind / so that we can all enjoy this channel. // 간절히 부탁드립니다 / 모든 팔로워가 이러한 점을 염두에 두시길 / 우리 모두 이 채널을 즐길 수 있도록 //

I always appreciate your time and support. //
항상 여러분의 시간과 성원에 감사드립니다 //

Please keep watching. // 계속 시청해 주시기 바랍니다 //

- comment ⓝ 댓글 · inappropriate ⓐ 부적절한
- relevant ⓐ 관련이 있는 · keep ~ in mind ~을 염두에 두다

안녕하세요, 여러분! 여러분이 가장 좋아하는 온라인 채널인 *With Ethan*에 다시 오신 것을 환영합니다. 항상 그렇듯이 저는 이 채널을 모든 연령대의 팔로워가 즐길 수 있는 공간으로 만들기 위해 노력하고 있습니다. 최근 댓글난에 어린 시청자에게 부적절한 언어 사례가 몇 가지 있었습니다. 또한 이 채널과 관련이 없는 댓글도 일부 있었습니다. 이런 종류의 댓글은 이런 채널에서 허용되지 않습니다. 우리 모두 이 채널을 즐길 수 있도록 모든 팔로워가 이러한 점을 염두에 두시길 간절히 부탁드립니다. 항상 여러분의 시간과 성원에 감사드립니다. 계속 시청해 주시기 바랍니다.

다음 글의 목적으로 가장 적절한 것은?
① 새로 개설한 온라인 채널을 홍보하려고 채널 홍보에 대한 내용이 아님
② 온라인 생방송 날짜 변경을 공지하려고 생방송 날짜 변경에 대한 언급은 없음
③ 부적절한 댓글을 쓰지 않도록 요청하려고
These kinds of comments are unacceptable ~ we can all enjoy this channel.
④ 온라인 채널 구독 연령 제한을 고지하려고
어린 시청자에게 부적절한 댓글을 달지 말라는 것이 연령 제한에 관한 내용이 아님
⑤ 온라인 구독자들의 요청 사항을 공유하려고
구독자의 요청이 아니라 운영자의 요청 사항임

외 정답? [정답률 80%]

자신이 운영하는 온라인 채널의 댓글에 최근 어린 시청자에게 부적절한 언어 사례가 있었다고 밝히며, 앞으로는 이러한 일이 다시 발생하지 않기를 부탁하는 내용이다.
▶ 따라서 글의 목적으로 가장 적절한 것은 ③이다.

외 오답?

① 채널 홍보에 대한 내용이 아니다.
② 생방송 날짜 변경에 대한 언급은 없다.
④ 어린 시청자에게 부적절한 댓글을 달지 말라는 것이지 연령 제한에 관한 내용이 아니다.
⑤ 구독자의 요청이 아니라 운영자의 요청 사항을 담은 글이다.

A 02 정답 ① ＊공원 재개장 행사 초대

Dear Custard Valley Park members, /
Custard Valley 공원 회원께 /

미래시제 수동태
Custard Valley Park's grand reopening event / will be held / on June 1st. //

Custard Valley 공원의 성대한 재개장 행사가 / 열릴 것입니다 / 6월 1일에 //

For this exciting occasion, / we are offering free admission / to all visitors / on the reopening day. //

이 신나는 행사를 위해 / 저희는 무료입장을 제공합니다 / 모든 방문객에게 / 재개장 당일 //

a food stand를 수식하는 현재분사구
There will be a food stand / selling ice cream and snacks. //

음식 노점이 있을 것입니다 / 아이스크림과 간식을 판매하는 //

We would like to invite you, our valued members, / to celebrate this event. // 단서 재개장 행사에 초대하고자 함

저희는 저희의 소중한 회원인 여러분을 초대하고 싶습니다 / 이 행사를 축하하기 위해 //

Please come and explore the park's new features / such as tennis courts and a flower garden. //

공원의 새로운 특별시설을 오셔서 둘러보세요 / 테니스 코트와 꽃 정원과 같은 //

Just relax / and enjoy the beautiful scenery. //
그저 긴장을 풀고 / 아름다운 경치를 즐기십시오 //

We are confident / that you will love the new changes, / and we
전치사 동명사구
are looking forward to seeing you soon. //

저희는 확신하며 / 새로운 변화를 매우 좋아하실 것으로 / 여러분을 곧 다시 뵙기를 고대하고 있습니다 //

Sincerely,
Katherine Carter
Park Management Team /
공원 관리 팀 Katherine Carter 드림 /

- occasion ⓝ 행사, 때 · admission ⓝ 입장
- food stand 음식 노점 · valued ⓐ 귀중한, 소중한
- celebrate ⓥ 축하하다 · feature ⓝ 특색 · scenery ⓝ 경치
- confident ⓐ 자신감 있는, 확신하는

Custard Valley 공원 회원께
6월 1일에 Custard Valley 공원의 성대한 재개장 행사가 열릴 것입니다. 이 신나는 행사를 위해 재개장 당일 모든 방문객에게 무료입장을 제공합니다. 아이스크림과 간식을 판매하는 음식 노점이 있을 것입니다. 이 행사를 축하하기 위해 우리의 소중한 회원인 여러분을 초대하고 싶습니다. 테니스 코트와 꽃 정원 등 공원의 새로운 특별시설을 오셔서 둘러보시기를 바랍니다. 그저 긴장을 풀고 아름다운 경치를 즐기십시오. 새로운 변화를 매우 좋아하실 것으로 확신하며 곧 다시 뵙기를 고대하고 있습니다.
공원 관리 팀 Katherine Carter 드림

다음 글의 목적으로 가장 적절한 것은?
① 공원 재개장 행사에 초대하려고 We would like to invite you, our valued members, to celebrate this event.
② 공원 운영 시간 변경을 공지하려고 운영 시간이 변경되었다는 언급은 없음
③ 공원 이용 규칙 준수를 당부하려고 이용 규칙은 언급되지 않음
④ 공원 입장 시 유의 사항을 안내하려고 유의 사항을 안내한 것이 아님
⑤ 공원 리모델링 사업 계획을 설명하려고 리모델링을 마치고 재개장함

외 정답? [정답률 97%]

- 6월 1일에 Custard Valley 공원의 성대한 재개장 행사가 열릴 것입니다.
- 이 행사를 축하하기 위해 우리의 소중한 회원인 여러분을 초대하고 싶습니다.

➡ 공원의 재개장 행사에 대해 알리며 회원을 초대하는 편지이므로 정답은 ①이다.

왜 오답 ?

② 운영 시간이 변경되었음을 알리는 것이 아니다.
③ 이용 규칙에 대한 언급은 없다.
④ 어떤 유의 사항에 대해 설명하는 것이 아니다.
⑤ 재개장 행사이므로 리모델링을 마쳤을 것이다.

A 03 정답 ① ＊Rosydale City 마라톤 대회 취소 공지

Dear Rosydale City Marathon Racers, /
Rosydale City 마라톤 대회 참가자분들께 /

We are really grateful to all of you / who have signed up for /
　　　　　　　　　　　　　　　　　주격 관계대명사

the 10th Rosydale City Marathon / that was scheduled for this
　　　　　　　　　　　　　　　　주격 관계대명사

coming Saturday at 10 a.m. //
모든 분께 진심으로 감사드립니다 / 등록해 주신 / 제10회 Rosydale City Marathon
대회에 / 이번 토요일 오전 10시로 예정되었던 //

Unfortunately, / as you may already know, / the weather
　　　　　　　　　　　목적어절을 이끄는 접속사

forecast says / that there is going to be a downpour / throughout

the race day. //
안타깝게도 / 이미 알고 계실 수도 있지만 / 일기 예보가 말해 줍니다 / 폭우가 쏟아질
것이라고 / 마라톤 대회 당일 내내 //

　　　　　　　　　　　목적어절을 이끄는 접속사
We truly hoped / that the race would go smoothly. //
저희는 진심으로 바랐습니다 / 대회가 순조롭게 진행되기를 //

　　　　가주어　　진주어절을 이끄는 접속사
However, / it is likely / that the heavy rain will make the roads /
　　　　　　동사 make의 목적격 보어
too slippery and dangerous for the racers / to run safely. //
하지만 / 가능성이 있습니다 / 폭우가 도로를 만들 / 대회 참가자들에게 너무 미끄럽고
위험하게 / 안전하게 달리기에 //

As a result, / we have decided / to cancel the race. //
그래서 / 저희는 결정했습니다 / 대회를 취소하기로 // **단서** 대회를 취소하기로 결정함
사이에 목적어절을 이끄는 접속사 that 생략
We hope you understand / and we promise to hold another race
/ in the near future. //
여러분의 양해를 바랍니다 / 그리고 다른 대회를 개최할 것을 약속드립니다 / 가까운 미래에 //

Sincerely, Martha Kingsley Race Manager /
대회 책임자 Martha Kingsley 드림 /

· sign up for ~에 등록하다　· scheduled ⓐ 예정된
· downpour ⓝ 폭우　· slippery ⓐ 미끄러운

Rosydale City Marathon 대회 참가자 여러분께,
이번 토요일 오전 10시로 예정되었던 제10회 Rosydale City Marathon
대회에 등록해 주신 모든 분께 진심으로 감사드립니다. 안타깝게도, 이미 알고
계실 수도 있지만, 일기 예보에 따르면 마라톤 대회 당일 내내 폭우가 쏟아질
것이라 합니다. 저희는 대회가 순조롭게 진행되기를 진심으로 바랐습니다.
하지만 폭우로 인해 대회 참가자들이 안전하게 달리기에는 도로가 너무
미끄럽고 위험해질 것 같습니다. 그래서 저희는 대회를 취소하기로 했습니다.
여러분의 양해를 부탁드리면서 가까운 미래에 다른 대회를 개최할 것을
약속드립니다.
대회 책임자 Martha Kingsley 드림

다음 글의 목적으로 가장 적절한 것은?

① 마라톤 경기 취소 사실을 공지하려고 폭우로 인한 마라톤 경기 취소 사실을 공지함
② 마라톤 경기 사전 행사 참여를 독려하려고
　마라톤 경기 사전 행사 참여를 독려하고 있지 않음
③ 마라톤 경기 참가비 환불 절차를 설명하려고
　참가비 환불 절차를 설명하는 내용이 없음
④ 마라톤 경기 참여 시 규칙 준수를 당부하려고
　마라톤 경기 참여 시 규칙 준수를 언급하지 않았음
⑤ 마라톤 경기 진행에 따른 도로 통제를 안내하려고
　마라톤 경기 진행에 따른 도로 통제를 위한 글이 아님

왜 정답 ? [정답률 99%]

Rosydale City Marathon 대회 당일 내내 폭우가 예보되어 마라톤 대회 참가자들의
안전을 위해 마라톤 대회를 취소하게 되었음을 공지하는 내용의 글이다.
▶ 따라서 글의 목적으로 가장 적절한 것은 ①이다.

왜 오답 ?

② 마라톤 경기 사전 행사 참여를 독려하고 있지 않다.
③ 마라톤 경기 참가비 환불 절차를 설명하는 글이 아니다.
④ 마라톤 경기 참여 시 규칙 준수를 당부하고 있지 않다.
⑤ 마라톤 경기 진행에 따른 도로 통제를 안내하고 있는 글이 아니다.

배지오 | 2025 수능 응시·성남 낙생고 졸

두 번째 문장에 City Marathon이라는 단어를 보고 주제가
마라톤이라는 것을 파악해야 돼. 그리고 다음 문장에서는
Unfortunately를 보고, 마라톤 행사에 차질이 생겼음을
예상할 수 있어. 그 이후에도 a downpour throughout the
race day를 보고 날씨로 인해 마라톤 행사에 차질이 생겼음을 파악할 수 있지.
마지막으로 As a result, we have decided to cancel the race. 부분을 통해
결국 마라톤 행사가 취소되었음을 알 수 있었어!

A 04 정답 ④ ＊Royal Ocean Cruises 독점 판촉 상품 안내

Dear Valued Members, / 소중한 고객님들께 /

We have exciting news / here at Royal Ocean Cruises! //
흥미진진한 소식이 있습니다 / 여기 저희 Royal Ocean Cruises에 //
　부사적 용법(목적)　　　　　　　　　　　　부사적 용법(감정의 원인)
To thank you for your loyalty, / we are thrilled / to offer you an

exclusive promotion! // **단서** 독점 판촉 상품을 제공하게 되어 기쁘다고 함
여러분의 충심에 대해 감사드리고자 / 저희는 매우 기쁩니다 / 여러분에게 독점 판촉 상품을
제공하게 되어 //
　　　　　　　　　　　　　　　　　　cruise를 수식하는 현재분사
Make a reservation / for any cruise / departing within the next

six months / and enjoy a 15% discount. //
예약하세요 / 어느 유람선 여행이든 / 향후 6개월 이내에 출발하는 / 그리고 15% 할인을
누리십시오 //

Additionally, / we are offering / a free specialty dining package /
　　　　　　　　　　　　　　　　　　　형용사적 용법
and a $20 coupon / to use at the onboard gift shop. //
게다가 / 저희는 제공하고 있습니다 / 무료 특식 패키지 / 그리고 20달러짜리 쿠폰을 / 선내
선물 가게에서 사용할 수 있는 //
부사적 용법(목적)
To take advantage of this offer, / simply go to our website / and

enter the promotion code 'ROC25'. //
이 제의를 이용하기 위해 / 그저 저희 홈페이지에 들어오세요 / 그리고 프로모션 코드
'ROC25'를 입력하세요 //

We look forward to welcoming you back aboard / for another

unforgettable journey. //
저희는 다시 승선하신 여러분을 환영하기를 학수고대하고 있습니다 / 또 한 번의 잊지 못할
여행을 위해 //

Thank you / for your continued loyalty and support. //
감사드립니다 / 지속적인 충심과 지지에 //

Sincerely, / 진심을 담아 /

Cindy Robins / Cindy Robins /

Customer Relations Manager / 고객 관계 매니저 /

· loyalty ⓝ 충심, 충성　· thrilled ⓐ 매우 기쁜
· exclusive ⓐ 독점적인　· reservation ⓝ 예약
· depart ⓥ 출발하다　· specialty ⓝ 특별 (사항)
· onboard ⓐ 선내의, 기내의　· advantage ⓝ 편의, 제의
· aboard ⓐⓓ 승선하여, 탑승하여　· unforgettable ⓐ 잊을 수 없는
· journey ⓝ 여행

소중한 고객님들께,
여기 저희 Royal Ocean Cruises에 흥미진진한 소식이 있습니다! 여러분의
충심에 대해 감사드리고자, 저희가 여러분에게 독점 판촉 상품을 제공하게 되어
매우 기쁩니다! 향후 6개월 이내에 출발하는 어느 유람선 여행이든 예약하시고
15% 할인을 누리십시오. 게다가 저희는 무료 특식 패키지와 선내 선물
가게에서 사용할 수 있는 20달러짜리 쿠폰을 제공하고 있습니다. 이 제의를

이용하고자 하시면, 저희 홈페이지에 들어오셔서 프로모션 코드 'ROC25'를 입력하기만 하세요. 저희는 또 한 번의 잊지 못할 여행을 위해 다시 승선하신 여러분을 환영하기를 학수고대하고 있습니다. 지속적인 충심과 지지에 감사드립니다.
고객 관계 매니저 Cindy Robins 드림

다음 글의 목적으로 가장 적절한 것은?

① 식사 메뉴 변경 사유를 설명하려고 무료 특식 패지키를 언급했을 뿐임
② 여행 후기 작성 참여를 독려하려고 여행 후기 작성 참여를 독려하는 내용이 아님
③ 여행 일정 변경 사항을 공지하려고 여행 일정 변경 사항 공지에 대한 내용은 없음
④ 여행 상품 판촉 행사를 안내하려고 여행사의 독점 상품 판촉 행사를 안내하고 있음
⑤ 고객 감사 행사 아이디어를 공모하려고 고객의 충심과 지지에 감사한다는 것으로 만든 오답

〉왜 정답? [정답률 90%]

여행사의 고객 관계 매니저가 고객에게 독점 판촉 상품에 관해 설명하며 구매를 권유하는 내용이다.

▶ 따라서 글의 목적으로 가장 적절한 것은 ④이다.

〉왜 오답?

① 무료 특식 패지키를 언급했을 뿐이고, 식사 메뉴 변경 사유를 설명하고 있지 않다.
② 여행 후기 작성 참여를 독려하지 않고 있다.
③ 여행 일정 변경 사항을 공지하는 것이 아니다.
⑤ 고객의 충심과 지지에 감사한다는 것으로 만든 오답이다.

A 05 정답 ② ＊연설자 제안 거절

I hope this email finds you well. //
이 이메일이 잘 전달되었기를 바랍니다 //

Thank you for considering me as a speaker / for the upcoming Digital Marketing Workshop. // **단서 1** 글쓴이를 디지털 마케팅 워크숍의 연설자로 고려함
연사로 고려해 주셔서 감사합니다 / 다가오는 디지털 마케팅 워크숍에서 //

I appreciate the invitation and your thoughtfulness. //
초대해 주신것과 배려에 감사드립니다 //

The workshop sounds like an amazing event, / and I would have loved to participate. // would have p.p. (유감)
워크숍은 정말 멋진 행사인 것 같고 / 참여하고 싶었습니다 //

목적어절을 이끄는 접속사
However, I regret to inform you / that I will be overseas on a business trip during the workshop. // **단서 2** 워크숍 기간 동안 출장을 감
하지만 아쉽게도 알려드립니다 / 워크숍 기간 동안 해외 출장이 있어 참석할 수 없음을 //

가주어 진주어절을 이끄는 접속사 (일이) 잘 풀리다
It is unfortunate that the timing does not work out. //
타이밍이 맞지 않아 안타깝습니다 //

단서 3 연설자로 참석할 수 없다고 함
Although I cannot attend as a speaker this time, / I remain hopeful for future opportunities where our schedules might coincide. // 관계부사
이번에는 연설자로 참석할 수 없지만 / 앞으로 일정이 맞는 기회가 있기를 희망합니다 //

I hope the workshop goes well. //
워크숍이 잘 진행되기를 바랍니다 //

- **appreciate** ⓥ 감사하다 · **invitation** ⓝ 초대
- **thoughtfulness** ⓝ 사려 깊음 · **overseas** ⓐ 해외의
- **work out** (일이) 잘 풀리다 · **attend** ⓥ 참석하다
- **opportunity** ⓝ 기회

이 이메일이 잘 전달되었기를 바랍니다. 다가오는 디지털 마케팅 워크숍에서 연설자로 고려해 주셔서 감사합니다. 초대해 주신것과 배려에 감사드립니다. 워크숍은 정말 멋진 행사인 것 같고, 참여하고 싶었습니다. 하지만 아쉽게도 워크숍 기간 동안 해외 출장이 있어 참석할 수 없음을 알려드립니다. 타이밍이 맞지 않아 안타깝습니다. 이번에는 연사로 참석할 수 없지만, 앞으로 일정이 맞는 기회가 있기를 희망합니다. 워크숍이 잘 진행되기를 바랍니다.

다음 글의 목적으로 가장 적절한 것은?

① 디지털 마케팅 워크숍에 참여를 독려하려고 워크숍 참여를 독려하고 있지 않음
② 연설자로 참석해 달라는 제안을 거절하려고 Although I cannot attend at a speaker this time
③ 워크숍의 변경된 장소를 안내하려고 워크숍 장소 변경에 대한 글은 아님
④ 행사가 취소되었음을 공지하려고 행사 취소를 공지하지 않음
⑤ 해외 출장 일정을 조정하려고 해외 출장 일정 조정에 대한 언급은 없음

〉왜 정답? [정답률 95%]

다가오는 디지털 마케팅 워크숍의 연설자로 초청 받았지만, 워크숍 기간 동안 출장이 있어 참석하지 못한다는 내용이다.

▶ 따라서 글의 목적으로 가장 적절한 것은 ②이다.

〉왜 오답?

① 디지털 마케팅 워크숍에 대한 언급은 있었으나, 참여를 독려하는 내용은 아니다.
③ 워크숍의 장소가 변경되었다는 내용은 없다.
④ 워크숍이 취소되었다는 내용이 아니라, 참석하지 못한다는 내용이다.
⑤ 출장 때문에 워크숍에 참석을 못한다고 했지, 일정을 조정하려는 내용은 아니다.

A 06 정답 ① ＊유연 근무제 실시 계획 안내

Dear Staff, / 직원 여러분에게 /

My name is Laura Miller, the Human Resources Manager. //
제 이름은 인사 관리자 Laura Miller입니다 //

~로 형용사적 용법 과거분사(area roadways 수식)
As part of our efforts / to reduce traffic on newly built area roadways, / we are starting to offer flextime working hours / to eligible employees. // **단서** 유연 근무 시간 제공을 시작함
명사적 용법
우리의 노력의 일부로 / 새로 건설된 지역 도로의 교통량을 줄이기 위한 / 우리는 유연 근무 시간 제공을 시작할 것입니다 / 자격이 있는 직원들에게 //

Under the plan, / staffers could begin work / 60 to 90 minutes before or after ordinary business hours, / adjusting their scheduled departure time accordingly. // 분사구문을 이끎 과거분사(departure time 수식)
그 계획하에 / 직원들은 일을 시작할 수 있습니다 / 통상 근무 시간의 60분에서 90분 전후에 / 그리고 그에 따라 예정된 출발 시간을 조정할 수 있습니다 //

수동태
All requests for flextime / must be submitted to departmental supervisors and will be approved / if they do not conflict / with the staffing needs of the company. // 미래시제 수동태
모든 유연 근무 요청은 / 부서의 관리자에게 제출되어야 하고 승인될 것입니다 / 상충되지 않는다면 / 회사의 인력 수요와 //

수동태
In addition, / flextime schedules will be reviewed every four months / to assure / that they do not adversely affect company goals. // 부사적용법(목적) 목적어절 접속사 affect: 영향을 미치다 / effect: 영향
또한 / 유연 근무 일정은 4개월마다 검토될 것입니다 / 확실히 하기 위해 / 회사 목표에 불리하게 영향을 미치지 않는 것을 //

Best regards, Laura Miller / Laura Miller 드림 /

- **flextime** ⓝ 유연 근무제 · **eligible** ⓐ ~할[가질] 수 있는
- **staffer** ⓝ 직원 · **submit** ⓥ 제출하다 · **supervisor** ⓝ 감독관
- **approve** ⓥ 승인하다, 찬성하다 · **adversely** ⓐⓓ 불리하게, 반대로

직원 여러분에게,
제 이름은 인사 관리자 Laura Miller입니다. 새로 건설된 지역 도로의 교통량을 줄이기 위한 우리의 노력의 일부로, 우리는 자격이 있는 직원들에게 유연 근무 시간 제공을 시작할 것입니다. 그 계획하에, 직원들은 통상 근무 시간의 60분에서 90분 전후에 일을 시작하여 그에 따라 예정된 출발 시간을 조정할 수 있습니다. 모든 유연 근무 요청은 부서의 관리자에게 제출되어야 하고 회사의 인력 수요와 상충되지 않는다면, 승인될 것입니다. 또한, 유연 근무 일정은 회사 목표에 불리하게 영향을 미치지 않는 것을 확실히 하기 위해 4개월마다 검토될 것입니다.
Laura Miller 드림

다음 글의 목적으로 가장 적절한 것은?

① 유연 근무제 실시 계획을 안내하려고
　we are starting to offer flextime working hours to eligible employees
② 직장 내 갈등 조정 기구 신설을 홍보하려고
　갈등 조정 기구에 대한 언급은 없음
③ 유연 근무제의 만족도 조사 참여를 독려하려고
　단순히 유연 근무제라는 단어를 넣어 만든 함정
④ 부서별 유연 근무 신청 승인 결과를 통보하려고
　유연 근무 신청 승인을 언급한 것으로 만든 오답
⑤ 교통량 감소를 위한 대중교통 이용을 장려하려고
　대중 교통 이용을 장려하지는 않았음

왜 정답? [정답률 96%]

유연 근무제를 새롭게 실시한다고 공지하며, 유연 근무 가능 시간, 유연 근무 요청 방법, 유연 근무 일정 검토 시기 등을 안내하고 있다.
▶ 따라서 글의 목적으로 가장 적절한 것은 ①이다.

왜 오답?

② 신설된 건 직장 내 갈등 조정 기구가 아니다.
③ 새롭게 도입된 유연 근무제에 대한 내용이지, 만족도 조사에 대한 내용은 아니다.
④ 유연 근무 신청 방법에 대한 내용은 있으나, 그 결과를 통보하는 것은 아니다. 주의
⑤ 새로 건설된 지역 도로의 교통량을 줄이기 위해 유연 근무제를 도입한다는 내용은 있으나 대중교통 이용을 장려하지는 않았다.

A 07 정답 ⑤ ＊영화 'Upagrah' 촬영 허가 요청

My name is Rohan Kaul, / the producer / of the upcoming film 'Upagrah.' //
제 이름은 Rohan Kaul이고 / 제작자입니다 / 곧 개봉할 영화 'Upagrah'의 //

'-와 관해'
I am reaching out to you / regarding a matter of importance / '-와 관련하여'
concerning the shooting of some scenes for our film. //
당신에게 연락을 드립니다 / 중요한 사항에 관해 / 저희 영화를 위한 일부 장면의 촬영과 관련하여 //

We have identified Gulab Park, Mumbai, / as an ideal location for these scenes. //
저희는 Mumbai의 Gulab 공원을 찾았습니다 / 이 장면들을 위한 이상적인 장소로 //

We are hoping to conduct this shoot / on 3rd June 2024, from 1p.m. to 6p.m. // 단서 1 특정 시간에 해당 장소에서 촬영하는 것을 희망함
저희는 이 촬영을 수행하기를 희망하고 있습니다 / 2024년 6월 3일 오후 1시부터 오후 6시까지 //

부사적 용법(목적)
We have chosen Monday for the shooting day / to minimize traffic issues and disruption to the public. //
저희는 월요일을 촬영일로 선택했습니다 / 교통 문제와 대중에게 끼칠 혼란을 최소화하기 위해 //

명사적 용법(promises의 목적어)
During the shoot, / our team promises to follow all rules and regulations, / ensuring no inconvenience is caused to the public. //
분사구문
촬영 동안에 / 저희 팀은 모든 규칙과 규정을 준수할 것을 약속드립니다 / 대중에게 어떠한 불편도 야기되지 않을 것을 확실히 하면서 //

단서 2 공원 내 촬영 허가를 구하고 있음
We would be so grateful / if you granted permission for the shoot / so that we can put the beautiful scenery of the park / in our film. //
부사절 접속사(목적)
우리는 매우 감사할 것입니다 / 촬영을 위한 허가를 해 주신다면 / 공원의 아름다운 배경을 담을 수 있도록 / 저희 영화에 //

We look forward to your response. //
당신의 답변을 고대합니다 //

- concerning prep ~에 관한[관련된]　• shooting ⓝ (영화) 촬영
- disruption ⓝ 혼란　• grant ⓥ 승인하다, 허락하다
- permission ⓝ 허락, 승인

제 이름은 Rohan Kaul이고 곧 개봉할 영화 'Upagrah'의 제작자입니다. 저희 영화를 위한 일부 장면의 촬영과 관련하여 중요한 사항에 관해 당신에게 연락을 드립니다. 저희는 이 장면들을 위한 이상적인 장소로 Mumbai의 Gulab

---

공원을 찾았습니다. 저희는 2024년 6월 3일 오후 1시부터 오후 6시까지 이 촬영을 수행하기를 희망하고 있습니다. 저희는 교통 문제와 대중에게 끼칠 혼란을 최소화하기 위해 월요일을 촬영일로 선택했습니다. 촬영 동안에, 저희 팀은 대중에게 어떠한 불편도 야기되지 않을 것을 확실히 하면서 모든 규칙과 규정을 준수할 것을 약속드립니다. 저희 영화에 공원의 아름다운 배경을 담을 수 있도록 촬영을 위한 허가를 해 주신다면 우리는 매우 감사할 것입니다. 당신의 답변을 고대합니다.

다음 글의 목적으로 가장 적절한 것은?

① 주말 영화 시사회에 초대하려고　시사회는 언급되지 않음
② 공원 이용 시간의 연장을 건의하려고　시간 연장이 아닌 촬영 허가를 얻고 있음
③ 촬영을 위한 장비 대여 방법을 문의하려고　관련 없음
④ 행사 운영을 위한 교통 통제를 요청하려고　교통 혼잡을 최소화할 수 있는 시간에 진행함
⑤ 영화 촬영을 위해 장소 사용 허가를 얻으려고
　We would be so grateful if you granted permission for the shoot

왜 정답? [정답률 91%]

영화 제작자인 Rohan Kaul은 Gulab 공원에서 영화 촬영을 희망한다며, 촬영을 위한 장소 사용 허가를 요청하고 있다. 따라서 글의 목적으로 가장 적절한 것은 ⑤이다.

왜 오답?

① 시사회는 언급되지 않았다.
② 시간 연장은 언급하지 않았다.
③ 장비가 아닌 장소 사용을 요청하고 있다.
④ 교통 혼잡을 최소화하겠다고 했지 통제해달라는 것이 아니다.

A 08 정답 ⑤ ＊다른 회사로의 이직 알림

가주어　　　　　　　진주어
It has been a privilege / to serve in this company / for the past four years. //
영광이었습니다 / 이 회사에서 근무한 것은 / 지난 4년간 //

The experiences and insights / I have gained / as a safety 사이에 목적격 관계대명사 생략
manager / have been invaluable. //
경험과 통찰력은 / 제가 얻었던 / 안전 관리자로서 / 귀중했습니다 //

However, / after careful consideration, / I have accepted a position / at another company / and will be leaving Lewis Ltd. // 미래진행시제
하지만 / 신중한 고려 후에 / 저는 직책을 수락하였고 / 다른 회사에서 / Lewis Ltd.를 떠날 것입니다 // 단서 다른 회사의 직책을 수락해 회사를 떠날 것이라 함

This was not an easy decision to make, / but I am confident / that my new role will help me / with my future goals. //
형용사적 용법　　　　명사절 접속사
이것이 내리기 쉬운 결정은 아니었지만 / 저는 확신합니다 / 저의 새로운 역할이 도움이 될 거라 / 제 미래의 목표에 //

My last day of work will be on April 30th. //
제 마지막 근무일은 4월 30일이 될 것입니다 //

부사적 용법(목적)
I will do all I can / to assist / in a smooth transfer of duties. //
제가 할 수 있는 모든 것을 다 할 것입니다 / 돕기 위해 / 매끄러운 인수인계를 //

I wish / both you and Lewis Ltd. / every good fortune. //
저는 빕니다 / 당신과 Lewis Ltd. 모두에게 / 행운이 가득하기를 //

- privilege ⓝ 영광, 특권　• insight ⓝ 통찰력
- invaluable ⓐ 귀중한

지난 4년간 이 회사에서 근무한 것은 영광이었습니다. 안전 관리자로서 제가 얻었던 경험과 통찰력은 귀중했습니다. 하지만, 신중한 고려 후에, 저는 다른 회사에서 직책을 수락하였고, Lewis Ltd.를 떠날 것입니다. 이것이 내리기 쉬운 결정은 아니었지만, 저는 저의 새로운 역할이 제 미래의 목표에 도움이 될 거라 확신합니다. 제 마지막 근무일은 4월 30일이 될 것입니다. 매끄러운 인수인계를 돕기 위해 제가 할 수 있는 모든 것을 다 할 것입니다. 저는 당신과 Lewis Ltd. 모두에게 행운이 가득하기를 빕니다.

다음 글의 목적으로 가장 적절한 것은?

① 업무에 대한 조언을 구하려고 업무에 대한 조언을 구하는 것이 아님

② 다른 부서로의 이동을 요청하려고 다른 부서로의 이동 요청을 하지는 않았음

③ 신규 채용 조건에 대해 안내하려고 신규 채용 조건에 대한 안내는 없음

④ 구직자를 위한 프로그램을 홍보하려고 구직자를 위한 프로그램 홍보가 아님

⑤ 다른 회사로 이직하게 되었음을 알리려고
I have accepted a position at another company and will be leaving Lewis Ltd.

왜 정답? [정답률 96%]

다른 회사에서 직책을 수락하여 Lewis Ltd.를 떠나려고 한다는 내용이다.
▶ 따라서 글의 목적으로 가장 적절한 것은 ⑤이다.

왜 오답?

① 업무에 대한 조언을 구하고 있지 않다.
② 다른 부서로의 이동을 요청하는 것이 아니다.
③ 신규 채용 조건에 대해 안내하는 내용이 아니다.
④ 구직자를 위한 프로그램을 홍보하고 있지 않다.

자이 쌤's Follow Me! —홈페이지에서 제공

A 09 정답 ③ *박물관 멤버십 회원을 위한 추가 혜택

Dear Ms. Larson, /
Larson 씨께 /

I am writing to you / with new information / about your current membership. //
저는 귀하께 글을 쓰고 있습니다 / 새로운 정보를 담아 / 귀하의 현재 멤버십에 대한 //

Last year, / you signed up for our museum membership / that provides special discounts. //
                                    선행사   주격 관계대명사
작년에 / 귀하께서는 저희 박물관 멤버십에 가입하셨습니다 / 특별 할인을 제공하는 //

As stated / in the last newsletter, / this year / we are happy /
to부정사(부사적 용법, 감정의 원인)의 진행태
to be celebrating our 50th anniversary. //
언급되었듯이 / 지난번 소식지에서 / 올해 / 저희는 기쁩니다 / 저희의 50주년을 기념하게 되어 //

                   간접목적어   직접목적어
So we would like to offer you / further benefits. //
그래서 저희는 귀하께 드리고 싶습니다 / 더 많은 혜택을 // **단서1** 멤버십 회원에게 50주년을 기념하여 더 많은 혜택을 드리고자 함

These include / free admission / for up to ten people / and 20% off museum merchandise / on your next visit. // **단서2** 추가 혜택에 대한 구체적인 안내 ①
이것들은 포함합니다 / 무료입장과 / 10명까지의 / 박물관 상품의 20퍼센트 할인을 / 귀하의 다음 방문 시에 //
                            미래 시제 수동태
You will also be invited / to all new exhibition openings / this year / at discounted prices. // **단서3** 추가 혜택에 대한 구체적인 안내 ②
귀하께서는 또한 초대될 것입니다 / 모든 새로운 전시회 개막식에 / 올해 / 할인된 가격으로 //
                        앞에 명사절 접속사가 생략됨
We hope / you enjoy these offers. //
저희는 바랍니다 / 귀하께서 이러한 제공을 누리시기를 //

For any questions, / please feel free to contact us. //
문의 사항이 있으시면 / 저희에게 언제든지 연락하십시오 //

Best regards,
Stella Harrison /
Stella Harrison 드림 /

- current ⓐ 현재의   - sign up for ~을 신청하다   - discount ⓝ 할인
- state ⓥ 명시하다, 진술하다   - newsletter ⓝ 소식지
- celebrate ⓥ 기념하다, 축하하다   - anniversary ⓝ 기념일
- offer ⓥ 제공하다   - further ⓐ 추가의   - benefit ⓝ 혜택
- include ⓥ 포함하다   - admission ⓝ 입장, 입장료   - up to ~까지
- merchandise ⓝ 상품   - exhibition ⓝ 전시회
- opening ⓝ 개막식   - contact ⓥ 연락하다

Larson 씨께
저는 귀하의 현재 멤버십에 대한 새로운 정보를 담아 귀하께 글을 씁니다. 작년에 귀하께서는 특별 할인을 제공하는 저희 박물관 멤버십에 가입하셨습니다. 지

난번 소식지에서 언급되었듯이, 올해 저희는 저희의 50주년을 기념하게 되어 기쁩니다. 그래서 저희는 귀하께 더 많은 혜택을 드리고 싶습니다. 여기에는 귀하의 다음 방문 시에 10명까지의 무료입장과 박물관 상품의 20퍼센트 할인이 포함됩니다. 귀하께서는 또한 할인된 가격으로 올해 모든 새로운 전시회 개막식에 초대될 것입니다. 저희는 귀하께서 이러한 제공을 누리시기를 바랍니다. 문의 사항이 있으시면 저희에게 언제든지 연락하십시오.
Stella Harrison 드림

다음 글의 목적으로 가장 적절한 것은?

① 박물관 개관 50주년 기념행사 취소를 공지하려고 행사를 취소한다는 공지가 아님

② 작년에 가입한 박물관 멤버십의 갱신을 요청하려고 작년에 멤버십에 가입했다는 언급으로 만든 오답

③ 박물관 멤버십 회원을 위한 추가 혜택을 알려 주려고 더 많은 혜택을 주고자 함

④ 박물관 기념품점에서 새로 판매할 상품을 홍보하려고 박물관 상품의 할인 혜택으로 만든 오답

⑤ 박물관 전시 프로그램에서 변경된 내용을 안내하려고 전시 프로그램이 변경되었다는 언급은 없음

왜 정답? [정답률 96%]

Larson 씨의 멤버십에 대한 새로운 정보를 담아 글을 쓴다면서 50주년을 맞아 Larson 씨에게 추가 혜택을 제공하고자 한다고 했다. 무료입장, 박물관 기념품의 20퍼센트 할인 등 멤버십 회원에게 주어지는 50주년 기념 추가 혜택에 대해 안내하는 것이므로 정답은 ③이다.

왜 오답?

① to be celebrating our 50th anniversary로 만든 오답이다. 50주년 기념행사를 취소한다는 내용은 없다. **함정**
② Larson 씨가 작년에 멤버십에 가입한 것은 맞지만, 멤버십의 갱신을 요청하는 것은 아니다.
④ 멤버십 추가 혜택을 통해 박물관 상품을 20퍼센트 할인 받을 수 있다고 안내한 것으로 만든 오답이다.
⑤ 전시 프로그램에 변경이 있다는 언급은 없다.

A 10 정답 ④ *수영장 추가 대여 요청

Dear Hylean Miller, /
Hylean Miller 씨께 /

Hello, I'm Nelson Perkins, / a teacher and swimming coach at Broomstone High School. //
                                동격
안녕하세요, 저는 Nelson Perkins이며 / Broomstone 고등학교 교사이자 수영 코치입니다 //

Last week, I made a reservation / for one of your company's swimming pools / for our summer swim camp. //
지난주에 저는 예약했습니다 / 귀사의 수영장 중 한 곳을 / 저희 여름 수영 캠프를 위해 //
                        구 형태의 전치사: ~ 때문에
However, due to its popularity, / thirty more students are coming to the camp / than we expected, / so we need one more swimming pool for them. // **단서1** 예상보다 많은 학생들의 참여로 수영장 한 곳이 더 필요하게 됨
하지만 그것의 인기로 인해 / 30명 더 많은 학생들이 캠프에 오게 되어 / 저희가 예상했던 것보다 / 저희는 그들을 위해 수영장 한 곳이 더 필요합니다 //

The rental section on your website says / that there are two other swimming pools / during the summer season: / the Splash Pool and the Rainbow Pool. //
                                            시간으로 나타내기 어려운 특정 기간에 쓰이는 전치사 during
귀사 웹사이트의 대여란에는 / (~라고) 되어 있습니다 / 두 곳의 다른 수영장이 있다고 / 여름철 동안 / Splash Pool과 Rainbow Pool //
                        불확실하거나 의문시되는 사실에 쓰이는 명사절 접속사
Please let me know / if an additional rental would be possible. //
저에게 알려주세요 / 추가 대여가 가능할지를 // **단서2** 수영장의 추가 대여가 가능한지를 알려 달라고 말함

Thank you in advance. //
미리 감사드립니다 //

Best Wishes,
Nelson Perkins /
Nelson Perkins 드림 /

- popularity ⓝ 인기   - additional ⓐ 추가의
- rental ⓝ 대여, 임대   - in advance 미리, 사전에

Hylean Miller 씨께

안녕하세요, 저는 Nelson Perkins이며 Broomstone 고등학교 교사이자 수영 코치입니다. 지난주에 저는 저희 여름 수영 캠프를 위해 귀사의 수영장 중 한 곳을 예약했습니다. 하지만 그것의 인기로 인해, 저희가 예상했던 것보다 학생들이 30명 더 캠프에 오게 되어, 저희는 그들을 위해 수영장 한 곳이 더 필요합니다. 귀사 웹사이트의 대여란에 보면 여름철 동안 두 곳의 다른 수영장이 있다고 나와 있는데, Splash Pool과 Rainbow Pool입니다. 추가 대여가 가능할지를 저에게 알려주세요. 미리 감사드립니다.

Nelson Perkins 드림

다음 글의 목적으로 가장 적절한 것은?

① 수영 캠프 참가 날짜를 변경하려고 캠프가 언제인지는 언급되지 않음
② 수영장 수용 가능 인원을 확인하려고 thirty more students로 만든 오답
③ 수영 캠프 등록 방법에 대해 알아보려고 Nelson Perkins는 수영 캠프를 개최하는 사람임
④ 수영장 추가 대여 가능 여부를 문의하려고 Please let me know if an additional rental would be possible.
⑤ 수영장 대여 취소에 따른 환불을 요청하려고 대여 취소가 아니라 추가 대여에 관한 문의임

왜 정답? [정답률 97%]

여름 수영 캠프를 개최하는 교사인 Nelson Perkins는 예상보다 30명 더 많은 학생들이 캠프에 참가하게 되었다며 수영장 한 곳을 추가로 대여할 수 있는지를 문의하고 있으므로 정답은 ④이다.

왜 오답?

① 수영 캠프가 언제 열리는지 그 날짜는 언급되지 않았다.
② 예상보다 30명 더 많은 학생들이 참가하게 되었다고만 했지, 수영장의 수용 가능 인원에 대해 문의한 것이 아니다.
③ 수영 캠프를 개최하고 관리하는 사람은 Hylean Miller가 아니라 편지를 쓴 Nelson Perkins이다.
⑤ 대여한 수영장을 취소하는 것이 아니라 오히려 추가로 수영장 한 곳을 더 예약하려는 상황이다.

A 11 정답 ② *자선 음악회에의 참여 요청

Dear Mr. Bernstein, /
Bernstein 씨께 /

My name is Thomas Cobb, / the marketing director of Calbary Hospital. //
저의 이름은 Thomas Cobb이며 / Calbary 병원의 마케팅부장입니다 //

Our hospital is planning / to hold a charity concert / on September 18th / in the Main Hall of our hospital. //
우리 병원은 계획하고 있습니다 / 자선 음악회를 개최하는 것을 / 9월 18일에 / 우리 병원의 대강당에서 //

We expect it to be helpful / in raising money / to cover the medical costs / of those in need. //
우리는 그 행사가 도움이 될 것으로 기대합니다 / 기금을 마련하는 데 / 의료비를 충당할 / 어려운 분들의 //

To make the concert more special, / we want to invite you / for the opening of the concert. // **단서1** 자선 음악회에 Mr. Bernstein을 초대하고자 함
그 음악회를 더 특별하게 만들고자 / 우리는 귀하를 초대하고 싶습니다 / 음악회의 개막식을 위해 //

단서2 Mr. Bernstein의 피아노 연주를 보며 모든 이가 매우 기뻐할 것이라고 말함

Your reputation / as a pianist / is well known, / and everyone will be very happy / to see your performance. //
귀하의 명성은 / 피아노 연주자로서 / 잘 알려져 있기에 / 모든 이가 매우 기뻐할 것입니다 / 귀하의 공연을 보며 //

Beautiful piano melodies will help create / an enjoyable experience / for the audience. //
아름다운 피아노 선율이 만드는 데 도움이 될 것입니다 / 즐거운 경험을 / 관객들에게 //

We look forward / to your positive reply. //
우리는 고대합니다 / 귀하의 긍정적인 답변을 //

Sincerely,
Thomas A. Cobb /
Thomas A. Cobb 드림 /

- director ⓝ 책임자   - charity ⓝ 자선   - raise ⓥ (자금을) 모으다
- reputation ⓝ 명성   - positive ⓐ 긍정적인   - reply ⓝ 답변

Bernstein 씨께

저의 이름은 Thomas Cobb이며, Calbary 병원의 마케팅부장입니다. 우리 병원은 9월 18일에 우리 병원 대강당에서 자선 음악회 개최를 계획하고 있습니다. 우리는 그 행사가 어려운 분들의 의료비를 충당할 기금을 마련하는 데 도움이 될 것으로 기대합니다. 그 음악회를 더 특별하게 만들고자, 우리는 음악회의 개막식을 위해 귀하를 초대하고 싶습니다. 피아노 연주자로서 귀하의 명성은 잘 알려져 있기에, 모든 이가 귀하의 공연을 보며 매우 기뻐할 것입니다. 아름다운 피아노 선율이 즐거운 경험을 만드는 데 관객들에게 도움이 될 것입니다. 우리는 귀하의 긍정적인 답변을 고대합니다.

Thomas A. Cobb 드림

다음 글의 목적으로 가장 적절한 것은?

① 의료비 지원이 필요한 이들을 위한 기부를 독려하려고 raising money to cover the medical costs of those in need로 만든 오답
② 자선 음악회 연주자로 참여해 줄 것을 요청하려고 피아노 연주자인 Mr. Bernstein에게 음악회에서 연주해 줄 것을 요청함
③ 피아노 독주회 관람 신청 방법을 문의하려고 Thomas Cobb이 음악회를 여는 것임
④ 병원 개관 기념행사 참가 방법을 안내하려고 개관을 기념하는 행사라는 언급은 없음
⑤ 병원 진료 시간이 변경된 것을 알려 주려고 진료 시간에 대한 안내가 아님

왜 정답? [정답률 93%]

병원의 마케팅부장인 Thomas Cobb이 피아노 연주자인 Mr. Bernstein을 자선 음악회 개막식에 초대하는 편지이다. Mr. Bernstein의 공연을 보며 모든 이들이 기뻐할 것이라고 한 것으로 보아 자선 음악회에서 연주해 줄 것을 부탁하는 것이므로 정답은 ②이다.

왜 오답?

① 자선 음악회가 어려움에 처한 사람들의 의료비를 충당할 기금을 마련하는 데 도움이 될 것이라고 했지, 편지로 의료비 지원을 위한 기부를 독려하는 것은 아니다. ⦿한정
③ Thomas Cobb이 Mr. Bernstein의 독주회를 관람하고자 하는 상황이 아니다.
④ 병원의 행사에 참가할 것을 요청하는 편지이다.
⑤ '병원'이라는 소재로 만든 오답이다. 진료 시간에 대한 언급은 없다.

A 12 정답 ③ *경연 전시회 장소 섭외

Dear Mr. Anderson: /
Anderson 씨께 /

My name is Sophia Willis, / Events Manager of the 2020 Caroline County Art Contest. //
저의 이름은 Sophia Willis이며 / 2020년 캐롤라인 카운티 예술 경연의 행사 기획자입니다 //

I am currently looking for a place / for this year's contest exhibition. // **단서1** 경연 전시회를 위한 장소를 찾고 있음
저는 현재 장소를 찾고 있습니다 / 올해의 경연 전시회를 위한 //

The Caroline County Art Contest has had over one hundred artworks / submitted to us / by local artists. // 주격 관계대명사와 be동사가 생략되고 남은 형용사구
캐롤라인 카운티 예술 경연에는 백 점이 넘는 예술 작품이 있습니다 / 저희에게 제출된 / 지역 예술가들에 의해 //

For the theme, / we wanted artists to explore / the natural world of Caroline County. // **단서2** 주어 동사 목적어 목적격 보어 Garden Café Gallery가 완벽한 장소라고 생각함
그 주제로 / 우리는 예술가들이 탐색하기를 원했습니다 / 캐롤라인 카운티의 자연 세계를 //

I believe / the Garden Café Gallery would be a perfect place / to host the event, / as your gallery is well-known / for its beautiful garden. // 형용사적 용법(place 수식) 이유의 부사절 접속사
저는 생각합니다 / Garden Café Gallery가 완벽한 장소가 될 것이라고 / 그 행사를 주최하기에 / 귀하의 갤러리가 잘 알려져 있으므로 / 그것의 아름다운 정원으로 //

The exhibition is usually held / throughout October, / and we very much hope / that we can rent a space for the exhibition / at the Garden Café Gallery / during this time. //

전시회는 보통 개최되며 / 10월 내내 / 우리는 간절히 바랍니다 / 우리가 전시 공간을 빌릴 수 있기를 / Garden Café Gallery에서 / 이 기간 동안 // 단서3 Garden Café Gallery의 전시 공간을 빌릴 수 있기를 간절히 바람

I look forward to your response. //
귀하의 답변을 고대합니다 //

Yours sincerely,
Sophia Willis /
Sophia Willis 드림 /

- currently ad 현재, 지금 · exhibition ⓝ 전시(회)
- artwork ⓝ 예술 작품 · submit ⓥ 출품하다, 제출하다
- local ⓐ 지역의 · theme ⓝ 주제, 테마 · explore ⓥ 탐험하다
- throughout prep ~ 동안 쭉, 내내 · rent ⓥ 빌리다, 임차하다
- response ⓝ 답변, 대답

Anderson 씨께

저의 이름은 Sophia Willis이며, 2020년 캐롤라인 카운티 예술 경연의 행사 기획자입니다. 저는 현재 올해의 경연 전시회를 위한 장소를 찾고 있습니다. 캐롤라인 카운티 예술 경연에 지역 예술가들이 백 점이 넘는 예술 작품을 출품하였습니다. 그 주제로, 우리는 예술가들이 캐롤라인 카운티의 자연 세계를 탐색하기를 원했습니다. 귀하의 Garden Café Gallery는 아름다운 정원으로 잘 알려져 있으므로, 이 행사를 주최하기에 완벽한 장소가 될 것이라고 저는 생각합니다. 전시회는 보통 10월 내내 개최되며, 우리는 이 기간 동안 Garden Café Gallery의 전시 공간을 빌릴 수 있기를 간절히 바랍니다. 귀하의 답변을 고대합니다.

Sophia Willis 드림

다음 글의 목적으로 가장 적절한 것은?

① 출품 작품 전시회에 초대하려고 전시회에 와 달라는 내용은 없음
② 작품 제출 방법의 변경을 안내하려고 ┐
③ 출품 작품 전시 장소 대여를 문의하려고 │ 작품 제출 방법이나 일정이
   Garden Café Gallery의 전시 공간을 빌릴 수 있기를 바란다며 편지를 썼음 │ 변경된다는 언급은 없음
④ 정원 박람회의 변경된 일정을 공지하려고 ┘
⑤ 지역 예술가들에게 작품 제출을 독려하려고 이미 작품을 제출받았음

왜 정답? [정답률 91%]

올해의 경연 전시회를 위한 장소를 찾고 있는 Sophia Willis는 Garden Café Gallery가 그 행사를 주최하기에 완벽한 장소가 될 것이라면서 Garden Café Gallery의 전시 공간을 빌릴 수 있기를 간절히 바란다는 내용으로 Anderson 씨에게 편지를 썼으므로 정답은 ③이다.

왜 오답?

① 전시회를 위한 공간을 빌릴 수 있기를 바란다는 내용이지, 전시회에 와 달라는 내용이 아니다.
② Mr. Anderson이 경연에 참여하여 작품을 제출하는 사람은 아니다.
④ Garden Café Gallery의 정원이 아름답다고 한 것으로 만든 오답이다. 정원 박람회가 아니라 예술 경연 전시회에 대한 내용이다.
⑤ 이미 지역 예술가들이 제출한 백 점이 넘는 예술 작품을 갖고 있다고 했다.

A 13 정답 ② * 온라인 과학 수업에 대한 강의 요청

Dear Ms. Green, /
Green 씨께 /

My name is Donna Williams, / a science teacher at Rogan High School. //
단서1 과학 교사들을 위한 특별 워크숍을 계획하고 있음
저의 이름은 Donna Williams이며 / Rogan 고등학교의 과학 교사입니다 //

I am planning a special workshop / for our science teachers. //
저는 특별 워크숍을 계획하고 있습니다 / 우리 학교의 과학 교사들을 위한 //

We are interested in learning / how to teach online science classes. //
동명사의 목적어로 쓰인 「의문사+to부정사」
저희는 배우는 것에 관심이 있습니다 / 온라인 과학 수업을 가르치는 방법을 //

I have been impressed with your ideas / about using internet 전치사 동명사구 platforms / for science classes. //
저는 귀하의 아이디어에 감명을 받았습니다 / 인터넷 플랫폼을 사용하는 것에 대한 / 과학 수업에 //

부사절 접속사(이유) 단서2 워크숍에서 특별 강연을 해줄 것을 부탁함
Since you are an expert / in online education, / I would like to ask
to ask의 목적어와 목적격 보어
you / to deliver a special lecture / at the workshop / scheduled for next month. //
앞에 주격 관계대명사와 be동사가 생략됨
귀하가 전문가이기에 / 온라인 교육에서 / 저는 귀하에게 부탁드리고자 합니다 / 특별 강연을 해주시기를 / 워크숍에서 / 다음 달로 계획된 //

will help의 목적어와 목적격 보어
I am sure / the lecture will help our teachers / manage successful online science classes, / and I hope / we can learn / from your insights. //
저는 확신합니다 / 그 강의가 저희 교사들을 도우리라고 / 성공적인 온라인 과학 수업을 해내도록 / 그리고 저는 희망합니다 / 저희가 배울 수 있기를 / 귀하의 통찰력으로부터 //

I am looking forward / to hearing from you. //
저는 고대하고 있겠습니다 / 귀하의 답변을 //

Sincerely,
Donna Williams /
Donna Williams 드림 /

- impress ⓥ 감명[감동]을 주다. (마음·기억 등에) 강하게 남다
- deliver ⓥ (연설·강연 등을) 하다 · lecture ⓝ 강의, 강연
- manage ⓥ 운영하다, (힘든 일을) 해내다 · insight ⓝ 통찰력, 식견, 이해

Green 씨께

저의 이름은 Donna Williams이며, Rogan 고등학교의 과학 교사입니다. 저는 우리 학교의 과학 교사들을 위한 특별 워크숍을 계획하고 있습니다. 저희는 온라인 과학 수업을 가르치는 방법을 배우는 데 관심이 있습니다. 저는 과학 수업에 인터넷 플랫폼을 사용하는 것에 대한 귀하의 아이디어에 감명을 받았습니다. 귀하가 온라인 교육의 전문가이기에, 저는 다음 달로 계획된 워크숍에서 귀하가 특별 강연을 해주시기를 부탁드리고자 합니다. 저는 그 강의가 저희 교사들이 성공적인 온라인 과학 수업을 해내도록 도우리라고 확신하며 귀하의 통찰력으로부터 저희가 배울 수 있기를 희망합니다. 귀하의 답변을 고대하고 있겠습니다.

Donna Williams 드림

다음 글의 목적으로 가장 적절한 것은?

① 과학 교육 정책 협의회 참여를 독려하려고 ┐
② 과학 교사 워크숍의 특강을 부탁하려고 │ 온라인 교육에 대한 특강을
   I would like to ask you to deliver a special lecture at the workshop │ 부탁함
③ 과학 교사 채용 계획을 공지하려고 │
   교사를 채용한다는 언급은 없음
④ 과학 교육 프로그램 개발을 요청하려고 ┘
⑤ 과학 교육 워크숍 일정의 변경을 안내하려고 the workshop scheduled for next month로 만든 오답

왜 정답? [정답률 90%]

과학 교사를 위한 특별 워크숍을 준비하고 있는 Donna Williams가 온라인 교육의 전문가인 Ms. Green에게 그 워크숍에서 특별 강연을 해 달라고 요청하는 편지이므로 정답은 ②이다.

왜 오답?

① 과학 교육 정책 협의회가 아니라 과학 교사들을 위한 특별 워크숍에 특별 강연자로 참석할 것을 요청하는 편지이다.
③ 새로 과학 교사를 채용한다는 언급은 없다.
④ Ms. Green에게 어떤 프로그램을 개발해 달라고 요청하는 것이 아니다.
⑤ 다음 달로 계획된 워크숍 일정에 변경 사항이 있다는 안내가 아니다.

A 14 정답 ③ *Millstown 출신인 Natalie Talley 응원

Dear Natalie Talley, /
Natalie Talley 씨께 /

My name is Olivia Spikes, / the mayor of Millstown. //
제 이름은 Olivia Spikes입니다 / Millstown의 시장인 //

Before you attend the world championships / next month, / on behalf of everyone in Millstown, / I wish to let you know / that we are supporting you all the way. //
당신이 세계 선수권 대회에 출전하기 전에 / 다음 달에 / Millstown의 모든 이를 대신하여 / 저는 당신에게 알려드리고 싶습니다 / 우리가 당신을 항상 응원하고 있음을 //

As you are the first famous figure skater / from Millstown, / we are all big fans of yours. //
당신은 최초의 유명한 피겨 스케이팅 선수이기에 / Millstown 출신의 / 우리는 모두 당신의 열렬한 팬입니다 //

Our community was so proud of you / for winning the national championships / last year. //
우리 지역 사회는 당신을 매우 자랑스럽게 생각했습니다 / 전국 선수권 대회에서 우승한 것에 대해 / 지난해에 //

Your amazing performance / really moved us all. //
당신의 놀라운 연기는 / 우리 모두를 진정 감동하게 했습니다 //

We all believe / that you are going to impress / the entire nation / again. //
우리 모두 믿습니다 / 당신이 감동하게 할 것이라고 / 온 나라를 / 다시 //

Your hometown supporters will cheer for you / whenever you perform on the ice. //
당신의 고향의 지지자들이 당신을 응원할 것입니다 / 당신이 빙판 위에서 연기할 때마다 //

Good luck! // 행운을 빕니다 //

Best wishes,
Olivia Spikes / Olivia Spikes 드림

- mayor ⓝ 시장, 구청장   • championship ⓝ 선수권 대회
- on behalf of ~을 대표[대신]하여   • national ⓐ 전국적인, 국가의
- move ⓥ 감동시키다   • impress ⓥ 감명을 주다   • entire ⓐ 전체의

Natalie Talley 씨께
제 이름은 Olivia Spikes이며, Millstown의 시장입니다. 다음 달 세계 선수권 대회에 출전하기 전에 Millstown의 모든 이를 대신하여 우리가 당신을 항상 응원하고 있음을 알려드리고 싶습니다. 당신은 Millstown 최초의 유명한 피겨 스케이팅 선수이기에 우리는 모두 당신의 열렬한 팬입니다. 우리 지역 사회는 당신이 지난해에 전국 선수권 대회에서 우승한 것을 매우 자랑스럽게 생각했습니다. 당신의 놀라운 연기는 우리 모두를 진정 감동하게 했습니다. 우리 모두 당신이 다시 온 나라를 감동하게 할 것이라고 믿습니다. 당신이 빙판 위에서 연기할 때마다 고향의 지지자들이 응원할 것입니다. 행운을 빕니다!
Olivia Spikes 드림

다음 글의 목적으로 가장 적절한 것은?
① 지역 사회 홍보 대사로 활동해 줄 것을 제안하려고
② 이웃 도시와 예정된 친선 경기 취소를 통보하려고
③ 지역 사회 출신 피겨 스케이팅 선수를 응원하려고
④ 시청에서 주관하는 연례 자선 행사를 홍보하려고
⑤ 피겨 스케이팅 경기장 건립을 위한 기부를 요청하려고

왜 정답? [정답률 96%]
Millstown의 시장인 Olivia Spikes가 Millstown 출신의 피겨 스케이팅 선수인 Natalie Talley에게 세계 선수권 대회를 앞두고 응원의 편지를 보내는 것이므로 정답은 ③이다.

왜 오답?
① Natalie Talley에게 Millstown의 홍보 대사가 되어 달라고 요청하는 것이 아니다.
②, ④ 이웃 도시와의 친선 경기나 연례 자선 행사에 대한 언급은 없다.
⑤ 피겨 스케이팅 경기장의 건립이나 건립을 위한 기부에 대한 내용은 없다.

A 15 정답 ① *추가 과정 개설 요청

To whom it may concern, /
관계자분께 /

My name is Daniel. //
제 이름은 Daniel입니다 //

Since I joined your youth sports program / several years ago, / I have really enjoyed swimming. //
제가 귀하의 청소년 스포츠 프로그램에 합류한 이후 / 몇 년 전에 / 저는 수영을 정말 즐겨 왔습니다 //

Thanks to your program, / I have become a good swimmer. //
귀하의 프로그램 덕분에 / 저는 수영을 잘하게 되었습니다 //

Now I want / to go one step further. //
이제 저는 원합니다 / 한 걸음 더 나아가기를 //

I like helping people / and hope to get a job / as a lifeguard / later. //
저는 사람들을 돕는 것을 좋아하고 / 취업하기를 희망합니다 / 구조원으로 / 나중에 //

So I tried to sign up / for your lifeguard training course / this summer. //
그래서 저는 등록하려고 했습니다 / 귀하의 구조원 양성 과정에 / 이번 여름에 //

But the course was so popular / that the registration closed / almost as soon as it opened. //
그러나 그 과정은 인기가 너무 많아 / 등록이 마감되었습니다 / 거의 그것이 개설되자마자 //

I couldn't register / and was really disappointed. //
저는 등록을 할 수 없었고 / 정말 실망했습니다 //

I heard / some of my friends couldn't, either. //
저는 들었습니다 / 제 친구 중 몇몇도 등록할 수 없었다고 //

I'm kindly asking you / to open an additional course. //
저는 귀하에게 정중히 요청합니다 / 추가 과정을 개설해 주시기를 //

I appreciate your consideration. // 고려해 주셔서 감사드립니다 //

Sincerely,
Daniel Smith / Daniel Smith 드림 /

- thanks to ~ 덕분에   • further ⓐⓓ 더 멀리에[로]
- lifeguard ⓝ 구조원   • sign up for ~에 등록하다[신청하다]
- registration ⓝ 등록   • additional ⓐ 추가적인
- appreciate ⓥ 감사하다   • consideration ⓝ 고려

관계자분께
제 이름은 Daniel입니다. 저는 몇 년 전에 귀하의 청소년 스포츠 프로그램에 합류한 이후 수영을 정말 즐겨 왔습니다. 귀하의 프로그램 덕분에 저는 수영을 잘하게 되었습니다. 이제 저는 한 걸음 더 나아가고 싶습니다. 저는 사람들을 돕는 것을 좋아하고 나중에 구조원으로 취업하기를 희망합니다. 그래서 저는 이번 여름에 귀하의 구조원 양성 과정에 등록하려고 했습니다. 그러나 그 과정은 인기가 너무 많아 거의 개설되자마자 등록이 마감되었습니다. 저는 등록을 할 수 없었고 정말 실망했습니다. 제 친구 중 몇몇도 등록할 수 없었다고 들었습니다. 저는 추가 과정을 개설해 주시기를 정중히 요청합니다. 고려해 주셔서 감사드립니다.
Daniel Smith 드림

다음 글의 목적으로 가장 적절한 것은?
① 구조원 양성 과정의 추가 개설을 요청하려고
② 구조원 양성 과정의 우수성을 홍보하려고
③ 동계 수영 강습 프로그램 수강을 신청하려고
④ 수영 강사 일자리가 있는지 문의하려고
⑤ 구조원 양성 과정의 등록 방법을 안내하려고

왜 정답? [정답률 94%]
이번 여름에 구조원 양성 과정에 등록하려고 했으나 강좌가 개설되자마자 마감되어 등록을 할 수 없었고, 그래서 추가 과정을 개설해 줄 것을 요청한다고 했으므로 정답은 ①이다.

─── 어법 특강

＊ 목적격 보어로 to부정사를 취하는 동사

• What caused you to change your mind?
(무엇이 네가 네 마음을 바꾸게 했니?)

• Her parents didn't want her to marry him.
(그녀의 부모님은 그녀가 그와 결혼하는 것을 원하지 않았다.)

• Students are not allowed to eat in class.
(학생들은 교실에서 먹는 것이 허용되지 않는다.)

– 준사역동사 help는 목적격 보어로 원형부정사나 to부정사를 취한다.

• I helped her to carry her suitcases up the stairs.
= I helped her carry her suitcases up the stairs.
(나는 그녀가 계단 위로 그녀의 짐가방을 옮기는 것을 도왔다.)

– 준사역동사 get은 목적격 보어로 to부정사를 취한다.

• I'll get Andrew to give you a call.
(내가 Andrew가 네게 전화하게 할게.)

• She couldn't get them to understand what she was saying.
(그녀는 그들이 그녀가 말하고 있는 것을 이해하게 할 수 없었다.)

A 16 정답 ① ＊웹툰 제작 온라인 강좌 수강생 모집 ───

I'm Charlie Reeves, / manager of Toon Skills Company. //
저는 Charlie Reeves이고 / Toon Skills Company의 경영자입니다 //
be interested in: ~에 관심 있는
If you're interested in new webtoon-making skills and
techniques, / this post is for you. // **단서 1** 웹툰 제작 기술과 기법에 관심이 있는
사람들을 위한 것이라고 했음
여러분이 새로운 웹툰 제작 기술과 기법에 관심이 있으시다면 / 이 게시물은 여러분을 위한 것입니다 //
현재완료의 결과적 용법   관계대명사의 계속적 용법
This year, / we've launched special online courses, / which
contain a variety of contents about webtoon production. //
올해 / 저희는 특별 온라인 강좌를 시작했는데 / 웹툰 제작에 관한 다양한 콘텐츠가 담겨
있습니다 // **단서 2** 웹툰 제작과 관련된 다양한 콘텐츠가 포함된 온라인 강좌를 홍보하고 있음
Each course consists of ten units / that help improve your
each+단수 명사+단수 동사   주격 관계대명사
drawing and story-telling skills. //
각 강좌는 10차시로 설계되어 있습니다 / 여러분의 그리기와 스토리텔링 기술을 향상하는 데
도움을 주는 //
Moreover, these courses are designed / to suit any level, from
beginner to advanced. //
게다가, 이 강좌들은 구성되어 있습니다 / 초급에서 고급까지 어떤 수준에도 맞게 //
It costs $45 for one course, / and you can watch your course / as
many times as you want for six months. // 비용은 한 강좌당 45달러이며 /
여러분은 여러분의 강좌를 보실 수 있습니다 / 6개월 동안 원하는 만큼 여러 번 //
Our courses with talented and experienced instructors / will
open up a new world of creativity for you. //
재능이 있고 노련한 강사들이 담당하는 저희 강좌는 / 여러분에게 창의력의 새로운 세계를
열어줄 것입니다 //
~할 시간이다
It's time to start / creating your webtoon world at https://
webtoonskills.com. //
이제 시작할 때입니다 / https://webtoonskills.com에서 여러분의 웹툰 세계를 창조하기 //

• launch ⓥ 시작하다, 개시하다　　• a variety of 다양한
• production ⓝ 제작　　• consist of ~로 구성되다
• advanced ⓐ 고급의　　• talented ⓐ 재능이 있는

저는 Charlie Reeves이고 Toon Skills Company의 경영자입니다. 여러분이 새로운 웹툰 제작 기술과 기법에 관심이 있으시다면, 이 게시물은 여러분을 위한 것입니다. 올해, 저희는 특별 온라인 강좌를 시작했는데, 웹툰 제작에 관한 다양한 콘텐츠가 담겨 있습니다. 각 강좌는 여러분의 그리기와 스토리텔링 기술을 향상하는 데 도움을 주는 10차시로 설계되어 있습니다. 게다가, 이 강좌들은 초급에서 고급까지 어떤 수준에도 맞게 구성되어 있습니다. 비용은 한 강좌당 45달러이며 여러분은 여러분의 강좌를 6개월 동안 원하는 만큼 여러 번 보실 수 있습니다. 재능이 있고 노련한 강사들이 담당하는 저희 강좌는 여러분에게 창의력의 새로운 세계를 열어줄 것입니다. 이제 https://webtoonskills.com에서 여러분의 웹툰 세계를 창조하기 시작할 때입니다.

다음 글의 목적으로 가장 적절한 것은?

① 웹툰 제작 온라인 강좌를 홍보하려고 If you're interested in new webtoon-making skills ~ a variety of contents about webtoon production.
② 웹툰 작가 채용 정보를 제공하려고 웹툰 작가를 채용하는 것은 아님
③ 신작 웹툰 공개 일정을 공지하려고 신작 웹툰 공개에 관한 언급은 없음
④ 웹툰 창작 대회에 출품을 권유하려고 웹툰 창작 대회에 관한 내용이 아님
⑤ 기초적인 웹툰 제작 방법을 설명하려고 웹툰 제작 방법 자체를 설명하는 글이 아님

> **왜** 정답 **?** [정답률 95%]

Toon Skills Company는 그리기와 스토리텔링 등 웹툰 제작과 관련된 온라인 강좌를 시작했다고 했다. 강좌의 비용과 수준 등을 안내하며 수강생을 모집하고 있다.
▶ 따라서 글의 목적으로 가장 적절한 것은 ①이다.

> **왜** 오답 **?**

② 웹툰 작가를 채용하는 것이 아니라 웹툰 제작 강좌의 수강생을 모집하는 글이다.
③ 신작 웹툰 공개에 관한 언급은 없었다.
④ 웹툰 창작 대회에 대한 내용이 아니다.
⑤ 웹툰 제작 방법을 알려주는 온라인 강좌를 홍보하는 글로, 웹툰 제작 방법 자체를 설명하고 있는 것은 아니다.

조수근 | 순천향대 의예과 2024년 입학·성남 태원고 졸

목적 파악 문제는 중간의 핵심 문장만 읽어도 정답을 고를 수 있어! 이 문제에서는 웹툰 제작에 관한 온라인 강좌를 시작했다는 세 번째 문장과 강좌의 구성 및 가격을 부연 설명하는 나머지 문장들을 조금만 읽어도 웹툰 제작과 관련된 강좌를 홍보하는 글이라는 것을 충분히 파악할 수 있지. 난 이런 유형의 문제에서 시간을 단축하는 것도 실력이라고 생각해!

─── 어법 특강

＊ 한정적 용법의 분사

(분사는 명사의 앞이나 뒤에서 그 명사를 수식하는 형용사의 역할을 할 수 있다.)

– 분사가 단독으로 수식할 때는 명사 앞에서 수식한다.

• Look at her shining face.
(그녀의 빛나는 얼굴을 좀 봐.)

• Tom broke the locked door.
(Tom이 그 잠긴 문을 부쉈다.)

– 분사에 수식어나 목적어, 보어 등이 있을 때는 명사 뒤에서 수식한다.

• She is picking up the leaves fallen on the ground.
(그녀는 바닥에 떨어진 나뭇잎들을 줍고 있다.)

A 17 정답 ① ＊교내 음식 모으기 운동 ───

Dear Friends, /
여러분께 /
Season's greetings. //
즐거운 크리스마스가 되길 바랍니다 //　　　**단서 1** 교내 음식 모으기 운동에 대한 내용임
As some of you already know, / we are starting the campus food
drive. //
여러분 중 일부는 이미 알고 있듯이 / 우리는 교내 음식 모으기 운동을 시작하고 있습니다 //

This is / how you participate. // 단서 2 참가 방법을 설명함
이것은 ~입니다 / 여러분이 참가하는 방법 //

You can bring your items for donation / to our booths. //
여러분은 기부할 음식물을 가져오면 됩니다 / 우리의 부스로 //

Our donation booths are located / in the lobbies of the campus libraries. //
우리의 기부 부스는 위치해 있습니다 / 교내 도서관 로비에 //

Just drop off the items there / during usual library hours / from December 4 to 23. //
전치사 / 명사구
그곳에 음식물을 갖다 놓기만 하세요 / 도서관의 정규 운영 시간에 / 12월 4일부터 23일까지 //

The donated food should be non-perishable / like canned meats and canned fruits. //
전치사 / 명사구
기부되는 음식은 상하지 않아야 합니다 / 통조림 고기와 통조림 과일 같이 //

복수 주어
Packaged goods / such as jam and peanut butter / are also good. //
복수 동사
포장된 제품 / 잼이나 땅콩버터 같은 / 또한 좋습니다 //

We will distribute the food / to our neighbors / on Christmas Eve. //
우리는 그 음식을 나눠줄 것입니다 / 우리의 이웃들에게 / 크리스마스이브에 //

We truly appreciate / your help. //
우리는 정말 고맙게 생각합니다 / 여러분의 도움을 //

Many blessings,
Joanna at Campus Food Bank /
많은 축복이 있기를, Campus Food Bank의 Joanna 올림 /

- greeting ⓝ 인사, 인사말
- drive ⓝ (조직적인) 운동
- participate ⓥ 참가[참여]하다
- donation ⓝ 기부, 기증
- usual ⓐ 평상시의, 보통의
- perishable ⓐ 잘 상하는[썩는]
- canned ⓐ 통조림으로 된
- distribute ⓥ 분배[배부]하다, 유통시키다
- truly ⓐⒹ 정말로, 진심으로
- appreciate ⓥ 고마워하다
- blessing ⓝ 축복

여러분께
즐거운 크리스마스가 되길 바랍니다. 여러분 중 일부는 이미 알고 있듯이, 우리는 교내 음식 모으기 운동을 시작하고 있습니다. 다음은 참가하는 방법입니다. 기부할 음식물을 우리 부스로 가져오면 됩니다. 우리 기부 부스는 교내 도서관 로비에 있습니다. 12월 4일부터 23일까지 도서관의 정규 운영 시간에 그곳에 음식물을 갖다 놓기만 하면 됩니다. 기부되는 음식은 통조림 고기와 통조림 과일 같은 상하지 않는 음식이어야 합니다. 잼이나 땅콩버터 같은 포장 제품도 좋습니다. 우리는 그 음식을 크리스마스이브에 우리의 이웃들에게 나눠줄 것입니다. 여러분의 도움을 정말 고맙게 생각합니다.
많은 축복이 있기를,
Campus Food Bank의 Joanna 올림

다음 글의 목적으로 가장 적절한 것은?
① 음식 기부에 참여하는 방법을 안내하려고 음식 모으기 운동에 참여하는 방법을 설명함
② 음식 배달 자원봉사 참여에 감사하려고 will distribute the food로 만든 오답
③ 도서관 이용 시간 변경을 공지하려고 도서관의 정규 운영 시간에 가져오라고 했음
④ 음식물 낭비의 심각성을 알려 주려고 음식을 낭비하지 말라는 것이 아님
⑤ 크리스마스 행사 일정을 문의하려고 크리스마스이브가 언급된 것으로 만든 오답

> 왜 정답? [정답률 89%]
교내 음식 모으기 운동을 시작하고 있다면서 참가 방법을 안내하고 있다. 음식물을 가져올 부스의 위치, 기부를 받는 기간, 기부할 수 있는 음식물이 무엇인지 등을 설명했으므로 정답은 ①이다.

> 왜 오답?
② 이웃들에게 나눠줄 것이라고 했지, 배달에 참여한 것에 대해 감사하는 것은 아니다.
③ '도서관의 정규 운영 시간'이 언급된 것으로 만든 오답이다.
④ 음식을 낭비하지 말라는 내용이 아니다.
⑤ '크리스마스이브'에 이웃들에게 나눠줄 것이라는 내용으로 만든 오답이다.

A 18 정답 ① *조류 관찰 클럽 가입 방법 문의

To whom it may concern, /
관계자분께 /

My name is Michael Brown. //
제 이름은 Michael Brown입니다 //

〈계속〉을 나타내는 현재완료
I have been a bird-watcher / since childhood. //
저는 조류 관찰자였습니다 / 어렸을 때부터 //

목적어로 동명사를 취하는 enjoy
I have always enjoyed / watching birds in my yard / and identifying them / by sight and sound. //
저는 항상 즐겼습니다 / 저의 뜰에서 새들을 관찰하고 / 그것들을 식별하는 것을 / 모습과 소리로 //

Yesterday, I happened to read an article / about your club. //
어제 저는 우연히 기사를 읽었습니다 / 귀하의 클럽에 대한 //

부사적 용법(감정의 원인)
I was surprised and excited / to find out about a community of
선행사 / 주격 관계대명사
passionate bird-watchers / who travel annually to go birding. //
저는 놀랐고 신이 났습니다 / 열정적인 조류 관찰자들의 공동체에 대해 알게 되어 / 조류 관찰을 하러 매년 여행하는 //

I would love to join your club, / but your website appears to be under construction. // 단서 1 조류 관찰 클럽에 가입하고 싶다고 말함
저는 귀하의 클럽에 가입하기를 몹시 원하지만 / 귀하의 웹 사이트가 공사 중인 것 같습니다 //

I could not find any information / except for this contact email address. //
전치사 * / 명사구 *
저는 어떤 정보도 찾을 수가 없었습니다 / 이 이메일 주소 외에 //

I would like to know / how to sign up for the club. //
저는 알고 싶습니다 / 클럽에 가입하는 방법을 // 단서 2 클럽에 가입하는 방법을 알고 싶음

I look forward to your reply. //
귀하의 답장을 기다리겠습니다 //

Sincerely,
Michael Brown / Michael Brown 드림 /

- identify ⓥ (신원 등을) 식별하다[확인하다]
- sight ⓝ 보기, 봄, 시력
- community ⓝ 공동체, 지역 사회
- passionate ⓐ 열정적인
- under ⓟⓡⓔⓟ ~ 중인
- construction ⓝ 건설, 공사

관계자분께
제 이름은 Michael Brown입니다. 저는 어렸을 때부터 조류 관찰자였습니다. 저는 항상 저의 뜰에서 새들을 관찰하고 모습과 소리로 그것들을 식별하는 것을 즐겼습니다. 어제 저는 우연히 귀하의 클럽에 대한 기사를 읽었습니다. 저는 조류 관찰을 하러 매년 여행하는 열정적인 조류 관찰자들의 공동체에 대해 알게 되어 놀랐고 신이 났습니다. 저는 귀하의 클럽에 가입하기를 몹시 원하지만, 귀하의 웹 사이트가 공사 중인 것 같습니다. 이 이메일 주소 외에 어떤 정보도 찾을 수가 없었습니다. 저는 클럽에 가입하는 방법을 알고 싶습니다. 귀하의 답장을 기다리겠습니다.
Michael Brown 드림

다음 글의 목적으로 가장 적절한 것은?
① 조류 관찰 클럽에 가입하는 방법을 문의하려고 I would like to know how to sign up for the club.
② 조류 관찰 시 주의해야 할 사항을 전달하려고 조류 관찰 클럽 관계자에게 보내는 이메일임
③ 조류 관찰 협회의 새로운 규정을 확인하려고
④ 조류 관찰과 관련된 웹 사이트를 소개하려고 협회나 규정, 장비에 대한 언급은 없음
⑤ 조류 관찰 시 필요한 장비를 알아보려고 website가 언급된 것으로 만든 오답

> 왜 정답? [정답률 98%]
어렸을 때부터 조류를 관찰해 온 Michael Brown이 우연히 조류 관찰 클럽에 대한 기사를 읽고 클럽에 가입하기를 원해서 이메일을 보내는 것이다.
후반부에서 클럽에 가입하는 방법을 알고 싶다고 했으므로 정답은 ①이다.

> 왜 오답?
② 조류 관찰 클럽의 관계자에게 클럽 가입 방법을 문의하는 이메일이다.
③, ⑤ 조류 관찰 협회나 규정, 관찰 장비에 대한 언급은 없다.
④ 조류 관찰 클럽의 웹 사이트가 언급된 것으로 만든 오답이다.

※ 전치사 vs. 접속사 ────── 어법 특강

- 전치사 뒤에는 명사상당어구가, 접속사 뒤에는 주어와 동사로 이루어진 절이 온다.

- During most of my interview I was calm and direct.
  명사구가 이어짐
  (인터뷰하는 대부분 동안 나는 침착하고 솔직했다.)

- Cats growl while they are asleep.
  절이 이어짐
  (고양이는 잠들어 있는 동안에 으르렁거린다.)

- Cancer is a global problem despite medical advances.
  명사구가 이어짐
  (의학적 발전에도 불구하고 암은 세계적인 문제이다.)

- Although we eat apples often, few of us know much about them.
  절이 이어짐
  (우리는 사과를 자주 먹지만 우리들 중 대부분은 사과에 대해서 많이 알고 있지 않다.)

※ 조류 독감 ────── 배경 지식

조류 독감은 닭, 오리, 야생 조류에서 조류 인플루엔자 바이러스의 감염으로 인해 발생하는 급성 바이러스성 전염병이며 드물게 사람에게서도 감염증을 일으킨다.

사람에게 전염될 수 있는 조류 인플루엔자 바이러스가 인체에 감염된 사례가 다수 보고되어 있고, 이 중 많은 경우는 조류 독감의 원인이 된 조류와 연관이 있는 사람들에서 발생하였으며, 사람-사람 간의 감염 가능성은 낮은 것으로 보인다.

하지만 인체에 감염된 경우 높은 사망률을 보여, 향후 조류 독감이 사람의 전염병으로 바뀔 가능성에 대해 세계 각국의 의학계가 주시하고 있다.

A 19 정답 ① ────── ★2등급 대비 [정답률 97%]

★교통안전 봉사 참여 요청

Dear Parents, /
학부모님께 /

My name is Danielle Hamilton, / and I am the principal of Techville High School. //
제 이름은 Danielle Hamilton이고 / 저는 Techville 고등학교 교장입니다 //

As you may know, / there is major road construction / scheduled to take place / in front of our school / next month. //
선행사(주격 관계대명사와 be동사는 생략됨)
아시다시피 / 큰 도로 공사가 있습니다 / 일어나기로 예정된 / 우리 학교 앞에서 / 다음 달에 //

This raises safety concerns. //
이것이 안전에 대한 염려를 불러일으킵니다 //

Therefore, / we are asking for parent volunteers / to help with directing traffic. //
형용사적 용법(parent volunteers 수식)
단서 교통정리를 도와줄 학부모 자원봉사자를 요청함
그래서 / 우리는 학부모 자원봉사자를 요청하고자 합니다 / 교통정리를 도와주실 //

The volunteer hours / are from 8:00 to 8:30 a.m. and from 4:30 to 5:00 p.m. / on school days. //
자원봉사 시간은 / 오전 8시부터 8시 30분, 오후 4시 30분부터 5시까지입니다 / 등교일에 //

If you are willing to take part / in the traffic safety volunteer group, / please email us / with your preferred schedule / at info@techville.edu. //
참여하실 의사가 있으시면 / 교통안전 자원 봉사단에 / 저희에게 이메일로 보내주시기 바랍니다 / 원하시는 일정과 함께 / info@techville.edu로 //

Your participation will be helpful / in building a safer school environment / for our students. //
전치사   동명사구
여러분의 참여는 도움이 될 것입니다 / 더 안전한 학교 환경을 만드는 데 / 우리 학생들을 위해 //

Thank you in advance / for your contributions. //
미리 감사드립니다 / 여러분의 기여에 //

Sincerely,
Danielle Hamilton /
Danielle Hamilton 드림 /

- road construction 도로 공사 · take place 발생하다
- raise concerns 염려를 불러일으키다 · volunteer ⓝ 자원 봉사
- direct traffic 교통정리를 하다 · take part 참여하다
- participation ⓝ 참여 · in advance 미리
- contribution ⓝ 기여

학부모님께
제 이름은 Danielle Hamilton이고 저는 Techville 고등학교 교장입니다. 아시다시피, 다음 달에 우리 학교 앞에서 큰 도로 공사가 있을 것으로 예정되어 있습니다. 이것이 안전에 대한 염려를 불러일으킵니다. 그래서 우리는 교통정리를 도와주실 학부모 자원봉사자를 요청하고자 합니다. 자원봉사 시간은 등교일 오전 8시부터 8시 30분, 오후 4시 30분부터 5시까지입니다. 교통안전 자원 봉사단에 참여하실 의사가 있으시면, info@techville.edu로 저희에게 원하시는 일정을 이메일로 보내주시기 바랍니다. 여러분의 참여는 우리 학생들을 위해 더 안전한 학교 환경을 만드는 데 도움이 될 것입니다. 여러분의 기여에 미리 감사드립니다.
Danielle Hamilton 드림

다음 글의 목적으로 가장 적절한 것은?

① 교통안전 봉사 참여를 요청하려고 we are asking for parent volunteers to help with directing traffic
② 자원봉사 교육 일정을 공지하려고 자원봉사자를 모집하려는 글임
③ 학교 시설 공사에 대한 양해를 구하려고 학교 시설 공사가 예정된 것은 아님
④ 학교 앞 도로 공사의 필요성을 설명하려고 왜 도로 공사를 하는지는 언급되지 않음
⑤ 등 · 하교 차량 안전 수칙 준수를 당부하려고
등 · 하교 시 지켜야 하는 수칙에 대한 내용이 아님

와 2등급? 선택지만으로는 주제를 확정짓기 어렵기에 글의 중반부까지는 읽어야 편지의 목적을 파악할 수 있는 2등급 대비 문제이다. 다만, 결론을 나타내는 연결어가 포함된 문장을 찾고 나면 어렵지 않게 글의 목적을 파악할 수 있다.

> 와 정답?

학교 앞에서 큰 도로 공사가 예정되어 있음
➡ 안전 문제 때문에 교통정리를 도울 학부모 자원봉사자를 요청하고자 함
▶ 편지를 쓴 목적은 ①

> 와 오답?

② 자원봉사자를 모집하는 편지이다.
③ 학교 시설에 공사를 하는 것이 아니라 학교 앞 도로에 공사가 예정된 것이다. 함정
④ 왜 공사를 하는지는 설명하지 않았다.
⑤ 등 · 하교 시간에 교통정리를 도와줄 자원봉사자를 요청한다고 했다.

────────────────────────────────── 어법 특강

✱ 도치 구문

– 강조하고자 하는 장소를 나타내는 부사(구)나 보어가 문두로 나올 경우에 주어와 동사의 도치가 일어난다. 이 경우 동사가 수 일치해야 하는 주어는 동사 뒤에 온다는 것에 유의해야 한다.

· **Among the trees** was a large tiger.
부사구로 인한 주어와 동사의 도치
(큰 호랑이 한 마리가 나무들 사이에 있었다.)

· **In the room** were round tables.
부사구로 인한 주어와 동사의 도치
(원형 탁자들이 방에 있었다.)

– 부정이나 부정을 의미하는 부사가 강조를 위해 문두에 올 경우에도 주어와 동사의 도치가 일어날 수 있다.

· **Never** did I dream that I could meet her.
일반동사가 있는 문장의 도치는 「do[does/did]+주어+동사원형」
(나는 내가 그녀를 만날 수 있을 거라고 꿈도 꾸지 않았다.)

· **Hardly** had she left home when it began to snow.
be동사나 조동사가 있는 문장의 도치는 be동사나 조동사와 주어의 순서를 바꿈
(그녀가 집을 나서자마자 눈이 오기 시작했다.)

A 20 정답 ② ⭐ 2등급 대비 [정답률 89%]

✱ 물품을 찾아갈 것을 통지함

We hope / this notice finds you / in good health and high spirits. //
저희는 바랍니다 / 이 통지가 귀하를 발견하기를 / 건강하고 기분 좋은 상태에서 //
to inform의 간접목적어와 직접목적어절 접속사
We are writing to inform you / that a package was delivered / to the Rosehill Apartment Complex / on October 9th, / specifically addressed to your home. //
저희는 귀하에게 알려 드리기 위해 글을 쓰고 있습니다 / 물품이 배달되었다는 것을 / Rosehill 아파트 단지로 / 10월 9일에 / 귀하의 집 주소가 분명하게 적힌 //
형용사적 용법(attempts 수식) ✱
However, despite multiple attempts / to deliver the package to you, / it has remained unclaimed / at our front desk / for an extended period. //
그런데 여러 번의 시도에도 불구하고 / 귀하에게 그 물품을 전달하려는 / 그것은 찾아가지 않은 채 남아 있습니다 / 저희 프런트 데스크에 / 장기간 //
가주어   진주어
As the management office, / it is our responsibility / to ensure the safekeeping of all delivered items / and help deliver them quickly / to the right residents. //
관리 사무실로서 / ~이 저희의 책임입니다 / 모든 배달된 물품을 안전하게 보관하고 / 그것들이 신속하게 전달되도록 돕는 것이 / 올바른 입주민에게 //
단서 관리 사무실을 방문하여 물품을 찾아갈 것을 요청함
Therefore, we kindly request / that you visit the management office / during our office hours / to claim your package. //
그런 까닭에 정중히 요청드립니다 / 귀하가 관리 사무실을 방문하셔서 / 저희의 업무 시간 동안에 / 귀하의 물품을 찾아가시기를 //
We genuinely appreciate your cooperation / in this matter. //
귀하의 협조에 진심으로 감사드립니다 / 이 문제와 관련하여 //

· notice ⓝ 통지   · address ⓥ 주소를 적다
· unclaimed ⓐ 찾아가지 않은   · for an extended period 오랫동안
· responsibility ⓝ 책임   · ensure ⓥ 보장하다
· resident ⓝ 입주민   · claim ⓥ 찾아가다   · genuinely ⓐⓓ 진심으로
귀하가 건강하고 기분 좋게 이 통지를 받으시기를 바랍니다. 10월 9일에 Rosehill 아파트 단지로, 귀하의 집 주소가 분명하게 적힌 물품이 배달되었다는 것을 귀하에게 알려 드리기 위해 글을 쓰고 있습니다. 그런데 귀하에게 그 물품을 전달하려고 여러 번 시도했지만, 그것은 저희 프런트 데스크에 장기간 찾아가지 않은 채 남아 있습니다. 모든 배달된 물품을 안전하게 보관하고 그것들이 신속하게 해당 입주민에게 전달되도록 돕는 것이 관리 사무실로서 저희의 책임입니다. 그런 까닭에, 귀하가 저희 업무 시간 동안에 관리 사무실을 방문하셔서 귀하의 물품을 찾아가시기를 정중히 요청드립니다. 이 문제와 관련하여 귀하의 협조에 진심으로 감사드립니다.

다음 글의 목적으로 가장 적절한 것은?
① 관리 사무실 공사 일정을 알리려고 관리 사무실을 공사한다는 언급은 없음
②배달된 물품을 찾아갈 것을 요청하려고 we kindly request ~ to claim your package
③ 잘못 찾아간 물품의 반납을 부탁하려고 물품을 찾아가지 않았음
④ 배달 물품의 도난 방지 조치를 설명하려고 도난과 관련된 언급은 없음
⑤ 관리 사무실 운영 시간 변경을 공지하려고 during our office hour로 만든 오답

2등급❓ 선택지가 물품과 관리 사무실이라는 두 갈래로 나뉘어 글의 주제를 한 번에 파악하기 어렵지만 결론을 나타내는 연결어가 포함된 문장 하나만 찾아도 목적을 쉽게 파악할 수 있는 2등급 대비 문제이다.

왜 정답❓
편지를 보낸 사람: 관리 사무실 직원
편지를 받는 사람: 특정 입주민
편지 내용: 편지를 받는 사람에게 배달된 물품을 관리 사무실에서 보관하고 있으니 찾아갈 것을 요청함
→ 글의 목적은 ②

왜 오답❓
① 관리 사무실이 공사에 들어간다는 언급은 없다.
③ 물품을 찾아가지 않은 것이 문제이다.
④ 배달 물품의 도난과 관련된 언급은 없다.
⑤ 관리 사무실의 운영 시간에 와서 물품을 찾아가라는 요청이다.

────────────────────────────────── 어법 특강

✱ 형용사적 용법의 to부정사

– 형용사적 용법의 to부정사는 명사나 대명사를 뒤에서 수식할 수 있다.
· I need someone to help me.
(나는 나를 도와줄 누군가가 필요하다.)
· Please give me something to sit on.
(제게 앉을 만한 것을 좀 주세요.)
· Eric has a lot of things to do.
(Eric은 해야 할 많은 일들이 있다.)
· Don't make a promise to buy me a computer.
(내게 컴퓨터를 사주겠다는 약속을 하지 마세요.)

A 어휘 Review 정답 ─── 문제편 p. 24

01 특색	11 on behalf of	21 national
02 부적절한	12 in advance	22 charity
03 대표하다	13 in regard to	23 moved
04 현재, 지금	14 drop off	24 reservation
05 인기	15 take part in	25 interpersonal
06 unclaimed	16 positive	26 confident
07 rental	17 rent	27 explore
08 aboard	18 mayor	28 relevant
09 further	19 advantage	29 genuinely
10 occasion	20 admission	30 impress

B 심경의 이해 문제편 p. 25~35

B 01 정답 ① *일몰을 보게 된 Jessica

The island tour bus / Jessica was riding on / was moving slowly / toward the ocean cliffs. //
섬 관광버스는 / Jessica가 타고 있는 / 천천히 움직이고 있었다 / 바다에 면한 절벽 쪽으로 //

Outside, the sky was getting dark. //
바깥에서는 하늘이 점점 어두워지고 있었다 // **단서 1** 차가 막혀서 일몰을 놓칠 거라며 걱정스럽게 한숨지었음

Jessica sighed with concern, / "I'm going to miss the sunset / because of the traffic." //
Jessica는 걱정스럽게 한숨이었다 / "나는 일몰을 놓칠 거야 / 교통 때문에" //

The bus arrived / at the cliffs' parking lot. //
버스가 도착했다 / 절벽의 주차장에 // 장소의 부사구

While the other passengers were gathering their bags, / Jessica quickly got off the bus / and she ran up the cliff / that was famous for its ocean views. //
다른 승객들이 자신들의 가방을 챙기는 동안 / Jessica는 재빨리 버스에서 내렸고 / 그녀는 절벽으로 뛰어 올라갔다 / 그것의 바다 전망으로 유명한 //

She was about to give up / when she got to the top. //
그녀는 막 포기하려 했다 / 그녀가 꼭대기에 도달했을 때 //

Just then / she saw the setting sun / and it still shone brightly in the sky. // **단서 2** 일몰을 보게 됨
바로 그때 / 그녀는 지는 해를 보았는데 / 그것은 여전히 하늘에서 밝게 빛났다 //

Jessica said to herself, / "The glow of the sun is so beautiful. //
It's even better / than I expected." // **단서 3** 자신이 기대했던 것보다 훨씬 더 아름다운 노을을 봤음
Jessica는 혼잣말을 했다 / "노을이 너무 아름다워 // 그건 훨씬 더 좋아 / 내가 기대했던 것보다"라고 //

• sigh ⓥ 한숨을 쉬다 • passenger ⓝ 승객 • glow ⓝ (은은한) 불빛

Jessica가 타고 있는 섬 관광버스는 바다에 면한 절벽 쪽으로 천천히 움직이고 있었다. 바깥에서는 하늘이 점점 어두워지고 있었다. Jessica는 "나는 교통 때문에 일몰을 놓칠 거야."라고 말하며 걱정스럽게 한숨지었다. 버스가 절벽의 주차장에 도착했다. 다른 승객들이 자신들의 가방을 챙기는 동안, Jessica는 재빨리 버스에서 내렸고 바다 전망으로 유명한 절벽으로 뛰어 올라갔다. 꼭대기에 도달했을 때 그녀는 막 포기하려 했다. 바로 그때 그녀는 지는 해를 보았는데, 그것은 여전히 하늘에서 밝게 빛났다. Jessica는 "노을이 너무 아름다워. 내가 기대했던 것보다 훨씬 더 좋아."라고 혼잣말을 했다.

다음 글에 드러난 Jessica의 심경 변화로 가장 적절한 것은?

① worried → delighted 노을을 못 볼까 봐 걱정하다가 보게 됨
 걱정스러운 → 매우 기쁜
② bored → confident 노을을 보면서 자신감을 느낀 것이 아님
 지루해하는 → 자신만만한
③ relieved → annoyed 안도하는 → 짜증이 난
 안도하는 → 짜증이 난
④ joyful → indifferent 전반부에서는 한숨을 쉬었음 ─ 아름다운 노을을 봐서 짜증이 나거나 우울한 것이 아님
 기쁜 → 무관심한
⑤ regretful → depressed
 후회하는 → 우울한

왜 정답? [정답률 96%]

차가 막혀서 해가 지는 광경을 놓칠 거라고 걱정스럽게 한숨짓던 Jessica는 버스가 주차장에 도착하자마자 절벽으로 뛰어 올라갔고, 마침내 자신이 기대했던 것보다 훨씬 더 아름다운 노을을 보게 되었으므로 정답은 ① '걱정스러운 → 매우 기쁜'이다.

왜 오답?

② 차가 막혀서 노을을 보지 못할까 봐 걱정하며 한숨 쉰 것이 지루함을 느끼는 것은 아니다.
③, ⑤ 자신이 기대했던 것보다 훨씬 더 아름다운 노을을 보게 되었는데 짜증이 나거나 우울하다는 것은 적절하지 않다.
④ 전반부에서는 걱정스럽게 한숨짓는 Jessica가 묘사되었다.

B 02 정답 ① *과학 프로젝트 아이디어에 도움을 준 누나

Timothy sat at his desk, / desperately turning the pages of his science book. // 분사구문
Timothy는 책상에 앉아 / 필사적으로 자신의 과학책 페이지를 넘겼다 //

His science project was due in a few days / and he had no idea where to start. // 의문사+to부정사 **단서 1** 과학 프로젝트에 대한 막막함으로 좌절스러움
그의 과학 프로젝트 마감일이 며칠 남지 않았는데 / 그는 어디서부터 시작해야 할지 막막했다 //

Finally, he closed his book, hit the table, and shouted, / "This is impossible!" //
마침내 그는 책을 덮고 테이블을 치며 외쳤다 / "이건 불가능해!"라고 //

His sister, Amelia, / drawn by the noise, / came into his room. // 분사구문
그의 누나 Amelia가 / 그 소리에 이끌려 / 그의 방으로 들어왔다 //

"Hey, little brother, can I help?" //
"이봐, 동생, 누나가 도와줄까" //

Timothy explained his situation / and Amelia immediately had a solution. //
Timothy가 자신의 상황을 설명하자 / Amelia는 즉시 해결책을 내놓았다 //

She knew / that Timothy enjoyed learning about environmental issues / and suggested / he do a project about climate change. // enjoy+동명사 / 주장, 요구, 명령, 제안을 나타내는 동사(+that)+주어(+should)+동사원형
그녀는 알았다 / Timothy가 환경 문제에 대해 배우는 것을 좋아한다는 것을 / 그리고 제안했다 / 그가 기후 변화에 관한 프로젝트를 할 것을 //

Timothy thought about the idea / and agreed that his sister was right. // Timothy는 그 아이디어를 생각해 본 후 / 누나의 말이 옳다고 동의했다 //

"Oh, Amelia, your idea is fantastic! // Thank you. // You are the best sister ever!" // **단서 2** 누나의 도움을 받게 되어 고마워함
"오, Amelia 누나, 누나의 아이디어는 정말 환상적이야 // 고마워 // 누나는 정말 최고의 누나야" //

• desperately ⓐⓓ 필사적으로 • due ⓐ 마감일이 된
• draw ⓥ 이끌다, 당기다 • immediately ⓐⓓ 즉시
• fantastic ⓐ 환상적인

Timothy는 책상에 앉아 필사적으로 자신의 과학책 페이지를 넘겼다. 그의 과학 프로젝트 마감일이 며칠 남지 않았는데 그는 어디서부터 시작해야 할지 막막했다. 마침내 그는 책을 덮고 테이블을 치며 "이건 불가능해!"라고 외쳤다. 그의 누나 Amelia가 그 소리에 이끌려 그의 방으로 들어왔다. "이봐, 동생, 누나가 도와줄까?" Timothy가 자신의 상황을 설명하자 Amelia는 즉시 해결책을 내놓았다. 그녀는 Timothy가 환경 문제에 대해 배우는 것을 좋아한다는 것을 알고 기후 변화에 관한 프로젝트를 해보라고 제안했다. Timothy는 그 아이디어를 생각해 본 후 누나의 말이 옳다고 동의했다. "오, Amelia 누나, 누나의 아이디어는 정말 환상적이야! 고마워. 누나는 정말 최고의 누나야!"

다음 글에 드러난 Timothy의 심경 변화로 가장 적절한 것은?

① frustrated → grateful 아이디어가 떠오르지 않아 좌절함 → 누나의 도움을 받고 고마워함
 좌절한 → 감사하는
② disappointed → envious 누나를 부러워하는 감정은 아님
 실망한 → 부러워하는
③ hopeful → thrilled 처음에는 아이디어가 떠오르지 않아 좌절하고 있었음
 희망에 찬 → 아주 신이 난
④ encouraged → ashamed 부끄러운 감정은 없음
 힘이 나는 → 부끄러운
⑤ fearful → indifferent 무관심한 감정을 느낄 상황이 아님
 두려워하는 → 무관심한

왜 정답? [정답률 95%]

전반부: Timothy는 과학 프로젝트 마감일이 얼마 남지 않았는데, 아이디어가 떠오르지 않았음 ▶ '좌절한'

후반부: 누나가 좋은 아이디어 제안을 해주어 고마움을 표했음 ▶ '감사하는'

▶ 따라서 Timothy의 심경 변화로 가장 적절한 것은 ① '좌절한 → 감사하는'이다.

왜 오답?

② 누나에게 감사해하는 것이지 부러워하는 감정은 아니다.
③ 전반부에서 아이디어가 떠오르지 않아 좌절하고 있었다.
④ 처음에는 좌절하는 심경이었으며 후반부에도 부끄러운 감정은 없다.
⑤ 전반부의 감정은 두려움이 아니며, 무관심한 감정을 느낄 상황도 아니다.

B 03 정답 ② *Valentine's Day 기념 식당 예약에 실패한 Peter

It was Valentine's Day on Friday / and Peter was certain / that
his wife, Amy, was going to love his surprise. //
금요일은 밸런타인데이였다 / 그리고 Peter는 확신했다 / 그의 아내인 Amy가 자신의 뜻밖의
선물을 정말 좋아할 것이라고 //

Peter had spent a long time / searching online for an event / that
would be a new way / to spend time with Amy. //
Peter는 오랜 시간을 보냈다 / 이벤트를 온라인에서 찾느라 / 새로운 방식이 될 / Amy와
시간을 보내는 //

He had finally found / the perfect thing for her. //
그는 마침내 찾아냈다 / 그녀에게 꼭 맞는 것을 //

She often told him / that she liked to go to places / she had never
visited before, / and he was absolutely sure / that she would
love / going to the new, five-star restaurant downtown. //
그녀는 그에게 자주 말했다 / 장소에 가보고 싶다고 / 전에 전혀 가 본 적이 없는 / 그리고 그는
전적으로 확신했다 / 그녀가 좋아할 것이라고 / 시내에 새로 생긴 5성급 레스토랑에 가는 것을 //

He smiled / as he called the restaurant / and asked for a
reservation for Friday. //
그는 미소를 지었다 / 그 레스토랑에 전화를 걸면서 / 그리고 금요일의 예약을 요청하며 //
단서 1 그는 그녀가 시내에 새로 생긴 식당에 가는 것을 좋아할 것으로 확신함

Unfortunately, / his smile quickly disappeared / when he was
told / that the restaurant was fully reserved. //
안타깝게도 / 그의 미소는 곧 사라졌다 / 그가 들었을 때 / 그 레스토랑의 예약이 꽉 찼다는
것을 //
단서 2 레스토랑의 예약이 꽉 찼다는 말을 듣고 미소가 사라짐

"That's too bad," / he said quietly. //
"너무 안타깝네요" / 그는 조용히 말했다 //

"I thought / that I had found the right place." //
"저는 생각했거든요 / 제가 딱 맞는 장소를 찾아냈다고" //

- absolutely [ad] 전적으로, 틀림없이   · five-star 최고급의
- downtown [ad] 시내에, 시내로   · reservation [n] 예약
- indifferent [a] 무관심한   · jealous [a] 질투하는
- embarrassed [a] 당황스러운

금요일은 밸런타인데이였고 Peter는 아내 Amy가 자신의 뜻밖의 선물을
정말 좋아할 것이라고 확신했다. Peter는 Amy와 시간을 보내는 새로운
방식이 될 이벤트를 온라인에서 찾느라 오랜 시간을 보냈다. 그는 마침내
그녀에게 꼭 맞는 것을 찾아냈다. 그녀는 전에 전혀 가 본 적이 없는 곳에
가보고 싶다고 그에게 자주 말했고, 그는 그녀가 시내에 새로 생긴 5성급
레스토랑에 가면 정말 좋아할 것이라고 전적으로 확신했다. 그는 그 레스토랑에
전화를 걸어 금요일의 예약을 요청하며 미소를 지었다. 안타깝게도, 그가 그
레스토랑의 예약이 꽉 찼다는 말을 들었을 때 그의 미소는 곧 사라졌다. 그는
"너무 안타깝네요."라고 조용히 말했다. "저는 딱 맞는 장소를 찾아냈다고
생각했거든요."

다음 글에 드러난 Peter의 심경 변화로 가장 적절한 것은?

① relaxed → indifferent 편안함을 느끼다가 무관심해지는 상황이 아님
편안한 → 무관심한
②confident → disappointed 식당을 좋아할 것으로 확신함 → 식당 예약이 끝나 실망함
확신하는 → 실망한
③ confused → satisfied 혼란스러움을 느끼다가 만족한 상황이 아님
혼란스러운 → 만족한
④ jealous → discouraged 낙담한 것은 맞지만 그 이전에 질투하는 심경은 언급되지 않음
질투하는 → 낙담한
⑤ embarrassed → joyful 당황하다가 기쁨을 느끼는 것이 아니라 오히려 실망했음
당황한 → 기쁜

왜 정답? [정답률 95%]

전반부: Peter가 Valentine's Day에 시내에 새로 생긴 5성급 식당에 아내를 데려갈
계획을 세우고 그녀가 그것을 정말 좋아할 것으로 확신함

후반부: 식당에 예약 전화를 하였으나 예약이 다 찼다는 응답을 듣고 실망함

▶ ②'확신하는' 심경에서 '실망한' 심경으로 변화함

왜 오답?

① 편안함을 느끼다가 무관심해지는 상황이 아니다.
③ 혼란스러움을 느끼다가 만족하게 되는 상황이 아니다.
④ 낙담한 것은 맞지만 그 이전에 질투를 하다가 낙담하게 되는 것이 아니다.
⑤ 당황했다가 기쁨을 느끼는 심경 변화는 일어나지 않았다.

백승준 | 2025 수능 응시 · 광주 광주숭원고 졸

심경 변화 문제는 쉬운 유형이니만큼 빠르게 풀어야 하는 문제야.
그러기 위해서 빠르게 글을 훑으며 심경을 나타내는 단어와
문장을 찾아내는 것이 중요해. 이 문제의 경우 첫 문장의 Peter
was certain과 역접의 연결사 Unfortunately 뒤에 오는 his
smile quickly disappeared로 정답이 ②인 걸 파악할 수 있지!

B 04 정답 ③ *항공기 탑승 시간에 늦을 뻔한 Sophie

The whole morning had been chaotic. //
아침 내내 혼란스러운 상태였다 //

Sophie's day began / with her alarm clock failing to ring, / which
had thrown her into an intense rush. //
Sophie의 하루는 시작되었다 / 그녀의 알람시계가 울리지 않으며 / 그것이 그녀를 격심한
서두름으로 던져넣었다 //

After terrible traffic, / her taxi finally arrived at the airport, /
where she was met with endless security lines. //
끔찍한 교통 체증 후에 / 그녀가 탄 택시가 마침내 공항에 도착했다 / 그곳에서 그녀는 끝없는
보안 검색 (대기) 줄과 마주하게 되었다 //

Sophie kept glancing at her watch / with each second feeling
like an hour. //
Sophie는 계속 자신의 시계를 힐끗힐끗 보았다 / 매 초가 한 시간처럼 느껴지는 가운데 //

Worried that she could not get to the boarding gate in time, / she
rushed through the crowds of people. //
시간 내에 탑승구에 도착할 수 없을까 봐 걱정하면서 / 그녀는 수많은 사람들을 뚫고
돌진했다 //
단서 1 시간 내에 도착할 수 없을까 봐 걱정함

Just then, / she heard an announcement / saying that her flight
had been "delayed." //
바로 그때 / 그녀는 안내 방송을 들었다 / 자신의 항공편이 '지연되었다'고 하는 //

Letting out a deep sigh, / she finally felt at ease. //
깊은 한숨을 내쉬며 / 그녀는 마침내 마음이 편해졌다 // **단서 2** 마음이 편해짐

With an unexpected hour to spare, / she would have time /
to relax and browse the airport shops before her journey. //
예상치 못한 한 시간의 여유가 생기면서 / 그녀는 시간을 갖게 되었다 / 여행 전에 긴장을 풀고
공항 상점들을 둘러볼 //

- chaotic [a] 혼란 상태의   · intense [a] 격심한
- security [n] 보안 (검색)   · glance [v] 힐끗힐끗 보다
- boarding gate 탑승구   · announcement [n] (안내) 방송
- unexpected [a] 예기치 못한   · browse [v] 둘러보다
- joyful [a] 즐거운   · indifferent [a] 무관심한
- satisfied [a] 만족스러워 하는

아침 내내 혼란스러운 상태였다. Sophie의 하루는 그녀의 알람시계가 울리지
않으며 시작되었는데, 그것이 그녀를 격심한 서두름으로 던져넣었다. 끔찍한
교통 체증 후에 그녀가 탄 택시가 마침내 공항에 도착했는데, 그곳에서 그녀는
끝없는 보안 검색 (대기) 줄과 마주하게 되었다. Sophie는 매 초가 한 시간처럼
느껴지는 가운데, 계속 자신의 시계를 힐끗힐끗 보았다. 시간 내에 탑승구에
도착할 수 없을까 봐 걱정하면서 그녀는 수많은 사람들을 뚫고 돌진했다. 바로
그때, 그녀는 자신의 항공편이 '지연되었다'고 하는 안내 방송을 들었다. 깊은
한숨을 내쉬며, 그녀는 마침내 마음이 편해졌다. 예상치 못한 한 시간의 여유가
생기면서, 그녀는 여행 전에 긴장을 풀고 공항 상점들을 둘러볼 시간을 갖게
되었다.

다음 글에 드러난 Sophie의 심경 변화로 가장 적절한 것은?

① calm → delighted 초반에 차분한 것과 반대 상황임
차분한 → 기쁜
② pleased → indifferent 기쁨을 느끼다가 무관심해지는 상황이 아님
기쁜 → 무관심한
③anxious → relieved 탑승 시간에 늦을까 봐 초조함 → 탑승 시간 지연으로 마음이 편해짐
초조한 → 안도하는
④ joyful → disappointed 초반에 즐거움을 느낄 상태가 아님
즐거운 → 실망한
⑤ bored → satisfied 지루한 상황은 없었음
지루한 → 만족한

정답 및 해설   **15**

전반부: Sophie가 교통 체증과 긴 보안 대기줄 때문에 탑승 시간에 늦을까 봐 매우 초조함

후반부: 탑승 시간이 지연되었다는 안내 방송을 듣고 마음이 편해짐

▶ ③ '초조한' 심경에서 '안도하는' 심경으로 변화함

왜 오답?

① 초반에 차분하다가 기쁜 감정을 느끼는 것으로 변하지 않았다.

② 기쁨을 느끼다가 무관심해지는 상황이 아니다.

④ 즐거움을 느끼다가 실망하게 되지 않았다.

⑤ 지루함을 느낄 상황은 없었다.

왜 정답? [정답률 96%]

전반부: 캠프파이어를 위한 장작을 구하러 나섰는데, 위협적인 곰을 보고 공포로 얼어붙었음

후반부: 곰이 관심없어하며 지나가자, Sarah는 참고 있던 숨을 내쉬며 극도의 안도감을 느낌

▶ ② '겁먹은' 심경에서 '안도한' 심경으로 변함

왜 오답?

① 곰과 마주하는 상황이 부러워할만한 상황이 아니며, 곰이 지나간 것에 후회를 느끼지도 않았다.

③ 곰을 보는 것을 열렬히 바라지도 않았고, 곰이 사라진 것에 무관심하지도 않았다.

④ 곰과 마주한 상황을 지루하게 여기지 않았다.

⑤ 곰을 밟을 때 흥분하지도 않았고, 곰이 가서 화가 난 상황도 아니다.

B 05 정답 ② ＊곰과 마주친 위험한 상황에서 벗어난 Sarah

출발하다
Setting out to find some wood for the campfire, / Sarah moved through the forest. //
캠프파이어를 위한 장작을 찾기 위해 나선 / Sarah는 숲 속으로 이동했다 //

Just then, she noticed an approaching danger / — a large, threatening bear. //
그때, 그녀는 다가오는 위험을 발견했다 / 크고 위협적인 곰을 //

Panic spread through her body. //
공포가 그녀를 휩싸였다 //

단서 1 공포로 얼어붙어서 소리도 지르지 못하는 지켜봄
Frozen and unable to shout, / she watched in horror. //
얼어붙어 소리조차 지를 수 없이 / 그녀는 공포에 질려 바라보았다 //

Her heart beat louder / with each step the bear took. //
그녀의 심장은 더 크게 뛰었다 / 곰이 한 걸음 한 걸음 내딛을 때마다 //

But then, as if by a miracle, / the bear paused, looked around, and, uninterested, turned away, / retreating into the shadows of the woods. //
분사구문
하지만 그때, 마치 기적처럼 / 곰이 잠시 멈추고 뒤를 돌아본 후, 관심을 잃고 돌아서서 / 숲의 그림자 속으로 물러났다 //

'무너지다'
When the bear had disappeared completely out of her sight, / her knees nearly gave way. //
곰이 완전히 그녀의 시야에서 사라졌을 때 / 그녀는 거의 주저앉을 지경이었다 //

Sarah could finally let out the breath / she had been holding. //
Sarah는 드디어 숨을 내쉴 수 있었다 / 참아왔던 //
과거완료 진행형

A wave of immense relief washed over her. //
거대한 안도감의 물결이 그녀를 휩감았다 // **단서 2** 곰이 사라지자 극도의 안도감을 느낌

· threatening ⓐ 위협적인   · freeze ⓥ 얼다
· retreat ⓥ 물러가다   · completely ⓐⓓ 완전히
· immense ⓐ 거대한, 엄청난   · relief ⓝ 안도

캠프파이어를 위한 장작을 찾기 위해 나선 Sarah는 숲 속으로 이동했다. 그때, 그녀는 다가오는 위험을 발견했다 – 크고 위협적인 곰을. 공포가 그녀를 휩싸였다. 얼어붙어 소리조차 지를 수 없이, 그녀는 공포에 질려 바라보았다. 곰이 한 걸음 한 걸음 내딛을 때마다 그녀의 심장은 더 크게 뛰었다. 하지만 그때, 마치 기적처럼, 곰이 잠시 멈추고 뒤를 돌아본 후, 관심을 잃고 돌아서서 숲의 그림자 속으로 물러났다. 곰이 완전히 그녀의 시야에서 사라졌을 때, 그녀는 거의 주저앉을 지경이었다. Sarah는 드디어 참아왔던 숨을 내쉴 수 있었다. 거대한 안도감의 물결이 그녀를 휩감았다.

다음 글에 드러난 Sarah의 심경 변화로 가장 적절한 것은?

① envious → regretful 곰과 마주하는 상황이 부러워하는 상황은 아님
부러워하는 → 후회하는
② frightened → relieved 곰 때문에 겁을 먹음 → 곰이 사라지자 안도감을 느낌
겁먹은 → 안도한
③ eager → indifferent 곰을 밟을 때 열렬한 감정을 느끼는 않음
열렬한 → 무관심한
④ bored → satisfied 지루해할만한 상황은 아님
지루해하는 → 만족하는
⑤ excited → furious 곰과 마주한 경험에서 신나는 감정을 느끼지 않음
신이 난 → 몹시 화가 난

B 06 정답 ⑤ ＊열심히 준비한 발표 자료가 쓸모없게 되어버린 Joshua

spend 시간 / 돈 -ing: ~하는 데 시간 / 돈을 쓰다
Joshua had spent ten weeks / crafting a presentation / for an upcoming meeting. //
Joshua는 10주를 보냈다 / 발표 자료를 만들며 / 곧 있을 회의를 위한 //

He had worked very hard / on analyzing data, making beautiful plots and projections, / and he had often stayed in the office past midnight / polishing his presentation. //
분사구문
그는 열심히 했고 / 데이터를 분석하고 훌륭한 도표와 전망을 작성하는 것을 / 자정이 넘도록 머물렀다 / 발표 자료를 다듬으며 //

단서 1 발표 자료 결과물에 기뻐하고 행복했음
He was delighted with the outcome / and happily e-mailed the presentation to his boss, / who was going to make the presentation / at the all-important meeting. //
계속적 용법의 관계대명사
그는 그 결과물에 기뻐했고 / 행복해하며 그 발표 자료를 자신의 상사에게 이메일로 보냈고 / 상사는 발표할 예정이었다 / 가장 중요한 회의에서 //

His boss e-mailed him back / a few hours later: /
그의 상사는 그에게 이메일로 답장을 보냈다 / 몇 시간 후 /

목적어절 접속사
"Sorry, Joshua, / but just yesterday we learned / that the deal is off. // "Joshua, 미안하지만 / 막 어제 우리는 알게 되었네 / 그 거래가 취소되었다는 것을 //
I did look at your presentation, / and it is an impressive and fine piece of work. // Well done."//
내가 자네의 발표 자료를 살펴보았는데 / 그것은 인상적이고 우수한 작품이더군 / 수고했네 //

목적어절 접속사   세상에 나오다, 빛을 보다
Joshua realized / that his presentation would never see the light of day. // Joshua는 깨달았다/ 그의 발표 자료가 세상에 나오지 못하리라는 것을 //

동격의 that
The fact / that all his effort had served no ultimate purpose / created a deep rift / between him and his job. //
문장의 본동사
그 사실은 / 그의 모든 노력이 궁극적인 목적을 달성하지 못했다는 / 깊은 틈을 만들었다 / 그와 그의 일 사이에 // **단서 2** 헛된 수고를 했다는 느낌으로 바뀜

go from A to B: A에서 B로 바뀌다
He'd quickly gone / from feeling useful and happy in his work / to feeling dissatisfied / and that his efforts were in vain. //
병렬 구조(dissatisfied와 that ~)
그는 빠르게 이동했다 / 자신의 일에 있어서 유능하고 행복하다는 느낌으로부터 / 불만족스럽고 / 자신의 노력이 헛되었다는 느낌으로 //

· craft ⓥ 공들여 만들다   · polish ⓥ 다듬다
· impressive ⓐ 인상적인   · rift ⓝ 균열   · in vain 헛된

Joshua는 곧 있을 회의를 위한 발표 자료를 만들며 10주를 보냈다. 그는 데이터를 분석하고 훌륭한 도표와 전망을 작성하는 것을 열심히 했고, 그는 종종 사무실에서 발표 자료를 다듬으며 자정이 넘도록 머물렀다. 그는 그 결과물에 기뻐했고 행복해하며 그 발표 자료를 자신의 상사에게 이메일로 보냈고, 상사는 가장 중요한 회의에서 발표할 예정이었다. 몇 시간 후 그의 상사는 그에게 이메일로 답장을 보냈다: "Joshua, 미안하지만 막 어제 우리는 그 거래가 취소되었다는 것을 알게 되었네. 내가 자네의 발표 자료를 살펴보았는데, 그것은 인상적이고 우수한 작품이더군. 수고했네." Joshua는 그의 발표 자료가 세상에 나오지 못하리라는 것을 깨달았다. 그의 모든 노력이 궁극적인 목적을 달성하지 못했다는 사실은 그와 그의 일 사이에 깊은 틈을 만들었다. 그는 자신의 일에 있어서 유능하고 행복하다는 느낌으로부터 불만족스럽고 자신의 노력이 헛되었다는 느낌으로 빠르게 이동했다.

다음 글에 드러난 Joshua의 심경 변화로 가장 적절한 것은?

① isolated → optimistic 발표 자료를 준비하면서 고립된 감정을 느낀 것은 아님
　고립된 　낙관적인
② curious → bored 발표 자료에 궁금증을 가진다는 내용은 없었음
　궁금해하는 　지루해하는
③ anxious → thrilled 발표 자료 준비에 불안하지 않음
　불안한 　아주 신이 난
④ terrified → relieved 발표 자료를 준비하는 것에서 겁을 먹지 않았음
　겁이 난 　안도하는
⑤ pleased → discouraged 발표 자료 결과에 기쁨을 느낌 → 쓸모없어지자 실망함
　기쁜 　낙담한

왜 정답? [정답률 95%]

전반부: Joshua는 중요한 회의에 쓰일 발표 자료를 열심히 준비했으며, 그 결과에 만족하며 발표 자료를 상사에게 전달함 ▶ '기쁜'

후반부: 발표 자료를 받은 상사가 거래가 취소되었다고 알려주자 헛된 노력을 했다는 생각에 실망하며 불만족스러움을 느낌 ▶ '낙담한'

▶ 따라서 Joshua의 심경 변화로 가장 적절한 것은 ⑤ '기쁜 → 낙담한'이다.

왜 오답?

① 발표 자료를 열심히 준비한 것에서 고립된 감정을 느끼지 않으며, 후반부에 낙관적으로 생각하지도 않았다.
② 후반부에 거래가 무산되었다는 소식을 듣고 지루해하지 않았다.
③ 발표 자료 준비를 하면서 불안감을 느끼지 않았으며, 후반부에는 신이 난 것이 아니라 오히려 그 반대였다.
④ 전반부에 발표 자료를 준비하면서 겁을 먹지 않았고, 후반부에 거래가 취소되었다는 소식에 안도하지도 않았다.

B 07 정답 ① ＊아는 문제가 하나도 없었던 이유

Charles was taking a quiz / in his math class. //
Charles는 퀴즈를 보고 있었다 / 수학 시간에 //
　　　　　　　　　　= the questions
He stared at the questions, / but they looked completely unfamiliar. //
그는 그 문제들을 유심히 살펴보았지만 / 그것들은 완전히 낯설게 보였다 //

Charles flipped through the pages of the quiz / for a while. //
Charles는 퀴즈 문제지를 넘겨 보았다 / 한동안 /
　　　　　　　　　　목적어절 접속사
His palms grew sweaty / as he realized that he didn't know a single answer. // **단서1** 답을 아는 문제가 없어서 손에 땀이 남
그의 손바닥에서 땀이 났다 / 그가 하나의 정답도 알지 못한다는 것을 깨닫고 //

A moment later, / a few other students began raising their hands. //
　　　　　　　　　　　　　　　　　　　　동명사구(began의 목적어)
잠시 후 / 몇몇 다른 학생들이 손을 들기 시작했다 //
　　　　　　　　　뒤에 목적어절 접속사 that 생략
One said, / "I don't think we ever learned / about the stuff on this quiz, / Mrs. Smith." //
한 학생이 말했다 / "제 생각에 저희는 한 번도 배운 적이 없는 것 같아요 / 이 퀴즈에 나오는 것들에 대해 / Smith 선생님"이라고 //

The teacher quickly looked over a copy of the quiz / and announced, /
　　　　　　　　　　　　　　　　病렬 구조(동사)
선생님은 퀴즈 문제지를 빠르게 살펴보았다 / 그리고 알렸다 /

"I'm sorry, class. // It appears that I have given you the wrong quiz by mistake. // We'll take the right quiz next class." //
"미안해요, 여러분 // 실수로 여러분에게 잘못된 문제지를 준 것 같아요 // 우리는 다음 시간에 올바른 퀴즈를 보겠습니다"라고 //
　　　　　　　　　　　　　　　명사절을 이끄는 관계대명사
As Charles heard what the teacher said, / the tension in his
　　　　　　　　명사적 용법(began의 목적어)
shoulders began to melt away. // **단서2** 시험이 미루어져서 안도감을 느낌
Charles는 선생님이 말씀하신 것을 듣자 / 어깨의 긴장이 차츰 사라지기 시작했다 //

- stare ⓥ 응시하다　· flip ⓥ 휙 젖히다　· palm ⓝ 손바닥
- sweaty ⓐ 땀투성이의　· melt away 차츰 사라지다
- sympathetic ⓐ 동정 어린

Charles는 수학 시간에 퀴즈를 보고 있었다. 그는 그 문제들을 유심히 살펴보았지만 그것들은 완전히 낯설게 보였다. Charles는 한동안 퀴즈 문제지를 넘겨 보았다. 그가 하나의 정답도 알지 못한다는 것을 깨닫고 그의

손바닥에서 땀이 났다. 잠시 후 몇몇 다른 학생들이 손을 들기 시작했다. 한 학생이 "Smith 선생님, 제 생각에 저희는 이 퀴즈에 나오는 것들을 한 번도 배운 적이 없는 것 같아요."라고 말했다. 선생님은 퀴즈 문제지를 빠르게 살펴보고 "미안해요, 여러분. 실수로 여러분에게 잘못된 문제지를 준 것 같아요. 우리는 다음 시간에 올바른 퀴즈를 보겠습니다."라고 알렸다. Charles는 선생님이 말씀하신 것을 듣자 어깨의 긴장이 차츰 사라지기 시작했다.

다음 글에 드러난 Charles의 심경 변화로 가장 적절한 것은?

① nervous → relieved His palms grew sweaty → the tension ~ melt away
　불안한 　안도하는
② relaxed → regretful 전반부에는 불안함을 느낌
　편안한 　후회하는
③ amazed → annoyed 후반부에는 짜증이 아닌 안도감이 들었음
　깜짝 놀란 　짜증 나는
④ indifferent → satisfied 전반부에는 불안함을 느낌
　무관심한 　만족한
⑤ shocked → sympathetic 동정 어린 감정을 느낄 대상이 없음
　충격받은 　동정 어린

왜 정답? [정답률 93%]

전반부: 시험지에 아는 문제가 하나도 없다는 것을 알아차리고 손바닥에 땀이 남
▶ '불안한'

후반부: 잘못된 시험지를 받은 것임을 알고 긴장이 사라지기 시작함
▶ '안도하는'

▶ 따라서 Charles의 심경 변화로 가장 적절한 것은 ① '불안한 → 안도하는'이다.

왜 오답?

② 시험 문제의 답을 하나도 알지 못했기 때문에 초반에는 불안함을 느꼈다.
③ 시험이 미루어져 안도감이 들었고 짜증이 나는 것은 아니다.
④ 초반에는 손바닥에 땀이 나는 등의 불안함을 느꼈다.
⑤ 동정 어린 감정을 느낄 대상은 나타나지 않았다.

B 08 정답 ② ＊물속에서 구조된 Anna

The piece of wreckage / Anna held on to / that served as a life preserver / had a window. // 　주어를 수식하는 부분
잔해 조각에는 / Anna가 매달려 있던 / 구명구로서의 역할을 했던 / 창문이 있었다 //

Now that there was light, / she looked through it and down into the water. //
이제 빛이 있어서 / 그녀는 그것을 통해 물속을 내려다보았다 //

She wished she hadn't. //
그녀는 그러지 말았어야 했다고 생각했다 //
　　　　　　　　　　명사(dark shapes)를 수식하는 분사
She spied dark shapes / moving beneath her. //
그녀는 어두운 형상을 보았다 / 자신의 아래에서 움직이는 //

What could they be? // Fish? // Sharks? //
그것들은 무엇일까 // 물고기 // 상어 //
단서1 공포심을 느낌
　　　　　　　　　　주어를 생략하지 않은 분사구문
Anna shook with fear, / her blood running cold. //
Anna는 공포심에 (몸을) 떨었고 / 그녀의 피는 차갑게 식어 갔다 //

The last bits of strength / were draining away from / her arms and upper body. //
마지막 남은 힘마저 / 빠져나가고 있었다 / 그녀의 팔과 상체에서 //

She did not know / how much longer she could hang on, / but then Anna glanced up / and couldn't believe what she saw. //
　　　　　　　　　　　　　　　　　　　= the thing which
그녀는 알 수 없었지만 / 얼마나 더 오래 버틸 수 있을지 / 그때 Anna가 흘깃 위를 쳐다보았고 / 그녀가 본 것을 믿을 수 없었다 //

A fishing boat was approaching / over the big waves. //
어선 한 척이 다가오고 있었다 / 큰 파도를 넘어 //

After being in the water for 3 hours, / she was finally rescued. //
3시간 동안 물속에 있다가 / 그녀는 마침내 구조되었다 //
　　　　　　　　　　　지각동사　　　　　　　　　　원형부정사
When she got on the boat, / she felt / a sense of relief spread through her body. // **단서2** 구조되어 안도감이 퍼져나가는 것을 느낌
그녀가 배에 올라탔을 때 / 그녀는 느꼈다 / 안도감이 그녀의 몸에 퍼져나가는 것을 //

- wreckage ⓝ 잔해, 난파
- life preserver (물에 빠진 사람들이 물에 떠 있게 하는) 구명구
- spy ⓥ 보다 • drain away 빠져나가다, 배출하다
- hang on 꽉 붙잡다 • glance ⓥ 홀깃 보다 • relief ⓝ 안도, 안심

Anna가 매달려 있던 (물에 빠진 사람들이 물에 떠 있게 하는) 구명구로서의 역할을 했던 잔해 조각에는 창문이 있었다. 이제 빛이 있어서 그녀는 그것을 통해 물속을 내려다보았다. 그녀는 그러지 말았어야 했다고 생각했다. 그녀는 자신의 아래에서 움직이는 어두운 형상을 보았다. 그것들은 무엇일까? 물고기? 상어? Anna는 공포심에 (몸을) 떨었고, 그녀의 피는 차갑게 식어 갔다. 마지막 남은 힘마저 팔과 상체에서 빠져나가고 있었다. 그녀는 얼마나 더 오래 버틸 수 있을지 알 수 없었지만, 그때 Anna가 홀깃 위를 쳐다보았고 그녀가 본 것을 믿을 수 없었다. 어선 한 척이 큰 파도를 넘어 다가오고 있었다. 3시간 동안 물속에 있다가, 그녀는 마침내 구조되었다. 그녀가 배에 올라탔을 때, 그녀는 안도감이 그녀의 몸에 퍼져나가는 것을 느꼈다.

다음 글에 드러난 Anna의 심경 변화로 가장 적절한 것은?

① eager → sorrowful 후반부에 슬픈 감정을 느끼는 상황이 아님
  열성적인 → 슬픈
②terrified → relieved 물 속에서 두려움을 느낌 → 구조되어 안도함
  무서워하는 → 안도하는
③ excited → confused 전반부가 신나는 상황은 아님
  신이 난 → 혼란스러운
④ indifferent → irritated 후반부에 짜증나는 감정으로 변한 상황이 아님
  무관심한 → 짜증난
⑤ confident → ashamed 자신감이 있거나 부끄러운 상황은 없었음
  자신만만한 → 부끄러운

왜 정답? [정답률 94%]

전반부: Anna는 물속에서 구명구에 매달려 공포심에 떨고 있었음
후반부: 어선에 의해 구조되어 안도감을 느낌
▶ ② '무서워하는' 심경에서 '안도하는' 심경으로 변화함

왜 오답?
① 후반부에 슬픈 감정을 느끼는 상황이 아니다.
③ 전반부에 신나는 감정을 느끼지 않았다.
④ 후반부에 짜증나는 감정으로 변한 상황이 아니다.
⑤ 자신감이나 부끄러움을 느낄 만한 상황은 언급되지 않았다.

자이 쌤's Follow Me! −홈페이지에서 제공

B 09 정답 ① *온라인 상담에 만족한 Natalie

부사절 접속사(~하면서)
As Natalie was logging in / to her first online counseling session, / she wondered, / "How can I open my heart / to the counselor / through a computer screen?"
Natalie는 접속하면서 / 자신의 첫 온라인 상담 시간에 / 그녀는 의문을 가졌다 / "내가 어떻게 나의 마음을 열 수 있을까 / 상담사에게 / 컴퓨터 화면을 통해"라는 //

부사절 접속사(이유)
Since the counseling center was a long drive away, / she knew / that this would save her / a lot of time. //
확정적인 사실을 말할 때 쓰는 명사절 접속사
상담 센터가 차로 오래 가야 하는 곳에 있었기 때문에 / 그녀는 알고 있었다 / 이것이 자신에게 절약해 줄 것임을 / 많은 시간을 //

불확실하거나 의문되는 사실에 대해 말할 때 쓰는 명사절 접속사
Natalie just wasn't sure / if it would be as helpful / as meeting her counselor / in person. // **단서1** 온라인 상담이 도움이 될 확신할 수 없었음
다만 Natalie는 확신할 수 없었다 / 그것이 도움이 될지 / 자신의 상담사를 만나는 것만큼 / 직접 //

부사절 접속사(일단 ~하자)   **단서2** 상담이 시작되자 걱정이 사라짐
Once the session began, / however, / her concerns went away. //
일단 상담이 시작되자 / 하지만 / 그녀의 걱정은 사라졌다 //

비교급 강조 부사
She actually started thinking / that it was much more convenient / than expected. // **단서3** 온라인 상담이 예상보다 훨씬 더 편리하다고 생각함
그녀는 실제로 생각하기 시작했다 / 그것이 훨씬 더 편리하다고 / 예상던 것보다 //

She felt / as if the counselor were in the room / with her. //
그녀는 느꼈다 / 마치 상담사가 방 안에 있는 것처럼 / 자신과 함께 //

As the session closed, / she told him with a smile, / "I'll definitely see you online again!" //
상담이 끝났을 때 / 그녀는 미소를 지으며 그에게 말했다 / "저는 당신을 온라인에서 꼭 다시 만날 거예요" //

- log in to ~에 접속하다 • counseling ⓝ 상담, 조언
- session ⓝ (특정한 활동을 위한) 시간[기간] • counselor ⓝ 상담사
- through prep ~을 통해 • in person 직접 • concern ⓝ 우려
- go away 없어지다 • actually ⓐⓓ 실제로 • convenient ⓐ 편리한
- expect ⓥ 예상하다 • as if 마치 ~인 것처럼 • definitely ⓐⓓ 분명히

Natalie는 자신의 첫 온라인 상담 시간에 접속하면서, "내가 컴퓨터 화면을 통해 상담사에게 어떻게 나의 마음을 열 수 있을까?"라는 의문을 가졌다. 상담 센터가 차로 오래 가야 하는 곳에 있었기 때문에, 그녀는 이것이 자신에게 많은 시간을 절약해 줄 것임을 알고 있었다. 다만 Natalie는 그것이 상담사를 직접 만나는 것만큼 도움이 될지 확신할 수 없었다. 하지만 일단 상담이 시작되자, 그녀의 걱정은 사라졌다. 그녀는 실제로 그것이 예상했던 것보다 훨씬 더 편리하다고 생각하기 시작했다. 그녀는 마치 상담사가 자신과 함께 방 안에 있는 것처럼 느꼈다. 상담이 끝났을 때, 그녀는 미소를 지으며 그에게 말했다. "저는 당신을 온라인에서 꼭 다시 만날 거예요!"

다음 글에 드러난 Natalie의 심경 변화로 가장 적절한 것은?

①doubtful → satisfied 확신하지 못하다가 엄청 편리하다고 생각하게 됨
  의심하는 → 만족한
② regretful → confused 후반부에는 온라인 상담에 대해 확신하게 됐음
  유감스러운 → 혼란스러운
③ confident → ashamed 부끄러움을 느낄 만한 일화가 아님
  자신만만한 → 부끄러운
④ bored → excited 온라인 상담이 따분하다고 생각한 것은 아님
  따분한 → 신이 난
⑤ thrilled → disappointed 온라인 상담에 무척 만족했음
  흥분한 → 실망한

왜 정답? [정답률 96%]

온라인 상담에 대해 처음에는 그것이 직접 상담사를 만나는 것만큼 도움이 될지 확신하지 못하고 의심했지만, 일단 상담이 시작되자 그러한 걱정이 사라지고 예상보다 훨씬 더 편리하다고 생각했으므로 정답은 ① '의심하는 → 만족한'이다.

왜 오답?
② 상담이 시작되자 온라인 상담이 예상보다 훨씬 더 편리하다고 생각했으므로 혼란스러워한 것이 아니다.
③ 온라인 상담에 대해 확신, 자신이 없던 것이지, 자신만만해 한 것이 아니다.
④ 온라인 상담의 효과에 대해 확신하지 못한 것이지, 온라인 상담이 따분하다고 생각한 것은 아니다.
⑤ 온라인 상담에 실망했다면 상담사에게 온라인에서 꼭 다시 만나자고 말하지 않았을 것이다.

B 10 정답 ① *안심한 Jennifer

부사절 접속사(때)
While the mechanic worked on her car, / Jennifer walked back and forth / in the waiting room. //
정비공이 그녀의 차를 수리하는 동안 / Jennifer는 왔다 갔다 했다 / 대기실에서 //

단서1 매우 근심스러웠음
She was deeply concerned / about how much it was going to cost / to get her car fixed. //
그녀는 매우 근심스러웠다 / 비용이 얼마나 들지에 대해 / 그녀의 차가 수리되는 데 //

Her car's engine had started making noises / and kept losing power / that morning, / and she had heard / that replacing an engine could be very expensive. //
동명사구 주어
그녀의 차의 엔진에서 소음이 나기 시작하고 / 계속 시동이 꺼졌다 / 그날 아침부터 / 그리고 그녀는 들었다 / 엔진 교체는 매우 비쌀 수 있다고 //

After a few minutes, / the mechanic came back into the waiting room. //
몇 분 후 / 정비공이 대기실로 돌아왔다 //

"I've got some good news. // It was just a dirty spark plug. // I already wiped it clean / and your car is as good as new." //

그는 "좋은 소식이 좀 있습니다 // 그냥 점화 플러그가 더러웠을 뿐입니다 // 제가 그것을 이미 깨끗하게 닦았고 / 손님의 차는 새 차처럼 깨끗합니다" //

He handed her the bill / and when she checked it, / the overall cost of repairs / came to less than ten dollars. //
주어   동사   간접목적어   직접목적어

그는 그녀에게 청구서를 건넸고 / 그녀가 확인해 보니 / 전체 수리 비용은 / 10달러도 되지 않았다 //

That was far less / than she had expected / and she felt at ease, /
was보다 앞선 시제를 나타내는 대과거
knowing she could easily afford it. // 단서2 안심했음

그것은 훨씬 적었으며 / 그녀가 예상했던 것보다 / 그녀는 안심했다 / 쉽게 감당할 수 있다는 사실을 알고 //

· mechanic ⓝ 정비공   · back and forth 왔다갔다
· deeply ⓐⓓ 매우, 깊이   · replace ⓥ 교체하다   · wipe ⓥ 닦다
· overall ⓐ 종합적인, 전체의   · at ease 걱정 없이, 편안한
· afford ⓥ 감당하다

정비공이 그녀의 차를 수리하는 동안 Jennifer는 대기실을 왔다 갔다 했다. 그녀는 차를 수리하는 데 비용이 얼마나 들지 매우 근심스러웠다. 그날 아침부터 차의 엔진에서 소음이 나기 시작하고 계속 시동이 꺼졌고, 엔진 교체는 매우 비쌀 수 있다는 말을 들었기 때문이다. 몇 분 후 정비공이 대기실로 돌아왔다. "좋은 소식이 좀 있습니다. 그냥 점화 플러그가 더러웠을 뿐입니다. 제가 이미 깨끗하게 닦았고, 손님 차는 새 차처럼 깨끗해졌습니다." 그는 그녀에게 청구서를 건넸고, 그녀가 확인해 보니 전체 수리 비용은 10달러도 되지 않았다. 예상했던 것보다 훨씬 적은 금액이었으며, 그녀는 쉽게 감당할 수 있다는 사실을 알고 안심했다.

다음 글에 드러난 Jennifer의 심경 변화로 가장 적절한 것은?

① worried → relieved deeply concerned → felt at ease
   걱정하는 → 안심한
② calm → terrified 후반부에서는 안심했음
   평온한 → 무서워하는
③ bored → thrilled 지루해서 왔다 갔다 한 것이 아님
   지루한 → 매우 흥분한
④ excited → scared 무서운 상황이 아님
   신이 난 → 겁을 먹은
⑤ disappointed → indifferent 좋은 소식을 들었음
   실망한 → 무관심한

⟩왜 정답? [정답률 97%]

전반부: 차를 수리하는 비용에 대해 매우 근심스러워했음
후반부: 생각보다 훨씬 적은 수리 비용에 안심했음
➡ 심경의 변화는 ① '걱정하는 → 안심한'!

⟩왜 오답?
② 전반부에는 초조하게 대기실 안에서 왔다 갔다 했다.
③ deeply concerned라고 했으므로 지루한 것이 아니다.
④ 정비공이 Jennifer를 무섭게 하는 상황이 아니다.
⑤ 정비공이 Jennifer에게 좋은 소식을 전했다.

B 11 정답 ③ *부상에서 회복한 David

부사절 접속사(때)
As he stepped / onto the basketball court, / David suddenly
┌병렬 구조┐   앞에 관계부사가 생략됨
thought of the day / he had gotten injured / last season / and froze. //

그가 들어서면서 / 농구 경기장으로 / David는 갑자기 그날을 생각하고는 / 그가 부상을 당했던 / 지난 시즌에 / 얼어붙었다 단서1 부상에서 회복한 후 첫 경기에서

불확실한 사실에 쓰이는 명사절 접속사   잘할 수 있을지 확신하지 못함
He was not sure / if he could play as well / as before the injury. //

그는 확신하지 못했다 / 그가 경기를 잘할 수 있을지 / 부상 전만큼 //

주어   동사   목적어   목적격 보어
A serious wrist injury / had caused him to miss / the rest of the season. //

심각한 손목 부상이 / 그로 하여금 놓치게 했다 / 그 시즌의 나머지를 //

= As he remembered the surgery
Remembering the surgery, / he said to himself, / "I thought / my basketball career was completely over." //

그 수술을 생각하며 / 그는 마음속으로 생각했다 / "나는 생각했어 / 내 농구 경력이 완전히 끝났다고" //

upon[on] -ing: ~하자마자 *
However, / upon hearing his fans' wild cheers, / he felt his body coming alive / and thought, /

하지만 / 그의 팬들의 열정적인 응원을 듣자 / 그는 그의 몸이 살아나는 것을 느꼈고 / 생각했다 /

"For sure, / my fans, friends, and family / are looking forward / to watching me play today." //
                      동명사 watching의 목적어와 목적격 보어

"분명히 / 나의 팬, 친구, 가족이 / 고대하고 있어 / 내가 오늘 경기하는 모습을 보는 것을"이라고 //
단서2 경기가 시작하자마자 에너지가 넘쳐흘렀음

As soon as the game started, / he was filled with energy. //

경기가 시작하자마자 / 그는 에너지가 넘쳐흘렀다 //
앞에 목적격 관계대명사가 생략됨
The first five shots / he attempted / went in the basket. //

첫 다섯 차례의 숫이 / 그가 시도한 / 바스켓으로 들어갔다 //

"I'm back! // I got this," / he shouted. // 단서3 다섯 번의 숫을 성공시킨 후
                                            "I'm back!"이라고 외침
"내가 돌아왔어 // 내가 이걸 해냈어" / 그는 외쳤다 //

· injure ⓥ 부상을 입다   · freeze ⓥ 얼어붙다   · serious ⓐ 심각한
· wrist ⓝ 손목   · surgery ⓝ 수술   · completely ⓐⓓ 완전히
· cheer ⓝ 환호(성)   · attempt ⓥ 시도하다

농구 경기장으로 들어서면서, David는 갑자기 지난 시즌 자신이 부상을 당했던 날을 생각하고는 얼어붙었다. 그는 자신이 부상 전만큼 경기를 잘할 수 있을지 확신하지 못했다. 심각한 손목 부상 때문에 그는 그 시즌의 나머지를 놓쳤다. 그 수술을 생각하며 그는 마음속으로 생각했다. "나는 내 농구 경력이 완전히 끝났다고 생각했어." 하지만 팬들의 열정적인 응원을 듣자, 그는 몸이 살아나는 것을 느꼈고 "분명히, 나의 팬, 친구, 가족이 내가 오늘 경기하는 모습을 보는 것을 고대하고 있어."라고 생각했다. 경기가 시작하자마자, 그는 에너지가 넘쳐흘렀다. 그가 시도한 첫 다섯 차례의 숫이 바스켓으로 들어갔다. "내가 돌아왔어! 내가 이걸 해냈어." 그는 외쳤다.

다음 글에 드러난 David의 심경 변화로 가장 적절한 것은?

① disappointed → unhappy
   실망한 → 슬픈   후반부에서는 에너지가 넘쳐흘렀음
② excited → indifferent
   흥분한 → 무관심한
③ anxious → confident 잘할 수 있을지 걱정하다가 자신감을 되찾음
   걱정스러운 → 자신만만한
④ impatient → calm shouted라고 했음
   조바심내는 → 차분한
⑤ eager → ashamed 첫 다섯 차례의 숫을 성공시킨 것이 부끄러운 일은 아님
   열의에 찬 → 부끄러워하는

⟩왜 정답? [정답률 95%]

부상에서 회복한 후 첫 경기에서 David는 처음에 자신이 전처럼 잘할 수 있을지 확신하지 못했다.
하지만 팬들의 응원을 듣자 자신의 몸이 살아남을 느꼈고 경기가 시작하자 에너지가 넘쳐흘렀으며 첫 다섯 번의 숫을 성공시킨 후 "I'm back!"이라고 외쳤으므로 정답은 ③ '걱정스러운 → 자신만만한'이다.

⟩왜 오답?
①, ② 후반부에서는 완전히 자신감을 회복했으므로 슬프거나 무관심한 심경이 아니다.
④ 전반부에서는 부상 전처럼 잘할 수 있을지 조바심을 냈다고도 할 수 있지만, 후반부에서 "I'm back!"이라고 '외쳤다'는 것으로 보아 차분한 것은 아니다.
⑤ David가 부끄러움을 느낄 만한 일은 글에 등장하지 않는다.

＊ 자주 쓰이는 동명사 표현

– upon[on] ~ing: ~하자마자
- Upon hearing the rumor, my heart began pounding.
  (그 소문을 듣자마자 내 가슴이 쿵쿵 뛰기 시작했다.)

– cannot help -ing: ~하지 않을 수 없다
- As I look back over my career, I cannot help smiling.
  = As I look back over my career, I cannot help but smile.
    (내 직장 생활을 돌아보면 난 웃지 않을 수 없다.)

– feel like -ing: ~을 하고 싶다
- Do you feel like going for a swim?
  (수영하러 가고 싶니?)

– be busy -ing: ~하느라 바쁘다
- Irina and Marcus were busy preparing for their wedding.
  (Irina와 Marcus는 그들의 결혼식을 준비하느라 바빴다.)

– It's no use -ing: (~해 봐야) 소용없다
- It is no use crying over spilt milk.
  (엎질러진 우유 앞에서 울어봐야 소용없다. (이미 엎질러진 물이다.))

B 12 정답 ⑤ ＊수포가 된 Evelyn의 탐험

It was Evelyn's first time to explore the Badlands of Alberta, /
앞에 주격 관계대명사와 be동사가 생략됨
famous across Canada / for its numerous dinosaur fossils. //
앨버타 주의 Badlands를 탐험하는 것이 Evelyn에게는 처음이었다 / 캐나다 전역에서 유명한 / 그곳의 수많은 공룡 화석으로 //

As a young amateur bone-hunter, / she was overflowing with
anticipation. // 단서1 자신의 평생에 걸친 꿈을 이루리라는 기대감으로 가득 차 있었음
젊은 아마추어 (공룡)뼈 발굴자로서 / 그녀는 기대감으로 가득 차 있었다 //

She had not travelled this far / for the bones / of common
(경험)을 나타내는 과거완료
dinosaur species. //
그녀는 이렇게 멀리까지 이동한 적이 없었다 / 뼈를 위해서 / 흔한 공룡 종의 //

Her life-long dream / to find rare fossils of dinosaurs / was
주어   형용사적 용법(dream 수식)   동사
about to come true. //
그녀의 평생에 걸친 꿈이 / 진기한 공룡 화석을 발견하고자 하는 / 막 실현되려고 하고 있었다 //

She began / eagerly searching for them. //
그녀는 시작했다 / 열심히 그것들을 찾기 // 준동사인 동명사는 부사의 수식을 받음

After many hours of wandering / throughout the deserted
lands, / however, / she was unsuccessful. //
여러 시간 헤매고 다닌 후에도 / 황량한 땅을 / 하지만 / 그녀는 성과를 얻지 못했다 //

Now, the sun was beginning to set, / and her goal was still far
beyond her reach. // 목적어로 to부정사나 동명사를 취하는 begin
이제 해가 지기 시작하고 있었고 / 그녀의 목표는 여전히 멀리 그녀의 손이 닿지 않는 곳에 있었다 //

Looking / at the slowly darkening ground / before her, / she
sighed to herself, /
바라보면서 / 천천히 어두워지는 지면을 / 그녀 앞의 / 그녀는 혼자 한숨을 쉬며 말했다 /

"I can't believe / I came all this way for nothing. // What a waste
of time!" // 단서2 먼 길을 와서 아무것도 얻지 못한 시간 낭비라며 한숨을 쉼
"난 믿을 수가 없어 / 내가 이렇게 먼 길을 와서 아무것도 얻지 못했다는 것을 // 무슨 시간 낭비란 말인가!" //

- explore ⓥ 탐험[탐사]하다, 연구하다
- numerous ⓐ 매우 많은, 다수로 이루어진 · fossil ⓝ 화석
- overflow ⓥ (마음이 ~으로) 넘치다, 범람하다
- anticipation ⓝ 예상, 예측, 기대 · common ⓐ 흔한, 공동의, 보통의
- species ⓝ 종(種) · life-long ⓐ 평생의, 긴 세월의
- rare ⓐ 보기 드문, 희귀한 · eagerly ⓐ 열심히, 간절히

- wander ⓥ 돌아다니다, 헤매다   · throughout (prep) 도처에, ~ 동안 내내
- deserted ⓐ 버림받은, 황폐한   · set ⓥ (해·달이) 지다
- reach ⓝ (닿을 수 있는) 거리[범위]
- darken ⓥ 어두워지다, 어둡게[우울하게] 만들다
- sigh ⓥ 한숨을 쉬다, 탄식하듯 말하다

캐나다 전역에서 그곳의 수많은 공룡 화석으로 유명한 앨버타 주의 Badlands를 탐험하는 것이 Evelyn에게는 처음이었다. 젊은 아마추어 (공룡)뼈 발굴자로서, 그녀는 기대감으로 가득 차 있었다. 그녀는 흔한 공룡 종의 뼈를 위해서 이렇게 멀리까지 이동한 적이 없었다. 진기한 공룡 화석을 발견하고자 하는 그녀의 평생에 걸친 꿈이 막 실현되려고 하고 있었다. 그녀는 열심히 그것들을 찾기 시작했다. 하지만 황량한 땅을 여러 시간 헤매고 다닌 후에도 그녀는 성과를 얻지 못했다. 이제 해가 지기 시작하고 있었고, 그녀의 목표는 여전히 멀리 그녀의 손이 닿지 않는 곳에 있었다. 천천히 어두워지는 그녀 앞의 지면을 바라보면서 그녀는 혼자 한숨을 쉬며 말했다. "이렇게 먼 길을 와서 아무것도 얻지 못하다니 믿을 수가 없어. 무슨 시간 낭비란 말인가!"

다음 글에 드러난 Evelyn의 심경 변화로 가장 적절한 것은?

① confused → scared
   혼란스러운 → 무서워하는
② discouraged → confident ──── 전반부에는 기대감으로 가득 차 있었음
   낙담한 → 자신에 찬
③ relaxed → annoyed Evelyn을 성가시게 하는
   느긋한 → 성가신   것은 등장하지 않았음
④ indifferent → depressed
   무관심한 → 낙심한
⑤ hopeful → disappointed 기대감으로 가득 찼다가 실망했음
   기대하는 → 실망스러운

〉왜 정답? [정답률 95%]

진기한 공룡 화석을 발견하는 것이 평생에 걸친 꿈인 젊은 아마추어 발굴자 Evelyn은 자신의 꿈이 이루어지리라는 기대감으로 가득 차서 Badlands를 탐험하기 시작했다. 하지만 해가 지기 시작할 때까지 아무것도 발견하지 못했고, 한숨을 쉬며 시간 낭비였다고 혼잣말을 했으므로 그녀의 심경은 ⑤ '기대하는'에서 '실망스러운'으로 변화했다고 할 수 있다.

〉왜 오답?

①, ③ Evelyn이 무서워하거나 성가셔 할 만한 상황은 등장하지 않는다.
② '낙담한'은 아무것도 찾지 못한 후반부에 느끼는 심경이다.
④ 후반부의 심경이 '낙심한'인 것은 맞지만, 전반부에는 꿈을 이루리라는 기대감으로 가득 찼으므로 무관심한 것이 아니다.

B 13 정답 ⑤ ＊메달을 따지 못한 Mark

Mark was participating / in freestyle swimming competitions /
in this Olympics. //   단서1 200미터에서 메달을 딸 수 있다는
Mark는 출전하고 있었다 / 자유형 수영 경기에 / 이번 올림픽에서 //   확고한 믿음이 있었음
                         동격절 접속사
He had a firm belief / that he could get a medal / in the 200m. //
그에게는 확고한 믿음이 있었다 / 그가 메달을 딸 수 있다는 / 200미터에서 //

Swimming was dominated by Americans / at the time, / so Mark
was dreaming / of becoming a national hero / for his country,
Britain. //
수영은 미국 선수들에 의해 지배되고 있었다 / 그 당시에 / 그래서 Mark는 꿈꾸고 있었다 / 국민적 영웅이 되는 것을 / 그의 조국인 영국의 //

That day, / Mark was competing / in his very last race / — the
final round of the 200m. // 과거진행시제
그날 / Mark는 출전하고 있었다 / 그의 정말 마지막 시합에 / 200미터 결승전 //
                         was보다 앞선 때를 나타내는 대과거
He had done his training / and was ready. //
그는 자신의 훈련을 다 했고 / 준비가 되었다 //

One minute and fifty seconds later, / it was all over. //
1분 50초 후에 / 다 끝났다 //

He had tried hard / and, at his best, / was ranked number four. //
그는 열심히 노력했고 / 최선을 다했지만 / 4등을 했다 //

He fell short of a bronze medal / by 0.49 of a second. //
그는 동메달에 미치지 못했다 / 0.49초 차이로 // **단서 2** 0.49초 차이로 동메달에 미치지 못함

And that was the end / of Mark's swimming career. //
그리고 그것이 끝이었다 / Mark의 수영 경력의 //

He was heartbroken. //
그는 상심했다 //

He had nothing left. //
그에게는 아무것도 남지 않았다 //

- competition ⓝ 경쟁, 대회, 시합 • firm ⓐ 확고한
- dominate ⓥ 장악하다 • national ⓐ 국가의, 전국적인
- compete ⓥ 경쟁하다, (시합 등에) 참가하다
- rank ⓥ (등급·등위·순위를) 매기다[평가하다]
- fall short of ~이 부족하다, ~에 못 미치다 • bronze ⓝ 청동
- heartbroken ⓐ 상심한

Mark는 이번 올림픽에서 자유형 수영 경기에 출전하고 있었다. 그에게는 200미터에서 메달을 딸 수 있다는 확고한 믿음이 있었다. 그 당시 수영은 미국 선수들이 장악하고 있어서, Mark는 조국인 영국의 국민적 영웅이 되는 것을 꿈꾸고 있었다. 그날 Mark는 그의 정말 마지막 시합인 200미터 결승전에 출전하고 있었다. 그는 자신의 훈련을 다 했고 준비가 되었다. 1분 50초 후에 다 끝났다. 그는 열심히 노력했고, 최선을 다했지만 4등을 했다. 그는 0.49초 차이로 동메달에 미치지 못했다. 그리고 그것이 Mark의 수영 경력의 끝이었다. 그는 상심했다. 그에게는 아무것도 남지 않았다.

다음 글에 드러난 Mark의 심경 변화로 가장 적절한 것은?

① worried → hopeful 후반부에는 상심했다고 했음
  걱정하는 희망에 찬
② grateful → fearful 메달을 따지 못했다는 것을 두려워한 것은 아님
  감사하는 두려워하는
③ pleased → jealous 1, 2, 3등을 질투했다는 언급은 없음
  기쁜 질투하는
④ indifferent → upset 메달을 따는 것에 무척 관심이 많았음
  무관심한 속상한
⑤ confident → disappointed had a firm belief → heartbroken
  자신감 있는 실망한

오답 정답? [정답률 89%]

전반부: 200미터에서 메달을 딸 수 있다는 확고한 믿음이 있었음 ▶ '자신감 있는'
후반부: 0.49초 차이로 동메달에 미치지 못했고, 상심했음 ▶ '실망한'
따라서 Mark의 심경 변화는 ⑤ '자신감 있는 → 실망한'이 적절하다.

오답?

① 메달을 못 딸까 봐 걱정한 것이 아니라 메달을 딸 것이라고 확신했다.
② 메달을 따지 못한 것에 대해 두려움을 느낀 것은 아니다.
③ 4등을 했지만 1, 2, 3등에 대해 질투했다는 언급은 없다.
④ 후반부에 속상한 심경인 것은 맞지만, 전반부에 무관심한 심경은 아니었다.

B 14 정답 ② ＊Susan의 딸 Carrie

Susan's daughter Carrie / is a special needs kid. //
Susan의 딸 Carrie는 / 특수 아동이다 //

She goes / to a special school, special camp, special therapists. //
그녀는 간다 / 특수 학교에, 특수 아동을 위한 캠프에, 특수 아동을 위한 치료사에게 //

One day, out of the blue, she asked Susan / if she could go get
a slice of pizza / on her own, / not far from their apartment. //
  주어 동사 간접목적어 직접목적어절 접속사
어느 날 느닷없이 그녀는 Susan에게 물었다 / 그녀가 피자 조각을 먹으러 가도 되는지 / 혼자서 / 아파트에서 멀지 않은 곳에 //

Anxious, Susan said, / "Well... why not get the pizza and bring
it home / to eat?" // **단서 1** 걱정하면서 피자를 사서 집에 가져와서 먹을 것을 권함
걱정하면서 Susan은 말했다 / "글쎄… 피자를 사서 집으로 가져오지 않고 / 먹기 위해"라고 //
  인용부 뒤에서 일어나는 주어와 동사의 도치
"No!" said Carrie, / sixteen at the time. //
"싫어요!" Carrie가 말했다 / 당시 16살이었던 //

"Other people eat at the pizza place, / and I want to, too!" //
"다른 사람들은 피자 가게에서 먹는데 / 저도 그렇게 하고 싶어요!" //

Susan **단서 2** 걱정이 되었음 was concerned, but said okay, / and Carrie went off by
herself / a block or two away. //
Susan은 걱정이 되었지만 허락했고 / Carrie는 혼자 떠났다 / 한두 블록 떨어진 곳으로 //

After a while, / Carrie came back, grinning. //
잠시 후 / Carrie는 씩 웃으며 돌아왔다 //

"You made it! // What made you want to do this?" / Susan
          목적격 보어로 원형부정사를 취하는 make
asked. //
"네가 해냈구나! // 왜 이렇게 하고 싶었던 것이니" / Susan이 물었다 //

Carrie had seen / her friend Izzy on TV talking / about his
글의 시제보다 앞선 시제를 나타내는 대과거
subway ride. //
Carrie는 봤었다 / 그녀의 친구 Izzy가 TV에서 이야기하는 것을 / 그의 지하철 탑승에 대해 //
        부사절 접속사(조건)
"I thought / if he could do it, / I could do it too." //
"저는 생각했어요 / 그가 그것을 할 수 있다면 / 저도 그것을 할 수 있다고" //

Susan's heart swelled, / realizing / her daughter was braver and
비교급 강조 부사
much more grown-up / than she thought. //
Susan의 가슴은 부풀어 올랐다 / 깨닫고 / 자신의 딸이 더 용감하고 훨씬 더 성장했다는 것을
/ 자신이 생각했던 것보다 // **단서 3** 딸이 생각보다 훨씬 더 용감하고
                성장했다는 것을 깨닫고 가슴이 부풂

- special needs kid 특수 아동 • therapist ⓝ 치료사
- out of the blue 느닷없이, 갑자기 • concerned ⓐ 걱정하는
- grin ⓥ 활짝 웃다 • swell ⓥ (감정이) 부풀다, 벅차다
- grown-up ⓝ 어른

Susan의 딸 Carrie는 특수 아동이다. 그녀는 특수 학교에, 특수 아동을 위한 캠프에, 특수 아동을 위한 치료사에게 간다. 어느 날, 느닷없이, 그녀는 그녀가 아파트에서 멀지 않은 곳에 혼자서 피자 한 조각을 먹으러 가도 되는지 Susan에게 물었다. 걱정하면서, Susan은 "글쎄… 피자를 사서 집으로 가져와서 먹지 않고?"라고 말했다. "싫어요!" 당시 16살이었던 Carrie가 말했다. "다른 사람들은 피자 가게에서 먹는데, 저도 그렇게 하고 싶어요!" Susan은 걱정이 되었지만 허락했고, Carrie는 한두 블록 떨어진 곳으로 혼자 떠났다. 잠시 후, Carrie는 씩 웃으며 돌아왔다. "네가 해냈구나! 왜 이렇게 하고 싶었던 것이니?" Susan이 물었다. Carrie는 TV에서 그녀의 친구 Izzy가 그의 지하철 탑승에 대해 이야기하는 것을 봤다. "저는 그가 그것을 할 수 있다면, 저도 그것을 할 수 있다고 생각했어요." Susan은 자신이 생각했던 것보다 자신의 딸이 더 용감하고 훨씬 더 성장했다는 것을 깨닫고 가슴이 부풀어 올랐다.

다음 글에 드러난 Susan의 심경 변화로 가장 적절한 것은?

① indifferent → thrilled 딸에게 무관심한 것이 아님
  무관심한 아주 흥분한
② worried → proud Anxious, worried에서 Susan's heart swelled
  걱정하는 자랑스러운
③ hopeful → regretful 허락한 것을 후회하는 것이 아님
  희망에 찬 후회하는
④ ashamed → satisfied 부끄러운 일을 한 것이 아님
  부끄러운 만족한
⑤ surprised → disappointed 딸에게 실망한 것이 아님
  놀란 실망한

오답 정답? [정답률 94%]

상황: 특수 아동인 딸이 혼자서 피자 한 조각을 먹으러 가도 되는지 물었음
전반부: 걱정이 되어 피자를 사서 집에 가져와서 먹을 것을 권함 → 딸이 싫다고 하자 걱정이 되었지만 허락했음
후반부: 웃으며 돌아온 딸을 보고, 딸이 생각보다 더 용감하고 성장했다는 것을 깨달음
▶ 전반부에서는 딸을 걱정하고, 후반부에서는 딸을 자랑스러워하므로 정답은
② '걱정하는 → 자랑스러워하는'

오답?

① 딸에게 무관심한 것이 전혀 아니다.
③ 처음에는 딸을 걱정했지, 잘 해낼 것이라는 희망에 찼던 것이 아니다.
④ Susan이 부끄러움을 느낄 만한 일은 없다.
⑤ 후반부에서는 무사히 돌아온 딸을 보고 가슴이 부풀었다고 했다.

✱ 관계대명사의 생략

– 목적격 관계대명사는 생략하는 경우가 많다.

• She was a celebrated actress (whom) he had known and loved.
  a celebrated actress를 선행사로 하는 목적격 관계대명사
  (그녀는 그가 알고 사랑했던 유명한 배우였다.)

• I've been thinking about those questions (which) you asked
  me last week. those questions를 선행사로 하는 목적격 관계대명사
  (나는 네가 내게 지난주에 물어본 그 질문들에 대해 생각해 오고 있다.)

• Davis is the most brilliant man (that) I've ever worked with.
  the most brilliant man을 선행사로 하는 목적격 관계대명사
  (Davis는 내가 지금껏 함께 일한 사람들 중 가장 똑똑한 사람이다.)

– 「주격 관계대명사+be동사」는 생략할 수 있다.

• Look at the singer (who is) performing on the stage!
  the singer를 선행사로 하는 주격 관계대명사와 be동사
  (무대에서 공연하고 있는 가수를 봐!)

• Bogart starred in the film *Casablanca* (which was) made in
  1942. the film *Casablanca*를 선행사로 하는 주격 관계대명사와 be동사
  (Bogart는 1942년에 만들어진 영화 《Casablanca》에 출연했다.)

• I want to speak to the person (who is) responsible for this.
  the person을 선행사로 하는 주격 관계대명사와 be동사
  (나는 이것에 책임이 있는 사람과 이야기하기를 원한다.)

✱ 폐소공포증(Claustrophobia)

폐소공포증은 특정공포증의 한 종류로,
주로 닫힌/밀폐된 공간(예, 엘리베이터,
터널, 비행기 등)에 있는 상황에 대해 지나친
두려움, 공포감을 특징적으로 나타내는
질환이다. 이러한 상황에 노출되면 거의
예외없이 지나친 공포를 보이는데, 공황
발작과 유사한 증상이 나타날 수 있다. 따라서
닫힌/밀폐된 공간에 가는 것을 피하려고 하며,
이러한 회피 행동으로 인하여 생활 범위가
제한되기도 한다.

B 15 정답 ② ✱ 예상외로 환상적이었던 탱고 콘서트 ―――

Sharon received a ticket / to an upcoming tango concert / from
her friend. //
Sharon은 표를 받았다 / 다가오는 탱고 콘서트의 / 자신의 친구로부터 //

While surfing the Internet, / she came across a review / for the
분사구문의 생략되지 않은 접속사
concert. //
인터넷을 검색하던 중 / 그녀는 우연히 논평을 발견했다 / 그 콘서트에 관한 //
                                    calling의 목적어   목적격 보어
The reviewer was harsh, / calling it "an awful performance." //
논평을 쓴 사람은 혹평했다 / 그것을 '끔찍한 공연'이라고 부르며 //

That raised in Sharon's mind the question / of whether it was
worthwhile to go, / but in the end, / she reluctantly decided / to
attend the concert. // 단서 1 콘서트가 갈 만한 가치가 있을지에 대해 의문을 가짐
그것은 Sharon의 마음속에 의문을 제기했다 / 과연 그것이 갈 만한 가치가 있을까 하는 / 하
지만 결국 / 그녀는 마지못해 마음먹었다 / 콘서트에 참석하기로 //
                                    주격 보어
The hall / located in the old town / was ancient and run-down. //
                       동사
홀은 / 구시가지에 위치한 / 아주 오래되고 황폐했다 //

Looking around, / Sharon again wondered / what kind of show
she could expect. // 단서 2 쇼가 어떨지에 대해 궁금해 함
주위를 둘러보며 / Sharon은 또다시 궁금했다 / 그녀가 어떤 쇼를 기대할 수 있을지 //
시간의 부사절 접속사
But as soon as the tango started, / everything changed. //
그러나 탱고가 시작되자마자 / 모든 것이 바뀌었다 // 주어   1형식 동사

The piano, guitar, flute, and violin magically flew out / in
harmony. //
피아노, 기타, 플루트, 바이올린이 마법처럼 흘러나왔다 / 화음을 이루며 //

The audience cheered. //
청중은 환호성을 질렀다   주어와 동사가 생략된 감탄문 단서 3 환상적인 음악이라며 소리침
"Oh my goodness! // What fantastic music!" // Sharon shouted. //
"어머나 // 얼마나 환상적인 음악인가" // Sharon은 소리쳤다 //

The rhythm and tempo were so energetic and sensational / that
            so ~ that S V: 너무 ~해서 …하다
they shook her body and soul. //
리듬과 박자가 너무 활기차고 선풍적이어서 / 그것들은 그녀의 몸과 마음을 뒤흔들었다 //

The concert was far beyond her expectations. //
그 콘서트는 그녀의 예상을 훨씬 뛰어넘었다 // 단서 4 콘서트가 예상을 훨씬 뛰어넘음

- **upcoming** ⓐ 다가오는, 곧 있을
- **surf** ⓥ 인터넷을 검색하다
- **come across** ~을 우연히 발견하다
- **harsh** ⓐ 혹독한, 가혹한
- **worthwhile** ⓐ ~할 가치가 있는
- **reluctantly** ⓐⓓ 마지못해
- **ancient** ⓐ 아주 오래된
- **run-down** ⓐ 황폐한
- **harmony** ⓝ 조화, 화합, 화음
- **energetic** ⓐ 활기찬
- **sensational** ⓐ 선풍적인
- **far** ⓐⓓ 훨씬, 아주

Sharon은 자신의 친구로부터 다가오는 탱고 콘서트 표를 받았다. 인터넷을 검
색하던 중 그녀는 그 콘서트에 관한 논평을 우연히 발견했다. 논평을 쓴 사람은
그것을 '끔찍한 공연'이라고 부르며 혹평했다. 그로 인해 Sharon의 마음속에 과
연 그것이 갈 만한 가치가 있을까 하는 의문이 생겼지만, 결국 그녀는 마지못해
콘서트에 참석하기로 마음먹었다. 구시가지에 위치한 홀은 아주 오래되고 황폐
했다. 주위를 둘러보며 Sharon은 어떤 쇼를 기대할 수 있을지 또다시 궁금했
다. 그러나 탱고가 시작되자마자 모든 것이 바뀌었다. 피아노, 기타, 플루트, 바
이올린이 마법처럼 화음을 이루며 흘러나왔다. 청중은 환호성을 질렀다. "어머
나! 얼마나 환상적인 음악인가!" Sharon은 소리쳤다. 리듬과 박자가 너무 활기
차고 선풍적이어서 그녀의 몸과 마음을 뒤흔들었다. 그 콘서트는 그녀의 예상을
훨씬 뛰어넘었다.

다음 글에 드러난 Sharon의 심경 변화로 가장 적절한 것은?

① excited → bored 리듬과 박자가 몸과 마음을 뒤흔듦
  신이 난 → 지루한
② doubtful → amazed 의문을 가졌던 콘서트가 예상을 훨씬 뛰어넘음
  확신이 없는 → 깜짝 놀란
③ calm → upset 예상외로 콘서트가 훌륭했음
  차분한 → 속상한
④ ashamed → grateful 친구가 표를 쳤다는 것으로 만든 오답
  부끄러운 → 고마워하는
⑤ envious → indifferent 환상적인 음악이라며 소리침
  부러워하는 → 무관심한

왜 정답? [정답률 92%]

친구로부터 표를 받은 탱고 콘서트에 대한 혹평을 발견하고 그 콘서트가 과연 갈
만한 가치가 있는지 의문을 가졌는데, 막상 가보니 리듬과 박자가 무척 활기차고
선풍적이어서 콘서트가 예상을 훨씬 뛰어넘었다고 했으므로 정답은 ② '확신이 없
는 → 깜짝 놀란'이다.

왜 오답?

① 콘서트가 시작되자 환호성을 질렀다고 했으므로 excited가 후반부의 심경이 되
  어야 한다.
③ 콘서트가 예상을 훨씬 뛰어넘도록 좋았으므로 속상하다는 것은 적절하지 않다.
④. ⑤ 전반부에 부끄럽거나 부러워할 만한 일은 언급되지 않았다.

B 16 정답 ① ✱ 새로운 직장에 첫 출근하는 David ―――

David was starting a new job in Vancouver, / and he was waiting
for his bus. //
David는 밴쿠버에서 새로운 일을 시작하게 되었고 / 자신이 탈 버스를 기다리고 있었다 //
                                          keep -ing: 계속 ~하다
He kept looking back and forth / between his watch / and
                                  뒤에 목적격 관계대명사 생략
the direction the bus would come from. //
그는 계속 번갈아 보았다 / 자신의 시계와 / 버스가 올 방향을 //

He thought, / "My bus isn't here yet. / I can't be late on my first day." //
그는 생각했다 / "내가 탈 버스가 아직 오지 않아 / 내가 첫날 지각할 수는 없어"라고 //

David couldn't feel at ease. //
David는 마음을 놓을 수가 없었다 // **단서 1** 버스가 오지 않아 새 직장에 지각할까 봐 초조함

When he looked up again, / he saw a different bus coming / that
was going right to his work. //
지각동사+목적어+목적격 보어(현재분사)
그가 다시 고개를 들어 보았을 때 / 그는 다른 버스가 오고 있는 것을 보았다 / 바로 자신의 직장으로 가는 // 주격 관계대명사

The bus stopped in front of him / and opened its door. //
분사구문
그 버스는 그의 앞에 섰고 / 문을 열었다 //

He got on the bus thinking, / "Phew! Luckily, this bus came just
in time / so I won't be late." //
그는 버스에 오르며 생각했다 / "후유! 다행히도 이 버스가 딱 맞춰 왔네 / 내가 지각하지 않도록" //

과거분사(수동의 의미로 seat 수식)
He leaned back on an unoccupied seat in the bus / and took a
deep breath, / finally able to relax. // **단서 2** 직장으로 가는 다른 버스에 제시간에 탑승해서 안도함
그는 버스의 빈 좌석에 등을 기대며 / 깊은 한숨을 내쉬었고 / 마침내 긴장을 풀 수 있었다 //

- back and forth 왔다갔다 · direction ⓝ 방향
- feel at ease 마음을 놓다, 안도하다 · lean back 상체를 뒤로 젖히다
- unoccupied ⓐ 빈, 비어 있는

David는 밴쿠버에서 새로운 일을 시작하게 되었고, 자신이 탈 버스를 기다리고 있었다. 그는 계속 자신의 시계와 버스가 올 방향을 번갈아 보았다. 그는 "내가 탈 버스가 아직 오지 않아. 내가 첫날 지각할 수는 없어."라고 생각했다. David는 마음을 놓을 수가 없었다. 그가 다시 고개를 들어 보았을 때, 그는 바로 자신의 직장으로 가는 다른 버스가 오고 있는 것을 보았다. 그 버스는 그의 앞에 섰고 문을 열었다. 그는 버스에 오르며, "후유! 다행히도 내가 지각하지 않도록 이 버스가 딱 맞춰 왔네."라고 생각했다. 그는 버스의 빈 좌석에 등을 기대며 깊은 한숨을 내쉬었고, 마침내 긴장을 풀 수 있었다.

다음 글에 드러난 'David'의 심경 변화로 가장 적절한 것은?
① nervous → relieved 마음을 놓을 수 없음 → 긴장을 풀
   초조한   안도한
② lonely → hopeful 버스를 기다리는 감정이 쓸쓸함은 아님
   쓸쓸한   희망찬
③ pleased → confused 다른 버스를 타고 안도한 감정이 당황함은 아님
   기쁜   당황한
④ indifferent → delighted 무관심한 감정은 없었음
   무관심한   즐거운
⑤ bored → thrilled 버스를 기다리는 상태는 지루한 것이 아니라 초조했음
   지루한   아주 신이 난

왜 정답? [정답률 96%]

전반부: David는 새 직장에 처음 출근하는 날, 버스가 오지 않아 지각할까 봐 마음을 놓을 수 없었음
후반부: 직장으로 가는 다른 버스가 제시간에 도착하여 빈 좌석에 앉아 긴장을 풂
▶ '초조한' 심경에서 '안도한' 심경으로 변화함

왜 오답?
② 전반부에 버스를 기다리는 감정이 쓸쓸한 감정은 아니다.
③ 후반부에 다른 버스를 타고 직장에 지각하지 않게 된 것이 당황한 감정은 아니다.
④ 무관심한 감정을 느낄 만한 일은 언급되지 않았다.
⑤ 전반부에 버스를 기다리는 상태는 지루한 감정이 아니다.

류이레 | 연세대 의예과 2024년 입학 · 광주대동고 졸
두 번째 문장에 나온 kept looking back and forth를 보면서
두리번거리는 거니까 부정적인 상황이라고 생각하고, 후반부에서
Luckily가 나오는 것을 보니 긍정적인 상황이라고 예상했어.
'부정 → 긍정'의 순서로 심경이 변화되는 선택지 중에서,
두리번거리면서 '초조한' 상황이었지만 다행히 버스가 와서 '안도하는' 상황으로
변화되는 선택지를 골랐어.

Ⓑ 17 정답 ③ *Jamie의 기운을 북돋운 Ken
Jamie와 능동 관계이므로 현재분사가 분사구문을 이끎
Putting all of her energy / into her last steps of the running race,
/ Jamie crossed the finish line. //
자신의 모든 에너지를 쏟으면서 / 자신의 달리기 경주의 마지막 스텝에 / Jamie는 결승선을 통과했다 // **단서 1** 자신의 개인 최고 기록을 깨지 못해 실망함

To her disappointment, / she had failed to beat / her personal
best time, / again. //
실망스럽게도 / 그녀는 깨는 데 실패했다 / 자신의 개인 최고 기록을 / 또 //

Jamie had pushed herself / for months / to finally break her
record, / but it was all for nothing.//
과거 이전부터 과거까지를 나타내는 과거완료
Jamie는 자신을 몰아붙였지만 / 몇 달 동안 / 기어코 자신의 기록을 깨기 위해 / 그것은 모두
수포로 돌아갔다 //

★Ken과 능동 관계이므로 현재분사가 분사구문을 이끎
Recognizing / how she felt /
알아차리고 / 그녀가 어떻게 느끼는지 /

about her failure, /
자신의 실패에 대해 / 자동사로 착각하기 쉬운 타동사

Ken, her teammate, approached her and said, /
그녀의 팀 동료인 Ken은 그녀에게 다가가 말했다 / 부사절 접속사(양보)

"Jamie, even though you didn't set a personal best time today, /
주어   동사(완전자동사)
your performances have improved dramatically. //
"Jamie, 비록 오늘 네가 개인 최고 기록을 세우지 않았지만 / 너의 경기력은 극적으로
향상되었어 //
주어   동사(완전자동사)
Your running skills / have progressed so much! // You'll
definitely break your personal best time / in the next race!" //
너의 달리기 기량이 / 아주 많이 발전했어 // 너는 분명히 너의 개인 최고 기록을 깰 거야 /
다음 경주에서 " // **단서 2** Ken의 말을 듣고 자신감을 느낌

After hearing his comments, / she felt confident about herself. //
그의 말을 들은 후 / 그녀는 자신에 대해 자신감을 느꼈다 //

Jamie, / now motivated to keep pushing for her goal, / replied
주어   동사(완전자동사)
with a smile. //
Jamie는 / 이제 자신의 목표를 계속 밀고 나갈 의욕을 갖게 된 / 미소를 지어 대답했다 //
단서 3 다음 경기에서 최고 기록을 깰 거라고 말함

"You're right! // Next race, / I'll beat my best time for sure!" //
"네 말이 맞아 // 다음 경주에서 / 나는 틀림없이 나의 최고 기록을 깰 거야" //

★ **분사구문의 수동태**
부사절이 수동태 문장인 경우 분사구문으로
바꿀 때 주절의 시제와 같으면 being p.p.,
주절의 시제보다 앞서면 having been
p.p.를 쓰는데, being이나 having been은
대개 생략된다.

- beat ⓥ 능가하다, (시합 등에서) 이기다 · dramatically ⓐ 극적으로
- progress ⓥ 진전을 보이다, 진행하다 · definitely ⓐ 분명히, 틀림없이
- confident ⓐ 자신감 있는 · motivate ⓥ 동기를 부여하다

Jamie는 자신의 모든 에너지를 달리기 경주의 마지막 스텝에 쏟으면서 결승선을 통과했다. 실망스럽게도, 그녀는 자신의 개인 최고 기록을 깨는 데 또 실패했다. Jamie는 기어코 자신의 기록을 깨기 위해 몇 달 동안 자신을 몰아붙였지만, 그것은 모두 수포로 돌아갔다. 그녀가 자신의 실패에 대해 어떻게 느끼는지 알아차린 그녀의 팀 동료인 Ken은 그녀에게 다가가 말했다.
"Jamie, 비록 오늘 네가 개인 최고 기록을 세우지 않았지만 너의 경기력은 극적으로 향상되었어. 너의 달리기 기량이 아주 많이 발전했어! 다음 경주에서 너는 분명히 너의 개인 최고 기록을 깰 거야!" 그의 말을 들은 후, 그녀는 자신에 대해 자신감을 느꼈다. 이제 자신의 목표를 계속 밀고 나갈 의욕을 갖게 된 Jamie는 미소를 지으며 대답했다. "네 말이 맞아! 다음 경주에서 나는 틀림없이 나의 최고 기록을 깰 거야!"

다음 글에 드러난 Jamie의 심경 변화로 가장 적절한 것은?
① indifferent → regretful 전반부에서는 To her disappointment라고 했음
   무관심한   후회하는
② pleased → bored Ken의 말을 듣고 지루해한 것이 아님
   기쁜   지루한
③ frustrated → encouraged 실망했다가 Ken의 격려를 듣고 자신감을 되찾음
   좌절한   용기를 얻은
④ nervous → fearful 초조하게 경기 결과를 기다리는 것이 아님
   초조한   무서워하는
⑤ calm → excited 차분한 → 신이 난
   차분한   신이 난

왜 정답? [정답률 92%]

자신의 개인 최고 기록을 깨지 못해서 실망한 Jamie에게 Ken이 격려의 말을 건넸고, Ken의 말을 듣고 난 Jamie가 자신감을 느끼며 다음 경기에서 자신이 최고 기록을 깰 거라고 확신한다고 말했으므로 정답은 ③ '좌절한 → 용기를 얻은'이다.

> **왜 오답?**

① 후반부에서는 자신감을 느꼈지, 후회한 것이 아니다.
② 자신의 최고 기록을 깨지 못한 것에 대해 실망한 것이 전반부의 심경이다.
④ Jamie가 두려움을 느낄 만한 상황은 아니다.
⑤ To her disappointment가 나타내는 심경은 침착함보다는 실망스러움이다.

조현준 | 전북대 의예과 2023년 입학·익산 이리고 졸

나는 이 문제를 듣기 문제가 방송에서 나올 때 짧은 시간을 모으고 할애해서 풀었어. 감정이 드러나는 단어 위주로 글의 앞부분과 뒷부분을 빠르게 읽어나갔지.
두 번째 문장에서 disappointment를 확인했고, 뒷부분에서 confident를 봤어. 실망이 자신감으로 바뀌었다는 상황을 파악한 후 선택지를 살펴보니까, 선택지 중 frustrated → encouraged가 내가 파악한 상황에 적절한 선택지였고, 자신 있게 그것을 정답으로 골랐어.

B 18 정답 ① *낯선 사람의 호의

I hurried to the bus terminal / to return home / for Christmas. //
나는 서둘러 버스 터미널로 갔다 / 집으로 돌아가기 위해 / 크리스마스를 보내려고 //

As soon as I arrived at the terminal, / **I saw my bus pulling**
주어 동사 목적어 목적격 보어
away. //
터미널에 도착하자마자 / 나는 내가 타야 하는 버스가 출발하고 있는 것을 보았다 //

I called out and ran after the bus, / but it was too late. //
나는 소리쳐 부르며 버스를 쫓아갔지만 / 너무 늦었다 //

단서1 실망감이 파도처럼 밀려듦
I felt a wave of disappointment wash over me / as I realized /
that I would have to wait three hours / for the next bus. //
나는 실망감이 나에게 파도처럼 밀려드는 것을 느꼈다 / 내가 알게 되었을 때 / 내가 세 시간을 기다려야 하리라는 것을 / 다음 버스를 //

과거 사실에 대한 확신: must have p.p. **단서2** 눈에 띄게 속상해 보였음
I must have been visibly upset / because a woman came over, /
took my arm, / and led me to the street. //
내가 눈에 띄게 속상해 보였음에 틀림없다 / 왜냐하면 한 여성이 다가와 / 내 팔을 잡고 / 나를 도로로 이끌었으므로 //

gave의 간접목적어와 직접목적어
She called a taxi / and gave the driver a five-dollar bill. //
그녀는 택시를 불러 / 기사에게 5달러짜리 지폐를 주었다 //

told의 목적어와 목적격 보어
She told him / to take me to the ferry terminal, / because the bus
made a stop there / before heading out onto the highway. //
그녀는 그에게 말했다 / 여객선 터미널까지 나를 데려다주라고 / 그 버스가 거기서 정차하기 때문에 / 고속도로로 나가기 전에 //

She also wished me a Merry Christmas, / and all I could do /
wished의 간접목적어와 직접목적어
was smile. //
그녀는 또한 내게 크리스마스를 잘 보내라고 말했고 / 내가 할 수 있었던 전부는 / 미소를 짓는 것뿐이었다 //

I couldn't believe / what she had done for me, / a complete
stranger! // **단서3** 낯선 사람인 자신을 위해 해준 일에 감동함
나는 믿기지 않았다 / 나를 위해 그녀가 해 준 일이 / 완전히 모르는 사람인 //

- **pull away** 출발하다 　 **disappointment** ⓝ 실망감
- **wash** ⓥ 밀려오다 　 **ferry terminal** 여객선 터미널
- **head out** 나가다 　 **complete** ⓐ 완전한

나는 크리스마스를 보내려고 집으로 돌아가기 위해 서둘러 버스 터미널로 갔다. 터미널에 도착하자마자, 나는 내가 타야 하는 버스가 출발하고 있는 것을 보았다. 나는 소리쳐 부르며 버스를 쫓아갔지만 너무 늦었다. 다음 버스를 타려면 세 시간을 기다려야 하리라는 것을 알게 되었을 때, 나는 실망감이 나에게 파도처럼 밀려드는 것을 느꼈다. 한 여성이 다가와 내 팔을 잡고 나를 도로로 이끈 것을 보니, 내가 눈에 띄게 속상해 보였음에 틀림없다. 그녀는 택시를 불러 기사에게 5달러짜리 지폐를 주었다. 그녀는 여객선 터미널까지

나를 데려다주라고 그에게 말했는데, 그 버스가 고속도로로 나가기 전에 거기서 정차하기 때문이었다. 그녀는 또한 내게 크리스마스를 잘 보내라고 말했고, 내가 할 수 있었던 것은 미소를 짓는 것뿐이었다. 나는 완전히 모르는 사람인 나를 위해 그녀가 해 준 일이 믿기지 않았다!

다음 글에 드러난 'I'의 심경 변화로 가장 적절한 것은?

① frustrated → touched 버스를 놓쳐서 속상함 → 낯선 이의 호의로 버스를 타게 됨
　좌절한 → 감동한
② jealous → proud 질투할 만한 대상이 없음
　질투하는 → 자랑스러운
③ thrilled → doubtful 호의를 의심하는 것이 아님
　짜릿한 → 의심하는
④ calm → regretful 호의를 받아들인 것을 후회하는 것이 아님
　차분한 → 후회하는
⑤ indifferent → sympathetic 낯선 이의 도움을 받았음
　무관심한 → 동정하는

> **왜 정답?** [정답률 92%]

전반부: 간발의 차로 타야 하는 버스를 놓치고, 다음 버스를 세 시간이나 기다려야 해서 실망하고 속상함

후반부: I가 떠난 버스를 탈 수 있도록 낯선 이가 택시를 잡아 택시비를 지불해 줌
➡ 전반부에는 '좌절한', 후반부에는 '감동한' 심경이므로 정답은 ①이다.

> **왜 오답?**

② I가 질투할 만한 대상이 글에 등장하지 않는다.
③ 낯선 이의 호의를 의심하는 상황이 아니다.
④ 버스를 눈앞에서 놓쳐서 실망하는 것이지, 차분한 것이 아니다.
⑤ I가 낯선 이를 동정하는 것이 아니다.

B 19 정답 ④ *Jenny가 그린 아빠 얼굴

"Daddy!" Jenny called, / waving a yellow crayon / in her little
hand. //
"아빠!" Jenny가 불렀다 / 노란색 크레용을 흔들며 / 그녀의 작은 손에 쥔 //

Nathan approached her, / wondering / why she was calling
1형식 동사로 착각하기 쉬운 3형식 동사 **단서1** Jenny가 왜 자신을 부르는지 궁금해함
him. //
Nathan은 그녀에게 다가갔다 / 궁금해하며 / 그녀가 왜 자신을 부르는지 //

Jenny, his three-year-old toddler, / was drawing a big circle / on
셀 수 없는 명사의 수량은 단위나 모양을 이용해서 나타냄
a piece of paper. //
그의 걸음마를 하는 세 살배기 Jenny는 / 큰 원을 그리고 있었다 / 종이 한 장에 //

"What are you doing, Sweetie?" / Nathan asked with interest. //
"뭘 하고 있니, 아가야?"라고 / Nathan은 관심을 가지고 물었다 //

She just kept drawing / without reply. //
그녀는 그저 계속 그림을 그렸다 / 대답 없이 //

목적어절을 이끄는 의문사
He continued watching her, / wondering / what she was
working on. // **단서2** Jenny가 무엇을 하고 있는지 궁금해함
그는 계속해서 그녀를 봤다 / 궁금해하면서 / 그녀가 무엇을 하고 있는지 //

선행사
She was drawing something / that looked like a face. //
그녀는 무언가를 그리고 있었다 / 얼굴처럼 보이는 //
주격 관계대명사절

When she finished it, / Jenny shouted, / "Look, Daddy!" //
그녀가 그것을 끝냈을 때 / Jenny는 외쳤다 / "보세요, 아빠!"라고 //

She held her artwork up / proudly. //
그녀는 자신의 작품을 들어 올렸다 / 자랑스럽게 //

= As he took ~
Taking a closer look, / Nathan recognized / that it was his face. //
자세히 보자 / Nathan은 알아차렸다 / 그것이 자신의 얼굴임을 //

The face had two big eyes and a beard / just like his. //
그 얼굴에는 두 개의 큰 눈과 수염이 있었다 / 그의 것과 똑같은 //
소유대명사

He loved Jenny's work. //
그는 Jenny의 작품이 마음에 들었다 // **단서3** Jenny의 그림을 보고 기쁨과 행복으로 가득 참

Filled with joy and happiness, / Nathan gave her a big hug. //
기쁨과 행복으로 가득 차 / Nathan은 그녀를 크게 껴안아 주었다 //

- **approach** ⓥ 다가가다[오다] 　 **toddler** ⓝ 아장아장 걷는 아이
- **reply** ⓝ 대답, 답장 　 **artwork** ⓝ 그림, (박물관의) 미술품
- **recognize** ⓥ 알아보다, 인정하다 　 **beard** ⓝ 턱수염

"아빠!" Jenny가 작은 손에 쥔 노란색 크레용을 흔들며 불렀다. Nathan은 그녀가 왜 자신을 부르는지 궁금해하며 그녀에게 다가갔다. 그의 걸음마를 하는 세 살배기 Jenny는 종이 한 장에 큰 원을 그리고 있었다. "뭘 하고 있니, 아가야?"라고 Nathan은 관심을 가지고 물었다. 그녀는 대답 없이 계속 그림을 그렸다. 그는 그녀가 무엇을 하고 있는지 궁금해하면서 계속해서 그녀를 봤다. 그녀는 얼굴처럼 보이는 것을 그리고 있었다.

그것을 끝냈을 때, Jenny는 "보세요, 아빠!"라고 외쳤다. 그녀는 자신의 작품을 자랑스럽게 들어 올렸다. 자세히 보자 Nathan은 그것이 자신의 얼굴임을 알아차렸다. 그 얼굴에는 그의 것과 똑같은 두 개의 큰 눈과 수염이 있었다. 그는 Jenny의 작품이 마음에 들었다. 기쁨과 행복으로 가득 찬 Nathan은 그녀를 크게 껴안아 주었다.

다음 글에 드러난 Nathan의 심경 변화로 가장 적절한 것은?

① sorrowful → relieved   전반부는 wondering이 핵심임
　슬픈 → 안도하는
② frustrated → satisfied   좌절감을 느낄 만한 상황이 아님
　좌절한 → 만족한
③ worried → scared   Jenny의 그림이 무서운 것은 아님
　걱정하는 → 무서워하는
④ curious → delighted   무엇을 그리는지 궁금하다가 기쁨으로 가득 참
　궁금한 → 기쁜
⑤ hopeful → disappointed   Filled with joy and happiness라고 했음
　기대하는 → 실망한

＞왜 정답? [정답률 96%]

딸이 왜 자신을 부르는지, 딸이 무엇을 하는 건지 궁금해하다가 딸이 그린 그림이 자신의 얼굴임을 알아차리고 기쁨과 행복으로 가득 찼다고 했으므로 정답은 ④ '궁금한 → 기쁜'이다.

＞왜 오답?

①, ② 아이가 그림을 그리는 모습을 보면서 슬픔이나 좌절을 느끼는 것이 아니다.
③ 아이가 그린 그림을 보고 무서움을 느낀 것은 아니다.
⑤ 아이의 그림을 기대했다가 결과물을 보고 실망하는 흐름이 아니다.

B 20 정답 ② ＊선생님의 말씀

Once again, / I had lost the piano contest / to my friend. //
또다시 / 나는 피아노 경연대회에서 졌다 / 내 친구에게 //

When I learned / that Linda had won, / I was deeply troubled and unhappy. //
부사절 접속사(시간)   명사절(목적어절) 접속사   learned보다 앞선 대과거   주절
내가 알게 되었을 때 / Linda가 우승했다는 것을 / 나는 매우 괴롭고 우울했다 //

My body was shaking / with uneasiness. // **단서 1** 불쾌감으로 몸이 떨림
내 몸은 떨리고 있었다 / 불쾌감으로 //
　　　주어　　　　2형식 동사　　주격 보어
My heart beat quickly / and my face became reddish. //
　　　　동사(완전자동사)
내 심장은 빠르게 뛰었고 / 내 얼굴은 불그스레해졌다 //

I had to run out of the concert hall / to settle down. //
나는 콘서트홀에서 뛰쳐나와야 했다 / 마음을 가라앉히기 위해 //
　　　　　　　　　　　　　　　　관계대명사가 이끄는 목적어절
＝ While I sat
Sitting on the stairs alone, / I recalled / what my teacher had said. //
홀로 계단에 앉아 / 나는 떠올렸다 / 나의 선생님께서 하신 말씀 //

"Life is about winning, / not necessarily about winning against others / but winning at being you. //
　　　　　　　　　　부분 부정: 반드시 ~인 것은 아님
"인생은 이기는 것과 관련이 있단다 / 반드시 다른 사람들과 싸워서 이기는 것과 관련이 있는 것이 아니라 / 자기 자신이 되는 것에서 이기는 것과 //
　　　　　　　　　　　　　명사적 용법(주격 보어)
And the way to win is / to figure out / who you are / and do your best." //
　　　　형용사적 용법(the way 수식)
그리고 이기는 방법은 ~이란다 / 알아내는 것 / 자신이 누군가를 / 그리고 자신의 최선을 다하는 것" //

He was absolutely right. //
선생님은 절대적으로 옳았다 // 형용사적 용법(reason 수식)
I had no reason / to oppose my friend. //
나는 이유가 없었다 / 내 친구를 적대할 //

Instead, I should focus / on myself and my own improvement. //
대신 나는 중점을 두어야 한다 / 나 자신과 나 자신의 발전에 //

I breathed out slowly. //
나는 천천히 숨을 내쉬었다 //

My hands were steady now. //
내 손은 이제 떨리지 않았다 //

At last, / my mind was at peace. // **단서 2** 마음이 편해짐
마침내 / 내 마음이 편해졌다 //

• deeply ⓐⓓ (대단히·몹시의 뜻으로) 깊이[크게]
• troubled ⓐ 걱정하는, 불안한, 괴로운   • uneasiness ⓝ 불안, 근심, 불쾌
• reddish ⓐ 발그레한, 불그스름한   • beat ⓥ (심장이) 고동치다
• settle down 진정되다, ~을 진정시키다   • recall ⓥ 상기하다, 기억해 내다
• figure out (생각한 끝에) ~을 이해하다[알아내다], (양·비용 등을) 계산[산출]하다
• absolutely ⓐⓓ 전적으로, 틀림없이   • oppose ⓥ 겨루다, 반대하다
• steady ⓐ 흔들림 없는, 안정된

또다시 나는 피아노 경연대회에서 내 친구에게 졌다. Linda가 우승했다는 것을 알게 되었을 때, 나는 매우 괴롭고 우울했다. 내 몸은 불쾌감으로 떨리고 있었다. 내 심장은 빠르게 뛰었고, 내 얼굴은 불그스레해졌다. 나는 마음을 가라앉히기 위해 콘서트홀에서 뛰쳐나와야 했다. 홀로 계단에 앉아, 나는 선생님께서 하신 말씀을 떠올렸다. "인생은 이기는 것과 관련이 있는데, 반드시 다른 사람들과 싸워서 이기는 것이 아니라 자기 자신이 되는 것에서 이기는 것과 관련이 있단다. 그리고 이기는 방법은 자신이 누군가를 알아내고 자신의 최선을 다하는 거란다." 선생님 말씀은 절대적으로 옳았다. 나는 내 친구를 적대할 이유가 없었다. 대신, 나는 나 자신과 나 자신의 발전에 중점을 두어야 한다. 나는 천천히 숨을 내쉬었다. 내 손은 이제 떨리지 않았다. 마침내 내 마음이 편해졌다.

다음 글에 드러난 'I'의 심경 변화로 가장 적절한 것은?

① grateful → sorrowful
　고마워하는 → 슬픈
② upset → calm
　심란한 → 차분한   불쾌감으로 떨리다가 마음이 편해짐
③ envious → doubtful
　부러워하는 → 의심하는   후반부에는 my mind was at peace라고 했음
④ surprised → disappointed
　놀란 → 실망한
⑤ bored → relieved
　따분한 → 안도한   심장이 빠르게 뛰었으므로 따분한 것이 아님

＞왜 정답? [정답률 88%]

전반부에는 피아노 경연대회에서 친구에게 또 졌다는 것을 알게 되어 불쾌감으로 몸이 떨리고 심장이 빠르게 뛰며 얼굴이 불그스레해졌다고 했다. 그러다가 선생님의 말씀을 떠올렸고, 이어 마음이 편해졌다고 했으므로 정답은 ② '심란한 → 차분한'이다.

＞왜 오답?

① 피아노 경연대회에서 친구에게 또 진 상황에서 처음에는 불쾌감을 느꼈으므로 고마워한다는 것은 적절하지 않다.   주의
③ 전반부의 심경이 친구를 부러워하는 것이라고 할 수는 있지만, 후반부에서 누군가 또는 무언가를 의심하는 것이 아니므로 정답이 아니다.
④ 실망감은 후반부가 아니라 전반부의 심경으로 적절하다.
⑤ 심장이 빠르게 뛰었다고 했으므로 전반부에 따분함을 느낀 것은 아니다.

B 21 정답 ① ＊Midtown 대신 Pland Zoo에 가게 됨

앞에 주격 관계대명사와 be동사가 생략됨
The day trip to Midtown / scheduled for today / was canceled / because the road leading there was blocked / by heavy snow. //
Midtown으로 가는 당일치기 여행은 / 오늘 예정된 / 취소되었다 / 그곳으로 가는 도로가 막혀서 / 폭설로 //

"Luck just didn't run my way. // Sightseeing in Midtown / was why I signed up for this trip ..." / Nancy said to herself, / with a long sigh. //
　　　　　　목적어로 쓰인 의문사절   **단서 1** 긴 한숨을 내쉬며 혼잣말을 함
"나한테 운이 따르지 않는군 / Midtown 관광이 / 내가 이 여행을 신청한 이유였는데…"라고 / Nancy는 혼잣말을 했다 / 긴 한숨을 내쉬며 //

She was thinking / of all the interesting sights / she wouldn't be able to enjoy. //
_{앞에 목적격 관계대명사가 생략됨}
그녀는 생각하고 있었다 / 온갖 흥미로운 명소들에 대해 / 자신이 즐길 수 없을 //

All of a sudden, / there was a knock at the door. //
갑자기 / 문을 두드리는 소리가 났다 //

"News! // We are going to the Pland Zoo / near the hotel. // We will meet in the lobby soon." //
_{미래를 나타내는 현재진행형}
"뉴스입니다 // 우리는 Pland 동물원에 갈 겁니다 / 호텔 근처에 있는 // 곧 로비에서 모일 겁니다" //

It was the voice / of her tour guide. //
그건 목소리였다 / 그녀의 여행 가이드의 //

She sprung off the couch / and started putting on her coat / in a hurry. //
_{목적어로 동명사나 to부정사를 취하는 start}
그녀는 소파에서 벌떡 일어나 / 외투를 입기 시작했다 / 서둘러 //

"The Pland Zoo! // That's on my bucket list! // What a turn of fortune!" / shouted Nancy. //
_{단서2 행운이 찾아왔다며 소리침}
"Pland 동물원이라고 / 그건 내 버킷 리스트에 있는 거잖아 // 이런 행운이 찾아오다니"라고 / Nancy는 소리쳤다 //

- day trip 당일치기 여행
- scheduled ⓐ 예정된
- sightseeing ⓝ 관광
- sign up 신청하다
- sigh ⓝ 한숨
- all of a sudden 갑자기
- spring off ~에서 벌떡 일어나다

오늘 예정된 Midtown으로 가는 당일치기 여행은 그곳으로 가는 도로가 폭설로 막혀 취소되었다. "나한테 운이 따르지 않는군. Midtown 관광이 내가 이 여행을 신청한 이유인데 …"라고 Nancy는 긴 한숨을 내쉬며 혼잣말을 했다. 그녀는 자신이 즐길 수 없을 온갖 흥미로운 명소들에 대해 생각하고 있었다. 갑자기 문을 두드리는 소리가 났다. "뉴스입니다! 우리는 호텔 근처에 있는 Pland 동물원에 갈 겁니다. 곧 로비에서 모일 겁니다." 그건 그녀의 여행 가이드의 목소리였다. 그녀는 소파에서 벌떡 일어나 서둘러 외투를 입기 시작했다. "Pland 동물원이라고! 그건 내 버킷 리스트에 있는 거잖아! 이런 행운이 찾아오다니!"라고 Nancy는 소리쳤다.

다음 글에 드러난 Nancy의 심경 변화로 가장 적절한 것은?

① disappointed → excited _{한숨을 내쉼 → 행운이 찾아왔다고 소리침}
   실망한 → 신이 난
② relieved → anxious _{여행이 취소되어 안도한 것이 아님}
   안도한 → 불안한
③ surprised → annoyed _{행운이 찾아온 것이 화가 날 일은 아님}
   깜짝 놀란 → 화가 난
④ ashamed → grateful _{부끄러움을 느낄 만한 일은 없음}
   부끄러운 → 감사한
⑤ indifferent → amazed _{여행을 신청한 이유라고 했음}
   무관심한 → 놀란

왜 정답? [정답률 97%]

전반부: 여행을 신청한 이유인 Midtown으로 가는 여행이 취소되어 긴 한숨을 내쉼
후반부: 버킷 리스트에 있는 Pland 동물원에 가게 되어 행운이 찾아왔다며 소리침
▶ ① '실망한' 심경에서 '신이 난' 심경으로 변화함

왜 오답?

② Midtown에 가지 못하게 되어 안도한 것이 아니다.
③ 깜짝 놀란 것은 후반부의 일이다.
④ 여행이 취소된 것이 부끄러운 일은 아니다.
⑤ Midtown으로의 여행이 취소된 것에 관심이 없던 것이 아니다.

B 22 정답 ① ＊한 시간 넘게 Reiner를 기다린 Annette ——

The day of the Five Mile Fun Walk / had arrived. //
_{주어}   _{동사(완전자동사)}
5마일 걷기 대회의 날이 / 도래했다 //

Annette had been waiting for Reiner / at the registration point / for over an hour. //
_{과거완료 진행형}
Annette는 Reiner를 기다리고 있었다 / 등록 장소에서 / 한 시간 넘게 //

There was still no sign of him. //
여전히 그의 모습은 보이지 않았다 //

_{might have p.p.: ~했을지도 모른다 ＊}
She started thinking / that something bad might have happened / to him. //
그녀는 생각하기 시작했다 / 나쁜 일이 일어났을지도 모른다고 / 그에게 //

Getting concerned, / she tried calling Reiner's phone again, / but there was no response. // _{단서1 Reiner가 한 시간 넘게 오지 않아 걱정하기 시작함}
걱정하면서 / 그녀는 다시 Reiner에게 전화를 하려고 했으나 / 아무런 응답이 없었다 //

At that moment, / she heard a voice / calling her name. //
그 순간 / 그녀는 목소리를 들었다 / 자신의 이름을 부르는 //

She found Reiner / coming toward her. //
그녀는 Reiner를 발견했다 / 자신을 향해 다가오는 //

"Thank goodness! // What happened?" / she asked. //
"정말 다행이다 // 어떻게 된 거야"라고 / 그녀가 물었다 //
_{생략 가능한 명사절 접속사}
He explained / that the traffic had been terrible. //
그는 설명했다 / 교통 체증이 끔찍했다고 //
_{결과를 나타내는 과거완료 시제}
What was worse, / he had left his phone at home. //
설상가상으로 / 그는 자신의 휴대 전화를 집에 두고 왔다 //

"I'm so sorry," he said. //
"정말 미안해"라고 그가 말했다 //

She started to relax. // _{단서2 Reiner가 안전하게 도착하자 긴장이 풀리기 시작함}
그녀는 긴장이 풀리기 시작했다 //

"I'm fine now. // As long as you're here and safe. // Why don't we go and register?" // _{조건의 부사절 접속사}
"나는 이제 괜찮아 // 네가 여기 안전하게 와 있는 한 // 우리 가서 등록할까?" //

They headed into the event / together. //
그들은 그 행사로 향했다 / 함께 //

- arrive ⓥ (어떤 순간이) 도래하다
- registration ⓝ 등록
- point ⓝ (특정한) 지점[장소]
- sign ⓝ 징후, 조짐, 기색, 흔적
- concerned ⓐ 걱정[염려]하는
- traffic ⓝ 차량들, 교통(량)
- terrible ⓐ 끔찍한
- relax ⓥ 긴장이 풀리다, 안심하다
- register ⓥ 등록하다
- head ⓥ (특정 방향으로) 가다[향하다]

5마일 걷기 대회의 날이 되었다. Annette는 등록 장소에서 한 시간 넘게 Reiner를 기다리고 있었다. 여전히 그의 모습은 보이지 않았다. 그녀는 그에게 나쁜 일이 일어났을지도 모른다고 생각하기 시작했다. 걱정하면서, 그녀는 다시 Reiner에게 전화를 하려고 했으나, 아무런 응답이 없었다. 그 순간, 그녀는 자신의 이름을 부르는 목소리를 들었다. 그녀는 Reiner가 자신을 향해 다가오는 것을 발견했다. "정말 다행이야! 어떻게 된 거야?"라고 그녀가 물었다. 그는 교통 체증이 끔찍했다고 설명했다. 설상가상으로, 그는 자신의 휴대 전화를 집에 두고 왔다. "정말 미안해."라고 그가 말했다. 그녀는 긴장이 풀리기 시작했다. "나는 이제 괜찮아. 네가 여기 안전하게 와 있으니까. 우리 가서 등록할까?" 그들은 함께 그 행사로 향했다.

다음 글에 드러난 Annette의 심경 변화로 가장 적절한 것은?

① worried → relieved _{Getting concerned → She started to relax.}
   걱정하는 → 안심한
② confident → nervous _{Reiner가 오지 않아 걱정함}
   자신감에 찬 → 불안해하는
③ calm → upset _{Reiner가 무사히 도착함}
   침착한 → 속상한
④ regretful → grateful _{후회할 일은 제시되지 않음}
   후회하는 → 고마워하는
⑤ bored → amazed _{걱정하다가 안심함}
   지루해하는 → 놀란

›왜 정답 ? [정답률 87%]

Annette는 등록 장소에서 한 시간 넘게 Reiner를 기다리면서 그에게 나쁜 일이 일어났을지도 모른다고 생각하며 걱정하다가 Reiner가 무사히 도착하자 긴장이 풀리기 시작했다고 했으므로 그녀의 심경 변화로 적절한 것은 ① '걱정하는 → 안심한'이다.

›왜 오답 ?

②, ③ Reiner가 무사히 도착하자 이제 괜찮다고 했으므로 불안해하거나 속상한 것이 아니다.

④, ⑤ 한 시간 넘게 Reiner를 기다리면서 그에게 나쁜 일이 생긴 것인지 걱정하고 있으므로 후회하거나 지루해하는 것이 아니다.

───── 어법 특강

＊ 과거에 대한 추측을 나타내는 「조동사(의 과거형)+have+p.p.」

– might have p.p.: ~했을지도 모른다
• He might have told me he was going to be late.
 (그가 늦을 거라고 내게 이야기했을지도 모른다.)

– could have p.p.: ~했을 수도 있다
• What was that noise? Could it have been the wind?
 (그 소리는 뭐였어? 바람이었을 수도 있을까?)

– should have p.p.: ~했어야 했다, ~했더라면 좋았을 텐데 (안 했다)
• I should have brought an umbrella.
 (나는 우산을 가져왔어야 했다.)

relax와 같이 심경을 나타내는 단어를 잘 살펴봐!

B 어휘 Review 정답 — 문제편 p. 36

01 턱수염	11 fall short of	21 scheduled
02 황폐한	12 in time	22 arrived
03 격심한	13 be supposed to-v	23 reluctantly
04 무관심한	14 in person	24 grown-up
05 장악하다	15 at ease	25 toddler
06 passenger	16 overall	26 sighed
07 disappointment	17 firm	27 glow
08 doubtful	18 immediately	28 attempted
09 calm	19 complete	29 headed
10 traffic	20 replacing	30 upcoming

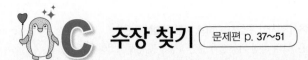

C 주장 찾기 문제편 p. 37~51

C 01 정답 ⑤ ＊인간의 오류 극복 능력을 활용하여 AI를 감독할 수 있다.

~하면서
As the world seems to be increasingly affected / by the ever-expanding influence / of machines in general / and artificial intelligence (AI) specifically, /
전 세계가 점점 더 영향을 받는 듯 보이면서 / 계속 확대되는 영향력에 의해 / 전반적으로 기계의 / 구체적으로 말하면 인공지능(AI)

either A or B: A 또는 B
many begin to imagine, with either fear or anticipation, / a
과거분사
future with a diminished role for human decision making. //
많은 사람은 두려움 속에 또는 기대를 품고 상상하기 시작한다 / 인간의 의사 결정 역할이 줄어드는 미래를 /
whether it be A or B: A이든 B이든
Whether it be due to the growing presence of AI assistants / or the emergence of self-driving cars, /
커지는 AI 비서의 존재감 때문이든 / 자율 주행 자동차의 등장 때문이든 /
the necessity of the role of humans / as the decision makers /
~로서
would appear to be in decline. //
인간 역할의 필요성은 / 의사 결정권자로서의 / 감소하는 듯 보일 것이다 //
수동태
After all, / our capacity for making mistakes / is well documented. //
어쨌든 / 실수를 저지르는 우리(= 인간)의 능력은 / 충분히 입증되었다 //
be to 부정사: 예정, 운명(~할 것이다)
However, perhaps the saving grace of human determination /
수동태
is to be found here as well. //
하지만, 아마도 인간 결단력의 장점은 / 또한 여기에서 발견될 것이다 //
거의 없는(부정)
Little evidence exists /
증거는 거의 존재하지 않는다 /
주격 관계대명사
that suggests modern AI's infallibility /
현재 AI의 무오류성을 시사하거나 /
or predicts it in the future. //
미래에 그것(= AI의 무오류성)을 예측하는 //

가주어 진주어절을 이끄는 접속사
It is crucial that, / in light of humanity's acceptance of our own fallibility, /
매우 중요하다 / 인류가 스스로 오류성을 인정한다는 점으로 미루어 볼 때 /
부사적 용법(결과)
we utilize our capacity to overcome such failures / to position ourselves / as the overseers of AI's own growth and applications
~로서
/ for the foreseeable future. //
단서 인간의 오류 극복 능력으로 AI를 감독하는 역할을 할 수 있다고 주장함
우리가 이러한 실패를 극복할 수 있는 능력을 활용하여 / 자리 잡는 것이 / AI 자체의 성장과 적용의 감독관으로서 / 가까운 미래에 //

[가주어와 진주어절: 주어 자리에 가주어 it을 쓰고 진주어절을 이끄는 접속사 that이 이끄는 진주어는 문장 뒤쪽으로 보낸다.]

• anticipation ⓝ 기대   • assistant ⓝ 비서, 조수, 보조원
• saving grace 장점, 미덕   • termination ⓝ 결단력
• infallibility ⓝ 무오류성   • crucial ⓐ 중대한, 결정적인
• utilize ⓥ 활용하다   • overseer ⓝ 감독관
• foreseeable future 가까운 미래

전 세계가 전반적으로 기계의 영향력, 구체적으로 말하면 인공지능(AI)의 계속 확대되는 영향력에 점점 더 영향을 받는 듯 보이면서, 많은 사람은 두려움 속에 또는 기대를 품고 인간의 의사 결정 역할이 줄어드는 미래를 상상하기 시작한다. 커지는 AI 비서의 존재감 때문이든, 자율 주행 자동차의 등장 때문이든, 의사 결정권자로서의 인간 역할의 필요성은 감소하는 듯 보일 것이다. 결국, 실수를 저지르는 우리의 능력은 충분히 입증되었다. 하지만, 아마도 인간 결단력의 장점 또한 여기에서 발견될 것이다. 현재 AI의 무오류성을 시사하거나 미래에 그것을 예측하는 증거는 거의 존재하지 않는다. 인류가 스스로 오류성을 인정한다는 점으로 미루어 볼 때, 우리가 이러한 실패를 극복할 수 있는 능력을 활용하여 가까운 미래에 AI 자체의 성장과 적용의 감독관으로서 자리 잡는 것이 매우 중요하다.

다음 글에서 필자가 주장하는 바로 가장 적절한 것은?

① 인간은 AI의 발전 가능성과 불안정성을 동시에 고려해야 한다.
  AI를 인간의 능력으로 감독할 수 있다는 것이 주요 내용임
② 인간은 창의력을 향상시키기 위해 AI에 의존하지 말아야 한다.
  창의력에 대한 내용은 언급되지 않았음
③ 실수를 보완하기 위해 인간은 AI의 활용 방안을 모색해야 한다.
  실수를 행하고 극복하는 것이 인간이 가진 장점이라고 했음
④ AI에 대한 학습을 통해 인간은 미래 사회 변화에 대비해야 한다.
  학습에 대한 언급은 없음
⑤ AI의 영향력 확산에 대비하여 인간은 오류 극복 능력을 활용해야 한다.
  인간의 오류 극복 능력으로 인공지능을 감독하는 역할을 할 수 있다고 주장하는 내용임

➤왜 정답? [정답률 72%]

- • 인공지능(AI)의 영향력이 점차 확대되면서 미래에는 인간의 의사 결정 능력이
   감소할 것으로 예측됨
  • 그러나 인간은 오류를 범하고 극복하는 능력이 있으므로, 이 능력을 활용해
   인공지능을 감독하는 역할을 해야 함 **단서**

▶ 인간의 오류 극복 능력으로 인공지능을 감독하는 역할을 할 수 있다고 주장하는
  내용이므로 정답은 ⑤이다.

➤왜 오답?

① AI를 인간의 능력으로 감독할 수 있다는 것이 주요 내용이다.
② 창의력에 대한 내용은 언급되지 않았다.
③ 실수를 행하고 극복하는 것이 인간이 가진 장점이며, 이를 이용해 AI를 감독하자는
  것이지 AI로 인간의 실수를 막자는 것이 아니다. **함정**
④ 학습에 대한 언급은 없다.

C 02 정답 ④ ＊창의성의 영역 간 활용

주어
Certain hindrances / to multifaceted creative activity / may lie / **동사(완전자동사)**
in premature specialization, /
어떤 방해 요인은 / 다면적인 창의적 활동에 대한 / 있을 수 있다 / 너무 이른 전문화에 /

i.e., having to choose the direction of education / or to focus on
 ──────────── 병렬 구조 ────────────
developing one ability / too early in life. //
즉 교육 방향을 선택해야 하거나 / 한 가지 능력 개발에 집중해야 하는 것에 / 인생의 너무
이른 시기에 //

However, / development of creative ability / in one domain
/ may enhance effectiveness / in other domains / that require
similar skills, / **단서1** 한 영역에서의 창의적 능력 개발은 다른 영역에서 효과를 높일 수 있음
그러나 / 창의적 능력 개발은 / 한 영역에서의 / 효과를 높일 수 있다 / 다른 영역에서 / 비슷한
기술을 필요로 하는 /

and flexible switching / between generality and specificity / **주어** is
helpful to productivity / in many domains. // **동사**
유연한 전환은 / 일반성과 특수성 사이의 / 생산성에 도움이 된다 / 많은 영역에서 //

Excessive specificity may result / in information / from outside
the domain / being underestimated and unavailable, / which
 계속적 용법의 주격 관계대명사
leads to fixedness of thinking, /
지나친 특수성은 결과를 낳을 수 있어서 / 정보가 / 해당 영역 외부로부터 오는 / 과소평가
되고 활용할 수 없게 되는 / 사고의 고정성으로 이어질 수 있다 /

whereas excessive generality causes / chaos, vagueness, and
부사적 접속사(대조) //
shallowness. //
지나친 일반성은 초래하는 반면 / 혼돈, 모호함, 얕음을 //

Both tendencies pose a threat / to the transfer of knowledge and
skills / between domains. //
두 가지 경향 모두 위협이 된다 / 지식과 기술 이전에 대한 / 영역 간 //

What should therefore be optimal / for the development of
 명사절 주어
cross-domain creativity / is support for young people / in taking
 단수 동사 **주격 보어①**
up creative challenges / in a specific domain /
그러므로 응당 최선인 것은 / 영역 간 창의성 개발을 위해 / 젊은이들을 지원하고 / 창의적인
도전을 하기 시작할 때 / 특정한 영역에서 /

단서2 최선인 것은 특정 영역에서의 창의적 도전을 다른
영역, 분야, 과업의 지식, 기술과 결합하도록 장려하는 것임
주격 보어②(동명사)
and coupling it with encouragement / to apply knowledge and
skills / in, as well as from, other domains, disciplines, and tasks. //
그것을 장려하는 것과 결합하는 것이다 / 지식과 기술을 적용하도록 / 다른 영역, 분야,
과업으로부터 나온 지식과 기술을 적용할 뿐만 아니라, 다른 영역, 분야, 과업에 //

- certain ⓐ 어떤, 무슨   • hindrance ⓝ 방해요인, 장애물
- multifaceted ⓐ 다면적인   • premature ⓐ 이른
- specialization ⓝ 전문화   • direction ⓝ 방향
- domain ⓝ 영역   • enhance ⓥ 높이다   • generality ⓝ 일반성
- specificity ⓝ 특수성   • productivity ⓝ 생산성
- excessive ⓐ 지나친   • underestimate ⓥ 과소평가하다
- unavailable ⓐ 손에 넣을 수 없는, 활용할 수 없는   • fixedness ⓝ 고정성
- chaos ⓝ 혼돈   • vagueness ⓝ 모호함   • shallowness ⓝ 얕음
- transfer ⓥ 이전하다   • optimal ⓐ 최선의   • couple ⓥ 연결하다
- discipline ⓝ 분야

다면적인 창의적 활동에 대한 어떤 방해 요인은 너무 이른 전문화, 즉 인생의
너무 이른 시기에 교육 방향을 선택하거나 한 가지 능력 개발에 집중해야 하는
것에 있을 수 있다. 그러나 한 영역에서의 창의적 능력 개발은 비슷한 기술을
필요로 하는 다른 영역에서 효과를 높일 수 있으며, 일반성과 특수성 사이의
유연한 전환은 많은 영역에서 생산성에 도움이 된다. 지나친 특수성은 해당
영역 외부로부터 오는 정보가 과소평가 되고 활용할 수 없게 되는 결과를 낳을
수 있어 사고의 고정성으로 이어지는 반면, 지나친 일반성은 혼돈, 모호함,
얕음을 초래한다. 두 가지 경향 모두 영역 간 지식과 기술 이전에 대한 위협이
된다. 그러므로 영역 간 창의성 개발을 위해 응당 최선인 것은 특정한 영역에서
창의적인 도전을 하기 시작할 때 젊은이들을 지원하고 그것을 다른 영역,
분야, 과업으로부터 나온 지식과 기술을 적용할 뿐만 아니라, 다른 영역, 분야,
과업에 지식과 기술을 적용하도록 장려하는 것과 결합하는 것이다.

다음 글에서 필자가 주장하는 바로 가장 적절한 것은?

① 창의성을 개발하기 위해서는 도전과 실패를 두려워하지 말아야 한다.
  창의성을 개발하는 방법을 설명한 것이 아님
② 전문 지식과 기술을 전수하려면 집중적인 투자가 선행되어야 한다.
  지식과 기술의 전수에 대한 내용이 아님
③ 창의적인 인재를 육성하기 위해 다양한 교육과정을 준비해야 한다.
  다양한 교육과정의 필요성은 언급되지 않음
④ 특정 영역에서 개발된 창의성이 영역 간 활용되도록 장려해야 한다.
  마지막 문장이 핵심 내용임
⑤ 조기 교육을 통해 특정 분야의 전문가를 지속적으로 양성해야 한다.
  너무 이른 전문화의 단점을 이야기했음

➤왜 정답? [정답률 83%]

> **첫 문장:** 다면적인 창의적 활동에 대한 방해 요인: 너무 이른 '전문화'
> **두 번째 문장:** 그러나(However) 한 영역에서의 창의적 능력 개발은
> 다른 영역에서 효과를 높일 수 있음 **단서1**
> **마지막 문장:** 영역 간 창의성 개발에 최선인 것: 특정 영역의 창의적
> 도전을 다른 영역, 분야, 과업의 지식, 기술과 결합하도록 장려하는 것
> **단서2**

➡ 너무 이른 전문화는 다면적인 창의적 활동을 방해한다. 한 영역에서 개발된
  창의성이 다른 영역에서도 적용되도록 해야 한다. 따라서 필자가 주장하는 바는
  ④이다.

➤왜 오답?

① 도전과 실패를 통해 창의성이 개발된다는 내용이 아니다.
② 전문 지식과 기술의 전수를 위한 선행 조건을 설명한 것이 아니다.
③ 다양한 교육과정의 필요성에 대해서는 언급되지 않았다.
⑤ 인생의 너무 이른 시기에 전문화되는 것을 부정적으로 바라보는 글이다.

C 03 정답 ① ＊학습 효과 증진에 도움이 되는 게임 개발의 필요성

We almost universally accept / that playing video games is at
목적어절을 이끄는 접속사
best a pleasant break / from a student's learning / and more often
what prevents a student / from accomplishing their goals. //

우리는 거의 보편적으로 받아들인다 / 비디오 게임을 하는 것이 기껏해야 즐거운 휴식이라고 /
학생의 학습으로부터 벗어나는 / 더 흔히는 학생을 방해하는 것이라고 / 목표를 이루는 것을 //

Games catch and hold attention / in a way / that few things can. //
way를 수식하는 관계부사

게임은 주의를 사로잡고 계속해서 유지한다 / 방식으로 / 다른 어떤 것도 거의 할 수 없는 //

And yet once they have our focus, / they rarely seem to offer
anything meaningful / to help students grow / in their lives
anything을 수식하는 형용사   help의 목적격 보어로 쓰인 동사원형
outside the games. //

하지만 일단 그것이 우리의 집중을 얻고 나면 / 그것은 거의 아무것도 제공하지 않는 것 같다 /
학생들이 성장하는 것을 돕는 / 게임 이외의 그들의 삶에서 //

While this may be true / for many games, / we are too easily
ignoring a valuable tool / that could be used / to enhance
주격 관계대명사
productivity / instead of derailing it. //

이것이 사실일 수도 있지만 / 많은 게임에 대해 / 우리는 가치 있는 도구를 너무 쉽게 무시하고
있다 / 사용될 수도 있는 / 생산성을 향상하는 데 / 저해하는 대신 //

Rather, / it is desirable / that we develop games / that connect to
가주어   진주어절을 이끄는 접속사   주격 관계대명사
the learning outcomes / we want for our students. //
사이에 outcomes를 수식하는 목적격 관계대명사 생략

오히려 / 바람직하다 / 우리가 게임을 개발하는 것이 / 학습 성과와 연결되는 / 우리가
학생들에게 원하는 //   [단서] 학습 성과와 연결되는 게임을 개발하는 것이 바람직함

This will enable educators / to take advantage of games'
attention commanding capacities / and allow our students / to
enjoy their games / while learning. //
접속사가 생략되지 않은 분사구문

이것은 교육자들을 가능하게 할 것이다 / 게임의 주의력 지배 능력을 활용할 수 있도록 /
그리고 학생들에게 허락할 것이다 / 게임을 즐기도록 / 학습하면서 //

- universally ⓐ 보편적으로 · accomplish ⓥ 이루다
- hold attention 주의를 유지하다 · enhance ⓥ 향상시키다
- productivity ⓝ 생산성 · derail ⓥ 탈선시키다, 망치다
- desirable ⓐ 바람직한 · connect to ~와 관련시키다[연결하다]
- outcome ⓝ 결과, 성과 · educator ⓝ 교육자
- take advantage of ~을 활용하다 · command ⓥ 지배하다, 지휘하다

우리는 거의 보편적으로 비디오 게임을 하는 것이 기껏해야 학생이 학습에서
잠시 벗어나는 즐거운 휴식이고, 더 흔히는 학생이 목표를 이루는 것을
방해하는 것이라 받아들인다. 게임은 다른 어떤 것도 거의 할 수 없는 방식으로
주의를 사로잡고 계속해서 유지한다. 하지만 일단 그것이 우리의 집중을 얻고
나면, 그것은 게임 이외의 삶에서 학생들이 성장하는 데 도움이 되는 의미
있는 무언가를 제공하는 경우는 거의 없는 것 같다. 많은 게임에 대해 이것이
사실일 수도 있지만, 우리는 생산성을 저해하는 대신 생산성을 향상하는 데
사용될 수도 있는 가치 있는 도구를 너무 쉽게 무시하고 있다. 오히려, 우리가
학생들에게 원하는 학습 성과와 연결되는 게임을 개발하는 것이 바람직하다.
이를 통해 교육자들은 게임의 주의력 지배 능력을 활용할 수 있게 되고, 우리
학생들은 학습하면서 게임을 즐길 수 있게 될 것이다.

다음 글에서 필자가 주장하는 바로 가장 적절한 것은?

① 학습 효과 증진에 활용될 수 있는 게임을 개발해야 한다.
　　학습 효과 증진에 활용될 수 있는 게임을 개발해야 한다는 것이 핵심 내용임
② 교육 현장에서 학습과 게임 활동을 적절하게 분배해야 한다.
　　학습과 게임 활동을 적절히 분배하라는 것이 아니라 학습과 연결된 게임을 개발하라는 것임
③ 학습 활동에 게임이 초래하는 집중력 저하를 경계해야 한다.
　　게임이 초래하는 학습 집중력 저하를 경계하라는 것이 필자의 주장은 아님
④ 여가 시간에 게임을 활용함으로써 학습 효율을 향상해야 한다.
　　여가 시간에 게임을 활용하라고 하지 않았음
⑤ 게임의 부정적 영향을 줄이기 위해 학습 공동체가 노력해야 한다.
　　게임의 부정적 영향을 줄이기 위한 학습 공동체의 노력은 언급되지 않음

▷왜 정답 ? [정답률 84%]

- 게임이 사람들의 주의 집중을 끄는 데 뛰어나지만 게임을 하는 것은 학생들의
  삶에서 성장에 도움이 되는 경우가 거의 없음
- 교육자들이 게임의 가치를 인정하고 학습 결과와 연결된 게임을 개발하여 게임의
  강력한 집중력 유도 능력을 활용하는 것이 바람직함

▶ 학습과 연결된 게임을 개발하여 게임의 집중력 유도 능력을 활용, 학생들이 즐기며
학습하도록 해야 한다는 것이 필자의 주장이므로 정답은 ①이다.

▷왜 오답 ?

② 학습과 게임 활동을 적절히 분배하라는 것이 아니라 학습과 연결된 게임을
　개발하라는 것이다.
③ 게임이 초래하는 학습 집중력 저하를 경계하라는 것이 필자의 주장은 아니다.
④ 여가 시간에 게임을 활용해 학습 효율을 향상시켜야 한다고 하지 않았다.
⑤ 게임의 부정적 영향을 줄이기 위한 학습 공동체의 노력은 언급되지 않았다.

한규진 | 2025 수능 응시 · 대구 계성고 졸

필자의 주장을 찾는다는 것은 곧 글의 주제를 찾는 것이라고 볼 수
있어. 해당 지문에서는 앞부분에 '비디오 게임'에 대한 부정적인
견해를 언급했지만, 중간에 while과 rather의 표현을 통해서
글의 기조를 바꾸고 있어. 또한 rather로 시작하는 문장에서는
desirable(바람직한)이라는 표현을 통해서 이 문장이 화자가 바라는 것임을 알 수
있어.

C 04 정답 ③ ＊소셜 미디어 사용자의 정보의 정확성과 신뢰성 확보

Truth is essential / for progress and the development of
접속사(이유)   전치사＋관계대명사
knowledge, / as it serves as the foundation / upon which reliable
and accurate understanding is built. //

진실은 필수적이다 / 진보와 지식의 발전에 / 그것이 토대의 역할을 하기 때문에 / 신뢰할 수
있고 정확한 이해가 이루어지는 //

However, / one of the greatest threats to the accumulation of
knowledge / can now be found / on social media platforms. //

그러나 / 지식 축적에 가장 큰 위협 중 하나가 / 이제 발견될 수 있다 / 소셜 미디어 플랫폼에서 //
접속사(~하면서)
As social media becomes / a primary source of information for
millions, / its unregulated nature / allows misinformation to
spread rapidly. //

소셜 미디어가 되면서 / 수백만 명에게 주 정보원이 / 그것의 규제받지 않는 특성이 / 오정보가
빠르게 퍼지게 허락한다 //

Social media users may unknowingly participate / in creating
and circulating misinformation, / which can influence elections,
계속적 용법의 관계대명사
/ cause violence, / and create widespread panic, / as seen in
병렬 구조   접속사(~하듯이): 주어와 동사가 생략된 분사구문이 따라옴
various global incidents. //

소셜 미디어 사용자는 자신도 모르게 참여할 수 있다 / 오정보를 만들고 유포하는 데 / 이는
선거에 영향을 미칠 수 있다 / 폭력을 유발하며 / 광범위한 공황 상태를 조성하고 / 다양한 전
세계적 사건에서 보이듯이 //
전치사(~로서)   가주어   진주어
As creators and consumers, / it is our responsibility / to take on
a greater role / in the enhancement of fact-checking protocols /
in order to ensure accuracy. // [단서 1] 소셜 미디어 정보의 정확성을 확보하기 위해
　　　　　　　　　　　　　　　　　더 큰 역할을 맡는 것이 우리의 역할이라고 함
(정보) 제작자이자 소비자로서 / 우리의 책무이다 / 더 큰 역할을 맡는 것이 / 사실 확인
프로토콜 강화에 / 정확성을 확보하기 위해 // [단서 2] 참여자들이 정보의 신뢰성을 보호하는
가주어   진주어절을 이끄는 접속사   것이 중요하다고 함
It is critical / that participants safeguard the reliability of
information, / supporting a more informed and rational public
분사구문
community. //

매우 중요하다 / 참여자들이 정보의 신뢰성을 보호하는 것이 / 더 사실 이해에 입각하고
합리적인 대중 커뮤니티를 지원하면서 //

- essential ⓐ 필수적인 · progress ⓝ 진보
- foundation ⓝ 토대, 기반 · reliable ⓐ 신뢰할 수 있는
- accurate ⓐ 정확한 · accumulation ⓝ 축적
- unregulated ⓐ 규제받지 않는 · unknowingly ⓐ 자신도 모르게
- participate in ~에 참여하다 · circulate ⓥ 유포하다
- violence ⓝ 폭력 · take on ~을 (떠)맡다
- enhancement ⓝ 강화 · safeguard ⓥ 보호하다
- informed ⓐ 사실 이해에 입각한, 정보에 근거한 · rational ⓐ 합리적인

진실은 진보와 지식의 발전에 필수적인데, 그것이 신뢰할 수 있고 정확한
이해가 이루어지는 토대의 역할을 하기 때문이다. 그러나 지식 축적에 가장 큰
위협 중 하나가 이제 소셜 미디어 플랫폼에서 발견될 수 있다. 소셜 미디어가

수백만 명에게 주 정보원이 되면서, 그것의 규제받지 않는 특성으로 인해 오정보가 빠르게 퍼지게 된다. 소셜 미디어 사용자는 자신도 모르게 오정보를 만들고 유포하는 데 참여할 수 있는데, 이는 다양한 전 세계적 사건에서 보이듯이 선거에 영향을 미치고, 폭력을 유발하며, 광범위한 공황 상태를 조성할 수 있다. (정보) 제작자이자 소비자로서, 정확성을 확보하기 위해 사실 확인 프로토콜 강화에 더 큰 역할을 맡는 것이 우리의 책무이다. 참여자들이 더 사실 이해에 입각하고 합리적인 대중 커뮤니티를 지원하면서 정보의 신뢰성을 보호하는 것이 매우 중요하다.

다음 글에서 필자가 주장하는 바로 가장 적절한 것은?

① 소셜 미디어 플랫폼을 운영할 때 사용자의 의견을 반영해야 한다.
　소셜 미디어 플랫폼 운영에 사용자 의견을 반영해야 한다고 하지 않았음
② 디지털 창작물의 저작권 보호에 관한 사회적 합의를 도출해야 한다.
　디지털 창작물 저작권 보호에 대한 내용이 아님
③ 소셜 미디어 사용자는 정보의 정확성과 신뢰성 확보를 위해 힘써야 한다.
　소셜 미디어 사용자로서 정보의 정확성과 신뢰성을 위해 역할을 해야 한다고 함
④ 광범위한 지식을 축적하기 위해 다양한 정보의 유통을 촉진해야 한다.
　광범위한 지식을 축적하기 위한 방법에 대한 언급은 없음
⑤ 소셜 미디어 기업은 개인 정보 보호를 위한 대책을 세워야 한다.
　단순히 '소셜 미디어'라는 단어를 넣어 만든 오답

왜 정답? [정답률 96%]

- 소셜 미디어에서의 오정보 확산이 문제가 됨
- (정보) 제작자이자 소비자로서의 소셜 미디어 사용자는 정보의 정확성과 신뢰성을 위해 큰 역할을 해야 함 단서1 단서2

▶ 소셜 미디어 사용자가 오정보를 만들고 유포해서 전 세계적으로 심각한 영향을 끼칠 수 있다고 하며, 정보의 정확성과 신뢰성 확보를 위해 힘써야 한다는 내용이다. 따라서 필자의 주장으로 가장 적절한 것은 ③이다.

왜 오답?

① 소셜 미디어 플랫폼 운영에 사용자 의견을 반영해야 한다고 하지 않았다.
② 디지털 창작물 저작권 보호에 대한 내용이 아니다.
④ 광범위한 지식을 축적하기 위한 방법에 대한 언급은 전혀 없다.
⑤ 소셜 미디어의 개인 정보 보호에 대한 내용이 아니다.

C 05 정답 ① * 초기 유년기에서 음악 실천의 장점

There are few universals in this world, / but among them are
　　　　　　도치된 주어의 병렬 구조
our love for our children and our love of music. //
이 세상에는 보편적인 것들이 거의 없지만 / 그것들 중에 우리 아이들에 대한 우리의 사랑과 음악에 대한 우리의 사랑이 있다 //

When we hold a baby in our arms, / comforting her with song, /
　　　　　　　　　　　　　　　　　분사구문
we are channelling the emotional power of music. //
우리가 아기를 우리 팔에 안고 / 그녀를 노래로 다독일 때 / 우리는 음악의 정서적 힘을 전하고 있다 //

We do so instinctively, / just as our ancestors did. //
우리는 본능적으로 그렇게 한다 / 꼭 우리 조상들이 했던 것처럼 //

Music can be a powerful parental ally / during the challenging child-rearing years. //
음악은 강력한 부모의 협력자가 될 수 있다 / 아이를 키우는 힘든 시기 동안 //

To successfully prepare our children for life in the twenty-first century, / we will need to nurture qualities / such as curiosity, imagination, empathy, creative entrepreneurship, and most of all resilience. //
21세기에서의 삶에 우리 아이들을 성공적으로 준비시키기 위해 / 우리는 자질들을 길러줘야 할 것이다 / 호기심, 상상력, 공감, 창의적 기업가 정신, 그리고 무엇보다도 회복력과 같은 //

Musical practice in early childhood / develops all of the above
단수 주어　　　　　　　　　　　　　　　　단수 동사
and more. //
초기 유년기에서 음악의 실천은 / 위의 모든 것과 그 이상을 발달시킨다 //
　　　　　　　　　　　　　　목적어절을 이끄는 접속사
Research has shown / that musical practice in early childhood / is beneficial not only for mental acuity / but for social and
　　　　　　　　　　not only A but (also) B: A뿐만 아니라 B도
emotional development as well. //
연구는 보여 준다 / 초기 유년기에서 음악의 실천은 / 정신의 예리함뿐만 아니라 / 사회적 그리고 정서적 발달에도 유익하다는 것을 // 단서1 초기 유년기에서 음악을 실천하면 정신의 예리함뿐만 아니라 사회적, 정서적 발달에도 유익함

Music is not just a hobby, a pleasant pastime; / it is an integral
　선행사를 포함하는 관계대명사　　　　　　　　　　　(= music)
part of what makes us happy, healthy, and whole. //
음악은 단지 취미, 즐거운 오락거리가 아니고 / 우리를 행복하고 건강하며 온전하게 만드는 것의 필수적인 부분이다 //

Indeed, if we want to do one thing to help our children develop / into emotionally, socially, intellectually, and creatively competent human beings, /
사실, 우리가 우리 아이들을 성장하도록 돕기 위해 한 가지를 하고 싶다면 / 정서적으로, 사회적으로, 지적으로, 그리고 창의적으로 유능한 인간으로 /

we should start the musical conversation / — the earlier the better. // 단서2 아이가 정서적, 사회적, 지적, 그리고 창의적으로 유능한 인간으로 성장시키는 데 도움을 주기 위해서는 최대한 빨리 음악을 접할 수 있도록 해야 함
우리는 음악의 대화를 시작해야 한다 / 더 빠를수록 더 좋다 //

- channel ⓥ 전하다, 보내다 　 • instinctively 쪠 본능적으로
- ancestor ⓝ 조상, 선조 　 • ally ⓝ 협력자
- child-rearing ⓝ 자녀 양육 　 • nurture ⓥ 양육하다, 길러주다
- quality ⓝ 질 　 • curiosity ⓝ 호기심 　 • empathy ⓝ 감정이입
- entrepreneurship ⓝ 기업가 정신 　 • childhood ⓝ 어린시절
- develop ⓥ 발달시키다 　 • beneficial ⓐ 유익한
- integral ⓐ 필수적인 　 • competent ⓐ 유능한
- conversation ⓝ 대화

이 세상에는 보편적인 것들이 거의 없지만, 그것들 중에 우리 아이들에 대한 우리의 사랑과 음악에 대한 우리의 사랑이 있다. 우리가 아기를 우리 팔에 안고, 그녀를 노래로 다독일 때, 우리는 음악의 정서적 힘을 전하고 있다. 꼭 우리 조상들이 했던 것처럼, 우리는 본능적으로 그렇게 한다. 음악은 아이를 키우는 힘든 시기 동안 강력한, 부모의 협력자가 될 수 있다. 21세기에서의 삶에 우리 아이들을 성공적으로 준비시키기 위해, 우리는 호기심, 상상력, 공감, 창의적 기업가 정신, 그리고 무엇보다도 회복력과 같은 자질들을 길러줘야 할 것이다. 초기 유년기에서 음악의 실천은 위의 모든 것과 그 이상을 발달시킨다. 연구는 초기 유년기에서 음악의 실천은 정신의 예리함뿐만 아니라 사회적 그리고 정서적 발달에도 유익하다는 것을 보여 준다. 음악은 단지 취미, 즐거운 오락거리가 아니고, 우리를 행복하고 건강하며 온전하게 만드는 것의 필수적인 부분이다. 사실, 우리가 우리 아이들을 정서적으로, 사회적으로, 지적으로, 그리고 창의적으로 유능한 인간으로 성장하도록 돕기 위해 한 가지를 하고 싶다면, 우리는 음악의 대화를 시작해야 한다. 더 빠를수록 더 좋다.

다음 글에서 필자가 주장하는 바로 가장 적절한 것은?

① 아이의 전인적 성장을 위해 어릴 때부터 음악을 접하게 해줘야 한다.
　정서적, 사회적, 지적, 그리고 창의적으로 유능한 사람이 되도록 하려면 어렸을 때부터 음악을 실천해야 함
② 음악이 단순한 취미 이상이 되려면 악기를 꾸준히 연습해야 한다.
　꾸준한 악기 연습에 대한 언급은 없음
③ 질 높은 음악 교육을 위해 이론과 실습을 병행해야 한다.
　이론과 실습을 병행해야 한다는 말은 나오지 않음
④ 음악을 아이 양육에 활용하려면 음악적 전문성이 있어야 한다.
　음악적 전문성을 강세야한다는 것은 글쓴이의 주장이 아님
⑤ 어린 연주자들에게도 재능을 발휘할 수 있는 기회가 주어져야 한다.
　어린 연주자들에게 기회를 제공해야한다는 내용은 아님

왜 정답? [정답률 97%]

- 21세기에서의 삶에 아이를 성공적으로 대비시키려면 호기심, 상상력, 공감 능력, 창의력 그리고 회복력을 갖추도록 해야 하고, 초기 유년기의 음악 실천이 이를 길러줄 수 있음 단서1
- 아이가 정서적, 사회적, 지적 그리고 창의적으로 유능한 인간으로 성장시키는 데 도움을 주기 위해서는 최대한 빨리 음악을 접할 수 있도록 해야 함 단서2

▶ 아이가 다방면으로의 역량을 기를 수 있도록 하기 위해서는 어릴 때부터 음악을 접해야 한다는 것이 필자의 주장이므로 정답은 ①이다.

왜 오답?

② 음악이 단순한 취미를 넘는다는 말은 있지만, 악기를 꾸준히 연습해야 한다는 말은 없다.
③ 음악 이론과 실습을 병행해야 한다는 말은 없다.
④ 아이 양육에 음악이 좋다는 내용이긴 하지만, 이를 위해 음악적 전문성을 갖춰야 한다는 내용은 아니다. 함정
⑤ 어린 연주자에게 기회를 줘야 한다는 언급은 없다.

C 06 정답 ① *작가로 성공하기 위한 방법으로서의 계속된 출간

Walk into a bookstore / and you'll see some authors have a
(앞에 목적어절 접속사 that 생략)
whole shelf. //
서점으로 걸어 들어가면 / 당신은 몇몇 작가들이 선반 전체를 차지하고 있는 것을 볼 것이다 //
복수 주어   복수 동사
Authors with just one book are hard to find / and it's the same
for digital shelf-space. //
단지 한 권의 책만 가지고 있는 작가들은 찾기 어렵고 / 이것은 디지털 선반 공간에서도
마찬가지이다 //

Look at the most loved and top-selling authors / and they all
have a lot of books. //
가장 사랑받고 가장 책이 잘 팔린 작가들을 보면 / 그들은 모두 많은 책을 가지고 있다 //

One book is not enough / to build a career as a fiction author / if
지시대명사(= to build a career as a fiction author)
that is a goal of yours. //
책 한 권은 그러기에 충분하지 않다 / 소설 작가로서 경력을 쌓는 것이 / (그것이) 당신의
목적이라면 //
                                지시형용사
So, don't obsess over that one book, / consider it just the
beginning, and get writing on the next one. //
그러므로, 그 책 한 권에 사로잡히지 말고 / 그것을 단지 시작이라고 여기고 다음 책을 쓰기
시작하라 //   단서 1 다음 책을 쓰기 시작하라는 조언을 함

Of course, / first-time authors don't want to hear this! //
물론 / 처음 쓴 작가는 이것을 듣기를 원하지 않는다 //
      뒤에 want to hear this 생략됨
I certainly didn't / when I put my first book out. //
나는 분명히 듣고 싶지 않았다 / 내가 처음 책을 내놓았을 때 //
                후치 수식 가능한 형용사(-ible, -able로 끝남)
I've tried every single marketing tool possible / and I still
          명사적 용법(목적어)
continue to experiment / with new forms. //
나는 가능한 모든 각각의 마케팅 수단을 시도해왔고 / 여전히 계속해서 실험한다 / 새로운
형태를 //
                동명사 주어   선행사를 포함한 관계대명사
But after 27 books, / writing more books / is what I personally
keep coming back to / as the best marketing tool / and the best
형용사적 용법(the best way 수식)
way / to increase my income as a writer. // 단서 2 책을 더 쓰는 것이
그러나 27권의 책 이후 / 더 많은 책을 쓰는 것이 / 내가 스스로 계속 되돌아가는 것이자 가장 좋은 방법
최고의 마케팅 수단으로서 / 그리고 가장 좋은 방법이다 / 작가로서 나의 수입을 증가시키는 //

Because every time a new book comes out, / more readers
discover the backlist. //
왜냐하면 새로운 책이 나올 때마다 / 더 많은 독자들이 이전에 출간된 도서 목록을 발견하기
때문이다 //

You also have another chance / to 'break out'. //
당신은 또한 또 다른 기회를 가진다 / '인기 작가가 될' //

- **author** ⓝ 필자, 작가   - **career** ⓝ 경력
- **obsess** ⓥ (생각이나 마음을) 사로잡다   - **income** ⓝ 수입
- **discover** ⓥ 발견하다

서점으로 걸어 들어가면 당신은 몇몇 작가들이 선반 전체를 차지하고 있는
것을 볼 것이다. 단지 한 권의 책만 가지고 있는 작가들은 찾기 어렵고 이것은
디지털 선반 공간에서도 마찬가지이다. 가장 사랑받고 가장 책이 잘 팔린
작가들을 보면 그들은 모두 많은 책을 가지고 있다. 소설 작가로서 경력을
쌓는 것이 당신의 목적이라면, 책 한 권은 그러기에 충분하지 않다. 그러므로,
그 책 한 권에 사로잡히지 말고, 그것을 단지 시작이라고 여기고, 다음 책을
쓰기 시작하라. 물론, 처음 쓴 작가는 이것을 듣기를 원하지 않는다! 나는
분명히 내가 처음 책을 내놓았을 때 듣고 싶지 않았다. 나는 가능한 한 모든
각각의 마케팅 수단을 시도해 왔고, 여전히 새로운 형태를 계속해서 실험한다.
그러나 27권의 책 이후, 더 많은 책을 쓰는 것이 최고의 마케팅 수단으로서
내가 스스로 계속 되돌아가는 것이자 작가로서 나의 수입을 증가시키는 가장
좋은 방법이다. 왜냐하면 새로운 책이 나올 때마다, 더 많은 독자들이 이전에
출간 된 도서 목록을 발견하기 때문이다. 당신은 또한 '인기 작가가 될' 또 다른
기회를 가진다.

다음 글에서 필자가 주장하는 바로 가장 적절한 것은?

① 작가로 성공하려면 계속해서 출간해야 한다.
writing more books is what I personally keep coming back to ~ as a writer.
② 좋은 글을 쓰려면 먼저 글을 많이 읽어야 한다.
글을 많이 읽으라는 내용은 없음
③ 자신의 경험을 글쓰기 소재로 적극 활용해야 한다.
경험을 활용한 글쓰기에 대해 말하지 않았음
④ 책을 홍보하기 위해 다양한 마케팅 수단을 마련해야 한다.
마케팅 수단 중 더 많은 책을 써야 한다는 것에 초점을 맞춘 글임
⑤ 작가별 전시에서 벗어나 새로운 도서 전시 방식을 시도해야 한다.
도서 전시 방식에 대한 언급은 없음

> **왜 정답?** [정답률 80%]

- 책이 잘 팔린 작가들은 모두 많은 책을 가지고 있음
- 글쓴이도 많은 마케팅 수단을 시도했으나, 계속 돌아가는 것이자 수입을
  증가시키는 가장 좋은 방법은 더 많은 책을 쓰는 것이라고 함

▶ 작가로 경험을 쌓고 성공을 하기 위해서는 더 많은 책을 써야 한다는 것이 필자의
주장이므로 정답은 ①이다.

> **왜 오답?**

② 글을 많이 읽어야 한다는 내용은 없었다.

③ 작가의 경험이 소개되어 있긴 해도 경험을 글쓰기 소재로 활용해야 한다는 내용은
없었다.

④ 글쓴이가 다양한 방법을 시도했으나 더 많은 책을 쓰는 것이 최고의 마케팅
수단이라 했으며, 다양한 수단을 활용해야 한다는 내용은 글의 초점이 아니다. [함정]

⑤ 도서 전시에 대한 언급은 없었다.

C 07 정답 ⑤ *중년의 결합 조직 부상 예방 방법

                              단수 주어
When you are middle-aged, / the risk of connective tissue
        단수 동사
injuries peaks / as decreased load tolerance combines / with
continued high activity levels. //
여러분이 중년이 되면 / 결합 조직 부상의 위험이 최고조에 달한다 / 감소된 하중을 견디는
힘이 결합하면서 / 계속된 높은 활동 수준과 //

The path of least resistance is to stop doing the things / that hurt
              (가장 무난한 방법)   명사적 용법(주격 보어)   주격 관계대명사
/ — avoid uncomfortable movements / and find easier forms of
exercise. //
가장 무난한 방법은 일들을 그만두는 것인데 / 아프게 하는 / 이를테면 불편한 움직임들을
피하며 / 더 쉬운 형태의 운동을 찾는 것이다 //
                                            명사절을 이끄는 관계대명사
However, that's the exact opposite / of what you should do. //
그러나 그것은 정확한 반대다 / 여러분이 해야 하는 것의 //

There is a path forward. // 앞으로 나아가는 길이 있다 //
                            동명사(involve의 목적어)   선행사
But it doesn't involve / following the typical pain management
advice / of rest, ice, and medicine, /
하지만 그것은 포함하지 않는데 / 전형적인 통증 관리 조언을 따르는 것을 / 휴식, 얼음찜질
및 의약품의 /

which multiple reviews have shown is not effective / for treating
계속적 용법의 관계대명사
age-related joint pain and dysfunction. //
다수의 비평은 이것이 효과적이지 않다는 것을 보여주었다 / 나이와 관련된 관절 통증과 기능
장애를 치료하는데 //

These methods do nothing more / than treat superficial
                              '~에 지나지 않는'
symptoms. //
이 방법들은 지나지 않는다 / 표면적인 증상을 치료하는 것에 //
                              명사적 용법(주격 보어)
The only practical solution is to strengthen your body / with
muscle training. // 단서 노화로 인해 약해진 신체를 위해서는 근육 운동이 필수적임
유일한 실질적인 해결책은 여러분의 신체를 강화하는 것이다 / 근육 훈련으로 //

Whether you've been training for a few years or a few decades,
/ or haven't ever stepped foot in the weight room, /
여러분이 몇 년이나 몇십 년 동안 운동을 해 왔든지 / 혹은 체력 단련실에 발을 디딘 적이 전혀
없든지 간에 /

it's not too late / to restore your body, build real strength, and
achieve your physical potential. //   병렬 구조
너무 늦지 않다 / 여러분의 몸을 회복하고, 실질적인 힘을 기르고 / 신체적인 잠재력을
실현하는 것은 //

- middle-aged ⓐ 중년의 • connective tissue 결합 조직
- peak ⓥ 절정에 달하다 • load tolerance 내하중(견딜 수 있는 무게)
- typical ⓐ 전형적인 • dysfunction ⓝ 기능 장애
- superficial ⓐ 피상적인 • weight room 체력 단련실
- restore ⓥ 회복시키다

여러분이 중년이 되면 감소된 하중을 견디는 힘이 계속된 높은 활동 수준과 결합하면서 결합 조직 부상의 위험이 최고조에 달한다. 가장 무난한 방법은 아프게 하는 일들을 그만두는 것인데 이를테면 불편한 움직임들을 피하며 더 쉬운 형태의 운동을 찾는 것이다. 그러나 그것은 여러분이 해야 하는 것의 정확한 반대다. 앞으로 나아가는 길이 있다. 하지만 그것은 휴식, 얼음찜질 및 의약품의 전형적인 통증 관리 조언을 따르는 것을 포함하지 않는데, 다수의 비평은 이것이 나이와 관련된 관절 통증과 기능 장애를 치료하는데 효과적이지 않다는 것을 보여 주었다. 이 방법들은 표면적인 증상을 치료하는 것에 지나지 않는다. 유일한 실질적인 해결책은 근육 훈련으로 여러분의 신체를 강화하는 것이다. 여러분이 몇 년이나 몇십 년 동안 운동을 해 왔든지 혹은 체력 단련실에 발을 디딘 적이 전혀 없든지 간에 여러분의 몸을 회복하고, 실질적인 힘을 기르고, 신체적인 잠재력을 실현하는 것은 너무 늦지 않다.

다음 글에서 필자가 주장하는 바로 가장 적절한 것은?

① 관절의 노화를 늦추기 위해 적절한 체중을 유지해야 한다. 체중과 관련 없음
② 근육을 강화하기 위해 다양한 강도의 운동을 병행해야 한다. 다양한 강도의 운동을 병행하자는 내용은 아님
③ 중년층은 근 손실 예방을 위해 식단을 철저히 관리해야 한다. 식단 관리를 주장하는 것이 아님
④ 노화와 관련된 관절 질환에는 치료보다 예방이 우선되어야 한다. 근육 훈련이 중요함
⑤ 중년에는 통증이 따르더라도 근력 운동으로 신체를 강화해야 한다. 노화가 옴에 따라 관절 통증을 느끼고 운동할 때 불편함을 느끼더라도 근력 운동은 해야함

오 정답? [정답률 85%]

- 중년이 되면 부상의 위험이 늘고 불편함이 느껴져서 쉬운 움직임 형태의 운동을 찾게 됨
- 휴식, 얼음찜질 및 의약품의 전형적인 통증 관리는 표면적인 치료임
- 유일한 실질적인 해결책은 근육 훈련임 **단서**

➡ 노화로 인해 약해진 신체를 단련하고 부상을 방지하기 위해서는 근육 훈련을 통한 신체 강화가 필수적이라는 내용의 글이다.
▶ 따라서 정답은 ⑤이다.

오 오답?

① 노화가 오면서 하중을 견디는 힘이 감소된다고 했으나 적절한 체중은 언급되지 않았다.
② 근력 강화를 위해 운동을 해야 하지만 다양한 강도로 해야 한다는 내용은 적절하지 않다. 함정
③ 철저한 식단 관리를 강조하는 것이 아니다.
④ 관절 질환의 치료가 표면적인 효과만 가지고 오기 때문에 운동을 해야 한다.

C 08 정답 ② ＊성인 학습자를 가르치는 교사의 역할

By definition, / adult learners have a self-concept / of being in charge of their own lives /
당연히 / 성인 학습자는 자아 개념을 가지고 있다 / 자기 자신의 삶을 책임진다는 /

and have a need / to be seen and treated / as being capable of taking responsibility [형용사적 용법] for their own learning. //
그리고 욕구를 가지고 있다 / 여겨지고 대우받고자 하는 / 책임을 질 수 있다고 / 자기 자신의 학습에 //

As such, / learners need to be given / the freedom and autonomy / to assume responsibility [형용사적 용법] for their own choices /
이처럼 / 학습자에게 주어져야 한다 / 자유와 자율성이 / 자기 자신의 선택을 책임져야 할 /

and to be proactive / in making decisions / that contribute to [주격 관계대명사(선행사: decisions)] their educational experiences. // [병렬 구조]
그리고 주도적이어야 한다 / 결정을 내릴 때 / 자신의 교육 경험에 기여하는 //

Rather than perform the role / of the "sage on the stage," / in working with adult learners, / the instructor's role should be the "guide on the side" /
역할을 수행하기보다는 / '강단 위의 현자'라는 / 성인 학습자를 가르칠 때 / 교사의 역할은 '옆에서의 안내자'이어야 한다 /

— a facilitator of learning, / and a coach or mentor / who works [주격 관계대명사(선행사: a coach or mentor)] alongside their learners / to promote achievement and academic [부사적 용법(목적)] success. // **단서** 성인 학습자를 가르칠 때 교사는 학습의 촉진자나 코치, 멘토여야 함 언급
학습의 촉진자 / 그리고 코치 또는 멘토 / 그들의 학습자와 함께 하는 / 성취와 학업적 성공을 촉진하기 위해 //

The facilitator role extends beyond course delivery, / and includes the broader pedagogical tasks / that will support [주격 관계대명사(선행사: tasks)] learners / on their growth /
촉진자의 역할은 강의 전달을 넘어 확장된다 / 그리고 더 폭넓은 교육적 과제를 포함한다 / 학습자를 지원할 / 그들의 성장에 대해 /

such as helping them effectively manage their time; / fostering engagement; / assigning meaningful and [병렬 구조] relevant learning activities; / and so on. //
그들(학습자)의 시간을 효과적으로 관리하도록 그들을 돕고 / 참여를 촉진하고 / 유의미하고 관련성이 있는 학습활동을 부여하는 / 등과 같이 //

- by definition 당연히, 말 그대로 • self-concept ⓝ 자아 개념
- responsibility ⓝ 책임 • as such 이처럼, 이와 같이
- assume ⓥ (권력·책임을) 맡다 • proactive ⓐ 주도적인
- contribute to ~에 기여하다 • facilitator ⓝ 촉진자
- alongside ⒫rep ~와 함께, ~와 동시에 • promote ⓥ 촉진하다
- achievement ⓝ 성취 • extend ⓥ 확장하다 • course ⓝ 강의
- growth ⓝ 성장 • foster ⓥ 촉진하다, 기르다
- engagement ⓝ 참여 • assign ⓥ 부여하다
- relevant ⓐ 관련 있는, 적절한

당연히, 성인 학습자는 자기 자신의 삶을 책임진다는 자아 개념을 가지고 있으며, 자기 자신의 학습에 책임을 질 수 있다고 여겨지고 대우받고자 하는 욕구를 가지고 있다. 이처럼 학습자에게 자기 자신의 선택을 책임져야 할 자유와 자율성이 주어져야 하고, (학습자는) 자신의 교육 경험에 기여하는 결정을 내릴 때 주도적일 필요가 있다. 성인 학습자를 가르칠 때 '강단 위의 현자' 역할을 수행하기보다는 교사의 역할은 '옆에서의 안내자' — 학습의 촉진자이자 성취와 학업적 성공을 촉진하기 위해 그들의 학습자와 함께 하는 코치 또는 멘토 — 이어야 한다. 촉진자의 역할은 강의 전달을 넘어 확장되고 그들(학습자)의 시간을 효과적으로 관리하도록 그들을 돕고, 참여를 촉진하고, 유의미하고 관련성이 있는 학습활동을 부여하는 등과 같이 그들의 성장에 대해 학습자를 지원할 더 폭넓은 교육적 과제를 포함한다.

다음 글에서 필자가 주장하는 바로 가장 적절한 것은?

① 학생들의 성취도를 측정할 수 있는 객관적인 평가 도구를 개발해야 한다. 학생들의 성취도를 측정할 수 있는 객관적 평가 도구 개발에 대한 언급은 없음
② 성인 학습자를 가르치는 교사는 촉진자의 역할을 수행해야 한다. 성인 학습자를 가르치는 교사는 촉진자의 역할을 수행해야 한다는 것이 필자의 주장임
③ 교사는 지식 전달을 최우선으로 하여 수업을 진행해야 한다. 교사는 지식 전달을 넘어 확장된 역할을 해야 한다고 함
④ 교사는 학생들의 연령에 상관없이 시각 자료를 활용해야 한다. 시각 자료 활용에 대한 언급은 없음
⑤ 성인 학습자는 새로운 것을 배울 때 더 많은 시간을 투자해야 한다. 성인 학습자의 시간 투자에 대한 언급은 없음

오 정답? [정답률 91%]

- 성인 학습자에게는 자신의 학습에 책임을 질 수 있는 자유와 자율성이 주어져야 함
- 교사는 성인 학습자의 학습을 촉진하는 역할을 수행해야 함

▶ 교사가 성인 학습자를 가르칠 때는 학습의 촉진자로서의 역할을 해야 한다는 것이 필자의 주장이므로 정답은 ②이다.

오 오답?

① 학생들의 성취도 측정을 위한 객관적 평가 도구 개발에 대한 언급은 없다.
③ 교사는 지식 전달을 넘어 확장된 역할(촉진자로서의 역할)을 해야 한다는 것이 필자의 주장이다. 함정
④ 시각 자료 활용에 대한 언급은 없다.
⑤ 성인 학습자가 새로운 것을 배울 때 더 많은 시간을 투자해야 한다는 언급은 없다.

C 09 정답 ① *과학자의 이미지 개선에 있어 대중문화의 역할

= new ideas 앞에 those를 선행사로 하는 주격 관계대명사와 be동사가 생략됨
New ideas, / such as those / inspired by scientific developments, / are often aired and critiqued / in our popular culture /
새로운 아이디어는 / ~한 것들과 같은 / 과학 발전에 영감을 받은 / 자주 방송되고 비판되는데 / 우리의 대중문화에서 /

앞에 목적격 관계대명사가 생략됨
as part of a healthy process of public debate, / and scientists sometimes deserve the criticism / they get. //
건전한 공개 토론 과정의 일부로 / 과학자들은 때로 비판을 받는 것이 마땅하다 / 자신들이 받는 //

단서1 과학자의 이미지를 개선하면 과학의 대중화가 크게 증진될 것임
But the popularization of science / would be greatly enhanced / by improving / the widespread images of the scientist. //
그러나 과학의 대중화는 / 크게 증진될 것이다 / 개선함으로써 / 널리 퍼진 과학자의 이미지를 //

주어
Part of the problem may be / that the majority of the people / who are most likely to write / novels, plays, and film scripts / were educated / in the humanities, / not in the sciences. //
그 문제의 일부는 ~일 수도 있다 / 사람들의 대다수가 / 쓸 가능성이 가장 높은 / 소설, 희곡, 그리고 영화 대본을 / 교육받았다는 것 / 인문학 분야에서 / 과학에서가 아니라 //

선행사
Furthermore, / the few scientists-turned-writers have used / their scientific training / as the source material for thrillers / that further damage / the image of science and scientists. //
주격 관계대명사
더욱이 / 작가로 전업한 몇 안 되는 과학자가 사용해왔다 / 자신들의 과학 교육을 / 스릴러물의 원자료로 / 더욱 해치는 / 과학과 과학자의 이미지를 //

We need more screenplays and novels / that present scientists / in a positive light. // 단서2 과학자를 긍정적으로 묘사하는 매체가 더 많아야 함
우리는 더 많은 영화 대본과 소설이 필요하다 / 과학자를 보여주는 / 긍정적인 관점에서 //

In our contemporary world, / television and film are particularly influential media, / and it is likely / that the introduction of more scientist-heroes would help / to make science more attractive. //
목적어로 to부정사와 원형부정사를 취하는 help
우리의 현대 세계에서 / 텔레비전과 영화는 특히 영향력 있는 매체여서 / ~할 것이다 / 더 많은 과학자 영웅들의 도입이 도움이 될 / 과학을 더 매력 있게 만드는 데 //

- inspire ⓥ 영감을 주다 · development ⓝ 발달 · air ⓥ 방송하다
- critique ⓥ 비평하다 · popular culture 대중문화
- healthy ⓐ 건전한, 건강한 · process ⓝ 과정, 절차
- public ⓐ 공개적인 · debate ⓝ 토론
- deserve ⓥ (보수·도움·벌 등을) 받아야 마땅하다 · criticism ⓝ 비판
- popularization ⓝ 대중화 · greatly ⓐ 크게
- enhance ⓥ 향상시키다 · improve ⓥ 개선하다
- widespread ⓐ 널리 퍼진 · majority ⓝ (특정 집단 내의) 대다수
- novel ⓝ 소설 · play ⓝ 희곡, 연극 · script ⓝ 대본
- humanities ⓝ 인문학 · furthermore ⓐ 뿐만 아니라
- few ⓐ (수가) 많지 않은 · source material 원자료
- further ⓐ 더, 게다가 · screenplay ⓝ 영화 대본
- present ⓥ 보여주다, 제시하다 · contemporary ⓐ 동시대의, 현대의
- particularly ⓐ 특히 · influential ⓐ 영향력 있는
- introduction ⓝ 도입, 전래 · attractive ⓐ 매력적인

과학 발전에 영감을 받은 아이디어와 같은 새로운 아이디어는 건전한 공개 토론 과정의 일부로 우리의 대중문화에서 자주 방송되고 비판되는데, 과학자들은 때로 자신들이 받는 비판을 받는 것이 마땅하다. 그러나 널리 퍼진 과학자의 이미지를 개선함으로써 과학의 대중화는 크게 증진될 것이다. 그 문제의 일부는 소설, 희곡, 그리고 영화 대본을 쓸 가능성이 가장 높은 사람들의 대다수가 과학에서가 아니라 인문학 분야에서 교육받았다는 것일 수도 있다. 더욱이 작가로 전업한 몇 안 되는 과학자가 자신들이 받은 과학 교육을 과학과 과학자의 이미지를 더욱 해치는 스릴러물의 원자료로 사용해왔다. 우리는 긍정적인 관점에서 과학자를 보여주는 더 많은 영화 대본과 소설이 필요하다. 우리의 현대 세계에서 텔레비전과 영화는 특히 영향력 있는 매체여서, 더 많은 과학자 영웅들의 도입이 과학을 더 매력 있게 만드는 데 도움이 될 것이다.

다음 글에서 필자가 주장하는 바로 가장 적절한 것은?

① 과학의 대중화를 위해 여러 매체에서 과학자를 긍정적으로 묘사해야 한다.
과학자의 이미지를 개선하면 과학의 대중화가 증진될 것임
② 작가로 전업한 과학자는 전공 지식을 작품에 사실적으로 반영해야 한다.
③ 공상 과학 작가로 성공하려면 과학과 인문학을 깊이 이해해야 한다.
과학이 아니라 인문학 분야에서 교육받았다는 것이 문제임
④ 과학의 저변 확대를 위해 영화 주인공으로 과학자가 등장해야 한다.
긍정적으로 묘사해야 한다는 것이 핵심임
⑤ 과학 정책 논의에 과학자뿐만 아니라 인문학도 참여해야 한다.
humanities로 만든 오답

왜 정답? [정답률 89%] 첫 문장은 과학자들이 때로 비판 받는 것이 마땅하다는 내용 꿀팁

역접의 연결어 But으로 시작한 두 번째 문장부터 과학자 이미지를 개선하면 과학의 대중화가 크게 증진될 것이고, 긍정적인 관점에서 과학자를 보여주는 더 많은 매체가 필요하다는 내용이 이어지는 것으로 보아 필자의 주장은 ①이다.

왜 오답?

② scientists-turned-writers가 언급된 것으로 만든 오답이다. 작가로 전업한 과학자들이 자신들의 과학적 지식으로 과학과 과학자의 이미지를 해치는 스릴러물을 만들어 낸다는 문제점을 지적했다.

③, ⑤ 대중 매체의 작가들이 과학이 아니라 인문학 교육을 받았다는 것이 문제의 일부라고 했다.

④ 단순히 과학자를 주인공으로 만들어야 한다는 것이 아니라, 과학자를 영웅으로 묘사해야 한다는 것이다.

C 10 정답 ① *교육의 바람직한 방법

선행사 관계부사
We live in a time / when everyone seems to be looking / for quick and sure solutions. //
우리는 시대에 살고 있다 / 모든 이가 찾고 있는 듯한 / 빠르고 확실한 해결책을 //

선행사
Computer companies have even begun / to advertise ways / in which computers can replace parents. //
관계부사 how를 대신하는 '전치사+관계대명사'
컴퓨터 회사들은 심지어 시작했다 / 방법을 광고하기를 / 컴퓨터가 부모를 대신할 수 있는 //

They are too late / — television has already done that. //
그들은 너무 늦었는데 / 텔레비전이 이미 그것을 해버렸다 //

Seriously, however, / in every branch of education, / including moral education, / 단서1 특정한 방식을 통해 아이들을 교육할 수 있다고 생각하는 것은 실수임
하지만 진지하게 / 교육의 모든 분야에서 / 도덕 교육을 포함한 /

we make a mistake / when we suppose / that a particular batch of content / or a particular teaching method / or a particular configuration of students and space / will accomplish our ends. //
or로 연결된 세 개의 주어
우리는 실수를 범한다 / 우리가 가정할 때 / 특정 내용 묶음이나 / 특정 교육 방법 / 또는 학생과 공간의 특정 배치가 / 우리의 목적을 성취할 것이라고 //

주격 보어로 쓰인 비교급 형용사가 both A and B(A와 B 둘 다)로 연결됨
The answer / is both harder and simpler. // 단서2 아이들과 생활하고 이야기 나누는 등의 일상을 통해 그들을 교육해야 함
정답은 / 더 어렵고 또한 더 단순하다 /

We, parents and teachers, have to live / with our children, / talk to them, / listen to them, / enjoy their company, /
우리, 부모와 교사는, 생활해야 하고 / 우리의 아이들과 / 그들과 이야기를 나눠야 하고 / 그들의 말에 귀 기울여야 하며 / 그들과 함께하는 것을 즐겨야 하고 /

병렬 구조
and show them / by what we do / and how we talk /
그들에게 보여주어야 한다 / 우리가 하는 것을 통해 / 그리고 우리가 말하는 방식을 통해 /

가주어   진주어   병렬 구조
that it is possible / to live / appreciatively or, at least, nonviolently / with most other people. //
~이 가능하다는 것을 / 사는 것이 / 감사하며 또는 최소한 비폭력적으로 / 대부분의 다른 사람들과 //

- solution ⓝ 해결책 · replace ⓥ 대신[대체]하다
- seriously ⓐ 진지하게, 심(각)하게
- branch ⓝ (지식의) 분야, 나뭇가지, 분점 · moral ⓐ 도덕과 관련된
- suppose ⓥ 가정하다 · batch ⓝ 묶음, 무리 · method ⓝ 방법
- configuration ⓝ 배치, 배열 · accomplish ⓥ 성취하다
- end ⓝ 목적 · company ⓝ 함께 있음
- appreciatively ⓐ 고마워하며 · nonviolently ⓐ 비폭력적으로

우리는 모든 이가 빠르고 확실한 해결책을 찾고 있는 듯한 시대에 살고 있다. 컴퓨터 회사들은 심지어 컴퓨터가 부모를 대신할 수 있는 방법을 광고하기 시작했다. 그들은 너무 늦었는데, 텔레비전이 이미 그것을 해버렸다. 하지만 진지하게, 도덕 교육을 포함한 교육의 모든 분야에서, 우리는 우리가 특정한 내용 묶음이나 특정 교육 방법 또는 학생과 공간의 특정 배치가 우리의 목적을 성취할 것이라고 가정할 때 실수를 범한다.

정답은 더 어렵고 또한 더 단순하다. 우리, 부모와 교사는, 우리의 아이들과 생활하고, 그들과 이야기를 나누고, 그들의 말에 귀 기울이며, 그들과 함께하는 것을 즐기고, 우리가 하는 것과 말하는 방식을 통해 그들에게 감사하며 살거나 최소한 대부분의 다른 사람들과 비폭력적으로 사는 것이 가능하다는 것을 보여주어야 한다.

다음 글에서 필자가 주장하는 바로 가장 적절한 것은?

① 교육은 일상에서 아이들과의 상호 작용을 통해 이루어져야 한다.
　　　　　　　　　　　　특정한 방식이 아이들을 교육할 것이라는 가정은 실수임
② 도덕 교육을 강화하여 타인을 배려하는 공동체 의식을 높여야 한다.
　　　　　　　　　　어떻게 교육해야 하는지를 주장하는 글임
③ 텔레비전의 부정적 영향을 줄이려는 사회적 노력이 있어야 한다.
　　television이 언급된 것으로 만든 오답
④ 다양한 매체를 활용하여 학교와 가정 교육의 한계를 보완해야 한다.
　　　　　　　　　다양한 매체를 활용해야 한다는 언급은 없음
⑤ 아이들의 온라인 예절 교육을 위해 적절한 콘텐츠를 개발해야 한다.
　　　　　　　　적절한 콘텐츠 개발이 필요하다는 것이 아님

왜 정답? [정답률 89%]

however 이후의 내용을 보면, 아이들을 교육하는 우리의 목적이 어떤 특별한 방법을 통해 성취될 것이라는 가정은 실수라고 했다. 이후로 우리는 아이들과 생활하고, 대화하며, 그들의 말에 귀 기울여야 하고, 우리가 하는 것과 말하는 방식을 통해 그들을 교육해야 한다는 내용이 이어지는데, 이는 어떤 특정한 수단으로 아이들을 교육하는 것이 아니라 일상에서 그들과 함께함으로써 그들을 교육해야 한다는 것이므로 정답은 **①**이다.

왜 오답?

② moral education이 언급된 것으로 만든 오답이다. 도덕 교육을 포함한 교육의 모든 분야에 대해 이야기하는 글이다.

③ television이 언급되긴 했지만, 텔레비전이 아이들에게 부정적인 영향을 미친다거나 그러한 부정적인 영향을 줄여야 한다는 것은 아니다.

④ 일상에서 아이들을 교육해야 한다는 것이지, 다양한 매체를 이용해야 한다는 것이 아니다.

⑤ 아이들에게 온라인 예절 교육이 필요하다거나 그러한 교육을 위해 적절한 콘텐츠를 개발해야 한다는 언급은 없다.

C 11 정답 ③ ＊기업이 소셜 미디어를 활용할 때 주의할 점

　　주어　　　　　　　　　　　　　앞에 주격 관계대명사와 be동사가 생략됨
One of the most common mistakes / made by organizations /
　　　　　　　　　　　　부사절 접속사(시간)
when they first consider / experimenting with social media /
가장 일반적인 실수 중 하나는 / 조직에 의해 저질러지는 / 그것들이 처음 고려할 때 / 소셜 미디어로 실험하는 것을 /
　　　　　주격 보어절 접속사　　　**단서1** 조직의 사업 목표에 충분히 중점을 두지 않는 것은 실수임
is / that they focus too much / on social media tools and platforms
동사
/ and not enough on their business objectives. //
~이다 / 그것들이 너무 지나치게 중점을 두고 / 소셜 미디어 도구와 플랫폼에 / 조직 자체의 사업 목표에는 충분히 중점을 두지 않는 것 //

The reality of success / in the social web for businesses / is / that
　　　　명사구 주어　　　　　　　　　　　　　　단수 동사
creating a social media program begins /
성공의 실제는 / 기업을 위한 소셜 웹에서의 / ~이다 / 소셜 미디어 프로그램을 고안하는 것이 시작된다는 것 /

not with insight / into the latest social media tools and channels
　　　　　　　　not A but B(A가 아니라 B인)로 with가 이끄는 전치사구가 연결됨
/ but with a thorough understanding / of the organization's own
goals and objectives. // **단서2** 소셜 웹에 성공하려면 조직의 목적, 목표에 대한 철저한 이해가 필요함
통찰력과 더불어서가 아니라 / 최신 소셜 미디어 도구와 채널에 대한 / 철저한 이해와 더불어 / 조직 자체의 목적과 목표에 대한 //

A social media program / is not merely the fulfillment of a vague
need / to manage a "presence" / on popular social networks /
　　　형용사적 용법(need 수식)
because "everyone else is doing it." //
소셜 미디어 프로그램은 / 그저 막연한 필요의 이행이 아니다 / '존재'를 관리할 / 인기 소셜 네트워크상에서 / '다른 모든 이가 하고 있기' 때문에 //

　　　명사구 주어　　　　　　　　단수 동사
"Being in social media" / serves no purpose in and of itself. //
'소셜 미디어에 있다는 것'은 / 그 자체로는 아무 쓸모도 없다 //　　'그것 자체는'

In order to serve any purpose at all, / a social media presence
　　　　　　　　　　　　　　　　'조금이라도'
/ must either solve a problem / for the organization and its
┌ either A or B(A 혹은 B)로 must에 이어지는 동사구가 연결됨
customers
조금이라도 어떤 목적에 도움이 되려면 / 소셜 미디어상의 존재는 / 문제를 해결하거나 / 조직과 조직의 고객을 위해
└or result in an improvement of some sort / (preferably a
measurable one). //
어떤 종류의 개선이라는 결과를 가져와야 한다 / (될 수 있으면 측정 가능한 결과) //

In all things, / purpose drives success. //
　　　　주어　　　　동사　　목적어
어떤 일이든 / 목적이 성공을 이끌어낸다 //

The world of social media / is no different. //
소셜 미디어의 세계도 / 다르지 않다 //

- common ⓐ 흔한, 공동의, 보통의　　· consider ⓥ 고려하다, 생각하다
- experiment ⓥ 실험하다, 시험 삼아 해 보다　　· objective ⓝ 목적, 목표
- reality ⓝ 현실, 사실, 실체　　· insight ⓝ 통찰력, 식견, 이해
- latest ⓐ 최신(식)의, 최근의　　· thorough ⓐ 철저한, 완전한
- merely ⓐⓓ 그저, 단지　　· fulfillment ⓝ (의무·직무 등의) 이행, 실천
- vague ⓐ (기억 등이) 희미한, 모호한
- presence ⓝ (특정한 곳에) 있음, 존재(함)
- serve ⓥ 도움이 되다, (상품·서비스를) 제공하다
- improvement ⓝ 향상, 개선　　· sort ⓝ 종류, 유형, 분류
- preferably ⓐⓓ 되도록이면, 가급적이면　　· measurable ⓐ 측정할 수 있는
- drive ⓥ (특정한 행동을 하도록) 만들다, 추진하다

조직이 소셜 미디어로 실험하는 것을 처음 고려할 때 범하는 가장 일반적인 실수 중 하나는 너무 지나치게 소셜 미디어 도구와 플랫폼에 중점을 두고 조직 자체의 사업 목표에는 충분히 중점을 두지 않는 것이다. 기업을 위한 소셜 웹에서의 성공의 실제는 소셜 미디어 프로그램을 고안하는 것이 최신 소셜 미디어 도구와 채널에 대한 통찰력이 아니라 조직 자체의 목적과 목표에 대한 철저한 이해와 더불어 시작된다는 것이다. 소셜 미디어 프로그램은 그저 '다른 모든 이가 하고 있기' 때문에 인기 소셜 네트워크상에서 '존재'를 관리해야 할 막연한 필요를 이행하는 것이 아니다. '소셜 미디어에 있다는 것'은 그 자체로는 아무 쓸모도 없다. 조금이라도 어떤 쓸모가 있으려면, 소셜 미디어상의 존재는 조직과 조직의 고객을 위해 문제를 해결하거나 어떤 종류의 개선이라는 결과(될 수 있으면 측정 가능한 결과)를 가져와야 한다. 어떤 일이든, 목적이 성공을 이끌어낸다. 소셜 미디어의 세계도 다르지 않다.

다음 글에서 필자가 주장하는 바로 가장 적절한 것은?

① 기업 이미지에 부합하는 소셜 미디어를 직접 개발하여 운영해야 한다.
　　　　　　　　　기업 이미지나 직접적인 개발, 운영에 대한 언급은 없음
② 기업은 사회적 가치와 요구를 반영하여 사업 목표를 수립해야 한다.
　　　　　　　　　　　사업 목표의 수립 방법을 설명한 것이 아님
③ 기업은 소셜 미디어를 활용할 때 사업 목표를 토대로 해야 한다.
　　　　　　　　　기업의 사업 목표에 충분히 중점을 두지 않는 것은 실수임
④ 소셜 미디어로 제품을 홍보할 때는 구체적인 정보를 제공해야 한다.
　　　　　　　　제품 홍보 방법에 대한 내용이 아님
⑤ 소비자의 의견을 수렴하기 위해 소셜 미디어를 적극 활용해야 한다.
　　　　　　　　소셜 미디어의 활용 목적은 언급되지 않음

왜 정답? [정답률 90%]　┌ '조직, 단체, 기구'를 의미하는 organizations를 '기업'으로 해석했음 **꿀팁**

기업이 소셜 미디어를 이용하는 것을 처음 고려할 때 저지르는 가장 일반적인 실수 중 하나가 조직 자체의 사업 목표에 충분히 중점을 두지 않는 것이라면서, 소셜 웹에서의 기업의 성공은 조직 자체의 목적과 목표에 대한 철저한 이해와 더불어 시작된다고 했으므로 필자는 **③**을 주장하는 것이다.

왜 오답?

① 기업의 이미지에 부합하는 소셜 미디어를 이용해야 한다거나, 그러한 소셜 미디어를 직접 개발하고 운영해야 한다는 언급은 없다.

② 소셜 미디어를 이용할 때 사업 목표를 고려해야 한다는 것이지, 사업 목표를 어떻게 수립해야 하는지를 설명한 것이 아니다.

④, ⑤ '소셜 미디어를 통한 제품 홍보 방법'이나 '소셜 미디어를 활용하는 목적'처럼 구체적이고 실질적인 소재를 다루는 글이 아니다. 소셜 미디어의 활용은 사업 목표에 부합해야 하고, 그 목표에 맞게 어떤 문제를 해결하거나 개선하는 결과를 가져와야 한다는, 다소 추상적인 내용의 글이다.

C 12 정답 ① *영역을 골라서 전문성을 키워라

동명사구 주어 / 단수 동사
Developing expertise carries / costs of its own. //
전문성을 개발하는 것은 수반한다 / 그 자체의 비용을 //

병렬 구조(전치사 like의 목적어로 쓰인 동명사)
We can become experts / in some areas, / like speaking a language or knowing our favorite foods, / simply by living our lives, /
전치사 by의 목적어(동명사)
우리는 전문가가 될 수 있다 / 어떤 분야에서는 / 언어를 말하거나 우리가 가장 좋아하는 음식을 아는 것과 같은 / 그냥 삶을 살아감으로써 /

but in many other domains / expertise requires / considerable training and effort. //
주어 / 동사 / 목적어
그러나 다른 많은 분야에서는 / 전문성이 요구한다 / 상당한 훈련과 노력을 //

What's more, / expertise is domain specific. //
게다가 / 전문성은 특정한 영역에만 국한된다 //

주어(선행사) 목적격 관계대명사
The expertise / that we work hard to acquire / in one domain / will carry over only imperfectly / to related ones, / and not at all to unrelated ones. //
동사
전문성은 / 우리가 얻기 위해 열심히 노력하는 / 한 영역에서 / 오직 불완전하게 이어질 뿐이다 / 관련 영역으로 그리고 관련이 없는 영역으로는 전혀 (이어지지 않을 것이다) //

양보의 부사절을 이끌어 '~이지만'
In the end, / as much as we may want to become experts / on everything / in our lives, / there simply isn't enough time / to do so. //
형용사적 용법(time 수식)
결국 / 우리가 전문가가 되기를 원한다고 해도 / 모든 것에서 / 우리 삶의 / 그저 충분한 시간이 없다 / 그렇게 할 //

Even in areas / where we could, / it won't necessarily be worth the effort. // **단서1** 모든 것에서 전문가가 될 수 있는 분야가 있더라도 그런 노력을 기울일 가치가 반드시 있는 것은 아님
분야에서조차도 / 우리가 그렇게 할 수 있는 / 노력을 기울일 가치가 반드시 있는 것은 아닐 것이다 /

진주어절 접속사
It's clear / that we should concentrate our own expertise / on those domains of choice / that are most common and/or important / to our lives, /
가주어
~은 분명하다 / 우리가 우리의 전문성을 집중해야만 하는 것은 / 선택 영역에 / 가장 흔하고/흔하거나 중요한 / 우리의 삶에 / **단서2** 우리 삶에 중요한 특정 영역을 선택해서 그것에 전문성을 집중해야 함
= domains
and those we actively enjoy / learning about and choosing from. //
그리고 우리가 적극적으로 즐기는 것에 / 배우고 선택하는 것을 //

- expertise ⓝ 전문 지식[기술] · domain ⓝ (지식·활동 등의) 영역[분야]
- considerable ⓐ 많은, 상당한 · effort ⓝ 수고, 애
- specific ⓐ 특정한, 구체적인 · acquire ⓥ 습득하다, 얻다
- imperfectly ⓐⓓ 불완전하게, 불충분하게
- worth ⓐ ~의 가치가 있는, ~할 가치가 있는 · clear ⓐ 분명한, 확실한
- concentrate ⓥ 집중하다, 전념하다, 집중시키다
- actively ⓐⓓ 활발히, 적극적으로

전문성을 개발하는 것은 그 자체의 비용을 수반한다. 우리는 언어를 말하거나 우리가 가장 좋아하는 음식을 아는 것과 같은 어떤 분야에서는 그냥 삶을 살아감으로써 전문가가 될 수 있지만, 다른 많은 분야에서는 전문성이 상당한 훈련과 노력을 요구한다. 게다가 전문성이란 특정한 영역에만 국한된다. 우리가 한 영역에서 얻기 위해 열심히 노력하는 전문성은 관련 영역으로 오직 불완전하게 이어질 뿐이며, 관련이 없는 영역으로는 전혀 이어지지 않을 것이다. 결국, 우리가 우리 삶의 모든 것에서 전문가가 되기를 원한다고 해도, 그저 그렇게 할 충분한 시간이 없다. 우리가 그렇게 할 수 있는 분야에서조차도, 노력을 기울일 가치가 반드시 있는 것은 아닐 것이다. 우리가 우리의 삶에 가장 흔하고/흔하거나 중요한 선택 영역과 우리가 배우고 선택하는 것을 적극적으로 즐기는 영역에 우리의 전문성을 집중해야만 하는 것은 분명하다.

다음 글에서 필자가 주장하는 바로 가장 적절한 것은?
① 자신에게 의미 있는 영역을 정해서 전문성을 키워야 한다.
선택 영역에 전문성을 집중해야 함
② 전문성 함양에는 타고난 재능보다 노력과 훈련이 중요하다.
재능과 노력을 비교한 것이 아님
③ 전문가가 되기 위해서는 다양한 분야에 관심을 가져야 한다.
특정 영역에서 전문성을 키우라는 주장임
④ 전문성을 기르기 위해서는 구체적인 계획과 실천이 필수적이다.
전문성을 기르는 방법을 설명한 것이 아님
⑤ 전문가는 일의 우선순위를 결정해서 업무를 수행해야 한다.
일의 우선순위의 중요성을 주장한 것이 아님

왜 정답? [정답률 88%] 모든 영역에서 전문성을 키울 수 있는 분야가 있더라도 굳이 그렇게 할 필요는 없다는 말임 **꿀팁**

전문성이 특정한 영역에만 국한된다고 한 이후로, 우리 삶의 모든 것에서 전문성을 키울 시간이 없고, 그렇게 할 수 있는 분야에서조차도 그러한 노력을 기울일 가치가 반드시 있지는 않을 거라고 했다. 삶에서 가장 흔하고/흔하거나 중요한 선택 영역, 자신이 배우고 선택하는 것을 적극적으로 즐기는 영역에 전문성을 집중해야 한다는 마지막 문장을 통해 필자의 주장이 ①임을 알 수 있다.

왜 오답?
② 전문성을 키우기 위해 상당한 훈련과 노력이 필요하다는 내용으로 만든 오답이다.
③ 다양한 영역이 아니라 특정 영역을 선택해서 전문성을 키우라는 주장이다.
④ 전문성을 어떻게 키우는지, 그 방법을 설명한 글이 아니다.
⑤ 일의 우선순위를 정해서 업무를 수행하는 것의 중요성을 이야기하는 것이 아니다.

C 13 정답 ① *논쟁 중에 믿음을 재조정할 필요성

동명사구 주어 / 단수 동사
There is no denying / that engaging in argument / carries certain significant risks. //
부인할 수 없다 / 논쟁에 참여하는 것이 / 어떤 중대한 위험을 수반한다는 것을 //

When we argue, / we exchange and examine reasons / with a view toward believing / what our best reasons say / we should believe; /
동명사 / 목적어(명사절)
우리가 논쟁할 때 / 우리는 논거를 교환하고 검토한다 / 믿으려고 / 우리의 최고의 논거가 말하는 것을 / 우리가 믿어야 한다고 / **단서1** 논쟁 중에 일어나는 일 ①: 우리의 논거가 부족하다는 것을 알게 됨

목적어절 접속사의 병렬 구조
sometimes we discover / that our current reasons fall short, / and that our beliefs are not well supported / after all. //
때로 우리는 알게 된다 / 우리의 현재 논거가 부족하다는 것과 / 우리의 믿음이 잘 뒷받침되지 않는다는 것을 / 결국 /

목적격 관계대명사
Or sometimes we discover / that a belief / that we had dismissed / as silly or obviously false / in fact enjoys / the support of highly compelling reasons. // **단서2** 논쟁 중에 일어나는 일 ②: 우리가 묵살했던 믿음이 매우 설득력 있는 논거를 갖는다는 것을 알게 됨
또는 이따금 우리는 알게 된다 / 믿음이 / 우리가 묵살했던 / 어리석다거나 명백히 틀렸다고 / 사실은 누린다는 것을 / 매우 설득력 있는 논거의 뒷받침을 //

복수 주어
On other occasions, / we discover / that the reasons / offered by those / with whom we disagree / measure up toe-to-toe / with our own reasons. //
복수 동사
다른 경우에 / 우리는 알게 된다 / 논거가 / 사람들에 의해 제시된 / 우리가 동의하지 않는 / 정면으로 맞붙어 겨룬다는 것을 / 우리 자신의 논거와 / **단서3** 이런 경우에는 우리의 믿음을 조정해야 함

In any of these situations, / an adjustment in our belief is called for; / we must change / what we believe, / or revise it, or replace it, / or suspend belief altogether. //
= what we believe
이런 상황 중 어느 경우에서든 / 우리의 믿음에 대한 조정이 요구된다 / 우리는 바꿔야 한다 / 우리가 믿는 것을 / 또는 그것을 수정하거나 대체하거나 / 믿음을 완전히 중지해야 한다 //

- deny ⓥ 부인[부정]하다 · engage in ~에 관여[참여]하다
- argument ⓝ 논쟁 · carry ⓥ (어떤 결과를) 수반하다
- significant ⓐ 중대한, 중요한 · argue ⓥ 언쟁을 하다, 다투다
- examine ⓥ 조사[검토]하다
- with a view toward ~하려고, ~할 목적으로
- fall short 부족하다, 모자라다 · dismiss ⓥ 묵살[일축]하다
- obviously ⓐⓓ 확실히, 분명히 · compelling ⓐ 설득력 있는
- measure up with ~과 겨루다 · toe-to-toe 정면으로 맞붙어
- adjustment ⓝ 조정 · call for ~을 요구하다
- revise ⓥ 변경[수정]하다 · suspend ⓥ 유예[중단]하다
- altogether ⓐⓓ 완전히, 전적으로

논쟁에 참여하는 것이 어떤 중대한 위험을 수반한다는 것을 부인할 수 없다. 논쟁할 때 우리는 우리가 믿어야 한다고 우리의 최고의 논거가 말하는 것을 믿으려고 논거를 교환하고 검토하는데, 때로 우리는 우리의 현재 논거가 부족하다는 것과 결국 우리의 믿음이 잘 뒷받침되지 않는다는 것을 알게 된다. 또는 이따금 우리가 어리석다거나 명백히 틀렸다고 묵살했던 믿음이 사실은

매우 설득력 있는 논거의 뒷받침을 누린다는 것을 알게 된다. 다른 경우에 우리와 의견이 다른 사람들이 제시한 논거가 우리 자신의 논거와 정면으로 맞붙어 겨룬다는 것을 알게 된다. 이런 상황 중 어느 경우에서든 우리의 믿음에 대한 조정이 요구되는데, 우리가 믿는 것을 바꾸거나 수정하거나 대체하거나 믿음을 완전히 중지해야 한다.

다음 글에서 필자가 주장하는 바로 가장 적절한 것은?

① 논쟁 중에 알게 된 바에 따라 자신의 믿음을 조정해야 한다.
　In any of these situations, an adjustment in our belief is called for
② 논쟁을 하기 전에 상대방의 주장을 면밀히 검토해야 한다.
　논쟁 중에 일어나는 일을 설명함
③ 논쟁에서 불리해지더라도 감정적으로 반응해서는 안 된다.
　감정적인 반응에 대한 언급은 없음
④ 의사 결정 시에는 충분한 시간을 갖고 신중하게 해야 한다.
　의사 결정 시 주의점에 대한 내용이 아님
⑤ 반대 의견을 제시할 때 상대의 논리적 허점을 공략해야 한다.
　내 믿음에 허점이 있다는 것을 알게 되는 경우임

＞오H 정답 ? ［정답률 91%］

· **논쟁할 때 일어나는 일: 1** 우리의 논거가 부족하고 우리의 믿음이 잘 뒷받침되지 않는다는 것을 알게 됨

　2 우리가 어리석거나 명백히 틀렸다고 묵살했던 믿음이 매우 설득력 있는 논거의 뒷받침을 누린다는 것을 알게 됨

· **이런 경우에 요구되는 일:** 우리의 믿음을 조정하는 것

　➡ 논쟁 중에 알게 되는 것을 반영하여 자신의 믿음을 조정해야 한다는 것이므로 정답은 ①이다.

＞오H 오답 ?

② '논쟁을 하기 전'이 아니라 '논쟁 중'에 알게 되는 것에 따라 자신의 믿음을 조정해야 한다는 주장이다.

③ 논쟁에서 감정적으로 반응하는 것의 문제점에 대해서는 이야기하지 않았다.

④ 의사 결정에 있어 충분한 시간과 신중함의 중요성을 강조하는 글이 아니다.

⑤ 논쟁을 하면서 내 의견에 논리적 허점이 발견되면 조정해야 한다는 내용이다.

C 14 정답 ④ ＊휴대전화와 떨어질 필요성

　　　　　　동명사구 주어　　　　　　　　　　　　　　　　단수 동사
Leaving behind technology / during intentional time alone / is essential / for the cognitive benefits, neurological repair, and spiritual clarity / that are the gifts of solitude. //
기술을 잊고 있는 것은 / 의도적인 혼자만의 시간에 / 필수적이다 / 인지적 이득, 신경학적 회복, 정신적 명료성을 위해 / 고독의 선물인 //

Multiple studies show / that anxiety is markedly reduced, / and we gain benefits / similar to solitude, /
여러 연구가 보여준다 / 불안감이 눈에 띄게 감소하고 / 우리가 이점을 얻는다는 것을 / 고독과 유사한 /

┌ not A but B(A가 아니라 B인)로 by가 이끄는 전치사구가 연결됨
not by simply turning our phones off / but by having them *not physically with us*. //
　　　　　단서 1 휴대전화와 물리적으로 떨어져 있어야
　　　　　　　　　고독과 유사한 이점을 얻음
단순히 우리의 휴대전화를 끔으로써가 아니라 / 그것을 '물리적으로 우리 곁에 있지 않게' 함으로써 //

　　　　단서 2 휴대전화를 접근하기 매우 불편한 곳에 보관할 것을 조언함
If a phone is essential for safety / during time alone, / then turn off alerts, / cover the screen / — just tape paper right over it — / and keep it somewhere / that is terribly inconvenient to access. //
　　　　　　　　　선행사　　　　주격 관계대명사
휴대전화가 안전을 위해 필수적이면 / 혼자 있는 시간에 / 알림을 끄고 / 화면을 가리고 / 그냥 종이를 바로 위에 붙여서 / 그것을 어딘가에 보관하라 / 접근하기 매우 불편한 //

I am always surprised / by how long it takes me to give up the impulse / to reach for my phone, / often for no reason at all, / other than to "just check." //
　　　　　　　　　형용사적 용법(the impulse 수식)
나는 항상 놀란다 / 내가 충동을 포기하는 데 얼마나 오랜 시간이 걸리는지에 / 나의 휴대전화에 손을 뻗고 싶은 / 종종 전혀 아무런 이유 없이 / '그냥 확인하는' 것 외에 //

Check what? //
무엇을 확인한다는 것인가 //

Always it is something / that can do without me / for the moment. //
　　　　　　　선행사　　주격 관계대명사
언제나 그것은 일이다 / 나 없이도 될 수 있는 / 지금 당장은 //

It is important / that we allow ourselves time / to free our minds / from even the possibility of constant connectivity, / to "normalize deactivation," /
가주어　　　진주어절 접속사　　　　　　　　　　형용사적 용법(time 수식)
~이 중요하다 / 우리가 우리 자신에게 시간을 허용하여 / 우리의 마음을 자유롭게 할 / 심지어 지속적 연결성의 가능성으로부터도 / '비활성화를 정상화하기' 위해 /

as herbalist Sophia Rose puts it, / allowing our overstimulated neuronal connections / to rest and reassemble. //
　　　　　　　　　　　put v. 표현[말]하다
식물학자 Sophia Rose가 표현하듯 / 우리의 과도하게 자극받은 신경 세포의 연결이 ~ 하도록 하는 것이 / 휴식을 취하고 다시 모이도록 //

- technology ⓝ 기술　　· intentional ⓐ 의도적인
- essential ⓐ 필수적인　　· neurological ⓐ 신경학적인
- repair ⓝ 회복　· spiritual ⓐ 정신적인　· clarity ⓝ 명료성
- solitude ⓝ 고독　· anxiety ⓝ 불안　· markedly 엔 두드러지게
- physically 엔 물리적으로　· access ⓥ 접근하다
- impulse ⓝ 충동　· free ⓥ 자유롭게 하다　· constant ⓐ 지속적인
- connectivity ⓝ 연결성　· normalize ⓥ 정상화하다
- deactivation ⓝ 비활성화　· reassemble ⓥ 다시 모으다

의도적인 혼자만의 시간에 기술을 잊고 있는 것은 고독의 선물인 인지적 이득, 신경학적 회복, 정신적 명료성을 위해 필수적이다. 여러 연구가 단순히 우리의 휴대전화를 끄는 것이 아니라 그것을 '물리적으로 우리 곁에 있지 않게' 함으로써, 불안감이 눈에 띄게 감소하고, 우리가 고독과 유사한 이점을 얻는다는 것을 보여준다. 혼자 있는 시간에 안전을 위해 휴대전화가 필수적이면, 알림을 끄고, 그냥 종이를 바로 위에 붙여서 화면을 가리고, 접근하기 매우 불편한 어딘가에 그것을 보관하라. 나는 '그냥 확인'하기 위한 것 외에 종종 전혀 아무런 이유 없이, 내가 나의 휴대전화에 손을 뻗고 싶은 충동을 포기하는 데 얼마나 오랜 시간이 걸리는지에 항상 놀란다. 무엇을 확인한다는 것인가? 언제나 그것은 지금 당장은 나 없이도 될 수 있는 일이다. 식물학자 Sophia Rose가 표현하듯 '비활성화를 정상화하기' 위해, 심지어 지속적 연결성의 가능성으로부터도 우리의 마음을 자유롭게 할 시간을 우리 자신에게 허용하여, 우리의 과도하게 자극받은 신경 세포의 연결이 휴식을 취하고 다시 모일 수 있도록 하는 것이 중요하다.

다음 글에서 필자가 주장하는 바로 가장 적절한 것은?

① 개인정보 유출을 막기 위해 휴대전화 보안을 강화해야 한다.
　개인정보나 보안에 관한 내용이 아님
② 물리적 고립 상황에 대응하기 위한 통신 기술을 개발해야 한다.
　for safety로 만든 오답
③ 업무에 집중하기 위해 근무 시간에 휴대전화 사용을 자제해야 한다.
　혼자만의 시간에 대한 내용임
④ 혼자 있는 시간의 이점을 얻으려면 휴대전화와 떨어져 있어야 한다.
　but by having them not physically with us
⑤ 고독감을 느끼지 않기 위해 사람들과 정서적인 연결을 지속해야 한다.
　고독의 선물에 대한 내용임

＞오H 정답 ? ［정답률 91%］

첫 문장: 의도적인 혼자만의 시간에 기술을 잊고 있는 것은 고독의 선물인 인지적 이득, 신경학적 회복, 정신적 명료성을 위해 필수적이다.
다음 문장: 여러 연구가 단순히 우리의 휴대전화를 끄는 것이 아니라 그것을 '물리적으로 우리 곁에 있지 않게' 함으로써, 불안감이 눈에 띄게 감소하고, 우리가 고독과 유사한 이점을 얻는다는 것을 보여준다.

➡ 첫 문장의 '기술을 잊는 것'에 대해 그다음 문장에서 구체적으로 설명한다.
고독의 선물을 얻는 데 필수적인 기술을 잊는 것: 단순히 휴대전화를 끄는 것이 아니라 휴대전화가 물리적으로 곁에 있지 않는 것
▶ 휴대전화가 곁에 없어야 고독과 유사한 이점을 얻는다는 것이므로 정답은 ④이다.

＞오H 오답 ?

① 휴대전화의 보안에 대해 주장하는 글이 아니다.
② 안전을 위해 휴대전화가 필수적인 상황이라면 휴대전화를 닿기 어려운 곳에 보관하라고 했다.
③ 의도적인 혼자만의 시간에 휴대전화를 멀리 떨어뜨려 놓으라는 주장이다.
⑤ 고독이 주는 선물을 얻기 위한 방법에 대해 이야기하는 글이다.

C 15 정답 ② ＊기업가 정신의 함양에 있어 대학의 역할

[prep] ~이 주어진다고 하면
Given the right conditions, / entrepreneurship can be fully woven / into the fabric of campus life, / greatly expanding its educational reach. //
분사구문(= while it greatly expands ~)
적절한 환경이 주어지면 / 기업가 정신은 완전히 짜일 수 있다 / 캠퍼스 생활의 구조로 / 그것의 교육적 범위를 크게 확장하면서 //

목적어 ─── 목적격 보어의 병렬 구조 ─ 동사
One study showed / that, within the workplace, / peers influence each other / to spot opportunities / and act on them: /
한 연구는 보여주었다 / 직장 내에서 / 동료들이 서로에게 영향을 미친다는 것을 / 기회를 포착하고 / 그에 따라 행동하도록 //

the+비교급, the+비교급: ~할수록 더욱 …한/하게
the more entrepreneurs you have / working together in an office, / the more likely their colleagues will catch the bug. //
당신이 더 많은 기업가들을 가질수록 / 사무실에서 함께 일하는 / 그들의 동료들이 병에 걸릴 가능성이 더 높다 //

주어
A study of Stanford University alumni found / that those / "who have varied work and educational backgrounds / are much more likely to start their own businesses /
동사   비교급
강조 부사
스탠퍼드대학교 동문들을 대상으로 한 연구는 발견했다 / 사람들이 / '다양한 업무 및 교육 배경을 가진 / 자기 자신의 사업을 시작할 가능성이 훨씬 더 높다는 것을 /

병렬 구조
than those / who have focused on one role at work / or concentrated in one subject at school." //
사람들보다 / 직장에서 한 가지 역할에 집중했거나 / 학교에서 한 가지 과목에 집중한' //

To cultivate an entrepreneurial culture, / colleges and universities need to offer students / a broad choice of experiences / and wide exposure to different ideas. // 단서 기업가적 문화를 배양하기 위해 대학이 학생들에게 알맞은 환경을 제공해야 함
기업가적 문화를 배양하기 위해 / 단과대학과 종합대학은 학생들에게 제공할 필요가 있다 / 폭넓은 경험의 선택과 / 다양한 아이디어에 대한 폭넓은 노출을 //

수단을 나타내는 「by+동명사」
They are uniquely positioned / to do this / by combining the resources / of academic programming, residential life, student groups, and alumni networks. //
그것들은 유일하게 자리 잡혀 있다 / 이것을 하도록 / 자원을 결합하여 / 학업 프로그램 기획, 주거 생활, 학생 집단, 동창회 네트워크라는 //

- **condition** ⓝ 상태, 환경, 상황 ・ **weave** ⓥ 짜다, 엮다
- **fabric** ⓝ 구조, 직물 ・ **expand** ⓥ 확장하다, 넓히다
- **reach** ⓝ 거리, 범위 ・ **peer** ⓝ 동료, 또래
- **spot** ⓥ 발견하다, 찾다, 알아채다
- **colleague** ⓝ (같은 직장이나 직종에 종사하는) 동료
- **catch the bug** 병에 걸리다 ・ **varied** ⓐ 다양한
- **concentrate** ⓥ 집중하다 ・ **cultivate** ⓥ 함양하다, 경작하다
- **exposure** ⓝ 접근, 노출 ・ **uniquely** ⓐⓓ 독특하게, 유일하게
- **residential** ⓐ 주거의

적절한 환경이 주어지면, 기업가 정신은 캠퍼스 생활의 구조로 완전히 짜여 들어가 그것의 교육적 범위를 크게 확장할 수 있다. 한 연구는, 기회를 포착하고 그에 따라 행동하도록 직장 내에서 동료들이 서로에게 영향을 미친다는 것을 보여주었다. 사무실에서 함께 일하는 기업가들이 많을수록, 그들의 동료들이 병에 걸릴(기업가 정신을 갖게 될) 가능성이 더 높다는 것이다. 스탠퍼드대학교 동문들을 대상으로 한 연구에서 '다양한 업무 및 교육 배경을 가진 사람들이 직장에서 한 가지 역할에 집중했거나 학교에서 한 가지 과목에 집중한 사람들보다 자기 자신의 사업을 시작할 가능성이 훨씬 더 높다'는 것을 발견했다. 기업가적 문화를 배양하기 위해, 단과대학과 종합대학에서는 학생들에게 폭넓은 경험의 선택과 다양한 아이디어를 폭넓게 접할 기회를 제공할 필요가 있다. 그것들은 학업 프로그램 기획, 주거 생활, 학생 집단, 동창회 네트워크라는 자원을 결합하여 이것을 할 수 있는 유일한 위치에 있다.

다음 글에서 필자가 주장하는 바로 가장 적절한 것은?
① 훌륭한 기업가가 되기 위해서 관심 있는 한 분야에 집중해야 한다.
다양한 업무, 교육 배경을 지닌 사람이 기업가가 될 가능성이 더 높음
② **대학은 학생들이 기업가 정신을 함양하도록 환경을 조성해야 한다.**
단과대학과 종합대학이 할 일을 제시함
③ 좋은 직장을 얻기 위해서 학업과 대외 활동에 충실해야 한다.
기업가 정신에 대한 내용임
④ 기업은 대학생들의 다양한 소모임 활동을 적극 지원해야 한다.
기업의 역할을 강조한 것이 아님
⑤ 대학생은 학업 성취를 위하여 경험과 생각의 폭을 넓혀야 한다.
기업가 정신의 함양이 목표임

왜 정답 ? [정답률 82%]
기업가 정신이 캠퍼스 생활, 즉 대학 생활의 구조로 짜여 들어갈 수 있다면서 단과대학과 종합대학은 기업가적 문화를 배양하기 위해 학생들에게 폭넓은 경험과 다양한 아이디어를 접할 수 있는 기회를 제공해야 한다고 했다. 학생들의 기업가 정신 함양에 있어 대학의 역할을 강조한 글이므로 정답은 ②이다.

왜 오답 ?
① 한 가지 역할, 한 가지 과목에 집중한 사람보다 다양한 업무, 다양한 교육 배경을 지닌 사람들이 기업가가 될 가능성이 훨씬 더 높다고 했다.
③, ⑤ 이 글에서 말하는 목적은 좋은 직장에 취업하는 것이나 학업의 성취가 아니라 기업가 정신을 함양하는 것이다.
④ 기업의 역할이 아니라 대학의 역할을 강조한 글이다.

C 16 정답 ③ ＊인류학의 질적 접근법

Anthropology has become relevant / for addressing global issues. // 단서 1 글로벌 문제를 다루는 데 인류학이 적절함
인류학은 적절해졌다 / 글로벌 문제를 다루는 데 //

명사적 용법(주격 보어)
This is not to deny / the vital role of 'hard' sciences / in addressing these problems. //
이것은 부정하는 것이 아니다 / '딱딱한' 과학의 중요한 역할을 / 이러한 문제를 다루는 데 있어 //

〈의도〉를 나타내는 be to-v 용법
However, / if we are to solve global problems / we need a new way of thinking / based in humanities and social sciences. //
그러나 / 우리가 글로벌 문제를 해결하려면 / 우리는 새로운 사고방식이 필요하다 / 인문학과 사회 과학에 기반한 //

가주어   진주어
It is impossible / to resolve global issues / merely by looking at numbers and statistics. //
~은 불가능하다 / 글로벌 문제를 해결하는 것은 / 단지 숫자와 통계를 보는 것만으로 //

Anthropology thus becomes crucial, / as a discipline and a profession / enabling the collection and interpretation / of 'thick data' — in addition to 'big data' — /
따라서 인류학은 중요해지고 / 학문과 전문 직업으로서 / 수집과 해석을 가능하게 하는 / '심층적 데이터'의 / '빅 데이터'에 더해 /
목적격 보어로 to부정사나 원형부정사를 취하는 준사역동사 help   앞에 관계대명사가 생략됨
and helps us to understand the world / we live in / more comprehensively. //
우리가 세상을 이해하도록 도와준다 / 우리가 살고 있는 / 더 포괄적으로 //

Why is a brand new and expensive 'smart' building a disaster? //
왜 새롭고 값비싼 '스마트' 건물이 재앙인가 //

What will happen / in the future / with passenger cars? //
무엇이 일어날 것인가 / 미래에 / 승용차에는 //

목적어로 동명사를 취하는 stop
In answering such questions, / we should stop / relying only on quantitative data analytics; / 단서 2 가장 중요한 결정은 인류학의 질적 접근법을 통해 얻은 정보를 토대로 이루어져야 함
그러한 질문에 대답할 때 / 우리는 멈추어야 한다 / 양적인 데이터 분석에만 의존하는 것을 /
instead, / the most important decisions should also be informed / by anthropological qualitative approaches / which provide / a more complete and nuanced picture / of people's lives. //
대신에 / 가장 중요한 결정은 또한 정보를 얻어야 한다 / 인류학의 질적 접근법을 통해 / 제공하는 / 더 온전하고 미묘한 그림을 / 사람들의 삶의 //

- **anthropology** ⓝ 인류학 ・ **relevant** ⓐ 적절한
- **address** ⓥ 다루다 ・ **vital** ⓐ 중요한 ・ **resolve** ⓥ 해결하다
- **statistics** ⓝ 통계 ・ **crucial** ⓐ 중대한, 결정적인
- **discipline** ⓝ 학문 ・ **profession** ⓝ 전문 직업
- **enable** ⓥ ~을 할 수 있게 하다 ・ **interpretation** ⓝ 해석
- **comprehensively** ⓐⓓ 완전히, 철저히
- **quantitative data** 양적 데이터 ・ **qualitative** ⓐ 질적인
- **approach** ⓝ 접근법 ・ **nuance** ⓝ 미묘한 차이, 뉘앙스

인류학은 글로벌 문제를 다루는 데 적절해졌다. 이것은 이러한 문제를 다루는 데 있어 '딱딱한' 과학의 중요한 역할을 부정하는 것이 아니다. 그러나 우리가 글로벌 문제를 해결하려면 우리는 인문학과 사회 과학에 기반한 새로운 사고방식이 필요하다. 단지 숫자와 통계를 보는 것만으로 글로벌 문제를 해결하는 것은 불가능하다. 따라서 인류학은 '빅 데이터' 외에도 '심층적 데이터'의 수집과 해석을 가능하게 하는 학문과 전문 직업으로서 중요해지고 우리가 살고 있는 세상을 우리가 더 포괄적으로 이해하도록 도와준다. 왜 새롭고 값비싼 '스마트' 건물이 재앙인가? 미래에 승용차는 어떻게 될 것인가? 그러한 질문에 대답할 때, 우리는 양적인 데이터 분석에만 의존하는 것을 멈추어야 한다. 대신에, 가장 중요한 결정은 또한 사람들의 삶의 더 온전하고 미묘한 그림을 제공하는 인류학의 질적 접근법을 통해 정보를 얻어야 한다.

다음 글에서 필자가 주장하는 바로 가장 적절한 것은?
① 광범위한 규모의 문제를 다룰 때는 처리 단계를 세분화해야 한다.
처리 단계의 세분화를 주장하는 것이 아님
② 실증적 자료를 토대로 해결할 수 있는 문제를 먼저 처리해야 한다.
문제 해결의 순서에 대한 내용이 아님
③ 글로벌 문제 해결을 위해 인류학의 질적 접근법을 활용해야 한다.
글로벌 문제를 다루는 데 인류학이 적절해졌음
④ 전 인류적 문제에 대한 질적 연구는 정량화된 수치에 기반해야 한다.
수치의 중요성은 언급되지 않음
⑤ 사회 문제의 포괄적 이해를 위해 자료를 반복적으로 검증해야 한다.
반복을 강조하는 것이 아님

>왜 정답? [정답률 89%]

> **첫 문장:** 인류학은 글로벌 문제를 다루는 데 적절해졌다. **단서 1**
> **마지막 문장:** 가장 중요한 결정은 인류학의 질적 접근법을 통해 정보를 얻어야 한다. **단서 2**

➡ 글로벌 문제를 해결할 때 인류학의 질적 접근법을 이용해서 정보를 얻어야 한다는 주장이므로 정답은 ③이다.

>왜 오답?
① 글로벌 문제를 '광범위한 규모의 문제'로 표현할 수는 있지만, 해당 문제를 다루는 처리 단계의 세분화를 주장하는 것은 아니다. (함정)
② 어떤 문제를 먼저 처리해야 하는지 등의 우선순위를 이야기하는 것이 아니다.
④ 단지 숫자와 통계를 보는 것만으로 글로벌 문제를 해결하는 것은 불가능하다고 했다.
⑤ 어떤 자료를 이용해야 하는지를 설명하는 것으로, 반복의 중요성에 대한 언급은 없다.

자이 쌤's Follow Me! —홈페이지에서 제공

C 17 정답 ② * 정신적 추진력의 중요성

복수 선행사 주격 관계대명사절의 복수 동사
Consider two athletes / who both want to play in college. //
두 명의 운동선수를 생각해 보라 / 둘 다 대학에서 뛰고 싶어 하는 //

둘 중 나머지 하나
One says / she has to work very hard / and the other uses goal
둘 중 하나
setting / to create a plan / to stay on track / and work on specific
추상적 의미의 장소에도 쓰이는 관계부사
skills / where she is lacking. // 선행사
한 명은 말하고 / 그녀가 매우 열심히 해야 한다고 / 다른 한 명은 목표 설정을 이용한다 / 계획을 세우기 위해 / 계획대로 계속 진전하고 / 특정 기술을 연마할 / 자신이 부족한 //

Both are working hard / but only the latter is working smart. //
둘 다 열심히 하고 있지만 / 후자만이 영리하게 하고 있다 //

It can be frustrating / for athletes to work extremely hard / but
가주어 to부정사의 의미상 주어 진주어
not make the progress / they wanted. //
~은 좌절감을 줄 수 있다 / 운동선수가 정말로 열심히 하지만 / 진전을 이루지 못하는 것은 / 자신이 원하는 //

명사절 주어 단수 동사
What can make the difference / is drive / — utilizing the mental
gear / to maximize gains / made in the technical and physical
areas. // **단서 1** 차이를 만드는 것은 정신적 장치, 즉 정신적 추진력임
차이를 만들어낼 수 있는 것은 / 추진력이다 / 정신적 장치를 활용하는 것 / 이점을 극대화하기 위해 / 기술과 신체 영역에서 이루어지는 //

Drive provides direction (goals), / sustains effort (motivation),
병렬 구조
/ and creates a training mindset / that goes beyond simply
working hard. // **단서 2** 정신적 추진력의 이점 ①
추진력은 방향(목표)을 제공하고 / 노력(동기 부여)을 유지하며 / 훈련의 마음가짐을 만든다 / 그냥 열심히 하는 것을 넘어서는 //

연속 동작을 나타내는 현재분사의 병렬 구조
Drive applies direct force / on your physical and technical gears,
/ strengthening and polishing them / so they can spin / with
vigor and purpose. // **단서 3** 정신적 추진력의 이점 ②
추진력은 직접적인 힘을 가하여 / 여러분의 신체와 기술 장치에 / 그것들을 강화하고 다듬는다 / 그것들이 회전할 수 있도록 / 활력과 목적을 가지고 //

목적격 보어(원형부정사)
While desire might make you spin those gears / faster and
주어 동사 목적어
harder / as you work out or practice, / drive is what built them
목적어 주격 보어절
/ in the first place. //
욕망은 여러분이 그러한 장치를 회전시키게 만들지도 모르지만 / 더 빨리 그리고 더 열심히 / 여러분이 운동을 하거나 연습할 때 / 추진력이 그것들을 만든 것이다 / 애초에 //

- athlete ⓝ (운동)선수 · on track 제대로 진행되고 있는
- specific ⓐ 구체적인, 특정한 · lack ⓥ 부족하다
- frustrating ⓐ 좌절감을 주는 · progress ⓝ 진전, 진행
- drive ⓝ 추진력, 투지 · utilize ⓥ 활용[이용]하다
- gear ⓝ (특정 목적용) 장치 · maximize ⓥ 극대화하다
- physical ⓐ 육체의, 물질의 · sustain ⓥ 지속하다, 존재하게 하다
- motivation ⓝ 동기 부여, 자극 · mindset ⓝ 사고방식, 태도
- strengthen ⓥ 강화하다 · polish ⓥ (좋아지도록) 다듬다
- desire ⓝ 욕구, 갈망 · spin ⓥ 돌다, 질주하다

둘 다 대학에서 뛰고 싶어 하는 두 명의 운동선수를 생각해 보라. 한 명은 매우 열심히 해야 한다고 말하고, 다른 한 명은 계획대로 계속 진전하고 자신이 부족한 특정 기술을 연마할 계획을 세우기 위해 목표 설정을 이용한다. 둘 다 열심히 하고 있지만 후자만이 영리하게 하고 있다. 운동선수가 정말로 열심히 하지만 자신이 원하는 진전을 이루지 못하는 것은 좌절감을 줄 수 있다. 차이를 만들어낼 수 있는 것은 추진력, 즉 기술과 신체 영역에서 이루어지는 이점을 극대화하기 위해 정신적 장치를 활용하는 것이다. 추진력은 방향(목표)을 제공하고, 노력(동기 부여)을 유지하며, 그냥 열심히 하는 것을 넘어서는 훈련의 마음가짐을 만든다. 추진력은 여러분의 신체와 기술 장치에 직접적인 힘을 가하여, 그것들이 활력과 목적을 가지고 회전할 수 있도록 그것들을 강화하고 다듬는다. 욕망은 여러분이 운동을 하거나 연습할 때 그러한 장치를 더 빨리, 그리고 더 열심히 회전시키게 만들지도 모르지만, 애초에 추진력이 그것들을 만든 것이다.

다음 글에서 필자가 주장하는 바로 가장 적절한 것은?
① 선수들의 훈련 방식은 장점을 극대화하는 방향으로 이루어져야 한다.
올바른 훈련 방식이 무엇인지 설명하는 것이 아님
② 선수들은 최고의 성과를 얻기 위해 정신적 추진력을 잘 활용해야 한다.
정신적 장치를 활용하는 것이 차이를 만듦
③ 선수들은 단기적 훈련 성과보다 장기적 목표 달성에 힘써야 한다.
단기적 훈련 성과와 장기적 목표 달성을 대조한 것이 아님
④ 선수들은 육체적 훈련과 정신적 훈련을 균형 있게 병행해야 한다.
정신적 추진력의 중요성을 주장함
⑤ 선수들은 수립한 계획을 실행하면서 꾸준히 수정하여야 한다.
계획을 적절히 수정하라는 조언이 아님

>왜 정답? [정답률 71%]

단순히 열심히 해야 한다고 말하는 선수와 목표를 설정하는 선수 중 후자만이 영리하게 하는 것이라면서, 차이를 만드는 것은 추진력, 즉 정신적 장치를 활용하는 것이라고 했다.
(정신적) 추진력을 통해 목표를 향한 방향을 잡고, 계속해서 동기를 부여 받아 노력하며, 그냥 열심히 하는 것을 넘어서는 훈련의 마음가짐을 갖는다는 설명과 (정신적) 추진력이 신체와 기술을 강화하고 다듬도록 직접적인 힘을 가한다는 설명을 통해 필자의 주장이 ②임을 알 수 있다.

>왜 오답?
① 훈련에 있어 정신적 추진력을 활용하라는 것이지, 장점을 극대화하는 훈련을 하라는 것은 아니다.
③ 단기적 훈련 성과보다 장기적 목표 달성이 더 중요하다는 언급은 없다.
④ 정신적으로도 훈련하라는 것이 아니라 정신적 장치, 즉 정신적 추진력을 활용하라는 것이다. (함정)
⑤ 목표를 설정하고 계획을 세우는 선수가 영리하게 훈련하는 것이라는 언급은 있지만, 수립한 계획을 수정해야 한다고 주장하는 것은 아니다.

38 자이스토리 영어 독해 실전

C 18 정답 ③ *불쾌감의 간접적 표현의 문제점

_{A as well as B: B뿐만 아니라 A도}
Occasionally / individuals do not merely come out as well as clearly state / what is troubling them / and instead select more indirect means / of expressing their annoyance. //
때때로 / 사람들은 분명히 말하지도 그저 드러내지도 않고 / 무엇이 자신을 괴롭히고 있는지를 / 대신 더 간접적인 수단을 선택한다 / 자신의 불쾌감을 표현하는 //

_{주격 관계대명사} _{선행사}
One companion might talk / to the various other / in a way / that is condescending / and also indicates underlying hostility. //
한 동료가 말할 수도 있다 / 다양한 다른 동료에게 / 방식으로 / 거들먹거리는 / 또한 기저에 있는 적개심을 나타내는 //

Numerous other times, / partners may mope and even frown / without genuinely dealing with an issue. //
다른 수많은 경우에도 / 상대방은 울적해하고 심지어 얼굴을 찡그릴 수도 있다 / 어떤 문제를 진정으로 다루지 않은 채 //

Companions may likewise merely prevent / discussing an issue /
마찬가지로 동료들도 그냥 막아버릴 수도 있다 / 어떤 문제에 대해 토론하는 것을 /

_{전치사구의 병렬 구조}
by swiftly switching over topics / when the subject turns up / or by being incredibly vague. //
신속하게 화제를 바꿈으로써 / 그 주제가 등장할 때 / 또는 믿을 수 없을 정도로 모호해짐으로써 //

단서1 짜증을 간접적으로 표현하는 것은 유용하지 않음
Such indirect ways / of expressing temper / are not useful /
그런 간접적인 방법은 / 짜증을 표현하는 / 유용하지 않다 /

_{이유의 부사절 접속사} _{don't provide의 간접목적어}
since they don't provide the individual / that is the target of the behaviors, / an idea / of exactly how to react. //
그것이 사람에게 제공하지 않기 때문이다 / 그런 행동의 대상이 되는 / 아이디어를 / 정확히 어떻게 반응해야 하는지에 대한 //

_{앞에 접속사 that이 생략됨} _{직접목적어}
They understand / their companion is irritated, / but the absence of directness leaves them / without advice / regarding what they can do / to solve the issue. // **단서2** 직접적으로 표현하지 않으면 문제가 해결되지 않음
_{부사적 용법(목적)}
그들은 이해한다 / 자신의 동료가 짜증이 나 있다는 것을 / 하지만 직접적인 표현의 부재는 그들을 남겨둔다 / 충고 없이 / 자신들이 무엇을 할 수 있는지에 관한 / 그 문제를 해결하기 위해 //

- occasionally ad 가끔, 때때로 · merely ad 단지, 그저
- come out 알려지다, 드러나다 · state ⓥ 말하다
- indirect ⓐ 간접적인 · means ⓝ 수단 · annoyance ⓝ 불쾌감
- companion ⓝ 동료 · indicate ⓥ 나타내다 · hostility ⓝ 적개심
- numerous ⓐ 수많은 · frown ⓥ 얼굴을 찡그리다
- genuinely ad 진정으로 · swiftly ad 신속히, 빨리
- switch over ~을 바꾸다 · turn up 등장하다, 나타나다
- incredibly ad 믿을 수 없을 정도로 · vague ⓐ 모호한
- temper ⓝ 짜증, 성질 · irritated ⓐ 짜증이 난
- absence ⓝ 없음, 부재 · regarding prep ~에 관하여

때때로 사람들은 무엇이 자신을 괴롭히고 있는지를 분명히 말하지도, 그저 드러내지도 않고, 대신 자신의 불쾌감을 표현하는 더 간접적인 수단을 선택한다. 한 동료가 거들먹거리는, 또한 기저에 있는 적개심을 나타내는 방식으로 다양한 다른 동료와 대화를 나눌 수도 있다. 다른 수많은 경우에도 상대방은 어떤 문제를 진정으로 다루지 않은 채 울적해하고 심지어 얼굴을 찡그릴 수도 있다. 마찬가지로 동료들 간에도 어떤 문제에 대해 토론하는 것을, 그 주제가 등장하면 신속하게 화제를 바꾸거나 믿을 수 없을 정도로 모호해짐으로써, 그냥 막아버릴 수도 있다. 짜증을 표현하는 그런 간접적인 방법은 유용하지 않은데, 그것이 그런 행동의 대상이 되는 사람에게 정확히 어떻게 반응해야 하는지에 대한 아이디어를 제공하지 않기 때문이다. 그들은 자신의 동료가 짜증이 나 있다는 것은 이해하지만 직접적인 표현이 없어서 자신들이 그 문제를 해결하기 위해 무엇을 할 수 있는지에 관한 충고가 없는 상태가 되게 된다.

다음 글에서 필자가 주장하는 바로 가장 적절한 것은?
① 이성보다 감정에 호소하여 상대방을 설득해야 한다.
_{상대를 설득하는 방법을 설명하는 것이 아님}
② 상대방의 기분을 상하게 하는 행동을 자제해야 한다.
_{상대의 기분을 상하게 하지 말라는 것이 아님}
③ 문제 해결을 위해서는 문제를 직접적으로 언급해야 한다.
_{짜증을 간접적으로 표현하지 말고 직접적으로 표현하면 문제가 해결됨}
④ 타인의 입장을 이해하려면 경청하는 자세를 가져야 한다.
_{경청하라고 조언하는 글이 아님}
⑤ 목표 달성을 방해하는 문제점을 지속적으로 파악해야 한다.
_{문제점을 직접적으로 표현하라는 주장임}

그렇다면 필자의 주장은 직접적으로 표현하라는 것임을 추론할 수 있음 **꿀팁**

왜 정답? [정답률 93%]

사람들이 자신의 불쾌감을 간접적으로 표현한다고 하면서, 그러한 간접적인 표현은 유용하지 않다고 했다. 또한, 직접적으로 표현하지 않는 것은 문제를 해결하기 위해 무엇을 할 수 있는지에 대한 단서를 주지 않는다고 한 것으로 보아 문제를 해결하기 위해서는 무엇이 문제인지를 직접적으로 표현해야 한다는 주장임을 알 수 있다. 따라서 정답은 ③이다.

왜 오답?

① 이성이나 감정에 대한 언급은 없으며 상대방을 설득하는 방법에 대해 이야기한 글이 아니다.
② 상대방에게 불쾌감을 주지 말라는 것이 아니다.
④ 다른 사람의 말을 경청할 것을 주장하는 글이 아니다.
⑤ 문제를 해결하기 위해서는 직접적으로 표현하라고 조언하는 글이다.

C 19 정답 ⑤ *조직에서 명시적 지침의 필요성

Values alone do not create and build culture. //
가치만으로는 문화가 창조되고 구축되지 않는다 //

_{동명사 주어(단수 취급)} _{단수 동사}
Living your values only some of the time / does not contribute / to the creation and maintenance of culture. //
일부 시간에만 가치에 따라 생활하는 것은 / 기여하지 않는다 / 문화의 창조와 유지에 //

_{동명사 주어(단수 취급)} _{단수 동사}
Changing values into behaviors / is only half the battle. //
가치를 행동으로 바꾸는 것은 / 전투의 절반에 불과하다 //

Certainly, this is a step in the right direction, / but those behaviors must then be shared and distributed / widely throughout the organization, /
물론, 이것은 올바른 방향으로 나아가는 단계이지만 / 그다음에 그러한 행동은 공유되고 배포되어야 한다 / 조직 전체에 널리 /

along with a clear and concise description of what is expected. // **단서** 조직 전체에 기대되는 가치관이 담긴 명확한 지침이 있어야 함
_{가주어} _{진주어}
기대되는 것에 대한 명확하고 간결한 설명과 함께 //
It is not enough / to simply talk about it. //
충분하지 않다 / 단순히 그것에 관해 이야기하는 것만으로는 //

_{가주어} _{진주어}
It is critical / to have a visual representation of the specific behaviors / that leaders and all people managers can use / to coach their people. //
_{목적격 관계대명사}
_{부사적 용법(목적)}
중요하다 / 특정 행동을 시각적으로 표현해 놓는 것이 / 리더와 모든 인력 관리자가 사용할 수 있는 / 자신의 팀을 지도하는 데 //

Just like a sports team has a playbook / with specific plays / designed to help them / perform well and win, /
_{과거분사(plays 수식)}
스포츠 팀이 플레이 북을 갖고 있는 것과 마찬가지로 / 특정 플레이를 담고 있는 / 도움이 되도록 고안된 / 좋은 성과를 내고 승리하는 데 /

your company should have a playbook / with the key shifts / needed to transform your culture into action / and turn your values into winning behaviors. //
_{과거분사(shifts 수식)}
_{병렬 구조}
여러분의 회사는 플레이 북을 갖고 있어야 한다 / 핵심적인 변화를 담은 / 여러분의 문화를 행동으로 바꾸고 / 여러분의 가치를 승리하는 행동으로 바꾸는 데 필요한 //

- contribute ⓥ 기여하다 · creation ⓝ 창작품
- maintenance ⓝ 유지 · concise ⓐ 간결한
- description ⓝ 설명, 기술 · critical ⓐ 중요한
- representation ⓝ 표현, 묘사
- playbook ⓝ 플레이 북(팀의 공격과 수비의 작전을 그림과 함께 기록한 책)
- shift ⓝ 변화 · transform ⓥ 바꾸다

가치만으로는 문화가 창조되고 구축되지 않는다. 일부 시간에만 가치에 따라 생활하는 것은 문화의 창조와 유지에 기여하지 않는다. 가치를 행동으로 바꾸는 것은 전투의 절반에 불과하다. 물론, 이것은 올바른 방향으로 나아가는

단계이지만, 그다음에 그러한 행동은 기대되는 것에 대한 명확하고 간결한 설명과 함께 조직 전체에 널리 공유되고 배포되어야 한다. 단순히 그것에 관해 이야기하는 것만으로는 충분하지 않다. 리더와 모든 인력 관리자가 자신의 팀을 지도하는 데 사용할 수 있는 특정 행동을 시각적으로 표현해 놓는 것이 중요하다. 스포츠 팀이 좋은 성과를 내고 승리하는 데 도움이 되도록 고안된 특정 플레이를 담고 있는 플레이 북을 갖고 있는 것과 마찬가지로, 여러분의 회사는 여러분의 문화를 행동으로 바꾸고 여러분의 가치를 승리하는 행동으로 바꾸는 데 필요한 핵심적인 변화를 담은 플레이 북을 갖고 있어야 한다.

다음 글에서 필자가 주장하는 바로 가장 적절한 것은?

① 조직 문화 혁신을 위해서 모든 구성원이 공유할 핵심 가치를 정립해야 한다.
   핵심 가치를 정립하는 것만으로는 충분하지 않다는 것이 필자의 주장임
② 조직 구성원의 행동을 변화시키려면 지도자는 명확한 가치관을 가져야 한다.
   지도자의 명확한 가치관에 관한 언급은 없음
③ 조직 내 문화가 공유되기 위해서 구성원의 자발적 행동이 뒷받침되어야 한다. 조직 내 문화가 공유되기 위해서는 명확한 지침이 필요하다는 것이 필자의 주장임
④ 조직의 핵심 가치 실현을 위해 구성원 간의 지속적인 의사소통이 필수적이다. 지속적인 의사소통에 관한 언급은 없음
⑤ 조직의 문화 형성에는 가치를 반영한 행동의 공유를 위한 명시적 지침이 필요하다. 스포츠 팀이 명확한 플레이 북을 갖고 있는 것처럼 조직도 핵심적인 변화를 담은 플레이 북이 있어야 함

⟩왜 정답 ? [정답률 76%]

- 조직의 문화가 구축되려면 단순히 가치를 논하거나 행동으로 바꾸기만으로는 충분하지 않음
- 조직에 요구되는 가치가 명확하게 담긴 플레이 북이 있어야 함

▶ 조직의 문화 형성에는 가치를 반영한 행동의 공유를 위한 명시적 지침이 필요하다는 것이 필자의 주장이므로 정답은 ⑤이다.

⟩왜 오답 ?

① 핵심 가치를 정립하는 것도 올바른 방향이지만, 그것만으로는 충분하지 않으며 명확한 지침이 수립되어야 한다는 것이 필자의 주장이다. 함정
② 지도자의 명확한 가치관에 관한 언급은 없다.
③ 구성원의 자발적 행동에 관한 내용은 없다.
④ 지속적인 의사소통에 관한 언급은 없다.

김아린 | 충남대 의예과 2024년 입학·대전한빛고 졸

필자의 주장 문제를 풀 때는 should, must, important, critical처럼 직접적으로 중요성을 나타내는 표현이 포함된 문장을 읽다 보면 금방 필자의 주장을 파악할 수 있어! 이 문제에서는 중반부에 must가 포함된 문장과 critical이 포함된 문장에 집중하는 것이지.
행동이 공유되어야 한다는 것과 특정 행동의 시각적 표현이 필요하다는 내용을 종합하면 ⑤이 답이라는 것을 쉽게 알 수 있을 거야.

C 20 정답 ① ＊타 문화의 이면을 보는 것의 중요성

동명사구 주어　단수 동사　동명사구 목적어
Becoming competent / in another culture / means / looking beyond behavior /
유능해진다는 것은 / 타 문화에 / 의미한다 / 행동 그 이상의 것을 살펴보는 것을 /

명사절 접속사　　목적어 역할을 하는 관계대명사절
to see / if we can understand / the attitudes, beliefs, and values / that motivate / what we observe. //
알아보기 위해 / 우리가 이해할 수 있는지를 / 태도, 신념, 가치를 / 이유가 되는 / 우리가 관찰하는 것의 //

By looking / only at the visible aspects of culture / — customs, clothing, food, and language — /
봄으로써 / 문화의 눈에 보이는 면만 / 관습, 의복, 음식, 언어 /

we develop a short-sighted view / of intercultural understanding / — just the tip of the iceberg, really. // 단서1 문화의 눈에 보이는 면만 보는 것은 빙산의 일각만 보는 것임
우리는 근시안적 시각을 키운다 / 타 문화 이해에 있어 / 정말로 빙산의 일각에 불과한 //

의도를 나타내는 'be동사+to부정사'
If we are to be successful / in our business interactions / with people / who have different values and beliefs / about how the world is ordered, / 전치사의 목적어로 쓰인 간접의문문
우리가 성공하고자 한다면 / 우리의 사업상의 교류에서 / 사람들과의 / 다른 가치와 신념을 가진 / 세상이 어떻게 질서를 세우는지에 대한 /

가주어　　진주어
then we must go below the surface / of what it means / to understand culture / and attempt to see / what Edward Hall calls the "hidden dimensions." // 단서2 우리는 문화를 이해한다는 것이 to see의 목적어절　　　의미하는 것의 이면을 들여다봐야 함
우리는 이면을 들여다봐야 하고 / ～이 의미하는 것의 / 문화를 이해한다는 것이 / 보려고 시도해야 한다 / Edward Hall이 '숨겨진 차원'이라고 부르는 것을 //

Those hidden aspects / are the very foundation of culture / and are the reason / why culture is actually more / than meets the eye. // 선행사　관계부사　　유사 관계대명사(비교급 문장에서 접속사와 주어·목적어·보어 역할을 겸할 수 있음)
그런 숨겨진 측면이 / 바로 문화의 근간이며 / 이유이다 / 문화가 실제로는 이상인 / 눈에 보이는 것 //

not A until B: B하고서야 비로소 A하다
We tend not to notice / those cultural norms / until they violate / what we consider / to be common sense, good judgment, or the nature of things. //
우리는 알아차리지 못하는 경향이 있다 / 그런 문화적 규범들을 / 그것들이 어길 때까지 / 우리가 여기는 것을 / 상식, 올바른 판단 또는 사물의 본질이라고 //

- **competent** ⓐ 능숙한, 만족할 만한
- **motivate** ⓥ 동기를 부여하다
- **observe** ⓥ 관찰하다, 목격하다
- **custom** ⓝ 관습, 풍습
- **short-sighted** ⓐ 근시안의
- **intercultural** ⓐ 다른 문화 간의
- **iceberg** ⓝ 빙산
- **surface** ⓝ 표면, 지면
- **attempt** ⓥ 시도하다
- **dimension** ⓝ 차원, 관점
- **foundation** ⓝ 토대, 기초
- **norm** ⓝ 규범, 표준
- **violate** ⓥ (법·합의 등을) 위반하다
- **judgment** ⓝ 판단, 심판

타 문화에 유능해진다는 것은 우리가 관찰하는 것의 이유가 되는 태도, 신념, 가치를 이해할 수 있는지 알아보기 위해 행동 그 이상의 것을 살펴보는 것을 의미한다. 문화의 눈에 보이는 면, 즉 관습, 의복, 음식, 언어만 봄으로써, 우리는 타 문화 이해에 있어 정말로 빙산의 일각에 불과한 근시안적 시각을 키운다. 세상이 어떻게 질서를 세우는지에 대한 다른 가치와 신념을 가진 사람들과의 사업상의 교류에서 성공하고자 한다면, 문화를 이해한다는 것이 의미하는 것의 그 이면을 들여다봐야 하고 Edward Hall이 '숨겨진 차원'이라고 부르는 것을 보려고 시도해야 한다. 그런 숨겨진 측면이 바로 문화의 근간이며 문화가 실제로는 눈에 보이는 것 이상인 이유이다. 우리는 그런 문화적 규범들이 우리가 상식, 올바른 판단 또는 사물의 본질이라고 여기는 것을 어기고 나서야 비로소 그것들을 알아차리는 경향이 있다.

다음 글에서 필자가 주장하는 바로 가장 적절한 것은?

① 타 문화 사람들과 교류를 잘하려면 그 문화의 이면을 알아야 한다.
   If we are to be successful ~ what Edward Hall calls the "hidden dimensions."
② 문화 배경이 다른 직원과 협업할 때 공정하게 업무를 나눠야 한다.
   공정한 업무 배분을 강조하는 것이 아님
③ 여러 문화에 대한 이해를 통해 공동체 의식을 길러야 한다.
   공동체 의식의 필요성에 대한 내용이 아님
④ 원만한 대인 관계를 위해서는 서로의 공통점을 우선 파악해야 한다.
   다른 문화를 이해하는 것에 대한 내용임
⑤ 문화적 갈등을 줄이려면 구성원 간의 소통을 활성화해야 한다.
   문화적 갈등의 해결책을 알려주는 것이 아님

⟩왜 정답 ? [정답률 94%]

관습이나 의복, 언어처럼 문화의 눈에 보이는 면만 보는 것은 타 문화를 이해하는 데 있어 근시안적인 시각을 키우는 것이라고 한 후, 타 문화 사람들과의 교류에서 성공하고자 한다면 문화를 이해한다는 것이 의미하는 것의 이면을 들여다봐야 한다고 했으므로 정답은 ①이다.

〈의무〉의 조동사 must가 포함된 문장이 정답의 핵심 단서! 꿀팁

왜 오답?

② 세상의 질서에 대해 다른 가치와 신념을 가진 사람들과의 사업상 교류에 대해 언급하긴 했지만, 공정한 업무 배분을 강조한 것은 아니다.

③ 타 문화의 이면을 알아야 한다는 주장이지, 타 문화의 이해를 통해 추구해야 하는 바를 설명하지는 않았다.

④ 타 문화의 사람들과의 사업상 교류에서 성공하기 위해 필요한 것을 설명하는 글로, 원만한 대인 관계를 위한 조언이 아니다.

⑤ 구성원 간의 소통이 아니라 다 문화의 이면을 아는 것의 중요성을 주장하는 글이다.

C 21 정답 ③ ＊성공 가능성에 대한 확률적 분석

At every step in our journey through life / we encounter junctions / with many different pathways / leading into the distance. //
＜소유·동반＞의 전치사
평생을 두고 우리 여정의 모든 단계에서 / 우리는 분기점을 만난다 / 많은 다른 길들이 있는 / 먼 곳으로 이어지는 //

Each choice involves uncertainty / about which path will get you / to your destination. //
단수 주어 단수 동사 ／ 전치사 about의 목적어절을 이끄는 의문형용사
각각의 선택은 불확실성을 포함한다 / 어떤 길이 여러분을 데려다줄지에 대한 / 여러분의 목적지로 //

Trusting our intuition / to make the choice / often ends up with us making a suboptimal choice. //
동명사구 주어 단수 동사
동명사 making의 의미상 주어
우리의 직관을 믿는 것은 / 선택을 하기 위해 / 흔히 우리가 차선의 선택을 하는 것으로 결국 끝난다 //

Turning the uncertainty into numbers / has proved a potent way / of analyzing the paths / and finding the shortcut / to your destination. //
동명사구 주어 단수 동사
병렬 구조 (of의 목적어(동명사))
단서 1 불확실성을 확률적으로 분석하는 것이 목적 달성에 도움이 됨
불확실성을 숫자로 바꾸는 것은 / 강력한 방법으로 입증되었다 / 길을 분석하는 / 그리고 지름길을 찾는 / 여러분의 목적지로 가는 // **단서 2** 확률적 분석은 위험을 효과적으로 관리하게 함

The mathematical theory of probability / hasn't eliminated risk, / but it allows us to manage that risk / more effectively. //
주어 동사 목적어 목적 보어
확률에 대한 수학적 이론은 / 위험을 제거하지는 않았지만 / 그것은 우리가 그 위험을 관리하게 한다 / 더 효과적으로 //

The strategy is / to analyze / all the possible scenarios / that the future holds / and then to see / what proportion of them lead / to success or failure. //
병렬 구조 (is의 주격 보어)
전략은 ~이다 / 분석하는 것 / 모든 가능한 시나리오를 / 미래가 안고 있는 / 그리고 나서 살펴보는 것 / 그것들의 얼마의 비율이 이어질지를 / 성공이나 실패로 //

This gives you / a much better map of the future / on which to base your decisions / about which path to choose. //
gives의 간접목적어와 직접목적어 the future to base on으로 해석
이것은 여러분에게 제공한다 / 미래에 대한 훨씬 더 좋은 지도를 / 여러분의 결정의 근거를 둘 / 어떤 길을 선택할 것인지에 관한 //

- encounter ⓥ 만나다, 경험하다 · uncertainty ⓝ 불확실성
- destination ⓝ 목적지 · intuition ⓝ 직관 · potent ⓐ 강력한
- shortcut ⓝ 지름길 · mathematical ⓐ 수학적인
- eliminate ⓥ 없애다, 제거하다 · proportion ⓝ 비율

평생을 두고 우리 여정의 모든 단계에서 우리는 먼 곳으로 이어지는 많은 다른 길들이 있는 분기점을 만난다. 각각의 선택은 어떤 길이 여러분의 목적지로 데려다줄지에 대한 불확실성을 포함한다. 선택을 하기 위해 우리의 직관을 믿는 것은 흔히 우리가 차선의 선택을 하는 것으로 결국 끝난다.

불확실성을 숫자로 바꾸는 것은 여러분의 목적지로 가는 길을 분석하고 지름길을 찾는 강력한 방법으로 입증되었다. 확률에 대한 수학적 이론은 위험을 제거하지는 않았지만, 우리가 그 위험을 더 효과적으로 관리하게 한다. 미래가 안고 있는 모든 가능한 시나리오를 분석한 다음, 그것들이 성공이나 실패로 이어질 비율이 얼마나 되는지를 살펴보는 것이 전략이다. 이것은 여러분이 어떤 길을 선택할 것인지에 관한 결정을 내릴 때 그 근거로 삼을 수 있는 미래에 대한 훨씬 더 좋은 지도를 여러분에게 제공한다.

다음 글에서 필자가 주장하는 바로 가장 적절한 것은?

① 성공적인 삶을 위해 미래에 대한 구체적인 계획을 세워야 한다.
분석의 중요성을 이야기함
② 중요한 결정을 내릴 때에는 자신의 직관에 따라 판단해야 한다.
직관보다 확률적 분석을 강조함
③ 더 나은 선택을 위해 성공 가능성을 확률적으로 분석해야 한다.
모든 시나리오를 분석하는 것이 전략임
④ 빠른 목표 달성을 위해 지름길로 가고자 할 때 신중해야 한다.
단순히 신중해야 한다는 것이 아님
⑤ 인생의 여정에서 선택에 따른 결과를 스스로 책임져야 한다.
선택과 책임에 대한 내용이 아님

왜 정답? [정답률 80%]

직관을 믿는 것과 불확실성을 숫자로 바꾸는 것을 대조하는 글이다. 불확실성을 확률적으로 분석하는 것은 목적지로 가는 지름길을 찾는 강력한 방법이고, 위험을 더 효과적으로 관리하게 한다는 것으로 보아 필자의 주장은 ③임을 알 수 있다.

왜 오답? 차선을 선택하는 것을 긍정적으로 이야기하는 글이 아님 꿀팁

① 성공하기 위해 불확실성을 확률적으로 분석해야 한다는 주장이다.
② 직관을 믿는 것은 흔히 결국 차선을 선택하는 것으로 끝난다고 했다. 주의
④ shortcut 등이 언급된 것으로 만든 오답이다. 단순히 신중해야 한다는 것이 아니라 확률적, 수학적으로 분석해야 한다는 것이 주장의 핵심이다.
⑤ 확률적 분석에 따라 선택해야 한다는 것이지, 선택에 대해 책임져야 한다는 언급은 없다.

장성욱 | 동아대 의예과 2023년 입학·부산 대연고 졸

주장이나 요지를 묻는 문제에서 글의 도입부나 마지막에 조동사 should 같이 당위성을 나타내는 표현이 있다면 그 부분만 읽고도 쉽게 풀 수 있지만, 이 문제는 그렇지 않아서 처음부터 읽었어.

글의 중간 부분에 불확실성을 숫자로 바꾼다는 내용이 나오는데, 여기서 숫자(numbers)가 뒷부분과 이어져서 '경우의 수' 또는 '확률' 등의 의미로 분석된다는 것을 파악했다면 정답을 고를 수 있어. 글의 초반부만 읽은 친구들은 Trusting our intuition이라는 말 때문에 ②을 오답으로 고르지 않았을까 해. 하지만 뒤의 내용을 더 읽어 보면 직관에 대해 부정적인 내용임을 알 수 있지.

어법 특강

＊ 목적격 보어로 to부정사를 취하는 동사

– ask, wish, want, tell, order, teach, allow 등의 동사는 목적격 보어로 to부정사를 취한다.

- I want you to call him right now.
  (나는 네가 당장 그에게 전화하기를 바란다.)
- Jennifer didn't allow Marshall to go out last night.
  (Jennifer는 Marshall이 어젯밤에 나가는 것을 허락하지 않았다.)
- Douglas asked us to join him.
  (Douglas는 우리에게 그와 함께할 것을 요청했다.)
- I told you to be here on time this morning.
  (내가 네게 오늘 아침에 제시간에 이곳에 오라고 말했잖아.)

＊자신감을 키우는 방법

Confident is not the same / as comfortable. //
자신감이 있다는 것은 같지 않다 / 맘이 편하다는 것과 //
주어
One of the biggest misconceptions / about becoming self-
동사 주격 보어절 접속사
confident / is that it means / living fearlessly. //
가장 큰 오해 중 하나는 / 자신감을 갖게 되는 것에 관한 / 그것이 의미한다는 것이다 / 두려움 없이 사는 것을 //
주어   동사
The key / to building confidence / is quite the opposite. //
핵심은 / 자신감 구축의 / 상당히 반대이다 //
to let의 목적격 보어(원형부사사)   선행사
It means / we are willing to let fear be present / as we do the
주격 관계대명사
things / that matter to us. //
이는 의미한다 / 우리가 두려움이 존재하도록 기꺼이 두는 것을 / 우리가 일을 할 때 / 우리에게 중요한 //

When we establish some self-confidence / in something, / it feels good. //
우리가 어느 정도의 자신감이 생기면 / 무언가에 대한 / 기분이 좋다 //

We want / to stay there and hold on to it. //
우리는 원한다 / 거기에 머물러서 고수하기를 //

But if we only go / where we feel confident, / then confidence never expands / beyond that. //
하지만 우리가 오직 간다면 / 자신감을 느끼는 곳으로만 / 그러면 자신감은 절대 확장되지 않는다 / 그 이상으로 //
앞에 목적격 관계대명사가 생략됨   단수 주어
If we only do the things / we know / we can do well, / fear of the
단수 동사   ┗앞에 명사절 접속사 that이 생략됨
new and unknown / tends to grow. //
우리가 일만 한다면 / 우리가 알고 있는 / 우리가 잘할 수 있다는 것을 / 새롭고 미지의 것에 대한 두려움은 / 커지는 경향이 있다 //
동명사구 주어   단수 동사
Building confidence inevitably demands / that we make friends with vulnerability / because it is the only way / to be without
형용사적 용법(the only way 수식)
confidence / for a while. //
자신감을 키우는 것은 필연적으로 요구한다 / 우리가 취약성과 친구가 되는 것을 / 그것이 유일한 방법이기 때문에 / 자신감 없이 지낼 수 있는 / 한동안 //

But the only way / confidence can grow / is when we are willing
앞에 관계부사가 생략됨
to be without it. //
하지만 유일한 방법은 / 자신감이 커질 수 있는 / 기꺼이 자신감 없이 지낼 때이다 //

When we can step into fear / and sit with the unknown, / it is the
┗━━━━━━━━ it is ~ that 강조 구문 ━━━━━━
courage of doing so / that builds confidence / from the ground
up. // **단서** 두렵고 낯선 것과 어울리는 용기가 자신감을 쌓음
우리가 두려움 속으로 들어가 / 미지의 것과 어울릴 수 있을 때 / 바로 그렇게 하는 용기가 / 자신감을 쌓는다 / 바닥에서부터 //

- confident ⓐ 자신감 있는
- misconception ⓝ 오해
- fearlessly ⓐⓓ 두려움 없이
- hold on to ~을 고수하다
- matter to ~에게 중요하다
- expand ⓥ 확장하다
- tend to ~하는 경향이 있다
- inevitably ⓐⓓ 불가피하게

자신감이 있다는 것은 맘이 편하다는 것과 같지 않다. 자신감을 갖게 되는 것에 관한 가장 큰 오해 중 하나는 그것이 두려움 없이 사는 것을 의미한다는 것이다. 자신감 구축의 핵심은 오히려 그 반대이다. 이는 우리가 우리에게 중요한 일을 할 때 두려움이 존재하도록 기꺼이 두는 것을 의미한다. 무언가에 대한 어느 정도의 자신감이 생기면 기분이 좋다. 우리는 거기에 머물러서 고수하고 싶어 한다. 하지만 우리가 자신감을 느끼는 곳으로만 간다면, 그런 경우 자신감은 그 이상으로 절대 확장되지 않는다. 우리가 잘할 수 있다고 알고 있는 일만 한다면, 새롭고 미지의 것에 대한 두려움은 커지는 경향이 있다. 자신감을 키우려면 필연적으로 취약성과 친구가 되어야 하는데 그것이 한동안 자신감 없이 지낼 수 있는 유일한 방법이기 때문이다. 하지만 자신감이 커질 수 있는 유일한 방법은 기꺼이 자신감 없이 지낼 때이다. 우리가 두려움 속으로 들어가 미지의 것과 어울릴 수 있을 때, 바닥에서부터 자신감을 쌓는 것은 바로 그렇게 하는 용기이다.

다음 글에서 필자가 주장하는 바로 가장 적절한 것은?

① 적성을 파악하기 위해서는 자신 있는 일을 다양하게 시도해야 한다.
　자신 있는 일만 하지 말라는 내용임
② 자신감을 키우기 위해 낯설고 두려운 일에 도전하는 용기를 가져야 한다.
　낯설고 두려운 것에 도전하는 용기가 자신감을 쌓음
③ 어려운 일을 자신 있게 수행하기 위해 사전에 계획을 철저히 세워야 한다.
　계획의 중요성을 언급한 것이 아님
④ 과도한 자신감을 갖기보다는 자신의 약점을 객관적으로 분석해야 한다.
　자신감을 갖기 위한 방법을 설명함
⑤ 자신의 경험과 지식을 바탕으로 당면한 문제에 자신 있게 대처해야 한다.
　자신감을 가지라는 조언이 아님

오 2등급 ? 선택지에서 반복되는 어구인 '자신 있는', '자신감' 등을 토대로 필자의 주장을 파악해야 하는 2등급 대비 문제이다. 필자의 주장을 묻는 문제의 대부분은 마지막 문장에 주장이 드러나기 마련이므로, 마지막 문장부터 읽는다면 오히려 쉽게 정답을 파악할 수 있다.

오 정답 ?

자신감에 대한 오해: 자신감이 있다는 것은 두려움 없이 사는 것을 의미함
자신감에 대한 진실: 두려움 속으로 들어가 미지의 것과 어울리려는 용기가 자신감을 쌓음
▶ ② 자신감을 키우려면 낯설고 두려운 일에 도전하려는 용기가 있어야 한다는 것이 필자의 주장

오 오답 ?

① 적성을 파악하기 위해 해야 하는 일을 설명한 글이 아니다.
③ 계획을 세우는 것의 중요성을 주장하는 것이 아니다.
④ 약점에 대한 객관적인 분석을 강조하는 내용이 아니다.
⑤ 자신감을 가지라는 주장이 아니라, 어떻게 하면 자신감을 갖게 되는지 설명한 것이다. [함정]

＊과학자가 지녀야 할 자질

The chemists Hans Ebel, Claus Bliefert, and William Russey
가주어
note: / "It goes without saying / that scientists need to be skillful
진주어절 접속사
readers. //
화학자 Hans Ebel과 Claus Bliefert, William Russey는 적는다 / "말할 필요가 없다 / 과학자가 숙련된 '독자'여야 한다는 것은 //
전치사   동명사①
Extensive reading is the principal key / to expanding one's
knowledge / and keeping up with developments in a
동명사②
discipline. //
다독은 주요한 비결이다 / 자신의 지식을 확장하고 / 학문에서의 발전에 뒤처지지 않는 //
명사절 주어   주격 보어절 접속사
However, what is often overlooked here is / that scientists are
단수 동사
also obliged / to be skillful writers. //
그러나 여기에서 흔히 간과되는 것은 ~이다 / 과학자는 또한 ~해야 한다는 것 / 숙련된 '필자'가 되어야 //
선행사, 주어   주격 관계대명사
Only the researcher / who is competent / in the art of written
communication / can play an active and effective role / in
동사
contributing to science." //
연구자만이 / 능숙한 / '글로 써서 하는' 의사소통 기술에 / 적극적이고 효과적인 역할을 할 수 있다 / 과학에 '기여하는' 데" // **단서 1** 과학자는 독자 중심의 사고방식으로 글을 써야 하고, 쓰기 행위에서도 읽기 행위를 염두에 두어야 함
From the perspective of readability, / moreover, / scientists should always write / with a reader-centered mentality; / even in the act of writing / they must be mindful / of the act of reading. //
가독성의 관점에서 / 더욱이 / 과학자는 항상 글을 써야 한다 / 독자 중심의 사고방식으로 / 심지어 글을 쓰는 행위에서도 / 그들은 염두에 두어야 한다 / 읽기 행위를 //
가주어   to understand의 의미상 주어 ＊
It would be beneficial for them to understand / how readers
read / in order to improve their writing. // 진주어
그들이 이해하는 것은 유익할 것이다 / 독자가 어떻게 읽는지를 / 그들의 글쓰기를 개선하려면 // **단서 2** 독자가 어떻게 읽는지를 이해하는 것이 글쓰기 개선에 도움이 됨

- chemist ⓝ 화학자　　• extensive ⓐ 광범위한
- discipline ⓝ 학문　　• overlook ⓥ 간과하다
- oblige ⓥ 의무를 다하다　　• competent ⓐ 능숙한
- contribute ⓥ 기여하다　　• perspective ⓝ 관점
- readability ⓝ 가독성　　• reader-centered ⓐ 독자 중심의
- mentality ⓝ 사고방식　　• mindful ⓐ 유의하는
- beneficial ⓐ 유익한

화학자 Hans Ebel과 Claus Bliefert, William Russey의 말에 따르면,
"과학자가 숙련된 '독자'여야 한다는 것은 말할 필요가 없다. 다독은 자신의
지식을 확장하고 학문에서의 발전에 뒤처지지 않는 주요한 비결이다. 그러나
여기에서 흔히 간과되는 것은 과학자는 또한 숙련된 '필자'가 되어야 한다는
것이다. '글로 써서 하는' 의사소통 기술에 능숙한 연구자만이 과학에 '기여하는'
데 적극적이고 효과적인 역할을 할 수 있다." 더욱이 가독성의 관점에서
과학자는 항상 독자 중심의 사고방식으로 글을 써야 하며, 심지어 글을 쓰는
행위에서도 읽기 행위를 염두에 두어야 한다. 그들의 글쓰기를 개선하려면
독자가 어떻게 읽는지 그들이 이해하는 것은 유익할 것이다.

다음 글에서 필자가 주장하는 바로 가장 적절한 것은?
① 과학자는 독자와 만나는 기회를 자주 가져야 한다.
　　자주 만나는 것에서 그치는 것이 아님
② 과학자는 독자의 관점에서 글을 쓸 줄 알아야 한다.
　　scientists should always write with a reader-centered mentality
③ 과학자는 다양한 의견에 개방적인 태도를 가져야 한다.
　　수용적인 태도를 이야기한 것이 아님
④ 과학자는 자기 연구 분야 이외의 책도 많이 읽어야 한다.
　　다독이 언급된 것으로 만든 오답
⑤ 과학자는 연구 결과가 사회에 미치는 영향을 인식해야 한다.
　　연구 결과에 대한 책임을 이야기하는 것이 아님

왜 2등급? 선택지에서 반복되는 어구인 '과학자'만으로는 필자의 주장을 예상할 수
없지만, 글의 마지막 부분에 초점을 맞추어 글을 읽다 보면 필자의 주장을 쉽게 파악할
수 있는 2등급 대비 문제이다.

왜 정답?

- **과학자에게 요구되는 자질**: 독자 중심의 사고방식으로 글을 쓰고, 글을 쓰는
  행위에서도 읽기 행위를 염두에 두는 숙련된 필자가 될 것
- **숙련된 필자가 되려면**: 독자가 어떻게 읽는지를 이해하는 것이 글쓰기를 개선하는
  데 도움이 됨
➡ 과학자는 독자의 관점에서 글을 써야 한다는 것이므로 정답은 ②이다.

왜 오답?
① 독자와의 만남을 넘어서, 독자의 관점에서 글을 써야 한다는 내용이다.
③ 개방적이고 수용적인 태도의 중요성에 대한 내용이 아니다.
④ 전반부에 다독이 주요한 비결이라고 한 것으로 만든 오답이다. 함정
⑤ 과학자가 가져야 하는 책임감에 대해 설명하는 것이 아니다.

글의 마지막 부분을 잘 살펴봐야
주장을 찾을 수 있어!

―――― 어법 특강

＊ to부정사의 의미상 주어

– 대부분 문장에서 행위자를 알 수 있는 경우를 제외하고, 「for+명사/목적격 대명
  사」를 to부정사 앞에 표시해 준다. (예외적으로, 사람의 성격이나 태도와 같은 형
  용사가 보어로 올 때 「of+명사/목적격 대명사」로 표시한다.)

• Here are some tips for you to remember.
  (여기 네가 기억할 몇 가지 팁이 있다.)

• It is important for everyone to take part equally in discussions.
  (모든 사람이 공평하게 논의에 참여하는 것이 중요하다.)

• This is big enough for my dog to wear.
  (이것은 우리 강아지가 입기에 충분히 크다.)

• It was stupid of you to make such a mistake.
  (네가 그런 실수를 한 것은 어리석었다.)

C 어휘 Review 정답

문제편 p. 52

01 좌절감을 주는	11 call for	21 argument
02 진전, 진행	12 matter to	22 addressing
03 영감을 주다	13 on track	23 deserve
04 배치	14 hold on to	24 obliged
05 필수적인	15 contribute to	25 competent
06 strengthen	16 assistants	26 athletes
07 spot	17 branch	27 fearlessly
08 concentrate	18 maximize	28 multiple
09 perspective	19 Reliable	29 expanding
10 circulate	20 iceberg	30 Excessive

D 밑줄 친 부분의 의미 찾기

문제편 p. 53~70

D 01 정답 ① *보석을 찾아주는 알고리즘

You may feel / there is something scary / about an algorithm /
현재분사 deciding의 목적어절
deciding / what you might like. //
여러분은 느낄 수 있다 / 뭔가 무서운 것이 있다고 / 알고리즘에 대해 / 결정하는 / 여러분이
좋아할지도 모르는 것을 //

Could it mean / that, if computers conclude / you won't like
형용사적 용법(the chance 수식)
something, / you will never get the chance / to see it? //
그것은 의미하는가 / 컴퓨터가 결론을 내린다면 / 당신이 뭔가를 좋아하지 않을 것이라고 /
당신이 기회를 결코 얻지 못하리라는 것을 / 그것을 볼 //

Personally, I really enjoy being directed / toward new music /
목적격 관계대명사   동명사의 수동태   선행사
that I might not have found by myself. //
개인적으로 나는 안내받는 것을 정말 좋아한다 / 새로운 음악 쪽으로 / 내가 스스로는
발견하지 못했을 //

I can quickly get stuck / in a rut / where I put on the same songs
선행사   관계부사
/ over and over. //
나는 빨리 갇힐 수 있다 / 틀에 / 내가 같은 노래를 재생하는 / 계속 반복해서 //

That's / why I've always enjoyed the radio. //
그것이 ~이다 / 내가 항상 라디오를 즐겨 듣는 이유 // 주격 보어로 쓰인 간접의문문

복수 주어
But the algorithms / that are now pushing and pulling me /
복수 동사
through the music library / are perfectly suited / to finding gems
/ that I'll like. // **단서 1** 알고리즘은 내가 좋아할 노래를 찾는 데 완벽하게 적합함
그러나 알고리즘은 / 지금 나를 밀고 당기고 있는 / 뮤직 라이브러리를 통해 / 완벽하게
적합하다 / 보석을 찾는 데 / 내가 좋아할 //

단수 주어   단수 동사 주격 보어절 접속사
My worry originally / about such algorithms / was / that they
might drive everyone / into certain parts of the library, / leaving
others lacking listeners. // **단서 2** 알고리즘이 모든 사람을
                        특정 음악으로만 몰아넣을까 봐 걱정함
원래 나의 걱정은 / 그런 알고리즘에 대한 / ~이었다 / 그것이 모든 사람을 몰아넣을 수
있다는 것 / 라이브러리의 특정 부분으로 / 나머지는 듣는 이들이 부족하게 하면서 //

Would they cause / a convergence of tastes? //
그것은 일으킬 것인가 / 취향의 수렴을 //

But thanks to the nonlinear and chaotic mathematics / usually
behind them, / this doesn't happen. // **단서 3** 걱정하는 일은 일어나지 않음
그러나 비선형적이고 불규칙적인 수학 덕분에 / 일반적으로 그 배후에 있는 / 이런 일은
발생하지 않는다 // **단서 4** 각자의 취향을 비교하여 갈라짐
                                                    = your likes
A small divergence / in my likes / compared to yours / can send
us off / into different far corners of the library. //
작은 갈라짐이 / 내가 좋아하는 것의 / 여러분의 것과 비교하여 / 우리를 보낼 수 있다 /
라이브러리의 서로 다른 저 멀리 떨어진 구석들로 //

• conclude ⓥ 결론을 내리다, 끝나다   • stuck ⓐ 움직일 수 없는, 갇힌
• suit ⓥ 어울리다, 맞다   • lack ⓥ 부족하다, 없다
• convergence ⓝ 집합점, 수렴   • nonlinear ⓐ 직선이 아닌
• chaotic ⓐ 혼돈 상태인

여러분은 여러분이 좋아할지도 모르는 것을 결정하는 알고리즘에 대해 뭔가
무서운 것이 있다고 느낄 수 있다. 그것은 당신이 뭔가를 좋아하지 않을
것이라고 컴퓨터가 결론을 내린다면 당신은 그것을 볼 기회를 결코 얻지 못할
수도 있다는 뜻인가? 개인적으로, 나는 스스로는 발견하지 못했을 새로운
음악 쪽으로 안내받는 것을 정말 좋아한다. 나는 같은 노래를 계속 반복해서
재생하는 틀에 빨리 갇힐 수 있다. 그래서 나는 항상 라디오를 즐겨 듣는다.
그러나 지금 뮤직 라이브러리를 통해 나를 밀고 당기고 있는 알고리즘은 내가
좋아할 보석을 찾는 데 완벽하게 적합하다. 원래 그런 알고리즘에 대한 나의
걱정은 모든 사람을 라이브러리의 특정 부분으로 몰아넣고 나머지는 듣는
이들이 부족하게 만들 수 있다는 것이었다. 그것은 취향의 수렴을 일으킬
것인가? 그러나 일반적으로 그 배후에 있는 비선형적이고 불규칙적인 수학
덕분에 이런 일은 발생하지는 않는다. 여러분이 좋아하는 것과 비교하여 내가
좋아하는 것의 작은 갈라짐이 우리를 라이브러리의 서로 다른 저 멀리 떨어진
구석들로 보낼 수 있다.

밑줄 친 **send us off into different far corners of the library**가 다음
글에서 의미하는 바로 가장 적절한 것은? [3점]

① **lead us to music selected to suit our respective tastes**
우리를 우리 각각의 취향에 맞도록 선택된 음악으로 이끌다   각각의 사람들이 좋아할 음악으로 안내함
② **enable us to build connections with other listeners**
우리가 다른 청취자들과 관계를 맺을 수 있게 하다   사람들이 관계를 맺는다는 것이 아님
③ **encourage us to request frequent updates for algorithms**
우리에게 알고리즘을 위한 잦은 업데이트를 요구하라고 권하다   업데이트를 필요로 한다는 언급은 없음
④ **motivate us to search for talented but unknown musicians**
재능이 있지만 알려지지 않은 음악가들을 찾도록 우리에게 동기를 주다   우리 스스로 찾는 것이 아님
⑤ **make us ignore our preferences for particular music genres**
우리가 특정 음악 장르에 대한 우리의 선호를 무시하도록 만들다   우리의 선호를 반영함

왜 정답? [정답률 55%] 뮤직 라이브러리의 특정 부분에만 사람들이 몰리는 일이
일어나지 않음, 즉 다양한 부분으로 사람들이 퍼짐

나를 내가 좋아할 음악으로 안내하는 알고리즘에 대해, 원래는 그것이 모든 사람을
특정 음악으로 몰아넣고 다른 음악은 듣는 사람이 부족하게 만들까 봐 걱정했지만,
그런 일은 일어나지 않는다고 했다.
내가 좋아하는 것과 다른 사람이 좋아하는 것이 갈라진다는 사실이 우리 각각을
뮤직 라이브러리의 다양한 부분으로 보낸다는 것은, 우리가 각각의 취향에 의해
우리가 좋아할 음악으로 안내받는다는 의미이므로 정답은 ① '우리를 우리 각각의
취향에 맞도록 선택된 음악으로 이끈다'이다.

왜 오답?

② my likes와 yours가 등장하긴 하지만, 나와 다른 청취자들이 어떤 관계를
맺는다는 내용이 아니다.
③ 알고리즘이 우리의 취향을 더 세밀하게 반영하여 안내할 수 있도록 잦은
업데이트가 필요하다는 등의 언급은 없다.
④ 우리로 하여금 스스로 새로운 음악을 찾도록 동기를 부여하는 것이 아니라
알고리즘이 우리를 우리가 좋아할 음악으로 안내하는 것에 대한 내용이다.
⑤ 우리의 선호를 반영하여 안내한다는 것이므로 글의 내용과 완전히 반대된다.
주의

D 02 정답 ⑤ *세계를 있는 그대로 볼 수는 없는 우리

Our view of the world / is not given to us / from the outside / in
a pure, objective form; /
세계에 대한 우리의 관점은 / 우리에게 주어지지 않는다 / 외부에서 / 순수하고 객관적인
형태로 / **단서 1** 우리의 세계관은 우리의 정신력, 문화적 관점, 가치관 등에 의해 형성됨
it is shaped / by our mental abilities, our shared cultural
perspectives and our unique values and beliefs. //
그것은 형성된다 / 우리의 정신 능력, 우리의 공유된 문화적 관점, 그리고 우리의 독특한
가치관과 신념에 의해 //

This is not to say / that there is no reality outside our minds / or
to say의 목적어절 이끄는 명사절 접속사의 병렬 구조
that the world is just an illusion. //
이것은 말하는 것이 아니다 / 우리의 마음 외부에 현실이 없다거나 / 세계는 환영에
불과하다고 //
            명사절 접속사   지시대명사
It is to say / that our version of reality is precisely that: / our
version, / not the version. //
그것은 말하는 것이다 / 현실에 대한 우리의 버전은 바로 그것이라고 / '우리의' 버전 /
'그' 버전이 아니라 //

There is no single, universal or authoritative version / that
                                            주격 관계대명사
makes sense, / other than as a theoretical construct. //
단일하거나, 보편적이거나 또는 권위 있는 버전은 없다 / 이치에 맞는 / 이론적 구성물로서가
아닌 // **단서 2** 우리는 정말로 있는 그대로가 아니라 우리에게 보이는 대로만 세계를 볼 수 있음
We can see the world / only as it appears to us, / not "as it truly
is," / because there is no "as it truly is" / without a perspective /
to give it form. //
우리는 세계를 볼 수 있다 / 그것이 우리에게 보이는 대로만 / '정말로 있는 그대로'가 아니라 /
'정말로 있는 그대로'란 없기 때문에 / 관점 없이 / 그것에 형태를 부여하는 //

Philosopher Thomas Nagel argued / that there is no "view from
nowhere," /
철학자 Thomas Nagel은 주장했다 / '입장이 없는 관점'은 없다고 /

since we cannot see the world / except from a particular
perspective, / and that perspective influences / what we see. //
〈이유〉의 부사절 접속사   지시형용사
우리는 세계를 볼 수 없기 때문에 / 특정한 관점에서를 제외하고는 / 그리고 그 관점이 영향을
미치기 때문에 / 우리가 보는 것에 // **단서 3** 우리는 우리의 렌즈를 통해서만 세계를 경험할 수 있음
We can experience the world / only through the human lenses /
that make it intelligible to us. //
우리는 세계를 경험할 수 있다 / 인간의 렌즈를 통해서만 / 그것을 우리가 이해할 수 있게
만드는 //

- pure ⓐ 순수한, 완전한　　· objective ⓐ 객관적인
- perspective ⓝ 관점, 시각　　· reality ⓝ 현실
- precisely ⓐⓓ 바로, 정확하게　　· universal ⓐ 보편적인, 일반적인
- authoritative ⓐ 권위적인　　· theoretical ⓐ 이론의, 이론적인
- construct ⓝ 생각, 건축물　　· philosopher ⓝ 철학자
- intelligible ⓐ (쉽게) 이해할 수 있는

세계에 대한 우리의 관점은 순수하고 객관적인 형태로 외부에서 우리에게
주어지는 것이 아니라, 그것은 우리의 정신 능력, 우리의 공유된 문화적 관점,
그리고 우리의 독특한 가치관과 신념에 의해 형성된다. 이것은 우리의 마음
외부에 현실이 없다거나 세계는 환영에 불과하다고 말하는 것이 아니다.
그것은 현실에 대한 우리의 버전은 바로 그것, 즉 '우리의' 버전이지 '그' 버전은
아니라고 말하는 것이다. 이론적 구성물로서가 아닌, 이치에 맞는 단일하거나,
보편적이거나 또는 권위 있는 버전은 없다. 우리는 세계를 '정말로 있는
그대로'가 아니라, 그것이 우리에게 보이는 대로만 볼 수 있는데, 왜냐하면
세계에 형태를 부여하는 관점 없이 '정말로 있는 그대로'란 없기 때문이다.
철학자 Thomas Nagel은 '입장이 없는 관점'은 없다고 주장했는데, 왜냐하면
우리는 특정한 관점에서 보는 경우를 제외하고는 세계를 볼 수 없고, 그 관점이
우리가 보는 것에 영향을 미치기 때문이다. 우리는 세계를 우리가 이해할 수
있게 만드는 인간의 렌즈를 통해서만 세계를 경험할 수 있다.

**밑줄 친 "view from nowhere"가 다음 글에서 의미하는 바로 가장 적절한
것은? [3점]**

① perception of reality affected by subjective views
주관적인 견해에 영향을 받는 현실 인식   밑줄 앞의 no에 주의해야 함
② valuable perspective most people have in mind ─ 대다수 또는 소수가
대부분의 사람이 염두에 두고 있는 가치 있는 관점 ┐ 가진 세계관에 대한
③ particular view adopted by very few people ─┘ 내용이 아님
극소수의 사람에게 채택된 특정한 견해
④ critical insight that defeats our prejudices
우리의 편견을 물리치는 비판적 통찰   편견을 버리려는 노력이 없음을 비판하는 것이 아님
⑤ unbiased and objective view of the world
편견이 없으면서 객관적인 세계관   '정말로 있는 그대로'라는 것은 없음

왜 정답? [정답률 59%] 주관적으로 형성된다는 것을 의미함 **꿀팁**

세계를 보는 우리의 관점은 외부에서 객관적인 형태로 주어지는 것이 아니라
우리의 정신, 문화, 가치관 등에 의해 형성된다면서 우리는 우리에게 보이는
대로만 세계를 볼 수 있고, 인간의 렌즈를 통해서만 세계를 경험할 수 있다고
했다.
이러한 글의 내용을 뒷받침하기 위해 Thomas Nagel의 말을 인용한 것이므로,
Thomas Nagel이 없다고 주장한 '입장이 없는 관점'은 ⑤ '편견이 없으면서
객관적인 세계관'이다.

왜 오답?

① '주관적인 견해에 영향을 받는 현실 인식'이 없다고(no) 말하는 것은 글과
정반대의 내용이 된다. **함정**
②, ③ 대다수가 가진 세계관 또는 극소수만이 채택하는 세계관에 대해서 설명하는
글이 아니다.
④ 우리가 우리의 렌즈를 통해 세계를 본다는 것이 편견을 의미한다고 할 수는
있지만, 그러한 편견을 버리려는 통찰이 없다는 등의 비판을 제기하는 글이
아니다.

D 03 정답 ③ ＊실용적, 이론적 지식을 모두 필요로 하는 건축가

rise의 과거(자동사)
The position of the architect / rose during the Roman Empire, /
as architecture symbolically became / a particularly important
political statement. //
건축가의 지위는 / 로마 제국 시대에 상승했는데 / 이는 건축이 상징적으로 되었기 때문이다 /
특히 중요한 정치적 성명이 //
Cicero classed the architect with the physician and the teacher /
「so+형용사+관사+명사」 어순 cf)「such+관사+형용사+명사」 어순
and Vitruvius spoke of "so great a profession as this." //
Cicero는 건축가를 의사와 교사와 같은 부류에 넣었으며 / Vitruvius는 '이토록 위대한 직업'
에 대해 말했다 // **단서 1** 건축은 실용적 지식과 이론적 지식 모두 필요로 함
Marcus Vitruvius Pollio, / a practicing architect during the rule
현재분사(architect 수식)
of Augustus Caesar, / recognized that architecture requires /
명사절 접속사
both practical and theoretical knowledge, /
Marcus Vitruvius Pollio는 / Augustus Caesar 통치 시기에 활동하던 건축가인 / 건축이
필요로 한다는 점을 인정했으며 / 실용적 지식과 이론적 지식을 모두 /
목적격 관계대명사 생략 현재분사(architect 수식)
and he listed the disciplines he felt the aspiring architect should
master: / literature and writing, draftsmanship, mathematics,
history, philosophy, music, medicine, law, and astronomy / — a
주격 관계대명사
curriculum that still has much to recommend it. //
그는 장차 건축가가 되려는 자가 숙달해야 한다고 생각한 학문 분야를 나열했는데 / 이는
문학과 작문, 제도, 수학, 역사, 철학, 음악, 의학, 법, 그리고 천문학이었고 / 이것은 여전히
많은 추천을 받는 교육과정이다 //
All of this study was necessary, he argued, / because architects
주격 관계대명사
who have aimed at acquiring manual skill without scholarship
현재완료
/ have never been able to reach a position of authority /
형용사적 용법(position 수식)
to correspond to their plans, / **단서 2** 학문 없이 손기술만 습득하는 건축가는
권위 있는 지위에 도달할 수 없음
그는 이 모든 학문이 필요하다고 주장했는데 / 그 이유는 학문 없이 손기술을 습득하려 한
건축가는 / 결코 권위 있는 지위에 도달할 수 없었던 반면 / 자신의 계획에 상응하는 /
those who: ~한 사람들
while those who have relied only upon theories and scholarship
/ were obviously "hunting the shadow, not the substance." //
오로지 이론과 학문에만 의존한 건축가는 / 분명히 '실체가 아닌 그림자를 쫓고 있었기'
때문이다 // **단서 3** 반대로 손기술 없이 이론과 학문에만 의존하는 건축가는
'실체가 아닌 그림자를 쫓고' 있음

- architect ⓝ 건축가　　· empire ⓝ 제국　　· architecture ⓝ 건축
- symbolically ⓐⓓ 상징적으로　　· statement ⓝ 성명
- class ⓥ 분류하다　　· physician ⓝ 의사　　· profession ⓝ 직업
- practice ⓥ 활동하다　　· practical ⓐ 실용적인
- theoretical ⓐ 이론적인　　· aspire ⓥ 열망하다
- draftsmanship ⓝ 제도　　· astronomy ⓝ 천문학
- manual ⓐ 손의　　· scholarship ⓝ 학문　　· authority ⓝ 권위
- correspond ⓥ 상응하다　　· substance ⓝ 실체

건축가의 지위는 로마 제국 시대에 상승했는데, 이는 건축이 상징적으로 특히
중요한 정치적 성명이 되었기 때문이다. Cicero는 건축가를 의사와 교사와
같은 부류에 넣었으며, Vitruvius는 '이토록 위대한 직업'에 대해 말했다.
Augustus Caesar 통치 시기에 활동하던 건축가인 Marcus Vitruvius
Pollio는 건축이 실용적 지식과 이론적 지식을 모두 필요로 한다는 점을
인정했으며, 그는 장차 건축가가 되려는 자가 숙달해야 한다고 생각한 학문
분야를 나열했는데, 이는 문학과 작문, 제도, 수학, 역사, 철학, 음악, 의학, 법,
그리고 천문학이었고, 이것은 여전히 많은 추천을 받는 교육과정이다. 그는 이
모든 학문이 필요하다고 주장했는데, 그 이유는 학문 없이 손기술을 습득하려
한 건축가는 결코 자신의 계획에 상응하는 권위 있는 지위에 도달할 수 없었던
반면, 오로지 이론과 학문에만 의존한 건축가는 분명히 '실체가 아닌 그림자를
쫓고 있었기' 때문이다.

건축 목표에 필요한 과목을 구별하는 것이 아니라, 모든 과목이 건축에 요구된다는 내용임
① seeking abstract knowledge emphasized by architectural
tradition 건축 전통이나 추상적 지식에 관한 언급은 없었음
건축 전통에 의해 강조되는 추상적 지식을 추구하기
② discounting the subjects necessary to achieve architectural goals
건축 목표를 달성하는 데 필요한 과목들을 무시하기
③ pursuing the ideals of architecture without the practical skills
실용적인 기술 없이 건축의 이상을 쫓기
기술 없이 이론만으로 건축의 이상을 쫓는 건축가들에 관한 설명임
④ prioritizing architecture's material aspects over its artistic ones
건축의 예술적 측면보다 물질적 측면을 우선시하기
건축가의 실용적, 이론적 지식에 관한 내용이므로, 예술적, 물질적 측면에 관한 언급은 없었음
⑤ following historical precedents without regard to current
standards 건축에 관한 현대 기준이나 역사적 선례와 같은 내용은 언급되지 않음
현재 기준을 고려하지 않고 역사적 선례를 따르기

> **왜 정답?** [정답률 52%]

1st 첫 부분과 밑줄 친 부분이 포함된 부분을 읽고, 글의 내용을 예상한다.

첫 부분	건축가의 지위는 로마 제국 시대에 상승했는데, 이는 건축이 상징적으로 특히 중요한 정치적 성명이 되었기 때문이다.
밑줄 친 부분이 포함된 부분	그는 이 모든 학문이 필요하다고 주장했는데, 그 이유는 학문 없이 손기술을 습득하려 한 건축가는 결코 자신의 계획에 상응하는 권위 있는 지위에 도달할 수 없었던 반면, 오로지 이론과 학문에만 의존한 건축가는 분명히 '실체가 아닌 그림자를 쫓고 있었기' 때문이다.

⇒ **첫 부분**: 로마 제국 당시 건축가의 지위가 상당히 중요하고 높았음
밑줄 친 부분이 포함된 부분: 건축가에게 필요한 학문을 나열한 후, 학문 없이 손기술만 습득하는 건축가는 권위에 도달할 수 없을 것이라 했고, 손기술 없이 학문에만 의존하는 건축가는 '실체가 아닌 그림자를 쫓고 있다'라고 표현함

⇒ 로마 제국 당시 건축가의 지위와 건축가에게 필요한 역량에 관한 고찰을 설명한 글이다. 밑줄 친 부분은 당시 건축가에게 필요하다고 인정되었던 여러 학문이 나열된 후, 이 모든 학문이 건축가에게 필요하다고 주장했음을 소개하고 있다. 이후에 학문 없이 손기술만 습득하려는 건축가를 부정적으로 바라보았으므로, 반대의 경우인 이론과 학문에만 의존하는 건축가 역시 부정적으로 바라보았을 것이다.

2nd 글의 나머지 부분을 읽고, 예상한 내용이 맞는지 확인한다.

- Marcus Vitruvius Pollio는 건축은 실용적 지식과 이론적 지식 모두 필요로 한다고 주장함 **단서 1**
- 학문 없이 손기술만 습득하는 건축가는 권위 있는 지위에 도달할 수 없음 **단서 2**
- 반대로 손기술 없이 이론과 학문에만 의존하는 건축가는 '실체가 아닌 그림자를 쫓고' 있음 **단서 3**

⇒ Marcus Vitruvius Pollio는 건축가에게는 실용적 지식과 이론적 지식 모두 요구된다고 주장했으며, 건축가에게 필요한 학문들을 나열한 후, 모든 학문이 필요하다고 했다. 따라서 이론과 기술 중 하나만을 추구하는 건축가를 부정적으로 평가하고 있다.

3rd 파악한 글의 내용을 종합하여 밑줄 친 부분의 의미를 파악한다.

로마 제국 당시 건축가의 지위가 상당히 높았으며, 건축가에게 요구되는 자질도 많았다는 내용이다. 구체적으로, Marcus Vitruvius Pollio는 건축에는 실용적 지식과 이론적 지식 모두 요구된다고 주장했다.
따라서 이론 없이 기술만 습득하는 건축가를 부정적으로 평가한 것과 마찬가지로, 기술 없이 이론에만 의존하는 건축가 역시 '실체가 아닌 그림자를 쫓고' 있다고 표현한 것의 의미는 ③ '실용적인 기술 없이 건축의 이상을 추구하기'이다.

| 선택지 분석 |

① seeking abstract knowledge emphasized by architectural tradition
건축 전통에 의해 강조되는 추상적 지식을 추구하기
건축 전통이나 추상적 지식에 관한 언급은 없었다.

② discounting the subjects necessary to achieve architectural goals
건축 목표를 달성하는 데 필요한 과목들을 무시하기
건축 목표에 필요한 과목을 구별하는 것이 아니라, 모든 과목이 건축에 요구된다는 내용이다.

③ pursuing the ideals of architecture without the practical skills
실용적인 기술 없이 건축의 이상을 추구하기
기술 없이 이론만으로 건축의 이상을 쫓는 건축가들에 관한 설명이다.

④ prioritizing architecture's material aspects over its artistic ones
건축의 예술적 측면보다 물질적 측면을 우선시하기
건축가의 실용적, 이론적 지식에 관한 내용이므로, 예술적, 물질적 측면에 관한 언급은 없었다.

⑤ following historical precedents without regard to current standards
현재 기준을 고려하지 않고 역사적 선례를 따르기
건축에 관한 현대 기준이나 역사적 선례와 같은 내용은 언급되지 않았다.

배지오 | 2025 수능 응시 · 성남 낙생고 졸

architect라는 단어가 반복되기 때문에 건축에 대한 글이라는 것을 알 수 있어. 더 나아가 건축이 로마 제국 시대에 정치적 성명의 역할을 했다는 것을 파악했다면 잘 한거야. 세 번째 recognized that architecture ~ theoretical knowledge 라는 문장에서 건축은 실용적 지식과 이론적 지식 모두를 필요로 한다고 주장해. 따라서 실용적 지식만을 갖춘 architects who have aimed at acquiring manual skill without scholarship과 이론적 지식만을 갖춘 those who have relied only upon theories 둘 다 불완전하다는 말이 나와야 하겠지!

D 04 정답 ③ * 인류학자들의 문화 집단 연구 방식

Around the turn of the twentieth century, / anthropologists
과거분사(선행사 anthropologists 수식)
trained in the natural sciences / began to reimagine /
20세기에 접어들면서 / 자연과학에서 훈련받은 인류학자들은 / 다시 생각하기 시작했다 /
간접의문문의 병렬 구조
what a science of humanity should look like / and how social
scientists ought to go / about studying cultural groups. //
인류학이 어떻게 보여야 하는지와 / 그리고 사회 과학자들이 어떻게 시작해야 하는지 / 문화 집단 연구를 //
insist that 주어(should) 동사원형: ~해야 한다고 주장하다
Some of those anthropologists insisted / that one should at least
spend significant time / actually observing and talking to / the
과거분사(선행사 people 수식) **단서 1** 연구 대상인 사람들을 직접 관찰하고 대화하며
people studied. // 시간을 할애해야 한다고 했음
그러한 인류학자들 중 일부는 주장했다 / 적어도 상당한 시간을 할애해야 한다고 / 실제로 관찰하고 대화하는 데 / 연구되는 사람들과 //
Early ethnographers such as Franz Boas and Alfred Cort
문장의 동사 ① 관계부사
Haddon / typically traveled to the remote locations / where
the people in question lived / and spent a few weeks to a few
문장의 동사 ②
months there. //
Franz Boas와 Alfred Cort Haddon과 같은 초기 민족지학자들은 / 일반적으로 외딴 지역으로 갔다 / 연구되고 있는 사람이 살고 있는 / 그리고 그곳에서 몇 주에서 몇 달을 보냈다 //
문장의 동사 ① 주격 관계대명사
They sought out a local Western host / who was familiar with
the people and the area / (such as a colonial official, missionary,
문장의 동사 ②
or businessman) / and found accommodations through them. //
그들은 서양인 호스트를 찾아내었다 / 주민들과 그 지역을 잘 알고 있는 / (식민지 관료, 선교사 혹은 사업가와 같이) / 그리고 그들을 통해 숙박 시설을 구했다 //
Although they did at times venture into the community /
without a guide, / they generally did not spend significant time
/ with the local people. // **단서 2** 민족지학자들은 현지인들과 상당한 시간을 보내지는
않았음
가끔은 그들은 정말이지 그 지역사회를 탐험하기도 했지만 / 가이드 없이 / 대개 그들은 상당한 시간을 보내지는 않았다 / 현지인들과 //
Thus, / their observations were primarily conducted / from their
verandas. //
그리하여 / 그들의 관찰은 주로 행해졌다 / 그들의 '베란다'에서 //

- anthropologist ⓝ 인류학자 · go about ~을 시작하다
- insist ⓥ 주장하다 · significant ⓐ 상당한, 중요한
- ethnographer ⓝ 민족지학자 · remote ⓐ 외딴

- in question 연구[논의]되고 있는　　・ seek out ~을 찾아내다
- colonial ⓐ 식민지의　　・ missionary ⓝ 선교사
- accommodation ⓝ 숙박 시설　　・ venture into ~을 탐험하다
- primarily ⓐⓓ 주로　　・ conduct ⓥ (특정한 활동을) 하다
- collaborative ⓐ 공동의　　・ struggle to ~하려고 애쓰다
- examine ⓥ 조사하다

20세기에 접어들면서, 자연과학에서 훈련받은 인류학자들은 인류학이 어떻게 보여야 하는지와 사회 과학자들이 문화 집단 연구를 어떻게 시작해야 하는지를 다시 생각하기 시작했다. 그러한 인류학자들 중 일부는 다른 건 몰라도 연구 대상인 사람들을 실제로 관찰하고 그들과 대화하는 데 상당한 시간을 할애해야 한다고 주장했다. Franz Boas와 Alfred Cort Haddon과 같은 초기 민족지학자들은 일반적으로 연구되고 있는 사람이 살고 있는 외딴 지역으로 가서 그곳에서 몇 주에서 몇 달을 보냈다. 그들은 (식민지 관료, 선교사 혹은 사업가와 같이) 주민들과 그 지역을 잘 알고 있는 그 지역 서양인 호스트를 찾아내어 그들을 통해 숙박 시설을 구했다. 가끔은 그들은 정말이지 가이드 없이 그 지역사회를 탐험하기도 했지만, 대개 그들은 현지인들과 상당한 시간을 보내지는 않았다. 그리하여 그들의 관찰은 주로 그들의 '베란다'에서 행해졌다.

밑줄 친 from their *verandas*가 다음 글에서 의미하는 바로 가장 적절한 것은?

　　　　　　　　　　　　　원주민과 관계를 구축하기 위해 노력하는 것과 반대임
① seeking to build long-lasting relationships with the natives
원주민과 오래 지속되는 관계를 구축하기 위해 노력하기
② participating in collaborative research with natural scientists
자연 과학자들과의 공동 연구에 참여하기　　자연 과학자들과 공동 연구에 참여하지 않았음
③ engaging in little direct contact with the people being studied
연구되고 있는 사람들과 직접적인 접촉을 거의 하지 않기　현지인들과는 거의 시간을 보내지 않았다고 했음
④ cooperating actively with Western hosts in the local community
지역사회에서 서양인 호스트와 적극적으로 협력하기　서양인 호스트를 통해 숙박 시설을 구했을 뿐임
⑤ struggling to take a wider view of the native culture examined
조사 대상인 원주민 문화에 관한 더 넓은 관점을 갖기 위해 애쓰기
　　　　　　　　　조사 대상인 원주민을 언급한 것으로 만든 함정

》왜 정답? [정답률 54%]

ㅏ • 인류학자들 중 일부는 연구 대상인 사람들을 직접 관찰하고 대화하며 시간을 할애해야 한다고 했음 단서 1
└ • 초기 민족지학자들이 연구를 할 때 현지인과 상당한 시간을 보내지 않았음 단서 2

➡ 자연과학에서 훈련받은 인류학자들은 연구 대상인 사람들을 직접 관찰하면서 소통하는 연구가 중요하다고 주장했다. 그러나 초기 민족지학자들은 연구 대상인 현지인과 직접 접촉하거나 시간을 보내지 않고 멀리서 지켜보기만 했다.

▶ 관찰이 주로 '그들의 베란다에서' 행해졌다는 말이 의미하는 바: ③ '연구되고 있는 사람들과 직접적인 접촉을 거의 하지 않기'

》왜 오답?

① 원주민과 오래 지속되는 관계를 구축하기 위해 노력하지 않았다.
② 자연 과학자들과 공동 연구에 참여했다는 내용은 없다.
④ 서양인 호스트를 통해 숙박 시설을 구한 것은 맞지만 밑줄 친 부분의 의미는 아니다. (▶◀ 이유: 민족지학자들이 서양인 호스트를 통해 숙박 시설을 구한 것을 확대 해석하면 안 됨)
⑤ 원주민을 언급했을 뿐, 문화에 대한 더 넓은 관점을 갖고자 애썼다는 것은 아니다.

D 05 정답 ① ＊대화에서 화자의 의도를 나타내는 단서를 알아차리는 것의 필요성

In improv, / the actors have no control / of the conversation or the direction it takes. //
즉흥 연극에서 / 배우들은 통제할 수 없다 / 대화나 대화의 방향을 //

They can only react / to the other actors' words or nonverbal communication. //
단서 1 즉흥 연극 배우들은 상대방의 몸짓 언어를 읽고 말의 행간을 읽는 데 전문가임
그들은 반응할 수 있을 뿐이다 / 다른 배우들의 말이나 비언어적 의사소통에 //

Because of this, / the actors become experts / at reading body language and reading between the lines of what is said. //
선행사를 포함한 관계대명사
이 때문에 / 배우들은 전문가가 된다 / 몸짓 언어를 읽고 발화의 행간을 읽는 데 //

If they are unable to do this, / they are left in the dark / and the
조건의 부사절 접속사
performance crumbles. //
만약 이것을 할 수 없다면 / 그들은 알지 못하는 상태에 있게 되며 / 공연은 무너진다 //

This applies to our daily conversations, / but we're usually too self-centered to notice. //
이것은 우리의 일상적인 대화에도 적용되지만 / 우리는 대개 너무 자기 중심적이어서 알아챌 수 없다 //
단서 2 우리도 즉흥 연극 배우처럼 해야 함

Just like the improv actors become adept / at picking up on the breadcrumbs of the conversation, / we need to do the same. //
즉흥 연극 배우들이 능숙해지는 것처럼 / 대화의 빵 부스러기를 알아차리는 데 / 우리는 똑같이 할 필요가 있다 //

When people want to talk about something specific, / rarely will
-thing으로 끝나는 대명사는 뒤에서 수식함
they come out and just say it. //
부정어 구문 도치(rarely+동사+주어)
사람들이 구체적인 무언가에 대해 말하기를 원할 때 / 그들은 좀처럼 나서서 그것을 말하지 않을 것이다 //

99 percent of people won't say, / "Hey, let's talk about my dog now. So...."//
99퍼센트의 사람들은 말하지 않을 것이다 / "이봐, 지금 내 강아지에 대해 말해보자. 그러니...."라고 //
단서 3 사람들은 말하고 싶은 것을 직접 말하기보다 암시할 것임

Instead, they will hint at it. // 대신에, 그들은 그것을 암시할 것이다 //

When they bring up a topic unprompted, / or ask questions about it, / they want to talk about it. //
그들이 남이 시키지 않은 상태에서 화제를 제시하거나 / 그것에 관해 질문할 때 / 그들은 그것에 대해 말하기를 원하는 것이다 //

Sometimes, / when the other person seems to not pick up on these signals, / they will keep redirecting the conversation / to
지시형용사
that specific topic. //
keep -ing: 계속 ~하다
때때로 / 상대방이 이 신호를 알아차리는 것처럼 보이지 않을 때 / 그들은 계속해서 대화를 다시 돌릴 것이다 / 그 특정 주제로 //

If they seem excited / whenever the topic comes up, / they want to talk about it. //
만약 그들이 신나 보인다면 / 그 화제가 나타날 때마다 / 그들은 그것에 대해 말하기를 원하는 것이다 //

- conversation ⓝ 대화　　・ nonverbal ⓐ 비언어적인
- apply to 적용하다　　・ pick up on 알아차리다
- specific ⓐ 구체적인　　・ unprompted ⓐ 자발적인
- roundabout ⓐ 둘러가는, 우회적인　　・ reveal ⓥ 밝히다, 드러내다
- intention ⓝ 의도　　・ distract ⓥ 방해하다
- unexpected ⓐ 예상치 못한

즉흥 연극에서, 배우들은 대화나 대화의 방향을 통제할 수 없다. 그들은 다른 배우들의 말이나 비언어적 의사소통에 반응할 수 있을 뿐이다. 이 때문에, 배우들은 몸짓 언어를 읽고 발화의 행간을 읽는 데 전문가가 된다. 만약 그들이 이것을 할 수 없다면, 그들은 알지 못하는 상태에 있게 되며 공연은 무너진다. 이것은 우리의 일상적인 대화에도 적용되지만, 우리는 대개 너무 자기 중심적이어서 알아챌 수 없다. 즉흥 연극 배우들이 대화의 빵 부스러기를 알아차리는 데 능숙해지는 것처럼, 우리는 똑같이 할 필요가 있다. 사람들이 구체적인 무언가에 대해 말하기를 원할 때, 그들은 좀처럼 나서서 그것을 말하지 않을 것이다. 99퍼센트의 사람들은 "이봐, 지금 내 강아지에 대해 말해보자. 그러니...."라고 말하지 않을 것이다. 대신에, 그들은 그것을 암시할 것이다. 그들이 남이 시키지 않은 상태에서 화제를 제시하거나 그것에 관해 질문할 때, 그들은 그것에 대해 말하기를 원하는 것이다. 때때로, 상대방이 이 신호를 알아차리는 것처럼 보이지 않을 때, 그들은 계속해서 대화를 그 특정 주제로 다시 돌릴 것이다. 만약 그들이 그 화제가 나타날 때마다 신나 보인다면, 그들은 그것에 대해 말하기를 원하는 것이다.

밑줄 친 the breadcrumbs of the conversation이 다음 글에서 의미하는 바로 가장 적절한 것은? [3점]

① roundabout hints revealing the speaker's intention
화자의 의도를 드러내는 우회적인 힌트　화자가 하고 싶은 말을 암시하는 단서를 드러낼 수 있다는 내용임
② opening words to make the topic more interesting
주제를 더 흥미롭게 만드는 시작의 말　　주제를 더 흥미롭게 한다는 내용은 없음
③ part of the conversation that distracts the listeners
청중을 산만하게 만드는 대화의 부분　　청자를 방해하는 것에 대한 내용이 아님
④ characteristics that are unique to the actors themselves
배우들만의 독특한 특징들　　배우들의 특징에 대한 언급은 없음
⑤ unexpected reactions of the audience to the performance
공연에 대한 관객의 예상치 못한 반응　　관객의 반응에 대한 내용이 아님

- 즉흥 연극 배우들은 대화를 이어나가기 위해 상대의 비언어적 표현을 알아차리고 말의 행간을 읽는 것에 전문가임 **단서 1**
- 일상 대화에서도 마찬가지로 상대의 의도를 드러내는 단서를 잘 알아차려야 함 **단서 2**

➡ 즉흥 연극 배우들이 '대화의 빵 부스러기(= 직접적으로 드러나지 않고 암시되어 있는 상대의 의도)'를 알아차리는 것에 능숙해지듯 우리도 그렇게 해야 한다는 것이 이 글의 중심 내용이다.

▶ 따라서 밑줄 친 부분은 ① '화자의 의도를 드러내는 우회적인 힌트'를 의미한다.

왜 오답?

② 주제를 더 흥미롭게 만드는 시작의 말에 대한 내용이 아니다.

③ 청자를 방해하는 대화의 부분에 대한 설명은 없다.

④ 배우의 독특한 특징에 대한 글이 아니다.

⑤ 관객이 공연에 대해 어떻게 반응하는지에 대한 언급은 없다.

D 06 정답 ② ＊번아웃은 '상태'가 아닌 '범위'로 간주해야 한다.

부사적 용법(목적)

To balance the need / for breadth (everyone feels a bit burned out) / and depth (some are so burned out, they can no longer do their jobs), / we ought to think of burnout / not as a *state* but as a *spectrum*. // **단서 1** 번아웃을 '상태'가 아니라 '범위'로 생각해야 함

필요의 균형을 맞추기 위해 / 폭(모두가 약간 지쳤다고 느낀다)과 깊이(일부는 너무 지쳐서 더는 일을 할 수 없다)에 대한 / 우리는 번아웃을 간주해야 한다 / '상태'가 아니라 '범위'로 //

In most public discussion of burnout, / we talk about workers who "are burned out," / as if that status were black and white. //

번아웃에 대한 대부분의 대중적 논의에서 / 우리는 '번아웃 된' 노동자에 대해 이야기한다 / 마치 그 상태가 흑백 상태인 것처럼 // **단서 2** 흑백 논리(대상을 둘 중 하나로 명확하게 나누는 것)로는 번아웃 경험의 다양성을 설명할 수 없음

A black-and-white view cannot account for / the variety of burnout experience, / though. //

흑백 논리의 관점은 설명할 수 없다 / 번아웃 경험의 다양성 / 그러나 //

If there is a clear line between burned out and not, / as there is with a lightbulb, /

번아웃 상태와 그렇지 않은 상태 사이에 명확한 경계가 있다면 / 전구의 경우 그런 것처럼 /

then we have no good way to categorize people / who say they are burned out / but still manage to do their work competently. //

사람들을 분류할 수 있는 좋은 방법이 없다 / 자신이 번아웃 되었다고 말하지만 / 여전히 유능하게 자기 일을 해내는 //

Thinking about burnout as a spectrum / solves this problem; / those who claim burnout but are not debilitated by it / are simply dealing with a partial or less-severe form of it. //

번아웃을 범위로 간주하는 것은 / 이러한 문제를 해결할 수 있는데 / 번아웃을 주장하지만 그것에 의해 쇠약해지지 않는 사람들은 / 그것의 부분적이거나 덜 심각한 형태를 다루고 있을 뿐이다 //

They are experiencing burnout / without *being* burned out. //

그들은 번아웃을 경험하고 있다 / 번아웃 '되고 있지' 않으면서 //

Burnout hasn't had the last word. // **단서 3** 앞에서 언급한 대로 생각하면 '번아웃 상태임에도 자기 일을 해내는 사람들(번아웃의 다양한 경험의 하나로 제시된 예시)'에 대한 분류를 할 수 있음

번아웃은 마지막 진술을 하지 않았다 //

- breadth ⓝ 폭, 너비   • burn out 에너지를 소진하다
- spectrum ⓝ 범위, 스펙트럼   • account for 설명하다
- categorize ⓥ 분류하다   • manage to 힘든 일을 겨우(간신히) 하다
- competently ⓐ 유능하게   • partial ⓐ 부분적인
- have[give, say] the last word 결정적 발언을 하다, 마지막 진술을 하다
- exhaustion ⓝ 탈진
- all-or-nothing ⓐ 양자택일의, 이것 아니면 저것인
- criterion ⓝ 기준 (복수형: criteria)   • applicable ⓐ 해당되는
- severity ⓝ 심각성

폭(모두가 약간 지쳤다고 느낀다)과 깊이(일부는 너무 지쳐서 더는 일을 할 수 없다)에 대한 필요의 균형을 맞추기 위해, 우리는 번아웃을 '상태'가 아니라 '범위'로 간주해야 한다. 번아웃에 대한 대부분의 대중적 논의에서, 우리는 '번아웃 된' 노동자에 대해, 마치 그 상태가 흑백 상태인 것처럼 이야기한다. 그러나, 흑백 논리의 관점은 번아웃 경험의 다양성을 설명할 수 없다. 전구의 경우 그런 것처럼, 번아웃 상태와 그렇지 않은 상태 사이에 명확한 경계가 있다면, 자신이 번아웃 되었다고 말하지만 여전히 유능케도 자기 일을 유능하게 해내는 사람들을 분류할 수 있는 좋은 방법이 없다. 번아웃을 범위로 간주하면 이러한 문제를 해결할 수 있는데, 번아웃을 주장하지만 그것에 의해 쇠약해지지 않는 사람은 그것의 부분적이거나 덜 심각한 형태를 다루고 있을 뿐이다. 그들은 번아웃 '되고 있지' 않으면서 번아웃을 경험하고 있다. 번아웃은 마지막 진술을 하지 않았다.

밑줄 친 Burnout hasn't had the last word.가 다음 글에서 의미하는 바로 가장 적절한 것은?

① Public discussion of burnout has not reached an end. 서두에 제시된 public discussion을 이용해 만든 오답
번아웃(= 탈진)을 범위로 간주하면, 번아웃의 다양한 경험과 정도를 설명할 수 있음
번아웃에 대한 대중적 논의는 아직 끝나지 않았다.

② There still exists room for a greater degree of exhaustion.
탈진의 정도가 더 클 수 있는 여지가 여전히 있다.

③ All-or-nothing criteria are applicable to burnout symptoms. 흑백
양자택일의 기준은 번아웃 증상에 적용 가능하다. (= 양자택일)로는 번아웃의 다양한 경험을 설명할 수 없음 논리

④ Exhaustion is overcome in different ways based on its severity.
탈진은 그것의 심각성을 기준으로 다양한 방법으로 극복된다. 탈진의 극복 방법은 언급되지 않음

⑤ Degrees of exhaustion are shaped by individuals' perceptions.
탈진의 정도는 개인의 인식에 의해 형성된다. 번아웃이 개인의 인식에 의해 형성된다는 말은 없음

왜 정답? [정답률 34%]

- 번아웃을 '상태'가 아니라 '범위'로 생각해야 함 **단서 1**
- 흑백 논리(대상을 둘 중 하나로 명확하게 나누는 것)로는 번아웃 경험의 다양성을 설명할 수 없음 **단서 2**
- 번아웃을 범위의 개념으로 생각하면 번아웃의 다양한 경험에 대한 분류를 할 수 있음 **단서 3**

➡ 번아웃을 '상태'로 간주(번아웃 vs 번아웃 아님 사이의 양자택일)하면 그 다양한 경험을 설명하기 어렵기 때문에, 번아웃은 '범위'로 이해해야 한다는 것이 글의 핵심이다.

▶ 따라서 밑줄 친 부분은 ② '탈진의 정도가 더 클 수 있는 여지가 여전히 있다.'를 의미한다.

왜 오답?

① 서두에 제시된 public discussion을 이용해 만든 오답일 뿐이다.
(▶◁ 이유: 대중적 논의는 이미 번아웃을 흑백 상태인 것처럼 이야기하고 있다고 언급되어 있음)

③ 흑백논리(= 양자택일)로는 번아웃의 다양한 경험을 설명할 수 없으므로, 번아웃 증상에 적용할 수 없다는 것이 글의 내용이다. 글의 주제와 반대되는 내용의 선택지이다.

④ 탈진의 극복 방법은 언급되지 않았다.

⑤ 번아웃을 명확한 상태보다는 다양한 범위로서 간주해야 한다는 것이지, '번아웃이 개인의 인식에 의해 형성된다'는 것은 논리적인 비약이다. 함정

D 07 정답 ⑤ ＊눈의 움직임과 시각 안정성

병렬 구조

Turn the lights out / and point the beam of a small flashlight / up into one of your eyes. //

조명을 끄고 / 작은 손전등의 빛줄기가 향하게 하라 / 여러분의 한쪽 눈 안을 //

Shake the beam around /

빛줄기를 이리저리 흔들어라 /

접속사가 생략되지 않은 분사구문
while moving your gaze up and down. //

여러분의 시선을 위아래로 움직이면서 //

You should catch glimpses /

여러분은 얼핏 보게 될 것이다 /

of what look like delicate branches. //

미세한 가지들처럼 보이는 것을 //

These branches are shadows of the blood vessels / that lie on top of your retina. //
주격 관계대명사

이 가지들은 혈관의 그림자들이다 / 여러분의 망막 위에 있는 //

★ **분사구문에서 접속사를 생략하지 않는 경우**
분사구문의 의미를 명확하게 나타내기 위해 접속사를 생략하지 않는 경우도 있다. (= ~ while you are moving gaze up and down.)

The vessels constantly cast shadows / as light streams into the eye, / but because these shadows never move, / the brain ceases responding to them. //
그 혈관들은 끊임없이 그림자를 드리우지만 / 빛이 눈으로 흘러들어 오는 동안 / 이 그림자들은 절대 움직이지 않기 때문에 / 뇌가 이것들에 반응하는 것을 멈춘다 //

Moving the flashlight beam around shifts the shadows / just
동명사구 주어(단수 취급)   단수 동사
enough to make them momentarily visible. //
손전등 빛줄기를 이리저리 움직이는 것은 그림자를 이동시킨다 / 그림자가 잠깐 눈에 보이게 할 만큼만 //

                              목적어절 접속사   cause의 목적어와 목적격 보어(to부정사)
Now you might wonder / if you could cause an image to fade / just by staring at something unmoving. //
이제 여러분은 궁금해할지도 모른다 / 이미지가 사라지도록 할 수 있는지 / 움직이지 않는 무언가를 단지 응시하는 것만으로도 //

But that is not possible / because the visual system constantly
                              계속적 용법의 주격 관계대명사
jiggles the eye muscles, / which prevents the perfect stabilization / of images of the world. // 단서1 눈 근육의 흔들림이 이미지의 완벽한 안정화를 막음
그러나 그것은 불가능하다 / 시각 체계가 끊임없이 눈의 근육을 가볍게 흔들고 있고 / 이것이 완벽한 안정화를 막기 때문에 / 세상의 이미지들의 //

These muscle movements are unbelievably small, / but their
                                                = these muscle movements'
effect is huge. //
이 근육의 움직임들은 믿을 수 없을 정도로 작지만 / 그 효과는 엄청나다 //

Without them, / we would go blind / by tuning out what we see / shortly after fixating our gaze! // 단서2 눈 근육의 흔들림 덕분에 시각적으로
볼 수 있음
그것들이 없으면 / 우리는 보지 못하게 될 것이다 / 보고 있는 것을 무시함으로써 / 시선을 고정한 직후에 //

It's an interesting notion: / Approximate perfection is better than perfect perfection. //
이것은 흥미로운 개념이다 / 근사치의 완벽함이 완벽한 완벽함보다 더 낫다 //

- beam ⓝ 빛줄기 • catch a glimpse 얼핏 보다
- delicate ⓐ 연약한 • blood vessel 혈관
- cast ⓥ (그림자를) 드리우다 • cease ⓥ 중단되다
- momentarily ⓐⒹ 잠깐, 곧 • stabilization ⓝ 안정화
- fixate ⓥ 정착[고정]시키다 • approximate ⓐ 거의 정확한, 근사치인
- blurry ⓐ 흐릿한 • sensitively ⓐⒹ 민감하게
- distortion ⓝ 왜곡 • shaky ⓐ 떨리는, 불안한

조명을 끄고 작은 손전등의 빛줄기가 여러분의 한쪽 눈 안을 향하게 하라. 여러분의 시선을 위아래로 움직이면서 빛줄기를 이리저리 흔들어라. 여러분은 미세한 가지들처럼 보이는 것을 얼핏 보게 될 것이다. 이 가지들은 여러분의 망막 위에 있는 혈관의 그림자들이다. 그 혈관들은 빛이 눈으로 흘러들어 오는 동안 끊임없이 그림자를 드리우지만, 이 그림자들은 절대 움직이지 않기 때문에 뇌가 이것들에 반응하는 것을 멈춘다. 손전등 빛줄기를 이리저리 움직이는 것은 그림자가 잠깐 눈에 보이게 할 만큼만 그림자를 이동시킨다. 이제 여러분은 움직이지 않는 무언가를 단지 응시하는 것만으로도 이미지가 사라지도록 할 수 있는지 궁금해할지도 모른다. 그러나 시각 체계가 끊임없이 눈의 근육을 가볍게 흔들고 있고 이것이 세상의 이미지들의 완벽한 안정화를 막기 때문에 그것은 불가능하다. 이 근육의 움직임들은 믿을 수 없을 정도로 작지만 그 효과는 엄청나다. 그것들이 없으면 우리는 시선을 고정한 직후에 보고 있는 것을 무시함으로써 보지 못하게 될 것이다! 이것은 흥미로운 개념이다. 근사치의 완벽함이 완벽한 완벽함보다 더 낫다.

밑줄 친 Approximate perfection is better than perfect perfection이 다음 글에서 의미하는 바로 가장 적절한 것은? [3점]

① What makes your vision blurry actually protects your eyes.
시야가 흐릿해지는 것이 실제로 당신의 눈을 보호한다. → 보호하는 것이 아님
② The more quickly an object moves, the more sensitively eyes react. 물체의 이동 속도를 말하는 것이 아님
물체가 더 빨리 움직일수록, 눈은 더 민감하게 반응한다.
③ Eyes exposed to intense light are subject to distortion of images.
강한 빛에 노출된 눈은 이미지가 왜곡될 수 있다. → 관련 없음
④ Constant adjustment of focusing makes your eye muscles tired.
지속적인 초점 조절은 눈의 근육을 피곤하게 한다. → 관련 없음
⑤Shaky eye-muscle movements let us see what the brain might ignore. 눈 근육의 떨림 덕분에 볼 수 있음
눈 근육의 떨림 운동은 뇌가 무시할 수도 있는 것을 우리가 볼 수 있게 한다.

왜 정답? [정답률 40%]

- 손전등의 빛줄기가 눈에 들어왔을 때 망막 위 혈관의 그림자들이 보임
- 혈관의 그림자들은 움직임을 통해 잠시 보이는데 작은 움직임은 뇌가 이미지를 완전히 무시하지 않게 하며, 시각 체계의 안정성을 막음 단서1

→ 시각 체계가 눈의 근육을 가볍게 흔들고 있고 이 작은 움직임 덕분에 시선을 고정한 직후에 보고 있는 것들을 무시하지 못하고 이로써 볼 수 있게 된다.

▶ 따라서 밑줄 친 부분은 ⑤ '눈 근육의 떨림 운동은 뇌가 무시할 수도 있는 것을 우리가 볼 수 있게 한다.'를 의미한다.

왜 오답?

① 시야가 흐릿해지는 행위가 눈을 실제로 보호한다는 내용은 관련이 없다.
② 물체 자체의 이동 속도가 아닌 눈의 근육에 관련된 내용이다.
③ 강한 빛으로 인한 이미지 왜곡은 전체 내용과 관련이 없다.
④ 초점을 조절하는 것으로 인해서 눈의 근육이 피곤하다는 것은 상관이 없는 내용이다.

D 08 정답 ⑤ * 인식된 가치가 주관적 경험에 미치는 영향 ——

주어를 이끄는 명사절 접속사
That perception is a construction / is not true / just of one's perception of sensory input, / such as visual and auditory information. //
인식이 구성이라는 것은 / 해당되는 것이 아니다 / 단지 감각적 투입에 대한 한 사람의 인식에만 / 시각 및 청각 정보와 같은 //

                                          ~도
It is true / of your social perceptions as well / — your perceptions / of the people you meet, / the food you eat, / and even of the products you buy. //
이것은 해당된다 / 여러분의 사회적 인식에도 / 여러분의 인식 / 여러분이 만나는 사람에 대한 / 여러분이 먹는 음식 / 그리고 심지어 여러분이 사는 제품 //

For example, / in a study of wine, / when wines were tasted blind, / there was little or no correlation / between the ratings of a wine's taste and its cost, /
예를 들어 / 와인에 대한 한 연구에서 / 와인이 조건을 숨긴 상태로 시음되었을 때 / 상관 관계가 거의 없거나 아예 없었다 / 와인의 맛에 대한 평가와 그것의 가격 간의 /

but there *was* a significant correlation / when the wines were labeled by price. // 단서1 와인의 가격을 알게 되면 맛과 가격 간의 유의미한 상관 관계가 있었음
그러나 유의미한 상관 관계가 '있었다' / 와인이 가격에 따라 라벨이 붙었을 때는 //

                                              목적어절 접속사
That wasn't because the subjects consciously believed / that the higher-priced wines should be the better ones / and thus revised / whatever opinion they had accordingly. //
이는 피험자들이 의식적으로 믿었기 때문은 아니었다 / 가격이 더 비싼 와인이 더 좋은 와인일 것이라고 / 그리고 따라서 수정했다 / 이에 따라 그들이 가졌던 어떠한 의견이든지 //

Or rather, / it wasn't true *just* at the conscious level. //
더 정확히 말하면 / 이것은 '단지' 의식적인 수준에서만 그런 것은 아니었다 //

                                    접속사
We know / because as the subjects were tasting the wine, / the researchers were imaging their brain activity, / and the imaging showed /
우리는 알 수 있다 / 왜냐하면 피험자들이 와인을 시음할 때 / 연구원들이 그들의 뇌 활동을 영상화했다 / 그리고 그 영상은 보여줬다 /

that drinking what they believed was an expensive glass of
목적어절 접속사   the thing which
wine / really did activate / their centers of taste for pleasure /
                                            주격 관계대명사(선행사: the same wine)
more than drinking a glass of the same wine / that had been labeled as cheaper. // 단서2 고가의 와인이라고 인식한 것을 마시는 것이 저렴하다고
인식한 와인을 마시는 것보다 더 만족감을 불러일으켰다고 함
그들이 고가의 와인 한 잔이라고 믿는 것을 마시는 것이 / 실제로 더 활성화했다 / 그들의 만족감을 담당하는 미각 중추를 / 같은 와인 한잔을 마시는 것보다 / 더 저렴하다고 라벨이 붙었던 //

That's related to the placebo effect. //
이는 플라세보 효과와 관련이 있다 //

Like pain, / taste is not just the product of sensory signals; / it depends also on psychological factors: / you don't just taste the wine; / you taste its price. //
통증과 같이 / 미각은 단순히 감각 신호의 산물일 뿐만 아니라 / 그것은 심리적 요인에도 좌우된다 / 여러분은 와인을 단순히 맛보는 것이 아니다 / 여러분은 그것의 가격을 맛보는 것이다 //

- perception ⓝ 인식, 지각　　• input ⓝ 투입, 입력
- auditory ⓐ 청각의　　• correlation ⓝ 상관 관계
- significant ⓐ 유의미한　　• label ⓥ 라벨[표]을 붙이다
- subject ⓝ 피험자　　• revise ⓥ 수정하다
- placebo effect 위약 효과(가짜 약이지만 약을 복용하고 있다는 데 대한 심리효과 따위로 실제 환자의 상태가 좋아지는 것)　　• psychological ⓐ 정신적인
- dismiss ⓥ 묵살하다

인식이 구성이라는 것은 단지 시각 및 청각 정보와 같은 감각적 투입에 대한 한 사람의 인식에만 해당되는 것이 아니다. 이것은 여러분의 사회적 인식, 즉 여러분이 만나는 사람, 여러분이 먹는 음식, 그리고 심지어 여러분이 사는 제품에 대한 여러분의 인식에도 해당된다. 예를 들어, 와인에 대한 한 연구에서 와인이 조건을 숨긴 상태로 시음되었을 때 와인의 맛에 대한 평가와 그것의 가격 간의 상관 관계가 거의 없거나 아예 없었지만, 와인이 가격에 따라 라벨이 붙었을 때는 유의미한 상관 관계가 '있었다'. 이는 피험자들이 가격이 더 비싼 와인이 더 좋은 와인일 것이라고 의식적으로 믿어서, 이에 따라 그들이 가졌던 어떠한 의견이든지 수정되었기 때문은 아니었다. 더 정확히 말하면, 이것은 '단지' 의식적인 수준에서만 그런 것이 아니었다. 우리는 알 수 있는데, 왜냐하면 피험자들이 와인을 시음할 때 연구원들이 그들의 뇌 활동을 영상화했고, 그 영상은 그들이 고가의 와인 한 잔이라고 믿는 것을 마시는 것이 더 저렴하다고 라벨이 붙었던 같은 와인 한잔을 마시는 것보다 그들의 만족감을 담당하는 미각 중추를 실제로 더 활성화했다는 것을 보여줬기 때문이다. 이는 플라세보 효과와 관련이 있다. 통증과 같이 미각은 단순히 감각 신호의 산물일 뿐만 아니라, 그것은 심리적 요인에도 좌우된다. 여러분은 와인을 단순히 맛보는 것이 아니다. 여러분은 그것의 가격을 맛보는 것이다.

다음 밑줄 친 you taste its price가 의미하는 바로 가장 적절한 것은?

① Customer ratings determine the price of a product.
고객 평가가 상품의 가격을 결정한다. 　고객 평가가 상품의 가격을 결정한다는 내용이 아님
② We fool ourselves into thinking our unplanned buying was reasonable. 무계획적인 소비가 합리적이었다는 생각으로 스스로를 속인다는 언급은 없음
우리는 우리의 무계획적인 소비가 합리적이었다는 생각으로 스스로를 속인다.
③ We immediately dismiss opposing opinions without any consideration. 반대 의견을 즉시 묵살한다는 내용이 아님
우리는 특별한 고려 없이 반대 의견을 즉시 묵살한다.
④ The brain shows consistent response regardless of personal preference. 뇌가 보여주는 지속적인 반응에 대한 내용이 아님
뇌는 개인적 선호에 관계 없이 지속적인 반응을 보여준다.
⑤ The perceived value of a product influences one's subjective experience of it. 상품에 대한 인식된 가치가 그것에 대한 경험을 좌우한다고 함
상품에 대한 인식된 가치가 그것에 대한 주관적 경험에 영향을 미친다.

왜 정답? [정답률 65%]

- 와인의 가격을 알게 되었을 때 맛과 가격 간 유의미한 상관 관계가 있음 단서1
- 고가로 인식한 와인을 마셨을 때 저렴하다고 인식한 와인을 마셨을 때보다 만족감이 증가함 단서2
➡ 와인이라는 상품에 대한 '인식'된 가치가 그 와인을 접했을 때의 경험(만족감)에 영향을 미침
▶ '여러분은 그것의 가격을 맛보는 것이다.'가 의미하는 바: ⑤ '상품에 대한 인식된 가치가 그것에 대한 주관적 경험에 영향을 미친다.'

왜 오답?

① 고객 평가가 상품의 가격을 결정한다는 내용이 아니다.
② 무계획적인 소비를 합리적인 것이라 생각하면서 스스로를 속인다는 언급은 없다.
③ 특별한 고려 없이 반대 의견을 즉시 묵살한다는 내용이 아니다.
④ 개인적 선호와 관계 없이 뇌가 보여주는 지속적인 반응에 대한 내용이 아니다.

D 09 정답 ③　＊막대 다발로 묘사되는 소유권

Lawyers sometimes describe ownership / as a *bundle of sticks*. //
변호사들은 때로는 소유권을 묘사한다 / 막대 다발로 //

This metaphor was introduced / about a century ago, / and it has dramatically transformed / the teaching and practice of law. //
이 비유는 도입되었고 / 약 1세기 전에 / 그것은 극적으로 변화시켰다 / 법학 교육과 실무를 //
　　　　　　　주어　동사　목적어 목적격 보어(원형부정사)
The metaphor is useful / because it helps us see ownership / as a grouping of interpersonal rights / that can be separated and put back together. // 단서1 소유권: 분리되고 다시 합쳐질 수 있는 대인 관계적 권리의 모음
그 비유는 유용하다 / 그것이 우리가 소유권을 보는 것을 도와주기 때문에 / 대인 관계적인 권리의 모음으로 / 분리될 수 있고 다시 합쳐질 수 있는 //

When you say *It's mine* / in reference to a resource, / often that means / you own a lot of the sticks / that make up the full bundle: /
　　　　　　　　　　　　　　주격 관계대명사
여러분이 '그것은 내 것이다'라고 말할 때 / 어떤 자원에 관해 / 흔히 그것은 의미한다 / 여러분이 많은 막대를 소유한다는 것을 / 전체 다발을 구성하는 //
　　　　　　　　　　　형용사적 용법(the right 수식)
the sell stick, the rent stick, the right to mortgage, license, give away, even destroy the thing. // 단서2 막대 다발을 구성하는 것: 판매할 권리 막대,
판매 막대, 임대 막대, 저당잡히고, 허가하고, 증여하며, 심지어 그것을 파괴할 권리 //

Often, though, we split the sticks up, / as for a piece of land: /
그러나 우리는 흔히 그 막대들을 분할한다 / 토지 한 면에 대해서처럼 / 분할하여 소유함
there may be / a landowner, a bank with a mortgage, a tenant with a lease, a plumber with a license to enter the land, an oil company with mineral rights. //
　　　　　　　　　　　　　　형용사적 용법의 to부정사구
　　　　　　　　　　　　　　(a license 수식)
~이 있을 수 있다 / 땅 주인, 저당권을 가진 은행, 임대차 계약을 맺은 세입자, 토지 진입 면허를 가진 배관공, 광물에 대한 권리를 가진 석유 회사가 //
단수 주어　　　　　단수 동사
Each of these parties owns / a stick in the bundle. //
이러한 각 당사자는 소유한다 / 그 다발의 막대 하나를 //

- ownership ⓝ 소유권　　• metaphor ⓝ 비유
- dramatically ⓐⓓ 극적으로　　• transform ⓥ 변화시키다
- interpersonal ⓐ 대인관계에 관련된　　• reference ⓝ 언급
- license ⓥ 허가하다　　• give away 증여하다　　• split up 분리하다
- lease ⓝ 임대차 계약　　• plumber ⓝ 배관공　　• party ⓝ 당사자
- obligation ⓝ 의무　　• priority ⓝ 우선권　　• aspect ⓝ 측면

변호사들은 때로는 소유권을 '막대 다발'로 묘사한다. 이 비유는 약 1세기 전에 도입되었고, 법학 교육과 실무를 극적으로 변화시켰다. 그 비유는 그것이 우리가 소유권을 분리될 수 있고 다시 합쳐질 수 있는 대인 관계적인 권리의 모음으로 보는 것을 도와주기 때문에 유용하다. 어떤 자원에 관해 '그것은 내 것이다.'라고 말할 때, 흔히 그것은 여러분이 전체 다발을 구성하는 많은 막대, 즉 판매 막대, 임대 막대, 저당잡히고, 허가하고, 증여하며, 심지어 그것을 파괴할 권리를 소유한다는 것을 의미한다. 그러나 우리는 흔히 토지 한 면에 대해서처럼 그 막대들을 분할한다. 즉 땅 주인, 저당권을 가진 은행, 임대차 계약을 맺은 세입자, 토지 진입 면허를 가진 배관공, 광물에 대한 권리를 가진 석유 회사가 있을 수 있다. 이러한 각 당사자는 그 다발의 막대 하나를 소유한다.

밑줄 친 a stick in the bundle이 다음 글에서 의미하는 바로 가장 적절한 것은? [3점]

① a legal obligation to develop the resource 권리에 대한 내용임
그 자원을 개발할 법적 의무
② a priority to legally claim the real estate 소유권이 분할됨
법적으로 그 부동산을 차지할 우선권
③ a right to use one aspect of the property 각각 소유권의 한 측면을 행사할
그 재산의 한 측면을 사용할 권리　　　　　　　　　　　　권리를 가짐
④ a building to be shared equally by tenants 임차인의 권리만 말하는 것이 아님
임차인들에 의해 동등하게 공유될 건물
⑤ a piece of land nobody can claim as their own 각각 소유권을 주장할 수 있음
아무도 자신의 것으로 주장할 수 없는 토지의 한 면

오H 정답 ? [정답률 59%]

> • **막대 다발로 묘사되는 소유권 첫 문장**: 소유권은 분리되고 다시 합쳐질 수 있는 대인 관계적 권리의 모음 **단서 1**
> • **소유권**: 어떤 자원을 판매할 권리, 임대할 권리, 저당잡힐 권리 등으로 구성되는데, 이 권리들은 흔히 분할됨 **단서 2 단서 3**

➡ 어떤 토지에 대해 땅 주인, 은행, 세입자, 배관공, 석유 회사가 각각 막대 하나를 소유한다.
　▶ 즉, 그 부동산에 대해 각각 분할된 권리를 갖는다는 의미이므로 정답은
　③ '그 재산의 한 측면을 사용할 권리'이다.

오H 오답 ?

① 법적 의무가 아니라 법적 권리가 분할된다는 내용이다.
② 각 당사자가 부동산에 대한 소유권을 분할하여 갖는다는 내용이다.
④ 임차인의 권리에 대해서만 이야기하는 글이 아니다.
⑤ 소유권이 분할되어 각각의 당사자가 자신의 권리를 주장할 수 있다.

D 10 정답 ⑤ *평판 덕분에 뿌린 대로 거두는 우리

Thanks to the power of reputation, / we help others / without expecting an immediate return. // **단서 1**
평판의 힘 덕분에 / 우리는 남들을 돕는다 / 즉각적인 보답을 기대하지 않고 //

If, / thanks to endless chat and intrigue, / the world knows / that you are a good, charitable guy, / then you boost your chance / of being helped by someone else / at some future date. //
만일 / 끝없는 잡담과 관심 덕분에 / 세상이 안다면 / 여러분이 선하고 관대한 사람임을 / 여러분은 여러분의 가능성을 높인다 / 다른 누군가에 의해 도움을 받을 / 미래의 어느 날에 //

The converse is also the case. //
그 역 또한 마찬가지이다 // **단서 2** 다른 사람에게 도움을 주지 않으면 도움을 받을 가능성이 낮아짐

I am less likely to get my back scratched, / in the form of a favor, / if it becomes known / that I never scratch anybody else's. //
나는 내 등이 긁어지게 할 가능성이 더 적어진다 / 호의의 형태로 / ~이 알려지면 / 내가 다른 누구의 등도 결코 긁어주지 않는다는 것이 //

Indirect reciprocity now means / something like /
간접적인 상호 호혜는 이제 의미한다 / ~와 같은 것을 /

"If I scratch your back, / my good example will encourage others / to do the same / and, with luck, / someone will scratch mine." //
"내가 너의 등을 긁어주면 / 나의 선한 모범이 다른 사람을 장려할 것이며 / 똑같이 하도록 / 운이 좋으면 / 누군가 내 등을 긁어줄 것이다" // **단서 3** 다른 사람에게 도움을 주면 나도 도움을 받을 것임

By the same token, / our behavior is endlessly shaped / by the possibility / that somebody else might be watching us / or might find out / what we have done. //
마찬가지로 / 우리의 행동은 끊임없이 형성된다 / 가능성에 의해 / 다른 누군가가 우리를 지켜보고 있거나 / 알아낼 수도 있다는 / 우리가 한 일을 //

We are often troubled / by the thought / of what others may think / of our deeds. //
우리는 흔히 걱정한다 / 생각으로 / 다른 사람이 어떻게 생각할지라는 / 우리의 행동에 대해 //

In this way, / our actions have consequences / that go far beyond any individual act of charity, / or indeed any act of mean-spirited malice. //
이런 식으로 / 우리의 행동은 결과를 초래한다 / 어떤 개별적인 자선 행위를 훨씬 넘어서는 / 또는 정말로 어떠한 비열한 악의의 행동을 //

We all behave differently / when we know / we live / in the shadow of the future. //
우리 모두는 다르게 행동한다 / 우리가 알면 / 우리가 산다는 것을 / 미래의 그늘 아래 //

That shadow is cast / by our actions / because there is always the possibility / that others will find out / what we have done. //
그 그늘은 드리워진다 / 우리의 행동에 의해 / 가능성이 항상 있기 때문에 / 다른 사람이 알아낼 / 우리가 한 일을 //

- reputation ⓝ 평판
- intrigue ⓝ 관심, 흥미
- boost ⓥ 북돋우다, 높이다
- converse ⓝ 정반대
- reciprocity ⓝ 호혜(互惠)
- encourage ⓥ 권장[장려]하다, 용기를 북돋우다
- by the same token 마찬가지로
- possibility ⓝ 가능성
- deed ⓝ 행동
- charity ⓝ 너그러움, 관용
- cast ⓥ (빛을) 발하다, (그림자를) 드리우다
- regardless of ~에 상관없이
- reap ⓥ 거두다, 수확하다
- immediate ⓐ 즉각적인, 당면한
- charitable ⓐ 관대한, 자선의
- chance ⓝ 가능성
- favor ⓝ 호의 · indirect ⓐ 간접적인
- shape ⓥ 형성하다
- trouble ⓥ 괴롭히다, 애 먹이다
- consequence ⓝ 결과
- mean-spirited ⓐ 비열한
- conflict ⓝ 갈등, 충돌
- ultimately ⓐⓓ 궁극적으로, 근본적으로
- sow ⓥ (씨를) 뿌리다[심다]

평판의 힘 덕분에, 우리는 즉각적인 보답을 기대하지 않고 남들을 돕는다. 만일 끝없는 잡담과 관심 덕분에 여러분이 선하고 관대한 사람임을 세상 사람들이 안다면, 여러분은 미래의 어느 날에 다른 누군가에 의해 도움을 받을 가능성을 높인다. 그 역 또한 마찬가지이다. 호의의 형태로, 내가 다른 누구의 등도 결코 긁어주지 않는다는 것이 알려지면, (누군가가) 내 등을 긁어줄 가능성은 더 적어진다. 간접적인 상호 호혜는 이제 "내가 너의 등을 긁어주면, 나의 선한 모범이 다른 사람을 똑같이 하도록 장려할 것이며, 운이 좋으면, 누군가 내 등을 긁어줄 것이다."와 같은 것을 의미한다. 마찬가지로, 우리의 행동은 다른 누군가가 우리를 지켜보고 있거나 우리가 한 일을 알아낼 수도 있다는 가능성에 의해 끊임없이 형성된다. 우리는 흔히 다른 사람이 우리의 행동을 어떻게 여길까라는 생각으로 걱정한다. 이런 식으로 우리의 행동은 어떤 개별적인 자선 행위나 정말로 어떠한 비열한 악의의 행동을 훨씬 넘어서는 결과를 초래한다. 우리가 미래의 그늘 아래 산다는 것을 알면 우리 모두는 다르게 행동한다. 다른 사람이 우리가 한 일을 알아낼 가능성이 항상 있기 때문에 그 그늘은 우리의 행동에 의해 드리워진다.

밑줄 친 live in the shadow of the future가 다음 글에서 의미하는 바로 가장 적절한 것은?

① are distracted by inner conflict 도울지 말지를 갈등하는 것이 아님
　내면의 갈등에 의해 산만해지다
② fall short of our own expectations 자신이나 타인의 기대에 대한 언급은 없음
　우리 자신의 기대에 미치지 못하다
③ seriously compete regardless of the results 타인을 돕는 것에 대한 내용임
　결과에 상관없이 진지하게 경쟁하다
④ are under the influence of uncertainty 도움을 받을지가 불확실하다는 것으로
　불확실성의 영향 아래에 있다　　　　　　　　　　　만든 오답
⑤ ultimately reap what we have sown 남을 도우면 내가 도움을 받을 가능성이
　궁극적으로 우리가 씨 뿌린 것을 거두다　　　　　높아짐

오H 정답 ? [정답률 33%]

> • 선하고 관대한 일을 함 → 선하고 관대한 사람이라는 평판을 얻음 → 미래의 어느 날에 다른 사람의 도움을 받을 가능성을 높임 **단서 1**
> • 남에게 도움을 주지 않음 → 남에게 도움을 주지 않는다는 것이 알려짐(평판) → 남에게 도움을 받을 가능성이 적어짐 **단서 2**

➡ 남을 도우면 미래에 남에게 도움을 받고, 남을 돕지 않으면 미래에 남에게 도움을 받지 못할 것임
　▶ 뿌린 대로 거둔다는 것이므로 '미래의 그늘 아래 산다'는 것은 ⑤ '궁극적으로 우리가 씨 뿌린 것을 거두다'라는 의미이다.

오H 오답 ?

① 남을 도울지 말지에 대한 내면의 갈등을 다룬 글이 아니다.
② 나의 행동이나 타인의 행동이 어떤 기준에 의해 평가된다는 언급은 없다.
③ 타인과의 경쟁이 아니라 타인을 돕는 것에 대해 이야기하는 글이다.
④ 내가 남을 도우면 남에게 도움을 받을 가능성이 높다고 한 것은 도움을 받을지, 받지 못할지가 불확실하다는 것을 이야기하기 위한 것이 아니다. (▶◀ 이유: 도움을 받을 가능성이 높다는 말과 도움을 받을 수 있는지 불확실하다는 말은 전혀 다른 말임)

D 11 정답 ② ＊빈 수신함보다 더 중요한 것

단수 주어
The single most important change / you can make / in your
                                     단수 동사
working habits / is to switch / to creative work first, / reactive
work second. // **단서1** 창조적인 일을 하는 것이 첫 번째이고, 대응하는 일이 나중임

가장 중요한 단 한 가지 변화는 / 여러분이 이룰 수 있는 / 여러분의 일하는 습관에서 / 전환하
는 것이다 / 창조적인 일을 첫 번째로 하고 / 대응적인 일을 두 번째로 하는 쪽으로 //

This means / blocking off a large chunk of time / every day / for
mean+동명사: ~을 의미하다 / mean+to부정사: ~을 의도하다
creative work / on your own priorities, / with the phone and
e-mail off. //

이것은 의미한다 / 많은 시간을 차단하는 것을 / 매일 / 창조적인 작업을 위해 / 여러분 자신의
우선순위에 따라 / 전화기와 이메일을 끈 채 //

'현재는 아니다'라는 것을 과거와 대조할 때 쓰이는 used to-v
I used to be / a frustrated writer. //

나는 ~였다 / 좌절감을 느끼는 작가 //

동명사구 주어
Making this switch / turned me / into a productive writer. //
                      동사   목적어

이러한 전환을 하는 것은 / 나를 변신시켰다 / 생산적인 작가로 //

Yet there wasn't a single day / when I sat down / to write an
              선행사   관계부사
article, blog post, or book chapter / without a string of people /
waiting for me / to get back to them. //

하지만 단 하루도 없었다 / 내가 앉은 / 기사나 블로그 게시글 혹은 책의 한 장을 쓰려고 / 일
련의 사람들 없이 / 나를 기다리는 / 그들에게 답장을 주기를 //

                                           부사절 접속사(시간)
It wasn't easy, / and it still isn't, / particularly when I get phone
messages / beginning / "I sent you an e-mail / *two hours ago…!*" //

그것은 쉽지 않았고 / 그것은 아직도 쉽지 않다 / 특히 내가 전화 메시지를 받을 때는 / 시작하
는 / "제가 당신에게 이메일을 보냈어요 / '2시간 전에'…!"라고 //

By definition, / this approach goes against the grain of others'
expectations / and the pressures / they put on you. //

당연히 / 이러한 접근 방식은 다른 사람들의 기대에 맞지 않는다 / 그리고 압박에 / 그들이 여
러분에게 가하는 //

It takes willpower / to switch off the world, / even for an hour. //
가주어   진주어

~은 의지가 필요하다 / 세상에 대한 스위치를 끄는 것은 / 단 한 시간 동안이라도 //

It feels uncomfortable, / and sometimes people get upset. //

그것은 불편한 느낌이 들고 / 때로 사람들이 기분 상하기도 한다 // **단서2** '빈 수신함'과 비교되는
것이 몇 사람을 실망하게 하는 것임
가주어   진주어
But it's better / to disappoint a few people / over small things,
to disappoint와 비교됨
/ than to abandon your dreams / for an empty inbox. //

그러나 ~이 더 낫다 / 몇 사람을 실망하게 하는 것이 / 사소한 것에 대해 / 여러분의 꿈을 포
기하는 것보다 / 빈 수신함을 위해 //

Otherwise, / you're sacrificing your potential / for the illusion
of professionalism. //

그렇게 하지 않으면 / 여러분은 자신의 잠재력을 희생할 것이다 / 전문성이라는 환상을 위해 //

────────────────────

- habit ⓝ 습관 ・ switch ⓥ 전환하다, 바꾸다
- reactive ⓐ 반응을 보이는 ・ block off ~을 막다[차단하다]
- chunk ⓝ 덩어리, 많은 양 ・ priority ⓝ 우선 사항, 우선권
- frustrated ⓐ 좌절감을 느끼는 ・ productive ⓐ 생산적인
- article ⓝ (신문·잡지의) 글, 기사 ・ a string of 여러 개의, 일련의

- particularly ⓐⓓ 특별히 ・ by definition 당연히, 분명히
- approach ⓝ 접근법, 처리 방법 ・ go against the grain 천성을 거스르다
- expectation ⓝ 예상, 기대 ・ pressure ⓝ 압박, 압력
- willpower ⓝ 의지력 ・ upset ⓥ 속상하게 만들다
- disappoint ⓥ 실망시키다 ・ abandon ⓥ 버리다, 포기하다
- inbox ⓝ 받은 편지함 ・ otherwise ⓐⓓ 그렇지 않으면
- sacrifice ⓥ 희생하다 ・ potential ⓝ 잠재력 ・ illusion ⓝ 환상
- professionalism ⓝ 전문성

여러분이 일하는 습관에서 이룰 수 있는 가장 중요한 단 한 가지 변화는 창조적
인 일을 첫 번째로 하고 대응적인 일은 두 번째로 하는 쪽으로 전환하는 것이
다. 이것은 전화기와 이메일을 끈 채, 여러분 자신의 우선순위에 따라 창조적인
작업을 위해 매일 많은 시간을 차단하는 것을 의미한다. 나는 좌절감을 느끼는
작가였다. 이러한 전환을 하는 것은 나를 생산적인 작가로 변신시켰다. 하지만
내가 그들에게 답장을 주기를 기다리는 사람들 없이 내가 기사나 블로그 게시글
혹은 책의 한 장을 쓰려고 앉은 날은 단 하루도 없었다. 그것은 쉽지 않았고, 특
히 "'2시간 전에' 당신에게 이메일을 보냈어요…!"라고 시작하는 전화 메시지를
받을 때는 아직도 쉽지 않다. 당연히, 이러한 접근 방식은 다른 사람들의 기대
와 그들이 여러분에게 가하는 압박에 맞지 않는다. 단 한 시간 동안이라도 세상
에 대한 스위치를 끄는 데는 의지가 필요하다. 그것은 불편한 느낌이 들고, 때로
사람들이 기분 상하기도 한다. 그러나 빈 수신함을 위해 여러분의 꿈을 포기하는
것보다, 사소한 것에 대해 몇 사람을 실망하게 하는 것이 더 낫다. 그렇게 하지
않으면, 여러분은 전문성이라는 환상을 위해 자신의 잠재력을 희생할 것이다.

밑줄 친 an empty inbox가 다음 글에서 의미하는 바로 가장 적절한 것은? [3점]

① following an innovative course of action
혁신적인 행동 방침을 따르는 것   혁신적인 행동 방침을 따르지 말라는 내용이 아님
② attempting to satisfy other people's demands
다른 사람들의 요구를 충족하려고 시도하는 것   대응을 요구하는 사람들에게 바로 대응하는 것을 의미함
③ completing challenging work without mistakes
도전적인 일을 실수 없이 완수하는 것   실수를 하는 것이 더 낫다는 내용이 아님
④ removing social ties to maintain a mental balance
정신적 균형을 유지하기 위해 사회적 유대를 제거하는 것   사람들과 아예 소통하지 말라는 것이 아님
⑤ securing enough opportunities for social networking
소셜 네트워킹을 위한 충분한 기회를 확보하는 것   소셜 네트워크에 대한 언급은 없음

▶왜 정답? [정답률 69%]   전화기, 이메일을 끄면 나의 대응을 요청하는
다른 사람들의 메시지가 쌓일 것임   [꿀팁]

첫 문장에서 창조적인 일을 하는 것이 가장 중요하고, 무언가에 대응하는 것은 그
다음이라고 했다. 두 번째 문장에 따르면 이는 창조적인 작업을 위해 전화기와 이
메일을 끈 채 많은 시간을 차단하는 것을 의미하는데, 다시 말하면, 나의 대응을 기
다리는 사람들을 실망하게 하더라도 창조적인 일을 하는 것이 더 낫다는 의미이다.
사람들에게 바로바로 대응해서 수신함을 빈 상태로 유지하는 것보다 대응하지 않
고 창조적인 일에 집중해서 사람들을 실망하게 하는 것이 더 낫다는 것이므로 '빈
수신함'이 의미하는 것은 ②'다른 사람들의 요구를 충족하려고 시도하는 것'이다.
바로 대답을 못 들으니까 실망함   [꿀팁]

▶왜 오답?

① 혁신적인 행동 방침을 따르지 않으면 사람들이 실망하겠지만, 그렇게 하는 것이
더 낫다는 내용이 아니다.

③ 어떤 일을 실수 없이 완수하는 것보다 실수를 함으로써 사람들을 실망하게 하는
것이 더 낫다는 것이 아니다.

④ 사람들에게 대응하는 것보다 창조적인 일을 하는 것이 더 먼저라면서 전화기와
이메일을 꺼서 사람들에게 대응하지 말라고는 했지만, 아예 사람들과의 사회적
유대를 제거하라는 것은 아니다.

⑤ '이메일'이 언급된 것으로 만든 오답이다. 소셜 네트워크가 글의 주요 소재인 것
은 아니다.

D 12 정답 ② ＊거시 경제학자의 어려움

Physicians and other natural scientists test their theories / using
controlled experiments. // **단서1** 의사, 자연 과학자는 통제된 실험을 통해
자신의 이론을 시험함
의사와 여타의 자연 과학자는 자신의 이론을 시험한다 / 통제된 실험을 통해 //

                                                      준부정어
Macroeconomists, however, have no laboratories / and little
형용사적 용법(ability 수식)
ability / to run economy-wide experiments of any kind. //

하지만 거시 경제학자에게는 실험실이 없고 / 능력이 거의 없다 / 경제 전반에 걸친 그 어떤
실험도 할 수 있는 // **단서2** 거시 경제학자에게는 실험실이 없고,
실험을 할 수 있는 능력이 거의 없음

Granted, they can study / different economies around the world,
등위접속사(그러나) 등위접속사(그래서)
/ but each economy is unique, / so comparisons are tricky. //
물론, 그들이 연구할 수는 있지만 / 전 세계의 다양한 경제를 / 각 경제가 고유해서 / 비교가
까다롭다 //

Controlled experiments also provide the natural sciences / with
available을 수식하는 부사(준부정어)
something seldom available to economists / — the chance, or
something을 수식하는 형용사
serendipitous, discovery (such as penicillin). //
또한 통제된 실험은 자연 과학에 제공한다 / 경제학자가 거의 얻을 수 없는 것을 / 뜻밖의 또는
우연히 하는 발견 (페니실린 같은) //
복수 주어 복수 동사
Macroeconomists / studying the U.S. economy / have only one
patient, / so they can't introduce particular policies / in a variety
of alternative settings. //
거시 경제학자에게는 / 미국 경제를 연구하는 / 환자가 한 명뿐이어서 / 그들은 특정 정책을
도입할 수 없다 / 다양한 다른 상황에서 //
단서3 거시 경제학자가 할 수 없는 것이 이어짐
You can't squeeze economies / into a test tube. //
당신은 경제를 집어넣을 수 없다 / 시험관에 //

Cries of "Eureka!" are seldom heard / from macroeconomists. //
"유레카!"라는 외침은 거의 들려오지 않는다 / 거시 경제학자에게서 //
단수 주어
An economy / consisting of hundreds of millions of individual
단수 동사
actors / is a complicated thing. //
경제는 / 수억 명의 개별 행위자로 구성된 / 복잡한 것이다 //

As Nobel Prize-winning physicist Murray Gell-Mann once
observed, / "Think / how hard physics would be / if particles
부사절 접속사(조건)
could think." //
노벨상을 수상한 물리학자 Murray Gell-Mann이 이전에 말했듯이 / "생각해 보라 /
물리학이 얼마나 어려울지 / 입자가 생각할 수 있다면" //

- physician ⓝ 의사 • macroeconomist ⓝ 거시경제학자
- economy-wide ⓐ 경제 전반에 걸친 • granted ⓐd 물론
- tricky ⓐ 까다로운 • penicillin ⓝ 페니실린
- alternative ⓐ (기존의 것과) 다른 • squeeze ⓥ 쥐어짜다
- complicated ⓐ 복잡한 • particle ⓝ 입자

의사와 여타의 자연 과학자는 통제된 실험을 통해 자신의 이론을 시험한다.
하지만 거시 경제학자에게는 실험실이 없고 경제 전반에 걸친 그 어떤 실험도
할 수 있는 능력이 거의 없다. 물론, 그들이 전 세계의 다양한 경제를 연구할
수는 있지만, 각 경제가 고유해서 비교가 까다롭다. 또한 통제된 실험은
경제학자가 거의 얻을 수 없는 것, 즉 뜻밖의 또는 우연히 하는 발견(페니실린
같은)을 자연 과학에 제공한다. 미국 경제를 연구하는 거시 경제학자에게는
환자가 한 명뿐이어서 다양한 다른 상황에서 특정 정책을 도입할 수 없다.
당신은 경제를 시험관에 집어넣을 수 없다. 거시 경제학자에게서 "유레카!"라는
외침은 거의 들려오지 않는다. 수억 명의 개별 행위자로 구성된 경제는 복잡한
것이다. 노벨상을 수상한 물리학자 Murray Gell-Mann이 이전에 말했듯이,
"입자가 생각할 수 있다면 물리학이 얼마나 어려울지 생각해 보라."

밑줄 친 squeeze economies into a test tube가 다음 글에서 의미하는 바
로 가장 적절한 것은?
① admit economists' contributions to the natural sciences
  자연 과학에 대한 경제학자들의 기여를 인정하다 경제학자의 기여를 설명하는 글이 아님
② conduct controlled experiments on the economy
  경제에 대해 통제된 실험을 수행하다 통제된 실험으로 이론을 시험하는 의사와 다른 점
③ employ complex economic theories
  복잡한 경제학 이론을 이용하다 '실험'과 관련된 내용임
④ share test results with other scientists
  다른 과학자들과 실험 결과를 공유하다 실험 자체를 할 수 없다는 내용임
⑤ collect economic data over a long period of time
  긴 기간에 걸쳐 경제적 데이터를 수집하다 자연 과학자는 짧은 기간의 데이터를 수집한다는 것이 아님

왜 정답? [정답률 74%]

밑줄 친 문장	당신은 경제를 시험관에 집어넣을 수 없다.
대조	의사와 여타의 자연 과학자: 통제된 실험을 통해 자신의 이론을 실험함
	거시 경제학자: 실험실이 없고, 거시 경제에 대해 그 어떤 실험도 할 수 있는 능력이 거의 없음

→ 밑줄 친 부분이 포함된 문장은 거시 경제학자가 할 수 없는 것(경제를 시험관에
집어넣는 것)을 설명한다. 이 글에서 설명하는 거시 경제학자가 할 수 없는 것은
경제에 대한 통제된 실험이다.
▶ 밑줄 친 부분이 포함된 문장은 거시 경제학자는 ② '경제에 대해 통제된 실험을
수행할 수 없다는 것을 의미함

왜 오답?
① 거시 경제학자가 자연 과학에 기여했다고 설명하는 글이 아니다.
③ 밑줄 친 부분은 거시 경제학자가 할 수 없는 것을 의미한다.
④ 실험을 할 수 있는지 여부에 대한 글이다.
⑤ 반대로 자연 과학자가 경제학자와는 다르게 '짧은' 기간에 수집된 데이터를
이용한다는 것이 아니다. 주의

D 13 정답 ② *최고는 좋음의 적

Gold plating in the project means / needlessly enhancing the
expected results, /
프로젝트에서 금도금은 의미한다 / 예상되는 결과를 불필요하게 향상하는 것을 /
선행사
namely, adding characteristics / that are costly, not required, /
주격 관계대명사의 병렬 구조
and that have low added value / with respect to the targets /
즉 특성을 추가하는 것 / 비용이 많이 들고 필요하지 않으며 / 부가 가치가 낮은 / 목표와
관련하여 /
— in other words, / giving more / with no real justification /
other than to demonstrate one's own talent. //
다시 말해 / 더 많은 것을 제공하는 것을 / 실질적인 명분이 없이 / 자신의 재능을 입증하는 것
외에는 // 단서1 프로젝트에서 금도금의 의미: 실질적인 명분 없이 자신의 재능을
입증하기 위해 더 많은 것을 제공하는 것
Gold plating is especially interesting / for project team
members, /
금도금은 특히 흥미롭다 / 프로젝트 팀원들에 대해서 /
부사절 접속사(이유)
as it is typical of projects / with a marked professional component
/ — in other words, projects / that involve specialists / with
선행사 주격 관계대명사
proven experience and extensive professional autonomy. //
그것이 프로젝트에서 일반적이기 때문에 / 전문적인 요소가 뚜렷한 / 다시 말해 프로젝트 /
전문가가 참여하는 / 검증된 경험과 폭넓은 전문적 자율성을 갖춘 //
형용사적 용법(an opportunity 수식)
In these environments / specialists often see the project as an
opportunity / to test and enrich their skill sets. //
이러한 환경에서 / 전문가들은 종종 프로젝트를 기회로 여긴다 / 자신의 다양한 능력을
테스트하고 강화할 //
There is therefore a strong temptation, / in all good faith, /
형용사적 용법(a strong temptation 수식)
to engage in gold plating, /
따라서 강한 유혹이 있다 / 선의로 / 금도금에 참여하려는 /
형용사적 용법(a strong temptation 수식)
namely, to achieve more or higher-quality work / that gratifies
the professional / but does not add value / to the client's
requests, /
병렬 구조
즉 더 많은 또는 더 높은 품질의 성과를 달성하려는 / 전문가를 만족시키는 / 하지만 가치를
더하지 않는 / 고객의 요청에 /
and at the same time / removes valuable resources / from the
project. // 단서2 고객에게 도움이 되는 성과가 아니라 전문가를 만족시키는 성과를 달성하려고 함
그리고 동시에 / 귀중한 자원을 없애는 / 프로젝트에서 //
As the saying goes, / "The best is the enemy of the good." //
속담에 있듯이 / '최고는 좋음의 적'이다 //

- gold plating 금도금 • needlessly ⓐd 불필요하게
- enhance ⓥ 향상시키다 • added value 부가 가치
- with respect to ~에 관하여 • in other words 다시 말해
- justification ⓝ 명분, 정당화 • other than ~외에
- demonstrate ⓥ 입증하다, 나타내다 • component ⓝ 요소
- enrich ⓥ 강화하다 • temptation ⓝ 유혹
- in all good faith 선의로

프로젝트에서 금도금은 예상되는 결과를 불필요하게 향상하는 것, 즉 비용이 많이 들고 필요하지 않으며 목표와 관련하여 부가 가치가 낮은 특성을 추가하는 것으로, 다시 말해 자신의 재능을 입증하는 것 외에는 실질적인 명분이 없는 더 많은 것을 제공하는 것을 의미한다. 금도금은 특히 프로젝트 팀원들에 대해서 흥미로운데, 이는 전문적인 요소가 뚜렷한 프로젝트, 다시 말해 검증된 경험과 폭넓은 전문적 자율성을 갖춘 전문가가 참여하는 프로젝트에서 일반적이기 때문이다. 이러한 환경에서 전문가들은 종종 프로젝트를 자신의 다양한 능력을 테스트하고 강화할 기회로 여긴다. 따라서 선의로 금도금에 참여하려는 유혹, 즉 전문가를 만족시키지만, 고객의 요청에 가치를 더하지 않는 동시에 프로젝트에서 귀중한 자원을 없애는 더 많은 또는 더 높은 품질의 성과를 달성하려는 유혹이 있다. 속담에 있듯이, '최고는 좋음의 적'이다.

밑줄 친 "The best is the enemy of the good."이 다음 글에서 의미하는 바로 가장 적절한 것은? [3점]

고객의 요청에 가치를 더하지 않는 성과를 추구함

① Pursuing perfection at work causes conflicts among team members. 팀원 간 갈등은 언급되지 않음
일에서 완벽을 추구하면 팀원 간 갈등이 일어난다.
② Raising work quality only to prove oneself is not desirable.
오로지 자신을 증명하기 위해 성과의 질을 올리는 것은 바람직하지 않다.
③ Inviting overqualified specialists to a project leads to bad ends.
프로젝트에 필요 이상의 자격을 갖춘 전문가를 끌어들이는 것은 나쁜 결과를 가져온다.
필요 이상의 자격을 갖춘 전문가라는 언급은 없음
④ Responding to the changing needs of clients is unnecessary.
고객의 변화하는 요구에 대응하는 것은 불필요하다. 부정적으로 언급한 내용임
⑤ Acquiring a range of skills for a project does not ensure success.
프로젝트에 필요한 다양한 기술을 습득한다고 해서 성공이 보장되는 것은 아니다.
다양한 기술에 대한 언급은 없음

왜 정답? [정답률 40%]

프로젝트에서 금도금의 의미: 순전히 자신의 재능을 입증하기 위해 비용이 많이 들고 필요하지 않으며 목표와 관련하여 부가 가치가 낮은 특성을 추가하는 것
전문가가 참여하는 프로젝트: 전문가를 만족시키지만, 고객의 요청에 가치를 더하지 않고, 프로젝트에서 귀중한 자원을 없애는 결과를 달성하려는 강한 유혹이 있음
⇒ 전문가가 자신의 재능을 입증하기 위해 전문가를 만족시키는 더 많은, 더 높은 품질의 성과를 추구하는 것이 프로젝트에 좋지 않은 영향을 미침
▶ '최고는 좋음의 적'이 의미하는 바: ② 오로지 자신을 증명하기 위해 성과의 질을 올리는 것은 바람직하지 않다.

왜 오답?

① 완벽을 추구하면 안 된다는 것이 아니다.
③ 전문가를 끌어들이는 것이 나쁜 결과를 가져온다는 것이 아니라 전문가가 자신의 재능을 입증하기 위해 필요 이상의 성과를 달성하려고 하는 것이 바람직하지 않다는 것이다.
④ 고객의 요청에 가치를 더하지 않는 성과를 부정적으로 이야기했다.
⑤ 다양한 기술을 습득한다는 언급은 없다.

D 14 정답 ④ *스트레스를 대처할 때 넓은 초점의 중요성

의문사절 주어 / 전치사의 의문사절 목적어
How you focus your attention / plays a critical role / in how you deal with stress. //
여러분이 여러분의 주의를 집중하는 방식은 / 중요한 역할을 한다 / 여러분이 스트레스에 대처하는 방식에 //

Scattered attention harms your ability to let go of stress, / because even though your attention is scattered, / it is narrowly focused, /
과거분사(attention 수식)
주의가 분산되면 스트레스를 해소하는 능력이 손상되는데 / 왜냐하면 여러분의 주의가 분산되더라도 / 그것이 좁게 집중되기 때문이다 /

for you are able to fixate / only on the stressful parts of your experience. //
이유의 접속사
여러분은 집착할 수 있으므로 / 여러분의 경험 중 스트레스가 많은 부분에만 //

When your attentional spotlight is widened, / you can more easily let go of stress. //
여러분의 주의의 초점이 넓어지면 / 여러분은 스트레스를 더 쉽게 해소할 수 있다 //

You can put in perspective / many more aspects of any situation / and not get locked into one part / that ties you down / to superficial and anxiety-provoking levels of attention. //
주격 관계대명사
여러분은 균형 있는 시각으로 볼 수 있으며 / 어떤 상황이라도 그 상황의 더 많은 측면을 / 한 부분에 갇히지 않을 수 있다 / 여러분을 옭아매는 / 피상적이고 불안을 유발하는 주의 수준으로 //

단서 1 초점이 좁으면 스트레스 수준이 높아지고, 초점이 넓으면 스트레스 수준이 낮아짐
A narrow focus heightens the stress level of each experience, / but a widened focus turns down the stress level / because you're better able to put / each situation into a broader perspective. //
초점이 좁으면 각 경험의 스트레스 수준이 높아지지만 / 초점이 넓으면 스트레스 수준이 낮아진다 / 여러분은 더 잘 볼 수 있기 때문에 / 각 상황을 더 넓은 시각으로 //

One anxiety-provoking detail / is less important than the bigger picture. //
비교급 구문
불안감을 유발하는 하나의 세부 사항은 / 더 큰 전체적인 상황보다 덜 중요하다 //

동명사 / 재귀대명사의 재귀적 용법
It's like transforming yourself / into a nonstick frying pan. //
그것은 여러분 자신을 변형시키는 것과 같다 / 들러붙지 않는 프라이팬으로 //

You can still fry an egg, / but the egg won't stick to the pan. //
여러분은 여전히 달걀을 부칠 수 있지만 / 그 달걀이 팬에 들러붙지 않을 것이다 //
단서 2 달걀이 팬에 들러붙지 않고도 달걀을 부칠 수 있다는 비유는 스트레스 상황에 좁게 초점을 맞춰 매달리지 않고도 스트레스를 대처할 수 있는 상태를 나타냄

- play a critical role 중요한 역할을 수행하다
- scatter ⓥ 분산시키다, 흩뜨리다
- let go of ~을 해소하다[놓아주다]
- fixate on ~에 집착하다
- perspective ⓝ 관점
- tie down to ~에 옭아매다
- superficial ⓐ 피상적인
- anxiety-provoking ⓐ 불안을 유발하는
- heighten ⓥ 높이다
- widened ⓐ 확장된
- turn down 약화하다
- nonstick ⓐ 들러붙지 않는

여러분이 여러분의 주의를 집중하는 방식은 여러분이 스트레스에 대처하는 방식에 중요한 역할을 한다. 주의가 분산되면 스트레스를 해소하는 능력이 손상되는데, 왜냐하면 여러분의 주의가 분산되더라도, 여러분은 여러분의 경험 중 스트레스가 많은 부분에만 집착할 수 있으므로, 그것이 좁게 집중되기 때문이다. 여러분의 주의의 초점이 넓어지면, 여러분은 스트레스를 더 쉽게 해소할 수 있다. 여러분은 어떤 상황이라도 그 상황의 더 많은 측면을 균형 있는 시각으로 볼 수 있으며, 피상적이고 불안을 유발하는 주의 수준으로 여러분을 옭아매는 한 부분에 갇히지 않을 수 있다. 초점이 좁으면 각 경험의 스트레스 수준이 높아지지만, 초점이 넓으면 여러분은 각 상황을 더 넓은 시각으로 더 잘 볼 수 있기 때문에 스트레스 수준이 낮아진다. 불안감을 유발하는 하나의 세부 사항은 더 큰 전체적인 상황보다 덜 중요하다. 그것은 여러분 자신을 들러붙지 않는 프라이팬으로 변형시키는 것과 같다. 여러분은 여전히 달걀을 부칠 수 있지만, 그 달걀이 팬에 들러붙지 않을 것이다.

밑줄 친 a nonstick frying pan이 다음 글에서 의미하는 바로 가장 적절한 것은? [3점]

① never being confronted with any stressful experiences in daily life 스트레스 상황에 직면하지 않는다는 내용은 언급되지 않음
일상생활에서 스트레스가 많은 어떤 경험에도 결코 직면하지 않는 것
② broadening one's perspective to identify the cause of stress
스트레스의 원인을 파악하기 위해 시각을 넓히는 것
시각을 넓힘으로써 스트레스 수준을 낮출 수 있다는 내용임
③ rarely confining one's attention to positive aspects of an experience
경험의 긍정적인 측면에 주의를 거의 제한하지 않는 것
경험의 긍정적인 측면에 관한 내용은 언급되지 않음
④ having a larger view of an experience beyond its stressful aspects
스트레스를 주는 측면을 넘어 경험에 대한 더 넓은 시각을 갖는 것
주의의 초점을 넓힘으로써 스트레스에만 얽매이지 않고 더 넓은 측면을 볼 수 있다는 내용임
⑤ taking stress into account as the source of developing a wide view 넓은 시각으로 스트레스를 대처할 수 있다는 내용임
넓은 시각을 개발하는 원천으로 스트레스를 고려하는 것

왜 정답? [정답률 61%]

- 주의를 집중하는 방식이 스트레스에 대처하는 방식에 영향을 미침
- 주의의 초점이 좁으면 스트레스 상황에 얽매이게 되어 스트레스 수준이 높아지지만, 주의의 초점이 넓으면 더 넓은 시각에서 상황을 바라볼 수 있으므로 스트레스 수준이 낮아짐 단서 1

→ 스스로를 '들러붙지 않는 프라이팬'으로 변형하여 달걀이 팬에 달라붙지 않고도 (= 스트레스 상황에 집착하지 않고도) 여전히 달걀을 부칠 수 있도록(= 스트레스에 대처할 수 있도록) 해야 함

▶ '들러붙지 않는 프라이팬'이 의미하는 바: ④ '스트레스를 주는 측면을 넘어 경험에 대한 더 넓은 시각을 갖는 것'

왜 오답?

① 스트레스 상황에 직면하지 않는다는 내용은 언급되지 않았다.

② 시각을 넓힘으로써 스트레스 수준을 낮출 수 있다는 내용이다. (이유: 시각을 넓히는 것이 스트레스의 '원인'을 파악하는 것이 아니라 '수준'을 낮추는 것임)

③ 경험의 긍정적인 측면에 관한 내용은 언급되지 않았다.

⑤ 스트레스가 넓은 시각의 원천이라는 내용이 아니라, 넓은 시각으로 스트레스를 대처할 수 있다는 내용이다.

조수근 | 순천향대 의예과 2024년 입학 · 성남 태원고 졸

대부분의 밑줄 문장은 맥락 없이 의미를 파악하기 힘들어. 달걀을 부칠 수 있지만 팬에 들러붙지 않는 것, 그리고 초점이 좁으면 스트레스가 높아지고 넓으면 스트레스 수준이 낮아진다고 했어. 앞 문장과 뒤 문장의 맥락을 고려해서 이 지문의 주제와 가장 근접한 내용의 선지를 고르면 생각보다 간단하게 풀 수 있을 거야.

D 15 정답 ⑤ *마지막으로 들어온 것이 제일 먼저 나간다

(부사절 접속사(대조))
While user habits are a boon / to companies / fortunate enough to generate them, /
(부사적 용법(fortunate enough 수식))
사용자 습관은 요긴한 것인 반면에 / 기업에게는 / 그것들을 만들어 낼 만큼 운 좋은 /

their existence inherently makes success less likely / for new innovations and startups / trying to disrupt the *status quo*. //
(주어, 동사, 목적어, 목적격 보어)
그것들의 존재는 본질적으로 성공을 덜 있음 직하게 만든다 / 새로운 혁신과 신생 기업에게 / '현재 상태'를 무너뜨리려는 //

(부사의 수식을 받는 동명사(준동사) 주어, 단수 동사)
The fact is, / successfully changing long-term user habits / is exceptionally rare. // 단서 1 장기적인 사용자 습관을 성공적으로 바꾸는 것은 대단히 드묾
사실은 ~이다 / 장기적인 사용자 습관을 성공적으로 바꾸는 것은 / 대단히 드물다 //

(동명사구 주어, 단수 동사)
Altering behavior requires / not only an understanding / of how to persuade people / to act /
(to persuade의 목적격 보어)
행동을 변화시키는 것은 필요로 한다 / 이해뿐만 아니라 / 사람들이 설득하는 방법에 대한 / 행동하도록 /

(requires와 병렬 구조, getting의 목적격 보어)
but also necessitates / getting them to repeat behaviors / for long periods, / ideally for the rest of their lives. //
또한 필요로 한다 / 그들이 행동 방식을 반복하도록 만드는 것을 / 오랫동안 / 이상적으로는 남은 인생 동안 //

Companies / that succeed in building a habit-forming business / are often associated / with game-changing, wildly successful innovation. //
(복수 주어, 복수 동사)
기업은 / 습관 형성 사업을 이루는 데 성공한 / 자주 관련된다 / 판도를 바꾸는, 크게 성공한 혁신과 //

(선행사, 주격 관계대명사)
But like any discipline, / habit design has rules / that define and explain / why some products change lives / while others do not. //
단서 2 우리의 마음이 예전의 사고방식과 행동 방식으로 되돌아가는 경향이 있어서 새로운 행동 방식은 짧은 반감기를 가짐
하지만 여느 분야와 마찬가지로 / 습관 설계에도 규칙이 있다 / 규명하고 설명하는 / 왜 어떤 제품들은 삶을 바꾸는지를 / 다른 것들은 그렇지 않은 반면에 //

(부사절 접속사(원인))
For one, / new behaviors have a short half-life, / as our minds tend to return / to our old ways of thinking and doing. //
한 예로 / 새로운 행동 방식은 짧은 반감기를 가진다 / 우리의 마음은 되돌아가는 경향이 있기 때문에 / 우리의 예전 사고방식과 행동 방식으로 //

Experiments show / that lab animals / habituated to new behaviors / tend to regress / to their first learned behaviors / over time. // 단서 3 새로운 행동 방식에 익숙해지더라도 시간이 지나면 처음의 행동 방식으로 돌아감
실험들이 보여준다 / 실험동물들이 / 새로운 행동 방식에 익숙해진 / 되돌아가는 경향이 있다는 것을 / 처음 학습된 그들의 행동 방식으로 / 시간이 지남에 따라 //

To borrow a term from accounting, / behaviors are LIFO / — "last in, / first out." //
회계에서 용어를 빌리자면 / 행동 방식은 LIFO이다 / '마지막으로 들어온 것이 / 제일 먼저 나간다' //

- existence ⓝ 존재, 실재
- inherently ⓐⓓ 본질적으로, 선천적으로
- innovation ⓝ 혁신
- startup ⓝ 신생 기업
- disrupt ⓥ 무너뜨리다, 방해하다
- status quo 현재 상태
- long-term 장기적인
- exceptionally ⓐⓓ 대단히
- rare ⓐ 드문
- alter ⓥ 바꾸다
- persuade ⓥ 설득하다
- necessitate ⓥ 필요로 하다
- ideally ⓐⓓ 이상적으로
- be associated with ~와 관련되다
- game-changing 판도를 바꾸는, 획기적인
- wildly ⓐⓓ 크게, 몹시
- discipline ⓝ 분야, 훈련
- half-life 반감기
- habituate ⓥ 익숙하게 만들다
- term ⓝ 용어, 기간
- accounting ⓝ 회계 (업무)

사용자 습관은 그것들을 만들어 낼 만큼 운 좋은 기업에게는 요긴한 것인 반면에, 그것들의 존재는 본질적으로 '현재 상태'를 무너뜨리려는 새로운 혁신과 신생 기업이 성공할 가능성을 더 적게 만든다. 사실, 장기적인 사용자 습관을 성공적으로 바꾸는 것은 대단히 드물다. 행동을 변화시키는 것은 사람들이 행동하도록 설득하는 방법에 대한 이해뿐만 아니라, 그들이 오랫동안, 이상적으로는 남은 인생 동안, 행동 방식을 반복하도록 만드는 것 역시 필요로 한다. 습관 형성 사업을 성공적으로 이룬 기업은 판도를 바꾸는, 크게 성공한 혁신과 자주 관련된다. 하지만 여느 분야와 마찬가지로, 습관 설계에도 어떤 제품들은 삶을 바꾸는 반면 다른 것들은 그렇지 않은 이유를 규명하고 설명하는 규칙이 있다. 한 예로 우리의 마음은 우리의 예전 사고방식과 행동 방식으로 되돌아가는 경향이 있기 때문에, 새로운 행동 방식은 짧은 반감기를 가진다. 새로운 행동 방식에 익숙해진 실험동물들이 시간이 지남에 따라 처음 학습된 행동 방식으로 되돌아가는 경향이 있다는 것을 여러 실험이 보여준다. 회계 용어를 빌리자면, 행동 방식은 LIFO이다. 즉, '마지막으로 들어온 것이, 제일 먼저 나간다.'

밑줄 친 last in, first out이 다음 글에서 의미하는 바로 가장 적절한 것은? [3점]

① The behavior witnessed first is forgotten first.
첫 번째로 목격된 행동이 첫 번째로 잊힌다. — 어떤 행동을 '목격'하는 것에 대한 언급은 없음

② Almost any behavior tends to change over time.
거의 모든 행동이 시간이 지나면 바뀌는 경향이 있다. — 새로운 습관의 짧은 반감기에 대한 내용임

③ After an old habit breaks, a new one is formed.
오래된 습관이 깨지고 난 후에 새로운 것이 형성된다. — 새로운 습관의 형성이 어렵다는 내용임

④ The habit formed last is the hardest to get rid of.
마지막으로 형성된 습관이 없애기 가장 어렵다.

⑤ The habit most recently acquired disappears soonest.
가장 최근에 얻어진 습관이 가장 빠르게 사라진다. — 마지막으로 형성된 습관이 가장 쉽게 사라진다는 내용임

왜 정답? [정답률 61%]

꿀팁: 새롭게 형성된 습관은 사라지고 예전의 습관은 남는다는 의미임

사용자 습관이 기업에 미치는 영향에 대해 설명하면서 장기적인 사용자 습관을 성공적으로 바꾸는 것은 대단히 드물다고 했다. 우리의 마음이 예전의 사고방식과 행동 방식으로 되돌아가는 경향이 있기 때문에 새로운 행동 방식은 짧은 반감기를 갖는다고 했고, 실험동물들이 새로운 행동 방식에 익숙해졌더라도 시간이 지나면 처음의 행동 방식으로 되돌아가는 경향이 있다고 한 것으로 보아 last in, first out(마지막으로 들어온 것이 제일 먼저 나간다)이 의미하는 바는 ⑤ '가장 최근에 얻어진 습관이 가장 빠르게 사라진다.'이다.

왜 오답?

① 습관의 '형성'에 대한 내용으로, 어떤 행동을 목격하고, 그것을 잊는 것에 대해 이야기하는 것이 아니다.

② 습관을 바꾸는 것이 어렵다는 것이므로 대부분의 행동이 바뀐다는 것은 적절하지 않다.

③ 새로운 습관이 형성되더라도 시간이 지나면 오래된 습관으로 되돌아간다는, 즉 새로운 습관이 사라진다는 내용이다.

④ 마지막으로 형성된 습관이 가장 오래 남는다는 의미가 되려면 last in, last out이라고 해야 한다.

Our brains light up / when our predicted reality and actual
reality match. // **단서1** 우리의 뇌는 예상과 현실이 일치하는 것을 좋아함
우리의 뇌는 환해진다 / 우리의 예상되는 현실과 실제 현실이 일치할 때 //
　　주어　　 　동사　 　　목적어
Our brains love / to be right. //
우리의 뇌는 좋아한다 / 맞기를 //
　　　　　　　　　　　　　단서2 현실이 예상과 다를 때는 위협을 느낌
We also don't like to be wrong, / and we feel threatened / when
our stereotyped predictions don't come true. //
우리는 또한 틀리기를 좋아하지 않으며 / 우리는 위협을 느낀다 / 우리의 고정 관념에 기반한
예측이 실현되지 않을 때 //
　　　　주어
Psychologist Wendy Mendes asked / White and Asian college
　　목적격 보어
students / to interact with Latino students / who had been hired
as actors / by the researchers. //
심리학자 Wendy Mendes는 요청했다 / 백인과 아시아인 대학생들에게 / 라틴계 학생들과
상호 작용하도록 / 배우로 고용된 / 연구원들에 의해 //
　　　　　　　　　　　　　　　재귀대명사(재귀적 용법)
Some of the Latino students / portrayed themselves / as
socioeconomically "high status," / with lawyer fathers, professor
mothers, and summers / spent volunteering in Europe. //
라틴계 학생들의 일부는 / 자신을 묘사했다 / 사회 경제적으로 '높은 계층'으로 / 변호사
아버지, 교수 어머니, 그리고 여름을 가진 / 유럽에서 자원봉사를 하며 보내는 //
Others portrayed themselves / as "low status," / with
unemployed parents and part-time summer jobs. //
다른 사람들은 자신을 묘사했다 / '낮은 계층'으로 / 실업자인 부모님과 여름에 아르바이트
일을 가진 //
　　　　　　　　명사절 접속사 부사절 접속사(때)
The researchers found / that when participants interacted / with
　　　　　　　　　선행사
the Latino students / who appeared to come from wealth / and
thus challenged American stereotypes, / ⌐주격 관계대명사절의 동사의 병렬 구조
연구원들은 알아냈다 / 참가자들이 상호 작용했을 때 / 라틴계 학생들과 / 부유한 가정
출신으로 보이고 / 그래서 미국인의 고정 관념에 이의를 제기하는 /
they responded physiologically / as if to a threat: / their blood
vessels constricted / and their heart activity changed. //
그들이 생리적으로 반응한다는 것을 / 마치 위협을 대하는 것처럼 / 그들의 혈관은 수축했고 /
그들의 심장 활동은 변했다 //
In these interactions, / participants also saw the students / who
violated stereotypes / as less likable. //
이러한 상호 작용에서 / 참가자들은 또한 학생들을 간주했다 / 고정 관념을 깨뜨린 / 덜 호감이
가는 것으로 //
　　　　　　　　주어
In this way, / stereotypes that are *descriptive* / can easily become
　　　　　　　　　　　　　　　　　　　　　　　동사
prescriptive. //
이러한 방식으로 / '기술적인' 고정 관념은 / 쉽게 '규범적이게' 될 수 있다 //
The phenomenon, / it turns out, / may have a neuroscientific
explanation: / it's an angry protest / from the brain's reward
system. //
그 현상은 / 판명된다 / 신경 과학적인 설명을 가질 수 있다고 / 그것은 격렬한 항의이다 / 뇌의
보상 체계로부터의 //

- light up 환해지다　・predict ⓥ 예상하다　・threaten ⓥ 협박하다
- stereotype ⓝ 고정관념　・psychologist ⓝ 심리학자
- portray ⓥ 묘사하다　・socioeconomically ⓐⓓ 사회경제적으로
- unemployed ⓐ 실직한　・appear ⓥ ~인 것 같다
- physiologically ⓐⓓ 생리적으로　・blood vessel 혈관
- constrict ⓥ 수축하다　・violate ⓥ 위반하다, 침해하다
- descriptive ⓐ 서술하는, 기술적인
- prescriptive ⓐ 지시하는, 규범적인　・phenomenon ⓝ 현상
- neuroscientific ⓐ 신경과학의　・protest ⓝ 항의
- conditioned to ~에 적응된

우리의 뇌는 우리의 예상되는 현실과 실제 현실이 일치할 때 환해진다. 우리의
뇌는 맞기를 좋아한다. 우리는 또한 틀리기를 좋아하지 않으며, 우리의 고정

관념에 기반한 예측이 실현되지 않을 때 우리는 위협을 느낀다. 심리학자
Wendy Mendes는 백인과 아시아인 대학생들에게 연구원들에 의해 배우로
고용된 라틴계 학생들과 상호 작용하도록 요청했다. 라틴계 학생들의 일부는
자신을 변호사 아버지, 교수 어머니, 그리고 유럽에서 자원봉사를 하며 보내는
여름을 가진 사회 경제적으로 '높은 계층'으로 묘사했다. 다른 사람들은 자신을
실업자인 부모님과 여름에 아르바이트 일을 가진 '낮은 계층'으로 묘사했다.
연구원들은 참가자들이 부유한 가정 출신으로 보이고 그래서 미국인의 고정
관념에 이의를 제기하는 라틴계 학생들과 상호 작용했을 때 그들이 마치 위협을
대하는 것처럼 생리적으로 반응한다는 것을 알아냈는데, 즉 그들의 혈관은
수축했고 그들의 심장 활동은 변했다. 이러한 상호 작용에서 참가자들은
또한 고정 관념을 깨뜨린 학생들을 덜 호감이 가는 것으로 간주했다. 이러한
방식으로 '기술적인' 고정 관념은 쉽게 '규범적이게' 될 수 있다. 그 현상은
신경 과학적인 설명을 가질 수 있다고 판명되는데, 즉 그것은 뇌의 보상
체계로부터의 격렬한 항의이다.

**밑줄 친 it's an angry protest from the brain's reward system이 다음 글에
서 의미하는 바로 가장 적절한 것은? [3점]**
① Our brain prefers actual reality to predicted reality. 　예상과 현실
우리의 뇌는 예상되는 현실보다 실제 현실을 더 좋아한다.　　　중에서의 선호를 이야기하는 것이 아님
② Humans have a tendency to deny that they are stereotyped.
인간은 그들이 정형화되어 있다는 것을 부인하는 경향이 있다.　　정형화되어 있음을 보여줌
③ Humans are conditioned to avoid people who resemble them.
인간은 그들을 닮은 사람들을 피하도록 길들여진다.　　닮았는지가 변수인 실험이 아님
④ Our brain dislikes when something goes against its prediction.
우리의 뇌는 무언가가 그것의 예상을 벗어나는 때를 싫어한다.　　예상이 틀리면 위협을 느낌
⑤ When dissatisfied, the brain operates to make itself feel better.
불만스러울 때, 뇌는 자신이 기분 좋아지게 만들도록 작동한다. 기분이 좋아지도록 뇌가 작동한다는 것이 아님

〉왜 정답? [정답률 62%]
주제문과 그 주제를 뒷받침하는 실험이 제시된 글이다.

> **주제문**: 우리의 뇌는 예상과 현실이 일치할 때 환해지고, 현실이 예상과 다를
> 때는 위협을 느낀다. **단서1** **단서2**
> **실험**: **1** 백인과 아시아인 대학생에게 라틴계 학생들과 상호 작용하도록 요청함
> **2** 라틴계 학생의 일부는 자신을 높은 계층으로 묘사하고, 나머지는 낮은
> 계층으로 묘사함
> **3** 높은 계층의 라틴계 학생과 상호 작용했을 때(자신의 예상(고정 관념)과
> 현실이 다를 때) 참가자는 생리적으로 위협을 받을 때처럼 반응하고, 그 학생이
> 덜 호감이 간다고 여김

➡ 이러한 현상에 대한 신경 과학적인 설명은 ④ '우리의 뇌는 무언가가 그것의 예상을
벗어나는 때를 싫어한다.'라고 할 수 있다.

〉왜 오답?
① 예상되는 현실과 실제 현실이 일치하지 않는 경우에 대한 이야기이다.
② 고정 관념에서 벗어나는 현실을 싫어한다는 것으로 보아, 정형화되어 있다고 할 수
있다.
③ 실험에 등장한 라틴계 학생이 참가자와 닮았는지가 실험의 변수인 것이 아니다.
⑤ 뇌가 좋아하지 않는 경우를 이야기한 것이지, 그 경우에 뇌가 어떻게 작동하는지를
설명한 것이 아니다.

D 17 정답 ④ ＊에디슨의 전깃불의 영향

Thomas Edison's name is synonymous / with invention, /
토머스 에디슨의 이름은 동의어이고 / 발명과 /
　　　　　　　　　　　　　　　⌐동격 ⌐
and his most famous invention, the electric light bulb, / is a
familiar symbol / for that flash of inspired genius / traditionally
associated with the inventive act. //
그의 가장 유명한 발명품인 전구는 / 친숙한 상징이다 / 그러한 영감을 받은 번득이는
천재성의 / 전통적으로 창의적 행위와 연관되는 //
　　　　　　　　　　　　　　　　　　동명사구
Besides being the exemplar / of the "bright idea," / however, /
　　전치사
Edison's electric light is worthy of study / for other reasons. //
표본이라는 것 외에도 / '총명한 아이디어'의 / 그러나 / 에디슨의 전깃불은 연구할 가치가
있다 / 다른 이유로 //

단수 주어   = the technical and economic importance

The technical and economic importance / of the light / and of
the electrical system / that surrounded it / matches / that of any
     = the light   단수 동사
other invention / 단서1 전깃불과 전기 시스템은 큰 기술적, 경제적 중요성을 지님
기술적, 경제적 중요성은 / 전깃불의 그리고 전기 시스템의 / 그 주변을 둘러싸고 있는 /
필적한다 / 다른 어떤 발명품의 그것에 /

we could name, / at least from the last two hundred years. //
우리가 열거할 수 있는 / 적어도 지난 200년 이래 //

The introduction and spread / of electric light and power / was
one of the key steps / in the transformation of the world / from
an industrial age, / characterized by iron and coal and steam, /
도입과 확산은 / 전깃불과 전력의 / 핵심 단계 중 하나였다 / 세상의 전환에 / 산업 시대에서
/ 철, 석탄, 증기로 특징지어지는 /
단서2 전깃불과 전력의 도입과 확산이 산업 시대에서
후기 산업 시대로의 전환에 있어 핵심 단계였음

to a post-industrial one, / in which electricity was joined /
     = where
by petroleum, light metals and alloys, and internal combustion
engines /
후기 산업 시대로의 / 전기가 결합되어 / 석유, 경금속과 합금 그리고 내연 기관에 의해 /
부사적 용법(결과)
to give the twentieth century / its distinctive form and
     to give의 간접목적어와 직접목적어
character. //
20세기에 부여한 / 그것의 특유한 형태와 특성을 //
주어   동사   목적어
Our own time still largely carries / the stamp of this age, /
however dazzled we may be / by the electronic, computerized,
복합 관계부사(아무리 ~할지라도)
and media wonders / of the twenty-first century. //
우리 자신의 시대는 여전히 대체로 지니고 있다 / 이 시대의 흔적을 / 우리가 아무리
감탄할지라도 / 전자의, 전산화된 그리고 미디어의 경이에 / 21세기의 //

- synonymous ⓐ 동의어의   • flash ⓝ 반짝임, 섬광
- inspired ⓐ (능력이) 탁월한, 영감을 받은   • associated ⓐ 관련된
- inventive ⓐ 창의[독창]적인   • exemplar ⓝ 대표적인 예, 본보기
- worthy ⓐ (~을 받을) 자격이 있는, 받을 만한   • surround ⓥ 둘러싸다
- match ⓥ 일치하다, 맞먹다   • introduction ⓝ 도입, 전래
- spread ⓝ 확산, 전파   • key ⓐ 핵심적인, 가장 중요한
- transformation ⓝ 전환, (완전한) 변화   • industrial ⓐ 산업[공업]의
- characterize ⓥ 특징이 되다, 특징짓다   • iron ⓝ 철, 쇠
- coal ⓝ 석탄   • steam ⓝ 증기   • post-industrial ⓐ 후기 산업의
- petroleum ⓝ 석유   • combustion ⓝ (물질의 화학적) 연소
- distinctive ⓐ 독특한, 뚜렷이 구별되는   • stamp ⓝ 흔적, 우표
- dazzle ⓥ 눈이 부시게 하다, 황홀하게 하다

토머스 에디슨의 이름은 발명과 동의어이고, 그의 가장 유명한 발명품인 전구는
전통적으로 창의적 행위와 연관되는, 그러한 영감을 받은 번득이는 천재성을
나타내는 친숙한 상징이다. 그러나 에디슨의 전깃불은 '총명한 아이디어'의
표본이라는 것 외에도 다른 이유로 연구할 가치가 있다. 전깃불과 그 주변을
둘러싸고 있는 전기 시스템의 기술적, 경제적 중요성은 적어도 지난 200년 이래
우리가 열거할 수 있는 다른 어떤 발명품의 기술적, 경제적 중요성에 필적한다.
전깃불과 전력의 도입과 확산은 세상이 철, 석탄, 증기를 특징으로 하는 산업
시대에서, 전기가 석유, 경금속과 합금 그리고 내연 기관과 결합해 20세기에
특유한 형태와 특성을 부여한, 후기 산업 시대로의 전환에 핵심 단계 중
하나였다. 우리가 21세기의 전자의, 전산화된 그리고 미디어의 경이에 아무리
감탄할지라도, 우리 자신의 시대는 여전히 대체로 <u>이 시대의 흔적을 지니고
있다.</u>

**밑줄 친 carries the stamp of this age가 다음 글에서 의미하는 바로 가장
적절한 것은? [3점]**

① combines creative ideas from various disciplines
   다양한 규율로부터 창의적인 아이디어들을 결합하다   전구의 발명이 언급된 것으로 만든 오답
② strives to overcome limitations of the industrial age
   산업 시대의 한계를 극복하려고 분투하다   산업 시대와 후기 산업 시대를 거쳐 21세기가 되었음
③ is a theoretical background for academic exploration
   학문적 탐험을 위한 이론적인 배경이다   21세기의 배경에 대해 이야기하는 것임
④ is under the influence of earlier electrical innovations
   이전의 전기적 혁명의 영향 하에 있다   전깃불과 전력이 여전히 영향을 미침
⑤ is dependent on resources reserved for future generations
   미래 세대를 위해 비축된 자원에 의존하다   비축된 자원에 대한 언급은 없음

왜 정답? [정답률 66%]

전깃불과 전기 시스템의 기술적, 경제적 중요성이 매우 크고, 전깃불과 전력의
도입과 확산이 산업 시대에서 후기 산업 시대로의 전환에 핵심이었다는 내용에
이어지면서 21세기 역시 여전히 그 시대의 흔적을 지니고 있다는 표현은 21세기
역시 ④ '이전의 전기적 혁명의 영향 하에 있다'는 것을 의미한다.
   Our own time이 21세기를 의미함 꿀팁

왜 오답?

① 우리가 전자적인, 전산화된, 미디어의 경이에 감탄하는 21세기 역시 후기 산업
시대와 마찬가지로 전깃불과 전력의 도입, 확산에 바탕을 둔다는 의미이다.
② 전깃불과 전력의 도입과 확산에 의해 산업 시대에서 후기 산업 시대로
전환되었다고 했다. 우리 자신의 시대는 21세기, 즉 후기 산업 시대에 이어지는
시대를 가리킨다.
③ 21세기가 또 다른 시대의 배경이 된다는 것이 아니라, 21세기로의 발전이
무엇에 의해 영향을 받았는지를 설명하는 것이다.
⑤ 현재 우리의 시대가 미래 세대가 사용할 자원에 의존하고 있다는 언급은 없다.

D 18 정답 ② ＊환경 저널리스트: 사자의 역사가

There is an African proverb / that says, / 'Till the lions have their
historians, / tales of hunting will always glorify / the hunter'. //
아프리카 속담이 있다 / 말하는 / "사자들이 자신들의 역사가를 가질 때까지 / 사냥 이야기는
언제나 미화할 것이다 / 사냥한 자를"이라고 //
     주격 보어 역할을 하는 전치사구
The proverb is / about power, control and law making. //
이 속담은 ~이다 / 권력, 통제, 법 제정에 관한 것 //

Environmental journalists have to play / the role of the 'lion's
historians'. //
환경 저널리스트는 수행해야 한다 / '사자의 역사가'의 역할을 //

They have to put across the point of view / of the environment /
전행사   주격 관계대명사
to people / who make the laws. //
그들은 관점을 이해시켜야 한다 / 환경에 대한 / 사람들에게 / 법을 만드는 //

They have to be the voice / of wild India. //
그들은 대변자가 되어야 한다 / 인도 야생 자연의 //

The present rate of human consumption / is completely
unsustainable. // 단서1 현재 인간의 지속 불가능한 소비를 비판함
인간의 현재 소비 속도는 / 완전히 지속 불가능하다 //

Forest, wetlands, wastelands, coastal zones, eco-sensitive zones,
     see A as B(A를 B로 여기다)의 수동태
/ they are all seen as disposable / for the accelerating demands /
of human population. //
숲, 습지, 황무지, 해안지대, 환경 민감 지역 / 그것들은 모두 마음대로 이용할 수 있는 것으로
여겨진다 / 가속화되고 있는 수요를 위해 / 인구의 //
     whether를 생략하고 주어와 동사를
     도치시켜 be it으로 쓸 수 있음
But to ask for any change / in human behaviour / — whether it
명사적 용법(주어)
be to cut down on consumption, / alter lifestyles / or decrease
     명사구 주어에 대한 단수 동사
population growth — / is seen as a violation / of human rights. //
그러나 어떤 변화든 요구하는 것은 / 인간의 행동에 / 그것이 소비를 줄이는 것이든 / 생활 방
식을 바꾸는 것이든 / 또는 인구 증가를 줄이는 것이든 / 침해로 여겨진다 / 인권의 //

But at some point / human rights become 'wrongs'. //
하지만 어느 시점에 / 인권은 '옳지 않은 것'이 된다 // 단서2 인권을 지키는 것, 즉 변화를 요구하지
     앞에 관계부사가 생략됨   않는 것이 옳지 않은 것이 됨
It's time / we changed our thinking / so that there is no difference
/ between the rights of humans and the rights of the rest of the
     부사절 접속사(목적)
environment. // 단서3 환경을 위해 우리의 생각을 바꿀 때임
~할 때이다 / 우리의 생각을 바꿀 / 차이가 없도록 / 인간의 권리와 나머지 환경의 권리 사이에 /
     진작 바뀌어야 하는데 바뀌지 않았다는 비난의 뉘앙스를 담은 과거형 동사 changed

- proverb ⓝ 속담   • historian ⓝ 사학자   • tale ⓝ 이야기, 소설
- glorify ⓥ 미화하다   • role ⓝ 역할   • put across ~을 이해시키다
- rate ⓝ 속도, 비율   • consumption ⓝ 소비[소모](량)
- completely ⓐⓓ 완전히, 전적으로   • unsustainable ⓐ 지속 불가능한
- wetland ⓝ 습지(대)   • wasteland ⓝ 황무지, 불모지
- coastal ⓐ 해안의   • sensitive ⓐ 세심한, 민감한
- disposable ⓐ 사용 후 버리게 되어 있는, 자유롭게 사용할 수 있는

- accelerate ⓥ 가속화하다 • cut down on ∼을 줄이다
- alter ⓥ 바꾸다, 고치다 • violation ⓝ 위반, 위배, 침입
- right ⓝ 권리, 권한 • uncover ⓥ 알아내다
- urge ⓥ 강력히 권고[촉구]하다 • shift ⓝ 변화
- underrepresent ⓥ 실제의 수량·정도보다 적게[낮게] 표시하다
- restrict ⓥ 제한[한정]하다

"사자들이 자신들의 역사를 가질 때까지, 사냥 이야기는 언제나 사냥한 자를 미화할 것이다."라는 아프리카 속담이 있다. 이 속담은 권력, 통제, 법 제정에 관한 것이다. 환경 저널리스트는 '사자의 역사가' 역할을 수행해야 한다. 그들은 법을 만드는 사람들에게 환경에 대한 관점을 이해시켜야 한다. 그들은 인도 야생 자연의 대변자가 되어야 한다. 현재 인간의 소비 속도는 완전히 지속 불가능하다.

숲, 습지, 황무지, 해안지대, 환경 민감 지역 모두 가속화되고 있는 인구의 수요를 위해 마음대로 이용할 수 있는 것으로 여겨진다. 그러나 소비를 줄이는 것이든, 생활 방식을 바꾸는 것이든, 인구 증가를 줄이는 것이든, 인간의 행동에 어떤 변화든 요구하는 것은 인권 침해로 여겨진다. 하지만 어느 시점에 인권은 '옳지 않은 것'이 된다. 인간의 권리와 나머지 환경의 권리 사이에 차이가 없도록 우리의 생각을 바꿀 때이다.

밑줄 친 the role of the 'lion's historians'가 다음 글에서 의미하는 바로 가장 적절한 것은?

① uncovering the history of a species' biological evolution
한 종의 생물학적 진화의 역사를 밝혀내는 것   진화의 역사를 밝혀내는 것이 아님
② urging a shift to sustainable human behaviour for nature
자연을 위한 인간의 지속 가능한 행동으로의 전환을 촉구하는 것   지속 불가능한 현재의 소비를 비판함
③ fighting against widespread violations of human rights
만연한 인권 침해에 맞서 싸우는 것   인권이 옳지 않은 것이라고 했음
④ rewriting history for more underrepresented people
더 부당하게 서술된 사람들을 위해서 역사를 다시 쓰는 것   사람이 아니라 자연을 위해 이야기하는 역할임
⑤ restricting the power of environmental lawmakers
환경법 제정자들의 권한을 제한하는 것   권한이 비대하다는 문제를 제기한 것이 아님

왜 정답? [정답률 57%]

사자의 역사가의 역할, 인도 야생 자연의 대변자, 즉 자연을 위해 일하는 역할을 의미함

환경 저널리스트가 수행해야 하는 역할이 무엇인지를 글을 통해 파악해야 한다. 현재 인간의 소비 속도는 완전히 지속 불가능한데, 이러한 인간의 행동에 변화를 요구하는 것이 인권의 침해로 여겨진다고 했다.

이때 인권이 '옳지 않은 것'이 된다는 것은 인간의 행동이 변화해야 한다는 의미이고, 마지막 문장에서 환경을 위해 우리의 생각을 바꿀 때라고 했으므로 환경 저널리스트가 수행해야 하는 역할은 ② '자연을 위한 인간의 지속 가능한 행동으로의 전환을 촉구하는 것'이다.

왜 오답?

① 환경 저널리스트가 해야 할 역할은 사자의 입장에서 사자를 대변하는 것이지, 어떤 종의 생물학적 진화의 역사를 밝혀내야 한다는 것이 아니다.
③ 숲, 습지 등의 자연을 마음대로 이용하는 인간의 권리가 어느 시점에서 '옳지 않은 것'이 된다고 했다.
④ 사람들의 무리를 나눈 것이 아니라 인간과 나머지 환경을 나누고, 환경 저널리스트들이 나머지 환경을 위한 역할을 수행해야 한다는 내용이다.
⑤ 환경법 제정자들의 권한을 문제 삼고, 그것을 해결해야 한다는 내용이 아니다.

D 19 정답 ⑤ * 소비주의와 자본주의에 대한 오해

단서1 소비주의는 자본 형성을 불가능하게 하기 때문에 자본주의를 불가능하게 만듦

Far from a synonym for capitalism, / consumerism makes
capitalism impossible / over the long term, / since it makes
capital formation / all but impossible. //
<small>makes의 목적어와 목적보어</small>
자본주의의 동의어이기는커녕 / 소비주의는 자본주의를 불가능하게 만든다 / 오랜 기간에
걸쳐 / 그것이 자본 형성을 만들기 때문에 / 사실상 불가능하게 //

A consumer culture / isn't a saving culture, / isn't a thrift
culture. //
소비문화는 / 저축 문화도 아니고 / 절약 문화도 아니다 //

It's too fixated / on buying the next toy / to ever delay
gratification, / to ever save and invest / for the future. //
<small>too+형용사/부사+to부정사: 너무 ∼해서 …할 수 없는</small>
그것은 너무 집착한다 / 다음 장난감을 사는 데 / 결코 욕구 충족도 미루지도 않고 / 결코
저축하고 투자하지도 않는다 / 미래를 위해 //

The point is elementary: / you can't have sustainable capitalism
/ without capital; / you can't have capital / without savings; /
요점은 기본적이다 / 여러분은 지속 가능한 자본주의를 가질 수 없다 / 자본이 없이는 /
여러분은 자본을 가질 수 없다 / 저축이 없이는 /

and you can't save / if you're running around / spending
everything / you've just earned. //
<small>〈조건〉의 부사절 접속사   앞에 목적격 관계대명사가 생략됨</small>
그리고 여러분은 저축할 수 없다 / 여러분이 돌아다닌다면 / 모든 것을 쓰면서 / 여러분이 방금
벌어들인 //

<small>so+형용사/부사+that+S+V: 너무 ∼해서 …하다</small>
But the confusion has grown so deep / that many people today
do not have the ears / to hear it. // **단서2** 혼동이 너무 깊어서 오늘날 많은 이들이
하지만 혼동은 너무 깊어져서 / 많은 이들이 오늘날 귀를 갖고 있지 않다 / 그것을 들을 //
<small>∼한다는 내용이 역접으로 연결됨</small>

Indeed, the policies of our nation's central bank / seem to
reinforce this habit /
실제로 우리나라의 중앙은행의 정책은 / 이런 습관을 강화하는 것 같다 /

by driving down interest rates / to near zero / and thereby
denying people a material reward /
<small>병렬 구조(by의 목적어)</small>
이자율을 끌어내림으로써 / 영에 가깝게 / 그리고 그로 인해 사람들에게 물질적 보상을 주기를
거부함으로써 /

— in the form of interest / on their banked savings — / for
foregoing consumption. //
이자의 형태로 / 그들의 은행 예금에 대한 / 소비를 단념하는 것에 대한 //

- far from 전혀 ∼이 아닌 • synonym ⓝ 동의어
- capitalism ⓝ 자본주의 • consumerism ⓝ 소비지상주의
- term ⓝ (지속되는·정해진) 기간 • capital ⓝ 자본금, 자산
- formation ⓝ 형성 • all but 사실상, 거의 • thrift ⓝ 절약
- elementary ⓐ 기본적인, 초보의 • sustainable ⓐ 지속 가능한
- saving ⓝ ((pl.)) 저축한 돈, 저금 • confusion ⓝ 혼란, 혼동
- policy ⓝ 정책, 방침 • reinforce ⓥ 강화하다, 증원하다
- interest ⓝ 이자, 이익 • deny ⓥ 부정하다, 거부하다
- material ⓐ 물질[물리]적인 • consumption ⓝ 소비[소모](량)

소비주의는 자본주의의 동의어이기는커녕 자본주의를 오랜 기간에 걸쳐 불가능하게 하는데, 이는 그것이 자본 형성을 사실상 불가능하게 하기 때문이다. 소비문화는 저축 문화도 아니고 절약 문화도 아니다. 그것은 다음 장난감을 사는 데 너무 집착한 나머지 결코 욕구 충족을 미루지도 않고, 미래를 위해 결코 저축하고 투자하지도 않는다.

요점은 기본적인데, 자본이 없이는 지속 가능한 자본주의가 있을 수 없고, 저축이 없이는 자본이 생길 수 없으며, 방금 벌어들인 모든 것을 쓰면서 돌아다닌다면 저축할 수 없다는 것이다. 하지만 혼동은 너무 깊어져서 많은 이들이 오늘날 그것을 들을 귀를 갖고 있지 않다. 실제로 우리나라의 중앙은행 정책은 이자율을 영에 가깝게 끌어내려, 그로 인해 사람들에게 그들의 은행 예금에 대한 이자의 형태로, 소비를 단념하는 것에 대한 물질적 보상을 주기를 거부함으로써 이런 습관을 강화하는 것 같다.

밑줄 친 do not have the ears to hear it이 다음 글에서 의미하는 바로 가장 적절한 것은? [3점]

<small>저축과 국가의 번영 사이의 관계에 대한 내용이 아님</small>
① disagree with the national policy of lowering interest rates
이자율을 낮추는 국가 정책에 반대하다   마지막 문장에 interest rates가 언급된 것으로 만든 오답
② ignore the fact that consumerism is a synonym for capitalism
소비주의가 자본주의의 동의어라는 사실을 무시하다   소비주의는 자본주의의 동의어가 아님
③ believe that consumerism doesn't really do much for well-being
소비주의가 실제로 행복을 위해 많은 것을 하지 않는다고 믿다   글과 상관없는 내용임
④ form a false assumption that savings can make nations prosper
저축이 국가를 번영하게 만들 수 있다는 잘못된 추정을 형성하다
⑤ fail to understand that consumption alone can't sustain
capitalism   소비주의가 자본주의를 불가능하게 한다는 것을 모름
소비만으로 자본주의를 지탱할 수 없다는 것을 이해하지 못하다

왜 정답? [정답률 44%]

소비주의는 자본 형성을 불가능하게 만들기 때문에 자본주의를 불가능하게 한다는 첫 문장 이후로 소비주의가 자본주의를 불가능하게 하는 것에 대한 구체적인 부연이 밑줄 친 부분이 포함된 문장의 바로 앞까지 이어진다.

역접의 연결어로 시작한 밑줄 친 부분이 포함된 문장은, 소비주의는 결코 자본주의의 동의어가 아닌데도 소비주의와 자본주의에 대한 혼동이 너무 깊어져서 많은 사람들이 '그것을 들을 귀를 갖고 있지 않다'는 의미이므로, 밑줄 친 부분이 의미하는 바는 ⑤ '소비만으로 자본주의를 지탱할 수 없다는 것을 이해하지 못하다'이다.

소비주의가 자본주의의 동의어가 아니며
소비주의가 자본주의를 불가능하게 한다는 것

⟩왜 오답 ?

① ④ 마지막 문장이 이자율에 관한 내용이라는 점으로 만든 오답이다. 〔확정〕
마지막 문장은 이자율을 영에 가깝게 만드는 국가 중앙은행의 정책으로
소비주의가 조장되어 자본주의가 불가능해진다는 의미이다.

② 소비주의가 자본주의의 동의어가 아니라는 것을 사람들이 모른다는 글이다.

③ 소비문화가 행복으로 이어지는지 또는 그렇지 않은지에 대해 이야기하는 것이
아니라 소비주의와 자본주의의 관계에 대한 글이다.

D 20 정답 ① *습관적인 문제 해결

수단을 나타내는 전치사 by와 그 목적어로 쓰인 동명사
By expecting / what's likely to happen next, / you prepare for
the few most likely scenarios / so that you don't have to figure
things out / while they're happening. //
시간의 부사절 접속사 / 목적의 부사절 접속사
예상함으로써 / 다음에 무슨 일이 일어날지 / 여러분은 가장 가능성이 높은 몇 가지 시나리오
에 대비한다 / 여러분이 상황을 파악할 필요가 없도록 / 그것들이 일어나는 동안에 //

It's therefore not a surprise / when a restaurant server offers you
a menu. //
가주어 / 진주어절 접속사
그러므로 ~은 놀랄 일이 아니다 / 음식점 종업원이 여러분에게 메뉴를 제공할 때는 //

When she brings you a glass / with a clear fluid in it, / you don't
have to ask / if it's water. //
시간의 부사절 접속사 / 명사절 접속사
그녀가 여러분에게 유리잔을 가져다줄 때 / 그 안에 투명한 액체가 담긴 / 여러분은 묻지 않아도
된다 / 그것이 물인지 //

After you eat, / you don't have to figure out / why you aren't
hungry anymore. //
여러분이 식사를 한 후에 / 여러분은 알아낼 필요가 없다 / 여러분이 왜 더 이상 배가 고프지
않은지 //

All these things are expected / and are therefore not problems
/ to solve. //
이 모든 것들은 예상되며 / 따라서 문제가 아니다 / 해결해야 할 //
명사절(목적어절) 가주어 진주어(to부정사)
Furthermore, / imagine how demanding it would be / to always
consider all the possible uses / for all the familiar objects / with
which you interact. //
선행사 / 「전치사+관계대명사」
더욱이 / ~이 얼마나 힘들 것인지 상상해 보라 / 모든 가능한 사용법들을 항상 고려하는 것이
/ 모든 친숙한 물건들에 대한 / 여러분이 상호 작용하는 //

Should I use my hammer / or my telephone / to pound in that nail? //
"내가 나의 망치를 사용해야 할까 / 아니면 나의 전화기를 / 저 못을 박기 위해서" //

On a daily basis, / functional fixedness is a relief, / not a curse. //
매일을 살아가는 데 있어서 / 기능적 고정성은 안도이다 / 저주가 아니라 //
목적어로 to부정사를 취하는 attempt
That's why you shouldn't even attempt / to consider / all your
options and possibilities. //
관계부사 단서1 '못을 박는 것 = 망치와 같은 기능적
고정성은 나쁜 게 아니라 좋은 것임
그것이 여러분이 시도조차 해서는 안 되는 이유이다 / 고려하는 것을 / 여러분의 모든 선택권
과 가능성을 //

You can't. //
그럴 수도 없다 단서2 모든 선택권과 가능성을 고려하려고 한다면 어떤 일도 끝낼 수 없을 것임

If you tried to, / then you'd never get anything done. //
여러분이 그렇게 하려고 한다면 / 여러분은 결코 그 어떤 일도 끝낼 수 없을 것이다 //

So don't knock the box. //
그러니 상자를 두드리지 말라 //
양보의 부사절 접속사 / 주어 동사 목적어
Ironically, / although it limits your thinking, / it also makes you
목적격 보어(형용사)
smart. //
역설적으로 / 비록 그것이 여러분의 사고를 제한하지만 / 그것은 또한 여러분을 똑똑하게 만
든다 //
동사 목적어 목적격 보어(to부정사)
It helps you / to stay one step ahead of reality. //
주어
그것은 여러분을 도와준다 / 현실보다 한발 앞서도록 //

- expect ⓥ 예상하다, 기대하다 · figure out ~을 알아내다
- fluid ⓝ 액체 · consider ⓥ 고려하다, 숙고하다
- familiar ⓐ 익숙한, 친숙한 · object ⓝ 물건, 물체
- interact ⓥ 상호 작용을 하다
- pound ⓥ (특히 요란한 소리를 내며 여러 차례) 치다[두드리다]
- nail ⓝ 못 · functional ⓐ 기능적인, 기능상의
- fixedness ⓝ 정착, 고착, 고정 · relief ⓝ 안도(감) · curse ⓝ 저주
- ironically ⓐⓓ 얄궂게도, 반어적으로

다음에 무슨 일이 일어날지 예상함으로써, 여러분은 그것들이 일어나는 동안에
상황을 파악할 필요가 없도록 가장 가능성이 높은 몇 가지 시나리오에 대비한
다. 그러므로 음식점 종업원이 여러분에게 메뉴를 제공하는 것은 놀랄 일이 아
니다. 그녀가 여러분에게 투명한 액체가 담긴 유리잔을 가져다줄 때, 여러분은
그것이 물인지 묻지 않아도 된다. 식사를 한 후에, 여러분은 왜 더 이상 배가 고
프지 않은지 알아낼 필요가 없다. 이 모든 것들은 예상되며 따라서 해결해야 할
문제가 아니다. 더욱이, 여러분이 상호 작용하는 모든 친숙한 물건들에 대한 모
든 가능한 사용법들에 대해 항상 고려하는 것이 얼마나 힘들 것인지 상상해 보
라. "저 못을 박기 위해서 나의 망치나 나의 전화기 중 어떤 것을 사용해야 할
까?" 매일을 살아가는 데 있어서, 기능적 고정성은 저주가 아니라 안도이다. 그
렇기 때문에 여러분은 여러분의 모든 선택권과 가능성을 고려하려는 시도조차
해서는 안 된다. 그럴 수도 없다. 여러분이 그렇게 하려고 한다면, 여러분은 결
코 그 어떤 일도 끝낼 수 없을 것이다. 그러니 상자를 두드리지 말라. 역설적으
로, 비록 그것이 여러분의 사고를 제한하지만, 그것은 또한 여러분을 똑똑하게
만든다. 그것은 여러분이 현실보다 한발 앞서도록 도와준다.

밑줄 친 don't knock the box가 다음 글에서 의미하는 바로 가장 적절한 것은?

①Deal with a matter based on your habitual expectations.
여러분의 습관적인 기대를 바탕으로 문제를 처리하라. 기능적 고정성으로 문제를 해결하라는 내용임

② Question what you expect from a familiar object.
여러분이 익숙한 물건으로부터 기대하는 것에 의문을 품으라. 문제를 해결할 때 익숙한 물건을 사용할 것

③ Replace predetermined routines with fresh ones.
미리 정해진 일상을 새로운 일상으로 교체하라. 늘 그래 왔던 것의 장점을 설명함

④ Think over all possible outcomes of a given situation.
주어진 상황의 모든 가능한 결과에 대해 숙고하라. 모든 가능성을 생각하려고 하지 말 것

⑤ Extend all the boundaries that guide your thinking to insight.
여러분의 사고를 통찰로 이끄는 모든 경계를 확대하라. 습관적 사고, 예상의 장점을 설명함

⟩왜 정답 ? [정답률 55%]

음식점 종업원이 우리에게 메뉴를 주는 것, 종업원이 가져다주는 유리잔에 든 투명
한 액체가 물이라는 것, 못을 박기 위해서는 망치를 사용한다는 것처럼 우리가 습
관적으로 예상하는 것들은 해결할 문제가 아니고, 이러한 기능적 고정성은 저주가
아니라 안도, 즉 이점이라고 했다. 만약 어떤 문제의 해결에 대해 모든 선택권과 가
능성을 고려하려고 한다면 그 어떤 일도 결코 끝마칠 수 없을 것이니 상자를 두드
리지 말라는 말은 문제 해결에 대한 모든 선택권과 가능성을 고려하지 말라는 의미,
즉 ① '여러분의 습관적인 기대를 바탕으로 문제를 처리하라.'는 의미이다.

⟩왜 오답 ?
굳이 시간을 들여 문제 해결 방법을 생각하는 것이 아니라 '못을
박으려면 = 망치'처럼 고정되어 있는 습관적 방법으로 해결하는 것 꿀팁

② 익숙한 물건을 익숙한 용도로 사용하라는 내용이라고 볼 수 있다.

③ 습관적으로, 익숙하게, 늘 그래 왔던 것의 이점을 설명하는 글이다.

④ 모든 선택권, 모든 가능성을 고려하는 것이 힘든 일이라는 내용이다.

⑤ 이미 습관적으로 알고 있는 사용법으로 물건을 사용하여 문제를 해결하라고 했
으므로 고정관념 등의 경계를 뛰어넘으라는 것은 적절하지 않다.

D 21 정답 ② *과학은 진화하고 뉴스는 일어난다

Journalists love to report studies / that are at the "initial
findings" stages /
선행사(관계부사는 생략됨)
언론인들은 연구들을 보도하기를 매우 좋아한다 / '초기 결과' 단계에 있는 /

— research / that claims to be the first time / anyone has
discovered a thing — / because there is newsworthiness / in
their novelty. // 단서1 언론인들은 최초의 발견이라고 주장하는 연구를 보도하는 것을
좋아하는데, 이는 그 '새로움'에 뉴스 가치가 있기 때문임
연구 / 최초라고 주장하는 / 누군가가 어떤 것을 발견한 / 뉴스 가치가 있기 때문에 / 그것들의
새로움에 //
전치사
But "first ever" discoveries are extremely vulnerable / to
동명사구
becoming undermined / by subsequent research. //
그러나 '사상 최초의' 발견들은 아주 취약하다 / 약화되는 것에 / 후속 연구에 의해 //
(시간)의 부사절
When that happens, / the news media often don't go back and
inform their audiences / about the change / — assuming they
even hear about it. // 단서2 그러나 후속 연구로 인해 기존에 보도한 연구에
변화가 있을 때는 그것을 보도하지 않음
그것이 일어날 때 / 뉴스 매체는 종종 돌아가서 그들의 독자들에게 알리지 않는다 / 변화에
관해 / 그들이 그것에 관해 심지어 듣는다고 가정한 채 //

Kelly Crowe, a CBC News reporter writes, / quoting one
epidemiologist, /
CBC News 기자인 Kelly Crowe는 쓴다 / 한 전염병학자의 말을 인용하며 /

"There is increasing concern / that in modern research, / false
findings may be the majority or even the vast majority / of
published research claims." //
　　　　　　동격절 접속사
"증가하는 염려가 있다 / 현대 연구에서 / 잘못된 결과가 다수 또는 심지어 대다수일 수도
있다는 / 게재된 연구 주장의"라고 //

She goes on to suggest / that journalists, / though blameworthy
　　　　　　　　　　　　　　복수 주어
for this tendency, / are aided and abetted / by the scientists /
소유격 관계대명사　　　　복수 동사　　　　　　　　　선행사
whose studies they cite. //

그녀는 이어서 시사한다 / 언론인들이 / 이러한 경향에 있어 비난받을 만하지만 / 방조된다고
/ 과학자들에 의해 / 그들(과학자들)의 연구를 그들(언론인들)이 인용하는 //

She writes / that the "conclusions" sections / in scientific
abstracts / can sometimes be overstated /
그녀는 쓴다 / '결론' 부분들이 / 과학 초록의 / 때때로 과장될 수 있다고 /
　　　　　　　　　형용사적 용법(an attempt 수식)　　　　선행사
in an attempt to draw attention / from prestigious academic
　　　　　　　　　　　　　　　주격 관계대명사
journals and media / who uncritically take their bait. //

관심을 끌기 위한 시도에서 / 명성 있는 학술지와 매체로부터 / 무비판적으로 그것들의 미끼를
무는 //

Even so, / Crowe ends her piece / by stressing / that there is
still an incompatibility / between the purposes and processes of
news and science: /
그럼에도 불구하고 / Crowe는 자신의 글을 끝맺는다 / 강조함으로써 / 여전히 상반된 점이
있다는 것을 / 뉴스와 과학의 목적과 과정 사이에는 /

Science 'evolves,' but news 'happens.' //
과학은 '진화하지만' / 뉴스는 '일어난다' //

- initial ⓐ 초기의, 처음의　　• claim ⓥ 주장하다, 요구하다 ⓝ 주장
- newsworthiness ⓝ 보도[뉴스] 가치가 있음　　• novelty ⓝ 신기함, 새로움
- vulnerable ⓐ 취약한, 상처받기 쉬운　　• undermine ⓥ 손상[약화]시키다
- subsequent ⓐ 그[이]다음의, 차후의　　• assume ⓥ 추정[상정]하다
- quote ⓥ 인용하다, 전달하다　　• majority ⓝ 다수, 대부분
- blameworthy ⓐ 탓할 만한, 책임이 있는　　• cite ⓥ 인용하다
- abstract ⓝ (책·연설·서류의) 개요
- overstate ⓥ 과장하다, 허풍을 떨다　　• draw ⓥ (마음을) 끌다
- prestigious ⓐ 명망 있는[높은], 일류의　　• uncritically ⓐⓓ 무비판적으로
- bait ⓝ 미끼　　• piece ⓝ (글·음악·미술 등의 작품) 한 점
- stress ⓥ 강조하다　　• incompatibility ⓝ 불일치, 양립할 수 없음

언론인들은 '초기 결과' 단계에 있는 연구들, 즉 누군가가 어떤 것을 발견한
최초라고 주장하는 연구를 보도하기를 매우 좋아하는데, 왜냐하면 그것들의
새로움에 뉴스 가치가 있기 때문이다. 그러나 '사상 최초의' 발견들은 후속
연구에 의해 약화되는 것에 아주 취약하다. 그것이 일어날 때 뉴스 매체는
그들의 독자들이 그것에 관해 심지어 듣는다고 가정한 채, 종종 돌아가서
그들에게 그 변화에 관해 알리지 않는다. CBC News 기자인 Kelly Crowe는
한 전염병학자의 말을 인용하며 "현대 연구에서 잘못된 결과가 게재된 연구
주장의 다수 또는 심지어 대다수일 수도 있다는 증가하는 염려가 있다."라고
쓴다. 그녀는 언론인들이 이러한 경향에 있어 비난받을 만하지만, 자신들이
인용하는 과학자들의 연구들이 그들에 의해 방조되고 있음을 이어서 시사한다.
그녀는 무비판적으로 그것들의 미끼를 무는 명성 있는 학술지와 매체로부터
관심을 끌기 위한 시도에서 과학 초록의 '결론' 부분들이 때때로 과장될 수
있다고 쓴다. 그럼에도 불구하고, Crowe는 뉴스와 과학의 목적과 과정
사이에는 여전히 상반된 점이 있다는 것, 즉 과학은 '진화하지만' 뉴스는
'일어난다'는 것을 강조함으로써 자신의 글을 끝맺는다.

밑줄 친 news 'happens'가 다음 글에서 의미하는 바로 가장 적절한 것은?
[3점]

① News follows the process of research more than the outcome.
　뉴스는 연구의 결과보다 과정을 더 많이 따른다.　　연구가 갖는 '새로움'에 뉴스 가치가 있는 것임
② News focuses not on how research changes but on the novelty
of it. 뉴스는 연구가 어떻게 바뀌는지가 아니라 그것의 새로움에 집중한다.
　　　　　　　　　　최초 연구의 새로움에 집중하고 후속 연구는 보도하지 않음
③ News attracts attention by criticizing false scientific discoveries.
　뉴스는 틀린 과학적 발견을 비판함으로써 주의를 끈다.　어떤 연구가 틀렸음을 보도하지 않음
④ Reporters give instant feedback to their viewers, unlike scientists.
　기자들은 과학자들과 달리 그들의 시청자들에게 즉각적인 피드백을 준다. 독자들에게 알리지 않는다고 했음
⑤ Reporters create and strengthen trust in the importance of
science. 기자들은 과학의 중요성에 대한 믿음을 만들어내고 강화한다. 기자가 과학이 중요하다고 믿게
　　　　　　　　　　　　　　　　　　　　　　　　　한다는 것이 아님

뉴스는 어떤 것을 **최초**로 발견했다고 주장하는 연구를 보도하는 것을 매우
좋아하는데, 이는 그러한 새로움에 뉴스 가치가 있기 때문이라는 것이 첫 문장의
내용이다.　**최초 = 새로움**　꿀팁
이러한 최초(라고 주장하는) 연구는 후속 연구에 의해 약화되기 쉬운데, 실제로
후속 연구로 인해 해당 연구가 약화되더라도 뉴스 매체는 그러한 변화를 보도하지
않는다는 내용이 역접의 연결어로 시작한 두 번째 문장부터 이어진다.
다시 말해, 뉴스는 연구의 새로움에는 많은 가치를 두지만, 그 연구가 어떻게
바뀌는지에 대해서는 관심을 갖지 않는다는 것이므로 정답은 ② '뉴스는 연구가
어떻게 바뀌는지가 아니라 그것의 새로움에 집중한다.'이다.

왜 오답?

① 연구의 결과와 과정 사이에서 무엇에 더 집중하는지를 이야기하는 것이
아니다. **최초 연구는 보도하고 후속 연구는 보도하지 않는다는 것이 핵심이다.** 주의

③, ④ 최초 연구의 새로움을 통해 주의를 끌며, 이미 보도한 최초 연구가 후속
연구에 의해 달라지더라도 그것을 알리지 않는다고 했다.

⑤ 기자들이 대중으로 하여금 과학이 중요하다고 믿게 만든다는 내용이 아니다.

D 22 정답 ① * 인간의 발달상의 분업

Humans already have / a longer period of protected immaturity
/ — a longer childhood — / than any other species. //
인간은 이미 갖는다 / 더 긴 기간의 보호받는 미성숙 상태를 / 더 긴 어린 시절 / 다른 어떤
종보다 //

Across species, / a long childhood is correlated / with an
evolutionary strategy / that depends on flexibility, intelligence,
　　　선행사　　　　　　주격 관계대명사 *
and learning. //
종 전체에서 / 긴 어린 시절은 상호 관련이 있다 / 진화 전략과 / 유연성, 지능, 그리고 학습에
의존하는 //

There is a developmental division of labor. //
발달상의 분업이 있다 //

Children get to learn freely / about their particular environment
/ without worrying about their own survival / — caregivers look
after that. //
아이들은 자유롭게 배우게 된다 / 자신의 특정 환경에 대해 / 자신의 생존에 대해 걱정하지
않고 / 보호자가 그것을 책임진다 //　　단서 1 어른: 어렸을 때 배운 것을 사용하여
　　　　　　　　　　　　　　　　　　　　　　삶의 과업을 수행함
　　　　　　　　　　use의 목적어절
Adults use / what they learned as children / to mate, hunt, and
generally succeed / as grownups / in that environment. //
어른들은 사용한다 / 자신이 어렸을 때 배운 것을 / 짝을 맺고, 사냥하고, 일반적으로 잘
해내기 위해 / 어른으로서 / 그 환경에서 //

Children are the R&D (research and development) department
/ of the human species. //
아이들은 R&D(연구와 개발) 부서이다 / 인류의 //

We grown-ups / are production and marketing. //
우리 어른들은 / 생산과 마케팅이다 //
　　　　　　　　　　　　　　babies를 수식하는 형용사구
We start out / as brilliantly flexible but helpless and dependent
babies, / great at learning everything / but terrible at doing just
about anything. //
우리는 시작한다 / 놀랍도록 유연하지만 무력하고 의존적인 아기로 / 모든 것을 배우는 데는
훌륭하지만 / 거의 어떤 것이든 하는 데에는 엉망인 //

We end up / as much less flexible but much more efficient
and effective adults, / not so good at learning / but terrific at
　　　　　　　　adults를 수식하는 형용사구
planning and acting. //
우리는 결국 ~이 된다 / 훨씬 덜 유연하지만 훨씬 더 효율적이고 효과적인 어른이 / 학습에는
그다지 능숙하지 않지만 / 계획과 실행은 매우 잘하는 //　　단서 2 어른: 계획과 실행은 매우 잘함

- immaturity ⓝ 미성숙　　• species ⓝ 종
- be correlated with ~와 상호 관련이 있다　　• evolutionary ⓐ 진화의
- strategy ⓝ 전략　　• flexibility ⓝ 유연성　　• intelligence ⓝ 지능
- developmental ⓐ 발달의　　• division of labor 분업

- succeed ⓥ 성공하다　　· dependent ⓐ 의존적인
- efficient ⓐ 효율적인　　· effective ⓐ 효과적인　　· agent ⓝ 행위자
- executive ⓝ 경영진, 이사　　· characteristic ⓝ 성격

인간은 이미 다른 어떤 종보다 더 긴 기간의 보호받는 미성숙 상태, 즉 더 긴 어린 시절을 갖는다. 종 전체에서, 긴 어린 시절은 유연성, 지능, 그리고 학습에 의존하는 진화 전략과 상호 관련이 있다. 발달상의 분업이 있다. 보호자가 아이들의 생존을 책임지기 때문에, 아이들은 자신의 생존에 대해 걱정하지 않고 자신의 특정 환경에 대해 자유롭게 배우게 된다. 어른들은 그 환경에서 짝을 맺고, 사냥을 하고, 어른으로서 일반적으로 잘 해내기 위해 자신이 어렸을 때 배운 것을 사용한다. 아이들은 인류의 R&D(연구와 개발) 부서이다. 우리 어른들은 생산과 마케팅 부서이다. 우리는 모든 것을 배우는 데는 훌륭하지만 거의 어떤 것이든 하는 데에는 엉망인, 놀랍도록 유연하지만 무력하고 의존적인 아기로 시작한다. 우리는 결국 학습에는 그다지 능숙하지 않지만 계획과 실행은 매우 잘하는, 훨씬 덜 유연하지만 훨씬 더 효율적이고 효과적인 어른이 된다.

밑줄 친 production and marketing이 다음 글에서 의미하는 바로 가장 적절한 것은? [3점]

Adults use what they learned as children ~ in that environment.

① agents who conduct the tasks of living with what they learned
　그들이 배운 것을 가지고 삶의 과업을 수행하는 행위자들
② executives who assign roles according to one's characteristics
　개인의 성격에 따라 역할을 배분하는 경영진들　　성격에 따른 분업이 아님
③ actors who realize their dreams by building better relations
　더 나은 관계를 맺음으로써 그들의 꿈을 실현하는 배우들　　관계를 통해 꿈을 실현한다는 언급은 없음
④ traders who contribute to economic development
　경제적 발전에 기여하는 거래자들　　경제적 발전에 대한 내용이 아님
⑤ leaders who express their thoughts to others
　그들의 생각을 다른 사람들에게 표현하는 지도자들　　성인과 아이가 대조되는 글임

왜 정답? [정답률 76%]

아이	· 인류의 연구/개발 부서 · 모든 것을 배우는 데는 훌륭하지만, 어떤 것이든 하는 데에는 엉망임
어른	· 인류의 생산/마케팅 부서 · 어렸을 때 배운 것을 이용하여 어른으로서 잘 해냄 · 학습에는 그다지 능숙하지 않지만, 계획과 실행은 매우 잘함

➡ 어른은 '생산과 마케팅 (부서)' = 어른은 ① '그들이 배운 것을 가지고 삶의 과업을 수행하는 행위자들'

왜 오답?

② 인간의 발달 과정에 따른 분업이 있다는 것이지, 성격에 따라 역할이 나뉜다는 것이 아니다. 함정
③ 관계를 통해 꿈을 실현한다는 언급은 없다.
④ 연구/개발 부서, 생산/마케팅 부서 등이 언급된 것으로 만든 오답이다.
⑤ 자신의 생각을 다른 사람에게 표현하는 것에 대한 내용이 아니다.

─── 어법 특강 ───

＊ **관계대명사의 생략**

- 목적격 관계대명사는 생략하는 경우가 많다.

· She was a celebrated actress (whom) he had known and loved.
　　　a celebrated actress를 선행사로 하는 관계대명사
　(그녀는 그가 알고 사랑했던 유명한 배우였다.)

- 「주격 관계대명사＋be동사」는 생략할 수 있다.

· Look at the singer (who is) performing on the stage!
　　　the singer를 선행사로 하는 관계대명사
　(무대에서 공연하고 있는 가수를 봐!)

D 23 정답 ④ ＊트로이의 목마였던 기술의 발전 ───

It seemed like a fair deal: / we would accept new technologies,
앞 절을 선행사로 하는 계속적 용법의 주격 관계대명사
/ which would modify our habits / and oblige us to adjust / to certain changes, /
그것은 공정한 거래처럼 보였다 / 우리는 새로운 기술을 받아들일 것이고 / 그것은 우리의 습관을 바꾸고 어쩔 수 없이 우리가 적응하게 할 것이었다 / 특정한 변화에 /

but in exchange / we would be granted / relief from the burden of work, / more security, / and above all, / the freedom to pursue our desires. // 단서1 새로운 기술의 대가로 우리의 욕망을 추구할(여가를 즐길) 자유를 얻을 것이었음 형용사적 용법 (the freedom 수식)
하지만 그 대가로 / 우리는 얻을 것이었다 / 일의 부담의 경감을 / 더 많은 보안을 / 그리고 무엇보다도 / 우리의 욕망을 추구할 자유를 //

The sacrifice was worth the gain; / there would be no regrets. //
그 희생에는 그 이득의 가치가 있었다 / 후회는 없을 것이었다 //

Yet it has become apparent / that this civilization of leisure / was, in reality, a Trojan horse. //
가주어　　　　　　　진주어절 접속사
그러나 ~이 명백해졌다 / 여가로 인한 이러한 생활의 개선은 / 실제로는 트로이 목마였다는 것이 //

Its swelling flanks hid / the impositions of a new type of enslavement. // 그것의 불룩한 옆구리는 숨겼다 / 새로운 형태의 노예화라는 부담을 //

The automatons are not as autonomous / as advertised. //
그 자동 장치는 자율적이지 않다 / 광고되는 것만큼　원급 비교

They need us. // 그것들은 우리를 필요로 한다 //
복수 주어
Those computers / that were supposed to do our calculations / for us / instead demand our attention: / for ten hours a day, / we are glued to their screens. // 단서2 하지만 우리는 하루에 10시간 동안
복수 동사　　　〈기간〉의 전치사　　　컴퓨터(새로운 기술) 화면에 붙어 있음
그 컴퓨터들은 / 우리의 계산을 해 주기로 되어 있던 / 우리를 위해 / 대신 우리의 주의를 요구한다 / 하루에 10시간 동안 / 우리는 그것들의 화면에 붙어 있다 //

Our communications / monopolize our time. //
우리의 통신은 / 우리의 시간을 독점한다 //
　　　　강조 용법의 재귀대명사
Time itself is accelerating. // 시간 자체가 빨라지고 있다 //

The complexity of the system / overwhelms us. //
그 시스템의 복잡성은 / 우리를 어쩔 줄 모르게 만든다 //

And leisure is often a costly distraction. //
그리고 여가는 종종 비용이 많이 드는 오락이다 //

- modify ⓥ 수정[변경]하다　　· oblige ⓥ 강요하다, 의무 지우다
- adjust ⓥ 적응하다, 조정하다　　· in exchange 그 대신
- grant ⓥ 주다, 부여[수여]하다, 승인[허락]하다　　· relief ⓝ 경감, 완화, 안심
- burden ⓝ 부담, 짐　　· above all 무엇보다도, 특히
- pursue ⓥ 추구하다, 계속하다　　· sacrifice ⓝ 희생(물)
- worth ⓐ ~할 가치가 있는　　· apparent ⓐ 분명한, 누가 봐도 알 수 있는
- civilization ⓝ 문명, 문명화　　· swell ⓥ 붓다, 부풀다
- imposition ⓝ (새로운 법률·세금 등의) 시행[도입], 부담
- enslavement ⓝ 노예화, 노예 상태　　· autonomous ⓐ 자율[자주]적인
- glue ⓥ (접착제로) 붙이다　　· monopolize ⓥ 독점하다
- accelerate ⓥ 가속화되다[하다]
- overwhelm ⓥ 어쩔 줄 모르게 만들다, 압도하다
- costly ⓐ 많은 돈이 드는, 대가[희생]가 큰　　· incorporate ⓥ 포함하다
- hierarchical ⓐ 계급[계층]에 따른

그것은 공정한 거래처럼 보였다. 우리는 새로운 기술을 받아들일 것이었고, 그것은 우리의 습관을 바꾸고 어쩔 수 없이 우리가 특정한 변화에 적응하게 할 것이었지만, 그 대가로 우리는 일의 부담의 경감, 더 많은 보안, 그리고 무엇보다도 우리의 욕망을 추구할 자유를 얻을 것이었다. 그 희생에는 그 이득의 가치가 있었다. 후회는 없을 것이었다. 그러나 여가로 인한 이러한 생활의 개선은 실제로는 트로이 목마였다는 것이 명백해졌다. 그것의 불룩한 옆구리는 새로운 형태의 노예화라는 부담을 숨겼다. 그 자동 장치는 광고되는 것만큼 자율적이지 않다. 그것들은 우리를 필요로 한다. 우리를 위해 계산을 해 주기로 되어 있던 그 컴퓨터들은 대신 우리의 주의를 요구한다. 하루에 10시간 동안 우리는 그것들의 화면에 붙어 있다. 우리의 통신은 우리의 시간을 독점한다. 시간 자체가 빨라지고 있다. 그 시스템의 복잡성은 우리를 어쩔 줄 모르게 만든다. 그리고 여가는 종종 비용이 많이 드는 오락이다.

밑줄 친 this civilization of leisure was, in reality, a Trojan horse가 다음 글에서 의미하는 바로 가장 적절한 것은? [3점]

① Doing leisure activities increased communication between colleagues. Our communications로 만든 오답
여가 활동을 하는 것이 동료들 사이의 의사소통을 증가시켰다.
② Labor was easily incorporated with leisure by the media.
노동은 미디어에 의해 쉽게 여가와 통합되었다. 여전히 노동을 해야 한다는 내용임
③ People's privacy was attacked because of low security.
사람들의 사생활이 낮은 보안 때문에 공격당했다. more security로 만든 오답
④Technology's promise for leisure actually made people less free.
여가에 대한 기술의 약속은 사실 사람들을 덜 자유롭게 만들었다. 하루 10시간을 컴퓨터 화면에 붙어 있음
⑤ Technological innovations did not improve hierarchical working culture. 계층적 업무 문화에 대한 언급은 없음
기술적 혁신은 계층적인 업무 문화를 향상하지 않았다.

> **왜 정답?** [정답률 72%] '여가를 즐길 자유'를 의미함 꿀팁

역접의 연결어 Yet을 사이에 두고, 새로운 기술을 받아들이는 대가로 우리는 우리의 욕망을 추구할 자유를 얻을 것이었지만, 사실 여가로 인한 이러한 생활의 개선이 트로이의 목마였다는 상반되는 내용이 이어진다.

우리에게 여가를 주기로 되어 있던 새로운 기술인 자동 장치는 광고만큼 자율적이지는 않아서 우리를 필요로 하고, 컴퓨터 역시 우리를 위해 계산을 해 주기로 되어 있었지만, 우리는 하루에 10시간 동안 컴퓨터 모니터에 붙어 있어야 한다는 것으로 보아 밑줄 친 부분의 의미는 ④ '여가에 대한 기술의 약속은 사실 사람들을 덜 자유롭게 만들었다.'이다.

> **왜 오답?** 새로운 기술이 우리를 필요로 한다는 것을 의미함 꿀팁

① 글의 후반부에서 우리의 통신(Our communications)이 우리의 시간을 독점한다고 한 것으로 만든 오답이다.
② 새로운 기술 덕분에 여가를 즐길 수 있게 될 줄 알았는데 전혀 그렇지 않다는 내용이다.
③ 새로운 기술이 가져올 것으로 생각했던 이점의 하나로 more security가 언급된 것으로 만든 오답이다. 사생활이 공격당했다는 내용은 없다.
⑤ 기술적 혁신이 계층적인 업무 문화에 어떤 영향을 미쳤는지에 대한 내용이 아니다.

D 24 정답 ⑤ ＊고객의 임무 완수를 돕는 부가 서비스

주어
Many ancillary businesses / that today seem almost core / at one
동사
time / started out as journey edges. //
많은 보조 사업들이 / 오늘날 거의 핵심인 것처럼 보이는 / 한때는 / 여정의 가장자리로 시작
했다 // 단서1 조립이나 설치와 같은 추가적인 서비스가 판매에 동반됨
For example, / retailers often boost sales / with accompanying
support / such as assembly or installation services. //
예를 들어 / 소매업자들은 흔히 판매를 북돋운다 / 동반 지원을 통해 / 조립이나 설치 서비스
와 같은 //
Think of a home goods retailer / selling an unassembled outdoor
└─ 병렬 구조 ─┐
grill / as a box of parts / and leaving its customer's mission
incomplete. // leaving의 목적어와 목적격 보어
가정용품 소매업자를 생각해 보라 / 조립되지 않은 야외 그릴을 판매하고 / 부품 상자로 / 고객
의 임무를 미완성 상태로 내버려 두는 // 단서2 야외 그릴의 판매와 함께 조립과 배달 서비스도 제공함
When that retailer also sells assembly and delivery, / it takes
another step in the journey / to the customer's true mission / of
cooking in his backyard. //
그 소매업자가 조립과 배달도 판매할 때 / 그것은 여정에서 또 다른 한 걸음을 내딛는다 / 그 고
객의 진정한 임무를 향한 / 자신의 뒤뜰에서 요리하는 것인 // 단서3 소프트웨어 판매에 추가되는
                                                      서비스들이 층층이 쌓임
Another example / is the business-to-business service contracts
/ that are layered / on top of software sales. //
또 다른 예는 / 기업 대 기업 간 서비스 계약이다 / 층층이 쌓이는 / 소프트웨어 판매에 더하여 //
Maintenance, installation, training, delivery, / anything at all /
                   주격 관계대명사절의 동사
that turns do-it-yourself / into a do-it-for-me solution / originally
주절의 동사
resulted /
유지, 설치, 교육, 배달 / 무엇이든 / 손수 하는 것을 바꿔주는 / 대신 해주는 해결책으로 / 원
래 생겨났다 /
             전치사   명사절(간접의문문) ＊
from exploring the edge / of where core products intersect / with
customer journeys. //
가장자리를 탐구함으로써 / 핵심 제품이 교차하는 곳의 / 고객의 여정과 //

· core ⓐ 핵심적인, 가장 중요한   · retailer ⓝ 소매업자
· boost ⓥ 북돋우다   · accompanying ⓐ 동반하는
· assembly ⓝ (기계 부품의) 조립   · installation ⓝ 설치
· home goods 가정용품   · incomplete ⓐ 미완성의
· contract ⓝ 계약(서)   · layer ⓥ 층층이 쌓다
· on top of ~뿐 아니라, ~ 외에도   · explore ⓥ 탐구하다
· component ⓝ 구성 요소, 부품   · breakthrough ⓝ 획기적 발전, 돌파구
· primary ⓐ 주된, 주요한, 기본적인

오늘날 거의 핵심인 것처럼 보이는 많은 보조 사업들이 한때는 여정의 가장자리로 시작했다. 예를 들어 소매업자들은 흔히 조립이나 설치 서비스와 같은 동반 지원을 통해 판매를 북돋운다. 조립되지 않은 야외 그릴을 부품 상자로 판매하고 고객의 임무를 미완성 상태로 내버려 두는 가정용품 소매업자를 생각해 보라. 그 소매업자가 조립과 배달도 판매할 때 그것은 자기네 뒤뜰에서 요리하는 것인 그 고객의 진정한 임무를 향한 여정에서 또 다른 한 걸음을 내딛는 것이다. 또 다른 예는 소프트웨어 판매에 더하여 층층이 쌓이는 기업 대 기업 간 서비스 계약이다. 유지, 설치, 교육, 배달, 손수 하는 것을 대신 해주는 해결책으로 바꿔주는 것은 무엇이든 원래 핵심 제품이 고객의 여정과 교차하는 곳의 가장자리를 탐구함으로써 생겨났다.

밑줄 친 journey edges가 다음 글에서 의미하는 바로 가장 적절한 것은?
[3점]

① requiring customers to purchase unnecessary goods
고객에게 불필요한 상품을 구매하도록 요구하는 것   불필요한 상품을 구매하게 하는 것이 아님
② decreasing customers' dependence on business services
비즈니스 서비스에 대한 고객의 의존도를 줄이는 것   고객이 손수 하는 것을 대신 해주는 것을 의미함
③ focusing more on selling end products than components
부품보다 최종 제품 판매에 더 중점을 두는 것   제품 판매에 더해지는 추가 지원을 이야기함
④ adding a technological breakthrough to their core products
그들의 핵심 제품에 기술의 획기적 발전을 추가하는 것 기술의 획기적 발전으로 고객을 만족시키는 것이 아님
⑤ providing extra services beyond customers' primary purchase
고객의 기본적인 구매를 넘어 추가 서비스를 제공하는 것   야외 그릴만 판매하는 것이 아니라 조립과 배달
                                                    서비스도 제공함

| 문제 풀이 순서 | [정답률 60%]

1st 밑줄 친 부분이 포함된 문장을 읽고, 글에서 찾아야 하는 것이 무엇인지 파악한다.

오늘날 거의 핵심인 것처럼 보이는 많은 보조 사업들이 한때는 여정의 가장자리로 시작했다.

⇒ 오늘날에는 거의 핵심인 것처럼 보이는 보조 사업들이 어떻게 시작됐는지가 이후로 이어질 것이다. 이어지는 예시를 종합하여 '여정의 가장자리'가 의미하는 바를 파악한다.

2nd For example 이후로 이어지는 예시의 내용을 확인한다.

· 예를 들어, 소매업자들은 흔히 조립이나 설치 서비스와 같은 동반 지원을 통해 판매를 북돋운다. 단서1
· 또 다른 예는 소프트웨어 판매에 더하여 층층이 쌓이는 기업 대 기업 간 서비스 계약이다. 단서2

⇒ 야외 그릴을 판매하는 것, 소프트웨어를 판매하는 것: 핵심 사업
야외 그릴의 조립이나 설치 서비스, 소프트웨어 판매에 더해지는 서비스 계약: 보조 사업'

3rd 1st 와 2nd 에서 파악한 바를 종합하여 정답을 찾는다.

보조 사업은 제품의 판매에 덧붙여 추가적인 서비스를 제공하는 것으로부터 시작된 것이므로 정답은 ⑤ '고객의 기본적인 구매를 넘어 추가 서비스를 제공하는 것'이다.

| 선택지 분석 |

① requiring customers to purchase unnecessary goods
고객에게 불필요한 상품을 구매하도록 요구하는 것
야외 그릴을 구매하는 고객에게 야외 그릴 외에 불필요한 상품을 구매하도록 한다는 내용이 아니다.

② decreasing customers' dependence on business services
비즈니스 서비스에 대한 고객의 의존도를 줄이는 것
고객이 할 일을 대신해서 해주는 추가 서비스의 제공을 이야기하는 글이므로 서비스에 대한 고객의 의존도를 높인다고 할 수 있다.

③ **focusing more on selling end products than components**
부품보다 최종 제품 판매에 더 중점을 두는 것
단순히 제품만 판매하는 것이 아니라 그 제품을 구매하는 고객의 최종적이고 진정한
임무의 완수를 위해 필요한 추가 서비스까지 판매한다는 내용이다.

④ **adding a technological breakthrough to their core products**
그들의 핵심 제품들에 기술의 획기적 발전을 추가하는 것
기술을 획기적으로 발전시켜서 고객을 만족시키는 것이 아니라 판매하는 제품과
관련된 여러 추가 서비스를 제공하는 것에 대한 내용이다.

⑤ **providing extra services beyond customers' primary purchase**
고객의 기본적인 구매를 넘어 추가 서비스를 제공하는 것
야외 그릴로 뒤뜰에서 요리를 한다는 고객의 진정한 임무를 향한 여정의 핵심이 야외
그릴 판매, 그 여정의 가장자리가 야외 그릴의 조립, 설치 서비스를 제공하는 것이다.

─── 어법 특강 ───

✻ 전치사의 목적어

– 전치사 뒤에 오는 단어나 어구를 전치사의 목적어라고 하는데, 주로 명사(구)나
  동명사, 명사절이 쓰인다.

• He has insisted on his innocence from the beginning.
  (그는 처음부터 자신의 무죄를 주장해 왔다.)

• He kept on saying 'Where are the kids?' over and over again.
  (그는 계속해서 '아이들은 어디에 있어?'라고 말했다.)

• Judith was surprised at what the news said.
  (Judith는 뉴스가 전한 것에 놀랐다.)

D 25 정답 ① ⭐ 2등급 대비 [정답률 68%]

✻ 자신을 되돌아보는 수단으로서의 일기

the personal diary와 능동 관계이므로 현재분사가 분사구문을 이끎
Coming of age / in the 18th and 19th centuries, / the personal
diary became a centerpiece / in the construction of a modern
subjectivity, /
발달한 상태가 되어 / 18세기와 19세기에 / 개인 일기는 중심물이 되었는데 / 근대적 주체성을
구축하는 데 / 장소의 부사구가 문두에 오면서 [단서 1] 일기를 통해 자아에 대한
이어지는 주어와 동사가 도치됨   이해에 이성과 비판이 적용됨
at the heart of which is / the application of reason and critique
/ to the understanding of world and self, / which allowed / the
계속적 용법의 주격 관계대명사
creation of a new kind of knowledge. //
그것의 중심에 (~이) 있고 / 이성과 비판의 적용이 / 세계와 자아에 대한 이해에 / 이는
가능하게 했다 / 새로운 종류의 지식의 창조를 //
전치사+관계대명사
선행사
Diaries were central media / through which enlightened and
free subjects / could be constructed. //
일기는 중심 매체였다 / 그것을 통해 계몽되고 자유로운 주체가 / 구성될 수 있는 //
They provided a space / where one could write daily / about her
선행사   관계부사
whereabouts, feelings, and thoughts. // [단서 2] 자신에 관한 통찰력과 이야기가
                                              만들어지고 주체성이 형성됨
그것은 공간을 제공했다 / 개인이 매일 쓸 수 있는 / 자신의 행방, 감정, 생각에 대해 //
전치사구의 병렬 구조
Over time and with rereading, / disparate entries, events, and
happenstances / could be rendered / into insights and narratives
              병렬 구조
about the self, / and allowed / for the formation of subjectivity. //
시간이 지남에 따라 그리고 다시 읽음으로써 / 이질적인 항목, 사건 및 우연이 / 만들어질 수
있었으며 / 자신에 관한 통찰력과 이야기로 / 허용했다 / 주체성의 형성을 //
It is in that context / that the idea / of "the self [as] both made
It is ~ that으로 강조되는 전치사구   동격의 전치사구
and explored with words" / emerges. //
바로 그러한 맥락에서 / 개념이 / '말로 만들어지고 또한 탐구되는 (것으로의) 자아'라는 /
나타난다 //
                                        과거의 동작을 나타내는 조동사
Diaries were personal and private; / one would write for
oneself, / or, in Habermas's formulation, / one would make
oneself public to oneself. //
일기는 개인적이고 사적이었다 / 사람들은 자신을 위해 쓰곤 했다 / 즉 Habermas의 명확한
표현을 빌리면 / 사람들은 자신을 자신에게 공개적으로 만들곤 했다 //
By making the self public / in a private sphere, / the self also
became an object / for self-inspection and self-critique. //
자아를 공적으로 만듦으로써 / 사적 영역에서 / 자아는 또한 대상이 되었다 / 자기 점검과 자기
비판의 // [단서 3] 일기를 통해 자아가 자기 점검과 자기 비판의 대상이 됨

• centerpiece ⓝ 중심물, 주목할 존재   • construction ⓝ 건설, 구성
• subjectivity ⓝ 주관성   • application ⓝ 적용
• reason ⓝ 이성, 사리(事理)   • critique ⓝ 비평하는 글, 평론
• enlighten ⓥ (설명하여) 이해시키다[깨우치다]
• whereabout ⓝ 소재, 행방   • entry ⓝ (사전·장부 등의 개별) 항목
• happenstance ⓝ (특히 좋은 결과로 이어지는) 우연   • insight ⓝ 통찰력
• narrative ⓝ 이야기, 묘사   • formation ⓝ 형성
• explore ⓥ 탐험하다   • emerge ⓥ 드러나다, 알려지다
• formulation ⓝ 정확한 표현[어구], 공식화
• sphere ⓝ (활동·영향·관심) 영역   • self-inspection ⓝ 자체 검사
• self-critique ⓝ 자기 비판   • means ⓝ 수단, 방법
• reflect on ~을 반성하다[되돌아보다]   • process ⓝ 과정
• alternate ⓐ 대신인, 번갈아 나오는   • ego ⓝ 자아
• selfhood ⓝ 자아, 개성

18세기와 19세기에 발달한 상태가 된 개인 일기는 근대적 주체성을 구축하는
데 중심물이 되었는데, 그것의 중심에는 세계와 자아에 대한 이해에 이성과
비판의 적용이 있고, 이는 새로운 종류의 지식을 창조할 수 있게 해주었다.
일기는 그것을 통해 계몽되고 자유로운 주체가 구성될 수 있는 중심 매체였다.
그것은 개인이 자신의 행방, 감정, 생각에 대해 매일 쓸 수 있는 공간을
제공했다.
시간이 지남에 따라 그리고 다시 읽음으로써, 이질적인 항목, 사건 및
우연이 자신에 관한 통찰력과 이야기로 만들어질 수 있었으며, 주체성의
형성을 가능하게 만들었다. '말로 만들어지고 또한 탐구되는 (것으로의)
자아'라는 개념이 나타나는 것은 바로 그러한 맥락에서이다. 일기는 개인적이고
사적이었다. 사람들은 자신을 위해 쓰곤 했는데, Habermas의 명확한 표현을
빌리면, 자신을 자신에게 공개적으로 만들곤 했다. 자아를 사적 영역에서
공적으로 만들면서, 자아는 또한 자기 점검과 자기 비판의 대상이 되었다.

**밑줄 친 make oneself public to oneself가 다음 글에서 의미하는 바로 가장
적절한 것은? [3점]**

① use writing as a means of reflecting on oneself
  글을 자신을 되돌아보는 수단으로 사용하고 일기를 통해 자아를 자기 점검과 자기 비판의 대상으로 만듦
② build one's identity by reading others' diaries
  타인의 일기를 읽음으로써 자신의 정체성을 확립하고   자신의 일기, 주체성,
③ exchange feedback in the process of writing   자아에 대한 내용임
  글 쓰는 과정에서 의견을 교환하고
④ create an alternate ego to present to others
  다른 사람에게 제시하기 위한 대체 자아를 창조하고
⑤ develop topics for writing about selfhood
  자아에 관한 글을 쓰기 위한 주제를 개발하고   '일기'라는 글의 소재로 만든 오답

오왜 2등급? Habermas의 표현에 나오는 public이라는 단어의 의미가 흔히
쓰이는 '공공의, 대중의'라는 의미가 아니라는 것을 파악해야 한다. 글을 이해했더라도
밑줄 친 부분의 해석을 잘못하면 틀리기 쉬운 2등급 대비 문제이다.

| 문제 풀이 순서 |

1st 밑줄 친 부분이 포함된 문장을 읽고, 의미를 예상한다.

> **일기**는 개인적이고 사적이었다. 사람들은 자신을 위해 쓰곤 했는데,
> Habermas의 명확한 표현을 빌리면, 자신을 자신에게 공개적으로 만들곤 했다.

➡ 개인적이고 사적인 기록인 '일기'에 대해 이야기하는 글이다. 자신을 자신에게
공개적으로 만든다는 것은 일기를 통해 자신을 되돌아본다는 의미이리라고 생각할
수 있다.

2nd 글의 나머지 부분에서 일기의 역할을 파악하여 정답을 찾는다.

> • **그것**의 중심에는 세계와 자아에 대한 이해에 이성과 비판의 적용이
>   있다. [단서 1]
> • 시간이 지남에 따라 그리고 다시 읽음으로써, 이질적인 항목, 사건 및 우연이
>   자신에 관한 통찰력과 이야기로 만들어질 수 있었으며, 주체성의 형성을
>   가능하게 만들었다. [단서 2]

자아에 대한 이해에 이성과 비판을 적용하는 것이 일기의 중심에 있다. 또한, 일기를 통해 자신에 관한 통찰력과 이야기가 만들어지고, 주체성이 형성된다. 그렇다면 밑줄 친 부분은 ① '글(일기)을 자신을 되돌아보는 수단으로 사용하곤' 했다는 의미이다.

> 자아를 사적 영역에서 공적으로 만들면서, 자아는 또한 자기 점검과 자기 비판의 대상이 되었다. 단서3

➡ '사적 영역 = 일기', '공적으로 만듦으로써 = 자신을 자신에게 공개함으로써'
마지막 문장 역시 일기를 통해 자아가 자기 점검과 자기 비판의 대상이 된다는 의미이므로, 정답은 ①이다.

| 선택지 분석 |

① use writing as a means of reflecting on oneself
글을 자신을 되돌아보는 수단으로 사용하곤
'자기 점검', '자기 비판'이 의미하는 바가 '자신을 되돌아보는 것'이다.

② build one's identity by reading others' diaries
타인의 일기를 읽음으로써 자신의 정체성을 확립하곤
자신의 행방, 감정, 생각에 대해 쓰는 일기를 통해 사람들이 자신을 돌아보고 주체성을 형성하게 되었다는 내용으로, 타인의 일기와 같이 다른 사람이 등장하는 글이 아니다.

③ exchange feedback in the process of writing
글 쓰는 과정에서 의견을 교환하곤
타인과의 의견 교환과 같이 다른 사람과 관련된 내용은 아니다.

④ create an alternate ego to present to others
다른 사람에게 제시하기 위한 대체 자아를 창조하곤
다른 사람과 관련 있는 글이 아니므로 대체 자아에 대한 것은 맞지 않다.

⑤ develop topics for writing about selfhood
자아에 관한 글을 쓰기 위한 주제를 개발하곤
'일기'라는 글의 소재로 만든 오답이다. 일기가 자신에 대한 글인 것은 맞지만, 자아에 대한 글의 주제를 개발했다는 등의 내용은 없다.

권주원 | 서울대 정치외교학부 2023년 입학·서울 배재고 졸
밑줄 친 문장의 의미를 묻는 유형은 글 전체의 주제를 추론하는 것뿐만 아니라 밑줄 친 문장의 해석 또한 유의해야 돼. 우선 이 글의 주제는 '일기의 자아 성찰적 기능'이야. 이 주제는 마지막 문장 By making the self public in a private sphere, the self also became an object for self-inspection and self-critique.에서 명확하게 드러나.
이 글의 주제는 금방 도출했지만 밑줄 친 문장의 해석은 시간이 조금 걸렸어. public이 일반적으로 쓰이는 '공공의, 대중의'라는 의미가 아니라 '공개되는'이라는 의미로 사용됐기 때문에 바로 정답을 찾기에는 조금 어려웠어. 밑줄 친 문장의 해석 또한 항상 유의해야 하는 유형임을 명심해!

D 26 정답 ②　　　　　　　⭐ 2등급 대비 [정답률 65%]

＊지도자가 해야 하는 일

Flicking / the collaboration light switch / is something / that leaders are uniquely positioned to do, / because several obstacles stand / in the way of people / voluntarily working alone. //
획 누르는 것은 / 협업의 전등 스위치를 / ～한 것이다 / 고유하게 지도자들이 해야 하는 위치에 있는 / 여러 장애물이 서 있기 때문에 / 사람들의 길에 / 자발적으로 혼자 일하는 //

For one thing, / the fear / of being left out of the loop / can keep them glued / to their enterprise social media. //
우선 / 두려움은 / 상황을 잘 모르고 혼자 남겨진다는 / 그들이 계속 매달리도록 할 수 있다 / 자신들의 기업 소셜미디어에 //

단서1 개인은 고립되는 것을 원하지 않음
Individuals don't want / to be — or appear to be — isolated. //
개인들은 원치 않는다 / 고립되거나 고립된 듯 보이는 것을 //

For another, / knowing / what their teammates are doing / provides a sense of comfort and security, /
또 다른 이유로는 / 아는 것이 / 자신들의 팀 동료들이 무엇을 하고 있는지 / 편안하고 안전하다는 느낌을 제공한다 /

---

because people can adjust their own behavior / to be in harmony / with the group. //
사람들은 그들 자신의 행동을 조정할 수 있기 때문에 / 조화를 이루도록 / 집단과 //

It's risky to go off on their own / to try something new / that will probably not be successful / right from the start. //
홀로 벗어나는 것은 위험천만하다 / 뭔가 새로운 것을 시도하기 위해 / 아마도 성공적이지 않을 / 바로 처음부터 //

But / even though it feels reassuring / for individuals to be hyperconnected, / 단서2 사람들과 연결되는 것이 안도감을 줌
하지만 / ～이 안도감이 든다고 느낄지라도 / 사람들이 과잉 연결되는 것이 /

it's better / for the organization / if they periodically go off / and think for themselves / and generate / diverse — if not quite mature — ideas. // 단서3 조직을 위해서는 개인이 주기적으로 혼자 일하는 것이 더 좋음
～이 더 좋다 / 조직을 위해 / 그들이 주기적으로 벗어나 / 스스로 생각하여 / 창안하는 것이 / 그다지 성숙하지는 않더라도 다양한 아이디어를 //

단서4 지도자의 임무는 전체에게 유익한 여건을 조성하는 것임
Thus, / it becomes the leader's job / to create conditions / that are good for the whole / by enforcing intermittent interaction /
따라서 / ～이 지도자의 임무가 된다 / 여건을 조성하는 것이 / 전체에게 유익한 / 간간이 일어나는 상호 작용을 시행함으로써 /

even when people wouldn't choose it for themselves, / without making it seem / like a punishment. //
사람들이 그것을 스스로 선택하지 않는 때에도 / 그것을 보이게 하지 않으면서 / 처벌처럼 //

- flick ⓥ (버튼·스위치를) 획 누르다　· collaboration ⓝ 협력, 협업
- obstacle ⓝ 장애물　· voluntarily ⓐⅾ 자발적으로
- out of the loop (상황을) 잘 알지 못하는　· enterprise ⓝ 기업, 회사
- individual ⓝ 개인　· isolate ⓥ 고립시키다
- security ⓝ 안전, 보안　· adjust ⓥ 조정하다　· risky ⓐ 위험한
- right ⓐⅾ 곧바로, 정확히, 꼭　· reassure ⓥ 안심시키다
- hyperconnected ⓐ 과잉 연결된　· periodically ⓐⅾ 주기적으로
- generate ⓥ 만들어 내다, 발생시키다　· diverse ⓐ 다양한
- mature ⓐ 성숙한　· enforce ⓥ 시행[집행]하다
- interaction ⓝ 상호 작용　· punishment ⓝ 처벌
- physical ⓐ 물리적인　· barrier ⓝ 장벽, 장애물
- norm ⓝ 규범, 표준　· prohibit ⓥ 금지하다, 방해하다
- cooperation ⓝ 협력　· devote ⓥ 전념하다, 헌신하다
- productivity ⓝ 생산성

협업의 전등 스위치를 획 누르는 것은 고유하게 지도자들이 해야 하는 위치에 있는 것인데, 자발적으로 혼자 일하는 사람들에게 여러 장애물이 방해되기 때문이다. 우선, 상황을 잘 모르고 혼자 남겨진다는 두려움은 그들이 계속 자신들의 기업 소셜미디어에 매달리도록 할 수 있다. 개인들은 고립되거나 고립된 듯 보이는 것을 원치 않는다. 또 다른 이유로는, 자신들의 팀 동료들이 무엇을 하고 있는지 아는 것이 편안하고 안전하다는 느낌을 제공하는데, 사람들은 그들 자신의 행동을 집단과 조화를 이루도록 조정할 수 있기 때문이다. 아마도 바로 처음부터 성공적이지 않을 뭔가 새로운 것을 시도하기 위해 홀로 벗어나는 것은 위험천만하다. 하지만 사람들이 과잉 연결되는 것이 안도감이 든다고 느낄지라도, 그들이 주기적으로 (조직을) 벗어나 스스로 생각하여 그다지 성숙하지는 않더라도 다양한 아이디어를 창안하는 것이 조직을 위해 더 좋다. 따라서, 사람이 그것을 스스로 선택하지 않는 때에도, 그것을 처벌처럼 보이게 하지 않으면서 간간이 일어나는 상호 작용을 시행함으로써, 전체에게 유익한 여건을 조성하는 것이 지도자의 임무가 된다.

밑줄 친 Flicking the collaboration light switch가 다음 글에서 의미하는 바로 가장 적절한 것은? [3점]

① breaking physical barriers and group norms that prohibit cooperation 협력을 방해하는 물리적 장벽과 집단 규범을 타파하는 것
협력을 유도하는 것과 반대되어야 함

② having people stop working together and start working individually 사람들이 함께 일하는 것을 멈추고 개인적으로 일하기 시작하도록 하는 것
조직을 벗어나 스스로 생각하게 해야 함

③ encouraging people to devote more time to online collaboration
사람들이 온라인 협업에 더 많은 시간을 할애하도록 격려하는 것　협업이 아니라 혼자 일하는 것이 지도자의 임무임

④ shaping environments where higher productivity is required
더 높은 생산성이 요구되는 환경을 조성하는 것　더 높은 생산성을 요구하는 것이 아님

⑤ requiring workers to focus their attention on group projects
직원들이 집단 프로젝트에 관심을 집중하도록 요구하는 것　집단성이 아니라 개인성을 촉진하는 것이 핵심임

왜 2등급? '협업의 전등 스위치를 휙 누르는 것'이라는 비유적 표현이 의미하는 바를 잘 파악해야 한다. 지도자가 해야 하는 일에 대해 말하며 나온 표현이라는 것을 이해하지 못하면 풀기 힘든 2등급 대비 문제이다.

| 문제 풀이 순서 |

1st 밑줄 친 부분이 포함된 문장을 읽고, 의미를 예상한다.

> 협업의 전등 스위치를 휙 누르는 것은 고유하게 지도자들이 해야 하는 위치에 있는 것인데, 여러 장애물이 자발적으로 혼자 일하는 사람들을 방해하기 때문이다.

➡ 지도자가 해야 하는 일로 '협업의 전등 스위치를 누르는 것'을 든 글이다. '협업의 전등 스위치를 휙 누르는 것'이 협업을 시작하게 한다는 것인지, 협업을 그만하게 한다는 것인지를 파악해야 한다.

▶ 여러 장애물이 자발적으로 혼자 일하는 사람을 방해한다는 것으로 보아 지도자가 나서서 혼자 일하게 해야 한다는 의미라고 예상할 수 있다.

2nd 글의 나머지 부분에서 지도자의 역할을 파악하여 정답을 찾는다.

> • 개인은 고립되거나 고립된 듯 보이는 것을 원치 않는다. 단서1
> • 하지만 사람들이 과잉 연결되는 것이 안도감이 든다고 느낄지라도, 단서2 그들이 주기적으로 (조직을) 벗어나 스스로 생각하여 그다지 성숙하지는 않더라도 다양한 아이디어를 창안하는 것이 조직을 위해 더 좋다. 단서3

➡ 개인이 조직을 벗어나 혼자서 아이디어를 창안하는 것이 조직을 위해 더 좋은데, 개인이 고립되는 것을 원치 않고, 사람들과 연결되는 것에서 안도감을 느낀다. 따라서 지도자가 나서서 ② '사람들이 함께 일하는 것을 멈추고 개인적으로 일하기 시작하도록 해야' 한다.

| 선택지 분석 |

① **breaking physical barriers and group norms that prohibit cooperation**
협력을 방해하는 물리적 장벽과 집단 규범을 타파하는 것
이 글에 제시된 지도자의 임무는 직원들이 협력을 하도록 유도하는 것이 아니다.

② **having people stop working together and start working individually**
사람들이 함께 일하는 것을 멈추고 개인적으로 일하기 시작하도록 하는 것
지도자의 임무는 전체 조직에 유익한 여건을 조성하는 것이고, 개인이 혼자서 일하는 것이 조직에 더 유익하다.

③ **encouraging people to devote more time to online collaboration**
사람들이 온라인 협업에 더 많은 시간을 할애하도록 격려하는 것
이 글에 제시된 지도자의 임무는 직원들이 조직을 벗어나 스스로 생각하도록 하는 것이다.

④ **shaping environments where higher productivity is required**
더 높은 생산성이 요구되는 환경을 조성하는 것
직원들에게 더 높은 생산성을 요구하는 환경을 조성해야 한다는 언급은 없다.

⑤ **requiring workers to focus their attention on group projects**
직원들이 집단 프로젝트에 관심을 집중하도록 요구하는 것
직원들이 집단 프로젝트에 집중하도록 요구하는 것이 아니라 반대로 개인적인 프로젝트를 진행하도록 요구하는 것이 이 글에서 설명하는 지도자의 임무이다.

─ 어법 특강 ─

※ to부정사의 의미상 주어

– 대부분 문장에서 행위자를 알 수 있는 경우를 제외하고, 「for+명사/목적격 대명사」를 to부정사 앞에 표시해 준다. (예외적으로, 사람의 성격이나 태도와 같은 형용사가 보어로 올 때 「of+명사/목적격 대명사」로 표시한다.)

• Here are some tips for you to remember.
(여기 네가 기억할 몇 가지 팁이 있다.)

• It is important for everyone to take part equally in discussions.
(모든 사람이 공평하게 논의에 참여하는 것이 중요하다.)

• This is big enough for my dog to wear.
(이것은 우리 강아지가 입기에 충분히 크다.)

• It was stupid of you to make such a mistake.
(네가 그런 실수를 한 것은 어리석었다.)

D 27 정답 ② ─────── **★ 1등급 대비 [정답률 61%]**

＊전문가에 대한 우리의 신뢰

Scientists have no special purchase / on moral or ethical decisions; /
과학자들은 특별한 강점이 없다 / 도덕적 혹은 윤리적 결정에 대한 /

a climate scientist is no more qualified / to comment on health care reform / than a physicist is / to judge the causes / of bee colony collapse. //
기후 과학자가 자격이 없는 것은 / 의료개혁에 대한 견해를 밝힐 / 물리학자가 자격이 없는 것과 같다 / 원인을 판단할 / 꿀벌 집단의 붕괴의 // 단서1

The very features / that create expertise / in a specialized domain / lead to ignorance / in many others. //
바로 그 특징이 / 전문 지식을 만들어 내는 / 전문화된 영역에서의 / 무지로 이어진다 / 많은 다른 영역에서의 //

In some cases / lay people / — farmers, fishermen, patients, native peoples — / may have relevant experiences / that scientists can learn from. // 단서2
어떤 경우에는 / 전문가가 아닌 사람들이 / 농부, 어부, 환자, 토착민 / 관련 경험을 가지고 있을 수 있다 / 과학자들이 배울 수 있는 //

Indeed, in recent years, / scientists have begun to recognize this: / the Arctic Climate Impact Assessment includes observations / gathered from local native groups. //
실제로 최근 들어 / 과학자들은 이 점을 인식하기 시작했다 / 북극 기후 영향 평가는 관찰을 포함한다 / 지역 토착 집단에게서 수집된 // 단서3

So our trust needs / to be limited, and focused. //
그러므로 우리의 신뢰는 ~할 필요가 있다 / 한정되고 초점이 맞춰질 //

It needs to be very *particular*. //
그것은 매우 '특정할' 필요가 있다 //

Blind trust will get us / into at least as much trouble / as no trust at all. // 단서4
맹목적 신뢰는 우리를 봉착하게 할 것이다 / 최소한 많은 문제에 / 신뢰가 전혀 없는 것만큼 //

But without some degree of trust / in our designated experts / — the men and women / who have devoted their lives / to sorting out tough questions / about the natural world / we live in /
하지만 어느 정도의 신뢰가 없으면 / 우리의 지정된 전문가들에 대한 / 남녀들 / 그들의 생애를 바친 / 어려운 질문들을 처리하는 데 / 자연 세계에 관한 / 우리가 사는 /

— we are paralyzed, / in effect / not knowing / whether to make ready / for the morning commute / or not. //
우리는 마비되어 / 사실상 / 알지 못한다 / 준비할지를 / 아침 통근을 위해 / 아니면 (준비하지) 말지를 //

• purchase ⓝ 유리한 입장, 강점　• moral ⓐ 도덕적인
• ethical ⓐ 윤리적인　• climate ⓝ 기후　• qualify ⓥ 자격이 있다
• comment on ~을 판단하다　• reform ⓝ (사회・제도 등의) 개혁[개정]
• colony ⓝ (동일 지역에 서식하는 동・식물의) 군집　• collapse ⓝ 붕괴, 외해
• very ⓐ (다른 아닌) 바로 그[이]　• expertise ⓝ 전문 지식
• specialized ⓐ 전문적인, 전문화된　• domain ⓝ (지식・활동의) 영역[분야]
• ignorance ⓝ 무지, 무식　• relevant ⓐ 관련 있는
• observation ⓝ 관찰, 주시　• assessment ⓝ 평가
• gather ⓥ 모으다, 수집하다　• blind ⓐ 맹목적인, 비논리적인
• designate ⓥ (특정한 자리나 직책에) 지정하다
• devote ⓥ (노력・시간・돈 등을) 바치다[쏟다]
• sort out ~을 처리하다[해결하다]

과학자들은 도덕적 혹은 윤리적 결정에 대한 특별한 강점이 없으며, 기후 과학자가 의료개혁에 대한 견해를 밝힐 자격이 없는 것은 물리학자가 꿀벌 집단의 붕괴 원인을 판단할 자격이 없는 것과 같다. 전문화된 영역에서의 전문 지식을 만들어 내는 바로 그 특징이, 많은 다른 영역에서의 무지로 이어진다. 어떤 경우에는, 농부, 어부, 환자, 토착민처럼 전문가가 아닌 사람들이 과학자들이 그것으로부터 배울 수 있는 관련 경험을 가지고 있을 수 있다. 실제로, 최근 들어

과학자들은 이 점을 인식하기 시작했는데, 북극 기후 영향 평가는 지역 토착 집단에게서 수집된 관찰을 포함한다. 그러므로 우리의 신뢰는 한정되고 초점이 맞춰질 필요가 있다. 그것은 매우 '특정할' 필요가 있다. 맹목적 신뢰는 최소한 신뢰가 전혀 없는 것만큼이나 우리를 문제에 봉착하게 할 것이다. 하지만 우리의 지정된 전문가들, 즉 우리가 사는 자연 세계에 관한 어려운 질문들을 처리하는 데 생애를 바친 남녀들에 대한 어느 정도의 신뢰가 없으면 우리는 마비되고, 사실상 아침 통근을 위해 준비할지 말지를 알지 못한다.

밑줄 친 whether to make ready for the morning commute or not이 다음 글에서 의미하는 바로 가장 적절한 것은? [3점]

① questionable facts that have been popularized by non-experts
의심스러운 사실이나 편향된 지식을 신뢰해도 된다는 것은 어색함.
비전문가에 의해 보급된 의심스러운 사실
② readily applicable information offered by specialized experts
전문화된 전문가들에 의해 제공된 쉽게 적용할 수 있는 정보 ← 전문 분야의 전문 지식과 대조됨
③ common knowledge that hardly influences crucial decisions
중대한 결정에 거의 영향을 주지 않는 일반 지식 일상적인 결정에 영향을 주는 전문가의 지식을 믿으라는 의미
④ practical information produced by both specialists and lay people
전문가와 전문가가 아닌 사람들 모두에 의해 생산된 실용적인 지식 언급된 lay people로 만든 오답
⑤ biased knowledge that is widespread in the local community
지역 공동체에 널리 퍼져 있는 편향된 지식

왜 1등급 ? '아침 통근을 위해 준비할지 말지'가 신뢰해야 하는 전문가의 지식을 가리킨다는 의미를 글을 읽으면서 파악해야 한다. 기후 과학자나 물리학자를 언급하며 설명하는 내용을 제대로 이해하지 못하면 풀기 힘든 문제이다.

| 문제 풀이 순서 |

1st 첫 문장과 밑줄 친 부분이 포함된 문장을 읽고, 글의 내용을 예상한다.

첫 문장	과학자들은 도덕적 혹은 윤리적 결정에 대한 특별한 강점이 없으며, 기후 과학자가 의료 개혁에 대한 견해를 밝힐 자격이 없는 것은 물리학자가 꿀벌 집단의 붕괴 원인을 판단할 자격이 없는 것과 같다.
밑줄 친 부분이 포함된 문장	**하지만** 우리의 지정된 전문가들, 즉 우리가 사는 자연 세계에 관한 어려운 질문들을 처리하는 데 생애를 바친 남녀들에 대한 어느 정도의 신뢰가 없으면 우리는 마비되고, 사실상 아침 통근을 위해 준비할지 말지를 알지 못한다.

→ 첫 문장: 과학자는 자신의 전문 분야에 대해서만 전문 지식을 갖고 있음
밑줄 친 부분이 포함된 문장: 우리가 사는 자연 세계에 관한 어려운 질문들을 처리하는 데 생애를 바친 남녀들(= 전문가)을 어느 정도 신뢰해야 함
▶ '전문가를 신뢰할 때는 매우 주의해야 한다. 하지만 전문가를 어느 정도 신뢰하지 않으면 우리는 마비된다.'라는 내용임을 예상할 수 있다.

2nd 글의 나머지 부분을 읽고, 예상한 내용이 맞는지 확인한다.

- 전문화된 영역에서의 전문 지식을 만들어 내는 바로 그 특징이 많은 다른 영역에서의 무지로 이어진다. **단서1**
- 그러므로 우리의 신뢰는 한정되고 초점이 맞춰질 필요가 있다. 그것은 매우 '특정할' 필요가 있다. **단서3**
- **하지만** 지정된 전문가들에 대한 어느 정도의 신뢰가 없으면 우리는 마비된다. **단서4**

→ 전문가에 대한 신뢰는 매우 한정되고 특정해야 한다. 하지만 전문가를 어느 정도 신뢰하지 않으면 마비된다. ▶ **1st**에서 예상한 흐름이 맞음

3rd 파악한 글의 내용을 종합하여 밑줄 친 부분의 의미를 파악한다.

'아침 통근을 위해 준비할지 말지'는 우리가 마비되지 않기 위해 어느 정도 신뢰해야 하는 전문가의 지식을 가리킨다. 따라서 정답은 ② '전문화된 전문가들에 의해 제공된 쉽게 적용할 수 있는 정보'이다.

| 선택지 분석 |

① questionable facts that have been popularized by non-experts
비전문가에 의해 보급된 의심스러운 사실
밑줄 친 부분이 포함된 문장은 우리가 어느 정도는 전문가를 신뢰해야 한다는 내용인데, 의심스러운 사실을 믿어야 한다는 것은 어색하다.

---

② readily applicable information offered by specialized experts
전문화된 전문가들에 의해 제공된 쉽게 적용할 수 있는 정보
단서1 문장을 통해 전문화된 영역에서의 전문 지식은 신뢰할 만하다는 것을 알 수 있다. '전문화된 영역에서의 전문 지식'이 곧 '전문화된 전문가들에 의해 제공된 정보'이다.

③ common knowledge that hardly influences crucial decisions
중대한 결정에 거의 영향을 주지 않는 일반 지식
'아침 통근을 위한 준비를 할지 말지'와 같은 일상적인 결정에 쉽게 적용되는 전문가의 지식, 정보를 신뢰하라는 의미이다.

④ practical information produced by both specialists and lay people
전문가와 전문가가 아닌 사람들 모두에 의해 생산된 실용적인 지식
전문가의 전문 지식을 매우 특정적으로 신뢰해야 하는 이유로 등장한, 전문가가 비전문가로부터 배우기도 한다는 내용으로 만든 오답이다.

⑤ biased knowledge that is widespread in the local community
지역 공동체에 널리 퍼져 있는 편향된 지식
편향된 지식을 믿어야 한다는 것은 어색하다.

D 28 정답 ④ ━━━━━━━ ⭐ 1등급 대비 [정답률 58%]

* 인터넷의 등장으로 약화된 집중력

In 1890, William James described attention / as "the taking (동명사) possession by the mind, in clear and vivid form, / of one out of what seem several simultaneously possible objects or trains of thought." //
1890년에 William James는 주의력을 기술했다 / '분명하고 선명한 형태로 차지하는 것'이라고 / '정신으로, 동시에 가능한 여러 대상들 혹은 생각의 맥락들 같은 것 중 하나를' //

관계대명사가 생략된 관계절(a choice 수식)
Attention is a choice we make / to stay on one task, one line of thinking, one mental road, / even as attractive off-ramps signal. // 동사(신호를 보내다)
주의력은 우리가 하는 선택이다 / 하나의 일, 하나의 사고 방식, 하나의 정신의 길에 머무르기 위해 / 심지어 매력적인 빠져나가는 길이 신호를 보내도 //

When we fail to make that choice / and allow ourselves to be frequently sidetracked, / we end up in "the confused, dazed, scatterbrained state" / that James said is the opposite of attention. //
주격 관계대명사   삽입어구
우리가 그 선택을 하지 못하고 / 우리 자신을 자주 곁길로 새게 할 때 / 우리는 '혼란스럽고, 멍하고, 정신이 산만한 상태'에 결국 처하게 된다 / James가 주의력의 반대라고 말한 //

동명사 주어
Staying on one road got much harder / when the internet arrived and moved much of our reading online. // **단서1** 인터넷의 등장으로 집중하는 것이 훨씬 더 어려워짐
한 길에 머무르는 것은 훨씬 더 어려워졌다 / 인터넷이 등장하고 우리 독서의 대부분을 온라인으로 이동시키자 //

관계대명사가 생략된 관계절
Every hyperlink is an off-ramp, / calling us to abandon the choice we made moments earlier. //
모든 하이퍼링크는 빠져나가는 길이며 / 우리가 잠깐(의 순간) 전에 한 선택을 포기하라고 우리를 부른다 //

Nicholas Carr, in his 2010 book, / grieved his lost ability to stay on one path. //
Nicholas Carr는 그의 2010년 저서에서 / 한 길에 머무르는 그의 능력을 잃어버린 것을 슬퍼했다 //

Life on the internet changed how his brain sought out information, / even when he was off-line trying to read a book. //
인터넷에서의 생활은 그의 뇌가 어떻게 정보를 찾아내는지를 바꾸었다 / 그가 오프라인에서 책을 읽으려고 노력하고 있었을 때조차 //
(= Life on the internet)
It reduced his ability to focus and reflect / because he now craved a constant stream of stimulation: //
이것은 그의 집중하고 성찰하는 능력을 감소시켰는데 / 그는 이제 끊임없는 자극의 흐름을 갈망하게 되었기 때문이다 // **단서2** 인터넷에서의 생활은 집중하고 성찰하는 능력을 감소시켰는데, 끊임없는 자극의 흐름을 원했기 때문임

"Once I was a scuba diver in the sea of words. / Now I zip along the surface like a guy on a Jet Ski." //
"한때 나는 언어의 바다 속 스쿠버 다이버였다 / 이제는 제트 스키를 타는 사람처럼 수면 위를 쌩하고 지나간다" //

- describe ⓥ 기술하다　　• possession ⓝ 소유
- simultaneously ⓐⓓ 동시에　　• sidetrack 곁길로 새게 하다
- scatterbrained ⓐ 침착하지 못한　　• abandon ⓥ 버리다, 포기하다
- constant ⓐ 끊임없는　　• stimulation ⓝ 자극
- convenience ⓝ 편의　　• restrain ⓥ 저지하다
- analyze ⓥ 분석하다　　• comprehend ⓥ 이해하다
- thoroughly ⓐⓓ 철저하게

1890년에 William James는 주의력을 '정신으로, 동시에 가능한 여러 대상들 혹은 생각의 맥락들 같은 것 중 하나를 분명하고 선명한 형태로 차지하는 것'이라고 기술했다. 주의력은 심지어 매력적인 빠져나가는 길이 신호를 보내도, 하나의 일, 하나의 사고 방식, 하나의 정신의 길에 머무르기 위해 우리가 하는 선택이다. 우리가 그 선택을 하지 못하고 우리 자신을 자주 곁길로 새게 할 때, 우리는 James가 주의력의 반대라고 말한 '혼란스럽고, 멍하고, 정신이 산만한 상태'에 결국 처하게 된다. 인터넷이 등장하고 우리 독서의 대부분을 온라인으로 이동시키자, 한 길에 머무르는 것은 훨씬 더 어려워졌다. 모든 하이퍼링크는 빠져나가는 길이며, 우리가 잠깐(의 순간) 전에 한 선택을 포기하라고 우리를 부른다. Nicholas Carr는 그의 2010년 저서에서 한 길에 머무르는 그의 능력을 잃어버린 것을 슬퍼했다. 인터넷에서의 생활은 그가 오프라인에서 책을 읽으려고 노력하고 있었을 때조차 그의 뇌가 어떻게 정보를 찾아내는 지를 바꾸었다. 이것은 그의 집중하고 성찰하는 능력을 감소시켰는데, 그는 이제 끊임없는 자극의 흐름을 갈망하게 되었기 때문이다. "한때 나는 언어의 바다 속 스쿠버 다이버였다. 이제는 제트 스키를 타는 사람처럼 수면 위를 쌩하고 지나간다."

밑줄 친 Now I zip along the surface like a guy on a Jet Ski가 다음 글에서 의미하는 바로 가장 적절한 것은? [3점]

① Ironically, the convenience of downloading digital creations restrains people's creativity. 사람의 창의력을 저해한다는 내용은 나오지 않음
　아이러니하게도, 디지털 창작물을 다운로드하는 편리함이 사람들의 창의력을 제한한다.
② By uncritically accepting information, we get trapped in a cycle of misunderstanding. 정보를 무비판적으로 받아들이게 된다는 내용이 초점이 아님
　비판적으로 정보를 수용하지 않으면, 우리는 오해의 악순환에 갇히게 된다.
③ People's attention is naturally drawn to carefully analyzed and well-presented data. 사람들이 잘 분석되고 제시된 데이터에 끌린다는 내용은 없음
　사람들은 신중하게 분석되고 잘 제시된 데이터에 자연스럽게 주목한다.
④ We now deal with the information in a skin-deep manner, constantly being distracted.
　우리는 이제 정보를 피상적으로 다루며, 끊임없이 주의가 분산되고 있다.
⑤ With the help of the internet, we comprehend the information quickly and thoroughly. 인터넷의 도움으로 정보를 철저하게 이해한다는 언급은 없음
　인터넷의 도움으로 우리는 정보를 빠르고 철저하게 이해한다.
　인터넷의 등장으로 과거와는 다르게 깊이 있는 성찰과 집중을 하지 못하고, 표면적인 정보만 끊임없이 찾게 됨

왜 1등급? '언어의 바다 속 스쿠버 다이버'나 '제트 스키를 타는 사람과 같이 비유적인 표현의 의미를 글을 읽으면서 잘 파악하지 못하면 풀기 힘든 1등급 대비 문제이다.

| 문제 풀이 순서 |

1st 밑줄 친 부분이 포함된 문장을 읽고, 글에서 찾아야 하는 것이 무엇인지 파악한다.
　"한때 나는 언어의 바다 속 스쿠버 다이버였다. 이제는 제트 스키를 타는 사람처럼 수면 위를 쌩하고 지나간다."

→ 예전에는 언어의 바다 속 스쿠버 다이버였지만, 이제는 제트 스키를 타는 사람처럼 수면 위를 쌩하고 지나간다고 했으므로, 과거와 다르게 어떻게 바뀌었는지를 파악해야 한다.

2nd 글의 나머지 부분을 읽고 정답의 근거들을 찾는다.
- 집중력은 곁길로 새지 않고 한 가지 일 / 사고방식 / 정신의 길에 머무를 수 있게 하는 것임
- 인터넷의 등장으로 이런 집중력은 많이 약해졌으며, 끊임없는 자극의 흐름을 찾게 됨 **단서1** **단서2**

→ 한 때 '언어의 바다 속 스쿠버다이버'였다는 말의 뜻은, 과거에는 깊이 있는 탐색과 사고를 할 수 있는 집중력이 있었다는 뜻이고, 지금 '제트스키를 타는 사람처럼 수면 위를 지나간다'라는 의미는 깊이는 없고 피상적인 정보만을 찾게 된다는 뜻이다.

3rd **1st** 와 **2nd** 에서 파악한 바를 종합하여 정답을 찾는다.

→ 과거에는 집중력이 있었지만 지금은 그런 집중력이 많이 약해졌고 피상적인 정보를 찾게 된다는 내용의 글이다. 따라서 정답은 ④ '우리는 이제 정보를 피상적으로 다루며, 끊임없이 주의가 분산되고 있다.'이다.

D

| 선택지 분석 |

① Ironically, the convenience of downloading digital creations restrains people's creativity.
아이러니하게도, 디지털 창작물을 다운로드하는 편리함이 사람들의 창의력을 제한한다.
글에 디지털 창작물을 다운로드 받는다는 말도, 창의력이 제한된다는 말도 없다.
② By uncritically accepting information, we get trapped in a cycle of misunderstanding.
비판적으로 정보를 수용하지 않으면, 우리는 오해의 악순환에 갇히게 된다.
집중에 대한 글이지, 오해의 악순환에 대한 언급은 없다.
③ People's attention is naturally drawn to carefully analyzed and well-presented data.
사람들은 신중하게 분석되고 잘 제시된 데이터에 자연스럽게 주목한다.
집중이 핵심 키워드이긴 하지만, 사람들이 잘 분석되고 소개된 데이터에 끌린다는 말은 없다.
④ We now deal with the information in a skin-deep manner, constantly being distracted.
우리는 이제 정보를 피상적으로 다루며, 끊임없이 주의가 분산되고 있다.
인터넷의 등장으로 과거와는 다르게 깊이 있는 성찰과 집중을 하지 못하고, 표면적인 정보만 끊임없이 찾게 된다는 내용의 글이다.
⑤ With the help of the internet, we comprehend the information quickly and thoroughly.
인터넷의 도움으로 우리는 정보를 빠르고 철저하게 이해한다.
인터넷의 등장이 악영향을 초래했다는 말이 핵심이지, 정보를 빠르고 철저하게 이해하도록 도움을 준다는 말은 아니다.

핵심 사업과 보조 사업을 잘 구분해야 밑줄 친 의미를 알 수 있어!

D 어휘 Review 정답　　　　　문제편 p. 71

01 평판	11 split up	21 immediate
02 수축하다	12 be correlated with	22 transformed
03 의무	13 compared to	23 immaturity
04 효율적인	14 in exchange	24 discipline
05 전략	15 a string of	25 reassuring
06 reality	16 stuck	26 temptation
07 complicated	17 pure	27 alternative
08 particle	18 convergence	28 theoretical
09 tricky	19 unemployed	29 violated
10 conclude	20 nonlinear	30 intelligible

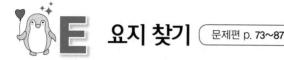
E 01　정답 ④　＊인간 의사소통의 평등성이 형성한 공유와 공조 가치

─ both A and B : A와 B 둘 다 ─
In both the ancient hunter-gatherer band / and our intimate speech communities today, / the diffusion of speech shaped values. //　단서1 언어의 확산은 어떠한 가치를 형성함
고대의 수렵·채집인 무리와 / 오늘날 우리의 친밀한 언어 공동체 둘 다에서 / 언어의 확산은 가치를 형성했다 //

　　주어　　동격의 접속사
The fact / that everyone was going to be able to speak and listen / had to be accommodated ethically, / and it was via a rough egalitarianism. //
그 사실 / 모든 사람이 말하고 들을 수 있을 것은 / 윤리적으로 수용되어야 했는데 / 그것은 개략적인 인류 평등주의를 통해서였다 //

In terms of communications, / people were equal and therefore /　단서2 의사소통 측면에서 인간은 평등함
가주어　　　that 생략
it was believed / they *should be* equal, / or at least relatively so. //
의사소통의 측면에서 / 사람들은 평등했고 그리고 그러므로 / 여겨졌다 / 그들은 평등'해야' 하거나, 적어도 비교적 그렇다(평등하다)고 //

By this code, / ancient Big Men were not allowed to act controllingly / and modern office managers / are not allowed to silence anyone at will. //
이러한 관례에 따라 / 고대의 '거물'은 통제적으로 행동하도록 허용되지 않았고 / 현대의 사무실 관리자는 / 마음대로 누구도 침묵시키도록 허용되지 않는다 //

Moreover, equal access to speech and hearing / promoted the notion /
게다가, 말하기와 듣기에 대한 평등한 접근은 / 생각을 촉진했다 /
동격의 접속사 ①　　　　　　　　　　　동격의 접속사 ②
that property should be held in common, / that goods and food
동격의 접속사 ③
in particular should be shared, / and that everyone had a duty / to take care of everyone else. //　단서3 의사소통의 평등은 공유, 상호협력의 가치를 촉진함
재산은 공동으로 소유되어야 하고 / 특히 물자와 식량은 공유되어야 하며 / 모든 사람은 의무가 있다는 / 다른 사람을 돌볼 //

　　　　　　　　　　　　비교급 more than
This was probably more true / among hunter-gatherers / than
= it is (true)
it is in the modern family, circle of friends, or workplace. //
이것은 아마도 더 사실이었을 것이다 / 수렵·채집인 사이에서 / 현대의 가족, 친구 사이, 또는 직장에서보다 //

　　　　　　　　　　　　　목적어절 접속사　　 주어
But even in these cases / we believe / that sharing and mutual
　　　　동사
aid are right and proper. //
하지만 이 경우에도 / 우리는 믿는다 / 공유와 상호 협력이 옳고 적절하다고 //

Remember, / if you bring something, / you should bring enough for everyone. //
기억하라 / 여러분이 무언가를 가져온다면 / 모두를 위해 충분히 가져와야 한다는 것을 //

- intimate ⓐ 친밀한　• speech community 언어 공동체
- accommodate ⓥ 수용하다　• ethically ⓐⓓ 윤리적으로
- code ⓝ 관례　• at will 마음대로　• promote ⓥ 촉진하다, 장려하다
- property ⓝ 재산, 소유물　• hunter-gatherer 수렵·채집인
- circle ⓝ (관심·직업 등으로 연결된 사람들의) …계[사회]
- mutual aid 상호 협력

고대의 수렵·채집인 무리와 오늘날 우리의 친밀한 언어 공동체 둘 다에서, 언어의 확산은 가치를 형성했다. 모든 사람이 말하고 들을 수 있을 것이라는 사실은 윤리적으로 수용되어야 했는데, 그것은 개략적인 인류 평등주의를 통해서였다. 의사소통의 측면에서 사람들은 평등했으므로, 그들은 평등'해야' 하거나 적어도 비교적 그렇다고 여겨졌다. 이러한 관례에 따라, 고대의 '거물'은 통제적으로 행동하도록 허용되지 않았고, 현대의 사무실 관리자는 마음대로 누구도 침묵시키도록 허용되지 않는다. 게다가, 말하기와 듣기에 대한 평등한 접근은 재산은 공동으로 소유되어야 하고, 특히 물자와 식량은 공유되어야 하며, 모든 사람은 다른 사람을 돌볼 의무가 있다는 생각을 촉진했다. 이것은

아마도 현대의 가족, 친구 사이, 또는 직장에서보다 수렵·채집인 사이에서 더 사실이었을 것이다. 하지만 이 경우에도, 우리는 공유와 상호 협력이 옳고 적절하다고 믿는다. 여러분이 무언가를 가져온다면, 모두를 위해 충분히 가져와야 한다는 것을 기억하라.

다음 글의 요지로 가장 적절한 것은?

① 수렵인과 현대인은 언어에 대한 유사한 가치를 가지고 있다.
　공유와 상호 협력에 대한 의무감은 수렵인에게서 더 높음
② 인간은 언어를 사용하여 자원을 보다 효율적으로 배분해 왔다.
　효율적인 자원의 배분은 언급되지 않음
③ 현대 사회는 고대 수렵 사회보다 평등한 체계에 의해 운영된다.
　각 사회의 체계가 얼마나 평등한지에 대한 내용은 없음
④ 인간 의사소통의 평등성은 공유와 공조 가치 기반을 형성했다.
　Moreover, equal access to speech and hearing promoted ~ to take care of everyone else.
⑤ 인간은 의사소통을 통해 자원을 공유하는 평등한 사회를 건설했다.
　의사소통을 통해 평등한 사회를 건설했다는 것은 논리의 비약임

왜 정답? [정답률 57%]

도입	언어의 확산은 가치를 형성함 단서1
의사소통의 특징이 가져온 가치	• 의사소통의 측면에서 사람들은 평등했으므로, 그들은 평등'해야' 하거나 적어도 비교적 그렇다고 여겨짐 단서2 • 말하기와 듣기에 대한 평등한 접근은, 재산은 공동으로 소유되어야 하고, 특히 물자와 식량은 공유되어야 하며, 모든 사람은 다른 사람을 돌볼 의무가 있다는 생각을 촉진함 단서3

→ 인간은 의사소통 측면에서 평등하므로 인간은 평등하며, 이 생각이 공유와 공조 가치를 촉진했다는 내용이다.
▶ 따라서 정답은 ④이다.

왜 오답?

① 공유와 상호 협력에 대한 의무감은 수렵인에게서 더 높다.
② 효율적인 자원의 분배는 언급되지 않았다.
③ 각 사회의 체계가 얼마나 평등한지는 언급되지 않은 내용이다.
⑤ 의사소통 평등성이 공유와 상호 협력의 가치를 촉진했다는 내용이지, 의사소통을 통해 평등한 사회를 건설했다는 것은 논리의 비약이다. 주의

E 02　정답 ⑤　＊가상 세계에서는 덜 방어적인 우리

When it comes to the Internet, / it just pays to be a little paranoid / (but not a lot). //
인터넷에 관한 한 / 약간 편집적이게 되는 것이 이득이 될 따름이다 / (많이는 아니고) //

Given the level of anonymity / with all that resides on the
　　　　　　가주어
Internet, / it's sensible / to question the validity of any data /
목적격 관계대명사　　　진주어
that you may receive. //　단서1 인터넷의 자료에 대해 타당성을 의심하는 것이 합리적임
익명성 수준을 고려할 때 / 인터넷에 있는 모든 것의 / ~이 합리적이다 / 어떤 자료든 그것의 타당성에 대해 의문을 제기하는 것이 / 여러분이 받을지도 모르는 //

Typically it's to our natural instinct / when we meet someone /
가주어
coming down a sidewalk / to place yourself / in some manner of
진주어
protective position, /
일반적으로 ~은 우리의 자연스러운 본능이다 / 우리가 누군가를 만날 때 / 인도를 따라 내려오는 / 여러분 스스로를 위치시키는 것은 / 어떤 방식의 방어적인 자세로 /

especially when they introduce themselves / as having known you, / much to your surprise. //
특히 그들이 자신을 소개할 때 / 여러분을 알고 있었다고 / 너무 놀랍게도 //

By design, we set up challenges / in which the individual must
　　　　　　　　　　　　　　　　관계부사 where로 바꿀 수 있음
validate / how they know us /
일부러 우리는 과제를 설정한다 / 그 사람이 입증해야만 하는 / 그들이 우리를 어떻게 아는지를 /

by presenting scenarios, names or acquaintances, or evidence / by which to validate / (that is, photographs). //
시나리오나, 이름이나 지인, 혹은 증거를 제시함으로써 / 그것으로 입증할 / (말하자면, 사진) //

Once we have received that information / and it has gone
부사절 접속사(조건)
through a cognitive validation, / we accept that person / as more
trustworthy. //
일단 우리가 그 정보를 받고 / 그것이 인지적 검증을 통과하면 / 우리는 그 사람을 받아들인다
/ 더 신뢰할 수 있다고 //

All this happens / in a matter of minutes / but is a natural defense
────────병렬 구조────────
mechanism / that we perform / in the real world. //
이 모든 것이 일어나지만 / 몇 분 안에 / 자연스러운 방어 기제이다 / 우리가 수행하는 / 현실
세계에서 //
단서2 우리는 가상 세계에서는
덜 방어적인 경향이 있음   형용사적 용법(a tendency 수식)
However, in the virtual world, / we have a tendency / to be less
defensive, / as there appears to be no physical threat / to our
well-being. //
부사절 접속사(이유)
하지만 가상 세계에서는 / 우리는 경향이 있다 / 덜 방어적인 / 물리적인 위협이 없는 것처럼
보이기 때문에 / 우리의 행복에 //

- reside ⓥ 살다, 거주하다   · sensible ⓐ 분별있는, 합리적인
- validity ⓝ 유효함, 타당성   · instinct ⓝ 본능
- protective ⓐ 방어적인   · challenge ⓝ 도전, 과제
- validate ⓥ 입증하다, 인증하다   · present ⓥ 제시하다
- acquaintance ⓝ 지인   · evidence ⓝ 증거
- cognitive ⓐ 인식의, 인지의   · trustworthy ⓐ 신뢰할 수 있는
- mechanism ⓝ 기제, 방법   · perform ⓥ 수행하다
- virtual ⓐ 가상의   · tendency ⓝ 경향, 성향

인터넷에 관한 한, (많이는 아니고) 약간 편집적이게 되는 것이 이득이 될
따름이다. 인터넷에 있는 모든 것의 익명성 수준을 고려할 때, 여러분이
받을지도 모르는 어떤 자료든 그것의 타당성에 대해 의문을 제기하는 것이
합리적이다. 일반적으로 우리가 인도를 따라 내려오는 누군가를 만날 때,
특히 너무 놀랍게도 그들이 여러분을 알고 있었다고 자신을 소개할 때,
여러분이 스스로 어떤 방식의 방어적인 자세를 취하는 것은 우리의 자연스러운
본능이다. 일부러 우리는 시나리오나, 이름이나 지인, 혹은 그것으로 입증할
증거 (말하자면, 사진)를 제시함으로써 그 사람이 우리를 어떻게 아는지를
입증해야만 하는 과제를 설정한다. 일단 우리가 그 정보를 받고 그것이 인지적
검증을 통과하면, 우리는 그 사람을 더 신뢰할 수 있다고 받아들인다. 이 모든
것이 몇 분 안에 일어나지만, 우리가 현실 세계에서 수행하는 자연스러운 방어
기제이다. 하지만, 가상 세계에서는 우리의 행복에 물리적인 위협이 없는
것처럼 보이기 때문에 우리는 덜 방어적인 경향이 있다.

다음 글의 요지로 가장 적절한 것은?
① 가상 세계 특유의 익명성 때문에 표현의 자유가 남용되기도 한다.
　인터넷상의 표현의 자유에 대한 언급은 없음
② 인터넷 정보의 신뢰도를 검증하는 기술은 점진적으로 향상되고 있다.
　신뢰도 검증 기술이 소재가 아님
③ 가상 세계에서는 현실 세계와 달리 자유로운 정보 공유가 가능하다.
　정보 공유의 자유로움에 대한 내용이 아님
④ 안전한 인터넷 환경 구축을 위해 보안 프로그램을 설치하는 것이 좋다.
　보안 프로그램 설치를 권하는 것이 아님
⑤ 방어 기제가 덜 작동하는 가상 세계에서는 신중한 정보 검증이 중요하다.
　어느 자료든 타당성에 의문을 제기하는 것이 합리적임

▷왜 정답? [정답률 85%]

첫 두 문장: 인터넷에서는 약간 편집적인 것이 이득이다. **단서1**
　　　　　　　인터넷상의 모든 자료에 있어 그 타당성을 의심하는 것
마지막 문장: 우리는 가상 세계에서는 덜 방어적인 경향이 있다. **단서2**

→ '우리는 가상 세계에서는 덜 방어적이다.' + '인터넷상의 모든 자료는 그 타당성에
의문을 제기하는 것이 합리적이다.' = 글의 요지: ⑤

▷왜 오답?

① 인터넷의 익명성 때문에 인터넷상의 모든 자료를 신중하게 검토해야 한다는
   것이다.
② 인터넷상의 정보를 검증하는 기술에 대해 설명하는 글이 아니다.
③ 가상 세계에서는, 현실 세계와 달리, 우리가 덜 방어적이라는 내용이다.
④ 보안 프로그램 설치의 필요성에 대해서는 언급되지 않았다.

E 03 정답 ② * 집단에서 협력하는 사람들의 특성

단서1 감정을 이해하는 능력은 집단 환경에서 중요함
The ability to understand emotions / — to have a diverse emotion
　　　　　　　　형용사적 용법(ability 수식)   앞의 to understand와 동격
vocabulary and to understand the causes and consequences of
emotion — / is particularly relevant in group settings. //
감정을 이해하는 능력 / 즉 다양한 감정 어휘를 가지고 있고 감정의 원인과 결과를 이해하는
능력은 / 특히 집단 환경에서 중요하다 //

Individuals who are skilled in this domain / are able to
　　　　　　　주격 관계대명사
express emotions, feelings and moods accurately / and thus,
　　　　　　　　　　　　　　　　　　　　　　　　　병렬 구조
may facilitate clear communication between co-workers. //
이 분야에 능숙한 사람들은 / 감정, 느낌, 그리고 기분을 정확하게 표현할 수 있으므로 /
동료들 간의 명확한 의사소통을 촉진할 수 있다 // **단서2** 이들은 동료들 간의 명확한
　　　　　　　　　　　　　　　　　　　　　　　　　　　　　　　　의사소통을 촉진함
Furthermore, / they may be more likely to act / in ways that
　　　　　　　　　　　　　　　 be likely to-v: ~할 가능성이 높다   주격 관계대명사
accommodate their own needs / as well as the needs of others /
(i.e. cooperate). //   **단서3** 이들은 타인의 필요도 수용하는 방식으로 행동함
더욱이 / 그들은 행동할 가능성이 더 높을 수도 있다 / 자신의 필요뿐만 아니라 / 타인의
필요도 수용하는 방식으로 / (즉, 협력) //

In a group conflict situation, for example, / a member with a
　　　　　　　　　　　형용사적 용법(ability 수식)
strong ability to understand emotion / will be able to express /
　　　　　　　　　　　　　　의문사절의 병렬 구조
how he feels about the problem / and why he feels this way. //
예를 들어, 집단 갈등 상황에서 / 감정을 이해하는 강력한 능력을 지닌 구성원은 / 표현할 수
있을 것이다 / 문제에 대해 자신이 어떻게 느끼는지 / 그리고 왜 그렇게 느끼는지를 //

He also should be able to take the perspective / of the other
　　　　　　　　　　　　　　　병렬 구조　　　　　　　의문사절
group members / and understand / why they are reacting in a
certain manner. //
또한 그는 관점을 취하여 / 다른 집단 구성원들의 / 이해할 수 있을 것이다 / 그들이 왜 특정한
방식으로 반응하는지 //

Appreciation of differences / creates an arena for open
　　　　　　　　　　　　　　　　　　병렬 구조
communication / and promotes constructive conflict resolution
and improved group functioning. //　　━━병렬 구조━━
다름에 대한 이해는 / 열린 의사소통을 위한 장을 만들고 / 건설적인 갈등 해결과 향상된 집단
기능을 촉진한다 //

- consequence ⓝ 결과   · relevant ⓐ 중요한, 의미 있는
- mood ⓝ 기분   · facilitate ⓥ 촉진하다
- accomodate ⓥ 수용하다   · perspective ⓝ 관점
- appreciation ⓝ 이해   · arena ⓝ 장, 터
- promote ⓥ 촉진하다   · constructive ⓐ 건설적인

감정을 이해하는 능력, 즉 다양한 감정 어휘를 가지고 있고 감정의 원인과
결과를 이해하는 능력은 특히 집단 환경에서 중요하다. 이 분야에 능숙한
사람들은 감정, 느낌, 그리고 기분을 정확하게 표현할 수 있으므로, 동료들
간의 명확한 의사소통을 촉진할 수 있다. 더욱이, 그들은 자신의 필요뿐만
아니라 타인의 필요도 수용하는 방식으로 행동(즉, 협력)할 가능성이 더
높을 수도 있다. 예를 들어, 집단 갈등 상황에서 감정을 이해하는 강력한
능력을 지닌 구성원은 문제에 대해 자신이 어떻게 느끼는지 그리고 왜 그렇게
느끼는지를 표현할 수 있을 것이다. 또한 그는 다른 집단 구성원들의 관점을
취하여 그들이 왜 특정한 방식으로 반응하는지 이해할 수 있을 것이다. 다름에
대한 이해는 열린 의사소통을 위한 장을 만들고 건설적인 갈등 해결과 향상된
집단 기능을 촉진한다.

다음 글의 요지로 가장 적절한 것은?
① 집단 구성원 간 갈등 해소를 위해 감정 조절이 중요하다.
　갈등 해소를 위한 감정 조절이 아니라, 감정을 잘 이해하는 사람들이 갈등 해결을 촉진한다는 내용임
② 감정 이해 능력은 집단 내 원활한 소통과 협력을 촉진한다.
　집단에 협력하는 사람들은 감정을 이해하는 능력을 가지고 있다는 내용임
③ 타인에 대한 공감 능력은 자신의 감정 표현 능력을 향상한다.
　감정을 잘 이해하는 것은 자신의 표현 능력을 향상하는 것이 아니라, 집단 환경에서 중요하다는 내용임
④ 감정 관련 어휘에 대한 지식은 공감 능력 발달의 기반이 된다.
　공감 능력이 발달할 수 있는 원인에 관한 설명은 언급되지 않음
⑤ 자신의 감정 상태에 대한 이해는 사회성 함양에 필수적 요소이다.
　자신의 감정만을 이해하는 것이 아니라, 상대의 감정까지 잘 읽어낼 수 있는 역량이 중요함

E 04 정답 ③ * 인간 사회에서만 나타나는 '도덕성'

Even though there is good reason / to consider a dog a sentient being / capable of making choices and plans — /
타당한 이유가 있더라도 / 개를 지각력 있는 존재로 간주할 / 선택과 계획을 할 수 있는 /

so that we might suppose / 'it could have conceived of acting otherwise' — / we're unlikely to think / it is wicked and immoral / for attacking a child. //
그래서 우리가 추정할 수도 있다 / 그것은 다른 방식으로 행동하는 것을 상상할 수 있었을 것이다'라고 / 우리는 생각할 것 같지는 않다 / 그것이 사악하고 부도덕하다고 / 아이를 공격하는 것에 관해 //

Moral responsibility is not some universal concept / like entropy or temperature — / something that applies equally, / and can be measured similarly, / everywhere in the cosmos. //
도덕적 책임은 보편적인 개념이 아니다 / 엔트로피나 온도 같은 / 즉 똑같이 적용되어 / 비슷하게 측정될 수 있는 / 우주 어디에서나 //

It is a notion / developed specifically for human use, / no more or less than languages are. //
그것은 개념이다 / 인간이 사용하기 위해 특별히 개발된 / 언어와 별반 다르지 않다 //

While sentience and volition are aspects of mind and agency, / morals are cultural tools / developed to influence social behaviour: / to cultivate the desirable / and discourage the harmful. // **단서1** 도덕성은 바람직한 것을 함양하고 해로운 것을 막기 위해 개발된 문화적 도구임
지각력과 의지가 마음 및 주체성의 측면인 반면 / 도덕성은 문화적 도구이다 / 사회적 행동에 영향을 미치기 위해 개발된 / 즉 바람직한 것을 함양하고 / 해로운 것을 막는 //

They are learnt, / not given at birth. //
그것들은 학습된다 / 태어날 때 주어지는 것이 아니라 //

It's possible, / indeed likely, / that we are born with a predisposition / to cooperate with others / — but only within human society / do we come to understand this / as *moral* behaviour. // **단서2** 오로지 인간 사회에서만 도덕적 행동으로 이해함
가능하다 / 실제로 가능성이 크다 / 우리가 성향을 가지고 태어난 것이 / 다른 사람과 협력하려는 / 그러나 오로지 인간 사회 내에서만 / 우리는 이것을 이해하게 된다 / '도덕적' 행동으로 //

- be capable of ~할 수 있다 · suppose ⓥ 추정하다
- conceive ⓥ 상상하다 · wicked ⓐ 사악한 · agency ⓝ 주체성
- moral ⓐ 도덕적(인); ⓝ 도덕성 · cultivate ⓥ 함양[배양]하다, 기르다
- desirable ⓐ 바람직한 · discourage ⓥ (못하게) 막다
- harmful ⓐ 해로운 · predisposition ⓝ 성향
- cooperate ⓥ 협력하다

개를 선택과 계획을 할 수 있는 지각력이 있는 존재로 간주하여, 이를테면 우리가 '그것은 다른 방식으로 행동하는 것을 상상할 수 있었을 것이다'라고 추정할 수도 있는 타당한 이유가 있더라도, 우리가 아이를 공격하는 것에 관해 그것이 사악하고 부도덕하다고 생각할 것 같지는 않다. 도덕적 책임은 엔트로피나 온도 같은 어떤 보편적인 개념, 즉 똑같이 적용되어 우주 어디에서나 비슷하게 측정될 수 있는 것이 아니다. 그것은 인간이 사용하기 위해 특별히 개발된 개념인데, 언어와 별반 다르지 않다. 지각력과 의지가 마음 및 주체성의 측면인 반면, 도덕성은 사회적 행동에 영향을 미치기 위해, 즉 바람직한 것을 함양하고 해로운 것을 막기 위해 개발된 문화적 도구이다. 그것들은 태어날 때 주어지는 것이 아니라 학습된다. 우리는 다른 사람과 협력하려는 성향을 가지고 태어날 수 있고 실제로 그럴 가능성이 크지만, 오로지 인간 사회 내에서만 우리는 이것을 '도덕적' 행동으로 이해하게 된다.

다음 글의 요지로 가장 적절한 것은?

① 도덕성은 자신의 선택에 대해 책임을 진다는 개념이다.
　도덕성의 개념을 정의하는 내용이 아님
② 동물과 인간을 구별하는 중요한 특징은 분별력과 언어이다.
　개를 언급하긴 했지만 동물과 인간을 구별하는 특징이 분별력과 언어라는 내용은 아님
③ 도덕성은 학습되는 문화적 도구로서 인간 사회에만 나타난다.
　도덕성은 문화적 도구로 학습되며 인간 사회에서만 나타난다고 함
④ 동물과 인간은 공통적으로 다른 개체와 협력하는 경향이 있다.
　동물이 다른 개체와 협력하려는 경향이 있다는 언급은 없음
⑤ 문화적 도구로서의 도덕성은 개체의 의사 결정에 영향을 미친다.
　도덕성이 문화적 도구라는 것으로 만든 함정

E 05 정답 ① * 실행과 경험을 통해 체득되고 전수되는 실용적 지식

Technical, book knowledge consists of / "formulated rules which are, or may be, deliberately learned." //
기술적, 책(에서 얻을 수 있는) 지식은 ~로 구성된다 / '의도적으로 배우거나, 그럴 수도 있는, 체계적으로 표현된 규칙들'로 //

Practical knowledge, on the other hand, / cannot be taught or learned but only transmitted and acquired. //
반면에 실용적 지식은 / 가르쳐지거나 배울 수 없으며 오직 전해지고 습득된다 //
(= Practical knowledge) **단서1** 실용적 지식은 가르치거나 배울 수 없고 전수되거나 체득될 수 밖에 없음

It exists only in practice. //
그것은 오직 실행 속에서만 존재한다 //

When we talk about practical knowledge, / we tend to use bodily metaphors. //
우리가 실용적 지식에 관해 이야기할 때 / 우리는 신체적 비유를 사용하는 경향이 있다 //
We say that somebody has a *touch* for doing some activity / — an ability to hit the right piano key / with just enough force and pace. //
우리는 누군가가 어떤 활동을 하기 위한 '솜씨'를 가지고 있다고 말한다 / 정확한 피아노 건반을 치는 능력을 / 딱 필요한 만큼의 힘과 속도로 //
We say that somebody has a *feel* for the game, / an intuition for how events are going to unfold, / an awareness of when you should plow ahead with a problem / and when you should put it aside before coming back to it. //
우리는 누군가가 게임에 대한 '감각'을 가지고 있다고 말한다 / 어떻게 사건들이 전개될지에 대한 직감 / 여러분이 문제를 밀고 나가야 할 때와 / 그것으로 되돌아오기 전까지 제쳐 두어야 할 때에 대한 인식 //
When the expert is using her practical knowledge, / she isn't thinking more; she is thinking less. //
전문가가 자신의 실용적 지식을 사용하고 있을 때 / 그녀는 더 생각하는 것이 아니다 / 그녀는 덜 생각한다 //
She has built up a repertoire of skills through habit / and has thereby extended the number of tasks she can perform / without conscious awareness. //
그녀는 습관을 통해 기술의 레퍼토리를 쌓아 왔고 / 그렇게 함으로써 그녀가 수행할 수 있는 과제의 수를 늘려 왔다 / 의식적 인식 없이 //
This sort of knowledge is built up through experience, / and it is passed along through shared experience. //
이러한 종류의 지식은 경험을 통해 쌓이고 / 그것은 공유된 경험을 통해 다음으로 전달된다 //

- consists of ~로 구성되다
- formulate ⓥ 표현[진술]하다
- deliberately ⓐⓓ 의도[계획]적으로
- practical ⓐ 실용적인
- transmit ⓥ 전송하다
- metaphor ⓝ 비유
- extend ⓥ 연장하다
- conscious ⓐ 의식적인

기술적, 책(에서 얻을 수 있는) 지식은 '의도적으로 배우거나, 그럴 수도 있는, 체계적으로 표현된 규칙들'로 구성된다. 반면에 실용적 지식은 가르쳐지거나 배울 수 없으며 오직 전해지고 습득된다. 그것은 오직 실행 속에서만 존재한다. 우리가 실용적 지식에 관해 이야기할 때, 우리는 신체적 비유를 사용하는 경향이 있다. 우리는 누군가가 어떤 활동을 하기 위한 '솜씨', 딱 필요한 만큼의 힘과 속도로 정확한 피아노 건반을 치는 능력을 가지고 있다고 말한다. 우리는 누군가가 게임에 대한 '감각', 어떻게 사건들이 전개될지에 대한 직감, 여러분이 문제를 밀고 나가야 할 때와 그것으로 되돌아오기 전까지 제쳐 두어야 할 때에 대한 인식을 가지고 있다고 말한다. 전문가가 자신의 실용적 지식을 사용하고 있을 때, 그녀는 더 생각하는 것이 아니다. 그녀는 덜 생각한다. 그녀는 습관을 통해 기술의 레퍼토리를 쌓아 왔고, 그렇게 함으로써 의식적 인식 없이 그녀가 수행할 수 있는 과제의 수를 늘려 왔다. 이러한 종류의 지식은 경험을 통해 쌓이고, 그것은 공유된 경험을 통해 다음으로 전달된다.

다음 글의 요지로 가장 적절한 것은?
① 실용적 지식은 실행과 경험을 통해 체득되고 전수된다.
실용적 지식은 배우거나 가르칠 수 없으며, 실행과 경험을 통해 체득되고 전수됨
② 직감에 의한 판단이 옳아 보여도 심사숙고의 과정은 필요하다.
직감에 의한 판단에 대한 심사숙고가 언급되지 않음
③ 기술적 지식을 완전히 이해해야만 이를 실제로 적용할 수 있다.
기술적 지식이 중심이 되는 글이 아님
④ 상황에 맞게 행동하게 하는 실용적 지식은 타고나는 능력이다.
실용적 지식은 경험을 통해 습득되는 것이지, 타고나는 능력이 아님
⑤ 실용적 지식과 기술적 지식의 균형 있는 학습이 중요하다.
실용적 지식과 기술적 지식의 균형을 강조한 글이 아님

왜 정답? [정답률 93%]
- 실용적 지식은 실천을 통해 체득될 수 있지, 가르치거나 배우는 것이 아님 단서1
- 실용적 지식을 갖춘 사람은 이를 사용할 때 기술의 레퍼토리를 형성했기에 의식적으로 하는 부분이 적음
- 실용적 지식은 경험을 통해 형성되고, 공유된 경험을 통해 전수됨 단서2
▶ 따라서 글의 요지는 '실용적 지식은 실행과 경험을 통해 체득되고 전수된다'는 것이므로 정답은 ①이다.

왜 오답?
② 실용적 지식에 직감이 포함되며, 심사숙고가 필요하다는 내용은 아니다.
③ 기술적 지식은 첫 문장에만 언급되었고, 나머지 글은 실용적 지식에 대한 것이다.
④ 실용적 지식은 계속된 연습과 실행을 통해 만들어지는 것이지, 타고나는 능력이란 말은 없다.
⑤ 실용적 지식과 기술적 지식 간의 균형에 대한 언급은 없다.

E 06 정답 ⑤ * 조직 행동 이해에 있어 관리자의 과학적 접근 부재의 실수 —

The relevance of science in understanding organizational behavior / can start with / asking this question: / Why do good managers make bad decisions? //
조직 행동을 이해하는 데 과학의 연관성은 / ~로 시작할 수 있다 / 이 질문을 묻는 것 / 왜 좋은 관리자가 나쁜 결정을 내리는가 //
Too often managers make mistakes / when it comes to fostering conditions / that inspire positive outcomes in the workplace, / such as performance, satisfaction, team cohesion, and ethical behavior. //
관리자들은 너무 자주 실수한다 / 조건을 조성하는 데 있어 / 직장에서 긍정적인 결과를 일으키게 하는 / 성과, 만족, 조직 응집력, 그리고 윤리적 행동과 같은 //
Why does this happen? // 왜 이런 일이 발생하는가 //
Part of the reason / is that rather than relying on a clearly validated set of scientific discoveries, / managers use less reliable sources of insight / such as feel, intuition, the latest trend, /
이유 중 일부는 / 정당성이 분명히 입증된 일련의 과학적 발견에 의존하기보다는 / 관리자는 덜 신뢰할 만한 통찰력의 원천을 사용한다는 것이다 / 직감, 직관, 최신 경향 /
what a highly paid consultant might say, / or what is being done in another company. // 단서1 관리자는 덜 신뢰할 만한 통찰력의 원천을 사용하기도 함
고액을 받는 컨설턴트가 말할 수도 있는 것 / 또는 다른 회사에서 일어나는 것과 같은 //
Like most of us, / managers tend to rely on their own strengths and experiences / when making choices / about how to get the best from others. //
대부분의 우리처럼 / 관리자들은 자기 자신의 장점과 경험에 의존하는 경향이 있다 / 선택할 때 / 다른 사람들로부터 가장 좋은 것을 얻어 내는 방법을 //
But what works for one manager / may not work for another. //
그러나 한 명의 관리자에게 효과가 있는 것이 / 다른 관리자에게는 효과가 없을지도 모른다 //
In the absence of a scientific approach, / managers tend to make mistakes, / offer ill-conceived incentives, misinterpret employee behavior, / and fail to account for the many possible explanations / for why employees might perform poorly. //
과학적 접근법이 부재하면 / 관리자들은 실수하고 / 잘못 생각해 낸 유인책을 제공하고, 직원들의 행동을 잘못 이해하고 / 많은 가능한 설명을 하는 데 실패한다 / 왜 직원들이 형편없이 일하는지에 대한 // 단서2 과학적 접근법이 없으면 관리자들은 조직 행동에 대한 판단을 제대로 하지 못함

- organizational ⓐ 구조적인
- forster ⓥ 강화하다, 조성하다
- condition ⓝ 조건
- inspire ⓥ 영감을 주다
- cohesion ⓝ 결속력
- ethical ⓐ 윤리적인
- validate ⓥ 입증하다, 인증하다
- absence ⓝ 부재
- misinterpret ⓥ 잘못 해석하다, 오해하다
- account for 설명하다, 차지하다

조직 행동을 이해하는 데 과학의 연관성은 이 질문을 묻는 것으로 시작할 수 있다. 왜 좋은 관리자가 나쁜 결정을 내리는가? 관리자들은 직장에서 성과, 만족, 조직 응집력, 그리고 윤리적 행동과 같은 긍정적인 결과를 일으키게 하는 조건을 조성하는 데 있어 너무 자주 실수한다. 왜 이런 일이 발생하는가? 이유 중 일부는 관리자가 정당성이 분명히 입증된 일련의 과학적 발견에 의존하기보다는 직감, 직관, 최신 경향, 고액을 받는 컨설턴트가 말할 수도 있는 것, 또는 다른 회사에서 일어나는 것과 같은 덜 신뢰할 만한 통찰력의 원천을 사용한다는 것이다. 대부분의 우리처럼 관리자들은 다른 사람들로부터

가장 좋은 것을 얻어 내는 방법을 선택할 때 자기 자신의 장점과 경험에 의존하는 경향이 있다. 그러나 한 명의 관리자에게 효과가 있는 것이 다른 관리자에게는 효과가 없을지도 모른다. 과학적 접근법이 부재하면, 관리자들은 실수하고, 잘못 생각해 낸 유인책을 제공하고, 직원들의 행동을 잘못 이해하고, 왜 직원들이 형편없이 일하는지에 대한 많은 가능한 설명을 하는 데 실패한다.

다음 글의 요지로 가장 적절한 것은?
① 직원들의 성과에 대한 다양한 평가 기준이 필요하다.
　직원의 성과를 평가하는 기준은 언급되지 않음
② 성공적인 관리자는 실패로부터 교훈을 이끌어 낸다.
　실패로부터 교훈을 이끌어 낸다는 내용이 요지가 아님
③ 직원 간의 목표 공유가 조직을 결속하는 데 효과적이다.
　조직을 결속하기 위해 직원 간 목표 공유가 효과적이라는 내용은 없음
④ 조직 문화의 혁신적 변화를 위해서는 관리자의 경험에 의한 직관이
　중요하다. 관리자의 경험에 의한 직관이 혁신적 변화를 이끌어내는 것이 아니라 판단 실수로
　이어질 수 있다고 했음
⑤ 조직 행동 이해에서 관리자가 과학적 접근법을 활용하지 않으면 잘못된
　판단을 할 수 있다. In the absence of a scientific approach, managers tend to
　make mistakes ~ perform poorly.

왜 정답? [정답률 83%]

전반부	관리자는 조직 행동을 이해하고 긍정적 결과를 가져올 수 있는 판단을 내리는 데에 실수를 하곤 함
중반부 이후	• 과학적으로 접근을 하기보다는 덜 신뢰할만한 통찰력의 원천을 사용하기 때문에 각종 결정 실수를 하게 됨 단서1 • 관리자들은 과학적 접근법이 없으면 조직 행동에 대한 판단을 제대로 하지 못함 단서2

▶ 따라서 글의 요지는 '조직 행동 이해에서 관리자가 과학적 접근법을 활용하지 않으면 잘못된 판단을 할 수 있다.'는 것이므로 정답은 ⑤이다.

왜 오답?
① 성과를 평가하는 기준이 필요하다는 것이 글의 요지가 아니다.
② 관리자가 경험으로부터 결정을 내린다는 내용은 있으나, 실패로부터 교훈을 이끌어
　낸다는 것이 요지는 아니다.
③ 직원 간 목표 공유에 대한 내용이 없으며, 이것이 조직 결속을 효과적으로 한다는
　내용도 없다.
④ 관리자의 경험에 의한 직관이 언급되었으나, 이런 결정 방식은 판단 실수로 이어질
　수 있다는 것이 글의 핵심 내용이다.

E 07 정답 ① *야생 보호 구역 보존과 경제적 가치

Most opposition to wilderness preservation / doesn't come
from environmentalists / but from corporate interests and
developers. //
　　　　　not A but B: A가 아니라 B
야생 보호 구역 보존에 대한 대부분의 반대는 / 환경론자들로부터가 아니라 / 기업 관계자와
개발자들로부터 나온다 //

When wild places are designated as wilderness, / they are closed
/ to most commercial activities and residential or infrastructure
development. //
야생의 지역이 야생 보호 구역으로 지정되면 / 그 지역은 금지된다 / 대부분의 상업 활동 및
주거 또는 기반 시설 개발이 //

There is thus frequently an economic cost / to wilderness
preservation. //
따라서 흔히 경제적인 비용이 존재한다 / 야생 보호 구역 보존에는 //

Some critics claim / that when wilderness and economic
interests clash, / economic interests should normally prevail. //
일부 비평가들은 주장한다 / 야생 보호 구역과 경제적 이익이 충돌할 때 / 경제적 이익이
일반적으로 우세해야 한다고 //

This argument, / even if it is sound, / won't exclude all wilderness
　　　　주어　　　　　　'타당한'　　　　　　동사
preservation efforts, / because some wilderness areas have little
economic value. //
이러한 주장은 / 비록 타당할지라도 / 모든 야생 보호 구역 보존 노력을 배제하지는 않을
것이다 / 일부 야생 보호 구역은 경제적인 가치가 거의 없기 때문에 //

But a deeper problem with the argument is / that it views nature
　　　　　　　　　　　　　　　　　　주격 보어절 접속사
/ from a human-focused and excessively economic point of
view. //
그러나 이 주장의 더 심층적인 문제점은 ~이다 / 그것이 자연을 본다는 것 / 인간 중심적이고
지나치게 경제적인 관점에서 //
동명사 주어(단수 취급)　　　　　　　　　　　　　Allowing의 목적격 보어
Allowing economic considerations to outweigh all other forms
of value / is inconsistent with the biocentric reasons / that
　　　　단수 동사　　　　　　　　　　　　　　　주격 관계대명사
support wilderness preservation. // 단서1 경제적인 고려 사항이 다른 형태의
　　　　　　　　　　　　　　　　　　　　　가치들을 능가하도록 두어서는 안 됨
경제적인 고려 사항이 모든 다른 형태의 가치를 능가하도록 두는 것은 / 생명 중심적인
이유들에 부합하지 않는다 / 야생 보호 구역 보존을 지지하는 //

Thus, / while it certainly makes sense / to weigh the economic
　　　　　　　　　　　　　가주어　　　　　진주어(to부정사)
costs of wilderness protection, / especially when such costs are
high, /
따라서 / 분명히 타당하지만 / 야생 보호 구역 보호의 경제적 비용을 따져 보는 것이 / 특히
그러한 비용이 높을 때 /
　　　　복수 주어　　　　　　　　　　　　현재분사구(values 수식)
the biocentric values underlying wilderness preservation
　　　　　　복수 동사
/ exclude viewing economic considerations / as the most
important. // 단서2 야생 보호 구역에 있어서 생명 중심적인 가치를 배제해서는 안 됨
야생 보호 구역 보존의 근본이 되는 생명 중심적인 가치는 / 경제적인 고려를 여기는 것을
배제한다 / 가장 중요한 것으로 //

- opposition ⓝ 반대　　　• wilderness ⓝ 황야, 황무지
- environmentalist ⓝ 환경 운동가　　• corporate ⓐ 기업의
- interest ⓝ 이익　　• designate ⓥ 지정하다
- residential ⓐ 거주지의　　• infrastructure ⓝ 사회 기반 시설
- clash ⓥ (의견 차이 등에 의해) 충돌하다　　• prevail ⓥ 만연하다
- exclude ⓥ 배제하다　　• outweigh ⓥ …보다 더 크다, 능가하다
- inconsistent ⓐ 부합하지 않는　　• biocentric ⓐ 생명을 중심으로 하는
- underlying ⓐ 근본적인

야생 보호 구역 보존에 대한 대부분의 반대는 환경론자들로부터가 아니라 기업 관계자와 개발자들로부터 나온다. 야생의 지역이 야생 보호 구역으로 지정되면 그 지역은 대부분의 상업 활동 및 주거 또는 기반 시설 개발이 금지된다. 따라서 야생 보호 구역 보존에는 흔히 경제적인 비용이 존재한다. 일부 비평가들은 야생 보호 구역과 경제적 이익이 충돌할 때 경제적 이익이 일반적으로 우세해야 한다고 주장한다. 이러한 주장은, 비록 타당할지라도, 일부 야생 보호 구역은 경제적인 가치가 거의 없기 때문에 모든 야생 보호 구역 보존 노력을 배제하지는 않을 것이다. 그러나 이 주장의 더 심층적인 문제점은 그것이 자연을 인간 중심적이고 지나치게 경제적인 관점에서 본다는 것이다. 경제적인 고려 사항이 모든 다른 형태의 가치를 능가하도록 두는 것은 야생 보호 구역 보존을 지지하는 생명 중심적인 이유들에 부합하지 않는다. 따라서 특히 그러한 비용이 높을 때 야생 보호 구역 보호의 경제적 비용을 따져 보는 것이 분명히 타당하지만, 야생 보호 구역 보존의 근본이 되는 생명 중심적인 가치는 경제적인 고려를 가장 중요한 것으로 여기는 것을 배제한다.

다음 글의 요지로 가장 적절한 것은?
① 야생 보호 구역 보존의 생명 중심적 가치는 경제적 고려에 우선한다.
　the biocentric values ~ as the most important
② 자연과의 공존을 고려한 상업 활동이 기업에 경제적 이익을 가져다준다.
　공존과 관련 없음
③ 야생 보호에 있어 우선적으로 고려하는 가치는 문화에 따라 다양하다.
　문화에 따라 다르다는 내용은 없음
④ 야생 보호는 경제적 가치와 상관없이 모든 생물에 똑같이 적용된다.
　관련 없음
⑤ 야생의 보호와 회복을 위한 비용 부담은 공동체 모두의 몫이다.
　책임 소재에 대해 이야기 하는 글이 아님

왜 정답? [정답률 70%]

- 경제적인 고려 사항이 모든 다른 형태의 가치를 능가하도록 두는 것은 야생 보호
　구역 보존을 지지하는 생명 중심적인 이유들에 부합하지 않는다. 단서1
- 야생 보호 구역 보존의 근본이 되는 생명 중심적인 가치는 경제적인 고려를 가장
　중요한 것으로 여기는 것을 배제한다. 단서2

➡ 일부 비평가들은 야생 보호 구역과 경제적 이익이 충돌할 때 경제적 이익이
　일반적으로 우세해야 한다고 주장하지만, 이는 야생 보호 구역 보존을 지지하는
　생명 중심적인 이유들에 부합하지 않는다고 주장하고 있다.

▶ 따라서 정답은 ①이다.

함축(된 의미)을 지니고 있지만, 모국어는 빈곤과 고난과 관련이 있다. 다른 사람들에게는 그 반대가 참이다 — 제2 외국어는 이민 후의 어려움, 차별, 그리고 친밀한 관계의 부재와 관련이 있지만, 모국어는 가족, 친구, 그리고 부모의 사랑과 관련이 있다. 그리고 많은 사람은 그 사이 어딘가에 있는데, 각 언어와 관련된 혼재되어 있는 긍정적이고 부정적인 경험들을 가지고 있다.

다음 글의 요지로 가장 적절한 것은?

① 다중 언어 환경은 모국어 학습 발달을 지연시킨다.
　다중 언어 환경이 모국어 학습 발달을 지연시킨다는 것은 요지가 아님
② 모국어 실력이 뛰어날수록 외국어를 습득하는 속도가 빠르다.
　다중 언어 사용자가 언급됐을 뿐 내용과 상관없음
③ 다중 언어 사용자는 사용하는 언어에 따라 다르게 느끼고 반응한다.
　a multilingual can quite literally feel ~ versus another
④ 부정적인 어휘가 긍정적인 어휘보다 감정에 미치는 영향이 크다.
　다중 언어 사용자가 사용하는 언어에 따라 다르게 느끼고 반응한다는 것이 글의 요지임
⑤ 긍정적인 감정을 나타내는 어휘량이 문화권마다 다르다.
　긍정적 감정을 나타내는 어휘량이 문화권마다 다르다는 내용이 아님

왜 정답? [정답률 92%]

첫 문장(주제문)	다중 언어 사용자는 사용하는 언어에 따라 다르게 느낌 **단서1**
중반까지	다중 언어 사용자는 다르게 느낀다고 말할 뿐만 아니라 사용하는 언어에 따라 반응과 판단이 다름 **단서2**

▶ 따라서 글의 요지는 '다중 언어 사용자는 사용하는 언어에 따라 다르게 느끼고 반응한다.'는 것이므로 정답은 ③이다.

왜 오답?　

① 다중 언어 환경이 모국어 발달을 지연시키는 것이 아니라, 다중 언어 사용자가 사용하는 언어에 따라 다르게 느끼고 반응한다는 것이 요지이다.
② 모국어 실력과 외국어 습득 속도 간 관계에 대한 내용이 아니다.
④ 부정적 어휘가 긍정적 어휘보다 감정에 미치는 영향이 크다는 것이 아니다.
⑤ 긍정적 감정을 나타내는 어휘량이 문화권마다 다르다는 것이 요지가 아니다.

왜 오답?

② 경제적 이익이 자연과의 공존으로 이뤄질 수 있다는 내용의 글이 아니다.
③ 경제적 고려를 최우선시하는 집단에 대한 언급이 있을 뿐이다.
④ 생물들 간에 차이를 두지 않고 동일하게 보호하자는 것이 글의 요지는 아니다.
⑤ 야생 보호와 회복을 위해서 공동체가 비용을 부담하자는 내용은 언급되지 않았다.

E 08 정답 ③ ＊사용하는 언어에 따라 다르게 느끼고 반응하는 다중 언어 사용자

Though it may seem extreme, / a multilingual can quite literally
　　　　　　　　　　접속사가 생략되지 않은 분사구문
feel differently / about people, events or things / when using one
language / versus another. // **단서1** 다중 언어 사용자는 사용하는 언어에 따라
　　　　　　　　　　　　　　　　　　　다르게 느낌
극단적으로 보일 수도 있지만 / 다중 언어 사용자는 말 그대로 꽤 다르게 느낄 수 있다 / 사람,
사건 또는 사물에 대해 / 한 언어를 사용할 때에 / 다른 언어를 사용할 때에 비해 //
　　핵심 주어(단수)
The likelihood of being rattled / by curse words or taboo words
　단수 동사
/ changes across native and second languages. //
당황할 가능성은 / 악담이나 금기어에 의해 / 모국어와 제2 외국어에 따라 달라진다 //

Speakers of multiple languages / not only report feeling different,
　　　not only A (but also) B: A뿐만 아니라 B도
/ but their bodies have different physiological reactions /
다중 언어 사용자는 / 다르게 느낀다고 말할 뿐만 아니라 / 그들의 신체는 서로 다른 생리적
반응을 보이고 /

and their minds make different emotionally driven decisions /
across languages. // **단서2** 다중 언어 사용자는 언어에 따라 반응과 판단이 다름
그들의 생각은 감정에 이끌린 서로 다른 판단을 내린다 / 언어에 따라 //

The exact relationship / between positive and negative emotions
and language / varies across people. //
정확한 관계는 / 긍정적, 그리고 부정적 감정과 언어 사이의 / 사람에 따라 다르다 //

For some, / the second language carries more positive
connotations / because it is associated / with freedom,
opportunity, financial well-being and escape from persecution, /
어떤 사람들에게는 / 제2 외국어가 더 긍정적인 함축(된 의미)을 지니고 있다 / 관련이 있기
때문에 / 자유, 기회, 재정적 풍요와 박해로부터의 탈출과 /
　반면에
whereas the native language is associated / with poverty and
hardship. //
반면에 모국어는 관련이 있다 / 빈곤과 고난과 //

For others, / the opposite is true / — the second language is
associated / with post-immigration challenges, discrimination
and lack of close relationships, /
다른 사람들에게는 / 그 반대가 참이다 / 제2 외국어는 관련이 있다 / 이민 후의 어려움, 차별,
그리고 친밀한 관계의 부재와

whereas the native language is associated / with family, friends
and parental love. //
반면에 모국어는 관련이 있다 / 가족, 친구, 그리고 부모의 사랑과 //
　　　　　　　　　　　　　　　　　　　　　　　분사구문
And many are somewhere in between, / having a mix of positive
and negative experiences / 명사(positive and negative experiences)를 수식하는 분사
associated with each language. //
그리고 많은 사람은 그 사이 어딘가에 있다 / 혼재되어 있는 긍정적이고 부정적인 경험들을
가지고 있다 / 각 언어와 관련된 //

• multilingual ⓐ 여러 언어를 하는　• likelihood ⓝ 가능성
• curse ⓝ 저주　• taboo ⓝ 금기　• physiological ⓐ 생리적인
• vary ⓥ 다르다　• financial ⓐ 재정의　• well-being ⓝ 풍요
• poverty ⓝ 빈곤　• hardship ⓝ 고난, 어려움
• discrimination ⓝ 차별　• parental ⓐ 부모의

극단적으로 보일 수도 있지만, 다중 언어 사용자는 한 언어를 사용할 때에 비해 다른 언어를 사용할 때 사람, 사건 또는 사물에 대해 말 그대로 꽤 다르게 느낄 수 있다. 악담이나 금기어에 당황할 가능성은 모국어와 제2 외국어에 따라 달라진다. 다중 언어 사용자는 언어에 따라 다르게 느낀다고 말할 뿐만 아니라, 그들의 신체는 서로 다른 생리적 반응을 보이고, 그들의 생각은 감정에 이끌린 서로 다른 판단을 내린다. 긍정적, 그리고 부정적 감정과 언어 사이의 정확한 관계는 사람에 따라 다르다. 어떤 사람들에게는 제2 외국어가 자유, 기회, 재정적 풍요와 박해로부터의 탈출과 관련이 있기 때문에 더 긍정적인

E 09 정답 ④ ＊면밀한 계획의 중요성

　　주어　　　　　　　　　　　　　　　　　　　　　동사
Contractors / that will construct a project / may place more
weight / on the planning process. //
도급업자들은 / 주택 단지를 건설하려는 / 더 많은 비중을 둘 수 있다 / 계획 과정에 //
Proper planning / forces detailed thinking / about the project. //
적절한 계획은 / 면밀한 사고를 하게 한다 / 그 건설 사업에 대해 //
It allows the project manager (or team) / to "build the project /
주어　동사　　　　　　　　　　목적어　　　　　　　목적격 보어
in his or her head." //
그것은 건설 사업 책임자(또는 팀)가 ~하게 한다 / '그 주택 단지를 지어 보게 / 자기 머릿속에' //
The project manager (or team) can consider / different
methodologies / thereby deciding / what works best / or what
　　　　　　　　　　　　　　　　　　　　　deciding의 목적어절의 병렬 구조
does not work at all. //
그 건설 사업 책임자(또는 팀)는 고려하고 / 여러 다른 방법론을 / 그에 의해 결정할 수 있다 /
어떤 것이 가장 잘 작동되는지 / 또는 어떤 것이 전혀 작동되지 않는지를 //
This detailed thinking / may be the only way / to discover
restrictions or risks / that were not addressed / in the estimating
process. // **단서1** 면밀한 사고를 통한 적절한 계획은 추정으로는
　　　　　　발견할 수 없는 제약이나 위험을 발견하는 유일한 방법임
이런 면밀한 사고는 / 유일한 방법일 수 있다 / 제약이나 위험을 발견하는 / 다뤄지지 못했던
/ 추정 과정에서 //
　　　가주어　　강조 부사　　　　진주어
It would be far better to discover / in the planning phase / that
　　　　　　비교급
a particular technology or material will not work / than in the
execution process. // **단서2** 실행 과정보다는 계획 단계에서 제약이나
　　　　　　　　　　　위험을 발견하는 것이 훨씬 더 나음
발견하는 것이 훨씬 더 나을 것이다 / 계획 단계에서 / 특정 기술이나 재료가 작동되지 않으리
라는 것을 / 실행 과정에서보다는 //
　　주어
The goal of the planning process / for the contractor / is to
　　　　　　　　　　　　　　　　　　　　　　　　　　동사
produce a workable scheme / that uses the resources efficiently
주격 관계대명사
/ within the allowable time and given budget. //
계획 과정의 목표는 / 도급업자에게 / 실행 가능한 계획을 만들어 내는 것이다 / 자원을 효율적
으로 사용하는 / 허용되는 시간과 주어진 예산 내에서 //

A well-developed plan does not guarantee / that the executing
process will proceed flawlessly / or that the project will even
succeed / in meeting its objectives. //
does not guarantee의 목적어절 접속사의 병렬 구조
잘 만들어진 계획이 보장하지는 않는다 / 실행 과정이 흠 없이 진행될 것이라거나 / 심지어 그
건설 사업이 성공할 것임을 / 그 목표를 달성하는 데 // **단서 3** 잘 만들어진 계획은 목표 달성
가능성을 크게 높임
It does, however, greatly improve / its chances. //
하지만 그것은 정말로 크게 높인다 / 그 가능성을 //

- contractor ⓝ 계약자, 도급업자   • construct ⓥ 건설하다
- project ⓝ 주택 계획, 주택 단지   • weight ⓝ 중요성, 무게
- process ⓝ 과정, 절차   • proper ⓐ 적절한
- force ⓥ 강요하다, ~하게 하다   • detailed ⓐ 상세한, 면밀한
- allow ⓥ 허락하다, 가능하게 하다   • methodology ⓝ 방법론
- thereby ⓐ 그렇게 함으로써   • discover ⓥ 발견하다
- restriction ⓝ 제약, 제한   • risk ⓝ 위험 (요소)
- address ⓥ (어려운 문제 등을) 다루다   • estimate ⓥ 추정하다
- far ⓐ 훨씬   • phase ⓝ 단계, 국면   • particular ⓐ 특정한
- material ⓝ 재료   • execution ⓝ 실행, 수행   • goal ⓝ 목표
- workable ⓐ 실행 가능한   • scheme ⓝ 계획   • resource ⓝ 자원
- efficiently ⓐ 능률적으로   • allowable ⓐ 허용되는
- given ⓐ (이미) 정해진, 주어진   • budget ⓝ 예산
- guarantee ⓥ 보장하다   • proceed ⓥ 진행하다
- flawlessly ⓐ 흠 없이   • meet ⓥ 충족시키다   • objective ⓝ 목표
- improve ⓥ 개선하다   • chance ⓝ 가능성

주택 단지를 건설하려는 도급업자들은 계획 과정에 더 많은 비중을 둘 수 있다.
적절한 계획은 그 건설 사업에 대해 면밀한 사고를 하게 한다. 그것은 건설 사
업 책임자(또는 팀)가 '그 주택 단지를 자기 머릿속에 지어 보게' 한다. 그 건설
사업 책임자(또는 팀)는 여러 다른 방법론을 고려함으로써 어떤 것이 가장 잘
작동되는지 또는 어떤 것이 전혀 작동되지 않는지를 결정할 수 있다. 이런 면밀
한 사고는 추정 과정에서 다뤄지지 못했던 제약이나 위험을 발견하는 유일한 방
법일 수 있다. 실행 과정보다는 계획 단계에서 특정 기술이나 재료가 작동되지
않으리라는 것을 발견하는 것이 훨씬 더 나을 것이다. 도급업자에게 계획 과정
의 목표는 허용되는 시간과 주어진 예산 내에서 자원을 효율적으로 사용하는 실
행 가능한 계획을 만들어 내는 것이다. 잘 만들어진 계획이, 실행 과정이 흠 없
이 진행될 것이라거나 심지어 그 건설 사업이 그 목표를 달성하는 데 성공할 것
이라고 보장하지는 않는다. 하지만 그것은 정말로 그 가능성을 크게 높인다.

다음 글의 요지로 가장 적절한 것은?
① 계획 수립 절차를 간소화하면 일의 진행 속도가 빨라진다.
　계획을 면밀히 세우라는 내용임
② 안정적인 예산 확보는 일의 원활한 진행을 위해 필수적이다.
　given budget으로 만든 오답
③ 사업 계획은 급변하는 상황에 따라 유연하게 변경될 수 있다.
　상황에 따라 계획을 변경하라는 것이 아님
④ 면밀한 계획 수립은 일의 효율성을 증대시키고 성공 가능성을 높인다.
　면밀한 계획 수립의 이점을 설명함
⑤ 대규모 사업에서는 지속적인 성장을 목표로 하는 세부 계획이 중요하다.
　지속적인 성장을 목표로 삼아야 한다는 것이 아님

왜 정답? [정답률 94%]
면밀한 사고를 통해 적절한 계획을 세우면 추정을 통해서는 발견되지 않는 제약이
나 위험을 발견할 수 있는데, 이러한 제약이나 오류를 실행 과정보다는 계획 단계
에서 발견하는 것이 훨씬 더 효율적이라고 했다. 마지막 두 문장에서는 잘 만들어
진 면밀한 계획이 목표 달성 성공을 보장하지는 않지만 성공할 가능성을 크게 높인
다고 했으므로 정답은 ④이다.

왜 오답?
① 계획 과정에 더 많은 비중을 두고 면밀한 사고를 통해 적절한 계획을 세우라는
　내용이다.
② 계획 과정의 목표를 설명하면서 given budget이 언급된 것으로 만든 오답이
　다. 예산 확보가 아니라 면밀한 계획의 수립이 필수적이라는 내용이다. **함정**
③ 상황에 따라 계획을 변경하는 유연성이 중요하다는 내용이 아니다.
⑤ 지속적인 성장을 목표로 세부적인 계획을 세우라는 것이 아니라, 면밀한 목표를
　세움으로써 목표 달성에 성공할 수 있다는 내용이다.

E 10 정답 ① *사회적 책임을 수반하는 전문직의 자율성*

Historically, / the professions and society have engaged / in
a negotiating process / intended to define / the terms of their
relationship. //
선행사(주격 관계대명사와 be동사는 생략됨)
역사적으로 / 전문직과 사회는 참여해 왔다 / 협상 과정에 / 규정하고자 의도된 / 그들의 관계
의 조건을 // *장소의 부사구가 문두로 오면서 주어와 동사가 도치됨*
At the heart of this process / is the tension / between the
professions' pursuit of autonomy / and the public's demand for
accountability. //
이 과정의 핵심에는 / 긴장이 있다 / 전문직의 자율성 추구 / 책임에 대한 공공의 요구 사이
의 // *granting의 의미상 주어 동명사 주어* **단서 1** 전문직에 권한과 특권을 부여한 것은
그들의 사회적 책임 완수를 전제로 함
Society's granting of power and privilege / to the professions /
동사
is premised / on their willingness and ability /
사회가 권한과 특권을 부여한 것은 / 전문직에 / 전제로 한다 / 그들의 자발성과 능력을 /
형용사적 용법(willingness and ability 수식)
to contribute to social well-being / and to conduct their affairs /
in a manner / consistent with broader social values. //
사회 복지에 기여하고 / 그들의 일을 수행하는 / 방식으로 / 더 넓은 사회적 가치와 일치하는 //
진주어절 접속사
It has long been recognized / that the expertise and privileged
가주어
position / of professionals / confer authority and power /
선행사
~이 오랫동안 인식되어 왔다 / 전문지식과 특권적 지위가 / 전문직의 / 권위와 권한을 준다
는 것이 /
that could readily be used / to advance their own interests / at
주격 관계대명사
the expense of those / they serve. //
쉽게 이용될 수 있는 / 그들 자신의 이익을 향상하기 위해 / 사람들을 희생시키고서 / 그들이
봉사하는 //
As Edmund Burke observed / two centuries ago, / "Men
are qualified / for civil liberty / in exact proportion / to their
형용사적 용법(disposition 수식)
disposition / to put moral chains / upon their own appetites." //
Edmund Burke가 말했듯이 / 두 세기 전에 / "인간은 자격이 부여된다 / 시민적 자유를 누
릴 / 정확히 비례해서 / 그들의 성향에 / 도덕적 사슬을 채우는 / 자신의 욕구에" //
Autonomy has never been a one-way street / and is never
granted / absolutely and irreversibly. // **단서 2** 자율성은 대가 없이 주어지기만
하는 것이 아님
자율성은 일방통행로였던 적이 없었으며 / 결코 주어지지 않는다 / 절대적이고 뒤집을 수 없게 //

- profession ⓝ 전문직   • engage in ~에 관여[참여]하다
- negotiate ⓥ 협상하다   • intend ⓥ 의도하다   • define ⓥ 규정하다
- terms ⓝ (합의·계약 등의) 조건   • tension ⓝ 긴장
- pursuit ⓝ 추구   • demand ⓝ 요구
- accountability ⓝ 책임, 의무   • grant ⓥ 부여하다, 승인하다
- willingness ⓝ 기꺼이 하는 마음   • contribute ⓥ 기여하다
- conduct ⓥ 수행하다   • affair ⓝ 일, 문제
- consistent ⓐ 일치하는, 일관된   • broad ⓐ 폭넓은, 넓은
- expertise ⓝ 전문 지식   • confer ⓥ 부여[수여]하다
- authority ⓝ 권한, 권위   • readily ⓐ 손쉽게
- at the expense of ~을 희생하면서   • observe ⓥ 말하다, 관찰하다
- qualify ⓥ 자격을 주다   • civil ⓐ 시민의   • liberty ⓝ 자유
- proportion ⓝ 비율   • disposition ⓝ 성향, 기질
- moral ⓐ 도덕적인   • appetite ⓝ 욕구, 식욕
- irreversibly ⓐ 돌이킬 수 없게

역사적으로 전문직과 사회는 그들의 관계의 조건을 규정하고자 의도된 협상 과
정에 참여해 왔다. 이 과정의 핵심에는 전문직의 자율성 추구와 책임에 대한 공
공의 요구 사이의 긴장이 있다. 사회가 전문직에 권한과 특권을 부여한 것은 사
회 복지에 기여하고 더 넓은 사회적 가치와 일치하는 방식으로 그들의 일을 수
행하는 그들의 자발성과 능력을 전제로 한다. 전문직의 전문지식과 특권적 지
위는 그들이 봉사하는 사람들을 희생시키고서 그들 자신의 이익을 향상하기 위
해 쉽게 이용될 수 있는 권위와 권한을 준다는 것이 오랫동안 인식되어 왔다.
Edmund Burke가 두 세기 전에 말했듯이, "인간은 자신의 욕구를 도덕적으
로 구속하는 그들의 성향에 정확히 비례해서 시민적 자유를 누릴 자격이 부여된
다." 자율성은 일방통행로였던 적이 없었으며 결코 절대적이고 뒤집을 수 없게
주어지지 않는다.

다음 글의 요지로 가장 적절한 것은?

① 전문직에 부여되는 자율성은 그에 상응하는 사회적 책임을 수반한다.
— 자율성은 그냥 주어지는 것이 아님
② 전문직의 권위는 해당 집단의 이익을 추구하는 데 이용되어 왔다.
— 글의 내용 중 일부로 만든 오답
③ 전문직의 사회적 책임을 규정할 수 있는 제도 정비가 필요하다.
— 제도 정비의 필요성은 언급되지 않음
④ 전문직이 되기 위한 자격 요건은 사회 경제적 요구에 따라 변화해 왔다.
— 전문직의 자격 요건 변화에 대한 글이 아님
⑤ 전문직의 업무 성과는 일정 수준의 자율성과 특권이 부여될 때 높아진다.
— 전문직에 주어지는 자율성에는 전제가 있다는 것이 핵심임

왜 정답? [정답률 85%]

전문직의 자율성 추구와 전문직의 책임에 대한 공공의 요구 사이의 긴장이 전문직과 사회의 협상 과정의 핵심이라고 한 이후에, 사회가 전문직에 권한과 특권을 부여한 것은 그들이 사회 복지에 기여하고 더 넓은 사회적 가치와 일치하는 방식으로 일할 것을 전제로 한다고 했다. 즉, 전문직에 부여되는 자율성은 그들이 사회적 책임을 다하는 것을 수반한다는 의미로, ①이 글의 요지이다.

왜 오답?

② 전문직의 전문지식과 특권적 지위가 그들 자신의 이익을 향상하기 위해 쉽게 이용될 수 있는 권위와 권한을 준다는 것이 오랫동안 인식되어 왔다는 문장이 있긴 하지만, 이는 전문직의 자율성에는 사회적 책임이 따른다는 것을 주장하는 글의 일부로서 제시된 것일 뿐이다.
③ 자율성이 부여된 전문직은 사회적 책임을 다해야 한다는 내용인 것은 맞지만, 그를 위해 제도를 정비해야 한다는 것은 아니다.
④ 전문직이 되기 위한 자격 요건이 변화한다는 언급은 없다.
⑤ 업무 성과 향상을 위해 전문직에 자율성과 특권을 부여해야 한다는 등의 내용이 아니다.

E 11 정답 ① *사회적 대응이 필요한 유해 환경 요인

Environmental hazards include / biological, physical, and
— = environmental hazards — 선행사 — 주격 관계대명사
chemical ones, / along with the human behaviors / that promote
or allow exposure. /
환경 위험 요인은 포함한다 / 생물학적, 물리적, 화학적 위험 요인을 / 인간의 행동과 함께 / 노출을 조장하거나 허용하는
단서1 피하기 어려운 환경적 위험 요인이 있음 부사적 용법(difficult 수식)
Some environmental contaminants are difficult / to avoid /
일부 환경오염 물질은 어렵다 / 피하기가 /
(the breathing / of polluted air, / the drinking / of chemically
contaminated public drinking water, / noise / in open public
spaces); /
(호흡 / 오염된 공기의 / 음용 / 화학적으로 오염된 공공 식수의 / 소음 / 개방된 공공장소에서의) /
단서2 이러한 환경적 위험 요인은 개인이 피하기 어려움
in these circumstances, / exposure is largely involuntary. //
이러한 상황에서 / 노출은 대개 자기도 모르게 이루어진다 //
Reduction or elimination of these factors / may require societal
action, / such as public awareness and public health measures. //
이러한 요인의 감소 또는 제거는 / 사회적 조치를 필요로 할 수도 있다 / 대중의 인식 및 공중 보건 조치와 같은 //
단서3 이러한 요인에 대해서 사회적 조치가 필요함
— 주어 — 동격절 접속사
In many countries, / the fact / that some environmental hazards
— 동사
are difficult / to avoid / at the individual level / is felt to be more
— 부사적 용법(difficult 수식) — 주격 관계대명사
morally egregious / than those hazards / that can be avoided. //
많은 국가에서 / 사실은 / 일부 환경적 위험 요인이 어렵다는 / 피하기 / 개인 수준에서 / 도덕적으로 더 나쁘다고 느껴진다 / 그러한 위험 요인보다도 / 피해질 수 있는 //
Having no choice but to drink water / contaminated with very
— or로 연결된 동명사구 주어
high levels of arsenic, / or being forced / to passively breathe in
tobacco smoke / in restaurants, /
어쩔 수 없이 물을 마실 수밖에 없는 것은 / 매우 높은 수준의 비소로 오염된 / 또는 강요당하는 것은 / 담배 연기를 수동적으로 들이마시도록 / 식당에서 /
— 단수 동사
outrages people more / than the personal choice / of whether an
— of의 목적어절을 이끄는 명사절 접속사
individual smokes tobacco. //
더 사람들을 화나게 한다 / 개인적인 선택보다 / 개인이 담배를 피울지에 대한 //
These factors are important / when one considers / how change
(risk reduction) happens. //
이러한 요인들은 중요하다 / 사람이 고려할 때 / 변화(위험 감소)가 어떻게 일어나는지를 //

· hazard ⓝ 위험 (요인)   · biological ⓐ 생물학적인
· physical ⓐ 물리적인   · chemical ⓐ 화학적인
· promote ⓥ 조장[촉진]하다   · exposure ⓝ (유해한 환경 등에의) 노출[접함]
· contaminant ⓝ 오염 물질   · breathing ⓝ 호흡
· polluted ⓐ 오염된, 더럽혀진   · chemically ⓐⓓ 화학적으로
· circumstance ⓝ 상황, 환경   · involuntary ⓐ 자기도 모르게 하는
· reduction ⓝ 감소   · elimination ⓝ 제거   · societal ⓐ 사회의
· public ⓐ 대중의, 공공의   · awareness ⓝ (중요성에 대한) 의식, 인식
· measure ⓝ 조치, 정책   · morally ⓐⓓ 도덕적으로
· arsenic ⓝ ((화학)) 비소(砒素)   · passively ⓐⓓ 수동적으로
· outrage ⓥ 격분[격노]하게 만들다

환경 위험 요인에는 노출을 조장하거나 허용하는 인간의 행동과 함께 생물학적, 물리적, 화학적 위험 요인이 포함된다. (오염된 공기의 호흡, 화학적으로 오염된 공공 식수의 음용, 개방된 공공장소에서의 소음처럼) 일부 환경오염 물질은 피하기가 어렵고, 이러한 상황에서 노출은 대개 자기도 모르게 이루어진다. 이러한 요인의 감소 또는 제거에는 대중의 인식 및 공중보건 조치와 같은 사회적 조치가 필요할 수도 있다. 많은 국가에서, 일부 환경적 위험 요인이 개인 수준에서 피하기 어렵다는 사실은 피할 수 있는 그 위험 요인보다도 도덕적으로 더 나쁘다고 느껴진다. 어쩔 수 없이 매우 높은 수준의 비소로 오염된 물을 마실 수밖에 없는 것이나, 식당에서 담배 연기를 수동적으로 들이마시도록 강요당하는 것은 개인이 담배를 피울지에 대한 개인적인 선택보다 더 사람들을 화나게 한다. 이러한 요인들은 변화(위험 감소)가 어떻게 일어나는지를 고려할 때 중요하다.

다음 글의 요지로 가장 적절한 것은?

① 개인이 피하기 어려운 유해 환경 요인에 대해서는 사회적 대응이 필요하다.
— Reduction or elimination of these factors may require societal action
② 환경오염으로 인한 피해자들에게 적절한 보상을 하는 것이 바람직하다.
— 보상에 대한 언급은 없음
③ 다수의 건강을 해치는 행위에 대해 도덕적 비난 이상의 조치가 요구된다.
— more morally egregious로 만든 오답
④ 환경오염 문제를 해결하기 위해서는 사후 대응이 중요하다.
— 환경적 위험 요인을 예방하는 것이 아님
⑤ 대기오염 문제는 인접 국가들과의 긴밀한 협력을 통해 해결할 수 있다.
— In many countries로 만든 오답

왜 정답? [정답률 84%]

일부 환경오염 물질에 대한 노출은 자기도 모르게 이루어지기 때문에 피하기가 어렵다면서 개인 수준에서 피하기 어려운 이러한 환경적 위험 물질을 감소시키거나 제거하는 데는 사회적 조치가 필요하다는 내용이므로 정답은 ①이다.

왜 오답?

② 오염된 공기의 호흡이나 화학적으로 오염된 공공 식수의 음용으로부터 피해를 입은 사람들에게 적절한 보상을 해야 한다는 것이 아니다.
③ 개인 수준에서 피하기 어려운 환경적 위험 요인에 대해서는 사회적인 조치가 필요하다는 내용으로, 다수의 건강을 해치는 행위에 사회적 조치를 해야 한다는 것이 아니다. 주의
④ 환경오염 문제에 있어서의 사후 대응과 예방을 대조하여 설명하는 글이 아니다.
⑤ 많은 국가에서 사람들이 일부 환경적 위험 요인은 개인 수준에서 피하기 어렵다는 사실을 피할 수 있는 위험 요인보다 도덕적으로 더 나쁘게 느낀다는 문장에서 언급된 many countries로 만든 오답이다. 국가 간 긴밀한 협력에 대한 언급은 없다.

E 12 정답 ④ *스포츠를 어떻게 정의하느냐가 미치는 영향

Official definitions of sport / have important implications. //
스포츠에 대한 공식적인 정의는 / 중요한 함의를 갖는다 //
When a definition emphasizes / rules, competition, and high
performance, /
단서1 스포츠에 대한 정의가 규칙, 경쟁, 높은 기량을 강조할 때 생기는 일을 설명함
정의가 강조할 때 / 규칙, 경쟁, 높은 기량을 /
— 병렬 구조
many people will be excluded from participation / or avoid
other physical activities / that are defined as "second class." //
많은 사람이 참여에서 배제되거나 / 다른 신체 활동을 피할 것이다 / '이류'로 정의되는 //
For example, / when a 12-year-old is cut / from an exclusive club
soccer team, /
예를 들어 / 12세의 선수가 잘리면 / 상위 클럽 축구팀에서 /

E

she may not want to play / in the local league / because she sees
^{see A as B: A를 B로 여기다}
_{rather than으로 연결된 명사구}
it / as "recreational activity" / rather than a real sport. //
그 선수는 뛰고 싶지 않을 수도 있다 / 지역 리그에서 / 왜냐하면 그 선수가 그것을 보기 때문
에 / '레크리에이션 활동'으로 / 진정한 스포츠라기보다 //
_{선행사} _{관계부사로 바꾸어 쓸 수 있는 「전치사+관계대명사」}
This can create a situation / in which most people are physically
inactive / at the same time / that a small number of people
_{관계부사}
perform / at relatively high levels / for large numbers of fans /
이것은 상황을 만들 수 있다 / 대부분의 사람이 신체적으로 활동적이지 않은 / 동시에 / 소수의
사람이 시합을 하는 / 상대적으로 높은 수준에서 / 많은 수의 팬을 위해 /
— a situation / that negatively impacts health / and increases
_{선행사} _{관계대명사}
health-care costs / in a society or community. //
상황 / 건강에 부정적인 영향을 주고 / 의료비를 증가시키는 / 사회나 지역사회에 //
When sport is defined / to include a wide range of physical
_{병렬 구조}
activities / that are played for pleasure / and integrated / into
local expressions of social life, / 단서2 스포츠의 정의가 즐거움을 위한 신체 활동을
포함할 때 생기는 일을 설명함
스포츠가 정의될 때 / 광범위한 신체 활동을 포함하도록 / 즐거움을 위해 행해지는 / 그리고 융
합될 때 / 사회생활의 지역적인 표현들로 /
physical activity rates will be high / and overall health benefits
are likely. //
신체 활동 비율이 높을 것이다 / 그리고 전반적인 건강상의 이점이 있을 수 있다 //

- -
- definition ⓝ 정의　　· implication ⓝ 함의, 내포된 뜻
- emphasize ⓥ 강조하다　　· exclude ⓥ 배제하다
- exclusive ⓐ 상위의, 상류의, 고급의　　· inactive ⓐ 활동적이지 않은
- relatively ⓐⓓ 상대적으로　　· negatively ⓐⓓ 부정적으로
- integrate ⓥ 융합하다, 통합하다　　· overall ⓐ 전반적인
- benefit ⓝ 이점　　· likely ⓐ 가능성이 있는

스포츠에 대한 공식적인 정의는 중요한 함의를 갖는다. 정의가 규칙, 경쟁, 높
은 기량을 강조할 때 많은 사람이 참여에서 배제되거나 '이류'로 정의되는 다른
신체 활동을 피할 것이다. 예를 들어 12세의 선수가 상위 클럽 축구팀에서 잘리
면 그 선수는 지역 리그에서 뛰고 싶지 않을 수도 있는데, 그 선수가 그것을 진
정한 스포츠라기보다 '레크리에이션 활동'으로 보기 때문이다. 이것은 소수의
사람이 많은 수의 팬을 위해 상대적으로 높은 수준의 시합을 하는 것과 동시에
대부분의 사람이 신체적으로 활동적이지 않은 상황, 즉 건강에 부정적인 영향을
주고 사회나 지역사회에 의료비를 증가시키는 상황을 만들 수 있다. 스포츠가
즐거움을 위해 행해지는 광범위한 신체 활동을 포함하도록 정의되고 사회생활
의 지역적인 표현들로 융합될 때 신체 활동 비율이 높을 것이고 전반적인 건강
상의 이점이 있을 수 있다.

다음 글의 요지로 가장 적절한 것은?
① 운동선수의 기량은 경기 자체를 즐길 때 향상된다.
　운동선수의 기량에 대한 글이 아님
② 공정한 승부를 위해 합리적인 경기 규칙이 필요하다.
　경기 규칙이 합리적일 때와 그렇지 않을 때를 설명한 것이 아님
③ 스포츠의 대중화는 스포츠 산업의 정의를 바꾸고 있다.
　스포츠에 대한 정의가 미치는 영향을 설명함
④ 스포츠의 정의는 신체 활동 참여와 건강에 영향을 미친다.
　스포츠에 대한 정의에 따라 많은 사람이 운동을 하거나 하지 않게 됨
⑤ 활발한 여가 활동은 원만한 대인 관계 유지에 도움이 된다.
　여가 활동과 대인 관계의 상관성을 설명한 것이 아님

>왜 정답? [정답률 70%]
스포츠에 대한 정의가 규칙, 경쟁, 높은 기량을 강조할 때는 많은 사람들이 스포츠
에 대한 참여에서 배제되거나 이류로 정의되는 신체 활동을 피하게 되어 건강에 부
정적인 영향을 주고 의료비를 증가시키는 상황이 야기될 수 있지만, 스포츠가 즐거
움을 위한 신체 활동을 포함하도록 정의되면 신체 활동 비율이 높고 전반적인 건강
상의 이점이 있을 것이라는 내용이므로 이 글의 요지는 ④이다.

>왜 오답?
① 운동선수의 기량 향상에 대해 설명한 글이 아니다.
② 합리적인 경기 규칙의 필요성을 다룬 내용이 아니다. ┌─영향을 미친다는 것인지,
③ 스포츠의 정의가 미치는 영향에 대한 글로, 스포츠의 대중화로 │영향을 받는다는 것인지를
  인해 스포츠 산 │반대로 파악하면 안 됨!
  업의 정의가 영향을 받는다는 것이 아니다. 꿀팁
⑤ 여가 활동과 대인 관계의 상관성에 대한 언급은 없다.

어법 특강
＊「전치사+관계대명사」와 관계부사
– 관계대명사가 전치사의 목적어로 쓰인 경우 「전치사+관계대명사」의 형태로 쓰거
  나, 전치사는 원래 있는 자리에 그대로 있을 수 있다. 선행사가 시간, 장소, 이유,
  방법을 나타낼 때 「전치사+관계대명사」는 관계부사 when, where, why, how로
  쓸 수 있다.
- I want to visit the town. + The movie was filmed in the town.
  (나는 그 마을에 가고 싶다.)　　　(그 영화는 그 마을에서 촬영되었다.)
- I want to visit the town in which the movie was filmed.
  _{전치사+관계대명사}
- I want to visit the town where the movie was filmed.
  _{관계부사(관계부사 앞에 전치사를 쓰면 안 된다.)}
  (나는 그 영화가 촬영되었던 그 마을에 가보고 싶다.)

E 13 정답 ⑤ ＊아이들의 성장에 있어 음악의 중요성

Music is a human art form, / an inseparable part of the human
experience / everywhere in the world. //
음악은 인간의 예술 형태이다 / 인간 경험에서 분리할 수 없는 부분 / 세계 어디에서나 //
Music is social, / and tightly woven into the tapestry of life, /
and young children are very much a part / of this multifaceted
fabric. //
음악은 사회적이며 / 삶의 색색의 실로 수놓은 장식 걸개에 촘촘히 짜여 들어가는데 / 어린아
이들이 매우 중요한 부분이다 / 이 다면적인 직물의 //
_{앞에 목적격 관계대명사가 생략됨}
The musical experiences / they have / provide opportunities /
_{형용사적 용법(opportunities 수식)}
for them to know / language, behaviors, customs, traditions,
_{to know의 의미상의 주어}
beliefs, values, stories, and other cultural nuances. //
음악적 경험은 / 그들이 갖는 / 기회를 제공한다 / 그들이 알 수 있는 / 언어, 행동, 관습, 전통,
믿음, 가치, 이야기, 그리고 다른 문화적 뉘앙스를 // 단서1 음악적 경험은 아이들이 사회 · 문화적
가치를 알 수 있는 기회를 제공함
_{접속사}
As they become musically skilled / through experiences / in
_{전치사}
song and instrumental music, / young children can also grow /
cultural knowledge and sensitivity. // 단서2 음악을 통해 아이들이 문화적 지식과
감수성을 기를 수 있음
그들이 음악적으로 숙련되면서 / 경험을 통해 / 노래와 기악곡에서의 / 어린아이들은 또한 기
를 수 있다 / 문화적 지식과 감수성을 //
Music is an extremely important aspect of culture, / shaping and
transmitting the above-mentioned aspects / that characterize
groups of people. //
음악은 문화의 극히 중요한 측면이며 / 위에서 언급한 측면들을 형성하고 전달한다 / 사람들
의 집단을 특징짓는 //
_{동명사구 주어}
Exposing young children / to the world's musical cultures /
_{단수 동사}
brings them into the cultural conversation, /
어린 아이들을 노출시키는 것은 / 세계의 음악 문화에 / 그들을 문화적 대화에 끌어들여 /
allowing them to learn / about self and others / in an artistically
_{명사적 용법(allowing의 목적격 보어)}
meaningful and engaging way. //
그들이 배우게 한다 / 자신과 다른 사람들에 대해 / 예술적으로 의미 있고 매력적인 방식으
로 //
_{선행사}
Prior to the development / of social biases and cultural
_{주격 관계대명사}
preferences / that all too easily turn into prejudices, /
발달에 앞서서 / 사회적 편향과 문화적 선호의 / 너무나도 쉽게 편견으로 변하는 /
_{주어} _{형용사적 용법(the opportunity 수식)}
the opportunity / to know people / through song, dance, and
instrument play /
기회는 / 사람들을 아는 / 노래, 춤, 악기 연주를 통해 /
_{동사 주격 보어 선행사 주격 관계대명사}
is a gift to all / who work for the well-balanced development /
of young children / into the responsible citizens / they will one
day become. // 단서3 음악은 아이들의 책임감 있는 시민으로의 균형 있는
발달을 가져오는 선물임
모든 이들에게 선물이다 / 균형 있는 발달을 위해 노력하는 / 어린아이들의 / 책임감 있는 시민
으로 / 그들이 언젠가 될 //

- -
- inseparable ⓐ 분리할 수 없는
- weave ⓥ (옷감 · 바구니 등을) 짜대[엮다], 짜서[엮어서] 만들다
- fabric ⓝ 직물, 천　　· skilled ⓐ 숙련된, 노련한
- sensitivity ⓝ 감수성　　· extremely ⓐⓓ 극도로, 극히
- aspect ⓝ 측면, 양상　　· transmit ⓥ 전달하다
- characterize ⓥ 특징짓다

- expose ⓥ 접하게[경험하게] 하다, (유해한 환경 등에) 노출시키다
- artistically ㏏ 예술[미술]적으로 ・ meaningful ⓐ 의미 있는, 중요한
- engaging ⓐ 호감이 가는, 매력적인 ・ prior to ~에 앞서, ~보다 먼저
- bias ⓝ 편향, 치우친 생각 ・ preference ⓝ 선호, 애호
- prejudice ⓝ 편견

음악은 인간의 예술 형태로서, 세계 어디에서나 인간 경험에서 분리할 수 없는 부분이다. 음악은 사회적이며, 삶의 색색의 실로 수놓은 장식 걸개에 촘촘히 짜여 들어가는데, 어린아이들이 이 다면적인 직물의 매우 중요한 부분이다. 그들이 갖는 음악적 경험은 그들이 언어, 행동, 관습, 전통, 믿음, 가치, 이야기, 그리고 다른 문화적 뉘앙스를 알 수 있는 기회를 제공한다. 노래와 기악곡에서의 경험을 통해 음악적으로 숙련되면서, 어린아이들은 또한 문화적 지식과 감수성을 기를 수 있다. 음악은 문화의 극히 중요한 측면이며, 사람들의 집단을 특징 짓는 위에서 언급한 측면들을 형성하고 전달한다. 어린 아이들을 세계의 음악 문화에 접하게 하는 것은 그들을 문화적 대화에 끌어들여, 예술적으로 의미 있고 매력적인 방식으로 자신과 다른 사람들에 대해 배우게 한다. 너무나도 쉽게 편견으로 변하는 사회적 편향과 문화적 선호의 발달에 앞서서, 노래, 춤, 악기 연주를 통해 사람들을 알 수 있는 기회를 갖게 하는 것은 어린아이들이 언젠가 될 책임감 있는 시민으로 균형 있게 발달하도록 해주기 위해 노력하는 모든 이들에게 선물이다.

다음 글의 요지로 가장 적절한 것은?
① 아이들의 균형 잡힌 성장을 위해서는 다양한 경험이 중요하다.
　음악적 경험의 중요성을 다룸
② 사회적 편견과 문화적 선호도는 서로 밀접하게 관련되어 있다.
　'음악'에 대한 언급이 있어야 함
③ 어린 나이에 다양한 음악에 노출되면 예술적 감각이 향상된다.
　예술적 감각의 향상이 목적이 아님
④ 음악을 포함한 예술은 특정 문화에 대한 당대의 사회적 시각을 반영한다.
　'아이들'에 대한 언급이 있어야 함
⑤ 음악은 아이들을 사회·문화적으로 균형 잡힌 시민으로 성장하게 해 준다.
　아이들의 책임감 있는 시민으로의 균형적 발달에 있어서의 음악의 중요성

▷왜 정답? [정답률 93%]

음악적 경험이 아이들에게 관습, 전통, 믿음 등의 사회·문화적 요소에 대해 알 수 있는 기회를 제공하며, 음악을 통해 아이들이 문화적 지식과 감수성을 기를 수 있다고 했다. 마지막 문장에서는 음악을 통해 사람들을 알 수 있는 기회가 아이들의 책임감 있는 시민으로의 균형 잡힌 발달을 위한 선물이라고 했으므로 이 글의 요지는 ⑤이다.

▷왜 오답?
① 다양한 경험이 아니라 음악적 경험의 중요성을 강조하는 글이다.
② 사회적 편견과 문화적 선호의 발달에 앞서 음악을 통해 사람들을 알 수 있는 기회를 아이들에게 주라는 것이 요지이다.
③ 예술적 감각의 향상을 위해 음악적 경험을 갖게 하라는 것이 아니다.
④ 예술 전반에 걸친 설명이 아니라 음악에 대해서만 이야기하는 글로, '아이들'에 관한 언급이 있어야 정답이 될 수 있다.

> 핵심 소재인 '음악'과 '아이들'이 요지에 꼭 포함되어야 함 [꿀팁]

E 14 정답 ⑤ ＊조세 입법에서 도덕적 목표 설정의 중요성

Historically, / drafters of tax legislation are attentive / to questions of economics and history, / and less attentive / to moral questions. //
역사적으로 / 조세 입법 입안자들은 주의를 기울이고 / 경제학과 역사 문제에 / 주의를 덜 기울인다 / 도덕적 질문에는 //

Questions of morality are often pushed to the side / in legislative debate, / labeled / too controversial, / too difficult to answer, / or, worst of all, / irrelevant to the project. //
　　　　　　　　　　　　　　　　　　부사적 용법(too difficult 수식)
도덕성에 관한 질문은 종종 옆으로 밀려나면서 / 입법 토론에서 / 분류된다 / 너무 논란이 많거나 / 답변하기 너무 어렵거나 / 아니면 최악의 경우 / 계획과 무관한 것으로 //

　　　　주어　　　　　　　　　　　　동사　　〈장소〉의 부사구
But, in fact, / the moral questions of taxation / are at the very heart / of the creation of tax laws. // [단서1] 조세의 도덕적 문제는 세법을 만드는 것의 핵심에 있음
하지만 사실 / 조세의 도덕적 문제는 / 핵심에 있다 / 세법의 창조의 //

Rather than irrelevant, / moral questions are fundamental / to the imposition of tax. // [단서2] 도덕적 질문은 세금 부과에 근본적임
무관한 것이 아니라 / 도덕적 질문은 근본적이다 / 세금 부과에 //

Tax is the application / of a society's theories / of distributive justice. //
　　　　　　　　　　〈소유·소속〉을 나타냄　　　　　〈주제·관련〉을 나타냄
세금은 적용이다 / 사회의 이론의 / 분배 정의에 대한 //

　　　　　　　　　　　　　　　　　　　　helping의 목적어와 목적격 보어
Economics can go a long way / towards helping a legislature determine /
　　　　　　　　'유용하다'
경제학은 큰 도움이 될 수 있지만 / 입법부가 결정하는 것을 돕는 것에 /
　　　　　　　　　　　　　　　　　　will help의 목적어로 쓰인 원형부정사
whether or not a particular tax law will help / achieve a
원형부정사 determine의 목적어절 접속사
particular goal, / but economics cannot, in a vacuum, identify the goal. //
　　　　　　　　　　　　　　　　　　　　　　'외부와 단절되어'
특정 세법이 도움이 될지 아닐지를 / 특정 목표를 달성하는 데 / 경제학만으로는 목표를 규명할 수 없다 // [단서3] 조세 정책의 수립은 도덕적 목표의 규명을 요구함

Creating tax policy requires / identifying a moral goal, / which is a task / that must involve / ethics and moral analysis. //
조세 정책을 만드는 것은 요구하는데 / 도덕적 목표를 규명하는 것을 / 그것은 과업이다 / 수반해야 하는 / 윤리학과 도덕적 분석을 //

- drafter ⓝ (계획·문서 등의) 입안자
- attentive ⓐ 주의를 기울이는, 신경을 쓰는 ・ moral ⓐ 도덕상의, 도의적인
- morality ⓝ 도덕(성) ・ legislative ⓐ 입법의, 입법부의
- debate ⓝ 토론, 논쟁 ・ controversial ⓐ 논란이 많은
- irrelevant ⓐ 무관심한, 상관없는 ・ taxation ⓝ 조세, 과세 제도
- fundamental ⓐ 근본적인, 핵심적인 ・ application ⓝ 적용, 응용, 신청(서)
- distributive ⓐ 분배의, 유통의 ・ justice ⓝ 정의, 공정성
- legislature ⓝ 입법 기관, 입법부 ・ identify ⓥ 확인하다, 발견하다
- policy ⓝ 정책, 방침 ・ ethics ⓝ 윤리학 ・ analysis ⓝ 분석

역사적으로, 조세 입법 입안자들은 경제학과 역사 문제에 주의를 기울이고 도덕적 질문에는 주의를 덜 기울인다. 도덕성에 관한 질문은 종종 입법 토론에서 옆으로 밀려나면서, 너무 논란이 많거나, 답변하기 너무 어렵거나, 아니면 최악의 경우, 계획과 무관한 것으로 분류된다. 하지만, 사실, 조세의 도덕적 문제는 세법을 만드는 핵심에 있다. 무관한 것이 아니라, 도덕적 질문은 세금 부과에 근본적이다. 세금은 사회의 분배 정의 이론을 적용한 것이다. 경제학은 입법부가 특정 세법이 특정 목표를 달성하는 데 도움이 될지를 결정하는 것을 돕는 것에 큰 도움이 될 수 있지만, 경제학만으로는 목표를 규명할 수 없다. 조세 정책을 만드는 것은 도덕적 목표를 규명하는 것을 요구하는데, 그것은 윤리학과 도덕적 분석을 수반해야 하는 과업이다.

다음 글의 요지로 가장 적절한 것은?
① 분배 정의를 실현하려면 시민 단체의 역할이 필요하다.
　시민 단체의 역할은 언급되지 않음
② 사회적 합의는 민주적인 정책 수립의 선행 조건이다.
　'세법'에 대한 걸림
③ 성실한 납세는 안정적인 정부 예산 확보의 기반이다.
　성실한 납세의 중요성에 대한 내용이 아님
④ 경제학은 세법을 개정할 때 이론적 근거를 제공한다.
　경제학의 역할을 강조하는 글이 아님
⑤ 세법을 만들 때 도덕적 목표를 설정하는 것이 중요하다.
　Creating tax policy requires identifying a moral goal

▷왜 정답? [정답률 92%]

조세 입법 입안자들이 경제학과 역사 문제에는 주의를 기울이지만 도덕적 질문에는 주의를 덜 기울인다면서, 사실 조세의 도덕적 문제가 세법을 만드는 것의 핵심에 있다고 했다.
또한 도덕적 질문은 세금 부과에 근본적이며, 조세 정책을 만드는 것은 도덕적 목표를 규명하는 것을 요구한다고 했으므로 정답은 ⑤이다.

▷왜 오답?
① a society's theories of distributive justice가 언급된 것으로 만든 오답이다. 시민 단체의 역할에 대해서는 언급되지 않았다.
② 일반적인 정책 수립에 대한 내용이 아니라, 조세 정책이라는 특정 정책에 대해 이야기하는 글이다.
③ 안정적인 정부 예산의 확보를 위해 성실히 납세해야 한다는 등의 내용이 아니다.
④ 조세 입법에 있어 경제학이 어떤 면에서는 큰 도움을 줄 수 있다는 언급으로 만든 오답이다. 해당 문장에서는 경제학만으로는 목표를 규명할 수 없다는 설명이 핵심이다. [주의]

E 15 정답 ⑤ ＊생태계 관리 시 고려할 사항

In order to be successful and equitable, / ecosystem management
〈의무〉를 나타내는 조동사
must be linked / to poverty reduction. // 단서1 생태계 관리는 빈곤 감소와
연결되어야 함
성공적이고 공평하기 위해서 / 생태계 관리는 연결되어야 한다 / 빈곤 감소와 //

Urban infrastructure projects / need to address the trade-offs
/ between conservation, livelihoods, and equitable distribution
of resources. //
도시 기반 시설 프로젝트는 / 교환을 다루어야 한다 / 보존, 생계, 그리고 자원의 공평한 분배
사이의 //

Historically there has been tension / when conservation models
부사절 접속사(때)   복수 주어
/ that create protected areas / are perceived / as inaccessible to
복수 동사
communities. //
역사적으로 긴장이 있어 왔다 / 보존 모델이 / 보호 구역을 만드는 / 인식될 때 / 지역사회에게
접근할 수 없는 것으로 //

Often, these models are implemented / at the expense / of poor
and marginalized residents / and users of resources / from the
areas. // 단서2 보호 구역을 만드는 보존 모델은 흔히 가난하고 소외된 거주자,
그 지역에서 나는 자원의 사용자의 희생으로 실행됨
흔히 이러한 모델은 실행된다 / 희생으로 / 가난하고 소외된 거주자의 / 그리고 자원의
사용자의 / 그 지역에서 나는 //

Social, economic, and environmental development programs /
전치사   명사구
have become obstacles / to sustainable development /
사회적인, 경제적인, 그리고 환경적인 개발 프로그램은 / 장애물이 되어 왔다 / 지속 가능한
발전의 /
형용사적 용법(the need 수식)
because there is no balance / between the need to protect
ecosystem services / and the desire to use resources / to address
형용사적 용법(the desire 수식)
community needs. //
균형이 없기 때문에 / 생태계 서비스를 보호할 필요성과 / 자원을 사용하려는 욕구 사이의 /
지역사회의 요구를 다루기 위해 //   단서3 지역사회는 자신이 선택할 수 있는 것들을
파악하여 협상하도록 허락되어야 함
Communities need to be allowed / to identify and negotiate
their own options / and to increase their flexibility / to cope with
unexpected change. //
지역사회는 허락되어야 한다 / 자신이 선택할 수 있는 것들을 파악하여 협상하고 / 자신의
유연성을 높이도록 / 예상치 못한 변화에 대처하는 //

- ecosystem ⓝ 생태계   · management ⓝ 관리
- be linked to ~와 연결되다   · infrastructure ⓝ 사회 기반 시설
- address ⓥ 다루다   · trade-off ⓝ 교환, 균형
- conservation ⓝ 보존   · livelihood ⓝ 생계
- distribution ⓝ 분배   · implement ⓥ 실행하다
- at the expense of ~의 희생으로   · marginalized ⓐ 소외된
- obstacle ⓝ 장애물   · sustainable ⓐ 지속 가능한
- identify ⓥ 확인하다   · negotiate ⓥ 협상하다
- flexibility ⓝ 유연성   · cope with ~에 대처하다
- unexpected ⓐ 예상치 못한

성공적이고 공평하기 위해서, 생태계 관리는 빈곤 감소와 연결되어야
한다. 도시 기반 시설 프로젝트는 보존, 생계, 그리고 자원의 공평한 분배
사이의 교환을 다루어야 한다. 역사적으로 보호 구역을 만드는 보존 모델이
지역사회에게 접근할 수 없는 것으로 인식될 때 긴장이 있어 왔다. 흔히,
이러한 모델은 가난하고 소외된 거주자와 그 지역에서 나는 자원의 사용자의
희생으로 실행된다. 생태계 서비스를 보호할 필요성과 지역사회의 요구를
다루기 위해 자원을 사용하려는 욕구 사이의 균형이 없기 때문에 사회적인,
경제적인, 그리고 환경적인 개발 프로그램은 지속 가능한 발전의 장애물이
되어 왔다. 지역사회가 자신이 선택할 수 있는 것들을 파악하여 협상하고
예상치 못한 변화에 대처할 수 있는 자신의 유연성을 높이도록 해야 한다.

다음 글의 요지로 가장 적절한 것은?

① 무분별한 도시 개발은 사회적 양극화를 심화한다.
생태계 관리에 대한 내용임
② 도시 기반 시설 확충 시 안정적인 재정 지원이 중요하다.
Urban infrastructure projects로 만든 오답
③ 인근 지역 간의 긴밀한 협력은 생태계 보존의 기반이 된다.
지역 간 협력이 중요하다는 것이 아님
④ 자원의 순환과 공정한 배분은 지속가능한 발전의 필수조건이다.
성공적이고 공평한 생태계 관리가 목표임
⑤ 생태계 관리 시 빈곤층을 포함한 지역사회의 요구를 고려할 필요가 있다.
가난하고 소외된 거주자의 희생으로 실행되는 것을 비판함

왜 정답? [정답률 55%]

첫 문장	성공적이고 공평하기 위해서, 생태계 관리는 빈곤 감소와 연결되어야 한다.
문제점	보호 구역을 만드는 것은 흔히 가난하고 소외된 거주자와 그 지역에서 나는 자원의 사용자의 희생으로 실행됨
해결 방안	지역사회는 자신이 선택할 수 있는 것들을 파악하여 협상하고 예상치 못한 변화에 대처하는 자신의 유연성을 높이도록 허락되어야 함

➡ 보호 구역 지정(생태계 관리)이 성공적이고 공평하려면 빈곤 감소와 연결되어야
하는데, 흔히 가난하고 소외된 거주자와 그 지역에서 나는 자원의 사용자의
희생으로 실행된다는 문제점이 있다.
▶ 보호 구역 지정에 있어 지역사회는 자신이 선택할 수 있는 것들을 파악하여
협상하도록 허락되어야 한다는 것이 글의 요지이므로 정답은 ⑤

왜 오답?

① 도시 개발이 가져오는 문제점에 대해 설명하는 글이 아니다.
② 생태계 관리에 있어 중요한 것이 무엇인지를 이야기하는 글이다.
③ 인근 지역 간의 긴밀한 협력이 중요하다는 내용은 없다.
④ 성공적이고 공평한 생태계 관리를 위해 필요한 것을 설명하는 글이다.

E 16 정답 ① ＊수동적 방관자에서 능동적 참여자로

Often overlooked, / but just as important a stakeholder, / is the
consumer / who plays a large role / in the notion of the privacy
동격의 전치사
paradox. //
흔히 간과되지만 / 못지않게 중요한 이해관계자는 / 소비자이다 / 큰 역할을 하는 / 개인정보
역설이라는 개념에서 //   복수 주어
Consumer engagement levels / in all manner of digital
experiences and communities / have simply exploded / — and
준부정어(거의 ~ 없는) 완전 부정어(전혀 ~ 없는) 복수 동사
they show little or no signs of slowing. //
소비자의 참여 수준은 / 모든 방식의 디지털 경험과 공동체에서 / 그야말로 폭발적으로 증가해
왔으며 / 둔화될 기미가 거의 또는 전혀 보이지 않는다 //
not only A but also B로 연결된 동격절 접속사 ①
There is an awareness / among consumers, / not only that their
personal data helps / to drive the rich experiences / that these
생략 가능한 목적격 관계대명사
companies provide, /
인식이 있다 / 소비자들 사이에서는 / 자신들의 개인정보가 도움이 된다는 것뿐만 아니라 /
풍부한 경험을 추진하는 데 / 이러한 회사들이 제공하는 /
앞에 목적격 관계대명사가 생략됨
but also that sharing this data is the price / you pay for these
동격절 접속사 ②
experiences, / in whole or in part. //
이 정보를 공유하는 것이 대가이기도 하다는 / 여러분이 이러한 경험에 대해 지불하는 /
전체로든 부분으로든   단서1 개인정보의 수집, 이용의 속성을 더 잘 이해하지
조건절의 if절을 대신하는 전치사   않으면 소비자는 취약하다는 느낌을 받게 됨
Without a better understanding / of the what, when, and why
of data collection and use, / the consumer is often left / feeling
vulnerable and conflicted. //
더 훌륭한 이해가 없다면 / 정보 수집 및 이용의 내용, 시기, 그리고 이유에 대한 / 소비자는
흔히 남겨진다 / 취약하고 갈등을 겪는다고 느끼도록 //

"I love this restaurant-finder app on my phone, / but what
happens to my data / if I press 'ok' / when asked / if that app
부사절 접속사   주어와 be동사가 생략됨 명사절 접속사
can use my current location?" //
'나는 내 전화기에 있는 이 식당 검색 앱이 마음에 드는데 / 내 정보에 무슨 일이 생기는 걸까 /
내가 'ok'를 누르면 / 질문받을 때 / 그 앱이 내 현재 위치를 이용할 수 있느냐고' //

Armed with tools / that can provide them options, / the consumer moves / from passive bystander to active participant. //
도구로 무장하여 / 그들에게 선택권을 제공할 수 있는 / 소비자는 이동한다 / 수동적 방관자에서 능동적 참여자로 // 단서2 선택권을 제공하는 도구로 무장함으로써 능동적 참여자가 됨

- notion ⓝ 개념, 생각
- privacy ⓝ 사생활, 비밀
- paradox ⓝ 역설
- engagement ⓝ 참여
- manner ⓝ 방식, 태도
- explode ⓥ 폭발하다
- awareness ⓝ (중요성에 대한) 의식[관심]
- rich ⓐ 풍부한
- conflicted ⓐ 갈등을 겪는
- current ⓐ 현재의
- armed ⓐ 무장한
- passive ⓐ 수동적인, 소극적인
- bystander ⓝ 구경꾼, 행인

흔히 간과되지만 못지않게 중요한 이해관계자는 개인정보 역설이라는 개념에서 큰 역할을 하는 소비자이다. 모든 방식의 디지털 경험과 공동체에서 소비자의 참여 수준은 그야말로 폭발적으로 증가해 왔으며, 둔화될 기미가 거의 또는 전혀 보이지 않는다. 소비자들 사이에서는 이러한 회사들이 제공하는 풍부한 경험을 추진하는 데 자신들의 개인정보가 도움이 된다는 것뿐만 아니라, 이 정보를 공유하는 것이 전체로든 부분으로든, 이러한 경험에 대해 지불하는 대가이기도 하다는 인식이 있다. 정보 수집 및 이용의 내용과 시기, 이유에 대해 더 잘 이해하지 못할 경우, 소비자는 흔히 취약하고 갈등을 겪는다는 느낌을 받게 된다. '내 전화기에 있는 이 식당 검색 앱이 마음에 드는데, 그 앱이 내 현재 위치를 이용할 수 있느냐고 물을 때 'ok'를 누르면 내 정보에 무슨 일이 생기는 걸까?' 그들에게 선택권을 제공할 수 있는 도구로 무장한 소비자는 수동적 방관자에서 능동적 참여자로 이동한다.

다음 글의 요지로 가장 적절한 것은?
① 개인정보 제공의 속성을 심층적으로 이해하면 주체적 소비자가 된다.
   이해를 못하면 취약하다는 느낌을 받게 됨
② 소비자는 디지털 시대에 유용한 앱을 적극 활용하는 자세가 필요하다.
③ 현명한 소비자가 되려면 다양한 디지털 데이터를 활용해야 한다.
   개인정보에 대한 글임
④ 기업의 디지털 서비스를 이용하면 상응하는 대가가 뒤따른다.
   the price you pay for these experiences로 만든 오답
⑤ 타인과의 정보 공유로 인해 개인정보가 유출되기도 한다.
   개인정보 유출을 우려하는 것이 아님

왜 정답? [정답률 62%]
개인정보의 수집 및 이용의 내용, 시기, 이유에 대해 더 잘 이해하지 못하면 소비자는 취약하고 갈등을 겪는다는 느낌을 받게 된다고 했다.
반대로 개인정보 수집의 속성을 더 잘 이해하고, 개인정보 제공 여부에 대한 선택권을 가짐으로써 소비자는 능동적 참여자가 될 수 있다고 했으므로 정답은 ①이다.

왜 오답?
②, ③ 현명한 소비자는 개인정보 제공의 속성을 잘 이해하고 자신에게 선택권을 제공하는 도구로 무장함으로써 수동적 방관자에서 능동적 참여자로 이동한다는 것이 핵심이다.
④ 우리의 개인정보는 회사에서 제공하는 경험에 대해 우리가 지불하는 대가이기도 하다는 것을 소비자들이 인식하고 있다는 언급으로 만든 오답이다. 주의
⑤ '개인정보'에 관한 내용인 것은 맞지만, 어떻게 해서 개인정보가 유출되는지를 설명한 것은 아니다.

E 17 정답 ② ＊인간 지능의 진화를 가져온 것

부사적 용법(목적)   선행사   주격 관계대명사
To overcome death / as the obstacle / that was hindering / the evolution of human intelligence, /
죽음을 극복하기 위해 / 장애물로서의 / 방해하고 있었던 / 인간 지능의 진화를 /
                          선행사   주격 관계대명사
our ancestors developed the killer app / that propelled our species forward, / ahead of all others: / namely, spoken and written language / in words and maths. //
우리 조상들은 킬러 앱을 개발했다 / 우리 종족을 앞으로 나아가게 했던 / 다른 모든 것들을 능가하여 / 즉 말과 글 / 말과 수학에서의 // 단서1 인간 지능이 진화하는 것을 방해하는 죽음을 극복한 것이 말과 글, 즉 의사소통임

I believe / communication was, and still is, / our most valuable invention. //
                                        was와 is의 주격 보어
나는 믿는다 / 의사소통이 ~이었고 여전히 ~이라고 / 우리의 가장 가치 있는 발명 // 단서2 의사소통이 인간의 가장 가치 있는 발명임
                병렬 구조(has helped의 목적격 보어로 쓰인 원형부정사)
It has helped us / preserve the knowledge, learning, discoveries and intelligence / we have gained / and pass them on / from person to person / and from generation to generation. //
그것은 우리에게 도움을 주어 왔다 / 지식, 학습, 발견 그리고 지능을 보존하고 / 우리가 얻어 온 / 그것들을 물려주도록 / 개인에서 개인으로 / 그리고 대대로 //
                Imagine의 목적어절 접속사
Imagine / if Einstein had had no way / of telling the rest of us / about his remarkable understanding / of the theory of relativity. // 단서3 의사소통은 인간이 얻은 지식, 발견, 지능 등이 후대에 이어지도록 도왔음
상상해 보라 / 만일 아인슈타인에게 방법이 없었다고 / 나머지 우리에게 말할 / 자신의 놀라운 이해에 대해 / 상대성 이론에 대한 //
                                형용사적 용법(abilities 수식)
In the absence of our incredible abilities / to communicate, / each and every one of us / would need to discover relativity / on his or her own. //
우리의 놀라운 능력의 부재 속에서 / 의사소통하는 / 우리 각자 모두가 / 상대성을 발견해야 할 것이다 / 스스로 //
복수 주어   복수 동사
Leaps of human intelligence have happened, / then, / as a response to the way / human society and culture developed. //
                    선행사(관계부사는 생략됨)
인간 지능의 도약은 발생해 왔다 / 그렇다면 / 방식에 대한 반응으로 / 인간 사회와 문화가 발전했던 //
A lot of our intelligence resulted / from our interaction with each other, / and not just in response / to our environments. //
상당한 우리의 지능은 기인했다 / 우리의 서로 간의 상호 작용에서 / 단지 반응뿐만 아니라 / 우리의 환경에 대한 //

- overcome ⓥ 극복하다
- obstacle ⓝ 장애(물)
- hinder ⓥ 방해하다
- evolution ⓝ 진화, 발전
- propel ⓥ 몰다, 밀다
- valuable ⓐ 귀중한
- preserve ⓥ 보존하다
- generation ⓝ 세대
- remarkable ⓐ 놀라운, 주목할 만한
- relativity ⓝ 상대성
- absence ⓝ 없음, 부재
- discover ⓥ 발견하다
- leap ⓝ 도약, 급증

인간 지능의 진화를 방해하고 있었던 장애물로서의 죽음을 극복하기 위해, 우리 조상들은 우리 종족을 다른 모든 것들을 능가하여 앞으로 나아가게 했던 킬러 앱, 즉 말과 수학에서의 말과 글을 개발했다. 나는 의사소통이 우리의 가장 가치 있는 발명이었고 지금도 여전히 그렇다고 믿는다. 그것은 우리가 얻어온 지식, 학습, 발견 그리고 지능을 보존하고 그것들을 개인에서 개인으로, 그리고 대대로 물려주도록 우리에게 도움을 주어 왔다. 만일 아인슈타인이 상대성 이론에 대한 자신의 놀라운 이해에 대해 나머지 우리에게 말할 방법이 없었다고 상상해 보라. 우리의 놀라운 의사소통 능력이 없을 때에는, 우리 각자 모두가 스스로 상대성을 발견해야 할 것이다. 그렇다면 인간 지능의 도약은 인간 사회와 문화가 발전했던 방식에 대한 반응으로 발생해 왔다. 상당한 우리의 지능은 단지 우리의 환경에 대한 반응뿐만 아니라, 서로 간의 상호 작용에서 기인했다.

다음 글의 요지로 가장 적절한 것은?
① 인간의 언어는 환경과의 상호 작용을 통해 발달한다.
   언어가 발달시킨 것에 대한 내용임
② 인간의 지능 발달은 상호 간 의사소통의 결과물이다.
   의사소통을 통해 인간 지능의 진화를 막는 장애물을 극복함
③ 과학의 발전은 인간 사회의 문화 보존에 필수적이다.
   상대성 이론이 언급된 것으로 만든 오답
④ 언어의 변화가 세대 간 의사소통의 단절을 초래한다.
   세대 간 의사소통을 통해 인간 지능이 진화함
⑤ 기술에 대한 의존이 인간의 학습 능력 발달을 저해한다.
   학습 능력의 발달을 방해하는 요소를 설명한 것이 아님

왜 정답? [정답률 87%]
인간 지능의 진화를 방해하는 죽음을 극복한 것이 말과 글, 즉 의사소통이라는 문장으로 글을 시작한 후, 의사소통은 인간이 지식, 학습, 발견, 지능 등을 다른 사람에게, 그리고 대대로 전달하도록 도왔다고 했다.
인간의 가장 가치 있는 발명이 의사소통이고, 우리 지능의 상당 부분이 서로 간의 상호 작용에서 기인했다고 했으므로 ②이 글의 요지임을 알 수 있다.

왜 오답?

① 인간의 언어가 인간의 지능을 발달시켰다는 것이지, 무엇이 인간의 언어를 ~~발달시키는지~~를 설명하는 것이 아니다. (한정)

③ 아인슈타인의 상대성 이론에 대한 언급은 의사소통이 인간 지능의 진화에 중요한 역할을 한다는 것을 보여주는 예시일 뿐이다.

④ 의사소통을 통해 지식, 학습, 발견, 지능을 보존하고 대대로 전달함으로써 인간 지능이 진화한다는 내용이다.

⑤ 인간이 기술에 과도하게 의존한다거나 그로 인해 학습 능력이 발달하지 못한다는 언급은 없다.

E 18 정답 ① *효율적인 배송 수단으로서의 자전거

Urban delivery vehicles can be adapted / to better suit / the density of urban distribution, / which often involves / smaller vehicles such as vans, / including bicycles. //
(계속적 용법의 주격 관계대명사)
도시의 배달 운송 수단은 개조될 수 있는데 / 더 잘 맞도록 / 도시 배치의 밀집 상태에 / 그것은 자주 포함한다 / 밴과 같은 더 작은 운송 수단을 / 자전거를 포함하여 /

The latter have the potential / to become a preferred 'last-mile' vehicle, / particularly in high-density and congested areas. //
(형용사적 용법(the potential 수식))
후자는 잠재력이 있다 / 선호되는 '최종 단계' 운송 수단이 될 / 특히 밀도가 높고 혼잡한 지역에서 // **단서1** 자전거(후자)는 밀도가 높고 혼잡한 지역(도시)에서 선호되는 운송 수단이 될 수 있음

In locations / where bicycle use is high, / such as the Netherlands, / delivery bicycles are also used / to carry personal cargo (e.g. groceries). //
(선행사) (관계부사)
지역에서 / 자전거 사용이 많은 / 네덜란드와 같이 / 배달 자전거는 또한 사용된다 / 개인 짐을 운반하기 위해 (예를 들어 식료품) /

Due to their low acquisition and maintenance costs, / cargo bicycles convey much potential / **단서2** 짐 자전거에는 많은 잠재력이 있음
(전치사) (명사구)
그것의 낮은 매입과 유지 비용 때문에 / 짐 자전거는 많은 잠재력을 전달한다 /

in developed and developing countries alike, / such as the *becak* (a three-wheeled bicycle) in Indonesia. //
선진국과 개발도상국에서 똑같이 / 인도네시아의 becak(바퀴가 세 개 달린 자전거)과 같이 //

Services / using electrically assisted delivery tricycles / have been successfully implemented / in France /
(복수 주어) (복수 동사 ①)
서비스는 / 전기 보조 배달용 세발자전거를 이용하는 / 성공적으로 시행되었고 / 프랑스에서 /

and are gradually being adopted / across Europe / for services / as varied as parcel and catering deliveries. //
(복수 동사 ②)
점차 도입되고 있다 / 유럽 전역에서 / 서비스를 위해 / 소포나 음식 배달만큼 다양한 //

Using bicycles / as cargo vehicles / is particularly encouraged /
(동명사구 주어) (단수 동사)
자전거를 사용하는 것은 / 화물 운송 수단으로 / 특히 장려된다 /

when combined / with policies / that restrict motor vehicle access / to specific areas / of a city, / such as downtown or commercial districts, / or with the extension of dedicated bike lanes. //
(병렬 구조)
결합될 때 / 정책과 / 자동차 접근을 제한하는 / 도시의 특정 지역에 / 도심이나 상업 지구처럼 / 또는 자전거 전용 도로의 확장과 /

- adapt ⓥ 개조하다 ・density ⓝ 밀도, 농도
- distribution ⓝ 분포, 배치 ・potential ⓝ 잠재력, 가능성
- congested ⓐ 붐비는, 혼잡한 ・cargo ⓝ 짐, 화물
- acquisition ⓝ 매입, 취득 ・maintenance ⓝ 유지
- convey ⓥ 운반하다, 전달하다 ・tricycle ⓝ 세발자전거
- implement ⓥ 시행하다 ・parcel ⓝ 소포
- catering ⓝ 음식 공급 ・district ⓝ 지역, 구역
- extension ⓝ 확장, 확대 ・dedicated ⓐ 전용의

도시의 배달 운송 수단은 도시 배치의 밀집 상태에 더 잘 맞도록 개조될 수 있다. 거기에는 자주 밴과 같은 더 작은 운송 수단을 포함하는데, 자전거도 포함된다. 후자는 특히 밀도가 높고 혼잡한 지역에서 선호되는 '최종 단계' 운송 수단이 될 잠재력이 있다. 네덜란드와 같이 자전거 사용이 많은 지역에서 배달 자전거는 또한 개인 짐(예를 들어 식료품)을 운반하기 위해 사용된다. 매입과 유지 비용이 낮아서 짐 자전거는 선진국에서 그리고 인도네시아의

becak(바퀴가 세 개 달린 자전거)과 같이 개발도상국에서 똑같이 많은 잠재력을 전달한다.

전기 보조 배달용 세발자전거를 이용하는 서비스는 프랑스에서 성공적으로 시행되었고 소포나 음식 배달만큼 다양한 서비스를 위해 유럽 전역에서 점차 도입되고 있다. 자전거를 화물 운송 수단으로 사용하는 것은 도심이나 상업 지구처럼 도시의 특정 지역에 자동차 접근을 제한하는 정책이나 자전거 전용 도로의 확장과 결합될 때 특히 장려된다.

다음 글의 요지로 가장 적절한 것은?

① 도시에서 자전거는 효율적인 배송 수단으로 사용될 수 있다.
두 번째 문장의 The latter가 자전거임
② 자전거는 출퇴근 시간을 줄이기 위한 대안으로 선호되고 있다.
배송(운송) 수단으로서의 자전거를 이야기함
③ 자전거는 배송 수단으로의 경제적 장단점을 모두 가질 수 있다.
단점은 언급되지 않음
④ 수요자의 요구에 부합하는 다양한 용도의 자전거가 개발되고 있다.
a three-wheeled bicycle로 만든 오답
⑤ 세계 각국에서는 전기 자전거 사용을 장려하는 정책을 추진하고 있다.
전기 자전거를 장려한다는 내용이 아님

왜 정답? [정답률 78%]

자전거는 특히 밀도가 높고 혼잡한 지역에서 선호되는 운송 수단이 될 잠재력이 있다면서, 낮은 구매 비용과 유지비 때문에 짐을 운반하는 자전거는 많은 잠재력을 가졌다고 했으므로 정답은 ①이다.

왜 오답?

② 출퇴근 수단이 아니라 배달 운송 수단으로서의 자전거의 장점을 이야기하는 글이다.

③ 자전거가 배송 수단으로 적합한 이유로 낮은 매입 비용과 유지비를 들었다. 자전거의 경제적 단점은 언급되지 않았다.

④ 인도네시아의 *becak* 등이 언급된 것으로 만든 오답이다. 운송 용도로서의 자전거의 이점에 대해 설명하는 글이다.

⑤ electrically assisted delivery tricycles, policies 등으로 만든 오답이다. 프랑스나 인도네시아의 전기 자전거 사용 장려 정책에 대해 설명하는 글이 아니다.

조현준 | 전북대 의예과 2023년 입학·익산 이리고 졸

난 글의 요지를 찾는 문제에서는 첫 문장을 완전히 파악하는 것이 중요하다고 생각해서 첫 문장을 자세히 봤어.
첫 문장을 보니 도시의 배송 수단에 관하여, 특히 자전거에 관해 얘기한다는 것을 알 수 있었고, 요지 파악 유형은 내용이 그렇게 어려운 편은 아니기에 속도를 붙여 읽었어.
좀 더 읽어보니 세계의 여러 지역에서 자전거가 도시에서의 배송 수단으로 사용된다는 내용이었지. 별다른 반전 없이 글이 끝났고, 이 글의 요지는 '자전거는 도시의 배송 수단 중 하나이다.'라는 것을 머릿속에 품고 선택지를 확인하니까 선택지에 비슷한 내용이 있더라고!

E 19 정답 ① *음악 비평의 변화

Prior to file-sharing services, / music albums landed exclusively / in the hands of music critics / before their release. //
파일 공유 서비스 이전에 / 음악 앨범은 독점적으로 들어갔다 / 음악 비평가들의 손에 / 그것의 발매 전에 /

These critics would listen to them / well before the general public could / and preview them / for the rest of the world / in their reviews. //
(병렬 구조)
이런 비평가들은 그것을 듣고 / 일반 대중이 들을 수 있기 훨씬 전에 / 그것에 대해 시사평을 쓰곤 했다 / 나머지 세상 사람들을 위해 / 자신의 비평에서 //

Once the internet made music easily accessible / and allowed even advanced releases to spread / through online social networks, / **단서1** 인터넷과 온라인 소셜 네트워크로 인해 음악 비평이 변화함
인터넷이 음악을 쉽게 접할 수 있게 만들자 / 그리고 심지어 미리 공개된 곡들이 퍼질 수 있게 하자 / 온라인 소셜 네트워크를 통해 /

availability of new music became democratized, / which meant
/ critics no longer had unique access. //

주어 / 동사 / 주격 보어 / 계속적 용법의 주격 관계대명사

신곡에 대한 입수 가능성이 민주화되었는데 / 이는 의미했다 / 비평가들이 더이상 유일한 접근
을 갖지 않는다는 것을 //

That is, / critics and laypeople alike could obtain new music /
simultaneously. //

즉 / 비평가와 비전문가가 똑같이 신곡을 얻을 수 있었다 / 동시에 //

Social media services also enabled people / to publicize their
views / on new songs, / list their new favorite bands / in their
social media bios, /

enabled의 목적격 보어(to부정사)의 병렬 구조

소셜 미디어 서비스는 또한 사람들이 ~할 수 있게 했다 / 자신의 견해를 알릴 수 있게 / 신곡에
대한 / 자신이 좋아하는 새로운 밴드의 목록을 작성할 수 있게 / 자신의 소셜 미디어 약력에 /

and argue over new music endlessly / on message boards. //

그리고 신곡을 놓고 끝없이 논쟁할 수 있게 / 메시지 게시판에서 //

The result was / that critics now could access / the opinions of the
masses / on a particular album / before writing their reviews. //

주격 보어절 접속사 / 전치사 / 동명사구

그 결과는 ~이었다 / 비평가들은 이제 접할 수 있었다는 것 / 대중의 의견을 / 특정 앨범에 관
한 / 자신의 비평을 쓰기 전에 //

단서 2 인터넷 이전 시대에는 음악 비평이 예술에 관한 여론을 인도했음

Thus, / instead of music reviews guiding popular opinion /
toward art / (as they did / in preinternet times), /

music reviews를 수식하는 현재분사구

그리하여 / 여론을 인도하는 음악 비평 대신에 / 예술에 관한 / (그것들이 그랬던 것처럼 / 인
터넷 이전 시대에) /

music reviews began to reflect / — consciously or subconsciously
— / public opinion. // 단서 3 이제는 음악 비평이 여론을 반영하기 시작했음

음악 비평은 반영하기 시작했다 / 의식적으로 혹은 잠재의식적으로 / 여론을 //

- prior to ~에 앞서, ~보다 먼저   • exclusively ad 배타적으로, 독점적으로
- critic ⓝ 비평가, 평론가   • release ⓝ (대중들에게) 발표[공개]
- well ad 아주, 상당히   • preview ⓥ 시사평을 쓰다, 사전 검토[조사]하다
- accessible ⓐ 접근[이용] 가능한
- advanced ⓐ 선진의, 고급[상급]의, 후기의
- spread ⓥ 퍼뜨리다, 확산시키다   • availability ⓝ 이용[입수] 가능성
- democratize ⓥ 민주화하다   • obtain ⓥ 얻다, 입수하다
- simultaneously ad 동시에, 일제히   • publicize ⓥ 광고하다, 알리다
- endlessly ad 끝없이, 무한히   • mass ⓝ ((pl.)) (일반) 대중
- particular ⓐ 특정한, 특별한
- consciously ad 의식[자각]하여, 의식적으로
- subconsciously ad 잠재의식적으로

파일 공유 서비스 이전에, 음악 앨범은 발매 전에 음악 비평가들의 손에 독점적
으로 들어갔다. 이런 비평가들은 일반 대중이 들을 수 있기 훨씬 전에 그것을
듣고 나머지 세상 사람들을 위해 자신의 비평에서 그것에 대해 시사평을 쓰곤
했다. 인터넷을 통해 음악을 쉽게 접할 수 있게 되고, 심지어 미리 공개된 곡들
이 온라인 소셜 네트워크를 통해 퍼질 수 있게 되자, 신곡을 접할 수 있는 것이
민주화되었는데, 이는 비평가들이 더이상 유일하게 접근하는 것이 아님을 의미
했다. 즉, 비평가와 비전문가가 똑같이 동시에 신곡을 얻을 수 있었다. 소셜 미
디어 서비스는 또한 사람들이 신곡에 대한 자신의 견해를 알리고, 자신의 소셜
미디어 약력에 자신이 좋아하는 새로운 밴드의 목록을 작성하고, 메시지 게시판
에서 신곡을 놓고 끝없이 논쟁할 수 있게 했다. 그 결과 비평가들은 이제 자신
의 비평을 쓰기 전에 특정 앨범에 관한 대중의 의견을 접할 수 있었다. 그리하
여 (인터넷 이전 시대에 그랬던 것처럼) 예술에 관한 여론을 인도하는 대신에,
음악 비평은 의식적으로 혹은 잠재의식적으로 여론을 반영하기 시작했다.

다음 글의 요지로 가장 적절한 것은?

① 미디어 환경의 변화로 음악 비평이 대중의 영향을 받게 되었다.
음악 비평 → 여론'이었던 것이 '여론 → 음악 비평'으로 바뀜
② 인터넷의 발달로 다양한 장르의 음악을 접하는 것이 가능해졌다.
음악 장르의 다양성은 언급되지 않음
③ 비평가의 음악 비평은 자신의 주관적인 경험을 기반으로 한다.
음악 비평의 기반을 설명한 것이 아님
④ 오늘날 새로운 음악은 대중의 기호를 확인한 후에 공개된다.
오늘날의 새로운 음악을 설명한 것이 아님
⑤ 온라인 환경의 대두로 음악 비평의 질이 전반적으로 상승하였다.
음악 비평의 질이 상승했는지 하락했는지는 알 수 없음

왜 정답? [정답률 79%]

인터넷 이전 시대에는 음악 비평가들이 일반 대중보다 훨씬 먼저, 독점적으로 음
악 앨범을 듣고 그것에 대한 시사평을 써서 예술, 음악에 대한 여론을 인도했는데,
인터넷이 음악을 쉽게 접할 수 있게 만들고, 온라인 소셜 네트워크를 통해 음악이
퍼질 수 있게 하자 음악 비평이 여론을 반영하기 시작했다는 내용이므로 정답은
①이다. 여론이 음악 비평에 영향을 미치기 시작했다는 의미임 꿀팁

왜 오답?

② 인터넷의 발달이 미친 영향에 대한 글인 것은 맞지만, 인터넷으로 인해 다양한
음악을 접하는 것이 가능해졌다는 내용은 아니다.
③ 비평가가 음악 비평을 하는 방식에 대해 설명한 글이 아니다.
④ 오늘날 새롭게 등장한 음악의 특징에 대해 이야기하는 것이 아니다. 글 곳곳에
release가 등장한 것으로 만든 오답이다.
⑤ 온라인 환경의 등장으로 음악 비평이 변화했다는 것이지, 구체적으로 음악 비평
의 질이 좋아졌는지 또는 나빠졌는지를 이야기하는 것은 아니다. 주의

E 20 정답 ① ＊고객의 브랜드 칭찬에 응답하는 것의 중요성

동명사 주어(단수 취급) / 단수 동사

Being able to prioritize your responses / allows you to connect
more deeply with individual customers, /

여러분의 응답에 우선순위를 매길 수 있는 것은 / 여러분이 개별 고객들과 더 깊은 관계를
맺을 수 있게 해 준다 / 단서 1 기업이 고객의 글에 우선순위를 매겨 응답하는 것은
고객과의 관계에 중요함

be it a one-off interaction around a particularly delightful or
upsetting experience, /

be it A or B = whether it be A or B (A든 B든 간에)

그것이 특별히 즐겁거나 화가 나는 경험에 대한 일회성 상호 작용이든 /

or the development of a longer-term relationship / with a
significantly influential individual / within your customer
base. //

장기적 관계의 발전이든 간에 / 상당히 영향력 있는 개인과의 / 여러분의 고객 기반 내에서 //

If you've ever posted a favorable comment / — or any comment,
for that matter — / about a brand, product or service, /

현재완료의 경험적 용법

만약 여러분이 호의적인 의견을 올려 본 적이 있다면 / 혹은 그 문제에 대해서 어떠한
의견이라도 / 어떤 브랜드, 제품 또는 서비스에 관해 /

think about what it would feel like / if you were personally
acknowledged / by the brand manager, for example, as a
result. //

가정법 과거(현재 사실과 반대): 「if+주어+동사의 과거형/were, 주어+조동사의 과거+동사원형」

기분이 어떨지 생각해 보라 / 개인적으로 인정의 반응을 얻는다면 / 그 브랜드 관리자로부터 /
그 결과, 예를 들어 //

In general, / people post / because they have something to say
/ — and because they want to be recognized for having said it. //

형용사적 용법 / 동명사의 완료형(과거 시제 표현)

일반적으로 / 사람들은 글을 올린다 / 할 말이 있기 때문에 / 그리고 그것을 말한 것에 대해
인정받기를 원하기 때문에 //

In particular, / when people post positive comments / they are
expressions of appreciation / for the experience that led to the
post. //

주격 관계대명사(선행사: the experience)

특히 / 사람들이 긍정적인 의견을 게시할 때 / 그것은 감사의 표현이다 / 그 게시물을 작성하게
만든 경험에 대한 //

While a compliment to the person standing next to you / is
typically answered with a response like "Thank You," / the sad
fact is / that most brand compliments / go unanswered. //

현재분사(the person 수식) / 명사절 접속사

여러분 옆에 서 있는 사람에 대한 칭찬은 / 보통 '감사합니다'와 같은 응답을 받지만 / 슬픈
사실은 ~이다 / 대부분의 브랜드 칭찬은 답을 받지 못한다는 것 //

These are lost opportunities / to understand what drove the
compliments / and create a solid fan based on them. //

형용사적 용법(opportunities 수식) / 의문사절을 이끎

이것은 기회를 잃은 것이다 / 무엇이 칭찬을 이끌어 냈는지 이해하고 / 그 칭찬을 바탕으로
하여 확고한 팬을 만들어 낼 수 있는 // 단서 2 고객의 긍정적인 칭찬에 응답하지 않는 것은 왜 칭찬을
받았는지 이해하거나 확고한 기업의 팬을 만들 기회를 잃는 것임

- **prioritize** ⓥ 우선순위를 매기다, 우선시하다 ・ **one-off** ⓐ 일회성의
- **upsetting** ⓐ 속상하게 하는 ・ **significantly** ⓐⓓ 상당히
- **influential** ⓐ 영향력 있는 ・ **customer base** 고객층
- **favorable** ⓐ 호의적인 ・ **acknowledge** ⓥ 감사하다, 인정하다
- **appreciation** ⓝ 감사 ・ **unanswered** ⓐ 답을 못한

여러분의 응답에 우선순위를 매길 수 있는 것은, 그것이 특별히 즐겁거나 화가 나는 경험에 대한 일회성 상호 작용이든, 여러분의 고객 기반 내에서 상당히 영향력 있는 개인과의 장기적 관계의 발전이든 간에, 여러분이 개별 고객들과 더 깊은 관계를 맺을 수 있게 해 준다. 만약 여러분이 어떤 브랜드, 제품 또는 서비스에 관해 호의적인 의견이나 혹은 그 문제에 대해서 어떠한 의견이라도 올려 본 적이 있다면, 그 결과, 예를 들어, 그 브랜드 관리자로부터 개인적으로 인정의 반응을 얻는다면 기분이 어떨지 생각해 보라. 일반적으로, 사람들은 할 말이 있기 때문에, 그리고 그것을 말한 것에 대해 인정받기를 원하기 때문에 글을 올린다. 특히, 사람들이 긍정적인 의견을 게시할 때 그것은 그 게시물을 작성하게 만든 경험에 대한 감사의 표현이다. 여러분 옆에 서 있는 사람에 대한 칭찬은 보통 '감사합니다'와 같은 응답을 받지만, 슬픈 사실은 대부분의 브랜드 칭찬은 답을 받지 못한다는 것이다. 이것은 무엇이 칭찬을 이끌어 냈는지 이해하고 그 칭찬을 바탕으로 하여 확고한 팬을 만들어 낼 수 있는 기회를 잃은 것이다.

다음 글의 요지로 가장 적절한 것은?

① 고객과의 관계 증진을 위해 고객의 브랜드 칭찬에 응답하는 것은 중요하다.
These are lost opportunities to understand ~ create a solid fan based on them.
② 고객의 피드백을 면밀히 분석함으로써 브랜드의 성공 가능성을 높일 수 있다. 긍정적인 피드백에 응답을 주는 것이 요지임
③ 신속한 고객 응대를 통해서 고객의 긍정적인 반응을 이끌어 낼 수 있다. 고객 응대를 '신속하게' 하는 것이 아니라 긍정적인 피드백에 응답을 주는 것이 요지임
④ 브랜드 매니저에게는 고객의 부정적인 의견을 수용하는 태도가 요구된다. 부정적 의견을 수용하는 것이 요지가 아님
⑤ 고객의 의견을 경청하는 것은 브랜드의 새로운 이미지 창출에 도움이 된다. 고객의 의견을 경청하는 방식은 긍정적인 피드백에 응답을 주는 것으로 소개됨

✍왜 정답 ? [정답률 86%]

첫 문장(주제문)	고객의 일회성 경험이든, 장기적 상호 작용이든, 응답에 우선순위를 매기는 것은 고객과의 관계에서 중요함
중반 이후	고객의 호의나 칭찬 등 긍정적인 의견에 반응하는 것은 작성자에게 인정받는 느낌을 주고 팬을 확보하는 기회가 됨

▶ 따라서 글의 요지는 '고객과의 관계 증진을 위해 고객의 브랜드 칭찬에 응답하는 것은 중요하다'이므로 정답은 ①이다.

✍왜 오답 ?

② 피드백을 면밀히 분석하는 것이 아니라, 긍정적인 피드백에 응답을 주는 것이 요지이다.
③ 고객 응대를 '신속하게' 하는 것이 아니라, 긍정적인 피드백에 응답을 주는 것이 요지이다.
④ 부정적 의견을 수용하는 것이 아니라, 긍정적 피드백에 응답을 주는 것이 요지이다.
⑤ 고객의 의견을 경청하는 방식은 구체적으로 긍정적인 피드백에 응답을 주는 것으로 소개되었다.

류이레 | 연세대 의예과 2024년 입학·광주대동고 졸

첫 문장에서 prioritize your responses라는 표현이 직접적으로 와닿지 않아서 처음에 잠깐 당황했던 문제였어. 그래도 지문에 나오는 예시들을 통해 고객의 의견에 대한 응답의 중요성을 강조한다는 걸 캐치하고 빠르게 후반부까지 읽었지. 결정적으로 지문 후반부에서 칭찬에 대해 답변이 되지 않는 것이 아쉽다고 하는 것을 보고, 첫 문장의 prioritize가 이해되어서 답을 고를 수 있었어.

E 21 정답 ① ⭐ 2등급 대비 [정답률 72%]

✱ **이민자의 권리에 대한 인식 변화 필요성**

The need / to assimilate / values and lifestyle of the host culture
/ has become a growing conflict. //
단수 주어 / 형용사적 용법(The need 수식) / 단수 동사
필요성이 / 동화시키는 / 주류 문화의 가치와 생활방식을 / 커지는 갈등이 되었다 //

Multiculturalists suggest / that there should be a model of
partial assimilation / in which immigrants retain / some of their
customs, beliefs, and language. // 생략 가능
다문화주의자들은 제안한다 / 부분 동화 모델이 있어야 한다고 / 이민자들이 유지하는 /
자신의 관습, 신념, 언어 중 일부를 [단서1] 갈등 해결을 위한 다문화주의자들의 제안: 이민자들이 자신의 일부 문화를 유지하는 부분 동화 모델이 필요함

There is pressure / to conform rather than to maintain / their
└형용사적 용법(pressure 수식)의 to부정사의 병렬 구조┘
cultural identities, / however, / and these conflicts are greatly
선행사
determined / by the community / to which one migrates. //
전치사+관계대명사
압력이 있다 / 유지하기보다는 순응해야 한다는 / 그들의 문화적 정체성을 / 그러나 / 그리고
이러한 갈등은 대개 결정된다 / 커뮤니티에 의해 / 이민자가 이주하는 //

These experiences are not new; / many Europeans experienced
exclusion and poverty / during the first two waves of
immigration / in the 19th and 20th centuries. //
이러한 경험은 새롭지 않다 / 많은 유럽인이 배제와 빈곤을 경험했다 / 첫 두 차례의 이민 물결
동안 / 19세기와 20세기에 //

Eventually, / these immigrants transformed this country /
선행사 주격 관계대명사
with significant changes / that included enlightenment and
acceptance of diversity. //
결국 / 이 이민자들은 이 나라를 탈바꿈시켰다 / 중대한 변화로 / 계몽과 다양성 수용을 포함한 //

People of color, / however, / continue to struggle / for
acceptance. //
유색인종들은 / 그러나 / 계속 안간힘을 쓰고 있다 / 받아들여지기 위해 //

Once again, / the challenge is to recognize / that other cultures
명사적 용법(주격 보어)
think and act differently / and that they have the right / to do
so. // [단서2] 과제: 다른 문화는 다르게 생각하고 행동하며, 그들에게는 그럴 권리가 있음을 인정하는 것
거듭 말하자면 / 어려운 과제는 인정하는 것이다 / 다른 문화는 다르게 생각하고 행동하며 /
그들에게 권리가 있다는 것을 / 그렇게 할 //

Perhaps, / in the not too distant future, / immigrants will no
longer be strangers / among us. //
아마도 / 그리 머지않아 / 이민자들이 더는 이방인이 아닐 것이다 / 우리 사이에서 //

- **assimilate** ⓥ 동화하다 ・ **host culture** 주류 문화
- **conflict** ⓝ 갈등 ・ **multiculturalist** ⓝ 다문화주의자
- **partial** ⓐ 부분적인 ・ **immigrant** ⓝ 이민자 ・ **retain** ⓥ 유지하다
- **conform** ⓥ 순응하다 ・ **be determined by** ~에 의해 결정되다
- **migrate** ⓥ 이주하다 ・ **exclusion** ⓝ 배제 ・ **poverty** ⓝ 빈곤
- **transform** ⓥ 변화시키다 ・ **enlightenment** ⓝ 계몽
- **diversity** ⓝ 다양성 ・ **people of color** 유색 인종

주류 문화의 가치와 생활방식에 동화되어야 하는 필요성 때문에 갈등이 커지고 있다. 다문화주의자들은 이민자들이 자신의 관습, 신념, 언어 중 일부를 유지하는 부분 동화 모델이 있어야 한다고 제안한다. 그러나 그들의 문화적 정체성을 유지하기보다는 순응해야 한다는 압력이 있는데, 이러한 갈등은 대개 이민자가 이주하는 커뮤니티에 따라 결정된다. 이러한 경험은 새로운 것이 아니며, 많은 유럽인이 19세기와 20세기의 첫 두 차례의 이민 물결 동안 배제와 빈곤을 경험했다. 결국 이 이민자들은 계몽과 다양성 수용을 포함한 중대한 변화로 이 나라를 탈바꿈시켰다. 그러나 유색인종들은 계속 받아들여지기 위해 안간힘을 쓰고 있다. 거듭 말하자면, 어려운 과제는 다른 문화는 다르게 생각하고 행동하며 그들이 그렇게 할 권리가 있다는 것을 인정하는 것이다. 아마도, 그리 머지않아 이민자들이 우리 사이에서 더는 이방인이 아닐 것이다.

다음 글의 요지로 가장 적절한 것은?

①이민자 고유의 정체성을 유지할 권리에 대한 공동체의 인식이 필요하다.
　the challenge is to recognize ~ and that they have the right to do so
② 이민자의 적응을 돕기 위해 그들의 요구를 반영한 정책 수립이 중요하다.
　정책적 해결책은 제시되지 않음
③ 이민자는 미래 사회의 긍정적 변화에 핵심적 역할을 수행할 수 있다.
　이민자를 받아들이는 자세에 대한 내용임
④ 다문화 사회의 안정을 위해서는 국제적 차원의 지속적인 협력이 요구된다.
　'이민자'라는 소재로 만든 오답
⑤ 문화적 동화는 장기적이고 체계적인 과정을 통해 점진적으로 이루어진다.
　문화적 동화의 과정을 설명한 것이 아님

─────────────

:왜: **2등급** ? assimilate, conform, enlightenment 등 생소한 어휘가 다수
사용되어 글의 요지 파악에 어려움을 겪을 수도 있는 2등급 대비 문제이다. 하지만
정작 글의 요지를 나타내는 단서 문장들은 어렵지 않은 단어로 이루어져 있으므로
차분히 글을 읽는다면 충분히 요지를 파악할 수 있다.

〉왜 정답 ?

> • **문제점**: 이민자가 주류 문화의 가치와 생활방식에 동화되어야 하는
> 　필요성이 갈등을 키움
> • **다문화주의자들의 제안**: 부분 동화 모델이 필요함
> 　↳ 이민자들이 자신의 관습, 신념, 언어 중 일부를 유지하며 주류 문화에 부분적으로 동화되는 것
> • **주어진 과제**: 다른 문화는 다르게 생각하고 행동하며, 그들에게는
> 　그렇게 할 권리가 있다는 것을 인정하는 것

▶ 글의 요지는 ①!

〉왜 오답 ?

② 특정 정책을 수립함으로써 이민자와의 문화적 갈등을 해결해야 한다는 내용이
아니다.
③ 이민자가 수행하는 역할은 언급되지 않았다.
④ '이민자'라는 소재로 만든 오답이다. 다른 문화에 대한 인정을 통해 다문화 사회를
안정시킬 수 있다는 내용이다.
⑤ 문화적 동화가 어떤 과정을 통해 이루어지는지를 설명한 글이 아니다.

E 22 정답 ① ──────── ★2등급 대비 [정답률 94%]

＊ 결말의 중요성

추상적 의미의 장소(선행사)　관계부사 ＊　＝only
Imagine a movie / where nothing but terrible things happen. //
영화를 상상해 보라 / 오로지 끔찍한 일만 일어나는 //

But, in the end, / everything works out. //
하지만 결국 / 모든 것이 잘 풀린다 //

Everything is resolved. //
모든 것이 해결된다 //

A sufficiently happy ending can change / the meaning of all the
previous events. // 단서 1 결말이 행복하다면 이는 오로지 끔찍하기만 했던
　　　　　　　　　 이전 사건의 의미를 바꿈
충분히 행복한 결말은 바꿀 수 있다 / 모든 이전 사건의 의미를 //
　　　　　　　　　　　prep. ~을 고려할 때
They can all be viewed / as worthwhile, / given that ending. //
그것들은 모두 보일 수 있다 / 가치 있다고 / 그 결말을 고려한다면 //

Now imagine / another movie. // 이제 상상해보라 / 또 다른 영화를 //

A lot of things / are happening. // 많은 일이 / 일어나고 있다 //

They're all exciting and interesting. // 그것들은 모두 신나고 흥미롭다 //

But there are a lot of them. // 하지만 그것들이 많이 있다 //
　　　　　　　　　　목적어로 to부정사나 동명사를 취하는 start
Ninety minutes in, / you start to worry. //
90분이 지나면서 / 여러분은 걱정하기 시작한다 //

"This is a great movie," / you think, / "but there are a lot of things
　　　　　　　　　　　　　 앞에 명사절 접속사 that이 생략됨
going on. // I sure hope / the filmmaker can pull it all together." //
"이것은 좋은 영화야" / 여러분은 생각한다 / "하지만 많은 일이 일어나고 있어 // 난 정말 바라
/ 영화 감독이 그 모든 것을 잘 정리할 수 있기를"이라고 //

But that doesn't happen. //
하지만 그런 일은 일어나지 않는다 //

────── 우측 컬럼 ──────

　　　　　　　　　　　　　　　　　　　　　단수 주어
Instead, the story ends, suddenly, unresolved, / or something
facile and clichéd / occurs. // 단수 동사
그 대신에, 이야기가 갑자기 해결되지 않은 채 끝나거나 / 지나치게 단순하고 상투적인 일이
/ 일어난다 // 단서 2 결말이 불만족스럽다면 이전에 영화에 완전히 몰입하고 영화를 즐겼다는 것을
　　　　　　　　　　　 의식하지 못하고 짜증 난 채로 영화관을 떠남

You leave deeply annoyed and unsatisfied / — failing to notice
/ that you were fully engaged and enjoying the movie / almost
the whole time / you were in the theatre. //
여러분은 몹시 짜증 나고 불만족스러운 채로 떠난다 / 의식하지 못하고 / 여러분이 완전히
몰입하여 영화를 즐기고 있었다는 것을 / 대부분의 시간 동안 / 여러분이 극장에 있었던 //

The present can change the past, / and the future can change
the present. //
현재는 과거를 바꿀 수 있고 / 미래는 현재를 바꿀 수 있다 //

• work out 잘 되어가다　　　• resolve ⓥ 해결하다
• sufficiently ⓐⓓ 충분히　　• worthwhile ⓐ 가치있는
• filmmaker ⓝ 영화감독　　• engage ⓥ 몰입하다

오로지 끔찍한 일만 일어나는 영화를 상상해 보라. 하지만 결국 모든 것이 잘
풀린다. 모든 것이 해결된다. 충분히 행복한 결말은 모든 이전 사건의 의미를
바꿀 수 있다. 그 결말을 고려한다면, 그것들은 모두 가치 있다고 볼 수 있다.
이제 또 다른 영화를 상상해보라. 많은 일이 일어나고 있다. 그것들은 모두
신나고 흥미롭다. 하지만 그것들이 많이 있다. 90분이 지나면서 여러분은
걱정하기 시작한다. "이것은 좋은 영화야. 하지만 많은 일이 일어나고 있어.
영화 감독이 그 모든 것을 잘 정리할 수 있으면 좋겠어."라고 여러분은
생각한다. 하지만 그런 일은 일어나지 않는다. 그 대신에, 이야기가 갑자기
해결되지 않은 채 끝나거나, 지나치게 단순하고 상투적인 일이 일어난다.
여러분은 극장에 있었던 시간 대부분 완전히 몰입하여 영화를 즐기고 있었다는
것을 의식하지 못하고 몹시 짜증 나고 불만족스러운 채로 떠난다. 현재는 과거를
바꿀 수 있고, 미래는 현재를 바꿀 수 있다.

다음 글의 요지로 가장 적절한 것은?

①결말에 따라 이전 상황에 대한 인식이 달라진다.
　현재(결말)가 과거(그동안의 사건)를 바꿀 수 있음
② 익숙하지 않은 이야기는 대중의 사랑을 받기 어렵다.
　대중의 취향을 설명한 글이 아님
③ 흥행에 성공한 영화가 항상 작품성이 뛰어난 것은 아니다.
　흥행 여부와 작품성의 관계는 글의 주제가 아님
④ 상황에 대한 집단의 평가는 개인의 평가에 영향을 끼친다.
　결말이 과정에 영향을 끼친다는 내용임
⑤ 같은 영화를 반복적으로 보는 것이 영화에 대한 이해를 높인다.
　n차 관람에 대한 내용이 아님

─────────────

:왜: **2등급** ? 결말에 관한 두 가지 경우를 잘 살펴보고 글의 요지를 도출해야 하는
2등급 대비 문제이다. 글의 처음와 끝에 글의 요지와 비슷한 핵심 문장이 있기 때문에
요지를 파악하기 쉽고 정답이 아닌 선택지 중에 헷갈릴 만한 선택지가 없어서 정답을
쉽게 찾을 수 있을 것이다.

〉왜 정답 ?

경우①	오로지 끔찍한 일만 일어나다가 결말에서 모든 것이 행복하게 해결됨 → 행복한 결말이 모든 이전의 (끔찍한) 사건의 의미를 바꿀 수 있음
경우②	신나고 흥미로운 많은 일이 일어나다가 해결되지 않은 채 끝나거나 지나치게 단순하고 상투적인 결말로 이어짐 → 이전의 많은 일을 몰입하여 즐겼다는 사실을 잊고 짜증 난 채로 영화관을 떠남

➡ 결말에 따라 이전에 일어난 일에 대한 인식이 달라진다는 것이므로 정답은 ①임

〉왜 오답 ?

② 익숙하지 않은 이야기와 익숙한 이야기를 대조하는 글이 아니다.
③ 어떤 영화가 흥행에 성공하는지를 설명한 것이 아니다.
④ 다수가 좋게 평가하면 안 좋게 평가했던 개인의 평가가 바뀐다는 내용은 없다.
⑤ 영화에 대한 이해도를 높이는 방법은 언급되지 않았다.

＊ 추상적 의미의 장소에도 사용되는 관계부사 where

– 장소를 나타내는 선행사에 쓰이는 관계부사 where는 case, point, example, circumstance 등의 추상적 의미의 장소에도 사용된다.

• The treatment will continue until the patient reaches the condition <u>where</u> he can walk safely.
(치료는 환자가 안전하게 걸을 수 있는 상태에 다다를 때까지 계속될 것이다.)

• You are saying that everyone should be equal, and that is the point <u>where</u> I disagree.
(당신은 모두가 평등해야 한다고 말하지만 그것이 내가 동의하지 않는 점이다.)

– 관계부사는 「접속사+부사」의 역할을 하며, 「전치사+관계대명사」로 바꿔 쓸 수 있다.

• The day <u>when</u> I arrived at New York was summer.
= on which
(내가 뉴욕에 도착했던 날은 여름이었다.)

핵심 문장을 찾아 요지를
파악하자!

E 어휘 Review 정답

문제편 p. 88

01 짜증나게 하다	11 prone to	21 legislature
02 본능	12 be capable of	22 explicitly
03 흠 없이	13 at the expense of	23 grasping
04 부분적인	14 engage in	24 Property
05 해결하다	15 irrelevant to	25 identify
06 broad	16 moral	26 Armed
07 ethics	17 affect	27 exclusion
08 worthwhile	18 cognitive	28 conceived
09 notion	19 manner	29 forces
10 bystander	20 fundamental	30 granted

F 주제 찾기 (문제편 p. 89~104)

F 01 정답 ② ＊문화적으로 구성되는 감정

Considerable work / by cultural psychologists and anthropologists / has shown /
(단수 주어 / 단수 동사)
주목할 만한 연구는 / 문화 심리학자들과 인류학자들에 의한 / 보였다 /

that there are indeed large and sometimes surprising differences / in the words and concepts / that different cultures have / for describing emotions, / **단서1** 서로 다른 문화가 감정을 묘사하기 위해 가진 어휘와 개념에는 큰 차이가 있음
정말로 크고, 때로는 놀랄 만한 차이가 있다는 것을 / 어휘와 개념에 / 서로 다른 문화가 가진 / 감정을 묘사하기 위해 /

as well as in the social circumstances / that draw out the expression of particular emotions. //
(복수 선행사 / 주격 관계대명사절의 복수 동사)
사회적 상황에서만이 아니라 / 특정한 감정의 표현을 끌어내는 //

However, / those data do not actually show / that different cultures have different emotions, /
하지만 / 그런 데이터가 실제로 보이지는 않는다 / 서로 다른 문화가 서로 다른 감정을 가지고 있다는 것을 /

if we think of emotions / as central, neurally implemented states. //
(ⓐ 중추 신경의)
만약 우리가 감정을 생각한다면 / 중추 신경의, 즉 신경계에서 실행되는 상태라고 //

As for, say, color vision, / they just say / that, despite the same internal processing architecture, /
(say의 목적어절 접속사 ① / 전치사 / 명사구)
예를 들어 색 식별에 대해 / 데이터들은 단지 말할 뿐이다 / 체내에서 일어나는 동일한 처리 구조에도 불구하고 /

how we interpret, categorize, and name emotions varies / according to culture / **단서2** 감정을 표현하는 것이 적절한 상황이 문화에 따라 다름
(명사절 주어 / 단수 동사)
우리가 감정을 해석하고 범주화하며 명명하는 방식은 다르고 / 문화에 따라 /

and that we learn in a particular culture the social context /
(say의 목적어절 접속사 ② / 선행사)
in which it is appropriate to express emotions. //
(관계부사 where로 바꿀 수 있음)
우리는 사회적 상황을 특정 문화에서 배운다는 것을 / 감정을 표현하는 것이 적절한 //

However, / the emotional states themselves / are likely to be quite invariant / across cultures. //
하지만 / 감정 상태 그 자체는 / 지극히 불변할 가능성이 있다 / 문화 전반에 걸쳐 //

In a sense, / we can think of a basic, culturally universal emotion set / that is shaped by evolution / and implemented in the brain, /
어떤 의미에서 / 우리는 기본적인, 문화적으로 보편적인 감정 모음을 생각할 수 있다 / 진화에 의해 형성되어 / 두뇌에서 실행되는 /

but the links / between such emotional states and stimuli, behavior, and other cognitive states / are plastic / and can be modified / by learning / in a specific cultural context. //
(복수 주어 / 복수 동사)
하지만 연관성은 / 그런 감정 상태와 자극, 행동, 그리고 다른 인지 상태 간의 / 바뀌기 쉽고 / 수정될 수 있다 / 학습에 의해 / 특정한 문화적 상황에서의 //

• considerable ⓐ 상당한, 주목할 만한 • psychologist ⓝ 심리학자
• indeed ⓐd 정말, 사실 • circumstance ⓝ (주변) 상황, 환경
• draw out ~을 끌어내다[뽑아내다]
• neurally ⓐd 신경(계)으로 • implement ⓥ 실행하다
• architecture ⓝ 건축, 구조 • categorize ⓥ 분류하다
• context ⓝ 맥락, 전후 사정 • invariant ⓐ 변함없는, 변치 않는
• evolution ⓝ 진화, 발전 • plastic ⓐ 형태를 바꾸기 쉬운, 가짜의
• modify ⓥ 수정하다, 조정하다

문화 심리학자들과 인류학자들의 주목할 만한 연구에 따르면 특정한 감정의 표현을 끌어내는 사회적 상황에서만이 아니라 감정을 묘사하기 위해 서로 다른 문화가 가진 어휘와 개념에 정말로 크고, 때로는 놀랄 만한 차이가 있다. 하지만 그런 데이터가 서로 다른 문화가 서로 다른 감정을 가지고 있다는 것을 실제로 보여주는 것은 아닌데, 만약 우리가 감정을 중추 신경의, 즉 신경계에서 실행되는 상태라고 생각한다면 말이다. 예를 들어 색 식별에 대해 데이터들은 체내에서 일어나는 동일한 처리 구조에도 불구하고, 우리가 감정을 해석하고,

범주화하며 명명하는 방식은 문화에 따라 다르고, 우리는 감정을 표현하는 것이
적절한 사회적 상황을 특정 문화에서 배운다는 것을 단지 말할 뿐이다.
하지만 감정 상태 그 자체는 문화 전반에 걸쳐 지극히 불변할 가능성이 있다.
어떤 의미에서 우리는 진화에 의해 형성되어 두뇌에서 실행되는 기본적인,
문화적으로 보편적인 감정 모음을 생각할 수 있지만, 그런 감정 상태와 자극,
행동, 그리고 다른 인지 상태 간의 연관성은 바뀌기 쉬워, 특정한 문화적
상황에서의 학습에 의해 수정될 수 있다.

다음 글의 주제로 가장 적절한 것은? [3점]

① essential links between emotions and behaviors
감정과 행동 간의 근본적 연관성   감정과 문화 간의 연관성에 대한 글
② culturally constructed representation of emotions
문화적으로 구성되는 감정 표현   감정 표현에 문화가 영향을 미침
③ falsely described emotions through global languages
세계 공용어를 통해 잘못 묘사되는 감정
④ universally defined emotions across academic disciplines
학문 분야 전반에 걸쳐 보편적으로 정의되는 감정
universal로 만든 오답
⑤ wider influence of cognition on learning cultural contexts
문화적 상황을 학습하는 데 미치는 인식의 더 광범위한 영향 감정 표현에 미치는 문화적 상황의 영향을 설명함

> 왜 정답? [정답률 63%]

서로 다른 문화가 감정을 묘사하기 위해 가진 어휘와 개념에는 큰 차이가 있다는
첫 문장만으로도 감정 표현이 문화적으로 구성된다는 내용임을 알 수 있다.
감정을 표현하는 것이 적절한 사회적 상황을 특정 문화에서 배운다는 설명 역시
문화가 감정 표현에 영향을 미친다는 의미이므로 정답은 ② '문화적으로 구성되는
감정 표현'이다.

> 감정을 표현하는 것이 적절한 사회적
> 상황이 문화에 따라 다르다는 의미임 꿀팁

> 왜 오답?

① 감정과 행동 간의 연관성이 아니라 감정 표현과 문화 간의 연관성을 설명한
글이다.

③ 세계 공용어를 통해 묘사됨으로써 잘못 묘사되는 특정 감정이 있다는 등의
내용이 아니다.

④ 문화적으로 보편적인 감정 모음을 생각할 수도 있지만, 그러한 감정 상태와
다른 인지 상태 사이의 연관성은 문화적 학습을 통해 쉽게 바뀐다고 했다.

⑤ 문화적 상황의 학습에 인식이 영향을 미친다는 것이 아니라, 감정 표현에
문화적 상황이 영향을 미친다는 것이다.

F 02 정답 ④ ＊박물관의 이윤 지향 경영의 결과

주격 관계대명사(선행사: pressures)
There are pressures within the museum / that cause it to
to emphasise의 목적어절
emphasise / what happens in the galleries / over the activities /
주격 관계대명사(선행사: the activities)
that take place in its unseen zones. //
박물관 '내부의' 압력이 있다 / 그것이 강조하게 만드는 / 갤러리에서 발생하는 것을 / 활동보다
/ 그것의 보이지 않는 구역에서 일어나는 단서 1 박물관이 수입을 늘리도록
선행사   관계부사   강요받는 경우에 일어나는 일
In an era / when museums are forced / to increase their earnings, /
시대에 / 박물관이 강요당하는 / 그것의 수입을 늘리도록

they often focus their energies / on modernising their galleries
병렬 구조
/ or mounting temporary exhibitions / to bring more and more
audiences through the door. //
그것은 흔히 자기 에너지를 집중시킨다 / 그것의 갤러리를 현대화하는 데 / 또는 일시적인
전시회를 시작하는 데 / 점점 더 많은 관객을 문으로 데려오기 위해 //

In other words, / as museums struggle to survive / in a
competitive economy, / their budgets often prioritise / those
parts of themselves / that are consumable: /
다시 말해서 / 박물관이 살아남기 위해 고군분투할 때 / 경쟁 경제에서 / 그것의 예산은 흔히
우선시한다 / 박물관 자체의 부분을 / 소비할 수 있는 //

infotainment in the galleries, goods and services in the cafes
and the shops. //
갤러리의 인포테인먼트, 카페와 상점의 상품과 서비스와 같은 //
부사절 접속사(양보)
The unlit, unglamorous storerooms, / if they are ever discussed,
/ are at best presented as service areas / that process objects / for
the exhibition halls. // 단서 2 저장실은 논의되더라도 기껏해야 전시할 물건을
처리하는 서비스 공간으로 제시됨
불이 켜져 있지 않은 매력 없는 저장실은 / 그것들이 논의가 된다고 해도 / 기껏해야 서비스
공간으로 제시된다 / 물건을 처리하는 / 전시 홀에 둘 //

And at worst, / as museums pour more and more resources /
into their publicly visible faces, /
그리고 최악의 경우 / 박물관이 점점 더 많은 자원을 쏟아붓기 때문에 / 공개적으로 보이는
겉면에 /
생략되지 않은 부사절의 주어
the spaces of storage may even suffer, / their modernisation
being kept on hold / or being given less and less space / to house
병렬 구조(space 수식)
the expanding collections / and serve their complex conservation
needs. // 단서 3 저장 공간은 현대화가 보류되거나 공간이 점점 더 작아짐
저장 공간은 더 나빠지지도 모른다 / 그것의 현대화가 보류되거나 / 점점 더 적은 공간이
주어지게 되어 / 확장되는 소장품을 보관하고 / 그것의 복잡한 보존상의 요구를 충족시킬 //

- emphasise ⓥ 강조하다   • era ⓝ 시대
- be forced to ~하도록 강요당하다   • earning ⓝ 획득, 소득
- modernise ⓥ 현대화하다   • mount ⓥ 시작하다
- competitive ⓐ 경쟁을 하는, 경쟁력 있는   • budget ⓝ 예산
- prioritise ⓥ 우선시하다   • consumable ⓐ 소비할 수 있는, 소비재의
- unlit ⓐ 불을 켜지 않은   • unglamorous ⓐ 매력적이지 못한, 따분한
- storage ⓝ 저장 공간   • conservation ⓝ 보호, 보존
- need ⓝ 욕구, 요구   • commitment ⓝ 헌신

박물관의 보이지 않는 구역에서 일어나는 활동보다 갤러리에서 발생하는 것을
강조하게 만드는 박물관 '내부의' 압력이 있다. 박물관의 수입을 늘리도록
박물관이 강요당하는 시대에, 박물관은 점점 더 많은 관객을 문으로 데려오기
위해 자기 갤러리를 현대화하거나 일시적인 전시회를 시작하는 데 흔히 자기
에너지를 집중시킨다. 다시 말해서, 박물관이 경쟁 경제에서 살아남기 위해
고군분투할 때, 그것의 예산은 흔히 갤러리의 인포테인먼트, 카페와 상점의
상품과 서비스와 같은 소비할 수 있는 박물관 자체의 부분을 우선시한다. 불이
켜져 있지 않은 매력 없는 저장실은, 그것들이 논의가 된다고 해도, 기껏해야
전시 홀에 둘 물건을 처리하는 서비스 공간으로 제시된다. 그리고 최악의
경우 박물관이 공개적으로 보이는 겉면에 점점 더 많은 자원을 쏟아붓기
때문에, 저장 공간의 현대화가 보류되거나 확장되는 소장품을 보관하고 그것의
복잡한 보존상의 요구를 충족시킬 공간이 점점 줄어들게 되어 저장 공간은 더
나빠지지도 모른다.

다음 글의 주제로 가장 적절한 것은? [3점]

① importance of prioritising museums' exhibition spaces
박물관 전시 공간을 우선시하는 것의 중요성   전시 공간의 우선시로 인한 악영향을 설명함
② benefits of diverse activities in museums for audiences
관객을 위한 박물관에서의 다양한 활동의 이점   the activities로 만든 오답
③ necessity of expanding storerooms for displaying objects
물건 전시를 위해 저장실을 확장할 필요성   저장실에 미치는 악영향을 설명함
④ consequences of profit-oriented management of museums
박물관의 이윤 지향 경영의 결과   저장 공간이 열악해짐
⑤ ways to increase museums' commitment to the public good
공공의 이익에 대한 박물관의 헌신을 늘리는 방법   박물관의 이윤 추구에 대한 글임

> 왜 정답? [정답률 56%]

- 박물관이 그것의 수입을 늘리도록 강요당하는 시대에 일어나는 일을 설명함
  단서 1

- 저장실은, 논의되더라도, 기껏해야 전시할 물건을 처리하는 서비스 공간으로
  제시될 뿐임 단서 2

- 저장 공간은 현대화가 보류되거나 공간이 점점 더 작아질 수 있음 단서 3

→ 박물관이 수입을 늘리는 것을 지향함으로써 저장 공간이 열악해질 수 있다는
내용이므로 정답은 ④ '박물관의 이윤 지향 경영의 결과'이다.

> 왜 오답?

① 박물관이 전시 공간을 우선시함으로써 일어나는 악영향에 대해 설명하는 글이다.

② 관객이 소비할 수 있는 부분을 우선시함으로써 저장 공간은 열악해질 수 있다는
내용이다.

③ 박물관의 이윤 추구가 저장실에 미치는 악영향을 설명한 것이지, 저장실을
확장해야 한다는 직접적인 언급은 없다. (▶◀ 이유: 저장실에 미치는 악영향을
저장실을 확장해야 한다는 것으로 확대 해석하면 안 됨)

⑤ 박물관이 공공의 이익에 기여해야 한다는 내용이 아니다.

F 03 정답 ① *산업화가 가져온 노동과 시간의 변화

The arrival of the Industrial Age / changed the relationship
among time, labor, and capital. // **단서 1** 산업 시대가 도래하면서 시간, 노동,
자본 사이의 관계가 변화함
산업 시대의 도래는 / 시간, 노동, 자본 사이의 관계를 변화시켰다 //

Factories could produce around the clock, / and they could
= produce around the clock
do so with greater speed and volume / than ever before. //
공장은 24시간 내내 생산할 수 있었고 / 더 빠른 속도와 더 많은 양으로 그렇게 할 수 있었다 /
이전 어느 때보다 //

A machine that runs twelve hours a day / will produce more
= a machine
widgets / than one that runs for only eight hours per day /
— and a machine that runs twenty-four hours per day / will
produce the most widgets of all. //
하루 12시간 가동되는 기계는 / 더 많은 제품을 생산할 것이고 / 하루 8시간만 가동되는
기계보다 / 하루 24시간 가동되는 기계는 / 모든 기계 중 가장 많은 제품을 생산할 것이다 //

As such, at many factories, / the workday is divided into eight-
                                                수동태
hour shifts, / so that there will always be people on hand /
부사적 용법(목적)
to keep the widget machines humming. // **단서 2** 공장의 기계화로 인간의
                                                         작업일은 8시간 근무 교대로 나뉨
따라서 많은 공장에서 / 작업일은 8시간 근무 교대로 나누어져서 / 언제나 인력이 배치되어
있을 것이다 / 제품(생산) 기계가 쉬지 않고 돌아가도록 // **단서 3** 산업화로 인해 인간은 노동한
                                                      시간만큼 많은 제품을 생산하고, 많은 돈을 벌게 되어 임금이 노력(시간)과 연계됨
Industrialization raised the potential value of every single work
          the 비교급 ~, the 비교급 ...: ~할수록 더 …하다
hour / — the more hours you worked, / the more widgets you
produced, / and the more money you made — / and thus wages
          수동태
became tied to effort and production. //
          과거분사(labor 수식)
산업화는 모든 개별 근무 시간의 잠재적 가치를 높였는데 / 더 많은 시간을 일했을수록 / 더
많은 제품을 생산했고 / 더 많은 돈을 벌었으며 / 이로써 임금은 노력과 생산량에 연계되었다 //

Labor, previously guided by harvest cycles, / became clock-
oriented, / and society started to reorganize / around new
principles of productivity. // **단서 4** 수확 시기(자연의 질서)를 따르던 노동이 시계와
                                          생산성을 중심으로 재조직됨
이전에는 수확 주기를 따르던 노동이 / 시계 중심이 되었고 / 사회는 재조직되기 시작했다 /
새로운 생산성의 원칙을 중심으로 //

- Industrial Age 산업 시대 • capital ⓝ 자본
- around the clock 24시간 내내 • shift ⓝ 교대 근무
- hum ⓥ 웅웅거리다, 활기가 넘치다 • industrialization ⓝ 산업화
- potential ⓐ 잠재적인 • wage ⓝ 임금
- reorganize ⓥ 재조직하다

산업 시대의 도래는 시간, 노동, 자본 사이의 관계를 변화시켰다. 공장은
24시간 내내 생산할 수 있었고, 이전 어느 때보다 더 빠른 속도와 더 많은
양으로 그렇게 할 수 있었다. 하루 12시간 가동되는 기계는 하루 8시간만
가동되는 기계보다 더 많은 제품을 생산할 것이고, 하루 24시간 가동되는
기계는 모든 기계 중 가장 많은 제품을 생산할 것이다. 따라서 많은 공장에서
작업일은 8시간 근무 교대로 나누어져서, 제품(생산) 기계가 쉬지 않고
돌아가도록 언제나 인력이 배치되어 있을 것이다. 산업화는 모든 개별 근무
시간의 잠재적 가치를 높였는데, 더 많은 시간을 일했을수록, 더 많은 제품을
생산했고, 더 많은 돈을 벌었으며, 이로써 임금은 노력과 생산량에 연계되었다.
이전에는 수확 주기를 따르던 노동이 시계 중심이 되었고, 사회는 새로운
생산성의 원칙을 중심으로 재조직되기 시작했다.

다음 글의 주제로 가장 적절한 것은?

① shift in the work-time paradigm brought about by
industrialization 산업화로 인해 야기된 일과 시간의 변화에 대한 내용임
산업화로 인해 야기된 일과 시간의 패러다임 변화
② effects of standardizing production procedures on labor markets
생산 절차의 표준화가 노동 시장에 미친 영향 생산 과정의 기계화가 노동 시간과 임금에 미친 영향을
                                            설명한 내용이므로, 생산 절차의 '표준화'와는 관련이 없음
③ influence of industrialization on the machine-human relationship
산업화가 기계와 인간의 관계에 미친 영향
산업화가 인간의 노동 시간과 임금에 미친 영향이지, '기계와 인간의 관계'에 미친 영향은 언급되지 않음
④ efficient ways to increase the value of time in the Industrial Age
산업 시대에 시간의 가치를 높이는 효율적인 방법 산업 시대가 도래하면서 시간에 따라 노동의 가치가
                                                부여되었다는 내용이지, '시간의 가치'를 높이는 방법에 관한 내용은 아님
⑤ problems that excessive work hours have caused for laborers
과도한 업무 시간이 노동자에게 초래한 문제 과도한 업무 시간으로 인해 발생한 문제에 관한 언급은 없음

- 산업 시대의 도래는 시간, 노동, 자본 사이의 관계를 변화시켰음 **단서 1**
- 많은 공장에서 작업일은 8시간 근무 교대로 나누어져서, 제품(생산) 기계가 쉬지
  않고 돌아가도록 언제나 인력이 배치되어 있을 것임 **단서 2**
- 산업화는 모든 개별 근무 시간의 잠재적 가치를 높였는데, 더 많은 시간을
  일했을수록, 더 많은 제품을 생산했고, 더 많은 돈을 벌었으며, 이로써 임금은
  노력과 생산량에 연계되었음 **단서 3**
- 수확 주기를 따르던 노동이 시계 중심이 되었고, 사회는 새로운 생산성의 원칙을
  중심으로 재조직되기 시작했음 **단서 4**

➡ 산업 시대가 도래하면서 시간, 노동, 자본 사이의 관계가 변화했다. 공장의 기계화로
인간의 작업일은 8시간 근무 교대로 나뉘게 되었으며, 산업화로 인해 인간은
노동한 시간만큼 기계를 돌릴 수 있고, 기계를 돌리는 만큼 생산량을 확보할 수 있게
되었다.
따라서 인간은 노동한 시간만큼 많은 제품을 생산하고, 또 그만큼 많은 돈을
벌게 되었다는 내용이다. 이는 임금이 노력(시간)과 연계되는 계기가 되었다.
이전에는 수확 시기(자연의 질서)를 따르던 노동이 시계와 생산성을 중심으로
재조직되었다고 설명하고 있으므로, 정답은 ① '산업화로 인해 야기된 일과 시간의
패러다임 변화'이다.

> 왜 오답 ?

② 생산 과정의 기계화가 노동 시간과 임금에 미친 영향을 설명한 내용이므로, 생산
절차의 '표준화'와는 관련이 없다.
③ 산업화가 인간의 노동 시간과 임금에 미친 영향이지, '기계와 인간의 관계'에 미친
영향은 언급되지 않았다.
④ 산업 시대가 도래하면서 시간에 따라 노동의 가치가 부여되었다는 내용이지,
'시간의 가치'를 높이는 방법에 관한 내용은 아니다.
⑤ 과도한 업무 시간으로 인해 발생한 문제에 관한 언급은 없었다.

한규진 | 2025 수능 응시 · 대구 계성고 졸

지문 초반에 '산업 시대의 도래'가 '시간, 노동, 자본 사이의 관계'를
'변화'시켰다고 했으니, 앞으로 글을 읽으면서 시간, 노동, 자본의
세 요소를 중심으로 '어떤 변화'가 있었는지를 주목해야겠다는
생각을 가져보자. 글 중간에 부정이나 대조의 표현 없이 글이
이어지고 있으므로, 마지막까지 산업 시대의 도래가 초래한 변화에 집중하면 돼.
특히 중간에 'the 비교급, the 비교급' 구문이 있는데 어떤 특성이 강하게 나타나는
것을 강조하는 표현이므로 여기에 무게를 두면 산업화가 시간에 영향을 미치는 것에
대한 이야기라는 걸 알 수 있어!

F 04 정답 ④ *특이한 것을 이해하기 위해 일상적인 것에 대해 질문 제기하기

         가주어   진주어
It is much more natural to be surprised / by unusual phenomena
        비교급을 강조하는 부사
like eclipses / than ordinary phenomena like falling bodies / or
the succession of night into day and day into night. //
놀라는 것이 훨씬 더 자연스럽다 / 일식과 같은 특이한 현상에 의해 / 낙하하는 물체 같은
평범한 현상보다 / 또는 밤이 낮으로, 낮이 밤으로 이어지는 것과 같은 //
                                   부사적 용법(목적)   주격 관계대명사
Many cultures invented gods / to explain these eclipses / that
                                                            관계절 없는
shocked, frightened, or surprised them; / but very few imagined
a god of falling bodies /
많은 문화는 신을 만들어 냈다 / 이러한 일식을 설명하기 위해 / 그들에게 충격, 공포, 또는
놀라움을 주었던 / 그러나 낙하하는 물체의 신을 상상했던 문화는 거의 없었다 /
            전치사+관계대명사   so 형용사/부사 that ...: 너무 ~해서 …하다
— to which they were so accustomed that they did not even
notice them. //
너무 익숙해서 심지어 알아차리지도 못했던 //
                                                      = reason
But the reason for eclipses / is ultimately the same / as that of the
succession of night and day: /
그러나 일식이 일어나는 이유는 / 궁극적으로 동일하다 / 밤과 낮이 연속되는 이유와 /
                                          계속적 용법의 관계대명사
the movement of celestial bodies, / which itself is based on the
Newtonian law of attraction / and how it explains / why things
                              let+목적어+목적격 보어(원형부정사)
fall / when we let them go. //
즉 천체의 움직임 / 그 자체로 뉴턴의 만유인력의 법칙에 기반하는 / 그리고 설명하는 방식 /
왜 물체가 떨어지는지 / 우리가 물체를 놓으면 //

For the physicist, / understanding the ordinary, the habitual,
핵심 주어
and the frequent / thus allows us to account for / the frightening
단서1 평범한 것을 이해하는 것이 기묘한 것을 설명할 수 있게 해줌
and the singular. //
그러므로 물리학자로 말할 것 같으면 / 평범한 것, 습관적인 것, 빈번한 것을 이해하는 것이 /
우리가 설명할 수 있게 해준다 / 무서운 것과 기묘한 것을 //
As such, / it was thus necessary / to ask "Why do things fall?" /
가주어   진주어①
and to have Newton's response /
진주어②
그와 같이 / 따라서 필요했다 / "물체는 왜 떨어지는가?"라고 질문하는 것 / 그리고 뉴턴식의
답을 하는 것 /
부사적 용법(목적) 단서2 평범한 것에 대해 질문을 던지는 것이 기괴한 현상을 이해하기 위해 필요함
to understand a broad range of much more bizarre phenomena
비교급을 강조하는 부사
/ occurring at every level of the universe. //
다양하고 폭넓은 훨씬 더 기괴한 현상들을 이해하기 위해서 / 우주의 모든 수준에서 일어나고
있는 //

- phenomena ⓝ 현상   · ordinary ⓐ 평범한
- succession ⓝ 연속   · frightened ⓐ 겁먹은
- accustomed ⓐ 익숙한   · physicist ⓝ 물리학자
- account for 설명하다   · notice ⓥ 알아차리다
- singular ⓐ 기묘한   · widespread ⓐ 광범위한
- mythical ⓐ 신화적인   · influence ⓝ 영향
- perception ⓝ 인식   · pose ⓥ (위협·문제 등을) 제기하다

낙하하는 물체나 밤이 낮으로, 낮이 밤으로 이어지는 것과 같은 평범한
현상보다 일식과 같은 특이한 현상에 놀라는 것이 훨씬 더 자연스럽다.
그들에게 충격, 공포, 또는 놀라움을 주었던 이러한 일식을 설명하기 위해 많은
문화에서 신을 만들어 냈지만, 너무 익숙해서 심지어 알아차리지도 못했던,
낙하하는 물체의 신을 상상했던 문화는 거의 없었다. 그러나 일식이 일어나는
이유는 밤과 낮이 연속되는 이유와 궁극적으로 동일한데, 즉 그 자체로 뉴턴의
만유인력의 법칙에 기반하는 천체의 움직임과 그것이 우리가 물체를 놓으면 왜
떨어지는지 설명하는 방식이다. 그러므로 물리학자로 말할 것 같으면, 평범한
것, 습관적인 것, 빈번한 것을 이해하여 우리가 무서운 것과 기묘한 것을
설명할 수 있게 해준다. 따라서 그와 같이, 우주의 모든 수준에서 일어나고
있는 다양하고 폭넓은 훨씬 더 기괴한 현상들을 이해하기 위해서, "물체는 왜
떨어지는가?"라고 질문하는 것과 뉴턴식의 답을 하는 것이 필요했다.

다음 글의 주제로 가장 적절한 것은? [3점]
특이한 것을 이해하기 위해 일상적인 것에 질문을 던지는 것이 필요함을 역설하는 내용
① widespread preference for mythical explanations over scientific
ones 신화적 설명에 대한 광범위한 선호가 있다고 하지 않았음
과학적 설명보다는 신화적 설명에 대한 광범위한 선호
② limitations of Newtonian law in explaining eclipse phenomena
일식 현상을 설명하는 데 있어 뉴턴 법칙의 한계   뉴턴 법칙이 언급된 것으로 만든 오답
③ influence of scientific interpretations on perceptions of reality
현실 인식에 대한 과학적 해석의 영향   현실 인식에 대한 과학적 해석의 영향을 다루지 않음
④ need to pose questions about the usual to understand the unusual
특이한 것을 이해하기 위해 일상적인 것에 대한 질문을 제기할 필요성
⑤ difficulty of drawing general conclusions from unusual phenomena
특이한 현상에서 일반적인 결론을 도출하는 것의 어려움
특이한 현상에서 일반적인 결론을 내는 것이 어렵다는 내용은 아님

왜 정답? [정답률 66%]

전반부	일식과 같은 특이한 현상이 일어나는 이유는 평범한 현상과 사실 동일함
후반부	• 물리학자는 평범한 것, 습관적인 것, 빈번한 것을 이해하여 우리가 무서운 것과 기묘한 것을 설명하게 해줌 단서1 • 다양하고 기괴한 현상을 이해하기 위해 평범한 현상에 대한 물음과 그것을 설명하기 위한 답이 필요함 단서2

▶ 따라서 이 글의 주제는 ④ '특이한 것을 이해하기 위해 일상적인 것에 대한 질문을
제기할 필요성'이다.

왜 오답?

① 과학적 설명보다는 신화적 설명에 대한 광범위한 선호를 이야기하는 글이 아니다.
② 뉴턴 법칙이 언급된 것으로 만든 오답일 뿐, 일식 현상을 설명하는 데 있어 뉴턴
   법칙의 한계에 대해 언급하지 않았다.
③ 일상적인 것을 언급하긴 했지만, 현실 인식에 대한 과학적 해석의 영향을 말하는
   글이 아니다.
⑤ 특이한 현상에서 일반적인 결론을 도출하는 것의 어려움에 대한 글이 아니다.

형용사적 용법(the human desire 수식)
The human desire to make pictures is deeply rooted. //
그림을 만드는 인간의 욕망은 깊게 뿌리를 내리고 있다 //
At least 64,000 years ago, / Neanderthals used colored oxide and
charcoal / to make paintings of large wild animals, tracings of
human hands, / and abstract patterns on cave and rock walls. //
명사구의 병렬 구조
적어도 6만 4천년 전에 / 네안데르탈인은 색깔이 있는 산화물과 목탄을 사용하여 / 커다란
야생 동물의 그림, 사람 손의 모사(模寫) / 그리고 동굴과 암벽에 추상적인 무늬를 만들었다 //
Today, people create images / with a multitude of mediums,
including photography. //
오늘날, 사람들은 그림을 만든다 / 사진 촬영을 포함한 다수의 도구로 //
What drives this picturemaking impulse? //
무엇이 이 그림을 만드는 충동을 이끄는가 //
Some make pictures for commercial reasons. //
어떤 사람들은 상업적인 이유로 그림을 만든다 //
Others create informational systems / or employ scientific
부사적 용법(목적)
imaging tools to visualize the unseen. //
다른 사람들은 정보 체계를 만들거나 / 보이지 않는 것을 시각화하기 위해 과학적 이미지화
도구를 사용한다 //
Artists use images expressionistically, / to conceptualize and
articulate / who they are and how they view the world. //
예술가들은 그림을 표현주의적으로 사용한다 / 개념화하고 분명하게 표현하기 위해서 /
그들이 누구인지 그리고 그들이 세상을 어떻게 바라보는지를 //
단서 그림을 만드는 근본적 동기는 보존하고 기념하려는 욕구임
However, the fundamental motive for making the vast majority
핵심 주어(단수)
of pictures / is a desire to preserve: / to document, and therefore
단수 동사
honor, specific people, events, and possessions of importance. //
그러나, 그림 대부분을 만드는 것에 대한 근본적인 동기는 / 보존하려는 욕구인데 / 기록하고,
그래서 중요성을 지닌 특정 사람들, 사건들, 그리고 소유물을 기념하려는 것이다 //
Regardless of purpose, the making of images persists / because
동명사
words alone cannot always provide a satisfactory way / to
describe and express our relationship to the world. //
목적과 관계없이, 그림 만드는 것은 지속되는데 / 말만으로는 만족할 만한 방법을 항상 제공할
수가 없기 때문이다 / 세상과 우리의 관계를 설명하고 표현하는 //
Pictures are an essential component / of how humans observe,
communicate, celebrate, comment, and, most of all, remember. //
그림은 가장 중요한 요소이다 / 인간이 어떻게 관찰하고, 소통하고, 기념하고, 논평하고,
무엇보다도 기억하는지의 //
What and how we remember shapes our worldview, / and
pictures can provide a stimulus to jog one's memory. //
주어
우리가 무엇을 그리고 어떻게 기억하느냐가 우리의 세계관을 형성하고 / 그림은 누군가의
기억을 되살리는 자극을 제공할 수 있다 //

- desire ⓝ 욕구   · rooted ⓐ ~에 뿌리[근원]를 둔
- abstract ⓐ 추상적인   · multitude ⓝ 다수
- visualize ⓥ 시각화하다 · conceptualize ⓥ 개념화하다
- fundamental ⓐ 근본적인 · preserve ⓥ 보존하다
- document ⓥ 기록하다   · persist ⓥ 계속[지속]되다
- satisfactory ⓐ 만족스러운, 충분한 · essential ⓐ 필수적인
- evaluation ⓝ 평가

그림을 만드는 인간의 욕망은 깊게 뿌리를 내리고 있다. 적어도 6만 4천년
전에, 네안데르탈인은 색깔이 있는 산화물과 목탄을 사용하여 동굴과 암벽에
커다란 야생 동물의 그림, 사람 손의 모사(模寫), 그리고 추상적인 무늬를
만들었다. 오늘날, 사람들은 사진 촬영을 포함한 다수의 도구로 그림을
만든다. 무엇이 이 그림을 만드는 충동을 이끄는가? 어떤 사람들은 상업적인
이유로 그림을 만든다. 다른 사람들은 정보 체계를 만들거나 보이지 않는
것을 시각화하기 위해 과학적 이미지화 도구를 사용한다. 예술가들은 그들이
누구인지 그리고 그들이 세상을 어떻게 바라보는지를 개념화하고 분명하게
표현하기 위해서 그림을 표현주의적으로 사용한다. 그러나, 그림 대부분을
만드는 것에 대한 근본적인 동기는 보존하려는 욕구인데, 기록하고, 그래서

중요성을 지닌 특정 사람들, 사건들, 그리고 소유물을 기념하려는 것이다. 목적과 관계없이, 그림 만드는 것은 지속되는데 말만으로는 세상과 우리의 관계를 설명하고 표현하는 만족할 만한 방법을 항상 제공할 수가 없기 때문이다. 그림은 인간이 어떻게 관찰하고, 소통하고, 기념하고, 논평하고, 무엇보다도 기억하는지의 가장 중요한 요소이다. 우리가 무엇을 그리고 어떻게 기억하느냐가 우리의 세계관을 형성하고 그림은 누군가의 기억을 되살리는 자극을 제공할 수 있다.

다음 글의 주제로 가장 적절한 것은?

인간은 중요한 것을 기념하고 보존하기 위해 그림을 만듦

① factors that influence the art evaluation process
예술 평가 과정에 영향을 미치는 요인

예술을 평가한다는 내용은 없음

② difference between commercial images and informative pictures
상업적 이미지와 정보 전달 이미지의 차이 상업적 이미지와 정보 전달 이미지를 대조하여 설명하는 글이 아님

③ explanation for the human desire of creating images to remember
기억하기 위해 이미지를 창조하려는 인간의 욕망에 대한 설명

④ benefits of written records in understanding our ancestors 그림에
조상을 이해하는 데 있어 글로 쓰여진 기록의 이점   대한 내용이지, 글로 쓰여진 기록에 대한 내용이 아님

⑤ change in the value of the same painting across history
역사 속에서 같은 그림의 가치 변화   한 그림이 시간이 지나면서 가치가 변했다는 내용이 아님

왜 정답? [정답률 89%]

• 아주 옛날부터 그림을 만들려는 인간의 욕망은 존재함

• 이러한 그림을 만드는 충동은 근본적으로 중요한 것을 기록하여 보존하려는 욕구임 **단서**

• 그림은 글만으로는 설명할 수 없는 세상과 우리의 관계를 표현하고, 우리가 무엇을 어떻게 기억하는지를 보여주는 중요한 요소임

⇒ 따라서 이 글의 주제로는 ③ '기억하기 위해 이미지를 창조하려는 인간의 욕망에 대한 설명'이 가장 적절하다.

왜 오답?

① 예술을 평가한다는 것에 대한 언급은 없다.

② 상업적 목적으로 그림을 만드는 사람이 있다는 언급은 있었으나, 이 글의 핵심 내용은 아니다.

④ 글로 쓰여진 기록이 아니라 그림이 이 글의 핵심이다.

⑤ 같은 그림이 시대의 흐름에 따라 가치가 어떻게 변화했는지에 대한 글이 아니다.

F 06 정답 ④ *문제의 본질에 따라 달라지는 정부의 접근 방식

목적격 관계대명사

Natural disasters and aging are two problems / that societies
현재완료진행형
have been dealing with for all of human history. //
자연재해와 노화는 두 문제이다 / 전 인류 역사에 걸쳐 사회가 다뤄온 //

Governments must respond to both, / but their dynamics are entirely different / and this has profound consequences / for the nature of the response. // **단서 1** (두 문제의) 역학이 다른 것이 반응의 본질에 큰 영향을 미침
정부는 두 가지 모두에 반응해야 하지만 / 그것들의 역학은 완전히 다르고 / 이것은 깊은 영향력을 가진다 / 반응의 본질에 //

Simply by plotting the aging slope, / policy makers go a long way / toward understanding the problem: / People get older / at a constant and reliable rate. //
단순히 노화 기울기를 그림으로써 / 정책 결정자들은 진척을 보인다 / 문제를 이해하는 데 / 사람들은 나이 들어간다 / 일정하고 신뢰할 만한 속도로 //

There can be disagreements / over how to solve the aging problem (this is political complexity), / but the nature of the problem is never in dispute. //
이견들이 있을 수 있으나 / 노화 문제를 해결하는 방법에 대한 (이것은 정치적 복잡성이다) / 문제의 본질은 절대로 논쟁의 여지가 없다 //

동명사 주어(단수)   과거분사(the number of people 수식)   단수 동사
Plotting the number of people / killed in natural disasters / does very little to advance understanding of this problem / other than emphasizing the randomness of natural disasters. //
사람들의 숫자를 그려 보는 것은 / 자연재해로 사망한 / 이 문제에 대한 이해를 거의 진척시키지 않는다 / 자연재해의 무작위성을 강조하는 것 외에는 //

동명사 주어
Preparing a policy response is, therefore, / much easier in some areas than in others. //
그러므로 정책 반응을 준비하는 것은 / 다른 영역보다 일부 영역에서 훨씬 더 쉽다 //

When inputs are reliable and easy to predict, / it greatly facilitates information processing / and allows for anticipatory problem-solving. // **단서 2** 문제(입력 정보)가 신뢰할 만하고 예측하기 쉬울 때의 정책 반응
입력 정보가 신뢰할 만하고 예측하기 쉬울 때 / 그것은 정보 처리를 크게 용이하게 하고 / 예측적 문제 해결을 가능하게 한다 //

When problems are causally complex and multivariate,
동명사 주어(단수)
/ determining the appropriate response / is a reactionary
단수 동사
endeavor. // **단서 3** 문제가 복잡하고 변수가 많을 때의 정책 반응
문제가 인과적으로 복잡하고 변수가 많을 때 / 적절한 반응을 결정하는 것은 / 반응적 노력이다 //

• plot ⓥ 표시하다 • slope ⓝ 기울기, 경사면
• emphasize ⓥ 강조하다 • facilitate ⓥ 용이하게 하다, 가능하게 하다
• anticipatory ⓐ 기대한, 예측한 • multivariate ⓐ 다변량의
• reactionary ⓐ 반응적인 • endeavor ⓝ 노력, 시도
• hasty ⓐ 급한, 서두르는 • comprehensive ⓐ 포괄적인, 종합적인

자연재해와 노화는 전 인류 역사에 걸쳐 사회가 다뤄온 두 문제이다. 정부는 두 가지 모두에 반응해야 하지만, 그것들의 역학은 완전히 다르고 이것은 반응의 본질에 깊은 영향력을 가진다. 단순히 노화 기울기를 그림으로써, 정책 결정자들은 문제를 이해하는 데 진척을 보인다. 사람들은 일정하고 신뢰할 만한 속도로 나이 들어간다. 노화 문제를 해결하는 방법에 대한 이견들이 있을 수 있으나, (이것은 정치적 복잡성이다) 문제의 본질은 절대로 논쟁의 여지가 없다. 자연재해로 사망한 사람들의 숫자를 그려 보는 것은 자연재해의 무작위성을 강조하는 것 외에는 이 문제에 대한 이해를 거의 진척시키지 않는다. 그러므로 정책 반응을 준비하는 것은 다른 영역보다 일부 영역에서 훨씬 더 쉽다. 입력 정보가 신뢰할 만하고 예측하기 쉬울 때, 그것은 정보 처리를 크게 용이하게 하고 예측적 문제 해결을 가능하게 한다. 문제가 인과적으로 복잡하고 변수가 많을 때, 적절한 반응을 결정하는 것은 반응적 노력이다.

다음 글의 주제로 가장 적절한 것은? [3점]

자연재해에 대한 언급은 있으나 성급한 결정이 위험하다는 내용은 없음

① risks of hasty decision-making during natural disasters
자연재해 발생 시 성급한 의사결정의 위험

② reasons for governmental concern about aging populations
노인 인구 증가에 대한 정부의 우려 이유 고령화에 대한 언급은 있으나, 정부의 걱정에 대한 내용은 없음

③ significance of studying the comprehensive history of policy making 정책 결정의 역사에 대한 글이 아님
정책 결정의 포괄적인 역사를 연구하는 것의 중요성

④ different approaches of governments depending on the nature of the problem their dynamics are entirely different ~ nature of the response
문제의 성격에 따른 정부의 다양한 접근 방식

⑤ advantages of anticipatory problem-solving in dealing with social problems 예측적 문제 해결의 장점이 언급은 되었으나, 이것의 장점에 대해 쓴 글이 아님
사회 문제 해결에 있어서 예측적 문제 해결의 장점

왜 정답? [정답률 42%]

핵심 문장	두 가지 사회적 문제는 역학이 다르고, 따라서 반응의 본질에도 영향을 미침 **단서 1**
예시 비교	• 노화는 일정하고 신뢰할 만한 속도로 일어나므로 단순한 노화 기울기 그림이 문제 이해에 큰 도움을 줌 **단서 2** • 하지만 자연재해는 같은 방식으로 접근하면 문제 이해에 거의 도움이 되지 않음 **단서 3**
구체적 설명	문제가 신뢰할 만하고 단순할 때와 인과적으로 복잡하고 변수가 많을 때의 정책 반응 준비는 다름

▶ 따라서 이 글의 주제는 ④ '문제의 성격에 따른 정부의 다양한 접근 방식'이 가장 적절하다.

왜 오답?

① 자연재해에 대한 언급은 있으나 성급한 결정으로 인한 위험에 대한 내용은 없다.

② 고령화에 대한 언급은 있으나, 이에 대해 정부가 걱정하는 이유가 없다.

③ 정책 수립의 역사에 대한 글이 아니다.

⑤ 입력 정보가 예측하기 쉽고 신뢰할 만하다면 예측적 문제 해결이 가능하다고 하지만, 이것의 장점을 설명하는 글은 아니다. 함정

While many city shoppers were clearly drawn to the notion /
of buying and eating foods associated with nature, / the nature
claimed by the ads / was no longer the nature / that created the
foods. //
도시의 구매자 대부분이 개념에 확실히 끌렸지만 / 자연과 관련이 있는 식품을 사고 먹는다는 /
광고가 주장하는 그 자연은 / 더는 그 자연이 아니었다 / 그 식품을 만들어 낸 //

단서 1 식품 광고의 '자연'은 광고의 부속물로서만 관련이 있음

Indeed, the nature claimed by many ads / was associated with
food products / only by the ads' attachment. //
실제로 많은 광고가 주장하는 자연은 / 식품 제품과 관련이 있었다 / '오직' 광고의 부속물로만 //

This is clearly a case of / what French sociologist Henri Lefebvre
has called "the decline of the referentials," /
이것이 분명하게 보이는 사례다 / 프랑스의 사회학자 Henri Lefebvre가 '지시성의 감소'라고
일컬었던 것 /

단서 2 자본주의의 영향을 받은 단어가 (원래의) 의미 있는 연관으로부터 분리되는 것임

or the tendency of words / under the influence of capitalism /
to become separated from meaningful associations. //
즉 단어들의 경향 / 자본주의의 영향을 받은 / 의미 있는 연관으로부터 분리되는 //

Increasingly, food ads helped shoppers become accustomed
to / new definitions of words such as "fresh" and "natural,"
definitions that could well be considered opposite of their
traditional meanings. //
단서 3 식품 광고의 '신선한', '자연스러운'이라는 단어는 기존과 정반대로 여겨지는 개념임
점차, 식품 광고는 구매자가 익숙해지도록 도왔는데 / '신선한', '자연스러운' 같은 단어의
새로운 개념에 / 어쩌면 기존 의미와 정반대로 여겨질 수 있는 정의였다 //

The new definitions better served / the needs of the emerging
industrial food system, / which could not supply foods / that
matched customary meanings and expectations. //
그 새로운 정의는 더 잘 부합했는데 / 신흥 식품 산업 시스템의 요구 / 그 시스템은 식품을
공급할 수 없었다 / 관례적인 의미와 기대에 부응하는 //

And they better met shoppers' desires, / although with
pretense. //
그래서 그 정의는 소비자들의 열망을 더 잘 충족했다 / 비록 겉치레이긴 하더라도 //

- attachment ⓝ 부속물, 부착 · decline ⓝ 감소, 하락
- referential ⓝ 지시성 · tendency ⓝ 경향
- capitalism ⓝ 자본주의 · association ⓝ 연관, 연상
- accustomed ⓐ 익숙한 · definition ⓝ 정의
- emerging ⓐ 신흥의, 새로 만들어진 · customary ⓐ 관례적인, 관습상의
- pretense ⓝ 겉치레, 가식 · reliability ⓝ 신뢰성

도시의 구매자 대부분이 자연과 관련이 있는 식품을 사고 먹는다는 개념에
확실히 끌렸지만, 광고가 주장하는 그 자연은 더는 그 식품을 만들어 낸 자연이
아니었다. 실제로 많은 광고가 주장하는 자연은 '오직' 광고의 부속물로만
식품 제품과 관련이 있었다. 이것이 프랑스의 사회학자 Henri Lefebvre가
'지시성의 감소'라고 일컬었던 것, 즉 자본주의의 영향을 받은 단어가 의미 있는
연관으로부터 분리되는 경향을 분명하게 보이는 사례다. 점차, 식품 광고는
구매자가 '신선한', '자연스러운' 같은 단어의 새로운 개념에 익숙해지도록
도왔는데, 어쩌면 기존 의미와 정반대로 여겨질 수 있을 정의였다. 그 새로운
정의는 신흥 식품 산업 시스템의 요구에 더 잘 부합했는데, 그 시스템은
관례적인 의미와 기대에 부응하는 식품을 공급할 수 없었다. 그래서 비록
겉치레이긴 하더라도 그 정의는 소비자들의 열망을 더 잘 충족했다.

다음 글의 주제로 가장 적절한 것은?
광고에서 쓰이는 단어의 뜻이 변화했다는 것이지 신뢰도 하락은 언급하고 있지 않음
① decline of reliability in the ads of natural foods
자연식품 광고의 신뢰도 하락
② changes in the senses of words linked to food ads
식품 광고와 관련된 단어 의미의 변화 자본주의의 영향으로 본래 의미로부터 분리되는 결과를 초래했음
③ influence of capitalism on the industrial food system
산업 식품 시스템에 대한 자본주의의 영향 산업 식품 시스템이나 자본주의는 주요 내용이 아님
④ various ways to attract customers in the food industry
식품 산업에서 고객을 유인하는 다양한 방법 고객을 유인하는 다양한 방법이 언급되어 있지 않음
⑤ necessity of meaningful word associations in commercials
상업 광고에서 유의미한 어휘 연관의 필요성 유의미한 어휘 연관의 필요성에 대해 언급하지 않았음

왜 정답? [정답률 42%]

⇒ 식품 광고에서 사용되는 단어는 자본주의의 영향으로 새로운 식품 산업 시스템의
요구에 더 잘 맞추어짐 → 이 단어는 소비자의 욕구를 충족시키는 방향으로
재정의되었음 → 이러한 현상은 단어가 원래의 의미에서 벗어나는 결과를 가져옴
▶ 따라서 글의 주제로 가장 적절한 것은 ② '식품 광고와 관련된 단어 의미의
변화'이다.

왜 오답?
① 광고에서 쓰이는 단어의 뜻이 변화했다는 것이지 신뢰도 하락으로 연결하고 있지
않다.
③ 산업 식품 시스템이나 자본주의는 주요 내용이 아니다.
④ 고객을 유인하는 다양한 방법이 언급되어 있지 않다.
⑤ 식품 광고에서 쓰이는 단어의 의미 변화에 대한 글이지, 유의미한 어휘 연관의
필요성에 대해 언급하지 않았다.

F **08** 정답 ⑤ *카페인과 뇌의 적응 반응

During the day, / a molecule called adenosine / builds up in
your brain. //
낮 동안에 / 아데노신이라고 불리는 분자가 / 여러분의 뇌에 쌓인다 //

Adenosine binds with receptors on nerve cells, or neurons, /
slowing down their activity / and making you feel drowsy. //
아데노신은 신경 세포들, 다시 말해 뉴런들의 수용체들과 결합해 / 그것들의 활동을 늦추고 /
여러분이 나른함을 느끼게 한다 //

But caffeine is also able to bind with these receptors, / and by
doing so / it blocks adenosine's effect, / making your neurons
fire more and keeping you alert. //
단서 1 카페인이 나른함을 느끼게 하는 아데노신의 효과를 차단함
그러나 카페인 역시 이 수용체들과 결합할 수 있고 / 그렇게 함으로써 / 그것이 아데노신의
효과를 차단하여 / 뉴런을 더 활성화시키고 여러분이 깨어 있도록 유지시킨다. /

Caffeine also activates a gland / at the base of your brain. //
카페인은 또한 분비선을 활성화시킨다 / 뇌 기저부의 //

This releases hormones / that tell the adrenal glands on your
kidneys to produce adrenaline, / causing your heart to beat
faster / and your blood pressure to rise. //
이것은 호르몬을 분비시켜 / 신장에 있는 부신이 아드레날린을 생산하도록 하는 / 여러분의
심장을 더욱 빨리 뛰게 하고 / 혈압이 올라가게 한다 //

If, however, your daily caffeine intake is consistent, / your brain
will adapt to it. //
단서 2 카페인을 일정하게 섭취하면 뇌는 이에 적응함
하지만 여러분의 하루 카페인 섭취량이 일정하다면 / 뇌가 이에 적응할 것이다 //

Your brain is like, / 'Okay, every morning I'm getting this
caffeine / that's binding to these receptors / and blocking
adenosine / from binding to them.' //
여러분의 뇌는 이와 같다 / '그래, 매일 아침 나는 이 카페인을 섭취하고 있군 / 이 수용체들과
결합해서 / 아데노신을 막는 / 그것들과 결합하는 것을' //

So your brain creates extra receptors / to give adenosine more of
an opportunity / to bind with them and have its usual effect. //
그래서 여러분의 뇌는 추가의 수용체들을 만들어 낸다 / 아데노신에게 더 많은 기회를 주기
위해 / 그것들(수용체)과 결합하여 평소의 효과를 낼 //

And more adenosine is also produced / to counteract the
caffeine. //
단서 3 카페인에 대응하기 위한 더 많은 아데노신이 생성됨
그리고 더 많은 아데노신이 또한 생성된다 / 카페인에 대응하기 위해 //

That's why it takes more and more caffeine / to have the same
effect. //
그것이 점점 더 많은 카페인이 필요한 이유다 / 같은 효과를 내기 위해서 //

- molecule ⓝ 분자 · bind with ~와 결합하다
- receptor ⓝ (인체의) 수용기[감각기] · nerve cell 신경 세포
- fire ⓥ (열의·관심 등이) 불타게 하다 · alert ⓐ 경계하는
- hormone ⓝ 호르몬 · adrenal ⓐ 신장 부근의

- intake ⓝ 섭취   · consistent ⓐ 거듭되는, 일정한
- counteract ⓥ 대응하다   · consequence ⓝ 결과
- deprivation ⓝ 박탈, 부족   · temptation ⓝ 유혹

낮 동안에 아데노신이라고 불리는 분자가 여러분의 뇌에 쌓인다. 아데노신은 신경 세포들, 다시 말해 뉴런들의 수용체들과 결합해 그것들의 활동을 늦추고 여러분이 나른함을 느끼게 한다. 그러나 카페인 역시 이 수용체들과 결합할 수 있고, 그렇게 함으로써 그것이 아데노신의 효과를 차단하여 뉴런을 더 활성화시키고 여러분이 깨어 있도록 유지시킨다. 카페인은 또한 뇌 기저부의 분비선을 활성화시킨다. 이것은 신장에 있는 부신이 아드레날린을 생산하도록 하는 호르몬을 분비시켜 여러분의 심장을 더욱 빨리 뛰게 하고 혈압이 올라가게 한다. 하지만 여러분의 하루 카페인 섭취량이 일정하다면 뇌가 이에 적응할 것이다. 여러분의 뇌는 이와 같다. '그래, 매일 아침 나는 이 수용체들과 결합해서 아데노신이 그것들과 결합하는 것을 막는 이 카페인을 섭취하고 있군.' 그래서 여러분의 뇌는 아데노신에게 그것들(수용체)과 결합하여 평소의 효과를 낼 더 많은 기회를 주기 위해 추가의 수용체들을 만들어 낸다. 그리고 카페인에 대응하기 위해 더 많은 아데노신이 또한 생성된다. 그것이 같은 효과를 내기 위해서 점점 더 많은 카페인이 필요한 이유다.

다음 글의 주제로 가장 적절한 것은?

① what your brain does for regular hormone production
정상적인 호르몬 생성을 위해 당신의 뇌가 하는 일   카페인이 미치는 영향에 관한 내용임
② consequences of sleep deprivation caused by caffeine
카페인으로 인한 수면 부족의 결과   수면 부족의 결과는 제시되지 않음
③ connection between brain health and hormone balance
뇌 건강과 호르몬 균형 사이의 관계   언급되지 않음
④ efforts to overcome the constant temptation of caffeine
카페인의 지속적인 유혹을 이기기 위한 노력   관련 없음
⑤ how your brain adapts to a steady caffeine consumption
당신의 뇌가 규칙적인 카페인 섭취에 적응하는 방법
카페인이 뇌에서 어떤 식으로 작용하는지 구체적으로 설명함

왜 정답? [정답률 82%]

낮 동안 피로를 느끼게 하는 아데노신이 뇌에 쌓임 → 카페인은 이를 차단하여 깨어 있도록 함 → 뇌가 이에 적응함 → 같은 효과를 내기 위해 더 많은 아데노신이 생성됨
▶ 뇌가 카페인에 어떻게 대응하는지를 설명하고 있으므로 주제는 ⑤ '당신의 뇌가 규칙적인 카페인 섭취에 적응하는 방법'이다.

왜 오답?

① 정상적인 호르몬 생성에 관한 내용이 아니고 카페인 섭취의 영향이 주된 내용이다.
② 카페인으로 인해 수면 부족이 일어난다는 내용은 언급되지 않았다.
③ 뇌 건강과 호르몬 사이의 상관관계는 전체 흐름과 관련이 없다.
④ 카페인을 지속적으로 섭취했을 때 발생할 수 있는 내용이 언급되어 있다.

F 09 정답 ① * 동일시하는 집단을 선호하는 경향

Sociologist Brooke Harrington said / if there was an $E=mc^2$ of social science, / it would be SD > PD, / "social death is more frightening than physical death." //
사회학자 Brooke Harrington은 말했다 / 사회 과학의 $E=mc^2$가 있다면 / 그것은 SD > PD 일 것이라고 / 즉 "사회적 죽음이 신체적 죽음보다 더 무섭다" //

This is why / we feel deeply threatened / when a new idea
　　　　　　　　　　　　= ideas 주격 관계대명사
challenges / the ones that have become part of our identity. //
이것은 이유이다 / 우리가 매우 위협적으로 느끼는 / 새로운 개념이 도전할 때 / 우리 정체성의 일부가 된 것들에 //

　　　　　　　　= ideas 주격 관계대명사(선행사: ones)
For some ideas, / the ones that identify us as members of a group, / we don't reason as individuals; / we reason as a member of a tribe. //
몇몇 견해에 대하여 / 우리가 한 집단의 구성원으로 우리를 동일시하는 / 우리는 개인으로서 판단하지 않는다 / 우리는 한 부족의 구성원으로서 판단한다 //

We want to seem trustworthy, / and reputation management as a trustworthy individual / often overrides most other concerns, / even our own mortality. //
우리는 믿음직스럽게 보이고 싶다 / 그리고 믿음직한 개인으로서의 평판 관리는 / 흔히 다른 모든 걱정보다 더 중요하다 / 심지어 우리 자신의 죽음보다 //

This is not entirely irrational. //
이것은 완전히 비이성적인 것이 아니다 //

　　　　　　　　　　　　　　　　　　　　　　동명사구 주어
A human alone in this world / faces a lot of difficulty, / but being alone in the world before modern times / was almost certainly a death sentence. //
　　　　　　　　　　　　　　단수 동사
이 세상에 홀로 있는 인간은 / 많은 어려움을 직면한다 / 하지만 근대 이전의 세상에서 혼자 있는 것은 / 거의 확실하게 사형 선고였다 //

　　　　　　　　　　　　　　　　형용사적 용법
So we carry with us an innate drive / to form groups, / join groups, / remain in those groups, / and oppose other groups. //
그래서 우리는 타고난 욕구를 가지고 있다 / 집단을 형성하고 / 집단에 합류하고 / 그 집단에 남아 있고 / 다른 집단에 반대하려는 //
단서 1 우리는 집단을 형성해 그곳에 속하려는 욕구를 가지고 있다고 했음
단서 2 '우리(= 집단)'를 편들기 시작한다고 했음
But once you can identify *them*, / you start favoring *us*; /
so much so that / given a choice / between an outcome that
= to the extent that 　분사구문을 이룸
favors both groups a lot /
하지만 일단 여러분이 '그들'을 인식할 수 있게 되면 / 여러분은 '우리'를 편들기 시작한다 / 매우 그러해서 / 선택이 주어졌을 때 / 양쪽 집단 모두를 크게 유리하게 하는 결과 /
= outcome
or one that favors both much less / but still favors yours more
　　　　　　　　　　　　　주격 관계대명사(선행사: one)
than theirs, / that's the one you will pick. //
또는 양측 모두에게 훨씬 덜 유리한 / 하지만 여전히 여러분의 집단을 그들보다 더 유리하게 하는 것(결과) 사이에 / 그것이 바로 여러분이 고르게 될 것이다 //

- sociologist ⓝ 사회학자   · tribe ⓝ 부족   · reputation ⓝ 평판
- trustworthy ⓐ 신뢰할 수 있는   · override ⓥ ~보다 더 중요하다
- mortality ⓝ 죽음   · irrational ⓐ 비이성적인
- death sentence 사형 선고   · drive ⓝ 욕구   · oppose ⓥ 반대하다
- favor ⓥ 편들다, 유리하게 하다   · objective ⓐ 객관적인

사회학자 Brooke Harrington은 사회 과학의 $E=mc^2$가 있다면, 그것은 SD > PD, 즉 "사회적 죽음이 신체적 죽음보다 더 무섭다."일 것이라고 말했다. 이것은 새로운 개념이 우리 정체성의 일부가 된 것들에 도전할 때 우리가 매우 위협적으로 느끼는 이유이다. 우리가 한 집단의 구성원으로 우리를 동일시하는 몇몇 견해에 대하여, 우리는 개인으로서 판단하지 않고, 우리는 한 부족의 구성원으로서 판단한다. 우리는 믿음직스럽게 보이고 싶고, 믿음직한 개인으로서의 평판 관리는 흔히 다른 모든 걱정, 심지어 우리 자신의 죽음보다 더 중요하다. 이것은 완전히 비이성적인 것이 아니다. 이 세상에 홀로 있는 인간은 많은 어려움을 직면하지만, 근대 이전의 세상에서 혼자 있는 것은 거의 확실하게 사형 선고였다. 그래서 우리는 집단을 형성하고, 집단에 합류하고, 그 집단에 남아 있고, 다른 집단에 반대하려는 타고난 욕구를 가지고 있다. 하지만 일단 여러분이 '그들'을 인식할 수 있게 되면, 여러분은 '우리'를 편들기 시작하는데, 매우 그러하므로, 양측 집단 모두를 크게 유리하게 하는 결과 또는 양측 모두에게 훨씬 덜 유리하게 하지만 여전히 여러분의 집단을 그들보다 더 유리하게 하는 것(결과) 사이에 선택이 주어졌을 때, 그것이 바로 여러분이 고르게 될 것이다.

다음 글의 주제로 가장 적절한 것은? [3점]

① tendency to prefer the group that one identifies with
동일시하는 집단을 선호하는 경향   우리는 동일시하는 집단을 선호하는 경향이 있다는 내용
② necessity of social isolation to build a reputation
평판을 쌓기 위한 사회적 고립의 필요성   사회적 고립이 아니라 집단에 속하는 것을 선호한다는 내용임
③ ways to ease one's irrational fear of crowds
군중에 대한 비합리적 공포심을 완화할 수 있는 방법   군중에 대한 비합리적 공포심 완화 방법에 대한 글이 아님
④ importance of forming groups with different interests
다른 관심사를 가진 집단을 형성하는 것의 중요성   다른 관심사를 가진 집단을 형성하는 것의 중요성에 대한 글이 아님
⑤ tips for staying objective during heated group discussions
과열된 집단 토론에서 객관성을 유지하는 방법   집단 토론에 대한 언급은 없음

왜 정답? [정답률 78%]

전반부	사회적 죽음을 두려워하고 사회적 평판을 중요시하는 우리의 경향
후반부	집단을 형성하고 집단에 속하기를 원하며 우리가 속한 그 집단을 편들기 시작함

▶ 따라서 이 글의 주제는 ① '동일시하는 집단을 선호하는 경향'이 가장 적절하다.

>왜 오답?

② 사회적 고립을 두려워하고 집단에 속하길 바란다는 내용의 글이지, 사회적 고립의 필요성을 역설한 글이 아니다.

③ 군중에 대한 비합리적 공포심을 완화하는 방법에 대한 글이 아니다.

④ 집단에 속하는 것을 선호한다고는 했지만, 다른 관심사를 가진 집단을 형성하는 것의 중요성에 대한 글은 아니다. 함정

⑤ 과열된 집단 토론에서 객관성을 유지하는 방법에 대한 글이 아니다.

F 10 정답 ⑤ *심미적 즐거움을 유발하는 것

In Kant's view, / geometrical shapes are too perfect / to induce (too ~ to-v: 너무 ~해서 …할 수 없는)
an aesthetic experience. // 단서1 기하학적 모양은 너무 완벽해서 심미적 경험을 유발할 수 없음
칸트의 관점에서 / 기하학적 모양은 너무 완벽하다 / 심미적 경험을 유발하기에 //

Insofar as they agree / with the underlying concept or idea / —
thus possessing the *precision* / that the ancient Greeks sought 선행사 목적격 관계대명사
and celebrated —
그것들이 일치하는 한 / 근본적인 개념이나 생각에 / 그래서 '정확성'을 갖는데 / 고대 그리스인들이 추구하고 찬양했던 / '~을 일으키다[낳다]'

geometrical shapes can be grasped, / but they do not give rise to emotion, / and, most importantly, / they do not move the imagination / to free and new (mental) lengths. //
기하학적 모양은 이해될 수는 있지만 / 감정을 불러일으키지 않으며 / 가장 중요하게 / 그것들은 상상력을 움직이게 하지 않는다 / 자유롭고 새로운 (정신적인) 범위로 //

Forms or phenomena, / on the contrary, / that possess a degree of 주어, 선행사 / 주격 관계대명사① / 주격 관계대명사②
immeasurability, / or that do not appear constrained, / stimulate the human imagination / 단서2 제약되어 보이지 않는 형태나 현상은 인간의 상상력을 자극함 동사
형태나 현상은 / 그와는 반대로 / 어느 정도의 헤아릴 수 없음을 갖거나 / 제약되어 보이지 않는 / 인간의 상상력을 자극한다 / 형용사적 용법(ability 수식)

— hence their ability / to induce a sublime aesthetic experience. //
그로 인한 그것들의 능력 / 숭고한 심미적인 경험을 유발하는 //

The pleasure / associated with experiencing / immeasurable 주어
objects / — indefinable or formless objects — / can be defined / 동사
as enjoying / one's own emotional and mental activity. //
즐거움은 / 경험하는 것과 연관된 / 헤아릴 수 없는 대상을 / 규정할 수 없거나 형태가 없는 대상 / 정의될 수 있다 / 즐기는 것으로 / 사람 자신의 감정적이고 정신적인 활동을 //

Namely, / the pleasure consists / of being challenged and struggling / to understand and decode the phenomenon / present to view. //
다시 말해 / 그 즐거움은 구성된다 / 도전 받고 애쓰는 것으로 / 현상을 이해하고 해독하려고 / 볼 수 있게 존재하는 // 부분을 나타내는 주어는 of 뒤의 명사에 동사를 일치시킴

Furthermore, / part of the pleasure comes / from having one's comfort zone (momentarily) violated. //
게다가 / 그 즐거움의 일부는 온다 / 사람의 안락구역을 (일시적으로) 벗어나는 데서 //

- induce ⓥ 유발[초래]하다
- insofar as ~하는 한
- underlying ⓐ 근본적인
- possess ⓥ 보유하다
- precision ⓝ 정확성
- seek ⓥ 추구하다((sought-sought))
- celebrate ⓥ 찬양하다, 축하하다
- grasp ⓥ 이해하다, 파악하다, 움켜잡다
- phenomenon ⓝ 현상((pl. phenomena))
- immeasurability ⓝ 헤아릴 수 없음
- constrain ⓥ 제한[제약]하다
- stimulate ⓥ 자극하다
- hence ⓐⓓ 그러므로, 이런 이유로
- associated ⓐ 관련된
- indefinable ⓐ 규정할 수 없는
- formless ⓐ 형태가 없는
- namely ⓐⓓ 다시 말해
- consist of ~으로 이루어지다[구성되다]
- struggle ⓥ 열심히 노력하다
- decode ⓥ 해독하다, 이해하다
- momentarily ⓐⓓ 잠깐, 일시적으로
- violate ⓥ 어기다, 위반하다
- diversity ⓝ 다양성
- inherent ⓐ 내재하는, 선천적인
- imperfection ⓝ 불완전 (상태)
- inclination ⓝ 경향, 성향

칸트의 관점에서 기하학적 모양은 너무 완벽해서 심미적 경험을 유발할 수 없다. 그것들이 근본적인 개념이나 생각에 일치하는 한, 그래서 고대 그리스인들이 추구하고 찬양했던 '정확성'을 갖는데, 기하학적 모양은 이해될 수는 있지만 감정을 불러일으키지 않으며 가장 중요하게 그것들은 상상력을 자유롭고 새로운 (정신적인) 범위로 움직이게 하지 않는다. 그와는 반대로, 어느 정도의 헤아릴 수 없음을 갖거나 제약되어 보이지 않는 형태나 현상은 인간의 상상력을 자극하기 때문에 숭고한 심미적인 경험을 유발할 수 있다. 헤아릴 수 없는 대상, 즉 규정할 수 없거나 형태가 없는 대상을 경험하는 것과 연관된 즐거움은 사람 자신의 감정적이고 정신적인 활동을 즐기는 것으로 정의될 수 있다. 다시 말해, 그 즐거움은 볼 수 있게 존재하는 현상을 이해하고 해독하려고 도전 받고 애쓰는 것으로 구성된다. 게다가, 그 즐거움의 일부는 사람의 안락구역을 (일시적으로) 벗어나는 데서 온다.

다음 글의 주제로 가장 적절한 것은? [3점]

① diversity of aesthetic experiences in different eras — 서로 다른 시대에 심미적인 경험의 다양성 / 시대에 따라 달라진다는 것이 아님
② inherent beauty in geometrically perfect shapes — 기하학적으로 완벽한 모양의 내재적 아름다움 / 완벽한 기하학적 모양이 아름답다는 것이 아님
③ concepts of imperfection in modern aesthetics — 현대 미학에서 불완전함의 개념 / 현대 미학에서의 불완전함의 개념을 설명한 것이 아님
④ natural inclination towards aesthetic precision — 심미적 정확성을 향한 자연스러운 경향 / 정확성을 갖는 기하학적 모양은 심미적 경험을 유발하지 않음
⑤ aesthetic pleasure from things unconstrained — 제약되지 않은 것으로부터 얻는 심미적 즐거움 / 제약되지 않은 형태나 현상이 인간의 상상력을 자극함

>왜 정답? [정답률 80%]

너무 완벽해서 심미적 경험을 유발할 수 없는 기하학적 모양은 이해는 될 수 있지만 감정을 불러일으키지 않고, 상상력을 자유롭고 새로운 정신적 영역으로 움직이게 하지 않는 반면에, 제약되어 보이지 않는 형태나 현상은 인간의 상상력을 자극하여 심미적인 경험을 유발한다는 내용이므로 주제로 적절한 것은 ⑤ '제약되지 않은 것으로부터 얻는 심미적 즐거움'이다. 글의 후반부는 헤아릴 수 없거나 규정할 수 없는, 또는 형태가 없는 대상을 경험하는 즐거움에 대한 구체적인 설명이다.

>왜 오답?

① 칸트의 시대와 오늘날의 심미적 경험이 다르다고 이야기하는 것이 아니다.

② 기하학적 모양은 너무 완벽해서 상상력을 자극하지 않는다는 것이지, 기하학적 모양이 내재적 아름다움을 지닌다는 것이 아니다. 함정

③ 칸트의 시대와 대조하여 현대 미학에서의 불완전함의 개념을 설명하는 것이 아니다.

④ precision은 기하학적 모양이 너무 완벽하고 '정확성'을 가져서 심미적 경험을 유발하지 않는다는 문장에서 언급되었다.

F 11 정답 ① *사회적 상호 작용을 통한 정보 처리

주어와 be동사(it is)가 생략된 부사절
Whenever possible, / we should take measures / to *re-socialize* the information / we think about. // 단서1 정보를 재사회화해야 함
가능할 때마다 / 우리는 조치를 취해야 한다 / 정보를 '재사회화'하는 / 우리가 생각하는 //
선행사(목적격 관계대명사 that은 생략됨)

The continual patter / we carry on in our heads / is in fact a kind of internalized conversation. //
지속적인 재잘거림은 / 우리가 머릿속에서 계속하는 / 사실 일종의 내면화된 대화이다 //
복수 주어
Likewise, / many of the written forms / we encounter at school and at work / — from exams and evaluations, / to profiles and case studies, / to essays and proposals — /
마찬가지로 / 서면 형식의 많은 것들이 / 우리가 학교와 직장에서 마주치는 / 시험과 평가에서 / 개요서와 사례 연구까지 / 에세이와 제안서에 이르기까지 /
복수 동사
are really social exchanges (questions, stories, arguments) / put on paper / and addressed / to some imagined listener or interlocutor. //
사실 사회적 교환(질문, 이야기, 논쟁)이다 / 종이에 쓰여 / 건네지는 / 가상의 어떤 청자나 대화자에게 //
전치사 동명사
There are significant advantages / to turning such interactions at a remove back / into actual social encounters. //
상당한 이점이 있다 / 조금 거리를 둔 그런 상호 작용을 다시 되돌리는 것에는 / 실제적인 사회적 만남으로 //

Research demonstrates / that the brain processes the "same" information differently, / and often more effectively, / when other human beings are involved / **단서2** 뇌는 다른 사람들이 관련될 때 똑같은 정보를 더 효과적으로 처리함

연구는 보여준다 / 뇌가 '똑같은' 정보를 다르게 처리한다는 것을 / 그리고 흔히 더 효과적으로 / 다른 사람들이 관련될 때 / 〈양보〉의 부사절 접속사

— whether we're imitating them, / debating them, / exchanging stories with them, / synchronizing and cooperating with them, / teaching or being taught by them. //

우리가 그들을 모방하고 있는지 / 그들과 논쟁하고 있는지 / 그들과 이야기를 교환하고 있는지 / 그들과 동조하면서 협력하고 있는지 / 그들을 가르치거나 그들에게 배우고 있든지 간에 //

We are inherently social creatures, / and our thinking benefits / from bringing other people / into our train of thought. //

우리는 본래 사회적 존재이고 / 우리의 생각은 이득을 본다 / 다른 사람을 끌어들이는 것으로부터 / 우리가 하는 일련의 생각으로 //

- measure ⓝ 조치, 정책
- continual ⓐ 거듭[반복]되는
- carry on ~을 계속하다
- internalized ⓐ 내면화된
- likewise ⓐ 똑같이, 또한
- encounter ⓥ 마주치다 ⓝ 만남, 접촉
- evaluation ⓝ 평가
- profile ⓝ 개요(서)
- argument ⓝ 논쟁, 언쟁
- exchange ⓝ 교환, 교류 ⓥ (이야기를) 주고받다
- address ⓥ 건네다, 보내다
- advantage ⓝ 유리한 점, 이점
- demonstrate ⓥ 입증[실증]하다
- effectively ⓐ 효과적으로, 실질적으로
- imitate ⓥ 모방하다, 본뜨다
- debate ⓥ 논쟁하다
- synchronize ⓥ 동시에 발생하다[움직이다]
- cooperate ⓥ 협력[협조]하다
- inherently ⓐ 본래
- via ⓟⓡⓔⓟ ~을 통해, ~을 경유하여[거쳐]
- cognitive ⓐ 인식[인지]의
- trait ⓝ 특성

가능할 때마다, 우리는 우리가 생각하는 정보를 '재사회화하는' 조치를 취해야 한다. 우리가 머릿속에서 계속하는 지속적인 재잘거림은 사실 일종의 내면화된 대화이다. 마찬가지로 시험과 평가에서, 개요서와 사례 연구, 에세이와 제안서에 이르기까지, 학교와 직장에서 우리가 마주치는 많은 문서가 사실 종이에 쓰여 가상의 어떤 청자나 대화자에게 건네는 사회적 교환(질문, 이야기, 논쟁)이다. 조금 거리를 둔 그런 상호 작용을 다시 실제적인 사회적 만남으로 되돌리는 것에는 상당한 이점이 있다. 다른 사람들이 관련될 때, 즉 우리가 그들을 모방하고 있는지, 그들과 논쟁하고 있든지, 그들과 이야기를 교환하고 있든지, 그들과 동조하면서 협력하고 있든지, 또는 그들을 가르치거나 그들에게 배우고 있든지 간에, 뇌가 '똑같은' 정보를 다르게, 그리고 흔히 더 효과적으로 처리한다는 것을 연구는 보여준다. 우리는 본래 사회적 존재이고 우리의 생각은 다른 사람을 우리가 하는 일련의 생각으로 끌어들이는 것으로부터 이득을 본다.

다음 글의 주제로 가장 적절한 것은? [3점]

① importance of processing information via social interactions
사회적 상호 작용을 통해 정보를 처리하는 것의 중요성   정보를 더 효과적으로 처리함
② ways of improving social skills through physical activities
신체적 활동을 통해 사회적 기술을 향상하는 방법   신체적 활동의 역할은 언급되지 않음
③ necessity of regular evaluations of cognitive functions
인지 기능의 정기적인 평가의 필요성   evaluations로 만든 오답
④ influence of personality traits on social interactions
성격적 특징이 사회적 상호 작용에 미치는 영향   사회적 상호 작용이 정보 처리에 미치는 영향임
⑤ socialization as a form of internalized social control
내면화된 사회적 통제라는 형태로서의 사회화   사회화의 종류를 설명한 것이 아님

왜 정답? [정답률 60%]

- 가능할 때마다 정보를 재사회화해야 한다. **단서1**
- 서면을 통한 상호 작용을 실제적인 사회적 만남으로 되돌리는 것에는 상당한 이점이 있다. **단서2**
  뇌는 다른 사람들이 관련될 때 똑같은 정보를 더 효과적으로 처리

➡ **사회화**: '인간의 상호 작용 과정'을 의미함
다른 사람들과 사회적으로 상호 작용할 때 정보를 더 효과적으로 처리한다는 것으로, ① '사회적 상호 작용을 통해 정보를 처리하는 것의 중요성'에 대해 이야기하는 글이다.

왜 오답?

② 신체적 활동이 사회적 기술을 향상한다는 내용이 아니다.
③ 서면 형식의 예시로 시험과 '평가'가 언급된 것으로 만든 오답이다. 인지 기능을 정기적으로 평가해야 한다는 언급은 없다. **주의**

④ 사회적 상호 작용이 정보 처리에 미치는 영향에 대해 설명한 글이다.
⑤ 사회화의 여러 형태 중 한 가지를 설명한 글이 아니다.

자이 쌤's Follow Me! —홈페이지에서 제공

F 12 정답 ① ＊개인 그 자체가 사회적 산물임

Conventional wisdom in the West, / influenced by philosophers / from Plato to Descartes, / credits individuals and especially geniuses / with creativity and originality. //
주어   주격 관계대명사와 be동사 생략   동사

서양의 통념은 / 철학자들의 영향을 받은 / 플라톤에서 데카르트에 이르는 / 개인, 특히 천재들에게 있다고 믿는다 / 창의력과 독창성이 //

Social and cultural influences and causes / are minimized, ignored, or eliminated / from consideration / at all. //

사회적, 문화적 영향과 원인은 / 최소화되거나 무시되거나 배제된다 / 고려로부터 / 완전히 //

Thoughts, original and conventional, / are identified with individuals, / and the special things / that individuals are and do / are traced / to their genes and their brains. //
주어   동사   동사   주어

사상은, 독창적이든 종래의 것이든 / 개인과 동일시되며 / 특별한 것은 / 개인이라는 존재와 개인이 하는 / 그 기원이 찾아진다 / 그 사람의 유전자와 두뇌에서 //

The "trick" here is to recognize / **단서1** 개개의 인간은 사회적 구성 그 자체이며 자신이 접해 온 사회적, 문화적 영향의 다양성을 구현하고 반영함
여기서 '요령'은 인식하는 것이다 / 명사적 용법(주격 보어)

that individual humans are social constructions themselves, / embodying and reflecting / the variety of social and cultural influences / they have been exposed to / during their lives. //

개개의 인간이 사회적 구성 그 자체이며 / 구현하고 반영한다는 것을 / 사회적, 문화적 영향의 다양성을 / 그들이 접해 온 / 그들의 생애 동안 / **단서2** 개인성은 특정한 사회적, 문화적 경험의 산물로 여겨짐

Our individuality is not denied, / but it is viewed as a product / of specific social and cultural experiences. //

우리의 개인성이 부인되는 것이 아니라 / 그것은 산물로 여겨진다 / 특정한 사회적, 문화적 경험의 // **단서3** 개인의 뇌 그 자체가 사회적인 것임
= and it is influenced

The brain itself is a social thing, / influenced / structurally and at the level of its connectivities / by social environments. //

뇌 그 자체가 사회적인 것이며 / 영향을 받는다 / 구조적으로 그리고 그것의 연결성 수준에서 / 사회 환경에 의한 //

The "individual" is a legal, religious, and political fiction / just as the "I" is a grammatical illusion. //

'개인'은 법적, 종교적, 그리고 정치적 허구이다 / '나'가 문법적 환상인 것과 마찬가지로 //

- conventional wisdom 통념
- philosopher ⓝ 철학자
- credit A with B A에게 B가 있다고 믿다
- minimize ⓥ 최소화하다
- eliminate ⓥ 배제하다
- be identified with ~와 동일시되다
- trace ⓥ (기원·원인을) 추적하다[(추적하여) 밝혀내다]
- construction ⓝ 구성물
- embody ⓥ 구현하다, 구체화하다
- reflect ⓥ 반영하다, 나타내다
- individuality ⓝ 개인성
- structurally ⓐ 구조적으로
- connectivity ⓝ 연결(성)
- fiction ⓝ 허구
- grammatical ⓐ 문법적인
- illusion ⓝ 환상, 착각
- inherent ⓐ 내재하는
- collectivity ⓝ 집단성
- separate ⓥ 구별하다
- acknowledgment ⓝ 인정, 시인
- interdependence ⓝ 상호 의존

플라톤에서 데카르트에 이르는 철학자들의 영향을 받은 서양의 통념은 개인, 특히 천재들에게 창의력과 독창성이 있다고 믿는다. 사회적, 문화적 영향과 원인은 최소화되거나 무시되거나 고려로부터 완전히 배제된다. 사상은, 독창적이든 종래의 것이든, 개인과 동일시되며, 개인이라는 특별한 존재와 개인이 하는 특별한 것은 그 사람의 유전자와 두뇌에서 그 기원을 찾는다. 여기서 '요령'은 개개의 인간이 사회적 구성 그 자체이며 그들이 생애 동안 접해 온 사회적, 문화적 영향의 다양성을 구현하고 반영한다는 것을 인식하는 것이다. 우리의 개인성이 부인되는 것이 아니라, 특정한 사회적, 문화적 경험의 산물로 여겨진다. 뇌 그 자체가 사회적인 것이며, 구조적으로, 그리고 그것의 사회 환경에 의한 연결성 수준에서 영향을 받는다. '나'가 문법적 환상인 것과 마찬가지로 '개인'은 법적, 종교적, 그리고 정치적 허구이다.

다음 글의 주제로 가장 적절한 것은? [3점]

① recognition of the social nature inherent in individuality
개인성에 내재한 사회적 속성의 인식　　개인성은 사회적, 문화적 경험의 산물임
② ways of filling the gap between individuality and collectivity
개인성과 집단성의 간극을 채우는 방법　　집단성은 언급되지 않음
③ issues with separating original thoughts from conventional ones
독창적인 생각과 종래의 생각을 구분하는 것과 관련된 문제　　original과 conventional로 만든 오답
④ acknowledgment of the true individuality embodied in human genes
인간 유전자에 구현된 진정한 개인성의 인정　　서양의 통념이 인식하는 바와 연결됨
⑤ necessity of shifting from individualism to interdependence
개인주의에서 상호 의존으로 전환할 필요성　　개인주의에 대한 내용이 아님

> 왜 정답 ? [정답률 86%]　　｜잘못된 통념을 부연 설명과 제시한 후 그것을 반박하는 사실을 설명하는 글의 구조｜ 꿀팁

서양의 통념은 사회적, 문화적 영향을 배제하고 창의력과 독창성이 개인에게서, 즉 개인의 유전자와 두뇌에서 나온다고 믿지만 사실은 개인 그 자체가 사회적 구성이며 사회적, 문화적 영향을 구현하고 반영한다는 내용이다. 우리의 개인성은 사회적, 문화적 경험의 산물이고, 개인의 뇌 그 자체가 사회적인 것이라는 설명으로 보아 이 글이 ① '개인성에 내재한 사회적 속성의 인식'에 대해 이야기하고 있음을 알 수 있다.

> 왜 오답 ?

② 개인성에 대한 내용인 것은 맞지만, 집단성에 대해서는 언급되지 않았다.

③ 서양의 통념에서는 사상이, 독창적인 사상이든 종래의 사상이든, 개인과 동일시 된다는 내용으로 만든 오답이다.

④ 서양의 통념은 독창성, 창의력이 개인에게, 즉 개인의 유전자, 개인의 두뇌에 있다고 믿지만 사실 개인성 자체가 사회적 산물이라는 것이 글의 핵심이다.

⑤ 개인성에 대해 이야기하는 글이라는 점으로 만든 오답이다. 개인주의를 설명한 것이 아니다.

F 13 정답 ④ ＊아동기 이후에도 계속되는 놀이에의 참여

Children can move effortlessly / between play and absorption in
　　　단수 주어
a story, / as if both are forms / of the same activity. //
아이들은 쉽게 이동할 수 있다 / 놀이와 이야기로의 몰입 사이를 / 마치 그 둘이 형태인 것처럼 / 같은 활동의 //

The taking of roles / in a narratively structured game of pirates
단수 동사
/ is not very different / than the taking of roles / in identifying
with characters / as one watches a movie. //
역할을 맡는 것은 / 이야기식 구조의 해적 게임에서 / 크게 다르지 않다 / 역할을 맡는 것과 / 등장인물과 동일시하며 / 사람들이 영화를 감상하면서 //
가주어
　단서 1 청소년기로 성장하면서 아동기의 놀이를 그만두는 것이 아님
It might be thought / that, as they grow towards adolescence,
　　　　　　　　　　진주절 접속사
people give up childhood play, / but this is not so. //
~라고 여겨질 수도 있지만 / 그들이 청소년기로 성장하면서 / 사람들이 아동기의 놀이를 그만둔다고 / 이는 그렇지 않다 //
　　　　　　　　　　　단서 2 그 기반과 흥미는 다양하게 바뀌어 발전함
Instead, / the bases and interests / of this activity / change and
develop / to playing and watching sports, / to the fiction of
plays, novels, and movies, / and nowadays to video games. //
대신에 / 기반과 흥미가 / 이런 활동의 / 바뀌어 발전한다 / 스포츠 활동과 관람으로 / 연극, 소설, 영화의 허구로 / 그리고 최근에는 비디오 게임으로 //
　　　to가 이끄는 전치사구의 병렬 구조
In fiction, / one can enter / possible worlds. //
　　　　　단수 주어
허구에서 / 사람들은 들어갈 수 있다 / 있을 법한 세계로 //

When we experience emotions / in such worlds, / this is not a
　　　　　　　　　　　　　　　　동격절 접속사
sign / that we are being incoherent or regressed. //
우리가 감정들을 경험할 때 / 그런 세계에서 / 이는 신호가 아니다 / 우리가 일관되지 않다거나 퇴행하고 있다는 //

It derives / from trying out metaphorical transformations / of
our selves / in new ways, / in new worlds, / in ways / that can
be moving and important / to us. //
　　　　　전치사구의 병렬 구조 ──　　주격 관계대명사
그것은 기인한다 / 은유적 변신을 시도하는 것에서 / 우리 자신의 / 새로운 방식으로 / 새로운 세계에서 / 방식으로 / 감동적이고 중요할 수 있는 / 우리에게 //

• effortlessly [ad] 쉽게, 노력하지 않고　• absorption [n] 몰두, 몰입
• role [n] 역할　• narratively [ad] 이야기식으로
• structure [v] 조직하다, 구조화하다　• identify with ~와 동일시하다
• towards [prep] ~쪽으로, ~를 향하여　• adolescence [n] 청소년기
• give up ~을 포기하다　• instead [ad] 대신에　• base [n] 기반, 기초
• develop [v] 발전하다　• fiction [n] 허구, 소설　• play [n] 연극, 희곡
• novel [n] 소설　• nowadays [ad] 요즘에는
• regress [v] 퇴행[퇴보]하다　• derive from ~에서 유래하다
• metaphorical [a] 은유[비유]의　• transformation [n] 변화, 변신
• self [n] 자아, 자신, 본모습

아이들은 놀이와 이야기로의 몰입 사이를 마치 그 둘이 같은 활동의 형태인 것처럼 쉽게 이동할 수 있다. 이야기식 구조의 해적 게임에서 역할을 맡는 것은 영화를 감상하면서 등장인물과 동일시하며 역할을 맡는 것과 크게 다르지 않다. 사람들이 청소년기로 성장하면서 아동기의 놀이를 그만둔다고 여겨질 수도 있겠지만, 이는 그렇지 않다. 대신에, 이런 활동의 기반과 흥미가 바뀌어 스포츠 활동과 관람으로, 연극, 소설, 영화의 허구로, 그리고 최근에는 비디오 게임으로 발전한다. 허구에서 사람들은 있을 법한 세계로 들어갈 수 있다. 우리가 그런 세계에서 감정들을 경험할 때 이는 우리가 일관되지 않다거나 퇴행하고 있다는 신호가 아니다. 그것은 새로운 방식으로, 새로운 세계에서, 우리에게 감동적이고 중요할 수 있는 방식으로 우리 자신의 은유적 변신을 시도하는 것에서 기인한다.

다음 글의 주제로 가장 적절한 것은? [3점]

① relationship between play types and emotional stability
놀이 유형과 정서적 안정 간의 관계　　놀이 유형에 따라 정서적 안정에 변화가 있다는 내용이 아님
② reasons for identifying with imaginary characters in childhood
아동기에 가상의 등장인물과 동일시하는 이유　　동일시하는 '이유'는 언급되지 않음
③ ways of helping adolescents develop good reading habits
청소년이 좋은 독서 습관을 개발하도록 돕는 방법　　좋은 독서 습관의 필요성 등이 등장하지 않음
④ continued engagement in altered forms of play after childhood
아동기 이후 변화된 형태의 놀이에의 지속적인 참여　　this is not so라고 했음
⑤ effects of narrative structures on readers' imaginations
이야기 구조가 독자의 상상력에 미치는 영향　　narratively structured가 언급된 것으로 만든 오답

> 왜 정답 ? [정답률 76%]

아이들에게는 놀이에서 역할을 맡는 것이나 어떤 이야기의 등장인물과 동일시하며 몰입하는 것이나 크게 다르지 않은데, 청소년기로 성장하면서 이러한 아동기의 놀이를 그만두는 것은 아니라면서 아동기 놀이의 기반과 흥미가 스포츠 활동과 관람으로, 연극, 소설, 영화의 허구로, 비디오 게임으로 바뀌어 발전한다고 했다. 이를 통해 이 글의 주제가 ④ '아동기 이후 변화된 형태의 놀이에의 지속적인 참여'임을 알 수 있다.

> 왜 오답 ?

① 놀이 유형이 정서적 안정에 영향을 미친다거나 반대로 정서적 안정이 놀이 유형에 영향을 미친다는 내용이 아니다.

② 영화와 같은 어떤 이야기를 감상하면서 등장인물과 동일시한다는 내용은 있지만, 그 이유를 설명한 것은 아니다.

③ 청소년이 좋은 독서 습관을 개발해야 한다고 주장하거나 그 방법을 설명하는 글이 아니다.

⑤ 이야기 구조와 독자의 상상력 사이에 어떤 관계가 있는지에 대한 설명은 없다.

F 14 정답 ② ＊정보 공개의 이점

　　단수 주어　　　　단서 1 (정보) 공개의 이점에 대해 이야기하는 글임
An important advantage of disclosure, / as opposed to more
aggressive forms / of regulation, / is its flexibility and respect /
for the operation of free markets. //　　단수 동사
공개의 중요한 이점은 / 더 공세적인 형태와는 반대로 / 규제의 / 그것의 유연성과 존중이다 / 자유 시장의 작용에 대한 //

Regulatory mandates are blunt swords; / they tend to neglect
　　　　　　　　　병렬 구조(문장의 동사)
diversity / and may have serious unintended adverse effects. //
규제하는 명령은 무딘 칼이다 / 그것들은 다양성을 무시하는 경향이 있으며 / 의도하지 않은 심각한 역효과를 발생시킬 수도 있다 //

For example, / energy efficiency requirements for appliances
　　　　　　　　　　선행사　　　주격 관계대명사 ①
/ may produce goods / that work less well / or that have
　　　　　　　목적격 관계대명사(선행사: characteristics)　　주격 관계대명사 ②
characteristics / that consumers do not want. //
예를 들어 / 가전제품에 대한 에너지 효율 요건은 / 제품을 만들어 낼 수도 있다 / 덜 잘 작동하거나 / 특성을 가진 / 소비자가 원하지 않는 //

Ⓕ

Information provision, by contrast, respects / freedom of
choice. // 단서2 정보 제공은 선택의 자유를 존중함

주어와 동사 사이에 삽입된 부사구

반대로 정보 제공은 존중한다 / 선택의 자유를 //

If automobile manufacturers are required / to measure and
publicize / the safety characteristics of cars, /

부사절 접속사(조건)

자동차 제조업체가 요청 받으면 / 측정하고 공개하도록 / 자동차의 안전 특성을 /

potential car purchasers can trade safety concerns / against
other attributes, / such as price and styling. //

잠재적인 자동차 구매자는 안전에 대한 우려를 맞바꿀 수 있다 / 다른 속성과 / 가격과 스타일 같은 /

If restaurant customers are informed of the calories / in their
meals, /

★부사절 접속사(조건)

식당 손님들이 칼로리를 알게 되면 / 그들의 식사에 들어 있는 /

those who want to lose weight /

주어

살을 빼고 싶은 사람들은 /

can make use of the information, /

동사

그 정보를 이용할 수 있다 /

leaving those / who are unconcerned about calories / unaffected. //

leaving의 목적어

사람들을 남겨 놓으며 / 칼로리에 신경 쓰지 않는 / 영향을 받지 않은 채로 //

leaving의 목적격 보어

Disclosure does not interfere with, / and should even promote,
/ the autonomy (and quality) / of individual decision-making. //

with와 should promote의 목적어

공개는 방해하지 않으며 / 심지어 촉진할 것이다 / 자율성(과 품질)을 / 개인 의사 결정의 //

단서3 (정보) 공개는 개인 의사 결정의 자율성과 품질을 촉진함

★ 접속사 if
if는 명사절 접속사로서 불확실하거나 의문시되는 사실에 대해 말할 때 쓰이기도 하고, 〈조건〉을 나타내는 부사절 접속사로 쓰이기도 한다.

- disclosure ⓝ (기업의) 정보 공개
- aggressive ⓐ 공격적인, 공세적인
- flexibility ⓝ 유연성, 융통성
- regulatory ⓐ 규제력을 지닌
- unintended ⓐ 의도하지 않은
- provision ⓝ 제공, 공급
- attribute ⓝ 속성, 자질
- as opposed to ~와는 대조적으로
- regulation ⓝ 규제, 단속
- operation ⓝ 작용, 운용, 수술
- blunt ⓐ 무딘
- appliance ⓝ (가정용) 기기, 가전제품
- potential ⓐ 잠재적인
- interfere ⓥ 방해하다, 간섭하다

공개의 중요한 이점은 규제의 더 공세적인 형태와는 반대로 자유 시장의 작용에 대한 유연성과 존중이다. 규제하는 명령은 무딘 칼인데, 그것들은 다양성을 무시하는 경향이 있으며, 의도하지 않은 심각한 역효과를 발생시킬 수도 있다. 예를 들어, 가전제품에 대한 에너지 효율 요건은 덜 잘 작동하거나 소비자가 원하지 않는 특성을 가진 제품을 만들어 낼 수도 있다.

반대로 정보 제공은 선택의 자유를 존중한다. 자동차 제조업체가 자동차의 안전 특성을 측정하고 공개해야 한다면, 잠재적인 자동차 구매자는 가격과 스타일 같은 다른 속성과 안전에 대한 우려를 맞바꿀 수 있다. 식당 손님들에게 식사에 들어 있는 칼로리를 알려주면, 살을 빼고 싶은 사람들은 그 정보를 이용할 수 있고, 칼로리에 신경 쓰지 않는 사람들은 영향을 받지 않은 채로 있게 된다. 공개는 개인 의사 결정의 자율성(과 품질)을 방해하지 않으며 심지어 촉진할 것이다.

다음 글의 주제로 가장 적절한 것은? [3점]

① steps to make public information accessible to customers
An important advantage of disclosure, respects freedom of choice
공공의 정보를 소비자가 이용할 수 있게 하는 절차   공공 정보에 대해서만 이야기하는 것이 아님
② benefits of publicizing information to ensure free choices
자유로운 선택을 보장하기 위해 정보를 공개하는 것의 이점
③ strategies for companies to increase profits in a free market
기업들이 자유 시장에서 이윤을 늘리는 전략들   이윤 증가를 위한 기업의 전략을 설명한 것이 아님
④ necessities of identifying and analyzing current industry trends
현재 산업 동향을 파악하고 분석할 필요성   현재의 산업 동향에 대한 언급은 없음
⑤ effects of diversified markets on reasonable customer choices
다양화된 시장이 합리적인 고객 선택에 미치는 영향   markets, choice가 언급된 것으로 만든 오답

왜 정답? [정답률 68%]

(정보) 공개의 중요한 이점은 자유 시장의 작용에 대한 유연성과 존중이라면서 규제와 달리 정보 제공은 선택의 자유를 존중한다고 했다.

마지막 문장에서는 (정보) 공개가 개인 의사 결정의 자율성뿐만 아니라 품질도 촉진할 것이라고 했으므로 이 글의 주제는 ② '자유로운 선택을 보장하기 위해 정보를 공개하는 것의 이점'이다.

왜 오답?

① 공공의 정보에 대해서만 이야기하는 글이 아니며, 정보 이용 절차 또한 언급되지 않았다.

③ 기업의 이윤 창출 전략에 대해서 설명한 글이 아니다.

④ 현재의 산업 동향을 분석해야 한다는 내용이 아니다.

⑤ 시장의 다양화가 고객의 선택에 미치는 영향을 설명한 것이 아니라 정보 공개가 고객의 선택에 도움이 된다는 내용이다.

장성욱 | 동아대 의예과 2023년 입학·부산 대연고 졸

글의 주제 유형이 3점으로 출제되는 경우는 드문데, 이번 수능에서 3점이었어. 하지만 지레 겁먹지 않는 게 중요해. 나는 주제나 제목 파악 유형을 풀 때 글을 처음부터 끝까지 읽고 글의 키워드를 파악해. 역접을 나타내는 어휘 뒤의 내용은 매우 중요하다는 사실도 잊으면 안 돼.

이 글에서는 by contrast가 포함된 문장이 중요한데, 여기서 정보 제공이 선택의 자유를 존중한다고 했으니, '정보 제공'과 '선택의 자유'가 이 글의 키워드야. 이어지는 문장들에서 이 키워드들에 대해 긍정적인 평가를 하고 있으니까 이 둘을 조합하면 정답은 ②이 될 수밖에 없어.

F 15 정답 ⑤ *과학 연구에서 패러다임의 기능적 측면

단서1 과학자들은 패러다임을 그저 '사용할' 뿐임

Scientists *use* paradigms / rather than believing them. //

= paradigms

과학자들은 패러다임을 '사용한다' / 그것들을 믿기보다는 //

The use of a paradigm in research / typically addresses related
problems /

단수 주어   단수 동사

연구에서 패러다임의 사용은 / 일반적으로 관련된 문제들을 다룬다 /

by employing / shared concepts, symbolic expressions,
experimental and mathematical tools and procedures, / and
even some of the same theoretical statements. //

사용함으로써 / 공유된 개념, 상징적 표현, 실험적이고 수학적인 도구와 절차를 / 그리고 심지어 동일한 이론적 진술의 일부를 //

Scientists need only understand / *how* to use these various
elements / in ways / that others would accept. //

조동사로 쓰인 need   선행사 목적격 관계대명사

과학자들은 이해할 필요가 있을 뿐이다 / 이러한 다양한 요소들을 사용하는 '방법'을 / 방식으로 / 다른 사람들이 받아들일 //

These elements of shared practice / thus need not presuppose
/ any comparable unity / in scientists' beliefs / about what they
are doing / when they use them. //

부사절(시간)   명사절(about의 목적어)

이러한 공유된 실행의 요소들은 / 따라서 전제로 할 필요는 없다 / 그 어떤 비슷한 통일성도 / 과학자들의 믿음에서 / 그들이 하고 있는 것에 관한 / 그들이 그것들을 사용할 때 //

Indeed, one role of a paradigm / is to enable scientists / to work
successfully /

명사적 용법   명사적 용법
(주격 보어)   (목적격 보어)

실제로 패러다임의 한 가지 역할은 / 과학자들이 ~하게 하는 것이다 / 성공적으로 일할 수 있게 /

단서2 패러다임은 과학자들로 하여금 그들이 하고 그에 대해 그들이 믿는 것을 설명하지 않고 성공적으로 일할 수 있게 함

without having to provide a detailed account / of what they are
doing / or what they believe about it. //

병렬 구조

상세한 설명을 제공할 필요 없이 / 그들이 무엇을 하고 있는지에 대한 / 또는 그들이 그것에 관해 무엇을 믿고 있는지에 대한 //

Thomas Kuhn noted / that scientists "can agree / in their
identification of a paradigm /

Thomas Kuhn이 언급했다 / 과학자들은 "의견이 일치할 수 있다 / 그들의 패러다임 '식별'에 있어서 /

단서3 과학자들은 패러다임에 대한 완전한 해석이나 이론적 설명이 없더라도 패러다임의 식별에 있어 의견의 일치를 보일 수 있음

without agreeing on, / or even attempting to produce, / a full
interpretation or *rationalization* / of it. //

agreeing on과 to produce의 공통된 목적어

동의하지 않고도 / 또는 심지어 만들어 내려고 시도조차 하지 않고도 / 완전한 '해석'이나 '이론적 설명'에 / 그것에 대한 //

Lack / of a standard interpretation / or of an agreed reduction to
rules / will not prevent a paradigm / from guiding research." //

주어   동사 prevent A from -ing: A가 ~하지 못하게 하다

없는 것은 / 표준적인 해석이나 / 규칙으로 축약되어 합의된 것이 / 패러다임을 막지는 못할 것이다 / 연구를 안내하는 것으로부터"라고 //

- address ⓥ (문제·상황 등에 대해) 고심하다[다루다]
- employ ⓥ (기술·방법 등을) 쓰다[이용하다] · symbolic ⓐ 상징적인
- mathematical ⓐ 수학적인
- procedure ⓝ (특히 어떤 일을 늘·제대로 하는) 절차[방법]
- theoretical ⓐ 이론적인 · statement ⓝ 진술 · element ⓝ 요소
- presuppose ⓥ 전제로 하다 · comparable ⓐ 비슷한
- unity ⓝ 통일성 · account ⓝ 설명, 기술
- identification ⓝ 식별, 확인 · attempt ⓥ 시도하다
- interpretation ⓝ 해석, 이해 · rationalization ⓝ 이론적 설명
- lack ⓝ 부족, 결핍 · standard ⓐ 표준적인, 기준이 되는

과학자들은 패러다임을 믿기보다는 그것을 '사용한다.' 연구에서 패러다임의 사용은 일반적으로 공유된 개념, 상징적 표현, 실험적이고 수학적인 도구와 절차, 그리고 심지어 동일한 이론적 진술의 일부를 사용함으로써 관련된 문제들을 다룬다. 과학자들은 다른 사람들이 받아들일 방식으로 이러한 다양한 요소들을 사용하는 '방법'을 이해하기만 하면 된다. 따라서 이러한 공유된 실행의 요소들은 과학자들이 그것들을 사용할 때 그들이 하고 있는 것에 관한 그들의 믿음에서 그 어떤 비슷한 통일성을 전제로 할 필요는 없다. 실제로, 패러다임의 한 가지 역할은 과학자들이 그들이 무엇을 하고 있는지 또는 그들이 그것에 관해 무엇을 믿고 있는지에 대한 상세한 설명을 제공할 필요 없이 성공적으로 일할 수 있게 하는 것이다.

Thomas Kuhn이 언급하기를, 과학자들은 "패러다임에 대한 완전한 '해석'이나 '이론적 설명'에 동의하거나, 심지어 그런 것을 만들어 내려고 시도조차 하지 않고도, 패러다임을 '식별'하는 데 있어서 의견이 일치할 수 있다. 표준적인 해석이나 규칙으로 축약되어 합의된 것이 없다 해도 패러다임이 연구를 안내하는 것을 막지는 못할 것이다."

다음 글의 주제로 가장 적절한 것은? [3점]
─ 패러다임의 기능적 사용에 대한 내용임
① difficulty in drawing novel theories from existing paradigms
  기존의 패러다임으로부터 새로운 이론을 도출하는 데 있어서의 어려움
② significant influence of personal beliefs in scientific fields
  과학 분야에서 개인 신념의 상당한 영향력 개인의 신념이 과학 분야에 영향을 미친다는 언급은 없음
③ key factors that promote the rise of innovative paradigms
  혁신적 패러다임의 출현을 고취하는 핵심 요인
④ roles of a paradigm in grouping like-minded researchers
  생각이 비슷한 연구원들을 분류하는 데 있어서 패러다임의 역할 패러다임이 연구원을 구분한다는 내용이 아님
⑤ functional aspects of a paradigm in scientific research
  과학 연구에서 패러다임의 기능적 측면 과학 연구의 편의를 위해 패러다임을 기능적으로 사용함

>왜 정답? [정답률 72%] 그냥 기능적인 측면에서만 사용함 꿀팁

과학자들이 연구에 패러다임을 사용하는 것에 관한 글로, 과학자들은 패러다임을 사용함으로써 자신이 하고 있는 것이나 그에 대해 자신이 믿고 있는 것을 설명할 필요 없이도 성공적으로 일할 수 있다고 했다. 패러다임을 사용하는 데 있어 그에 대한 과학자들의 믿음이 통일될 필요가 없다고 했고, Thomas Kuhn의 말을 인용하여 과학자들은 패러다임에 대한 완전한 해석이나 이론적 설명이 없더라도 패러다임의 식별에 있어 의견이 일치할 수 있다고 했다. 이를 종합하면 과학 연구를 위해 기능적 측면에서만 패러다임을 사용한다는 것이므로 글의 주제는 ⑤ '과학 연구에서 패러다임의 기능적 측면'이 적절하다.

>왜 오답?

①, ③ 과학 연구에서 패러다임을 기능적 측면에서 사용한다는 내용의 글이다. 기존의 패러다임에서 새로운 이론을 도출한다거나 혁신적 패러다임의 출현을 촉진하는 요인을 설명하는 글이라면 단순한 기능적 측면이 아니라 더 중요한 의미를 갖는 요소로서 패러다임을 이야기했을 것이다.

② scientists' beliefs, what they believe about it 등이 언급된 것으로 만든 오답이다. 개인의 신념이 과학 분야에 상당한 영향을 미친다는 내용이 아니다.

④ 패러다임이 생각이 비슷한 연구원들을 분류한다는 것이 아니라, 과학자들의 의견이 패러다임 식별에서 일치할 수 있다는 것이다.

F 16 정답 ① *문제를 개인화하는 것이 미치는 영향

Facing large-scale, long-term change / can seem overwhelming. //
복수 주어
대규모의 장기적인 변화에 직면하는 것은 / 대응할 수 없는 것처럼 보인다 //
Problems / like global contagion or economic inequality / are
so ~ that S V: 너무 ~해서 …하다   복수 동사
so complex / that it can be hard to believe / any intervention
might make a difference. //
문제는 / 세계적인 전염이나 경제적 불평등 같은 / 너무 복잡해서 / 믿기가 어려울 수 있다 /
어떠한 개입이 변화를 가져올 것이라고 //
Working through fears / of what could be / depends on
동명사구 주어   단수 동사
전치사 on의 동명사구 목적어
connecting / with the abstract. //
두려움을 극복하는 것은 / 무슨 일이 있을지에 대한 / 연결하는 것에 달려 있다 / 추상적인
것과 [단서1] 거대한 문제(기후 변화)를 우리의 현실과 연결하면 개념적 생각이 구체적인 감정으로 바뀜
Linking / issues like climate change, / for example, / with the
realities / of our own neighborhoods, jobs, and relationships, /
translates conceptual ideas / into concrete emotions. //
연결하는 것은 / 기후 변화와 같은 문제를 / 예를 들어 / 현실과 / 우리 자신의 이웃, 직업
그리고 관계라는 / 개념적인 생각을 바꾼다 / 구체적인 감정으로 //
주어
Thinking / of how the beaches we love might disappear, / how
more frequent floods might destroy our homes, /
생각하는 것은 / 우리가 사랑하는 해변이 어떻게 사라질 것인지 / 더 빈번한 홍수가 어떻게
우리의 집을 파괴할 것인지 /
or how we might have to move / to flee mounting wildfire risk,
동사
/ evokes feelings / like anger, sadness, or guilt / — feelings / that
inspire us to act. // [단서2] 구체적인 감정: 우리가 행동하도록 자극하는 감정
혹은 어떻게 우리가 이동해야 할지에 대해 / 증가하는 산불 위험에서 달아나기 위해 / 감정을
불러일으킨다 / 분노, 슬픔 혹은 죄책감 같은 / 감정 / 우리가 행동하도록 자극하는 //
A recent study found / that when people feel personally affected
/ by potential climatic change, / [단서3] 잠재적인 기후 변화가 개인적으로 영향을
미친다고 느낄 때
최근의 한 연구는 발견했다 / 사람들이 개인적으로 영향을 받는다고 느낄 때 / 잠재적인 기후
변화에 의해 / [단서4] 기후 변화의 해결을 위해 실제로 행동할 가능성이 높아짐
they are more likely to support / carbon reduction efforts / and
push for proactive policies. //
그들이 지지할 가능성이 더 높다는 점을 / 탄소 감소 노력을 / 그리고 예방적인 정책을 요구할 //
동명사구 주어   단수 동사
Forming emotional connections / to potential futures / helps us
목적격 보어(원형부정사)   목적어
move / from denial and despair / to action. //
감정적인 연결을 형성하는 것은 / 잠재적인 미래와의 / 우리가 이동하도록 도와준다 / 부정과
절망에서 / 행동으로 //

- overwhelming ⓐ 압도적인, 저항하기 힘든 · contagion ⓝ 전염
- intervention ⓝ 개입 · abstract ⓐ 추상적인
- conceptual ⓐ 개념의, 구상의 · concrete ⓐ 사실에 의거한, 구체적인
- flee ⓥ 도망가다 · mounting ⓐ 증가하는 · evoke ⓥ 떠올려주다
- guilt ⓝ 죄책감 · climate change 기후 변화
- proactive ⓐ 예방적인 · denial ⓝ 부정 · despair ⓝ 절망
- remote ⓐ 외딴, 동떨어진 · impact ⓝ 영향
- contribution ⓝ 기여

대규모의 장기적인 변화에 직면하는 것은 대응할 수 없는 것처럼 보인다. 세계적인 전염이나 경제적 불평등 같은 문제는 너무 복잡해서 어떠한 개입이 변화를 가져올 것이라고 믿기가 어려울 수 있다. 무슨 일이 있을지에 대한 두려움을 극복하는 것은 추상적인 것과 연결하는 것에 달려 있다. 예를 들어 기후 변화와 같은 문제를 우리 자신의 이웃, 직업 그리고 관계라는 현실과 연결하는 것은 개념적인 생각을 구체적인 감정으로 바꾼다. 우리가 사랑하는 해변이 어떻게 사라질 것인지, 더 빈번한 홍수가 어떻게 우리의 집을 파괴할 것인지 혹은 증가하는 산불 위험에서 달아나기 위해 어떻게 우리가 이동해야 할지에 대해 생각하는 것은 분노, 슬픔 혹은 죄책감 같은 감정, 즉 우리가 행동하도록 자극하는 감정을 불러일으킨다. 최근의 한 연구는 사람들이 잠재적인 기후 변화에 의해 개인적으로 영향을 받는다고 느낄 때 그들이 탄소 감소 노력을 지지하고 예방적인 정책을 요구할 가능성이 더 높다는 점을 발견했다. 잠재적인 미래와의 감정적인 연결을 형성하는 것은 우리가 부정과 절망에서 행동으로 이동하도록 도와준다.

다음 글의 주제로 가장 적절한 것은?

① **effectiveness of making remote problems personal**
동떨어진 문제들을 개인적으로 만드는 것의 효과적임 　우리의 현실과 연결하면 개념적인 생각이 구체적인 감정이 됨
② **impacts of negative tone in news on problem solving**
뉴스의 부정적인 어조가 문제 해결에 미치는 영향 　뉴스의 어조에 대한 내용이 아님
③ **contribution of experts to solving large-scale problems**
대규모 문제들을 해결하는 데 있어 전문가들의 기여 　대규모 문제를 개인화하는 것의 이점임
④ **limits of personal intervention in minimizing climate change**
기후 변화를 최소화하는 데 있어 개인적 개입의 한계 　'기후 변화'는 예시일 뿐임
⑤ **risks of attempting to predict events with limited information**
제한된 정보로 사건을 예측하는 것을 시도하는 것의 위험들 　예측의 위험성을 설명하는 것이 아님

✦왜 정답? [정답률 61%]

대규모의 장기적인 문제에 대응하는 방법으로 개인화를 든 글이다.

> • 기후 변화 문제를 우리의 현실과 연결하는 것(개인화)은 개념적인 생각을 구체적인 감정, 우리가 행동하도록 자극하는 감정으로 바꾼다. 단서1 단서2
> • 기후 변화로 인해 개인적으로 영향을 받는다고 느낄(개인화) 때 사람들은 실제적인 행동을 할 가능성이 크다. 단서3 단서4

➡ 기후 변화와 같이 와 닿지 않는 대규모의 장기적인 변화를 우리의 직접적인 현실과 연결하는 것이 우리로 하여금 실제로 행동하게 만든다는 내용이다.

▶ 따라서 이 글의 주제는 ① '동떨어진 문제들을 개인적으로 만드는 것의 효과적임'이다.

✦왜 오답?

② 뉴스가 기후 변화를 어떤 어조로 보도하는지가 그 문제에 대한 우리의 인식이나 행동에 어떤 영향을 미치는지 설명한 것이 아니다.
③ 기후 변화 해결을 위해 전문가들이 어떤 기여를 하는지는 언급되지 않았다.
④ 개인적인 개입을 활성화하기 위한 방법을 설명하는 글이다.
⑤ 완전한 정보를 기반으로 사건을 예측해야 한다는 내용이 아니다.

F 17 정답 ① *농업에서 경험적 관찰 사용의 한계

단서1 농부는 무엇이 이익이 되는지에 대한 관찰에 근거하여 결정함

Environmental learning occurs / when farmers base decisions /
주어　　　　　동사(완전자동사)　　　　(시간)의 부사절 접속사
on observations of "payoff" information. //
환경적 학습은 발생한다 / 농부들이 결정의 근거를 둘 때 / '이익' 정보에 관한 관찰에 //

They may observe / their own or neighbors' farms, / but it is the it is ~ (that) 강조 구문
empirical results / they are using / as a guide, / not the neighbors themselves. // 단서2 이는 경험적 결과를 지침으로 사용하는 것임
그들은 관찰할 수도 있다 / 자기 자신이나 이웃의 농장을 / 하지만 바로 경험적 결과를 / 그들은 사용하고 있다 / 지침으로 / 이웃 자체가 아니라 /

They are looking at farming activities / as experiments / and
병렬 구조
assessing such factors / as relative advantage, compatibility with existing resources, difficulty of use, and "trialability" /
그들은 농업 활동을 보고 / 실험으로 / 그러한 요인을 평가하고 있다 / 상대적 이점, 기존 자원과의 양립성, 사용의 어려움, 그리고 '시험 가능성'과 같은 /

— how well / can it be experimented with. //
얼마나 잘 / 그것이 실험될 수 있는가 //

But that criterion of "trialability" turns out / to be a real problem; /
하지만 그 '시험 가능성'의 기준은 밝혀진다 / 진짜 문제인 것으로 /

it's true / that farmers are always experimenting, / but working
가주어　　진주어절 접속사
farms are / very flawed laboratories. // 단서3 경작되고 있는 농장은 매우 결함이 있는 실험실임
~은 사실이다 / 농부들이 항상 실험하고 있다는 것은 / 하지만 경작되고 있는 농장은 ~이다 / 매우 결함이 있는 실험실 //

Farmers cannot set up / the controlled conditions of professional test plots / in research facilities. //
농부는 마련할 수 없다 / 전문적인 시험 구성의 통제된 조건을 / 연구 시설에서 //

Farmers also often confront / complex and difficult-to-observe
부사적 용법(hard 수식)
phenomena / that would be hard to manage / even if they could (양보)의 부사절 접속사
run / controlled experiments. // 단서4 통제된 실험을 할 수 있다고 하더라도 관리하기 힘든 현상에 자주 직면함
농부는 자주 직면하기도 한다 / 복잡하고 관찰하기 어려운 현상에 / 관리하기 힘든 / 그들이 운영할 수 있다고 해도 / 통제된 실험을 //

Moreover farmers can rarely acquire / payoff information / on
부사어
more than a few of the production methods / they might use, /
게다가 농부는 거의 얻을 수 없고 / 이익 정보를 / 몇 가지 생산 방법을 넘어서는 것에 관한 / 자신이 사용할 수 있는 /

which makes the criterion of "relative advantage" hard / to
measure. // makes의 목적어와 목적격 보어
이는 '상대적 이점'의 기준을 어렵게 만든다 / 측정하기에 //

• **base** ⓥ (~에) 근거[기초]를 두다　• **observation** ⓝ 관찰, 감시, 의견
• **payoff** ⓝ 이득, 보상, 분배　• **assess** ⓥ 평가하다
• **factor** ⓝ 요인, 인자　• **advantage** ⓝ 이점, 장점
• **resource** ⓝ 자원, 재료　• **trialability** ⓝ 시험 (사용) 가능성
• **flaw** ⓥ 망가뜨리다, 파기하다　• **laboratory** ⓝ 실험실
• **plot** ⓝ (소설·영화 등의) 구성, 줄거리
• **facility** ⓝ ((pl.)) (생활의 편리를 위한) 시설[기관]
• **confront** ⓥ 정면으로 부딪치다, 맞서다
• **phenomenon** ⓝ 현상(pl. phenomena)　• **acquire** ⓥ 습득하다, 취득하다

환경적 학습은 농부들이 '이익' 정보에 관한 관찰에 근거하여 결정할 때 발생한다. 그들은 자기 자신이나 이웃의 농장을 관찰할 수도 있지만, 그들이 지침으로 삼고 있는 것은 이웃 자체가 아니라 바로 경험적 결과이다. 그들은 농업 활동을 실험으로 보고 상대적 이점, 기존 자원과의 양립성, 사용의 어려움, 그리고 '시험 가능성', 즉 그것이 얼마나 잘 실험될 수 있는가와 같은 요인을 평가하고 있다. 하지만 그 '시험 가능성'의 기준은 진짜 문제인 것으로 밝혀지는데, 농부들이 항상 실험한다는 것은 사실이지만, 경작되고 있는 농장은 매우 결함이 있는 실험실이다. 농부는 연구 시설에서 전문적인 시험 구성의 통제된 조건을 마련할 수 없다. 통제된 실험을 할 수 있다고 해도, 농부는 관리하기 힘들고 복잡하고 관찰하기 어려운 현상에 자주 직면하기도 한다. 게다가 농부는 자신이 사용할 수 있는 몇 가지 생산 방법을 넘어서는 것에 관한 이익 정보를 거의 얻을 수 없고, 이는 '상대적 이점'의 기준을 측정하기 어렵게 만든다.

다음 글의 주제로 가장 적절한 것은? [3점]

① **limitations of using empirical observations in farming**
농업에서 경험적 관찰을 사용하는 것의 한계 　농부가 경험적 관찰을 근거로 결정하는 것의 한계를 설명함
② **challenges in modernizing traditional farming equipment**
기존 농업 장비를 현대화하는 데 있어서의 난제 　농업 장비의 현대화가 어렵다는 것이 아님
③ **necessity of prioritizing trialability in agricultural innovation**
농업 혁신에서 시험 가능성을 우선 처리해야 할 필요성 　trialability로 만든 오답
④ **importance of making instinctive decisions in agriculture**
농업에서 본능적 결정을 하는 것의 중요성 　경험적 관찰에 근거한 결정에 대한 설명임
⑤ **ways to control unpredictable agricultural phenomena**
예측할 수 없는 농업 현상을 통제하는 방법 　농업 현상을 통제하는 방법을 알려주는 것이 아님

✦왜 정답? [정답률 73%]

농부는 자신의 농장이나 이웃의 농장에서 무엇이 이익이 되는지 관찰하여 결정을 내리는데, 이는 경험적 결과를 지침으로 사용하는 것이라고 했다.
하지만 경작되고 있는 농장은 매우 결함이 있는 실험실이며, 통제된 실험을 할 수 있더라도 농부는 관리하기 힘들고 복잡하고 관찰하기 어려운 현상에 자주 직면한다는 내용이 이어지는 것으로 보아 정답은 ① '농업에서 경험적 관찰을 사용하는 것의 한계'이다.

✦왜 오답?

② 기존의 농업 장비를 현대화하는 것이 어렵다는 내용이 아니다.
③ 글에 언급된 trialability를 이용하여 만든 오답이다. 농업 혁신에 있어 시험 가능성을 우선 처리하는 것이 중요하다고 말하는 글이 아니다.
④ 농부의 본능적 결정이 아니라 경험적 관찰에 의한 결정에 한계가 있다는 점을 설명하는 글이다. 주의
⑤ 농부는 '통제된' 조건을 마련할 수 없다는 문장이나 '통제된' 실험을 할 수 있더라도 관찰하기 어려운 현상에 자주 직면한다는 문장에 등장한 controlled로 만든 오답이다. 함정

F 18 정답 ③ *인간에게 부적합한 과제의 할당

주어 **단서1** 어려움이 발생하는 상황을 설명함
Difficulties arise / when we do not think of people and machines
동사(완전자동사) 부사절 동사 ①
/ as collaborative systems, /
어려움이 발생한다 / 우리가 사람과 기계를 생각하지 않을 때 / 협업 시스템으로 /

but assign / whatever tasks can be automated / to the machines
/ and leave the rest / to people. //
복합 관계형용사가 이끄는 명사절
(= any tasks that can be automated)
그러나 할당할 때 / 자동화될 수 있는 작업은 무엇이든 / 기계에 / 그 나머지를 맡길 때 / 사람들에게 //
부사절 동사 ②, ③

동명사 requiring의 목적어와 목적격 보어
This ends up requiring people to behave / in machine-like
선행사
fashion, / in ways / that differ from human capabilities. //
주격 관계대명사
이것은 결국 사람들에게 행동할 것을 요구하게 된다 / 기계와 같은 방식으로 / 방식으로 / 인간의 능력과 다른 //
주어 동사 목적어 목적격 보어
단서2 우리가 잘하지 못하는 과제를 할당함 ①
We expect people to monitor machines, / which means /
keeping alert for long periods, / something we are bad at. //
우리는 사람들이 기계를 감시하기를 기대하는데 / 이는 의미한다 / 오랫동안 경계를 게을리하지 않는 것을 / 우리가 잘하지 못하는 것 //
주어 동사 목적어 목적격 보어 앞에 목적격 관계대명사가 생략됨
단서3 우리가 잘하지 못하는 과제를 할당함 ②
We require people to do / repeated operations / with the
extreme precision and accuracy / required by machines, / again
something we are not good at. // 앞에 목적격 관계대명사가 생략됨
우리는 사람들에게 할 것을 요구한다 / 반복적인 작업을 / 극도의 정밀함과 정확성을 가지고 / 기계에 의해 요구되는 / 또한 우리가 잘하지 못하는 것 //

When we divide up / the machine and human components of a
task / in this way, /
우리가 나눌 때 / 어떤 과제의 기계적 구성 요소와 인간적 구성 요소를 / 이런 식으로 /

we fail to take advantage / of human strengths and capabilities
병렬 구조 선행사 관계부사
/ but instead rely upon areas / where we are genetically,
biologically unsuited. // **단서4** 인간에게 유전적으로, 생물학적으로 부적합한 영역에 의존하는 문제에 대해 이야기함
우리는 이용하지 못한다 / 인간의 강점과 능력을 / 그러나 그 대신 영역에 의존한다 / 우리가 유전적으로, 생물학적으로 부적합한 //

Yet, when people fail, / they are blamed. //
하지만 사람들이 실패할 때 / 그들은 비난을 받는다 //

- arise ⓥ 생기다, 발생하다 · collaborative ⓐ 공동의
- assign ⓥ (일·책임 등을) 맡기다[배정하다], 할당하다
- automate ⓥ 자동화하다 · fashion ⓝ (행동·문화 등의) 방식
- capability ⓝ 역량, 능력 · monitor ⓥ 감시하다
- alert ⓐ 기민한, 주의를 게을리하지 않는 · extreme ⓐ 극도의, 극심한
- precision ⓝ 정확(성), 정밀(성) · accuracy ⓝ 정확(성)
- divide up ~을 분배하다 · component ⓝ (구성) 요소, 부품
- take advantage of ~을 이용하다 · strength ⓝ 힘, 기운, 강점, 장점
- rely upon ~에 의존[의지]하다 · genetically ⓐⓓ 유전적으로, 유전자 상으로
- biologically ⓐⓓ 생물학적으로 · unsuited ⓐ 부적합한, 어울리지 않는
- overcome ⓥ 극복하다 · allocate ⓥ 할당하다
- unfit ⓐ 부적합한 · pursue ⓥ 추구하다

우리가 사람과 기계를 협업 시스템으로 생각하지 않고 자동화될 수 있는 작업은 무엇이든 기계에 할당하고 그 나머지를 사람들에게 맡길 때 어려움이 발생한다. 이것은 결국 사람들에게 기계와 같은 방식으로, 즉 인간의 능력과 다른 방식으로 행동할 것을 요구하게 된다. 우리는 사람들이 기계를 감시하기를 기대하는데, 이는 오랫동안 경계를 게을리하지 않는 것을 의미하며, 그것은 우리가 잘하지 못하는 것이다.
우리는 사람들에게 기계에 의해 요구되는 극도의 정밀함과 정확성을 가지고 반복적인 작업을 할 것을 요구하는데, 이 또한 우리가 잘하지 못하는 것이다. 우리가 이런 식으로 어떤 과제의 기계적 구성 요소와 인간적 구성 요소를 나눌 때, 우리는 인간의 강점과 능력을 이용하지 못하고, 그 대신 우리가 유전적으로, 생물학적으로 부적합한 영역에 의존한다. 하지만, 사람들이 실패할 때, 그들은 비난을 받는다.

다음 글의 주제로 가장 적절한 것은? [3점]
① difficulties of overcoming human weaknesses to avoid failure
실패를 피하기 위해 인간의 약점을 극복하는 것의 어려움 인간이 잘하지 못하는 것을 극복한다는 내용이 아님
② benefits of allowing machines and humans to work together
기계와 인간이 함께 일하는 것의 이점 이점이 아니라 문제점에 대한 내용임
③ issues of allocating unfit tasks to humans in automated systems
자동화된 시스템에서 인간에게 부적합한 과제를 할당하는 것의 문제 인간이 잘하지 못하는 과제를 부여함
④ reasons why humans continue to pursue machine automation
인간이 기계의 자동화를 계속 추구하는 이유 기계의 자동화를 추구하는 이유는 언급되지 않음
⑤ influences of human actions on a machine's performance
인간의 행동이 기계의 성능에 미치는 영향 기계의 성능에 대한 언급은 없음

> 왜 정답? [정답률 69%] | 인간이 유전적으로, 생물학적으로 부적합한 영역 | 꿀팁
자동화될 수 있는 작업은 모두 기계에 할당하고, 나머지를 사람들에게 맡길 때 어려움이 발생한다는 첫 문장 이후로, 사람들에게 그들이 잘하지 못하는 과제(오랫동안 경계를 게을리하지 않으며 기계를 감시하는 것, 극도의 정밀함과 정확성을 가지고 반복적인 작업을 하는 것)를 할 것을 기대한다는 구체적인 문제점을 제시했으므로 정답은 ③ '자동화된 시스템에서 인간에게 부적합한 과제를 할당하는 것의 문제'이다.
of는 〈소유·소속〉이 아니라 〈동격〉을 나타내는 전치사로 쓰였음 | 꿀팁

> 왜 오답?
① 인간이 잘하지 못하는 것을 극복하는 것이 어렵다는 내용이 아니다.
② 기계와 인간이 함께 일하는 자동화된 시스템에서 기계가 할 일과 인간이 할 일을 나누는 잘못된 방식에 대해 이야기하는 글이다.
④ 기계의 자동화를 계속해서 추구한다거나 그 이유가 무엇인지에 대해서 설명하는 글이 아니다.
⑤ 인간의 행동에 따라 기계의 성능이 달라진다는 내용은 없다.

F 19 정답 ② *산림 자원의 비시장적 가치

Managers of natural resources typically face / market incentives
주격 관계대명사(선행사: market incentives)
that provide financial rewards for exploitation. //
천연자원의 관리자는 일반적으로 직면한다 / 이용에 대한 재정적 보상을 제공하는 시장 인센티브에 //

For example, / owners of forest lands have a market incentive /
to cut down trees /
예를 들어 / 삼림 지대의 소유자는 시장 인센티브를 가지고 있다 / 나무를 베어 내는 /
cut down과 manage 병렬 연결
rather than manage the forest / for carbon capture, wildlife
habitat, flood protection, and other ecosystem services. //
숲을 관리하기보다는 / 탄소 포집, 야생 동물 서식지, 홍수 방어 및 다른 생태계 도움을 위해 //
provide A with B: A에게 B를 제공하다 = provide B for A
These services provide the owner with no financial benefits, /
and thus are unlikely to influence management decisions. //
이러한 (생태계) 도움은 소유자에게 어떠한 재정적 이익도 제공하지 않는다 / 따라서 관리 결정에 영향을 미칠 것 같지 않다 // **단서1** 생태계 도움을 위해 숲을 관리하는 것은 소유자에게 재정적 이익을 가져다주지 않음

But the economic benefits provided by these services, / based
과거분사
on their non-market values, / may exceed the economic value
of the timber. //
그러나 이러한 도움이 제공하는 경제적 이익은 / 그것의 비시장적 가치에 근거하여 / 목재의 경제적 가치를 초과할 수도 있다 //

For example, / a United Nations initiative has estimated / that the
명사절 접속사
economic benefits of ecosystem services / provided by tropical
과거분사(services 수식)
forests, including climate regulation, water purification, and
erosion prevention, / **단서2** 숲을 관리하는 것의 경제적 이익(비시장적 이익)이 시장의 이익보다 3배 이상 큼
예를 들어 / 유엔의 한 계획은 추정했다 / 생태계 도움의 경제적 이익이 / 기후 조절, 수질 정화 및 침식 방지를 포함하여 열대 우림이 제공하는 /

are over three times greater per hectare / than the market
benefits. //
헥타르당 3배보다 더 크다고 / 시장 이익보다 //
동명사 주어(단수 취급) 단수 동사
Thus cutting down the trees / is economically inefficient, / and
형용사적 용법(signal 수식)
markets are not sending the correct "signal" / to favor ecosystem
services over extractive uses. // **단서3** 비시장적 가치를 고려했을 때 나무를 베는 것은 비효율적이지만, 시장은 이를 간과하고 있음
따라서 나무를 베는 것은 / 경제적으로 비효율적인데 / 시장은 올바른 '신호'를 보내지 않고 있다 / 채취하는 사용보다 생태계 도움을 선호하게 하는 //

F

정답 및 해설 **97**

- market incentive 시장 인센티브 • carbon capture 탄소 포집
- habitat ⓝ 서식지 • ecosystem ⓝ 생태계 • exceed ⓥ 초과하다
- initiative ⓝ 계획 • estimate ⓥ 추정하다 • tropical ⓐ 열대의
- regulation ⓝ 규제 • purification ⓝ 정화 • erosion ⓝ 침식
- hectare ⓝ 헥타르(땅 면적의 단위) • favor ~ over … ~를 …보다 선호하다
- extractive ⓐ 채취의, 채광의

천연자원의 관리자는 일반적으로 이용에 대한 재정적 보상을 제공하는 시장 인센티브에 직면한다. 예를 들어, 삼림 지대의 소유자는 탄소 포집, 야생 동물 서식지, 홍수 방어 및 다른 생태계 도움을 위해 숲을 관리하기보다는 나무를 베어 내는 시장 인센티브를 가지고 있다. 이러한 (생태계) 도움은 소유자에게 어떠한 재정적 이익도 제공하지 않으므로, 관리 결정에 영향을 미칠 것 같지 않다. 그러나 이러한 도움이 제공하는 경제적 이익은, 그것의 비시장적 가치에 근거하여, 목재의 경제적 가치를 초과할 수도 있다. 예를 들어, 유엔의 한 계획은 기후 조절, 수질 정화 및 침식 방지를 포함하여 열대 우림이 제공하는 생태계 도움의 경제적 이익이 시장 이익보다 헥타르당 3배보다 더 크다고 추정했다. 따라서 나무를 베는 것은 경제적으로 비효율적인데, 시장은 채취하는 사용보다 생태계 도움을 선호하게 하는 올바른 '신호'를 보내지 않고 있다.

다음 글의 주제로 가장 적절한 것은?

생태계 도움의 시장 가치는 이미 나무를 베는 것과 비교하여 제시됨
① necessity of calculating the market values of ecosystem services
생태계 도움의 시장 가치 계산의 필요성
② significance of weighing forest resources' non-market values
산림 자원의 비시장적 가치를 따져 보는 것의 의의
산림 자원을 관리하는 것이 생태계 도움에 미치는 비시장적 가치가 있음
③ impact of using forest resources to maximize financial benefits
재정적 이익을 극대화하기 위해 산림 자원을 이용하는 것의 영향
산림을 이용하게 되는 현상만 소개했고 구체적인 영향은 언급되지 않음
④ merits of balancing forests' market and non-market values
숲의 시장 가치와 비시장 가치의 균형을 맞추는 장점
숲의 시장 가치가 비시장 가치보다 중시되는 현상을 소개한 글임
⑤ ways of increasing the efficiency of managing natural resources
천연자원 관리의 효율성을 높이는 방법
천연자원 관리의 효율성은 언급되지 않음

왜 정답 ? [정답률 55%]

문제 상황: 천연자원 관리자는 생태계 도움을 위해 숲을 관리하는 것에서 시장 인센티브를 받기 어려움

추정 결과: 삼림 지대를 관리함으로써 얻게 되는 경제적 가치가, 파괴함으로써 얻게 되는 경제적 가치보다 3배 이상 큼

▶ 따라서 이 글의 주제는 ② '산림 자원의 비시장적 가치를 따져 보는 것의 의의'가 가장 적절하다.

왜 오답 ?

① 생태계 도움의 시장 가치는 이미 나무를 베는 것과 비교하여 제시되었으며, 이를 계산하는 것이 필요하다는 내용이 아니다.
③ 재정적 이익을 위해 삼림을 관리하기보다는 이용하게 되는 현상만 소개했지, 구체적인 영향은 언급되지 않았다.
④ 숲의 시장 가치가 비시장 가치보다 중시되는 현상을 소개한 글이므로, 둘의 균형을 맞추는 내용은 언급되지 않았다.
⑤ 천연자원 관리의 효율성에 대한 내용은 없다.

김아린 | 충남대 의예과 2024년 입학 · 대전한빛고 졸

주제 문제에서는 특히 선지의 첫 단어들이 중요한데, ① '필요성'이라면 명확한 주장, ② '의의'라면 중요성을 암시하는 설명, ③ '영향'이라면 특정 현상의 결과, ④ '장점들'과 ⑤ '방법들'처럼 복수 명사면 해당하는 '여러' 내용이 글에 나타났는지 확인해야 해.
이 문제에선 ecosystem service가 어떤 재정적 이익도 제공하지 않는다고 했지만 But 뒤에서 글의 흐름이 바뀌는 것과, Thus로 시작하는 결론 문장을 통해 산림 자원이 재정적 이익 외에 다른 가치를 가진다는 주제를 잘 찾아낸다면 정답을 고를 수 있을 거야.

F 20 정답 ① ⭐ 2등급 대비 [정답률 78%]

＊고대 매장지에서 발견된 불평등의 증거

앞 문장의 내용을 받는 so가 문두로 오면서 도치 구문이 이어짐
Just as today some jobs are better / than others, / so would they have been / in early societies / with their blossoming towns and eventually cities, /
오늘날 어떤 직업이 더 나은 것처럼 / 다른 직업보다 / 직업은 마찬가지였을 것이다 / 초기 사회에서도 / 번창하는 마을과 종국에는 도시가 있었던 /
with+(대)명사+분사 구문에서 more 앞에 being이 생략됨
with some roles more dangerous / and some having more plentiful access / to food or other resources. //
어떤 역할은 더 위험하고 / 어떤 역할은 더 많은 접근권을 가지면서 / 식량이나 다른 자원들에 //
생략 가능한 명사절 접속사
The archeological record shows / that soon after the appearance / of towns, agriculture, and surpluses, / some burials start to look different / from others. //
고고학적 기록은 보인다 / 출현 직후에 / 마을과 농업, 잉여물의 / 일부 매장지는 다르게 보이기 시작한다 / 다른 매장지와 //
단서1 고고학적 기록이 보여줌: 어떤 사람은 귀중품과 함께 매장되고, 어떤 사람은 공동묘지에 매장됨
Some individuals are buried / with more precious goods (metals, weapons, and maybe even art), /
어떤 사람들은 매장되고 / 더 많은 귀중품(금속과 무기, 아마도 심지어 예술품)과 함께 /
some are in group graves / and some by themselves, / and still others don't even seem to be buried at all. // **단서2** 어떤 사람은 홀로 매장되고, 어떤 사람은 전혀 매장되지도 못함
어떤 사람들은 집단 무덤에 매장되고 / 어떤 사람들은 홀로 / 또 다른 어떤 사람들은 전혀 매장되지도 않은 것처럼 보인다 //
복수 주어   복수 동사   to show의 간접목적어와 직접목적어
The bones from the burials / start to show us differences / as well / — chemical and isotope analyses / of teeth and long bones / reveal /
매장지에서 나온 뼈도 / 우리에게 차이점을 보여 주기 시작한다 / 또한 / 화학적, 동위 원소 분석은 / 치아와 긴뼈에 대한 / 보여 준다 /
that some members of groups / were getting more protein or minerals / than others; / **단서3** 일부 구성원이 다른 구성원보다 더 많은 단백질이나 무기질을 섭취함
집단의 일부 구성원들이 / 더 많은 단백질이나 무기질을 섭취하고 있었다는 것을 / 다른 구성원들보다 /
some have more evidence / of diseases and greater physical injuries / from their labors. // **단서4** 일부 구성원은 노동으로 인해 더 큰 신체적 부상을 당했음
일부에게는 더 많은 증거가 있다 / 질병 및 더 큰 신체적 부상의 / 그들의 노동으로 인한 //
Early on these differences are small, / but by 5,000 to 7,000 years ago / they are becoming quite pronounced. //
초기에는 이런 차이가 작았지만 / 5,000년에서 7,000년 전 즈음에는 / 그 차이가 상당히 뚜렷해지고 있다 //

- blossoming ⓐ 번창하는 • appearance ⓝ 출현
- resource ⓝ 자원 • agriculture ⓝ 농업 • burial ⓝ 매장지
- bury ⓥ 매장하다 • protein ⓝ 단백질 • mineral ⓝ 무기질
- pronounce ⓥ 뚜렷하게 하다

오늘날 어떤 직업이 다른 직업보다 더 나은 것처럼, 번창하는 마을과 종국에는 도시가 있었던 초기 사회에서도 직업은 마찬가지였을 텐데, 어떤 역할은 더 위험하고 어떤 역할은 식량이나 다른 자원들에 더 많은 접근권을 가졌을 것이다. 고고학적 기록에 따르면 마을과 농업, 잉여물이 나타난 직후에, 일부 매장지는 다른 매장지와 다르게 보이기 시작한다. 어떤 사람들은 더 많은 귀중품(금속과 무기, 아마도 심지어 예술품)과 함께 매장되고, 어떤 사람들은 집단 무덤에 매장되고, 어떤 사람들은 홀로 매장되며, 또 다른 어떤 사람들은 전혀 매장되지도 않은 것처럼 보인다. 매장지에서 나온 뼈도 또한 우리에게 차이점을 보여 주기 시작하는데, 치아와 긴뼈에 대한 화학적, 동위 원소 분석은 집단의 일부 구성원들이 다른 구성원들보다 더 많은 단백질이나 무기질을 섭취하고 있었고, 일부에게는 질병 및 그들의 노동으로 인한 더 큰 신체적 부상의 더 많은 증거가 있다는 것을 보여 준다. 초기에는 이런 차이가 작았지만, 5,000년에서 7,000년 전 즈음에는 그 차이가 상당히 뚜렷해지고 있다.

다음 글의 주제로 가장 적절한 것은? [3점]

① the evidence of social inequality found in ancient burials
고대 매장지에서 발견된 사회적 불평등의 증거 ┌ 일부가 다른 구성원보다 더 잘 먹음을 보여주는 증거
② scientific efforts to preserve ancient remains
고대 유적을 보존하려는 과학적 노력 ┌ 유적 보존에 대한 글이 아님
③ attempts to overcome inequality in history
역사에서 불평등을 극복하려는 시도 ┌ 불평등했음을 보여주는 증거를 설명함
④ cultural differences in the concept of better jobs
더 나은 직업이라는 개념에 있어 문화적 차이 ┌ 첫 문장으로만 만든 오답
⑤ ancient agricultural methods passed down to the present
현재로 전해진 고대의 농업 기술 ┌ 농업 기술을 설명하는 글이 아님

왜 2등급? 선택지와 첫 문장을 통해 핵심 소재에 대한 힌트를 얻지 못하면, 뒤에 이어지는 고고학적 기록에 대한 내용이 왜 나오는지 알 수 없을 것이므로 풀기 힘든 2등급 대비 문제이다.

| 문제 풀이 순서 |

1st 선택지와 첫 문장을 통해 핵심 소재를 확인하고 글의 내용을 예상한다.

선택지	거의 모든 선택지에 '고대', '불평등'과 같은 표현들이 등장한다.
첫 문장	오늘날 어떤 직업이 다른 직업보다 더 나은 것처럼, 번창하는 마을과 중국에는 도시가 있었던 초기 사회에서도 직업은 마찬가지였을 텐데, 어떤 역할은 더 위험하고 어떤 역할은 식량이나 다른 자원들에 더 많은 접근권을 가졌을 것이다.

➡ 이 글은 고대의 불평등과 관련된 내용일 것이다.

➡ 오늘날 더 나은 직업이 있는 것처럼, 초기 사회에서도 그랬을 것이라고 했으므로 이런 불평등에 대한 내용이 나올 것을 예상할 수 있다.

2nd 글의 나머지 부분에서 내용을 파악하고 주제를 찾는다.

- 어떤 사람들은 더 많은 귀중품(금속과 무기, 아마도 심지어 예술품)과 함께 매장되고, 어떤 사람들은 집단 무덤에 매장되고, 어떤 사람들은 홀로 매장되며, 또 다른 어떤 사람들은 전혀 매장되지도 않은 것처럼 보인다. **단서 1**
- 치아와 긴뼈에 대한 화학적, 동위 원소 분석은 집단의 일부 구성원들이 다른 구성원들보다 더 많은 단백질이나 무기질을 섭취하고 있었고, 일부에게는 질병 및 그들의 노동으로 인한 더 큰 신체적 부상의 더 많은 증거가 있다는 것을 보여 준다. **단서 2** **단서 3**

➡ 고고학적 기록에서 어떤 사람은 귀중품과 함께 매장되고, 어떤 사람은 집단 무덤에 매장되고, 어떤 사람은 홀로 매장되고, 또 어떤 사람은 아예 매장되지도 않았다고 했다. **단서 1** 일부 구성원이 다른 구성원보다 더 많은 단백질이나 무기질을 섭취했고, **단서 2** 일부 구성원은 노동으로 인한 더 큰 신체적 부상을 당했다고 했다. **단서 3**
모두 고고학적 기록이 고대 사회에서도 불평등이 존재했음을 보여 주는 것이므로 글의 주제로 ① '고대 매장지에서 발견된 사회적 불평등의 증거'가 가장 적절하다.

| 선택지 분석 |

① **the evidence of social inequality found in ancient burials**
고대 매장지에서 발견된 사회적 불평등의 증거
고고학적 기록이 고대 사회에서도 불평등이 존재했음을 보여 주는 내용이다.

② **scientific efforts to preserve ancient remains**
고대 유적을 보존하려는 과학적 노력
고대 유적에서 드러난 고대 사회의 불평등을 설명하는 글이다.

③ **attempts to overcome inequality in history**
역사에서 불평등을 극복하려는 시도
고대 사회도 불평등했다는 글로, 그 불평등을 극복하려는 시도에 대한 언급은 없다.

④ **cultural differences in the concept of better jobs**
더 나은 직업이라는 개념에 있어 문화적 차이
고대 사회에도 직업간 불평등이 존재했다는 의미라고 할 수 있다.

⑤ **ancient agricultural methods passed down to the present**
현재로 전해진 고대의 농업 기술
농업 기술에 대해 설명하는 글이 아니다.

＊소셜 네트워킹 서비스의 부정적인 영향들

선행사, 뒤에 주격 관계대명사와 be동사가 생략됨
For those of any age / with an existing network of friendships / built up in the three-dimensional world, /
어떠한 연령대의 사람에게나 / 친구 관계의 기존의 네트워크를 가진 / 3차원 세계에서 구축된 /
social networking sites can be a happy extension of communication, / along with email, video calls, or phone calls, /
부사절 접속사(때)
when face-to-face time together just isn't possible. //
소셜 네트워킹 사이트는 소통의 행복한 연장선이 될 수 있다 / 이메일, 영상 통화, 또는 전화 통화와 함께 / 함께 대면하는 시간이 단지 실현 가능하지 않을 때 //

The danger comes / when a fake identity is both tempting and
선행사
possible / through relationships / that are *not* based / on real,
주격 관계대명사
three-dimensional interaction, /
위험이 발생한다 / 가짜 정체성이 유혹적이고도 가능할 때 / 관계를 통해 / 기반하지 '않은' / 현실의 3차원적 상호 작용에 / ┌ <때>를 나타내는 부사절 접속사의 병렬 구조
and/or when the most important things in your life are / the secondhand lives of others / rather than personal experiences. //
그리고/또는 여러분의 삶에서 가장 중요한 것이 ~일 때 / 다른 사람들의 간접적인 삶 / 개인적인 경험이라기보다 //

Living in the context of the screen / might suggest / false norms
동명사의 전치사
of desirable lifestyles / full of friends and parties. //
화면의 맥락 안에서 사는 것은 / 암시할지 모른다 / 바람직한 생활 방식이라는 잘못된 기준을 / 친구들과 파티들로 가득 찬 // **단서 1** 평범한 사람이 소셜 네트워킹 사이트의 생활 방식을 추종함에 따라 필연적으로 자존감이 떨어짐
As ordinary human beings follow / the activities of these golden individuals, / self-esteem will inevitably drop; /
평범한 인간들이 추종함에 따라 / 이러한 특별한 개인들의 활동을 / 자존감은 필연적으로 떨어질 것이다 /
yet the constant narcissistic obsession with the self / and its inadequacies / will dominate. //
그러나 자신에 대한 끊임없는 자아도취적 집착과 / 그것의 부적절함이 / 지배력을 발휘할 것이다 // **단서 2** 악순환: 소셜 네트워킹의 결과로 자존감이 떨어질수록 소셜 네트워킹의 매력이 더 커짐
We can imagine a vicious circle / where the more your identity
선행사(추상적 의미의 장소) 관계부사
is harmed / as a result of social networking / and the more inadequate you feel, /
우리는 악순환을 상상할 수 있다 / 여러분의 정체성이 더 많이 손상될수록 / 소셜 네트워킹의 결과로 / 그리고 여러분이 더 많이 부족하다고 느낄수록 /
the greater the appeal of a medium / where you don't need to
선행사(추상적 의미의 장소) 관계부사
communicate with people / face-to-face. //
매체의 매력이 더 커지는 / 여러분이 사람들과 소통할 필요가 없는 / 얼굴을 맞대고 //

- three-dimensional ⓐ 3차원의 · extension ⓝ 연장선
- along with ~와 함께 · identity ⓝ 정체성
- tempting ⓐ 유혹적인 · interaction ⓝ 상호작용
- secondhand ⓐ 간접의 · context ⓝ 맥락 · norm ⓝ 기준
- golden ⓐ 특별한 · self-esteem ⓝ 자존감
- inevitably ⓐⓓ 필연적으로, 불가피하게 · obsession ⓝ 집착
- inadequacy ⓝ 부적절함 · dominate ⓥ 지배하다
- vicious circle 악순환

3차원 세계에서 구축된 친구 관계의 기존의 네트워크를 가진 어떠한 연령대의 사람에게나, 소셜 네트워킹 사이트는 함께 대면하는 시간이 단지 실현 가능하지 않을 때, 이메일, 영상 통화, 또는 전화 통화와 함께 소통의 행복한 연장선이 될 수 있다. 현실의 3차원적 상호 작용에 기반하지 '않은' 관계를 통해 가짜 정체성이 유혹적이고도 가능할 때, 그리고/또는 여러분의 삶에서 가장 중요한 것이 개인적인 경험이라기보다 다른 사람들의 간접적인 삶일 때 위험이 발생한다. 화면의 맥락 안에서 사는 것은 친구들과 파티들로 가득 찬 바람직한 생활 방식이라는 잘못된 기준을 암시할지 모른다. 평범한 인간들이 이러한 특별한 개인들의 활동을 추종함에 따라 자존감이 필연적으로 떨어질 것이다. 그러나 자신에 대한 끊임없는 자아도취적 집착과 그것의 부적절함이 지배력을 발휘할 것이다. 소셜 네트워킹의 결과로 여러분의 정체성이 더 많이 손상되고 여러분이 더 많이 부족하다고 느낄수록, 우리는 여러분이 사람들과 얼굴을 맞대고 소통할 필요가 없는 매체의 매력이 더 커지는 악순환을 상상할 수 있다.

① negative effects of social networking services on self-perception
자아 인식에 미치는 소셜 네트워킹 서비스의 부정적인 영향들   자존감이 떨어짐
② unknown risks to personal well-being from internet addiction
인터넷 중독으로부터 오는 개인적인 안녕에 대한 알려지지 않은 위험들   인터넷 중독은 너무 광범위함
③ software features to make virtual lives more realistic
가상의 삶을 더욱 현실적으로 만드는 소프트웨어 특징들   소프트웨어의 특징을 설명한 것이 아님
④ efforts to increase face-to-face interaction for social bonds
사회적 유대감을 위한 대면 상호 작용을 증가하려는 노력들   문제점을 설명하는 글임
⑤ difficulties of filtering out fake information on social media
소셜 미디어에서 가짜 정보를 걸러내는 것의 어려움들   가짜 정보라는 문제점을 설명한 것이 아님

왜 2등급? 접속사 없이 내용이 전환되므로 문맥 위주로 지문을 유심히 살펴봐야 하는 문제였다. 하지만 첫 번째 문장을 제외한 모든 문장에서 not, false, drop, inadequacies, vicious 등 부정적인 어감의 단어들과 identity, self-esteem 등 자아 인식과 관련된 단어들을 종합하면 '소셜 네트워킹 서비스가 자아 인식에 부정적인 영향을 미친다'라는 주제를 쉽게 파악할 수 있다.

| 문제 풀이 순서 |

1st 글의 앞부분에서 중심 화제를 제시했는지 확인하고 글의 내용을 예상한다.

> • … 소셜 네트워킹 사이트는 … 소통의 행복한 연장선이 될 수 있다.
> • 현실의 3차원적 상호 작용에 기반하지 '않은' 관계를 통해 가짜 정체성이 유혹적이고도 가능할 때, 그리고/또는 여러분의 삶에서 가장 중요한 것이 개인적인 경험이라기보다 다른 사람들의 간접적인 삶일 때 위험이 발생한다.

➡ 첫 번째 문장에서 소셜 네트워킹 서비스가 소통의 행복한 연장선이 될 수 있다고 하며 긍정적인 기능을 제시했다. 하지만 바로 다음 문장에서 가짜 정체성이 가능하고 간접적인 삶이 중요해질 때 '위험'이 발생한다고 하며 부정적인 영향을 언급했다.

➡ 소셜 네트워킹 서비스의 부정적인 영향에 관한 내용이 이어질 것이다.

2nd 글을 읽으면서 세부적인 내용들을 파악해서 주제를 고른다.

> • 평범한 인간들이 이러한 특별한 개인들의 활동을 추종함에 따라 자존감은 필연적으로 떨어질 것이다. **단서 1**
> • 소셜 네트워킹의 결과로 여러분의 정체성이 더 많이 손상되고 여러분이 더 많이 부족하다고 느낄수록, … 매체의 매력이 더 커지는 악순환을 상상할 수 있다. **단서 2**

➡ 소셜 네트워킹 서비스를 이용하는 평범한 인간들은 자존감이 떨어지고, 정체성이 더 많이 손상되고, 더 많이 부족하다고 느끼는 등 여러 부정적인 영향을 받는다고 했다. 즉, 자아 인식에 있어서 부정적인 영향을 받지만, 그럴수록 매체의 매력이 더 커지는 악순환이 발생한다고 했다.

▶ 따라서 ① '자아 인식에 미치는 소셜 네트워킹 서비스의 부정적인 영향들'이 이 글의 주제로 가장 적절하다.

| 선택지 분석 |

① **negative effects of social networking services on self-perception**
자아 인식에 미치는 소셜 네트워킹 서비스의 부정적인 영향들
소셜 네트워킹 서비스로 인해 자존감이 떨어진다는 문제점을 이야기하고 있다.

② **unknown risks to personal well-being from internet addiction**
인터넷 중독으로부터 오는 개인적인 안녕에 대한 알려지지 않은 위험들
인터넷 중독이 아니라 현실의 상호 작용에 기반하지 않고 소셜 네트워킹 서비스를 통해 사람들과 관계를 맺는 것의 문제점을 이야기하는 글이다.

③ **software features to make virtual lives more realistic**
가상의 삶을 더욱 현실적으로 만드는 소프트웨어 특징들
소프트웨어를 통해 가상의 삶이 더욱 현실적이 된다는 내용이 아니다.

④ **efforts to increase face-to-face interaction for social bonds**
사회적 유대감을 위한 대면 상호 작용을 증가하려는 노력
대면 상호 작용이 아닌 소셜 네트워킹을 통해 상호 작용의 문제점을 이야기하는 글이다.

⑤ **difficulties of filtering out fake information on social media**
소셜 미디어에서 가짜 정보를 걸러내는 것의 어려움들
소셜 미디어의 문제점 중 가짜 정보를 설명하는 것이 아니다.

F 22 정답 ⑤ ━━━━━━━━ ⭐ 1등급 대비 [정답률 66%]

＊문제 해결책에 영향을 미치는 문제 구조화

Problem framing amounts to defining / *what* problem you are proposing to solve. // **단서 1** 문제 구조화는 어떤 문제를 해결하려는 것인지를 정의하는 것임
'문제 구조화'는 정의하는 것에 해당한다 / 여러분이 '어떤' 문제를 해결하려고 하는지 //

This is a critical activity / because the frame / you choose /
앞에 목적격 관계대명사가 생략됨
strongly influences your understanding / of the problem, /
이것은 중대한 활동이다 / 왜냐하면 구조가 / 여러분이 선택하는 / 여러분의 이해에 강하게 영향을 미치며 / 그 문제에 대한 / **단서 2** 문제 구조가 해결책으로의 접근법을 결정함
thereby conditioning your approach / to solving it. //
그로 인해 여러분의 접근 방식을 결정하기 때문에 / 그것을 해결하는 것으로의 // 형용사적 용법 (ways 수식)
For an illustration, / consider Thibodeau and Broditsky's series
관계부사 where로 바꾸어 쓸 수 있음
of experiments / in which they asked people for ways / to reduce crime in a community. // **단서 3** 해결하려는 문제를 바이러스로 정의하는지, 짐승으로 정의하는지에 따라 제안하는 해결책이 크게 달라짐
하나의 예로 / Thibodeau와 Broditsky의 일련의 실험에 대해 생각해 보라 / 그들이 사람들에게 방법을 물어본 / 지역사회 내의 범죄를 줄이는 //
생략 가능한 명사절 접속사
They found / that the respondents' suggestions changed significantly / depending / on whether the metaphor / used to describe crime / was as a virus or as a beast. //
앞에 주격 관계대명사와 be동사가 생략됨
그들은 발견했다 / 응답자들의 제안이 크게 달라진다는 것을 / (~에) 따라 / 은유가 / 범죄를 묘사하는 데 사용된 / 바이러스였는지 혹은 짐승이었는지에 //
주어   people 수식   a metaphor 수식
People / presented with a metaphor / comparing crime to a
a virus 수식
virus / invading their city /
사람들은 / 은유를 제공받은 / 범죄를 바이러스에 비유하는 / 자신들의 도시에 침입하는 /
동사
emphasized prevention and addressing the root causes / of the problem, / such as eliminating poverty and improving education. //
예방과 근본 원인을 해결하는 것을 강조했다 / 문제의 / 빈곤을 없애고 교육을 향상시키는 것 같은 //
주어
On the other hand, / people / presented with the beast metaphor
동사
/ focused on remediations: / increasing the size / of the police force and prisons. //
반면에 / 사람들은 / 짐승의 은유를 제공받은 / 교정 조치에 초점을 맞추었다 / 규모를 늘리는 것 / 경찰력과 교도소의 //

• framing ⓝ 구조화   • amount to ~에 해당하다, ~과 마찬가지이다
• propose ⓥ 작정[의도]하다   • critical ⓐ 대단히 중요한
• thereby ⓐⓓ 그렇게 함으로써
• condition ⓥ 결정하다, 좌우하다, 영향을 미치다
• approach ⓝ 접근법, 연구법   • illustration ⓝ 실례, 보기
• metaphor ⓝ 은유   • invade ⓥ 침입[침략]하다
• eliminate ⓥ 제거하다, 없애다   • remediation ⓝ 교정 (조치)
• preventive ⓐ 예방적인   • measure ⓝ 조치, 정책

'문제 구조화'는 여러분이 '어떤' 문제를 해결하려고 하는지 정의하는 것에 해당한다. 여러분이 선택하는 구조가 그 문제에 대한 여러분의 이해에 강하게 영향을 미치며, 그로 인해 그것을 해결하는 것으로의 여러분의 접근 방식을 결정하기 때문에 이것은 중대한 활동이다. 하나의 예로, 사람들에게 지역사회 내의 범죄를 줄이는 방법을 물어본 Thibodeau와 Broditsky의 일련의 실험에 대해 생각해 보라. 그들은 범죄를 묘사하는 데 사용된 은유가 바이러스였는지 혹은 짐승이었는지에 따라 응답자들의 제안이 크게 달라진다는 것을 발견했다. 범죄를 자신들의 도시에 침입하는 바이러스에 비유하는 은유를 제공받은 사람들은 빈곤을 없애고 교육을 향상시키는 것 같은, 예방과 문제의 근본 원인 해결을 강조했다. 반면에 짐승의 은유를 제공받은 사람들은 경찰력과 교도소의 규모를 늘리는 것, 즉 교정 조치에 초점을 맞추었다.

다음 글의 주제로 가장 적절한 것은?

① importance of asking the right questions for better solutions
더 나은 해결책을 위해 올바른 질문을 하는 것의 중요성
질문에 따라 올바르거나 틀린 해결책이 나오는 것이 아님

② difficulty of using a metaphor to find solutions to a problem
문제에 대한 해결책을 찾기 위해 은유를 사용하는 것의 어려움   metaphor가 언급된 것으로 만든 오답

③ reasons why problem framing prevents solutions from appearing
문제 구조화가 해결책의 출현을 막는 이유   문제 구조화가 해결책이 나오지 못하게 하는 것은 아님

④ usefulness of preventive measures in reducing community crime
지역사회 범죄를 줄이는 데 있어서 예방 조치의 유용성   지역사회 범죄는 예시로 든 내용임

⑤ effect of problem framing on approaching and solving problems
문제 구조화가 문제 접근 및 해결에 미치는 영향   문제 구조화를 어떻게 하는지에 따라 접근 방식과 해결책이 달라짐

왜 1등급? 첫 문장의 '문제 구조화'라는 개념부터 와닿지 않아서 지문 파악이 어렵겠다는 선입견을 가질 수도 있지만, 의외로 두 번째 문장을 통해 주제를 쉽게 짐작할 수 있다. 또한 주어진 예시에 이를 대입하면 더욱 쉽게 주제를 확정지을 수 있는 2등급 대비 문제였다.

| 문제 풀이 순서 |

1st 선택지와 첫 문장을 통해 핵심 소재를 확인하고 글의 내용을 예상한다.

선택지	거의 모든 선택지에 '문제', '해결', '해결책'과 같은 표현들이 등장한다.
첫 문장	'문제 구조화'는 여러분이 '어떤' 문제를 해결하려고 하는지 정의하는 것에 해당한다. **단서1**

→ 이 글은 문제 해결을 위한 '문제 구조화'에 관한 내용일 것이다. (단서)

→ 첫 문장만으로는 '문제 구조화'에 대해 명확히 알기 어려우므로 이와 관련된 부연 설명 및 예시가 이어질 것이라고 예상할 수 있다. (발상)

2nd 글의 나머지 부분에서 내용을 파악하고 주제를 찾는다.

• 여러분이 선택하는 구조가 그 문제에 대한 여러분의 이해에 강하게 영향을 미치며, 그로 인해 그것을 해결하는 것으로의 여러분의 접근 방식을 결정하기 때문에 이것은 중대한 활동이다. **단서2**

• 그들은 범죄를 묘사하는 데 사용된 은유가 바이러스였는지 혹은 짐승이었는지에 따라 응답자들의 제안이 크게 달라진다는 것을 발견했다. **단서3**

→ '문제 구조화'가 문제 이해에 강한 영향을 미치며 해결로 향하는 접근 방식을 결정하므로 중요하다고 했다. **단서2** 또한 예시로서 범죄 묘사에 사용되는 은유를 제시했는데, 은유(= 구조)가 달라짐에 따라 응답자들의 제안(= 해결책)도 달라졌다는 내용이므로 **단서3** 글의 주제는 ⑤ '문제 구조화가 문제 접근 및 해결에 미치는 영향'이 가장 적절하다.

| 선택지 분석 |

① **importance of asking the right questions for better solutions**
더 나은 해결책을 위해 올바른 질문을 하는 것의 중요성
문제를 어떻게 정의하느냐에 따라 해결책이 달라진다는 것이지, 질문에 따라 올바르거나 틀린 해결책이 나온다는 것이 아니다.

② **difficulty of using a metaphor to find solutions to a problem**
문제에 대한 해결책을 찾기 위해 은유를 사용하는 것의 어려움
해결책을 찾는 데 은유를 사용하는 것이 어렵다는 내용이 아니다.

③ **reasons why problem framing prevents solutions from appearing**
문제 구조화가 해결책의 출현을 막는 이유
문제 구조화에 따라 해결책이 달라진다는 것이지, 문제 구조화가 해결책이 나오지 못하게 한다는 것이 아니다.

④ **usefulness of preventive measures in reducing community crime**
지역사회 범죄를 줄이는 데 있어서 예방 조치의 유용성
지역사회 범죄 문제에 대한 문제 구조화에 따라 두 가지 해결책이 나온다는 것은 주제를 설명하기 위한 예시일 뿐이다.

⑤ **effect of problem framing on approaching and solving problems**
문제 구조화가 문제 접근 및 해결에 미치는 영향
문제 구조화에 따라 문제 접근과 해결 방식이 달라진다는 내용이다.

F 23 정답 ⑤ ● 1등급 대비 [정답률 62%]

＊청취자를 끌어들이려는 시도의 결과

The primary purpose / of commercial music radio broadcasting / is to deliver an audience / to a group of advertisers and sponsors. //
주어   동사   주격 보어
주된 목적은 / 상업적 음악 라디오 방송의 / 청취자를 인도하는 것이다 / 광고주와 후원자 집단에 //
부사적 용법(목적) ＊

To achieve commercial success, / that audience must be as large as possible. // **단서1** 상업적 음악 라디오 방송이 상업적 성공을 달성하려면 대규모의 청취자를 끌어들여야 함
상업적 성공을 달성하기 위해서는 / 그 청취자는 가능한 한 대규모여야 한다 //

More than any other characteristics / (such as demographic or psychographic profile, / purchasing power, / level of interest, / degree of satisfaction, / quality of attention / or emotional state), /
다른 어떤 특성보다도 / (인구 통계학적 또는 심리 통계학적 개요 / 구매력 / 관심 수준 / 만족도 / 주목의 질 / 또는 정서 상태 같은) /

the quantity of an audience / aggregated as a mass / is the most significant metric / for broadcasters / seeking to make music radio / for profitable ends. //
주어   동사
청취자의 크기는 / 집단으로 모인 / 가장 중요한 측정 기준이다 / 방송 진행자에게 / 음악 라디오를 만들고자 하는 / 수익 목적을 위해 //

As a result, / broadcasters attempt / to maximise their audience size / by playing music / that is popular, /
결과적으로 / 방송 진행자는 애쓴다 / 청취자의 규모를 극대화하려고 / 음악을 틀어서 / 인기 있는 / **단서2** 그 결과 방송 진행자는 특정 음악을 틀어서 청취자의 규모를 극대화하려고 애씀

or — at the very least — music / that can be relied upon / not to cause audiences / to switch off their radio / or change the station. //
└─ to cause의 목적격 보어의 병렬 구조 ─┘
또는 적어도 음악 / 믿길 수 있는 / 청취자가 ~하게 하지 않을 거라고 / 그들의 라디오를 끄거나 / 방송국을 바꾸게 //

Audience retention is a key value / (if not the key value) / for many music programmers / and for radio station management. //
청취자 보유는 하나의 핵심 가치이다 / (유일한 핵심 가치는 아니더라도) / 많은 음악 프로그램 제작자에게 / 그리고 라디오 방송국 경영진에 //

In consequence, / a high degree of risk aversion / frequently marks out / the 'successful' radio music programmer. //
그 결과 / 높은 수준의 모험 회피는 / 흔히 구분 짓는다 / '성공한' 라디오 음악 프로그램 제작자를 // **단서3** 라디오 음악 프로그램 제작자는 높은 수준으로 모험을 회피하게 됨

Playlists are restricted, / and often very small. //
방송 목록은 한정되고 / 흔히 매우 적다 //

• primary ⓐ 주된   • demographic ⓐ 인구 통계학적인
• psychographic ⓐ 심리 통계학적인   • profile ⓝ 개요, 윤곽
• emotional state 정서 상태   • metric ⓝ 측정 기준
• profitable ⓐ 수익성이 있는   • attempt ⓥ 시도하다
• maximise ⓥ 극대화하다   • retention ⓝ 보유, 유지

상업적 음악 라디오 방송의 주된 목적은 청취자를 광고주와 후원자 집단에 인도하는 것이다. 상업적 성공을 달성하기 위해서는, 그 청취자는 가능한 한 대규모여야 한다. (인구 통계학적 또는 심리 통계학적 개요, 구매력, 관심 수준, 만족도, 주목의 질, 또는 정서 상태 같은) 다른 어떤 특성보다도, 집단으로 모인 청취자의 크기는 음악 라디오가 수익 목적에 이바지하게 하고자 하는 방송 진행자에게 가장 중요한 측정 기준이다. 결과적으로 방송 진행자는 인기 있는 음악, 또는 – 적어도 – 청취자가 라디오를 끄거나 방송국을 바꾸게 하지 않을 것으로 믿기는 음악을 틀어 청취자의 규모를 극대화하려고 애쓴다. 청취자 보유는 많은 음악 프로그램 제작자에게, 그리고 라디오 방송국 경영진에 (유일한 핵심 가치는 아니더라도) 하나의 핵심 가치이다. 그 결과 높은 수준의 모험 회피는 흔히 '성공한' 라디오 음악 프로그램 제작자를 구분 짓는다. 방송 목록은 한정되고 흔히 매우 적다.

다음 글의 주제로 가장 적절한 것은?

① features of music playlists appealing to international audiences
국제적 청중의 관심을 끄는 음악 방송 목록의 특징　상업적 음악 방송에 대한 내용임
② influence of advertisers on radio audiences' musical preferences
광고주가 라디오 청중의 음악적 선호에 미치는 영향
③ difficulties of increasing audience size in radio music programmes 청중 규모 확대를 추구한 결과를 설명함　광고주가 청중의 음악적 선호에
라디오 음악 프로그램에서 청중 규모 확대의 어려움　　영향을 미친다는 것이 아님
④ necessity of satisfying listeners' diverse needs in the radio business 청취자의 요구를 충족시키는 것이 목적이 아님
라디오 사업에서 청취자의 다양한 요구를 충족시킬 필요성
⑤outcome of music radio businesses' attempts to attract large audiences 인기 있는 음악만 틂
음악 라디오 사업의 대규모 청취자를 끌어들이려는 시도의 결과

왜 1등급? 첫 문장에서 음악 라디오 방송의 목적이 나오고 그 뒤로는 방송 제작자가 청취자를 끌어들이려는 시도가 언급된다. 다만 글 전체를 읽으면서 그 주제가 단순히 청취자를 끌어들이는 '시도'가 아니라, 그 시도의 '결과'라는 것을 파악해야 한다. 글 앞부분의 단편적인 정보만으로는 정답이 아닌 선택지를 가려내기 어려운 1등급 대비 문제였다.

| 문제 풀이 순서 |

1st 글의 중심 내용을 이해하는 데 중요한 내용이 앞부분에 나오는지 확인한다.

- 상업적 음악 라디오 방송의 주된 목적은 청취자를 광고주와 후원자 집단에 인도하는 것이다.
- 상업적 성공을 달성하기 위해서는, 그 청취자는 가능한 한 대규모여야 한다. **단서1**

→ 앞부분에서 상업적 음악 라디오 방송의 목적이 광고주와 후원자 집단에 청취자를 인도하는 것이라고 하며, 상업적 성공을 위해서는 청취자가 대규모여야 한다고 했다.
→ 상업적 음악 라디오 방송의 성공을 위해 청취자를 대규모로 모으려는 시도에 관한 내용이 이어질 것이다.

2nd 글의 나머지 부분에 나오는 관련된 내용을 파악한다.

- 결과적으로 방송 진행자는 인기 있는 … 음악을 틀어 청취자의 규모를 극대화하려고 애쓴다. **단서2**
- 그 결과 높은 수준의 모험 회피는 흔히 '성공한' 라디오 음악 프로그램 제작자를 구분 짓는다. **단서3**
- 방송 목록은 한정되고 흔히 매우 적다.

→ 앞에서 예상한 대로, 방송 진행자가 인기 있는 음악을 재생하여 청취자의 규모를 극대화하려고 애쓴다는, 즉 청취자를 대규모로 모으려는 시도가 있었다. **단서2**
→ '성공한' 라디오 음악 프로그램 제작자는 높은 수준의 모험 회피를 한다고 했는데, **단서3** 여기서 '모험'이 뜻하는 것은 '인기 있는 한정된 음악이 아니라 그보다 많은 수의 인기가 없는 음악을 재생하는 것'이다. 즉, 성공한 제작자는 인기 있는 음악만 재생하여 이러한 모험을 회피한다.
→ 마지막 문장에는 그 결과로 방송 목록이 한정되고 매우 적게 되는 부정적인 결과가 제시되었다.

3rd 글의 알맞은 주제를 고른다.

→ **2nd**에서 파악한 글의 내용을 종합하면 이 글의 주제는 '음악 라디오 사업이 대규모의 청취자를 끌어들이려고 시도하면서 제한된 음악만을 재생하게 된다는 부정적인 결과'이다.
따라서 이 글의 주제로 가장 적절한 것은 ⑤ '음악 라디오 사업의 대규모 청취자를 끌어들이려는 시도의 결과'이다.

| 선택지 분석 |

① features of music playlists appealing to international audiences
국제적 청중의 관심을 끄는 음악 방송 목록의 특징
상업적 성공을 추구하는 음악 방송의 특징을 이야기하는 글이다.

② influence of advertisers on radio audiences' musical preferences
광고주가 라디오 청중의 음악적 선호에 미치는 영향
광고주와 후원자가 음악 방송에 미치는 영향을 설명하는 것이지, 광고주가 청중의 음악적 선호에 영향을 미친다는 것이 아니다.

③ difficulties of increasing audience size in radio music programmes
라디오 음악 프로그램에서 청중 규모 확대의 어려움
청중 규모의 확대를 목표로 하기 때문에 일어나는 일을 설명했다.

④ necessity of satisfying listeners' diverse needs in the radio business
라디오 사업에서 청취자의 다양한 요구를 충족시킬 필요성
청취자의 다양한 요구를 충족시켜야 한다는 언급은 없다.

⑤outcome of music radio businesses' attempts to attract large audiences
음악 라디오 사업의 대규모 청취자를 끌어들이려는 시도의 결과
음악 라디오 사업이 대규모의 청취자를 끌어들이려고 시도하면서 제한된 음악만을 재생하게 된다는 부정적인 결과가 나타났다는 내용이다.

── 어법 특강

＊ to부정사의 명사, 형용사, 부사적 용법

- to부정사는 문장에 따라 명사, 형용사, 부사의 역할을 한다.

1. 명사적 용법 : '~ 하는 것'의 의미로 주어, 목적어, 보어 역할을 한다.
- He could not afford to buy a new bag.
（그는 새 가방을 살 여유가 없었다.）
- It is wrong to fight with your brother.
（너의 남동생과 싸우는 것은 옳지 않다.）

2. 형용사적 용법: 명사를 수식하며 '~할'이라는 의미로 해석하면 된다.
- I have a lot of homework to do today.
（나는 오늘 해야 할 숙제가 많다.）

3. 부사적 용법: 문맥에 따라 다양한 의미를 가지는데, 보통 '~하기 위해서, ~하려고'라는 의미의 목적으로 많이 쓰인다. 그 외에 (감정의) 원인, 결과, 조건 등의 의미를 가진다.
- What can we do to save energy?
（에너지를 절약하기 위해 우리는 무엇을 할 수 있을까?）

F 어휘 Review 정답 ──── 문제편 p. 105

01 평범한	11 account for	21 accustomed
02 경향	12 carry on	22 illustration
03 연속	13 addressed to	23 frequent
04 퇴행하다	14 be associated with	24 emerging
05 개입	15 be forced to	25 incoherent
06 underlying	16 modernise	26 grasped
07 evolution	17 extension	27 implemented
08 notice	18 blossoming	28 confront
09 critical	19 archeological	29 inevitably
10 resource	20 agriculture	30 retention

G 01 정답 ① *예술에서 그림자의 역사적 발전

As far back as 32,000 years ago, / **단서1** 선사시대 동굴 벽화의 그림자 prehistoric cave artists skillfully used modeling shadows / to give their horses and bison volume. //
부사적 용법(목적)
무려 3만 2천 년 전으로 거슬러 올라가 / 선사시대 동굴 예술가들은 모형화한 그림자를 능숙하게 사용했다 / 자신의 말과 들소 그림에 입체감을 주기 위해 //

A few thousand years ago / ancient Egyptian and then ancient Greek art / presented human forms in shadow-style silhouette. // **단서2** 고대 이집트, 고대 그리스 미술의 그림자
수천 년 전 / 고대 이집트와 그 이후 고대 그리스 예술은 / 그림자 스타일의 실루엣으로 인간 형태를 나타냈다 //

not A until B: B하고 나서야 비로소 A하다
But cast shadows do not appear in Western art / until about 400 BCE in Athens. //
그러나 서양 예술에서 그림자 드리우기는 등장하지 않는다 / 기원전 400년경까지도 아테네에서 //

과거완료
It was only after shadows had become an established, /
It ~ that 강조 구문(only after ~ representation을 강조)
if controversial, / part of representation / that classical writers
삽입어구
claimed / that art itself had begun with the tracing of a human
과거완료
shadow. //
그림자가 자리 잡게 되고 난 이후였다 / 논란의 여지는 있으나 / (그림자가) 표현의 확고한 한 부분으로 / 고전 저술가들이 주장한 것은 / 예술 자체가 인간 그림자의 모사와 더불어 시작되었다고 //

단서3 그리스와 로마인들은 그림자 표현 방식을 전환시킴
Greeks and Romans were the first / to make the transition from
from A to B: A에서 B로
modeling shadows to cast shadows, /
그리스인과 로마인은 최초였다 / 그림자를 모형화하는 방식에서 그림자를 드리우는 방식으로 전환한 /

주격 관계대명사(선행사 a practice)　implied의 목적어①　implied의 목적어②
a practice that implied / a consistent light source, / a fixed point
implied의 목적어③
of view, / and an understanding of geometric projection. //
이는 함축하는 관행이었다 / 일관된 광원 / 고정된 시점 / 기하학적 투영에 대한 이해를 //

선행사를 포함하는 관계대명사
In fact, / what we might now call "shadow studies" / — the exploration of shadows in their various artistic representations
동사
/ — has its roots in ancient Athens. //
사실 / 현재 우리가 '그림자 연구'라고 부를 수도 있을 것 / 즉 다양한 예술적 표현에서 그림자에 관해 탐구하는 것은 / 고대 아테네에 그 뿌리를 두고 있다 //

단서4 그 이후 그림자의 묘사 방식은 계속 발전해왔음
Ever since, / the practice of portraying shadows / has evolved
현재완료
along with critical analysis of them, /
그 이후로 / 그림자를 묘사하는 방식은 / 그림자에 대한 비판적 분석과 더불어 발전해왔다 /

현재완료
as artists and theoreticians have engaged in an ongoing debate / about the significance of shadow representation. //
예술가와 이론가가 지속적인 논쟁을 벌임에 따라 / 그림자 표현의 중요성에 대한 //

- prehistoric ⓐ 선사시대의　• bison ⓝ 들소　• volume ⓝ 부피, 양
- silhouette ⓝ 실루엣, 그림자 그림　• cast shadows 그림자 드리우기
  ((물체(캐릭터)를 입체적으로 보이게 하기 위해 그림 밑에 그림자 색을 붙여 넣는 것))
- established ⓐ 확립된　• controversial ⓐ 논란의 여지가 있는
- tracing ⓝ 모사, 투사　• transition ⓝ 전환, 이행, 변천
- portray ⓥ 그리다, 묘사하다　• theoretician ⓝ 이론가
- engage in ~에 종사하다　• ongoing ⓐ 지속적인

무려 3만 2천 년 전으로 거슬러 올라가, 선사시대 동굴 예술가들은 자신의 말과 들소 그림에 입체감을 주기 위해 모형화한 그림자를 능숙하게 사용했다. 수천 년 전 고대 이집트와 그 이후 고대 그리스 예술은 그림자 스타일의 실루엣으로 인간 형태를 나타냈다. 그러나 서양 예술에서 그림자 드리우기는 기원전 400년경이 되어서야 아테네에서 등장한다. 고전 저술가들이 예술 자체가 인간 그림자의 모사와 더불어 시작되었다고 주장한 것은 그림자가, 논란의 여지는 있으나, 표현의 확고한 한 부분으로 자리 잡게 되고 난 이후였다. 그리스인과

로마인은 최초로 그림자를 모형화하는 방식에서 그림자를 드리우는 방식으로 전환했는데, 이는 일관된 광원, 고정된 시점, 기하학적 투영에 대한 이해를 함축하는 관행이었다. 사실 현재 우리가 '그림자 연구'라고 부를 수도 있을 것, 즉 다양한 예술적 표현에서 그림자에 관해 탐구하는 것은 고대 아테네에 그 뿌리를 두고 있다. 그 이후로 예술가와 이론가가 그림자 표현의 중요성에 대한 지속적인 논쟁을 벌임에 따라 그림자를 묘사하는 방식은 그림자에 대한 비판적 분석과 더불어 발전해 왔다.

다음 글의 제목으로 가장 적절한 것은? [3점]
미술에서 그림자가 역사적으로 어떻게 발전해왔는지를 서술한 글임
① The Journey of Shadows in Art from Prehistoric Caves Onward
선사시대 동굴에서 이어져 온 예술 속 그림자의 여정
② Portrayals of Human Shadows from the Artistic Perspective
예술적 관점에서 본 사람 그림자의 묘사　사람 그림자만을 예술적 관점으로 다룬 글이 아님
③ Representing Shadows as a Key Part of Contemporary Art
현대 예술의 핵심 요소로 그림자 표현하기　그림자 표현하기를 현대 예술만의 핵심 요소로 표현하지 않음
④ What Are the Primary Challenges for Shadow Painters?
그림자 화가에게 주요 과제란 무엇인가?　그림자 화가의 어려움에 대한 내용이 아님
⑤ Unique Views on Shadows: From Cave Artists to Romans
그림자에 대한 독특한 관점: 동굴 예술가부터 로마인까지
독특한 관점은 언급되지 않았으며, 로마인까지만의 역사를 다룬 글이 아님

왜 정답? [정답률 56%]

선사시대 동굴 벽화	모형화한 그림자를 능숙하게 사용함
고대 이집트, 고대 그리스	그림자 스타일의 실루엣으로 인간 형태를 나타냄
그리스, 로마	그림자를 모형화하는 방식에서 그림자를 드리우는 방식으로 전환 → 일관된 광원, 고정된 시점, 기하학적 투영에 대한 이해를 나타냄
그 이후	그림자를 묘사하는 방식은 그림자에 대한 비판적 분석과 함께 발전해옴

➡ 예술에서 그림자를 표현하는 방식은 선사시대 동굴 벽화에서 시작하여 고대 이집트와 고대 그리스를 거쳐 아테네와 로마에 이르러 모형화하는 방식에서 그림자를 드리우는 방식으로 변화하였으며, 그 이후 계속 발전해왔다.

▶ 따라서 글의 제목으로 가장 적절한 것은 ① '선사시대 동굴에서 시작된 예술 속 그림자의 여정'이다.

왜 오답?
② 사람의 그림자만을 지엽적으로 다룬 글이 아니다. 함정
③ 그림자 표현하기를 현대 예술만의 핵심 요소로 표현하지 않았다.
④ 미술 속 그림자의 역사에 대한 글이지, 그림자 화가의 어려움에 대한 내용이 아니다.
⑤ 그림자에 대한 독특한 관점은 언급되지 않았으며, 로마인까지만의 역사를 다룬 글이 아니다.

G 02 정답 ① *하이퍼 모빌리티의 단점

단수 주어　동격절 접속사
Hyper-mobility / — the notion / that more travel at faster speeds / covering longer distances / generates greater economic success — /
하이퍼 모빌리티는 / 개념 / 더 빠른 속도의 더 많은 여행이 / 더 먼 거리를 이동하는 / 더 큰 경제적 성공을 만든다는 **단서1** 하이퍼 모빌리티는 도시 지역의 두드러진 특징임
단수 동사　선행사　관계부사
seems to be a distinguishing feature of urban areas, / where more than half of the world's population / currently reside. //
도시 지역의 두드러진 특징인 것으로 보인다 / 세계 인구의 절반보다 더 많은 사람이 / 현재 거주하는 //

By 2005, / approximately 7.5 billion trips were made / each day / in cities worldwide. //
2005년까지 / 약 75억 건의 이동이 이루어졌다 / 매일 / 전 세계 도시에서 //

In 2050, / there may be three to four times as many passenger-
원급 비교를 이용한 배수 표현
kilometres travelled / as in the year 2000, / infrastructure and
생략되지 않은 부사절의 주어
energy prices permitting. //
2050년에는 / 서너 배 더 많은 이동된 인킬로미터가 있을지도 모른다 / 2000년보다 / 사회 기반 시설 및 에너지 가격이 하락하는 한 //

Freight movement could also rise / more than threefold / during the same period. //

화물 이동도 증가할 수 있다 / 세 배보다 더 많이 / 같은 기간 동안 //

Mobility flows have become a key dynamic of urbanization, / with the associated infrastructure invariably constituting / the backbone of urban form. //

이동성 흐름은 도시화의 핵심 동력이 되었다 / 관련 사회 기반 시설이 변함없이 구성하면서 / 도시 형태의 중추를 //

Yet, / despite the increasing level of urban mobility worldwide, / access to places, activities and services / has become increasingly difficult. // **단서2** 증가하는 도시 이동성 수준에도 불구하고 장소,

그러나 / 전 세계적으로 증가하는 도시 이동성 수준에도 불구하고 / 장소, 활동 및 서비스에 대한 접근은 / 점점 더 어려워졌다
부정어가 문두로 나가면서 가주어와 동사가 도치됨

Not only is it less convenient / — in terms of time, cost and comfort — / to access locations in cities, /
진주어
~이 덜 편리할 뿐만 아니라 / 시간, 비용 및 편안함 측면에서 보면 / 도시에서 장소에 접근하는 것이 /

단서3 하이퍼 모빌리티로 인한 부정적인 영향을 부연함
but the very process of moving around in cities / generates a number of negative externalities. //

도시에서 돌아다니는 바로 그 과정이 / 많은 부정적인 외부 효과를 발생시킨다 //

Accordingly, / many of the world's cities face / an unprecedented accessibility crisis, / and are characterized / by unsustainable mobility systems. // **단서4** 많은 도시가 전례 없는 접근성 위기를 직면하고,
동사의 병렬 구조   지속 불가능한 이동성 시스템을 특징으로 함

그에 따라 / 세계의 많은 도시는 직면하고 / 전례 없는 접근성 위기를 / 특징지어진다 / 지속 불가능한 이동성 시스템으로 //

- notion ⓝ 개념 • generate ⓥ 만들다
- distinguishing ⓐ 두드러진, 특색있는 • feature ⓝ 특징
- reside ⓥ 살다, 거주하다 • freight ⓝ 화물 • threefold ⓐ 3배의
- dynamic ⓝ 동력 • urbanization ⓝ 도시화
- invariably ⓐd 변함없이 • constitute ⓥ ~을 구성하다
- backbone ⓝ 중추 • mobility ⓝ 이동성
- increasingly ⓐd 점점 더 • in terms of ~의 면에서
- externality ⓝ 외부 효과, 외부성 • unprecedented ⓐ 전례없는
- crisis ⓝ 위기 • unsustainable ⓐ 지속 불가능한
- winding ⓐ 구불구불한 • inevitable ⓐ 불가피한

더 먼 거리를 더 빠른 속도로 더 많이 이동하는 것이 더 큰 경제적 성공을 만든다는 개념인 하이퍼 모빌리티는 현재 세계 인구의 절반보다 더 많은 사람이 거주하는 도시 지역의 두드러진 특징인 것으로 보인다. 2005년까지 전 세계 도시에서 매일 약 75억 건의 이동이 이루어졌다. 2050년에는 사회 기반 시설 및 에너지 가격이 허락하는 한, 2000년보다 서너 배 더 많은 인킬로미터를 이동할지도 모른다. 화물 이동도 같은 기간 세 배보다 더 많이 증가할 수 있다. 이동성 흐름은 관련 사회 기반 시설이 변함없이 도시 형태의 중추를 구성하면서 도시화의 핵심 동력이 되었다. 그러나 전 세계적으로 증가하는 도시 이동성 수준에도 불구하고, 장소, 활동 및 서비스에 대한 접근은 점점 더 어려워졌다. 시간, 비용 및 편안함 측면에서 보면, 도시에서 장소에 접근하는 것이 덜 편리할 뿐만 아니라, 도시에서 돌아다니는 바로 그 과정이 많은 부정적인 외부 효과를 발생시킨다. 그에 따라 세계의 많은 도시는 전례 없는 접근성 위기를 직면하고 지속 불가능한 이동성 시스템을 특징으로 한다.

다음 글의 제목으로 가장 적절한 것은?

① Is Hyper-mobility Always Good for Cities?
하이퍼 모빌리티는 도시에 항상 이로운가? 이롭지 않은 점을 설명함
② Accessibility: A Guide to a Web of Urban Areas
접근성: 도시 지역망의 가이드 접근성 자체에 대한 설명이 아님
③ A Long and Winding Road to Economic Success
경제적 성공으로 가는 길고 구불불한 길 첫 문장으로 만든 오답
④ Inevitable Regional Conflicts from Hyper-mobility
하이퍼 모빌리티로 인한 불가피한 지역 갈등 지역 갈등에 대한 언급은 없음
⑤ Infrastructure: An Essential Element of Hyper-mobility
사회 기반 시설: 하이퍼 모빌리티의 필수 요소 infrastructure and energy prices permitting으로 만든 오답

도입	하이퍼 모빌리티(더 먼 거리를 더 빠른 속도로 더 많이 이동하는 것이 더 큰 경제적 성공을 만든다는 개념)는 도시 지역의 두드러진 특징임 **단서1**
반전	• **그러나(Yet)** 증가하는 도시 이동성 수준에도 불구하고 장소, 활동 및 서비스에 대한 접근은 점점 더 어려워졌음 **단서2** → 도시에서 장소에 접근하는 것이 시간, 비용 및 편안함 측면에서 덜 편리할 뿐만 아니라, 도시에서 돌아다니는 바로 그 과정이 많은 부정적인 외부 효과를 발생시킴 **단서3** → **그에 따라(Accordingly)** 세계의 많은 도시는 접근성 위기를 직면하고, 지속 불가능한 이동성 시스템을 특징으로 함 **단서4**

→ Yet 이후의 내용이 글의 핵심이다.
하이퍼 모빌리티가 도시 지역의 특징이고, 이동성의 흐름이 도시화의 핵심 동력이지만, 도시에서 돌아다니는 바로 그 과정이 많은 부정적인 외부 효과도 발생시킨다고 했다.

▶ 따라서 정답은 ① '하이퍼 모빌리티는 도시에 항상 이로운가?'이다.

왜 오답 ?

② 접근성이 도시 지역망의 가이드 역할을 한다는 등의 내용이 아니다.
③ 하이퍼 모빌리티의 개념을 설명하면서 economic success를 언급한 것으로 만든 오답이다.
④ 하이퍼 모빌리티로 인한 단점을 설명한 것은 맞지만, 지역 갈등이라는 구체적인 문제점을 설명한 것은 아니다. 주의
⑤ 하이퍼 모빌리티를 실현하는 데 사회 기반 시설이 필수적이라는 것을 설명하는 글이 아니다.

G 03 정답 ⑤ * 자신을 드러내는 현대적인 방식인 셀피

─── not A but B: A가 아니라 B ───
The selfie resonates / not because it is new, / but because it expresses, develops, expands, and intensifies / the long history of the self-portrait. // **단서1** 셀피는 새로워서가 아니라 자화상의 오랜 역사를 발전시키고

셀피가 공명하는 이유는 / 그것이 새롭기 때문이 아니라 / 표현하고 발전시키며 확장하고 강화하기 때문이다 / 자화상의 오랜 역사를 //

The self-portrait showed to others / the status of the person depicted. //
과거분사(person 수식)

자화상은 다른 사람들에게 보여 주었다 / 그려진 사람의 지위를 //

관계대명사절을 이끎 have come to-v: ~하게 되다
In this sense, / what we have come to call our own "image" / — the interface of the way we think we look / and the way others see us — / is the first and fundamental object of global visual culture. //

이런 의미에서 / 우리가 자신의 '이미지'라고 부르게 된 것은 / 즉 우리가 생각하는 우리의 모습과 / 다른 사람들이 우리를 보는 방식의 접점이라고 / 세계적 시각 문화의 첫 번째이자 근본적인 대상이다 //

단서2 셀피는 우리가 바라는 대로 표현되거나 되지 않을 내면의 감정들과의 긴장 관계 속에서 일상적인 모습을 담아냄
The selfie depicts / the drama of our own daily performance of ourselves / in tension with our inner emotions / that may or may not be expressed as we wish. //
재귀적 용법   주격 관계대명사

셀피는 그린다 / 우리 자신의 일상적 수행의 드라마를 / 우리의 내면적 감정과 긴장 관계에 있는 / 우리가 바라는 대로 표현될 수도 있고 그렇지 않을 수도 있는 //

At each stage of the self-portrait's expansion, / more and more people have been able to depict themselves. //
현재완료   재귀적 용법

자화상 확장의 각 단계에서 / 점점 더 많은 사람이 자신을 그릴 수 있게 되었다 //

Today's young, urban, networked majority / has reworked the history of the self-portrait / to make the selfie / into the first visual signature of the new era. // **단서3** 현대인들은 셀피를 새 시대의 첫 시각적
현재완료   부사적 용법(목적)   특징으로 만들고 자화상의 역사를 다시 씀

오늘날의 젊고, 도시에 살며, 네트워크로 연결된 대다수는 / 자화상의 역사를 다시 만들었다 / 셀피를 만들기 위해 / 새로운 시대의 첫 번째 시각적 특징으로 //

- selfie ⓝ 셀피(셀카)   · expand ⓥ 확장하다
- intensify ⓥ 강화하다   · self-portrait ⓝ 자화상
- interface ⓝ 접점   · fundamental ⓐ 근본적인
- tension ⓝ 긴장   · inner ⓐ 내면의   · signature ⓝ 서명, 특징
- era ⓝ 시대

셀피가 공명하는 이유는 그것이 새롭기 때문이 아니라, 자화상의 오랜 역사를 표현하고 발전시키며 확장하고 강화하기 때문이다. 자화상은 그려진 사람의 지위를 다른 사람들에게 보여 주었다. 이런 의미에서, 우리가 자신의 '이미지', 즉 우리가 생각하는 우리의 모습과 다른 사람들이 우리를 보는 방식의 접점이라고 부르게 된 것은 세계적 시각 문화의 첫 번째이자 근본적인 대상이다. 셀피는 우리가 바라는 대로 표현될 수도 있고 그렇지 않을 수도 있는 우리의 내면적 감정과 긴장 관계에 있는, 우리 자신의 일상적 수행의 드라마를 그린다. 자화상 확장의 각 단계에서 점점 더 많은 사람이 자신을 그릴 수 있게 되었다. 오늘날의 젊고, 도시에 살며, 네트워크로 연결된 대다수는 셀피를 새로운 시대의 첫 번째 시각적 특징으로 만들기 위해 자화상의 역사를 다시 만들었다.

다음 글의 제목으로 가장 적절한 것은?

① Are Selfies Just a Temporary Trend in Art History?
셀피는 단지 미술사의 일시적 유행인가?   셀피가 일시적 유행일 것이라는 내용은 언급되지 않음
② Fantasy or Reality: Your Selfie Is Not the Real You
환상 또는 현실: 당신의 셀피는 진정한 당신이 아니다   셀피는 자신의 '이미지'를 보여주는 수단이라고
했으므로, 이를 진정한 당신이 아니라고 표현하는 것은 적절하지 않음
③ The Selfie: A Symbol of Self-oriented Global Culture
셀피: 자기 지향적인 세계 문화의 상징   셀피는 자신이 생각하는 자신의 모습과 타인에게 보여지는
모습의 접점을 찾는 과정이므로, '자기 지향적인' 특성은 아니며, 세계 문화에 관한 언급은 없음
④ The End of Self-portraits: How Selfies Are Taking Over   자화상의
자화상의 종말: 셀피가 어떻게 지배하고 있는가   특징이 현대에 들어 셀피로 확장되고 발전되었다는 내용임
⑤ Selfies, the Latest Innovation in Representing Ourselves
셀피, 우리 자신을 표현하는 최신 혁신   자신을 드러내는 현대적인 방식인 셀피에 대한 글임

왜 정답? [정답률 42%]

- **주제**: 셀피는 새로워서가 아니라 자화상의 오랜 역사를 발전시키고 확장해 가기 때문에 우리에게 반향을 불러일으킴 단서1
  - 셀피는 우리가 바라는 대로 표현되거나 되지 않을 내면의 감정들과의 긴장 관계 속에서 일상적인 모습을 담아냄 단서2
  - 현대인들은 셀피를 새 시대의 첫 시각적 특징으로 만들고 자화상의 역사를 다시 씀 단서3

▶ 셀피는 예전에 자신의 '이미지'를 보여주기 위해 그렸던 자화상을 현대적 특징에 맞게 발전된 형태라고 설명하고 있으므로, 글의 제목으로 가장 적절한 것은 ⑤ '셀피, 우리 자신을 표현하는 최신 혁신'이다.

왜 오답?

① 셀피가 일시적 유행일 것이라는 내용은 언급되지 않았다.
② 셀피는 자신의 '이미지'를 보여주는 수단이라고 했으므로, 이를 진정한 당신이 아니라고 표현하는 것은 적절하지 않다.
③ 셀피는 자신이 생각하는 자신의 모습과 타인에게 보여지는 모습의 접점을 찾는 과정이므로, '자기 지향적인' 특성은 아니며, 세계 문화에 관한 언급은 더더욱 없었다.
④ 자화상이 종말했다는 내용이 아니라, 자화상의 특징이 현대에 들어 셀피로 확장되고 발전되었다는 내용이다. 함정

배지오 | 2025 수능 응시 · 성남 낙생고 졸

첫 문장을 보고 셀피 혹은 자화상을 주제로 파악했어야 해. In this sense 이후의 문장에서 자화상을 통해 우리가 자신 스스로가 보는 자신의 모습과 타인이 보는 나의 모습을 알 수 있고 그 사이에 접점이 있음을 말해줘. 마지막 문장에서 Today's young, urban, networked majority들이 self-portrait를 통해 자화상의 역사를 다시 만들었다는 것을 보아, 오늘날은 셀피가 자화상의 역할을 구현하고 있음을 파악하고 답을 구할 수 있었어.

G 04 정답 ④   * 일정한 주기를 두고 반복되는 사무실 디자인

G

관계부사
There are good reasons / why open-office plans have gained currency, / but open offices may not be the plan of choice / for all times. //
그럴 만한 이유가 있다 / 개방형 사무실 계획이 유행하는 데는 / 그러나 개방형 사무실이 선택할 수 있는 계획은 아닐 수도 있다 / '언제라도' //

Instead, / the right plan seems to be building / a culture of change. //
대신에 / 올바른 계획은 구축하는 것인 듯하다 / 변화의 문화를 //

부사절을 이끄는 종속접속사(아무리 ~하더라도)
Overly rigid habits and conventions, / no matter how well-considered or well-intentioned, / threaten innovation. //
지나치게 굳은 관례와 관습은 / 아무리 깊이 고려되거나 의도가 좋다 하더라도 / 혁신을 위협한다 //

핵심 주어
The crucial take-away / from analyzing office plans over time /
보어절을 이끄는 접속사
is that the answers keep changing. //
매우 중요한 핵심은 / 시간이 지남에 따른 사무실 계획을 분석할 때 / 답이 계속 바뀐다는 것이다 //

보어절을 이끄는 접속사
It might seem / that there is a straight line of progress, / but it's a myth. //
보일 수도 있다 / 일직선으로 발전하는 것처럼 / 그러나 이는 근거 없는 믿음이다 //

분사구문을 이끎
Surveying office spaces / from the past eighty years, / one can
선행사(cycle)를 수식하는 주격 관계대명사
see a cycle / that repeats. // 단서1 사무실 공간에서 반복되는 주기를 확인할 수 있음
사무실 공간을 조사해 보면 / 지난 80년의 / 주기를 확인할 수 있다 / 반복되는 //

핵심 주어
Comparing the offices of the 1940s / with contemporary office
목적어절을 이끄는 접속사
spaces / shows that they have circled back around /
1940년대의 사무실을 비교하는 것이 / 현대의 사무실 공간과 / 다시 크게 한 바퀴 돌아왔음을 보여준다 /
단서2 현대와 과거 사무실을 비교하면 사무실 스타일이 다시 돌아왔음을 알 수 있다고 함
to essentially the same style, / via a period in the 1980s / when
관계부사
partitions and cubicles were more the norm. //
본질적으로 동일한 스타일로 / 1980년대를 거쳐 / 칸막이벽과 작은 개인 방이 훨씬 더 일반적이었던 //

The technologies and colors may differ, / but the 1940s and
pillars를 수식하는 분사
2000s plans are alike, / right down to the pillars / running down the middle. //
기술과 색상은 다를 수 있지만 / 1940년대와 2000년대의 계획은 비슷하다 / 바로 기둥까지 그렇다 / 중앙을 따라 내려오는 //

- open-office ⓝ 개방형 사무실   · currency ⓝ 유행
- rigid ⓐ 굳은   · convention ⓝ 관습   · crucial ⓐ 매우 중요한
- take-away ⓝ 핵심, 요점   · progress ⓝ 발전
- contemporary ⓐ 현대의   · partition ⓝ 칸막이벽
- cubicle ⓝ 작은 개인 방   · alike ⓐ 비슷한
- cost-efficient ⓐ 비용 효율적인   · incorporate ⓥ 통합하다
- retro ⓐ 복고풍의

개방형 사무실 계획이 유행하는 데는 그럴 만한 이유가 있지만, 개방형 사무실이 '언제라도' 선택할 수 있는 계획은 아닐 수도 있다. 대신에, 올바른 계획은 변화의 문화를 구축하는 것인 듯하다. 지나치게 굳은 관례와 관습은, 아무리 깊이 고려되거나 의도가 좋다 하더라도 혁신을 위협한다. 시간이 지남에 따른 사무실 계획을 분석할 때 매우 중요한 핵심은 답이 계속 바뀐다는 것이다. 일직선으로 발전하는 것처럼 보일 수 있지만 이는 근거 없는 믿음이다. 지난 80년의 사무실 공간을 조사해 보면, 반복되는 주기를 확인할 수 있다. 1940년대의 사무실과 현대의 사무실 공간을 비교해 보면 칸막이벽과 작은 개인 방이 훨씬 더 일반적이었던 1980년대를 거쳐, 다시 본질적으로 동일한 스타일로 크게 한 바퀴 돌아왔음을 알 수 있다. 기술과 색상은 다를 수 있지만, 1940년대와 2000년대의 계획은 비슷한데, 바로 중앙을 따라 내려오는 기둥까지 그렇다.

다음 글의 제목으로 가장 적절한 것은?

① Why Are Open-office Plans So Cost-efficient?
왜 개방형 사무실 계획이 매우 비용 효율적인가?　개방형 사무실이 언급된 것으로 만든 함정
② How to Incorporate Retro Styles into Office Spaces
복고 스타일을 사무실 공간에 섞어 넣는 방법　복고 스타일을 사무실에 섞는 방법은 나오지 않음
③ An Office Divided: Why Partitions Limit Productivity　칸막이벽이 더
분할된 사무실: 칸막이벽이 생산성을 제한하는 이유　일반적이었던 때가 있었다는 언급 있음
④ Office Designs: What Goes Around Comes Around　시간이 지남에 따른
사무실 디자인: 유행은 돌고 돈다　사무실 계획을 분석해 보면 반복되는 주기를 확인해 볼 수 있음
⑤ Tips for Managing Contemporary Office Spaces
현대의 사무실 공간 관리를 위한 요령　현대의 사무실 공간 관리 요령에 대한 글이 아님

왜 정답? [정답률 77%]

전반부	시간이 지남에 따른 사무실 계획을 분석해 보면 반복되는 주기를 확인해 볼 수 있음 **단서 1**
후반부	개방형 사무실 계획이 유행하고 있지만 올바른 (사무실) 계획은 변화의 문화를 구축하는 것임 **단서 2**

▶ 사무실 계획(디자인)은 반복되는 주기를 가지고 있다는 내용이므로 ④ '사무실 디자인: 유행은 돌고 돈다'가 글의 제목으로 가장 적절하다.

왜 오답?

① 개방형 사무실이 비용 효율적이라는 내용이 아니다.
② 복고 스타일을 사무실 공간에 섞는 방법이 언급되지 않았다.
③ 칸막이벽이 더 일반적이었던 때가 있었다는 언급만 있을 뿐, 칸막이벽이 생산성을 제한하는 것에 대한 내용은 없다.
⑤ 현대의 사무실 공간 관리 요령에 대한 글이 아니다.

G 05 정답 ③ ＊유사한 신념을 가진 집단이 개인의 정체성에 미치는 영향

소유격 관계대명사
We naturally gravitate toward people / whose views and beliefs
　　　　　　　　　　　　분사구문을 이끎 선행사를 포함한 관계대명사
are similar to our own, / seeking what the eighteenth-century
moral philosopher Adam Smith called "a certain harmony of
minds."//
우리는 자연스럽게 사람들에게 자연히 끌리며 / 견해와 신념이 우리 자신의 것과 유사한 / 18
세기 도덕 철학자 Adam Smith가 '마음의 특정한 조화'라고 불렀던 것을 추구한다 //
동명사 주어(단수 취급)　　　　　주격 관계대명사　　　　　단수 동사
Spending time with people who share our opinions / reinforces
our group identity, / strengthening trust, cooperation, equality,
　　　　　　　　　　분사구문을 이끎
and productivity. //
우리의 의견을 공유하는 사람들과 시간을 보내는 것은 / 우리의 집단 정체성을 보강하여 /
신뢰, 협력, 평등, 그리고 생산성을 강화한다 //
　　　　　　　　　　　　　　　　not just/only A but (also) B: A뿐만 아니라 B도
Our shared reality grounds us / not just in our common
perceptions / but in similar feelings and worldviews. //
우리의 공유된 현실은 근거를 두게 한다 / 단지 우리의 공통의 인식뿐만 아니라 / 유사한
감정과 세계관에 //
This helps to preserve / our core values and beliefs about
ourselves. //
이는 지키는 데 도움이 된다 / 우리의 핵심적인 가치와 자신에 대한 신념을 //
It also provides us with meaning and a feeling of self-worth. //
또한, 그것은 우리에게 의미와 자아 존중감을 제공한다 //
　　　　　　　　　　　　　　　　주격 관계대명사
And with each decision or interaction / that confirms our tribe's
common experience, / we get rewarded with the hormonal
앞에 관계대명사가 생략된 관계절 **단서 1** 공통된 경험을 확인받는 결정이나 상호 작용으로부터
happiness we crave. // 우리는 호르몬의 행복을 느낌
그리고 각 결정이나 상호 작용으로 / 우리 부족의 공통의 경험을 견고하게 하는 / 우리는
우리가 갈망하는 호르몬의 행복으로 보상받는다 //
Our perception of ourselves is a mixture / of our own unique
characteristics and our sense of belonging to our in-groups. //
우리 자신에 대한 우리의 인식은 혼합이다 / 우리 자신의 고유한 특성과 우리의 내집단에 대한
소속감의 // **단서 2** 스스로에 대한 인식은 자신의 고유한 특성과 내집단에 대한 소속감의 혼합임
　　　　　　　　　　　　　　　　　　　　　　so ~ that ...: 너무 ~해서 …하다
In fact, / our personal identity is so closely interwoven with our
social identity / that our brains can't tell them apart. //
실제로 / 우리의 개인 정체성은 우리의 사회 정체성과 너무 밀접하게 뒤섞여서 / 우리 뇌는
그것들을 분간할 수 없다 //

If I put you in a scanner and ask you to talk about yourself / and
then about the groups to which you feel the closest affinity, / it
will activate the same neural networks in your brain. //
만약 내가 여러분을 스캐너에 넣고 여러분 자신에 대해 이야기하게 한 다음 / 여러분이 가장
가까운 유사성을 느끼는 집단에 대해 이야기하게 한다면 / 그것은 여러분의 뇌에서 동일한
신경망을 활성화할 것이다 //

- cooperation ⓝ 협력　　　・equality ⓝ 평등
- perception ⓝ 인식　　　・core ⓐ 핵심적인
- self-worth ⓝ 자아 존중감, 자부심　・confirm ⓥ 견고하게 하다
- hormonal ⓐ 호르몬의　　　・crave ⓥ 갈망[열망]하다
- characteristic ⓝ 특성　　　・belong to ~에 속하다
- activate ⓥ 활성화시키다　　　・breed ⓥ 새끼를 낳다, 초래하다
- mutual ⓐ 상호간의　　・sympathy ⓝ 동정　・resolve ⓥ 해결하다

우리는 자연스럽게 견해와 신념이 우리 자신의 것과 유사한 사람들에게 자연히 끌리며, 18세기 도덕 철학자 Adam Smith가 '마음의 특정한 조화'라고 불렀던 것을 추구한다. 우리의 의견을 공유하는 사람들과 시간을 보내는 것은 우리의 집단 정체성을 보강하여, 신뢰, 협력, 평등, 그리고 생산성을 강화한다. 우리의 공유된 현실은 단지 우리의 공통의 인식뿐만 아니라 유사한 감정과 세계관에 근거를 두게 한다. 이는 우리의 핵심적인 가치와 자신에 대한 신념을 지키는 데 도움이 된다. 또한, 그것은 우리에게 의미와 자아 존중감을 제공한다. 그리고 우리 부족의 공통의 경험을 견고하게 하는 각 결정이나 상호 작용으로 우리는 우리가 갈망하는 호르몬의 행복으로 보상받는다. 우리 자신에 대한 우리의 인식은 우리 자신의 고유한 특성과 우리의 내집단에 대한 소속감의 혼합이다. 실제로 우리의 개인 정체성은 우리의 사회 정체성과 너무 밀접하게 뒤섞여서 우리 뇌는 그것들을 분간할 수 없다. 만약 내가 여러분을 스캐너에 넣고 여러분 자신에 대해 이야기하게 한 다음 여러분이 가장 가까운 유사성을 느끼는 집단에 대해 이야기하게 한다면, 그것은 여러분의 뇌에서 동일한 신경망을 활성화할 것이다.

다음 글의 제목으로 가장 적절한 것은? [3점] 자신과 의견이 비슷한 사람들과의 상호
작용으로 행복을 느끼며, 개인의 정체성 형성에
① The Secret to Becoming a Unique Individual 내집단의 소속감이 기여함
독특한 개인이 되는 비밀　　　　　독특한 개인이 되는 방법에 대한 글이 아님
② Societal Conflict: Shared Reality Breeding Mutual Distrust
사회적 갈등: 공유된 현실이 상호 불신을 초래하다　사회적 갈등에 대한 언급은 없음
③ Our Identity Shaped by Shared Views: Comfort of Like Minds
공유된 관점에 의해 형성된 우리의 정체성: 같은 생각을 가진 사람들의 편안함
④ Sympathy: Key to Resolving Disharmony in the Workplace
동정심: 직장에서 불화를 해결하는 열쇠　직장에서의 불화에 대한 내용이 전혀 언급되지 않음
⑤ How We Balance Personal Identity with Social Identity 개인 정체성과
개인 정체성과 사회적 정체성의 균형 맞추기　사회적 정체성간의 균형에 대한 내용이 글의 핵심이 아님

왜 정답? [정답률 84%]

- 우리는 우리와 신념과 관점이 비슷한 사람에게 끌리며, 이런 사람들과 상호 작용하는 것은 신뢰, 협력, 평등, 생산성을 강화하는 등 우리 집단의 정체성을 보강함
- 이런 공통된 인식, 세계관, 감정을 가진 집단에서의 상호 작용은 자신에 대한 신념을 지키고 자아 존중감을 제공하는 것에 도움을 주고, 행복함을 느끼게 해줌 **단서 1**
- 개인의 정체성은 고유한 특징과 사회 정체성의 혼합임 **단서 2**

▶ 따라서 비슷한 의견의 사람과 상호 작용할 때 긍정적 감정을 느끼며 개인 정체성과도 밀접한 연관성이 있다는 내용을 담은 ③ '공유된 관점에 의해 형성된 우리의 정체성: 같은 생각을 가진 사람들의 편안함'이 제목으로 적절하다.

왜 오답?

① 독특한 개인이 되는 방법이 초점이 되는 글이 아니다.
② 글에서 공유된 현실을 부정적으로 보지 않았으며, 사회적 갈등에 대한 언급도 없다.
④ 동정심이 핵심이 되는 글이 아니며, 직장에서의 불화에 대한 언급도 없다.
⑤ 개인의 정체성과 사회적 정체성에 대한 내용이 있으나, 이 둘 간의 균형을 맞춰야 한다는 글은 아니다.

5형식 동사+목적어+목적격 보어(to부정사)
A scholar Eve Tuck urges researchers to move away from / what she calls "damage-based research," /

학자 Eve Tuck은 연구자들에게 멀어질 것을 촉구한다 / 그녀가 "피해 기반 연구"라고 부르는 것으로부터 /

주격 관계대명사
or "research that operates, even benevolently, from a theory of
주격 관계대명사
change / that establishes harm or injury / in order to achieve reparation." //

또는 "선의일지라도 변화의 이론으로부터 작동하는 연구 / 손상이나 피해를 정하는 / 보상을 얻기 위하여" //

분사구문을 이끎   주격 관계대명사
Citing studies in education / that sought to increase resources for marginalized youths / by documenting the "illiteracies" of indigenous youths and youths of color, /

교육에서의 연구를 인용하면서 / 소외된 청년들을 위한 자원을 증가시키려고 노력한 / 토착 청년들과 유색 청년들의 "문맹"을 기록함으로써 /

목적어절 접속사
Tuck explains / that damage-based research is a popular
전치사+관계대명사   수동태
mechanism / by which "pain and loss are documented / in order to obtain particular political or material gains." //

Tuck은 설명한다 / 피해 기반 연구가 인기 있는 메커니즘이라고 / "고통과 손실이 기록되는 / 특정 정치적 또는 물질적 이득을 얻기 위하여" //

접속사
While damage-based studies have proven successful / in attaining political or material gains / in the form of funding,
과거분사
attention, and increased awareness / related to the struggles of marginalized communities, /

[단서] 피해 기반 연구가 선의롭거나 뚜렷이 이득이 되는 상황에서조차 소외된 공동체에 지속적 폭력을 가함

피해 기반 연구가 성공적으로 입증되어 왔지만 / 정치적 또는 물질적 이득을 얻는 데 있어 / 자금 조성, 주의, 그리고 증가된 인식의 형태로 / 소외된 공동체의 고군분투에 관한 /

Tuck points researchers to the ongoing violence / damage-based research inflicts on marginalized communities, / even under benevolent or perceivably beneficial circumstances. //

Tuck은 연구자들에게 지속적인 폭력을 지적한다 / 피해 기반 연구가 소외된 공동체에 가하는 / 심지어 선의로운 또는 뚜렷이 이득이 되는 상황에서조차 //

과거분사(the many issues 수식)
Among the many issues associated with damage-based research / are the underlying assumptions / this type of work makes and
동격의 that이 생략된 절
sustains / about marginalized people; /

피해 기반 연구와 관련된 많은 문제 중에 / 저변의 전제들이 있다 / 이러한 유형의 연구가 만들어 내고 지속시키는 / 소외된 사람들에 대해 /

namely, that marginalized communities lack / communication, civility, intellect, desires, assets, innovation, and ethics. //

즉, 소외된 공동체는 결핍되어 있다는 것이다 / 의사소통, 시민성, 지적 능력, 욕구, 자산, 혁신, 그리고 윤리 의식이 //

- **benevolently** @ 호의적으로 · **illiteracy** ⓝ 문맹
- **attain** ⓥ 얻다 · **inflict on** ~에 영향을 주다, 타격을 주다
- **sustain** ⓥ 살아가게 하다, 지속시키다 · **civility** ⓝ 시민성
- **privileged** @ 특권을 가진 · **backfire** ⓥ 부작용을 낳다
- **diversity** ⓝ 다양성

학자 Eve Tuck은 연구자들에게 그녀가 "피해 기반 연구", 또는 "선의일지라도 보상을 얻기 위하여 손상이나 피해를 정하는 변화의 이론으로부터 작동하는 연구"라고 부르는 것으로부터 멀어질 것을 촉구한다. 토착 청년들과 유색 청년들의 "문맹"을 기록함으로써 소외된 청년들을 위한 자원을 증가시키려고 노력한 교육에서의 연구를 인용하면서, Tuck은 피해 기반 연구가 "특정 정치적 또는 물질적 이득을 얻기 위하여 고통과 손실이 기록되는" 인기 있는 메커니즘이라고 설명한다. 피해 기반 연구가 자금 조성, 주의, 그리고 소외된 공동체의 고군분투에 관한 증가된 인식의 형태로 정치적 또는 물질적 이득을 얻는 데 있어 성공적으로 입증되어 왔지만, Tuck은 연구자들에게 피해 기반 연구가 심지어 선의로운 또는 뚜렷이 이득이 되는 상황에서조차 소외된 공동체에 가하는 지속적인 폭력을 지적한다. 피해 기반 연구와 관련된 많은 문제 중에 이러한 유형의 연구가 소외된 사람들에 대해 만들어 내고 지속시키는 저변의 전제들이 있다. 즉, 소외된 공동체는 의사소통, 시민성, 지적 능력, 욕구, 자산, 혁신, 그리고 윤리 의식이 결핍되어 있다는 것이다.

다음 글의 제목으로 가장 적절한 것은?

① Marginalized Yesterday, Privileged Today
소외된 어제, 특권을 누리는 오늘   예전에 소외된 사람들이 지금은 특권을 가진다는 내용이 아님

② How Damage-Based Research Can Backfire 좋은 의도에도 불구하고 소외된
피해 기반 연구가 역효과를 낼 수 있는 방법   집단에게 피해를 미칠 수 있다고 했음

③ Research: An Endless Journey to the Truth 연구에 대한 내용이지만
연구: 진리를 향한 끝없는 여정   연구를 통해 진리를 추구하고자 하는 내용이 핵심은 아님

④ Different Era, Different Education for Minority Youth 시대가 바뀜에
소수 민족 청소년을 위한 다른 시대, 다른 교육   따라 소수 민족 청소년을 위한 교육이 달라진다는 내용은 없음

⑤ The Growth of Diversity Among Younger Generations
젊은 세대의 다양성 성장   젊은 세대의 다양성이 증가한다는 내용이 아님

왜 정답? [정답률 75%]

전반 내용	피해 기반 연구는 소외된 집단의 정치적 혹은 물질적 이득을 위해 그들의 고통과 손실을 기록하는 연구임
후반 내용	피해 기반 연구는 의도가 선하고 뚜렷하게 이득이 되는 상황이더라도 소외된 집단에게 해를 끼칠 수 있음 **[단서]**

▶ 피해 기반 연구가 좋은 의도에도 불구하고 소외된 집단에게 피해를 미칠 수 있다는 내용을 담은 ② '피해 기반 연구가 역효과를 낼 수 있는 방법'이 글의 제목으로 가장 적절하다.

왜 오답?

① 예전에 소외된 사람들이 지금은 특권을 갖게 되었다는 것이 아니다.

③ 연구에 대한 내용이지만, 연구를 통해 진리를 추구하고자 하는 내용이 핵심은 아니다. **주의**

④ 시대에 따라 소수 집단 청소년의 교육이 달라진다는 내용이 아니다.

⑤ 젊은 세대에서 다양성이 증가한다는 언급은 없다.

G 07 정답 ④ *물속에서의 색상 변화와 바다 생물의 색깔

앞에 being 생략   단수 주어
When viewed from space, / one of the Earth's most commanding
단수 동사
features / is the blueness of its vast oceans. // **[단서1]** 바다의 푸르름에 대해 설명함

우주에서 보았을 때 / 지구의 가장 인상적인 특징들 중 하나는 / 드넓은 바다의 푸르름이다 //

Small amounts of water do not indicate / the color of these large bodies of water; / when pure drinking water is examined in a glass, / it appears clear and colorless. //

적은 양의 물은 나타내지 않고 / 이러한 많은 양의 물의 색을 / 깨끗한 식수가 유리잔 속에서 검사될 때 / 그것은 맑고 무색인 것처럼 보인다 //

Apparently a relatively large volume of water is required / to reveal the blue color. //

분명 비교적 많은 양의 물이 필요하다 / 파란색을 드러내기 위해서는 //

Why is this so? // 이것은 왜 그런 것일까 //

When light penetrates water, / it experiences both absorption and scattering. //

빛이 물을 관통할 때 / 그것은 흡수와 산란 둘 다를 겪는다 // **[단서2]** 물 분자는 적외선을 강하게 흡수함

Water molecules strongly absorb infrared / and, to a lesser
병렬 구조(absorb의 목적어)
degree, red light. //

물 분자는 적외선을 강하게 흡수하고 / 더 적은 정도로 붉은빛을 (흡수한다) // **[단서3]** 물 분자는 짧은 파장을 산란시킴

At the same time, / water molecules are small enough to scatter
분사구문
shorter wavelengths, / giving water its blue-green color. //

동시에 / 물 분자는 더 짧은 파장을 산란시키기에 충분히 작아서 / 물에 청록색을 부여한다 //

The amount of long-wavelength absorption / is a function of
the 비교급, the 비교급: ~하면 할수록, 더 …하다
depth; / the deeper the water, / the more red light is absorbed. //

장파장 흡수의 양은 / 수심의 작용이다 / 즉, 물이 더 깊을수록 / 더 많은 붉은빛이 흡수된다 //

단수 동사①
At a depth of 15m, / the intensity of red light drops / to 25% of
단수 동사②
its original value / and falls to zero / beyond a depth of 30m. //

15미터 수심에서는 / 붉은빛의 강도가 떨어지고 / 기존 값의 25%로 / 0으로 떨어진다 / 30미터 이상의 수심에서는 //

과거분사구(Any object 수식)   수동태 동사
Any object viewed at this depth / is seen in a blue-green light. //

이 수심에서 보이는 모든 물체는 / 청록빛 내에서 보인다 //

For this reason, / red inhabitants of the sea, / such as lobsters and crabs, / appear black to divers / not carrying a lamp. //
현재분사구(divers 수식)
이러한 이유로 / 바다의 붉은색 서식 동물들은 / 바닷가재와 게와 같은 / 잠수부들에게는 검게 보인다 / 램프를 들고 있지 않은 //

- commanding ⓐ 인상적인 · vast ⓐ 방대한
- indicate ⓥ 나타내다 · examine ⓥ 조사하다
- apparently ⓐⓓ 겉보기에는, 외관상으로는 · absorption ⓝ 흡수
- scattering ⓝ 분산 · absorb ⓥ 흡수하다 · scatter ⓥ 흩뿌리다
- wavelength ⓝ 파장 · depth ⓝ 깊이 · intensity ⓝ 강도
- inhabitant ⓝ 서식 동물 · deceptive ⓐ 기만적인
- microorganism ⓝ 미생물

우주에서 보았을 때 지구의 가장 인상적인 특징들 중 하나는 드넓은 바다의 푸르름이다. 적은 양의 물은 이러한 많은 양의 물의 색을 나타내지 않고, 깨끗한 식수가 유리잔 속에서 검사될 때 그것은 맑고 무색인 것처럼 보인다. 파란색을 드러내기 위해서는 분명 비교적 많은 양의 물이 필요하다. 이것은 왜 그런 것일까? 빛이 물을 관통할 때 그것은 흡수와 산란 둘 다를 겪는다. 물 분자는 적외선을 강하게 흡수하고 더 적은 정도로 붉은빛을 흡수한다. 동시에 물 분자는 더 짧은 파장을 산란시키기에 충분히 작아서 물에 청록색을 부여한다. 장파장 흡수의 양은 수심의 작용이다. 즉, 물이 더 깊을수록 더 많은 붉은빛이 흡수된다. 15미터 수심에서는 붉은빛의 강도가 기존 값의 25%로 떨어지고 30미터 이상의 수심에서는 0으로 떨어진다. 이 수심에서 보이는 모든 물체는 청록빛 내에서 보인다. 이러한 이유로 바닷가재와 게와 같은 바다의 붉은색 서식 동물들은 램프를 들고 있지 않은 잠수부들에게는 검게 보인다.

다음 글의 제목으로 가장 적절한 것은?

① We Should Go Green with the Ocean Exploration
우리는 해양 탐사를 친환경적으로 해야 한다   해양 탐사 방법에 대한 글이 아님
② Various Tones of Water Our Deceptive Eyes Show Us
우리의 기만적인 눈이 보여 주는 다양한 색조의 물   우리의 눈 때문에 푸른빛으로 보는 것이 아님
③ How Deep-Sea Microorganisms Affect the Ocean's Color
심해 미생물이 바다의 색깔에 미치는 영향   미생물들에 의해 바다 색이 정해지는 것이 아님
④ Why So Blue: The Science Behind the Color of Earth's Oceans
왜 그렇게 푸른빛일까: 지구의 바다 색깔에 숨겨진 과학   바닷물의 색이 푸른 이유를 설명함
⑤ The Bigger Volume Water Has, the Lower Temperature It Gets
물의 부피가 클수록, 물의 온도는 낮아진다   언급되지 않음

왜 정답? [정답률 81%]

지구의 가장 인상적인 특징들 중 하나는 드넓은 바다의 푸르름임

이유 ①: 물 분자는 적외선은 강하게, 붉은빛을 적게 흡수함

이유 ②: 물 분자는 더 짧은 파장을 산란시키기에 충분히 작아서 물에 청록색을 부여함

▶ 바다의 푸르름에 대해 설명하고 있으므로 글의 제목으로 가장 적절한 것은 ④ '왜 그렇게 푸른빛일까: 지구의 바다 색깔에 숨겨진 과학'이다.

왜 오답?

① 해양 탐사에 있어서 친환경적인 방법을 채택해야 한다는 내용은 언급되지 않았다.
② 우리의 시각 때문에 물의 색을 다양하게 보는 것이 아니다.
③ 바닷물의 색은 심해 미생물들이 아닌 빛과 물 분자의 속성에 의해 정해진다.
⑤ 물의 부피와 온도는 언급되지 않았다.

G 08 정답 ⑤ *시간의 경계를 넘어 행동하는 우리

Distance in time is like / distance in space. //
시간 속에서의 거리는 같다 / 공간 속에서의 거리와 //

People matter / even if they live thousands of miles away. //
사람들은 중요하다 / 그들이 수천 마일 떨어져서 살더라도 //

Likewise, / they matter / even if they live thousands of years hence. //
마찬가지로 / 그들은 중요하다 / 그들이 지금부터 수천 년 후에 살더라도 //

In both cases, / it's easy / to mistake distance for unreality, / to treat the limits of what we can see / as the limits of the world. //
가주어   진주어의 병렬 구조   = the thing which
두 경우 모두 / 쉽다 / 거리를 비현실성으로 착각하는 것이 / 우리가 볼 수 있는 것의 한계를 취급하는 것이 / 세상의 한계로 //

But just as the world does not stop / at our doorstep or our country's borders, / neither does it stop / with our generation, or the next. //
부정어구에 의한 도치   단서 1 시간에 따라 세상이 멈추는 것 아님
하지만 세상이 멈추지 않는 것처럼 / 우리의 문 앞이나 우리 국가의 경계에서 / 그것은 멈추지 않는다 / 우리의 세대나 다음 세대에서 //

These ideas are common sense. // 이러한 생각들은 상식이다 //

A popular proverb says, / "A society grows great / when old men plant trees / under whose shade they will never sit." //
소유격 관계대명사
한 유명한 속담은 말한다 / "사회는 크게 성장한다 / 노인들이 나무를 심을 때 / 그 그늘에 결코 앉지 못할" //

When we dispose of radioactive waste, / we don't say, / "Who cares / if this poisons people centuries from now?" //
우리가 방사성 폐기물을 버릴 때 / 우리는 말하지 않는다 / "누가 상관하겠는가 / 이것이 지금으로부터 수백 년 후의 사람들을 해치든" //

Similarly, / few of us who care about climate change or pollution / do so / solely for the sake of people alive today. //
주격 관계대명사
비슷하게 / 기후 변화나 오염에 신경 쓰는 우리들 중 사람은 거의 없다 / 그렇게 하는 / 단지 오늘날 살아 있는 사람들을 위해서 //

We build museums and parks and bridges / that we hope will last for generations; /
주격 관계대명사(museums and parks and bridges 수식)
우리는 박물관과 공원과 다리를 만든다 / 대대로 지속되기를 바라는 /

we invest in schools and longterm scientific projects; / we preserve paintings, traditions, languages; / we protect beautiful places. //
우리는 학교와 장기적인 과학 프로젝트에 투자한다 / 우리는 그림, 전통, 언어를 보존한다 / 우리는 아름다운 장소를 보호한다 //
단서 2 우리는 현재와 미래 사이에 명확한 선을 긋지 않고 둘 다 영향을 끼친다고 함

In many cases, / we don't draw clear lines / between our concerns for the present and the future / — both are in play. //
많은 경우 / 우리는 명확한 선을 긋지 않는다 / 현재와 미래에 대한 우리의 걱정 사이에 / 둘 다 영향을 끼친다 //

- matter ⓥ 중요하다 · hence ⓐⓓ 이런 이유로 · doorstep ⓝ 문간
- proverb ⓝ 속담 · shade ⓝ 그늘 · dispose of ~을 버리다
- solely ⓐⓓ 단지, 오로지 · for the sake of ~을 위해서
- preserve ⓥ 보존하다, 유지하다 · in play 작용하여, 영향을 끼치는
- management ⓝ 관리 · infrastructure ⓝ 사회 기반 시설

시간 속에서의 거리는 공간 속에서의 거리와 같다. 사람들이 수천 마일 떨어져서 살더라도 그들은 중요하다. 마찬가지로, 그들이 지금부터 수천 년 후에 살더라도 그들은 중요하다. 두 경우 모두, 거리를 비현실성으로 착각하고 우리가 볼 수 있는 것의 한계를 세상의 한계로 취급하기 쉽다. 하지만 세상이 우리의 문 앞이나 우리 국가의 경계에서 멈추지 않는 것처럼, 그것은 우리의 세대나 다음 세대에서 멈추지 않는다. 이러한 생각들은 상식이다. 한 유명한 속담은 "사회는 노인들이 그 그늘에 결코 앉지 못할 나무를 심을 때 크게 성장한다."라고 한다. 우리가 방사성 폐기물을 버릴 때, 우리는 "이것이 지금으로부터 수백 년 후의 사람들을 해치든 누가 상관하겠는가?"라고 말하지 않는다. 비슷하게, 기후 변화나 오염에 신경 쓰는 우리들 중 단지 오늘날 살아 있는 사람들을 위해서 그렇게 하는 사람은 거의 없다. 우리는 대대로 지속되기를 바라는 박물관과 공원과 다리를 만들고, 우리는 학교와 장기적인 과학 프로젝트에 투자하고, 우리는 그림, 전통, 언어를 보존하고, 우리는 아름다운 장소를 보호한다. 많은 경우, 우리는 현재와 미래에 대한 우리의 걱정 사이에 명확한 선을 긋지 않는다 — 둘 다 영향을 끼친다.

다음 글의 제목으로 가장 적절한 것은?

① How to Be Present: Discover the Benefits of Here and Now
현재를 사는 방법: 지금 여기의 이점을 발견하라   지금 여기의 이점을 발견하라는 내용의 글이 아님
② The Power of Time Management: The Key to Success
시간 관리의 힘: 성공의 열쇠   시간 관리의 힘에 대해 언급하고 있지 않음
③ Why Is Green Infrastructure Eventually Cost-Effective?
친환경 기반 시설이 왜 결국 비용 효율적인가?   친환경 기반 시설에 대한 글이 아님
④ Solving Present-Day Problems from Past Experiences
과거 경험으로부터 현재의 문제 해결하기   과거 경험에서 현재 문제를 해결하는 것에 대한 언급은 없음
⑤ How We Act Beyond the Bounds of Time
우리는 어떻게 시간의 경계를 넘어 행동하는가
우리가 현재와 미래 사이에 명확한 선을 긋지 않고 시간의 경계를 넘어 행동한다고 함

전반부	세상은 우리 세대나 다음 세대에서 멈추는 것이 아님 (시간에 따라 세상이 멈추지 않음) 단서1
후반부	• 나무 심기, 기후 변화나 오염 문제, 박물관이나 학교 등 기반 시설에 투자하는 것은 모두 오늘만을 위해서가 아님 • 우리는 현재와 미래 사이에 명확한 선을 긋지 않음 단서2

▶ 우리가 현재와 미래, 즉 시간 사이에 명확한 선을 긋지 않고 그 경계를 넘어 행동한다는 내용이므로 ⑤ '우리는 어떻게 시간의 경계를 넘어 행동하는가'가 제목으로 적절하다.

왜 오답?

① 지금 여기의 이점을 발견하라는 내용의 글이 아니다.

② 시간 관리의 힘에 대해 언급하고 있지 않다.

③ 친환경 기반 시설에 대한 글이 아니다.

④ 과거 경험에서 현재 문제를 해결하는 것에 대한 언급이 없다.

G 09 정답 ① *인간과 로봇의 혼합팀

단서1 로봇을 서로 도움을 주고받는 인간-기계 팀의 일부로 다루는 접근법에 대한 내용임

The approach, *joint cognitive systems*, treats a robot / as part of a human-machine team / where the intelligence is synergistic, / arising from the contributions of each agent. //
'결합 인지 시스템' 접근법은 로봇을 다룬다 / 인간-기계 팀의 일부로 / 지력이 서로 도움을 주는 / 각 행위자의 기여로 생겨나는 //

The team consists / of at least one robot and one human / and is often called a *mixed team* / because it is a mixture of human and robot agents. //
그 팀은 구성되고 / 적어도 로봇 하나와 인간 한 명으로 / 흔히 '혼합팀'이라고 불린다 / 그것이 인간 행위자와 로봇 행위자가 혼합된 것이기 때문에 //

Self-driving cars, / where a person turns on and off the driving, / is an example of a joint cognitive system. //
자율주행차는 / 사람이 주행을 켜고 끄는 / 결합 인지 시스템의 한 예이다 //

Entertainment robots are examples of mixed teams / as are robots for telecommuting. //
오락용 로봇은 혼합팀의 예이다 / 재택근무를 위한 로봇이 그런 것처럼 //

The design process concentrates / on how the agents will cooperate and coordinate with each other / to accomplish the team goals. //
설계 과정은 집중한다 / 그 행위자들이 어떻게 서로 협력하고 조정하는지에 / 팀의 목표를 달성하기 위해 //

Rather than treating robots / as peer agents / with their own completely independent agenda, /
로봇을 다루기보다는 / 동료 행위자로 / 그들 자체의 완전히 독립된 과제를 가진 /

joint cognitive systems approaches treat robots as helpers / such as service animals or sheep dogs. // 단서2 이 접근법은 로봇을 도움을 주는 존재로 다룸
결합 인지 시스템 접근법은 로봇을 도움을 주는 존재로 다룬다 / 도우미 동물이나 양몰이 개처럼 //

In joint cognitive system designs, / artificial intelligence is used / along with human-robot interaction principles /
결합 인지 시스템 설계에서 / 인공 지능이 사용된다 / 인간-로봇 상호작용 원리와 함께 /

to create robots / that can be intelligent enough / to be good team members. //
로봇을 만들기 위해 / 충분히 똑똑할 수 있는 / 훌륭한 팀 구성원이 될 만큼 //

- **joint** ⓐ 공동의, 합동의   • **intelligence** ⓝ 지능
- **synergistic** ⓐ (반응·효과 등이) 상승[상조]적인
- **contribution** ⓝ 기여, 이바지   • **agent** ⓝ 행위자, 대리인
- **telecommute** ⓥ (컴퓨터 등의) 통신 시설을 이용하여 재택근무하다
- **concentrate** ⓥ 집중하다, 모으다   • **coordinate** ⓥ 조정하다, 조직화하다

- **accomplish** ⓥ 완수하다, 성취하다   • **peer** ⓝ (나이 등이 비슷한) 또래
- **independent** ⓐ 독립적인   • **agenda** ⓝ 의제, 안건
- **artificial** ⓐ 인공의   • **intelligent** ⓐ 지능적인, 지능이 있는

'결합 인지 시스템' 접근법은 로봇을 지력이 서로 도움을 주고, 각 행위자의 기여로 생겨나는 인간-기계 팀의 일부로 다룬다. 그 팀은 적어도 로봇 하나와 인간 한 명으로 구성되고 그 팀이 인간 행위자와 로봇 행위자가 혼합된 것이기 때문에 흔히 '혼합팀'이라고 불린다. 사람이 주행을 켜고 끄는 자율주행차는 결합 인지 시스템의 한 예이다. 오락용 로봇은 재택근무를 위한 로봇이 그런 것처럼 혼합팀의 예이다. 설계 과정은 그 행위자들이 팀의 목표를 달성하기 위해 어떻게 서로 협력하고 조정하는지에 집중한다. 결합 인지 시스템 접근법은 로봇을 그들 자체의 완전히 독립된 과제를 가진 동료 행위자로 다루기보다는 로봇을 도우미 동물이나 양몰이 개처럼 도움을 주는 존재로 다룬다. 결합 인지 시스템 설계에서, 훌륭한 팀 구성원이 될 만큼 충분히 똑똑할 수 있는 로봇을 만들기 위해 인공 지능이 인간-로봇 상호작용 원리와 함께 사용된다.

다음 글의 제목으로 가장 적절한 것은?

① Better Together: Human and Machine Collaboration
함께 하는 것이 더 낫다: 인간과 기계의 공동 작업   로봇을 도움을 주는 존재로 봄
② Can Robots Join Forces to Outperform Human Teams?
로봇은 인간 팀을 능가하기 위해 세력을 규합할 수 있을까?   로봇의 반란에 대한 내용이 아님
③ Loss of Humanity in the Human and Machine Conflict
인간과 기계 간의 갈등에서 인간성의 상실   인간-기계를 도움을 주고받는 관계로 봄
④ Power Off: When and How to Say No to Robot Partners
전원 끄기: 로봇 파트너에게 아니라고 말할 시점과 방법   혼합팀을 긍정적으로 보는 접근법임
⑤ Shifting from Service Animals to Robot Assistants of Humans
도우미 동물에서 인간을 돕는 로봇 조력자로의 이동   service animals로 만든 오답

왜 정답? [정답률 76%]

로봇을 서로 도움을 주고받는 인간-기계 팀의 일부로 다루는 결합 인지 시스템 접근법에 대해 설명하는 글로, 이 접근법은 로봇을 도움을 주는 존재로 다룬다고 했으므로 제목으로 ① '함께 하는 것이 더 낫다: 인간과 기계의 공동 작업'이 적절하다.

왜 오답?

② 로봇이 인간을 능가할 수 있다거나 그렇게 하기 위해 세력을 규합할 수 있는지 없는지에 대해 설명한 것이 아니다.

③, ④ 로봇을 인간과 도움을 주고받는 존재로 여기는 접근법에 대한 글이므로 로봇에 대한 부정적인 견해를 담은 제목은 적절하지 않다.

⑤ 결합 인지 시스템 접근법은 로봇을 도우미 동물처럼 도움을 주는 존재로 다룬다고 했지, 도우미 동물을 로봇으로 대체한다는 것이 아니다. 주의

G 10 정답 ⑤ *즉흥적 혁신의 특징

The most innovative teams are those / that can restructure themselves / in response / to unexpected shifts / in the environment; /
가장 혁신적인 팀들은 팀들이다 / 스스로 재구성할 수 있는 / 대응하여 / 예기치 않은 변화에 / 환경에 있어 /

they don't need a strong leader / to tell them / what to do. //
그 팀들은 강력한 리더를 필요로 하지 않는다 / 그들에게 말하는 / 무엇을 해야 할지를 //

Moreover, / they tend to form spontaneously; / when like-minded people find each other, / a group emerges. //
게다가 / 그 팀들은 자발적으로 형성되는 경향이 있다 / 생각이 비슷한 사람들이 서로 발견할 때 / 집단이 생겨난다 //

The improvisational collaboration / of the entire group / translates moments / of individual creativity / into group innovation. //
즉흥적인 협업은 / 집단 전체의 / 순간을 바꾼다 / 개인의 창의성의 / 집단 혁신으로 //

Allowing the space / for this self-organizing emergence / to occur / is difficult / for many managers /
여지를 허용하는 것은 / 이러한 자발적으로 조직하는 출현이 / 일어날 / 어렵다 / 많은 관리자들에게 /

because the outcome isn't controlled / by the management team's agenda / and is therefore less predictable. //
왜냐하면 그 결과는 통제되지 않으며 / 관리팀의 일정에 의해 / 따라서 덜 예측 가능하기 때문에 //

단서 1 대부분의 기업 관리자는 큰 그림에서 시작해서 세부 사항으로 내려가는 것을 좋아함

Most business executives like / to start with the big picture / and then work out the details. //
to start와 병렬 구조(to는 생략됨)
대부분의 기업 관리자들은 좋아한다 / 큰 그림에서 시작하고 / 그다음에 세부 사항을 해결하는 것을 //

단서 2 대부분의 기업 관리자는 큰 그림에서 시작해서 세부 사항으로 내려가는 것을 좋아해서 즉흥적 혁신은 대개 공식적 조직 밖에서 일어남

That's / why so many of the best examples / of improvised innovation / take place / outside of formal organizations. //
그것이 ~이다 / 왜 그렇게 많은 가장 좋은 사례가 / 즉흥적 혁신의 / 일어나는지 / 공식적 조직 밖에서 //

In improvisational innovation, / teams start / with the details / and then work up to the big picture. //
핵심 문장: 즉흥적 혁신에 있어 팀은 세부 사항에서 시작하여 차츰 큰 그림에 이름
즉흥적 혁신에 있어 / 팀은 시작하고 / 세부 사항에서 / 차츰 큰 그림에 이른다 //

It's riskier and less efficient, / but when a successful innovation emerges, / it's often very surprising and imaginative. //
그것은 더 위험하고 덜 효율적이지만 / 성공적인 혁신이 일어나면 / 그것은 흔히 매우 놀랍고 창의적이다 //

- restructure ⓥ 재구성하다, 개혁하다 · shift ⓝ 변화
- spontaneously ⓐ 자발적으로 · like-minded ⓐ 생각[뜻]이 비슷한
- emerge ⓥ 생겨나다 · improvisational ⓐ 즉흥적인
- collaboration ⓝ 공동 작업, 협력 · translate ⓥ 바꾸다
- emergence ⓝ 출현 · outcome ⓝ 결과
- agenda ⓝ 의사 일정, 의제 · predictable ⓐ 예측할 수 있는
- executive ⓝ 경영진, 간부 · improvised ⓐ 즉흥의
- efficient ⓐ 효율적인 · conflicting ⓐ 모순되는, 상충되는

가장 혁신적인 팀들은 예기치 않은 환경의 변화에 대응하여 스스로 재구성할 수 있는 팀들이며, 그 팀들은 그들에게 무엇을 해야 할지를 말하는 강력한 리더를 필요로 하지 않는다. 게다가, 그 팀들은 자발적으로 형성되는 경향이 있는데, 생각이 비슷한 사람들이 서로를 발견할 때, 집단이 생겨난다. 집단 전체의 즉흥적인 협업은 개인의 창의성의 순간을 집단 혁신으로 바꾼다. 이러한 자발적으로 조직하는 (집단의) 출현이 일어날 여지를 허용하는 것은 많은 관리자에게 어려운 일인데, 왜냐하면 그 결과는 관리팀의 일정에 의해 통제되지 않으며, 따라서 덜 예측 가능하기 때문이다. 대부분의 기업 관리자들은 큰 그림에서 시작하고 그다음에 세부 사항을 해결하는 것을 좋아한다. 그것이 왜 즉흥적 혁신의 그렇게 많은 가장 좋은 사례가 공식적 조직 밖에서 일어나는지의 이유이다. 즉흥적 혁신을 할 때, 팀은 세부 사항에서 시작하고 차츰 큰 그림에 이르게 된다. 그것은 더 위험하고 덜 효율적이지만, 성공적인 혁신이 일어나면 그것은 흔히 매우 놀랍고 창의적이다.

다음 글의 제목으로 가장 적절한 것은?

① The Start of Innovation: A Leader's Big Picture
혁신의 시작: 리더의 큰 그림 혁신적인 팀은 강력한 리더를 필요로 하지 않는다고 했음
② Unpredictable Changes: Challenges to Innovation
예측할 수 없는 변화: 혁신에 대한 도전 혁신에 있어 어려운 점이 무엇인지 설명한 것이 아님
③ Conflicting Ideas Lead to the Ultimate Innovation
상충하는 아이디어들이 궁극적인 혁신으로 이어진다 즉흥적 혁신은 세부 사항에서 시작한다는 내용임
④ Weakness of Improvisational Teams in Emergencies
위급 상황에서 즉흥적인 팀의 약점 즉흥적인 팀의 약점에 대한 언급은 없음
⑤ Improvised Innovation Emerges from the Bottom Up
즉흥적인 혁신은 상향식에서 나온다 세부 사항에서 시작하여 큰 그림에 이름

왜 정답? [정답률 71%] 반의어인 '하향식'은 top down이라고 하며, 어떤 일이나 정책이 위에서 결정되어 아래로 전달되는 방식을 의미함 꿀팁

가장 좋은 즉흥적 혁신의 많은 사례는 공식적인 조직 밖에서 이루어진다고 했는데, 공식적인 조직이란, 큰 그림에서 시작하여 세부 사항을 해결하는 것을 좋아하는 관리자가 있는 하향식 조직을 말한다. 이는 곧 즉흥적 혁신이 세부 사항에서 시작하여 큰 그림에 이르는 조직에서 이루어진다는 것을 의미하므로 ⑤ '즉흥적인 혁신은 상향식에서 나온다'가 이 글의 제목으로 적절하다.

왜 오답? 가장 혁신적인 팀은 리더를 필요로 하지 않고, 생각이 비슷한 개개인이 모여 자발적으로 팀이 형성된다는 것 역시 상향식이라고 할 수 있음 꿀팁

① 가장 혁신적인 팀은 무엇을 해야 하는지 말하는 강력한 리더를 필요로 하지 않는다고 했으므로 글의 내용과 상반되는 제목이다.

② 첫 문장에 unexpected shifts in the environment가 언급된 것으로 만든 오답이다. 예측할 수 없는 변화 때문에 혁신에 어려움을 겪는다는 등의 내용이 아니다. 함정

③ 즉흥적인 혁신에 있어 팀은 세부 사항에서부터 시작하여 차츰 큰 그림에 이른다는 내용이다. 충돌하는 아이디어들이 궁극적인 혁신으로 이어진다는 언급은 없다.

④ 즉흥적인 팀의 장점을 설명한 글로, 위급 상황이나 즉흥적인 팀의 약점에 대해서는 설명하지 않았다.

G 11 정답 ① *작은 것에서 시작하는 에너지 수확

Every day / an enormous amount of energy is created / by the movement of people and animals, / and by interactions of people / with their immediate surroundings. //
전치사구의 병렬 구조
매일 / 막대한 양의 에너지가 만들어진다 / 사람들과 동물들의 움직임에 의해 / 그리고 사람들의 상호 작용에 의해 / 그들의 인접 환경과의 //

This is usually in very small amounts / or in very dispersed environments. //
단서 1 매일 막대한 양의 에너지가 매우 적은 양으로 매우 분산된 환경에서 만들어짐
이것은 보통 매우 적은 양으로 일어난다 / 혹은 매우 분산된 환경 속에서 //

Virtually all of that energy is lost / to the local environment, / and historically there have been no efforts / to gather it. //
형용사적 용법(efforts 수식)
사실상 그 에너지 전부가 소실되고 / 주변 환경으로 / 역사적으로 노력이 없었다 / 그것을 모으려는 //

It may seem odd / to consider finding ways / to "collect" energy / that is given off all around us /
가주어 명사적 용법(진주어) 형용사적 용법(ways 수식)
~이 이상하게 보일지도 모른다 / 방법을 찾는 것을 고려하는 것이 / 에너지를 '모으는' / 우리 주변에서 방출되는 /

— by people simply walking / or by walking upstairs and downstairs / or by riding stationary/exercise bicycles, / for example —
사람들이 단순히 걸음으로써 / 혹은 계단을 오르내림으로써 / 혹은 고정된/실내 운동용 자전거를 탐으로써 / 예를 들어 //

단서 2 우리 주변에서 발생하는 작은 에너지를 모으는 방법을 찾는 것이 에너지 수확의 본질

but that is the general idea and nature / of energy harvesting. //
하지만 그것이 일반적인 발상이고 본질이다 / 에너지 수확의 //

The broad idea of energy harvesting is / that there are many places / at which small amounts of energy are generated / — and often wasted — /
에너지 수확의 대략적인 발상은 ~이다 / 장소가 많다는 것 / 소량의 에너지가 생성되는 / 그리고 흔히 버려지는 /

단서 3 에너지 수확의 대략적인 발상: 생성되는 소량의 에너지가 수집되면 실용적으로 이용될 수 있음

and when collected, / this can be put to some practical use. //
그리고 수집되면 / 이것이 실용적으로 이용될 수 있다는 것 //
주어 동사(완전자동사)

Current efforts have begun, / aimed at collecting such energy / in smaller devices / which can store it, / such as portable batteries. //
현재의 노력은 시작되었다 / 모으는 것을 목표로 해서 / 더 작은 장치에 / 그것을 저장할 수 있는 / 그러한 에너지를 휴대용 배터리와 같이 //

- enormous ⓐ 막대한, 거대한 · immediate ⓐ 인접한
- surroundings ⓝ 환경 · dispersed ⓐ 분산된
- virtually ⓐ 사실상, 거의 · odd ⓐ 이상한 · give off ~을 방출하다
- stationary ⓐ 움직이지 않는, 정지된 · nature ⓝ 천성, 본성
- broad ⓐ (폭이) 넓은, 일반[개괄]적인 · generate ⓥ 생성하다
- put ~ to use ~을 이용하다 · store ⓥ 저장하다
- portable ⓐ 휴대[이동]가 쉬운, 휴대용의
- fulfill ⓥ (약속·요구 등을) 이행하다[충족시키다]

매일 막대한 양의 에너지가 사람들과 동물들의 움직임에 의해, 그리고 사람들과 그들의 인접 환경의 상호 작용에 의해 만들어진다. 이것은 보통 매우 적은 양으로 혹은 매우 분산된 환경 속에서 일어난다. 사실상 그 에너지 전부가

주변 환경으로 소실되고, 역사적으로 그것을 모으기 위한 노력이 없었다. 예를 들어, 사람들이 단순히 걷거나, 계단을 오르내리거나, 고정된/실내 운동용 자전거를 탐으로써 우리 주변에서 방출되는 에너지를 '모으는' 방법을 찾는 것을 고려하는 것이 이상하게 보일지도 모르지만, 그것이 에너지 수확의 일반적인 발상이고 본질이다. 에너지 수확의 대략적인 발상은 소량의 에너지가 생성되는, 그리고 흔히 버려지는, 장소가 많다는 것이며, 수집되면 이를 실용적으로 이용할 수 있다는 것이다. 현재의 노력은 그러한 에너지를 휴대용 배터리와 같이 그것을 저장할 수 있는 더 작은 장치에 모으는 것을 목표로 해서 시작되었다.

다음 글의 제목으로 가장 적절한 것은?

① Energy Harvesting: Every Little Helps
  에너지 수확: 모든 작은 도움들 ……… 작은 에너지를 모으는 것이 에너지 수확의 본질임
② Burning Waste for Energy Is Harmful
  에너지를 얻기 위해 쓰레기를 태우는 것은 해롭다 …… 쓰레기를 태워서 에너지를 얻는다는 언급은 없음
③ Is Renewable Energy Really Green?
  재생 가능한 에너지가 정말 친환경적인가? …… 에너지의 친환경성에 대한 내용이 아님
④ Pros and Cons of Energy Harvesting
  에너지 수확의 장단점 …… 에너지 수확이란 무엇인가에 대한 내용임
⑤ Can Natural Energy Sources Fulfill the Demand?
  천연 에너지 자원이 수요를 충족시킬 수 있는가? …… 에너지 수요에 대한 언급은 없음

왜 정답? [정답률 76%]

❶ 매일 막대한 양의 에너지가 매우 적은 양으로, 매우 분산된 환경에서 만들어진다. 단서1

❷ 이러한 에너지를 모으는 방법을 찾는 것이 에너지 수확의 본질이다. 단서2

❸ 생성되는 소량의 에너지가 수집되면 실용적으로 이용될 수 있다는 것이 에너지 수확의 대략적인 발상이다. 단서3

▶ 작은 에너지를 모으는 것이 에너지 수확의 본질이라는 것이므로 정답은 ① '에너지 수확: 모든 작은 도움들'이다.

왜 오답?

② 쓰레기를 태워서 에너지를 얻는 것의 단점을 설명한 것이 아니다.
③ 친환경적인 에너지에 대한 오해를 다룬 글이 아니다.
④ 에너지 수확의 정의, 본질에 대해 설명한 글이다.
⑤ 천연 에너지나 에너지 수요에 대한 언급은 없다.

G 12 정답 ② ＊관계의 깨짐은 곧 새로운 시작을 의미한다 ─

When you break up / with a partner or close friend, / the natural response / (after having a good cry, obviously) / is to blame yourself.
여러분이 헤어지는 경우에 / 파트너나 친한 친구와 / 자연스러운 반응은 / (분명히, 실컷 운 다음에) / 여러분 자신을 탓하는 것이다 //

You wonder / what you did wrong / and what you might have done differently. //
여러분은 궁금해한다 / 무엇을 잘못했고 / 여러분이 무엇을 다르게 할 수 있었을지 //

Bonds can help us reach / a more balanced perspective; /
결합 관계는 우리가 도달하도록 도와줄 수 있다 / 더 균형 잡힌 관점에 /

there are some bonds / that were simply never meant to last, / even if they played an essential role / in your evolution / to this point. //
일부 결합 관계가 있다 / 결코 절대 지속되기로 되어 있지 않았을 / 그것들이 중요한 역할을 했을지라도 / 여러분의 진화에서 / 이 시점까지 //

Perhaps the most valuable thing / is to know / that seeing bonds break / doesn't have to break us. //
어쩌면 가장 중요한 것은 / 아는 것이다 / 결합 관계가 깨지는 것을 보는 것이 / 우리를 무너뜨릴 필요는 없다는 것을 // 단서1 화학: 원자의 결합에서의 변화는 새로운 결합 가능성에 대한 여지를 만드는 것임

In chemistry, / by definition, / a change in the atomic bonding / is not just the end of one state, / but the beginning of another: / creating the space / for new bonding potential. //
화학에서 / 본질적으로 / 원자 결합에서의 변화는 / 단지 한 상태의 끝이 아니라 / 또 다른 상태의 시작이다 / 여지를 만드는 것 / 새로운 결합 가능성에 대한 //

The same is true for us / as humans. //
우리에게도 마찬가지이다 / 인간인 단서2 이는 인간에게도 마찬가지임

It might take a cup of warm milk / to reset us and give us comfort / after a relationship has broken down. //
~은 따뜻한 우유 한 잔이 필요할지도 모른다 / 우리를 원래 상태로 되돌리고 우리에게 위안을 주는 것은 / 관계가 깨진 후에 //

But / however many bonds / we see / come apart, /
하지만 / 아무리 많은 결합 관계가 / 우리가 보더라도 / 깨지는 것을 /

we will always retain / one of our most human abilities: / to connect afresh, find new friends and love again. //
우리는 항상 보유할 것이다 / 우리의 가장 인간적인 능력 중 하나를 / 새롭게 관계 맺고, 새 친구들을 찾으며, 다시 사랑하는 것 // 단서3 아무리 많은 관계가 깨지더라도 우리는 항상 새롭게 관계 맺을 것임

- obviously [ad] 분명히 · bond [n] 결합 관계 · perspective [n] 관점
- evolution [n] 진화 · chemistry [n] 화학
- by definition 본질적으로 · atomic bonding 원자 결합
- potential [n] 가능성 · come apart 분리되다 · retain [v] 보유하다
- afresh [ad] 새롭게

여러분이 파트너나 친한 친구와 헤어지는 경우에, 자연스러운 반응(분명히, 실컷 운 다음에)은 여러분 자신을 탓하는 것이다. 여러분은 무엇을 잘못했고 무엇을 다르게 할 수 있었을지 궁금해한다. 결합 관계는 우리가 더 균형 잡힌 관점에 도달하도록 도와줄 수 있는데, 이 시점까지 여러분의 진화에서 중요한 역할을 했을지라도 결코 절대 지속되기로 되어 있지 않았을 일부 결합 관계가 있다. 어쩌면 가장 중요한 것은 결합 관계가 깨지는 것을 본다고 해서 우리가 무너질 필요는 없다는 것을 아는 것이다. 화학에서, 본질적으로 원자 결합에서의 변화는 단지 한 상태의 끝이 아니라 또 다른 상태의 시작, 즉 새로운 결합 가능성에 대한 여지를 만드는 것이다. 인간인 우리에게도 마찬가지이다. 관계가 깨진 후에 우리를 원래 상태로 되돌리고 우리에게 위안을 주기 위해서는 따뜻한 우유 한 잔이 필요할지도 모른다. 하지만 아무리 많은 결합 관계가 깨지는 것을 보더라도, 우리는 우리의 가장 인간적인 능력 중 하나를 항상 보유할 것인데, 즉 새롭게 관계 맺고, 새 친구들을 찾으며, 다시 사랑하는 것이다.

다음 글의 제목으로 가장 적절한 것은?

① Relationships: The Older, The Better
  관계: 오래될수록 더 좋은 …… 관계의 깨짐에 대한 글임
② A Break in a Bond: A New Beginning
  결합 관계의 깨짐: 새로운 시작 …… 결합의 깨짐은 새로운 결합의 여지를 만듦
③ Shared Experiences Make Strong Bonds
  공유된 경험이 강한 결합 관계를 만든다 …… 결합의 요소에 대한 글이 아님
④ A Friend in Need, A Friend Indeed
  어려울 때 친구가 진정한 친구 …… 우정이 깨졌을 때에 대한 내용임
⑤ Two Heads Are Better Than One
  두 사람이 한 사람보다 낫다 …… 힘을 합치는 것에 대한 내용이 아님

왜 정답? [정답률 91%]

- 화학에서 원자의 결합에서의 변화는 또 다른 상태의 시작으로, 새로운 결합 가능성에 대한 여지를 만듦 단서1
- 위에서 설명한 원자의 결합에서의 변화는 인간인 우리에게도 마찬가지임 단서2
- 아무리 많은 결합 관계가 깨지더라도 우리는 항상 새롭게 관계 맺고, 새 친구를 찾으며, 다시 사랑할 것임 단서3

➡ 관계가 깨진다는 것은 새로운 관계가 시작된다는 의미라는 내용이므로, 제목은 ② '결합 관계의 깨짐: 새로운 시작'이 적절함

왜 오답?

① '관계가 깨졌을 때', '새로운 관계의 시작'에 대한 내용이다.
③ 관계를 강화하는 요소에 대해 설명한 것이 아니다.
④ 관계의 진정성을 결정하는 요소에 대한 언급은 없다.
⑤ 혼자보다 여럿이 낫다는 것을 설명하는 글이 아니다.

G 13 정답 ① *웹 기반 저널리즘의 특징

Before the web, / newspaper archives were largely the musty
domain / of professional researchers and journalism students. //
웹 이전에 / 신문 기록 보관소는 주로 곰팡내 나는 영역이었다 / 전문적 연구원과 언론학과
학생의

Journalism was, by definition, current. //
저널리즘은 당연히 최신에 관한 것이었다 //

단서 1 웹 기반 저널리즘은 저널리즘의 유통 기한을 크게 늘렸음

The general accessibility of archives / has greatly extended / the
shelf life of journalism, / with older stories now regularly cited /
to provide context / for more current ones. // with+(대)명사+분사:
~가 …한된 채로
자료 보관소의 일반적 접근 가능성은 / 크게 늘렸다 / 저널리즘의 유통 기한을 / 더 오래된
기사가 이제는 자주 인용되면서 / 맥락을 제공하기 위해 / 더 최신 기사에 //

With regard / to how meaning is made / of complex issues /
선행사(주격 관계대명사와 be동사는 생략됨)
encountered in the news, /
관련하여 / 의미가 어떻게 형성되는가와 / 복잡한 이슈에 관해 / 뉴스에서 마주치는 /

this departure can be understood / as a readiness / by online
news consumers / to engage / with the underlying issues and
형용사적 용법(a readiness 수식)
contexts of the news /
이 새로운 출발은 이해될 수 있다 / 준비로 / 온라인 뉴스 소비자에 의한 / 관여할 / 뉴스의
기저 이슈와 맥락에 /

that was not apparent in, or even possible for, / print
consumers. //
명백하지 않았던 또는 심지어 가능하지 않았던 / 인쇄물 소비자에게는 //

One of the emergent qualities of online news, / determined / in
단수 주어
part by the depth / of readily accessible online archives, /
온라인 뉴스의 떠오르는 특성 중 하나는 / 결정되는 / 부분적으로는 깊이로 / 쉽게 접근할 수
있는 온라인 기록 보관소의 /

seems to be the possibility / of understanding news stories
단수 동사
/ as the manifest outcomes / of larger economic, social and
cultural issues / rather than short-lived and unconnected media
spectacles. // 단서 2 온라인 뉴스의 특성 중 하나는 더 큰 맥락에서 뉴스 기사를 이해할 가능성임
가능성인 듯 보인다 / 뉴스 기사를 이해할 / 분명한 결과로 / 더 큰 경제적, 사회적, 문화적
이슈의 / 수명이 짧고 연결성이 없는 미디어 구경거리가 아니라 //

- domain ⓝ 영역
- journalism ⓝ 저널리즘 (기사거리를 모으고 기사를 쓰는 일)
- by definition 당연히 · accessibility ⓝ 접근성
- extend ⓥ 연장하다 · shelf life 유통기한 · cite ⓥ 인용하다
- readiness ⓝ 준비 · engage ⓥ 참여하다
- underlying ⓐ 기저의 · apparent ⓐ 분명한
- emergent ⓐ 명백한, 뚜렷한 · manifest ⓐ 분명한
- short-lived ⓐ 수명이 짧은 · spectacle ⓝ 구경거리

웹 이전에 신문 기록 보관소는 주로 전문적 연구원과 언론학과 학생의 곰팡내
나는 영역이었다. 저널리즘은 당연히 최신에 관한 것이었다. 자료 보관소의
일반적 접근 가능성은 더 오래된 기사가 이제는 자주 더 최신 기사에 맥락을
제공하기 위해 인용되면서, 저널리즘의 유통 기한을 크게 늘리게 되었다.
뉴스에서 마주치는 복잡한 이슈에 관해 의미가 어떻게 형성되는가와 관련하여,
이 새로운 출발은 온라인 뉴스 소비자가 인쇄물 소비자에게는 명백하지 않았던,
또는 심지어 가능하지 않았던, 뉴스의 기저 이슈와 맥락에 관여할 준비로
이해될 수 있다. 온라인 뉴스의 떠오르는 특성 중 하나는, 부분적으로는 쉽게
접근할 수 있는 온라인 기록 보관소의 깊이로 결정되는데, 뉴스 기사가 수명이
짧고 연결성이 없는 미디어 구경거리가 아니라 더 큰 경제적, 사회적, 문화적
이슈의 분명한 결과로 이해될 가능성인 듯 보인다.

다음 글의 제목으로 가장 적절한 것은? [3점]

① Web-based Journalism: Lasting Longer and Contextually Wider
웹 기반 저널리즘: 더 오래 지속되고 맥락상 더 넓다   웹 기반 저널리즘의 특징을 설명함
② With the Latest Content, Online News Beats Daily Newspapers!
최신 콘텐츠로 온라인 뉴스는 일간 신문을 능가한다!   이전 콘텐츠를 인용함
③ How Online Media Journalists Reveal Hidden Stories Behind
News   저널리스트는 언급되지 않음
온라인 미디어 저널리스트가 뉴스 배경에 숨겨진 이야기를 밝히는 방식
④ Let's Begin a Journey to the Past with Printed Newspapers!
인쇄된 신문으로 과거로의 여행을 시작하자!   온라인 뉴스를 통해 과거로 여행함
⑤ Present and Future of Journalism in the Web World
웹 세계 저널리즘의 현재와 미래   인쇄물 소비자와 온라인 뉴스 소비자를 대조함

왜 정답? [정답률 54%]

인쇄물을 통한 저널리즘	· 최신 이슈를 다룸 · 뉴스의 기저 이슈와 맥락이 명백하지 않고, 소비자가 그에 관여할 수 없음
웹 기반 저널리즘	· 최신 기사에 오래된 기사가 인용됨 → 저널리즘의 유통 기한이 크게 늘어남 · 뉴스 기사를 더 큰 경제적, 사회적, 문화적 이슈의 결과로 이해할 수 있음 → 기사를 더 큰 맥락에서 이해할 수 있음

→ 웹 기반 저널리즘의 특징을 담은 ① '웹 기반 저널리즘: 더 오래 지속되고 맥락상 더
넓다'가 제목으로 적절하다.

왜 오답?

② 최신 뉴스에 오래된 기사를 인용한다는 온라인 뉴스의 특징을 설명하는 글이다.
③ 온라인 미디어 저널리스트가 사용하는 방식을 설명한 것이 아니다.
④ 인쇄물을 통한 저널리즘은 최신 이슈를 다룬다고 했다.
⑤ 웹에 기반한 저널리즘이 가져온 변화에 대한 글이다.

G 14 정답 ① *우리가 진정 구해야 하는 것

양보의 부사절 접속사(~이지만, ~하긴 하지만)
As much as we like to think of ourselves / as being different
and special, / humans are a part of Earth's biosphere, / created
전치사 within과 by의 목적어
within and by it. //
우리는 우리 자신을 생각하고 싶어 하지만 / 다르고 특별한 존재인 것으로 / 인간은 지구
생물권의 일부이다 / 그것 내에서 그것에 의해 창조된 //

Ultimately, / it is the living, breathing elements / of this world /
it is ~ that 구문으로 need의 목적어가 강조됨
that we need / more than inanimate supplies, / such as coal, gas,
or bauxite ore. //
궁극적으로 / 살아 숨 쉬는 요소를 / 이 세상의 / 우리는 필요로 한다 / 무생물 공급품보다 더
많이 / 석탄, 가스, 또는 보크사이트 광석과 같은 //

We can live / without cars or beer cans, / but we cannot / without
뒤에 live가 생략됨
food and oxygen. //
우리는 살 수 있지만 / 자동차나 맥주 캔 없이 / 우리는 그럴 수 없다 / 식량과 산소가 없이 //

As nations around the globe try / to band together / to attack
부사절 접속사
the problems / of greenhouse gas emissions / and the shrinking
availability / of fresh drinking water, /
전 세계 국가가 애쓰는 중에도 / 협력하려 / 문제를 공략하기 위해 / 온실가스의 배출과 /
줄어들고 있는 가용성이라는 / 신선한 식수의 /

in all corners of the world / thousands of species quietly go
extinct. //
세계 곳곳에서 / 수천 종의 생물이 조용히 멸종하고 있다 //

E. O. Wilson, / the renowned Harvard biologist, / recently
앞에 목적격 관계대명사가 생략됨*
presented the problem / our species faces / in a succinct law: /
E. O. Wilson은 / 하버드 대학교의 저명한 생물학자인 / 최근에 문제를 제시했다 / 우리
인간이 직면하고 있는 / 간결한 법칙으로 /

동격
"If you save the living environment, / the biodiversity / that
we have left, / you will also automatically save / the physical
environment, too. // 단서 생물 다양성을 구하면 물리적 환경까지 구하는 것임
'만약 여러분이 살아있는 환경을 구한다면 / 생물 다양성 / 우리가 남겨 둔 / 여러분은 또한
자동으로 구할 것이다 / 물리적 환경도 //

But if you only save the physical environment, / you will ultimately lose both." //

하지만 여러분이 물리적 환경만 구한다면 / 결국 여러분은 두 가지 모두를 잃게 될 것이다' //

- ultimately ⓐ 궁극적으로, 결국   - element ⓝ 요소, 성분
- inanimate ⓐ 무생물의   - coal ⓝ 석탄   - oxygen ⓝ 산소
- globe ⓝ 지구, 세계   - band together (무엇을 달성하기 위해) 함께 뭉치다
- greenhouse ⓝ 온실   - emission ⓝ 배출
- shrink ⓥ 줄어들다, 오그라들다   - availability ⓝ 이용할 수 있음, 가능성
- species ⓝ 종(種)   - extinct ⓐ 멸종된   - renowned ⓐ 유명한
- biologist ⓝ 생물학자   - present ⓥ 제시하다, 보여 주다
- face ⓥ 직면하다   - biodiversity ⓝ 생물 다양성
- automatically ⓐ 자동적으로   - physical ⓐ 물리적인, 신체의

우리는 우리 자신을 다르고 특별한 존재인 것으로 생각하고 싶어 하지만, 인간은 지구 생물권 내에서 그것에 의해 창조된 생물권의 일부이다. 궁극적으로, 석탄, 가스, 또는 보크사이트 광석과 같은 무생물 공급품보다 우리에게 더 필요한 것은 이 세상의 살아 숨 쉬는 요소이다. 우리는 자동차나 맥주 캔 없이는 살 수 있지만, 식량과 산소가 없으면 살 수 없다. 전 세계 국가가 온실가스의 배출을 줄어들고 있는 신선한 식수의 가용성 문제를 공략하기 위해 협력하려 애쓰는 중에도, 세계 곳곳에서 수천 종의 생물이 조용히 멸종하고 있다. 하버드 대학교의 저명한 생물학자인 E. O. Wilson은 우리 인간이 직면하고 있는 문제를 간결한 법칙으로 최근에 제시했다. '만약 여러분이 살아있는 환경, 즉 우리가 남겨 둔 생물 다양성을 구한다면, 여러분은 자동으로 물리적 환경도 구할 것이다. 하지만 물리적 환경만 구한다면, 결국 두 가지 모두를 잃게 될 것이다.'

다음 글의 제목으로 가장 적절한 것은?

① Save Biodiversity to Save the Earth 살아있는 환경을 구하라고 했음
  지구를 구하기 위해 생물 다양성을 구하라
② Invasive Alien Species Threaten Biodiversity
  급속히 퍼지는 외래종이 생물 다양성을 위협한다   무엇이 생물 다양성을 위협하는지는 언급되지 않음
③ Potentiality and Utilization of Renewable Energy
  재생 가능한 에너지의 잠재력과 이용   석탄, 가스 등이 언급된 것으로 만든 오답
④ Tackling Climate Change Has a Long Way to Go
  기후 변화와 씨름하는 것은 갈 길이 멀다   기후 변화를 말하는 것이 아님
⑤ Worldwide Efforts to Protect Endangered Species
  위기에 처한 종을 보호하려는 전 세계적인 노력   thousands of species quietly go extinct로 만든 오답

왜 정답? [정답률 87%]

전 세계 국가의 노력에도 불구하고 세계 곳곳에서 수천 종의 생물이 멸종하는 것에 대해 E. O. Wilson이 한 말은 우리가 생물 다양성, 즉 살아있는 환경을 구하는 것이 물리적 환경 역시 구하는 것이라는 내용이다.

다시 말해, 지구를 구하기 위해 석탄, 가스, 또는 보크사이트 광석과 같은 물리적 환경이 아니라 생물 다양성을 구하라는 것이므로 제목은 ① '지구를 구하기 위해 생물 다양성을 구하라'가 적절하다.

> bauxite ore가 무엇인지 모르더라도 그것이 석탄과 가스처럼 무생물 공급품의 일종이라는 것만 파악할 수 있으면 정답을 찾는 데 아무 문제가 없음 꿀팁

왜 오답?

② 생물 다양성을 보호해야 지구가 보호된다는 내용이지, 무엇이 생물 다양성을 해치는 요인인지를 설명한 것은 아니다.
③ 재생 가능한 에너지를 이용함으로써 지구를 구한다는 내용이 아니다.
④ greenhouse gas emissions 등이 등장하는 것으로 만든 오답으로, 기후 변화에 대해 설명하는 글이 아니다.
⑤ 전 세계 국가들의 노력에도 불구하고 세계 곳곳에서 수천 종의 생물이 조용히 멸종하고 있다는 문제점을 어떻게 해결할 수 있는지에 대해 설명하는 글이다.

어법 특강

✽ 관계대명사의 생략

- 목적격 관계대명사는 생략하는 경우가 많다.
- She was a celebrated actress (whom) he had known and loved.
  a celebrated actress를 선행사로 하는 관계대명사
  (그녀는 그가 알고 사랑했던 유명한 배우였다.)

- 「주격 관계대명사+be동사」는 생략할 수 있다.
- Look at the singer (who is) performing on the stage!
  the singer를 선행사로 하는 관계대명사
  (무대에서 공연하고 있는 가수를 봐!)

G 15 정답 ① ✽무엇이 환경에 먼저 적응하는가

A common error / in current Darwinian thinking / is the assumption / that "selfish genes" are the prime mover / in evolution. //
단수 주어 / 단수 동사 / 동격절 접속사

흔한 오류는 / 현재의 다윈적 사고에서 / 가정이다 / "이기적인 유전자"가 원동력이라는 / 진화에서 //

In strict Darwinism / the prime mover is environmental threat. //
엄격한 다윈설에서 / 원동력은 환경적 위협이다 //

In the absence of threat, / natural selection tends / to *resist* change. //
위협이 없을 때 / 자연 선택은 경향이 있다 / 변화에 '저항하는' //

It is un-biological / to "explain" behavioural change / as *resulting / from* genetic change or the *ex vacuo* emergence / of domain-specific brain modules. //
가주어 / 진주어

~은 생물학적으로 맞지 않다 / 행동의 변화를 '설명하는' 것은 / '기인하는' 것으로 / 유전적 변화나 '무(無)에서의' 출현에서 / 영역별 뇌 모듈의 //

Evolutionary psychologists surely know / why brains evolved: / as Cosmides and Tooby point out, / brains are found / only in animals / that move. //
의문사 why가 이끄는 목적어절 / 선행사 / 관계대명사

진화 심리학자들은 확실히 안다 / 왜 뇌가 진화했는지 / Cosmides와 Tooby가 지적하듯이 / 뇌는 발견된다 / 동물에서만 / 움직이는 //

Brains are behavioural organs, / and behavioural adaptation, / being immediate and non-random, / is vastly more efficient / than genetic adaptation. // 단서1 유전적 적응보다 행동 적응이 훨씬 더 효율적임
뇌는 행동 기관이며 / 행동 적응이 / 즉각적이고 무작위적이지 않은 / 훨씬 더 효율적이다 / 유전적 적응보다 //

So, / in animals with brains, / behavioural change is the usual first response / to environmental threat. // 단서2 행동 변화가 첫 번째 대응임
그러므로 / 뇌를 가진 동물에게 / 행동 변화는 보통의 첫 번째 대응이다 / 환경 위협에 대한 //

If the change is successful, / genetic adaptation to the new behaviour / will follow more gradually. // 단서3 행동 변화에 대한 유전적 적응이 뒤따름
그 변화가 성공적이면 / 새로운 행동에 대한 유전적 적응이 / 더 점진적으로 뒤따를 것이다 //

Animals do not evolve carnivore teeth and then decide / it might be a good idea / to eat meat. //
진주어 / 가주어

동물들은 육식 동물의 이빨을 진화시키고 나서 결정하지 않는다 / ~이 좋은 생각일 수도 있다고 / 고기를 먹는 것이 //

- assumption ⓝ 가정, 가설   - prime mover 원동력
- evolution ⓝ 진화   - absence ⓝ 없음, 부재   - resist ⓥ 저항하다
- genetic ⓐ 유전의   - emergence ⓝ 출현   - evolve ⓥ 진화하다
- point out ~을 지적하다[가리키다]   - organ ⓝ (신체 내의) 장기[기관]
- adaptation ⓝ 적응   - immediate ⓐ 즉각적인
- vastly ⓐ 대단히, 엄청나게   - response ⓝ 대응, 응답
- gradually ⓐ 점진적으로, 서서히   - superior ⓐ 우월한

현재의 다윈적 사고에서 흔히 볼 수 있는 오류는 "이기적인 유전자"가 진화의 원동력이라는 가정이다. 엄격한 다윈설에서 원동력은 환경적 위협이다. 위협이 없을 때, 자연 선택은 변화에 '저항하는' 경향이 있다. 행동의 변화를 유전적 변화나 영역별 뇌 모듈의 '무(無)에서의' 출현에서 '기인하는' 것으로 '설명하는' 것은 생물학적으로 맞지 않다. 진화 심리학자들은 왜 뇌가 진화했는지 확실히 안다. Cosmides와 Tooby가 지적하듯이, 뇌는 움직이는 동물에서만 발견된다. 뇌는 행동 기관이며, 즉각적이고 무작위적이지 않은 행동 적응이 유전적 적응보다 훨씬 더 효율적이다. 그러므로 뇌를 가진 동물에게 행동 변화는 환경 위협에 대한 보통의 첫 번째 대응이다. 그 변화가 성공적이면, 새로운 행동에 대한 유전적 적응이 더 점진적으로 뒤따를 것이다. 동물들은 육식 동물의 이빨을 진화시키고 나서 고기를 먹는 것이 좋은 생각일 수도 있다고 결정하지 않는다.

다음 글의 제목으로 가장 적절한 것은?

① Which Adapts First, Behaviour or Genes?
행동 또는 유전자 중 어느 것이 먼저 적응하는가?　　행동 적응이 유전적 적응보다 먼저 일어남
② The Brain Under Control of Selfish Genes
이기적인 유전자의 통제 하에 있는 뇌　　진화의 원동력이 이기적인 유전자라는 것은 흔한 오류임
③ Why Animals Eat Meat: A Story of Survival
동물들이 고기를 먹는 이유: 생존의 이야기　　예시로 든 내용임
④ Genes Always Win the Battle Against Nature!
유전자는 항상 자연과의 싸움에서 승리한다　　유전자의 자연과의 싸움에 대한 내용이 아님
⑤ The Superior Efficiency of Genetic Adaptation
유전적 적응의 뛰어난 효율성　　행동 적응이 훨씬 더 효율적임

왜 정답? [정답률 69%]

행동의 변화를 유전적 변화에서 기인하는 것으로 설명하는 것은 생물학적으로 맞지 않다고 하면서, 즉각적이고 무작위적이지 않은 행동 적응이 유전적 적응보다 훨씬 더 효율적이며, 환경에 맞게 행동이 먼저 변화하고 유전적 적응이 뒤따른다고 이야기하고 있으므로 정답은 ① '행동 또는 유전자 중 어느 것이 먼저 적응하는가?'이다.

> 제목에서 의문을 제시하고 글에서 그 의문에 대답함 꿀팁

왜 오답?

② selfish genes가 언급된 것으로 만든 오답이다. 진화에 있어 이기적인 유전자가 원동력이라는 가정은 흔한 오류라고 했다. 함정

③ 마지막 문장에 언급된 육식 동물에 관한 내용은 주제를 뒷받침하는 예시일 뿐이므로 제목으로 삼기에는 너무 지엽적이다.

④ 유전적 적응과 행동 적응을 비교, 대조해서 설명하는 글로, 유전자와 자연의 싸움은 언급되지 않았다.

⑤ 유전적 적응보다 행동 적응이 훨씬 더 효율적이라고 했다.

G 16 정답 ⑤ *동물 모방 의식과 동굴 예술 이해하기*

단서 1 동굴 예술을 이해하기 위해 여전히 동물에 그림을 그리는 현존하는 수렵-채집 사회에 관심을 둠

In making sense of cave art, / anthropologists have turned / to surviving hunter-gatherer societies / that continue to paint inside caves, /
　　　　　　선행사　　　　　　주격 관계대명사
동물 예술을 이해하는 데 있어 / 인류학자들은 관심을 두었다 / 현존하는 수렵-채집 사회에 / 동물 내부에 그림을 그리는 것을 계속하는 /
　　　　　　계속적 용법의 주격 관계대명사
particularly the San peoples, / who live in communities / across
　　선행사
a wide region of southern Africa. // **단서 2** San 족의 상세한 동물 모방이
특히 San 족에 / 그들은 공동체를 이루며 산다 / 남부 　인류학자를 매료시킴
아프리카의 넓은 지역에 걸쳐 //
　명사절 주어
What began to fascinate anthropologists / who studied the San /
단수 동사
was their detailed imitations of the animals / they hunt. //
인류학자들을 매료시키기 시작했던 것은 / San 족을 연구한 / 동물들에 대한 그들의 상세한 모방이었다 / 그들이 사냥하는 //

The hunters, in some sense, become animals / in order to make inferences /
사냥꾼들은 어떤 의미에서 동물이 된다 / 추론하기 위해 / ★전치사 about의 목적어로 쓰인 간접의문문
about how their prey might behave. //
자신의 사냥감이 어떻게 행동할 수 있을지에 관해 //

> ★ **간접의문문**
> 의문문이 다른 문장에서 주어, 목적어, 보어 등의 역할을 할 수 있는데, 이때 어순은 「의문사+S+V」이다.

This spills over / into ritual. // **단서 3** 동물 모방이 의식으로 번짐
이것이 번진다 / 의식으로 //

The San use hyperventilation and rhythmic movement / to create states of altered consciousness / as part of a shamanistic culture. //
San 족은 과호흡과 리듬 있는 동작을 사용하여 / 변환된 의식 상태를 만든다 / 주술적인 문화의 일부로 //

In the final stage of a trance, / Lewis-Williams writes, /
무아지경의 마지막 단계에서 / Lewis-Williams는 적는다 /

'people sometimes feel themselves / to be turning into animals / and undergoing / other frightening or exalting transformations'. //
　　　　　　　　　　　feel이 〈인지〉의 의미를 나타낼 때는 목적격 보어로
　　　　　　　　　　　상태를 나타내는 동사의 to부정사가 쓰일 수 있음
'사람들은 때때로 자신을 느낀다 / 동물로 변하고 있다고 / 그리고 겪고 있다고 / 두렵게 하거나 의기양양하게 하는 다른 변신을'이라고 //

For anthropologist Kim Hill, / identifying and observing
　형용사적 용법(animals 수식)　　　　　　형용사적 용법(those 수식)
animals / to eat / and those / to escape /
인류학자 Kim Hill에게 / 동물을 알아보고 관찰하는 것은 / 먹을 / 그리고 동물을 / 피할 /

---

might merge into 'a single process' / that sees animals / as having humanlike intentions / that 'can influence and be influenced'. //
'단일 과정'으로 합쳐질 수도 있다 / 동물을 보는 / 인간과 같은 의도를 가진 것으로 / '영향을 미칠 수 있고 영향을 받을 수 있는' //

- anthropologist ⓝ 인류학자
- fascinate ⓥ 마음을 사로잡다
- spill over into ~로 번지다
- rhythmic ⓐ 리듬의, 주기적인
- consciousness ⓝ 의식, 자각
- undergo ⓥ 겪다, 받다
- identify ⓥ 알아보다, 확인하다
- merge ⓥ 합치다, 합병하다
- intention ⓝ 의도, 목적
- region ⓝ 지역, 지방
- inference ⓝ 추론(한 것)
- ritual ⓝ 의식, 의례
- altered ⓐ 바뀐
- shamanistic ⓐ 샤머니즘적인, 주술적인
- transformation ⓝ 변화, 탈바꿈
- observe ⓥ 관찰하다, 목격하다
- humanlike ⓐ 인간 같은, 인간적인
- dawn ⓝ 새벽, (어떤 일의) 시작

동굴 예술을 이해할 때, 인류학자들은 동굴 내부에 계속 그림을 그리는 현존하는 수렵-채집 사회, 특히 San 족에 관심을 두었는데, 그들은 남부 아프리카의 넓은 지역에 걸쳐 공동체를 이루며 산다. San 족을 연구한 인류학자들을 매료시키기 시작했던 것은 사냥하는 동물들에 대한 그들의 상세한 모방이었다. 사냥꾼들은 자신의 사냥감이 어떻게 행동할 수 있을지에 관해 추론하기 위해 어떤 의미에서 동물이 된다. 이것이 의식으로 번진다.

San 족은 주술적인 문화의 일부로 과호흡과 리듬 있는 동작을 사용하여 변환된 의식 상태를 만든다. Lewis-Williams는 무아지경의 마지막 단계에서 '사람들은 때때로 자신이 동물로 변하고 있으며, 두렵게 하거나 의기양양하게 하는 다른 변신을 겪고 있다고 느낀다.'라고 적는다. 인류학자 Kim Hill에게, 먹을 동물과 피해야 할 동물을 알아보고 관찰하는 것은 동물을 '영향을 미칠 수 있고 영향을 받을 수 있는', 인간과 같은 의도를 가진 것으로 보는 '단일 과정'으로 합쳐질 수도 있다.

다음 글의 제목으로 가장 적절한 것은?

① Cave Paintings: The Dawn of Human Creativity
동굴 그림: 인류의 창의성의 시작　　창의성에 대한 언급은 없음
② Early Humans' Communication Through Cave Art
동굴 예술을 통한 초기 인류의 의사소통　　동굴 예술을 통해 초기 인류가 의사소통했다는 것이 아님
③ Hardships of Early Humans Depicted in Cave Art
동굴 예술에 묘사된 초기 인류의 고난　　인류의 고난은 언급되지 않음
④ Shamanistic Culture for Paying Honor to Ancestors
조상에게 경의를 표하는 주술적 문화　　a shamanistic culture로 만든 오답
⑤ Animal Imitation Rituals and Understanding Cave Art
동물 모방 의식과 동굴 예술 이해하기　　동굴 예술을 이해하기 위해 San 족에 관심을 뒀고, San 족의 동물 모방에 매료됨

왜 정답? [정답률 79%]

동굴 예술을 이해하는 데 있어 인류학자들은 여전히 동굴 내부에 그림을 그리는 현존하는 수렵-채집 사회, 특히 San족에 관심을 뒀고, San 족의 상세한 동물 모방이 인류학자들을 매료시켰다고 했다.

이후로 이러한 모방이 의식으로 번진다면서 의식에 대해 구체적으로 부연하는 내용이 이어지므로 제목으로 적절한 것은 ⑤ '동물 모방 의식과 동굴 예술 이해하기'이다.

왜 오답?

① 동굴 그림에 나타난 초기 인류의 창의성에 대한 내용이 아니다.

② 초기 인류가 의사소통을 위해 동굴 예술을 이용했다는 언급은 없다.

③ 동굴 내부에 구체적으로 무엇을 그렸는지에 대한 정확한 설명은 없다.

④ 동물 모방 의식에 대한 부연 설명에 등장한 a shamanistic culture로 만든 오답이다. 조상에게 경의를 표하는 의식에 대한 내용은 없다.

G 17 정답 ② ＊공백 채우기 원리

Melody is one of the primary ways / that our expectations are
관계부사 how를 대신해서 쓰임
controlled / by composers. //
멜로디는 주요한 방법 중 하나이다 / 우리의 기대가 통제되는 / 작곡가들에 의해 //

Music theorists have identified a principle / called gap fill; / in
앞에 주격 관계대명사와 be동사가 생략됨
a sequence of tones, / if a melody makes a large leap, / either up
or down, / the next note should change direction. //
음악 이론가들은 원리를 밝혀냈다 / 공백 채우기라고 불리는 / 일련의 음조에서 / 멜로디가
크게 도약한다면 / 위나 아래로 / 다음 음은 방향을 바꿔야 한다 //

A typical melody includes / a lot of stepwise motion, / that is,
adjacent tones / in the scale. //
전형적인 멜로디는 포함한다 / 많은 단계적 움직임을 / 즉 인접한 음조를 / 음계에서 //

If the melody makes a big leap, / theorists describe a tendency /
for the melody to "want" to return / to the jumping-off point; /
형용사적 용법(a tendency 수식)   형용사적 용법(way 수식)
to want의 의미상 주어
this is another way / to say /   단서1 크게 도약한 멜로디는 출발점으로
                                        돌아가기를 원하는 경향이 있음
멜로디가 크게 도약하면 / 이론가들은 경향을 설명한다 / 멜로디가 돌아가기를 '원하는' /
출발점으로 / 이것은 또 다른 방법이다 / 말하는 /

that our brains expect / that the leap was only temporary, / and
복수 명사(주어, 선행사)
tones / that follow / need to bring us closer and closer / to our
         주격 관계대명사절과 문장의 복수 동사
starting point, or harmonic "home." //
단서2 우리의 뇌는 그 도약이 일시적이며, 이어지는 음조는 우리를 출발점으로 데려다줘야 한다고 기대함
우리의 뇌가 기대한다는 것을 / 그 도약이 일시적이었을 뿐이며 / 음조는 / 뒤따르는 / 우리를
점점 더 가까이 데려다줄 필요가 있다고 / 우리의 출발점, 즉 음악적 '고향'으로 //

In "Over the Rainbow," / the melody begins / with one of the
largest leaps / we've ever experienced / in a lifetime of music
listening: / an octave. //
'Over the Rainbow'에서 / 멜로디는 시작한다 / 가장 큰 도약 중 하나로 / 우리가 지금까지
경험한 / 음악 감상을 한 일생에서 / 옥타브 //

This is a strong schematic violation, / and so the composer
rewards and soothes us / by bringing the melody back toward
home again, /   단서3 크게 도약한 멜로디에 대해 작곡가는 멜로디를
                       고향을 향해 가져옴으로써 우리를 보상하고 달램
이것은 강력한 도식적 위반이고 / 그래서 작곡가는 우리를 보상하고 달랜다 / 멜로디를 고향을
향해 다시 가져옴으로써 /

but not by too much / because he wants to continue / to build
                     wants의 목적어
tension. //   to continue의 목적어
하지만 너무 많이 하지는 않는다 / 그가 계속하기를 원하기 때문에 / 긴장감을 조성하는 것을 //

The third note of this melody / fills the gap. //
이 멜로디의 세 번째 음이 / 그 공백을 채운다 //

- primary ⓐ 주요한   · expectation ⓝ 기대
- composer ⓝ 작곡가   · identify ⓥ 밝혀내다
- a sequence of 일련의   · leap ⓝ 도약   · note ⓝ 음정
- typical ⓐ 전형적인   · stepwise ⓐ 단계적인   · tone ⓝ 음조
- scale ⓝ 음계   · theorist ⓝ 이론가   · tendency ⓝ 경향
- temporary ⓐ 일시적인   · harmonic ⓐ 화성의
- octave ⓝ 옥타브   · schematic ⓐ 도식적인   · violation ⓝ 위반
- soothe ⓥ 달래다   · tension ⓝ 긴장

멜로디는 우리의 기대가 작곡가들에 의해 통제되는 주요한 방법 중 하나이다.
음악 이론가들은 공백 채우기라고 불리는 원리를 밝혀냈다. 일련의 음조에서,
멜로디가 위나 아래로 크게 도약한다면, 다음 음은 방향을 바꿔야 한다.
전형적인 멜로디는 많은 단계적 움직임, 즉, 음계에서 인접한 음조를 포함한다.
멜로디가 크게 도약하면 이론가들은 멜로디가 출발점으로 돌아가기를 '원하는'
경향을 설명한다. 이것은 그 도약이 일시적이었을 뿐이며, 뒤따르는 음조는
우리를 우리의 출발점, 즉 음악적 '고향'으로 점점 더 가까이 데려다줄 필요가
있다고 우리의 뇌가 기대한다는 것을 말하는 또 다른 방법이다. 'Over the
Rainbow'에서, 멜로디는 음악 감상을 한 일생에서 우리가 지금까지 경험한
가장 큰 도약 중 하나인 옥타브로 시작한다. 이것은 강력한 도식적 위반이고,
그래서 작곡가는 멜로디를 고향을 향해 다시 가져옴으로써 우리를 보상하고
달래지만, 계속해서 긴장감을 조성하기를 원하기 때문에 너무 많이 하지는
않는다. 이 멜로디의 세 번째 음이 그 공백을 채운다.

다음 글의 제목으로 가장 적절한 것은?

① How Awesome Repetition in Melody Can Be!
   멜로디의 반복이 얼마나 멋질 수 있는지!   멜로디의 도약에 대한 내용임
② Why a Big Leap Melody Tends to Go Back Home
   크게 도약한 멜로디가 고향으로 돌아가는 경향이 있는 이유   우리 뇌의 기대 때문임을 설명함
③ Lyrics of Songs: Key Controller of Our Emotions
   노래의 가사: 우리의 감정의 핵심적인 통제자   노래 가사에 대한 설명이 아님
④ Should Composers Consider Their Potential Audience?
   작곡가들은 그들의 잠재적인 청중을 고려해야 하는가?   잠재적인 청중에 대한 고려는 언급되지 않음
⑤ Misunderstanding of Composers' Intention with Melody
   작곡가들의 의도된 멜로디에 대한 오해   '오해'를 설명하는 글이 아님

왜 정답? [정답률 75%]

공백 채우기 원리	일련의 음조에서 멜로디가 위나 아래로 크게 도약하면 다음 음은 방향을 바꿔야 함
이유	우리의 뇌는 그 도약이 일시적이었을 뿐이고 뒤따르는 음조는 우리를 출발점(음악적 고향)으로 데려다줄 필요가 있다고 기대함
예시	Over the Rainbow에서 작곡가는 큰 도약 이후에 멜로디를 고향을 향해 다시 가져옴으로써 우리를 보상하고 달램

➡ 멜로디가 크게 도약한 이후 다음 음이 음악적 고향을 향하는 이유에 대해 설명하는
글이다.
　▶ 따라서 제목으로 적절한 것은 ② '크게 도약한 멜로디가 고향으로 돌아가는
　경향이 있는 이유'

왜 오답?

① 멜로디의 반복이 아니라 멜로디의 도약 이후에 이어지는 다음 음의 경향에 대한
글이다.
③ 첫 문장에 등장한 controlled로 만든 오답이다. 노래의 가사에 대한 언급은 없다.
④ 청중의 기대가 원인이라는 내용으로, 잠재적인 청중을 고려해야 한다는 것이
아니다.
⑤ 작곡가들의 멜로디에 대해 청중이 오해한다는 내용은 없다.

G 18 정답 ① ＊침팬지의 자기 자신을 위한 팀워크

Chimpanzees are known / to hunt and eat red colobus
                                    to hunt and eat의 목적어
monkeys. //
침팬지는 알려져 있다 / 붉은콜로부스 원숭이를 사냥하고 먹는 것으로 //

Although a solo male typically initiates a hunt, / others often
(양보)의 부사절 접속사
join in, / and hunting success is much higher / when chimps
                              비교급 강조 부사
hunt as a group / rather than individually. //
                  비교의 두 대상
비록 혼자인 수컷이 일반적으로 사냥을 시작하지만 / 다른 것들이 종종 함께하며 / 사냥
성공률은 훨씬 더 높다 / 침팬지들이 집단으로서 사냥할 때 / 개별적으로보다는 // 둘 중 하나

During the hunt, / chimpanzees adopt different roles: / one male
might flush the monkeys / from their refuge, / while another
blocks the escape route. //   둘 중 나머지 하나
사냥 동안 / 침팬지들은 다른 역할들을 맡는다 / 한 수컷은 원숭이들을 몰아낼지도 모른다 /
그것들의 은신처에서 / 다른 침팬지가 탈출로를 막는 동안 //

Somewhere else, / an ambusher hides, / ready to make his
deadly move. //   앞에 being이 생략됨
어딘가 다른 곳에서는 / 복병이 숨어서 / 자신의 치명적인 동작을 하려고 준비한다 //

Although this sounds a lot like teamwork, / recent work offers /
a simpler interpretation. //
비록 이것이 매우 팀워크처럼 들리지만 / 최근의 연구는 제공한다 / 더 단순한 해석을 //

Chimps are more likely to join others / for hunts / because larger
hunting groups increase / each individual's chance / of catching
a monkey /   단서1 침팬지가 단체로 사냥하는 것은 그것이 원숭이를
               사냥할 각 개체의 가능성을 증가시키기 때문임
침팬지들은 다른 침팬지들에게 합류하기가 더 쉽다 / 사냥을 위해 / 더 큰 사냥 집단이
증가시키기 때문에 / 각 '개체'의 가능성을 / 원숭이 한 마리를 잡을 /

— they aren't interested / in collective goals. //
그들은 관심이 없다 / 집단적인 목표에는 //

The appearance of specialised roles / in the hunt / may also be an illusion: /
전문화된 역할들의 출현은 / 사냥에서의 / 역시 착각일지도 모른다 /
〈장소〉를 나타내는 부사절 접속사
a simpler explanation is / that each chimp places himself / where
주격 보어절 접속사　　　　　단수 취급하는 each
his own chance of catching a monkey is highest, / relative to the
앞에 목적격 관계대명사가 생략됨
positions / the others have already taken. //
더 단순한 설명은 ~이다 / 각 침팬지가 자기 자신을 배치한다는 것 / 원숭이를 잡을 자신의
가능성이 가장 높은 곳에 / 위치와 비교하여 / 다른 침팬지들이 이미 차지한 //
　　　　　　　　　　　　　단수 동사
Collaboration in chimps / seems to emerge / from an 'every
chimp for himself' mentality. // 단서2 침팬지들의 협력은
　　　　　　　　　　　　　　　　　자기 스스로를 위한 행동일 뿐임
침팬지들의 협력은 / 나타나는 것처럼 보인다 / '자기 자신을 위하는 모든 침팬지'라는
사고방식에서 //

- initiate ⓥ 개시하다, 착수시키다　· individually ⓐ𝑑 개별적으로
- adopt ⓥ 취하다, 채택하다　· flush from ~에서 쫓아내다
- block ⓥ 방해하다, 막다　· route ⓝ 길, 경로
- deadly ⓐ 치명적인, 죽음의　· interpretation ⓝ 해석
- collective ⓐ 집단적인　· appearance ⓝ 출현, 나타남
- specialized ⓐ 전문화된, 전문적인　· illusion ⓝ 환상, 착각
- collaboration ⓝ 협력, 합작　· emerge ⓥ 나오다, 생겨나다
- mentality ⓝ (개인·집단의) 사고방식

침팬지는 붉은콜로부스 원숭이를 사냥하고 먹는 것으로 알려져 있다. 비록 혼자인 수컷이 일반적으로 사냥을 시작하지만, 다른 것들이 종종 함께하며, 사냥 성공률은 침팬지들이 개별적으로보다는 집단으로서 사냥할 때 훨씬 더 높다. 사냥 동안 침팬지들은 다른 역할들을 맡는데, 다른 침팬지가 탈출로를 막는 동안 한 수컷(침팬지)은 원숭이들을 그것들의 은신처에서 몰아낼지도 모른다. 어딘가 다른 곳에서는 복병이 숨어서 자신의 치명적인 동작을 하려고 준비한다. 비록 이것이 매우 팀워크처럼 들리지만, 최근의 연구는 더 단순한 해석을 제공한다. 침팬지들은 더 큰 사냥 집단이 각 '개체'의 원숭이가 한 마리를 잡을 가능성을 증가시키기 때문에 사냥을 위해 다른 침팬지들에 합류하기가 더 쉽다. 그들은 집단적인 목표에는 관심이 없다. 사냥에서의 전문화된 역할들의 출현 역시 착각일지도 모르는데, 더 단순한 설명은 각 침팬지가 다른 침팬지들이 이미 차지한 위치와 비교하여 원숭이를 잡을 자신의 가능성이 가장 높은 곳에 자기 자신을 배치한다는 것이다. 침팬지들의 협력은 '자기 자신을 위하는 모든 침팬지'라는 사고방식에서 나타나는 것처럼 보인다.

다음 글의 제목으로 가장 적절한 것은?
① Chimps' Group Hunt: It's All about Myself, Not Ourselves
침팬지의 단체 사냥: 그것은 우리가 아니라 나에 관한 것이다　자기를 위해 단체로 사냥하는 것임
② Obstacles to Chimps in Assigning Roles for Group Hunting
단체 사냥을 위해 역할을 배정하는 데 있어서 침팬지들에게의 장애물　침팬지에게 어려움이 있다는 언급은 없음
③ How One Selfish Chimp Can Ruin a Cooperative Group Hunt
한 마리의 이기적인 침팬지가 협력적인 단체 사냥을 망칠 수 있는 방식　이기적인 이유로 단체 사냥이 일어남
④ Hunting in Concert with Other Chimps Determines Social Status!
다른 침팬지들과 협력하여 사냥하는 것이 사회적 지위를 결정한다!　침팬지의 사회적 지위에 대한 언급은 없음
⑤ Which Are Better Hunters, Cooperative or Competitive Chimps?
누가 더 나은 사냥꾼인가, 협력하는 침팬지인가 유능한 침팬지인가?　두 종류의 침팬지를 대조한 것이 아님

왜 정답? [정답률 75%]
침팬지들은 단체로 협력하여 사냥을 하는데, 팀워크처럼 보이는 이것은 사실 단체 사냥이 원숭이를 사냥할 각 개체의 가능성을 증가시키기 때문에 일어나는 일이라는 내용이다.
마지막 문장에서도 모든 침팬지들이 자기 자신을 위한다는 사고방식에서 침팬지들의 협력이 나타나는 것처럼 보인다고 했으므로 정답은 ① '침팬지의 단체 사냥: 그것은 우리가 아니라 나에 관한 것이다'이다.

왜 오답?
② 한 침팬지가 원숭이들을 은신처에서 몰아내고, 다른 한 침팬지는 탈출로를 막으며, 또 다른 침팬지는 숨어서 치명적인 동작을 준비하는 등의 단체 사냥에 있어서의 역할을 나누는 데 어려움이 있다는 언급은 없다.
③ 이기적인 침팬지가 있으면 단체 사냥이 실패한다는 것이 아니라, 침팬지들이 모두 이기적인 이유로 단체 사냥에 참가한다는 것이다.
④ 단체 사냥에서 맡는 역할에 따라 침팬지의 사회적 지위가 결정된다는 등의 언급은 없다.
⑤ 침팬지가 협력하여 단체로 사냥하는 원인에 대한 내용이지, 협력적인 침팬지와 유능한 침팬지를 대조한 것이 아니다.

G 19 정답 ⑤ ＊과잉 관광의 문제 요소

The concept of overtourism / rests on a particular assumption / about people and places / common in tourism studies and the social sciences in general. //
　　　　　　　　　　　　앞에 주격 관계대명사와 be동사가 생략됨
과잉 관광의 개념은 / 특정한 가정에 기초한다 / 사람과 장소에 관한 / 관광학과 사회 과학
전반에서 흔히 볼 수 있는 // 단서1 과잉 관광에서 사람과 장소는 명확하게 정의되고
　　　　　　　　　　　　　　　　경계가 정해진 것으로 여겨짐
Both are seen / as clearly defined and demarcated. //
둘은 모두 여겨진다 / 명확하게 정의되고 경계가 정해진 것으로 //
People are framed as bounded social actors / either playing the
role of hosts or guests. // either A or B: A와 B 둘 중 하나
사람들은 경계가 확실한 사회적 행위자로 구성된다 / 주인이나 손님의 역할을 하는 //
Places, in a similar way, / are treated as stable containers with clear boundaries. //
장소는 비슷한 방식으로 / 명확한 경계가 있는 안정적인 용기로 취급된다 //
Hence, places can be full of tourists / and thus suffer from overtourism. //
그러므로 장소는 관광객으로 가득 찰 수 있고 / 따라서 과잉 관광으로 고통받을 수 있다 //
　　　　　　　　　　　　　가주어　　　의미상 주어　　진주어
But what does it mean / for a place to be full of people? //
하지만 무엇을 의미하는가 / 어떤 장소가 사람으로 가득 차 있다는 것은 //
Indeed, there are examples of particular attractions / that have
　　　　　　　　　　　　　주격 관계대명사(선행사: particular attractions)
limited capacity / and where there is actually no room for more
　　　　　　　　　　　　　　관계부사
visitors. //
사실, 특정 명소의 예가 있다 / 제한된 수용력을 가지고 있고 / 더 많은 방문객을 수용할
공간이 실제로 없는 //
This is not least the case with some man-made constructions /
such as the Eiffel Tower. // = especially
이것은 특히 일부 인공 건축물의 경우이다 / 에펠탑과 같은 // 단서2 과잉 관광의 피해지로 묘사
　　　　　　　　　　　　　　　　　　　　　　되는 곳들은 문제 요소가 복잡함
However, with places such as cities, regions or even whole
countries / being promoted as destinations / and described as
　　　　　　　　　현재분사의 수동태
victims of overtourism, / things become more complex. //
　　　　　　　　　　　　　promoted와 described 병렬 연결
그러나 도시, 지역 또는 심지어 국가 전체와 같은 장소에서는 / 목적지로 홍보되고 / 과잉
관광의 피해지로 묘사되는 / 상황이 더 복잡해진다 //
　　　　　　　선행사를 포함하는 관계대명사
What is excessive or out of proportion / is highly relative / and
might be more related to other aspects than physical capacity, /
과도하거나 균형이 안 맞는 것은 / 매우 상대적이며 / 물리적 수용력 이외의 다른 측면과 더
관련이 있을 수도 있다 /
such as natural degradation and economic leakages / (not to
mention politics and local power dynamics). //
자연적 저하와 경제적 유출과 같은 / (정치 및 지방 권력 역학은 말할 것도 없이) //
　　　　　　　　　　　　단서3 과잉 관광이라는 개념은 상대적이며, 사람과 장소 등 물리적 수용력 외에도
　　　　　　　　　　　　자연적 저하, 경제적 유출 등의 문제가 복합적으로 작용함

- overtourism ⓝ 과잉 관광(지역 규모에 비해 너무 많은 관광객이 오는 현상)
- rest on ~에 기초하다　· assumption ⓝ 가정
- frame as ~로 규정하다　· bounded ⓐ 경계가 확실한
- boundary ⓝ 경계　· attraction ⓝ 관광 명소
- capacity ⓝ 수용력　· destination ⓝ 목적지　· victim ⓝ 피해자
- out of proportion 균형이 안 맞는　· degradation ⓝ (질적) 저하
- leakage ⓝ 유출　· dynamics ⓝ 역학

과잉 관광의 개념은 관광학과 사회 과학 전반에서 흔히 볼 수 있는 사람과 장소에 관한 특정한 가정에 기초한다. 둘(사람과 장소)은 모두 명확하게 정의되고 경계가 정해진 것으로 여겨진다. 사람들은 주인이나 손님의 역할을 하는 경계가 확실한 사회적 행위자로 구성된다. 장소는 비슷한 방식으로, 명확한 경계가 있는 안정적인 용기로 취급된다. 그러므로 장소는 관광객으로 가득 찰 수 있고, 따라서 과잉 관광으로 고통받을 수 있다. 하지만 어떤 장소가 사람으로 가득 차 있다는 것은 무엇을 의미하는가? 사실, 제한된 수용력을 가지고 있고 더 많은 방문객을 수용할 공간이 실제로 없는 특정 명소의 예가 있다. 이것은 특히 에펠탑과 같은 일부 인공 건축물의 경우이다. 그러나 장소가 목적지로 홍보되고 과잉 관광의 피해지로 묘사되는 도시, 지역 또는 심지어

국가 전체와 같은 장소에서는 상황이 더 복잡해진다. 과도하거나 균형이 안 맞는 것은 매우 상대적이며 자연적 저하와 경제적 유출(정치 및 지방 권력 역학은 말할 것도 없이)과 같은, 물리적 수용력 이외의 다른 측면과 더 관련이 있을 수도 있다.

다음 글의 제목으로 가장 적절한 것은? [3점]

① The Solutions to Overtourism: From Complex to Simple
   과잉 관광의 해결책: 복잡함으로 단순함으로   과잉 관광의 해결책을 설명하는 글이 아님
② What Makes Popular Destinations Attractive to Visitors?
   무엇이 인기 있는 목적지를 방문객에게 매력적으로 만드는가?
   인기 있는 목적지의 매력 요소에 대한 언급은 없었음
③ Are Tourist Attractions Winners or Losers of Overtourism?
   관광 명소는 과잉 관광의 승자가 아니면 패자인가?   관광 명소의 승패를 설명하는 글이 아님
④ The Severity of Overtourism: Much Worse than Imagined
   과잉 관광의 심각성: 상상했던 것보다 훨씬 더 나쁘다   과잉 관광이 심각하다는 내용의 글이 아님
⑤ Overtourism: Not Simply a Matter of People and Places
   과잉 관광: 단순히 사람과 장소의 문제가 아니다
   과잉 관광의 문제 요소는 단순히 사람과 장소뿐만이 아님

왜 정답? [정답률 70%]

통념	• 과잉 관광은 사람과 장소의 개념이 명확하게 정의되고 경계가 정해진 것으로 여겨지기 때문에, 특정 관광지가 관광객으로 가득 차면 과잉 관광으로 고통받는 것으로 여겨짐 • 특히 에펠탑 등 인공 건축물의 경우, 제한된 수용력을 가진 경우가 있음
반박	• 과잉 관광의 피해지로 묘사되는 곳들은 상황이 복잡함 • 과잉이라는 개념은 상대적이며, 자연적 저하, 경제적 유출 등 사람과 장소의 물리적 수용력 외에 다른 측면과도 관련이 있음

▶ 과잉 관광의 문제 요소를 사람과 장소에 국한하지 않아야 한다는 내용을 담은
⑤ '과잉 관광: 단순히 사람과 장소의 문제가 아니다'가 제목으로 적절함

왜 오답?

① 과잉 관광의 해결책을 단순화해야 한다는 내용의 글이 아니다.
② 인기 있는 목적지의 매력 요소에 대한 언급은 없었다.
③ 과잉 관광의 문제 요소를 다룬 글로, 관광 명소의 승패를 설명하는 글이 아니다. 함정
④ 과잉 관광이 심각하다는 내용의 글이 아니다.

 조수근 | 순천향대 의예과 2024년 입학·성남 태원고 졸

나는 이 문제를 '소거법'으로 풀었어! 먼저 지문에 등장한 적도 없는 소재의 선지를 지워보는 거야. 해결책이나 심각한 현상 등이 구체적으로 제시되지는 않았으니 ①과 ④ 정도가 지워질 거야. 그리고 지문의 주제와 관련이 없는 선지를 지우는 거지. 이 문제에서는 공통적으로 관광 명소에 초점을 맞추는 ②과 ③을 지울 수 있어. 글의 내용으로부터 제목을 바로 도출할 수 있으면 좋겠지만, 이 문제처럼 그렇지 못한 경우도 있으니 필요하다면 '소거법'도 적극적으로 활용해보자!

------ 배경 지식 ------

＊소수민족문제

복수민족국가에서 소수민족이 불이익을 받거나 불평등한 처지에 놓여 있는 경우에 발생하는 일련의 문제를 말한다. 국제법상으로는 하나의 국가 안에서 인종, 종교, 언어, 풍습 등을 달리하는 소수민족의 권리를 보호하는 것을 소수자 보호의 원칙으로 중시하고 있다. 제1차 세계대전 후에는 국제연맹의 보장 아래 동유럽을 주축으로 한 유럽 13개국과 튀르키예가 소수민족보호조약을 체결하였고, 제2차 세계대전 후 이 문제는 인권옹호 문제의 일부분으로서 국제연합의 보장하에 있다.

소수민족 보호의 방법에는 여러 종류가 있는데, 단지 일반 국민과 평등한 대우를 한다는 데 그치지 않고, 그 소수민족이 전통적으로 유지하고 있는 종교나 언어, 풍습 등의 존중을 포함한다. 나라에 따라서는 정치상으로도 일정한 자치권을 인정하거나 연방제를 택하기도 한다.

G 20 정답 ① ＊완벽하게 정확한 지식으로 나아가는 과정

단서1 인간의 지식은 과거에도, 현재에도 완벽하게 정확하지 않음
(정상에 도달하지 못했음)

The discovery / that man's knowledge is not, *and never has been,* perfectly accurate / has had a humbling and perhaps a calming effect / upon the soul of modern man. //
주어 동격절 접속사 동사
발견은 / 인간의 지식이 완벽하게 정확하지 않고 결코 완벽하게 정확'했던 적이 없다'는 / 겸허하게 하고 아마도 진정시키는 효과를 가져왔다 / 현대 인간의 영혼에 //

The nineteenth century, / as we have observed, / was the last / to believe / that the world, / as a whole as well as in its parts, / could ever be perfectly known. //
주어 동사 주격 보어 형용사적 용법(the last 수식)
19세기는 / 우리가 목격했듯이 / 마지막이었다 / 믿은 / 세계가 / 그것의 부분들뿐만 아니라 전체로서 / 언제나 완벽하게 알려질 수 있다고 //

동사의 병렬 구조
We realize now / that this is, and always was, impossible. //
우리는 이제 깨닫는다 / 이것이 불가능하며, 언제나 불가능했다는 것을 //

We know within limits, / not absolutely, / even if the limits can usually be adjusted / to satisfy our needs. //
양보의 부사절 접속사
우리는 한계 내에서 안다 / 완전히 아니라 / 비록 그 한계가 보통 조정될 수 있을지라도 / 우리의 필요를 충족시키기 위해 //
단서2 (정상을 알지 못하는) 불확실성으로부터 더 위대한 목표, 달성 가능해 보이는 목표가 나타남

Curiously, / from this new level of uncertainty / even greater goals emerge / and appear to be attainable. //
동사① 동사② 주어
의아스럽게도 / 이 새로운 수준의 불확실성으로부터 / 훨씬 더 위대한 목표가 나타나고 / 달성 가능해 보인다 //

Even if we cannot know the world / with absolute precision, / we can still control it. //
비록 우리가 세계를 알 수 없을지라도 / 절대적인 정확성을 가지고 / 우리는 여전히 그것을 제어할 수 있다 //

Even our inherently incomplete knowledge / seems to work / as powerfully as ever. //
심지어 우리의 본질적으로 불완전한 지식조차도 / 작동하는 것처럼 보인다 / 그 어느 때만큼이나 강력하게 //

In short, / we may never know precisely / how high is the highest mountain, / but we continue to be certain / that we can get to the top nevertheless. //
단서3 가장 높은 산의 정상을 정확히 알지는 못하지만 그곳에 갈 수 있음을 확신함
간단히 말해 / 우리는 결코 정확히 알 수 없을 것이다 / 가장 높은 산이 얼마나 높은지 / 그러나 우리는 계속 확신한다 / 그런데도 우리가 정상에 도달할 수 있다는 것을 //

- accurate ⓐ 정확한
- observe ⓥ 보다, 목격하다
- adjust ⓥ 조정하다
- curiously ⓐⓓ 호기심에서, 이상하게도, 기묘하게도
- attainable ⓐ 달성 가능한
- precision ⓝ 정확, 정밀
- summit ⓝ 정상, 꼭대기
- yet to-v 아직 ~하지 않은
- integrate ⓥ 통합하다
- humble ⓥ 겸허하게 하다
- absolutely ⓐⓓ 완전히, 전적으로
- satisfy ⓥ (필요·욕구 등을) 충족하다[채우다]
- absolute ⓐ 완전한, 완벽한
- inherently ⓐⓓ 본질적으로
- integrate ⓥ 통합하다
- onward ⓐ 앞으로[계속 이어서] 나아가는

인간의 지식이 완벽하게 정확하지 않고 결코 완벽하게 정확'했던 적이 없다'는 발견은 현대 인간의 영혼에 겸허하게 하고 아마도 진정시키는 효과를 가져왔다. 우리가 목격했듯이, 19세기는 세계가 그것의 부분들뿐만 아니라 전체로서, 언제나 완벽하게 알려질 수 있다고 믿은 마지막 시기였다. 우리는 이제 이것이 불가능하며, 언제나 불가능했다는 것을 깨닫는다. 우리는 완전히 아는 것은 아니라 한계 내에서, 비록 그 한계가 보통 우리의 필요를 충족시키기 위해 조정될 수 있을지라도 안다. 의아스럽게도 이 새로운 수준의 불확실성으로부터 훨씬 더 위대한 목표가 나타나고 달성 가능해 보인다. 비록 우리가 세계를 절대적인 정확성을 가지고 알 수 없을지라도, 우리는 여전히 그것을 제어할 수 있다. 심지어 우리의 본질적으로 불완전한 지식조차도 그 어느 때만큼이나 강력하게 작동하는 듯 보인다. 간단히 말해, 우리는 가장 높은 산이 얼마나 높은지 결코 정확하게 알 수 없을 테지만, 우리는 그런데도 우리가 정상에 도달할 수 있다는 것을 계속 확신한다.

왜 정답? [정답률 65%] 비유적 표현을 이용한 제목을 추론해야 함 꿀팁

인간의 지식이 과거에도, 현재에도 완벽하게 정확하지 않다는 첫 문장과 이를 산에 비유하여 가장 높은 산이 얼마나 높은지를 우리가 정확히 알 수 없다고 한 마지막 문장을 통해 완벽한 지식, 즉 정상에 도달하지 못했다는 의미를 추론할 수 있다. 정상에 도달하는 것이 불가능하다는 것을 깨달았지만, 정확히 알지 못하는 불확실성으로부터 나타난 더 위대한 목표를 달성 가능하다고 생각하면서 정상에 도달할 수 있음을 확신한다는 것은 정상, 즉 지식으로 가는 과정을 강조하는 것으로 볼 수 있으므로 제목으로 ① '아직 도달되지 않은 정상: 지식을 향해 나아가는 여정'이 적절하다.

왜 오답?

② 산의 정상은 '완전하게 정확한 지식'을 의미하는 비유적인 표현이다. 그 정상을 넘는 것이 목표라는 내용은 등장하지 않았다.

③ 단편적인 지식들을 모아 완전한 지식을 얻게 된다는 내용이 아니다.

④ uncertainty가 언급된 것으로 만든 오답이다. 불확실성을 극복하는 공동체 의식 등에 대해 설명한 글이 아니다. 주의

⑤ 지식 기반 사회가 양면적인 특성을 지닌다는 등의 내용은 없다.

자이 쌤's Follow Me! -홈페이지에서 제공

G 21 정답 ① ✱노년의 사회 지각

부사절 접속사(양보)
Although cognitive and neuropsychological approaches emphasize / the losses / with age / that might impair social perception, /
　　　　　선행사　　　　　주격 관계대명사
인식적 접근법과 신경심리학적 접근법이 강조하긴 하지만 / 상실을 / 노화에 따른 / 사회 지각을 훼손할지도 모르는

단서 1 노화로 인한 사회 지각에 어떤 이득이나 질적 변화가 있을 수 있음
motivational theories indicate / that there may be / some gains or qualitative changes. //
동기 이론은 보여준다 / 있을 수 있다는 것을 / 어떤 이득이나 질적 변화가 //

Charles and Carstensen review / a considerable body of evidence / indicating / that, as people get older, / they tend /
Charles와 Carstensen은 재검토한다 / 상당한 양의 증거를 / 보여주는 / 사람들은 나이가 들면서 / 그들이 (~하는) 경향이 있다는 것을

to prioritize / close social relationships, / focus more / on achieving emotional well-being, / and attend more / to positive emotional information / while ignoring negative information. //
　병렬 구조(focus, attend 앞에 to가 생략됨)　　　　while they ignore
우선시하는 / 친밀한 사회적 관계를 / 더 주력하는 / 정서적 행복을 성취하는 데 / 그리고 더 주목하는 / 긍정적인 정서적 정보에 / 부정적인 정보는 무시하는 반면에 //

These changing motivational goals / in old age / have implications / for attention to and processing of social cues / from the environment. //
　　　　　　　　　　　　　　　　전치사 to와 of의 목적어
이런 변화하는 동기 부여상의 목표는 / 노년의 / 영향을 미친다 / 사회적 신호에 주목하고 (그것을) 처리하는 것에 / 주변 환경으로부터의 //

　　　　　　주격 보어 역할을 하는 'of+추상 명사'가 문두로 가면서 주어와 동사가 도치됨
Of particular importance / in considering emotional changes / in old age / is the presence / of a positivity bias: /
특히 중요(하다) / 정서적 변화를 고려할 때 / 노년의 / 존재가 ~하다 / 긍정 편향의 //

that is, a tendency / to notice, attend to, and remember / more positive / compared to negative information. //
　　　　　　　　　　　　　　　　　형용사적 용법(a tendency 수식)
즉 경향 / 인지하고, 주목하고, 기억하는 / 더 많은 긍정적 (정보를) / 부정적 정보에 비해 //
　단수 주어
The role of life experience / in social skills / also indicates / that older adults might show gains / in some aspects / of social perception. // **단서 2** 인생 경험을 통해 노인이 사회 지각의 일부 측면에서 이득을 얻을 수도 있음
　단수 동사
인생 경험의 역할이 / 사회적 기술에 관한 / 또한 보여준다 / 노년의 성인이 이득을 얻을 수 있다는 것을 / 일부 측면에서 / 사회 지각의 //

- neuropsychological ⓐ 신경심리학적인
- approach ⓝ 접근법, 처리 방법　　• emphasize ⓥ 강조하다
- loss ⓝ 상실, 분실　　• perception ⓝ 인식, 지각
- motivational ⓐ 동기의, 동기를 주는　　• theory ⓝ 이론
- indicate ⓥ 나타내다, 보이다　　• gain ⓝ 이득, 이점
- qualitative ⓐ 질적인　　• considerable ⓐ 상당한
- body ⓝ 많은 양[모음]　　• evidence ⓝ 증거
- prioritize ⓥ 우선순위를 매기다　　• close ⓐ 친(밀)한, 가까운
- focus on ~에 주력하다　　• achieve ⓥ 성취하다
- emotional ⓐ 감정의　　• attend ⓥ 주의를 기울이다
- ignore ⓥ 무시하다　　• goal ⓝ 목표
- implication ⓝ 영향, 결과, 암시　　• process ⓥ 처리하다
- cue ⓝ 신호　　• environment ⓝ 환경　　• particular ⓐ 특별한
- presence ⓝ 존재(함)　　• bias ⓝ 편향, 편견　　• tendency ⓝ 경향, 성향
- notice ⓥ 의식하다, 주목하다　　• compared to ~와 비교하여
- role ⓝ 역할　　• aspect ⓝ 측면, 양상

인식적 접근법과 신경심리학적 접근법이 사회 지각을 손상시킬지도 모르는 노화에 따른 상실을 강조하긴 하지만, 동기 이론은 어떤 이득이나 질적 변화가 있을 수 있다는 것을 보여준다. Charles와 Carstensen은 사람들은 나이가 들면서 친밀한 사회적 관계를 우선시하고, 정서적 행복을 성취하는 데 더 주력하고, 긍정적인 정서적 정보에 더 주목하는 반면에 부정적인 정보는 무시하는 경향이 있다는 것을 보여주는 상당한 양의 증거를 재검토한다. 노년의 이런 변화하는 동기 부여상의 목표는 주변 환경으로부터의 사회적 신호에 주목하고 그것을 처리하는 것에 영향을 미친다. 노년의 정서적 변화를 고려할 때 특히 중요한 것은 긍정 편향, 즉 부정적 정보에 비해 더 많은 긍정적 정보를 인지하고, 주목하고, 기억하는 경향의 존재이다. 사회적 기술에 관한 인생 경험의 역할 또한 노년의 성인이 사회 지각의 일부 측면에서 이득을 얻을 수 있다는 것을 보여준다.

왜 정답? [정답률 77%]　　although가 이끄는 양보의 부사절은 주절을 강조하는 도구임 꿀팁

인식적 접근법과 신경심리학적 접근법은 사회 지각을 손상시킬지도 모르는 노화에 따른 상실을 강조하지만, 이와 달리 동기 이론은 어떤 이득이 있을 수 있음을 보여준다고 한 첫 문장 이후로 사람들이 나이가 들수록 사회 지각에 있어 부정적인 것보다 긍정적인 것에 주목하는 긍정 편향이 존재한다는 내용이 이어진다. 마지막 문장에서는 인생 경험을 통해 노년의 성인이 사회 지각의 일부 측면에서 이득을 얻을 수도 있다고 했으므로 제목은 ① '노년의 사회 지각: 전부 나쁜 소식은 아니다!'가 적절하다.

왜 오답?

②, ⑤ positive, negative 등의 단어가 언급된 것으로 만든 오답이다. 노화가 진행됨에 따라 부정적인 것보다 긍정적인 것에 주목한다는 이점이 있다는 것이지, 부정적인 것을 떨치라거나 긍정적으로 생각하고 행동해서 노화를 되돌리라는 것이 아니다.

③ 노화에 따른 현상을 설명한 것이지, 노년에 크게 성취한 사람들의 특징을 이야기하는 것이 아니다.

④ 나이를 먹으면 긍정 편향이 생긴다고 했다. 긍정 편향이란 부정적 정보보다는 긍정적 정보를 더 많이 인지하고 기억하는 것으로, 객관적이라고는 할 수 없다.

G 22 정답 ③ *목성의 위성들의 위치

There was once a certain difficulty / with the moons of Jupiter / that is worth remarking on. //
한때 어떤 어려움이 있었다 / 목성의 위성들에는 / 주목할 만한 가치가 있는 //
　　　　　　　　　　　　　　　　　　　　　　계속적 용법의 주격 관계대명사
These satellites were studied very carefully / by Roemer, / who noticed / that the moons sometimes seemed to be ahead of schedule, / and sometimes behind. //
　　　　　　　　　　　　　　　선행사
이 위성들은 매우 면밀히 연구되었는데 / Roemer에 의해 / 그는 알아차렸다 / 위성이 때로는 예정보다 앞서는 것처럼 보였다는 것을 / 때로는 뒤처지고 //

They were *ahead* / when Jupiter was particularly *close* to the earth / and they were *behind* / when Jupiter was *farther* from the earth. // 단서1 목성의 위성들이 때에 따라 앞서거나 뒤처지는 것으로 관찰됨
그것들은 '앞섰다' / 목성이 지구에 특히 '가까울' 때는 / 그리고 그것들은 '뒤처졌다' / 목성이 지구에서 '더 멀' 때는 //

This would have been a very difficult thing / to explain / according to the law of gravitation. //
이것은 매우 어려운 것이었을 것이다 / 설명하기에 / 중력의 법칙에 따라 //

If a law does not work / even in *one place* / where it ought to, / it is just wrong. //
　　　　　　　　　　　　　선행사　　관계부사
법칙이 작용하지 않는다면 / '한 곳'에서라도 / 그것이 그래야 하는 / 그것은 그냥 틀리다 //

But / the reason for this discrepancy / was very simple and beautiful: / 단서2 목성의 위성들이 그렇게 보이는 이유를 설명함
하지만 / 이 불일치의 이유는 / 매우 간단하고 아름다웠다 /

it takes a little while / to *see* the moons of Jupiter / because of the time / it takes light to travel / from Jupiter to the earth. //
선행사(목적격 관계대명사는 생략됨)
약간의 시간이 걸린다 / 목성의 위성들을 '보는' 데 / 시간 때문에 / 빛이 이동하는 데 걸리는 / 목성에서 지구로 //

　　　　　　　　부사절(때)　　　　　　　　주절
When Jupiter is closer to the earth / the time is a little less, / and
　　　　　　　　부사절(때)　　　　　　　주절
when it is farther from the earth, / the time is more. //
목성이 지구에 더 가까울 때는 / 그 시간이 조금 더 짧으며 / 지구에서 더 멀 때는 / 그 시간이 더 길다 //

This is why moons appear / to be, on the average, a little ahead or a little behind, / depending on whether they are closer to or farther / from the earth. //
　　　　　　　　　　　전치사 on의 목적어절을 이끄는 명사절 접속사
이것이 위성들이 보이는 이유이다 / 대체로 조금 앞서거나 조금 뒤처지는 것처럼 / 더 가깝거나 더 먼지에 따라 / 지구로부터 //

- remark ⓝ 주목 · satellite ⓝ 위성
- particularly ⓐⓓ 특히, 특별히 · average ⓐ 평균의, 일반적인, 보통의
- gravitational ⓐ 중력의 · illusion ⓝ 환영 · obstacle ⓝ 장애물
- technology ⓝ 기술

한때 목성의 위성들에는 주목할 만한 가치가 있는 어떤 어려움이 있었다. 이 위성들은 Roemer에 의해 매우 면밀히 연구되었는데, 그는 위성들이 때로는 예정보다 앞서고 때로는 뒤처지는 것처럼 보였다는 것을 알아차렸다. 그것들은 목성이 지구에 특히 '가까울' 때는 '앞섰고' 목성이 지구에서 '더 멀' 때는 '뒤처졌다'. 이것은 중력의 법칙에 따라 설명하기 매우 어려운 것이었을 것이다. 법칙이 작용해야 하는 '한 곳'에서라도 작용하지 않는다면 그것은 그냥 틀린 것이다. 하지만 이 불일치의 이유는 매우 간단하고 아름다웠는데, 그것은 빛이 목성에서 지구로 이동하는 데 걸리는 시간 때문에 목성의 위성들을 '보는' 데 약간의 시간이 걸린다는 것이다. 목성이 지구에 더 가까울 때는 그 시간이 조금 더 짧으며 지구에서 더 멀 때는 그 시간이 더 길다. 이것이 위성들이 지구에 더 가깝거나 더 먼지에 따라 대체로 조금 앞서거나 조금 뒤처지는 것처럼 보이는 이유이다.

다음 글의 제목으로 가장 적절한 것은?
① The Difficulty of Proving the Gravitational Law
중력의 법칙을 증명하는 것의 어려움　　　　the law of gravitation으로 만든 오답
② An Illusion Created by the Shadow of the Moon
달의 그림자에 의해 만들어진 환영　　　　환영에 대한 언급은 없음
③ Why Aren't Jupiter's Moons Observed Where They Should Be?
목성의 위성들은 왜 그것들이 관찰되어야 하는 곳에서 관찰되지 않는가? 빛의 이동 시간 때문이라고 설명함
④ Obstacles in Measuring Light's Speed: Limits of Past Technology
빛의 속도를 측정하는 데 있어 장애물들: 과거 기술의 한계들　빛의 속도를 측정하는 것에 대한 내용이 아님
⑤ Ahead and Behind: Moons Change Their Position by Themselves
앞서고 뒤처지다: 위성들은 스스로 자신의 위치를 바꾼다　　실제로 위치가 바뀌는 것이 아님

왜 정답? [정답률 63%]

의문점: 목성의 위성들이 때에 따라 예정보다 앞서거나 뒤처지는 것처럼 보였음
→ 목성이 지구에 가까울 때는 앞서고, 지구에서 더 멀 때는 뒤처졌음

이 현상의 이유: 빛이 목성에서 지구로 이동하는 데 약간의 시간이 걸리기 때문임
→ 목성이 지구에 더 가까울 때는 그 시간이 더 짧고, 지구에서 더 멀 때는 그 시간이 더 길

▶ 그래서 목성의 위성들이 지구로부터의 거리에 따라 앞서거나 뒤처지는 것처럼 보인다는 내용이다. 따라서 제목은 ③ '목성의 위성들은 왜 그것들이 관찰되어야 하는 곳에서 관찰되지 않는가?'가 적절하다.

왜 오답?

① '중력의 법칙'이 언급되긴 하지만, 그것을 증명하는 것이 어렵다는 내용은 아니다.
② '환영'에 대한 내용은 등장하지 않는다.
④ 빛이 이동하는 데 걸리는 시간 때문에 일어나는 현상을 설명하는 것이지, 빛의 속도 측정에 대한 내용은 아니다.
⑤ 목성의 위성들이 위치를 바꾸는 것이 아니라, 위치가 바뀐 것처럼 보이는 이유를 설명하는 글이다. 주의

G 23 정답 ⑤　　　　　　　　　　　★ 2등급 대비 [정답률 78%]

*독립적으로 작동하는 뇌의 시각 체계

　　　　　복수 주어　　　　　　　　　　　　　　복수 동사
Different parts of the brain's visual system / get information / on a need-to-know basis. //
뇌 시각 시스템의 다양한 부분들은 / 정보를 얻는다 / 꼭 필요한 때 꼭 필요한 것만 알려주는 방식으로 //

　　　　　　　　　　　　　help의 목적어와 목적격 보어　　　부정관사
Cells / that help your hand muscles / reach out to an object /
복수 주어
need to know / the size and location of the object, / but they
복수 동사　　　　　　　　　　　　　　　　　정관사
don't need to know / about color. //
세포들은 / 여러분의 손 근육을 돕는 / 어떤 물체에 닿도록 / 알아야 하지만 / 그 물체의 크기와 위치를 / 그것들은 알 필요는 없다 / 색깔에 대해 //

They need to know a little about shape, / but not in great detail. //
그것들은 모양에 대해 약간 알아야 하지만 / 매우 자세히는 아니다 //

Cells / that help you / recognize people's faces / need to be
복수 주어　　　　　　　　　　　　　　　　　　　　복수 동사
extremely sensitive / to details of shape, / but they can pay less attention / to location. //
세포들은 / 여러분을 돕는 / 사람의 얼굴을 인식하도록 / 극도로 예민해야 하지만 / 모양의 세부 사항에 / 그것들은 신경을 덜 쓸 수 있다 / 위치에는 //

It is natural to assume / that anyone who sees an object /
가주어　　　　　　　진주어　　　　단수 주어
sees everything about it / — the shape, color, location, and
단수 동사
movement. //
추정하는 것은 당연하다 / 어떤 물체를 보는 사람은 누구든 / 그것에 관한 모든 것을 본다고 / 모양, 색깔, 위치, 움직임 //

However, / one part of your brain sees its shape, / another sees color, / another detects location, / and another perceives movement. // 단서 뇌의 부분마다 보는 것이 다름 → 뇌세포의 시각적 인식이 분리되고 독립적임
하지만 / 여러분 뇌의 한 부분은 그것의 모양을 보고 / 다른 한 부분은 색깔을 보며 / 또 다른 부분은 위치를 감지하고 / 또 다른 한 부분은 움직임을 인식한다 //

Consequently, / after localized brain damage, / it is possible /
　　　　　　　진주어　　　전치사　　　명사구　　　가주어
to see certain aspects of an object / and not others. //
따라서 / 국부적 뇌 손상 후 / ~이 가능하다 / 물체의 특정한 측면은 보면서 / 다른 측면은 볼 수 없는 것이 //

　　　　　　　　　　　　　　　　　　가목적어　　　　진목적어
Centuries ago, / people found it difficult to imagine / how someone could see an object / without seeing / what color it is. //
　　　　　　　　　　　　　　　　　동명사 seeing의 목적어(간접의문문)
수 세기 전 / 사람들은 상상하기가 어렵다는 것을 알았다 / 어떻게 누군가가 어떤 물체를 볼 수 있는지를 / 못 보면서 / 그것이 무슨 색깔인지 //

Even today, / you might find it surprising to learn / about people /
가목적어   진목적어
심지어 오늘날에도 / 여러분은 알게 되는 것이 놀랍다고 생각할 수 있다 / 사람들에 대해 /
who see an object / without seeing / where it is, / or see it /
                    동명사 seeing의 목적어절 접속사
without seeing / whether it is moving. //
물체를 보는 / 보지 못하면서 / 그것이 어디에 있는지 / 또는 그것을 보는 / 보지 못하면서 / 그것이 움직이고 있는지 //

- basis ⓝ 근거, 기반
- extremely ⓐⓓ 극도로, 극히
- sensitive ⓐ 세심한, 민감한
- detect ⓥ 감지하다
- perceive ⓥ 감지[인지]하다
- betray ⓥ 배신하다, 등지다
- exemplify ⓥ 전형적인 예가 되다
- perception ⓝ 인식

뇌 시각 시스템의 다양한 부분들은 꼭 필요한 때 꼭 필요한 것만 알려주는 방식으로 정보를 얻는다. 여러분의 손 근육이 어떤 물체에 닿도록 돕는 세포들은 그 물체의 크기와 위치를 알아야 하지만 색깔에 대해 알 필요는 없다. 그것들(그 세포들)은 모양에 대해 약간 알아야 하지만, 매우 자세히는 아니다. 여러분이 사람의 얼굴을 인식하도록 돕는 세포들은 모양의 세부 사항에 극도로 예민해야 하지만, 위치에는 신경을 덜 쓸 수 있다.

어떤 물체를 보는 사람은 누구든 모양, 색깔, 위치, 움직임 등 그것에 관한 모든 것을 본다고 추정하는 것은 당연하다. 하지만, 여러분 뇌의 한 부분은 그것의 모양을 보고, 다른 한 부분은 색깔을 보며, 또 다른 부분은 위치를 감지하고, 또 다른 한 부분은 움직임을 인식한다. 따라서 국부적 뇌 손상 후 물체의 특정한 측면은 보면서 다른 측면은 볼 수 없는 것이 가능하다. 수 세기 전, 사람들은 어떻게 누군가가 그것이 무슨 색깔인지 못 보면서 그 물체를 볼 수 있는지 상상하기가 어렵다는 것을 알았다. 심지어 오늘날에도, 여러분은 물체가 어디에 있는지 보지 못하면서 그것을 보거나, 또는 그것이 움직이고 있는지 보지 못하면서 그것을 보는 사람들에 대해 알게 되면 놀라워할 수 있다.

다음 글의 제목으로 가장 적절한 것은?

① Visual Systems Never Betray Our Trust!
시각 체계는 결코 우리의 신뢰를 저버리지 않는다!   모든 것을 볼 거라는 추정이 틀렸음
② Secret Missions of Color-Sensitive Brain Cells
색에 예민한 뇌세포의 비밀 임무   색깔을 인식하는 뇌세포에 대한 자세한 설명이 아님
③ Blind Spots: What Is Still Unknown About the Brain
맹점: 뇌에 관해 아직 알려지지 않은 것   뇌의 시각 시스템의 특징을 설명하는 글임
④ Why Brain Cells Exemplify Nature's Recovery Process
뇌세포가 자연의 회복 과정의 전형적 예가 되는 이유   뇌세포의 회복 과정은 언급되지 않음
⑤ Separate and Independent: Brain Cells' Visual Perceptions
분리되고 독립적인: 뇌세포의 시각적 인식   각각의 뇌세포가 서로 다른 것을 봄

2등급? 글의 중간에서 However로 시작하는 문장을 통해 주제를 파악하기 쉽다. 하지만 지문에 자주 등장한 단어인 '뇌세포', '시각' 등이 여러 선택지에 공통으로 포함되어 헷갈릴 수 있을 것이다.

| 문제 풀이 순서 |

1st 글의 앞부분에서 중심 화제를 제시했는지 확인하고 글의 내용을 예상한다.

> 뇌 시각 시스템의 다양한 부분들은 꼭 필요한 때 꼭 필요한 것만 알려주는 방식으로 정보를 얻는다.

➡ 뇌 시각 시스템을 언급하면서 그것의 다양한 부분들이 필요한 때에 필요한 정보만 알려준다는 내용이 나온다.
➡ 뇌 시각 시스템의 구체적인 작동 방식과 관련된 내용이 이어질 것이다.

2nd 글을 읽으면서 세부적인 내용들을 파악해서 답을 고른다.

> • 하지만, 여러분 뇌의 한 부분은 그것의 모양을 보고, 다른 한 부분은 색깔을 보며, 또 다른 부분은 위치를 감지하고, 또 다른 한 부분은 움직임을 인식한다. **단서**

➡ 뇌의 부분들이 모양, 색깔, 위치, 움직임 등 각각 다른 정보를 인식한다고 했다. 그 뒤에는 국부적 뇌 손상의 증상과 물체를 단편적으로 인식하는 현상을 언급하는데, 이들은 뇌세포가 독립적으로 기능하기에 가능한 현상들이다.

▶ 따라서 ⑤ '분리되고 독립적인: 뇌세포의 시각적 인식'이 이 글의 제목으로 가장 적절하다.

| 선택지 분석 |

① **Visual Systems Never Betray Our Trust!**
시각 체계는 결코 우리의 신뢰를 저버리지 않는다!
우리는 어떤 물체를 보는 사람은 그 물체에 관한 모든 것을 본다고 추정하지만 사실 뇌의 각각의 부분이 보는 것은 독립적이고 분리되어 있다는 내용이다.

② **Secret Missions of Color-Sensitive Brain Cells**
색에 예민한 뇌세포의 비밀 임무
색깔을 인식하는 뇌세포에 대해서만 설명하는 글이 아니다.

③ **Blind Spots: What Is Still Unknown About the Brain**
맹점: 뇌에 관해 아직 알려지지 않은 것
뇌의 시각 시스템이 어떻게 작동하는지를 알려주는 글이다.

④ **Why Brain Cells Exemplify Nature's Recovery Process**
뇌세포가 자연의 회복 과정의 전형적 예가 되는 이유
뇌세포의 회복 과정을 다루거나 그것이 자연의 회복 과정을 보여주는 예시라고 설명하는 글이 아니다.

⑤ **Separate and Independent: Brain Cells' Visual Perceptions**
분리되고 독립적인: 뇌세포의 시각적 인식
뇌세포마다 시각적 인식이 분리되어 있어 각기 다른 정보를 인식하고, 독립적으로 기능한다고 한다.

권주원 | 서울대 정치외교학부 2023년 입학·서울 배재고 졸

제목은 글의 주제를 갖고 만드는 것이기 때문에 전체 글을 관통하는 하나의 흐름을 잡아 주제를 찾으면 쉽게 풀려. 그리고 이 문제는 첫 문장에서 주제를 제시하고 시작하기 때문에 글을 읽으면서 a need-to-know basis가 의미하는 바만 정확히 파악한다면 쉽게 정답을 찾을 수 있어. 두 번째 문장부터 확인하면, a need-to-know basis는 우리 뇌의 시각 세포가 각자에게 필요한 것만 인지한다는 것을 의미하므로 정답은 ⑤이야!

G 24 정답 ①   ☆ 2등급 대비 [정답률 71%]

＊수리는 기계가 못함

등위접속사 and로 연결된 주어는 원칙적으로 복수형 동사 사용   복수 동사
Mending and restoring objects / often require even more creativity / than original production. //
                                                    비교급 강조 부사
물건을 고치고 복원하는 것은 / 흔히 훨씬 더 많은 창의력을 필요로 한다 / 최초 제작보다 //

The preindustrial blacksmith made things to order / for people in his immediate community; /
                                    make to order: 주문에 따라 만들다
산업화 이전의 대장장이는 주문에 따라 물건을 만들었다 / 그와 가까운 마을의 사람들을 위해 /

customizing the product, / modifying or transforming it /
동명사구 주어   단수 동사
according to the user, / was routine. //
제품을 주문 제작하는 것은 / 그것을 수정하거나 변형하여 / 사용자에게 맞게 / 일상적이었다 //

Customers would bring things back / if something went wrong;
                                    부사절 접속사(조건)
/ repair was thus / an extension of fabrication. //
고객들은 다시 가져오곤 했다 / 뭔가 잘못되면 / 따라서 수리는 ~이었다 / 제작의 연장 //

With industrialization / and eventually with mass production, /
                동명사구 주어
making things became / the province of machine tenders / with limited knowledge. //
동사   주격 보어
산업화로 / 그리고 결국 대량 생산으로 / 물건을 만드는 것은 되었다 / 기계 관리자의 영역이 / 제한된 지식을 지닌 //   **단서1** 제작과 비교하여 수리는 전체와 설계자의 의도에 대한 더 큰 이해가 필요함

But repair continued to require / a larger grasp of design and materials, / an understanding of the whole / and a comprehension of the designer's intentions. //
그러나 수리는 계속해서 필요로 했다 / 설계와 재료에 대한 더 큰 이해를 / 전체에 대한 이해 / 설계자 의도에 대한 이해 //

"Manufacturers all work / by machinery / or by vast subdivision of labour / and not, so to speak, by hand," / an 1896 *Manual of Mending and Repairing* explained. //
                                                    '말하자면, 이를테면'
"제조업자들은 모두 일한다 / 기계로 / 또는 방대한 분업으로 / 말하자면 수작업으로가 아니라"라고 / 1896년의 *Manual of Mending and Repairing*은 설명했다 //

"But all repairing *must* be done / by hand. //
"그러나 모든 수리는 '행해져야 한다' / 손으로 **단서 2** 모든 수리는 여전히 손으로 행해져야 함

We can make every detail / of a watch or of a gun / by machinery, / but the machine cannot mend it / when broken, / much less a clock or a pistol!" //
주어와 동사(it is)가 생략된 부사절 '하물며[더구나]' '~은 아니다'
우리는 모든 세부적인 것을 만들 수 있지만 / 손목시계나 총의 / 기계로 / 기계는 그것을 고칠 수 없으며 / 고장 났을 때 / 시계나 권총은 말할 것도 없다" //

- mend ⓥ 고치다, 수리하다 · restore ⓥ 복원하다, 복구하다
- creativity ⓝ 창의력, 독창성 · original ⓐ 원래의, 최초의
- preindustrial ⓐ 산업화 이전의, 산업 혁명 전의
- blacksmith ⓝ 대장장이
- immediate ⓐ (시간적·공간적으로) 아주 가까운, 직속[직계]의
- customize ⓥ 주문 제작하다 · modify ⓥ (더 알맞도록) 수정[변경]하다
- transform ⓥ (외양·모양을) 변형하다 · routine ⓐ 일상적인, 보통의
- extension ⓝ 연장(선) · fabrication ⓝ 제작, 제조
- industrialization ⓝ 산업화 · mass ⓐ 대량의, 대규모의
- province ⓝ 영역, 분야 · tender ⓝ 관리자, 감시인
- grasp ⓝ (~에 대한) 이해[파악] · comprehension ⓝ 이해
- intention ⓝ 의도, 계획 · manufacturer ⓝ (대규모의) 제조업자[회사]
- subdivision ⓝ 세분, 다시 나눔 · labour ⓝ (육체적인) 노동[작업]
- pistol ⓝ 권총, 회전 탄창이 없는 소형의 총

물건을 고치고 복원하는 것에는 흔히 최초 제작보다 훨씬 더 많은 창의력이 필요하다. 산업화 이전의 대장장이는 가까이에 사는 마을 사람들을 위해 주문에 따라 물건을 만들었고, 사용자에게 맞게 그것을 수정하거나 변형하여 제품을 주문 제작하는 것이 일상적이었다. 고객들은 뭔가 잘못되면 물건을 다시 가져오곤 했고, 따라서 수리는 제작의 연장이었다. 산업화와 결국 대량 생산이 이루어지면서, 물건을 만드는 것은 제한된 지식을 지닌 기계 관리자의 영역이 되었다. 그러나 수리에는 설계와 재료에 대한 더 큰 이해, 즉 전체에 대한 이해와 설계자 의도에 대한 이해가 계속해서 요구되었다. 1896년의 Manual of Mending and Repairing의 설명에 따르면, "제조업자들은 모두 기계나 방대한 분업으로 일하고, 말하자면 수작업으로 일하지는 않는다." "그러나 모든 수리는 손으로 '해야 한다.' 우리는 기계로 손목시계나 총의 모든 세부적인 것을 만들 수 있지만, 고장 났을 때 기계는 그것을 고칠 수 없으며, 시계나 권총은 말할 것도 없다!"

다음 글의 제목으로 가장 적절한 것은?

① Still Left to the Modern Blacksmith: The Art of Repair
현대 대장장이에게 여전히 남겨진 것: 수리의 기술
기계가 시계나 권총의 부품을 만들 수는 있지만 그것을 고치지는 못함
② A Historical Survey of How Repairing Skills Evolved
수리의 기술이 어떻게 발전했는가에 관한 역사적 개괄
수리 기술의 발전 과정을 설명한 것이 아님
③ How to Be a Creative Repairperson: Tips and Ideas
창의적 수리공이 되는 방법: 조언과 아이디어
수리공이 되는 방법을 설명한 것이 아님
④ A Process of Repair: Create, Modify, Transform!
수리의 과정: 만들고, 수정하고, 변형하라!
수리의 구체적인 과정은 등장하지 않음
⑤ Can Industrialization Mend Our Broken Past?
산업화가 우리의 부서진 과거를 고칠 수 있을까?
industrialization, when broken으로 만든 오답

왜 2등급 ? 모든 선택지가 '수리'에 관한 내용이어서 정답을 쉽게 가려내기 힘들었을 것이다. 그러나 마지막에서 두 번째 문장에 주목하면 **단서** 주제를 쉽게 파악할 수 있을 것이다. **발상**

| 문제 풀이 순서 |

1st 선택지와 첫 문장을 통해 핵심 소재를 확인하고 글의 내용을 예상한다.

선택지	거의 모든 선택지에 '수리'와 같은 표현이 등장한다.
첫 문장	물건을 고치고 복원하는 것에는 흔히 최초 제작보다 훨씬 더 많은 창의력이 필요하다.

→ 이 글은 창의력의 관점에서 물건 제작과 물건 수리·복원을 대조하는 내용일 것이다.

→ 첫 문장을 통해 물건의 수리·복원에 많은 창의력이 요구되는 이유가 이어질 것임을 짐작할 수 있다.

2nd 글의 나머지 부분에서 내용을 파악하고 정답을 찾는다.

- 그러나 수리에는 설계와 재료에 대한 더 큰 이해, 즉 전체에 대한 이해와 설계자 의도에 대한 이해가 계속해서 요구되었다. **단서 1**
- '그러나 모든 수리는 손으로 해야 한다.' **단서 2**

→ 수리에는 전체와 설계자의 의도에 대한 이해가 요구되며 모든 수리는 사람의 손으로 이루어져야 한다고 했다. 물건 제작은 제한된 지식을 지닌 기계 관리자의 영역이 되었지만, 여전히 수리는 설계와 재료에 대한 더 큰 이해를 지닌 사람의 손으로 행해져야 한다는 내용이므로 ① '현대 대장장이에게 여전히 남겨진 것: 수리의 기술'이 제목으로 가장 적절하다.

| 선택지 분석 |

①Still Left to the Modern Blacksmith: The Art of Repair
현대 대장장이에게 여전히 남겨진 것: 수리의 기술
물건 수리는 기계가 아니라 여전히 인간의 수작업이 필요하다는 내용이다.

② A Historical Survey of How Repairing Skills Evolved
수리의 기술이 어떻게 발전했는가에 관한 역사적 개괄
과거에 대한 언급은 산업화 이전에는 대장장이가 제작도, 수리도 했다는 내용 뿐이다.
수리의 기술이 과거부터 어떻게 발전해 왔는지를 설명한 것이 아니다.

③ How to Be a Creative Repairperson: Tips and Ideas
창의적 수리공이 되는 방법: 조언과 아이디어
어떻게 하면 창의적인 수리공이 될 수 있는지를 알려주는 내용이 아니다.

④ A Process of Repair: Create, Modify, Transform!
수리의 과정: 만들고, 수정하고, 변형하라!
수리는 여전히 사람이 손으로 해야 한다는 내용으로, 과거에는 대장장이가 물건을 만들고 수정하거나 변형했다고 했지만, 수리의 구체적인 과정은 언급되지 않았다.

⑤ Can Industrialization Mend Our Broken Past?
산업화가 우리의 부서진 과거를 고칠 수 있을까?
preindustrial, industrialization, when broken 등이 언급된 것으로 만든 오답이다. 우리의 과거가 부서졌다거나 산업화가 그것을 고칠 수 있다는 등의 내용은 없다.

G 25 정답 ③   ✪ 1등급 대비 [정답률 70%]

* 시민 참여를 감소시키는 정부 서비스

주어   동사   주격 보어
The world has become / a nation of laws and governance / that has introduced / a system of public administration and management / to keep order. //
세상은 되었다 / 법과 통치의 나라가 / 도입한 / 공공 행정과 관리의 체계를 / 질서를 유지하기 위해 //

With this administrative management system, / urban institutions of government have evolved / to offer increasing levels of services / to their citizenry, /
이런 행정적인 관리 체계로 / 도시의 정부 기관들은 진화했다 / 증대되는 수준의 서비스를 제공하도록 / 자신의 시민에게 /

provided / through a taxation process and/or fee for services / (e.g., police and fire, street maintenance, utilities, waste management, etc.). //
제공되는 / 과세 과정 그리고/또는 서비스 수수료를 통해 / (예를 들면, 치안과 소방, 도로 유지·보수, 공익사업, 쓰레기 관리 등) //

주어   동사   목적어
Frequently this has displaced / citizen involvement. //
빈번하게 이것은 대체했다 / 시민 참여를 **단서 1** 정부가 서비스를 제공하는 것이 시민 참여를 대체함

Money for services / is not a replacement / for citizen responsibility and public participation. //
서비스를 위해 내는 돈은 / 대체물이 아니다 / 시민의 책임과 공적인 참여에 대한 //

Responsibility of the citizen / is slowly being supplanted / by government being the substitute provider. //
수동태의 진행형
시민의 책임이 / 서서히 대체되고 있다 / 대체 제공자가 되는 정부에 의해 //

Consequentially, / there is a philosophical and social change / in
attitude and sense of responsibility / of our urban-based society
/ to become involved. //
단수 동사 / 단수 주어
결과적으로 / 철학적이고 사회적인 변화가 있다 / 책임의 태도와 의식에서 / 도시를 기반으로
하는 우리 사회의 / 참여해야 하는

단서 2 서비스를 제공하는 정부에 의해 적극적인 참가자가
되어야 한다는 시민의 책임감이 줄어들고 있음

The sense of community / and associated responsibility of all
형용사적 용법(responsibility 수식)
citizens / to be active participants / is therefore diminishing. //
공동체 의식과 / 모든 시민의 관련된 책임감은 / 적극적인 참가자가 되어야 한다는 / 그래서 줄
어들고 있다 //

단서 3 정부가 시민의 참여를 대신하는 것은 심각한 영향을 미칠 수 있음

Governmental substitution / for citizen duty and involvement /
can have serious implications. //
정부의 대체는 / 시민의 의무와 참여에 대한 / 심각한 영향을 미칠 수 있다 //

형용사적 용법(the nations 수식)
This impedes / the nations of the world / to be responsive
/ to natural and man-made disasters / as part of global
preparedness. //
이것은 방해한다 / 전 세계의 국가들을 / 반응하는 / 자연재해와 인재에 / 전반적인 준비 태세
의 일부로

- governance ⓝ 통치   • administration ⓝ 행정(업무)
- administrative ⓐ 행정[관리]상의   • urban ⓐ 도시의
- institution ⓝ 기관, 단체   • evolve ⓥ 진화하다
- citizenry ⓝ 시민들   • taxation ⓝ 과세
- maintenance ⓝ 보수, 유지   • utility ⓝ (수도·전기·가스 등의) 공익사업
- frequently ⓐ 자주   • displace ⓥ 대체하다
- involvement ⓝ 관여, 참여   • replacement ⓝ 대체, 교체
- responsibility ⓝ 책임   • substitute ⓝ 대체재[물]
- consequentially ⓐ 결과적으로   • philosophical ⓐ 철학의
- associated ⓐ 관련된   • diminish ⓥ 줄어들다
- substitution ⓝ 대체, 대리   • duty ⓝ 의무
- implication ⓝ 영향, 결과   • responsive ⓐ 반응하는
- sound ⓐ 건전한   • contemporary ⓐ 현대의, 당대의

세상은 질서를 유지하기 위해 공공 행정과 관리의 체계를 도입한 법과 통치의
나라가 되었다. 이런 행정적인 관리 체계로, 도시의 정부 기관들은 자신의 시민
에게, 과세 과정 그리고/또는 (예를 들면, 치안과 소방, 도로 유지·보수, 공익
사업, 쓰레기 관리 등) 서비스 수수료를 통해 제공되는, 증대되는 수준의 서비
스를 제공하도록 진화했다. 빈번하게 이것은 시민 참여를 대체했다. 서비스를
위해 내는 돈은 시민의 책임과 공적인 참여를 대체하는 게 아니다. 대체 제공자
가 되는 정부가 서서히 시민의 책임을 대체하고 있다. 결과적으로, 도시를 기반
으로 하는 우리 사회가 참여해야 하는 책임의 태도와 의식에서 철학적이고 사
회적인 변화가 있다. 공동체 의식과 적극적인 참가자가 되어야 한다는 모든 시
민의 관련된 책임감은 그래서 줄어들고 있다. 시민의 의무와 참여를 정부가 대
신하는 것은 심각한 영향을 미칠 수 있다. 이것은 전반적인 준비 태세의 일부로
자연재해와 인재에 반응하는 전 세계의 국가들을 방해한다.

다음 글의 제목으로 가장 적절한 것은?

① A Sound Citizen Responsibility in a Sound Government
건전한 정부에 건전한 시민의 책임감(이 깃든다) 정부가 건전해야 시민의 책임감이 건전하다는 내용이 아님
② Always Better than Nothing: The Roles of Modern Government
없는 것보다 항상 더 낫다: 현대 정부의 역할   정부의 서비스 제공이 갖는 악영향을 설명함
③Decreased Citizen Involvement: A Cost of Governmental
줄어든 시민 참여: 정부 서비스의 대가
Services 정부의 서비스 제공이 시민 참여를 감소시킴
④ Why Does Global Citizenship Matter in Contemporary Society?
현대 사회에서 세계 시민권은 왜 중요한가?   세계 시민권에 대한 언급은 없음
⑤ How to Maximize Public Benefits of Urban-Based Society
도시를 기반으로 하는 사회의 공적인 혜택을 최대화하는 방법   공적 서비스가 커지는 것을 경계함

왜 1등급? 글 전반적으로 정부, 공공행정, 시민 참여 등의 단어가 등장하여
생소하다고 느낄 수 있다. **단서** '정부 서비스의 증가'와 '시민 참여의 감소'라는 각각의
현상을 파악하고 이들이 어떤 결과를 낳게 되었는지 파악해야 주제를 도출할 수 있을
것이다. **발상**

| 문제 풀이 순서 |

1st 글의 중심 내용을 이해하는 데 중요한 내용이 앞부분에 나오는지 확인한다.

이런 행정적인 관리 체계로, 도시의 정부 기관들은 자신의 시민에게, …
증대되는 수준의 서비스를 제공하도록 진화했다. 빈번하게 이것은 시민
참여를 대체했다. **단서 1**

➡ 앞부분에서 정부는 공공 행정과 관리 체계를 통해 시민에게 더 많은 서비스를
제공하도록 진화했지만, 이것이 시민 참여를 대체했다고 했다.

2nd 글의 나머지 부분에 나오는 관련된 내용을 파악한다.

- 공동체 의식과 적극적인 참가자가 되어야 한다는 모든 시민의 관련된
책임감은 그래서 줄어들고 있다. **단서 2**
- 시민의 의무와 참여를 정부가 대신하는 것은 심각한 영향을 미칠 수 있다.
단서 3

➡ 정부 서비스가 증가하면서 시민 참여를 대체함에 따라, 참가자로서 시민의
책임감이 줄어들었다고 했으며, 이는 심각한 영향을 미칠 수 있다고 했다.
정부 서비스가 증가하면서 시민의 참여가 감소하는 현상에 대해 우려하는
내용이다.

3rd 글의 주제에 알맞은 제목을 고른다.

➡ **2nd** 에서 파악한 글의 내용을 종합하면 이 글의 주제는 '정부 서비스 증가에 따른
시민 참여 감소'이다.
▶ 따라서 이 글의 제목으로 가장 적절한 것은 ③ '줄어든 시민 참여: 정부 서비스의
대가'이다.

| 선택지 분석 |

① **A Sound Citizen Responsibility in a Sound Government**
건전한 정부에 건전한 시민의 책임감 (이 깃든다)
정부가 건전하지 않아서 시민 참여가 줄어든다는 것이 아니다.

② **Always Better than Nothing: The Roles of Modern Government**
없는 것보다 항상 더 낫다: 현대 정부의 역할
오늘날 정부가 서비스를 제공하는 것에 의해 시민의 참여가 줄어들고 있음을 지적하는
글로, 정부의 서비스 제공을 경계하는 글이다.

③**Decreased Citizen Involvement: A Cost of Governmental Services**
줄어든 시민 참여: 정부 서비스의 대가
정부 서비스가 시민의 참여를 대체하면서 시민들의 책임감이 줄어들었다고 했다.

④ **Why Does Global Citizenship Matter in Contemporary Society?**
현대 사회에서 세계 시민권은 왜 중요한가?
the nations of the world, global preparedness가 언급된 것으로 만든
오답이다. 세계 시민권에 대한 언급은 없다.

⑤ **How to Maximize Public Benefits of Urban-Based Society**
도시를 기반으로 하는 사회의 공적인 혜택을 최대화하는 방법
오늘날 정부가 서비스를 제공하는 것에 의해 시민의 참여가 줄어들고 있음을 지적하는
글로, 정부의 서비스 제공을 경계하는 글이다.

G 26 정답 ② ⎯⎯⎯⎯⎯⎯ ✪ 1등급 대비 [정답률 86%]

＊음악 연주에서 변화의 가치

not only A but also B(A뿐만 아니라 B도)로 주어가 연결됨
Not only musicians and psychologists, / but also committed
music enthusiasts and experts / often voice the opinion /
음악가와 심리학자뿐만 아니라 / 열성적인 음악 애호가와 전문가도 / 흔히 의견을 표현한다 /

동격절 접속사
that the beauty of music lies / in an expressive deviation / from
the exactly defined score. // 단서1 음악의 아름다움은 정해진 악보대로
음악의 아름다움은 있다는 / 표현상 벗어나는 데 / 정확히 정해진 악보로부터 / 표현되지 않는 데 있음
복수 주어   동사①   동사②
Concert performances / become interesting and gain in attraction
/ from the fact / that they go far beyond the information / printed
in the score. // 동격절 접속사   단서2 콘서트 공연은 악보에 인쇄된 정보를 훨씬
콘서트 공연은 / 흥미로워지고 매력을 얻는다 / 사실에서 / 그것이 정보를 훨씬 뛰어넘는다는 점에서 흥미로워지고 매력을 얻음
/ 악보에 인쇄된 //
〈주제·관계〉를 나타내는 전치사
In his early studies / on musical performance, / Carl Seashore
discovered / that musicians only rarely play / two equal notes /
in exactly the same way. //
자신의 초기 연구에서 / 음악 연주에 관한 / Carl Seashore는 발견했다 / 음악가는 거의
연주하지 않는다는 것을 / 두 개의 동등한 음을 / 정확히 같은 방식으로 //
Within the same metric structure, / there is a wide potential of
variations / in tempo, volume, tonal quality and intonation. //
같은 미터 구조 내에서 / 광범위한 변화 가능성이 있다 / 박자, 음량, 음질 및 인토네이션에
있어   주어   동사①   동사②
Such variation is based / on the composition / but diverges from
it individually. //
이러한 변화는 기초한다 / 작품에 / 하지만 개별적으로 그것으로부터 갈라진다 //
주어   동사 목적어 목적격 보어
We generally call this 'expressivity'. //
우리는 일반적으로 이것을 '표현성'이라고 부른다 // 단서3 음악가마다 다르게 표현하기
목적어절을 이끄는 의문사   때문에 우리가 흥미를 잃지 않음
This explains / why we do not lose interest / when we hear
〈시간의〉
different artists perform / the same piece of music. // 부사절 접속사
이것은 설명한다 / 왜 우리가 / 흥미를 잃지 않는지를 / 우리가 서로 다른 예술가가 연주하는
것을 들을 때 / 같은 음악을 // 지각동사 hear의 목적격 보어
가주어   to repeat의 의미상 주어
It also explains / why it is worthwhile / for following generations
진주어
to repeat / the same repertoire. // 단서4 음악가마다 다르게 표현하기 때문에 다음
이것은 또한 설명한다 / 왜 ~이 가치 있는지를 / 다음 세대가 반복하는 것이 / 같은 연주 세대가 같은 작품을 반복하는 것이 가치 있음
목록을 //
주어   동사 목적어 목적격 보어
New, inspiring interpretations help us / to expand our
understanding, / which serves / to enrich and animate the music
scene. // 새롭고 영감을 주는 해석은 우리에게 도움을 주는데 / 우리의 이해를 넓히도록 /
이는 도움이 된다 / 음악계를 풍부하게 하고 활기를 불어넣는 데 //

- psychologist ⓝ 심리학자   · commit ⓥ 전념하다, (그릇된 일을) 저지르다
- enthusiast ⓝ 열렬한 지지자   · expressive ⓐ (생각·감정을) 나타내는
- score ⓝ 악보, 점수   · metric ⓐ 미터법의
- potential ⓐ 잠재적인, 가능성이 있는   · variation ⓝ 변화, 변형
- tempo ⓝ (음악의) 박자, 속도   · tonal ⓐ 음색의, 음조의
- composition ⓝ 구성 요소, (음악·미술) 작품
- diverge ⓥ 갈라지다, 나뉘다   · individually ⓐ 개별적으로
- expressivity ⓝ 표현성, 표현의 풍부함   · worthwhile ⓐ 가치[보람] 있는
- repertoire ⓝ 연주[노래] 목록   · interpretation ⓝ 해석, 이해, 설명
- enrich ⓥ 풍요롭게 하다, 강화하다   · animate ⓥ 생기를 불어넣다

음악가와 심리학자뿐만 아니라, 열성적인 음악 애호가와 전문가도 음악의
아름다움은 정확히 정해진 악보로부터 표현상 벗어나는 데 있다는 의견을 흔히
표현한다. 콘서트 공연은 악보에 인쇄된 정보를 훨씬 뛰어넘는다는 사실에서
흥미로워지고 매력을 얻는다. 음악 연주에 관한 자신의 초기 연구에서, Carl
Seashore는 음악가가 정확히 같은 방식으로 두 개의 동등한 음을 연주하는
경우가 거의 없다는 것을 발견했다. 같은 미터 구조 내에서, 박자, 음량, 음질
및 인토네이션에 있어 광범위한 변화 가능성이 있다. 이러한 변화는 작품에
기초하지만, 개별적으로 그것으로부터 갈라진다. 우리는 일반적으로 이것을
'표현성'이라고 부른다. 이것은 서로 다른 예술가가 같은 음악을 연주하는 것을
들을 때 왜 우리가 흥미를 잃지 않는지를 설명한다. 이것은 또한 다음 세대가
같은 연주 목록을 반복하는 것이 왜 가치 있는지를 설명한다. 새롭고 영감을
주는 해석은 우리가 이해를 넓히는 데 도움을 주는데, 이 이해는 음악계를
풍부하게 하고 활기를 불어넣는 데 도움이 된다.

다음 글의 제목으로 가장 적절한 것은?

① How to Build a Successful Career in Music Criticism
음악 비평에서 성공적인 이력을 이루는 방법   음악 비평에 대한 내용이 아님
②Never the Same: The Value of Variation in Music Performance
절대 같지 않음: 음악 연주에서 변화의 가치   같은 작품을 다르게 연주하는 것의 가치를 설명함
③ The Importance of Personal Expression in Music Therapy
음악 요법에서 개인적 표현의 중요성   음악 요법은 언급되지 않음
④ Keep Your Cool: Overcoming Stage Fright When Playing Music
냉정을 유지하라: 음악 연주 시 무대 공포증을 극복하기   무대 공포증을 극복하는 방법을 알려주는 것이 아님
⑤ What's New in the Classical Music Industry?
클래식 음악 산업에서 무엇이 새로운가?   음악 산업이 아니라 음악에 대한 글임

왜 1등급 ? 첫 번째 문장에 주제가 제시되어 있지만, 단서 여러 단서를 종합하여
더 구체적으로 이를 파악해야 풀 수 있었을 것이다. 발상

| 문제 풀이 순서 |

1st 글의 중심 내용을 이해하는 데 중요한 내용이 앞부분에 나오는지 확인한다.

> 음악가와 심리학자뿐만 아니라, 열성적인 음악 애호가와 전문가도
> 음악의 아름다움은 정확히 정해진 악보로부터 표현상 벗어나는 데
> 있다는 의견을 흔히 표현한다. 단서1

➡ 음악 분야의 전문가들이 음악의 아름다움은 정확히 정해진 악보로부터 표현상
벗어나는 데 있다는 의견을 표현한다고 했다.

2nd 글의 나머지 부분에 나오는 관련된 내용을 파악한다.

> · 콘서트 공연은 악보에 인쇄된 정보를 훨씬 뛰어넘는다는 사실에서
>   흥미로워지고 매력을 얻는다. 단서2
> · 이것은 서로 다른 예술가가 같은 음악을 연주하는 것을 들을 때 왜 우리가
>   흥미를 잃지 않는지를 설명한다. 단서3
> · 이것은 또한 다음 세대가 같은 연주 목록을 반복하는 것이 왜 가치 있는지를
>   설명한다. 단서4

➡ 콘서트 공연은 악보에 인쇄된 정보를 뛰어넘는다는 점에서 흥미롭다고 했다. 또한
같은 음악과 연주 목록이더라도 예술가마다, 그리고 세대마다 변화 가능성이
있으므로 흥미롭고 가치 있다고 했다.

▶ 정해진 악보를 벗어나 변화를 주는 음악 연주의 가치에 대한 내용이다.

3rd 글의 주제에 알맞은 제목을 고른다.

➡ 이 글의 주제는 '음악 연주에서 변화의 가치'이므로 글의 제목으로 가장 적절한 것은
② '절대 같지 않음: 음악 연주에서 변화의 가치'이다.

| 선택지 분석 |

① How to Build a Successful Career in Music Criticism
음악 비평에서 성공적인 이력을 이루는 방법
음악 비평가로서 어떻게 하면 성공적인 이력을 이루는지 등을 알려주는 글이 아니다.

②Never the Same: The Value of Variation in Music Performance
절대 같지 않음: 음악 연주에서 변화의 가치
음악의 아름다움은 정해진 악보대로 연주하는 것이 아니라 변화하는 연주에 있다고
했다.

③ The Importance of Personal Expression in Music Therapy
음악 요법에서 개인적 표현의 중요성
연주에 있어 개인적 표현이 중요하다는 내용인 것은 맞지만, 그것이 음악 요법에 있어
중요하다는 글이 아니다.

④ Keep Your Cool: Overcoming Stage Fright When Playing Music
냉정을 유지하라: 음악 연주 시 무대 공포증을 극복하기
음악 연주에 관한 글인 것은 맞지만, 음악을 연주할 때 냉정을 유지함으로써 무대
공포증을 극복할 수 있다는 내용이 아니다.

⑤ What's New in the Classical Music Industry?
클래식 음악 산업에서 무엇이 새로운가?
following generations 등이 언급된 것으로 클래식 음악을 연상할 수는 있지만,
클래식 음악 산업에 대해 이야기하는 글이 아니다.

G 어휘 Review 정답

문제편 p. 124

01 악보, 점수	11 flush from	21 established
02 저장하다	12 in terms of	22 currency
03 보유하다	13 spill over into	23 tension
04 논란의 여지가 있는	14 focus on	24 accurate
05 굳은	15 back around	25 absence
06 implication	16 enormous	26 significance
07 volume	17 inherently	27 domain
08 apparent	18 response	28 analyzing
09 substitution	19 various	29 diverges
10 improvised	20 agents	30 Artificial

H 도표의 이해

문제편 p. 125~139

H 01 정답 ⑤ * 유럽 상위 4개국의 재생에너지 발전 용량

The graph above shows / the top four European countries / with the most renewable energy generation capacity / in 2011 and in 2020. //

위의 그래프는 보여 준다 / 유럽의 상위 4개국을 / 가장 많은 재생에너지 발전 용량을 가진 / 2011년과 2020년에 //

① Each / of the four countries in the graph / had a higher capacity / to generate renewable energy / in 2020 / than its respective capacity / in 2011. // 4개국 모두 2020년의 그래프가 더 높음

각각은 / 그래프에 있는 4개국의 / 더 높은 용량을 가졌다 / 재생에너지를 발전하는 / 2020년에 / 그것의 각각의 용량보다 / 2011년에 //

② Germany's capacity to generate renewable energy / in 2011 / reached more than 50.0 gigawatts, / which was also the case / in 2020. // 독일: 2011년에 67.4, 2020년에 131.7로 두 해 모두 50이 넘음 계속적 용법의 주격 관계대명사

독일의 재생에너지 발전 용량은 / 2011년에 / 50.0기가와트가 넘는 수준에 달했으며 / 이는 마찬가지였다 / 2020년에도 //

③ Among the countries above, / Spain ranked in second place / in terms of renewable energy generation capacity / in 2011 / and remained in second place / in 2020. // 스페인: 2011년에도, 2020년에도 2위임

상기 국가 중 / 스페인은 2위에 있었고 / 재생에너지 발전 용량 면에서 / 2011년에 / 2위를 유지했다 / 2020년에도 //

④ The renewable energy generation capacity of Italy / in 2020 / was lower / than that of Spain / in the same year. // 2020년: 이탈리아는 55.3, 스페인은 59.1

이탈리아의 재생에너지 발전 용량은 / 2020년에 / 더 낮았다 / 스페인의 그것보다 / 같은 해에 //

⑤ The renewable energy generation capacity of France / was higher / than that of Italy / in both 2011 and 2020(→ 2020). // 단서 2011년에는 이탈리아가 더 높았음

프랑스의 재생에너지 발전 용량은 / 더 높았다 / 이탈리아의 그것보다 / 2011년과 2020년 모두(→ 2020년에) //

• renewable ⓐ 재생할 수 있는   • generation ⓝ (전기ㆍ열 등의) 발생
• capacity ⓝ 능력, 용량   • respective ⓐ 각각의

위의 그래프는 2011년과 2020년에 가장 많은 재생에너지 발전 용량을 가진 유럽의 상위 4개국을 보여 준다. ① 그래프에 있는 4개국은 각각 2020년 재생에너지 발전 용량이 각각의 2011년 용량보다 더 높았다. ② 독일의 2011년 재생에너지 발전 용량은 50.0기가와트가 넘는 수준에 달했으며, 이는 2020년에도 마찬가지였다. ③ 상기 국가 중, 스페인은 2011년 재생에너지 발전 용량 면에서 2위에 있었고, 2020년에도 2위를 유지했다. ④ 2020년 이탈리아의 재생에너지 발전 용량은 같은 해 스페인의 용량보다 더 낮았다. ⑤ 프랑스의 재생에너지 발전 용량은 2011년과 2020년 모두(→ 2020년에) 이탈리아의 용량보다 더 높았다.

다음 도표의 내용과 일치하지 않는 것은?

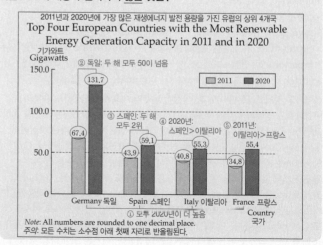

2011년과 2020년에 가장 많은 재생에너지 발전 용량을 가진 유럽의 상위 4개국
Top Four European Countries with the Most Renewable Energy Generation Capacity in 2011 and in 2020

Note: All numbers are rounded to one decimal place.
주의: 모든 수치는 소수점 아래 첫째 자리로 반올림된다.

주제를 먼저 찾고 제목으로 표현해보자!

오왜 정답? [정답률 96%]

프랑스와 이탈리아를 비교하면, 2011년에는 이탈리아가 40.8기가와트로 34.8기가와트인 프랑스보다 더 높으므로, 2011년과 2020년 모두 프랑스의 재생에너지 발전 용량이 이탈리아의 재생에너지 발전 용량보다 더 높았다고 한 ⑤은 도표와 일치하지 않는다.

오왜 오답?

① 제시된 4개국 모두 2020년의 그래프가 2011년의 그래프보다 더 길다.
② 독일의 재생에너지 발전 용량은 2011년에 67.4기가와트, 2020년에 131.7기가와트로 두 해 모두 50기가와트가 넘는다.
③ 스페인은 2011년과 2020년 모두 2위를 기록했다.
④ 2020년에 이탈리아는 55.3기가와트, 스페인은 59.1기가와트로, 이탈리아의 재생에너지 발전 용량이 더 낮았다.

H 02 정답 ③ ＊거주민 특허 출원 통계 ─────

The above tables show / the resident patent applications per million population / for the top 6 origins / in 2009 and in 2019. //
위의 표들은 보여준다 / 인구 100만 명당 거주민 특허 출원을 / 상위 6개 출처에 대한 / 2009년과 2019년에 //

① The Republic of Korea, Japan, and Switzerland, / the top three origins in 2009, / maintained their rankings in 2019. //
대한민국과 일본, 스위스는 / 2009년에 상위 3개 출처였던 / 2019년에도 자신들의 순위를 유지했다
└2009년과 2019년 모두 1위는 한국, 2위는 일본, 3위는 스위스

② Germany, / which sat fourth on the 2009 list / with 891 resident patent applications per million population, /
독일: 2009년 4위
독일은 / 2009년 명단에서 4위를 차지했던 / 인구 100만 명당 891건의 거주민 특허 출원으로 /
fell to fifth place on the 2019 list / with 884 resident patent applications per million population. // 독일: 2019년 884로 5위
2019년 명단에서 5위로 떨어졌다 / 인구 100만 명당 884건의 거주민 특허 출원으로 //

③ The U.S. fell / from fifth place on the 2009 list / to sixth place on the 2019 list, /
〔단서〕 미국: 2009년 733으로 5위, 2019년 869로 6위 → 건수는 증가함
미국은 떨어졌는데 / 2009년 명단에서 5위였다가 / 2019년 명단에서 6위로 /
showing a decrease(→ an increase) / in the number of resident patent applications per million population. //
감소(→ 증가)를 보였다 / 인구 100만 명당 거주민 특허 출원 건수에서 //

④ Among the top 6 origins / which made the list in 2009, / Finland was the only origin / which did not make it again in 2019. // 2009년에 6위였던 핀란드가 2019년에는 순위에 없음
상위 6개 출처들 중에서 / 2009년에 명단에 들었던 / 핀란드가 유일한 출처였다 / 2019년에 다시 순위에 들지 못한 //

⑤ On the other hand, / China, / which did not make the list of the top 6 origins / in 2009, / sat fourth on the 2019 list / with 890 resident patent applications per million population. //
주어 2009년에는 중국이 없었는데 2019년에는 중국이 890으로 4위
반면에 / 중국은 / 상위 6개 출처 명단에 오르지 못한 / 2009년에 / 2019년 명단에서 4위를 차지했다 / 인구 100만 명당 890건의 거주민 특허 출원 건수로 //

- **resident** ⓝ 거주자, 주민 · **patent** ⓝ 특허(권)
- **application** ⓝ 신청(서) · **population** ⓝ 인구
- **origin** ⓝ (사람의) 출신, 기원 · **maintain** ⓥ 유지하다

위의 표들은 2009년과 2019년에 상위 6개 출처에 대한 인구 100만 명당 거주민 특허 출원을 보여준다. ① 2009년에 상위 3개 출처였던 대한민국과 일본, 스위스는 2019년에도 자신들의 순위를 유지했다. ② 인구 100만 명당 891건의 거주민 특허 출원으로 2009년 명단에서 4위를 차지했던 독일은 인구 100만 명당 884건의 거주민 특허 출원으로 2019년 명단에서 5위로 떨어졌다. ③ 미국은 2009년 명단에서 5위였다가 2019년 명단에서 6위로 떨어졌는데, 인구 100만 명당 거주민 특허 출원 건수에서 감소(→ 증가)를 보여 주었다. ④ 2009년에 명단에 들었던 상위 6개 출처들 중에서, 핀란드가 2019년에 다시 순위에 들지 못한 유일한 출처였다. ⑤ 반면에, 2009년에 상위 6개 출처 명단에 오르지 못한 중국은 인구 100만 명당 거주민 특허 출원 건수가 890건으로 2019년 명단에서 4위를 차지했다.

다음 표의 내용과 일치하지 않는 것은?

Resident Patent Applications per Million Population for the Top 6 Origins, in 2009 and in 2019
2009년과 2019년에 상위 6개 출처에 대한 인구 100만 명당 거주민 특허 출원

2009 인구 100만 명당 거주민 특허 출원			**2019** 인구 100만 명당 거주민 특허 출원		
Rank 순위	Origin 출처	Resident patent applications per million population	Rank 순위	Origin 출처	Resident patent applications per million population
1	Republic of Korea	2,582	1	Republic of Korea	3,319
2	Japan	2,306	2	Japan	1,943
3	Switzerland	975	3	Switzerland	1,122
4	Germany	891	4	China	890
5	U.S.	733	5	Germany	884 순위는 떨어졌지만
6	Finland	609	6	U.S.	869 건수는 증가함

Note: The top 6 origins were included if they had a population greater than 5 million and if they had more than 100 resident patent applications.
주의: 상위 여섯 개 출처는 5백만 명보다 더 큰 인구와 100건보다 많은 거주민 특허 출원이 있는 경우에 포함되었다.

오왜 정답? [정답률 93%] 〔함정〕

미국이 2009년에 5위였다가 2019년에 6위로 떨어진 것은 맞지만, 거주민 특허 출원 건수는 733건에서 869건으로 증가했으므로 특허 출원 건수에서 감소를 보였다고 설명한 ③은 표와 일치하지 않는다.

오왜 오답?

① 2009년과 2019년 모두 1위는 한국, 2위는 일본, 3위는 스위스이다.
② 독일은 2009년에 891건으로 4위였다가 2019년에 884건으로 5위로 떨어졌다.
④, ⑤ 핀란드는 2009년에 6위였는데 2019년에는 순위에 들지 못했다. 반대로 2009년에 순위에 들지 못했던 중국이 2019년에 890건으로 4위를 차지했다.

H 03 정답 ④ ＊미국 영화 제작 현장에 고용된 역할별 여성 비율 ─

과거분사(women 수식)
The graph above shows / the percentages of women / employed behind the scenes / on the top 100 U.S. films / by role / in 2020, 2021, and 2022. //
위 그래프는 보여 준다 / 여성의 비율을 / 제작 현장에 고용된 / 미국 상위 100개 영화의 / 역할별로 / 2020년, 2021년, 그리고 2022년에 //

① For each of the three years, / the percentage of women employed as producers on the top 100 U.S. films / was the highest / as compared with the percentages of each of the other three roles. // '제작자' 비율은 2020년, 2021년, 2022년 각각에서 모두 네 역할 중 가장 높음
~와 비교하여
세 개 연도 각각에서 / 상위 100개 미국 영화의 제작자로 고용된 여성의 비율이 / 가장 높았다 / 다른 세 가지 역할 각각의 비율과 비교하여

과거분사(women 수식)
② The percentage of women employed as directors / on the top 100 U.S. films / in 2021 / was lower than in 2020 / but higher than in 2022. // '감독' 비율은 2021년에 12퍼센트로, 2020년의 16퍼센트보다 낮고, 2022년의 11퍼센트보다 높음
감독으로 고용된 여성의 비율은 / 상위 100개 미국 영화에서 / 2021년에 / 2020년보다는 더 낮았지만 / 2022년보다는 더 높았다 // '작가' 비율은 2020년 12퍼센트에서 2021년 16퍼센트로 4퍼센트포인트, 이후 2022년 17퍼센트로 1퍼센트포인트 증가함

③ The percentage of women employed as writers / on the top 100 U.S. films / increased by 4 percentage points / from 2020 to 2021 / and by 1 percentage point / from 2021 to 2022. //
과거분사(women 수식)
작가로 고용된 여성의 비율은 / 상위 100개 미국 영화에서 / 4퍼센트 포인트가 증가했고 / 2020년에서 2021년까지는 / 1퍼센트 포인트가 증가했다 / 2021년에서 2022년까지는

④ The percentage of women employed as editors / on the top 100 U.S. films / was less(→ more) than 20% / in each of the three years. // 〔단서〕 '편집자' 비율은 2021년에 21퍼센트로 20퍼센트보다 높음
편집자로 고용된 여성의 비율은 / 상위 100개 미국 영화에서 / 각각 20퍼센트보다 더 낮았다 (→ 더 높았다) / 세 개 연도에서 //

⑤ In 2022, / the percentage of women employed as producers / on the top 100 U.S. films / was the same as that in 2020. //

'제작자' 비율은 2022년과 2020년 모두 28퍼센트로 같음
= the percentage of women employed as producers

2022년에 / 제작자로 고용된 여성의 비율은 / 상위 100개 미국 영화에서 / 2020년의 비율과 같았다 //

• employ ⓥ 고용하다　• director ⓝ 감독　• writer ⓝ 작가
• editor ⓝ 편집자　• producer ⓝ 제작자

위 그래프는 2020년, 2021년, 그리고 2022년에 미국 상위 100개 영화의 제작 현장에 고용된 여성의 비율을 역할별로 보여 준다. ① 세 개 연도 각각에서, 상위 100개 미국 영화의 제작자로 고용된 여성의 비율이 다른 세 가지 역할 각각의 비율과 비교하여 가장 높았다. ② 2021년에 상위 100개 미국 영화에서 감독으로 고용된 여성의 비율은, 2020년보다는 더 낮았지만 2022년보다는 더 높았다. ③ 상위 100개 미국 영화에서 작가로 고용된 여성의 비율은 2020년에서 2021년까지는 4퍼센트 포인트가 증가했고, 2021년에서 2022년까지는 1퍼센트 포인트가 증가했다. ④ 상위 100개 미국 영화에서 편집자로 고용된 여성의 비율은 세 개 연도에서 각각 20퍼센트보다 더 낮았다(→ 더 높았다). ⑤ 2022년에 상위 100개 미국 영화에서 제작자로 고용된 여성의 비율은 2020년의 비율과 같았다.

다음 도표의 내용과 일치하지 <u>않는</u> 것은?

제작 현장에 고용된 여성의 비율
Percentages of Women Employed Behind the Scenes on Top 100 U.S. Films by Role in 2020, 2021, and 2022
미국 상위 100개 영화의 2020년, 2021년, 2022년 역할별로

> **왜** 정답? [정답률 96%]

④ '편집자' 비율은 세 개 연도에서 모두 20퍼센트보다 낮았다고 했으나, 2020년과 2022년에는 18퍼센트로 20퍼센트보다 낮았던 반면, 2021년에 21퍼센트로 20퍼센트보다 높다. 따라서 세 개 연도 모두 20퍼센트보다 낮았다는 ④은 도표의 내용과 일치하지 않는다.

> **왜** 오답?

① '제작자' 비율은 2020년, 2021년, 2022년 각각에서 모두 네 역할 중 가장 높아서 가장 그래프가 길다.
② '감독' 비율은 2021년에 12퍼센트로, 2020년의 16퍼센트보다 낮고, 2022년의 11퍼센트보다 높다.
③ '작가' 비율은 2020년 12퍼센트에서 2021년 16퍼센트로 4퍼센트포인트, 이후 2022년 17퍼센트로 1퍼센트포인트 증가했다.
⑤ '제작자' 비율은 2022년과 2020년 모두 28퍼센트로 같다.

백승준 | 2025 수능 응시 · 광주 광주숭원고 졸

도표 문제는 특정 정보와 연결된 구체적인 수치를 바탕으로 선택지의 정답 여부를 판단해야 하므로 1 percentage point, 20%와 같은 수치나, less, same, higher, increased와 같은 단어들에 주목하여 빠르게 도표와 비교하는 것이 중요해. 또 The percentage of women employed와 같이 도표의 주제가 반복되는 경우가 많으니 이는 무시하고 Director, Writer와 같은 도표의 변인에 집중하여 읽는다면 빠르게 정답을 찾아낼 수 있을 거야.

H 04 정답 ⑤　＊4개국의 가상 현실과 증강 현실에 친숙한 응답자 비율

The graph above shows / the percentages of respondents / who were familiar with the concept of virtual reality (VR) /

주격 관계대명사
위 그래프는 보여준다 / 응답자 비율을 / 가상 현실(VR)의 개념에 친숙한 /

and those who were familiar with the concept of augmented reality (AR) / in four countries in 2022. //
~하는 사람들
그리고 증강 현실(AR)의 개념에 친숙한 응답자 비율을 / 2022년에 4개국에서 //

핵심 주어
① For each country, / the percentage of respondents familiar with VR / was greater / than the percentage of respondents familiar with AR. //
각 국가별로 VR에 친숙한 응답자 비율이 AR에 친숙한 응답자 비율보다 높음
각 국가별로 / VR에 친숙한 응답자 비율이 / 더 높았다 / AR에 친숙한 응답자 비율보다 //

핵심 주어
② The country / with the highest percentage of respondents familiar with AR / was South Korea. //
AR에 친숙한 응답자 비율이 가장 높은 국가는 70퍼센트로 한국임
국가는 / AR에 친숙한 응답자 비율이 가장 높은 / 한국이었다 //

③ The country with the largest gap / between the percentage of respondents familiar with VR / and that of respondents familiar with AR / was Canada. //
= percentage
VR에 친숙한 응답자와 AR에 친숙한 응답자의 격차는 캐나다가 31퍼센트로 가장 큼
격차가 가장 큰 국가는 / VR에 친숙한 응답자 비율과 / AR에 친숙한 응답자 비율의 / 캐나다였다 //

④ In Japan, / the percentage of respondents familiar with VR / was greater / than 60%. //
일본은 VR에 친숙한 응답자 비율이 67퍼센트로 60퍼센트보다 높음
일본에서는 / VR에 친숙한 응답자 비율이 / 더 높았다 / 60퍼센트보다 //

⑤ The percentage of respondents familiar with VR / and that of respondents familiar with AR / were lower in Switzerland / than in Japan, / respectively. (→ The percentage of respondents familiar with VR was lower in Switzerland than in Japan, but that of respondents familiar with AR was not.) //
VR에 친숙한 응답자 비율과 / AR에 친숙한 응답자 비율은 / 스위스에서 더 낮았다 / 일본보다 / 각각 단서 스위스의 AR에 친숙한 응답자 비율(46퍼센트)은 일본(43퍼센트)보다 높음

• respondent ⓝ 응답자　• familiar with ~에 친숙한
• concept ⓝ 개념　• respectively ⓐⓓ 각각

위 그래프는 2022년 4개국에서 가상 현실(VR)의 개념에 친숙한 응답자 비율과 증강 현실(AR)의 개념에 친숙한 응답자 비율을 보여준다. ① 각 국가별로 VR에 친숙한 응답자 비율이 AR에 친숙한 응답자 비율보다 더 높았다. ② AR에 친숙한 응답자 비율이 가장 높은 국가는 한국이었다. ③ VR에 친숙한 응답자 비율과 AR에 친숙한 응답자 비율의 격차가 가장 큰 국가는 캐나다였다. ④ 일본에서는 VR에 친숙한 응답자 비율이 60퍼센트를 넘었다. ⑤ VR에 친숙한 응답자 비율과 AR에 친숙한 응답자 비율은 각각 일본보다 스위스에서 더 낮았다. (→ 스위스의 VR에 친숙한 응답자 비율은 일본보다 낮았지만, AR에 친숙한 응답자 비율은 그렇지 않았다.)

다음 도표의 내용과 일치하지 <u>않는</u> 것은?

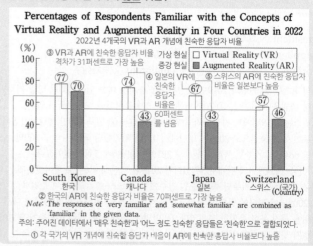

Percentages of Respondents Familiar with the Concepts of Virtual Reality and Augmented Reality in Four Countries in 2022
2022년 4개국의 VR과 AR 개념에 친숙한 응답자 비율

Note: The responses of "very familiar" and "somewhat familiar" are combined as "familiar" in the given data.
주의: 주어진 데이터에서 '매우 친숙한'과 '어느 정도 친숙한' 응답들은 '친숙한'으로 결합되었다.

> **왜 정답?** [정답률 95%]

⑤ 스위스의 VR에 친숙한 응답자 비율은 57퍼센트로 일본의 비율 67퍼센트보다
낮은 것이 맞지만, 스위스의 AR에 친숙한 응답자 비율은 46퍼센트로 일본의 비율
43퍼센트보다 높다. 따라서 스위스의 VR에 친숙한 응답자 비율과 AR에 친숙한
응답자 비율이 모두 일본보다 낮다고 하는 것은 적절하지 않다.

> **왜 오답?**

① 각 국가별로 VR에 친숙한 응답자 비율이 AR에 친숙한 응답자 비율보다 높다.
② 한국의 AR에 친숙한 응답자 비율은 70퍼센트로 가장 높다.
③ 캐나다의 VR에 친숙한 응답자 비율은 74퍼센트, AR에 친숙한 응답자 비율은
43퍼센트로 그 격차가 31퍼센트포인트로 가장 높다.
④ 일본의 VR에 친숙한 응답자 비율은 67퍼센트로 60퍼센트를 넘는다.

H 05 정답 ③ ＊머신 러닝 기능을 갖춘 스마트 앱에 대한 인식과 사용 현황

The above graph shows awareness and usage / of smartphone
applications featuring machine learning in 2017. //
위 그래프는 인식과 사용 현황을 보여준다 / 2017년에 머신 러닝 기능을 갖춘 스마트폰 앱에
대한 //

① In each of the five surveyed applications, / the percentage of
respondents demonstrating awareness / was higher than that of
＝the percentage
respondents demonstrating usage. // 모든 앱에서 '인지' 항목의 비율이 '사용'
항목의 비율보다 높음
조사된 다섯 개의 앱 각각에 대해 / 인지하고 있는 응답자의 비율이 / 사용하고 있다는
응답자의 비율보다 높았다 //
┌ 텍스트 예측이 '인지' 항목과 '사용' 항목 둘 다에서
│ 가장 높은 응답자 비율을 기록함
② Predictive text had the highest percentages of respondents /
in both awareness and usage, / among the five applications. //
텍스트 예측이 응답자의 비율이 가장 높았다 / 인지와 사용 모두에서 / 다섯 개의 앱 중에서 //

③ The percentage of respondents displaying awareness of
voice search / was(→ was not) more than four times that of
＝voice search **[단서]** 음성 검색의 '인지' 비율은 31퍼센트로, '사용' 비율인
respondents using it. 9퍼센트의 네 배 이상 높지 않음
음성 검색을 인지하고 있다는 응답자의 비율이 / 사용한다는 응답자의 비율보다 네 배 이상
높았다(→ 높지 않았다) //
음성 텍스트 변환의 '인지' 비율은 25퍼센트로 이메일 분류 '인지' 비율인 23퍼센트보다 높고,
반대로 음성 텍스트 변환의 '사용' 비율은 7퍼센트로 이메일 분류의 '사용' 비율인 12퍼센트보다 낮음
④ Voice-to-text showed a higher percentage of the respondents
reporting awareness of it / than email classification, / while this
was not the case in their usage. //
음성 텍스트 변환은 인지하고 있다는 응답자의 비율은 높았지만 / 이메일 분류보다 / 사용하고
있다는 응답자의 비율에서는 그렇지 않았다 //

⑤ The percentage of respondents showing usage of automated
photo classification / was less than half of the percentage of
those showing awareness of it. // 자동 사진 분류의 '사용' 비율은 9퍼센트로,
'인지' 비율인 20퍼센트의 절반에 못 미침
자동 사진 분류에 대한 사용 비율은 / 인지 비율의 절반에도 미치지 못했다 //

- **awareness** ⓝ 인식　　・**feature** ⓥ 포함하다
- **demonstrate** ⓥ 입증하다　　・**predictive** ⓐ 예측의
- **classification** ⓝ 분류

위 그래프는 2017년 머신러닝 기능을 갖춘 스마트폰 앱에 대한 인식과 사용
현황을 보여준다. ① 조사된 다섯 개의 앱 각각에 대해, 인지하고 있다는
응답자의 비율이 사용하고 있다는 응답자의 비율보다 높았다. ② 다섯 개의 앱
중에서 텍스트 예측이 인지와 사용 모두에서 응답자의 비율이 가장 높았다.
③ 음성 검색을 인지하고 있다는 응답자의 비율이 사용한다는 응답자의
비율보다 네 배 이상 높았다(→ 높지 않았다). ④ 음성 텍스트 변환은 이메일
분류보다 인지하고 있다는 응답자의 비율은 높았지만, 사용하고 있다는
응답자의 비율에서는 그렇지 않았다. ⑤ 자동 사진 분류에 대한 사용 비율은
인지 비율의 절반에도 미치지 못했다.

다음 도표의 내용과 일치하지 않는 것은?

2017년에 머신 러닝 기능을 갖춘 스마트폰 앱의 인지와 사용

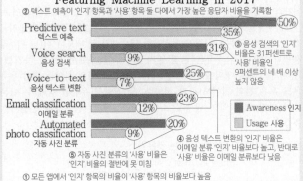

Awareness and Usage of Smartphone Applications
Featuring Machine Learning in 2017

② 텍스트 예측이 '인지' 항목과 '사용' 항목 둘 다에서 가장 높은 응답자 비율을 기록함

Predictive text 텍스트 예측 — 50% / 35%
Voice search 음성 검색 — 31% / 9%
Voice-to-text 음성 텍스트 변환 — 25% / 7%
Email classification 이메일 분류 — 23% / 12%
Automated photo classification 자동 사진 분류 — 20% / 9%

③ 음성 검색의 '인지' 비율은 31퍼센트로, '사용' 비율인 9퍼센트의 네 배 이상 높지 않음

■ Awareness 인지
□ Usage 사용

④ 음성 텍스트 변환의 '인지' 비율은 이메일 분류 '인지' 비율보다 높고, 반대로 '사용' 비율은 이메일 분류보다 낮음

⑤ 자동 사진 분류의 '사용' 비율은 '인지' 비율의 절반에 못 미침

① 모든 앱에서 '인지' 항목의 비율이 '사용' 항목의 비율보다 높음

(H)

> **왜 정답?** [정답률 95%]

③ 음성 검색 앱의 '인지' 비율은 31퍼센트로, '사용' 비율인 9퍼센트의 4배가 되지
않는다. 따라서 음성 검색을 인지하고 있다는 응답자의 비율이 사용한다는
응답자의 비율보다 네 배 이상 높았다는 것은 적절하지 않다.

> **왜 오답?**

① 모든 앱에 대해 '인지' 비율이 '사용' 비율보다 높다.
② 텍스트 예측 앱이 '인지' 비율은 50퍼센트, '사용' 비율은 35퍼센트로 모든 앱 중에서
가장 높은 응답자 비율을 보인다.
④ 음성 텍스트 변환 앱의 '인지' 비율은 25퍼센트이고, 이는 이메일 분류 앱의 '인지'
비율인 23퍼센트보다 높다. 반면 음성 텍스트 변환 앱의 '사용' 비율은 7퍼센트로,
이는 이메일 분류 앱의 '사용' 비율인 12퍼센트보다 낮다.
⑤ 자동 사진 분류 앱의 '사용' 비율은 9퍼센트로, 같은 앱의 '인지' 비율인 20퍼센트의
절반이 되지 않는다.

H 06 정답 ② ＊낙농 우유와 식물성 우유의 환경 발자국

The above graph shows / the environmental footprints /
~ 면에서
in terms of greenhouse gas emissions (measured per kilogram)
and freshwater use (measured per liter) / of dairy and the four
plant-based milks in 2018. //
위 그래프는 보여준다 / 환경 발자국을 / (킬로그램당 측정된) 온실가스 배출과 (리터당
측정된) 담수 사용 면에서 / 2018년 낙농 우유와 4가지의 식물성 우유의 //
낙농 우유의 온실가스 배출량은 3.15kg, 담수 사용량은 628.2L로 가장 많음
① Dairy milk had the largest environmental footprint / of both
greenhouse gas emissions and freshwater use. //
낙농 우유는 가장 큰 환경 발자국을 남겼다 / 온실가스 배출과 담수 사용 모두에서 //

② Rice milk used more(→ less) than ten times / the amount of
목적격 관계대명사 대동사(＝used) 쌀 우유는 담수량이 269.81L이고, 콩 우유는
fresh water that soy milk did. 27.81L로, 쌀 우유의 담수량은 10배 미만임
쌀 우유는 열 배보다 더(→ 덜) 많이 사용했다 / 콩 우유가 사용한 담수량의 //

③ Oat milk ranked fourth / in both environmental footprint
categories. // 귀리 우유는 0.9kg의 온실가스 배출량, 48.24L의 담수량을 가지고 있으며,
전체 우유 중 4위임
귀리 우유는 4위를 차지했다 / 환경 발자국의 두 범주에서 //

④ In the category of greenhouse gas emissions, / the gap
between A and B: A와 B 사이
between soy milk and oat milk / was less than the gap between
oat milk and almond milk. // 콩 우유와 귀리 우유의 온실가스 배출량 차이가 더 작음
온실가스 배출 영역에서 / 콩 우유와 귀리 우유 간의 차이는 / 귀리 우유와 아몬드 우유 간의
차이보다 더 적었다 //

⑤ Among plant-based milks, / almond milk consumed the
largest amount of freshwater, / yet emitted the least amount of
식물성 우유들 중에서 / 아몬드 우유가 담수량 371.46L로 가장 많고,
greenhouse gas. // 온실가스 배출량은 0.7kg으로 가장 적음
식물성 우유들 중에서 / 아몬드 우유가 가장 많은 양의 담수를 소비했지만 / 가장 적은 양의
온실가스를 배출했다 //

- greenhouse gas 온실가스 • emission ⓝ 배출
- freshwater ⓝ 담수

위 그래프는 2018년 낙농 우유와 4가지의 식물성 우유의 (킬로그램당 측정된) 온실가스 배출과 (리터당 측정된) 담수 사용 면에서 환경 발자국을 보여준다. ① 낙농 우유는 온실가스 배출과 담수 사용 모두에서 가장 큰 환경 발자국을 남겼다. ② 쌀 우유는 콩 우유가 사용한 담수량의 열 배보다 더(→ 덜) 많이 사용했다. ③ 귀리 우유는 환경 발자국의 두 범주에서 4위를 차지했다. ④ 온실가스 배출 영역에서, 콩 우유와 귀리 우유 간의 차이는 귀리 우유와 아몬드 우유 간의 차이보다 더 적었다. ⑤ 식물성 우유들 중에서, 아몬드 우유가 가장 많은 양의 담수를 소비했지만, 가장 적은 양의 온실가스를 배출했다.

다음 도표의 내용과 일치하지 않는 것은?

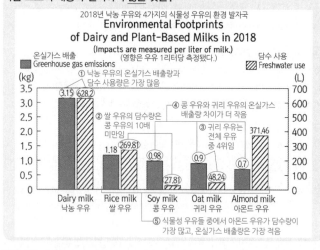

2018년 낙농 우유와 4가지의 식물성 우유의 환경 발자국
Environmental Footprints of Dairy and Plant-Based Milks in 2018
(Impacts are measured per liter of milk.)
(영향은 우유 1리터당 측정됐다.)

▶ 오답 ? [정답률 43%]

② 쌀 우유는 담수량이 269.81L이고, 콩 우유는 27.81L로, 쌀 우유의 담수량은 10배 미만이므로 10배보다 더 많다고 한 것은 적절하지 않다.

▶ 오답 ?

① 낙농 우유의 온실가스 배출량은 3.15kg, 담수 사용량은 628.2L로 가장 많다.
③ 귀리 우유는 0.9kg의 온실가스 배출량, 48.24L의 담수량을 가지고 있으며, 전체 우유 중 4위이다.
④ 콩 우유와 귀리 우유의 온실가스 배출량 차이는 0.08kg이고, 귀리 우유와 아몬드 우유의 온실가스 배출량 차이는 0.2kg으로, 콩 우유와 귀리 우유의 온실가스 배출량 차이가 더 작다.
⑤ 식물성 우유들 중에서 아몬드 우유가 담수량 371.46L로 가장 많고, 온실가스 배출량은 0.7kg으로 가장 적다.

H 07 정답 ③ * 독서가 개인 취미 중 하나라고 응답한 각국의 남녀 비율

The above graph, / based on a survey conducted in 2023, / shows the share of respondents / who say reading is one of their personal hobbies / according to their gender group in five countries. //
위 도표는 / 2023년에 수행된 한 설문조사에 근거한 것으로 / 응답자의 비율을 보여준다 / 독서가 개인 취미 중 하나라고 답한 / 5개국에서 성별 집단에 따라 //

① Among the countries shown in the graph, / Spain had the largest share of females / who said reading was one of their hobbies, / which was 58%. //
도표에 나온 나라 중 / 스페인이 여성의 비율이 가장 높았는데 / 독서가 취미 중 하나라고 답한 / 비율은 58퍼센트였다 //

② The gap between the share of females and that of males / who selected reading as one of their hobbies / was larger in Germany than in Mexico. // 남녀 비율 차이가 독일이 20퍼센트포인트, 멕시코는 10퍼센트포인트로 독일이 멕시코보다 더 컸음
남녀 간의 비율 차이는 / 독서를 취미 중 하나로 고른 / 독일이 멕시코보다 더 컸다 //

③ The share of males / who selected reading as one of their hobbies in Mexico / was 41%, / which was smaller(→ larger) than that in the United States. // 멕시코의 남성 응답자 비율은 41퍼센트로 미국의 남성 응답자 비율인 30퍼센트보다 더 높음
남성의 비율은 / 멕시코에서 독서를 취미 중 하나로 고른 / 41퍼센트였는데 / 이는 미국에서보다 더 낮았다(→ 더 높았다) //

④ The share of females / who selected reading as one of their hobbies in the United States / was larger than that in South Korea. // 미국의 여성 응답자 비율인 44퍼센트는 한국의 31퍼센트보다 더 높음
여성의 비율은 / 미국에서 독서를 취미 중 하나로 고른 / 한국에서보다 더 높았다 //

⑤ As for South Korea, / the share of respondents / who selected reading as one of their hobbies / was the smallest among the countries / shown in the graph for each gender, respectively. //
한국의 경우 / 응답자의 비율이 / 독서를 취미 중 하나로 고른 / 도표에 나온 나라 중 가장 낮았다 / 남녀 각각 도표에 나온 // 한국의 남녀 응답 비율은 각각 가장 적음

- conduct ⓥ 수행하다 • share ⓝ 지분, 비율
- respondent ⓝ 응답자 • respectively ⓐⓓ 각각

위 도표는 2023년에 수행된 한 설문조사에 근거한 것으로, 5개국에서 독서가 개인 취미 중 하나라고 답한 응답자의 비율을 성별 집단에 따라 보여준다. ① 도표에 나온 나라 중 스페인이 독서가 취미 중 하나라고 답한 여성의 비율이 가장 높았는데, 58퍼센트였다. ② 독서를 취미 중 하나로 고른 남녀 간의 비율 차이는 독일이 멕시코보다 더 컸다. ③ 멕시코에서 독서를 취미 중 하나로 고른 남성의 비율은 41퍼센트였는데, 이는 미국에서보다 더 낮았다(→ 더 높았다). ④ 미국에서 독서를 취미 중 하나로 고른 여성의 비율은 한국에서보다 더 높았다. ⑤ 한국의 경우, 독서를 취미 중 하나로 고른 응답자의 비율이 남녀 각각 도표에 나온 나라 중 가장 낮았다.

다음 도표의 내용과 일치하지 않는 것은?

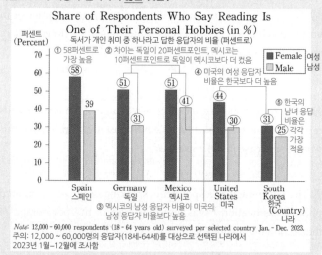

Share of Respondents Who Say Reading Is One of Their Personal Hobbies (in %)
독서가 개인 취미 중 하나라고 답한 응답자의 비율 (퍼센트로)

Note: 12,000 - 60,000 respondents (18 - 64 years old) surveyed per selected country Jan. - Dec. 2023.
주의: 12,000 ~ 60,000명의 응답자(18세-64세)를 대상으로 선택된 나라에서 2023년 1월~12월에 조사함

▶ 오답 ? [정답률 94%]

③ 멕시코의 남성 응답자 비율은 41퍼센트로 미국의 남성 응답자 비율인 30퍼센트보다 더 높으므로 더 낮다고 한 것은 적절하지 않다.

▶ 오답 ?

① 스페인의 독서를 취미 중 하나로 하는 여성 응답자의 비율은 58퍼센트이며, 가장 높다.
② 남녀 비율 차이는 독일이 20퍼센트포인트, 멕시코는 10퍼센트포인트로 격차는 독일이 멕시코보다 크다.
④ 미국의 여성 응답자 비율은 44퍼센트이며, 31퍼센트인 한국보다 더 높다.
⑤ 한국의 남녀 응답 비율은 제시된 국가 중에서 각각 가장 적다.

H 08 정답 ④ *연령대별 챗봇 플랫폼 선호도 분석

The above graph shows / the percentage of preferable chatbot
platforms / by age / categorized by Generation Z, Millennials,
and Generation X. // <u>과거분사(age 수식)</u>
위 그래프는 보여 준다 / 선호하는 챗봇 플랫폼의 비율을 /
연령대별로 / Z세대, 밀레니얼 세대 그리고 X세대로 분류된 //

① Millennials and Generation X had the highest percentage
of respondents / <u>who preferred</u> Desktop Websites / while
　　　　　　　　주격 관계대명사
Generation Z had the highest percentage / for Messenger
Apps. // 가장 선호하는 챗봇 플랫폼 - 밀레니얼 세대, X세대: 데스크톱 웹사이트 / Z세대: 메신저 앱
밀레니얼 세대와 X세대는 가장 높은 비율을 가졌다 / 데스크톱 웹사이트를 선호하는 / 반면 Z
세대는 응답자의 가장 높은 비율을 가졌다 / 메신저 앱에 대해 //

② In Generation Z, / the percentage of respondents / who
　　　　　　　　　　단수 주어　　　　　　　　　　　주격 관계대명사
preferred Mobile Apps / <u>was</u> more than twice / that of those
　　　　　　　　　　단수 동사
who preferred Voice Assistant Devices. // 모바일 앱(78)은 음성 지원 장치
(33)의 두 배(66) 이상임
Z세대 내에서 / 응답자의 비율은 / 모바일 앱을 선호하는 / 두 배보다 더 높았다 / 음성 지원
장치를 선호하는 응답자 비율의 //

③ Messenger Apps was the only platform / where the percentage
　　　　　　　　　　　　　　　　　　　　　관계부사
of respondents' preference for it / sank lower and lower / from
Generation Z, to Millennials, to Generation X. //
메신저 앱은 유일한 플랫폼이었다 / 그것에 대한 응답자의 선호 비율이 / 점점 더 낮아진 /
Z세대, 밀레니얼 세대, X세대로 갈수록 // **단서** 모바일 앱의 격차(11)은 음성 지원 장치의
격차(13)보다 더 작음

④ The percentage point gap / between Millennial and
Generation X respondents / who preferred Mobile Apps / was
larger(→ smaller) than the percentage point gap / between
= Millennial and Generation X respondents
the same two groups for Voice Assistant Devices. //
비율 수치 격차는 / 밀레니얼 세대와 X세대의 응답자의 / 모바일 앱을 선호하는 / 비율 수치
격차보다 더 컸다(→ 더 작았다) / 음성 지원 장치에 대한 동일한 두 집단 사이의 //
모바일 웹사이트는 모든 연령 집단에서 가장 낮은 선호도를 보임

⑤ The percentage of respondents / who preferred Mobile
Websites / was the lowest / in all the age groups. //
응답자들의 비율은 / 모바일 웹사이트를 선호하는 / 가장 낮았다 / 모든 연령 집단에서 //

• preferable ⓐ 선호되는　　• respondent ⓝ 응답자
• sink ⓥ 가라앉다

위 그래프는 Z세대, 밀레니얼 세대 그리고 X세대로 분류된 연령대별로
선호하는 챗봇 플랫폼의 비율을 보여 준다. ① 밀레니얼 세대와 X세대는
데스크톱 웹사이트를 선호하는 응답자의 가장 높은 비율을 가진 반면 Z세대는
메신저 앱에 대해 가장 높은 비율을 가졌다. ② Z세대 내에서, 모바일 앱을
선호하는 응답자의 비율은 음성 지원 장치를 선호하는 응답자 비율의 두 배보다
더 높았다. ③ 메신저 앱은 Z세대, 밀레니얼 세대, X세대로 갈수록 그것에
대한 응답자의 선호 비율이 점점 더 낮아진 유일한 플랫폼이었다. ④ 모바일
앱을 선호하는 밀레니얼 세대와 X세대의 응답자의 비율 수치 격차는 음성 지원
장치에 대한 동일한 두 집단 사이의 비율 수치 격차보다 더 컸다(→ 더 작았다).
⑤ 모바일 웹사이트를 선호하는 응답자들의 비율은 모든 연령 집단에서 가장
낮았다.

다음 도표의 내용과 일치하지 <u>않는</u> 것은?

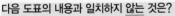

① 밀레니얼 세대와
X세대는 데스크톱
웹사이트, Z세대는
메신저 앱을 가장
선호함

연령대별로 선호하는 챗봇 플랫폼
Preferable Chatbot Platforms by Age
2019년의 전 세계 사용자
worldwide users in 2019
③ Z세대(83)>밀레니얼 세대(76)>X세대(46)

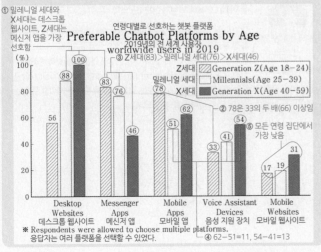

Z세대 ▨ Generation Z (Age 18–24)
밀레니얼 세대 ▢ Millennials (Age 25–39)
X세대 ■ Generation X (Age 40–59)

② 78은 33의 두 배(66) 이상임
⑤ 모든 연령 집단에서
가장 낮음

Desktop Messenger Mobile Voice Assistant Mobile
Websites Apps Apps Devices Websites
데스크톱 웹사이트 메신저 앱 모바일 앱 음성 지원 장치 모바일 웹사이트
※ Respondents were allowed to choose multiple platforms.
응답자는 여러 플랫폼을 선택할 수 있었다. ④ 62−51=11, 54−41=13

왜 정답? [정답률 85%]

모바일 앱: 밀레니얼 세대(51), X세대(62) → 11퍼센트포인트 차이
음성 지원 장치: 밀레니얼 세대(41), X세대(54) → 13퍼센트포인트 차이
따라서 모바일 앱에서의 격차가 음성 지원 장치보다 크다고 한 ④이 일치하지 않는다.

왜 오답?

① 가장 높은 비율은 밀레니얼 세대와 X세대는 데스크톱 웹사이트, Z세대는 메신저
　 앱이다.
② 모바일 앱(78)은 음성 지원 장치(33)의 두 배(66) 이상이다.
③ 메신저 앱에 대한 선호도는 Z세대(83)>밀레니얼 세대(76)>X세대(46)이다.
⑤ 모바일 웹사이트는 모든 연령 집단에서 가장 낮은 선호도(17, 19, 31)를 보인다.

H 09 정답 ⑤ *반려동물 개체 수의 변화

The above graph shows / the pet population changes / from
1980 to 2020. // 반려견의 개체 수는 2000년을 제외하고
반려묘의 개체 수보다 더 많거나 동일함
위 그래프는 보여준다 / 반려동물 개체 수의 변화를 / 1980년부터 2020년까지의 //

① The population of pet dogs / was higher than or equal to /
　　　　　　　　　　　　　= the population
that of pet cats / except for the year 2000. //
반려견의 개체 수는 / 더 많거나 동일했다 / 반려묘의 그것보다 / 2000년을 제외하고 //

② In 1990, / the difference between the population of pet dogs
　　　　　　　between A and B: A와 B 차이　　　　　1990년에 반려견과 반려묘 개체 수
and pet cats / was less than 1 million. // 차이는 60만으로 100만보다 적음
1990년에 / 반려견과 반려묘의 개체 수 사이의 차이는 / 100만보다 적었다 //

③ In 2020, / the population of pet dogs / reached its highest
point, / yet it was still less / than double the number of pet dogs
in 1980. // 2020년 반려견 개체 수: 900만, 1980년 반려견 개체 수: 560만으로 두 배보다는 적음
2020년에 / 반려견의 개체 수가 / 그것의 정점에 도달했다 / 그것은 여전히 적었다 /
1980년도 반려견의 수의 두 배보다는 //

④ The population of pet cats / reached its highest population of
8 million in 2000, / and it was the same in 2010. //
반려묘의 개체 수는 / 2000년에 그것의 가장 높은 개체 수인 800만에 도달했고 /
2010년에도 똑같았다 // 2000년 반려묘 개체 수: 800만, 2010년 반려묘 개체 수: 800만으로 동일

⑤ Although the population of pet cats decreased / from 2010 to
2020, / the population of pet cats in 2020 / still exceeded(→ did
　　　　　= the population
not exceeded) / that of pet dogs in 2020. //
단서 2020년 반려묘 개체 수: 750만, 2020년 반려견 개체 수: 900만으로 초과하지 못함
비록 반려묘의 개체 수가 감소했지만 / 2010년부터 2020년까지 / 2020년에 반려묘 개체
수는 / 여전히 초과했다(→ 초과하지 못했다) / 2020년도 반려견의 그것을 //

• population ⓝ 개체 수, 인구　　• except for ~을 제외하고는
• decrease ⓥ 감소하다　　• exceed ⓥ 초과하다

위 그래프는 1980년부터 2020년까지의 반려동물 개체 수의 변화를 보여준다.
① 2000년을 제외하고 반려견의 개체 수가 반려묘의 그것보다 더 많거나
동일했다. ② 1990년에 반려견과 반려묘의 개체 수 사이의 차이는 100만
보다 적었다. ③ 2020년에 반려견의 개체 수가 그것의 정점에 도달했지만,
그것은 여전히 1980년도 반려견의 수의 두 배보다는 적었다. ④ 반려묘의 개체
수는 2000년에 그것의 가장 높은 개체 수인 800만에 도달했고, 2010년에도
똑같았다. ⑤ 비록 반려묘의 개체 수가 2010년부터 2020년까지 감소했지만,
2020년에 반려묘 개체 수는 여전히 2020년도 반려견의 그것을 초과했다(→
초과하지 못했다).

다음 도표의 내용과 일치하지 <u>않는</u> 것은?

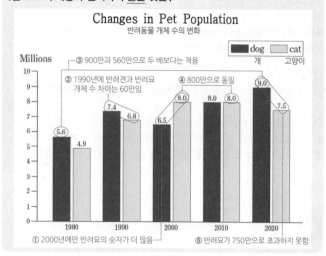

Changes in Pet Population
반려동물 개체 수의 변화

③ 900만과 560만으로 두 배보다는 적음
② 1990년에 반려견과 반려묘 개체 수 차이는 60만임
④ 800만으로 동일
① 2000년에만 반려묘의 숫자가 더 많음
⑤ 반려묘가 750만으로 초과하지 못함

▷**오H 정답**? [정답률 85%]

⑤ 2020년의 반려묘 개체 수는 750만, 2020년 반려견 개체 수는 900만으로 2020년의 반려묘 개체 수는 반려견 개체 수를 초과하지 못했다. 따라서 2020년에 반려묘 개체 수는 여전히 2020년도 반려견의 그것보다 초과했다고 하는 것은 적절하지 못하다.

▷**오H 오답**?

① 반려견의 개체 수는 2000년을 제외하고 반려묘의 개체 수보다 많거나 동일하다.

② 1990년에 반려견과 반려묘 개체 수 차이는 60만으로 100만보다 적다.

③ 2020년의 반려견 개체 수는 900만, 1980년의 반려견 개체 수는 560만으로 2020년의 반려견 개체 수는 1980년 반려견 개체 수의 두 배보다는 적다.

④ 2000년의 반려묘 개체 수는 800만, 2010년의 반려묘 개체 수도 800만으로 동일하다.

H 10 정답 ④ *때때로 또는 자주 적극적으로 뉴스를 회피한 비율 —

The above graph shows / the percentages of the respondents in five countries / who sometimes or often actively avoided news / in 2017, 2019, and 2022. //
주격 관계대명사
위 도표는 보여준다 / 다섯 개 국가의 응답자 비율을 / 때때로 또는 자주 적극적으로 뉴스를 회피한 / 2017년, 2019년 및 2022년에 //

① For each of the three years, / Ireland showed the highest percentage of the respondents / who sometimes or often actively avoided news, / among the countries in the graph. //
주격 관계대명사   아일랜드는 세 해 모두 가장 높음
세 해 각각에 대해 / 아일랜드가 응답자의 가장 높은 비율을 보여주었다 / 때때로 또는 자주 적극적으로 뉴스를 회피한 / 도표의 국가 중 //

② In Germany, / the percentage of the respondents who sometimes or often actively avoided news / was less than 30% in each of the three years. // 독일은 세 해 모두 30퍼센트보다 낮음
주격 관계대명사
독일의 경우 / 때때로 또는 자주 적극적으로 뉴스를 회피한 응답자 비율이 / 세 해 각각 30퍼센트보다 낮았다 //

③ In Denmark, / the percentage of the respondents / who sometimes or often actively avoided news in 2019 / was higher than that in 2017 / but lower than that in 2022. //
the percentage of ~ avoided news
덴마크는 2019년에는 15퍼센트로, 2017년의 14퍼센트보다 높고 2022년의 20퍼센트보다 낮음
덴마크의 경우 / 응답자 비율이 / 2019년에 때때로 또는 자주 적극적으로 뉴스를 회피한 / 2017년의 비율보다 더 높았으나 / 2022년의 그것보다는 더 낮았다 //

④ In Finland, / the percentage of the respondents / who sometimes or often actively avoided news in 2019 / was lower than that in 2017, / which was also(→ not) true for Japan. //
주격 관계대명사의 계속적 용법
단서 일본은 2019년에는 11퍼센트로 2017년의 6퍼센트보다 높으므로 일본도 마찬가지라는 표현은 틀림
핀란드의 경우 / 응답자 비율아 / 2019년에 때때로 또는 자주 적극적으로 뉴스를 회피한 / 2017년의 그것보다 더 낮았으며 / 이는 일본도 마찬가지였다(→ 일본은 아니었다) //

---

⑤ In Japan, / the percentage of the respondents who sometimes or often actively avoided news / did not exceed 15% in each of the three years. // 일본은 세 해 모두 15퍼센트보다 낮음
일본의 경우 / 때때로 또는 자주 적극적으로 뉴스를 회피한 응답자 비율이 / 세 해 각각 15퍼센트를 넘지 않았다 //

- **respondent** ⓝ 응답자   - **actively** ⓐⓓ 적극적으로
- **exceed** ⓥ 넘다

위 도표는 2017년, 2019년 및 2022년에 때때로 또는 자주 적극적으로 뉴스를 회피한 다섯 개 국가의 응답자 비율을 보여준다. ① 세 해 각각에 대해, 아일랜드가 도표의 국가 중, 때때로 또는 자주 적극적으로 뉴스를 회피한 응답자의 가장 높은 비율을 보여주었다. ② 독일의 경우, 때때로 또는 자주 적극적으로 뉴스를 회피한 응답자 비율이 세 해 각각 30퍼센트보다 낮았다. ③ 덴마크의 경우, 2019년에 때때로 또는 자주 적극적으로 뉴스를 회피한 응답자 비율이 2017년의 비율보다 더 높았으나 2022년의 그것보다는 더 낮았다. ④ 핀란드의 경우, 2019년에 때때로 또는 자주 적극적으로 뉴스를 회피한 응답자 비율이 2017년의 그것보다 더 낮았으며, 이는 일본도 마찬가지였다(→ 일본은 아니었다). ⑤ 일본의 경우, 때때로 또는 자주 적극적으로 뉴스를 회피한 응답자 비율이 세 해 각각 15퍼센트를 넘지 않았다.

다음 도표의 내용과 일치하지 <u>않는</u> 것은?

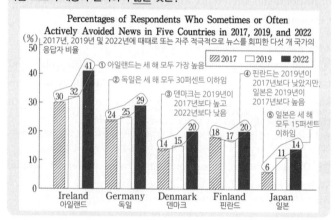

Percentages of Respondents Who Sometimes or Often Actively Avoided News in Five Countries in 2017, 2019, and 2022
(%) 2017년, 2019년 및 2022년에 때때로 또는 자주 적극적으로 뉴스를 회피한 다섯 개 국가의 응답자 비율

① 아일랜드는 세 해 모두 가장 높음
② 독일은 세 해 모두 30퍼센트 이하임
③ 덴마크는 2019년이 2017년보다 높고 2022년보다 낮음
④ 핀란드는 2019년이 2017년보다 낮았지만, 일본은 2019년이 2017년보다 높음
⑤ 일본은 세 해 모두 15퍼센트 이하임

▷**오H 정답**? [정답률 95%]

④ 핀란드는 2019년에 17퍼센트로, 2017년의 18퍼센트보다 낮은 것은 맞지만, 일본은 2019년에 11퍼센트로, 2017년의 6퍼센트보다 높다. 따라서 일본도 핀란드와 마찬가지라는 표현은 적절하지 않다.

▷**오H 오답**?

① 아일랜드는 2017년에는 30퍼센트, 2019년에는 32퍼센트, 2022년에는 41퍼센트로 세 해 모두 가장 높다.

② 독일은 2017년에는 24퍼센트, 2019년에는 25퍼센트, 2022년에는 29퍼센트로 세 해 모두 30퍼센트보다 낮다.

③ 덴마크는 2019년에는 15퍼센트로, 2017년의 14퍼센트보다 높고 2022년의 20퍼센트보다 낮다.

⑤ 일본은 2017년에는 6퍼센트, 2019년에는 11퍼센트, 2022년에는 14퍼센트로 세 해 모두 15퍼센트보다 낮다.

류이레 | 연세대 의예과 2024년 입학·광주대동고 졸

여기서는 ④의 which was also true for Japan이라는 부분이 틀린 부분이었어. 도표 문제는 빠르게 맥락을 눈치채고 도표의 필요한 내용을 신속하게 뽑아내어 선지와 연결하는 것이 중요해. 그리고 도표 문제에서 percentage와 percentage point라는 단어가 등장하는데, 이 중 percentage point는 퍼센트 값들 사이의 차이를 뜻하는 말이니까 퍼센트 값들에 대한 해석을 할 때 참고해!

H 11 정답 ② ＊아시아 태평양 지역의 행선지 도시

The table above shows / the top seven destination cities / in the Asia-Pacific region / in 2018 /
위 표는 보여준다 / 상위 7개 행선지 도시를 / 아시아 태평양 지역의 / 2018년에 /

by international overnight arrivals, / with additional information / on the average spend per day / in those cities. //
숙박하는 해외 방문객으로 / 추가 정보와 함께 / 일일 평균 소비에 관한 / 그 도시들에서의 //

① Bangkok was the top destination / in the Asia-Pacific region / with 22.8 million international overnight arrivals, / 방콕: 2,280만 명으로 1위
방콕은 최고의 행선지였고 / 아시아 태평양 지역에서 / 2,280만 명의 숙박하는 해외 방문객으로 /

immediately followed by Singapore / with 14.7 million international overnight arrivals. // 싱가포르: 1,470만 명으로 2위
싱가포르가 바로 그 뒤를 이었다 / 1,470만 명의 숙박하는 해외 방문객으로 //

② Kuala Lumpur was ranked in third place / based on the number of international overnight arrivals, / and the average spend per day / in this city / was more(→ less) than $150. // '~에 근거하여'
쿠알라룸푸르는 3위에 올랐고 / 숙박하는 해외 방문객 수를 바탕으로는 / 일일 평균 소비는 / 이 도시에서의 / 150달러보다 더 많았다(→ 더 적었다) // 단서 쿠알라룸푸르가 1,380만 명으로 3위인 것은 맞지만, 일일 평균 소비는 142달러임

③ Tokyo was ranked in fourth place / for the number of international overnight arrivals, / and the average spend per day / in this city / was $196. // 도쿄: 1,290만 명으로 4위이고 일일 평균 소비는 196달러
도쿄는 4위에 올랐고 / 숙박하는 해외 방문객 수로는 / 일일 평균 소비는 / 이 도시에서의 / 196달러였다 //

④ The number of international overnight arrivals / in Seoul / was larger than that of Osaka. // 서울은 1,130만 명. 오사카는 1,010만 명 단수 주어＊ 단수 동사＊
숙박하는 해외 방문객 수는 / 서울에서 / 오사카의 그것보다 더 많았다 //

⑤ Phuket was the only city / where the number of international overnight arrivals was less / than 10 million, / and the average spend per day / in this city / was $247. // 푸켓: 990만 명. 일일 평균 소비는 247달러 선행사 관계부사
푸켓은 유일한 도시였고 / 숙박하는 해외 방문객 수가 더 적은 / 1,000만 명보다 / 일일 평균 소비는 / 이 도시에서의 / 247달러였다 //

• destination ⓝ 행선지, 목적지 • overnight ⓐ 숙박의, 일박의
• arrival ⓝ 도착(한 사람[것]) • region ⓝ 지역, 지방
• additional ⓐ 추가의 • immediately ⓐⓓ 바로, 즉시

위 표는 숙박하는 해외 방문객 및 행선지 도시에서의 일일 평균 소비에 관한 추가 정보로 2018년 아시아 태평양 지역의 상위 7개 행선지 도시를 보여준다. ① 방콕은 2,280만 명의 숙박하는 해외 방문객으로 아시아 태평양 지역에서 최고의 행선지였고, 싱가포르가 1,470만 명의 숙박하는 해외 방문객으로 바로 그 뒤를 이었다. ② 쿠알라룸푸르는 숙박하는 해외 방문객 수를 바탕으로는 3위에 올랐고, 이 도시에서의 일일 평균 소비는 150달러보다 더 많았다(→ 더 적었다). ③ 도쿄는 숙박하는 해외 방문객 수로는 4위에 올랐고, 이 도시에서의 일일 평균 소비는 196달러였다. ④ 서울의 숙박하는 해외 방문객 수는 오사카의 숙박하는 해외 방문객 수보다 더 많았다. ⑤ 푸켓은 숙박하는 해외 방문객 수가 1,000만 명이 되지 않은 유일한 도시였고, 이 도시에서의 일일 평균 소비는 247달러였다.

다음 표의 내용과 일치하지 <u>않는</u> 것은?

Top 7 Asia-Pacific Destinations (2018)
상위 7개 아시아 태평양 행선지 (2018년)

Rank 순위	Destination 행선지	International Overnight Arrivals (million) 숙박하는 해외 방문객(백만 명)	Average Spend per Day (USD) 일일 평균 소비(미국 달러)
1	Bangkok	22.8 가장 많음	$184
2	Singapore	14.7 두 번째로 많음	$272
3	Kuala Lumpur	13.8 세 번째로 많음	$142 150달러를 넘지 않음
4	Tokyo	12.9 네 번째로 많음	$196
5	Seoul	11.3 오사카보다 많음	$155
6	Osaka	10.1	$223
7	Phuket	9.9 천만 명보다 적음	$247

왜 정답? [정답률 94%]

숙박하는 해외 방문객 수를 기준으로 하면 쿠알라룸푸르가 1,380만 명으로 3위인 것은 맞지만, 그 도시에서의 일일 평균 소비는 142달러이므로 150달러보다 많다고 한 ②은 표의 내용과 일치하지 않는다.

왜 오답?

① 방콕이 2,280만 명으로 1위이고, 싱가포르는 1,470만 명으로 2위이다.
③ 도쿄는 1,290만 명으로 4위이고, 일일 평균 소비는 196달러이다.
④ 서울의 숙박하는 해외 방문객 수는 1,130만 명이고, 오사카는 1,010만 명이다.
⑤ 푸켓의 숙박하는 해외 방문객 수는 990만 명이고, 일일 평균 소비는 247달러이다.

── 어법 특강 ──

＊ a number of ～/the number of ～의 수 일치
– 「a number of(많은) + 복수 명사」는 복수 취급한다.
• A number of people are waiting in the line.
(많은 사람들이 줄을 서서 기다리고 있다.)
– 「The number of(~의 수) + 복수 명사」는 단수 취급한다.
• The number of victims is increasing every month.
(피해자의 수가 매달 증가하고 있다.)

H 12 정답 ② ＊연령대별 독서 양상

주어(선행사)＊ 생략 가능한 주격 관계대명사와 be동사 앞에 주격 관계대명사와 be동사가 생략됨
The above graph, / which was based on a survey / conducted in 2019, / shows the percentages of U.S. adults / by age group /
위의 그래프는 / 조사에 근거한 / 2019년에 실시된 / 미국 성인의 비율을 보여준다 / 연령대별로 /

who said / they had read (or listened to) a book / in one or more of the formats / — print books, e-books, and audiobooks — / in the previous 12 months. //
말한 / 그들이 책을 읽었(거나 들었)다고 / 한 가지 이상의 형식으로 / 활자본, 전자책, 오디오북 / 지난 12개월 동안 //

① The percentage of people / in the 18-29 group / who said / they had read a print book / was 74%, / which was the highest / among the four groups. // 활자본: 18~29세가 74퍼센트로 가장 높음 주어 동사
사람들의 비율은 / 18~29세 연령대 / 말한 / 그들이 활자본을 읽었다고 / 74퍼센트였는데 / 이는 가장 높았다 / 네 개의 연령대 중에서 // 단서 활자본: 50~64세는 59퍼센트, 65세 이상은 63퍼센트

② The percentage of people / who said / they had read a print book / in the 50-64 group / was higher(→ lower) / than that in the 65 and up group. // 주어 동사
사람들의 비율은 / 말한 / 그들이 활자본을 읽었다고 / 50~64세 연령대에서 / 더 높았다(→ 더 낮았다) / 65세 이상 연령대에서의 그것보다 //

③ While 34% of people in the 18-29 group said / they had read an e-book, / the percentage of people / who said so / was below 20% / in the 65 and up group. // 전자책: 18~29세는 34퍼센트, 65세 이상은 17퍼센트 부사절 접속사(대조)
18~29세 연령대의 34퍼센트의 사람들이 말한 반면에 / 그들이 전자책을 읽었다고 / 사람들의 비율이 / 그렇게 말한 / 20퍼센트 미만이었다 / 65세 이상 연령대에서는 //

④ In all age groups, / the percentage of people / who said / they had read an e-book / was higher / than that of people / who said / they had listened to an audiobook. // 네 개의 연령대 모두에서 전자책의 비율이 오디오북의 비율보다 더 높음
모든 연령대에서 / 사람들의 비율은 / 말한 / 그들이 전자책을 읽었다고 / 더 높았다 / 사람들의 그것보다 / 말한 / 그들이 오디오북을 들었다고 //

⑤ Among the four age groups, / the 30-49 group had the highest percentage of people / who said / they had listened to an audiobook. // 오디오북: 30~49세가 27퍼센트로 가장 높음
네 개의 연령대 중에서 / 30~49세 연령대가 가장 높은 사람들의 비율을 가졌다 / 말한 / 그들이 오디오북을 들었다고 //

- above ⓐ 위의, 앞서 말한 • based on ~에 근거하여
- survey ⓝ (설문) 조사 • conduct ⓥ (특정한 활동을) 하다
- previous ⓐ 이전의 • among prep ~ 중에
- consumption ⓝ 소비(량) • format ⓝ (전반적인) 구성 방식, 형식

2019년에 실시된 조사에 근거한 위의 그래프는 지난 12개월 동안 활자본, 전자책, 오디오북 중 한 가지 이상의 형식으로 책을 읽었(거나 들었)다고 말한 미국 성인의 비율을 연령대별로 보여준다. ① 활자본을 읽었다고 말한 18~29세 연령대 사람들의 비율은 74퍼센트였는데, 이는 네 개의 연령대 중에서 가장 높았다. ② 50~64세 연령대에서 활자본을 읽었다고 말한 사람들의 비율은 65세 이상 연령대의 비율보다 더 높았다(→ 더 낮았다). ③ 18~29세 연령대의 34퍼센트의 사람들이 전자책을 읽었다고 말한 반면에, 65세 이상 연령대에서는 그렇게 말한 사람들의 비율이 20퍼센트 미만이었다. ④ 모든 연령대에서, 전자책을 읽었다고 말한 사람들의 비율은 오디오북을 들었다고 말한 사람들의 비율보다 더 높았다. ⑤ 네 개의 연령대 중에서, 30~49세 연령대에서 오디오북을 들었다고 말한 사람들의 비율이 가장 높았다.

다음 도표의 내용과 일치하지 않는 것은?

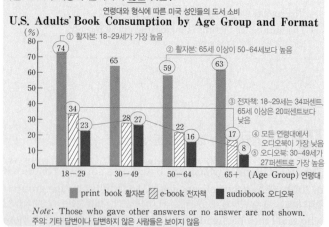

연령대와 형식에 따른 미국 성인들의 도서 소비
U.S. Adults' Book Consumption by Age Group and Format

① 활자본: 18~29세가 가장 높음
② 활자본: 65세 이상이 50~64세보다 높음
③ 전자책: 18~29세는 34퍼센트, 65세 이상은 20퍼센트보다 낮음
④ 모든 연령대에서 오디오북이 가장 낮음
⑤ 오디오북: 30~49세가 27퍼센트로 가장 높음

■ print book 활자본 ▨ e-book 전자책 ■ audiobook 오디오북

Note: Those who gave other answers or no answer are not shown.
주의: 기타 답변이나 답변하지 않은 사람들은 보이지 않음

왜 정답? [정답률 92%]

활자본을 읽었다고 말한 사람들의 비율은 50~64 연령대가 59퍼센트, 65세 이상이 63퍼센트로, 65세 이상이 더 높다. 따라서 ②의 higher를 반의어인 lower로 바꿔야 도표와 일치한다.

왜 오답?

① 활자본을 읽었다고 말한 사람들의 비율은 18~29세가 74퍼센트로 가장 높다.
③ 전자책을 읽었다고 말한 사람들의 비율은 18~29세는 34퍼센트, 65세 이상은 17퍼센트로 20퍼센트 미만이다.
④ 네 개의 연령대에서 모두 오디오북의 그래프보다 전자책의 그래프가 더 길다.
⑤ 오디오북에 관해서는 30~49세 그래프가 27퍼센트로 가장 길다.

--- 어법 특강

✽ 주어와 동사의 수 일치

- 주어 뒤에 전치사구, 분사구, 관계사절이 붙어서 길어지면 진짜 동사를 찾아서 해석하기가 어렵다. 이때 수식어구와 진짜 주어, 동사를 구분해야 한다.

• Children [with permission from their parents] are able to join
복수 주어   복수 동사
the special summer camp.
(부모님의 허락을 받은 아이들은 특별한 여름 캠프에 참가할 수 있다.)

• Health problems [related to using smartphones too much and
복수 주어
too often] give you more stress.
복수 동사
(스마트폰을 너무 많이 그리고 너무 자주 사용하는 것과 관련된 건강 문제들은 여러분에게 더 스트레스를 준다.)

• Making a list of situations [that make you feel shy] helps
단수 주어(동명사구)   단수 동사
overcome shyness.
(당신을 부끄럽게 느끼도록 만드는 상황들의 목록을 만드는 것은 수줍음을 극복하는 데 도움을 준다.)

H 13 정답 ④ ✽미국인의 연령대별 선호 주거지 유형

The above graph shows / the percentages of Americans' preferred type of place to live / by age group, / based on a 2020 survey. //
위의 그래프는 보여준다 / 미국인이 선호하는 거주지 유형의 비율을 / 연령대별로 / 2020년 조사를 기반으로 //

각각의 연령 그룹에서 읍내/시골 지역의 그래프가 가장 길   최상급 비교
① In each of the three age groups, / Town/Rural Area was the most preferred type of place to live. //
세 연령대 각각에서 / 읍내/시골 지역이 가장 선호되는 거주지 유형이었다 //

                                      주어
② In the 18-34 year-olds group, / the percentage of those / who
                                      동사
preferred Big/Small City / was higher than that of those / who preferred Suburb of Big/Small City. //   18-34세 그룹에서 대/소도시는 33%, 대/소도시의 근교는 27%
18~34세 연령층에서는 / 사람들의 비율이 / 대도시/소도시를 선호하는 / 사람들의 비율보다 더 높았다 / 대도시/소도시의 근교를 선호하는 //   35-54세 그룹에서 대/소도시의 근교는 27%, 대/소도시는 24%

③ In the 35-54 year-olds group, / the percentage of those / who preferred Suburb of Big/Small City / exceeded that of those / who preferred Big/Small City. //   = the percentage
35~54세 연령층에서는 / 사람들의 비율이 / 대도시/소도시의 근교를 선호하는 / 사람들의 비율을 앞질렀다 / 대도시/소도시를 선호하는 //

단서 55세 이상 연령대에서 대/소도시는 26%, 대/소도시의 근교는 22%
④In the 55 year-olds and older group, / the percentage of those / who chose Big/Small City(→ Suburb of Big/Small City) / among the three preferred types of place to live / was the lowest. //
55세 이상 연령층에서는 / 사람들의 비율이 / 대도시/소도시(→ 대도시/소도시의 근교)를 선택한 / 세 가지 선호하는 거주지 유형 중에서 / 가장 낮았다 // 도표의 모든 그래프가 20%보다 높음

단수 주어
⑤ Each percentage / of the three preferred types of place to live / was higher than 20% / across the three age groups. //
단수 동사
각각의 비율은 / 세 가지 선호하는 거주지 유형의 / 20퍼센트보다 더 높았다 / 세 연령대에 걸쳐 //

• suburb ⓝ 교외, 근교 • exceed ⓥ 넘어서다

위의 그래프는 2020년 조사를 기반으로 연령대별로 미국인이 선호하는 거주지 유형의 비율을 보여준다. ① 각기 세 연령대에서 읍내/시골 지역이 가장 선호되는 거주지 유형이었다. ② 18~34세 연령층에서는 대도시/소도시를 선호하는 비율이 대도시/소도시의 근교를 선호하는 비율보다 더 높았다. ③ 35~54세 연령층에서는 대도시/소도시의 근교를 선호하는 비율이 대도시/소도시를 선호하는 비율을 앞질렀다. ④ 55세 이상 연령층에서는 세 가지 선호하는 거주지 유형 중에서 대도시/소도시(→ 대도시/소도시의 근교)를 선택한 비율이 가장 낮았다. ⑤ 세 가지 선호하는 거주지 유형의 각각의 비율은 세 연령대에 걸쳐 20퍼센트보다 더 높았다.

다음 도표의 내용과 일치하지 않는 것은?

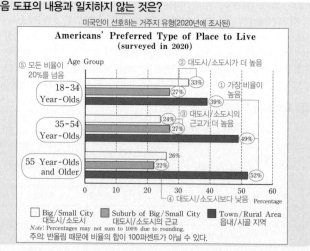

미국인이 선호하는 거주지 유형(2020년에 조사된)
Americans' Preferred Type of Place to Live
(surveyed in 2020)

⑤ 모든 비율이 20%를 넘음
② 대도시/소도시가 더 높음
① 가장 비율이 높음
③ 대도시/소도시의 근교가 더 높음
④ 대도시/소도시보다 낮음

18-34 Year-Olds: 33%, 27%, 39%
35-54 Year-Olds: 24%, 27%, 49%
55 Year-Olds and Older: 26%, 22%, 52%

□ Big/Small City 대도시/소도시
▨ Suburb of Big/Small City 대도시/소도시의 근교
■ Town/Rural Area 읍내/시골 지역
Note: Percentages may not sum to 100% due to rounding.
주의: 반올림 때문에 비율의 합이 100퍼센트가 아닐 수 있다.

왜 정답? [정답률 94%]

55세 이상 그룹에서 가장 낮은 비율을 차지한 것은 22퍼센트의 대도시/소도시의 근교이므로 대도시/소도시를 선택한 사람들의 비율이 가장 낮았다고 설명한 ❹은 도표와 일치하지 않는다.

왜 오답?

❶ 각각의 연령 그룹에서 가장 긴 그래프는 읍내/시골 지역이다.
❷ 18~34세 그룹에서 대도시/소도시는 33퍼센트이고, 대도시/소도시의 근교는 27퍼센트이므로 대도시/소도시의 비율이 더 높다.
❸ 35~54세 그룹에서 대도시/소도시의 근교는 27퍼센트로, 24퍼센트인 대도시/소도시를 능가한다.
❺ 세 연령 그룹의 모든 비율이 20퍼센트보다 높다.

조현준 | 전북대 의예과 2023년 입학·익산 이리고 졸

도표 문제를 풀 때 가장 먼저 해야 할 일은 도표의 제목과 구성 요소를 확인하는 거야. 굳이 도표 전체를 먼저 확인할 필요는 없어. 글을 읽으면서 도표의 각 부분을 확인해서 각 선택지 문장이 제대로 된 설명을 하고 있는지 파악하면 되거든.
보통 숫자를 틀리게 서술하거나, 집단 간의 비교가 틀리거나, 집단 내에서의 잘못된 비교를 하니까, 어떤 집단의 어떤 수치를 가리키는지 정확히 파악해야 해. 이 문제는 Big/Small City와 Suburb of Big/Small City를 비교할 때 헷갈리지 않는 게 중요했어.

H 14 정답 ③ *태양에너지 산업에 추가된 노동자의 수

The table above shows seven U.S. states / ranked by the number of workers added / in the solar industry / between 2015 and 2020, /
위 표는 미국의 일곱 개 주를 보여주고 / 추가된 노동자의 수에 따라 순위가 매겨진 / 태양에너지 산업에 / 2015년에서 2020년 사이에 /

and provides information / on the corresponding growth percentage / in each state. //
정보를 제공한다 / 그에 상응하는 증가율에 관한 / 각 주의 //

❶ During this period, / Florida, / which ranked first / with regard to the number of workers added, / exhibited 71% growth. //
이 기간에 / 플로리다는 / 1위였던 / 추가된 노동자의 수에 있어서 / 71퍼센트의 성장을 보였다 //

❷ The number of workers added / in Utah / was more / than twice the number of workers added / in Minnesota. //
추가된 노동자의 수는 / 유타에서 / 더 많았다 / 추가된 노동자 수의 두 배보다 / 미네소타에서 //

❸ Regarding Texas and Virginia, / each state showed / less than 50% growth. // 단서 텍사스는 44퍼센트, 버지니아는 120퍼센트의 성장을 보였음
텍사스와 버지니아에 관해서는 / 각 주는 보였다 / 50퍼센트 미만의 성장을 //

❹ New York added more than 1,900 workers, / displaying 24% growth. // 뉴욕: 1,964명, 24퍼센트
뉴욕은 1,900명이 넘는 노동자를 추가했다 / 24퍼센트의 성장을 보이면서 //

❺ Among these seven states, / Pennsylvania added the lowest number of workers / during this period. // 펜실베이니아가 1,810명으로 가장 적음
이 일곱 개 주 가운데 / 펜실베이니아는 가장 적은 수의 노동자를 추가했다 / 이 기간에 //

- solar ⓐ 태양열을 이용한
- with regard to ~에 관해서
- regarding prep ~에 관해
- corresponding ⓐ 상응하는
- exhibit ⓥ 보여주다
- display ⓥ 나타내다

위 표는 2015년에서 2020년 사이에 태양에너지 산업에 추가된 노동자의 수에 따라 순위를 매긴 미국의 일곱 개 주를 보여주고, 그에 상응하는 각 주의 증가율에 관한 정보를 제공한다. ① 이 기간에 추가된 노동자의 수에 있어서 1위였던 플로리다는 71퍼센트의 성장을 보였다. ② 유타에서 추가된 노동자의 수는 미네소타에서 추가된 노동자 수의 두 배보다 더 많았다. ③ 텍사스와 버지니아에 관해서는, 각 주는 50퍼센트 미만의 성장을 보였다. ④ 뉴욕은 24퍼센트의 성장을 보이면서, 1,900명이 넘는 노동자를 추가했다. ⑤ 이 일곱 개 주 가운데 펜실베이니아는 이 기간에 가장 적은 수의 노동자를 추가했다.

다음 표의 내용과 일치하지 않는 것은?

2015년과 2020년 사이에 태양에너지 산업에 가장 많은 노동자가 추가된 미국의 주들
U.S. States That Added the Most Solar Industry Workers Between 2015 and 2020

Rank 순위	State 주	Number of Workers Added 추가된 노동자의 수	Growth Percentage (%) 성장률
①	Florida	4,659	71
2	Utah	4,246	158
3	Texas	3,058	44
4	Virginia	2,352	120
5	Minnesota	2,003	101
6	New York	1,964	24
7	Pennsylvania	1,810	72

① 71퍼센트 성장한 플로리다가 1위임
③ 버지니아는 120퍼센트로 50퍼센트보다 높음
④ 뉴욕은 1,964명과 24퍼센트임
⑤ 펜실베이니아는 1,810명으로 7위임
② 유타(4,246명)>미네소타의 두 배(2,003×2=4,006명)

왜 정답? [정답률 91%]

텍사스가 44퍼센트로 50퍼센트 미만의 성장을 보인 것은 맞지만, 버지니아는 120퍼센트로 50퍼센트가 넘는 성장을 보였으므로 ③은 표와 일치하지 않는다.

왜 오답?

① 플로리다가 71퍼센트의 성장을 보이며 1위를 차지했다.
② 유타의 추가된 노동자는 4,246명으로, 미네소타의 2,003명의 두 배보다 더 많았다.
④ 뉴욕은 1,964명을 추가하여 24퍼센트의 성장을 보였다.
⑤ 펜실베이니아는 가장 적은 수인 1,810명을 추가하여 일곱 개 주 중에서 7위를 차지했다.

H 15 정답 ④ *2015년과 2025년의 세계 중산층의 점유율

The above graphs show / the percentage share of the global middle class / by region / in 2015 / and its projected share / in 2025. //
위의 그래프들은 보여준다 / 세계 중산층의 점유율을 / 지역별로 / 2015년에 / 그리고 그것의 예상되는 점유율을 / 2025년에 //

① It is projected / that the share of the global middle class / in Asia Pacific / will increase / from 46 percent in 2015 / to 60 percent in 2025. // 아시아 태평양: 2015년에 46%, 2025년에 60%
~이 예상된다 / 세계 중산층 점유율은 / 아시아 태평양 지역의 / 증가할 것이 / 2015년에 46퍼센트에서 / 2025년에는 60퍼센트로 //

② The projected share of Asia Pacific / in 2025, / the largest / among the six regions, / is more than three times / that of Europe / in the same year. // 2025년: 아시아 태평양은 60%, 유럽은 16%
아시아 태평양 지역의 예상 점유율은 / 2025년의 / 가장 큰 / 여섯 개의 지역 중에서 / 세 배보다 더 많다 / 유럽의 예상 점유율의 / 같은 해 //

③ The shares of Europe and North America / are both projected to decrease, /
유럽과 북미 지역의 점유율은 / 둘 다 감소할 것으로 예상된다 / 유럽은 2015년에 24%, 2025년에 16%

from 24 percent in 2015 to 16 percent in 2025 / for Europe, / and from 11 percent in 2015 to 8 percent in 2025 / for North America. //
2015년에 24퍼센트에서 2025년에 16퍼센트로 / 유럽은 / 그리고 2015년에 11퍼센트로부터 2025년에 8퍼센트로 / 북미 지역은 // 북미는 2015년에 11%, 2025년에 8%

④ Central and South America is not expected(→ expected) / to change from 2015 to 2025 / in its share of the global middle class. // 단서 중남미: 2015년에 9%, 2025년에 7%

중남미 지역은 예상되지 않는다(→ 예상된다) / 2015년에서 2025년까지 변화할 것으로 / 세계 중산층 점유율에 있어서 //
사하라 사막 이남의 아프리카: 2015년과 2025년에 4%

⑤ In 2025, / the share of the Middle East and North Africa / will be larger / than that of sub-Saharan Africa, / as it was in 2015. //

2025년에 / 중동 및 북아프리카의 점유율은 / 더 클 것이다 / 사하라 사막 이남의 아프리카의 점유율보다 / 2015년에 그랬듯이 //
뒤에 larger than that of sub-Saharan Africa가 생략됨

• share ⓝ 점유율, 지분   • middle class 중산층   • region ⓝ 지역
• project ⓥ 예상하다, 추정하다

위의 그래프들은 지역별로 2015년 세계 중산층의 점유율과 2025년에 예상되는 점유율을 보여준다. ① 아시아 태평양 지역의 세계 중산층 점유율은 2015년에 46퍼센트에서 2025년에는 60퍼센트로 증가할 것으로 예상된다. ② 2025년의 아시아 태평양 지역의 예상 점유율은 여섯 개의 지역 중에서 가장 크며, 같은 해 유럽의 예상 점유율의 세 배보다 더 많다. ③ 유럽과 북미 지역의 점유율은, 유럽은 2015년에 24퍼센트로부터 2025년에 16퍼센트로, 북미 지역은 2015년에 11퍼센트로부터 2025년에 8퍼센트로, 둘 다 감소할 것으로 예상된다. ④ 중남미 지역은 세계 중산층 점유율에 있어서 2015년에서 2025년까지 변화할 것으로 예상되지 않는다(→ 예상된다). ⑤ 2015년에 그랬듯이, 2025년에 중동 및 북아프리카의 점유율은 사하라 사막 이남의 아프리카의 점유율보다 더 클 것이다.

다음 도표의 내용과 일치하지 않는 것은?
⑤ 중동 및 북아프리카: 2015, 2025년에 6퍼센트>
사하라 이남 아프리카: 2015, 2025년에 4퍼센트

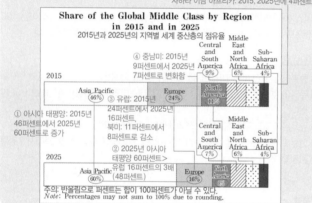

Share of the Global Middle Class by Region
in 2015 and in 2025
2015년과 2025년의 지역별 세계 중산층의 점유율

④ 중남미: 2015년 9퍼센트에서 2025년 7퍼센트로 변화함

① 아시아 태평양: 2015년 46퍼센트에서 2025년 60퍼센트로 증가

③ 유럽: 2015년 24퍼센트에서 2025년 16퍼센트, 북미: 11퍼센트에서 8퍼센트로 감소

② 2025년 아시아 태평양 60퍼센트>
유럽 16퍼센트의 3배

Note: Percentages may not sum to 100% due to rounding.
주의: 반올림으로 퍼센트는 합이 100퍼센트가 아닐 수 있다.

왜 정답? [정답률 90%]

도표에 따르면 중남미는 2015년에는 9퍼센트였고, 2025년에는 7퍼센트로 예상된다. 따라서 변화할 것으로 예상되지 않는다고 한 ④은 도표와 일치하지 않는다.

왜 오답?
not을 뺀 긍정문으로 바꾸어야 도표와 일치함 꿀팁

① 아시아 태평양은 2015년에는 46퍼센트였고, 2025년에는 60퍼센트로 예상되므로 증가할 것으로 예상된다는 설명은 적절하다.
② 2025년에 아시아 태평양은 60퍼센트이고, 유럽은 16퍼센트이므로, 아시아 태평양이 유럽의 세 배인 48퍼센트보다 더 크다.
③ 유럽은 2015년에 24퍼센트, 2025년에 16퍼센트이고, 북미는 2015년에 11퍼센트, 2025년에 8퍼센트이므로 감소할 것으로 예상된다는 설명은 도표와 일치한다.
⑤ 중동 및 북아프리카는 2015년과 2025년에 6퍼센트이고, 사하라 사막 이남의 아프리카는 2015년과 2025년에 4퍼센트이므로, 2015년과 2025년에 중동 및 북아메리카가 사하라 사막 이남의 아프리카보다 비율이 더 컸고, 더 클 것이라는 설명은 적절하다.

H 16 정답 ④ *2015년 산업별 전 세계 플라스틱 폐기물 발생량

The above table shows / global plastic waste generation / by industry / in 2015. //
위 표는 보여준다 / 전 세계 플라스틱 폐기물 발생을 / 산업별 / 2015년에 //

① The sector / that generated plastic waste most / was packaging, / accounting for 46.69% / of all plastic waste generated. // 포장 부문이 46.69퍼센트로 발생량이 가장 많음
주어   주격 보어   동사

부문 / 플라스틱 폐기물을 가장 많이 발생시킨 / 포장 부문으로 / 46.69퍼센트를 차지했다 / 발생된 전체 플라스틱 폐기물의 //

② The textiles sector generated / 38 million tons of plastic waste, / or 12.58% of the total plastic waste / generated. // 섬유 부문: 3,800만 톤, 12.58퍼센트
동격의 접속사

섬유 부문은 발생시켰다 / 3,800만 톤의 플라스틱 폐기물을 / 즉 총 플라스틱 폐기물의 12.58퍼센트를 / 발생된 // 소비자·기관 부문: 3,700만 톤, 운송 부문: 1,700만 톤

③ The consumer and institutional products sector generated / 37 million tons of plastic waste, / and the amount was more than twice that of plastic waste / the transportation sector generated. //
앞에 목적격 관계대명사가 생략됨 *

소비자·기관 제품 부문은 발생시켰는데 / 3,700만 톤의 플라스틱 폐기물을 / 그 양은 플라스틱 폐기물량의 두 배가 넘었다 / 운송 부문이 발생시킨 //

④ The electrical and electronic sector generated / just as much plastic waste / as the building and construction sector did, /
전기·전자 부문은 발생시켰는데 / 꼭 (~만큼) 많은 플라스틱 폐기물을 / 건축·건설 부문이 발생시킨 만큼 // 단서 전기·전자 부문: 1,300만 톤/4.3퍼센트, 건축·건설 부문: 1,300만 톤/4.3퍼센트

each sector accounting for 8.60%(→ 4.30%) / of the total plastic waste generation. //
각 부문은 8.60퍼센트(→ 4.30퍼센트)를 차지했다 / 총 플라스틱 폐기물 발생량의 //

⑤ Only one million tons of plastic waste were generated / in the industrial machinery sector, / representing less than 0.50% / of the total plastic waste generated. // 산업용 기계 부문: 100만 톤, 0.33퍼센트
단 100만 톤의 플라스틱 폐기물만 발생되었는데 / 산업용 기계 부문에서는 / 이것은 0.50퍼센트에 못 미친다 / 발생된 총 플라스틱 폐기물의 //

• table ⓝ 표, 목록   • global ⓐ 세계적인, 지구의
• generation ⓝ 발생   • industry ⓝ 산업   • sector ⓝ 부문
• packaging ⓝ 포장   • account for ~을 차지하다
• institutional ⓐ 기관의   • industrial ⓐ 산업[공업]의
• machinery ⓝ (특히 큰 기계를 집합적으로 가리켜) 기계(류)
• represent ⓥ (~에) 해당[상당]하다   • round ⓥ 반올림[반내림]하다
• sum ⓥ 합계하다, 합계가 ~이 되다

위 표는 2015년의 산업별 전 세계 플라스틱 폐기물 발생을 보여준다. ① 플라스틱 폐기물을 가장 많이 발생시킨 부문은 포장 부문으로, 발생된 총 플라스틱 폐기물의 46.69퍼센트를 차지했다. ② 섬유 부문은 3,800만 톤의 플라스틱 폐기물, 즉 발생된 총 플라스틱 폐기물의 12.58퍼센트를 발생시켰다. ③ 소비자·기관 제품 부문은 3,700만 톤의 플라스틱 폐기물을 발생시켰는데, 그 양은 운송 부문이 발생시킨 플라스틱 폐기물량의 두 배가 넘는 것이었다. ④ 전기·전자 부문은 건축·건설 부문이 발생시킨 플라스틱 폐기물과 똑같은 양을 발생시켰는데, 각 부문은 총 플라스틱 폐기물 발생량의 8.60퍼센트(→ 4.30퍼센트)를 차지했다. ⑤ 산업용 기계 부문에서는 단 100만 톤의 플라스틱 폐기물만 발생되었는데, 이것은 발생된 총 플라스틱 폐기물의 0.50퍼센트에 못 미친다.

왜 정답? [정답률 83%]

전기·전자 부문과 건축·건설 부문의 플라스틱 폐기물 발생량이 똑같은 것은 맞지만, 각각의 비율이 4.3퍼센트이므로 각 부문이 8.6퍼센트를 차지했다고 설명한 ④은 표와 일치하지 않는다.

왜 오답?
each에 주의! 꿀팁

① 포장 부문이 46.69퍼센트로 가장 많은 플라스틱 폐기물을 발생시켰다.
② 섬유 부문은 전체 폐기물의 12.58퍼센트, 3,800만 톤을 발생시켰다.
③ 소비자·기관 제품 부문은 3,700만 톤, 운송 부문은 1,700만 톤의 플라스틱 폐기물을 발생시켰으므로, 소비자·기관 제품 부문이 두 배 넘게 발생시킨 것이다.
⑤ 산업용 기계 부문은 100만 톤으로 0.33퍼센트를 차지했으므로 0.5퍼센트보다 적다.

다음 표의 내용과 일치하지 <u>않는</u> 것은?

Global Plastic Waste Generation by Industry in 2015
2015년의 산업별 전 세계 플라스틱 폐기물 발생

Market Sectors 시장 부문		Million Tons	%
Packaging 포장		141 가장 많은 발생량	46.69
Textiles 섬유	3,800만 톤, 12.58퍼센트	38	12.58
Consumer and Institutional Products 소비자와 기관 제품	두 배 넘게	37	12.25
Transportation 운송	차이 남	17	5.63
Electrical and Electronic 전기와 전자	동일함	13	4.30
Building and Construction 건축과 건설		13	4.30
Industrial Machinery 산업용 기계	0.5보다 작음	1	0.33
Others 기타		42	13.91
Total 총계		302	100

Note: Due to rounding, the percentages may not sum to 100%.
참고: 반올림으로 인해 백분율 합계가 100퍼센트가 아닐 수 있다.
각각 4.3퍼센트

— 어법 특강 —

＊ 관계대명사의 생략

– 목적격 관계대명사는 생략하는 경우가 많다.
• She was a celebrated actress (whom) he had known and loved.
  a celebrated actress를 선행사로 하는 관계대명사
  (그녀는 그가 알고 사랑했던 유명한 배우였다.)

– 「주격 관계대명사＋be동사」는 생략할 수 있다.
• Look at the singer (who is) performing on the stage!
  the singer를 선행사로 하는 관계대명사
  (무대에서 공연하고 있는 가수를 봐!)

H 17 정답 ⑤ ＊소매 판매의 온라인 점유율

The graph above shows / the online shares of retail sales / for each of six countries / in 2012 and in 2019. //
위 도표는 보여 준다 / 소매 판매의 온라인 점유율을 / 여섯 나라 각각의 / 2012년과 2019년에 //

The online share of retail sales refers / to the percentage of retail sales / conducted online / in a given country. //
앞에 주격 관계대명사와 be동사가 생략됨
소매 판매의 온라인 점유율은 말한다 / 소매 판매의 비율을 / 온라인으로 이루어진 / 주어진 나라에서 //

① For each country, / its online share of retail sales / in 2019 / was larger / than that in 2012. // 모든 나라의 오른쪽 그래프가 왼쪽 그래프보다 더 길 = online share of retail sales
각 나라에서 / 소매 판매의 온라인 점유율은 / 2019년의 / 더 컸다 / 2012년의 그것보다 //

② Among the six countries, / the UK owned the largest online share of retail sales / with 19.7% / in 2019. // 2019년의 그래프는 영국이 19.7%로 가장 길
= Of
여섯 나라 중에서 / 영국은 가장 큰 소매 판매의 온라인 점유율을 가졌다 / 19.7퍼센트로 / 2019년에 //

③ In 2019, / the U.S. had the second largest online share of retail sales / with 16.5%. // 2019년 그래프가 두 번째로 긴 것은 16.5%의 미국임
2019년에 / 미국은 두 번째로 큰 소매 판매의 온라인 점유율을 가졌다 / 16.5퍼센트로 //

④ In 2012, / the online share of retail sales / in the Netherlands / was larger / than that in France, / whereas the reverse was true / in 2019. // 2012년에 네덜란드는 5.7%, 프랑스는 5.4%이고, 2019년에는 네덜란드가 9.9%, 프랑스가 10.9%
= online share of retail sales
2012년에 / 소매 판매의 온라인 점유율은 / 네덜란드의 / 더 컸다 / 프랑스의 그것보다 / 그 반대가 사실이었지만 / 2019년에는 //

단서 2019년에 스페인은 5.4%
⑤ In the case of Spain and Italy, / the online share of retail sales / in each country / was less than 5.0% / both in 2012 and in 2019. //
스페인과 이탈리아의 경우에 / 소매 판매의 온라인 점유율이 / 각국에서 / 5.0퍼센트보다 더 적었다 / 2012년과 2019년 둘 다에서 //

• share ⓝ 점유율, 몫 • retail ⓐ 소매의, 소매상의
• refer to ~을 나타내다, ~와 관련이 있다 • conduct ⓥ (특정한 활동을) 하다
• own ⓥ 소유하다 • whereas [conj] ~한 반면에 • reverse ⓝ (정)반대
• case ⓝ (특정한 상황의) 경우, 사례

위 도표는 2012년과 2019년에 여섯 나라 각각의 소매 판매의 온라인 점유율을 보여 준다. 소매 판매의 온라인 점유율은 주어진 나라에서 온라인으로 이루어진 소매 판매의 비율을 말한다. ① 각 나라에서 2019년의 소매 판매의 온라인 점유율은 2012년의 그것보다 더 컸다. ② 여섯 나라 중에서 영국은 2019년에 19.7 퍼센트로 가장 큰 소매 판매의 온라인 점유율을 가졌다. ③ 2019년에 미국은 16.5퍼센트로 소매 판매의 온라인 점유율이 두 번째로 컸다. ④ 2012년에 네덜란드의 소매 판매의 온라인 점유율은 프랑스의 그것보다 더 컸지만, 2019년에는 그 반대였다. ⑤ 스페인과 이탈리아의 경우에, 각국에서 소매 판매의 온라인 점유율이 2012년과 2019년 둘 다에서 5.0퍼센트보다 더 적었다.

다음 도표의 내용과 일치하지 <u>않는</u> 것은?

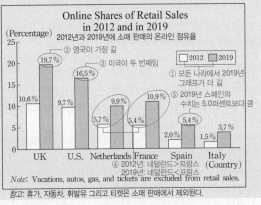

Online Shares of Retail Sales in 2012 and in 2019
(Percentage) 2012년과 2019년에 소매 판매의 온라인 점유율

- ② 영국이 가장 김
- ③ 미국이 두 번째임
- ① 모든 나라에서 2019년 그래프가 더 김
- ⑤ 2019년 스페인의 수치는 5.0퍼센트보다 큼

UK 10.6% / 19.7%, U.S. 9.7% / 16.5%, Netherlands 5.7% / 9.9%, France 5.4% / 10.9%, Spain 2.0% / 5.4%, Italy 1.5% / 3.7% (Country)
④ 2012년: 네덜란드＞프랑스, 2019년: 네덜란드＜프랑스
□ 2012 ▨ 2019

Note: Vacations, autos, gas, and tickets are excluded from retail sales.
참고: 휴가, 자동차, 휘발유 그리고 티켓은 소매 판매에서 제외된다.

＞왜 정답＞ [정답률 88%]

스페인의 2019년 수치가 5.4퍼센트이므로, 2012년과 2019년에 스페인과 이탈리아의 수치가 5.0퍼센트보다 더 적었다고 한 ⑤은 도표와 일치하지 않는다.

＞왜 오답＞

① 6개국 모두 2012년 그래프보다 2019년 그래프가 더 길다.
②, ③ 2019년에 가장 큰 수치는 19.7퍼센트의 영국, 두 번째로 큰 수치는 16.5퍼센트의 미국이다.
④ 2012년에는 네덜란드가 5.7퍼센트, 프랑스가 5.4퍼센트로 네덜란드가 더 컸지만, 2019년에는 네덜란드가 9.9퍼센트, 프랑스가 10.9퍼센트로 프랑스가 더 컸다.

— 배경 지식 —

＊ 도매(wholesale)

소매가 개인적으로 소비하는 최종 소비자에 대한 판매인 데 반해 도매는 최종 소비자에 대한 판매 이외의 모든 판매를 포괄하는 개념이다.

도매와 소매의 개념 구분은 그 거래 규모와 거래 건수, 거래 대상 품목 등에 의해 규정되는 것이 아니라 일반적으로 판매처의 성격에 의해 규정된다. 예를 들면 문방구 상인이 연필을 개인적으로 사용하는 최종 소비자에게 판매하는 경우는 소매지만, 사무용으로 사용하는 사무실이나 제조업자에게 판매하는 경우는 도매가 된다. 따라서 같은 업자가 같은 상품을 판매하는 경우라 하더라도 소매가 될 수도 있고, 도매가 될 수도 있다.

H 18 정답 ④ ＊지역별 세계 항공기 승객 수의 점유율

The graph above shows / the share of the global air passenger
traffic / by region / in 2015 / and its projected share / in 2040. //
the global air passenger traffic을 가리키는 소유격 대명사
위의 도표는 보여준다 / 세계 항공기 승객 수의 점유율을 / 지역별로 / 2015년의 / 그리고
그것의 예상되는 점유율을 / 2040년의 //

① Asia Pacific had the highest share of 34 percent / among the
six regions / in 2015 / *병렬 구조* and is expected / to have the highest share
/ in 2040. // 아시아 태평양: 2015년에 34%로 1위, 2040년에도 1위
아시아 태평양 지역은 34퍼센트로 가장 높은 점유율을 가졌고 / 6개 지역 중 / 2015년에 /
예상된다 / 가장 높은 점유율을 가질 것으로 / 2040년에도 //

② Europe is projected / to rank second in 2040, / with its share /
less than half / of that of Asia Pacific / that year. //
유럽은 예상되고 / 2040년에 2위일 것이다 / 그것의 예상 점유율로 / 절반에 미치지 못하는 /
아시아 태평양의 그것의 / 그해의 // —— 유럽: 2040년에 20%로 2위, 2040년에 아시아 태평양은 47%

③ The shares of Europe and North America / are both expected
to decrease / from 2015 to 2040, / the decrease of the latter being
= North America
greater / than that of the former. // 유럽: 27% → 20%, 북미: 24% → 15%
= Europe
유럽과 북미의 점유율은 / 모두 감소할 것으로 예상되는데 / 2015년부터 2040년까지 /
후자의 감소 폭은 더 클 것이다 / 전자의 그것보다 //
단수 주어
④ The share of Middle East and North Africa / in 2040 / is
단수 동사
projected / to be more(→ less) than double that of 2015, /
중동과 북아프리카의 점유율이 / 2040년에 / 예상된다 / 2015년의 그것의 두 배가 넘을(→
넘지 않을) 것으로 / *단서* 중동&북아프리카: 2015년 5%, 2040년 9%
부사절 접속사(대조)
while in Latin America and Caribbean, / the share will decline
slightly / from 2015 to 2040. // 라틴 아메리카&카리브해 지역: 2015년 8%, 2040년 7%
라틴 아메리카와 카리브해 지역에서는 / 점유율이 약간 감소할 것인 반면에 / 2015년부터
2040년까지 //
주어, 선행사 *주격 관계대명사*
⑤ Sub-Saharan Africa, / which had the lowest share in 2015 /
동사
among the regions, / with 2 percent, / will be the only region / to
keep the same share in 2040. // 사하라 사막 이남의 아프리카: 2015년에 2%로 꼴찌,
2040년에도 2%
사하라 사막 이남의 아프리카는 / 2015년에 가장 낮은 점유율을 가졌던 / 그 지역들 중에서 /
2퍼센트로 / 유일한 지역일 것이다 / 2040년에 같은 점유율을 유지하는 //

- -

- share ⓝ 점유율　　• passenger traffic 여객 수송　　• region ⓝ 지역
- projected ⓐ 예상되는　　• decrease ⓥ 감소하다
- decline ⓥ 감소하다

위의 도표는 2015년 지역별 세계 항공기 승객 수의 점유율과 2040년에
그것(지역별 세계 항공기 승객 수)의 예상되는 점유율을 보여준다. ① 아시아
태평양 지역은 6개 지역 중 2015년에 34퍼센트로 가장 높은 점유율을 가졌고
2040년에도 가장 높은 점유율을 가질 것으로 예상된다. ② 유럽은 2040년에
2위일 것으로 예상되고, 그 예상 점유율은 그해의 아시아 태평양 지역
점유율의 절반에 미치지 못할 것이다. ③ 유럽과 북미의 점유율은 2015년부터
2040년까지 모두 감소할 것으로 예상되며, 후자의 감소 폭은 전자의 그것(감소
폭)보다 클 것으로 예상된다. ④ 2040년에 중동과 북아프리카의 점유율이
2015년의 그것(중동과 북아프리카의 점유율)의 두 배가 넘을(→ 넘지 않을)
것으로 예상되는 반면에, 라틴 아메리카와 카리브해 지역에서는 2015년부터
2040년까지 점유율이 약간 감소할 것이다. ⑤ 2015년에 그 지역들 중에서
2퍼센트로 가장 낮은 점유율을 가졌던 사하라 사막 이남의 아프리카는
2040년에는 같은 점유율을 유지하는 유일한 지역이 될 것이다.

다음 도표의 내용과 일치하지 않는 것은?

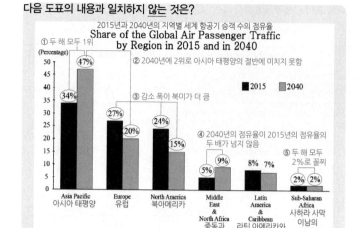

2015년과 2040년의 지역별 세계 항공기 승객 수의 점유율
**Share of the Global Air Passenger Traffic
by Region in 2015 and in 2040**

① 두 해 모두 1위
② 2040년에 2위로 아시아 태평양의 절반에 미치지 못함
③ 감소 폭이 북미가 더 큼
④ 2040년의 점유율이 2015년의 점유율의 두 배가 넘지 않음
⑤ 두 해 모두 2%로 꼴찌

> **왜 정답?**　[정답률 94%]

④ 중동과 북아프리카의 점유율: 2015년에 5%, 2040년에 9%
→ 2040년의 점유율이 2015년의 점유율의 두 배가 넘지 않으므로 ④의 more를
less로 바꿔야 한다.

> **왜 오답?**

① 아시아 태평양은 2015년에 34%로 1위, 2040년에도 1위이다.
② 유럽은 2040년에 20%로 2위, 2040년에 아시아 태평양은 47%로 아시아
　태평양의 절반에 미치지 못한다.
③ 유럽은 27%에서 20%로 감소, 북미는 24%에서 15%로 감소해서 감소 폭이
　북미가 더 크다.
⑤ 사하라 사막 이남의 아프리카: 2015년에 2%로 꼴찌, 2040년에도 2%

H 19 정답 ④ ＊나이 그룹별 낮잠 통계

The above graph shows / the nap length / and the number of
nap days per year / by age group. //
위 도표는 보여준다 / 낮잠 길이와 / 1년당 낮잠을 잔 날의 수를 / 나이 그룹별로 //
완전자동사
① As people get older, / the nap length consistently decreases, /
but that is not the case / with the number of nap days per year. //
사람들은 나이가 들수록 / 낮잠 길이가 꾸준히 감소하지만 / 그것은 사실이 아니다 / 1년당
낮잠을 잔 날의 수의 경우 // 오른쪽으로 갈수록 시간의 길이(mins)는 짧아지고,
날짜의 수(days)는 들쑥날쑥함
② The 18 to 24 age group, / which has the longest nap length, /
단수 주어
naps over 30 minutes longer / than the 55 and older age group,
단수 동사 / which has the shortest nap length. // 낮잠의 길이: 18-24세는 78.3분,
55세 이상은 43.4분
18세에서 24세 그룹은 / 가장 긴 낮잠 길이를 가진 / 30분 더 길게 낮잠을 잔다 / 55세 이상
그룹보다 / 가장 짧은 낮잠 길이를 가진 //
③ As for the number of nap days per year, / the 55 and older age
group / has the most days, 135.7 days, / *부사절 접속사(대조)* whereas the 25 to 34 age
group has / the fewest days, 84.8 days. //
1년당 낮잠을 잔 날의 수에 대해서는 / 55세 이상 그룹이 / 135.7일로 가장 많은 일수를
가졌다 / 25세에서 34세 그룹이 가진 반면에 / 84.8일로 가장 적은 일수를 //
④ The 35 to 44 age group is ranked third / in the nap length,
/ and second(→ third) / in the number of nap days per year. //
35세에서 44세 그룹은 세 번째 순위이다 / 낮잠 길이에서 / 그리고 두 번째(→ 세 번째) 순위
1년당 낮잠을 잔 날의 수에서 // *단서* 35-44세: 낮잠 길이는 3위, 낮잠을 잔 날의 수도 3위
⑤ The nap length and the number of nap days per year / of the
45 to 54 age group / are lower than those / of the 35 to 44 age
group. // 45-54세는 46.9분, 86.8일이고, 35-44세는 55분, 91.3일
낮잠 길이와 1년당 낮잠을 잔 날의 수는 / 45세에서 54세 그룹의 / 그것보다 더 낮다 /
35세에서 44세 그룹의 //

- -

- consistently ⓐⒹ 꾸준하게　　• as for ~에 대하여
- rank ⓥ 순위를 매기다

위 도표는 각 나이 그룹별로 1년 동안의 낮잠 길이와 낮잠을 잔 날짜가
며칠인지를 보여준다. ① 사람들은 나이가 들수록, 낮잠 길이가 꾸준히
감소하지만, 1년 동안 낮잠을 잔 날짜의 경우는 그렇지 않다. ② 가장 긴 낮잠
길이를 가진 18세에서 24세 그룹은 가장 짧은 낮잠 길이를 가진 55세 이상
그룹보다 30분 넘게 낮잠을 잔다. ③ 1년 동안 낮잠을 잔 날짜에 대해서는,
25세에서 34세 그룹이 84.8일로 가장 적은 일수를 가진 반면에, 55세 이상
그룹이 135.7일로 가장 많은 일수를 가졌다. ④ 35세에서 44세 그룹은 낮잠
길이가 세 번째로 높고, 1년 동안 낮잠을 잔 날짜는 두 번째(→ 세 번째)이다.
⑤ 45세에서 54세 그룹의 낮잠 길이와 1년 동안 낮잠을 잔 날짜는 35세에서
44세 그룹보다 더 적다.

다음 도표의 내용과 일치하지 <u>않는</u> 것은?

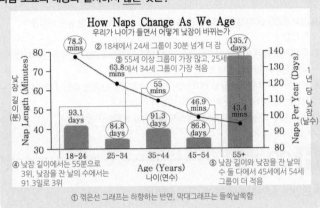

How Naps Change As We Age
우리가 나이가 들면서 어떻게 낮잠이 바뀌는가
② 18세에서 24세 그룹이 30분씩 더 잠
③ 55세 이상 그룹이 가장 많고, 25세에서 34세 그룹이 가장 적음
④ 낮잠 길이에서는 55분으로 3위, 낮잠을 잔 날의 수에서는 91.3일로 3위
⑤ 낮잠 길이와 낮잠을 잔 날의 수 둘 다에서 45세에서 54세 그룹이 더 적음
① 꺾은선 그래프는 하향하는 반면, 막대그래프는 들쑥날쑥함

>왜 정답? [정답률 93%]

35세에서 44세 그룹: 낮잠 길이에서는 55분으로 3위, 낮잠을 잔 날의 수에서는
91.3일로 3위
▶ 1년당 낮잠을 잔 날의 수에서 2위라고 한 ④은 도표와 일치하지 않음

>왜 오답?

① 꺾은선 그래프는 오른쪽으로 갈수록 하향하는 반면, 막대그래프는 들쑥날쑥하다.
② 18세에서 24세 그룹은 78.3분을 자고, 55세 이상 그룹은 43.4분을 자므로, 전자가
  30분 넘게 더 잔다.
③ 1년당 낮잠을 잔 날의 수: 55세 이상 그룹이 135.7일로 가장 많고, 25세에서 34세
  그룹이 84.8일로 가장 적다.
⑤ 45세에서 54세 그룹과 35세에서 44세 그룹을 비교하면, 낮잠 길이와 낮잠을 잔
  날의 수 둘 다에서 45세에서 54세 그룹이 더 적다.

H 20 정답 ④ ＊2021년과 2050년의 치매 환자 수 ─────

The graph above shows the number / of dementia patients per
1,000 inhabitants / in six European countries / in 2021 and in
2050 / (The number in 2050 / is estimated). //
위의 그래프는 수를 보여 준다 / 거주자 1,000명당 치매 환자의 / 6개 유럽 국가에서의 /
2021년과 2050년의 / (2050년의 숫자는 / 예측된 것이다) //

단수 주어
① By 2050, / the number of dementia patients per 1,000 people /
단수 동사
is expected to increase / by more than 10 / in all given countries
compared / to 2021. // 6개 국가 모두 2021년보다 2050년의 수치가 10 넘게 많음
2050년까지 / 1,000명당 치매 환자 수는 / 증가할 것으로 예측된다 / 10명 넘게 / 모든
주어진 국가들에서 / 2021년에 비해 //   2021년과 2050년 둘 다 이탈리아의 수치가 가장 높음

② In 2021, / Italy recorded / the highest proportion of dementia
= Italy
patients / out of the six countries / and it is expected to do so /
in 2050 / as well. //   = record the highest proportion of dementia patients ~
2021년에는 / 이탈리아가 기록했다 / 가장 높은 치매 환자 비율을 / 6개 국가 중에 / 그리고
그것은 그러할 것으로 예측된다 / 2050년에도 / 역시 //

단수 주어   단수 동사
③ The proportion of dementia patients / in Spain / was lower
than that of Germany / in 2021, / but is expected to exceed / that
of Germany / in 2050. // 2021년: 스페인 21 < 독일 22 2050년: 스페인 41 > 독일 36
치매 환자 비율은 / 스페인에서 / 독일의 그것보다 낮았지만 / 2021년에는 / 초과할 것으로
예측된다 / 독일의 그것을 / 2050년에는 //   **단서** 2021년: 스위스&네덜란드 18
                                        2050년: 스위스 33, 네덜란드 33
④ Switzerland and the Netherlands had / the same proportion
of dementia patients / in 2021, / and by 2050 / those proportions
are both projected / to more(→ less) than double. //
스위스와 네덜란드는 가지고 있었으며 / 동일한 치매 환자 비율을 / 2021년에 / 2050년까지
/ 그 비율은 둘 다 예상된다 / 두 배가 넘을(→ 넘지 않을) 것으로 //

⑤ Among the six countries, / Belgium shows the smallest gap /
between the number of dementia patients per 1,000 inhabitants
/ in 2021 and in 2050. // 2021년과 2050년의 격차: 벨기에가 12로 가장 적음
6개 국가 중 / 벨기에는 가장 적은 격차를 보인다 / 거주자 1,000명당 치매 환자 수 사이의 /
2021년과 2050년에 //

· ·
• dementia ⓝ 치매   • inhabitant ⓝ 주민
• estimate ⓥ 추정하다, 예측하다   • proportion ⓝ 부분, 비율
• exceed ⓥ 넘다, 넘어서다   • project ⓥ 계획하다, 예상하다

위의 그래프는 6개 유럽 국가의 2021년과 2050년의 거주자 1,000명당
치매 환자 수를 보여 준다(2050년의 숫자는 예측된 것이다). ① 2050년까지
1,000명당 치매 환자 수는 모든 주어진 국가들에서 2021년에 비해 10명 넘게
증가할 것으로 예측된다. ② 2021년에는 이탈리아가 6개 국가 중에 가장
높은 치매 환자 비율을 기록했고 2050년에도 역시 그러할 것으로 예측된다.
③ 스페인에서 치매 환자 비율은 2021년에는 독일의 그것보다 낮았지만
2050년에는 독일의 그것을 초과할 것으로 예측된다. ④ 스위스와 네덜란드는
2021년에 동일한 치매 환자 비율을 가지고 있었으며 2050년까지 둘 다 그
비율이 두 배가 넘을(→ 넘지 않을) 것으로 예상된다. ⑤ 6개 국가 중 벨기에는
2021년과 2050년 사이의 거주자 1,000명당 치매 환자 수에서 가장 적은 격차를
보인다.

다음 도표의 내용과 일치하지 <u>않는</u> 것은?

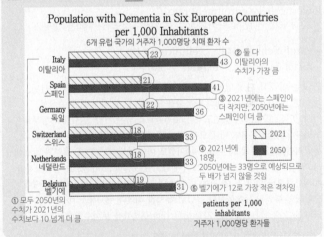

Population with Dementia in Six European Countries per 1,000 Inhabitants
6개 유럽 국가의 거주자 1,000명당 치매 환자 수
② 둘 다 이탈리아의 수치가 가장 큼
③ 2021년에는 스페인이 더 작지만, 2050년에는 스페인이 더 큼
④ 2021년에 18명, 2050년에는 33명으로 예상되므로 두 배가 넘지 않을 것임
⑤ 벨기에가 12로 가장 적은 격차임
① 모두 2050년의 수치가 2021년의 수치보다 10 넘게 더 큼
☐ 2021 ■ 2050
patients per 1,000 inhabitants
거주자 1,000명당 환자들

Italy 이탈리아 23 / 43
Spain 스페인 21 / 41
Germany 독일 22 / 36
Switzerland 스위스 18 / 33
Netherlands 네덜란드 18 / 33
Belgium 벨기에 19 / 31

>왜 정답? [정답률 90%]

④ 스위스와 네덜란드가 2021년에 18명으로 동일한 치매 환자 비율인 것은 맞다.
  하지만 2050년에는 33명으로 예상되므로, 두 배가 넘을 것이라는 설명은 도표와
  맞지 않는다.

>왜 오답?

① 주어진 국가 모두에서 2050년의 수치가 2021년의 수치보다 10 넘게 더 크다.
② 2021년과 2050년 둘 다 이탈리아의 수치가 가장 크다.
③ 스페인과 독일의 수치는, 2021년에는 스페인이 더 작지만, 2050년에는 스페인이
  더 크다.
⑤ 2021년과 2050년의 격차는 이탈리아와 스페인은 20, 독일은 14, 스위스와
  네덜란드는 15, 벨기에는 12이다.

H

＊미국의 인종/민족별 대학 등록률

The table above shows / the college enrollment rates of 18- to 24-year-olds / from five racial/ethnic groups / in the U.S. / in 2011, 2016, and 2021. //
위 표는 보여준다 / 18세에서 24세 사람들의 대학 등록률을 / 다섯 인종/민족 집단의 / 미국 내 / 2011년, 2016년, 그리고 2021년에 //

세 해 모두 아시아인의 비율이 가장 높음
① Among the five groups, / Asians exhibited the highest college
관계대명사
enrollment rate / with more than 50% / in each year / listed in the table. //
앞에 주격 관계대명사와 be동사가 생략됨
다섯 집단 중에서 / 아시아인은 가장 높은 대학 등록률을 보였다 / 50퍼센트를 넘는 / 연도마다 / 표에 열거된 /

백인: 2011년 45, 2016년 42, 2021년 38퍼센트이고, 세 해 모두 두 번째로 높은 비율
② Whites were the second highest / in terms of the college enrollment rate / among all the groups / in all three years, /
부사절 접속사(대조)
while the rate dropped below 40% / in 2021. //
백인은 두 번째로 높았다 / 대학 등록률에 있어 / 모든 집단 중에서 / 3년 내내 / 그 비율은 40퍼센트 아래로 떨어진 반면에 / 2021년에 //

③ The college enrollment rates / of both Blacks and Hispanics(→ Blacks) / were higher than 35% / but lower than 40% / in 2011 and in 2021. // **단서** 흑인: 2011년 37퍼센트, 2021년 37퍼센트 히스패닉: 2011년 35퍼센트, 2021년 33퍼센트
대학 등록률이 / 흑인과 히스패닉 둘 다(→ 흑인)의 / 35퍼센트보다 높았지만 / 40퍼센트보다 낮았다 / 2011년과 2021년에 //

2016년: 히스패닉 39퍼센트, 흑인 36퍼센트
선행사
④ Among the years / displayed in the table, / 2016 was the
관계부사
only year / when the college enrollment rate of Hispanics / was
= the college enrollment rate
higher than that of Blacks. //
연도 중 / 표에 나타난 / 2016년은 유일한 해였다 / 히스패닉의 대학 등록률이 / 흑인의 그것보다 높았던 //

세 해 모두 아메리칸 인디언/알래스카 원주민의 비율이 가장 낮음
⑤ In each year, / American Indians/Alaska Natives showed / the lowest college enrollment rate. //
매년 / 아메리칸 인디언/알래스카 원주민은 보여주었다 / 가장 낮은 대학 등록률을 //

・enrollment ⓝ 등록   ・ethnic ⓐ 민족의
・racial ⓐ 인종의   ・exhibit ⓥ 보이다

위 표는 미국 내 다섯 인종/민족 집단의 18세에서 24세 사람들의 2011년, 2016년, 그리고 2021년 대학 등록률을 보여준다. ① 다섯 집단 중에서 아시아인은 표에 열거된 연도마다 50퍼센트를 넘는 가장 높은 대학 등록률을 보였다. ② 백인은 3년 내내 모든 집단 중에서 대학 등록률이 두 번째로 높았지만, 2021년에 그 비율은 40퍼센트 아래로 떨어졌다. ③ 흑인과 히스패닉 둘 다(→ 흑인)의 2011년과 2021년에 대학 등록률이 35퍼센트보다 높았지만 40퍼센트보다 낮았다. ④ 표에 나타난 연도 중, 2016년은 히스패닉의 대학 등록률이 흑인의 등록률보다 높았던 유일한 해였다. ⑤ 매년, 아메리칸 인디언/알래스카 원주민은 가장 낮은 대학 등록률을 보여주었다.

다음 도표의 내용과 일치하지 않는 것은?

미국 내 인종/민족의 18세에서 24세 사람들의
College Enrollment Rates of 18- to 24-year-olds
2011년, 2016년, 그리고 2021년 대학 등록률
by Race/Ethnicity in the U.S. in 2011, 2016, and 2021

종/민족 / 연도 Year Race/Ethnicity	2011	2016	2021
백인 White	45%	42%	38%
흑인 Black	37%	36%	37%
히스패닉 Hispanic	35%	39%	33%
아시아인 Asian	60%	58%	61%
아메리칸 인디언/알래스카 원주민 American Indian/ Alaska Native	24%	19%	28%

② 백인은 항상 두 번째로 높았지만, 2021년에 40퍼센트 아래로 떨어졌음
③ 히스패닉의 비율은 35퍼센트보다 높지 않았음
① 아시아인은 세 해 모두 가장 높은 비율을 보임
⑤ 매년 가장 낮은 대학 등록률을 보여주었음
④ 2016년은 히스패닉의 대학 등록률이 흑인의 등록률보다 높았던 유일한 해였음

Note: Rounded figures are displayed.
참고: 반올림 숫자가 표시된다.

왜 2등급? both라는 표현이 등장하여 두 그룹의 대학 등록률을 동시에 살펴봐야 해서 헷갈릴 수도 있는 2등급 대비 문제이다. 표에서 every, all, both 등 여러 그룹의 수치를 나타내는 표현이 등장한다면 그 중 하나라도 설명과 일치하지 않는 수치가 있는지 꼼꼼히 살펴봐야 한다.

왜 정답?
③ 2021년에 히스패닉의 비율은 33퍼센트로, 35퍼센트보다 낮다. 2011년에도 35퍼센트로, 35퍼센트보다 높지 않다. 따라서 흑인과 히스패닉 둘 다가 아니라 흑인의 비율만 2011년과 2021년에 37퍼센트로, 35퍼센트보다 높다.

왜 오답?
① 아시아인은 60퍼센트, 58퍼센트, 61퍼센트로 세 해 모두 가장 높은 비율을 차지했다.
② 두 번째로 높은 비율을 차지한 것은 세 해 모두 백인인데, 2021년에는 38퍼센트로, 40퍼센트 미만으로 떨어졌다.
④ 히스패닉과 흑인의 비율을 비교하면, 2011년과 2021년에는 흑인의 비율이 더 높았는데, 2016년에는 히스패닉의 비율이 더 높았다.
⑤ 세 해 모두 아메리칸 인디언/알래스카 원주민의 비율이 가장 낮다.

＊관광에 참여한 EU-28 인구의 점유율

The above graph shows / the share of the EU-28 population / participating in tourism / in 2017 / by age group and destination category. //
위의 그래프는 보여준다 / EU-28 인구의 점유율을 / 관광에 참여한 / 2017년에 / 연령대와 목적지 범주별로 //

다섯 개 그래프 모두에서 No Trips의 비율이 30이 넘음
① The share of people / in the No Trips category / was over 30%
단수 주어 ＊
/ in each of the five age groups. // 단수 동사 ＊
사람들의 비율은 / 여행 안 함 범주에 있는 / 30퍼센트가 넘었다 / 다섯 연령 집단 각각에서 //

② The percentage of people / in the Outbound Trips Only category / was higher in the 25 – 34 age group / than in the 35 –
비교급 비교
44 age group. // Outbound Trips Only: 25~34세 15.2, 35~44세 11.8
사람들의 비율은 / 오로지 외국 여행 범주에 있는 / 25~34세 연령 집단에서 더 높았다 / 35~44세 연령 집단보다 //

③ In the 35 – 44 age group, / the percentage of people / in the Domestic Trips Only category / was 34.2%. // Domestic Trips Only: 35~44세 34.2
35~44세 연령 집단에서 / 사람들의 비율은 / 오로지 국내 여행 범주에 있는 / 34.2퍼센트였다 //

④ The percentage of people / in the Domestic & Outbound Trips category / was lower(→ higher) in the 45 – 54 age group / than in the 55 – 64 age group. // **단서** Domestic & Outbound Trips: 45~54세 23.3, 55~64세 22.5이므로 45~54세가 더 높음
사람들의 비율은 / 국내외 여행 범주에 속하는 / 45~54세 연령 집단에서 더 낮았다(→ 더 높았다) / 55~64세 연령 집단에서보다 //

⑤ In the 65 or over age group, / the percentage of people / in the No Trips category / was more than 50%. // No Trips: 65세 52.6
65세 이상 연령 집단에서 / 사람들의 비율은 / 여행 안 함 범주에 속하는 / 50퍼센트가 넘었다 //

・share ⓝ 점유율, 몫, 지분   ・population ⓝ 인구
・participate ⓥ 참여하다   ・destination ⓝ 목적지
・percentage ⓝ 비율

위의 그래프는 2017년에 관광에 참여한 EU-28 인구의 점유율을 연령대와 목적지 범주별로 보여준다. ① 여행 안 함 범주에 있는 사람들의 비율은 다섯 연령 집단 각각에서 30퍼센트가 넘었다. ② 오로지 외국 여행 범주에 있는 사람들의 비율은 35~44세 연령 집단보다 25~34세 연령 집단에서 더 높았다. ③ 35~44세 연령 집단에서 오로지 국내 여행 범주에 있는 사람들의 비율은 34.2퍼센트였다. ④ 국내외 여행 범주에 속하는 사람들의 비율은 55~64세 연령 집단보다 45~54세 연령 집단에서 더 낮았다(→ 더 높았다). ⑤ 65세 이상 연령 집단에서 여행 안 함 범주에 속하는 사람들의 비율은 50퍼센트가 넘었다.

다음 도표의 내용과 일치하지 <u>않는</u> 것은?

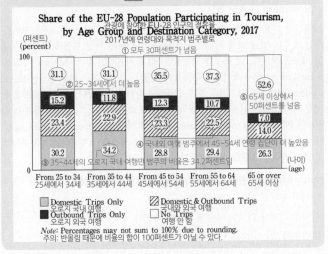

Share of the EU-28 Population Participating in Tourism,
관광에 참여한 EU-28 인구의 점유율
by Age Group and Destination Category, 2017
2017년에 연령대와 목적지 범주별로

① 모두 30퍼센트가 넘음
② 25~34세에서 더 높음
⑤ 65세 이상에서 50퍼센트를 넘음
④ 국내외 여행 범주에서 45~54세 연령 집단이 더 높았음
③ 35~44세의 오로지 국내 여행만 범주의 비율은 34.2퍼센트임

□ Domestic Trips Only 오로지 국내 여행
▨ Domestic & Outbound Trips 국내외 여행
■ Outbound Trips Only 오로지 외국 여행
□ No Trips 여행 안 함

Note: Percentages may not sum to 100% due to rounding.
주의: 반올림 때문에 비율의 합이 100퍼센트가 아닐 수 있다.

2등급? 그래프를 구성하는 그룹 중에 Domestic, Outbound, 그리고 이 둘을 묶은 'Domestic & Outbound'로 구성되어 있어 그룹을 명확히 구분해야 하는 2등급 대비 문제이다. 그래프 문제에서 비교해야 하는 자료들의 그래프 비중이 비슷하다면, 수치도 꼼꼼히 살펴보면서 비교해야 한다.

오H 정답?
④ 국내와 외국 여행 범주의 비율은 45~54세에서 23.3퍼센트, 55~64세에서 22.5퍼센트이다.
▶ 45~54세의 비율이 더 높으므로 lower를 반의어인 higher로 바꿔야 한다.

오H 오답?
① 여행 안 함 범주의 비율은 각각 31.1, 31.1, 35.5, 37.3, 52.6퍼센트로 모두 30퍼센트가 넘는다.
② 오로지 외국 여행 범주의 비율은 35~44세에서 11.8, 25~34세에서 15.2퍼센트이다.
③ 35~44세의 오로지 국내 여행 범주의 비율은 34.2퍼센트이다.
⑤ 65세 이상에서 여행 안 함 범주의 비율은 52.6퍼센트이다.

─── 어법 특강

＊ 주어-동사 수 일치

– most, half, part, the rest, 분수, 퍼센트 등의 〈부분·수량〉을 나타내는 표현이 주어부에 쓰이면, 동사는 of 뒤에 오는 명사의 수에 일치시킨다.
• Most of us feel good. (우리 대부분은 기분이 좋다.)
　　　　복수 명사 복수 동사
• Most of the work is done. (일의 대부분이 끝났다.)
　　　　단수 명사 단수 동사

H 어휘 Review 정답

문제편 p. 140

01 거주자, 주민	11 account for	21 exceeded
02 친숙한	12 as for	22 corresponding
03 특허(권)	13 except for	23 emissions
04 목적지	14 make the list	24 maintained
05 능력, 용량	15 in terms of	25 respectively
06 decline	16 population	26 share
07 table	17 indifferent	27 whereas
08 region	18 projected	28 males
09 ethnic	19 renewable	29 enrollment
10 select	20 solar	30 quarter

I 내용 불일치

문제편 p. 141~155

I 01 정답 ③ ＊위대한 지질학자 William Buckland

William Buckland (1784–1856) was well known / as one of the greatest geologists / in his time. //
William Buckland(1784-1856)는 잘 알려져 있었다 / 가장 위대한 지질학자 중 한 사람으로 / 그의 시대에 //

①의 단서 태어난 곳은 화석이 풍부했음
His birthplace, Axminster in Britain, was rich with fossils, / and as a child, / he naturally became interested in fossils / while collecting them. //
그의 출생지인 영국의 Axminster에는 화석이 풍부했고 / 어릴 때 / 그는 자연스럽게 화석에 관심을 갖게 되었다 / 화석을 수집하면서 //

In 1801, / Buckland won a scholarship / and was admitted to Corpus Christi College, Oxford. //
1801년에 / Buckland는 장학금을 받고 / Oxford의 Corpus Christi College에 입학하였다 //

②의 단서 John Kidd의 강의를 들으며 자신의 과학 지식을 발전시켰음
He developed his scientific knowledge there / while attending John Kidd's lectures / on mineralogy and chemistry. //
그는 거기서 자신의 과학 지식을 발전시켰다 / John Kidd의 강의를 들으면서 / 광물학과 화학에 관한 //

③의 단서 Kidd가 사임한 후에 후임자로 임명되었음
After Kidd resigned his position, / Buckland was appointed his successor / at the college. //
Kidd가 자신의 직위에서 사임한 후에 / Buckland가 그의 후임자로 임명되었다 / 대학에서 //

④의 단서 자신의 강의에서 대축척 지질학 지도를 사용했음
Buckland used / representative samples and large-scale geological maps / in his lectures, / which made his lectures more lively. //
앞 절 전체를 선행사로 하는 계속적 용법의 관계대명사
Buckland는 사용했는데 / 대표 표본과 대축척 지질학 지도를 / 자신의 강의에서 / 그것이 그의 강의를 더 활기차게 만들었다 //

⑤의 단서 1824년에 거대 생물 뼈의 발견을 발표했음
In 1824, / he announced the discovery / of the bones of a giant
주어　동사　목적어　　목적격 보어
creature, / and he named it *Megalosaurus*, or 'great lizard'. //
동격의 전치사
1824년에 / 그는 발견을 발표했으며 / 거대한 생물의 뼈의 / 그는 그것을 Megalosaurus 즉 '거대한 도마뱀'이라고 이름 붙였다 //

He won the prize from the Geological Society / due to his
전치사　명사구
achievements in geology. //
그는 지질학회로부터 상을 받았다 / 지질학에서의 그의 업적으로 //

• geologist ⓝ 지질학자　• birthplace ⓝ 출생지, 발생지
• fossil ⓝ 화석　• scholarship ⓝ 장학금
• admit ⓥ 가입[입학]을 허락하다　• lecture ⓝ 강의, 강연
• mineralogy ⓝ 광물학　• chemistry ⓝ 화학
• resign ⓥ 사직[사임]하다　• appoint ⓥ 지명하다, 정하다
• successor ⓝ 후임자, 계승자　• representative ⓐ 대표적인 사례가 되는
• large-scale ⓐ 광범위한, 대규모의　• geological ⓐ 지질학의
• lizard ⓝ 도마뱀　• achievement ⓝ 업적, 성취
• geology ⓝ 지질학

William Buckland(1784-1856)는 그의 시대에 가장 위대한 지질학자 중 한 사람으로 잘 알려져 있었다. 그의 출생지인 영국의 Axminster에는 화석이 풍부했고, 어릴 때 그는 화석을 수집하면서 자연스럽게 화석에 관심을 갖게 되었다. 1801년에 Buckland는 장학금을 받고 Oxford의 Corpus Christi College에 입학하였다. 그는 거기서 광물학과 화학에 관한 John Kidd의 강의를 들으면서 자신의 과학 지식을 발전시켰다. Kidd가 자신의 직위에서 사임한 후에, Buckland가 대학에서 그의 후임자로 임명되었다. Buckland는 자신의 강의에서 대표 표본과 대축척 지질학 지도를 사용했는데, 그것이 그의 강의를 더 활기차게 만들었다. 1824년에, 그는 거대한 생물의 뼈를 발견했다고 발표했으며, 그는 그것을 Megalosaurus 즉 '거대한 도마뱀'이라고 이름 붙였다. 그는 지질학에서의 그의 업적으로 지질학회로부터 상을 받았다.

William Buckland에 관한 다음 글의 내용과 일치하지 <u>않는</u> 것은?

① 태어난 곳이 화석이 풍부하였다.
His birthplace, Axminster in Britain, was rich with fossils
② John Kidd의 강의를 들으며 자신의 과학 지식을 발전시켰다.
He developed his scientific knowledge there while attending John Kidd's lectures
③ John Kidd의 사임 전에 그의 후임자로 임명되었다.
After Kidd resigned his position, Buckland was appointed his successor
④ 자신의 강의에서 대축척 지질학 지도를 사용하였다.
Buckland used representative samples and large-scale geological maps in his lectures
⑤ 1824년에 거대 생물 뼈의 발견을 발표하였다.
In 1824, he announced the discovery of the bones of a giant creature

왜 정답? [정답률 92%]

Kidd가 사임한 후에 그의 후임자로 임명되었으므로(After Kidd resigned his position, Buckland was appointed his successor) ③은 글과 일치하지 않는다.

왜 오답?

① 태어난 곳은 화석이 풍부했다. (His birthplace, Axminster in Britain, was rich with fossils)
② John Kidd의 강의를 들으며 자신의 과학 지식을 발전시켰다. (He developed his scientific knowledge there while attending John Kidd's lectures)
④ 자신의 강의에서 대축척 지질학 지도를 사용했다. (Buckland used ~ large-scale geological maps in his lectures)
⑤ 1824년에 거대 생물 뼈의 발견을 발표했다. (In 1824, he announced the discovery of the bones of a giant creature)

I 02 정답 ⑤ *영국 예술가 Henry Moore

Henry Moore (1898–1986), / one of the most significant British artists / of the 20th century, / was the seventh child / of a coal miner. // **①의 단서** 석탄 광부의 일곱 번째 자녀였음
Henry Moore(1898~1986)는 / 가장 중요한 영국 예술가 중 한 명인 / 20세기의 / 일곱 번째 자녀였다 / 석탄 광부의 //

Henry Moore showed a talent for art / from early on / in school. // **②의 단서** 학창 시절에 일찍이 예술에 재능을 보였음
Henry Moore는 예술에 재능을 보였다 / 일찍이 / 학창 시절에 //

After World War I, / during which he volunteered for army service, / Moore began to study sculpture / at the Leeds School of Art. //
선행사 「전치사+관계대명사」
제1차 세계대전 후에 / 그가 군 복무를 자원했던 / Moore는 조각을 공부하기 시작했다 / Leeds School of Art에서 // **③의 단서** 런던에 있는 Royal College of Art에 들어갔고 거기서 학위를 취득했음

Then, he entered the Royal College of Art / in London / and earned his degree there. //
그 후 그는 Royal College of Art에 들어갔고 / 런던에 있는 / 거기서 자신의 학위를 취득했다 // **④의 단서** 그의 조각은 독특한 방식으로 신체 형태를 나타냄

His sculptures, / known around the world, / present the forms of the body / in a unique way. //
복수 주어 복수 동사
그의 조각은 / 전 세계적으로 알려진 / 신체 형태를 나타낸다 / 독특한 방식으로 //

One of his artistic themes / was mother-and-child / as shown in Madonna and Child / at St. Matthew's Church in Northampton. //
단수 주어 단수 동사
그의 예술적 주제 중 하나는 / 엄마와 아이였다 / 〈Madonna and Child〉에서 보이듯이 / Northampton의 St. Matthew's 교회에 있는 // **⑤의 단서** 경제적인 성공을 거두었음

He achieved financial success / from his hard work / and established the Henry Moore Foundation / to support / education and promotion of the arts. //
그는 경제적인 성공을 거두었고 / 각고의 노력으로 / Henry Moore 재단을 세웠다 / 후원하기 위해 / 예술 교육과 증진을 //

- significant ⓐ 중요한 · coal ⓝ 석탄 · miner ⓝ 광부
- sculpture ⓝ 조각(품)
- earn ⓥ (그럴 만한 자격·자질이 되어서 ~을) 얻다[받다]
- degree ⓝ 학위, ((단위)) 도 · artistic ⓐ 예술적인

- establish ⓥ 설립하다 · foundation ⓝ 토대, 기반, 재단
- promotion ⓝ 증진, 촉진

20세기의 가장 중요한 영국 예술가 중 한 명인 Henry Moore(1898~1986)는 석탄 광부의 일곱 번째 자녀였다. Henry Moore는 학창 시절에 일찍이 예술에 재능을 보였다. 군 복무를 자원했던 제1차 세계대전 후에, Moore는 Leeds School of Art에서 조각을 공부하기 시작했다. 그 후, 그는 런던에 있는 Royal College of Art에 들어갔고 거기서 자신의 학위를 취득했다. 전 세계적으로 알려진 그의 조각은 신체 형태를 독특한 방식으로 나타낸다. 그의 예술적 주제 중 하나는 Northampton의 St. Matthew's 교회에 있는 〈Madonna and Child〉에서 보이듯이 엄마와 아이였다. 그는 각고의 노력으로 경제적인 성공을 거두었고 예술 교육과 증진을 후원하기 위해 Henry Moore 재단을 세웠다.

Henry Moore에 관한 다음 글의 내용과 일치하지 <u>않는</u> 것은?

① 석탄 광부의 일곱 번째 자녀였다.
was the seventh child of a coal miner
② 학창 시절에 일찍이 예술에 재능을 보였다.
Henry Moore showed a talent for art from early on in school.
③ 런던에 있는 Royal College of Art에서 학위를 취득했다.
Then, he entered the Royal College of Art in London and earned his degree there.
④ 그의 조각은 신체 형태를 독특한 방식으로 나타낸다.
His sculptures, ~ present the forms of the body in a unique way.
⑤ 경제적으로 성공을 거두지 못했다.
He achieved financial success

왜 정답? [정답률 97%]

경제적인 성공을 거두었고(He achieved financial success) Henry Moore 재단을 설립했다고 했으므로 ⑤은 글과 일치하지 않는다.

왜 오답?

① 석탄 광부의 일곱 번째 자녀였다. (was the seventh child of a coal miner)
② 학창 시절에 일찍이 예술에 재능을 보였다. (Henry Moore showed a talent for art from early on in school.)
③ 런던에 있는 Royal College of Art에서 학위를 취득했다. (Then, he entered the Royal College of Art in London and earned his degree there.)
④ 그의 조각은 신체 형태를 독특한 방식으로 나타낸다. (His sculptures, ~ present the forms of the body in a unique way.)

I 03 정답 ④ *스포츠 방송인 Dick Enberg의 일생

Dick Enberg was one / of America's most beloved sports broadcasters. //
형용사(broadcasters 수식)
Dick Enberg는 한 명이었다 / 미국의 가장 사랑받는 스포츠 방송인 중 //

He was born in Michigan in 1935. //
그는 1935년에 미시간에서 태어났다 // **①의 단서** Michigan에서 태어났음

In the early 1960s, / he became an assistant professor at San Fernando Valley State College, / where he also served as a coach of its baseball team. // **②의 단서** 대학 야구팀 코치했음
관계부사
1960년대 초에 / 그는 San Fernando Valley 주립 대학의 조교수가 되었으며 / 그곳에서 그는 그 대학의 야구팀 코치로도 활동했다 //

Afterwards, / he began a full-time sportscasting career / in Los Angeles. //
후에 / 그는 전업 스포츠 방송 일을 시작했다 / 로스앤젤레스에서 //

In 1973, / he became the first U.S. sportscaster / ever to visit China. // **③의 단서** 중국을 방문한 첫 미국인 스포츠 캐스터였음
형용사적 용법(sportscaster 수식)
1973년에 / 그는 최초의 미국 스포츠 방송 진행자가 되었다 / 역사상 중국을 방문한 //

He joined NBC Sports in 1975 / and remained with the network for about 25 years, / covering such big events as the Olympics. //
병렬 구조 분사구문
그는 1975년에 NBC 스포츠에 합류하여 / 그 방송국에 약 25년간 남아 있었고 / 올림픽과 같은 대규모 행사를 보도했다 //

He later worked for other major sports broadcasting stations. //
그는 후에 다른 주요 스포츠 방송국에서 일했다 //

He made his last live broadcast in 2016 / and died the following
　　　　　　　　　　　병렬 구조
year at the age of 82. // **④의 단서** 마지막 생방송 후 3년 뒤가 아니라 1년 뒤에 사망하였음
그는 2016년에 자신의 마지막 생방송을 했고 / 그 다음 해에 82세의 나이로 사망했다 //

He served as Chairman / of the American Sportscaster
Association / for more than three decades. //
그는 회장직을 역임했다 / 미국 스포츠 캐스터 협회의 / 30년 넘게 //
　　　　　　　　　　병렬 구조
Enberg was also a best-selling writer / and won Emmy Awards
　　　　　　　　　　　　　　　　　　　　　　　　　　　　수상하였음 Emmy Awards를
/ as a sportscaster, a writer, and a producer. //
Enberg는 또한 베스트셀러 작가였으며 / 에미상을 수상했다 / 스포츠 방송 진행자, 작가,
그리고 제작자로 //

- beloved ⓐ 사랑받는　　　- broadcaster ⓝ 방송인
- assistant professor 조교수　　　- cover ⓥ 보도하다
- broadcasting station 방송국　　　- chairman ⓝ 회장

Dick Enberg는 미국의 가장 사랑받는 스포츠 방송인 중 한 명이었다. 그는
1935년에 미시간에서 태어났다. 1960년대 초에, 그는 San Fernando Valley
주립 대학의 조교수가 되었으며, 그곳에서 그는 그 대학의 야구팀 코치로도
활동했다. 후에 그는 로스앤젤레스에서 전업 스포츠 방송 일을 시작했다.
1973년에 그는 역사상 중국을 방문한 최초의 미국 스포츠 방송 진행자가
되었다. 그는 1975년에 NBC 스포츠에 합류하여 그 방송국에 약 25년간 남아
있었고, 올림픽과 같은 대규모 행사를 보도했다. 그는 후에 다른 주요 스포츠
방송국에서 일했다. 그는 2016년에 자신의 마지막 생방송을 했고 그 다음 해에
82세의 나이로 사망했다. 그는 30년 넘게 미국 스포츠 캐스터 협회의 회장직을
역임했다. Enberg는 또한 베스트셀러 작가였으며, 스포츠 방송 진행자, 작가,
그리고 제작자로 에미상을 수상했다.

Dick Enberg에 관한 다음 글의 내용과 일치하지 않는 것은?

① Michigan에서 태어났다.
　He was born in Michigan in 1935.
② 대학 야구팀 코치였다. he became an assistant professor at San Fernando
　Valley State College, where he also served as a coach of its baseball team
③ 중국을 방문한 첫 미국인 스포츠 캐스터였다.
　he became the first U.S. sportscaster ever to visit China
④ 마지막 생방송 후 3년 뒤에 사망하였다.
　He made his last live broadcast in 2016 and died the following year
⑤ Emmy Awards를 수상하였다.
　won Emmy Awards

>왜 정답? [정답률 98%]

④ 그는 2016년에 마지막 생방송을 하고 그 다음 해에 사망했다고 했으므로 (He
　made his last live broadcast in 2016 and died the following year) ④은
　글의 내용과 일치하지 않는다.

>왜 오답?

① Michigan에서 태어났다. (He was born in Michigan in 1935.)
② 대학 야구팀 코치였다. (he became an assistant professor at San
　Fernando Valley State College, where he also served as a coach of its
　baseball team)
③ 중국을 방문한 첫 미국인 스포츠 캐스터였다. (he became the first U.S.
　sportscaster ever to visit China)
⑤ Emmy Awards를 수상하였다. (won Emmy Awards)

한규진 | 2025 수능 응시 · 대구 계성고 졸

이 문제를 시간을 줄이면서 푸는 꿀팁은 지문을 먼저 다 읽는 것이
아니라, 선택지를 먼저 보는 거야! 선택지를 먼저 보고 지문을
훑으면서 Michigan에서 태어났는지, 대학 야구팀 코치였는지 등
해당 내용이 지문에 있는지만 확인해도 충분히 답을 찾을 수 있어.
이렇게 하면 불필요한 부분을 해석하는 데 낭비하는 시간을 확보할 수 있으니까 꼭
도전해봐!

Ⅰ 04 정답 ② ＊예술가이자 교육자였던 György Kepes ─────

　　　　　　　　　　　　　　　　　　　　artist and educator를 수식하는 분사
György Kepes was an artist and educator / born in Selyp,
Hungary in 1906. //
György Kepes는 예술가이자 교육자였다 / 1906년에 헝가리 Selyp에서 태어난 //

He studied painting / at the Royal Academy of Fine Arts / in
Budapest, Hungary. // **①의 단서** 헝가리에서 회화를 공부함
그는 회화를 공부했다 / 왕립 미술 아카데미에서 / 헝가리 Budapest의 //

Then, / he studied design and film / in Berlin, Germany. //
그 후 / 그는 디자인과 영화를 공부했다 / 독일 Berlin에서 //

He went to the United States in 1937, / and about a decade
later, / he started teaching visual design / at the Massachusetts
Institute of Technology (MIT). // **②의 단서** MIT에서 시각 디자인을 가르치기
　　　　　　　　　　　　　　　　시작한 것은 1937년이 아니라 10년 후임
그는 1937년 미국으로 갔다 / 그리고 약 10년 후 / 그는 시각 디자인을 가르치기 시작했다 /
매사추세츠 공과대학(MIT)에서 //

He founded the Center for Advanced Visual Studies at MIT /
부사적 용법(결과)
to form a community / composed of artists and scientists. //
그는 MIT에 고급 시각 연구 센터를 설립했다 / 그리고 커뮤니티를 만들었다 / 예술가와
과학자들로 구성된 //

His exhibition in 1951 titled *The New Landscape* / became the
　　　　　　　　　　　　　　　　　　　　　　계속적 용법의 관계대명사
basis of his book *The New Landscape in Art and Science*, / which
was published several years later. // **③의 단서** 전시회를 기반으로 책을 출간했음
1951년 '새로운 풍경'이라는 제목으로 열린 그의 전시회는 / 그의 저서 '예술과 과학의 새로운
풍경'의 기반이 되었다 / 몇 년 후에 출간된 //
　　　　　　　　　　　　　　　　　　　주격 관계대명사
In the book, / he presented images / that were not previously
　　　　　　　　　　　　　　　　　　분사구문
available, / captured by the latest scientific devices. //
그 책에서 / 그는 이미지를 선보였다 / 이전에는 볼 수 없었던 / 최신 과학 기기로 포착된 //
　　　　　　　　핵심 주어(단수)　　　　　　　　　　단수 동사
In 1995, / a museum to house his works / was established / in
Eger, Hungary. // **④의 단서** 작품을 소장하기 위한 박물관이 설립됨
1995년 / 그의 작품을 소장하기 위한 박물관이 / 설립되었다 / 헝가리 Eger에 //

He was a great pioneer / in connecting art and technology. //
그는 위대한 선구자였다 / 예술과 기술을 연결하는 데 있어 // **⑤의 단서** 예술과 기술을 연결하는 데
　　　　　　　　　　　　　　　　　　　　　　　　　　　　　　　있어서 위대한 선구자였음

- decade ⓝ 10년　　　- found ⓥ 설립하다　　　- exhibition ⓝ 전시회
- basis ⓝ 기반, 기초　　　- capture ⓥ 포착하다
- previously ⓐⓓ 이전에　　　- establish ⓥ 설립하다

György Kepes는 1906년 헝가리 Selyp에서 태어난 예술가이자 교육자였다.
그는 헝가리 Budapest의 왕립 미술 아카데미에서 회화를 공부했다. 그 후
그는 독일 Berlin에서 디자인과 영화를 공부했다. 그는 1937년 미국으로
건너가 약 10년 후 매사추세츠 공과대학(MIT)에서 시각 디자인을 가르치기
시작했다. 그는 MIT에 고급 시각 연구 센터를 설립하여 예술가와 과학자들로
구성된 커뮤니티를 만들었다. 1951년 '새로운 풍경'이라는 제목으로 열린 그의
전시회는 몇 년 후 출간된 그의 저서 '예술과 과학의 새로운 풍경'의 기반이
되었다. 그 책에서 그는 최신 과학 기기로 포착한, 이전에는 볼 수 없었던
이미지를 선보였다. 1995년 그의 작품을 소장하기 위한 박물관이 헝가리
Eger에 설립되었다. 그는 예술과 기술을 연결하는 데 있어 위대한 선구자였다.

György Kepes에 관한 다음 글의 내용과 일치하지 않는 것은?

① 헝가리에서 그림을 공부했다.
　He studied painting at the Royal Academy of Fine Arts in Budapest, Hungary.
② 1937년에 MIT에서 시각 디자인을 가르치기 시작했다.
　He went to the United States in 1937 ~ at the Massachusetts Institute of Technology (MIT).
③ 그의 전시회를 기반으로 책이 출판되었다.
　His exhibition in 1951 titled *The New Landscape* became the basis of his book
④ 그의 작품을 소장하기 위한 박물관이 설립되었다.
　In 1995, a museum to house his works was established in Eger, Hungary.
⑤ 예술과 기술을 연결하는 데 있어 위대한 개척자였다.
　He was a great pioneer in connecting art and technology.

>왜 정답? [정답률 65%]

② 1937년에 MIT에서 시각 디자인을 가르치기 시작한 것이 아니라 10년 후인
　1947년에 가르치기 시작했다. (He went to the United States in 1937,
　and about a decade later, he started teaching visual design at the
　Massachusetts Institute of Technology (MIT).)

>왜 오답?

① 헝가리에서 그림을 공부했다. (He studied painting at the Royal Academy of Fine Arts in Budapest, Hungary.)

③ 그의 전시회를 기반으로 책이 출판되었다. (His exhibition in 1951 titled *The New Landscape* became the basis of his book)

④ 그의 작품을 소장하기 위한 박물관이 설립되었다. (In 1995, a museum to house his works was established in Eger, Hungary.)

⑤ 예술과 기술을 연결하는 데 있어서 위대한 개척자였다. (He was a great pioneer in connecting art and technology.)

I 05 정답 ⑤ *미국의 유명한 공인 Will Rogers의 일생

Will Rogers (1879-1935) / was a famous American public figure. //
Will Rogers(1879-1935)는 / 미국의 유명한 공인이었다 //
①의 단서 여덟 번째 아이로 태어났음
He was born as the eighth child. // 그는 여덟 번째 아이로 태어났다 //
When he was young, / he was clever and mature / but he dropped out of school after the 10th grade. //
어렸을 때 / 그는 영리하고 어른스러웠지만 / 10학년을 마치고 학교를 중퇴했다 //
②의 단서 카우보이와 말에 매우 관심이 있었음
He was very interested in cowboys and horses, / and he even learned how to do rope tricks. //
그는 카우보이와 말에 매우 관심이 많았고 / 심지어 밧줄로 묘기하는 방법까지 배웠다 //
He left the U.S. in 1902 / and worked as a cowboy and roping artist / in South Africa and Australia. //
1902년에 그는 미국을 떠나 / 카우보이와 로핑 아티스트로 일했다 / 남아프리카공화국과 호주에서 //
③의 단서 미국에 돌아온 후 50편이 넘는 영화에 출연했음
After returning to the U.S., / he appeared in more than 50 movies / and was often heard on the radio as an entertainer. //
미국으로 돌아온 후 / 그는 50편 이상의 영화에 출연했으며 / 라디오에 자주 엔터테이너로 나왔다 //
④의 단서 뛰어난 신문 칼럼니스트였음
He was also an outstanding newspaper columnist with his wit and humor, / writing more than 4,000 columns. //
그는 또한 재치와 유머를 겸비한 뛰어난 신문 칼럼니스트로서 / 4,000편이 넘는 칼럼을 썼다 //
He unfortunately died / at the height of his career in 1935. //
그는 안타깝게도 세상을 떠났다 / 경력이 한창일 때인 1935년에 //
⑤의 단서 생전이 아니라 사망 이후에 그의 동상이 U.S. Capitol에 설치되었음
Rogers was so popular / that after his death / his statue was installed in the U.S. Capitol. //
Rogers는 인기가 많았다 / 사망 후 / 미국 국회의사당에 그의 동상이 설치될 정도로 //
He will be remembered / as a great American of many talents. //
그는 기억될 것이다 / 많은 재능을 가진 위대한 미국인으로 //

- public figure 공인, 유명 인사   • mature @ 어른스러운
- drop out of ~을 중퇴하다   • trick ⓝ 묘기, 마술
- outstanding @ 뛰어난   • columnist ⓝ 정기 기고가, 칼럼니스트
- wit ⓝ 재치   • at the height of ~이 한창일 때에
- install ⓥ 설치하다

Will Rogers(1879~1935)는 미국의 유명한 공인이었다. 그는 여덟 번째 아이로 태어났다. 어렸을 때 그는 영리하고 어른스러웠지만 10학년을 마치고 학교를 중퇴했다. 그는 카우보이와 말에 매우 관심이 많았고 심지어 밧줄로 묘기하는 방법까지 배웠다. 1902년에 그는 미국을 떠나 남아프리카공화국과 호주에서 카우보이와 로핑 아티스트로 일했다. 미국으로 돌아온 후, 그는 50편 이상의 영화에 출연했으며 라디오에 자주 엔터테이너로 나왔다. 그는 또한 재치와 유머를 겸비한 뛰어난 신문 칼럼니스트로서 4,000편이 넘는 칼럼을 썼다. 그는 안타깝게도 경력이 한창일 때인 1935년에 세상을 떠났다. Rogers는 사망 후 미국 국회의사당에 그의 동상이 설치될 정도로 인기가 많았다. 그는 많은 재능을 가진 위대한 미국인으로 기억될 것이다.

Will Rogers에 관한 다음 글의 내용과 일치하지 않는 것은?

① 여덟 번째 아이로 태어났다.
He was born as the eighth child.
② 카우보이와 말에 매우 관심이 있었다.
He was very interested in cowboys and horses
③ 미국에 돌아온 후 50편이 넘는 영화에 출연했다.
After returning to the U.S., he appeared in more than 50 movies
④ 뛰어난 신문 칼럼니스트였다.
He was also an outstanding newspaper columnist
⑤ 생전에 그의 동상이 U.S. Capitol에 설치되었다.
after his death his statue was installed in the U.S. Capitol.

>왜 정답? [정답률 91%]

⑤ 생전이 아니라 사망 이후에 그의 동상이 U.S. Capitol에 설치되었다. (after his death his statue was installed in the U.S. Capitol)

>왜 오답?

① 여덟 번째 아이로 태어났다. (He was born as the eighth child.)

② 카우보이와 말에 매우 관심이 있었다. (He was very interested in cowboys and horses)

③ 미국에 돌아온 후 50편이 넘는 영화에 출연했다. (After returning to the U.S., he appeared in more than 50 movies)

④ 뛰어난 신문 칼럼니스트였다. (He was also an outstanding newspaper columnist)

I 06 정답 ⑤ *고고학자 Mary Douglas Leakey의 일생

수동태
Mary Douglas Leakey was born in 1913 in London, England / in a family of scholars and researchers. // **①의 단서** 1913년에 영국 런던에서 태어남
Mary Douglas Leakey는 1913년에 영국 런던에서 태어났다 / 학자와 연구자의 집안에서 //
주격 관계대명사
Her father, who was an artist, / took her to see the stone tools / being studied by French prehistorians. //
예술가였던 그녀의 아버지는 / 그녀를 데리고 석기를 보러 갔다 / 프랑스 선사학자들이 연구하고 있던 //
This sparked her interest in archaeology. //
이것은 고고학에 대한 그녀의 흥미를 불러 일으켰다 //
When she was just 17 years old, / she served as an illustrator at a dig in England. // **②의 단서** 17살이었을 때 영국에 있는 발굴지에서 삽화가로 일함
그녀가 단지 17세일 때 / 그녀는 영국에 있는 발굴지에서 삽화가로 일했다 //
Shortly after marrying Louis Leakey, / she left for East Africa with her husband. // **③의 단서** 그녀는 남편과 함께 동아프리카로 떠났음
Louis Leakey와 결혼하고 얼마 되지 않아 / 그녀는 그녀의 남편과 함께 동아프리카로 떠났다 //
Together, they made important fossil discoveries. //
함께, 그들은 중요한 화석들을 발견했다 // **④의 단서** 1948년에 Proconsul africanus의 두개골 화석의 일부를 찾음
In 1948, / Mary found a partial skull fossil of *Proconsul africanus* / on Rusinga Island in Lake Victoria. //
1948년 / Mary는 Proconsul africanus의 두개골 화석의 일부를 찾았다 / Lake Victoria에 있는 Rusinga Island에서 //
목적격 관계대명사
In 1959 in Tanzania, / she discovered the skull of an early hominin / that her husband named *Zinjanthropus boisei*, / which is now known as *Paranthropus boisei*. //
1959년 탄자니아에서 / 그녀는 초기 호미닌(분류학상 인간의 조상으로 분류되는 종족)의 두개골을 발견했다 / 그녀의 남편이 Zinjanthropus boisei라고 이름 붙인 / 지금은 Paranthropus boisei라고 알려진 //
Even after her husband's death in 1972, / Mary continued her work in Africa. //
1972년 그녀의 남편의 사망 이후에도 / Mary는 아프리카에서 그녀의 일을 계속했다 //
Mary died in 1996, in Nairobi, Kenya. //
Mary는 1996년 케냐 나이로비에서 사망했다 // **⑤의 단서** 1996년에 케냐 나이로비에서 사망함

- prehistorian ⓝ 선사학자   • spark ⓥ 촉발시키다
- archaeology ⓝ 고고학   • serve as ~의 역할을 하다, 일하다

Mary Douglas Leakey는 1913년에 영국 런던에서 학자와 연구자의 집안에서 태어났다. 예술가였던 그녀의 아버지는 그녀를 데리고 프랑스 선사학자들이 연구하고 있던 석기를 보러 갔다. 이것은 고고학에 대한 그녀의 흥미를 불러 일으켰다. 그녀가 단지 17세일때, 그녀는 영국에 있는 발굴지에서 삽화가로 일했다. Louis Leakey와 결혼하고 얼마 되지 않아, 그녀는 그녀의 남편과 함께 동아프리카로 떠났다. 함께, 그들은 중요한 화석들을 발견했다. 1948년에, Mary는 Lake Victoria에 있는 Rusinga Island에서 Proconsul africanus의 두개골 화석의 일부를 찾았다. 1959년 탄자니아에서 그녀는 그녀의 남편이 Zinjanthropus boisei라고 이름 붙인, 지금은 Paranthropus boisei라고 알려진 초기 호미닌(분류학상 인간의 조상으로 분류되는 종족)의 두개골을 발견했다. 1972년 그녀의 남편의 사망 이후에도, Mary는 아프리카에서 그녀의 일을 계속했다. Mary는 1996년 케냐 나이로비에서 사망했다.

Mary Douglas Leakey에 관한 다음 글의 내용과 일치하지 <u>않는</u> 것은?
① 1913년에 영국 런던에서 태어났다.
  Mary Douglas Leakey was born in 1913 in London, England
② 17세의 나이에 영국에 있는 발굴지에서 삽화가로 일했다.
  When she was just 17 years old ~ dig in England.
③ 그녀의 남편과 함께 동아프리카로 떠났다.
  she left for East Africa with her husband
④ 1948년에 *Proconsul africanus*의 두개골 화석의 일부를 찾았다.
  In 1948, Mary found a partial skull fossil of Proconsul africanus
⑤ 1972년에 케냐 나이로비에서 사망했다.
  Mary died in 1996, in Nairobi, Kenya.

> **왜 정답?** [정답률 95%]
⑤ 1972년에는 Mary가 아닌 그녀의 남편이 사망했으며, Mary는 1996년 케냐 나이로비에서 사망했다. (Mary died in 1996, in Nairobi, Kenya.)

> **왜 오답?**
① 1913년에 영국 런던에서 태어났다. (Mary Douglas Leakey was born in 1913 in London, England)
② 17세의 나이에 영국에 있는 발굴지에서 삽화가로 일했다. (When she was just 17 years old, she served as an illustrator at a dig in England.)
③ 그녀의 남편과 함께 동아프리카로 떠났다. (she left for East Africa with her husband)
④ 1948년에 Lake Victoria에 있는 Rusinga Island에서 Proconsul africanus의 두개골 화석의 일부를 찾았다. (In 1948, Mary found a partial skull fossil of Proconsul africanus)

I 07 정답 ④ * John Carew Eccles의 일생

John Carew Eccles was born / on 27 January 1903 in Melbourne, Australia. //
John Carew Eccles는 태어났다 / Australia의 Melbourne에서 1903년 1월 27일에 //
계속적 용법의 관계대명사
Both his parents were school teachers, / who home-schooled him until he was 12. //
①의 단서 부모님은 그를 12세까지 홈스쿨링 시킴
부모님 모두 학교 선생님이었고 / 그를 12세까지 홈스쿨링 시켰다 //

In 1915, Eccles began his secondary schooling / and after four years, / prior to entering the University of Melbourne, / ~에 앞서 / he studied science and mathematics / for another year at Melbourne High School. //
②의 단서 Melbourne High School에서 과학과 수학을 공부함
1915년에 Eccles는 중등교육을 시작했고 / 4년 뒤에 / University of Melbourne에 입학하기 전에 / 과학과 수학을 공부했다 / Melbourne High School에서 한 해 더 //

He completed his medical course in February 1925, / and left Melbourne for Oxford the same year. //
그는 의학 과정을 1925년 2월에 끝마쳤고 / 같은 해에 Melbourne에서 Oxford로 갔다 //
③의 단서 Sir Charles Sherrington의 연구 조교를 했음
From 1928 to 1931 / he was a research assistant to Sir Charles Sherrington, / and published eight papers conjointly. //
1928년부터 1931년까지 / 그는 Sir Charles Sherrington의 연구 조교였고 / 공동으로 출판된 8개의 논문이 있었다 //

Returning to Australia with his family in 1937, / he gave lectures 분사구문 to third-year medical students / at the University of Sydney from 1938 to 1940. //
그의 가족들과 1937년에 Australia로 돌아와서 / 그는 의대 3학년 학생들에게 강의를 했다 / University of Sydney에서 1938년부터 1940년까지 //

④의 단서 1963년 노벨 생리 · 의학상의 공동 수상자였음
Eccles was the co-winner of the Nobel Prize in Physiology or Medicine / along with A.L. Hodgkin and A.F. Huxley in 1963. //
Eccles는 노벨 생리·의학상의 공동 수상자였다 / 1963년에 A.L. Hodgkin, A.F. Huxley와 함께 //
⑤의 단서 은퇴 후에 Switzerland로 이주함
In 1975, he voluntarily retired / and moved to Switzerland / to dedicate himself to work on the mind-brain problem. //
1975년에 그는 자발적으로 은퇴했고 / Switzerland로 이주해서 / 정신과 두뇌의 문제에 관한 연구에 전념했다 //

- complete ⓥ 끝내다, 완성하다   · assistant ⓝ 조수
- publish ⓥ 출판하다   · conjointly ⓐⓓ 결합하여, 공동으로
- dedicate oneself to ~ ~에 전념하다

John Carew Eccles는 Australia의 Melbourne에서 1903년 1월 27일에 태어났다. 부모님 모두 학교 선생님이었고 그를 12세까지 홈스쿨링 시켰다. 1915년에 Eccles는 중등교육을 시작했고 4년 뒤에, University of Melbourne에 입학하기 전에, 과학과 수학을 Melbourne High School에서 한 해 더 공부했다. 그는 의학 과정을 1925년 2월에 끝마쳤고, 같은 해에 Melbourne에서 Oxford로 갔다. 1928년부터 1931년까지 그는 Sir Charles Sherrington의 연구 조교였고, 공동으로 출판된 8개의 논문이 있었다. 그의 가족들과 1937년에 Australia로 돌아와서, 그는 University of Sydney에서 의대 3학년 학생들에게 1938년부터 1940년까지 강의를 했다. Eccles는 1963년에 A.L. Hodgkin, A.F. Huxley와 함께 노벨 생리 · 의학상의 공동 수상자였다. 1975년에 그는 자발적으로 은퇴했고 Switzerland로 이주해서 정신과 두뇌의 문제에 관한 연구에 전념했다.

John Carew Eccles에 관한 다음 글의 내용과 일치하지 <u>않는</u> 것은?
① 12세까지 홈스쿨링을 받았다. who home-schooled him until he was 12.
  Both his parents were school teachers,
② Melbourne High School에서 과학과 수학을 공부했다.
  he studied science and mathematics for another year at Melbourne High School
③ Sir Charles Sherrington의 연구 조교였다.
  he was a research assistant to Sir Charles Sherrington   Eccles was the co-winner
④ 1963년에 노벨 생리 · 의학상을 단독으로 수상했다. of the Nobel Prize in
  Physiology or Medicine along with A.L. Hodgkin and A.F. Huxley in 1963.
⑤ 은퇴하고 Switzerland로 이주했다.
  he voluntarily retired and moved to Switzerland

> **왜 정답?** [정답률 94%]
④ 1963년에 노벨 생리·의학상을 단독으로 수상한 것이 아니라, A.L. Hodgkin, A.F. Huxley와 함께 노벨 생리·의학상을 공동 수상했다. (Eccles was the co-winner of the Nobel Prize in Physiology or Medicine along with A.L. Hodgkin and A.F. Huxley in 1963.)

> **왜 오답?**
① 12세까지 홈스쿨링을 받았다. (Both his parents were school teachers, who home-schooled him until he was 12.)
② Melbourne High School에서 과학과 수학을 공부했다. (he studied science and mathematics for another year at Melbourne High School)
③ Sir Charles Sherrington의 연구 조교였다. (he was a research assistant to Sir Charles Sherrington)
⑤ 은퇴하고 Switzerland로 이주했다. (he volutarily retired and moved to Switzerland)

I 08 정답 ③ * José Saramago의 생애와 문학적 업적

José Saramago was born in 1922 / to a family of farmers / in a little village north of Lisbon. //
José Saramago는 1922년에 태어났다 / 농부의 가정에서 / Lisbon 북쪽의 작은 마을에 있는 //
①의 단서 재정적인 이유로 고등학교 공부를 그만둠
For financial reasons / he abandoned his high-school studies /
병렬 구조(동사)
and worked as a mechanic. //
재정적인 이유로 / 그는 고등학교 공부를 그만두었고 / 정비공으로 일을 했다 //
②의 단서 독서에 흥미가 생겨 공립 도서관을 자주 방문하기 시작함
At this time, / he acquired a taste for reading / and started
명사적 용법(started의 목적어)
to frequent a public library in Lisbon / in his free time. //
이때 / 그는 독서에 흥미가 생겨 / Lisbon에 있는 공립 도서관을 자주 방문하기 시작했다 / 여가 시간에 //

After trying different jobs in the civil service, / he worked for a publishing company for twelve years / and then as an editor of the newspaper 'Diário de Notícias.' // **③의 단서** 출판사에서 일한 후 편집자로 일함
공직에서 여러 가지 일을 해 본 뒤에 / 그는 출판사에서 12년간 일한 후 / 신문사 'Diário de Notícias'의 편집자로 일했다 //

Between 1975 and 1980 / Saramago supported himself as a translator, / but after his literary successes in the 1980s / he devoted himself to his own writing. // *재귀 용법의 재귀대명사* himself *devote A to B: A를 B에 바치다*
1975년부터 1980년까지 / Saramago는 번역가로 생계를 유지했지만 / 1980년대의 문학적인 성공 이후로는 / 자신의 글쓰기에 몰두했다 //

He achieved worldwide recognition in 1982 / with the humorous love story *Baltasar and Blimunda*, / a novel set in 18th-century Portugal. // **④의 단서** 포르투갈이 배경으로 소설로 세계적인 인정을 받음
그는 1982년에 세계적인 인정을 받았다 / 해학적인 사랑 이야기 'Baltasar and Blimunda'로 / 18세기 포르투갈을 배경으로 한 소설인 //

Saramago's oeuvre totals 30 works, / and comprises not only novels but also poetry, essays and drama. // *병렬 구조(동사)* **⑤의 단서** 소설뿐 아니라 시, 수필, 희곡 또한 집필함
Saramago의 전체 작품은 총 30편에 이르고 / 소설뿐만 아니라 시, 수필, 희곡 등도 포함한다 //

- **abandon** ⓥ 그만두다
- **mechanic** ⓝ 정비공
- **frequent** ⓥ 자주 다니다
- **civil service** (정부의) 공무원[행정] 조직[업무]
- **recognition** ⓝ 인정
- **humorous** ⓐ 재미있는, 해학적인

José Saramago는 1922년에 Lisbon 북쪽의 작은 마을에 있는 농부의 가정에서 태어났다. 그는 재정적인 이유로 고등학교 공부를 그만두었고 정비공으로 일을 했다. 이때, 그는 독서에 흥미가 생겨 여가 시간에 Lisbon에 있는 공립 도서관을 자주 방문하기 시작했다. 공직에서 여러 가지 일을 해 본 뒤에 그는 출판사에서 12년간 일한 후, 신문사 'Diário de Notícias'의 편집자로 일했다. 1975년부터 1980년까지 Saramago는 번역가로 생계를 유지했지만 1980년대의 문학적인 성공 이후로는 자신의 글쓰기에 몰두했다. 그는 18세기 포르투갈을 배경으로 한 소설인 해학적인 사랑 이야기 'Baltasar and Blimunda'로 1982년에 세계적인 인정을 받았다. Saramago의 전체 작품은 총 30편에 이르고 소설뿐만 아니라 시, 수필, 희곡 등도 포함한다.

José Saramago에 관한 다음 글의 내용과 일치하지 않는 것은?

① 재정적인 이유로 고등학교 공부를 그만두었다.
For financial reasons he abandoned his highschool studies
② 독서에 흥미가 생겨 공립 도서관을 자주 방문하기 시작했다.
he acquired a taste for reading and started to frequent a public library
③ 신문사의 편집자로 일한 후 출판사에서 12년간 일했다.
he worked ~ and then as an editor of the newspaper 'Diário de Notícias'
④ 포르투갈이 배경인 소설로 세계적인 인정을 받았다.
He achieved worldwide recognition in 1982 ~ Portugal.
⑤ 소설뿐 아니라 시, 수필, 희곡 또한 집필하였다.
comprises not only novels but also poetry, essays and drama

왜 정답? [정답률 91%]

출판사에서 12년간 일한 후, 신문사의 편집자로 일했다고 했으므로 (he worked for a publishing company for twelve years and then as an editor of the newspaper 'Diário de Notícias.') 반대로 말한 ③이 글의 내용과 일치하지 않는다.

왜 오답?

① 재정적인 이유로 고등학교 공부를 그만두었다. (For financial reasons he abandoned his highschool studies)
② 독서에 흥미가 생겨 공립 도서관을 자주 방문하기 시작했다. (he acquired a taste for reading and started to frequent a public library)
④ 포르투갈이 배경인 소설로 세계적인 인정을 받았다. (He achieved worldwide recognition in 1982 ~ Portugal.)
⑤ 소설뿐 아니라 시, 수필, 희곡 또한 집필하였다. (comprises not only novels but also poetry, essays and drama)

I 09 정답 ④ *노벨 화학상을 수상한 Ilya Prigogine*

Ilya Prigogine was born into a Jewish family / in Moscow. //
Ilya Prigogine은 한 유대인 가정에서 태어났다 / 모스크바의 //

In 1921, / he and his family left Russia, / eventually settling in Belgium. // *분사구문* **①의 단서** 1921년에 그와 그의 가족이 러시아를 떠남
1921년에 / 그와 그의 가족은 러시아를 떠났으며 / 마침내 벨기에에 정착했다 // **②의 단서** 부모님은 그가 변호사가 되길 권함

His parents encouraged him / to become a lawyer, / and he first studied law / at the Free University of Brussels. //
그의 부모님은 그에게 권했다 / 변호사가 되기를 / 그는 처음에 법학을 공부했다 / Free University of Brussels에서 //

It was then / that he became interested / in psychology and behavioral research. // *it ~ that 강조 구문*
바로 그 때였다 / 그가 관심을 가지게 된 것이 / 심리학과 행동 연구에 //

In turn, / reading about these subjects / sparked his interest in chemistry / since chemical processes affect the mind and body. //
다음에는 / 이러한 주제에 관해 읽는 것은 / 화학에 대한 그의 관심을 유발했다 / 이는 화학적 작용이 정신과 신체에 영향을 미치기 때문이었다 //

He eventually dropped out of law school. //
그는 결국 법대를 중퇴했다 //

Prigogine then studied chemistry and physics / at the same time / at the Free University of Brussels. // **③의 단서** Free University of Brussels에서 화학과 물리학을 동시에 공부함
Prigogine은 그 후에 화학과 물리학을 공부했다 / 동시에 / Free University of Brussels에서 //

He obtained the equivalent of a master's degree / in both fields / in 1939, /
그는 석사 학위에 상응하는 것을 취득했다 / 두 분야에서 / 1939년에 /

and he obtained a PhD in chemistry / in 1941 / at the Free University of Brussels, / where he accepted the position of professor / in 1947. // *관계부사* where **④의 단서** 1941년이 아니라 1947년에 교수직을 수락함
그리고 그는 화학 박사 학위를 취득했다 / 1941년에 / Free University of Brussels에서 / 그곳에서 그는 교수직을 수락했다 / 1947년에 //

Considered one of the founders of complexity science, / Ilya Prigogine was awarded / the Nobel Prize in Chemistry / in 1977. // *분사구문* **⑤의 단서** 1977년에 노벨 화학상을 수상함
복잡계 과학의 창시자 중 한 명으로 여겨지는 / Ilya Prigogine은 수상했다 / 노벨 화학상을 / 1977년에 //

- **settle** ⓥ 정착하다
- **behavioral** ⓐ 행동에 관한
- **in turn** 결국
- **drop out of** ~에서 중퇴하다
- **obtain** ⓥ 얻다
- **founder** ⓝ 창시자, 설립자
- **complexity science** 복잡계 과학

Ilya Prigogine은 모스크바의 한 유대인 가정에 태어났다. 1921년에 그와 그의 가족은 러시아를 떠났으며, 마침내 벨기에에 정착했다. 그의 부모님은 그가 변호사가 되기를 권했고, 그는 처음에 Free University of Brussels에서 법학을 공부했다. 그가 심리학과 행동 연구에 관심을 가지게 된 것은 바로 그 때였다. 다음에는, 이러한 주제에 관해 읽는 것은 화학에 대한 그의 관심을 유발했는데, 이는 화학적 작용이 정신과 신체에 영향을 미치기 때문이었다. 그는 결국 법대를 중퇴했다. Prigogine은 그 후에 Free University of Brussels에서 화학과 물리학을 동시에 공부했다. 1939년에 그는 두 분야에서 석사 학위에 상응하는 것을 취득했고, 1941년에 그는 Free University of Brussels에서 화학 박사 학위를 취득했으며, 그곳에서 그는 1947년에 교수직을 수락했다. 복잡계 과학의 창시자 중 한 명으로 여겨지는 Ilya Prigogine은 1977년에 노벨 화학상을 수상했다.

Ilya Prigogine에 관한 다음 글의 내용과 일치하지 않는 것은?

① 1921년에 그와 그의 가족은 러시아를 떠났다.
In 1921, he and his family left Russia
② 부모님은 그가 변호사가 되기를 권했다.
His parents encouraged him to become a lawyer
③ Free University of Brussels에서 화학과 물리학을 동시에 공부했다.
Prigogine then studied chemistry and physics at the same time at the Free University of Brussels.
④ 1941년에 Free University of Brussels의 교수직을 수락했다.
he accepted the position of professor in 1947
⑤ 1977년에 노벨 화학상을 수상했다.
Ilya Prigogine was awarded the Nobel Prize in Chemistry in 1977.

>왜 정답? [정답률 95%]

④ 1941년에 Free University of Brussels의 교수직을 수락한 것이 아니라 1947년에 수락했다. (he accepted the position of professor in 1947)

>왜 오답?

① 1921년에 그와 그의 가족은 러시아를 떠났다. (In 1921, he and his family left Russia)

② 부모님은 그가 변호사가 되기를 권했다. (His parents encouraged him to become a lawyer)

③ Free University of Brussels에서 화학과 물리학을 동시에 공부했다. (Prigogine then studied chemistry and physics at the same time at the Free University of Brussels.)

⑤ 1977년에 노벨 화학상을 수상했다. (Ilya Prigogine was awarded the Nobel Prize in Chemistry in 1977.)

I 10 정답 ④ ＊프랑스 영화감독 Jean Renoir

Jean Renoir (1894 – 1979), a French film director, / was born in Paris, France. //
프랑스 영화감독인 Jean Renoir(1894~1979)는 / 프랑스 파리에서 태어났다 //

①의 단서 유명 화가인 Pierre-Auguste Renoir의 아들이었음
He was the son / of the famous painter Pierre-Auguste Renoir. //
그는 아들이었다 / 유명 화가 Pierre-Auguste Renoir의 //

He and the rest of the Renoir family / were the models / of many of his father's paintings. //
그와 나머지 Renoir 가족은 / 모델이었다 / 그의 아버지의 그림 다수의 //

②의 단서 제1차 세계대전이 발발했을 때 프랑스 군에 복무 중이었음
At the outbreak of World War I, / Jean Renoir was serving in the French army / but was wounded in the leg. // 병렬 구조
제1차 세계대전이 발발했을 때 / Jean Renoir는 프랑스 군에 복무 중이었지만 / 다리에 부상을 입었다 //

In 1937, / he made *La Grande Illusion*, / one of his better-known films. // ③의 단서 1937년에 La Grande Illusion을 만들었음
1937년에 / 그는 La Grande Illusion을 만들었다 / 자신의 더 잘 알려진 영화 중 하나인 //

It was enormously successful / but was not allowed / to show in Germany. // 능동태 문장의 목적격 보어
그것은 엄청나게 성공적이었지만 / 허용되지 않았다 / 독일에서 상영하도록 //

During World War II, / when the Nazis invaded France in 1940, / he went to Hollywood in the United States / and continued his career there. // ④의 단서 제2차 세계대전 중에 미국 할리우드로 갔음
전치사 · 부사절 접속사 · 부사절
제2차 세계대전 중 / 1940년에 나치가 프랑스를 침공했을 때 / 그는 미국 할리우드로 가서 / 그곳에서 경력을 이어갔다 //

⑤의 단서 Academy Honorary Award를 포함하여 많은 상을 받았음
He was awarded numerous honors and awards / throughout his career, / including the Academy Honorary Award in 1975 / for his lifetime achievements / in the film industry. //
그는 수많은 명예상과 상을 받았다 / 그의 경력을 통틀어 / 1975년 아카데미 공로상을 포함하여 / 평생의 업적을 인정받아 / 영화계에서 //

Overall, Jean Renoir's influence / as a film-maker and artist / endures. // 동사(완전자동사) · 주어
전반적으로 Jean Renoir의 영향력은 / 영화 제작자이자 예술가로서 / 지속되고 있다 //

- film director ⓝ 영화 감독
- outbreak ⓝ 발생
- serve ⓥ 복무하다, 제공하다
- army ⓝ 군대
- wound ⓥ 상처를 입히다
- enormously 🄰🄳 엄청나게, 대단히
- successful ⓐ 성공한, 출세한
- award ⓥ 수여하다
- throughout 🄿🄰🄴🄿 ~동안, 도처에
- lifetime ⓝ 일생, 생애
- achievement ⓝ 업적
- influence ⓝ 영향력
- endure ⓥ 오래가다, 지속되다

프랑스 영화감독인 Jean Renoir(1894~1979)는 프랑스 파리에서 태어났다. 그는 유명 화가 Pierre-Auguste Renoir의 아들이었다. 그와 나머지 Renoir 가족은 아버지의 그림 다수의 모델이었다. 제1차 세계대전이 발발했을 때, Jean

---

Renoir는 프랑스 군에 복무 중이었지만, 다리에 부상을 입었다. 1937년에 그는 자신의 더 잘 알려진 영화 중 하나인 La Grande Illusion을 만들었다. 그것은 엄청나게 성공적이었지만 독일에서는 상영이 허용되지 않았다. 제2차 세계대전 중, 1940년에 나치가 프랑스를 침공했을 때 그는 미국 할리우드로 가서 그곳에서 경력을 이어갔다. 그는 영화계에서 평생의 업적을 인정받아 1975년 아카데미 공로상을 포함하여 경력을 통틀어 수많은 명예상과 상을 받았다. 전반적으로, 영화 제작자이자 예술가로서 Jean Renoir의 영향력은 지속되고 있다.

Jean Renoir에 관한 다음 글의 내용과 일치하지 않는 것은?

① 유명 화가의 아들이었다. He was the son of the famous painter Pierre-Auguste Renoir.

② 제1차 세계대전이 발발했을 때 프랑스 군에 복무 중이었다.
At the outbreak of World War I, Jean Renoir was serving in the French army

③ *La Grande Illusion*을 1937년에 만들었다.
In 1937, he made La Grande Illusion

④ 제2차 세계대전 내내 프랑스에 머물렀다.
During World War II, ~ he went to Hollywood in the United States

⑤ Academy Honorary Award를 수상하였다.
He was awarded numerous honors and awards ~ including the Academy Honorary Award

>왜 정답? [정답률 96%]

④ 제2차 세계대전 중에 미국 할리우드로 갔다. (During World War II, ~ he went to Hollywood in the United States)

>왜 오답?

① 유명 화가의 아들이었다. (He was the son of the famous painter Pierre-Auguste Renoir.)

② 제1차 세계대전이 발발했을 때 프랑스 군에 복무 중이었다. (At the outbreak of World War I, Jean Renoir was serving in the French army)

③ *La Grande Illusion*을 1937년에 만들었다. (In 1937, he made *La Grande Illusion*)

⑤ Academy Honorary Award를 수상하였다. (He was awarded numerous honors and awards ~ including the Academy Honorary Award)

I 11 정답 ③ ＊위대한 장거리 선수인 Emil Zátopek

Emil Zátopek, a former Czech athlete, / is considered / one of the greatest long-distance runners ever. //
전직 체코 육상선수인 Emil Zátopek은 / 여겨진다 / 역대 가장 위대한 장거리 선수 중 한 명이라고 //

①의 단서 독특한 달리기 스타일로 유명했음
He was also famous / for his distinctive running style. //
그는 또한 유명했다 / 그의 독특한 달리기 스타일로 //

②의 단서 신발 공장에서 일한 적이 있음
While working in a shoe factory, / he participated in a 1,500-meter race / and won second place. //
While he worked
신발 공장에서 일하는 동안 / 그는 1,500미터 경주에 참가해서 / 2등을 했다 //

After that event, / he took a more serious interest / in running / and devoted himself to it. // 병렬 구조 ③의 단서 헬싱키 올림픽에서 올림픽 기록을 깼음
그 일 이후로 / 그는 더 진지한 흥미를 느끼게 되어 / 달리기에 / 그것에 전념했다 //

At the 1952 Olympic Games in Helsinki, / he won three gold medals / in the 5,000-meter and 10,000-meter races and in the marathon, / breaking Olympic records / in each. //
1952년 헬싱키 올림픽 대회에서 / 그는 세 개의 금메달을 땄는데 / 5,000미터, 1만 미터 종목과 마라톤에서 / 올림픽 기록을 깼다 / 각 종목에서 //

선행사 · 주격 관계대명사(계속적 용법)
He was married to Dana Zátopková, / who was an Olympic gold medalist, too. // ④의 단서 Dana Zátopková와 결혼했는데 그녀도 올림픽 금메달리스트였음
그는 Dana Zátopková와 결혼했는데 / 그녀 또한 올림픽 금메달리스트였다 //

Zátopek was also noted / for his friendly personality. //
Zátopek은 또한 유명했다 / 그의 다정한 성격으로 //

In 1966, / Zátopek invited Ron Clarke, / a great Australian runner / who had never won an Olympic gold medal, / to an athletic meeting in Prague. //
1966년에 / Zátopek은 Ron Clarke를 초대했다 / 위대한 호주 달리기 선수인 / 올림픽 금메달을 딴 적이 없었던 / 프라하에서 열린 체전에 //

After the meeting, / he gave Clarke / one of his gold medals / as
a gift. // **⑥의 단서** 자신의 금메달들 중 하나를 Ron Clarke에게 줬음
그 대회 후에 / 그는 Clarke에게 주었다 / 자신의 금메달들 중 하나를 / 선물로 //

- **former** ⓐ 과거의, 이전의, 전자의 · **Czech** ⓐ 체코의
- **athlete** ⓝ (운동) 선수 · **consider A B** A를 B로 여기다
- **long-distance** ⓐ 장거리의 · **distinctive** ⓐ 독특한, 특유의
- **factory** ⓝ 공장 · **participate in** ~에 참가하다
- **race** ⓝ 달리기 (시합), 경주 · **win** ⓥ (경기 등에서 이겨) 따다[타다]
- **serious** ⓐ 진지한, 심각한 · **devote** ⓥ (노력 · 시간을) 바치다
- **break** ⓥ (기록을) 깨다 · **record** ⓝ 기록 · **noted for** ~로 유명한
- **personality** ⓝ 성격 · **athletic** ⓐ 육상(경기)의

전직 체코 육상선수인 Emil Zátopek은 역대 가장 위대한 장거리 선수 중 한 명이라고 여겨진다. 그는 또한 그의 독특한 달리기 스타일로 유명했다. 신발 공장에서 일하는 동안 그는 1,500미터 경주에 참가해서 2등을 했다. 그 일 이후로 그는 달리기에 더 진지한 흥미를 느끼게 되어 그것에 전념했다. 1952년 헬싱키 올림픽 대회에서 그는 5,000미터, 1만 미터 종목과 마라톤에서 세 개의 금메달을 땄는데, 각 종목에서 올림픽 기록을 깼다. 그는 Dana Zátopková와 결혼했는데, 그녀 또한 올림픽 금메달리스트였다. Zátopek은 또한 그의 다정한 성격으로 유명했다. 1966년에, Zátopek은 올림픽 금메달을 딴 적이 없었던 위대한 호주 달리기 선수인 Ron Clarke를 프라하에서 열린 체전에 초대했다. 그 대회 후에 그는 Clarke에게 자신의 금메달들 중 하나를 선물로 주었다.

Emil Zátopek에 관한 다음 글의 내용과 일치하지 않는 것은?
① 독특한 달리기 스타일로 유명했다.
　He was also famous for his distinctive running style.
② 신발 공장에서 일한 적이 있다.
　While working in a shoe factory
③ 1952년 Helsinki 올림픽에서 올림픽 기록을 깨지 못했다.
　At the 1952 Olympic Games in Helsinki, ~ breaking Olympic records in each.
④ 올림픽 금메달리스트인 Dana Zátopková와 결혼했다.
　He was married to Dana Zátopková, who was an Olympic gold medalist, too.
⑤ 자신의 금메달 중 하나를 Ron Clarke에게 주었다.
　After the meeting, he gave Clarke one of his gold medals as a gift.

왜 정답? [정답률 96%]
1952년 헬싱키 올림픽에서 5,000미터, 1만 미터 마라톤에서 금메달을 땄고, 각 종목에서 올림픽 기록을 깼다고(At the 1952 Olympic Games in Helsinki, ~ breaking Olympic records in each.) 했으므로 ③은 글과 일치하지 않는다.

왜 오답?
① 자신의 독특한 달리기 스타일로 유명했다. (He was also famous for his distinctive running style.)
② 신발 공장에서 일하는 동안 1,500미터 경주에 참가해서 2등을 했다. (While working in a shoe factory)
④ 올림픽 금메달리스트인 Dana Zátopková와 결혼했다. (He was married to Dana Zátopková, who was an Olympic gold medalist, too.)
⑤ 프라하에서 열린 체전 이후에 자신의 금메달들 중 하나를 Ron Clarke에게 주었다. (After the meeting, he gave Clarke one of his gold medals as a gift.)

I 12 정답 ③ ＊Donato Bramante의 생애

Donato Bramante, / born in Fermignano, Italy, / began to paint
/ early in his life. //
Donato Bramante는 / 이탈리아의 Fermignano에서 태어난 / 그림을 그리기 시작했다 /
인생에서 일찍이 //
His father encouraged him / to study painting. //
그의 아버지는 그를 격려했다 / 그림을 공부하도록 //
Later, he worked / as an assistant of Piero della Francesca / in
Urbino. // **①의 단서** Piero della Francesca의 조수로 일했음
나중에 그는 일했다 / Piero della Francesca의 조수로 / Urbino에서 //

Around 1480, / he built several churches / in a new style / in
Milan. // **②의 단서** Milan에서 새로운 양식의 교회들을 건축했음
1480년경 / 그는 몇 개의 교회를 건축했다 / 새로운 양식으로 / Milan의 //
He had a close relationship / with Leonardo da Vinci, / and they
worked together / in that city. //
그는 친근한 관계를 맺었으며 / Leonardo da Vinci와 / 그들은 함께 작업했다 / 그 도시에서 //
Architecture became his main interest, / but he did not give up
painting. // **③의 단서** 건축이 주된 관심사가 되었지만 그림 그리기를 포기하지 않았음
건축이 그의 주요한 관심사가 되었지만 / 그는 그림을 포기하지 않았다 //
Bramante moved to Rome / in 1499 / and participated in Pope
Julius II's plan / for the renewal of Rome. //
Bramante는 Rome으로 이주해서 / 1499년에 / 교황 Julius 2세의 계획에 참여했다 /
Rome 재개발을 위한 // **④의 단서** Pope Julius II의 Rome 재개발 계획에 참여했음
He planned / the new Basilica of St. Peter in Rome / — one
of the most ambitious building projects / in the history of
humankind. //
그는 구상했다 / Rome의 St. Peter(성 베드로 대성당)의 새로운 바실리카를 / 가장 야심 찬
건축 프로젝트 중 하나 / 인류 역사에서 //
Bramante died on April 11, 1514 / and was buried in Rome. //
Bramante는 1514년 4월 11일에 사망했으며 / Rome에 묻혔다 //
His buildings influenced other architects / for centuries. //
그의 건축물들은 다른 건축가들에게 영향을 끼쳤다 / 여러 세기 동안 //
⑤의 단서 그의 건축물들이 다른 건축가들에게 영향을 미쳤음

- **encourage** ⓥ 격려하다, 권장하다 · **assistant** ⓝ 조수, 보조원
- **architecture** ⓝ 건축 (양식) · **renewal** ⓝ 재개발
- **ambitious** ⓐ 어마어마한, 야심 찬 · **architect** ⓝ 건축

이탈리아의 Fermignano에서 태어난 Donato Bramante는 인생에서 일찍이 그림을 그리기 시작했다. 그의 아버지는 그림을 공부하도록 그를 격려했다. 나중에, 그는 Urbino에서 Piero della Francesca의 조수로 일했다. 1480년경, 그는 Milan의 몇 개의 교회들을 새로운 양식으로 건축했다. 그는 Leonardo da Vinci와 친근한 관계를 맺었으며, 그들은 그 도시에서 함께 작업했다. 건축이 그의 주요한 관심사가 되었지만, 그는 그림을 포기하지 않았다. Bramante는 1499년에 Rome으로 이주해서 교황 Julius 2세의 Rome 재개발 계획에 참여했다. 그는 Rome의 성 베드로 대성당의 새로운 바실리카를 구상했는데, 그것은 인류 역사상 가장 야심 찬 건축 프로젝트 중 하나였다. Bramante는 1514년 4월 11일에 사망했으며 Rome에 묻혔다. 그의 건축물들은 여러 세기 동안 다른 건축가들에게 영향을 끼쳤다.

Donato Bramante에 관한 다음 글의 내용과 일치하지 않는 것은?
① Piero della Francesca의 조수로 일했다.
　he worked as an assistant of Piero della Francesca
② Milan에서 새로운 양식의 교회들을 건축했다.
　he built several churches in a new style in Milan
③ 건축에 주된 관심을 갖게 되면서 그림 그리기를 포기했다.
　Architecture became his main interest, but he did not give up painting.
④ Pope Julius II의 Rome 재개발 계획에 참여했다.
　participated in Pope Julius II's plan for the renewal of Rome
⑤ 그의 건축물들은 다른 건축가들에게 영향을 끼쳤다.
　His buildings influenced other architects

왜 정답? [정답률 95%]
건축이 그의 주된 관심사가 되었지만 그는 그림 그리기를 포기하지 않았다고 (Architecture became his main interest, but he did not give up painting.) 했으므로 ③은 글과 일치하지 않는다.

왜 오답?
① Piero della Francesca의 조수로 일했다. (he worked as an assistant of Piero della Francesca)
② Milan에서 새로운 양식의 교회들을 건축했다. (he built several churches in a new style in Milan)
④ Pope Julius II의 Rome 재개발 계획에 참여했다. (participated in Pope Julius II's plan for the renewal of Rome)
⑤ 그의 건축물들은 다른 건축가들에게 영향을 끼쳤다. (His buildings influenced other architects)

I 13 정답 ⑤ * 템스 터널의 아버지

Marc Isambard Brunel (1769–1849) is best known / for the design and construction / of the Thames Tunnel. //
Marc Isambard Brunel(1769~1849)은 가장 잘 알려져 있다 / 설계와 건설로 / 템스 터널의 //

Originally born in France, / Brunel escaped to the United States / during the French Revolution. // **①의 단서** 프랑스 혁명 중에 미국으로 달아났음
전치사 * 명사구
원래 프랑스에서 태어나 / Brunel은 미국으로 달아났다 / 프랑스 혁명 중에 //

He later moved / to London. //
그는 후에 거처를 옮겼다 / 런던으로 //

When the Napoleonic Wars were at their height, / he invented machines / for making boots. // **②의 단서** 부츠를 만드는 기계를 발명했음
시간의 부사절 접속사 * 명사구
나폴레옹 전쟁이 한창일 때 / 그는 기계를 발명했다 / 부츠를 만드는 //

During the Napoleonic Wars, / Brunel's factory supplied British troops / with boots. // **③의 단서** 그의 공장이 영국 군대에 부츠를 공급했음
전치사 * 명사구
나폴레옹 전쟁 중에 / Brunel의 공장은 영국 군대에 공급했다 / 부츠를 //

After the Wars ended, however, / the government stopped buying his boots / and he went out of business. //
부사절 접속사 * 완전한 절
그러나 전쟁이 끝난 후 / 정부는 그의 부츠를 사는 것을 멈췄고 / 그는 파산했다 //

A few years later, / Brunel was imprisoned / for several months / because of his debt. // **④의 단서** 빚 때문에 감옥에 수감되었음
전치사 * 명사구
몇 년 후 / Brunel은 감옥에 수감되었다 / 몇 달 동안 / 그의 빚 때문에 //

At that time, / London was very much divided / by the River Thames / and needed more ways / for people and goods to move across it. //
to move의 의미상의 주어   형용사적 용법 (ways 수식)
그 당시 / 런던은 매우 많이 나뉘어 있었고 / 템스강에 의해 / 더 많은 방법을 필요로 했다 / 사람과 상품이 강을 가로질러 건너는 //

In 1825, / Brunel designed a tunnel / under the river. //
1825년에 / Brunel은 터널을 설계했다 / 강 밑에 //

The Thames Tunnel officially opened / on 25 March 1843, / and Brunel, / despite being in ill health, / attended the opening ceremony. // **⑥의 단서** 개통식에 참석했음
전치사 * 동명사구
템스 터널은 공식적으로 개통했고 / 1843년 3월 25일에 / Brunel은 / 건강이 좋지 않음에도 불구하고 / 개통식에 참석했다 //

- construction ⓝ 건설   · escape ⓥ 달아나다, 탈출하다
- at one's height ~가 한창일 때   · supply ⓥ 공급하다
- troop ⓝ 군대   · go out of business 파산하다
- imprison ⓥ 감옥에 수감하다   · debt ⓝ 빚, 부채
- goods ⓝ 상품, 제품   · officially ⓐⓓ 공식적으로
- opening ceremony 개통식

Marc Isambard Brunel(1769~1849)은 템스 터널의 설계와 건설로 가장 잘 알려져 있다. 원래 프랑스에서 태어난 Brunel은 프랑스 혁명 중에 미국으로 달아났다. 그는 후에 런던으로 거처를 옮겼다. 나폴레옹 전쟁이 한창일 때, 그는 부츠를 만드는 기계를 발명했다. 나폴레옹 전쟁 중에, Brunel의 공장은 영국 군대에 부츠를 공급했다. 그러나 전쟁이 끝난 후, 정부는 그의 부츠를 더 이상 사지 않았고 그는 파산했다. 몇 년 후, Brunel은 빚 때문에 몇 달 동안 감옥에 수감되었다. 그 당시, 런던은 템스강에 의해 매우 많이 나뉘어 있었고 사람과 상품이 강을 가로질러 건너는 더 많은 방법을 필요로 했다. 1825년, Brunel은 강 밑에 터널을 설계했다. 템스 터널은 1843년 3월 25일에 공식적으로 개통했고, Brunel은 건강이 좋지 않았음에도 불구하고 개통식에 참석했다.

Marc Isambard Brunel에 관한 다음 글의 내용과 일치하지 않는 것은?

① 프랑스 혁명 중에 미국으로 달아났다.
Brunel escaped to the United States during the French Revolution
② 부츠를 만드는 기계를 발명하였다.
he invented machines for making boots
③ 그의 공장은 영국 군대에 부츠를 공급한 적이 있다.
Brunel's factory supplied British troops with boots
④ 빚 때문에 감옥에 수감되었다.
Brunel was imprisoned for several months because of his debt
⑤ Thames Tunnel 개통식에 아파서 참석하지 못했다.
Brunel, despite being in ill health, attended the opening ceremony

왜 정답 ? [정답률 94%]

마지막 문장에서 건강이 좋지 않음에도 불구하고 개통식에 참석했다고(Brunel, despite being in ill health, attended the opening ceremony) 했으므로 ⑤은 글의 내용과 일치하지 않는다.

왜 오답 ?

① 원래 프랑스에서 태어났는데 프랑스 혁명 중에 미국으로 탈출했다. (Brunel escaped to the United States during the French Revolution)
② 나폴레옹 전쟁이 한창일 때 부츠를 만드는 기계를 발명했다. (he invented machines for making boots)
③ 그의 공장은 나폴레옹 전쟁 중에 영국 군대에 부츠를 공급했다. (Brunel's factory supplied British troops with boots)
④ 전쟁이 끝난 후 빚 때문에 몇 달 동안 감옥에 수감되었다. (Brunel was imprisoned for several months because of his debt)

― 어법 특강

＊ 전치사 vs. 접속사
- 전치사 뒤에는 명사 상당어구가, 접속사 뒤에는 주어와 동사로 이루어진 절이 온다.

- <u>During</u> most of my interview I was calm and direct.
  명사구가 이어짐
  (인터뷰하는 대부분 동안 나는 침착하고 솔직했다.)

- Cats growl <u>while</u> they are asleep.
  절이 이어짐
  (고양이는 잠들어 있는 동안에 으르렁거린다.)

- Cancer is a global problem <u>despite</u> medical advances.
  명사구가 이어짐
  (의학적 발전에도 불구하고 암은 세계적인 문제이다.)

- <u>Although</u> we eat apples often, few of us know much about them.
  절이 이어짐
  (우리는 사과를 자주 먹지만 우리들 중 대부분은 사과에 대해서 많이 알고 있지 않다.)

I 14 정답 ⑤ * Ann Bancroft의 탐험

Ann Bancroft was born / in Minnesota, U.S. //
Ann Bancroft는 태어났다 / 미국 Minnesota에서 //

Bancroft grew up in rural Minnesota / in what she described as a family of risk-takers. // **①의 단서** Minnesota의 시골에서 성장했음
전치사   명사절
Bancroft는 Minnesota의 시골에서 성장했다 / 그녀가 모험을 좋아하는 사람의 가정이라고 묘사한 곳에서 //

Although she struggled with a learning disability, / she graduated from St. Paul Academy / and became a physical education teacher. // **②의 단서** St. Paul Academy를 졸업하고 체육 교사가 되었음
부사절 접속사(양보)
비록 그녀는 학습 장애로 어려움을 겪었지만 / 그녀는 St. Paul Academy를 졸업하고 / 체육 교사가 되었다 //

③의 단서 1986년에 교직을 그만두었음
Bancroft resigned her teaching position / in 1986 / in order to participate / in the Will Steger International Polar Expedition. //
Bancroft는 교직을 그만두었다 / 1986년에 / 참여하기 위해 / Will Steger International Polar Expedition에 //

The group departed from Ellesmere Island / on March 6, / and after 56 days, / she and five other team members arrived / at the North Pole / by dogsled. // **④의 단서** Ellesmere섬에서 출발한 지 56일 후에 북극에 도달했음
그 탐험대는 Ellesmere섬에서 출발했고 / 3월 6일에 / 56일 후에 / 그녀와 다섯 명의 다른 팀원은 도달했다 / 북극에 / 개 썰매를 타고 //

She thus became the first woman / to reach the North Pole / by sled and on foot. //
형용사적 용법(the first woman 수식)
그래서 그녀는 최초의 여성이 되었다 / 북극에 도달한 / 썰매와 도보로 //

In November 1992, / she led three other women / on the American Women's Expedition to Antarctica. // **⑥의 단서** 세 명의 여성 대원과 남극에 갔음
1992년 11월에 / 그녀는 세 명의 다른 여성을 이끌었다 / 남극으로 가는 American Women's Expedition에서 //

It took them 67 days / to reach the South Pole on skis / and Bancroft became the first woman / to have stood at both poles. //
to부정사의 완료형
67일이 걸렸고 / 그들이 스키를 타고 남극에 가기까지 / Bancroft는 최초의 여성이 되었다 / 양극에 선 //

- risk-taker ⓝ 모험을 좋아하는 사람   • struggle ⓥ 어려움을 겪다
- learning disability 학습 장애   • resign ⓥ 그만두다
- expedition ⓝ 원정   • North Pole 북극   • sled ⓝ 썰매
- on foot 도보로   • Antarctica ⓝ 남극

Ann Bancroft는 미국 Minnesota에서 태어났다. Bancroft는 Minnesota의 시골에서, 그녀가 모험을 좋아하는 사람의 가정이라고 묘사한 곳에서 성장했다. 비록 그녀는 학습 장애로 어려움을 겪었지만, St. Paul Academy를 졸업하고 체육 교사가 되었다. Will Stegar International Polar Expedition에 참여하기 위해 Bancroft는 1986년에 교직을 그만두었다. 그 탐험대는 3월 6일에 Ellesmere섬에서 출발했고, 56일 후에 그녀와 다섯 명의 다른 팀원은 개 썰매를 타고 북극에 도달했다. 그래서 그녀는 썰매와 도보로 북극에 도달한 최초의 여성이 되었다. 1992년 11월에 그녀는 남극으로 가는 American Women's Expedition에서 세 명의 다른 여성을 이끌었다. 그들이 스키를 타고 남극에 가기까지 67일이 걸렸고, Bancroft는 양극에 선 최초의 여성이 되었다.

Ann Bancroft에 관한 다음 글의 내용과 일치하지 않는 것은?

① Minnesota의 시골에서 자랐다.
Bancroft grew up in rural Minnesota
② St. Paul Academy를 졸업하고 체육 교사가 되었다.
she graduated from St. Paul Academy and became a physical education teacher
③ 1986년에 교직을 그만두었다.
Bancroft resigned her teaching position in 1986
④ Ellesmere섬에서 출발한 지 56일 후에 북극에 도달했다.
The group departed from Ellesmere Island on March 6, and after 56 days,
~ arrived at the North Pole
⑤ 세 명의 남자 대원과 남극까지 스키를 타고 갔다.
she led three other women on the American Women's Expedition to Antarctica

왜 정답? [정답률 95%]

⑤ 남자 대원이 아니라 세 명의 여자 대원과 남극에 갔다. (she led three other women on the American Women's Expedition to Antarctica)

왜 오답?

① Minnesota의 시골에서 자랐다. (Bancroft grew up in rural Minnesota)
② St. Paul Academy를 졸업하고 체육 교사가 되었다. (she graduated from St. Paul Academy and became a physical education teacher)
③ 1986년에 교직을 그만두었다. (Bancroft resigned her teaching position in 1986)
④ Ellesmere섬에서 출발한 지 56일 후에 북극에 도달했다. (The group departed from Ellesmere Island on March 6, and after 56 days, ~ arrived at the North Pole)

I 15 정답 ⑤ ＊Charles Rosen의 일생

주어   동사
Charles Rosen, / a virtuoso pianist and distinguished writer, / was born in New York / in 1927. //
Charles Rosen은 / 거장 피아니스트이자 저명한 작가인 / 뉴욕에서 태어났다 / 1927년에 //

Rosen displayed a remarkable talent / for the piano / from his early childhood. // ①의 단서 어려서부터 피아노에 재능을 보였음
Rosen은 주목할 만한 재능을 보였다 / 피아노에 / 어린 시절부터 //
선행사(관계부사는 생략됨)
In 1951, / the year he earned / his doctoral degree in French literature / at Princeton University, / Rosen made both his New York piano debut and his first recordings. // ②의 단서 프랑스 문학으로 박사 학위를 받았음
1951년에 / 그가 받은 해인 / 불문학 박사 학위를 / 프린스턴 대학교에서 / Rosen은 뉴욕에서 피아노 데뷔도 했고 첫 음반의 녹음도 했다 //

To glowing praise, / he appeared / in numerous recitals and orchestral concerts / around the world. //
열렬한 찬사 속에 / 그는 출연했다 / 수많은 독주회와 오케스트라 연주회에 / 전 세계적으로 //

Rosen's performances impressed / some of the 20th century's most well-known composers, / who invited him / to play their music. // ③의 단서 유명 작곡가들로부터 그들의   invited의 목적어와 목적격 보어
작품 연주를 요청받았음
Rosen의 연주는 감명을 주었고 / 20세기의 가장 유명한 작곡가들 중 일부에게 / 그들은 그에게 요청했다 / 자기들의 곡을 연주해 달라고 //

Rosen was also the author / of many widely admired books / about music. //
Rosen은 또한 저자였다 / 널리 칭송받는 많은 저서의 / 음악에 관한 //

His most famous book, *The Classical Style*, / was first published in 1971 / and won the U.S. National Book Award / the next year. // ④의 단서 The Classical Style이 처음으로 출판되고 다음 해에 상을 받았음
그의 가장 유명한 책은 The Classical Style은 / 1971년에 처음 출판되었고 / U.S. National Book Award를 수상했다 / 이듬해에 //
주어
This work, / which was reprinted / in an expanded edition / in 1997, / remains a landmark / in the field. //
동사
이 저작은 / 재판(再版)되었고 / 증보판으로 / 1997년에 / 획기적인 것으로 남아 있다 / 그 분야에서 //
생략되지 않은 부사절 접속사   ⑤의 단서 피아니스트로서 공연을 계속하면서 글쓰기에 매진함
While writing extensively, / Rosen continued to perform as a pianist / for the rest of his life / until he died in 2012. //
폭넓게 글쓰기를 하면서 / Rosen은 피아니스트로서 공연을 계속했다 / 여생 동안 / 2012년에 사망할 때까지 //

- virtuoso ⓝ 거장, 명장   • distinguished ⓐ 저명한, 성공한
- doctoral degree 박사 학위   • recital ⓝ 독주회
- landmark ⓝ 획기적인 것   • extensively ⓐd 폭넓게

거장 피아니스트이자 저명한 작가인 Charles Rosen은 1927년 뉴욕에서 태어났다. Rosen은 어린 시절부터 피아노에 주목할 만한 재능을 보였다. 프린스턴 대학교에서 불문학 박사 학위를 받은 1951년, Rosen은 뉴욕에서 피아노 데뷔도 했고 첫 음반의 녹음도 했다. 열렬한 찬사 속에, 그는 전 세계적으로 수많은 독주회와 오케스트라 연주회에 출연했다. Rosen의 연주는 20세기의 가장 유명한 작곡가들 중 일부에게 감명을 주었고, 그들은 Rosen에게 자기들의 곡을 연주해 달라고 요청했다. Rosen은 또한 널리 칭송받는 많은 음악 저서의 저자였다. 그의 가장 유명한 책은 The Classical Style은 1971년에 처음 출판되고 이듬해에 U.S. National Book Award를 수상했다. 이 저작은 1997년에 증보판으로 재판(再版)되었고, 이 분야에서 획기적인 것으로 남아있다. 폭넓게 글쓰기를 하면서, Rosen은 2012년 사망할 때까지 여생 동안 피아니스트로서 공연을 계속했다.

Charles Rosen에 관한 다음 글의 내용과 일치하지 않는 것은?

① 어려서부터 피아노에 재능을 보였다.
Rosen displayed a remarkable talent for the piano from his early childhood.
② 프랑스 문학으로 박사 학위를 받았다.
he earned his doctoral degree in French literature
③ 유명 작곡가들로부터 그들의 작품 연주를 요청받았다.
some of the 20th century's most well-known composers, who invited him to play their music
④ *The Classical Style*이 처음으로 출판되고 다음 해에 상을 받았다.
was first published in 1971 and won the U.S. National Book Award the next year
⑤ 피아니스트 활동을 중단하고 글쓰기에 매진하였다.
While writing extensively, Rosen continued to perform as a pianist

왜 정답? [정답률 96%]

⑤ 광범위하게 글쓰기를 하면서 피아니스트로서 공연을 계속했다. (While writing extensively, Rosen continued to perform as a pianist)

왜 오답?

① 어려서부터 피아노에 재능을 보였다. (Rosen displayed a remarkable talent for the piano from his early childhood.)
② 프랑스 문학으로 박사 학위를 받았다. (he earned his doctoral degree in French literature)
③ 유명 작곡가들로부터 그들의 작품 연주를 요청받았다. (Rosen's performances impressed some of the 20th century's most well-known composers, who invited him to play their music.)
④ The Classical Style이 처음으로 출판되고 다음 해에 상을 받았다. (was first published in 1971 and won the U.S. National Book Award the next year)

I 16 정답 ③ ＊Leon Festinger의 생애

Leon Festinger was an American social psychologist. //
Leon Festinger는 미국의 사회 심리학자였다 //

He was born in New York City / in 1919 / to a Russian immigrant
family. // **①의 단서** 러시아인 이민자 가정에서 태어났음
전치사　　　　　　　명사구
그는 New York City에서 태어났다 / 1919년에 / 러시아인 이민자 가정에 //

As a graduate student / at the University of Iowa, / Festinger
was influenced / by Kurt Lewin, a leading social psychologist. //
대학원생으로서 / Iowa 대학교의 / Festinger는 영향을 받았다 / 대표적인 사회 심리학자
Kurt Lewin의 //
생략되지 않은 부사절 접속사　　**②의 단서** 사회 심리학자인 Kurt Lewin의 영향을 받음

After graduating from there, / he became a professor / at the
Massachusetts Institute of Technology / in 1945. //
그곳에서 졸업한 후 / 그는 교수가 되었다 / Massachusetts 공과대학의 / 1945년에 //
　　　　　　　　　　　　　선행사　　　　계속적 용법의 관계부사
He later moved to Stanford University, / where he continued /
his work in social psychology. // **③의 단서** Stanford University에서
　　　　　　　　　　　　　　　　　　　사회 심리학 연구를 계속함
이후 그는 Stanford University로 옮겨 / 그곳에서 그는 계속했다 / 그의 사회 심리학
연구를 //
　　　주어　　　　　　　　　　　동사　간접목적어　직접목적어
His theory of social comparison / earned him a good
reputation. //
그의 사회 비교 이론은 / 그에게 훌륭한 명성을 얻어 주었다 //

Festinger actively participated / in international scholarly
cooperation. // **④의 단서** 국제 학술 협력에 활발히 참여함
Festinger는 적극적으로 참여했다 / 국제 학술 협력에 //
　　　　　　　　　　　　　　　　　　⑤의 단서 1970년대 후반에
　　　　　　　　　　　　　　　　　　역사 분야로 관심을 돌림
In the late 1970s, / he turned his interest / to the field of history. //
1970년대 후반에 / 그는 그의 관심을 돌렸다 / 역사 분야로 //

He was one / of the most cited psychologists / of the twentieth
century. //
그는 한 명이었다 / 가장 많이 인용된 심리학자 중 / 20세기의 //

Festinger's theories still play an important role / in psychology
/ today. //
　　　복수 주어　　　　　복수 동사
Festinger의 이론은 여전히 중요한 역할을 한다 / 심리학에서 / 오늘날에도 //

- immigrant ⓝ 이민자, 이주민　　・ leading ⓐ 선두의, 가장 중요한
- comparison ⓝ 비교, 비유　　・ earn ⓥ (돈을) 벌다, (자격이 되어서) 얻다
- actively ⓐⓓ 활발하게, 적극적으로　　・ scholarly ⓐ 학자의, 전문적인
- cooperation ⓝ 협력, 협조　　・ theory ⓝ 학설, 이론

Leon Festinger는 미국의 사회 심리학자였다. 그는 1919년 New
York City에서 러시아인 이민자 가정에서 태어났다. Iowa 대학교의
대학원생으로서, Festinger는 대표적인 사회 심리학자 Kurt Lewin의 영향을
받았다. 그곳에서 졸업한 후, 그는 1945년에 Massachusetts 공과대학의
교수가 되었다. 이후 그는 Stanford University로 옮겨 그곳에서 자신의
사회 심리학 연구를 계속했다. 자신의 사회 비교 이론으로 그는 훌륭한 명성을
얻었다. Festinger는 국제 학술 협력에 적극적으로 참여했다. 1970년대 후반,
그는 역사 분야로 자신의 관심을 돌렸다. 그는 가장 많이 인용된 20세기의
심리학자 중 한 명이었다. Festinger의 이론은 오늘날에도 여전히 심리학에서
중요한 역할을 한다.

Leon Festinger에 관한 다음 글의 내용과 일치하지 <u>않는</u> 것은?

① 러시아인 이민자 가정에서 태어났다.
　He was born in New York City in 1919 to a Russian immigrant family.
② 사회 심리학자 Kurt Lewin에게 영향을 받았다.
　Festinger was influenced by Kurt Lewin, a leading social psychologist
③ Stanford University에서 사회 심리학 연구를 중단했다.
　Stanford University, where he continued his work in social psychology
④ 국제 학술 협력에 활발하게 참여했다.
　Festinger actively participated in international scholarly cooperation.
⑤ 1970년대 후반에 역사 분야로 관심을 돌렸다.
　In the late 1970s, he turned his interest to the field of history.

⟩왜 정답 ? [정답률 98%]

Stanford University에서 자신의 사회 심리학 연구를 계속했다고(Stanford
University, where he continued his work in social psychology) 했으므로
③은 글과 일치하지 않는다.

⟩왜 오답 ?

① 러시아인 이민자 가정에서 태어났다. (He was born in New York City in
1919 to a Russian immigrant family.)
② 사회 심리학자 Kurt Lewin에게 영향을 받았다. (Festinger was influenced
by Kurt Lewin, a leading social psychologist)
④ 국제 학술 협력에 활발하게 참여했다. (Festinger actively participated in
international scholarly cooperation.)
⑤ 1970년대 후반에 역사 분야로 관심을 돌렸다. (In the late 1970s, he turned
his interest to the field of history.)

I 17 정답 ② ＊최초의 중국계 미국인 영화배우

Anna May Wong is considered / the first Chinese-American
movie star / in Hollywood. //
Anna May Wong은 여겨진다 / 최초의 중국계 미국인 영화배우로 / Hollywood에서 //
①의 단서 전업 배우가 되기 위해 고등학교를 중퇴했음
She dropped out of high school / to pursue a full-time acting
career / and, at 17, / she played her first leading role / in The Toll
of the Sea. //
그녀는 고등학교를 중퇴했고 / 전업 배우가 되기 위해 / 17세에 / 그녀의 첫 번째 주요한
역할을 연기했다 / 'The Toll of the Sea'에서 //

Reviewers praised her extraordinary acting / but her ethnicity
　　　　　┌ prevent A from B: A가 B하는 것을 막다 ┐
prevented U.S. filmmakers / from casting her as a leading lady. //
평론가들은 그녀의 놀랄만한 연기를 칭송했지만 / 그녀의 민족성이 미국 영화제작자들을
막았다 / 그녀에게 주요한 여성 배역을 맡기는 것으로부터 //
　　　　　　　　　　선행사　　　　　　　계속적 용법의 관계부사
Frustrated, Wong left for Europe in 1928, / where she had main
roles / in many notable films. // **②의 단서** 유럽으로 떠나 많은 영화에서
　　　　　　　　　　　　　주요한 역할을 맡음
좌절한 채 Wong은 1928년에 유럽으로 떠났고 / 그곳에서 그녀는 주요한 역할을 맡았다 /
많은 저명한 영화에서 //
부사절 접속사(때)
When American studios wanted fresh European talent / in the
1930s, / Wong's new prestige immediately led / to a main role
on Broadway. //
미국 스튜디오들이 참신한 유럽 인재들을 원했을 때 / 1930년대에 / Wong의 새로운 명성은
곧 이어졌다 / Broadway의 주요한 역할로 //

She returned to America / and used her influence / to advocate
for better film opportunities / for Chinese-Americans. //
그녀는 미국으로 돌아가서 / 자신의 영향력을 사용하여 / 더 좋은 영화 기회를 지지했다 /
중국계 미국인을 위한 //　　　　**③의 단서** 자신의 영화 의상 판매 수입금을 기부했음
In 1938, / she sold her movie costumes / and donated the money
from the sale / to organizations / supporting Chinese refugees. //
1938년에 / 그녀는 자신의 영화 의상을 판매하고 / 그 판매 수입금을 기부했다 / 단체에 /
중국 난민을 지원하는 //　　　　**④의 단서** 반아시아적 태도에 대항하는 연설을 했음
During World War II, / she gave political speeches / against the
anti-Asian attitudes / in the U.S. //
2차 세계대전 동안 / 그녀는 정치적 연설을 했다 / 반아시아적 태도에 대항하는 / 미국에서의 //
　　　　　　　　　　　　　　　형용사적 용법(the first Asian American 수식)
In 2022, / she became the first Asian American / to appear on
U.S. currency / — a century after she landed her first leading
role. // **⑤의 단서** 미국 화폐에 등장한 최초의
　　　　아시아계 미국인이 되었음
2022년에 / 그녀는 최초의 아시아계 미국인이 되었다 / 미국 화폐에 등장한 / 그녀가 그녀의
첫 번째 주요한 역할을 얻은 지 한 세기 후 //

- drop out 탈퇴하다, 중퇴하다　　・ pursue a career 경력을 추구하다
- leading role 주연　　・ reviewer ⓝ 평론가　　・ praise ⓥ 칭찬하다
- extraordinary ⓐ 놀라운, 비범한　　・ ethnicity ⓝ 인종
- prevent A from B A를 B로부터 막다　　・ cast ⓥ 배역을 맡기다
- frustrated ⓐ 좌절한　　・ talent ⓝ 인재　　・ prestige ⓝ 명성
- notable ⓐ 주목할 만한, 저명한　　・ advocate ⓥ 지지하다
- donate ⓥ 기부하다　　・ refugee ⓝ 난민　　・ currency ⓝ 화폐

Anna May Wong은 Hollywood에서 최초의 중국계 미국인 영화배우로 여겨진다. 그녀는 전업 배우가 되기 위해 고등학교를 중퇴했고 17세에 'The Toll of the Sea'에서 처음으로 주요한 역할을 연기했다. 평론가들은 그녀의 놀랄만한 연기를 칭송했지만 그녀의 민족성은 미국 영화제작자들이 그녀에게 주요한 여성 배역을 맡기는 것을 막았다. 좌절한 채, Wong은 1928년에 유럽으로 떠났고, 그곳에서 그녀는 많은 저명한 영화에서 주요한 역할을 맡았다. 1930년대 미국 스튜디오들이 참신한 유럽 인재들을 원했을 때, Wong의 새로운 명성은 곧 Broadway의 주요한 역할로 이어졌다. 그녀는 미국으로 돌아가서 자신의 영향력을 사용하여 중국계 미국인의 더 좋은 영화 기회를 지지했다. 1938년에, 그녀는 자신의 영화 의상을 판매하고 그 판매 수입금을 중국 난민을 지원하는 단체에 기부했다. 2차 세계대전 동안, 그녀는 미국에서의 반아시아적 태도에 대항하는 정치적 연설을 했다. 2022년에, 그녀는 미국 화폐에 등장한 최초의 아시아계 미국인이 되었는데, 그것은 그녀가 처음으로 주요한 역할을 얻은 지 한 세기 후였다.

Anna May Wong에 관한 다음 글의 내용과 일치하지 <u>않는</u> 것은?

① 전업 배우가 되기 위해 고등학교를 중퇴했다.
　She dropped out of high school to pursue a full-time acting career
② 유럽에서는 영화에 출연하지 못했다.
　Wong left for Europe in 1928, where she had main roles in many notable films
③ 자신의 영화 의상 판매 수입금을 기부했다.
　she sold her movie costumes and donated the money from the sale
④ 반아시아적 태도에 대항하는 연설을 했다.
　she gave political speeches against the anti-Asian attitudes
⑤ 미국 화폐에 등장한 최초의 아시아계 미국인이 되었다.
　she became the first Asian American to appear on U.S. currency

>왜 정답? [정답률 90%]

② 유럽으로 떠나 많은 저명한 영화에서 주요한 역할을 맡았다. (Wong left for Europe in 1928, where she had main roles in many notable films)

>왜 오답?

① 전업 배우가 되기 위해 고등학교를 중퇴했다. (She dropped out of high school to pursue a full-time acting career)
③ 자신의 영화 의상 판매 수입금을 기부했다. (she sold her movie costumes and donated the money from the sale)
④ 반아시아적 태도에 대항하는 연설을 했다. (she gave political speeches against the anti-Asian attitudes)
⑤ 미국 화폐에 등장한 최초의 아시아계 미국인이 되었다. (she became the first Asian American to appear on U.S. currency)

I 18 정답 ② ＊물리학자 Charles H. Townes의 일생

Charles H. Townes, / one of the most influential American
physicists, / was born in South Carolina. //
Charles H. Townes는 / 가장 영향력 있는 미국의 물리학자 중 한 사람인 / South Carolina에서 태어났다 //

In his childhood, / he grew up on a farm, / studying the stars in
the sky. // **①의 단서** 어린 시절에 농장에서 성장함
어린 시절에 / 그는 농장에서 성장했다 / 하늘의 별들을 연구하면서 //

He earned his doctoral degree / from the California Institute of
Technology in 1939, / and then he took a job at Bell Labs in New
York City. // **②의 단서** 박사 학위를 받기 전이 아니라 후에 Bell Labs에서 일함
그는 박사 학위를 받았다 / 1939년에 California Institute of Technology에서 / 그 후 뉴욕시에 있는 Bell Labs에서 일자리를 얻었다 //

After World War II, / he became an associate professor of physics
/ at Columbia University. //
제2차 세계 대전 후에 / 그는 물리학 부교수가 되었다 / Columbia 대학교에서 //

In 1958, / Townes and his co-researcher / proposed the concept
of the laser. // **③의 단서** 1958년에 레이저의 개념을 제안함
1958년에 / Townes와 그의 동료 연구자는 / 레이저의 개념을 제안했다 //

Laser technology won quick acceptance / in industry and
research. //
레이저 기술은 빠르게 인정을 받았다 / 산업과 연구에서 //

He received the Nobel Prize in Physics / in 1964. //
그는 노벨 물리학상을 받았다 / 1964년에 **④의 단서** 1964년에 노벨 물리학상을 수상함
be involved in: ~에 관여하다

He was also involved in Project Apollo, / the moon landing
project. // **⑤의 단서** 달 착륙 프로젝트에 관여함
그는 또한 아폴로 계획에 관여했다 / 달 착륙 프로젝트인 //

His contribution is priceless / because the Internet and all digital
media would be unimaginable / without the laser. //
그의 공헌은 대단히 귀중하다 / 인터넷과 모든 디지털 미디어는 상상할 수 없을 것이기 때문에 / 레이저 없이는 //

- physicist ⓝ 물리학자 ・ institute ⓝ 기관
- associate professor 부교수 ・ acceptance ⓝ 인정
- contribution ⓝ 공헌, 기여 ・ priceless ⓐ 대단히 귀중한
- unimaginable ⓐ 상상할 수 없는

가장 영향력 있는 미국의 물리학자 중 한 사람인 Charles H. Townes는 South Carolina에서 태어났다. 어린 시절에 그는 하늘의 별들을 연구하면서 농장에서 성장했다. 1939년에 그는 California Institute of Technology에서 박사 학위를 받았고 그 후 뉴욕시에 있는 Bell Labs에서 일자리를 얻었다. 제2차 세계 대전 후에 그는 Columbia 대학교에서 물리학 부교수가 되었다. 1958년에 Townes와 그의 동료 연구자는 레이저의 개념을 제안했다. 레이저 기술은 산업과 연구에서 빠르게 인정을 받았다. 1964년에 그는 노벨 물리학상을 받았다. 그는 또한 달 착륙 프로젝트인 아폴로 계획에 관여했다. 인터넷과 모든 디지털 미디어는 레이저 없이는 상상할 수 없을 것이기 때문에 그의 공헌은 대단히 귀중하다.

Charles H. Townes에 관한 다음 글의 내용과 일치하지 <u>않는</u> 것은?

① 어린 시절에 농장에서 성장하였다.
　In his childhood, he grew up on a farm
② 박사 학위를 받기 전에 Bell Labs에서 일했다.
　He earned his doctoral degree ~ and then he took a job at Bell Labs in New York City.
③ 1958년에 레이저의 개념을 제안하였다.
　In 1958, Townes and his co-researcher proposed the concept of the laser.
④ 1964년에 노벨 물리학상을 수상하였다.
　He received the Nobel Prize in Physics in 1964.
⑤ 달 착륙 프로젝트에 관여하였다.
　He was also involved in Project Apollo, the moon landing project.

>왜 정답? [정답률 94%]

② California Institute of Technology에서 박사 학위를 받기 전이 아니라 후에 뉴욕시에 있는 Bell Labs에서 일했다. (He earned his doctoral degree from the California Institute of Technology in 1939, and then he took a job at Bell Labs in New York City.)

>왜 오답?

① 어린 시절에 농장에서 성장하였다. (In his childhood, he grew up on a farm)
③ 1958년에 레이저의 개념을 제안하였다. (In 1958, Townes and his co-researcher proposed the concept of the laser.)
④ 1964년에 노벨 물리학상을 수상하였다. (He received the Nobel Prize in Physics in 1964.)
⑤ 달 착륙 프로젝트에 관여하였다. (He was also involved in Project Apollo, the moon landing project.)

김아린 | 충남대 의예과 2024년 입학・대전한빛고 졸

내용 일치 문제에서 시간 절약 해야하는 거 알지? 4번 선지나 5번 선지가 답인 경우가 많아서 난 보통 밑에서부터 거꾸로 확인하는 편인데 이번엔 2번 선지가 답이라 살짝 당황했어. 이번 문제에서는 특히 '이전'이나 '이후' 등 선후 관계가 정답의 단서였어. 이 경우는 단어 하나로 선후 관계가 좌우되어서 글을 대충 읽으면 놓치기 쉬우니까 반드시 꼼꼼히 확인해!

I 19 정답 ⑤ *20세기의 사회학자 Niklas Luhmann

Niklas Luhmann, / a renowned sociologist of the twentieth century, / was born / in Lüneburg, Germany / in 1927. //
〈장소〉와 〈시간〉을 나타내는 전치사
Niklas Luhmann은 / 20세기의 유명한 사회학자인 / 태어났다 / 독일 Lüneburg에서 / 1927년에 //

After World War II, / he studied law / at the University of Freiburg / until 1949. // **①의 단서** 제2차 세계 대전 이후에 법을 공부했음
제2차 세계 대전 후 / 그는 법학을 공부했다 / University of Freiburg에서 / 1949년까지 //
선행사
Early in his career, / he worked for the State of Lower Saxony, / where he was in charge of educational reform. //
관계부사
그의 경력 초기에 / 그는 State of Lower Saxony에서 일했는데 / 그곳에서 그는 교육 개혁을 담당했다 // **②의 단서** State of Lower Saxony에서 교육 개혁을 담당했음

In 1960–1961, / Luhmann had the chance to study sociology / at Harvard University, /
선행사   형용사적 용법(the chance 수식)
1960년에서 1961년에 / Luhmann은 사회학을 공부할 기회가 있었는데 / Harvard University에서 / **③의 단서** Harvard University에 있을 때 Talcott Parsons의 영향을 받았음
관계부사
where he was influenced by Talcott Parsons, / one of the most famous social system theorists. //
그곳에서 그는 Talcott Parsons의 영향을 받았다 / 가장 유명한 사회 체계 이론가 중 한 명이었던 //

Later, Luhmann developed / his own social system theory. //
나중에 Luhmann은 개발했다 / 자기 자신의 사회 체계 이론을 //

In 1968, / he became a professor of sociology / at the University of Bielefeld. //
1968년에 / 그는 사회학 교수가 되었다 / University of Bielefeld에서 //

He researched a variety of subjects, / including mass media and law. // **④의 단서** 다양한 주제에 관해 연구했음
그는 다양한 주제를 연구했다 / 대중 매체와 법을 포함한 //
부사적 용법(difficult 수식)
Although his books are known / to be difficult to translate, / they have in fact been widely translated / into other languages. // **⑤의 단서** 그의 책은 번역하기가 어렵다고 알려짐
비록 그의 책들이 알려져 있지만 / 번역하기에 어렵다고 / 그것들은 사실 널리 번역되었다 / 다른 언어들로 //

- renowned ⓐ 유명한   • sociologist ⓝ 사회학자
- theorist ⓝ 이론가   • translate ⓥ 번역[통역]하다

　20세기의 유명한 사회학자 Niklas Luhmann은 1927년 독일 Lüneburg에서 태어났다. 제2차 세계 대전 후, 그는 University of Freiburg에서 1949년까지 법학을 공부했다. 경력 초기에 그는 State of Lower Saxony에서 일했는데, 그곳에서 그는 교육 개혁을 담당했다.
　1960년에서 1961년에 Luhmann은 Harvard University에서 사회학을 공부할 기회가 있었는데, 그곳에서 그는 가장 유명한 사회 체계 이론가 중 한 명이었던 Talcott Parsons의 영향을 받았다. 나중에 Luhmann은 자기 자신의 사회 체계 이론을 개발했다. 1968년에 그는 University of Bielefeld에서 사회학 교수가 되었다. 그는 대중 매체와 법을 포함한 다양한 주제를 연구했다. 비록 그의 책들이 번역하기 어렵다고 알려져 있지만, 그것들은 사실 다른 언어들로 널리 번역되었다.

Niklas Luhmann에 관한 다음 글의 내용과 일치하지 않는 것은?

① 제2차 세계 대전 이후에 법을 공부했다.
　After World War II, he studied law
② State of Lower Saxony에서 교육 개혁을 담당했다.
　he worked for the State of Lower Saxony, where he was in charge of educational reform
③ Harvard University에 있을 때 Talcott Parsons의 영향을 받았다.
　at Harvard University, where he was influenced by Talcott Parsons
④ 다양한 주제에 관해 연구했다.
　He researched a variety of subjects
⑤그의 책은 번역하기가 쉽다고 알려져 있다.
　his books are known to be difficult to translate

>왜 정답? [정답률 97%]

그의 책은 번역하기 어렵다고 알려져 있다고(his books are known to be difficult to translate) 했으므로 ⑤은 글과 일치하지 않는다.

>왜 오답?

① 제2차 세계 대전 이후에 법을 공부했다. (After World War II, he studied law)
② State of Lower Saxony에서 교육 개혁을 담당했다. (he worked for the State of Lower Saxony, where he was in charge of educational reform)
③ Harvard University에 있을 때 Talcott Parsons의 영향을 받았다. (at Harvard University, where he was influenced by Talcott Parsons)
④ 다양한 주제에 관해 연구했다. (He researched a variety of subjects)

장성욱 | 동아대 의예과 2023년 입학·부산 대연고 졸
내용의 일치/불일치 문제도 듣기 문제와 비슷하게 선택지의 순서와 글에 제시되는 내용의 순서가 같은 경우가 대부분이야. 정답이 글의 뒷부분에 있는 경우가 많지만, 나는 정확하게 풀기 위해 ①부터 차례대로 대조하는 방법으로 문제를 풀어. 나머지 선택지는 모두 글과 일치하는데, ⑤은 글에서는 difficult라고 했는데 선택지에서는 easy라고 했어! 쉬운 유형이지만 방심하면 실수할 수 있으니까 차분하게 푸는 게 중요해.

I

I 20 정답 ⑤ *경제학자 Frank Hyneman Knight

①의 단서 20세기의 가장 영향력 있는 경제학자들 중 한 명
Frank Hyneman Knight was one / of the most influential economists / of the twentieth century. //
Frank Hyneman Knight는 한 명이었다 / 가장 영향력 있는 경제학자들 중 / 20세기의 //

After obtaining his Ph.D. in 1916 / at Cornell University, / Knight taught / at Cornell, the University of Iowa, and the University of Chicago. //
= After he obtained
1916년에 박사 학위를 받은 뒤에 / Cornell 대학교에서 / Knight는 가르쳤다 / Cornell, Iowa 대학교, Chicago 대학교에서 // **②의 단서** 경력의 대부분을 University of Chicago에서 보냄
Knight spent most of his career / at the University of Chicago. //
Knight는 경력의 대부분을 보냈다 / Chicago 대학교에서 //

Some of his students at Chicago / later received the Nobel Prize. // **③의 단서** 그의 학생들 중 몇 명이 나중에 노벨상을 받음
Chicago에서 그의 학생들 중 몇 명은 / 나중에 노벨상을 받았다 //

Knight is known as the author / of the book *Risk, Uncertainty and Profit*, / a study of the role of the entrepreneur / in economic life. // **④의 단서** Risk, Uncertainty and Profit의 저자로 알려져 있음
동격
Knight는 저자로 알려져 있다 / 〈Risk, Uncertainty and Profit〉이라는 책의 / 기업가의 역할에 대한 연구인 / 경제생활에서 //
앞에 주격 관계대명사와 be동사가 생략됨
He also wrote a brief introduction to economics / entitled *The Economic Organization*, / which became a classic of microeconomic theory. //
그는 또한 짧은 경제학 개론서를 썼는데 / 〈The Economic Organization〉이라는 제목의 / 그것은 미시 경제학 이론의 고전이 되었다 //

But Knight was much more than an economist; / he was also a social philosopher. //
비교급 강조 부사
하지만 Knight는 경제학자 훨씬 이상이었다 / 그는 또한 사회 철학자이기도 했다 //

Later in his career, / Knight developed his theories / of freedom, democracy, and ethics. //
그의 경력의 후반기에 / Knight는 자신의 이론을 발전시켰다 / 자유, 민주주의, 그리고 윤리에 대한 //
= After he retired
After retiring in 1952, / Knight remained active / in teaching and writing. // **⑥의 단서** 은퇴 후에도 가르치는 일에 적극적이었음
1952년에 은퇴한 후에도 / Knight는 여전히 적극적이었다 / 가르치기와 글쓰기에 //

- **influential** ⓐ 영향력 있는, 영향력이 큰
- **economist** ⓝ 경제학자, 경제 전문가   • **economic** ⓐ 경제의, 경제성이 있는
- **brief** ⓐ 짧은, 간단한   • **introduction** ⓝ 입문서, 도입, 소개
- **economics** ⓝ 경제학   • **entitle** ⓥ 제목을 붙이다
- **classic** ⓝ 고전, 명작   • **microeconomic** ⓐ 미시(微視) 경제학의
- **philosopher** ⓝ 철학자   • **democracy** ⓝ 민주주의
- **ethics** ⓝ 윤리학, 도덕   • **retire** ⓥ 은퇴[퇴직]하다
- **active** ⓐ 활동적인, 적극적인

Frank Hyneman Knight는 20세기의 가장 영향력 있는 경제학자들 중 한 명이었다. 1916년에 Cornell 대학교에서 박사 학위를 받은 뒤에, Knight는 Cornell, Iowa 대학교, Chicago 대학교에서 가르쳤다. Knight는 경력의 대부분을 Chicago 대학교에서 보냈다. Chicago에서 그의 학생들 중 몇 명은 나중에 노벨상을 받았다. Knight는 경제생활에서 기업가의 역할에 대한 연구인 〈Risk, Uncertainty and Profit〉이라는 책의 저자로 알려져 있다. 그는 또한 〈The Economic Organization〉이라는 제목의 짧은 경제학 개론서를 썼는데, 그것은 미시 경제학 이론의 고전이 되었다. 하지만 Knight는 경제학자를 훨씬 넘어 사회 철학자이기도 했다. 경력의 후반기에 Knight는 자유, 민주주의, 그리고 윤리에 대한 자신의 이론을 발전시켰다. 1952년에 은퇴한 후에도 Knight는 가르치기와 글쓰기에 여전히 적극적이었다.

Frank Hyneman Knight에 관한 다음 글의 내용과 일치하지 않는 것은?

① 20세기의 가장 영향력 있는 경제학자들 중 한 명이었다.
  one of the most influential economists of the twentieth century
② 경력의 대부분을 University of Chicago에서 보냈다.
  Knight spent most of his career at the University of Chicago.
③ 그의 학생들 중 몇 명은 나중에 노벨상을 받았다.
  Some of his students at Chicago later received the Nobel Prize.
④ Risk, Uncertainty and Profit의 저자로 알려져 있다.
  Knight is known as the author of the book Risk, Uncertainty and Profit
⑤ 은퇴 후에는 가르치는 일은 하지 않고 글 쓰는 일에 전념했다.
  After retiring in 1952, Knight remained active in teaching and writing.

〉왜 정답? [정답률 90%]

1952년에 은퇴한 이후에도 가르치는 일과 글 쓰는 일에 적극적이었다고(After retiring in 1952, Knight remained active in teaching and writing.) 했으므로 ⑤은 글과 일치하지 않는다.

〉왜 오답?

① 20세기의 가장 영향력 있는 경제학자들 중 한 명이었다. (one of the most influential economists of the twentieth century)
② Knight는 경력의 대부분을 University of Chicago에서 보냈다. (Knight spent most of his career at the University of Chicago.)
③ 그의 학생들 중 몇 명이 나중에 노벨상을 받았다. (Some of his students at Chicago later received the Nobel Prize.)
④ Knight는 Risk, Uncertainty and Profit의 저자로 알려져 있다. (Knight is known as the author of the book Risk, Uncertainty and Profit)

Ⅰ 21 정답 ④ * 인테리어 전문가 Josef Frank

주어   ①의 단서 Vienna University of Technology에서 건축학을 공부했음
Josef Frank, / born in Austria of Jewish heritage, / studied architecture / at the Vienna University of Technology. //
  동사
Josef Frank는 / 유태인 혈통으로 오스트리아에서 태어난 / 건축학을 공부했다 / Vienna University of Technology에서 //

He then taught / at the Vienna School of Arts and Crafts / from 1919 to 1925. //
  from A to B : (시간적·공간적으로) A에서 B까지
그는 그러고 나서 가르쳤다 / Vienna School of Arts and Crafts에서 / 1919년부터 1925년까지 //

②의 단서 건축가 동료들과 함께 인테리어 디자인 회사를 설립했음
He founded an interior design firm / together with some architect colleagues / in 1925. //
그는 인테리어 디자인 회사를 설립했다 / 몇몇 건축가 동료들과 함께 / 1925년에 //

③의 단서 비엔나 모더니즘의 가장 중요한 인물 중 한 명이었음
He was one / of early Vienna modernism's most important figures, / but already in the beginning of the 1920s / he started to question / modernism's growing pragmatism. //
그는 한 명이었다 / 초기 비엔나 모더니즘의 가장 중요한 인물 중 / 하지만 이미 1920년대 초에 / 그는 의문을 제기하기 시작했다 / 모더니즘의 고조되는 실용주의에 //

주부정어(거의 ~ 않는)
He had little appreciation / for the French architect Le Corbusier's belief / that a house should be "a machine for living in." //
  동격절 접속사
그는 거의 공감하지 않았다 / 프랑스 건축가 Le Corbusier의 신념에 / 집이 '생활을 위한 기계'여야 한다는 //

④의 단서 당시의 표준화된 인테리어 디자인 경향에 반대함
He was against the standardized interior design trend / of the time, / fearing / that it would make people all too uniform. //
그는 표준화된 인테리어 디자인 경향에 반대했고 / 당시의 / 두려워했다 / 그것이 사람들을 너무 획일적으로 만들 것을 //

⑤의 단서 나치의 차별을 피해 스웨덴으로 가서 시민권을 얻었음
He moved to Sweden / with his Swedish wife / in 1933 / to escape growing Nazi discrimination / and gained citizenship in 1939. //
그는 스웨덴으로 가서 / 스웨덴인 아내와 함께 / 1933년에 / 심해지는 나치의 차별을 피해 / 1939년에 시민권을 얻었다 //

He was the most prestigious designer / at his Stockholm design company. //
그는 가장 명성 있는 디자이너였다 / 자신의 스톡홀름의 디자인 회사에서 //

In addition to his architectural work / he created numerous designs / for furniture, fabric, wallpaper and carpet. //
그의 건축 작업 외에도 / 그는 수많은 디자인을 만들었다 / 가구, 직물, 벽지 그리고 카펫의 //

- **heritage** ⓝ 유산, 혈통   • **architecture** ⓝ 건축학
- **found** ⓥ 설립하다, 세우다   • **firm** ⓝ 회사   • **figure** ⓝ 인물
- **pragmatism** ⓝ 실용주의   • **appreciation** ⓝ 감탄, 공감
- **standardize** ⓥ 표준화하다   • **uniform** ⓐ 획일적인
- **discrimination** ⓝ 차별   • **citizenship** ⓝ 시민권
- **prestigious** ⓐ 명망 있는, 일류의   • **fabric** ⓝ 직물

유태인 혈통으로 오스트리아에서 태어난 Josef Frank는 Vienna University of Technology에서 건축학을 공부했다. 그는 그러고 나서 1919년부터 1925년까지 Vienna School of Arts and Crafts에서 가르쳤다. 1925년에 그는 몇몇 건축가 동료들과 함께 인테리어 디자인 회사를 설립했다. 그는 초기 비엔나 모더니즘의 가장 중요한 인물 중 한 명이었지만 이미 1920년대 초에 모더니즘의 고조되는 실용주의에 의문을 제기하기 시작했다. 그는 집이 '생활을 위한 기계'여야 한다는 프랑스 건축가 Le Corbusier의 신념에 거의 공감하지 않았다. 그는 당시의 표준화된 인테리어 디자인 경향에 반대했고 그것이 사람들을 너무 획일적으로 만들 것을 두려워했다. 그는 심해지는 나치의 차별을 피해 1933년에 스웨덴인 아내와 함께 스웨덴으로 가서 1939년에 시민권을 얻었다. 그는 자신의 스톡홀름의 디자인 회사에서 가장 명성 있는 디자이너였다. 그의 건축 작업 외에도 그는 가구, 직물, 벽지 그리고 카펫의 수많은 디자인을 만들었다.

Josef Frank에 관한 다음 글의 내용과 일치하지 않는 것은?

① Vienna University of Technology에서 건축학을 공부했다.
  studied architecture at the Vienna University of Technology
② 건축가 동료들과 함께 인테리어 디자인 회사를 설립했다.
  He founded an interior design firm together with some architect colleagues
③ 초기 비엔나 모더니즘의 가장 중요한 인물 중 한 명이었다.
  He was one of early Vienna modernism's most important figures
④ 당시의 표준화된 인테리어 디자인 경향을 옹호했다.
  He was against the standardized interior design trend of the time
⑤ 나치의 차별을 피해 스웨덴으로 가서 시민권을 얻었다.
  He moved to Sweden ~ and gained citizenship in 1939.

〉왜 정답? [정답률 93%]

④ 당신의 표준화된 인테리어 경향에 반대했다. (He was against the standardized interior design trend of the time)

〉왜 오답?

① Vienna University of Technology에서 건축학을 공부했다. (studied architecture at the Vienna University of Technology)
② 건축가 동료들과 함께 인테리어 디자인 회사를 설립했다. (He founded an interior design firm together with some architect colleagues)
③ 초기 비엔나 모더니즘의 가장 중요한 인물 중 한 명이었다. (He was one of early Vienna modernism's most important figures)
⑤ 나치의 차별을 피해 스웨덴으로 가서 시민권을 얻었다. (He moved to Sweden ~ to escape growing Nazi discrimination and gained citizenship in 1939.)

I 22 정답 ③ * 심리학자 William McDougall

Born in Lancashire, England, in 1871, / William McDougall left his mark / on experimental and physiological psychology. //
1871년에 영국 Lancashire에서 태어나 / William McDougall은 자신의 발자취를 남겼다 / 실험 심리학과 생리 심리학에 //
부사구문의 생략되지 않은 접속사　**①의 단서** Cambridge University에서 자연과학 학위를 받음
After receiving a degree in natural sciences / in Cambridge University, / he became interested / in human behavior. //
자연과학 학위를 받은 후에 / Cambridge University에서 / 그는 관심을 갖게 되었다 / 인간 행동에 //
주어　　　동사　　　목적어　　목적격 보어(to부정사의 수동형)
He believed / human behavior to be based on three abilities / — intellect, emotion, and will. // **②의 단서** 인간 행동이 세 가지 능력에 근거한다고 믿었음
그는 믿었다 / 인간 행동이 세 가지 능력에 근거한다고 / 지력, 감정, 그리고 의지 //
Being a hardworking scholar, / he held academic positions / in several universities in England. //
= As he was a hardworking scholar
성실한 학자여서 / 그는 교수직을 얻었다 / 영국에 있는 여러 대학에서 //
He also wrote many books on psychology / including the well-known *Introduction to Social Psychology*. //
그는 또한 심리학에 관한 많은 책을 썼다 / 유명한 〈Introduction to Social Psychology〉를 포함하여 //
In 1920, / he published *The Group Mind* / opposing mechanistic interpretations / of human behavior. //
1920년에 / 그는 〈The Group Mind〉를 출간했다 / 기계론적인 해석에 반대하면서 / 인간 행동에 관한 //
주절의 주어와 똑같은 주어와 be동사가 생략된 부사절 *
However, *The Group Mind* was poorly received / when published. // **③의 단서** 〈The Group Mind〉는 출판되었을 때 제대로 인정받지 못했음
하지만 〈The Group Mind〉는 제대로 인정받지 못했다 / 출판되었을 때 //
부사적 용법(결과)
Somewhat disappointed, / he moved to the United States / in the same year / to be a professor at Harvard University. //
다소 실망한 나머지 / 그는 미국으로 옮겨 가 / 같은 해에 / Harvard University에서 교수가 되었다 //
선행사　　　계속적 용법의 관계부사
Seven years later, / he moved to Duke University, / where he developed a psychology department / and continued various research. // **④의 단서** Duke University로 옮겨서 다양한 연구를 계속함
7년 후에 / 그는 Duke University로 옮겼고 / 거기에서 심리학과를 만들고 / 다양한 연구를 계속했다 //
⑤의 단서 오늘날 심리학자들이 그의 지적 업적을 기림
Today many people read his books, / and psychologists celebrate his intellectual achievements. //
오늘날 많은 사람이 그의 책을 읽고 / 심리학자들은 그의 지적 업적을 기린다 //

- leave one's mark on ~에 발자취를 남기다
- physiological ⓐ 생리적인 ・ degree ⓝ 학위
- intellect ⓝ 지적 능력, 지력 ・ will ⓝ 의지
- hardworking ⓐ 근면한, 부지런히 일하는 ・ scholar ⓝ 학자
- academic position 교수직 ・ oppose ⓥ 반대하다
- mechanistic ⓐ 기계론적인 ・ interpretation ⓝ 해석
- poorly ⓐ𝒹 좋지 못하게, 저조하게 ・ somewhat ⓐ𝒹 다소, 약간
- department ⓝ 학과, 부서 ・ celebrate ⓥ 찬양하다, 기리다
- intellectual ⓐ 지능의, 지적인 ・ achievement ⓝ 업적

1871년에 영국 Lancashire에서 태어난 William McDougall은 실험 심리학과 생리 심리학에 자신의 발자취를 남겼다. Cambridge University에서 자연과학 학위를 받은 후에 그는 인간 행동에 관심을 갖게 되었다. 그는 인간 행동이 지력, 감정, 그리고 의지라는 세 가지 능력에 근거한다고 믿었다. 성실한 학자여서 그는 영국에 있는 여러 대학에서 교수직을 얻었다. 그는 또한 유명한 〈Introduction to Social Psychology〉를 포함하여 심리학에 관한 많은 책을 썼다. 1920년에 그는 인간 행동에 관한 기계론적인 해석에 반대하면서 〈The Group Mind〉를 출간했다. 하지만 〈The Group Mind〉는 출판되었을 때 제대로 인정받지 못했다. 다소 실망한 나머지 그는 같은 해에 미국으로 옮겨 가 Harvard University에서 교수가 되었다. 7년 후에 그는 Duke University로 옮겼고, 거기에서 심리학과를 만들고 다양한 연구를 계속했다. 오늘날 많은 사람이 그의 책을 읽고, 심리학자들은 그의 지적 업적을 기린다.

William McDougall에 관한 다음 글의 내용과 일치하지 <u>않는</u> 것은?

① Cambridge University에서 학위를 받았다.
After receiving a degree in natural sciences in Cambridge University
② 인간 행동이 세 가지 능력에 근거한다고 믿었다.
He believed human behavior to be based on three abilities
③ *The Group Mind*는 출판되었을 때 매우 인정받았다.
However, *The Group Mind* was poorly received when published.
④ Duke University에서 다양한 연구를 계속하였다.
Seven years later, he moved to Duke University, ~ continued various research.
⑤ 오늘날 심리학자들은 그의 지적 업적을 기린다.
Today ~ psychologists celebrate his intellectual achievements.

> 왜 정답 ? [정답률 89%]

출판되었을 때는 제대로 인정받지 못했다고(However, *The Group Mind* was poorly received when published.) 했으므로 ③은 글의 내용과 일치하지 않는다.

> 왜 오답 ?

① Cambridge University에서 자연과학 학위를 받았다. (After receiving a degree in natural sciences in Cambridge University)
② 인간 행동이 세 가지 능력에 근거한다고 믿었다. (He believed human behavior to be based on three abilities)
④ Duke University로 옮긴 후 다양한 연구를 계속하였다. (Seven years later, he moved to Duke University, ~ continued various research.)
⑤ 오늘날 심리학자들은 그의 지적 업적을 기린다. (Today ~ psychologists celebrate his intellectual achievements.)

---- 어법 특강

＊ 부사절에서 「주어＋be동사」의 생략

– 시간, 조건, 양보를 나타내는 부사절에서 부사절의 주어가 주절의 주어와 같고 동사가 be동사일 때, 부사절의 주어와 be동사는 생략 가능하다.
・ He was crossing the street while looking at his smartphone.
　　　　　　　　　　　　　　앞에 주어와 be동사가 생략됨
　(그 소년은 스마트폰을 쳐다보면서 길을 건너고 있었다.)
・ If disturbed, the bird may abandon the nest.
　앞에 주어와 be동사가 생략됨
　(방해받는다면 새는 둥지를 버릴지도 모른다.)
・ Though small, the rooms were pleasant and airy.
　　　앞에 주어와 be동사가 생략됨
　(방들은 비록 작지만 쾌적하고 바람이 잘 통했다.)

I 어휘 Review 정답 　　　　　　　문제편 p. 156

01 폭넓게	11 at one's height	20 outbreak
02 원정	12 be rich with	21 actively
03 조각(품)	13 noted for	22 will
04 협력, 협조	14 drop out	23 resigned
05 설립하다	15 leave one's mark on	24 uniform
06 prestige	16 fossils	25 wounded
07 geologist	17 decade	26 appointed
08 devote	18 lectures	27 leading
09 promotion	19 standardized	28 notable
10 debt		29 struggled

J 01 정답 ④ *유성 보기 행사

Shooting Star Viewing Event /
유성 보기 행사 /

Would you like to watch the rare shooting star, / coming on Sunday, July 24? //
희귀한 유성을 보고 싶으신가요 / 7월 24일 일요일에 오는 //

The Downtown Central Science Museum is the perfect spot / to catch the vivid view! //
형용사적 용법 (spot 수식)
Downtown Central Science Museum은 최적의 장소입니다 / 그 생생한 광경을 포착하는 //

Registration /
등록 / **①의 단서** 등록은 온라인으로만 가능함

• Online only — www.dcsm.org /
온라인으로만 가능 — www.dcsm.org /

• From July l to July 14 /
7월 1일부터 7월 14일까지 /

②의 단서 참가자는 50명으로 제한됨
• The number of participants / will be limited to 50. //
참가자 수는 / 50명으로 제한될 것입니다 //

Schedule on July 24 /
7월 24일 일정 /

• 8:00 p.m.: / Participants will gather at the hall / and then move to the rooftop. // **③의 단서** 참가자들이 홀에서 모인 다음 옥상으로 이동하는 것은 오후 8시임
오후 8시: / 참가자들은 홀에서 모이고 / 그다음 옥상으로 이동할 것입니다 //

• 8:30 p.m.: / Guides will explain / how to observe the shooting star. // will explain의 목적어로 쓰인 「의문사+to부정사」
오후 8시 30분: / 안내원들이 설명할 것입니다 / 유성을 관측하는 방법을 //

• 9:00 p.m. – 11:00 p.m.: / We will share / the experience of the shooting star. //
오후 9시~오후 11시: / 우리는 공유할 것입니다 / 유성을 본 경험을 //

Notes /
공지 사항 / **④의 단서** 기상 상황으로 행사가 취소되면 문자 메시지를 통해 공지될 것임

• If the event is cancelled / due to the weather conditions, / notice will be given / via text message. //
행사가 취소되면 / 기상 상황으로 인해 / 공지가 주어질 것입니다 / 문자 메시지를 통해 //

• Outside food and drinks / are not allowed. //
외부 음식과 음료는 / 허용되지 않습니다 // **⑤의 단서** 외부 음식과 음료는 허용되지 않음

• rare ⓐ 드문, 희귀한 • spot ⓝ (특정한) 곳, 장소
• vivid ⓐ 선명한, 생생한 • limit ⓥ 제한[한정]하다
• rooftop ⓝ (건물의) 옥상 • observe ⓥ 관측하다, 관찰하다
• notice ⓝ 안내문, 공지 사항 • via ⓟⓡⓔⓟ ~을 통하여

유성 보기 행사

7월 24일 일요일에 오는, 희귀한 유성을 보고 싶으신가요? Downtown Central Science Museum은 그 생생한 광경을 포착하는 최적의 장소입니다!
등록
• 온라인으로만 가능 — www.dcsm.org
• 7월 1일부터 7월 14일까지
• 참가자 수는 50명으로 제한될 것입니다.
7월 24일 일정
• 오후 8시: 참가자들은 홀에서 모인 다음에 옥상으로 이동할 것입니다.
• 오후 8시 30분: 안내원들이 유성을 관측하는 방법을 설명할 것입니다.
• 오후 9시~오후 11시: 우리는 유성을 본 경험을 공유할 것입니다.
공지 사항
• 행사가 기상 상황으로 인해 취소될 경우, 문자 메시지를 통해 공지될 것입니다.
• 외부 음식과 음료는 허용되지 않습니다.

Shooting Star Viewing Event에 관한 다음 안내문의 내용과 일치하는 것은?
① 현장 등록이 가능하다. Online only
② 참가 인원에 제한이 없다. The number of participants will be limited to 50.
③ 참가자들은 오후 9시에 홀에서 모여 옥상으로 이동할 것이다.
8:00 p.m.: Participants will gather at the hall and then move to the rooftop.
④ 기상 상황으로 인한 행사 취소 시 문자 메시지로 공지될 것이다.
If the event is cancelled due to the weather conditions, notice will be given via text message.
⑤ 외부 음식과 음료는 허용된다. Outside food and drinks are not allowed.

>왜 정답? [정답률 96%]

만약 기상 상황으로 인해 행사가 취소되면 문자 메시지를 통해 공지될 것이라고(If the event is cancelled due to the weather conditions, notice will be given via text message.) 했으므로 ④이 안내문과 일치한다.

>왜 오답?

① 등록은 온라인으로만 가능하다. (Online only)
② 참가 인원은 50명으로 제한될 것이다. (The number of participants will be limited to 50.)
③ 오후 8시에 참가자들이 홀에서 모여 옥상으로 이동할 것이다. (8:00 p.m.: Participants will gather at the hall and then move to the rooftop.)
⑤ 외부 음식과 음료는 허용되지 않는다. (Outside food and drinks are not allowed.)

J 02 정답 ④ *Mary 고등학교 외국어 프로그램

Mary High School Foreign Language Program /
Mary 고등학교 외국어 프로그램 /

Would you like to learn / about another culture? //
여러분은 배우고 싶으신가요 / 다른 문화에 관해 //

동명사구 주어 단수 동사 형용사적 용법(way 수식)
Learning a new language / is the best way / to do it. //
새로운 언어를 배우는 것이 / 가장 좋은 방법입니다 / 그것을 하는 //

Please come and enjoy / our new foreign language classes. //
방문하셔서 즐기세요 / 저희 새로운 외국어 수업을 // **①의 단서** 하나만 선택할 수 있음

Languages: Arabic, French, Spanish / (A student can choose only one.) //
언어: 아랍어, 프랑스어, 스페인어 / (한 학생은 하나만 선택할 수 있습니다) //

Dates and Times: September 13, 2021 — October 29, 2021 /
날짜 및 시간: 2021년 9월 13일 ~ 2021년 10월 29일 / **②의 단서** 월요일부터 금요일까지임

Monday to Friday, 4:00 p.m. — 6:00 p.m. /
월요일부터 금요일까지, 오후 4시 ~ 오후 6시 /

Registration: / Available / from September 1 to September 5 / on our website (www.maryhighs.edu) /
등록: / 가능함 / 9월 1일부터 9월 5일까지 / 저희 웹사이트(www.maryhighs.edu)에서 /

Tuition Fee: $50 / (Full payment is required / when registering.) // **③의 단서** 등록 시 전액 납부해야 함
수업료: 50달러 / (전액 납부가 요구됩니다 / 등록 시) /

부사절 접속사(조건)
Refund Policy: / If you cancel on or before September 5, / your payment will be refunded. // **④의 단서** 9월 5일 이전에 취소하면 전액 환불됨
환불 방침: / 여러분이 9월 5일이나 그 이전에 취소하시면 / 여러분의 대금이 환불될 것입니다 //

For more information about the classes, / feel free to contact us at (215) 8393-6047 / or email us at info@maryhighs.edu. //
수업에 대한 더 많은 정보를 원하시면 / 자유롭게 저희에게 (215) 8393-6047로 연락하시거나 / info@maryhighs.edu로 저희에게 이메일을 보내세요 // **⑤의 단서** 전화로도 문의할 수 있음

• tuition ⓝ 수업, 교습, 수업료 • fee ⓝ 요금, 수수료
• full ⓐ 완전한, 모든 • payment ⓝ 지불, 납입 • refund ⓥ 환불하다
• policy ⓝ 방침 • contact ⓥ 연락하다

Mary 고등학교 외국어 프로그램

여러분은 다른 문화에 관해 배우고 싶으신가요? 새로운 언어를 배우는 것이 그것을 하는 가장 좋은 방법입니다. 방문하셔서 저희 새로운 외국어 수업을 즐기세요.

언어: 아랍어, 프랑스어, 스페인어 (한 학생은 하나만 선택할 수 있습니다.)
날짜 및 시간: 2021년 9월 13일 ~ 2021년 10월 29일
월요일부터 금요일까지, 오후 4시 ~ 오후 6시
등록: 9월 1일부터 9월 5일까지 저희 웹사이트(www.maryhighs.edu)에서 가능함
수업료: 50달러 (등록 시에 전액 납부가 요구됩니다.)
환불 방침: 9월 5일이나 그 이전에 취소하시면 대금이 환불될 것입니다.
수업에 대한 더 많은 정보를 원하시면, 자유롭게 저희에게 (215) 8393-6047로 연락하시거나 info@maryhighs.edu로 이메일을 보내세요.

Mary High School Foreign Language Program에 관한 다음 안내문의 내용과 일치하는 것은?

① 학생은 두 개의 언어를 선택할 수 있다. A student can choose only one.

② 수업은 주말에 진행된다. Monday to Friday

③ 수업료는 등록 시 전액 납부하지 않아도 된다.
　　　　　　　　　　　Full payment is required when registering.

④ 9월 5일까지 취소하면 환불받을 수 있다.
　If you cancel on or before September 5, your payment will be refunded.

⑤ 수업 관련 문의는 이메일을 통해서만 할 수 있다.
　For more information about the classes, feel free to contact us at (215) 8393-6047

왜 정답? [정답률 96%]

9월 5일이나 그 이전에 취소하면 환불될 것이라고(If you cancel on or before September 5, your payment will be refunded.) 했으므로 ④이 안내문과 일치한다.

왜 오답?

① 한 학생이 한 언어만 선택할 수 있다. (A student can choose only one.)
② 월요일부터 금요일까지(Monday to Friday) 진행된다.
③ 등록 시 전액 납부가 요구된다. (Full payment is required when registering.)
⑤ 수업과 관련하여 전화로도 문의할 수 있다. (For more information about the classes, feel free to contact us at (215) 8393-6047)

J 03 정답 ③ * Adenville 시티 패스 카드 안내

Adenville City Pass Card / Adenville 시티 패스 카드 /

The Adenville City Pass Card / is a public transportation card /
　　　　현재분사(tourists 수식)　　　　　**①의 단서** 관광객을 위한 대중교통 카드임
for tourists visiting Adenville. //
Adenville 시티 패스 카드는 / 대중교통 카드입니다 / Adenville을 방문하는 관광객을 위한 //

Service Range / 서비스 범위 /

• Adenville-based subway lines / Adenville 기반의 지하철 노선 /
• Adenville-licensed buses / Adenville 면허의 버스 /
　　　　　　　　　　　　수동태
※ This card cannot be used / for city tour buses. //
이 카드는 사용될 수 없습니다 / 시티 투어 버스에 // **②의 단서** 시티 투어 버스에는 사용할 수 없음

Card Type / 카드 유형 /

	Price 가격	Additional Benefit 추가 혜택
1-Day 1일권	$10 10달러	10% off admission for major tourist attractions **③의 단서** 5일 패스 카드뿐만 아니라 1일, 3일 패스 카드에도 주요 관광지 입장료 할인 혜택이 제공됨 주요 관광지 입장료 10퍼센트 할인
3-Day 3일권	$25 25달러	
5-Day 5일권	$40 40달러	

과거분사(cards 수식)
※ Unused cards are refundable / within 30 days of the purchase
date. // **④의 단서** 미사용 카드는 구입일로부터 30일 이내에 환불이 가능함
미사용 카드는 환불할 수 있습니다 / 구입일 30일 이내에 //

Purchase Information / 구매 정보 /
　　　　　　　　　　　수동태
• Physical cards can be purchased / at subway stations. //
실물 카드는 구입할 수 있습니다 / 지하철역에서 //
　　　　　　　　　　수동태
• Mobile cards can be purchased / on the A-Transit app. //
모바일 카드는 구입할 수 있습니다 / A-Transit 앱에서 // **⑤의 단서** 모바일 카드는 A-Transit 앱에서 구입할 수 있음

• additional ⓐ 추가적인　　• admission ⓝ 입장료
• refundable ⓐ 환불할 수 있는　• physical ⓐ 물리적인, 실물의

Adenville 시티 패스 카드

Adenville 시티 패스 카드는 Adenville을 방문하는 관광객을 위한 대중교통 카드입니다.

서비스 범위
• Adenville 기반의 지하철 노선
• Adenville 면허의 버스
※ 이 카드는 시티 투어 버스에 사용될 수 없습니다.

카드 유형

	가격	추가 혜택
1일권	10달러	주요 관광지 입장료 10퍼센트 할인
3일권	25달러	
5일권	40달러	

※ 미사용 카드는 구입일 30일 이내에 환불할 수 있습니다.

구매 정보
• 실물 카드는 지하철역에서 구입할 수 있습니다.
• 모바일 카드는 A-Transit 앱에서 구입할 수 있습니다.

Adenville City Pass Card에 관한 다음 안내문의 내용과 일치하지 않는 것은?

① 관광객을 위한 대중교통 카드이다.
　The Adenville City Pass Card is a public transportation card for tourists
② 시티 투어 버스에는 사용할 수 없다.
　※ This card cannot be used for city tour buses.
③ 5일 패스 카드에만 주요 관광지 입장료 할인 혜택이 제공된다.
　10% off admission for major tourist attractions
④ 미사용 카드는 구입일로부터 30일 이내에 환불이 가능하다.
　※ Unused cards are refundable within 30 days of the purchase date.
⑤ 모바일 카드는 A-Transit 앱에서 구입할 수 있다.
　Mobile cards can be purchased on the A-Transit app.

왜 정답? [정답률 98%]

③ 주요 관광지 입장료 할인 혜택은 5일 패스 카드뿐만 아니라 1일, 3일 패스 카드에도 제공된다고 했으므로 (10% off admission for major tourist attractions) ③은 안내문의 내용과 일치하지 않는다.

왜 오답?

① 관광객을 위한 대중교통 카드이다. (The Adenville City Pass Card is a public transportation card for tourists)
② 시티 투어 버스에는 사용할 수 없다. (※ This card cannot be used for city tour buses.)
④ 미사용 카드는 구입일로부터 30일 이내에 환불이 가능하다. (※ Unused cards are refundable within 30 days of the purchase date.)
⑤ 모바일 카드는 A-Transit 앱에서 구입할 수 있다. (Mobile cards can be purchased on the A-Transit app.)

배지오 | 2025 수능 응시 · 성남 낙생고 졸

이런 유형의 문제는 주어진 글을 읽기보다 바로 선택지로 넘어가야 빨리 풀 수 있어. 선택지를 먼저 읽고, 바로 글로 올라가서 근거를 하나씩 찾아 나가면 돼. 예를 들어, 두 번째 선택지에서 카드를 시티 투어 버스에는 사용할 수 없다고 하니, 위로 올라가서 Service Range를 보면, 정말 시티 투어에는 사용할 수 없음을 명시한 것을 확인할 수 있지.

J

J 04 정답 ③ ＊Luckwood 눈 축제 안내문

Luckwood Snow Festival / Luckwood 눈 축제 /
<u>부사적 용법(~하게 되어, 이유)</u>
We're happy to announce / the 15th annual Luckwood Snow
Festival. // **①의 단서** 1년마다 열리는 연례 축제임
저희는 알려 드리게 되어 기쁩니다 / 제15회 연례 Luckwood 눈 축제를 //
<u>부사적 용법(목적)</u>
Come to the festival / to enjoy winter activities. //
축제에 오세요 / 동계 활동을 즐기러 //

When & Where / 언제 & 어디서 /
②의 단서 7일 간 진행됨
• January 24th – 30th (7 days), / from 9 a.m. to 8 p.m. //
1월 24일부터 30일까지(7일간) / 오전 9시부터 오후 8시까지 //

• Luckwood Park / Luckwood 공원 /

Special Activities / 특별 활동 /
• Snow Sculpture Contest: / 11 teams will participate. //
눈 조각 경연 / 11개 팀이 참가할 것입니다 // **③의 단서** 눈 조각 경연에는 11개 팀이 참가할 것임

• Fun in the Snow: / Kids can enjoy snow tunnels and snow
slides. //
눈 속 즐거움 / 아이들은 눈 터널과 눈 미끄럼틀을 즐길 수 있습니다 //

Transportation / 교통 /
④의 단서 주차는 가능하지 않음
• Parking is not available / (Use public transportation and/or
shuttle bus service). //
주차는 할 수 없습니다 / (대중교통과/또는 셔틀버스 서비스를 이용하세요) //
<u>자동사</u>
• The shuttle bus runs / between Luckwood Subway Station
and Luckwood Park / (One-way fare: $1, cash only). //
셔틀버스는 운행합니다 / Luckwood 지하철역과 Luckwood 공원 사이를 / (편도 요금: 1
달러, 현금만 받음) // **⑤의 단서** 셔틀버스 이용은 편도에 1달러로 유료임

※ For more information, / please visit www.lwsnow.org.//
더 많은 정보를 원하시면 / 웹사이트 www.lwsnow.org를 방문하세요 //

• annual ⓐ 연례의   • sculpture ⓝ 조각
• slide ⓝ 미끄럼틀   • transportation ⓝ 교통

Luckwood 눈 축제

저희는 제15회 연례 Luckwood 눈 축제를 알려 드리게 되어 기쁩니다. 동계
활동을 즐기러 축제에 오세요.
언제 & 어디서
• 1월 24일부터 30일까지(7일간) 오전 9시부터 오후 8시까지
• Luckwood 공원
특별 활동
• 눈 조각 경연: 11개 팀이 참가할 것입니다.
• 눈 속 즐거움: 아이들은 눈 터널과 눈 미끄럼틀을 즐길 수 있습니다.
교통
• 주차는 할 수 없습니다(대중교통과/또는 셔틀버스 서비스를 이용하세요).
• 셔틀버스는 Luckwood 지하철역과 Luckwood 공원 사이를 운행합니다
  (편도 요금: 1달러, 현금만 받음).
※ 더 많은 정보를 원하시면, 웹사이트 www.lwsnow.org를 방문하세요.

Luckwood Snow Festival에 관한 다음 안내문의 내용과 일치하는 것은?
① 2년에 한 번 열린다.
the 15th annual Luckwood Snow Festival
② 열흘 동안 진행된다.
January 24th–30th (7 days)
③ 눈 조각 경연에는 11개 팀이 참가할 것이다.
Snow Sculpture Contest: 11 teams will participate.
④ 주차가 가능하다.
Parking is not available
⑤ 셔틀버스 이용은 무료이다.
(One-way fare: $1, cash only)

왜 정답? [정답률 98%]
③ 눈 조각 경연에는 11개 팀이 참가할 것이라고 했으므로 (Snow Sculpture
Contest: 11 teams will participate.) ③은 안내문의 내용과 일치한다.

왜 오답?
① 2년에 한 번이 아니라 1년마다 열리는 연례 축제이다. (the 15th annual
Luckwood Snow Festival)
② 열흘 동안 진행되는 것이 아니라 7일 간 진행된다. (January 24th – 30th
(7 days))
④ 주차는 가능하지 않다. (Parking is not available)
⑤ 셔틀버스 이용은 무료가 아니라 편도에 1달러로 유료다. (One-way fare: $1,
cash only)

백승준 | 2025 수능 응시·광주 광주숭원고 졸

안내문 문제는 선택지를 먼저 읽고 이를 안내문과 비교해서 답을
판단하는 게 유리한 유형이야. 쉬운 유형이라 정답률이 높지만
그럼에도 연습을 통해 어떤 부분에서 정보가 제시되고 정답을
찾을 수 있는지 익숙해지는 것이 중요해. 이 문제의 경우엔
안내문에서 정보가 When & Where, Special Activities, Transportation처럼
크게 구분되어 있기에 선택지에 해당하는 정보의 대략적인 위치를 확인할 수 있지.

J 05 정답 ③ ＊Teverley 대학교 캠퍼스 방문의 날

University of Teverley Campus Visit Day /
Teverley 대학교 캠퍼스 방문의 날 /
<u>명사절 접속사</u>
Do you want to see / if the University of Teverley is the right fit
for you? // 알아보고 싶으신가요 / Teverley 대학교가 여러분에게 딱 알맞은지 //
Come to our annual campus visit event / for prospective
students / on Thursday, September 26th. //
연례 캠퍼스 방문 행사에 오세요 / 입학 희망 학생들을 위한 / 9월 26일 목요일에 //
Participants / 참가 대상 /
①의 단서 고등학교 3학년 학생만 참여할 수 있음
• 3rd-year high school students only / 고등학교 3학년 학생 한정 /
Meeting Time & Place / 만남 시간과 장소 /
• The auditorium at the Student Center / at 9:30 a.m. /
학생회관 강당 / 오전 9시 30분 /
Schedule / 일정 /
• 10:00 a.m.: / Presentation on the admissions process /
오전 10시 / 입학 절차에 관한 소개 / **②의 단서** 입학 절차에 관한 소개가 오전 10시에 있을 예정임
• 10:30 a.m.: / Campus tour / 오전 10시 30분 / 캠퍼스 투어 /
<u>free lunch를 수식하는 분사</u>
• 12:00 p.m.: / Free lunch / provided at the students' cafeteria /
낮 12시 / 무료 점심 / 학생 식당에서 제공되는 / **③의 단서** 점심이 무료로 제공될 것임
• 1:00 p.m.: / Q&A with the student tour staff /
오후 1시 / 학생 투어 담당 직원과의 질의응답 /
<u>미래시제 수동태</u>
※ After the event, / a T-shirt with our university logo / will be
given out / as a gift. // **④의 단서** 티셔츠가 선물로 주어질 것임
행사 종료 후 / 우리 대학 로고가 새겨진 티셔츠가 / 주어질 것입니다 / 선물로 //
Registration / 등록 /
• Register / by 6 p.m., / September 17th, / on our website, www.
teverley.edu. // **⑤의 단서** 등록은 학교 웹사이트에서 함
등록하세요 / 오후 6시까지 / 9월 17일 / 저희 웹사이트 www.teverley.edu에서 //

• fit ⓝ 알맞은 것, 적합한 것   • annual ⓐ 연례의
• prospective student 입학 희망 학생   • admission ⓝ 입학
• registration ⓝ 등록

Teverley 대학교 캠퍼스 방문의 날

Teverley 대학교가 여러분에게 딱 알맞은지 알아보고 싶으신가요? 9월 26일
목요일에 열리는 입학 희망 학생들을 위한 연례 캠퍼스 방문 행사에 오세요.
참가 대상
• 고등학교 3학년 학생 한정
만남 시간과 장소
• 오전 9시 30분 학생회관 강당

일정
- 오전 10시: 입학 절차에 관한 소개
- 오전 10시 30분: 캠퍼스 투어
- 낮 12시: 학생 식당에서 무료 점심 제공
- 오후 1시: 학생 투어 담당 직원과의 질의응답
- ※ 행사 종료 후 우리 대학 로고가 새겨진 티셔츠가 선물로 주어질 것입니다.

등록
- 9월 17일 오후 6시까지 저희 웹사이트 www.teverley.edu에서 등록하세요.

University of Teverley Campus Visit Day에 관한 다음 안내문의 내용과 일치하지 <u>않는</u> 것은?

① 고등학교 3학년 학생만 참여할 수 있다.
3rd-year high school students only
② 입학 절차에 관한 소개가 예정되어 있다.
10:00 a.m.: Presentation on the admissions process
③ 점심은 무료로 제공되지 않는다.
12:00 p.m.: Free lunch provided at the students' cafeteria
④ 티셔츠가 선물로 주어질 것이다.
a T-shirt with our university logo will be given out as a gift
⑤ 등록은 학교 웹사이트에서 한다.
Register by 6 p.m., September 17th, on our website, www.teverley.edu.

⟩왜 정답? [정답률 97%]

③ 점심은 무료로 제공된다고 했다. (12:00 p.m.: Free lunch provided at the students' cafeteria)

⟩왜 오답?

① 고등학교 3학년 학생만 참여할 수 있다. (3rd-year high school students only)
② 입학 절차에 관한 소개가 예정되어 있다. (10:00 a.m.: Presentation on the admissions process)
④ 티셔츠가 선물로 주어질 것이다. (a T-shirt with our university logo will be given out as a gift)
⑤ 등록은 학교 웹사이트에서 한다. (Register by 6 p.m., September 17th, on our website, www.teverley.edu.)

J 06 정답 ⑤ * 2024 녹색 미래 웹툰 공모전

2024 Green Future Webtoon Contest / 2024 녹색 미래 웹툰 공모전 /
Showcase your creativity and artistic talents / by creating a
주격 관계대명사
webtoon / that captures your vision of a cleaner environment. //
여러분의 창의력과 예술적 재능을 뽐내 보세요 / 웹툰을 제작하여 / 더 깨끗한 환경에 대한
여러분의 비전을 포착한 //

Theme: / Renewable energy for a green future /
주제 / 친환경 미래를 위한 재생 에너지 / **①의 단서** 주제는 친환경 미래를 위한 재생 에너지임

Submission Details / 출품 세부 정보 /
미래시제 수동태
- **Submissions will be accepted** / from October 1st to November 30th. // **②의 단서** 출품은 10월 1일부터 접수됨
출품작은 접수됩니다 / 10월 1일부터 11월 30일까지 //

- **Submissions should be uploaded** / to our website. //
출품작은 업로드되어야 합니다 / 저희 웹사이트에 //

- **Each participant is allowed** / to submit only one webtoon. //
각 참가자는 허용됩니다 / 한 개의 웹툰만 제출하도록 // **③의 단서** 참가자는 웹툰 하나만 제출 가능함

Prizes / 상금 /

	Number of winners 수상자 수	Prize money(per winner) 상금(수상자 당)
1st prize 1등	1	$3,000
2nd prize 2등 **④의 단서** 2등 수상자는 2명임	2	$2,000
3rd prize 3등	3	$1,000

- The winners will be decided / by the selection committee /
and will be announced / on December 30th. // **⑤의 단서** 수상자는 선정 위원회에서 결정함
수상자는 결정될 것입니다 / 선정 위원회에서 / 그리고 발표될 것입니다 / 12월 30일에 //

- ※ For more information, / visit our website, www.grnftr.org. //
더 많은 정보를 원하시면 / 저희 웹사이트 www.grnftr.org를 방문하세요 //

- showcase ⓥ 뽐내다
- capture ⓥ 포착하다
- renewable ⓐ 재생 가능한
- submission ⓝ 출품, 출품작
- submit ⓥ 제출하다
- selection committee 선정 위원회

2024 녹색 미래 웹툰 공모전
더 깨끗한 환경에 대한 여러분의 비전을 포착한 웹툰을 제작하여 여러분의 창의력과 예술적 재능을 뽐내 보세요.
주제: 친환경 미래를 위한 재생 에너지
출품 세부 정보
- 출품작은 10월 1일부터 11월 30일까지 접수합니다.
- 출품작은 저희 웹사이트에 업로드해야 합니다.
- 각 참가자는 한 개의 웹툰만 제출할 수 있습니다.
상금

	수상자 수	상금(수상자 당)
1등	1	$3,000
2등	2	$2,000
3등	3	$1,000

- 수상자는 선정 위원회에서 결정되며 12월 30일에 발표될 것입니다.
- ※ 더 많은 정보를 원하시면, 저희 웹사이트 www.grnftr.org를 방문하세요.

2024 Green Future Webtoon Contest에 관한 다음 안내문의 내용과 일치하는 것은?

① 주제는 농업 기술의 미래이다.
Theme: Renewable energy for a green future
② 출품은 11월 30일부터이다.
Submissions will be accepted from October 1st to November 30th.
③ 각 참가자는 두 개의 웹툰을 제출할 수 있다.
Each participant is allowed to submit only one webtoon.
④ 2등상은 세 명에게 주어진다.
2nd prize Number of winners - 2
⑤ 수상자는 선정 위원회에서 결정될 것이다.
The winners will be decided by the selection committee

⟩왜 정답? [정답률 96%]

⑤ 수상자는 선정 위원회에서 결정될 것이라고 했다. (The winners will be decided by the selection committee)

⟩왜 오답?

① 주제는 친환경 미래를 위한 재생 에너지이다. (Theme: Renewable energy for a green future)
② 출품은 10월 1일부터이다. (Submissions will be accepted from October 1st to November 30th.)
③ 각 참가자는 한 개의 웹툰만 제출할 수 있다. (Each participant is allowed to submit only one webtoon.)
④ 2등상은 두 명에게 주어진다. (2nd prize Number of winners – 2)

J 07 정답 ⑤ * 야생 동물 구조 센터 여름 일자리

Summer Job at Wildlife Rescue Center /
야생 동물 구조 센터 여름 일자리 / **①의 단서** Mount Donovahn으로부터 구조된 동물을 돌봄
We are looking for summer workers / who will take care of the
과거분사   주격 관계대명사(전행사 workers)
animals / rescued from Mount Donovahn. //
여름 근무자를 모집합니다 / 동물들을 돌봐줄 / Mount Donovahn에서 구조된 //

Schedule / 일정 /
- Dates: August 1st to 31st / 날짜: 8월 1일부터 31일까지 /
- Hours: 10 a.m. – 4 p.m. / 시간: 오전 10시 ~ 오후 4시 /
- ※ On rainy days, / working hours may change. //
우천 시에는 / 근무 시간이 변경될 수 있습니다 // **②의 단서** 우천 시 업무 시간이 변경될 수 있음

Requirements / 자격 요건 /
뒤에 who are 생략
- Only those aged 18 and over / can apply. //
18세 이상만 / 지원할 수 있습니다 // **③의 단서** 18세 이상만 지원할 수 있음

- Previous experience with animals /
이전에 동물과 관련된 경험이 있어야 합니다 /

Tasks / 업무 /

- Preparing food for animals and feeding them /
동물 먹이 준비 및 먹이 주기 /

- Writing reports about animals /
동물에 대한 보고서 작성하기 / **④의 단서** 동물에 관한 보고서를 작성함

- Summer workers will get training / from our caretakers. //
여름 근무자는 교육을 받게 됩니다 / 사육사로부터 //

- Free shuttle bus service will be ~~수동태~~ provided / twice a day. //
무료 셔틀 버스 서비스가 제공됩니다 / 하루에 두 번 // **⑤의 단서** 무료 셔틀 버스 서비스가
하루에 두 번 제공됨

To learn more about the summer job, / please visit our website,
www.dwildliferescue.org. //
여름 일자리에 대해 더 알아보려면 / 저희 웹사이트(www.dwildliferescue.org)를
방문하세요 //

- wildlife ⓝ 야생 동물   • previous ⓐ 이전의
- feed ⓥ 먹이를 주다   • caretaker ⓝ 사육사, 돌보는 사람

야생 동물 구조 센터 여름 일자리

Mount Donovahn에서 구조된 동물들을 돌봐줄 여름 근무자를 모집합니다.

일정
- 날짜: 8월 1일부터 31일까지
- 시간: 오전 10시 ~ 오후 4시
※ 우천 시에는 근무 시간이 변경될 수 있습니다.

자격 요건
- 18세 이상만 지원할 수 있습니다.
- 이전에 동물과 관련된 경험이 있어야 합니다.

업무
- 동물 먹이 준비 및 먹이 주기
- 동물에 대한 보고서 작성하기
- 여름 근무자는 사육사로부터 교육을 받게 됩니다.
- 무료 셔틀 버스 서비스가 하루에 두 번 제공됩니다.

여름 일자리에 대해 더 알아보려면, 저희 웹사이트 (www.dwildliferescue.
org)를 방문하세요.

Summer Job at Wildlife Rescue Center에 관한 다음 안내문의 내용과 일치하지 않는 것은?

① Mount Donovahn으로부터 구조된 동물을 돌본다.
  who will take care of the animals rescued from Mount Donovahn
② 우천 시 업무 시간이 변경될 수 있다.
  On rainy days, working hours may change.
③ 18세 이상만 지원할 수 있다.
  Only those aged 18 and over can apply.
④ 동물에 관한 보고서를 작성한다.
  Writing reports about animals
⑤ 무료 셔틀 버스 서비스가 하루에 세 번 제공된다.
  Free shuttle bus service will be provided twice a day.

왜 정답? [정답률 96%]

⑤ 무료 셔틀 버스 서비스가 하루에 세 번이 아니라 두 번 제공된다. (Free shuttle
  bus service will be provided twice a day.)

왜 오답?

① Mount Donovahn으로부터 구조된 동물을 돌본다. (who will take care of
  the animals rescued from Mount Donovahn)
② 우천 시 업무 시간이 변경될 수 있다. (On rainy days, working hours may
  change.)
③ 18세 이상만 지원할 수 있다. (Only those aged 18 and over can apply.)
④ 동물에 관한 보고서를 작성한다. (Writing reports about animals)

J 08 정답 ④ ＊LCU 지리 현장 학습

LCU Geography Field Trip / LCU 지리 현장 학습 /
Lionsford City University is offering a one-day geography field ~~현재진행형으로 가까운 미래를 표현함~~
trip / on June 17th. // **①의 단서** 2일 동안이 아닌 일일 지리 현장 학습임
Lionsford City University는 일일 지리 현장 학습을 제공합니다 / 6월 17일에 //
We believe / it is **one of the finest field trips in the country.** // ~~one of+최상급+복수 명사: 가장 ~한 것들 중 하나~~
저희는 생각합니다 / 이 현장 학습이 국내 최고의 현장 학습 중 하나라고 //
Participants: / **First-year students** ~~현재분사~~ **majoring in geography** //
참가 대상 / 지리학을 전공하는 1학년 학생 // **②의 단서** 지리학 전공 1학년 학생들이 참여할 수 있음

Course Options / 코스 옵션 /

A	B
Exploring the landscape while hiking Mount Belena	Examining coastal features along Lionsford Beach
Belena 산을 하이킹하며 풍경 탐험하기	**③의 단서** B코스에서 Lionsford Beach 해안의 특징을 조사함 Lionsford 해변을 따라 해안 특징 살펴보기

Participation Fee: / $70 per person (lunch included) /
참가비 / 1인당 70달러(점심 포함) / **④의 단서** 참가비에 점심이 포함되어 있음

How to Apply / 지원 방법 /

- **Email the application** to geography@lcu.edu / **or drop it off at**
  the department office. // **⑤의 단서** 지원서는 이메일과 사무실 직접 제출
  두 가지 방법이 가능함
  지원서를 이메일(geography@lcu.edu)로 보내거나 / 학과 사무실에 제출하세요 //

- **Deadline: June 4th** / 마감일: 6월 4일 /

※ **For further information,** / **please contact us at 607-223-2127.** //
더 많은 정보를 원하시면 / 607-223-2127로 문의하시기 바랍니다 //

- field trip 현장 학습   • fine ⓐ 좋은, 질 높은   • coastal ⓐ 해안의
- feature ⓝ 특징, 특색   • include ⓥ 포함하다
- department ⓝ 부서

LCU 지리 현장 학습

Lionsford City University는 6월 17일에 일일 지리 현장 학습을 제공합니다.
저희는 이 현장 학습이 국내 최고의 현장 학습 중 하나라고 생각합니다.
참가 대상: 지리학을 전공하는 1학년 학생
코스 옵션

A	B
Belena 산을 하이킹하며 풍경 탐험하기	Lionsford 해변을 따라 해안 특징 살펴보기

참가비: 1인당 70달러(점심 포함)
지원 방법
- 지원서를 이메일(geography@lcu. edu)로 보내거나 학과 사무실에 제출하세요.
- 마감일: 6월 4일
※ 더 많은 정보를 원하시면 607-223-2127로 문의하시기 바랍니다.

LCU Geography Field Trip에 관한 다음 안내문의 내용과 일치하는 것은?

① 2일 동안 진행된다.
  a one-day geography field trip on June 17th
② 모든 전공의 학생들이 참여할 수 있다.
  First-year students majoring in geography
③ A코스에서는 Lionsford Beach 해안의 특징을 조사한다.
  B: Examining coastal features along Lionsford Beach
④ 참가비에 점심이 포함되어 있다.
  Participation Fee: $70 per person (lunch included)
⑤ 지원서는 이메일로만 제출이 가능하다.
  Email the application to geography@lcu.edu or drop it off at the department office.

왜 정답? [정답률 94%]

④ 참가비에 점심이 포함되어 있다. (Participation Fee: $70 per person (lunch
  included))

왜 오답?

① 2일 동안 진행된다. (a one-day geography field trip on June 17th)
② 모든 전공의 학생들이 참여할 수 있다. (First-year students majoring in geography)
③ A코스에서는 Lionsford Beach 해안의 특징을 조사한다. (B: Examining coastal features along Lionsford Beach)
⑤ 지원서는 이메일로만 제출이 가능하다. (Email the application to geography@lcu.edu or drop it off at the department office.)

J 09 정답 ③ * "Be Active" 공동체 챌린지

2024 "Be Active" Community Challenge /
2024 "Be Active" 공동체 챌린지 /

The "Be Active" Community Challenge invites all of you. //
"Be Active" 공동체 챌린지에 여러분을 초대합니다 //

Let's get moving this fall! // 올 가을, 함께 움직여 보아요 //
①의 단서 챌린지 기간은 10월 1일부터 10월 31일까지임
• **When**: October 1 – October 31 / 기간: 10월 1일 – 10월 31일 /

• **How It Works**: / 진행 방법 /

- Keep track of the number of minutes / you were active every day. // 분 단위로 기록하세요 / 매일 활동한 시간을 //
②의 단서 모든 종류의 운동이 인정됨
- Every kind of exercise counts: / jogging, dancing, football, etc. // 모든 종류의 운동이 인정됩니다 / 조깅, 춤, 축구, 등 //

• **Tracking Your Progress**: / 진행 상황 기록 /

- Log your active minutes daily / on the "Be Active" app. // 매일 활동 시간을 기록하세요 / "Be Active" 앱에 //
③의 단서 총합 시간의 제출 기한은 11월 1일 오전 10시임
- Deadline for submitting your total time / is November 1, 10:00 a.m. // 총합 시간을 제출하는 마감일은 / 11월 1일 오전 10시입니다 //

• **Entry Fees**: $10 (12 years and under are FREE.) /
참가비: 10달러 (12세 이하 무료) / **④의 단서** 12세 이하는 참가비가 무료임

• **Rewards and Recognition**: / 보상 및 표창 /

- The three participants / who recorded the highest total time / will win a prize. // 세 명의 참가자 / 총 활동 시간이 가장 많은 / 상을 받습니다 //
⑤의 단서 우승자는 온라인으로 발표될 것임
- Winners will be announced online. //
수상자는 온라인으로 발표됩니다 //

• track ⓥ 기록하다 • log ⓥ (일지에) 기록하다
• deadline ⓝ 마감일 • submit ⓥ 제출하다 • record ⓥ 기록하다
• announce ⓥ 발표하다

2024 "Be Active" 커뮤니티 챌린지

"Be Active" 커뮤니티 챌린지에 여러분을 초대합니다.
올 가을, 함께 움직여 보아요!
• 기간: 10월 1일 – 10월 31일
• 진행 방법:
매일 활동한 시간을 분 단위로 기록하세요.
모든 종류의 운동이 인정됩니다: 조깅, 춤, 축구 등.
• 진행 상황 추적:
"Be Active" 앱에 매일 활동 시간을 기록하세요.
총합 시간을 제출하는 마감일은 11월 1일 오전 10시입니다.
• 참가비: $10 (12세 이하 무료)
• 보상 및 표창:
총 활동 시간이 가장 많은 세 명의 참가자가 상을 받습니다.
수상자는 온라인으로 발표됩니다.

2024 "Be Active" Community Challenge에 관한 다음 안내문의 내용과 일치하지 않는 것은?

① 기간은 10월 1일부터 10월 31일까지이다.
When: October 1 – October 31
② 모든 종류의 운동이 인정된다.
Every kind of exercises counts
③ 총합 시간의 제출 기한은 11월 1일 오후 10시이다.
Deadline for submitting your total time is November 1, 10:00 a.m.
④ 12세 이하는 참가비가 무료이다.
12 years and under are FREE
⑤ 우승자는 온라인으로 발표될 것이다.
Winners will be announced online

왜 정답? [정답률 95%]

③ 총합 시간의 제출 기한은 오후 10시가 아니라 오전 10시이다. (Deadline for submitting your total time is November 1, 10:00 a.m.)

왜 오답?

① 기간은 10월 1일부터 10월 31일까지이다. (When: October 1 – October 31)
② 모든 종류의 운동이 인정된다. (Every kind of exercises counts)
④ 12세 이하는 참가비가 무료이다. (12 years and under are FREE)
⑤ 우승자는 온라인으로 발표될 것이다. (Winners will be announced online)

J 10 정답 ④ * Heritage 호텔 숙박 안내

Heritage Hotel Stay Information / Heritage Hotel 숙박 안내 /
Dear guests, please read the following / to ensure your safety and comfort during your stay. //
부사적 용법(목적)
고객님들께, 다음 내용을 읽어주시기 바랍니다 / 귀하의 안전과 편안함을 위해 //

• **Check in & Check out** / 체크인 & 체크아웃 /

- Room check in is from 2 p.m. // 객실 체크인은 오후 2시부터 가능합니다 //

- Room check out is until 12 p.m. // 객실 체크아웃은 오후 12시까지입니다 //

• **During the Stay** / 숙박 중 / **①의 단서** 객실 체크아웃은 오후 12시까지임

- Used towels are changed every other day. //
사용한 수건은 이틀에 한 번 교체됩니다 // **②의 단서** 사용한 수건은 이틀에 한 번 교체됨

- Free Wi-Fi is available ONLY in the lobby. //
무료 와이파이는 로비에서만 이용 가능합니다 // **③의 단서** 무료 와이파이는 로비에서만 이용 가능함

- Two bottles of water are provided for FREE. //
무료로 생수 두 병이 제공됩니다 // **④의 단서** 무료로 생수 두 병이 제공됨

• **Facilities** / 시설 /

- The gym and business center are open 24 hours. //
헬스장과 비즈니스 센터는 24시간 운영됩니다 //

- The parking lot is in front of the hotel. //
주차장은 호텔 앞에 위치해 있습니다 // **⑤의 단서** 주차장은 호텔 앞에 있음

• following ⓐ 다음에 나오는 • ensure ⓥ 반드시 …하게[이게] 하다
• available ⓐ 이용할 수 있는 • parking lot 주차장

Heritage 호텔 숙박 정보

고객님들께, 귀하의 안전과 편안함을 위해 다음 내용을 읽어 주시기 바랍니다.
• 체크인 & 체크아웃
객실 체크인은 오후 2시부터 가능합니다.
객실 체크아웃은 오후 12시까지입니다.
• 숙박 중
사용한 수건은 이틀에 한 번 교체됩니다.
무료 Wi-Fi는 로비에서만 이용 가능합니다.
무료로 생수 두 병이 제공됩니다.
• 시설
헬스장과 비즈니스 센터는 24시간 운영됩니다.
주차장은 호텔 앞에 위치해 있습니다.

Heritage Hotel Stay Information에 관한 다음 안내문의 내용과 일치하는 것은?

① 객실 체크아웃은 오후 2시까지이다.
  Room check out is until 12 p.m.
② 사용한 수건은 매일 교체된다.
  Used towels are changed every other day.
③ 무료 와이파이는 호텔 전체에서 이용 가능하다.
  Free Wi-Fi is available ONLY in the lobby.
④ 물 두 병이 무료로 제공된다.
  Two bottles of water are provided for FREE.
⑤ 주차장은 호텔 뒤편에 있다.
  The parking lot is in front of the hotel.

>왜 정답? [정답률 89%]

④ 무료로 생수 두 병이 제공된다고 했다. (Two bottles of water are provided for FREE.)

>왜 오답?

① 객실 체크아웃은 오후 12시까지이다. (Room check out is until 12 p.m.)
② 사용한 수건은 이틀에 한 번 교체된다. (Used towels are changed every other day.)
③ 무료 와이파이는 로비에서만 이용 가능하다. (Free Wi-Fi is available ONLY in the lobby.)
⑤ 주차장은 호텔 앞에 있다. (The parking lot is in front of the hotel.)

J 11 정답 ④ * Dolphin Tours

Dolphin Tours / Dolphin Tours /

Come join Dolphin Tours / sailing from Golden Bay / and dive into the enchanting world of marine life. //
현재분사(Dolphin Tours 수식)
Dolphin Tour에 참여하고 / Golden Bay에서 항해하는 / 해양 생물의 매력적인 세계로 뛰어드세요 //

Daily Tour Times / 일일 투어 시간 /

• 11 a.m., 2 p.m., & Sunset / 오전 11시, 오후 2시 & 일몰 /
  ①의 단서 각 투어는 2시간이 소요됨
※ Each tour lasts two hours. // 각 투어는 2시간이 소요됩니다 //
  each+단수 명사+단수 동사

Tickets & Booking / 티켓 & 예약 /

• Adult (ages 12 and over): $20 / 성인 (12세 이상): 20달러 /
  ②의 단서 11세 이하 어린이는 티켓이 무료임
• Child (ages 11 and under): Free / 어린이 (11세 이하): 무료 /
• Reserve your tickets on our website at www.dolphintourgb. com. // 티켓은 저희 웹사이트인 www.dolphintourgb.com에서 예약하세요 //

Activities / 활동 /
                            과거분사(Dolphin watching 수식)
• Dolphin watching guided by a marine biologist /
해양 생물학자가 안내하는 돌고래 관찰 / ③의 단서 해양 생물학자가 돌고래 관찰을 안내함
• Swimming with dolphins (Optional) / 돌고래와 수영하기 (선택 사항) /

Notices / 공지 /

• Reservations are required for all activities. //
모든 활동은 예약이 필요합니다 // ④의 단서 모든 활동은 예약이 필요함

• Children must be accompanied by a parent or guardian. //
어린이는 부모나 보호자를 동반해야 합니다 // ⑤의 단서 어린이는 부모나 보호자를 동반해야 함

• In the case of cancellation due to bad weather, / a full refund will be provided. // 기상 악화로 취소될 경우 / 전액 환불됩니다 //

• enchanting ⓐ 매력적인, 황홀케 하는 • accompany ⓥ 동행하다
• guardian ⓝ 후견인 • refund ⓝ 환불

Dolphin Tours
Golden Bay에서 항해하는 Dolphin Tour에 참여하고 해양 생물의 매력적인 세계로 뛰어드세요.
일일 투어 시간
• 오전 11시, 오후 2시 & 일몰
※ 각 투어는 2시간이 소요됩니다.

티켓 & 예약
• 성인 (12세 이상): 20달러
• 어린이 (11세 이하): 무료
• 티켓은 저희 웹사이트인 www.dolphintourgb.com에서 예약하세요.
활동
• 해양 생물학자가 안내하는 돌고래 관찰
• 돌고래와 수영하기 (선택 사항)
공지
• 모든 활동은 예약이 필요합니다.
• 어린이는 부모나 보호자를 동반해야 합니다.
• 기상 악화로 취소될 경우, 전액 환불됩니다.

Dolphin Tours에 관한 다음 안내문의 내용과 일치하지 않는 것은?

① 각 투어는 2시간이 소요된다.
  Each tour lasts two hours.
② 11세 이하의 어린이는 무료로 참가할 수 있다.
  Child (ages 11 and under): Free
③ 해양 생물학자가 돌고래 관찰을 안내한다.
  Dolphin watching guided by a marine biologist
④ 일부 활동은 예약 없이 참여할 수 있다.
  Reservations are required for all activities.
⑤ 어린이는 부모나 보호자를 동반해야 한다.
  Children must be accompanied by a parent or guardian.

>왜 정답? [정답률 95%]

④ 모든 활동은 예약을 해야 하므로 일부 활동은 예약 없이 참여할 수 있다는 내용은 일치하지 않는다. (Reservations are required for all activities.)

>왜 오답?

① 각 투어는 2시간이 소요된다. (Each tour lasts two hours.)
② 11세 이하의 어린이는 무료로 참가할 수 있다. (Child (ages 11 and under): Free)
③ 해양 생물학자가 돌고래 관찰을 안내한다. (Dolphin watching guided by a marine biologist)
⑤ 어린이는 부모나 보호자를 동반해야 한다. (Children must be accompanied by a parent or guardian.)

J 12 정답 ② * 2024 Celton 수학의 밤

2024 Celton Math Night / 2024 Celton 수학의 밤 /

Celton High School invites students / to experience how math connects to the real world! //
                            목적격 보어
Celton High School은 학생 여러분을 초대합니다 / 수학이 어떻게 실생활과 연관되는지 경험할 수 있도록 //

Students will search supermarket aisles / for answers to math questions / on their activity sheets. //
학생들은 슈퍼마켓 통로를 탐색할 것입니다 / 수학 문제의 답을 구하기 위해 / 활동지에 있는 //

Who: Teams of 10th and 11th Grade Students /
대상: 10학년과 11학년 학생으로 구성된 팀 /

Where: Jay Supermarket / 장소: Jay Supermarket /
  ①의 단서 5시에 시작해서 7시에 종료됨
When: July 26th, 5 p.m. – 7 p.m. / 일시: 7월 26일 오후 5시~오후 7시 /

Event Information / 행사 정보 /
  ②의 단서 각 팀은 3명의 학생으로 구성되어야 함
• Each team should consist of 3 students. //
각 팀은 3명의 학생으로 구성되어야 합니다 //
  ③의 단서 계산기 반입이 허용됨
• Bringing a calculator is allowed. // 계산기 반입이 허용됩니다 //
  동명사 주어   형용사적 용법(the first team 수식)
• A prize will not be given / to the first team to finish the activity sheet. // ④의 단서 활동지를 먼저 완성하는 팀에게는 상이 주어지지 않음
상이 주어지지 않습니다 / 활동지를 먼저 완성하는 팀에게 //
It's not a race. // 이 행사는 경주가 아닙니다 //
                                                       늦어도 ~까지는
• Sign up for the event at www.celtonmath.com / no later than July 24th. // ⑤의 단서 7월 24일까지 홈페이지에서 행사에 등록해야 함
www.celtonmath.com에서 행사에 등록하세요 / 7월 24일까지 //

※ For more information, / please contact us at (512)1654-9783 or visit our website. //
더 많은 정보를 원하시면 / (512)1654-9783으로 연락하거나 저희 웹사이트에 방문하세요 //

2024 Celton 수학의 밤

Celton High School은 수학이 어떻게 실생활과 연관되는지 경험할 수 있도록 학생 여러분을 초대합니다! 학생들은 활동지에 있는 수학 문제의 답을 구하기 위해 슈퍼마켓 통로를 탐색할 것입니다.

대상: 10학년과 11학년 학생으로 구성된 팀
장소: Jay Supermarket
일시: 7월 26일 오후 5시~오후 7시
행사 정보
• 각 팀은 3명의 학생으로 구성되어야 합니다.
• 계산기 반입이 허용됩니다.
• 활동지를 먼저 완성하는 팀에게 상이 주어지지 않습니다. 이 행사는 경주가 아닙니다.
• www.celtonmath.com에서 7월 24일까지 행사에 등록하세요.
※ 더 많은 정보를 원하시면, (512)1654-9783으로 연락하거나 저희 웹사이트에 방문하세요.

2024 Celton Math Night에 관한 다음 안내문의 내용과 일치하는 것은?

① 오후 5시에 종료된다.
　When: July 26th, 5 p.m. – 7 p.m.
② 각 팀은 3명의 학생으로 구성되어야 한다.
　Each team should consist of 3 students.
③ 계산기 반입이 허용되지 않는다.
　Bringing a calculator is allowed.
④ 가장 먼저 활동지를 완성하는 팀이 상을 받는다.
　A prize will not be given to the first team to finish the activity sheet.
⑤ 7월 26일까지 등록해야 한다.
　Sign up for the event at www.celtonmath.com no later than July 24th.

왜 정답? [정답률 97%]

② 각 팀은 3명의 학생으로 구성되어야 한다고 했다. (Each team should consist of 3 students.)

왜 오답?

① 오후 5시에 시작해서 7시에 종료된다. (When: July 26th, 5 p.m., – 7 p.m.)
③ 계산기 반입이 허용된다. (Bringing a calculator is allowed.)
④ 행사는 경주가 아니므로 활동지를 가장 먼저 완성해도 상을 받지 않는다. (A prize will not be given to the first team to finish the activity sheet.)
⑤ 7월 24일까지 홈페이지에 등록해야 한다. (Sign up for the event at www.celtonmath.com no later than July 24th.)

J 13 정답 ④ ＊Scottish 당일 여행 패키지

Scottish Day Trip Package / Scottish 당일 여행 패키지 /
형용사적 용법(the chance 수식)
Don't miss the chance / to soak up the spirit of Scotland! //
기회를 놓치지 마세요 / Scotland의 정신을 만끽할 //
단수 주어　　　　　　　　　　단수 동사
A full-day trip through the Highlands / is waiting for you. //
Highlands를 두루 다니는 종일 여행이 / 당신을 기다리고 있습니다 //

Schedule / 일정 /
• Departs at 7 a.m. / from the Highland Tours office /
오전 7시에 출발함 / Highland Tours 사무실에서 /
• Returns around 9 p.m. / to the original departure point //
오후 9시경에 돌아옴 / 원래 출발지로 / **①의 단서** 출발하는 장소와 돌아오는 장소가 같음

Details / 세부 사항 / **②의 단서** 한 그룹당 40명까지 참여할 수 있음
• Max of 40 people / per group / 최대 40명 / 그룹당 /
• Minimum age: / 5 years old / 최소 연령 / 5세 /
• Price: / $150 per person / 가격 / 1인당 150달러 /
• **Booking** / 예약 /
• Only online booking is available. //
온라인 예약만 이용 가능합니다 //

일단 ~하면
• You will receive an email / once your booking is confirmed. //
당신은 이메일을 받게 될 것입니다 / 예약이 확정되면 // **③의 단서** 예약이 확정되면 이메일을
받을 것임
• For a refund, / cancel at least two days before the tour departs. // **④의 단서** 환불을 위해서는 출발하기 최소 이틀 전까지 취소해야 함
환불을 위해서는 / 투어가 출발하기 최소 이틀 전까지 취소하세요 //

Note / 유의 사항 /
주격 관계대명사
• The tour will not hold back / for tourists who arrive at the departure point late. // **⑤의 단서** 출발지에 늦게 도착하는 여행자를 기다려 주지 않음
투어는 기다리지 않습니다 / 출발지에 늦게 도착하는 여행자를 //

Scottish 당일 여행 패키지

Scotland의 정신을 만끽할 기회를 놓치지 마세요!
Highlands를 두루 다니는 종일 여행이 당신을 기다리고 있습니다.

일정
• Highland Tours 사무실에서 오전 7시에 출발함
• 원래 출발지로 오후 9시경에 돌아옴
세부 사항
• 그룹당 최대 40명
• 최소 연령: 5세
• 가격: 1인당 150달러
예약
• 온라인 예약만 이용 가능합니다.
• 예약이 확정되면 당신은 이메일을 받게 될 것입니다.
• 환불을 위해서는 투어가 출발하기 최소 이틀 전까지 취소하세요.
유의 사항
• 투어는 출발지에 늦게 도착하는 여행자를 기다리지 않습니다.

Scottish Day Trip Package에 관한 다음 안내문의 내용과 일치하지 않는 것은?

① 출발하는 장소와 돌아오는 장소가 같다.
　Returns around 9 p.m. to the original departure point
② 한 그룹당 40명까지 참여할 수 있다.
　Max of 40 people per group
③ 예약이 확정되면 이메일을 받을 것이다.
　You will receive an email once your booking is confirmed.
④ 환불을 위해서는 출발 하루 전까지 취소해야 한다.
　For a refund, cancel at least two days before the tour departs.
⑤ 출발지에 늦게 도착하는 여행자를 기다려 주지 않는다.
　The tour will not hold back for tourists who arrive at the departure point late.

왜 정답? [정답률 96%]

환불을 위해서는 투어가 출발하기 최소 이틀 전까지 취소하라고 했으므로 (For a refund, cancel at least two days before the tour departs.) 하루 전까지라고 한 ④이 안내문의 내용과 일치하지 않는다.

왜 오답?

① 출발하는 장소와 돌아오는 장소가 같다. (Returns around 9 p.m. to the original departure point)
② 한 그룹당 40명까지 참여할 수 있다. (Max of 40 people per group)
③ 예약이 확정되면 이메일을 받을 것이다. (You will receive an email once your booking is confirmed.)
⑤ 출발지에 늦게 도착하는 여행자를 기다려 주지 않는다. (The tour will not hold back for tourists who arrive at the departure point late.)

J 14 정답 ④ ＊Jr. Chef Class 안내

JR. CHEF CLASS / with Chef Scott Gomez /
JR. CHEF 교실 / 'Scott Gomez 셰프와 함께하는' /
Professional Chef Scott Gomez offers cooking classes / to provide your children / with hands-on experience and happy memories. //
전문 셰프 Scott Gomez가 요리 교실을 제공합니다 / 여러분의 아이들에게 선사할 / 직접 체험과 행복한 기억을 //

현재완료
He has picked pizza for the menu / this week. //
그는 메뉴로 피자를 택했습니다 / 이번 주의 // **❶의 단서** 이번 주의 메뉴는 셰프가 택함

Details / 세부 사항 /

• Date: / Tuesday, May 14th, 2024 / 날짜 / 2024년 5월 14일 화요일 /

• Place: / Rosehill Community Center Cafeteria /
장소 / Rosehill 주민 센터 식당 /

• Available for children ages 6 – 12 /
6세부터 12세까지의 아이들이 이용 가능 /

Cost / 비용 /
❷의 단서 20달러에 앞치마가 포함됨
• **$20 per child includes / all ingredients, chef hat and apron. //**
아이당 20달러는 포함합니다 / 모든 재료, 요리사 모자 그리고 앞치마를 //

Schedule / 일정 /

Time / Contents / 시간 / 내용 /

5:00 – 5:20 p.m. / rolling pizza dough /
오후 5시 ~ 5시 20분 / 피자 반죽 밀기 / **❸의 단서** 피자 반죽 밀기는 20분간 진행

5:20 – 6:00 p.m. / topping and baking /
오후 5시 20분 ~ 6시 / 토핑 얹기와 굽기 /

6:00 – 6:30 p.m. / plating and serving /
오후 6시 ~ 6시 30분 / 접시에 담기와 차려 내기 /

Note / 유의 사항 /

• Call 876–725–7501 / to register. //
876-725-7501로 연락하세요 / 등록을 위해서는 //

• **A parent or guardian must stay on site / during class. //**
부모 혹은 보호자는 수업 동안 현장에 머물러야 합니다 // **❹의 단서** 부모 혹은 보호자는
수업 동안 현장에 머물러야 함
• Since parking space is limited, / using public transportation is
부사절 접속사(이유)
recommended. // **❺의 단서** 주차 공간이 제한적임
주차 공간이 제한적이기 때문에 / 대중교통을 이용하는 것이 권장됩니다 //

• hands-on ⓐ 직접 해 보는 • apron ⓝ 앞치마
• guardian ⓝ 보호자 • public transportation 대중교통 수단

'Scott Gomez 셰프와 함께하는' JR. CHEF 교실

전문 셰프 Scott Gomez가 여러분의 아이들에게 직접 체험과 행복한 기억을 선사할 요리 교실을 제공합니다. 그는 이번 주의 메뉴로 피자를 택했습니다.

세부 사항
• 날짜: 2024년 5월 14일 화요일
• 장소: Rosehill 주민 센터 식당
• 6세부터 12세까지의 아이들이 이용 가능

비용
• 아이당 20달러는 모든 재료, 요리사 모자 그리고 앞치마를 포함합니다.

일정

시간	내용
오후 5시 ~ 5시 20분	피자 반죽 밀기
오후 5시 20분 ~ 6시	토핑 얹기와 굽기
오후 6시 ~ 6시 30분	접시에 담기와 차려 내기

유의 사항
• 등록을 위해서는 876-725-7501로 연락하세요.
• 부모 혹은 보호자는 수업 동안 현장에 머물러야 합니다.
• 주차 공간이 제한적이기 때문에 대중교통을 이용하는 것이 권장됩니다.

Jr. Chef Class에 관한 다음 안내문의 내용과 일치하는 것은?
① 이번 주의 메뉴는 아이들이 택한다.
  He has picked pizza for the menu this week.
② 비용에는 앞치마가 포함되지 않는다.
  $20 per child includes all ingredients, chef hat and apron.
③ 피자 반죽 밀기는 30분간 진행된다.
  5:00 – 5:20 p.m. rolling pizza dough
④ 부모 혹은 보호자는 수업 동안 현장에 머물러야 한다.
  A parent or guardian must stay on site during class.
⑤ 충분한 주차 공간이 확보되어 있다.
  Since parking space is limited

> **왜 정답 ?** [정답률 95%]

부모 혹은 보호자는 수업 동안 현장에 머물러야 한다고 했으므로 (A parent or guardian must stay on site during class.) 안내문의 내용과 일치하는 것은 ④이다.

> **왜 오답 ?**

① 이번 주의 메뉴는 셰프가 피자로 택했다. (He has picked pizza for the menu this week.)
② 비용에는 앞치마가 포함된다. ($20 per child includes all ingredients, chef hat and apron.)
③ 피자 반죽 밀기는 20분간 진행된다. (5:00 — 5:20 p.m. rolling pizza dough)
⑤ 주차 공간이 제한적이다. (Since parking space is limited)

J 15 정답 ④ *전자 금고 사용자 매뉴얼

Electronic Safe User Manual / 전자 금고 사용자 매뉴얼 /

OPENING THE SAFE FOR THE FIRST TIME / 처음으로 금고 열기 /

Upon first use, / users should open the safe / with the emergency
key. // **❶의 단서** 처음 금고를 열 때는 비상 열쇠가 필요함
처음 사용 시 / 사용자는 금고를 열어야 합니다 / 비상 열쇠로 //

INSERTING THE BATTERIES / 건전지 넣기 /

• Insert four AA batteries, / and the green light will flash. //
AA 건전지 네 개를 넣으면 / 녹색 불이 깜빡일 것입니다 // **❷의 단서** 건전기 네 개를 넣으면

• If both the green light and the red light are on, / replace the
batteries. // **❸의 단서** 녹색과 빨간색 불이 둘 다 켜져 있으면 건전지 교체 필요
만약 녹색 불과 빨간색 불 둘 다 켜져 있으면 / 건전지를 교체하십시오 //

SETTING A PASSWORD / 비밀번호 설정하기 /
with+명사+형용사: ~가 …한 채로
• With the door open, / press the reset button. //
문을 연 채로 / 재설정(리셋) 버튼을 누르십시오 //

Then, / input a four-digit password / and press the **"enter"**
button. //
그런 다음 / 네 자리 비밀번호를 입력하십시오 / 그리고 '입력' 버튼을 누르십시오 //

• When the new password is set, / the green light will flash
twice. // **❹의 단서** 새 비밀번호가 설정되면 녹색 불이 세 번이 아니라 두 번 깜빡임
새로운 비밀번호가 설정되면 / 녹색 불이 두 번 깜빡일 것입니다 //

OPENING THE DOOR WITH A PASSWORD / 비밀번호로 문 열기 /

Input your password / and press the **"enter"** button. //
여러분의 비밀번호를 입력하십시오 / 그리고 '입력' 버튼을 누르십시오 //

CAUTION: / A wrong password input / will set off an alarm. //
주의 / 잘못된 비밀번호의 입력은 / 경보음을 울릴 것입니다 // **❺의 단서** 잘못된 비밀번호 입력은
경보음을 울림
• safe ⓝ 금고 • insert ⓥ 넣다 • flash ⓥ 깜빡이다, 번쩍이다, 빛나다
• replace ⓥ 교체하다, 대신하다 • set off (경보 장치를) 울리다

전자 금고 사용자 매뉴얼

처음으로 금고 열기
처음 사용 시 사용자는 비상 열쇠로 금고를 열어야 합니다.

건전지 넣기
• AA 건전지 네 개를 넣으면, 녹색 불이 깜빡일 것입니다.
• 만약 녹색 불과 빨간색 불 둘 다 켜져 있으면, 건전지를 교체하십시오.

비밀번호 설정하기
• 문을 연 채로 재설정(리셋) 버튼을 누르십시오. 그런 다음, 네 자리 비밀번호를 입력한 후 '입력' 버튼을 누르십시오.
• 새로운 비밀번호가 설정되면, 녹색 불이 두 번 깜빡일 것입니다.

비밀번호로 문 열기
여러분의 비밀번호를 입력하고 '입력' 버튼을 누르십시오.
주의: 잘못된 비밀번호의 입력은 경보음을 울릴 것입니다.

Electronic Safe User Manual에 관한 다음 안내문의 내용과 일치하지 <u>않는</u> 것은?

① 처음으로 금고를 열 때는 비상 열쇠를 사용해야 한다.
Upon first use, users should open the safe with the emergency key.
② AA 건전지 네 개를 넣으면, 녹색 불이 깜빡일 것이다.
Insert four AA batteries, and the green light will flash.
③ 녹색과 빨간색 불이 둘 다 켜져 있으면, 건전지를 교체해야 한다.
If both the green light and the red light are on, replace the batteries.
④ 새로운 비밀번호가 설정되면, 녹색 불이 세 번 깜빡일 것이다.
When the new password is set, the green light will flash twice.
⑤ 잘못된 비밀번호의 입력은 경보음을 울릴 것이다.
A wrong password input will set off an alarm.

>왜 정답? [정답률 97%]

④ 새로운 비밀번호가 설정되면, 녹색 불이 세 번이 아니라 두 번 깜빡인다고 했다.
(When the new password is set, the green light will flash twice.)

>왜 오답?

① 처음으로 금고를 열 때는 비상 열쇠를 사용해야 한다. (Upon first use, users should open the safe with the emergency key.)
② AA 건전지 네 개를 넣으면, 녹색 불이 깜빡일 것이다. (Insert four AA batteries, and the green light will flash.)
③ 녹색과 빨간색 불이 둘 다 켜져 있으면, 건전지를 교체해야 한다. (If both the green light and the red light are on, replace the batteries.)
⑤ 잘못된 비밀번호의 입력은 경보음을 울릴 것이다. (A wrong password input will set off an alarm.)

J 16 정답 ② *세계 시의 날 경연 대회

World Poetry Day Competition / 세계 시의 날 경연 대회 /
In honor of World Poetry Day, / let's experience the power of words / with our poetry competition! //
세계 시의 날을 기념하여 / 말의 힘을 경험해 봅시다 / 우리의 시 경연 대회에서 //

Competition Details / 대회 상세 정보 /
①의 단서 주제는 예상못한 순간들임
• Theme: Unexpected Moments / 주제 : 예상치 못한 순간들 /
②의 단서 마감일은 3월 21일임
• Deadline: March 21, 2024 (World Poetry Day) /
마감일 : 2024년 3월 21일 (세계 시의 날) /
• Age: Only those who are under age 18 / can participate. //
연령 : 오직 18세 미만만 / 참여할 수 있다 ③의 단서 18세 미만만 참여할 수 있음

Special Opportunities / 특별한 기회 /
our poetry workshop을 수식하는 분사
• Poetry Workshop: All participants can join our poetry workshop / led by well-known poets. // ④의 단서 시 워크숍에는 모든
시 워크숍 : 모든 참가자는 시 워크숍에 참여할 수 있습니다 / 유명한 시인들이 이끄는 // 참가자가 참여할 수 있음

How to Participate / 참여 방법 /
your poem을 수식하는 분사
• Compose your poem / inspired by the theme. //
자신의 시를 창작하십시오 / 주제에 영감을 받은 //
• You can submit your piece / only through E-mail at administer@worldpoetry.org. // ⑥의 단서 작품은 이메일로만 제출할 수 있음
여러분은 여러분의 작품을 제출할 수 있습니다 / 이메일 administer@worldpoetry.org로만 //

• poetry ⓝ 시 • competition ⓝ 경연 대회 • theme ⓝ 주제
• unexpected ⓐ 예상치 못한 • deadline ⓝ 마감일
• opportunity ⓝ 기회 • participant ⓝ 참가자
• well-known ⓐ 유명한 • compose ⓥ 창작하다

세계 시의 날 경연 대회
세계 시의 날을 기념하여 우리의 시 경연 대회에서 말의 힘을 경험해 봅시다!
대회 상세 정보
• 주제 : 예상치 못한 순간들
• 마감일 : 2024년 3월 21일 (세계 시의 날)
• 연령 : 오직 18세 미만만 참여할 수 있다.

특별한 기회
• 시 워크숍 : 모든 참가자는 유명한 시인들이 이끄는 시 워크숍에 참여할 수 있습니다.
참여 방법
• 주제에 영감을 받아 자신의 시를 창작하십시오
• 여러분은 여러분의 작품을 이메일 administer@worldpoetry.org로만 제출할 수 있습니다.

World Poetry Day Competition에 관한 다음 안내문의 내용과 일치하는 것은?

① 주제는 예상했던 순간들이다.
Theme: Unexpected Moments
② 마감일은 2024년 3월 21일이다.
Deadline: March 21, 2024
③ 18세 이상도 대회에 참가할 수 있다.
Only those who are under age 18 can participate.
④ 대회에서 수상한 사람들만 워크숍에 참석할 수 있다.
All participants can join our poetry workshop led by well-known poets.
⑤ 작품은 직접 또는 이메일로 제출할 수 있다.
You can submit your piece only through E-mail

>왜 정답? [정답률 96%]

② 마감일은 2024년 3월 21일이다. (Deadline: March 21, 2024)

>왜 오답?

① 주제는 예상치 못했던 순간들이다. (Theme: Unexpected Moments)
③ 18세 미만만 대회에 참가할 수 있다. (Only those who are under age 18 can participate.)
④ 모든 참가자가 워크숍에 참석할 수 있다. (All participants can join our poetry workshop led by well-known poets.)
⑤ 작품은 이메일로만 제출할 수 있다. (You can submit your piece only through E-mail)

J 17 정답 ③ *노래하는 Tommy

Singing Tommy /
노래하는 Tommy /
Congratulations! // Tommy is now your singing friend. //
축하합니다 // Tommy는 이제 여러분의 노래하는 친구입니다 //
부사적 용법(목적)
Read these instructions / to learn / how to play with and care for him. //   to learn의 목적어 역할을 하는 「의문사+to부정사」
이 사용 설명서를 읽으세요 / 배우기 위해 / 그와 함께 놀고 그를 돌보는 방법을 //
Tommy sings to you / anytime, anywhere. //
Tommy는 여러분에게 노래를 불러 줍니다 / 언제 어디서나 //
An Internet connection is not required / to play the songs! //
인터넷 연결이 요구되지 않습니다 / 노래를 재생하기 위해 ①의 단서 인터넷 연결 없이도
노래가 재생됨
Before Use /
사용 전 /
film을 수식하는 현재분사구
1. Remove the protective film / covering Tommy's eyes. //
보호 필름을 제거하세요 / Tommy의 눈을 덮고 있는 //
2. Insert two AA batteries / into the battery box / and press the power button. // ②의 단서 두 개의 AA 건전지를 넣음
AA 건전지 두 개를 넣고 / 배터리 칸에 / 전원 단추를 누르세요 //
3. Choose your volume setting: / LOW volume or HIGH volume. //
소리 크기 설정을 선택하세요 / '낮은' 소리 크기 또는 '높은' 소리 크기 //
Operation /
작동 /
1. Play / - Touch Tommy's right ear / to start a song. //
재생 / Tommy의 오른쪽 귀를 건드리세요 / 노래를 시작하려면 //
2. Stop / - Press Tommy's hat / to stop the song. //
중지 / Tommy의 모자를 누르세요 / 노래를 멈추려면 // ③의 단서 모자를 누르면 노래가 멈춤
3. Control /
조절 /

J

④의 단서 다섯 곡의 노래 중에서 선택함

- Choose / from five songs. //

선택하세요 / 다섯 곡의 노래 중에서 //

- Push Tommy's badge / to skip to the next song. //

Tommy의 배지를 누르세요 / 다음 노래로 건너뛰려면 //

Caution /

주의사항 / ⑤의 단서 방수가 되지 않음

Tommy is not waterproof. //

Tommy는 방수가 되지 않습니다 //

to부정사의 부정은 to 앞에 부정어를 씀

Be careful / not to get Tommy wet! //

조심하세요 / Tommy가 물에 젖게 하지 않도록 //

- instruction ⓝ ((pl.)) 사용 설명서 · care for ~을 돌보다
- remove ⓥ 제거하다, 없애다 · protective ⓐ 보호하는, 보호용의
- insert ⓥ 넣다, 삽입하다 · skip ⓥ 건너뛰다, 생략하다
- caution ⓝ (위험에 대한) 경고[주의]문 · waterproof ⓐ 방수의

노래하는 Tommy

축하합니다! Tommy는 이제 여러분의 노래하는 친구입니다. 그와 함께 놀고 그를 돌보는 방법을 배우기 위해 이 사용 설명서를 읽으세요. Tommy는 언제 어디서나 여러분에게 노래를 불러 줍니다. 노래를 재생하기 위해 인터넷에 연결될 필요가 없습니다!

사용 전

1. Tommy의 눈을 덮고 있는 보호 필름을 제거하세요.

2. 배터리 칸에 AA 건전지 두 개를 넣고 전원 단추를 누르세요.

3. 소리 크기 설정을 선택하세요. '낮은' 소리 크기 또는 '높은' 소리 크기

작동

1. 재생

− Tommy의 오른쪽 귀를 건드리면 노래를 시작합니다.

2. 중지

− Tommy의 모자를 누르면 노래를 멈춥니다.

3. 조절

− 다섯 곡의 노래 중에서 선택하세요.

− Tommy의 배지를 누르면 다음 노래로 건너뜁니다.

주의사항

Tommy는 방수가 되지 않습니다. Tommy가 물에 젖지 않게 조심하세요!

Singing Tommy 사용에 관한 다음 안내문의 내용과 일치하지 않는 것은?

① 인터넷에 연결되지 않아도 노래를 재생할 수 있다. An Internet connection is not required to play the songs!

② 사용 전에 두 개의 AA 건전지를 넣어야 한다. Before use–Insert two AA batteries

③ 모자를 누르면 노래가 시작된다. Press Tommy's hat to stop the song.

④ 다섯 곡의 노래 중에 선택할 수 있다. Choose from five songs.

⑤ 방수가 되지 않는다. Tommy is not waterproof.

> **왜 정답?** [정답률 95%]

모자를 누르면 노래가 멈춘다고(Press Tommy's hat to stop the song.) 했으므로 ③은 안내문의 내용과 일치하지 않는다. 노래를 시작하려면 오른쪽 귀를 건드리라고 했다.

> **왜 오답?**

① 노래를 재생하는 데 인터넷 연결이 요구되지 않는다. (An Internet connection is not required to play the songs!)

② 사용 전에(Before use) AA 건전지 두 개를 넣으라고(Insert two AA batteries) 했다.

④ 다섯 곡의 노래 중에서 선택한다. (Choose from five songs.)

⑤ 방수가 되지 않으므로(Tommy is not waterproof.) 물에 젖지 않게 조심해야 한다.

J 18 정답 ⑤ ＊Wing Cheese Factory 견학 안내 ━━━━

Wing Cheese Factory Tour /

Wing Cheese Factory 견학 /

Attention, / all cheese lovers! //

주목해 주세요 / 모든 치즈 애호가 여러분 //

Come and experience / our historic cheese-making process / at the Wing Cheese Factory. //

오셔서 경험하세요 / 우리의 유서 깊은 치즈 제조 과정을 / Wing Cheese Factory에서 //

Look around, taste, and make! //

구경하고, 맛보고, 만드세요 //

Participation /

참가 /

- Adults: $30, / Children: $10 / (Ages 3 and under: Free) /

어른: 30달러 / 어린이: 10달러 / (3세 이하: 무료) / ①의 단서 참가비에 치즈 만들기 비용이 포함됨

- The fee includes / cheese tasting and making. //

참가 요금은 포함합니다 / 치즈 시식과 만들기를 // ②의 단서 참가 신청은 6월 30일까지

- Sign up for the tour / at www.cheesewcf.com / by June 30. //

견학을 신청하세요 / www.cheesewcf.com에서 / 6월 30일까지 // 동작이나 상태의 완료 기한을 나타내는 전치사

Tour Schedule /

견학 일정 / ③의 단서 공장의 역사에 관한 비디오를 시청함

- 10:00 a.m.: / Watch a video / about the factory's history /

오전 10시: / 비디오 시청 / 공장의 역사에 대한 /

- 10:30 a.m.: / Factory tour and cheese tasting /

오전 10시 30분: / 공장 견학과 치즈 시식 /

- 11:30 a.m.: / Cheese making /

오전 11시 30분: / 치즈 만들기 /

Note /

참고 사항 / ④의 단서 참가자는 치즈 모양의 열쇠고리를 15달러에 살 수 있음

- Participants can buy / a cheese-shaped key chain / for $15. //

참가자는 구입할 수 있습니다 / 치즈 모양의 열쇠고리를 / 15달러에 //

- No photography is allowed / inside the factory. //

사진 촬영은 허용되지 않습니다 / 공장 안에서 // ⑤의 단서 공장 안에서는 사진 촬영이 허용되지 않음

- We are closed / on Saturdays, Sundays, and holidays. //

우리는 영업하지 않습니다 / 토요일, 일요일, 그리고 공휴일에는 //

- factory ⓝ 공장 · historic ⓐ 역사적으로 중요한, 역사적인
- process ⓝ 과정, 절차 · taste ⓥ 맛보다
- participation ⓝ 참가, 참여 · fee ⓝ 요금 · include ⓥ 포함하다
- sign up for ~을 신청하다 · participant ⓝ 참가자
- allow ⓥ 허락[허용]하다 · holiday ⓝ 공휴일

Wing Cheese Factory 견학

주목해 주세요, 모든 치즈 애호가 여러분! Wing Cheese Factory에 오셔서 우리의 유서 깊은 치즈 제조 과정을 경험하세요. 구경하고, 맛보고, 만드세요!

참가

- 어른: 30달러, 어린이: 10달러 (3세 이하: 무료)
- 참가 요금에는 치즈 시식과 만들기가 포함됩니다.
- 6월 30일까지 www.cheesewcf.com에서 견학을 신청하세요.

견학 일정

- 오전 10시: 공장의 역사에 대한 비디오 시청
- 오전 10시 30분: 공장 견학과 치즈 시식
- 오전 11시 30분: 치즈 만들기

참고 사항

- 참가자는 치즈 모양의 열쇠고리를 15달러에 구입할 수 있습니다.
- 공장 안에서 사진 촬영은 허용되지 않습니다.
- 토요일, 일요일, 그리고 공휴일에는 영업하지 않습니다.

Wing Cheese Factory Tour에 관한 다음 안내문의 내용과 일치하지 <u>않는</u> 것은?

① 참가비에는 치즈 만들기 비용이 포함된다.
The fee includes cheese tasting and making.
② 참가 신청은 6월 30일까지 해야 한다.
Sign up for the tour at www.cheesewcf.com by June 30.
③ 공장의 역사에 대한 비디오를 보는 일정이 있다.
10:00 a.m.: Watch a video about the factory's history
④ 참가자는 치즈 모양의 열쇠고리를 15달러에 살 수 있다.
Participants can buy a cheese-shaped key chain for $15.
⑤ 공장 안에서 사진 촬영이 허용된다.
No photography is allowed inside the factory.

> **왜** 정답 ? [정답률 97%]

공장 안에서는 사진 촬영이 허용되지 않는다고(No photography is allowed inside the factory.) 했으므로 ⑤이 안내문과 일치하지 않는다.

> **왜** 오답 ?

① 참가 요금에는 치즈 시식과 만들기가 포함된다. (The fee includes cheese tasting and making.)
② 견학 신청은 6월 30일까지이다. (Sign up for the tour at www.cheesewcf.com by June 30.)
③ 오전 10시에 공장의 역사에 대한 비디오를 시청한다. (10:00 a.m.: Watch a video about the factory's history)
④ 참가자는 치즈 모양의 열쇠고리를 15달러에 구입할 수 있다. (Participants can buy a cheese-shaped key chain for $15.)

J 19 정답 ⑤ ＊2022 K-차 문화 프로그램 ━━━

2022 K-Tea Culture Program /
2022 K-차 문화 프로그램 /
Evergreen Tea Society invites you / to the second annual K-Tea Culture Program! //
Evergreen 차 협회는 여러분을 초대합니다 / 제2회 연례 K-차 문화 프로그램에 //
Come and enjoy / a refreshing cup of tea / and learn / about traditional Korean tea culture. //
오셔서 즐기세요 / 상쾌한 차 한 잔을 / 그리고 배우세요 / 전통적인 한국의 차 문화에 관해 //
Program Includes: /
프로그램은 포함합니다: /
1) Watching a short video / about the history of Korean tea culture / ①의 단서 한국의 차 문화 역사에 관한 짧은 영상을 시청함
짧은 영상 시청하기를 / 한국의 차 문화 역사에 관한 /
2) Observing a demonstration / of a traditional Korean tea-ceremony (*dado*) / ②의 단서 한국 전통 다도 시연을 봄
시연 보기를 / 한국 전통의 차 의식('다도')의 /
3) Participating in the ceremony / yourself /
그 의식에 참가하기를 / 직접 /
4) Tasting / a selection of teas / along with cookies / ③의 단서 쿠키와 함께 차를 맛봄
맛보기를 / 엄선된 여러 차를 / 쿠키와 함께 /
When: Saturday, September 24, 3:00 p.m. – 5:00 p.m. /
일시: 9월 24일 토요일 오후 3시 ~ 오후 5시 /
Where: Evergreen Culture Center /
장소: Evergreen 문화 센터 /
Participation Fee: $20 per person / (traditional teacup included) / ④의 단서 참가비에 전통 찻잔이 포함됨
참가비: 1인당 20달러 / (전통 찻잔이 포함됨) /
Reservations should be made online (www.egtsociety.or.kr) / at least one day before your visit. // ⑤의 단서 예약은 적어도 방문 하루 전에 해야 함
예약은 온라인(www.egtsociety.or.kr)으로 이루어져야 합니다 / 적어도 여러분의 방문 하루 전에 //

・ refreshing ⓐ 신선한, 상쾌하게 하는
・ demonstration ⓝ (제품 등의) 시연, 입증
・ selection ⓝ 선발(된 것들), 선택 ・ reservation ⓝ 예약

2022 K-차 문화 프로그램

Evergreen 차 협회는 여러분을 제2회 연례 K-차 문화 프로그램에 초대합니다!
오셔서 상쾌한 차 한 잔을 즐기면서 전통적인 한국의 차 문화에 관해 배우세요.
프로그램은 포함합니다:
1) 한국의 차 문화 역사에 관한 짧은 영상 시청하기를
2) 한국 전통의 차 의식('다도')의 시연 보기를
3) 직접 그 의식에 참가하기를
4) 엄선된 여러 차를 쿠키와 함께 맛보기를
일시: 9월 24일 토요일 오후 3시 ~ 오후 5시
장소: Evergreen 문화 센터
참가비: 1인당 20달러 (전통 찻잔이 포함됨)
예약은 적어도 방문 하루 전에 온라인(www.egtsociety.or.kr)으로 이루어져야 합니다.

2022 K-Tea Culture Program에 관한 다음 안내문의 내용과 일치하지 <u>않는</u> 것은?

① 한국의 차 문화 역사에 관한 영상을 시청한다. Watching a short video about the history of Korean tea culture
② 한국 전통 다도 시연을 본다. Observing a demonstration of a traditional Korean tea-ceremony (*dado*)
③ 쿠키와 함께 차를 맛본다. Tasting a selection of teas along with cookies
④ 참가비에는 전통 찻잔이 포함되어 있다. traditional teacup included
⑤ 예약은 방문 일주일 전까지 해야 한다. Reservations should be made ~ at least one day before your visit.

> **왜** 정답 ? [정답률 97%]

예약은 최소한 방문 하루 전에 해야 한다고(Reservations should be made ~ at least one day before your visit.) 했으므로 ⑤은 안내문과 일치하지 않는다.

> **왜** 오답 ?

① 한국의 차 문화 역사에 관한 영상을 시청한다. (Watching a short video about the history of Korean tea culture)
② 한국 전통 다도 시연을 본다. (Observing a demonstration of a traditional Korean tea-ceremony (*dado*))
③ 쿠키와 함께 차를 맛본다. (Tasting a selection of teas along with cookies)
④ 참가비에는 전통 찻잔이 포함된다. (traditional teacup included)

J 20 정답 ③ ＊Springfield 과학 발명 경연 대회 ━━━

Springfield Science Invention Contest /
Springfield 과학 발명 경연 대회 /
Springfield High School invites all students / to participate in the Springfield Science Invention Contest. // 주어 동사 목적어 목적격 보어
Springfield 고등학교는 모든 학생들을 초대합니다 / Springfield 과학 발명 경연 대회에 참가하도록 // ①의 단서 매년 개최되는 대회임
In this annual contest, / you have the opportunity / to invent a useful object / and show your creativity! // 형용사적 용법 (the opportunity 수식)
매년 개최되는 이 경연 대회에서 / 여러분은 기회를 갖습니다 / 유용한 물건을 발명하고 / 여러분의 창의성을 보여 줄 //
Details /
세부 사항 /
・ Judging criteria are creativity and usefulness / of the invention. // ②의 단서 심사 기준: 발명품의 창의성과 유용성
심사 기준은 창의성과 유용성입니다 / 발명품의 //
・ Participants must enter / in teams of four / and can only join one team. //
참가자는 참가해야 하며 / 네 명의 팀으로 / 오직 한 팀에만 참여할 수 있습니다 //
・ Submission is limited / to one invention per team. //
제출은 제한됩니다 / 한 팀당 하나의 발명품으로 // ③의 단서 한 팀당 하나의 발명품 제출
Prizes /
상품 /

④의 단서 1등 상품: 50달러 상품권

- 1st Place — $50 gift certificate /

1등 — 50달러 상품권 /

- 2nd Place — $30 gift certificate /

2등 — 30달러 상품권 /

- 3rd Place — $10 gift certificate /

3등 — 10달러 상품권 /

Note /

주의 사항 /

⑤의 단서 발명품은 과학 실험실로 제출

- Inventions must be submitted / to the science lab / by October 1, 2020. //

발명품은 제출되어야 합니다 / 과학 실험실로 / 2020년 10월 1일까지 //

For more information, / visit www.hsspringfield.edu. //

더 많은 정보를 원하시면 / www.hsspringfield.edu를 방문하십시오 //

- participate in ~에 참여[참가]하다   • annual ⓐ 매년의
- object ⓝ 물건   • creativity ⓝ 창의력, 창의성
- criterion ⓝ 기준(pl. criteria)   • submission ⓝ 제출(물)
- gift certificate 상품권   • submit ⓥ 제출하다

Springfield 과학 발명 경연 대회

Springfield 고등학교는 모든 학생들이 Springfield 과학 발명 경연 대회에 참가하도록 초대합니다. 매년 개최되는 이 경연 대회에서, 여러분은 유용한 물건을 발명하고 여러분의 창의성을 보여 줄 기회를 갖게 됩니다!

세부 사항
- 심사 기준은 발명품의 창의성과 유용성입니다.
- 참가자는 네 명이 한 팀으로 참가해야 하며 오직 한 팀에만 참여할 수 있습니다.
- (발명품) 제출은 한 팀당 하나의 발명품으로 제한됩니다.

상품
- 1등 – 50달러 상품권
- 2등 – 30달러 상품권
- 3등 – 10달러 상품권

주의 사항
- 발명품은 2020년 10월 1일까지 과학 실험실로 제출해야 합니다.

더 많은 정보를 원하시면, www.hsspringfield.edu를 방문하십시오.

Springfield Science Invention Contest에 관한 다음 안내문의 내용과 일치하지 않는 것은?

① 매년 개최되는 대회이다. this annual contest
② 심사 기준은 발명품의 창의성과 유용성이다. Judging criteria are creativity and usefulness of the invention.
③ 발명품은 한 팀당 두 개까지 제출할 수 있다. Submission is limited to one invention per team.
④ 1등은 50달러 상품권을 받는다. 1st Place — $50 gift certificate
⑤ 발명품은 과학 실험실로 제출해야 한다. Inventions must be submitted to the science lab

〉왜 정답? [정답률 97%]

발명품 제출은 한 팀당 하나로 제한된다고(Submission is limited to one invention per team.) 했으므로 ③은 안내문의 내용과 일치하지 않는다.

〉왜 오답?

① 매년 열리는 대회이다. (this annual contest)
② 심사 기준은 발명품의 창의성과 유용성이다. (Judging criteria are creativity and usefulness of the invention.)
④ 1등 상품은 50달러 상품권이다. (1st Place — $50 gift certificate)
⑤ 발명품은 과학 실험실로 제출되어야 한다. (Inventions must be submitted to the science lab)

J 21 정답 ⑤ ＊Treehouse 드라이브 인 영화의 밤

Treehouse Drive-in Movie Night /

Treehouse 드라이브 인 영화의 밤 /

Looking / for a fun night out with the family? //

찾고 있나요 / 가족과 함께 외출하는 즐거운 하룻밤을 //

Come / with your loved ones / and enjoy / our first drive-in movie night of 2021! //   **①의 단서** 2021년에 첫 번째로 열리는 행사임

오셔서 / 여러분의 사랑하는 이들과 함께 / 즐기세요 / 우리의 2021년 첫 번째 드라이브 인 영화의 밤을 //

미래 시제 수동태
All money / from ticket sales / will be donated / to the local children's hospital. //   **②의 단서** 지역 아동 병원에 기부될 것임

모든 돈은 / 티켓 판매로부터의 / 기부될 것입니다 / 지역 아동 병원에 //

Featured Film: *Dream Story* /

특집 영화: Dream Story /

Date: June 13, 2021 / 일자: 2021년 6월 13일 /

Place: Treehouse Parking Lot / 장소: Treehouse 주차장 /

Showtimes / 상영 시각 /

- First Screening: 7:30 p.m. /   **③의 단서** 첫 번째 상영은 오후 7시 30분임

첫 번째 상영: 오후 7시 30분 /

- Second Screening: 10:00 p.m. /

두 번째 상영: 오후 10시 /

Tickets: $30 per car /   **④의 단서** 티켓 가격은 자동차 한 대당 30달러임

티켓: 자동차 한 대당 30달러 /

Additional Information / 추가 정보 /

- 50 parking spots are available / (The gate opens / at 6 p.m.). //

50개의 주차 공간이 이용 가능합니다 / (문은 엽니다 / 오후 6시에) //

- Ice cream and hot dogs are sold / on site. //

아이스크림과 핫도그가 판매됩니다 / 현장에서 //   **⑤의 단서** 현장에서 아이스크림과 핫도그가 판매됨

- Make your reservation online / at www.tdimn.com. //

온라인으로 예약하세요 / www.tdimn.com에서 //

- drive-in ⓐ 자동차를 탄 채 이용할 수 있는   • donate ⓥ 기부하다
- local ⓐ 지역의, 현지의   • feature ⓥ 특별히 포함하다
- parking lot 주차장   • showtime ⓝ 상영 시간
- screening ⓝ (영화) 상영   • additional ⓐ 추가의
- spot ⓝ (특정한) 곳[자리]   • available ⓐ 이용할 수 있는
- on site 현장에서, 현지에서   • reservation ⓝ 예약

Treehouse 드라이브 인 영화의 밤

가족과 함께 외출하는 즐거운 하룻밤을 찾고 있나요? 여러분의 사랑하는 이들과 함께 오셔서 우리의 2021년 첫 번째 드라이브 인 영화의 밤을 즐기세요! 티켓 판매에서 오는 모든 돈은 지역 아동 병원에 기부될 것입니다.

특집 영화: Dream Story
일자: 2021년 6월 13일
장소: Treehouse 주차장
상영 시각
- 첫 번째 상영: 오후 7시 30분
- 두 번째 상영: 오후 10시
티켓: 자동차 한 대당 30달러
추가 정보
- 50개의 주차 공간이 이용 가능합니다(문은 오후 6시에 엽니다).
- 아이스크림과 핫도그가 현장에서 판매됩니다.
- www.tdimn.com에서 온라인으로 예약하세요.

Treehouse Drive-in Movie Night에 관한 다음 안내문의 내용과 일치하는 것은?

① 2021년에 두 번째로 열리는 행사이다. our first drive-in movie night of 2021
② 티켓 판매 수입금 전액은 어린이 도서관에 기부될 것이다. to the local children's hospital
③ 첫 번째 상영 시작 시간은 오후 10시이다. First Screening: 7:30 p.m.
④ 티켓 가격은 자동차 한 대당 50달러이다. Tickets: $30 per car
⑤ 아이스크림과 핫도그가 현장에서 판매된다. Ice cream and hot dogs are sold on site.

>왜 정답? [정답률 96%]

현장에서 아이스크림과 핫도그가 판매된다고(Ice cream and hot dogs are sold on site.) 했으므로 ⑤가 안내문과 일치한다.

>왜 오답?

① 2021년의 첫 번째 드라이브 인 영화의 밤 행사이다. (our first drive-in movie night of 2021)

② 티켓 판매 수익금 전액은 지역 아동 병원에 기부될 것이다. (to the local children's hospital)

③ 첫 번째 상영은 오후 7시 30분이다. (First Screening: 7:30 p.m.)

④ 티켓은 자동차 한 대당 30달러이다. (Tickets: $30 per car)

J 22 정답 ② *2021년 씽씽 자동차 그리기 대회

2021 Whir Car Drawing Contest for Kids /
2021년 어린이들을 위한 씽씽 자동차 그리기 대회 /

Theme: Family /
주제: 가족 /

Does your child love cars? //
여러분의 자녀는 자동차를 좋아하나요 // *to think and draw의 의미상 주어*

Take this opportunity / for your child to think / about what they love / and draw it. // *형용사적 용법(opportunity 수식)*
이번 기회를 잡으세요 / 여러분의 자녀가 생각하고 / 자신이 아주 좋아하는 것에 관해 / 그리고 그것을 그리는 //

will enjoy와 learn from의 목적어
They will definitely enjoy / and learn from this contest! //
그들은 틀림없이 (이 대회를) 즐기고 / 이 대회로부터 배울 것입니다 //

Details /
세부 사항 / **①의 단서** 10개의 출품작이 선정되며 각각 50달러의 상품권이 수여됨

• **Ten entries are chosen, / and each is awarded a $50 gift certificate.** //
10개의 출품작이 선정되며 / 각각은 50달러의 상품권이 수여됩니다 //

• **Drawing skills are not considered / in judging.** //
그림 기술은 고려되지 않습니다 / 심사에서 // **②의 단서** 심사에서 그림 기술은 고려되지 않음

Submission /
제출 /

• **Take a photo / of your child's drawing.** //
사진으로 찍으십시오 / 여러분 자녀의 그림을 //

• **Visit our website (www.whircar4kids.com) / and upload the photo / by October 3.** // **③의 단서** 자녀의 그림을 찍어 웹사이트에 업로드해야 함
저희 웹사이트(www.whircar4kids.com)를 방문하여 / 사진을 업로드하십시오 / 10월 3일까지 //

Note /
참고 사항 / **④의 단서** 그림에는 가족과 자동차가 포함되어야 함

• **The drawing should contain / your family and a car.** //
그림은 포함해야 합니다 / 여러분의 가족과 자동차를 //

• **Participants must be 3 to 7 years old.** //
참가자는 3세에서 7세까지여야 합니다 // **⑤의 단서** 참가자는 3세에서 7세까지여야 함

Please visit our website / to learn more. //
저희 웹사이트를 방문하십시오 / 더 많은 것을 아시려면 //

• whir ⓝ 씽씽 하는 소리 • theme ⓝ 주제, 테마
• definitely ⓐⓓ 틀림없이, 분명히 • entry ⓝ 출품작, 출전, 참가
• gift certificate 상품권 • judging ⓝ 심사
• submission ⓝ (서류 등의) 제출, 항복
• contain ⓥ 포함하다, ~이 들어 있다 • participant ⓝ 참가자

2021년 어린이들을 위한 씽씽 자동차 그리기 대회

주제: 가족

여러분의 자녀는 자동차를 좋아하나요? 여러분의 자녀가 자신이 아주 좋아하는 것에 관해 생각하고 그것을 그리는 이번 기회를 잡으세요. 그들은 틀림없이 이 대회를 즐기고 그것으로부터 배울 것입니다!

세부 사항

• 10개의 출품작이 선정되며, 각각 50달러의 상품권이 수여됩니다.
• 그림 기술은 심사에서 고려되지 않습니다.

제출

• 여러분 자녀의 그림을 사진으로 찍으십시오.
• 저희 웹사이트(www.whircar4kids.com)를 방문하여 10월 3일까지 사진을 업로드하십시오.

참고 사항

• 그림에 여러분의 가족과 자동차가 포함되어야 합니다.
• 참가자는 3세에서 7세까지여야 합니다.

더 많은 것을 아시려면 저희 웹사이트를 방문하십시오.

2021 Whir Car Drawing Contest for Kids에 관한 다음 안내문의 내용과 일치하지 않는 것은?

① 출품작 중 10개를 선정해서 시상한다. Ten entries are chosen, and each is awarded a $50 gift certificate.

② 그림 기술이 심사에서 고려된다. Drawing skills are not considered in judging.

③ 그림을 찍은 사진을 웹사이트에 업로드해야 한다. Take a photo of your child's drawing. ~ and upload the photo

④ 그림은 가족과 차를 포함해야 한다. The drawing should contain your family and a car.

⑤ 참가자의 나이는 3세에서 7세까지로 제한된다. Participants must be 3 to 7 years old.

>왜 정답? [정답률 97%]

그림 기술은 심사에서 고려되지 않는다고(Drawing skills are not considered in judging.) 했으므로 ②은 안내문과 일치하지 않는다.

>왜 오답?

① 10개의 출품작이 선정되며 각각 50달러의 상품권이 수여된다. (Ten entries are chosen, and each is awarded a $50 gift certificate.)

③ 자녀의 그림을 사진 찍어서 웹사이트에 업로드하라고 했다. (Take a photo of your child's drawing. ~ and upload the photo)

④ 그림에는 가족과 자동차가 포함되어야 한다. (The drawing should contain your family and a car.)

⑤ 참가자는 3세에서 7세까지여야 한다. (Participants must be 3 to 7 years old.)

J 23 정답 ③ *Goldbeach SeaWorld 하룻밤 행사

Goldbeach SeaWorld Sleepovers /
Goldbeach SeaWorld 하룻밤 행사 /

Do your children love / marine animals? //
여러분의 자녀는 좋아하나요 / 해양 동물들을 //

A sleepover at Goldbeach SeaWorld / will surely be an exciting overnight experience / for them. //
Goldbeach SeaWorld에서의 하룻밤 행사는 / 분명히 신나는 하룻밤 동안의 경험이 될 것입니다 / 그들에게 //

Join us / for a magical underwater sleepover. //
우리와 함께하십시오 / 환상적인 수중 하룻밤 행사를 //

Participants /
참가자 / **①의 단서** 8세에서 12세 아이들이 대상임

- **Children ages 8 to 12** /
8세~12세의 아동 / *조동사가 포함된 수동태: 조동사+be p.p.*

- **Children must be accompanied / by a guardian.** //
아동은 동반되어야 합니다 / 보호자에 의해 // **②의 단서** 토요일 오후 5시부터 일요일 오전 10시까지임

When: / Saturdays 5 p.m. / to Sundays 10 a.m. / in May, 2022 /
일시: / 매주 토요일 오후 5시부터 / 매주 일요일 오전 10시까지 / 2022년 5월에 //

Activities: / guided tour, underwater show, and photo session with a mermaid /
활동: / 가이드 투어, 수중 쇼, 인어와 사진 찍는 시간 /

Participation Fee /
참가비 /

- $50 per person / (dinner and breakfast included) /
③의 단서 참가비에 아침 식사가 포함됨
1인당 50달러 / (저녁 식사 및 아침 식사 포함) /
Note /
참고 사항 /
- Sleeping bags and other personal items / will not be provided. //
미래 시제 수동태의 부정
침낭 및 기타 개인용품은 / 제공되지 않을 것입니다 //
④의 단서 모든 활동이 실내에서 진행됨
- All activities / take place indoors. //
모든 활동은 / 실내에서 이루어집니다 //
동명사구 주어   단수 동사
⑤의 단서 밤 10시부터 아침 7시까지는 사진 촬영이 허용되지 않음
- Taking photos is not allowed / from 10 p.m. to 7 a.m. /
사진 촬영이 허용되지 않습니다 / 오후 10시부터 오전 7시까지는 //

For more information, / you can visit our website at www.goldbeachseaworld.com. //
더 많은 정보를 원하시면 / 우리 웹사이트 www.goldbeachseaworld.com을 방문하실 수 있습니다 //

- sleepover ⓝ (아이들이나 청소년들이 한 집에 모여) 함께 자며 놀기, 밤샘 파티
- marine ⓐ 해양의, 바다의   • surely ⓐⓓ 분명히, 틀림없이
- overnight ⓐ 하룻밤 동안의   • underwater ⓐ 수중의
- accompany ⓥ 동반하다, 동행하다   • guardian ⓝ 보호자
- session ⓝ (특정한 활동을 위한) 시간[기간]   • mermaid ⓝ 인어
- indoors ⓐⓓ 실내에서

Goldbeach SeaWorld 하룻밤 행사
여러분의 자녀는 해양 동물들을 좋아하나요? Goldbeach SeaWorld에서의 하룻밤 행사는 그들에게 분명히 신나는 하룻밤 동안의 경험이 될 것입니다. 환상적인 수중 하룻밤 행사를 우리와 함께하십시오.
참가자
− 8세~12세의 아동
− 아동은 보호자를 동반하여야 합니다.
일시: 2022년 5월 매주 토요일 오후 5시부터 일요일 오전 10시까지
활동: 가이드 투어, 수중 쇼, 인어와 사진 찍는 시간
참가비
1인당 50달러(저녁 식사 및 아침 식사 포함)
참고 사항
− 침낭 및 기타 개인용품은 제공되지 않을 것입니다.
− 모든 활동은 실내에서 이루어집니다.
− 오후 10시부터 오전 7시까지는 사진 촬영이 허용되지 않습니다.
더 많은 정보를 원하시면 우리 웹사이트 www.goldbeachseaworld.com을 방문하실 수 있습니다.

Goldbeach SeaWorld Sleepovers에 관한 다음 안내문의 내용과 일치하는 것은?
① 7세 이하의 어린이가 참가할 수 있다. Children ages 8 to 12
② 평일에 진행된다. Saturdays 5 p.m. to Sundays 10 a.m.
③ 참가비에 아침 식사가 포함된다. dinner and breakfast included
④ 모든 활동은 야외에서 진행된다. All activities take place indoors.
⑤ 사진 촬영은 언제든지 할 수 있다. Taking photos is not allowed from 10 p.m. to 7 a.m.

왜 정답? [정답률 96%]
참가비는 한 사람당 50달러인데 저녁 식사와 아침 식사가 포함된다고(dinner and breakfast included) 했으므로 ③이 안내문과 일치한다.

왜 오답?
① 8세에서 12세 아이들이 대상이다. (Children ages 8 to 12)
② 토요일 오후 5시부터 일요일 오전 10시까지 진행된다. (Saturdays 5 p.m. to Sundays 10 a.m.)
④ 모든 활동은 실내에서 진행된다. (All activities take place indoors.)
⑤ 밤 10시부터 아침 7시까지는 사진 촬영이 허용되지 않는다. (Taking photos is not allowed from 10 p.m. to 7 a.m.)

J 24 정답 ③ * 2023 Cierra 농구 주간 캠프

2023 Cierra Basketball Day Camp /
2023 Cierra 농구 주간 캠프 /
Cierra Basketball Day Camp provides opportunities / for teens
형용사적 용법(opportunities 수식)
to get 의 의미상 주어
to get healthy and have fun. //
Cierra 농구 주간 캠프는 기회를 제공합니다 / 십 대들이 건강해지고 즐길 //
Come and learn a variety of skills / from the experts! //
오셔서 다양한 기술을 배우세요 / 전문가들로부터 //   ①의 단서 전문가들로부터 다양한 기술을 배움
Site & Dates /
장소 & 일자 /
• Cierra Sports Center /
Cierra 스포츠 센터 /
• July 17th – July 21st /
7월 17일~7월 21일 /
Ages & Level: 13 – 18 years, for beginners only /
연령 및 수준: 13~18세, 초보자만을 대상으로 함 /   ②의 단서 초보자만을 대상으로 함
Camp Activities /
캠프 활동 /
• Skill Drills: 1:00 p.m. – 2:00 p.m. /
기술 연습: 오후 1시~오후 2시 /
• Team Games: 2:30 p.m. – 3:30 p.m. /
팀 경기: 오후 2시 30분~오후 3시 30분 /   ③의 단서 팀 경기는 오후 2시 30분에 시작함
• Free Throw Shooting Contests: 4:00 p.m. – 5:00 p.m. /
자유투 슈팅 대회: 오후 4시~오후 5시 /
Registration & Cost /
등록 & 비용 /
④의 단서 온라인으로 등록함
• Register online / at www.crrbbcamp.com. //
온라인 등록하세요 / www.crrbbcamp.com에서 //
• $40 (Full payment is required / when registering. //)
40달러(완불하셔야 합니다 / 등록 시 //)
미래 시제 수동태
※ A towel will be provided / for free. // ⑤의 단서 수건이 무료로 제공됨
※ 수건이 제공될 것입니다 / 무료로 //

• provide ⓥ 제공하다   • opportunity ⓝ 기회
• variety of 형형색색의, 다양한   • expert ⓝ 전문가
• registration ⓝ 등록

2023 Cierra 농구 주간 캠프
Cierra 농구 주간 캠프는 십 대들이 건강해지고 즐길 기회를 제공합니다.
오셔서 전문가들로부터 다양한 기술을 배우세요!
장소 & 일자
• Cierra 스포츠 센터
• 7월 17일~7월 21일
연령 및 수준: 13~18세, 초보자만을 대상으로 함
캠프 활동
• 기술 연습: 오후 1시~오후 2시
• 팀 경기: 오후 2시 30분~오후 3시 30분
• 자유투 슈팅 대회: 오후 4시~오후 5시
등록 & 비용
• www.crrbbcamp.com에서 온라인 등록하세요.
• 40달러(등록 시 완불하셔야 합니다.)
※ 수건이 무료로 제공될 것입니다.

2023 Cierra Basketball Day Camp에 관한 다음 안내문의 내용과 일치하지 않는 것은?
① 전문가들로부터 다양한 기술을 배울 수 있다. Come and learn a variety of skills from the experts!
② 초급자만을 대상으로 한다. for beginners only
③ 팀 경기는 오후 1시에 시작한다. Team Games: 2:30 p.m. – 3:30 p.m.
④ 온라인으로 등록할 수 있다. Register online
⑤ 수건이 무료로 제공될 것이다. A towel will be provided for free.

> **왜 정답?** [정답률 97%]

③ 팀 경기는 오후 2시 30분에 시작한다. (Team Games: 2:30 p.m. — 3:30 p.m.)

> **왜 오답?**

① 와서 전문가들로부터 다양한 기술을 배우라고 했다. (Come and learn a variety of skills from the experts!)

② 초급자만을 대상으로 한다. (for beginners only)

④ 온라인으로 등록하라고 했다. (Register online)

⑤ 수건이 무료로 제공될 것이다. (A towel will be provided for free.)

J 25 정답 ⑤ ＊2020 범죄와 탐정 과학 워크숍

2020 Crime & Spy Science Workshop /
2020 범죄와 탐정 과학 워크숍 /

Come learn / to be a top detective! //
와서 배우세요 / 최고의 탐정이 되는 것을 //

병렬 구조

In this workshop, / you will investigate crime scenes / and learn
to부정사가 병렬 구조를 이룰 때 뒤에 오는 to부정사의 to는 흔히 생략됨
skills / necessary / to become a detective / and solve mysteries! //
이 워크숍에서 / 여러분은 범죄 현장을 조사하고 / 기술을 배울 것입니다 / 필요한 / 탐정이 되어 / 미스터리를 해결하는 데 //

When & Where /
일시와 장소 / **①의 단서** 2020년 8월 18일에 진행됨

• 9 a.m. to 3 p.m. / on Tuesday, August 18, 2020 /
오전 9시부터 오후 3시 / 2020년 8월 18일 화요일 /

• Conference Room #103, ZBU Student Union /
ZBU 학생회관 회의실 103호 /

Who: Ages 14 and up /
대상: 14세 이상 / **②의 단서** 참가비에 보험이 포함되지 않음

Participation Fee: $20 / (insurance not included) /
참가비: 20달러 / (보험은 포함되어 있지 않음) /

Registration /
등록 / **③의 단서** 등록은 전화나 이메일로 함

• Call 555-540-0421, or email spyscience@zbu.edu /
by Wednesday, July 29, 2020. //
555-540-0421로 전화하시거나 spyscience@zbu.edu로 이메일을 보내세요 / 2020년 7월 29일 수요일까지 //

Preparations /
준비 /
형용사적 용법(a bag 수식)＊
• Bring comfortable shoes and a bag / to carry detective tools. //
편한 신발과 가방을 가져오세요 / 탐정 도구를 갖고 다닐 //

• Lunch and snacks are provided. //
점심과 간식은 제공됩니다 // **④의 단서** 점심과 간식이 제공됨

You will learn /
여러분은 배울 것입니다 /

• how to find / traces of suspects. //
찾는 방법을 / 용의자의 흔적을 //

• how to manage / the scene of a crime. //
관리하는 방법을 / 범죄 현장을 //

• how to choose / the right tools. //
선택하는 방법을 / 적절한 도구를 // **⑤의 단서** 적절한 도구를 선택하는 방법을 배움

• detective ⓝ 탐정   • investigate ⓥ 조사하다
• scene ⓝ 현장, 장면   • necessary ⓐ 필요한, 필연적인
• conference ⓝ 회의, 학회   • insurance ⓝ 보험   • trace ⓝ 흔적
• suspect ⓝ 용의자   • right ⓐ 적절한, 적당한

2020 범죄와 탐정 과학 워크숍
와서 최고의 탐정이 되는 것을 배우세요! 이 워크숍에서 여러분은 범죄 현장을 조사하고 탐정이 되어 미스터리를 해결하는 데 필요한 기술을 배울 것입니다!
일시와 장소
•2020년 8월 18일 화요일 오전 9시부터 오후 3시
•ZBU 학생회관 회의실 103호

대상: 14세 이상
참가비: 20달러 (보험은 포함되어 있지 않음)
등록
•2020년 7월 29일 수요일까지 555-540-0421로 전화하시거나 spyscience@zbu.edu로 이메일을 보내세요.
준비
•편한 신발과 탐정 도구를 갖고 다닐 가방을 가져오세요.
•점심과 간식은 제공됩니다.
배울 내용
•용의자의 흔적을 찾는 방법
•범죄 현장을 관리하는 방법
•적절한 도구를 선택하는 방법

2020 Crime & Spy Science Workshop에 관한 다음 안내문의 내용과 일치하는 것은?

① 이틀 동안 진행된다. 9 a.m. to 3 p.m. on Tuesday, August 18, 2020

② 참가비에 보험이 포함되어 있다. Participation Fee: $20 (insurance not included)

③ 등록은 이메일로만 할 수 있다. Call 555-540-0421, or email spyscience@zbu.edu

④ 점심과 간식은 제공되지 않는다. Lunch and snacks are provided.

⑤ 적절한 도구를 선택하는 방법을 배울 것이다. how to choose the right tools

> **왜 정답?** [정답률 94%]

배울 내용에 적절한 도구를 선택하는 방법(how to choose the right tools)도 포함되어 있으므로 ⑤가 이 안내문의 내용과 일치한다.

> **왜 오답?**

① 2020년 8월 18일 오전 9시부터 오후 3시까지, 하루 동안 진행된다. (9 a.m. to 3 p.m. on Tuesday, August 18, 2020)

② 참가비에는 보험이 포함되지 않는다. (Participation Fee: $20 (insurance not included))

③ 등록은 전화나 이메일로 가능하다. (Call 555-540-0421, or email spyscience@zbu.edu)

④ 점심과 간식이 제공된다. (Lunch and snacks are provided.)

─── 어법 특강 ───

＊ 형용사적 용법의 to부정사
– 형용사적 용법의 to부정사는 명사나 대명사를 뒤에서 수식할 수 있다.
• I need someone to help me.
(나는 나를 도와줄 누군가가 필요하다.)
• Please give me something to sit on.
(제게 앉을 만한 것을 좀 주세요.)
• Eric has a lot of things to do.
(Eric은 해야 할 많은 일들이 있다.)

J 26 정답 ④ ＊Cornhill 종이컵 사용 않기 챌린지

Cornhill No Paper Cup Challenge /
Cornhill 종이컵 사용 않기 챌린지 /
주어   동사   목적어 목적격 보어
Cornhill High School invites you / to join the "No Paper Cup Challenge." //
Cornhill 고등학교는 여러분을 초대합니다 / '종이컵 사용 않기 챌린지'에 참여하도록 //
주어   동사   목적어 목적격 보어
This encourages you / to reduce your use of paper cups. //
이 행사는 여러분을 권장합니다 / 여러분의 종이컵 사용을 줄이도록 //

Let's save the earth together! //
함께 지구를 구합시다 //

How to Participate /
참여 방법 / **①의 단서** 텀블러를 사용하는 자신의 동영상을 촬영함
전치사
1) After being chosen, / record a video / showing you are using
a tumbler. // 동명사구
선택된 후에 / 동영상을 녹화하십시오 / 여러분이 텀블러를 사용하고 있는 것을 보여주는 //

2) Choose the next participant / by saying his or her name / in the video. //
②의 단서 동영상을 학교 웹사이트에 업로드함
다음 참가자를 선택하십시오 / 그 사람의 이름을 말하여 / 동영상에서 //

3) Upload the video / to our school website / within 24 hours. //
동영상을 업로드하십시오 / 우리 학교 웹사이트에 / 24시간 이내에 //

※ The student council president will start the challenge / on December 1st, 2021. // ③의 단서 학생회장이 챌린지를 시작할 것임
학생회장이 챌린지를 시작할 것입니다 / 2021년 12월 1일에 //

Additional Information /
추가 정보 /
④의 단서 챌린지는 2주 동안 진행될 것임
• The challenge will last / for two weeks. //
챌린지는 계속될 것입니다 / 2주 동안 //

• All participants will receive T-shirts. //
모든 참가자는 티셔츠를 받을 것입니다 // ⑤의 단서 모든 참가자가 티셔츠를 받을 것임

If you have questions about the challenge, / contact us at cornhillsc@chs.edu. //
챌린지에 관한 질문이 있다면 / cornhillsc@chs.edu로 저희에게 연락하십시오 //

• encourage ⓥ 권장하다, 고무하다   • reduce ⓥ 줄이다
• participate ⓥ 참가하다, 참여하다   • participant ⓝ 참가자
• additional ⓐ 추가의

Cornhill 종이컵 사용 않기 챌린지
Cornhill 고등학교는 '종이컵 사용 않기 챌린지'에 여러분을 초대합니다. 이 행사는 여러분이 종이컵의 사용을 줄이도록 권장합니다. 함께 지구를 구합시다!
참여 방법
1) 선택된 후에, 여러분이 텀블러를 사용하고 있는 것을 보여주는 동영상을 녹화하십시오.
2) 동영상에서 그 사람의 이름을 말하여 다음 참가자를 선택하십시오.
3) 24시간 이내에 우리 학교 웹사이트에 동영상을 업로드하십시오.
※ 학생회장이 2021년 12월 1일에 챌린지를 시작할 것입니다.
추가 정보
• 챌린지는 2주 동안 진행될 것입니다.
• 모든 참가자는 티셔츠를 받을 것입니다.
챌린지에 관한 질문이 있다면 cornhillsc@chs.edu로 저희에게 연락하십시오.

Cornhill No Paper Cup Challenge에 관한 다음 안내문의 내용과 일치하지 않는 것은?
① 참가자는 텀블러를 사용하는 자신의 동영상을 찍는다. record a video showing you are using a tumbler
② 참가자가 동영상을 업로드할 곳은 학교 웹사이트이다. Upload the video to our school website
③ 학생회장이 시작할 것이다. The student council president will start the challenge
④ 두 달 동안 진행될 예정이다. The challenge will last for two weeks.
⑤ 참가자 전원이 티셔츠를 받을 것이다. All participants will receive T-shirts.

> 왜 정답? [정답률 93%]
두 달이 아니라 2주 동안(for two seeks) 진행되는 것이므로 ④은 안내문과 일치하지 않는다.

> 왜 오답?
① 텀블러를 사용하는 자신의 동영상을 찍으라고 했다. (record a video showing you are using a tumbler)
② 동영상을 학교 웹사이트에 업로드하라고 했다. (Upload the video to our school website)
③ 학생회장이 시작할 것이다. (The student council president will start the challenge)
⑤ 모든 참가자가 티셔츠를 받을 것이다. (All participants will receive T-shirts.)

J 27 정답 ④   *2023 Greenfield City Run

2023 Greenfield City Run /
2023 Greenfield City Run /

Are you eager for the race / that can awaken the running spirit within you? //
선행사   주격 관계대명사
여러분은 경주를 열망하나요 / 여러분 안에 있는 달리기에 대한 열정을 깨울 수 있는 //

Maybe the Greenfield City Run is best / for you. //
아마 Greenfield City Run이 가장 좋을 거예요 / 여러분에게 //

• **When**: Sunday, November 5 /
일시: 11월 5일 일요일 /

– Assembly time is 9:00 a.m. // ①의 단서 집합 시간: 오전 9시
집합 시간은 오전 9시입니다 //

– Start time is 9:30 a.m. //
시작 시간은 오전 9시 30분입니다 //

• **Where**: Riverside Park /
장소: Riverside 공원 /

②의 단서 2km 종목은 아이들만 참가
• **Races**: 2km, 5km, 10km (The 2km race is only for kids.) //
경주 목록: 2 km, 5 km, 10 km (2 km 경주는 아이들만 참가 가능합니다) //

• **Registration /**
등록 /
주어   동사   시간의 부사구
– Registration starts / on October 16. //
등록은 시작합니다 / 10월 16일에 // ③의 단서 등록: 10월 16일에 시작함

– The registration fees depend on the date / you sign up. //
등록비는 날짜에 따라 다릅니다 / 여러분이 등록한 // ④의 단서 등록비: 등록 날짜에 따라 다름

$30: October 16 – November 4 / $40: November 5 /
30달러: 10월 16일 – 11월 4일 / 40달러: 11월 5일 /

– Register online / at www.finishrace.com. //
온라인으로 등록하세요 / www.finishrace.com에서 //

• **Activities /**
활동 /

– Coffee and Cookie Fair & Outdoor Charity Bazaar /
커피와 쿠키 박람회 & 야외 자선 바자회 // ⑤의 단서 야외 자선 바자회가 있음

For more information, / call (516) 703–1737. //
더 많은 정보를 원하시면 / (516) 703–1737로 전화 주세요 //

• eager ⓥ 열망하다   • awaken ⓥ 깨우다
• charity bazaar 자선 바자회

2023 Greenfield City Run
여러분 안에 있는 달리기에 대한 열정을 깨울 수 있는 경주에 대한 열망이 있나요? 아마 Greenfield City Run이 여러분에게 가장 좋을 거예요.
• 일시: 11월 5일 일요일
– 집합 시간은 오전 9시입니다.
– 시작 시간은 오전 9시 30분입니다.
• 장소: Riverside 공원
• 경주 목록: 2 km, 5 km, 10 km (2 km 경주는 아이들만 참가 가능합니다.)
• 등록
– 등록은 10월 16일부터 시작합니다.
– 등록비는 여러분이 서명한 날짜에 따라 다릅니다.
30달러: 10월 16일 – 11월 4일 / 40달러: 11월 5일
– www.finishrace.com에서 온라인으로 등록하세요.
• 활동
커피와 쿠키 박람회 & 야외 자선 바자회
더 많은 정보를 원하시면, (516) 703–1737로 전화 주세요.

2023 Greenfield City Run에 관한 다음 안내문의 내용과 일치하지 않는 것은?
① 집합 시간은 오전 9시이다. Assembly time is 9:00 a.m.
② 2km 종목은 아이들만 참가할 수 있다. The 2km race is only for kids.
③ 등록은 10월 16일부터 시작된다. Registration starts on October 16.
④ 날짜와 상관없이 등록비는 동일하다. The registration fees depend on the date you sign up.
⑤ 야외 자선 바자회가 있다. Outdoor Charity Bazaar

>왜 정답 ? [정답률 98%]

④ 등록한 날짜에 따라 등록비는 다르다. (The registration fees depend on the date you sign up.)

>왜 오답 ?

① 집합 시간은 오전 9시이다. (Assembly time is 9:00 a.m.)
② 2km 종목은 아이들만 참가할 수 있다. (The 2km race is only for kids.)
③ 등록은 10월 16일부터 시작된다. (Registration starts on October 16.)
⑤ 야외 자선 바자회가 있다. (Outdoor Charity Bazaar)

J 28 정답 ② * 보수 공사 공지

Renovation Notice /
보수 공사 공지 /

★ **형용사 vs. 부사**
형용사는 명사를 수식하고, 부사는 명사 외에 형용사, 동사, 부사를 수식한다.
동사에서 파생한 준동사 역시 부사의 수식을 받는다.

At the Natural Jade Resort, /
Natural Jade 리조트에서 /

현재진행형 동사 are improving을 수식하는 부사

we are continually improving our facilities / to better serve our guests. //
우리는 계속해서 시설을 개선하고 있습니다 / 투숙객들에게 더 나은 서비스를 제공하기 위해 //

미래진행 시제
Therefore, we will be renovating / some areas of the resort, / according to the schedule below. //
그래서 우리는 보수 공사를 하려고 합니다 / 리조트의 몇몇 구역을 / 아래 일정에 따라 //

Renovation Period: / November 21 to December 18, 2022 /
보수 공사 기간: / 2022년 11월 21일부터 12월 18일까지 / ①의 단서 2022년 11월 21일부터임

• Renovations will take place / every day / from 9:00 a.m. to 5:00 p.m. / ②의 단서 보수 공사는 매일 진행될 것임
보수 공사는 진행됩니다 / 매일 / 오전 9시부터 오후 5시까지 //

Areas to be Closed: / Gym and indoor swimming pool /
폐쇄될 구역: / 체육관과 실내 수영장 / ③의 단서 폐쇄될 구역은 체육관과 수영장

Further Information /
추가정보 / ④의 단서 모든 야외 레저 활동은 평소와 같이 가능할 것임

• All outdoor leisure activities / will be available / as usual. //
모든 야외 여가 활동은 / 이용 가능할 것입니다 / 평소와 같이 //

• Guests will receive a 15% discount / for all meals in the restaurant. //
투숙객들은 15퍼센트의 할인을 받을 것입니다 / 식당의 모든 식사에 대해 //

• Guests may use the tennis courts / for free. // ⑥의 단서 손님은 테니스장을 무료로 이용할 수 있음
투숙객들은 테니스장을 이용할 수 있습니다 / 무료로 //

We will take all possible measures / to minimize / noise and any other inconvenience. //
부사적 용법(목적)
저희는 가능한 모든 조치를 취할 것입니다 / 최소화하기 위해 / 소음과 다른 불편함을 //

We sincerely appreciate your understanding. //
이해해 주셔서 진심으로 감사드립니다 //

- renovation ⓝ 보수, 개조   - minimize ⓥ 최소화하다
- inconvenience ⓝ 불편(함)   - sincerely ⓐⓓ 진심으로
- appreciate ⓥ 고마워하다

보수 공사 공지

Natural Jade 리조트는 투숙객들에게 더 나은 서비스를 제공하기 위해 계속해서 시설을 개선하고 있습니다. 그래서 우리는 아래 일정에 따라 리조트의 몇몇 구역을 보수 공사를 하려고 합니다.

보수 공사 기간: 2022년 11월 21일부터 12월 18일까지
• 보수 공사는 매일 오전 9시부터 오후 5시까지 진행됩니다.
폐쇄될 구역: 체육관과 실내 수영장
추가정보
• 모든 야외 여가 활동은 평소와 같이 이용 가능할 것입니다.
• 투숙객들은 식당의 모든 식사에 대해 15퍼센트의 할인을 받을 것입니다.
• 투숙객들은 테니스장을 무료로 이용할 수 있습니다.
저희는 소음과 다른 불편함을 최소화하기 위해 가능한 모든 조치를 취할 것입니다.
이해해 주셔서 진심으로 감사드립니다.

다음 Renovation Notice의 내용과 일치하지 않는 것은?

① 보수 공사는 2022년 11월 21일에 시작된다. November 21 to December 18, 2022
② 보수 공사는 주말에만 진행될 것이다. Renovations will take place every day
③ 체육관과 실내 수영장은 폐쇄될 것이다. Areas to be Closed: Gym and indoor swimming pool
④ 모든 야외 레저 활동은 평소와 같이 가능할 것이다. All outdoor leisure activities will be available as usual.
⑤ 손님은 무료로 테니스장을 이용할 수 있다. Guests may use the tennis courts for free.

>왜 정답 ? [정답률 97%]

보수 공사는 매일 진행될 것이라고(Renovations will take place every day) 했으므로 ②은 안내문과 일치하지 않는다.

>왜 오답 ?

① 보수 공사는 2022년 11월 21일부터 12월 18일까지이다. (November 21 to December 18, 2022)
③ 체육관과 실내 수영장은 폐쇄될 것이다. (Areas to be Closed: Gym and indoor swimming pool)
④ 모든 야외 레저 활동은 평소와 같이 가능할 것이다. (All outdoor leisure activities will be available as usual.)
⑤ 손님은 무료로 테니스장을 이용할 수 있다. (Guests may use the tennis courts for free.)

권주원 | 서울대 정치외교학부 2023년 입학·서울 배재고 졸

실용문 일치/불일치 유형은 빠르게 푸는 것이 중요해! 수능에서 나는 이 문제를 빨리 풀기 위해 지시문보다 선택지를 먼저 확인했어. 일치하지 않는 것을 고르는 것이기 때문에 먼저 나는 선택지에서 '모든 ~' 혹은 '-만'처럼 예외의 형태로 부정되기 쉬운 표현을 찾았어.
이 문제에서는 ②과 ④에 '주말에만', '모든 야외 레저 활동'이 등장하는데, 순서대로 안내문에서 관련된 내용을 찾아 확인했어. 그리고 정답이 ②임을 곧바로 확인할 수 있었지. 이런 접근법을 사용하면 시간을 크게 아낄 수 있어.

J 29 정답 ③ * 시 창작 기초 워크숍

Poetry Writing Basics Workshop /
시 창작 기초 워크숍 /
병렬 구조 *
Join our Poetry Writing Basics Workshop / and meet the poet, Ms. Grace Larson! //
저희의 시 창작 기초 워크숍에 참여하여 / 시인 Grace Larson 씨를 만나십시오 //

All students of George Clarkson University / are invited. //
George Clarkson 대학교의 모든 학생들이 / 초대됩니다 // ①의 단서 오후에 진행됨

When: / Thursday, September 24, 2020 (1:00 p.m. — 4:00 p.m.) /
언제 / 2020년 9월 24일 목요일 (오후 1시 ~ 오후 4시) /

Where: / Main Seminar Room, 1st Floor, Student Union /
어디서 / 학생회관 1층 메인 세미나실 / ②의 단서 1층에서 열림

After an introduction / to the basic techniques of poetry writing, / you will: /
소개 후에 / 시 창작의 기초 기법에 대한 / 여러분은 ~할 것입니다 /

1. Write your own poem. //
여러분 자신의 시를 창작할 // ③의 단서 자신의 시를 창작하여 낭독할 것임

2. Read it aloud / to the other participants. //
그것을 큰 소리로 읽을 / 다른 참가자들에게 //

3. Receive expert feedback / from Ms. Larson. //
전문가의 피드백을 받을 / Larson 씨로부터 //

Registration Fee: $10 /
등록비: 10달러 /

전치사의 병렬 구조 ※ ④의 단서 18일까지 등록하면 7달러임

※ Register on or before September 18 / and pay only $7. //
9월 18일이나 그 전에 등록하시고 / 7달러만 내십시오 //

Any related inquiries should be sent / via email / to studentun@georgeclarkson.edu. // ⑤의 단서 모든 문의는 이메일을 통해 해야 함
관련된 모든 문의는 보내져야 합니다 / 이메일을 통해 / studentun@georgeclarkson.edu로 //

- poetry ⓝ (집합적으로) 시
- poet ⓝ 시인
- introduction ⓝ 소개, 도입
- poem ⓝ (한 편의) 시
- aloud ad 큰 소리로
- participant ⓝ 참가자, 참여자
- receive ⓥ 받다, 받아들이다
- expert ⓐ 전문가의, 전문적인
- registration fee 등록비
- inquiry ⓝ 문의
- via prep ~을 통해, ~을 거쳐

시 창작 기초 워크숍

저희의 시 창작 기초 워크숍에 참여하여 시인 Grace Larson 씨를 만나십시오!
George Clarkson 대학교의 모든 학생들을 초대합니다.
언제: 2020년 9월 24일 목요일(오후 1시 ~ 오후 4시)
어디서: 학생회관 1층 메인 세미나실
시 창작의 기초 기법에 대한 소개 후에, 여러분은
1. 여러분 자신의 시를 창작할 것입니다.
2. 그 시를 다른 참가자들에게 큰 소리로 읽을 것입니다.
3. Larson 씨로부터 전문가의 피드백을 받을 것입니다.
등록비: 10달러
※ 9월 18일이나 그 전에 등록하시고 7달러만 내십시오.
관련된 모든 문의는 studentun@georgeclarkson.edu로 이메일을 통해 보내주셔야 합니다.

Poetry Writing Basics Workshop에 관한 다음 안내문의 내용과 일치하는 것은?

① 목요일 오전에 진행된다. 1:00 p.m. — 4:00 p.m.
② 학생회관 3층에서 열린다. 1st Floor
③ 참가자는 자신이 창작한 시를 낭독할 것이다. Write your own poem., Read it aloud to the other participants.
④ 9월 18일까지는 등록비가 10달러이다. Register on or before September 18 and pay only $7.
⑤ 관련 문의는 이메일로 할 수 없다. Any related inquiries should be sent via email

왜 정답? [정답률 93%]

자신의 시를 창작하여 그것을 다른 참가자들에게 큰 소리로 읽을 것이라고(Write your own poem., Read it aloud to the other participants.) 했으므로 ③이 안내문의 내용과 일치한다.

왜 오답?

① 목요일 오후 1시부터 4시까지(1:00 p.m. — 4:00 p.m.) 진행된다.
② 학생회관 1층에서(1st Floor) 열린다.
④ 9월 18일이나 그 전에 등록하면 7달러이다. (Register on or before September 18 and pay only $7.)
⑤ 모든 관련 문의는 이메일을 통해 보내져야 한다. (Any related inquiries should be sent via email)

어법 특강

※ 병렬 구조를 이루는 등위접속사

– 등위접속사 and, but, or, so 등은 두 개 이상의 단어, 구, 절을 연결한다. 이때 동일한 품사와 문법적으로 같은 성분을 연결해야 한다.

- Don't forget to prepare a cutting board and a knife. 단어와 단어를 연결
(도마와 칼을 준비할 것을 잊지 마세요.)
- You can squeeze oranges by hand, but it's easier if you use a squeezer. 문장과 문장을 연결
(당신은 손으로 오렌지를 짤 수 있지만, 압착기를 사용하면 더 쉬워요.)
- Anyone caught faces a huge fine, but this has not discouraged selling their seats. 문장과 문장을 연결
(잡히면 누구나 엄청난 벌금에 처해지지만, 이것은 입장권을 파는 것을 막지는 못한다.)

J 30 정답 ⑤ *2022 Sunbay 고등학교 자선 음악회

2022 Sunbay High School Benefit Concert /
2022 Sunbay 고등학교 자선 음악회 /

Sunbay High School students will be holding / their benefit concert for charity. // 미래진행형과 현재진행형이 미래를 나타내기도 함
Sunbay 고등학교 학생들이 엽니다 / 그들의 자선 음악회를 // ①의 단서 수익금 전액이 지역 아동 병원에 기부될 것임

All profits will be donated / to the local children's hospital. //
수익금 전액은 기부될 것입니다 / 지역 아동 병원에 //

Come and enjoy / your family and friends' performances. //
오셔서 즐기세요 / 여러분의 가족과 친구의 공연을 //

Date & Time: / Thursday, June 30, 2022 at 6 p.m. /
일시: / 2022년 6월 30일 목요일 오후 6시 /

Place: / Sunbay High School's Vision Hall /
장소: / Sunbay 고등학교의 Vision Hall / ②의 단서 장소: Sunbay 고등학교의 Vision Hall

Events /
행사 /

- singing, dancing, drumming, and other musical performances /
노래 부르기, 춤추기, 드럼 치기, 그리고 다른 음악 공연들 / ③의 단서 Sunbay 고등학교를 졸업한 가수의 특별 공연이 있음
- special performance by singer Jonas Collins, / who graduated from Sunbay High School / 선행사 주격 관계대명사
가수 Jonas Collins의 특별 공연 / Sunbay 고등학교를 졸업한 /

Tickets /
티켓 /

- $3 per person /
1인당 3달러 / ④의 단서 오후 5시부터 티켓을 구입할 수 있음
- available to buy / from 5 p.m. / at the front desk of Vision Hall /
구입 가능 / 오후 5시부터 / Vision Hall의 접수대에서 /

Other Attractions /
다른 관심을 끌 만한 것들 / ⑤의 단서 동아리 학생들의 작품이 전시되지만 구입할 수는 없음

- club students' artwork on display, / but not for purchase /
동아리 학생들의 예술 작품이 전시되나 / 구입이 가능하지는 않음 /
- free face-painting /
무료 얼굴 페인팅 /

For more information about the concert, / feel free to contact us at concert@sunbayhighs.edu. //
음악회에 관해 더 많은 정보를 원하시면 / 자유롭게 concert@sunbayhighs.edu로 저희에게 연락하세요 //

- benefit ⓝ (모금을 위한) 자선 행사
- charity ⓝ 자선
- profit ⓝ (금전적) 이익, 수익
- donate ⓥ 기부하다, 기증하다
- local ⓐ 지역의, 현지의
- performance ⓝ 공연, 연주
- attraction ⓝ 흥미를 끄는 것[장소], 매력
- display ⓝ 전시, 진열
- purchase ⓝ 구입, 구매

2022 Sunbay 고등학교 자선 음악회

Sunbay 고등학교 학생들이 자선 음악회를 엽니다. 수익금 전액은 지역 아동 병원에 기부될 것입니다. 오셔서 여러분의 가족과 친구의 공연을 즐기세요.
일시: 2022년 6월 30일 목요일 오후 6시
장소: Sunbay 고등학교의 Vision Hall
행사
- 노래 부르기, 춤추기, 드럼 치기, 그리고 다른 음악 공연들
- Sunbay 고등학교를 졸업한 가수 Jonas Collins의 특별 공연

티켓
- 1인당 3달러
- Vision Hall의 접수대에서 오후 5시부터 구입 가능

다른 관심을 끌 만한 것들
- 동아리 학생들의 예술 작품이 전시되나, 구입이 가능하지는 않음
- 무료 얼굴 페인팅

음악회에 관해 더 많은 정보를 원하시면 자유롭게 concert@sunbayhighs.edu로 저희에게 연락하세요.

2022 Sunbay High School Benefit Concert에 관한 다음 안내문의 내용과 일치하지 <u>않는</u> 것은?

① 수익금 전액은 지역 아동 병원에 기부될 것이다.
　All profits will be donated to the local children's hospital.
② Sunbay 고등학교의 Vision Hall에서 열린다.
　Place: Sunbay High School's Vision Hall.
③ Sunbay 고등학교를 졸업한 가수의 특별 공연이 있다.
　special performance by singer Jonas Collins, who graduated from Sunbay High School
④ 티켓은 오후 5시부터 살 수 있다.
　available to buy from 5 p.m.
⑤ 동아리 학생들의 전시 작품은 구입이 가능하다.
　club students' artwork on display, but not for purchase

> 왜 정답 ? [정답률 97%]

동아리 학생들의 작품이 전시되기는 하지만 구입할 수는 없다고(club students' artwork on display, but not for purchase) 했으므로 ⑤이 안내문과 일치하지 않는다.

> 왜 오답 ?

① 수익금 전액은 지역 아동 병원에 기부될 것이다. (All profits will be donated to the local children's hospital.)
② Sunbay 고등학교의 Vision Hall에서 열린다. (Place: Sunbay High School's Vision Hall)
③ Sunbay 고등학교를 졸업한 가수의 특별 공연이 있다. (special performance by singer Jonas Collins, who graduated from Sunbay High School)
④ 티켓은 오후 5시부터 살 수 있다. (available to buy from 5 p.m.)

J 31 정답 ② ＊Brushwood 국립 공원 투어 프로그램

Brushwood National Park Tour Program /
Brushwood 국립 공원 투어 프로그램 /
형용사적 용법(a great way 수식)
Walking in nature is a great way / to stay fit and healthy. //
자연 속에서 걷는 것은 좋은 방법입니다 / 체력과 건강을 유지하는
　　　　　　　　　　　　　　　　생략되지 않은 부사절 접속사
Enjoy free park walks / with our volunteer guides, / while
appreciating / the beautiful sights and sounds of the forest. //
무료 공원 산책을 즐기요 / 우리의 자원봉사 안내자와 함께 / 감상하면서 / 숲의 아름다운 풍경과 소리를 //
　　①의 단서 자원봉사 안내자와 함께함

Details /
세부 정보 /
　②의 단서 평일에 운영함
• Open on weekdays / from March to November /
평일에 운영함 / 3월부터 11월까지 /
• Easy walk along the path / for one hour / (3 km) /
길을 따라 편안하게 걷기 / 1시간 동안 / (3km) /
• Groups of 15 to 20 / per guide /
15명 내지 20명으로 이루어진 그룹 / 가이드당 /

Registration /
등록 /
• Scan the QR code / to sign up for the tour. //
QR 코드를 스캔하여 / 투어에 신청하십시오. // ③의 단서 QR 코드를 스캔하여 신청함

Note /
참고 사항 /
　　　조동사가 포함된 수동태: 조동사+be p.p.
• A bottle of water will be provided / to each participant. //
물이 한 병씩 제공될 것입니다 / 가 참가자에게 ④의 단서 각 참가자에게 물이
　　　조동사가 포함된 수동태: 조동사+be p.p.　한 병씩 제공될 것임
• Children under 12 must be accompanied / by an adult. //
12세 미만 어린이는 동행되어야 합니다 / 어른에 의해 /
• Tours may be canceled / due to weather conditions. //
투어가 취소될 수도 있습니다 / 날씨로 인해 / ⑤의 단서 날씨로 인해 취소될 수 있음
※ If you have any questions, / please email us at
brushwoodtour@parks.org. //
※ 궁금한 점이 있으면 / brushwoodtour@parks.org로 저희에게 이메일을 보내주십시오 //

• appreciate ⓥ 감상하다　• accompany ⓥ 동행하다
• participant ⓝ 참가자　• registration ⓝ 등록

Brushwood 국립 공원 투어 프로그램

자연 속에서 걷는 것은 체력과 건강을 유지하는 좋은 방법입니다. 우리의 자원봉사 안내자와 함께 무료 공원 산책을 즐기며, 숲의 아름다운 풍경과 소리를 감상하십시오.

세부 정보
• 3월부터 11월까지 평일에 운영함
• 1시간 동안 길을 따라 편안하게 걷기 (3km)
• 가이드당 15명 내지 20명으로 이루어진 그룹

등록
• QR 코드를 스캔하여 투어에 신청하십시오.

참고 사항
• 각 참가자에게 물이 한 병씩 제공될 것입니다.
• 12세 미만 어린이는 어른과 동행해야 합니다.
• 날씨로 인해 투어가 취소될 수도 있습니다.
※ 궁금한 점이 있으면, brushwoodtour@parks.org로 저희에게 이메일을 보내주십시오.

Brushwood National Park Tour Program에 관한 다음 안내문의 내용과 일치하지 <u>않는</u> 것은?

① 자원봉사 안내자가 동행한다. with our volunteer guides
② 주말에 진행된다. Open on weekdays
③ QR 코드를 스캔하여 신청한다. Scan the QR code to sign up for the tour.
④ 각 참가자에게 물이 한 병씩 제공될 것이다. A bottle of water will be provided to each participant.
⑤ 날씨에 따라 취소될 수 있다. Tours may be canceled due to weather conditions.

> 왜 정답 ? [정답률 92%]

② 평일에 운영된다. (Open on weekdays)

> 왜 오답 ?

① 자원봉사 안내자가 동행한다. (with our volunteer guides)
③ QR 코드를 스캔하여 신청한다. (Scan the QR code to sign up for the tour.)
④ 각 참가자에게 물이 한 병씩 제공될 것이다. (A bottle of water will be provided to each participant.)
⑤ 날씨에 따라 취소될 수 있다. (Tours may be canceled due to weather conditions.)

J 32 정답 ③ ＊Turtle Island 보트 투어

Turtle Island Boat Tour /
Turtle Island 보트 투어 /
The fantastic Turtle Island Boat Tour / invites you to the beautiful sea world. //
환상적인 Turtle Island 보트 투어가 / 아름다운 바다 세계로 여러분을 초대합니다 //

Dates: From June 1 to August 31, 2024 /
날짜: 2024년 6월 1일부터 8월 31일까지 /

Tour Times /
투어 시간 /

Weekdays 주중	1 p.m. – 5 p.m. 오후 1시 ~ 오후 5시
Weekends 주말 ①의 단서 주말에는 하루에 두 번 운영됨	9 a.m. – 1 p.m. 오전 9시 ~ 오후 1시
	1 p.m. – 5 p.m. 오후 1시 ~ 오후 5시

※ Each tour lasts four hours. //
각각의 투어는 네 시간 동안 진행됩니다 //

Tickets & Booking /
표와 예약 /
• $50 per person for each tour /
투어별로 1인당 50달러 /
(Only those aged 17 and over can participate.) //
17세 이상인 사람만 참가할 수 있습니다 // ②의 단서 17세 이상만 참가할 수 있음

- Bookings must be completed / no later than 2 days before the
day of the tour. // 늘어도 ❸의단서 예약은 늦어도 투어 이틀 전에 완료되어야 하므로 당일 예약은 불가능함
예약은 완료되어야 합니다 / 늦어도 투어 당일 이틀 전에 //

- No refunds after the departure time /
출발 시각 이후에는 환불 불가 ❹의단서 출발 시간 이후에는 환불이 불가능함

each+단수 명사+단수 동사
- Each tour group size is limited / to 10 participants. //
각각의 투어 그룹 규모는 제한됩니다 / 10명의 참가자로 //

Activities /
활동 /

- Snorkeling with a professional diver /
전문 다이버와 함께 하는 스노클링 / ❻의단서 전문 다이버와 함께 하는 스노클링 활동이 있음

- Feeding tropical fish /
열대어에게 먹이 주기 /

※ Feel free to explore our website, www.snorkelingti.com. //
저희 웹사이트인 www.snorkelingti.com을 마음껏 탐색하세요 //

- no later than 늦어도 ~까지는   - refund ⓝ 환불
- feed ⓥ 먹이를 주다

Turtle Island 보트 투어

환상적인 Turtle Island 보트 투어가 아름다운 바다 세계로 여러분을
초대합니다.
날짜: 2024년 6월 1일부터 8월 31일까지
투어 시간

주중	오후 1시 ~ 오후 5시
주말	오전 9시 ~ 오후 1시
	오후 1시 ~ 오후 5시

※ 각각의 투어는 네 시간 동안 진행됩니다.
표와 예약
- 투어별로 1인당 50달러
  (17세 이상인 사람만 참가할 수 있습니다.)
- 예약은 늦어도 투어 당일 이틀 전에 완료되어야 합니다.
- 출발 시각 이후에는 환불 불가
- 각각의 투어 그룹 규모는 10명의 참가자로 제한됩니다.
활동
- 전문 다이버와 함께 하는 스노클링
- 열대어에게 먹이 주기
※ 저희 웹사이트인 www.snorkelingti.com을 마음껏 탐색하세요.

Turtle Island Boat Tour에 관한 다음 안내문의 내용과 일치하지 않는 것은?
① 주말에는 하루에 두 번 운영된다. Weekends 9 a.m. – 1 p.m., 1 p.m. – 5 p.m.
② 17세 이상만 참가할 수 있다. Only those aged 17 and over can participate.
③ 당일 예약이 가능하다. Bookings must be completed no later than 2 days before the day of the tour.
④ 출발 시간 이후에는 환불이 불가능하다. No refunds after the departure time
⑤ 전문 다이버와 함께 하는 스노클링 활동이 있다.
Snorkeling with a professional diver

꿈왜 정답? [정답률 97%]
③ 예약은 늦어도 투어 이틀 전에 완료되어야 하므로 당일 예약은 불가능하다.
(Bookings must be completed no later than 2 days before the day of
the tour.)

꿈왜 오답?
① 주말에는 하루에 두 번 운영된다. (Weekends 9 a.m. – 1 p.m.,
1 p.m. – 5 p.m.)
② 17세 이상만 참가할 수 있다. (Only those aged 17 and over can
participate.)
④ 출발 시간 이후에는 환불이 불가능하다. (No refunds after the departure
time)
⑤ 전문 다이버와 함께 하는 스노클링 활동이 있다. (Snorkeling with a
professional diver)

조수근 | 순천향대 의예과 2024년 입학·성남 태원고 졸

안내문의 세부 내용 파악 문제는 선지를 먼저 읽고, 그 선지와
관련된 내용만 안내문에서 찾아내면 빠르게 풀 수 있어! 이
문제에서는 ③의 '당일 예약'이라는 단어를 보고 지문에서 다른
부분은 볼 필요도 없이 Booking이 나타난 문장만 바로 확인하는
거야. 늦어도 투어 당일 이틀 전에 예약이 완료되어야 한다고 했으니 당일 예약은
불가능하다는 것을 알 수 있지.

J 33 정답 ④ ＊Oyster Bay Town 유아 스포츠 프로그램

2023 Oyster Bay Town Toddler Sports Program /
2023 Oyster Bay Town 유아 스포츠 프로그램 /

The Town's Toddler Sports Program will return / this spring on
April 7th. //
Town의 유아 스포츠 프로그램이 돌아올 것입니다 / 올해 봄 4월 7일에 //

❶의단서 6주간의 프로그램임
This 6-week program offers sports classes / at the Youth Center
/ for children aged 3 and 4. //
6주간의 이 프로그램은 스포츠 수업을 제공합니다 / Youth Center에서 / 세 살과 네 살
아동을 위해 //

주어, 선행사   주격 관계대명사   ❷의단서 매주 한 개의 수업을 선택해야 함
- Parents / who sign their toddler up for the program / must
choose one class per week, / per child. //   동사
부모는 / 프로그램에 그들의 유아를 등록시키는 / 매주 한 개의 수업을 선택해야 합니다 / 아동
한 명당 //

Classes will take place on: /
수업은 다음과 같이 실시될 것입니다 /   ❸의단서 수업은 수요일과 목요일 오전에 있음

Wednesdays 10 a.m. or 11 a.m. / & Fridays 10 a.m. or 11 a.m. /
수요일 오전 10시 또는 오전 11시 / 그리고 금요일 오전 10시 또는 오전 11시 /

- Registration will take place ONLINE / at www.obtown.org /
starting Friday, March 24th, at 9 a.m. // ❹의단서 등록은 3월 24일 오전 9시부터
온라인으로 실시됨
등록은 '온라인으로' 실시될 것입니다 / www.obtown.org에서 / 3월 24일 금요일 오전 9
시부터 //

Fee /
참가비 /

- $75 / per resident child / ❻의단서 지역 거주 아동은 75달러임
75달러 / 지역 거주 아동 한 명당 /

- $90 / for any non-resident child /
90달러 / 지역 비거주 아동은 누구라도 /

For more information, / call (516) 797-1234. //
더 많은 정보를 원하시면 / (516) 797-1234로 전화하세요 //

- oyster ⓝ 굴   - toddler ⓝ (아장아장 걷는) 유아
- sign up for ~을 신청[가입]하다   - take place 개최되다, 일어나다
- resident ⓝ 주민

2023 Oyster Bay Town 유아 스포츠 프로그램

Town의 유아 스포츠 프로그램이 올해 봄 4월 7일에 돌아올 것입니다. 6주간의
이 프로그램은 세 살과 네 살 아동을 위해 Youth Center에서 스포츠 수업을
제공합니다.
- 프로그램에 유아를 등록시키는 부모는 아동 한 명당 매주 한 개의 수업을
  선택해야 합니다. 수업은 다음과 같이 실시될 것입니다:
  수요일 오전 10시 또는 오전 11시 그리고 금요일 오전 10시 또는 오전 11시
- 등록은 3월 24일 금요일 오전 9시부터 www.obtown.org에서 '온라인으로'
  실시될 것입니다.
참가비
– 지역 거주 아동 한 명당 75달러
– 지역 비거주 아동은 누구라도 90달러
더 많은 정보를 원하시면, (516) 797-1234로 전화하세요.

2023 Oyster Bay Town Toddler Sports Program에 관한 다음 안내문의 내용과 일치하는 것은?

① 7주간 진행되는 프로그램이다. This 6-week program

② 참가 아동마다 매주 두 개의 수업을 선택해야 한다. must choose one class per week

③ 수업은 수요일과 금요일 오후에 있다. Wednesdays 10 a.m. or 11 a.m. & Fridays 10 a.m. or 11 a.m.

④ 등록은 3월 24일 오전 9시에 시작될 것이다. Registration will take place ~ starting Friday, March 24th, at 9 a.m.

⑤ 지역 거주 아동의 참가비는 90달러이다. $75 per resident child

>왜 정답? [정답률 90%]

④ 등록은 3월 24일 금요일 오전 9시부터 온라인으로 실시될 것이다. (Registration will take place ~ starting Friday, March 24th, at 9 a.m.)

>왜 오답?

① 6주간의 프로그램이다. (This 6-week program)

② 매주 한 개의 수업을 선택해야 한다. (must choose one class per week)

③ 수요일과 금요일 오전에 있다. (Wednesdays 10 a.m. or 11 a.m. & Fridays 10 a.m. or 11 a.m.)

⑤ 지역 거주 아동의 참가비는 75달러이다. ($75 per resident child)

J 34 정답 ④ *아이들을 위한 창의적인 미술 강좌

Creative Art Class for Kids /
아이들을 위한 창의적인 미술 강좌 /

Want to encourage / your child's artistic talent? //
북돋고 싶으신가요 / 여러분의 자녀의 예술적 재능을 //

Color World Art Center is going to have art classes / for kids / from A to B: (시간적·공간적) A부터 B까지 from June 1st to August 31st. // ①의 단서 6월부터 8월까지 진행됨
Color World 아트 센터는 미술 강좌를 열 예정입니다 / 아이들을 위한 / 6월 1일부터 8월 31일까지 //

Class Programs & Schedule /
강좌 프로그램 & 일정 /

- Clay Arts: Ages 4 – 6, Every Monday /
점토 미술: 4~6세, 매주 월요일 /

- Cartoon Drawing: Ages 7 – 9, Every Thursday /
만화 그리기: 7~9세, 매주 목요일 / ②의 단서 만화 그리기 강좌는 매주 목요일임

- Watercolors: Ages 10 – 12, Every Friday /
수채화: 10~12세, 매주 금요일 /

Class Time: 4 p.m. – 6 p.m. / ③의 단서 강좌는 오후에 열림
강좌 시간: 오후 4시~오후 6시 /

Monthly Fee /
월 수강료 /

- $30 per child (snacks included) / ④의 단서 월 수강료에 간식이 포함됨
아동당 30달러(간식 포함) /

- Family discounts are available / (10% discount for each child). //
가족 할인이 가능합니다 / (각 아동당 10퍼센트 할인) //

Notes /
참고 사항 /

- Only 10 kids are allowed / per class. // ⑤의 단서 강좌당 아동 10명으로 제한됨
10명의 아동만 허용됩니다 / 강좌당 //
선행사   목적격 관계대명사
- Kids should wear clothes / that they don't mind getting dirty. //
아이들은 옷을 입어야 합니다 / 더러워져도 그들이 신경 쓰지 않는 //

※ Sign up at Color World Art Center. //
Color World 아트 센터에서 등록하세요 //

- -

- encourage ⓥ 격려하다, 북돋우다 - talent ⓝ 재능
- monthly fee 월 수강료 - include ⓥ 포함하다
- discount ⓝ 할인 - allow ⓥ 허락하다, 용납하다
- mind ⓥ 언짢아하다, 신경쓰다

아이들을 위한 창의적인 미술 강좌

자녀의 예술적 재능을 키워주고 싶으신가요? Color World 아트 센터는 6월 1일부터 8월 31일까지 아이들을 위한 미술 강좌를 열 예정입니다.

강좌 프로그램 & 일정

- 점토 미술: 4~6세, 매주 월요일
- 만화 그리기: 7~9세, 매주 목요일
- 수채화: 10~12세, 매주 금요일

강좌 시간: 오후 4시~오후 6시

월 수강료

- 아동당 30달러(간식 포함)
- 가족 할인(각 아동당 10퍼센트 할인)이 가능합니다.

참고 사항

- 강좌당 10명의 아동만 허용됩니다.
- 아이들은 더러워져도 신경 쓰지 않는 옷을 입어야 합니다.

※ Color World 아트 센터에서 등록하세요.

Creative Art Class for Kids에 관한 다음 안내문의 내용과 일치하는 것은?

① 6월부터 9월까지 진행된다. from June 1st to August 31st

② 만화 그리기 강좌가 월요일마다 있다. Cartoon Drawing: Ages 7 – 9, Every Thursday

③ 모든 강좌는 오전에 열린다. Class Time: 4 p.m. – 6 p.m.

④ 월 수강료에 간식이 포함되어 있다. $30 per child (snacks included)

⑤ 강좌당 수강 아동 수에 제한이 없다. Only 10 kids are allowed per class.

>왜 정답? [정답률 96%]

④ 월 수강료 30달러에 간식이 포함된다. ($30 per child (snacks included))

>왜 오답?

① 6월부터 8월까지 진행된다. (from June 1st to August 31st)

② 만화 그리기 강좌는 매주 목요일이다. (Cartoon Drawing: Ages 7 – 9, Every Thursday)

③ 강좌 시간은 오후 4시부터 6시까지이다. (Class Time: 4 p.m. – 6 p.m.)

⑤ 강좌당 10명의 아동만 허용된다. (Only 10 kids are allowed per class.)

J 35 정답 ⑤ *WGHS 지리 사진 대회

WGHS Geography Photo Contest /
WGHS 지리 사진 대회 /

The event / you've been waiting for all this year / is finally
앞에 목적격 관계대명사가 생략됨
here! //
행사가 / 여러분이 올해 내내 기다려온 / 드디어 돌아왔습니다 //

Please join / Wood Gate High School's 10th annual Geography
Photo Contest. // ①의 단서 제10회 연례 대회임
참가하십시오 / Wood Gate 고등학교의 제10회 연례 지리 사진 대회에 //

Guidelines /
지침 /

- Participants should use / the theme of the "Beauty of Rivers
Crossing Our City." // ②의 단서 사용해야 하는 주제가 정해져 있음
참가자는 사용해야 합니다 / '우리의 도시를 가로지르는 강들의 아름다움'이라는 주제를 //

- Submissions are limited / to one photo / per person. //
출품작은 제한됩니다 / 사진 한 장으로 / 1인당 //

- Files should not be larger / than 50 MB. //
파일 용량은 더 크면 안 됩니다 / 50MB보다 // ③의 단서 파일은 50MB를 초과하면 안 됨

Schedule /
일정 /

	When 언제	Where 어디서
Submission 제출	October 2 - October 8 10월 2일 ~ 10월 8일	Email: geography@woodgate.edu 이메일: geography@woodgate.edu
Voting 투표	October 11 - October 13 ④의 단서 투표는 10월 11일부터 13일까지임 10월 11일 ~ 10월 13일	School Website: https://www.woodgate.edu 학교 웹 사이트: https://www.woodgate.edu
Exhibition 전시	October 16 - October 20 10월 16일 ~ 10월 20일	Main Lobby 메인 로비

Note /
참고 사항 /
_{앞에 주격 관계대명사와 be동사가 생략됨}
- The top 10 photos / selected by students / will be exhibited. //
상위 10개의 사진이 / 학생들이 선정한 / 전시될 것입니다 // ⑤의 단서 학생들이 선정한 상위 10개
사진이 전시될 것임
※ For more information, / visit the geography teacher's room. //
더 많은 정보를 얻으려면 / 지리 교사실을 방문하십시오 //

- geography ⓝ 지리 • annual ⓐ 매년의, 연례의
- submission ⓝ 제출 • voting ⓝ 투표 • exhibition ⓝ 전시

WGHS 지리 사진 대회

여러분이 올해 내내 기다려온 행사가 드디어 돌아왔습니다! Wood Gate
고등학교의 제10회 연례 지리 사진 대회에 참가하십시오.

지침
- 참가자는 '우리의 도시를 가로지르는 강들의 아름다움'이라는 주제를
사용해야 합니다.
- 출품작은 1인당 사진 한 장으로 제한됩니다.
- 파일 용량은 50MB보다 더 크면 안 됩니다.

일정

	언제	어디서
제출	10월 2일 ~ 10월 8일	이메일: geography@woodgate.edu
투표	10월 11일 ~ 10월 13일	학교 웹 사이트: https://www.woodgate.edu
전시	10월 16일 ~ 10월 20일	메인 로비

참고 사항
- 학생들이 선정한 상위 10개의 사진이 전시될 것입니다.
※ 더 많은 정보를 얻으려면, 지리 교사실을 방문하십시오.

WGHS Geography Photo Contest에 관한 다음 안내문의 내용과 일치하는 것은?
① 처음으로 개최되는 대회이다. 10th annual Geography Photo Contest
② 출품 사진 주제에 제한이 없다. Participants should use the theme of the "Beauty of Rivers Crossing Our City."
③ 100 MB 크기의 파일을 제출할 수 있다. Files should not be larger than 50 MB.
④ 투표는 일주일간 실시된다. October 11 - October 13
⑤ 학생들이 선정한 사진들이 전시될 것이다.
The top 10 photos selected by students will be exhibited.

>왜 정답 ? [정답률 96%]
⑤ 학생들이 선정한 상위 10개 사진이 전시될 것이다. (The top 10 photos selected by students will be exhibited.)

>왜 오답 ?
① 제10회 연례 사진 대회이다. (10th annual Geography Photo Contest)
② '우리의 도시를 가로지르는 강들의 아름다움'이라는 주제를 사용해야 한다.
(Participants should use the theme of the "Beauty of Rivers Crossing Our City.")
③ 파일은 50MB를 초과하면 안 된다. (Files should not be larger than 50 MB.)
④ 투표는 10월 11일부터 10월 13일까지이다. (October 11 - October 13)

City of Sittka Public Bike Sharing Service /
Sittka시 공공 자전거 공유 서비스 /
Are you planning / to explore the city? //
계획하고 계신가요 / 도시를 답사하는 것을 //
This is the eco-friendly way / to do it! // _{형용사적 용법(way 수식)}
이것이 친환경적인 방법입니다 / 그것을 하는 //
Rent /
대여 /
- Register anywhere / via our easy app. //
어디서든 등록하세요 / 저희의 쉬운 앱을 통해 //
- Payment can be made / only by credit card. //
요금 지불은 행해질 수 있습니다 / 신용 카드로만 // ①의 단서 신용 카드로만 결제가 가능함
Fee /
요금 /
- Free / for the first 30 minutes /
무료 / 처음 30분 동안 / ②의 단서 처음 30분은 무료임
- One dollar / per additional 30 minutes /
1달러 / 추가 30분마다 /
Use /
사용 / ③의 단서 자전거의 QR 코드를 스캔해서 이용함
- Choose a bike / and scan the QR code on the bike. //
자전거를 선택하고 / 그 자전거의 QR 코드를 스캔하세요 //
- Helmets are not provided. //
헬멧은 제공되지 않습니다 // ④의 단서 헬멧이 제공되지 않음
Return /
반납 / _{앞에 주격 관계대명사와 be동사가 생략됨}
- Return the bike / to the Green Zone / shown on the app. //
자전거를 반납하세요 / Green Zone으로 / 앱에 보이는 //
- Complete the return / by pressing the OK button / on the
bike. // ⑥의 단서 자전거의 OK 버튼을 눌러서 반납을 완료함
반납을 완료하세요 / OK 버튼을 눌러서 / 자전거의 //

- explore ⓥ 탐사[탐험]하다, 탐구하다 • register ⓥ 등록하다, 기록하다
- via prep ~을 통해, (어떤 장소를) 경유하여[거쳐] • payment ⓝ 지급, 지불
- additional ⓐ 추가의 • complete ⓥ 완료하다, 끝마치다

Sittka시 공공 자전거 공유 서비스
도시를 답사할 계획이신가요?
이것이 그것을 하는 친환경적인 방법입니다!
대여
- 저희의 쉬운 앱을 통해 어디서든 등록하세요.
- 요금 지불은 신용 카드로만 할 수 있습니다.
요금
- 처음 30분은 무료입니다.
- 추가 30분마다 1달러입니다.
사용
- 자전거를 선택하고 그 자전거의 QR 코드를 스캔하세요.
- 헬멧은 제공되지 않습니다.
반납
- 앱에 보이는 Green Zone으로 자전거를 반납하세요.
- 자전거의 OK 버튼을 눌러 반납을 완료하세요.

City of Sittka Public Bike Sharing Service에 관한 다음 안내문의 내용과 일치하지 않는 것은?
① 신용 카드 결제만 가능하다. Payment can be made only by credit card.
② 처음 30분은 무료이다. Free for the first 30 minutes
③ 자전거의 QR 코드를 스캔해서 이용한다. scan the QR code on the bike
④ 헬멧이 제공된다. Helmets are not provided.
⑤ 자전거의 OK 버튼을 눌러서 반납을 완료한다. Complete the return by pressing the OK button on the bike.

⊃왜 정답? [정답률 90%]

헬멧은 제공되지 않는다고(Helmets are not provided.) 했으므로 ④은 안내문과 일치하지 않는다.

⊃왜 오답?

① 결제는 신용 카드로만 가능하다. (Payment can be made only by credit card.)

② 처음 30분은 무료이다. (Free for the first 30 minutes)

③ 자전거의 QR 코드를 스캔해서 이용한다. (scan the QR code on the bike)

⑤ 자전거의 OK 버튼을 눌러서 반납을 완료한다. (Complete the return by pressing the OK button on the bike.)

J 37 정답 ⑤ *Bluehill 사과 줍기

Bluehill Apple Picking /
Bluehill 사과 줍기 /

Take home a bag / full of apples / fresh from the orchard. //
가방을 집으로 가져가세요 / 사과들이 가득한 / 과수원에서 갓 나온 //

This year, / unfortunately, / apple pie eating contests will not be held / due to time constraints. // ①의 단서 애플파이 먹기 대회는 열리지 않음
올해에는 / 안타깝게도 / 애플파이 먹기 대회는 열리지 않을 것입니다 / 시간 제약 때문에 //

• **Date**: Saturday, October 21, 2023 /
일시: 2023년 10월 21일 토요일 /

• **Time** /
시간 /

– Departure: 8:15 a.m. for pre-trip meeting /
출발: 오전 8시 15분에 여행 전 모임 /
미래 시제를 나타내는 현재형 동사
Buses leave / at 8:30 a.m. SHARP! //
버스는 떠납니다 / 오전 8시 30분 정각에 // ②의 단서 버스는 오전 8시 30분에 떠남

– Return: Approximately 7:00 p.m. /
도착: 대략 오후 7시 /

• **Price**: $20 per person / (transportation included, / meals not included) / ③의 단서 식사는 포함되지 않음
가격: 1인당 $20 (교통비 포함 / 식사 미포함) /
④의 단서 사전 예약이 필요함
• Pre-registration is required / at www.blueapple.com. //
사전 예약이 필요합니다 / www.blueapple.com에서 //
조동사를 포함한 수동태
– 12 years and under / must be accompanied by adults. //
12살 이하는 / 반드시 어른들을 동반해야 합니다 // ⑤의 단서 12살 이하는 어른을 동반해야 함

• orchard ⓝ 과수원　• unfortunately ⓐⓓ 불행하게도
• constraint ⓝ 제약　• pre-registration ⓝ 사전예약
• accompany ⓥ 동반하다

Bluehill 사과 줍기

과수원에서 갓 나온 사과들이 가득한 가방을 집으로 가져가세요. 올해, 불행하게도, 사과 파이 먹기 대회는 시간 제약 때문에 열리지 않을 것입니다.
• 일시: 2023년 10월 21일 토요일
• 시간
– 출발: 오전 8시 15분에 여행 전 모임
　　　　버스는 오전 8시 30분 정각에 떠납니다!
– 도착: 대략 오후 7시
• 가격: 1인당 $20 (교통비 포함, 식비 미포함)
• www.blueapple.com에서 사전예약이 필요합니다
– 12살 이하는 반드시 어른들과 함께 다녀야 합니다.

Bluehill Apple Picking에 관한 다음 안내문의 내용과 일치하는 것은?
① 애플파이 먹기 대회가 열릴 예정이다. apple pie eating contests will not be held
② 버스는 오전 8시 15분에 출발한다. Buses leave at 8:30 a.m. SHARP!
③ 참가비에 식사가 포함되어 있다. meals not included
④ 사전 등록은 필요 없다. Pre-registration is required
⑤ 12세 이하는 성인이 동반해야 한다. 12 years and under must be accompanied by adults.

⊃왜 정답? [정답률 96%]

⑤ 12세 이하는 성인이 동반해야 한다. (12 years and under must be accompanied by adults.)

⊃왜 오답?

① 애플파이 먹기 대회가 열리지 않는다. (apple pie eating contests will not be held)

② 버스는 오전 8시 30분에 출발한다. (Buses leave at 8:30 a.m. SHARP!)

③ 참가비에 식사가 포함되어 있지 않다. (meals not included)

④ 사전 등록이 필요하다. (Pre-registration is required)

J 38 정답 ③ *빅 데이터 전문가와 함께하는 직업의 날

Career Day with a Big Data Expert /
빅 데이터 전문가와 함께하는 직업의 날 /

Meet a Big Data expert / from a leading IT company! //
빅 데이터 전문가를 만나 보십시오 / 선도적인 IT 기업의 //
미래진행형
Jill Johnson, / famous data analyst and bestselling author, / will be visiting Sovenhill High School / to give a lecture on careers / related to Big Data. //
Jill Johnson은 / 유명한 데이터 분석가이자 베스트셀러 작가인 / Sovenhill 고등학교를 방문하여 / 직업에 대한 강의를 할 것입니다 / 빅 데이터에 관련된 //

Participation: /
참가: / ①의 단서 Sovenhill 고등학교 학생만 참여할 수 있음
- Sovenhill High School students only /
Sovenhill 고등학교 학생만 참여 가능 /
- Limited / to 50 students / ②의 단서 학생 50명으로 제한됨
제한됨 / 50명의 학생으로 /

When & Where: /
일시 및 장소: /
- October 15, / 10:00 a.m. to 11:30 a.m. /
10월 15일 / 오전 10시부터 오전 11시 30분까지 /
- Library /
도서관 / ③의 단서 QR 코드를 스캔하여 신청서를 작성함
Registration: Scan the QR code / to fill in the application form. //
등록: QR 코드를 스캔하여 / 신청서를 작성하세요 //

Note: /
주의사항: / ④의 단서 강의 중 음료수를 마시는 것은 허용되지 않음
- Drinking beverages is not permitted / during the lecture. //
음료수를 마시는 것은 허용되지 않습니다 / 강의 중에 //
미래시제 수동태
- The lecture will be followed / by a Q&A session. //
강의는 이어질 것입니다 / 질의응답 시간으로 //
- All participants will receive / a free copy of the lecturer's book. // ⑤의 단서 모든 참석자가 강연자의 책을 무료로 받음
모든 참석자는 받을 것입니다 / 강연자의 무료 책 한 부를 //

• analyst ⓝ 분석가　• author ⓝ 작가, 저자　• lecture ⓝ 강의, 강연
• participation ⓝ 참가, 참여　• registration ⓝ 등록, 신고
• application ⓝ 신청(서)　• beverage ⓝ (물 외의) 음료
• permit ⓥ 허용[허락]하다　• participant ⓝ 참가자

빅 데이터 전문가와 함께하는 직업의 날

선도적인 IT 기업의 빅 데이터 전문가를 만나 보십시오! 유명한 데이터 분석가이자 베스트셀러 작가인 Jill Johnson은 Sovenhill 고등학교를 방문하여 빅 데이터 관련 직업에 대한 강의를 할 것입니다.
참가:
– Sovenhill 고등학교 학생만 참여 가능
– 학생 50명까지 제한됨
일시 및 장소:
– 10월 15일 오전 10시부터 오전 11시 30분까지
– 도서관

J

등록: QR 코드를 스캔하여 신청서를 작성하세요.
주의사항:
– 강의 중에 음료수를 마시는 것은 허용되지 않습니다.
– 강의 후에 질의응답 시간이 이어질 것입니다.
– 모든 참석자는 강연자의 책 한 부를 무료로 받을 것입니다.

Career Day with a Big Data Expert에 관한 다음 안내문의 내용과 일치하는 것은?

① 학부모도 참여할 수 있다. Sovenhill High School students only
② 참석 인원에 제한이 없다. Limited to 50 students
③ QR 코드를 스캔하여 신청서를 작성한다. Scan the QR code to fill in the application form.
④ 강연 중에 음료수를 마실 수 있다. Drinking beverages is not permitted during the lecture.
⑤ 참석자 중 일부만 강연자의 책을 무료로 받는다. All participants will receive a free copy of the lecturer's book.

왜 정답? [정답률 97%]

등록 방법을 안내하면서 QR 코드를 스캔하여 신청서를 작성하라고(Scan the QR code to fill in the application form.) 했으므로 ③이 안내문과 일치한다.

왜 오답?

① Sovenhill 고등학교 학생만 참여할 수 있다. (Sovenhill High School students only)
② 학생 50명으로 제한된다. (Limited to 50 students)
④ 강연 중 음료수를 마시는 것은 허용되지 않는다. (Drinking beverages is not permitted during the lecture.)
⑤ 모든 참석자가 강연자의 책 한 부를 무료로 받는다. (All participants will receive a free copy of the lecturer's book.)

J 39 정답 ④ ＊국제 가면 축제

International Mask Festival /
국제 가면 축제 /

Would you like to appreciate masks / from all over the world? //
여러분은 가면을 감상하고 싶으신가요 / 전 세계로부터의 //

Visit Maywood Hills Museum / and enjoy their beauty! //
Maywood Hills 박물관을 방문해서 / 그것들의 아름다움을 즐기세요 //

When: Every Tuesday to Sunday in April / (10:00 a.m. – 8:00 p.m.) / ①의 단서 매주 화요일부터 일요일까지 운영됨
기간: 4월 매주 화요일부터 일요일까지 / (오전 10시 – 오후 8시) /

Admission Price: $10 per person /
입장료: 1인당 $10 /

Event Information /
행사 정보 /

– Booth A: Exhibition of masks / from 25 countries /
부스 A: 가면 전시회 / 25개국으로부터의 /

– Booth B: Mask making activity / (reservation required) /
부스 B: 가면 만들기 활동 / (예약이 필요함) / ②의 단서 가면 만들기 활동은 예약이 필요함

Details /
세부 사항 /

– Audio guides are available in Booth A / and are included / in the admission price. // ③의 단서 오디오 가이드는 입장료에 포함되어 있음
오디오 가이드가 부스 A에서 이용 가능하고 / 포함되어 있습니다 / 입장료에 //

– After making a mask / in Booth B, / you can take it home / as a souvenir. // ④의 단서 만든 가면을 기념품으로 집에 가져갈 수 있음
가면을 만들고 난 후에 / 부스 B에서 / 여러분은 그것을 집에 가져갈 수 있습니다 / 기념품으로 //
⑤의 단서 관련 문의는 이메일이나 전화로 받음
Any related inquiries are welcome / via email (maskfestival@maywood.org) or phone call (234-567-7363). //
관련 문의는 받습니다 / 이메일(maskfestival@maywood.org)이나 전화(234-567-7363)를 통해 //

• international ⓐ 국제적인　• appreciate ⓥ 감상하다
• admission price 입장료　• exhibition ⓝ 전시회
• souvenir ⓝ 기념품　• inquiry ⓝ 질문, 문의

국제 가면 축제

전 세계의 가면을 감상하고 싶으신가요? Maywood Hills 박물관을 방문해서 그것들의 아름다움을 즐기세요!
기간: 4월 매주 화요일부터 일요일까지 (오전 10시 – 오후 8시)
입장료: 1인당 $10
행사 정보
– 부스 A: 25개국의 가면 전시회
– 부스 B: 가면 만들기 활동(예약이 필요함)
세부 사항
– 부스 A에서는 오디오 가이드가 이용 가능하고 입장료에 포함되어 있습니다.
– 부스 B에서 가면을 만들고 난 후에 그것을 기념품으로 집에 가져갈 수 있습니다.
관련 문의는 이메일(maskfestival@maywood.org)이나 전화(234-567-7363)를 통해 받습니다.

International Mask Festival에 관한 다음 안내문의 내용과 일치하는 것은?

① 화요일에는 축제가 운영되지 않는다. Every Tuesday to Sunday
② 가면 만들기 활동은 예약 없이 참여할 수 있다. Mask making activity (reservation required)
③ 오디오 가이드는 입장료에 포함되지 않는다. Audio guides are available in Booth A and are included in the admission price.
④ 만든 가면은 기념품으로 집에 가져갈 수 있다. After making a mask in Booth B, you can take it home as a souvenir.
⑤ 관련 문의는 전화로만 가능하다. Any related inquiries are welcome via email (maskfestival@maywood.org) or phone call (234-567-7363).

왜 정답? [정답률 95%]

④ 가면을 만든 후에 그것을 기념품으로 집에 가져갈 수 있다. (After making a mask in Booth B, you can take it home as a souvenir.)

왜 오답?

① 매주 화요일부터 일요일까지 운영된다. (Every Tuesday to Sunday)
② 가면 만들기 활동은 예약이 필요하다. (Mask making activity (reservation required))
③ 오디오 가이드는 입장료에 포함된다. (Audio guides are available in Booth A and are included in the admission price.)
⑤ 관련 문의는 이메일이나 전화로 가능하다. (Any related inquiries are welcome via email (maskfestival@maywood.org) or phone call (234-567-7363).)

J 40 정답 ④ ＊Jason의 사진 교실

Jason's Photography Class /
Jason의 사진 교실 /
「with+목적어+과거분사」: ～가 …된 채로
Are you tired of taking pictures / with your camera set to "Auto"? //
사진을 촬영하는 데 싫증이 나셨나요 / 여러분의 카메라가 '자동'으로 설정된 채로 //

Do you want to create / more professional-looking photos? //
만들어 내고 싶으신가요 / 더 전문가처럼 보이는 사진을 //

You won't want / to miss this opportunity. //
여러분은 원하지 않으실 겁니다 / 이 기회를 놓치는 것을 //

• Date: / Saturday, December 19 /
날짜 / 12월 19일, 토요일 /

• Time: / 1:30 p.m. – 5:30 p.m. / ①의 단서 오후에 시작함
시간 / 오후 1시 30분 – 오후 5시 30분 /

• Place: / Thrombon Building, Room 2 on the first floor / ②의 단서 1층에서 진행됨
장소 / Thrombon 빌딩, 1층 2호실 /

• Tuition Fee: / $50 (snacks provided) /
수업료 / 50달러 (간식 제공됨) /

- Level: / Beginner / **③의 단서** 초급자 수준임
수준 / 초급자 / 형용사적 용법(Topics 수식)
- Topics / to Be Covered: /
주제 / 다뤄지는 /
  – Equipment Selection / – Lighting Techniques /
장비 선정 / 조명 기술 /
  – Color Selection / – Special Effects / **④의 단서** 특수 효과를 다룸
색상 선정 / 특수 효과 / **⑤의 단서** 8명으로 제한됨
- Class size is limited to eight, / so don't delay! //
학급의 규모가 8명으로 제한되니 / 미루지 마세요 //

Visit our web site at www.eypcap.com / to register. //
저희 웹 사이트 www.eypcap.com을 방문하세요 / 등록하려면 //

- professional ⓐ 직업[직종]의, 전문적인   • tuition ⓝ 수업, 교습
- cover ⓥ 다루다, 포함하다   • equipment ⓝ 장비, 용품
- lighting ⓝ 조명 (시설)   • delay ⓥ 미루다, 연기하다

Jason의 사진 교실
'자동'으로 설정된 여러분의 카메라로 사진을 촬영하는 데 싫증이 나셨나요? 더 전문가처럼 보이는 사진을 만들어 내고 싶으신가요? 이 기회를 놓치고 싶지 않으실 겁니다.
- 날짜: 12월 19일, 토요일
- 시간: 오후 1시 30분 – 오후 5시 30분
- 장소: Thrombon 빌딩, 1층 2호실
- 수업료: 50달러 (간식 제공됨)
- 수준: 초급자
- 다루는 주제: – 장비 선정 – 조명 기술 – 색상 선정 – 특수 효과
- 학급의 규모가 8명으로 제한되니, 미루지 마세요!
등록을 위해 저희 웹 사이트 www.eypcap.com을 방문하세요.

Jason's Photography Class에 관한 다음 안내문의 내용과 일치하는 것은?
① 오전에 시작된다. 1:30 p.m. – 5:30 p.m.
② 3층에서 진행된다. on the first floor
③ 중급자 수준이다. Beginner
④ 다루는 주제 중 하나는 특수 효과이다. Special Effects
⑤ 수강 학생 수에는 제한이 없다. Class size is limited to eight

〉**왜** 정답 ? [정답률 86%]
사진 교실에서 다루는 주제에 특수 효과(Special Effects)가 있으므로 ④이 안내문과 일치한다.

〉**왜** 오답 ?
① 오전이 아니라 오후 1시 30분에 시작된다. (1:30 p.m. – 5:30 p.m.)
② 3층이 아니라 1층에서 진행된다. (on the first floor)
③ 중급자 수준이 아니라 초급자 수준이다. (Beginner)
⑤ 강좌는 8명으로 제한된다. (Class size is limited to eight)

J 41 정답 ② *2023 Oakfield Mini Marathon

2023 Oakfield Mini Marathon /
2023 Oakfield Mini Marathon /

Join the 2023 Oakfield Mini Marathon / to celebrate / the opening of Central Park in our town! //
2023 Oakfield Mini Marathon에 참가하세요 / 축하하기 위한 / 우리 동네의 Central Park의 개장을 //

Runners, joggers, and walkers are all welcome. //
달리는 사람, 조깅하는 사람, 걷는 사람 모두 환영합니다 //

When: Saturday, October 21, starting at 8:30 a.m. /
언제: 10월 21일 토요일, 오전 8시 30분 시작 /

Where: Start at Gate 1 of Central Park / and finish in the parking lot / **①의 단서** Central Park의 Gate 1에서 출발
어디서: Central Park의 Gate 1에서 출발 / 그리고 주차장에서 종료 /

Who: Ages 13 and above / **②의 단서** 13세 이상이 참여함
누가: 13세 이상 /

Distance: 10km /
거리: 10km /

Participation Fee: $5 per person /
참가비: 1인당 5달러 / **③의 단서** 참가비는 1인당 5달러

Registration /
등록 /

- Online only (www.oakfieldminimarathon.com) /
온라인으로만 가능 (www.oakfieldminimarathon.com) /
- September 1 to 30 /
9월 1일부터 30일까지 / **④의 단서** 등록은 9월 1일부터 30일까지
부사절접속사(조건)
※ If you finish the race, / you will receive a T-shirt and an e-certificate. // **⑤의 단서** 경주를 완주하면 티셔츠를 받음
※ 경주를 완주하시면 / 티셔츠와 전자증명서를 받게 됩니다 //

For more information, / visit our website. //
더 많은 정보를 원하시면 / 저희 웹사이트를 방문하세요 //

- celebrate ⓥ 기념하다   • opening ⓝ 개장   • parking lot 주차장
- participation fee 참가비   • registration ⓝ 등록

2023 Oakfield Mini Marathon
우리 동네의 Central Park의 개장을 축하하기 위한 2023 Oakfield Mini Marathon에 참가하세요! 달리는 사람, 조깅하는 사람, 걷는 사람 모두 환영합니다.
언제: 10월 21일 토요일, 오전 8시 30분 시작
어디서: Central Park의 Gate 1에서 출발 및 주차장에서 종료
누가: 13세 이상
거리: 10km
참가비: 1인당 5달러
등록
- 온라인으로만 가능 (www.oakfieldminimarathon.com)
- 9월 1일부터 30일까지
※ 경주를 완주하시면, 티셔츠와 전자증명서를 받게 됩니다. 더 많은 정보를 원하시면, 저희 웹사이트를 방문하세요.

2023 Oakfield Mini Marathon에 관한 다음 안내문의 내용과 일치하는 것은?
① Central Park 주차장에서 출발한다. Start at Gate 1 of Central Park
② 13세 이상 참여할 수 있다. Ages 13 and above
③ 참가비는 무료이다. Participation Fee: $5 per person
④ 9월 1일까지 등록해야 한다. September 1 to 30
⑤ 등록을 하면 티셔츠를 받는다. If you finish the race, you will receive a T-shirt and an e-certificate.

〉**왜** 정답 ? [정답률 91%]
② 13세 이상 참여할 수 있다. (Ages 13 and above)

〉**왜** 오답 ?
① Central Park의 Gate 1에서 출발한다. (Start at Gate 1 of Central Park)
③ 참가비는 1인당 5달러이다. (Participation Fee: $5 per person)
④ 등록은 9월 1일부터 30일까지이다. (September 1 to 30)
⑤ 경주를 완주하면 티셔츠를 받는다. (If you finish the race, you will receive a T-shirt and an e-certificate.)

J 42 정답 ④ ＊2022 Valestown 재활용 포스터 대회

2022 Valestown Recycles Poster Contest /
2022 Valestown 재활용 포스터 대회 /

Join this year's Valestown Recycles Poster Contest / and show off your artistic talent! //
병렬 구조
올해의 Valestown 재활용 포스터 대회에 참가하여 / 여러분의 예술적 재능을 뽐내세요 //

Guidelines /
지침 /
❶의 단서 Valestown의 고등학생만 참여할 수 있음
- Participation is only for high school students in Valestown. //
참가는 Valestown의 고등학생만 가능합니다 //

- Participants should use / the theme of "Recycling for the Future." // **❷의 단서** 참가자는 정해진 주제를 사용해야 함
참가자들은 사용해야 합니다 / '미래를 위한 재활용'이라는 주제를 //

Submission Format /
출품작 형식 /
- File type: PDF only / **❸의 단서** PDF 양식만 허용됨
파일 형식: PDF만 가능 /

- Maximum file size: 40MB /
최대 파일 크기: 40MB /

Judging Criteria /
심사 기준 / **❹의 단서** 심사 기준에 창의성이 포함됨
- Use of theme / - Creativity / - Artistic skill
주제 활용 / 창의성 / 예술적 기술

Details /
세부 사항 / **❺의 단서** 출품은 1인당 하나의 포스터로 제한됨
- Submissions are limited / to one poster per person. //
출품작은 제한됩니다 / 1인당 한 장의 포스터로 //

- Submissions should be uploaded to the website / by 6 p.m.,
(의무)의 조동사   완료 기한을 나타내는 전치사
December 19. //
출품작은 웹 사이트에 업로드되어야 합니다 / 12월 19일 오후 6시까지 //

- Winners will be announced / on the website / on December 28. //
수상자는 발표될 것입니다 / 웹 사이트에 / 12월 28일에 //

For more information, / please visit www.vtco.org. //
더 많은 정보를 원하면 / www.vtco.org를 방문하십시오 //

- show off ~을 자랑하다, 뽐내다 · talent ⓝ 재주, 재능
- submission ⓝ 제출 · format ⓝ 방식
- maximum ⓐ 최대[최고]의 · criterion ⓝ 기준(pl. criteria)

2022 Valestown 재활용 포스터 대회

올해의 Valestown 재활용 포스터 대회에 참가하여 여러분의 예술적 재능을 뽐내세요!
지침
- Valestown의 고등학생만 참가할 수 있습니다.
- 참가자들은 '미래를 위한 재활용'이라는 주제를 사용해야 합니다.
출품작 형식
- 파일 형식: PDF만 가능
- 최대 파일 크기: 40MB
심사 기준
- 주제 활용   - 창의성   - 예술적 기술
세부 사항
- 출품작은 1인당 한 장의 포스터로 제한됩니다.
- 출품작은 12월 19일 오후 6시까지 웹 사이트에 업로드되어야 합니다.
- 수상자는 12월 28일에 웹 사이트에 발표될 것입니다.
　　　더 많은 정보를 원하면 www.vtco.org를 방문하십시오.

2022 Valestown Recycles Poster Contest에 관한 다음 안내문의 내용과 일치하는 것은?

① Valestown의 모든 학생들이 참여할 수 있다. Participation is only for high school students in Valestown.
② 참가자는 포스터의 주제 선정에 제약을 받지 않는다. Participants should use the theme of "Recycling for the Future."
③ 출품할 파일 양식은 자유롭게 선택 가능하다. File type: PDF only
④ 심사 기준에 창의성이 포함된다. Creativity
⑤ 1인당 출품할 수 있는 포스터의 수에는 제한이 없다. Submissions are limited to one poster per person.

＞왜 정답？ [정답률 96%]
심사 기준에는 주제의 사용과 창의성(Creativity), 예술적 기술이 포함되므로 ④이 안내문과 일치한다.

＞왜 오답？
① Valestown의 고등학생만 참여할 수 있다. (Participation is only for high school students in Valestown.)
② 참가자는 정해진 주제를 사용해야 한다. (Participants should use the theme of "Recycling for the Future.")
③ 파일은 PDF 양식만 허용된다. (File type: PDF only)
⑤ 출품은 1인당 하나의 포스터로 제한된다. (Submissions are limited to one poster per person.)

조현준 | 전북대 의예과 2023년 입학·익산 이리고 졸
이 유형은 선택지가 한글로 되어 있기 때문에 선택지를 먼저 읽고 필요한 부분을 안내문에서 찾아 읽는 것을 추천해. 또, 모르는 단어가 있어도 한글로 된 선택지를 보고 뜻을 알아차릴 수도 있지.
이번 문제는 Creativity라는 단어만 제대로 확인하면 정답을 찾을 수 있었어!

J 43 정답 ③ ＊2023 Eastland 고등학교 비디오 클립 경연대회

2023 Eastland High School Video Clip Contest /
2023 Eastland 고등학교 비디오 클립 경연대회 /
명령문
Shoot and share your most memorable moments / with your teachers and friends! //
가장 기억할 만한 순간들을 찍어 공유하세요 / 선생님과 친구들과 //

Guidelines /
참가 요령 /
• Theme: "Joyful Moments" in Our Growing Community /
주제: 우리가 성장하는 공동체에서 '즐거운 순간들' / **❶의 단서** 출품작의 주제가 정해져 있음
미래 시제 수동태 ＊
• Submissions will be accepted / from December 1 to December 14. // **❷의 단서** 2주 동안 동영상을 접수할 예정임
출품작은 접수될 예정입니다 / 12월 1일부터 12월 14일까지 //

• Submissions should be uploaded / to our school website. //
출품작은 업로드되어야 합니다 / 우리 학교 웹사이트에 //

- Video length cannot exceed three minutes. //
동영상의 길이는 3분을 초과할 수 없습니다 // **❸의 단서** 출품할 동영상의 길이는 3분을
초과할 수 없음
- Entries are limited to one per student. //
출품작은 학생 1인당 1개로 제한됩니다 // **❹의 단서** 출품작은 학생 1인당 한 개로 제한됨

Prizes /
시상 /
• 1st place: $100 gift card, 2nd place: $50 gift card /
1등: 100달러 상품권, 2등: 50달러 상품권 /
미래 시제 수동태
• Winning videos will be posted to our school's app. //
수상한 동영상은 우리 학교 앱에 게시될 예정입니다 //

• The prize winners will be chosen / by the school art teachers. //
수상자는 선정될 것입니다 / 학교 미술 선생님들에 의해 // **❺의 단서** 학교 미술 선생님들이
수상자를 선정할 것임
※ For more information, / visit the school website. //
더 많은 정보를 원하시면 / 학교 웹사이트를 방문하세요 //

• shoot ⓥ 촬영하다 • memorable ⓐ 기억할 만한
• theme ⓝ 주제 • submission ⓝ 출품(작)
• entry ⓝ 출품(작), 응모

2023 Eastland 고등학교 비디오 클립 경연대회

선생님, 친구들과의 가장 기억할 만한 순간들을 찍어 공유하세요!

참가 요령
• 주제: 우리가 성장하는 공동체에서 '즐거운 순간들'
• 출품작은 12월 1일부터 12월 14일까지 접수될 예정입니다.
• 출품작은 우리 학교 웹사이트에 업로드되어야 합니다.
– 동영상의 길이는 3분을 초과할 수 없습니다.
– 출품작은 학생 1인당 1개로 제한됩니다.

시상
• 1등: 100달러 상품권, 2등: 50달러 상품권
• 수상한 동영상은 우리 학교 앱에 게시될 예정입니다.
• 수상자는 학교 미술 선생님들에 의해 선정될 것입니다.
※ 더 많은 정보를 원하시면 학교 웹사이트를 방문하세요.

2023 Eastland High School Video Clip Contest에 관한 다음 안내문의 내용과 일치하는 것은?
① 출품작의 주제가 정해져 있지 않다.
　Theme: "Joyful Moments" in Our Growing Community
② 한 달 동안 동영상을 접수할 예정이다.
　Submissions will be accepted from December 1 to December 14.
③ 출품할 동영상의 길이는 3분을 초과할 수 없다.
　Video length cannot exceed three minutes.
④ 출품작은 학생 1인당 두 개로 제한된다. Entries are limited to one per student.
⑤ 학생회가 수상자를 선정할 것이다.
　The prize winners will be chosen by the school art teachers.

왜 정답? [정답률 97%]
③ 출품할 동영상의 길이는 3분을 초과할 수 없다고 했다. (Video length cannot exceed three minutes.)

왜 오답?
① 출품작의 주제는 정해져 있다. (Theme: "Joyful Moments" in Our Growing Community)
② 2주 동안 동영상을 접수할 예정이다. (Submissions will be accepted from December 1 to December 14.)
④ 출품작은 학생 1인당 한 개로 제한된다. (Entries are limited to one per student.)
⑤ 학교 미술 선생님들이 수상자를 선정할 것이다. (The prize winners will be chosen by the school art teachers.)

류이레 | 연세대 의예과 2024년 입학 · 광주대동고 졸
28번 문제는 제시된 자료와 '일치'하는 내용을 고르는 문제야. 이 문제에서는 제시문의 중반부에 나온 Video length cannot exceed three minutes.라는 문장과 ③이 일치하기 때문에 사실 쉽게 답을 고를 수 있는 문제였어. 도표, 자료 문제는 단순한 매칭 문제니까 듣기평가 도중에 해결해서 독해 시간을 확보하는 걸 추천해!

─── 어법 특강 ───

✱ 수동태의 시제

수동태 과거	was/were+과거분사
수동태 진행	is/are+being+과거분사
	was/were+being+과거분사
수동태 완료	have[has]+been+과거분사
	had+been+과거분사
수동태 조동사	조동사+be+과거분사

01 구입, 구매	11 care for	21 rooftop
02 선명한, 생생한	12 sign up for	22 profits
03 이전의	13 on site	23 beverages
04 분석가	14 be limited to	24 announced
05 동반하다	15 due to	25 via
06 benefit	16 featured	26 mind
07 rare	17 display	27 at least
08 observe	18 spot	28 participants
09 refreshing	19 process	29 Submission
10 tuition	20 university	30 limited

J

K 빈칸 완성하기 〔문제편 p. 185~234〕

K 01 정답 ⑤ ＊사진이 장소에 미친 영향

Prior to photography, / **places did not travel well.** //
사진이 나오기 전에는 / 장소들이 잘 이동하지 않았다 //
부사절 접속사(대조)
<u>While</u> painters have always lifted |particular places / out of their
particular places를 가리키는 / 소유격/목적격 대명사
'dwelling' / and transported them elsewhere, /
화가들이 항상 특정한 장소를 들어 올려 / 그것의 '거주지' 밖으로 / 그것을 다른 곳으로 이동시켜 왔지만 /
부사적 용법(time-consuming 수식)
paintings were time-consuming to produce, / relatively difficult
부사적 용법(difficult 수식)
to transport / and one-of-a-kind. // **단서 1** 그림은 장소를 이동시키는 데 어려움이 많았음
그림은 제작에 시간이 많이 걸렸고 / 상대적으로 운반이 어려웠고 / 단품 수주 생산이었다 //

The multiplication of photographs especially took place / with
the introduction of the half-tone plate / in the 1880s /
사진의 증가는 특히 이루어졌다 / 하프톤 판의 도입으로 / 1880년대 /

that made possible the mechanical reproduction of photographs
made의 목적격 보어와 목적어
/ in newspapers, periodicals, books and advertisements. //
사진의 기계적인 복제를 가능하게 한 / 신문, 정기간행물, 책 그리고 광고에서 //

Photography became coupled / to consumer capitalism / and
the globe was now offered / 'in limitless quantities, / figures,
landscapes, events /
사진은 결합하게 되었고 / 소비자 자본주의와 / 이제 세계는 제공받았다 / '무제한의 양으로 / 인물, 풍경, 사건들을 /

which had not previously been utilised either at all, / or only as
pictures / for one customer'. //
이전에는 전혀 사용되지 않았거나 / 그림으로만 사용되었던 / 단 한 명의 고객을 위한' //

With capitalism's arrangement of the world / as a 'department
store', /
자본주의가 세계를 정리함에 따라 / '백화점'으로 / **단서 2** 사진을 통해 표현물이 세계적 규모로 확산 및 유통됨
'the proliferation and circulation of representations ... achieved
/ a spectacular and virtually inescapable global magnitude'. //
'표현물의 확산과 유통은 … 달성했다 / 극적이고 사실상 피할 수 없는 세계적 규모를' //

Gradually photographs became / cheap mass-produced objects
/ that made the world visible, aesthetic and desirable. //
made의 목적어와 목적격 보어
점차 사진은 되었다 / 값싼 대량생산품이 / 세계를 가시적이고, 미적이며, 탐나게 만드는 //

Experiences were 'democratised' / by translating them into
cheap images. //
수단을 나타내는 「by+동명사」
경험들은 '대중화'되었다 / 그것을 저렴한 이미지로 바꿈으로써 //

Light, small and mass-produced photographs / became dynamic
vehicles / for the spatiotemporal circulation of places. //
가볍고 작고 대량으로 제작된 사진은 / 역동적인 수단이 되었다 / 장소의 시공간적 순환을 위한 // **단서 3** 사진은 장소의 시공간적 순환을 위한 역동적인 수단이 되었음

- prior to ~ 이전에 • lift ~ out of ~을 들어서 벗어나게 하다
- dwelling ⓝ 거주지 • transport ⓥ 이동시키다
- time-consuming ⓐ 시간이 많이 걸리는
- one-of-a-kind 단 하나뿐인 것 • multiplication ⓝ 증가, 증식
- take place 이루어지다 • periodical ⓝ 정기 간행물
- capitalism ⓝ 자본주의 • globe ⓝ 세계 • limitless ⓐ 무제한의
- circulation ⓝ 순환 • virtually ⓐⓓ 사실상
- democratise ⓥ 민주화하다 • spatiotemporal ⓐ 시공간적인

사진이 나오기 전에는 **장소들이 잘 이동하지 않았다**. 화가들이 항상 특정한 장소를 그것의 '거주지'에서 벗어나게 해 다른 곳으로 이동시켜 왔지만, 그림은 제작에 시간이 많이 걸렸고, 상대적으로 운반이 어려웠고, 단품 수주 생산이었다. 사진의 증가는 특히, 신문, 정기간행물, 책 그리고 광고에서

사진의 기계적인 복제를 가능하게 한 1880년대 하프톤 판의 도입으로 이루어졌다. 사진은 소비자 자본주의와 결합하게 되었고 이제 세계는 '이전에는 전혀 사용되지 않았거나 단 한 명의 고객을 위한 그림으로만 사용되었던 인물, 풍경, 사건들을 무제한의 양으로 제공받았다'. 자본주의가 세계를 '백화점'으로 정리함에 따라, '표현물의 확산과 유통은... 극적이고 사실상 피할 수 없는 세계적 규모를 달성했다'. 점차 사진은 세계를 가시적이고, 미적이며, 탐나게 만드는 값싼 대량생산품이 되었다. 경험들은 그것을 저렴한 이미지로 바꿈으로써 '대중화'되었다. 가볍고 작고 대량으로 제작된 사진은 장소의 시공간적 순환을 위한 역동적인 수단이 되었다.

다음 빈칸에 들어갈 말로 가장 적절한 것을 고르시오. [3점]

① paintings alone connected with nature 자연과의 연관성에 대한 내용이 아님
그림만이 자연과 연관되었다
② painting was the major form of art 예술로서의 사진의 역할을 설명하지 않음
그림은 예술의 주요한 형식이었다
③ art held up a mirror to the world 예술이 세상을 반영했다는 것이 아님
예술은 세상을 비추는 거울이 되었다
④ desire for travel was not strong 그림과 사진을 통한 장소의 이동을 대조하는 글임
여행을 위한 욕구가 강하지 않았다
⑤ places did not travel well 장소를 시공간적으로 순환시킨 사진과 대조됨
장소들이 잘 이동하지 않았다

> 왜 정답? [정답률 25%]

사진이 나오기 이전	화가가 그림을 통해 장소를 이동시켰으나, 그림은 제작에 시간이 많이 걸리고, 운반이 어려우며, 단품 수주 생산이라는 어려움이 있음
하프톤 판의 도입	사진의 기계적인 복제가 가능해지고, 표현물의 확산과 유통이 세계적인 규모를 달성함
사진의 역할	장소의 시공간적 순환을 위한 역동적인 수단이 됨

→ 사진이 나오기 이전과 이후의 상황이 대조되는 글이다.
빈칸 문장은 사진이 나오기 이전의 상황을 설명한다.
▶ 마지막 문장에서 사진이 장소의 시공간적 순환을 위한 역동적인 수단이 되었다고 했으므로, 빈칸 문장은, 사진이 나오기 전에는 ⑤ '장소들이 잘 이동하지 않았다'는 내용이 되어야 한다.

> 왜 오답?

① 사진이 표현물의 확산과 유통에 미친 영향을 설명하는 글이다.
② 예술의 형식으로서 그림과 사진의 차이를 설명하는 것이 아니다.
③ 예술의 역할은 언급되지 않았다.
④ 사진이나 그림이 여행 욕구에 미친 영향이 글의 주요 내용은 아니다.

K 02 정답 ⑤ ＊문학이 외국어 학습에 도움을 주는 방식

Literature can be helpful / in the language learning process /
전치사
because of the **personal involvement** / it fosters in readers. //
앞에 목적격 관계대명사 생략
문학은 도움이 될 수 있다 / 언어 학습 과정에 / 개인적 몰입 때문에 / 그것이 독자에게 촉진하는 //

Core language teaching materials / must concentrate on / how
의문사절을 이끎
a language operates / both as a rule-based system and as a
sociosemantic system. // ├─ both A and B: A와 B 둘 다 ─┤
핵심 언어 교육 자료는 / 중점을 두어야 한다 / 언어가 어떻게 작동하는지에 / 규칙 기반 체계이자 사회의미론적인 체계로서 //

Very often, / the process of learning / is essentially analytic,
piecemeal, / and, at the level of the personality, / fairly
superficial. //
매우 흔히 / 학습 과정은 / 본질적으로 분석적이고 단편적이며 / 개인의 수준에서는 / 상당히 피상적이다 // **단서 1** 문학에 몰입하며 상상력을 발휘하는 것은 외국어 체계의 기계적인 측면을 넘어 초점을 전환하도록 해줌
Engaging imaginatively with literature / enables learners to
동명사 주어(단수 취급) / 단수동사
shift the focus of their attention / beyond the more mechanical
aspects / of the foreign language system. //
상상력을 발휘하여 문학에 몰입함으로써 / 학습자는 주의의 초점을 전환할 수 있게 된다 / 더 기계적인 측면 너머로 / 외국어 체계의 //

When a novel, play or short story / is explored over a period of
time, / the result is / that the reader begins to 'inhabit' the text. //
소설, 희곡, 혹은 단편 소설이 / 일정 기간 탐구되면 / 그 결과로 ~한다 / 독자는 그 글에
'깃들기' 시작 //

He or she is drawn / into the book. //
그 독자는 빨려 들어간다 / 책 속으로 //

Pinpointing / what individual words or phrases may mean /
becomes less important / than pursuing the development of the
story. //
정확히 집어내는 것은 / 개별 단어나 어구가 무엇을 의미할 수도 있는지 / 덜 중요해진다 /
이야기 전개를 따라가는 것보다 //

단서 2 독자는 책에 빨려 들어가며 점차 언어 하나하나의 의미에 집착하기보다는 이야기의 전개나 등장인물의 감정에 더 관심을 두게 됨

The reader is eager to find out / what happens as events unfold;
/ he or she feels close / to certain characters / and shares their
emotional responses. //
독자는 간절히 알아내고 싶어 하고 / 사건이 전개되면서 무슨 일이 일어나는지 / 그 독자는
친밀감을 느끼며 / 특정 등장인물들과 / 그들의 감정적 반응을 공유한다 //

The language becomes 'transparent' / — the fiction draws the
whole person / into its own world. // **단서 3** 문학은 독자 전체를 자신의 세계로 끌어들여 언어가 투명해지도록 만듦
언어는 '투명'해지는데 / 소설은 그 사람 전체를 끌어들인다 / 그 자신의 세계로 //

- literature ⓝ 문학   · foster ⓥ 촉진하다, 강화하다
- concentrate on ~에 중점을 두다   · piecemeal ⓐ 단편적인
- superficial ⓐ 피상적인   · inhabit ⓥ ~에 깃들다, ~에 거주하다
- pinpoint ⓥ 정확히 찾아내다   · unfold ⓥ 전개되다
- insight ⓝ 통찰력   · sensibility ⓝ 감성[감수성]
- alternative ⓐ 대안적인   · involvement ⓝ 몰입

문학은 그것이 독자에게 촉진하는 **개인적 몰입** 때문에 언어 학습 과정에 도움이
될 수 있다. 핵심 언어 교육 자료는 언어가 규칙 기반 체계이자 사회의미론적인
체계로서 어떻게 작동하는지에 중점을 두어야 한다. 매우 흔히, 학습 과정은
본질적으로 분석적이고 단편적이며, 개인의 수준에서는 상당히 피상적이다.
상상력을 발휘하여 문학에 몰입함으로써 학습자는 주의의 초점을 외국어
체계의 더 기계적인 측면 너머로 전환할 수 있게 된다. 소설, 희곡, 혹은 단편
소설이 일정 기간 탐구되면, 그 결과로 독자는 그 글에 '깃들기' 시작한다. 그
독자는 책 속으로 빨려 들어간다. 개별 단어나 어구가 무엇을 의미할 수도
있는지 정확히 집어내는 것은 이야기 전개를 따라가는 것보다 덜 중요해진다.
독자는 사건이 전개되면서 무슨 일이 일어나는지 간절히 알아내고 싶어 하고,
그 독자는 특정 등장인물들과 친밀감을 느끼며 그들의 감정적 반응을 공유한다.
언어는 '투명'해지는데, 소설은 그 사람 전체를 그 자신의 세계로 끌어들인다.

다음 빈칸에 들어갈 말로 가장 적절한 것을 고르시오.

① linguistic insight 문학은 언어를 오히려 투명하게 만들어서 문학의 세계로 끌어들인다고 했음
언어적 통찰력
② artistic imagination 문학은 상상을 통해 독자를 문학의 세계로 몰입하게 만든다는 내용이지,
예술적 상상력   문학 자체의 예술적 상상력이 언어 학습을 돕는다는 내용은 아님
③ literary sensibility 문학적 감수성에 관한 내용은 언급되지 않음
문학적 감수성
④ alternative perspective 문학이 다른 관점을 제공한다는 것이 아님
대안적 관점
⑤ personal involvement 문학은 독자가 문학의 세계에 개인적으로 몰입하게 함으로써
개인적 몰입   외국어 학습에 도움을 줌

왜 정답? [정답률 38%]

1st 빈칸이 포함된 문장을 읽고, 빈칸에 들어갈 말에 대한 단서를 얻는다.

빈칸 문장	문학은 그것이 독자에게 촉진하는 _____ 때문에 언어 학습 과정에 도움이 될 수 있다.

→ 글의 첫 부분에 밑줄이 있으므로, 글의 전체적인 주제를 다루는 부분이며, 이어질
내용을 토대로 문학의 '이러한 특징' 덕분에 언어 학습 과정에 도움이 될 것이라는
내용임

▶ 빈칸을 채우려면 글에서 소개된 내용을 통해 문학이 언어 학습에 어떻게 도움을
주는지를 찾아야 한다.

2nd 글을 마저 읽으며 빈칸에 들어갈 적절한 말을 찾는다.

보통의 언어 교육 자료는 언어의 규칙, 체계 등 피상적이고 분석적인 측면만을 다룸 →
하지만 문학에 몰입하며 상상력을 발휘하는 것은 외국어 체계의 기계적인 측면을 넘어
초점을 전환하도록 해줌 → 독자는 책에 빨려 들어가며 점차 언어 하나하나의 의미에
집착하기보다는 이야기의 전개나 등장인물의 감정에 더 관심을 두게 됨 → 문학은
독자 전체를 자신의 세계로 끌어들여 언어가 투명해지도록 만듦

▶ 언어를 교육할 때 우리가 흔히 사용하는 자료는 언어의 사회의미론적 체계를
다루는 분석적, 단편적 자료이고, 이로 인해 학습자는 피상적으로 언어를 학습할
수밖에 없다. 하지만 문학은 독자를 책에 빨려 들어가게 만들며 점차 단어 하나하나의
의미가 중요하지 않게 만들어 준다.
즉, 문학은 독자를 자신의 세계로 이끌어 이야기의 전개나 등장인물의 감정에 더
초점을 맞추게 함으로써 언어를 투명하게 만든다는 것이다. 따라서 문학이 외국어
학습에 도움을 주는 방식은 독자가 문학에 개인적으로 몰입하게 함이므로, 정답은
⑤ '개인적 몰입'이다.

| 선택지 분석 |

① **linguistic insight**
언어적 통찰력
문학은 언어를 오히려 투명하게 만들어서 문학의 세계로 끌어들인다고 했으므로,
언어적 통찰력은 빈칸과 상반되는 표현이다.

② **artistic imagination**
예술적 상상력
문학은 상상을 통해 독자를 문학의 세계로 몰입하게 만든다는 내용이지, 문학 자체의
예술적 상상력이 언어 학습을 돕는다는 내용은 아니다.

③ **literary sensibility**
문학적 감수성
문학적 감수성에 관한 내용은 언급되지 않았다.

④ **alternative perspective**
대안적 관점
문학이 다른 관점을 제공한다는 것이 아니라, 주인공의 감정을 공유하고 그들의
세계에 몰입하도록 만들어 준다는 내용이다.

⑤ **personal involvement**
개인적 몰입
문학은 독자가 문학의 세계에 개인적으로 몰입하게 함으로써 외국어 학습에 도움을 준다.

백승준 | 2025 수능 응시 · 광주 광주숭원고 졸
나는 빈칸 문제에서 빈칸이 있는 문장을 먼저 읽고 빈칸에서
요구하는 정보를 파악한 후 그걸 의식하며 지문을 읽어나가. 이
문제에서는 문학을 읽는 독자가 얻는 능력을 찾으면 되겠지.
지문을 읽어보면 Engaging imaginatively나 inhabit the text
같은 부분에서 힌트를 얻을 수 있었지. 글 전반적으로도 큰 반전 없이 진행되어서
쉽게 답을 찾을 수 있던 문제였어. 또한, 3번째 문장(Very often ~ superficial.)과
문학을 통한 언어 학습의 이점을 대조하며 읽으면 쉽게 글의 주제를 이해할 수
있었지.

K 03 정답 ⑤ ＊역할과 관행을 확립함으로써 생산적인 활동을 촉진하는 규칙

과거분사(rules 수식)
Centralized, formal rules / can **facilitate productive activity /
by establishing roles and practices**. //
중앙 집권화되고 공식적인 규칙은 / 생산적인 활동을 촉진할 수 있다 / 역할과 관행을
확립함으로써 //

The rules of baseball don't just regulate the behavior of the
players; / they determine the behavior / that constitutes playing
the game. // 주격 관계대명사
야구 규칙은 그저 선수들의 행동을 규제하는 것만이 아니라 / 행동을 결정한다 / 경기하는
것을 구성하는 //

prevent A from B: A를 B로부터 막다
Rules do not prevent people from playing baseball; / they create
the very **practice** / that allows people to play baseball. //
the very+명사: 바로 그 명사
규칙은 사람들이 야구를 하지못하게 막는 게 아니라 / 바로 그 관행을 만들어 낸다 / 사람들이
야구를 할 수 있게 하는 // **단서 1** 야구 규칙은 행동을 규제하는 것이 아니라 경기를 구성하는
행동을 결정하여 경기가 진행되도록 함

A score of music imposes rules, / but it also creates a pattern of

conduct / that enables people to produce music. //
주격 관계대명사 enable+목적어+목적격 보어(to 부정사)

악보는 규칙을 부과하지만 / 그것은 또한 행동 양식을 만들어 내기도 한다 / 사람들이 음악을
만들 수 있게 하는 // **단서 2** 악보는 음악에 규칙을 부과하지만, 음악을 만들 수 있게 하기도 함

Legal rules that enable the formation of corporations, / that
                              rules를 수식하는 that절의 병렬 구조
enable the use of wills and trusts, / that create negotiable

instruments, / and that establish the practice of contracting /

기업의 형성을 가능하게 하는 법규 / 유언장과 신탁금의 사용을 가능하게 하는 법규 / 양도성
증권을 만들어 내는 법규 / 계약의 관행을 확립하는 법규는 /
문장의 본동사   practices를 선행사로 하는 관계대명사
all make practices / that create new opportunities for

individuals. // **단서 3** 모든 법규들은 새로운 기회를 창출하는 관행을 만듦
모두 관행을 만든다 / 사람들을 위해 새로운 기회를 만들어 내는 //
                     주격 관계대명사   목적격 관계대명사 생략
And we have legal rules / that establish roles / individuals play

within the legal system, / such as judges, trustees, partners, and

guardians. //

그리고 우리에게는 법규가 있다 / 역할을 확립하는 / 법률 시스템 내에서 개인이 수행하는 /
판사, 신탁 관리자, 동업자, 후견인과 같은 //
                     주격 관계대명사
True, / the legal rules that establish these roles / constrain the
                                 주격 관계대명사
behavior of individuals / who occupy them, / but rules also
                   강조적 용법(생략 가능)
create the roles themselves. // **단서 4** 개인의 역할을 확립하는 법규는 사람들의 행동을
                                      제약하지만, 동시에 그 역할을 만들어 내기도 함
물론 / 이러한 역할을 확립하는 법규는 / 사람들의 행동을 제약하지만 / 그 역할을 차지하는 /
규칙 스스로가 또한 역할을 만들어 내기도 한다 //

Without them / an individual would not have the opportunity /
                           형용사적 용법(opportunity 수식)
to occupy the role. //

그것들이 없다면 / 개인은 기회를 갖지 못할 것이다 / 역할을 차지할 //

- centralize ⓥ 중앙집권화하다   - constitute ⓥ 구성하다
- impose ⓥ 부과하다   - will ⓝ 유언장   - trust ⓝ 신탁금
- negotiable ⓐ 절충 가능한   - trustee ⓝ 신탁 관리자
- guardian ⓝ 후견인   - occupy ⓥ 차지하다
- reinforce ⓥ 강화하다

중앙 집권화되고 공식적인 규칙은 **역할과 관행을 확립함으로써 생산적인
활동을 촉진할** 수 있다. 야구 규칙은 그저 선수들의 행동을 규제하는 것만이
아니라, 경기하는 것을 구성하는 행동을 결정한다. 규칙은 사람들이 야구를
하지 못하게 막는 게 아니라, 사람들이 야구를 할 수 있게 하는 바로 그 관행을
만들어 낸다. 악보는 규칙을 부과하지만, 그것은 또한 사람들이 음악을 만들
수 있게 하는 행동 양식을 만들어 내기도 한다. 기업의 형성을 가능하게 하는
법규, 유언장과 신탁금의 사용을 가능하게 하는 법규, 양도성 증권을 만들어
내는 법규, 계약의 관행을 확립하는 법규는 모두 사람들을 위해 새로운 기회를
만들어 내는 관행을 만든다. 그리고 우리에게는 판사, 신탁 관리자, 동업자,
후견인과 같은 법률 시스템 내에서 개인이 수행하는 역할을 확립하는 법규가
있다. 물론, 이러한 역할을 확립하는 법규는 그 역할을 차지하는 사람들의
행동을 제약하지만, 규칙 스스로가 또한 역할을 만들어 내기도 한다. 그것들이
없다면 개인은 역할을 차지할 기회를 갖지 못할 것이다.

다음 빈칸에 들어갈 말로 가장 적절한 것을 고르시오. [3점]

① categorize one's patterns of conduct in legal and productive
   ways 행동 양식을 분류한다는 내용은 언급되지 않음
   합법적이고 생산적인 방식으로 행동 양식을 분류할
                                      규칙이 각자의
② lead people to reevaluate their roles and practices in a society
   사람들이 사회에서 자기 역할과 행동을 재평가하도록 이끌   역할과 행동을 재평가한다는 내용은 아님
③ encourage new ways of thinking which promote creative ideas
   창의적인 생각을 촉진하는 새로운 사고방식을 장려할   창의적인 사고방식에 관한 내용은 언급되지 않음
④ reinforce one's behavior within legal and established contexts
   합법적이고 확립된 맥락 내에서 자기의 행동을 강화할
⑤ facilitate productive activity by establishing roles and
   practices   합법적이고 확립된 규칙을 통해 자신의 행동을 강화한다는 내용은 아님
   역할과 관행을 확립함으로써 생산적인 활동을 촉진할
   공식적인 규칙은 역할이나 관행을 설정해 줌으로써 생산적인 활동을 가능하게 함

왜 정답? [정답률 34%]

1st 빈칸이 포함된 문장을 읽고, 빈칸에 들어갈 말에 대한 단서를 얻는다.

빈칸 문장	중앙 집권화되고 공식적인 규칙은 _____ 수 있다.

→ 글의 첫 부분에 밑줄이 있으므로, 글의 전체적인 주제를 다루는 부분이며, 이어질
내용을 토대로 중앙 집권화되고 공식적인 규칙이 무엇을 할 수 있는지에 관한
내용임

▶ 빈칸을 채우려면 글에서 소개된 내용을 통해 공식적인 규칙들이 어떤 특징을
가지는지를 찾아야 한다.

2nd 글을 마저 읽으며 빈칸에 들어갈 적절한 말을 찾는다.

예시 1) 야구 규칙은 행동을 규제하는 것이 아니라 경기를 구성하는 행동을 결정하여
경기가 진행되도록 함 → 예시 2) 악보는 음악에 규칙을 부과하지만, 음악을 만들 수
있게 하기도 함 → 예시 3) 모든 법규들은 새로운 기회를 창출하는 관행을 만듦 → 예시
4) 개인의 역할을 확립하는 법규는 사람들의 행동을 제약하지만, 동시에 그 역할을
만들어 내기도 함

▶ 중앙 집권화되고 공식적인 규칙들은 어떤 역할을 할 수 있는가에 관한 글이다.
주제문 이후 이어지는 문장에서 여러 구체적인 사례들이 제시되고 있다. 야구는
규칙을 통해 선수들이 하지 못할 행동을 규제하기도 하지만, 규칙이 있어서 경기가
진행된다.

악보는 음악을 어떻게 연주하라는 규칙을 부과하지만, 음악을 만들 수 있게 하기도
한다. 또한 모든 법규는 새로운 기회를 창출하는 관행을 만들며, 개인의 역할을
확립하는 법규는 개인마다 어떤 행동을 해야 하는지 제약하지만 동시에 그 역할을
만들어 내기도 한다.

즉, 공식적인 규칙들은 역할과 관행을 확립해 줌으로써 오히려 그것을 가능하게
한다는 내용이므로, 정답은 ⑤ '역할과 관행을 확립함으로써 생산적인 활동을
촉진할'이다.

| 선택지 분석 |

① **categorize one's patterns of conduct in legal and productive
ways**
합법적이고 생산적인 방식으로 행동 양식을 분류할
행동 양식을 분류한다는 내용은 언급되지 않았다.

② **lead people to reevaluate their roles and practices in a society**
사람들이 사회에서 자기 역할과 행동을 재평가하도록 이끌
규칙은 사람들이 각자의 역할과 행동을 할 수 있도록 해준다는 내용이지, 그것을
재평가한다는 내용은 아니다.

③ **encourage new ways of thinking which promote creative ideas**
창의적인 생각을 촉진하는 새로운 사고방식을 장려할
창의적인 사고방식에 관한 내용은 언급되지 않았다.

④ **reinforce one's behavior within legal and established contexts**
합법적이고 확립된 맥락 내에서 자기의 행동을 강화할
합법적이고 확립된 규칙을 통해 생산적인 활동이 가능하다는 내용이지, 자신의 행동을
강화한다는 내용은 아니다.

⑤ **facilitate productive activity by establishing roles and practices**
역할과 관행을 확립함으로써 생산적인 활동을 촉진할
공식적인 규칙은 역할이나 관행을 설정해 줌으로써 생산적인 활동을 가능하게 한다.

백승준 | 2025 수능 응시 · 광주 광주숭원고 졸

이 문제는 빈칸에 '규칙의 특징'이 들어가야 함을 금방 파악할 수
있을 거야. 해석하기 매우 어려운 문장은 없지만, 말하고자 하는
바를 명확하게 파악하지 못했고 정답에 근접해 보이는 ①, ④,
⑤ 선택지가 비슷해 보여서 답을 고르기에 곤란했던 문제였어.
그래서 나는 선택지별로 오답의 여지가 있는 부분을 파악하여 소거법으로 이 문제를
해결했어. 글에서 반복되는 말이 '규칙이 ~를 확립한다.'였기에 ①, ④에서 각각
categorize와 reinforce가 부적절하다고 생각하여 답을 ⑤으로 선택했지.

K 04 정답 ② *빛에 의해 갇혀 있는 나방

There has been a lot of discussion / on why moths are attracted to light. //
많은 논의가 있어 왔다 / 나방이 왜 빛에 끌리는지에 관한 //

목적어절을 이끄는 접속사
The consensus seems to hold / that moths are not so much attracted to lights / as they are **trapped** by them. //
not so much A as B: A라기보다는 B에 가까운
합의인 것처럼 보인다 / 나방이 빛에 끌리는 것이 아니라 / 빛에 의해 갇힌다는 것이 //

단서 1 빛은 곤충이 방향을 잃고 제자리를 맴돌게 하는 특성이 있음
주격 관계대명사
The light becomes a sensory overload / that disorients the insects / and sends them into a holding pattern. //
관계대명사절의 동사 ②   관계대명사절의 동사 ①
빛은 감각 과부하를 일으킨다 / 곤충이 방향을 잃게 하는 / 그리고 그것이 제자리를 맴돌게 하는 //

hypothesis를 수식하는 분사   목적어절을 이끄는 접속사
A hypothesis called the Mach band theory suggests / that moths see a dark area around a light source / and head for it / to escape the light. //
that절의 동사 ①   that절의 동사 ②
마하 밴드 이론이라는 가설은 보여준다 / 나방이 광원 주변의 어두운 영역을 본다고 / 그리고 그쪽으로 향한다고 / 빛을 피하고자 //

목적어절을 이끄는 접속사
Another theory suggests / that moths perceive the light / coming from a source as a diffuse halo / with a dark spot in the center. //
또 다른 이론은 보여준다 / 나방이 빛을 인식한다는 것을 / 광원에서 나오는 널리 퍼진 광륜(光輪)으로 / 중앙에 어두운 점이 있는 //

The moths, / attempting to escape the light, /
나방은 / 빛을 피하려고 애쓰면서 /

fly toward that imagined "portal," /
★분사구문
상상 속의 '입구'를 향해 날아간다 /

bringing them closer to the source. //
★분사구문
그래서 광원에 더 가까이 다가가게 된다 //

> **분사구문의 다양한 의미**
> 부사절의 주어가 주절의 주어와 같으면 부사절의 주어를 생략하고 분사구문을 만들 수 있다. 분사구문은 시간, 이유, 조건, 양보, 동시동작 등 다양한 의미를 나타낸다.

단서 2 빛에 가까워지면서 나방은 입구에 도달하기 위해 어쩔 수 없이 빛 주위를 맴돌게 됨
As they approach the light, / their reference point changes / and they circle the light hopelessly / trying to reach the portal. //
분사구문
빛에 가까워지면서 / 나방의 기준점이 바뀌고 / 나방은 어쩔 도리 없이 빛 주위를 맴돈다 / 입구에 도달하기 위해 //

moths를 수식하는 분사
Everyone is familiar with moths / circling their porch lights. //
누구나 나방에 익숙하다 / 현관 불빛을 맴도는 // 단서 3 나방은 빛의 끌어당김에서 벗어나려고 애씀

Their flight appears to have no purpose, / but they are, it is believed, / trying to escape / the pull of the light. //
나방의 비행은 아무런 목적이 없는 것처럼 보인다 / 그러나 그들은 여겨진다 / 벗어나려고 애쓰고 있는 것으로 / 빛의 끌어당김에서 //

- **consensus** ⓝ 합의
- **overload** ⓝ 과부하
- **send ~ into a holding pattern** ~가 제자리를 맴돌게 하다
- **hypothesis** ⓝ 가설
- **perceive** ⓥ 인식하다
- **halo** ⓝ 광륜(光輪), 후광
- **reference point** 기준점, 참조점
- **target** ⓥ 겨냥하다
- **sensory** ⓐ 감각의
- **disorient** ⓥ 방향을 잃게 하다
- **escape** ⓥ 달아나다, 탈출하다
- **diffuse** ⓐ 널리 퍼진, 분산된
- **portal** ⓝ 입구, 정문
- **porch** ⓝ 현관
- **trap** ⓥ 가두다
- **reject** ⓥ 거부하다

나방이 왜 빛에 끌리는지에 관한 많은 논의가 있어 왔다. 나방이 빛에 끌리는 것이 아니라 빛에 의해 **갇힌다**는 것이 합의인 것처럼 보인다. 빛은 감각 과부하를 일으켜 곤충이 방향을 잃게 하고 그것이 제자리를 맴돌게 한다. 마하 밴드 이론이라는 가설에 따르면, 나방은 광원 주변의 어두운 영역을 보고 빛을 피하고자 그쪽으로 향한다. 또 다른 이론은 나방이 광원에서 나오는 빛을 중앙에 어두운 점이 있는, 널리 퍼진 광륜(光輪)으로 인식한다는 것을 보여 준다. 나방은 빛을 피하려고 애쓰면서, 상상 속의 '입구'를 향해 날아가 광원에 더 가까이 다가가게 된다. 빛에 가까워지면서 나방의 기준점이 바뀌고 나방은 입구에 도달하기 위해 어쩔 도리 없이 빛 주위를 맴돈다. 누구나 현관 불빛을 맴도는 나방에 익숙하다. 나방의 비행은 아무런 목적이 없는 것처럼 보이지만, 그들은 빛의 끌어당김에서 벗어나려고 애쓰고 있는 것으로 여겨진다.

다음 빈칸에 들어갈 말로 가장 적절한 것을 고르시오.

① warmed 나방이 빛에 의해 데워진다는 내용은 없음
  데워진
②**trapped** 나방이 빛에 끌리는 것이 아니라 빛에 의해 갇히게 되는 것이라는 내용임
  갇힌
③ targeted 나방이 빛을 피하려고 애쓴다는 것이지 겨냥되었다고 하지 않음
  겨냥된
④ protected 나방이 빛에 의해 보호되고 있다는 언급은 없음
  보호된
⑤ rejected 나방이 빛에 의해 거부당하는 것이 아니라 벗어나려고 애쓰는 것임
  거부된

> **왜 정답?** [정답률 66%]

빈칸 문장	나방이 빛에 끌리는 것이 아니라 빛에 의해 _____는 것이 합의인 것처럼 보인다.

→ 빈칸에는 나방이 빛에 끌리는 것이 아니라 빛에 의해 어떻게 되는지가 들어가야 한다.

- 빛은 감각 과부하를 일으켜 곤충이 방향을 잃게 하고 그것이 제자리를 맴돌게 한다. 단서 1
- 빛에 가까워지면서 나방의 기준점이 바뀌고 나방은 입구에 도달하기 위해 어쩔 도리 없이 빛 주위를 맴돈다. 단서 2
- 그들은 빛의 끌어당김에서 벗어나려고 애쓰고 있는 것으로 여겨진다. 단서 3

→ 나방이 빛에 끌리기 때문에 빛 주위를 맴도는 것이 아니라 빛의 특성(곤충이 방향을 잃고 제자리를 맴돌게 만드는)에 의해 빛을 피하지 못하고 입구를 찾는 것처럼 그 주변을 계속 맴돌게 된다는 내용의 글이다.
  ▶ 그러므로 나방은 빛에 끌리는 것이 아니라 빛에 의해 갇히는 것이라고 할 수 있으므로 ② '갇힌'이 정답이다.

> **왜 오답?**

① 나방이 빛에 의해 데워진다는 내용은 없다.
③ 나방이 빛을 피하려고 애쓴다는 것이지 빛에 의해 겨냥되었다고 하지 않았다.
④ 나방이 빛에 의해 보호되고 있다는 언급은 없다.
⑤ 나방이 빛에 의해 거부당하는 것이 아니라 벗어나려고 애쓰는 것이다.

K 05 정답 ② *시각 정보에 비해 더 큰 청각 정보에 대한 민감도

We are **less forgiving of technical sound mistakes** / than we are of visual ones. //
우리는 음향에 관한 기술적인 실수를 덜 용서한다 / 시각적인 것보다 //

We notice and dislike / breaks in audio, defects in audio, and static in audio. // 단서 1 우리는 오디오의 끊김, 결함 및 잡음을 인지하고 싫어함
우리는 알아차리고 싫어한다 / 오디오의 끊김, 결함, 및 잡음을 //

단서 2 오디오보다 시각 자료의 흠에 덜 예민함
A bit less so for things on the visual side. //
시각적인 면에 있는 것들에 대해서는 조금 덜 그렇다 //

For example, / if a video has some scan lines in it, / within a short period, / you will start to ignore them. //
명사적 용법 (= scan lines)
예를 들어 / 만약 일부 주사선(스캔 라인)이 비디오에 있다면 / 짧은 기간 내에 / 당신은 그것을 무시하기 시작할 것이다 //

If the visual signal streams in 1080 instead of 4k, / eventually you'll get used to it. //
get used to ~: ~에 익숙해지다
만약 시각적인 신호가 4k가 아니라 1080으로 스트리밍된다면 / 결국 당신은 그것에 익숙해질 것이다 //

However / if there is static in the audio, / you will want to shut it off / rather than endure the whole program. //
그러나 / 만약 오디오에 잡음이 있다면 / 당신은 그것을 꺼버리고 싶을 것이다 / 전체 프로그램을 견디기보다 //

Or if the audio continues to drop out, / you also will barely be able to tolerate it. //
또는 오디오가 계속 중단된다면 / 당신은 또한 그것을 참기 어려울 것이다 //

In fact, / probably more than any other aspect of filmmaking, / it is via the audio / that people determine silently to themselves, /
└ it is ~ that ... 강조 구문 ┘
사실 / 아마도 영화 제작의 다른 어떤 측면보다 / 오디오를 통해서이다 / 사람들이 조용히 결정하는 것은 /

"Good, professional quality" or "low-budget student production" / as soon as the film begins. //
"훌륭하고 전문적인 품질" 또는 "저예산 학생 작품"이라고 / 영화가 시작되자마자 //

These reactions are not just from seasoned filmmakers and educators, / but the instinctual, natural reaction of all audiences. //
└ not A but B: A가 아니라 B ┘
이러한 반응은 숙련된 영화 제작자와 교육자들로부터만 오는 것이 아니라 / 모든 관객들의 본능적이면서 자연스러운 반응이다 //

• defect ⓝ 결함   • static ⓝ 잡음   • ignore ⓥ 무시하다
• endure ⓥ 참다, 견디다   • via prep 경유하여
• determine ⓥ 결정하다   • seasoned ⓐ 노련한
• instinctual ⓐ 본능적인   • forgive ⓥ 용서하다
• forgetful ⓐ 잘 잊는   • desirous ⓐ 바라는

우리는 시각적인 것보다 **음향에 관한 기술적인 실수를 덜 용서**한다. 우리는 오디오의 끊김, 결함, 및 잡음을 알아차리고 싫어한다. 시각적인 면에 있는 것들에 대해서는 조금 덜 그렇다. 예를 들어, 만약 일부 주사선(스캔 라인)이 비디오에 있다면, 당신은 짧은 기간 내에 그것을 무시하기 시작할 것이다. 만약 시각적인 신호가 4k가 아니라 1080으로 스트리밍된다면, 결국 당신은 그것에 익숙해질 것이다. 그러나, 만약 오디오에 잡음이 있다면, 당신은 전체 프로그램을 견디기보다 그것을 꺼버리고 싶을 것이다. 또는 오디오가 계속 중단된다면, 당신은 또한 그것을 참기 어려울 것이다. 사실, 영화 제작의 다른 어떤 측면보다, 아마도 영화가 시작되자마자 사람들이 "훌륭하고 전문적인 품질" 또는 "저예산 학생 작품"이라고 조용히 결정하는 것은 오디오를 통해서이다. 이러한 반응은 숙련된 영화 제작자와 교육자들로부터만 오는 것이 아니라, 모든 관객들의 본능적이면서 자연스러운 반응이다.

다음 빈칸에 들어갈 말로 가장 적절한 것을 고르시오.

① less aware of the sound techniques in film 사람들은 시각 정보보다
영화의 음향 기법에 대한 인식이 덜하다   청각 정보에 더 민감하다는 내용이지, 그 반대는 아님
②less forgiving of technical sound mistakes
음향에 관한 기술적인 실수를 덜 용서한다   음향/소리와 관련된 실수를 더 예민하게 알아차리고 더 싫어함
③ more forgetful of auditory experiences
청각적 경험을 잊어버리기 더 쉽다   청각 경험을 시각 경험보다 더 잘 잊는다는 말은 없음
④ less desirous of sound effects 시각 효과에 비해 음향 효과를 덜 원한다는 내용이 아님
음향 효과에 대한 욕구가 덜하다
⑤ more in need of hearing aids 보청기에 대한 언급은 아예 없음
보청기의 필요성이 더 크다

왜 정답? [정답률 51%]

빈칸 문장	우리는 시각적인 것보다 _____ 한다.
빈칸 뒤 문장	시각 자료와 상반된 오디오(청각 자료)라는 소재를 언급하며 오디오보다 시각 자료의 홈에 덜 예민하다고 함 단서1, 단서2

➡ 우리는 오디오에서의 문제를 시각 자료에서의 문제보다 더 잘 알아차리고 싫어한다는 것이 핵심이다. 영상에서 주사선이 있거나 화질이 좀 떨어져도(시각 자료 결함) 금새 적응하지만, 오디오에 잡음이 있거나 계속 중단되면 참기 힘들어한다는 예시로 이를 뒷받침해주고 있다.
▶ 그러므로 시각적인 것보다 ②'음향에 관한 기술적인 실수를 덜 용서'한다고 하는 것이 적절하다.

왜 오답?

① 후반부에 영화 제작에 대한 내용은 언급되나 사람들은 시각 자료보다 오디오에 더 민감하다는 것이 이 글의 핵심이다.→ 주의
③ 청각 경험을 시각 경험보다 더 잘 잊는다는 내용은 없다.
④ 시각 효과에 비해 음향 효과를 덜 원한다는 언급은 없다.
⑤ 청각이나 시각 보조기에 대한 언급은 전혀 없다.

K 06 정답 ② *사회의 계층과 색상 사용의 역사

As colors came to take on / meanings and cultural significance / within societies, / attempts were made / to **restrict** their use. //
= colors'
색들이 갖게 됨에 따라 / 의미와 문화적인 의의를 / 사회 내에서 / 시도들이 이루어졌다 / 그것들의 사용을 제한하는 //

The most extreme example of this phenomenon / was the sumptuary laws. //
이 현상의 가장 극단적인 예시는 / 사치 금지법이었다 //

While these were passed in ancient Greece and Rome, / and examples can be found in ancient China and Japan, /
결과 절을 잇는 등위접속사
이것은 고대 그리스와 로마에서 통과되었고 / 실례들이 고대 중국과 일본에서 발견될 수 있지만 /

they found their fullest expressions in Europe / from the mid-twelfth century, / before slowly disappearing in the early modern period. //
접속사가 생략되지 않은 분사구문
그것은 유럽에서 가장 완전하게 표출되었다 / 12세기 중반부터 / 초기 근대에 서서히 사라지기 전에 //

단서1 법을 통해서 신분에 따라 사용할 수 있는 것들을 특정함
Such laws could touch on / anything from diet to dress and furnishings, / and sought to enforce social boundaries / by encoding the social classes into a clear visual system: /
└ 병렬 구조(동사) ┘   from A to B: A부터 B까지
그러한 법들은 관여할 수 있었고 / 식단에서 의복과 가구까지 어떤 것에도 / 사회적인 경계선을 강요하는 것을 추구했다 / 사회적인 계층을 분명한 시각적 체계로 부호화함으로써 /

the peasants, in other words, should eat and dress like peasants; / craftsmen should eat and dress like craftsmen. //
즉, 다시 말해서 농부는 농부처럼 먹고 입어야 하고 / 기술자는 기술자처럼 먹고 입어야 한다 //

단서2 색은 사회적 언어에서 중대한 기표였음(제한했음)
Color was a vital signifier in this social language / — dull, earthy colors like russet were explicitly confined / to the poorest rural peasants, / while bright ones like scarlet were the preserve of a select few. //
부사절 접속사 (대조)
색은 이 사회적 언어에서 중대한 기표였는데 / 황갈색과 같은 칙칙한 흙색은 명시적으로 국한한 반면 / 가장 가난한 시골 농부들에게 / 진홍색과 같은 밝은색들은 선택된 소수의 전유물이었다 //

• sumptuary law 사치 금지법   • pass ⓥ (투표로 법안 등을) 통과시키다
• touch on ~에 관해 언급하다, 관여하다   • furnishing ⓝ 가구
• enforce ⓥ (법률 등을) 시행하다   • boundary ⓝ 경계
• encode ⓥ 부호화하다   • peasant ⓝ 소작농
• craftsman ⓝ 공예가   • signifier ⓝ 기표   • earthy ⓐ 흙의
• russet ⓝ 적갈색   • explicitly ad 명백하게
• confine ⓥ 국한시키다   • scarlet ⓝ 진홍색   • preserve ⓝ 전유물

색들이 사회 내에서 의미와 문화적인 의의를 갖게 됨에 따라 그것들의 사용을 **제한하는** 시도들이 이루어졌다. 이 현상의 가장 극단적인 예시는 사치 금지법이었다. 이것은 고대 그리스와 로마에서 통과되었고 실례들이 고대 중국과 일본에서 발견될 수 있지만, 그것은 초기 근대에 서서히 사라지기 전에 12세기 중반부터 유럽에서 가장 완전하게 표출되었다. 그러한 법들은 식단에서 의복과 가구까지 어떤 것에도 관여할 수 있었고 사회적인 계층을 분명한 시각적 체계로 부호화함으로써 사회적인 경계선을 강요하는 것을 추구했다. 즉, 다시 말해서 농부는 농부처럼 먹고 입어야 하고 기술자는 기술자처럼 먹고 입어야 한다. 색은 이 사회적 언어에서 중대한 기표였는데, 황갈색과 같은 칙칙한 흙색은 가장 가난한 시골 농부들에게 명시적으로 국한된 반면 진홍색과 같은 밝은색들은 선택된 소수의 전유물이었다.

다음 빈칸에 들어갈 말로 가장 적절한 것을 고르시오.

① export 수출은 언급되지 않은 내용임
수출하다
②restrict 신분에 따라 색 사용을 제한하는 예가 이어짐
제한하다
③ conceal 숨기는 것이 아니고 제한을 당함
숨기다
④ liberate 반대되는 내용
해방하다
⑤ tolerate 용인되지 않음
용인하다

>왜 정답 ? [정답률 59%]

- 그러한 법들은 식단에서 의복과 가구까지 어떤 것에도 관여할 수 있었고 사회적인 계층을 분명한 시각적 체계로 부호화함으로써 사회적인 경계선을 강요하는 것을 추구했다. 단서 1
- 색은 이 사회적 언어에서 중대한 기표였는데, 황갈색과 같은 칙칙한 흙색은 가장 가난한 시골 농부들에게 명시적으로 국한된 반면 진홍색과 같은 밝은 색들은 선택된 소수의 전유물이었다. 단서 2

➡ 신분에 따라 색이 국한된다는 내용이므로 색들의 사용을 ② '제한하는' 시도가 있었다고 해야 한다.

>왜 오답 ?

① 색을 사용하는 방법이 다른 나라에 퍼진 것은 아니다.
③ 숨기는 것이 아니고 제한을 해서 한정된 색만 사용할 수 있게 했다.
④ 해방하는 것은 내용과 반대되는 표현이다.
⑤ 자유로운 색의 사용이 용인되지 않는 사회 상황이었다.

K 07 정답 ③ *긍정적인 경험이 판매에 미치는 영향

Running a business / that sells goods and services to consumers
/ requires / getting to know the products / they like. //
사업을 운영하는 것은 / 소비자에게 상품과 서비스를 판매하는 / 필요로 한다 / 제품을 알아가는 것을 / 그들이 좋아하는 //

More than that, / however, / you want to **link positive experiences / to the products / they purchase.** //
그 이상으로 / 그러나 / 여러분은 긍정적인 경험을 연결하기를 원한다 / 제품에 / 그들이 구매하는 //

단서 1 쉽게 문의할 수 있고 좋은 상태로 빨리 얻을 수 있었던 제품과 판매자를 좋게 생각함

In traditional or online sales, / people are bound to favorably regard / the vendor and product / that they could easily inquire about / and quickly acquire / in good order. //
전통적인 판매나 온라인 판매에서 / 사람들은 좋게 생각할 수밖에 없다 / 제품과 판매자를 / 그들이 쉽게 문의할 수 있고 / 빨리 얻을 수 있는 / 좋은 상태로 //

Using the product / can increase or decrease their satisfaction, / and they will remember / to repurchase products / that meet and exceed their expectations. // 단서 2 소비자는 자신의 기대를 충족시키고 뛰어넘었던 제품을 재구매할 것임
제품을 사용하는 것은 / 그들의 만족도를 증가시키거나 감소시킬 수 있으며 / 그들은 기억할 것이다 / 제품을 재구매할 것을 / 그들의 기대를 충족시키고 뛰어넘는 //

단서 3 전통적인 상점은 진열과 개인 서비스로 쇼핑 경험을 즐겁게 만듦으로써 구매를 유도함
Traditional stores make the shopping experience pleasant / by their displays and personal service. //
전통적인 상점은 쇼핑 경험을 즐겁게 만든다 / 그것의 진열과 개인 서비스로 //

Internet retailers lead buyers / to products / they want / through speedy searches and clicks. //
인터넷 소매업체는 구매자를 유도한다 / 제품으로 / 그들이 원하는 / 빠른 검색과 클릭을 통해 //

A new online selling method / that can generate / millions of dollars in purchases / within a few minutes / is livestream selling. //
새로운 온라인 판매 방법은 / 창출할 수 있는 / 수백만 달러의 구매를 / 몇 분 안에 / 실시간 스트리밍 판매이다 //

That's / when hosts / streaming their shows live / demonstrate a product /
그것은 ~이다 / 호스트가 ~하는 때(이다) / 그들의 쇼를 실시간으로 스트리밍하는 / 제품을 시연하고 /

and even interactively receive comments and answer questions / from their viewers / through the power of social media. //
심지어 양방향으로 의견을 받고 질문에 답하는 / 그들의 시청자로부터 / 소셜 미디어의 힘을 통해 //

If they like the product, / they buy it immediately / through an e-commerce feature on the platform. //
그들은 그 제품이 마음에 들면 / 그들은 즉시 그것을 구매한다 / 플랫폼의 전자 상거래 기능을 통해 //

Buyers say / that the experience is so convenient, / it is like talking to a friend. //
구매자는 말한다 / 경험이 매우 편리하고 / 그것은 친구에게 이야기하는 것과 같다고 //

- be bound to 의무가 있다 • favorably (ad) 호의적으로
- regard (v) 여기다, 생각하다 • vendor (n) 판매자
- inquire (v) 문의하다 • acquire (v) 얻다 • satisfaction (n) 만족
- exceed (v) 넘다, 넘어서다 • retailer (n) 소매업자
- generate (v) 발생시키다, 만들어내다
- livestream selling 실시간 스트리밍 판매
- demonstrate (v) 보여주다, 입증하다 • immediately (ad) 즉시
- convenient (a) 편리한, 간편한 • rare (a) 드문, 희귀한
- examine (v) 조사하다 • convince (v) 설득하다
- must-have 꼭 필요한

소비자에게 상품과 서비스를 판매하는 사업을 운영하는 것은 그들이 좋아하는 제품을 알아가는 것을 필요로 한다. 그러나 그 이상으로 여러분은 **긍정적인 경험을 그들이 구매하는 제품에 연결하는** 것이 좋다. 전통적인 판매나 온라인 판매에서 사람들은 쉽게 문의할 수 있고 좋은 상태로 빨리 얻을 수 있는 제품과 판매자를 좋게 생각할 수밖에 없다. 제품을 사용하는 것은 그들의 만족도를 증가시키거나 감소시킬 수 있으며, 그들은 기대를 충족시키고 뛰어넘는 제품을 재구매할 것을 기억할 것이다. 전통적인 상점은 그것의 진열과 개인 서비스로 쇼핑 경험을 즐겁게 만든다. 인터넷 소매업체는 빠른 검색과 클릭을 통해 구매자를 그들이 원하는 제품으로 유도한다. 몇 분 안에 수백만 달러의 구매를 창출할 수 있는 새로운 온라인 판매 방법은 실시간 스트리밍 판매이다. 그것은 그들의 쇼를 실시간으로 스트리밍하는 호스트가 제품을 시연하고 심지어 소셜 미디어의 힘을 통해 양방향으로 그들의 시청자로부터 의견을 받고 질문에 답하는 경우이다. 그들은 그 제품이 마음에 들면 플랫폼의 전자 상거래 기능을 통해 즉시 그것을 구매한다. 구매자는 경험이 매우 편리하고, 그것은 친구에게 이야기하는 것과 같다고 말한다.

다음 빈칸에 들어갈 말로 가장 적절한 것을 고르시오. [3점]

① provide rare items that can draw others' eyes
   다른 사람들의 눈길을 사로잡을 수 있는 희귀한 품목을 제공하다 판매 제품의 희귀성에 대한 언급은 없음
② maximize the profit through competitive incentives
   경쟁력 있는 장려책을 통해 수익을 극대화하다 장려책에 대한 내용은 없음
③ link positive experiences to the products they purchase
   긍정적인 경험을 그들이 구매하는 제품에 연결하다 소비자는 좋은 경험을 했던 제품을 구매함
④ examine the current state of digital marketing technologies
   디지털 마케팅 기술의 현재 상태를 조사하다 온라인 판매가 언급된 것으로 만든 오답
⑤ convince yourself the product is a must-have in their lives
   제품이 그들의 삶에서 꼭 필요하다고 스스로 설득하다 필수품이라는 인식을 심어야 한다는 언급은 없음

>왜 정답 ? [정답률 51%]

빈칸 문장의 앞 문장	소비자에게 상품과 서비스를 판매하는 사업을 운영하는 것은 소비자가 좋아하는 제품을 알아가는 것을 필요로 한다.
빈칸 문장	그러나 그 이상으로 여러분은 _____ 하는 것이 좋다.
빈칸 문장의 뒤 문장	• 사람들은 그들이 쉽게 문의할 수 있고, 좋은 상태로 빨리 얻을 수 있던 제품과 판매자를 좋게 생각한다. 단서 1 • 사람들은 그들의 기대를 충족시키고 뛰어넘은 제품을 재구매할 것이다. 단서 2 • 전통적인 상점은 진열과 개인 서비스로 쇼핑 경험을 즐겁게 만든다. 단서 3

➡ 소비자에게 상품과 서비스를 판매하기 위해 소비자가 좋아하는 제품을 아는 것 이상으로 무엇을 해야 하는지가 빈칸에 들어가야 한다. ➡ 빈칸 문장의 앞 문장+빈칸 문장
소비자는 자신이 긍정적으로 경험했던 제품을 재구매하며, 전통적인 상점은 (판매를 위해) 쇼핑 경험을 즐겁게 만든다고 했다.
▶ 따라서 이 글에서 말하는 판매 전략은 ③ '긍정적인 경험을 그들이 구매하는 제품에 연결하는' 것이다.

>왜 오답 ?

① 판매하는 제품이 특이해야 한다는 언급은 없다.
② 경쟁력 있는 장려책을 통한 판매 촉진에 대한 내용이 아니다.
④ 온라인 판매에 대해 구체적으로 설명한 것으로 만든 오답이다.
⑤ 제품의 필요성을 납득시킨다는 언급은 없다.

"What's in a name? //
"이름에는 무엇이 있는가 //
주어(선행사)
That / which we call a rose, / by any other name / would smell
목적격 관계대명사   동사
as sweet." //
그것은 / 우리가 장미라고 부르는 / 다른 어떤 이름으로도 / 향기가 똑같이 달콤할 것이다" //

This thought of Shakespeare's / points up a difference / between
roses and, say, paintings. //
셰익스피어의 이 생각은 / 차이를 강조한다 / 장미와 이를테면 그림 사이의 //

Natural objects, / such as roses, / are not **interpreted**. //
자연물은 / 장미와 같은 / 해석되지 않는다 // 단서1 자연은 의미와 메시지를
지닌 매개체로 여겨지지 않음

They are not taken as vehicles / of meanings and messages. //
그것들은 매개체로 받아들여지지 않는다 / 의미와 메시지의 //

They belong to no tradition, / strictly speaking / have no style,
                    세 개의 동사의 병렬 구조
/ and are not understood / within a framework of culture and
convention. // 단서2 자연물은 문화와 관습의 틀 안에서 이해되지 않음
그것들은 어떤 전통에도 속하지 않고 / 엄밀히 말하면 / 양식이 없으며 / 이해되지 않는다 / 문
화와 관습의 틀 안에서 //

Rather, they are sensed and savored / relatively directly, /
without intellectual mediation, / 단서3 자연물은 지적인 매개 없이 감지되고 음미됨
오히려 그것들은 감지되고 음미된다 / 비교적 직접적으로 / 지적인 매개 없이 /

and so / what they are called, / either individually or collectively,
단수 동사   명사절 주어
/ has little bearing / on our experience of them. //
따라서 / 그것들이 불리는 이름은 / 개별적으로든 집합적으로든 / 거의 관계가 없다 / 그것들
에 대한 우리의 경험과는 //

What a work of art is titled, / on the other hand, / has a significant
effect / on the aesthetic face / it presents / and on the qualities /
we correctly perceive / in it. //   전치사구의 병렬 구조
미술 작품에 붙여지는 제목은 / 반면에 / 상당한 영향을 미친다 / 미학적 측면에 / 그것이 제시
하는 / 그리고 특징에 / 우리가 올바르게 인지하는 / 그 속에서 //

목적격 관계대명사 생략
A painting of a rose, / by a name / other than the one it has, /
might very well smell different, / aesthetically speaking. //
장미 한 송이의 그림은 / 이름으로 / 그것이 가지고 있는 것과는 다른 / 아마 향기가 다를 것이
다 / 미학적으로 말하면 //

주어 ①   주어 ②
The painting / titled *Rose of Summer* / and an indiscernible
painting / titled *Vermillion Womanhood* /
그림과 / 〈Rose of Summer〉라는 제목의 / 식별하기 어려운 그림은 / 〈Vermillion
Womanhood〉라는 제목의 /

복수 동사
are physically, but also semantically and aesthetically, distinct
objects of art. //
물리적으로 또한 의미적으로나 미학적으로도 별개의 미술품이다 //

- point up ~을 강조하다   - vehicle ⓝ 매개체, 매개물
- strictly speaking 엄밀히 말해서   - framework ⓝ 틀
- convention ⓝ 관습   - mediation ⓝ 매개, 중개, 조정
- collectively 〔ad〕 집합적으로
- have little bearing on ~과 거의 관계가 없다   - aesthetic ⓐ 미(학)적인
- face ⓝ 측면   - present ⓥ 제시하다, 나타내다
- quality ⓝ 특성, 특징   - correctly 〔ad〕 올바르게
- perceive ⓥ 인지[인식]하다   - other than ~을 제외하고, ~과 다른
- might (very) well 아마 ~일 것이다   - distinct ⓐ 별개의

"이름에는 무엇이 들어 있는가? 우리가 장미라고 부르는 그것은 다른 어떤 이름
으로 부른다 해도 향기가 똑같이 달콤할 것이다." 셰익스피어의 이 생각은 장미
와, 이를테면 그림의 차이를 강조한다. 장미와 같은 자연물은 **해석되지** 않는다.
그것들은 의미와 메시지의 매개체로 받아들여지지 않는다. 그것들은 어떤 전통
에도 속하지 않고, 엄밀히 말하면 양식이 없으며, 문화와 관습의 틀 안에서 이해
되지 않는다. 오히려 그것들은 지적인 매개 없이 비교적 직접적으로 감지되고 음
미되며, 따라서 개별적으로든 집합적으로든, 그것들이 불리는 이름은 그것들에
대한 우리의 경험과는 거의 관계가 없다. 반면에 미술 작품에 붙여지는 제목은

그것이 제시하는 미학적 측면과 그 속에서 우리가 올바르게 인지하는 특징에 상
당한 영향을 미친다. 가지고 있는 이름과는 다른 이름으로 불리는 장미 한 송이
의 그림은, 미학적으로 말하면, 아마 향기가 다를 것이다. 〈Rose of Summer〉
라는 제목의 그림과 〈Vermillion Womanhood〉라는 제목의 식별하기 어려운
그림은 물리적으로, 또한 의미적으로나 미학적으로도 별개의 미술품이다.

다음 빈칸에 들어갈 말로 가장 적절한 것을 고르시오.
① changed 자연물, 미술품 자체가 바뀐다는   ② classified 자연물이나 미술품의 분류에
  바뀌는   것이 아님   분류되다   관한 글이 아님
③ preserved 미술품은 보존된다는 언급은 없음 ④ controlled '통제'에 관한 내용이 아님
  보존되다   통제되다
⑤ interpreted 자연물은 문화와 관습의 틀 안에서 '이해되지' 않음
  해석되지

▶왜 정답 ? [정답률 52%]
자연물의 이름이 갖는 의미와 미술품의 이름이 갖는 의미를 대조하는 글로, 자연물
인 장미는 다른 어떤 이름으로 불리든 똑같이 달콤한 향기가 나지만, 장미 그림은
그 제목에 따라 향기가 다르다고 했다. 빈칸 문장은 자연물을 설명하는데, 자연물
은 의미와 메시지를 지닌 매개체로 여겨지지 않고, 문화와 관습의 틀 안에서 이해
되지 않으며, 지적인 매개 없이 직접적으로 감상된다는 내용이 이어지는 것으로 보
아 자연물은 ⑤ '해석되지' 않는다는 의미로 빈칸 문장을 완성하는 것이 적절하다.

▶왜 오답 ?
미술품은 의미와 메시지를 지니고 있고, 그것이
문화와 관습의 틀 안에서 이해됨(해석됨)   꿀팁
① 자연물은 이름에 따라 그 자연물의 특성이 바뀌지 않지만 미술품은 제목이 그
  미술품에 큰 영향을 미친다는 내용이다. 자연물이나 미술품 자체가 바뀌거나 바
  뀌지 않는다는 것이 아니라 이름, 제목에 의해 그것이 영향을 받는지, 그렇지 않
  은지를 설명한 글이다.
② 자연물과 미술품의 분류에 대한 글이 아니다.
③ 자연물은 보존되지 않고 미술품은 보존된다는 내용이 아니다.
④ 자연물이나 미술품의 통제와 관련된 언급은 없다.

단서1 '날고 있는 말'의 사례가 무엇을 확신시키는지를 파악해야 함
If you are unconvinced / that **our beliefs influence** / **how we**
interpret facts, / consider the example of the "flying horse." //
만약 여러분이 확신하지 못한다면 / 우리의 믿음이 영향을 미친다는 것을 / 우리가 사실을
해석하는 방식에 / '날고 있는 말'의 사례를 생각해보라 //

주어
Depictions of galloping horses / from prehistoric times up until
the mid-1800s /
질주하는 말의 묘사는 / 선사 시대부터 1800년대 중반까지 /

동사   목적격 보어
typically showed horses' legs splayed / while galloping, / that
is, / the front legs reaching far ahead / as the hind legs stretched
far behind. //
전형적으로 말의 다리가 벌어져 있는 것을 보였다 / 질주하는 동안 / 즉 / 멀리 앞으로 내딛는
앞다리 / 뒷다리를 뒤로 멀리 뻗은 채 //

주격 보어로 쓰인 간접의문문
People just "knew" / that's how horses galloped, / and that is /
how they "saw" them galloping. // 단서2 말이 질주하는 방식이라고 믿는 대로
말이 질주하는 것을 봤음
사람들은 그저 '알고 있었고' / 그것이 말이 질주하는 방식이라고 / 그것이 ~이다 / 그들이
말이 질주하는 것을 '보았던' 방식 //

Cavemen *saw* them / this way, /   ★ 도치 구문
동굴 거주인들은 그것들을 '보았고' / 이런 식으로 /   so, neither, nor가 앞 문장의
                                           내용을 받아 맨 앞으로 나올 때는
Aristotle *saw* them / this way, /   주어와 동사의 위치가 도치된다.
아리스토텔레스도 그것들을 '보았으며' / 이런 식으로 /   앞에 나온 saw them을 so로
★앞 내용을 받는 so가 문두에 오면서 주어와 동사가 도치됨 받았기 때문에 주어와 대동사
and so did Victorian gentry. //   did가 도치되었다.
빅토리아 시대의 상류층도 그랬다 //

But all of that ended / when, in 1878, Eadweard Muybridge
published / a set of twelve pictures / he had taken / of a galloping
horse /   앞에 목적격 관계대명사가 생략됨
그러나 그 모든 것은 끝이 났다 / 1878년에 Eadweard Muybridge가 공개했을 때 / 한
세트로 된 열두 장의 사진을 / 자신이 찍은 / 질주하는 한 마리 말의 /
(published보다 앞선 때를 나타내는 대과거)

in the space of less than half a second / using twelve cameras /
_{앞에 주격 관계대명사와 be동사가 생략됨}
hooked to wire triggers. //
0.5초도 안 되는 사이에 / 열두 대의 카메라를 사용하여 / 와이어 트리거에 연결된 //
단서 3 사실 말은 앞에서 설명한 방식과는 다른 방식으로 질주함
Muybridge's photos showed clearly / that a horse goes
completely airborne / in the third step of the gallop / with its
legs *collected* beneath it, / not splayed. // 「with+(대)명사+분사」 형태의
분사구문에서 being은 종종 생략됨
Muybridge의 사진은 분명히 보였다 / 말이 완전히 공중에 뜬 채 간다는 것을 / 질주의 세
번째 걸음에서 / 그것의 다리들이 밑에 '모아진' 상태로 / 벌어진 상태가 아니라 //

It is called / the moment of suspension. //
그것은 불린다 / 부유의 순간이라고 //

Now even kids draw horses galloping / this way. //
지금은 아이들도 말이 질주하는 것을 그린다 / 이런 식으로 //

- unconvinced ⓐ 확신하지 못하는   - depiction ⓝ 묘사, 서술
- prehistoric ⓐ 선사 시대의   - typically ⓐⓓ 일반적으로, 보통
- hind ⓐ 뒤의   - hook ⓥ 갈고리로 걸다   - airborne ⓐ 하늘에 떠 있는
- suspension ⓝ 공중에 떠 있기, (일시적) 정지   - adhere to ~을 고수하다
- intuition ⓝ 직감, 직관

만약 여러분이 우리의 믿음이 우리가 사실을 해석하는 방식에 영향을
미친다는 것을 확신하지 못한다면, '날고 있는 말'의 사례를 생각해보라. 선사
시대부터 1800년대 중반까지 질주하는 말의 묘사는 질주하는 동안 말의 다리가
벌어져 있는 것을, 즉 뒷다리를 뒤로 멀리 뻗은 채 앞다리를 멀리 앞으로
내딛는 모습을 전형적으로 보였다. 사람들은 그것이 말이 질주하는 방식이라고
그저 '알고 있었고', 그것이 그들이 말이 질주하는 것을 '보았던' 방식이다. 동굴
거주인들은 그것들을 이런 식으로 '보았고', 아리스토텔레스도 그것들을 이런
식으로 '보았으며', 빅토리아 시대의 상류층도 그랬다.

그러나 그 모든 것은 1878년 Eadweard Muybridge가 와이어 트리거에
연결된 열두 대의 카메라를 사용하여 0.5초도 안 되는 사이에 자신이 찍은, 한
세트로 된 열두 장의 질주하는 한 마리 말의 사진을 공개했을 때 끝이 났다.
Muybridge의 사진은 말이 질주의 세 번째 걸음에서 그것의 다리들이 벌어진
상태가 아니라, 밑에 '모아진' 상태로 완전히 공중에 뜬 채 간다는 것을 분명히
보였다. 그것은 부유의 순간이라고 불린다. 지금은 아이들도 이런 식으로
질주하는 말을 그린다.

다음 빈칸에 들어갈 말로 가장 적절한 것을 고르시오. [3점]
① our beliefs influence how we interpret facts
  우리의 믿음이 우리가 사실을 해석하는 방식에 영향을 미친다   말이 질주하는 방식을 믿는 대로 봄
② what we see is an illusion of our past memories
  우리가 보는 것은 우리의 과거 기억의 환영이다   동굴 거주인 등이 언급된 것으로 만든 오답
③ even photographs can lead to a wrong visual perception
  사진조차 잘못된 시각적 인식으로 이어질 수 있다   사진으로 사실을 보여줌
④ there is no standard by which we can judge good or bad
  우리가 좋고 나쁨을 판단할 수 있는 기준이 없다   좋고 나쁨의 판단에 대한 내용이 아님
⑤ we adhere to our intuition in spite of irresistible evidence
  우리는 압도적인 증거에도 불구하고 우리의 직감을 고수한다   1878년에 끝났음

왜 정답? [정답률 44%]
'무엇을 확신하지 못한다면 → '날고 있는 말'의 사례를
생각해보라 → 그럼 '무엇'을 확신하게 될 것이다'라는 흐름   꿀팁

빈칸 문장의 내용으로 보아 빈칸에는 '날고 있는 말'의 사례가 '무엇'을
확신시키는지가 들어가야 한다.
1878년 이전에는 사람들이 질주하는 말의 다리가 벌어진다고 믿었고,
그 믿음대로 질주하는 말을 보았는데, 사실을 있는 그대로 보여주는 도구 꿀팁
1878년에 공개된 Muybridge의 사진은 사실 질주하는 말의 다리는 벌어진
상태가 아니라 모아진 상태로 공중에 떠 있다는 것을 보였다는 내용이다.
다시 말해, 말이 질주하는 방식이라는 정해진 사실을 자신이 믿는 대로
해석했다는 의미이므로, '날고 있는 말'이 확신시키는 것은 ① '우리의 믿음이
우리가 사실을 해석하는 방식에 영향을 미친다'는 것이다.

왜 오답?
② 동굴 거주인, 아리스토텔레스, 빅토리아 시대의 상류층 등이 언급된 것으로
   만든 오답이다. 우리가 보는 것에는 우리의 믿음이 반영된다는 내용이다.
③ 이 글에서 사진은 사실을 일깨우는 수단으로 사용되었다. 주의
④ 말이 질주하는 방식이 좋고 나쁨을 판단하는 기준과 연관된다는 것은 타당하지
   않다.
⑤ 1878년에 증거가 등장한 이후로는 모든 것이 끝났다고 했다.

K 10 정답 ① *정신적 모델의 확장

Learning is *constructive*, / not *destructive*. //
학습은 '건설적'이다 / '파괴적'이지 않고
앞에 명사절 접속사 that이 생략됨
This means / we don't **replace** mental models / — we simply
expand / upon them. //
이것은 의미한다 / 우리가 정신적 모델을 교체하지 않는다는 것을 / 우리는 단지 확장한다 /
그것을 기반으로 //
부사적 용법(목적)
To understand / what I mean, / think back to your childhood. //
이해하기 위해서 / 내가 의미하는 것을 / 여러분의 어린 시절을 회상해 보아라 //

There was likely a time / when you believed in Santa Claus;
선행사   관계부사
/ your mental model accepted him / and your predictions
accounted / for his existence. //
때가 있었을 것이다 / 여러분이 산타클로스를 믿었던 / 여러분의 정신적 모델은 그를
받아들였고 / 여러분의 예측은 설명했다 / 그의 존재를 //

At some point, however, / you came to recognize / he was
앞에 명사절 접속사 that이 생략됨
fictitious / and you updated your mental model accordingly. //
하지만 어느 순간 / 여러분은 인식하게 되었고 / 그가 가상이라는 것을 / 그에 따라 여러분의
정신적 모델을 갱신했다 //

At that moment, / you didn't suddenly forget everything /
about Santa Claus. // **단서 1** 이전의 믿음을 잃어버린 것이 아님
그 순간 / 여러분은 갑자기 모든 것을 잊어버린 것은 아니다 / 산타클로스에 대한 //

To this day, / you can still recognize him, / speak of him / and
embrace young children's belief in him. //
오늘날까지 / 여러분은 여전히 그를 인식하고 / 그에 대해 말하고 / 그에 대한 어린아이들의
믿음을 받아들일 수 있다 // **단서 2** 이전의 모델 대신 새로운 모델을 받아들인 것이
아니라 새로운 정보를 추가한 것임
In other words, / you didn't destroy your old mental model, /
you simply added new information / to it. //
다시 말해 / 여러분은 여러분의 이전의 정신적 모델을 파괴한 것이 아니라 / 단순히 새로운
정보를 추가했을 뿐이다 / 그것에 //

By building upon old mental models / we are able to maintain
/ ties to the past, / foster a deeper understanding of concepts /
이전의 정신적 모델을 기반으로 함으로써 / 우리는 유지할 수 있고 / 과거와의 연결을 / 개념에
대한 더 깊은 이해를 촉진할 수 있으며 / 병렬 구조(to부정사가 병렬 구조를 이룰 때
뒤에 오는 to는 흔히 생략됨)
and develop an ever-expanding pool of information / to draw
upon / in order to continually adapt / to an ever-evolving world. //
끊임없이 확장하는 정보 저장소를 개발할 수 있다 / 활용할 / 계속해서 적응하기 위해 /
끊임없이 진화하는 세계에 //

- constructive ⓐ 건설적인   - destructive ⓐ 파괴적인
- mental ⓐ 정신적인   - expand ⓥ 확장하다   - think back 회상하다
- prediction ⓝ 예측   - account for 설명하다
- embrace ⓥ 안다, 받아들이다   - belief ⓝ 믿음
- in other words 다시 말해   - build upon ~을 기반으로 하다
- maintain ⓥ 유지하다   - tie ⓝ 연결   - foster ⓥ 양육하다
- ever-evolving ⓐ 계속 진화하는

학습은 '파괴적'이지 않고 '건설적'이다. 이것은 우리가 정신적 모델을
교체하지 않는다는 것을 의미한다. 우리는 단지 그것을 기반으로 확장한다.
내가 의미하는 것을 이해하기 위해서, 여러분의 어린 시절을 회상해 보아라.
여러분이 산타클로스를 믿었던 때가 있었을 것이다. 여러분의 정신적 모델은
그를 받아들였고 여러분의 예측은 그의 존재를 설명했다. 하지만 어느 순간,
여러분은 그가 가상이라는 것을 인식하게 되었고 그에 따라 여러분의 정신적
모델을 갱신했다. 그 순간, 여러분은 갑자기 산타클로스에 대한 모든 것을
잊어버린 것은 아니다. 오늘날까지, 여러분은 여전히 그를 인식하고, 그에
대해 말하고, 그에 대한 어린아이들의 믿음을 받아들일 수 있다. 다시 말해,
여러분은 여러분의 이전의 정신적 모델을 파괴한 것이 아니라, 단순히 그것에
새로운 정보를 추가했을 뿐이다. 이전의 정신적 모델을 기반으로 함으로써
우리는 과거와의 연결을 유지할 수 있고, 개념에 대한 더 깊은 이해를 촉진할
수 있으며, 끊임없이 진화하는 세계에 계속해서 적응하기 위해 활용할 끊임없이
확장하는 정보 저장소를 개발할 수 있다.

다음 빈칸에 들어갈 말로 가장 적절한 것을 고르시오.

① replace 이전 모델을 새로운 모델로 바꾸는 것이 아님
  교체하다
② imagine 산타클로스를 상상하는 것이 아님
  상상하다
③ predict your predictions로 만든 오답
  예측하다
④ analyze 산타클로스에 대한 믿음을 분석한다는 언급은 없음
  분석하다
⑤ imitate 타인 등을 모방한다는 내용은 없음
  모방하다

왜 정답? [정답률 77%]

빈칸 문장	우리는 정신적 모델을 ＿＿＿＿＿＿하지 않는다. 우리는 그것을 기반으로 확장한다.
예시	이전의 정신적 모델: 산타클로스의 존재를 믿음 → 산타클로스가 가상이라는 것을 인식하고 정신적 모델을 갱신함 → 산타클로스에 대한 이전의 정신적 모델을 없앤 것이 아니라 새로운 정보를 추가한 것임

➡ 산타클로스가 존재한다는 이전의 정신적 모델을 산타클로스는 가상이라는 새로운 정신적 모델로 ① '교체한' 것이 아니라, 이전의 정신적 모델에 새로운 정보를 추가했을 뿐이라는 내용이다.

왜 오답?

② 산타클로스가 가상의 인물이라는 점으로 만든 오답이다. 함정
③ your predictions accounted for his existence로 만든 오답이다.
④ 산타클로스의 존재를 믿은 정신적 모델을 분석한다는 언급은 없다.
⑤ 모방과 관련된 내용은 없다.

K 11 정답 ① ✱똑똑한 우리의 다리 ——————

Research with human runners / challenged conventional wisdom / and found /
주어 / 동사① / 동사②
달리는 사람에 관한 연구는 / 사회적 통념에 이의를 제기하고 / 알아냈다 /

that the ground-reaction forces / at the foot / and the shock / transmitted up the leg and through the body / after impact with the ground /
목적어절 접속사
지면 반발력 / 발에 작용하는 / 그리고 충격은 / 다리 위로 몸을 통해 전달되는 / (발이) 땅에 부딪히고 난 후에 /

varied little / as runners moved / from extremely compliant / to extremely hard running surfaces. // 단서1
부사절 접속사
거의 달라지지 않는다는 것을 / 달리는 사람이 옮겨갔을 때 / 매우 말랑말랑한 (활주면에서) / 매우 단단한 활주면으로 //
말랑말랑한 활주면에서 달릴 때와 매우 단단한 활주면에서 달릴 때를 대조함

As a result, / researchers gradually began to believe / that runners are subconsciously able / to adjust leg stiffness / prior to foot strike /
to believe의 목적어절 접속사
결과적으로 / 연구자들은 점차 믿기 시작했다 / 달리는 사람은 잠재의식적으로 ~할 수 있다고 / 다리의 경직도를 조정할 / 발이 (땅에) 닿기 전에 /

based on their perceptions / of the hardness or stiffness of the surface / on which they are running. //
「전치사+관계대명사」 선행사
자신의 인식을 바탕으로 / 지표면의 경도나 경직도에 대한 / 자신이 달리고 있는 //

This view suggests / that runners create soft legs / that soak up impact forces / when they are running / on very hard surfaces
선행사 주격 관계대명사
이 견해는 암시한다 / 달리는 사람은 푹신한 다리를 만들고 / 충격력을 흡수하는 / 그들이 달리고 있을 때는 / 매우 단단한 지표면에서 /

and stiff legs / when they are moving along / on yielding terrain. //
단단한 다리를 (만드는 것을) / 그들이 움직일 때는 / 물렁한 지형에서 //

As a result, / impact forces / passing through the legs / are strikingly similar / over a wide range of running surface types. //
복수 주어 impact forces를 수식하는 현재분사구 복수 동사
그 결과 / 충격력은 / 다리를 통해 전해지는 / 놀랄 만큼 비슷하다 / 아주 다양한 활주면 유형에 걸쳐서 //
단서2 다양한 활주면 유형에 걸쳐 다리를 통해 전해지는 충격은 놀랄 만큼 비슷함

Contrary to popular belief, / running on concrete / is not more damaging to the legs / than running on soft sand. //
동명사구 주어 단수 동사
통념과는 반대로 / 콘크리트 위를 달리는 것은 / 다리에 더 해롭지 않다 / 푹신한 모래 위를 달리는 것보다 //

• challenge ⓥ 이의를 제기하다
• conventional wisdom 사회적[일반적] 통념
• ground-reaction force 지면 반발력 • transmit ⓥ 전달하다
• impact ⓝ 부딪힘, 충돌, 충격 • extremely ⓐⓓ 극도로, 극히
• gradually ⓐⓓ 점진적으로, 서서히 • subconsciously ⓐⓓ 잠재의식적으로
• adjust ⓥ 조정하다 • stiffness ⓝ 경직도, 뻣뻣한 정도
• prior to ~에 앞서, 먼저 • strike ⓝ 치기, 때리기, 차기
• perception ⓝ 인식, 지각 • hardness ⓝ 경도(硬度), 단단함
• soak up ~을 흡수하다 • yielding ⓐ 물렁한, 유연한
• strikingly ⓐⓓ 놀랄 만큼 • a wide range of 아주 다양한
• contrary to ~와 반대로

달리는 사람에 관한 연구는 사회적 통념에 이의를 제기하고 발에 작용하는 지면 반발력과 발이 땅에 부딪히고 난 후에 다리 위로 몸을 통해 전달되는 충격은 달리는 사람이 매우 말랑말랑한 활주면에서 매우 단단한 활주면으로 옮겨갔을 때 **거의 달라지지 않는다**는 것을 알아냈다. 결과적으로 연구자들은 점차 달리는 사람은 자신이 달리고 있는 지표면의 경도나 경직도에 대한 자신의 인식을 바탕으로 발이 땅에 닿기 전에 다리의 경직도를 잠재의식적으로 조정할 수 있다고 믿기 시작했다. 이 견해에 따르면, 달리는 사람은 매우 단단한 지표면에서 달리고 있을 때는 충격력을 흡수하는 푹신한 다리를 만들고 물렁한 지형에서 움직일 때는 단단한 다리를 만든다. 그 결과 다리를 통해 전해지는 충격력은 아주 다양한 활주면 유형에 걸쳐서 놀랄 만큼 비슷하다. 통념과는 반대로, 콘크리트 위를 달리는 것은 푹신한 모래 위를 달리는 것보다 다리에 더 해롭지 않다.

다음 빈칸에 들어갈 말로 가장 적절한 것을 고르시오. [3점]

① varied little strikingly similar와 같은 표현 ② decreased a lot
  거의 달라지지 않았다 많이 감소했다
③ suddenly peaked 놀랄 만큼 비슷함 ④ gradually appeared
  갑자기 최고조에 달했다 점차 나타났다 충격이 없다가 생기는 것이 아님
⑤ were hardly generated
  거의 발생되지 않았다 충격이 없다는 내용이 아님

왜 정답? [정답률 42%]

콘크리트 위를 달리는 것이 푹신한 모래 위를 달리는 것보다 다리에 더 해롭다는 사회적 통념에 이의를 제기하는 연구에 대한 내용이다. 매우 말랑한 활주면에서 달릴 때의 충격과 매우 단단한 활주면에서 달릴 때의 충격을 대조하는 문장에 빈칸이 있는데, 글의 후반부에서 아주 다양한 활주면 유형에 걸쳐 다리를 통해 전해지는 충격이 놀랄 만큼 비슷하다고 했으므로 빈칸 문장에서는 활주면이 말랑할 때나 단단할 때나 다리로 전해지는 충격은 ① '거의 달라지지 않는다'라고 해야 한다.

왜 오답? little이 준부정어로서 '거의 ~하지 않는'이라는 의미라는 것에 주의해야 함! 꿀팁

②, ③ 활주면 유형이 달라지더라도 다리로 전해지는 충격은 놀랄 만큼 비슷하다고 했으므로 충격이 많이 감소했다거나 갑자기 최고조에 달했다고 하는 것은 적절하지 않다.
④ 충격이 없다가 생겨나는 것이 아니다.
⑤ 충격이 없다는 내용이 아니다. hardly 역시 준부정어로 '거의 ~하지 않는'이라는 뜻임 꿀팁

어법 특강

✱「전치사+관계대명사」와 관계부사

– 관계대명사가 전치사의 목적어로 쓰인 경우 「전치사+관계대명사」의 형태로 쓰거나, 전치사는 원래 있는 자리에 그대로 있을 수 있다. 선행사가 시간, 장소, 이유, 방법을 나타낼 때 「전치사+관계대명사」는 관계부사 when, where, why, how로 쓸 수 있다.

• I want to visit the town. + The movie was filmed in the town.
  (나는 그 마을에 가보고 싶다.) (그 영화는 그 마을에서 촬영되었다.)
• I want to visit the town in which the movie was filmed.
  전치사+관계대명사
• I want to visit the town where the movie was filmed.
  관계부사(관계부사 앞에 전치사를 쓰면 안 된다)
  (나는 그 영화가 촬영되었던 그 마을에 가보고 싶다.)

Even when we do something / as apparently simple as picking up a screwdriver, / our brain automatically **adjusts / what it considers body / to include the tool.** // 선행사를 포함하는 목적격 관계대명사 ＊
우리가 무언가를 할 때조차도 / 나사돌리개를 집는 것만큼 겉으로 보기에 간단한 / 우리의 뇌는 무의식적으로 조정한다 / 그것이 신체라고 간주하는 것을 / 도구를 포함하도록 //

We can literally feel things / with the end of the screwdriver. //
우리는 말 그대로 사물을 느낄 수 있다 / 나사돌리개의 끝부분으로 //

When we extend a hand, / holding the screwdriver, / we automatically take the length of the latter into account. //
우리가 손을 뻗을 때 / 나사돌리개를 들고 / 우리는 무의식적으로 후자의 길이를 계산에 넣는다 //
단서 1 나사돌리개를 들고 손을 뻗을 때 후자(나사돌리개)의 길이까지 계산에 넣음

We can probe difficult-to-reach places / with its extended end, / and comprehend / what we are exploring. //
└─병렬 구조─┘
우리는 도달하기 어려운 곳을 탐색할 수 있고 / 그것의 확장된 끝을 가지고, 이해할 수 있다 / 우리가 탐색하고 있는 것을 //

선행사(목적격 관계대명사는 생략됨)
Furthermore, / we instantly regard the screwdriver / we are holding / as "our" screwdriver, / and get possessive about it. //
regard A as B: A를 B로 여기다
게다가 / 우리는 즉시 나사돌리개를 간주한다 / 우리가 들고 있는 / '우리의' 나사돌리개로 / 그리고 그것에 대해 소유욕을 갖게 된다 //
비교급 강조
We do the same / with the much more complex tools / we use, / in much more complex situations. //
앞에 목적격 관계대명사가 생략됨
우리는 똑같이 한다 / 훨씬 더 복잡한 도구에도 / 우리가 사용하는 / 훨씬 더 복잡한 상황에서도 //
주어   동사
The cars / we pilot / instantaneously and automatically become ourselves. // 단서 2 우리가 이용하는 도구인 자동차가 우리 자신이 됨
자동차는 / 우리가 조종하는 / 순간적이면서도 무의식적으로 우리 자신이 된다 //

Because of this, / when someone bangs his fist / on our car's hood / after we have irritated him / at a crosswalk, / we take it personally. //
부사절 접속사   주절
이것 때문에 / 누군가가 자신의 주먹으로 칠 때 / 우리 자동차의 덮개를 / 우리가 그를 짜증나게 한 후에 / 건널목에서 / 우리는 그것을 인신공격적으로 받아들인다 //

This is not always reasonable. //
이것은 항상 합리적인 것은 아니다 //

Nonetheless, / without the extension of self into machine, / it would be impossible to drive. //
진주어   가주어
그렇더라도 / 기계까지로 자신을 확장하지 않으면 / 운전하는 것은 불가능할 것이다 //

- apparently ⓐⓓ 겉으로 보기에 · screwdriver ⓝ 나사돌리개, 드라이버
- automatically ⓐⓓ 자동적으로, 무의식적으로 · adjust ⓥ 조정하다
- literally ⓐⓓ 말 그대로 · extend ⓥ (팔·다리 등을) 뻗다, 확장하다
- take ~ into account ~을 계산에 넣다 · comprehend ⓥ 이해하다
- instantly ⓐⓓ 즉시, 즉각 · possessive ⓐ 소유욕이 강한
- pilot ⓥ 조종하다 · instantaneously ⓐⓓ 순간적으로 · fist ⓝ 주먹
- hood ⓝ 모자, (자동차 등의) 덮개 · irritate ⓥ 짜증나게 하다
- personally ⓐⓓ 인신공격적으로, (개인적인) 모욕감을 주도록
- reasonable ⓐ 합리적인 · nonetheless ⓐⓓ 그렇기는 하지만, 그렇더라도
- utility ⓝ 유용, 효용

우리가 나사돌리개를 집는 것만큼 겉으로 보기에 간단한 일을 할 때조차도, 우리의 뇌는 무의식적으로 **그것이 신체라고 간주하는 것을 도구를 포함하도록 조정한다.** 우리는 말 그대로 나사돌리개의 끝부분으로 사물을 느낄 수 있다. 나사돌리개를 들고 손을 뻗을 때, 우리는 무의식적으로 후자(나사돌리개)의 길이를 계산에 넣는다. 우리는 그것의 확장된 끝을 가지고 도달하기 어려운 곳을 탐색할 수 있고, 우리가 탐색하고 있는 것을 이해할 수 있다. 게다가, 우리는 즉시 우리가 들고 있는 나사돌리개를 '우리의' 나사돌리개로 간주하고, 그것에 대해 소유욕을 갖게 된다. 우리는 훨씬 더 복잡한 상황에서도 우리가 사용하는 훨씬 더 복잡한 도구를 두고도 똑같이 한다. 우리가 조종하는 자동차는 순간적이면서도 무의식적으로 우리 자신이 된다. 이것 때문에 우리가 건널목에서 누군가를 짜증나게 한 후에, 그 사람이 우리 자동차의 덮개를 주먹으로 칠 때, 우리는 그것을 인신공격적으로 받아들인다. 이것은 항상 합리적인 것은 아니다. 그렇더라도, 기계까지로 자신을 확장하지 않으면 운전하는 것은 불가능할 것이다.

다음 빈칸에 들어갈 말로 가장 적절한 것을 고르시오. [3점]

① recalls past experiences of utilizing the tool
그 도구를 활용했던 지난 경험을 떠올린다 　나사돌리개를 활용했던 지난 경험은 언급되지 않음
② recognizes what it can do best without the tool
그 도구 없이 그것이 가장 잘할 수 있는 것을 인식한다 　나사돌리개를 통해 할 수 있는 일이 이어짐
③ judges which part of our body can best be used
우리 신체의 어느 부분이 가장 잘 활용될 수 있는지를 판단한다 　신체를 활용하는 내용이 아님
④ perceives what limits the tool's functional utility
무엇이 그 도구의 기능적 활용을 제한하는지를 인식한다 　도구의 활용이 제한된다는 예시는 없음
⑤ adjusts what it considers body to include the tool
그것이 신체라고 간주하는 것을 도구를 포함하도록 조정한다 　나사돌리개와 자동차가 우리 자신이 됨

> 왜 정답 ? [정답률 47%]

나사돌리개를 집을 때 우리의 뇌가 어떻게 반응하는지를 빈칸에 넣어야 한다. 나사돌리개를 들고 손을 뻗을 때 나사돌리개의 길이까지 계산에 넣는다는 것은 나사돌리개까지 우리의 손으로 인식한다는 의미이고, 자동차를 예시로 든 내용에서는 자동차가 순간적이고 무의식적으로 우리 자신이 된다고 했다. 마지막 문장에서는 자신을 기계까지로 확장한다고 했으므로 빈칸 문장은 우리의 뇌가 ⑤ '그것이 신체라고 간주하는 것을 도구를 포함하도록 조정한다'는 내용이 되어야 한다.
it이 가리키는 것이 our brain임 꿀팁

> 왜 오답 ?

① 나사돌리개를 우리의 신체 일부로 인식하는 예시를 든 것이지, 그것을 활용했던 지난 경험에 대해서는 언급되지 않았다. 주의
② 도구를 이용할 때 우리의 뇌가 그 도구를 우리의 신체로 간주한다는 내용이다.
③ 신체를 활용하는 것에 대한 내용이 아니다.
④ 나사돌리개나 자동차의 기능적 활용을 제한하는 것에 대해서는 언급되지 않았다.

─ 어법 특강

＊ 선행사를 포함하는 관계대명사 what

- 다른 관계대명사가 형용사절을 이끄는 반면 what은 명사절을 이끈다.
- No one knows exactly <u>what</u> happened.
(일어난 일을 아무도 정확히 모른다.)
- She showed me <u>what</u> she had bought.
(그녀는 내게 자신이 산 것을 보여줬다.)
- I haven't even thought about <u>what</u> I'm going to wear to the dinner.
(난 저녁식사에 입고 갈 것에 대해서 생각조차 하지 않았다.)
- <u>What</u> annoys me is the way he boasts about <u>what</u> he's done.
(나를 짜증나게 하는 것은 그가 자신이 한 것에 대해 자랑하는 방식이다.)

단수 주어   단수 동사
A commonality / between conceptual and computer art / was the suppression of authorial presence. // 단서 1 개념 예술과 컴퓨터 예술의 공통점이 빈칸에 들어가야 함
공통점은 / 개념 예술과 컴퓨터 예술의 / 작가의 존재에 대한 억제였다 //

Conceptual artists decoupled the relationship / between the art object and artist / by mitigating / all personal signs of invention. //
└〈수단〉의 전치사
개념 예술가들은 관계를 분리했다 / 예술품과 예술가 사이의 / 완화함으로써 / 창작의 모든 개인적인 흔적을 // 단서 2 개념 예술: 창작의 모든 개인적인 흔적을 완화하여 예술품과 예술가 사이의 관계를 분리함

The artist became detached / from the idea of personalized draftsmanship / by installing a predetermined system / — a type of instruction / for another to follow. //
to follow의 의미상 주어   형용사적 용법(a type of instruction 수식)
예술가는 분리되었다 / 개인화된 제도공의 솜씨라는 개념으로부터 / 미리 정해진 시스템을 설치함으로써 / 일종의 지침 / 다른 사람이 따르는 //

That way / there was, as Sol LeWitt states, no "dependence / on the skill of the artist / as a craftsman." //
그런 식으로 / Sol LeWitt가 말하듯이 '의존'이 없었다 / '예술가의 솜씨에의 / 공예가로서' //

Effectively / any person could carry out the instructions. //
사실상 / 누구나 그 지침을 수행할 수 있었다 //
선행사(추상적 의미의 장소)
The same process was at work / in computer art, / where artists devised / a predetermined drawing algorithm / for the computer automaton / to carry out the instruction. //
단서 3 컴퓨터 예술에서도 같은 과정이 이루어짐   관계부사
to carry out의 의미상 주어
같은 과정이 이루어졌는데 / 컴퓨터 예술에서도 / 거기서 예술가는 고안했다 / 미리 정해진 그리기 알고리즘을 / 컴퓨터 자동 장치가 / 그 지침을 수행하도록 //

The human agent initiated / the conceptual form, / and a machine actuated it. //

인간 행위자는 창안했고 / 개념적 형태를 / 기계는 이를 작동시켰다 //

Likewise, / the computer artwork lacked / any autographic mark, trace of spontaneity, or artistic authenticity. //

마찬가지로 / 컴퓨터 예술품에는 결여되어 있었다 / 어떠한 자필의 흔적도, 자발성의 흔적도, 또는 예술적 진정성도 //

과거의 습관을 나타내는 조동사

The plotter arm would replace the human arm / in the production process. //

플로터의 팔은 인간의 팔을 대체하곤 했다 / 생산 과정에서 //

- commonality ⓝ 공통점 • conceptual ⓐ 개념의
- decouple ⓥ 분리시키다 • object ⓝ 물체 • detach ⓥ 떼다
- invention ⓝ 발명, 창작 • personalized ⓐ 개인화된
- draftsmanship ⓝ 제도공의 기술 • install ⓥ 설치하다
- predetermined ⓐ 미리 정해진 • instruction ⓝ 지침
- state ⓥ 말하다 • dependence ⓝ 의존
- effectively ⓐⓓ 효율적으로 • carry out 수행하다
- algorithm ⓝ 알고리즘 • automaton ⓝ 자동 장치
- agent ⓝ 행위자 • initiate ⓥ 시작하다 • artwork ⓝ 예술품
- trace ⓥ 추적하다 • spontaneity ⓝ 자발성
- authenticity ⓝ 진정성

개념 예술과 컴퓨터 예술의 공통점은 **작가의 존재가 감춰지는 것**이었다. 개념 예술가들은 창작의 모든 개인적인 흔적을 완화함으로써 예술품과 예술가 사이의 관계를 분리했다. 예술가는 다른 사람이 따르는 일종의 지침인 미리 정해진 시스템을 설치함으로써 개인화된 제도공의 솜씨라는 개념으로부터 분리되었다. 그런 식으로 Sol LeWitt가 말하듯이 '공예가로서 예술가의 솜씨에 대한 의존'이 없었다. 사실상 누구나 그 지침을 수행할 수 있었다. 같은 과정이 컴퓨터 예술에서도 이루어졌는데, 예술가는 컴퓨터 자동 장치가 그 지침을 수행하도록 미리 정해진 그리기 알고리즘을 고안했다. 인간 행위자는 개념적 형태를 창안했고, 기계는 이를 작동시켰다. 마찬가지로, 컴퓨터 예술품에는 어떠한 자필의 흔적도, 자발성의 흔적도, 또는 예술적 진정성도 결여되어 있었다. 플로터의 팔은 생산 과정에서 인간의 팔을 대체하곤 했다.

다음 빈칸에 들어갈 말로 가장 적절한 것을 고르시오. [3점]

① the suppression of authorial presence 예술품과 예술가 사이의 관계가 분리됨
  작가의 존재에 대한 억제
② the rejection of meaningless repetition 의미 없는 반복과 관련된 언급은 없음
  의미 없는 반복의 거부
③ the elevation of ordinary objects to art
  평범한 물체의 예술로의 승격 어떤 것이 예술이 되는지에 대한 내용이 아님
④ the preference of simplicity to elaboration
  정교함보다 단순함에 대한 선호 정교함과 단순함이 대조되는 것이 아님
⑤ the tendency of artists to work in collaboration
  협력하여 작업하려는 예술가들의 경향 예술가의 협력에 대한 언급은 없음

왜 정답? [정답률 30%]

빈칸 문장	개념 예술과 컴퓨터 예술의 공통점은 _____ 이었다.
개념 예술	개념 예술가들은 창작의 모든 개인적인 흔적을 완화하여 예술품과 예술가 사이의 관계를 분리했음 **단서2**
컴퓨터 예술	컴퓨터 예술에서도 개념 예술과 같은 과정이 이루어졌음 **단서3**

➡ 빈칸에는 개념 예술과 컴퓨터 예술의 공통점(A commonality)이 들어가야 한다.
  ▶ 개념 예술에서 예술품과 예술가 사이의 관계가 분리되었다고 했고, 컴퓨터 예술에서도 그와 같은 과정이 이루어졌다고 했으므로 둘의 공통점은 ① '작가의 존재에 대한 억제'이다.

왜 오답?

② 두 예술에서 의미 없는 반복이 거부되었다는 등의 언급은 없다.
③ 평범한 물체가 예술이 된다는 내용이 아니다.
④ 정교함과 단순함이 대조되는 글이 아니다.
⑤ 예술가의 협력에 대해서는 언급되지 않았다.

K 14 정답 ④ ＊사람이 도로를 바라보는 자기중심적 방식 ——

주격 관계대명사
Everyone who drives, walks, or swipes a transit card in a city / views herself / as a transportation expert / from the moment / 사이에 관계부사 when이 생략됨
she walks out the front door. //

도시에서 운전하거나 걷거나 교통 카드를 판독기에 통과시키는 모든 사람은 / 자신을 여긴다 / 교통 전문가로 / 순간부터 / 현관문을 나서는 //

And how she views the street / **tracks pretty closely / with how she gets around**. //

그리고 그 사람이 도로를 바라보는 방식은 / 매우 밀접하게 일치한다 / 그 사람이 돌아다니는 방식과 //

find+목적어+목적격 보어(-ing)
That's why we find / so many well-intentioned and civic-minded citizens / arguing past one another. //

그런 이유로 우리는 보게 된다 / 선의의 시민 의식을 가진 매우 많은 사람이 / 서로를 지나치며 언쟁하는 것을 //

At neighborhood meetings in school auditoriums, / and in back rooms at libraries and churches, / 병렬 구조

학교 강당에서 열리는 주민 회의에서 / 도서관과 교회의 뒷방에서 /

local residents across the nation gather / for often-contentious discussions / about transportation proposals / 주격 관계대명사 that would change a city's streets. //

전국의 지역 주민들이 모인다 / 흔한 논쟁적인 토론을 하려고 / 교통 제안에 대한 / 도시의 거리를 바꿀 //

And like all politics, / all transportation is local and intensely personal. // **단서1** 교통은 지역적이고 '개인적'이라고 함

그리고 모든 정치와 마찬가지로 / 모든 교통은 지역적이고 지극히 개인적이다 //

주격 관계대명사
A transit project / that could speed travel / for tens of thousands of people / can be stopped /

교통 프로젝트는 / 이동 속도를 높일 수 있는 / 수만 명의 / 중단될 수 있다 /

동격절을 이끄는 접속사
by objections to the loss of a few parking spaces / or by the simple fear / that the project won't work. //

몇 개의 주차 공간 상실에 대한 반대에 의해 / 또는 단순한 두려움에 의해 / 프로젝트가 효과가 없을 것이라는 //

It's not a challenge / of the data or the traffic engineering or the planning. //

그것은 과제가 아니다 / 데이터나 교통 공학 또는 계획의 //

Public debates about streets / are typically rooted / in emotional assumptions / **단서2** 도로에 대한 대중의 생각은 그 변화가 자신의 통근이나 주차, 안전함에 대한 믿음 등에 어떠한 영향을 미칠지에 대한 감정적인 추정에 뿌리를 둠

도로에 대한 대중 토론은 / 뿌리를 두고 있다 / 감정적인 추정에 /

형용사적 용법
about how a change will affect / a person's commute, / ability to park, / belief about what 선행사를 포함한 관계대명사 is safe and what isn't, / or the bottom line of a local business. //

보통 변화가 어떤 영향을 미칠지에 대한 / 개인의 통근에 / 주차 능력에 / 안전한 것과 안전하지 않은 것에 대한 믿음에 / 또는 지역 사업체의 순익에 //

- transit card 교통 카드 • transportation ⓝ 교통, 운송
- well-intentioned ⓐ 선의의 • civic-minded ⓐ 시민 의식이 있는
- auditorium ⓝ 강당 • across the nation 전국의
- discussion ⓝ 토론 • intensely ⓐⓓ 지극히, 몹시
- objection ⓝ 반대 • engineering ⓝ 공학
- be rooted in ~에 뿌리를 두다 • assumption ⓝ 추정, 가정
- bottom line 순익

도시에서 운전하거나 걷거나 교통 카드를 판독기에 통과시키는 모든 사람은 현관문을 나서는 순간부터 자신을 교통 전문가로 여긴다. 그리고 그 사람이 도로를 바라보는 방식은 **그 사람이 돌아다니는 방식과 매우 밀접하게 일치한다.** 그런 이유로 우리는 선의의 시민 의식을 가진 매우 많은 사람이 서로를 지나치며 언쟁하는 것을 보게 된다. 학교 강당에서 열리는 주민 회의에서, 도서관과 교회의 뒷방에서, 전국의 지역 주민들이 모여 도시의 거리를 바꿀 교통 제안에 대해 흔히 논쟁적인 토론을 벌인다. 그리고 모든 정치와

마찬가지로, 모든 교통은 지역적이고 지극히 개인적이다. 수만 명의 이동 속도를 높일 수 있는 교통 프로젝트는 몇 개의 주차 공간 상실에 대한 반대나 프로젝트가 효과가 없을 것이라는 단순한 두려움 때문에 중단될 수 있다. 그것은 데이터나 교통 공학 또는 계획의 과제가 아니다. 도로에 대한 대중 토론은 보통 변화가 개인의 통근, 주차 능력, 안전한 것과 안전하지 않은 것에 대한 믿음, 또는 지역 사업체의 순익에 어떤 영향을 미칠지에 대한 감정적인 추정에 뿌리를 두고 있다.

다음 빈칸에 들어갈 말로 가장 적절한 것을 고르시오. [3점]

① relies heavily on how others see her city's streets
다른 사람이 그 사람의 도시 도로를 어떻게 보느냐에 크게 의존한다
② updates itself with each new public transit policy
각각의 새로운 대중교통 정책에 맞춰 자체를 업데이트한다
③ arises independently of the streets she travels on
그 사람이 이동하는 도로와 관계없이 발생한다
④ tracks pretty closely with how she gets around
그 사람이 돌아다니는 방식과 매우 밀접하게 일치한다
⑤ ties firmly in with how her city operates
그 사람의 도시가 운영되는 방식과 긴밀하게 연계되어 있다

> 다른 사람이 도로를 어떻게 보느냐에 의존한다고 하지 않음
> 도로를 바라보는 방식을 업데이트한다는 내용이 아님
> 그 사람이 이동하는 도로와 관계없이 발생 새로운 대중교통 정책에 맞춰 자체를 업데이트한다고 했음
> 그 사람이 돌아다니는 방식과 매우 밀접하게 일치한다고 했음
> 도시가 운영되는 방식이 영향을 미치는 것이 아님

왜 정답? [정답률 25%]

빈칸 문장	(도시에서 다니는) 모든 사람이 도로를 바라보는 방식은 '무엇'이다.

➡ 빈칸에는 도시에서 돌아다니는 사람들이 갖는 도로 정책이나 교통에 대한 생각에 영향을 미치는 것이 들어가야 한다.

- 모든 교통은 지역적이고 지극히 개인적이다. **단서1**
- 도로에 대한 대중 토론은 보통 변화가 개인의 통근, 주차 능력, 안전한 것과 안전하지 않은 것에 대한 믿음, 또는 지역 사업체의 순익에 어떤 영향을 미칠지에 대한 감정적인 추정에 뿌리를 두고 있다. **단서2**

➡ 도시에서 운전하거나 걷거나 교통 카드를 판독기에 통과시키는 모든 사람은 개인적인 관점에서 교통 제안을 하며, 결국 사람이 도로를 바라보는 방식은 자기중심적 추정에 뿌리를 두고 있다는 내용의 글이다.

▶ 빈칸에 들어갈 말로 가장 적절한 것은 ④ '그 사람이 돌아다니는 방식과 매우 밀접하게 일치한다'이다.

왜 오답?

① 다른 사람이 도로를 어떻게 보느냐가 아니라 자신의 관점에 크게 의존한다고 했다.
② 새로운 대중교통 정책에 맞춰 도로를 바라보는 방식을 업데이트한다는 내용의 글이 아니다.
③ 단순히 '이동'과 '도로'를 넣어 만든 오답일 뿐, 도로를 바라보는 방식이 이동하는 도로와 관계없이 발생한다고 한 것이 아니다. **주의**
⑤ 도로를 바라보는 방식이 도시가 운영되는 방식에 의해 영향을 받는 것이 아니다.

류이레 | 연세대 의예과 2024년 입학 · 광주대동고 졸

이번 수능에서 33번과 함께 가장 어려운 문제 중 하나였어. 이 지문은 빈칸 뒤 문장을 읽으면서 시민들이 논쟁하는 이유가 빈칸에 들어가야 한다는 사실을 캐치해야 했는데 그 과정이 많이 어려웠어.

이에 대한 구체적인 근거는 It's not a challenge ~문장부터 계속 나타나. 변화가 시행될 수 없는 요인으로 '감정적인 가정'을 언급하고 있거든. 다시 말해 도시의 변화가 과학에 기인하지 않는다는 것이지. 그래서 사람들의 일상적인 삶을 지칭하는 ④이 답이야.

K 15 정답 ② *고통스러운 자각에서 벗어나고 싶은 마음

— as ~ as 원급 비교 * —
Even as mundane a behavior as watching TV / may be a
to escape의 의미상 주어
way / for some people / to **escape** / **painful self-awareness** /
through distraction. //
형용사적 용법(a way 수식)
TV를 보는 것처럼 평범한 행동일지라도 / 방법일 수 있다 / 어떤 사람들이 / 벗어나는 / 고통 스러운 자각에서 / 주의를 딴 데로 돌리는 것을 통해 //

주어   동사①
To test this idea. / Sophia Moskalenko and Steven Heine / gave
간접목적어   직접목적어
participants false feedback / about their test performance, /
이 생각을 검증하기 위해 / Sophia Moskalenko와 Steven Heine은 / 참가자들에게 거 짓 피드백을 주었고 / 그들의 시험 성적에 관한 /

동사②   목적어
and then seated each one / in front of a TV set / to watch a video
전치사
/ as the next part of the study. //
그런 다음 각각 앉혔다 / TV 앞에 / 비디오를 시청하도록 / 연구의 다음 부분으로 //

When the video came on, / showing nature scenes / with a
musical soundtrack, /
비디오가 나오자 / 자연의 장면을 보여주는 / 음악 사운드트랙과 함께 /

the experimenter exclaimed / that this was the wrong video
병렬 구조
/ and went / supposedly to get the correct one, / leaving the
접속사
participant alone / as the video played. //
실험자는 소리쳤고 / 이것이 잘못된 비디오라고 / 갔다 / 아마도 제대로 된 것을 가지러 / 참가 자를 홀로 남겨두고 / 비디오가 재생될 때 //

선행사
The participants / who had received failure feedback / watched
주격 관계대명사   선행사 주격 관계대명사
the video / much longer / than those / who thought / they had
비교급 강조 부사   **단서1** 자신이 시험에 실패했다는 피드백을 받은
succeeded. //   참가자가 훨씬 더 오래 비디오를 시청함
참가자들은 / 실패라는 피드백을 받았던 / 비디오를 시청했다 / 훨씬 더 오래 / 참가자들보다 / 생각하는 / 자신이 성공했다고 **단서2** TV 시청을 통해 고통스러운 자각을 효과적으로 완화할 수 있음
The researchers concluded / that distraction / through television
선행사(주격 관계대명사와 be동사는 생략됨)
viewing / can effectively relieve the discomfort /
연구원들은 결론지었다 / 주의를 딴 데로 돌리는 것이 / 텔레비전 시청을 통해 / 불편함을 효과 적으로 완화할 수 있다고 /

associated with painful failures or mismatches / between the
self and self-guides. //
고통스러운 실패나 불일치와 관련된 / 자신과 자기 안내 지침 사이의 //   형용사적 용법
(wish 수식)
In contrast, / successful participants had little wish / to be
준부정어
distracted / from their self-related thoughts! // (거의 ~ 없는)
이와 대조적으로 / 성공한 참가자들은 거의 바라지 않았다 / 주의가 딴 데로 돌려지기를 / 자기 자신과 관련된 생각에서 // **단서3** 자각이 고통스럽지 않은 사람은 주의를 딴 데로 돌리고 싶어 하지 않음

- experimenter ⓝ 실험자   • exclaim ⓥ 소리치다, 외치다
- supposedly ⓐⓓ 아마, 추정하건대   • conclude ⓥ 결론을 내리다
- distraction ⓝ 주의를 딴 데로 돌리기   • relieve ⓥ 완화하다
- discomfort ⓝ 불편   • mismatch ⓝ 불일치   • peer ⓝ 동료
- escape ⓥ 벗어나다, 탈출하다   • self-awareness ⓝ 자기 인식
- constructive ⓐ 건설적인   • intense ⓐ 강렬한, 극심한
- self-reflection ⓝ 자기반성

TV를 보는 것처럼 평범한 행동일지라도 그 행동은 어떤 사람들이 **주의를 딴 데 로 돌리는 것을 통해 고통스러운 자각에서 벗어나는** 방법일 수 있다. 이 생각을 검증하기 위해, Sophia Moskalenko와 Steven Heine은 참가자들에게 그들의 시험 성적에 관한 거짓 피드백을 주었고, 그런 다음 연구의 다음 부분으로 각각 TV 앞에 앉아 비디오를 시청하게 했다. 음악 사운드트랙과 함께 자연의 장면을 보여주는 비디오가 나오자, 실험자는 이것이 잘못된 비디오라고 소리쳤고, 아마도 제대로 된 것을 가지러 가면서, 참가자를 비디오가 재생될 때 홀로 남겨두 었다. (시험 성적에 관하여) 실패라는 피드백을 받았던 참가자들은 자신이 성공 했다고 생각하는 참가자들보다 훨씬 더 오래 비디오를 시청했다. 연구원들은 텔 레비전 시청을 통해 주의를 딴 데로 돌리는 것이 고통스러운 실패나 자신과 자 기 안내 지침 사이의 불일치와 관련된 불편함을 효과적으로 완화할 수 있다고 결론지었다. 이와 대조적으로, 성공한 참가자들은 자기 자신과 관련된 생각에 서 주의가 딴 데로 돌려지기를 거의 바라지 않았다!

다음 빈칸에 들어갈 말로 가장 적절한 것을 고르시오.
① ignore uncomfortable comments from their close peers
　가까운 동료의 불편한 지적을 무시하는　　　　　동료가 지적하는 상황을 실험한 것이 아님
②escape painful self-awareness through distraction
　주의를 딴 데로 돌리는 것을 통해 고통스러운 자각에서 벗어나는　TV를 봄으로써 자신이 시험에
③ receive constructive feedback from the media　실패했다는 자각을 벗어남
　미디어에서 건설적인 피드백을 받는　　　　　TV를 통해 건설적인 피드백을 얻는다는 것이 아님
④ refocus their divided attention to a given task
　분열된 집중력을 주어진 과업에 다시 집중시키는　　TV 시청을 통해 주의를 분산시키는 것임
⑤ engage themselves in intense self-reflection
　스스로를 강력한 자기반성에 참여시키는　　TV를 보면서 강력하게 자기반성을 한다는 것이 아님

▶왜 정답? [정답률 43%]
빈칸 문장에 이어지는 실험 내용을 보면, 시험에 실패했다는 피드백을 받은 참가자, 즉 고통스러운 자각을 마주한 참가자들이 시험에 성공했다고 생각하는 참가자들보다 훨씬 더 오래 비디오를 시청했고, 이러한 결과를 가지고 연구원들은 TV 시청을 통해 주의를 딴 데로 돌리는 것이 불편함을 효과적으로 완화할 수 있다는 결론을 내렸다고 했다. 따라서 빈칸 문장은 TV를 보는 것과 같은 평범한 행동일지라도 어떤 사람들이 ② '주의를 딴 데로 돌리는 것을 통해 고통스러운 자각에서 벗어나는' 방법일 수 있다는 내용이 되어야 한다. ┌자신이 시험에 실패했다는 🍯팁
　　　　　　　　　　　　　　　　　　└고통스러운 자각

▶왜 오답?
① 참가자 중 일부가 시험에 실패했다는 피드백을 받는 상황을 실험한 것이지, 동료로부터 불편한 지적을 받는 상황을 실험한 것이 아니다.
③ TV 시청을 통해 건설적인 피드백을 받는다는 결론을 내린 것이 아니다.
④ TV를 시청함으로써 주의를 딴 데로 돌려서 자신이 시험에 실패했다는 고통스러운 자각에서 벗어나는 것이다. 주의
⑤ TV를 보면서 시험에 실패한 자신을 반성한다는 것이 아니다.

──────────── 어법 특강 ────────────

＊as ~ as 원급 비교
– as ~ as는 두 비교 대상이 동등함을 나타내며, '…만큼 ~한[하게]'라고 해석하면 된다. 이때 첫 번째 as는 부사로, as와 as 사이에는 부사의 수식을 받는 형용사나 부사가 들어가야 한다.
• This cookie is as big as my face.
　(이 쿠키는 내 얼굴만큼 크다.)
–「배수사+as ~ as」구문은 '…의 몇 배만큼 ~한[하게]'라는 의미로 쓴다.
• Your office is twice as big as my room.
　(네 사무실이 내 방보다 두 배만큼 크다.)

K 16 정답 ④ ＊동물이 무해한 자극을 대하는 방식 ──────
　동명사 주어　　　　　　　　　　'~에 직면하여, ~의 면전에서'
Enabling animals to operate / in the presence of harmless
　　　　단수 동사
stimuli / is an almost universal function / of learning. //
동물이 움직일 수 있게 하는 것은 / 무해한 자극 앞에서 / 거의 보편적인 기능이다 / 학습의 //

Most animals innately avoid objects / they have not previously
　　　　　　　　　　　　선행사(목적격 관계대명사는 생략됨)　〈경험〉을 나타내는 현재완료
encountered. //
대부분의 동물은 선천적으로 대상을 피한다 / 그들이 이전에 마주친 적 없는 //

Unfamiliar objects may be dangerous; / treating them with
　　　　　　　　　　　단수 동사　　　　　　　동명사구 주어
caution / has survival value. //
익숙하지 않은 대상은 위험할 수 있다 / 그것을 조심해서 다루는 것은 / 생존가(生存價)를 갖는다 //

　　　　　단서1 익숙하지 않은 자극에 대한 신중함이 지속되면 오히려 해가 될 수 있음
If persisted in, / however, / such careful behavior could interfere
/ with feeding and other necessary activities / to the extent / that
　　　　　　　　　　　　　　　　　　　　선행사　　관계부사
the benefit of caution / would be lost. //
지속된다면 / 그러나 / 그러한 신중한 행동은 방해할 수도 있다 / 먹이 섭취와 다른 필요한 활동을 / 정도로 / 조심해서 얻는 이익이 / 소실될 //

A turtle / that withdraws / into its shell / at every puff of wind /
　주어
or whenever a cloud casts a shadow / would never win races, /
　　　　　　　　　　　　　　　　　　동사
not even with a lazy rabbit. //
거북은 / 움츠리는 / 자신의 등껍질 속으로 / 바람이 조금 불 때마다 / 또는 구름이 그림자를 드리울 때마다 / 결코 경주에서 이기지 못할 것이다 / 게으른 토끼와의 (경주라도) //
　　부사적용법(목적)
To overcome this problem, / almost all animals habituate / to
　　　　　　　선행사　　주격 관계대명사
safe stimuli / that occur frequently. //
이 문제를 극복하기 위해 / 거의 모든 동물은 익숙해져 있다 / 안전한 자극에 / 자주 발생하는 //

단서2 낯선 자극이 무해하다고 판단되면 동물은 자신의 활동을 계속할 것임
Confronted by a strange object, / an inexperienced animal / may
freeze or attempt to hide, / but if nothing unpleasant happens, /
　　　　　　　　　　　　부사절 접속사(조건)
sooner or later / it will continue its activity. //
낯선 대상에 직면하면 / 경험이 없는 동물은 / 얼어붙거나 숨으려고 할 수도 있지만 / 불쾌한 일이 일어나지 않으면 / 머잖아 / 그것은 자신의 활동을 계속할 것이다 //

The possibility also exists / that an unfamiliar object may be
　　　　　　　　　　　　　The possibility의 동격절 접속사
useful, / so if it poses no immediate threat, / a closer inspection
〈결과〉의 등위절 접속사
may be worthwhile. //
가능성도 있으므로 / 익숙하지 않은 대상이 유용할 / 그것이 즉각적인 위협을 주지 않는다면 / 더 자세히 살펴보는 것이 가치가 있을 수도 있다 //

• universal ⓐ 보편적인, 일반적인　• avoid ⓥ (회)피하다, 모면하다
• object ⓝ 물건, 물체　• previously ⓐⓓ 이전에, 사전에
• encounter ⓥ 마주치다, 맞닥뜨리다　• treat ⓥ 다루다, 대하다
• caution ⓝ 조심　• persist ⓥ 집요하게[끈질기게] 계속하다
• interfere ⓥ 방해하다, 간섭하다　• feed ⓥ 먹을 것을 먹다
• necessary ⓐ 필요한, 필연적인　• activity ⓝ 활동
• extent ⓝ 정도　• benefit ⓝ 이득, 혜택
• withdraw ⓥ (뒤로) 물러나다　• shell ⓝ 껍데기, 껍질
• puff ⓝ (훅 날아오는 작은 양의) 공기[연기]
• cast ⓥ (빛을) 발하다, (그림자를) 드리우다　• overcome ⓥ 극복하다
• habituate ⓥ 습관이 되다, 길들이다　• occur ⓥ 일어나다, 발생하다
• confront ⓥ 마주치다, 직면하게 만들다　• strange ⓐ 낯선, 이상한
• inexperienced ⓐ 경험이 부족한, 미숙한　• freeze ⓥ 얼다, 얼어붙다
• attempt ⓥ 시도하다　• hide ⓥ 숨다, 감추다
• sooner or later 조만간, 머지않아　• possibility ⓝ 가능성, 가능함
• exist ⓥ 존재하다, 있다　• pose ⓥ (위협·문제 등을) 제기하다
• immediate ⓐ 즉각적인, 당면한　• threat ⓝ 위협
• close ⓐ 철저한, 면밀한　• inspection ⓝ 검사
• worthwhile ⓐ ~할 가치가 있는　• weigh ⓥ 따져 보다, 저울질하다
• predict ⓥ 예측하다　• operate ⓥ 움직이다, 작동하다
• stimulus ⓝ 자극((pl. stimuli))　• surrounding ⓐ 주위의

동물이 무해한 자극 앞에서 움직일 수 있게 하는 것은 학습의 거의 보편적인 기능이다. 대부분의 동물은 선천적으로 이전에 마주친 적 없는 대상을 피한다. 익숙하지 않은 대상은 위험할 수 있으므로, 그것을 조심해서 다루는 것은 생존가(生存價)를 갖는다. 그러나 그러한 신중한 행동이 지속된다면, 그 행동은 조심해서 얻는 이익이 소실될 정도로 먹이 섭취와 다른 필요한 활동을 방해할 수도 있다. 바람이 조금 불 때마다, 또는 구름이 그림자를 드리울 때마다 등껍질 속으로 움츠리는 거북은 게으른 토끼와의 경주라도 결코 이기지 못할 것이다. 이 문제를 극복하기 위해, 거의 모든 동물은 자주 발생하는 안전한 자극에 익숙해져 있다. 낯선 대상에 직면하면, 경험이 없는 동물은 얼어붙거나 숨으려고 할 수도 있지만, 불쾌한 일이 일어나지 않으면 그것은 머잖아 활동을 계속할 것이다. 익숙하지 않은 대상이 유용할 가능성도 있으므로, 그것이 즉각적인 위협을 주지 않는다면, 더 자세히 살펴보는 것이 가치가 있을 수도 있다.

다음 빈칸에 들어갈 말로 가장 적절한 것을 고르시오. [3점]
① weigh the benefits of treating familiar things with care
　익숙한 것을 조심해서 다루는 것의 이점을 따져 봄　　신중한 행동이 계속되면 해가 됨
② plan escape routes after predicting possible attacks
　있을법한 공격을 예측한 이후에 퇴로를 계획함　　낯선 자극이 무해할 때의 행동에 대한 내용임
③ overcome repeated feeding failures for survival
　생존을 위해 반복된 먹이 섭취의 실패를 극복함　　먹이 섭취의 실패를 극복한다는 언급은 없음
④operate in the presence of harmless stimuli
　무해한 자극 앞에서 움직임　　낯선 자극에 직면하여 불쾌한 일이 일어나지 않으면 활동을 계속함
⑤ monitor the surrounding area regularly
　주변 지역을 정기적으로 감시할　　자주 발생하는 안전한 자극에는 익숙함

▶왜 정답? [정답률 42%]　　＝ '불쾌한 일이 일어나지 않으면' 🍯팁
동물이 낯선 자극을 조심해서 다루는 것은 생존에 도움이 되지만, 그러한 신중한 행동이 지속되면 조심해서 얻는 이익이 없어질 만큼 먹이 섭취와 같은 다른 활동이 방해 받을 수 있다고 했다. 그래서 낯선 자극에 직면했을 때 그것이 무해하다고 밝혀지면 동물은 자신의 활동을 계속할 것이고, 나아가 낯선 자극을 더 자세히 살펴보는 것이 가치가 있을 수 있다는 내용이 이어진다. 따라서 빈칸 문장에서 설명하는 학습의 거의 보편적인 기능은 동물이 ④ '무해한 자극 앞에서 움직일' 수 있게 하는 것이다.

① 낯선 자극을 신중히 다루는 것도 지속되면 해가 된다고 했다. 따라서 동물로 하여금 익숙한 것을 조심히 다루는 이점을 따져 볼 수 있게 한다는 것은 글의 내용에 맞지 않는다.

② 동물이 낯선 자극에 직면했을 때 있을법한 공격을 예측하고 퇴로를 계획한다는 언급은 없다. 낯선 자극에 직면했을 때 그것이 무해하다고 밝혀지면 자신의 행동을 계속하도록 학습된다는 것이 핵심이다.

③ 동물이 학습을 통해 먹이 섭취의 반복적인 실패를 극복한다는 내용이 아니다.

⑤ 거의 모든 동물이 자주 발생하는 안전한 자극에는 익숙해져 있다고 했으므로 자신에게 익숙한 주변 지역을 정기적으로 감시한다는 것은 글의 내용에 맞지 않는다. 동물이 주변 지역을 정기적으로 감시하도록 학습된다는 언급도 없다. [주의]

K 17 정답 ② ＊아리스토텔레스와 생각이 다른 헤겔

In Hegel's philosophy, / even though there is interaction and interrelation / between the universal and the individual, / **the universal still has more priority / than the individual**. //
부사절 접속사(양보)
헤겔의 철학에서 / 비록 상호 작용과 상호 관계가 있긴 하지만 / 보편자와 개별자 사이에 / 보편자는 여전히 더 많은 우위를 갖는다 / 개별자보다 //

For Hegel, / individuals are not distinguished / in terms of Reason. //
헤겔에게 / 개인은 '이성'의 관점에서는 구별되지 않는다 //

In *Philosophy of Right* / Hegel stresses particularity and universality / as follows: "A man, / who acts perversely, / exhibits particularity. //
동사   목적어   주어, 선행사   주격 관계대명사절
Philosophy of Right에서 / 헤겔은 특수성과 보편성을 강조한다 / 다음과 같이 / '사람은 / 별나게 행동하는데 / 특수성을 보인다 //

The rational is the highway / on which everyone travels, / and no one is specially marked." //
관계부사 where로 바꿀 수 있음
이성적인 것은 고속 도로이며 / 모든 사람이 이동하는 / 아무도 특별하게 표시되지 않는다' //

Here, / Hegel maintains / that individuals can be differentiated / from each other / in terms of their acts / but they are not differentiated / with respect to reason. //
생략 가능한 목적어절 접속사
여기서 / 헤겔은 주장한다 / 개인이 구별될 수 있지만 / 서로 / 그들의 행동의 관점에서는 / 그들은 구별되지 않는다고 / 이성의 측면에서는 //

There are specific thoughts, / but they are finally resolved / into the universal. // [단서1] 헤겔의 철학에서 특수한 생각(개별자)은 결국 보편자로 귀착됨
특수한 생각은 있지만 / 그것들은 결국 귀착된다 / 보편자로 //

One might say / that Hegel seems to focus on the individual / like Aristotle /
생략 가능한 목적어절 접속사
[단서3] 개별자를 제일 실체로, 보편자를 제이 실체로 여기는 아리스토텔레스와 대조됨
혹자는 말할 수도 있다 / 헤겔이 개별자에만 초점을 맞춘 것으로 보인다고 / 아리스토텔레스처럼 / [단서2] 헤겔은 보편자를 근본적인 것으로 다룸

but in reality, / he subtly treats the universal / as fundamental / whereas Aristotle considers / the individual as primary substance / and universal as secondary substance; /
하지만 실제로 / 그는 미묘하게 보편자를 다룬다 / 근본적인 것으로 / 아리스토텔레스가 여기는 반면 / 개별자를 제일(第一) 실체로 / 보편자를 제이(第二) 실체로 /

in so doing / Aristotle emphasizes the universal / to be subordinate / to the individual / in contrast to Hegel. //
그렇게 하는 것을 통해 / 아리스토텔레스는 보편자를 강조한다 / 종속된다고 / 개별자에게 / 헤겔과는 반대로 // [단서4] 보편자가 개별자에게 종속된다는 아리스토텔레스와 반대됨

- philosophy ⓝ 철학
- interaction ⓝ 상호 작용
- interrelation ⓝ 상호 관계
- priority ⓝ 우위
- distinguish ⓥ 구별하다
- in terms of ~의 면에서, ~에 관하여
- stress ⓥ 강조하다
- particularity ⓝ 특수성
- universality ⓝ 보편성
- highway ⓝ 고속도로
- differentiate ⓥ 구별하다
- with respect to ~에 관하여
- subtle ⓐ 미묘한
- fundamental ⓐ 근본적인, 필수적인
- substance ⓝ 물질, 실체
- emphasize ⓥ 강조하다
- subordinate ⓐ 종속된
- in contrast to ~와 반대로, 대조적으로
- deduce ⓥ 추론하다

헤겔의 철학에서 비록 보편자와 개별자 사이에 상호 작용과 상호 관계가 있긴 하지만 보편자는 여전히 개별자보다 더 많은 우위를 갖는다. 헤겔에게 개인은 '이성'의 관점에서는 구별되지 않는다. Philosophy of Right에서 헤겔은 다음과 같이 특수성과 보편성을 강조한다. '사람은 별나게 행동하는데, 특수성을 보인다. 이성적인 것은 모든 사람이 이동하는 고속 도로이며, 아무도 특별하게 표시되지 않는다.' 여기서 헤겔은 개인이 그들의 행동의 관점에서는 서로 구별될 수 있지만 이성의 측면에서는 구별되지 않는다고 주장한다. 특수한 생각은 있지만 그것들은 결국 보편자로 귀착된다. 혹자는 헤겔이 아리스토텔레스처럼 개별자에만 초점을 맞춘 것으로 보인다고 말할 수도 있지만 아리스토텔레스가 개별자를 제일(第一) 실체로, 보편자를 제이(第二) 실체로 여기고, 그렇게 하는 것을 통해 헤겔과는 반대로 보편자가 개별자에게 종속된다고 강조하는 것과는 달리 실제로 그(헤겔)는 미묘하게 보편자를 근본적인 것으로 다룬다.

다음 빈칸에 들어갈 말로 가장 적절한 것을 고르시오. [3점]

① an individual stands alone apart from the universe
개인은 세계와 떨어져 분리되어 있다   보편자와 개별자에 대한 내용임
② the universal still has more priority than the individual
보편자는 여전히 개별자보다 더 많은 우위를 갖는다   아리스토텔레스와 반대되는 내용
③ universal truth cannot be the key to individual problems
보편적인 진실은 개인적인 문제의 해결책이 될 수 없다   보편자를 강조함
④ individuals can't deduce universal principles from reality itself
개인은 스스로 현실에서 보편적인 원칙을 추론할 수 없다   보편자를 추론하는 것이 아님
⑤ every individual should have his or her own particular universe
모든 개인은 자신만의 특별한 세계를 가져야 한다   특수성보다 보편성을 강조함

> 왜 오답 ? [정답률 42%]

빈칸 문장	헤겔의 철학에서, 비록 보편자와 개별자 사이에 상호 작용과 상호 관계가 있긴 하지만, _____.

→ 보편자와 개별자 사이에 상호 작용과 상호 관계가 있다는 내용이 양보의 접속사 even though로 이어졌다. → 빈칸은 부사절과 대조되는, 보편자와 개별자 사이에 상하 관계가 있다는 등의 문맥이어야 함

> - 특수한 생각(개별자)은 결국 보편자로 귀착된다. [단서1]
> - 헤겔은, 아리스토텔레스와 달리, 사실 보편자를 근본적인 것으로 다룬다. [단서2]
> - 아리스토텔레스: 개별자를 제일 실체로, 보편자를 제이 실체로 여김, 보편자는 개별자에게 종속된다고 강조. [단서3] [단서4]

→ 헤겔은 보편자보다 개별자를 강조하는 아리스토텔레스와 대조된다.

▶ 그러므로 빈칸에 들어갈 헤겔의 철학은 ② '보편자는 여전히 개별자보다 더 많은 우위를 갖는다'이다.

> 왜 오답 ?

① 보편자와 개별자의 관계에 대한 헤겔의 생각이 빈칸에 들어가야 한다.
③ 보편자를 개별자보다 우위에 두는 것이 헤겔의 생각이다.
④ 보편자를 추론할 수 있는지 여부를 다룬 것이 아니다.
⑤ 개인의 자신만의 특별한 세계는 '개별자'를 의미한다고 볼 수 있으므로, 이 글에서 설명하는 헤겔의 생각과는 거리가 멀다. [함정]

K 18 정답 ⑤ 😊 2등급 대비 [정답률 51%]

＊뉴스의 표현 방식의 변화

News, / especially in its televised form, / is constituted / not only by its choice of topics and stories / but by its **verbal and visual idioms or modes of address**. //
not only A but (also) B로 전치사구가 연결됨
뉴스는 / 특히 텔레비전으로 방송되는 형태에서 / 구성된다 / 그것의 주제와 이야기 선택에 의해서뿐만 아니라 / 그것의 언어적, 시각적 표현 양식이나 전달 방식에 의해서도 //

Presentational styles have been subject to a tension / between an informational-educational purpose and the need / to engage us entertainingly. //
형용사적 용법(the need 수식)
표현 방식은 긴장 상태에 영향을 받아 왔다 / 정보 제공 및 교육적 목적과 필요성 사이의 / 재미있게 우리의 주의를 끌 //

While current affairs programmes are often 'serious' / in tone /
부사절 접속사(대조)
sticking to the 'rules' of balance, / more popular programmes
adopt / a friendly, lighter, idiom /

시사 프로그램들이 흔히 '진지'하지만 / 어조에 있어 / 균형이라는 '규칙'을 고수하면서 / 더 대중적인 프로그램들은 채택한다 / 친근하고 더 가벼운 표현 양식을 /

in which we are invited to consider / the impact of particular
관계부사 where로 바꾸어 쓸 수 있음
news items / from the perspective / of the 'average person in
the street'. //

그 안에서 우리가 고려하도록 초대되는 / 특정 뉴스 기사의 영향을 / 관점에서 / '거리에서 만나는 보통 사람'의 //

Indeed, / contemporary news construction / has come to rely / on an increased use / of faster editing tempos / and 'flashier' presentational styles / 단서 2 '더 현란한' 표현 방식, 즉 시각적 전달 방식에 대해 설명함

사실 / 현대의 뉴스 구성은 / 의존하게 되었다 / 더 많은 이용에 / 더 빠른 편집 속도와 / '더 현란한' 표현 방식의 /

including the use / of logos, sound-bites, rapid visual cuts / and the 'star quality' of news readers. //

이용을 포함한 / 로고, 짤막한 방송용 어구, 빠른 시각적 편집 화면의 / 그리고 뉴스 독자의 '스타성'의 //

Popular formats can be said / to enhance understanding / by
an audience를 수식하는 현재분사
engaging an audience / unwilling to endure / the longer verbal orientation / of older news formats. //

대중적인 구성은 말해질 수 있다 / 이해를 높인다고 / 시청자의 주의를 끎으로써 / 견딜 의사가 없는 / 더 장황한 언어적 지향을 / 낡은 뉴스 구성 방식의 //

However, / they arguably work to reduce understanding / by failing to provide / the structural contexts / for news events. //

하지만 / 그것은 거의 틀림없이 이해를 감소시키는 효과가 있다 / 제공하지 못함으로써 / 구조적 맥락을 / 뉴스 사건에 관한 //

- televised ⓐ 텔레비전으로 방송되는　• constitute ⓥ 구성하다, 이루다
- be subject to ~의 영향을 받다
- tension ⓝ (필요·이해의 차이로 인한) 긴장[갈등] 상태
- informational ⓐ 지식을 주는, 정보를 제공하는
- engage ⓥ 끌어들이다, 참여시키다　• entertainingly ⓐ 재미있게
- current affairs (현재의 정치적·사회적 사건들인) 시사(時事)
- stick to ~을 고수하다[지키다]
- adopt ⓥ (특정한 방식이나 자세를) 채택하다[취하다]
- idiom ⓝ 어법, 표현 양식　• impact ⓝ 영향
- perspective ⓝ 관점, 시각　• contemporary ⓐ 현대의, 당대의
- construction ⓝ 구성　• rely ⓥ 의존하다, 믿다
- edit ⓥ 편집하다, 수정하다　• flashy ⓐ 현란한, 호화스러운
- enhance ⓥ 높이다, 증진하다　• unwilling ⓐ 꺼리는, 마지못해 하는
- endure ⓥ 견디다, 참다　• verbal ⓐ 언어의, 구두의
- orientation ⓝ 지향　• arguably ⓐ 아마 틀림없이, 주장하건대
- structural ⓐ 구조적인, 구조상의

뉴스, 특히 텔레비전으로 방송되는 형태는 그것이 선택하는 주제와 이야기뿐만 아니라 그것의 **언어적, 시각적 표현 양식이나 전달 방식**에 의해서도 구성된다. 표현 방식은 정보 제공 및 교육적 목적과 재미있게 우리의 주의를 끌 필요성 사이의 긴장 상태에 영향을 받아 왔다. 시사 프로그램들이 흔히 균형이라는 '규칙'을 고수하면서 어조가 '진지'하지만, 더 대중적인 프로그램들은 친근하고 더 가벼운 표현 양식을 채택하는데, 그 표현 양식에서 우리는 '거리에서 만나는 보통 사람'의 관점에서 특정 뉴스 기사의 영향을 고려하도록 초대된다. 사실, 현대의 뉴스 구성은 로고, 짤막한 방송용 어구, 빠른 시각적 편집 화면, 그리고 뉴스 독자의 '스타성'을 이용하는 것을 포함한 더 빠른 편집 속도와 '더 현란한' 표현 방식을 더 많이 이용하는 것에 의존하게 되었다. 대중적인 구성은 더 장황한 언어를 지향하는 낡은 뉴스 구성 방식을 견딜 의사가 없는 시청자의 주의를 끌어서 이해를 높인다고 할 수 있다. 하지만 그것은 뉴스 사건에 관한 구조적 맥락을 제공하지 못함으로써 거의 틀림없이 이해를 감소시키는 효과가 있다.

다음 빈칸에 들어갈 말로 가장 적절한 것을 고르시오.

① coordination with traditional display techniques
전통적인 표현 기법과의 조화　　　older news formats가 언급된 것으로 만든 오답
② prompt and full coverage of the latest issues
최신 쟁점에 대한 신속하고도 완전한 취재　　취재의 신속성과 완전성에 대한 언급은 없음
③ educational media contents favoured by producers
제작자가 선호하는 교육용 매체 내용　　informational-educational로 만든 오답
④ commitment to long-lasting news standards
오래도록 지속하는 뉴스 기준에 대한 책임　　뉴스의 기준에 대한 내용이 아님
⑤ verbal and visual idioms or modes of address
언어적, 시각적 표현 양식이나 전달 방식 친근하고 가벼운 어조, 시각적으로 더 현란한 표현 방식을 설명함

────────

왜 2등급? 뉴스의 구성 요소가 주제나 이야기 말고 또 어떤 것이 있는지 찾아야 하는 것을 첫 문장을 읽고 바로 파악해야 한다. 글을 읽으면서 무엇을 찾아야 하는지 첫 문장에서 힌트를 얻지 못하면 풀기 힘든 2등급 대비 문제이다.

| 문제 풀이 순서 |

1st 빈칸이 포함된 문장을 읽고, 글에서 찾아야 하는 것이 무엇인지 확인한다.

> News, especially in its televised form, is constituted not only by its choice of topics and stories but by its
> _____.
>
> 뉴스는, 특히 텔레비전으로 방송되는 형태에서, 그것의 주제와 이야기 선택에 의해서뿐만 아니라 그것의 _____에 의해서도 구성된다.

➡ 뉴스의 구성 요소를 설명하는 글로, 주제와 이야기 외에 또 무엇으로 뉴스가 구성되는지를 파악해야 한다.

2nd 글에서 설명하는 뉴스의 구성 요소를 확인한다.

- 시사 프로그램들이 흔히 어조가 진지하지만, 더 대중적인 프로그램들은 친근하고 더 가벼운 표현 양식을 채택한다. 단서 1
- 현대의 뉴스 구성은 로고, 빠른 시각적 편집 화면 등을 포함한 더 빠른 편집 속도와 더 현란한 표현 방식을 이용하는 것에 의존하게 되었다. 단서 2

➡ 시사 프로그램은 어조가 진지하고, 대중적인 프로그램은 어조가 친근하고 가볍다. 현대의 뉴스는 빠른 시각적 편집 화면, 더 현란한 표현 방식을 이용한다.
▶ '어조=언어적', '화면=시각적'
따라서 첫 문장은 〈뉴스가 ⑤ '언어적, 시각적 표현 양식이나 전달 방식'에 의해서도 구성된다〉는 내용이어야 한다.

| 선택지 분석 |

① coordination with traditional display techniques
전통적인 표현 기법과의 조화
낡은 뉴스 구성 방식의 장황한 언어적 지향과 오늘날의 뉴스의 표현 방식에 대해 이야기하기는 했지만, 그 둘을 조화시킨다는 언급은 없다.

② prompt and full coverage of the latest issues
최신 쟁점에 대한 신속하고도 완전한 취재
뉴스가 글의 소재라는 점으로 만든 오답이다. 취재의 신속성과 완전성이 강조된다는 등의 내용이 아니다.

③ educational media contents favoured by producers
제작자가 선호하는 교육용 매체 내용
뉴스의 표현 방식이 정보 제공 및 교육적 목적과 재미, 흥미로움 사이의 긴장 상태로부터 영향을 받는다는 언급으로 만든 오답이다.

④ commitment to long-lasting news standards
오래도록 지속하는 뉴스 기준에 대한 책임
오래도록 지속하는 뉴스 기준이나 그것에 대한 뉴스의 전념, 책임에 대해서는 언급되지 않았다.

⑤ verbal and visual idioms or modes of address
언어적, 시각적 표현 양식이나 전달 방식
idiom에 '관용구, 숙어' 외에 '표현 양식'이라는 뜻이 있다. address의 '연설, 강연'이라는 뜻에서 modes of address가 '전달 방식'이라는 의미임을 추론해야 한다.

* 엄청나게 불완전한 고고학 기록

분사구문의 생략되지 않은 접속사
When examining / the archaeological record of human culture, /
(일반적인) 사람[사람들]
one has to consider / that it is vastly **incomplete**. //
살펴볼 때 / 인류 문화의 고고학 기록을 / 사람들은 고려해야 한다 / 그것이 엄청나게 불완전
하다는 것을 // 단서1 인류 문화의 많은 측면은 고고학적으로
식별하기가 어려움   have의 목적어로 쓰인 간접의문문
Many aspects of human culture have / what archaeologists
describe / as low archaeological visibility, / meaning / they are
부사적용법(difficult 수식)
difficult / to identify archaeologically. //
인류 문화의 많은 측면은 지니고 있는데 / 고고학자들이 말하는 것을 / 낮은 고고학적 가시성
이라고 / 이것은 의미한다 / 그것들이 어렵다는 것을 / 고고학적으로 식별하기에 //
Archaeologists tend to focus / on tangible (or material) aspects
of culture: / things / that can be handled and photographed, /
such as tools, food, and structures. //
고고학자들은 초점을 맞추는 경향이 있다 / 문화의 유형적인 (혹은 물질적인) 측면에 / ~한 것
들 / 다뤄지고 사진을 찍힐 수 있는 / 도구, 음식, 구조물처럼 // 단서2 문화의 무형적 측면은
동명사 주어   더 많은 추론이 필요함
Reconstructing / intangible aspects of culture / is more difficult,
앞에 조동사 should가 생략됨   단수 동사
/ requiring / that one draw more inferences / from the tangible. //
재구성하는 것은 / 문화의 무형적 측면을 / 더 어려워서 / 요구한다 / 사람들이 더 많은 추론을
끌어내는 것을 / 유형적인 것에서 //
가주어   의미상 주어
It is relatively easy, / for example, / for archaeologists /
진주어
to identify / and draw inferences about technology and diet /
from stone tools and food remains. //
~은 비교적 쉽다 / 예를 들어 / 고고학자들이 / (기술과 식습관을) 식별하고 / 기술과 식습관에
관한 추론을 도출하기는 / 석기와 음식 유물로부터 //
Using / the same kinds of physical remains / to draw inferences
동명사 주어
/ about social systems / and what people were thinking about /
단수 동사   단서3 무형적인 측면에 대해서는 어쩔 수 없이
is more difficult. //   더 많은 추론이 있음
사용하는 것은 / 같은 종류의 물질적인 유물을 / 추론을 도출하기 위해 / 사회 체계에 관한 /
그리고 사람들이 무엇에 대해 생각하고 있었는지에 관한 / 더 어렵다 //
Archaeologists do it, / but there are necessarily more inferences /
고고학자들은 그렇게 하지만 / 더 많은 추론이 어쩔 수 없이 있다 /
involved in getting / from physical remains / recognized as trash
from A to B: A에서 B까지
/ to making interpretations / about belief systems. //
physical remains를
도달하는 것과 관련된 / 물리적 유물로부터 / 쓸모없는 것으로 인식되는 / 해석하는 것에 / 신
념 체계에 관해 //   수식하는 과거분사구

- examine ⓥ 조사[검토]하다   - consider ⓥ 고려하다, 여기다
- vastly ⓐ 엄청나게   - aspect ⓝ 측면
- visibility ⓝ 가시성, 눈에 잘 보임   - identify ⓥ 확인하다, 알아보다
- tangible ⓐ 유형의, 만질 수 있는   - reconstruct ⓥ 재구성하다
- intangible ⓐ 무형의, 만질 수 없는   - draw ⓥ (결론·생각 등을) 도출하다
- inference ⓝ 추론   - relatively ⓐ 상대적으로, 비교적
- diet ⓝ 식습관   - remains ⓝ 유물, 유적
- necessarily ⓐ 어쩔 수 없이, 필연적으로   - interpretation ⓝ 해석

인류 문화의 고고학 기록을 살펴볼 때, 사람들은 그것이 엄청나게 **불완전하다는**
것을 고려해야 한다. 인류 문화의 많은 측면은 고고학자들이 낮은 고고학적 가
시성이라고 말하는 것을 지니고 있는데, 이것은 그것들이 고고학적으로 식별하
기 어렵다는 것을 의미한다. 고고학자들은 문화의 유형적인 (혹은 물질적인) 측
면, 즉 도구, 음식, 구조물처럼 다루고 사진을 찍을 수 있는 것들에 초점을 맞추
는 경향이 있다. 문화의 무형적 측면을 재구성하는 것은 더 어려워서, 사람들은
유형적인 것에서 더 많은 추론을 끌어내야 한다. 예를 들어, 고고학자들이 석기
와 음식 유물로부터 기술과 식습관을 식별하고 그것에 관한 추론을 도출하기는
비교적 쉽다. 같은 종류의 물질적인 유물을 사용하여 사회 체계와 사람들이 무
엇에 대해 생각하고 있었는지에 관한 추론을 도출하는 것은 더 어렵다. 고고학
자들은 그렇게 하지만, 쓸모없는 것으로 인식되는 물리적 유물로부터 신념 체계
에 관한 해석에 도달하는 것과 관련된 더 많은 추론이 어쩔 수 없이 있다.

다음 빈칸에 들어갈 말로 가장 적절한 것을 고르시오.

① outdated 고고학적 기록이 시대에 뒤떨어진다는 것이 아님
  구식인
② factual 고고학적 기록이 허구인지 사실인지를 논하는 것이 아님
  사실에 기반을 둔
③ incomplete 고고학적 기록을 바탕으로 많은 추론이 필요함
  불완전한
④ organized ┐
  체계적인   │ 체계적이고 상세하다면 굳이 추론할 필요가 없을 것임
⑤ detailed ┘
  상세한

⊙₩ 2등급 ? 고고학 기록이 식별하기 어렵고, 추론이 필요하다는 것을 설명하는
내용을 잘 이해해야 한다. 첫 문장에 빈칸이 있으므로 이후에 나오는 고고학 기록의
이런 특성을 파악하지 못하면 풀기 힘든 2등급 대비 문제이다.

| 문제 풀이 순서 |

1st 빈칸이 포함된 문장을 읽고, 글에서 찾아야 하는 것이 무엇인지 확인한다.

> When examining the archaeological record of human
> culture, one has to consider that ⓘ it is vastly _____
>
> 인류 문화의 고고학 기록을 살펴볼 때, 사람들은 그것이 엄청나게 _____
> 하다는 것을 고려해야 한다.

➡ it이 가리키는 것은 앞에 나온 the archaeological record이다.
글에서 인류 문화의 고고학 기록이 어떤 특성을 갖는지 확인하여 빈칸을 채워야
한다.

2nd 글에서 설명하는 고고학 기록의 특성을 확인한다.

- 인류 문화의 많은 측면은 고고학자들이 낮은 고고학적 가시성이라고 말하는
  것을 지니고 있는데, 이것은 그것들이 고고학적으로 식별하기 어렵다는 것을
  의미한다. 단서1
- 문화의 무형적 측면을 재구성하는 것은 더 어려워서, 사람들은 유형적인
  것에서 더 많은 추론을 끌어내야 한다. 단서2
- 쓸모없는 것으로 인식되는 물리적 유물로부터 신념 체계에 관한 해석에
  도달하는 것과 관련된 더 많은 추론이 어쩔 수 없이 있다. 단서3

➡ 고고학 기록의 '식별하기 어렵다', '추론이 필요하다'는 특성에 대해 설명하는
글이다.
추론: 어떤 근거를 갖고 미루어 생각하는 것
▶ 근거(고고학적 기록)가 ③ '불완전하기' 때문에 미루어 생각하는 것임

| 선택지 분석 |

① outdated
  구식인
고고학적 기록이 불완전하긴 하지만 그래도 고고학적 기록을 토대로 추론을 한다는
내용이 이어지므로 구식이어서 더는 쓸모가 없다는 의미를 내포하는 outdated는
적절하지 않다.

② factual
  사실에 기반을 둔
고고학적 기록이 허구인지 아니면 사실에 기반을 둔 것인지에 대해 이야기하는 것이
아니다. 굳이 말하자면 사실에 기반을 두었다고 가정하기 때문에 그것을 토대로
추론하는 것이겠지만, 글의 핵심은 그것이 아니다.

③ incomplete
  불완전한
인류 문화의 고고학 기록이 완전하다면 기록을 바탕으로 추론하는 것이 아니라 기록을
통해 알게 될 것이다.

④ organized
  체계적인
고고학적 기록이 충분히 체계적이라면 많은 추론이 필요하지 않을 것이다.

⑤ detailed
  상세한
고고학적 기록이 충분히 상세하다면 많은 추론이 필요하지 않을 것이다.

＊글쓰기에 있어 가장 큰 위험 중 하나

<u>단수 주어</u> **단서1** 글쓰기에 있어 가장 큰 위험 중 하나가 무엇인지 설명함
One of the great risks of writing <u>is</u> / that even the simplest of
　　　　　　　　　　　　　　　단수 동사　주격 보어절의 주어
choices / regarding wording or punctuation / 주격 보어절 접속사
글쓰기의 가장 큰 위험 중 하나는 ~이다 / 가장 사소한 선택조차 / 단어 선택이나 구두점과
관련한 /
주격 보어절의 동사
can sometimes **prejudice your audience** / **against you** / in ways
주격 관계대명사　　　　　　　　　　　　　　　　　선행사
/ that may seem unfair. //
때때로 청중에게 편견을 갖게 할 수 있다는 것 / 여러분에 대해 / 방식으로 / 부당해 보일 수 있는 //

For example, / look again at the old grammar rule / forbidding
the splitting of infinitives. // the old grammar rule을 수식하는 현재분사구
예를 들어 / 옛날 문법 규칙을 다시 보라 / 부정사를 분리하는 것을 금지하는 //

After decades of telling students / to never split an infinitive /
(something just done in this sentence), / telling의 목적격 보어(to부정사)
학생들에게 수십 년 동안 말한 후에 / 부정사를 결코 분리하지 말라고 / (바로 이 문장에서 행
해진 것) /

most composition experts now acknowledge / that a split
infinitive is *not* a grammar crime. // 동사 split의 과거분사
대부분의 작문 전문가들은 이제 인정한다 / 분리된 부정사가 문법적으로 끔찍한 일이 '아니라
는' 점을 //

Suppose / you have written a position paper / trying to convince
your city council / of the need to hire security personnel / for the
library, /
가정해 보라 / 여러분이 의견서를 작성했고 / 시의회를 납득시키려고 하는 / 보안 요원을 고용
할 필요를 / 도서관을 위한 / 부분을 나타내는 표현이 주어에 포함되면
　　　　　　　　　　　　　of 뒤의 명사의 수에 동사를 일치시킴＊
and half of the council members / — the people / you wish to
convince — / remember their eighth-grade grammar teacher's
warning / about splitting infinitives. // 복수 동사
시의회 의원 중 절반이 / 사람들인 / 여러분이 납득시키고 싶어 하는 / 자신들의 8학년 문법 교
사의 경고를 기억한다고 / 부정사를 분리하는 것에 대한 //

How will they respond / when you tell them, / in your
introduction, / 시간의 부사절 접속사
그들은 어떻게 반응할까 / 여러분이 그들에게 말할 때 / 여러분의 도입부에서 /

that librarians are compelled "to always accompany" visitors /
to the rare book room / because of the threat of damage? //
전치사　　　　　명사구
도서관 사서는 방문객과 '항상 동행해야' 한다고 / 희귀 서적 자료실에 / 손상의 위협 때문에 //

How much of their attention / have you suddenly lost / because
of their automatic recollection / of what is now a nonrule? //
전치사의 목적어절
얼마나 많은 그들의 관심을 / 여러분이 갑작스럽게 잃었는가 / 그들이 자동으로 떠올린 것 때
문에 / 지금은 규칙이 아닌 것을 / 진주어의 병렬 구조
가주어　　　　　　　　　　　　　(offend 앞에 to가 생략됨)
It is possible, / in other words, / to write correctly / and still
offend your readers' notions / of your language competence. //
~이 가능하다 / 다른 말로 하면 / 올바르게 글을 쓰면서도 / 그런데도 독자의 생각에 불쾌감을
주는 것이 / 여러분의 언어 능력에 대한 // **단서2** 올바르게 글을 썼음에도 불구하고 글쓴이의 언어
　　　　　　　　　　　　　　　　　능력에 대한 독자의 생각에 불쾌감을 줄 수 있음

- **risk** ⓝ 위험, 위험 요소　・ **regarding** prep ~에 관하여[대하여]
- **wording** ⓝ (글・연설에서, 특히 신중히 골라 쓴) 단어 선택
- **offend** ⓥ 불쾌하게 하다　・ **prejudice** ⓥ 편견을 갖게 하다
- **unfair** ⓐ 부당한　・ **forbid** ⓥ 금지하다　・ **split** ⓥ 분리하다, 나누다
- **composition** ⓝ 작문, 작품, 작곡　・ **acknowledge** ⓥ 인정하다
- **crime** ⓝ 끔찍한 일, 범죄　・ **position paper** 의견서, 성명서
- **convince** ⓥ 납득시키다　・ **council** ⓝ 의회
- **security personnel** 보안 요원　・ **compel** ⓥ 강요[강제]하다
- **accompany** ⓥ 동반하다, 동행하다　・ **rare** ⓐ 희귀한, 드문
- **automatic** ⓐ 자동의, 무의식적인　・ **recollection** ⓝ 회상, 기억
- **notion** ⓝ 생각, 개념　・ **competence** ⓝ 능력
- **reveal** ⓥ 드러내다, 밝히다　・ **distort** ⓥ 왜곡하다
- **comprehension** ⓝ 이해력　・ **fierce** ⓐ 격렬한, 맹렬한

글쓰기의 가장 큰 위험 중 하나는 단어 선택이나 구두점과 관련한 가장 사소한
선택조차 부당해 보일 수 있는 방식으로 때때로 **청중이 여러분에 대해 편견을
갖게 할** 수 있다는 것이다. 예를 들어 부정사를 분리하는 것을 금지하는 옛날 문
법 규칙을 다시 보라. 학생들에게 (바로 이 문장에서 행해진 것인) 부정사를 분
리하지 말라고 수십 년 동안 말한 후에, 이제 대부분의 작문 전문가들은 분리된
부정사가 문법적으로 끔찍한 일이 '아니라는' 점을 인정한다. 여러분이 시의회에
도서관을 위한 보안 요원을 고용할 필요를 납득시키려고 하는 의견서를 작성했
고, 여러분이 납득시키고 싶어 하는 사람들인 시의회 의원 중 절반이 자신들의
8학년 문법 교사가 부정사를 분리하는 것에 대해 경고한 내용을 기억한다고 하
자. 여러분이 도입부에서, 손상의 위협 때문에 도서관 사서는 희귀 서적 자료실
에 방문객과 '항상 동행해야' 한다고 그들에게 말할 때 그들은 어떻게 반응할까?
지금은 규칙이 아닌 것을 그들이 자동으로 떠올린 것 때문에 여러분이 그들의
관심을 얼마나 많이 갑작스럽게 잃었는가? 다른 말로 하면, 올바르게 글을 쓰면
서도 여러분의 언어 능력에 대한 독자의 생각에 불쾌감을 주는 것이 가능하다.

다음 빈칸에 들어갈 말로 가장 적절한 것을 고르시오.
① reveal your hidden intention 숨겨진 의도에 대한 언급은 없음
　여러분의 숨겨진 의도를 드러낼
② distort the meaning of the sentence 의도된 의미가 왜곡되는 예시가 아님
　문장의 의미를 왜곡할
③ prejudice your audience against you 글쓴이의 언어 능력에 대해 오해하게 됨
　여러분의 청중이 여러분에 대해 편견을 갖게 할
④ test your audience's reading comprehension 글쓴이에 대한 오해가 핵심임
　여러분의 청중의 독해력을 시험할
⑤ create fierce debates about your writing topic 논쟁이 생긴다는 내용은 없음
　여러분의 작문 주제에 관한 열띤 논쟁을 만들어 낼

왜 1등급? to always accompany라고 쓰는 것이 글쓴이의 언어 능력을
부당하게 평가하도록 만들 수 있다는 것을 잘 이해해야 한다. 부정사를 분리하는 규칙
등 예시의 내용을 잘 이해했더라도 이것을 잘 녹여내어 빈칸에 들어갈 말을 찾는 것이
쉽지 않은 1등급 대비 문제이다.

| 문제 풀이 순서 |

1st 밑줄 친 부분이 포함된 문장을 읽고, 의미를 예상한다.

> One of the great risks of writing is that even the simplest
> of choices regarding wording or punctuation can
> sometimes ＿＿＿＿＿＿＿＿＿＿ in ways that may seem
> unfair.
> 글쓰기의 가장 큰 위험 중 하나는 단어 선택이나 구두점과 관련한 가장 사소한
> 선택조차 때때로 부당해 보일 수 있는 방식으로 ＿＿＿＿＿＿ 할 수 있다는
> 것이다.

➡ 글쓰기의 가장 큰 위험 중 하나가 무엇인지 설명하는 글이다.
　단어 선택이나 구두점과 관련한 사소한 선택이 어떤 결과를 초래하는지를 나머지
　글에서 파악해야 한다.

2nd For example 이후로 등장하는 예시의 내용을 파악한다.

> ・부정사를 분리하지 말라는 것은 예전의 규칙으로, 지금은 적용되지 않는다.
> ・시의회 의원 중 절반이 그 규칙을 기억하는 상황에서 그들을 설득하는
> 　보고서에 to always accompany라고 부정사를 분리하여 썼다.
> ・더 이상 규칙이 아닌 규칙 때문에 시의회 의원의 관심을 잃게 된다.

➡ 부정사를 분리하지 말라는 것은 더 이상 적용되지 않는 예전의 규칙이다. 그러므로
　to always accompany라고 쓰는 것도 올바르다. 하지만 예전의 규칙을
　기억하는 독자는 글쓴이가 규칙을 모른다고 생각할 것이고, 글에 대한 관심을
　거둔다.
　▶ 이 글에서 말하는 글쓰기의 위험: 독자가 글쓴이의 글쓰기 능력을 부당하게
　평가할 수도 있음

3rd 글의 나머지 부분을 읽고, 정답을 찾는다.

| 마지막 문장 | 다른 말로 하면, 올바르게 글을 쓰면서도 여러분의 언어 능력에 대한 독자의 생각에 불쾌감을 주는 것이 가능하다. **단서2** |

→ to always accompany라고 쓰는 것과 같은 사소한 선택으로 글쓴이의 언어 능력이 부당한 평가를 받을 수도 있다.

▶ 단어 선택이나 구두점과 관련한 가장 사소한 선택조차 부당해 보일 수 있는 방식으로 ③ '청중이 여러분에 대해 편견을 갖게 할 수 있다.

| 선택지 분석 |

① reveal your hidden intention
여러분의 숨겨진 의도를 드러낼
특정 단어나 구두점이 글쓴이의 숨겨진 의도를 드러내는 예시가 아니다.

② distort the meaning of the sentence
문장의 의미를 왜곡할
글쓴이의 의도가 왜곡된다는 내용은 없다.

③ prejudice your audience against you
여러분의 청중이 여러분에 대해 편견을 갖게 할
'부당하게 평가하다'를 '편견을 갖다'라고 표현했다.

④ test your audience's reading comprehension
여러분의 청중의 독해력을 시험할
to always accompany가 독자의 독해력을 시험하는 것이 아니다.

⑤ create fierce debates about your writing topic
여러분의 작문 주제에 관한 열띤 논쟁을 만들어 낼
사소한 선택이 논쟁을 일으킨다는 것이 글쓰기의 가장 큰 위험 중 하나라는 내용이 아니다.

───── 어법 특강 ─────

＊ 주어-동사 수 일치

− most, half, part, the rest, 분수, 퍼센트 등의 〈부분·수량〉을 나타내는 표현이 주어부에 쓰이면, 동사는 of 뒤에 오는 명사의 수에 일치시킨다.
· Most of us feel good. (우리 대부분은 기분이 좋다.)
　　　복수 명사　복수 동사
· Most of the work is done. (일의 대부분이 끝났다.)
　　　단수 명사　단수 동사

K 21 정답 ① ＊주관적 경험과 환경은 결합하여 결정에 영향을 준다.

Because the environment plays a significant role / in aiding meaningful internal processes, / subjective experience and the environment / act as a 'coupled system.' **단서1** '외부 환경'과 '개인의 주관적 경험'은 결합된 시스템으로 작용함
환경이 중요한 역할을 하기 때문에 / 의미 있는 내적 과정을 돕는 데 / 주관적 경험과 환경은 / '결합된 시스템'으로 작용한다 //

This coupled system can be seen / as a complete cognitive system of its own. //
이 결합된 시스템은 여겨질 수 있다 / 그 자체로 하나의 완전한 인지 시스템으로 //

In this manner, / subjective experience is extended into the external environment / and vice versa; /
이런 방식으로 / 주관적 경험은 외부 환경으로 확장되고 / 그 반대의 경우도 마찬가지여서 /

the external environment with its disciplinary objects / such as institutional laws and equipment / becomes mental institutions / that affect our subjective experience and solutions. //
규율 객체를 지닌 외부 환경은 / 제도적 법률과 장비와 같은 / 정신적 제도가 된다 / 우리의 주관적 경험과 해결책에 영향을 미치는 **단서2** 제도적 법률과 장비와 같은 규율을 갖춘 외부의 환경은 '빈칸'하는 정신적 제도가 됨

A subjectively held belief / attains the status of objectivity / when the belief is socially shared. //
주관적으로 가지고 있는 믿음은 / 객관성의 지위를 얻는다 / 그 믿음이 사회적으로 공유될 때 //

That is, even if we are trained / as hard-nosed health care rationalists, or no-nonsense bureaucrats, or data-driven scientists, /
즉, 우리가 훈련되어 있다고 해도 / 엄격한 의료 합리주의자, 혹은 현실적인 관료, 혹은 데이터 기반의 과학자로서 /

---

research has shown / that our decisions are influenced by various institutional practices. // **단서3** 제도적 관행은 우리의 결정에 영향을 미침
연구는 증명해왔다 / 우리의 결정은 다양한 제도적 관행의 영향을 받는다고 //

They include / bureaucratic structures and procedures, / the architectural design of health care institutions, / the rules of evidence and the structure of allowable questions in a courtroom trial, /
그것(제도적 관행)은 포함한다 / 관료적 구조와 절차 / 의료 기관의 건축 설계 / 법정 재판에서 증거 규칙과 허용되는 질문의 구조 /

the spatial arrangement of kindergartens and supermarkets, / and a variety of conventions and practices / designed to manipulate our emotions. //
유치원과 슈퍼마켓의 공간 배치 / 그리고 다양한 관습과 관행을 / 우리의 감정을 다루기 위해 고안된 //

· significant ⓐ 중요한 · aid ⓥ 돕다 · internal ⓐ 내적인, 내부의
· subjective ⓐ 주관적인 · couple ⓥ 결합하다
· cognitive ⓐ 인지의 · extend ⓥ 확장하다
· external ⓐ 외부의, 외적인 · disciplinary ⓐ 규율의
· institutional ⓐ 제도적인, 제도상의 · attain ⓥ 얻다
· status ⓝ 지위, 중요도 · hard-nosed ⓐ 엄격한, 냉철한
· no-nonsense ⓐ 현실적인 · data-driven ⓐ 데이터 기반의
· procedure ⓝ 절차 · architectural ⓐ 건축학의
· allowable ⓐ 허용되는 · courtroom ⓝ 법정 · trial ⓝ 재판
· spatial ⓐ 공간의 · arrangement ⓝ 배치
· convention ⓝ 관습 · manipulate ⓥ 다루다, 조작하다
· advocate ⓝ 지지자, 옹호자 · comprise ⓥ ~으로 구성되다

환경이 의미 있는 내적 과정을 돕는 데 중요한 역할을 하기 때문에, 주관적 경험과 환경은 '결합된 시스템'으로 작용한다. 이 결합된 시스템은 자체로 하나의 완전한 인지 시스템으로 볼 수 있다. 이런 방식으로 주관적 경험은 외부 환경으로 확장되고 그 반대의 경우도 마찬가지여서, 제도적 법률과 장비와 같은 규율 객체를 지닌 외부 환경은 우리의 주관적 경험과 해결책에 영향을 미치는 정신적 제도가 된다. 주관적으로 가지고 있는 믿음이 사회적으로 공유될 때 그 믿음은 객관성의 지위를 얻는다. 즉, 우리가 엄격한 의료 합리주의자, 혹은 현실적인 관료, 혹은 데이터 기반의 과학자로 훈련되어 있다고 해도, 연구에 따르면 우리의 결정은 다양한 제도적 관행의 영향을 받는다. 그것에는 관료적 구조와 절차, 의료 기관의 건축 설계, 법정 재판에서 증거 규칙과 허용되는 질문의 구조, 유치원과 슈퍼마켓의 공간 배치, 그리고 우리의 감정을 다루기 위해 고안된 다양한 관습과 관행이 포함된다.

다음 빈칸에 들어갈 말로 가장 적절한 것을 고르시오. [3점]
외부의 환경과 우리의 경험이 서로 결합하여 영향을 준다는 내용의 글임

① affect our subjective experience and solutions
우리의 주관적 경험과 해결책에 영향을 미치는
② serve as advocates for independent decision-making 독립적이라는
독립적인 의사 결정에 대한 옹호자의 역할을 하는 것은 영향을 받지 않는다는 것이므로 글의 내용과 반대임
③ position social experience within the cognitive system 빈칸 뒤에
인지 시스템 내에 사회적 경험을 배치하는 제시되는 '사회적 공유'라는 어구를 연결시켜 만든 오답
④ comprise subjective interpretations of the environment
환경에 대한 주관적 해석을 구성하는 외부 환경과 주관적 경험은 서로 영향을 주고받는 관계임
⑤ facilitate the construction of our concept of subjectivity
주관성 개념의 형성을 촉진하는 주관성과 외부 환경이 합쳐져 정신적 제도가 만들어지는 것임

왜 정답? [정답률 35%]

빈칸 앞 내용	'외부 환경'과 '개인의 주관적 경험'은 결합하여 인지 시스템으로 작용함 **단서1**
빈칸 문장	제도적 법률과 장비와 같은 규율을 갖춘 외부의 환경은 ＿＿＿ 하는 정신적 제도가 됨
빈칸 뒤 내용	제도적 관행은 우리의 결정에 영향을 미침 **단서3**

→ 외부 환경과 주관적 경험은 서로 영향을 주고받는 '결합된 시스템'으로 작용하여, 주관적 경험은 외부 환경으로 확장되며, 외부 환경은 우리의 주관적 경험에 영향을 미친다고 했다.

▶ 제도적 법률과 장비와 같은 규율을 갖춘 외부의 환경은 '~하는' 정신적 제도가 된다고 했으므로 빈칸에 들어갈 말로 가장 적절한 것은 ① '우리의 주관적 경험과 해결책에 영향을 미치는'이다.

>왜 오답?

② 독립적이라는 것은 영향을 받지 않는다는 것이므로 글의 내용과 반대이다.

③ 빈칸 뒤에 제시되는 '주관적 믿음의 사회적 공유'라는 어구를 변형하여 만든 **주의** 오답이며, 외부 환경과 주관적 경험은 종속적 관계가 아니다.

④ 외부 환경과 주관적 경험은 종속적 관계가 아니라 서로 영향을 주고받는 관계이다.

⑤ 정신적 제도가 주관성 형성을 촉진하는 것이 아니라 주관성과 외부 환경이 합쳐져 정신적 제도가 만들어지는 것이다.

K 22 정답 ③ *교육을 통해 얻는 정신적 해방

Education, at its best, / teaches more than just knowledge. //
교육은 최고의 모습에서는 / 단순한 지식 이상을 가르친다 //
단서 1 교육은 비판적 사고, 즉 감정적 압박에 굴복하지 않는 것을 가르침
It teaches critical thinking: / the ability to stop and think before
acting, / to avoid succumbing to emotional pressures. //
└─────── 병렬 구조 ───────┘
그것은 비판적 사고를 가르친다 / 즉 행동하기 전에 멈추어 생각할 수 있는 / 감정적 압박에 굴복하는 것을 피하는 능력을 //

This is not thought control. // 이것은 사고 통제가 아니다 //
   the very+명사: 바로 그 '명사'
It is the very reverse: / mental liberation. //
그것은 바로 정반대인 / 정신적 해방이다 //

Even the most advanced intellectual / will be imperfect at this
skill. // 심지어 가장 지적으로 발달한 사람조차도 / 이 기능은 불완전할 것이다 //
                         free A from B: A를 B로부터 해방시키다
But even imperfect possession of it / frees a person from the
burden / of being 'stimulus-driven', / constantly reacting / to
                                        └── 분사구문을 이끎 ──┘
the immediate environment, / the brightest colours or loudest
sounds. //
하지만 그것을 불완전하게나마 소유하는 것은 / 부담에서 사람을 벗어나게 한다 / '자극에 유도'되는 것에 대한 / 끊임없이 반응하면서 / 인접한 주변 환경, 가장 밝은색이나 가장 큰 소리에 //
단서 2 자극과 반응, 본능과 감정에 따라 사는 것은 쉽고, 사고는 노력을 필요로 함
Being driven by heuristic responses, / living by instinct and
동명사 주어(동명사의 수동태, 단수 취급)   주어 동명사와 동격
emotion all the time, / is a very easy way to live, / in many ways:
                        └── 단수 동사
/ thought is effortful, / especially for the inexperienced. //
경험적인 반응에 의해 유도되는 것 / 즉 항상 본능과 감정에 따라 사는 것은 / 매우 쉬운 삶의 방식인데 / 여러 면에서 / 사고는 노력을 필요로 한다 / 특히 경험이 없는 사람들에게는 //

But emotions are also exhausting, / and short-term reactions
                   현재분사(감정을 당하는 것이 아니라 유발함)
may not, in the long term, / be the most beneficial for health
and survival. //
그러나 감정도 또한 지치게 하고 / 단기적인 반응은 장기적으로 볼 때 / 건강과 생존에 가장 유익하지 않을 수도 있다 //
단서 3 감정에 의존하며 사는 것은 눈앞의 편리함을 위해 장기적으로 해로운 일을 하는 것과 마찬가지임
Just as we reach for burgers / for the sake of convenience, /
just as A, so B: A처럼 B 역시 그러하다
storing up the arterial fat / which may one day kill us, / so our
└── 분사구문을 이끎
reliance on feelings / can do us great harm. //
우리가 햄버거에 손을 뻗어 / 편리함을 얻으려고 / 동맥 지방을 축적하는 것처럼 / 언젠가 우리의 목숨을 앗아갈지도 모르는 / 우리가 감정에 의존하는 것은 / 우리에게 큰 해를 끼칠 수 있다 //

- reverse ⓝ 정반대   · liberation ⓝ 해방
- possession ⓝ 소유   · stimulus-driven ⓐ 자극 유발의
- heuristic ⓐ 체험적인   · instinct ⓝ 본능   · reliance ⓝ 의존
- intensify ⓥ 심화시키다   · burden ⓝ 부담, 짐
- inevitability ⓝ 필연성

교육은 최고의 모습에서는 단순한 지식 이상을 가르친다. 그것은 비판적 사고, 즉 행동하기 전에 멈추어 생각할 수 있는, 감정적 압박에 굴복하는 것을 피하는 능력을 가르친다. 이것은 사고 통제가 아니다. 그것은 바로 정반대인 정신적 해방이다. 심지어 가장 지적으로 발달한 사람조차도 이 기능은 불완전할 것이다. 하지만 그것을 불완전하게나마 소유하는 것은 인접한 주변 환경, 가장 밝은색이나 가장 큰 소리에 끊임없이 반응하면서 '자극에 유도'되는 것에 대한 **부담에서 사람을 벗어나게 한다.** 경험적인 반응에 의해 유도되는 것, 즉 항상

본능과 감정에 따라 사는 것은 여러 면에서 매우 쉬운 삶의 방식인데, 사고는 특히 경험이 없는 사람들에게는 노력을 필요로 한다. 그러나 감정도 또한 지치게 하고, 단기적인 반응은 장기적으로 볼 때 건강과 생존에 가장 유익하지 않을 수도 있다. 우리가 편리함을 얻으려고 햄버거에 손을 뻗어 언젠가 우리의 목숨을 앗아갈지도 모르는 동맥 지방을 축적하는 것처럼, 우리가 감정에 의존하는 것은 우리에게 큰 해를 끼칠 수 있다.

다음 빈칸에 들어갈 말로 가장 적절한 것을 고르시오.

① intensifies people's danger   비판적 사고는 사람들이 자극이나 감정에서 벗어나게
   사람들의 위험을 심화시킨다   해준다고 했으므로 글의 내용과 상반됨
② enhances our understanding
   우리의 이해를 증진한다   자극에 유도되는 것에 대한 이해를 증진한다는 내용은 아님
③ frees a person from the burden   교육은 비판적 사고를 가르침으로써 사람들이
   부담에서 사람을 벗어나게 한다   자극에 유도되지 않도록 해준다는 내용임
④ allows us to accept the inevitability
   어찌할 수 없음을 받아들이도록 해준다   자극에 유도되는 부담으로부터 자유롭게 해준다는 내용임
⑤ requires one to have the experience
   경험을 해보기를 요구한다   자극에 유도되는 것을 직접 경험해보라는 내용은 아님

> **왜 정답?** [정답률 23%]

1st 빈칸이 포함된 문장을 읽고, 빈칸에 들어갈 말에 대한 단서를 얻는다.

빈칸 문장	하지만 그것을 불완전하게나마 소유하는 것은 인접한 주변 환경, 가장 밝은색이나 가장 큰 소리에 끊임없이 반응하면서 '자극에 유도'되는 것에 대한 _____.

→ '하지만(but)'으로 시작하는 문장에 빈칸이 있으므로, 이전 내용을 전환하는 부분이며, 이어질 내용을 토대로 비판적 사고를 가지고 있다는 것은 자극에 유도되는 것에 대해 우리를 '어떻게' 만들어 주는지에 관한 내용임

▶ 빈칸을 채우려면 글에서 소개된 내용을 통해 비판적 사고가 자극으로 유도되는 것을 어떻게 해주는지를 찾아야 한다.

2nd 글을 마저 읽으며 빈칸에 들어갈 적절한 말을 찾는다.
교육은 비판적 사고, 즉 감정적 압박에 굴복하지 않는 것을 가르침 → 이러한 비판적 사고는 정신적 해방으로, 우리를 감정에 의해 유도되는 것으로부터 해방해 줌
자극과 반응, 본능과 감정에 따라 사는 것은 쉽고, 사고는 노력을 필요로 함 → 감정에 의존하며 사는 것은 눈앞의 편리함을 위해 장기적으로 해로운 일을 하는 것과 마찬가지임

▶ 교육의 정점은 학생들에게 비판적 사고, 즉 감정적 압박에 굴복하지 않는 법을 가르치는 것이다. 이러한 비판적 사고는 정신적 해방이라고 말할 수 있으며, 그것이 정신적 해방인 이유가 자극과 관련해 무엇인지를 빈칸에서 묻고 있다.
빈칸 이후, 자극과 반응, 감정 등에 따라 사는 것은 쉽고, 비판적으로 사고하며 사는 것은 노력을 필요로 한다고 설명했다. 그리고 감정에 의존하며 사는 것은 단기적인 편의를 위해 장기적으로 해로운 일을 저지르는 것과 마찬가지라고 비유했다.
따라서 교육을 통해 비판적 사고를 기르는 것은 '자극에 유도되는 것'으로부터 우리를 벗어날 수 있도록 해준다는 내용이므로, 정답은 ③ '부담에서 사람을 벗어나게 한다'이다.

| 선택지 분석 |

① **intensifies people's danger**
   사람들의 위험을 심화시킨다
비판적 사고는 사람들이 자극이나 감정에서 벗어나게 해주므로, 자극에 유도될 위험을 심화시킨다는 말은 글의 내용과 상반된다.

② **enhances our understanding**
   우리의 이해를 증진한다
자극에 유도되는 것에 대한 이해를 증진한다는 내용은 아니다.

③ **frees a person from the burden**
   부담에서 사람을 벗어나게 한다
교육은 비판적 사고를 가르침으로써 사람들이 자극에 유도되지 않도록 해준다는 내용이다.

④ **allows us to accept the inevitability**
   어찌할 수 없음을 받아들이도록 해준다
자극에 유도되는 것이 어찌할 수 없는 것이 아니라, 자극에 유도되는 부담으로부터 자유롭게 해준다는 내용이다.

⑤ **requires one to have the experience**
   경험을 해보기를 요구한다
자극에 유도되는 것을 직접 경험해보라는 내용은 아니다.

한규진 | 2025 수능 응시·대구 계성고 졸

앞부분에 추상적이고 어렵게만 느껴지는 이야기들을 늘어놓고 중간에 But 표현까지 들어 있어 난이도가 있게 느껴지지만, 후반부에 '단기적인 반응은 장기적으로 볼 때 건강과 생존에 가장 유익한 것이 아닐 수도 있다'라는 문장을 통해서 빈칸과 연관된 stimulus-driven을 부정적으로 인식하고 있다는 것을 알 수 있어. 이렇게 단서를 차근차근 찾아가면서 선택지를 빈칸에 대입하지 말고 먼저 능동적으로 빈칸에 무슨 내용이 들어갈지를 생각해보는 게 좋아.

K 23 정답 ② ＊자신의 관심을 소비하는 관심 경제

단서 1 가장 수익성이 높은 사업은 자신의 관심을 소비하는 관심 경제임

We are famously living in the era of the attention economy, /
관계부사
where the largest and most profitable businesses in the world /
주격 관계대명사
are those that *consume* my attention. //

우리는 잘 알려져 있는 바와 같이 관심 경제의 시대에 살고 있다 / 세상에서 가장 크고
수익성이 가장 높은 사업은 / 나의 관심을 '소비하는' 사업인 //

be dedicated to -ing: ~에 전념하다
The advertising industry / is literally dedicated to capturing the
conscious hours of my life / and selling them to someone else. //
병렬 구조

광고 산업은 / 말 그대로 내 삶의 의식적인 시간을 포착하여 / 다른 누군가에게 그것을
판매하는 데 전념한다 // **단서 2** 광고 산업은 자신이 의식하는 시간이나 대상을 포착하여
누군가에게 관심을 판매하는 것임

It might seem magical / that so many exciting and useful
가주어   진주어절을 이끄는 접속사
software systems / are available to use for free, /

아주 멋지게 보일 수도 있지만 / 너무나 많은 흥미롭고 유용한 소프트웨어 시스템을 / 무료로
사용할 수 있는 것이 /

가주어   진주어절을 이끄는 접속사 부사절 접속사   의문사
but it is now conventional wisdom / that if you can't see who
is paying for something / that appears to be free, / then **the real**
주격 관계대명사
product being sold is you. //

이제 일반 통념이다 / 누가 비용을 지불하고 있는지 알 수 없다면 / 무료인 것처럼 보이는 것에
대해 / 그렇다면 팔리고 있는 진짜 제품은 바로 당신이라는 것은 //
단서 3 우리는 타인과 관계를 맺을 때, 우리의 관심을 끌도록 고안된 인공지능 추천 시스템의 영향을 받음

Our creative engagement with other people / is mediated by AI-
주격 관계대명사   수동태
based recommendation systems / that are designed to trap our
attention / through the process that Nick Seaver calls *captology*, /
목적격 관계대명사

다른 사람들과 맺는 우리의 창의적 관계는 / AI 기반 추천 시스템의 영향을 받는다 / 우리의
관심을 붙잡도록 고안된 / Nick Seaver가 'captology'라고 부르는 과정을 통해 /

분사구문으로 의미상 과거분사(work 수식)
keeping us attending to work / sold by one company rather than
another, / replacing the freedom of personal exploration with
algorithm-generated playlists / or even algorithm-generated
art. // **단서 4** 인공지능 추천 시스템은 우리가 특정 회사에 관심을 쏟게 하고,
자신이 탐색할 자유를 알고리즘이 만들어낸 상품으로 대체시킴
제품에 우리가 계속 관심을 쏟게 하고 / 딴 회사가 아니라 어떤 한 회사에 의해 판매되는 /
개인적 탐색의 자유를 대체하며 / 알고리즘이 생성한 재생 목록이나 / 심지어 알고리즘이
생성한 예술로 //

- profitable ⓐ 수익성이 있는 · conscious ⓐ 의식하는, 자각하는
- conventional wisdom 일반 통념 · mediate ⓥ 영향을 주다, 중재하다
- trap ⓥ 가두다, 붙잡다 · violate ⓥ 침해하다
- sponsor ⓥ 후원하다

우리는 잘 알려져 있는 바와 같이 세상에서 가장 크고 수익성이 가장 높은 사업은 나의 관심을 '소비하는' 사업인 관심 경제의 시대에 살고 있다. 광고 산업은 말 그대로 내 삶의 의식적인 시간을 포착하여 다른 누군가에게 그것을 판매하는 데 전념한다. 너무나 많은 흥미롭고 유용한 소프트웨어 시스템을 무료로 사용할 수 있는 것이 아주 멋지게 보일 수도 있지만, 무료인 것처럼 보이는 것에 대해 누가 비용을 지불하고 있는지 알 수 없다면, 그렇다면 **팔리고 있는 진짜 제품은 바로 당신이라는 것**은 이제 일반 통념이다. 다른 사람들과 맺는 우리의 창의적 관계는 Nick Seaver가 'captology'라고 부르는 과정을 통해 우리의 관심을 붙잡고, 딴 회사가 아니라 어떤 한 회사에 의해 판매되는 제품에 우리가 계속 관심을 쏟게 하고, 개인적 탐색의 자유를 알고리즘이 생성한 재생 목록이나 심지어 알고리즘이 생성한 예술로 대체하도록 고안된 AI 기반 추천 시스템의 영향을 받는다.

다음 빈칸에 들어갈 말로 가장 적절한 것을 고르시오. [3점]

① all of your attention has already been spent
모든 관심이 이미 지출된 것이 아니라, 무료로 제품을 이용하는 상황에서도 자신의 관심이라는 대가를
당신의 모든 관심은 이미 지출되었다는 것임   지불하고 있다는 내용임
② the real product being sold is you 무료로 보이지만 아무도 대가를 지불하고 있지
팔리고 있는 진짜 제품은 바로 당신이라는 것 않다면, 이때 팔리고 있는 진짜 제품은 당신의 관심사임
③ your privacy is being violated
당신의 사생활이 침해되고 있다는 것   사생활 침해와 관련된 내용은 언급되지 않음
④ the public may be sponsoring you
대중이 당신을 후원하고 있을지도 모른다는 것   대중의 후원과 관련된 내용은 언급되지 않음
⑤ you owe the benefits to your friend AI
당신은 당신의 친구인 인공지능에 그 혜택을 빚지고 있다는 것
제품을 무료로 이용하는 것이 인공지능 덕분이라는 내용이 아님

> **왜 정답?** [정답률 41%]

1st 빈칸이 포함된 문장을 읽고, 빈칸에 들어갈 말에 대한 단서를 얻는다.

빈칸 문장	너무나 많은 흥미롭고 유용한 소프트웨어 시스템을 무료로 사용할 수 있는 것이 아주 멋지게 보일 수도 있지만, 무료인 것처럼 보이는 것에 대해 누가 비용을 지불하고 있는지 알 수 없다면, 그렇다면 ＿＿＿＿＿＿＿은 이제 일반 통념이다.

→ 유용한 소프트웨어 시스템을 무료로 사용할 수 있지만, 누가 비용을 지불하고 있는지 알 수 없는 상황이라면 어떤 생각을 해야 하는지를 묻고 있음
  ▶ 빈칸을 채우려면 글에서 소개된 내용을 통해 우리는 누구도 값을 지불하지 않는 무료 제품을 어떻게 생각해야 하는지를 찾아야 한다.

2nd 글을 마저 읽으며 빈칸에 들어갈 적절한 말을 찾는다.

가장 수익성이 높은 사업은 자신의 관심을 소비하는 관심 경제임 → 광고 산업은 자신이 의식하는 시간이나 대상을 포착하여 누군가에게 그 관심을 판매하는 것임 → 무료로 보이지만 누구도 값을 지불하지 않는다면, 진짜 팔리고 있는 것은 자신의 관심임 → 우리는 타인과 관계를 맺을 때, 우리의 관심을 끌도록 고안된 인공지능 추천 시스템의 영향을 받음 → 즉, 인공지능 추천 시스템은 우리가 특정 회사에 관심을 쏟게 하고, 자신이 탐색할 자유를 알고리즘이 만들어 낸 상품으로 대체시킴
  ▶ 관심 경제는 자신의 관심을 소비하는 사업이며, 광고 산업은 자신이 무엇에 몰두하는지를 포착하여 누군가에게 그 관심을 판매하는 것이다. 즉, 우리가 무료로 제공받고 있다고 생각하는 제품에 실제로 우리는 우리의 관심사와 관련된 정보를 대가로 지불하고 있다.

마지막 문장에서 우리는 타인과 관계를 맺을 때, 나의 관심을 끌 만한 대상을 인공지능 추천 시스템이 제안하는 세상에 살고 있다고 했다. 우리의 관심을 소비하여 무료로 제품을 이용하거나 특정 제품을 추천받게 되는 것이다.
따라서 관심 경제에서는 자신의 관심을 대가로 지불하여 상품이나 서비스를 얻게 되므로, 정답은 ② '팔리고 있는 진짜 제품은 바로 당신이라는 것'이다.

| 선택지 분석 |

① all of your attention has already been spent
당신의 모든 관심은 이미 지출되었다는 것
모든 관심이 이미 지출된 것이 아니라, 무료로 제품을 이용하는 상황에서도 자신의 관심이라는 대가를 지불하고 있다는 내용이다.

② the real product being sold is you
팔리고 있는 진짜 제품은 바로 당신이라는 것
무료로 보이지만 아무도 대가를 지불하고 있지 않다면, 이때 팔리고 있는 진짜 제품은 당신의 관심사이다.

③ your privacy is being violated
당신의 사생활이 침해되고 있다는 것
사생활 침해와 관련된 내용은 언급되지 않았다.

④ the public may be sponsoring you
대중이 당신을 후원하고 있을지도 모른다는 것
대중의 후원과 관련된 내용은 언급되지 않았다.

⑤ you owe the benefits to your friend AI
당신은 당신의 친구인 인공지능에 그 혜택을 빚지고 있다는 것
제품을 무료로 이용하는 것이 인공지능 덕분이라는 내용이 아니라, 제품을 무료로 이용하는 대신 인공지능 추천 시스템에 의해 영향을 받게 된다는 내용이다.

K

배지오 | 2025 수능 응시·성남 낙생고 졸

첫 문장에서 우리는 현재 개인의 관심을 소비하는 사업인 관심 경제 시대에 살고 있음을 알려줘. 이후 문장에서는 관심 경제에 대한 구체적인 설명이 나오고 빈칸의 앞부분에서 it is now conventional wisdom that이라고 언급하며 빈칸에 들어갈 말이 앞의 내용과 동일선상에 있겠구나를 추리하면 돼. 이 문제의 경우에도 앞 문장의 내용을 제대로 해석하지 못했더라도, 뒤에 by AI-based recommendation systems, with algorithm-generated playlists 등을 보고, 아, 사람들의 관심을 사업의 자원으로 사용하는 관심 경제에 대한 이야기구나를 파악한다면 보기에서 쉽게 답을 고를 수 있을 거야.

통신 기술의 사용을 결정하는 요인 중 하나는 장비와 인력에 들어가는 투자의 종류, 즉, 누가 투자를 하고, 그들이 수익으로 무엇을 기대하는지이다. 투자가 반드시 **다수의 사람에게 가장 적합한** 통신 형태일 것이라는 보장은 없다. 투자 기금의 소유권은 상업적 조직의 수중에 있는 경향이 있으므로, 통신 기간 시설의 현대화는 오로지 잠재적 수익성을 바탕으로 이루어진다. 아프리카 대륙 전역에 걸친 광섬유 통신 케이블 설치를 예로 들어보자. 여러 아프리카 국가가 그 개발에 관여하고 있지만, 그것의 운영 구조는 이용에 대한 대가를 지급할 수 있는 국가들을 우선할 것이다. 교육과 정보를 위해 그것을 이용하고 싶어 할 수도 있는 많은 국가는 그것이 자국에 너무 비쌀 뿐만 아니라 단순히 이용할 수 없다는 것을 알게 될지도 모른다. 그 개발이 지역 사회의 수요보다는 투자 기회에 의해 주도되었다는 것은 의심의 여지가 있을 수 없다.

다음 빈칸에 들어갈 말로 가장 적절한 것을 고르시오. [3점]

① require minimal cost and effort to maintain 유지 관리에 최소한의 비용과 노력이
유지 관리에 최소한의 비용과 노력이 필요한   필요한 통신 형태일 것이란 보장은 없다는 내용이 아님
② are most appropriate for the majority of people   투자가 반드시 다수의
다수의 사람에게 가장 적합한   사람에게 가장 적합한 통신 형태를 만드는 보장은 없다고 함
③ are in line with current standards and global norms
현재 표준 및 글로벌 규범과 부합하는   현재 표준 및 글로벌 규범과 관련 없음
④ employ some of the most advanced technologies
가장 진보된 기술 중 일부를 사용하는   통신 시설의 현대화에 대해 언급한 것으로 만든 오답
⑤ promote the commercial interests of companies   투자가 기업의 업적
기업의 상업적 이익을 촉진하는   이익을 촉진하는 통신 형태를 보장한다고 했으므로 반대임

K 24 정답 ② ＊상업적 이익을 추구하는 투자로 결정되는 통신 기술 현대화

factors를 수식하는 분사
One of the factors / determining the use of technologies of
investments를 수식하는 분사
communication / will be the kinds of investments / made in
equipment and personnel; / who makes them, / and what they
expect in return. //
요인들 중 하나는 / 통신 기술의 사용을 결정하는 / 투자의 종류일 것이다 / 장비와 인력에 들어가는 / 즉, 누가 투자를 하고 / 그들이 수익으로 무엇을 기대하는지 //

There is no guarantee / that the investment will necessarily be
주격 관계대명사
in forms of communication / that **are most appropriate for the**
majority of people. //
보장은 없다 / 투자가 반드시 통신 형태일 것이라는 / 다수의 사람에게 가장 적합한 //
단서 1 통신 시설의 투자 기금이 상업적 조직의 것이므로, 통신 시설 현대화는 수익성을 바탕으로 함

Because the ownership of investment funds tends to / be in the
hands of commercial organisations, /
투자 기금의 소유권은 경향이 있기 때문에 / 상업적 조직의 수중에 있는 /

the modernisation of communications infrastructure only takes
place / on the basis of potential profitability. //
통신 기간 시설의 현대화는 오로지 이루어진다 / 잠재적 수익성을 바탕으로 //

Take, for example, / the installation of fibre-optic
communications cable / across the African continent. //
예로 들어보자 / 광섬유 통신 케이블 설치를 / 아프리카 대륙 전역에 걸친 //
= many
A number of African nations / are involved in the development
~하는 사람들
/ but its operational structures will be oriented / to those who
can pay for access. // **단서 2** 통신 케이블 운영은 이용 대가를 지급할 수 있는 국가를
우선시할 것임
여러 아프리카 국가가 / 그 개발에 관여되어 있다 / 그러나 그것의 운영 구조는 우선할 것이다
/ 이용에 대한 대가를 지급할 수 있는 국가들을 //
주격 관계대명사
Many states / that might wish to use it for education and
find의 목적격 보어인 형용사 ①
information / may not only find it too expensive / but also
find의 목적격 보어인 형용사 ②
simply unavailable to them. //
많은 국가들 / 교육과 정보를 위해 그것을 이용하고 싶어 할 수도 있는 / 그것이 너무 비쌀
뿐만이 아니라는 것을 알게 될지도 모른다 / 자국에 단순히 이용할 수 없다는 것도 //

There can be no doubt / that the development has been led /
by investment opportunity / rather than community demand. //
의심의 여지가 있을 수 없다 / 그 개발이 주도되었다는 것은 / 투자 기회에 의해 / 지역 사회의
수요보다는 // **단서 3** 개발이 지역 사회를 위해서라기 보다 투자 기회에 의해 주도됨

- investment ⓝ 투자   · equipment ⓝ 장비
- personnel ⓝ 인력, 직원   · return ⓝ 수익   · guarantee ⓝ 보장
- appropriate ⓐ 적합한   · majority ⓝ 대다수
- ownership ⓝ 소유권   · organisation ⓝ 조직
- modernisation ⓝ 현대화   · infrastructure ⓝ 기간 시설
- profitability ⓝ 수익성   · installation ⓝ 설치
- continent ⓝ 대륙   · oriented to ~을 우선하는
- in line with ~와 일치하다 · current ⓐ 현재의
- advanced ⓐ 진보된

왜 정답? [정답률 44%]

- 투자 기금의 소유권은 상업적 조직의 수중에 있는 경향이 있으므로, 통신 기간 시설의 현대화는 오로지 잠재적 수익성을 바탕으로 이루어진다. **단서 1**
- 그것의 운영 구조는 이용에 대한 대가를 지급할 수 있는 국가들을 우선할 것이다. **단서 2**
- 그 개발이 지역 사회의 수요보다는 투자 기회에 의해 주도되었다는 것은 의심의 여지가 있을 수 없다. **단서 3**

➡ 통신 시설 개발은 지역 사회의 수요보다는 투자 기금을 댄 상업적 조직의 이해 관계에 따라 주도되고 있다는 내용의 글이다. 따라서 통신 시설에 대한 투자가 반드시 지역 사회의 많은 사람들의 이용을 위한 것이라고 보장할 수는 없다.
▶ 빈칸에는 투자가 어떠한 통신 형태일 것이라는 보장이 없는지가 들어가야 한다. 그러므로 투자가 반드시 ② '다수의 사람에게 가장 적합한' 통신 형태일 것이라는 보장이 없다고 하는 것이 적절하다.

왜 오답?

① 투자가 유지 관리에 최소한의 비용과 노력이 필요한 통신 형태일 것이란 보장은 없다는 내용이 아니다.
③ 현재 표준 및 글로벌 규범과 관련 없는 내용이다.
④ 통신 시설의 현대화에 대해 언급한 것으로 만든 오답일 뿐, 가장 진보된 기술 중 일부를 사용하는 통신 형태일 것이란 보장은 없다는 내용은 아니다.
⑤ 투자가 기업의 상업적 이익을 촉진하는 통신 형태를 보장할 리가 없다는 것이 **주의** 아니라 오히려 보장한다는 내용이다.

K 25 정답 ③ ＊타인과의 정서적 유대를 통해 개인이 형성된다고 한 Rousseau

주어를 이끄는 명사절 접속사
That people need other people / is hardly news, / but for Rousseau
/ this dependence extended / far beyond companionship or even
love, / into the very process of becoming human. //
사람이 다른 사람을 필요로 한다는 것은 / 거의 새로울 게 없다 / 그러나 Rousseau에게는 /
이러한 의존이 이르렀다 / 동료 관계나 심지어 사랑을 넘어 / 인간이 되는 바로 그 과정에까지 //
단서 1 Rousseau는 사람은 만들어지며 특히 잠재성 실현을 위해서는 다른 사람들의 관여가 필수라고 함
Rousseau believed / that people are not born but made, / every
목적어절을 이끄는 접속사
individual a bundle of potentials / whose realization requires /
소유격 관계대명사
the active involvement of other people. //
Rousseau는 믿었다 / 사람은 태어나는 것이 아니라 만들어진다고 / 모든 개인은 잠재성
꾸러미라고 / 이 잠재성의 실현은 필요하다고 / 다른 사람의 적극적인 관여가 //
단서 2 자기 계발은 사회적 과정이라 함
Self-development is a social process. // 자기 계발은 사회적 과정이다 //
Self-sufficiency is an impossible fantasy. // 자족은 불가능한 환상이다 //

Much of the time / Rousseau wished passionately / ^{목적어절을 이끄는 접속사}that it were not: / *Robinson Crusoe* was a favorite book, / and he yearned to be free / from the pains and uncertainties of social life. //
대부분 시간을 / Rousseau는 열렬히 바랐다 / 그것이 그렇지 않기를 / Robinson Crusoe는 좋아하는 책이었고 / 그는 벗어나기를 갈망했다 / 그는 사회생활의 고통과 불확실성에서 //

But his writings document / with extraordinary clarity / **the shaping of the individual by his emotional attachments**. //
그러나 그의 저작은 기록한다 / 보기 드문 명료함으로 / 정서적 유대에 의해 개인이 형성되는 과정을 //

"Our sweetest existence / is relative and collective, / and our true *self* is not entirely within us." //
"우리의 가장 달콤한 존재는 / 상대적이고 집단적이다 / 그리고 우리의 진정한 '자아'는 우리 안에 전혀 있지 않다" //

^{it is ~ that ... 강조 구문}
^{목적격 관계대명사}
And it is kindness / — which Rousseau analyzed / under the rubric of *pitié*, / ^{계속적 용법의 관계대명사}which translates as "pity" /
그리고 친절이다 / Rousseau가 분석한 / 'pitié'라는 항목 아래에 / '연민'으로 번역되는 /

but is much closer to "sympathy" / as Hume and Smith defined it / — that is the key to this collective existence. //
그러나 '공감'에 훨씬 더 가까운 / Hume과 Smith가 정의한 것처럼 / 이러한 집단적 존재의 핵심인 것은 //

- extend ⓥ (~에) 이르다, 미치다 · companionship ⓝ 동료 관계
- involvement ⓝ 관여 · self-development ⓝ 자기 계발
- self-sufficiency ⓝ 자족 · passionately ⓐⓓ 열렬하게
- yearn ⓥ 갈망하다, 동경하다 · uncertainty ⓝ 불확실성
- document ⓥ 기록하다 · extraordinary ⓐ 보기 드문, 뛰어난
- clarity ⓝ 명료함 · attachment ⓝ 유대, 애착
- existence ⓝ 존재 · relative ⓐ 상대적인
- collective ⓐ 집단적인 · entirely ⓐⓓ 아주, 완전히
- rubric ⓝ 항목 · sympathy ⓝ 공감, 동정
- philosophical ⓐ 철학적인 · self-reliant ⓐ 자립적인
- wholeheartedly ⓐⓓ 진정으로, 전적으로

사람이 다른 사람을 필요로 한다는 것은 거의 새로울 게 없지만, Rousseau에게는 이러한 의존이 동료 관계나 심지어 사랑을 넘어 인간이 되는 바로 그 과정에까지 이르렀다. Rousseau는 사람은 태어나는 것이 아니라 만들어진다고, 모든 개인은 잠재성 꾸러미라고, 이 잠재성을 실현하기 위해서는 다른 사람의 적극적인 관여가 필요하다고 믿었다. 자기 계발은 사회적 과정이다. 자족은 불가능한 환상이다. Rousseau는 대부분 시간을 그것이 그렇지 않기를 열렬히 바랐는데, *Robinson Crusoe*는 좋아하는 책이었고, 그는 사회생활의 고통과 불확실성에서 벗어나기를 갈망했다. 그러나 그의 저작은 보기 드문 명료함으로 정서적 유대에 의해 개인이 형성되는 과정을 기록한다. "우리의 가장 달콤한 존재는 상대적이고 집단적이며, 우리의 진정한 '자아'는 우리 안에 있는 것이 전혀 아니다." 그리고 이러한 집단적 존재의 핵심은 친절인데, Rousseau는 이를 'pitié'라는 항목 아래에 분석하였고, 이는 '연민'으로 번역되지만, Hume과 Smith가 정의한 '공감'에 훨씬 더 가깝다.

다음 빈칸에 들어갈 말로 가장 적절한 것을 고르시오. [3점]
^{Rousseau가 인간 본성을 이해하기 위한 철학적 연구의 필요성을 이야기한 것이 아님}
① the necessity of philosophical study to understand human nature
인간 본성을 이해하기 위한 철학적 연구의 필요성
② the development of self-sufficiency through literary works
문학 작품을 통한 자족의 개발 　　　Rousseau가 좋아하는 책이 언급된 것으로 만든 오답
③ the shaping of the individual by his emotional attachments
정서적 유대에 의해 개인이 형성되는 과정　다른 사람과의 관계, 사회적 과정을 통해 개인이 형성된다고 함
④ the making of the self-reliant man through his struggles
투쟁을 통해 자립적인 사람 만들기　　　　투쟁을 통해 자립적인 사람을 만든다는 내용이 아님
⑤ the difficulty of trusting other people wholeheartedly
다른 사람을 진심으로 신뢰하는 것의 어려움
　　　　　　　다른 사람을 진심으로 신뢰하는 것의 어려움에 대한 언급은 없음

왜 정답? [정답률 32%]

1st 빈칸이 포함된 문장을 읽고, 빈칸에 들어갈 말에 대한 단서를 얻는다.

| 빈칸 문장 | 그러나 그의 저작은 보기 드문 명료함으로 _____을 기록한다. |

→ 빈칸에는 그(Rousseau)의 저작이 무엇을 기록하는 지가 들어가야 한다.

2nd 글의 앞부분을 읽고, 빈칸에 들어갈 적절한 말을 찾는다.

앞부분 주요 내용	• Rousseau는 사람은 태어나는 것이 아니라 만들어진다고, 모든 개인은 잠재성 꾸러미고 이 잠재성을 실현하기 위해서는 다른 사람의 적극적인 관여가 필요하다고 믿었다. 단서1 • 자기 계발은 사회적 과정이다. 단서2
빈칸 문장의 앞 문장	Robinson Crusoe는 그(Rousseau)가 좋아하는 책이었고, 사회생활의 고통과 불확실성에서 벗어나기를 갈망했음

→ Rousseau는 인간의 자기 계발은 사회적 과정으로서 인간이 형성되고 잠재성을 실현하는 과정에 다른 사람의 관여가 반드시 필요하다고 했다.
▶ 빈칸에는 그(Rousseau)의 저작이 기록한 것이 들어가야 함

3rd **2nd** 에서 이해한 내용을 선택지에서 고른다.

Rousseau는 인간의 잠재성을 실현하는 과정에서 다른 사람의 관여가 필요하고, 친절이나 공감이 핵심적인 역할을 한다고 보는 내용의 글이다.
그러므로 그(Rousseau)가 명료하게 기록한 내용은 ③ '정서적 유대에 의해 개인이 형성되는 과정'이라고 하는 것이 적절하다.

| 선택지 분석 |

① the necessity of philosophical study to understand human nature
인간 본성을 이해하기 위한 철학적 연구의 필요성
Rousseau가 인간 본성을 이해하기 위한 철학적 연구의 필요성을 이야기한 것이 아니다.

② the development of self-sufficiency through literary works
문학 작품을 통한 자족의 개발
Rousseau가 좋아하는 책이 언급된 것으로 만든 오답일 뿐이다.

③ the shaping of the individual by his emotional attachments
정서적 유대에 의해 개인이 형성되는 과정
Rousseau는 다른 사람과의 관계, 사회적 과정을 통해 개인이 형성된다고 보았다는 내용의 글이다.

④ the making of the self-reliant man through his struggles
투쟁을 통해 자립적인 사람 만들기
투쟁을 통해 자립적인 사람을 만든다는 내용이 아니다.

⑤ the difficulty of trusting other people wholeheartedly
다른 사람을 진심으로 신뢰하는 것의 어려움
다른 사람을 진심으로 신뢰하는 것의 어려움에 대한 언급은 없다.

K 26 정답 ③ ＊디지털 환경에서의 정보 콘텐츠 보존

^{접속사가 생략되지 않은 분사구문}
When trying to establish / what is meant by digital preservation, / the first question that must be addressed is: / what are you actually trying to preserve? //
정립하려고 할 때 / 디지털 보존이 의미하는 바를 / 가장 먼저 다루어야 할 질문은 ~이다 / '실제로 무엇을 보존하려고 하는가?' //

^{선행사}　　　　　^{관계부사(뒤에 완전한 절이 옴)}
This is clear in the analog environment / where the information content is inextricably fixed to the physical medium. //
이것(무엇을 보존하려 하는지)은 / 아날로그 환경에서는 분명하다 / 정보 콘텐츠가 물리적 매체에 풀 수 없게 고정된 //
단서1 아날로그 환경에서는 보존하고자 하는 것이 분명함

In the digital environment, / 단서2 디지털 환경이므로 앞서 제시된 아날로그 환경 the medium is not part of the (매체 자체를 보존함)과는 반대되는 내용이 나와야 함 **message**. //
디지털 환경에서는 / 매체가 메시지의 일부가 아니다 //

A bit stream looks the same to a computer / regardless of the
^{앞에 목적격 관계대명사 생략}　　　　　^{수동태}
media it is read from. // 단서3 비트 스트림(보존해야 할 정보)은 그것이 읽히는 매체와 관계없이 동일하게 보이므로, 원본 이동 장치의 보존은 그 중요성이 줄어들고 있음
비트 스트림은 컴퓨터에서 동일하게 보인다 / 그것이 읽히는 매체와 관계없이 //

A physical carrier is necessary, / but as long as the source media can be read, / bit-perfect copies can be made cheaply and easily on other devices, /
물리적 이동 장치가 필요하다 / 하지만 원본 매체를 읽을 수 있는 한 / 다른 기기에서도 비트 단위의 완벽한 복사본을 저렴하고 쉽게 만들 수 있어서 /

분사구문(결과)
making the preservation of the original carrier of diminishing
~~of+추상명사=형용사~~
importance. //
원본 이동 장치의 보존은 그 중요성이 줄어들고 있다 //
이유를 나타내는 접속사   주격 관계대명사(선행사 the physical media)
As the physical media / that carry digital information / are quite
delicate / relative to most analog media, /
물리적 매체는 ~ 때문에 / 디지털 정보를 전달하는 / 상당히 취약하기 / 대부분의 아날로그
매체에 비해 /
가주어   진주어절을 이끄는 접속사
it is expected / that digital information will necessarily need to
be migrated / from one physical carrier to another / as part of the
ongoing preservation process. //
예상된다 / 디지털 정보를 옮겨야 할 필요가 있을 것으로 / 한 물리적 이동 장치에서 다른 이동
장치로 / 지속적인 보존 과정의 일환으로 //
not A but B : A가 아니라 B
It is not the media itself / but the information on the media / that
needs to be preserved. //   **It that 강조 구문   단서 4 보존되어야 하는 것은 매체가 아닌 매체에 담긴 정보임**
매체 자체가 아니라 / 매체에 담긴 정보이다 / 보존해야 하는 것은 //

- preservation ⓝ 보존   · address ⓥ 다루다, 해결하다
- analog ⓐ 아날로그의   · medium ⓝ 매체, 수단 (복수형: media)
- bit stream 비트 스트림(비트 단위로 전송하는 데이터)
- regardless of ~와 관계없이   · device ⓝ 장치, 기기
- carrier ⓝ 운반 용기   · delicate ⓐ 취약한
- migrate ⓥ 옮기다, 이동하다

디지털 보존이 의미하는 바를 정립하려고 할 때 가장 먼저 다루어야 할 질문은
'실제로 무엇을 보존하려고 하는가?'이다. 이는 정보 콘텐츠가 물리적 매체에
풀 수 없게 고정된 아날로그 환경에서는 분명하다. 디지털 환경에서는 매체가
메시지의 일부가 아니다. 비트 스트림은 그것이 읽히는 매체와 관계없이
컴퓨터에서 동일하게 보인다. 물리적 이동 장치가 필요하지만, 원본 매체를
읽을 수 있는 한, 다른 기기에서도 비트 단위의 완벽한 복사본을 저렴하고
쉽게 만들 수 있어서 원본 이동 장치의 보존은 그 중요성이 줄어들고 있다.
디지털 정보를 전달하는 물리적 매체는 대부분의 아날로그 매체에 비해 상당히
취약하기 때문에, 지속적인 보존 과정의 일환으로 디지털 정보를 한 물리적
이동 장치에서 다른 이동 장치로 옮겨야 할 필요가 있을 것으로 예상된다.
보존해야 하는 것은 매체 자체가 아니라 매체에 담긴 정보이다.

다음 빈칸에 들어갈 말로 가장 적절한 것을 고르시오.

① platform 정보 기술과 관련된 단어를 이용하여 만든 오답
플랫폼
② storage '매체'와 '저장'은 이 글에서 반대되는 내용을 나타내지 않음
저장
③ message 매체는 보존하고자 하는 메시지의 일부(즉 고정된 것)가 아니라는 내용임
메시지
④ challenge 어려움에 대해 언급되지 않음
어려움
⑤ transformation 단순히 정보 기술과 관련된 단어로 만든 함정
변환

⟩왜 정답 ? [정답률 15%]

빈칸 문장의 앞 문장	아날로그 환경에서는 정보가 매체에 고정되어 있으므로, 보존하고자 하는 대상이 명확함 (매체를 보존한다는 것) **단서 1**
빈칸 문장	디지털 환경에서는 매체가 _____의 일부가 아니다.
빈칸 문장의 뒤 문장	비트 스트림(보존해야 할 정보)은 그것이 읽히는 매체와 관계없이 동일하게 보이므로, 원본 이동 장치의 보존은 그 중요성이 줄어들고 있음 **단서 3**

➡ 빈칸에는 앞에서 언급된 아날로그 환경과는 대조적인 내용이 나와야 한다.
아날로그 환경과는 반대로 디지털 환경에서는 '정보가 매체에 고정되어 있지
않다'는 내용이 와야 할 것이다.
또한, 디지털 환경의 메시지에 해당하는 비트 스트림은 매체와 관계없이 동일하게
보인다고 했다.
▶ 따라서 디지털 환경에서 매체는 ③ '메시지'의 일부가 아닌 것이다.

⟩왜 오답 ?

① 정보 기술과 관련된 단어를 이용하여 만든 오답이다.
② '매체'와 '저장'은 이 글에서 반대되는 내용을 나타내지 않고, 빈칸에는 오히려
매체와 반대되는 개념인 '내용, 메시지'가 와야 한다.
④ 이 글에서는 어려움에 대해 언급되지 않았다.
⑤ 정보 기술과 관련된 '변환'이라는 단어로 만든 함정일 뿐이다.

🅚 27 정답 ① *점차 어려워지는 과학적, 기술적 발전 ————

After we make some amount of scientific and technological
progress, / does further progress get easier or harder? //
우리가 어느 정도의 과학적 그리고 기술적 발전을 이룬 후에 / 더 이상의 발전은 더
쉬워지는가 혹은 더 어려워지는가 //
~처럼 보이다
Intuitively, it seems like it could go either way / because there
복수 동사(뒤의 주어에 일치)
are two competing effects. //
직관적으로, 어느 쪽이든 될 수 있을 것처럼 보이는데 / 두 가지 경쟁하는 영향이 있기
때문이다 //
On the one hand, we "stand on the shoulders of giants": /
5형식 동사 make+목적어+목적격 보어
previous discoveries can make future progress easier. //
한편으로는, 우리는 '거인의 어깨에 서 있는데' / 즉 이전의 발견이 미래의 발전을 더 쉽게 만들
수 있다 //
단서 1 우리는 쉬운 발견을 먼저하고 남은 발견은 더 어려움
On the other hand, /
다른 한편으로는 /

> ★ **주격 관계대명사 that**
> 선행사가 사람, 동물, 사물일
> 때 주격 관계대명사로
> that을 쓸 수 있다. 주격
> 관계대명사는 관계대명사절
> 안에서 주어의 역할을 한다.

we "pick the low-hanging fruit": /
우리는 '낮게 매달려 있는 과일을 따는데' /
we make the easy discoveries first, /
즉 우리는 쉬운 발견을 먼저 해서 /
★주격 관계대명사
so those that remain are more difficult. //
남아 있는 것들은 더 어렵다 //
뒤에 invented the wheel 생략 가주어
You can only invent the wheel once, / and once you have, / it's
진주어
harder to find a similarly important invention. //
여러분은 바퀴를 한 번만 발명할 수 있고 / 일단 그러고 나면 / 비슷하게 중요한 발명을 찾기란
더 어렵다 //
Though both of these effects are important, / when we look at
the data / it's the latter effect that **predominates**. //
이 두 영향 모두 중요하지만 / 데이터를 보면 / 지배하는 것은 바로 후자의 영향이다 //
Overall, past progress makes future progress harder. //
대체로, 과거의 발전은 미래의 발전을 더 어렵게 한다 // **단서 2 과거의 진보는 미래 진보를 어렵게 함**
It's easy to see this qualitatively / by looking at the history of
innovation. //
이것을 질적으로 아는 것은 쉽다 / 혁신의 역사를 살펴봄으로써 //
Consider physics. // 물리학을 고려해 보라 //
In 1905, his "miracle year," / Albert Einstein revolutionized
분사구문을 이끎
physics, / describing the photoelectric effect, Brownian motion,
the theory of special relativity, and his famous equation,
$E=mc^2$. //
그의 '기적의 해'인 1905년에 / 알버트 아인슈타인은 물리학에 대변혁을 일으켰는데 / 광전
효과, 브라운 운동, 특수 상대성 이론, 그리고 그의 유명한 공식 $E=mc^2$을 기술하였다 //
He was twenty-six at the time and did all this / while working
접속사가 생략되지 않은 분사구문
as a patent clerk. //
그는 그 당시 26살이었고 이 모든 것을 했다 / 특허 사무원으로 일하며 //
Compared to Einstein's day, / progress in physics is now much
비교급 강조 부사
harder to achieve. //
아인슈타인의 시대와 비교하여 / 이제 물리학에서 발전은 이루기가 훨씬 더 어렵다 //

- progress ⓝ 발전, 진전   · predominate ⓥ 지배적이다
- qualitatively 〔ad〕 질적으로   · physics ⓝ 물리학
- revolutionize ⓥ 대변혁[혁신]을 일으키다

- **photoelectric** ⓐ 광전자를 이용한   • **theory** ⓝ 이론
- **relativity** ⓝ 상대성 이론, 상대성   • **equation** ⓝ 방정식
- **scatter** ⓥ (흩)뿌리다   • **vary** ⓥ 다르다
- **vanish** ⓥ 없어지다   • **fade** ⓥ 바래다, 희미해지다

우리가 어느 정도의 과학적 그리고 기술적 발전을 이룬 후에, 더 이상의 발전은 더 쉬워지는가 혹은 더 어려워지는가? 직관적으로, 어느 쪽이든 될 수 있을 것처럼 보이는데, 두 가지 경쟁하는 영향이 있기 때문이다. 한편으로는, 우리는 '거인의 어깨에 서 있는데,' 즉 이전의 발견이 미래의 발전을 더 쉽게 만들 수 있다. 다른 한편으로는, 우리는 '낮게 매달려 있는 과일을 따는데,' 즉 우리는 쉬운 발견을 먼저 해서 남아 있는 것들은 더 어렵다. 여러분은 바퀴를 한 번만 발명할 수 있고, 일단 그러고 나면, 비슷하게 중요한 발명을 찾기란 더 어렵다. 이 두 영향 모두 중요하지만, 데이터를 보면 **지배하는** 것은 바로 후자의 영향이다. 대체로, 과거의 발전은 미래의 발전을 더 어렵게 한다. 혁신의 역사를 살펴봄으로써 이것을 질적으로 아는 것은 쉽다. 물리학을 고려해 보라. 그의 '기적의 해'인 1905년에, 알버트 아인슈타인은 물리학에 대변혁을 일으켰는데, 광전 효과, 브라운 운동, 특수 상대성 이론, 그리고 그의 유명한 공식 $E=mc^2$을 기술하였다. 그는 그 당시 26살이었고, 특허 사무원으로 일하며 이 모든 것을 했다. 아인슈타인의 시대와 비교하여, 이제 물리학에서 발전은 이루기가 훨씬 더 어렵다.

다음 빈칸에 들어갈 말로 가장 적절한 것을 고르시오.

① **predominates** 갈수록 발명이 어려워진다는 것이 지배적이라는 내용임
  지배하는
② **scatters** 어려운 발명만 남아 있다는 영향이 흩어진다는 내용은 아님
  흩어지는
③ **varies** 남아 있는 것은 어려운 발명이라는 영향이 다양하다는 것이 아님
  다양한
④ **vanishes** 후자의 영향이 사라진다는 내용은 글의 내용과 반대임
  사라지는
⑤ **fades** 후자의 영향이 희미해진다는 내용은 글의 내용과 반대됨
  희미해지는

왜 정답? [정답률 66%]

빈칸 문장	이 두 영향 모두 중요하지만, 데이터를 보면 _____ 것은 바로 후자의 영향이다.

→ 후자의 영향이 '어떠하다'를 선택지에서 찾아야 한다. 이를 위해서는 후자의 영향이 무엇인지, 그리고 이것이 어떠한지를 글에서 찾아야 한다.

- 다른 한편으로는, 우리는 '낮게 매달려 있는 과일을 따는데,' 즉 우리는 쉬운 발견을 먼저 해서 남아있는 것들은 더 어렵다. **단서 1**
- 대체로, 과거의 발전은 미래의 발전을 더 어렵게 한다. **단서 2**

→ 후자의 영향은 쉬운 발견을 먼저했기에 어려운 발견만 남아서 갈수록 진보는 더 어려워질 것이라는 내용이며, 빈칸 문장 바로 다음 문장에서 과거의 발전은 미래의 발전을 더 어렵게 한다고 했다.

▶ 따라서 빈칸에 들어갈 말로 가장 적절한 것은 ① '지배하는'이다.

왜 오답?

② 남아있는 발견은 어렵다는, 후자의 영향이 흩어진다는 내용은 적절하지 않다.
③ 후자의 영향이 다양하다는 것이 아니다.
④ 후자의 영향이 사라진다는 것은 글의 요지와 반대되는 내용이다.
⑤ 후자의 영향이 희미해진다는 것은 글의 핵심 내용과 반대된다.

K 28 정답 ① ＊식충식물의 독특한 먹이 유인 전략

복수 주어
Insect-eating plants' unique strategies / for catching live prey /
복수 동사
have long captured the public imagination. //
식충식물의 독특한 전략들은 / 살아 있는 먹이를 잡기 위한 / 오랫동안 대중의 상상력을
사로잡아 왔다 //

「전치사+관계대명사」
But even within this strange group, / in which food-trapping
mechanisms have evolved multiple times independently, /
= strategies
some unusual ones stand out. //
그러나 심지어 이상한 무리 안에서조차 / 먹이를 가두는 기제가 여러 번 독립적으로 진화해 온
/ 이 몇몇 특이한 것들이 두드러진다 //

동격
According to Ulrike Bauer, / an evolutionary biologist, / the
visually striking pitcher plant *Nepenthes gracilis*, / for example, /
can **exploit external energy for a purpose**. //
Ulrike Bauer에 따르면 / 진화 생물학자인 / 시각적으로 인상적인 낭상엽 식물인
Nepenthes gracilis는 / 예를 들어 / 어떤 목적을 위해 외부의 에너지를 이용할 수 있다 //

This species' pitcher has a rigid, horizontal lid / with an exposed
주격 관계대명사   **분사구문**
underside / that produces nectar, / luring insects to land on it. //
이 종의 주머니 모양의 잎은 단단하고 수평으로 된 뚜껑을 갖고 있는데 / 노출된 아랫면을
지닌 / 꿀을 생산하는 / 그것은 곤충들이 그 면에 앉도록 유혹한다 //

When a raindrop strikes the lid's top, / the lid jolts downward
병렬 구조
/ and throws any unsuspecting visitor / into digestive juices
below. //
빗방울이 뚜껑의 윗면을 칠 때 / 뚜껑은 아래쪽으로 흔들려서 / 의심하지 않고 있는 어떤
방문객도 떨구어 버린다 / 아래의 소화액으로 //

Researchers used x-ray scans / to analyze cross sections of
the pitchers / when the lid is raised, lowered, and in a neutral
position. //
연구원들은 엑스선 정밀 검사를 사용했다 / 주머니 모양의 잎의 단면을 분석하기 위해 /
뚜껑이 올려질 때, 내려질 때 그리고 중립 위치에 있을 때의 //

Their results revealed a structural weak point / in the pitcher's
neck: /
그것의 결과는 구조상의 약한 부분을 밝혀냈다 / 주머니 모양의 잎의 목 부분에서 /

when a raindrop hits the lid, / the weak spot folds in / and forces
forces의 목적격 보어
the lid to quickly move downward, / similar to a diving board. //
즉 빗방울이 뚜껑을 칠 때 / 그 약한 지점은 안으로 접히고 / 뚜껑이 아래로 빠르게 움직이도록
만드는데 / 그것은 다이빙 보드와 비슷하다 // **단서 1** 빗방울의 도움을 받아
방문객(곤충)을 가둠

The weak point makes / the pitcher's body / bend and bounce
makes의 목적격 보어 (원형부정사)
back in a specific, consistent way, /
그 약한 부분은 하도록 한다 / 주머니 모양의 잎의 몸통이 / 휘었다가 일정하고 일관된
방식으로 튀어서 되돌아오도록 /
동명사구 (전치사의 목적어)
so the lid rises back up / without bouncing too far / — unlike a
typical leaf's chaotic vibration / when struck by rain. //
그래서 그 뚜껑은 다시 올라온다 / 너무 멀리 튀지 않고 / 보통의 잎의 무질서한 흔들림과 달리
/ 비에 맞을 때 // **단서 2** 비에 맞을 때 순간적으로 휘어 먹이를 포획하고 이후 모양을 회복함

- **insect-eating plant** 식충식물   • **stand out** 눈에 띄다
- **rigid** ⓐ 뻣뻣한, 단단한   • **horizontal** ⓐ 수평의
- **lure** ⓥ 꾀다, 유혹하다   • **unsuspecting** ⓐ 의심하지 않는
- **digestive juice** 소화액   • **cross section** 횡단면, 단면도
- **neutral** ⓐ 중립의(위치에 있는)   • **structural** ⓐ 구조상의
- **diving board** 다이빙 도약대   • **chaotic** ⓐ 혼돈 상태의
- **vibration** ⓝ 진동   • **exploit** ⓥ 이용하다
- **modify** ⓥ 수정하다, 바꾸다

식충식물의 살아 있는 먹이를 잡기 위한 독특한 전략들은 오랫동안 대중의 상상력을 사로잡아 왔다. 그러나 심지어 먹이를 가두는 기제가 여러 번 독립적으로 진화해 온 이 이상한 무리 안에서조차 몇몇 특이한 것들이 두드러진다. 진화 생물학자인 Ulrike Bauer에 따르면 예를 들어 시각적으로 인상적인 낭상엽 식물인 Nepenthes gracilis는 **어떤 목적을 위해 외부의 에너지를 이용**할 수 있다. 이 종의 주머니 모양의 잎은 꿀을 생산하는 노출된 아랫면을 지닌 단단하고 수평으로 된 뚜껑을 갖고 있는데, 그것은 곤충들이 그 면에 앉도록 유혹한다. 빗방울이 뚜껑의 윗면을 칠 때, 뚜껑은 아래쪽으로 흔들려서 의심하지 않고 있는 어떤 방문객도 아래의 소화액으로 떨구어 버린다. 연구원들은 뚜껑이 올려질 때, 내려질 때 그리고 중립 위치에 있을 때의 주머니 모양의 잎의 단면을 분석하기 위해 엑스선 정밀 검사를 사용했다. 그것의 결과는 주머니 모양의 잎의 목 부분에서 구조상의 약한 부분을 밝혀냈다. 즉 빗방울이 뚜껑을 칠 때 그 약한 지점은 안으로 접히고, 뚜껑이 아래로 빠르게 움직이도록 만드는데, 그것은 다이빙 보드와 비슷하다. 그 약한 부분은 주머니 모양의 잎의 몸통을 휘었다가 특정하고 일관된 방식으로 튀어서 되돌아오도록 해서, 비에 맞을 때 보통의 잎의 무질서한 흔들림과 달리 그 뚜껑은 너무 멀리 튀지 않고 다시 올라온다.

다음 빈칸에 들어갈 말로 가장 적절한 것을 고르시오. [3점]

① exploit external energy for a purpose
외부 에너지인 빗방울을 통해서 먹이를 잡음
어떤 목적을 위해 외부의 에너지를 이용하다
② hide itself with help of the environment 숨는 것은 아님
환경의 도움을 받아 자신을 숨기다
③ coordinate with other plants to trap insects 관련 없음
곤충을 포획하기 위해 다른 식물들과 협력하다
④ change its shape to absorb more rain water 흡수하기 위한 것이 아님
더 많은 비를 흡수하기 위해 모양을 변형하다
⑤ modify its hunting strategy on a regular basis
정기적으로 사냥 전략을 수정하다   사냥 전략의 변화는 언급되지 않음

| 문제 풀이 순서 | [정답률 40%]

1st 빈칸이 포함된 문장을 읽고, 빈칸에 들어갈 말에 대한 단서를 얻는다.

빈칸 문장 앞	그러나 심지어 먹이를 가두는 기제가 여러 번 독립적으로 진화해 온 이 이상한 무리 안에서조차 몇몇 특이한 것들이 두드러진다.
빈칸 문장	진화 생물학자인 Ulrike Bauer에 따르면 예를 들어 시각적으로 인상적인 낭상엽 식물인 'Nepenthes gracilis'는 _____ 할 수 있다.

→ 먹이를 잡기 위한 Nepenthes gracilis의 독특한 전략이 빈칸에 들어갈 것이다.
▶ 나머지 부분을 읽으며 Nepenthes gracilis의 먹이 잡기 전략이 무엇인지 파악한다.

2nd 글의 나머지 부분을 읽고, Nepenthes gracilis의 먹이 잡기 전략을 파악한다.

• 빗방울이 뚜껑의 윗면을 칠 때, ~ 방문객도 아래의 소화액으로 떨어져 버린다. 단서1
• ~ 비에 맞을 때 ~ 그 뚜껑은 너무 멀리 튀지 않고 다시 올라온다. 단서2

→ Nepenthes gracilis는 빗방울의 도움을 받아 방문객(곤충)을 가두고, 먹이를 포획한 후 모양을 회복함

3rd 2nd 에서 이해한 내용을 선택지에서 고른다.

빗방울(외부의 에너지)을 이용해 먹이를 포획하는 Nepenthes gracilis의 전략을 소개하고 있는 빈칸에는 ① '어떤 목적을 위해 외부의 에너지를 이용하다'가 들어가는 것이 알맞다.

| 선택지 분석 |

① exploit external energy for a purpose
어떤 목적을 위해 외부의 에너지를 이용하다
외부 에너지인 빗방울을 통해서 먹이를 잡는 Nepenthes gracilis의 독특한 전략을 소개하고 있다.

② hide itself with help of the environment
환경의 도움을 받아 자신을 숨기다
환경의 도움으로 숨는 것은 아니다.

③ coordinate with other plants to trap insects
곤충을 포획하기 위해 다른 식물들과 협력하다
협력하는 내용은 나오지 않는다.

④ change its shape to absorb more rain water
더 많은 비를 흡수하기 위해 모양을 변형하다
비를 더 많이 흡수하기 위함이 아니다.

⑤ modify its hunting strategy on a regular basis
정기적으로 사냥 전략을 수정하다
Nepenthes gracilis가 전략을 수정하지는 않았다.

K 29 정답 ① ＊언어 기술의 숙달에 따른 변화 ────────

From about ages eight through sixteen, / our manual dexterity has strengthened / through continually improving eye-hand coordination. //
약 8세부터 16세까지 / 우리의 손재주는 강화되어 왔다 / 눈과 손의 협응을 지속적으로 향상시키면서 //

There is considerable improvement / in handwriting skills. //
상당한 향상이 있다 / 필기 능력에 //

We gain mastery / over the mechanics of language. //
우리는 숙달을 얻는다 / 언어의 기술에 대한 //

We also gradually eliminate / the logical gaps in our stories / — characteristic of our earlier stage of perception /
우리는 또한 점차적으로 제거한다 / 우리 이야기의 논리적 공백을 / 우리의 초기 지각 단계의 특징인 /
접속사
— as intense preoccupation with the whole vision / gives way / to preoccupation with correctness. // 단서1 정확성에 집착하게 되면서 초기
전체 시각에 대한 강렬한 집착이 / 바뀌면서 / 정확성에 대한 집착으로 //   단계의 특징인 논리적 공백을 제거한다고 함

As a result, / our writing and oral storying / become increasingly conventional and literal, / 단서2 글쓰기와 구술이 상투적이며
그 결과 / 우리의 글쓰기와 구술은 / 점점 더 상투적이며 사실에 충실하게 된다 /   사실에 충실하게 된다고 함

with an accompanying **loss** of the spontaneity and originality /
주격 관계대명사(the spontaneity and originality 수식)
that characterized our earlier efforts. //
즉흥성과 독창성의 손실을 수반하면서 / 우리의 초기 노력의 특징이었던 //

At this stage /
이 단계에서 /

our vocabulary is firmly grounded. //
우리의 어휘는 확고하게 기반을 갖는다 //
★사이에 목적격 관계대명사 생략
We use words /
우리는 단어를 사용한다 /

everyone else uses. //
모든 사람이 사용하는 // 단서3 모든 사람이 사용하는 단어를 사용함
형용사적 용법   부사적 용법(목적)
We have little need / to invent metaphors / to communicate. //
우리는 필요가 거의 없다 / 은유를 지어낼 / 의사소통하기 위해 //
목적어를 이끄는 접속사   mass를 수식하는 분사
By now / we know / that a star is "a hot gaseous mass floating in space" / in contrast to our innocent stage, / when we noticed, / "Look that star is like a flower without a stem!" //
이제 / 우리는 알고 있다 / 별이 "우주를 떠다니는 뜨거운 기체 덩어리"라는 것을 / 순진한 단계와 대조하여 / 우리가 말했던 / "봐 저 별은 줄기가 없는 꽃과 같아."라고 //

★ 목적격 관계대명사의 생략
관계대명사절에서 목적어 역할을 하는 목적격 관계대명사는 생략될 수 있다. 선행사인 words 뒤에 uses의 목적어 역할을 하는 목적격 관계대명사 that이 생략되었다.

- continually ad 지속적으로   - coordination n 협응, 협조
- handwriting n 필기   - mastery n 숙달, 통달
- eliminate v 제거하다   - logical a 타당한, 논리적인
- characteristic n 특징   - earlier a 초기의   - intense a 강렬한
- preoccupation n 집착   - whole a 전체의, 온전한
- give way to ~로 바뀌다   - correctness n 정확성
- conventional a 상투적인, 관습적인
- literal a 사실에 충실한, 글자 그대로의   - accompanying a 수반하는
- originality n 독창성   - characterize v 특징짓다
- firmly ad 단호히, 확고히   - grounded a 현실에 기반을 둔
- metaphor n 은유(법)   - by now 이제
- gaseous a 기체의   - mass n 덩어리   - float v 떠다니다
- in contrast with[to] ~와 대조를 이루어   - innocent a 순진한
- stem n 줄기

약 8세부터 16세까지, 우리의 손재주는 눈과 손의 협응을 지속적으로 향상시키면서 강화되어 왔다. 필기 능력에 상당한 향상이 있다. 우리는 언어의 기술에 대한 숙달을 얻는다. 우리는 또한 전체 시각에 대한 강렬한 집착이 정확성에 대한 집착으로 바뀌면서 — 우리의 초기 지각 단계의 특징인 — 우리 이야기의 논리적 공백을 점차적으로 제거한다. 그 결과, 우리의 글쓰기와 구술은 점점 더 상투적이며 사실에 충실하게 되고, 우리의 초기 노력의 특징이었던 즉흥성과 독창성의 **손실**을 수반하게 된다. 이 단계에서 우리의 어휘는 확고하게 기반을 갖는다. 우리는 모든 사람이 사용하는 단어를 사용한다. 우리는 의사소통하기 위해 은유를 지어낼 필요가 거의 없다. 이제 우리는 "봐 저 별은 줄기가 없는 꽃과 같아!"라고 말했던 순진한 단계와 대조하여, 별이 "우주를 떠다니는 뜨거운 기체 덩어리"라는 것을 알고 있다.

다음 빈칸에 들어갈 말로 가장 적절한 것을 고르시오.

① loss 글쓰기와 구술이 초기의 즉흥성과 독창성을 손실하고 상투적이며 사실에 충실하게 된다고 함
손실
② sense 글쓰기와 구술이 즉흥성과 독창성의 감각을 수반하는 것이 아니라 이를 잃게 된다는 내용임
감각
③ increase 즉흥성과 독창성의 증가를 수반한다는 것과 반대되는 내용임
증가
④ recovery 즉흥성과 독창성을 회복하는 것이 아니라 잃게 됨
회복
⑤ demonstration 글쓰기와 구술이 즉흥성과 독창성을 입증한다는 내용이 아님
입증

왜 정답? [정답률 45%]

빈칸 문장	그 결과, 우리의 글쓰기와 구술은 점점 더 상투적이며 사실에 충실하게 되고, 우리의 초기 노력의 특징이었던 즉흥성과 독창성의 _____을 수반하게 된다.

➡ 빈칸에는 글쓰기와 구술에서 초기 노력이었던 즉흥성과 독창성이 어떻게 되었는지가 들어가야 한다.

┌ • 전체 시각에 대한 강렬한 집착이 정확성에 대한 집착으로 바뀌면서, 우리의 초기 지각 단계의 특징인 이야기의 논리적 공백을 점차적으로 제거하게 된다. **단서 1**
│ • 우리의 글쓰기와 구술은 점점 더 상투적이며 사실에 충실하게 된다. **단서 2**
└ • 우리는 모든 사람이 사용하는 단어를 사용한다. **단서 3**

➡ 정확성에 대한 집착이 생겨나면서 초기 지각 단계의 특징인 이야기의 논리적 공백이 제거되며, 글쓰기와 구술은 점점 더 상투적이며 사실에 충실하게 된다고 했다. 또한, 이제는 모든 사람이 사용하는 단어를 사용하게 된다는 내용의 글이다.
 ▶ 그러므로 글쓰기와 구술에서 사실에 충실하고 다른 사람들이 사용하는 단어를 사용하기 위해 초기 노력이었던 즉흥성과 독창성은 '사라지게' 된다고 하는 것이 적절하므로 ① '손실'이 정답이다.

왜 오답?

② 글쓰기와 구술이 즉흥성과 독창성의 감각을 수반한다는 내용이 아니다.
③ 글쓰기와 구술이 즉흥성과 독창성의 증가를 수반한다는 것과 오히려 반대되는 내용이다.
④ 글쓰기와 구술이 즉흥성과 독창성의 회복을 수반한다는 언급은 없다.
⑤ 글쓰기와 구술이 즉흥성과 독창성을 입증한다는 내용의 글이 아니다.

K 30 정답 ① ＊이타적인 행위를 하는 사람들의 도덕성 ─────

The commonsense understanding / of the moral status of altruistic acts / conforms to / how most of us think about our responsibilities toward others. //
상식적인 이해는 / 이타적인 행위의 도덕적 상태에 대한 / ~에 따른다 / 우리 대부분이 다른 사람들을 향한 우리의 책임에 대해 어떻게 생각하는지 //

We tend to get offended / when someone else or society determines for us / how much of what we have should be given away; / **단서 1** 일반적으로 다른 사람이나 사회가 무언가를 결정해 주는 것을 불쾌하게 여기는 경향이 있다고 함
우리는 불쾌하게 여기는 경향이 있다 / 다른 누군가 또는 사회가 우리를 대신하여 결정하면 / 우리가 가진 것의 얼마만큼을 나누어줘야 하는지를 /

we are adults / and should have the right / to make such [형용사적 용법] decisions for ourselves. //
우리는 성인이다 / 그리고 권리가 있어야 한다 / 스스로 그러한 결정을 내릴 //

Yet, / when interviewed, / altruists known for making the largest [접속사가 생략되지 않은 분사구문] [altruists를 수식하는 분사] sacrifices / — and bringing about the greatest benefits to their [동명사의 병렬 구조] recipients / — assert just the opposite. // **단서 2** 이타주의자들은 (앞 내용과) 정반대의 주장을 함
하지만 / 인터뷰를 하면 / 가장 큰 희생을 한 것으로 알려진 이타주의자들은 / 그리고 그들의 수혜자에게 가장 큰 이익을 가져다주는 것으로 / 정반대의 주장을 한다 //

They insist / that they **had absolutely no choice but to act / as** [목적절 접속사] **they did**. //
그들은 주장한다 / 그들이 전적으로 (그렇게) 행동할 수밖에 없었다고 / 자신들이 그랬던 것처럼 // **단서 3** 이타적인 사람들은 누구나 똑같은 일을 했을 것이며 자신들의 행동이 찬사를 받을 만하지 않다고 일관되게 주장함

Organ donors, and everyday citizens / who risk their own lives [주격 관계대명사(Organ donors, and everyday citizens 수식)] to save others in mortal danger / are remarkably consistent / in [주어 Organ donors, and everyday citizens에 수 일치] their explicit denials /
장기 기증자들과 평범한 시민들은 / 치명적인 위험에 처한 다른 사람들을 구하기 위해 자기 자신의 목숨을 거는 / 놀랍게 일관된다 / 그들의 명백한 부인에서 /

that they have done anything deserving of high praise / as well [동격의 접속사] as in their assurance / that anyone in their shoes should have done exactly the same thing. //
should have p.p.: ~했어야 했다
자신이 찬사를 받을 만한 어떤 일을 했다는 것에 대한 / 그들의 확신에서뿐만 아니라 / 자신의 입장에 처한 사람이라면 누구나 정확하게 똑같은 것을 했을 것이라는 //

To be sure, / it seems / that the *more* altruistic someone is, / └── the 비교급 ~, the 비교급 …: ~할수록 더 …하다 ──┘ the more they are likely to insist /
확실히 / 보인다 / 누군가가 '더' 이타적일수록 / 그들은 주장할 가능성이 더 높다 / [목적어절 접속사]

that they have done no more than all of us would be expected to do, / lest we shirk our basic moral obligation to humanity. //
[접속사(~하지 않도록)]
우리 모두가 할 것으로 기대되는 만큼만 했을 뿐이라고 / 우리가 인류에 대한 우리의 기본적인 도덕적 의무를 회피하지 않도록 //

─────────────────────────

• commonsense ⓐ 상식적인   • moral status 도덕적 지위
• conform ⓥ 따르다   • responsibility ⓝ 책임
• offend ⓥ 기분 상하게 하다, 불쾌하게 여겨지다   • determine ⓥ 결정하다
• sacrifice ⓝ 희생   • benefit ⓝ 이익   • recipient ⓝ 수혜자
• assert ⓥ 주장하다   • organ donor 장기 기증자
• mortal ⓐ 치명적인   • remarkably ⓐⓓ 놀랍게도
• explicit ⓐ 명백한   • denial ⓝ 부인, 부정
• deserving ⓐ (도움·보답·칭찬 등을) 받을 만한[자격이 있는]
• assurance ⓝ 확신   • in one's shoes ~의 입장에서
• obligation ⓝ 의무   • humanity ⓝ 인류
• appreciation ⓝ 감탄, 찬사   • in return 대신에, 답례로
• inapplicable ⓐ 적용되지 않는, 사용할 수 없는

이타적인 행위의 도덕적 상태에 대한 상식적인 이해는 우리 대부분이 다른 사람들을 향한 우리의 책임에 대해 어떻게 생각하는지에 따른다. 우리는 다른 누군가 또는 사회가 우리를 대신하여 우리가 가진 것의 얼마만큼을 나누어줘야 하는지를 결정하면 그것을 불쾌하게 여기는 경향이 있다. 우리는 성인이고 스스로 그러한 결정을 내릴 권리가 있어야 한다. 하지만, 인터뷰를 하면, 가장 큰 희생을 하고, 그들의 수혜자에게 가장 큰 이익을 가져다주는 것으로 알려진 이타주의자들은 정반대의 주장을 한다. 그들은 그들이 **자신들이 그랬던 것처럼 전적으로 (그렇게) 행동할 수밖에 없었다**고 주장한다. 치명적인 위험에 처한 다른 사람들을 구하기 위해 자기 자신의 목숨을 거는 장기 기증자들과 평범한 시민들은 자신의 입장에 처한 사람이라면 누구나 정확하게 똑같은 것을 했을 것이라는 그들의 확신에서뿐만 아니라 자신이 찬사를 받을 만한 어떤 일을 했다는 것에 대한 그들의 명백한 부인에서도 놀랍게 일관된다. 확실히, 누군가가 '더' 이타적일수록, 그들은 우리가 인류에 대한 우리의 기본적인 도덕적 의무를 회피하지 않도록, 우리 모두가 할 것으로 기대되는 만큼만 했을 뿐이라고 주장할 가능성이 더 높아 보인다.

다음 빈칸에 들어갈 말로 가장 적절한 것을 고르시오.

① had absolutely no choice but to act as they did 그 입장에 처하면 자신들처럼 행동할 수밖에 없다는 주장을 하고 있음
자신들이 그랬던 것처럼 전적으로 (그렇게) 행동할 수밖에 없었다
② should have been rewarded financially
재정적으로 보상을 받았어야 했다   재정적으로 보상을 받았어야 한다고 하지 않음
③ regretted making such decisions 이러한 결정을 후회한다는 언급은 없음
이러한 결정을 한 것을 후회했다
④ deserved others' appreciation in return
보답으로 다른 사람들의 인정을 받을 만했다   오히려 다른 사람들의 찬사를 부인한다고 했음
⑤ found the moral obligations inapplicable in risky situations
위험한 상황에서 도덕적 의무감이 적용되지 않는다는 것을 발견했다
위험한 상황에서 도덕적 의무감이 적용되지 않는다는 것을 발견했다는 내용이 아님

왜 정답? [정답률 47%]

• 우리는 다른 누군가 또는 사회가 우리를 대신하여 결정하면 그것을 불쾌하게 여기는 경향이 있다. **단서 1**
• 하지만, 이타주의자들은 정반대의 주장을 한다. **단서 2**
• 이타주의자들은 자신의 입장에 처한 사람이라면 누구나 정확하게 똑같은 것을 했을 것이며 자신이 찬사를 받을 만한 어떤 일을 했다는 것에 대해 일관되게 부인한다. **단서 3**

➡ 사람들은 일반적으로 자신이 스스로 결정하지 못하는 상황을 불쾌해하지만 이타주의자들은 이와 정반대의 주장을 하는데, 그 정반대의 주장이란 바로 자신의 입장이라면 누구나 (선택권 없이) 정확하게 똑같은 일을 했으리라는 것이다.
 ▶ 빈칸에는 그들(이타주의자들)이 무엇이라고 주장했는지가 들어가야 하므로 ① '자신들이 그랬던 것처럼 전적으로 (그렇게) 행동할 수밖에 없었다'고 하는 것이 적절하다.

> **왜 오답?**

② 재정적으로 보상을 받았어야 한다고 하지 않았다.

③ 이러한 결정을 후회한다는 언급은 없다. **주의**

④ 다른 사람들의 인정을 바라는 것이 아니라 오히려 다른 사람들의 찬사를 부인한다고 했다.

⑤ 위험한 상황에서 도덕적 의무감이 적용되지 않는다는 것을 발견했다는 내용이 아니다.

K 31 정답 ③ ＊스토아학파의 철학: 통제 불가능한 것에 대한 대응 방법

Epictetus wrote, / "A man's master is / he who is able to confirm

<small>주격 관계대명사(he 수식)</small>

or remove / whatever that man seeks or shuns." //

<small>~는 무엇이든지</small>

Epictetus는 썼다 / "사람의 주인은 ~이다 / 확인하거나 제거할 수 있는 사람이다."라고 / 그 사람이 추구하거나 피하는 것 무엇이든지를 //

If you depend on no one except yourself / to satisfy your desires,

<small>부사적 용법(목적)</small>

/ you will have no master other than yourself / and you will be

free. //

만일 여러분이 여러분 자신 외에 누구에게도 의존하지 않는다면 / 자신의 욕망을 만족시키기 위해 / 여러분은 여러분 자신 외에 주인이 없을 것이고 / 여러분은 자유로울 것이다 //

Stoic philosophy was about that / — taking charge of your life, /

<small>분사구문을 이끎</small> <small>주격 관계대명사(things 수식)</small>

learning to work on those things that are within your power to

accomplish or change /

스토아 철학은 ~ 것에 관한 것이었다 / 여러분의 삶을 책임지고 / 성취하거나 변화하기 위해 여러분의 힘 안에 있는 것들에 노력하는 것과 / **단서 1** 스토아 학파는 여러분이 할 수 없는

<small>learning에 연결 사이에 목적격 관계대명사 생략 것에 에너지를 낭비하지 말라고 함</small>

and not to waste energy on things you cannot. //

여러분이 할 수 없는 것들에 에너지를 낭비하지 않는 것을 배우는 //

In particular, / the Stoics warned against / **reacting emotionally**

to what is outside your control. //

특히 / 스토아학파는 ~에 대해 경고했다 / 여러분의 통제 밖에 있는 것에 대해 감정적으로 반응하는 것 //

Often, Epictetus argued, / it's not our circumstances that get us

<small>┌── it ~ that 강조 구문 ──┐</small>

down / but rather the judgments we make about them. //

<small>사이에 목적격 관계대명사 생략</small>

흔히, Epictetus는 주장했다 / 우리를 낙담시키는 것은 우리의 상황이 아니라 / 오히려 그것들에 대해 우리가 내리는 판단이라고 //

Consider anger. // 분노를 생각해보라 //

We don't get angry at the rain / if it spoils our picnic. //

우리는 그것에 화가 나지 않는다 / 비가 우리의 소풍을 망친다 해도 //

That would be silly / because we can't do anything about the

rain. //

<small>**단서 2** 비만큼이나 그 사람을 통제하거나 바꿀 수 없기 때문에 둘 다 똑같이 어리석다고 함</small>

그것은 어리석은 짓인데 / 우리가 비에 대해 아무것도 할 수 없기 때문이다 //

But we often do get angry / if someone mistreats us. //

하지만 우리는 흔히 정말 화가 난다 / 누군가가 우리를 나쁘게 대한다면 //

We usually can't control or change that person / any more than

we can stop the rain, / so that is equally silly. //

우리는 대개 그 사람을 통제하거나 바꿀 수도 없으므로 / 우리가 비를 멈출 수 없는 것처럼 / 그것은 마찬가지로 어리석다 //

<small>가주어 진주어</small>

More generally, / it is just as pointless / to tie our feelings of

well-being to altering another individual's behavior / as it is

<small>just as ~ as ...: ~만큼이나 ~하다 가주어</small>

<small>진주어</small>

to tie them to the weather. //

더 일반적으로 / 무의미하다 / 우리의 안녕에 관한 감정을 다른 개인의 행동을 바꾸는 것에 연결하는 것 / 그것들을 날씨에 연결하는 것만큼이나 //

Epictetus wrote, / "If it concerns anything not in our control, / be

<small>목적어절 접속사</small>

prepared to say that it is nothing to you." // **단서 3** 통제 안에 있지 않다면

<small>아무것도 아니라고 함</small>

Epictetus는 썼다 / "만약 그것이 우리의 통제 안에 있지 않은 것과 관련이 있다면 / 그것은 당신에게 아무것도 아니라고 말할 준비를 하라."고 //

· satisfy ⓥ 만족시키다 · desire ⓝ 욕구

· take charge of ~을 책임지다 · accomplish ⓥ 완수하다, 성취하다

· circumstance ⓝ 상황 · judgment ⓝ 판단 · spoil ⓥ 망치다

· mistreat ⓥ 학대하다 · equally ⓐⓓ 마찬가지로

· pointless ⓐ 무의미한 · well-being ⓝ 안녕, (건강과) 행복

· alter ⓥ 바꾸다, 변경하다 · concern ⓥ 영향을 미치다

· argument ⓝ 논쟁 · react ⓥ 반응하다

· comprehend ⓥ 이해하다 · rationalize ⓥ 합리화하다

Epictetus는 "사람의 주인은 그 사람이 추구하거나 피하는 것 무엇이든지를 확인하거나 제거할 수 있는 사람이다."라고 썼다. 만일 여러분이 자신의 욕망을 만족시키기 위해 여러분 자신 외에 누구에게도 의존하지 않는다면, 여러분은 여러분 자신 외에 주인이 없을 것이고 여러분은 자유로울 것이다. 스토아 철학은 여러분의 삶을 책임지고, 성취하거나 변화하기 위해 여러분의 힘 안에 있는 것들에 노력하는 것과 여러분이 할 수 없는 것들에 에너지를 낭비하지 않는 것을 배우는 것에 관한 것이었다. 특히, 스토아학파는 **여러분의 통제 밖에 있는 것에 대해 감정적으로 반응하는 것**에 대해 경고했다. 흔히, Epictetus는 우리를 낙담시키는 것은 우리의 상황이 아니라 오히려 그것들에 대해 우리가 내리는 판단이라고 주장했다. 분노를 생각해보라. 우리는 비가 우리의 소풍을 망친다 해도, 그것에 화가 나지 않는다. 그것은 어리석은 짓인데, 우리가 비에 대해 아무것도 할 수 없기 때문이다. 하지만 우리는 누군가가 우리를 나쁘게 대한다면 흔히 정말 화가 난다. 우리가 비를 멈출 수 없는 것처럼 우리는 대개 그 사람을 통제하거나 바꿀 수도 없으므로, 그것은 마찬가지로 어리석다. 더 일반적으로, 우리의 안녕에 관한 감정을 다른 개인의 행동을 바꾸는 것에 연결하는 것은, 그것들을 날씨에 연결하는 것만큼이나 무의미하다. Epictetus는 "만약 그것이 우리의 통제 안에 있지 않은 것과 관련이 있다면, 그것은 당신에게 아무것도 아니라고 말할 준비를 하라."고 썼다.

다음 빈칸에 들어갈 말로 가장 적절한 것을 고르시오. [3점]

① making an argument without enough evidence

<small>충분한 증거 없이 주장을 하는 것 충분한 증거 없이 주장을 하는 것에 대한 언급은 없음</small>

② listening to others' opinions without judgment

<small>판단 없이 다른 사람의 의견을 듣는 것 판단 없이 다른 사람의 의견을 들으라고 하지 않았음</small>

③ reacting emotionally to what is outside your control 통제할 수 없는

<small>여러분의 통제 밖에 있는 것에 대해 감정적으로 반응하는 것 것에 에너지를 쏟지 말라고 함</small>

④ pretending to have comprehended when you have not

<small>여러분이 이해하지 못했을 때 이해한 척 하는 것 이해하지 못했을 때 이해한 척 하라는 언급은 없음</small>

⑤ rationalizing to yourself that the situation is out of control

<small>그 상황이 통제 불가능하다는 것을 여러분 스스로에게 합리화하는 것 상황이 통제 불가능함을 합리화하는 것을 경고하는 내용이 아님</small>

> **왜 정답?** [정답률 53%]

빈칸 문장	특히, 스토아학파는 _____에 대해 경고했다.

➡ 빈칸에는 스토아학파가 무엇에 대해 경고했는지가 들어가야 한다.

· 스토아 철학은 여러분이 할 수 없는 것들에 에너지를 낭비하지 않는 것을 배우는 것이었다. **단서 1**

· 비를 멈출 수 없는 것처럼 그 사람을 통제하거나 바꿀 수도 없으므로 마찬가지로 어리석다. **단서 2**

· 만약 그것이 우리의 통제 안에 있지 않은 것과 관련이 있다면, 그것은 당신에게 아무것도 아니라고 말할 준비를 하라. **단서 3**

➡ 스토아 철학에서는 자신이 통제할 수 없는 것들(비 또는 다른 사람)에 에너지를 낭비하지 말라고 가르쳤으며, 통제 안에 있지 않은 것이라면 아무것도 아니라고 말할 수 있어야 한다고 했다.

▶ 그러므로 스토아 학파들이 ③ '여러분의 통제 밖에 있는 것에 대해 감정적으로 반응하는 것'에 대해 경고했다고 하는 것이 적절하다.

> **왜 오답?**

① 충분한 증거 없이 주장을 하는 것에 대한 언급은 없다.

② 판단 없이 다른 사람의 의견을 들으라고 하지 않았다.

④ 이해하지 못했을 때 이해한 척 하라고 언급하지 않았다.

⑤ 상황이 통제 불가능함을 스스로에게 합리화하는 것을 경고하는 내용이 아니다.

(▶◀ 이유: 통제 불가능한 상황을 합리화하라는 것이 아니라 신경 쓰지 말라는 내용임)

K 32 정답 ② * 전략적 자기 무지

Some of the most insightful work / on information seeking /
emphasizes "strategic self-ignorance," /
가장 통찰력 있는 연구 중 일부는 / 정보 탐색에 관한 / '전략적 자기 무지'를 강조하는데 /
앞에 주격 관계대명사와 be동사가 생략됨
understood / as "the use of ignorance / as an excuse / to engage
excessively / in pleasurable activities / that may be harmful / to
one's future self." // 단서1 미래에 해로울 수도 있는 즐거운 활동을 하기
위한 핑계로 무지를 전략적으로 사용함
이는 이해된다 / '무지의 사용으로 / 핑계로서 / 과도하게 하기 위한 / 즐거운 활동을 / 해로울
수도 있는 / 자신의 미래 자아에' 부사절 접속사(조건)
The idea here is / that if people are present-biased, / they might
명사절(주격 보어) 접속사
avoid information / that would **make current activities less**
주격 관계대명사
attractive /
여기서의 생각은 ~이다 / 만약 사람들이 현재에 편향되어 있다면 / 그들은 정보를 피할 수도
있다는 것 / 현재의 활동을 덜 매력적으로 만들 단서2 정보가 죄책감이나 수치심을 유발하고 그러한
활동을 하지 말라고 충고할 것이기 때문에 정보를 피함
— perhaps because it would produce guilt or shame, / perhaps
because it would suggest / an aggregate trade-off / that would
counsel against engaging / in such activities. //
아마도 그것이 죄책감이나 수치심을 유발할 것이기 때문에 / 아마도 그것이 제안할 것이기 때
문에 / 총체적 절충을 / 관여하지 말라고 충고할 / 그러한 활동에 //
간접목적어 직접목적어
St. Augustine famously said, / "God give me chastity —
주어   동사
tomorrow." //
성 아우구스티누스는 유명한 말을 했다 / "하나님 제게 정결을 내일 주시옵소서"라는 //
Present-biased agents think: / "Please let me know the risks
— tomorrow." //
현재에 편향되어 있는 행위자들은 생각한다 / "제가 위험을 내일 알게 해주세요"라고 //
Whenever people are thinking / about engaging in an activity /
= No matter when
with short-term benefits but long-term costs, / they might prefer
to delay / receipt of important information. //
사람들이 생각하고 있을 때마다 / 활동을 하려고 / 단기적인 혜택은 있지만 장기적인 대가가
있는 / 그들은 미루는 것을 선호할 수도 있다 / 중요한 정보의 수신을 //
The same point might hold / about information / that could
make people sad or mad: / "Please tell me / what I need to know
/ — tomorrow." 단서3 슬프게 하거나 화나게 할 수 있는 정보를 아는 것을 미룸
똑같은 점이 있을 수 있다 / 정보에 관해서도 / 사람들을 슬프게 하거나 화나게 할 수 있는 /
"제게 말해 주세요 / 제가 알아야 할 것을 / 내일" //

- insightful ⓐ 통찰력 있는 · seek ⓥ 찾다, 추구하다
- emphasize ⓥ 강조하다 · strategic ⓐ 전략적인
- self-ignorance 자기 무지 · excuse ⓝ 핑계, 변명
- engage in ~에 참여[관여]하다 · excessively ⓐⓓ 지나치게, 과도하게
- pleasurable ⓐ 즐거운 · harmful ⓐ 해로운
- present-biased 현재에 편향되어 있는 · avoid ⓥ 피하다, 모면하다
- guilt ⓝ 죄책감 · shame ⓝ 수치심, 창피 · trade-off 절충, 균형
- counsel ⓥ 조언[충고]하다, 상담하다
- agent ⓝ 행위자, (일정 권한을 가진) 대리인[점] · risk ⓝ 위험
- benefit ⓝ 혜택 · prefer ⓥ 선호하다 · delay ⓥ 미루다
- receipt ⓝ 수령, 받기, 인수 · mad ⓐ 몹시 화가 난

정보 탐색에 관한 가장 통찰력 있는 연구 중 일부는 '전략적 자기 무지'를 강조하
는데, 이는 '자신의 미래 자아에 해로울 수도 있는 즐거운 활동을 과도하게 하
기 위한 핑계로서의 무지의 사용'으로 이해된다. 여기서의 생각은, 만약 사람들
이 현재에 편향되어 있다면, 현재의 활동을 덜 매력적으로 만들 정보를 피할 수
도 있다는 것인데, 아마도 그것이 죄책감이나 수치심을 유발할 것이고, 그러한
활동을 하지 말라고 충고할 총체적 절충을 제안할 것이기 때문일 것이다. 성 아
우구스티누스는 "하나님 제게 정결을 내일 주시옵소서."라는 유명한 말을 했다.
현재에 편향되어 있는 행위자들은 "제가 위험을 내일 알게 해주세요."라고 생각
한다. 사람들이 단기적인 혜택은 있지만 장기적인 대가가 있는 활동을 하려고
생각하고 있을 때마다, 그들은 중요한 정보의 수신을 미루는 것을 선호할 수도
있다. 사람들을 슬프게 하거나 화나게 할 수 있는 정보에 관해서도 똑같은 점이
있을 수 있다. "제가 알아야 할 것을 내일 말해 주세요."

다음 빈칸에 들어갈 말로 가장 적절한 것을 고르시오.
① highlight the value of preferred activities   선호되는 활동의 가치를 떨어뜨리는
정보임
선호되는 활동의 가치를 강조할
②make current activities less attractive   현재의 활동을 하는 것에 대해 수치심을
유발하는 정보임
현재의 활동을 덜 매력적으로 만들
③ cut their attachment to past activities   '현재'의 활동에 대한 내용임
과거 활동에 대한 자신들의 애착을 끊을
④ enable them to enjoy more activities   그들로 하여금 그 활동을 하지 못하게 하는
정보임
그들로 하여금 더 많은 활동을 즐기게 할
⑤ potentially become known to others   타인이 관련되는 것은 아님
다른 사람들에게 잠재적으로 알려지게 될

> 왜 정답 ? [정답률 39%] 지금은 즐거운 어떤 활동이 미래에는
해로울 수 있음을 알기를 피하는 것

전략적 자기 무지란 미래의 자신에게 해로울 수 있는, 그러나 현재에는 즐거운 활
동을 하기 위한 핑계로서 무지를 사용하는 것을 말한다. 다시 말해, 그러한 활동을
하는 것에 대해 죄책감이나 수치심을 유발하거나 그 활동을 하지 말 것을 제안하는
정보를 일부러 피하는 것을 의미하므로 이러한 정보가 어떤 정보인지를 설명하는
빈칸에는 ② '현재의 활동을 덜 매력적으로 만들'이 들어가야 한다.

> 왜 오답 ?
① 선호되는, 즉 현재 하고 싶은 활동의 가치를 떨어뜨리는 정보를 피하는 것이다.
③, ⑤ 현재의 활동이 갖는 부정적인 영향에 대한 정보를 일부러 피하는 것이지, 과
거의 활동이나 다른 사람들과 관련되는 것이 아니다.
④ 미래에는 해롭지만 현재에는 즐거운 활동을 하지 못하게 하는 정보를 말한다.

K 33 정답 ② * 소비의 변화

People have always needed to eat, / and they always will. //
사람들은 항상 먹을 것이 필요했으며 / 그들은 항상 그럴 것이다 // 뒤에 need to eat이 생략됨
Rising emphasis / on self-expression values / does not put an
단수 주어   단수 동사
end / to material desires. //
늘어나는 강조가 / 자기표현 가치에 관한 / 마침표를 찍지는 않는다 / 물질적 욕구에 //
But prevailing economic orientations / are gradually being
reshaped. // ── 수동태의 현재진행형 ──
하지만 우세한 경제적 방향성이 / 서서히 재형성되고 있다 //
People / who work in the knowledge sector / continue to seek
복수 주어   복수 동사
high salaries, /
사람들은 / 지식 부문에서 일하는 / 계속 높은 급료를 추구하지만 /
but they place equal or greater emphasis / on doing stimulating
work / and being able to follow their own time schedules. //
그들은 동등한 또는 더 큰 중점을 둔다 / (아주 흥미로워) 자극이 되는 일을 하는 것에 / 그리고
그들 자신의 시간 계획을 따르는 것에 //
Consumption is becoming progressively less determined / by
the need for sustenance / and the practical use of the goods
consumed. //
소비는 점진적으로 덜 결정된다 / 생존에 대한 필요에 의해 / 소비되는 재화의 실용적 사용에
의해 //
단서1 음식의 가치가 '어떤' 측면에 의해 결정되는지가 빈칸에 필요함
People still eat, / but a growing component of food's value / is
determined / by its **nonmaterial** aspects. //
사람들은 여전히 먹지만 / 음식 가치의 증가하는 구성 요소가 / 결정된다 / 그것의 비물질적인
측면에 의해 //
단서2 음식의 가치: 흥미로운 경험을 제공, 독특한 생활 방식을 접할 기회
People pay a premium / to eat exotic cuisines / that provide an
부사적 용법(목적)   주격 관계대명사의 병렬 구조
interesting experience / or that symbolize a distinctive life-style. //
사람들은 할증금을 낸다 / 이국적인 요리를 먹고자 / 흥미로운 경험을 제공하는 / 또는 독특한
생활 방식을 상징하는 //
The publics of postindustrial societies / place growing emphasis
/ on "political consumerism," / such as boycotting goods / whose
production violates / ecological or ethical standards. //
선행사   소유격
관계대명사
탈공업화 사회의 대중은 / 점점 더 많은 중점을 둔다 / '정치적 소비주의'에 / 상품의 구매를
거부하는 것과 같은 / 그 생산이 위반하는 / 생태적 또는 윤리적 기준을 //
Consumption is less and less a matter of sustenance / and more
and more a question of life-style / — and choice. //
비교급 and 비교급: 점점 더 ~한/하게
소비는 점점 덜 생존의 문제이며 / 점점 더 생활 방식의 문제(이다) / 그리고 선택(의 문제이다) //

- emphasis ⓝ 강조
- value ⓥ 소중하게 생각하다
- orientation ⓝ 방향성
- reshape ⓥ 모양을 고치다, 재형성하다
- salary ⓝ 급료
- stimulating ⓐ 자극이 되는
- consumption ⓝ 소비
- progressively ⓐⓓ 계속해서, 점진적으로
- determine ⓥ 결정하다
- sustenance ⓝ 자양물, 지속, 생존
- practical ⓐ 현실적인, 실용적인
- component ⓝ 구성요소
- nonmaterial ⓐ 비물질적인
- aspect ⓝ 측면
- exotic ⓐ 이국적인
- symbolize ⓥ 상징하다
- distinctive ⓐ 독특한
- postindustrial ⓐ 탈공업화의
- boycott ⓥ 구매를 거부하다
- violate ⓥ 위반하다
- ecological ⓐ 생태적인
- ethical ⓐ 윤리적인

사람들은 항상 먹을 것이 필요했으며, 또 항상 그럴 것이다. 자기표현 가치에 관한 늘어나는 강조가 물질적 욕구를 끝내지는 않는다. 하지만 우세한 경제적 방향성이 서서히 재형성되고 있다. 지식 부문에서 일하는 사람들은 계속 높은 급료를 추구하지만, 그들은 (아주 흥미로워) 자극이 되는 일을 하는 것과 그들 자신의 시간 계획을 따르는 것에 동등한 또는 더 큰 중점을 둔다. 소비는 점진적으로 생존에 대한 필요와 소비되는 재화의 실용적 사용에 의해 덜 결정된다. 사람들은 여전히 먹지만, 음식 가치의 증가하는 구성 요소가 그것의 **비물질적인** 측면에 의해 결정된다. 사람들은 흥미로운 경험을 제공하거나 독특한 생활 방식을 상징하는 이국적인 요리를 먹고자 할증금을 낸다. 탈공업화 사회의 대중은 생산이 생태적 또는 윤리적 기준을 위반하는 상품의 구매를 거부하는 것과 같은 '정치적 소비주의'에 점점 더 많은 중점을 둔다. 소비는 점점 덜 생존의 문제이며 점점 더 생활 방식, 그리고 선택의 문제이다.

다음 빈칸에 들어갈 말로 가장 적절한 것을 고르시오.

① quantitative 음식의 양이 중요하다는 것이 아님
   양적인
②**nonmaterial** 흥미로운 경험, 독특한 생활 방식을 접하는 것
   비물질적인
③ nutritional 음식의 영양적 측면에 대한 내용이 아님
   영양의
④ invariable 변하지 않는 음식을 추구한다는 것이 아님
   불변의
⑤ economic high salaries로 만든 오답
   경제적인

왜 정답? [정답률 52%]

빈칸 문장	사람들은 여전히 먹지만, 음식 가치의 증가하는 구성 요소가 그것의 _____한 측면에 의해 결정된다.

➡ 음식의 가치가 그것의 '어떤' 측면에 의해 결정되는지를 파악해야 한다.

빈칸 문장의 뒤 문장	사람들은 흥미로운 경험을 제공하거나 독특한 생활 방식을 상징하는 이국적인 요리를 먹고자 할증금을 낸다.

➡ 흥미로운 경험을 제공하거나 독특한 생활 방식을 상징하는 이국적인 요리를 먹기 위해 더 많은 돈을 지불한다.
다시 말해, 음식의 가치는 그것이 제공하는 흥미로운 경험, 독특한 생활 방식을 접할 기회에 있다.
▶ 이는 음식의 가치가 ② '비물질적인' 측면에 의해 결정된다는 것을 보여준다.

왜 오답?

① 음식의 양에 가치를 두는 것이 아니다.
③ '음식'이라는 소재에서 연상되는 '영양'으로 만든 오답이다.
④ 음식의 변하지 않는 측면을 중시한다는 언급은 없다.
⑤ economic, salaries, consumption 등의 어휘가 등장한 것으로 만든 오답이다.
   음식의 경제적인 측면을 위해 할증금을 지불하는 것이 아니다.

K 34 정답 ① ＊주관적인 뉴스 선정 ——————

There is a difference / between a newsworthy event and news. //
차이가 있다 / 뉴스 가치가 있는 사건과 뉴스 간에는 //
부분 부정: 반드시 ~인 것은 아닌
A newsworthy event / will not necessarily become news, / just as news is often about an event / that is not, in itself, newsworthy. //
뉴스 가치가 있는 사건이 / 반드시 뉴스가 되지는 않을 것이다 / 뉴스가 종종 사건에 관한 것이듯이 / 그 자체로는 뉴스 가치가 없는 //

선행사   생략 가능한 주격 관계대명사와 be동사
We can define news as an event / that is recorded in the news
전치사 of의 목적어 역할을 하는 명사절
media, / regardless of whether it is about a newsworthy event. //
우리는 뉴스를 사건으로 규정할 수 있다 / 뉴스 매체에 기록되는 / 그것이 뉴스 가치가 있는 사건에 대한 것인지와 상관없이 //

The very fact of its transmission means / that it is regarded as
            주어   동사   주격 보어절 접속사
news, /
그것의 전송이라는 바로 그 사실이 의미한다 / 그것이 뉴스로 간주됨을 /

even if we struggle to understand / why that particular story
(양보)의 부사절 접속사
has been selected / from all the other events / happening at the
          주격 관계대명사절의 복수 동사   복수 선행사
same time / that have been ignored. //
비록 우리가 이해하려고 몹시 애쓸지라도 / 그 특정 이야기가 선정된 이유를 / 다른 모든 일들 중에서 / 같은 시기에 발생한 / 무시된 **단서 1** 일부 사람들에게 뉴스 가치가 있어 보이는 모든 사건이
뉴스가 되는 것은 아니라는 내용이 결과의 연결어로 이어짐
News selection is **subjective** / so not all events /
                                   부분 부정: 모두 ~안 것은 아님
seen as newsworthy / by some people / will make it to the news. //
뉴스 선정은 주관적이어서 / 모든 사건이 (~하지는 않는다) / 뉴스 가치가 있어 보이는 / 일부 사람들에게 / 뉴스가 되지는 않는다 //

                                          선행사   관계부사
All journalists are familiar with the scenario / where they are approached / by someone / with the words 'I've got a great story for you'. //
모든 기자들은 시나리오에 익숙하다 / 그들이 접근 당하는 / 누군가에 의해 / '내가 당신을 위한 엄청난 이야기를 가지고 있어'라는 말로 //

For them, / it is a major news event, / but for the journalist / it might be something to ignore. // **단서 2** 누군가에게는 주요한 뉴스 사건이지만
                                                                        다른 사람에게는 무시할 만한 사건임
그들에게는 / 그것이 주요한 뉴스 사건이지만 / 기자에게는 / 그것이 무시할 만한 것일 수도 있다 //

- newsworthy ⓐ 뉴스 가치가 있는, 뉴스거리가 되는
- define ⓥ 정의하다, 규정하다
- regardless of ~에 상관없이[구애받지 않고]
- transmission ⓝ 방송, 전송, 전염
- struggle ⓥ 분투하다, 애쓰다
- ignore ⓥ 무시하다
- major ⓐ 주요한, 중대한

뉴스 가치가 있는 사건과 뉴스 간에는 차이가 있다. 뉴스가 종종 그 자체로는 뉴스 가치가 없는 사건에 관한 것이듯이, 뉴스 가치가 있는 사건이 반드시 뉴스가 되지는 않을 것이다. 우리는 그것이 뉴스 가치가 있는 사건에 대한 것인지와 상관없이, 뉴스를 뉴스 매체에 기록되는 사건으로 규정할 수 있다. 비록 그 특정 이야기가 같은 시기에 발생하였지만 선정되지 못한 다른 모든 일들 중에서 선정된 이유를 우리가 이해하려고 몹시 애쓸지라도, 그것의 전송이라는 바로 그 사실이 그것이 뉴스로 간주됨을 의미한다. 뉴스 선정은 **주관적**이어서 일부 사람들에게 뉴스 가치가 있어 보이는 모든 사건이 뉴스가 되지는 않는다. 모든 기자들은 누군가가 '내가 당신을 위한 엄청난 이야기를 가지고 있어'라는 말로 접근하는 시나리오에 익숙하다. 그들에게는 그것이 주요한 뉴스 사건이지만, 기자에게는 그것이 무시할 만한 것일 수도 있다.

다음 빈칸에 들어갈 말로 가장 적절한 것을 고르시오.

①**subjective** 사람마다 생각이 다름
   주관적인
② passive 누가 시켜서 뉴스로 만드는 것이
   수동적인   아님
③ straightforward 뉴스 선정이 간단하다는
   복잡하지 않은   것이 아님
④ consistent 사람마다 다르므로 일관적이지
   일관적인   않음
⑤ crucial 뉴스 선정이 중요하다는 내용이 아님
   중요한

왜 정답? [정답률 67%]

뉴스 가치가 있는 사건과 뉴스 사이에는 차이가 있다면서 뉴스 가치가 있는 사건이 반드시 뉴스가 되지는 않는다는 내용으로 글을 시작한 후, 누군가에게는 뉴스 가치가 있어 보이는 사건이 기자나 다른 사람에게는 무시할 만한 사건일 수도 있다고 한 것으로 보아 뉴스 선정이 ① '주관적이라는' 점을 설명하는 글이다.

왜 오답?

② 뉴스 선정을 능동적으로 하는지 아니면 누가 시켜서 수동적으로 하는지를 설명하는 것이 아니다.
③ 어떤 복잡하지 않은 기준으로 뉴스를 선정한다는 내용이 아니다.
④ 사람마다 뉴스를 선정하는 기준이 다르다는 내용이므로 일관적인 것과는 정반대이다. **주의**
⑤ 뉴스 선정이 중요하다는 것을 설명하는 것이 아니다.

K 35 정답 ③ ＊사회적으로 규제되는 노동력 공유 정산

In labor-sharing groups, / people contribute labor to other people / on a regular basis / (for seasonal agricultural work / such as harvesting) /
노동력 공유 집단에서 / 사람들은 다른 사람들에게 노동력을 제공한다 / 정기적으로 / (계절적인 농사일을 위해 / 수확과 같은) /

or on an irregular basis / (in the event of a crisis / such as the need to rebuild a barn / damaged by fire). //
앞에 주격 관계대명사와 be동사가 생략됨
혹은 비정기적으로 / (위기 상황 발생시 / 헛간을 다시 지어야 하는 것과 같은 / 화재로 손상된) //

Labor sharing groups are part / of what has been called a "moral economy" / since no one keeps formal records / on how much any family puts in or takes out. //
부사절 접속사(이유)　단서 1 노동력 공유 집단은 '도덕적 경제'라고 불리는 것의 일부임
노동력 공유 집단은 일부이다 / '도덕적 경제'라고 불려 온 것의 / 아무도 공식적인 기록을 남기지 않으므로 / 어떤 가족이 얼마나 많이 투입하거나 가져갔는지에 대해 //

Instead, / accounting is **socially regulated**. //
대신에 / 정산은 사회적으로 규제된다//

선행사(주격 관계대명사와 be동사는 생략됨)
The group has a sense of moral community / based on years of trust and sharing. //
단서 2 노동력 공유가 사회적 응집성을 구성하는 주요 경제적 요소임
그 집단은 도덕적 공동체 의식을 가지고 있다 / 다년간의 신뢰와 나눔을 바탕으로 하는 //

In a certain community of North America, / labor sharing is a major economic factor / of social cohesion. //
북미의 특정 지역 사회에서는 / 노동력 공유가 주요 경제적 요소이다 / 사회적 응집성의 //

When a family needs a new barn / or faces repair work / that
부사절 접속사(때)　선행사　주격
requires group labor, / a barn-raising party is called. // 관계대명사
한 가족이 새 헛간을 필요로 할 때 / 또는 수리 작업에 직면할 때 / 단체 노동력을 요하는 / 헛간 조성 모임이 소집된다 //

Many families show up / to help. //
여러 가족이 온다 / 도우러 //

Adult men provide manual labor, / and adult women provide food / for the event. //
성인 남성은 육체노동을 제공하고 / 성인 여성은 음식을 제공한다 / 행사를 위한 //

Later, / when another family needs help, / they call on the same people. //
나중에 / 다른 가족이 도움이 필요할 때 / 그들은 같은 사람들을 부른다 //

- contribute ⓥ 제공하다, 기여하다 • labor ⓝ 노동력
- on a regular basis 정기적으로 • agricultural ⓐ 농업의
- harvest ⓥ 수확하다 • crisis ⓝ 위기 상황
- rebuild ⓥ 다시 세우다, 다시 조립하다 • barn ⓝ 헛간
- accounting ⓝ 회계 • regulate ⓥ 규제하다 • repair ⓥ 수리하다
- manual ⓐ 육체노동의, 수동의 • call on 요청하다
- legally ⓐ 법적으로

노동력 공유 집단에서 사람들은 정기적으로(수확과 같은 계절적인 농사일을 위해) 혹은 비정기적으로(화재로 손상된 헛간을 다시 지어야 하는 것과 같은 위기 상황 발생시) 다른 사람들에게 노동력을 제공한다. 아무도 어떤 가족이 얼마나 많이 투입하고 얼마나 많이 가져갔는지에 대해 공식적인 기록을 남기지 않으므로, 노동력 공유 집단은 '도덕적 경제'라고 불려 온 것의 일부이다. 대신에, 정산은 **사회적으로 규제된다**. 그 집단은 다년간의 신뢰와 나눔을 바탕으로 하는 도덕적 공동체 의식을 가지고 있다. 북미의 특정 지역 사회에서는 노동력 공유가 사회적 응집성의 주요 경제적 요소이다. 한 가족이 새 헛간이 필요하거나 단체 노동력을 요하는 수리 작업에 직면할 때, 헛간 조성 모임이 소집된다. 여러 가족이 도우러 온다. 성인 남성은 육체노동을 제공하고, 성인 여성은 행사를 위한 음식을 제공한다. 나중에, 다른 가족이 도움이 필요할 때, 그들은 같은 사람들을 부른다.

다음 빈칸에 들어갈 말로 가장 적절한 것을 고르시오.

① legally established 도덕적으로 정산됨
　법적으로 확립된다
② regularly reported 보고의 대상이 없음
　정기적으로 보고된다
③ socially regulated 도움을 받으면 도움을 줘야 한다는 도덕적 기준
　사회적으로 규제된다
④ manually calculated 수동 계산인지 자동 계산인지가 핵심이 아님
　수동으로 계산된다
⑤ carefully documented 기록을 남기지 않는다고 했음
　신중하게 문서화된다

왜 정답? [정답률 56%]

빈칸 문장과 그 앞뒤 문장	아무도 어떤 가족이 얼마나 많이 투입하거나 가져갔는지에 대해 공식적인 기록을 남기지 않으므로, 노동력 공유 집단은 '도덕적 경제'라고 불려 온 것의 일부이다. 대신에, 정산은 _____. 그 집단은 다년간의 신뢰와 나눔을 바탕으로 하는 도덕적 공동체 의식을 가지고 있다.

➡ 어떤 가족이 얼마나 많이 투입하거나 가져갔는지에 대한 공식적인 기록이 없는데, 노동력 공유의 정산이 어떻게 이루어지는지가 빈칸에 들어가야 한다.

➡ '도덕적 경제', '도덕적 공동체 의식'이 언급된 것으로 보아, 정산이 도덕적 기준에 의해 이루어짐을 알 수 있다.
도덕: 사회의 구성원들이 양심, 사회적 여론, 관습 등에 비추어 스스로 마땅히 지켜야 할 행동 준칙이나 규범

이어지는 문장	노동력 공유가 사회적 응집성의 주요 경제적 요소이다.

▶ 노동력 공유를 통해 사회적으로 응집된다는 것이므로, 정산은 ③ '사회적으로 규제된다'고 할 수 있다.

왜 오답?

① 법적으로가 아니라 도덕적으로 정산된다는 것을 설명하는 글이다.
② a regular basis, an irregular basis 등이 언급된 것으로 만든 오답이다.
④ 누가 얼마의 도움을 주고받았는지가 구체적으로 계산되지 않는다.
⑤ 아무도 공식적인 기록을 남기지 않는다고 했다.

K 36 정답 ② ＊바우어새의 예술 감상

Animals arguably make art. //
동물은 거의 틀림없이 예술을 만든다 //
복수 주어

복수 동사
The male bowerbirds of New Guinea and Australia / dedicate huge fractions / of their time and energy /
전치사　동명사구
뉴기니와 오스트레일리아의 수컷 바우어새는 / 큰 부분을 바친다 / 그들의 시간과 에너지의 /

to creating elaborate structures / from twigs, flowers, berries, beetle wings, and even colorful trash. //
정교한 구조물을 만드는 데 / 나뭇가지, 꽃, 딸기류, 딱정벌레 날개 그리고 심지어 다채로운 잡동사니로부터 //

These are the backdrops / to their complex mating dances, /
계속적 용법의 주격 관계대명사 전치사　명사구
which include / acrobatic moves and even imitations / of other species. //
이것들은 배경이며 / 그들의 복잡한 짝짓기 춤을 위한 / 그것은 포함한다 / 그 춤은 곡예 동작과 심지어 모방까지 / 다른 종들의 //

앞에 목적격 관계대명사가 생략됨
What's most amazing / about the towers and "bowers" / they
단수 동사　주격 보어절 접속사
construct / is that they aren't stereotyped / like a beehive or hummingbird nest. //
가장 놀라운 점은 / 탑과 '바우어'의 / 그들이 지은 / 그것들이 정형화되어 있지 않다는 것이다 / 벌집이나 벌새 둥지처럼 //

Each one is different. //
각각의 것은 다르다 //

주어
Artistic skill, / along with fine craftsbirdship, / is rewarded by
동사
the females. //
예술적 기술은 / 새의 정교한 장인 정신과 함께 / 암컷에 의해 보상받는다 //

정답 및 해설 **211**

Many researchers suggest / these displays are used by the
females / to gauge the cognitive abilities / of her potential

mates, / 단서1 바우어가 잠재적 짝의 능력을 측정하는 데 사용된다고 말함
~~suggest가 제안의 의미로 쓰인 것이 아님~~
많은 연구원들은 말한다 / 이 과시가 암컷에 의해 이용된다고 / 인지적 능력을 측정하기
위해서 / 자신의 잠재적 짝의 /

but Darwin thought / that she was actually attracted / to their

beauty. // 단서2 사실은 바우어의 아름다움 그 자체에 끌린 것이라고 생각함
하지만 다윈은 생각했다 / 암컷이 실제로 끌렸다고 / 그것들의 '아름다움'에 //

In other words, / the bowers **aren't simply signals** / of mate

quality; /
다시 말해 / 바우어는 단순히 신호만인 것은 아니다 / 짝의 자질의 /

they are appreciated by the females / for their own sake, / much
부사절 접속사(~처럼)
as we appreciate / a painting or a bouquet of spring flowers. //
그것들은 암컷에 의해 감상된다 / 그 자체의 목적을 위해 / 우리가 감상하는 것처럼 / 그림이나
봄꽃 한 다발을 //

A 2013 study looked / at whether bowerbirds / that did better
          명사절 접속사   주격 관계대명사
on cognitive tests / were more successful / at attracting mates. //
2013년의 한 연구는 살펴보았다 / 바우어새가 / 인지 검사에서 더 잘했던 / 더
성공적이었는지를 / 짝을 유혹하는 데 //

They were not, / suggesting / whatever the females are looking
              〈부정〉의 부사절을 이끄는 복합 관계대명사
for, / it isn't a straightforward indicator / of cognitive ability. //
그들은 그러지 않았고 / 이것은 시사한다 / 암컷이 찾는 것이 무엇이든지 / 그것이 직접적인
지표는 아니라는 것을 / 인지 능력의 //

- • arguably [ad] 거의 틀림없이 • dedicate ⓥ 바치다, 전념하다
- • fraction ⓝ 부분, 분수 • elaborate ⓐ 정교한, 정성을 들인
- • twig ⓝ 나뭇가지 • backdrop ⓝ 배경 • acrobatic ⓐ 곡예의
- • imitation ⓝ 모방 • beehive ⓝ 벌집 • hummingbird ⓝ 벌새
- • gauge ⓥ 측정하다 • cognitive ⓐ 인식의
- • appreciate ⓥ 감상하다 • for one's own sake 자신을 위해
- • straightforward ⓐ 간단한, 솔직한 • indicator ⓝ 지표
- • reproduction ⓝ 번식 • aggressiveness ⓝ 공격성

동물은 거의 틀림없이 예술을 만든다. 뉴기니와 오스트레일리아의 수컷
바우어새는 나뭇가지, 꽃, 딸기류, 딱정벌레 날개 그리고 심지어 다채로운
잡동사니로부터 정교한 구조물을 만드는 데 그들의 시간과 에너지의 큰 부분을
바친다. 이것들은 그들의 복잡한 짝짓기 춤을 위한 배경이며 그 춤은 곡예
동작과 심지어 다른 종들의 모방까지 포함한다. 그들이 지은 탑과 '바우어'의
가장 놀라운 점은 그것들이 벌집이나 벌새 둥지처럼 정형화되어 있지 않다는
것이다. 각각의 것은 다르다. 새의 정교한 장인 정신과 함께 예술적 기술은
암컷에 의해 보상받는다. 많은 연구원들은 이 과시가 자신의 잠재적 짝의
인지적 능력을 측정하기 위해서 암컷에 의해 이용된다고 말하지만, 다윈은
암컷이 실제로 그것들의 '아름다움'에 끌렸다고 생각했다. 다시 말해, 바우어는
단순히 짝의 자질의 신호만인 것은 아니다. 그것들은 우리가 그림이나 봄꽃
한 다발을 감상하는 것처럼 그 자체의 목적을 위해 암컷에 의해 감상된다.
2013년의 한 연구는 인지 검사에서 더 잘했던 바우어새가 짝을 유혹하는 데
더 성공적이었는지를 살펴보았다. 그들은 그러지 않았고, 이것은 암컷이 찾는
것이 무엇이든지 그것이 인지 능력의 직접적인 지표는 아니라는 것을 시사한다.

다음 빈칸에 들어갈 말로 가장 적절한 것을 고르시오.

① block any possibility of reproduction 번식을 위해 짝을 고르는 데 사용되기도 함
  번식의 어떠한 가능성도 차단한다
② aren't simply signals of mate quality
  단순히 짝의 자질의 신호만인 것은 아니다 짝의 인지적 능력을 측정하기 위한 것만이 아님
③ hardly sustain their forms long enough
  그들의 형태를 충분히 길게 지속하지 않는다 그들의 형태에 대한 언급은 없음
④ don't let the mating competition overheat
  짝짓기 경쟁이 과열되게 하지 않는다 짝짓기 경쟁의 과열은 언급되지 않음
⑤ can be a direct indicator of aggressiveness
  공격성의 직접적인 지표일 수 있다 바우어가 공격성을 나타내는 것은 아님

왜 정답? [정답률 61%]

빈칸 문장의 앞 문장	**많은 연구원**: 이 과시(바우어)는 암컷이 잠재적 짝의 인지적 능력을 측정하는 데 사용됨 **다윈**: 사실 암컷은 바우어의 아름다움 그 자체에 끌리는 것임
빈칸 문장	다시 말해(In other words), 바우어는 _____. 우리가 그림이나 봄꽃 한 다발을 감상하는 것처럼 암컷은 그것을 감상한다.

⇒ 빈칸 앞 문장에서 많은 연구원의 생각(암컷은 바우어를 잠재적 짝의 인지적 능력을
측정하는 데 사용함)을 뒤집는 다윈의 의견(암컷은 바우어의 아름다움 그 자체에
끌리는 것임)이 제시된다.

In other words로 연결되는 빈칸 문장 역시 앞 문장과 같은 문맥이어야 한다.

▶ 따라서 빈칸에 들어갈 말은 ② '단순히 짝의 자질의 신호만인 것은 아니다'가
적절하다.

왜 오답?

① 바우어가 짝을 찾는 데 아예 사용되지 않는다는 것이 아니며, 짝짓기를 막는다는
내용도 아니다.

③ 바우어의 형태가 정형화되어 있지 않다는 등의 언급은 있으나, 바우어의 형태가
글의 주제인 것은 아니다. (▶ 이유: 바우어의 형태는 일부 내용이므로 글의 중심
내용과 구분해야 함)

④ 바우어를 통해 짝짓기 경쟁이 과열되지 않는다는 내용은 없다.

⑤ 바우어새의 공격성에 대한 언급은 없다.

K 37 정답 ⑤ ＊학습에 더 의존적인 먹이 찾기

              복수 주어
Innate behaviors / used for finding food, / such as grazing,
                                    복수 동사
scavenging, or hunting, / are more dependent on learning / than
비교의 두 대상
behaviors / used to consume food. // 단서1 먹이를 먹는 행동보다 먹이를 찾는
                                     행동이 학습에 더 의존적임
내재된 행동은 / 먹이를 찾는 데 사용되는 / 풀을 뜯어 먹기, 동물 사체를 찾아다니기, 또는
사냥하기와 같이 / 학습에 더 의존적이다 / 행동보다 / 음식을 먹는 데 사용되는 /
                                       to부정사의 수동태(to be p.p.)
Mating, nesting, eating, and prey-killing behaviors / tend to be
governed more / by instinct. // 단서2 먹이를 죽이거나 먹는 행동은 본능에 더 지배됨
짝짓기, 둥지 틀기, 먹기, 그리고 먹이를 죽이는 행동은 / 더 지배되는 경향이 있다 / 본능에
의해
          단수 주어   단수 동사
The greater dependence on learning / to find food / makes
animals in the wild / **more flexible and able to adapt / to a
variety of environments**. //
학습에의 더 큰 의존은 / 먹이를 찾기 위해 / 야생의 동물들을 만든다 / 더 유연하고 적응할 수
있게 / 다양한 환경에
주어, 선행사(뒤에 주격 관계대명사와 be동사 생략됨)   동사
Behaviors / used to kill or consume food / can be the same / in
any environment. // 단서3 먹이를 죽이거나 먹는 행동은 어떤 환경에서도 동일함
행동은 / 먹이를 죽이거나 먹기 위해 사용되는 / 동일할 수 있다 / 어떤 환경에서도 //

Ernst Mayr, an evolutionary biologist, / called these different
behavioral systems / "open" or "closed" to the effects of
experience. //
진화 생물학자인 Ernst Mayr는 / 이러한 다른 행동 체계들을 칭했다 / 경험의 영향에 대해
'개방적' 또는 '폐쇄적'이라고 /
주어   동사
A lion / hunting her prey / is an example of an open system. //
사자는 / 사냥감을 사냥하는 / 개방적 체계의 한 예이다 //

The hunting female lion / recognizes her prey from a distance /
and approaches it carefully. //
사냥하는 암사자는 / 멀리서 먹이를 알아보고 / 조심스럽게 그것에게 다가간다 //

Charles Herrick, a neurobiologist, wrote, / "the details of the
복수 동사(완전자동사)   앞에 관계부사가 생략됨
hunt vary / every time she hunts. //
신경 생물학자인 Charles Herrick은 썼다 / "사냥의 세부적인 것들은 다르다 / 그것이
사냥할 때마다 //

Therefore / no combination of simple reflex arcs / laid down in
the nervous system / will be adequate / to meet / the infinite
_{부사적 용법(adequate 수식)}
variations of the requirements / for obtaining food." //
따라서 / 단순한 반사궁들의 어떤 조합도 / 신경계에 있는 / 충분하지 않을 것이다"라고 /
충족시키기에 / 요건의 무한한 변화를 / 먹이를 획득하기 위한 //

- innate ⓐ 내재된 · graze ⓥ 풀을 뜯다
- dependent on ~에 의존하는 · consume ⓥ 섭취하다
- mating ⓝ 짝짓기 · nest ⓥ 둥지를 틀다 · prey ⓝ 먹이
- tend to ~하는 경향이 있다 · governed ⓐ 지배되는
- instinct ⓝ 본능 · flexible ⓐ 유연한 · behavioral ⓐ 행동의
- neurobiologist ⓝ 신경 생물학자 · evolutionary ⓐ 진화의
- vary ⓥ 서로 다르다 · combination ⓝ 결합
- nervous system ⓝ 신경계 · adequate ⓐ 적합한
- infinite ⓐ 무한한 · requirement ⓝ 요건

풀을 뜯어 먹기, 동물 사체를 찾아다니기, 또는 사냥하기와 같이, 먹이를 찾는
데 사용되는 내재된 행동은 음식을 먹는 데 사용되는 행동보다 학습에 더
의존적이다. 짝짓기, 둥지 틀기, 먹기, 그리고 먹이를 죽이는 행동은 더 본능에
의해 지배되는 경향이 있다. 먹이를 찾기 위해 학습에 더 크게 의존하는 것은
야생의 동물들을 <u>더 유연하게 그리고 다양한 환경에 적응할 수 있게</u> 한다.
먹이를 죽이거나 먹기 위해 사용되는 행동은 어떤 환경에서도 동일할 수 있다.
진화 생물학자인 Ernst Mayr는 이러한 다른 행동 체계들을 경험의 영향에
대해 '개방적' 또는 '폐쇄적'이라고 칭했다. 사냥감을 사냥하는 사자는 개방적
체계의 한 예이다. 사냥하는 암사자는 멀리서 먹이를 알아보고 조심스럽게
그것에게 다가간다. 신경 생물학자인 Charles Herrick은 "사냥할 때 세부적인
것들은 그것이 사냥할 때마다 다르다. 따라서 신경계에 있는 단순한 반사궁들의
어떤 조합도 먹이를 획득하기 위한 요건의 무한한 변화를 충족시키기에
충분하지 않을 것이다."라고 썼다.

다음 빈칸에 들어갈 말로 가장 적절한 것을 고르시오. [3점]

① less cooperative with others in their community
그들의 집단에서 다른 개체들과 덜 협력적이게   동물의 협력에 대한 언급은 없음
② less focused on monitoring predators' approaches
포식자의 접근을 추적 관찰하는 데 덜 집중하게   사냥하는 암사자로 만든 오답
③ more intelligent to build their natural surroundings
그들의 자연 환경을 구축하기에 더 총명하게   환경에 적응하는 것임
④ more sensitive to visual information than any other stimuli
다른 어떤 자극보다 시각적 정보에 더 민감하게   정보의 종류에 대한 내용이 아님
⑤ more flexible and able to adapt to a variety of environments
더 유연하고 다양한 환경에 적응할 수 있게   어떤 환경에서도 동일한 행동과 대조됨

왜 정답? [정답률 49%]

빈칸 문장	먹이를 찾는 데 학습에 더 크게 의존하는 것은 야생의 동물을 _____ 하게 만든다.
먹이를 죽이거나 먹는 행동	본능에 지배되는 경향이 있음 **단서2** → 어떤 환경에서도 동일할 수 있음 **단서3**
먹이를 찾는 행동	· 학습에 더 의존적임 **단서1** → ?

➡ 먹이를 찾는(사냥하는) 행동과 먹이를 죽이거나 먹는 행동이 대조되는 글이다.
  먹이를 죽이거나 먹는 행동: 본능에 지배되므로 어떤 환경에서도 동일할 수 있음
  먹이를 찾는 행동: 학습에 더 의존함 → 환경이 달라지면 학습하는 바도 달라짐
  ▶ 학습에 더 크게 의존하는 것은 동물을 ⑤ '더 유연하게 그리고 다양한 환경에
  적응할 수 있게' 만드는 것이다.

왜 오답?

① 사냥을 위한 동물의 협력에 대한 내용은 없다.
② 사냥하는 암사자를 언급한 것으로 만든 오답이다.
③ 자신을 둘러싼 자연 환경에 맞게 학습한다는 내용이다.
④ 자극, 정보의 종류에 대해 설명하는 글이 아니다.

K 38 정답 ② ＊상징의 사용, 나아가 글자의 발달

In the classic model of the Sumerian economy, / the temple
_{주어}
functioned / as an administrative authority / governing
_{동사}   _{an administrative authority를 수식하는 현재분사구}
commodity production, collection, and redistribution. //
수메르 경제의 전형적 모델에서 / 사원은 기능했다 / 행정 당국으로서 / 상품의 생산, 수집, 그
리고 재분배를 관장하는 //

The discovery of administrative tablets / from the temple
complexes at Uruk / suggests /
행정용 (점토)판의 발견은 / Uruk의 사원 단지에서 나온 / 시사한다 /

that token use and consequently writing evolved / as a tool / of
_{생략 가능한 명사절 접속사}   _{주어}   _{완전자동사}
centralized economic governance. //
상징의 사용, 그리고 결과적으로 글자가 발달했다는 것을 / 도구로서 / 중앙 집권화된 경제 지
배의 //

Given the lack of archaeological evidence / from Uruk-period
_{prep ~을 고려해 볼 때}
domestic sites, / it is not clear / whether individuals also used
_{가주어}   _{진주어절 접속사}
the system / for **personal agreements**. //
고고학적 증거의 부족을 고려하면 / Uruk 시기 가정집의 터에서 나온 / ~은 명확하지 않다 /
개인들이 또한 그 체계를 사용했는지는 / 사적인 합의를 위해 //

For that matter, / it is not clear / how widespread literacy was /
_{가주어}   _{진주어절}
at its beginnings. //
그 문제와 관련하여 / ~은 명확하지 않다 / 읽고 쓰는 능력이 얼마나 널리 퍼져 있었는지는 /
그것의 초기에 //

The use / of identifiable symbols and pictograms / on the early
_{주어}
tablets / is consistent with administrators /
사용은 / 인식 가능한 기호와 그림 문자의 / 초기의 판에서의 / 행정가들과 일치한다 /

needing a lexicon / that was mutually intelligible / by literate
_{선행사}   _{주격 관계대명사}
and nonliterate parties. //
어휘 목록을 필요로 했던 / 서로 이해될 수 있는 / 읽고 쓸 줄 아는 측과 읽고 쓸 수 없는 측
에 의해 //
_{과거 사실에 대한 강한 추측을 나타내는 must have p.p.}
As cuneiform script became more abstract, / literacy must have
_{부사절 접속사}   _{부사적 용법(목적)}
become increasingly important / to ensure / one understood /
what he or she had agreed to. // **단서** 읽고 쓰는 능력이 중요해진 것은 자신이 합의한
것을 이해한다는 것을 확실히 하기 위해서임
쐐기 문자가 더욱 추상적으로 되면서 / 읽고 쓰는 능력이 점점 더 중요해졌음이 틀림없다 / 확
실히 하기 위해 / 한 사람이 이해한다는 것을 / 자신이 합의했던 것을 //

- temple ⓝ 신전, 사원 · function ⓥ 기능하다, 작용하다
- administrative ⓐ 관리[행정]상의 · authority ⓝ 당국, 권한
- govern ⓥ 통치하다, 다스리다, 지배하다 · commodity ⓝ 상품, 물품
- redistribution ⓝ 재분배, 재배급 · discovery ⓝ 발견, 발견된 것[사람]
- complex ⓝ (건물) 단지, (관련 있는 것들의) 덩어리[집합체]
- token ⓝ 표시, 징표 · consequently 🇦🇩 그 결과, 따라서
- evolve ⓥ (점진적으로) 발달[진전]하다 · centralize ⓥ 중앙 집권화하다
- governance ⓝ 지배, 관리 · domestic ⓐ 국내의, 가정(용)의
- literacy ⓝ 글을 읽고 쓸 줄 아는 능력
- identifiable ⓐ 인식 가능한, 알아볼 수 있는 · pictogram ⓝ 그림 문자
- consistent ⓐ 일치하는, 한결같은 · mutually 🇦🇩 서로, 상호 간에
- literate ⓐ 글을 읽고 쓸 줄 아는
- party ⓝ 정당, 단체, (소송·계약 등의) 당사자
- abstract ⓐ 관념적인, 추상적인 · ensure ⓥ 반드시 ~하게 하다, 보장하다
- religious ⓐ 종교의 · communal ⓐ 공동의, 공용의

수메르 경제의 전형적 모델에서 사원은 상품의 생산, 수집, 그리고 재분배를 관
장하는 행정 당국으로서 기능했다. Uruk의 사원 단지에서 나온 행정용 (점토)
판의 발견은 상징의 사용, 그리고 결과적으로 글자가 중앙 집권화된 경제 지배
의 도구로 발달했다는 것을 시사한다. Uruk 시기 가정집의 터에서 나온 고고학
적 증거가 부족하다는 것을 고려하면, 개인들이 또한 **사적인 합의**를 위해 그 체
계를 사용했는지는 명확하지 않다. 그 문제와 관련하여, 읽고 쓰는 능력이 그것
의 초기에 얼마나 널리 퍼져 있었는지 명확하지 않다. 초기의 판에서의 인식 가
능한 기호와 그림 문자의 사용은 행정가들이 읽고 쓸 줄 아는 측과 읽고 쓸 수
없는 측이 서로 이해할 수 있는 어휘 목록이 필요했던 것과 일치한다. 쐐기 문
자가 더욱 추상적으로 되면서, 읽고 쓰는 능력이 자신이 합의했던 것을 이해한
다는 것을 확실히 하기 위해 점점 더 중요해졌음이 틀림없다.

① religious events 사원(temple) 등이 언급된 것으로 만든 오답임
   종교 행사
②personal agreements 자신이 합의한 것을 이해한다는 것을 확실히 하기 위해
   사적인 합의 상징과 글자를 사용함
③ communal responsibilities 공동으로 책임진다는 등의 내용은 언급되지 않음
   공동 책임
④ historical records 역사적 기록을 위해 판에 기록한 것이 아님
   역사적 기록
⑤ power shifts governing이 언급된 것으로 만든 오답
   권력 이동

> **왜 정답?** [정답률 57%]

빈칸 문장은 개인들도 '무엇'을 위해 그 체계를 사용했는지가 명확하지 않다는 내용이다. 행정가, 행정 당국은 '어떤 목적'을 위해 그 체계를 사용했는데, 개인들도 그 목적으로 사용했는지는 명확하지 않다는 것이므로 행정가, 행정 당국의 그 체계의 사용 목적을 확인해야 한다. '그 체계'란 앞 문장에 나온 상징, 나아가 글자의 사용을 가리키는데, 마지막 문장에서 자신이 합의한 것을 이해하고 있다는 것을 확실히 하기 위해 읽고 쓰는 능력이 점점 더 중요해졌다고 했으므로, 그 체계를 사용한 목적은 ② '사적인 합의'라고 할 수 있다.

> **왜 오답?**

①, ④ 종교 행사나 역사적 기록을 위해 상징, 나아가 글자를 사용했다는 것이 아니다.
③, ⑤ 공동의 책임이나 권력의 이동에 대해서는 언급되지 않았다.

K 39 정답 ② ＊혁명의 승리파와 과학의 혁명적 재구성

The revolution's victorious party can claim / to have resolved / the fundamental anomalies of the old paradigm /
혁명의 승리파는 주장할 수 있다 / 해결해 왔고 / 낡은 패러다임의 근본적인 변칙을 / ┗to부정사의 완료형(to have p.p.)
and to have renewed / the prospects for successful research / governed by shared assumptions. //
새롭게 해 왔다고 / 성공적인 연구의 전망을 / 공유된 가정에 의해 좌우된 //

Indeed, / the new community typically rewrites the textbooks, / and retells its own history, / to reflect this point of view. //
┗━━━병렬 구조━━━┛   부사적 용법(목적)
실제로 / 새로운 공동체는 전형적으로 교과서를 다시 쓰고 / 자신의 역사를 다시 이야기한다 / 이러한 관점을 반영하기 위해 //

But from the standpoint / of the losers, or even of those / who
                                                       선행사   주격 관계대명사
look on impartially, / 단서 1 혁명 승리파의 재작성: 변화의 장점을 평가하는 중립적인 기준이
                       없음 → 진보에 대한 진정한 주장이 없는 변화로 보일 수 있음
그러나 관점에서 / 패배자들이나 심지어 사람들의 / 공정하게 바라보는 //

such rewritings might seem to mark change / without any
                                          선행사
genuine claim to progress, / because there is no neutral standard
┗전치사+관계대명사┛
/ by which to assess / the merits of the change. //
그러한 재작성은 변화를 나타내는 것처럼 보일지 모른다 / 진보에 대한 진정한 주장 없이 / 중립적인 기준이 없기 때문에 / 그것으로 평가하는 / 그 변화의 장점을 //

The resulting body of knowledge / is in any case not cumulative, /
그 결과적인 지식의 체계는 / 어떠한 경우에도 누적되지 않는다 /
부사절 접속사(이유)
since much / of what was previously known / (or merely
          주어
believed) / had to be excluded / without ever having been
                동사
conclusively refuted. ┗동명사의 완료형 수동태(having been p.p.)
왜냐하면 많은 부분이 / 이전에 알려졌던 것의 / (또는 단순히 믿어졌던 것의) / 배제되어야 했기 때문에 / 한 번도 확실하게 반박되어 보지 않은 채 //
단서 2 과학의 혁명적 재구성에 대해 진리를 지향하는 것으로 말할 수 없음
One likewise cannot plausibly talk / about revolutionary
reconstitutions of science / as aiming toward truth, /
마찬가지로 우리는 그럴듯하게 말할 수 없다 / 과학의 혁명적 재구성에 대해 / 진리를 지향하는 것으로 /
등위접속사(이유) ┓ 단서 3 혁명 승리파의 재작성과 마찬가지의 이유임
for similarly, / there can be no **impartial formulation of**
standards / for its assessment. //
왜냐하면 비슷하게도 / 기준의 공정한 공식화는 있을 수 없기 때문에 / 그것을 평가하기 위한 //

주어
The available justification of scientific knowledge / after revolutions, / couched in new terms / according to newly
                                              동사
instituted standards, / may well be sufficient, /
과학 지식의 유효한 정당화는 / 혁명 이후의 / 새로운 용어로 표현된 / 새로 제정된 기준에 따라 / 충분할 것 같다 /

but perhaps / only because these standards and terms / are now inevitably our own. //
하지만 아마도 / 단지 이러한 기준과 용어가 / 이제 불가피하게 우리 자신의 것이기 때문일 것이다 //

- revolution ⓝ 혁명   · victorious ⓐ 승리한   · claim ⓥ 주장하다
- resolve ⓥ 해결하다   · fundamental ⓐ 근본적인
- prospect ⓝ 전망   · paradigm ⓝ 패러다임
- assumption ⓝ 가정   · point of view 관점
- standpoint ⓝ 관점   · impartially ⓐⓓ 공정하게
- genuine ⓐ 진정한   · progress ⓝ 진보   · neutral ⓐ 중립의
- assess ⓥ 평가하다   · cumulative ⓐ 누적되는
- exclude ⓥ 배제하다   · conclusively ⓐⓓ 결론적으로
- justification ⓝ 정당화   · inevitably ⓐⓓ 불가피하게

혁명의 승리파는 낡은 패러다임의 근본적인 변칙을 해결해 왔고 공유된 가정에 의해 좌우된 성공적인 연구의 전망을 새롭게 해 왔다고 주장할 수 있다. 실제로, 새로운 공동체는 이러한 관점을 반영하기 위해 전형적으로 교과서를 다시 쓰고, 자신의 역사를 다시 이야기한다. 그러나 패배자들이나, 심지어 공정하게 바라보는 사람들의 관점에서, 그러한 재작성은 진보에 대한 진정한 주장 없이 변화를 나타내는 것처럼 보일지 모르는데, 왜냐하면 그 변화의 장점을 평가하는 중립적인 기준이 없기 때문이다. 이전에 알려졌던 것(또는 단순히 믿어졌던 것)의 많은 부분이 한 번도 확실하게 반박되어 보지 않은 채 배제되어야 했기 때문에, 그 결과적인 지식의 체계는 어떠한 경우에도 누적되지 않는다. 마찬가지로 우리는 과학의 혁명적 재구성을 진리를 지향하는 것으로 그럴듯하게 말할 수 없는데, 왜냐하면 비슷하게도 **과학의 평가를 위한 기준의 공정한 공식화**는 있을 수 없기 때문이다. 새로 제정된 기준에 따라 새로운 용어로 표현된 혁명 이후의 과학 지식의 유효한 정당화는 충분할 것 같으나, 아마도 단지 이러한 기준과 용어가 이제 불가피하게 우리 자신의 것이기 때문일 것이다.

다음 빈칸에 들어갈 말로 가장 적절한 것을 고르시오. [3점]

① official connection between scientists and policy makers
   과학자들과 정책 입안자들 사이의 공식적인 연관성   공식적으로 연관되었다는 말이 아님
② impartial formulation of standards for its assessment
   과학의 평가를 위한 기준의 공정한 공식화   변화의 장점을 평가하는 중립적인 기준과 같은 의미
③ incomplete terms to describe the reconstitutions
   재구성을 묘사하는 불완전한 용어들   용어의 문제가 아님
④ easy process to learn about new scientific theories
   새로운 과학적 이론들에 대해 배우는 쉬운 과정   혁명의 승리파와 연관되어야 함
⑤ strong belief that scientific progress benefits everyone
   과학적 발전이 모두에게 이롭다는 강한 믿음   '기준'과 관련된 언급이 포함되어야 함

> **왜 정답?** [정답률 43%]

혁명의 승리파	교과서를 다시 쓰고, 자신의 역사를 다시 이야기함 → 그러나 그러한 재작성은 진보에 대한 진정한 주장이 없는 변화로 보일 수 있음 단서 1 → 왜냐하면 그 변화의 장점을 평가하는 중립적인 기준이 없기 때문임
과학의 혁명적 재구성	마찬가지로(likely) 진리를 지향하는 것으로 말할 수 없음 → 왜냐하면, 유사하게(similarly), _____이 있을 수 없기 때문임

→ 혁명의 승리파가 가져온 변화가, 그 변화의 장점을 평가하는 중립적인 기준이 없기 때문에 진정한 주장이 없는 변화로 보일 수 있는 것처럼, 과학의 혁명적 재구성 역시 ② '과학의 평가를 위한 기준의 공정한 공식화'가 있을 수 없으므로 그것이 진리를 지향한다고 말할 수 없다는 내용이다.

왜 오답?

① 과학의 혁명적 재구성과 혁명의 승리파가 행한 재작성의 공통점을 설명하는 글이지, 과학자와 정책 입안자 사이에 공식적인 연관성이 있다는 내용이 아니다.

(▶◀ 이유: 혁명의 승리파를 단순히 정책 입안자와 연결시키면 안 되고, 글에 나온 내용에만 근거해 생각해야 함)

③ 용어가 불완전하기 때문이라는 언급은 없다.

④ 혁명의 승리파에 대해 이야기하는 글의 전반부에 해당 내용에 관한 언급이 없다.

⑤ 과학적 발전의 이점에 대한 믿음이 없어서 일어나는 일이 아니다.

K 40 정답 ④ ＊제2차 세계대전 이후의 변화

In the post-World War II years after 1945, / unparalleled
economic growth / fueled a building boom and a massive
migration / from the central cities / to the new suburban areas. //
1945년 이후 제2차 세계대전 이후 시절에 / 유례없는 경제 성장은 / 건축 붐과 대규모 이주를 부추겼다 / 중심 도시에서 / 새로운 교외 지역으로의 //

The suburbs were far more dependent / on the automobile,
/ signaling the shift / from primary dependence on public
transportation / to private cars. //
교외 지역은 훨씬 더 많이 의존했고 / 자동차에 / 전환을 알렸다 / 대중교통에 대한 주된 의존에서 / 자가용으로의 //

Soon this led / to the construction of better highways and
freeways / and the decline and even loss / of public
transportation. //
이것은 곧 이어졌다 / 더 나은 고속도로와 초고속도로의 건설과 / 감소, 심지어 쇠퇴까지로 / 대중교통의 //

With all of these changes / came a **privatization** of leisure. //
이러한 모든 변화와 함께 / 여가의 사유화가 이루어졌다 //

As more people owned their own homes, / with more space
inside / and lovely yards outside, /
더 많은 사람이 자신의 집을 소유함에 따라 / 내부 공간은 더 넓어지고 / 외부 정원은 더 아름다운 /

their recreation and leisure time / was increasingly centered /
around the home or, at most, the neighborhood. //
그들의 휴양과 여가 시간은 / 점점 더 집중되었다 / 집이나 기껏해야 이웃에 //

One major activity / of this home-based leisure / was watching
television. //
한 가지 주요 활동은 / 이러한 가정에 기반한 여가의 / TV를 시청하는 것이었다 //

No longer did one have to ride the trolly / to the theater / to
watch a movie; / similar entertainment was available / for free /
and more conveniently / from television. //
더 이상 전차를 타고 갈 필요가 없었다 / 극장까지 / 영화를 보기 위해 / 유사한 오락(물)이 이용 가능하게 되었다 / 무료로 / 그리고 더 편리하게 / 텔레비전을 통해 //

- fuel ⓥ 기름을 끼얹다; 부추기다
- massive ⓐ 대규모의
- central city 중심 도시
- suburban area 교외 지역
- suburb ⓝ 교외
- dependent on ~에 의존하는
- automobile ⓝ 자동차
- signal ⓥ 신호를 주다, 알리다
- shift ⓝ 전환
- public transportation 대중 교통
- freeway ⓝ 초고속도로
- decline ⓝ 감소
- loss ⓝ 쇠퇴
- leisure ⓝ 여가

1945년 이후 제2차 세계대전 이후 시절에 유례없는 경제 성장은 건축 붐과 중심 도시에서 새로운 교외 지역으로의 대규모 이주를 부추겼다. 교외 지역은 자동차에 훨씬 더 많이 의존했고, 대중교통에 대한 주된 의존에서 자가용으로의 전환을 알렸다. 이것은 곧 더 나은 고속도로와 초고속도로의 건설과 대중교통의 감소, 심지어 쇠퇴까지로 이어졌다. 이러한 모든 변화와 함께 여가의 사유화가 이루어졌다. 더 많은 사람이 내부 공간은 더 넓어지고 외부 정원은 더 아름다운 자신의 집을 소유함에 따라 그들의 휴양과 여가 시간은 점점 더 집이나 기껏해야 이웃에 집중되었다. 이러한 가정에 기반한 여가의 한 가지 주요 활동은 TV를 시청하는 것이었다. 더 이상 영화를 보기 위해 전차를 타고 극장까지 갈 필요가 없었고, 유사한 오락(물)이 텔레비전을 통해 무료로 그리고 더 편리하게 이용 가능하게 되었다.

다음 빈칸에 들어갈 말로 가장 적절한 것을 고르시오.

① downfall 몰락 어떻게 여가를 즐겼는지가 이어짐
② uniformity 획일성 모든 사람이 같은 여가를 즐겼다는 것이 아님
③ restoration 회복 이전에는 여가를 즐기지 못했다는 언급은 없음
④ privatization 사유화 가정에 기반한 여가를 즐기게 됨
⑤ customization 맞춤화 TV 시청이 맞춤 여가는 아님

왜 정답? [정답률 58%]

제2차 세계대전 이후의 변화	대중교통에서 자가용으로 전환됨
	• 휴양과 여가 시간이 집, 기껏해야 이웃에 집중됨
	• 극장에 가지 않고 집에서 텔레비전으로 유사한 오락(물)을 즐김

→ 대중교통에서 자가용으로 전환된 것처럼, 여가도 개인적으로 즐기게 되었다는 내용이다.

▶ 따라서 빈칸에는 ④ '사유화'가 적절하다.

왜 오답?

① 제2차 세계대전 이후로 사람들이 여가를 즐기지 않았다는 내용이 아니다.

② 다양한 여가를 즐겼다거나, 여가의 종류가 획일화되었다는 언급은 없다. 모든 사람들이 여가 시간에 TV를 시청했다는 의미가 아니라는 점에 주의해야 한다.

③ 이전에는 여가를 즐기지 못했다가 제2차 세계대전 이후로 여가를 즐기게 되었다는 말은 없다.

⑤ 여가 활동의 예시로 등장한 TV 시청이 맞춤화된 여가는 아니다.

K 41 정답 ④ ＊눈에 잘 띄지 않는 진보의 과정

Protopia is a state of becoming, / rather than a destination. //
프로토피아는 생성의 상태이다 / 목적지라기보다는 //

It is a process. //
그것은 과정이다 //

In the protopian mode, / things are better today / than they were
yesterday, / although only a little better. //
프로토피아적인 방식에서 / 상황이 오늘 더 낫다 / 그것이 어제 그랬던 것보다 / 비록 그저 약간 더 나을 뿐이라도 //

It is / incremental improvement or mild progress. //
그것은 ~이다 / 점진적인 개선이나 가벼운 진보 //

The "pro" in protopian stems / from the notions / of process and
progress. //
프로토피아적이라는 말에서 '프로'는 비롯된다 / 개념에서 / 과정과 진보라는 //

This subtle progress / is not dramatic, not exciting. //
이 미묘한 진보는 / 극적이지도 않고 자극적이지도 않다 //

It is easy to miss / because a protopia generates / almost as many
new problems / as new benefits. //
그것은 놓치기 쉽다 / 프로토피아는 발생시키기 때문에 / 거의 ~만큼 많은 새로운 문제를 / 새로운 이점만큼 //

The problems of today were caused / by yesterday's
technological successes, / and the technological solutions / to
today's problems / will cause the problems of tomorrow. //
오늘의 문제는 유발되었고 / 어제의 기술적 성공에 의해 / 기술적 해결책은 / 오늘의 문제에 대한 / 내일의 문제를 유발할 것이다 //

This circular expansion / of both problems and solutions / **hides
a steady accumulation** / **of small net benefits** / **over time.** //
이런 순환적 팽창은 / 문제와 해결책 둘 다의 / 꾸준한 축적을 보이지 않게 한다 / 작은 순이익의 / 시간이 지남에 따라 //

Ever since the Enlightenment and the invention of science, /
we've managed to create / a tiny bit more / than we've destroyed
each year. //
계몽주의와 과학의 발명 이래로 줄곧 / 우리는 가까스로 만들어 냈다 / 조금 더 많은 것을 / 우리가 매년 파괴해 온 것보다 //

But that few percent positive difference is compounded / over
decades / into what we might call civilization. //
그러나 그 작은 몇 퍼센트의 긍정적인 차이는 조합된다 / 수십 년에 걸쳐 / 우리가 문명이라고
부를 수 있는 것으로

Its benefits never star / in movies. // 단서4 그 순이익은 결코 돋보이지 않음
그것의 장점은 결코 주연을 맡아 돋보이지 않는다 / 영화에서 //

- state ⓝ 상태　　　・becoming ⓝ ((철학)) 생성　　　・destination ⓝ 목적지
- mode ⓝ 방식　　　・mild ⓐ (정도가) 심하지 않은, 가벼운
- stem from ~에서 비롯되다　　　・notion ⓝ 개념
- progress ⓝ 진전, 진척　　　・subtle ⓐ 미묘한　　　・dramatic ⓐ 극적인
- generate ⓥ 발생시키다　　　・technological ⓐ 기술적인
- circular ⓐ 순환적인　　　・expansion ⓝ 팽창, 확장
- Enlightenment ⓝ ((the)) 계몽주의　　　・civilization ⓝ 문명
- star ⓥ 주연을 맡아 돋보이다　　　・accumulation ⓝ 축적
- conceal ⓥ 감추다, 숨기다

프로토피아는 목적지라기보다는 생성의 상태이다. 그것은 과정이다. 프로토피아적인 방식에서는 어제보다 오늘, 비록 그저 약간 더 나아졌을 뿐이라도, 상황이 더 낫다. 그것은 점진적인 개선이나 가벼운 진보이다. 프로토피아적이라는 말에서 '프로'는 과정과 진보라는 개념에서 비롯된다. 이 미묘한 진보는 극적이지도 않고 자극적이지도 않다. 프로토피아는 거의 새로운 이점만큼 많은 새로운 문제를 발생시키기 때문에 그것을 놓치기 쉽다. 오늘의 문제는 어제의 기술적 성공이 가져온 것이고, 오늘의 문제에 대한 기술적 해결책은 내일의 문제를 유발할 것이다. 문제와 해결책 둘 다의 이런 순환적 팽창은 **시간이 지남에 따라 작은 순이익의 꾸준한 축적을 보이지 않게 한다.** 계몽주의와 과학의 발명 이래로 줄곧, 우리는 매년 파괴해 온 것보다 조금 더 많은 것을 가까스로 만들어 냈다. 그러나 그 작은 몇 퍼센트의 긍정적인 차이는 수십 년에 걸쳐 우리가 문명이라고 부를 수 있는 것으로 조합된다. 그것의 장점은 영화에서 주연을 맡아 돋보이는 법이 없다.

다음 빈칸에 들어갈 말로 가장 적절한 것을 고르시오. [3점]

① conceals the limits of innovations at the present time
　현재의 혁신의 한계를 감춘다　　　　내일의 문제를 유발함 = 한계를 드러냄
② makes it difficult to predict the future with confidence
　자신감 있게 미래를 예측하는 것을 어렵게 만든다　　미래의 예측과 관련된 내용이 아님
③ motivates us to quickly achieve a protopian civilization
　프로토피아적인 문명을 빨리 이루도록 우리에게 동기를 부여한다　프로토피아는 목적지가 아니라 과정임
④ hides a steady accumulation of small net benefits over time
　시간이 지남에 따라 작은 순이익의 꾸준한 축적을 보이지 않게 한다　놓치기 쉬운 점진적인 개선을 이룸
⑤ produces a considerable change in technological successes
　기술적 성공에 상당한 변화를 만든다　　　　　작은 몇 퍼센트의 차이임

왜 정답? [정답률 53%]

프로토피아는 어제보다 오늘이 약간 더 나은 점진적인 개선인데, 거의 새로운 개선만큼 많은 새로운 문제를 발생시키기 때문에 이러한 진보(개선)는 놓치기 쉽다고 했다. 어제의 문제를 해결한 오늘의 기술적 성공에 의해 내일의 문제가 유발되는 이러한 순환적 팽창은 파괴해 온 것보다 조금 더 많은 것을 만들어 내어 작은 순이익을 쌓아 가는, 즉 점진적인 개선이나 진보를 놓치기 쉽게, 또 결코 돋보이지 않게 한다는 내용이므로 빈칸에는 ④ '시간이 지남에 따라 작은 순이익의 꾸준한 축적을 보이지 않게 한다'가 적절하다. 작은 몇 퍼센트의 긍정적 차이 〈꿀팁〉

왜 오답?

① 오늘의 해결책이 내일의 문제를 유발할 것이라고 했으므로, 현재의 혁신의 한계를 드러내는 것이라고 할 수 있다.
② 미래를 예측하는 것과 관련된 내용이 아니다.
③ 프로토피아는 목적지가 아니라 과정이라고 했으므로, 프로토피아적인 문명의 달성이 목적인 것도 아니다.← 주의
⑤ 작은 몇 퍼센트의 긍정적인 차이라고 했으므로, 상당한 변화라고 하는 것은 적절하지 않다.

K 42 정답 ①　＊수용된 이전의 사상에서 도출되는 새로운 사상

가주어　　　　　　진주어
It is important / to recognise the interdependence / between
individual, culturally formed actions / and the state of cultural
integration. //
~은 중요하다 / 상호 의존성을 인식하는 것은 / 개별적이고 문화적으로 형성된 행동과 / 문화
적 통합의 상태 사이의 //

지시형용사
People work / within the forms / provided by the cultural
　　　　　　　　　　　목적격 관계대명사　　　　　　　선행사
patterns / that they have internalised, / however contradictory
these may be. //　　　　　　　　　　　　　= no matter how
사람들은 일한다 / 형태 내에서 / 문화적 패턴에 의해 제공되는 / 자신이 내면화한 / 이것들이
아무리 모순되더라도 // 단서1 사상은 이전에 수용된 사상의 결과로 도출되고, 이런 방식으로
　　　　　　　　　　　　　　　　　문화적 혁신과 발견이 가능함
Ideas are worked out / as logical implications or consequences
/ of other accepted ideas, / and it is in this way / that cultural
innovations and discoveries are possible. // it is ~ that
사상은 도출되고 / 논리적 영향이나 결과로 / 다른 수용된 사상의 / 이러한 방식으로 / 문화적　강조 구문
혁신과 발견이 가능하다 //

New ideas are discovered / through logical reasoning, /
새로운 사상은 발견되지만 / 논리적 추론을 통해 / 단서2 새로운 사상은 그 전제가 되는 사상을
　　　　　　　　　　　　　　　　　　　　　　　　　수용했기 때문에 가능한 것임
but such discoveries are inherent in and integral / to the
conceptual system / and are made possible / only because of the
acceptance of its premises. //
그러한 발견은 내재 및 내장되어 있고 / 개념 체계에 / 가능해진다 / 오직 그 전제의 수용 때문
에 // 단서3 새로운 소수를 발견한 것은 사용되고
　　　　　　　　　　　　　있는 특정 숫자 체계에서 비롯된 결과임
For example, / the discoveries of new prime numbers / are 'real'
consequences / of the particular number system / employed. //
예를 들어 / 새로운 소수의 발견은 / '실제' 결과이다 / 그것은 특정 숫자 체계의 / 사용되고 있
는 //

Thus, / cultural ideas show / 'advances' and 'developments' /
because they **are outgrowths** / of previous ideas. //
따라서 / 문화적 사상은 보여준다 / '진보'와 '발전'을 / 그것이 이전 사상의 결과물이기 때문
에 //

　　　단수 주어　　　　　　　　　　　　　　　　선행사
The cumulative work of many individuals / produces a corpus
of knowledge / within which certain 'discoveries' become　단수 동사
possible or more likely. // 「전치사+관계대명사」
많은 개인의 축적된 작업은 / 집적된 지식을 생산한다 / 그것으로 특정 '발견'이 가능해지거나
가능성이 높아지는 //
　　　　　　　　　　　　　　　　　could have p.p.: ~했을 수도 있다
Such discoveries are 'ripe' / and could not have occurred earlier
/ and are also likely to be made simultaneously / by numbers of
individuals. //
그러한 발견은 '알맞게 익고' / 더 일찍 발생할 수 없었을 것이며 / 또한 동시에 이루어질 가능
성이 있다 / 다수의 개인에 의해 //

- recognise ⓥ 인식하다, 알아보다　　・interdependence ⓝ 상호 의존
- individual ⓝ 개인　　・integration ⓝ 통합
- internalise ⓥ (사상・태도 등을) 내면화하다
- contradictory ⓐ 모순되는　　・logical ⓐ 논리적인, 타당한
- implication ⓝ 영향, 결과, 함축　　・consequence ⓝ 결과
- discovery ⓝ 발견　　・reasoning ⓝ 추론, 추리
- inherent ⓐ 내재하는
- integral ⓐ 내장된, 일부로서 포함되어 있는, 필수적인
- conceptual ⓐ 개념의　　・premise ⓝ 전제
- prime number 소수(素數)　　・cumulative ⓐ 누적되는
- ripe ⓐ 익은, 숙성한　　・outgrowth ⓝ 결과물, 파생물
- abstract ⓐ 추상적인　　・basis ⓝ 근거, 기반
- universalism ⓝ 보편성

개별적이고 문화적으로 형성된 행동과 문화적 통합의 상태 사이의 상호 의존성을 인식하는 것은 중요하다. 사람들은 아무리 모순되더라도 자신이 내면화한 문화적 패턴에 의해 제공되는 형태 내에서 일한다. 사상은 다른 수용된 사상의 논리적 영향이나 결과로 도출되고, 이러한 방식으로 문화적 혁신과 발견이 가능하다. 새로운 사상은 논리적 추론을 통해 발견되지만, 그러한 발견은 개념 체계에 내재 및 내장되어 있고, 오직 그 전제를 수용하기 때문에 가능해진다. 예를 들어, 새로운 소수의 발견은 사용되고 있는 특정 숫자 체계의 '실제' 결과이다. 따라서, 문화적 사상은 그것이 **이전 사상의 결과물이기** 때문에 '진보'와 '발전'을 보여준다. 많은 개인의 축적된 작업은 특정 '발견'이 가능해지거나 가능성이 높아지는 집적된 지식을 생산한다. 그러한 발견은 (이루어지기에) '알맞게 익고', 더 일찍 발생할 수 없었을 것이며, 또한 다수의 개인에 의해 동시에 이루어질 가능성이 있다.

다음 빈칸에 들어갈 말로 가장 적절한 것을 고르시오. [3점]

① are outgrowths of previous ideas
이전 사상의 결과이기   문화적 혁신과 발견은 이전에 수용된 사상의 결과로 도출됨
② stem from abstract reasoning ability
추상적 추론 능력에서 비롯되기   추상적 추론 능력으로 문화적 진보가 이루어진다는 예시가 아님
③ form the basis of cultural universalism
문화적 보편성의 토대를 형성하기   문화적 사상이 발전한 결과가 문화적 보편성이라는 것이 아님
④ emerge between people of the same age
같은 시대의 사람들 사이에서 출현하기   같은 시대의 사람들 사이에서 문화적 사상이 발전한다는 언급은 없음
⑤ promote individuals' innovative thinking
개인들의 혁신적 사고를 촉진하기   무엇이 문화적 사상의 진보의 토대인지를 설명하는 글임

왜 정답? [정답률 51%]

> 2, 3, 5, 7, 11처럼 1과 그 수 자신 이외의
> 자연수로는 나눌 수 없는 자연수   꿀팁

새로운 사상은 이전에 수용된 사상의 논리적 영향의 결과로 도출되고, 이러한 방식으로 문화적 혁신과 발견이 가능한 것이라고 하면서, 새로운 소수의 발견은 이전에 사용되고 있던 특정 숫자 체계로부터의 결과라는 예시를 들었다. 다시 말해, 문화적 사상의 진보와 발전은 그 이전에 수용된 사상의 결과라는 것이므로 빈칸에는 ① '이전 사상의 결과물이기'가 적절하다.

왜 오답?

② 문화적 사상의 진보가 추상적 추론 능력을 통해 이루어진다는 것이 아니라 이전의 사상의 영향과 결과로 이루어진다는 내용이다.

③, ⑤ 문화적 사상의 진보와 발전이 무엇을 토대로 이루어지는지를 설명한 것이지, 문화적 사상의 진보와 발전이 다른 무언가의 토대가 되고 촉진한다는 것이 아니다.

④ 같은 시대의 사람들 사이에서 일어나기 때문에 문화적 사상이 진보하고 발전하는 것이라는 언급은 없다.

K 43 정답 ② ＊단어 태그의 한계

Many people create and share pictures and videos / on the
       동사의 병렬 구조   목적어의 병렬 구조
Internet. // 많은 사람이 사진과 비디오를 만들고 공유한다 / 인터넷에서 //
  주어   동사   주격 보어(동명사구)
The difficulty is / finding what you want. //
어려운 점은 ~이다 / 여러분이 원하는 것을 찾는 것 //

Typically, people want to search / using words / (rather than,
say, example sketches). //
일반적으로 사람들은 검색하기를 원한다 / 단어를 사용하여 / (가령, 예시 스케치 대신) //
                                                                가주어
Because most pictures don't come with words attached, / it is
           진주어   선행사   주격 관계대명사
natural / to try and build tagging systems / that tag images /
with relevant words. //
대부분의 사진은 첨부된 단어와 같이 오지 않기 때문에 / ~은 자연스럽다 / 태그 시스템을
시도하고 만들려는 것은 / 이미지를 태그하는 / 관련 단어로 //

The underlying machinery is straightforward / — we apply /
                                            동사의 병렬 구조
image classification and object detection methods / and tag the
image / with the output words. //
기본적인 시스템은 간단하다 / 우리는 적용하고 / 이미지 분류와 개체 감지 방법을 /
이미지를 태그한다 / 출력된 단어로 //

But tags aren't **a comprehensive description / of what is
happening in an image.** //
하지만 태그는 포괄적인 설명이 아니다 / 이미지에서 일어나고 있는 일에 대한 //
가주어   진주어   단서 1 태그는 누가 무엇을 하고 있는지를 포착하지 못함
It matters / who is doing what, / and tags don't capture this. //
~이 중요하다 / 누가 무엇을 하고 있는지가 / 그리고 태그는 이것을 포착하지 못한다 //
                                    동명사구 주어
For example, / tagging a picture / of a cat in the street / with the
object categories "cat", "street", "trash can" and "fish bones" /
예를 들어 / 사진을 태그하는 것은 / 거리에 있는 고양이의 / '고양이', '거리', '쓰레기통', '물고기
뼈'의 개체 범주로 /
  단수 동사   단서 2 고양이가 무엇을 하고 있는지는 태그를 통해 알 수 없음
leaves out the information / that the cat is pulling the fish bones
/ out of an open trash can / on the street. // 정보를 빠뜨리게 된다 / 그
고양이가 물고기 뼈를 빼내고 있다는 / 열린 쓰레기통에서 / 거리에 있는 //

- typically ⓐⅾ 일반적으로 · attach ⓥ 첨부하다
- relevant ⓐ 관련 있는 · underlying ⓐ 기본적인
- machinery ⓝ 시스템 · straightforward ⓐ 간단한
- classification ⓝ 분류 · object ⓝ 개체 · detection ⓝ 감지
- method ⓝ 방법 · output ⓝ 출력 · capture ⓥ 포착하다

많은 사람이 인터넷에서 사진과 비디오를 만들고 공유한다. 어려운 점은 여러분이 원하는 것을 찾는 것이다. 일반적으로 사람들은 (가령, 예시 스케치 대신) 단어를 사용하여 검색하기를 원한다. 대부분의 사진에는 단어가 첨부되어 있지 않기 때문에 이미지에 관련 단어를 태그하는 태그 시스템을 시도하고 만들려는 것은 자연스러운 일이다. 기본적인 시스템은 간단한데, 이미지 분류와 개체 감지 방법을 적용하고 출력된 단어로 이미지를 태그한다. 하지만 태그는 **이미지에서 일어나고 있는 일에 대한 포괄적인 설명**이 아니다. 누가 무엇을 하고 있는지가 중요한데, 태그는 이것을 포착하지 못한다. 예를 들어, 거리에 있는 고양이의 사진을 '고양이', '거리', '쓰레기통', '물고기 뼈'의 개체 범주로 태그하는 것은 그 고양이가 거리에 있는 열린 쓰레기통에서 물고기 뼈를 빼내고 있다는 정보를 빠뜨리게 된다.

다음 빈칸에 들어갈 말로 가장 적절한 것을 고르시오.
┌ 사진을 분류하는 데 있어서의 역할에 대한 내용이 아님
① a set of words that allow users to identify an individual object
사용자가 개별 개체를 식별할 수 있게 하는 단어의 집합   부정어 not에 주의해야 함
② a comprehensive description of what is happening in an image
이미지에서 일어나고 있는 일에 대한 포괄적인 설명   누가 무엇을 하고 있는지를 설명하지 못함
③ a reliable resource for categorizing information by pictures
사진으로 정보를 분류할 수 있는 신뢰할 만한 자원
④ a primary means of organizing a sequential order of words
단어의 순차적 순서를 구성하는 주요 수단   이미지와 관련된 내용임
⑤ a useful filter for sorting similar but not identical images
유사하지만 동일하지 않은 이미지를 분류하는 데 유용한 필터   태그를 통한 이미지 분류는 언급되지 않음

왜 정답? [정답률 55%]

글의 앞부분	이미지를 관련 단어로 태그하는 태그 시스템을 시도하고 만드는 것은 자연스러움
빈칸 문장	그러나(But) 태그는 _____이 아님
빈칸 뒤 문장	태그는 누가 무엇을 하고 있는지를 포착하지 못함
예시	거리에 있는 고양이의 사진을 '고양이', '거리', '쓰레기통', '물고기 뼈'로 태그하는 것은, 고양이가 거리에 있는 열린 쓰레기통에서 물고기 뼈를 빼내고 있다는 정보를 나타내지 못함

➡ 역접의 연결어 But으로 시작한 빈칸 문장부터 글의 흐름이 전환된다.
태그는 누가 무엇을 하고 있는 이미지인지를 포착하지 못한다는 설명과 그 예시가 빈칸 문장에 이어진다.

▶ 따라서 빈칸 문장은 태그가 ② '이미지에서 일어나고 있는 일에 대한 포괄적인 설명'이 아니라는 내용이어야 한다.

왜 오답?

① 태그를 통해 어떤 이미지인지 대강은 알 수 있다.

③ 태그가 나타내는 정보가 불완전하다는 것이지, 태그를 통해 정보나 사진을 분류한다는 등의 내용은 아니다. 확정

④ 이미지에 단어를 태그하는 것에 대해 설명하는 글이다.

⑤ 이어지는 예시가 이미지를 분류하는 내용이 아니다.

K 44 정답 ③ ＊너무 낙관적인 우리
                형용사적 용법(reason 수식)
There's reason to worry / that an eyes-on-the-prize mentality /
could be a mistake. //
우려할 이유가 있다 / 자기 목표에 몰두하는 사고방식이 / 잘못일 수 있다고 //
                                 가주어   진주어
Lots of research shows / that we tend to be over-confident /
about how easy it is / to be self-disciplined. //
많은 연구는 보여준다 / 우리는 과신하는 경향이 있다는 것을 / ~이 얼마나 쉬운지에 관해 /
자기 훈련이 된다는 것이 //

This is / why so many of us optimistically buy expensive gym
                                병렬 구조
memberships / when paying per-visit fees would be cheaper, /
이것이 ~이다 / 우리 중 매우 많은 사람이 낙관적으로 값비싼 체육관 회원권을 사는 이유 /
방문당 이용료를 내는 것이 더 저렴할 때 /
                                앞에 목적격 관계대명사가 생략됨
register for online classes / we'll never complete, / and purchase
family-size chips on discount / to trim our monthly snack
                                     부사적 용법(목적)
budget, /
온라인 강좌에 등록하는 (이유) / 우리가 결코 다 끝내지 않을 / 그리고 할인하는 대형 과자를
사서 / 우리의 한 달 치 간식 예산을 줄이기 위해 /

부사적 용법(결과)
only to consume every last crumb / in a single sitting. //
결국 한 번에 마지막 부스러기까지 다 먹는 (이유) / 앉은 자리에서 //

We think / "future me" will be able to make good choices, / but too often / "present me" gives in to temptation. //
우리는 생각하지만 / '미래의 내'가 좋은 선택을 할 수 있을 거라고 / 너무나 자주 / '현재의 나'는 유혹에 굴복한다 //

형용사적 용법(ability 수식)
People have a remarkable ability / to **ignore** their own failures. //
사람들에게는 놀라운 능력이 있다 / 자신의 실패를 무시하는 //

단서 거듭 실패할 때도 실수로부터 배우기보다 자신의 능력에 관해 장밋빛 낙관주의를 유지함

Even when we flounder again and again, / many of us manage to maintain / a rosy optimism / about our ability / to do better next time / rather than learning from our past mistakes. //
형용사적 용법(ability 수식)
우리가 거듭 실패할 때도 / 우리 중 많은 사람은 용케 유지한다 / 장밋빛 낙관주의를 / 우리의 능력에 관해 / 다음에는 더 잘 거라는 / 우리의 과거의 실수로부터 배우기보다는 //

형용사적 용법(reason 수식)
We cling / to fresh starts and other reasons / to stay upbeat, /
우리는 매달리고 / 새로운 시작과 다른 이유들에 / 낙관적인 태도를 유지할 /

which may help us / get out of bed in the morning / but can prevent us / from approaching change / in the smartest possible way. //
may help의 목적어와 목적격 보어(원형부정사)
그것이 우리를 도울지는 모르지만 / 아침에 침대에서 일어나도록 / 우리를 막을 수 있다 / 변화에 접근하는 것으로부터 / 가능한 가장 영리한 방식으로 //

- eyes-on-the-prize ⓐ 자기 목표에 몰두하는 · mentality ⓝ 사고방식
- over-confident ⓐ 과신하는 · self-disciplined ⓐ 자기 훈련이 되는
- optimistically ⓐⓓ 낙관적으로 · per-visit fee 방문 당 이용료
- trim ⓥ 줄이다 · in a single sitting 앉은 자리에서
- give in to ~에 굴복하다 · temptation ⓝ 유혹
- remarkable ⓐ 놀라운 · manage to ~하기 위해 애쓰다
- rosy ⓐ 장밋빛의 · optimism ⓝ 낙관주의

자기 목표에 몰두하는 사고방식이 잘못일 수 있다고 우려할 이유가 있다. 많은 연구에 따르면, 우리는 자기 훈련이 된다는 것이 얼마나 쉬운지에 관해 과신하는 경향이 있다. 이것이 우리 중 매우 많은 사람이 낙관적으로 방문당 이용료를 내는 것이 더 저렴할 텐데도 값비싼 체육관 회원권을 사고, 다 끝내지도 못할 온라인 강좌에 등록하며, 우리의 한 달 치 간식 예산을 줄이기 위해 할인하는 대형 과자를 사서 결국 앉은 자리에서 한 번에 마지막 부스러기까지 다 먹는 이유이다. 우리는 '미래의 내'가 좋은 선택을 할 수 있을 거라고 생각하지만, 너무나 자주 '현재의 나'는 유혹에 굴복한다. 사람들에게는 자신의 실패를 <u>무시하는</u> 놀라운 능력이 있다. 거듭 실패하면서도 우리 중 많은 사람은 우리의 과거의 실수로부터 배우기보다는 다음에는 더 잘 거라는 우리의 능력에 관해 장밋빛 낙관주의를 용케 유지한다. 우리는 새로운 시작과 낙관적인 태도를 유지할 다른 이유들에 매달리고, 그것이 아침에 우리가 침대에서 일어나는 데 도움이 될지는 모르지만 가능한 가장 영리한 방식으로 우리가 변화에 접근하는 것을 막을 수 있다.

다음 빈칸에 들어갈 말로 가장 적절한 것을 고르시오.

① criticize 실수에 대해 비판적으로 접근하는 것이 아님
비판하다
② remind 실수를 생각한다면 실수에서 배울 것임
상기시키다
③ ignore 거듭된 실패에도 실수에서 배우지 않고 장밋빛으로 생각함
무시하다
④ detect 실수를 발견하더라도 무시한다는 내용임
탐지하다
⑤ overestimate 실수를 과소평가하는 능력임
과대평가하다

>왜 정답? [정답률 70%]

빈칸 문장	사람들에게는 자신의 실패를 '~하는' 놀라운 능력이 있다.
빈칸 뒤 문장	거듭 실패할 때도 우리 중 많은 사람은 과거의 실수에서 배우기보다 자신의 능력에 관해 장밋빛 낙관주의를 유지한다.

⇒ 거듭 실패할 때도 실수로부터 배우지 않고 자신의 능력에 관해 장밋빛 낙관주의를 유지하는 능력에 대해 말했다.
▶ 즉 자신의 실패를 ③ '무시하는' 능력을 말한다.

>왜 오답?

① 자신이 실수했다는 사실에 비판적으로 접근하는 것이 아니다.
② 실수에 많은 주의를 기울이지 않는다는 내용이다.
④ 실수했다는 것을 알면서도 자신의 능력을 과대평가한다는 내용이다.
⑤ 실수를 과소평가하는 능력에 더 가깝다.

K **45** 정답 ⑤ *생태 건강이 붕괴하는 상황

keeping의 목적어와 목적격 보어
Ecological health depends / on keeping the surface of the earth rich / in humus and minerals / so that it can provide a foundation / for healthy plant and animal life. //
〈목적〉의 부사절 접속사
생태 건강은 달려 있다 / 지표면을 풍부한 상태로 유지하는 데 / 부식토와 광물에 있어 / 그것이 토대를 제공할 수 있도록 / 동식물의 건강한 삶을 위한 // **단서 1** 지표면의 상태에 달린 생태 건강이 붕괴하는 상황을 찾아야 함

The situation is disrupted / if the soil loses these raw materials / or if great quantities of contaminants are introduced / into it. //
〈조건〉의 부사절 접속사   〈조건〉의 부사절 접속사
그 상황은 붕괴된다 / 토양이 이러한 원료를 잃거나 / 다량의 오염 물질이 유입되면 / 그것에 //

When man goes / beneath the surface of the earth / and drags out minerals or other compounds / that did not evolve / as part of this system, / then problems follow. //
병렬 구조
인간이 가면 / 지표면 아래로 / 그리고 광물이나 다른 화합물을 끄집어내면 / 변하지 않은 / 이 시스템의 일부로 / 그러면 문제가 뒤따른다 //

The mining of lead and cadmium / are examples of this. //
납과 카드뮴의 채굴이 / 이것의 예이다 //

Petroleum is also a substance / that has been dug / out of the bowels of the earth / and introduced into the surface ecology / by man. //
병렬 구조
석유 또한 물질이다 / 채굴되어 / 지구의 내부 밖으로 / 지표 생태계에 유입된 / 인간에 의해 // **단서 2** 석유는 인간이 지표면 아래의 광물이나 다른 화합물을 지표 생태계로 끄집어내면 문제가 발생한다는 것을 보여주는 예시임

Though it is formed / from plant matter, / the highly reduced carbon compounds / that result / are often toxic / to living protoplasm. //
〈양보〉의 부사절 접속사   주격 관계대명사절
비록 그것이 형성되지만 / 식물로부터 / 고도로 환원된 탄소 화합물은 / 그로 인해 생기는 / 종종 유독하다 / 살아 있는 원형질에 // **단서 3** 지구 내부에서 채굴되어 지표면으로 유입된 석유는 종종 유독함

In some cases / this is true of even very tiny amounts, / as in the case of "polychlorinated biphenyls," / a petroleum product / which can cause cancer. //
몇몇 경우에는 / 심지어 매우 적은 양일 때도 이러하다 / '폴리염화 바이페닐'의 경우에서처럼 / 석유 생성 물질인 / 암을 유발할 수 있는 //

- ecological ⓐ 생태계의 · surface ⓝ 표면, 수면
- foundation ⓝ 토대, 기초 · disrupt ⓥ 방해하다, 지장을 주다
- raw ⓐ 날것의, 가공되지 않은 · quantity ⓝ 양, 수량
- contaminant ⓝ 오염 물질 · drag out ~을 끄집어내다
- compound ⓝ 화합물, 혼합물 · mine ⓥ 채굴하다, 캐다
- lead ⓝ ((화학)) 납 · petroleum ⓝ 석유 · substance ⓝ 물질, 본질
- bowel ⓝ 창자, 가장 깊은 곳 · introduce ⓥ (처음으로) 들여오다, 시작하다
- ecology ⓝ 생태계, 생태학 · matter ⓝ 물질, 성분 · carbon ⓝ 탄소
- toxic ⓐ 유독성의

생태 건강은 지표면이 동식물의 건강한 삶을 위한 토대를 제공할 수 있도록 그것을 부식토와 광물이 풍부한 상태로 유지하는 데 달려 있다. 토양이 이러한 원료를 잃거나 **다량의 오염 물질이 그것에 유입되면** 그 상황은 붕괴된다.

인간이 지표면 아래로 가서, 이 시스템의 일부로 변하지 않은 광물이나 다른 화합물을 끄집어내면, 문제가 뒤따른다. 납과 카드뮴의 채굴이 이것의 예이다. 석유 또한 인간에 의해 지구의 내부에서 채굴되어 지표 생태계에 유입된 물질이다. 비록 그것이 식물로부터 형성되지만, 그로 인해 생기는 고도로 환원된 탄소 화합물은 살아 있는 원형질에 유독한 경우가 많다. 암을 유발할 수 있는 석유 생성 물질인 '폴리염화 바이페닐'의 경우에서처럼, 몇몇 경우에는 심지어 매우 적은 양일 때도 이러하다.

다음 빈칸에 들어갈 말로 가장 적절한 것을 고르시오.

① the number of plants on it increases too rapidly
그것에 있는 식물의 수가 너무 빠르게 증가하다
② it stops providing enough nourishment for humans
그것이 인간을 위한 충분한 영양분을 제공하기를 멈추다
③ climate change transforms its chemical components
기후 변화가 그것의 화학적 구성요소를 바꾸다
④ alien species prevail and deplete resources around it
외래종이 만연하여 그것 주변의 자원을 대폭 감소시키다
⑤ great quantities of contaminants are introduced into it
다량의 오염 물질이 그것에 유입되다

동식물의 건강한
삶을 위한 토대를
제공한다는
언급으로 만든
오답

기후 변화는 언급되지 않음

지표면으로 유입된 다량의 지구 내부의 광물이나 화합물이 문제임

> **왜** 정답? [정답률 32%]

지표면의 상태에 달린 생태 건강이 붕괴하는 조건을 설명하는 부사절에 빈칸이 있다.

인간이 지표면 아래의 광물이나 다른 화합물을 (지표면으로) 끄집어내면 문제가 뒤따른다면서, 인간에 의해 채굴되어 지표 생태계에 유입된 물질의 예시로 납과 카드뮴, 석유를 들었다. 그중 석유를 구체적으로 부연했는데, 살아 있는 원형질에 종종 유독하다면서 석유 생성 물질인 폴리염화 바이페닐이 암을 유발할 수 있다고 했다.

따라서 생태 건강이 붕괴하는 조건은 ⑤ '다량의 오염 물질이 그것(지표면)에 유입되면'이다.

> 지표면 아래에서 채굴되어 지표면으로 유입된 납, 카드뮴, 석유가 지표면 입장에서는 오염 물질 **꿀**팁

> **왜** 오답?

①, ② 동식물의 건강한 삶을 위한 토대를 제공할 수 있도록 지표면이 부식토와 광물이 풍부한 상태로 유지되어야 한다는 첫 문장으로 만든 오답이다.
③, ④ 기후 변화나 외래종이 지표면에 영향을 미친다는 언급은 없다.

K 46 정답 ② *수많은 사람들이 서로와 접촉하는 도시

People have always wanted / to be around other people / and
병렬 구조(have wanted의 목적어)
to learn from them. //
사람들은 항상 원해 왔다 / 다른 사람들 주위에 머무르며 / 그들로부터 배우기를 //

Cities have long been dynamos of social possibility, / foundries
단서 1 어휘의 혁신은 항상 도시에서 시작되었는데,
of art, music, and fashion. //
이는 많은 사람들이 서로 접촉한 결과물임
도시는 오랫동안 사회적 가능성의 발전기였다 / 예술, 음악, 패션의 주물 공장 //
단수 주어   단수 동사
Slang, or, if you prefer, "lexical innovation," / has always started
in cities / — an outgrowth / of all those different people / so
frequently exposed / to one another. //
속어, 또는 여러분이 선호한다면 '어휘의 혁신'은 / 항상 도시에서 시작되었다 / 결과물 그
모든 별의별 사람의 / 그렇게도 빈번히 접촉된 / 서로에게 //

It spreads outward, / in a manner / not unlike transmissible
주격 관계대명사   선행사
disease, / which itself typically "takes off" in cities. //
그것은 외부로 퍼져나가는데 / 방식으로 / 전염성 질병과 다르지 않은 / 그것 자체도 보통
도시에서 '이륙한다' // 재귀대명사(강조 용법)
부사절의 주어, 선행사(관계부사는 생략됨)
If, / as the noted linguist Leonard Bloomfield argued, / the way
부사절의 동사 **단서 2** 언어 혁신은 가장 많은 사람들이 가장 많은 사람들의
/ a person talks / is a "composite result / of what he has heard
말을 듣고 가장 많은 다른 사람들에게 말한 곳에서 일어남
before," /
만약 / 저명한 언어학자 Leonard Bloomfield가 주장하듯 / 방식이 / 한 사람이 말하는 /
'합성한 결과물'이라면 / 그가 전에 들었던 것의 /
부사절 접속사(장소)
then language innovation would happen / where the most
people heard and talked / to the most other people. //
언어 혁신은 일어날 것이다 / 가장 많은 사람이 귀를 기울이고 말한 곳에서 / 가장 많은 다른
사람들에게 //

Cities drive taste change / because they **offer the greatest**
선행사
exposure / to other people, /
도시는 취향 변화를 이끄는데 / 곳이 가장 많은 접촉을 제공하기 때문에 / 다른 사람들과의 /

who not surprisingly are often the creative people / cities seem
주격 관계대명사   선행사(목적격 관계대명사는 생략됨)
to attract. //
그들은 놀랄 것도 없이 흔히 창의적인 사람들이다 / 도시가 끌어들이는 듯 보이는 //

Media, / ever more global, ever more far-reaching, / spread
복수 주어   복수 동사
language faster / to more people. //
미디어는 / 그 어느 때보다 더 전방위적이고, 그 어느 때보다 더 멀리까지 미치는 / 언어를 더
빨리 퍼뜨린다 / 더 많은 사람에게 //

• dynamo ⓝ ((pl.)) 발전기   • slang ⓝ 속어, 은어
• outgrowth ⓝ 결과물   • expose ⓥ 노출하다, 접하게 하다
• spread ⓥ 퍼지다, 퍼뜨리다   • outward ⓐⓓ 외부로
• transmissible ⓐ 전염성의   • noted ⓐ 저명한, 잘 알려진
• linguist ⓝ 언어학자   • composite ⓐ 합성의, 복합의
• drive ⓥ 추진하다, 몰아붙이다   • far-reaching ⓐ 멀리까지 미치는

사람들은 항상 다른 사람들 주위에 머무르며 그들로부터 배우기를 원해 왔다. 도시는 오랫동안 사회적 가능성의 발전기, 즉 예술, 음악, 패션의 주물 공장이었다. 속어, 또는 여러분이 선호한다면 '어휘의 혁신'은 항상 도시에서 시작되었는데, 그 모든 별의별 사람이 그렇게도 빈번히 서로에게 접촉한 결과물이다. 그것은 전염성 질병과 다르지 않은 방식으로 외부로 퍼져나가는데, 그 전염성 질병 자체도 보통 도시에서 '이륙한다.'

저명한 언어학자 Leonard Bloomfield가 주장하듯, 한 사람이 말하는 방식이 '그가 전에 들었던 것을 합성한 결과물'이라면, 언어 혁신은 가장 많은 사람이 가장 많은 다른 사람의 말을 듣고 가장 많은 다른 사람에게 말한 곳에서 일어날 것이다. 도시는 그곳이 다른 사람들과의 가장 많은 접촉을 제공하기 때문에 취향 변화를 이끄는데, 그들은 놀랄 것도 없이 흔히 도시가 끌어들이는 듯 보이는 창의적인 사람들이다. 그 어느 때보다 더 전방위적이고, 그 어느 때보다 더 멀리까지 미치는 미디어는 언어를 더 빨리 더 많은 사람에게 퍼뜨린다.

다음 빈칸에 들어갈 말로 가장 적절한 것을 고르시오.

① provide rich source materials for artists
예술가들에게 풍부한 원재료를 공급하기   타인과의 빈번한 접촉이 핵심임
② offer the greatest exposure to other people
다른 사람들과의 가장 많은 접촉을 제공하기   그 모든 별의별 사람들의 그렇게도 빈번한 접촉의 결과물
③ cause cultural conflicts among users of slang
속어 사용자들 사이에서 문화 갈등을 초래하기   문화 갈등에 대한 내용이 아님
④ present ideal research environments to linguists
언어학자들에게 이상적인 연구 환경을 제공하기   the noted linguist로 만든 오답
⑤ reduce the social mobility of ambitious outsiders
야심 찬 외부인의 사회 이동을 줄이기   사회 이동에 대해서는 언급되지 않음

> **왜** 정답? [정답률 68%]

어휘의 혁신은 항상 도시에서 시작되었는데, 그것은 많은 사람들이 서로에게 빈번히 접촉한 결과물이라고 했다.

빈칸 문장의 바로 앞 문장에서도 언어 혁신이 가장 많은 사람들이 가장 많은 다른 사람들의 말을 듣고, 가장 많은 사람들에게 말한 곳에서 일어날 것이라고 했으므로, > 다른 사람들과 많이 접촉하는 곳, 즉 도시 **꿀**팁

도시가 취향 변화를 이끄는 이유는 도시가 ② '다른 사람들과의 가장 많은 접촉을 제공하기' 때문이라고 하는 것이 적절하다.

> **왜** 오답?

① 첫 문장에서 도시가 예술의 주물 공장이라고 한 것으로 만든 오답이다.
③ 도시에서 시작된 속어가 문화 갈등을 초래한다는 내용은 없다.
④ 저명한 언어학자인 Leonard Bloomfield의 주장이 인용된 것으로 만든 오답이다. **함정**
⑤ '외부인'이나 '사회 이동'에 대해서는 언급되지 않았다.

장성욱 | 동아대 의예과 2023년 입학·부산 대연고 졸

많은 학생들이 어려워하는 빈칸 유형이지만 이번 문제는 그리 어렵지는 않았어. 나는 소거법을 이용해서 빈칸 문제를 푸는데, 글을 한번 읽은 후 이 글이 하고 싶은 말을 파악한 다음, 키워드와 중심 내용을 뽑아내는 거야. 이 글의 핵심은 도시(cities)에서 다른 사람과의 접촉, 노출이 발생한다는 거야. all those different people ~ exposed to one another 등의 표현으로 이러한 키워드를 찾을 수 있지. 이렇게 찾은 키워드에 맞는 선택지는 다른 사람들과의 가장 많은 접촉, 노출을 제공한다는 ②이야.

K 47 정답 ① *큰 그림을 보는 우리의 조상들

A connection with ancestors, / especially remote ones, / is useful
단수 주어
/ for getting a wide-angled, philosophical view of life. //
단수 동사
조상들과의 관계는 / 특히 먼 조상들과의 관계 / 유용하다 / 삶에 대한 폭넓은 철학적 관점을
얻는 데 //

Whereas our immediate ancestors are notably skilled / at
부사절 접속사(대조)
helping us / with the "little pictures," / namely the particular,
the trees / — say, a problem with a boss — /
우리의 직계 조상들은 특히 능숙하지만 / 우리를 도와주는 데 / '작은 그림'에 대해 / 즉 특정한
것, 나무들 / 말하자면, 상사와의 문제 /

our remote ones are best / for seeing the "Big Picture," / namely
the general, the forest / — say, the meaning of our job. //
우리의 먼 조상들은 가장 알맞다 / '큰 그림'을 보는 것에 / 즉 일반적인 것, 숲 / 말하자면
직업의 의미 //

As modern people rush around / blowing small problems out
of proportion, / thus contributing to a global anxiety epidemic, /
현대인들은 바쁠 때 / 작은 문제를 어울리지 않게 부풀리며 / 그래서 세계적인 불안 확산의
원인이 되면서 /

ancestral spirits have a broader perspective / that can **calm the**
선행사   주격 관계대명사
disquieted soul. //
조상들에게는 더 넓은 시야가 있다 / 불안한 영혼을 진정시킬 수 있는 //

When it comes to a trivial problem, / for example, / they'll just
tell us, / "This too will pass." // **단서 1** 작은 문제들에 있어 조상들은 우리에게
"이 또한 지나갈 것이다"라고 말할 것임
사소한 문제에 관한 한 / 예를 들어 / 그들은 그저 우리에게 말할 것이다 / "이 또한 지나갈
것이다"라고 //

They appreciate / how rapidly and often things change. //
그들은 이해한다 / 상황이 얼마나 빨리 그리고 자주 변하는지를 //

According to American anthropologist Richard Katz, / for
instance, /
미국 인류학자 Richard Katz에 따르면 / 예를 들어 /

Fijians say / that from the ancestral viewpoint / whatever looks
생략 가능한 명사절 접속사   명사절(주어)을 이끄는 복합 관계대명사
unfortunate / may turn out to be fortunate after all: /
피지 사람들은 말한다 / 조상의 관점에서 볼 때 / 불운해 보이는 무엇이든 / 결국은 운 좋은
것으로 판명될 수 있다고 /

"What may seem to be a horrible outcome / ... is seen in another
명사절 주어
light / by the ancestors." //
단수 동사
"끔찍한 결과로 보일지도 모르는 것은 / … 또 다른 관점으로 보인다 / 조상들에게는" //

The ancestors, / it might be said, / keep their heads / when
everyone around them / is losing theirs. //
조상들은 / 말해질 수 있다 / 자신들의 평정심을 유지한다고 / 그들 주변의 모든 사람이 /
평정심을 잃고 있을 때도 // **단서 2** 조상들은 주변 모든 사람이 평정심을 잃을 때도 평정심을 유지함

- remote ⓐ 먼 · wide-angled ⓐ 폭넓은
- philosophical ⓐ 철학적인 · immediate ⓐ 직접적인
- notably [ad] 특히 · rush around 서두르다
- blow out of proportion 과장하다 · contribute to ~의 원인이 되다
- anxiety ⓝ 불안 · ancestral ⓐ 선조의 · perspective ⓝ 시야
- calm ⓥ 진정시키다 · disquieted ⓐ 불안한
- when it comes to ~에 관한 한 · trivial ⓐ 사소한
- appreciate ⓥ 이해하다 · unfortunate ⓐ 불운한
- turn out 판명되다 · keep one's head 평정심을 유지하다
- lose one's head 평정심을 잃다

조상들과의 관계, 특히 먼 조상들과의 관계는, 삶에 대한 폭넓은 철학적 관점을
얻는 데 유용하다. 우리의 직계 조상들은 '작은 그림', 즉 특정한 것, 나무들을,
말하자면, 상사와의 문제, 도와주는 데 특히 능숙하지만, 우리의 먼 조상들은
'큰 그림', 즉 일반적인 것, 숲, 말하자면 직업의 의미와 같은 것을 보는 것에
가장 알맞다. 현대인들은 바쁘게 작은 문제를 어울리지 않게 부풀리며,
세계적인 불안 확산의 원인이 될 때, 조상들은 **불안한 영혼을 진정시킬** 수 있는
더 넓은 시야가 있다. 예를 들어, 사소한 문제에 관한 한, 그들은 그저 우리에게

"이 또한 지나갈 것이다."라고 말할 것이다. 그들은 상황이 얼마나 빨리 그리고
자주 변하는지를 이해한다. 예를 들어, 미국 인류학자 Richard Katz에 따르면
피지 사람들은 조상의 관점에서 볼 때, 불운해 보이는 무엇이든 결국은 운
좋은 것으로 판명될 수 있다고 말한다. "끔찍한 결과로 보일지도 모르는 것은
… 조상들에게는 또 다른 관점으로 보인다." 조상들은 주변의 모든 사람이
평정심을 잃고 있을 때도, 자신들의 평정심을 유지한다고 할 수 있다.

다음 빈칸에 들어갈 말로 가장 적절한 것을 고르시오.

① calm the disquieted soul 이 또한 지나갈 것이라고 말해줌
불안한 영혼을 진정시키다
② boost cooperation in the community 공동체, 협력에 대한 내용이 아님
공동체에서 협력을 신장시키다
③ make us stick to the specific details 작은 문제에 호들갑 떨지 않게 함
우리로 하여금 특정한 세부 사항을 고수하게 하다
④ result in a waste of time 긍정적인 면을 이야기하는 글임
시간 낭비를 야기하다
⑤ complicate situations 작은 문제를 부풀리는 것은 현대인임
상황을 복잡하게 하다

왜 정답? [정답률 55%]

빈칸 문장	현대인이 작은 문제를 부풀리며 세계적인 불안 확산의 원인이 될 때, 조상들에게는 '무엇'할 수 있는 더 넓은 시야가 있다.
빈칸 뒤 문장	사소한 문제에 대해 그들은 그저 우리에게 "이 또한 지나갈 것이다"라고 말할 것임 불안을 진정시키는 말
마지막 문장	조상들은 그들 주변의 모든 사람이 평정심을 잃을 때도 평정심을 유지한다고 할 수 있다.

➡ 사소한 문제를 부풀려 불안을 확산시키는 현대인과 조상이 대조되는 글이다.
▶ 사소한 문제를 겪는 현대인에게 "이 또한 지나갈 것이다"라고 말할 것이라는
빈칸 뒤 문장을 통해, 조상들에게 ① '불안한 영혼을 진정시킬' 수 있는 더 넓은
시야가 있다는 내용임을 알 수 있다.

왜 오답?

② 공동체나 협력에 대해 이야기하는 글이 아니다.
③ 특정한 세부 사항과 같은 사소한 문제에 대해 '이 또한 지나갈 것이다'라고 말한다는
내용이다. (▶◀ 이유: 조상들이 불안을 진정시키는 말을 할 것이라고 했으므로
오히려 반대 내용임)
④ 조상들의 긍정적인 면에 대해 이야기하는 글이다.
⑤ 상황을 복잡하게 하는 것은 사소한 문제를 부풀리는 현대인이다.

K 48 정답 ① *다른 대우를 필요로 할 수도 있는 평등

이유의 부사절 접속사
Since human beings are at once both similar and different, / they
should be treated equally / because of both. //
인간은 동시에 비슷하기도 하고 다르기도 해서 / 그들은 동등하게 대우받아야 한다 / 둘 다 때
문에 //
주어(선행사) 주격 관계대명사   not A but B: A가 아니라 B인
Such a view, / which grounds equality / not in human uniformity
/ but in the interplay / of uniformity and difference, /
그러한 견해는 / 평등의 기초를 두는 / 인간의 획일성이 아니라 / 상호 작용에 / 획일성과 차이에 /
동사①
builds difference / into the very concept of equality, / breaks
동사②
the traditional equation of equality / with similarity, / and is
immune / to monist distortion. //
동사③
차이를 포함시키고 / 평등이라는 바로 그 개념에 / 전통적인 평등의 동일시를 깨뜨리며 / 유사
성과의 / 면한다 / 일원론적 왜곡을 /
앞 내용을 받는 so가 문두에 오면서 주어와 동사가 도치됨
Once the basis of equality changes / so does its content. //
일단 평등의 기초가 바뀌면 / 그것의 내용도 그러하다 //

Equality involves equal freedom or opportunity / to be different,
목적어
/ and treating human beings equally / requires us to take into
동명사구 주어   단수 동사
account / both their similarities and differences. //
목적격 보어
평등은 동등한 자유나 기회를 포함하고 / 서로 다를 수 있는 / 인간을 동등하게 대하는 것은 /
우리가 고려하도록 요구한다 / 그들의 유사성과 차이점 둘 다를 //

When the latter are not relevant, / equality entails uniform or
= differences
identical treatment; / when they are, / it requires differential
= differences are relevant
treatment. // **단서 1** 차이점이 관련이 있을 때는 평등이 차이가 있는
대우를 필요로 함
후자가 관련이 없을 때 / 평등은 균일하거나 똑같은 대우를 내포한다 / 그것들이 관련이 있을
때 / 그것은 차이를 나타내는 대우를 필요로 한다 //
이유의 부사절 접속사
Equal rights do not mean identical rights, / for individuals
with different cultural backgrounds and needs / might **require**
different rights / **to enjoy equality** **단서 2** 차이점이 관련이 있는 경우임
평등한 권리는 똑같은 권리를 의미하지 않는데 / 왜냐하면 서로 다른 문화적 배경과 요구를 가
진 개인들이 / 다른 권리를 요구할지도 모르기 때문이다 / 평등을 누릴 수 있도록 /
in respect / of whatever happens to be the content / of their
rights. //
~에 관해서 / 우연히 내용이 되는 어떤 것에든 / 그들의 권리의 //
Equality involves / not just rejection of irrelevant differences /
as is commonly argued, / but also full recognition / of legitimate
= differences
and relevant ones. // not just A but also B: A뿐만 아니라 B도
평등은 포함한다 / 무관한 차이들에 대한 거부뿐만 아니라 / 흔히 주장되듯이 / 완전한 인정도
/ 합법적이고 관련 있는 차이들에 대한 //

- at once 동시에   - treat ⓥ (특정한 태도로) 대하다
- ground A in B A의 기초를 B에 두다   - uniformity ⓝ 획일성
- interplay ⓝ 상호 작용   - build A into B A를 B에 포함시키다
- concept ⓝ 개념   - equation ⓝ 동일시
- immune ⓐ (질병이나 공격 등을) 면한   - distortion ⓝ 왜곡
- content ⓝ 내용   - take ~ into account ~을 고려하다
- the latter 후자   - relevant ⓐ 관련이 있는
- identical ⓐ 동일한, 똑같은   - differential ⓐ 차이를 나타내는
- in respect of ~에 관해서   - rejection ⓝ 거부
- legitimate ⓐ 합법적인, 합당한   - abandon ⓥ 버리다, 포기하다

인간은 동시에 비슷하기도 하고 다르기도 해서 둘 다 때문에 동등하게 대우받아
야 한다. 평등의 기초를 인간의 획일성이 아니라 획일성과 차이의 상호 작용에
두는 그러한 견해는 평등이라는 바로 그 개념에 차이를 포함시키고, 전통적으
로 평등을 유사성과 동일시하는 것을 깨뜨리며, 일원론적 왜곡을 면한다. 일단
평등의 기초가 바뀌면 그것의 내용도 바뀐다. 평등은 서로 다를 수 있는 동등한
자유나 기회를 포함하고, 인간을 동등하게 대하는 것은 우리가 그들의 유사성
과 차이점을 둘 다 고려하도록 요구한다. 후자(차이점)가 관련이 없을 때 평등
은 균일하거나 똑같은 대우를 내포하고, 차이점이 관련이 있을 때 그것은 차이
를 나타내는 대우를 필요로 한다. 평등한 권리는 똑같은 권리를 의미하지 않는
데, 서로 다른 문화적 배경과 요구를 가진 개인들이 우연히 그들의 권리의 내용
이 되는 어떤 것이든 그것에 관해서 **평등을 누릴 수 있도록 다른 권리를 요구할**
지도 모르기 때문이다. 평등은 흔히 주장되듯이 무관한 차이들에 대한 거부뿐만
아니라 합법적이고 관련 있는 차이들에 대한 완전한 인정도 포함한다.

다음 빈칸에 들어갈 말로 가장 적절한 것을 고르시오. [3점]
① require different rights to enjoy equality 차이점이 관련 있는 상황에 대한 설명임
   평등을 누릴 수 있도록 다른 권리를 요구할
② abandon their own freedom for equality 자유를 포기한다는 내용은 없음
   평등을 위해 자신의 자유를 포기할
③ welcome the identical perception of inequality 불평등에 대한 언급은 없음
   불평등에 관한 동일한 인식을 기꺼이 받아들일
④ accept their place in the social structure more easily
   사회 구조에서 자신의 위치를 더 쉽게 받아들일   자신에 대한 대우를 받아들인다는 내용이 아님
⑤ reject relevant differences to gain full understanding
   온전한 이해를 얻기 위해 관련 있는 차이점을 거부할   평등에 있어 차이점을 고려하라는 내용임

> **왜** 정답 ? [정답률 50%]

빈칸 문장의 '똑같은 '권리'를 앞 문장의
'똑같은 '대우'와 연결시켜서 생각할 수 있음 **꿀팁**

빈칸 문장의 앞 문장에 등장한 the latter는 그 앞 문장에 나온 similarities와
differences 중에서 후자, 즉 differences를 가리킨다. differences(차이점)가 관
련 없을 때는 평등이 똑같은 대우를 내포하지만, 차이점이 관련이 있을 때는 평등
이 차이가 있는 대우를 필요로 한다고 했다. 빈칸 문장에서는 서로 다른 문화적 배
경과 요구를 가진 개인들, 즉 차이점이 관련이 있는 경우를 설명하므로 평등이 서
로 다른 대우를 필요로 한다는 내용과 연결되어야 한다. 따라서 빈칸에는 ① '평등
을 누릴 수 있도록 다른 권리를 요구할'이 들어가야 한다.

> **왜** 오답 ?

② 평등이 서로 다를 수 있는 동등한 자유나 기회를 포함할 수 있다고 했지, 평등을
   위해 자유를 포기한다는 내용은 없다.
③ 평등에 대한 내용으로, 불평등이 무엇인지 그 인식에 관한 설명은 없다.
④ 차이점이 관련되는 상황에서는 평등이 차이가 있는 대우를 요구한다는 것이지,
   어떤 대우를 받아들이는 것에 대한 설명은 아니다.
⑤ 평등이라는 개념에 차이점을 거부, 배제하는 것이 아니라 고려 대상에 포함시킨
   다는 내용이다.

K 49 정답 ② *공간을 분할하는 인간과 동물

More than just *having* territories, / animals also *partition* them. //
그저 영역을 '갖는' 것을 넘어서 / 동물은 또한 그것을 '분할한다' //
And this insight turned out / to be particularly useful / for zoo
husbandry. //
그리고 이러한 통찰은 밝혀졌다 / 특히 유용한 것으로 / 동물원 관리에 /
선행사   목적격 관계대명사
An animal's territory has an internal arrangement / that Heini
Hediger compared / to the inside of a person's house. //
동물의 영역에는 내부 배치가 있다 / Heini Hediger가 비유한 / 사람의 집 내부에 //
Most of us assign separate functions / to separate rooms, / but
even if you look at a one-room house / you will find / the same
internal specialization. // **단서 1** 우리는 (공간이 구분되어 있지 않더라도)
                        각 공간에 별도의 기능을 할당함
우리 대부분은 별도의 기능을 할당한다 / 별도의 방에 / 하지만 여러분이 원룸 주택을
살펴봐도 / 여러분은 발견할 것이다 / 동일한 내부의 전문화를 //
In a cabin or a mud hut, or even a Mesolithic cave / from 30,000
                전치사 In의 목적어의 병렬 구조
years ago, / **단서 2** 각 공간에 별도의 기능을 할당하는 예시
오두막이나 진흙 오두막, 혹은 심지어 중석기 시대의 동굴 안에도 / 3만 년 전의 /
this part is for cooking, / that part is for sleeping; / this part is for
making tools and weaving, / that part is for waste. //
이 부분은 요리를 위한 것이고 / 저 부분은 잠을 자기 위한 것이다 / 이 부분은 도구 제작과
직조를 위한 것이고 / 저 부분은 폐기물을 위한 것이다 //
We keep / **a neat functional organization**. //
우리는 유지한다 / 정돈된 기능적 체계를 //
To a varying extent, / other animals do the same. //
다양한 정도로 / 다른 동물들도 같은 행동을 한다 // 본동사로 쓰인 do
                                            뒤에 반복되는 동사 is가 생략됨
A part of an animal's territory / is for eating, / a part for sleeping,
/ a part for swimming or wallowing, /
동물의 영역 중 일부는 / 먹기 위한 것이고 / 일부는 잠을 자기 위한 것이며 / 일부는
헤엄치거나 뒹굴기 위한 것이고 /
a part may be set aside / for waste, / depending on the species
of animal. //
일부는 남겨질 수도 있다 / 폐기물을 위해 / 동물의 종에 따라 //

- territory ⓝ 영역, 영토   - partition ⓥ 분할하다, 나누다
- insight ⓝ 통찰력, 이해   - arrangement ⓝ 배치, 배열
- assign ⓥ (일·책임 등을) 맡기다, (가치·기능 등을) 부여하다
- separate ⓐ 분리된, 관련 없는   - specialization ⓝ 특수[전문]화
- cabin ⓝ 오두막집, 객실   - weave ⓥ (옷감을) 짜다[엮다]
- neat ⓐ 정돈된, 깔끔한   - functional ⓐ 기능적인, 가동되는
- varying ⓐ 가지각색의, 바뀌는   - extent ⓝ 정도, 규모
- wallow ⓥ (물·진흙 등의 속에서) 뒹굴다   - set aside 따로 떼어 두다

그저 영역을 '갖는' 것을 넘어서, 동물은 또한 영역을 '분할한다'. 그리고 이러한
통찰은 동물원 관리에 특히 유용한 것으로 밝혀졌다. 동물의 영역에는 Heini
Hediger가 사람의 집 내부에 비유한 내부 배치가 있다. 우리 대부분은 별도의
방에 별도의 기능을 할당하지만, 원룸 주택을 살펴봐도 동일한 내부의 전문화를
발견할 것이다. 오두막이나 진흙 오두막, 혹은 심지어 3만 년 전의 중석기
시대의 동굴 안에도, 이 부분은 요리를 위한 것이고, 저 부분은 잠을 자기 위한
것이며, 이 부분은 도구 제작과 직조를 위한 것이고, 저 부분은 폐기물을 위한
것이다. 우리는 **정돈된 기능적 체계**를 유지한다. 다양한 정도로, 다른 동물들도
같은 행동을 한다. 동물의 종에 따라, 동물의 영역 중 일부는 먹기 위한 것이고,
일부는 잠을 자기 위한 것이며, 일부는 헤엄치거나 뒹굴기 위한 것이고, 일부는
폐기물을 위해 남겨질 수도 있다.

다음 빈칸에 들어갈 말로 가장 적절한 것을 고르시오.

왜 정답? [정답률 74%]

빈칸 문장의 앞부분을 보면, 우리는 각 공간에 각각의 기능을 할당하는데,
이는 공간이 구분되어 있지 않은 원룸 주택인 경우에도 마찬가지라는 설명이
등장하고, 각각의 공간에 요리, 수면, 도구 제작과 직조, 폐기물 처리 등의 기능을
할당하는 구체적인 예시가 이어진다.
이를 통해 이 글에서 설명하는 우리가 유지하는 것이 ② '정돈된 기능적 체계'임을
알 수 있다.

왜 오답?

① 우리가 가까운 이웃에게 관심을 갖는다는 내용이 아니다. '주거 공간'이라는
　글의 소재에서 자연스럽게 연상되는 '이웃'을 포함하여 오답의 함정을 [함정]
　만들었다.
③ 우리와 동물이 비상용품의 비축량을 일정하게 유지한다는 내용이 아니다.
④ 잠재적 경쟁자에 대해서는 전혀 언급되지 않았다.
⑤ 각 공간에 별도의 기능을 할당한다는 것이지, 일상을 엄격하게 지킨다는 것은
　아니다.

K 50 정답 ④ ＊팬덤의 즐거움의 원천

Fans feel / for feeling's own sake. //
팬은 느낀다 / 감정 그 자체를 //

They make meanings / beyond what seems to be on offer. //
　　　　　　　　　　전치사　　　　　　　　명사절
그들은 의미를 만든다 / 제공되는 것으로 보이는 것을 넘어서는 //

They build identities and experiences, / and make artistic
　　　동사①　　　　　　　　　　　　　　　　　　동사②
creations of their own / to share with others. //
그들은 정체성과 경험을 만들고 / 그들 자신의 예술적 창작물을 만든다 / 다른 사람들과
공유하기 위해 //
　　　　　　　　　　　　　　　　　　분사구문을 이끄는 현재분사①
A person can be an individual fan, / feeling / an "idealized
connection with a star, / strong feelings of memory and
nostalgia," /
한 사람은 개인적인 팬이 되어 / 느끼며 / '어떤 스타와 이상적인 관계를 / 기억과 향수의 강한
감정'을 /
　　分사구문을 이끄는 현재분사②
and engaging in activities / like "collecting to develop a sense
of self." //　　[단서1] 개인적인 경험은 공유된 애착을 지닌 사람들이 애정의
　　　　　　　　　　대상을 중심으로 교제하는 사회적 상황에서 깊이 새겨짐
그리고 활동을 할 수 있다 / '자아감 형성을 위해 수집하기'와 같은 //

But, more often, / individual experiences are embedded / in
　선행사　　　　　　　관계부사
social contexts / where other people / with shared attachments /
socialize around the object / of their affections. //
그러나 더 흔히 / 개인적인 경험은 깊이 새겨진다 / 사회적인 상황에서 / 다른 사람들이 /
공유된 애착을 지닌 / 대상을 중심으로 교제하는 / 그들의 애정의 //

Much of the pleasure of fandom / **comes from being connected
/ to other fans**. //　　　　주어부에 부분을 나타내는 표현이 쓰이면
　　　　　　　　　　　　　of 뒤의 명사에 동사의 수를 일치시킴
팬덤의 많은 즐거움은 / 연결되는 것에서 온다 / 다른 팬들에게 //

In their diaries, / Bostonians of the 1800s described / being
part of the crowds / at concerts / as part of the pleasure of
attendance. // [단서2] 콘서트에 모인 군중의 일부가 되는 것이 참석의 즐거움의 일부임
그들의 일기에서 / 1800년대의 보스턴 사람들은 묘사했다 / 군중의 일부가 되는 것을 /
콘서트에서 / 참석의 즐거움의 일부로 //
　　　　　　　　　　　　동격절 접속사　　　명사절 주어
A compelling argument can be made / that what fans love / is
less the object of their fandom /　　　　　　　　　　단수 동사
강력한 주장이 제기될 수 있다 / 팬이 사랑하는 것은 / 그들의 팬덤의 대상이라기보다 /

than the attachments to (and differentiations from) one another
/ that those affections afford. // [단서3] 팬들이 사랑하는 것은 그들의 서로에 대한
　　　　　　　　　　　　　　　애착과 서로 간의 차이라고 강력히 주장할 수 있음
서로에 대한 애착(그리고 서로 간의 차이)이라는 / 그 애정이 제공하는 //

・on offer 제공되는, 이용할[살] 수 있는　・identity ⓝ 정체성, 신원
・idealize ⓥ 이상화하다　　・nostalgia ⓝ 향수(鄕愁)
・context ⓝ 맥락, 문맥　　・attachment ⓝ 애착, 믿음
・socialize ⓥ (사람들과) 어울리다, 사회화하다
・affection ⓝ 애착, 보살핌　・attendance ⓝ 출석, 참석
・argument ⓝ 논쟁, 주장　　・differentiation ⓝ 차별, 구별
・afford ⓥ 제공하다

팬은 감정 그 자체를 느낀다. 그들은 제공되는 것으로 보이는 것을 넘어서는
의미를 만든다. 그들은 정체성과 경험을 만들고, 다른 사람들과 공유하기 위해
그들 자신의 예술적 창작물을 만든다. 한 사람은 개인적인 팬이 되어, '어떤
스타와 이상적인 관계, 기억과 향수의 강한 감정'을 느끼며, '자아감 형성을 위해
수집하기'와 같은 활동을 할 수 있다. 그러나 더 흔히 개인적인 경험은 애착을
공유하는 다른 사람들이 그들의 애정의 대상을 중심으로 교제하는 사회적인
상황에서 깊이 새겨진다. 팬덤의 많은 즐거움은 **다른 팬들에게 연결되는 것에서
온다**. 1800년대의 보스턴 사람들은 그들의 일기에서 콘서트에 모인 군중의
일부가 되는 것을 참석의 즐거움의 일부로 묘사했다. 팬이 사랑하는 것은 그들의
팬덤의 대상이라기보다 그 애정이 제공하는 서로에 대한 애착(그리고 서로 간의
차이)이라는 강력한 주장이 제기될 수 있다.

다음 빈칸에 들어갈 말로 가장 적절한 것을 고르시오.
　　애착의 대상으로부터 즐거움을 얻는다는 것이 아님

왜 정답? [정답률 65%] [역접의 연결어 But을 통해!] [꿀팁]

빈칸 문장의 앞 문장에서 글의 내용이 전환되면서, 공유된 애착을 지닌 사람들,
즉 같은 대상을 사랑하는 팬들이 그 대상을 중심으로 교제하는 사회적 상황에서
개인적인 경험이 깊이 새겨진다고 했다.
빈칸 문장 이후로는, 콘서트에 모인 군중의 일부가 되는 것이 즐거움의 일부이고,
팬들이 사랑하는 것은 팬덤의 대상이라기보다 팬들의 서로에 대한 애착일 수
있다는 내용이 이어지므로, 이 글은 팬덤의 많은 즐거움이 ④ '다른 팬들에게
연결되는 것에서 온다'는 점을 설명하는 것이다.

왜 오답?

①, ②, ⑤ 팬덤의 즐거움이 그들의 애착의 대상인 스타로부터 오는 것이 아니라
　같은 대상을 좋아하는 사람들과의 교제로부터 온다는 내용이다.
③ 애착의 대상과 팬이 나이 들수록, 혹은 세월이 흐를수록 즐거움이 커진다는
　내용은 없다.

K 51 정답 ④ ＊형식주의자의 특징

　　주어
The critic / who wants to write about literature / from a formalist
perspective / must first be a close and careful reader /
　　　　　　　　　동사
비평가 / 문학에 관하여 쓰고자 하는 / 형식주의자의 관점에서 / 먼저 면밀하고도 주의 깊은
독자가 되어야 한다 /
　　　　　　　주격 관계대명사절의 동사①
who examines all the elements of a text individually / and
주격 관계대명사절의 동사②　　　　　　　　　　부사적 용법(결과)
questions / how they come together to create a work of art. //
글의 모든 요소를 개별적으로 검토하고 / 질문하는 / 그것들이 모여 예술 작품을 만드는
방식에 대해 //　　주어
Such a reader, / who respects the autonomy of a work, / achieves
　　　　　　　　　　　　　　　　　　　　　　　　　　　동사
an understanding of it / by **looking inside it, / not outside it or
beyond it**. //
그러한 독자는 / 작품의 자율성을 존중하는 / 그것에 대한 이해를 달성한다 / 그것의 내부를
들여다봄으로써 / 그것의 외부나 그것을 넘어서가 아니라 //

Instead of examining / historical periods, author biographies, or
literary styles, / for example, / [단서1] 글 자체가 아닌 외적인 요소를 검도하지 않음
검토하는 대신 / 역사상의 시대, 작가의 전기, 또는 문학적 양식을 / 예를 들어

he or she will approach a text / with the assumption / that it
is a self-contained entity / and that he or she is looking for the
governing principles / that allow the text to reveal itself. //
그 사람은 글에 접근할 것이다 / 추정으로 / 글이 자족적인 실체이며 / 자신은 지배적인 원칙을
찾고 있다는 / 그 글이 스스로를 드러내도록 해주는 //
단서2 글은 자기 스스로를 충족시키는
실체라는 추정으로 글에 접근함

For example, / the correspondences / between the characters
in James Joyce's short story "Araby" and the people / he knew
personally / may be interesting, /
예를 들어 / 관련성은 / James Joyce의 단편 소설인 〈Araby〉 속의 등장인물들과
사람들과의 / 그가 개인적으로 알았던 / 흥미로울 수도 있겠지만 /

but for the formalist / they are less relevant / to understanding
/ how the story creates meaning / than are other kinds of
information / that the story contains within itself. //
그 형식주의자에게 / 그것들은 덜 관련되어 있다 / 이해하는 데 / 그 이야기가 의미를
만들어내는 방식을 / 다른 종류의 정보가 그런 것보다 / 이야기가 그 안에 포함하고 있는 //
단서3 〈Araby〉를 이해하는 데 있어 외적인 요소는 〈Araby〉 안에 포함된 정보보다 덜 관련되어 있음

- literature ⓝ (특정 분야의) 문헌, 문학
- formalist ⓝ 형식주의자, 이론주의자 · autonomy ⓝ 자율성, 자주성
- biography ⓝ 전기(傳記) · literary ⓐ 문학적인, 문학의
- assumption ⓝ 가정, 추정 · self-contained ⓐ 자족적인, 자립하는
- entity ⓝ 독립체 · correspondence ⓝ 관련성, 서신, 편지
- relevant ⓐ 관련 있는, 적절한 · contain ⓥ 포함하다, 함유하다

형식주의자의 관점에서 문학에 관하여 쓰고자 하는 비평가는 먼저 글의 모든
요소를 개별적으로 검토하고 그것들이 모여 예술 작품을 만드는 방식에
대해 질문하는 면밀하고도 주의 깊은 독자가 되어야 한다. 작품의 자율성을
존중하는 그러한 독자는 **그것의 외부나 그것을 넘어서가 아니라 그것의 내부를
들여다봄**으로써 그것에 대한 이해를 달성한다. 예를 들어, 역사상의 시대,
작가의 전기, 또는 문학적 양식을 검토하는 대신, 그 사람은 글이 자족적인
실체이며, 자신은 그 글이 스스로를 드러내도록 해주는 지배적인 원칙을 찾고
있다는 추정으로 글에 접근할 것이다. 예를 들어, James Joyce의 단편 소설인
〈Araby〉 속의 등장인물들과 그가 개인적으로 알았던 사람들과의 관련성은
흥미로울 수도 있겠지만, 그 형식주의자에게 그것들은 그 이야기가 그 안에
포함하고 있는 다른 종류의 정보보다 이야기가 의미를 만들어내는 방식을
이해하는 데 덜 관련되어 있다.

다음 빈칸에 들어갈 말로 가장 적절한 것을 고르시오.

① putting himself or herself both inside and outside it 작품의 안팎을 대조하는 것임
   그 자신을 그것의 안과 밖 모두에 놓음
② finding a middle ground between it and the world 내부에 집중함
   그것과 세상 사이에서 중간 위치를 찾음
③ searching for historical realities revealed within it 역사적 사실을 다룬
   그 안에서 드러난 역사적인 사실을 찾아봄 글에 국한하는 것이 아님
④ looking inside it, not outside it or beyond it 작품 자체의 내용에 집중함
   그것의 외부나 그것을 넘어서가 아니라 그것의 내부를 들여다봄
⑤ exploring its characters' cultural relevance 외부적 요소를 배제함
   그것의 등장인물들의 문화적 관련성을 탐구함

왜 정답? [정답률 47%]   필요한 것을 자기 스스로 충족시키는 것을 의미함 **꿀팁**

형식주의자는 어떤 글을 검토할 때 그 글이 쓰인 역사적 시대나 작가의 전기,
문학적 양식 등의 외적인 요소를 고려하는 대신, 글은 자족적인 실체라는 추정으로
글에 접근할 것이라는 내용이다.
이에 대한 예로, 단편 소설 〈Araby〉의 등장인물과 작가가 개인적으로 알았던
사람들과의 관련성은 흥미로울 수는 있지만, 〈Araby〉를 이해하는 데는 〈Araby〉
안에 포함된 정보보다 덜 중요하다고 했다.
이를 통해 형식주의자의 특징이 ④ '작품의 외부나 작품을 넘어서가 아니라 작품의
내부를 들여다봄'으로써 작품을 이해한다는 것임을 알 수 있다.

왜 오답?

①, ② 작품 내부와 외부를 대조하여 내부에 집중한다는 내용이다. 내부와 외부를
   모두 고려한다거나 그 사이의 중간 위치를 찾는다는 것이 아니다. **주의**
③ 작품 내부에 드러나는 내용이 구체적으로 무엇인지에 대해서는 언급하지
   않았다.
⑤ James Joyce의 단편 소설인 〈Araby〉를 예시로 들어 설명한 부분으로 만든
   오답이다. 외적인 요소인 '문화적 관련성'을 중점적으로 다룬 글이 아니다.

K 52 정답 ① *신피질의 특징

단서1 신피질은 '거의' 아무것도 모르는 채로 태어남(일부는 이미 아는 상태로, 즉 정해진 상태로 태어남)
When you are born, / your neocortex knows almost nothing. //
여러분이 태어날 때 / 여러분의 신피질은 거의 아무것도 모른다 //

It doesn't know / any words, / what buildings are like, / how
to use a computer, / or what a door is / and how it moves on
hinges. //
그것은 알지 못한다 / 어떠한 단어도 / 건물이 무엇과 같은지 / 컴퓨터를 어떻게 사용하는지 /
혹은 문이 무엇이며 / 그것이 경첩에서 어떻게 움직이는지를 //

It has to learn / countless things. //
그것은 배워야 한다 / 무수한 것을 //

The overall structure of the neocortex / is not random. //
신피질의 전체적인 구조는 / 무작위가 아니다 //

Its size, / the number of regions / it has, / and how they are
connected together / is largely determined / by our genes. //
그것의 크기 / 영역들의 수 / 그것이 가진 / 그리고 어떻게 그것들이 함께 연결되는지는 / 주로
결정된다 / 우리의 유전자에 의해 //

For example, / genes determine / what parts of the neocortex are
connected / to the eyes, / what other parts are connected / to the
ears, / and how those parts connect / to each other. //
예를 들어 / 유전자는 결정한다 / 신피질의 어떤 부분들이 연결되는지 / 눈에 / 어떤 다른
부분들이 연결되는지 / 귀에 / 그리고 어떻게 그 부분들이 연결되는지를 / 서로에 //

Therefore, / we can say / that the neocortex is structured / at
birth / to see, hear, and even learn language. //
그러므로 / 우리는 말할 수 있다 / 신피질은 구조화된다고 / 태어날 때 / 보고 듣고 심지어
언어를 배우도록 //
단서2 보고 듣고 언어를 배우도록 결정된 채로 태어남

But it is also true / that the neocortex doesn't know / what it will
see, / what it will hear, / and what specific languages it might
learn. //
하지만 ~이 또한 사실이다 / 신피질은 모른다는 것이 / 그것이 무엇을 볼지를 / 그것이 무엇을
들을지를 / 그리고 그것이 어떤 특정한 언어를 배울지를 //
단서3 무엇을 보고 들을지, 어떤 언어를 배울지는 모르는 채로 태어남

We can think of the neocortex / as starting life / **having some
built-in assumptions / about the world** / but knowing nothing
in particular. //
우리는 신피질을 생각할 수 있다 / 생을 시작하는 것으로 / 어떤 내재된 가정을 가졌지만 /
세상에 대한 / 특정하게 아는 것은 없이 //

Through experience, / it learns / a rich and complicated model
of the world. //
경험을 통해 / 그것은 배운다 / 풍부하고 복잡한 세상 모형을 //

- hinge ⓝ (문ㆍ뚜껑 등의) 경첩 · countless ⓐ 무수한, 셀 수 없이 많은
- overall ⓐ 전반적인 · structure ⓝ 구조, 구성 ⓥ 구조화하다, 조직하다
- random ⓐ 임의의, 무작위의 · determine ⓥ 결정하다
- gene ⓝ 유전자 · complicated ⓐ 복잡한

여러분이 태어날 때, 여러분의 신피질은 거의 아무것도 모른다. 그것은 어떠한
단어도, 건물이 어떤지, 컴퓨터를 어떻게 사용하는지, 혹은 문이 무엇이며
그것이 경첩에서 어떻게 움직이는지를 알지 못한다. 그것은 무수한 것을 배워야
한다. 신피질의 전체적인 구조는 무작위가 아니다. 그것의 크기, 그것이 가지고
있는 영역들의 수, 그리고 어떻게 그것들이 함께 연결되는지는 우리의 유전자에
의해 주로 결정된다. 예를 들어, 유전자는 신피질의 어떤 부분들이 눈과
연결되는지, 어떤 다른 부분들이 귀와 연결되는지, 그리고 어떻게 그 부분들이
서로 연결되는지를 결정한다. 그러므로 우리는 신피질은 태어날 때 보고 듣고
심지어 언어를 배우도록 구조화된다고 말할 수 있다. 하지만 신피질은 그것이
무엇을 볼지, 그것이 무엇을 들을지, 그리고 그것이 어떤 특정한 언어를 배울지
모른다는 것 또한 사실이다. 우리는 신피질이 **세상에 대한 어떤 내재된 가정을
가졌지만** 특정하게 아는 것은 없이 생을 시작하는 것으로 생각할 수 있다.
경험을 통해 그것은 풍부하고 복잡한 세상 모형을 배운다.

다음 빈칸에 들어갈 말로 가장 적절한 것을 고르시오.

① having some built-in assumptions about the world
세상에 대한 어떤 내재된 가정을 가졌지만　　유전자에 의해 전체적인 구조는 결정된 채로 태어남
② causing conflicts between genes and environments
유전자와 환경 사이에 충돌을 야기하지만　　유전자와 환경의 충돌에 대한 내용이 아님
③ being able to efficiently reprocess prior knowledge
이전의 지식을 효율적으로 다시 처리할 수 있지만　　지식의 재처리가 가능하다는 언급은 없음
④ controlling the structure and processing power of the brain
뇌의 구조와 처리 능력을 제어하지만　　신피질의 기능에 대한 설명이 아님
⑤ fighting persistently against the determined world of genes
유전자라는 정해진 세상에 맞서 끊임없이 싸우지만　　유전자와 맞서 싸우는 것이 아님

▷왜 정답? [정답률 44%]

> 아예 아무것도 모른다면 부사 almost를 쓰지 않았을 것임 **꿀팁**

우리의 신피질은 '거의 아무것도' 모르는 채로 태어난다는 첫 문장은 신피질이 대부분은 모르는 채로 태어나지만 결정된 채로 태어나는 것도 있다는 것을 의미한다.

신피질은 태어날 때 보고 듣고 언어를 배우도록 구조화되지만 무엇을 보고 들을지, 어떤 언어를 배울지는 모른다는 것으로 보아 빈칸 문장은 신피질이 ① '세상에 대한 어떤 내재된 가정을 가졌지만' 특정하게 아는 것은 없이 태어난다는 내용이 되어야 한다.

▷왜 오답?

② 유전자의 영향을 받는지, 아니면 환경의 영향을 받는지를 대조해서 설명하는 글이 아니다.

③, ④ 신피질이 이전의 지식을 다시 처리할 수 있다거나 뇌의 구조와 처리 능력을 제어한다는 언급은 없다. **함정**

⑤ genes가 언급된 것으로 만든 오답이다. 신피질의 전체적인 구조가 유전자에 의해서 결정된다고 했지, 신피질이 유전자에 맞선다는 내용은 없다.

K 53 정답 ③ ＊시계의 잔인한 힘

〈대조〉의 부사절 접속사
While early clocks marked / only the hour or quarter-hour, / by 1700 / most clocks had acquired minute hands, / and by 1800 / second hands were standard. //
초기 시계는 표시했던 반면 / 오직 정각이나 15분씩만을 / 1700년경에는 / 대부분의 시계가 분침을 얻었고 / 1800년경에는 / 초침이 표준이었다 //

형용사적 용법(ability 수식)
This unprecedented ability / to measure time precisely / **found its most authoritarian expression / in the factory clock**, / which became a prime weapon / of the Industrial Revolution. //
이러한 전례 없는 능력은 / 시간을 정확하게 측정하는 / 그것의 가장 권위적인 모습으로 나타났고 / 공장 시계에서 / 이는 주요 무기가 되었다 / 산업 혁명의 //

주어
As the historian of technology Lewis Mumford argued, / "the clock, / not the steam engine, / is the key-machine / of the modern industrial age." //
동사　　주격 보어
기술 역사가 Lewis Mumford가 주장했듯이 / "시계가 / 증기 기관이 아닌 / 핵심 기계이다 / 근대 산업 시대의" //

Soon factory workers were clocking in, / filling out timesheets, / and being punished for lateness. //
과거진행형을 완성하는 현재분사구의 병렬 구조
곧 공장 노동자들은 출근 시간을 기록하고 있었고 / 근무 시간 기록표를 기입하고 있었고 / 지각에 대해 처벌받고 있었다 //

'with+(대)명사+과거분사', 분사구문
With time sliced / into smaller and smaller periods, /
시간이 분할되면서 / 점점 더 작은 시간으로 /

business owners could measure / the speed of their workers / down to the second, / and gradually increase the pace / of the production line. // **단서1** 시간을 초 단위로 측정할 수 있게 되면서 사업주들은 노동자의 속도를 측정하고 생산 라인의 속도를 증가시킬 수 있게 되었음
병렬 구조
사업주들은 측정할 수 있었고 / 자신들의 노동자들의 속도를 / 초에 이르기까지 / 속도를 점진적으로 증가시킬 수 있었다 / 생산 라인의 //

Workers / who tried to reject this strict control / by "going slow" / were swiftly fired. // **단서2** 정확한 시계를 통한 고용주의 통제를 거부하는 노동자는 빠르게 해고되었음
주어
노동자들은 / 이러한 엄격한 통제를 거부하려 노력했던 / '태업함'으로써 / 빠르게 해고되었다 //

The cruel power of the clock fed / the growing culture of utilitarian efficiency, / so brilliantly depicted / by Charles Dickens / in his 1854 novel *Hard Times*, /
선행사
시계의 잔인한 힘은 충족시켰으며 / 커지는 공리주의적 효율성 문화를 / 이는 너무나도 훌륭하게 묘사되었는데 / Charles Dickens에 의해 / 그의 1854년 소설 〈Hard Times〉에서 /

---

where the office of Mr. Gradgrind / contained "a deadly
관계부사
statistical clock in it, / which measured every second / with a
선행사　　관계대명사
beat / like a rap upon a coffin-lid." //
여기에서 Gradgrind 씨의 사무실은 / '치명적인 통계 시계를 그 안에 갖고 있었다 / 매 초를 측정하는 / 똑딱거리는 소리와 함께 / 관 뚜껑을 두드리는 것 같은' //

- mark ⓥ 표시하다　　・quarter-hour ⓝ 15분(간)
- acquire ⓥ 얻다, 습득하다　　・hand ⓝ (시계) 바늘
- unprecedented ⓐ 전례 없는　　・measure ⓥ 측정하다, 재다
- precisely ⓐⓓ 정확하게　　・find expression in ～의 모습으로 나타나다
- prime ⓐ 주된, 중요한　　・argue ⓥ 주장하다, 논증하다
- clock in 출근 시간을 기록하다　　・timesheet ⓝ 출퇴근 시간 기록 용지
- slice ⓥ 얇게 베다[썰다]　　・pace ⓝ 속도　　・reject ⓥ 거절[거부]하다
- swiftly ⓐⓓ 신속히, 빨리　　・fire ⓥ 해고하다　　・cruel ⓐ 잔혹한, 잔인한
- feed ⓥ (필요・욕구 등을) 충족시키다　　・brilliantly ⓐⓓ 훌륭하게
- depict ⓥ 묘사하다　　・contain ⓥ 포함하다　　・deadly ⓐ 치명적인
- statistical ⓐ 통계의, 통계(학)상의

초기 시계는 오직 정각이나 15분씩만을 표시했던 반면, 1700년경에는 대부분의 시계가 분침을 얻었고, 1800년경에는 초침이 표준이었다. 시간을 정확하게 측정하는 이러한 전례 없는 능력은 **공장 시계에서 그것의 가장 권위적인 모습으로 나타났고**, 이는 산업 혁명의 주요 무기가 되었다. 기술 역사가 Lewis Mumford가 주장했듯이, "증기 기관이 아닌 시계가 근대 산업 시대의 핵심 기계이다." 곧 공장 노동자들은 출근 시간을 기록하고 있었고, 근무 시간 기록표를 기입하고 있었고, 지각에 대해 처벌받고 있었다. 시간이 점점 더 작은 시간(단위)으로 분할되면서 사업주들은 자신들의 노동자들의 속도를 초에 이르기까지 측정할 수 있었고, 생산 라인의 속도를 점진적으로 증가시킬 수 있었다. 이러한 엄격한 통제를 '태업함'으로써 거부하려 노력했던 노동자들은 빠르게 해고되었다. 시계의 잔인한 힘은 커지는 공리주의적 효율성 문화를 충족시켰으며, 이는 Charles Dickens의 1854년 소설 〈Hard Times〉에서 그에 의해 너무나도 훌륭하게 묘사되었는데, 여기에서 Gradgrind 씨의 사무실은 "관 뚜껑을 두드리는 것 같은 똑딱거리는 소리와 함께 매 초를 측정했던 치명적인 통계 시계를 그 안에" 갖고 있었다.

다음 빈칸에 들어갈 말로 가장 적절한 것을 고르시오. [3점]

① allowed workers to climb up the ladder of social class
노동자들이 사회적 계급의 사다리를 올라가도록 허용했다　　정확한 시계는 고용주에게 유리했음
② liberated workers but imprisoned employers in a time trap
노동자들을 자유롭게 했지만 고용주들을 시간의 덫에 감금했다　노동자에게 유리하고 고용주에게 불리한 것이 아님
③ found its most authoritarian expression in the factory clock
공장 시계에서 그것의 가장 권위적인 모습으로 나타났다　　고용주가 노동자를 통제하는 수단으로 이용됨
④ veiled the violent nature and the discipline of measured time
측정된 시간의 폭력적인 본성과 규율을 감췄다　　시계의 잔인한 힘을 설명하는 글임
⑤ paved the way for workers to control manufacturing machines
노동자들이 생산 기계를 통제하는 길을 닦았다　　노동자의 기계 통제에 영향을 미친 것이 아님

▷왜 정답? [정답률 34%]

정확한 시계의 등장이 어떤 영향을 미쳤는지를 살펴봐야 하는데, 빈칸 문장 이후의 내용을 보면, 산업 혁명의 무기가 된 정확한 시간 측정으로 고용주는 노동자의 작업 속도를 초 단위로 측정할 수 있게 되었고, 생산 라인의 속도를 증가시킬 수 있게 되었다고 했다.

이러한 통제를 거부하는 노동자는 빠르게 해고되었다는 것으로 보아, 빈칸 문장은 시간을 정확하게 측정하는 능력이 ③ '공장 시계에서 그것의 가장 권위적인 모습으로 나타났다'는 내용이 되는 것이 적절하다.

▷왜 오답?

① 정확한 시계의 등장으로 인한 고용주의 통제를 거부하는 노동자가 빠르게 해고되었다고 했으므로 노동자가 사회적 계급의 사다리를 올라가게 되었다는 것은 적절하지 않다.

② 정확한 시계가 고용주에게 유리하고 노동자에게 불리하게 작용했다는 글의 내용과 반대이다.

④ '시계의 잔인한 힘'이라고 표현한 것으로 보아 시간의 폭력적인 본성과 규율을 드러냈다고 하는 것이 더 적절하다. **주의**

⑤ 정확한 시간을 알게 됨으로써 노동자가 기계를 통제하게 되었다는 내용이 아니다.

K 54 정답 ① * 적극적인 행위자인 인간

Gordon Allport argued / that history records many individuals
(주격 관계대명사)
/ who were not content with an existence / that offered them /
(선행사) (주격 관계대명사)
little variety, a lack of psychic tension, and minimal challenge. //
Gordon Allport는 주장했다 / 역사가 많은 개개인을 기록한다고 / 존재에 만족하지 않았던
/ 그들에게 제공한 / 거의 없는 다양성, 심적 긴장의 결핍, 그리고 최소한의 도전을 //

Allport considers it normal / to be pulled forward / by a vision
(주어) (동사) (가목적어) (목적격 보어) (진목적어)
of the future / that awakened / within persons / their drive / to
alter the course of their lives. //
(형용사적 용법: their drive 수식)
Allport는 ~을 정상이라고 여긴다 / 앞으로 이끌어지는 것을 / 미래에 대한 통찰력에 의해 /
일깨운 / 인간의 내면에서 / 그들의 욕구를 / 자기 삶의 행로를 바꾸려는 //

He suggests / that people possess a need / to invent motives and
(형용사적 용법: a need 수식)
purposes / that would consume their inner energies. //
그는 말한다 / 사람들이 욕구를 지니고 있다고 / 동기와 목적을 만들어 내려는 / 그들의
내면의 에너지를 소모할 // **단서1** 사람들은 동기와 목적을 만들어 내려는 욕구를 지니고 있음

Similarly, Erich Fromm proposed a need / on the part of humans
(형용사적 용법: a need 수식)
/ to rise above the roles of passive creatures / in an accidental if
not random world. // **단서2** 인간에게는 수동적인 피조물의 역할을 벗어나려는 욕구가 있음
마찬가지로 Erich Fromm은 욕구를 제시했다 / 인간 측의 / 수동적인 피조물의 역할을
넘어서려는 / 마구잡이는 아니더라도 우연한 세계에서 //

To him, / humans are driven / to transcend / the state of merely
having been created; / **단서3** 인간은 단지 창조된 상태를 넘어서도록 이끌림
그에게 / 인간은 이끌린다 / 넘어서도록 / 단지 창조된 상태를 /

instead, humans seek / to become the creators, / the active
(동격)
shapers of their own destiny. // **단서4** 자신의 운명의 적극적인
행위자가 되는 것을 추구함
대신에 인간은 추구한다 / 창조자가 되는 것을 / 자신의 운명의 적극적인 행위자 //

Rising / above the passive and accidental nature of existence,
(주어) (동사①)
/ humans generate their own purposes / and thereby provide
(동사②)
themselves / with a true basis of freedom. //
넘어서서 / 존재의 수동적이고 우연한 본질을 / 인간은 자신만의 목적을 만들어 내고 / 그렇게
함으로써 자신에게 제공한다 / 자유의 진정한 토대를 //

- argue ⓥ 주장하다, 다투다
- content ⓐ (가진 것에) 만족하는
- existence ⓝ 실재, 존재
- lack ⓝ 부족, 결핍
- psychic ⓐ 마음의, 초자연적인
- tension ⓝ 긴장 (상태)
- minimal ⓐ 최소의, 아주 적은
- awaken ⓥ (감정을) 불러일으키다, 깨우다
- drive ⓝ 욕구, 추진력 ⓥ (특정한 행동을 하도록) 만들다
- alter ⓥ 바꾸다, 변하다
- possess ⓥ 지니다, 소유하다
- motive ⓝ 동기, 이유
- consume ⓥ (연료·에너지·시간을) 소모하다
- propose ⓥ 제안하다
- passive ⓐ 수동적인
- accidental ⓐ 우연한, 돌발적인
- merely ⓐⓓ 단지, 그저
- seek ⓥ 추구하다, 찾다
- active ⓐ 적극적인
- shaper ⓝ 만드는 사람
- generate ⓥ 만들어 내다, 발생하다
- thereby ⓐⓓ 그렇게 함으로써
- basis ⓝ 기반, 이유

Gordon Allport는 다양성이 거의 없고 심적 긴장이 결핍되어 있으며 최소한의
도전을 제공한 존재에 만족하지 않았던 많은 개개인을 역사가 기록한다고
주장했다. Allport는 인간의 내면에서 **자기 삶의 행로를 바꾸려는** 욕구를
일깨운 미래에 대한 통찰력에 의해 앞으로 나아가게 되는 것을 정상이라고
여긴다. 그는 사람들이 내면의 에너지를 소모할 동기와 목적을 만들어 내려는
욕구를 지니고 있다고 말한다. 마찬가지로 Erich Fromm은 마구잡이는
아니더라도 우연한 세계에서 수동적인 피조물의 역할을 넘어서려는 인간 측의
욕구를 제시했다. 그에게, 인간은 단지 창조된 상태를 넘어서도록 이끌리며,
대신에 창조자, 즉 자신의 운명의 적극적인 행위자가 되는 것을 추구한다.
존재의 수동적이고 우연한 본질을 넘어서서 인간은 자신만의 목적을 만들어
내고 그렇게 함으로써 자신에게 자유의 진정한 토대를 제공한다.

다음 빈칸에 들어갈 말로 가장 적절한 것을 고르시오. [3점]

① alter the course of their lives 자신의 운명을 적극적으로 개척하고자 함
자기 삶의 행로를 바꾸려는
② possess more than other people 욕심이 많은 인간에 대한 내용이 아님
다른 사람들보다 더 많이 소유하려는
③ suppress their negative emotions 긍정적이고자 한다는 언급은 없음
자신의 부정적인 감정을 억누르려는
④ sacrifice themselves for noble causes 인간이 대의명분을 위해 희생한다는 내용이
숭고한 대의명분을 위해 자신을 희생하려는 아님
⑤ show admiration for supernatural power 초자연적인 힘은 등장하지 않음
초자연적인 힘에 대해 존경심을 보이려는

왜 정답? [정답률 51%]

Gordon Allport와 Erich Fromm의 주장에 따르면, 인간은 동기와 목적을 만들어
내려는 욕구를 지녔고, 수동적인 피조물의 역할을 넘어서도록 이끌리며, 자신의
운명을 적극적으로 창조하는 행위자가 되는 것을 추구한다.
이렇게 존재의 수동적이고 우연한 본질을 넘어서서 인간은 자신의 목적을
만들어 내고, 스스로에게 자유의 진정한 토대를 제공한다고 했으므로, Allport가
정상이라고 여기는 것은 ① '자기 삶의 행로를 바꾸려는' 인간의 욕구를 일깨우는
미래에 대한 통찰력에 의해 앞으로 나아가게 되는 것이다.

왜 오답?

②, ③ 인간의 다른 사람들보다 더 많이 소유하려는 욕구나 부정적인 감정을
억누르려는 욕구에 대한 내용이 아니다.
④ 인간에게 숭고한 대의명분을 위해 스스로를 희생하려는 욕구가 있다는 언급은
없다.
⑤ '초자연적인 힘'은 '수동적인 피조물' 등의 표현에서 연상할 수 있는 오답이다.

K 55 정답 ③ * 비슷한 사람들과 함께하는 전략의 제한

Choosing similar friends / can have a rationale. //
비슷한 친구들을 선택하는 것은 / 논리적 근거를 가질 수 있다 //

Assessing the survivability of an environment / can be risky / (if
an environment turns out to be deadly, / for instance, / it might
(앞에 관계부사가 생략됨) (비인칭 주어)
be too late / by the time you found out), /
어떤 환경에서의 생존 가능성을 평가하는 것은 / 위험할 수 있다 / (어떤 환경이 치명적인 것으
로 판명되면 / 예를 들어 / 너무 늦을 수도 있다 / 그 사실을 알 때쯤에는) /
(형용사적 용법: the desire 수식)
so humans have evolved the desire / to associate with similar
(형용사적 용법: a way 수식)
individuals / as a way / to perform this function efficiently. //
그래서 인간은 욕구를 진화시켜 왔다 / 유사한 개인들과 함께하고자 하는 / 한 방법으로서 / 이
기능을 효율적으로 수행하기 위한 //
(선행사) (주격 관계대명사)
This is especially useful / to a species / that lives / in so many
different sorts of environments. //
이것은 특히 유용하다 / 종에게 / 사는 / 매우 다양한 종류의 환경에 //

However, / the carrying capacity of a given environment /
places a limit / on this strategy. // **단서1** 나무가 거의 없다면 나무집에서 사는
사람들이 함께할 수 없고, 망고가 부족하면 망고만
그러나 / 주어진 환경의 수용 능력은 / 제한을 둔다 / 이 전략에 // 먹는 사람들이 함께할 수 없음

If resources are very limited, / the individuals / who live in a
(동사) (주어(선행사)) (주격 관계대명사)
particular place / cannot all do the exact same thing /
자원이 매우 한정되어 있다면 / 개인이 / 특정 장소에 사는 / 모두 똑같은 것을 할 수는 없다 /
(for example, / if there are few trees, / people cannot all live in
tree houses, / or if mangoes are in short supply, / people cannot
all live / solely on a diet of mangoes). //
(예를 들어 / 나무가 거의 없다면 / 사람들이 모두 나무집에 살 수는 없다 / 또는 망고의 공급
이 부족하면 / 사람들이 모두 살 수는 없다 / 오직 망고를 먹는 식단으로) //
(명사적 용법(주격 보어))
A rational strategy would therefore sometimes be to avoid /
similar members of one's species. // **단서2** 환경의 수용 능력으로 인해 자신의
종의 비슷한 구성원을 피하게 됨
그러므로 합리적인 전략은 때때로 '피하는' 것일 것이다 / 자신의 종의 비슷한 구성원을 //

- **rationale** ⓝ 근본적 이유, 논리적 근거　　• **assess** ⓥ 평가하다, 가늠하다
- **survivability** ⓝ 생존 가능성　　• **risky** ⓐ 위험한
- **deadly** ⓐ 생명을 앗아가는, 치명적인
- **associate** ⓥ 연상하다, 결부[연관] 짓다　　• **exact** ⓐ 정확한, 정밀한
- **short** ⓐ 부족한, ~이 없는　　• **live on** ~을 먹고 살다
- **solely** ⓓ 오로지, 단독으로　　• **diverse** ⓐ 다양한
- **means** ⓝ 수단, 방법　　• **suitable** ⓐ 적합한, 적절한
- **tie** ⓝ 유대 (관계), 결속

비슷한 친구들을 선택하는 것은 논리적 근거를 가질 수 있다. 어떤 환경에서의 생존 가능성을 평가하는 것은 위험할 수 있어서 (예를 들어, 어떤 환경이 치명적인 것으로 판명되면, 그 사실을 알 때쯤에는 너무 늦을 수도 있다), 인간은 이 기능을 효율적으로 수행하기 위한 한 방법으로서 유사한 개인들과 함께하고자 하는 욕구를 진화시켜 왔다. 이것은 매우 다양한 종류의 환경에 사는 종에게 특히 유용하다. 그러나 주어진 환경의 수용 능력은 **이 전략에 제한을 둔다**. 자원이 매우 한정되어 있다면, 특정 장소에 사는 개인이 모두 똑같은 것을 할 수는 없다 (예를 들어, 나무가 거의 없다면, 사람들이 모두 나무집에 살 수는 없으며, 또는 망고의 공급이 부족하면, 사람들이 모두 오직 망고를 먹는 식단으로 살 수는 없다). 그러므로 합리적인 전략은 때때로 자신의 종의 비슷한 구성원을 '피하는' 것일 것이다.

다음 빈칸에 들어갈 말로 가장 적절한 것을 고르시오.
① exceeds the expected demands of a community
　공동체의 예상 수요를 초과한다　　나무와 망고가 부족한 경우를 예로 들었음
② is decreased by diverse means of survival
　다양한 생존 수단에 의해 감소된다　　환경의 수용 능력이 감소하는 경우를 설명한 것이 아님
③ places a limit on this strategy
　이 전략에 제한을 둔다　　비슷한 사람들을 피하는 것이 전략인 경우를 설명함
④ makes the world suitable for individuals
　세상을 개인들에게 적합하게 만든다　　개인이 환경에 적응하는 것임
⑤ prevents social ties to dissimilar members
　비슷하지 않은 구성원의 사회적 유대를 막는다　　비슷한 구성원과의 유대를 막는 경우라고 할 수 있음

왜 정답? [정답률 46%]

인간이 어떤 환경에서의 생존 가능성을 평가하는 방법(전략)으로서 비슷한 사람들과 함께하고자 하는 욕구를 진화시켜 왔다는 내용에 역접으로 연결된 문장에 빈칸이 있다. 빈칸 문장 이후의 내용을 보면, 나무가 거의 없는 환경에서는 나무집에서 사는 (비슷한) 사람들이 모여 살 수 없고, 망고가 부족한 환경에서는 망고만 먹고 사는 (비슷한) 사람들이 모여 살 수 없다고 했다. 즉, 주어진 환경의 수용 능력이 제한된 경우에는, 앞에서 설명한 것과는 다르게 자신의 종의 비슷한 구성원을 피하는 것이 전략이라고 했으므로 빈칸에는 ③ '이 전략에 제한을 둔다'가 들어가야 한다.

왜 오답?

［비슷한 사람들과 함께하는 생존 전략］ 꿀팁

① 나무와 망고가 부족한 환경을 예로 들었으므로 주어진 환경의 수용 능력이 수요를 초과한다는 것은 정답과 정반대이다.
② 환경의 수용 능력이 감소되는 경우를 설명한 것이 아니다.
④ 주어진 환경으로 인한 인간의 생존 전략의 변화에 대해 이야기하는 글이다.
⑤ 비슷한 구성원과의 유대를 막는 경우라고 할 수 있다.

K 56 정답 ② ＊영화 음악의 친숙한 구조가 갖는 효과 ─────

A musical score within any film / can add an additional layer
　　　　　　　　　　　　　　　관계대명사의 계속적 용법
/ to the film text, / which goes beyond / simply imitating the
　　　　앞 명사를 수식하는 과거분사
action viewed. //

어떤 영화 속에서든 악보는 / 추가적인 층을 추가할 수 있다 / 영화 텍스트에 / 그것은 넘어선다 / 보이는 연기를 단순히 흉내 내는 것을 //

In films / that tell of futuristic worlds, / composers, / much like
　　　　　주격 관계대명사
sound designers, / have added freedom / to create a world / that
　　　　　　　　　　　　　　　　　　　　　　　　　　주격 관계대명사
is unknown and new to the viewer. //

영화에서 / 미래 세계에 관해 말하는 / 작곡가는 / 사운드 디자이너와 꼭 마찬가지로 / 자유를 추가해 왔다 / 세계를 창조할 수 있는 / 관객에게 알려지지 않은 새로운 //

However, / unlike sound designers, / composers often shy
away from / creating unique pieces / that reflect these new
　　　　　　　　　　　병렬 구조　　주격 관계대명사
worlds /

그러나 / 사운드 디자이너와 달리 / 작곡가는 흔히 피한다 / 독특한 곡을 만들어 내는 것을 / 이러한 새로운 세계를 반영하는 /

and often present musical scores / that possess familiar
　　　　　　　　　　　　　　　　　　　주격 관계대명사
structures and cadences. //

그리고 흔히 악보를 제시한다 / 친숙한 구조와 박자를 가진 //
　　　　　가주어　　　　진주어
While it is possible / that this may interfere with creativity / and
a sense of space and time, / it in fact **aids in viewer / access to
the film**. //

가능성이 있지만 / 창의성을 저해할 / 그리고 시공간 감각을 / 사실 그것은 관객에게 도움이 된다 / 영화에 접근하는 데 //

단서 1 친숙한 악보를 통해 알아볼 수 있는 맥락을 제공함
Through recognizable scores, / visions of the future or a galaxy
far, far away / can be placed / within a recognizable context. //

알아볼 수 있는 악보를 통해 / 미래나 멀고 먼 은하계에 대한 비전은 / 놓일 수 있다 / 알아볼 수 있는 맥락 안에 //

Such familiarity allows the viewer / to be placed / in a
comfortable space /

그러한 친숙함은 관객에게 허락한다 / 놓이도록 / 편안한 공간에 /
so that ~: ~할 수 있도록, 그래서 ~하다
so that the film may then lead the viewer / to what is an
unfamiliar, but acceptable vision of a world / different from
their own. // 단서 2 친숙한 악보가 관객들에게 편안함을 제공하고, 이를 통해 영화를 낯설지만
　　　　　　　　　　　　　받아들일 수 있는 비전으로 인식하게 됨
그러면 영화는 관객을 인도할 수 있을 것이다 / 낯설지만 받아들일 수 있는 비전으로 / 그들 자신의 것과 다른 세계에 관한 //

- **futuristic** ⓐ 미래의　　• **composer** ⓝ 작곡가
- **shy away from** ~을 피하다　　• **piece** ⓝ 작품, 곡
- **possess** ⓥ 가지다, 보유하다　　• **structure** ⓝ 구조
- **interfere with** ~을 저해[방해]하다　　• **recognizable** ⓐ 알아볼 수 있는
- **galaxy** ⓝ 은하계　　• **familiarity** ⓝ 친숙함
- **acceptable** ⓐ 받아들일 수 있는

어떤 영화 속에서든 악보는 영화 텍스트에 추가적인 층을 추가할 수 있는데, 그것은 보이는 연기를 단순히 흉내 내는 것을 넘어선다. 미래 세계에 관해 말하는 영화에서, 작곡가는 사운드 디자이너와 꼭 마찬가지로, 관객에게 알려지지 않은 새로운 세계를 창조할 수 있는 자유를 추가해 왔다. 그러나 사운드 디자이너와 달리, 작곡가는 흔히 이러한 새로운 세계를 반영하는 독특한 곡을 만들어 내는 것을 피하고, 친숙한 구조와 박자를 가진 악보를 흔히 제시한다. 이는 창의성과 시공간 감각을 저해할 가능성이 있지만, 사실 그것은 **관객이 영화에 접근하는 데 도움이 된다**. 알아볼 수 있는 악보를 통해 미래나 멀고 먼 은하계에 대한 비전은 알아볼 수 있는 맥락 안에 놓일 수 있다. 그러한 친숙함을 통해 관객은 편안한 공간에 놓이게 되고, 그러면 영화는 관객을 그들 자신의 것과 다른 세계에 관한 낯설지만 받아들일 수 있는 비전으로 인도할 수 있을 것이다.

다음 빈칸에 들어갈 말로 가장 적절한 것을 고르시오.
　　　　　　　　　　　　　　음악의 친숙함이 줄거리를 친숙함에서 자유롭게 한다는 내용이 아님
① frees the plot of its familiarity
　줄거리를 그것의 친숙함에서 자유롭게 하다　　영화 음악의 친숙함을 통해 관객이 영화에
② aids in viewer access to the film　접근하는 데 도움을 준다는 내용임
　관객이 영화에 접근하는 데 도움이 된다
③ adds to an exotic musical experience　낯선 다른 세계를 언급한 것으로 만든 오답
　이국적인 음악 경험을 늘린다
④ orients audiences to the film's theme　영화의 주제로 향하게 한다고는 하지 않음
　관객을 영화의 주제로 향하게 한다
⑤ inspires viewers to think more deeply
　관객이 더 깊이 생각할 수 있도록 고취한다
　　　　　친숙한 영화 음악이 관객을 더 깊이 생각할 수 있게 만든다는 내용은 없음

왜 정답? [정답률 45%]

빈칸 문장	(영화 음악의 친숙한 구조는) 창의성과 시공간 감각을 저해할 수도 있지만, 사실은 '무엇이다.'
빈칸 뒤 문장	친숙한 악보는 알아볼 수 있는 맥락을 제공함 **단서1**
마지막 문장	이러한 친숙함을 통해 관객은 편안한 공간에 놓여, 미래 세계를 낯설지만 받아들일 수 있는 비전으로 보게 됨 **단서2**

➡ 영화 속 음악의 친숙한 구조는 알아볼 수 있는 맥락을 제공한다고 했고, 이를 통해 관객은 편안한 공간에 놓여, 미래 세계를 낯설지만 받아들일 수 있는 비전으로 보게 된다고 했다.

▶ 그러므로 친숙한 영화 음악은 ② '관객이 영화에 접근하는 데 도움이 된다'고 하는 것이 적절하다.

왜 오답?

① 음악의 친숙함이 줄거리를 친숙함에서 자유롭게 한다는 내용이 아니다.
③ 낯선 다른 세계를 언급했을 뿐, 이국적인 음악 경험에 대한 내용은 없다.
④ 음악의 친숙한 구조가 영화의 '주제'로 향하게 한다고는 하지 않았다. **주의**
⑤ 음악의 친숙함이 관객으로 하여금 더 깊이 생각할 수 있도록 한다는 내용이 아니다.

김아린 | 충남대 의예과 2024년 입학·대전한빛고 졸

빈칸 문제를 풀 때는 빈칸 앞뒤에도 집중을 해야 하는데, 여기선 it in fact라고 적혀있지? 그러면 앞 문장에서 it이 가리키는 걸 찾고 그 내용을 그대로 연결시키는 거야. 작곡가들이 친숙한 악보를 만든다는 내용이 앞에 나오고 빈칸 뒤에 such familiarity로 부연 설명해주고 있으니까 이 둘을 조합하면 ②이 정답이라는 것을 금방 찾을 수 있어! 빈칸 문제를 풀기 위해서는 빈칸 앞뒤에 있는 기능어들에 주목해보자!

K 57 정답 ⑤ ＊환경이나 맥락이 빠진 감정의 불확정성

전치사+관계대명사
There have been psychological studies / in which subjects were shown / photographs of people's faces / and asked to identify / the expression or state of mind / evinced. //
심리학 연구가 있었다 / 피실험자에게 보여준 / 사람들의 얼굴 사진을 / 그리고 파악하도록 요청한 / 표정이나 마음 상태를 / 분명히 나타나는 //

The results are invariably very mixed. //
그 결과는 언제나 매우 엇갈린다 //

In the 17th century / the French painter and theorist Charles Le Brun / drew a series of faces / illustrating the various emotions /
목적격 관계대명사
that painters could be called upon to represent. //
17세기에 / 프랑스의 화가이자 이론가인 Charles Le Brun은 / 일련의 얼굴 그림을 그렸다 / 다양한 감정을 분명히 보여주는 / 화가가 표현해 달라고 요청받을 수 있는 //

선행사를 포함하는 관계대명사
What is striking about them is / that **any number of them could be substituted** / **for one another** / **without loss**. //
보어절을 이끄는 접속사
그 그림들에서 놀라운 점은 / 어떤 수의 얼굴 그림이든 대체될 수 있었다는 것이다 / 서로 / 손실 없이 //

형용사적 용법(any setting or context 수식)
What is missing in all this is / any setting or context / to make the emotion determinate. // **단서**
make+목적어+목적격 보어(동사원형)
이 모든 것에서 빠진 것은 / 어떤 환경이나 맥락이다 / 감정을 확정적인 것으로 만드는 // (위에서 언급한 그림들에서) 빠진 것이 감정을 뚜렷하게 보여주는 환경이나 맥락임

We must know / who this person is, / who these other people
병렬 구조
are, / what their relationship is, / what is at stake in the scene, /
병렬 구조
and the like. //
우리는 알아야 한다 / 이 사람이 누구인지 / 다른 이 사람들이 누구인지 / 그들은 어떤 관계인지 / 그 장면에서 관건이 무엇인지 / 그리고 기타 등등을 //

In real life as well as in painting / we do not come across / just faces; / we encounter people / in particular situations /
그림에서뿐만 아니라 실생활에서도 / 우리는 우연히 마주치는 것이 아니다 / 단지 얼굴만 / 우리는 사람들을 마주친다 / 특정한 상황에서 /

---

and our understanding of people / cannot somehow be
병렬 구조
precipitated and held isolated /
그리고 사람들에 대한 우리의 이해는 / 그럭저럭 촉발되어 보유되고 괴리될 수 없다 /

from the social and human circumstances / in which they, and
전치사+관계대명사
we, live and breathe and have our being. //
사회적, 인간적 상황으로부터 / 그들과 우리가 살아 숨 쉬고 존재하는 //

- **psychological** ⓐ 심리학의 • **subject** ⓝ 피실험자
- **identify** ⓥ 확인하다, 파악하다 • **state of mind** 마음 상태
- **invariably** ⓐⓓ 언제나, 변함없이 • **theorist** ⓝ 이론가
- **illustrate** ⓥ 분명히 보여주다, 그려넣다
- **call upon to-v** ~하도록 요청하다 • **striking** ⓐ 놀라운
- **determinate** ⓐ 확정적인 • **at stake** 관건이 되는
- **encounter** ⓥ 마주치다 • **isolated** ⓐ 고립된, 괴리된

피실험자에게 사람들의 얼굴 사진을 보여주고 분명히 나타나는 표정이나 마음 상태를 파악하도록 요청하는 심리학 연구가 있었다. 그 결과는 언제나 매우 엇갈린다. 17세기에 프랑스의 화가이자 이론가인 Charles Le Brun은 화가가 표현해 달라고 요청받을 수 있는 다양한 감정을 분명히 보여주는 일련의 얼굴 그림을 그렸다. 그 그림들에서 놀라운 점은 **어떤 수의 얼굴 그림이든 손실 없이 서로 대체될 수 있었다는 것이다.** 이 모든 것에서 빠진 것은 감정을 확정적인 것으로 만드는 어떤 환경이나 맥락이다. 우리는 이 사람이 누구인지, 다른 이 사람들이 누구인지, 그들은 어떤 관계인지, 그 장면에서 관건이 무엇인지 등을 알아야 한다. 그림에서뿐만 아니라 실생활에서도 우리는 단지 얼굴만 우연히 마주치는 것이 아니며, 우리는 특정한 상황에서 사람들을 마주치고, 사람들에 대한 우리의 이해는 그들과 우리가 살아 숨 쉬고 존재하는 사회적, 인간적 상황으로부터 괴리된 채 그럭저럭 촉발되어 보유될 수는 없다.

다음 빈칸에 들어갈 말로 가장 적절한 것을 고르시오. [3점]

① all of them could be matched consistently with their intended emotions
모든 얼굴 그림이 의도된 감정과 일관되게 일치할 수 있었다 글의 내용과 정반대임
② every one of them was illustrated with photographic precision
모든 얼굴 그림이 사진과 같이 정밀하게 그려졌다
모든 얼굴 그림이 사진과 같이 정밀하게 그려졌다는 내용은 없음
③ each of them definitively displayed its own social narrative
얼굴 그림 각각이 자체의 사회적 이야기를 명확하게 보여주었다 사회적 이야기와 관련된 내용이 아님
④ most of them would be seen as representing unique characteristics
얼굴 그림 대부분이 고유한 특징을 나타내는 것으로 여겨질 것이다
얼굴 그림이 나타내는 고유의 특징에 대한 글이 아님
⑤ any number of them could be substituted for one another without loss 확정적으로 보여줄 수 없어 얼굴 그림이 서로 대체될 수 있었다는 내용임
어떤 수의 얼굴 그림이든 손실 없이 서로 대체될 수 있었다

왜 정답? [정답률 18%]

빈칸 문장	그 (얼굴) 그림들에서 놀라운 점은 '무엇'이다.
빈칸 뒤 문장	이 모든 것에서 빠진(없는) 것은 감정을 확정적인 것으로 만드는 어떤 환경이나 맥락이다. **단서**

➡ 환경이나 맥락이 있어야 얼굴에 나타나는 감정이 확실해진다는 내용의 글이다. 얼굴 그림들에서 빠진 것은 감정을 확정적인 것으로 만드는 어떤 환경이나 맥락이라고 했다. 그러므로 얼굴 그림들은 환경이나 맥락 없이 그려졌기 때문에 감정이 확정적인 것으로 드러나지 않아 서로 대체될 수 있었다는 것을 알 수 있다.

▶ 따라서 빈칸에는 ⑤ '어떤 수의 얼굴 그림이든 손실 없이 서로 대체될 수 있었다'가 들어가야 한다.

왜 오답?

① 모든 얼굴 그림이 의도된 감정과 일관되게 일치할 수 있었다는 내용은 글의 내용과 오히려 정반대이다. **함정**
② 모든 얼굴 그림이 사진과 같이 정밀하게 그려졌다는 내용은 없었다.
③ 얼굴 그림이 각각의 사회적 이야기를 보여주고 있다는 내용의 글이 아니다.
④ 얼굴 그림이 나타내는 고유의 특징에 대한 글이 아니다.

K 58 정답 ⑤ — 2등급 대비 [정답률 41%]

＊기후 변화에 있어 시간 구분의 문제점

We understand / that the segregation of our consciousness / into present, past, and future / is both a fiction and an oddly self-referential framework; /
understand의 목적어절 접속사 / 주어 / 동사 / 주격 보어가 both A and B로 연결됨
우리는 이해한다 / 우리의 의식을 분리하는 것이 / 현재, 과거, 미래로 / 허구이며 또한 이상하게도 자기 지시적인 틀이라는 것을 /

your present was part of your mother's future, / and your children's past / will be in part your present. //
여러분의 현재는 여러분 어머니의 미래의 일부였고 / 여러분 자녀의 과거는 / 부분적으로 여러분의 현재일 것이다 //

Nothing is generally wrong / with structuring our consciousness of time / in this conventional manner, / and it often works well enough. //
주어 / 동사(완전자동사)
일반적으로 잘못된 것이 전혀 없으며 / 시간에 대한 우리의 의식을 구조화하는 것에는 / 이러한 전통적인 방식으로 / 그것은 흔히 충분히 효과적이다 //

In the case of climate change, / however, / the sharp division of time / into past, present, and future /
단수 주어
기후 변화의 경우 / 그러나 / 시간의 분명한 구분은 / 과거, 현재, 미래로 /
단수 동사① / 단수 동사②
has been desperately misleading / and has, most importantly, hidden / from view / the extent of the responsibility / of those of us alive now. //
has hidden의 목적어
[단서 1] 기후 변화의 경우에는 시간을 과거, 현재, 미래로 분명히 구분하는 것이 우리의 책임 범위를 보이지 않게 숨겨 왔음
심하게 오도해 왔으며 / 가장 중요하게는 숨겨 왔다 / 시야로부터 / 책임 범위를 / 지금 살아 있는 우리들의 //

The narrowing of our consciousness of time / smooths the way /
주어 / 동사
시간에 대한 우리의 의식을 좁히는 것은 / 길을 닦는다 /

to divorcing ourselves / from responsibility for developments / in the past and the future / with which our lives are in fact deeply intertwined. //
전치사 / 동명사구
[단서 2] 시간에 대한 의식을 좁히는 것은 발전에 대한 책임으로부터 우리를 단절시킴
우리를 단절시키는 것으로의 / 발전에 대한 책임으로부터 / 과거와 미래의 / 사실 우리의 삶이 깊이 뒤얽혀 있는 //

In the climate case, / it is not that **we face the facts but then deny / our responsibility**. //
기후의 경우 / 우리가 사실을 직면하면서도 부인하는 것이 문제가 아니다 / 우리의 책임을 //

It is that the realities are obscured / from view / by the partitioning of time, / and so questions of responsibility / toward the past and future / do not arise naturally. //
복수 주어 / 복수 동사
문제는 현실이 흐릿해지고 / 시야로부터 / 시간을 나눔으로써 / 그래서 책임에 관한 질문이 / 과거와 현재를 향한 / 자연스럽게 생겨나지 않는 것이다 //

- consciousness ⓝ 의식
- oddly ⓐ𝖽 이상하게
- framework ⓝ 틀, 골조
- structure ⓥ 구조화하다
- conventional ⓐ 전통적인
- manner ⓝ 방식
- division ⓝ 구분
- desperately ⓐ𝖽 심하게, 극도로
- mislead ⓥ (사실을) 오도[호도]하다
- extent ⓝ 범위
- smooth ⓥ 매끄럽게[반반하게] 하다
- divorce ⓥ 단절시키다, 분리하다
- partition ⓥ 나누다, 분할하다
- arise ⓥ 생겨나다

우리는 우리의 의식을 현재, 과거, 미래로 분리하는 것이 허구이며 또한 이상하게도 자기 지시적인 틀이라는 것을 이해하는데, 여러분의 현재는 여러분 어머니의 미래의 일부였고 여러분 자녀의 과거는 여러분 현재의 일부일 것이라는 것이다. 시간에 대한 우리의 의식을 이러한 전통적인 방식으로 구조화하는 것에는 일반적으로 잘못된 것이 전혀 없으며 그것은 흔히 충분히 효과적이다.

그러나 기후 변화의 경우, 시간을 과거, 현재, 미래로 분명하게 구분하는 것은 심하게 오도해 왔으며 가장 중요하게는 지금 살아 있는 우리들의 책임 범위를 시야로부터 숨겨 왔다. 시간에 대한 우리의 의식을 좁히는 것은 사실 우리의 삶이 깊이 뒤얽혀 있는 과거와 미래의 발전에 대한 책임으로부터 우리를 단절시키는 길을 닦는다. 기후의 경우, **우리가 사실을 직면하면서도 우리의 책임을 부인하는** 것이 문제가 아니다. 문제는 시간을 나눔으로써 현실이 시야로부터 흐릿해지고 그래서 과거와 현재의 책임에 관한 질문이 자연스럽게 생겨나지 않는 것이다.

다음 빈칸에 들어갈 말로 가장 적절한 것을 고르시오. [3점]

① all our efforts prove to be effective and are thus encouraged
우리의 모든 노력이 효과적인 것으로 밝혀지고 따라서 장려되는 → 노력한다는 언급은 없음
② sufficient scientific evidence has been provided to us
충분한 과학적인 증거가 우리에게 제공되어 온 → 기후 변화의 증거에 대한 언급은 없음
③ future concerns are more urgent than present needs
미래의 우려가 현재의 필요보다 더욱 긴급한 → 미래에 대해 우려해야 함
④ our ancestors maintained a different frame of time
우리의 조상들이 다른 시간적 틀을 유지 → 과거, 현재, 미래의 다른 틀은 언급되지 않음
⑤ we face the facts but then deny our responsibility
우리가 사실을 직면하면서도 우리의 책임을 부인하는 → 책임에 대한 질문 자체가 생겨나지 않는다는 것과 대조됨

🔍 2등급 ❓ 기후 변화에 있어 과거, 현재, 미래로 시간을 구분하는 것이 문제임을 말하는 글이다. 빈칸에는 문제인 것과 대조되는 것이 들어가야 함을 파악하지 못하면 풀기 힘든 2등급 대비 문제이다.

| 문제 풀이 순서 |

1st 역접의 연결어가 포함된 문장부터 확인한다.

> In the case of climate change, however, the sharp division of time into past, present, and future has been desperately misleading and has, most importantly, hidden from view the extent of the responsibility of those of us alive now.
> 그러나 기후 변화의 경우, 시간을 과거, 현재, 미래로 분명하게 구분하는 것은 심하게 오도해 왔으며, 가장 중요하게는 지금 살아 있는 우리들의 책임 범위를 시야로부터 숨겨 왔다. **[단서 1]**

→ 앞부분은 기후 변화 외의 경우에는 시간을 과거, 현재, 미래로 구분하는 것이 문제없다는 내용일 것이다.
→ 기후 변화에 있어서는 시간을 과거, 현재, 미래로 구분하는 것이 우리의 책임 범위를 보이지 않게 한다. → 시간을 과거, 현재, 미래로 구분해서는 안 됨
　▶ 기후의 경우를 설명하는 문장에 빈칸이 있으므로, 중요한 것은 앞부분이 아니라 이후의 내용임

2nd 기후 변화의 경우에 과거, 현재, 미래로 구분하는 문제점이 이어질 것이다.

> The narrowing of our consciousness of time smooths the way to divorcing ourselves from responsibility for developments in the past and the future with which our lives are in fact deeply intertwined.
> 시간에 대한 우리의 의식을 좁히는 것은 사실 우리의 삶이 깊이 뒤얽혀 있는 과거와 미래의 발전에 대한 책임으로부터 우리를 단절시키는 길을 닦는다. **[단서 2]**

→ 시간에 대한 의식을 좁히는 것 = 시간을 과거, 현재, 미래로 구분하는 것
　→ 과거와 미래에 대한 책임으로부터 우리를 단절시킴
　▶ 글의 주제: 기후 변화에 있어 시간을 과거, 현재, 미래로 구분하는 것이 문제임

In the climate case, it is not that _____.
기후의 경우, _____하는 것이 문제가 아니다.

→ 문제인 것(시간을 과거, 현재, 미래로 나누어 우리의 책임 범위를 보이지 않게 하는 것)과 대조되는 것이 빈칸에 들어가야 한다.

▶ 기후의 경우에는 ⑤ '우리가 사실을 직면하면서도 우리의 책임을 부인하는' 것이 문제가 아니라 시간을 과거, 현재, 미래로 나눔으로써 책임에 대한 질문 자체가 생겨나지 않게 하는 것이 문제임

| 선택지 분석 |

① all our efforts prove to be effective and are thus encouraged
우리의 모든 노력이 효과적인 것으로 밝혀지고 따라서 장려되는
기후에 있어 우리가 노력한다거나 그 노력이 효과적인 것으로 밝혀졌다는 언급은 없다.

② sufficient scientific evidence has been provided to us
충분한 과학적인 증거가 우리에게 제공되어 온
기후 변화를 알려주는 과학적 증거에 대한 내용이 아니다.

③ future concerns are more urgent than present needs
미래의 우려가 현재의 필요보다 더욱 긴급한
기후 변화 책임에 대한 질문 자체가 생겨나지 않는다는 문제점을 지적한 글로, 미래에 대해 우려해야 한다는 의미로 볼 수 있다.

④ our ancestors maintained a different frame of time
우리의 조상들이 다른 시간적 틀을 유지한
past가 등장하는 것으로 만든 오답이다. 우리의 선조가 과거, 현재, 미래와는 다른 시간적 틀을 유지했다는 내용은 없다.

⑤ we face the facts but then deny our responsibility
우리가 사실을 직면하면서도 우리의 책임을 부인하는
정답을 찾는 직접적인 근거가 글에 드러나지는 않는다. 기후 변화에 대한 책임 자체가 보이지 않게 된다는 것과 가장 논리적으로 대조되는 선택지가 정답이다.

조현준 | 전북대 의예과 2023년 입학·익산 이리고 졸

이 문제는 앞부분이 이해하기 쉬워서 쭉쭉 읽어나갔어. 글의 앞부분은 '시간에 대한 의식을 나누는 방법'에 대한 내용이었는데, 글의 중간에 등장하는 however를 기점으로 중심 화제가 기후 변화로 바뀌고, 기후 변화의 경우에는 평소와 같은 '시간 분할법'을 사용하면 우리에게 책임감이 보이지 않는다는 문제가 발생한다는 점을 지적했어.
이 문제에서는 빈칸 문장과 바로 다음 문장이 it is not that ~, it is that ~이라는 같은 구조로 되어 있다는 게 큰 단서였어. 빈칸 문장에는 not이 포함되고, 그다음 문장에는 포함되지 않았으니까 마지막 문장과 반대되는 내용이 빈칸 문장에 들어가야 한다는 생각으로 정답을 골랐지.

K 59 정답 ① ⚙ 2등급 대비 [정답률 66%]

✽공유지 문제의 해결책에 있어 중요한 점

생략 가능한 명사절(목적어절 접속사)
Elinor Ostrom found / that there are several factors / critical to bringing about stable institutional solutions / to the problem of the commons. //
Elinor Ostrom은 알게 되었다 / 몇 가지 요인이 있음을 / 안정적인 제도적 해결책을 가져오는 데 중요한 / 공유지의 문제에 대한 //

주어
She pointed out, / for instance, / that the actors / affected by the rules / for the use and care of resources / must have the right /
형용사적 용법(the right 수식)
to **participate in decisions / to change the rules**. //
그녀는 지적했다 / 예를 들어 / 행위자는 / 규칙의 영향을 받는 / 자원의 이용 및 관리에 대한 / 권리를 가져야 한다고 / 결정에 참여할 / 규칙을 변경하는 //

For that reason, / the people / who monitor and control / the behavior of users / should also be users / and/or have been given a mandate / by all users. //
동사 단서1 이용자의 행동을 감시하고 통제하는 사람은 모든 이용자에 의해 위임을 받았어야 함
그러한 이유로 / 사람들은 / 감시하고 통제하는 / 이용자의 행동을 / 또한 이용자이고/이용자이거나 / 위임을 받았어야 한다 / 모든 이용자에 의해 //

This is a significant insight, / as it shows / that prospects are
부사절 접속사(이유)
poor / for a centrally directed solution / to the problem of the commons / coming from a state power /
이것은 중요한 통찰이다 / 그것이 보여주기 때문에 / 전망이 열악하다는 것을 / 중앙 (정부) 지향적 해결책의 / 공유지 문제에 대한 / 국가 권력에서 나오는 /

in comparison with a local solution / for which users assume
선행사   전치사+관계대명사
personal responsibility. //
지역적인 해결책에 비해 / 이용자가 개인적 책임을 지는 //

Ostrom also emphasizes / the importance of democratic decision processes / and that all users must be given access / to local forums / 단서2 Ostrom이 강조하는 것은 민주적 의사결정 과정과 모든 이용자에게 문제의 해결 과정에 참여할 권리가 주어져야 한다는 것임
Ostrom은 또한 강조한다 / 민주적 의사결정 과정의 중요성과 / 모든 이용자에게 접근권이 주어져야 한다는 것을 / 지역 포럼에의 /

for solving problems and conflicts / among themselves. //
문제와 갈등을 해결하기 위한 / 그들 사이의 //

Political institutions / at central, regional, and local levels / must
주어
allow users / to devise their own regulations / and independently
동사
목적어   목적격 보어
ensure observance. //
정치 기관들은 / 중앙, 지방 및 지역 차원의 / 이용자가 ~할 수 있게 해야 한다 / 자체 규정을 고안하고 / 독립적으로 준수를 보장할 수 있게 //

- critical ⓐ 중요한, 중대한 · bring about ~을 불러일으키다[유발하다]
- stable ⓐ 안정적인 · institutional ⓐ 제도적인
- point out ~을 지적하다 · resource ⓝ 자원
- monitor ⓥ 감시하다, 관리하다 · significant ⓐ 중요한, 의미 있는
- insight ⓝ 통찰(력), 안식(眼識) · prospect ⓝ (성공할) 전망
- centrally ⓐⓓ 중심에, 중앙에 · state power 공권력, 국가 권력
- in comparison with ~에 비해서 · assume ⓥ (권력·책임을) 지다[맡다]
- responsibility ⓝ 책임, 책무 · emphasize ⓥ 강조하다
- democratic ⓐ 민주적인 · conflict ⓝ 갈등, 충돌
- institution ⓝ (대학·은행 등과 같은) 기관[단체], 협회
- devise ⓥ (계획·방법 등을) 고안하다
- ensure ⓥ 보장하다, 반드시 ~하게[이게] 하다 · observance ⓝ 준수, 엄수

Elinor Ostrom은 공유지의 문제에 대한 안정적인 제도적 해결책을 가져오는 데 중요한 몇 가지 요인이 있음을 알게 되었다. 예를 들어, 그녀는 자원의 이용 및 관리 규칙의 영향을 받는 행위자는 규칙을 변경하는 결정에 참여할 권리를 가져야 한다고 지적했다. 그러한 이유로 이용자의 행동을 감시하고 통제하는 사람들 또한 이용자이고/이용자이거나 모든 이용자에 의해 위임을 받았어야 한다. 이것은 중요한 통찰인데, 이용자가 개인적 책임을 지는 지역적인 해결책에 비해 국가 권력에서 나오는 공유지 문제에 대한 중앙 (정부) 지향적 해결책의 전망이 열악하다는 것을 그것이 보여주기 때문이다. Ostrom은 또한 민주적 의사결정 과정의 중요성과 모든 이용자에게 그들 사이의 문제와 갈등을 해결하기 위한 지역 포럼에 참여할 권한이 주어져야 한다고 강조한다. 중앙, 지방 및 지역 차원의 정치 기관들은 이용자가 자체 규정을 고안하고 독립적으로 준수할 수 있도록 해야 한다.

다음 빈칸에 들어갈 말로 가장 적절한 것을 고르시오. [3점]
① participate in decisions to change the rules
규칙을 변경하는 결정에 참여할   문제의 해결 과정에 참여할 권한이 주어져야 함
② claim individual ownership of the resources
자원에 대한 개인의 소유권을 주장할   개인 소유의 자원이 아니라 공유지에 대한 내용임
③ use those resources to maximize their profits ┐ 공유지를 마음대로 이용할
자신의 이익을 최대화하기 위해 그 자원을 이용할   권리가 주어져야
④ demand free access to the communal resources ┘ 한다는 것이 아님
공동 자원에 대한 자유로운 이용 권한을 요구할
⑤ request proper distribution based on their merits
자신의 능력을 바탕으로 적당한 분배를 요청할   공유지를 분배하는 것에 대한 언급은 없음

Elinor Ostrom이 공유지 문제에 대한 해결책으로 무엇이 중요하다고 생각하는지 파악해야 한다. 예시가 나오는 빈칸 문장 뒤에 나오는 글의 내용을 잘 포함하는 선택지를 찾아야 하는 2등급 대비 문제이다.

| 문제 풀이 순서 |

1st 빈칸이 포함된 문장을 읽고, 글에서 찾아야 하는 것이 무엇인지 확인한다.

> She pointed out, for instance, that the actors affected by the rules for the use and care of resources must have the right _____.
> 예를 들어, 그녀는 자원의 이용 및 관리에 대한 규칙의 영향을 받는 행위자는 _____한 권리를 가져야 한다고 지적했다.

→ 자원의 이용 및 관리 규칙의 영향을 받는 행위자가 어떤 권리를 가져야 하는지를 파악해야 한다.
 She는 앞 문장에 나온 Elinor Ostrom을 가리킨다. Elinor Ostrom이 생각하는 공유지 문제를 해결하는 데 중요한 요인이 무엇인지 설명하는 글이다.

2nd 공유지 문제를 해결하는 데 있어 Ostrom이 중요하다고 생각하는 요인을 찾는다.

> • 이용자의 행동을 감시하고 통제하는 사람들 또한 이용자이고/이용자이거나 모든 이용자에 의해 위임을 받았어야 한다. **단서 1**
> • Ostrom은 또한 민주적 의사결정 과정의 중요성과 모든 이용자에게 그들 사이의 문제와 갈등을 해결하기 위한 지역 포럼에 참여할 권한이 주어져야 한다고 강조한다. **단서 2**

→ **단서 1** <이용자의 행동을 감시하고 통제하는 사람을 결정하는 과정에 모든 이용자가 참여해야 한다>는 것을 의미한다.
 단서 2 <모든 이용자가 문제 해결 과정에 참여해야 한다>라는 의미이다.
 ▶ Elinor Ostrom이 지적한 것은 <규칙의 영향을 받는 행위자는 ① '규칙을 변경하는 결정에 참여할' 권리를 가져야 한다>는 것이다.

| 선택지 분석 |

① **participate in decisions to change the rules**
 규칙을 변경하는 결정에 참여할
 민주적: '국민이 모든 결정의 중심에 있는 것'을 의미한다.

② **claim individual ownership of the resources**
 자원에 대한 개인의 소유권을 주장할
 여러 사람이 이용하는 공유지에 대해 개인에게 문제 해결 과정에 참여할 권리를 주는 것이지, 자원에 대한 소유권을 주장한다는 것은 자연스럽지 않다.

③ **use those resources to maximize their profits**
 자신의 이익을 최대화하기 위해 그 자원을 이용할
 공유지 문제의 해결책을 만드는 데 있어 개인에게 자신의 이익을 최대화하기 위해 공동 자원을 이용할 권리를 주어야 한다는 것은 적절하지 않다.

④ **demand free access to the communal resources**
 공동 자원에 대한 자유로운 이용 권한을 요구할
 공유지 문제의 해결책을 만드는 데 있어 개인에게 자신의 이익을 최대화하기 위해 공동 자원을 자유롭게 이용할 권한을 주어야 한다는 것은 적절하지 않다.

⑤ **request proper distribution based on their merits**
 자신의 능력을 바탕으로 적당한 분배를 요청할
 개인의 능력에 따라 공유지를 개인에게 분배해야 한다는 언급은 없다.

K 60 정답 ② ✪ 2등급 대비 [정답률 36%]

＊다-다-다-덤의 다양한 변화

Development can get very complicated and fanciful. //
전개부는 매우 복잡하고 별날 수가 있다 //
A fugue by Johann Sebastian Bach / illustrates / how far this process could go, /
 주어   동사   목적어
Johann Sebastian Bach의 푸가는 / 보여준다 / 이 과정이 어느 정도까지 갈 수 있을지를 /
when a single melodic line, / sometimes just a handful of notes, / was all / that the composer needed /
하나의 멜로디 라인이 / 때로는 단지 소수의 음표가 / 전부였을 때 / 그 작곡가가 필요한 /

to create a brilliant work / containing lots of intricate development / within a coherent structure. //
훌륭한 작품을 만들기 위해 / 많은 복잡한 전개부를 포함하는 / 일관된 구조 내에서 //
Ludwig van Beethoven's famous Fifth Symphony / provides an exceptional example /
Ludwig van Beethoven의 유명한 5번 교향곡은 / 이례적일 정도로 우수한 예를 제공한다 /
of how much mileage / a classical composer can get / out of a few notes and a simple rhythmic tapping. //
얼마나 많은 이익을 / 클래식 작곡가가 얻어낼 수 있는지에 대한 / 몇 개의 음표와 단순하며 리듬감 있는 두드림에서 // **단서 1** 베토벤의 5번 교향곡은 몇 개의 음표와 단순한 두드림에서 작곡가가 많은 이익을 얻는다는 것을 보여줌
 단수 주어
The opening da-da-da-DUM / that everyone has heard somewhere or another / **appears in an incredible variety of ways** /
 단수 동사
시작 부분의 다-다-다-덤은 / 모든 사람들이 어디선가 들어본 / 엄청나게 다양한 방식으로 나타난다 /
 ┌─ not only A but (also) B로 연결된 명사구 ─┐
throughout not only the opening movement, / but the remaining three movements, / like a kind of motto or a connective thread. //
시작 악장뿐만 아니라 / 나머지 3악장 내내 / 일종의 주제구나 연결 끈처럼 //
Just as we don't always see / the intricate brushwork / that goes into the creation of a painting, /
 부분 부정: 항상 ~인 것은 아닌
우리가 항상 보는 것이 아니듯이 / 복잡한 붓놀림을 / 그림 작품 하나를 완성하는 데 들어가는 /
we may not always notice / how Beethoven keeps finding fresh uses / for his motto / **단서 2** 우리가 항상 알아보는 못하지만 베토벤은 자신의 주제구를 계속해서 새롭게 사용함
 may not notice의 목적어절 접속사 ①
우리는 항상 알아보지는 못할 수도 있다 / Beethoven이 어떻게 계속 새로운 사용을 찾는지를 / 자신의 주제구에 대한 /
 may not notice의 목적어절 접속사 ②
or how he develops his material / into a large, cohesive statement. //
또는 그가 그의 제재를 어떻게 전개하는지를 / 거대하고 응집력 있는 진술로 //
 앞에 목적격 관계대명사가 생략됨
But a lot of the enjoyment / we get from that mighty symphony / stems from the inventiveness behind it, / the impressive development of musical ideas. //
그러나 즐거움의 많은 부분은 / 그 강력한 교향곡에서 우리가 얻는 / 그 이면의 독창성에서 비롯된다 / 음악적 아이디어의 인상적인 전개 //

- fanciful ⓐ 별난, 기발한 • illustrate ⓥ 분명히 보여주다, 실증하다
- melodic ⓐ 운율의 • a handful of 소수의, 한 줌의
- composer ⓝ 작곡가 • brilliant ⓐ 훌륭한, 눈부신
- symphony ⓝ 교향곡 • exceptional ⓐ 특출한, 예외적인
- mileage ⓝ (특정 상황에서 얻을 수 있는) 이득, 사용(량)
- tap ⓥ (가볍게) 톡톡 두드리다
- movement ⓝ (큰 음악 작품의) 한 부분, 움직임
- motto ⓝ 좌우명, ((음악)) 주제구 • thread ⓝ 실, (이야기의) 맥락
- brushwork ⓝ (화가의) 화법[붓놀림] • cohesive ⓐ 화합[결합]하는
- statement ⓝ 표현, 서술 • mighty ⓐ 웅장한, 힘센
- stem ⓥ 유래하다, 생기다 • inventiveness ⓝ 독창적임

전개부는 매우 복잡하고 별날 수가 있다. Johann Sebastian Bach의 푸가는 하나의 멜로디 라인, 때로는 단지 소수의 음표가 그 작곡가가 일관된 구조 내에서 많은 복잡한 전개부를 포함하는 훌륭한 작품을 만들기 위해 필요한 전부였을 때, 이 과정이 어느 정도까지 갈 수 있을지를 보여준다. Ludwig van Beethoven의 유명한 5번 교향곡은 클래식 작곡가가 몇 개의 음표와 단순하며 리듬감 있는 두드림에서 얼마나 많은 이익을 얻어낼 수 있는지에 대한 이례적일 정도로 우수한 예를 제공한다. 모든 사람들이 어디선가 들어본 시작 부분의 다-다-다-덤은 일종의 주제구나 연결 끈처럼, 시작 악장뿐만 아니라 나머지 3악장 내내 **엄청나게 다양한 방식으로 나타난다**. 우리가 그림 작품 하나를 완성하는 데 들인 복잡한 붓놀림을 항상 보는 것이 아니듯이, Beethoven이 자신의 주제구를 어떻게 계속 새롭게 사용하는 것을 찾는지 또는 그의 제재를 거대하고 응집력 있는 진술로 어떻게 전개하는지를 항상 알아보지는 못할 수도 있다. 그러나 그 강력한 교향곡에서 우리가 얻는 즐거움의 많은 부분은 그 이면의 독창성, 즉 음악적 아이디어의 인상적인 전개에서 비롯된다.

③ **provides extensive musical knowledge creatively**
광범위한 음악적 지식을 창의적으로 제공한다

다음 빈칸에 들어갈 말로 가장 적절한 것을 고르시오. [3점]

① makes the composer's musical ideas contradictory
작곡가의 음악적 아이디어를 모순되게 만든다   음악적 아이디어의 모순에 대한 언급은 없음

②appears in an incredible variety of ways
엄청나게 다양한 방식으로 나타난다   베토벤은 다-다-다-덤을 계속 새롭게 사용함

③ provides extensive musical knowledge creatively
광범위한 음악적 지식을 창의적으로 제공한다   다-다-다-덤이 음악적 지식을 제공하는 것은 아님

④ remains fairly calm within the structure
구조 내에서 상당히 조용하게 남아 있다   계속 새롭게 활용됨

⑤ becomes deeply associated with one's own enjoyment
스스로의 즐거움과 깊이 관련된다   a lot of the enjoyment로 만든 오답

왜 2등급 ? Bach의 푸가, Beethoven의 5번 교향곡의 예시를 통해
'다-다-다-덤'에 대해 설명하는 내용을 잘 파악해야 한다. 다소 생소한
'다-다-다-덤'이라는 표현 때문에 어렵다고 생각할 수 있는 2등급 대비 문제이다.

| 문제 풀이 순서 |

1st 빈칸이 포함된 문장을 읽고, 글에서 찾아야 하는 것이 무엇인지 확인한다.

> The opening da-da-da-DUM that everyone has heard
> somewhere or another _____ throughout not
> only the opening movement, but the remaining three
> movements, like a kind of motto or a connective thread.
> 모든 사람들이 어디선가 들어본 시작 부분의 다-다-다-덤은 일종의 주제구나 연결
> 끈처럼 시작 악장뿐만 아니라 나머지 3악장 내내 _____.

➡ 먼저 '시작 부분의 다-다-다-덤'이 가리키는 것이 무엇인지 앞부분에서 확인해야
한다.

2nd 빈칸 문장 앞뒤를 읽고, 무슨 내용인지 파악한다.

빈칸 앞앞 문장	Bach의 푸가는 하나의 멜로디 라인, 때로는 단지 소수의 음표가 그 작곡가가 일관된 구조 내에서 많은 복잡한 전개부를 포함하는 훌륭한 작품을 만들기 위해 필요한 전부였을 때, 이 과정이 어느 정도까지 갈 수 있을지를 보여준다.
빈칸 앞 문장	Beethoven의 유명한 5번 교향곡은 클래식 작곡가가 몇 개의 음표와 단순하며 리듬감 있는 두드림에서 얼마나 많은 이익을 얻어낼 수 있는지에 대한 이례적일 정도로 우수한 예를 제공한다. **단서 1**
빈칸 다음 문장	우리는 Beethoven이 자신의 주제구를 어떻게 계속 새롭게 사용하는 것을 찾는지 또는 그의 제재를 거대하고 응집력 있는 진술로 어떻게 전개하는지를 항상 알아보지는 못할 수도 있다. **단서 2**

➡ **Bach의 푸가:** 하나의 멜로디 라인, 소수의 음표만으로 많은 일관된 구조 내에서
복잡한 전개부를 포함한 훌륭한 작품을 만든 사례
➡ **빈칸 문장의 '시작 부분의 다-다-다-덤':** Beethoven의 5번 교향곡에 등장하는
멜로디
Beethoven의 5번 교향곡: 몇 개의 음표와 단순하고 리듬감 있는 두드림으로
많은 이익을 얻는 사례
➡ Beethoven은 다-다-다-덤(자신의 주제구)을 계속 새롭게 사용하고, 거대하고
응집력 있는 진술로 전개한다.
▶ 〈시작 부분의 다-다-다-덤이 시작 악장뿐만 아니라 3악장 내내, 5번 교향곡 내내
② '엄청나게 다양한 방식으로 나타난다'〉는 것을 의미함

| 선택지 분석 |

① **makes the composer's musical ideas contradictory**
작곡가의 음악적 아이디어를 모순되게 만든다
다-다-다-덤을 다양하게 사용하는 음악적 아이디어의 인상적인 전개에서 우리가
즐거움을 얻는다는 내용이다.

②**appears in an incredible variety of ways**
엄청나게 다양한 방식으로 나타난다
우리가 항상 알아차리지는 못하지만 Beethoven은 다-다-다-덤(자신의 주제구)을
계속 새롭게 사용하고, 거대하고 응집력 있는 진술로 전개한다.

---

③ **provides extensive musical knowledge creatively**
광범위한 음악적 지식을 창의적으로 제공한다
광범위한 음악적 지식을 창의적으로 청자에게 제공하는 것이 아니라 이를 활용하여
다-다-다-덤을 계속 새롭게 사용하는 것이라고 할 수 있다.

④ **remains fairly calm within the structure**
구조 내에서 상당히 조용하게 남아 있다
몇 개의 음표와 단순한 두드림을 계속 새롭게 사용하여 훌륭한 작품을 만들어낸다는
것이지, 몇 개의 음표와 단순한 두드림이 두드러지지 않는다는 것이 아니다.

⑤ **becomes deeply associated with one's own enjoyment**
스스로의 즐거움과 깊이 관련된다
다-다-다-덤이 그 자체로 우리에게 즐거움을 주는 것이 아니라 그것을 계속 새롭게
사용하는 베토벤의 독창성에서 즐거움의 많은 부분이 비롯된다는 것이다.

K 61 정답 ② 💥 1등급 대비 [정답률 35%]

＊**제조업자들의 생각**

Manufacturers design their innovation processes / around the
way / they think / the process works. // (삽입절)
제조업자들은 자신들의 혁신 과정을 설계한다 / 방식에 맞춰 / 자신들이 생각하기에 /
그 과정이 작동되는 //

The vast majority of manufacturers still think / that product (think의 목적어절 접속사 ①)
development and service development / are always done by
manufacturers, /
제조업자의 대다수는 여전히 생각한다 / 제품 개발과 서비스 개발은 / 항상 제조업자들에 의해
이루어진다고 /

and that their job / is always to find a need and fill it / rather (think의 목적어절 접속사 ②) (명사적 용법(주격 보어))
than to sometimes find and commercialize an innovation / that
lead users have already developed. //
그리고 자신들의 일은 / 항상 필요를 발견하고 그것을 채우는 것이라고 / 가끔 혁신을
발견하고 상업화하기보다는 / 시장 경향을 선도하는 사용자가 이미 개발한 /

Accordingly, / manufacturers have set up / market-research (have set up의 목적어 ①)
departments / to explore the needs of users / in the target
market, / **단서 1** 제조업자가 직접 표적 시장 사용자들의
필요를 탐구하는 시장 연구 부서를 설치함
그래서 / 제조업자들은 설치해 왔다 / 시장 연구 부서를 / 사용자들의 필요를 탐구하기 위한 /
표적 시장에서 /

product-development groups / to think up suitable products / to (have set up의 목적어 ②)
address those needs, / and so forth. //
제품 개발 집단을 / 적절한 제품을 고안하기 위한 / 그러한 필요에 대처하기에 / 그리고 기타
등등을 //

The needs and prototype solutions of lead users / — if
encountered at all — / are typically rejected / as outliers of no
interest. // **단서 2** 제조업자는 시장 경향을 선도하는 사용자의 필요와 해결책을 대체로 거부함
시장 경향을 선도하는 사용자의 필요와 시제품 해결책은 / 만일 정말 마주치기라도 한다면 /
대체로 거부된다 / 전혀 흥미롭지 않고 해당 범위에서 많이 벗어나는 것으로 //

Indeed, / when lead users' innovations do enter / a firm's (일반동사 enter를 강조함)
product line /
정말로 / 시장 경향을 선도하는 사용자의 혁신이 정말로 들어가게 될 때 / 한 회사의 제품
라인에 / = lead users' innovations

— and they have been shown / to be the actual source / of many
major innovations / for many firms — / they typically arrive / = lead users' innovations
with a lag / and by an unusual and unsystematic route. //
그리고 그것은 알려졌는데 / 실질적인 원천이 되는 것으로 / 여러 주요 혁신의 / 많은 회사의 /
그것은 대체로 도착한다 / 지연과 함께 / 그리고 이례적이고 비체계적인 경로를 통해 //

- manufacturer ⓝ 제조재[사]   - innovation ⓝ 혁신, 쇄신
- vast ⓐ (범위·크기 등이) 방대한   - majority ⓝ (특정 집단 내에서) 다수
- commercialize ⓥ 상업화하다   - accordingly ⓐⓓ 그런 이유로, 그에 맞춰
- department ⓝ (조직의) 부서   - explore ⓥ 탐험하다, 탐구하다
- suitable ⓐ 적합한, 적절한
- address ⓥ (어려운 문제 등을) 다루다, 처리하다   - and so forth ~ 등등
- prototype ⓝ 원형, 시제품   - encounter ⓥ 맞닥뜨리다
- reject ⓥ 거부[거절]하다   - outlier ⓝ 영외 거주자, 분리물
- firm ⓝ 회사   - unsystematic ⓐ 비체계적인   - route ⓝ 길, 노선

제조업자들은 자신들이 생각하기에 그 과정이 작동되는 방식에 맞춰 자신들의 혁신 과정을 설계한다. 제조업자의 대다수는 제품 개발과 서비스 개발은 항상 제조업자들에 의해 이루어지며, 자신들의 일은 가끔 **시장 경향을 선도하는 사용자가 이미 개발한** 혁신을 발견하고 상업화하기보다는 항상 필요를 발견하고 그것을 채우는 것이라고 여전히 생각한다. 그래서, 제조업자들은 표적 시장 사용자들의 필요를 탐구하기 위한 시장 연구 부서, 그러한 필요에 대처하기에 적절한 제품을 고안하기 위한 제품 개발 집단 및 기타 등등을 설치해 왔다. 시장 경향을 선도하는 사용자의 필요와 시제품 해결책은, 만일 정말 마주치기라도 한다면, 대체로 전혀 흥미롭지 않고 해당 범위에서 많이 벗어나는 것으로 거부된다. 정말로, 시장 경향을 선도하는 사용자의 혁신이 한 회사의 제품 라인에 정말로 들어가게 될 때, 그리고 그것은 많은 회사의 여러 주요 혁신의 실질적인 원천이 되는 것으로 알려졌는데, 그것은 대체로 지연 후에 이례적이고 비체계적인 경로를 통해 도착한다.

다음 빈칸에 들어갈 말로 가장 적절한 것을 고르시오. [3점]

① lead users tended to overlook 시장 경향을 선도하는 사용자의 해결책을 거부함
시장 경향을 선도하는 사용자가 간과하는 경향이 있던
② lead users have already developed 자신들이 직접 필요를 발견하고 충족시켜야 한다는 생각과 대조됨
시장 경향을 선도하는 사용자가 이미 개발한
③ lead users encountered in the market if encountered at all로 만든 오답
시장 경향을 선도하는 사용자가 시장에서 마주친
④ other firms frequently put into use 다른 회사가 실행한 혁신이 아니라 lead
다른 회사들이 자주 실행한 users의 혁신을 거부함
⑤ both users and firms have valued 여러 번 언급된 users, firm으로 만든 오답
사용자와 회사 둘 다 소중하게 여긴

왜 1등급❓ 제조업자들이 자신들의 일이 아니라고 생각하는 것을 글에서 찾아야 빈칸에 들어갈 말을 고를 수 있다. 제조업자들의 생각과 대조되는 것을 제조업자들의 생각으로 헷갈리면 틀리기 쉬운 1등급 대비 문제이다.

| 문제 풀이 순서 |

1st 빈칸이 포함된 문장을 읽고, 글에서 찾아야 하는 것이 무엇인지 확인한다.

> The vast majority of manufacturers still think that product development and service development are always done by manufacturers, and that their job is always to find a need and fill it rather than to sometimes find and commercialize an innovation that _____.
> 제조업자의 대다수는 여전히 제품 개발과 서비스 개발은 항상 제조업자들에 의해 이루어지고, 자신들의 일은 가끔 _____한 혁신을 발견하고 상업화하기보다는 항상 필요를 발견하고 그것을 충족시키는 것이라고 생각한다.

→ 제조업자가 생각하는 자신의 일: 제품 개발과 서비스 개발, 필요를 발견하고 충족시키기 ↔ 가끔 _____한 혁신을 발견하고 상업화하는 것은 자신의 일이 아니라고 생각함

2nd 글의 나머지 부분에서 제조업자의 생각을 파악한다.

빈칸 앞 문장	제조업자들은 자신들이 생각하기에 그 과정이 작동되는 방식에 맞춰 자신들의 혁신 과정을 설계한다.
빈칸 다음 문장	제조업자들은 표적 시장 사용자들의 필요를 탐구하기 위한 시장 연구 부서, 그러한 필요에 대처하기에 적절한 제품을 고안하기 위한 제품 개발 집단 및 기타 등등을 설치해 왔다. **단서 1**

→ **1** 다른 사람이 아니라 제조업자 자신이 생각하는 대로 혁신 과정을 설계한다.
2 제조업자가 표적 시장 사용자의 필요를 조사하고, 그 필요에 대처한다.
▶ 제조업자는 사용자가 무엇을 필요로 하는지 '직접' 조사하여 대처하고, 자신이 생각하는 대로 혁신 과정을 설계함

3rd 제조업자가 자신의 일이라고 생각하는 것과 대조되는 것을 찾는다.

빈칸 다다음 문장	시장 경향을 선도하는 사용자의 필요와 시제품 해결책은, 만일 정말 마주치기라도 한다면, 대체로 전혀 흥미롭지 않고 해당 범위에서 많이 벗어나는 것으로 거부된다. **단서 2**

→ 제조업자는 시장 경향을 선도하는 사용자의 시제품 해결책을 거부한다.
▶ 제조업자는 ②'시장 경향을 선도하는 사용자가 이미 개발한' 혁신을 발견하고 상업화하는 것은 자신의 일이 아니라고 생각함

| 선택지 분석 |

① **lead users tended to overlook**
시장 경향을 선도하는 사용자가 간과하는 경향이 있던
시장 경향을 선도하는 사용자가 간과한 혁신을 거부하는 것이 아니라 그들이 만들어낸 해결책, 혁신을 거부하는 것이다.

② **lead users have already developed**
시장 경향을 선도하는 사용자가 이미 개발한
직접 혁신을 발견하고 상업화하는 것이 제조업자가 생각하는 자신의 일이다.

③ **lead users encountered in the market**
시장 경향을 선도하는 사용자가 시장에서 마주친
'제조업자들이 직접 혁신을 이루려 한다는 것'과 좀 더 정확하게 대조되는 것은 '시장 경향을 선도하는 사용자가 이미 개발한 혁신을 발견하고 상업화하는 것'이지, 시장 경향을 선도하는 사용자가 단순히 시장에서 마주친 혁신을 이용하는 것이 아니다.

④ **other firms frequently put into use**
다른 회사들이 자주 실행한
시장 경향을 선도하는 사용자의 혁신을 제조업자들은 대체로 거부하지만, 실제로 그러한 혁신이 회사의 제품 라인에 적용되면 여러 주요 혁신의 실질적인 원천이 된다는 마지막 문장에 firm이 언급된 것으로 만든 오답이다.

⑤ **both users and firms have valued**
사용자와 회사 둘 다 소중하게 여긴
마찬가지로 firm이라는 단어를 넣어 만든 오답으로 빈칸에 들어갈 말로 적절하지 않다.

K 62 정답 ① ─────── ⚙ 1등급 대비 [정답률 34%]

＊개별적 행동이 군집의 노동력을 조절함

단수 주어   수식 받는 a honeybee colony와 수동 관계
The entrance to a honeybee colony, / often referred to as the
dancefloor, / is a market place for information / about the state
          단수 동사
of the colony / and the environment outside the hive. //
꿀벌 군집의 입구는 — 흔히 댄스 플로어라고 불리는 / 정보를 위한 시장이다 / 군집의 상태에 관한 / 그리고 벌집 밖의 환경(에 관한) //
동명사 주어   단수 동사
Studying / interactions on the dancefloor / provides us / with a
                                                          '많은'
number of illustrative examples /   the number of: ~의 수
연구하는 것은 / 댄스 플로어에서의 상호 작용을 / 우리에게 제공한다 / 많은 예증이 되는 예들을 /
                        주어
of how individuals / changing their own behavior / in response
to local information / **allow the colony to regulate** / **its**
                        동사   목적어   목적격 보어
workforce. //
어떻게 개체들이 / 그것들 자신의 행동을 바꾸는 / 지엽적인 정보에 반응하여 / 군집으로 하여금 조절하게 하는지에 대한 / 그것의 노동력을 //
                                                주어, 선행사
For example, / upon returning to their hive / honeybees / that
             upon+동명사: ~하자마자   주격 관계대명사
have collected water / search out a receiver bee / to unload their
                                                      동사
water to / within the hive. //
예를 들어 / 자신들의 벌집으로 돌아오자마자 / 꿀벌들은 / 물을 가져온 / 받을 벌을 찾는다 / 자신들의 물을 넘겨줄 / 벌집 안에서 //
If this search time is short / then the returning bee is more likely
to perform / a waggle dance / to recruit others / to the water
                                부사적 용법(목적)
source. //
만약 이 찾는 시간이 짧으면 / 그 돌아오는 벌은 수행할 가능성이 더 크다 / 8자 춤을 / 다른 벌들을 모집하기 위해 / 물이 있는 곳으로 //
Conversely, / if this search time is long / then the bee is more
              목적어로 동명사를 취하는 give up
likely to give up / collecting water. //
반대로 / 이 찾는 시간이 길면 / 그 벌은 포기할 가능성이 더 크다 / 물을 가지러 가는 것을 //
Since receiver bees will only accept water / if they require it, /
부사절 접속사(이유)   either A or B로 연결된 부사구
either for themselves / or to pass on to other bees and brood, /
받는 벌들은 오직 물을 받을 것이므로 / 그들이 그것을 필요로 할 때 / 자신들을 위해서든 / 또는 다른 벌들과 애벌레들에게 전해주기 위해서든 /
this unloading time is correlated / with the colony's overall
need of water. //
이러한 물을 넘겨주는 시간은 상관관계가 있다 / 군집의 전반적인 불 수요와 //

Thus / the individual water forager's response / to unloading
time / (up or down) / regulates water collection / in response to
the colony's need. // **단서** 물을 넘겨주는 시간에 대한 개별적인 물 조달자의 반응이
군집의 수요에 맞추어 물 수집(량)을 조절함

따라서 / 개별적인 물 조달자의 반응은 / 물을 넘겨주는 시간에 대한 / (시간이 늘어나든 혹은
줄어들든 간에) / 물 수집(량)을 조절한다 / 군집의 수요에 맞춰서 //

- colony ⓝ 군집, 집단 · hive ⓝ 벌집
- illustrative ⓐ 예증이 되는, 분명히 보여주는 · regulate ⓥ 규제[조절]하다
- unload ⓥ 넘겨주다 · workforce ⓝ 노동력
- respective ⓐ 각각의

흔히 댄스 플로어라고 불리는 꿀벌 군집의 입구는 군집의 상태와 벌집 밖의
환경에 관한 정보를 (교환하기) 위한 시장이다. 댄스 플로어에서의 상호 작용을
연구하는 것은 우리에게 지엽적인 정보에 반응하여 그것들 자신의 행동을
바꾸는 개체들이 어떻게 **군집이 그것의 노동력을 조절하게 하는지**에 대한 많은
예증이 되는 예들을 제공한다.

예를 들어, 물을 가져온 꿀벌들은 자신들의 벌집으로 돌아오자마자 벌집
안에서 자신들의 물을 넘겨줄 받을 벌을 찾는다. 만약 이 찾는 시간이 짧으면,
그 돌아오는 벌은 물이 있는 곳으로 데려갈 다른 벌들을 모집하기 위해 8자
춤을 출 가능성이 더 크다. 반대로, 이 찾는 시간이 길면 그 벌은 물을 가지러
가는 것을 포기할 가능성이 더 크다. 물을 받는 벌들은 자신들을 위해서든
다른 벌들과 애벌레들에게 전해주기 위해서든, 물이 필요할 때만 물을 받을
것이므로, 이러한 물을 넘겨주는 시간은 군집의 전반적인 물 수요와 상관관계가
있다. 따라서 (시간이 늘어나든 혹은 줄어들든 간에) 물을 넘겨주는 시간에 대한
개별적인 물 조달자의 반응은 군집의 수요에 맞춰서 물 수집(량)을 조절한다.

다음 빈칸에 들어갈 말로 가장 적절한 것을 고르시오. [3점]

① allow the colony to regulate its workforce
군집으로 하여금 군집의 노동력을 조절하게 하는지 .... 물 수집에 투입되는 벌의 수가 조절됨
② search for water sources by measuring distance
거리를 측정하여 물이 있는 곳을 찾는지 .... 물이 있는 곳까지의 거리가 중요한 것이 아님
③ decrease the colony's workload when necessary
필요할 때 군집의 작업 부담을 줄이는지 .... 물 수집량을 늘릴 수도 있음
④ divide tasks according to their respective talents
자신들 각자의 재능에 따라 일을 나누는지 .... 재능에 따른 분업에 대한 내용이 아님
⑤ train workers to acquire basic communication patterns
기본적인 의사소통 패턴을 습득하도록 일벌들을 훈련하는지 .... 8자 춤을 춘다는 것으로 만든 오답

왜 1등급? 예시로 나온, 물을 가져온 벌이 군집에 물이 필요한 경우와 필요하지
않은 경우에 어떻게 하는지를 파악하는 것이 문제를 푸는 열쇠이다. 이 단서를 잘
이해해서 문제를 풀어야 하는 1등급 대비 문제이다.

| 문제 풀이 순서 |

1st 빈칸 문장이나 그 앞뒤 문장에 쓰인 연결어나 지시어를 확인한다.

빈칸 다음 문장	For example, upon returning to their hive honeybees that have collected water search out a receiver bee to unload their water to within the hive. 예를 들어, 자신들의 벌집으로 돌아오자마자 물을 가져온 꿀벌들은 벌집 안에서 자신들의 물을 넘겨줄 받을 벌을 찾는다.

➡ For example은 앞서 설명한 것을 구체적인 예시를 통해 뒷받침할 때 쓰이는
연결어이다.
　▶ 예시의 내용을 파악하면 그 앞부분, 즉 빈칸 문장이 어떤 내용이어야 하는지 알
　수 있음

2nd 이어지는 문장을 읽고, 예시의 내용을 파악한다.

물을 갖고 돌아온 벌은 벌집 안에서 물을 넘겨 받을 벌을 찾는다.
벌집 안의 벌은 물이 필요할 때만 물을 받을 것이다.

찾는 시간이 짧으면 물을 가져온 벌은 물을 가지러 갈 벌을 모집하기 위해 8자 춤을 춘다.	찾는 시간이 길면 물을 가져온 벌은 물을 가지러 가는 것을 포기한다.

그러므로 물을 넘겨주는 데 드는 시간은 군집의 물 수요와 관계가 있다.
따라서 물을 넘겨주는 시간에 대한 개별적인 물 조달자의 반응은 군집의
수요에 맞춰 물 수집(량)을 조절한다. **단서**

➡ 벌집 안의 벌은 군집에 물이 필요하면 물을 넘겨 받고, 필요하지 않으면 넘겨 받지
않는다.
　➡ **1** 군집에 물이 필요한 경우: 물을 가져온 벌이 물을 넘겨줄 벌을 찾는 시간이
　짧음, 그러면 그 벌은 물을 가지러 갈 벌을 모집함
　➡ **2** 군집에 물이 필요하지 않은 경우: 물을 가져온 벌이 물을 벌을 찾는 시간이 긺,
　그러면 그 벌은 물을 가지러 가는 것을 포기함

3rd 확인한 예시의 내용에 맞게 빈칸 문장을 완성한다.

> Studying interactions on the dancefloor provides us with
> a number of illustrative examples of how individuals
> changing their own behavior in response to local
> information _____.
> 댄스 플로어에서의 상호 작용을 연구하는 것은 우리에게 지엽적인 정보에 반응하여
> 그것들 자신의 행동을 바꾸는 개체들이 어떻게 _____에 대한 많은 예증이
> 되는 예들을 제공한다.

➡ 개별적인 물 조달자(개체)가 물을 넘겨줄 벌을 찾는 시간(지엽적인 정보)에
따라 다르게 반응함으로써 군집의 벌들(노동력)이 물을 가지러 가는지 여부가
결정된다는 내용이다.
　▶ 댄스 플로어(꿀벌 군집의 입구)에서의 상호 작용을 연구하는 것은, 지엽적인
　정보에 반응하여 자신의 행동을 바꾸는 개체가 어떻게 ① '군집으로 하여금 그것의
　노동력을 조절하게 하는지'를 알려줌

| 선택지 분석 |

① **allow the colony to regulate its workforce**
군집으로 하여금 군집의 노동력을 조절하게 하는지
'물을 가져온 벌=개체', '물을 넘겨줄 벌을 찾는 시간=지엽적인 정보', '물을 가지러 갈지
말지=노동력 조절'

② **search for water sources by measuring distance**
거리를 측정하여 물이 있는 곳을 찾는지
to the water source가 언급된 것으로 만든 오답이다. 물이 있는 곳을 어떻게
찾는지를 설명하는 것이 아니다.

③ **decrease the colony's workload when necessary**
필요할 때 군집의 작업 부담을 줄이는지
군집에 물이 필요한 경우에는 물을 수집하러 나가는 벌의 수를 늘릴 것이므로 정답이
될 수 없다.

④ **divide tasks according to their respective talents**
자신들 각자의 재능에 따라 일을 나누는지
각각의 벌들이 서로 다른 일을 수행한다는 언급은 없다.

⑤ **train workers to acquire basic communication patterns**
기본적인 의사소통 패턴을 습득하도록 일벌들을 훈련하는지
8자 춤을 추어서 물을 가지러 갈 벌들을 모집한다는 내용으로 만든 오답이다.

권주원 I 서울대 정치외교학부 2023년 입학·서울 배재고 졸

처음 이 문제를 접했을 때 내가 주목한 건 a market
place for information이었는데, 이 단어를 보자마자
'정보의 교환'을 통해 '무엇'이 이루어질 것이다.'라는 주제를
대강 유추할 수 있었거든.
그리고 예시를 읽으면서 주목했던 건 search time과 물의 공급량 간의
상관관계였는데, search time이 짧으면 물의 공급량이 늘고, 길면 물의
공급량이 감소한다는 상관관계를 통해 주제를 바로 알아낼 수 있었지. '아,
정보의 교환으로 물과 같은 자원의 공급이 변하는구나. 다시 말해서, 자원
수집에 쓰이는 노동력이 변하는구나!'라고 말이야. 그리고 이 주제는 마지막
문장에서 명확하게 드러났고, 이 단서들을 활용해서 비교적 쉽게 정답을
구한 문제였어.

K 63 정답 ④ * 19세기 후반의 변화

There was nothing modern / about the idea / of men making
 동격의 전치사
women's clothes / — we saw them doing it / for centuries in
주어 동사 목적어 목적격 보어
the past. //
현대적인 것이 전혀 없었다 / 생각에 대해서는 / 여자 옷을 만드는 남자라는 / 우리는 그들이
그것을 하는 것을 보았다 / 과거 여러 세기 동안 //

In the old days, however, / the client was always primary / and
her tailor was an obscure craftsman, / perhaps talented but
perhaps not. // 하지만 옛 시절에는 / 고객이 항상 주됐고 / 그녀의 재단사는 무명의
장인이었다 / 재능이 있었을 수도 있고 그렇지 않았을 수도 있는 //

She had her own ideas / like any patron, / there were no fashion
plates, /
그녀는 자기 자신의 생각이 있었고 / 여느 후원자처럼 / 유행하는 옷의 본이 없었으며 /

and the tailor was simply at her service, / perhaps with helpful
전치사
suggestions / about what others were wearing. //
명사절
재단사는 그저 그녀의 생각에 따랐다 / 아마도 도움이 되는 제안을 가지고 / 다른 사람들이
입고 있는 것에 관한 //

Beginning in the late nineteenth century, / with the hugely
successful rise / of the artistic male couturier, /
19세기 후반에 시작하여 / 매우 성공적인 부상과 함께 / 예술적인 남성 고급 여성복
디자이너의 / it was ~ who 구문으로 강조된 문장의 주어 동사 became이 생략됨
it was the designer / who became celebrated, / and the client
elevated / by his inspired attention. //
바로 디자이너가 / 유명해졌고 / 고객은 치켜세워졌다 / 그의 영감 어린 관심에 의해 //

In a climate of admiration / for male artists and their female
creations, / the dress-designer first flourished / as the same sort
of creator. // 단서 의상 디자이너가 남성 예술가와 같은 종류의 창작자로서 번영함
찬탄의 분위기 속에서 / 남성 예술가와 여성을 위한 그들의 창작물에 대한 / 의상 디자이너는
처음으로 번영했다 / 같은 종류의 창작자로서 //
동격의 접속사 선행사
Instead of the old rule / that dressmaking is a craft, / **a modern**
connection / between dress-design and art / was invented /
주격 관계대명사
that had not been there before. // 옛 규칙 대신에 / 의상 제작은 공예라는 /
현대적 연결이 / 의상 디자인과 예술 사이의 / 만들어졌다 / 예전에는 없던 //

- client ⓝ 의뢰인, 고객 • primary ⓐ 주된, 기본적인, 초기의
- tailor ⓝ 재단사 • craftsman ⓝ (수)공예가, 장인(匠人)
- talented ⓐ (타고난) 재능이 있는 • suggestion ⓝ 제안, 암시
- rise ⓝ 성공, 출세 • elevate ⓥ (정도를) 높이다, (들어)올리다
- climate ⓝ 기후, 분위기 • admiration ⓝ 감탄, 존경
- flourish ⓥ 번창하다

남자가 여자 옷을 만든다는 생각에는 현대적인 것이 전혀 없었는데, 우리는
과거 여러 세기 동안 그들이 그것을 하는 것을 보았다. 하지만 옛 시절에는
고객이 항상 주됐고 그녀의 재단사는 재능이 있었을 수도 있고 그렇지 않았을
수도 있는 무명의 장인이었다. 그녀는 여느 후원자처럼 자기 자신의 생각이
있었고, 유행하는 옷의 본이 없었으며, 재단사는 아마도 다른 사람들이 입고
있는 것에 관한 도움이 되는 제안을 가지고 그저 그녀의 생각에 따랐다.
예술적인 남성 고급 여성복 디자이너의 매우 성공적인 부상과 함께 19세기
후반에 시작하여, 유명해진 것은 바로 디자이너였고, 고객은 그의 영감 어린
관심에 의해 치켜세워졌다. 남성 예술가와 여성을 위한 그들의 창작물에 대한
찬탄의 분위기 속에서, 의상 디자이너는 처음으로 같은 종류의 창작자로서
번영했다. 의상 제작은 공예라는 옛 규칙 대신에, 예전에는 없던 <u>의상 디자인과
예술 사이의 현대적 연결</u>이 만들어졌다.

다음 빈칸에 들어갈 말로 가장 적절한 것을 고르시오. [3점]

① a profitable industry driving fast fashion 패스트 패션에 대한 언급은 없음
패스트 패션을 주도하는 수익성 있는 산업
② a widespread respect for marketing skills
마케팅 기술에 대한 광범위한 존중 마케팅 기술이 존중받게 되었다는 것이 아님
③ a public institution preserving traditional designs
전통 디자인을 보존하는 공공 기관 공공 기관은 등장하지 않음
④ a modern connection between dress-design and art
의상 디자인과 예술 사이의 현대적 연결 의상 디자이너가 예술가와 같은 종류의 창작자가 됨
⑤ an efficient system for producing affordable clothing
적정 가격의 의류를 생산하기 위한 효율적인 체계 의류의 가격에 대한 내용은 없음

왜 정답? [정답률 48%]

글을 통해 예전에는 없던 '무엇'이 만들어졌는지 파악해서 빈칸에 들어갈 말을
골라야 한다.
과거에 재단사는 그저 고객의 생각에 따라 옷을 만드는 무명의 장인이었지만,
19세기 후반에 고급 여성복을 디자인하는 예술적인 남성 디자이너가 매우
성공적으로 부상했고, 의상 디자이너는 여성을 위한 창작물을 창작하는 남성
예술가와 같은 종류의 창작자로서 번영했다고 했다.
그러므로 의상 제작은 공예라는 옛 규칙 대신에 등장한 것은 ④ '의상 디자인과
예술 사이의 현대적 연결'이다.

왜 오답? '물건을 만드는 기술에 관한 재주'라는 뜻으로,
'(수)공예가, 장인'이 '예술가, 창작자'와 대조되는 글임 꿀팁

①, ⑤ 의류 산업의 수익성이나 의류의 적정 가격에 대한 내용이 아니다.
② 마케팅 기술이 과거에는 제대로 존중받지 못하다가 존중받게 되었음을
설명하는 글이 아니다.
③ 전통 디자인이나 그것을 보존하기 위한 공공 기관에 대한 언급은 없다.

K 64 정답 ① * 도시의 질을 측정하는 머물기 활동의 정도

so+형용사/부사+that절: 너무 ~해서 …하다
City quality is so crucial for optional activities / that the extent
of staying activities can often be used / as a measuring stick for
the quality of the city / as well as of its space. //
도시의 질은 선택적 활동에 매우 중요하다 / 그래서 머물기 활동의 정도가 흔히 사용될 수
있다 / 도시의 질을 측정하는 잣대로 / 도시의 공간뿐만 아니라 //

Many pedestrians in a city / are not necessarily an indication of
단서1 머물기 활동의 정도가 도시의
good city quality / 질을 측정하는 잣대일 수 있음
도시의 많은 보행자가 / 반드시 좋은 도시 질의 지표인 것은 아니다 /
people을 수식하는 분사
— many people walking around / can often be a sign / of
insufficient transit options / or long distances between the
various functions in the city. //
걸어서 돌아다니는 많은 사람은 / 흔히 징표일 수 있다 / 부족한 운송 선택권 / 또는 도시 내
다양한 기능 간의 먼 거리의 //
가주어 진주어절을 이끄는 접속사
Conversely, / it can be claimed / that a city in which many
전치사+관계대명사(= where)
people are not walking / often indicates good city quality. //
반대로 / 주장될 수 있다 / 많은 사람이 걷지 않는 도시가 / 흔히 좋은 도시의 질을 나타낸다고 //
it is ~ that … 강조 구문
In a city like Rome, / it is the large number of people / standing
병렬 구조(people을 수식하는 분사)
or sitting in squares / rather than walking / that is conspicuous. //
로마와 같은 도시에서 / 많은 사람이 / 광장에서 서 있거나 앉아 있는 / 걷기보다는 / 눈에
띄는 것은 // 단서2 로마와 같은 도시에는 서 있거나 앉아 있는 사람이 많음

And it's not due to necessity / but rather that **the city quality is**
so inviting. //
그런데 이것은 필요성 때문이 아니다 / 그 도시의 질이 매우 매력적이기 때문이다 //
가주어 진주어
It is hard / to keep moving in city space / with so many
temptations / to stay. // 단서3 도시에 머물게 만드는 유혹이 많아 움직이기 어려움
어렵다 / 도시 공간에서 계속 움직이는 것은 / 너무 많은 유혹이 있는 / 머무르게 하는 //
주어와 동사 도치 목적격 관계대명사
In contrast / are many new quarters and complexes / that many
people walk through / but rarely stop or stay in. //
반대로 / 새로운 구역과 단지가 있다 / 많은 사람이 걸어서 지나가는 / 그러나 거의 멈추거나
머무르지 않는 //

- crucial ⓐ 중요한 • optional ⓐ 선택의 • extent ⓝ 정도
- pedestrian ⓝ 보행자 • indication ⓝ 지표, 표시
- insufficient ⓐ 부족한, 불충분한 • transit ⓝ 운송
- function ⓝ 기능 • conversely ⓐ 반대로
- conspicuous ⓐ 눈에 띄는 • inviting ⓐ 매력적인, 유혹적인
- temptation ⓝ 유혹 • quarter ⓝ 구역, 지구
- complex ⓝ (건물) 단지 • occupy ⓥ 차지하다
- public transportation 대중 교통 • administrative ⓐ 행정의
- concentrate ⓥ 집중하다, 모으다

도시의 질은 선택적 활동에 매우 중요해서, 머물기 활동의 정도가 흔히 도시의 공간뿐만 아니라 도시의 질을 측정하는 잣대로 사용될 수 있다. 도시의 많은 보행자가 반드시 도시의 질이 좋다는 지표인 것은 아니며, 걸어서 돌아다니는 많은 사람은 흔히 부족한 운송 선택권 또는 도시 내 다양한 기능 간의 먼 거리의 징표일 수 있다. 반대로, 많은 사람이 걷지 않는 도시는 흔히 좋은 도시의 질을 나타낸다고 주장될 수 있다. 로마와 같은 도시에서 눈에 띄는 것은 걷기보다는 광장에 서 있거나 앉아 있는 많은 사람이다. 그런데 이것은 필요성 때문이 아니라, **그 도시의 질이 매우 매력적이기** 때문이다. 도시 공간에는 머무르게 하는 유혹이 너무 많아서 계속 움직이기 어렵다. 반대로 많은 사람이 걸어서 지나가지만 거의 멈추거나 머무르지 않는 많은 새로운 구역과 단지가 있다.

다음 빈칸에 들어갈 말로 가장 적절한 것을 고르시오.

① the city quality is so inviting 그 도시에 서 있거나 앉아 있는 사람이 많은 것은 도시의 질이 좋기 때문이라고 함
② public spaces are already occupied 공공장소가 이미 점유되었기 / 도시에 서 있거나 앉아 있는 사람이 있다는 것으로 만든 함정
③ public transportation is not available 대중교통을 이용할 수 없기 / 대중교통을 이용할 수 없기 때문에 도시에 머무는 것이 아님
④ major tourist spots are within walking distance 주요 관광지가 도보 거리 내에 있기 / 주요 관광지가 도보 거리 내에 있어서 도시에 머문다는 내용이 아님
⑤ the city's administrative buildings are concentrated 도시의 행정 건물이 밀집되어 있기 / 도시의 행정 건물이 밀집되어 있다는 언급은 없음

왜 정답? [정답률 35%]

| 빈칸 문장 | 그런데 이것은 필요성 때문이 아니라, _____ 때문이다. |

➡ 빈칸에는 이것(앉아 있는 사람이 많은 것)이 필요성 때문이 아니라 무엇 때문인지가 들어가야 한다.

- • 머물기 활동의 정도가 도시의 질을 측정하는 잣대로 사용될 수 있다. **단서 1**
- • 로마와 같은 도시에는 광장에 서 있거나 앉아 있는 사람이 많다. **단서 2**
- • 도시 공간에는 머무르게 하는 유혹이 너무 많아서 계속 움직이기 어렵다. **단서 3**

➡ 머물기 활동의 정도가 도시의 질을 측정할 수 있는데, 로마와 같은 도시에서 광장에 서 있거나 앉아 있는 사람이 많은 이유는 그 도시에 머무르게 하는 유혹이 너무 많아서, 즉 도시의 질이 좋아서 계속 움직이기 어렵기 때문이라고 한다.

▶ 그러므로 도시에 사람들이 앉아 있는 이유로는 ① '그 도시의 질이 매우 매력적이기' 때문이라고 하는 것이 적절하다.

왜 오답?

② 도시에 서 있거나 앉아 있는 사람이 있다는 것으로 만든 함정으로, 공공장소가 이미 점유되었기 때문에 많은 사람들이 도시에 머문다는 내용은 없다.
③ 대중교통을 이용할 수 없기 때문에 도시에 머무는 것이 아니다.
④ 주요 관광지가 도보 거리 내에 있어서 도시에 머무는 것이라고 하지 않았다.
⑤ 도시의 행정 건물이 밀집되어 있다는 언급은 없다.

K 65 정답 ① ＊창의성을 위해 아이디어를 평가하고 선택하는 과정의 필요성

Creativity is commonly defined / ~로서 as the production of ideas / that are both novel (original, new) and useful (appropriate, 주격 관계대명사 └both A and B: A와 B 둘 다┘ feasible). //
창의성은 흔히 정의된다 / 아이디어를 생산하는 것으로 / 참신하고(독창적이고, 새로운) 유용한(적절하고, 실현 가능한) //

복수 주어 주격 관계대명사 복수 동사
Ideas that are original but not useful / are irrelevant, / and ideas that are useful but not original / are unremarkable. //
독창적이지만 유용하지 않은 아이디어는 / 무의미하고 / 유용하지만 독창적이지 않은 아이디어는 / 특별한 것이 없다 //

동명사 주어(단수 취급)
While this definition is widely used in research, / an important aspect of creativity / is often ignored. / Generating creative ideas 단수 동사 **단서 1** 창의적 아이디어 생성 자체가 rarely is the final goal. // 최종 목표인 경우는 거의 없음
이러한 정의가 연구에서 널리 사용되지만 / 창의성의 중요한 측면이 / 흔히 간과되는데 / 창의적인 아이디어를 생성하는 것이 최종 목표인 경우는 거의 없다는 것이다 //

주어 단수 동사
Rather, to successfully solve problems or innovate / requires 주격 관계대명사 one or a few good ideas / that really work, and work better than previous approaches. //
오히려, 문제를 성공적으로 해결하거나 혁신하는 것에는 / 하나 또는 몇 개의 좋은 아이디어가 필요하다 / 실제로 작동하고, 이전 접근 방식보다 더 잘 작동하는 //

주장, 요구, 명령, 제안을 나타내는 동사(+that)+주어(+should)+동사원형
This requires / that people evaluate the products of their own or 동사① each other's imagination, /
이것은 필요로 한다 / 사람들은 자기 자신 또는 서로의 상상력 산물을 평가하고 /

동사② and choose those ideas that seem promising enough to develop 동사③ further, / and abandon those that are unlikely to be successful. //
더 발전시킬 수 있을 정도로 유망해 보이는 아이디어를 선택하며 / 성공 가능성이 작은 것들은 포기해야 한다 // **단서 2** 아이디어 생성 이후 평가, 선택의 과정이 필요함

Thus, being creative / **does not stop with idea generation**. //
따라서 창의적인 것은 / 아이디어 생성에서 멈추지 않는다 //

단수 주어 단수 동사
In fact, the ability to generate creative ideas / is essentially useless / if these ideas subsequently die a silent death. //
사실, 창의적인 아이디어를 생성하는 능력은 / 본질적으로 쓸모가 없다 / 이러한 아이디어가 이후 조용히 죽어 없어진다면 // **단서 3** 아이디어가 생성만 되고 사라진다면 쓸모가 없음 (= 생성 이후의 평가와 선택의 과정이 중요)

- • commonly ⓐⓓ 흔히 • novel ⓐ 참신한 • original ⓐ 독창적인
- • appropriate ⓐ 적절한 • feasible ⓐ 실현 가능한
- • irrelevant ⓐ 무의미한 • unremarkable ⓐ 특별한 것이 없는, 평범한
- • ignore ⓥ 간과하다 • innovate ⓥ 혁신하다
- • evaluate ⓥ 평가하다 • abandon ⓥ 포기하다, 버리다
- • essentially ⓐⓓ 본질적으로, 근본적으로 • subsequently ⓐⓓ 나중에
- • practical ⓐ 실용적인, 현실적인 • frequently ⓐⓓ 자주
- • give way to ~에 굽히다 • tension ⓝ 긴장 상태

창의성은 참신하고(독창적이고, 새로운) 유용한(적절하고, 실현 가능한) 아이디어를 생산하는 것으로 흔히 정의된다. 독창적이지만 유용하지 않은 아이디어는 무의미하고, 유용하지만 독창적이지 않은 아이디어는 특별한 것이 없다. 이러한 정의가 연구에서 널리 사용되지만, 창의성의 중요한 측면이 흔히 간과되는데, 창의적인 아이디어를 생성하는 것이 최종 목표인 경우는 거의 없다는 것이다. 오히려, 문제를 성공적으로 해결하거나 혁신하기 위해서는, 실제로 작동하고 이전 접근 방식보다 더 잘 작동하는 하나 또는 몇 개의 좋은 아이디어가 필요하다. 이를 위해 사람들은 자기 자신 또는 서로의 상상력 산물을 평가하고, 더 발전시킬 수 있을 정도로 유망해 보이는 아이디어를 선택하며, 성공 가능성이 작은 것들은 포기해야 한다. 따라서 창의적인 것은 **아이디어 생성에서 멈추지 않는다.** 사실, 창의적인 아이디어를 생성하는 능력은 이러한 아이디어가 이후 조용히 죽어 없어진다면 본질적으로 쓸모가 없다.

다음 빈칸에 들어갈 말로 가장 적절한 것을 고르시오.

① does not stop with idea generation 아이디어 생성에서 멈추지 않는다 / 아이디어 생성 후 이를 평가하고 선택하는 과정이 있어야 한다는 내용임
② rarely originates from practical ideas 아이디어가 유용하게 쓰이게 하기 위함 / 실용적인 아이디어에서 비롯되는 경우는 거의 없다 / 평가 및 선택이 필요하다고 했으므로 반대 내용임
③ is often regarded as a shortcut to innovation 혁신으로 가는 지름길로 흔히 간주된다 / 지름길보다는 거쳐야 하는 과정을 제시하고 있음
④ frequently gives way to unanticipated success 예상치 못한 성공에 자주 자리를 내어준다 / 예상치 못한 성공은 언급된 바 없음
⑤ brings out tension between novelty and relevancy 독창성과 유의미성 사이에 긴장을 불러일으킨다 / 창의적인 것과 독창성을 연결시켜 만든 오답

왜 정답? [정답률 35%]

- • 창의적 아이디어 생성 자체가 최종 목표인 경우는 거의 없음 **단서 1**
- • 아이디어 생성 이후 평가, 선택의 과정이 필요함 **단서 2**
- • 아이디어가 생성만 되고 사라진다면 쓸모가 없음(= 생성 이후의 평가와 선택의 과정이 중요함) **단서 3**

➡ 창의적인 것은 단순히 창의적인 아이디어를 생성하는 것으로 끝나지 않고, 생성된 아이디어를 평가하고 선택하는 과정이 필요하다는 내용의 글이다.

▶ 따라서 빈칸에 들어갈 말로 가장 적절한 것은 ① '아이디어 생성에서 멈추지 않는다'이다.

왜 오답?

② 아이디어가 유용하게 쓰이고자 하기 위해 아이디어 평가 및 선택이 필요한 내용이므로 이것은 글의 내용과 반대라고 볼 수 있다. **주의**
③ 지름길보다는 거쳐야 하는 과정을 제시하고 있다.
④ 예상치 못한 성공은 언급된 바 없다.
⑤ 창의적인 것과 독창성을 연결시켜 만든 오답일 뿐이다.

K 66 정답 ② ＊유전자와 뇌의 신경 경로의 산물인 행동

Behavior is, for the most part, / a product of genes and brain neuropathways. // **단서1** 행동은 대부분 유전자와 뇌의 신경 경로의 산물임
행동은, 대부분 ~이다 / 유전자와 뇌의 신경 경로의 산물 //

Consider the elegant chemistry at work / when living organisms move, think, behave, and act. //
정교한 화학 작용을 고려해 보라 / 살아 있는 유기체가 움직이고, 생각하고, 처신하고, 행동할 때 작용하는 //

Certainly, the environment is a factor here / because it can influence *how* we act. //
관계부사
틀림없이, 환경은 여기서 하나의 요소인데 / 그것이 우리가 '행동하는 방식'에 영향을 미칠 수 있기 때문이다 //

An analogy would illustrate this adequately. //
한 가지 비유가 이것을 적절히 설명할 수 있을 것이다 //

Think of the environment as gasoline, and our body as the engine. // 환경을 휘발유로, 우리 몸을 엔진으로 생각해 보라 //

Truly, the engine does not run without the gasoline, / but all the intricate parts of the engine are the product of *physical architecture*, /
엄밀히, 엔진은 휘발유 없는 작동하지 않지만 / 엔진의 모든 복잡한 부품들은 '물리적 구조'의 산물인데
등위접속사 and로 연결된 과거분사
designed and assembled for a reactive purpose / long before the gasoline is injected. //
반응을 보이려는 목적으로 설계되고 조립되었다 / 휘발유가 주입되기 훨씬 이전에 //
(= inject less gas)
Inject more gas and the engine accelerates, / less, and it slows. //
더 많은 휘발유를 주입하면, 엔진이 빨라지고 / 더 적은 (휘발유를 주입하면), 그것은 느려진다 //

The same is true for an organism. // 유기체에서도 마찬가지이다 //

Behavior is a *response* to the environment. //
행동은 환경에 대한 '반응'이다 //
지시형용사
We have 'free will,' / but the ultimate characteristic of that response can only act / with respect to the architecture of our genes and our brain. // **단서2** 반응의 궁극적 특성은 우리 유전자와
~에 관하여
뇌의 구조에 관해서만 작용 가능함
우리는 '자유 의지'를 가지고 있지만 / 그 반응의 궁극적인 특성은 작용할 수 있다 / 우리의 유전자와 우리의 뇌의 구조와 관해서만 //

In other words, the environment can, effectively, accelerate or slow down a potential behavior, /
다시 말해, 환경은 잠재적인 행동을 효과적으로 빨라지게 하거나 늦출 수 있지만 /
지시형용사
but the engine for that behavior **is already built and functional**; / therefore, the environment is but a catalyst. //
그 행동을 위한 엔진은 이미 구축되었고 가동된다 / 따라서, 환경은 단지 촉매일 뿐이다 //

- behavior ⓝ 행동　　・elegant ⓐ 우아한
- influence ⓥ 영향을 미치다　　・analogy ⓝ 비유, 유사점
- illustrate ⓥ 설명하다　　・adequately ⓐ 적절히
- intricate ⓐ 복잡한　　・architecture ⓝ 구조, 건축
- assemble ⓥ 조립하다　　・reactive ⓐ 반응을 하는
- inject ⓥ 주입하다　　・accelerate ⓥ 가속화하다
- malfunction ⓥ 제대로 작동하지 않다　　・periodically ⓐ 주기적으로

행동은, 대부분, 유전자와 뇌의 신경 경로의 산물이다. 살아 있는 유기체가 움직이고, 생각하고, 처신하고, 행동할 때 작용하는 정교한 화학 작용을 고려해 보라. 틀림없이, 환경은 여기서 하나의 요소인데 그것이 우리가 '행동하는 방식'에 영향을 미칠 수 있기 때문이다. 한 가지 비유가 이것을 적절히 설명할 수 있을 것이다. 환경을 휘발유로, 우리 몸을 엔진으로 생각해 보라. 엄밀히, 엔진은 휘발유 없는 작동하지 않지만, 엔진의 모든 복잡한 부품들은 '물리적 구조'의 산물인데, 휘발유가 주입되기 훨씬 이전에 반응을 보이려는 목적으로 설계되고 조립되었다. 더 많은 휘발유를 주입하면, 엔진이 빨라지고, 더 적은

(휘발유를 주입하면), 그것은 느려진다. 유기체에서도 마찬가지이다. 행동은 환경에 대한 '반응'이다. 우리는 '자유 의지'를 가지고 있지만, 그 반응의 궁극적인 특성은 우리의 유전자와 우리의 뇌의 구조와 관해서만 작용할 수 있다. 다시 말해, 환경은 잠재적인 행동을 효과적으로 빨라지게 하거나 늦출 수 있지만, 그 행동을 위한 엔진은 **이미 구축되었고 가동된다**. 따라서 환경은 단지 촉매일 뿐이다.

다음 빈칸에 들어갈 말로 가장 적절한 것을 고르시오.

① malfunctions even with correct input 행동을 하게 하는 물리적 구조인 엔진이
올바른 입력에도 불구하고 오작동한다　　올바른 입력에도 고장난다는 말이 아님
② is already built and functional
이미 구축되었고 가동된다　　행동을 하게 하는 엔진은 이미 만들어져 있다는 내용임
③ tends to shut down periodically
주기적으로 자동으로 꺼지는 경향이 있다　　행동을 하게 하는 엔진이 때때로 멈춘다는 내용이 아님
④ runs in an unpredictable manner
예측할 수 없는 방식으로 작동한다　　엔진이 예측 불가능한 방식으로 작동된다는 의미가 아님
⑤ is subject to change without notice
사전 통보 없이 변경될 수 있다　　예고 없이 엔진이 바뀔수도 있다는 언급은 없음

▷왜 정답? [정답률 69%]

첫번째 문장	행동은, 대부분, 유전자와 뇌의 신경 경로의 산물이다. **단서1**
빈칸 앞 문장	우리는 '자유 의지'를 가지고 있지만, 그 반응의 궁극적인 특성은 우리의 유전자와 우리의 뇌의 구조와 관해서만 작용할 수 있다. **단서2**
빈칸 문장	다시 말해, 환경은 잠재적인 행동을 효과적으로 빨라지게 하거나 늦출 수 있지만, 그 행동을 위한 엔진은 _____. 따라서 환경은 단지 촉매일 뿐이다.

➡ 첫 번째 문장에서 행동은 유전자와 뇌 신경 경로의 산물이라고 했으며, 빈칸 앞 문장에서도 이 내용을 다시 언급하고 있다. 또한, 비유에서 휘발유가 주입되기 훨씬 이전부터 엔진은 반응을 보이려는 목적으로 미리 설계된 '물리적 구조'의 산물이라고 했다.
　▶ 따라서 행동의 엔진은 ② '이미 구축되었고 가동된다'고 하는 것이 가장 적절하다.

▷왜 오답?

① 엔진에 올바른 입력을 했음에도 오작동한다는 내용은 없다.
③ 엔진이 주기적으로 꺼진다는 내용이 아니다.
④ 엔진이 예측 불가능한 방식으로 작동한다는 의미가 아니다.
⑤ 엔진이 사전 통보 없이 바뀔 수도 있다는 언급은 없다.

K 67 정답 ② ＊의도된 행동에 대한 유아의 모방 학습

The social-cognitive revolution at 1 year of age / sets the stage for infants' second year of life, / in which they begin to imitatively learn the use of all kinds of tools, artifacts, and symbols. //
전치사+관계대명사
1살의 나이에 사회 인지의 혁명은 / 유아들의 생애 두번째 해를 위한 발판을 설정하는데 / 그때 그들은 모든 종류의 도구, 인공물, 그리고 기호의 사용을 모방하여 배우기 시작한다 //

For example, in a study by Meltzoff (1988), / 14-month-old children observed / an adult bend at the waist and touch its head to a panel, / thus turning on a light. //
분사구문을 이끎　　목적격 보어의 병렬 구조
예를 들어, Meltzoff(1988)의 한 연구에서 / 14개월 된 아이들은 관찰했다 / 한 어른이 허리를 구부리고 자신의 머리를 패널에 갖다 대어 / 전등을 켜는 것을 //

'방금 남이 한 대로 따라하다'
They followed suit. // 그들은 이 방식을 따라 했다 //

Infants engaged in this somewhat unusual and awkward behavior, / even though it would have been easier and more natural for them / simply to push the panel with their hand. //
가주어
의미상 주어　　진주어
유아들은 이 다소 이상하고 어색한 행동을 하기 시작했다 / 그들에게 더 쉽고 자연스러웠을 것임에도 불구하고 / 단순히 그들의 손으로 패널을 누르는 것이 //
보어절을 이끄는 접속사
One interpretation of this behavior is / that infants understood that the adult had the goal of illuminating the light /
목적어절을 이끄는 접속사
이 행동에 대한 한 가지 해석은 ~이나 / 유아들이 그 어른이 불을 켜는 목표를 가지고 있다는 것을 이해했다는 것 /

and then chose one means for doing so, / from among other possible means, / and if they had the same goal, they could choose the same means. // (= the infants)

단서1 유아들은 어른의 목표를 이해했고, 자기도 같은 목표를 가진다면 같은 수단을 선택할 수 있다는 것을 이해함
그리고 나서 그렇게 하기 위한 수단 하나를, 가능한 다른 수단들 중에서, 골랐다는 것과 / 만약 그들이 같은 목표를 가진다면, 그들은 같은 수단을 선택할 수 있다는 것을 //

Similarly, Carpenter et al. (1998) found / that 16-month-old infants will imitatively learn from a complex behavioral sequence / only those behaviors that appear intentional, / ignoring those that appear accidental. // 관계대명사
단서2 의도가 담긴 것처럼 보이는 행동만 모방하여 배우고, 실수처럼 보이는 것들은 무시함
마찬가지로, Carpenter et al.(1998)은 알아냈다 / 16개월 된 유아들은 복잡한 행동의 연달아 일어남으로부터 모방하여 배울 것이고 / 의도적이라고 보이는 그런 행동들만 / 뜻하지 않아 보이는 것들은 무시한다는 것을 //

Young children do not just imitate the limb movements of other persons, / they attempt to **reproduce other persons' intended actions in the world**. //
어린아이들은 단순히 다른 사람들의 팔다리의 움직임을 모방하는 것이 아니라 / 그들은 세상에서 다른 사람들의 의도된 행동들을 재현하려고 시도한다 //

- imitatively [ad] 모방하여 • symbol [n] 상징
- awkward [a] 어색한 • interpretation [n] 해석
- illuminate [v] 밝히다 • mean [n] 수단 • complex [a] 복잡한
- sequence [n] 순서[차례] • intentional [a] 의도적인
- accidental [a] 우연한, 뜻하지 않은 • reproduce [v] 재현하다
- unprecedented [a] 전례 없는 • coincide [v] 일치하다

1살의 나이에 사회 인지의 혁명은 유아들의 생애 두번째 해를 위한 발판을 설정하는데, 그때 그들은 모든 종류의 도구, 인공물, 그리고 기호의 사용을 모방하여 배우기 시작한다. 예를 들어, Meltzoff(1988)의 한 연구에서, 14개월 된 아이들은 한 어른이 허리를 구부리고 자신의 머리를 패널에 갖다 대어, 전등을 켜는 것을 관찰했다. 그들은 이 방식을 따라 했다. 유아들은 단순히 그들의 손으로 패널을 누르는 것이 그들에게 더 쉽고 자연스러웠을 것임에도 불구하고, 이 다소 이상하고 어색한 행동을 하기 시작했다. 이 행동에 대한 한 가지 해석은 유아들이 그 어른이 불을 켜는 목표를 가지고 있었고 그리고 나서 그렇게 하기 위한 수단 하나를, 가능한 다른 수단들 중에서, 골랐다는 것과 만약 그들이 같은 목표를 가진다면, 그들은 같은 수단을 선택할 수 있다는 것을 이해했다는 것이다. 마찬가지로, Carpenter et al.(1998)은 16개월 된 유아들은 복잡한 행동의 연달아 일어남으로부터 의도적이라고 보이는 그런 행동들만 모방하여 배울 것이고, 뜻하지 않아 보이는 것들은 무시한다는 것을 알아냈다. 어린아이들은 단순히 다른 사람들의 팔다리의 움직임을 모방하는 것이 아니라, 그들은 세상에서 다른 사람들의 의도된 행동들을 재현하려고 시도한다.

다음 빈칸에 들어갈 말로 가장 적절한 것을 고르시오. [3점]
가족에게 어색하게 보이려고 타인의 행동을 모방한다는 내용은 아님
① avoid looking awkward in the eyes of family members
가족들의 눈에 어색하게 보이지 않도록 하려고
② reproduce other persons' intended actions in the world 타인의 행동의 의도를 파악하고,
세상에서 다른 사람들의 의도된 행동들을 재현하려고 의도가 같으면 그 행동을 모방한다는 내용임
③ accept the value of chance incidents that turn out helpful
유용하게 드러나는 우연한 사건의 가치를 받아들이려고 우연한 사건의 가치를 받아들인다는 내용은 아님
④ behave in an unprecedented way that others have missed
다른 사람들이 놓친 전례없는 방식으로 행동하려고
⑤ undermine any goal that does not coincide with their own
자신의 목표와 일치하지 않는 목표를 약화시키려고 타인의 행동을 모방한다는 내용의 글이지,
목표를 약화시킨다는 내용은 없음 전례없는 행동을 한다는 내용이 초점이 아님

> **왜 정답?** [정답률 59%]

빈칸 앞 내용	• 유아들은 어른의 목표를 이해했고, 자기도 같은 목표를 가진다면 같은 수단을 선택할 수 있다는 것을 이해함 단서1 • 16개월 된 유아들은 복잡한 행동 중 의도적이라고 보이는 행동만 모방 학습하며, 의도가 없는 것처럼 보이는 것들은 무시한다는 것을 알아낸 연구 결과 단서2
빈칸 문장	어린아이들은 단순히 다른 사람들의 팔다리 움직임을 모방하는 것이 아니라, 그들은 _____ 시도한다.

⇒ 유아는 사람의 행동을 무조건 따라하는 것이 아니라, 행동의 의도와 목적을 이해하고, 자신의 목적과 같으면 그 행동을 모방한다는 내용의 글이다.
▶ 따라서 빈칸에는 ② '세상에서 다른 사람들의 의도된 행동들을 재현하려고'가 들어가야 한다.

> **왜 오답?**
① 유아가 가족의 눈에 어떻게 보이는지 신경쓴다는 내용은 나오지 않는다.
③ 자신의 목적을 달성하는 데 도움이 될 것 같은 행동을 모방한다는 내용이긴 하지만, 우연한 사건의 가치를 받아들인다는 내용은 아니다. 함정
④ 다른 사람이 놓친 방식으로 행동하려고 한다는 언급은 없다.
⑤ 자신의 목표와 일치하지 않는 목표를 약화시킨다는 내용이 아니다.

K 68 정답 ② *과학에서 틀림을 입증하는 것의 중요함 ———

As an ideal of intellectual inquiry and a strategy for the advancement of knowledge, / the scientific method is essentially a monument to the utility of error. // 단서1 과학적 방식은 본질적으로 오류의 유용성을 보여줌
지적 탐구의 이상이자 지식의 발전을 위한 전략으로서 / 과학적 방법은 본질적으로 오류의 유용성을 보여주는 기념비이다 //

Most of us gravitate toward trying to prove our beliefs, / to the extent that we bother investigating their validity at all. // ~할 정도까지
우리 대부분은 우리의 믿음을 입증하려고 노력하는 것에 자연히 끌리는데 / 우리가 그것들의 타당성을 굳이 조사하려 해야만 (조사)하는 정도까지 그러하다 //

But scientists gravitate toward falsification; / as a community if not as individuals, / they seek to disprove their beliefs. //
그러나 과학자들은 반증에 자연히 끌리며 / 개인으로서는 아니더라도 공동체로서 / 그들은 자신의 믿음이 그릇됨을 입증하려고 한다 //

Thus, the defining feature of a hypothesis / is that it has the potential to be proven wrong / (which is why it must be both testable and tested), / 보어절을 이끄는 접속사 관계대명사 both A and B: A 와 B 둘 다
따라서 가설의 본질적인 의미를 규정하는 특징은 / 그것이 틀리다고 입증될 가능성을 가진다는 것이며 / (이는 그것(가설)이 반드시 검증 가능할 수도 있어야 하고 검증되기도 해야 한다는 이유이다.) /

and the defining feature of a theory / is that it hasn't been proven wrong yet. // 보어절을 이끄는 접속사
이론의 본질적인 의미를 규정하는 특징은 / 그것이 아직 틀리다고 입증되지 않았다는 것이다 //
(= can be proven wrong)
But the important part is that it can be / — no matter how much evidence appears to confirm it, / no matter how many experts endorse it, / no matter how much popular support it enjoys. //
그러나 중요한 부분은 그것은 그렇게 될 수 있다는 것이다 / 아무리 많은 증거가 그것(이론) 이 옳음을 증명하는 것 같더라도 / 아무리 많은 전문가가 그것을 지지하더라도 / 아무리 큰 대중의 지지를 그것이 받더라도 //

In fact, not only *can* any given theory be proven wrong; / sooner or later, it probably will be. //
사실, 어떤 주어진 이론도 틀리다고 입증'될 수 있을' 뿐만 아니라 / 조만간 그것은 아마도 그렇게 될 것이다 //
(= is proven wrong)
And when it is, / the occasion will mark the success of science, not its failure. // 단서2 어떤 주어진 이론이 틀렸다고 입증되었을 때, 그것은 과학의 성공을 나타낼 것임
그리고 그것이 그렇게 될 때 / 그 경우는 그것(과학)의 실패가 아닌, 과학의 성공을 나타낼 것이다 //

This was the crucial insight of the Scientific Revolution: / that the advancement of knowledge depends on / current theories **collapsing in the face of new insights and discoveries**. //
이것은 과학 혁명의 중대한 통찰력이었는데 / 지식의 발전은 ~에 달려 있다 / 새로운 통찰과 발견들 앞에서 붕괴하는 현재 이론 //

- **strategy** ⓝ 전략　　• **advancement** ⓝ 발전
- **monument** ⓝ 기념비　　• **utility** ⓝ 유용성
- **prove** ⓥ 입증하다　　• **extent** ⓝ 정도[규모]
- **bother** ⓥ 신경 쓰다, 애를 쓰다　　• **investigate** ⓥ 조사하다
- **validity** ⓝ 유효함, 타당성　　• **falsification** ⓝ 반증
- **hypothesis** ⓝ 가설　　• **expert** ⓝ 전문가　　• **mark** ⓥ 나타내다
- **crucial** ⓐ 중대한, 결정적인　　• **collapse** ⓥ 붕괴하다
- **temporal** ⓐ 시간의

지적 탐구의 이상이자 지식의 발전을 위한 전략으로서, 과학적 방법은 본질적으로 오류의 유용성을 보여주는 기념비이다. 우리 대부분은 우리의 믿음을 입증하려고 노력하는 것에 자연히 끌리는데, 우리가 그것들의 타당성을 굳이 조사하려 해야만 (조사하는) 정도까지 그러하다. 그러나 과학자들은 반증에 자연히 끌리며, 개인으로서는 아니더라도 공동체로서, 그들은 자신의 믿음이 그릇됨을 입증하려고 한다. 따라서 가설의 본질적인 의미를 규정하는 특징은 그것이 틀리다고 입증될 가능성을 가진다는 것이며(이는 그것(가설)이 반드시 검증 가능할 수도 있어야 하고 검증되기도 해야 한다는 이유이다.) 이론의 본질적인 의미를 규정하는 특징은 그것이 아직 틀리다고 입증되지 않았다는 것이다. 그러나 중요한 부분은 아무리 많은 증거가 그것(이론)이 옳음을 증명하는 것 같더라도, 아무리 많은 전문가가 그것을 지지하더라도, 아무리 큰 대중의 지지를 그것이 받더라도, 그것은 그렇게 될 수 있다는 것이다. 사실, 어떤 주어진 이론도 틀리다고 입증'될 수 있을' 뿐만 아니라, 조만간 그것은 아마도 그렇게 될 것이다. 그리고 그것이 그렇게 될 때, 그 경우는 그것(과학)의 실패가 아닌, 과학의 성공을 나타낼 것이다. 이것은 과학 혁명의 중대한 통찰력이었는데, 지식의 발전은 **새로운 통찰과 발견들 앞에서 붕괴하는** 현재 이론에 달려 있다.

다음 빈칸에 들어갈 말로 가장 적절한 것을 고르시오.

시·공간적 제약과 상관없이 항상 사실인 이론은 글이 말하고자 하는 바와 반대임
① holding true regardless of temporal and spatial constraints
시간적, 공간적 제약에 관계없이 항상 사실인
② collapsing in the face of new insights and discoveries ←새로운 통찰과 발견 앞에서
새로운 통찰과 발견 앞에서 붕괴하는　틀렸다는 것이 증명되면서 과학적 성공을 거두었다고 했음
③ shifting according to scientists' pursuit of reputation
과학자들의 명성 추구에 따라 변화하는　과학자들의 명성 추구에 따라 현재 이론이 변화한다는 내용은 없음
④ being exposed to the public and enjoying popularity
대중에게 노출되어 인기를 누리는　대중에게 인기를 누리는 이론은 이 글의 핵심이 아님
⑤ leaving no chance of error and failure
오류와 실패의 여지를 남기지 않는　글이 전하고자 하는 바와 정반대임

왜 정답?　[정답률 52%]

첫 문장	과학적 방식은 본질적으로 오류의 유용성을 보여주는 기념비이다. **단서 1**
빈칸 앞 문장	어떤 주어진 이론이 틀렸다고 입증되었을 때, 그것은 과학의 실패가 아닌, 과학의 성공을 나타낼 것이다. **단서 2**
빈칸 문장	이것은 과학 혁명의 중대한 통찰력이었는데, 지식의 발전은 ＿＿＿＿＿＿ 현재 이론에 달려 있다.

➡ 빈칸에는 지식의 발전이 어떤 특성을 갖춘 현재 이론에 달려 있는지가 들어가야 하고, 첫 번째 문장과 빈칸 앞 문장에서 과학에서의 오류나 틀린 것은 실패가 아니라 과학 발전에 성공함을 보여주는 것이라고 했다.

▶ 따라서 빈칸에 들어갈 말로 가장 적절한 것은 ② '새로운 통찰과 발견들 앞에서 붕괴하는'이다.

왜 오답?

① 이론은 결국 틀릴 수 있다는 것이 이 글의 핵심이며, 시·공간적 제약과 상관없이 항상 사실인 이론에 대한 내용은 글이 말하고자 하는 바와 반대이다.
③ 과학자들이 이론을 통해 명성을 추구한다는 내용은 언급되지 않았다.
④ 아무리 큰 대중의 지지를 받더라도 이론은 틀릴 수 있다는 내용은 나왔지만, 대중에게 노출되어 인기를 누리는 이론이 글의 초점은 아니다.
⑤ 어떤 과학적 이론도 결국에는 틀렸다고 입증될 가능성이 높다고 했으므로, 현재 이론이 오류와 실패의 여지를 남기지 않는다는 것은 글의 내용과 정반대이다.

K 69 정답 ③　＊동기부여를 위한 의식적 환경 통제 ————

Motivation doesn't have to be accidental. //
동기는 우연적일 필요는 없다 / **단서 1** 동기부여는 우연적일 필요는 없음

For example, / you don't have to wait for hours / until a certain
　　　　　　　　　주격 관계대명사
song that picks up your spirits comes on the radio. //
예를 들면 / 당신은 몇 시간 동안 기다릴 필요는 없다 / 기분을 좋게 하는 특정한 노래가 라디오에서 나올 때까지 //

You can control / what songs you hear. //
　　　　　　　　　의문형용사
당신은 통제할 수 있다 / 자신이 듣는 노래를 //
　　　　　　　　　주격 관계대명사
If there are certain songs / that always lift you up, / make a mix
of those songs / and have it ready to play in your car. //
만약 특정한 노래가 있다면 / 항상 당신을 기분 좋게 만드는 / 이런 노래들의 모음을 만들고 / 당신의 차에서 그것을 틀 준비를 해라 //

Go through all of your music / and create a "greatest motivational hits" playlist for yourself. //
당신의 모든 음악을 찾아보고 / 스스로 "최고의 동기부여 히트곡" 목록을 만들어라 //

Use the movies, too. // 또한 영화도 이용해라 //

How many times do you leave a movie / feeling inspired and ready to take on the world? //
당신은 몇 번이나 영화관을 나오는가 / 감명받고 세상에 맞설 준비가 된 상태로 //
복합관계부사(~할 때마다)
Whenever that happens, / put the name of the movie in a special
　　　　　　　　목적격 관계대명사
notebook / that you might label "the right buttons." //
그런 일이 일어날 때마다 / 특별한 노트에 그 영화의 이름을 적어놓아라 / "적절한 버튼"이라고 이름 붙인 //

Six months to a year later, / you can watch the movie / and get the same inspired feeling. //
6개월에서 1년 후에 / 당신은 그 영화를 볼 수 있고 / 똑같이 감명받은 기분을 느낄 수 있다 //
　　　　　주격 관계대명사　　　　　　비교급 강조 부사
Most movies that inspire us are even better / the second time
around. // 우리에게 감명을 주는 대부분의 영화는 훨씬 더 좋다 / 두 번째에 //
　　　　　비교급 강조 부사
You have much more control over your environment / than you
realize. // **단서 2** 환경을 스스로 통제할 수 있음
당신은 자신의 환경을 더 많이 통제할 수 있다 / 당신이 깨닫는 것보다 //

You can begin **programming** yourself consciously / to be
　　　　　　　　'더욱더'
more and more focused and motivated. //
당신은 의식적으로 스스로를 프로그래밍하기 시작할 수 있다 / 더욱더 집중하고 동기부여될 수 있도록 //

- **motivation** ⓝ 동기　　• **accidental** ⓐ 우연한, 돌발적인
- **label** ⓥ 이름을 붙이다　　• **consciously** ⓐⓓ 의식적으로
- **isolate** ⓥ 고립시키다, 격리하다　　• **deny** ⓥ 부정하다
- **silence** ⓥ 침묵을 지키다

동기는 우연적일 필요는 없다. 예를 들면, 당신은 라디오에서 기분을 좋게 하는 특정한 노래가 나올 때까지 몇 시간 동안 기다릴 필요는 없다. 당신은 자신이 듣는 노래를 통제할 수 있다. 만약 항상 당신을 기분 좋게 만드는 특정한 노래가 있다면, 이런 노래들의 모음을 만들고 당신의 차에서 그것을 틀 준비를 해라. 당신의 모든 음악을 찾아보고 "최고의 동기부여 히트곡" 목록을 스스로 만들어라. 또한 영화도 이용해라. 당신은 몇 번이나 감명받고 세상에 맞설 준비가 된 상태로 영화관을 나오는가? 그런 일이 일어날 때마다, "적절한 버튼"이라고 이름 붙인 특별한 노트에 그 영화의 이름을 적어놓아라. 6개월에서 1년 후에, 당신은 그 영화를 볼 수 있고 똑같이 감명받은 기분을 느낄 수 있다. 우리에게 감명을 주는 대부분의 영화는 두 번째에 훨씬 더 좋다. 당신이 깨닫는 것보다 자신의 환경을 더 많이 통제할 수 있다. 당신은 더욱더 집중하고 동기부여될 수 있도록 의식적으로 스스로를 **프로그래밍하기** 시작할 수 있다.

다음 빈칸에 들어갈 말로 가장 적절한 것을 고르시오.

① isolating 스스로를 고립시킴으로써 동기부여를 한다는 내용이 아님
격리하기
② denying 스스로를 거부해야 한다는 언급은 없음
거부하기
③ programming 동기부여를 위해서 스스로 환경 통제를 할 수 있다는 내용임
프로그래밍하기
④ silencing 의식적으로 침묵해야 한다는 내용이 아님
침묵시키기
⑤ questioning 스스로를 의심해야 한다는 언급은 없음
의심하기

첫 문장	• 동기부여는 우연일 필요가 없음 단서1
빈칸 문장의 앞부분	• 동기를 부여하는 음악과 영화를 모아뒀다가 필요할 때 다시 듣고 보는 등 동기 부여를 위해 주변 환경을 스스로 통제할 수 있음 단서2
빈칸 문장	더욱더 집중하고 동기부여될 수 있도록 의식적으로 스스로를 _____ 시작할 수 있다.

→ 빈칸에는 동기부여를 위해 스스로 무엇을 시작할 수 있는지가 들어가야 한다. 동기는 우연하지 않아도 되며 동기를 불러일으키는 노래 모음집을 만들거나 동기 부여를 해준 영화를 기록했다가 필요할 때 다시 듣고 보면 스스로를 동기부여할 수 있다고 했다. 이는 환경을 통제함으로써 스스로에게 동기를 부여할 수 있다는 것을 의미한다.

▶ 환경을 통제함으로써 스스로 무엇인가를 하고 싶게 만들 수 있다는 내용이 핵심이며, 더 집중하고 동기부여 받기 위해서는 의식적으로 스스로 '프로그래밍하기' 시작할 수 있다는 내용으로 이어져야 하므로 ③이 정답이다.

◦왜 오답 ?

① 스스로를 고립시킴으로써 동기부여를 한다는 내용이 아니다.
② 동기부여를 위해 무엇인가를 할 수 있다는 내용이지, 스스로를 거부해야 한다는 내용은 아니다.
④ 의식적으로 침묵해야 한다는 내용은 없다.
⑤ 스스로를 의심해야 한다는 내용은 아예 언급되지 않았다.

K 70 정답 ③ *순환적인 제품 생산의 필요성

목적어절 접속사 / 관계부사 how 생략(the way와 같이 쓸 수 없음)
Businesses are realizing / that the way they operate and the
형용사적 용법(ability 수식)
impact they have on the environment / greatly impacts their
ability to maintain customers. //

기업은 깨닫고 있다 / 그들이 운영하는 방식과 그들이 환경에 미치는 영향이 / 고객을 유지하는 능력에 큰 영향을 미친다는 것을 //

동명사 주어 ┌───from A to B: A에서 B까지───┐
Transitioning from a linear way of producing products to a
문장의 동사
circular one / won't be necessary only from an environmental
perspective, / but from a social and economic perspective as
well. // 단서1 순환적인 제품 생산 방식으로 바꾸는 것은 사회적이고 경제적인 관점에서도 필요함

제품을 생산하는 선형적인 방식에서 순환적인 것으로 이행하는 것은 / 환경적인 관점에서뿐만 아니라 ~ 필요할 것이다 / 사회적이고 경제적인 관점에서 또한 //

부사적 용법(목적)
To minimize the negative impact on the environment, /
관계대명사가 생략된 관계절(relationship 수식)
businesses will need to adjust the relationship they have with
부사적 용법(목적)
customers / to maximize the value of the products they create. //

환경에 대한 부정적인 영향을 최소화하기 위해서 / 기업은 고객과의 관계를 조정할 필요가 있을 것이다 / 그들이 만드는 제품의 가치를 극대화하기 위해 //

동명사의 의미상 주어 동명사
Rather than businesses viewing success / as the number of
products made per year, / they will instead base their bottom
line / on the number of products *kept in use* per year. //

기업이 성공을 간주하기보다는 / 연간 생산되는 제품의 수라고 / 그들은 그들의 손익을 기초시킬 것이다 / 연간 사용 상태로 유지되는 제품의 수에 //

의미상 주어
Though waste certainly creates a demand / for companies
형용사적 용법(demand 수식) 동명사 주어
to continue selling new products, / eliminating waste doesn't
have to eliminate demand. //

비록 폐기물은 분명히 수요를 창출하지만 / 회사가 신제품을 계속 판매해야 하는 / 폐기물을 제거하는 것이 수요를 제거하는 것일 필요는 없다 //

By prolonging the ownership of a product / rather than selling
it, / new business opportunities emerge / in the world of
maintenance and repair. //

제품의 소유 상태를 연장시킴으로써 / 제품을 판매하는 것이 아니라 / 새로운 사업상의 기회가 나타난다 / 유지 및 수리의 세계에서 //

단서2 폐기물을 제거함으로써 기존 제품에 대한 서비스의 필요성이 증가함
Though eliminating waste minimizes the need for new products,
/ it certainly increases the need / to service existing products. //

비록 폐기물을 제거하는 것이 신제품에 대한 필요성을 최소화하지만 / 그것은 필요성을 분명히 증가시킨다 / 기존 제품에 대한 서비스를 제공해야 할 //

목적어절 접속사
The circular economy will demand / that new business models
focus on **maintaining products / rather than on making new
products**. //

순환 경제는 요구할 것이다 / 새로운 비즈니스 모델들이 제품을 유지하는 것에 초점을 맞출 것을 / 신제품을 만드는 것보다 //

- operate ⓥ 운영하다 • linear ⓐ 일직선의
- perspective ⓝ 시각 • minimize ⓥ 최소화하다
- maximize ⓥ 극대화하다 • eliminate ⓥ 지우다
- prolong ⓥ 연장하다 • ownership ⓝ 소유권
- profit ⓝ 이익, 수익 • frequently ⓐⓓ 자주

기업은 그들이 운영하는 방식과 그들이 환경에 미치는 영향이 고객을 유지하는 능력에 큰 영향을 미친다는 것을 깨닫고 있다. 제품을 생산하는 선형적인 방식에서 순환적인 것으로 이행하는 것은 환경적인 관점에서뿐만 아니라 사회적이고 경제적인 관점에서 또한 필요할 것이다. 환경에 대한 부정적인 영향을 최소화하기 위해서, 기업은 그들이 만드는 제품의 가치를 극대화하기 위해 고객과의 관계를 조정할 필요가 있을 것이다. 기업이 성공을 연간 생산되는 제품의 수라고 간주하기보다는, 그들의 손익을 연간 사용 상태로 유지되는 제품의 수에 기초시킬 것이다. 비록 폐기물은 분명히 회사가 신제품을 계속 판매해야 하는 수요를 창출하지만, 폐기물을 제거하는 것이 수요를 제거하는 것일 필요는 없다. 제품을 판매하는 것이 아니라 제품의 소유 상태를 연장시킴으로써, 유지 및 수리의 세계에서 새로운 사업상의 기회가 나타난다. 비록 폐기물을 제거하는 것이 신제품에 대한 필요성을 최소화하지만, 그것은 기존 제품에 대한 서비스를 제공해야 할 필요성을 분명히 증가시킨다. 순환 경제는 새로운 비즈니스 모델들이 신제품을 만드는 것보다 제품을 유지하는 것에 초점을 맞출 것을 요구할 것이다.

다음 빈칸에 들어갈 말로 가장 적절한 것을 고르시오.
순환 경제는 기업이 생산보다는 기존 제품의 유지 및 수리에 초점을 두게 할 것임
① returning much of their profits back to society
수익의 대부분을 사회에 환원하는 것 기업의 수익을 사회에 환원해야 한다는 내용이 핵심이 아님
② producing user-friendly items to meet customers' needs 새로운
고객의 필요를 충족하기 위해 사용자 친화적인 제품을 생산하는 것 제품을 생산하는 것이 초점이 아님
③ maintaining products rather than on making new products
신제품을 만드는 것보다 제품을 유지하는 것
④ creating a new demand at the expense of the environment
환경을 희생하면서 새로운 수요를 창출하는 것 환경을 희생하면서 새로운 수요를 만든다는 내용은 아님
⑤ encouraging consumers to express their opinions frequently
소비자가 의견을 자주 표현하도록 장려하는 것 순환 경제의 초점은 소비자의 의견 표현이 아님

◦왜 정답 ? [정답률 48%]

전반부	순환적인 제품 생산 방식으로 바꾸는 것은 사회적이고 경제적인 관점에서도 필요함 단서1
빈칸 앞 문장	낭비를 제거하는 것은 새로운 제품에 대한 수요를 줄이긴 하지만, 확실히 기존 제품의 유지 및 보수에 대한 요구를 증가시킬 것임 단서2
빈칸 문장	순환 경제는 새로운 비즈니스 모델들이 _____에 초점을 맞출 것을 요구할 것이다.

→ 사회적이고 경제적인 관점에서 기업이 선택하게 될 순환적 제품 생산 방식에서는 폐기물을 줄이고 기존의 상품을 오랫동안 쓸 수 있도록 할 것이라는 내용의 글이다. 생산한 제품을 계속 쓸 수 있도록 하는 순환적인 생산 방식은 새로운 제품에 대한 수요보다는 제품을 오래 쓸 수 있도록 지원해주는 서비스에 대한 수요가 증가할 것이다. 순환 경제에서 새로운 기업 모델은 이런 부분에 초점을 맞출 것이다.

▶ 따라서 빈칸에는 ③ '신제품을 만드는 것보다 제품을 유지하는 것'이 들어가야 한다.

◦왜 오답 ?

① 사회적 관점에 대한 글이긴 하지만, 사회에 기업의 이익을 돌려줘야 한다는 것이 핵심은 아니다.
② 새로운 제품을 생산하는 것에 초점을 맞추는 내용은 글의 내용과 반대된다.
④ 환경을 희생하면서 새로운 수요를 만든다는 내용이 아니라 순환 경제는 사회경제적 관점뿐만 아니라 환경적 관점에서도 필요하다는 내용이다.
⑤ 순환 경제의 초점은 소비자의 의견 표현이 아니다.

K 71 정답 ⑤　＊어린 나무가 오래 살 수 있도록 도와주는 어미 나무

The term *Mother Tree* comes from forestry. //
어미나무(모수)라는 용어는 임업에서 유래한다 //
가주어　　　　　　　　　　　진주어절을 이끄는 접속사
It has been clear for centuries / that tree parents play such an
such ~that ... : 매우 ~해서 …하다
important role / in raising their offspring / that they can be
compared to human parents. //
수 세기 동안 분명했다 / 부모인 나무가 매우 중요한 역할을 하기에 / 그것의 자손을 기르는 데
/ 그것이 인간 부모에 비유될 수 있다는 것은 //

A mother tree identifies / which neighboring seedlings are hers
의문형용사
/ using her roots. //
어미나무는 식별한다 / 근처에 있는 어떤 묘목이 그것의 자손인지를 / 그것의 뿌리를
사용하여 //

She then, via delicate connections, / supports the seedlings
with a solution of sugar, / a process similar to a human mother
nursing her child. //
그러고는 그것은 섬세한 연결을 통해 / 당 용액으로 묘목을 부양한다 / 인간 어머니가 아이를
수유하는 것과 유사한 과정으로 //

단서 1 묘목들의 성장을 억제하는 그늘은 부모가 제공하는 또 다른 돌봄의 형태임
Shade provided by parents is another form of care, / as it curbs
과거분사(shade 수식)　　　　　　　현재분사(youngsters 수식) (= parents)
the growth of youngsters / living under their crowns. //
부모에 의해 제공되는 그늘은 또 다른 돌봄의 형태이다 / 묘목들의 성장을 억제하기 때문에 /
수관 아래에서 살고 있는 //

단서 2 그늘 없이는 빠르게 자라서 비교적 금방 소진될 것임
Without the shade and exposed to full sunlight, / the young
without 가정법
trees would shoot up / and expand the width of their trunks so
so that 강조 구문에서 that이 생략됨
quickly / they'd be exhausted after just a century or two. //
그늘 없이 완전한 햇빛에 노출된 상태에서는 / 어린 나무들은 급속히 자라 / 나무 몸통의
너비를 너무 빨리 확장시켜 / 그것들은 단지 한두 세기 후에 소진될 것이다 //

If, however, / the young trees stand strong in the shadows for
decades — or even centuries / — they can live to a great age. //
그러나, 만약 / 어린 나무들이 수십 년 동안 혹은 심지어 수 세기 동안 그늘 속에 굳건하게 서
있다면 / 그것들은 장수할 것이다 //

Shade means / less sunlight and therefore considerably less
sugar. //
그늘은 의미한다 / 더 적은 햇빛 그리고 따라서 상당히 더 적은 당을 //

**The slow pace of life / gently imposed by the mother tree / is
no accident**, / as generations of foresters have observed. //
느린 삶의 속도는 / 어미나무에 의해 부드럽게 부과되는 / 우연이 아니다 / 수 세대의 산림
감독관들이 관찰했듯이 //
선행사를 포함하는 관계대명사
To this day, they talk of what is known in German / as
erzieherischer Schatten or "instructive shade."//
오늘날까지, 그들은 독일어로 알려진 것에 대해 이야기한다 / erzieherischer Schatten
또는 '교육적 그늘'이라고 //

- offspring ⓝ 자식　・identify ⓥ 식별하다, 구분하다
- seedling ⓝ 묘목　・delicate ⓐ 연약한　・curb ⓥ 억제하다
- expand ⓥ 확장하다　・trunk ⓝ (나무의) 몸통
- exhausted ⓐ 기진맥진한　・considerably ⓐⓓ 상당히
- instructive ⓐ 교육적인, 유익한

어미나무(모수)라는 용어는 임업에서 유래한다. 부모인 나무가 그것의 자손을
기르는 데 매우 중요한 역할을 하기에 그것이 인간 부모에 비유될 수 있다는
것은 수 세기 동안 분명했다. 어미나무는 근처에 있는 어떤 묘목이 그것의
자손인지를 그것의 뿌리를 사용하여 식별한다. 그러고는 그것은 인간 어머니가
아이를 수유하는 것과 유사한 과정으로, 섬세한 연결을 통해 당 용액으로
묘목을 부양한다. 부모에 의해 제공되는 그늘은 수관 아래에서 살고있는
묘목들의 성장을 억제하기 때문에 또 다른 돌봄의 형태이다. 그늘 없이 완전한
햇빛에 노출된 상태에서는, 어린 나무들은 급속히 자라 나무 몸통의 너비를
너무 빨리 확장시켜 그것들은 단지 한두 세기 후에 소진될 것이다. 그러나 만약
어린 나무들이 수십 년 동안 혹은 심지어 수 세기 동안 그늘 속에 굳건하게 서
있다면, 그것들은 장수할 것이다. 그늘은 더 적은 햇빛 그리고 따라서 상당하게

더 적은 당을 의미한다. 수 세대의 산림 감독관들이 관찰했듯이, **어미나무에
의해 부드럽게 부과되는 느린 삶의 속도는 우연이 아니다.** 오늘날까지 그들은
독일어로 erzieherischer Schatten 또는 '교육적 그늘'이라고 알려진 것에 대해
이야기한다.

다음 빈칸에 들어갈 말로 가장 적절한 것을 고르시오. [3점]
　　　　　　　　　　　　　　그늘이 열을 식히는 역할을 한다고 글에서 언급하지 않음
① One can pleasantly cool down under the shade of large trees
큰 나무의 그늘 아래에서 쾌적하게 더위를 식힐 수 있다
② The trees manage to extend their roots towards the water source
나무가 물 근원 쪽으로 뿌리를 뻗는다
③ The attempts to outgrow neighboring seedlings are likely to
succeed 이웃 묘목과 경쟁한다는 내용은 없음
이웃 묘목을 이기려는 시도는 성공할 가능성이 높다
④ Mother trees provide shade to accelerate the growth of their
offspring 성장 속도를 억제하여 오래 살 수 있도록 그늘을 제공하는 것임
어미 나무는 자식 나무의 성장을 촉진하기 위해 그늘을 제공한다
⑤ The slow pace of life gently imposed by the mother tree is no
accident 어미 나무가 제공하는 그늘에 의해 어린 나무는 느리지만 튼튼하게 성장함
어미 나무에 의해 부드럽게 부과되는 느린 삶의 속도는 우연이 아니다
　　어미 나무가 자기 자손을 파악하기 위해 뿌리를 썼다는 내용만 있지, 수원으로 뿌리를 뻗는다는 내용이
　　아님

왜 정답? [정답률 32%]

1st 빈칸이 포함된 문장을 읽고, 빈칸에 들어갈 말에 대한 단서를 얻는다.

빈칸 문장	수 세대의 산림 감독관들이 관찰한 내용은 　　　　　 이다.

➡ 빈칸에는 위에 나온 내용을 통해 산림 감독관들이 내린 결론에 대한 내용이
들어가야 한다.

2nd 글의 나머지 부분을 읽고, 빈칸에 들어갈 적절한 말을 찾는다.

앞부분 주요 내용	・부모 나무가 제공하는 그늘은 또 다른 돌봄의 형태로, 어린 나무의 성장을 억제한다. **단서 1** ・그늘 없이는 너무 빨리 자라 한 두 세기 후에 소진되지만 그늘 아래에서는 튼튼하게 장수할 수 있다. **단서 2**

➡ 부모 나무가 제공하는 그늘은 또 다른 돌봄의 형태로, 어린 나무의 성장을 억제하고,
그늘 아래에서는 튼튼하게 장수할 수 있다고 했다.
▶ 빈칸에는 산림 감독관들이 관찰해서내린 결론이 들어가야 함

3rd **2nd** 에서 이해한 내용을 선택지에서 고른다.

어미 나무는 뿌리를 통해 자기 자손을 구분하여 당 용액을 제공하고 그늘을 제공해서
성장 속도를 억제하여 오래 살 수 있게 하는 등 어린 나무의 성장에 중요한 역할을
한다는 내용의 글이다.
빈칸에 들어갈 말로 가장 적절한 것은 ⑤ '어미 나무에 의해 부드럽게 부과되는 느린
삶의 속도는 우연이 아니다'이다.

| 선택지 분석 |

① **One can pleasantly cool down under the shade of large trees**
큰 나무의 그늘 아래에서 쾌적하게 더위를 식힐 수 있다
나무 그늘에 대한 내용은 있으나 열을 식히는 역할이 초점이 되는 것은 아니다.

② **The trees manage to extend their roots towards the water
source**
나무가 물 근원 쪽으로 뿌리를 뻗는다
뿌리에 대한 언급은 있으나 어미 나무가 자신의 자손을 파악하기 위해 사용하는
것이지, 물의 근원으로 뿌리를 뻗는다는 내용은 없다.

③ **The attempts to outgrow neighboring seedlings are likely to
succeed**
이웃 묘목을 이기려는 시도는 성공할 가능성이 높다
이웃 묘목과 경쟁을 한다는 언급은 없다.

④ **Mother trees provide shade to accelerate the growth of their
offspring**
어미 나무는 자식 나무의 성장을 촉진하기 위해 그늘을 제공한다
성장 속도를 가속화하는 것이 아니라, 성장을 억제하여 오래 살 수 있도록 해주는
역할을 한다.

⑤ **The slow pace of life gently imposed by the mother tree is no
accident**
어미 나무에 의해 부드럽게 부과되는 느린 삶의 속도는 우연이 아니다
어미 나무가 제공하는 그늘에 의해 어린 나무는 느리지만 튼튼하게 성장한다는 내용의
글이다.

K 72 정답 ① *뇌의 공간 인식과 시간 연관성

John Douglas Pettigrew, / a professor of psychology at the
University of Queensland, / found /
John Douglas Pettigrew는 / Queensland 대학의 심리학 교수인 / 알아냈다 /
목적어절 접속사   '~ 함으로써'
that the brain manages the external world / by dividing it into
separate regions, / the *peripersonal* and the *extrapersonal* / —
basically, near and far. //
뇌가 외부 세계를 다룬다는 것을 / 그것(외부 세계)을 별개의 부분들로 나눔으로써 /
'주변의'와 '외부의' / 요컨대 '가깝다'와 '멀다'라는 //
                              복합관계대명사
Peripersonal space includes / whatever is in arm's reach; /
                    앞에 목적격 관계대명사 생략
things you can control right now / by using your hands. //
주변 공간은 포함한다 / 팔이 닿는 범위 내에 있는 모든 것 / 즉 당장 여러분이 통제할 수 있는
것들을 / 여러분의 손을 사용함으로써 //

This is the world of what's real, / right now. //
이것은 실제의 세계이다 / 지금 당장 // 단서1 '주변' 공간은 지금 당장의 세계임
                                                  복합관계대명사
Extrapersonal space refers to everything else / — whatever
                        부사절 접속사(조건)
you can't touch / unless you move beyond your arm's reach, /
부사절 접속사(양보)
whether it's three feet or three million miles away. //
외부 공간은 그 외 모든 것을 가리키는데 / 만질 수 없는 모든 것이다 / 자신의 팔이 닿는
범위를 넘어서서 움직이지 않으면 / 즉 3피트든 3백만 마일 밖이든 여러분이 //

This is the realm of possibility. //
이것은 가능성의 영역이다 // 단서2 '외부' 공간은 가능성의 영역임
                                              another fact 수식
With those definitions in place, / another fact follows, / obvious
but useful: / any interaction in the extrapersonal space must
occur in the future. // 단서3 외부 공간에서의 모든 상호 작용은 미래에 일어남
그러한 정의들이 자리 잡은 상태에서 / 또 하나의 사실이 따라온다 / 뻔하지만 유용한 / 즉,
외부 공간에서의 모든 상호 작용은 미래에 일어나야만 한다는 것이다 //

Or, to put it another way, / **distance is linked to time**. //
또는, 달리 말하면 / 거리는 시간과 연관되어 있다 //

For instance, / if you're in the mood for a peach, / but the closest
= peach
one is sitting in a bin at the corner market, / you can't enjoy it
now. //
예를 들어 / 만약 여러분이 복숭아를 원하지만 / 가장 가까운 것이 모퉁이 가게의 상자에
있다면 / 여러분은 지금 그것을 즐길 수 없다 //

You can only enjoy it in the future, / after you go get it. //
여러분은 오직 미래에 즐길 수 있다 / 즉 그것을 사러 간 후에 //

- psychology ⓝ 심리학   - external ⓐ 외부의
- separate ⓐ 분리된   - realm ⓝ 영역
- in the mood for ~가 마음에 내켜서   - bin ⓝ (흔히 뚜껑이 달린 저장용) 통

Queensland 대학의 심리학 교수인 John Douglas Pettigrew는 뇌가
그것(외부 세계)을 '주변의'와 '외부의', 요컨대 '가깝다'와 '멀다'라는 별개의
부분들로 나눔으로써 외부 세계를 다룬다는 것을 알아냈다. 주변 공간은 팔이
닿는 범위 내에 있는 모든 것, 즉 여러분의 손을 사용함으로써 당장 여러분이
통제할 수 있는 것들을 포함한다. 이것은 지금 당장 실제의 세계이다. 외부
공간은 그 외 모든 것을 가리키는데, 즉 3피트든 3백만 마일 밖이든 여러분이
자신의 팔이 닿는 범위를 넘어서서 움직이지 않으면 만질 수 없는 모든 것이다.
이것은 가능성의 영역이다. 그러한 정의들이 자리 잡은 상태에서 뻔하지만
유용한 또 하나의 사실이 따라온다. 즉, 외부 공간에서의 모든 상호 작용은
미래에 일어나야만 한다는 것이다. 또는, 달리 말하면, **거리는 시간과 연관되어
있다**. 예를 들어 만약 여러분이 복숭아를 원하지만 가장 가까운 것이 모퉁이
가게의 상자에 있다면, 여러분은 지금 그것을 즐길 수 없다. 여러분은 오직
미래에 즉 그것을 사러 간 후에 즐길 수 있다.

다음 빈칸에 들어갈 말로 가장 적절한 것을 고르시오.

① distance is linked to time 지금 당장 실제의 세계와 가능성의 영역
  거리는 시간과 연관되어 있다
② the past is out of your reach 과거를 바꿀 수 없다는 내용은 관련이 없음
  과거는 여러분의 손길을 벗어난 곳에 있다
③ what is going to happen happens 운명론적인 내용은 흐름상 부적절함
  일어날 일은 일어난다
④ time doesn't flow in one direction 관련 없음
  시간은 한 방향으로만 흐르지 않는다
⑤ our brain is attracted to near objects 관련 없음
  우리의 뇌는 가까운 물체에 끌린다

왜 정답? [정답률 69%]

- 외부 세계는 '주변의'와 '외부의'로 나뉨
- **주변 공간**: 지금 당장 실제의 세계 단서1
- **외부 공간**: 가능성의 영역 단서2,
        외부 공간에서의 모든 상호 작용은 미래에 일어나야만 함 단서3
즉, 단순한 거리 이외에도 현시점에 할 수 있는 것과 없는 것에는 차이가 존재한다.
▶ 이를 달리 말하면, ① '거리는 시간과 연관되어 있다'고 할 수 있다.

왜 오답?

② 과거는 이미 지난 일이라 손쓸 수 없다는 내용은 아니다.
③ 운명론적인 이야기에 대한 이야기는 아니다.
④ 시간이 다양한 방향으로 흐른다는 내용을 다루고 있지는 않다.
⑤ 가까운 물체에 더 친밀감을 느낀다는 내용이 핵심은 아니다.

K 73 정답 ② *생체 발광을 통한 물고기들의 생존 전략

Many fish generate their own light / in a biological firework
              과거분사구(a biological firework display 수식)
display / called bioluminescence. //
많은 물고기들은 자체의 빛을 생성한다 / 생물학적인 불꽃놀이로 / 생체 발광이라고 불리는 //
                                        주격 관계대명사
The lanternfish creates beams / that sweep the sea like
headlamps. // 단서1 랜턴피시는 빛줄기를 생성해 바다를 비춤
랜턴피시는 빛줄기를 만들어 낸다 / 헤드라이트처럼 바다를 싹 비추는 //
                                          주격 관계대명사
The dragonfish produces wavelengths / that only it can see, /
분사구문을 이끄는 현재분사
leaving its victims unaware of the approaching threat. //
드래곤피시는 파장을 생산해서 / 자신만이 볼 수 있는 / 다가오는 위협을 먹잇감이 인식하지
못하게 한다 //
        단서2 드래곤피시는 파장을 생산해 먹잇감이 알아차리지 못하도록 함
In contrast, / the anglerfish hopes / its prey will notice and be
                    뒤에 목적어절 접속사that 생략
lured toward its rod-like bioluminescent barbel; / its fierce jaws
stay hidden in the shadows. // 단서3 앵글러피시는 발광 수염으로 먹잇감을 유인함
대조적으로 / 앵글러피시는 바라는데 / 먹이가 자신의 막대 모양의 생체 발광 수염을 알아채고
그것에 유인되기를 / 그것의 사나운 턱이 그림자에 감춰져 있다 //

Bioluminescence is also used to frustrate predators. //
생체 발광은 또한 포식자들을 좌절시키는 데 사용된다 //

A species from the spookfish family relies on / a bellyful of
                                    형용사적 용법(bacteria 수식)
symbiotic, glowing bacteria / to save it from becoming a meal. //
스푸크피시과(科)의 한 종은 의존한다 / 배에 가득 찬 공생하는 빛나는 박테리아에 /
식사거리가 되는 것으로부터 그것을 지켜주는 / 단서4 스푸크피시과의 한 종은 박테리아를
                                          통해 자신을 보호함
It uses the same concept / developed by the US Navy during
                        과거분사구(concept 수식)
World War II / to make bomber aircraft difficult to see. //
그것은 동일한 발상을 사용한다 / 제2차 세계 대전 중에 미국 해군에 의해 개발된 / 폭격기를
보기 어렵게 만들기 위해 //

Just as Project Yehudi designed planes / with under-wing
spotlights, / the fish's glowing belly conceals its silhouette /
against sunlight / to hide it / from watching eyes below. //
Yehudi 프로젝트가 비행기를 설계한 것처럼 / 날개 아랫면에 환한 조명이 있는 / 그 물고기의
빛나는 복부는 자신의 실루엣을 숨긴다 / 태양 빛에 대비되는 / 그것을 감춰서 / 아래에서
주시하는 눈들로부터 //

In this fish-eat-fish world, / survival is **a game of hide-and-seek
      주격 관계대명사
/ that prioritizes the sense of sight**. //
물고기가 물고기를 잡아먹는 이 세상에서 / 생존은 숨바꼭질 게임이다 / 시각을 우선시하는 //

- biological ⓐ 생물학적인   - bioluminescence ⓝ 생물 발광
- sweep ⓥ 쓸다   - victim ⓝ 피해자   - threat ⓝ 위협
- rod-like ⓐ 막대 형태의   - fierce ⓐ 사나운   - jaw ⓝ 턱
- predator ⓝ 포식자   - a bellyful of 배에 가득한
- bomber aircraft 폭격기   - spotlight ⓝ 환한 조명
- conceal ⓥ 숨기다   - silhouette ⓝ 외형[윤곽], 실루엣
- subtle ⓐ 미묘한   - illumination ⓝ 빛, 발광

많은 물고기들은 생체 발광이라고 불리는 생물학적인 불꽃놀이로 자체의 빛을 생성한다. 랜턴피시는 헤드라이트처럼 바다를 쫙 비추는 빛줄기를 만들어 낸다. 드래곤피시는 자신만이 볼 수 있는 파장을 생산해서 다가오는 위협을 먹잇감들이 인식하지 못하게 한다. 대조적으로 앵글러피시는 먹이가 자신의 막대 모양의 생체 발광 수염을 알아채고 그것에 유인되기를 바라는데, 그것(앵글러피시)의 사나운 턱이 그림자에 감춰져 있다. 생체 발광은 또한 포식자들을 좌절시키는 데 사용된다. 스푸크피시과(科)의 한 종은 식사거리가 되는 것으로부터 그것을 지켜주는 배에 가득 찬 공생하는 빛나는 박테리아에 의존한다. 그것은 폭격기를 보기 어렵게 만들기 위해 제2차 세계 대전 중에 미국 해군에 의해 개발된 동일한 발상을 사용한다. Yehudi 프로젝트가 날개 아랫면에 환한 조명이 있는 비행기를 설계한 것처럼, 그 물고기의 빛나는 복부는 태양 빛에 대비되는 자신의 실루엣을 감춰서 아래에서 주시하는 눈들로부터 그것을 숨긴다. 물고기가 물고기를 잡아먹는 이 세상에서 생존은 **시각을 우선시하는 숨바꼭질 게임**이다.

다음 빈칸에 들어갈 말로 가장 적절한 것을 고르시오. [3점]
① dependent upon communication within the same species
동일 종 내 의사소통에 의존하는   의사소통은 언급되지 않음
② a game of hide-and-seek that prioritizes the sense of sight
시각을 우선시하는 숨바꼭질 게임   발광을 통해 생존함
③ up to the ability to detect the subtle dance of sound waves
음파의 미묘한 움직임을 감지하는 능력에 달린   음파가 중요한 것이 아님
④ a competition to imitate the illumination of different species
다양한 종의 발광을 모방하는 경쟁   인간의 발명품과 물고기의 발광을 비교해서 설명함
⑤ a war where wider vision means better chances to catch prey
더 넓은 시야가 먹잇감을 더 많이 잡을 가능성이 높은 전투   넓은 시야를 강조하는 것이 아님

왜 정답? [정답률 59%]

- 예시 ①: 랜턴피시는 헤드라이트처럼 바다를 쫙 비추는 빛줄기를 만들어 냄 **단서1**
- 예시 ②: 드래곤피시는 자신만이 볼 수 있는 파장을 생산해서 다가오는 위협을 먹잇감들이 인식하지 못하게 함 **단서2**
- 예시 ③: 앵글러피시는 사나운 턱은 그림자에 감춘 채 생체 발광 수염으로 먹이를 유인함 **단서3**
- 예시 ④: 스푸크피시과(科)의 한 종은 배에 가득 찬 빛나는 박테리아에 의존함 (빛나는 복부는 태양 빛에 대비되는 자신의 실루엣을 감춰서 아래에서 주시하는 눈들로부터 그것을 숨김) **단서4**

▶ 눈속임을 통해 생존하는 다양한 물고기의 예시를 들고 있다. 따라서 물고기가 물고기를 잡아먹는 이 세상에서 생존은 ② '시각을 우선시하는 숨바꼭질 게임'이라고 하는 것이 적절하다.

왜 오답?
① 동일 종들끼리 서로 소통하며 생존을 돕는 내용은 언급되지 않았다.
③ 음파를 감지하는 능력에 관한 내용은 없었다.
④ 다양한 종의 발광을 서로 모방한다는 내용은 관련이 없다.
⑤ 시야가 넓을수록 사냥에 유리한 것이 아니고, 시각적 요소인 발광을 통해서 생존을 한다는 내용이다. 함정

K 74 정답 ① *일본이 주행 신호등 색상을 변경한 배경

used to-v: (과거에) ~했다   주격 관계대명사(a color word 수식)
Japanese used to have a color word, *ao*, / that spanned both green and blue. //
예전에 일본어에는 'ao'라는 색상 단어가 있었는데 / 이는 초록색과 파란색 모두에 걸쳐 있었다 //

In the modern language, / however, / *ao* has come to be restricted mostly to blue shades, / and green is usually expressed by the word *midori*. // —**단서1** 현대에 'ao'는 파란색을 의미함
현대어에서는 / 하지만 / 'ao'가 주로 파란색 색조로 한정되었고 / 초록색은 보통 'midori'라는 단어로 표현된다 //

When the first traffic lights were imported from the United States / and installed in Japan / in the 1930s, / they were just as green as anywhere else. //
과거형 동사의 병렬 구조
최초의 신호등이 미국으로부터 수입되었을 때 / 그리고 일본에 설치되었을 때 / 1930년대에 / 그것들은 다른 곳에서와 마찬가지로 초록색이었다 //

Nevertheless, / in common parlance / the go light was called *ao shingoo*, / perhaps because the three primary colors on Japanese artists' palettes are / traditionally *aka*(red), *kiiro*(yellow), and *ao*. // **단서2** 일반적으로 주행 신호(초록색)는 'ao shingoo'라고 불림
그럼에도 불구하고 / 일반적인 용어로 / 주행 신호가 'ao shingoo'라고 불렸는데 / 아마도 일본 화가들의 팔레트의 3원색이 ~이기 때문일 것이다 / 전통적으로 'aka'(빨간색), 'kiiro'(노란색), 그리고 'ao' //

The label *ao* for a green light / did not appear so out of the ordinary at first, / because of the remaining associations / of the word *ao* with greenness. //
~때문에
초록색 신호등에 'ao'라는 라벨이 / 처음에는 그리 이상하게 보이지 않았다 / 남아 있는 연관성 때문에 / 단어 'ao'와 초록색 간에 //

But over time, / the difference / between the green color / and the dominant meaning of the word *ao* / began to feel awkward. //
하지만 시간이 지나면서 / 차이가 / 초록색과 'ao' 단어의 주된 의미 사이의 / 어색하게 느껴지기 시작했다 **단서3** 초록색과 'ao'라는 단어의 의미 간 괴리 때문에 어색하게 느껴지기 시작함

Nations that are less assertive / might have opted for the solution / of simply changing the official name of the go light / to *midori*. //
주격 관계대명사(nations 수식)   might have p.p: ~했을지도 모른다
덜 단호한 나라들은 / 해결책을 선택했을지도 모른다 / 간단하게 주행 신호의 공식 명칭을 바꾸는 'midori'로 //

Not so the Japanese. // 일본은 그렇게 하지 않았다 //

Rather than alter the name to fit reality, / the Japanese government announced / in 1973 / that **reality should be altered to fit the name**: /
announce that 주어 (should) 동사원형: ~해야 한다고 발표하다
이름을 현실에 맞추어 변경하는 대신 / 일본 정부는 발표했다 / 1973년에 / 이름에 맞추어 현실을 변경하기로 /

henceforth, / go lights would be a color / that better corresponded to the dominant meaning of *ao*. // **단서4** 주행 신호가 'ao'라는 단어의 지배적 의미에 맞는 색상이 됨
주격 관계대명사(a color 수식)
그 이후로 / 주행 신호등은 색상이 되었다 / 'ao'의 주된 의미에 더 잘 부합하는 //

- span ⓥ 걸치다   • restrict ⓥ 제한하다   • traffic light 신호등
- import ⓥ 수입하다   • install ⓥ 설치하다
- traditionally ⓐⓓ 전통적으로   • out of the ordinary 특이한, 색다른
- dominant ⓐ 주된   • awkward ⓐ 어색한, 불편한
- assertive ⓐ 단호한   • opt ⓥ 택하다   • henceforth ⓐⓓ ~ 이후로
- correspond ⓥ 부합하다   • ban ⓥ 금하다

예전에 일본어에는 'ao'라는 색상 단어가 있었는데, 이는 초록색과 파란색 모두에 걸쳐 있었다. 하지만 현대어에서는 'ao'가 주로 파란색 색조로 한정되었고, 초록색은 보통 'midori'라는 단어로 표현된다. 1930년대에 최초의 신호등이 미국으로부터 수입되고 일본에 설치되었을 때, 그것들은 다른 곳에서와 마찬가지로 초록색이었다. 그럼에도 불구하고, 일반적인 용어로 주행 신호가 'ao shingoo'라고 불렸는데, 아마도 일본 화가들의 팔레트의 3원색이 전통적으로 'aka'(빨간색), 'kiiro'(노란색), 그리고 'ao'이기 때문일 것이다. 단어 'ao'와 초록색 간에 남아 있는 연관성 때문에, 초록색 신호등에 'ao'라는 라벨이 처음에는 그리 이상하게 보이지 않았다. 하지만 시간이 지나면서, 초록색과 'ao' 단어의 주된 의미 사이의 차이가 어색하게 느껴지기 시작했다. 덜 단호한 나라들은 간단하게 주행 신호의 공식 명칭을 'midori'로 바꾸는 해결책을 선택했을지도 모른다. 일본은 그렇게 하지 않았다. 이름을 현실에 맞추어 변경하는 대신, 1973년에 일본 정부는 **이름에 맞추어 현실을 변경하기로** 발표했다. 그 이후로, 주행 신호등은 'ao'의 주된 의미에 더 잘 부합하는 색상이 되었다.

다음 빈칸에 들어갈 말로 가장 적절한 것을 고르시오. [3점]
① reality should be altered to fit the name
이름에 맞추어 현실을 변경하기로   'ao'라는 이름에 맞추어 현실(신호등 색)을 변경하였다는 내용임
② language reflected what people had in mind
언어가 사람들의 생각을 반영했다고   언어가 사람들의 생각을 반영했다고 발표한 것이 아님
③ the go light should follow the global standard
주행 신호는 국제 표준을 따라야 한다고   주행 신호를 언급한 것으로 만든 오답
④ the use of the word *ao* for go light would be banned   주행 신호에 'ao'
주행 신호에 'ao' 단어를 사용하는 것이 금지되어야 할 것이라고   단어를 사용하는 것을 금지하지 않음
⑤ they would not change the color of go light in any way
그들은 주행 신호의 색을 어떤 식으로든 변경하지 않을 것이라고
주행 신호의 색을 변경하지 않은 것이 아니라 그 반대임

왜 정답? [정답률 35%]

1st 빈칸이 포함된 문장을 읽고, 빈칸에 들어갈 말에 대한 단서를 얻는다.

빈칸 문장	이름을 현실에 맞추어 변경하는 대신, 1973년에 일본 정부는 _____ 발표했다.

➡ 빈칸 문장은 Rather than ~(~ 대신)으로 시작하면서 '이름을 현실에 맞추어 변경하는 대신'이라고 했다. 따라서 빈칸에는 이와 반대되는 내용이 들어갈 것이다.

2nd 글의 나머지 부분을 읽고, 빈칸에 들어갈 적절한 말을 찾는다.

앞부분 주요 내용	• 현대어에서는 'ao'가 주로 파란색 색조로 한정됨 **단서1** • 일반적인 용어로 주행 신호가 'ao shingoo'라고 불렸음 **단서2**
빈칸 문장의 앞 부분	• 시간이 지나면서, 초록색과 'ao' 단어의 주된 의미 사이의 차이가 어색하게 느껴지기 시작함 **단서3**
빈칸 문장의 뒤 부분	• 주행 신호등은 'ao'의 주된 의미에 더 잘 부합하는 색상이 되었음 **단서4**

➡ 현대어에서는 'ao'가 파란색을 의미하는데 초록색인 주행 신호가 'ao shingoo'로 불리고 있어 주행 신호의 색과 'ao'라는 단어의 의미 사이에 괴리가 생겼고, 이를 해결하여 주행 신호등이 'ao(신호등의 이름)'의 의미에 잘 부합하는 색(파란색)으로 변경되었다는 내용이다.

▶ 빈칸에는 일본 정부가 이름을 변경하는 대신 무엇을 발표했는지가 들어가야 함

3rd **2nd**에서 이해한 내용을 선택지에서 고른다.

일본이 주행 신호등의 색상을 변경한 배경에 대한 내용의 글이다.
따라서 일본 정부가 이름을 변경하는 대신 ① '이름에 맞추어 현실을 변경하기로' 했다고 하는 것이 적절하다.

│ 선택지 분석 │

① **reality should be altered to fit the name**
　이름에 맞추어 현실을 변경하기로
시간이 지나면서 초록색과 'ao' 단어의 주된 의미 사이의 차이가 어색하게 느껴지게 되자, 일본이 주행 신호등의 이름을 변경하는 대신 색상을 변경한 배경에 대해 말하는 내용이다.

② **language reflected what people had in mind**
　언어가 사람들의 생각을 반영했다고
언어가 사람들의 생각을 반영했다고 발표한 것이 아니다.

③ **the go light should follow the global standard**
　주행 신호는 국제 표준을 따라야 한다고
주행 신호가 국제 표준을 따라야 한다는 언급은 없다.

④ **the use of the word ao for go light would be banned**
　주행 신호에 'ao' 단어를 사용하는 것이 금지되어야 할 것이라고
주행 신호에 'ao' 단어를 사용하는 것을 금지하고자 하지 않았다.

⑤ **they would not change the color of go light in any way**
　그들은 주행 신호의 색을 어떤 식으로든 변경하지 않을 것이라고
주행 신호의 색을 변경하지 않은 것이 아니라 오히려 그 반대이다.

K 75 정답 ③ ＊부차적인 학문이 된 수집

<u>주어</u>
The growth / of academic disciplines and sub-disciplines, / such as art history or palaeontology, / and of particular figures / such as the art critic, /
성장은 / 학과와 하위 학과의 / 미술사학이나 고생물학과 같은 / 그리고 특정 인물의 / 미술평론가와 같은 /

<u>동사</u>　<u>목적어(원형부정사)</u>
helped produce principles and practices / for selecting and organizing / what was worthy of keeping, / though it remained a struggle. //
원칙과 관행을 도출하는 것에 도움이 되었다 / 선택하고 정리하기 위한 / 지킬 가치가 있는 것을 / 비록 힘든 일로 남게 되었지만 //

<u>부사절 접속사(~함에 따라)</u>
Moreover, / as museums and universities drew further apart / toward the end of the nineteenth century, /
게다가 / 박물관과 대학이 더욱 멀어지면서 / 19세기 말엽에 /

<u>부사절 접속사(~함에 따라)</u>
and as the idea of objects / as a highly valued route / to knowing the world / went into decline, /
그리고 물체라는 개념이 / 매우 가치 있는 경로로서 / 세상을 알게 되는 / 쇠퇴하면서 /

<u>주어</u>　<u>동사</u>　<u>목적어(to부정사)</u>
collecting began to lose its status / as a worthy intellectual pursuit, / especially in the sciences. // **단서1** 수집은 특히 과학에서 가치 있는 지적 활동으로서의 지위를 잃기 시작했음
수집은 그 지위를 잃기 시작했다 / 가치 있는 지적 활동으로서 / 특히 과학에서 //

The really interesting and important aspects / of science / were increasingly those invisible / to the naked eye, /
참으로 흥미롭고 중요한 측면은 / 과학의 / 점점 더 보이지 않는 것들이었고 / 육안에 /

and the classification of things collected / no longer promised to produce / cutting-edge knowledge. // **단서2** 수집된 것들에 대한 분류는 더이상 최첨단의 지식을 생산할 가망이 없었음
수집된 것들에 대한 분류는 / 더이상 생산할 가망이 없었다 / 최첨단의 지식을 //

The term "butterfly collecting" / could come to be used / with the adjective "mere" / to indicate / a pursuit of **secondary** academic status. //
'나비 채집'이라는 용어는 / 사용될 수 있었다 / '한낱'이라는 형용사와 / 나타내는 데 / 부차적인 학문적 지위의 추구를 //

- growth ⓝ 성장　• academic ⓐ 학업의, 학과의
- discipline ⓝ 지식[학문] 분야, 학과　• sub- pref 「아래」,「하위」
- particular ⓐ 특정한　• figure ⓝ 인물, 사람　• critic ⓝ 평론가
- principle ⓝ 원칙, 원리　• practice ⓝ 관행, 관례
- select ⓥ 선발[선택]하다　• organize ⓥ 정리하다, 체계화하다
- worthy ⓐ (~을 받을) 자격이 있는, 받을 만한　• remain ⓥ 계속 ~이다
- struggle ⓝ 힘든 일, 투쟁　• moreover ⓐⓓ 게다가
- draw apart (~으로부터) 떨어져[사라져] 가다　• further ⓐⓓ 더 멀리에[로]
- toward prep 무렵, ~쯤　• object ⓝ 물건, 대상
- valued ⓐ 귀중한, 평가된　• route ⓝ 길, 경로　• decline ⓝ 감소
- status ⓝ 지위, 신분　• intellectual ⓐ 지적인
- pursuit ⓝ 추구, (시간과 에너지를 들여서 하는) 일[활동]　• aspect ⓝ 측면
- increasingly ⓐⓓ 점점 더　• invisible ⓐ 보이지 않는
- naked ⓐ 아무것도 걸치지 않은, 벌거벗은　• classification ⓝ 분류
- promise ⓥ ~의 조짐을 보이다　• cutting-edge ⓐ 최첨단의
- knowledge ⓝ 지식　• mere ⓐ ~에 불과한　• indicate ⓥ 나타내다

미술사학이나 고생물학과 같은 학과와 하위 학과의 성장, 그리고 미술평론가와 같은 특정 인물의 성장은 비록 힘든 일로 남게 되었지만, 지킬 가치가 있는 것을 선택하고 정리하기 위한 원칙과 관행의 도출에 도움이 되었다. 게다가, 19세기 말엽에 박물관과 대학이 더욱 멀어지면서, 그리고 세상을 알게 되는 매우 가치 있는 경로로서 물체라는 개념이 쇠퇴하면서, 수집은 특히 과학에서 가치 있는 지적 활동으로서의 지위를 잃기 시작했다. 과학의 참으로 흥미롭고 중요한 측면은 점점 더 육안에 보이지 않는 것들이었고, 수집된 것들에 대한 분류는 더 이상 최첨단의 지식을 생산할 가망이 없었다. '나비 채집'이라는 용어는 '한낱'이라는 형용사와 **부차적인** 학문적 지위의 추구를 나타내는 데 사용될 수 있었다.

다음 빈칸에 들어갈 말로 가장 적절한 것을 고르시오.

① competitive 경쟁력이 없었다는 내용임　② novel 새롭게 등장한 것이 아님
　　경쟁하는　　　　　　　　　　　　　　　　새로운
③ secondary 가치 있는 지적 활동으로서의　④ reliable 신뢰와 관련된 내용이 아님
　　부차적인　지위를 잃었음　　　　　　　　　신뢰할 수 있는
⑤ unconditional 가치 있는 학문으로서의 지위를
　　무조건적인　잃었다는 내용임

왜 정답? [정답률 65%]

수집이 가치 있는 지적 활동으로서의 지위를 잃었고, 수집된 것들을 분류하는 것은 더이상 최첨단 지식을 생산하리라는 보장이 없었다는 것으로 보아 수집 활동을 나타내는 '나비 채집'이라는 용어는 '한낱'이라는 형용사와 함께 ③ '부차적인' 학문적 지위의 추구를 나타내는 데 사용될 수 있었다는 내용으로 글을 마무리하는 것이 적절하다.

왜 오답?

① '나비 채집'과 같은 수집이 학문으로서의 경쟁력이 없어졌다는 내용이다.

② 수집이 과거에는 도움이 되는 학문이었으나 현재는 가치 있는 지적 학문으로서의 지위를 잃었음을 설명하는 글이다.

④ 수집이 쇠퇴했음을 설명하는 글이므로, '신뢰할 수 있는'이라는 형용사는 적절하지 않다.

⑤ '한낱'이라는 형용사와 함께 사용된다는 것은 그 중요성이 떨어졌다는 것을 의미한다. '무조건적인 학문적 지위의 추구'와 관련된 언급은 없다.
　　 주의

양보의 부사절(whatever가 be동사의 주격 보어일 때 be동사는 생략할 수 있음)
Whatever their differences, / scientists and artists begin / with
the same question: / *can you and I see the same thing / the same
way? // If so, how? //
그들의 차이점이 무엇이든 / 과학자와 예술가는 시작한다 / 똑같은 질문으로 / '당신과 내가
똑같은 것을 볼 수 있을까 / 똑같은 방식으로 // 만약 그렇다면 어떻게' //

The scientific thinker looks for features of the thing / that can be
stripped of subjectivity /
과학적 사고를 하는 사람은 사물의 특징을 찾는다 / 주관성이 박탈될 수 있는 /

                  선행사   주격 관계대명사   소유격 관계대명사
— ideally, / those aspects / that can be quantified / and whose
values will thus never change / from one observer to the next. //
이상적으로는 / 그런 측면들 / 정량화될 수 있고 / 그래서 그것의 가치가 전혀 달라지지 않을 /
관찰자마다 //

In this way, / he arrives at a reality / independent of all observers. //
이런 식으로 / 그 사람은 현실에 도달한다 / 모든 관찰자로부터 독립적인 //

                                                부사적 용법(목적)
The artist, on the other hand, relies / on the strength of her
artistry / to effect a marriage / between her own subjectivity and
=subjectivity
that of her readers. // 단서1 예술가는 자신의 주관성과 독자의 주관성의 결합을 이루려고 함
한편 예술가는 의지한다 / 자신의 예술적 솜씨의 힘에 / 결합을 이루기 위해 / 자기 자신의
주관성과 자기 독자의 그것 간의 //

                                강한 추측을 나타내는 조동사
To a scientific thinker, / this must sound like magical thinking: /
과학적 사고를 하는 사람에게 / 이것은 틀림없이 마술적인 사고처럼 들릴 것이다 /

                                앞에 관계부사가 생략됨
*you're saying / you will imagine something so hard / it'll pop into
someone else's head / exactly the way / you envision it? //
'당신은 말하고 있는 것인가 / 당신이 뭔가를 매우 열심히 상상해서 / 다른 누군가의 머릿속에
그것이 떠오를 것이라고 / 바로 그 방식대로 / 당신이 마음속으로 그것을 그리는' //

The artist has sought the opposite / of the scientist's observer-
independent reality. // 단서2 과학자: 관찰자로부터의 독립을 추구함,
                          예술가: 과학자와 정반대인 것을 추구함
예술가는 정반대인 것을 추구해 왔다 / 과학자의 관찰자로부터 독립적인 현실과 //

She creates a reality / dependent upon observers, / indeed a
관계부사 where로 바꾸어 쓸 수 있음   to부정사의 목적의 의미를 강조함
reality / in which **human beings must participate** / in order for
it to exist at all. // 단서3 관찰자가 필요한 현실을 만듦   to exist의
                                                      의미상 주어
그 사람은 현실을 만들어 낸다 / 관찰자에게 의존하는 / 다시 말하면 현실 / 인간들이
참여해야만 하는 / 그것이 존재할 수라도 있으려면 //

- feature ⓝ 특색, 특징   - strip of ~을 빼앗다
- subjectivity ⓝ 주관성   - aspect ⓝ 측면
- quantify ⓥ 양을 나타내다, 수량화하다   - observer ⓝ 관찰자
- artistry ⓝ 예술적 기교   - envision ⓥ 마음속에 그리다
- seek ⓥ 추구하다   - participate ⓥ 참여하다
- maintain ⓥ 유지하다   - harmonize ⓥ 조화를 이루다
- disengage ⓥ 분리하다, 풀다

과학자와 예술가의 차이점이 무엇이든, 그들은 똑같은 질문, 즉 '당신과 내가
똑같은 것을 똑같은 방식으로 볼 수 있을까? 만약 그렇다면 어떻게?'라는
질문으로 시작한다. 과학적 사고를 하는 사람은 주관성이 박탈될 수 있는
사물의 특징, 즉 이상적으로는 정량화될 수 있고 그래서 그것의 가치가
관찰자마다 전혀 달라지지 않을 그런 측면을 찾는다. 이런 식으로, 그
사람은 모든 관찰자로부터 독립적인 현실에 도달한다. 다른 한편, 예술가는
자기 자신의 주관성과 자기 독자의 주관성 간의 결합을 이루기 위해 자신의
예술적 솜씨의 힘에 의지한다. 과학적 사고를 하는 사람에게, 이것은
틀림없이 마술적인 사고처럼 들릴 것이다. 즉 '당신이 뭔가를 매우 열심히
상상해서 그것에 대해 당신이 마음속으로 그리는 바로 그대로 다른 누군가의
머릿속에 그것이 떠오를 것이라고 당신은 말하고 있는 것인가?' 예술가는
과학자의 관찰자로부터 독립적인 현실과 정반대인 것을 추구해 왔다. 예술가는
관찰자에게 의존하는 현실, 다시 말하면, 그것이 존재할 수라도 있으려면
인간들이 참여해야만 하는 현실을 만들어 낸다.

다음 빈칸에 들어갈 말로 가장 적절한 것을 고르시오. [3점]
① human beings must participate 다른 사람들이 포함되어야 함
  인간들이 참여해야만 하는
② objectivity should be maintained subjectivity에 대한 내용임
  객관성이 유지되어야 하는
③ science and art need to harmonize 과학과 예술의 차이를 대조함
  과학과 예술이 조화를 이룰 필요가 있는
④ readers remain distanced from the arts 독자의 주관성과 결합하는 현실을 추구함
  독자가 예술로부터 거리를 둠
⑤ she is disengaged from her own subjectivity 자신의 주관성도 포함되어야 함
  예술가가 자신의 주관성에서 벗어난

> 왜 정답? [정답률 34%]

| 대조 | **과학자**: 모든 관찰자로부터 독립적인, 그들로부터 영향을 받지 않는 현실(주관성이 박탈되는 사물의 특징)에 도달하고자 함 |
| | **예술가**: 자신의 예술가적 솜씨를 통해 자신의 주관성과 독자의 주관성이 결합되는 것을 추구함 |

→ 과학자와 예술가가 대조되는 글이다. 빈칸 문장이 과학자를 설명하는 문장인지,
예술가를 설명하는 문장인지 파악해서 빈칸을 채워야 한다.

| 빈칸 문장 | 예술가는 관찰자에게 의존하는 현실, 다시 말하면, 그것이 존재할 수라도 있으려면 _____ 현실을 만들어 낸다. |

→ 예술가가 만들어 내는 현실을 설명하는 문장이다.
  ▶ '관찰자에게 의존하는 현실'이란 관찰자, 즉 다른 사람을 필요로 하는 현실이라는
  의미이므로, 이를 다르게 표현하려면 ① '인간들이 참여해야만 하는'이 가장
  적절하다.

> 왜 오답?
② '객관성'은 과학자가 추구하는 현실이라고 할 수 있다.
③ 과학과 예술의 조화가 아니라 과학자가 추구하는 바와 예술가가 추구하는 현실을
  대조하는 글이다.
④ 예술가적 솜씨를 통해 예술가의 주관성과 독자의 주관성이 결합되는 것을
  추구한다.
⑤ 독자의 주관성뿐만 아니라 예술가의 주관성도 결합 요소이다.

                            단수 주어
One of the common themes / of the Western philosophical
tradition / is the distinction / between sensual perceptions and
rational knowledge. //
    단수 동사
공통된 주제 중 하나는 / 서양의 철학적 전통의 / 구별이다 / 감각적 지각과 합리적 지식
사이의 //

Since Plato, / the supremacy of rational reason / is based on
the assertion / that it is able to extract true knowledge / from
experience. //   동격절 접속사
플라톤 이래로 / 합리적 이성의 우월성은 / 주장에 근거한다 / 그것이 참된 지식을 얻어낼 수
있다는 / 경험에서 //

As the discussion in the *Republic* helps / to explain, / perceptions
are inherently unreliable and misleading / because the senses
are subject / to errors and illusions. // 단서1 지각은 본질적으로 신뢰할 수 없고
                                            오해의 소지가 있음
*Republic*에서의 논의가 도움이 되듯이 / 설명하는 데 / 지각은 본질적으로 신뢰할 수 없고
오해의 소지가 있다 / 감각은 영향을 받기 때문에 / 오류와 착각에 //
                                            형용사적 용법(the tools 수식)
Only the rational discourse has the tools / to overcome illusions
/ and to point towards true knowledge. // 단서2 합리적 담론만이 착각을
                                            극복하고 참된 지식을 가리킬 수 있음
오직 합리적 담론만이 도구를 가지고 있다 / 착각을 극복하고 / 참된 지식을 가리키는 //

For instance, / perception suggests / that a figure in the distance
is smaller / than it really is. //
예를 들어 / 지각은 보여 준다 / 멀리 있는 어떤 형체가 더 작다는 것을 / 실제로 그것이 그런
것보다 //

Yet, / the application of logical reasoning will reveal / that
the figure only appears small / because it obeys / the laws of
geometrical perspective. //
하지만 / 논리적 추론의 적용은 드러낼 것이다 / 그 형체는 작게 보일 뿐이라는 것을 / 그것이
따르기 때문에 / 기하학적 원근법을 //

Nevertheless, / even after the perspectival correction is applied /
부사절 접속사(때)
and reason concludes / that perception is misleading, /
그럼에도 불구하고 / 원근 보정을 적용한 후에도 / 그리고 이성이 결론을 내린 후에도 / 지각이
오해의 소지가 있다고 **단서3** 원근 보정을 적용해도, 지각은 오해의 소지가 있다고
이성이 결론을 내려도 여전히 작게 보임
the figure still *appears* small, / and the truth of the matter is
revealed / not **in the perception of the figure** / but in its rational
┌── not A but B(A가 아니라 B)로 연결된 전치사구 ──┐
representation. //
그 형체는 여전히 작게 '보이고' / 문제의 진실은 드러난다 / 형체의 지각에서가 아닌 / 그것의
합리적 재현에서 //

- tradition ⓝ 전통 · distinction ⓝ 구별 · perception ⓝ 지각
- sensual ⓐ 감각의 · supremacy ⓝ 패권, 우위
- assertion ⓝ 주장 · inherent ⓐ 내재하는, 본질적으로
- unreliable ⓐ 믿을 수 없는 · illusion ⓝ 오해, 환상
- figure ⓝ 형체 · application ⓝ 적용 · perspective ⓝ 관점
- conclude ⓥ 결론을 내리다 · representation ⓝ 묘사, 나타낸 것

서양의 철학적 전통의 공통된 주제 중 하나는 감각적 지각과 합리적 지식
사이의 구별이다. 플라톤 이래로, 합리적 이성의 우월성은 그것이 경험에서
참된 지식을 얻어낼 수 있다는 주장에 근거한다. Republic에서의 논의가
설명에 도움이 되듯이, 감각은 오류와 착각의 영향을 받기 때문에 지각은
본질적으로 신뢰할 수 없고 오해의 소지가 있다. 오직 합리적 담론만이 착각을
극복하고 참된 지식을 가리키는 도구를 가지고 있다. 예를 들어, 지각은 멀리
있는 어떤 형체가 실제보다 더 작다는 것을 보여 준다. 하지만, 논리적 추론을
적용하면 그 형체는 기하학적 원근법을 따르기 때문에 작게 보일 뿐이라는
것이 드러날 것이다. 그럼에도 불구하고, 원근 보정을 적용하여 이성이 지각이
오해의 소지가 있다는 결론을 내린 후에도, 그 형체는 여전히 작게 '보이고',
문제의 진실은 **형체의 지각이 아닌 그것의 합리적 재현에서** 드러난다.

다음 빈칸에 들어갈 말로 가장 적절한 것을 고르시오. [3점]
① as the outcome of blindly following sensual experience
감각적인 경험을 맹목적으로 따르는 것의 결과로   감각적 '지각'에 대한 내용임
② by moving away from the idea of perfect representation
완벽한 재현이라는 생각에서 벗어남으로써   완벽한 재현이 잘못됐다는 것이 아님
③ beyond the limit of where rational knowledge can approach
합리적 지식이 접근할 수 있는 곳의 한계 너머에서   합리적 지식의 우월성을 설명함
④ through a variety of experiences rather than logical reasoning
논리적 추론이라기보다 다양한 경험을 통해   경험의 우월성을 설명하는 것이 아님
⑤ not in the perception of the figure but in its rational representation
형체의 지각이 아닌 그것의 합리적 재현에서   지각과 합리적 지식이 대조됨

K 78 정답 ① *유머를 통해 얻고자 하는 것

Humour involves / not just practical disengagement / but
┌── not just A but (also) B(A뿐만 아니라 B도)로 연결된 목적어 ──┘
cognitive disengagement. //
유머는 포함한다 / 실제적인 이탈뿐만 아니라 / 인식의 이탈도 //
부사절 접속사(조건)   부사구가 be동사와 과거분사 사이에 삽입됨
As long as something is funny, / we are for the moment not
concerned / with whether it is real or fictional, true or false. //
어떤 것이 재미있다면 / 우리는 잠깐 관심을 두지 않는다 / 그것이 진짜인지 허구인지, 진실인
지 거짓인지에 // **단서1** 유머를 들을 땐 그것이 진짜인지 허구인지에 관심을 두지 않음
This is why we give considerable leeway / to people / telling
people을 수식하는 현재분사구
funny stories. //
이것이 우리가 상당한 여지를 주는 이유이다 / 사람들에게 / 재미있는 이야기를 하는 //
If they are getting extra laughs / by exaggerating / the silliness of
병렬 구조
a situation / or even by making up a few details, /
만약 그들이 추가 웃음을 얻고 있다면 / 과장함으로써 / 상황의 어리석음을 / 또는 심지어 몇
가지 세부 사항을 꾸며냄으로써 /
we are happy to grant them comic licence, / a kind of poetic
licence. //
우리는 그들에게 기꺼이 희극적 파격을 허락한다 / 일종의 시적 파격 //
주어
Indeed, / someone / listening to a funny story / who tries to
correct the teller /   **단서2** 유머를 정확한 정보로 바로잡는 사람은
방해하지 말라는 말을 들을 것임
실제로 / 누군가는 / 재미있는 이야기를 듣고 있는 / 말하는 사람을 바로잡으려고 하는 /
— 'No, he didn't spill the spaghetti / on the keyboard and the
monitor, / just on the keyboard' — / will probably be told / by
동사(미래 시제 수동태)
the other listeners / to stop interrupting. //
'아니야, 그는 스파게티를 쏟지 않았어 / 키보드와 모니터에 / 키보드에만 (쏟았어)' / 아마 들을
것이다 / 듣고 있는 다른 사람들에게서 / 방해하는 것을 멈추라고 //
선행사
The creator of humour is putting ideas / into people's heads / for
the pleasure / those ideas will bring, / not to provide **accurate**
앞에 목적격 관계대명사가 생략됨
information. //
유머를 만드는 사람은 생각을 집어넣고 있다 / 사람들의 머릿속에 / 재미를 위해서 / 그 생각이
가져올 / 정확한 정보를 제공하기 위해서가 아니라 //

- disengagement ⓝ 이탈, 자유, 해방
- be concerned with ~에 관심을 두다 · fictional ⓐ 허구적인
- considerable ⓐ 상당한, 많은
- exaggerate ⓥ 과장하다, 지나치게 강조하다
- silliness ⓝ 어리석음, 우둔한 짓 · make up ~을 꾸며내다[지어내다]
- grant ⓥ 부여하다, 허락하다 · licence ⓝ (창작상의) 파격, 허용
- poetic ⓐ 시적인 · correct ⓥ (남의 실수를) 바로잡다[지적하다]
- spill ⓥ 쏟다, 흘리다 · interrupt ⓥ 방해하다, 중단하다

유머는 실제적인 이탈뿐만 아니라 인식의 이탈도 포함한다. 어떤 것이 재미있다
면, 우리는 잠깐 그것이 진짜인지 허구인지, 진실인지 거짓인지에 관심을 두지
않는다. 이것이 우리가 재미있는 이야기를 하는 사람들에게 상당한 여지를 주는
이유이다. 만약 그들이 상황의 어리석음을 과장하거나 심지어 몇 가지 세부 사
항을 꾸며서라도 추가 웃음을 얻고 있다면, 우리는 그들에게 기꺼이 희극적 파
격, 일종의 시적 파격을 허락한다. 실제로, 재미있는 이야기를 듣고 있는 누군
가가 '아니야, 그는 스파게티를 키보드와 모니터에 쏟은 것이 아니라 키보드에
만 쏟았어.'라며 말하는 사람을 바로잡으려고 하면 그는 아마 듣고 있는 다른 사
람들에게서 방해하지 말라는 말을 들을 것이다. 유머를 만드는 사람은 사람들의
머릿속에 생각을 집어넣고 있는데, 그 생각이 가져올 재미를 위해서이지, **정확
한** 정보를 제공하기 위해서가 아니다.

다음 빈칸에 들어갈 말로 가장 적절한 것을 고르시오.

① accurate 진짜인지 허구인지 관심을
정확한 두지 않음
② detailed
상세한
③ useful
유용한
④ additional 추가적인 정보를 달라고
추가적인 요청한 예시가 아님
⑤ alternative 정확한 정보로 바로잡는
대안적인 예시를 들었음

>왜 정답? [정답률 54%] 정확한 정보를 제공하는지 그렇지 않은지 꿀팁

어떤 것이 재미있다면 우리는 그것이 진짜인지 허구인지, 진실인지 거짓인지에 관심을 두지 않는다면서, 유머를 듣던 누군가가 정확한 정보(스파게티를 키보드와 모니터에 쏟은 것이 아니라 키보드에만 쏟았다는 것)로 유머를 바로잡으려고 하면 다른 사람들이 그에게 방해하지 말라고 할 것이라고 했다. 따라서 마지막 문장은 유머가 ① '정확한' 정보가 아니라 재미를 위한 것이라는 의미가 되어야 한다.

>왜 오답?

②, ④ 유머를 말하는 사람을 방해하는 사람이 정확한 정보를 요청하는 것이지, 상세한 정보나 추가적인 정보를 요청하는 것이 아니다.

③, ⑤ 스파게티를 키보드와 모니터에 쏟은 것이 아니라 키보드에만 쏟았다고 바로잡는 것이 유용하거나 대안적인 정보를 요청하는 것은 아니다.

K 79 정답 ② ＊생태계를 파괴하지 말아야 하는 이유

Genetic engineering / followed by cloning / to distribute / many
주어
identical animals or plants / is sometimes seen / as a threat / to
동사
the diversity of nature. //

유전 공학은 / 복제로 이어지는 / 퍼뜨리기 위한 / 많은 똑같은 동물이나 식물을 / 때때로 여겨진다 / 위협으로 / 자연의 다양성에 대한 //
현재완료 진행형 단서 1 인간은 자연의 다양성을
파괴해 왔음
However, / humans have been replacing / diverse natural
habitats / with artificial monoculture / for millennia. //

그러나 / 인간은 대체해 오고 있다 / 다양한 자연 서식지를 / 인위적인 단일 경작으로 / 수천 년 동안 //
'완료'를 나타내는 현재완료 수동태
Most natural habitats / in the advanced nations / have already
been replaced / with some form of artificial environment / based
on mass production or repetition. //

대부분의 자연 서식지는 / 선진국에 있는 / 이미 대체되었다 / 어떤 형태의 인위적인 환경으로 / 대량 생산 또는 반복에 기반을 둔 //
주격 보어 형용사적 용법
The real threat to biodiversity / is surely the need / to convert (the need 수식)
주어 동사
ever more of our planet / into production zones / to feed the
부사적 용법(목적)
ever-increasing human population. //

생물 다양성에 대한 진정한 위협은 / 확실히 필요성이다 / 지구의 더욱더 많은 부분을 전환해야 할 / 생산지대로 / 계속 늘어나는 인구에 식량을 공급하기 위해서 //
준동사(거의 ~하지 않는)
The cloning and transgenic alteration / of domestic animals /
makes little difference / to the overall situation. //

복제와 이식 유전자에 의한 변형은 / 가축의 / 거의 변화를 주지 않는다 / 전반적인 상황에 //

Conversely, / the renewed interest in genetics / has led to a
growing awareness /

반대로 / 유전학에 관한 새로워진 관심은 / 증가하는 인식으로 이어졌다 /
동격절 접속사 주격 관계대명사
that there are many wild plants and animals / with interesting
or useful genetic properties / that could be used / for a variety of
as-yet-unknown purposes. // 단서 2 아직 알려지지 않은 목적을 위해 이용될 수 있는
많은 야생 동식물이 있다는 인식이 증가함
많은 야생 동식물이 있다는 / 흥미롭거나 유용한 유전적 특성을 가진 / 이용될 수 있는 / 아직 알려지지 않은 다양한 목적을 위해서 //
동격절 접속사
This has led in turn to a realization / that we should avoid /
destroying natural ecosystems /

이것은 결국 깨달음으로 이어졌다 / 우리가 피해야 한다는 / 자연 생태계를 파괴하는 것을 /

because they may harbor tomorrow's drugs / against cancer,
malaria, or obesity. // 단서 3 암 등의 질병에 대항하는 약을 품고 있을 가능성이 있다면
그것을 파괴하는 것을 피해야 할 것임
그것이 미래의 약을 품고 있을 수도 있기 때문에 / 암, 말라리아 또는 비만에 대항하는 //

• genetic engineering 유전 공학 • cloning ⓝ 복제
• distribute ⓥ 퍼뜨리다 • identical ⓐ 똑같은 • threat ⓝ 위협
• diversity ⓝ 다양성 • habitat ⓝ 서식지
• artificial ⓐ 인위적인, 인공적인 • millennium ⓝ 천년(pl. millennia)
• mass ⓐ 대량의, 대규모의 • biodiversity ⓝ 생물의 다양성
• convert ⓥ 전환하다 • transgenic ⓐ 이식 유전자에 의한
• alteration ⓝ 변형 • conversely ⓐⓓ 정반대로, 역으로
• renewed ⓐ 재개된, 새로워진 • property ⓝ 특성
• harbor ⓥ (계획ㆍ생각 등을) 품다 • obesity ⓝ 비만

많은 똑같은 동물이나 식물을 퍼뜨리기 위한 복제로 이어지는 유전 공학은 때때로 자연의 다양성에 대한 위협으로 여겨진다. 그러나 인간은 수천 년 동안 인위적인 단일 경작으로 다양한 자연 서식지를 대체해 오고 있다. 선진국에 있는 대부분의 자연 서식지는 대량 생산 또는 반복에 기반을 둔 어떤 형태의 인위적인 환경으로 이미 대체되었다. 생물 다양성에 대한 진정한 위협은 계속 늘어나는 인구에 식량을 공급하기 위해서 지구의 더욱더 많은 부분을 생산지대로 전환해야 할 필요성임이 확실하다. 가축의 복제와 이식 유전자에 의한 변형은 전반적인 상황에 거의 변화를 주지 않는다. 반대로, 유전학에 관한 새로워진 관심은 아직 알려지지 않은 다양한 목적을 위해서 이용될 수 있는 흥미롭거나 유용한 유전적 특성을 가진 많은 야생 동식물이 있다는 인식을 점점 키웠다. 이것은 결국 자연 생태계가 암, 말라리아 또는 비만을 치료하는 미래의 약을 품고 있을 수도 있기 때문에 **우리가 자연 생태계를 파괴하는 것을 피해야 한다**는 깨달음으로 이어졌다.

다음 빈칸에 들어갈 말로 가장 적절한 것을 고르시오.

① ecological systems are genetically programmed
생태계는 유전적으로 프로그램되어 있다 생태계가 유전적으로 정해져 있다는 내용이 아님
② we should avoid destroying natural ecosystems
우리가 자연 생태계를 파괴하는 것을 피해야 한다 유용하게 쓰일 수도 있으므로 파괴하면 안 됨
③ we need to stop creating genetically modified organisms
우리가 유전자 변형 유기체를 만드는 것을 중단할 필요가 있다 유전자 변형 유기체의 문제점을 설명한 것이 아님
④ artificial organisms can survive in natural environments
인위적인 유기체는 자연환경에서 생존할 수 있다 복제된 유기체의 생존 여부를 언급한 것이 아님
⑤ living things adapt themselves to their physical environments
살아있는 것들은 자신의 물리적 환경에 적응한다 유기체의 환경 적응에 대한 내용이 아님

>왜 정답? [정답률 59%] 앞부분은 유전 공학이 자연의 다양성(생물 다양성)에 대한 위협이라는 내용임 꿀팁

Conversely를 기준으로 내용이 전환되고 있다. 빈칸이 포함된 뒷부분은 아직 알려지지 않은 다양한 목적(암, 말라리아, 비만의 치료를 예로 듦)에 이용될 수 있는 유용한 유전적 특성을 가진 많은 야생 동식물이 있다는 인식이 증가했다는 내용이다. 이러한 인식의 증가는 결국 야생 동식물을 파괴하면 안 된다는 깨달음, 즉 ② '우리가 자연 생태계를 파괴하는 것을 피해야 한다'는 깨달음으로 이어졌을 것이다.

>왜 오답?

① 생태계가 유전적으로 정해져 있다는 것이 아니라 생태계, 즉 많은 동식물의 유전적 특성이 어떤 유용한 목적으로 이용될 수 있는지를 다 알지 못하기 때문에 생태계의 파괴를 피해야 한다는 내용이다.

③ 유전자 변형 유기체를 만드는 것의 문제점이 아니라 다양한 자연 서식지를 인위적인 단일 경작지로 바꾸지 말아야 하는 이유를 인식하게 된 것이다.

④ 유전 공학으로 복제된 똑같은 동물이나 식물이 자연환경에 적응할 수 있는지 여부를 설명한 글이 아니다.

⑤ 유기체의 환경 적응에 대한 내용이 아니다.

K 80 정답 ① ＊우리의 경험에 의해 만들어지는 뇌

Thanks to newly developed neuroimaging technology, / we
now have access / to the specific brain changes / that occur
선행사 주격 관계대명사
during learning. //

새롭게 개발된 신경 촬영 기술 덕분에 / 우리는 이제 접근할 수 있다 / 특정한 뇌 변화에 / 학습 중에 일어나는 // 양보의 부사절 접속사
Even though all of our brains contain / the same basic
structures, / our neural networks are as unique / as our
fingerprints. // 단서 1 우리의 뇌(신경망)는 우리의 지문만큼이나 개인에 따라 독특함
우리들의 뇌 모두는 가지고 있음에도 불구하고 / 같은 기본 구조를 / 우리의 신경망은 (~만큼)
독특하다 / 우리의 지문만큼이나 //

The latest developmental neuroscience research has shown / that the brain is much more malleable / throughout life / than previously assumed; /

비교급 강조 부사

가장 최근의 발달 신경 과학 연구는 보여 준다 / 뇌가 훨씬 더 순응성이 있다는 것을 / 평생 동안 / 이전에 가정된 것보다 // **단서 2** 뇌는 자신의 처리 과정, 자신의 환경, 자신의 상황에 반응하여 발달함

it develops / in response / to its own processes, / to its immediate and distant "environments," / and to its past and current situations. //

전치사구의 병렬 구조

그것은 발달한다 / 반응하여 / 자기 자신의 처리 과정에 / 자신에게 인접한 '환경'과 멀리 떨어진 '환경'에 / 그리고 자신의 과거와 현재의 상황에 //

The brain seeks to create meaning / through establishing or refining / existing neural networks. //

동명사 establishing과 refining의 목적어

뇌는 의미를 창조하려고 한다 / 확립하거나 개선하는 것을 통해 / 기존의 신경망을 //

When we learn a new fact or skill, / our neurons communicate / to form networks of connected information. //

우리가 새로운 사실이나 기술을 배울 때 / 우리의 뉴런들은 소통한다 / 연결된 정보망을 형성하기 위해 // **단서 3** 새로운 사실이나 기술을 배울 때 연결된 정보망이 형성됨

동명사구 주어   단수 동사

Using this knowledge or skill / results in structural changes / to allow similar future impulses to travel / more quickly and efficiently / than others. //

to allow의 목적격 보어 **단서 4**

이러한 지식이나 기술을 사용하는 것은 / 구조적 변화를 가져온다 / 미래의 유사한 자극이 이동하게 하는 / 더 빠르고 효율적으로 / 다른 것들보다 // 배운 지식이나 기술을 사용하는 것이 (뇌의) 구조적 변화를 가져옴

High-activity synaptic connections / are stabilized and strengthened, / while connections with relatively low use / are weakened and eventually pruned. //

대조의 부사절 접속사

고활동성 시냅스 연결이 / 안정화되고 강화된다 / 상대적으로 적게 사용되는 연결은 (~하는) 반면에 / 약해져서 결국에는 잘리는 //

In this way, / our brains are **sculpted** / **by our own history of experiences**. //

이런 식으로 / 우리의 뇌는 만들어진다 / 우리 자신의 경험의 이력에 의해 //

- newly [ad] 최근에, 새로
- specific [a] 특정한, 구체적인
- neuroscience [n] 신경 과학
- previously [ad] 미리, 사전에
- in response to ~에 응하여[답하여]
- distant [a] 먼, 떨어져 있는
- refine [v] 정제하다, 개선하다
- result in ~을 낳다[야기하다]
- efficiently [ad] 효율적으로, 유효하게
- strengthen [v] 강화하다, 더 튼튼하게 하다
- relatively [ad] 비교적, 상대적으로
- eventually [ad] 결국
- initial [a] 처음의, 초기의
- twin [v] 결부시키다, 밀접하게 연결시키다
- portray [v] 그리다, 묘사하다
- access [n] 입장, 접근
- fingerprint [n] 지문
- throughout [prep] 도처에, ~ 동안 내내
- assume [v] 추정하다, 가정하다
- immediate [a] 즉각적인, 당면한
- establish [v] 설립하다, 확립하다
- neural [a] 신경의
- impulse [n] 자극, 충격
- stabilize [v] 안정시키다
- weaken [v] 약화시키다
- sculpt [v] 조각하다, 형상[형태]을 만들다
- gear [v] 적응시키다, 맞게 조정하다
- organ [n] (인체 내의) 장기

새롭게 개발된 신경 촬영 기술 덕분에, 우리는 이제 학습 중에 일어나는 특정한 뇌 변화에 접근할 수 있다. 우리들의 뇌 모두는 같은 기본 구조를 가지고 있음에도 불구하고, 우리의 신경망은 우리의 지문만큼이나 독특하다. 가장 최근의 발달 신경 과학 연구는 뇌가 이전에 가정했던 것보다 평생 동안 훨씬 더 순응성이 있다는 것을 보여 주며, 그것은 자기 자신의 처리 과정에, 자신에게 인접한 '환경'과 멀리 떨어진 '환경'에, 자신의 과거와 현재의 상황에 반응하여 발달한다. 뇌는 기존의 신경망을 확립하거나 개선하여 의미를 창조하려고 한다. 우리가 새로운 사실이나 기술을 배울 때, 우리의 뉴런들은 연결된 정보망을 형성하기 위해 소통한다. 이러한 지식이나 기술을 사용하는 것은 미래의 유사한 자극이 다른 것들보다 더 빠르고 효율적으로 이동하게 하는 구조적 변화를 가져온다. 고활동성 시냅스 연결이 안정화되고 강화되는 반면에, 상대적으로 적게 사용되는 연결은 약해져서 결국에는 잘린다. 이런 식으로, 우리의 뇌는 **우리 자신의 경험의 이력에 의해 만들어진다**.

다음 빈칸에 들어갈 말로 가장 적절한 것을 고르시오. [3점]

① sculpted by our own history of experiences 개인의 지문만큼 독특함
   우리 자신의 경험의 이력에 의해 만들어진다
② designed to maintain their initial structures 구조적 변화를 겪는다고 했음
   그것의 최초의 구조를 유지하도록 설계된다
③ geared toward strengthening recent memories
   최근의 기억을 강화하도록 조정된다   최근의 기억이 아니라 구조가 변화하는 것이 아님
④ twinned with the development of other organs
   다른 장기의 발달과 밀접히 연결된다   뇌 이외의 다른 장기는 언급되지 않음
⑤ portrayed as the seat of logical and creative thinking
   논리적이고 창의적인 사고가 일어나는 장소로 그려진다   뇌가 창의적인 사고의 근원이라는 내용이 아님

왜 정답? [정답률 54%]   신경망도 결국 뇌를 의미함 꿀팁

우리의 뇌는 모두 같은 기본 구조를 갖고 있긴 하지만, 신경망은 지문만큼이나 개인에 따라 독특하고, 우리의 뇌가 자신의 처리 과정, 자신이 처한 환경과 상황에 반응하여 발달한다고 했다. 우리가 새로운 사실이나 기술을 배울 때 연결된 정보망이 형성되고, 배운 지식과 기술을 사용하는 것이 (뇌의) 구조적 변화를 가져온다는 것은 개인이 배우는 것에 따라 뇌의 구조가 달라진다는 의미이므로 우리의 뇌가 ① '우리 자신의 경험의 이력에 의해 만들어진다'는 내용이 되도록 빈칸을 완성해야 한다.

왜 오답?

② 안정화되고 강화되는 연결이 있기도 하고 약해져서 결국 잘리는 연결도 있는 것처럼 구조적 변화가 일어난다고 했으므로 최초의 구조를 유지한다는 것은 적절하지 않다.

③ 고활동성 시냅스 연결이 강화된다고 했지, 최근의 기억이 강화된다는 것은 아니다.

④ 뇌와 다른 장기의 밀접한 연결에 대한 내용이 아니다.

⑤ 논리적, 창의적 사고가 일어나는 장소로서 뇌를 설명한 것이 아니다.

K 81 정답 ④ *시대를 너무 앞서갔던 Mendel의 발견

주어, 선행사   주격 관계대명사   동사

An invention or discovery / that is too far ahead of its time / is worthless; / no one can follow. //

발명이나 발견은 / 시대를 너무 앞서간 / 가치가 없다 / 누구도 따라갈 수 없다 //

invites의 목적어와 목적격 보어   전치사   명사절

Ideally, / an innovation opens up only the next step / from what is known / and invites the culture / to move forward one hop. //

이상적으로 / 혁신은 단지 다음 단계만을 가능하게 하고 / 알려진 것으로부터 / 그 문화에 요청한다 / 한 걸음 앞으로 나아가도록 // **단서 1** 이상적인 혁신은 한 걸음 오직 다음 단계만을 가능하게 함

병렬 구조

An overly futuristic, unconventional, or visionary invention / can fail initially /

지나치게 미래지향적이거나 관행을 벗어나는 혹은 비현실적인 발명은 / 처음에는 실패할 수도 있다 /

(it may lack / essential not-yet-invented materials / or a critical market / or proper understanding) /

(그것은 부족할 수 있다 / 아직 발명되지 않은 필수적인 재료나 / 중요한 시장 / 또는 적절한 이해가) /

fail과 병렬 구조

yet succeed later, / when the ecology of supporting ideas catches up. //

하지만 나중에 성공할 수도 있다 / 아이디어를 뒷받침하는 생태 환경이 따라잡을 때 //

Gregor Mendel's 1865 theories of genetic heredity / were correct / but ignored for 35 years. //

〈기간〉의 전치사 **단서 2** Mendel의 이론은 너무 앞서가서 35년 동안 무시됐음

Gregor Mendel의 1865년 유전 이론은 / 옳았지만 / 35년 동안 무시되었다 //

His sharp insights were not accepted / because they did not explain the problems / biologists had at the time, /

앞에 목적격 관계대명사가 생략됨

그의 날카로운 통찰력은 받아들여지지 않았다 / 그것들이 문제들을 설명하지 않았기 때문에 / 생물학자들이 그 당시에 가졌던 /

nor did his explanation operate / by known mechanisms, / so his discoveries were out of reach / even for the early adopters. //

부정어가 문두로 오면서 주어와 동사가 도치됨

그의 설명 역시 작동하지 않았기 때문에 / 알려진 메커니즘에 의해 / 그의 발견은 이해하기 어려웠다 / 얼리 어답터들에게도 //

생략 가능한 목적격 관계대명사

Decades later / science faced the urgent questions / that Mendel's discoveries could answer. // **단서 3** 수십 년이 지나고 Mendel의 발견이 이상적인 혁신이 됨

수십 년 후 / 과학은 긴급한 질문에 직면했다 / Mendel의 발견이 답할 수 있는 //

Now his insights / **were only one step away**. //

이제 그의 통찰력은 / 단 한 걸음만 떨어져 있었다 //

Within a few years of one another, / three different scientists
each independently rediscovered / Mendel's forgotten work, /
선행사
계속적 용법의 관계대명사
which of course had been there all along. //
서로 몇 년 간격으로 / 세 명의 다른 과학자들이 각각 독립적으로 재발견했는데 / Mendel의
잊혀진 연구를 / 물론 그것은 줄곧 그곳에 있었다 //

- ahead of ~보다 앞선　　・ worthless ⓐ 가치가 없는
- ideally ⓐ 이상적으로　　・ open up ~을 가능하게 하다
- futuristic ⓐ 미래지향적인　　・ unconventional ⓐ 관습에 얽매이지 않는
- visionary ⓐ 비현실적인　　・ initially ⓐⓓ 처음에는
- critical ⓐ 중요한　　・ catch up 따라잡다　　・ genetic ⓐ 유전의
- insight ⓝ 통찰력
- early adopter 얼리 어답터(신제품을 먼저 사서 써 보는 사람)
- urgent ⓐ 긴급한　　・ independently ⓐⓓ 독립적으로

시대를 너무 앞서간 발명이나 발견은 가치가 없는데, 누구도 따라갈 수
없기 때문이다. 이상적으로, 혁신은 알려진 것으로부터 단지 다음 단계만을
가능하게 하고, 그 문화가 한 걸음 앞으로 나아가도록 요청한다. 지나치게
미래지향적이거나 관행을 벗어나는 혹은 비현실적인 발명은 처음에는 실패할
수도 있지만(아직 발명되지 않은 필수적인 재료나 중요한 시장 또는 적절한
이해가 부족할 수 있다) 아이디어를 뒷받침하는 생태 환경이 따라잡을 때
나중에 성공할 수도 있다. Gregor Mendel의 1865년 유전 이론은 옳았지만
35년 동안 무시되었다. 그의 날카로운 통찰력은 생물학자들이 그 당시에
가졌던 문제들을 설명하지 않았기 때문에 받아들여지지 않았고, 그의 설명
역시 알려진 메커니즘에 의해 작동하지 않았기 때문에 그의 발견은 얼리
어답터들에게도 이해하기 어려웠다. 수십 년 후 과학은 Mendel의 발견이 답할
수 있는 긴급한 질문에 직면했다. 이제 그의 통찰력은 **단 한 걸음만 떨어져
있었다.** 서로 몇 년 간격으로, 세 명의 다른 과학자들이 각각 독립적으로
Mendel의 잊혀진 연구를 재발견했는데, 물론 그 연구는 줄곧 그곳에 있었다.

다음 빈칸에 들어갈 말로 가장 적절한 것을 고르시오. [3점]
① caught up to modern problems Mendel의 연구는 줄곧 그곳에 있었음
　현대의 문제를 따라잡았다
② raised even more questions Mendel의 발견이 답할 수 있음
　훨씬 더 많은 의문을 제기했다
③ addressed past and current topics alike 과거에는 무시되었음
　과거와 현재의 주제를 동일하게 다루었다
④ were only one step away 이상적인 혁신은 오직 다음 단계만을 가능하게 함
　단 한 걸음만 떨어져 있었다
⑤ regained acceptance of the public 수용된 적이 없음
　대중에게 다시 수용되었다

▷왜 정답? [정답률 22%]

글의 앞부분	• 이상적인 혁신은 오직 다음 단계만을 가능하게 하고, 한 걸음 앞으로 나아갈 것을 요청함 • 지나치게 앞서간 발명/발견은 처음에는 실패할 수 있지만 나중에 성공할 수도 있음
예시	이제(수십 년 후) Mendel의 통찰력은 ＿＿＿＿＿＿＿했다.
빈칸 문장	• Gregor Mendel의 1865년 유전 이론은 옳았지만, 당시에는 받아들여지지 않았음 • 수십 년 후 과학은 Mendel의 발견이 답할 수 있는 질문에 직면했음

⇒ 당시에는 인정받지 못했던 Mendel의 발견이 수십 년이 지난 후에 성공한,
　이상적인 혁신이 되었다는 내용이다.

▶ 이상적인 혁신이란 오직 다음 단계만을 가능하게 한다고 했으므로 Mendel의
　혁신을 설명하는 빈칸에는 ④ '단 한 걸음만 떨어져 있었다'가 적절하다.

▷왜 오답?

① Mendel의 발견이 현대의 문제를 따라잡은 게 아니라, 생태 환경이 Mendel의
　아이디어를 따라잡은 것이다. (◀◀ 이유: Mendel의 1865년 유전 이론은 35년
　동안 무시된 상태로 있었음)
② 긴급한 질문에 Mendel의 발견이 답할 수 있었다.
③ 과거의 문제들은 설명하지 않았다.
⑤ 수용된 적이 없으므로 regained는 적절하지 않다.

K 82 정답 ② ＊텍스트가 의미하는 것

과거분사
Over the last decade / the attention / given to how children learn
to read / has foregrounded / the nature of *textuality*, /
지난 10년 동안 / 관심은 / 어린이가 읽는 법을 배우는 방법에 관한 / 전면으로 불러왔다 /
'텍스트성'의 본질 /
전치사＋관계대명사(선행사 ways 수식)
and of the different, interrelated ways / in which readers of all
make＋목적어＋목적격보어(동사원형)
ages / make texts mean. //
그리고 다양하고 상호 연관된 방식의 / 모든 나이의 독자가 / 텍스트를 의미하게 하는 //

'Reading' now applies / to a greater number of representational
forms / than at any time in the past: / pictures, maps, screens,
design graphics and photographs are all regarded / as text. //
이제 '읽기'는 적용된다 / 훨씬 더 많은 표현 형식에 / 과거 어느 시대보다 / 그림, 지도, 화면,
디자인 그래픽, 사진이 모두 여겨진다 / 텍스트로 //
단서 1 이제 읽기는 훨씬 더 많은
표현 형식에 적용됨
과거분사
In addition to the innovations / made possible in picture books /
by new printing processes, / design features also predominate /
in other kinds, / such as books of poetry and information texts. //
혁신에 더해 / 그림책에서 가능해진 / 새로운 인쇄 공정에 의해 / 디자인적 특징이 두드러진다
/ 다른 종류에서도 / 시집이나 정보 텍스트와 같은 //

Thus, / reading becomes / a more complicated kind of
interpretation /
이처럼 / 읽기는 된다 / 더 복잡한 종류의 해석이 /
＝reading
than it was when children's attention was focused / on the
printed text, / with sketches or pictures as an adjunct. //
어린이들의 주의가 집중될 때보다 / 인쇄된 텍스트에 / 스케치나 그림을 부속물로 가질
때보다 //
단서 2 읽기는 인쇄된 텍스트보다 더 복잡한 종류의 해석이 됨

Children now learn / from a picture book / that words and
목적어절을 이끄는 접속사
illustrations complement and enhance each other. //
이제 어린이들은 배운다 / 그림책을 통해 / 글과 삽화가 서로를 보완하여 향상한다는 것을 //

Reading is not simply **word recognition**. //
읽기는 단순히 단어 인식이 아니다 //
선행사를 포함하는 관계대명사
Even in the easiest texts, / what a sentence 'says' / is often not /
what it means. // 단서 3 문장이 말하는 것이 의미하는 것은 아님
아무리 쉬운 텍스트에서도 / 문장이 '말하는 것'은 / 흔히 아니다 / 그 문장이 의미하는 것이 //

- foreground ⓥ 특히 중시하다　　・ textuality ⓝ 텍스트성
- interrelated ⓐ 상호 연관된　　・ representational ⓐ 표현의, 나타내는
- predominate ⓥ 두드러지다, 지배적이다　　・ illustration ⓝ 삽화
- complement ⓥ 보완하다　　・ enhance ⓥ 높이다, 향상하다

지난 10년 동안 어린이가 읽는 법을 배우는 방법에 관한 관심은 '텍스트성'의
본질과 모든 나이의 독자가 텍스트를 의미하게 하는 다양하고 상호 연관된
방식의 본질을 전면으로 불러왔다. 이제 '읽기'는 과거 어느 시대보다 훨씬
더 많은 표현 형식에 적용되는데, 그림, 지도, 화면, 디자인 그래픽, 사진이
모두 텍스트로 여겨진다. 새로운 인쇄 공정에 의해 그림책에서 가능해진
혁신에 더해, 시집이나 정보 텍스트와 같은 다른 종류에서도 디자인적 특징이
두드러진다. 이처럼, 읽기는 어린이들의 주의가 인쇄된 텍스트에 집중되고
스케치나 그림이 부속물일 때보다 더 복잡한 종류의 해석이 된다. 이제
어린이들은 그림책을 통해 글과 삽화가 서로를 보완하여 향상한다는 것을
배운다. 읽기는 단순히 **단어 인식**이 아니다. 아무리 쉬운 텍스트에서도 흔히
문장이 '말하는 것'이 그 문장이 의미하는 것이 아니다.

다음 빈칸에 들어갈 말로 가장 적절한 것을 고르시오.
① knowledge acquisition 읽기가 단순히 지식 습득이 아니라는 내용은 아님
　지식 습득
② word recognition 읽기는 단순히 인쇄된 단어를 인식하는 것이 아니라는 내용임
　단어 인식
③ imaginative play 읽기가 창의적 놀이가 아니라는 언급은 아예 없음
　창의적인 놀이
④ subjective interpretation 더 복잡한 종류의 해석이 된다고 했음
　주관적인 해석
⑤ image mapping 사진, 그림 등이 언급된 것으로 만든 오답
　이미지 맵핑

>왜 정답? [정답률 77%]

빈칸 문장	읽기는 단순히 '~'이 아니다.

➡ 빈칸에는 읽기가 단순히 무엇이 아니라고 하는지가 들어가야 한다.

- 이제 '읽기'는 과거 어느 시대보다 훨씬 더 많은 표현 형식에 적용된다. **단서 1**
- 읽기는 어린이들의 주의가 인쇄된 텍스트에 집중되고 스케치나 그림이 부속물일 때보다 더 복잡한 종류의 해석이 된다. **단서 2**
- 아무리 쉬운 텍스트에서도 흔히 문장이 '말하는 것'이 그 문장이 의미하는 것이 아니다. **단서 3**

➡ 이제는 글뿐만 아니라 그림, 지도, 화면, 디자인 그래픽, 사진이 모두 텍스트로 여겨지므로 읽기 또한 이러한 다양한 표현 방식에 적용되고 읽기가 인쇄된 텍스트에 집중하는 것보다 더 복잡한 종류의 해석이 되며, 문장이 말하는 것이 문장이 의미하는 것은 아니라는 내용의 글이다.

▶ 그러므로 읽기는 단순한 '단어 인식'이 아니라는 것이 되어야 하므로 ②가 정답이다.

>왜 오답?

① 읽기가 단순히 지식 습득이 아니라고 하지 않았다.
③ 읽기가 창의적인 놀이가 아니라는 내용은 나오지 않았다.
④ 더 복잡한 종류의 해석이 된다고 했으므로 빈칸에 들어갈 말로 적절하지 않다.
⑤ 사진, 그림 등이 언급된 것으로 만든 오답일 뿐, 읽기가 단순히 이미지 맵핑은 아니라는 내용이 아니다.

류이레 | 연세대 의예과 2024년 입학·광주대동고 졸

이 문제에서는 '글을 읽는 방법을 배우는 것'을 화제로 글이 시작되고 바로 필자의 생각이 나타나는데, 필자는 그림이나 지도와 같은 요소들이 글과 높은 관련성을 지니는 것으로 인식된다고 했어.

Thus 뒤에서 '읽기'가 그림과 같은 부속물들과 함께 있는 대상을 해석하는 복잡한 과정이라고 하며 주장을 끝맺지. 이를 토대로 '필자는 글을 읽는 과정을 단순한 글자 인식으로 여기지 않는구나!'라고 생각했고, 빈칸 앞의 not에 유의하며 정답을 고를 수 있었지.

K 83 정답 ① * 진정한 철학자가 관심을 둔 것

단수 주어
One of the criticisms of Stoicism / by modern translators and teachers / **단수 동사** is the amount of repetition. //

스토아 철학에 대한 비판 중 하나는 / 현대 번역가들과 교사들에 의한 / 반복의 정도이다 //

Marcus Aurelius, for example, has been dismissed / by **동명사의 부정형: 동명사 앞에 부정어를 씀** academics / as not being original / because his writing resembles / **writing** that of other, earlier Stoics. //

예를 들어 Marcus Aurelius는 무시되었다 / 학자들에 의해 / 독창적이지 않다고 / 그의 글이 닮았기 때문에 / 다른 앞선 스토아 철학자들의 그것과 //

This criticism misses the point. //
이러한 비판은 핵심을 놓친다 // **단서 1** 독창적이지 않다는 비판은 핵심을 놓치는 것임

Even before Marcus's time, / Seneca was well aware / that there was a lot of borrowing and overlap / among the philosophers. //
Marcus 시대 이전에도 / Seneca는 잘 알고 있었다 / 많은 차용과 중복이 있다는 것을 / 철학자들 사이에 //

That's because real philosophers weren't concerned / with authorship, / but only what worked. // **단서 2** 진정한 철학자는 차용과 중복에 관심이 없고 효과가 있는지에만 관심을 둠
그것은 왜냐하면 진정한 철학자들이 관심을 두지 않았고 / 원저라는 것에 / 오직 효과가 있는 것에만 (관심을 두었기 때문이다) //

주어 **동사** More important, / they believed / that what was said / mattered less / than what was done. // **단서 3** 말로 한 것보다 행동으로 한 것이 더 중요함
더 중요한 것은 / 그들은 믿었다 / 말해진 것이 / 덜 중요하다고 / 행해진 것보다 //

And this is true now / as it was then. //
그리고 이것은 지금도 사실이다 / 그것이 그때 그랬던 것처럼 //

You're welcome / to take all of the words / of the great philosophers / **병렬 구조** and use them / to your own liking / (they're dead; / they don't mind). //
여러분은 원한다면 ~해도 된다 / 모든 말을 가져다가 / 위대한 철학자들의 / 그것들을 사용해도 / 자신의 취향에 맞게 / (그들은 죽었다 / 그들은 개의치 않는다) //

Feel free to make adjustments and improvements / as you like. //
맘껏 수정하고 개선하라 / 여러분이 원하는 대로 //

Adapt them / to the real conditions / of the real world. //
그것을 적용하라 / 실제 여건에 맞게 / 실제 세계의 //

The way to prove / that you truly understand / what you speak **주어** **형용사적 용법(The way 수식)** and write, / that you truly are original, / is to **put them into** **동사 명사적 용법(주격 보어)** **practice**. //
증명하는 방법은 / 여러분이 참으로 이해하고 있다는 것을 / 자신이 말하고 쓴 것을 / 여러분이 진정으로 독창적이라는 것을 / 그것들을 실행에 옮기는 것이다 //

- criticism ⓝ 비판 • repetition ⓝ 반복 • dismiss ⓥ 무시하다
- borrowing ⓝ 차용 • overlap ⓝ 중복
- philosopher ⓝ 철학자 • authorship ⓝ 원저자
- matter ⓥ 문제가 되다 • feel free to 마음대로 ~하다
- adjustment ⓝ 수정 • improvement ⓝ 개선
- adapt ⓥ 적용하다 • put ... into practice ~을 실행에 옮기다

현대 번역가들과 교사들이 스토아 철학을 비판하는 것 중 하나는 반복의 정도이다. 예를 들어, Marcus Aurelius는 그의 글이 다른 앞선 스토아 철학자들의 글과 닮았기 때문에 독창적이지 않다고 학자들에 의해 무시되었다. 이러한 비판은 핵심을 놓친다. Marcus 시대 이전에도 Seneca는 철학자들 사이에 많은 차용과 중복이 있다는 것을 잘 알고 있었다. 그것은 진정한 철학자들이 원저자라는 것에 관심을 두지 않고 오직 효과가 있는 것에만 관심을 두었기 때문이다. 더 중요한 것은, 그들은 말로 한 것이 행동으로 한 것보다 덜 중요하다고 믿었다는 점이다. 그리고 이것은 그때처럼 지금도 사실이다. 원한다면 위대한 철학자들의 모든 말을 가져다가 자신의 취향에 맞게 사용해도 된다(그들은 죽었으니 개의치 않는다). 원하는 대로 맘껏 수정하고 개선하라. 그것을 실제 세계의 실제 여건에 맞게 적용하라. 여러분이 자신이 말하고 쓴 것을 참으로 이해하고 있다는 것, 자신이 진정으로 독창적이라는 것을 증명하는 방법은 **그것들을 실행에 옮기는** 것이다.

다음 빈칸에 들어갈 말로 가장 적절한 것을 고르시오. [3점]

① **put them into practice** what was said mattered less than what was done
그것들을 실행에 옮기다
② **keep your writings to yourself** 진정한 철학자는 차용과 중복에 관심을 두지 않음
여러분의 글을 여러분만 알고 숨기다
③ **combine oral and written traditions** 전통을 결합하라는 것이 아님
구두로 그리고 글로 전해진 전통을 결합하다
④ **compare philosophical theories** 철학 이론 간의 비교에 대한 언급은 없음
철학적 이론들을 비교하다
⑤ **avoid borrowing them** 마음껏 차용하라는 내용임
그것들을 차용하는 것을 피하다

>왜 정답? [정답률 45%]

- 앞선 철학자들을 차용하고 독창적이지 않다고 Marcus Aurelius를 비판하는 것은 핵심을 놓치는 것임 **단서 1**
- 진정한 철학자는 원저자라는 것에 관심을 두지 않고, 오직 효과가 있는 것에만 관심을 두었음 **단서 2**
- 말로 한 것보다 행동으로 한 것이 더 중요함 **단서 3**

➡ 차용과 중복, 독창성이 중요한 것이 아니라 실제로 행하는 것이 중요하다고 말하는 글이다.
▶ 따라서 빈칸에는 ① '그것들을 실행에 옮기다'가 적절하다.

>왜 오답?

② 자신의 글이 차용되지 않도록 주의하라는 내용이 아니다.
③ 스토아 철학자, Marcus 시대 등이 언급된 것으로 만든 오답이다.
④ 철학적 이론들을 비교하는 것이 중요하다는 내용이 아니다.
⑤ 원하는 대로 차용하라고 했다.

K 84 정답 ③ *언어가 인식에 미치는 영향

단수 주어 **단서1** 우리가 사용하는 말이 우리가 인식하는 방식에 영향을 미침
The way / we perceive / the colors of the rainbow, and the
앞에 목적격 관계대명사가 생략됨
universe in general, / is influenced / by the words / we use / to
단수 동사
describe them. //
방식은 / 우리가 인식하는 / 무지개의 색깔들, 그리고 우주 일반을 / 영향을 받는다 / 말들에
의해 / 우리가 사용하는 / 그것들을 묘사하기 위해

This is not limited / to visual perception / but also applies / to
is limited와 applies가 not (only) A but also B로 연결됨
smell, taste, touch, our perception of time and countless other
human experiences. //
이것은 국한되는 것이 아니라 / 시각적인 인식에 / 또한 적용된다 / 후각, 미각, 촉각, 시간에
대한 우리의 인식, 수많은 여타 인간의 경험에도 //

비교급 강조 부사
A wine or Scotch connoisseur, / for example, / has a much richer
vocabulary at their disposal / to describe the fullness, finish,
flavors and aroma of the drink, / **단서2** 와인이나 스카치위스키 감정가는 훨씬 더
풍부한 어휘를 마음대로 사용함
와인이나 스카치위스키 감정가는 / 예를 들어 / 훨씬 더 풍부한 어휘를 마음대로 사용하고 / 그
음료의 풍부함, 끝맛, 맛과 향을 묘사하는 데 /

형용사적 용법(ability 수식)
which in turn improves their ability / to recognize and remember
subtle differences / of which a non-expert may be unaware. //
그것이 결국 그들의 능력을 향상시킨다 / 미묘한 차이를 인식하고 기억하는 / 비전문가라면
모를 수 있는 // **단서3** 그들의 어휘가 미묘한 차이를 인식하는 그들의 능력을 향상시킴

Similarly, / a chef or perfumer has at their disposal labels / for
flavors and smells / that allow them / to perceive, differentiate
among, prepare and remember / subtle variations. //
마찬가지로 / 요리사나 조향사는 라벨을 마음대로 사용한다 / 맛과 향에 대한 / 그들로 하여금
~하게 하는 / 인지하고, 구별하며, 준비하고, 기억하게 / 미묘한 차이를 //
복수 주어
The labels / that we have at our disposal / influence / how we see
복수 동사
the world around us. // **단서4** 우리가 사용하는 라벨(말)이 우리가
세상을 인식하는 방식에 영향을 미침
라벨이 / 우리가 마음대로 사용하는 / 영향을 준다 / 우리가 우리 주변의 세상을 보는 방식에 //

Regardless of where you place the limits / of linguistic effects /
on cognition, /
한계를 어디에 두느냐와 상관없이 / 언어적 영향의 / 인식에 미치는 /

there is evidence / that at least some of the things / that we
동격절 접속사
perceive and remember / differ / depending on **what labels we
use**. //
증거가 있다 / 적어도 ~한 것의 일부는 / 우리가 인식하고 기억하는 / 달라진다는 / 우리가
무슨 라벨을 사용하느냐에 따라 //

- perceive ⓥ 인식하다 · perception ⓝ 인식
- apply ⓥ 적용하다 · countless ⓐ 수많은
- fullness ⓝ 풍부함 · in turn 결국 · subtle ⓐ 미묘한
- perfumer ⓝ 조향사 · at one's disposal 마음대로
- differentiate ⓥ 구별하다 · variation ⓝ 차이
- regardless of ~에 관계없이 · linguistic ⓐ 언어적인

우리가 무지개의 색깔들, 그리고 우주 일반을 인식하는 방식은 그것들을
묘사하기 위해 우리가 사용하는 말들에 의해 영향을 받는다. 이것은 시각적인
인식에 국한되는 것이 아니라 후각, 미각, 촉각, 시간에 대한 우리의 인식,
수많은 여타 인간의 경험에도 적용된다. 예를 들어 와인이나 스카치위스키
감정가는 그 음료의 풍부함, 끝맛, 맛과 향을 묘사하는 데 훨씬 더 풍부한
어휘를 마음대로 사용하고 그것이 결국 비전문가라면 모를 수 있는 미묘한
차이를 인식하고 기억하는 그들의 능력을 향상시킨다. 마찬가지로 요리사나
조향사는 미묘한 차이를 인지하고, 구별하며, 준비하고, 기억할 수 있게 해
주는, 맛과 향에 대한 라벨을 마음대로 사용한다. 우리가 마음대로 사용하는
라벨이 우리가 우리 주변의 세상을 보는 방식에 영향을 준다. 인식에 미치는
언어적 영향의 한계를 어디에 두느냐와 상관없이 적어도 우리가 인식하고
기억하는 것의 일부는 **우리가 무슨 라벨을 사용하느냐**에 따라 달라진다는
증거가 있다.

다음 빈칸에 들어갈 말로 가장 적절한 것을 고르시오. [3점]

① where we purchase them 구입과 관련된 내용이 아님
우리가 그것들을 어디에서 구입하느냐
② how expensive they are 와인의 가격에 미치는 영향은 언급되지 않음
그것들이 얼마나 비싸느냐
③ what labels we use '라벨'이 곧 '언어', '어휘'를 의미함
우리가 무슨 라벨을 사용하느냐
④ how persuasive ads are 무지개, 우주 일반에도 적용되어야 함
광고가 얼마나 설득력 있느냐
⑤ who makes the products '라벨'의 의미를 잘못 이해한 것임
누가 그 제품을 만드느냐

> **왜 정답?** [정답률 71%]

빈칸 문장	우리가 인식하고 기억하는 것의 일부는 '무엇'에 따라 달라진다.

→ 빈칸에는 우리의 인식과 기억에 영향을 미치는 것이 들어가야 함

- 우리가 무지개의 색깔, 우주를 인식하는 방식은 그것들을 묘사하는 데 우리가 사용하는 말에 영향을 받는다. **단서1**
- 와인이나 스카치위스키 감정가는 음료를 묘사하는 데 훨씬 더 풍부한 어휘를 사용하고, 이는 미묘한 차이를 인식하는 그들의 능력을 향상시킨다. **단서2 단서3**
- 우리가 사용하는 라벨이 우리가 주변 세상을 인식하는 방식에 영향을 미친다. **단서4**

→ 와인의 맛과 향에 붙이는 '라벨', 즉 와인의 맛과 향을 묘사하는 '어휘'가 와인의 맛과
향을 '인식하고 기억하는' 능력에 영향을 미친다는 내용이다.
▶ 그러므로 우리의 인식과 기억에 미치는 것은 ③ '우리가 어떤 라벨을
사용하느냐'이다.

> **왜 오답?**

① some of the things는 물건만 가리키는 것이 아니다.
② 가격이 인식에 영향을 미친다는 언급은 없다.
④ 광고가 미치는 영향에 대해서는 전혀 이야기하지 않았다.
⑤ 와인, 스카치위스키뿐만 아니라 무지개, 우주 일반도 언급되었다는 사실을
기억해야 한다. 함정

K 85 정답 ② *우리의 뇌의 시각적 전략

주어 동사 **단서1** 우리는 대부분 우리가 볼
것이라고 기대하는 것을 봄
A large part / of what we see / is what we expect / to see. //
많은 부분은 / 우리가 보는 것의 / 우리가 기대하는 것이다 / 볼 것이라고 // 주격 보어

This explains / why we "see" faces and figures / in a flickering
목적격절을 이끄는 의문사
campfire, / or in moving clouds. //
이것은 설명한다 / 왜 우리가 얼굴과 형상을 '보는지'를 / 흔들리는 모닥불에서 / 또는 움직이
는 구름 속에서 //
주격 보어절을 이끄는 의문사
This is why Leonardo da Vinci advised artists / to discover their
주어 동사 목적어 목적격 보어
motifs / by staring at patches on a blank wall. //
이것이 Leonardo da Vinci가 화가들에게 권한 이유이다 / 그들의 모티프를 찾으라고 / 빈
벽의 부분들을 응시함으로써 //

A fire provides a constant flickering change / in visual
information / that never integrates / into anything solid / and
병렬 구조 allows의 목적격 보어
thereby allows the brain to engage / in a play of hypotheses. //
불은 지속적으로 흔들리는 변화를 제공하고 / 시각 정보에 있어 / 절대 통합되지 않는다 / (형
태가) 확실한 어떤 것에도 / 그렇게 함으로써 뇌가 참여할 수 있게 한다 / 가설 놀이에 //

On the other hand, / the wall does not present us with very
much / in the way of visual clues, /
반면에 / 벽은 우리에게 그다지 많이 주지 않고 / 시각적인 단서라고 할 만한 것을 /

and so the brain begins to make / more and more hypotheses /
병렬 구조
and desperately searches for confirmation. // **단서2** 뇌가 가설을 세우고
가설을 확인해주는 것을 찾음
그래서 뇌는 세우기 시작하고 / 점점 더 많은 가설을 / 필사적으로 확인을 모색한다 //

A crack in the wall / looks a little like the profile of a nose /
and suddenly a whole face appears, / or a leaping horse, / or a
dancing figure. //
뒤에 appears가 생략됨
벽에 난 금이 / 코의 옆모습과 약간 닮아 / 갑자기 얼굴 전체가 나타나거나 / 또는 도약하는 말
이 / 또는 춤추는 형상이 (나타나기도 한다) // 주어
동사 주격 보어(동명사)
In cases like these / the brain's visual strategies are **projecting
images / from within the mind / out onto the world**. //
이와 같은 경우에 / 뇌의 시각적 전략은 이미지를 투영하는 것이다 / 마음속으로부터 / 세계로

- figure ⓝ 형상, 인물   · motif ⓝ 모티프, 주제   · stare at ~을 응시하다
- patch ⓝ (특히 주변과는 다른 조그만) 부분
- constant ⓐ 끊임없는, 거듭되는   · integrate ⓥ 통합되다
- solid ⓐ 확실한, 단단한   · thereby ⓐⅾ 그렇게 함으로써
- engage in ~에 참여하다   · hypothesis ⓝ 가설
- in the way of (의문문이나 부정문에서) ~라고 할 만한 것이
- desperately ⓐⅾ 절망적으로, 필사적으로   · confirmation ⓝ 확인
- crack ⓝ (무엇이 갈라져 생긴) 금   · profile ⓝ 옆모습, 옆얼굴
- leap ⓥ 뛰다, 뛰어오르다[넘다]   · strategy ⓝ 전략
- distract ⓥ (정신이) 집중이 안 되게[산만하게] 하다
- project ⓥ (빛·영상 등을) 비추대[투영하다]   · strengthen ⓥ 강화하다

우리가 보는 것의 많은 부분은 우리가 볼 것이라 기대하는 것이다. 이것은 왜 우리가 흔들리는 모닥불이나 움직이는 구름 속에서 얼굴과 형상을 '보는지'를 설명한다. 이것이 Leonardo da Vinci가 화가들에게 빈 벽의 부분들을 응시함으로써 그들의 모티프를 찾으라고 권한 이유이다. 불은 (형태가) 확실한 어떤 것에도 절대 통합되지 않는 시각 정보에 있어 지속적으로 흔들리는 변화를 제공하고, 그렇게 함으로써 뇌가 가설 놀이에 참여할 수 있게 한다. 반면에, 벽은 우리에게 시각적인 단서라고 할 만한 것을 그다지 많이 주지 않고, 그래서 뇌는 점점 더 많은 가설을 세우기 시작하고 필사적으로 확인을 모색한다. 벽에 난 금이 코의 옆모습과 약간 닮아 갑자기 얼굴 전체가 나타나거나, 도약하는 말 또는 춤추는 형상이 나타나기도 한다. 이와 같은 경우에 뇌의 시각적 전략은 마음속으로부터 이미지를 세계로 투영하는 것이다.

다음 빈칸에 들어갈 말로 가장 적절한 것을 고르시오. [3점]
특정 정보를 무시하는 것에 대한 언급은 없음
① ignoring distracting information unrelated to visual clues
시각적 단서와 관련이 없는 정신을 산만하게 하는 정보를 무시하는 것
②projecting images from within the mind out onto the world
이미지를 마음속으로부터 세계로 투영하는 것   뇌에서 가설을 세우고 그 가설을 확인해주는 것을 찾음
③ categorizing objects into groups either real or imagined
사물을 실제이거나 상상한 그룹으로 범주화하여 분류하는 것   사물을 분류하는 것에 대한 내용이 아님
④ strengthening connections between objects in the real world
현실 세계에서 사물들 간의 관련성을 강화하는 것   사물들 간의 관련성을 강화한다는 언급은 없음
⑤ removing the broken or missing parts of an original image
원래의 상(像)에서 부서지거나 유실된 부분을 제거하는 것   crack으로 만든 오답

왜 정답? [정답률 50%]   = 우리가 볼 것이라고 기대하는 이미지 / = 우리 마음에 있는 이미지 꿀팁

첫 문장에서부터 우리가 보는 것의 대부분이 우리가 볼 것이라고 기대하는 것이라고 했는데, 이것이 우리의 뇌가 만든 이미지를 바깥세상으로 투영한다는 의미임을 추론해야 한다. 시각적 단서를 별로 주지 않는 벽을 보면서 우리의 뇌는 가설을 세우고, 그것을 확인해주는 것을 찾는다는 후반부의 내용 역시 ② '이미지를 마음속으로부터 세계로 투영하는 것'이 우리 뇌의 전략임을 의미한다.

왜 오답?
① 우리의 뇌가 어떤 정보를 무시하는 것이 아니라 오히려 마음속에 있는 정보를 실제 세계에서 찾아내는 것이다.
③ 사물들을 범주화하거나 분류한다는 내용이 아니다.
④ 사물들 간의 관련성에 대한 언급은 없다.
⑤ crack이 언급된 것으로 만든 오답이다. 우리의 뇌가 원래의 상에서 부서지거나 유실된 부분을 제거한다는 것은 언급되지 않았다.

K 86 정답 ② ＊교육 기술의 성공적인 통합
전치사 by의 목적어로 쓰인   단서1 교육 기술의 성공적인 통합은 사용자가 그것을
동명사 being의 의미상 주어   학습, 교육, 수행의 촉진자로 여길 때 일어남
Successful integration of an educational technology / is marked / by that technology being regarded by users /
교육 기술의 성공적인 통합은 / 나타난다 / 그 기술이 사용자에 의해 여겨지는 것에 의해 /

as an unobtrusive facilitator / of learning, instruction, or performance. //   단서2 기술의 사용에서 교육적 목적으로
눈에 띄지 않는 촉진자로 / 학습이나 교육, 또는 수행의 //   초점이 옮겨갈 때 성공적인 통합으로 여겨질 수 있음
When the focus shifts / from the technology being used / to the educational purpose / that technology serves, /   from A to B: A에서 B로
초점이 옮겨갈 때 / 사용되고 있는 기술에서 / 교육적 목적으로 / 기술이 이바지하는 /

then that technology is becoming / a comfortable and trusted element, / and can be regarded / as being successfully integrated. //   병렬 구조   전치사 as의 목적어로 쓰인 동명사구
그 기술은 되고 있다 / 편안하고 신뢰할 수 있는 요소가 / 그리고 여겨질 수 있다 / 성공적으로 통합되고 있다고 //

준부정어: 거의 없는
Few people give a second thought / to the use of a ball-point pen   양보의 부사절 접속사
/ although the mechanisms involved vary /
재고하는 사람들은 거의 없다 / 볼펜 사용법에 대해 / 그 관련된 구조가 다양하지만 /

— some use a twist mechanism / and some use a push button on top, / and there are other variations as well. //
어떤 것들은 돌리는 방법을 사용하고 / 또 어떤 것들은 위에 달린 누름단추를 사용하며 / 그리고 다른 변형들도 있다 //

Personal computers have reached / a similar level of familiarity / for a great many users, / but certainly not for all. //
개인용 컴퓨터는 도달했다 / 비슷한 수준의 친숙함에 / 아주 많은 사용자들에게 / 그러나 분명 모두에게 그렇지는 않다 //

New and emerging technologies often introduce / both fascination and frustration / with users. //
새롭고 떠오르는 기술은 흔히 경험하게 한다 / 매력과 좌절감 둘 다를 / 사용자들에게 //
부사절 접속사(~하는 한)
As long as **the user's focus is / on the technology itself / rather than its use** / in promoting learning, instruction, or performance, /
사용자의 초점이 있는 한 / 기술 그 자체에 / 그것의 사용이 아니라 / 학습, 교육 또는 수행을 촉진하는 데 있어서 /   단서3 기술이 성공적으로 통합되었다고 볼 수 없는 경우를 빈칸에서 설명함

then one ought not to conclude / that the technology has been successfully integrated / — at least for that user. //   현재완료 수동태(완료)
결론 내려서는 안 된다 / 그 기술이 성공적으로 통합되었다고 / 적어도 그 사용자에게는 //

- integration ⓝ 통합   · facilitator ⓝ 일을 용이하게 하는 것[사람], 촉진자
- vary ⓥ 서로[각기] 다르다   · twist ⓝ 돌리기, 비틀기
- variation ⓝ 변화, 변형   · familiarity ⓝ 익숙함, 친근함
- certainly ⓐⅾ 틀림없이, 분명히   · emerging ⓐ 신흥의, 떠오르는
- introduce ⓥ (모르던 것을) 소개하다[접하게 하다]
- fascination ⓝ 매력, 매혹   · frustration ⓝ 불만, 좌절감
- outdated ⓐ 구식인   · involuntarily ⓐⅾ 모르는 사이에, 본의 아니게
- misuse ⓝ 남용, 오용   · persist ⓥ 계속[지속]되다

교육 기술의 성공적인 통합은 그 기술이 사용자에 의해 학습이나 교육, 또는 수행의 눈에 띄지 않는 촉진자로 여겨지는 것으로 나타난다. 사용되고 있는 기술에서 기술이 이바지하는 교육적 목적으로 초점이 옮겨갈 때, 그 기술은 편안하고 신뢰할 수 있는 요소가 되고 있으며, 성공적으로 통합되고 있다고 여겨질 수 있다. 어떤 것들은 돌리는 방법을 사용하고, 또 어떤 것들은 위에 달린 누름단추를 사용하며, 그리고 다른 변형된 방법들도 있을 정도로 그 구조가 다양하지만, 볼펜 사용법에 대해 재고하는 사람들은 거의 없다. 개인용 컴퓨터는 아주 많은 사용자들에게 (볼펜과) 비슷한 수준의 친숙함에 도달했지만, 분명 모두에게 그렇지는 않다. 새롭게 떠오르는 기술은 흔히 사용자들에게 매력과 좌절감 둘 다를 경험하게 한다. 학습, 교육 또는 수행을 촉진하는 데 있어서 **사용자의 초점이 기술의 사용이 아니라 기술 그 자체에 맞춰져 있는** 한, 적어도 그 사용자에게는 그 기술이 성공적으로 통합되었다는 결론을 내려서는 안 된다.

교육적 목적으로 옮겨가야 성공적으로 통합되는 것임
다음 빈칸에 들어갈 말로 가장 적절한 것을 고르시오. [3점]
① the user successfully achieves familiarity with the technology
사용자가 성공적으로 그 기술에 대한 친숙함을 얻는   familiarity가 언급된 것으로 만든 오답
②the user's focus is on the technology itself rather than its use
사용자의 초점이 기술의 사용이 아니라 기술 그 자체에 맞춰져 있는
③ the user continues to employ outdated educational techniques
사용자가 계속 구식의 교육 기술을 사용하는   교육 기술이 구식인지 여부는 언급되지 않음
④ the user involuntarily gets used to the misuse of the technology
사용자가 무의식적으로 그 기술의 오용에 익숙해지는   기술의 오용이라는 내용이 아님
⑤ the user's preference for interaction with other users persists
다른 사용자와의 상호 작용에 대한 사용자의 선호가 지속되는   다른 사용자와의 상호 작용에 대한 언급은 없음

왜 정답? [정답률 48%]

처음 두 문장에서 기술의 성공적인 통합은 그 기술이 사용자에 의해 학습이나 교육, 수행의 촉진자로 여겨질 때 나타나고, 기술의 사용에서 기술의 교육적 목적으로 초점이 옮겨갈 때 성공적으로 통합되고 있는 것이라고 했다. 빈칸 문장은 기술이 성공적으로 통합되었다고 결론 지을 수 없는 경우를 설명하는데, 이는 사용자의 초점이 학습, 교육, 수행을 촉진하는 데 있어서의 기술의 사용이 아니라 기술 그 자체에 맞춰져 있는 경우이므로 빈칸에는 ② '사용자의 초점이 기술의 사용이 아니라 기술 그 자체에 맞춰져 있는'이 들어가야 한다.   즉, 개인용 컴퓨터에서 개인용 컴퓨터의 사용법으로 초점을 이동시키지 못한 경우를 의미 꿀팁

① 개인용 컴퓨터가 볼펜과 비슷한 수준의 친숙함에 도달했다는 내용으로 만든 오답이다.

③ 구식의 교육 기술을 비판하는 것이 아니다. 교육 기술이 교육적 목적으로 사용되는지 여부가 핵심이다. 함정

④ 기술의 오용에 무의식적으로 익숙해지는 것을 성공적인 통합으로 볼 수 없다는 내용이 아니다.

⑤ 다른 사용자와의 상호 작용에 대해서는 언급되지 않았다.

K 87 정답 ⑤ * 소멸한 컴퓨터 아티스트

Young contemporary artists / who employ digital technologies / in their practice / rarely make reference to computers. //
주어 / 준부정어 / 동사
젊은 현대 미술가들은 / 디지털 기술을 이용하는 / 자기 일에 / 컴퓨터를 거의 언급하지 않는다 //

For example, / Wade Guyton, / an abstractionist / who uses a word processing program and inkjet printers, / does not call himself a computer artist. // 단서1 젊은 현대 미술가인 Wade Guyton은 스스로를 컴퓨터 아티스트라고 부르지 않음
주어 / 목적어 / 목적격 보어 / 동사
예를 들어 / Wade Guyton은 / 추상파 화가인 / 워드 프로세싱 프로그램과 잉크젯식 프린터를 사용하는 / 자신을 컴퓨터 아티스트라고 부르지 않는다 //

Moreover, / some critics, / who admire his work, / are little concerned / about his extensive use of computers / in the art-making process. //
준부정어
게다가 / 몇몇 비평가들은 / 그의 작품을 높이 평가하는 / 거의 신경 쓰지 않는다 / 그의 광범위한 컴퓨터 사용에 관해 / 예술 창작 과정에서 //

This is a marked contrast / from three decades ago / when artists / who utilized computers / were labeled by critics / — often disapprovingly — / as computer artists. //
주어 / 동사
이것은 뚜렷한 대조이다 / 30년 전과 / 미술가들이 / 컴퓨터를 활용하는 / 비평가들에 의해 명명되었던 / 자주 탐탁지 않게 / 컴퓨터 아티스트라고 // 단서2 30년 전에는 컴퓨터를 활용하는 미술가들을 컴퓨터 아티스트라고 명명했음

For the present generation of artists, / the computer, or more appropriately, the laptop, / is one /
현세대의 미술가들에게 / 컴퓨터 혹은 더욱 적절히는 휴대용 컴퓨터는 / 하나이다 /

in a collection of integrated, portable digital technologies / that link their social and working life. //
일련의 통합된, 휴대 가능한 디지털 기술 중 / 그들의 사회생활과 직업 생활을 연결하는 //

With tablets and cell phones / surpassing personal computers / in Internet usage, /
with+(대)명사+현재분사: ~이 …한 채로
태블릿 컴퓨터와 휴대 전화가 / 개인용 컴퓨터를 능가하고 / 인터넷 사용에서 /

and as slim digital devices resemble nothing / like the room-sized mainframes and bulky desktop computers / of previous decades, / 단서3 오늘날의 디지털 기기들은 예전의 컴퓨터 같지 않음
〈이유〉의 부사절 접속사
그리고 얇은 디지털 기기들이 전혀 닮지 않았으므로 / 방 크기의 중앙 컴퓨터와 부피가 큰 탁상용 컴퓨터와 / 수십 년 전의 /

it now appears / that the computer artist is finally extinct. //
가주어 / 진주어절 접속사
오늘날에는 ~으로 보인다 / 컴퓨터 아티스트가 결국 소멸한 것으로 //

• contemporary ⓐ 현대의, 동시대의
• employ ⓥ (기술 · 방법 등을) 쓰다[이용하다]
• practice ⓝ (의사 · 변호사 등 전문직 종사자의) 업무
• reference ⓝ 언급, 참조   • abstractionist ⓝ 추상파 화가
• critic ⓝ 비평가, 평론가   • admire ⓥ 칭찬하다, 감탄하다
• marked ⓐ 뚜렷한   • contrast ⓝ 차이, 대조
• label ⓥ 꼬리표를 붙이다, (~라고) 분류하다
• disapprovingly ⓐⓓ 못마땅하여, 비난하여
• appropriately ⓐⓓ 적당하게, 알맞게   • integrate ⓥ 통합하다
• portable ⓐ 휴대가 쉬운, 휴대용의   • surpass ⓥ 능가하다, 뛰어넘다
• resemble ⓥ 닮다, 비슷하다   • bulky ⓐ 부피가 큰

자기 일에 디지털 기술을 이용하는 젊은 현대 미술가들은 컴퓨터를 거의 언급하지 않는다. 예를 들어, 워드 프로세싱 프로그램과 잉크젯식 프린터를 사용하는 추상파 화가인 Wade Guyton은 자신을 컴퓨터 아티스트라고 부르지 않는다. 게다가, 그의 작품을 높이 평가하는 몇몇 비평가들은 예술 창작 과정에서 그의 광범위한 컴퓨터 사용에 관해 거의 신경 쓰지 않는다. 이것은 컴퓨터를 활용하는 미술가들이 비평가들에 의해, 자주 탐탁지 않게, 컴퓨터 아티스트라고 명명되었던 30년 전과 뚜렷이 대조된다. 현세대의 미술가들에게 컴퓨터, 혹은 더욱 적절히는 휴대용 컴퓨터는, 그들의 사회생활과 직업 생활을 연결하는 일련의 통합된, 휴대 가능한 디지털 기술 중 하나이다. 인터넷 사용에서 태블릿 컴퓨터와 휴대 전화가 개인용 컴퓨터를 능가하는 상황에서, 그리고 얇은 디지털 기기들이 수십 년 전의 방 크기의 중앙 컴퓨터와 부피가 큰 탁상용 컴퓨터와 전혀 닮지 않았으므로, 오늘날에는 컴퓨터 아티스트가 결국 소멸한 것으로 보인다.

다음 빈칸에 들어갈 말로 가장 적절한 것을 고르시오.

① awake 깨어 있는   컴퓨터 아티스트가 있었던 것은 30년 전임
② influential 영향력 있는   컴퓨터를 사용하든 말든 상관하지 않음
③ distinct 뚜렷이 다른   뚜렷이 다른 게 아니라 사라졌음
④ troublesome 골칫거리의   디지털 기술을 이용하는 것이 자연스러움
⑤ extinct 소멸한   30년 전에는 있었지만 오늘날에는 없음

➤왜 정답? [정답률 37%]

30년 전에는 컴퓨터를 활용하는 미술가들을 컴퓨터 아티스트라고 명명했지만, 오늘날 디지털 기술을 이용하는 젊은 현대 미술가들은 컴퓨터를 거의 언급하지 않고, Wade Guyton은 디지털 기술을 이용하더라도 자신을 컴퓨터 아티스트라고 부르지 않는다고 했다.

또한, 오늘날의 디지털 기기들은 예전의 컴퓨터와 전혀 닮지 않았고, 인터넷 사용에 있어 태블릿과 휴대 전화가 개인용 컴퓨터를 능가한다고 한 것으로 보아 마지막 문장은 컴퓨터 아티스트가 오늘날에는 결국 ⑤ '소멸한' 것으로 보인다는 내용이 되어야 한다.

➤왜 오답?

① 30년 전, 수십 년 전과 달리 오늘날에는 컴퓨터 아티스트가 존재하지 않는다는 내용이다.

② 워드 프로세싱 프로그램 등의 디지털 기술을 이용하더라도 스스로를 컴퓨터 아티스트라고 부르지 않는다고 했으므로 컴퓨터 아티스트가 영향력을 갖는 것이 아니다.

③ 컴퓨터 아티스트가 30년 전과 뚜렷이 대조되는 것이 아니라 더이상 존재하지 않는 것이다.

④ 오늘날에는 디지털 기술을 이용하는 것에 거의 신경 쓰지 않는다고 했으므로 컴퓨터 아티스트가 골칫거리라는 말은 글에 맞지 않는다.

K 88 정답 ② * 원시 자연이라는 허황된 생각

Concepts of nature / are always cultural statements. //
자연에 대한 개념은 / 항상 문화적 진술이다 //

This may not strike Europeans / as much of an insight, / for Europe's landscape is so much of a blend. //
much of a(n): 대단한, 심한, 지독한 / 부사절 접속사(이유)
이것은 유럽인들에게 인상을 주지 않을 수도 있다 / 대단한 통찰이라는 / 유럽의 풍경은 너무나 많이 혼합되어 있기 때문에 // 크게[대단히] ~한

But in the new worlds / — 'new' at least to Europeans — / the distinction appeared much clearer / not only to European settlers and visitors / but also to their descendants. //
비교급 강조 부사 / not only A but also B(A뿐만 아니라 B도)로 연결된 전치사구
그러나 새로운 세계에서 / 적어도 유럽인들에게는 '새로운' / 그 차이는 훨씬 더 분명해 보였다 / 유럽 정착민과 방문객뿐만 아니라 / 그들의 후손에게도 //

For that reason, / they had the fond conceit / of primeval nature / uncontrolled by human associations / which could later find expression / in an admiration for wilderness. //
선행사 / 주격 관계대명사
그런 이유로 / 그들은 허황된 생각을 갖고 있었다 / 원시 자연이라는 / 인간과의 연관에 의해 통제되지 않는 / 후에 표현을 찾을 수 있었던 / 황야에 대한 감탄에서 //

Ecological relationships certainly have / their own logic /
생태학적 관계는 확실히 가지고 있었고 / 그 나름의 논리를 /

and in this sense / 'nature' can be seen to have / a self-regulating but not necessarily stable dynamic / independent of human intervention. // **단서1** 자연이 인간의 개입과 무관한 역동성을 가지고 있다는 내용에 역접으로 연결됨
이런 의미에서 / '자연'은 가지고 있다고 보일 수 있다 / 자율적이지만 반드시 안정적이지는 않은 역동성을 / 인간의 개입과 무관하게 //

But / the context for ecological interactions / **has increasingly been set / by humanity**. //
그러나 / 생태학적 상호 작용의 맥락은 / 점점 더 설정되어 왔다 / 인류에 의해 //
may not determine의 목적어절
We may not determine / how or what a lion eats / but we certainly can regulate / where the lion feeds. //
can regulate의 목적어절
우리는 정하지 못할 수도 있지만 / 사자가 어떻게 또는 무엇을 먹는지는 / 우리는 확실히 규제할 수 있다 / 사자가 어디에서 먹이를 먹을지는 // **단서2** 사자가 어디에서 먹이를 먹는지 인간이 규제할 수 있음

- concept ⓝ 개념 · cultural ⓐ 문화와 관련된 · statement ⓝ 진술
- strike A as B A에게 B라는 인상을 주다 · insight ⓝ 통찰력
- landscape ⓝ 풍경 · blend ⓝ 혼합(물) · distinction ⓝ 차이, 구분
- settler ⓝ 정착민 · descendant ⓝ 후손, 자손
- fond ⓐ 허황된, 좋아하는 · uncontrolled ⓐ 통제되지 않은
- association ⓝ 연관(성), 협회 · expression ⓝ 표현, 표정
- admiration ⓝ 감탄, 존경 · wilderness ⓝ 황야, 황무지
- ecological ⓐ 생태계[학]의 · certainly ⓐⓓ 분명히, 틀림없이
- logic ⓝ 논리 · self-regulating ⓐ 자체적으로 규제하는
- not necessarily 반드시 ~은 아닌 · stable ⓐ 안정된
- dynamic ⓝ 역동성 · independent of ~와는 관계없이
- intervention ⓝ 개입, 중재, 조정 · context ⓝ 맥락, 전후 사정
- interaction ⓝ 상호 작용 · determine ⓥ 결정하다, 알아내다
- regulate ⓥ 규제[통제]하다

자연에 대한 개념은 항상 문화적 진술이다. 이것은 유럽인들에게 대단한 통찰이라는 인상을 주지 않을 수도 있는데, 유럽의 풍경은 너무나 많이 혼합되어 있기 때문이다. 그러나 새로운, 적어도 유럽인들에게는 '새로운', 세계에서, 그 차이는 유럽 정착민과 방문객뿐만 아니라 그들의 후손에게도 훨씬 더 분명해 보였다. 그런 이유로, 그들은 후에 황야에 대한 감탄에서 표현을 찾을 수 있었던 인간과의 연관에 의해 통제되지 않는 원시 자연이라는 허황된 생각을 갖고 있었다. 생태학적 관계는 확실히 그 나름의 논리를 가지고 있었고, 이런 의미에서 '자연'은 인간의 개입과 무관하게, 자율적이지만 반드시 안정적이지는 않은 역동성을 가지고 있다고 볼 수 있다. 그러나 생태학적 상호 작용의 맥락은 **점점 더 인류에 의해 설정되어 왔다**. 우리는 사자가 어떻게 또는 무엇을 먹는지는 정하지 못할 수도 있지만, 사자가 어디에서 먹이를 먹을지는 확실히 규제할 수 있다.

다음 빈칸에 들어갈 말로 가장 적절한 것을 고르시오. [3점]

① has supported new environment-friendly policies
새로운 친환경적인 정책을 지지해 왔다 '정책'과 관련된 내용이 아님
② has increasingly been set by humanity
점점 더 인류에 의해 설정되어 왔다 인간의 개입과 무관하다는 것과 반대되는 내용
③ inspires creative cultural practices
창의적인 문화적 관행을 고취한다 cultural statements로 만든 오답
④ changes too frequently to be regulated
너무 자주 바뀌어 규제될 수 없다 생태학적 상호 작용의 맥락이 자주 바뀐다는 것이 아님
⑤ has been affected by various natural conditions
다양한 자연의 조건에 의해 영향을 받아 왔다 '인간'의 영향을 받는다는 것임

왜 정답? [정답률 56%]

자연이 인간의 개입과 무관하게 자율적인 (그러나 반드시 안정적이지는 않은) 역동성을 가지고 있는 것으로 보일 수 있다는 내용에 역접의 연결어 But으로 이어진 것으로 보아 빈칸 문장은 생태학적 상호 작용의 맥락이 ② '점점 더 인류에 의해 설정되어 왔다'는 내용이 되어야 한다. 이어지는 문장에서도 사자가 어떻게, 무엇을 먹는지는 인간의 개입 없이 결정되지만, 사자가 먹이를 어디에서 먹는지는 인간이 규제할 수 있다고 했다. 꿀팁 but으로 이어지는 내용이 핵심이며, 낮은 가능성을 나타내는 조동사 may와 부사 certainly의 수식을 받는 조동사 can이 대조됨

왜 오답?

① 자연에 대한 인간의 개입에 관련된 내용인 것은 맞지만, 정책을 통한 인간의 개입을 설명하는 것은 아니다.
③ 자연에 대한 개념이 항상 문화적 진술(cultural statements)이라고 한 첫 문장으로 만든 오답이다.
④ 이어지는 문장에서 생태학적 상호 작용의 맥락이 인간에 의해 규제됨을 보여주는 예시를 들었으므로 정답이 될 수 없다.
⑤ 생태학적 상호 작용의 맥락이 자연적 조건의 영향을 받는다는 것이 아니라 인간의 영향을 받는다는 내용이다.

꿀팁 for example 등의 연결어가 등장하지는 않지만, 내용상 앞 문장에 대한 예시임

K 89 정답 ④ ⭐ 2등급 대비 [정답률 62%]

* 장소와 노래를 연관시키는 유럽 울새

Emma Brindley has investigated / the responses of European robins / to the songs of neighbors and strangers. //
전치사   명사구
Emma Brindley는 조사해 왔다 / 유럽 울새의 반응을 / 이웃 새와 낯선 새의 노래에 대한 //

Despite the large and complex song repertoire / of European robins, / they were able to discriminate / between the songs of neighbors and strangers. //
크고 복잡한 노래 목록에도 불구하고 / 유럽 울새의 / 그것은 구별할 수 있었다 / 이웃 새와 낯선 새의 노래를 //

When they heard / a tape recording of a stranger, / they began to sing sooner, /
부사절 접속사(시간)
그것이 들었을 때 / 낯선 새의 테이프 녹음 소리를 / 그것은 더 빨리 노래를 부르기 시작했고 /

sang more songs, / and overlapped their songs / with the playback / more often / than they did / on hearing a neighbor's song. //
began ~, sang ~, overlapped ~를 대신하는 대동사
더 많은 노래를 불렀으며 / 자기 노래를 겹치게 불렀다 / 재생된 노래와 / 더 자주 / 그것이 그랬던 것보다 / 이웃 새의 노래를 들었을 때 //

As Brindley suggests, / the overlapping of song / may be an aggressive response. //
Brindley가 말하는 것처럼 / 노래를 겹치게 하는 것은 / 공격적인 반응일 수도 있다 //

However, / this difference / in responding to neighbor versus stranger / occurred /
동사(완전자동사) *
그러나 / 이러한 차이는 / 이웃 새와 낯선 새에 대한 반응의 / 발생했다 / **단서1** 이웃 새와 낯선 새에 대한 반응의 차이는 이웃 새의 노래가 특정 장소에서 재생되었을 때만 발생함

only when the neighbor's song was played / by a loudspeaker / placed at the boundary / between that neighbor's territory and the territory of the bird / being tested. //
이웃 새의 노래가 재생되었을 때만 / 확성기로 / 경계에 놓인 / 그 이웃 새의 영역과 새의 영역 사이의 / 실험되고 있는 // **단서2** 같은 이웃 새의 노래가 다른 장소에서 재생되면 낯선 새의 울음으로 취급되었음

If the same neighbor's song was played / at another boundary, / one / separating the territory / of the test subject / from another neighbor, / it was treated / as the call of a stranger. //
같은 이웃 새의 노래가 재생되었을 경우 / 다른 경계에서 / 경계 / 영역을 분리하는 / 실험 대상의 / 또 다른 이웃 새에게서 / 그것은 취급되었다 / 낯선 새의 울음으로 //

Not only does this result demonstrate / that **the robins associate locality / with familiar songs**, / but it also shows / that the choice of songs / used in playback experiments / is highly important. //
부정어가 문두로 나간 도치 구문
이 결과는 입증할 뿐만 아니라 / 울새가 장소를 연관시킨다는 것을 / 친숙한 노래와 / 그것은 또한 보여준다 / 노래의 선택이 / 재생 실험에 사용되는 / 매우 중요하다는 것을 //

- investigate ⓥ 조사[연구]하다   • response ⓝ 반응, 대답
- despite (prep) ~에도 불구하고   • complex ⓐ 복잡한
- repertoire ⓝ (할 수 있는) 모든 것[목록]
- discriminate ⓥ 식별하다, 차별하다   • recording ⓝ 녹음(된 것)
- overlap ⓥ 겹치게 하다, 포개지다   • playback ⓝ 재생(된 내용)
- suggest ⓥ 말하다, (뜻을) 비치다   • aggressive ⓐ 공격적인
- versus (prep) ~에 비해   • occur ⓥ 발생하다, 일어나다
- loudspeaker ⓝ 확성기   • boundary ⓝ 경계(선)
- separate ⓥ 분리하다, 나누다   • subject ⓝ 연구[실험] 대상
- treat ⓥ 대하다, 취급하다   • demonstrate ⓥ 입증하다
- highly (ad) 매우

Emma Brindley는 이웃 새와 낯선 새의 노래에 대한 유럽 울새의 반응을 조사해 왔다. 유럽 울새의 크고 복잡한 노래 목록에도 불구하고, 그것은 이웃 새와 낯선 새의 노래를 구별할 수 있었다. 낯선 새의 테이프 녹음 소리를 들었을 때, 그것은 이웃 새의 노래를 들었을 때 그랬던 것보다, 더 빨리 노래를 부르기 시작했고, 더 많은 노래를 불렀으며, 더 자주 자기 노래를 재생된 노래와 겹치게 불렀다. Brindley가 말하는 것처럼, 노래를 겹치게 하는 것은 공격적인 반응일 수도 있다. 그러나 이웃 새와 낯선 새에 대한 반응의 이러한 차이는, 그 이웃 새의 영역과 실험되고 있는 새의 영역 사이의 경계에 놓인 확성기로 이웃 새의 노래가 재생되었을 때만 발생했다. 같은 이웃 새의 노래가 다른 경계, 즉 실험 대상의 영역을 또 다른 이웃 새에게서 분리하는 경계에서 재생되었을 경우, 그것은 낯선 새의 울음으로 취급되었다. 이 결과는 **울새가 장소를 친숙한 노래와 연관시킨다**는 것을 입증할 뿐만 아니라, 또한 재생 실험에 사용되는 노래의 선택이 매우 중요하다는 것을 보여준다.

다음 빈칸에 들어갈 말로 가장 적절한 것을 고르시오. [3점]

① variety and complexity characterize the robins' songs
   다양성과 복잡성이 울새 노래의 특징이다   울새의 노래가 가진 특징을 설명하는 글이 아님
② song volume affects the robins' aggressive behavior
   노래의 음량이 울새의 공격적 행동에 영향을 미친다   an aggressive response로 만든 오답
③ the robins' poor territorial sense is a key to survival
   울새의 보잘것없는 영역 감각이 생존의 열쇠이다   울새는 뛰어난 영역 감각을 갖고 있음
④ the robins associate locality with familiar songs
   울새가 장소를 친숙한 노래와 연관시킨다   장소에 따라 이웃 새의 노래에 대한 반응이 달라짐
⑤ the robins are less responsive to recorded songs
   울새는 녹음된 노래에 대해서는 관심을 덜 보인다   둘 다 녹음된 노래였음

왜 2등급? 빈칸 문장을 제외한 글 전체를 통해 실험 내용을 파악한 뒤에 결론을 빈칸에 넣어야 한다. 빈칸 문장에서 '재생 실험에 사용되는 노래의 선택'이 언급되는데, **단서** 이것 외에도 다른 '무엇'이 입증되는지 파악해야 할 것이다. **발상** 글의 일부 내용으로 구성한 오답이 다수 있어 충분히 헷갈릴 수 있는 2등급 대비 문제이다.

| 문제 풀이 순서 |

1st 빈칸이 포함된 문장의 내용을 파악하고, 빈칸에 들어갈 말에 대한 단서를 얻는다.

빈칸 문장	Not only does this result demonstrate that _____, but it also shows that the choice of songs used in playback experiments is highly important. 이 결과는 _____는 것을 입증할 뿐만 아니라, 또한 재생 실험에 사용되는 노래의 선택이 매우 중요하다는 것을 보여준다.

➡ 빈칸 문장은 '이 결과'가 '무엇'하다는 것을 입증한다는 내용이며, not only A but also B 구조를 이루면서 '무엇'뿐만 아니라 재생 실험에 사용된 노래의 선택이 중요하다고 했다.
글의 나머지 부분에서 '이 결과'가 어떤 것이며, 이를 통해 '무엇'을 입증하는지 확인한다.

2nd 글의 내용을 종합해서 빈칸에 들어갈 적절한 말을 찾는다.

- 그러나 이웃 새와 낯선 새에 대한 반응의 이러한 차이는, 그 이웃 새의 영역과 실험되고 있는 새의 영역 사이의 경계에 놓인 확성기로 이웃 새의 노래가 재생되었을 때만 발생했다. **단서 1**
- 같은 이웃 새의 노래가 다른 경계, 즉 실험 대상의 영역을 또 다른 이웃 새에게서 분리하는 경계에서 재생되었을 경우, 그것은 낯선 새의 울음으로 취급되었다. **단서 2**

➡ 다섯 번째 문장에서 새의 영역 사이 경계에 놓인 확성기로 이웃 새의 노래가 재생되었을 때만 울새의 반응에 차이가 있었다고 했다.
빈칸이 포함된 문장 앞에는 같은 이웃 새의 노래이더라도 다른 경계에서 재생될 경우, 낯선 새의 울음으로 취급되었다는 내용이 나온다.
이는 곧 이웃 새의 노래가 특정 장소에서 재생될 때만 이웃으로 인식한다는 것이다.
▶ 빈칸 문장은 <이 결과는 ④ '울새가 장소를 친숙한 노래와 연관시킨다'는 것을 입증할 뿐만 아니라, …>라는 내용이 되어야 함

3rd 글의 내용을 다시 한번 정리하며 정답이 맞는지 확인한다.

➡ 유럽 울새는 같은 이웃 새의 노래이더라도 특정 장소가 아닌 다른 장소에서 들릴 경우, 낯선 새의 울음으로 취급한다는 내용이다. 따라서 빈칸에 들어갈 말로 가장 적절한 것은 ④ '울새가 장소를 친숙한 노래와 연관시킨다'이다.

| 선택지 분석 |

① **variety and complexity characterize the robins' songs**
   다양성과 복잡성이 울새 노래의 특징이다
Emma Brindley의 실험을 통해 울새의 노래가 다양하고 복잡하다는 것을 알 수 있는 것이 아니다.

② **song volume affects the robins' aggressive behavior**
   노래의 음량이 울새의 공격적 행동에 영향을 미친다
노래를 겹치게 하는 것이 공격적인 반응일 수도 있다는 언급으로 만든 오답이다.
노래의 음량과 울새의 공격적인 행동의 연관성을 보여주는 실험이 아니다.

③ **the robins' poor territorial sense is a key to survival**
   울새의 보잘것없는 영역 감각이 생존의 열쇠이다
제시된 실험을 통해 울새의 영역 감각이 뛰어나다는 것을 알 수 있다. 또한, 울새의 생존 방식에 대한 언급은 없다.

④ **the robins associate locality with familiar songs**
   울새가 장소를 친숙한 노래와 연관시킨다
같은 이웃 새의 노래가 다른 장소에서 재생될 때는 낯선 새의 울음으로 취급되었다고 했으므로 '장소를 친숙한 노래와 연관시킨다'는 것을 입증한다고 할 수 있다.

⑤ **the robins are less responsive to recorded songs**
   울새는 녹음된 노래에 대해서는 관심을 덜 보인다
이웃 새와 낯선 새의 노래가 모두 녹음된 것이었으므로 실험의 변수가 될 수 없다.

---- 어법 특강 ----

＊1형식 동사, 2형식 동사, 3형식 동사

- John is in the backyard. (1형식 동사)
  (John은 뒷마당에 있다.)

- John is my cousin. (2형식 동사)
  (John은 내 사촌이다.)

- I need something sharp. That screwdriver will do. (1형식 동사)
  (나는 날카로운 것이 필요하다. 저 드라이버가 도움이 될 것이다.)

- I do yoga twice a week. (3형식 동사)
  (나는 일주일에 두 번 요가를 한다.)

- Designer clothes don't sell much in the smaller towns. (1형식 동사)
  (디자이너 의상은 더 작은 동네에서는 많이 팔리지 않는다.)

- My uncle buys and sells antiques for a living. (3형식 동사)
  (내 삼촌은 생계를 위해 골동품을 사고판다.)

＊심리학은 정원, 문학은 황무지

In trying to explain / how different disciplines attempt / to understand autobiographical memory /
설명하려고 노력하는 것에 있어 / 서로 다른 학문이 어떻게 시도하는지를 / 자전적 기억을 이해하는 것을 /

the literary critic Daniel Albright said, / "Psychology is a garden, / literature is a wilderness." // **단서1** 심리학은 정원이고, 문학은 황무지임
문학평론가 Daniel Albright는 말했다 / '심리학은 정원이고 / 문학은 황무지이다'라고 //

He meant, / I believe, / that psychology seeks / to make patterns, / find regularity, / and ultimately impose order / on human experience and behavior. // **단서2** 심리학은 인간의 경험과 행동에 질서를 부여하는 것을 추구함
그는 의미했다 / 내가 믿기에 / 심리학은 추구한다는 것을 / 패턴을 만들고 / 규칙성을 찾으며 / 궁극적으로 질서를 부여하는 것을 / 인간의 경험과 행동에 //

Writers, by contrast, dive / into the unruly, untamed depths / of human experiences. // **단서3** 작가(문학)는 인간 경험의 제멋대로 굴고, 길들지 않은 깊이를 파고듦
반면에 작가는 파고든다 / 제멋대로 굴고, 길들지 않은 깊이를 / 인간 경험의 //

What he said / about understanding memory / can be extended / to our questions / about young children's minds. //
그가 말한 것 / 기억을 이해하는 것에 관해 / 확장될 수 있다 / 우리의 질문으로 / 어린아이의 마음에 관한 //

If we psychologists are too bent / on identifying the orderly pattern, / the regularities of children's minds, /
만약 우리 심리학자들이 너무 열중한다면 / 질서 있는 패턴을 밝히는 데 / 즉 아이 마음의 규칙성을 /

we may miss / an essential and pervasive characteristic / of our topic: / the child's more unruly and imaginative ways / of talking and thinking. // **단서4** 심리학자가 아이 마음의 규칙성을 밝히는 데 너무 열중하면 아이의 제멋대로 굴고 상상력이 풍부한 방식을 놓칠 수 있음
우리는 놓칠 수도 있다 / 본질적이고 널리 퍼져 있는 특성을 / 우리 주제의 / 아이의 더 제멋대로 굴고 상상력이 풍부한 방식 / 말하고 생각하는 //

It is not only the developed writer or literary scholar / who seems drawn / toward a somewhat wild and idiosyncratic way of thinking; / young children are as well. //
비단 성숙한 작가나 문학 연구가뿐만 (~한 것이) 아니다 / 끌리는 것처럼 보이는 / 다소 거칠고 색다른 사고방식에 / 어린아이도 역시 그렇다 //

The psychologist / interested in young children / may have to venture / a little more often / **into the wilderness** / in order to get a good picture / of how children think. //
심리학자는 / 어린아이에게 관심이 있는 / 위험을 무릅쓰고 가야 할지도 모른다 / 조금 더 자주 / 황무지로 / 상황을 잘 파악하기 위해 / 아이가 어떻게 생각하는지에 관한 //

- discipline ⓝ 지식 분야, 학과목 · autobiographical ⓐ 자서전적인
- literary ⓐ 문학의, 문학적인 · wilderness ⓝ 황야, 버려진 땅
- regularity ⓝ 규칙적임, 정기적임 · impose ⓥ 도입하다, 부과하다
- untamed ⓐ 길들지 않은 · depth ⓝ 깊이
- orderly ⓐ 정돈된, 질서 있는 · essential ⓐ 필수적인, 본질적인
- imaginative ⓐ 창의적인, 상상력이 풍부한 · scholar ⓝ 학자, 장학생
- somewhat ⓐ 어느 정도, 다소 · venture ⓥ (위험을 무릅쓰고) 가다

서로 다른 학문이 자전적 기억을 어떻게 이해하려고 하는지 설명하려고 노력할 때, 문학평론가 Daniel Albright는 '심리학은 정원이고, 문학은 황무지이다.'라고 말했다. 내가 믿기에, 그는 심리학은 패턴을 만들고, 규칙성을 찾으며, 궁극적으로 인간의 경험과 행동에 질서를 부여하는 것을 추구한다는 것을 의미했다. 반면에, 작가는 제멋대로 굴고, 길들지 않은 인간 경험의 깊이를 파고든다. 기억을 이해하는 것에 관해 그가 말한 것은 어린아이의 마음에 관한 우리의 질문으로 확장될 수 있다. 만약 우리 심리학자들이 질서 있는 패턴, 즉 아이 마음의 규칙성을 밝히는 데 너무 열중한다면, 우리는 우리 주제의 본질적이고 널리 퍼져 있는 특성, 즉 아이가 지닌 더 제멋대로 굴고 상상력이 풍부한 말하기 방식과 생각하기 방식을 놓칠 수도 있다. 다소 거칠고

색다른 사고방식에 끌리는 것처럼 보이는 것은 비단 성숙한 작가나 문학 연구가뿐만이 아니라, 어린아이도 역시 그렇다. 어린아이에게 관심이 있는 심리학자는 아이가 어떻게 생각하는지에 관한 상황을 잘 파악하기 위해 조금 더 자주 위험을 무릅쓰고 황무지로 가야 할지도 모른다.

다음 빈칸에 들어갈 말로 가장 적절한 것을 고르시오. [3점]

① venture a little more often into the wilderness 작가의 특징을 띠어야 함
위험을 무릅쓰고 조금 더 자주 황무지로 가야
② help them recall their most precious memories 아이로 하여금 어떤 기억을
그들이 자신의 가장 소중한 기억을 떠올리도록 도와야 떠올리게 해야 한다는 것이 아님
③ better understand the challenges of parental duty 부모의 의무는 언급되지 않음
부모의 의무라는 난제를 더 잘 이해해야
④ disregard the key characteristics of children's fiction '문학', '작가'로 만든 오답
아동 소설의 핵심 특징을 무시해야
⑤ standardize the paths of their psychological development 표준화는 규칙성의 발견과 연관됨
그들의 심리발달 경로를 표준화해야

왜 2등급? 선택지에 비유적인 표현이 사용되어 곧바로 정답을 유추하기 어려운 2등급 대비 문제이다. 글의 전반부를 통해 '문학=황무지=불규칙성'이라는 관계를 정립한 후, 단서 '심리학자들이 아이가 지닌 불규칙적 사고방식을 놓치면 안 된다'라는 글의 주장을 찾아내야 할 것이다. 발상 그렇다면 어린아이의 사고방식을 파악하려면 '황무지로 가야 한다'라는 정답을 찾을 수 있다.

| 문제 풀이 순서 |

1st 빈칸이 포함된 문장의 내용을 파악하고, 빈칸에 들어갈 말에 대한 단서를 얻는다.

빈칸 문장	The psychologist interested in young children may have to ＿＿＿＿＿＿＿＿ in order to get a good picture of how children think. 어린아이에게 관심이 있는 심리학자는 아이가 어떻게 생각하는지에 관한 상황을 잘 파악하기 위해 ＿＿＿＿＿＿할지도 모른다.

→ 어린아이에게 관심이 있는 '심리학자'를 언급하며 아이가 어떻게 생각하는지에 관한 상황을 파악하려면 '무엇'을 할지도 모른다고 했다. 글의 나머지 부분에서 심리학자들이 어린아이의 사고 과정을 파악하기 위해 '무엇'을 할지 확인한다.

2nd 글의 내용을 종합해서 빈칸에 들어갈 적절한 말을 찾는다.

- '심리학은 정원이고, 문학은 황무지이다.' **단서1**
- 그는 심리학은 패턴을 만들고, 규칙성을 찾으며, 궁극적으로 인간의 경험과 행동에 질서를 부여하는 것을 추구한다는 것을 의미했다. **단서2**
- 반면에, 작가는 제멋대로 굴고, 길들지 않은 인간 경험의 깊이를 파고든다. **단서3**
- 만약 우리 심리학자들이 … 아이 마음의 규칙성을 밝히는 데 너무 열중한다면, 우리는 …, 즉 아이가 지닌 더 제멋대로 굴고 상상력이 풍부한 말하기 방식과 생각하기 방식을 놓칠 수도 있다. **단서4**

→ '심리학=정원', '문학=황무지'라는 관계를 찾아낼 수 있다. **단서1**
한편 심리학이 규칙성을 찾는다는 것 **단서2**, 작가(문학)가 제멋대로 구는 특성, 즉 불규칙성을 파악한다는 것 **단서3**을 알 수 있다.
이를 종합하면 '심리학=정원=규칙성', '문학=황무지=불규칙성'이라는 관계가 정립된다.
이어서 심리학자들이 아이 마음의 규칙성에만 열중하면 불규칙적인 생각하기 방식을 놓칠 수 있다고 했다. **단서4**
▶ 빈칸 문장은 〈어린아이에게 관심이 있는 심리학자는 … ① '조금 더 자주 위험을 무릅쓰고 황무지로 가야' 할지도 모른다.〉라는 내용이 되어야 함

3rd 글의 내용을 다시 한번 정리하며 정답이 맞는지 확인한다.

→ 이 글은 어린아이의 심리의 불규칙성에 관한 내용이다. 심리학자들은 규칙성을 추구하지만, 어린아이의 심리를 연구하는 심리학자들은 규칙성에 집착하지 않고 불규칙성, 즉 황무지로 나아가야 한다는 것이다.
▶ 따라서 빈칸에 들어갈 말로 가장 적절한 것은 ① '위험을 무릅쓰고 조금 더 자주 황무지로 가야'이다.

① **venture a little more often into the wilderness**
위험을 무릅쓰고 조금 더 자주 황무지로 가야
어린아이의 심리를 연구하는 심리학자들은 아이의 불규칙적인 사고방식을 연구하는
것을 놓치지 말아야 한다는 내용이다.

② **help them recall their most precious memories**
그들이 자신의 가장 소중한 기억을 떠올리도록 도와야
아이의 사고방식을 파악하기 위해 심리학자가 아이로 하여금 어떤 기억을 떠올리게
해야 한다는 것이 아니다.

③ **better understand the challenges of parental duty**
부모의 의무라는 난제를 더 잘 이해해야
아이의 사고방식을 연구하는 심리학자가 주의해야 하는 점을 설명한 것으로,
심리학자가 부모의 의무를 더 잘 이해해야 한다는 것은 아니다.

④ **disregard the key characteristics of children's fiction**
아동 소설의 핵심 특징을 무시해야
작가처럼 인간 경험의 제멋대로 굴고 길들지 않은 깊이를 파고들어야 한다는
것이므로, 아동 소설의 핵심 특징을 무시해야 한다는 것은 아니다.

⑤ **standardize the paths of their psychological development**
그들의 심리발달 경로를 표준화해야
표준화한다는 것은 규칙성을 발견하고자 하는 심리학자의 특징과 비슷한 의미이다. 이
글은 심리학자가 작가의 특징을 띠어야 한다고 주장하는 것이다.

K 91 정답 ②　　　　　　　　⚡ 2등급 대비 [정답률 53%]

✱ 스포츠 저널리스트가 겪는 역설

형용사의 후치 수식을 받는 -thing
There is something deeply paradoxical / about the professional
status of sports journalism, / especially in the medium of
print. // **단서1** 스포츠 저널리즘의 전문적 지위에 관한 역설에 대해 이야기하는 글임
매우 역설적인 것이 있다 / 스포츠 저널리즘의 전문적 지위에 관해서 / 특히 인쇄 매체에서//

In discharging their usual responsibilities / of description and
　　　　　　　　　　　　　복수 주어
commentary, / reporters' accounts of sports events / are eagerly
　　　　　　　　　　　　　　　　　　　　복수 동사
consulted by sports fans, / **단서2** 스포츠 팬들은 스포츠 기자들의 기사를 열심히 찾아 읽음
그들의 통상적인 책무를 이행하는 것에 있어 / 설명과 논평이라는 / 스포츠 경기에 관한
기자들의 설명은 / 스포츠 팬들에 의해 열심히 찾아진다 /

while in their broader journalistic role / of covering sport / in its
many forms, / sports journalists are among the most visible / of
all contemporary writers. // the+형용사: 사람을 나타내는 복수 보통명사
반면에 그들의 더 폭넓은 저널리스트의 역할에서 / 스포츠를 취재하는 / 여러 형식으로 /
스포츠 저널리스트는 가장 눈에 띄는 이들 가운데 있다 / 동시대의 모든 작가 중에서 //

The ruminations / of the elite class / of 'celebrity' sports
　　　　　　　　　seek after와 같은 구동사는 하나의 동사로 취급하여 수동태로 전환함
journalists / are much sought after / by the major newspapers, /
생각은 / 엘리트 계층의 / '유명인급' 스포츠 저널리스트 중 / 많이 추구되고 / 주요 신문사들에
의해 / 주어가 생략되지 않음(독립 분사구문)

their lucrative contracts being the envy of colleagues / in other
'disciplines' of journalism. //
그들의 돈을 많이 버는 계약은 동료들의 선망 대상이 된다 / 저널리즘의 다른 '부문'에 있는 //
　　　　　　　　　　　　　　　　　　　　　　　　　　선행사
Yet sports journalists do not have a standing / in their profession
/ that corresponds to the size / of their readerships or of their
주격 관계대명사
pay packets, / **단서3** 하지만 스포츠 기자는 독자 수나 급여 액수의 크기에
　　　　　　　　상응하는 지위를 누리지 못함
그러나 스포츠 저널리스트는 지위를 누리지 못한다 / 그들의 전문성에서의 / 크기에 상응하는
/ 그들의 독자 수나 급여 액수의 /

with the old saying / (now reaching the status of cliché) / that
sport is the 'toy department of the news media' / 동격절 접속사
옛말과 더불어 / (이제는 상투적인 문구의 지위에 이르는) / 스포츠는 '뉴스 매체의 장난감
부서'라는 / **단서4** 스포츠 기자는 그들이 하는 일의 가치를 묵살하는 말로 지위를 누리지 못함
still readily to hand / as a dismissal of the worth / of what sports
journalists do. //　　　　　　　　　전치사 of의 목적어로 쓰인 명사절
여전히 쉽게 건네지는 / 가치를 묵살하는 말로 / 스포츠 저널리스트들이 하는 일의 //

This reluctance / to take sports journalism seriously / produces
단수 주어　　　　형용사적 용법(reluctance 수식)　　　　　　단수 동사
the paradoxical outcome / that sports newspaper writers / are
　　　　　　　　준부정어　　동격절 접속사
much read but little **admired**. //
이러한 꺼림은 / 스포츠 저널리즘을 진지하게 여기기를 / 역설적인 결과를 낳는다 / 스포츠
신문 작가들이 / 많이 읽히지만 거의 존경받지 못하는 //

- **paradoxical** ⓐ 역설적인
- **commentary** ⓝ 해설, 논평
- **eagerly** ⓐⓓ 열렬히, 열심히
- **cover** ⓥ 다루다, 취재하다
- **discipline** ⓝ 분야, 부문
- **correspond** ⓥ 상응하다
- **pay packet** 급여 봉투
- **reluctance** ⓝ 꺼림, 내키지 않음
- **censor** ⓥ 검열하다

- **description** ⓝ 설명, 서술
- **account** ⓝ 말, 설명
- **consult** ⓥ 찾아보다
- **contemporary** ⓐ 동시대의
- **standing** ⓝ 지위
- **readership** ⓝ (특정 신문 등의) 독자 수[층]
- **dismissal** ⓝ 묵살, 일축
- **admire** ⓥ 존경하다, 선망하다

스포츠 저널리즘의 전문적 지위에 관해서, 특히 인쇄 매체에서, 매우
역설적인 것이 있다. 기자들이 설명하고 논평하는 통상적으로 자신이
맡은 일을 이행할 때, 스포츠 팬들이 스포츠 경기에 관한 기자들의 설명을
열심히 찾아보는 반면, 여러 형식으로 스포츠를 취재하는 그들의 더 폭넓은
저널리스트의 역할에서 스포츠 저널리스트는 동시대의 모든 작가 중에서 가장
눈에 띄는 이들 가운데 있다.
'유명인급' 스포츠 저널리스트 중 엘리트 계층의 생각은 주요 신문사들이
많이 원하고, 그들의 돈을 많이 버는 계약은 저널리즘의 다른 '부문'에 있는
동료들의 선망 대상이 된다. 그러나 스포츠 저널리스트는 스포츠는 스포츠
저널리스트들이 하는 일의 가치를 묵살하는 말로 여전히 쉽게 건네지는 '뉴스
매체의 장난감 부서'라는 (이제는 상투적인 문구의 지위에 이르는) 옛말과
더불어 그들의 독자 수나 급여 액수의 크기에 상응하는 그들의 전문성에서의
지위를 누리지 못한다. 이렇게 스포츠 저널리즘을 진지하게 여기기를 꺼리는
것은 스포츠 신문 작가들이 많이 읽히지만 거의 **존경받지** 못하는 역설적인
결과를 낳는다.

다음 빈칸에 들어갈 말로 가장 적절한 것을 고르시오.

① paid 많은 돈을 번다고 했음　　　　② admired 전문성에서의 지위를 누리지 못함
　　돈을 받지　　　　　　　　　　　　　　　존경받지
③ censored 기사 검열에 대한 내용이 아님　④ challenged
　　검열되지　　　　　　　　　　　　　　　의문이 제기되지
⑤ discussed
　　논의되지　　　스포츠 기자의 의견에 의문을 제기하거나 그것을 논의한다는 언급은 없음

와 2등급? 각각의 문장이 너무 길어서 정확히 해석하기가 무척 어려운 글이다.
하지만 첫 문장을 읽고 '스포츠 저널리즘의 전문적 지위에 관한 역설'이 이 글의
소재임을 파악한 후, **단서** 스포츠 저널리스트의 설명(기사)이 스포츠 팬들에 의해
열심히 읽힌다는 것과 (그럼에도 불구하고) 스포츠 저널리스트가 그들의 전문성에서의
지위를 누리지 못한다는 것만 파악하면 정답을 찾는 것은 어렵지 않을 것이다. **발상**

| 문제 풀이 순서 |

1st 빈칸이 포함된 문장의 내용을 파악하고, 빈칸에 들어갈 말에 대한 단서를 얻는다.

빈칸 문장	This reluctance to take sports journalism seriously produces the paradoxical outcome that sports newspaper writers are much read but little _____. 이렇게 스포츠 저널리즘을 진지하게 여기기를 꺼리는 것은 스포츠 신문 작가들이 많이 읽히지만 거의 _____ 못하는 역설적인 결과를 낳는다.

➡ 스포츠 저널리즘을 진지하게 여기기를 꺼리는 현상은 스포츠 신문 작가들이 거의
'무엇'하지 못하는 역설적인 결과를 낳는다고 했다. 글의 나머지 부분에서 앞서 말한
현상이 스포츠 신문 작가들에게 어떤 부정적인 영향을 미치는지 확인한다.

2nd Yet으로 시작하는 문장에서 글의 흐름이 계속 전환되는 것에 주목한다.

- 스포츠 저널리즘의 전문적 지위에 관해서, 특히 인쇄 매체에서, 매우 역설적인 것이 있다. 단서 1
- 스포츠 팬들이 스포츠 경기에 관한 기자들의 설명을 열심히 찾아보는 … 단서 2
- 그러나(Yet) 스포츠 저널리스트는 … 그들의 독자 수나 급여 액수의 크기에 상응하는 그들의 전문성에서의 지위를 누리지 못한다. 단서 3
- 스포츠는 스포츠 저널리스트들이 하는 일의 가치를 묵살하는 말로 … 단서 4

→ 글의 전반부는 스포츠 저널리즘의 전문적 지위는 역설적이라고 하며 스포츠 저널리즘이 선망되는 측면을 보여준다. 단서 1 단서 2

역접의 연결어 Yet으로 이어지는 후반부에서 스포츠 기자는 전문성에 상응하는 지위를 누리지 못하며, 그들이 하는 일의 가치를 묵살하는 옛말이 쉽게 건네진다고 했다. 단서 3 단서 4

즉, 스포츠 저널리즘이 선망되기도 하지만 역설적으로 그 일의 가치를 인정받지 못한다는 내용의 글이다.

▶ 빈칸 문장은 〈스포츠 저널리즘을 진지하게 여기기를 꺼리는 것은 스포츠 신문 작가들이 많이 읽히지만 거의 ② '존경받지' 못하는 역설적인 결과를 낳는다.〉라는 내용이 되어야 함

3rd 글의 내용을 다시 한번 정리하며 정답이 맞는지 확인한다.

→ 이 글은 선망받기도 하면서 인정받지 못하는 스포츠 저널리즘의 역설적인 지위에 관한 내용이다. 스포츠 저널리즘의 가치를 묵살하는 경향과 전문성의 지위를 누리지 못하는 현상으로 인해 스포츠 신문 작가들이 많이 읽히면서도 존경받지 못한다는 내용이 자연스럽다.

▶ 따라서 빈칸에 들어갈 말로 가장 적절한 것은 ② '존경받지'이다.

| 선택지 분석 |

① paid
돈을 받는
스포츠 저널리스트의 돈을 많이 버는 계약이 다른 부문에 있는 동료들의 선망의 대상이 된다고 했다.

②admired
존경받지
스포츠 신문 작가들은 그들의 전문성을 인정받지 못하므로 존경받지 못하는 것과 같다.

③ censored
검열되지
스포츠 기사가 많이 읽히지만, 이들이 검열된다는 내용이 아니다.

④ challenged
의문이 제기되지
스포츠 기사가 많이 읽히지만, 이들에게 의문이 제기된다는 내용이 아니다.

⑤ discussed
논의되지
스포츠 기사가 많이 읽히지만, 이들이 논의되지 않는다는 내용이 아니다.

조현준 | 전북대 의예과 2023년 입학·익산 이리고 졸

일단 글의 앞부분에서 스포츠 뉴스 기사는 인기가 많다는 내용임을 파악했는데, 중간에 역접의 연결어인 Yet과 함께 글의 분위기가 바뀌었어.

스포츠 뉴스 기자들은 a standing을 갖지 못한다는 내용인데, standing은 지위라는 뜻이야. 이 뜻을 알았다면 정답을 쉽게 찾았겠지만, 나는 그렇지 못했어. 하지만 글의 첫 문장에 단서가 있더라. 첫 문장은 스포츠 저널리즘의 the professional status의 역설적 상황을 이야기하는데, 다행히 status의 뜻은 알고 있었기 때문에 standing의 의미를 추론했고, 인기가 많다는 것과 역설 관계에 있는 정답을 찾을 수 있었어. 모르는 단어가 있다고 당황하지 않는 게 중요해!

＊ 엠바고(embargo)

엠바고의 본래 뜻은 '선박의 억류 혹은 통상 금지'이나, 언론에서는 '어떤 뉴스 기사를 일정 시간까지 그 보도를 유보하는 것'을 말한다. 즉, 뉴스를 발표하는 시간을 일시적으로 제한하는 것이다.

취재 대상이 기자를 상대로 보도 자제를 요청하거나, 기자실에서 기자들 사이 합의에 따라 일정 시점까지 보도를 자제하겠다는 약속이며 국가 안보 사항 등 조기 보도할 경우 문제가 생기는 경우에 보도를 유보한다. 언론에서의 엠바고는 크게 보충 취재용 엠바고, 조건부 엠바고, 공공이익을 위한 엠바고, 관례적 엠바고의 네 가지 유형으로 나뉜다.

K 92 정답 ② ✪ 1등급 대비 [정답률 50%]

＊과학과 역사의 차이

Precision and determinacy are a necessary requirement / for all meaningful scientific debate, /
정확성과 확정성은 필요조건이며 / 모든 의미 있는 과학 토론을 위한 /
주어
and progress in the sciences / is, to a large extent, the ongoing
비교급·최상급 강조 부사   동사
주격 보어
process / of achieving ever greater precision. //
과학에서의 발전은 / 상당 부분 계속 진행 중인 과정이다 / 훨씬 더 높은 정확성을 달성하는 //
put a premium on: ~을 중시[장려]하다
But historical representation puts a premium / on a proliferation
of representations, /
그러나 역사적 진술은 중요시한다 / 진술의 증식을 /   단서 1 역사적 진술은 하나의 진술을 정제하는 것이 아니라
다양한 진술의 생성, 즉 진술의 증식을 중요시함
not A but B(A가 아니라 B)로 on이 이끄는 전치사구가 연결됨
hence not on the refinement of one representation / but on the
production / of an ever more varied set of representations. //
한 가지 진술의 정제가 아니라 / 생성을 / 훨씬 더 다양한 진술 집합의 //

Historical insight is not a matter / of a continuous "narrowing
not A but B로 Historical insight를 설명하는 주격 보어가 연결됨
down" / of previous options, / not of an approximation of the
truth, /
역사적 통찰은 문제가 아니라 / 지속적인 '줄여 가기'의 / 이전에 선택한 것들의 / 진리에 근접함의 문제가 아니라 /
but, on the contrary, is an "explosion" / of possible points of
view. //   단서 2 역사적 통찰은 가능한 관점들의 폭발적 증가임
반대로 '폭발적 증가'이다 / 가능한 관점들의 //

It therefore aims / at the unmasking of previous illusions / of
determinacy and precision / by the production / of new and
alternative representations, /   단서 3 새롭고 대안적인 진술을 만들어 내서 이전의
확정성과 정확성의 정체를 드러냄
그러므로 그것은 목표로 한다 / 이전에 가진 환상의 정체를 드러내는 것을 / 확정성과 정확성에 대해 / 생성에 의해 / 새롭고 대안적인 진술의 /
rather than으로 at이 이끄는 전치사구가 연결됨
rather than at achieving truth / by a careful analysis / of what
was right and wrong / in those previous representations. //
진리를 획득하는 것이 아니라 / 신중한 분석에 의해 / 무엇이 옳고 틀렸는지에 대한 / 이전의 진술에서 //
단서 4 역사적 통찰은 외부인에게는 더 큰 혼란을 만들어 내는 과정으로 보일 수 있음
And from this perspective, / the development of historical
insight / may indeed be regarded / by the outsider / as a process
of creating / ever more confusion, /   regard A as B(A를 B로 여기다)의 수동태
그리고 이러한 관점에서 보면 / 역사적 통찰의 발전은 / 진정 여겨질 수도 있다 / 외부인에 의해 / 만들어 내는 과정으로 / 훨씬 더 큰 혼란을 //

a continuous questioning / of **certainty and precision** / **seemingly achieved already**, / rather than, / as in the sciences, / an ever greater approximation / to the truth. //
_{rather than으로 as의 목적어가 연결됨}
지속적인 의문 제기 / 확실성과 정확성에 대한 / 이미 획득한 것처럼 보이는 / ~보다는 / 과학에서처럼 / 훨씬 더 큰 근접(보다는) / 진리에 //

- precision ⓝ 정확성   • determinacy ⓝ 확정성, 결정된 상태
- necessary requirement 필요조건   • meaningful ⓐ 의미 있는, 중요한
- progress ⓝ 발전, 진보   • to a large extent 상당 부분
- ongoing ⓐ 진행 중인   • achieve ⓥ 달성하다, 성취하다
- representation ⓝ 진술, 설명, 묘사   • refinement ⓝ 정제, 정련
- varied ⓐ 다양한   • insight ⓝ 통찰(력), 안식(眼識)
- continuous ⓐ 계속되는, 지속적인   • narrow down 좁히다, 줄이다
- approximation ⓝ 근접, 근사   • explosion ⓝ 폭발적인 증가
- unmask ⓥ 정체를 밝히다, 가면을 벗기다   • illusion ⓝ 환상, 착각
- alternative ⓐ 대안적인, 대체의   • analysis ⓝ 분석, 해석
- regard ⓥ 여기다, 평가하다   • confusion ⓝ 혼란, 혼동

정확성과 확정성은 모든 의미 있는 과학 토론을 위한 필요조건이며, 과학에서의 발전은 상당 부분, 훨씬 더 높은 정확성을 달성하는 계속 진행 중인 과정이다. 그러나 역사적 진술은 진술의 증식을 중요시하는데, 이는 한 가지 진술의 정제가 아닌, 훨씬 더 다양한 진술 집합의 생성에 중요성을 두는 것이다. 역사적 통찰은 이전에 선택한 것들을 지속해서 '줄여 가는' 것의 문제, 즉 진리에 근접함의 문제가 아니라, 반대로 가능한 관점들의 '폭발적 증가'이다. 그러므로 그것은 이전의 진술에서 무엇이 옳고 틀렸는지에 대한 신중한 분석에 의해 진리를 획득하는 것이 아니라, 새롭고 대안적인 진술의 생성에 의해 확정성과 정확성에 대해 이전에 가진 환상의 정체를 드러내는 것을 목표로 한다. 그리고 이러한 관점에서 보면, 역사적 통찰의 발전은 과학에서처럼 진리에 훨씬 더 많이 근접함보다는, 훨씬 더 큰 혼란을 만들어 내는 과정, 즉 **이미 획득한 것처럼 보이는 확실성과 정확성**에 대한 지속적인 의문 제기로 외부인에게 진정 여겨질 수도 있다.

다음 빈칸에 들어갈 말로 가장 적절한 것을 고르시오. [3점]
① criteria for evaluating historical representations
_{역사적 진술을 평가하는 기준   역사적 진술을 평가하는 기준에 의문을 제기하는 것처럼 보이는 과정이 아님}
②certainty and precision seemingly achieved already
_{이미 획득한 것처럼 보이는 확실성과 정확성   이미 진술이 있는데 또다른 진술을 생성함}
③ possibilities of alternative interpretations of an event
_{어떤 사건에 대한 대안적 해석의 가능성   대안적 해석의 가능성을 믿기 때문에 진술의 증식을 중시하는 것임}
④ coexistence of multiple viewpoints in historical writing
_{역사 저술에서 여러 관점의 공존   여러 관점이 공존한다고 생각하기 때문에 진술의 증식을 중시하는 것임}
⑤ correctness and reliability of historical evidence collected
_{수집된 역사적 증거의 정확성과 신뢰성   더 큰 혼란을 만들어 내는 과정처럼 보여야 함}

왜 1등급? 과학과 역사의 차이라는 추상적인 내용을 다루는 데다가, 구체적인 예시 없이 설명이 이어지고 있다. **단서** 이런 문제일수록 서로 비교되는 대상이 각각 어떤 특징을 지니는지 명확히 구분해야 한다. **발상** 최종적으로 빈칸에서 묻는 대상이 무엇인지 파악하고 그 대상의 특징을 중심으로 글을 읽다 보면 정답을 찾을 수 있을 것이다.

| 문제 풀이 순서 |

1st 먼저 빈칸이 포함된 문장을 읽고, 빈칸에 들어갈 말에 대한 단서를 얻는다.

빈칸 문장	And from this perspective, the development of historical insight may indeed be regarded by the outsider as a process of creating ever more confusion, a continuous questioning of _____ rather than, as in the sciences, an ever greater approximation to the truth. **단서4** 그리고 이러한 관점에서 보면, 역사적 통찰의 발전은 과학에서처럼 진리에 훨씬 더 많이 근접함보다는, 훨씬 더 큰 혼란을 만들어 내는 과정, 즉 _____에 대한 지속적인 의문 제기로 외부인에게 진정 여겨질 수도 있다.

➡ rather than을 사용하여 '역사적 통찰'과 '과학'을 비교하며, 역사적 통찰은 '무엇'에 대한 지속적인 의문 제기로 간주되는 반면, 과학은 진리에 근접함으로 간주된다고 했다. 빈칸 문장 처음에 제시된 '이러한 관점'이 무엇인지, 역사적 통찰이 '무엇'에 대해 지속적인 의문을 제기하는지 찾아야 한다.

2nd **1st** 에서 찾은 단서를 염두에 두고, 빈칸 문장의 앞부분부터 확인한다.

> • 그러나 역사적 진술은 진술의 증식을 중요시하는데, 이는 한 가지 진술의 정제가 아닌, 훨씬 더 다양한 진술 집합의 생성에 중요성을 두는 것이다. **단서1**
> • 역사적 통찰은 … 가능한 관점들의 '폭발적 증가'이다. **단서2**
> • 그러므로(therefore) 그것은 … 새롭고 대안적인 진술의 생성에 의해 확정성과 정확성에 대해 이전에 가진 환상의 정체를 드러내는 것을 목표로 한다. **단서3**

➡ 역사적 진술은 진술의 증식을 중요시하고, 역사적 통찰은 가능한 관점들의 '폭발적 증가'라고 했다. **단서1 단서2**
Therefore를 사용하여 위에 진술한 내용들을 종합하며, 그것(역사적 통찰)은 새롭고 대안적인 진술을 만들어내며 과학의 필요조건인 확정성과 정확성의 정체를 드러내는 것이 목표라고 했다. **단서3**
빈칸 문장을 보면 역사적 통찰의 발전 과정이 혼란을 만드는 과정이라 언급하는데, 이는 역사적 통찰과 대조되는 의견이므로, this perspective는 '과학'의 관점임을 알 수 있다. 결국 과학에 관점에서 볼 때, 역사적 통찰이 지속적인 의문을 제기하는 것은 과학의 특성일 것이다.
▶ 빈칸 문장은 〈② '이미 획득한 것처럼 보이는 확실성과 정확성'에 대한 지속적인 의문 제기로 외부인에게 진정 여겨질 수도 있다.〉라는 내용이 되어야 함

3rd 글의 내용을 다시 한번 정리하며 정답이 맞는지 확인한다.

➡ 역사적 통찰은 가능한 관점과 진술을 증가시키며 과학이 가진 환상의 정체를 드러낸다고 했다. 즉, 과학의 관점에서 역사적 통찰은 과학의 필요조건에 의문을 제기할 것이므로, 빈칸에 들어갈 말로 ②이 가장 적절하다.

| 선택지 분석 |

① **criteria for evaluating historical representations**
역사적 진술을 평가하는 기준
역사적 진술을 평가하는 기준에 대해 지속적으로 의문을 제기함으로써 역사적 통찰이 발전한다고 외부인이 생각할 만한 내용은 언급되지 않았다.

②**certainty and precision seemingly achieved already**
이미 획득한 것처럼 보이는 확실성과 정확성
역사적 통찰이 과학의 필요조건인 확실성과 정확성에 대해 의문을 제기한다는 내용이다.

③ **possibilities of alternative interpretations of an event**
어떤 사건에 대한 대안적 해석의 가능성
어떤 역사적 사건에 대한 대안적 해석이 가능하고, 역사 저술에 있어 다수의 관점이 공존할 수 있다고 생각하기 때문에 역사적 통찰의 발전이 진술의 증식을 중시한다고 볼 수 있다. 이러한 역사적 통찰의 발전이 대안적 해석의 가능성과 여러 관점의 공존에 대해 지속적으로 의문을 제기하는 것으로 보이지는 않을 것이다.

④ **coexistence of multiple viewpoints in historical writing**
역사 저술에서 여러 관점의 공존
어떤 역사적 사건에 대한 대안적 해석이 가능하고, 역사 저술에 있어 다수의 관점이 공존할 수 있다고 생각하기 때문에 역사적 통찰의 발전이 진술의 증식을 중시한다고 볼 수 있다. 이러한 역사적 통찰의 발전이 대안적 해석의 가능성과 여러 관점의 공존에 대해 지속적으로 의문을 제기하는 것으로 보이지는 않을 것이다.

⑤ **correctness and reliability of historical evidence collected**
수집된 역사적 증거의 정확성과 신뢰성
수집된 역사적 증거의 정확성과 신뢰성에 지속적인 의문을 제기하는 것은 합리적인 발전 과정이지, 더 큰 혼란을 만들어 내는 과정으로 보이지는 않을 것이다.

K 93 정답 ④ ────── ⭐1등급 대비 [정답률 22%]

*음악의 기본적인 인식에는 일관성이 존재함

형용사적 용법(Any attempt 수식)
Any attempt / to model musical behavior or perception in a general way / is filled with difficulties. //
어떤 시도이든 / 일반적인 방식으로 음악적 행동이나 인식의 모형을 만들려는 것은 / 어려움으로 가득 차 있다 //

with regard to ~ : ~와 관련하여
With regard to models of perception, / the question arises /
the question을 수식하는 긴 수식어구를 뒤로 보냄
of whose perception we are trying to model / — even if we confine ourselves to a particular culture and historical environment. //
인식의 모형과 관련하여 / 의문이 생긴다 / 우리가 누구의 인식을 모형으로 만들려고 하고 있는지에 관한 / 우리가 특정 문화와 역사적 환경에 국한하더라도 //

Surely the perception of music varies greatly / between listeners of different levels of training; /
분명, 음악에 대한 인식은 크게 다르다 / 다양한 수준의 훈련을 받은 청취자마다 /
be devoted to+명사 / 동명사(to는 전치사): ~에 할애하다
indeed, a large part of music education is devoted / to developing and enriching (and therefore likely changing) these listening processes. //
사실, 음악 교육의 큰 부분은 할애되고 있다 / 이러한 청취 과정을 개발하고 풍부하게 하는 (따라서 변화시킬 가능성이 있는) 데에 //
단서 1 음악 청취자 간에 비교적 일관성이 있다고 믿는 측면에 관심을 두고자 함

While this may be true, / I am concerned here with fairly basic aspects of perception / — particularly meter and key — / which
주격 관계대명사
삽입어구   동사
I believe are relatively consistent across listeners. //
이것이 사실일 수도 있지만, / 나는 여기서는 인식의 아주 기본적인 측면에 관심을 두고 있다 / 특히 박자 및 조성과 같이 / 청취자 간에 비교적 일관성이 있다고 내가 믿고 있는 //

목적어절 접속사
Anecdotal evidence suggests, for example, / that most people are able to "find the beat" / in a typical folk song or classical piece. // 단서 2 대부분의 사람들은 '박자'라는 것을 찾을 수 있다(일관성이 있는 측면에 대한 예시)
예를 들어 일화적 증거가 있다 / 대부분의 사람은 '박자를 찾을' 수 있다는 / 전형적인 민요나 클래식 곡에서 //

목적어절 접속사
This is not to say / that there is complete uniformity in this regard / — there may be occasional disagreements, even among experts, / as to how we hear the tonality or meter of a piece. //
~에 관하여   간접의문문
이것이 의미하는 것은 아니다 / 이 점에 있어 완전한 일치가 있다는 것을 / 심지어 전문가들 사이에서도 이따금 의견 차이가 있을 수도 있다 / 곡의 음조나 박자를 듣는 방법에 대해 //
단서 3 빈칸 문장은 But으로 시작했으므로 앞과 대조되는 내용이 와야 함
But I believe / **the commonalities between us far outweigh / the differences.** //
하지만 나는 믿는다 / 우리 사이의 공통점이 훨씬 더 크다 / 차이점보다 //

- perception ⓝ 인식, 지각   · arise ⓥ 생기다, 일어나다
- confine ⓥ 국한하다   · be devoted to ~에 할애되다
- enrich ⓥ 풍부하게 하다   · meter ⓝ 박자   · key ⓝ (장·단조의) 조성
- relatively ⓐ 비교적, 상대적으로   · consistent ⓐ 일관성이 있는
- typical ⓐ 전형적인   · uniformity ⓝ 일치, 통일성
- occasional ⓐ 이따금의   · tonality ⓝ 조성
- emerge ⓥ 드러나다   · narrow ⓥ 좁히다
- fundamental ⓐ 근본적인   · diversity ⓝ 다양성

일반적인 방식으로 음악적 행동이나 인식의 모형을 만들려는 시도는 어떤 것이든 어려움으로 가득 차 있다. 인식의 모형과 관련하여, 우리가 특정 문화와 역사적 환경에 국한하더라도, 우리가 누구의 인식을 모형으로 만들려고 하고 있는지에 관한 의문이 생긴다. 분명, 음악에 대한 인식은 다양한 수준의 훈련을 받은 청취자마다 크게 다르며, 사실, 음악 교육의 큰 부분은 이러한 청취 과정을 개발하고 풍부하게 하는(따라서 변화시킬 가능성이 있는) 데 할애되고 있다. 이것이 사실일 수도 있지만, 나는 여기서는 인식의 아주 기본적인 측면, 특히 박자 및 조성과 같이 청취자 간에 비교적 일관성이 있다고 내가 믿고 있는 측면에 관심을 두고 있다. 예를 들어, 대부분의 사람은 전형적인 민요나 클래식 곡에서 '박자를 찾을' 수 있다는 일화적 증거가 있다. 이것이 이 점에 있어 완전한 일치가 있다는 것을 의미하는 것은 아니고, 전문가들 사이에서도 곡의 음조나 박자를 듣는 방법에 대해 이따금 의견 차이가 있을 수도 있다. 하지만 나는 **우리 사이의 공통점이 차이점보다 훨씬 더 크다**고 믿는다.

다음 빈칸에 들어갈 말로 가장 적절한 것을 고르시오. [3점]
일관성을 찾으려고 하는 것은 맞지만 이를 위한 헌신은 논리의 비약임
① our devotion to narrowing these differences will emerge
이 차이를 좁히려는 우리의 헌신이 드러날 것이다
② fundamental musical behaviors evolve within communities
기본적인 음악적 행동은 공동체 내에서 진화한다 '행동'이 아니라 주로 음악적 '인식'에 대해 다루고 있음
③ these varied perceptions enrich shared musical experiences 다양한
이러한 다양한 인식은 공유된 음악적 경험을 풍부하게 한다   인식과는 반대되는 내용이 제시되어야 함
④ the commonalities between us far outweigh the differences 음악의
우리 사이의 공통점이 차이점보다 훨씬 더 크다   기본적인 인식의 측면에는 비교적 일관성이 있다고 함
⑤ diversity rather than uniformity in musical processes counts
음악적 과정에서 일치보다는 다양성이 중요하다
음악의 인식 측면에서 일관적인 요소가 있다는 것을 주장하는 글의 내용과 반대임

왜 1등급? 글에 나오는 어휘들의 난이도는 높지 않지만, 필자의 입장과 반대의 입장이 교차되면서 나오고 있다. 단서 따라서 어떤 것이 필자의 입장인지 정확히 파악해야 할 것이다. 발상 글을 읽으면서 음악의 기본적인 인식에는 일관성이 존재한다는 필자의 입장을 잘 집어내야 하는 1등급 문제였다.

| 문제 풀이 순서 |

1st 빈칸이 포함된 문장을 읽고, 빈칸에 들어갈 말에 대한 단서를 얻는다.

빈칸 문장	하지만, 나는 ＿＿＿＿＿＿＿＿＿＿고 믿는다.

➡ 빈칸 문장은 반대되는 내용을 연결하는 But(하지만)으로 시작했다. 따라서 앞과 대조되는 내용이 와야 하므로 글의 앞부분의 내용을 정확히 파악해야 한다.

2nd 글의 앞부분을 읽고, 빈칸에 들어갈 적절한 말을 찾는다.

앞부분 주요 내용	개인차로 인해 일반적인 음악적 인식 모형을 만드는 것은 어렵지만, 음악의 기본적인 인식(박자 및 조성과 같은 요소)에는 일관성이 존재함 단서 1
예시	대부분의 사람은 전형적인 민요나 클래식 곡에서 '박자'를 찾을 수 있다는 일화적 증거가 있음 단서 2
빈칸 문장의 앞 문장	음악의 인식에 완벽한 일치가 있는 것은 아니고, 의견 차이가 있을 수 있음

➡ 글의 서술 방식이 '반대 입장을 인정하지만, 나의 의견은 이러하다'는 패턴으로 반대 입장과 주장하는 바가 교차로 반복되고 있다.
음악적 행동이나 인식의 모형을 만들려는 시도는 개인차로 인해 어려움이 있지만, 음악에 대한 기본적인 인식 측면에서는 비교적 일관성이 있다는 주장을 담은 글이다.

▶ 빈칸 문장은 〈앞의 내용과 반대로, 나는 우리 사이의 공통점이 차이점보다 더 크다고 믿는다.〉는 내용이 되어야 함

3rd **2nd** 에서 이해한 내용을 선택지에서 고른다.

음악에 대한 기본적인 인식 측면에서는 비교적 일관성이 있다는 내용의 글이다. 따라서 빈칸에 들어갈 말로 가장 적절한 것은 ④ '우리 사이의 공통점이 차이점보다 훨씬 더 크다'이다.

| 선택지 분석 |

① **our devotion to narrowing these differences will emerge**
이 차이를 좁히려는 우리의 헌신이 드러날 것이다
차이를 좁히고 일관성을 찾으려고 하는 것은 맞지만 '헌신'은 논리적으로 어색하다.

② **fundamental musical behaviors evolve within communities**
기본적인 음악적 행동은 공동체 내에서 진화한다
'행동'이 아니라 주로 음악적 '인식'에 대해 다루고 있으며, 공동체에서의 진화는 언급되지 않았다.

③ **these varied perceptions enrich shared musical experiences**
이러한 다양한 인식은 공유된 음악적 경험을 풍부하게 한다
빈칸은 But으로 시작되므로 앞에 나온 '다양한 인식'과는 반대되는 내용이 제시되어야 한다.

④ **the commonalities between us far outweigh the differences**
우리 사이의 공통점이 차이점보다 훨씬 더 크다
음악의 기본적인 인식의 측면에는 비교적 일관성이 있다는 주장을 하는 글이다.

⑤ **diversity rather than uniformity in musical processes counts**
음악적 과정에서 일치보다는 다양성이 중요하다
필자는 음악의 인식 측면에서 일관적인 요소가 있다는 것을 주장하므로 이것은 글의 내용과 반대이다.

K 어휘 Review 정답

01 이해하다	11 regardless of	21 delicate
02 추론하다	12 and so forth	22 flourished
03 적절한	13 contrary to	23 wilderness
04 언급, 참조	14 in terms of	24 dramatic
05 사소한	15 head for	25 discriminate
06 commercialize	16 route	26 exceptional
07 integrate	17 supremacy	27 tangible
08 precisely	18 attendance	28 untamed
09 conceal	19 constant	29 cumulative
10 biography	20 forbid	30 urgent

빈칸 문장이 But으로
시작하는 것에 주목하자!

L 흐름에 맞지 않는 문장 찾기

L 01 정답 ③ *동물의 의사 결정

다음 글에서 전체 흐름과 관계 없는 문장은?

단서 1 상대를 공격할지 아니면 도망칠지 갈등하는 상황에 처한 동물에 관한 글임

The animal / in a conflict / between attacking a rival and fleeing / may initially not have sufficient information / to enable it to make a decision straight away. //

주어 / 동사 / to enable의 목적어와 목적격 보어

동물은 / 갈등하는 / 상대를 공격하는 것과 도피하는 것 사이에서 / 처음에는 충분한 정보를 갖지 못할 수도 있다 / 그것이 즉시 결정을 내릴 수 있게 할 //

① If the rival is likely to win the fight, / then the optimal decision / would be to give up immediately and not risk getting injured. //

병렬 구조 (risk 앞에 to가 생략됨)

상대가 싸움에서 이길 것 같다면 / 최적의 결정은 / 즉시 포기하고 부상당할 위험을 무릅쓰지 않는 것일 것이다 //

② But if the rival is weak and easily defeatable, / then there could be considerable benefit / in going ahead and obtaining / the territory, females, food or whatever is at stake. //

하지만 상대가 약하고 쉽게 이길 만하다면 / 상당한 이익이 있을 수 있다 / 싸워서 얻는 것에 / 영역, 암컷, 먹이 또는 성패가 달린 것은 무엇이든 // 복합 관계대명사 이끄는 obtaining의 목적어절

③ Animals / under normal circumstances / maintain a very constant body weight / and they eat and drink enough / for their needs / at regular intervals. // 단서 2 평상시 동물의 특징을 설명함

(동물은 / 보통의 상황에서 / 매우 일정한 체중을 유지하며 / 그들은 충분히 먹고 마신다 / 자신들에게 필요한 만큼 / 규칙적인 간격으로 //)

④ By taking a little extra time / to collect information about the opponent, /

약간의 추가 시간을 들임으로써 / 상대에 대한 정보를 수집하는 데 /

the animal is more likely to reach a decision / that maximizes its chances of winning / than if it takes a decision / without such information. //

주격 관계대명사 / 선행사

그 동물은 결정에 도달할 가능성이 더 크다 / 그것의 이길 가능성을 최대화하는 / 그것이 결정을 내리는 경우보다 / 그러한 정보 없이 //

⑤ Many signals are now seen / as having this information gathering or 'assessment' function, /

see A as B(A를 B로 간주하다)의 수동태

오늘날 많은 신호들이 간주되어 / 이러한 정보 수집 또는 '평가' 기능을 갖는 것으로 /

directly contributing / to the mechanism of the decision-making process / by supplying vital information / about the likely outcomes / of the various options. //

연속 동작의 분사구문을 이끄는 현재분사

직접적으로 기여한다 / 의사 결정 과정의 메커니즘에 / 매우 중요한 정보를 제공함으로써 / 가능한 결과에 관한 / 다양한 선택의 //

- conflict ⓝ 갈등 · flee ⓥ 달아나다 · initially ⓐⓓ 처음에
- sufficient ⓐ 충분한 · straight away 즉시, 지체 없이
- optimal ⓐ 최고[최적]의 · considerable ⓐ 상당한, 많은
- obtain ⓥ 얻다, 구하다 · territory ⓝ 영토, 지역
- at stake 위태로운, 성패가 달려 있는 · circumstance ⓝ 환경, 상황
- constant ⓐ 끊임없는, 변함없는 · interval ⓝ 간격, 사이
- opponent ⓝ 상대, 반대자 · maximize ⓥ 극대화하다, 최대한 활용하다
- assessment ⓝ 평가 · vital ⓐ 필수적인
- likely ⓐ 예상되는, 그럴듯한 · outcome ⓝ 결과

상대를 공격하는 것과 도피하는 것 사이에서 갈등하는 동물은 처음에는 즉시 결정을 내릴 수 있게 할 충분한 정보를 갖지 못할 수도 있다. ① 상대가 싸움에서 이길 것 같다면, 최적의 결정은 즉시 포기하고 부상당할 위험을 무릅쓰지 않는 것일 것이다. ② 하지만 상대가 약하고 쉽게 이길 만하다면, 싸워서 영역, 암컷, 먹이 또는 성패가 달린 것은 무엇이든 얻는 것에 상당한 이익이 있을 수 있다. (③ 보통의 상황에서 동물은 매우 일정한 체중을 유지하며, 그들은 규칙적인 간격으로 자신들에게 필요한 만큼 충분히 먹고 마신다.) ④ 상대에 대한 정보를 수집하는 데 약간의 추가 시간을 들임으로써,

그 동물은 그러한 정보 없이 결정을 내리는 경우보다 이길 가능성을 최대화하는 결정에 도달할 가능성이 더 크다. ⑤ 오늘날 많은 신호들이 이러한 정보 수집 또는 '평가' 기능을 갖는 것으로 간주되어, 다양한 선택의 가능한 결과에 관한 매우 중요한 정보를 제공함으로써 의사 결정 과정의 메커니즘에 직접적으로 기여한다.

> **왜** 정답 ? [정답률 82%] 싸울지 도망칠지 결정하는 것을 말함 꿀팁

첫 문장을 통해 이 글이 상대와 싸울지 아니면 도망칠지 갈등하는 상황에 처한 동물에 대해 설명한다는 것을 알 수 있다. 이어지는 내용은 약간의 추가 시간을 들임으로써 정보를 수집하여 결정을 내리면 정보 없이 결정을 내리는 것보다 더 좋은 결정을 내릴 수 있다는 것으로, 보통의 상황에서 동물이 일정한 체중을 유지한다는 ③은 전체 글의 흐름에 맞지 않는다.

> **왜** 오답 ?

①, ② 각각 도망치기로 결정하는 것과 상대를 공격하기로 결정하는 것에 대해 부연하는 문장이다.

④ 처음에는 충분한 정보를 갖지 못할 수 있다고 설명한 첫 문장과 연결되는 내용으로, 약간의 추가 시간을 들여서 정보를 수집하면 좋은 결정을 내릴 가능성이 더 커진다는 설명이다.

⑤ 오늘날에는 많은 신호들이 앞에서 설명한 정보 수집이나 평가의 기능을 갖는 것으로 간주되고 의사 결정에 기여한다는 내용으로, '의사 결정에 영향을 미치는 정보 수집'이라는 글의 소재와 연결된다.

* 글의 흐름

도입	상대를 공격할지 도망칠지 갈등하는 동물은 처음에는 결정을 내리기에 충분한 정보를 갖지 못할 수도 있음
대조	상대가 이길 것 같다면 최적의 결정은 즉시 (싸움을) 포기하는 것임
	상대를 쉽게 이길 것 같다면 싸워서 얻는 것에 상당한 이익이 있을 수 있음
부연	상대에 대한 정보를 수집하는 데 약간의 추가 시간을 들임으로써 최적의 결정에 도달할 수 있음

L 02 정답 ④ * 수정 확대가족

다음 글에서 전체 흐름과 관계 없는 문장은?

Kinship ties / continue to be important / today. //
친족 유대 관계는 / 계속 중요하다 / 오늘날에도 //
앞에 관계부사가 생략됨
In modern societies / such as the United States / people frequently have family get-togethers, /
현대 사회에서 / 미국과 같은 / 사람들이 자주 가족 모임을 갖는 /
they telephone their relatives regularly, / and they provide their kin / with a wide variety of services. //
provide A with B: A에게 B를 제공하다
그들은 자신의 친척에게 자주 전화하고 / 그들은 자신의 친척에게 제공한다 / 아주 다양한 도움을 //
① Eugene Litwak has referred to this pattern of behaviour / as the 'modified extended family'. // 단서1 수정 확대가족 구조의 특징을 설명함
Eugene Litwak은 이 행동 양식을 표현했다 / '수정 확대가족'이라고 //
② It is an extended family structure / because multigenerational ties are maintained, /
그것은 확대가족 구조이지만 / 다세대의 유대 관계가 유지되기 때문에 /
but it is modified / because it does not usually rest on co-residence / between the generations / and most extended families do not act / as corporate groups. //
그것은 수정된다 / 그것이 일반적으로 공동 거주에 기초를 두지 않고 / 세대 간 / 대부분의 확대가족이 기능하지는 않기 때문에 / 공동 집단으로서 //
③ Although modified extended family members often live / close by, /
부사절 접속사(양보)
비록 수정 확대가족의 구성원들이 흔히 살기는 하지만 / 가까이 /

the modified extended family does not require / geographical proximity / and ties are maintained / even when kin are separated / by considerable distances. //
부사절 접속사(시간)
수정 확대가족은 필요로 하지 않으며 / 지리적 근접을 / 유대 관계는 유지된다 / 친척이 떨어져 있더라도 / 상당한 거리에 의해 단서2 수정 확대가족 구조가 갖는 특징이 아님
(④ The oldest member of the family / makes the decisions / on
= however
important issues, / no matter how far away family members live / from each other. //)
(그 가족의 최고 연장자가 / 결정을 내린다 / 중요한 문제에 관해서는 / 가족 구성원들이 아무리 멀리 떨어져 살지라도 / 서로에게서 //)
⑤ In contrast to the traditional extended family / where kin
선행사   관계부사
always live / in close proximity, /
전통적인 확대가족과는 대조적으로 / 친척이 항상 사는 / 아주 가까이에서 /
the members of modified extended families / may freely move away from kin / to seek opportunities / for occupational advancement. // 수정 확대가족의 구성원들은 / 친척에게서 자유로이 멀리 이주해 가서 / 기회를 추구할 수도 있다 / 직업상의 발전을 위한 //

- kinship ⓝ 친족 · tie ⓝ ((pl.)) 유대 관계 · modern ⓐ 현대의
- frequently ⓐⓓ 자주 · get-together (비격식적인) 모임
- relative ⓝ 친척 · regularly ⓐⓓ 자주, 규칙적으로
- refer to ~을 언급[표현]하다 · behaviour ⓝ 행동
- modified ⓐ 수정된 · extend ⓥ 확대하다 · structure ⓝ 구조
- multigenerational ⓐ 다세대의 · maintain ⓥ 유지하다
- rest on ~에 기초하다 · co-residence 공동 거주
- corporate ⓐ 공동의 · close ⓐⓓ 가까이 · require ⓥ 필요로 하다
- geographical ⓐ 지리(학)적인 · separate ⓥ 분리하다
- considerable ⓐ 상당한, 많은 · distance ⓝ 거리
- decision ⓝ 결정 · in contrast ~와 대조적으로
- traditional ⓐ 전통적인 · away from ~에서 떠나서
- seek ⓥ 찾다, 추구하다 · opportunity ⓝ 기회
- occupational ⓐ 직업의 · advancement ⓝ 발전

친족 유대 관계는 오늘날에도 계속 중요하다. 사람들이 자주 가족 모임을 갖는 미국과 같은 현대 사회에서, 그들은 자신의 친척에게 자주 전화하고, 아주 다양한 도움을 제공한다. ① Eugene Litwak은 이 행동 양식을 '수정 확대가족'이라고 표현했다. ② 그것은 다세대의 유대 관계가 유지되기 때문에 확대가족 구조이지만, 일반적으로 세대 간 공동 거주에 기초를 두지 않고 대부분의 확대가족이 공동 집단으로서 기능하지는 않기 때문에 수정 확대가족 구조이다. ③ 비록 수정 확대가족의 구성원들이 흔히 가까이 살기는 하지만, 수정 확대가족은 지리적 근접이 필요치 않으며, 유대 관계는 친척이 상당한 거리에 의해 떨어져 있더라도 유지된다. (④ 가족 구성원들이 서로에게서 아무리 멀리 떨어져 살지라도, 중요한 문제에 관해서는 그 가족의 최고 연장자가 결정을 내린다.) ⑤ 친척이 항상 아주 가까이에서 사는 전통적인 확대가족과는 대조적으로, 수정 확대가족의 구성원들은 친척에게서 자유로이 멀리 이주해 가서 직업상의 발전을 위한 기회를 추구할 수도 있다.

> **왜** 정답 ? [정답률 83%]

현대 사회의 수정 확대가족 구조의 특징을 설명하는 글로, 다세대의 유대 관계가 유지된다는 점에서 확대가족이지만, 지리적으로 근접한 곳에 거주하는 것이 필요치 않기 때문에 수정 확대가족이라는 것이 글의 핵심이다. 그런데 ④는 가족 구성원들이 떨어져 살더라도 중요한 문제에 관한 결정은 가족의 최고 연장자가 내린다는 내용으로, 수정 확대가족 구조가 갖는 특징을 설명한 문장이 아니다.

> **왜** 오답 ?

① 과거의 확대가족과는 다르면서도 비슷한 현대 사회의 가족 구조를 수정 확대가족이라고 부른다는 내용으로, 수정 확대가족의 특징에 대한 설명을 시작하는 문장이다.

② 수정 확대가족과 기존의 확대가족의 특징을 설명하여 오늘날의 가족 구조가 어떤 특징 때문에 '수정된 확대가족'인지를 설명한다.

③, ⑤ 기존의 확대가족 구조와 달리 공동 거주에 기초를 두지 않는다는 수정 확대가족의 특징을 좀 더 자세히 설명하는 문장이다.

＊ 글의 흐름

도입	친족 유대 관계는 오늘날에도 계속 중요함
전개	Eugene Litwak은 오늘날의 확대가족이 다세대의 유대 관계를 유지하기는 하지만 공동 집단으로서 기능하지 않기 때문에 '수정 확대가족'이라고 설명함
부연	수정 확대가족은 지리적 근접이 필요치 않고 상당한 거리로 서로 떨어져 있어도 유대 관계는 유지됨
결론	수정 확대가족 구성원들은 친척에게서 멀리 이주해 가서 직업상의 발전을 추구할 수 있음

L 03 정답 ④ ＊교통수단의 발달이 스포츠 관광에 미치는 영향

다음 글에서 전체 흐름과 관계 없는 문장은?

단서1 스포츠 관광의 확대는 교통수단의 발전에 영향을 받았음
The expansion of sports tourism / in the twentieth century / has
been influenced / by further developments in transportation. //
　　　　현재완료의 수동태
스포츠 관광의 확대는 / 20세기의 / 영향을 받았다 / 교통수단이 더욱 발전되는 것에 //

Just as the railways revolutionized travel / in the nineteenth
just as A, so B: A와 마찬가지로 B도
century, / so the automobile produced even more dramatic
　　　　　　　　　　　　　비교급 강조
changes / in the twentieth. //
철도가 여행에 혁신을 일으켰던 것과 꼭 마찬가지로 / 19세기에 / 자동차가 훨씬 더 극적인
변화를 일으켰다 / 20세기에 //

① The significance of the car / in the development of sport and
　　　　　　　　　　　현재완료
tourism / generally has attracted considerable coverage / and it
　현재완료
has had no less an impact / on sports tourism specifically. //
자동차의 중요성은 / 스포츠와 관광의 발전에서의 / 일반적으로 상당한 주목을 끌었으며 /
못지않은 영향을 미쳤다 / 구체적으로는 스포츠 관광에 //
　　　뒤에 부사절의 주어와 be동사 생략
② Although originally invented / towards the end of the
nineteenth century, / it started to become a mass form of
transport / in the 1920s in the USA / and rather later in Britain. //
자동차는 원래 발명되었지만 / 19세기 말에 접어들면서 / 대중적인 교통수단이 되기 시작했다
/ 1920년대에 미국에서 / 그리고 상당히 더 늦게 영국에서 //

③ Apart from its convenience and flexibility, / the car has the
additional advantages / of affording access to many areas /
　과거분사(areas 수식)
not served by public transport,
자동차는 편리함과 유연성 외에도 / 추가적인 장점이 있다 / 많은 지역에 접근하게 해 준다는 /
대중교통이 제공되지 않는 /
　　A as well as B: B뿐만 아니라 A도
/ as well as allowing the easy transport / of luggage and
equipment. // **단서2** 자동차는 대중교통이 제공되지 않는 많은 지역에 접근하게 해줌
쉽게 운송해 준다는 것과 더불어 / 짐과 장비를 //

(④ The expansion of reasonably priced, good quality
　　　　　　　　　　　　　　과거분사(accomodation 수식)
accommodation / associated with tourism growth / has also
　현재완료　　　　　　　　　　　과거분사(restaurants 수식)
facilitated the growth / of locally based restaurants. //)
(가격이 합리적이고 질이 좋은 숙박 시설의 확대는 / 관광업 성장과 연관된 / 또한 성장을
촉진했다 / 현지에 기반을 둔 식당의 // **단서3** 관광업이 지역의 숙박 시설과 식당의
　　　　　　　　　　　　　　성장을 촉진한다는 내용은 관계 없음
⑤ As a result, / it was invaluable / for the development of many
　　　　　　　　　　　　　　　= forms 주격 관계대명사
forms of sports tourism / but especially those which require the
transportation of people and equipment / to relatively remote
locations. //
그 결과 / 그것은 매우 유용했다 / 여러 형태의 스포츠 관광 형태가 발전하는 데 / 특히 사람과
장비를 운송해야 하는 스포츠 관광 형태가 / 비교적 먼 곳으로 //

- expansion ⓝ 확장　　　　• revolutionize ⓥ 혁신을 일으키다
- significance ⓝ 중요성　　　• considerable ⓐ 상당한
- apart from ~외에도　　　　• flexibility ⓝ 유연성, 신축성
- equipment ⓝ 장비　　　　　• reasonably ⓐⓓ 합리적으로
- invaluable ⓐ 매우 유용한, 귀중한

20세기의 스포츠 관광의 확대는 교통수단이 더욱 발전되는 것에 영향을 받았다. 철도가 19세기에 여행에 혁신을 일으켰던 것과 꼭 마찬가지로, 자동차가 20세기에 훨씬 더 극적인 변화를 일으켰다. ① 스포츠와 관광의 발전에서의 자동차의 중요성은 일반적으로 상당한 주목을 끌었으며, 구체적으로는 스포츠 관광에 못지않은 영향을 미쳤다. ② 자동차는 원래 19세기 말에 접어들면서 발명되었지만, 1920년대에 미국에서, 그리고 상당히 더 늦게 영국에서 대중적인 교통수단이 되기 시작했다. ③ 자동차는 편리함과 유연성 외에도 짐과 장비를 쉽게 운송해 준다는 것과 더불어 대중교통이 제공되지 않는 많은 지역에 접근하게 해 준다는 추가적인 장점이 있다. (④ 관광업 성장과 연관된 가격이 합리적이고 질이 좋은 숙박 시설의 확대는 또한 현지에 기반을 둔 식당의 성장을 촉진했다.) ⑤ 그 결과, 그것은 여러 형태의 스포츠 관광, 특히 사람과 장비를 비교적 먼곳으로 운송해야 하는 스포츠 관광 형태가 발전하는 데 매우 유용했다.

왜 정답·오답? [정답률 66%]

글의 앞부분: 20세기의 스포츠 관광의 확대는 교통수단이 더욱 발전되는 것에 영향을 받았다. 철도가 19세기에 여행에 혁신을 일으켰던 것과 꼭 마찬가지로, 자동차가 20세기에 훨씬 더 극적인 변화를 일으켰다.

➡ 철도가 19세기 여행에 혁신을 일으켰던 것처럼, 자동차는 20세기의 스포츠 관광에 큰 변화를 불러왔다.

① 스포츠와 관광의 발전에서의 자동차의 중요성은 일반적으로 상당한 주목을 끌었으며, 구체적으로는 스포츠 관광에 못지않은 영향을 미쳤다.

➡ 스포츠와 관광이 발전하는 데 있어 자동차는 매우 중요하며, 구체적으로 스포츠 관광에 못지않은 영향을 미쳤다고 했다.
앞부분에서 자동차가 스포츠 관광에 변화를 불러왔다는 내용에 이어, 스포츠와 관광 및 스포츠 관광의 발전에 자동차가 중요하다고 설명하고 있는 흐름이다.
▶ ①은 무관한 문장이 아님

② 자동차는 원래 19세기 말에 접어들면서 발명되었지만, 1920년대에 미국에서, 그리고 상당히 더 늦게 영국에서 대중적인 교통수단이 되기 시작했다.

➡ 자동차가 대중적인 교통수단이 되기 시작했다고 언급했다. 20세기에 스포츠 관광에 자동차가 큰 영향을 미쳤다는 내용을 구체화하기 위해 자동차가 20세기에 대중적인 교통수단이 되었다고 설명하는 문장이므로 자연스럽게 이어진다.
▶ ②은 무관한 문장이 아님

③ 자동차는 편리함과 유연성 외에도 짐과 장비를 쉽게 운송해 준다는 것과 더불어 대중교통이 제공되지 않는 많은 지역에 접근하게 해 준다는 추가적인 장점이 있다.

➡ 자동차는 짐과 장비를 쉽게 운송해 주고, 대중교통이 제공되지 않는 많은 지역에 접근하도록 해준다고 했다. 자동차가 스포츠 관광 발달에 어떻게 영향을 주었는지를 설명하는 흐름이다.
▶ ③은 무관한 문장이 아님

④ 관광업 성장과 연관된 가격이 합리적이고 질이 좋은 숙박 시설의 확대는 또한 현지에 기반을 둔 식당의 성장을 촉진했다.

➡ 관광업이 지역의 숙박 시설과 식당의 성장을 촉진했다는 내용은 지금까지 이야기한 내용과 전혀 관계 없는 것이다.
▶ ④은 무관한 문장임

⑤ 그 결과, 그것은 여러 형태의 스포츠 관광, 특히 사람과 장비를 비교적 먼곳으로 운송해야 하는 스포츠 관광 형태가 발전하는 데 매우 유용했다.

➡ 그 결과, 스포츠 관광의 발전에 자동차가 매우 유용하다고 했다. 자동차가 먼 지역을 이동하고, 장비를 쉽게 운송한다는 장점을 ③에서 언급한 이후, 이 이유로 스포츠 관광의 발전에 영향을 미쳤다고 설명하는 흐름이다.
▶ ④이 빠져야 자연스러운 흐름이 됨, ⑤은 무관한 문장이 아님

＊ 글의 흐름

주제	자동차의 발달은 스포츠 관광의 발전에 큰 변화를 불러옴
원인	자동차는 짐과 장비를 쉽게 운송해 주고, 대중교통이 미치지 않는 곳까지 쉽게 이동할 수 있도록 해 줌
결과	스포츠 관광의 발전에 자동차가 매우 유용한 역할을 함

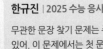

한규진 | 2025 수능 응시 · 대구 계성고 졸

무관한 문장 찾기 문제는 주제 찾기와 연결되어 있다고 할 수 있어. 이 문제에서는 첫 문장에서 '20세기의 스포츠 관광 확대는 교통수단이 더욱 발전하는 데에 영향을 받았다'라고 했으니까, '스포츠 관광 확대'와 '교통수단의 발전'을 포인트로 잡고 글을 읽어내려갈 수 있어. 계속 글이 이어지다가 3번 문장에서 갑자기 '숙박 시설의 확대와 식당의 성장'이라는 다소 뜬금없는 내용이 등장한다는 것이 느껴지면 성공이야!

L 04 정답 ④ ＊판매업자의 물품 확보를 위한 조직망

다음 글에서 전체 흐름과 관계 없는 문장은?

The best dealers offer / a much broader service / than merely
having their goods on display / and 'selling from stock'. //
최고의 판매업자는 제공한다 / 훨씬 더 폭넓은 서비스를 / 단지 상품을 전시하는 것보다 /
그리고 '재고로 있는 것을 판매하는 것'보다 //

Once they know / the needs of a particular collector / they can
actively seek specific items / to fill gaps in the collection. //
일단 그들이 알게 되면 / 특정 수집가의 필요를 / 그들은 적극적으로 특정 물품을 찾을 수 있다
/ 소장품의 빈틈을 채우려 //

① Because it is their business, / to which they devote themselves
full-time, / they will inevitably have a much wider network /
than any non-professional collector can ever develop. //
그것이 그들의 사업이기 때문에 / 그들이 전업으로 하는 / 그들은 훨씬 더 넓은 조직망을
필연적으로 갖출 것이다 / 여태껏 어느 비전문 수집가가 구축할 수 있는 것보다도 //

② As a matter of course / they can enquire about the availability
of pieces / from dealers in other cities / and, most crucially in
some categories, / from overseas. //
당연히 / 그들은 작품의 구매 가능 여부를 문의할 수 있다 / 그들은 다른 도시의
판매업자들에게 / 그리고 가장 중요하게 일부 범주에서는 / 해외의 판매업자들에게도 //

③ They will be routinely informed / of news of all auctions and
important private sales, /
그들은 정례적으로 정보를 받을 것이다 / 모든 경매와 중요한 개인 판매 소식에 대해 /

and should be well-enough connected / to hear occasionally of
items / which are not yet quite on sale / but might be available
for a certain price. //
그리고 충분히 연결망을 갖추고 있을 것이다 / 물품에 대해 가끔 소식을 들을 수 있도록 / 아직
판매되지 않은 / 그러나 특정 가격에 구매할 수 있을 //

④ The main advantage / of buying from a dealer / is getting
personalised service / on your purchases. //
주요 이점은 / 판매업자로부터 구매하는 것의 / 개인화된 서비스를 받는 것이다 / 구매품에
대해 //

⑤ In turn, / they can circulate their own contacts / with 'want-
lists' of desired items or subjects, / multiplying their client
collectors' chances of expanding their collections. //
결과적으로 / 그들은 자신들이 연락하는 이들에게 배포할 수 있다 / 원하는 물품이나 대상의
'필요 품목표'를 / 자신들의 고객 수집가의 소장품 확장 기회를 배가할 수 있다 //

• **stock** ⓝ 재고 • **specific** ⓐ 특정한 • **collection** ⓝ 소장품
• **devote** ⓥ (~에) 바치다, 기울이다
• **full-time** ⓐ 전업의, 전시간(근무, 노동)의
• **inevitably** ⓐ𝒹 필연적으로 • **as a matter of course** 당연히
• **enquire** ⓥ 문의하다 • **availability** ⓝ 구매 가능 여부, 이용 가능성
• **crucially** ⓐ𝒹 중요하게 • **routinely** ⓐ𝒹 정례적으로, 일상적으로
• **occasionally** ⓐ𝒹 가끔 • **purchase** ⓝ 구매
• **circulate** ⓥ 배포하다, 돌리다 • **multiply** ⓥ 배가하다, 늘리다
• **expand** ⓥ 확장하다

최고의 판매업자는 단지 상품을 전시하고 '재고로 있는 것을 판매하는 것'보다 훨씬 더 폭넓은 서비스를 제공한다. 특정 수집가의 필요를 알게 되면, 그들은 소장품의 빈틈을 채우려 특정 물품을 적극적으로 찾을 수 있다. ① 그것이 그들이 전업으로 하는 사업이기 때문에, 그들은 여태껏 어느 비전문 수집가가 구축할 수 있는 것보다도 훨씬 더 넓은 조직망을 필연적으로 갖출 것이다. ② 당연히 그들은 다른 도시의 판매업자들에게, 그리고 가장 중요하게 일부 범주에서는 해외의 판매업자들에게도 작품의 구매 가능 여부를 문의할 수 있다. ③ 그들은 모든 경매와 중요한 개인 판매 소식에 대해 정례적으로 정보를 받을 것이며, 아직 판매되지 않았지만 특정 가격에 구매할 수 있을 물품에 대해 가끔 소식을 들을 수 있도록 충분히 연결망을 갖추고 있을 것이다. (④ 판매업자로부터 구매하는 것의 주요 이점은 구매품에 대해 개인화된 서비스를 받는 것이다.) ⑤ 결과적으로, 그들은 원하는 물품이나 대상의 '필요 품목표'를 자신들이 연락하는 이들에게 배포하여, 자신들의 고객 수집가의 소장품 확장 기회를 배가할 수 있다.

왜 정답·오답? [정답률 78%]

첫 문장: 최고의 판매업자는 단지 상품을 전시하고 '재고로 있는 것을 판매하는 것'보다 훨씬 더 폭넓은 서비스를 제공한다. 특정 수집가의 필요를 알게 되면, 그들은 소장품의 빈틈을 채우려 특정 물품을 적극적으로 찾을 수 있다.

→ 판매업자는 특정 구매자가 필요로 하는 물품을 적극적으로 찾아줄 수 있다는 내용으로 특정 물품을 적극적으로 찾는 것에 대한 부연 설명이 뒤따를 것임

① 그것이 그들이 전업으로 하는 사업이기 때문에, 그들은 여태껏 어느 비전문 수집가가 구축할 수 있는 것보다도 훨씬 더 넓은 조직망을 필연적으로 갖출 것이다.

→ 훨씬 더 넓은 조직망을 필연적으로 갖출 것이라고 하며 앞 문장에서 언급한 특정 물품을 적극적으로 찾는 방법을 제시했다. ▶ ①은 무관한 문장이 아님

② 당연히(As a matter of course) 그들은 다른 도시의 판매업자들에게, 그리고 가장 중요하게 일부 범주에서는 해외의 판매업자들에게도 작품의 구매 가능 여부를 문의할 수 있다.

→ 앞 문장에서 언급한 더 넓은 조직망을 사용해 다른 도시나 해외의 판매업자에게 작품의 구매 여부를 문의할 수 있다고 말하고 있다.
▶ ②은 무관한 문장이 아님

③ 그들은 모든 경매와 중요한 개인 판매 소식에 대해 정례적으로 정보를 받을 것이며, 아직 판매되지 않았지만 특정 가격에 구매할 수 있을 물품에 대해 가끔 소식을 들을 수 있도록 충분히 연결망을 갖추고 있을 것이다.

→ ①에서 언급한 더 넓은 조직망을 활용하여 물품을 구입하는 것에 대한 정보를 교환하는 것에 대해 추가적으로 설명하고 있다.
▶ ③은 무관한 문장이 아님

④ 판매업자로부터 구매하는 것의 주요 이점은 구매품에 대해 개인화된 서비스를 받는 것이다.

→ 판매업자가 물품 확보를 위해 조직망을 활용하는 것에 대해 이야기하는 것과는 다르게 판매업자의 이점을 구매품에 대한 개인화된 서비스를 받는 것이라고 언급하고 있다. ▶ ④은 무관한 문장임

⑤ 결과적으로(In turn), 그들은 원하는 물품이나 대상의 '필요 품목표'를 자신들이 연락하는 이들에게 배포하여, 자신들의 고객 수집가의 소장품 확장 기회를 배가할 수 있다.

→ ③의 내용에 이어서 원하는 물품이나 대상의 필요 품목표를 연락하는 이들에게 배포하여 확보할 수 있다고 말하고 있다.
▶ ④이 빠져야 자연스러운 흐름이 됨

＊글의 흐름

도입	최고의 판매업자는 폭넓은 서비스를 제공, 구매자를 위해 특정 물품을 적극적으로 찾을 수 있음
설명	물품 확보를 위한 넓은 조직망을 갖춤
부연	다른 도시나 해외 판매업자에게 문의 가능하고, 물품에 대한 여러 정보를 받을 수 있음
결론	자신들이 원하는 물품 확보 가능성을 조직망을 활용해 높일 수 있음

L 05 정답 ④ ＊새가 노래를 학습하는 단계

다음 글에서 전체 흐름과 관계 <u>없는</u> 문장은?

Avian song learning occurs in two stages: / first, songs must
be memorized / and, second, they must be practiced. //
조류의 노래 학습은 두 단계로 이루어지는데 / 첫째로는, 노래를 암기해야 하고 / 둘째로는,
노래를 연습해야 한다 // **단서 1** 조류의 노래 학습은 암기와 연습이라는 두 단계로 이루어짐

In some species these two events overlap, / but in others
memorization can occur / before practice by several months,
/ providing an impressive example of long-term memory
storage. //
일부 종에서는 이 두 가지 일이 겹치기도 하지만 / 다른 종에서는 암기가 이루어질 수 있는데 /
연습 전 몇 달 동안 / 이는 장기 기억 저장의 인상적인 예시를 제공한다 //

① The young bird's initial efforts / to reproduce the memorized
song / are usually not successful. //
어린 새의 초기의 노력은 / 암기한 노래를 재현하려는 / 대체로 성공적이지 못하다 //

② These early songs may have / uneven pitch, irregular tempo, /
and notes that are out of order or poorly reproduced. //
이러한 초기의 노래에는 있을 수도 있다 / 고르지 않은 음정과 불규칙한 박자 / 그리고 순서가
맞지 않거나 제대로 재현되지 않은 음이 //

③ However, sound graphs of songs recorded / over several
weeks or months / reveal /
히지만 녹음된 노래의 음향 그래프를 보면 / 몇 주 또는 몇 달에 걸쳐(녹음된) / 보여준다 /
that during this practice period / the bird fine-tunes his
efforts / until he produces an accurate copy of the memorized
template. //
이 연습 기간 동안 / 새가 미세 조정의 노력을 기울인다는 것을 / 암기된 본보기를 정확하게
모방할 때까지 //
단서 2 지금까지 제시된 새의 노래 학습에 대한 내용은 선호나 한계점과는 관련이 없음

(④ An important idea to emerge from the study of birdsong / is
that song learning is shaped by preferences and limitations. //)
(새소리 연구를 통해 드러날 수 있는 중요한 아이디어는 / 노래 학습은 선호하는 것과
한계점에 의해 형성된다는 것이다 //)
단서 3 새가 노래를 연습하며 정확도를 높이기 위해 미세 조정을 하는 ③ 문장의 내용을 가리킴

⑤ This process requires hearing oneself sing; / birds are unable
to reproduce memorized songs / if they are deafened / after
memorization but before the practice period. //
이 과정에서는 자신이 노래하는 것을 들어야 하는데 / 새들은 암기된 노래를 재현할 수 없다 /
만약 귀가 먹으면 / 새들이 암기하는 한 후이지만 연습 기간 전이라면 //

- memorize ⓥ 암기하다   - overlap ⓥ 겹치다
- storage ⓝ 저장, 보관   - reproduce ⓥ 재현하다
- uneven ⓐ 고르지 않은   - pitch ⓝ 음정   - irregular ⓐ 불규칙인
- tempo ⓝ 박자   - note ⓝ 음, 음표   - fine-tune ⓐ 미세 조정을 하다
- accurate ⓐ 정확한   - template ⓝ 본보기
- emerge ⓥ 드러나다, 판명되다   - deafen ⓥ 귀를 먹게 만들다

조류의 노래 학습은 두 단계로 이루어지는데, 첫째로는, 노래를 암기해야 하고
둘째로는, 노래를 연습해야 한다. 일부 종에서는 이 두 가지 일이 겹치기도
하지만, 다른 종에서는 연습 전 몇 달 동안 암기가 이루어질 수 있는데, 이는
장기 기억 저장의 인상적인 예를 제공한다. ① 어린 새가 암기한 노래를
재현하려는 초기의 노력은 대체로 성공적이지 못하다. ② 이러한 초기의
노래에는 고르지 않은 음정과 불규칙한 박자, 그리고 순서가 맞지 않거나
제대로 재현되지 않은 음이 있을 수도 있다. ③ 하지만 몇 주 또는 몇 달에 걸쳐
녹음된 노래의 음향 그래프를 보면, 이 연습 기간 동안 새가 암기된 본보기를
정확하게 모방할 때까지 미세 조정의 노력을 기울인다는 것을 알 수 있다.
(④ 새소리 연구를 통해 드러날 수 있는 중요한 아이디어는 노래 학습은
선호하는 것과 한계점에 의해 형성된다는 것이다.) ⑤ 이 과정에서는 자신이
노래하는 것을 들어야 하는데, 만약 새들이 암기한 후이지만 연습 기간 전에
귀가 먹으면 암기된 노래를 재현할 수 없다.

왜 정답·오답? [정답률 83%]

글의 앞부분: 조류의 노래 학습은 두 단계로 이루어지는데, 첫째로는, 노래를
암기해야 하고 둘째로는, 노래를 연습해야 한다. 일부 종에서는 이 두 가지 일이
겹치기도 하지만, 다른 종에서는 연습 전 몇 달 동안 암기가 이루어질 수 있는데,
이는 장기 기억 저장의 인상적인 예를 제공한다.
➡ 조류가 노래를 학습하는 두 단계(암기, 연습)의 구체적인 설명이 뒤따를 것이다.

① 어린 새가 암기한 노래를 재현하려는 초기의 노력은 대체로 성공적이지
못하다.
➡ 새가 노래를 학습하는 과정의 첫 단계가 제시된다.
▶ ①은 무관한 문장이 아님

② 이러한 초기의 노래(These early songs)에는 고르지 않은 음정과
불규칙한 박자, 그리고 순서가 맞지 않거나 제대로 재현되지 않은 음이
있을 수도 있다.
➡ '이러한 초기의 노래'는 ①에서 제시된 초기의 노력과 연결되므로 자연스러운
흐름이다.
▶ ②은 무관한 문장이 아님

③ 하지만(However) 몇 주 또는 몇 달에 걸쳐 녹음된 노래의 음향
그래프를 보면, 이 연습 기간 동안 새가 암기된 본보기를 정확하게 모방할
때까지 미세 조정의 노력을 기울인다는 것을 알 수 있다.
➡ 반대 내용을 연결하는 However(하지만)가 오는데, 암기 이후 연습하는 과정과
관련된 내용이면서 However로 연결 가능한 문장이 이어진다.
▶ ③은 무관한 문장이 아님

④ 새소리 연구를 통해 드러날 수 있는 중요한 아이디어는 노래 학습은
선호하는 것과 한계점에 의해 형성된다는 것이다.
➡ 현재까지 제시된 새의 노래 학습 과정은 이 문장에서 말하는 선호나 한계점과는
관련이 없다.
▶ ④이 무관한 문장임

⑤ 이 과정(This process)에서는 자신이 노래하는 것을 들어야 하는데,
만약 새들이 암기한 후이지만 연습 기간 전에 귀가 먹으면 암기된 노래를
재현할 수 없다.
➡ ⑤의 '이 과정(This process)'은 ③에서 제시된 '미세 조정의 노력'을 가리킨다.
▶ ④이 빠져야 자연스러운 흐름이 되므로 ⑤은 무관한 문장이 아님

＊ 글의 흐름

도입	새의 노래 학습은 암기와 연습이라는 두 단계로 이루어짐
설명	초기의 암기는 불완전한 노래지만 계속 연습하면서 미세 조정을 통해 노래를 정확하게 재현할 수 있게 됨
부연	연습하면서 자신의 노래를 들어야 미세 조정이 가능함

L 06 정답 ③ ＊새로운 시스템 사용에 있어 사회적 목표와 개인적 목표의 불일치

다음 글에서 전체 흐름과 관계 <u>없는</u> 문장은?

It is important to remember / that to achieve acceptance and
use of new technologies systems, / the personal importance
to the users / has to be valued more highly than the degree of
innovation. //
기억하는 것이 중요하다 / 새로운 기술/시스템의 수용과 사용을 달성하기 위해서는 /
사용자들에게 개인적 중요성이 / 혁신의 정도보다 더욱 높이 평가되어야 한다는 점을 //

However, policies and political goals / are often confused with
the driver's personal goals. //
그러나 정책들과 정치적 목표들은 / 종종 운전자의 개인적 목표들과 혼동된다 //

① Societal goals and individual goals / do not necessarily
coincide. // **단서 1** 사회적 목표와 개인적 목표는 반드시 일치하지는 않음
사회적 목표들과 개인적 목표들은 / 반드시 일치하지는 않는다 //

② For example, / the policy goal / behind ISA (Intelligent Speed Adaptation; a system which warns the drivers when they
주격 관계대명사
exceed the speed limit, and may even prevent them from doing
동사구의 병렬 구조
so) /
예를 들어 / 정책 목표는 / ISA (지능형 속도 적응 시스템, 즉 운전자들이 제한 속도를 초과할 때 그들에게 경고하고 심지어 그들이 그렇게 하는 것을 방지할 수 있는 시스템) 뒤에 있는 /

could be to increase traffic safety / or to increase speed limit compliance. //
교통안전을 증진하거나 / 제한 속도 준수를 증진하는 것일 수 있다 //

③ Some drivers have a goal to collect many classic cars, /
형용사적 용법
although it has little impact on their use of new speed adaptation
systems. // 단서2 일부 운전자들이 클래식 자동차를 수집하는 목표를 가지고 있다는 것은
관계없는 내용임
일부 운전자들은 많은 클래식 자동차를 수집하는 목표를 가지고 있지만 / 이는 그들의 새로운 속도 적응 시스템들의 사용에는 거의 영향이 없다 //

④ These goals might not be relevant to some drivers, / for example, due to their feeling that safety measures are redundant /
이러한 목표들은 일부 운전자들에게는 관련이 없을 수 있는데 / 예를 들어, 안전 조치가 불필요하다는 그들의 느낌 때문에

because of their own personal driving skills / or because speeding is not seen as a 'real crime'. // 단서3 이러한 목표, 즉, 정책 목표는 일부
운전자들에게는 관련이 없을 수 있음
그들 자신의 개인적인 운전 기술 때문에 / 혹은 속도위반이 '진짜 범죄'로 보이지 않기 때문이다 //

⑤ Nevertheless, they might find / that the system helps them
help+목적어+목적격 보어(to부정사)
to avoid speeding tickets / or they want to use the system / simply because they have a general interest in innovative systems. // 그럼에도 불구하고, 그들은 알게 될 수도 있고 / 그 시스템이 속도위반 딱지를 피하는 것을 도와준다는 것을 / 혹은 그들은 그 시스템을 사용하고 싶어 한다 / 단순히 그들이 혁신적인 시스템에 대한 일반적인 관심을 가졌기 때문에 //

- achieve ⓥ 성취하다, 달성하다   • policy ⓝ 정책
- warn ⓥ 경고하다   • exceed ⓥ 넘다   • adaptation ⓝ 적응
- relevant ⓐ 관련 있는   • measure ⓝ 조치
- innovative ⓐ 혁신적인

새로운 기술/시스템의 수용과 사용을 달성하기 위해서는 사용자들에게 개인적 중요성이 혁신의 정도보다 더욱 높이 평가되어야 한다는 점을 기억하는 것이 중요하다. 그러나 정책들과 정치적 목표들은 종종 운전자의 개인적 목표들과 혼동된다. ① 사회적 목표들과 개인적 목표들은 반드시 일치하지는 않는다. ② 예를 들어, ISA(지능형 속도 적응 시스템, 즉 운전자들이 제한 속도를 초과할 때 그들에게 경고하고 심지어 그들이 그렇게 하는 것을 방지할 수 있는 시스템) 뒤에 있는 정책 목표는 교통안전을 증진하거나 제한 속도 준수를 증진하는 것일 수 있다. (③ 일부 운전자들은 많은 클래식 자동차를 수집하는 목표를 가지고 있지만, 이는 그들의 새로운 속도 적응 시스템들의 사용에는 거의 영향이 없다.) ④ 이러한 목표들은 일부 운전자들에게는 관련이 없을 수 있는데, 예를 들어, 그들 자신의 개인적인 운전 기술 때문에 안전 조치가 불필요하다는 그들의 느낌 때문에 혹은 속도위반이 '진짜 범죄'로 보이지 않기 때문이다. ⑤ 그럼에도 불구하고, 그들은 그 시스템이 속도위반 딱지를 피하는 것을 도와준다는 것을 알게 될 수도 있고 혹은 단순히 그들이 혁신적인 시스템에 대한 일반적인 관심을 가졌기 때문에 그들은 그 시스템을 사용하고 싶어 한다.

정답·오답? [정답률 77%]

첫 두 문장: 새로운 기술/시스템의 수용과 사용을 달성하기 위해서는 사용자들에게 개인적 중요성이 혁신의 정도보다 더욱 높이 평가되어야 한다는 점을 기억하는 것이 중요하다. 그러나 정책들과 정치적 목표들은 종종 운전자의 개인적 목표들과 혼동된다.

→ 새로운 기술/시스템에 대한 정책들과 정치적 목표들이 개인적 목표들과 어떤 방식으로 혼동되는지에 대한 구체적인 설명이나 예시가 뒤따를 것이다.

― ① 사회적 목표들과 개인적 목표들은 반드시 일치하지는 않는다.

→ 앞 문장의 정치적 목표와 개인적 목표들이 혼동된다는 내용을 반복하고 있다.
▶ ①은 무관한 문장이 아님

---

② 예를 들어(For example), ISA(지능형 속도 적응 시스템, 즉 운전자들이 제한 속도를 초과할 때 그들에게 경고하고 심지어 그들이 그렇게 하는 것을 방지할 수 있는 시스템) 뒤에 있는 정책 목표는 교통안전을 증진하거나 제한 속도 준수를 증진하는 것일 수 있다.

→ 앞 문장에서 말한 사회적 목표와 개인적 목표 중 사회적 목표(정책/정치적 목표)에 대한 구체적 예시를 들고 있다.
▶ ②은 무관한 문장이 아님

③ 일부 운전자들은 많은 클래식 자동차를 수집하는 목표를 가지고 있지만, 이는 그들의 새로운 속도 적응 시스템들의 사용에는 거의 영향이 없다.

→ 앞에서 지능형 속도 적응 시스템에 대한 언급은 있었으나, 클래식 자동차를 수집하는 목표가 있는 운전자와 이들의 시스템 사용에 대한 내용으로 이어지는 것은 어색하다.
▶ ③이 무관한 문장임

④ 이러한 목표들(These goals)은 일부 운전자들에게는 관련이 없을 수 있는데, 예를 들어, 그들 자신의 개인적인 운전 기술 때문에 안전 조치가 불필요하다는 그들의 느낌 때문에 혹은 속도위반이 '진짜 범죄'로 보이지 않기 때문이다.

→ '이러한 목표들(These goals)'은 ②에서 언급된 정책 목표(= 사회적 목표)이며, 주어진 문장과 ①에서 말한 개인적 목표와 사회적 목표의 다름을 뒷받침해주는 예시가 된다.
▶ ③이 빠져야 자연스러운 흐름이 됨, ④은 무관한 문장이 아님

⑤ 그럼에도 불구하고, 그들(They)은 그 시스템이 속도위반 딱지를 피하는 것을 도와준다는 것을 알게 될 수도 있고 혹은 단순히 그들이 혁신적인 시스템에 대한 일반적인 관심을 가졌기 때문에 그들은 그 시스템을 사용하고 싶어 한다.

→ 여기서 '그들(They)'은 운전자를 뜻하며, 정책 목표와 개인적 목표가 다를지라도 시스템을 사용한다는 설명이 이어지고 있다.
▶ ⑤은 무관한 문장이 아님

＊글의 흐름

도입	새로운 기술의 수용과 사용을 위해서는 혁신의 정도보다 사용자들의 개인적 중요성이 높게 평가되어야 하는데, 종종 정책과 정치적 목표들이 개인적 목표들과 혼동됨
예시 ① (사회적 목표)	지능형 속도 적응 시스템의 정책 목표는 교통 안전 증진 혹은 제한 속도 준수 증진일 수 있음
예시 ② (개인적 목표)	운전자들의 개인적 목표와 일치하지 않을 수 있지만, 속도 위반 딱지를 피하게 해주거나 혁신적 시스템에 관심이 있어서 시스템을 사용하고 싶을 수 있음

L 07 정답 ③ ＊알고리즘에 맡겨지는 개인화

다음 글에서 전체 흐름과 관계 없는 문장은? [3점]

In a context in which / the cultural obligation to produce the
전치사+관계대명사
self / as a distinctive authentic individual / is difficult to fulfill, /
상황에서 / 자아를 만들어야 하는 문화적 의무가 / 독특하고 진정한 개인으로서의 / 이행되기 어려운

the burdensome work of individualizing the self / is turned over increasingly to algorithms. // 단서1 자아를 개인화하는 것은 알고리즘에
넘겨짐
자아를 개인화하는 부담스러운 작업은 / 점점 더 알고리즘에 넘겨진다 //

① The "personalization" that is promised on every front /
단수 주어   주격 관계대명사
— in the domains of search, shopping, health, news, advertising, learning, music, and entertainment — /
모든 전면에서 약속되는 "개인화"는 / 검색, 쇼핑, 건강, 뉴스, 광고, 학습, 음악, 그리고 오락의 영역에서 /

단수 동사
depends on ever more refined algorithmic constructions of individuality. //
그 어느 때보다 더 정교한 개성의 알고리즘적 구성에 달려 있다 //

② 가주어   진주어
As it becomes more difficult / to produce our digital selves as unique individuals, / we are increasingly being produced as unique individuals from the outside. //
더 어려워지면서 / 우리의 디지털 자아를 고유한 개인으로 만들어내는 것이 / 우리는 점점 더 외부에서부터 고유한 개인으로 만들어지고 있다 //

(③ 가주어   진주어
When AI algorithms learn more about our identities, / it becomes essential / to safeguard this information and ensure
목적어절 접속사
/ that individuals have control and consent / over the data
과거분사
collected about them. //) **단서 2** 우리에 대한 정보를 보호하고 수집된 데이터에 대한 통제권과 동의를 가져야 한다는 것은 관계 없는 내용임
인공지능 알고리즘이 우리의 자아에 대해서 더 많이 배울 때 / 필수적인 것으로 되고 있다 / 이 정보를 보호하고 확실히 하는 것이 / 개인들이 통제권과 동의를 가짐을 / 그들에 대해 수집된 데이터에 대한 //

④ Individuality is redefined / from a cultural practice and
from A to B: A에서 B로
reflexive project to an algorithmic process. //
개성은 재정의된다 / 문화적 관행이자 성찰적 과제에서 알고리즘적 과정으로 //

⑤ Our unique selfhood is no longer something / for which we are wholly responsible; / it is algorithmically guaranteed. //
우리의 고유한 자아는 더이상 무언가가 아니다 / 우리가 전적으로 책임지는 / 그것은 알고리즘적으로 보장된다 //

- obligation ⓝ 의무   - distinctive ⓐ 독특한
- authentic ⓐ 진짜의   - fulfill ⓥ 충족하다, 이행하다
- personalization ⓝ 개인화 - refined ⓐ 정제된
- construction ⓝ 구조   - essential ⓐ 필수적인
- consent ⓝ 합의, 동의   - individuality ⓝ 특성, 개성
- reflexive ⓐ 성찰적인

독특하고 진정한 개인으로서의 자아를 만들어야 하는 문화적 의무가 이행되기 어려운 상황에서, 자아를 개인화하는 부담스러운 작업은 점점 더 알고리즘에 넘겨진다. ① 모든 전면—검색, 쇼핑, 건강, 뉴스, 광고, 학습, 음악, 그리고 오락의 영역—에서 약속되는 "개인화"는 그 어느 때보다 더 정교한 개성의 알고리즘적 구성에 달려 있다. ② 우리의 디지털 자아를 고유한 개인으로 만들어내는 것이 더 어려워지면서, 우리는 점점 더 외부에서부터 고유한 개인으로 만들어지고 있다. (③ 인공지능 알고리즘이 우리의 자아에 대해서 더 많이 배울 때, 이 정보를 보호하고 개인들이 그들에 대해 수집된 데이터에 대한 통제권과 동의를 가짐을 확실히 하는 것이 필수적인 것으로 되고 있다.) ④ 개성은 문화적 관행이자 성찰적 과제에서 알고리즘적 과정으로 재정의된다. ⑤ 우리의 고유한 자아는 더 이상 우리가 전적으로 책임지는 무언가가 아니다. 그것은 알고리즘적으로 보장된다.

왜 정답·오답? [정답률 53%]

첫 문장: 진정한 개인으로서의 자아를 만들어야 하는 것이 어려워진 상황에서 자아를 개인화하는 작업은 알고리즘에 점차 넘겨진다.
→ 개인화와 알고리즘의 관계와 관련된 내용이 나올 것이다.

① 모든 전면—검색, 쇼핑, 건강, 뉴스, 광고, 학습, 음악, 그리고 오락의 영역—에서 약속되는 "개인화"는 그 어느 때보다 더 정교한 개성의 알고리즘적 구성에 달려 있다.
→ 모든 면에서 개인화는 알고리즘에 달려 있다는 내용으로, 앞 문장과 이어지는 내용이다.
▶ ①은 무관한 문장이 아님

② 우리의 디지털 자아를 고유한 개인으로 만들어내는 것이 더 어려워지면서, 우리는 점점 더 외부에서부터 고유한 개인으로 만들어지고 있다.
→ 개인이 고유하게 자신만의 디지털 자아를 만드는 것이 어려워지면서 외부에서부터 만들어지고 있다는 내용으로, 여기서 '외부'는 앞의 알고리즘과 비슷한 의미로 쓰였으므로 자연스럽게 이어진다.
▶ ②은 무관한 문장이 아님

③ 인공지능 알고리즘이 우리의 자아에 대해서 더 많이 배울 때, 이 정보를 보호하고 개인들이 그들에 대해 수집된 데이터에 대한 통제권과 동의를 가짐을 확실히 하는 것이 필수적인 것으로 되고 있다.
→ 앞 내용과 달리 글의 초점이 인공지능 알고리즘에 의해 수집된 데이터에 대한 개인의 통제권과 동의 및 정보 보호에 있다고 말하고 있다.
▶ ③이 무관한 문장임

④ 개성은 문화적 관행이자 성찰적 과제에서 알고리즘적 과정으로 재정의된다.
→ 개성, 즉, 개인화는 알고리즘적 과정으로 재정의되고 있다는 내용으로, ②의 내용이 이어지고 있다.
▶ ③이 빠져야 자연스러운 흐름이 됨, ④은 무관한 문장이 아님

⑤ 우리의 고유한 자아는 더 이상 우리가 전적으로 책임지는 무언가가 아니다. 그것은 알고리즘적으로 보장된다.
→ 우리의 고유한 자아는 알고리즘적으로 보장된다는 내용으로, ④의 내용에 이어서 같은 맥락이 이어지고 있다.
▶ ⑤은 무관한 문장이 아님

* 글의 흐름

도입	자아를 개인화하는 부담스러운 작업은 점점 더 알고리즘에 넘겨지고 있음
전개	모든 전면에서 약속되는 "개인화"는 그 어느 때보다 더 정교한 개성의 알고리즘적 구성에 달려 있음
부연	우리는 점점 더 외부에서부터 고유한 개인으로 만들어지고 있음
결론	고유한 자아는 더 이상 우리가 전적으로 책임지는 무언가가 아니고, 알고리즘적으로 보장됨

L 08 정답 ③ *인류의 공통 조상과 생존의 어려움

다음 글에서 전체 흐름과 관계 없는 문장은?

The human race traces back / to a surprisingly small number of
'거슬러 올라가다'
common ancestors. //
인류는 거슬러 올라간다 / 놀랄 만큼 적은 수의 공통 조상으로 //

It has been documented / that the entire human race can be
가주어   진주어절 접속사
traced back / to only seven different mothers, / and one of these
절과 절을 잇는 등위접속사
women / is a common ancestor to roughly 40% of the human species. //
밝혀졌다 / 전체 인류가 거슬러 올라갈 수 있고 / 단 7명의 다른 어머니들로 / 이 여성들 중 한 명은 / 대략 인간 종의 40%의 공통 조상이라고 //

Why is this? // 이것은 왜일까 //

The simple answer is / that humans are extremely good at dying
주격 보어절 접속사
and at wiping each other out. // **단서 1** 인간은 서로를 몰살함
간단한 답은 ~이다 / 인간이 죽는 것과 서로를 몰살하는 것에 몹시 능숙하다는 것 //

① History has had many successful rulers and conquerors /
주격 관계대명사
who have got rid of entire populations, /
역사적으로 많은 성공적인 통치자들과 정복자들이 존재해 왔으며 / 전체 인구를 제거한 /
절과 절을 잇는 등위접속사
and even beyond that, / our species has wiped out plenty of
주격 관계대명사
similar humanoid lines / that existed on this earth. //
심지어 그것을 넘어 / 우리 종은 수많은 비슷한 인간에 가까운 계통들을 몰살해 왔다 / 이 지구에 존재했던 // **단서 2** 네안데르탈인과 데니소바인 또한 몰살된 것으로 추정됨

주어
② Scientific finds have so far discovered / a number of other
humanoid species / that once shared the earth with us, / some of
계속적 용법의 목적격 관계대명사
which include Neanderthals and Denisovans. //
과학적 발견들은 지금까지 발견해 왔는데 / 많은 인간에 가까운 종들을 / 한때 우리와 지구를 공유했던 / 그들 중 몇몇은 네안데르탈인과 데니소바인을 포함한다 //

③ There are still no clear examples / of Neanderthals attempting [attempting의 의미상 주어] to expressively symbolize / real-life elements such as animals or people / in creative works. //) **단서 3** 네안데르탈인은 지구에서 사라진 종들의 예시로 언급되었음
(명백한 사례는 아직까지 없다 / 네안데르탈인이 표현적으로 상징화하려고 시도한 / 동물이나 사람과 같은 실재의 요소들을 / 창의적인 작품에 //)

④ Yet of these lines, / only homo sapiens have survived, / only the modern humans. //
그러나 이 계통들 중에서 / 오직 호모사피엔스 살아남았다 / 즉 현대의 인간들만이 //

⑤ That itself shows / how difficult it is / for a species to survive and thrive long-term / on this planet. // [가주어 / 의미상 주어 / 진주어]
그 자체가 보여 준다 / 얼마나 어려운지를 / 한 종이 살아남아 장기적으로 번영하는 것이 / 이 행성에서 //

- human race 인류
- trace back to …의 기원[유래]이 …까지 거슬러 올라가다
- roughly [ad] 대략 · wipe out 몰살하다, ~을 완전히 파괴하다
- ruler [n] 통치자 · conqueror [n] 정복자
- expressively [ad] 표현적으로 · symbolize [v] 상징하다
- thrive [v] 번성하다

인류는 놀랄 만큼 적은 수의 공통 조상으로 거슬러 올라간다. 전체 인류가 단 7명의 다른 어머니들로 거슬러 올라갈 수 있고 이 여성들 중 한 명은 대략 인간 종의 40%의 공통 조상이라고 밝혀졌다. 이것은 왜일까? 간단한 답은 인간이 죽는 것과 서로를 몰살하는 것에 몹시 능숙하다는 것이다. ① 역사적으로 전체 인구를 제거한 많은 성공적인 통치자들과 정복자들이 존재해 왔으며, 심지어 그것을 넘어 우리 종은 이 지구에 존재했던 수많은 비슷한 인간에 가까운 계통들을 몰살해 왔다. ② 과학적 발견들은 지금까지 한때 우리와 지구를 공유했던 많은 인간에 가까운 종들을 발견해 왔는데, 그들 중 몇몇은 네안데르탈인과 데니소바인을 포함한다. (③ 네안데르탈인이 동물이나 사람과 같은 실재의 요소들을 창의적인 작품에 표현적으로 상징화하려고 시도한 명백한 사례는 아직까지 없다.) ④ 그러나 이 계통들 중에서 오직 호모사피엔스, 즉 현대의 인간들만이 살아남았다. ⑤ 그 자체가 한 종이 이 행성에서 살아남아 장기적으로 번영하는 것이 얼마나 어려운지를 보여 준다.

왜 정답·오답? [정답률 74%]

글의 앞부분: 인류는 놀랄 만큼 적은 수의 공통 조상으로 거슬러 올라간다. 전체 인류가 단 7명의 다른 어머니들로 거슬러 올라갈 수 있고 이 여성들 중 한 명은 대략 인간 종의 40%의 공통 조상이라고 밝혀졌다. 이것은 왜일까? 간단한 답은 인간이 죽는 것과 서로를 몰살하는 것에 몹시 능숙하다는 것이다.

→ 인간들이 서로를 몰살하는 것이 능숙하다는 것에 관한 구체적인 설명이 뒤따를 것이다.

① 역사적으로 전체 인구를 제거한 많은 성공적인 통치자들과 정복자들이 존재해 왔으며, 심지어 그것을 넘어 우리 종은 이 지구에 존재했던 수많은 비슷한 인간에 가까운 계통들을 몰살해 왔다.

→ 우리 종은 수많은 비슷한 인간에 가까운 계통들을 몰살해 왔다는 내용이 이어진다.
▶ ①은 무관한 문장이 아님

② 과학적 발견들은 지금까지 한때 우리와 지구를 공유했던 많은 인간에 가까운 종들을 발견해 왔는데, 그들 중 몇몇은 네안데르탈인과 데니소바인을 포함한다.

→ 인간이 몰살시킨 구체적인 사례를 들며, 앞 문장을 뒷받침하고 있다.
▶ ②은 무관한 문장이 아님

③ 네안데르탈인이 동물이나 사람과 같은 실재의 요소들을 창의적인 작품에 표현적으로 상징화하려고 시도한 명백한 사례는 아직까지 없다.

→ 네안데르탈인이 상징을 창의적 작품에 사용했다는 내용은 관련이 전혀 없다.
▶ ③이 무관한 문장임

④ 그러나 이 계통들 중에서 오직 호모사피엔스, 즉 현대의 인간들만이 살아남았다.

→ 인간들끼리 서로 몰살시킨 결과 현대 인간들의 조상인 호모사피엔스만 살아남았다고 설명하므로 앞의 내용에서 이어진다.
▶ ③이 빠지면 자연스러운 흐름이 되므로 ④은 무관한 문장이 아님

---

⑤ 그 자체가 한 종이 이 행성에서 살아남아 장기적으로 번영하는 것이 얼마나 어려운지를 보여 준다.

→ 한 종만이 살아남았다는 앞 내용에 이어, 그것이 어려운 일임을 설명한다.
▶ ⑤은 무관한 문장이 아님

* 글의 흐름

도입	인간들은 서로를 몰살하는 것에 능숙함
부연	인류 역사상 인간은 자신과 비슷한 계통들을 몰살시켰음
전개	인간들끼리의 몰살 결과 호모사피엔스만 살아남음
부연	몰살을 뚫고 현대까지 자손을 퍼뜨린 일이 쉽지는 않았을 것임

L 09 정답 ④ * 다른 영어 사용자와 일하면서 겪게 되는 언어적 차이

다음 글에서 전체 흐름과 관계 없는 문장은?

No doubt / students collaborating with other speakers of [사이에 접속사 that 생략 / students를 수식하는 분사] English / might encounter language variances, / which may [관계대명사의 계속적 용법] interfere with intentionality. // **단서 1** 다른 영어 사용자와 일하면 언어적 차이에 마주칠 수밖에 없음을 언급함
의심의 여지가 없다 / 영어로 말하는 다른 사용자와 공동으로 일하는 학생들이 / 언어적 차이와 마주칠 수도 있다는 것은 / 그것은 의도성에 방해가 될 수도 있다 //

① To address such disparities, / Horner, Lu, Royster, and [부사적 용법(목적)] Trimbur (2011) call for a "translingual approach" /
이러한 차이를 다루기 위해 / Horner, Lu, Royster, Trimbur(2011)는 '초언어적 접근법'을 요구한다 /
in which language varieties are not perceived as barriers, / but [= where] [not A but B: A가 아니라 B] as avenues for meaning making. //
언어의 다양성이 장벽으로 인식되는 것이 아니라 / 의미 창출의 수단으로(인식되는) //

② Similarly, / Galloway and Rose (2015) study of Global Englishes found / that exposure to other Englishes / helps [목적어절 접속사 / help+동사원형] normalize language differences. //
마찬가지로 / 글로벌 영어들에 대한 Galloway와 Rose(2015)의 연구가 발견했다 / 다른 영어들에 대한 노출이 / 언어 차이를 표준화하는 데 도움이 된다는 사실을 //

③ Educators have to work with students / to examine phrases, [부사적 용법(목적)] expressions, and other ranges of English language use /
교육자들은 학생들과 함께해야 한다 / 구문, 표현 그리고 영어 사용의 다른 범주를 검토하기 위해 / **단서 2** 언어적 차이의 오류나 열등한 지위가 아니라 여러 차이점의 범주를 검토해야 함
for their rhetorical and communicative possibilities / and not their perceived errors or inferior status. //
그것들의 수사적, 의사소통적 가능성을 위한 / 그것들의 인식되는 오류나 열등한 지위가 아니라 //

④ Committing an error means / unintentionally saying what [= the thing which] isn't true, / so any linguistic or perspective error should be avoided / at all cost. //) **단서 3** 언어적 오류를 무슨 수를 써서라도 피해야 한다고 함 (앞 문장들과 다른 내용)
오류를 범한다는 것은 의미한다 / 사실이 아닌 것을 의도치 않게 말하는 것을 / 그래서 그 어떤 언어적 또는 관점적 오류는 피해야 한다 / 무슨 수를 써서라도 //

⑤ After all, / students are constantly reading texts / and listening to speakers / whose Englishes do not necessarily conform to / [소유격 관계대명사] what is considered standard / in their own communities. // [= the thing which]
결국 / 학생들은 계속해서 글을 읽고 / 화자의 말을 듣는다 / (그것)들의 영어는 반드시 일치하지는 않는다 / 표준으로 여겨지는 것과 / 그들 자신의 공동체에서 //

- collaborate [v] 협력하다 · encounter [v] 마주치다
- variance [n] 차이, 불일치 · interfere [v] 방해하다
- intentionality [n] 의도성
- address [v] (문제·상황 등에 대해) 고심하다[다루다]
- translingual [a] 초언어적인 · barrier [n] 장벽
- avenue [n] 수단; 큰 길 · exposure [n] 노출
- normalize [v] 표준화하다, 정상화하다 · examine [v] 조사하다
- constantly [ad] 끊임없이 · considered [a] 중히 여겨지는, 깊이 생각한
- community [n] 주민, 공동체

영어로 말하는 다른 사용자와 공동으로 일하는 학생들이 언어적 차이와 마주칠 수도 있다는 것은 의심의 여지가 없고, 그것은 의도성에 방해가 될 수도 있다. ① 이러한 차이를 다루기 위해 Horner, Lu, Royster, Trimbur(2011)는 언어의 다양성이 의미 창출의 장벽이 아니라 수단으로 인식되는 '초언어적 접근법'을 요구한다. ② 마찬가지로, 글로벌 영어들에 대한 Galloway와 Rose(2015)의 연구가 다른 영어들에 대한 노출이 언어 차이를 표준화하는 데 도움이 된다는 사실을 발견했다. ③ 교육자들은 그것들의 인식되는 오류나 열등한 지위가 아니라 그것들의 수사적, 의사소통적 가능성을 위한 구문, 표현 그리고 영어 사용의 다른 범주를 검토하기 위해 학생들과 함께해야 한다. (④ 오류를 범한다는 것은 사실이 아닌 것을 의도치 않게 말하는 것을 의미하고, 그래서 그 어떤 언어적 또는 관점적 오류는 무슨 수를 써서라도 피해야 한다.) ⑤ 결국, 학생들은 계속해서 글을 읽고 화자의 말을 듣는데, 그(것)들의 영어는 그들 자신의 공동체에서 표준으로 여겨지는 것과 반드시 일치하지는 않는다.

왜 정답·오답? [정답률 80%]

첫 문장: 영어로 말하는 다른 사용자와 공동으로 일하는 학생들이 언어적 차이와 마주칠 수도 있다는 것은 의심의 여지가 없고, 그것은 의도성에 방해가 될 수도 있다.

➡ 학생들이 마주치는 언어적 차이 혹은 언어적 차이를 다루는 방법에 대한 설명이 뒤따를 것임

① 이러한 차이(such disparities)를 다루기 위해 Horner, Lu, Royster, Trimbur(2011)는 언어의 다양성이 의미 창출의 장벽이 아니라 수단으로 인식되는 '초언어적 접근법'을 요구한다.

➡ 언어적 차이를 다루기 위해 언어의 다양성을 의미 창출의 수단으로 보는 접근법이 요구된다고 하며 앞 문장에서 언급한 언어적 차이를 다루는 방법을 제시했다.
▶ ①은 무관한 문장이 아님

② 마찬가지로(Similarly), 글로벌 영어들에 대한 Galloway와 Rose(2015)의 연구가 다른 영어들에 대한 노출이 언어 차이를 표준화하는 데 도움이 된다는 사실을 발견했다.

➡ 다른 영어들에 대한 노출이 언어 차이를 표준화한다고 하며 언어적 차이를 다루는 방법을 추가적으로 제시하고 있다.
▶ ②은 무관한 문장이 아님

③ 교육자들은 그것들의 인식되는 오류나 열등한 지위가 아니라 그것들의 수사적, 의사소통적 가능성을 위한 구문, 표현 그리고 영어 사용의 다른 범주를 검토하기 위해 학생들과 함께해야 한다.

➡ 앞 문장에 이어 교육자들이 학생들과 함께 다른 영어들이 갖는 차이를 표준화하고 검토하는 방법을 말하고 있다.
▶ ③은 무관한 문장이 아님

④ 오류를 범한다는 것은 사실이 아닌 것을 의도치 않게 말하는 것을 의미하고, 그래서 그 어떤 언어적 또는 관점적 오류는 무슨 수를 써서라도 피해야 한다.

➡ 앞 문장에서 언어 차이에 의한 오류가 열등한 것이 아니며 언어 차이를 표준화하는 방식을 제시한 것과 달리 언어적 오류를 반드시 피해야 한다고 말하고 있다.
▶ ④은 무관한 문장임

⑤ 결국(After all), 학생들은 계속해서 글을 읽고 화자의 말을 듣는데, 그(것)들의 영어는 그들 자신의 공동체에서 표준으로 여겨지는 것과 반드시 일치하지는 않는다.

➡ ③의 내용에 이어서 학생들의 영어가 표준과 반드시 일치하지는 않는다고 언급하고 있다.
▶ ④이 빠져야 자연스러운 흐름이 됨

* 글의 흐름

도입	다른 영어 사용 시 발생하는 언어적 차이
전개	언어적 차이를 다양한 의미 창출의 수단으로 보는 접근법을 소개하고, 다른 영어에 대한 노출이 언어적 차이를 표준화한다고 함
부연	교육자들이 학생들과 함께 다른 영어들이 갖는 차이를 표준화하고 검토하는 방법 소개
결론	학생들의 영어가 표준과 반드시 일치하지는 않음

268 자이스토리 영어 독해 실전

L 10 정답 ④ * 사회적 증거의 원리

다음 글에서 전체 흐름과 관계 없는 문장은?

According to the principle of social proof, / one way / individuals determine appropriate behavior / for themselves / in a situation /
사회적 증거의 원리에 따르면 / 한 가지 방법은 / 사람들이 적합한 행동을 결정하는 / 자신에게 / 어떤 상황에서 **단서1** 다른 사람들의 행동을 기준으로 적합한 행동을 결정함
is to examine / the behavior of others there / — especially similar others. //
살펴보는 것이다 / 그곳에 있는 다른 사람들의 행동을 / 특히 유사한 다른 사람들 //
It is ~ that으로 강조되는 부사구
① It is through social comparison / with these referent others / that people validate the correctness / of their opinions and decisions. //
바로 사회적 비교를 통해서 이다 / 선택하는 데 모델 역할을 하는 이러한 다른 사람들과의 / 사람들이 올바름을 확인하는 것은 / 자신의 의견과 결정의 //
② Consequently, / people tend to behave / as their friends and peers have behaved. //
그 결과 / 사람들은 행동하는 경향이 있다 / 친구들과 동료들이 행동해 온 것처럼 //
단수 주어
③ Because the critical source of information / within the principle of social proof / is the responses of referent others, /
단수 동사
왜냐하면 정보의 중요한 원천은 / 사회적 증거의 원리 안에서 / 선택하는 데 모델 역할을 하는 다른 사람들의 반응이기 때문에 /
<추측>을 나타내는 조동사
compliance tactics / that employ this information / should be especially effective / in collectivistically oriented nations and persons. //
순응 전술은 / 이러한 정보를 이용하는 / 특히 효과적일 것이다 / 집단주의 지향의 국가와 사람들에게 //
<장소>의 부사절 접속사 **단서2** 개인화된 자아가 중심이자 기준인 경우를 설명함
④ That is, / where the individualized self is / both the focus and the standard, / one's own behavioral history / should be heavily weighted / in subsequent behavior. //)
(다시 말해 / 개인화된 자아가 ~인 경우에 / 중심이자 기준 / 자기 자신의 행동 이력은 / 크게 비중이 더해질 것이다 / 후속 행동에서 //)
주어 동사
⑤ Some evidence / in this regard / comes from a study /
어떤 증거는 / 이 점과 관련하여 / 연구에서 나온다 /
목적어절 접속사 주격 관계대명사
showing / that advertisements / that promoted group benefits / were more persuasive / in Korea (a collectivistic society) / than in the United States (an individualistic society). //
보여 주는 / 광고가 / 집단 혜택을 홍보하는 / 더 설득력이 있었다는 것을 / 한국(집단주의 사회)에서 / 미국(개인주의 사회)에서보다 //

- principle ⓝ 원리 · proof ⓝ 증거
- determine ⓥ 알아내다, 결정하다 · appropriate ⓐ 적합한
- examine ⓥ 조사[검토]하다 · comparison ⓝ 비교
- validate ⓥ 확인하다 · consequently ⓐⓓ 그 결과, 결과적으로
- peer ⓝ 동료, 또래 · critical ⓐ 중요한 · compliance ⓝ 순응
- employ ⓥ 이용하다 · oriented ⓐ ~을 지향하는
- behavioral ⓐ 행동의, 행동에 관한 · weight ⓥ 비중을 더하다
- subsequent ⓐ 그[이] 다음의, 차후의 · evidence ⓝ 증거, 증언
- in this regard 이와 관련하여 · promote ⓥ 홍보하다
- persuasive ⓐ 설득력이 있는 · collectivistic ⓐ 집단주의의
- individualistic ⓐ 개인주의의

사회적 증거의 원리에 따르면, 어떤 상황에서 사람들이 자신에게 적합한 행동을 결정하는 한 가지 방법은 그곳에 있는 다른 사람들의 행동, 특히 유사한 다른 사람들의 행동을 살펴보는 것이다. ① 사람들이 자신의 의견과 결정의 올바름을 확인하는 것은 바로 선택하는 데 모델 역할을 하는 이러한 다른 사람들과의 사회적 비교를 통해서이다. ② 그 결과, 사람들은 친구들과 동료들이 행동해 온 것처럼 행동하는 경향이 있다. ③ 사회적 증거의 원리 안에서 정보의

중요한 원천은 선택하는 데 모델 역할을 하는 다른 사람들의 반응이기 때문에, 이러한 정보를 이용하는 순응 전술은 집단주의 지향의 국가와 사람들에게 특히 효과적일 것이다. (④ 다시 말해, 개인화된 자아가 중심이자 기준인 경우에, 자기 자신의 행동 이력은 후속 행동에서 크게 비중이 더해질 것이다.)
⑤ 이 점과 관련하여 어떤 증거는 집단 혜택을 홍보하는 광고가 미국(개인주의 사회)에서보다 한국(집단주의 사회)에서 더 설득력이 있었다는 것을 보여 주는 연구에서 나온다.

왜 정답·오답? [정답률 62%]

첫 문장: 어떤 상황에서 자신에게 적합한 행동을 결정하는 한 방법은 그곳에 있는 다른 사람들의 행동을 살펴보는 것이다.

→ 이 글은 주변 사람들의 행동을 살펴봄으로써 자신의 적합한 행동을 결정한다는 내용임

① 사람들은 선택하는 데 모델 역할을 하는 이러한 다른 사람들(these referent others)과의 사회적 비교를 통해 자신의 의견과 결정이 올바른지 판단한다.

→ these referent others가 가리키는 것: 앞 문장에 등장한, '그 곳에 있는 다른 사람들'
첫 문장에 이어 ①에서도, 다른 사람들의 행동과 비교하여 자신의 행동, 의견, 결정이 적합한지를 판단한다는 내용이 이어진다.
▶ ①은 무관한 문장이 아님

② 그 결과(Consequently) 사람들은 친구들과 동료들이 행동해 온 것처럼 행동하는 경향이 있다.

→ consequently는 그 앞에 원인이, 그 뒤에 결과가 온다.
다른 사람들과의 사회적 비교를 통해 자신의 의견과 결정이 올바른지 판단한다. → 다른 사람들의 의견과 결정이 올바른 것이다. → 그렇다면 다른 사람들과 똑같이 행동할 것이다.
▶ ①과 ②은 consequently로 이어지기에 자연스러우므로 ②은 무관한 문장이 아님

③ 다른 사람들의 반응을 정보의 중요한 원천으로 이용하는 전술은 집단주의를 지향하는 국가와 사람들에게 효과적일 것이다.

→ 다른 사람들이 행동하는 것처럼 행동하게 하는 전술은 집단주의를 추구하는 국가와 사람들에게 효과적일 것이라는 흐름이다.
▶ ③은 무관한 문장이 아님

④ 다시 말해(That is), 개인화된 자아가 중심이자 기준인 경우에는 자기 자신의 행동 이력이 후속 행동에서 큰 비중을 차지할 것이다.

→ that is는 앞에 나온 내용을 다른 말로 하거나 요약할 때 쓰인다.
앞부분: 다른 사람들의 행동이 중심이자 기준인 경우
④: 자기 자신의 행동이 중심이자 기준인 경우 ▶ ④이 무관한 문장임

⑤ 집단 혜택을 홍보하는 광고는 개인주의 사회인 미국에서보다 집단주의 사회인 한국에서 더 설득력이 있었다.

→ 집단주의를 지향하는 국가와 사람들에게 더 효과적일 것이라는 ③을 뒷받침하는 연구를 ⑤에서 소개한다. ▶ ④이 빠져야 자연스러운 흐름이 됨

---

* 글의 흐름

도입	사람들이 적합한 행동을 결정하는 한 가지 방법은 유사한 다른 사람들의 행동을 살펴보는 것임
부연	사람들이 자신의 결정의 올바름을 확인하는 것은 이러한 다른 사람들과의 사회적 비교를 통해서임
결과	사람들은 친구들과 동료들이 행동해 온 것처럼 행동하는 경향이 있음
설명	어떤 증거는 집단 혜택을 홍보하는 광고가 미국에서보다 한국에서 더 설득력이 있었다는 것을 보여 주는 연구에서 나옴

L 11 정답 ③ * 이주 결정에 대한 경제학적 관점

다음 글에서 전체 흐름과 관계 없는 문장은?

A variety of theoretical perspectives / provide insight / into immigration. //
단서 1 이주에 대한 경제학적 관점은 행위자들이 효용 극대화에 참여한다고 상정하는 것임
다양한 이론적 관점은 / 통찰을 제공한다 / 이주에 대한
학과 이름, 병명, 운동 이름 등의 복수형 명사가 주어일 때는 단수 동사를 씀
Economics, / which assumes / that actors engage / in utility maximization, / represents one framework. //
경제학은 / 상정하는 / 행위자들이 참여한다고 / 효용 극대화에 / 하나의 틀을 제시한다 //
가주어
① From this perspective, / it is assumed / that individuals are
진주어절 접속사 ①
rational actors, / i.e., that they make migration decisions /
진주어절 접속사 ①
이런 관점에서는 / ~이라고 추정된다 / 개인은 합리적인 행위자라고 / 즉 그들은 이주 결정을 내린다고 /
based on their assessment / of the costs as well as benefits / of
B as well as A: A뿐만 아니라 B도
remaining in a given area / versus the costs and benefits / of leaving. //
자신의 평가에 근거하여 / 비용 및 편익에 대한 / 특정한 지역에 남는 것의 / 비용과 편익 모두에 비한 / 떠나는 것의 //
동사 may include와 전치사 to의 공통된 목적어
② Benefits may include / but are not limited / to short-term and long-term monetary gains, safety, and greater freedom / of cultural expression. //
편익은 포함할 수도 있지만 / 국한되지는 않는다 / 단기적 및 장기적인 금전적 이득, 안전, 더 큰 자유에 / 문화적 표현의 //
주어   동사
③ People with greater financial benefits / tend to use their money / to show off their social status / by purchasing luxurious items. // 단서 2 사람들이 효용 극대화의 관점에서 이주 결정을 내린다는 것과 관계 없음
(더 큰 금전적 혜택이 있는 사람들은 / 자신의 돈을 쓰는 경향이 있다 / 자신의 사회적 지위를 과시하기 위해 / 사치품을 구입함으로써 //)
④ Individual costs include / but are not limited / to the expense of travel, /
개인적 비용은 포함하지만 / 국한되지는 않는다 / 이동 비용에 /
uncertainty of living in a foreign land, / difficulty of adapting / to a different language, / uncertainty about a different culture, / and the great concern / about living in a new land. //
타지에서 사는 것의 불확실성에 / 적응하는 것의 어려움에 / 다른 언어에 / 다른 문화에 대한 불확실성에 / 그리고 큰 염려에 / 새로운 지역에서 사는 것에 대한 //
⑤ Psychic costs / associated / with separation from family,
주어
friends, / and the fear of the unknown / also should be taken into account / in cost-benefit assessments. //
동사
심리적 비용은 / 관련된 / 가족, 친구와의 이별과 / 그리고 미지의 것에 대한 두려움과 / 또한 고려되어야 한다 / 비용-편익 평가에서 //

- theoretical ⓐ 이론적인 · perspective ⓝ 관점 · insight ⓝ 통찰
- immigration ⓝ 이주, 이민 · assume ⓥ 추정[상정]하다
- utility ⓝ 효용 · maximization ⓝ 극대화
- represent ⓥ 제시하다 · rational ⓐ 합리적인
- migration ⓝ (사람·동물의 대규모) 이주, 이동 · assessment ⓝ 평가
- versus ⓟ ~ 대(對) · monetary ⓐ 금전(상)의

- show off ~을 과시하다 · status ⓝ 지위 · luxurious ⓐ 사치스러운
- expense ⓝ 비용 · uncertainty ⓝ 불확실성 · adapt ⓥ 적응하다
- associated ⓐ 관련된 · separation ⓝ 헤어짐
- take ~ into account ~을 고려하다

다양한 이론적 관점은 이주에 대한 통찰을 제공한다. 행위자들이 효용 극대화에 참여한다고 상정하는 경제학은 하나의 틀을 제시한다. ① 이런 관점에서는 개인은 합리적인 행위자라고, 즉 그들은 특정한 지역을 떠나는 것의 비용 및 편익과 대비하여 남는 것의 비용과 편익 모두에 대한 자신의 평가에 근거하여 이주 결정을 내린다고 추정된다. ② 편익은 단기적 및 장기적인 금전적 이득, 안전, 문화적 표현의 더 큰 자유를 포함할 수도 있지만 이에 국한되지는 않는다. (③ 더 큰 금전적 혜택이 있는 사람들은 사치품을 구입함으로써 자신의 사회적 지위를 과시하기 위해 돈을 쓰는 경향이 있다.) ④ 개인적 비용은 이동 비용, 타지에서 사는 것의 불확실성, 다른 언어에 적응하는 것의 어려움, 다른 문화에 대한 불확실성, 새로운 지역에서 사는 것에 대한 큰 염려를 포함하지만 이에 국한되지는 않는다. ⑤ 가족, 친구와의 이별과 미지의 것에 대한 두려움과 관련된 심리적 비용 또한 비용-편익 평가에서 고려되어야 한다.

> **왜 정답?** [정답률 79%]

이주에 대한 경제학적 관점에 대해 설명하는 글로, 경제학은 행위자들의 효용 극대화 측면에서 이주를 설명한다는 내용이다.
즉, '특정 지역에 남는 것의 비용과 편익 vs. 그곳을 떠나는 것의 비용과 편익'에 대한 자신의 판단에 근거하여 이주 결정을 내리는 것으로, 편익에 포함되는 요소와 비용에 포함되는 요소에 대한 구체적인 설명이 이어진다. ③은 더 큰 금전적 혜택을 가진 사람들의 사치품 구입 목적을 설명하는, 경제학에서 바라보는 이주 결정과 관계 없는 문장이다.

> **왜 오답?**

① 이주 결정에 있어 행위자가 효용 극대화에 참여하는 것이 구체적으로 무슨 의미인지를 설명하는 문장이다.
② 앞 문장에서 두 가지 경우의 비용과 편익을 비교하여 결정을 내린다고 했고, 편익에 포함되는 요소가 무엇인지 설명하는 문장이 이어지는 것이다.
④, ⑤ 앞에서 편익에 포함되는 요소를 설명했고, 이어서 비용에 포함되는 요소가 무엇인지 설명하는 것이다.

* 글의 흐름

도입	경제학에서는 개인이 특정 지역을 떠나는 것과 떠나지 않는 것의 비용과 편익 평가에 근거하여 이주를 결정한다고 상정함
부연 ①	편익에는 단기 및 장기적인 금전적 이득, 안전, 문화적 표현의 더 큰 자유가 포함됨
부연 ②	비용에는 이동 비용, 타지 생활의 불확실성과 염려, 다른 언어에의 적용 등이 포함됨
	비용 측면에서는 가족, 친구와의 이별과 미지의 것에 대한 두려움과 관련된 심리적 비용도 고려되어야 함

L 12 정답 ④ * 정보 시스템의 도입이 가져온 변화

다음 글에서 전체 흐름과 관계 없는 문장은?

Since their introduction, / information systems have substantially changed the way / business is conducted. //
그것의 도입 이래로 / 정보 시스템은 방식을 상당히 변화시켜 왔다 / 사업이 수행되는 //

① This is particularly true / for business / in the shape and form of cooperation / between firms / that involves an integration of value chains / across multiple units. // **단서1** 정보 시스템의 도입이 기업 간 협력 형태의 사업에 가져온 변화에 대한 글임
이는 특히 해당된다 / 사업에 / 협력의 형태와 유형의 / 기업 간의 / 가치 체인의 통합을 수반하는 / 다수의 부문에 걸쳐 //

not only A but also B로 동사구가 연결됨
② The resulting networks / do not only cover / the business units / of a single firm / but typically also include multiple units / from different firms. //
그 결과로 나타나는 네트워크는 / 포함할 뿐만 아니라 / 사업 부문 / 단일 기업의 / 보통 여러 부문을 포함하기도 한다 / 서로 다른 기업의 //

③ As a consequence, / firms do not only need to consider / their internal organization / in order to ensure / sustainable business performance; /
결과적으로 / 기업은 고려할 필요가 있을 뿐만 아니라 / 그들 내부 조직을 / 보장하기 위해 / 지속 가능한 사업 성과를 /
'~을 고려하다'
they also need to take into account / the entire ecosystem of units / surrounding them. //
그것들은 또한 고려할 필요도 있다 / 부문들의 전체 생태계를 / 자신들을 둘러싸고 있는 //

④ Many major companies are fundamentally changing / their business models / by focusing on profitable units / and cutting off less profitable ones. // **단서 2** 많은 주요 기업이 수익성 있는 부문에 집중하고 수익성 낮은 부문은 잘라내고 있다는 내용임
(많은 주요 기업들은 근본적으로 변화시키고 있다 / 자신들의 사업 모델을 / 수익성이 있는 부문에는 집중하고 / 수익성이 낮은 부문은 잘라냄으로써 //

to allow의 목적어와 목적격 보어
⑤ In order to allow these different units / to cooperate successfully, / the existence of a common platform / is crucial. //
이 서로 다른 부문들이 ~하게 하기 위해서는 / 성공적으로 협력하게 / 공동 플랫폼의 존재가 / 매우 중요하다 //

- introduction ⓝ 도입, 전래 · substantially ⓐⓓ 상당히, 많이
- conduct ⓥ (업무 등을) 수행하다[처리하다] · cooperation ⓝ 협력, 협동
- firm ⓝ 기업, 회사 · involve ⓥ 수반하다 · integration ⓝ 통합
- multiple ⓐ 다수의, 다양한 · resulting ⓐ 결과로 초래된[나타난]
- cover ⓥ 포함하다 · ensure ⓥ 보장하다, 확실하게 하다
- sustainable ⓐ (오랫동안) 지속[유지] 가능한 · entire ⓐ 전체의, 온
- surround ⓥ 둘러싸다, 에워싸다 · fundamentally ⓐⓓ 근본적으로, 완전히
- profitable ⓐ 수익성이 있는, 이득이 되는 · cut off ~을 잘라내다
- cooperate ⓥ 협력하다, 협조하다 · existence ⓝ 존재

정보 시스템은 도입 이래로 사업이 수행되는 방식을 상당히 변화시켜 왔다. ① 이는 특히 다수의 부문에 걸쳐 가치 체인의 통합을 수반하는 기업 간의 협력 형태와 유형의 사업에 해당된다. ② 그 결과로 나타나는 네트워크는 단일 기업의 사업 부문을 포함할 뿐만 아니라 서로 다른 기업의 여러 부문을 보통 포함하기도 한다. ③ 결과적으로, 기업은 지속 가능한 사업 성과를 보장하기 위해 그들 내부 조직을 고려할 필요가 있을 뿐만 아니라, 자신들을 둘러싸고 있는 부문들의 전체 생태계를 고려할 필요도 있다. (④ 많은 주요 기업들은 수익성이 있는 부문에는 집중하고 수익성이 낮은 부문은 잘라냄으로써 자신들의 사업 모델을 근본적으로 변화시키고 있다.) ⑤ 이 서로 다른 부문들이 성공적으로 협력할 수 있도록 하기 위해서는 공동 플랫폼의 존재가 매우 중요하다.

> **왜 정답?** [정답률 78%]

정보 시스템의 도입이 여러 부문에 걸친 가치 체인의 통합을 수반하는 기업 간의 협력 형태의 사업에 특히 상당한 변화를 가져왔다는 내용의 글로, 기업은 그 내부 조직뿐 아니라 자신을 둘러싼 부문들의 전체 생태계를 고려할 필요가 있게 되었다고 했다. 그런데 ④은 많은 주요 기업들이 수익성 있는 부문에는 집중하고 수익성 낮은 부문은 잘라내고 있다는 내용으로, 기업의 내부와 외부를 모두 고려해야 한다는 내용인 전체 글의 흐름에 맞지 않는다.

> **왜 오답?**

① 정보 시스템의 도입이 사업의 수행 방식을 상당히 변화시켰는데, 이것이 특히 다수의 부문에 걸친 가치 체인의 통합을 수반하는 기업 간의 협력 형태의 사업에서 두드러진다는 내용이다.
② 정보 시스템의 도입이 기업 간의 협력 형태에 변화를 가져온 결과로 등장하는 네트워크에 대한 설명이 자연스럽게 이어진다.
③ 앞 문장에서 설명한 네트워크가 한 기업의 사업 부문뿐 아니라 서로 다른 기업의 여러 부문을 포함하기도 해서 일어나는 일들에 대한 부연 설명이다.
⑤ 앞에서 설명한 한 기업을 둘러싼 부문들의 전체 생태계가 성공적으로 협력하려면 공동 플랫폼이 꼭 있어야 한다는 내용으로 이어진다.

* 글의 흐름

도입	정보 시스템은 가치 체인을 공유하는 기업 간의 협력 사업에 변화를 가져옴
부연	네트워크는 단일 기업뿐만 아니라 여러 기업의 사업 부문을 포함함
결론	기업은 내부 조직뿐만 아니라 주변의 전체 생태계를 고려해야 함
부연	기업들이 서로 성공적으로 협력하기 위해서는 공동 플랫폼이 매우 중요함

L 13 정답 ③ *언어는 현실을 정확히 나타낼 수 있는가

다음 글에서 전체 흐름과 관계 없는 문장은?

단수 주어 / 단수 동사
One of the branches of postmodernism examines / the structure
of language / and how it is used. //
포스트모더니즘의 분파 중 하나는 살펴본다 / 언어의 구조와 / 그것이 어떻게 사용되는지를 //

동격절 접속사
It challenges the assumption / that language can be precisely
used / to represent reality. // 단서1 언어가 현실을 정확히 나타낼 수 있다는 가정에 이의를 제기하는 포스트모더니즘의 분파를 설명하는 글임
그것은 가정에 이의를 제기한다 / 언어가 정확하게 사용될 수 있다는 / 현실을 나타내는 데 //

부사절 접속사(이유)
① Meanings of words are ambiguous, / as words are only signs
or labels / given to concepts / (what is signified) /
단어의 의미는 모호하다 / 왜냐하면 단어는 단지 기호 또는 표호이고 / 개념에 주어진 / (의미되는 바) /

and therefore there is no necessary correspondence / between
the word and the meaning, / the signifier and the signified. //
따라서 필연적인 상응이 존재하지 않기 때문에 / 단어와 그 의미 사이에 / 기표(記標)와 기의(記意) //

선행사 관계부사 where로 바꿀 수 있음
② The use of signs (words) and their meaning / can vary /
depending on the flow of the text / in which they are used, /
기호(단어)의 사용과 그것의 의미는 / 다양할 수 있고 / 텍스트의 흐름에 따라 / 그것이 사용되는 /

부사적 용법(목적)
leading to the possibility of 'deconstructing' text / to reveal its
underlying inconsistencies. //
이것은 텍스트를 '해체할' 가능성으로 이어진다 / 그것의 기저에 있는 불일치성을 드러내기 위해 //

주어 완전자동사 단서2 오직 언어를 통해 현실을 있는 그대로 인식할 수 있다는 내용임
③ Reality exists / outside of our thoughts, / and it is only
it is ~ that 강조 구문
through language / that we are able to perceive the natural
world / as it really is. //)
(현실은 존재한다 / 우리의 사고 밖에 / 그리고 오직 언어를 통해서 / 우리는 자연 세계를 인식할 수 있다 / 그것을 정말 있는 그대로 //)

주격 관계대명사
④ This approach can be applied / to all forms of representation /
— pictures, films, etc. / that gain added or alternative meanings
/ by the overlaying of references / to previous uses. //
이러한 접근법은 적용될 수 있다 / 모든 형태의 표상에 / 사진, 영화 등 / 추가된 혹은 대안적인 의미를 얻는 / 외연을 덧씌움으로써 / 이전의 사용에 //

선행사 계속적 용법의 관계부사
⑤ This can be seen / particularly in the media, / where it is
가주어
difficult to distinguish the real / from the unreal / — everything
is representation, / there is no reality. //
이것은 보여질 수 있는데 / 특히 미디어에서 / 여기에서는 실제를 구별하기가 어렵다 / 가상으로부터 / 모든 것은 표상이고 / 현실은 없다 //

- branch ⓝ 분파, 분점   - examine ⓥ 조사하다, 검토하다
- structure ⓝ 구조   - assumption ⓝ 가정
- precisely ⓐⓓ 정확히   - ambiguous ⓐ 애매모호한
- signify ⓥ 의미하다, 중요하다   - correspondence ⓝ 상응, 관련성
- signifier ⓝ 기표   - signified ⓝ 기의   - vary ⓥ 각기 다르다
- deconstruct ⓥ 해체하다   - underlying ⓐ 근본적인, 기저에 있는
- inconsistency ⓝ 불일치성, 모순되는 부분   - perceive ⓥ 인식하다
- alternative ⓐ 대안적인, 대체의   - overlay ⓥ 덮어씌우다, 더하다
- reference ⓝ 외연, 언급   - distinguish ⓥ 구별하다

포스트모더니즘의 분파 중 하나는 언어의 구조와 그것이 어떻게 사용되는지를 살펴본다. 그것은 언어가 현실을 나타내는 데 정확하게 사용될 수 있다는 가정에 이의를 제기한다. ① 단어는 단지 개념(의미되는 바)에 주어진 기호 또는 표호이고 따라서 단어와 그 의미, 즉 기표(記標)와 기의(記意) 사이에는 필연적인 상응이 존재하지 않기 때문에 단어의 의미는 모호하다. ② 기호(단어)의 사용과 그것의 의미는 그것이 사용되는 텍스트의 흐름에 따라 다양할 수 있고, 이것은 그것의 기저에 있는 불일치성을 드러내기 위해 텍스트를 '해체할' 가능성으로 이어진다. (③ 현실은 우리의 사고 밖에 존재하고 우리가 자연 세계를 정말 있는 그대로 인식할 수 있는 것은 오직 언어를 통해서이다.) ④ 이러한 접근법은 모든 형태의 표상, 즉 외연을 이전의 사용에 덧씌움을 통해 추가된 혹은 대안적인 의미를 얻는 사진, 영화 등에 적용될 수 있다. ⑤ 이것은 특히 미디어에서 보여질 수 있는데, 여기에서는 실제와 가상을 구별하기가 어려우며 모든 것은 표상이고 현실은 없다.

> **왜 정답·오답?** [정답률 61%]

첫 문장: 포스트모더니즘의 분파 중 하나는 언어의 구조와 그것이 어떻게 사용되는지를 살펴본다. 그것은 언어가 현실을 나타내는 데 정확하게 사용될 수 있다는 가정에 이의를 제기한다.

→ 언어가 현실을 정확히 나타낼 수 있다는 가정에 이의를 제기하는 포스트모더니즘의 한 분파를 설명하는 글임

① 단어는 단지 개념(의미되는 바)에 주어진 기호 또는 표호이고 따라서 단어와 그 의미, 즉 기표(記標)와 기의(記意) 사이에는 필연적인 상응이 존재하지 않기 때문에 단어의 의미는 모호하다.

→ 단어와 그것이 의미하는 것 사이에는 필연적인 상응이 존재하지 않는다. (언어의 자의성) 그러므로 단어의 의미는 모호하다.
언어, 즉 단어가 현실을 정확하게 나타낼 수 없다는 주장을 뒷받침하는 근거이다.
▶ ①은 무관한 문장이 아님

② 기호(단어)의 사용과 그것의 의미는 그것이 사용되는 텍스트의 흐름에 따라 다양할 수 있고, 이것은 그것의 기저에 있는 불일치성을 드러내기 위해 텍스트를 '해체할' 가능성으로 이어진다.

→ 단어는 그것이 사용되는 텍스트의 흐름에 따라 다양한 의미를 가질 수 있다.
단어와 그것이 의미하는 것 사이에 필연적인 상응이 존재하지 않는다는 앞 문장과 같은 흐름이다.
▶ ②은 무관한 문장이 아님

③ 현실은 우리의 사고 밖에 존재하고 우리가 자연 세계를 정말 있는 그대로 인식할 수 있는 것은 오직 언어를 통해서이다.

→ 우리는 언어를 통해서만 자연 세계(현실)를 있는 그대로 인식할 수 있다.
언어가 현실을 정확하게 나타낼 수 없음을 설명하는 앞부분과 반대되는 내용이다.
▶ ③이 무관한 문장임

④ 이러한 접근법(This approach)은 모든 형태의 표상, 즉 외연을 이전의 사용에 덧씌움을 통해 추가된 혹은 대안적인 의미를 얻는 사진, 영화 등에 적용될 수 있다.

→ 단어와 그것이 의미하는 바의 관계가 사진이나 영화 등의 모든 형태의 표상에 적용될 수 있다는 내용은 ②에 자연스럽게 이어진다.
▶ ③이 빠져야 자연스러운 흐름이 됨, ④은 무관한 문장이 아님

⑤ 이것(This)은 특히 미디어에서 보여질 수 있는데, 여기에서는 실제와 가상을 구별하기가 어려우며 모든 것은 표상이고 현실은 없다.

→ 주어인 This가 가리키는 것이 ④에 등장한다. 이전의 사용에 외연을 덧씌워서 추가적인 혹은 대안적인 의미를 얻는 분야가 특히 미디어라는 설명이다.
▶ ⑤은 무관한 문장이 아님

정답 및 해설 **271**

도입	언어가 현실을 나타내는 데 정확하게 사용될 수 있다는 가정에 이의를 제기하는 포스트모더니즘의 분파가 있음
근거	기표(記標)와 기의(記意) 사이에는 필연적인 상응이 존재하지 않기 때문에 단어의 의미는 모호함
설명	기호(단어)의 사용과 의미는 텍스트의 흐름에 따라 다양할 수 있음
부연	이러한 접근법은 사진, 영화 등에 적용될 수 있는데, 실제와 가상을 구별하기가 어려우며 모든 것은 표상임

L 14 정답 ④ *식품의 장기 보관 방법

다음 글에서 전체 흐름과 관계 없는 문장은?

Except for grains and sugars, / most foods / humans eat / are
perishable. //
└주절과 동일한 주어와 be동사가 생략된 부사절
앞에 목적격 관계대명사가 생략됨
곡물과 설탕을 제외하고 / 대부분의 식품은 / 인간이 먹는 / 부패하기 쉽다 //

They deteriorate in palatability, spoil, or become unhealthy /
when stored / for long periods. // **단서1** 식품은 장기간 보관될 때 좋지 않게 변함
그것들은 맛이 나빠지거나 상하거나 건강에 좋지 않게 된다 / 보관될 때 / 장기간 //

① Surplus animal and crop harvests, / however, / can be saved
for future use / if appropriate methods of preservation are
used. // **단서2** 적절한 보존 방법을 통해 나중에 사용하도록 보관될 수 있음 →
적절한 보존 방법에 대한 설명이 이어질 것임
잉여의 동물 및 농작물 수확물은 / 하지만 / 나중에 사용하기 위해 남겨질 수 있다 / 적절한
보존 방법이 사용되면 /

② The major ways of preserving foods / are canning, freezing,
  복수 주어   복수 동사
drying, salting, and smoking. //
식품을 보존하는 것의 주요 방법은 / 통조림 가공, 냉동, 건조, 염장, 그리고 훈제이다 //

③ With all methods / the aim is to kill or restrict / the growth of
harmful microbes / or their toxins /
                    명사적 용법(주격 보어)의 to부정사의 병렬 구조
모든 방법에서 / 목표는 없애거나 제한하는 것이다 / 해로운 미생물의 성장이나 / 그것들의
독소를 /

and to slow or inactivate enzymes / that cause undesirable
changes / in food palatability. //
그리고 효소를 늦추거나 비활성화하는 것이다 / 바람직하지 않은 변화를 초래하는 / 음식의 맛에 //

④ Palatability is not static: / it is always changing, / based on
the state of the individual, / especially in regard to the time / of
food consumption. //) **단서3** 음식의 맛이 음식 섭취 시간, 개인의 상태에 따라
변한다는 것은 식품의 보존 방법과 관계 없음
(맛은 그대로 있지 않는다 / 그것은 늘 변한다 / 개인의 상태에 따라 / 특히 시간과 관련하여 /
음식 섭취의) //

⑤ For further protection / during long periods of storage, /
preserved food is placed / either in sterile metal cans or glass
  수동태를 완성하는 과거분사의 병렬 구조
jars / or frozen / in airtight paper or plastic containers. //
추가적인 보호를 위해 / 장기간 보관하는 동안 / 보존되는 음식은 담긴다 / 멸균한 금속 캔
또는 유리병에 / 또는 냉동된다 / 밀폐된 종이 또는 플라스틱 용기에 넣어져 //

- grain ⓝ 곡물   - perishable ⓐ 잘 상하는
- deteriorate ⓥ 악화되다   - spoil ⓥ 상하다, 못쓰게 만들다
- surplus ⓐ 잉여의, 과잉의   - crop ⓝ 농작물
- harvest ⓝ 수확, 추수   - preserve ⓥ 보존하다, 지키다
- restrict ⓥ 제한하다, 통제하다   - microbe ⓝ 미생물   - toxin ⓝ 독소
- inactivate ⓥ 비활성화하다   - static ⓐ 고정된, 정지 상태의
- in regard to ~에 대한   - airtight ⓐ 밀폐된

곡물과 설탕을 제외하고, 인간이 먹는 대부분의 식품은 부패하기 쉽다.
장기간 보관될 때, 그것들은 맛이 나빠지거나, 상하거나, 건강에 좋지 않게
된다. ① 하지만 적절한 보존 방법이 사용되면 잉여의 동물 및 수확한 농작물은
나중에 사용하기 위해 남겨질 수 있다. ② 식품을 보존하는 주요 방법은 통조림
가공, 냉동, 건조, 염장, 그리고 훈제이다.
 ③ 모든 방법에서 목표는 해로운 미생물의 성장이나 그것들의 독소를
없애거나 제한하고 음식의 맛에 바람직하지 않은 변화를 초래하는 효소의

작용을 늦추거나 비활성화하는 것이다. (④ 맛은 그대로 있지 않은데, 특히
음식 섭취 시간과 관련하여 개인의 상태에 따라 늘 변한다.) ⑤ 장기간
보관하는 동안 추가적인 보호를 위해, 보존되는 음식은 멸균한 금속 캔 또는
유리병에 담기거나 밀폐된 종이 또는 플라스틱 용기에 넣어 냉동된다.

> 왜 정답 ? [정답률 83%]

 글의 첫 세 문장은 인간이 먹는 대부분의 식품은 부패하기 쉽고 장기간 보관되면
좋지 않게 변하지만, 적절한 보존 방법이 사용되면 보관될 수 있다는 내용이다.
 이후로 적절한 보존 방법에 대한 구체적인 부연 설명이 이어지는데, ④은 맛이
개인의 상태, 음식 섭취 시간에 따라 늘 변한다는 것을 설명하는 문장으로,
식품의 보관 방법에 대한 나머지 문장들과 관련이 없다.

> 왜 오답 ?

① 인간이 먹는 대부분의 식품이 장기간 보관되기 어렵다는 앞부분의 내용과
  적절한 보존 방법이 사용되면 보관될 수 있다는 내용이 however로 자연스럽게
  이어진다.
②, ③, ⑤ 식품의 보관을 가능하게 하는 적절한 보존 방법에 대한 구체적인 부연
  설명을 하는 문장들로, 글이 자연스럽게 흘러간다.

* 글의 흐름

도입	인간이 먹는 대부분의 식품은 부패하기 쉬워서 장기간 보관되기 어려움
반전	하지만 적절한 보존 방법이 사용되면 보관될 수 있음
부연	주요 보존 방법은 통조림 가공, 냉동, 건조, 염장, 훈제로, 이 모든 방법의 목표는 해로운 미생물의 성장이나 그것들의 독소를 없애거나 제한하는 것임
	또, 음식을 멸균한 금속 캔이나 유리병에 담거나 밀폐된 종이나 플라스틱 용기에 넣어 냉동할 수도 있음

L 15 정답 ③ *특정 지역의 역사를 탐구할 때

다음 글에서 전체 흐름과 관계 없는 문장은?

                                    형용사적 용법(place 수식)
The written word / is the obvious, and easiest, place / to start /
when exploring local history, / if only to see / what has already
been written / on the subject. // **단서1** 특정 지역의 역사를 탐구하는 책을
쓰는 것에 대한 내용임
쓰인 이야기는 / 분명한 그리고 가장 쉬운 곳이다 / 시작하기에 / 특정 지역의 역사를 탐구할
때 / 보기만 한다면 / 이미 쓰인 것을 / 주제에 관해 //

Local history books have been written / for centuries / and are
                                    └──── 병렬 구조 ────┘
very variable / in quality. //
특정 지역의 역사책은 쓰여 왔고 / 수 세기에 걸쳐 / 매우 가변적이다 / 질적으로 //

① These books / will certainly not mention your ancestor / by
name / unless they played a particularly prominent part / in the
                 = if not
development of the locality / in question. //
이러한 책들은 / 여러분의 조상을 확실히 언급하지 않을 것이다 / 이름으로 / 만약 그들이 특히
두드러진 역할을 하지 않았다면 / 그 특정 지역의 발달에서 / 연구 중인 //

② However, they do provide information / about how a place
             <강조>의 조동사
changed / over time, / who the major personalities were / and
           선행사   주격 관계대명사
the significant events / that occurred there; /
그러나 그것들은 정보를 정말로 제공한다 / 어떻게 한 장소가 변화했는지 / 시간에 걸쳐 / 누가
주요 인물들이었는지 / 그리고 중요한 사건들에 대해 / 그곳에서 일어난 /
                        앞에 주격 관계대명사와 be동사가 생략됨
or at least those / selected by the author / for inclusion. //
또는 적어도 ~한 것들 / 작가에 의해서 선택된 / 포함하기 위해 //

③ If the author is writing / from his personal experiences, / he
                            능동태 문장의 목적격 보어
must be allowed / to spend more energy / on adding creative
twists / to a story / that already exists. //) **단서2** 역사책을 쓰는 것과 창의적인
비틀기를 더하는 것은 관련이 없음
(만약에 작가가 쓰고 있다면 / 자신의 개인적인 경험으로부터 / 그가 ~하도록 해야 한다 / 더
많은 에너지를 쓰도록 / 창의적인 비틀기를 더하는 데 / 어떤 이야기에 / 이미 존재하는 //)

④ Unless a book is extremely large / or the district chosen is very small, /
the district를 수식하는 과거분사
만약에 어떤 책이 극도로 광범위하거나 / 선택된 지역이 매우 작지 않다면 /

then the author must choose very carefully / what he is to
<예정>을 나타내는 「be+to부정사」
include / and their priorities may not be the same / as all their readers. //
그때 작가는 매우 신중하게 선택해야 하고 / 그가 포함할 것을 / 그들의 우선 사항은 같지 않을지도 모른다 / 그들의 모든 독자와 //

선행사(주격 관계대명사와 be동사가 생략됨)
⑤ It is well worth reading / some or preferably all of the books /
선행사　목적격 관계대명사
written about a locality / that your ancestors lived in. //
읽는 것은 충분히 가치가 있다 / 몇몇 또는 되도록이면 모든 책을 / 특정 지역에 대해 쓰인 / 여러분의 조상이 살았던 //

- obvious ⓐ 분명한　・ written ⓐ 쓰여진　・ variable ⓐ 가변적인
- mention ⓥ 언급하다　・ prominent ⓐ 중요한, 눈에 띄는
- locality ⓝ 지역　・ in question 연구 중인
- personality ⓝ 성격, 인물　・ significant ⓐ 중요한
- occur ⓥ 발생하다　・ twist ⓝ 비틀기　・ extremely ⓐⓓ 극도로
- district ⓝ 지역　・ priority ⓝ 우선 순위　・ preferably ⓐⓓ 되도록

주제에 관해 이미 쓰인 것을 보기만 한다면, 쓰인 이야기는 특정 지역의 역사를 탐구할 때 시작하기에 분명한 그리고 가장 쉬운 곳이다. 특정 지역의 역사책들은 수 세기에 걸쳐 쓰여 왔고 질적으로 매우 가변적이다. ① 이러한 책들은 만약 연구 중인 그 특정 지역의 발달에서 그들(여러분의 조상)이 특히 두드러진 역할을 하지 않았다면 여러분의 조상을 이름으로 확실히 언급하지 않을 것이다. ② 그러나 그것들은 어떻게 한 장소가 시간에 걸쳐 변화했는지, 누가 주요한 인물들이었는지 그리고 그곳에서 일어난 중요한 사건들, 또는 적어도 포함하기 위해 작가에 의해서 선택된 것들에 대한 정보를 정말로 제공한다. (③ 만약에 작가가 자신의 개인적인 경험으로부터 쓰고 있다면, 그가 이미 존재하는 어떤 이야기에 창의적인 비틀기를 더하는 데 더 많은 에너지를 쓰도록 해야 한다.) ④ 만약에 어떤 책이 극도로 광범위하거나 선택된 지역이 매우 작지 않다면, 그때 작가는 그가 포함할 것을 매우 신중하게 선택해야 하고 그들의 우선 사항은 그들의 모든 독자와 같지 않을지도 모른다. ⑤ 여러분의 조상이 살았던 특정 지역에 대해 쓰인 몇몇 또는 되도록이면 모든 책을 읽는 것은 충분히 가치가 있다.

왜 정답·오답? [정답률 68%]

첫 문장: 주제에 관해 이미 쓰인 것을 보기만 한다면, 쓰인 이야기는 특정 지역의 역사를 탐구할 때 시작하기에 분명한 그리고 가장 쉬운 곳이다. 특정 지역의 역사책들은 수 세기에 걸쳐 쓰여 왔고 질적으로 매우 가변적이다.

➡ 특정 지역의 역사를 탐구할 때 이미 쓰인 특정 지역의 역사책을 토대로 하는 것이 가장 쉽다는 내용이다.
  ▶ 이미 쓰인 역사책을 어떻게 활용할지에 대한 글이라고 예상할 수 있음

①
이러한 책들(These books)은 만약 연구 중인 그 특정 지역의 발달에서 그들이 특히 두드러진 역할을 하지 않았다면 여러분의 조상을 이름으로 확실히 언급하지 않을 것이다.

➡ These books가 가리키는 것이 앞 문장에 등장한 '특정 지역의 역사책'이다. 앞 문장에서 설명한 책들의 특징을 설명하는 문장이므로 앞뒤 흐름이 자연스럽다.
  ▶ ①은 무관한 문장이 아님

②
그러나(However) 그것들은 어떻게 한 장소가 시간에 걸쳐 변화했는지, 누가 주요한 인물들이었는지 그리고 그곳에서 일어난 중요한 사건들, 또는 적어도 포함하기 위해 작가에 의해서 선택된 것들에 대한 정보를 정말로 제공한다.

➡ 앞 문장에서는 그러한 책들이 언급하지 않는 것에 대해 설명했고, 뒤 문장에서는 그러한 책들이 제공하는 정보에 대해 설명한다. 반대되는 내용이 역접의 연결어로 자연스럽게 이어진다.
  ▶ ②은 무관한 문장이 아님

③
만약에 작가가 자신의 개인적인 경험으로부터 쓰고 있다면, 그가 이미 존재하는 어떤 이야기에 창의적인 비틀기를 더하는 데 더 많은 에너지를 쓰도록 해야 한다.

➡ 이미 존재하는 역사책을 이용하여 특정 지역의 역사에 관해 탐구하는 것에 대한 글이다.
  역사를 탐구하는 데 있어 '창의적인 비틀기'를 더한다는 것은 앞뒤가 맞지 않는다.
  ▶ ③이 무관한 문장임

④
만약에 어떤 책이 극도로 광범위하거나 선택된 지역이 매우 작지 않다면, 그때 작가는 그가 포함할 것을 매우 신중하게 선택해야 하고 그들의 우선 사항은 그들의 모든 독자와 같지 않을지도 모른다.

➡ 탐구하고자 하는 지역에 대해 이미 쓰인 이야기를 참고할 때 주의해야 하는 점을 이야기하는 문장으로, 주제에 맞는 내용이다.
  ▶ ③이 빠져야 자연스러운 흐름이 됨, ④은 무관한 문장이 아님

⑤
여러분의 조상이 살았던 특정 지역에 대해 쓰인 몇몇 또는 되도록이면 모든 책을 읽는 것은 충분히 가치가 있다.

➡ 특정 지역의 역사를 탐구할 때 그 지역에 대해 쓰인 기존의 책을 읽는 것에 충분한 가치가 있다는 내용이다. 글의 결론으로 자연스러운 흐름이다.
  ▶ ⑤은 무관한 문장이 아님

* 글의 흐름

도입	특정 지역의 역사를 탐구할 때 이미 쓰인 특정 지역의 역사책을 토대로 하는 것이 가장 쉬움
설명	이러한 책들은 그 특정 지역의 발달에서 조상이 두드러진 역할을 하지 않았다면 이름으로 확실히 언급하지 않을 것임
역접	그곳에서 일어난 중요한 사건들, 또는 적어도 포함하기 위해 작가에 의해서 선택된 것들에 대한 정보를 제공함
부연	조상이 살았던 특정 지역에 대해 쓰인 되도록이면 모든 책을 읽는 것은 충분히 가치가 있음

L 16 정답 ③ ＊상품으로 여겨지는 경관

다음 글에서 전체 흐름과 관계 없는 문장은?

In a highly commercialized setting / such as the United States, / it is not surprising / that many landscapes are seen / as
가주어　진주어절 접속사
commodities. // **단서1** 경관이 상품으로 여겨지는 것에 대한 글
고도로 상업화된 환경에서는 / 미국처럼 / ~이 놀랍지 않다 / 많은 경관이 여겨지는 것이 / 상품으로 //

In other words, / they are valued / because of their market
=landscapes
potential. //
다시 말해 / 그것들은 가치 있게 여겨진다 / 그것들의 시장 잠재력 때문에 //

Residents develop an identity / in part based / on how the
전치사 on의 목적어절을 이끄는 의문사
landscape can generate income / for the community. //
주민들은 정체성을 발전시킨다 / 부분적으로 기초하여 / 경관이 어떻게 소득을 창출할 수 있는가에 / 지역 사회를 위해 //

① This process involves / more than the conversion / of the natural elements / into commodities. //
이 과정은 포함한다 / 전환 그 이상을 / 자연적인 요소의 / 상품으로 //

② The landscape itself, / including the people and their sense of self, / takes on the form of a commodity. //
단수 주어 / *단수 동사*
경관 자체가 / 사람들과 그들의 자아의식을 포함하여 / 상품의 형태를 띤다 //

③ Landscape protection in the US / traditionally focuses / on protecting areas of wilderness, / typically in mountainous regions. // **단서2** 경관 보호의 방식에 대해 설명함
(미국에서 경관 보호는 / 전통적으로 초점을 둔다 / 황무지 지역을 보호하는 데 / 일반적으로 산악지대에 있는 //)

④ Over time, / the landscape identity can evolve / into a sort of "logo" / that can be used / to sell the stories of the landscape. //
선행사 / *주격 관계대명사*
시간이 흐르면서 / 경관 정체성은 발전할 수 있다 / 일종의 '로고'로 / 사용될 수 있는 / 경관에 대한 이야기를 판매하기 위해 //

⑤ Thus, / California's "Wine Country," Florida's "Sun Coast," or South Dakota's "Badlands" / shape /
복수 주어 / *복수 동사*
따라서 / California의 'Wine Country(포도주의 고장)', Florida의 'Sun Coast(태양의 해변)', 혹은 South Dakota의 'Badlands(악지)'는 / 형성한다 /
how both outsiders and residents perceive a place, / and these labels build a set of expectations / associated with the culture of those / who live there. //
shape의 목적어절을 이끄는 의문사 / *주격 관계대명사+be동사」 생략*
외지인과 거주자가 모두 장소를 인식하는 방식을 / 그리고 이런 호칭들은 일련의 기대치를 형성한다 / 사람들의 문화와 관련된 / 그곳에 사는 //

- highly @d 크게, 대단히
- setting ⓝ 환경, 장소
- commercialized @ 상업화된
- commodity ⓝ 상품, 일용품
- value ⓥ 소중하게[가치 있게] 여기다
- potential ⓝ 가능성, 잠재력
- resident ⓝ 거주자, 주민
- identity ⓝ 정체성
- generate ⓥ 창출하다, 만들어 내다
- conversion ⓝ 전환, 변환
- element ⓝ 요소, 성분
- take on (성질·기운 등을) 띠다
- wilderness ⓝ 황무지
- typically @d 보통, 일반적으로
- mountainous @ 산이 많은, 산악의
- region ⓝ 지방, 지역
- evolve ⓥ 발전하다, 진화하다
- a sort of 일종의
- perceive ⓥ 인식하다
- associated with ~와 관련된

미국처럼 고도로 상업화된 환경에서는 많은 경관이 상품으로 여겨지는 것이 놀랍지 않다. 다시 말해 경관은 그것들의 시장 잠재력 때문에 가치 있게 여겨진다. 주민들은 경관이 지역 사회를 위해 어떻게 소득을 창출할 수 있는가에 부분적으로 기초하여 정체성을 발전시킨다. ① 이 과정에는 자연의 요소를 상품으로 전환하는 것 그 이상의 것이 포함된다. ② 사람들과 그들의 자아의식을 포함하여 경관 자체가 상품의 형태를 띤다. (③ 미국에서 경관 보호는 일반적으로 산악지대에 있는 황무지 지역을 보호하는 데 전통적으로 초점을 둔다.) ④ 시간이 흐르면서 경관 정체성은 경관에 대한 이야기를 판매하기 위해 사용될 수 있는 일종의 '로고'로 발전할 수 있다. ⑤ 따라서 California의 'Wine Country(포도주의 고장)', Florida의 'Sun Coast(태양의 해변)', 혹은 South Dakota의 'Badlands(악지)'는 외지인과 거주자가 모두 장소를 인식하는 방식을 형성하며, 이런 호칭들은 그곳에 사는 사람들의 문화와 관련된 일련의 기대치를 형성한다.

⟩왜 정답? [정답률 73%]

미국과 같이 고도로 상업화된 환경에서는 경관이 상품으로 여겨진다는 첫 문장 이후로 경관이 상품으로 여겨지는 것과 관련된 설명이 이어지고 있다. 그런데 ③은 미국의 경관 보호 방식에 대한 내용으로, 상품으로 여겨지는 경관에 대한 설명이 아니므로 글의 전체 흐름에 맞지 않는다.

> '경관'이라는 소재만 같고 전혀 다른 이야기를 함 **꿀팁**

⟩왜 오답?

①, ② 경관이 상품으로 여겨지는 것은 단순히 자연적인 요소를 상품으로 전환하는 것이 아니라 주민들의 자아의식을 포함하여 경관 그 자체가 상품의 형태를 띠는 것이라는 설명이다.

④, ⑤ 일종의 로고로 사용될 수 있는 경관 정체성에 대해 California의 'Wine Country(포도주의 고장)', Florida의 'Sun Coast(태양의 해변)', South Dakota의 'Badlands(악지)'를 예로 들어 설명했다.

----

* 글의 흐름

도입	고도로 상업화된 환경에서는 많은 경관이 상품으로 여겨짐
전개 ①	경관이 상품으로 여겨지는 과정은 자연적인 요소가 상품으로 전환되는 것 이상을 포함하는데, 주민들의 자아의식을 포함하여 경관 그 자체가 상품의 형태를 띰
전개 ②	경관 정체성은 경관에 대한 이야기를 판매하는 데 이용될 수 있는 '로고'로 발전할 수 있음
예시	경관 정체성이 로고로 발전한 예시: California의 'Wine Country', Florida의 'Sun Coast', South Dakota의 'Badlands'

L 17 정답 ④ * 매우 창의적인 사람들의 어린 시절

다음 글에서 전체 흐름과 관계 없는 문장은?

단서1 매우 창의적인 사람들이 겪을 어린 시절의 특징을 설명하는 글임
Several common themes were found / in the highly creative individuals / regarding their early experiences and education. //
몇 가지 공통된 주제들이 발견되었다 / 매우 창의적인 사람들 사이에서 / 어릴 적 경험과 교육에 관하여 //

In early childhood / their families accorded them a great deal of respect / and allowed them / to explore on their own / and develop a strong sense of personal autonomy. //
accorded의 간접목적어와 직접목적어 / *병렬 구조(allowed의 목적격 보어)*
어린 시절에 / 그들의 가족들은 그들을 많이 존중해 주었고 / 그들이 ~하게 했다 / 스스로 탐구하고 / 강한 개인적 자율성을 발달시키게 //

① There was also a lack of extreme emotional closeness / with parents. //
극도의 정서적 친밀감도 없었다 / 부모와의 //

② There was little evidence / of intensely negative experiences; / for example / there was, / relative to the times in which they lived, / very little physical punishment for transgressions. //
준부정어
증거가 거의 없었다 / 심하게 부정적인 경험에 대한 / 예를 들어 / ~이 있었다 / 부모가 살았던 시대에 비해 / 일탈에 대한 신체적 처벌이 거의 없는 //

③ Nor, on the positive side, was there evidence / of extremely intense bonds of the sort / that can smother independence. //
부정어 nor가 문두로 가면서 주어와 동사가 도치됨
긍정적인 측면에서도 증거가 없었다 / ~한 종류의 극도로 강렬한 유대감의 / 독립성을 억누를 수 있는 //
단서2 핵가족과 확대 가족 사이의 차이점을 이야기함
(④ There was more competition / among brothers and sisters / for parental love / in nuclear families / than in extended families. //)
(경쟁이 더 많았다 / 형제자매간에 / 부모의 사랑을 두고 / 핵가족에서 / 확대 가족에서보다 //)

⑤ On balance, / for those / who would grow up to be highly creative, /
모든 것을 감안할 때 / 사람들의 경우 / 매우 창의적인 사람으로 성장하는 /
relationships with parents / were relatively easy / and, in later life, / pleasant and friendly / rather than intensely intimate. //
복수 주어 / *복수 동사*
부모와의 관계가 / 비교적 편안했고 / 나이가 들어서는 / 즐겁고 친했다 / 몹시 친밀했다기보다는 //

- accord ⓥ 부합하게 하다
- a great deal of 많은
- on one's own 스스로
- intensely @d 심하게
- relative to ~에 비하여
- punishment ⓝ 처벌
- bond ⓝ 유대감
- sort ⓝ 분류
- independence ⓝ 독립성
- competition ⓝ 경쟁
- parental @ 부모의
- nuclear family 핵가족
- extended family 대가족
- on balance 모든 것을 감안하여
- relatively @d 상대적으로
- intimate @ 친밀한

매우 창의적인 사람들 사이에서 어릴 적 경험과 교육에 관하여 몇 가지 공통된 주제들이 발견되었다. 어린 시절에 그들의 가족들은 그들을 많이 존중해 주었고 그들이 스스로 탐구하고 강한 개인적 자율성을 발달시키게 했다.

① 또한, 부모와의 극도의 정서적 친밀감도 없었다. ② 심하게 부정적인 경험에 대한 증거가 거의 없었는데, 예를 들어, 부모가 살았던 시대에 비해, 일탈에 대한 신체적 처벌은 거의 없었다. ③ 긍정적인 측면에서도, 독립성을 억누를 수 있는 것과 같은 종류의 극도로 강렬한 유대감의 증거도 없었다. (④ 확대 가족에서보다 핵가족에서 부모의 사랑을 두고 형제자매간에 경쟁이 더 많았다.) ⑤ 모든 것을 감안할 때, 매우 창의적인 사람으로 성장하는 사람들의 경우 부모와의 관계가 몹시 친밀했다기보다는 비교적 편안했고, 나이가 들어서는 즐겁고 친했다.

왜 정답·오답? [정답률 81%]

첫 문장: 매우 창의적인 사람들 사이에서 어릴 적 경험과 교육에 관하여 몇 가지 공통된 주제들이 발견되었다. 어린 시절에 그들의 가족들은 그들을 많이 존중해 주었고 그들이 스스로 탐구하고 강한 개인적 자율성을 발달시키게 했다.

→ 매우 창의적인 사람들이 보낸 어린 시절의 특징에 대해 설명하는 글이다.
　▶ 그들의 가족들이 그들을 많이 존중했고, 스스로 탐구하며 강한 개인적 자율성을 발달시키게 했다는 특징과 관련된 내용이 이어질 것이다.

① 또한(also), 부모와의 극도의 정서적 친밀감도 없었다.

→ also는 앞부분과 같은 맥락의 내용이 이어질 때 쓰이는 부사이다.
　스스로 탐구하고, 강한 개인적 자율성을 발달시켰다는 것과 부모와의 극도의 정서적 친밀감이 없었다는 것은 같은 맥락이다.
　▶ ①은 무관한 문장이 아님

② 심하게 부정적인 경험에 대한 증거가 거의 없었는데, 예를 들어, 부모가 살았던 시대에 비해, 일탈에 대한 신체적 처벌은 거의 없었다.

→ 매우 창의적인 사람들의 어린 시절의 특징을 설명하는 문장이다.
　바로 앞 문장과의 연관성은 떨어져 보일 수 있지만, 여전히 글의 주제(매우 창의적인 사람들이 보낸 어린 시절의 특징)에 맞는 문장이다.
　▶ ②은 무관한 문장이 아님

③ 긍정적인 측면에서도, 독립성을 억누를 수 있는 것과 같은 종류의 극도로 강렬한 유대감의 증거도 없었다.

→ **앞 문장:** 신체적 처벌과 같은 부정적인 경험을 했다는 증거가 거의 없음
　뒤 문장: 긍정적인 측면에서도 독립성을 억누를 만한 극도의 강렬한 유대감의 증거도 없음
　긍정적이든 부정적이든 부모와의 극도의 친밀감이 없다는 설명이 앞뒤로 자연스럽게 이어진다.
　▶ ③은 무관한 문장이 아님

④ 확대 가족에서보다 핵가족에서 부모의 사랑을 두고 형제자매간에 경쟁이 더 많았다.

→ 확대 가족과 핵가족이 보이는 차이점을 설명하는 문장이다. 매우 창의적인 사람들이 지닌 어린 시절의 특징을 설명하는 글에 맞지 않는 문장이다.
　▶ ④이 무관한 문장임

⑤ 모든 것을 감안할 때, 매우 창의적인 사람으로 성장하는 사람들의 경우 부모와의 관계가 몹시 친밀했다기보다는 비교적 편안했고, 나이가 들어서는 즐겁고 친했다.

→ 부모와의 극도의 정서적 친밀감이 없었다는 글의 내용을 종합하여 결론 짓는 문장이다.
　▶ ④이 빠져야 자연스러운 흐름이 됨. ⑤은 무관한 문장이 아님

* **글의 흐름**

도입	매우 창의적인 사람들은 어린 시절에 가족들이 그들을 많이 존중해 주었고 강한 개인적 자율성을 발달시키게 했음
설명 ①	부모와의 극도의 정서적 친밀감도 없었고 심하게 부정적인 경험에 대한 증거가 거의 없었음
설명 ②	긍정적인 측면에서도, 극도로 강렬한 유대감의 증거도 없었음
결론	매우 창의적인 사람으로 성장하는 사람들의 경우 부모와의 관계가 비교적 편안했음

L 18 정답 ③ * 빨리 말하는 것이 가져올 수 있는 언어적 위험

다음 글에서 전체 흐름과 관계 없는 문장은?

Speaking fast is a high-risk proposition. //
빨리 말하는 것은 위험 부담이 큰 일이다 // **단서 1** 빨리 말하는 것은 위험 부담이 큼

It's nearly impossible / to maintain the ideal conditions / to be
가주어　　　　　　　　진주어　　　　　　　　　형용사적 용법
persuasive, well-spoken, and effective / when the mouth is
traveling well over the speed limit. //
거의 불가능하다 / 이상적 조건을 유지하는 것은 / 설득력 있고, 말을 잘하며, 효과적인 / 입이 속도 제한을 훨씬 초과하여 움직일 때 //

① Although we'd like to think / that our minds are sharp
　　　　　　　　　　　　　　　　　명사절 접속사
/ enough to always make good decisions with the greatest
efficiency, / they just aren't. //
　　　　　　　대동사
우리는 생각하고 싶겠지만 / 우리의 정신이 예리하다고 / 항상 최고의 효율로 좋은 결정을 내릴 수 있을 정도로 / 그것은 정말 그렇지 않다 //

② In reality, / the brain arrives at an intersection of four or five
possible things to say / and sits idling for a couple of seconds, /
　　　　　　　　　　분사구문의 병렬 구조
considering the options. // **단서 2** 선택지가 많아지면 뇌(정신)는 빈둥거리며 시간을 보냄
　　　　　　　　　　　　　　　　　（① 문장의 예시）
실제로 / 뇌는 말할 가능성이 있는 것을 4~5가지가 교차하는 지점에 도달하면 / 몇 초 동안 빈둥거리며 / 선택지를 고려한다 //

③ Making a good decision helps you speak faster / because
　　　　　　　　　　　　help+목적어+목적격 보어(원형부정사)
it provides you with more time / to come up with your
responses. //) **단서 3** 좋은 결정을 내리면 빨리 말할 수 있음(앞 문장들과 다른 내용)
(좋은 결정을 내리면 여러분은 더 빨리 말할 수 있다 / 시간이 더 많아지기 때문에 / 응답을 생각해 낼 //)

④ When the brain stops sending navigational instructions back
to the mouth / and the mouth is moving too fast to pause, /
　　　　　　　　　　　　　　　　　　　too + 부사 + to-v
that's when you get a verbal fender bender, / otherwise known
관계부사　　　　　　　　　　　　　　　　　　과거분사
as filler. //
뇌가 입에 향해 지시를 다시 보내는 것을 멈추었는데 / 입은 너무 빨리 움직여 멈출 수 없을 때 / 이때가 바로 여러분이 가벼운 언어적 장애를 겪게 되는 시간이다 / 또는 필러라고도 하는 것을 //

⑤ Um, ah, you know, and like are what your mouth does / when
it has nowhere to go. //
'음, 아, 알다시피, 그러니까'는 입이 하는 행동이다 / 갈 곳이 없을 때 //

- proposition ⓝ 일, 문제　　　· maintain ⓥ 유지하다
- persuasive ⓐ 설득력이 있는　　　· sharp ⓐ 예리한
- efficiency ⓝ 효율성　　　· intersection ⓝ 교차하는 지점
- idle ⓥ 빈둥거리다　　　· come up with ~을 생각해 내다
- navigational ⓐ 항해의　　　· instruction ⓝ 지시
- fender bender 가벼운 접촉 사고

빨리 말하는 것은 위험 부담이 큰 일이다. 입이 속도 제한을 훨씬 초과하여 움직일 때 설득력 있고, 말을 잘하며, 효과적인 이상적 조건을 유지하는 것은 거의 불가능하다. ① 우리는 우리의 정신이 항상 최고의 효율로 좋은 결정을 내릴 수 있을 정도로 예리하다고 생각하고 싶겠지만, 그것은 정말 그렇지 않다. ② 실제로 뇌는 말할 가능성이 있는 것들 4~5가지가 교차하는 지점에 도달하면

몇 초 동안 빈둥거리며 선택지를 고려한다. (③ 좋은 결정을 내리면 응답을 생각해 낼 시간이 더 많아지기 때문에, 여러분은 더 빨리 말할 수 있다.) ④ 뇌가 입에 향해 지시를 다시 보내는 것을 멈추었는데 입은 너무 빨리 움직여 멈출 수 없을 때, 이때가 바로 여러분이 가벼운 언어적 장애, 또는 필러라고도 하는 것을 겪게 되는 시간이다. ⑤ '음, 아, 알다시피, 그러니까'는 입이 갈 곳이 없을 때 하는 행동이다.

> **왜 정답 · 오답?** [정답률 80%]

첫 두 문장: 빨리 말하는 것은 위험 부담이 큰 일이다. 입이 속도 제한을 훨씬 초과하여 움직일 때 설득력 있고, 말을 잘하며, 효과적인 이상적 조건을 유지하는 것은 거의 불가능하다.

➡ 빨리 말하는 것이 지닌 위험 부담에 대한 구체적인 설명이 뒤따를 것이다.

① 우리는 우리의 정신이 항상 최고의 효율로 좋은 결정을 내릴 수 있을 정도로 예리하다고 생각하고 싶겠지만, 그것은 정말 그렇지 않다.

➡ 우리의 정신은 항상 또렷하지 않다는 주장에 대한 예시가 나올 것이다.
▶ ①은 무관한 문장이 아님

② 실제로 뇌는 말할 가능성이 있는 것들 4~5가지가 교차하는 지점에 도달하면 몇 초 동안 빈둥거리며 선택지를 고려한다.

➡ 특정 상황에서 뇌(정신)가 빈둥거리며 시간을 보낸다고 말하며, 앞 문장을 뒷받침하고 있다.
▶ ②는 무관한 문장이 아님

③ 좋은 결정을 내리면 응답을 생각해 낼 시간이 더 많아지기 때문에, 여러분은 더 빨리 말할 수 있다.

➡ 앞 내용과 달리 부정적인 진술이 갑자기 사라졌고, '빨리 말하다'가 앞 내용과 달리 원인이 아닌 결과로 등장하고 있다.
▶ ③이 무관한 문장임

④ 뇌가 입에 향해 지시를 다시 보내는 것을 멈추었는데 입은 너무 빨리 움직여 멈출 수 없을 때, 이때가 바로 여러분이 가벼운 언어적 장애, 또는 필러라고도 하는 것을 겪게 되는 시간이다.

➡ 뇌가 빈둥거리며 시간을 보내고 있기에 입에게 지시를 보내지 않는다고 풀어 설명하고, 첫 문장의 빨리 말하는 것으로 인해 발생하는 장애(위험 부담)를 소개하면서 ②의 내용이 이어지고 있다.
▶ ③이 빠져야 자연스러운 흐름이 됨, ④은 무관한 문장이 아님

⑤ '음, 아, 알다시피, 그러니까'는 입이 갈 곳이 없을 때 하는 행동이다.

➡ 앞의 내용에 이어서 장애의 구체적인 사례를 나열하고 있다.
▶ ⑤은 무관한 문장이 아님

＊글의 흐름

도입	빨리 말하는 것은 위험 부담이 큼
부연	뇌는 선택지가 많아지면 고민하는 시간이 길어짐
전개	뇌가 선택지를 고민하는 동안 입은 계속 움직이면 가벼운 언어적 장애를 겪음
부연	'음, 아, 알다시피, 그러니까'가 그 장애의 발현임

김아린 | 충남대 의예과 2024년 입학·대전한빛고 졸

일단 첫 문장과 ① 문장을 읽으면서 글의 소재를 찾아보자. 빠르게 말하는 것에 대해 부정적으로 이야기했어. ②, ④ 문장에선 우리의 뇌에 대해 이야기하고 있지. 그런데 갑자기 ③ 문장에서 뜬금없이 '좋은 결정이 빠르게 말하는 데에 도움이 된다.'라고 하며 글이 어색하게 단절되는 게 느껴지지?
글의 소재를 찾고 앞뒤 문장 간 연결 관계를 확인하면서 읽으면 글이 어색하게 끊기는 지점을 쉽게 찾을 수 있을 거야!

L 19 정답 ④ ＊교외나 시골에 사는 것이 과연 친환경적인가 —

다음 글에서 전체 흐름과 관계 없는 문장은?

One / of the most widespread, and sadly mistaken, environmental myths is /
하나는 / 가장 널리 퍼져 있고 아쉽게도 잘못된 환경에 대한 근거 없는 통념 중 ~이다 /

that living "close to nature" / out in the country or in a leafy suburb / is the best "green" lifestyle. //
'자연과 가까이' 사는 것이 / 시골이나 잎이 우거진 교외에서 / 최고의 '친환경적인' 생활 방식이다 //
단서 1 시골이나 교외에서 자연과 가까이 사는 것이 최고의 친환경적인 생활 방식이라는 것은 근거 없는 통념임

Cities, on the other hand, are often blamed / as a major cause / of ecological destruction / — artificial, crowded places / that suck up precious resources. //
반면에 도시들은 자주 비난받는다 / 주요 원인으로 / 생태 파괴의 / 인공적이고 혼잡한 장소로서 / 귀중한 자원을 빨아먹는 //

Yet, / when you look at the facts, / nothing could be farther from the truth. //
그러나 / 여러분이 사실들을 살펴보면 / 아무것도 진실에서 더 멀리 있을 수 없다 //

① The pattern of life / in the country and most suburbs / involves long hours in the automobile / each week, /
생활양식은 / 시골과 대부분의 교외의 / 자동차 안에서 오랜 시간 동안 있는 것을 포함한다 / 매주 /

burning fuel and pumping out exhaust / to get to work, / buy groceries, / and take kids to school and activities. //
연료를 소모하고 배기가스를 뿜어내면서 / 출근하기 위해 / 식료품을 사기 위해 / 그리고 아이들을 학교와 활동에 데리고 가기 위해 //

② City dwellers, on the other hand, have the option / of walking or taking transit / to work, shops, and school. //
반면에 도시 거주자들은 선택권이 있다 / 걸어가거나 대중교통을 타는 / 일터, 상점, 학교로 //

③ The larger yards and houses / found outside cities / also create an environmental cost / in terms of energy use, water use, and land use. //
더 큰 마당과 집들도 / 도시 밖에서 발견되는 / 또한 환경적인 대가를 만들어 낸다 / 에너지 사용, 물 사용, 토지 사용 측면에서 //
단서 2 도시 거주자들이 시골에 정착하는 경향에 대한 내용이 아님

④ This illustrates the tendency / that most city dwellers get tired of urban lives / and decide to settle in the countryside. //)
(이는 경향을 보여준다 / 대부분의 도시 거주자들이 도시 생활에 지쳐서 / 시골에서 정착하기로 하는 //)

⑤ It's clear / that the future of the Earth depends / on more people gathering together / in compact communities. //
~은 분명하다 / 지구의 미래가 달린 것은 / 더 많은 사람들이 모이는 것에 / 밀집한 공동체들 속에 //

- widespread ⓐ 널리 퍼진 · sadly ⓐ(ad) 애석하게도, 불행히
- mistaken ⓐ 틀린, 잘못된 · myth ⓝ 근거 없는 통념, 잘못된 믿음
- leafy ⓐ 잎이 무성한, 녹음이 우거진 · suburb ⓝ 교외
- ecological ⓐ 생태계[학]의, 생태상의 · destruction ⓝ 파괴, 파멸
- artificial ⓐ 인공[인조]의 · suck up ~을 빨아먹다[빨아들이다]
- precious ⓐ 귀한, 소중한 · exhaust ⓝ 배기가스
- dweller ⓝ 거주자 · transit ⓝ 대중교통
- in terms of ~의 측면에서 · illustrate ⓥ 보여주다
- tendency ⓝ 성향, 경향 · get tired of ~에 싫증이 나다
- urban ⓐ 도시의, 도회지의 · settle ⓥ 정착하다

가장 널리 퍼져 있고 아쉽게도 잘못된, 환경에 대한 근거 없는 통념 중 하나는 시골이나 잎이 우거진 교외에서 '자연과 가까이' 사는 것이 최고의 '친환경적인' 생활 방식이라는 것이다. 반면에 도시들은 귀중한 자원을 빨아먹는 인공적이고 혼잡한 장소로서 자주 생태 파괴의 주요 원인으로 비난받는다. 그러나 사실들을 살펴보면, 그것은 전혀 진실이 아니다. ① 시골과 대부분의 교외의 생활양식은 매주 출근하고, 식료품을 사고, 아이들을 학교와 활동에 데리고 가기 위해 연료를 소모하고 배기가스를 뿜어내면서 자동차 안에서 오랜 시간 동안 있는 것을 포함한다. ② 반면에 도시 거주자들은 일터, 상점, 학교로 걸어가거나 대중교통을 타기로 선택할 수 있다. ③ 도시 밖에서 발견되는 더 큰 마당과 집들도 또한 에너지 사용, 물 사용, 토지 사용 측면에서 환경적인 대가를 야기한다. (④ 이는 대부분의 도시 거주자들이 도시 생활에 지쳐서 시골에서 정착하기로 하는 경향을 보여준다.) ⑤ 지구의 미래가 더 많은 사람들이 밀집한 공동체들 속에 모이는 것에 달린 것은 분명하다.

> **왜 정답?** [정답률 64%]
> 〔통념을 제시하고 그것을 뒤집는 진실을 설명하는 전개 방식!〕 〔꿀팁〕

교외나 시골에서 자연 가까이 사는 것이 친환경적인 생활 방식이라는 생각은 근거 없는 통념이라는 글이다. 교외에 사는 것보다 도시에 사는 것이 오히려 환경에 더 이롭다는 내용이 이어지는데, ④은 도시 생활에 지친 도시 거주자들이 시골에 정착하기로 결정하는 경향에 대해 이야기하므로 전체 글의 흐름에 맞지 않는다.

> **왜 오답?**

① 시골이나 교외의 생활 양식이 환경에 좋지 않음을 이야기하는 문장이다.
② 도시 거주자들의 생활 방식이 오히려 환경에 이롭다는 내용이다.
③ 교외에서의 거주가 야기하는 또 다른 환경적 대가에 대해 설명한다.
⑤ 밀집한 공동체 속에서, 즉 도시에서 사는 것이 지구의 미래를 위해 더 낫다는 결론을 내리는 문장이다.

* 글의 흐름

통념	시골이나 교외에서 자연과 가까이 사는 것이 최고의 친환경적인 생활 방식임
반전	시골과 교외의 거주자들은 연료를 소모하고 배기가스를 뿜는 자동차를 많이 이용하고, 에너지 사용이나 물 사용, 토지 사용의 측면에서도 환경적 대가를 야기함
결론	더 많은 사람들이 밀집한 공동체들 속에 모이는 것에 지구의 미래가 달려 있음은 분명함

L 20 정답 ④ ＊재해로부터 회복하는 식물의 특별한 능력

다음 글에서 전체 흐름과 관계 없는 문장은?

〈이유〉의 부사절 접속사
Because plants tend to recover / from disasters / more quickly than animals, / they are essential / to the revitalization of damaged environments. //
식물은 회복하는 경향이 있기 때문에 / 재해로부터 / 동물보다 더 빨리 / 그것은 필수적이다 / 손상된 환경의 소생에 //

형용사적 용법(ability 수식)
Why do plants have this preferential ability / to recover from disaster? // 단서1 식물이 가진 재해로부터 회복하는 능력에 대해 설명하는 글임
왜 식물에게는 이런 특별한 능력이 있을까 / 재해로부터 회복하는 //

It is largely because, unlike animals, they can generate / new organs and tissues / throughout their life cycle. //
주격 보어절을 이끄는 접속사
그것은 대체로 그들이 동물과 달리 생성할 수 있기 때문이다 / 새로운 장기와 조직을 / 그들의 생애 주기 내내 //

주격 보어 역할을 하는 전치사구
① This ability is due to the activity / of plant meristems /
이러한 능력은 활동 때문이다 / 식물의 분열 조직(分裂組織)의 /

— regions of undifferentiated tissue / in roots and shoots / that can, in response to specific cues, differentiate / into new tissues and organs. //
조동사와 동사 사이에 삽입된 부사구
미분화 세포 조직 부위 / 뿌리와 싹에 있는 / 특정 신호에 반응하여 분화할 수 있는 / 새로운 세포 조직과 기관으로 //

〈조건〉의 부사절 접속사
② If meristems are not damaged / during disasters, / plants can recover / and ultimately transform / the destroyed or barren environment. //
분열 조직(分裂組織)이 손상되지 않으면 / 재해 시에 / 식물은 회복해서 / 궁극적으로 변화시킬 수 있다 / 파괴되거나 척박한 환경을 //

〈시간〉의 부사절 접속사
③ You can see this phenomenon / on a smaller scale / when a tree struck by lightning forms / new branches / that grow from the old scar. //
선행사　주격 관계대명사
여러분은 이러한 현상을 볼 수 있다 / 더 작은 규모로 / 번개 맞은 나무가 형성할 때 / 새로운 가지를 / 오래된 상처에서 자라나는 //

④ In the form of forests and grasslands, / plants regulate the cycling of water / and adjust / the chemical composition of the atmosphere. // 단서2 식물의 재해로부터 회복하는 능력이 아닌 다른 능력을 설명함
(숲과 초원의 형태로 / 식물은 물의 순환을 조절하고 / 조정한다 / 대기의 화학적 구성을 //)

구 형태의 전치사
⑤ In addition to regeneration or resprouting of plants, / disturbed areas can also recover / through reseeding. //
명사구
식물의 재생이나 재발아 외에도 / 교란된 지역은 또한 회복할 수 있다 / 재파종을 통해서 //

- essential ⓐ 필수적인, 근본적인
- preferential ⓐ 우선권[특혜]을 주는, 특혜인
- organ ⓝ (인체 내의) 장기[기관] • tissue ⓝ ((생물)) 조직
- shoot ⓝ (새로 돋아난) 순[싹] • barren ⓐ 척박한, 열매가 안 열리는
- scale ⓝ 규모, 범위 • scar ⓝ 흉터, 상처
- composition ⓝ 구성 (요소) • atmosphere ⓝ (지구의) 대기, 분위기
- regeneration ⓝ ((생물)) 재생, 부흥 • resprout ⓥ 재발아하다
- disturb ⓥ 방해하다, 불안하게 만들다
- reseed ⓥ 다시 씨를 뿌리다, 자생하다

식물은 동물보다 더 빨리 재해로부터 회복하는 경향이 있기 때문에 손상된 환경의 소생에 필수적이다. 왜 식물에게는 재해로부터 회복하는 이런 특별한 능력이 있을까? 그것은 대체로 식물이 동물과 달리 생애 주기 내내 새로운 장기와 조직을 생성할 수 있기 때문이다. ① 이러한 능력은 식물의 분열 조직(分裂組織), 즉 특정 신호에 반응하여 새로운 세포 조직과 기관으로 분화할 수 있는, 뿌리와 싹에 있는 미분화 세포 조직 부위의 활동 때문이다. ② 재해 시에 분열 조직(分裂組織)이 손상되지 않으면, 식물은 회복해서 파괴되거나 척박한 환경을 궁극적으로 변화시킬 수 있다. ③ 번개 맞은 나무가 오래된 상처에서 자라나는 새로운 가지를 형성할 때 더 작은 규모로 이러한 현상을 볼 수 있다. (④ 숲과 초원의 형태로, 식물은 물의 순환을 조절하고 대기의 화학적 구성을 조정한다.) ⑤ 식물의 재생이나 재발아 외에도, 교란된 지역은 재파종을 통해서도 회복할 수 있다.

> **왜 정답?** [정답률 80%]

첫 세 문장으로 보아 재해로부터 회복하는 식물의 특별한 능력에 대해 설명하는 글인데, ④은 식물의 재해로부터 회복하는 능력이 아니라 물의 순환을 조절하고 대기의 화학적 구성을 조정하는 능력을 설명하고 있으므로 글의 전체 흐름에 맞지 않는다.
'식물의 능력'이라는 글의 소재는 일치하지만, 글의 구체적인 주제와는 맞지 않는다.

> **왜 오답?**

①, ② 재해로부터 회복하는 식물의 능력이 무엇 때문에 가능한지 설명한 후, 이러한 능력 때문에 가능한 일을 이야기하는 문장이다.
③ 앞 문장에서 말한 현상을 좀 더 작은 규모로 확인할 수 있는 구체적인 경우를 제시하는 문장으로, 앞 문장과 자연스러운 흐름으로 이어진다.
⑤ 앞에서 설명한 식물의 재생, 재발아 외에 식물을 재파종함으로써 교란된 환경을 회복시킬 수 있다는 내용으로, 파괴된 환경을 회복시키는 식물의 능력에 대해 추가적으로 설명하는 문장이다.

L 21 정답 ③ * 조직 구성원을 결속하는 공유된 웃음

다음 글에서 전체 흐름과 관계 <u>없는</u> 문장은?

단서1 공유된 사건에 대해 웃는 것을 통해 직원들이 단합된다는 내용의 글임

Workers are united / by laughing at shared events, / even ones /
= events
that may initially spark anger or conflict. //

직원들은 단합된다 / 공유된 사건에 대해 웃음으로써 / 심지어 사건에도 / 처음에는 분노나 갈등을 불러일으킬 수 있는 //

Humor reframes potentially divisive events / into merely
"laughable" ones / which are put in perspective / as subservient
to unifying values / held by organization members. //

유머는 어쩌면 불화를 일으킬 수 있는 사건을 재구성한다 / 그저 '재미있는' 사건으로 / (제대로) 이해되는 / 통합 가치에 도움이 된다고 / 조직 구성원들에 의해 간직되는 //

Repeatedly recounting humorous incidents / reinforces unity /
동명사구 주어   단수 동사
동명사를 수식하는 부사
based on key organizational values. //

유머러스한 사건들을 되풀이해서 이야기하는 것은 / 단합을 강화한다 / 조직의 핵심 가치에 근거를 둔 //

① One team told repeated stories / about a dumpster fire, /
something that does not seem funny / on its face, /

어떤 팀이 되풀이되는 이야기를 말했는데 / 극도로 혼란스러운 상황에 대해 / 재미있어 보이지 않는 것 / 표면적으로는 /

주어
but the reactions of workers / motivated to preserve safety /
    동사   목적어
sparked laughter / as the stories were shared multiple times / by
multiple parties in the workplace. //

그러나 직원들의 반응이 / 안전을 지켜야겠다고 동기가 부여된 / 웃음을 자아냈다 / 그 이야기가 여러 번 공유되면서 / 직장의 여러 당사자에 의해 //

② Shared events / that cause laughter / can indicate a sense of
부사절 접속사(이유)
belonging / since "you had to be there" /

공유된 사건들은 / 웃음을 유발하는 / 소속감을 나타낼 수 있는데 / 이는 '여러분은 그곳에 있어야 했기' 때문이다 /

부사적 용법(목적)   = were not there and do not see the humor in them
to see the humor in them, / and non-members were not and do
not. //

그것들 속의 유머를 이해하려면 / 그리고 조직 구성원이 아닌 사람들은 그러지 않아서 그러지 않기 (때문이다) //
단서2 광고 방송이 유머러스한 요소를 포함하는 경향이 있다는 내용

③ Since humor can easily capture people's attention, /
commercials tend to contain humorous elements, / such as
funny faces and gestures. //)

(유머는 사람들의 관심을 쉽게 사로잡을 수 있기 때문에 / 광고 방송은 유머러스한 요소들을 포함하는 경향이 있다 / 웃긴 얼굴과 몸짓 같은 //)

④ Instances of humor / serve to enact bonds / among
organization members. //

유머의 사례는 / 유대감을 만드는 역할을 한다 / 조직 구성원들 간의 //

⑤ Understanding the humor may even be required / as an
동명사구 주어
informal badge of membership / in the organization. //

심지어 유머를 이해하는 것은 요구될 수도 있다 / 구성원임을 나타내는 비공식적 신분증으로 / 조직에서 //

- unite ⓥ 통합[결속]시키다 • initially ⓐⓓ 처음에
- conflict ⓝ 갈등, 충돌 • reframe ⓥ 다시 구성하다
- potentially ⓐⓓ 가능성 있게, 잠재적으로 • divisive ⓐ 분열을 초래하는
- merely ⓐⓓ 그저, 한낱 • in perspective 진상을 올바르게, 올바른 균형으로
- unify ⓥ 통합[통일]하다 • recount ⓥ 이야기하다, 말하다

- reinforce ⓥ 강화하다, 보강하다 • unity ⓝ 통합, 통일
- key ⓐ 가장 중요한, 핵심적인
- dumpster fire 재앙, 극도로 혼란스러운 상황
- preserve ⓥ 지키다, 보호하다 • spark ⓥ 촉발시키다, 유발하다
- multiple ⓐ 많은, 다수[복수]의
- party ⓝ 정당, 단체, (소송·계약 등의) 당사자
- indicate ⓥ 나타내다, 보여주다 • capture ⓥ 사로잡다, 포착하다
- commercial ⓝ (텔레비전·라디오의) 광고 (방송)
- enact ⓥ (법을) 제정하다, 일으키다 • bond ⓝ 유대, 결속
- informal ⓐ 격식에 얽매이지 않는, 비공식의

직원들은 공유된 사건, 심지어 처음에는 분노나 갈등을 불러일으킬 수 있는 사건에 대해서도 웃음으로써 단합된다. 유머는 어쩌면 불화를 일으킬 수 있는 사건을, 조직 구성원들에 의해 간직되는 통합 가치에 도움이 된다고 (제대로) 이해되는 그저 '재미있는' 사건으로 재구성한다. 유머러스한 사건들을 되풀이해서 자세히 이야기하는 것은 조직의 핵심 가치에 근거를 둔 단합을 강화한다. ① 어떤 팀이 극도로 혼란스러운 상황에 관한 되풀이되는 이야기를 말했는데, 표면적으로는 재미있어 보이지 않는 것이지만, 그 이야기가 직장의 여러 당사자에 의해 여러 번 공유되면서 안전을 지켜야겠다고 동기가 부여된 직원들의 반응이 웃음을 자아냈다. ② 웃음을 유발하는 공유된 사건은 소속감을 나타낼 수 있는데, 이는 그 사건 속의 유머를 이해하려면 '여러분은 그곳에 있어야 했기' 때문이고 조직 구성원이 아닌 사람들은 그곳에 없어서 유머를 이해하지 못하기 때문이다. (③ 유머는 사람들의 관심을 쉽게 사로잡을 수 있기 때문에, 광고 방송은 웃긴 얼굴과 몸짓 같은, 유머러스한 요소들을 포함하는 경향이 있다.) ④ 유머의 사례는 조직 구성원들 간의 유대감을 만드는 역할을 한다. ⑤ 심지어 유머를 이해하는 것은 조직 구성원임을 나타내는 비공식적 신분증으로 요구될 수도 있다.

> 왜 정답? [정답률 73%]

어떤 공유된 사건에 대해 웃음으로써 직원들이 단합된다는 첫 문장에 이어 계속해서 조직의 구성원임을 나타내는 신분증과도 같은 역할을 하는 '공유된 사건에 대한 웃음'에 대해 설명하는 글이다. 그런데 ③은 웃긴 얼굴과 몸짓 같은 유머러스한 요소들을 포함하는 경향이 있는 광고 방송에 대해 설명하므로 글의 전체 흐름에 맞지 않는다.

> 왜 오답?

① 표면적으로는, 즉 외부인이 보기에는 재미있어 보이지 않는 사건에 대해서도 같은 조직 내의 직원들은 웃을 수 있다는 내용이다.

② 웃음을 유발하는 공유된 사건들이 소속감을 나타낼 수 있음을 설명하는 문장이다.

④, ⑤ 유머의 사례가 조직 구성원 간의 유대감을 만들고, 나아가 그 조직의 유머를 이해하는 것이 조직 구성원임을 나타내는 신분증으로 기능할 수도 있다는 내용으로 전체 흐름에 적절하다.

* 글의 흐름

도입	직원들은 공유된 사건에 대해 웃음으로써 단합됨
부연	유머는 불화를 일으킬 수 있는 사건도 재미있는 사건으로 재구성하고, 이를 되풀이해서 이야기하는 것은 조직의 단합을 강화함
전개	웃음을 유발하는 공유된 사건들은 소속감을 나타냄
부연	유머의 사례가 조직 구성원들 간의 유대감을 만들고, 유머를 이해하는 것은 조직에서 구성원임을 나타내는 비공식적 신분증으로 요구될 수 있음

L 22 정답 ③ * 경력 초기의 교사에게 필요한 기술

다음 글에서 전체 흐름과 관계 <u>없는</u> 문장은?

Actors, singers, politicians and countless others / recognise the
      수단, 방법
power of the human voice / as a means of communication /
      생략 가능한 주격 관계대명사와 be동사
beyond the simple decoding of the words / that are used. //

배우, 가수, 정치가, 그리고 무수한 다른 사람은 / 사람 목소리의 힘을 인정한다 / 의사소통의 수단으로서의 / 단어의 단순한 해독을 넘어서는 / 사용된 //

동명사 주어 ┌── 병렬 구조(Learning의 목적어) ──┐
Learning / to control your voice and use it / for different purposes
/ is, therefore, one of the most important skills / to develop / as
단수 동사
an early career teacher. // **단서 1** 교사로서 다양한 목적으로 목소리를 통제하고
사용하는 것을 배우는 것이 중요함
배우는 것은 / 여러분의 목소리를 통제하고 그것을 사용하는 것을 / 다양한 목적을 위해 /
따라서 가장 중요한 기술 중 하나이다 / 개발할 / 경력 초기의 교사로서 //

① The more confidently / you give instructions, / the higher the
the+비교급, the+비교급: ~할수록 더욱 ···한/하게
chance / of a positive class response. //
더 자신 있게 / 여러분이 설명할수록 / 확률이 더 높다 / 긍정적인 학급 반응의 //

② There are times / when being able to project your voice loudly
      동사   선행사 관계부사 동명사구 주어
/ will be very useful / when working in school, /
경우가 있으며 / 목소리를 크게 내보낼 수 있는 것이 / 매우 유용할 / 학교에서 일할 때 /

and knowing / that you can cut through a noisy classroom,
동명사 주어   단수 동사   형용사적 용법(skill 수식)
dinner hall or playground / is a great skill to have. //
아는 것은 / 여러분이 시끄러운 교실, 구내식당이나 운동장을 가를 수 있다는 것을 / 갖출
훌륭한 기술이다 //
to address의 〈목적〉의 의미를 강조   **단서 2** 학교 내의 소음 문제에 대한 대처 방법을 설명함
③ In order to address / serious noise issues in school, / students,
parents and teachers should search for a solution / together. //)
(대처하기 위해서는 / 학교 내의 심각한 소음 문제에 / 학생, 학부모, 교사가 해결책을 찾아야
한다 / 함께 //)
                                       앞에 should가 생략됨
④ However, I would always advise / that you use your loudest
voice / incredibly sparingly / and avoid shouting / as much as
                        use와 병렬 구조 목적어로 동명사를 취하는 avoid
possible. //
그러나 나는 항상 조언하고자 한다 / 여러분이 가장 큰 목소리를 쓰고 / 놀랍도록 드물게 /
소리치는 것을 피해야 한다고 / 최대한 //

⑤ A quiet, authoritative and measured tone / has so much more
              비교의 두 대상
impact / than slightly panicked shouting. //
조용하고도 권위가 있으며 침착한 어조는 / 그렇게나 훨씬 더 큰 효과를 갖는다 / 약간 당황한
고함보다 //

- -

- countless @d 무수한, 셀 수 없이 많은   · recognise ⓥ 인정하다
- decode ⓥ (암호를) 해독하다   · instruction ⓝ 지시, 설명
- address ⓥ 대처하다   · incredibly @d 놀랍도록
- sparingly @d 드물게, 인색하게   · authoritative @ 권위가 있는
- measured @ 침착한   · tone ⓝ 어조   · panicked @ 당황한

배우, 가수, 정치가, 그리고 무수한 다른 사람은 사용된 단어의 단순한
해독을 넘어서는 의사소통의 수단으로서의 사람 목소리의 힘을 인정한다.
따라서 여러분의 목소리를 통제하고 그것을 다양한 목적을 위해 사용하는 것을
배우는 것은 경력 초기의 교사로서 개발할 가장 중요한 기술 중 하나이다.
① 여러분이 더 자신 있게 설명할수록, 긍정적인 학급의 반응이 나올 확률은
더 높다. ② 목소리를 크게 내보낼 수 있는 것이 학교에서 일할 때 매우 유용할
경우가 있으며, 여러분이 시끄러운 교실, 구내식당이나 운동장을 가를 수
있다는 것을 아는 것은 갖춰야 할 훌륭한 기술이다. (③ 학교 내의 심각한 소음
문제에 대처하기 위해서는 학생, 학부모, 교사가 함께 해결책을 찾아야 한다.)
④ 그러나, 나는 가장 큰 목소리는 놀랍도록 드물게 쓰고 소리치는 것을 최대한
피해야 한다고 항상 조언하고자 한다. ⑤ 조용하고도 권위가 있으며 침착한
어조는 약간 당황한 고함보다 그렇게나 훨씬 더 큰 효과를 갖는다.

> **왜 정답?** [정답률 82%]
사람의 목소리의 힘에 대해 이야기하면서 다양한 목적으로 목소리를 통제하고
사용하는 것을 배우는 것이 경력 초기의 교사로서 개발해야 하는 중요한 기술 중
하나라고 했다.
이후로 교사의 목소리 사용에 대해 부연하는 내용이 이어지는데, ③은 학교 내의
소음 문제에 대처하는 방법을 설명한 문장으로, 전체 글의 흐름에 맞지 않는다.

> **왜 오답?**
①, ② 교사가 목소리를 통제하고 다양한 목적으로 목소리를 사용할 줄 아는 것의
이점에 대한 구체적인 부연이 이어지는 문장이다.
④, ⑤ 큰 목소리를 낼 수 있다는 것이 유용한 경우를 설명한 앞 문장과 반대되는
내용이 역접의 연결어 However로 이어진다.

> 조용하고도 권위가 있으며 침착한 어조가 고함보다 훨씬 더
> 큰 효과가 있으므로, 소리치는 것을 최대한 피하라는 조언 **꿀팁**

- -

* 글의 흐름

도입	다양한 목적으로 목소리를 통제하고 사용하는 것을 배우는 것이 교사로서 개발할 가장 중요한 기술 중 하나임
대조	학교에서 일할 때 큰 목소리를 낼 수 있다는 것이 매우 유용한 경우가 있음
	하지만 조용하고도 권위 있는, 침착한 어조가 고함보다 훨씬 더 큰 효과가 있으므로 소리치는 것을 최대한 피해야 함

장성욱 | 동아대 의예과 2023년 입학·부산 대연고 졸

무관한 문장은 보통 선택지가 아닌 문장에서 어떤 키워드와
주제문을 주고, 키워드는 같지만 주제에서는 벗어난
문장을 정답으로 제시하는 경우가 많아. 첫 문장을 보니까
이 글의 키워드는 '목소리(voice)'이고, 주제는 '경력 초기의 교사에게
중요한 목소리에 관한 기술'이더라고. 모든 문장이 키워드와
주제의 큰 틀
안에서 벗어나지 않는데, 다만 ③ 문장만 noise 이야기가 나오면서 갑자기
해결책을 찾는다는 등 엉뚱한 맥락으로 이어지고 있어. 혹시 loud voice와
noise가 비슷하다고 느낄 수도 있겠지만, 주제와 아예 다른 내용이기
때문에 정답을 쉽게 찾을 수 있는 문제야.

L 23 정답 ③ ── ⭐ 2등급 대비 [정답률 81%]

* 전문가와 초보자의 차이

다음 글에서 전체 흐름과 관계 없는 문장은?

단서 1 초보자에 비해 전문가가 가진 강점에 대해 설명하는 글임
Interestingly, experts do not suffer / as much as beginners /
= when they perform
when performing complex tasks / or combining multiple tasks. //
흥미롭게도 전문가들은 어려움을 겪지 않는다 / 초보자만큼 / 복잡한 과제를 수행하거나 /
많은 과제를 결합할 때 //

Because experts have extensive practice / within a limited
domain, / the key component skills / in their domain / tend to be
              복수 주어
highly practiced and more automated. //
                        복수 동사
전문가는 광범위한 연습을 하기 때문에 / 제한된 영역 내에서 / 핵심 구성 기술은 / 그들의
영역에서의 / 고도로 숙련되고 더 자동화되어 있는 경향이 있다 //

① Each of these highly practiced skills / then demands /
        단수 주어   단수 동사
relatively few cognitive resources, / effectively lowering the
total cognitive load / that experts experience. //
고도로 숙련된 이러한 각각의 기술은 / 그래서 필요로 하여 / 비교적 적은 인지 자원을 / 총
인지 부하를 효과적으로 낮춘다 / 전문가가 경험하는 //

② Thus, / experts can perform complex tasks / and combine
multiple tasks relatively easily. //
따라서 / 전문가는 복잡한 과제를 수행하고 / 많은 과제를 결합할 수 있다 / 비교적 쉽게 //
                      단서 2 초보자의 강점이 furthermore로 연결되는 문맥이 아님
③ Furthermore, / beginners are excellent / at processing the
tasks / when the tasks are divided and isolated. //)
(게다가 / 초보자는 탁월하다 / 과제를 처리하는 데 / 과제가 분할되고 분리될 때 //)

④ This is not because they necessarily have / more cognitive
            접속사(뒤에 완전한 절이 옴)
resources / than beginners; /
이것은 그들이 반드시 가지고 있기 때문인 것은 아니다 / 더 많은 인지적 자원을 / 초보자보다 /

rather, because of the high level of fluency / they have achieved
        구 형태의 전치사(뒤에 명사구가 옴)
/ in performing key skills, / they can do more / with what they
have. //
오히려 높은 수준의 능숙함 때문에 / 그들이 달성한 / 핵심 기술을 수행하면서 / 그들은 더
많은 것을 할 수 있다 / 자신들이 가지고 있는 것으로 //

⑤ Beginners, on the other hand, have not achieved / the same degree of fluency and automaticity / in each of the component skills, /
반면에 초보자는 달성하지 못했으며 / 동일한 수준의 능숙함과 자동성을 / 각각의 구성 기술에서 /

and thus they struggle to combine skills / that experts combine / with relative ease and efficiency. //
선행사 주격 관계대명사
따라서 그들은 기술을 결합하려고 애쓴다 / 전문가가 결합하는 / 비교적 쉽고 효율적으로 //

- expert ⓝ 전문가 • extensive ⓐ 광범위한
- domain ⓝ 영역, 범위 • component ⓝ 요소, 부품
- automate ⓥ 자동화하다 • cognitive ⓐ 인식의, 인지의
- load ⓝ 부하, 짐 • process ⓥ 처리하다, 가공하다
- isolate ⓥ 격리하다, 분리하다 • necessarily ⓐⓓ 어쩔 수 없이, 필연적으로
- fluency ⓝ 유창성, 능숙도 • struggle ⓥ 애쓰다, 고군분투하다
- relative ⓐ 비교상의, 상대적인

흥미롭게도, 전문가들은 복잡한 과제를 수행하거나 많은 과제를 결합할 때 초보자만큼 어려움을 겪지 않는다. 전문가는 제한된 영역 내에서 광범위한 연습을 하기 때문에, 그들의 영역에서의 핵심 구성 기술은 고도로 숙련되고 더 자동화되어 있는 경향이 있다. ① 그래서 고도로 숙련된 이러한 각각의 기술은 비교적 적은 인지 자원을 필요로 하여, 전문가가 경험하는 총 인지 부하를 효과적으로 낮춘다. ② 따라서 전문가는 비교적 쉽게 복잡한 과제를 수행하고 많은 과제를 결합할 수 있다. (③ 게다가, 초보자는 과제가 분할되고 분리될 때 그것을 처리하는 데 탁월하다.) ④ 이것은 그들이 반드시 초보자보다 더 많은 인지적 자원을 가지고 있기 때문인 것은 아니며, 오히려 핵심 기술을 수행하면서 달성한 높은 수준의 능숙함 때문에 그들은 자신들이 가지고 있는 것으로 더 많은 것을 할 수 있다. ⑤ 반면에, 초보자는 각각의 구성 기술에서 동일한 수준의 능숙함과 자동성을 달성하지 못했으며, 따라서 그들은 전문가가 비교적 쉽고 효율적으로 결합하는 기술을 결합하려고 애쓴다.

왜 2등급❓ 전문가와 초보자를 비교하는 글에서, 초보자라는 그럴 듯한 소재가 오답 문장에도 포함되어 충분히 헷갈릴 수도 있는 2등급 대비 문제이다.

왜 정답•오답❓

첫 문장: 흥미롭게도, 전문가들은 복잡한 과제를 수행하거나 많은 과제를 결합할 때 초보자만큼 어려움을 겪지 않는다. 전문가는 제한된 영역 내에서 광범위한 연습을 하기 때문에, 그들의 영역에서의 핵심 구성 기술은 고도로 숙련되고 더 자동화되어 있는 경향이 있다.

⇒ 초보자에 비해 전문가가 갖는 강점에 대해 설명하는 글이다.

①
그래서 고도로 숙련된 이러한 각각의 기술은 비교적 적은 인지 자원을 필요로 하여, 전문가가 경험하는 총 인지 부하를 효과적으로 낮춘다.

⇒ 전문가가 가진 기술 덕분에 전문가는 초보자보다 낮은 인지 부하를 경험한다는 내용으로, 전문가의 강점을 설명한다.
▶ ①은 무관한 문장이 아님

②
따라서(Thus) 전문가는 비교적 쉽게 복잡한 과제를 수행하고 많은 과제를 결합할 수 있다.

⇒ 앞 문장에서 설명한 것 때문에 전문가가 비교적 쉽게 과제를 수행할 수 있다는 내용으로, 앞뒤 문장이 Thus로 자연스럽게 연결된다.
▶ ②은 무관한 문장이 아님

③
게다가(Furthermore), 초보자는 과제가 분할되고 분리될 때 그것을 처리하는 데 탁월하다.

⇒ furthermore는 앞에서 설명한 것에 대한 추가적 요소를 덧붙일 때 쓰이는 부사이다.
앞에서는 전문가가 갖는 강점에 대해 설명했는데, 이어지는 내용은 초보자의 강점에 대한 것이므로 ③이 글의 흐름에 맞지 않는다.
▶ ③이 무관한 문장임

④
이것은(This) 그들이 반드시 초보자보다 더 많은 인지적 자원을 가지고 있기 때문인 것은 아니며, 오히려 핵심 기술을 수행하면서 달성한 높은 수준의 능숙함 때문에 그들은 자신들이 가지고 있는 것으로 더 많은 것을 할 수 있다.

⇒ This가 가리키는 것은 ③이 아니라 ②의 내용이다. 따라서 ③이 무관한 문장임을 더욱 확실히 알 수 있다.
▶ ③이 빠져야 자연스러운 흐름이 됨, ④은 무관한 문장이 아님

⑤
반면에(on the other hand), 초보자는 각각의 구성 기술에서 동일한 수준의 능숙함과 자동성을 달성하지 못했으며, 따라서 그들은 전문가가 비교적 쉽고 효율적으로 결합하는 기술을 결합하려고 애쓴다.

⇒ on the other hand는 상반되는 내용을 이을 때 쓰이는 연결어이다.
앞 문장의 전문가에 대한 내용과, 이어지는 문장의 초보자의 내용이 on the other hand로 매끄럽게 이어진다.
▶ ⑤은 무관한 문장이 아님

* 글의 흐름

도입	전문가들은 복잡한 과제를 수행하거나 많은 과제를 결합할 때 초보자만큼 어려움을 겪지 않음
설명	고도로 숙련된 기술은 비교적 적은 인지 자원을 필요로 하여, 전문가가 경험하는 총 인지 부하를 효과적으로 낮춤
부연	핵심 기술을 수행하면서 달성한 높은 수준의 능숙함 때문에 그들은 더 많은 것을 할 수 있음
역접	초보자는 동일한 수준의 능숙함을 달성하지 못했으므로 전문가가 쉽게 효율적으로 결합하는 기술을 결합하려고 애씀

L 24 정답 ③ ─────── ⭐ 2등급 대비 [정답률 68%]

＊재택근무의 발전

다음 글에서 전체 흐름과 관계 없는 문장은?

부사절 접속사(양보)
Although organizations are offering telecommuting programs / in greater numbers than ever before, / acceptance and use of these programs / are still limited / by a number of factors. //
복수 주어
복수 동사
조직들이 더 많은 수의 재택근무 프로그램을 제공하고 있지만 / 과거 어느 때보다 / 이러한 프로그램의 수용과 이용은 / 여전히 제한된다 / 많은 요인에 의해 //

① These factors include / manager reliance on face-to-face management practices, / lack of telecommuting training within an organization, / misperceptions of and discomfort with flexible workplace programs, /
이들 요인은 포함한다 / 대면 관리 관행에 대한 관리자의 의존을 / 조직 내 재택근무 교육 부족을 / 유연한 직장 프로그램에 대한 오해와 불편함을 /

and a lack of information / about the effects of telecommuting / on an organization's bottom line. //
그리고 정보 부족을 / 재택근무의 영향에 대한 / 조직의 최종 결산 결과에 미치는 //
전치사   명사구
② Despite these limitations, / at the beginning of the 21st century, / a new "anytime, anywhere" work culture / is emerging. //
이러한 한계에도 불구하고 / 21세기 초에는 / '언제 어디서나' 일할 수 있는 새로운 업무 문화가 / 등장하고 있다 // **단서 1** 재택근무가 직면한 한계에도 불구하고 재택근무 문화가 등장하고 있음

(③ Care must be taken / to select employees / whose
_{선행사} _{소유격 관계대명사}
personal and working characteristics / are best suited for
telecommuting. //)
단서 2 재택근무가 아니라 직원 선발 방법에 대한 내용임
(주의를 기울여야 한다 / 직원을 선발하기 위해 / 개인적 그리고 업무적 특성이 / 재택근무에
가장 적합한 //)

④ Continuing advances in information technology, / the
expansion of a global workforce, / and increased desire /
_{형용사적 용법(increased desire 수식)}
to balance work and family /
정보 기술의 지속적인 발전 / 글로벌 노동력의 확대 / 그리고 욕구의 증가 / 일과 가정
사이에서 균형을 이루려는 /
_{선행사} _{주격 관계대명사}
are only three of the many factors / that will gradually reduce the
current barriers / to telecommuting / as a dominant workforce
development. //
많은 요인 중 세 가지에 불과하다 / 현재의 장벽을 점진적으로 낮출 / 재택근무에 대한 /
지배적인 노동력 개발로서 //

⑤ With implications / for organizational cost savings, /
_{부사구}
especially with regard / to lower facility costs, increased
employee flexibility, and productivity, /
영향과 함께 / 조직 비용 절감에 대한 / 특히 관련하여 / 더 낮은 시설 비용, 증가된 직원의
유연성, 그리고 생산성과 /
_{주절}
telecommuting is increasingly of interest / to many
organizations. //
재택근무는 점점 더 관심사가 되고 있다 / 많은 조직의 //

- acceptance ⓝ 수용   · factor ⓝ 요인   · reliance ⓝ 의존
- face-to-face 대면의   · misperception ⓝ 오해, 오인
- discomfort ⓝ 불편함   · flexible ⓐ 유연한
- bottom line 최종 결산 결과   · limitation ⓝ 한계
- emerge ⓥ 등장하다   · be suited for ~에 적합하다
- advance ⓝ 진보   · expansion ⓝ 확대   · workforce ⓝ 노동력
- balance ⓥ 균형을 맞추다   · barrier ⓝ 장벽
- dominant ⓐ 지배적인   · implications ⓝ 영향
- with regard to ~에 관련하여

조직들이 과거 어느 때보다 더 많은 수의 재택근무 프로그램을 제공하고
있지만, 이러한 프로그램의 수용과 이용은 여전히 많은 요인에 의해 제한된다.
① 이들 요인에는 대면 관리 관행에 대한 관리자의 의존, 조직 내 재택근무
교육 부족, 유연한 직장 프로그램에 대한 오해와 불편함, 그리고 재택근무가
조직의 최종 결산 결과에 미치는 영향에 대한 정보 부족 등이 있다. ② 이러한
한계에도 불구하고, 21세기 초에는, '언제 어디서나' 일할 수 있는 새로운 업무
문화가 등장하고 있다. (③ 개인적 그리고 업무적 특성이 재택근무에 가장
적합한 직원을 선발하기 위해 주의를 기울여야 한다.) ④ 정보 기술의 지속적인
발전, 글로벌 노동력의 확대, 일과 가정 사이에서 균형을 이루려는 욕구의
증가는 지배적인 노동력 개발로서 재택근무에 대한 현재의 장벽을 점진적으로
낮출 많은 요인 중 세 가지에 불과하다. ⑤ 특히 더 낮은 시설 비용, 증가된
직원의 유연성, 그리고 생산성과 관련하여 조직 비용 절감에 대한 영향과 함께,
재택근무는 점점 더 많은 조직의 관심사가 되고 있다.

왜 2등급？ 오답에도 '재택근무'라는 핵심 소재가 포함되어 있어서 집중해서 읽지
않으면 헷갈릴 수 있는 2등급 대비 문제이다. 재택근무를 제한하는 요인을 설명하는
흐름에서, 재택근무에 적합한 직원을 선발해야 한다는 문장은 어색하다는 점을 잘
포착해야 한다.

왜 정답·오답？

첫 문장: 조직들이 과거 어느 때보다 더 많은 수의 재택근무 프로그램을
제공하고 있지만, 이러한 프로그램의 수용과 이용은 여전히 많은 요인
(a number of factors)에 의해 제한된다.

→ 조직들이 이전보다 많은 재택근무 프로그램을 제공하지만 여전히 그 이용은 많은
요인에 의해 제한받는다는 내용이다.
▶ 재택근무 프로그램의 수용과 이용을 제한하는 요인에 대한 구체적인 설명이
이어질 것임

①
이들 요인(These factors)에는 대면 관리 관행에 대한 관리자의 의존,
조직 내 재택근무 교육 부족, 유연한 직장 프로그램에 대한 오해와
불편함, 그리고 재택근무가 조직의 최종 결산 결과에 미치는 영향에
대한 정보 부족 등이 있다.

→ 앞 문장에 등장한 '많은 요인'에 어떤 것들이 포함되는지를 구체적으로 설명하므로
앞 문장에 자연스럽게 연결되고 있다.
▶ ①은 무관한 문장이 아님

②
이러한 한계(these limitations)에도 불구하고, 21세기 초에는, '언제
어디서나' 일할 수 있는 새로운 업무 문화가 등장하고 있다.

→ 앞 문장에서 설명한 재택근무가 직면한 한계를 these limitations로 가리키며,
이러한 한계에도 불구하고 재택근무가 새로운 업무 문화로 등장하고 있다는
내용이다. 지시형용사 these를 통해 앞뒤 문장이 자연스럽게 이어진다.
▶ ②은 무관한 문장이 아님

③
개인적 그리고 업무적 특성이 재택근무에 가장 적합한 직원을 선발하기
위해 주의를 기울여야 한다.

→ 앞부분은 재택근무가 직면한 여러 한계에도 불구하고 재택근무가 새로운 업무
문화로 등장하고 있다는 내용이다. 그렇다면 이후로는 왜 이런 현상이 일어나고
있는지에 대한 설명이 이어지는 것이 적절하고, 기업의 직원 선발 방법에 대해
설명하는 글이 아니다.
▶ ③이 무관한 문장임

④
정보 기술의 지속적인 발전, 글로벌 노동력의 확대, 일과 가정 사이에서
균형을 이루려는 욕구의 증가는 재택근무에 대한 현재의 장벽(the
current barriers)을 점진적으로 낮출 많은 요인 중 세 가지에
불과하다.

→ 정보 기술의 지속적인 발전, 글로벌 노동력의 확대, 일과 가정 사이에서 균형을
이루려는 욕구의 증가 등의 요인 때문에 재택근무 문화가 증가하고 있다는
내용이다.
앞에서 설명한 한계를 the current barriers로 가리키며 앞뒤 내용을 자연스럽게
연결한다.
▶ ③이 빠져야 자연스러운 흐름이 됨, ④은 무관한 문장이 아님

⑤
특히 더 낮은 시설 비용, 증가한 직원의 유연성, 그리고 생산성과
관련하여 조직 비용 절감에 대한 영향과 함께, 재택근무는 점점 더 많은
조직의 관심사가 되고 있다.

→ 앞 문장에서 설명한 요인 외에 재택근무를 증가시키는 추가적인 요인을 설명한다.
재택근무 문화가 등장하고 있는 요인에 대해 앞뒤 문장에서 자연스럽게 설명하고
있다.
▶ ⑤은 무관한 문장이 아님

＊ 글의 흐름

도입	조직들이 어느 때보다 더 많은 수의 재택근무 프로그램을 제공하고 있지만, 여전히 많은 요인에 의해 제한됨
설명 ①	여러 한계에도 불구하고, 21세기 초에는 새로운 업무 문화가 등장하고 있음
설명 ②	정보 기술의 지속적인 발전 등의 요인 때문에 재택근무 문화가 증가하고 있음
부연	재택근무는 점점 많은 조직의 관심사가 되고 있음

L 어휘 Review 정답

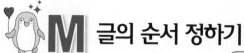

M 글의 순서 정하기

M 01 정답 ① * 호주에서 경관 관리를 위한 의도적인 불 지르기

Wildfire is a natural phenomenon / in many Australian environments. //
산불은 자연스러운 현상이다 / 호주의 많은 환경에서 //

단서 1 호주 원주민에 의해 오랜 기간 행해졌던 의도적 불 지르기를 설명함

The intentional setting of fire / to manage the landscape / was practised by Aboriginal people for millennia. //
의도적으로 불을 지르는 일은 / 경관을 관리하기 위해 / 수천 년 동안 호주 원주민들에 의해 행해졌다 //

(A) However, the pattern of burning that stockmen introduced / was unlike previous regimes. //
하지만 목축업자들이 도입한 불 지르기 방식은 / 이전 양식과는 달랐다 //

단서 2 주어진 글에서 말한, 기존의 호주 원주민의 방식과 다른 목축업자들의 방식을 소개함

When conditions allowed, / they would set fire to the landscape / as they moved their animals out for the winter. //
여건이 허락되면 / 그들은 경관에 불을 지르곤 했다 / 그들은 겨울에 자신들의 가축을 외부로 이동시켜 //

This functioned to clear woody vegetation / and also stimulated new plant growth in the following spring. //
이는 숲이 우거진 초목을 없애는 역할을 했고 / 또한 이듬해 봄에 새로운 식물의 성장을 촉진했다 //

(B) Although grasses were the first kinds of plants / to recolonize the burnt areas / they were soon succeeded by further woody plants and shrubs. //
첫 번째 식물류는 풀이었지만 / 불에 탄 지역에 다시 대량 서식한 / 목본성 식물과 관목이 곧 그것들의 뒤를 이었다 //

단서 3 불을 지른 후 의도했던 대로 어린 새싹이 먼저 자랐지만, 그 이후 통제하고자 했던 목본성 식물과 관목이 다시 자라남

About the only strategy to prevent such regrowth / was further burning / — essentially using fire to control the consequences of using fire. //
그러한 재성장을 막기 위한 거의 유일한 전략은 / 불을 더 지르는 것이었는데 / 본질적으로는 불을 사용하여 불을 사용한 결과를 통제하는 것이었다 //

(C) The young shoots were a ready food source / for their animals when they returned. //
어린 새싹은 준비된 먹을 수 있는 식량원이었다 / 그들의 동물들이 돌아왔을 때 //

단서 4 '그들의 동물들'은 (A)에서 말한 목축업자들의 동물을 지칭함

However, the practice also tended to reinforce the scrubby growth / it was intended to control. //
하지만, 그 관행은 우거진 관목의 성장을 강화하는 경향도 있었다 / 그것(그 관행)이 통제하고자 했던 //

- intentional ⓐ 의도적인   • aboriginal ⓐ 호주 원주민의
- millennia ⓝ (millennium의 복수형) 천년   • stockman ⓝ 목축업자
- woody ⓐ 숲이 우거진   • vegetation ⓝ 초목
- stimulate ⓥ 자극하다   • recolonize ⓥ 다시 대량 서식하다
- woody plant 목본성 식물(木本性 植物)   • shrub ⓝ 관목(灌木)
- shoot ⓝ 새싹, 순   • reinforce ⓥ 강화하다

산불은 호주의 많은 환경에서 자연스러운 현상이다. 경관을 관리하기 위해 의도적으로 불을 지르는 일은 수천 년 동안 호주 원주민들에 의해 행해졌다. (A) 하지만 목축업자들이 도입한 불 지르기 방식은 이전 양식과는 달랐다. 여건이 허락되면, 그들은 겨울에 자신들의 가축을 외부로 이동시켜, 경관에 불을 지르곤 했다. 이는 숲이 우거진 초목을 없애는 역할을 했고, 또한 이듬해 봄에 새로운 식물의 성장을 촉진했다. (C) 어린 새싹은 그들의 동물들이 돌아왔을 때 준비된 먹을 수 있는 식량원이었다. 하지만, 그 관행은 또한 통제하고자 했던 우거진 관목의 성장을 강화하는 경향도 있었다. (B) 불에 탄 지역에 다시 대량 서식한 첫 번째 식물류는 풀이었지만, 목본성 식물과 관목이 곧 그것들의 뒤를 이었다. 그러한 재성장을 막기 위한 거의 유일한 전략은 불을 더 지르는 것이었는데, 본질적으로는 불을 사용하여 불을 사용한 결과를 통제하는 것이었다.

핵심 소재가 포함된 문장의 함정에 빠지지 말자!

주어진 글 다음에 이어질 글의 순서로 가장 적절한 것을 고르시오.

① (A) ― (C) ― (B)
② (B) ― (A) ― (C) ┐
③ (B) ― (C) ― (A) ┘ (B)는 풀이 자란 후에 다시 불을 지르게 됐다는 내용이 나오는 결말임
④ (C) ― (A) ― (B) ┐ (C)에서 어린 새싹을 언급하려면 (A)에서 새로운 식물의 성장을
⑤ (C) ― (B) ― (A) ┘ 촉진했다는 내용이 먼저 나와야 함

호주 원주민들은 경관을 관리하기 위해 의도적 불지르기를 했음 - 목축업자들은 겨울에 동물을
이동시킨 후 불을 질렀음 - 어린 새싹은 동물의 식량원이 되었으나 원래 없애고자 했던 나무의 성장이
강화됨 - 풀이 자란 이후 뒤이어 다시 나무가 자라게 되었고, 불을 더 질러야 했음

| 문제 풀이 순서 | [정답률 15%]

1st 각 문단의 내용을 파악하고, 글의 논리적인 순서를 추론한다.

┌ **주어진 글:** 산불은 호주의 많은 환경에서 자연스러운 현상이다. 경관을
│ 관리하기 위해 의도적으로 불을 지르는 일은 수천 년 동안 호주 원주민들에
└ 의해 행해졌다.

⇒ **주어진 글 뒤:** 호주에서 경관을 관리하기 위한 의도적 불 지르기는 이미 원주민들이
오랜 기간 해왔던 것이었다고 했으므로, **단서** 원주민들이 오랫동안 해왔던 이
방식을 설명하거나, 원주민의 방식과는 다르게 새로운 방식을 소개할 것이다. **발상**

┌ **(A)** **하지만(However)** 목축업자들이 도입한 불 지르기 방식은 이전
│ 양식과는 달랐다. 여건이 허락되면, 그들은 겨울에 자신들의 가축을 외부로
│ 이동시켜, 경관에 불을 지르곤 했다. 이는 숲이 우거진 초목을 없애는
└ 역할을 했고, 또한 이듬해 봄에 새로운 식물의 성장을 촉진했다.

⇒ **(A) 앞:** 반대 내용을 연결하는 However(하지만)로 문장이 시작했고,
목축업자들의 불 지르기 방식은 이전 양식과는 달랐다는 내용이 나온다.
▶ 주어진 글에 목축업자들의 방식과 다른 이전 양식인 호주 원주민에 대한
내용이 나옴 (순서: 주어진 글 → (A))
(A) 뒤: 이동한 동물들은 어떻게 되었으며, 우거진 나무가 없어진 자리에 어떤
새로운 식물이 자랐는지 나올 것이다.

┌ **(B)** 불에 탄 지역에 다시 대량 서식한 첫 번째 식물류는 풀이었지만, 목본성
│ 식물과 관목이 곧 그것들의 뒤를 이었다. 그러한 재성장을 막기 위한 거의
│ 유일한 전략은 불을 더 지르는 것이었는데, 본질적으로는 불을 사용하여
└ 불을 사용한 결과를 통제하는 것이었다.

⇒ **(B) 앞:** 풀이 자란 이후 다시 나무가 자라게 되었다는 내용이므로, 없애고자 했던
나무의 성장을 언급했던 내용이 앞에 와야 한다.
▶ (B) 앞에 (C)가 와야 함 (순서: (C) → (B))
(B) 뒤: 나무가 다시 자라게 되어 불을 지른 자리에 다시 불을 지르게 된다고 했다.
▶ (B)가 마지막에 올 확률이 큼

┌ **(C)** 어린 새싹은 [그들의 동물들(their animals)]이 돌아왔을 때 준비된
│ 먹을 수 있는 식량원이었다. 하지만, 그 관행은 또한 통제하고자 했던
└ 우거진 관목의 성장을 강화하는 경향도 있었다.

⇒ **(C) 앞:** '그들의 동물들(their animals)'은 (A)에서 말한 목축업자들의 동물들을
가리킨다. ▶ 순서: (A) → (C)
(C) 뒤: 원래 없애고자 했던 나무의 성장이 다시 강화되는 경향이 있었다고
했으므로, 앞에서 살펴본 것처럼 이와 관련된 내용인 (B)가 이어질 것이다.
▶ 순서: 주어진 글 → (A) → (C) → (B)

2nd 글이 한눈에 들어오도록 정리하여 정답을 확인한다.

주어진 글: 호주에서 경관을 관리하기 위한 의도적 불 지르기는 이미 원주민들이 오랜
기간 해왔던 것이었다.
→ **(A):** 목축업자들이 도입한 불 지르기 방식은 이전 양식(원주민)과는 달랐다. 겨울에
동물을 이동시킨 후 불을 질렀다.
→ **(C):** 동물이 돌아왔을 때 새로 자란 어린 새싹은 동물의 식량원이 되었다. 그러나
원래 없애고자 했던 나무의 성장이 다시 강화되는 경향이 있었다.
→ **(B):** 풀이 자란 이후 뒤이어 다시 나무가 자라게 되었고, 불을 더 질러야 했다.
▶ 주어진 글 다음에 이어질 글의 순서는 (A) → (C) → (B)이므로 정답은 ①임

M 02 정답 ④ *복잡해지는 컴퓨터 소프트웨어

The growing complexity of computer software / has direct
단수 주어   단수 동사
implications / for our global safety and security, /
컴퓨터 소프트웨어 증가하는 복잡성은 / 직접적인 영향을 준다 / 우리의 전 세계적인
안전과 보안에 /
particularly as the physical objects / upon which we
부사절 접속사(~함에 따라)   주어, 선행사   전치사+관계대명사
depend — things like cars, airplanes, bridges, tunnels, and
동사
implantable medical devices — / transform themselves / into
동사
computer code. //
특히 물리적 대상이 ~함에 따라 / 우리가 의존하는 / 자동차, 비행기, 교량, 터널, 이식형
의료 기기와 같은 것들 / 그 자신을 변화시킴에 (따라) / 컴퓨터 코드로 //

(A) As all this code grows / in size and complexity, / so too do /
the number of errors and software bugs. //
이 모든 코드가 증가함에 따라 / 크기와 복잡성에서 / 또한 그렇다 / 오류와 소프트웨어 버그
수 // **단서 1** 자동차와 비행기와 같은 물리적 사물들이 크고 복잡한 코드로
변함에 따라 오류와 소프트웨어 버그의 수도 증가함
According to a study / by Carnegie Mellon University, /
commercial software typically has twenty to thirty bugs / for
every thousand lines of code /
연구에 따르면 / Carnegie Mellon 대학교에 의한 / 상용 소프트웨어에는 20~30개의
버그가 있다 / 보통 코드 1,000줄당 /
— 50 million lines of code means / 1 million to 1.5 million
to부정사의 수동태
potential errors / to be exploited. //
5천만 줄의 코드는 의미한다 / 1백만~150만 개의 잠재적 오류를 / 악의적으로 이용되는 //

(B) This is the basis / for all malware attacks / that take advantage
to get의 목적어와 목적격 보어
of these computer bugs / to get the code to do something / it was
not originally intended to do. // **단서 2** 버그에 대해 언급된 (A) 뒤에 이어져야 함
이것이 근간이다 / 모든 악성 소프트웨어 공격의 / 이 컴퓨터 버그를 이용하는 / 코드가 ~한
것을 하도록 / 그것이 원래 하도록 의도되지 않았던 //

As computer code grows more elaborate, / software bugs
flourish / and security suffers, / with increasing consequences
for society at large. //
컴퓨터 코드가 더 정교해짐에 따라 / 소프트웨어 버그는 창궐하고 / 보안은 악화된다 / 사회
전반에 미치는 증가하는 영향으로 //

(C) Physical things are increasingly becoming / information
technologies. // **단서 3** 주어진 글에서 말한 the physical objects에 대한 부연 설명이 이어짐
물리적 사물은 점점 더 되어가고 있다 / 정보 기술이 //
Cars are "computers / we ride in," / and airplanes are nothing
선행사(목적격 관계대명사는 생략됨)
more than "flying Solaris boxes / attached to bucketfuls of
선행사(주격 관계대명사와 be동사는 생략됨)
industrial control systems." //
자동차는 '컴퓨터'이고 / 우리가 타는 / 비행기는 '비행 솔라리스 박스'에 불과하다 / 수많은
산업 제어 시스템에 부착된 //

- complexity ⓝ 복잡성 · implication ⓝ 영향, 함축
- implantable ⓐ 체내에 삽입되는 · transform ⓥ 변화시키다
- commercial ⓐ 상업의 · intend ⓥ 의도하다
- elaborate ⓐ 정교한 · flourish ⓥ 번성하다, 창궐하다
- consequence ⓝ 결과

컴퓨터 소프트웨어 복잡성의 증가는 전 세계의 안전과 보안에 직접적인 영향을
주는데, 우리가 의존하는 물리적 대상, 즉 자동차, 비행기, 교량, 터널, 이식형
의료 기기와 같은 것들이 컴퓨터 코드로 변해감에 따라 특히 그렇다. (C)
물리적 사물은 점점 더 정보 기술이 되어가고 있다. 자동차는 '우리가 타는
컴퓨터'이고, 비행기는 '수많은 산업 제어 시스템에 부착된 비행 솔라리스
박스'에 불과하다. (A) 이 모든 코드가 크기와 복잡성이 증가함에 따라, 오류와
소프트웨어 버그 수 또한 증가한다. Carnegie Mellon 대학교의 연구에
따르면, 상용 소프트웨어에는 보통 코드 1,000줄당 20~30개의 버그가 있어서,
5천만 줄의 코드는 1백만~150만 개의 잠재적 오류가 악의적으로 이용될 수
있다는 것을 의미한다. (B) 이것이 코드가 원래 하도록 의도되지 않았던 것을

하도록 이 컴퓨터 버그를 이용하는 모든 악성 소프트웨어 공격의 근간이다. 컴퓨터 코드가 더 정교해짐에 따라, 소프트웨어 버그는 창궐하고 보안은 악화되어, 사회 전반에 미치는 영향이 커진다.

주어진 글 다음에 이어질 글의 순서로 가장 적절한 것을 고르시오.

① (A) — (C) — (B) 코드가 증가한다는 내용을 다룬 (C)가 (A) 앞에 필요함
② (B) — (A) — (C) these computer bugs가 가리키는 것이 주어진 글에 없음
③ (B) — (C) — (A) 컴퓨터 소프트웨어의 증가하는 복잡성은 전 세계의 안전과 보안에 직접적인 영향을 줌 - 물리적 사물은 점점 정보 기술이 되어 가고 있음 - 코드가 크고 복잡해짐에 따라 오류와 소프트웨어 버그의 수도 증가함 - 보안은 악화되며 사회 전반에 더 큰 영향을 미침
④ (C) — (A) — (B)
⑤ (C) — (B) — (A) these computer bugs가 가리키는 것은 (A)에 등장함

| 문제 풀이 순서 | [정답률 58%]

1st 각 문단의 내용을 파악하고, 글의 논리적인 순서를 추론한다.

> **주어진 글:** 컴퓨터 소프트웨어 복잡성의 증가는 전 세계의 안전과 보안에 직접적인 영향을 주는데, 우리가 의존하는 물리적 대상, 즉 자동차, 비행기, 교량, 터널, 이식형 의료 기기와 같은 것들이 컴퓨터 코드로 변해감에 따라 특히 그렇다.

⇒ 이 글은 컴퓨터 소프트웨어가 점점 복잡해지면서 전 세계의 안전과 보안에 영향을 미친다는 내용일 것이다.
주어진 글 뒤: 자동차, 비행기 등의 물리적 대상이 컴퓨터 코드로 변해감에 따른 구체적 과정이 이어질 것이다.

> **(A):** 이 모든 코드가 크기와 복잡성이 증가함에 따라, 오류와 소프트웨어 버그 수 또한 증가한다. Carnegie Mellon 대학교의 연구에 따르면, 상용 소프트웨어에는 보통 코드 1,000줄당 20~30개의 버그가 있어서, 5천만 줄의 코드는 1백만~150만 개의 잠재적 오류가 악의적으로 이용될 수 있다는 것을 의미한다.

⇒ 물리적 대상이 코드로 변하고, 그 코드가 크고 복잡해짐에 따라 오류와 소프트웨어 버그의 수 또한 증가한다는 내용이다.
(A) 앞: 물리적 대상이 코드로 변한다는 내용이 있어야 한다.
▶ 주어진 글이 (A) 앞에 올 수 있음
(A) 뒤: 증가하는 오류와 소프트웨어 버그가 악의적으로 이용될 수 있고, 나아가 전 세계의 안전과 보안에 직접적인 영향을 준다는 결론으로 이어지리라고 예상할 수 있다.

> **(B):** 이것이 코드가 원래 하도록 의도되지 않았던 것을 하도록 이 컴퓨터 버그(these computer bugs)를 이용하는 모든 악성 소프트웨어 공격의 근간이다. 컴퓨터 코드가 더 정교해짐에 따라, 소프트웨어 버그는 창궐하고 보안은 악화되어, 사회 전반에 미치는 영향이 커진다.

⇒ **(B) 앞:** these computer bugs가 가리킬 만한 것이 (B) 앞에 있어야 한다.
▶ (A)에서 소프트웨어 버그에 대한 설명이 제시되었으므로 (A)가 (B) 앞에 옴 (순서: (A) → (B))
(B) 뒤: 컴퓨터 코드가 더 정교해짐에 따라 소프트웨어 버그가 창궐하고 보안이 악화되어, 사회 전반에 큰 영향을 미친다는 내용으로, (B)가 글의 결론에 해당한다.
▶ (B)가 마지막에 올 확률이 큼

> **(C):** 물리적 사물은 점점 더 정보 기술이 되어가고 있다. 자동차는 '우리가 타는 컴퓨터'이고, 비행기는 '수많은 산업 제어 시스템에 부착된 비행 솔라리스 박스'에 불과하다.

⇒ 자동차와 비행기를 예시로 들어, 물리적 사물이 컴퓨터 코드로 변하는 것을 부연 설명한다.

(C) 앞: 물리적 대상이 컴퓨터 코드로 변한다고 설명한 주어진 문장이 (C) 앞에 필요하다.
▶ (C) 앞에 주어진 문장이 와야 함 (순서: 주어진 글 → (C))
(C) 뒤: (A)에서 살펴본 것처럼, (A) 앞에는 물리적 대상이 코드로 변한다는 내용이 있어야 한다.
▶ (C) 뒤에는 (A)가 와야 함 (순서: 주어진 글 → (C) → (A) → (B))

2nd 글이 한눈에 들어오도록 정리하여 정답을 확인한다.

주어진 글: 컴퓨터 소프트웨어의 증가하는 복잡성은 전 세계의 안전과 보안에 직접적인 영향을 주는데, 특히 물리적 대상이 컴퓨터 코드로 변함에 따라 그렇다.

→ **(C):** 자동차, 비행기와 같은 물리적 사물은 점점 더 정보 기술이 되어 가고 있다.

→ **(A):** 이러한 코드가 크고 복잡해짐에 따라 오류와 소프트웨어 버그의 수도 증가한다.

→ **(B):** 컴퓨터 코드가 더 정교해짐에 따라 소프트웨어 버그는 창궐하고 보안은 악화되며 사회 전반에 더 큰 영향을 미친다.

▶ 주어진 글 다음에 이어질 글의 순서는 (C) → (A) → (B)이므로 정답은 ④임

M 03 정답 ⑤ * 평판 자본과 시장 규제 집행 가능성 간 관계

단서1 시장 규제 집행 가능성은 계약 위반 시 가치가 떨어질 수 있는 평판 자본을 구축한 경우에 더 크다고 언급함
The potential for market enforcement is greater / when contracting parties have developed reputational capital / that [주격 관계대명사] can be devalued when contracts are violated. //
시장 규제 집행 가능성은 더 크다 / 계약 당사자들이 평판 자본을 구축한 경우에 / 계약 위반 시 가치가 떨어질 수 있는 //

(A) Similarly, / a landowner can undermaintain / fences, ditches, and irrigation systems. // **단서2** (B)의 마지막 문장에 이어서, 마찬가지로 지주는 울타리, 도랑 등을 제대로 관리하지 않을 수 있음
마찬가지로 / 지주는 제대로 관리하지 않을 수 있다 / 울타리, 도랑, 관개 시스템을 //

Accurate assessments of farmer and landowner behavior / will be made / over time, /
농부와 지주의 행동에 대한 정확한 평가는 / 이루어질 것이다 / 시간이 지남에 따라 /

and those farmers and landowners / who attempt to gain at [주격 관계대명사] each other's expense / will find / that others may refuse to deal with them / in the future. // [목적어절을 이끄는 접속사]
그리고 그러한 농부와 지주 / 상대방의 비용으로 이익을 취하려고 시도하는 / 알게 될 것이다 / 다른 사람들이 그들과 거래하는 것을 거부할 수도 있다는 것을 / 향후 //

단서3 시간이 지나면서 지주들은 농부들을 간접적으로 감시하게 됨
(B) Over time / landowners indirectly monitor farmers / by observing the reported output, / the general quality of the soil, / and any unusual or extreme behavior. //
시간이 지나면서 / 지주들은 농부들을 간접적으로 감시한다 / 보고된 생산량을 관찰함으로써 / 토양의 전반적인 질 / 그리고 어떤 보기 드물거나 극단적인 행동 //

Farmer and landowner reputations act / as a bond. //
농부와 지주의 평판은 역할을 한다 / 계약의 //

In any growing season / a farmer can reduce effort, / overuse soil, / or underreport the crop. // [병렬 구조]
어떤 한 재배 철에 / 농부는 노력을 줄일 수 있다 / 토양을 과도하게 사용하거나 / 또는 작물을 축소 보고하거나 //

단서4 농부와 지주들이 평판을 쌓아 나감(주어진 글에서 언급한 평판 자본의 예시)
(C) Farmers and landowners develop reputations / for honesty, fairness, / producing high yields, / and consistently [분사구문의 병렬 구조] demonstrating / that they are good at what they do. // [목적어절을 이끄는 접속사]
농부와 지주는 평판을 쌓아 나간다 / 정직함과 공정함에 대한 / 높은 수확량을 생산하면서 / 그리고 지속적으로 입증하면서 / 자신이 하는 일을 잘한다는 것을 //

In small, close-knit farming communities, / reputations are well known. //
소규모의 긴밀히 맺어진 농업 공동체에서는 / 평판이 잘 알려져 있다 //

- **enforcement** ⓝ 집행　　• **party** ⓝ 당사자
- **reputational capital** 평판 자본　　• **devalue** ⓥ 평가 절하하다
- **undermaintain** ⓥ 제대로 관리하지 않다　　• **assessment** ⓝ 평가
- **expense** ⓝ 비용　　• **extreme** ⓐ 극적인　　• **reputation** ⓝ 평판
- **overuse** ⓥ 남용하다　　• **underreport** ⓥ (소득·수입 등을) 적게 신고하다
- **yield** ⓝ 수확량　　• **demonstrate** ⓥ 입증하다
- **close-knit** ⓐ 긴밀히 맺어진

시장 규제 집행 가능성은 계약 당사자들이 계약 위반 시 가치가 떨어질 수 있는 평판자본을 구축한 경우에 더 크다. (C) 농부와 지주는 높은 수확량을 생산하고, 자신이 하는 일을 잘한다는 것을 지속적으로 입증하면서 정직함과 공정함에 대한 평판을 쌓아 나간다. 소규모의 긴밀히 맺어진 농업 공동체에서는 평판이 잘 알려져 있다. (B) 시간이 지나면서 지주들은 보고된 생산량, 토양의 전반적인 질, 어떤 보기 드물거나 극단적인 행동을 관찰하여 농부들을 간접적으로 감시한다. 농부와 지주의 평판은 계약의 역할을 한다. 어떤 한 재배 철에 농부는 노력을 줄이거나 토양을 과도하게 사용하거나 작물을 축소 보고할 수 있다. (A) 마찬가지로, 지주는 울타리, 도랑, 관개 시스템을 제대로 관리하지 않을 수 있다. 농부와 지주의 행동에 대한 정확한 평가는 시간이 지남에 따라 이루어질 것이고, 상대방의 비용으로 이익을 취하려고 시도하는 농부와 지주는 다른 사람들이 향후 그들과의 거래를 거부할 수도 있다는 것을 알게 될 것이다.

주어진 글 다음에 이어질 글의 순서로 가장 적절한 것을 고르시오.

① (A) — (C) — (B) (A)의 Similarly로 이어질 수 있는 내용이 주어진 글에 없음
② (B) — (A) — (C) ┐ (B)에서 시간이 지나면서 지주는 농부를 감시하고, 농부는 부정직한
③ (B) — (C) — (A) ┘ 행동을 할 수 있다고 했으므로 (B) 앞에는 시간이 지나기 이전 농부와 지주에 대한 설명이 나와야 함
④ (C) — (A) — (B) (A)의 Similarly는 (B)의 마지막 문장에 이어짐
⑤ (C) — (B) — (A) 계약 당사자가 평판 자본을 구축한 경우 시장 규제 집행의 가능성이 더 큼 - 농부와 지주가 평판을 쌓아 감 - 시간이 지나면서 지주는 농부를 감시하는데, 농부가 부정직하게 행동할 수 있음 - 마찬가지로 지주도 부정직하게 행동할 수 있는데, 결국 이런 사람들은 향후 거래를 거부당할 것임

| 문제 풀이 순서 | [정답률 57%]

1st 각 문단의 내용을 파악하고, 글의 논리적인 순서를 추론한다.

┌ **주어진 글**: 시장 규제 집행 가능성은 계약 당사자들이 계약 위반 시 가치가
└ 떨어질 수 있는 평판 자본을 구축한 경우에 더 크다.
➡ 계약 당사자가 평판 자본을 구축한 경우 시장 규제 집행의 가능성이 더 크다는 내용을 제시하고 있다. (단서)

주어진 글 뒤: 계약 당사자가 평판 자본을 구축한 경우 시장 규제 집행의 가능성이 더 크다는 내용을 설명하는 예시가 이어질 것이다. (발상)

┌ (A) 마찬가지로(Similarly), 지주는 울타리, 도랑, 관개 시스템을 제대로
│ 관리하지 않을 수 있다. 농부와 지주의 행동에 대한 정확한 평가는 시간이
│ 지남에 따라 이루어질 것이고, 상대방의 비용으로 이익을 취하려고
│ 시도하는 농부와 지주는 다른 사람들이 향후 그들과의 거래를 거부할 수도
└ 있다는 것을 알게 될 것이다.
➡ **(A) 앞**: '마찬가지로(Similarly)'가 쓰인 것으로 보아 울타리 등을 제대로 관리하지 않는 지주처럼 농부가 무언가를 제대로 하지 않는 것에 관한 내용이 제시되었을 것이다. ▶ 주어진 글이 (A) 앞에 올 수 없음

(A) 뒤: 상대방 비용으로 이익을 취하려고 하는 농부와 지주가 맞이하게 되는 결론이 마지막에 제시되었으므로 (A)가 글의 마지막에 올 확률이 높다.
▶ (A)가 글의 마지막에 올 확률이 높음

┌ (B) 시간이 지나면서(Over time) 지주들은 보고된 생산량, 토양의
│ 전반적인 질, 어떤 보기 드물거나 극단적인 행동을 관찰하여 농부들을
│ 간접적으로 감시한다. 농부와 지주의 평판은 계약의 역할을 한다. 어떤 한
│ 재배 철에 농부는 노력을 줄이거나 토양을 과도하게 사용하거나 작물을
└ 축소 보고할 수 있다.
➡ **(B) 앞**: '시간이 지나면서(Over time)'라고 했으므로 앞에는 이전에 지주와 농부 사이에 어떤 일이 발생하였는지가 제시되어야 한다.
▶ 주어진 글이 (B) 앞에 올 수 없음

(B) 뒤: 농부가 노력을 줄이는 등의 행동을 하는 것에 대한 지주의 반응이나 결과가 이어질 것이다. ▶ 순서: (B) → (A)

┌ (C) 농부와 지주는 높은 수확량을 생산하고, 자신이 하는 일을 잘한다는
│ 것을 지속적으로 입증하면서 정직함과 공정함에 대한 평판을 쌓아 나간다.
└ 소규모의 긴밀히 맺어진 농업 공동체에서는 평판이 잘 알려져 있다.
➡ **(C) 앞**: 농부와 지주가 서로 일을 잘 하는 것을 입증하면서 정직함과 공정함에 대한 평판을 쌓아 나간다고 언급하고 있으므로, 계약 당사자의 평판 자본에 대해 설명한 주어진 글 다음에 (C)가 이어져 예시를 제시하는 것으로 보는 것이 적절하다.
▶ 순서: 주어진 글 → (C)
(C) 뒤: 농부와 지주 사이 평판에 어떤 변화가 발생하는지 추가적인 정보가 제시될 것이다. 이 내용이 (B)에 있다. ▶ 순서: 주어진 글 → (C) → (B) → (A)

2nd 글이 한눈에 들어오도록 정리하여 정답을 확인한다.

주어진 글: 계약 당사자가 평판 자본을 구축한 경우 시장 규제 집행의 가능성이 더 크다.
➡ **(C)**: 하나의 예로 농부와 지주가 서로 평판을 쌓아 간다.
➡ **(B)**: 시간이 지나면서 지주는 농부를 감시하는데, 농부가 부정직하게 행동할 수 있다.
➡ **(A)**: 마찬가지로 지주도 부정직하게 행동할 수 있는데, 결국 이런 사람들은 향후 거래를 거부당할 것이다.
▶ 주어진 글 다음에 이어질 글의 순서는 (C) → (B) → (A)이므로 정답은 ⑤임

배지오 | 2025 수능 응시·성남 낙생고 졸
난 (A), (B), (C) 각각에서 말하고자 하는 바를 한국어로 정리한 다음, 어떻게 연결해야 논리적으로 말이 될지 생각한 뒤 각 문단을 이어봐. 주제를 파악한 이후에, 나는 접속사, 연결사와 대명사에 신경 쓰면서 순서를 맞춰나갔어. 이 문제의 경우, Similarly, Over time에 주목했지. 처음에는 농부와 지주 모두 긍정적이게 행동을 한다는 (C)가 와야 할 거야. (B)에서 시간이 지나 농부들이 부정적이게 행동을 할 것임을 언급했고 이와 마찬가지로 지주도 부정적인 행동을 할 수 있다는 흐름이 자연스럽기 때문에 (A)가 마지막에 와야 하지.

M 04 정답 ③ ＊일렬로 선 새들의 관찰 조정력과 감정 전염

Watch the birds / in your backyard. // 새를 관찰해보라 / 뒷마당의 //

If one bird startles and flies off, / others will follow, / not 문자구문을 이룸
waiting around to assess / whether the threat is real. //
새 한 마리가 놀라 날아오르면 / 다른 새들도 뒤따를 것이다 / 판단하기 위해 기다리지 않고 / 그 위협이 진짜인지 아닌지를 / **단서1** 새 한 마리가 날아오르면 다른 새들도 뒤따르는 것을 감정 전염에 감염되었다고 설명하고 있음

They have been infected / by emotional contagion. //
그것들은 감염되었다 / 감정 전염에 //

(A) Marc wondered / 명사절 접속사 whether the birds in line were more fearful / because they didn't know / what their flockmates were doing. // **단서2** (C)의 마지막에 이어지는 내용으로, 줄을 선 새들이 더 두려워하는 이유에 대해 궁금해 함
Marc는 궁금해했다 / 줄을 선 새들이 더 두려운 것은 아닌지 / 그들이 모르기 때문에 / 자기 무리가 무엇을 하는지 //

Emotional contagion would have been impossible / for individual grosbeaks in the linear array / except with their nearest neighbors. //
감정 전염은 불가능했을 것이다 / 선형 배열에 있는 개개의 콩새류에 / 가장 가까운 곳에 있는 이웃을 제외하고는 //

(B) In a long-term research project / 목적격 관계대명사 that Marc did with some of his students / on patterns of antipredatory scanning / by western evening grosbeaks, /
장기 연구 프로젝트에서 / Marc가 자신의 학생 몇 명과 함께 진행한 / 포식자 회피 관찰 패턴에 관한 / 서양 콩새류의 /

단서 3 Marc의 연구에서 원을 그리고 있는 새들이 일렬로 서 있는 새들보다 더 많은 관찰 조정력을 보이는 것 발견함

목적어절을 이끄는 접속사

they found / that birds in a circle showed / more coordination in

주어와 동사 도치   주격 관계대명사

scanning / than did birds who were feeding in a line. //

그들은 발견했다 / 원을 그리고 있는 새들이 보인다는 것을 / 관찰에 더 많은 조정력을 / 일렬로 먹이를 먹고 있는 새보다 //

계속적 용법의 관계대명사

(C) The birds in a line, / who could only see their nearest

접속사가 생략되지 않은 분사구문

neighbor, / not only were less coordinated / when scanning, /

일렬로 늘어선 새들은 / 가장 가까운 이웃만 볼 수 있었는데 / 조정력이 떨어졌을 뿐만 아니라 / 관찰할 때 /

단서 4 일렬로 줄을 선 새들이 더 조정력이 떨어졌고 더 긴장한 상태였음

but also were more nervous, / changing their body and head

분사구문을 이끎

positions / significantly more than grosbeaks in a circle, /

where it was possible for each grosbeak / to see every other

관계부사   가주어   의미상 주어   진주어

grosbeak. //

더 긴장한 상태였고 / 몸과 머리 위치를 바꾸었는데 / 원을 그리고 있는 콩새들보다 훨씬 더 많이 / 그곳에서는 각각의 콩새에게 가능했다 / 다른 모든 콩새를 보는 것이 //

- startle ⓥ 놀래다   - infect ⓥ 감염시키다   - contagion ⓝ 전염
- linear ⓐ (직)선의   - antipredatory ⓐ 포식자 회피의
- scan ⓥ 살피다, 훑어보다   - coordination ⓝ (신체) 조정력
- significantly ⓐd 상당히

뒷마당의 새를 관찰해보라. 새 한 마리가 놀라 날아오르면 다른 새들도 위협의 진위를 판단하기 위해 기다리지 않고 뒤따를 것이다. 그것들은 감정 전염에 감염되었다. (B) Marc가 자신의 학생 몇 명과 함께 진행한 서양 콩새류의 포식자 회피 관찰 패턴에 관한 장기 연구 프로젝트에서, 그들은 일렬로 먹이를 먹고 있는 새보다 원을 그리고 있는 새들이 관찰에 더 많은 조정력을 보인다는 사실을 발견했다. (C) 일렬로 늘어선 새들은, 가장 가까운 이웃만 볼 수 있었는데, 관찰할 때 조정력이 떨어졌을 뿐만 아니라 더 긴장한 상태였고 원을 그리고 있는 콩새들보다 몸과 머리 위치를 훨씬 더 많이 바꾸었는데, 원을 그린 상태에서는 각각의 콩새가 다른 모든 콩새를 볼 수 있었다. (A) Marc는 줄을 선 새들이 자기 무리가 무엇을 하는지 모르기 때문에 더 두려운 것은 아닌지 궁금해했다. 감정 전염은 선형 배열에 있는 개개의 콩새류에 가장 가까운 곳에 있는 이웃을 제외하고는 불가능했을 것이다.

주어진 글 다음에 이어질 글의 순서로 가장 적절한 것을 고르시오. [3점]

① (A) — (C) — (B)　(A) 앞에는 일렬로 선 새들이 두려워하거나 불안해했다는 내용이 제시되어야 하므로 주어진 글이 올 수 없음
② (B) — (A) — (C)　(C)의 마지막에 이어지는 내용(줄을 선 새들이 더 두려워하는 이유에 대해 궁금해 함)이 (A)에 나오므로 뒤에 와야 함
③ (B) — (C) — (A)　새 한 마리가 날아오르면 다른 새들도 뒤따르는 것을 감정 전염에 감염되었다고 함 - 일렬로 선 새보다 원을 그리고 있는 새들이 더 많은 조정력을 보임 - 일렬로 늘어선 새들은 가장 가까운 이웃만 볼 수 있었고 관찰 조정력이 떨어짐 - 줄을 선 새들은 무엇을 하는지 모르기 때문에 더 두려웠을 것이며, 감정 전염은 선형 배열의 이웃들끼리만 가능함
④ (C) — (A) — (B)
⑤ (C) — (B) — (A)
(B)가 Marc의 연구 프로젝트를 처음으로 소개하는 내용을 제시하고 있으므로 (C) 뒤에 올 수 없음

| 문제 풀이 순서 | [정답률 34%]

1st 각 문단의 내용을 파악하고, 글의 논리적인 순서를 추론한다.

주어진 글: 뒷마당의 새를 관찰해보라. 새 한 마리가 놀라 날아오르면 다른 새들도 위협의 진위를 판단하기 위해 기다리지 않고 뒤따를 것이다. 그것들은 감정 전염에 감염되었다.

➡ 새 한 마리가 놀라 날아오르면 다른 새들도 위협의 진위를 떠나 뒤따르는 것을 감정 전염에 감염되었다고 설명하고 있다. **단서**

주어진 글 뒤: 새들의 감정 전염에 대한 구체적인 예시가 제시될 것이다. **발상**

(A) Marc는 줄을 선 새들이 자기 무리가 무엇을 하는지 모르기 때문에 더 두려운 것은 아닌지 궁금해했다. 감정 전염은 선형 배열에 있는 개개의 콩새류에 가장 가까운 곳에 있는 이웃을 제외하고는 불가능했을 것이다.

➡ **(A) 앞:** Marc는 일렬로 줄을 선 새들이 자기 무리가 무엇을 하는지 몰라서 더 두려운 것인지 궁금해 했다고 했으므로, 줄지어 있는 새들이 두려워했다는 사실이 앞에 제시되어야 (A)에서 그 이유에 대해 궁금해했다는 내용이 이어질 수 있다.
  ▶ 주어진 글이 (A) 앞에 올 수 없음

(A) 뒤: 감정 전염이 가장 가까운 곳에 있는 이웃을 제외하고는 불가능했을 것이라는 결론을 제시하고 있으므로 (A)가 글의 마지막에 올 확률이 큼
  ▶ (A)가 글의 마지막에 올 확률이 큼

(B) Marc가 자신의 학생 몇 명과 함께 진행한 서양 콩새류의 포식자 회피 관찰 패턴에 관한 장기 연구 프로젝트에서, 그들은 일렬로 먹이를 먹고 있는 새보다 원을 그리고 있는 새들이 관찰에 더 많은 조정력을 보인다는 사실을 발견했다.

➡ **(B) 앞:** Marc가 학생들과 서양 콩새류의 포식자 회피 관찰 패턴에 대해 연구했다고 했으므로, Marc의 연구를 예시로 드는 것에 대한 배경이나 단서가 제시되어야 할 것이다. ▶ 순서: 주어진 글 → (B)
(B) 뒤: 일렬로 먹이를 먹고 있는 새보다 원을 그리고 있는 새들이 관찰에 더 많은 조정력을 보이는 것에 대한 부연 설명이 이어질 것이다.

(C) 일렬로 늘어선 새들은, 가장 가까운 이웃만 볼 수 있었는데, 관찰할 때 조정력이 떨어졌을 뿐만 아니라 더 긴장한 상태였고 원을 그리고 있는 콩새들보다 몸과 머리 위치를 훨씬 더 많이 바꾸었는데, 원을 그린 상태에서는 각각의 콩새가 다른 모든 콩새를 볼 수 있었다.

➡ **(C) 앞:** 일렬로 서 있는 새들과 원을 그리고 있는 새들이 차이를 보인다는 내용이 제시되어야, 그 사실에 대해 부연 설명을 하고 있는 (C)가 이어질 수 있다.
  ▶ 순서: (B) → (C)
(C) 뒤: 일렬로 늘어선 새들과 원을 그리고 있는 새들의 차이에 대한 부연 설명이나 이에 대한 연구자의 결론 등이 이어지는 것이 자연스러울 것이다. 이 내용이 (A)에 있다. ▶ 순서: 주어진 글 → (B) → (C) → (A)

2nd 글이 한눈에 들어오도록 정리하여 정답을 확인한다.

주어진 글: 새 한 마리가 놀라 날아오르면 다른 새들도 위협의 진위를 떠나 뒤따르는 것은 감정 전염에 감염된 것이다.

➡ **(B):** Marc의 연구에서, 일렬로 먹이를 먹는 새보다 원을 그리고 있는 새들이 관찰에 더 많은 조정력을 보인다는 사실을 발견했다.

➡ **(C):** 일렬로 늘어선 새들은 가장 가까운 이웃만 볼 수 있었고 관찰 조정력이 떨어졌으며, 원을 그린 상태에서는 각각의 콩새가 다른 모든 콩새를 볼 수 있었다.

➡ **(A):** 줄을 선 새들이 자기 무리가 무엇을 하는지 모르기 때문에 더 두려웠을 것이며, 감정 전염은 선형 배열의 가장 가까운 곳에 있는 이웃을 제외하고는 불가능했을 것이다.

▶ 주어진 글 다음에 이어질 글의 순서는 (B) → (C) → (A)이므로 정답은 ③임

백승준 | 2025 수능 응시·광주 광주숭원고 졸

이 문제는 '순서 배열' 문제이고 3점짜리 문제지만 생각보다 쉽게 접근했어. 글의 제재가 호기심에 따른 관찰과 그에 따른 분석이었기에 순서가 명확할 것이라 생각했지. 주어진 글에서 특정 현상을 제시했으니 이에 관하여 연구를 제시한 (B)가 와야 한다고 생각했어. 다음으로 (A)와 (C)를 훑어보았는데, (A)에서 제시된 Marc의 궁금증은 (B)와 (C)에서 제시된 관찰에 대한 추가적인 궁금증이라 생각했고 또, (A)의 마지막 부분에서 곧바로 궁금증에 대한 가설을 제시했기에 (A)가 마지막 순서인 것을 알 수 있었지.

M 05 정답 ⑤ ＊새로운 정보가 추가될 때 기존 패턴을 조정하는 정도

단서 1 학습이 사실의 목록을 축적하는 문제라면 새로운 정보가 제공되더라도 아무런 차이가 없을 것임

If learning were simply a matter / of accumulating lists of

facts, / then it shouldn't make any difference /

학습이 단순히 문제라면 / 사실의 목록을 축적하는 / 아무런 차이가 없을 것이다 /

주격 관계대명사

if we are presented / with information that is just a little bit

beyond what we already know / or totally new information. //

우리가 제공받은 아니든 / 이미 알고 있는 것을 조금 넘어서는 정보를 / 또는 완전히 새로운 정보를 //

단서 2 그러나 완전히 새로운 것을 이해하려고 하면 이미 가진 패턴의 단위를 더 크게 조정해야 함

(A) If we are trying to understand something totally new,

however, / we need to make larger adjustments / to the units of

차이에 목적격 관계대명사 생략

the patterns we already have, /

그러나 완전히 새로운 것을 이해하려고 한다면 / 우리는 더 큰 조정을 해야 한다 / 이미 가지고 있는 패턴의 단위를 /

계속적 용법의 관계대명사
which requires changing / the strengths of large numbers of connections in our brain, / and this is a difficult, tiring process. //
이것은 변경을 필요로 한다 / 우리 뇌의 수많은 연결 강도를 / 이것은 어렵고 피곤한 과정이다 //

(B) The adjustments are clearly smallest / when the new information is only slightly new / — when it is compatible / with what we already know, / 단서3 약간만 새로운 정보가 추가될 때는 조정이 적음
조정은 분명히 가장 적다 / 새로운 정보가 약간만 새로운 것일 때 / 즉 그것이 양립할 때 / 우리가 이미 알고 있는 것과 /
접속사(그래서 ~하다)
so that the old patterns need / only a little bit of adjustment /
부사적 용법(목적)
to accommodate the new knowledge. //
그래서 기존 패턴이 필요로 한다 / 약간의 조정만을 / 새로운 지식을 수용하기 위해 //

(C) Each fact would simply be stored separately. //
각 사실은 단순히 개별적으로 저장될 것이다 // 단서4 주어진 글에 언급한 '사실'이 연결됨

According to connectionist theory, / however, / our knowledge is organized / into patterns of activity, /
연결주의 이론에 따르면 / 그러나 / 우리의 지식은 조직된다 / 활동 패턴으로 /
접속사(~할 때마다)
and each time we learn something new / we have to modify the old patterns / so as to keep the old material / while adding the new information. //
접속사 뒤에 주어와 be동사 생략
그리고 우리가 새로운 것을 배울 때마다 / 기존 패턴을 수정해야 한다 / 이전 자료를 유지하기 위해 / 새로운 정보를 추가하면서 //

- accumulate ⓥ 축적하다, 쌓다 • adjustment ⓝ 조정
- unit ⓝ 단위 • strength ⓝ 힘 • slightly ⓐⓓ 약간
- compatible ⓐ 양립될 수 있는 • accommodate ⓥ 수용하다
- store ⓥ 저장하다 • separately ⓐⓓ 개별적으로
- organize ⓥ 조직하다 • modify ⓥ 수정하다
- material ⓝ 자료, 재료

학습이 단순히 사실의 목록을 축적하는 문제라면, 우리가 이미 알고 있는 것을 조금 넘어서는 정보가 제공되거나 완전히 새로운 정보가 제공되더라도 아무런 차이가 없을 것이다. (C) 각 사실은 단순히 개별적으로 저장될 것이다. 그러나 연결주의 이론에 따르면, 우리의 지식은 활동 패턴으로 조직되며, 우리가 새로운 것을 배울 때마다 새로운 정보를 추가하면서 이전 자료를 유지하기 위해 기존 패턴을 수정해야 한다. (B) 새로운 정보가 약간만 새로운 것일 때, 즉 그것이 우리가 이미 알고 있는 것과 양립할 수 있어서, 새로운 지식을 수용하기 위해 기존 패턴을 약간만 조정하면 될 때 조정은 분명 가장 적다. (A) 그러나 완전히 새로운 것을 이해하려고 한다면, 우리는 이미 가지고 있는 패턴의 단위를 더 크게 조정해야 하는데, 이를 위해서는 우리 뇌의 수많은 연결 강도를 변경해야 하며, 이것은 어렵고 피곤한 과정이다.

주어진 글 다음에 이어질 글의 순서로 가장 적절한 것을 고르시오. [3점]

① (A) — (C) — (B) (A)는 글의 마무리에 해당하는 내용이므로 맨 마지막에 와야 함
② (B) — (A) — (C) ┐ 주어진 글에서 언급한 '사실'이 (C)의 첫 문장에서 연결됨
③ (B) — (C) — (A) ┐ 학습이 사실의 목록을 축적하는 문제라면 새로운 정보가 제공되더라도 아무런 차이가 없을 것임 - 연결주의 이론에
④ (C) — (A) — (B) ┤ 따르면 새로운 것을 배울 때마다 기존 패턴을 수정해야 함 -
⑤ (C) — (B) — (A) ┘ 약간만 새로운 것일 때는 기존 패턴을 약간만 조정하면 됨 - 완전히 새로운 것을 이해할 때는 더 큰 조정이 필요함
 (A)에서 그러나 완전히 새로운 것을 이해할 때 더 큰 조정이 필요하다고 했으므로 (A) 앞에는 약간만 새로운 것을 배우는 것에 대한 (B)가 와야 함

| 문제 풀이 순서 | [정답률 44%]

1st 각 문단의 내용을 파악하고, 글의 논리적인 순서를 추론한다.

주어진 글: 학습이 단순히 사실의 목록을 축적하는 문제라면, 우리가 이미 알고 있는 것을 조금 넘어서는 정보가 제공되거나 완전히 새로운 정보가 제공되더라도 아무런 차이가 없을 것이다.

→ 학습이 단순히 사실의 목록을 축적하는 문제라면 새로운 정보를 제공받더라도 아무런 차이가 없을 것이라고 설명하고 있다. (단서)

주어진 글 뒤: 아무런 차이가 없는 경우라면 각 사실이 단순히 저장될 것이라는 내용이 이어질 것이다. (발상)

(A) 그러나(however) 완전히 새로운 것을 이해하려고 한다면, 우리는 이미 가지고 있는 패턴의 단위를 더 크게 조정해야 하는데, 이를 위해서는 우리 뇌의 수많은 연결 강도를 변경해야 하며, 이것은 어렵고 피곤한 과정이다.

→ **(A) 앞:** '그러나(however)'가 쓰인 것으로 보아 완전히 새로운 것을 이해하려고 한다는 내용과 반대되는 내용이 제시되었을 것이다.
▶ 주어진 글이 (A) 앞에 올 수 없음
(A) 뒤: 뇌의 수많은 연결 강도를 변경해야 하는데 이것은 어려운 과정이라고 했으므로 이에 대한 부연 설명이 이어지거나 (A)가 글의 마지막일 확률이 높음

(B) 새로운 정보가 약간만 새로운 것일 때, 즉 그것이 우리가 이미 알고 있는 것과 양립할 수 있어서, 새로운 지식을 수용하기 위해 기존 패턴을 약간만 조정하면 될 때 조정은 분명 가장 적다.

→ **(B) 앞:** 새로운 정보에 대한 언급이 앞에 있어야 할 것이다.
(B) 뒤: 기존 패턴을 약간만 조정하면 된다는 말로 마무리되었으므로, 뒤에 이와 반대되는 내용이 이어질 것이다. ▶ 순서: (B) → (A)

(C) 각 사실(Each fact)은 단순히 개별적으로 저장될 것이다. 그러나 연결주의 이론에 따르면, 우리의 지식은 활동 패턴으로 조직되며, 우리가 새로운 것을 배울 때마다 새로운 정보를 추가하면서 이전 자료를 유지하기 위해 기존 패턴을 수정해야 한다.

→ **(C) 앞:** 각 사실이 단순히 개별적으로 저장될 것이라고 말하는 배경이 나와야 한다. 학습이 단순히 사실의 목록을 축적하는 문제라면 새로운 정보를 제공받더라도 아무런 차이가 없을 것이라고 이야기한 주어진 글이 앞에 나오는 것이 자연스럽다.
▶ 순서: 주어진 글 → (C)
(C) 뒤: 새로운 정보를 추가할 때 패턴을 수정하는 것에 대한 상세한 부연 설명이 이어져야 할 것이므로 (B)가 와야 한다.
▶ 순서: 주어진 글 → (C) → (B) → (A)

2nd 글이 한눈에 들어오도록 정리하여 정답을 확인한다.

주어진 글: 학습이 단순히 사실의 목록을 축적하는 문제라면 새로운 정보를 제공받더라도 아무런 차이가 없을 것이다.

→ **(C):** 각 사실은 개별적으로 저장될 것이지만, 새로운 정보가 추가될 때 기존 패턴을 수정해야 한다.

→ **(B):** 추가되는 새로운 정보가 약간만 새로운 것일 때는 기존 패턴을 약간만 조정한다.

→ **(A):** 그러나 완전히 새로운 것을 이해하려고 한다면 패턴의 단위를 더 크게 조정해야 하고 이것은 어려운 과정이다.
▶ 주어진 글 다음에 이어질 글의 순서는 (C) → (B) → (A)이므로 정답은 ⑤임

Ⓜ 06 정답 ③ *동물의 건강을 지키는 능력

The generally close connection / between health and what animals want / exists /
일반적으로 밀접한 관계가 / 건강과 동물이 원하는 것 사이에 / 존재한다 /
복수 주어
because wanting to obtain the right things / and wanting to avoid the wrong ones / are major ways / in which animals keep themselves healthy. // 단서1 동물은 올바른 것은 얻고 잘못된 것은 피하려고 함
복수 동사 / 전치사+관계대명사
왜냐하면 올바른 것을 얻고자 하는 것과 / 잘못된 것을 피하고자 하는 것은 / 주요한 방법이기 때문이다 / 동물이 자신의 건강을 유지하는 //

접속사(~할 수 있도록)
(A) They can take pre-emptive action / so that the worst never happens. // 단서2 (C)의 마지막에 언급한 '동물들(They)'이 최악의 상황을 피하려고
주격 관계대명사
그들은 선제 조치를 취할 수 있다 / 최악의 상황이 발생하지 않도록 //
They start to want / things that will be necessary / for their health and survival / not for now / but for some time in the future. //
그들은 원하기 시작한다 / 필요할 것들을 / 건강과 생존에 / 지금이 아니라 / 미래 언젠가의 //

(B) Animals have evolved / many different ways of maintaining
their health / and then regaining it again / once it has been
damaged, / **단서3** 동물들이 건강을 유지하고 건강이 손상되었을 때 되찾는 방법을 많이 개발함
동물은 발달시켜 왔다 / 건강을 유지하는 많은 다양한 방법을 / 그러고는 건강을 되찾는 /
건강이 손상되었을 때 //
such as an ability to heal wounds / when they are injured /
and an amazingly complex immune system / for warding off
infection. //
상처를 치유하는 능력과 같은 / 다쳤을 때 / 그리고 놀랍도록 복잡한 면역 체계와 같은 /
감염을 막기 위한 //
단서4 동물은 부상과 질병이 발생하기 전에 대처하는 능력도 뛰어남
(C) Animals are equally good, / however, / at dealing with
injury and disease / before they even happen. //
동물은 똑같이 뛰어나다 / 그러나 / 부상과 질병에 대처하는 능력도 / 발생하기 전에 //
They have evolved / a complex set of mechanisms / for
anticipating and avoiding danger altogether. //
동물은 발달시켜 왔다 / 복잡한 메커니즘을 / 위험을 예측하고 완전히 피하기 위한 //

- obtain ⓥ 얻다 · pre-emptive ⓐ 선제의
- evolve ⓥ 발달[진전]하다[시키다] · maintain ⓥ 유지하다
- survival ⓝ 생존 · regain ⓥ 되찾다 · damage ⓥ 손상을 주다
- heal ⓥ 치유하다 · wound ⓝ 상처 · complex ⓐ 복잡한
- immune system 면역 체계 · ward off 피하다, 물리치다
- infection ⓝ 감염 · anticipate ⓥ 예측하다

올바른 것을 얻고자 하는 것과 잘못된 것을 피하고자 하는 것은 동물이 자신의
건강을 유지하는 주요한 방법이기 때문에 건강과 동물이 원하는 것 사이에는
일반적으로 밀접한 관계가 존재한다. (B) 동물은 다쳤을 때 상처를 치유하는
능력과 감염을 막기 위한 놀랍도록 복잡한 면역 체계와 같은, 건강을 유지하고
그리고는 건강이 손상되었을 때 이를 되찾는 많은 다양한 방법을 발달시켜
왔다. (C) 그러나 동물은 부상과 질병이 발생하기 전에 대처하는 능력도 똑같이
뛰어나다. 동물은 위험을 예측하고 완전히 피하기 위한 복잡한 메커니즘을
발달시켜 왔다. (A) 그들은 최악의 상황이 발생하지 않도록 선제 조치를 취할
수 있다. 그들은 지금이 아니라 미래 언젠가의 건강과 생존에 필요할 것들을
원하기 시작한다.

주어진 글 다음에 이어질 글의 순서로 가장 적절한 것을 고르시오.

① (A) — (C) — (B) (A)는 동물의 선제 조치에 대한 이야기로 글의 마무리 내용임
② (B) — (A) — (C) (C)의 마지막에 언급한 동물들이 (A)에서 They로 이어짐
③ (B) — (C) — (A) 동물은 올바른 것은 얻고 잘못된 것은 피하려고 함 - 동물은 건강을
유지하고 건강이 손상되었을 때 되찾는 많은 방법을 발달시킴 -
부상과 질병이 발생하기 전 예측하는 능력도 뛰어남 - 선제 조치를
취해 미래의 건강에 필요할 것들을 원하기 시작함
④ (C) — (A) — (B) (C)는 '그러나' 동물이 부상과 질병 전에 예측하는 능력도 뛰어나다고
⑤ (C) — (B) — (A) 했으므로 (B) 뒤에 이어져야 함

| 문제 풀이 순서 | [정답률 62%]

1st 각 문단의 내용을 파악하고, 글의 논리적인 순서를 추론한다.

┌ **주어진 글:** 올바른 것을 얻고자 하는 것과 잘못된 것을 피하고자 하는 것은
│ 동물이 자신의 건강을 유지하는 주요한 방법이기 때문에 건강과 동물이
└ 원하는 것 사이에는 일반적으로 밀접한 관계가 존재한다.

➡ 동물은 건강을 위해 올바른 것은 얻고자 하고 잘못된 것은 피하고자 한다고
했다. **단서**
주어진 글 뒤: 건강을 위해 동물이 올바른 것은 얻고 잘못된 것은 피하고자 하는
구체적인 설명이 이어질 것이다. **발상**

┌ (A) **그들(They)**은 최악의 상황이 발생하지 않도록 선제 조치를 취할 수
│ 있다. 그들은 지금이 아니라 미래 언젠가의 건강과 생존에 필요할 것들을
└ 원하기 시작한다.

➡ **(A) 앞:** 선제 조치를 취한다는 것에 대한 배경 설명이나 관련된 내용이 언급되어야
한다.
▶ 주어진 글이 (A) 앞에 올 수 없음
(A) 뒤: 미래의 건강과 생존에 필요할 것들에 대해 부연 설명하거나 (A)가 글의
마지막일 확률이 높다.

┌ (B) 동물은 다쳤을 때 상처를 치유하는 능력과 감염을 막기 위한 놀랍도록
│ 복잡한 면역 체계와 같은, 건강을 유지하고 그러고는 건강이 손상되었을 때
└ 이를 되찾는 많은 다양한 방법을 발달시켜 왔다.

➡ **(B) 앞:** 동물이 건강을 위해 올바른 것(건강)은 얻고 잘못된 것(건강 손상)은
피하려고 한다는 내용이 나와야 한다.
▶ 순서: 주어진 글 → (B)
(B) 뒤: 건강이 손상되었을 때 되찾는 다양한 방법을 발달시켜 왔다고 이미
언급했으므로 화제가 전환될 가능성이 있다.
▶ (C)가 이어질 확률이 큼

┌ (C) [그러나(however)] 동물은 부상과 질병이 발생하기 전에 대처하는
│ 능력도 똑같이 뛰어나다. 동물은 위험을 예측하고 완전히 피하기 위한
└ 복잡한 메커니즘을 발달시켜 왔다.

➡ **(C) 앞:** '그러나'가 쓰였으므로 앞 내용과 역접 관계에 있어야 한다. 부상과 질병이
발생하기 '전에' 대처하는 능력도 뛰어나다고 했으므로 이와 상반되는 내용이
나와야 할 것이다.
▶ 순서: (B) → (C)
(C) 뒤: 위험을 예측하고 피하기 위한 메커니즘의 사례나 부연 설명이 이어져야
하므로 (A)가 이어질 것이다.
▶ 순서: 주어진 글 → (B) → (C) → (A)

2nd 글이 한눈에 들어오도록 정리하여 정답을 확인한다.

주어진 글: 건강과 동물이 원하는 것 사이에는 밀접한 관계가 존재한다.
➡ **(B):** 상처 치유 능력, 면역 체계 등 동물이 건강을 유지하고 되찾는 방법을 발달시켜
왔다.
➡ **(C):** 부상과 질병이 발생하기 전에 대처하는 능력도 똑같이 뛰어나다.
➡ **(A):** 동물이 미래의 건강과 생존에 대비해 선제 조치를 취할 수 있다.
▶ 주어진 글 다음에 이어질 글의 순서는 (B) → (C) → (A)이므로 정답은 ③임

M 07 정답 ③ ＊조직의 학습을 지원하는 인적 자원 관리

a number of+복수 명사 / 선행사
There are a number of human resource management practices
주격 관계대명사
/ that are necessary to support organizational learning. //
여러 가지 인적 자원 관리 관행이 있다 / 조직의 학습을 지원하는 데 필요한 //
단서1 조직 학습 지원에 필요한 여러 인적 관리 관행이 있음

단서2 '그들'은 (C)의 마지막에 언급한 human resource development professionals임
(A) Their role should be to assist, consult, and advise teams / on
how best to approach learning. //
그들의 역할은 팀을 지원하고, 상담하고, 조언하는 것이어야 한다 / 학습에 가장 잘 접근하는
방법에 대해 //
They must be able to develop / new mechanisms for cross-
training peers — team members — / and new systems for
전치사+동명사
capturing and sharing information. //
그들은 개발할 수 있어야 한다 / 동료, 즉 팀원을 두 가지 이상의 일이 가능하도록 훈련시키기
위한 새로운 기법과 / 정보를 수집하고 공유하기 위한 새로운 시스템을 //
To do this, / human resource development professionals / must
be able to think systematically / and understand how to promote
동사① 동사②
learning / within groups and across the organization. //
이를 이행하기 위해 / 인적 자원 개발 전문가는 / 체계적으로 사고하고 / 학습을 촉진하는
방법을 이해할 수 있어야 한다 / 집단 내 및 조직 전체에서 //
단서3 주어진 글에서 언급한 인적 관리에 대한 예시를 들어 여러 가지 인적 관리 관행들을 설명함
(B) For example, / performance evaluation and reward systems
주어
that reinforce long-term performance / and the development
주격 관계대명사
and sharing of new skills and knowledge / are particularly
동사(performance evaluation ~ and knowledge가 주어)
important. //
예컨대 / 장기적인 성과를 강화하는 업무 평가 및 보상 시스템 / 그리고 새로운 기술과 지식의
개발 및 공유가 / 특히 중요하다 //
In addition, / the human resource development function may
be dramatically changed / to keep the emphasis on continuous
learning. //
또한 / 인적 자원 개발 기능은 획기적으로 변경될 수도 있다 / 지속적인 학습에 계속 중점을
두도록 //

단세 4 (B)의 마지막에 언급한 학습과 관련해서 학습 조직에 대한 내용이 이어짐

(C) In a learning organization, / every employee must take the responsibility / for acquiring and transferring knowledge. //
학습 조직 내에서 / 모든 직원은 책임을 져야 한다 / 지식 습득과 전수에 대한 //

Formal training programs, / developed in advance and delivered according to a preset schedule, / are insufficient / to address shifting training needs / and encourage timely information sharing. //
형식적인 교육 프로그램은 / 사전에 개발되어 미리 정해진 일정에 따라 제공되는 / 충분하지 않다 / 변화하는 교육적 요구에 대응하고 / 시기적절한 정보 공유를 촉진하기에는 //

Rather, human resource development professionals / must become learning facilitators. //
오히려 인적 자원 개발 전문가가 / 학습의 촉진자가 되어야 한다 //

- human resource(s) management 인적 자원 관리((구성원의 잠재적 능력을 육성, 개발하여 조직의 전략적 목표를 달성하는 데 기여하는 활동))
- practice ⓝ 관행 · organizational learning 조직 학습(組織 學習)
- assist ⓥ 지원하다, 돕다 · mechanism ⓝ 기법
- cross-train ⓥ 두 가지 이상의 일이 가능하도록 훈련시키다 · peer ⓝ 동료
- systemically ⓐⓓ 조직적으로 · function ⓝ 기능
- dramatically ⓐⓓ 극적으로, 획기적으로 · emphasis ⓝ 중점, 강조
- transfer ⓥ 전수하다 · preset ⓐ 미리 조절한
- insufficient ⓐ 충분하지 않은 · address ⓥ 대응[대처]하다
- shifting ⓐ 변화하는 · timely ⓐ 시기적절한
- facilitator ⓝ 촉진자

조직의 학습을 지원하는 데 필요한 여러 가지 인적 자원 관리 관행이 있다. (B) 예컨대, 장기적인 성과를 강화하는 업무 평가 및 보상 시스템, 그리고 새로운 기술과 지식의 개발 및 공유가 특히 중요하다. 또한, 지속적인 학습에 계속 중점을 두도록 인적 자원 개발 기능을 획기적으로 변경할 수도 있다. (C) 학습 조직 내 모든 직원은 지식 습득과 전수에 대한 책임을 져야 한다. 사전에 개발되어 미리 정해진 일정에 따라 제공되는 형식적인 교육 프로그램은 변화하는 교육적 요구에 대응하고 시기적절한 정보 공유를 촉진하기에는 충분하지 않다. 오히려 인적 자원 개발 전문가가 학습의 촉진자가 되어야 한다. (A) 그들의 역할은 학습에 가장 잘 접근하는 방법에 대해 팀을 지원하고, 상담하고, 조언하는 것이어야 한다. 그들은 동료, 즉 팀원을 두 가지 이상의 일이 가능하도록 훈련시키기 위한 새로운 기법과 정보를 수집하고 공유하기 위한 새로운 시스템을 개발할 수 있어야 한다. 이를 이행하기 위해, 인적 자원 개발 전문가는 체계적으로 사고하고 집단 내 및 조직 전체에서 학습을 촉진하는 방법을 이해할 수 있어야 한다.

주어진 글 다음에 이어질 글의 순서로 가장 적절한 것을 고르시오. [3점]

① (A) — (C) — (B) (A)의 '그들'이 가리키는 것이 주어진 글에 없음
② (B) — (A) — (C) (C)의 human resource development professionals가 (A)의 '그들'이므로 (A)가 뒤에 와야 함
③ (B) — (C) — (A)
④ (C) — (A) — (B) (B)의 마지막에 언급한 학습과 관련해서 학습 조직에 대한 내용이 (C)에 이어지므로 맨 앞에 올 수 없음
⑤ (C) — (B) — (A)
ㄴ 조직(회사)의 학습 지원에 필요한 여러 인적 자원 관리 관행이 있음 - 여러 가지 조직 내에서의 제도와 시스템이 있음 - 형식적 프로그램보다는 인적 자원 개발 전문가가 학습 촉진자가 되어야 함 - 인적 자원 개발 전문가가 학습을 촉진하기 위해 해야 하는 역할과 자질을 설명함

| 문제 풀이 순서 | [정답률 23%]

1st 각 문단의 내용을 파악하고, 글의 논리적인 순서를 추론한다.

주어진 글: 조직의 학습을 지원하는 데 필요한 여러 인적 자원 관리 관행이 있다.

➡ **주어진 글 뒤:** 조직(회사)의 학습 지원에 필요한 인적 자원 관리 관행이 있다고 했으므로, 단서 조직(회사)의 학습 지원과 인적 자원 관리가 이 글의 주요 내용이 될 것이다. 발상

(A) 그들의(Their) 역할은 학습에 가장 잘 접근하는 방법에 대해 팀을 지원하고, 상담하고, 조언하는 것이어야 한다. 그들은(They) 동료, 즉 팀원을 두 가지 이상의 일이 가능하도록 훈련시키기 위한 새로운 기법과 정보를 수집하고 공유하기 위한 새로운 시스템을 개발할 수 있어야 한다. 이를 이행하기 위해, 인적 자원 개발 전문가는 체계적으로 사고하고 집단 내 및 조직 전체에서 학습을 촉진하는 방법을 이해할 수 있어야 한다.

➡ **(A) 앞:** '그들'이라고 지칭할 수 있는 대상이 제시되어야 한다.
  ▶ 주어진 글은 '그들이' 해야 하는 역할이 아니라 관행에 대해 설명하고 있으므로 (A) 앞에 올 수 없음
  (A) 뒤: 인적 자원 개발 전문가에게 필요한 자질을 이야기하고 있으므로 이와 관련된 내용이 이어지거나 글의 마무리일 수 있다.

○ **(B)** 예컨대(For example), 장기적인 성과를 강화하는 업무 평가 및 보상 시스템, 그리고 새로운 기술과 지식의 개발 및 공유가 특히 중요하다. 또한, 지속적인 학습에 계속 중점을 두도록 인적 자원 개발 기능을 획기적으로 변경할 수도 있다.

➡ **(B) 앞:** '예컨대(For example)'라고 했으므로 설명하고 있는 대상이나 개념이 앞에 제시되어야 한다. 따라서 조직(회사)의 학습 지원에 필요한 인적 자원 관리 관행이 있다고 언급한 주어진 글이 앞에 와야 한다.
  ▶ 순서: 주어진 글 → (B)
  (B) 뒤: 인적 자원 관리 관행에서 지속적 학습을 위한 인적 자원 개발 기능의 획기적 변경으로 초점이 바뀌었으므로, 이에 대한 설명이 나와야 한다.
  ▶ (A)에 이런 내용이 없으므로 (C)가 뒤에 올 확률이 큼

○ **(C)** 학습 조직 내 모든 직원은 지식 습득과 전수에 대한 책임을 져야 한다. 사전에 개발되어 미리 정해진 일정에 따라 제공되는 형식적인 교육 프로그램은 변화하는 교육적 요구에 대응하고 시기적절한 정보 공유를 촉진하기에는 충분하지 않다. 오히려 인적 자원 개발 전문가가 학습의 촉진자가 되어야 한다.

➡ **(C) 앞:** 조직 내 학습에 대한 내용이 앞에 나와야 하는데, 이 내용이 (B)에 있었으므로 (B)가 앞에 와야 한다.
  ▶ 순서: (B) → (C)
  (C) 뒤: 구체적으로 인적 자원 개발 전문가가 어떻게 학습의 촉진자가 되어야 하는지 설명해야 한다. (A)에서 언급한 '그들'이 바로 이 '인적 자원 개발 전문가들(human resource development professionals)'이다.
  ▶ 순서: 주어진 글 → (B) → (C) → (A)

2nd 글이 한눈에 들어오도록 정리하여 정답을 확인한다.

주어진 글: 조직(회사)의 학습 지원에 필요한 여러 인적 자원 관리 관행이 있다.

➡ **(B):** 예를 들어 여러 가지 조직 내에서의 제도와 시스템이 있다. 또한 인적 자원 개발 기능을 획기적으로 변경할 수도 있다.

➡ **(C):** 모든 직원은 학습에 대한 책임이 있음을 강조하며, 기존의 정해진 프로그램은 충분하지 않다. 형식적 프로그램보다는 인적 자원 개발 전문가가 학습 촉진자가 되어야 한다.

➡ **(A):** 인적 자원 개발 전문가가 학습을 촉진하기 위해 해야 하는 역할과 자질을 설명하고 있다.

▶ 주어진 글 다음에 이어질 글의 순서는 (B) → (C) → (A)이므로 정답은 ③임

Ⓜ 08 정답 ② ＊다시 계발할 수 있는, 행동으로부터 감정을 추론할 수 있는 능력

단세 1 말하는 것을 배우기 전에 어떻게 사람들의 행동으로부터 감정들을 추론하는지를 흡수함
From infancy, / even before we learn to speak, / we absorb / how to infer people's emotions from their behaviors. //
유아기부터 / 심지어 우리가 말하는 것을 배우기 전에 / 우리는 흡수한다 / 어떻게 사람들의 감정들을 그들의 행동으로부터 추론하는지를 //

(A) Some people, however, have a talent for detecting emotions, / even when they're unspoken. //
하지만, 어떤 사람들은 감정들을 감지하는 재능을 가지고 있다 / 심지어 그것들이 입 밖에 내어지지 않을 때도 // 단세 2 (B)의 내용과는 다르게 어떤 사람들은 입 밖에 내어지지 않을 때도 감정을 감지하는 재능을 갖고 있다는 내용

We all know people like this: / Friends who seem to intuit when we're feeling down, / even if we haven't said anything; /
우리 모두는 이와 같은 사람들을 안다 / 우리가 마음이 울적한 때를 직관으로 아는 것처럼 보이는 친구들 / 우리가 어떤 것도 말하지 않았더라도 /

managers who sense when a kind word is needed / to help us get over the hump at work. //
우리가 직장에서 친절한 말이 필요한 때를 감지하는 매니저들 / 고비를 넘기는 것을 돕기 위해 //

단서 3 나이가 들면서 '이 능력'(행동으로부터 감정을 추론하는 능력)이 쇠퇴할 수 있음

(B) As we grow older, however, / this capacity can atrophy. //
하지만, 우리가 나이가 들면서 / 이 능력은 쇠퇴할 수 있다 //

We start to pay increasing attention / to what people say rather than what they do, / to the point where we can fail to notice nonlinguistic clues. //
우리는 점점 더 느는 주의를 기울이기 시작하여 / 사람들이 무엇을 하는지보다 무엇을 말하는지에 / 비언어적인 단서들을 알아차리지 못하는 정도에 이른다 //

Spoken language is so information rich / that it lulls us into
└─ so ~ that...: 너무 ~해서 …하다 ─┘
ignoring hints / that someone might be, say, upset / and instead
   동격의 that   예를 들어
focus on their words / when they say, It's nothing. I feel fine. //
구어는 정보가 매우 풍부해서 / 힌트들을 우리가 무시하게 하고 / 그것은 누군가가, 예를 들어, 화가 났을 수 있다는 / 그들의 말에 대신 집중한다 / 그들이 '아무것도 아니야. 나는 괜찮아.' 라고 말할 때 //

단서 4 '이러한 사람들'(행동으로부터 감정을 추론하는 사람들)을 대단히 관찰력이 있거나 세심하다고 추측하는 것은 당연함

(C) It's natural / to assume these people are unusually observant,
    가주어   진주어
or uncommonly sensitive. //
당연하다 / 이러한 사람들이 대단히 관찰력이 있거나, 굉장히 세심하다고 추측하는 것은 //

Sometimes they are. // 때때로 그들은 그러하다 //

But years of research indicates / this is a skill anyone can develop. //
하지만 수년간의 연구는 보여 준다 / 이것이 누구나 계발할 수 있는 기술이라는 것을 //

We can learn to identify the nonverbal clues / that indicate
                                    주격 관계대명사
someone's true emotions / and use these hints to understand what they are feeling. //
우리는 비언어적 단서들을 알아보는 것을 배울 수 있고 / 누군가의 진짜 감정들을 보여 주는 / 이 힌트들을 사용하여 그들이 무엇을 느끼고 있는지 이해할 수 있다 //

- infancy ⓝ 유아기   - absorb ⓥ 흡수하다   - infer ⓥ 추론하다
- detect ⓥ 감지하다   - capacity ⓝ 능력   - ignore ⓥ 무시하다
- observant ⓐ 관찰력 있는   - sensitive ⓐ 예민한, 세심한
- identify ⓥ 알아보다   - nonverbal ⓐ 비언어적인

유아기부터, 심지어 우리가 말하는 것을 배우기 전에, 우리는 어떻게 사람들의 감정들을 그들의 행동으로부터 추론하는지를 흡수한다. (B) 하지만, 우리가 나이가 들면서 이 능력은 쇠퇴할 수 있다. 우리는 사람들이 무엇을 하는지보다 무엇을 말하는지에 점점 더 느는 주의를 기울이기 시작하여, 비언어적인 단서들을 알아차리지 못하는 정도에 이른다. 구어는 정보가 매우 풍부해서 그것은 누군가가, 예를 들어, 화가 났을 수 있다는 힌트들을 우리가 무시하게 하고 그들이 '아무것도 아니야. 나는 괜찮아.'라고 말할 때 그들의 말에 대신 집중한다. (A) 하지만, 어떤 사람들은 심지어 그것들이 입 밖에 내어지지 않을 때도 감정들을 감지하는 재능을 가지고 있다. 우리 모두는 이와 같은 사람들(우리가 어떤 것도 말하지 않았더라도 우리가 마음이 울적한 때를 직관으로 아는 것처럼 보이는 친구들, 우리가 직장에서 고비를 넘기는 것을 돕기 위해 친절한 말이 필요한 때를 감지하는 매니저들)을 안다. (C) 이러한 사람들이 대단히 관찰력이 있거나, 굉장히 세심하다고 추측하는 것은 당연하다. 때때로 그들은 그러하다. 하지만 수년간의 연구는 이것이 누구나 계발할 수 있는 기술이라는 것을 보여 준다. 우리는 누군가의 진짜 감정들을 보여 주는 비언어적 단서들을 알아보는 것을 배울 수 있고 이 힌트들을 사용하여 그들이 무엇을 느끼고 있는지 이해할 수 있다.

주어진 글 다음에 이어질 글의 순서로 가장 적절한 것을 고르시오.

① (A) — (C) — (B) ──(A)에서 말하는, 입 밖에 내어지지 않을 때도 감정을 감지하는 재능을 갖고 있는 사람들이 있다는 내용의 반대가 주어진 글에 나오지 않음
② (B) — (A) — (C)
③ (B) — (C) — (A) ──(B)의 내용과 다르게 감정을 감지하는 재능을 갖고 있는 사람들의 내용이 (A)에 이어짐
④ (C) — (A) — (B)
⑤ (C) — (B) — (A) ──(C)에서 언급된 '이런 사람들'에 대한 내용이 주어진 글에 없음

유아기때부터 사람들의 행동에서 감정을 추론할 수 있는 능력이 있음 - 나이 들면서 이 능력은 쇠퇴할 수 있으며, 언어적 단서에만 의존하게 됨 - 어떤 사람들은 말을 하지 않아도 감정을 알아채는 능력이 있음 - 이런 사람들이 유독 세심하고 관찰력 있는 것일 수도 있지만, 이는 누구나 계발할 수 있는 기술임

| 문제 풀이 순서 | [정답률 53%]

1st 주어진 글을 통해 글의 핵심 소재를 파악하고 전개 방향을 예측한다.

주어진 글: 유아기부터, 심지어 우리가 말하는 것을 배우기 전에, 우리는 어떻게 사람들의 감정들을 그들의 행동으로부터 추론하는지를 흡수한다. **단서**

➡ 유아기 때 우리는 사람의 행동으로부터 감정을 추론하는 방법을 흡수한다고 했다. 따라서 사람의 감정을 행동으로부터 추론하는 방법/능력에 대한 추가 설명이 나올 것이다. **발상**

2nd 각 문단의 내용을 파악하고, 글의 논리적인 순서를 추론한다.

(A) 하지만(however), 어떤 사람들은 심지어 그것들이 입 밖에 내어지지 않을 때도 감정들을 감지하는 재능을 가지고 있다. 우리 모두는 이와 같은 사람들(우리가 어떤 것도 말하지 않았더라도 우리가 마음이 울적한 때를 직관으로 아는 것처럼 보이는 친구들, 우리가 직장에서 고비를 넘기는 것을 돕기 위해 친절한 말이 필요한 때를 감지하는 매니저들)을 안다.

➡ **(A) 앞:** '하지만(however)'이 왔기 때문에 앞에서는 이런 재능을 일반적으로는 갖고 있지 않다는 내용이 올 것이다.
▶ 주어진 글이 (A) 앞에 올 수 없음
(A) 뒤: 말을 하지 않아도 감정을 알아채는 사람들에 대한 추가 설명이 나올 것이다.

(B) 하지만(however), 우리가 나이가 들면서 이 능력(this capacity)은 쇠퇴할 수 있다. 우리는 사람들이 무엇을 하는지보다 무엇을 말하는지에 점점 더 느는 주의를 기울이기 시작하여, 비언어적인 단서들을 알아차리지 못하는 정도에 이른다. 구어는 정보가 매우 풍부해서 그것은 누군가가, 예를 들어, 화가 났을 수 있다는 힌트들을 우리가 무시하게 하고 그들이 '아무것도 아니야. 나는 괜찮아.'라고 말할 때 그들의 말에 대신 집중한다.

➡ **(B) 앞:** '이 능력(this capacity)'을 가리키는 내용이 있어야 한다. '이 능력'은 주어진 문장에서 설명한, 사람의 행동으로부터 감정을 추론하는 능력으로, 어렸을 때는 갖고 있는 능력이다.
▶ 순서: 주어진 문장 → (B)
(B) 뒤: 이 능력을 다시 갖출 수 있는 방법이나, 이 능력을 갖춘 사람들에 대한 내용이 나올 것이다. (A)에서 이와 반대되는 내용이 however로 이어지며, 입 밖에 내지 않아도 감정들을 감지하는 재능을 가진 사람들에 대한 내용이 나온다.
▶ 순서: (B) → (A)

(C) 이러한 사람들(these people)이 대단히 관찰력이 있거나, 굉장히 세심하다고 추측하는 것은 당연하다. 때때로 그들은 그러하다. 하지만 수년간의 연구는 이것이 누구나 계발할 수 있는 기술이라는 것을 보여 준다. 우리는 누군가의 진짜 감정들을 보여 주는 비언어적 단서들을 알아보는 것을 배울 수 있고 이 힌트들을 사용하여 그들이 무엇을 느끼고 있는지 이해할 수 있다.

➡ **(C) 앞:** '이러한 사람들(these people)'에 대한 내용이 나와야 하며, 이는 (A)에서 말로 하지 않아도 감정을 알아채는 사람들을 뜻한다.
▶ 순서: (A) → (C)
(C) 뒤: 어떤 방식으로 이러한 기술을 기를 수 있는지에 대한 내용이 나오거나 글이 마무리될 것이다.
▶ 순서: 주어진 글 → (B) → (A) → (C)

3rd 글이 한눈에 들어오도록 정리하여 정답을 확인한다.

주어진 글: 유아기때부터 사람들의 행동에서 감정을 추론할 수 있는 능력이 있다.
➡ **(B):** 하지만 나이 들면서 이 능력은 쇠퇴할 수 있으며, 감정을 파악하는 데 언어적 단서에만 의존하게 된다.
➡ **(A):** 하지만 어떤 사람들은 여전히 말을 하지 않아도 감정을 알아채는 능력이 있다.
➡ **(C):** 이런 사람들이 유독 세심하고 관찰력 있는 것일 수도 있지만, 이는 누구나 계발할 수 있는 기술이다.
▶ 주어진 글 다음에 이어질 글의 순서는 (B) → (A) → (C)이므로 정답은 ②임

사역동사+목적어+목적격 보어(동사원형) 접속사
Some epistemic feelings let us know / that we know. //
어떤 인식론적 느낌들은 우리에게 알게 한다 / 우리가 안다는 것을 //

These include / the feeling of knowing, the feeling of certainty,
and the feeling of correctness. //
이것들은 포함한다 / 안다는 느낌, 확신의 느낌, 그리고 정확함의 느낌을 //
단서 1 안다는 느낌, 확신의 느낌, 그리고 정확함의 느낌을 포함하는 인식론적 느낌은 우리가 안다는
사실을 알게 함

선행사를 포함하는 관계대명사
(A) Other epistemic feelings alert our attention / to what we do
not yet know. // **단서 2** 다른 인식론적 느낌은 우리가 아직 알지 못하는 것을 알게 해 줌
다른 인식론적 느낌들은 우리의 주의를 환기시킨다 / 우리가 아직 알지 못하는 것에 //

Curiosity, awe, and wonder / fall into this category. //
호기심, 경외감, 그리고 놀라움이 / 이 범주에 속한다 //

As with the feelings of knowing, / we can ask whether feelings
of not-yet-knowing are necessarily right. //
안다는 느낌들에서 그렇듯이 / 우리는 아직 알지 못한다는 느낌들이 반드시 맞는지 물을 수
있다 //
동사를 강조하는 do동사
It does seem that if you wonder at something, / there is
주격 관계대명사
something that prompted you to wonder. //
여러분이 무언가를 궁금해한다면 정말로 있는 것처럼 보인다 / 여러분을 궁금해하게 한
무언가가 // **단서 3** 이 느낌((A)의 마지막에 말한 내용)은 현재 지식 체계가 궁금해하는 것을
해결하는 데 충분하지 않다는 것을 알려줌
(B) This feeling alerts you to the fact / that your current body of
동격의 that
knowledge / — the schemas, heuristics, and other information
앞에 관계대명사 생략된 관계절
you use / — did not prepare you for the thing you wonder at. //
이 느낌은 여러분에게 사실에 주의를 환기시킨다 / 여러분의 현재 지식 체계, 즉 스키마,
휴리스틱, 그리고 여러분이 사용하는 다른 정보가 / 여러분이 궁금해하는 것에 대해 여러분을
준비시키지 않았다는 //

As such, wonder is a useful emotion, / because it points to gaps
in what you thought you knew. // 이처럼
이처럼 놀라움은 유용한 감정인데 / 그것은 여러분이 알고 있었다 생각했던 것에 빈 곳을
가리키기 때문이다 // **단서 4** 주어진 글에 대한 예시임
(C) For example, you feel sure / that "1666" is the answer to the
목적어절을 이끄는 접속사
question, / "When did the Great Fire of London occur?" //
예를 들어, 여러분은 확신한다 / 질문에 '1666년'이 답이라고 / "런던 대화재는 언제
발생했습니까?"라는 //
동명사
Feeling that you know, even that you are sure, / is not unfailing. //
여러분이 안다고, 심지어 확신한다고, 느끼는 것이 / 언제나 변함없는 것은 아니다 //

We can be mistaken in those feelings. //
우리는 그런 느낌들에서 잘못 알고 있을 수 있다 //

- include ⓥ 포함하다 • correctness ⓝ 정확함
- alert ⓥ 주의를 환기시키다 • awe ⓝ 경외감
- wonder ⓝ 놀라움 • prompt ⓥ 유도하다, 촉발하다
- point to 가리키다

어떤 인식론적 느낌들은 우리에게 우리가 안다는 것을 알게 한다. 이것들은
안다는 느낌, 확신의 느낌, 그리고 정확함의 느낌을 포함한다. (C) 예를
들어, 여러분은 "런던 대화재는 언제 발생했습니까?"라는 질문에 '1666년'이
답이라고 확신한다. 여러분이 안다고, 심지어 확신한다고, 느끼는 것이 언제나
변함없는 것은 아니다. 우리는 그런 느낌들에서 잘못 알고 있을 수 있다.
(A) 다른 인식론적 느낌들은 우리가 아직 알지 못하는 것에 우리의 주의를
환기시킨다. 호기심, 경외감, 그리고 놀라움이 이 범주에 속한다. 안다는
느낌들에서 그렇듯이 우리는 아직 알지 못한다는 느낌들이 반드시 맞는지
물을 수 있다. 여러분이 무언가를 궁금해한다면 여러분을 궁금해하게 한
무언가가 정말로 있는 것처럼 보인다. (B) 이 느낌은 여러분에게 여러분의
현재 지식 체계, 즉 스키마, 휴리스틱, 그리고 여러분이 사용하는 다른 정보가
여러분이 궁금해하는 것에 대해 여러분을 준비시키지 않았다는 사실에 주의를
환기시킨다. 이처럼 놀라움은 유용한 감정인데 그것은 여러분이 알고 있었다
생각했던 것에 빈 곳을 가리키기 때문이다.

주어진 글 다음에 이어질 글의 순서로 가장 적절한 것을 고르시오. [3점]

① (A) — (C) — (B)   (A)에서 말하는 다른 인식론적 느낌들은 (C)의 마지막에 이어지는 내용
② (B) — (A) — (C)   (B)의 '이 느낌'으로 가리키는 것이 주어진 글에 언급되지 않음
③ (B) — (C) — (A)   안다는 느낌, 확신의 느낌과 확신의 느낌에 대한 예시는 인식론적
                  느낌임 - 안다는 느낌과 확신의 느낌에 대한 예시를 소개하고, 이런
                  느낌이 항상 옳은 것은 아님 - 다른 인식론적 느낌들은 우리가 아직
④ (C) — (A) — (B)   알지 못하는 것에 우리의 주의를 환기시킴 - 호기심은 궁금해하는
⑤ (C) — (B) — (A)   것에 대한 답을 찾기에 현재 지식 체계가 부족하다는 점을 알려줌
                  (B)의 '이 느낌'은 (A)의 마지막에 말한 느낌을 가리킴

| 문제 풀이 순서 | [정답률 54%]

1st 각 문단의 내용을 파악하고, 글의 논리적인 순서를 추론한다.

주어진 글: 어떤 인식론적 느낌들은 우리에게 우리가 안다는 것을 알게
한다. 이것들은 안다는 느낌, 확신의 느낌, 그리고 정확함의 느낌을
포함한다.

➡ 안다는 느낌, 확신의 느낌, 그리고 정확함의 느낌은 우리가 안다는 사실을 알게
해주는 인식론적 느낌이다. **단서**
주어진 글 뒤: 이런 느낌에 대한 예시나 추가 설명이 이어질 것이다. **발상**

(A) 다른 인식론적 느낌들(Other epistemic feelings)은 우리가 아직
알지 못하는 것에 우리의 주의를 환기시킨다. 호기심, 경외감, 그리고
놀라움이 이 범주에 속한다. 안다는 느낌들에서 그렇듯이 우리는 아직
알지 못한다는 느낌들이 반드시 맞는지 물을 수 있다. 여러분이 무언가를
궁금해한다면 여러분을 궁금해하게 한 무언가가 정말로 있는 것처럼
보인다.

➡ **(A) 앞:** '다른' 인식론적 느낌이라 했으므로, 앞에 어떠한 인식론적 느낌에 대한
언급이 있어야 하고, '안다는 느낌들에서 그렇듯이' 이런 느낌이 반드시 맞는지
의문을 던질수 있다고 했으므로, (A) 앞에는 이런 내용도 나와야 한다.
▶ 주어진 글이 (A) 앞에 올 수 없음
(A) 뒤: 호기심, 경외감, 그리고 놀라움과 관련된 예시나 추가 설명이 이어질
것이다.

(B) 이 느낌(This feeling)은 여러분에게 여러분의 현재 지식 체계,
즉 스키마, 휴리스틱, 그리고 여러분이 사용하는 다른 정보가 여러분이
궁금해하는 것에 대해 여러분을 준비시키지 않았다는 사실에 주의를
환기시킨다. 이처럼 놀라움은 유용한 감정인데 그것은 여러분이 알고
있었다 생각했던 것에 빈 곳을 가리키기 때문이다.

➡ **(B) 앞:** '이 느낌(This feeling)'에 대한 내용이 앞에서 언급되어야 하고, 뒤
문장에서 '이 느낌'이 놀라움이라는 것을 알려줬으므로 놀라움이 등장하는 (A)가
(B) 앞에 와야 한다. ▶ 순서: (A) → (B)
(B) 뒤: 놀라움 말고 다른 느낌에 대한 설명이 이어지거나, 인식론적 느낌을 모두
설명했기에 글이 마무리될 수도 있다. ▶ (B)가 마지막에 올 확률이 큼

(C) 예를 들어(For example), 여러분은 "런던 대화재는 언제
발생했습니까?"라는 질문에 '1666년'이 답이라고 확신한다. 여러분이
안다고, 심지어 확신한다고, 느끼는 것이 언제나 변함없는 것은 아니다.
우리는 그런 느낌들에서 잘못 알고 있을 수 있다.

➡ **(C) 앞:** 안다는 느낌, 확신의 느낌에 대한 예시이다. 이런 느낌은 주어진 글에
언급되었으므로 주어진 글이 (C)의 앞에 올 것이다. ▶ 순서: 주어진 글 → (C)
(C) 뒤: 이런 느낌이 틀린 이유나 구체적 설명이 오거나, 다른 인식론적 느낌이
소개될 수도 있다. ▶ 순서: 주어진 글 → (C) → (A) → (B)

2nd 글이 한눈에 들어오도록 정리하여 정답을 확인한다.

주어진 글: 안다는 느낌, 확신의 느낌, 그리고 정확함의 느낌은 우리가 안다는 사실을
알게 해주는 인식론적 느낌이다.

➡ **(C):** 안다는 느낌과 확신의 느낌의 예시를 소개하며, 이런 느낌이 항상 옳은 것은
아니다.

➡ **(A):** 호기심, 경외감, 그리고 놀라움은 다른 인식론적 느낌인데, 이는 우리가 아직
알지 못하는 것에 우리의 주의를 환기시킨다. 이런 느낌은 항상 옳은지 의문을 품을
수 있다.

➡ **(B):** 호기심은 궁금해하는 것에 대한 답을 찾기에 현재 지식 체계가 부족하다는
점을 알려주고, 이는 우리가 안다고 생각했던 것에서 빈 곳을 알려주는 유용한
것이다.

▶ 주어진 글 다음에 이어질 글의 순서는 (C) → (A) → (B)이므로 정답은 ④임

단서 1 테크노크라시는 기술적 의사결정에 두 가지 방법 중 하나로 영향을 미침
Technocracy can be thought / to influence technological decision-making / in one of two ways. //
테크노크라시는 생각될 수 있다 / 기술적 의사결정에 영향을 미치는 것으로 / 두 가지 방법 중 하나로 //

(A) This is because policy-makers work within the constraints / set by the experts / and *choose from the options* / *those experts provide.* //
과거분사(the constraints 수식)
단서 2 정책 결정자들은 전문가들이 설정된 제약 내에서 결정을 내림
(정치가와 전문가가 구분됨)
이것은 정책 결정자들은 제약 내에서 일하고 / 전문가들에 의해 설정된 / 선택지들 중에서 고르기 때문이다 / 그러한 전문가들이 제공하는 //

The technocratic element is clear: / experts set the agenda / and political judgements are parasitic on the judgements of experts. //
테크노크라시적 요소는 명확하다 / 전문가들은 의제를 설정하고 / 정치적 판단은 전문가들의 판단에 기생한다 //

(B) An idealized science and technology replaces politics / and technical experts become the decision-makers, / planning and organizing societies / according to whatever scientific principles the evidence supports. //
병렬 구조
단서 3 주어진 글에서 말한 테크노크라시와 관련된 내용
이상화된 과학과 기술은 정치를 대체하고 / 기술 전문가들이 의사결정자가 되어 / 사회를 계획하고 조직한다 / 증거가 뒷받침하는 과학적 원칙이면 무엇이든지 그에 따라 //

This form of technocracy is rarely found in practice. //
이러한 형태의 테크노크라시는 실제로는 거의 발견되지 않는다 //

(C) In contrast, / a more moderate form / in which experts advise and politicians decide / is found in many democratic societies. //
전치사+관계대명사(= 관계부사 where)
이와 대조적으로 / 더 온건한 형태는 / 전문가들이 조언하고 정치가들이 결정하는 / 많은 민주주의 사회에서 발견된다 //
단서 4 테크노라시가 기술적 의사 결정에 영향을 미치는 다른 방식을 소개함: 의사결정자가 정치인임

Also called the 'decisionist model', / this form of technocracy institutionalizes a division of labour / based on the distinction between facts and values / and allows specialist experts to wield significant power. //
병렬 구조
5형식 동사+목적어+목적격 보어(to부정사)
'결정론자 모델'이라고도 불리는 / 이러한 형태의 테크노크라시는 노동 분업을 제도화하고 / 사실과 가치 사이에서의 구별에 기초한 / 특정 분야의 전문가들이 상당한 권력을 휘두를 수 있도록 한다 //

- constraint ⓝ 제약　　• element ⓝ 요소
- idealized ⓐ 이상화된　　• organize ⓥ 조직하다
- democratic ⓐ 민주적인　　• institutionalize ⓥ 제도화하다
- labour ⓝ 노동　　• wield ⓥ 행사하다, 휘두르다
- significant ⓐ 중요한

테크노크라시는 두 가지 방법 중 하나로 기술적 의사결정에 영향을 미치는 것으로 생각될 수 있다. (B) 이상화된 과학과 기술은 정치를 대체하고 기술 전문가들이 의사결정자가 되어, 증거가 뒷받침하는 과학적 원칙이면 무엇이든지 그에 따라 사회를 계획하고 조직한다. 이러한 형태의 테크노크라시는 실제로는 거의 발견되지 않는다. (C) 이와 대조적으로, 전문가들이 조언하고 정치가들이 결정하는 더 온건한 형태는 많은 민주주의 사회에서 발견된다. '결정론자 모델'이라고도 불리는 이러한 형태의 테크노크라시는 사실과 가치 사이에서의 구별에 기초한 노동 분업을 제도화하고 특정 분야의 전문가들이 상당한 권력을 휘두를 수 있도록 한다. (A) 이것은 정책 결정자들은 전문가들에 의해 설정된 제약 내에서 일하고 그러한 전문가들이 제공하는 선택지들 중에서 고르기 때문이다. 테크노크라시적 요소는 명확하다: 전문가들은 의제를 설정하고 정치적 판단은 전문가들의 판단에 기생한다.

주어진 글 다음에 이어질 글의 순서로 가장 적절한 것을 고르시오. [3점]

① (A) — (C) — (B)　(A)에서는 정책 결정자가 전문가들이 설정한 제약 내에서 일해야 한다는 이유가 나오기 때문에 주어진 글 다음에 올 수 없음
② (B) — (A) — (C)　(C)에서 소개되는 테크노크라시 형태가 전문가와 정책 결정자의 역할이 나눠져 있다는 내용이 있기에 (A)보다 먼저 나와야 함
③ (B) — (C) — (A)
④ (C) — (A) — (B)　(C)는 '이와 대조적으로'로 시작하고 있으므로 대조적으로 여길만한
⑤ (C) — (B) — (A)　내용이 없는 주어진 글 다음에 오지 못함

테크노크라시의 두가지 형태가 있음 - 전문가가 정책 결정까지 하는 형태는 잘 사용되지 않음 - 전문가와 정치가가 나눠진 온건한 형태는 많이 발견됨 - 정치가는 전문가가 제공한 선택지들 중에서 고르기 때문임

| 문제 풀이 순서 | [정답률 45%]

1st 각 문단의 내용을 파악하고, 글의 논리적인 순서를 추론한다.

주어진 글: 테크노크라시는 두 가지 방법 중 하나로 기술적 의사결정에 영향을 미치는 것으로 생각될 수 있다.

➡ 테크노크라시는 기술적 의사결정에 두 가지 방법 중 하나로 영향을 미친다. **단서**
주어진 글 뒤: 테크노크라시가 기술적 의사결정에 영향을 미치는 첫 번째 방법을 소개할 것이다. **발상**

(A) 이것(This)은 정책 결정자들은 전문가들에 의해 설정된 제약 내에서 일하고 그러한 전문가들이 제공하는 선택지들 중에서 고르기 때문이다. 테크노크라시적 요소는 명확하다: 전문가들은 의제를 설정하고 정치적 판단은 전문가들의 판단에 기생한다.

➡ **(A) 앞:** '이것(This)'이 가리키는 것이 앞에 나와야 하고, 전문가가 설정한 의제와 제약 내에서 정책 결정자가 결정을 내리기 때문이라고 하고 있으므로, 이와 관련된 방법이 이전에 소개되었을 것이다.
▶ 주어진 글이 (A) 앞에 올 수 없음
(A) 뒤: 글의 맥락상 이유에 대한 것이므로 마무리 내용일 가능성이 크다.

(B) 이상화된 과학과 기술은 정치를 대체하고 기술 전문가들이 의사결정자가 되어, 증거가 뒷받침하는 과학적 원칙이면 무엇이든지 그에 따라 사회를 계획하고 조직한다. 이러한 형태의 테크노크라시는 실제로는 거의 발견되지 않는다.

➡ **(B) 앞:** 주어진 글처럼 기술적 의사결정에 영향을 미친다는 포괄적인 내용이 와야 할 것이다.
▶ 순서: 주어진 글 → (B)
(B) 뒤: 실제로 많이 발견되는 테크노크라시의 두 번째 형태를 소개할 것이다.
▶ (B)가 (A) 앞에 올 수 없음

(C) 이와 대조적으로(In contrast), 전문가들이 조언하고 정치가들이 결정하는 더 온건한 형태는 많은 민주주의 사회에서 발견된다. '결정론자 모델'이라고도 불리는 이러한 형태의 테크노크라시는 사실과 가치 사이에서의 구별에 기초한 노동 분업을 제도화하고 특정 분야의 전문가들이 상당한 권력을 휘두를 수 있도록 한다.

➡ **(C) 앞:** '이와 대조적으로(In contrast)'라고 했으므로 테크노크라시의 다른 형태가 앞에서 소개되었을 것이다. 이 내용이 (B)에 나왔다.
▶ 순서: (B) → (C)
(C) 뒤: 전문가들이 권력을 휘두를 수 있는 이유에 대해 나올 것이다.
▶ 순서: 주어진 글 → (B) → (C) → (A)

2nd 글이 한눈에 들어오도록 정리하여 정답을 확인한다.

주어진 글: 테크노크라시는 두가지 형태 중 하나로 기술적 의사결정에 영향을 미친다.
➡ **(B):** 기술이 정치를 대신하고 전문가들이 의사결정자가 되는 테크노크라시의 형태는 실제로 거의 발견되지 않는다.
➡ **(C):** 사회에서 더 많이 발견되는 온건한 형태의 테크노크라시는 전문가와 정치가의 역할을 구분하고 전문가에게 상당한 권력을 준다.
➡ **(A):** 전문가에게 상당한 권력이 있는 이유는 정치가는 전문가가 제공하는 선택지 중에서 고르는 의사결정을 하기 때문이다.
▶ 주어진 글 다음에 이어질 글의 순서는 (B) → (C) → (A)이므로 정답은 ③임

Land use change can be good or bad / for the climate. //
토지 이용 변화는 좋을 수도 나쁠 수도 있다 / 기후에 //

단서 1 식물은 광합성을 통해 이산화탄소와 물을 탄수화물로 전환함
Plants use photosynthesis / to convert carbon dioxide from
부사적 용법
the air and water to carbohydrates. //
식물은 광합성을 사용하여 / 공기로부터의 이산화탄소와 물을 탄수화물로 전환한다 //

단서 2 (B)의 마지막에 언급한 내용이 '그러한 상황'으로 이어지고, 미생물은 저장된 탄소를 소비하고
이산화탄소로 내뿜음
(A) In those conditions / microorganisms consume carbon /
that has been stored in the soil and in plants and animals, / and
주격 관계대명사
respire that stored carbon back to atmosphere as CO₂. //
그러한 상황에서 / 미생물들은 탄소를 소비하고 / 흙과 식물들과 동물들에 저장된 / 그 저장된
탄소를 다시 대기로 이산화탄소로서 내뿜는다 //

If the original ecosystem was a forest, / much of the carbon
stored in the trees / may also be converted to CO₂ through
burning. //
만약에 원래 생태계가 숲이었다면 / 나무에 저장된 탄소의 많은 부분은 / 또한 화재를 통해
이산화탄소로 전환될지 모른다 //

단서 3 '그 남은 탄소'는 바이오매스와 토양 안에 저장됨
(B) That extra carbon is stored in living biomass / like tree trunks
and soil bacteria and fungi, / and as carbon compounds in the
전치사구의 병렬 구조
soil. //
그 남는 탄소는 살아있는 바이오매스 안에 저장된다 / 나무 몸통, 토양 박테리아, 균류와 같은
/ 그리고 탄소 화합물로서 토양 안에 //

But when actions like deforestation or plowing / severely
disturb a plant community, /
그러나 산림파괴나 경작과 같은 행동들이 / 식물 군집을 심각하게 교란할 때 /

the remaining plants cannot photosynthesize / enough to feed
themselves, / plus all the animals and microorganisms / that
주격 관계대명사
depend on them. //
남아있는 식물들은 광합성을 할 수 없게 된다 / 충분히 자신들을 먹일 만큼 / 그에 더해서 모든
동물들과 미생물들을 먹일 만큼 / 그들에게 의존하는

단서 4 '그러한 탄수화물'은 주어진 글에서 언급한 것을 가리키며, 동물과 미생물을 위한 식량뿐만
아니라 식물에게 필요한 에너지와 기본 구성요소를 제공함
(C) Those carbohydrates provide / the energy plants need to
앞에 관계대명사가 생략된 관계절
live, / and the building blocks for plant growth, / as well as food
A as well as B: B 뿐만 아니라 A도
for animals and microorganisms. //
그러한 탄수화물은 제공한다 / 식물이 살아가기 위해 필요한 에너지와 / 식물 성장을 위한
기본 구성요소를 / 동물과 미생물들을 위한 식량뿐만 아니라 //

In healthy ecosystems / the plants pull more carbon out of the
atmosphere / than they, and the animals and microorganisms
주격 관계대명사   (= plants)
that consume them, need. //
건강한 생태계에서 / 식물들은 대기로부터 더 많은 탄소를 끌어온다 / 그것들이, 그리고
그것들을 소비하는 동물들과 미생물들이 필요로 하는 것보다 더 (많은 탄소를) //

- photosynthesis ⓝ 광합성   - convert ⓥ 전환하다
- carbon dioxide 이산화탄소   - carbohydrate ⓝ 탄수화물
- microorganism ⓝ 미생물   - consume ⓥ 소비하다
- respire ⓥ 호흡하다, (나무가 공기를) 내뿜다   - atmosphere ⓝ 대기, 공기
- biomass ⓝ 바이오매스 연료(메탄·수소로 만든 합성 연료)
- fungi ⓝ 균류   - compound ⓝ 화합물
- deforestation ⓝ 산림파괴   - plowing ⓝ 경작
- severely ⓐⓓ 심각하게   - disturb ⓥ 교란하다, 방해하다

토지 이용 변화는 기후에 좋을 수도 나쁠 수도 있다. 식물은 광합성을 사용하여
공기로부터의 이산화탄소와 물을 탄수화물로 전환한다. (C) 그러한 탄수화물은
동물과 미생물들을 위한 식량뿐만 아니라 식물이 살아가기 위해 필요한
에너지와 식물 성장을 위한 기본 구성요소를 제공한다. 건강한 생태계에서
식물들은 그것들이, 그리고 그것들을 소비하는 동물들과 미생물들이 필요로
하는 것보다 더 많은 탄소를 대기로부터 끌어온다. (B) 그 남는 탄소는 나무
몸통, 토양 박테리아, 균류와 같은 살아있는 바이오매스 안에, 그리고 탄소
화합물로서 토양 안에 저장된다. 그러나 산림파괴나 경작과 같은 행동들이

식물 군집을 심각하게 교란할 때, 남아있는 식물들은 자신들과, 그에 더해서
그들에게 의존하는 모든 동물들과 미생물들을 먹일 만큼 충분히 광합성을 할
수 없게 된다. (A) 그러한 상황에서 미생물들은 흙과 식물들과 동물들에 저장된
탄소를 소비하고, 그 저장된 탄소를 다시 대기로 이산화탄소로서 내뿜는다.
만약에 원래 생태계가 숲이었다면, 나무에 저장된 탄소의 많은 부분은 또한
화재를 통해 이산화탄소로 전환될지 모른다.

주어진 글 다음에 이어질 글의 순서로 가장 적절한 것을 고르시오.

① (A) — (C) — (B)   (A)의 시작인 미생물이 탄소를 소비하고 이산화탄소를 배출하게 되는
'그러한 상황'에 해당하는 내용이 주어진 글에 없음
② (B) — (A) — (C)
(B)의 '그 남는 산소'에 대한 내용은 주어진 글에 없음
③ (B) — (C) — (A)
④ (C) — (A) — (B)   식물은 광합성으로 이산화탄소를 탄수화물로 만듦 - 건강한
생태계에서는 식물이 필요 이상의 탄소를 흡수하고 저장함 - 생태계가
훼손된 경우 식물은 충분한 광합성을 못함 - 미생물은 저장된 탄소를
⑤ (C) — (B) — (A)   사용하고 이산화탄소로 대기에 방출함
(A)의 '그러한 상황'에 해당하는 내용(식물 군집이 심각하게 교란되는 상황)은 (B)에 있으므로
(B) 뒤에 와야 함

| 문제 풀이 순서 | [정답률 44%]

1st 각 문단의 내용을 파악하고, 글의 논리적인 순서를 추론한다.

주어진 글: 토지 이용 변화는 기후에 좋을 수도 나쁠 수도 있다. 식물은
광합성을 사용하여 공기로부터의 이산화탄소와 물을 탄수화물로 전환한다.

➡ 식물은 광합성을 통해 이산화탄소와 물을 탄수화물로 전환한다. **단서**
주어진 글 뒤: 첫 번째 문장에서 기후를 언급했으므로 광합성과 이산화탄소에 대한
내용이 이어질 것이다. **발상**

(A) 그러한 상황에서(In those conditions) 미생물들은 흙과 식물들과
동물들에 저장된 탄소를 소비하고, 그 저장된 탄소를 다시 대기로
이산화탄소로서 내뿜는다. 만약에 원래 생태계가 숲이었다면, 나무에
저장된 탄소의 많은 부분은 또한 화재를 통해 이산화탄소로 전환될지
모른다.

➡ **(A) 앞:** 미생물이 탄소를 소비하고 이산화탄소로 내뿜는 '그러한 상황(In those
conditions)'에 대한 내용이 나올 것이다.
▶ 주어진 글이 (A) 앞에 올 수 없음
(A) 뒤: 글이 마무리되거나 대기 중에 방출된 이산화탄소가 기후에 어떻게 영향을
미칠지 등에 대한 내용이 올 것이다.
▶ (A)가 마지막에 올 확률이 큼

(B) 그 남는 탄소(That extra carbon)는 나무 몸통, 토양 박테리아,
균류와 같은 살아있는 바이오매스 안에, 그리고 탄소 화합물로서 토양 안에
저장된다. 그러나 산림파괴나 경작과 같은 행동들이 식물 군집을 심각하게
교란할 때, 남아있는 식물들은 자신들과, 그에 더해서 그들에게 의존하는
모든 동물들과 미생물들을 먹일 만큼 충분히 광합성을 할 수 없게 된다.

➡ **(B) 앞:** '그 남는 탄소(That extra carbon)'가 가리킬 수 있는 것, 즉 탄소가 남는
상황에 대한 내용이 있어야 한다.
▶ 주어진 글이나 (A)가 앞에 올 수 없으므로 (C)가 올 가능성이 큼
(B) 뒤: 자기 자신과 모든 동물 및 미생물을 먹일 만큼 충분히 광합성을 할 수
없게 되는 경우 발생하는 일이 이어질 것이다. (A)에서 '그러한 상황(In those
conditions)'이라고 하며 이 내용이 이어진다.
▶ 순서: (B) → (A)

(C) 그러한 탄수화물(Those carbohydrates)은 동물과 미생물들을 위한
식량뿐만 아니라 식물이 살아가기 위해 필요한 에너지와 식물 성장을 위한
기본 구성요소를 제공한다. 건강한 생태계에서 식물들은 그것들이, 그리고
그것들을 소비하는 동물들과 미생물들이 필요로 하는 것보다 더 많은
탄소를 대기로부터 끌어온다.

➡ **(C) 앞:** 식물이 탄수화물을 만든다는 내용처럼 탄수화물에 대한 언급이 있어야
한다.
▶ 순서: 주어진 글 → (C)
(C) 뒤: 필요보다 더 많이 끌어온 탄소를 어떻게 하는지에 대한 내용이 이어져야
한다. 앞에서 예상했던 것처럼 (B)가 뒤에 와야 한다.
▶ 순서: 주어진 글 → (C) → (B) → (A)

2nd 글이 한눈에 들어오도록 정리하여 정답을 확인한다.

주어진 글: 식물은 광합성을 통해 이산화탄소와 물을 탄수화물로 전환한다.

→ **(C):** 탄수화물은 식물의 성장을 위한 에너지와 기본 구성요소를 제공하며, 건강한 생태계에서는 식물이 필요 이상의 탄소를 대기로부터 가져온다.

→ **(B):** 그 남은 탄소는 바이오매스와 토양 내에 저장되지만, 생태계가 훼손되는 경우에는 광합성을 충분히 하지 못한다.

→ **(A):** 이 경우, 미생물은 탄소를 소비하고 이산화탄소를 배출하며, 저장된 탄소는 화재를 통해 이산화탄소로 전환될 수 있다.

▶ 주어진 글 다음에 이어질 글의 순서는 (C) → (B) → (A)이므로 정답은 ⑤임

M 12 정답 ③ ＊시간 여행과 철학적 사고 실험

> 주어 　주격 관계대명사
> Philosophers / who seek to understand the nature of time /
> 　동사
> might consider the possibility of time travel. //
> 철학자들은 / 시간의 본질을 이해하고자 하는 / 시간 여행의 가능성을 고려할지도 모른다 //
> But there are no real-life cases of time travel. //
> 그러나 시간 여행의 실제 사례는 없다 // **단서 1** 시간 여행이 실제 일어난 사례는 없음

(A) It seems that something must happen / to prevent you from doing this, / **단서 2** (C)에서 말한 시간 여행을 가서 개입하는 것을 가리킴
무슨 일이 일어나야 하는 것처럼 보이는데 / 여러분이 그렇게 하는 것을 막기 위해 /

because if you were to succeed, / you would not exist / and so you would not have been able to go back in time. //
왜냐하면 만약 여러분이 성공한다면 / 여러분은 존재하지 않을 것이고 / 그래서 여러분은 시간을 거슬러 갈 수 없었을 것이기 때문이다 //

As a result of thinking through these sorts of cases, / some philosophers claim / that the very notion of time travel makes no sense. //
이러한 종류의 사례들을 통해 생각한 결과 / 일부 철학자들은 주장한다 / 시간 여행이라는 바로 그 개념이 말이 되지 않는다고 // **단서 3** 주어진 글의 시간 여행이 실제 일어난 사례가 없는 것을 가리킴

(B) In situations such as this, / philosophers often construct thought experiments / — imagined scenarios / 　　주격 관계대명사 that bring out the thoughts and presuppositions / underlying people's judgments. // 　　현재분사구(the thoughts and presuppositions 수식)
이와 같은 상황들에서 / 철학자들은 종종 사고 실험을 구성한다 / 즉 상상의 시나리오를 / 생각과 전제를 끌어내는 / 사람들의 판단의 기초가 되는 //

Sometimes these scenarios are drawn / from books, movies, and television. //
때때로 이러한 시나리오들은 얻어진다 / 책, 영화 그리고 텔레비전으로부터 //

Other times, / philosophers just make up their own scenarios. //
다른 때에는 / 철학자들이 그냥 자신들만의 시나리오를 지어낸다 // **단서 4** (B)의 책, 영화 등에서 시나리오를 얻는 경우와 지어내는 경우를 가리킴

(C) Either way, / the point is to put such concepts to the test. //
어느 쪽이든 / 요점은 그러한 개념들을 시험해 보는 것이다 //

In the case of time travel, for example, / a common thought 　　명사적 용법(주격 보어)
experiment is to imagine / what would happen /
예를 들어 시간 여행의 경우 / 일반적인 사고 실험은 상상하는 것이다 / 어떤 일이 일어났을지를 /

if you went back in time / and found yourself in a position 　　형용사적 용법(a position 수식)
to interfere / in such a way that you were never born. //
만약 여러분이 시간을 거슬러 가서 / 개입할 위치에 있는 자신을 발견한다면 / 여러분이 결코 태어나지 않았다는 식으로 //

- **philosopher** ⓝ 철학자　・**go back in time** 시간을 거슬러 가다
- **sort** ⓝ 분류　・**notion** ⓝ 개념, 생각　・**construct** ⓥ 구성하다
- **presupposition** ⓝ 예상　・**interfere** ⓥ 간섭하다

시간의 본질을 이해하고자 하는 철학자들은 시간 여행의 가능성을 고려할지도 모른다. 그러나 시간 여행의 실제 사례는 없다. (B) 이와 같은 상황들에서 철학자들은 사고 실험, 즉 사람들의 판단의 기초가 되는 생각과 전제를

끌어내는 상상의 시나리오를 종종 구성한다. 때때로 이러한 시나리오들은 책, 영화 그리고 텔레비전으로부터 얻어진다. 다른 때에는 철학자들이 그냥 자신들만의 시나리오를 지어낸다. (C) 어느 쪽이든, 요점은 그러한 개념들을 시험해 보는 것이다. 예를 들어 시간 여행의 경우 일반적인 사고 실험은 만약 여러분이 시간을 거슬러 가서 여러분이 결코 태어나지 않았다는 식으로 개입할 위치에 있는 자신을 발견한다면 어떤 일이 일어났을지를 상상하는 것이다. (A) 여러분이 그렇게 하는 것을 막기 위해 무슨 일이 일어나야 하는 것처럼 보이는데, 왜냐하면 만약 여러분이 성공한다면, 여러분은 존재하지 않을 것이고 그래서 여러분은 시간을 거슬러 갈 수 없었을 것이기 때문이다. 이러한 종류의 사례들을 통해 생각한 결과, 일부 철학자들은 시간 여행이라는 바로 그 개념이 말이 되지 않는다고 주장한다.

주어진 글 다음에 이어질 글의 순서로 가장 적절한 것을 고르시오.

① (A) — (C) — (B) ┐ 막아야 하는 상황이 주어진 글과 (B)에 없음
② (B) — (A) — (C) ┐
③ (B) — (C) — (A) │ (B) 철학자들은 기존 자료, 자신의 상상력에 기반해서 시나리오를 구성함 - (C) 다양한 시나리오에 개입한 것을 상상하며 사고 실험을 진행함 - (A) 일부 철학자들은 시간 여행의 개념을 부정함
④ (C) — (A) — (B) ┐
⑤ (C) — (B) — (A) ┘ '어느 쪽이든'으로 언급할 상황이 주어진 글에 없음

| 문제 풀이 순서 | [정답률 57%]

1st 각 문단의 내용을 파악하고, 글의 논리적인 순서를 추론한다.

┌ **주어진 글:** 시간의 본질을 이해하고자 하는 철학자들은 시간 여행의
└ 가능성을 고려할지도 모른다. 그러나 시간 여행의 실제 사례는 없다.

⇒ **주어진 글 뒤:** 시간 여행의 실제 사례는 없다는 사실에 대응하는 내용이 이어질 것이다. **발상**

┌ **(A):** 여러분이 그렇게(this) 하는 것을 막기 위해 무슨 일이 일어나야
│ 하는 것처럼 보이는데, 왜냐하면 만약 여러분이 성공한다면, 여러분은
│ 존재하지 않을 것이고 그래서 여러분은 시간을 거슬러 갈 수 없었을 것이기
│ 때문이다. 이러한 종류의 사례들을 통해 생각한 결과, 일부 철학자들은
└ 시간 여행이라는 바로 그 개념이 말이 되지 않는다고 주장한다.

⇒ **(A) 앞:** 우리가 존재하기 위해 막아야 하는 것(this)이 주어진 글에는 나오지 않는다.
　▶ 주어진 글 바로 다음에 (A)가 이어질 수 없음
(A) 뒤: 주어진 글에서 주장한 바를 다시 정리하고 있으므로, 주어진 글과 (A) 사이에 뒷받침하는 내용이 나오고 (A)는 글의 마지막에 올 것이다.

┌ **(B):** 이와(this) 같은 상황들에서 철학자들은 사고 실험, 즉 사람들의
│ 판단의 기초가 되는 생각과 전제를 끌어내는 상상의 시나리오를 종종
│ 구성한다. 때때로 이러한 시나리오들은 책, 영화 그리고 텔레비전으로부터
└ 얻어진다. 다른 때에는 철학자들이 그냥 자신들만의 시나리오를 지어낸다.

⇒ **(B) 앞:** '이와(this)' 같은 상황들이 가리키는 것은 주어진 글의 시간 여행의 실제 사례가 없다는 것이다.
　▶ 순서: 주어진 글 → (B)
(B) 뒤: 시나리오를 얻는 두 방법에 대한 설명이 이어질 것이다.
　▶ (C)에 그러한 내용이 있을 것이고 (B) 뒤에 이어질 것임
　(순서: 주어진 글 → (B) → (C))

┌ **(C):** 어느 쪽이든(Either way), 요점은 그러한 개념들을 시험해 보는
│ 것이다. 예를 들어 시간 여행의 경우 일반적인 사고 실험은 만약 여러분이
│ 시간을 거슬러 가서 여러분이 결코 태어나지 않았다는 식으로 개입할
└ 위치에 있는 자신을 발견한다면 어떤 일이 일어났을지를 상상하는 것이다.

⇒ **(C) 앞:** '어느 쪽이든(Either way)'으로 가리킬 만한 상황이 앞에 와야 한다.
　▶ (B)에 책, 영화 등에서 시나리오를 얻는 경우와 지어내는 경우가 나옴
　(순서: 주어진 글 → (B) → (C))
(C) 뒤: 개입할 수 있는 가능성이 나오므로 그것을 막아야 한다는 내용이 이어질 것이다.
　▶ (A)에서 이를 this로 가리킴 (순서: 주어진 글 → (B) → (C) → (A))

주어진 글: 시간 여행은 가능할 수 있지만 아직 실제 이루어진 사례가 없다.

→ **(B)**: 철학자들은 다양한 시나리오를 구성할 때 기존의 자료, 자신의 상상력에 의존한다.

→ **(C)**: 다양한 시나리오에 개입한 것을 가정하고 상상하는 방식으로 사고 실험이 진행된다.

→ **(A)**: 실험의 결과 일부 철학자들은 시간 여행의 개념이 성립되지 않는다고 주장한다.

▶ 주어진 글 다음에 이어질 글의 순서는 (B) → (C) → (A)이므로 정답은 ③임

Ⓜ 13 정답 ④ *수면 중 감각 차단과 시상의 역할

A universal indicator of sleep / is the loss of external awareness. //
수면의 한 보편적인 지표는 / 외부 인식의 상실이다 //

You are no longer conscious / of all that surrounds you, / at least not explicitly. //
주격 관계대명사
여러분은 더 이상 의식하지 않는다 / 자신을 둘러싸고 있는 모든 것을 / 최소한 겉으로 보기에는 //

단서 1 수면 상태에도 감각 정보를 인식함

In actual fact, / your ears are still 'hearing'; / your eyes, though closed, are still capable of 'seeing.' //
분사구문
실상은 / 여러분의 귀는 여전히 '듣고' 있고 / 눈은, 감겨 있지만, 여전히 '보는 것'이 가능하다 //

단서 2 its는 (C)의 시상을 가리킴

(A) Should they be granted its permission to pass, / they are sent to the cortex at the top of your brain, / where they are
= If they should   계속적 용법의 관계부사
consciously perceived. //
그것들이 그것(시상)의 통행 허가를 받게 된다면 / 그것들은 여러분의 뇌 상부에 있는 대뇌피질로 보내지는데 / 거기서 그것들은 의식적으로 지각된다 //

By locking its gates shut, / the thalamus imposes a sensory
by -ing: ~함으로써
blackout in the brain, / preventing onward travel of those
                        분사구문을 이끄는 현재분사
signals to the cortex. //
그것의 문을 닫아 잠금으로써 / 시상은 뇌에 감각 정전을 가하고 / 그 신호들의 대뇌피질을 향한 전진 이동을 막는다 //

단서 3 시상이 신호들을 대뇌피질로 보내지 않은 결과

(B) As a result, / you are no longer consciously aware / of the information broadcasts / being transmitted from your outer
                                        현재분사구(information broadcasts 수식)
sense organs. //
그 결과 / 여러분은 더 이상 의식적으로 인식하지 못한다 / 정보 방송을 / 외부 감각 기관으로부터 전송되고 있는 //

At this moment, your brain has lost / waking contact with the outside world. //
이 순간 여러분의 뇌는 잃었다 / 외부 세계와의 깨어 있는 접촉을 //

Said another way, / you are now asleep. //
다른 말로 하면 / 여러분은 지금 잠이 든 것이다 //

단서 4 수면 상태에도 감각 정보를 인식한다는 것을 의미함

(C) All these signals still flood / into the center of your brain / while you sleep, / but they are blocked / by a perceptual
                                        과거분사구(barricade 수식)   과거분사(a structure 수식)
barricade / set up in a structure called the thalamus. //
이 모든 신호들은 흘러 들어가지만 / 뇌의 중심부로 / 여러분이 자는 동안 여전히 / 그것들은 차단된다 / 지각의 바리케이드에 의해 / 시상이라고 불리는 조직에 설치된 //

The thalamus decides / which sensory signals are allowed through its gate, / and which are not. //
시상은 결정한다 / 그것의 문을 통해 어떤 감각 신호들이 들여보내질지 / 어떤 것들이 그렇지 않을지를 //

- universal ⓐ 보편적인 · indicator ⓝ 지표
- awareness ⓝ 의식 · grant permission 허가하다
- impose ⓥ 부과하다 · blackout ⓝ 일시적인 의식[시력/기억] 상실
- onward ⓐ 앞으로[계속 이어서] 나아가는 · outer ⓐ 바깥의
- sense organ 감각 기관 · perceptual ⓐ 지각의
- barricade ⓝ 장애물, 바리케이드

수면의 한 보편적인 지표는 외부 인식의 상실이다. 여러분은 자신을 둘러싸고 있는 모든 것을, 최소한 겉으로 보기에는, 더 이상 의식하지 않는다. 실상은 여러분의 귀는 여전히 '듣고' 있고, 눈은, 감겨 있지만, 여전히 '보는 것'이 가능하다. (C) 이 모든 신호들은 여러분이 자는 동안 여전히 뇌의 중심부로 흘러 들어가지만, 그것들은 시상이라고 불리는 조직에 설치된 지각의 바리케이드에 의해 차단된다. 시상은 그것의 문을 통해 어떤 감각 신호들이 들여보내질지, 어떤 것들이 그렇지 않을지를 결정한다. (A) 그것들이 그것의 통행 허가를 받게 된다면, 그것들은 여러분의 뇌 상부에 있는 대뇌피질로 보내지는데, 거기서 그것들은 의식적으로 지각된다. 그것의 문을 닫아 잠금으로써 시상은 뇌에 감각 정전을 가하고, 그 신호들의 대뇌피질을 향한 전진 이동을 막는다. (B) 그 결과 여러분은 외부 감각 기관으로부터 전송되고 있는 정보 방송을 더 이상 의식적으로 인식하지 못한다. 이 순간 여러분의 뇌는 외부 세계와의 깨어 있는 접촉을 잃었다. 다른 말로 하면, 여러분은 지금 잠이 든 것이다.

주어진 글 다음에 이어질 글의 순서로 가장 적절한 것을 고르시오. [3점]

① (A) — (C) — (B) 통행 허가의 주체가 주어진 글과 (B)에 나오지 않음
② (B) — (A) — (C)
③ (B) — (C) — (A) ┘ (B)의 '그 결과'와 주어진 글이 연결되지 않음
④ (C) — (A) — (B)
⑤ (C) — (B) — (A) (B)의 '그 결과'와 (C)는 연결되지 않음
(C) 시상이라는 조직에 어떤 신호가 뇌로 들어갈지 결정함 - (A) 시상이 감각 신호를 대뇌피질로 보내지 않을 수도 있음 - (B) 그렇게 되면 외부 정보를 인식하지 못하게 되며 이는 곧 수면 상태임

| 문제 풀이 순서 | [정답률 44%]

1st 각 문단의 내용을 파악하고, 글의 논리적인 순서를 추론한다.

주어진 글: 수면의 한 보편적인 지표는 외부 인식의 상실이다. 여러분은 자신을 둘러싸고 있는 모든 것을, 최소한 겉으로 보기에는, 더 이상 의식하지 않는다. 실상은 여러분의 귀는 여전히 '듣고' 있고, 눈은, 감겨 있지만, 여전히 '보는 것'이 가능하다.

→ **주어진 글 뒤**: 감지된 정보들이 수면 중에는 어떻게 처리되는지가 나와야 한다. **발상**

(A): 그것들이 그것(its)의 통행 허가를 받게 된다면, 그것들은 여러분의 뇌 상부에 있는 대뇌피질로 보내지는데, 거기서 그것들은 의식적으로 지각된다. 그것의 문을 닫아 잠금으로써 시상은 뇌에 감각 정전을 가하고, 그 신호들의 대뇌피질을 향한 전진 이동을 막는다.

→ **(A) 앞**: 통행 허가를 내리는 주체가 주어진 글에 등장하지 않는다.
▶ 주어진 글 바로 다음에 (A)가 이어질 수 없음
(A) 뒤: 신호들의 이동을 막는 것의 결과가 나와야 한다.

(B): 그 결과(As a result) 여러분은 외부 감각 기관으로부터 전송되고 있는 정보 방송을 더 이상 의식적으로 인식하지 못한다. 이 순간 여러분의 뇌는 외부 세계와의 깨어 있는 접촉을 잃었다. 다른 말로 하면, 여러분은 지금 잠이 든 것이다.

→ **(B) 앞**: 외부 감각 기관이 보내는 정보 방송을 인식하지 못하는 이유가 나와야 한다. ▶ (A)에 시상이 신호들을 막는다는 내용이 있고, 그것이 정보 방송을 인식하지 못하는 이유가 될 수 있음 (순서: (A) → (B))
(B) 뒤: 수면에 대한 설명이 이어지거나 (B)가 글의 결론일 것이다.
▶ (B)가 마지막에 올 확률이 높음

(C): 이 모든 신호들(All these signals)은 여러분이 자는 동안 여전히 뇌의 중심부로 흘러 들어가지만, 그것들은 시상이라고 불리는 조직에 설치된 지각의 바리케이드에 의해 차단된다. 시상은 그것의 문을 통해 어떤 감각 신호들이 들여보내질지, 어떤 것들이 그렇지 않을지를 결정한다.

→ **(C) 앞**: 뇌의 중심부로 흘러 들어가는 '이 모든 신호들(All these signals)'에 관한 내용이 나와야 한다.
▶ 주어진 글에서 언급한 수면 상태에서도 여전히 '듣고 보는 것'을 가리킴 (순서: 주어진 글 → (C))
(C) 뒤: 시상이 통과시킨 감각 신호와 통과시키지 않은 감각 신호들이 각각 어떻게 되는지 이어질 것이다.
▶ (A)에 해당 내용이 나오므로 (A)가 (C) 뒤에 이어질 것임 (순서: 주어진 글 → (C) → (A) → (B))

2nd 글이 한눈에 들어오도록 정리하여 정답을 확인한다.

주어진 글: 수면 중 감각들이 비활성화된 것 같지만 여전히 감각들이 어느 정도 살아 있다.

→ **(C):** 시상이라는 조직이 이를 차단하여 어떤 신호가 뇌로 들어갈지 결정한다.

→ **(A):** 시상이 감각 신호를 대뇌피질로 보내는 것을 결정하면, 해당 신호들은 의식적으로 인식되며, 시상이 문을 닫아 잠그면 감각의 전달을 막고 대뇌피질로의 처리를 막는다.

→ **(B):** 그 경우, 외부 감각에서 오는 정보를 의식적으로 인식하지 못하게 되며, 이는 수면 상태임을 의미한다.

▶ 주어진 글 다음에 이어질 글의 순서는 (C) → (A) → (B)이므로 정답은 ④임

M 14 정답 ② ＊무의식적, 의식적 능력의 결합이 요구되는 창의적인 일

Different creative pursuits / require varying degrees of unconscious flexible thinking, /
서로 다른 창의적인 일들은 / 다양한 정도의 무의식적이고 유연한 사고를 요구한다 /

in combination with varying degrees of the conscious ability /
형용사적 용법
to adjust it and shape it / through analytical thinking. //
다양한 정도의 의식적인 능력과 함께 결합하여 / 그것을 조정하고 그것을 형성하는 / 분석적인 사고를 통해서 // **단서 1** 창의적인 일에는 무의식적, 의식적 능력의 결합이 요구됨

In music, / for example, / at one end of the creative spectrum / are improvisational artists, / such as jazz musicians. //
음악에서 / 예를 들어 / 창의적인 스펙트럼의 한끝에는 / 즉흥 연주가들이 있다 / 재즈 음악가와 같은 //

(A) On the other end of the spectrum / are those who compose complex forms, / such as a symphony or concerto, /
스펙트럼의 다른 끝에는 / 복잡한 형식을 작곡하는 자들이 있다 / 심포니와 콘체르토와 같은 //
not jus A but also B: A 뿐만 아니라 B도
that require / not just imagination but also careful planning and
주격 관계대명사(forms 수식)
exacting editing. // **단서 2** 스펙트럼의 다른 끝에는 복잡한 형식을 작곡하는 자들이 있음
요구하는 / 상상력뿐만이 아니라 신중한 계획과 고된 편집을 //

We know, / for example, / through his letters and the reports of others, /
우리는 안다 / 예를 들어 / 그의 편지와 다른 이들의 기록을 통해 /

that even Mozart's creations did not appear spontaneously, /
know의 목적어절을 이끄는 접속사
wholly formed in his consciousness, / as the myths about him
creations를 수식하는 분사   접속사
portray. //
심지어 모차르트의 창작물 또한 즉흥적으로 발생한 것이 아니라는 것을 / 그의 의식에서 완전히 만들어졌다는 것을 / 그에 관한 전설이 그려 내듯 //

(B) They have to be particularly talented / at lowering their
동명사의 병렬 구조
inhibitions / and letting in their unconsciously generated ideas. // **단서 3** 그들(즉흥 연주가들)은 무의식적 생각을 받아들이는 데 재능이 있음
그들은 특히 재능이 있다 / 그들의 억제를 낮추는 것에 / 그리고 무의식적으로 생성된 생각들을 받아들이는 것에 //

And although the process of learning the fundamentals of jazz / would require a high degree of analytical thought, / that thinking style is not as big a factor / during the performance. //
그리고 비록 재즈의 원리를 배우는 과정이 / 높은 정도의 분석적 사고를 요구할지라도 / 그러한 사고방식은 그렇게 큰 요인이 아니다 / 공연 중에 // **단서 4** 그(모차르트)는 생각을 분석하고 재작업하는 데 긴 시간을 보냄

(C) Instead, / he spent long, hard hours / analyzing and
주격 관계대명사(ideas 수식)
reworking the ideas / that arose in his unconscious, /
대신 / 그는 길고 힘든 시간을 보냈다 / 생각들을 분석하고 재작업하는 데 / 무의식에 떠오른 /

much as a scientist does / when producing a theory / from a
접속사가 생략되지 않은 분사구문
germ of insight. //
과학자가 그러하듯 / 이론을 만들어 낼 때 / 통찰력의 기원으로부터 //

In Mozart's own words: / "I immerse myself in music... / I think
동명사의 병렬 구조
about it all day long / — I like experimenting — studying — reflecting..." //
모차르트의 말처럼 / "나는 음악에 몰두한다 / 나는 그것에 대해 하루 종일 생각한다 / 나는 시도하고 — 공부하고 — 성찰하는 것…을 좋아한다" //

• pursuit ⓝ 일, 연구 • varying ⓐ 다양한 • flexible ⓐ 유연한
• combination ⓝ 조합 • adjust ⓥ 적응하다, 조절하다
• analytical ⓐ 분석적인 • spectrum ⓝ 범위, 스펙트럼
• concerto ⓝ 협주곡 • exacting ⓐ 고된
• spontaneously ⓐⓓ 자발적으로 • consciousness ⓝ 의식
• myth ⓝ 전설 • portray ⓥ 그리다, 묘사하다 • inhibition ⓝ 억제
• fundamental ⓝ 원리, 기초 • theory ⓝ 이론
• germ ⓝ 기원, 싹틈 • reflect ⓥ 깊이 생각하다, 심사숙고하다

서로 다른 창의적인 일들은 다양한 정도의 무의식적이고 유연한 사고를 분석적인 사고를 통해서 그것을 조정하고 그것을 형성하는 다양한 정도의 의식적인 능력과 함께 결합하여 요구한다. 예를 들어, 음악에서 창의적인 스펙트럼의 한끝에는 재즈 음악가와 같은 즉흥 연주가들이 있다. (B) 그들은 그들의 억제를 낮추고 무의식적으로 생성된 생각들을 받아들이는 것에 특히 재능이 있다. 그리고 비록 재즈의 원리를 배우는 과정이 높은 정도의 분석적 사고를 요구할지라도, 그러한 사고방식은 공연 중에 그렇게 큰 요인이 아니다. (A) 스펙트럼의 다른 끝에는 심포니와 콘체르토와 같은, 상상력뿐만이 아니라 신중한 계획과 고된 편집을 요구하는 복잡한 형식을 작곡하는 자들이 있다. 예를 들어, 우리는 그의 편지와 다른 이들의 기록을 통해, 심지어 모차르트의 창작물 또한, 그에 관한 전설이 그려 내듯 즉흥적으로 발생한 것이 아니라 그의 의식에서 완전히 만들어졌다는 것을 안다. (C) 대신, 그는 과학자가 통찰력의 기원으로부터 이론을 만들어 낼 때 그러하듯, 그의 무의식에 떠오른 생각들을 분석하고 재작업하는 데 길고 힘든 시간을 보냈다. 모차르트의 말대로, "나는 음악에 몰두한다… 나는 그것에 대해 하루 종일 생각하고, 나는 시도하고 — 공부하고 — 성찰하는 것…을 좋아한다."

주어진 글 다음에 이어질 글의 순서로 가장 적절한 것을 고르시오. [3점]

① (A) — (C) — (B) (A)는 즉흥 연주가들에 대한 설명이 아니라 의식에서 비롯된 복잡한 형식을 작곡하는 자들에 관한 내용이므로 주어진 글에 이어질 수 없음

② (B) — (A) — (C) 창의적인 일은 무의식적 능력과 의식적 능력이 함께 필요함 - 즉흥 연주가들은 무의식적 사고에 재능이 있음 - 반면에 의식에서 비롯된 복잡한 형식을 작곡하는 자들이 있음 - 무의식에서 떠오른 생각들을 분석하고 재작업함

③ (B) — (C) — (A)

④ (C) — (A) — (B) (C)는 (A)에 대한 부연 설명이므로 주어진 글 다음에 올 수 없음

⑤ (C) — (B) — (A) (C)는 의식을 사용하여 복잡한 형식의 곡을 만드는 작곡가들에 대한 부연 설명이므로 (B)가 아니라 (A) 뒤에 이어져야 함

| 문제 풀이 순서 | [정답률 37%]

1st 각 문단의 내용을 파악하고, 글의 논리적인 순서를 추론한다.

주어진 글: 서로 다른 창의적인 일들은 다양한 정도의 무의식적이고 유연한 사고를 분석적인 사고를 통해서 그것을 조정하고 그것을 형성하는 다양한 정도의 의식적인 능력과 함께 결합하여 요구한다. 예를 들어, 음악에서 창의적인 스펙트럼의 한끝에는 재즈 음악가와 같은 즉흥 연주가들이 있다.

→ 창의적인 일은 무의식적 능력과 의식적 능력이 함께 필요하다고 설명하면서 예시로 재즈 음악가 같은 즉흥 연주가들을 제시하고 있다. (단서)

주어진 글 뒤: 재즈 음악가 같은 즉흥 연주가들에 대한 설명이 이어질 것이다. (발상)

(A): 스펙트럼의 다른 끝에는 심포니와 콘체르토와 같은, 상상력뿐만이 아니라 신중한 계획과 고된 편집을 요구하는 복잡한 형식을 작곡하는 자들이 있다. 예를 들어, 우리는 그의 편지와 다른 이들의 기록을 통해, 심지어 모차르트의 창작물 또한, 그에 관한 전설이 그려 내듯 즉흥적으로 발생한 것이 아니라 그의 의식에서 완전히 만들어졌다는 것을 안다.

→ **(A) 앞:** 주어진 글은 재즈 음악가 같은 즉흥 연주가들을 제시했으므로, 즉흥 연주가들에 대한 설명이 이어져야 하는데 (A)는 그런 내용이 아니다.
▶ 주어진 글이 (A) 앞에 올 수 없음
(A) 뒤: 모차르트의 창작물이 의식에서 만들어졌다는 것에 대한 부연 설명이 이어질 것이다.

(B): 그들(They)은 그들의 억제를 낮추고 무의식적으로 생성된 생각들을 받아들이는 것에 특히 재능이 있다. 그리고 비록 재즈의 원리를 배우는 과정이 높은 정도의 분석적 사고를 요구할지라도, 그러한 사고방식은 공연 중에 그렇게 큰 요인이 아니다.

→ **(B) 앞:** '그들'이 가리키는 내용이 있어야 한다. They는 주어진 글에서 재즈 음악가와 같은 즉흥 연주가들을 가리킨다.
▶ 순서: 주어진 문장 → (B)

(B) 뒤: 무의식적 능력을 사용하는 연주가들의 이야기가 마무리되었으므로 의식적 사고를 사용하는 것에 대한 이야기가 나올 것이다.

▶ (A)가 이어질 확률이 큼

(C): 대신, 그(he)는 과학자가 통찰력의 기원으로부터 이론을 만들어 낼 때 그러하듯, 그의 무의식에 떠오른 생각들을 분석하고 재작업하는 데 길고 힘든 시간을 보냈다. 모차르트의 말대로, "나는 음악에 몰두한다… 나는 그것에 대해 하루 종일 생각하고, 나는 시도하고 — 공부하고 — 성찰하는 것…을 좋아한다."

➡ **(C) 앞:** '그'가 가리키는 내용이 있어야 한다. he는 (A)의 모차르트를 가리키며, 모차르트가 의식을 사용하여 분석한다는 내용이므로 (A) 뒤에 이어지는 것이 자연스럽다.

▶ 순서: (A) → (C)

(C) 뒤: 모차르트에 대한 설명이 이어지거나 (C)가 글의 마지막일 확률이 높다.

▶ 순서: 주어진 글 → (B) → (A) → (C)

2nd 글이 한눈에 들어오도록 정리하여 정답을 확인한다.

주어진 글: 창의적 작업은 무의식적, 의식적 노력의 결합을 요구한다.

→ **(B):** 재즈 음악가와 같은 즉흥 연주가들은 무의식적 생각을 잘 받아들인다.

→ **(A):** 반면 복잡한 형식을 작곡하는 자들이 있고, 모차르트의 창작물 또한 의식을 사용한다.

→ **(C):** 모차르트는 과학자가 이론을 만들어 내는 것처럼 무의식에 떠오른 생각들을 분석하고 음악에 대해 공부한다.

▶ 주어진 글 다음에 이어질 글의 순서는 (B) → (A) → (C)이므로 정답은 ②임

M 15 정답 ⑤ * 지속 가능한 도시 계획에 대한 두 가지 접근 방식

Today, / historic ideas about integrating nature and urban/
suburb space / find expression in various interpretations /
of sustainable urban planning. // **단서1** 지속 가능한 도시 계획에 대해 언급함
오늘날 / 자연과 도시/교외 공간의 통합에 대한 역사적인 생각들은 / 다양한 해석의
모습으로 나타난다 / 지속 가능한 도시 계획에 대한 //

(A) But Landscape Urbanists find / that these designs do not
prioritize the natural environment / and often involve diverting
streams / and disrupting natural wetlands. //
그러나 경관 도시론자들은 알게 되었다 / 이러한 설계가 자연환경을 우선시하지 않는다는
것을 / 그리고 흔히 하천의 우회를 수반한다는 것을 / 자연 습지 파괴와 //

Still others, / such as those advocating / for "just sustainabilities"
or "complete streets," / find /
그럼에도 불구하고 다른 사람들은 / 예를 들어 주장하는 이들은 / '정당한 지속 가능성'이나
'완전 도로(보행, 자전거 및 자동차 모두 안전하게 접근하고 이동할 수 있도록 설계된 도로)'를
/ 알게 되었다 //

that both approaches are overly idealistic / and neither pays
enough attention to the realities / of social dynamics and
systemic inequality. // **단서2** 두 가지 접근 방식이 모두 문제가 있다고 함
두 접근 방식 모두 지나치게 이상주의적이라는 것을 / 그리고 또한 현실에 충분한 주의를
기울이지 않는다는 것을 / 사회적 역학 관계와 구조적 불평등의 //

(B) However, / critics claim / that Landscape Urbanists prioritize
aesthetic and ecological concerns / over human needs. //
그러나 / 비판가들은 주장한다 / 경관 도시론자들이 미적 그리고 생태적 관심사를
우선시한다고 / 인간의 필요보다 // **단서3** 경관 도시론자들의 주장과 비판이 있음

In contrast, / New Urbanism is an approach / that was
popularized in the 1980s / and promotes / walkable streets,
compact design, and mixed-use developments. // **단서4** 신도시론이라는
대조적으로 / 신도시론은 접근법이다 / 1980년대에 대중화된 / 그리고 장려한다 / 걸을 수
있는 거리, 고밀도 디자인, 그리고 복합 용도 개발을 //   다른 접근 방식을 제시함

(C) However, / the role of social justice / in these approaches /
remains highly controversial. //
그러나 / 사회 정의의 역할은 / 이러한 접근 방식에서 / 논란의 소지가 많이 남아 있다 //

For example, / Landscape Urbanism is a relatively recent
planning approach / that advocates for native habitat designs /
예를 들어 / 경관 도시론은 비교적 최근에 등장한 계획 접근 방식이다 / 자연 서식지 설계를
옹호하는

that include diverse species and landscapes / that require very
low resource use. // **단서5** 경관 도시론의 주장/내용을 제시하고 있음
다양한 종과 경관을 포함하는 / 매우 적은 자원 사용을 필요로 하는 //

- integrate ⓥ 통합시키다   • suburban ⓐ 교외의
- interpretation ⓝ 해석   • sustainable ⓐ 지속 가능한
- Landscape Urbanist 경관 도시론자   • prioritize ⓥ 우선시하다
- disrupt ⓥ 방해하다   • wetland ⓝ 습지
- advocate ⓥ 주장하다, 옹호하다   • overly ⓐⓓ 지나치게
- idealistic ⓐ 이상주의적인   • dynamics ⓝ 역학 관계
- inequality ⓝ 불평등   • aesthetic ⓐ 미적인
- popularize ⓥ 대중화시키다   • controversial ⓐ 논란의 소지가 있는
- relatively ⓐⓓ 비교적   • habitat ⓝ 서식지   • diverse ⓐ 다양한

오늘날, 자연과 도시/교외 공간의 통합에 대한 역사적인 생각들은 지속 가능한 도시 계획에 대한 다양한 해석의 모습으로 나타난다. (C) 그러나 이러한 접근 방식에서 사회 정의의 역할은 논란의 소지가 많이 남아 있다. 예를 들어, 경관 도시론은 매우 적은 자원 사용을 필요로 하고 다양한 종과 경관을 포함하면서 자연 서식지 설계를 옹호하는 비교적 최근에 등장한 계획 접근 방식이다. (B) 그러나 비판가들은 경관 도시론자들이 인간의 필요보다 미적, 그리고 생태적 관심사를 우선시한다고 주장한다. 대조적으로 신도시론은 1980년대에 대중화된 접근법이고 걸을 수 있는 거리, 고밀도 디자인, 그리고 복합 용도 개발을 장려한다. (A) 그러나 경관 도시론자들은 이러한 설계가 자연환경을 우선시하지 않으며, 하천의 우회와 자연 습지 파괴를 흔히 수반한다는 것을 알게 되었다. 그럼에도 불구하고 다른 사람들은, 예를 들어 '정당한 지속 가능성'이나 '완전 도로(보행, 자전거 및 자동차 모두 안전하게 접근하고 이동할 수 있도록 설계된 도로)'를 주장하는 이들은 두 접근 방식 모두 지나치게 이상주의적이며, 사회적 역학 관계와 구조적 불평등의 현실에 충분한 주의를 기울이지 않는다는 것을 알게 되었다.

주어진 글 다음에 이어질 글의 순서로 가장 적절한 것을 고르시오.

① (A) — (C) — (B)   (A) 앞에 두 가지 접근 방식이 모두 제시되어야 하는데 주어진 글에 없음

② (B) — (A) — (C)   (B)에 경관 도시론자들에 대한 비판이 제시되므로 (B) 앞에는 경관 도시론의 주장이 언급된 (C)가 와야 함

③ (B) — (C) — (A)

④ (C) — (A) — (B)   지속 가능한 도시 계획에 대한 다양한 해석이 존재함 - 경관 도시론은 매우 적은 자원으로 다양한 종과 경관을 포함하는 자연 서식지 설계 옹호 방식 - 이와 대조적으로 대중화된 접근 방식인 신도시론이 있음

⑤ (C) — (B) — (A)   두 접근 방식이 모두 문제가 있다고 이야기하는 사람이 있음
(A)에서 두 접근 방식이 모두 문제가 있다고 했으므로 (A) 앞에 두 가지 접근 방식이 나와야 함

| 문제 풀이 순서 | [정답률 48%]

1st 각 문단의 내용을 파악하고, 글의 논리적인 순서를 추론한다.

주어진 글: 오늘날, 자연과 도시/교외 공간의 통합에 대한 역사적인 생각들은 지속 가능한 도시 계획에 대한 다양한 해석의 모습으로 나타난다.

➡ 지속 가능한 도시 계획에 대한 다양한 해석이 존재한다고 언급했다. **단서**

주어진 글 뒤: 지속 가능한 도시 계획에 대한 여러 방안이 제시될 것이다. **발상**

(A): 그러나 경관 도시론자들은 이러한 설계(these designs)가 자연환경을 우선시하지 않으며, 하천의 우회와 자연 습지 파괴를 흔히 수반한다는 것을 알게 되었다. 그럼에도 불구하고 다른 사람들은, 예를 들어 '정당한 지속 가능성'이나 '완전 도로(보행, 자전거 및 자동차 모두 안전하게 접근하고 이동할 수 있도록 설계된 도로)'를 주장하는 이들은 두 접근 방식(both approaches) 모두 지나치게 이상주의적이며, 사회적 역학 관계와 구조적 불평등의 현실에 충분한 주의를 기울이지 않는다는 것을 알게 되었다.

➡ **앞 문장:** 경관 도시론자들은 이러한 설계가 자연환경을 우선시하지 않는 등의 문제가 있다고 함

뒤 문장: 두 접근 방식 모두 지나치게 이상주의적인 등의 문제가 있다고 함

(A) 앞: '이러한 설계', '두 접근 방식'이 가리키는 내용이 나와야 한다.
▶ 주어진 글이 (A) 앞에 올 수 없음

(A) 뒤: 두 접근 방식이 가진 문제에 대한 해결책이 나오거나 (A)가 글의 마지막일 확률이 높다.

(B): 그러나(However) 비판가들은 경관 도시론자들이 인간의 필요보다 미적, 그리고 생태적 관심사를 우선시한다고 주장한다. 대조적으로 신도시론은 1980년대에 대중화된 접근법이고 걸을 수 있는 거리, 고밀도 디자인, 그리고 복합 용도 개발을 장려한다.

➡ **(B) 앞:** 비판가들은 경관 도시론자들의 접근법이 미적, 생태적 관심사를 우선시한다고 했으므로 경관 도시론의 주장이 제시되어야 한다.
▶ 순서: (C) → (B)

(B) 뒤: 대조적으로 신도시론이라는 대중화된 접근법이 제시됐으므로 신도시론에 대한 부연 설명이나 추가 정보가 제시될 것이다.
▶ (A)가 이어질 확률이 큼

(C): 그러나 이러한 접근 방식(these approaches)에서 사회 정의의 역할은 논란의 소지가 많이 남아 있다. 예를 들어, 경관 도시론은 매우 적은 자원 사용을 필요로 하고 다양한 종과 경관을 포함하면서 자연 서식지 설계를 옹호하는 비교적 최근에 등장한 계획 접근 방식이다.

➡ **(C) 앞:** '이러한 접근 방식'이 가리키는 내용이 있어야 한다. these approaches는 지속 가능한 도시 계획에 대한 다양한 해석들을 의미하므로 주어진 글 뒤에 이어지는 것이 자연스럽다.
▶ 순서: 주어진 글 → (C)

(C) 뒤: 경관 도시론에 대한 부연 설명이나 추가 정보가 제시될 것이다.
▶ 순서: 주어진 글 → (C) → (B) → (A)

2nd 글이 한눈에 들어오도록 정리하여 정답을 확인한다.

주어진 글: 지속 가능한 도시 계획에 대한 여러 해석이 존재한다.
→ **(C):** 경관 도시론은 다양한 종과 경관을 포함한 자연 서식지 설계를 옹호하는 접근 방식이다.
→ **(B):** 경관 도시론에 대한 비판 존재, 신도시론이라는 대중적 접근 방식이 있다.
→ **(A):** 경관 도시론자들은 신도시론을 비판, 다른 사람들은 두 접근 방식 모두를 비판한다.
▶ 주어진 글 다음에 이어질 글의 순서는 (C) → (B) → (A)이므로 정답은 ⑤임

자이 쌤's Follow Me! – 홈페이지에서 제공

M 16 정답 ① * 블랙홀 같은 랜드마크

> Spatial reference points are larger / than themselves. //
> 공간 기준점은 더 크다 / 자기 자신보다 //
> This isn't really a paradox: / landmarks are themselves, / but they also define neighborhoods / around themselves. //
> 이것은 그다지 역설이 아니다 / 랜드마크는 그 자체이기도 하지만 / 그것은 또한 주변 지역을 규정한다 / 자기 자신 주변의 //

(A) In a paradigm / that has been repeated / on many campuses, / researchers first collect / a list of campus landmarks / from students. //
현재완료 수동태
한 전형적인 예에서 / 반복되어 온 / 많은 대학 캠퍼스에서 / 연구원들은 먼저 수집한다 / 캠퍼스 랜드마크의 목록을 / 학생들에게서 //
Then they ask another group of students / to estimate the distances / between pairs of locations, / **단서1** 쌍으로 이루어진 장소 사이의 거리를 추정하라고 요청함
그런 다음 그들은 다른 학생 집단에게 요청한다 / 거리를 추정하라고 / 쌍으로 이루어진 장소 사이의 /
some to landmarks, / some to ordinary buildings / on campus. //
단서2 거리 추정에 관한 이 비대칭이 가리키는 예시가 선행되어야 함
어떤 장소에서 랜드마크까지 / 어떤 장소에서 평범한 건물까지 / 캠퍼스에 있는 //

(B) This asymmetry of distance estimates violates / the most elementary principles of Euclidean distance, / that the distance / from A to B / must be the same / as the distance / from B to A. //
주어 / **동사** / **동격절 접속사**
거리 추정에 관한 이 비대칭은 위배된다 / 가장 기초적인 유클리드 거리 법칙에 / 거리는 / A에서부터 B까지의 / 같아야 한다는 / 거리와 / B에서부터 A까지의 //

부분 부정(반드시 ~는 아닌)
Judgments of distance, / then, / are not necessarily coherent. //
거리에 관한 추정은 / 그렇다면 / 반드시 일관적이지는 않다 //

(C) The remarkable finding is / that distances / from an ordinary location / to a landmark / are judged shorter / than distances / from a landmark / to an ordinary location. //
주격 보어절 접속사 **주어** **동사**
주목할 만한 결과는 ~이다 / 거리가 / 평범한 장소에서 / 랜드마크까지의 / 더 짧다고 판단된다는 것 / 거리보다 / 랜드마크에서 / 평범한 장소까지의 //
So, / people would judge the distance / from Pierre's house / to the Eiffel Tower / to be shorter / than the distance / from the Eiffel Tower / to Pierre's house. //
목적어 **보어** **단서3** 거리를 추정하라는 요청 결과 '평범한 장소 → 랜드마크'가 '랜드마크 → 평범한 장소'보다 더 짧다고 판단됨
그래서 / 사람들은 거리를 판단할 것이다 / Pierre의 집에서 / 에펠탑까지의 / 더 짧다고 / 거리보다 / 에펠탑에서 / Pierre의 집까지의 //
Like black holes, / landmarks seem to pull ordinary locations / toward themselves, / but ordinary places do not. //
뒤에 seem to pull landmarks toward themselves가 생략됨
블랙홀처럼 / 랜드마크는 평범한 장소를 끌어들이는 것처럼 보이지만 / 자기 자신을 향해 / 평범한 장소들은 그렇지 않다 //

- **spatial** ⓐ 공간의 · **reference point** 기준(점) · **paradox** ⓝ 역설
- **landmark** ⓝ 주요 지형지물 · **define** ⓥ 규정하다
- **paradigm** ⓝ 전형적인 예 · **repeated** ⓐ 반복되는
- **researcher** ⓝ 연구원 · **estimate** ⓥ 추정하다 ⓝ 추정
- **distance** ⓝ 거리 · **ordinary** ⓐ 평범한, 보통의
- **violate** ⓥ 위반하다 · **elementary** ⓐ 기본적인
- **principle** ⓝ 원칙 · **judgement** ⓝ 추정, 판단
- **not necessarily** 반드시 ~은 아닌 · **coherent** ⓐ 일관성이 있는
- **remarkable** ⓐ 주목할 만한 · **finding** ⓝ 결과

공간 기준점은 자기 자신보다 더 크다. 이것은 그다지 역설이 아닌데, 랜드마크는 그 자체이기도 하지만, 또한 자기 자신 주변 지역을 규정한다. (A) 많은 대학 캠퍼스에서 반복되어 온 한 전형적인 예에서, 연구원들은 먼저 학생들에게서 캠퍼스 랜드마크의 목록을 수집한다. 그런 다음, 그들은 다른 학생 집단에게 쌍으로 이루어진 장소 사이의 거리, 즉 캠퍼스에 있는 어떤 장소에서 랜드마크까지, 어떤 장소에서 평범한 건물까지의 거리를 추정하라고 요청한다. (C) 주목할 만한 결과는 평범한 장소에서 랜드마크까지의 거리가 랜드마크에서 평범한 장소까지의 거리보다 더 짧다고 판단된다는 것이다. 그래서 사람들은 Pierre의 집에서 에펠탑까지의 거리가 에펠탑에서 Pierre의 집까지의 거리보다 더 짧다고 판단할 것이다. 블랙홀처럼, 랜드마크는 평범한 장소를 자기 자신을 향해 끌어들이는 것처럼 보이지만, 평범한 장소들은 그렇지 않다. (B) 거리 추정에 관한 이 비대칭은, A에서부터 B까지의 거리는 B에서부터 A까지의 거리와 같아야 한다는 가장 기초적인 유클리드 거리 법칙에 위배된다. 그렇다면, 거리에 관한 추정은 반드시 일관적이지는 않다.

주어진 글 다음에 이어질 글의 순서로 가장 적절한 것을 고르시오.

① (A) — (C) — (B) ← 학생들에게 쌍으로 이루어진 장소 사이의 거리를 추정하라고 요청함
'평범한 장소 → 랜드마크'가 '랜드마크 → 평범한 장소'보다 더 짧다고 판단됨
거리에 관한 추정이 반드시 일관적이지는 않음
② (B) — (A) — (C)
③ (B) — (C) — (A) } This asymmetry of distance estimates가 가리키는 것이 주어진 글에 없음
④ (C) — (A) — (B)
⑤ (C) — (B) — (A) } 결과를 설명하기 전에 무엇을 요청했는지가 먼저 나와야 함

| 문제 풀이 순서 | [정답률 70%]

1st 각 문단의 내용을 파악하고, 글의 논리적인 순서를 추론한다.

> **주어진 글:** 공간 기준점은 자기 자신보다 더 크다. 이것은 그다지 역설이 아닌데, 랜드마크는 그 자체이기도 하지만, 또한 자기 자신 주변 지역을 규정한다. **단서**

➡ **주어진 글 뒤:** 랜드마크와 같은 공간 기준점이 자기 자신보다 더 크다는 것을 보여주는 구체적인 사례가 등장할 것이다. **발상**

(A): 많은 대학 캠퍼스에서 반복되어 온 한 전형적인 예에서, 연구원들은 먼저 학생들에게서 캠퍼스 랜드마크의 목록을 수집한다. 그런 다음, 그들은 다른 학생 집단에게 쌍으로 이루어진 장소 사이의 거리, 즉 캠퍼스에 있는 어떤 장소에서 랜드마크까지, 어떤 장소에서 평범한 건물까지의 거리를 추정하라고 요청한다.

➡ **(A) 앞:** 랜드마크가 자기 자신보다 더 크다는 것을 보여주는 연구에 대한 설명이 (A)에서 시작된다.
▶ 주어진 글 뒤에 (A)가 이어짐 (순서: 주어진 글 ➝ (A))
(A) 뒤: 어떤 장소에서 랜드마크까지의 거리, 어떤 장소에서 평범한 건물까지의 거리를 추정한 결과가 (A) 뒤에 이어져야 한다.

(B): 거리 추정에 관한 이러한 비대칭(This asymmetry)은, A에서부터 B까지의 거리는 B에서부터 A까지의 거리와 같아야 한다는 가장 기초적인 유클리드 거리 법칙에 위배된다. 그렇다면, 거리에 관한 추정은 반드시 일관적이지는 않다.

➡ **(B) 앞:** '이러한 비대칭'이 가리키는 바가 (B) 앞에 있어야 한다.
▶ (A)에는 거리 추정에 비대칭이 있다는 내용이 없음
(B) 뒤: 학생들에게 거리를 추정하라고 요청한 결과 비대칭이 있었고, 이를 통해 거리에 관한 추정이 반드시 일관적이지는 않다는 결론을 내린 것이라고 예상할 수 있다. ▶ (B)는 글의 결론일 것임

(C): 주목할 만한 결과는 평범한 장소에서 랜드마크까지의 거리가 랜드마크에서 평범한 장소까지의 거리보다 더 짧다고 판단된다는 것이다. 그래서 사람들은 Pierre의 집에서 에펠탑까지의 거리가 에펠탑에서 Pierre의 집까지의 거리보다 더 짧다고 판단할 것이다. 블랙홀처럼, 랜드마크는 평범한 장소를 자기 자신을 향해 끌어들이는 것처럼 보이지만, 평범한 장소들은 그렇지 않다.

➡ **(C) 앞:** (C)에서는 사람들이 거리를 어떻게 추정했는지를 설명한다. (A)에서 거리를 추정하라고 요청한 결과를 (C)에서 이야기하는 것이다.
▶ 순서: 주어진 글 ➝ (A) ➝ (C)
(C) 뒤: 사람들이 Pierre의 집에서 에펠탑까지의 거리가 에펠탑에서 Pierre의 집까지의 거리보다 더 짧다고 판단한 것을 (B)에서 '이 비대칭'이라고 가리킨 것이다.
▶ (C) 뒤에 (B)가 와야 함 (순서: 주어진 글 ➝ (A) ➝ (C) ➝ (B))

2nd 글이 한눈에 들어오도록 정리하여 정답을 확인한다.

주어진 글: 랜드마크와 같은 공간 기준점은 그 자체뿐 아니라 주변 지역까지 규정함으로써 자기 자신보다 더 크다.
➝ **(A):** 연구원은 학생들에게 어떤 장소에서 랜드마크까지, 어떤 장소에서 평범한 건물까지의 거리를 추정하라고 요청한다.
➝ **(C):** 평범한 장소(Pierre의 집)에서 랜드마크(에펠탑)까지의 거리가 랜드마크(에펠탑)에서 평범한 장소(Pierre의 집)까지의 거리보다 더 짧다고 판단된다.
➝ **(B):** 거리 추정에 관한 이 비대칭은 유클리드 거리 법칙에 위배된다.
▶ 주어진 글 다음에 이어질 글의 순서는 (A) ➝ (C) ➝ (B)이므로 정답은 ①임

* 글의 흐름

도입	랜드마크는 그 자체이기도 하지만 주변 지역을 규정하기 때문에 공간 기준점은 자기 자신보다 더 큼
실험 과정	연구원들은 학생들에게 캠퍼스의 어떤 장소에서 랜드마크까지, 어떤 장소에서 평범한 건물까지의 거리를 추정하라고 요청함
실험 결과	평범한 장소에서 랜드마크까지의 거리가 랜드마크에서 평범한 장소까지의 거리보다 더 짧다고 추정됨
결론	유클리드 거리 법칙에 위배되는 거리 추정에 관한 비대칭은 거리에 관한 추정이 반드시 일관성이 있는 것은 아니라는 것을 보여줌

A firm is deciding / whether to invest / in shipbuilding. //
한 회사가 결정하고 있다 / 투자할지를 / 조선업에 // 문장에서 주로 목적어 역할을 하는 「의문사+to부정사」

If it can produce / at sufficiently large scale, / it knows / the venture will be profitable. //
앞에 명사절 접속사 that이 생략됨
만약 그것이 생산할 수 있다면 / 충분히 대규모로 / 그것은 알고 있다 / 모험이 수익성이 있으리라는 것을 //

단서1 두 가지 결과 중 하나 선행사 관계부사 where를 대신하는 「전치사+관계대명사」
(A) There is a "good" outcome, / in which both types of investments are made, / and both the shipyard and the steelmakers / end up profitable and happy. //
'좋은' 결과가 있는데 / 그 결과 내에서는 두 가지 투자 형태가 모두 이루어지고 / 조선소와 제강업자 모두 / 결국 이득을 얻고 만족하게 된다 //

Equilibrium is reached. //
균형이 이루어진다 //
선행사 관계부사 where를 대신하는 「전치사+관계대명사」
Then there is a "bad" outcome, / in which neither type of investment is made. //
그다음에 '나쁜' 결과가 있는데 / 그 결과 내에서는 어떤 투자 형태도 이루어지지 않는다 //

This second outcome also is an equilibrium / because the decisions / not to invest / reinforce each other. //
형용사적 용법(the decisions 수식)
이 두 번째 결과 또한 균형이 이루어진 것인데 / 왜냐하면 결정 / 투자하지 않겠다는 / 서로를 강화하기 때문이다 //

(B) Assume / that shipyards are the only potential customers / of steel. //
가정하라 / 조선소가 유일한 잠재적 소비자라고 / 강철의 //
형용사적 용법(a shipyard 수식)
Steel producers figure / they'll make money / if there's a shipyard / to buy their steel, / but not otherwise. // **단서2** 잠재적 강철 투자자들의 생각
강철 생산자들은 생각한다 / 자신이 돈을 벌 것이고 / 조선소가 있으면 / 자신의 강철을 구매할 / 그렇지 않으면 돈을 벌지 못하리라고 //
= they'll not make money if there's not a shipyard

Now we have two possible outcomes / — what economists call "multiple equilibria." //
이제 우리는 가능한 두 가지 결과를 갖는다 / 경제학자들이 '복수 균형'이라고 부르는 것 //

(C) But one key input / is low-cost steel, / and it must be produced nearby. //
조동사가 포함된 수동태(「조동사+be p.p.」)
하지만 한 가지 핵심 투입 요소는 / 저가의 강철이고 / 그것은 근처에서 생산되어야 한다 //

The company's decision / boils down to this: / if there is a steel factory close by, / invest in shipbuilding; / otherwise, don't invest. // **단서3** 조선업에 대한 투자를 고민하는 한 회사의 결정
= if there is not a steel factory close by
그 회사의 결정은 / 결국 다음과 같이 된다 / 만약 근처에 강철 공장이 있다면 / 조선업에 투자하고 / 그렇지 않으면 투자하지 마라 //

Now consider / the thinking of potential steel investors / in the region. //
이제 고려해 보라 / 잠재적 강철 투자자들의 생각을 / 그 지역에 있는 //

- firm ⓝ 회사 · invest ⓥ 투자하다 · shipbuilding ⓝ 조선(업)
- sufficiently ⓐⓓ 충분히 · scale ⓝ 규모 · venture ⓝ (사업상의) 모험
- profitable ⓐ 수익성이 있는 · outcome ⓝ 결과
- investment ⓝ 투자 · shipyard ⓝ 조선소
- steelmaker ⓝ 제강업자 · end up 결국 ~이 되다
- equilibrium ⓝ 균형, 평형 (pl. equilibria) · reach ⓥ ~에 이르다
- reinforce ⓥ 강화하다 · assume ⓥ 가정하다
- potential ⓐ 잠재적인 · steel ⓝ 강철
- figure ⓥ (~일 거라고) 생각하다 · otherwise ⓐⓓ 그렇지 않으면
- economist ⓝ 경제학자 · key ⓐ 핵심적인
- input ⓝ 투입 · boil down to 결국 ~이 되다 · factory ⓝ 공장
- close ⓐⓓ 가까이 · investor ⓝ 투자자 · region ⓝ 지역

한 회사가 조선업에 투자할지를 결정하고 있다. 만약 충분히 대규모로 생산할 수 있다면, 그것은 그 모험이 수익성이 있으리라는 것을 알고 있다. (C) 하지만 한 가지 핵심 투입 요소는 저가의 강철이고, 그것은 근처에서 생산되어야 한다.

M

그 회사의 결정은 결국 다음과 같이 된다. 만약 근처에 강철 공장이 있다면, 조선업에 투자하고, 그렇지 않으면 투자하지 마라. 이제 그 지역에 있는 잠재적 강철 투자자들의 생각을 고려해 보라. (B) 조선소가 유일한 잠재적 강철 소비자라고 가정하라. 강철 생산자들은 자신의 강철을 구매할 조선소가 있으면 자신이 돈을 벌 것이고, 그렇지 않으면 돈을 벌지 못하리라고 생각한다. 이제 우리는 경제학자들이 '복수 균형'이라고 부르는 것이 가능한 두 가지 결과를 갖는다. (A) '좋은' 결과가 있는데, 그 결과 내에서는 두 가지 투자 형태가 모두 이루어지고, 조선소와 제강업자 모두 결국 이득을 얻고 만족하게 된다. 균형이 이루어진다. 그다음에 '나쁜' 결과가 있는데, 그 결과 내에서는 어떤 투자 형태도 이루어지지 않는다. 이 두 번째 결과 또한 균형이 이루어진 것인데, 왜냐하면 투자하지 않겠다는 결정이 서로를 강화하기 때문이다.

주어진 글 다음에 이어질 글의 순서로 가장 적절한 것을 고르시오. [3점]

① (A) — (C) — (B) — 두 가지 결과가 발생한다는 (B)가 각각의 결과를 구체적으로 설명하는 (A)보다 앞에 있어야 함
② (B) — (A) — (C) — 주어진 글에는 강철 투자자에 대한 언급이 없음
③ (B) — (C) — (A)
④ (C) — (A) — (B) — 조선업 투자와 강철 투자자의 생각을 모두 설명한 후에 그로 인한 결과가 이어져야 함
⑤ (C) — (B) — (A) — 근처에 강철 공장이 있어야 조선업에 투자함–강철을 구입할 조선소가 있어야 강철에 투자함–조선업 투자와 강철 투자가 둘 다 이뤄지든지 둘 다 이뤄지지 않든지 하는 두 가지 결과가 생김

| 문제 풀이 순서 | [정답률 59%]

1st 각 문단의 내용을 파악하고, 글의 논리적인 순서를 추론한다.

> **주어진 글:** 한 회사가 조선업에 투자할지를 결정하고 있다. 만약 충분히 대규모로 생산할 수 있다면, 그것은 그 모험이 수익성이 있으리라는 것을 알고 있다. (단서)

⇒ **주어진 글 뒤:** 조선업 투자에 있어서 고려해야 할 요소와 관련된 내용이 이어질 것이다. (발상)

> **(A):** '좋은' 결과가 있는데, 그 결과 내에서는 두 가지 투자 형태가 모두 이루어지고, 조선소와 제강업자 모두 결국 이득을 얻고 만족하게 된다. (단서1) 균형이 이루어진다. 그다음에 '나쁜' 결과가 있는데, 그 결과 내에서는 어떤 투자 형태도 이루어지지 않는다. 이 두 번째 결과 또한 균형이 이루어진 것인데, 왜냐하면 투자하지 않겠다는 결정이 서로를 강화하기 때문이다.

⇒ **(A) 앞:** 두 가지 투자 형태가 이루어지는지, 그리고 균형이 이루어지는지에 따라 '좋은' 결과와 '나쁜' 결과로 나뉜다는 내용으로, 이와 관련된 언급이 앞에 먼저 나와야 한다.
▶ (A) 앞에 주어진 글이 올 수 없음
(A) 뒤: 어떤 것의 결과에 대해 언급하고 있으므로 글을 마무리하는 문단일 것이다.
▶ (A)가 마지막에 올 확률이 높음

> **(B):** 조선소가 유일한 잠재적 강철 소비자라고 가정하라. 강철 생산자들은 자신의 강철을 구매할 조선소가 있으면 자신이 돈을 벌 것이고, 그렇지 않으면 돈을 벌지 못하리라고 생각한다. (단서2) 이제 우리는 경제학자들이 '복수 균형'이라고 부르는 것이 가능한 두 가지 결과를 갖는다.

⇒ **(B) 앞:** 강철 생산자들의 결정에 관한 내용으로, 강철에 대한 투자와 관련된 내용이 나와야 한다.
▶ (B) 앞에 주어진 글이 올 수 없음
(B) 뒤: 복수 균형의 두 가지 결과에 관한 내용이 (A)에 나온다.
▶ (B) 뒤에 (A)가 와야 함 (순서: (B) → (A))

> **(C):** 하지만 한 가지 핵심 투입 요소는 저가의 강철이고, 그것은 근처에서 생산되어야 한다. 그 회사의 결정은 결국 다음과 같이 된다. 만약 근처에 강철 공장이 있다면, 조선업에 투자하고, 그렇지 않으면 투자하지 마라. (단서3) 이제 그 지역에 있는 잠재적 강철 투자자들의 생각을 고려해 보라.

⇒ **(C) 앞:** 조선업에 투자하려는 회사의 결정에 관하여 언급하므로, 주어진 글 다음에 이어져야 한다.
▶ (C) 앞에 주어진 글이 와야 함 (순서: 주어진 글 → (C))
(C) 뒤: 강철 투자자들의 생각을 고려해 보라고 했는데, 강철 생산자들의 결정에 관한 내용이 (B)에 나온다.
▶ (C) 뒤에 (B)가 와야 함 (순서: 주어진 글 → (C) → (B) → (A))

2nd 글이 한눈에 들어오도록 정리하여 정답을 확인한다.

주어진 글: 조선업에 투자하려는 회사는 대규모로 생산할 경우, 수익성이 있다.
→ **(C):** 강철 공장이 주변에 있다면 투자하고, 그렇지 않으면 투자하지 마라.
→ **(B):** 강철 생산자들은 소비자인 조선소가 근처에 있으면 돈을 벌고, 그렇지 않으면 돈을 벌지 못한다고 생각한다. 여기서 '복수 균형'인 두 가지 결과를 갖는다.
→ **(A):** 좋은 결과는 두 가지 투자가 모두 이루어지는 것이고 나쁜 결과는 어떤 투자도 이루어지지 않는 것이다.
▶ 주어진 글 다음에 이어질 글의 순서는 (C) → (B) → (A)이므로 정답은 ⑤임

＊글의 흐름

조건 ①	한 회사가 조선업에 투자할지 결정하고 있음: 근처에 강철 공장이 있는 경우에만 회사는 조선업에 투자함
조건 ②	강철 생산자: 잠재적 소비자인 조선소가 있어야만 돈을 벌 것임
결론	'복수 균형'이라고 부르는 것이 가능한 두 가지 결과가 생김
부연	두 가지 투자 형태 모두 이루어지는 '좋은' 결과에서는 조선소와 제강업자 모두 이득을 얻고 만족하는 균형
	어떤 투자도 이루어지지 않는 '나쁜' 결과에서는 투자하지 않겠다는 결정이 서로를 강화하여 균형을 이룸

M 18 정답 ⑤ ＊기업이 친환경 제품에 투자하지 않는 이유

Green products involve, / in many cases, / higher ingredient costs / than those of mainstream products. // (단서1) 친환경 제품의 부정적인 면을 설명함
친환경 제품은 수반한다 / 많은 경우 / 더 높은 원료비를 / 주류 제품의 그것보다 //

(단서2) 성공적인 주류 제품을 보유한 기업들은 이미 알려지고 수익성 있는 다량의 제품에 투자하고자 함
(A) They'd rather put money and time / into known, profitable, high-volume products / that serve populous customer segments /
그들은 돈과 시간을 투자하고 싶어 한다 / 이미 알려지고 수익성이 있는 다량의 제품에 / 다수의 고객 계층의 요구를 충족하는 / 'rather ~ than …,'으로 연결된 전치사구

than into risky, less-profitable, low-volume products / that may serve current noncustomers. //
위험하고 수익성이 더 낮은 소량의 제품보다는 / 현재 고객이 아닌 사람들의 요구를 충족할 수 있는 //

Given that choice, / these companies may choose to leave / the green segment of the market / to small niche competitors. //
prep ~을 고려할 때
그런 선택을 고려하면 / 이들 기업은 남겨두는 선택을 할 수 있다 / 시장의 친환경 부문을 / 소규모 틈새 경쟁업체들에게 // (단서3) 친환경 제품의 부정적인 면에 대한 설명이 완료됨

(B) Even if the green product succeeds, / it may cannibalize / the company's higher-profit mainstream offerings. //
부사절 접속사(양보)
친환경 제품이 성공하더라도 / 그것은 잡아먹을 수 있다 / 기업의 고수익 주류 제품을 //

Given such downsides, / companies / serving mainstream consumers / with successful mainstream products / face / what seems like an obvious investment decision. //
주어 동사 목적어 (관계대명사절)
이런 부정적인 면들을 고려하면 / 기업들은 / 주류 소비자의 요구를 충족하는 / 성공적인 주류 제품으로 / 직면한다 / 뻔한 투자 결정처럼 보이는 것에 / (단서4) 친환경 제품의 또다른 부정적인 면을 설명함

(C) Furthermore, / the restrictive ingredient lists and design criteria / that are typical of such products / 주어(명사구)
게다가 / 제한 성분 목록과 디자인 기준이 / 그런 제품에서 일반적인 /

may make green products inferior / to mainstream products /
_{동사} _{목적어} _{목적격 보어}
on core performance dimensions / (e.g., less effective cleansers). //
친환경 제품을 더 열등하게 만들 수 있다 / 주류 제품보다 / 핵심 성능 측면에서 / (예를 들어,
덜 효과적인 세척제) //

In turn, / the higher costs and lower performance / of some
products /
결과적으로 / 더 높은 비용과 더 낮은 성능은 / 일부 제품의 /

attract only a small portion of the customer base, / leading to
_{= and then they lead}
lower economies of scale / in procurement, manufacturing, and
distribution. //
고객층의 오직 적은 부분만 유인해서 / 더 낮은 규모의 경제를 초래한다 / 조달, 제조, 유통에서 //

- -

- ingredient ⓝ 성분   - mainstream ⓐ 주류의
- profitable ⓐ 수익성이 있는   - volume ⓝ (~의) 양
- populous ⓐ 다수의   - given that ~을 고려하면
- niche ⓝ (시장의) 틈새   - offering ⓝ 제품
- downside ⓝ 부정적인 면   - obvious ⓐ 뻔한
- restrictive ⓐ 제한하는   - criterion ⓝ 기준((pl. criteria))
- typical ⓐ 일반적인   - inferior ⓐ (~보다) 열등한   - core ⓐ 핵심적인
- dimension ⓝ 차원   - economies of scale 규모의 경제
- distribution ⓝ 유통

많은 경우, 친환경 제품은 주류 제품의 원료비보다 더 높은 원료비를 수반한다.
(C) 게다가 그런 제품에서 일반적인 제한 성분 목록과 디자인 기준이 친환경 제
품을 주류 제품보다 핵심 성능 측면에서 더 열등하게 만들 수 있다(예를 들어,
덜 효과적인 세척제). 결과적으로, 일부 제품의 더 높은 비용과 더 낮은 성능은
고객층의 오직 적은 부분만 유인해서, 조달, 제조, 유통에서 더 낮은 규모의 경
제를 초래한다. (B) 친환경 제품이 성공하더라도 기업의 고수익 주류 제품을 잡
아먹을 수 있다. 이런 부정적인 면들을 고려하면, 성공적인 주류 제품으로 주류
소비자의 요구를 충족하는 기업들은 뻔한 투자 결정처럼 보이는 것에 직면한다.
(A) 그들은 현재 고객이 아닌 사람들의 요구를 충족할 수 있는 위험하고 수익성
이 더 낮은 소량의 제품보다는, 다수의 고객 계층의 요구를 충족하는, 이미 알
려지고 수익성이 있는 다량의 제품에 돈과 시간을 투자하고 싶어 한다. 그런 선
택을 고려하면, 이들 기업은 소규모 틈새 경쟁업체들에게 시장의 친환경 부문을
남겨두는 선택을 할 수 있다.

주어진 글 다음에 이어질 글의 순서로 가장 적절한 것을 고르시오.

① (A) — (C) — (B) (A)의 They가 가리킬 만한 것이 주어진 글에 없음

② (B) — (A) — (C) ⎤
③ (B) — (C) — (A) ⎦ (B)는 친환경 제품의 부정적인 면이 모두 설명된 이후에 와야 함

④ (C) — (A) — (B) (A)의 They가 가리키는 것은 (B)에 등장한 companies임

⑤ (C) — (B) — (A)
친환경 제품은 주류 제품보다 원료비가 더 높음 – 친환경 제품은 주류 제품보다 핵심 성능 측면에서
열등함 – 이런 단점을 고려하면 성공적인 주류 제품으로 주류 고객을 만족시키는 기업들은 돈과 시간을
기존의 주류 제품에 투자하고자 함 – 이들 기업은 소규모 경쟁업체들에게 시장의 친환경 부문을 남겨둠

| 문제 풀이 순서 | [정답률 60%]

1st 각 문단의 내용을 파악하고, 글의 논리적인 순서를 추론한다.

┌───┐
│ **주어진 글:** 많은 경우, 친환경 제품은 주류 제품의 원료비보다 더 높은 │
│ 원료비를 수반한다. **단서1** │
└───┘

➡ **주어진 글 뒤:** 주류 제품보다 더 높은 원료비를 수반한다는 친환경 제품의 부정적인
면과 관련된 내용이 이어질 것이다.

┌───┐
│ **(A): 그들(They)**은 현재 고객이 아닌 사람들의 요구를 충족할 수 있는 │
│ 위험하고 수익성이 더 낮은 소량의 제품보다는, 다수의 고객 계층의 │
│ 요구를 충족하는, 이미 알려지고 수익성이 있는 다량의 제품에 돈과 │
│ 시간을 투자하고 싶어 한다. **단서2** 그런 선택을 고려하면, 이들 기업은 │
│ 소규모 틈새 경쟁업체들에게 시장의 친환경 부문을 남겨두는 선택을 할 │
│ 수 있다. │
└───┘

➡ **(A) 앞:** **1** They로 가리키는 사람들이 앞에 나왔을 것이다.

2 (A)에서는 They가 다수 고객의 요구를 충족하는 제품에 투자하고 싶어 한다고
설명하므로 (A) 앞에는 이들 기업이 그렇게 결정한 원인이 나와야 한다.

▶ 주어진 글에 기업의 결정에 관한 내용이 없으므로 (A) 앞에 주어진 글이 올 수
없음

(A) 뒤: 앞에서 언급한 기업들이 소규모 경쟁업체들에게 친환경 부문을 남겨둘 수
있다고 하며 문단의 내용이 마무리된다.

▶ (A)가 마지막에 올 확률이 높음

┌───┐
│ **(B):** 친환경 제품이 성공하더라도 기업의 고수익 주류 제품을 잡아먹을 │
│ 수 있다. 이런 부정적인 면들(such downsides)을 고려하면, │
│ 성공적인 주류 제품으로 주류 소비자의 요구를 충족하는 기업들은 뻔한 │
│ 투자 결정처럼 보이는 것에 직면한다. **단서3** │
└───┘

➡ **(B) 앞:** '이런 부정적인 면들'을 통해, 주어진 글 외에도 친환경 제품의 부정적인
면이 더 있음을 알 수 있다. 따라서 주어진 글 외에 친환경 제품의 부정적인 면이
추가로 언급된 문단이 이어져야 한다.

▶ (B) 앞에 주어진 글이 올 수 없음

(B) 뒤: 주류 제품으로 주류 소비자의 요구를 충족하는 기업들의 투자 결정이
뻔하다고 했다. 이 기업들은 (A)에 언급되는 They이며 그들의 결정에 관한
세부사항이 (A)에 나온다.

▶ (B) 뒤에 (A)가 와야 함 (순서: (B) → (A))

┌───┐
│ **(C):** 게다가(Furthermore) 그런 제품에서 일반적인 제한 성분 │
│ 목록과 디자인 기준이 친환경 제품을 주류 제품보다 핵심 성능 │
│ 측면에서 더 열등하게 만들 수 있다(예를 들어, 덜 효과적인 세척제). │
│ **단서4** 결과적으로, 일부 제품의 더 높은 비용과 더 낮은 성능은 │
│ 고객층의 오직 적은 부분만 유인해서, 조달, 제조, 유통에서 더 낮은 │
│ 규모의 경제를 초래한다. │
└───┘

➡ **(C) 앞:** Furthermore는 부연 설명을 나타내는 연결어이므로 (C)보다 앞서 친환경
제품의 부정적인 면이 언급되어야 한다.

▶ (C) 앞에 주어진 글이 와야 함 (순서: 주어진 글 → (C))

(C) 뒤: In turn을 통해 친환경 제품의 부정적인 면에 관한 내용을 마무리한다.
이어서 친환경 제품의 두 가지 부정적인 면들을 언급하는 (B)가 뒤에 나와야 한다.

▶ (C) 뒤에 (B)가 와야 함 (순서: 주어진 글 → (C) → (B) → (A))

2nd 글이 한눈에 들어오도록 정리하여 정답을 확인한다.

주어진 글: 친환경 제품은 주류 제품보다 높은 원료비를 수반한다.

→ **(C):** 친환경 제품은 주류 제품보다 성능 측면에서 열등할 수 있다.

→ **(B):** 이러한 부정적인 면들을 고려하면 주류 제품을 생산하는 기업들의 결정은
뻔하다.

→ **(A):** 그런 기업들은 수익성이 높은 제품에 투자할 것이며 친환경 제품은 소규모
경쟁업체들에게 남겨질 것이다.

▶ 주어진 글 다음에 이어질 글의 순서는 (C) → (B) → (A)이므로 정답은 ⑤임

* 글의 흐름

원인 ①	친환경 제품은 주류 제품보다 원료비가 더 많이 들고 핵심 성능 측면에서 열등할 수 있음
원인 ②	친환경 제품이 성공하더라도 주류 제품의 수익성을 잡아먹을 수 있음
결과	기업들은 위험하고 수익성이 낮은 친환경 제품보다 이미 알려지고 수익성이 높은 주류 제품에 투자하고자 함
부연	기업들은 소규모 틈새 기업에 시장의 친환경 부문을 남겨두는 선택을 할 수 있음

The fossil record provides / evidence of evolution. //
화석 기록은 제공한다 / 진화의 증거를 //
　　　　앞에 목적격 관계대명사가 생략됨
The story / the fossils tell / is one of change. //
이야기는 / 화석이 전하는 / 변화에 관한 것이다 //
　　선행사　　　　　　　　주격 관계대명사
Creatures existed / in the past / that are no longer with us. //
생물들이 존재했다 / 과거에는 / 더는 우리와 함께하지 않는 //

Sequential changes are found / in many fossils / showing
the change of certain features / over time / from a common
ancestor, / as in the case of the horse. //
일련의 변화가 발견된다 / 많은 화석에서 / 특정 특징의 변화를 보여주는 / 시간이 지남에 따라
/ 공통의 조상으로부터 / 말의 경우에서처럼 //
　　　　　　　　　　　　　　　　　　문장의 시제보다 앞선 때를 나타내는
　　　　　　　　　　　　　　　　　　완료형 to부정사

(A) If multicelled organisms were indeed found / to have
evolved / before single-celled organisms, / then the theory of
evolution would be rejected. // 단서1 (B)의 the opposite가
　　　　　　　　　　　　　　　　　　의미하는 바를 구체적으로 설명함
다세포 생물이 정말로 밝혀진다면 / 진화한 것으로 / 단세포 생물 이전에 / 진화론은 거부될
것이다 //

A good scientific theory always allows / for the possibility of
rejection. //
좋은 과학 이론은 항상 허용한다 / 거부의 가능성을 //

The fact / that we have not found such a case / in countless
주어　　동격절 접속사
examinations / of the fossil record / strengthens the case for
　　　　　　　　　　　　　　　　　　동사
evolutionary theory. //
사실은 / 우리가 그러한 경우를 발견하지 못했다는 / 수많은 조사에서 / 화석 기록에 대한 /
진화론을 위한 논거를 강화한다 // 단서2 단세포 생물이 다세포 생물 이전에
　　　　　　　　　　　　　　　　진화했다는 진화론의 예측을 가리킴
(B) The fossil record supports this prediction / — multicelled
organisms are found / in layers of earth / millions of years after
the first appearance / of single-celled organisms. //
화석 기록은 이 예측을 뒷받침한다 / 다세포 생물은 발견된다 / 지구 지층에서 / 최초 출현
수백만 년 후의 / 단세포 생물의 //

Note / that the possibility always remains / that the opposite
목적어절 접속사　　　　　　　　　　　　동격절 접속사
could be found. //
주목하라 / 가능성은 항상 남아 있다는 점에 / 그 반대가 발견될 단서3 주어진 글에서 화석이
　　　　　　　　　　　　　　　　　　진화의 증거를 제공한다고 했음
(C) Apart from demonstrating / that evolution did occur, / the
fossil record also provides / tests of the predictions / made from
　　　　　　　　　　　　　　　앞에 주격 관계대명사와 be동사가 생략됨
evolutionary theory. //
증명하는 것 외에도 / 진화가 정말 일어났다는 것을 / 화석 기록은 또한 제공한다 / 예측에
대한 테스트를 / 진화론에서 만들어진 단서4 단세포 생물, 다세포 생물의
　　　　　　　　　　　　　　　　진화에 대한 예시가 시작됨
For example, / the theory predicts / that single-celled organisms
evolved / before multicelled organisms. //
예를 들어 / 그 이론은 예측한다 / 단세포 생물이 진화했다고 / 다세포 생물 이전에 //

• evidence ⓝ 증거, 흔적　　• creature ⓝ 생물, 생명이 있는 존재
• sequential ⓐ 순차적인, 잇따라 일어나는　　• feature ⓝ 특색, 특징
• ancestor ⓝ 조상, 선조　　• organism ⓝ 유기체, 생물(체)
• evolve ⓥ 진화하다, 발달하다　　• reject ⓥ 거부[거절]하다
• countless ⓐ 셀 수 없이 많은　　• examination ⓝ 조사, 검토
• evolutionary ⓐ 진화의　　• prediction ⓝ 예측, 예견
• layer ⓝ 층, 겹　　• appearance ⓝ 출현, 나타남
• opposite ⓝ 반대(되는 것)　　• demonstrate ⓥ 입증하다, 보여주다

화석 기록은 진화의 증거를 제공한다. 화석이 전하는 이야기는 변화에 관한
것이다. 더는 우리와 함께하지 않는 생물들이 과거에는 존재했다. 말의
경우에서처럼 시간이 지남에 따라 공통의 조상으로부터 특정 특징의 변화를
보여주는 많은 화석에서 일련의 변화가 발견된다. (C) 진화가 정말 일어났다는
것을 증명하는 것 외에도, 화석 기록은 또한 진화론에서 만들어진 예측에 대한
테스트를 제공한다. 예를 들어, 진화론은 단세포 생물이 다세포 생물 이전에
진화했다고 예측한다. (B) 화석 기록은 이 예측을 뒷받침하는데, 다세포 생물은
단세포 생물이 최초로 출현한 수백만 년 후의 지구 지층에서 발견된다.

그 반대가 발견될 가능성은 항상 남아 있다는 점에 주목하라. (A) 다세포
생물이 단세포 생물보다 먼저 진화한 것으로 정말로 밝혀진다면, 진화론은
거부될 것이다. 좋은 과학 이론은 항상 거부의 가능성을 허용한다. 화석 기록에
대한 수많은 조사에서 그러한 경우를 발견하지 못했다는 사실은 진화론을 위한
논거를 강화한다.

주어진 글 다음에 이어질 글의 순서로 가장 적절한 것을 고르시오.

① (A) — (C) — (B) 다세포, 단세포 생물의 진화에 대한 내용은 (C)에서 시작됨

② (B) — (A) — (C)
　　　　　　　　　　(B)의 this prediction이 가리키는 것이 (C)에 있음
③ (B) — (C) — (A)

④ (C) — (A) — (B) (C)에서 설명한 진화론의 예측을 (B)에서 이어서 설명함

⑤ (C) — (B) — (A)
　　화석 기록은 진화의 증거를 제공함 – 화석 기록은 진화를 증명할 뿐 아니라 진화론의 예측을
　　테스트하기도 함 – 진화론은 단세포 생물이 다세포 생물 이전에 진화했다고 예측함 – 화석 기록
　　이 예측을 뒷받침하지만 그 반대가 발견될 가능성도 항상 있음 – 그 반대가 발견되면 진화론은
　　거부될 것임

| 문제 풀이 순서 | [정답률 55%]

1st 각 문단의 내용을 파악하고, 글의 논리적인 순서를 추론한다.

주어진 글: 화석 기록은 진화의 증거를 제공한다. 화석이 전하는
이야기는 변화에 관한 것이다. 더는 우리와 함께하지 않는 생물들이
과거에는 존재했다. 말의 경우에서처럼 시간이 지남에 따라 공통의
조상으로부터 특정 특징의 변화를 보여주는 많은 화석에서 일련의
변화가 발견된다.

➡ 주어진 글 뒤: 화석 기록은 진화의 증거를 제공하며 변화에 관한 이야기를 전한다고
했으므로 단서 생물의 진화와 관련된 내용이 이어질 것이다. 발상

(A): 다세포 생물이 단세포 생물보다 먼저 진화한 것으로 정말로
밝혀진다면, 진화론은 거부될 것이다. 단서1 좋은 과학 이론은 항상
거부의 가능성을 허용한다. 화석 기록에 대한 수많은 조사에서 그러한
경우를 발견하지 못했다는 사실은 진화론을 위한 논거를 강화한다.

➡ (A) 앞: 다세포 생물이 단세포 생물보다 먼저 진화한 것으로 밝혀진다는 가정을
언급하므로, 이와 관련된 내용이 앞에 먼저 나와야 한다.
▶ (A) 앞에 주어진 글이 올 수 없음
(A) 뒤: 화석 기록에 대한 수많은 조사에서 거부의 가능성을 발견하지 못했다는
사실이 진화론의 논거를 강화한다는 결론을 내리고 있다.
▶ (A)가 마지막에 올 확률이 높음

(B): 화석 기록은 이 예측(this prediction)을 뒷받침하는데, 다세포
생물은 단세포 생물이 최초로 출현한 수백만 년 후의 지구 지층에서
발견된다. 단서2 그 반대가 발견될 가능성은 항상 남아 있다는 점에
주목하라.

➡ (B) 앞: this prediction, 즉, 다세포 생물이 단세포 생물보다 나중의 지층에서
발견된다는 예측이 등장한다. 따라서 (B) 앞에는 단세포 생물이 다세포 생물 이전에
진화했다는 내용이 나와야 한다.
▶ (B) 앞에 주어진 글이 올 수 없음
(B) 뒤: 화석 기록이 밝히는 사실의 반대가 발견될 가능성이 항상 남아 있다고 했다.
다세포 생물이 단세포 생물보다 먼저 진화한다는 가정이 (A)에 나온다.
▶ (B) 뒤에 (A)가 와야 함 (순서: (B) → (A))

(C): 진화가 정말 일어났다는 것을 증명하는 것 외에도(Apart
from), 화석 기록은 또한 진화론에서 만들어진 예측에 대한 테스트를
제공한다. 단서3 예를 들어(For example), 진화론은 단세포 생물이
다세포 생물 이전에 진화했다고 예측한다. 단서4

➡ **(C) 앞:** 화석 기록이 진화를 증명하는 것 외에도 진화론의 예측에 대한 테스트를 제공한다는 내용으로, 화석 기록이 진화의 증거를 제공한다는 내용이 앞에 나와야 한다,
   ▶ (C) 앞에 주어진 글이 와야 함 (순서: 주어진 글 → (C))
   (C) 뒤: For example을 사용하여 '진화론은 단세포 생물이 다세포 생물보다 이전에 진화했다고 예측한다'라는 예시가 나오므로, (B)의 this prediction으로 이어지는 것이 자연스럽다.
   ▶ (C) 뒤에 (B)가 와야 함 (순서: 주어진 글 → (C) → (B) → (A))

2nd 글이 한눈에 들어오도록 정리하여 정답을 확인한다.

주어진 글: 화석 기록은 진화의 증거를 제공한다.
→ **(C):** 화석 기록은 진화론의 예측에 대한 테스트를 제공한다.
→ **(B):** 화석 기록이 진화론의 예측을 뒷받침하지만 반대의 가능성도 남아 있다.
→ **(A):** 진화론의 예측을 반증하면 진화론은 거부된다.
   ▶ 주어진 글 다음에 이어질 글의 순서는 (C) → (B) → (A)이므로 정답은 ⑤임

* 글의 흐름

도입	화석 기록은 진화의 증거를 제공할 뿐만 아니라 진화론의 예측에 대한 테스트도 제공함
부연	진화론은 단세포 생물이 다세포 생물 이전에 진화했다고 예측함
	화석 기록은 진화론의 이러한 예측을 뒷받침함
결론	하지만 그 반대가 발견될 가능성이 항상 남아 있고, 정말 발견된다면 진화론은 거부될 것임

Ⓜ 20 정답 ② *개인용 가정 도우미로서의 소셜 로봇

Recently, / a number of commercial ventures / have been launched / that offer social robots / as personal home assistants,
최근에 / 많은 상업적인 벤처 기업들이 / 진출해 왔는데 / 소셜 로봇을 제공하는 / 개인용 가정 도우미로 /
단서1 많은 기업들이 개인용 가정 도우미로 소셜 로봇을 제공함
perhaps eventually to rival / existing smart-home assistants. //
아마도 결국 경쟁할 것이다 / 기존의 스마트홈 도우미와 //

(A) They might be motorized / and can track the user / around the room, / giving the impression / of being aware of the people / in the environment. //
그것들은 동력화될 수 있으며 / 사용자를 추적할 수 있는데 / 실내에서 / 이는 인상을 준다 / 사람들을 감지한다는 / 환경 내의 //
단서2 뚜렷한 사회적 존재감을 갖고, 사회적 존재감이 소셜 로봇에게만 있는 기회를 제공함
Although personal robotic assistants provide services / similar to those of smart-home assistants, / their social presence offers an opportunity / that is unique to social robots. //
개인용 로봇 도우미는 서비스를 제공하긴 하지만 / 스마트홈 도우미의 그것과 비슷한 / 그들의 사회적 존재감은 기회를 제공한다 / 소셜 로봇에게만 특유한 //

(B) Personal robotic assistants are devices / that have no physical manipulation or locomotion capabilities. //
개인용 로봇 도우미는 장치이다 / 신체 조작이나 이동 능력이 없는 //
단서3 개인용 로봇 도우미에 대해 구체적으로 설명하기 시작함
Instead, / they have a distinct social presence / and have visual features / suggestive of their ability / to interact socially, / such as eyes, ears, or a mouth. //
대신에 / 그것들은 뚜렷한 사회적 존재감을 갖고 / 시각적 특징을 갖는다 / 그것들의 능력을 암시하는 / 사회적으로 상호 작용을 할 수 있는 / 눈, 귀 또는 입과 같은 //
단서4 사회적 존재감을 가진 소셜 로봇에게만 있는 기회의 예시

(C) For instance, / in addition to playing music, / a social personal assistant robot would express /
예를 들어 / 음악을 재생할 뿐만 아니라 / 소셜 개인용 도우미 로봇은 표현한다 /
its engagement with the music / so that users would feel / like they are listening to the music / together with the robot. //
그것의 음악과의 교감을 / 사용자가 느끼도록 / 그들이 그 음악을 듣는 것처럼 / 로봇과 함께 //

These robots can be used / as surveillance devices, / act as communicative intermediates, /
이들 로봇은 사용될 수 있거나 / 보안 감시 장치로 / 통신 매개체의 역할을 하거나 /
engage in richer games, / tell stories, / or be used / to provide encouragement or incentives. //
더 다채로운 게임에 참여하거나 / 이야기를 들려주거나 / 사용될 수 있다 / 격려나 동기를 제공하는 데 //

- commercial ⓐ 상업적인 • launch ⓥ 시작하다, 출시하다
- assistant ⓝ 조수, 도우미 • eventually ⓐⓓ 결국
- motorize ⓥ 동력화하다 • device ⓝ 장치
- manipulation ⓝ 조작, 조종 • capability ⓝ 능력
- distinct ⓐ 뚜렷한 • suggestive of ~을 암시하는
- engagement ⓝ 참여, 교감 • intermediate ⓝ 매개[중재]자
- rich ⓐ 다채로운 • encouragement ⓝ 격려
- incentive ⓝ 동기, 장려[우대]책

최근에, 소셜 로봇을 개인용 가정 도우미로 제공하는 많은 상업적인 벤처 기업들이 진출해 왔는데, 아마도 결국 기존의 스마트홈 도우미와 경쟁할 것이다. (B) 개인용 로봇 도우미는 신체 조작이나 이동 능력이 없는 장치이다. 대신에, 그것들에게는 뚜렷한 사회적 존재감이 있고 눈, 귀 또는 입과 같은 사회적 상호 작용을 할 수 있는 능력을 암시하는 시각적 특징을 가지고 있다. (A) 그것들은 동력화될 수 있으며 실내에서 사용자를 추적할 수 있는데, 환경 내의 사람들을 감지한다는 인상을 준다. 개인용 로봇 도우미는 스마트홈 도우미와 비슷한 서비스를 제공하긴 하지만, 그들의 사회적 존재감은 소셜 로봇에게만 특유한 기회를 제공한다. (C) 예를 들어, 소셜 개인용 도우미 로봇은 음악을 재생할 뿐만 아니라 사용자가 로봇과 함께 그 음악을 듣는 것처럼 느끼도록 음악과의 교감을 표현한다. 이들 로봇은 보안 감시 장치로 사용될 수 있거나, 통신 매개체의 역할을 하거나, 더 다채로운 게임에 참여하거나, 이야기를 들려주거나, 격려나 동기를 제공하는 데 사용될 수 있다.

주어진 글 다음에 이어질 글의 순서로 가장 적절한 것을 고르시오. [3점]

① (A) — (C) — (B) 그들에게 사회적 존재감이 있다는 언급이 (A) 앞에 있어야 함
② (B) — (A) — (C)
③ (B) — (C) — (A) (A)의 an opportunity에 대한 예시가 (C)에 등장함
④ (C) — (A) — (B) (C)에 등장한 예시가 기존의 스마트홈 도우미와 개인용 로봇 도우미의 경쟁을 보여주는 것이 아님
⑤ (C) — (B) — (A)
최근 많은 기업들이 개인용 가정 도우미로 소셜 로봇을 제공함 - 개인용 로봇 도우미는 뚜렷한 사회적 존재감을 가짐 - 그들의 사회적 존재감이 소셜 로봇에게만 있는 기회를 제공함 - 예를 들어, 소셜 개인용 도우미 로봇은 사용자가 로봇과 함께 음악을 듣는 것처럼 느끼게 하는 음악과의 교감이 있음

| **문제 풀이 순서** | [정답률 56%]

1st 각 문단의 내용을 파악하고, 글의 논리적인 순서를 추론한다.

주어진 글: 최근에, 소셜 로봇을 개인용 가정 도우미로 제공하는 많은 상업적인 벤처 기업들이 진출해 왔는데, 아마도 결국 기존의 스마트홈 도우미와 경쟁할 것이다. **단서1**

➡ **주어진 글 뒤:** 소셜 로봇과 스마트홈 도우미 사이의 경쟁에 관한 내용이 이어질 것이다.

(A): 그것들(They)은 동력화될 수 있으며 실내에서 사용자를 추적할 수 있는데, 환경 내의 사람들을 감지한다는 인상을 준다. 개인용 로봇 도우미는 스마트홈 도우미와 비슷한 서비스를 제공하긴 하지만, 그들의 사회적 존재감은 소셜 로봇에게만 특유한 기회를 제공한다. **단서2**

➡ **(A) 앞:** 동력화되고 실내에서 사용자를 추적할 수 있는 무언가가 They로 앞에 언급되었을 것이다.
   ▶ 주어진 글에 이 내용이 없으므로 (A) 앞에 주어진 글이 올 수 없음
   (A) 뒤: 소셜 로봇에게만 제공되는 특유한 기회에 관한 내용이 이어질 것이다.

정답 및 해설 **303**

(B): 개인용 로봇 도우미는 신체 조작이나 이동 능력이 없는 장치이다. **단서3** 대신에, 그것들에게는 뚜렷한 사회적 존재감이 있고 눈, 귀 또는 입과 같은 사회적 상호 작용을 할 수 있는 능력을 암시하는 시각적 특징을 가지고 있다.

→ **(B) 앞:** 개인용 로봇 도우미에 대해 구체적으로 설명하기 시작하는 내용으로, 개인용 가정 도우미로서 소셜 로봇은 주어진 글에서 처음 언급된다.
  ▶ (B) 앞에 주어진 글이 와야 함
  (B) 뒤: 개인용 로봇 도우미를 They로 지칭하며 동력화되고 실내에서 사용자를 추적할 수 있다는 내용이 (A)에 나온다.
  ▶ (B) 뒤에 (A)가 와야 함 (순서: (B) → (A))

(C): 예를 들어(For instance), 소셜 개인용 도우미 로봇은 음악을 재생할 뿐만 아니라 사용자가 로봇과 함께 그 음악을 듣는 것처럼 느끼도록 음악과의 교감을 표현한다. **단서4** 이들 로봇은 보안 감시 장치로 사용될 수 있거나, 통신 매개체의 역할을 하거나, 더 다채로운 게임에 참여하거나, 이야기를 들려주거나, 격려나 동기를 제공하는 데 사용될 수 있다.

→ **(C) 앞:** For instance는 예시를 나타내는 연결어로, (A)의 마지막에 언급된 사회적 존재감의 예시로서 로봇이 음악과의 교감을 표현하는 것을 제시했다.
  ▶ (C) 앞에 (A)가 와야 함 (순서: 주어진 글 → (B) → (A) → (C))

2nd 글이 한눈에 들어오도록 정리하여 정답을 확인한다.

주어진 글: 최근 개인용 가정 도우미로 많이 제공되는 소셜 로봇이 기존의 스마트홈 도우미와 경쟁할 것이다.
→ **(B):** 개인용 로봇 도우미는 움직일 수 없지만 사회적 존재감을 갖는다.
→ **(A):** 개인용 로봇 도우미의 사회적 존재감은 소셜 로봇에게 특유의 기회를 제공한다.
→ **(C):** 소셜 로봇은 사용자와 교감을 표현하는 등 여러 목적으로 활용될 수 있다.
▶ 주어진 글 다음에 이어질 글의 순서는 (B) → (A) → (C)이므로 정답은 **②**임

＊ 글의 흐름

도입	최근 많은 벤처 기업들이 소셜 로봇을 개인용 가정 도우미로 제공함
부연	개인용 로봇 도우미는 신체 조작이나 이동 능력은 없지만, 환경 내에서 사람들을 감지한다는 인상을 주며 뚜렷한 사회적 존재감을 가짐
전개	사회적 존재감은 소셜 로봇만 갖는 기회를 제공함
예시	음악을 재생할 뿐만 아니라 사용자가 로봇과 함께 음악을 듣는 것처럼 느끼도록 교감을 표현함

━━━━━ 배경 지식 ━━━━━

＊ 로봇 3원칙(three laws of robotics)

1942년 Isaac Asimov의 공상 과학 소설 〈Runaround〉에서 처음 언급된 로봇의 안전 준칙으로, 로봇이 따라야 할 세 가지 원칙은 다음과 같다.

첫째, 로봇은 인간에게 해를 가하거나, 혹은 행동하지 않음으로써 인간에게 해를 끼치지 않는다. 둘째, 로봇은 첫 번째 원칙에 위배되지 않는 한 인간이 내리는 명령에 복종해야 한다. 셋째, 로봇은 첫 번째와 두 번째 원칙을 위배하지 않는 선에서 로봇 자신의 존재를 보호해야 한다. 1985년 아시모프는 위 원칙에 인류 집단 안전을 위한 0번째 법칙으로 '로봇은 인류에게 해를 가하거나, 해를 끼치는 행동을 하지 않음으로써 인류에게 해를 끼치지 않는다'를 추가하였다.

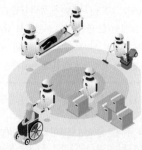

M 21 정답 ② ＊가격 인상의 효과

According to the market response model, / it is increasing prices / that drive providers to search / for new sources, / innovators to substitute, / consumers to conserve, / and alternatives to emerge. //
it is ~ that 강조 구문
목적어와 목적격 보어 ② drive의 목적격 보어 ①
목적어와 목적격 보어 ④ 목적어와 목적격 보어 ③
시장 반응 모형에 따르면 / 바로 가격의 인상이 / 공급자가 찾게 하고 / 새로운 공급원을 / 혁신가가 대용하게 하고 / 소비자가 아껴 쓰게 하고 / 대안이 생기게 한다 //

(A) Many examples / of such "green taxes" / exist. //
복수 주어   복수 동사(완전자동사)
많은 예가 / 그러한 '환경세'의 / 존재한다 //

Facing / landfill costs, labor expenses, / and related costs / in the provision of garbage disposal, / for example, / **단서1** 폐기물 처리 서비스에 세금을 부과한 예시가 시작됨
직면하여 / 쓰레기 매립 비용, 인건비에 / 그리고 관련된 비용에 / 쓰레기 처리의 제공에 / 예를 들어
'~을 처리하다'
some cities have required households / to dispose of all waste / in special trash bags, / purchased by consumers themselves, / and often costing a dollar or more / each. //
special trash bags를 수식하는 과거분사구와 현재분사구
일부 도시는 가정에 요구해 왔다 / 모든 폐기물을 처리하라고 / 특별 쓰레기봉투에 담아 / 소비자에 의해 직접 구입된 / 흔히 1달러 또는 그 이상씩 드는 / 각각 **단서2** 주어진 글에서 언급한 가격 인상의 방법으로 세금의 부과를 설명하기 시작함

(B) Taxing certain goods or services, / and so increasing prices, / should result / in either decreased use of these resources / or creative innovation / of new sources or options. //
either A or B로 연결된 전치사 in의 목적어
특정 재화나 서비스에 과세하는 것은 / 그래서 가격을 인상하는 것은 / 낳을 것이다 / 이러한 자원의 감소된 사용이나 / 창조적 혁신을 / 새로운 공급원 또는 선택사항의 //

The money / raised through the tax / can be used / directly by the government / either to supply services / or to search for alternatives. //
either A or B로 연결된 목적을 나타내는 부사적 용법의 to부정사구
돈은 / 세금을 통해 조성된 / 사용될 수 있다 / 정부에 의해 직접 / 서비스를 공급하기 위해서나 / 대안을 모색하기 위해 //
단서3 소비자가 직접 구입하는 약 1달러가 드는 쓰레기봉투에 폐기물을 처리할 것을 요구한 결과
(C) The results have been greatly increased / recycling and more careful attention / by consumers / to packaging and waste. //
그 결과는 크게 증가시켜 왔다 / 재활용과 더 세심한 주의를 / 소비자에 의한 / 포장과 폐기물에 //

By internalizing the costs of trash / to consumers, / there has been an observed decrease / in the flow of garbage / from households. //
쓰레기 비용을 자기 것으로 하게 함으로써 / 소비자에게 / 관찰된 감소가 있어 왔다 / 쓰레기의 흐름에 / 가정에서 나오는 //

───────────────────

• drive ⓥ (사람을 특정한 방식의 행동을 하도록) 만들다
• innovator ⓝ 혁신가, 도입자 • substitute ⓥ 대용하다, 대체하다
• conserve ⓥ 아껴 쓰다, 보존하다 • alternative ⓝ 대안, 대안이 되는 것
• emerge ⓥ 생겨나다, 모습을 드러내다
• green tax 환경세(환경을 오염시키거나 파괴하는 행위자에게 부과하는 세금)
• landfill ⓝ 쓰레기 매립 • labor expense 인건비
• provision ⓝ 제공, 공급 • disposal ⓝ (무엇을 없애기 위한) 처리, 처분
• household ⓝ (한 집에 사는 사람들을 일컫는) 가정
• innovation ⓝ 혁신, 쇄신
• internalize ⓥ (문화·사상 등을) 자신의 것으로 만들다[내면화하다]
• flow ⓝ 흐름

시장 반응 모형에 따르면, 바로 가격의 인상이 공급자가 새로운 공급원을 찾게 하고, 혁신가가 대용하게 하고, 소비자가 아껴 쓰게 하고, 대안이 생기게 한다. (B) 특정 재화나 서비스에 과세하여 가격이 인상되면 이러한 자원의 사용의 감소나 새로운 공급원 또는 선택사항의 창조적 혁신을 낳을 것이다. 세금을 통해 조성된 돈은 정부가 서비스를 공급하거나 대안을 모색하는 데 직접 사용할 수 있다. (A) 그러한 '환경세'의 많은 예가 존재한다. 예를 들어, 쓰레기 매립 비용, 인건비, 쓰레기 처리를 제공하는 데 관련된 비용에 직면하여 일부 도시는 모든 폐기물을 소비자가 직접 구입한, 각각 흔히 1달러 또는 그 이상씩 드는 특별 쓰레기봉투에 담아 처리하도록 가정에 요구해 왔다. (C) 그 결과는 재활용과 포장과 폐기물에 대한 소비자의 더 세심한 주의를 크게 증가시켜 왔다. 소비자에게 쓰레기 비용을 자기 것으로 하게 함으로써, 가정에서 나오는 쓰레기의 흐름에 감소가 관찰되어 왔다.

주어진 글 다음에 이어질 글의 순서로 가장 적절한 것을 고르시오.

① (A) — (C) — (B) 주어진 글에는 '세금'에 대한 언급이 없으므로 such green taxes라고 할 수 없음
② (B) — (A) — (C) 가격 인상이 변화를 가져오는 요인임 – 재화나 서비스에 과세하여 가격을 인상함 – 일부 도시가 과세를 통해 폐기물 처리를 위한 가격을 인상함 – 그 결과 재활용, 포장과 폐기물에 대한 소비자의 주의가 크게 증가함
③ (B) — (C) — (A)
④ (C) — (A) — (B) 폐기물에 대한 소비자의 주의가 크게 증가한 원인은 (A)에 등장함
⑤ (C) — (B) — (A)

| 문제 풀이 순서 | [정답률 59%]

1st 각 문단의 내용을 파악하고, 글의 논리적인 순서를 추론한다.

주어진 글: 시장 반응 모형에 따르면, 바로 가격의 인상이 공급자가 새로운 공급원을 찾게 하고, 혁신가가 대용하게 하고, 소비자가 아껴 쓰게 하고, 대안이 생기게 한다.

→ **주어진 글 뒤:** 시장 반응 모형에서 가격 인상의 영향에 대한 설명이 이어질 것이다.

(A): 그러한 '환경세'의 많은 예가 존재한다. 예를 들어(for example), 쓰레기 매립 비용, 인건비, 쓰레기 처리를 제공하는 데 관련된 비용에 직면하여 일부 도시는 모든 폐기물을 소비자가 직접 구입한, 각각 흔히 1달러 또는 그 이상씩 드는 특별 쓰레기봉투에 담아 처리하도록 가정에 요구해 왔다. **단서 1**

→ **(A) 앞:** 환경세의 예를 드는 내용으로, 환경세에 대한 설명이 앞에 나와야 한다.
▶ 주어진 글에 이 내용이 없으므로 (A) 앞에 주어진 글이 올 수 없음
(A) 뒤: For example은 예시를 나타내는 연결어로, 폐기물 처리 서비스에 세금을 부과한 내용이다. 그에 따른 결과가 뒤에 이어지는 것이 자연스럽다.

(B): 특정 재화나 서비스에 과세하여 가격이 인상되면 이러한 자원의 사용의 감소나 새로운 공급원 또는 선택사항의 창조적 혁신을 낳을 것이다. **단서 2** 세금을 통해 조성된 돈은 정부가 서비스를 공급하거나 대안을 모색하는 데 직접 사용할 수 있다.

→ **(B) 앞:** 과세로 가격이 인상되면 자원 사용이나 공급원 등에 변화가 생기고, 모인 세금은 정부의 서비스 공급에 사용된다는 내용으로, 가격 인상의 결과를 언급한 주어진 글에 이어진다.
▶ (B) 앞에 주어진 글이 와야 함 (순서: 주어진 글 → (B))
(B) 뒤: 정부의 과세에 대한 예시로서 '환경세'가 (A)에 나온다.
▶ (B) 뒤에 (A)가 와야 함 (순서: 주어진 글 → (B) → (A))

(C): 그 결과(The results)는 재활용과 포장과 폐기물에 대한 소비자의 더 세심한 주의를 크게 증가시켜 왔다. **단서 3** 소비자에게 쓰레기 비용을 자기 것으로 하게 함으로써, 가정에서 나오는 쓰레기의 흐름에 감소가 관찰되어 왔다.

→ **(C) 앞:** The results(그 결과)는 재활용에 대한 소비자의 주의를 증가시켰다고 했다. 즉, 소비자가 직접 특별 쓰레기봉투에 폐기물을 담아 처리하도록 가정에 요구한 것을 나타낸다.
▶ (C) 앞에 (A)가 와야 함 (순서: 주어진 글 → (B) → (A) → (C))

2nd 글이 한눈에 들어오도록 정리하여 정답을 확인한다.

주어진 글: 가격이 인상되면 공급자, 혁신가, 소비자의 행동이 변화한다.
→ **(B):** 과세로 인해 가격이 인상되면 시장에 변화가 나타나고, 그 세금은 정부의 서비스 공급 또는 대안 모색에 사용될 수 있다.
→ **(A):** 환경세의 예시로 폐기물 처리 서비스에 세금을 부과한 것이 있다.
→ **(C):** 환경세는 폐기물에 대한 주의를 증가시키고 쓰레기 배출을 감소시켰다.
▶ 주어진 글 다음에 이어질 글의 순서는 (B) → (A) → (C)이므로 정답은 ②임

＊글의 흐름

도입	가격이 오르면 공급자는 새로운 공급원을 찾고, 혁신가는 대응하고, 소비자는 절약하고, 대안은 생겨날 것임
부연	과세를 통해 가격을 인상하면 가격이 오른 그 재화나 서비스의 사용이 감소되거나 새로운 창조적 혁신이 등장할 것임
예시	일부 도시에서 소비자에게 쓰레기봉투를 구입해 쓰레기를 처리하도록 함으로써 쓰레기 처리 서비스에 세금을 부과하여 가격을 인상함
결과	가정에서 나오는 쓰레기에 대한 소비자의 세심한 주의가 증가하고 쓰레기의 흐름이 감소함

M 22 정답 ⑤ ＊아리스토텔레스의 eudaimoniā

Aristotle explains / that the Good for human beings / consists in *eudaimoniā* /
아리스토텔레스는 설명한다 / 인간을 위한 '선'은 / eudaimoniā에 있다고 /
(a Greek word / combining eu meaning "good" / with *daimon* meaning "spirit," / and most often translated / as "happiness"). //
　　　　　　a Greek word를 수식하는 현재분사와 과거분사
(그리스어 단어 / '좋다'라는 의미인 eu를 결합한 / '영혼'이라는 의미의 daimon과 / 가장 흔히 번역되는 / '행복'이라고) //

(A) It depends only on knowledge / of human nature and other worldly and social realities. // **단서 1** 신이나 형이상학적이고 보편적인 도덕규범에 관한 지식에 의존하지 않는다는 설명에 이어짐
그것은 오직 지식에만 의존한다 / 인간 본성과 여타의 세속적이고 사회적인 현실에 대한 //
　　　　　　　　선행사
For him / it is the study / of human nature and worldly existence
　　　　　주격 관계대명사
/ that will disclose the relevant meaning / of the notion of *eudaimoniā*. //
그에게 있어 / 그것은 연구이다 / 인간 본성과 세속적 존재에 대한 / 적절한 의미를 밝힐 / eudaimoniā라는 개념의 //
　　　　　　　　　　　　　　　　　　부사절 접속사(대조)
(B) Some people say / it is worldly enjoyment / while others say / it is eternal salvation. // **단서 2** 행복이 무엇인지에 대해 사람마다 서로 다른 견해를 갖는다는 데 대한 부연
어떤 사람들은 말한다 / 그것이 세속적인 쾌락이라고 / 다른 사람들은 말하는 반면 / 그것이 영원한 구원이라고 //
Aristotle's theory / will turn out to be "naturalistic" / in that it does not depend / on any theological or metaphysical knowledge. //
아리스토텔레스의 이론은 / '자연적'이라고 판명될 것이다 / 그것이 의존하지 않는다는 점에서 / 어떤 신학이나 형이상학적 지식에도 //
It does not depend on knowledge / of God / or of metaphysical and universal moral norms. // **단서 3** 그것이 무엇에 의존하는지가 이어져야 함
그것은 지식에 의존하지 않는다 / 신에 관한 / 또는 형이상학적, 보편적 도덕규범에 관한 //
　　부사절 접속사(대조)　　　　　　　　　　　　　　　had argued의 목적어절 접속사
(C) Whereas he had argued / in a purely formal way / that the Good was that / to which we all aim, / he now gives a more substantive answer: /
그는 주장했지만 / 순전히 형식적으로 / '선'은 그것이라고 / 우리 모두가 목표로 하는 / 그는 이제 더 실질적인 답을 한다 / **단서 4** 인간을 위한 선은 eudaimoniā에 있고, eudaimoniā는 '행복'을 의미한다고 했음
that this universal human goal / is happiness. //
이 보편적인 인간의 목표는 / 행복이라는 것 //
However, / he is quick to point out / that this conclusion is still somewhat formal / since different people have different views
　　　　　　　　　　　부사절 접속사(원인)
/ about what happiness is. // **단서 5** 어떤 사람들은 세속적 쾌락이 행복이라고 생각하고, 다른 사람들은 영원한 구원이 행복이라고 생각함
하지만 / 그는 재빨리 지적한다 / 이 결론이 여전히 다소 형식적이라고 / 사람마다 서로 다른 견해를 가지고 있기 때문에 / 행복이 무엇인지에 대해 //

• consist in ~에 있다　　• worldly ⓐ 세속적인, 속세의
• existence ⓝ 존재　　• disclose ⓥ 밝히다, 드러내다
• relevant ⓐ 적절한, 타당한　　• notion ⓝ 개념

- enjoyment ⓝ 즐거움, 기쁨　· eternal ⓐ 영원한
- naturalistic ⓐ 자연주의적인　· metaphysical ⓐ 형이상학의
- universal ⓐ 보편적인　· norm ⓝ 규범
- point out ~을 지적하다[말하다]　· conclusion ⓝ 결론, (최종적인) 판단
- somewhat ⓐd 어느 정도, 약간

아리스토텔레스는 인간을 위한 '선'은 eudaimoniā('좋다'라는 의미인 eu와 '영혼'이라는 의미의 daimon을 결합하여, '행복'이라고 가장 흔히 번역되는 그리스어 단어)에 있다고 설명한다. (C) 그는 순전히 형식적으로 '선'은 우리 모두가 목표로 하는 것이라고 주장했지만, 그는 이제 이 보편적인 인간의 목표는 행복이라는 더 실질적인 답을 한다. 하지만, 그는 사람마다 행복이 무엇인지에 대해 서로 다른 견해를 가지고 있기 때문에 이 결론이 여전히 다소 형식적이라고 재빨리 지적한다. (B) 어떤 사람들은 그것을 세속적인 쾌락이라고 말하지만, 다른 사람들은 그것을 영원한 구원이라고 말한다. 아리스토텔레스의 이론은 어떤 신학이나 형이상학적 지식에도 의존하지 않는다는 점에서 '자연적'이라고 판명될 것이다. 그것은 신에 대한 지식이나 형이상학적, 보편적 도덕규범에 관한 지식에 의존하지 않는다. (A) 그것은 오직 인간 본성과 여타의 세속적이고 사회적인 현실에 대한 지식에만 의존한다. 그에게 있어 그것은 eudaimoniā라는 개념의 적절한 의미를 밝힐 인간 본성과 세속적 존재에 대한 연구이다.

(C)에는 그것이 의존하지 않는 것에 대한 내용이 없음

주어진 글 다음에 이어질 글의 순서로 가장 적절한 것을 고르시오.

① (A) — (C) — (B) 그것이 의존하지 않는 것에 대한 내용이 (A) 앞에 있어야 함
② (B) — (A) — (C)
③ (B) — (C) — (A) (B)의 '그것'이 가리키는 것이 (B) 앞에 있어야 함
④ (C) — (A) — (B)
⑤ (C) — (B) — (A)

아리스토텔레스는 인간을 위한 선이 '행복'을 뜻하는 eudaimoniā에 있다고 설명함 - 사람마다 행복에 대한 견해가 서로 다름 - 어떤 사람은 행복이 세속적 쾌락이라고, 다른 사람들은 행복이 영원한 구원이라고 생각함, 아리스토텔레스의 이론은 신학이나 형이상학적 지식에 의존하지 않음 - 그것은 인간 본성과 세속적이고 사회적인 현실에 의존함

| 문제 풀이 순서 | [정답률 44%]

1st 각 문단의 내용을 파악하고, 글의 논리적인 순서를 추론한다.

> **주어진 글:** 아리스토텔레스는 인간을 위한 선이 eudaimoniā에 있다고 설명한다. eudaimoniā는 eu(좋다)와 daimon(영혼)을 결합한, '행복'이라고 번역되는 그리스어 단어다.

→ **주어진 글 뒤:** 주어진 글은 인간을 위한 선은 곧 행복이라는 의미이므로, 단서 이에 대한 구체적인 부연이 이어질 것이다. 발상

> **(A):** 그것(It)은 오직 인간 본성과 여타의 세속적이고 사회적인 현실에 대한 지식에만 의존한다. 그에게 있어 그것은 eudaimoniā라는 개념의 적절한 의미를 밝힐 인간 본성과 세속적 존재에 대한 연구이다.

→ **(A) 앞:** '그것(It)'이 의존하는 것, 인간 본성과 여타의 세속적이고 사회적인 현실에 대한 지식과 대조되는 것에 대한 설명이 있어야 한다.
　▶ 주어진 글에는 그것이 무엇에 의존하는지가 등장하지 않음
　(A) 뒤: 아리스토텔레스가 그것이 무엇인지 결론을 내리는 것으로 보아 (A)가 글의 결론이라고 예상할 수 있다.
　▶ (A)는 마지막에 올 확률이 큼

> **(B):** 어떤 사람들은 그것이 세속적인 쾌락이라고 말하고, 다른 사람들은 그것이 영원한 구원이라고 말한다. 아리스토텔레스의 이론은 신에 관한 또는 형이상학적이고 보편적인 도덕규범에 관한 지식에 의존하지 않는다.

→ **(B) 앞:** 그것이 무엇인지에 대한 생각이 사람마다 다르다는 설명이 (B) 앞에 있고, (B)에서 그것을 구체적으로 부연하는 흐름이 되어야 한다.
　▶ 주어진 글이나 (A)에는 사람마다 생각이 다르다는 언급이 없음
　(B) 뒤: (A)의 '인간 본성과 여타의 세속적이고 사회적인 현실'과 대조되는 것이 (B)의 '신에 관한, 형이상학적이고 보편적인 도덕규범'이다.
　▶ (B) 뒤에 (A)가 와야 함 (순서: (B) → (A))

> **(C):** 그는 순전히 형식적으로 선은 우리 모두가 목표로 하는 것이라고 주장했지만, 이제는 보편적인 인간의 목표가 행복이라는 더 실질적인 대답을 한다. 이 결론은 여전히 형식적인데, 사람마다 행복이 무엇인지에 대해 서로 다른 견해를 갖고 있기 때문이다.

→ **(C) 앞:** 보편적인 인간의 목표가 행복이라고 말하기에 앞서, 인간을 위한 선은 eudaimoniā에 있고, eudaimoniā는 '행복'을 뜻한다는 내용이 있어야 한다.
　(C) 뒤: (B)의 '그것'이 가리키는 것이 바로 '행복'이다.
　<(C) 사람마다 행복이 무엇인지에 대한 견해가 다름 → (B) 어떤 사람들은 행복이 세속적 쾌락이라고 말하고, 다른 사람들은 행복이 영원한 구원이라고 말함>
　▶ (C) 뒤에 (B)가 있어야 함 (순서: 주어진 글 → (C) → (B) → (A))

2nd 글이 한눈에 들어오도록 정리하여 정답을 확인한다.

주어진 글: 아리스토텔레스는 인간을 위한 '선'은 eudaimoniā에 있다고 설명하는데, eudaimoniā는 '행복'을 뜻하는 그리스어 단어이다.

→ **(C):** 아리스토텔레스는 이 보편적인 인간의 목표가 행복이라는 답을 하지만, 행복이 무엇인지에 대해 사람마다 견해가 서로 다르므로 이 결론은 여전히 다소 형식적이다.

→ **(B):** 어떤 사람은 행복이 세속적인 쾌락이라고 말하고, 다른 사람들은 행복이 영원한 구원이라고 말한다. 아리스토텔레스의 이론은 그것이 신에 관한, 형이상학적이고 보편적인 도덕규범에 관한 지식에 의존하지 않는다는 점에서 '자연적'이라고 판명될 것이다.

→ **(A):** 그것은 오직 인간 본성과 여타의 세속적이고 사회적인 현실에 대한 지식에만 의존한다.

▶ 주어진 글 다음에 이어질 글의 순서는 (C) → (B) → (A)이므로 정답은 ⑤임

M 23 정답 ⑤ *허구의 세계가 현실 세계를 벗어나는 측면

In spite of the likeness / between the fictional and real world, / the fictional world deviates / from the real one / in one important respect. // **단서1** 허구의 세계와 현실 세계의 차이점에 대해 설명하는 글임
유사성에도 불구하고 / 허구의 세계와 현실의 세계 사이의 / 허구의 세계는 벗어난다 / 현실 세계로부터 / 하나의 중요한 측면에서 //

단서2 (B)에서 설명한 '또다른 의식'이 바로 작가의 의식을 가리킴
(A) The author has selected the content / according to his own worldview / and his own conception of relevance, /
작가는 내용을 선정했다 / 자신의 세계관에 따라 / 그리고 적절성에 대한 자신의 개념에 (따라) /
in an attempt / to be neutral and objective / or convey a subjective view / on the world. //
형용사적 용법(an attempt 수식)의 to부정사의 병렬 구조
시도에서 / 중립적이고 객관적이려는 / 또는 주관적인 견해를 전달하려는 / 세계에 대한 //
Whatever the motives, / the author's subjective conception of the world / stands / between the reader and the original, untouched world / on which the story is based. //
뒤에 are가 생략됨(whatever가 be동사의 주격 보어일 때 be동사는 생략 가능)
전치사+관계대명사　선행사
동기가 무엇이든 / 세계에 대한 작가의 주관적인 개념은 / 서 있다 / 독자와 원래의 손대지 않은 세계 사이에 / 이야기의 기반이 되는 //
명사구　전치사+관계대명사
(B) Because of the inner qualities / with which the individual is endowed / through heritage and environment, /
전치사
내적 특성 때문에 / 개인이 부여받은 / 유산과 환경을 통해 **단서3** (C)에서 설명한 a human mind가 작동하는 방식을 설명함
단수 주어
the mind functions / as a filter; / every outside impression / that passes through it / is filtered and interpreted. //
단수 동사
그러한 정신은 기능한다 / 여과기로서 / 모든 외부의 인상이 / 그것을 통과하는 / 걸러지고 해석된다 // **단서4** 문학, 즉 허구의 세계에 대해
앞에 목적격 관계대명사가 생략됨
역접의 연결어로 설명하기 시작함
However, / the world / the reader encounters / in literature / is already processed and filtered / by another consciousness. //
그러나 / 세계는 / 독자가 접하는 / 문학에서 / 이미 처리되고 여과되어 있다 / 또다른 의식에 의해 // **단서5** 현재의 세계, 즉 현실 세계에 대해 설명하기 시작함
주어　동사 '이론상으로는'
(C) The existing world / faced by the individual / is in principle an infinite chaos / of events and details / before it is organized / by a human mind. //
주격 보어
현재의 세계는 / 개인이 직면하는 / 이론상으로는 무한한 혼돈 상태이다 / 사건들과 세부 사항들의 / 그것이 조직되기 전에는 / 인간의 정신에 의해 //

This chaos only gets processed and modified / when perceived / by a human mind. //
주어와 be동사가 생략된 부사절
이 혼돈 상태는 오직 처리되고 수정된다 / 인식될 때 / 인간의 정신에 의해 //

- likeness ⓝ 유사성, 닮음 · fictional ⓐ 허구의, 가상의
- respect ⓝ (측)면, 점, 사항 · content ⓝ (책·프로그램 등의) 내용
- worldview ⓝ 세계관 · conception ⓝ 개념, 생각
- relevance ⓝ 적절성, 타당성 · neutral ⓐ 중립적인
- objective ⓐ 객관적인 · convey ⓥ (생각·감정 등을) 전달하다[전하다]
- subjective ⓐ 주관적인 · motive ⓝ 동기, 이유
- stand ⓥ (어떤 상태·관계·입장에) 있다
- untouched ⓐ 손을 대지 않은, 본래 그대로의 · inner ⓐ 내적인, 내면의
- quality ⓝ 특성, 특징 · function ⓥ 역할을 하다, 기능하다
- impression ⓝ (사람·사물로부터 받는) 인상[느낌]
- interpret ⓥ (의미를) 설명[해석]하다 · encounter ⓥ 접하다, 마주하다
- literature ⓝ 문학 (작품) · process ⓥ 처리하다, 가공하다
- consciousness ⓝ 의식 · existing ⓐ 기존의, 현재 존재하는
- infinite ⓐ 한계가 없는, 무한한 · chaos ⓝ 혼돈, 혼란
- modify ⓥ (더 알맞도록) 수정[변경]하다 · perceive ⓥ 인식하다, 인지하다

허구의 세계와 현실의 세계 사이의 유사성에도 불구하고 허구의 세계는 하나의 중요한 측면에서 현실 세계로부터 벗어난다. (C) 개인이 직면하는 현재의 세계는 이론상으로는 인간의 정신에 의해 조직되기 전에는 사건들과 세부 사항들의 무한한 혼돈 상태이다. 이 혼돈 상태는 인간의 정신에 의해 인식될 때만 처리되고 수정된다. (B) 개인이 유산과 환경을 통해 부여받은 내적 특성 때문에 그러한 정신은 그것을 통과하는 모든 외부의 인상이 걸러지고 해석되는 여과기로 기능한다. 그러나 문학에서 독자가 접하는 세계는 이미 또다른 의식에 의해 처리되고 여과되어 있다. (A) 작가는 중립적이고 객관적이려는 또는 세계에 대한 주관적인 견해를 전달하려는 시도에서 자신의 세계관과 적절성에 대한 자신의 개념에 따라 내용을 선정했다. 동기가 무엇이든, 세계에 대한 작가의 주관적인 개념은 독자와 이야기의 기반이 되는 원래의 손대지 않은 세계 사이에 존재한다.

주어진 글 다음에 이어질 글의 순서로 가장 적절한 것을 고르시오. [3점]

① (A) — (C) — (B) ──(B)에서 독자가 문학에서 접하는 세계에 대한 설명이 역접의 연결어로 이어짐
② (B) — (A) — (C) ──주어진 글에는 '정신'에 대한 언급이 없음
③ (B) — (C) — (A)
④ (C) — (A) — (B) ──허구의 세계는 중요한 측면에서 현실 세계와 다름 – 현실 세계는 개인의
⑤ (C) — (B) — (A) ──정신에 의해서만 걸러지고 해석됨 – 그러나 문학의 세계는 작가의 의식에 의해 이미 처리되고 여과되어 있음

| 문제 풀이 순서 | [정답률 59%]

1st 각 문단의 내용을 파악하고, 글의 논리적인 순서를 추론한다.

주어진 글: 허구의 세계와 현실의 세계 사이의 유사성에도 불구하고 허구의 세계는 하나의 중요한 측면에서 현실 세계로부터 벗어난다. **단서 1**

➡ **주어진 글 뒤:** 허구의 세계가 현실 세계에서 벗어나는 측면이 무엇인지에 대해 나올 것이다.

(A): 작가(The author)는 중립적이고 객관적이려는 또는 세계에 대한 주관적인 견해를 전달하려는 시도에서 자신의 세계관과 적절성에 대한 자신의 개념에 따라 내용을 선정했다. **단서 2** 동기가 무엇이든, 세계에 대한 작가의 주관적인 개념은 독자와 이야기의 기반이 되는 원래의 손대지 않은 세계 사이에 존재한다.

➡ **(A) 앞:** 작가는 견해를 전달하려는 시도에서 자신의 개념에 따라 내용을 선정했다는 내용이다. 주어진 글 뒤에는 허구 세계와 현실 세계 사이의 차이점이 나와야 하는데, 문학의 세계, 즉 허구 세계를 설명하는 (A)가 먼저 나올지, 현실 세계를 설명하는 글이 먼저 나올지 확정하기 어렵다.
▶ (A) 앞에 주어진 글이 올 수도 있지만, (B), (C)도 확인해야 함
(A) 뒤: 문학 세계에서 작가가 독자와 원래(현실) 세계 사이에 존재한다는 내용으로 추가적인 내용으로 이어지는 단서가 없다.
▶ (A)가 마지막에 올 확률이 높음

(B): 개인이 유산과 환경을 통해 부여받은 내적 특성 때문에 그러한 정신(the mind)은 그것을 통과하는 모든 외부의 인상이 걸러지고 해석되는 여과기로 기능한다. **단서 3** 그러나(However) 문학에서 독자가 접하는 세계는 이미 또다른 의식에 의해 처리되고 여과되어 있다. **단서 4**

➡ **(B) 앞:** 외부의 인상을 거르고 해석하는 여과기로서의 the mind에 대해 앞에 나와야 한다. 주어진 글에는 외부의 인상을 거르고 해석한다는 내용이 나오지 않는다.
▶ (B) 앞에 주어진 글이 올 수 없음
(B) 뒤: however는 반대되는 내용을 나타내는 연결어이므로, 현실 세계와 다른 문학의 세계를 설명하는 내용이 이어져야 한다. 문학의 세계에서는 작가의 주관적 개념이 독자와 원래 세계 사이에 존재한다는 내용이 (A)에 나온다.
▶ (B) 뒤에 (A)가 와야 함 (순서: (B) → (A))

(C): 개인이 직면하는 현재의 세계는 이론상으로는 인간의 정신에 의해 조직되기 전에는 사건들과 세부 사항들의 무한한 혼돈 상태이다. **단서 5** 이 혼돈 상태는 인간의 정신에 의해 인식될 때만 처리되고 수정된다.

➡ **(C) 앞:** 현실 세계에 대한 설명을 시작하는 내용이다. (A) 앞에 (B)가 나오므로, 현실 세계와 문학 세계 사이의 차이점이 있다고 언급하는 주어진 글에 이어서 현실 세계를 먼저 설명하는 흐름이 된다.
▶ (C) 앞에 주어진 글이 와야 함 (순서: 주어진 글 → (C))
(C) 뒤: a human mind가 (B)에 등장하는 the mind를 지칭하므로, (B)가 뒤에 이어져야 한다.
▶ (C) 뒤에 (B)가 와야 함 (순서: 주어진 글 → (C) → (B) → (A))

2nd 글이 한눈에 들어오도록 정리하여 정답을 확인한다.

주어진 글: 현실 세계와 문학 세계 사이에 중요한 차이점이 있다.
➡ **(C):** 현실 세계는 인간의 정신으로 걸러지고 해석된다.
➡ **(B):** 인간의 정신은 외부의 인상을 해석하는 여과기로 기능하지만, 문학의 세계는 또다른 의식에 의해 여과되어 있다.
➡ **(A):** 작가는 자신의 개념에 따라 내용을 선정하고, 작가의 주관적 개념은 독자와 현실 세계 사이에 존재한다.
▶ 주어진 글 다음에 이어질 글의 순서는 (C) → (B) → (A)이므로 정답은 ⑤임

* 글의 흐름

도입	허구의 세계는 하나의 중요한 측면에서 현실 세계와 다름
현실 세계	현재의 세계는 사건들과 세부 사항들의 무한한 혼돈 상태이고, 인간의 정신이 인식할 때만 처리되고 수정됨
	인간의 정신은 모든 외부의 인상을 거르고 해석하는 여과기로 기능함
허구의 세계	문학의 세계는 작가의 세계관과 개념에 따라 내용이 선정되어 처리된, 이미 여과된 세계임
	작가의 정신은 손대지 않은 원래의 세계와 독자 사이에 존재함

M 24 정답 ④ * 고정 관념의 효율성

The intuitive ability / to classify and generalize / is undoubtedly a useful feature / of life and research, /
형용사적 용법(The intuitive ability 수식)
직관적인 능력은 / 분류하고 일반화하는 / 의심할 여지 없이 유용한 특징이다 / 삶과 연구에 / **단서 1** 분류하고 일반화하는 능력은 일반화를 고정 관념화하는 우리의 경향과 같은 많은 대가를 수반
but it carries a high cost, / such as in our tendency / to stereotype generalizations / about people and situations. //
형용사적 용법(our tendency 수식)
그러나 그것은 많은 대가를 수반한다 / 우리의 경향에 있어서와 같이 / 일반화를 고정 관념화하는 / 사람과 상황에 대한 //

(A) Intuitively and quickly, / **단서 2** 우리는 직관적이고 빠르게, 즉 효율적으로 사물을 차이에 따라 분류함 we mentally sort things into groups / based on what we perceive the differences between them to be, / and that is the basis for stereotyping. //
perceive의 목적어와 목적격 보어

직관적이고 빠르게 / 우리는 정신적으로 사물을 그룹으로 분류하며 / 우리가 그것들 간에 차이라고 인식하는 것에 기초해 / 그것이 고정 관념의 기초이다 //

Only afterwards / do we examine (or not examine) more
준부사어가 문두로 나가면서 주어와 동사가 도치됨
evidence / of how things are differentiated, / and the degree and significance / of the variations. //

그 후에야 / 우리는 더 많은 증거를 조사한다 (또는 조사하지 않는다) / 사물이 어떻게 차별화되는지에 대한 / 그리고 정도와 중요성에 대한 / 그 차이의 //

(B) Our brain performs these tasks / efficiently and automatically, / usually without our awareness. // **단서 3** 우리의 뇌는 효율적이고 자동으로 사물을 차이에 의하여 인식하고 분류함

우리의 뇌는 이러한 일을 수행한다 / 효율적이고 자동으로 / 대개 우리가 인식하지 못하는 사이에 //

The real danger of stereotypes / is not their inaccuracy, / but
단수 주어   단수 동사
their lack of flexibility / and their tendency / to be preserved, /
형용사적 용법(their tendency 수식)
even when we have enough time / to stop and consider. //
형용사적 용법(enough time 수식)

고정 관념이 진정 위험한 것은 / 그것들의 부정확성이 아니라 / 그것들의 유연성 부족과 / 경향이다 / 유지되려는 / 우리가 시간이 충분할 때조차도 / 멈추어 생각할 //

(C) For most people, / the word stereotype arouses / negative connotations: / it implies a negative bias. //

대부분 사람에게 / 고정 관념이라는 단어는 불러일으킨다 / 부정적인 함축을 / 그것은 부정적인 편견을 암시한다 //

But, in fact, stereotypes do not differ / in principle / from all other generalizations; / generalizations about groups of people / are not necessarily always negative. // **단서 4** 그러나 고정 관념이 반드시 항상 부정적인 것은 아님

그러나 사실 고정 관념은 다르지 않다 / 원칙적으로 / 모든 다른 일반화와 / 사람들의 집단에 대한 일반화가 / 반드시 항상 부정적인 것은 아니다 //

- classify ⓥ 분류하다
- generalize ⓥ 일반화하다
- undoubtedly ⓐⓓ 의심할 여지 없이
- feature ⓝ 특징
- tendency ⓝ 경향
- stereotype ⓝ 고정 관념 ⓥ 고정 관념화하다
- mentally ⓐⓓ 정신적으로
- sort ⓥ 분류하다
- based on ~에 기초하여
- perceive ⓥ 인식하다
- afterwards ⓐⓓ 그 후에
- differentiate ⓥ 차별화하다
- significance ⓝ 중요성
- variation ⓝ 변화
- perform ⓥ 수행하다
- awareness ⓝ 인식
- inaccuracy ⓝ 부정확성
- flexibility ⓝ 유연성
- arouse ⓥ 불러일으키다
- imply ⓥ 암시하다
- bias ⓝ 편견
- differ in ~에 대해 다르다

분류하고 일반화하는 직관적인 능력은 의심할 여지 없이 삶과 연구에 유용한 특징이지만, 그것은 사람과 상황에 대한 일반화를 고정 관념화하는 경향에 있어서와 같이 많은 대가를 수반한다. (C) 대부분 사람에게, 고정 관념이라는 단어는 부정적인 함축을 불러일으키는데, 즉 그것은 부정적인 편견을 암시한다. 그러나 사실 고정 관념은 원칙적으로 모든 다른 일반화와 다르지 않으며, 사람들의 집단에 대한 일반화가 반드시 항상 부정적인 것은 아니다. (A) 직관적이고 빠르게, 우리는 사물 간에 차이가 있다고 인식하는 것에 기초해 정신적으로 그들을 그룹으로 분류하며, 그것이 고정 관념의 기초이다. 그 후에야 우리는 사물이 어떻게 차별화되는지, 그리고 그 차이의 정도와 중요성에 대한 더 많은 증거를 조사한다 (또는 조사하지 않는다). (B) 우리의 뇌는, 대개 우리가 인식하지 못하는 사이에, 이러한 일을 효율적이고 자동으로 수행한다. 고정 관념이 진정 위험한 것은 그것들의 부정확성이 아니라, 우리가 멈추어 생각할 시간이 충분할 때조차도, 그것들의 유연성 부족과 유지되려는 경향이다.

주어진 글 다음에 이어질 글의 순서로 가장 적절한 것을 고르시오.

① (A) — (C) — (B) ┐ 주어진 글은 고정 관념을 부정적으로 보고, (A)는 고정 관념의 효율성에 대해 이야기함
② (B) — (A) — (C) ┐ (B)의 these tasks가 가리키는 것이 주어진 글에 없음
③ (B) — (C) — (A) ┐ 분류하고 일반화하는 능력은 유용하지만, 사람과 상황에 대한 일반화를 고정 관념화하는 대가를 수반함 - 사실 고정 관념이 반드시 항상 부정적인 것은 아님 - 사물을 그룹으로 분류하는데, 그것이 고정 관념의 기초임 - 고정 관념의 진정한 위험성은 유연성 부족과 유지되려는 경향임
④ (C) — (A) — (B)
⑤ (C) — (B) — (A) ┘
고정 관념의 진정한 위험성을 설명한 (B)가 고정 관념이 항상 부정적인 것은 아니라는 글의 결론으로 적절함

| 문제 풀이 순서 | [정답률 54%]

1st 각 문단의 내용을 파악하고, 글의 논리적인 순서를 추론한다.

주어진 글: 분류하고 일반화하는 직관적인 능력은 의심할 여지 없이 삶과 연구에 유용한 특징이지만, 그것은 사람과 상황에 대한 일반화를 고정 관념화하는 경향에 있어서와 같이 많은 대가를 수반한다.

→ 분류하고 일반화하는 직관적인 능력이 사람과 상황에 대한 일반화를 고정 관념화하는 등의 대가를 수반한다는 내용이다. **단서**
주어진 글 뒤: 고정 관념을 부정적으로 바라보는 내용이 나왔으므로 이와 관련된 내용이 이어질 것이다. **발상**

(A): 직관적이고 빠르게(Intuitively and quickly), 우리는 사물 간에 차이가 있다고 인식하는 것에 기초해 정신적으로 그것들을 그룹으로 분류하며, 그것이 고정 관념의 기초이다. 그 후에야 우리는 사물이 어떻게 차별화되는지, 그리고 그 차이의 정도와 중요성에 대한 더 많은 증거를 조사한다(또는 조사하지 않는다).

→ '직관적이고 빠르게' 차이가 있는 사물을 그룹으로 분류하고(고정 관념의 기초), 그 후에 그것들이 어떻게 차별화되는지 등에 대한 더 많은 증거를 조사한다고 했다.
(A) 앞: 분류하는 것(고정 관념의 기초)의 효율성(직관적이고 빠르게)을 이야기하므로, 고정 관념을 부정적으로 바라보는 내용은 올 수 없다.
▶ 주어진 글이 (A) 앞에 올 수 없음
(A) 뒤: 고정 관념의 효율성에 대한 추가적인 설명이 이어질 것이다.

(B): 우리의 뇌는, 대개 우리가 인식하지 못하는 사이에, 이러한 일 (these tasks)을 효율적이고 자동으로 수행한다. 고정 관념이 진정 위험한 것은 그것들의 부정확성이 아니라, 우리가 멈추어 생각할 시간이 충분할 때조차도, 그것들의 유연성 부족과 유지되려는 경향이다.

→ **앞 문장:** 고정 관념의 효율성 → 우리의 뇌는 '이러한 일'을 효율적이고 자동으로 수행함
뒤 문장: 고정 관념의 진정한 위험성 → 고정 관념의 부정확성이 아니라 유연성 부족과 유지되려는 경향임
(B) 앞: 고정 관념의 효율성을 보여주는 these tasks가 가리키는 내용이 있어야 한다. these tasks는 (A)에서 설명한, 직관적이고 빠르게 이루어지는 고정 관념화를 가리킨다.
▶ (B) 앞에 (A)가 와야 함 (순서: (A) → (B))
(B) 뒤: 고정 관념의 유연성 부족과 유지되려는 경향에 대한 구체적인 설명이 이어지거나 (B)가 글의 결론일 것이다.
▶ (B)가 마지막에 올 확률이 큼

(C): 대부분 사람에게, 고정 관념이라는 단어는 부정적인 함축을 불러일으키는데, 즉 그것은 부정적인 편견을 암시한다. 그러나(But) 사실 고정 관념은 원칙적으로 모든 다른 일반화와 다르지 않으며, 사람들의 집단에 대한 일반화가 반드시 항상 부정적인 것은 아니다.

앞 문장: 고정 관념은 부정적인 편견을 암시함

뒤 문장: 그러나 고정 관념이 항상 부정적인 것은 아님

(C) 앞: 고정 관념을 부정적으로 바라본 주어진 글이 와야 한다.

▶ 주어진 글이 (C) 앞에 와야 함 (순서: 주어진 글 → (C))

(C) 뒤: 고정 관념이 항상 부정적인 것은 아니라는 점을 구체적으로 설명하는 문단이 필요하다.

▶ (C) 뒤에 (A)가 와야 함 (순서: 주어진 글 → (C) → (A) → (B))

2nd 글이 한눈에 들어오도록 정리하여 정답을 확인한다.

주어진 글: 분류하고 일반화하는 능력은 유용하지만, 그것은 사람과 상황에 대한 일반화를 고정 관념화하는 우리의 경향과 같은 대가를 수반한다.

→ **(C)**: 고정 관념은 부정적인 편견을 암시하지만, 사실 고정 관념이 반드시 항상 부정적인 것은 아니다.

→ **(A)**: 우리는 직관적이고 빠르게 차이에 기초하여 사물을 그룹으로 분류하는데, 그것이 고정 관념의 기초이다. 그런 다음 사물이 어떻게 차별화되는지, 그 차이의 정도와 중요성에 대한 더 많은 증거를 조사하거나 조사하지 않는다.

→ **(B)**: 우리의 뇌는 이러한 일을 효율적이고 자동으로 수행한다. 고정 관념의 진정한 위험성은 그것의 부정확성이 아니라 유연성 부족과 유지되려는 경향이다.

▶ 주어진 글 다음에 이어질 글의 순서는 (C) → (A) → (B)이므로 정답은 ④임

M 25 정답 ② *문법적 성 차이가 미치는 영향

Shakespeare wrote, / "What's in a name? // That / which we call a rose / by any other name / would smell as sweet." //
셰익스피어는 썼다 / "이름 안에 무엇이 있는가? // 그것은 / 우리가 장미라고 부르는 / 그 어떤 다른 이름으로도 / 그만큼 달콤한 냄새가 날 것이다"라고 // **단서 1** 셰익스피어의 말이 인용됨

(A) Take the word *bridge*. //
'다리'라는 단어를 보자 // **단서 2** Boroditsky의 연구 결과를 뒷받침하는 예시가 시작됨

In German, / *bridge* (die brücke) is a feminine noun; / in Spanish, / *bridge* (el puente) is a masculine noun. //
독일어로 / '다리'(die brücke)는 여성 명사이다 / 스페인어로 / '다리'(el puente)는 남성 명사이다 //

Boroditsky found / that when asked to describe a bridge, / native German speakers used words / like *beautiful*, *elegant*, *slender*. //
Boroditsky는 알아냈다 / 다리를 묘사하라는 요청을 받았을 때 / 독일어 원어민이 단어를 사용한다는 사실을 / '아름다운', '우아한', '날씬한' 같은 //

When native Spanish speakers were asked / the same question, / they used words / like *strong*, *sturdy*, *towering*. //
스페인어 원어민이 질문받았을 때 / 같은 질문을 / 그들은 단어를 사용했다 / '강한', '튼튼한', '우뚝 솟은' 같은 //

(B) According to Stanford University psychology professor Lera Boroditsky, / that's not necessarily so. //
Stanford 대학교의 심리학 교수인 Lera Boroditsky에 따르면 / 그것이 반드시 그렇지는 않다 // **단서 3** 셰익스피어가 쓴 것이 반드시 그렇지는 않다는 것을 보여주는 내용이 이어짐

Focusing on the grammatical gender differences / between German and Spanish, /
문법적 성 차이에 초점을 맞추어 / 독일어와 스페인어 간의 /

Boroditsky's work indicates / that the gender / our language assigns to a given noun / influences us / to subconsciously give that noun / characteristics of the grammatical gender. //
Boroditsky의 연구는 나타낸다 / 성은 / 우리의 언어가 특정 명사에 부여하는 / 우리에게 영향을 미친다는 것을 / 무의식적으로 그 명사에 부여하도록 / 문법적 성의 특성을 //

(C) This worked / the other way around / as well. //
이것은 마찬가지였다 / 반대의 경우에도 / 또한 // **단서 4** 독일어에서는 여성형이고, 스페인어에서는 남성형인 단어가 앞에 등장해야 함

The word *key* is masculine / in German / and feminine in Spanish. //
'열쇠'라는 단어는 남성형이고 / 독일어에서는 / 스페인어에서는 여성형이다 //

When asked to describe a key, / native German speakers used words / like *jagged*, *heavy*, *hard*, *metal*. //
열쇠를 묘사하라는 요청을 받았을 때 / 독일어 원어민은 단어를 사용했다 / '뾰족뾰족한', '무거운', '단단한', '금속의' 같은 //

Spanish speakers used words / like *intricate*, *golden*, *lovely*. //
스페인어 사용자는 단어를 사용했다 / '정교한', '황금빛의', '사랑스러운' 같은 //

- feminine ⓐ 여성의 · masculine ⓐ 남성의 · sturdy ⓐ 튼튼한
- towering ⓐ 우뚝 솟은 · gender ⓝ 성 · indicate ⓥ 나타내다
- assign ⓥ 부여하다 · subconsciously ⓐⓓ 무의식적으로
- characteristics ⓝ 특성

셰익스피어는 "이름 안에 무엇이 있는가? 우리가 장미라고 부르는 것은 그 어떤 다른 이름으로 불러도 그만큼 달콤한 냄새가 날 것이다."라고 썼다. (B) Stanford 대학교의 심리학 교수인 Lera Boroditsky에 따르면, 그것이 반드시 그렇지는 않다. 독일어와 스페인어 간의 문법적 성 차이에 초점을 맞춘 Boroditsky의 연구에 따르면, 우리의 언어가 특정 명사에 부여하는 성은 우리가 무의식적으로 그 명사에 문법적 성의 특성을 부여하도록 영향을 미친다. (A) '다리'라는 단어를 보자. 독일어로 '다리'(die brücke)는 여성 명사이지만, 스페인어로 '다리'(el puente)는 남성 명사이다. Boroditsky는 독일어 원어민이 다리를 묘사하라는 요청을 받았을 때, '아름다운', '우아한', '날씬한' 같은 단어를 사용한다는 사실을 알아냈다. 같은 질문을 받았을 때, 스페인어 원어민은 '강한', '튼튼한', '우뚝 솟은' 같은 단어를 사용했다. (C) 이것은 반대의 경우에도 마찬가지였다. '열쇠'라는 단어는 독일어에서는 남성형이고 스페인어에서는 여성형이다. 독일어 원어민이 열쇠를 묘사하라는 요청을 받았을 때, '뾰족뾰족한', '무거운', '단단한', '금속의' 같은 단어를 사용했다. 스페인어 사용자는 '정교한', '황금빛의', '사랑스러운' 같은 단어를 사용했다.

주어진 글 다음에 이어질 글의 순서로 가장 적절한 것을 고르시오.

① (A) — (C) — (B) 남성 명사, 여성 명사라는 개념이 왜 등장하는지가 (A) 앞에 필요함
② (B) — (A) — (C)
③ (B) — (C) — (A) '다리'가 나온 뒤에 '열쇠'가 나와야 함
④ (C) — (A) — (B) ┐ This가 가리키는 것이 셰익스피어의 말이 아님
⑤ (C) — (B) — (A) ┘

똑같은 사물에 서로 다른 이름을 붙이더라도 그 사물의 특징은 바뀌지 않는다는 의미인 셰익스피어의 말을 인용함 - 셰익스피어의 말이 틀렸음을 보여주는 Lera Boroditsky의 연구 - 다리를 묘사하라고 했을 때 독일어 원어민과 스페인어 원어민이 사용하는 단어가 다름 - '열쇠'라는 단어 같은 반대의 경우에도 마찬가지였음

| 문제 풀이 순서 | [정답률 55%]

1st 각 문단의 내용을 파악하고, 글의 논리적인 순서를 추론한다.

주어진 글: 셰익스피어는 "이름 안에 무엇이 있는가? 우리가 장미라고 부르는 것은 그 어떤 다른 이름으로 불러도 그만큼 달콤한 냄새가 날 것이다."라고 썼다.

→ 셰익스피어의 말은 똑같은 사물에 서로 다른 이름을 붙이더라도 그 사물의 특징은 바뀌지 않는다는 의미이다.

주어진 글 뒤: 셰익스피어의 이 말을 뒷받침하는 내용이나 이것이 틀렸음을 보여주는 내용이 이어질 것이다.

(A): '다리'라는 단어를 보자. 독일어로 '다리'(die brücke)는 여성 명사이지만, 스페인어로 '다리'(el puente)는 남성 명사이다. Boroditsky는 독일어 원어민이 다리를 묘사하라는 요청을 받았을 때, '아름다운', '우아한', '날씬한' 같은 단어를 사용한다는 사실을 알아냈다. 같은 질문을 받았을 때, 스페인어 원어민은 '강한', '튼튼한', '우뚝 솟은' 같은 단어를 사용했다.

→ 다리를 묘사하라는 요청을 받았을 때,
'다리'가 여성 명사인 독일어 원어민: '아름다운', '우아한', '날씬한' 같은 단어를 사용함
'다리'가 남성 명사인 스페인어 원어민: '강한', '튼튼한', '우뚝 솟은' 같은 단어를 사용함

(A) 앞: 셰익스피어의 말을 반박하는 예시라는 것은 알 수 있지만, 주어진 글에 곧바로 이어지기에는 부족하다.

▶ 주어진 글이 (A) 앞에 올 수 없음

(A) 뒤: '다리' 외의 또 다른 예시가 등장하거나 '다리'와 달리 셰익스피어의 말을 뒷받침하는 예시가 등장할 수 있다.

(B): Stanford 대학교의 심리학 교수인 Lera Boroditsky에 따르면, 그것(that)이 반드시 그렇지는 않다. 독일어와 스페인어 간의 문법적 성 차이에 초점을 맞춘 Boroditsky의 연구에 따르면, 우리의 언어가 특정 명사에 부여하는 성은 우리가 무의식적으로 그 명사에 문법적 성의 특성을 부여하도록 영향을 미친다.

→ 셰익스피어의 말이 틀렸음을 보여주는 Lera Boroditsky의 연구: 특정 명사에 부여하는 성이 그 명사에 문법적 성의 특성을 부여하도록 영향을 미침
(B) 앞: that이 가리키는 것이 셰익스피어의 말이므로 주어진 글에 (B)가 이어져야 한다.
▶ 순서: 주어진 글 → (B)
(B) 뒤: 특정 명사의 문법적 성이 그 명사에 그 문법적 성의 특성을 부여하도록 영향을 미친다는 것을 보여주는 예시가 (A)의 '다리'이다.
▶ 순서: 주어진 글 → (B) → (A)

(C): 이것은 반대의 경우에도 마찬가지였다. '열쇠'라는 단어는 독일어에서는 남성형이고 스페인어에서는 여성형이다. 독일어 원어민이 열쇠를 묘사하라는 요청을 받았을 때, '뾰족뾰족한', '무거운', '단단한', '금속의' 같은 단어를 사용했다. 스페인어 사용자는 '정교한', '황금빛의', '사랑스러운' 같은 단어를 사용했다.

→ '열쇠'는, '다리'와 반대로, 독일어에서는 남성형이고, 스페인어에서는 여성형이다.
(C) 앞: '다리'와 반대의 경우를 설명하므로 (C) 앞에는 (A)가 와야 한다.
▶ 순서: 주어진 글 → (B) → (A) → (C)

2nd 글이 한눈에 들어오도록 정리하여 정답을 확인한다.

주어진 글: 셰익스피어는 "이름 안에 무엇이 있는가? 우리가 장미라고 부르는 것은 그 어떤 다른 이름으로 불러도 그만큼 달콤한 냄새가 날 것이다."라고 썼다.
→ **(B):** 그것이 반드시 그렇지는 않은데, 우리의 언어가 특정 명사에 부여하는 성이 우리로 하여금 그 명사에 문법적 성의 특성을 부여하도록 영향을 미친다.
→ **(A):** '다리'는 독일어에서는 여성 명사이지만, 스페인어에서는 남성 명사이다. 독일어 원어민은 다리를 묘사하라는 요청을 받았을 때, '아름다운', '우아한', '날씬한' 같은 단어를 사용하고, 스페인어 원어민은 '강한', '튼튼한', '우뚝 솟은' 같은 단어를 사용했다.
→ **(C):** 이는 반대의 경우에도 마찬가지이다. '열쇠'는 독일어에서는 남성형이고 스페인어에서는 여성형이다. 독일어 원어민이 열쇠를 묘사하라는 요청을 받았을 때, '뾰족뾰족한', '무거운', '단단한', '금속의' 같은 단어를 사용하고, 스페인어 사용자는 '정교한', '황금빛의', '사랑스러운' 같은 단어를 사용했다.
▶ 주어진 글 다음에 이어질 글의 순서는 (B) → (A) → (C)이므로 정답은 ②임

M 26 정답 ③ *얼굴이 붉어지는 것의 역할

Darwin saw blushing / as uniquely human, / representing an
　　　　　see A as B: A를 B로 여기다
involuntary physical reaction / caused by embarrassment and
self-consciousness / in a social environment. // **단서 1** 얼굴이 붉어지는 것은 사회적 환경에서 일어나는 신체 반응임
다윈은 얼굴이 붉어지는 것을 여겼다 / 특별나게 인간적인 것으로 / 무의식적인 신체 반응을 나타내는 것 / 당혹감과 자의식에 의해 야기되는 / 사회적 환경에서 //

(A) Maybe our brief loss of face benefits / the long-term cohesion
　　　　　　　　　　　　　　단수 주어　　　　　단수 동사
of the group. //
아마도 우리가 잠시 체면을 잃는 것이 도움이 될 수 있을 것이다 / 집단의 장기적인 결속에 //

Interestingly, / if someone blushes / after making a social
mistake, / they are viewed / in a more favourable light / than
　　　비교의 부사 대상어
those / who don't blush. // **단서 2** 얼굴이 붉어지는 것은 실수에 대한 사과의 표시이므로 얼굴이 붉어지면 호의적인 시각을 받음
흥미롭게도 / 누군가 얼굴을 붉히면 / 사회적 실수를 저지른 후 / 그들은 바라봐진다 / 더 호의적인 시각으로 / 사람들보다 / 얼굴을 붉히지 않는 //

(B) If we feel awkward, embarrassed or ashamed / when we are
alone, / we don't blush; / **단서 3** 주어진 글의 사회적 환경과 혼자 있는 경우가 대조됨
우리가 어색하거나 부끄럽거나 창피하다고 느끼더라도 / 우리가 혼자 있을 때 / 우리는 얼굴이 붉어지지 않는다 /

it seems to be caused / by our concern / about what others are
　　　　　to부정사의 수동태(to be p.p.)
thinking of us. //
그것은 야기되는 것으로 보인다 / 우리의 염려에 의해 / 다른 사람들이 우리를 어떻게 생각할지에 대한 //

Studies have confirmed / that simply being told / you are
　　　　　　　　　　　　　　　　　　　　동명사의 수동태(being p.p.)
blushing / brings it on. //
연구들은 확인했다 / 단지 듣는 것만으로도 / 여러분이 얼굴이 붉어진다고 / 그것을 야기한다는 것을 //

We feel / as though others can see / through our skin and into
our mind. //
우리는 느낀다 / 다른 사람들이 들여다볼 수 있는 것처럼 / 우리의 피부를 꿰뚫어 우리의 마음을 //

(C) However, / while we sometimes want to disappear / when
　　　　　　부사절 접속사(대조)　　　　　　　　　　　부사절 접속사(때)
we involuntarily go bright red, /
그러나 / 우리가 때로 사라지고 싶어 하지만 / 우리가 자신도 모르는 사이에 얼굴이 새빨개질 때 /

psychologists argue / that blushing actually serves / a positive
social purpose. // **단서 4** 얼굴이 붉어지는 것이 실제로는 긍정적인 사회적 목적에 부합한다는 심리학자의 주장을 소개함
심리학자들은 주장한다 / 얼굴이 붉어지는 것이 실제로는 부합한다고 / 긍정적인 사회적 목적에 //

When we blush, / it's a signal to others / that we recognize / that
　　　　　　　　　　　　　　　　　　　　동격절 접속사
a social norm has been broken; / it is an apology for a faux pas. //
우리가 얼굴이 붉어질 때 / 그것은 다른 사람에게 보내는 신호이다 / 우리가 인정한다는 / 사회적 규범이 깨졌다는 것을 / 그것은 실수에 대한 사과이다 //

- blush ⓥ 얼굴을 붉히다　　• involuntary ⓐ 원치 않는, 자기도 모르게 하는
- embarrassment ⓝ 어색함, 쑥스러움
- self-consciousness ⓝ 자의식　　• brief ⓐ 짧은
- cohesion ⓝ 화합, 응집력　　• favourable ⓐ 좋은, 호의적인
- awkward ⓐ 어색한, 곤란한　　• bring on ~을 야기하다
- psychologist ⓝ 심리학자　　• recognize ⓥ 인정하다
- norm ⓝ 규범

다윈은 얼굴이 붉어지는 것을 특별나게 인간적인 것으로, 사회적 환경에서 당혹감과 자의식에 의한 무의식적인 신체 반응을 나타내는 것으로 여겼다. (B) 우리가 혼자 있을 때는 어색하거나 부끄럽거나 창피하다고 느끼더라도 얼굴이 붉어지지 않는데, 얼굴이 붉어지는 것은 우리가 다른 사람들이 우리를 어떻게 생각할지에 대해 염려하기 때문인 것으로 보인다. 연구에 따르면 단지 얼굴이 붉어진다는 말을 듣는 것만으로도 얼굴이 붉어진다는 것이 확인되었다. 우리는 다른 사람들이 우리의 피부를 꿰뚫어 우리의 마음을 들여다볼 수 있는 것처럼 느낀다. (C) 그러나 우리가 때로 자신도 모르는 사이에 얼굴이 새빨개질 때 사라지고 싶어 하지만, 심리학자들은 얼굴이 붉어지는 것이 실제로는 긍정적인 사회적 목적에 부합한다고 주장한다. 얼굴이 붉어질 때, 그것은 사회적 규범을 어겼다는 것을 우리가 인정한다는 것을 다른 사람에게 알리는 신호이자 실수에 대한 사과이다. (A) 아마도 우리가 잠시 체면을 잃는 것이 집단의 장기적인 결속에 도움이 될 수 있을 것이다. 흥미롭게도 누군가가 사회적 실수를 저지른 후 얼굴을 붉히면, 우리는 그 사람을 얼굴을 붉히지 않는 사람보다 더 호의적인 시각으로 바라보게 된다.

주어진 글 다음에 이어질 글의 순서로 가장 적절한 것을 고르시오.

① (A) — (C) — (B) 적절한 글의 흐름과 정반대
② (B) — (A) — (C) 실수에 대한 언급은 (C)에서 먼저 등장함
③ (B) — (C) — (A)
④ (C) — (A) — (B)
⑤ (C) — (B) — (A) 주어진 글과 (C)는 However로 이어질 만한 내용이 아님

└─ 얼굴이 붉어지는 것은 당혹감과 자의식에 의해 야기되는 무의식적인 신체 반응임 — 얼굴이 붉어지는 것은 혼자 있을 때는 일어나지 않음 — 얼굴이 붉어지는 것은 긍정적인 사회적 목적에 부합함 — 사회적 실수를 저지른 후 얼굴을 붉히면 더 호의적인 시각으로 바라봐짐

1st 각 문단의 내용을 파악하고, 글의 논리적인 순서를 추론한다.

주어진 글: 다윈은 얼굴이 붉어지는 것을 특별나게 인간적인 것으로, 사회적 환경에서 당혹감과 자의식에 의한 무의식적인 신체 반응을 나타내는 것으로 여겼다.

→ **주어진 글 뒤:** 얼굴이 붉어지는 것이 사회적 환경에서 어떤 역할을 하는지에 대한 설명이 이어지는 글일 것이다.

(A): 아마도 우리가 잠시 체면을 잃는 것이 집단의 장기적인 결속에 도움이 될 수 있을 것이다. 흥미롭게도 누군가가 사회적 실수를 저지른 후 얼굴을 붉히면, 우리는 그 사람을 얼굴을 붉히지 않는 사람보다 더 호의적인 시각으로 바라보게 된다.

→ '잠시 체면을 잃는 것'은 '얼굴이 붉어지는 것'을 의미한다. 얼굴이 붉어지는 것이 사회적 환경에서 긍정적인 역할을 한다는 내용이다.

(A) 앞: 주어진 글에서는 얼굴이 붉어지는 것이 사회적 환경에서 어떤 역할을 한다는 것을 암시하기만 했으므로, 주어진 글 바로 뒤에 (A)가 이어지는 것은 어색하다.

▶ 주어진 글 뒤에 (A)가 올 수 없음

(A) 뒤: 얼굴을 붉히는 것이 집단의 장기적인 결속에 도움이 될 수 있다는 것으로 보아, 얼굴을 붉히는 것의 사회적 역할을 설명한 글의 결론일 것이라고 예상할 수 있다.

▶ (A)가 마지막에 올 확률이 큼

(B): 우리가 혼자 있을 때는 어색하거나 부끄럽거나 창피하다고 느끼더라도 얼굴이 붉어지지 않는데, 얼굴이 붉어지는 것은 우리가 다른 사람들이 우리를 어떻게 생각할지에 대해 염려하기 때문인 것으로 보인다. 연구에 따르면 단지 얼굴이 붉어진다는 말을 듣는 것만으로도 얼굴이 붉어진다는 것이 확인되었다. 우리는 다른 사람들이 우리의 피부를 꿰뚫어 우리의 마음을 들여다볼 수 있는 것처럼 느낀다.

→ **(B) 앞:** 사회적 환경에서는 얼굴이 붉어지지만 혼자 있을 때는 얼굴이 붉어지지 않는다는 두 내용이 대조되도록 주어진 문장이 (B) 앞에 필요하다.

▶ (B) 앞에 주어진 글이 와야 함 (순서: 주어진 글 → (B))

(B) 뒤: (B)에서 얼굴이 붉어지는 원인(우리는 다른 사람들이 우리를 어떻게 생각할지 염려하기 때문)에 대해 설명했다. 이제 얼굴을 붉히는 것의 사회적 역할에 대한 내용이 이어질 것이다.

▶ (B) 뒤에 (A)가 이어질 수도 있음

(C): 그러나(However) 우리가 때로 자신도 모르는 사이에 얼굴이 새빨개질 때 사라지고 싶어 하지만, 심리학자들은 얼굴이 붉어지는 것이 실제로는 긍정적인 사회적 목적에 부합한다고 주장한다. 얼굴이 붉어질 때, 그것은 사회적 규범을 어겼다는 것을 우리가 인정한다는 것을 다른 사람에게 알리는 신호이자 실수에 대한 사과이다.

→ 얼굴이 붉어지는 것이 사실 긍정적인 사회적 목적에 부합한다는 내용이 However로 이어진다.

(C) 앞: 다른 사람들이 우리를 어떻게 생각할지 염려해서 얼굴이 붉어지지만, 사실 얼굴이 붉어지는 것은 긍정적인 사회적 역할을 한다는 흐름이다.

▶ (B) 뒤에 (C)가 와야 함 (순서: 주어진 글 → (B) → (C))

(C) 뒤: 얼굴이 붉어지는 것은 실수에 대한 사과를 표시하는 것이므로, 실수를 저지른 후 얼굴을 붉히면 더 호의적인 시선을 받는 것이다.

▶ (C) 뒤에 (A)가 와야 함(순서: 주어진 글 → (B) → (C) → (A))

2nd 글이 한눈에 들어오도록 정리하여 정답을 확인한다.

주어진 글: 얼굴이 붉어지는 것은 특별히 인간적인 것으로, 사회적 환경에서 당혹감과 자의식에 의해 야기되는 무의식적인 신체 반응이다.

→ **(B):** 얼굴이 붉어지는 것은 다른 사람들이 우리를 어떻게 생각할지에 대한 염려 때문이므로, 혼자 있을 때는 일어나지 않는다.

→ **(C):** 얼굴이 붉어지는 것은 실수에 대한 사과의 신호로, 긍정적인 사회적 목적에 부합한다.

→ **(A):** 사회적 실수를 저지른 후 얼굴을 붉히면 사과를 한 것이므로 더 호의적인 시각으로 바라봐진다.

▶ 주어진 글 다음에 이어질 글의 순서는 (B) → (C) → (A)이므로 정답은 ③임

M 27 정답 ⑤ *기록 증거로서의 미술의 위치 결정

It can be difficult / to decide the place of fine art, / such as
가주어   진주어
oil paintings, watercolours, sketches or sculptures, / in an
archival institution. //
~은 어려울 수 있다 / 미술의 위치를 정하는 것은 / 유화, 수채화, 스케치, 또는 조각과 같은 / 기록 보관 기관에서 //

(A) The best archival decisions / about art / do not focus on
territoriality / (this object belongs / in my institution / even
                          형용사적 용법(the resources 수식)   양보의
though I do not have the resources / to care for it) /
                                                      부사절 접속사
최선의 기록 보관 결정은 / 미술에 관한 / 영토권에 초점을 두지 않는다 / (이 물건은 속해 있다 / 내 기관에 / 내게 자원이 없더라도 / 그것을 돌볼) /
└─ 전치사구의 병렬 구조
or on questions / of monetary value or prestige / (this object
raises the cultural standing / of my institution). //
또는 문제에 (초점을 두지 않는다) / 금전적 가치나 위신의 / (이 물건은 문화적 지위를 높인다 / 내 기관의) //   **단서 1** 최선의 기록 보관 결정이 무엇인지 결론 내림
The best decisions focus / on what evidential value exists / and
                          └─전치사의 목적어 역할을 하는 명사절의 병렬 구조─┘
what is best / for the item. //
최선의 결정은 초점을 맞춘다 / 어떤 증거 가치가 존재하고 / 무엇이 최선인지에 / 그 품목을
위해 //   **단서 2** 앞에 미술이 지니는 미적 가치 외의 또 다른 가치가 있어야 함
(B) But art can also carry aesthetic value, / which elevates the
job of evaluation / into another realm. //   계속적 용법의 주격 관계대명사
그러나 미술은 또한 미적 가치를 지닐 수 있는데 / 그것은 감정이라는 일을 격상시킨다 / 다른 영역으로 //

Aesthetic value and the notion of artistic beauty / are important
considerations, / but they are not / what motivates archival
preservation / in the first instance. //   주격 보어절을 이끄는 관계대명사
미적 가치와 예술적 아름다움의 개념은 / 중요한 고려사항이다 / 하지만 그것들은 ~이 아니다
/ 기록 보존의 동기를 부여하는 것이 / 우선으로 //   **단서 3** 기록 증거로서의 미술의 가치를 이야기함
(C) Art can serve / as documentary evidence, / especially
when the items were produced / before photography became
시간의 부사절 접속사
common. //
미술은 도움이 될 수 있다 / 기록 증거로서 / 특히 그 품목들이 생산되었을 때 / 사진 촬영이 흔해지기 전에 //

Sketches of soldiers on a battlefield, / paintings of English
country villages / or portraits of Dutch townspeople /
전쟁터에 있는 군인들의 스케치 / 영국 시골 마을의 그림 / 또는 네덜란드 시민들의 초상화는 /
can provide the only visual evidence / of a long-ago place,
                          └─long-ago의 수식을 받는 명사의 병렬 구조─┘
person or time. //
유일한 시각적 증거를 제공할 수 있다 / 옛날의 장소, 사람 또는 시절의 //

- -

- fine art 미술   - oil painting 유화   - watercolour ⓝ 수채화
- sculpture ⓝ 조각(품)   - institution ⓝ 기관
- territoriality ⓝ 영토권   - monetary ⓐ 금전적인
- standing ⓝ 지위   - evidential ⓐ 증거의   - aesthetic ⓐ 미적인
- elevate ⓥ 격상시키다, 높이다   - evaluation ⓝ 감정, 평가
- notion ⓝ 개념, 관념, 생각   - consideration ⓝ 사려, 숙고, 고려 사항
- motivate ⓥ 이유[원인]가 되다, 동기를 부여하다   - preservation ⓝ 보존
- serve ⓥ 도움이 되다, 기여하다   - documentary ⓐ 기록의
- portrait ⓝ 초상화, 인물 사진   - townspeople ⓝ 시민

유화, 수채화, 스케치, 또는 조각과 같은 미술의 위치를 기록 보관 기관에서 정하는 것은 어려울 수 있다. (C) 미술은, 특히 사진 촬영이 흔해지기 전에 그 품목들이 생산되었을 때, 기록 증거의 역할을 할 수 있다. 전쟁터에 있는 군인들의 스케치, 영국 시골 마을의 그림 또는 네덜란드 시민들의 초상화는 옛날의 장소, 사람 또는 시절의 유일한 시각적 증거를 제공할 수 있다. (B) 그러나 미술은 또한 미적 가치를 지닐 수 있는데, 그것은 감정이라는 일을 다른 영역으로 격상시킨다. 미적 가치와 예술적 아름다움의 개념은 중요한 고려사항이지만, 그것들은 기록 보존의 동기를 우선으로 부여하는 것은 아니다. (A) 미술에 관한 최선의 기록 보관 결정은 영토권(이 물건은 내게 그것을 돌볼 자원이 없더라도 내 기관에 속해 있다)이나 금전적 가치나 위신의 문제(이 물건은 내 기관의 문화적 지위를 높인다)에 초점을 두지 않는다. 최선의 결정은 어떤 증거 가치가 존재하고 그 품목을 위해 무엇이 최선인지에 초점을 맞춘다.

주어진 글 다음에 이어질 글의 순서로 가장 적절한 것을 고르시오. [3점]

① (A) — (C) — (B)   최선의 기록 보관 결정이 무엇인지 결론 내리는 (A)가 맨 앞이나 중간에 오는 것은 어색함

② (B) — (A) — (C)

③ (B) — (C) — (A)   (B) 앞에 미적 가치 외의 미술의 또 다른 가치가 있어야 함

④ (C) — (A) — (B)

⑤ (C) — (B) — (A)   (C) 미술은 기록 증거로서의 가치가 있음 – (B) 미술에는 또한 미적 가치가 있음 – (A) 기록 증거로서의 미술의 위치에 대한 최선의 결정을 설명함

| 문제 풀이 순서 | [정답률 55%]

1st 각 문단의 내용을 파악하고, 글의 논리적인 순서를 추론한다.

> **주어진 글:** 유화, 수채화, 스케치, 또는 조각과 같은 미술의 위치를 기록 보관 기관에서 정하는 것은 어려울 수 있다.

➡ **주어진 글 뒤:** 기록 보관 기관에서 미술의 위치를 어떻게 정하는지에 관한 내용이 이어질 것이다.

> **(A):** 미술에 관한 최선의 기록 보관 결정은 영토권(이 물건은 내게 그것을 돌볼 자원이 없더라도 내 기관에 속해 있다)이나 금전적 가치나 위신의 문제(이 물건은 내 기관의 문화적 지위를 높인다)에 초점을 두지 않는다. 최선의 결정은 어떤 증거 가치가 존재하고 그 품목을 위해 무엇이 최선인지에 초점을 맞춘다. **단서 1**

➡ **(A) 앞:** 미술에 관한 여러 기록 보관 결정 중에서 최선의 결정에 관한 내용으로, 기록 보관 결정에 대한 내용이 앞에 먼저 나와야 한다.
▶ 주어진 글에 이 내용이 없으므로 (A) 앞에 주어진 글이 올 수 없음
(A) 뒤: 최선의 결정에 관한 내용이므로 글의 결론일 가능성이 크다.
▶ (A)가 마지막에 올 확률이 높음

> **(B):** 그러나 미술은 또한(also) 미적 가치를 지닐 수 있는데, 그것은 감정이라는 일을 다른 영역으로 격상시킨다. **단서 2** 미적 가치와 예술적 아름다움의 개념은 중요한 고려사항이지만, 그것들은 기록 보존의 동기를 우선으로 부여하는 것은 아니다.

➡ **(B) 앞:** 연결어 also로 앞에 언급된 내용과 더불어 새로운 내용을 제시하는데, 미술이 미적 가치를 지니는 것 말고 다른 가치를 지닌다는 내용이 앞에 나와야 한다.
▶ (B) 앞에 주어진 글이 올 수 없음
(B) 뒤: 미술의 미적 가치도 중요하지만, 우선적인 기록 보존 동기는 아니라고 했으므로 기록 보관 결정에 있어 다른 고려사항이 뒤에 이어져야 한다. 기록 보관 결정이 영토권, 금전적 가치, 위신 등에 초점을 두지 않는다는 내용이 (A)에 나온다.
▶ (B) 뒤에 (A)가 와야 함 (순서: (B) → (A))

> **(C):** 미술은, 특히 사진 촬영이 흔해지기 전에 그 품목들이 생산되었을 때, 기록 증거의 역할을 할 수 있다. **단서 3** 전쟁터에 있는 군인들의 스케치, 영국 시골 마을의 그림 또는 네덜란드 시민들의 초상화는 옛날의 장소, 사람 또는 시절의 유일한 시각적 증거를 제공할 수 있다.

➡ **(C) 앞:** 미술이 기록 증거의 역할을 한다는 내용으로, 미술의 위치 중 하나를 제시한다. 기록 보관 기관에서 미술의 위치를 정하기 어렵다는 내용의 주어진 글이 앞에 나와야 한다.
▶ (C) 앞에 주어진 글이 와야 함 (순서: 주어진 글 → (C))
(C) 뒤: 미술이 기록 증거의 역할은 물론이고 미적 가치도 지닌다는 흐름이므로, 미술의 미적 가치를 언급하는 (B)가 뒤에 나와야 한다.
▶ (C) 뒤에 (B)가 와야 함 (순서: 주어진 글 → (C) → (B) → (A))

2nd 글이 한눈에 들어오도록 정리하여 정답을 확인한다.

주어진 글: 기록 보관 기관에서 미술의 위치를 정하는 것은 어렵다.
→ **(C):** 미술은 기록 증거의 역할을 할 수 있다.
→ **(B):** 미술은 또한 미적 가치를 지니지만 이것이 우선적인 기록 보존 동기가 되진 않는다.
→ **(A):** 미술에 관한 최선의 기록 보관 결정은 최선의 증거 가치에 초점을 맞춘다.
▶ 주어진 글 다음에 이어질 글의 순서는 (C) → (B) → (A)이므로 정답은 ⑤임

＊ 글의 흐름

도입	기록 보관 기관에서 미술품의 위치를 결정하는 것은 어려울 수 있음
부연 ①	미술은 기록 증거로서 도움이 될 수 있음
부연 ②	미술에는 기록 증거로서의 가치 외에도 미적 가치도 있을 수 있지만, 이것이 기록 보존의 동기를 우선적으로 부여하는 것은 아님
결론	최선의 기록 보관 결정은 어떤 증거 가치가 존재하고 무엇이 그 품목을 위해 최선인지에 초점을 맞춤

M 28 정답 ③ ＊상상력을 수반하는 우리의 인식

Our perception always involves / some imagination. //
우리의 인식은 항상 수반한다 / 얼마간의 상상력을 //

It is more similar to painting / than to photography. //
그것은 그림과 더 비슷하다 / 사진보다는 //

And, according to the confirmation effect, / we blindly trust
the reality / we construct. //   앞에 목적격 관계대명사가 생략됨 ＊
그리고, 확증 효과에 따르면 / 우리는 현실을 맹목적으로 신뢰한다 / 자신이 구축하는 //

(A) You will see / that the majority of us are quite ignorant /
   전치사   명사절
about what lies around us. // **단서 1** 다른 사람과 함께 있을 때 그에게 그 현장에 대해 질문하면 알게 되는 사실
여러분은 알게 될 것이다 / 우리 대다수가 상당히 무지하다는 것을 / 우리 주변에 놓여 있는 것에 대해 //

This is not so puzzling. //
이것은 그렇게 이해하기 어렵지 않다 //

The most extraordinary fact is / that we completely disregard
   주어   동사   주격 보어절 접속사
this ignorance. //
가장 놀라운 사실은 ~이다 / 우리가 이 무지를 완전히 무시한다는 것 //

(B) This is best witnessed / in visual illusions, / which we
   선행사   계속적 용법의 목적격 관계대명사
perceive with full confidence, / as if there were no doubt / that
we are portraying reality faithfully. //
이것은 가장 잘 목격되는데 / 시각적 착각들에서 / 우리는 그것을 온전히 자신 있게 인식한다 / 마치 의심의 여지가 없는 것처럼 / 우리가 현실을 충실하게 묘사하고 있다는 것에 //

   단수 주어
One interesting way of discovering this / — in a simple game /
that can be played at any moment — / is the following. //
   단수 동사
이것을 발견하는 한 가지 흥미로운 방법은 / 간단한 게임에서 / 언제든지 행해질 수 있는 / 다음과 같다 // **단서 2** 이것을 발견하는 구체적인 방법을 설명한 문단이 이어져야 함

(C) Whenever you are with another person, / ask him or her
   복합 관계부사   병렬 구조
to close their eyes, / and start asking questions / about what is
nearby / **단서 3** (B)에서 말한 한 가지 흥미로운 방법을 설명하기 시작함
여러분이 다른 사람과 함께 있을 때마다 / 그 사람에게 눈을 감으라고 요청하고 / 질문하기 시작하라 / 근처에 있는 것에 대해 /

— not very particular details / but the most striking elements
of the scene. //
그 현장의 아주 구체적인 세부 사항이 아니라 / 가장 눈에 띄는 요소들 //

What is the color of the wall? //
벽의 색깔은 무엇인가 //

Is there a table in the room? //
방에 테이블이 있는가 //

Does that man have a beard? //
저 남자는 턱수염이 있는가 //

- perception ⓝ 인식 ・imagination ⓝ 상상
- confirmation effect 확증 효과 ・blindly ⓐⓓ 맹목적으로
- construct ⓥ 구축하다 ・ignorant ⓐ 무지한
- puzzling ⓐ 이해하기 어려운 ・extraordinary ⓐ 놀라운
- disregard ⓥ 무시하다 ・ignorance ⓝ 무지
- portray ⓥ 묘사하다 ・faithfully ⓐⓓ 충실하게
- striking ⓐ 눈에 띄는 ・element ⓝ 요소 ・beard ⓝ 턱수염

우리의 인식은 항상 얼마간의 상상력을 수반한다. 그것은 사진보다는 그림과 더 비슷하다. 그리고, 확증 효과에 따르면, 우리는 자신이 구축하는 현실을 맹목적으로 신뢰한다. (B) 이것은 시각적 착각들에서 가장 잘 목격되는데, 마치 우리가 현실을 충실하게 묘사하고 있다는 것에 의심의 여지가 없는 것처럼 우리는 그것을 온전히 자신 있게 인식한다. 언제든지 할 수 있는 간단한 게임에서 이것을 발견하는 한 가지 흥미로운 방법은 다음과 같다. (C) 여러분이 다른 사람과 함께 있을 때마다, 그 사람에게 눈을 감으라고 요청하고, 근처에 있는 것, 즉 그 현장의 아주 구체적인 세부 사항이 아니라 가장 눈에 띄는 요소들에 대해 질문하기 시작하라. 벽의 색깔은 무엇인가? 방에 테이블이 있는가? 저 남자는 턱수염이 있는가? (A) 여러분은 우리 대다수가 우리 주변에 놓여 있는 것에 대해 상당히 무지하다는 것을 알게 될 것이다. 이것은 그렇게 이해하기 어렵지 않다. 가장 놀라운 사실은 우리가 이 무지를 완전히 무시한다는 것이다.

주어진 글 다음에 이어질 글의 순서로 가장 적절한 것을 고르시오. [3점]

① (A) ― (C) ― (B) 무엇을 통해 알게 되는지가 (A) 앞에 필요함
② (B) ― (A) ― (C) 같이 있는 사람에게 현장에 대해 질문함으로써 알게 되는 것임
③ (B) ― (C) ― (A)
④ (C) ― (A) ― (B) ┐ (B)에서 '다음과 같다'고 했으므로 방법을 설명하는
⑤ (C) ― (B) ― (A) ┘ (C) 앞에 (B)가 필요함

― 우리는 현실을 상상력을 수반하여 인식하고, 이러한 인식을 맹목적으로 신뢰함 - 이것을 발견하는 흥미로운 방식은 다음과 같음 - 다른 사람과 함께 있을 때 그 현장의 가장 눈에 띄는 요소들을 질문하라고 했음 - 대다수가 주변에 놓여 있는 것에 대해 상당히 무지하다는 것을 알게 될 것임

| 문제 풀이 순서 | [정답률 64%]

1st 각 문단의 내용을 파악하고, 글의 논리적인 순서를 추론한다.

주어진 글: 우리의 인식은 항상 얼마간의 상상력을 수반한다. 그것은 사진보다는 그림과 더 비슷하다. 그리고, 확증 효과에 따르면, 우리는 자신이 구축하는 현실을 맹목적으로 신뢰한다.

→ 우리는 현실을 사진처럼 정확하게 인식하는 것이 아니라 얼마간의 상상력을 수반하여 인식하고, 나아가 이러한 인식을 맹목적으로 신뢰한다는 내용이다.
주어진 글 뒤: 우리가 현실을 인식하는 방식에 대한 구체적인 설명이 이어질 것이다.

(A): 여러분은 우리 대다수가 우리 주변에 놓여 있는 것에 대해 상당히 무지하다는 것을 알게 될 것이다(will see). 이것은 그렇게 이해하기 어렵지 않다. 가장 놀라운 사실은 우리가 이 무지를 완전히 무시한다는 것이다.

→ 어떤 실험의 결과로 우리가 알게 될 것(우리가 우리 주변에 놓여 있는 것에 대해 상당히 무지하다는 사실)을 설명한다.
(A) 앞: 실험의 과정 등 구체적인 실험 내용이 (A) 앞에 있어야 하는데, 주어진 글은 그러한 내용이 아니다.
▶ 주어진 글이 (A) 앞에 올 수 없음
(A) 뒤: 실험 결과를 이야기하는 문단이므로 글의 결론임을 알 수 있다.
▶ (A)가 마지막에 올 확률이 큼

(B): 이것(This)은 시각적 착각들에서 가장 잘 목격되는데, 마치 우리가 현실을 충실하게 묘사하고 있다는 것에 의심의 여지가 없는 것처럼 우리는 그것을 온전히 자신 있게 인식한다. 언제든지 할 수 있는 간단한 게임에서 이것을 발견하는 한 가지 흥미로운 방법은 다음과 같다.

→ **(B) 앞:** 주어진 글에서 설명한 현상이 가장 잘 목격되는 상황을 설명하는 문단으로, This가 가리키는 것이 주어진 글에서 설명한 내용이다.
▶ 순서: 주어진 글 → (B)
(B) 뒤: 이것을 발견하는 한 방법이 다음과 같다고 했으므로, 이후로는 그 방법에 대해 설명할 것이다.

(C): 여러분이 다른 사람과 함께 있을 때마다, 그 사람에게 눈을 감으라고 요청하고, 근처에 있는 것, 즉 그 현장의 아주 구체적인 세부 사항이 아니라 가장 눈에 띄는 요소들에 대해 질문하기 시작하라. 벽의 색깔은 무엇인가? 방에 테이블이 있는가? 저 남자는 턱수염이 있는가?

→ **(C) 앞:** (B)에서 다음과 같다고 말한 '방법'을 구체적으로 설명한 문단이다.
▶ 순서: 주어진 글 → (B) → (C)
(C) 뒤: 같이 있는 사람에게 그 현장의 눈에 띄는 요소에 대해 질문한 결과를 통해 우리가 우리 주변에 놓여 있는 것에 대해 상당히 무지하다는 사실을 알게 될 것이라는 흐름이다.
▶ 순서: 주어진 글 → (B) → (C) → (A)

2nd 글이 한눈에 들어오도록 정리하여 정답을 확인한다.

주어진 글: 우리의 인식은 얼마간의 상상력을 수반하며, 우리는 현실에 대한 우리의 인식을 맹목적으로 신뢰한다.
→ **(B):** 이것을 발견하는 한 가지 흥미로운 방식은 다음과 같다.
→ **(C):** 다른 사람과 함께 있을 때 그 사람에게 그 현장의 가장 눈에 띄는 요소들을 질문하라.
→ **(A):** (그러면) 우리 대다수가 우리 주변에 놓여 있는 것에 대해 상당히 무지하다는 것을 알게 될 것이고, 가장 놀라운 것은 우리가 이 무지를 완전히 무시한다는 것이다.
▶ 주어진 글 다음에 이어질 글의 순서는 (B) → (C) → (A)이므로 정답은 ③임

────── 어법 특강

✱ 관계대명사의 생략

- 목적격 관계대명사는 생략하는 경우가 많다.
- She was a celebrated actress (whom) he had known and loved.
  a celebrated actress를 선행사로 하는 관계대명사
  (그녀는 그가 알고 사랑했던 유명한 배우였다.)

- 「주격 관계대명사+be동사」는 생략할 수 있다.
- Look at the singer (who is) performing on the stage!
  the singer를 선행사로 하는 관계대명사
  (무대에서 공연하고 있는 가수를 봐!)

Ⓜ 29 정답 ⑤ ＊똑똑한 식물 ─────

Plants show / finely tuned adaptive responses / when nutrients are limiting. //
　　　　　　　　　　　　　　　　부사절 접속사(때)
식물은 보인다 / 미세하게 조정된 적응 반응을 / 영양분이 제한적일 때 //

Gardeners may recognize yellow leaves / as a sign / of poor nutrition and the need for fertilizer. //
정원사는 노란 잎을 인식할 수도 있다 / 신호로 / 영양 부족과 비료가 필요하다는 //

　　　　　　　복수 동사
(A) In contrast, / plants / with a history of nutrient abundance /
복수 주어
are risk averse / and save energy. // **단서 1** 영양분이 풍부했던 이력을 가진 식물에 대한 내용이 In contrast로 이어짐
반대로 / 식물은 / 영양분이 풍부했던 이력을 가진 / 위험을 회피하고 / 에너지를 절약한다 //

At all developmental stages, / plants respond / to environmental

changes or unevenness / so as to be able to use their energy / for

〈목적〉의 의미를 강조하는 so as to-v

growth, survival, and reproduction, /

모든 발달 단계에서 / 식물은 반응한다 / 환경 변화나 불균형에 / 에너지를 사용할 수 있도록 /

성장, 생존, 번식에 /

= they limit

while limiting / damage and nonproductive uses / of their

valuable energy. //

제한하는 동시에 / 손상과 비생산적인 사용을 / 귀중한 에너지의 //

생략 가능한 목적어절 접속사

(B) Research in this area has shown / that plants are constantly

aware / of their position in the environment, / in terms of both

space and time. //

이 분야의 연구는 보여주었다 / 식물은 지속적으로 인식한다는 것을 / 환경에서 자신의 위치를

/ 공간과 시간 모두의 측면에서 //

주격 관계대명사   주격 관계대명사절의 복수 동사   _{단서 2} 다양한 영양소 가용성을 경험한 식물의 경우를 설명함

Plants / that have experienced / variable nutrient availability / in

복수 주어, 선행사

the past / tend to exhibit risk-taking behaviors, / such as spending

복수 동사

energy / on root lengthening / instead of leaf production. //

식물은 / 경험한 / 다양한 영양소 가용성을 / 과거에 / 위험을 감수하는 행동을 보이는 경향이

있다 / 에너지를 소비하는 것과 같은 / 뿌리 길이를 연장하는 데 / 잎 생산 대신 //

(C) But if a plant does not have a caretaker / to provide

부사절 접속사(조건)   형용사적 용법(a caretaker 수식)

supplemental minerals, /

그러나 식물에게 관리자가 없다면 / 보충하는 미네랄을 공급해 줄 /

it can proliferate or lengthen its roots / and develop root hairs /

부사적 용법(목적)

to allow foraging / in more distant soil patches. //

그것은 뿌리를 증식하거나 길게 늘리고 / 뿌리털을 발달시킬 수 있다 / 구하러 다닐 수 있도록

/ 더 먼 토양에서 //

Plants can also use their memory / to respond / to histories

of temporal or spatial variation / in nutrient or resource

availability. // _{단서 3} 영양이나 자원 가용성의 변화에 대응하기 위해

식물이 자신의 기억을 사용할 수도 있다고 설명함

식물은 또한 자신의 기억을 사용할 수 있다 / 대응하기 위해 / 시간적 또는 공간적 변화의

역사에 / 영양 혹은 자원 가용성의 //

- finely [ad] 미세하게   • tune [v] 조정하다
- adaptive response 적응 반응   • gardener [n] 정원사
- poor nutrition 영양 실조   • in contrast 반대로
- abundance [n] 풍부   • risk averse 위험을 회피하는
- developmental [a] 발달의   • unevenness [n] 불균형
- so as to-v ~하기 위하여   • reproduction [n] 번식
- nonproductive [a] 비생산적인   • constantly [ad] 지속적으로
- availability [n] 가용성   • risk-taking [a] 위험을 감수하는
- lengthen [v] 연장하다   • supplemental [a] 보충의
- proliferate [v] 증식시키다   • patch [n] 작은 땅, 지대
- temporal [a] 시간의   • spatial [a] 공간의

식물은 영양분이 제한적일 때 미세하게 조정된 적응 반응을 보인다. 정원사는

노란 잎을 영양 부족과 비료가 필요하다는 신호로 인식할 수도 있다.

(C) 그러나 식물에 보충하는 미네랄을 공급해 줄 관리자가 없다면, 그것은 더

먼 토양에서 구하러 다닐 수 있도록 뿌리를 증식하거나 길게 늘리고 뿌리털을

발달시킬 수 있다. 식물은 또한 영양 혹은 자원 가용성의 시간적 또는 공간적

변화의 역사에 대응하기 위해 자신의 기억을 사용할 수 있다.

(B) 이 분야의 연구는 식물은 공간과 시간 모두의 측면에서 환경에서 자신의

위치를 지속적으로 인식한다는 것을 보여주었다. 과거에 다양한 영양소

가용성을 경험한 식물은 잎 생산 대신 뿌리 길이를 연장하는 데 에너지를

소비하는 것과 같은 위험을 감수하는 행동을 보이는 경향이 있다.

(A) 반대로, 영양분이 풍부했던 이력을 가진 식물은 위험을 회피하고 에너지를

절약한다. 모든 발달 단계에서 식물은 성장, 생존, 번식에 에너지를 사용할

수 있도록 환경 변화나 불균형에 반응하는 동시에, 귀중한 에너지의 손상과

비생산적인 사용을 제한한다.

주어진 글 다음에 이어질 글의 순서로 가장 적절한 것을 고르시오. [3점]

① (A) — (C) — (B) (A)에서 설명하는 식물이 정원사가 없는 식물이 아님

② (B) — (A) — (C) ┐ (B)의 this area가 가리키는 것이 주어진 글에 없음

③ (B) — (C) — (A) ┘

④ (C) — (A) — (B) (B)의 다양한 영양소 가용성을 경험한 식물이 (A)의 영양분이 풍부했던 이력을 가진 식물보다 먼저 나와야 함

⑤ (C) — (B) — (A)

┌ 정원사는 노란 잎을 신호로 인식하여 비료를 식물에 제공할 것임 - 관리자가 없는 식물은 뿌리를 ┐

│ 증식하거나 길게 늘릴 것임 - 다양한 영양소 가용성을 경험한 식물은 뿌리 길이를 연장하는 데 │

└ 에너지를 소비하는 경향이 있음 - 영양분이 풍부했던 경험을 가진 식물은 위험을 회피함 ┘

| 문제 풀이 순서 | [정답률 42%]

1st 각 문단의 내용을 파악하고, 글의 논리적인 순서를 추론한다.

┌─────────────────────────────────────┐
│ **주어진 글:** 식물은 영양분이 제한적일 때 미세하게 조정된 적응 반응을 │
│ 보인다. 정원사는 노란 잎을 영양 부족과 비료가 필요하다는 신호로 │
│ 인식할 수도 있다. │
└─────────────────────────────────────┘

⇒ 영양분이 제한적일 때 식물이 보이는 적응 반응을 보이는데 노란 잎을 보면

영양사는 영양과 비료를 제공할 것이라는 내용이다. _{단서}

주어진 글 뒤: 정원사가 식물을 관리해주는 것과 관련된 내용이 이어질 것이다. _{발상}

┌─────────────────────────────────────┐
│ (A): 반대로(In contrast), 영양분이 풍부했던 이력을 가진 식물은 │
│ 위험을 회피하고 에너지를 절약한다. 모든 발달 단계에서 식물은 │
│ 성장, 생존, 번식에 에너지를 사용할 수 있도록 환경 변화나 불균형에 │
│ 반응하는 동시에, 귀중한 에너지의 손상과 비생산적인 사용을 │
│ 제한한다. │
└─────────────────────────────────────┘

⇒ **(A) 앞:** 영양분이 풍부하지 않았던 이력을 가진 식물의 적응 반응을 설명한 문단이

필요하다.

▶ 주어진 글이 (A) 앞에 올 수 있음

(A) 뒤: 서로 다른 이력을 가진 식물의 적응 반응을 대조하는 글로, 두 번째 식물의

반응을 설명한 (A)가 글의 결론일 수 있다.

▶ (A)가 글의 결론일 가능성이 더 큼

┌─────────────────────────────────────┐
│ (B): 이 분야(this area)의 연구는 식물은 공간과 시간 모두의 측면에서 │
│ 환경에서 자신의 위치를 지속적으로 인식한다는 것을 보여주었다. │
│ 과거에 다양한 영양소 가용성을 경험한 식물은 잎 생산 대신 뿌리 │
│ 길이를 연장하는 데 에너지를 소비하는 것과 같은 위험을 감수하는 │
│ 행동을 보이는 경향이 있다. │
└─────────────────────────────────────┘

⇒ **(B) 앞:** 식물이 공간과 시간 모두의 측면에서 환경에서의 자신의 위치를

지속적으로 인식한다는 것을 보여주는 연구가 어떤 분야의 연구인지, 즉 this

area가 가리키는 내용이 (B) 앞에 있어야 한다.

▶ 주어진 글이나 (A)에는 해당 분야가 언급되지 않음

(B) 뒤: (A)에서 설명한 '영양분이 풍부했던 이력을 가진 식물'과 대조되는 '과거에

다양한 영양소 가용성을 경험한 식물'이 (B)에 등장하므로 (A) 앞에 (B)가 있어야

한다.

▶ (A) 앞에 (B)가 와야 함 (순서: (B) → (A))

┌─────────────────────────────────────┐
│ (C): 그러나(But) 식물에 보충하는 미네랄을 공급해 줄 관리자가 │
│ 없다면, 그것은 더 먼 토양에서 구하러 다닐 수 있도록 뿌리를 │
│ 증식하거나 길게 늘리고 뿌리털을 발달시킬 수 있다. 식물은 또한 영양 │
│ 혹은 자원 가용성의 시간적 또는 공간적 변화의 역사에 대응하기 위해 │
│ 자신의 기억을 사용할 수 있다. │
└─────────────────────────────────────┘

⇒ **(C) 앞:** 식물에게 보충하는 미네랄을 공급해 줄 관리자가 없는 경우와 대조되는

경우가 (C) 앞에 필요한데, 주어진 글이 정원사가 있는 경우를 설명했다.

▶ 주어진 글이 (C) 앞에 와야 함 (순서: 주어진 글 → (C))

(C) 뒤: 식물은 자신의 기억, 경험을 사용하여 대응할 수 있다고 한 후, 두 가지 서로 다른 경험을 한 식물을 예로 들어 구체적으로 설명하는 흐름이 되어야 한다.

▶ (C) 뒤로 (B)와 (A)가 차례로 이어져야 함 (순서: 주어진 글 → (C) → (B) → (A))

2nd 글이 한눈에 들어오도록 정리하여 정답을 확인한다.

주어진 글: 정원사는 노란 잎을 영양 부족과 비료가 필요하다는 신호로 인식하여 그것을 식물에 제공할 것이다.

→ (C): 그러나 관리자가 없는 식물은 뿌리를 증식하거나 길게 늘이고, 뿌리털을 발달시켜 더 먼 토양에서 미네랄을 구할 것이다. 식물은 또한 자신의 기억을 사용하여 영양이나 자원 가용성의 변화에 대응할 수 있다.

→ (B): 다양한 영양소 가용성을 경험한 식물은 잎 생산 대신 뿌리 길이를 연장하는 데 에너지를 소비하는 경향이 있다.

→ (A): 반대로 영양분이 풍부했던 경험을 가진 식물은 위험을 회피하고 에너지를 절약한다.

▶ 주어진 글 다음에 이어질 글의 순서는 (C) → (B) → (A)이므로 정답은 ⑤임

M 30 정답 ⑤ * 에너지 효율을 위한 투자의 비용

> Experts have identified / a large number of measures / that
> 선행사   주격 관계대명사
> promote energy efficiency. //
> 전문가들은 찾아냈다 / 다수의 대책을 / 에너지 효율을 증진하는 //
>
> Unfortunately / many of them are not cost effective. //
> 유감스럽게도 / 그중 많은 수는 비용 효율적이지 않다 //   단서1 비용 효율성이 에너지 효율을 위한 투자에 근본적인 필요조건임
>
> This is a fundamental requirement / for energy efficiency
> investment / from an economic perspective. //
> 이것은 근본적인 필요조건이다 / 에너지 효율을 위한 투자에 / 경제적 관점에서 //
> 단서2 국가의 에너지 효율 수준을 높이는 것이 개인적인 차원에도 직접적인 영향을 미침
> (A) And this has direct repercussions / at the individual level: /
> 그리고 이것은 직접적인 영향을 미친다 / 개인적 차원에서 /
>
> households can reduce / the cost of electricity and gas bills, /
>   병렬구조
> and improve their health and comfort, / while companies can
> increase / their competitiveness and their productivity. //
> 가정은 줄일 수 있고 / 전기 비용과 가스 요금을 / 그들의 건강과 안락함을 증진할 수 있다 / 회사는 증대시킬 수 있는 한편 / 자체 경쟁력과 생산성을 //
>
> Finally, / the market for energy efficiency / could contribute to
> the economy / through job and firms creation. //
>   전치사   명사구
> 결국 / 에너지 효율 시장은 / 경제에 이바지할 수 있다 / 일자리와 기업 창출을 통해 //
>   형용사적 용법(externalities 수식)
> (B) There are significant externalities / to take into account / and
> there are also macroeconomic effects. //   단서3 비용 효율성의 산정이 쉽지 않다는 내용에 대한 부연 설명
> 상당한 외부 효과가 있고 / 고려해야 할 / 거시 경제적 효과도 있다 //
>   동명사구 주어
> For instance, / at the aggregate level, / improving the level
> of national energy efficiency / has positive effects / on
>   단수 동사
> macroeconomic issues /
> 예를 들어 / 집합적 차원에서 / 국가의 에너지 효율 수준을 높이는 것은 / 긍정적인 영향을 미친다 / 거시 경제적 문제에 /
>
> such as energy dependence, climate change, health, national
> competitiveness / and reducing fuel poverty. //
> 에너지 의존도, 기후 변화, 보건, 국가 경쟁력과 같은 / 그리고 연료 빈곤을 줄이는 것(과 같은) //
> 단서4 '그러한' 비용 효율성의 산정이 쉽지 않다는 내용으로 However로 연결됨
> (C) However, / the calculation of such cost effectiveness is not
>   of의 목적어로 쓰인 동명사의 병렬 구조 *
> easy: / it is not simply a case / of looking at private costs / and
> comparing them / to the reductions achieved. //
> 그러나 / 그러한 비용 효율성의 산정은 쉽지 않다 / 그것은 단순히 경우가 아니다 / 사적 비용을 살펴보고 / 그것을 비교하는 / 달성한 절감액과 //

- identify ⓥ (신원 등을) 확인하다[알아보다]   • measure ⓝ 조치, 정책
- promote ⓥ 촉진하다, 홍보하다   • efficiency ⓝ 효율(성), 능률
- fundamental ⓐ 근본[본질]적인, 핵심적인   • investment ⓝ 투자(액)
- perspective ⓝ 관점, 시각   • competitiveness ⓝ 경쟁력, 경쟁적인 것
- productivity ⓝ 생산성   • externality ⓝ 외부 효과
- take ~ into account ~을 고려하다[계산에 넣다]
- macroeconomic ⓐ 거시 경제의   • dependence ⓝ 의존, 의지
- calculation ⓝ 계산, 산출   • reduction ⓝ 감소, 할인

전문가들은 에너지 효율을 증진하는 다수의 대책을 찾아냈다. 유감스럽게도 그중 많은 수는 비용 효율적이지 않다. 이것은 경제적 관점에서 에너지 효율을 위한 투자에 근본적인 필요조건이다. (C) 그러나 그러한 비용 효율성의 산정은 쉽지 않은데, 그것은 단순히 사적 비용을 살펴보고 그것을 달성한 절감액과 비교하는 경우가 아니기 때문이다. (B) 고려해야 할 상당한 외부 효과가 있고 거시 경제적 효과도 있다. 예를 들어 집합적 차원에서, 국가의 에너지 효율 수준을 높이는 것은 에너지 의존도, 기후 변화, 보건, 국가 경쟁력, 연료 빈곤을 줄이는 것과 같은 거시 경제적 문제에 긍정적인 영향을 미친다. (A) 그리고 이것은 개인적 차원에서 직접적인 영향을 미치는데, 즉 가정은 전기 비용과 가스 요금을 줄이고 그들의 건강과 안락함을 증진할 수 있는 한편, 회사는 자체 경쟁력과 생산성을 증대시킬 수 있다. 결국, 에너지 효율 시장은 일자리와 기업 창출을 통해 경제에 이바지할 수 있다.

주어진 글 다음에 이어질 글의 순서로 가장 적절한 것을 고르시오. [3점]

① (A) — (C) — (B) (A)의 this가 가리키는 것이 주어진 글에 없음
② (B) — (A) — (C) ┐
③ (B) — (C) — (A) ┘ 상당한 외부 효과 때문에 비용 효율성 산정이 어려운 것임
④ (C) — (A) — (B) 예를 들어 설명하기 시작하는 (B)가 (A)보다 먼저 와야 함
⑤ (C) — (B) — (A)
└ 비용 효율성이 에너지 효율을 위한 투자의 필요조건임 – (C) 하지만 비용 효율성 산정은 쉽지 않음 – (B) 상당한 외부 효과와 거시 경제적 효과가 있기 때문에 산정이 어려움 – (A) 국가 차원에서 에너지 효율 수준을 높이는 것이 개인적 차원에서도 영향을 미침

| 문제 풀이 순서 | [정답률 48%]

1st 각 문단의 내용을 파악하고, 글의 논리적인 순서를 추론한다.

> **주어진 글:** 전문가들은 에너지 효율을 증진하는 다수의 대책을 찾아냈다. 유감스럽게도 그중 많은 수는 비용 효율적이지 않다. 이것은 경제적 관점에서 에너지 효율을 위한 투자에 근본적인 필요조건이다. 단서1

→ 주어진 글 뒤: 에너지 효율을 위한 투자의 비용 효율성에 관한 내용이 이어질 것이다.

> **(A):** 그리고 이것은(this) 개인적 차원에서 직접적인 영향을 미치는데, 즉 가정은 전기 비용과 가스 요금을 줄이고 그들의 건강과 안락함을 증진할 수 있는 한편, 회사는 자체 경쟁력과 생산성을 증대시킬 수 있다. 단서2 결국, 에너지 효율 시장은 일자리와 기업 창출을 통해 경제에 이바지할 수 있다.

→ (A) 앞: this가 개인적 차원에서 직접적인 영향을 미치고, 가정의 건강과 회사의 경쟁력을 증대시킨다는 내용이다. this가 '무엇'인지에 대해 앞에 나와야 한다.
▶ 주어진 글에 이 내용이 없으므로 (A) 앞에 주어진 글이 올 수 없음
(A) 뒤: 결론을 나타내는 부사인 Finally가 나온다.
▶ (A)가 마지막에 올 확률이 높음

> **(B):** 고려해야 할 상당한 외부 효과가 있고 거시 경제적 효과도 있다. 단서3 예를 들어 집합적 차원에서, 국가의 에너지 효율 수준을 높이는 것은 에너지 의존도, 기후 변화, 보건, 국가 경쟁력, 연료 빈곤을 줄이는 것과 같은 거시 경제적 문제에 긍정적인 영향을 미친다.

→ (B) 앞: 고려해야 할 외부 효과와 거시 경제적 효과가 있다는 내용으로, '무엇'을 하기 전에 이러한 효과들을 고려해야 하는지 앞에 나와야 한다.
▶ (B) 앞에 주어진 글이 올 수 없음
(B) 뒤: 국가의 에너지 효율 수준을 높이는 것이 거시 경제적 문제에 긍정적 영향을 미친다는 내용으로, 개인적 차원에서도 건강과 안락함을 증진한다는 등의 긍정적인 영향을 미친다는 내용이 (A)에 나온다. 즉, (A)의 this는 '국가의 에너지 효율 수준을 높이는 것'이다.
▶ (B) 뒤에 (A)가 와야 함 (순서: (B) → (A))

(C): 그러나(However) 그러한 비용 효율성의 산정은 쉽지 않은데, 그것은 단순히 사적 비용을 살펴보고 그것을 달성한 절감액과 비교하는 경우가 아니기 때문이다. **단서 4**

→ **(C) 앞:** 역접의 연결어 However로 시작하며 비용 효율성의 산정이 쉽지 않다고 설명하는 내용이다. 비용 효율성이 에너지 효율을 위한 투자에 필요조건이지만 이를 산정하는 것은 어렵다는 흐름이 되어야 한다.
 ▶ (C) 앞에 주어진 글이 와야 함 (순서: 주어진 글 → (C))
 (C) 뒤: 비용 효율성을 산정하는 것이 어려운 이유를 설명하기 위해 고려해야 할 다른 요소, 즉 상당한 외부 효과와 거시 경제적 효과가 (B)에 나온다.
 ▶ (C) 뒤에 (B)가 와야 함 (순서: 주어진 글 → (C) → (B) → (A))

2nd 글이 한눈에 들어오도록 정리하여 정답을 확인한다.

주어진 글: 에너지 효율 투자에서 비용 효율성이 필요조건이다.
→ **(C):** 비용 효율성의 산정이 쉽지 않다.
→ **(B):** 이를 위해 고려해야 할 상당한 외부 효과와 거시 경제적 효과가 있다. 국가의 에너지 효율 수준을 높이면 거시 경제적 문제에 긍정적 영향을 미친다.
→ **(A):** 이는 개인적 차원에서도 직접적인 영향을 미친다.
 ▶ 주어진 글 다음에 이어질 글의 순서는 (C) → (B) → (A)이므로 정답은 **⑤**임

* 글의 흐름

도입	에너지 효율을 위한 투자에 비용 효율성은 근본적인 필요조건임
전개	하지만 고려해야 할 상당한 외부 효과가 있고, 거시 경제적 효과 때문에 비용 효율성의 산정은 쉽지 않음
예시	국가의 에너지 효율 수준을 높이는 것은 거시 경제적 문제에 긍정적인 영향을 미치는데, 이것은 개인적 차원에도 직접적인 영향을 미침

─── 어법 특강 ───

* 전치사의 목적어

– 전치사 뒤에 오는 단어나 어구를 전치사의 목적어라고 하는데, 주로 명사(구)나 동명사, 명사절이 쓰인다.

• He has insisted on his innocence from the beginning.
 (그는 처음부터 자신의 무죄를 주장해 왔다.)

• He kept on saying 'Where are the kids?' over and over again.
 (그는 계속해서 '아이들은 어디에 있어?'라고 말했다.)

• Judith was surprised at what the news said.
 (Judith는 뉴스가 전한 것에 놀랐다.)

M 31 정답 ④ ***제국주의화의 두 가지 요소**

Representation is control. //
표현은 지배력이다 //
(주어) (형용사적 용법(The power 수식)) (동사) (주격 보어)
The power / to represent the world / is the power / to represent
 / us in it or it in us, / (형용사적 용법(the power 수식))
힘은 / 세상을 표현하는 / 힘이다 / 표현하는 / 그것 속에 있는 우리 또는 우리 속에 있는 그것을 /
(부사절 접속사(이유))
for the final stage of representing merges / the representor
and the represented / into one. //
표현하기의 최종 단계는 병합하기 때문에 / 표현하는 것과 표현되는 것을 / 하나로 //
(복수 주어) (복수 동사)
Imperializing cultures produce / great works of art (great
representations) / which can be put to work intellectually
(주격 관계대명사)
/ as armies and trading houses work / militarily and
 단서 1 제국주의화하는 문화는 지적으로 작동할 수 있는 훌륭한 예술 작품을 생산함
economically. //
제국주의화하는 문화는 생산한다 / 훌륭한 예술 작품을 (훌륭한 표현) / 지적으로 작동할 수 있는 / 군대와 무역 회사가 작동하는 것과 마찬가지로 / 군사적, 경제적으로 //

─────────────────

(주격 보어절 접속사)   (부사절 접속사(조건))
(A) That is because / unless we can control the world
intellectually / by maps / we cannot control it / militarily or
economically. // **단서 2** 식민지화의 유럽이 위대한 지도 제작자들의 유럽이기도 했던 이유
그것은 ~ 때문이다 / 우리가 세상을 지적으로 지배할 수 없다면 / 지도로 / 우리는 그것을 지배할 수 없기 (때문이다) / 군사적으로나 경제적으로 //

Mercator, Molière, Columbus and Captain Cook / imperialized
in different ways, /
메르카토르, 몰리에르, 콜럼버스 그리고 쿡 선장은 / 서로 다른 방식으로 제국주의화했지만 /
but they all imperialized, / and ultimately the effectiveness of
one / depended upon and supported / the effectiveness of all
the others. // (upon과 supported의 목적어)
그들은 모두 제국주의화했고 / 궁극적으로 하나의 유효성은 / 의존하고 뒷받침했다 / 다른 모든 것들의 유효성에 // **단서 3** 유럽과 유사한 점을 보이는 미국의 현대 식민지화 형태에 대한 내용이 시작

(B) Similarly / the US form of contemporary colonization, /
(주어)
which involves / occupying economies and political parties /
rather than physical territories, /
마찬가지로 / 미국의 현대 식민지화 형태는 / 포함하는 / 경제와 정당을 차지하는 것을 / 물리적 영토라기보다는 /
(동사)
is accompanied / by the power of both Hollywood and the
satellite / to represent the world / to and for the US. // (to와 for의 목적어)
동반된다 / 할리우드와 인공위성 둘 다의 힘에 의해 / 세계를 표현하기 위해 / 미국에 그리고 미국을 위해 //

─── 원급 비교 ───
(C) Shakespeare, Jane Austen and maps / were as important / to
 (주어와 동사가 도치됨)
English Imperial power / as was the East India Company, the
British army and the churches of England. //
셰익스피어, 제인 오스틴 그리고 지도는 / ~만큼 중요했다 / 영국 제국의 힘에 / 동인도 회사, 영국 군대 그리고 영국의 교회가 그런 만큼 // **단서 4** 식민지화의 유럽이 위대한 예술의 유럽이기도 했던 것은 우연이 아님
It is no coincidence / that modern Europe, / the Europe of
colonization, / was also the Europe of "great art," /
우연이 아니다 / 현대 유럽이 / 식민지화의 유럽인 / '위대한 예술'의 유럽이기도 했다는 것은 /
and no coincidence either / that it was the Europe / of great map
makers. // **단서 5** 지도에 대한 언급이 등장함
또한 우연이 아니다 / 그것이 유럽이었다는 것도 / 위대한 지도 제작자들의 //

• representation ⓝ 표현   • merge ⓥ 합병하다
• imperialize ⓥ 제국주의화하다   • intellectually ⓐⓓ 지적으로
• depend upon ~에 의존하다   • contemporary ⓐ 현대의
• accompany ⓥ 동반하다   • coincidence ⓝ 우연의 일치, 우연
• colonization ⓝ 식민지화

표현은 지배력이다. 세상을 표현하는 힘은 그것 속에 있는 우리 또는 우리 속에 있는 그것을 표현하는 힘인데, 표현하기의 최종 단계는 표현하는 것과 표현되는 것을 하나로 병합하기 때문이다. 제국주의화하는 문화는 군대와 무역 회사가 군사적, 경제적으로 작동하는 것과 마찬가지로 지적으로 작동할 수 있는 훌륭한 예술 작품(훌륭한 표현)을 생산한다. (C) 셰익스피어, 제인 오스틴 그리고 지도는 동인도 회사, 영국 군대 그리고 영국의 교회만큼 영국 제국의 힘에 중요했다. 식민지화의 유럽인 현대 유럽이 '위대한 예술'의 유럽이기도 했다는 것은 우연이 아니며, 위대한 지도 제작자들의 유럽이었다는 것도 우연이 아니다. (A) 그것은 우리가 지도로 세상을 지적으로 지배할 수 없다면 군사적으로나 경제적으로 지배할 수 없기 때문이다. 메르카토르, 몰리에르, 콜럼버스 그리고 쿡 선장은 서로 다른 방식으로 제국주의화했지만 그들은 모두 제국주의화했고 궁극적으로 하나의 유효성은 다른 모든 것들의 유효성에 의존하고 그것을 뒷받침했다. (B) 마찬가지로 물리적 영토라기보다는 경제와 정당을 차지하는 것을 포함하는 미국의 현대 식민지화 형태는 세계를 미국에 그리고 미국을 위해 표현하기 위해 할리우드와 인공위성 둘 다의 힘을 동반한다.

주어진 글 다음에 이어질 글의 순서로 가장 적절한 것을 고르시오. [3점]

① (A) — (C) — (B) (A)의 That이 가리키는 것이 (C)에 등장함
② (B) — (A) — (C)
③ (B) — (C) — (A) — 유럽에 대한 설명이 끝난 후에 (B)가 이어져야 함
 — 제국주의화하는 문화가 훌륭한 예술 작품을 생산함 - 셰익스피어와 제인 오스틴, 식민지화의 유럽 등의 예시 - 지도로 세상을 지적으로 지배할 수
④ (C) — (A) — (B) 없다면 군사적으로나 경제적으로 지배할 수 없음 - 미국의 현대 식민지화
⑤ (C) — (B) — (A) 형태는 할리우드(문화)와 인공위성(지도)을 동반
 (C)와 (A)가 유럽, (B)가 미국에 대한 내용임

1st 각 문단의 내용을 파악하고, 글의 논리적인 순서를 추론한다.

주어진 글: 표현은 지배력이다. 세상을 표현하는 힘은 그것 속에 있는 우리 또는 우리 속에 있는 그것을 표현하는 힘인데, 표현하기의 최종 단계는 표현하는 것과 표현되는 것을 하나로 병합하기 때문이다. 제국주의화하는 문화는 군대와 무역 회사가 군사적, 경제적으로 작동하는 것과 마찬가지로 지적으로 작동할 수 있는 훌륭한 예술 작품(훌륭한 표현)을 생산한다.

➡ **주어진 글 뒤:** 제국주의화하는 문화가 지적으로 작동할 수 있는 훌륭한 예술 작품을 생산한다는 것에 대한 부연 설명이 이어져야 한다.

(A): 그것(That)은 우리가 지도로 세상을 지적으로 지배할 수 없다면 군사적으로나 경제적으로 지배할 수 없기 때문이다. 메르카토르, 몰리에르, 콜럼버스 그리고 쿡 선장은 서로 다른 방식으로 제국주의화했지만 그들은 모두 제국주의화했고 궁극적으로 하나의 유효성은 다른 모든 것들의 유효성에 의존하고 그것을 뒷받침했다.

➡ **(A) 앞:** 주어인 That이 가리키는 것이 (A) 앞에 있어야 한다.
That이 가리키는 것: 우리가 지도로 세상을 지적으로 지배할 수 없다면 군사적으로나 경제적으로 지배할 수 없기 때문에 일어나는 일
▶ 주어진 글에는 이에 해당하는 내용이 없음
(A) 뒤: 하나의 유효성이 다른 모든 것의 유효성에 의존하고 또 그것을 뒷받침한다는 데 대한 구체적인 설명이 이어질 것이다.

(B): 마찬가지로(Similarly) 물리적 영토라기보다는 경제와 정당을 차지하는 것을 포함하는 미국의 현대 식민지화 형태는 세계를 미국에 그리고 미국을 위해 표현하기 위해 할리우드와 인공위성 둘 다의 힘에 의해 동반된다.

➡ **(B) 앞:** 유사한 사례를 연결하는 부사 similarly로 문단이 시작되었다. 따라서 (B) 앞에는 미국의 현대 식민지화 형태와 유사성을 보이는 사례가 있어야 한다. (B)는 미국의 현대 식민지화 형태는 할리우드(문화)와 인공위성(지도)을 동반한다는 내용이다.
▶ 주어진 글에는 '지도'에 대한 언급이 없음
(B) 뒤: 두 개의 사례를 제시하는 글이라고 예상한다면, Similarly로 시작하여 또 하나의 사례를 설명하는 (B)가 글의 결론에 해당할 것이다.
▶ (B)가 마지막에 올 확률이 큼

(C): 셰익스피어, 제인 오스틴 그리고 지도는 동인도 회사, 영국 군대 그리고 영국의 교회만큼 영국 제국의 힘에 중요했다. 식민지화의 유럽인 현대 유럽이 '위대한 예술'의 유럽이기도 했다는 것은 우연이 아니며, 위대한 지도 제작자들의 유럽이었다는 것도 우연이 아니다.

➡ **(C) 앞:** 셰익스피어와 제인 오스틴은 훌륭한 예술 작품을 만들어 내는 예술가를 가리킨다. 또한 식민지화의 유럽이 위대한 예술의 유럽이었다는 설명 역시 제국주의화하는 문화는 훌륭한 예술 작품을 생산한다는 주어진 글과 이어진다.
▶ (C) 앞에 주어진 글이 와야 함 (순서: 주어진 글 → (C))
(C) 뒤: 식민지화의 유럽이 위대한 지도 제작자들의 유럽이었던 것은 지도가 식민지화에 중요했기 때문이다. 지도의 중요성은 (A)에 제시된다.
▶ (C) 뒤에 (A)가 와야 함 (순서: 주어진 글 → (C) → (A) → (B))

2nd 글이 한눈에 들어오도록 정리하여 정답을 확인한다.

주어진 글: 제국주의화하는 문화는 지적으로 작동할 수 있는 훌륭한 예술 작품을 생산한다.
➡ **(C):** 식민지화의 유럽이 위대한 예술의 유럽이기도 했다는 것은 우연이 아니다. 그것이 위대한 지도 제작자들의 유럽이었다는 것도 우연이 아니다.

➡ **(A):** 그것은 우리가 지도로 세상을 지적으로 지배할 수 없다면, 군사적으로나 경제적으로 지배할 수 없기 때문이다.

➡ **(B):** 미국의 현대 식민지화 형태는, 식민지화의 유럽과 유사하게, 할리우드(문화)와 인공위성(지도)을 동반한다.

▶ 주어진 글 다음에 이어질 글의 순서는 (C) → (A) → (B)이므로 정답은 ④임

M 32 정답 ④ *상황에 따라 달라지는 협상의 다양한 목적

Negotiation can be defined / as an attempt to explore / and reconcile conflicting positions / in order to reach an acceptable outcome. // 단서1 협상의 정의를 설명함　부사적 용법 (목적)
협상은 정의될 수 있다 / 상충하는 입장을 탐색하고 / 화해시키려는 시도라고 / 수용할 수 있는 결과에 도달하기 위해 //

(A) Areas of difference can and do frequently remain, / and will perhaps be the subject of future negotiations, / or indeed remain irreconcilable. // 일반동사(remain) 강조
이견이 있는 영역은 남을 수 있고, 실제로 자주 남으며 / 아마도 향후 협상의 주제가 되거나 / 실제로 화해할 수 없는 상태로 남게 될 것이다 //

단서2 협의에 이르지 못하면 공개적인 설명으로 갈등을 다스리기도 함

In those instances / in which the parties have highly antagonistic or polarised relations, / the process is likely to be dominated by the exposition, / very often in public, of the areas of conflict. // 전치사+관계대명사　be likely to-v: ~할 가능성이 있다
그런 경우에 / 당사자들이 매우 적대적이거나 양극화된 관계를 맺고 있는 / 그 과정은 설명에 의해 지배될 가능성이 있다 / 갈등 영역에 대한 아주 흔히 공개적인 //

(B) In these and sometimes other forms of negotiation, / negotiation serves functions / other than reconciling conflicting interests. // 단서3 이러한 형태의 협상에서는 협상이 중재가 아닌 다른 기능을 수행함
이러한 형태의 협상과 때로는 다른 형태의 협상에서 / 협상은 기능을 수행한다 / 상충하는 이익을 화해시키는 것이 아닌 //

These will include / delay, publicity, diverting attention / or seeking intelligence about the other party and its negotiating position. //
이러한 것들에는 포함될 것이다 / 지연, 홍보, 주의를 돌리거나 / 상대방과 그쪽의 협상 입장에 관한 정보를 구하는 것이 //

주격 관계대명사(선행사: the outcome)
(C) Whatever the nature of the outcome, / which may actually favour one party more than another, / the purpose of negotiation / is the identification of areas of common interest and conflict. //
그 결과의 성격이 무엇이든 / 실제로 다른 당사자보다 한쪽 당사자에게 더 유리할 수도 있는 / 협상의 목적은 / 공통의 이익과 갈등의 영역을 밝히는 것이다 //

In this sense, / depending on the intentions of the parties, / the areas of common interest / may be clarified, refined and given negotiated form and substance. // 단서4 협상의 목적은 공통의 이익과 갈등을 정의하고 협의를 이루는 것임
이러한 의미에서 / 당사자들의 의도에 따라 / 공통의 이익 영역은 / 명확해지고, 정제되며, 협의가 이뤄진 형식과 실체가 주어질 수 있다 //

- negotiation ⓝ 협상　　• explore ⓥ 탐색하다
- conflicting ⓐ 상충하는　　• acceptable ⓐ 수용할 수 있는
- outcome ⓝ 결과　　• irreconsilable ⓐ 화해할 수 없는
- party ⓝ 당사자　　• polarise ⓥ 양극화를 초래하다
- dominate ⓥ 지배하다　　• publicity ⓝ 홍보
- divert ⓥ 방향을 바꾸게 하다　　• intelligence ⓝ 정보, 기밀
- identification ⓝ (실체를) 밝힘, 확인　　• intention ⓝ 의도
- clarify ⓥ 명확하게 하다　　• refine ⓥ 정제하다
- substance ⓝ 실체

협상은 수용할 수 있는 결과에 도달하기 위해 상충하는 입장을 탐색하고 화해시키려는 시도라고 정의될 수 있다. (C) 실제로 다른 당사자보다 한쪽 당사자에게 더 유리할 수도 있는, 그 결과의 성격이 무엇이든, 협상의 목적은 공통의 이익과 갈등의 영역을 밝히는 것이다. 이러한 의미에서 당사자들의 의도에 따라 공통의 이익 영역은 명확해지고, 정제되며, 협의가 이뤄진 형식과

실체가 주어질 수 있다. (A) 이견이 있는 영역은 남을 수 있고, 실제로 자주 남으며, 아마도 향후 협상의 주제가 되거나 실제로 화해할 수 없는 상태로 남게 될 것이다. 당사자들이 매우 적대적이거나 양극화된 관계를 맺고 있는 그런 경우에, 그 과정은 갈등 영역에 대한 아주 흔히 공개적인 설명에 의해 지배될 가능성이 있다. (B) 이러한 형태의 협상과 때로는 다른 형태의 협상에서, 협상은 상충하는 이익을 화해시키는 것이 아닌 기능을 수행한다. 이러한 것들에는 지연, 홍보, 주의를 돌리거나 상대방과 그쪽의 협상 입장에 관한 정보를 구하는 것이 포함될 것이다.

주어진 글 다음에 이어질 글의 순서로 가장 적절한 것을 고르시오.

① (A) — (C) — (B)   (A)는 협상의 결과로 이견이 발생한 경우를 설명하므로 주어진 글 뒤에 올 수 없음
② (B) — (A) — (C)   (C)는 협상의 본래 목적을 설명하고 있으므로 협의에 이르지 못해 협상의 목적이 달라진다는 (A)와 (B)보다 먼저 나와야 함
③ (B) — (C) — (A)
④ (C) — (A) — (B)
⑤ (C) — (B) — (A)   (B)는 협의에 이르지 못한 협상의 구체적인 목적을 설명하고 있으므로 (A) 뒤에 이어져야 함

- 협상은 상충하는 입장을 중재하는 것이 목적임 - 협상을 통해 당사자 간의 합의를 끌어내는 것이 목적임 - 이견이 발생한 경우, 협상의 과정은 공개적인 설명으로 지배될 수 있음 - 이러한 협상의 목적은 더 이상 중재가 아님

| 문제 풀이 순서 | [정답률 38%]

1st 각 문단의 내용을 파악하고, 글의 논리적인 순서를 추론한다.

> **주어진 글**: 협상은 수용할 수 있는 결과에 도달하기 위해 상충하는 입장을 탐색하고 화해시키려는 시도라고 정의될 수 있다.

⇒ 협상은 상충하는 입장을 중재하는 과정으로 정의하고 있다. (단서)
주어진 글 뒤: 협상의 기능과 목적 등에 관한 내용이 이어질 것이다. (발상)

> (A) 이견이 있는 영역은 남을 수 있고, 실제로 자주 남으며, 아마도 향후 협상의 주제가 되거나 실제로 화해할 수 없는 상태로 남게 될 것이다. 당사자들이 매우 적대적이거나 양극화된 관계를 맺고 있는 그런 경우에, 그 과정은 갈등 영역에 대한 아주 흔히 공개적인 설명에 의해 지배될 가능성이 있다.

⇒ **앞 문장**: 협상 후에도 합의나 화해가 이뤄지지 않을 수 있음
뒤 문장: 당사자 간의 적대적인 관계가 유지된다면, 협상의 과정은 공개적인 설명에 의해 좀 더 객관적으로 다스려질 수 있음
(A) 앞: 이견이 발생한 상황을 소개하고 있으므로, 그 이전에 협상의 결과로 합의가 이루어진 상황을 소개했을 것이다.
▶ 주어진 글이 (A) 앞에 올 수 없음
(A) 뒤: 합의가 이루어지지 않아 공개적인 설명으로 협상을 다스릴 때 어떤 특징이 있는지 이어질 것이다.

> (B) 이러한 형태의 협상과 때로는 다른 형태의 협상에서(In these and sometimes other forms of negotiation), 협상은 상충하는 이익을 화해시키는 것이 아닌 기능을 수행한다. 이러한 것들에는 지연, 홍보, 주의를 돌리거나 상대방과 그쪽의 협상 입장에 관한 정보를 구하는 것이 포함될 것이다.

⇒ **앞 문장**: 이러한 형태의 협상에서는 협상의 목적이 화해가 아님
뒤 문장: 이 경우, 협상의 목적은 지연, 홍보, 주의 분산, 정보 탐색 등이 됨
(B) 앞: '이러한 형태의 협상'이 가리키는 내용이 있어야 한다. these negotiations는 (A)에서 설명한 당사자 간의 합의에 이르지 못한 협상을 가리킨다.
▶ 순서: (A) → (B)
(B) 뒤: 합의에 이르지 못한 협상의 구체적인 형태가 이어지거나 (B)가 글의 결론일 것이다.
▶ (B)가 마지막에 올 확률이 큼

> (C) 실제로 다른 당사자보다 한쪽 당사자에게 더 유리할 수도 있는, 그 결과의 성격이 무엇이든, 협상의 목적은 공통의 이익과 갈등의 영역을 밝히는 것이다. 이러한 의미에서 당사자들의 의도에 따라 공통의 이익 영역은 명확해지고, 정제되며, 협의가 이뤄진 형식과 실체가 주어질 수 있다.

⇒ **앞 문장**: 협상의 결과가 어떻든 간에, 협상의 목적은 공통의 이익과 갈등 영역을 밝히는 것임
뒤 문장: 이러한 의미에서 협상의 결과로 공통의 이익을 위한 협의가 이루어짐
(C) 앞: 협상의 개념과 당사자 간 협의를 한다는 것의 의미가 무엇인지 나와야 함
▶ 순서: 주어진 글 → (C)

2nd 글이 한눈에 들어오도록 정리하여 정답을 확인한다.

주어진 글: 협상은 상충하는 입장을 중재하는 과정으로 정의된다.

⇒ **(C)**: 협상의 목적은 공통의 이익과 갈등의 영역을 밝히는 것이고, 이러한 의미에서 협상의 결과로 공통의 이익을 위한 협의가 이루어진다.

⇒ **(A)**: 협상 후에도 당사자 간의 협의가 이뤄지지 않을 수 있으며, 당사자들의 관계가 적대적이거나 양극화된 경우, 협상의 과정은 갈등에 관한 공개적인 설명으로 지배될 것이다.

⇒ **(B)**: 이러한 협상(협의가 이루어지지 않은 이후)에는 협상의 목적이 중재가 아닌 지연, 홍보, 주의 분산, 정보 탐색 등이다.

▶ 주어진 글 다음에 이어질 글의 순서는 (C) → (A) → (B)이므로 정답은 ④임

조수근 | 순천향대 의예과 2024년 입학·성남 태원고 졸

이 문제의 핵심은 글의 범주 파악이야. 주어진 글은 협상의 정의, (C)는 협상의 목적에 대한 내용인 반면 (A)와 (B)는 협상에서 이견이 있는 경우에 대한 내용임을 알 수 있어. 즉, 주어진 글 다음에 (C)가 이어진다는 것이지.

그다음에 나는 ④와 ⑤의 순서로 각각 지문을 읽어보고 더 자연스러운 걸 찾았어. 복잡하게 다음 순서를 생각하는 것보다 두 경우로 모두 읽어보는 게 더 편하더라고. 무식해 보이지만, 순서 문제라면 이런 접근법이 오히려 지름길이 될 수도 있다는 걸 잊지 마!

M 33 정답 ② * 전쟁의 목적은 무엇인가

The objective of battle, / to "throw" the enemy / and to make
〔주어〕
him defenseless, / may temporarily blind commanders and
〔동사〕
even strategists / to the larger purpose of war. // 〔단서 1〕 전쟁의 더 큰 목적이 간과된다고 설명함
전투의 목표는 / 적군을 '격멸하고' / 그를 무방비 상태로 만드는 것 / 일시적으로 지휘관과
심지어 전략가까지도 보지 못하게 할 수도 있다 / 전쟁의 더 큰 목적을 //
nor가 문두로 오면서 주어와 동사가 도치됨
War is never an isolated act, / nor is it ever only one decision. //
전쟁은 결코 고립된 행위가 아니며 / 또한 그것은 결코 단 하나의 결정도 아니다 //
〔부사적 용법(목적)〕
(A) To be political, / a political entity or a representative of a
political entity, / whatever its constitutional form, / has to have
an intention, / a will. //
정치적으로 되려면 / 정치적 실체나 정치적 실체의 대표자는 / 그것의 체제상의 형태가 무엇이
든지 / 의도가 있어야 한다 / 의지 //
That intention / has to be clearly expressed. //
그 의도는 / 분명히 표현되어야 한다 // 〔단서 2〕 의도가 분명히 표현되어야 한다고 말함
(B) In the real world, / war's larger purpose / is always a political
purpose. // 〔단서 3〕 전쟁의 더 큰 목적이 무엇인지 설명함
현실 세계에서 / 전쟁의 더 큰 목적은 / 항상 정치적 목적이다 //
It transcends / the use of force. // 그것은 초월한다 / 물리력의 사용을 //
This insight was famously captured / by Clausewitz's most
famous phrase, / "War is a mere continuation of politics / by
other means." //
이 통찰은 멋지게 포착되었다 / Clausewitz의 가장 유명한 한마디에 의해 / "전쟁은 단지 정
치를 계속하는 것에 불과하다 / 다른 수단으로"라는 //

(C) And one side's will has to be transmitted / to the enemy /
at some point / during the confrontation / (it does not have to
be publicly communicated). //
　　　전치사　　　　　　　명사구
그리고 한쪽의 의지는 전달되어야 한다 / 적에게 / 어느 시점에 / 대치하는 동안 / (그것이 공
개적으로 전달될 필요는 없다) //

　　　　　　　　　　　　　　　　　　　조동사가 포함된 수동태
A violent act and its larger political intention / must also be
attributed to one side / at some point / during the confrontation. //
폭력 행위와 그것의 더 큰 정치적 의도는 / 또한 한쪽의 탓으로 돌려져야 한다 / 어느 시점에
/ 대치하는 동안 //

History does not know of acts of war / without eventual
attribution. // 역사는 전쟁 행위에 대해 알지 못한다 / 궁극적인 귀인이 없는 //

- objective ⓝ 목적, 목표　　· defenseless ⓐ 무방비의, 방어할 수 없는
- temporarily ⓐⓓ 일시적으로, 임시로
- blind ⓥ 눈이 멀게 만들다, 앞이 안 보이게 만들다, 맹목적이 되게 만들다
- commander ⓝ 지휘관, 사령관　　· strategist ⓝ 전략가
- representative ⓝ 대표(자), 대리인
- constitutional ⓐ 헌법(상)의, 구조상의　　· intention ⓝ 의사, 의도
- will ⓝ 의지(력)　　· clearly ⓐⓓ 분명히, 또렷하게　　· force ⓝ 물리력, 힘
- insight ⓝ 통찰력　　· capture ⓥ 사로잡다, 포착하다
- phrase ⓝ 구절, 관용구　　· continuation ⓝ 계속, 지속, 연속
- means ⓝ 수단, 방법　　· transmit ⓥ 전달하다, 알리다
- confrontation ⓝ 대립, 대치　　· publicly ⓐⓓ 공공연하게, 공개적으로
- attribute to ~의 덕분[탓]으로 돌리다　　· eventual ⓐ 궁극[최종]적인

전투의 목표, 즉 적군을 '격멸하고' 무방비 상태로 만드는 것은 일시적으로 지휘
관과 심지어 전략가까지도 전쟁의 더 큰 목적을 보지 못하게 할 수도 있다. 전
쟁은 결코 고립된 행위가 아니며, 또한 결코 단 하나의 결정도 아니다. (B) 현실
세계에서 전쟁의 더 큰 목적은 항상 정치적 목적이다. 그것은 물리력의 사용을
초월한다. 이 통찰은 "전쟁은 다른 수단으로 단지 정치를 계속하는 것에 불과하
다."라고 한 Clausewitz의 가장 유명한 한마디에 의해 멋지게 포착되었다. (A)
정치적으로 되려면, 정치적 실체나 정치적 실체의 대표자는, 체제상의 형태가
무엇이든지, 의도, 즉 의지가 있어야 한다. 그 의도는 분명히 표현되어야 한다.
(C) 그리고 한쪽의 의지는 대치하는 동안 어느 시점에 적에게 전달되어야 한다
(그것이 공개적으로 전달될 필요는 없다). 폭력 행위와 그것의 더 큰 정치적 의
도 또한 대치하는 동안 어느 시점에 한쪽의 탓으로 돌려져야 한다. 역사는 궁극
적인 귀인이 없는 전쟁 행위에 대해 알지 못한다.

주어진 글 다음에 이어질 글의 순서로 가장 적절한 것을 고르시오.

① (A) ― (C) ― (B) 주어진 글에 등장한 전쟁의 더 큰 목적을 (B)에서 설명함
② (B) ― (A) ― (C) (B) 전쟁의 더 큰 목적은 정치적인 목적임 – (A) 정치적이 되려면 의도, 의지가
　　　　　　　　　　있어야 함 – (C) 그리고 한쪽의 의지는 적에게 전달되어야 함
③ (B) ― (C) ― (A) 의지가 전달되어야 한다는 내용 전에 의지가 있어야 한다는 내용이 필요함
④ (C) ― (A) ― (B) ┐
⑤ (C) ― (B) ― (A) ┘ (C)는 주어진 글과 and로 연결될 만한 내용이 아님

| 문제 풀이 순서 |　[정답률 50%]

1st 각 문단의 내용을 파악하고, 글의 논리적인 순서를 추론한다.

주어진 글: 전투의 목표, 즉 적군을 '격멸하고' 무방비 상태로 만드는 것은
일시적으로 지휘관과 심지어 전략가까지도 전쟁의 더 큰 목적을 보지
못하게 할 수도 있다. 단서1 전쟁은 결코 고립된 행위가 아니며, 또한
결코 단 하나의 결정도 아니다.

→ **주어진 글 뒤:** 전쟁의 목적은 전투의 목표만으로는 설명이 되지 않으며, 전쟁이
고립된 행위가 아니고 하나의 결정이 아니라고 했다. 단서 따라서 전쟁의 목적에
관한 설명이 구체적으로 이어질 것이다. 발상

(A): 정치적으로 되려면, 정치적 실체나 정치적 실체의 대표자는,
체제상의 형태가 무엇이든지, 의도, 즉 의지가 있어야 한다. 그 의도는
분명히 표현되어야 한다. 단서2

→ **(A) 앞:** '무엇'이 정치적으로 되는지에 대한 설명이 앞에 있어야 하는데, 주어진
글에서는 해당 내용을 찾을 수 없다.
▶ (A) 앞에 주어진 글이 올 수 없음
(A) 뒤: 의도(의지)가 분명히 표현되어야 한다는 내용으로, 의도의 표현과 관련된
내용이 뒤에 이어질 것이다.

(B): 현실 세계에서 전쟁의 더 큰 목적은 항상 정치적 목적이다.
단서3 그것은 물리력의 사용을 초월한다. 이 통찰은 "전쟁은 다른
수단으로 단지 정치를 계속하는 것에 불과하다."라고 한 Clausewitz
의 가장 유명한 한마디에 의해 멋지게 포착되었다.

→ **(B) 앞:** 전쟁의 더 큰 목적은 정치적 목적이라 했으며, 이는 주어진 글에서 언급한
전쟁의 목적을 구체적으로 언급한 것이다.
▶ (B) 앞에 주어진 글이 와야 함 (순서: 주어진 글 → (B))
(B) 뒤: 정치적 목적에 관한 내용에 이어서, 정치적으로 되려면 의도가 있어야
한다는 (A)가 이어지는 것이 자연스럽다.
▶ (B) 뒤에 (A)가 와야 함 (순서: 주어진 글 → (B) → (A))

(C): 그리고 한쪽의 의지는 대치하는 동안 어느 시점에 적에게
전달되어야 한다(그것이 공개적으로 전달될 필요는 없다). 단서4 폭력
행위와 그것의 더 큰 정치적 의도 또한 대치하는 동안 어느 시점에
한쪽의 탓으로 돌려져야 한다. 역사는 궁극적인 귀인이 없는 전쟁
행위에 대해 알지 못한다.

→ **(C) 앞:** 의지가 적에게 전달되어야 한다는 내용으로, '의도(의지)의 분명한 표현'을
언급한 (A) 다음에 이어지는 것이 자연스럽다.
▶ (C) 앞에 (A)가 와야 함 (순서: 주어진 글 → (B) → (A) → (C))

2nd 글이 한눈에 들어오도록 정리하여 정답을 확인한다.

주어진 글: 전쟁은 전투의 목적을 넘어서는 더 큰 목적이 있다.

→ **(B):** 전쟁의 목적은 정치적 목적이다.
→ **(A):** 정치적이 되려면 의도(의지)가 있어야 하며 이는 분명히 표현되어야 한다.
→ **(C):** 한쪽의 의지는 대치 과정에서 적에게 전달되어야 한다.
▶ 주어진 글 다음에 이어질 글의 순서는 (B) → (A) → (C)이므로 정답은 ②임

＊ 글의 흐름

도입	적군을 격멸하는 전투의 목표로 인해 전쟁의 더 큰 목적을 간과하게 될 수도 있음
전개	전쟁의 더 큰 목적은 정치적 목적임
부연 ①	정치적으로 되려면 정치적 실체나 그 대표자는 의도(의지)가 있어야 하고, 그 의도는 분명히 표현되어야 함
부연 ②	그리고 한쪽의 의지는 적에게 전달되어야 하며 폭력 행위와 그것의 더 큰 정치적 의도는 한쪽의 탓으로 돌려져야 함

━━━ 배경 지식 ━━━

＊ 세계대전
　제1차 세계대전은 1914년 7월 28일 오스트리아가 세르비아에 대한
선전포고를 하면서 시작되었다. 1918년 11월 11일 독일의 항복으로 끝난
세계적 규모의 전쟁이다.
　제2차 세계대전은 1939년부터 1945년까지 유럽, 아시아, 북아프리카,
태평양 등지에서 독일, 이탈리아, 일본을
중심으로 한 추축국과 영국, 프랑스, 미국,
소련, 중국 등을 중심으로 한 연합국
사이에 벌어진 세계 규모의 전쟁이다.
지금까지의 인류 역사에서 가장 큰
인명과 재산 피해를 낳은 전쟁이다.

M 34 정답 ② *don't보다 효과가 좋은 do

It raises much less reactance / to tell people / what to do / than
to tell them / what not to do. //
~이 훨씬 더 적은 저항을 일으킨다 / 사람들에게 말하는 것이 / 할 것을 / 그들에게 말하는
것보다 / 하지 말 것을 //

Therefore, advocating action should lead / to higher
compliance / than prohibiting action. //
그러므로 행동을 지지하는 것은 이어질 것이다 / 더 높은 준수로 / 행동을 금지하는 것보다 //

단서1 (B)에 등장한 연구원의 말을 가리킴

(A) This is a prescription / that is rife with danger, / failing to
provide an implementation rule / and raising reactance. //
이는 지시이다 / 위험으로 가득한 / 실행 규칙을 제공하지 못하고 / 저항을 높이는 //

Much better is to say, / "To help make sure / that other people
provide answers / as useful as yours have been, /
말하는 것이 훨씬 더 좋다 / "확실히 하도록 돕기 위해 / 다른 사람들이 응답을 제공하는 것을
/ 당신의 것이 그런 만큼 유용한 /

when people ask you / about this study, / please tell them / that
you and another person answered some questions / about each
other." //
사람들이 당신에게 질문할 때 / 이 연구에 대해 / 그들에게 말해 주세요 / 당신과 다른 사람이
몇 가지 질문에 대답했다고 / 서로에 대한"이라고 //

(B) For example, / researchers have a choice / of how to debrief
research participants / in an experiment / involving some
deception or omission of information. // **단서2** 주어진 글에서 말한 것을 보여주는 예시가 시작됨
예를 들어 / 연구원들은 선택의 여지가 있다 / 연구 참여자들에게 비밀 준수 의무를 지우는
방법에 대한 / 실험에서 / 정보의 어떤 속임이나 생략과 관련한 //

Often researchers attempt / to commit the participant to silence,
/ saying / "Please don't tell other potential participants / that
feedback from the other person / was false." //
연구원들은 자주 시도한다 / 참여자에게 침묵의 의무를 지우려고 / 말하면서 / "다른 잠재적인
참여자들에게 말하지 마세요 / 상대방으로부터의 피드백이 / 거짓이었다고"라고 //

(C) Similarly, I once saw / a delightful and unusual example / of
this principle / at work in an art gallery. // **단서3** 또 다른 사례를 설명함
유사하게 나는 이전에 보았다 / 즐겁고 특이한 사례를 / 이 원칙이 / 미술관에서 작동하고
있는 //

A fragile acrylic sculpture had a sign / at the base / saying,
"Please touch with your eyes." //
깨지기 쉬운 아크릴 조각품은 팻말을 가지고 있었다 / 밑면에 / "눈으로 만져주세요"라고 쓰여
있는 //

The command was clear, / yet created much less reactance in me
/ than "Don't touch!" would have. //
그 지시는 명확했지만 / 나에게는 훨씬 더 적은 저항을 만들어 냈다 / "손대지 마세요"가
그랬을 것보다 //

- raise ⓥ 불러일으키다, 자아내다 - advocate ⓥ 지지하다, 옹호하다
- compliance ⓝ (법·명령 등의) 준수, (명령 등에) 따름
- prohibit ⓥ 금지하다 - prescription ⓝ 처방(전), 지시
- implementation ⓝ 이행, 수행 - deception ⓝ 속임, 기만
- omission ⓝ 생략, 누락
- commit ⓥ (그릇된 일을) 저지르다, (~할 것을) 의무 지우다
- silence ⓝ 침묵, 고요 - potential ⓐ 가능성이 있는, 잠재적인
- false ⓐ 틀린, 사실이 아닌 - delightful ⓐ 정말 기분 좋은
- at work 작용하고 있는 - fragile ⓐ 부서지기[손상되기] 쉬운
- acrylic ⓐ 아크릴로 만든 - sculpture ⓝ 조각(품), 조소
- command ⓝ 명령

사람들에게 하지 말 것을 말하기보다 할 것을 말하는 것이 훨씬 더 적은
저항을 일으킨다. 그러므로 행동을 지지하는 것은 행동을 금지하는 것보다 더
높은 준수로 이어질 것이다. (B) 예를 들어 연구원들은 정보의 어떤 속임이나
생략과 관련한 실험에서 연구 참여자들에게 비밀 준수 의무를 지우는 방법에
대한 선택의 여지가 있다. 연구원들은 자주 "다른 잠재적인 참여자들에게

상대방으로부터의 피드백이 거짓이었다고 말하지 마세요."라고 말하면서
참여자에게 침묵(비밀 엄수)의 의무를 지우려고 시도한다. (A) 이는 실행
규칙을 제공하지 못하고 저항을 높이는 위험으로 가득한 지시이다. "다른
사람들이 당신의 응답이 그런 만큼 유용한 응답을 제공하는 것을 확실히 하도록
돕기 위해, 사람들이 이 연구에 대해 당신에게 질문할 때, 당신과 다른 사람이
서로에 대한 몇 가지 질문에 대답했다고 그들에게 말해 주세요."라고 말하는
것이 훨씬 더 좋다. (C) 유사하게, 나는 이전에 미술관에서 이 원칙이 작동하고
있는 즐겁고 특이한 사례를 보았다. 깨지기 쉬운 아크릴 조각품 밑면에 "눈으로
만져주세요."라는 팻말이 있었다. 그 지시는 명확하지만, 나에게는 "손대지
마세요!"가 그랬을 것보다 훨씬 더 적은 저항을 만들어 냈다.

주어진 글 다음에 이어질 글의 순서로 가장 적절한 것을 고르시오. [3점]

① (A) — (C) — (B) (A)의 This가 가리키는 것이 주어진 글에 없음
② (B) — (A) — (C)
③ (B) — (C) — (A) 첫 번째 사례가 (B)와 (A)에 등장함
④ (C) — (A) — (B) ─ 미술관에서의 사례가 나오기 전에 (B)와 (A)의 사례가 등장해야 함
⑤ (C) — (B) — (A)

할 것을 말하는 것이 하지 말 것을 말하는 것보다 훨씬 더 적은 저항을 일으킴 –
사례 ① 연구 참여자들에게는 말하지 말라는 지시보다 말하라는 지시가 훨씬 더 좋다 –
사례 ② '만지지 마세요'보다 '눈으로 만지세요'가 더 적은 저항을 만들어 냄

| 문제 풀이 순서 | [정답률 63%]

1st 각 문단의 내용을 파악하고, 글의 논리적인 순서를 추론한다.

> 주어진 글: 사람들에게 하지 말 것을 말하기보다 할 것을 말하는 것이
> 훨씬 더 적은 저항을 일으킨다. 그러므로 행동을 지지하는 것은 행동을
> 금지하는 것보다 더 높은 준수로 이어질 것이다.

→ **주어진 글 뒤:** 행동을 지지하는 것이 금지하는 것보다 훨씬 더 저항이 적다는
내용으로, **단서** 이에 대한 구체적인 내용이나 예시가 이어질 것이다. **발상**

> (A): 이는(This) 실행 규칙을 제공하지 못하고 저항을 높이는 위험으로
> 가득한 지시이다. **단서1** "다른 사람들이 당신의 응답이 그런 만큼
> 유용한 응답을 제공하는 것을 확실히 하도록 돕기 위해, 사람들이 이
> 연구에 대해 당신에게 질문할 때, 당신과 다른 사람이 서로에 대한 몇
> 가지 질문에 대답했다고 그들에게 말해 주세요."라고 말하는 것이 훨씬
> 더 좋다.

→ **(A) 앞:** 실행 규칙을 제공하지 못하고 저항을 높이는 지시인 This가 무엇인지 앞에
나와야 한다. 주어진 글에는 부정적인 지시에 관한 내용은 나오지 않는다.
▶ (A) 앞에 주어진 글이 올 수 없음
(A) 뒤: 의도(의지)가 분명히 표현되어야 한다는 내용으로, 의도의 표현과 관련된
내용이 뒤에 이어질 것이다.

> (B): 예를 들어(For example) 연구원들은 정보의 어떤 속임이나
> 생략과 관련한 실험에서 연구 참여자들에게 비밀 준수 의무를 지우는
> 방법에 대한 선택의 여지가 있다. **단서2** 연구원들은 자주 "다른
> 잠재적인 참여자들에게 상대방으로부터의 피드백이 거짓이었다고
> 말하지 마세요."라고 말하면서 참여자에게 침묵(비밀 엄수)의 의무를
> 지우려고 시도한다.

→ **(B) 앞:** For example은 예시를 나타내는 연결어이며 '하지 말라고 말하는 것'의
예시이므로, 행동을 금지하는 것에 대해 처음 언급한 주어진 글에 이어지는 것이
자연스럽다.
▶ (B) 앞에 주어진 글이 와야 함 (순서: 주어진 글 → (B))
(B) 뒤: '하지 말라고 말하는 것'을 This로서 위험으로 가득찬 지시라고 언급하는
(A)가 이어져야 한다.
▶ (B) 뒤에 (A)가 와야 함 (순서: 주어진 글 → (B) → (A))

(C): 유사하게(Similarly), 나는 이전에 미술관에서 이 원칙이
작동하고 있는 즐겁고 특이한 사례를 보았다. 단서3 깨지기 쉬운 아크릴
조각품 밑면에 "눈으로 만져주세요."라는 팻말이 있었다. 그 지시는
명확했지만, 나에게는 "손대지 마세요!"가 그랬을 것보다 훨씬 더 적은
저항을 만들어 냈다.

→ (C) 앞: Similarly는 앞의 내용과 비슷한 내용을 부연 설명하는 연결어이므로
행동을 지지하는 말을 하는 것이 훨씬 더 좋다는 사례를 제시한 (A) 뒤에 이어지는
것이 자연스럽다.
▶ (C) 앞에 (A)가 와야 함 (순서: 주어진 글 → (B) → (A) → (C))

2nd 글이 한눈에 들어오도록 정리하여 정답을 확인한다.

주어진 글: 행동을 지지하는 것이 금지하는 것보다 훨씬 더 저항이 적다.
→ **(B):** 비밀 준수 의무를 부과하는 실험에서 연구자들은 두 가지 선택의 여지가 있다.
→ **(A):** 행동을 금지하는 말은 저항을 높일 위험이 있다.
→ **(C):** 미술관에서도 마찬가지로 이 원칙이 적용된다.
▶ 주어진 글 다음에 이어질 글의 순서는 (B) → (A) → (C)이므로 정답은 ②임

* 글의 흐름

도입	사람들에게 할 것을 말하는 것이 하지 말 것을 말하는 것보다 훨씬 더 적은 저항을 일으킴
예시 ①	연구 참여자들에게 무언가를 말하지 말라고 하는 것보다 말하라고 지시하는 것이 훨씬 더 좋음
예시 ②	'만지지 마세요'보다 '눈으로만 만지세요'라는 지시가 훨씬 더 적은 저항을 일으킴

M 35 정답 ④ *우리의 시선을 다른 곳으로 돌리는 전략

One common strategy and use / of passive misdirection / in
the digital world / comes through the use of repetition. //
한 가지 흔한 전략과 사용은 / 인식하지 못한 채 시선을 다른 곳으로 돌리게 하는 것에 대한
/ 디지털 세계에서 / 반복의 이용을 통해 이루어진다 // 단서1 (C)에 등장한 온라인

(A) This action is repeated over and over / to navigate their web
browsers / to the desired web page or action / until it becomes
an almost immediate, reflexive action. //
이 동작은 여러 번 되풀이하여 반복된다 / 그들의 웹 브라우저를 조종해 가기 위해 / 원하는 웹
페이지나 동작으로 / 그것이 거의 즉각적이고 반사적인 동작이 될 때까지 //

Malicious online actors take advantage of this behavior / to
distract the user / from carefully examining / the details of the
web page /
악의적인 온라인 행위자들은 이러한 행동을 이용한다 / 사용자의 관심을 다른 곳으로 돌리려고
/ 주의 깊게 검토하는 것으로부터 / 웹 페이지의 세부 사항을 /

that might tip off the user / that there is something amiss / about
the website. //
사용자에게 귀띔해 주는 / 어떤 잘못된 것이 있다고 / 웹사이트에 //

(B) The website is designed / to focus the user's attention / on
the action / the malicious actor wants them to take / (e.g., click
a link) / 단서2 (A)에 등장한 Malicious online actors를
정관사 the를 이용한 the malicious actor로 가리킴
그 웹사이트는 설계된다 / 사용자의 관심을 집중시키도록 / 행동에 / 악의적인 행위자가
그들이 수행하기를 원하는 / (예를 들어, 링크를 클릭하는 것) /

and to draw their attention away from any details / that might
suggest to the user / that the website is not / what it appears to
be on the surface. //
그리고 세부 사항으로부터 그들의 주의를 돌리도록 / 사용자에게 암시할 수 있는 / 웹사이트가
~이 아니라는 것을 / 그것이 겉으로 보이는 것이 //

(C) This digital misdirection strategy relies / on the fact / that
online users / utilizing web browsers / to visit websites / have
quickly learned /
이러한 디지털상에서 시선을 다른 곳으로 돌리게 하는 전략은 의존한다 / 사실에 / 온라인
사용자가 / 웹 브라우저를 사용하는 / 웹사이트를 방문하기 위해 / 빠르게 배웠다는 / 단서3 주어진 글에서 설명한 디지털 세계에서 시선을 다른 곳으로 돌리게 하는 전략을 가리킴

that the most basic ubiquitous navigational action is / to click on
a link or button / presented to them on a website. //
가장 기본적이고 어디에서나 하는 탐색 동작이 ~이라는 것을 / 링크나 버튼을 클릭하는 것 /
웹사이트에서 그들에게 제시되는 //

- common ⓐ 흔한, 공동의   • strategy ⓝ 계획, 전략
- passive ⓐ 수동적인, 소극적인
- misdirection ⓝ 잘못된 지시[지도], 엉뚱한 곳으로 보내기
- repetition ⓝ 반복   • over and over 반복해서, 여러 번 되풀이하여
- navigate ⓥ 길을 찾다, 조종하다   • immediate ⓐ 즉각적인, 당면한
- reflexive ⓐ 반사적인, 반응하는   • malicious ⓐ 악의적인, 적의 있는
- take advantage of ~을 이용하다
- distract ⓥ (주의를) 딴 데로 돌리게 하다, 집중이 안 되게 하다
- examine ⓥ 조사[검토]하다, 검사[진찰]하다
- tip off ~에게 제보하다[귀띔하다]   • amiss ⓐ 잘못된
- draw away from (주의 등을) ~로부터 돌리다
- surface ⓝ 표면, 지면, 수면   • utilize ⓥ 활용[이용]하다
- ubiquitous ⓐ 어디에나 있는, 아주 흔한   • navigational ⓐ 항해(술)의

디지털 세계에서 인식하지 못한 채 시선을 다른 곳으로 돌리게 하는 것에
대한 한 가지 흔한 전략과 사용은 반복을 이용하여 이루어진다. (C) 이러한
디지털상에서 시선을 다른 곳으로 돌리게 하는 전략은 웹사이트를 방문하기
위해 웹 브라우저를 사용하는 온라인 사용자가 가장 기본적이고 어디에서나
하는 탐색 동작이 웹사이트에서 그들에게 제시되는 링크나 버튼을 클릭하는
것이라는 것을 빠르게 배웠다는 사실에 의존한다. (A) 이 동작은 원하는 웹
페이지나 동작으로 그들의 웹 브라우저를 조종해 가기 위해, 그것이 거의
즉각적이고 반사적인 동작이 될 때까지 여러 번 되풀이하여 반복된다. 악의적인
온라인 행위자들은 웹사이트에 어떤 잘못된 것이 있다고 사용자에게 귀띔해
주는 웹 페이지의 세부 사항을 주의 깊게 검토하는 것으로부터 사용자의 관심을
다른 곳으로 돌리려고 이러한 행동을 이용한다. (B) 그 웹사이트는 악의적인
행위자가 사용자들이 수행하기를 원하는 행동에 사용자의 관심을 집중시키고
(예를 들어, 링크를 클릭하는 것) 사용자에게 웹사이트가 겉으로 보이는 것이
아니라는 것을 암시할 수 있는 세부 사항으로부터 주의를 돌리도록 설계된다.

주어진 글 다음에 이어질 글의 순서로 가장 적절한 것을 고르시오.

① (A) — (C) — (B) (A)의 This action이 가리키는 것이 주어진 글에 없음
② (B) — (A) — (C) ┐주어진 글에는 악의적인 행위자에 대한 언급이 없음
③ (B) — (C) — (A) ┘
④ (C) — (A) — (B)
⑤ (C) — (B) — (A) 악의적인 행위자가 처음 등장하는 (A)가 (B)보다 앞에 있어야 함
┌ 디지털 세계에서 인식하지 못한 채 시선을 다른 곳으로 돌리게 하는 전략은 반복을 이용하여
이루어짐 - 이 전략은 웹사이트를 방문하기 위해 웹 브라우저를 이용하는 온라인 사용자가 링크나
버튼을 클릭하는 것이 가장 기본적인 탐색 동작이라는 것을 빠르게 배웠다는 사실에 의존함 -
악의적인 행위자들은 웹 페이지의 세부 사항을 주의 깊게 검토하지 못하도록 링크나 버튼을
클릭하는 이러한 행동을 이용함 - 그러한 웹 페이지, 웹사이트는 악의적인 행위자가 사용자들이
수행하기를 원하는 행동에 사용자의 관심을 집중시키도록 설계됨

| 문제 풀이 순서 | [정답률 47%]

1st 각 문단의 내용을 파악하고, 글의 논리적인 순서를 추론한다.

주어진 글: 디지털 세계에서 인식하지 못한 채 시선을 다른 곳으로
돌리게 하는 것에 대한 한 가지 흔한 전략과 사용은 반복을 이용하여
이루어진다.

→ **주어진 글 뒤:** 디지털 세계에서 사용자의 시선을 돌리는 전략은 반복을 이용해서
이루어진다는 내용으로, 단서 반복을 어떻게 이용하는지에 대한 설명이
구체적으로 이어질 것이다. 발상

(A): 이 동작(This action)은 원하는 웹 페이지나 동작으로 그들의 웹 브라우저를 조종해 가기 위해, 그것이 거의 즉각적이고 반사적인 동작이 될 때까지 여러 번 되풀이하여 반복된다. **단서 1** 악의적인 온라인 행위자들은 웹사이트에 어떤 잘못된 것이 있다고 사용자에게 귀띔해 주는 웹 페이지의 세부 사항을 주의 깊게 검토하는 것으로부터 사용자의 관심을 다른 곳으로 돌리려고 이러한 행동을 이용한다.

→ **(A) 앞:** This action이 무엇인지 앞에 나와야 한다.
  ▶ (A) 앞에 주어진 글이 올 수 없음
  (A) 뒤: 악의적인 온라인 행위자들이 사용자의 관심을 세부 사항 검토로부터 돌린다는 내용으로, 그것이 어떻게 이루어지는지에 관한 내용이 이어질 것이다.

(B): 그 웹사이트는 악의적인 행위자(malicious actor)가 사용자들이 수행하기를 원하는 행동에 사용자의 관심을 집중시키고(예를 들어, 링크를 클릭하는 것) 사용자에게 웹사이트가 겉으로 보이는 것이 아니라는 것을 암시할 수 있는 세부 사항으로부터 주의를 돌리도록 설계된다. **단서 2**

→ **(B) 앞:** (A)에서 처음 등장한 Malicious online actors를 정관사 the를 이용하여 다시 언급했다. 세부 사항으로부터 사용자들의 주의를 돌리는 구체적인 방법에 관한 내용으로, 이에 대해 처음 언급하는 (A) 뒤에 이어지는 것이 자연스럽다.
  ▶ (B) 앞에 (A)가 와야 함 (순서: (A) → (B))
  (B) 뒤: 온라인상의 악의적인 행위자가 사용자의 관심을 돌리는 내용으로 마무리되며, 뒤에 다른 내용이 이어질 여지가 없다.
  ▶ (B)가 마지막에 올 확률이 높음

(C): 이러한 디지털상에서 시선을 다른 곳으로 돌리게 하는 전략(this digital misdirection strategy)은 웹사이트를 방문하기 위해 웹 브라우저를 사용하는 온라인 사용자가 가장 기본적이고 어디에서나 하는 탐색 동작이 웹사이트에서 그들에게 제시되는 링크나 버튼을 클릭하는 것이라는 것을 빠르게 배웠다는 사실에 의존한다. **단서 3**

→ **(C) 앞:** 주어진 글에 언급된 '디지털 세계에서 시선을 다른 곳으로 돌리는 전략'을 '이러한 ~ 전략'으로 다시 언급했다.
  ▶ (C) 앞에 주어진 글이 와야 함 (순서: 주어진 글 → (C))
  (C) 뒤: 디지털상에서 시선을 다른 곳으로 돌리는 전략은 온라인 사용자가 링크나 버튼을 클릭하는 것을 이용한다는 내용으로, 클릭하는 것을 This action으로 지칭한 (A)가 뒤에 이어지는 것이 자연스럽다.
  ▶ (C) 뒤에 (A)가 와야 함 (순서: 주어진 글 → (C) → (A) → (B))

2nd 글이 한눈에 들어오도록 정리하여 정답을 확인한다.

주어진 글: 디지털 세계에서 사용자의 시선을 돌리는 전략은 반복을 이용해서 이루어진다.
  → **(C):** 이러한 전략은 사용자가 링크나 버튼을 클릭하는 것이 기본적인 동작이라는 점에 의존한다.
  → **(A):** 악의적인 온라인 행위자들은 사용자의 관심을 웹사이트에서 다른 곳으로 돌리기 위해 클릭하는 행동을 이용한다.
  → **(B):** 그러한 웹사이트는 악의적인 행위자가 사용자의 관심을 링크를 클릭하는 것과 같은 행동에 집중시키도록 설계된다.
  ▶ 주어진 글 다음에 이어질 글의 순서는 (C) → (A) → (B)이므로 정답은 ④임

＊ 글의 흐름

도입	디지털 세계에서 사용자의 시선을 돌리는 전략은 반복을 이용해서 이루어짐
부연	이러한 전략은 사용자가 웹사이트에서 그들에게 제시되는 링크나 버튼을 클릭하는 것이 가장 기본적인 탐색 동작이라는 것을 배웠다는 사실에 의존함
	악의적인 온라인 행위자들은 사용자의 관심을 웹사이트에서 다른 곳으로 돌리기 위해 링크나 버튼을 클릭하는 이러한 행동을 이용함
	그러한 웹사이트는 악의적인 행위자가 사용자가 수행하기를 원하는 링크를 클릭하는 것과 같은 행동에 사용자의 관심을 집중시키도록 설계됨

M 36 정답 ⑤ ＊미래가 있다는 것을 알고 있긴 하지만

Humans are unique / in the realm of living beings / in knowing
_{앞에 명사절 접속사 that이 생략됨}
/ there is a future. //
인간은 고유하다 / 생물의 영역에서 / 안다는 점에서 / 미래가 있다는 것을 //

If people experience worry and hope, /
사람들이 걱정과 희망을 경험한다면 /

it is because they realize / the future exists, / that it can be better or worse, / and that the outcome depends / to some extent / on them. // **단서 1** 인간은 미래가 존재하고, 미래가 더 좋거나 나쁠 수 있으며, _{그 결과가 어느 정도 자신에게 달려 있음을 앎}
그것은 그들이 깨닫기 때문이다 / 미래가 존재한다는 것을 / 그것이 더 좋거나 나쁠 수 있다는 것을 / 그리고 그 결과가 달려 있다는 것을 / 어느 정도 / 자신에게 //

단서 2 미래와 잘 지내는 것이 쉬운 일이 아니라고 말한 (B)의 마지막 문장을 가리킴
(A) That is / why we so often have / a poor relationship with
_{주격 보어절의 동사 ①}
the future /
그것이 ~이다 / 우리가 매우 자주 갖는 이유 / 미래와 좋지 않은 관계를 /

and are either more fearful / than we need to be / or allow
_{주격 보어절의 동사 ②}　　　　　　　　　　　　　　　　　　_{주격 보어절의 동사 ③}
ourselves to hope / against all evidence; /
그리고 더 두려워하거나 / 우리가 그럴 필요가 있는 것보다 / 또는 자신에게 희망을 허락하는 / 모든 증거에 반하여 /

we worry / excessively or not enough; / we fail / to predict the
future / or to shape it / as much as we are able. //
_{병렬 구조(fail의 목적어)}
우리는 걱정한다 / 과도하게 또는 충분치 않게 / 우리는 실패한다 / 미래를 예측하는 것에 / 또는 그것을 만들어 내는 것에 / 우리가 할 수 있는 만큼 //

(B) The future, on the other hand, must be imagined / in
advance / **단서 3** 미래는 항상 불확실하다는　　**조동사가 포함된 수동태**
_{내용이 on the other hand로 이어짐}
반면에 미래는 상상되어야 한다 / 미리 /

　　★ **조동사가 포함된 수동태**
　　조동사가 포함된 동사의 수동태는 「조동사 + be p.p.」의 형태로 나타낸다. 조동사 must에 imagine의 수동태인 be imagined가 더해져 '상상되어야 한다'라는 의미를 완성했다.

and, for that very reason, /
그리고 바로 그 이유 때문에 /

is always uncertain. //
항상 불확실하다 //

Getting along with the future / is not an easy task, / nor is it one
_{= where}　　　　　　　　　　　　　　　　　　　　　　　　_{nor가 문두로 오면서}
/ in which instinct prevents us from blunders. //　　_{주어와 동사가 도치됨}
미래와 잘 지내는 것은 / 쉬운 일이 아니며 / 그것은 일도 아니다 / 본능이 우리를 큰 실수로부터 막아 주는 // **단서 4** 주어진 글에서 인간이 알고 있다고 말한 것들을 가리킴

(C) But having this knowledge does not imply / that they know
/ what to do with it. // _{문장에서 주로 목적어 역할을 하는 「의문사＋to부정사」}
하지만 이 지식을 갖고 있다는 것이 의미하지는 않는다 / 그들이 알고 있다는 것을 / 그것으로 무엇을 할지를 //

People often repress / their awareness of the future / because
_{동명사구 주어　　　　　　　　　　　　　단수 동사　　　　　　　선행사}
thinking about it distorts / the comfort of the now, /
사람들은 종종 억누른다 / 미래에 대한 자신의 인식을 / 미래에 대해 생각하는 것이 왜곡하기 때문에 / 현재의 안락함을 /

which tends to be more powerful / than the future / because it is
_{계속적 용법의 주격 관계대명사}
present / and because it is certain. //
그리고 그것은 더 강력한 경향이 있다 / 미래보다 / 그것이 존재하고 있기 때문에 / 그리고 그것이 확실하기 때문에 //

- realm ⓝ 영역, 범위　　• outcome ⓝ 결과　　• extent ⓝ 정도, 규모
- excessively ⓐⓓ 지나치게, 매우　　• predict ⓥ 예측하다
- uncertain ⓐ 불확실한, 불분명한　　• instinct ⓝ 본능, 직감
- imply ⓥ 암시하다, 의미하다　　• repress ⓥ 참다, 억누르다
- awareness ⓝ 의식, 관심　　• distort ⓥ (형체를) 비틀다, (사실을) 왜곡하다

인간은 미래가 있다는 것을 안다는 점에서 생물의 영역에서 고유하다. 사람들이 걱정과 희망을 경험한다면, 그것은 그들이 미래가 존재하고, 그것이 더 좋거나 나쁠 수 있고, 그 결과가 어느 정도 자신에게 달려 있다는 것을 깨닫기 때문이다. (C) 하지만 이것을 알고 있다는 것이 그들이 그것으로 무엇을 할지 알고 있다는 것을 의미하지는 않는다. 사람들은 미래에 대한 인식을 억누르는 경우가 많고, 그 이유는 미래에 대해 생각하는 것이 현재의 안락함을 왜곡하기 때문인데, 그것은 존재하고 있고 확실하기 때문에 미래보다 더 강력한 경향이 있다.

(B) 반면에 미래는 미리 상상되어야 하며, 바로 그 이유로 항상 불확실하다. 미래와 잘 지내는 것은 쉬운 일이 아니며, 본능이 우리가 큰 실수를 저지르지 않게 막아 주는 일도 아니다. (A) 그것이 우리가 매우 자주 미래와 좋지 않은 관계를 갖게 되고, 그럴 필요가 있는 것보다 더 두려워하거나 모든 증거에 반하여 스스로에게 희망을 허락하는 이유인데, 우리는 과도하게 또는 충분치 않게 걱정하며, 우리가 할 수 있는 만큼 미래를 예측하거나 만들어 내지 못한다.

주어진 글 다음에 이어질 글의 순서로 가장 적절한 것을 고르시오.
① (A) — (C) — (B)　—(A)의 That이 가리키는 것은 (B)에 등장함
② (B) — (A) — (C)
③ (B) — (C) — (A)　—미래가 불확실하다는 것과 상반된 내용이 주어진 글에 없음
④ (C) — (A) — (B)　인간은 미래가 있다는 것을 앎 – 그러한 지식을 가졌더라도 인간은 미래에 대해 생각하는 것이 확실한 현재의 안락함을 왜곡하기 때문에 미래에 대한 인식을 억누름 – 현재와 반대로 미래는 항상 불확실하며 미래와 잘 지내는 것은 쉬운 일이 아님 – 그래서 우리는 자주 미래와 좋지 않은 관계를 맺음
⑤ (C) — (B) — (A)

| 문제 풀이 순서 | [정답률 49%]

1st 각 문단의 내용을 파악하고, 글의 논리적인 순서를 추론한다.

주어진 글: 인간은 미래가 있다는 것을 안다는 점에서 생물의 영역에서 고유하다. 사람들이 걱정과 희망을 경험한다면, 그것은 그들이 미래가 존재하고, 그것이 더 좋거나 나쁠 수 있고, 그 결과가 어느 정도 자신에게 달려 있다는 것을 깨닫기 때문이다. 단서1

→ **주어진 글 뒤:** 인간이 미래의 존재를 인식한다는 것과 관련된 내용이 이어질 것이다.

(A): 그것이(That) 우리가 매우 자주 미래와 좋지 않은 관계를 갖게 되고, 그럴 필요가 있는 것보다 더 두려워하거나 모든 증거에 반하여 스스로에게 희망을 허락하는 이유인데, 우리는 과도하게 또는 충분치 않게 걱정하며, 우리가 할 수 있는 만큼 미래를 예측하거나 만들어 내지 못한다. 단서2

→ **(A) 앞:** 우리가 미래와 좋지 않은 관계를 갖게 한다는 That이 무엇을 지칭하는지 앞에 나와야 한다.
　▶ (A) 앞에 주어진 글이 올 수 없음
(A) 뒤: 우리는 미래를 예측하거나 만들어 내지 못한다는 결론으로 글을 마무리하고 있다.
　▶ (A)가 마지막에 올 확률이 높음

(B): 반면에(On the other hand) 미래는 미리 상상되어야 하며, 바로 그 이유로 항상 불확실하다. 미래와 잘 지내는 것은 쉬운 일이 아니며, 본능이 우리가 큰 실수를 저지르지 않게 막아 주는 일도 아니다. 단서3

→ **(B) 앞:** 앞의 내용과 반대되는 내용을 언급할 때 쓰이는 On the other hand가 나오므로 미래는 불확실하다는 내용과 반대되는 내용이 앞에 나와야 한다.
　▶ (B) 앞에 주어진 글이 올 수 없음

(B) 뒤: 미래와 잘 지내는 것이 쉽지 않으며 미래가 우리의 실수를 막아 주지 않는다는 내용으로, 이는 우리가 미래와 좋지 않은 관계를 갖게 하는 것이므로 (A)의 That에 해당한다.
　▶ (B) 뒤에 (A)가 와야 함 (순서: (B) → (A))

(C): 하지만 이것을 알고 있다는 것이(this knowledge) 그들이 그것으로 무엇을 할지 알고 있다는 것을 의미하지는 않는다. 단서4 사람들은 미래에 대한 인식을 억누르는 경우가 많고, 그 이유는 미래에 대해 생각하는 것이 현재의 안락함을 왜곡하기 때문인데, 그것은 존재하고 있고 확실하기 때문에 미래보다 더 강력한 경향이 있다.

→ **(C) 앞:** this knowledge는 우리가 미래에 대해 알고 있다는 것을 의미하며, 이는 주어진 글에서 처음 나온다.
　▶ (C) 앞에 주어진 글이 와야 함 (순서: 주어진 글 → (C))
(C) 뒤: 현재의 확실함이 미래보다 강력하여 미래에 대한 인식을 억누르는 경우가 많다는 내용으로, On the other hand로 '미래는 불확실하다'라는 반대 내용을 언급하는 (B)가 뒤에 이어지는 것이 자연스럽다.
　▶ (C) 뒤에 (B)가 와야 함 (순서: 주어진 글 → (C) → (B) → (A))

2nd 글이 한눈에 들어오도록 정리하여 정답을 확인한다.

주어진 글: 인간은 미래의 존재를 인식한다.
→ **(C):** 하지만 미래를 인식하는 것이 미래의 일을 안다는 것은 아니며, 현재의 확실함이 미래에 대한 인식을 억누른다.
→ **(B):** 미래는 불확실하며 미래와 잘 지내는 것은 쉽지 않다.
→ **(A):** 이는 우리가 미래를 예측하거나 만들지 못하게 한다.
　▶ 주어진 글 다음에 이어질 글의 순서는 (C) → (B) → (A)이므로 정답은 ⑤임

＊ 글의 흐름

도입	인간은 미래가 존재하고, 그것이 더 좋거나 나쁠 수 있다는 것과 그 결과가 어느 정도 자신에게 달려 있음을 앎
반전	그러나 그것을 안다는 것이 그것으로 무엇을 할지를 안다는 것을 의미하지는 않음
부연	인간은 미래에 대해 생각하는 것이 확실한 현재의 안락함을 왜곡하기 때문에 미래에 대한 인식을 억누르며, 미래와 잘 지내는 것은 쉬운 일이 아니기 때문에 자주 미래와 좋지 않은 관계를 맺음

Ⓜ 37 정답 ② ＊인간은 정말 만물의 척도인가

In the fifth century B.C.E., / the Greek philosopher Protagoras pronounced, / "Man is the measure / of all things." //
기원전 5세기에 / 그리스의 철학자 Protagoras는 선언했다 / "인간이 척도이다 / 만물의"라고 //
단서1 인간이 만물의 기준이라는 생각

In other words, / we feel entitled / to ask the world, / "What good are you?" //
다시 말해서 / 우리는 자격이 있다고 느낀다 / 세상에 물어볼 / "당신은 무슨 쓸모가 있는가?"라고 //

(A) Abilities / said to "make us human" / — empathy, communication, grief, toolmaking, and so on — /
복수 주어
능력들은 / '우리를 인간답게 만든다'고 일컬어지는 / 공감, 의사소통, 슬픔, 도구 만들기 등 /
복수 동사
all exist / to varying degrees / among other minds / sharing the world with us. // 단서2 우리가 간과하는 것들 중 하나　　minds를 수식하는 형용사구
모두 존재한다 / 다양한 정도로 / 다른 지력을 지닌 존재들 사이에 / 우리와 세상을 공유하는 //
Animals with backbones / (fishes, amphibians, reptiles, birds, and mammals) / all share / the same basic skeleton, organs, nervous systems, hormones, and behaviors. //
복수 주어　　　　　　　　　　　　복수 동사
척추를 가진 동물들은 / (어류, 양서류, 파충류, 조류, 그리고 포유류) / 모두 공유한다 / 동일한 기본 골격, 장기, 신경계, 호르몬, 행동을 //

(B) We assume / that we are the world's standard, / that all
things should be compared / to us. // **단서3** 주어진 글에 나온, 인간이 만물의 척도라는 생각과 동일한 맥락

<u>assume의 목적어절 접속사</u>

우리는 추정한다 / 우리가 세상의 기준이라고 / 모든 것이 비교되어야 한다고 / 우리와 //

Such an assumption makes us / overlook a lot. //

그런 추정은 우리로 하여금 ~하게 한다 / 많은 것을 간과하게 //

(C) Just as different models of automobiles each have / an
engine, drive train, four wheels, doors, and seats, /

다양한 자동차의 모델들이 각각 가지고 있는 것과 마찬가지로 / 엔진, 동력 전달 체계, 네 바퀴, 문, 좌석을 /

we differ mainly / in terms / of our outside contours and a few
internal tweaks. // **단서4** we는 (A)에 나온 척추동물들을 가리킴

우리는 주로 다르다 / 측면에서 / 우리의 외부 윤곽과 몇 가지 내부적인 조정의 //

But like naive car buyers, / most people see only / animals' varied
exteriors. //

전치사   명사구

하지만 순진한 자동차 구매자들처럼 / 대부분의 사람들은 오직 본다 / 동물들의 다양한 겉모습만을 //

- pronounce ⓥ 선언하다 · measure ⓝ 척도
- entitled to-v ~할 자격이 있는 · empathy ⓝ 감정이입, 공감
- grief ⓝ 슬픔 · backbone ⓝ 척추, 등뼈 · amphibian ⓝ 양서류
- reptile ⓝ 파충류 · mammal ⓝ 포유류 · skeleton ⓝ 골격
- organ ⓝ (인체 내의) 장기[기관] · nervous system 신경계
- standard ⓝ 기준, 표준 · overlook ⓥ 간과하다
- drive train 동력 전달 체계 · internal ⓐ 내부의 · naive ⓐ 순진한
- exterior ⓝ 겉모습

기원전 5세기에, 그리스의 철학자 Protagoras는 "인간이 만물의 척도이다."라고 선언했다. 다시 말해서, 우리는 세상을 향해 "당신은 무슨 쓸모가 있는가?"라고 물어볼 자격이 있다고 느낀다. (B) 우리는 우리가 세상의 기준이라고, 즉 모든 것이 우리와 비교되어야 한다고 추정한다. 그런 추정은 우리로 하여금 많은 것을 간과하게 한다. (A) '우리를 인간답게 만든다'고 일컬어지는 능력들, 즉 공감, 의사소통, 슬픔, 도구 만들기 등은 모두 우리와 세상을 공유하는 다른 지력을 지닌 존재들에게도 다양한 정도로 존재한다. 척추동물(어류, 양서류, 파충류, 조류, 그리고 포유류)은 모두 동일한 기본 골격, 장기, 신경계, 호르몬, 행동을 공유한다. (C) 다양한 자동차의 모델들이 각각 엔진, 동력 전달 체계, 네 바퀴, 문, 좌석을 가지고 있는 것과 마찬가지로, 우리는 주로 우리의 외부 윤곽과 몇 가지 내부적인 조정의 측면에서 다르다. 하지만 순진한 자동차 구매자들처럼, 대부분의 사람들은 오직 동물들의 다양한 겉모습만을 본다.

주어진 글 다음에 이어질 글의 순서로 가장 적절한 것을 고르시오.

인간이 만물의 척도라는 생각이 많은 것을 간과하게 한다는 내용인 (B)가 주어진 글과 (A) 사이에 있어야 함
① (A) — (C) — (B)
② (B) — (A) — (C) — (B) 인간이 만물의 척도라는 생각은 우리로 하여금 많은 것을 간과하게 만듦
(A) 인간을 포함한 척추동물들은 동일한 기본 골격, 장기 등을 공유함
(C) 우리는 단지 외부 윤곽과 몇몇 내부적인 조정 측면에서 다를 뿐임
③ (B) — (C) — (A)
④ (C) — (A) — (B) (C)의 we가 가리키는 대상이 (A)에 등장하므로 (C)보다 (A)가 앞에 와야 함
⑤ (C) — (B) — (A)

| 문제 풀이 순서 | [정답률 52%]

1st 각 문단의 내용을 파악하고, 글의 논리적인 순서를 추론한다.

주어진 글: 기원전 5세기에, 그리스의 철학자 Protagoras는 "인간이 만물의 척도이다."라고 선언했다. 다시 말해서, 우리는 세상을 향해 "당신은 무슨 쓸모가 있는가?"라고 물어볼 자격이 있다고 느낀다. **단서1**

➡ **주어진 글 뒤:** 인간이 만물의 척도라는 주장에 관한 내용이 이어질 것이다.

(A): '우리를 인간답게 만든다고' 일컬어지는 능력들, 즉 공감, 의사소통, 슬픔, 도구 만들기 등은 모두 우리와 세상을 공유하는 다른 지력을 지닌 존재들에게도 다양한 정도로 존재한다. **단서2** 척추동물 (어류, 양서류, 파충류, 조류, 그리고 포유류)은 모두 동일한 기본 골격, 장기, 신경계, 호르몬, 행동을 공유한다.

➡ **(A) 앞:** 인간의 고유한 능력으로 일컬어지는 것들이 지력을 지닌 다른 존재들에게도 존재한다는 내용으로, 인간이 만물의 척도라는 주장이 잘못되었다는 증거에 해당한다. 따라서 이러한 주장이 잘못되었다는 내용이 앞에 나와야 한다.
  ▶ (A) 앞에 주어진 글이 올 수 없음
(A) 뒤: 인간을 포함한 척추동물은 모두 동일한 내부 구조를 공유한다는 내용으로, 이에 관한 구체적인 설명이나 예시가 뒤에 이어질 것이다.

(B): 우리는 우리가 세상의 기준이라고, 즉 모든 것이 우리와 비교되어야 한다고 추정한다. **단서3** 그런 추정은 우리로 하여금 많은 것을 간과하게 한다.

➡ **(B) 앞:** 인간이 세상의 기준이며 모든 것이 인간과 비교되어야 한다는 내용으로, "인간이 만물의 척도이다."라는 Protagoras의 주장이 나타난 주어진 글에 이어지는 것이 자연스럽다.
  ▶ (B) 앞에 주어진 글이 와야 함 (순서: 주어진 글 → (B))
(B) 뒤: 인간이 세상의 기준이라는 추정이 무엇을 간과하게 하는지 이어져야 하는데, 인간의 고유한 능력이 다른 존재들에게도 있다는 내용이 (A)에 나온다.
  ▶ (B) 뒤에 (A)가 와야 함 (순서: 주어진 글 → (B) → (A))

(C): 다양한 자동차의 모델들이 각각 엔진, 동력 전달 체계, 네 바퀴, 문, 좌석을 가지고 있는 것과 마찬가지로, 우리는 주로 우리의 외부 윤곽과 몇 가지 내부적인 조정의 측면에서 다르다. **단서4** 하지만 순진한 자동차 구매자들처럼, 대부분의 사람들은 오직 동물들의 다양한 겉모습만을 본다.

➡ **(C) 앞:** 자동차를 예로 들어, 다양한 자동차의 모델들이 큰 틀에서는 동일하지만 외부 윤곽과 내부적인 조정에서 다르다는 내용이며, 인간이 동물들과 동일한 내부 구조를 공유한다는 내용이 나오는 (A) 뒤에 이어지는 것이 자연스럽다.
  ▶ (C) 앞에 (A)가 와야 함 (순서: 주어진 글 → (B) → (A) → (C))

2nd 글이 한눈에 들어오도록 정리하여 정답을 확인한다.

주어진 글: 인간이 만물의 척도라는 주장이 있었다.
➡ **(B):** 인간이 세상의 기준이라는 추정은 우리에게 많은 것을 간과하게 한다.
➡ **(A):** 인간의 능력은 고유하지 않으며 인간은 다른 척추동물과 동일한 내부 구조를 갖는다.
➡ **(C):** 인간은 외부 윤곽과 몇 가지 내부적인 조정의 측면에서 다를 뿐이지만 대부분의 사람들은 동물들의 다양한 겉모습만 본다.
▶ 주어진 글 다음에 이어질 글의 순서는 (B) → (A) → (C)이므로 정답은 ②임

* 글의 흐름

도입	우리는 우리가 세상의 기준이고, 모든 것이 우리와 비교되어야 한다고 추정함
반박	하지만 그러한 추정은 우리로 하여금 많은 것을 간과하게 만듦
부연	우리를 인간답게 만든다고 일컬어지는 능력들은 사실 다른 지력을 지닌 존재들에게도 존재하고, 척추동물들은 모두 동일한 기본 골격, 장기, 신경계 등을 공유함
결론	우리는 주로 외부 윤곽과 몇 가지 내부적인 조정의 측면에서 다를 뿐이지만 대부분의 사람들은 동물들의 다양한 겉모습만을 봄

The fruit ripening process brings / about the softening of cell walls, / sweetening and the production of chemicals / that give colour and flavour. //
선행사 / 주격 관계대명사
과일 숙성 과정은 가져온다 / 세포벽의 연화를 / 감미 그리고 화학 물질의 생산 / 색과 맛을 주는 //

The process is induced / by the production of a plant hormone / called ethylene. //
주격 관계대명사와 be동사가 생략됨
그 과정은 유도된다 / 식물 호르몬의 생산에 의해 / 에틸렌이라고 불리는 //

조건의 부사절 접속사
(A) If ripening could be slowed down / by interfering / with ethylene production or with the processes / that respond to ethylene, /
전치사구의 병렬 구조
숙성이 늦춰질 수 있다면 / 방해함으로써 / 에틸렌 생산 또는 과정을 / 에틸렌에 반응하는 /

fruit could be left on the plant / until it was ripe and full of flavour / but would still be in good condition / when it arrived at the supermarket shelf. // 단서1
숙성을 늦춤으로써 맛도 좋고 시간의 부사절 접속사 / 상태도 좋은 과일을 얻을 수 있음
과일은 식물에 붙어 있을 수 있다 / 그것이 익어서 맛이 가득 찰 때까지 / 하지만 여전히 좋은 상태를 유지할 것이다 / 그것이 슈퍼마켓 선반에 도착했을 때 // 단서2
수확된 토마토와 다른 과일들을 가리킴
(B) In some countries / they are then sprayed with ethylene / before sale to the consumer / to induce ripening. //
전치사 / 명사구
일부 국가에서는 / 그런 다음 그것들은 에틸렌으로 살포된다 / 소비자에게 판매하기 전에 / 숙성을 유도하기 위해 //

주어 / 접속사 / 완전한 절 / 동사
However, / fruit / picked before it is ripe / has less flavour / than fruit / picked ripe / from the plant. //
그러나 / 과일은 / 그것이 익기 전에 수확된 / 맛이 덜하다 / 과일보다 / 익은 상태로 수확된 / 식물에서 //

Biotechnologists therefore saw an opportunity / in delaying / the ripening and softening process in fruit. //
전치사 / 동명사
따라서 생명공학자들은 기회를 엿보았다 / 지연하는 데 있어서 / 과일의 숙성 및 연화 과정을 //

주격 보어절 접속사
(C) The problem for growers and retailers is / that ripening is followed sometimes quite rapidly / by deterioration and decay / and the product becomes worthless. //
주어 / 동사
재배자나 소매업자에게 문제는 ~이다 / 숙성이 때로는 아주 빠르게 뒤따라진다는 것 / 품질 저하와 부패에 의해 / 그리고 제품이 가치 없게 된다는 것 //
수동태를 완성하는 과거분사
Tomatoes and other fruits / are, therefore, usually picked and transported / when they are unripe. // 단서3
토마토와 다른 과일들은 일반적으로 익지 않을 때 수확되어 운송됨
토마토와 다른 과일은 / 그러므로 일반적으로 수확되어 운송된다 / 그것들이 익지 않았을 때 //

- ripening ⓝ 숙성   - bring about ~을 야기하다[초래하다]
- softening ⓝ 연화   - chemical ⓝ 화학 물질   - flavour ⓝ 맛, 풍미
- induce ⓥ 유도하다   - interfere with ~을 방해하다
- spray ⓥ 살포하다   - biotechnologist ⓝ 생명공학자
- delay ⓥ 지연하다   - decay ⓝ 부패   - worthless ⓐ 가치가 없는
- transport ⓥ 운송하다

과일 숙성 과정은 세포벽의 연화, 즉 감미, 색과 맛을 주는 화학 물질의 생산을 가져온다. 그 과정은 에틸렌이라고 불리는 식물 호르몬의 생산에 의해 유도된다. (C) 재배자와 소매업자에게 문제는 숙성 이후에 때로는 아주 빠르게 품질 저하와 부패가 뒤따라서 제품이 가치 없게 된다는 것이다. 그러므로 토마토와 다른 과일은 일반적으로 익지 않았을 때 수확되어 운송된다. (B) 일부 국가에서는 그런 다음 숙성을 유도하기 위해 소비자에게 판매하기 전에 에틸렌을 그것들에 살포한다. 그러나 익기 전에 수확된 과일은 식물에서 익은 상태로 수확된 과일보다 맛이 덜하다. 따라서 생명공학자들은 과일의 숙성 및 연화 과정을 지연하는 데 있어서 기회를 엿보았다. (A) 에틸렌 생산을 방해하거나 에틸렌에 반응하는 과정을 방해함으로써 숙성을 늦출 수 있다면, 과일은 익어서 맛이 가득 찰 때까지 식물에 붙어 있을 수 있지만, 슈퍼마켓 선반에 도착했을 때에도 여전히 좋은 상태를 유지할 것이다.

주어진 글 다음에 이어질 글의 순서로 가장 적절한 것을 고르시오. [3점]

① (A) — (C) — (B) (A) 앞에는 과일 숙성을 늦춰야 하는 문제 상황이 언급되어 있어야 함
② (B) — (A) — (C)
③ (B) — (C) — (A) (B)의 they가 가리키는 것이 주어진 글에 없음
④ (C) — (A) — (B) 익기 전에 수확되면 맛이 덜하다는 내용이 (A) 앞에 있어야 함
⑤ (C) — (B) — (A) (C) 숙성 이후 빠르게 품질이 저하되고 부패되어 토마토 등은 익기 전에 수확됨 – (B) 익기 전에 수확된 과일은 맛이 덜함 – (A) 두 문제점을 해결하는 방법을 제시함

| 문제 풀이 순서 | [정답률 49%]

1st 각 문단의 내용을 파악하고, 글의 논리적인 순서를 추론한다.

> **주어진 글:** 과일 숙성 과정은 세포벽의 연화, 즉 감미, 색과 맛을 주는 화학 물질의 생산을 가져온다. 그 과정은 에틸렌이라고 불리는 식물 호르몬의 생산에 의해 유도된다.

→ **주어진 글 뒤:** 과일의 숙성 과정은 에틸렌이라는 식물 호르몬이 생산되면서 유도되고 감미를 가져온다는 내용으로, 단서 이에 관한 구체적인 과정이나 문제 사항이 이어질 것이다. (발상)

> **(A):** 에틸렌 생산을 방해하거나 에틸렌에 반응하는 과정을 방해함으로써 숙성을 늦출 수 있다면, 과일은 익어서 맛이 가득 찰 때까지 식물에 붙어 있을 수 있지만, 슈퍼마켓 선반에 도착했을 때에도 여전히 좋은 상태를 유지할 것이다. 단서1

→ **(A) 앞:** 과일의 숙성으로 인해 좋은 상태를 유지하기 힘들다는 내용이 앞에 나와야 한다.
▶ (A) 앞에 주어진 글이 올 수 없음
(A) 뒤: 에틸렌 생산 및 반응 과정을 방해하여 과일 숙성을 늦춘다면 좋은 상태를 오래 유지한다는 설명으로, 특정 과정의 마무리 단계에 해당한다.
▶ (A)가 마지막에 올 확률이 높음

> **(B):** 일부 국가에서는 그런 다음 숙성을 유도하기 위해 소비자에게 판매하기 전에 에틸렌을 그것들에(they) 살포한다. 단서2 그러나 익기 전에 수확된 과일은 식물에서 익은 상태로 수확된 과일보다 맛이 덜하다. 따라서 생명공학자들은 과일의 숙성 및 연화 과정을 지연하는 데 있어서 기회를 엿보았다.

→ **(B) 앞:** 숙성을 유도하기 위해 (그 위에) 에틸렌이 살포된다는 they가 무엇인지 앞에 나와야 한다.
▶ (B) 앞에 주어진 글이 올 수 없음
(B) 뒤: 생명공학자들이 과일의 숙성 및 연화 과정을 지연하는 데 있어서 기회를 엿보았다는 내용으로, 에틸렌 생산을 방해하여 숙성을 늦춘다는 가정이 (A)에 나온다.
▶ (B) 뒤에 (A)가 와야 함 (순서: (B) → (A))

> **(C):** 재배자와 소매업자에게 문제는 숙성 이후에 때로는 아주 빠르게 품질 저하와 부패가 뒤따라서 제품이 가치 없게 된다는 것이다. 그러므로 토마토와 다른 과일은 일반적으로 익지 않았을 때 수확되어 운송된다. 단서3

→ **(C) 앞:** 숙성 이후의 빠른 품질 저하에 관한 내용으로, 과일의 숙성 과정에 대해 처음으로 언급하는 주어진 글이 앞에 나와야 자연스럽다.
▶ (C) 앞에 주어진 글이 와야 함 (순서: 주어진 글 → (C))
(C) 뒤: 토마토와 다른 과일이 익지 않았을 때 수확되어 운송된다는 내용으로, (B)에서 이 과일들을 they로 지칭하며, 그것들 위에 에틸렌이 살포된다고 했다.
▶ (C) 뒤에 (B)가 와야 함 (순서: 주어진 글 → (C) → (B) → (A))

2nd 글이 한눈에 들어오도록 정리하여 정답을 확인한다.

주어진 글: 과일 숙성 과정은 연화와 감미를 가져오고, 이는 에틸렌의 생산에 의해 유도된다.

→ **(C):** 숙성 이후에 빠르게 품질이 저하되므로 토마토 등은 익기 전에 수확되어 운송된다.

→ **(B):** 익기 전에 수확되면 맛이 덜하므로 생명공학자들은 숙성 지연의 기회를 엿보았다.

→ **(A):** 에틸렌 생산을 방해하여 숙성을 늦춘다면 수확 전부터 좋은 상태를 유지할 것이다.

▶ 주어진 글 다음에 이어질 글의 순서는 (C) → (B) → (A)이므로 정답은 ⑤임

＊ 글의 흐름

도입	과일의 숙성 과정과 식물 호르몬인 에틸렌에 대한 소개
문제점 ①	숙성 이후 때로 아주 빠르게 품질 저하와 부패가 뒤따름
문제점 ②	문제점 ①의 해결을 위해 익기 전에 수확하지만, 익기 전에 수확된 과일은 맛이 덜함
해결책	에틸렌의 생산 또는 에틸렌에 반응하는 과정을 방해해서 과일의 숙성을 늦추면 두 문제를 해결할 수 있음

M 39 정답 ⑤ ＊로크를 이용한 운하 건설

When two natural bodies of water stand / at different levels,
(통명사구 주어)
/ building a canal / between them / presents a complicated
(단수 동사)
engineering problem. // **단서1** 수위에 차이가 있는 두 자연 수역에 운하를
건설하는 것이 복잡한 공학적 문제를 만들어 냄
두 곳의 자연 수역이 있을 때 / 서로 다른 수위에 / 운하를 건설하는 것은 / 그것들 사이에 /
복잡한 공학적 문제를 만들어 낸다 /

단서2 로크 안에서 위쪽 물 높이까지 들어 올려진 배가 열린 문을 통과해 상류로 진입함
(A) Then the upper gates open / and the ship passes through. //
그리고 나면 위쪽 문이 열리고 / 배가 통과한다 //

For downstream passage, / the process works / the opposite
way. //
앞에 전치사 in이 생략됨
하류 통행의 경우 / 그 과정은 작동한다 / 정반대로 //

The ship enters the lock / from the upper level, / and water is
1형식 동사로 착각하기 쉬운 3형식 동사
pumped / from the lock / until the ship is in line / with the lower
level. //
배가 로크로 들어오고 / 위쪽 수위로부터 / 물이 양수된다 / 로크로부터 / 배가 직선을 이룰
때까지 / 더 낮은 수위와 // **단서3** 선박이 상류로 올라가는 경우에 로크가
(시간)의 부사절 접속사   어떻게 작동하는지를 설명하기 시작함
(B) When a vessel is going upstream, / the upper gates stay
closed / as the ship enters the lock / at the lower water level. //
선박이 상류로 올라가고 있을 때는 / 위쪽 문은 닫혀 있다 / 배가 로크에 들어서는 동안 / 더
낮은 수위에 있는 //

The downstream gates are then closed / and more water is
pumped / into the basin. //
그리고 나서 하류의 문이 닫히고 / 더 많은 물이 양수된다 / 웅덩이 안으로 //

The rising water lifts the vessel / to the level / of the upper body
of water. // **단서4** 로크 안으로 양수된 물이 선박을 위쪽의 물 높이까지 들어 올림
상승하는 물이 선박을 들어 올린다 / 수준까지 / 위쪽의 물의 //
앞에 주격 관계대명사와 be동사가 생략됨
(C) To make up for the difference in level, / engineers build one
or more water "steps," / called locks, / that carry ships or boats
up or down / between the two levels. // **단서5** 공학자들이 주어진 글에서
소개한 문제를 해결하는 방법을 설명함
수위의 차이를 보전하기 위해 / 공학자들은 하나 이상의 물 '계단'을 만든다 / 로크라고 불리는
/ 배나 보트를 위아래로 운반하는 / 두 수위 사이에서 //
주어   동사   주격 보어
A lock is an artificial water basin. //
로크는 인공적인 물웅덩이이다 //

It has a long rectangular shape / with concrete walls and a pair
of gates / at each end. //
그것은 긴 직사각형 모양을 갖는다 / 콘크리트 벽과 한 쌍의 문이 있는 / 양 끝에 //

(우측 단)

- body ⓝ 많은 양[모음]   · stand ⓥ (특정 조건 · 상황에) 있다
- canal ⓝ 운하, 수로   · downstream ⓐ (강) 하류의
- passage ⓝ 뱃길, 통행, 통로   · opposite ⓐ 반대의, 다른 편의
- in (a) line with ～와 일직선을 이루는   · vessel ⓝ (대형) 선박
- upstream ⓐⓓ 상류로   · basin ⓝ 물웅덩이, 대야
- artificial ⓐ 인공의, 인위적인   · concrete ⓐ 콘크리트로 된

두 곳의 자연 수역이 서로 다른 수위에 있을 때, 그것들 사이에 운하를 건설하는 것은 복잡한 공학적 문제를 만들어 낸다. (C) 수위의 차이를 보전하기 위해 공학자들은 두 수위 사이에서 배나 보트를 위아래로 운반하는, 로크라고 불리는 하나 이상의 물 '계단'을 만든다. 로크는 인공적인 물웅덩이이다. 그것은 콘크리트 벽과 양 끝에 한 쌍의 문이 있는 긴 직사각형 모양을 하고 있다. (B) 선박이 상류로 올라가고 있을 때는, 배가 더 낮은 수위에 있는 로크에 들어서는 동안 위쪽 문은 닫혀 있다. 그리고 나서 하류의 문이 닫히고 더 많은 물이 웅덩이 안으로 양수된다. 상승하는 물이 선박을 위쪽의 물 높이 수준까지 들어 올린다. (A) 그리고 나면 위쪽 문이 열리고 배가 통과한다. 하류 통행의 경우, 그 과정은 정반대로 작동한다. 배가 위쪽 수위로부터 로크로 들어오고, 배가 더 낮은 수위와 일치할 때까지 물이 로크로부터 양수된다.

주어진 글 다음에 이어질 글의 순서로 가장 적절한 것을 고르시오.

① (A) ― (C) ― (B) 상승하는 물이 배를 위쪽 수위까지 들어 올리고 나면(Then) 위쪽 문이 열리는 것임
② (B) ― (A) ― (C) ┐정관사가 쓰인 the lock보다 부정관사가 쓰인 a lock이 앞에 있어야 함
③ (B) ― (C) ― (A) ┘
④ (C) ― (A) ― (B) (A)에서 상류로 이동하는 선박에 대한 내용이 마무리됨
⑤ (C) ― (B) ― (A) 서로 다른 수위의 두 수역에 운하를 건설하는 것은 복잡한 공학적 문제를 야기함 ─로크라고 불리는 물 계단을 통해 수위의 차이를 극복함 ─로크를 통해 선박이 상류로, 또 하류로 이동하는 과정을 설명함

| 문제 풀이 순서 | [정답률 69%]

1st 각 문단의 내용을 파악하고, 글의 논리적인 순서를 추론한다.

주어진 글: 두 곳의 자연 수역이 서로 다른 수위에 있을 때, 그것들 사이에 운하를 건설하는 것은 복잡한 공학적 문제를 만들어 낸다. **단서1**

→ **주어진 글 뒤:** 서로 다른 수위의 자연 수역 사이에 운하를 건설하는 과정에서 발생하는 문제에 관하여 이어질 것이다.

(A): 그리고 나면(Then) 위쪽 문이 열리고 배가 통과한다. **단서2** 하류 통행의 경우, 그 과정은 정반대로 작동한다. 배가 위쪽 수위로부터 로크로 들어오고, 배가 더 낮은 수위와 일치할 때까지 물이 로크로부터 양수된다.

→ **(A) 앞:** Then이 나오려면 위쪽 문이 열리고 배가 통과하기 전의 과정이 앞에 나와야 한다. 주어진 글에는 운하 건설의 공학적 문제에 대한 세부 사항이 없다.
▶ (A) 앞에 주어진 글이 올 수 없음
(A) 뒤: 하류 통행의 과정을 설명하며 문단이 마무리된다.
▶ (A)가 마지막에 올 확률이 높음

(B): 선박이 상류로 올라가고 있을 때는, 배가 더 낮은 수위에 있는 로크에 들어서는 동안 위쪽 문은 닫혀 있다. **단서3** 그리고 나서 하류의 문이 닫히고 더 많은 물이 웅덩이 안으로 양수된다. 상승하는 물이 선박을 위쪽의 물 높이 수준까지 들어 올린다. **단서4**

→ **(B) 앞:** 선박의 이동에 관한 언급이 있어야 하는데 주어진 글에서는 운하 건설에 관해서만 언급했다.
▶ (B) 앞에 주어진 글이 올 수 없음
(B) 뒤: 선박이 상류로 올라가고 있을 때, 양수되는 물이 선박을 물 높이까지 들어 올린다는 내용이며, 이후에 위쪽 문이 열리고 배가 통과한다는 내용이 (A)에 나온다.
▶ (B) 뒤에 (A)가 와야 함 (순서: (B) → (A))

(C): 수위의 차이를 보전하기 위해 공학자들은 두 수위 사이에서 배나 보트를 위아래로 운반하는, 로크라고 불리는 하나 이상의 물 '계단'을 만든다. **단서5** 로크는 인공적인 물웅덩이이다. 그것은 콘크리트 벽과 양 끝에 한 쌍의 문이 있는 긴 직사각형 모양을 하고 있다.

→ **(C) 앞:** 수위의 차이를 보전하기 위해 수위 사이에서 배나 보트를 운반하는 로크라는 물 계단을 소개하는 내용이다. 두 곳의 자연 수역이 서로 다른 수위에 있는 경우가 주어진 글에서 언급되었다.
  ▶ **(C) 앞에 주어진 글이 와야 함** (순서: 주어진 글 → (C))
  (C) 뒤: 서로 다른 수위 사이에서 배나 보트를 운반하는 로크에 대한 소개에 이어서, 선박의 이동 과정을 처음 설명하는 (B)가 뒤에 오는 것이 자연스럽다.
  ▶ **(C) 뒤에 (B)가 와야 함** (순서: 주어진 글 → (C) → (B) → (A))

2nd 글이 한눈에 들어오도록 정리하여 정답을 확인한다.

주어진 글: 서로 다른 수위의 두 자연 수역에 운하를 건설하는 것은 공학적으로 복잡하다.
→ **(C):** 로크라는 물 계단을 통해 두 수위 사이에서 배나 보트를 운반할 수 있다.
→ **(B):** 선박의 상류 통행 과정
→ **(A):** 선박의 하류 통행 과정
▶ 주어진 글 다음에 이어질 글의 순서는 (C) → (B) → (A)이므로 정답은 ⑤임

＊ 글의 흐름

도입	서로 다른 수위의 두 자연 수역에 운하를 건설하는 것은 공학적으로 복잡한데, '로크'라는 물 계단을 만들어 문제를 해결할 수 있음
부연	선박이 상류로 이동할 때: 선박이 낮은 수위에 있는 로크에 들어오고, 로크 안으로 물이 양수되어 선박이 높은 수위까지 들어 올려지면 로크의 위쪽 문이 열리고 선박이 통과함
	선박이 하류로 이동할 때: 상류로 이동할 때와 정반대의 과정으로 선박이 이동됨

M 40 정답 ④ ＊역경과 정신 건강 사이의 곡선 관계

Studies of people / struggling with major health problems / (복수 주어)
show / that the majority of respondents report / they derived (복수 동사) (목적절 접속사)
benefits / from their adversity. //
사람들에 대한 연구는 / 중대한 건강 문제를 해결하려고 노력하는 / 보여준다 / 대다수의 응답자가 보고한다는 것을 / 그들이 이익을 얻었다고 / 그들의 역경에서 //
Stressful events sometimes force people / to develop new (주어) (동사) (목적어) (목적어)
skills, / reevaluate priorities, / learn new insights, / and
acquire new strengths. // (목적격 보어(to부정사)의 병렬 구조)
스트레스를 주는 사건들은 때때로 사람들로 하여금 ～하게 한다 / 새로운 기술을 개발하고 / 우선순위를 재평가하고 / 새로운 통찰을 배우고 / 새로운 강점을 얻게 //

(A) High levels of adversity / predicted poor mental health, / as expected, /
높은 수준의 역경은 / 나쁜 정신 건강을 예측했지만 / 예상된 대로 /
but people / who had faced intermediate levels of adversity / (주어) (준부정어)
were healthier than those / who experienced little adversity, / (동사)
하지만 사람들은 / 중간 수준의 역경에 직면했던 / 사람들보다 더 건강했는데 / 역경을 거의 경험하지 않았던 /
suggesting / that moderate amounts of stress / can foster resilience. //
이것은 보여준다 / 적당한 양의 스트레스가 / 회복력을 촉진할 수 있음을 //

A follow-up study found a similar link / between the amount of lifetime |adversity| and subjects' responses / to laboratory stressors. // **단서1** 첫 번째 연구에 이어지는 후속 연구에 대한 설명이 시작됨
후속 연구는 비슷한 관계를 발견했다 / 생애에서 겪은 역경의 양과 피실험자의 반응 사이에서 / 실험 중 주어진 스트레스 요인에의 //

(B) Intermediate levels of adversity / were predictive of the greatest resilience. //
중간 수준의 역경이 / 가장 큰 회복력을 예측했다 **단서2** 두 연구 결과를 종합하여 글의 결론을 내림
Thus, / having to deal with a moderate amount of stress / (동명사구 주어) (동사)
may build resilience / in the face of future stress. //
따라서 / 적당한 양의 스트레스를 해결하기 위해 노력해야 하는 것은 / 회복력을 기를 수도 있다 / 미래에 스트레스를 직면할 때의 //
(C) In other words, / the adaptation process / initiated by stress / (앞에 주격 관계대명사와 be동사가 생략됨)
can lead to personal changes / for the better. //
다시 말해 / 적응 과정은 / 스트레스에 의해 시작된 / 개인적 변화를 가져올 수 있다 / 더 나은 쪽으로의 // **단서3** 주어진 글의 내용을 뒷받침하는 첫 번째 연구에 대해 이야기함
One study / that measured participants' exposure / to thirty-(주어)
seven major negative events / found a curvilinear relationship / (동사)
between lifetime adversity and mental health. //
한 연구는 / 참가자들의 노출을 측정한 / 서른일곱 가지 주요 부정적인 사건에의 / 곡선 관계를 발견했다 / 생애에서 겪은 역경과 정신 건강 사이의 //

- struggle with ～으로 고투하다, ～을 해결하려고 노력하다
- major ⓐ 주된, 주요한   · respondent ⓝ 응답자
- derive A from B A를 B에서 얻다   · adversity ⓝ 역경
- reevaluate ⓥ 재평가하다   · priority ⓝ 우선순위   · insight ⓝ 통찰
- acquire ⓥ 얻다   · strength ⓝ 강점, 장점, 힘
- intermediate ⓐ 중간의   · moderate ⓐ 적당한
- foster ⓥ 촉진하다, 키우다   · follow-up 후속의, 뒤따르는
- laboratory ⓝ 실험실 ⓐ 실험(실)의   · intermediate ⓐ 중간의, 중급의
- predictive ⓐ 예측[예견]의   · deal with ～을 처리하다[다루다]
- in the face of ～에 직면하여   · adaptation ⓝ 적응
- initiate ⓥ 개시되게 하다, 착수시키다   · measure ⓥ 측정하다, 재다
- exposure ⓝ (유해한 환경 등에의) 노출, (직접) 경험[체험]함, 접함
- curvilinear ⓐ 곡선으로 이루어진

중대한 건강 문제를 해결하려고 노력하는 사람들에 대한 연구는 대다수의 응답자가 자신이 겪은 역경에서 이익을 얻었다고 보고한다는 것을 보여준다. 스트레스를 주는 사건들은 때때로 사람들이 새로운 기술을 개발하고, 우선순위를 재평가하고, 새로운 통찰을 배우고 새로운 강점을 얻게 한다.
(C) 다시 말해, 스트레스에 의해 시작된 적응 과정은 더 나은 쪽으로의 개인적 변화를 가져올 수 있다. 참가자들의 서른일곱 가지 주요 부정적인 사건 경험을 측정한 한 연구는 생애에서 겪은 역경과 정신 건강 사이의 곡선 관계를 발견했다.
(A) 높은 수준의 역경은 예상대로 나쁜 정신 건강을 예측했지만, 중간 수준의 역경에 직면했던 사람들은 역경을 거의 경험하지 않았던 사람들보다 더 건강했는데, 이것은 적당한 양의 스트레스가 회복력을 촉진할 수 있음을 보여준다. 후속 연구는 생애에서 겪은 역경의 양과 피실험자들이 실험 중 주어진 스트레스 요인에 반응하는 것 사이에서 비슷한 관계를 발견했다.
(B) 중간 수준의 역경이 가장 큰 회복력을 예측했다. 따라서 적당한 양의 스트레스를 해결하기 위해 노력해야 하는 것은 미래에 스트레스를 직면할 때의 회복력을 기를 수도 있다.

주어진 글 다음에 이어질 글의 순서로 가장 적절한 것을 고르시오.

① (A) — (C) — (B) A follow-up study 전에 One study가 나와야 함
② (B) — (A) — (C) ┐(B)에는 글의 결론이 포함되어 있음
③ (B) — (C) — (A)┘
  역경이 사람들로 하여금 새로운 강점을 얻게 함 – (C) 첫 번째 연구에 대한
④ (C) — (A) — (B) 내용 – (A) 첫 번째 연구 결과와 후속 연구에 대한 언급 – (B) 후속 연구의 결과와 글의 결론
⑤ (C) — (B) — (A)
  후속 연구에 대한 결과가 (B)에 제시됨

M

1st 각 문단의 내용을 파악하고, 글의 논리적인 순서를 추론한다.

주어진 글: 중대한 건강 문제를 해결하려고 노력하는 사람들에 대한 연구는 대다수의 응답자가 자신이 겪은 역경에서 이익을 얻었다고 보고한다는 것을 보여준다. 스트레스를 주는 사건들은 때때로 사람들이 새로운 기술을 개발하고, 우선순위를 재평가하고, 새로운 통찰을 배우고 새로운 강점을 얻게 한다.

➡ **주어진 글 뒤:** 스트레스를 주는 사건들이 주는 이익에 관한 내용으로, [단서] 그러한 사건들이 어떻게 이익이 되는지에 대한 설명이 이어질 것이다. [발상]

(A): 높은 수준의 역경은 예상대로 나쁜 정신 건강을 예측했지만, 중간 수준의 역경에 직면했던 사람들은 역경을 거의 경험하지 않았던 사람들보다 더 건강했는데, 이것은 적당한 양의 스트레스가 회복력을 촉진할 수 있음을 보여준다. 후속 연구(A follow-up study)는 생애에서 겪은 역경의 양과 피실험자들이 실험 중 주어진 스트레스 요인에 반응하는 것 사이에서 비슷한 관계를 발견했다. [단서 1]

➡ **(A) 앞:** 역경의 수준별로 정신 건강을 측정하는 연구의 결과를 나타내므로, 실험을 소개하는 내용이 앞에 나와야 한다.
▶ (A) 앞에 주어진 글이 올 수 없음
(A) 뒤: 생애에서 겪은 역경의 양과 스트레스 요인에 대한 반응 사이의 관계를 밝히는 후속 연구에 관한 내용이 이어질 것이다.

(B): 중간 수준의 역경이 가장 큰 회복력을 예측했다. 따라서(Thus) 적당한 양의 스트레스를 해결하기 위해 노력해야 하는 것은 미래에 스트레스를 직면할 때의 회복력을 기를 수도 있다. [단서 2]

➡ **(B) 앞:** (A)의 두 번째 문장에 나타난 후속 연구의 결과를 설명하는 내용으로, (A) 뒤에 이어지는 것이 자연스럽다.
▶ (B) 앞에 (A)가 와야 함 (순서: (A) → (B))
(B) 뒤: 후속 연구의 결과로 글이 마무리된다.
▶ (B)가 마지막에 올 확률이 높음

(C): 다시 말해(In other words), 스트레스에 의해 시작된 적응 과정이 더 나은 쪽으로의 개인적 변화를 가져올 수 있다. 참가자들의 서른일곱 가지 주요 부정적인 사건 경험을 측정한 한 연구(One study)는 생애에서 겪은 역경과 정신 건강 사이의 곡선 관계를 발견했다. [단서 3]

➡ **(C) 앞:** In other words를 사용하여 주어진 글의 내용을 다시 요약한다.
▶ (C) 앞에 주어진 글이 와야 함 (순서: 주어진 글 → (C))
(C) 뒤: 생애에서 겪은 역경과 정신 건강 사이의 관계를 연구한 One study의 결과가 (A)에 나타난다.
▶ (C) 뒤에 (A)가 와야 함 (순서: 주어진 글 → (C) → (A) → (B))

2nd 글이 한눈에 들어오도록 정리하여 정답을 확인한다.

주어진 글: 스트레스를 주는 사건들은 사람들에게 이익을 가져다준다.
➡ **(C):** 스트레스에 의해 시작된 적응 과정은 더 나은 쪽으로의 개인적 변화를 가져올 수 있다.
➡ **(A):** 적당한 수준의 스트레스가 회복력을 촉진할 수 있다.
➡ **(B):** 중간 수준의 역경이 가장 큰 회복력을 예측했다.
▶ 주어진 글 다음에 이어질 글의 순서는 (C) → (A) → (B)이므로 정답은 ④임

---

* 글의 흐름

도입	역경을 통해 이익을 얻음
부연 ①	첫 번째 연구: 참가자들의 서른일곱 가지 주요 부정적인 사건 경험을 측정함
부연 ②	후속 연구: 생애에서 겪은 역경의 양과 실험 중 주어진 스트레스 요인에 대한 반응에서 비슷한 관계를 발견함
결론	적당량의 스트레스를 해결하기 위해 노력해야 하는 것은 미래에 스트레스를 직면할 때의 회복력을 기를 수 있음

M 41 정답 ④ *규범의 발생과 순응 양상

동명사의 의미상 주어
Norms emerge in groups / as a result of people conforming to the behavior of others. //
동명사(전치사 of의 목적어)
규범은 집단에서 생겨난다 / 사람들이 다른 사람들의 행동에 순응하는 결과로 //

Thus, the start of a norm occurs / when one person acts in a particular manner / in a particular situation / because she thinks she ought to. // [단서 1] 규범은 한 사람이 특정 상황에서 하는 특정 행동 방식에서 시작됨
따라서 규범의 시작은 발생한다 / 한 사람이 특정 방식으로 행동할 때 / 특정 상황에서 / 자신이 그래야 한다고 생각하여 //

[단서 2] 최초의 행동을 했던 사람은 그 행동을 다른 사람들에게 지시함
(A) Thus, she may prescribe the behavior to them / by uttering the norm statement in a prescriptive manner. //
by -ing: ~함으로써
따라서 그 사람은 그들에게 행동을 지시할 수도 있다 / 지시하는 방식으로 규범 진술을 말함으로써 //

명사절 접속사
Alternately, she may communicate / that conformity is desired in other ways, such as by gesturing. //
다른 방식으로는 그 사람은 전달할 수도 있다 / 몸짓과 같은 것으로 순응이 요망된다는 것을 //

In addition, she may threaten to sanction them / for not behaving as she wishes. //
동명사의 부정형
게다가 제재를 가하겠다고 그들에게 위협할 수도 있다 / 자신이 원하는 대로 행동하지 않으면 //

This will cause some / to conform to her wishes / and act as she acts. //
병렬 구조
이것은 일부 사람들을 만들 것이다 / 그 사람의 바람에 순응하고 / 그 사람이 행동하는 대로 행동하도록 //

사역동사+목적어+목적격 보어(과거분사)
(B) But some others will not need / to have the behavior prescribed to them. // [단서 3] 다른 어떤 사람들에게는 행동에 대한 지시가 필요 없음
그러나 다른 일부 사람들에게는 필요가 없을 것이다 / 그 행동이 자신에게 지시되게 할 //

명사절 접속사
They will observe the regularity of behavior / and decide on their own / that they ought to conform. //
그들은 행동의 규칙성을 관찰하고 / 스스로 결정할 것이다 / 자신이 순응해야 할지를 //

They may do so / for either rational or moral reasons. //
그들은 그렇게 할 수도 있다 / 이성적 또는 도덕적 이유로 //

a number of: 여러, 다양한
(C) Others may then conform to this behavior / for a number of reasons. // [단서 4] this behavior이 가리키는 행동은 주어진 문장에서 한 사람이 특정 방식으로 했던 행동임
그런 다음 다른 사람들은 이 행동에 순응할 수도 있다 / 여러 가지 이유로 //

주격 관계대명사   명사절 접속사
The person who performed the initial action / may think that others ought to behave / as she behaves / in situations of this sort. //
최초의 행동을 한 사람은 / 다른 사람들이 행동해야 한다고 생각할 수도 있다 / 자신이 행동하는 것처럼 / 이런 종류의 상황에서 //

• norm ⓝ 규범   • conform to ~에 순응하다
• prescribe ⓥ 지시하다, 규정하다   • utter ⓥ 말하다
• prescriptive ⓐ 지시하는   • alternately 🔒 다른 방식으로
• conformity ⓝ 순응   • regularity ⓝ 규칙성
• rational ⓐ 이성적인   • moral ⓐ 도덕적인

규범은 사람들이 다른 사람들의 행동에 순응하는 결과로 집단에서 생겨난다. 따라서 규범의 시작은 한 사람이 특정 상황에서 자신이 그래야 한다고 생각하여 특정 방식으로 행동할 때 발생한다. (C) 그런 다음 다른 사람들은 여러 가지 이유로 이 행동에 순응할 수도 있다. 최초의 행동을 한 사람은 다른 사람들이 이런 종류의 상황에서 자신이 행동하는 것처럼 행동해야 한다고 생각할 수도 있다. (A) 따라서 그 사람은 지시하는 방식으로 규범 진술을 말함으로써 그들에게 행동을 지시할 수도 있다. 다른 방식으로는 몸짓과 같은 것으로 순응이 요망된다는 것을 전달할 수도 있다. 게다가 자신이 원하는 대로 행동하지 않으면 그들에게 제재를 가하겠다고 위협할 수도 있다. 이것은 일부 사람들을 그 사람의 바람에 순응하고 그 사람이 행동하는 대로 행동하도록 만들 것이다. (B) 그러나 다른 일부 사람들에게는 그 행동이 자신에게 지시되게 할 필요가 없을 것이다. 그들은 행동의 규칙성을 관찰하고 자신이 순응해야 할지를 스스로 결정할 것이다. 그들은 이성적 또는 도덕적 이유로 그렇게 할 수도 있다.

주어진 글 다음에 이어질 글의 순서로 가장 적절한 것을 고르시오. [3점]

① (A) — (C) — (B) (A)의 시작인 '따라서(Thus)'에 해당하는 원인은 주어진 글에 없음
② (B) — (A) — (C) (B)는 '규범에 순응하지 않는 사람들'을 설명하고 있으므로, 이와 역접을 이루는 '규범에 순응하는 사람'에 대한 설명인 (A)보다 뒤에 와야 함
③ (B) — (C) — (A)
④ (C) — (A) — (B) (A)의 시작인 '따라서(Thus)'에 해당하는 원인은 '처음 행동했던 사람이 다른 사람들도 그 행동을 따라 하기를 바라기' 때문이므로 (C) 뒤에 이어져야 함
⑤ (C) — (B) — (A)

규범은 한 사람이 특정 상황에서 특정 방식으로 행동할 때 발생함 - 그 행동을 다른 사람들이 순응하면서 처음 행동을 했던 사람은 다른 사람들도 그렇게 행동해야 한다고 생각함 - 처음 행동한 사람은 지시 등으로 다른 사람들이 자신의 행동에 순응하도록 만듦 - 일부 사람들은 규범에 순응할지를 스스로 결정함

| 문제 풀이 순서 | [정답률 37%]

1st 각 문단의 내용을 파악하고, 글의 논리적인 순서를 추론한다.

주어진 글: 규범은 사람들이 다른 사람들의 행동에 순응하는 결과로 집단에서 생겨난다. 따라서 규범의 시작은 한 사람이 특정 상황에서 자신이 그래야 한다고 생각하여 특정 방식으로 행동할 때 발생한다.

➡ 규범은 한 사람이 특정 상황에서 특정 방식으로 행동할 때 발생한다. [단서]
주어진 글 뒤: 특정 행동 방식으로 시작된 규범이 어떻게 퍼져나가는지에 관한 내용이 이어질 것이다. [발상]

(A) 따라서(Thus) 그 사람은 지시하는 방식으로 규범 진술을 말함으로써 그들에게 행동을 지시할 수도 있다. 다른 방식으로는 몸짓과 같은 것으로 순응이 요망된다는 것을 전달할 수도 있다. 게다가 자신이 원하는 대로 행동하지 않으면 그들에게 제재를 가하겠다고 위협할 수도 있다. 이것은 일부 사람들을 그 사람의 바람에 순응하고 그 사람이 행동하는 대로 행동하도록 만들 것이다.

➡ **앞부분:** 처음 행동을 했던 사람은 다른 사람도 자신과 같은 행동을 하도록 명시적으로 지시하거나 몸짓 등으로 전달할 수 있음
뒷부분: 혹은 제재를 가하는 방식으로 자신의 행동대로 순응하도록 만들 것임
(A) 앞: 처음 행동을 했던 사람이 다른 사람도 자신의 행동을 따라하기를 바란다는 내용이 제시되어야 한다.
▶ 주어진 글이 (A) 앞에 올 수 없음
(A) 뒤: 이를 통해 다른 사람들이 처음 행동에 순응하는 경우를 설명했으므로, 이와 대조되는 내용이 역접으로 이어질 수 있다.

(B) 그러나(But) 다른 일부 사람들에게는 그 행동이 자신에게 지시되게 할 필요가 없을 것이다. 그들은 행동의 규칙성을 관찰하고 자신이 순응해야 할지를 스스로 결정할 것이다. 그들은 이성적 또는 도덕적 이유로 그렇게 할 수도 있다.

➡ **앞부분:** 그러나 일부 사람들은 자신에게 행동이 지시되는 것을 불필요하다고 생각함
뒷부분: 그들은 행동의 규칙성을 관찰하고 이성적, 도덕적인 근거로 이에 순응할지를 스스로 결정함
(B) 앞: (B)에서는 다른 사람들은 이러한 행동 지시가 필요하지 않고, 여기에 마냥 순응하지는 않는다고 했다. 따라서 '그러나(But)'로 이어질 수 있는 내용인 행동 지시에 순응하는 사람들에 관한 내용이 나와야 한다.
▶ 순서: (A) → (B)
(B) 뒤: 규범을 따르지 않는 사람들에 대한 구체적인 설명이 이어지거나 (B)가 글의 결론일 것이다.
▶ (B)가 마지막에 올 확률이 큼

(C) 그런 다음 다른 사람들은 여러 가지 이유로 이 행동(this behavior)에 순응할 수도 있다. 최초의 행동을 한 사람은 다른 사람들이 이런 종류의 상황에서 자신이 행동하는 것처럼 행동해야 한다고 생각할 수도 있다.

➡ **앞부분:** 한 사람이 시작했던 '이 행동'을 다른 사람들도 따라 하기 시작함
뒷부분: 처음 그 행동을 한 사람은 다른 사람들도 그렇게 행동해야 한다고 생각함
(C) 앞: 다른 사람들도 순응하기 시작한 '이 행동(this behavior)'에 관한 내용이 나와야 한다. 이 행동은 주어진 문장에서 한 사람이 특정 상황에서 했던 특정 행동 방식을 가리킨다.
▶ 순서: 주어진 글 → (C)
(C) 뒤: 처음 행동을 했던 사람은 다른 사람들도 같은 행동을 해야 한다고 생각하므로 어떻게 규범을 퍼뜨릴지에 대한 내용이 이어질 것이다.
▶ 순서: 주어진 글 → (C) → (A) → (B)

2nd 글이 한눈에 들어오도록 정리하여 정답을 확인한다.

주어진 글: 규범은 한 사람이 특정 상황에서 특정 방식으로 행동할 때 발생한다.
→ **(C):** 한 사람이 시작했던 '이 행동'을 다른 사람들도 따라 하기 시작하면서 규범이 발생하고, 처음 그 행동을 한 사람은 다른 사람들도 그렇게 행동해야 한다고 생각한다.
→ **(A):** 따라서 처음 행동을 했던 사람은 지시, 제스처, 제재 등을 활용해 다른 사람도 자신과 같은 행동을 하도록 만든다.
→ **(B):** 그러나 다른 일부 사람들은 그 행동이 자신에게 지시되는 것이 필요하지 않다. 그들은 행동의 규칙성을 관찰하고 이에 순응할지를 스스로 결정한다.
▶ 주어진 글 다음에 이어질 글의 순서는 (C) → (A) → (B)이므로 정답은 ④임

류이레 | 연세대 의예과 2024년 입학·광주대동고 졸

순서 문제를 풀 때 각 문단의 지시어나 연결어 등을 먼저 체크하되, 내용도 같이 고려해서 정답을 고르는 것이 좋아. 이 문제에서는 one person, she, some others, Others 등의 지시어와 Thus, But, then 등의 연결어가 보이네.
규범의 시작을 언급하는 주어진 글 뒤에는 규범에 순응하는 여러 이유가 있고 그중 하나로 최초 행위자의 의도를 언급하는 (C)가 이어져야 해. 그 뒤에는 다른 이유로서 규범의 지시를 통한 순응을 언급하는 (A)와 그러한 지시 없이 이성적, 도덕적 이유로 인한 순응을 언급하는 (B)가 이어지는 것이 자연스럽지.

* 매몰 비용에 대한 인간의 경향이 갖는 장단점

In economics, / there is a principle / known as the *sunk cost*
fallacy. //
_{앞에 주격 관계대명사와 be동사가 생략됨}
경제학에서 / 원리가 있다 / '매몰 비용 오류'라고 알려진 //

The idea is / that when you are invested and have ownership
_{주어 · 동사 · 부사절 접속사}
/ in something, / you overvalue that thing. //
그 생각은 ~이다 / 여러분이 투자하고 소유권을 가지면 / 어떤 것에 / 여러분은 그것을
지나치게 중시한다는 것 // **단서1** 그저 많이 투자했기 때문에 끔찍한
관계를 유지할 때 할 수 있는 가장 현명한 일 _{주격 보어로 쓰인 to부정사의 to는 흔히 생략됨}

(A) Sometimes, / the smartest thing / a person can do / is quit. //
때로는 / 가장 현명한 일은 / 한 사람이 할 수 있는 / 중지하는 것이다 //

Although this is true, / it has also become a tired and played-out
argument. //
이것이 진실이더라도 / 그것은 또한 식상하고 효력이 떨어진 주장이 되었다 //
_{부분 부정: 항상 ~인 것은 아님}
Sunk cost doesn't always have to be a bad thing. //
매몰 비용이 언제나 나쁜 것이어야 하는 것은 아니다 // **단서2** 매몰 비용의 장점에 대한
내용이 이어져야 함

(B) This leads people / to continue on paths or pursuits / that
should clearly be abandoned. // **단서3** 자신이 투자하고 소유한 것을 지나치게
중시하기 때문에 계속 따르고 추구하게 됨
이것은 사람들이 ~하게 한다 / 계속 경로를 따르거나 추구를 하게 / 분명히 버려져야 하는 //

For example, / people often remain in terrible relationships /
simply because they've invested / a great deal of themselves /
into them. //
예를 들어 / 사람들은 자주 끔찍한 관계에 남아 있다 / 그저 그들이 투자했기 때문에 / 자신의
많은 것을 / 그것에 //

Or / someone may continue pouring money / into a business /
_{주격 관계대명사} _{선행사}
that is clearly a bad idea / in the market. //
또는 / 누군가는 계속 돈을 쏟아부을지도 모른다 / 사업에 / 분명히 나쁜 아이디어인 /
시장에서 //

(C) Actually, / you can leverage this human tendency / to your
benefit. // **단서4** 매몰 비용을 득이 되도록 이용하는 경우를 설명함
실제로 / 여러분은 이 인간적인 경향을 이용할 수 있다 / 여러분에게 득이 되도록 //

Like someone invests a great deal of money / in a personal
_{앞에 명사절 접속사 that이 생략됨}
trainer / to ensure / they follow through on their commitment, /
누군가가 많은 돈을 투자하는 것처럼 / 개인 트레이너에게 / 확실히 하기 위해 / 그들이 자신의
약속을 끝까지 완수하는 것을 /

you, too, can invest a great deal up front / to ensure / you stay
_{앞에 목적격 관계대명사가 생략됨}
on the path / you want to be on. //
여러분 또한 선지급으로 많은 것을 투자할 수 있다 / 확실히 하기 위해 / 여러분이 경로에
머무는 것을 / 여러분이 있고 싶은 //

- economics ⓝ 경제학 · principle ⓝ 원칙, 원리
- sink ⓥ 가라앉다 · fallacy ⓝ 오류, 틀린 생각
- ownership ⓝ 소유(권) · overvalue ⓥ 지나치게 가치를 두다
- played-out ⓐ 영향력[효력]이 다 된 · argument ⓝ 논쟁, 언쟁
- pursuit ⓝ 추구, 추적 · abandon ⓥ 버리다, 포기하다
- tendency ⓝ 경향, 추세 · commitment ⓝ 전념, 약속

경제학에서 '매몰 비용 오류'라고 알려진 원리가 있다. 여러분이 어떤 것에
투자하고 소유권을 가지면, 그것을 지나치게 중시한다는 생각이다.
(B) 이것은 사람들이 분명히 그만두어야 하는 경로를 계속 따르거나 추구를
계속하게 한다. 예를 들어, 사람들은 그저 자신의 많은 것을 그 관계에
투자했기 때문에 자주 끔찍한 관계에 남아 있다. 또는, 누군가는 시장에서
분명히 나쁜 아이디어인 사업에 계속 돈을 쏟아부을지도 모른다.
(A) 때로는 한 사람이 할 수 있는 가장 현명한 일은 중지하는 것이다. 이것이
진실이더라도, 그것은 또한 식상하고 효력이 떨어진 주장이 되었다. 매몰
비용이 언제나 나쁜 것이어야 하는 것은 아니다.
(C) 실제로, 여러분은 이 인간적인 경향을 여러분에게 득이 되도록 이용할
수 있다. 확실히 자신이 자신의 약속을 끝까지 완수하기 위해 많은 돈을 개인
트레이너에게 투자하는 사람처럼, 여러분 또한 여러분이 있고 싶은 경로에
확실히 있기 위해 선지급으로 많은 것을 투자할 수 있다.

주어진 글 다음에 이어질 글의 순서로 가장 적절한 것을 고르시오. [3점]

① (A) — (C) — (B) 그저 중지하는 것이 가장 현명한 일인 사례가 (B)에 등장함
② (B) — (A) — (C)
③ (B) — (C) — (A) 매몰 비용이 항상 나쁜 것은 아니라는 문장 뒤에 구체적인 사례가 나와야 함
④ (C) — (A) — (B)
⑤ (C) — (B) — (A) — 부정적인 면을 먼저 설명하고 긍정적인 면도 있다고 덧붙이는 흐름임
자신이 투자한 것을 지나치게 중시함 - 그래서 분명히 버려야 하는 경로를 계속 따르게 됨 - 이 경우 할 수
있는 가장 현명한 일은 중지하는 것임 - 매몰 비용이 항상 나쁜 것은 아님 - 자신의 약속을 완수하기 위해
개인 트레이너에게 계속 많은 돈을 투자하는 것은 긍정적임

오H 2등급 ❓ '매몰 비용 오류'의 개념에 대한 설명을 이해하고, 단점과 장점을 말하는
글의 흐름을 파악하지 못하면 풀기 힘든 2등급 대비 문제이다.

| 문제 풀이 순서 |

1st 주어진 글을 통해 글의 핵심 소재를 파악하고 전개 방향을 예측한다.

> **주어진 글:** 경제학에서 '매몰 비용 오류'라고 알려진 원리가 있다.
> 여러분이 어떤 것에 투자하고 소유권을 가지면, 그것을 지나치게
> 중시한다는 생각이다.

➡ **소재:** 매몰 비용 오류 **단서**
전개 방향: 매몰 비용이 우리에게 어떤 영향을 미치는지, 긍정적인 영향인지 또는
부정적인 영향인지 등에 대한 내용이 이어질 것이다. **발상**

2nd 각 문단의 내용을 파악하고, 글의 논리적인 순서를 추론한다.

> **(A):** 때로는 한 사람이 할 수 있는 가장 현명한 일은 중지하는 것이다.
> 이것이 진실이더라도, 그것은 또한 식상하고 효력이 떨어진 주장이
> 되었다. 매몰 비용이 언제나 나쁜 것이어야 하는 것은 아니다.

➡ **(A) 앞:** 중지하는 것이 가장 현명한 일인 상황이 (A) 앞에 있어야 한다.
▶ 주어진 글에는 그러한 상황이 등장하지 않으므로, (A) 앞에 주어진 글이 올 수
없음
(A) 뒤: 매몰 비용이 긍정적인 영향을 미치는 경우에 대한 예시 또는 구체적인
부연이 이어질 것이다.
▶ (A) 앞에는 매몰 비용이 부정적인 영향을 미치는 경우가 있어야 함

> **(B):** 이것(This)은 사람들이 분명히 그만두어야 하는 경로를 계속
> 따르거나 추구를 계속하게 한다. 예를 들어, 사람들은 그저 자신의
> 많은 것을 그 관계에 투자했기 때문에 자주 끔찍한 관계에 남아 있다.
> 또는, 누군가는 시장에서 분명히 나쁜 아이디어인 사업에 계속 돈을
> 쏟아부을지도 모른다.

➡ **(B) 앞:** 매몰 비용 때문에 분명히 그만두어야 하는 것을 계속하는 것이다. 즉,
'이것(This)'이 가리키는 것이 주어진 글에서 설명한 '매몰 비용 오류'이다.
▶ (B) 앞에 주어진 글이 와야 함 (순서: 주어진 글 → (B))
(B) 뒤: 많은 것을 투자했기 때문에 끔찍한 관계를 지속하거나 나쁜 사업에 계속
투자하는 상황에서 할 수 있는 가장 현명한 일이 중지하는 것이다.
▶ (B) 뒤에 (A)가 와야 함 (순서: 주어진 글 → (B) → (A))

> **(C):** 실제로, 여러분은 이 인간적인 경향을 여러분에게 득이 되도록
> 이용할 수 있다. 확실히 자신이 자신의 약속을 끝까지 완수하기
> 위해 많은 돈을 개인 트레이너에게 투자하는 사람처럼, 여러분 또한
> 여러분이 있고 싶은 경로에 확실히 있기 위해 선지급으로 많은 것을
> 투자할 수 있다.

➡ **(C) 앞:** (A) 뒤에 이어질 것으로 예상한 내용이 (C)에 등장한다.
〈(A) 매몰 비용 오류가 항상 나쁜 것은 아니다. → (C) 개인 트레이너에게 많은 돈을
투자하면 운동하기로 한 자신과의 약속을 완수할 수 있다.〉라는 흐름이다.
▶ 순서: 주어진 글 → (B) → (A) → (C)

3rd 글이 한눈에 들어오도록 정리하여 정답을 확인한다.

주어진 글: 매몰 비용 오류로 인해 우리는 어떤 것에 투자하고 소유권을 가지면 그것을 지나치게 중시한다.

→ **(B):** 매몰 비용 때문에 사람들은 분명히 그만두어야 하는 것을 계속한다. (매몰 비용의 부정적인 영향)

→ **(A):** 매몰 비용이 언제나 나쁜 것은 아니다. (흐름 전환: 부정적인 영향 → 긍정적인 영향)

→ **(C):** 많은 돈을 개인 트레이너에게 투자함으로써 자신과의 약속(운동)을 끝까지 완수할 수 있다. (매몰 비용의 긍정적인 영향)

▶ 주어진 글 다음에 이어질 글의 순서는 (B) → (A) → (C)이므로 정답은 ②임

* 글의 흐름

도입	인간은 자신이 투자하고 소유한 것을 지나치게 중시하는 경향이 있음
대조	단점: 분명히 버려져야 하는 경로를 계속 따르거나 끔찍한 관계에 남아 있음
	장점: 개인 트레이너에게 많은 돈을 투자하여 자신의 약속을 끝까지 완수하도록 함

Ⓜ 43 정답 ② ⭐ 2등급 대비 [정답률 60%]

* 적응적 가소성

A fascinating species of water flea / exhibits a kind of flexibility / that evolutionary biologists call *adaptive plasticity*. //
생략 가능한 목적격 관계대명사 동격의 전치사 call의 목적격 보어
물벼룩이라는 매혹적인 종은 / 일종의 유연성을 보여준다 / 진화생물학자들이 '적응적 가소성'이라고 부르는 //

단서 1 자신을 둘러싼 물에 포식자의 화학적 특성이 없으면 보호 장치를 발달시키지 않는 것을 가리킴

(A) That's a clever trick, / because producing spines and a helmet / is costly, / in terms of energy, /
주격 보어(형용사) 동명사구 주어 단수 동사
그것은 영리한 묘책이다 / 왜냐하면 가시돌기와 머리 투구를 만드는 것은 / 비용이 많이 들고 / 에너지 면에서 /
and conserving energy is essential / for an organism's ability / to survive and reproduce. //
동명사구 주어 단수 동사
에너지를 보존하는 것은 핵심적이기 때문이다 / 유기체의 능력을 위해 / 살아남고 생식하는 //

The water flea only expends the energy / needed to produce spines and a helmet / when it needs to. //
물벼룩은 오직 에너지를 소모한다 / 가시돌기와 머리 투구를 만드는 데 필요한 / 그것이 그래야 할 때만 // **단서 2** a kind of flexibility에 대한 구체적 설명이 시작됨
└ 뒤에 expend the energy needed ~가 생략됨

(B) If the baby water flea is developing / into an adult / in water / that includes the chemical signatures of creatures / that prey on water fleas, /
선행사 주격 관계대명사 선행사 주격 관계대명사
만일 새끼 물벼룩이 발달하고 있으면 / 성체로 / 물에서 / 생물의 화학적인 고유한 특징을 포함하는 / 물벼룩을 잡아먹고 사는 /
it develops a helmet and spines / to defend itself against predators. //
부사적 용법(목적)
그것은 머리 투구와 가시돌기를 발달시킨다 / 자신을 포식자로부터 지키기 위해 //

If the water around it doesn't include / the chemical signatures of predators, / the water flea doesn't develop / these protective devices. // **단서 3** 물에 포식자의 흔적이 없으면 보호 장치를 발달시키지 않는 게 '영리한 묘책'임
만일 그것을 둘러싼 물이 포함하지 않으면 / 포식자의 화학적인 고유한 특징을 / 그 물벼룩은 발달시키지 않는다 / 이러한 보호 장치를 //

(C) So it may well be that this plasticity is an adaptation: / a trait / that came to exist in a species / because it contributed / to reproductive fitness. // **단서 4** 가소성이 유기체의 생식에 이바지하기 때문에 생긴 특징이라는 내용이 so로 연결됨
(결과)의 등위접속사
그러므로 이러한 가소성은 아마 적응일 것이다 / 특징 / 생물 종에 존재하게 된 / 그것이 이바지하기 때문에 / 생식적 적합성에 //

There are many cases, / across many species, / of adaptive plasticity. //
많은 사례가 있다 / 많은 종에 걸쳐 / 적응적 가소성의 //

Plasticity is conducive to fitness / if there is sufficient variation / in the environment. //
부사절 접속사(조건)
가소성은 적합성에 도움이 된다 / 충분한 차이가 있을 때 / 환경에 //

- exhibit ⓥ (특징 등을) 보이다 · flexibility ⓝ 유연성
- trick ⓝ 묘책, 속임수 · in terms of ~라는 면에서
- conserve ⓥ 보존하다 · organism ⓝ 유기체
- reproduce ⓥ 생식하다, 재생산하다
- signature ⓝ (고유성을 잘 나타내는) 특징 · prey on ~을 먹이로 하다
- predator ⓝ 포식자 · protective ⓐ 방어하는
- adaptation ⓝ 적응 · trait ⓝ 특성, 특징
- reproductive ⓐ 생식의, 번식의 · fitness ⓝ 적합성
- variation ⓝ 차이, 변화

　물벼룩이라는 매혹적인 종은 진화생물학자들이 '적응적 가소성'이라고 부르는 일종의 유연성을 보여준다. (B) 만일 새끼 물벼룩이 물벼룩을 잡아먹고 사는 생물의 화학적인 고유한 특징을 포함하는 물에서 성체로 발달하고 있으면, 그것은 자신을 포식자로부터 지키기 위해 머리 투구와 가시돌기를 발달시킨다. 만일 자신을 둘러싼 물이 포식자의 화학적인 고유한 특징을 포함하지 않으면, 그 물벼룩은 이러한 보호 장치를 발달시키지 않는다.

　(A) 그것은 영리한 묘책인데, 에너지 면에서 가시돌기와 머리 투구를 만드는 것은 비용이 많이 들고 에너지를 보존하는 것은 살아남고 생식하는 유기체의 능력을 위해 핵심적이기 때문이다. 물벼룩은 오직 필요할 때만 가시돌기와 머리 투구를 만드는 데 필요한 에너지를 소모한다. (C) 그러므로 이러한 가소성은 아마 적응일 텐데, 즉 그것은 생식적 적합성에 이바지하기 때문에 생물 종에 존재하게 된 특징이다. 많은 종에 걸쳐 적응적 가소성의 많은 사례가 있다. 가소성은 환경에 충분한 차이가 있을 때 적합성에 도움이 된다.

주어진 글 다음에 이어질 글의 순서로 가장 적절한 것을 고르시오.
(A)의 That이 가리키는 것이 (B)에 있음
① (A) ― (C) ― (B) 물벼룩은 '적응적 가소성'이라고 불리는 유연성을 보임 – 물벼룩은 필요할 때만 보호 장치를 발달시킴 – 보호 장치를 발달시키는 것은 에너지 면에서 많은
② (B) ― (A) ― (C) 비용이 듦 – 에너지 보존은 생식 능력에 핵심적임 – 따라서 가소성은 그것이 생식에 이바지하기 때문에 존재하게 된 특징임
③ (B) ― (C) ― (A) (A)에 (C)의 원인이 등장함
④ (C) ― (A) ― (B) 물벼룩의 유연성에 대한 구체적인 설명이 (B)에서 시작됨
⑤ (C) ― (B) ― (A)

왜 2등급? 물벼룩의 '적응적 가소성'이라는 생소한 개념을 정확하게 이해하여 글의 흐름을 파악해야 하는 2등급 대비 문제이다. 새끼 물벼룩의 유연성에 대한 글의 흐름을 지시대명사 등의 단서를 통해 찾아야 한다.

| 문제 풀이 순서 |

1st 주어진 글을 통해 글의 핵심 소재를 파악하고 전개 방향을 예측한다.

> **주어진 글:** 물벼룩이라는 매혹적인 종은 진화생물학자들이 '적응적 가소성'이라고 부르는 일종의 유연성을 보여준다.

→ **소재:** 물벼룩의 적응적 가소성 **단서**
전개 방향: 물벼룩이 보이는 적응적 가소성, 즉 유연성에 대한 구체적인 부연이 이어질 것이다. **발상**

2nd 각 문단의 내용을 파악하고, 글의 논리적인 순서를 추론한다.

> (A): 그것(That)은 영리한 묘책인데, 에너지 면에서 가시돌기와 머리 투구를 만드는 것은 비용이 많이 들고 에너지를 보존하는 것은 살아남고 생식하는 유기체의 능력을 위해 핵심적이기 때문이다. 물벼룩은 오직 필요할 때만 가시돌기와 머리 투구를 만드는 데 필요한 에너지를 소모한다.

→ **(A) 앞:** '그것(That)'이 가리키는 것을 찾아 (A) 앞에 위치시켜야 한다.
❶ 가시돌기와 머리 투구를 만드는 데 많은 에너지가 든다. ❷ 에너지를 보존하는 것은 유기체의 생존과 번식에 핵심적이다.

1과 **2**를 통해, '영리한 묘책'인 '그것(That)'은 꼭 필요하지 않은 경우에는 가시돌기와 머리 투구를 만들지 않는 것이라고 예상할 수 있다.

▶ 주어진 글에는 가시돌기나 머리 투구가 전혀 언급되지 않으므로 (A) 앞에 주어진 글이 올 수 없음

(A) 뒤: 오직 필요할 때만 가시돌기와 머리 투구를 만드는 물벼룩의 적응적 가소성이 의미하는 바, 즉 글의 결론이 이어질 것이다.

> **(B):** 만일 새끼 물벼룩이 물벼룩을 잡아먹고 사는 생물의 화학적인 고유한 특징을 포함하는 물에서 성체로 발달하고 있으면, 그것은 자신을 포식자로부터 지키기 위해 머리 투구와 가시돌기를 발달시킨다. 만일 자신을 둘러싼 물이 포식자의 화학적인 고유한 특징을 포함하지 않으면, 그 물벼룩은 이러한 보호 장치를 발달시키지 않는다.

➡ **(B) 앞:** 주어진 글에서 소개한 물벼룩의 적응적 가소성을 (B)에서 부연한다. <주어진 글: 물벼룩은 적응적 가소성(유연성)을 보인다. ➡ (B): 새끼 물벼룩은 자신이 자라고 있는 환경에 따라 보호 장치를 발달시키기도 하고, 발달시키지 않기도 하는 유연성을 보인다.>라는 흐름이다. ▶ 순서: 주어진 글 ➡ (B)

(B) 뒤: (A)의 '그것(That)'이 가리키는 것이 (B)에 등장한다. <(B) 자신을 둘러싼 물에 포식자의 화학적인 고유한 특징이 없으면 새끼 물벼룩은 가시돌기와 머리 투구를 발달시키지 않는다. ➡ (A) 가시돌기와 머리 투구를 만드는 데는 많은 에너지가 드는데, 에너지를 보존하는 것이 생존과 번식에 핵심적이므로 '그것'은 영리한 묘책이다.>라는 흐름이다. ▶ 순서: 주어진 글 ➡ (B) ➡ (A)

> **(C):** 그러므로 이러한 가소성은 아마 적응일 텐데, 즉 그것은 번식적 적합성에 이바지하기 때문에 생물 종에 존재하게 된 특징이다. 많은 종에 걸쳐 적응적 가소성의 많은 사례가 있다. 가소성은 환경에 충분한 차이가 있을 때 적합성에 도움이 된다.

➡ **(C) 앞:** 가소성이 번식에 이바지하기 때문에 존재하게 된 특성이라는 결론을 내리려면 앞에서 가소성이 번식에 이바지하는 것을 보여주는 사례를 제시해야 한다.

▶ (C) 앞에 적응적 가소성이 번식에 이바지한다는 것을 보여주는 내용이 포함된 (B)와 (A)가 있어야 한다. (순서: 주어진 글 ➡ (B) ➡ (A) ➡ (C))

(C) 뒤: 주어진 글, (B), (A)는 물벼룩이 보여주는 적응적 가소성을 이야기하는데, (C)는 많은 종에서 적응적 가소성이 나타난다는 내용이다.

▶ 물벼룩의 사례로 적응적 가소성을 설명한 후 이러한 적응적 가소성이 많은 종에서 나타난다는 결론을 내리는 흐름이다.

3rd 글이 한눈에 들어오도록 정리하여 정답을 확인한다.

주어진 글: 물벼룩은 '적응적 가소성'이라고 불리는 일종의 유연성을 보인다.

➡ **(B):** 새끼 물벼룩은 자신의 주변 환경에 포식자의 고유한 특징이 포함되어 있으면 머리 투구와 가시돌기를 발달시킨다. 주변 환경에 포식자의 특징이 없으면 보호 장치를 발달시키지 않는다.

➡ **(A):** 새끼 물벼룩의 이러한 유연성은 영리한 묘책이다. 왜냐하면 보호 장치를 발달시키는 데는 에너지가 많이 드는데, 에너지를 보존하는 것이 생존과 번식에 핵심적이기 때문이다.

➡ **(C):** 이러한 가소성은 번식에 이바지하기 때문에 존재하게 된 특성이고, 많은 종에게 나타난다.

▶ 주어진 글 다음에 이어질 글의 순서는 (B) ➡ (A) ➡ (C)이므로 정답은 ②임

＊ 글의 흐름

도입	물벼룩은 '적응적 가소성'이라고 불리는 일종의 유연성을 보임
부연 ①	새끼 물벼룩이 성체로 발달하고 있는 물에 포식자의 화학적 특징이 포함되어 있으면 물벼룩은 보호 장치를 발달시킴
	물에 그러한 화학적 특징이 없으면 보호 장치를 발달시키지 않음
부연 ②	보호 장치를 발달시키는 데 많은 에너지가 들고, 에너지 보존이 생식에 핵심적이므로 물벼룩이 보이는 이러한 가소성은 영리한 묘책임
결론	가소성은 그것이 생식에 이바지하기 때문에 존재하게 된 특징임

권주원 | 서울대 정치외교학부 2023년 입학·서울 배재고 졸

순서 찾기 유형을 풀 때 나는 (A)보다 (B)와 (C)를 먼저 읽는데, 이 문제에서도 (C)의 첫 문장은 주어진 글과 전혀 연결되지 않아서 (B)가 첫 번째로 이어진다고 가정하고 (A)를 읽었어.

역시 (A)의 That은 (B)의 마지막 문장을 가리키는 거였고, (C)는 adaptive plasticity를 water flea의 사례에서 다양한 종으로 확장하는 내용이니까 마지막에 오는 문단이라고 생각했어!

M 44 정답 ④ ⭐ 2등급 대비 [정답률 43%]

＊승소 시 보수 약정

> The most commonly known form / of results-based pricing / is a practice / called *contingency pricing*, / used by lawyers. //
> 〈앞에 주격 관계대명사와 be동사가 생략됨〉
> 가장 일반적으로 알려진 형태는 / 결과 기반 가격 책정 중 / 관행이다 / '승소 시 보수 약정'이라고 불리는 / 변호사에 의해 사용되는 //

(A) Therefore, / only an outcome in the client's favor / is compensated. // **단서 1** 의뢰인이 승소할 때만 보수가 지불되는 이유가 앞에 있어야 함
따라서 / 의뢰인에게 유리한 결과만 / 보수가 지불된다 //

From the client's point of view, / the pricing makes sense / in part / because most clients in these cases / are unfamiliar with and possibly intimidated by law firms. //
〈전치사 with와 by의 목적어〉
의뢰인의 관점에서 보면 / 그 가격 책정은 타당하다 / 부분적으로는 / 왜냐하면 이러한 소송의 의뢰인 대부분이 / 법률 사무소에 익숙하지 않고 아마도 겁을 먹을 수 있기 때문에 //

Their biggest fears / are high fees for a case / that may take years / to settle. //
〈선행사〉 〈주격 관계대명사〉
그들의 가장 큰 두려움은 / 소송에 대한 높은 수수료이다 / 몇 년이 걸릴 수 있는 / 해결하는 데 //
단서 2 승소 시 보수 약정을 통해 의뢰인의 가장 큰 두려움이 해결됨
〈전치사 동명사구〉

(B) By using contingency pricing, / clients are ensured / that they pay no fees / until they receive a settlement. //
승소 시 보수 약정을 사용함으로써 / 의뢰인은 보장받는다 / 그들이 수수료를 지불하지 않는다는 것을 / 그들이 합의금을 받을 때까지 //

In these and other instances of contingency pricing, / the economic value of the service / is hard to determine / before the service, /
〈부사적 용법(hard 수식)〉
승소 시 보수 약정의 이런 경우와 여타 경우에서 / 서비스의 경제적 가치는 / 결정하기 어렵고 / 서비스 전에 /
〈선행사〉 〈주격 관계대명사〉 〈명사적 용법 (allows의 목적격 보어)〉

and providers develop a price / that allows them to share / the risks and rewards / of delivering value to the buyer. //
공급자는 가격을 만든다 / 그들이 나누게 하는 / 위험과 보상을 / 구매자에게 가치를 전달하는 것의 //

(C) Contingency pricing is the major way / that personal injury and certain consumer cases are billed. //
〈선행사〉 〈관계부사〉
승소 시 보수 약정은 주요 방식이다 / 개인 상해 및 특정 소비자 소송에 대해 비용이 청구되는 //

In this approach, / lawyers do not receive fees or payment / until the case is settled, / when they are paid a percentage of the money / that the client receives. //
〈계속적 용법의 관계부사〉 〈선행사〉 〈목적격 관계대명사〉
이 방식에서 / 변호사는 수수료나 지불금을 받지 않는데 / 소송이 해결될 때까지 / 그때 그들은 금액의 일정 비율을 받는다 / 의뢰인이 받는 //
단서 3 승소 시 보수 약정 방식에서는 의뢰인이 받는 금액의 일정 비율을 변호사가 지불 받음

- price ⓥ 값을 매기다[정하다]
- compensate ⓥ 보수[급여]를 지불하다
- make sense 타당하다
- settle ⓥ 해결하다, 합의를 보다
- ensure ⓥ 보장하다
- settlement ⓝ 합의(금)
- bill ⓥ 비용을 청구하다
- payment ⓝ 지불금

결과 기반 가격 책정 중 가장 일반적으로 알려진 형태는 변호사가 사용하는 '승소 시 보수 약정'이라고 불리는 관행이다. (C) 승소 시 보수 약정은 개인 상해 및 특정 소비자 소송에 대해 비용이 청구되는 주요 방식이다. 이 방식에서 변호사는 소송이 해결될 때까지 수수료나 지불금을 받지 않는데, 그때 그들은 의뢰인이 받는 금액의 일정 비율을 받는다. (A) 따라서 의뢰인에게 유리한 결과만 보수가 지불된다. 의뢰인의 관점에서 보면, 이러한 소송의 의뢰인 대부분이 법률 사무소에 익숙하지 않고 아마도 겁을 먹을 수 있다는 부분적인 이유로 그 가격 책정은 타당하다. 그들의 가장 큰 두려움은 해결하는 데 몇 년이 걸릴 수 있는 소송에 대한 높은 수수료이다.

(B) 승소 시 보수 약정을 사용함으로써 의뢰인은 합의금을 받을 때까지 수수료를 지불하지 않도록 보장받는다. 승소 시 보수 약정의 이런 경우와 여타 경우에서 서비스의 경제적 가치는 서비스 전에 결정하기 어렵고, 공급자는 구매자에게 가치를 전달하는 위험과 보상을 그들이 나눌 수 있게 하는 가격을 만든다.

주어진 글 다음에 이어질 글의 순서로 가장 적절한 것을 고르시오. [3점]

① (A) — (C) — (B) (A) 앞에는 의뢰인에게 유리한 결과만 보상되는 원인이 필요함
② (B) — (A) — (C)
③ (B) — (C) — (A) (B)의 두 번째 문장의 these가 가리킬 만한 경우가 주어진 글에 없음
④ (C) — (A) — (B) 승소 시 보수 약정에서는 변호사가 의뢰인이 받는 금액의 일정 비율을 받음 – 그래서 의뢰인이 합의금을 받는 경우에만 (변호사의) 보수가 지불됨 – 승소 시 보수 약정을 통해 의뢰인은 합의금을 받을 때까지 수수료를
⑤ (C) — (B) — (A) 지불하지 않도록 보장됨

(왜)2등급? '승소 시 보수 약정'이 무엇인지를 확실하게 이해해야 글의 흐름을 파악할 수 있는 2등급 대비 문제이다. 이 개념과 그에 대한 설명이 이어지는 흐름을 자연스럽게 이어지도록 해야 한다.

| 문제 풀이 순서 |

1st 주어진 글을 통해 글의 핵심 소재를 파악하고 전개 방향을 예측한다.

주어진 글: 결과 기반 가격 책정 중 가장 일반적으로 알려진 형태는 변호사가 사용하는 '승소 시 보수 약정'이라고 불리는 관행이다.

→ **소재:** 승소 시 보수 약정 (단서)
전개 방향: 승소 시 보수 약정이 어떤 방식인지 구체적으로 설명하는 내용이 이어질 것이다. 또한, 승소 시 보수 약정이 갖는 장단점이 추가될 수도 있다. (발상)

2nd 각 문단의 내용을 파악하고, 글의 논리적인 순서를 추론한다.

(A): 따라서(Therefore) 의뢰인에게 유리한 결과만 보수가 지불된다. 의뢰인의 관점에서 보면, 이러한 소송의 의뢰인 대부분이 법률 사무소에 익숙하지 않고 아마도 겁을 먹을 수 있다는 부분적인 이유로 그 가격 책정은 타당하다. 그들의 가장 큰 두려움은 해결하는 데 몇 년이 걸릴 수 있는 소송에 대한 높은 수수료이다.

→ **(A) 앞:** therefore는 인과 관계를 나타내는 연결어로, 앞에는 원인, 뒤에는 결과가 온다. 그러므로 (A) 앞에는 의뢰인에게 유리한 결과만 보수가 지불되는 원인이 있어야 한다.
▶ 주어진 글이 (A) 앞에 올 수 없음
(A) 뒤: 승소 시 보수 약정의 장점에 대한 글이라면, 의뢰인의 가장 큰 두려움이 승소 시 보수 약정 방식을 통해 해소된다는 내용이 이어질 것이다.

(B): 승소 시 보수 약정을 사용함으로써 의뢰인은 합의금을 받을 때까지 수수료를 지불하지 않도록 보장받는다. 승소 시 보수 약정의 이런 경우와 여타 경우에서 서비스의 경제적 가치는 서비스 전에 결정하기 어렵고, 공급자는 구매자에게 가치를 전달하는 위험과 보상을 그들이 나눌 수 있게 하는 가격을 만든다.

→ **(B) 앞:** (A)에서 설명한 의뢰인의 가장 큰 두려움이 승소 시 보수 약정을 사용함으로써 해소된다.

〈(A) 의뢰인의 가장 큰 두려움은 해결에 몇 년이 걸릴 수 있는 소송에 대한 높은 수수료이다. → (B) 승소 시 보수 약정을 사용함으로써 의뢰인은 합의금을 받을 때까지 수수료를 지불하지 않도록 보장받는다.〉라는 흐름이다.
▶ (B) 앞에 (A)가 와야 함 (순서: (A) → (B))
(B) 뒤: 앞에서 설명한 변호사가 사용하는 승소 시 보수 약정 방식 외에 다른 경우에도 결과 기반 가격 책정 방식이 적용된다는 내용이다.
▶ (B)가 글의 결론에 해당함

(C): 승소 시 보수 약정은 개인 상해 및 특정 소비자 소송에 대해 비용이 청구되는 주요 방식이다. 이 방식에서 변호사는 소송이 해결될 때까지 수수료나 지불금을 받지 않는데, 그때 그들은 의뢰인이 받는 금액의 일정 비율을 받는다.

→ **(C) 앞:** 주어진 글에서 '승소 시 보수 약정' 관행을 소개한 후 (C)에서 승소 시 보수 약정 방식을 구체적으로 설명하기 시작한다.
▶ 순서: 주어진 글 → (C)
(C) 뒤: 승소 시 보수 약정 방식에서 변호사는 의뢰인이 받는 금액의 일정 비율을 받는다. 그래서(Therefore) 의뢰인에게 유리한 결과가 나올 때만 변호사에게 보수가 지불되는 것이다.
▶ (C)가 원인, (A)가 결과 (순서: 주어진 글 → (C) → (A) → (B))

3rd 글이 한눈에 들어오도록 정리하여 정답을 확인한다.

주어진 글: 결과 기반 가격 책정 중 가장 일반적으로 알려진 형태는 변호사가 사용하는 '승소 시 보수 약정' 관행이다.
→ **(C):** 승소 시 보수 약정 방식에서 변호사는 소송이 해결될 때까지 보수를 받지 않으며, 소송이 해결될 때 의뢰인이 받는 금액의 일정 비율을 받는다.
→ **(A):** 따라서 의뢰인에게 유리한 결과가 나올 때만 변호사에게 보수가 지불된다. 의뢰인에게 가장 큰 두려움은 해결에 몇 년이 걸릴 수 있는 소송에 대한 높은 수수료이다.
→ **(B):** 승소 시 보수 약정을 사용함으로써 의뢰인은 합의금을 받을 때까지 수수료를 지불하지 않도록 보장받아 그러한 두려움이 해소된다.
▶ 주어진 글 다음에 이어질 글의 순서는 (C) → (A) → (B)이므로 정답은 ④임

＊ 글의 흐름

도입	결과 기반 가격 책정 중에서 가장 일반적으로 알려진 형태는 변호사에 의해 사용되는 승소 시 보수 약정임
부연	승소 시 보수 약정 방식에서 변호사는 의뢰인이 받는 금액의 일정 비율을 받으므로 의뢰인에게 유리한 결과만 보상됨
	의뢰인의 가장 큰 두려움은 해결하는 데 몇 년이 걸릴 수 있는 소송에 대한 높은 수수료인데, 승소 시 보수 약정을 사용하면 그 두려움이 해소됨

조현준 | 전북대 의예과 2023년 입학·익산 이리고 졸
순서 찾기 유형에서 나는 주어진 글을 가장 유심히 보는데, 주어진 글은 contingency pricing이 중심 소재였어. 그리고서 (A), (B), (C)의 첫 문장을 읽어서 순서를 알아내는데, 주어진 글에 the client에 대한 정보가 안 나왔기에 (A), (B)는 첫 순서가 될 수 없다고 판단했지. (C)를 읽고 나는 contingency pricing을 '후지급제'라고 생각했고, Therefore를 통해 (A)가 (C) 뒤에 이어진다는 걸 알았어. 그리고 마지막으로 other instances로 확장하는 내용이 포함된 (B)가 오는 거지. 내용이 어렵다면 '후지급제'처럼 나만의 말로 바꾸는 게 쉽게 이해하는 데 도움이 될 수 있어.

＊문화의 작동 방식

> Culture operates / in ways / we can consciously consider and discuss / but also in ways / of which we are far less cognizant. // 단서1 문화는 우리가 인식하는 방식으로도 작동하고, 훨씬 덜 인식하는 방식으로도 작동함
> 문화는 작동한다 / 방식으로 / 우리가 의식적으로 고려하고 논의할 수 있는 / 또한 방식으로도 / 우리가 훨씬 덜 인식하는 //

(A) In some cases, / however, / we are far less aware / of why we believe a certain claim to be true, / 단서2 우리가 훨씬 덜 알고 있는 경우에 대한 설명이 역접으로 이어짐
어떤 경우에는 / 하지만 / 우리는 훨씬 덜 알고 있다 / 왜 우리가 어떤 주장을 사실이라고 믿는지에 대해 /

or how we are to explain / why certain social realities exist. //
또는 어떻게 우리가 설명할 것인지에 대해 / 왜 어떤 사회적 현실이 존재하는지를 //

Ideas / about the social world / become part of our worldview / without our necessarily being aware /
관념은 / 사회적 세계에 대한 / 우리 세계관의 일부가 된다 / 우리가 반드시 알고 있지 않은 상태에서도 /

of the source of the particular idea / or that we even hold the idea at all. // 단서2 우리가 의식적으로 이해하는 경우에 대해 설명하기 시작함
특정한 관념의 출처에 대해서 / 혹은 우리가 심지어 그 관념을 갖고 있다는 것조차 //

(B) When we have / to offer / an account of our actions, / we consciously understand / which excuses might prove acceptable, / given the particular circumstances / we find ourselves in. //
우리가 제시해야 할 때 / 우리의 행동에 대한 설명을 / 우리는 의식적으로 이해한다 / 어떤 변명이 용인되는 것으로 판명될 수도 있는지를 / 특정한 상황 하에 / 우리가 처한 //

In such situations, / we use cultural ideas / as we would use a particular tool. // 단서3 우리는 우리가 특정 도구를 사용하는 것처럼 문화적 관념을 사용함
그런 상황에서 / 우리는 문화적 관념을 사용한다 / 우리가 특정 도구를 사용하는 것처럼 //

(C) We select the cultural notion / as we would select a screwdriver: / certain jobs call for a Phillips head / while others require an Allen wrench. // 단서4 (B)의 a particular tool을 a screwdriver라는 구체적인 예시를 들어 부연함
우리는 문화적 개념을 선택한다 / 우리가 스크루드라이버를 선택하는 것처럼 / 어떤 일은 십자드라이버 헤드를 필요로 한다 / 다른 일은 육각 렌치를 필요로 하는 반면에 //

Whichever idea we insert / into the conversation / to justify our actions, / the point is / that our motives are discursively available / to us. //
우리가 어떤 생각을 넣든 / 대화에 / 우리의 행동을 정당화하기 위해 / 요점은 ~이다 / 우리의 동기가 만연하게 이용 가능하다는 것 / 우리에게 //

They are not hidden. //
그것들은 숨겨져 있지 않다 //

- consciously ⓐⓓ 의식적으로 · claim ⓝ 주장, 권리
- worldview ⓝ 세계관 · necessarily ⓐⓓ 어쩔 수 없이, 필연적으로
- account ⓝ 설명, 해석 · excuse ⓝ 변명, 이유 · prove ⓥ 증명하다
- acceptable ⓐ 용인되는, 허용할 수 있는 · circumstance ⓝ 환경, 상황
- notion ⓝ 개념, 생각 · call for ~을 요구하다
- insert ⓥ 끼워 넣다, 삽입하다 · justify ⓥ 정당화하다, 해명하다
- motive ⓝ 동기, 이유

문화는 우리가 의식적으로 고려하고 논의할 수 있는 방식뿐만 아니라 우리가 훨씬 덜 인식하는 방식으로도 작동한다. (B) 우리의 행동에 대해 설명을 제시해야 할 때, 우리는 우리가 처한 특정한 상황 하에 어떤 변명이 용인되는 것으로 판명될 수도 있는지를 의식적으로 이해한다. 그런 상황에서 우리는 특정 도구를 사용하는 것처럼 문화적 관념을 사용한다. (C) 우리는 스크루드라이버를 선택하는 것처럼 문화적 개념을 선택한다. 어떤 일은 십자드라이버 헤드를 필요로 하지만 다른 일은 육각 렌치를 필요로 한다. 우리의 행동을 정당화하기 위해 대화에 어떤 생각을 넣든, 요점은 우리의 동기가 우리에게 만연하게 이용 가능하다는 것이다. 그것들은 숨겨져 있지 않다. (A) 하지만 우리는 어떤 경우에는 왜 우리가 어떤 주장을 사실이라고

믿는지 또는 어떤 사회적 현실이 존재하는 이유를 어떻게 우리가 설명할 것인지에 대해 훨씬 덜 알고 있다. 사회적 세계에 대한 관념은 우리가 특정한 관념의 출처에 대해서 혹은 심지어 우리가 그 관념을 갖고 있다는 것조차 반드시 알고 있지 않은 상태에서도 우리 세계관의 일부가 된다.

주어진 글 다음에 이어질 글의 순서로 가장 적절한 것을 고르시오. [3점]

① (A) — (C) — (B) 주어진 글과 (A)가 서로 반대되는 내용인 것은 아님
② (B) — (A) — (C) 스크루드라이버를 선택하는 것은 (B)와 연결되는 내용임
③ (B) — (C) — (A)
④ (C) — (A) — (B) (B)의 마지막 문장에 등장함 a particular tool에 대한 예시가
⑤ (C) — (B) — (A) a screwdriver임

└ 문화는 우리가 의식적으로 고려하고 논의할 수 있는 방식으로도 작동하고 우리가 훨씬 덜 인식하는 방식으로도 작동함 - 우리의 행동에 대한 설명을 제시해야 할 때는 특정 도구를 사용하는 것처럼 의식적으로 문화적 관념을 사용함 - 이는 우리가 필요에 따라 십자드라이버 헤드나 육각 렌치를 선택하는 것과 같음 - '하지만' 어떤 경우에는 우리는 훨씬 덜 알고 있음

왜 1등급? 핵심 소재인 문화의 두 가지 작동 방식을 설명하는 내용인데, 이 작동 방식을 이해하지 못하면 풀기 힘든 1등급 대비 문제이다. 그러나 반대 내용을 연결하는 however와 같은 연결어를 잘 활용하면 의외로 쉽게 풀 수 있는 문제이다.

| 문제 풀이 순서 |

1st 주어진 글을 통해 글의 핵심 소재를 파악하고 전개 방향을 예측한다.

> **주어진 글:** 문화는 우리가 의식적으로 고려하고 논의할 수 있는 방식뿐만 아니라 우리가 훨씬 덜 인식하는 방식으로도 작동한다.

➡ **소재:** 문화의 작동 방식 단서
전개 방향: 문화의 두 가지 작동 방식(우리가 의식하는 작동 방식, 우리가 덜 의식하는 작동 방식)에 대해 구체적으로 설명할 것이다. 발상

2nd 각 문단의 내용을 파악하고, 글의 논리적인 순서를 추론한다.

> (A): 하지만(however) 우리는 어떤 경우에는 왜 우리가 어떤 주장을 사실이라고 믿는지 또는 어떤 사회적 현실이 존재하는 이유를 어떻게 우리가 설명할 것인지에 대해 훨씬 덜 알고 있다. 사회적 세계에 대한 관념은 우리가 특정한 관념의 출처에 대해서 혹은 심지어 우리가 그 관념을 갖고 있다는 것조차 반드시 알고 있지 않은 상태에서도 우리 세계관의 일부가 된다.

➡ **(A) 앞:** 역접의 연결어 however는 앞뒤에 반대되는 내용이 온다.
문화의 두 가지 작동 방식 중 (A)에서 설명하는 것은 우리가 덜 의식하는 작동 방식에 대해 설명한다. 따라서 (A) 앞에는 우리가 의식하는 방식으로 문화가 작동하는 사례가 있어야 한다.
▶ 주어진 글과 (A)는 서로 반대되는 내용이 아니므로 (A) 앞에 주어진 글이 올 수 없음
(A) 뒤: however로 보아, (A) 앞에서 첫 번째 작동 방식을 설명하고, 그와 반대되는 작동 방식을 (A)에서 설명하는 흐름이다.
▶ (A)가 마지막에 올 확률이 높음

> (B): 우리의 행동에 대해 설명을 제시해야 할 때, 우리는 우리가 처한 특정한 상황 하에 어떤 변명이 용인되는 것으로 판명될 수도 있는지를 의식적으로 이해한다. 그런 상황에서 우리는 특정 도구를 사용하는 것처럼 문화적 관념을 사용한다.

➡ **(B) 앞:** 주어진 글에서 문화의 작동 방식 두 가지를 소개한 후, (B)에서 그중 한 가지(우리가 의식하는 작동 방식)를 설명하기 시작한다.
▶ however가 (A)에 포함되어 있으므로 (B)보다 앞에 (A)가 올 수는 없음 (순서: 주어진 글 ➡ (B))
(B) 뒤: 특정 도구를 사용하는 것처럼 문화적 관념을 사용하는 것에 대한 구체적인 예시가 이어질 것이다.
▶ (A)에는 특정 도구에 대한 언급이 없음

(C): 우리는 [스크루드라이버]를 선택하는 것처럼 문화적 개념을 선택한다. 어떤 일은 십자드라이버 헤드를 필요로 하지만 다른 일은 육각 렌치를 필요로 한다. 우리의 행동을 정당화하기 위해 대화에 어떤 생각을 넣든, 요점은 우리의 동기가 우리에게 만연하게 이용 가능하다는 것이다. 그것들은 숨겨져 있지 않다.

→ **(C) 앞:** (B)에 등장한 '특정 도구'의 구체적인 예시가 '스크루드라이버'이다.
▶ 순서: 주어진 글 → (B) → (C)
(C) 뒤: 주어진 글에서 문화의 두 가지 작동 방식을 소개함 → (B)와 (C)에서 그중 한 가지 작동 방식(우리가 의식하는 작동 방식)을 설명함
▶ 우리가 덜 의식하는 작동 방식을 설명하는 (A)가 (C) 뒤에 역접으로 이어짐
(순서: 주어진 글 → (B) → (C) → (A))

3rd 글이 한눈에 들어오도록 정리하여 정답을 확인한다.

주어진 글: 문화는 우리가 의식하는 방식으로도 작동하고, 우리가 훨씬 덜 인식하는 방식으로도 작동한다.

→ **(B):** 특정 상황에서 우리는 의식적으로 문화를 이해하고 특정 도구를 사용하는 것처럼 문화적 관념을 사용한다.

→ **(C):** 우리는 스크루드라이버를 선택하는 것처럼 문화적 개념을 선택하여 사용한다.

→ **(A):** 하지만 사회적 세계에 대한 관념은 우리가 의식하지 않는 상태에서도 작동한다.

▶ 주어진 글 다음에 이어질 글의 순서는 (B) → (C) → (A)이므로 정답은 ③임

* 글의 흐름

도입	문화는 우리가 의식적으로 고려하고 논의할 수 있는 방식으로도 작동하고, 우리가 훨씬 덜 인식하는 방식으로도 작동함
부연	우리의 행동에 대해 설명을 제시해야 할 때는 우리가 특정 도구를 사용하는 것처럼 문화적 개념을 선택함
	하지만 사회적 세계에 대한 관념은 우리가 잘 알고 있지 않은 상태에서도 작동함

M 46 정답 ⑤ ★ 1등급 대비 [정답률 35%]

*수면의 질에 대한 실제 생물학적 척도

There was a moment / in research history / when scientists wondered / (관계부사)
순간이 있었다 / 연구의 역사에서 / 과학자들이 궁금해한 /

if the measure of choice / — total minutes of sleep — / was the (명사절 접속사)
wrong way / of looking at the question / of why sleep varies (동격의 전치사)
so considerably / across species. //
선택된 척도가 / 전체 수면 시간 / 잘못된 방법인지 / 문제를 보는 / 왜 수면이 그렇게 많이 다른지에 대한 / 종에 따라 //

Instead, / they suspected / that assessing sleep *quality*, / (동명사구 주어)
rather than *quantity* (time), / would shed some light / on the (동사) (목적어)
mystery. //
대신, / 그들은 생각했다 / 수면의 '질'을 평가하는 것이 / 수면의 '양'(시간)이 아닌 / 밝힐 것이라고 / 그 비밀을 //

단서1 can 뒤에 obtain the real biological measure of sleep quality가 생략됨
(A) When we can, / our understanding of the relationship (주어)
/ between sleep quantity and quality / across the animal kingdom /
우리가 할 수 있을 때 / 관계에 대한 우리의 이해가 / 수면의 양과 질 사이의 / 동물계 전체에 걸쳐 / (동사)

will likely explain / what currently appears to be an incomprehensible map / of sleep-time differences. //
설명할 것이다 / 현재에는 이해할 수 없는 지도로 보이는 것을 / 수면 시간 차이의 //

(B) In truth, / the way / quality is commonly assessed / in these
주어(선행사, 관계부사 how는 생략됨) *
investigations / (degree of unresponsiveness **단서2** 수면의 질과 수면 시간이 반비례하지 / to the outside 않음을 발견한 것에 대한 부연 설명
world / and the continuity of sleep) /
사실 / 방법은 / 질이 일반적으로 평가되는 / 이러한 연구에서 / (무반응의 정도와 / 외부 세계에 대한 / 수면의 연속성) / (동사)

is probably a poor index / of the real biological measure / of sleep quality: / one that we cannot yet obtain / in all these species. //
아마도 부족한 지표이다 / 실제 생물학적 척도에 대한 / 수면 질의 / 우리가 아직 얻을 수 없는 것 / 이 모든 종들에 대해 // (주어)

(C) That is, / species / with superior quality of sleep / should be (동사)
able to accomplish all / they need / in a shorter time, / and vice versa. // **단서3** 수면 시간이 아니라 수면의 질을 평가하는 것이 수면의 비밀을 밝힐 것이라는 생각을 구체적으로 부연함
즉 / 종들은 / 우수한 수면의 질을 가진 / 모든 것을 성취할 수 있을 것이고 / 그들에게 필요한 / 더 짧은 시간 안에 / 그 반대의 경우도 마찬가지이다 //

It was a great idea, / with the exception / that, if anything, / (동격절 접속사) '오히려'
we've discovered the opposite relationship: / those that sleep (동사) (주어)
more / have deeper, "higher"-quality sleep. //
그것은 좋은 아이디어였다 / ~을 제외하면 / 오히려 / 우리가 정반대의 관계를 발견했다는 것을 / 잠을 더 많이 자는 종들이 / 더 깊고 '더 높은' 질의 수면을 취한다 //

- measure ⓝ 척도 • vary ⓥ 서로 다르다 • considerably ⓐⓓ 상당히
- species ⓝ 종(생물 분류의 기초 단위) • suspect ⓥ 추측하다
- assess ⓥ 평가하다 • quantity ⓝ 양, 수량
- shed ⓥ (빛·소리·냄새 등을) 발산하다 • currently ⓐⓓ 현재
- incomprehensible ⓐ 이해할 수 없는 • investigation ⓝ 연구, 조사
- degree ⓝ 정도 • unresponsiveness ⓝ 무반응
- continuity ⓝ 연속성 • index ⓝ 지표 • biological ⓐ 생물학의
- obtain ⓥ 얻다 • superior ⓐ 우수한 • accomplish ⓥ 성취하다
- vice versa 반대의 경우도 마찬가지 • exception ⓝ 제외, 예외
- opposite ⓐ 정반대의

연구의 역사에서 과학자들이 전체 수면 시간이라는 선택된 척도가 왜 수면이 종에 따라 그렇게 많이 다른지에 대한 문제를 보는 잘못된 방법인지 궁금해한 적이 있었다. 대신, 그들은 수면의 '양'(시간)이 아닌 수면의 '질'을 평가하는 것이 그 비밀을 밝힐 것이라고 생각했다. (C) 즉, 수면의 질이 우수한 종들은 더 짧은 시간 안에 필요한 모든 것을 성취할 수 있을 것이고, 그 반대의 경우도 마찬가지이다. 그것은 우리가 오히려 잠을 더 많이 자는 종들이 더 깊고 '더 높은' 질의 수면을 취한다는 정반대의 관계를 발견했다는 것을 제외하면 좋은 아이디어였다. (B) 사실, 이러한 연구에서 질이 일반적으로 평가되는 방법(외부 세계에 대한 무반응의 정도와 수면의 연속성)은 아마도 우리가 이 모든 종들에 대해 아직 얻을 수 없는 수면 질의 실제 생물학적 척도에 대한 부족한 지표이다. (A) 우리가 할 수 있을 때, 동물계 전체에 걸쳐 수면의 양과 질 사이의 관계에 대한 우리의 이해가 현재에는 수면 시간 차이의 이해할 수 없는 지도로 보이는 것을 설명할 수 있을 것이다.

주어진 글 다음에 이어질 글의 순서로 가장 적절한 것을 고르시오. [3점]

① (A) — (C) — (B) (A)의 can은 (B)의 cannot과 이어짐
② (B) — (A) — (C) — 수면의 질을 평가하는 방법이 부족함을 보여주는
③ (B) — (C) — (A) (C)가 (B) 앞에 있어야 함
④ (C) — (A) — (B) 현재는 cannot이지만 미래에 can이 되면 비밀을 풀 것이라는 흐름임
⑤ (C) — (B) — (A) 수면의 질을 평가하는 것이 수면의 비밀을 설명할 것이라고 생각함-수면의 질이 우수할수록 수면 시간이 적어진다는 생각이었지만 이와 정반대의 관계를 발견했음-수면의 질을 측정하는 현재의 지표는 부족하고, 실제 생물학적 척도는 아직 얻을 수 없음-얻을 수 있을 때 우리는 동물계 전체의 수면의 양과 질 사이의 관계를 이해할 수 있음

1등급? 여러 종들의 수면이 왜 그렇게 많이 다른지에 대한 연구의 한계를 설명하는 글로, 소재 자체가 까다로워 쉽게 이해할 수 없는 글이다. 각 문단의 첫머리에 등장한 When we can, In truth, That is가 문단들의 순서를 추론하는 단서가 되지만, 그것만으로는 정답을 찾을 수 없고, 정확히 이해한 각 문단의 내용을 토대로 자연스러운 글의 흐름을 파악해야 한다.

1st 주어진 글을 통해 글의 핵심 소재를 파악하고 전개 방향을 예측한다.

> **주어진 글:** '종에 따라 수면이 왜 그렇게 많이 다른지'라는 문제를 '전체 수면 시간'이라는 척도를 통해 보는 것이 잘못된 방법은 아닌지 궁금해한 과학자들이 있었고, 그들은 수면의 양이 아니라 수면의 질을 평가하는 것이 그 비밀을 밝힐 것으로 생각했다. (단서)

➡ 주어진 글 이후로 그 과학자들의 생각을 좀 더 구체적으로 설명할 것이다. 나아가 그 생각이 과연 옳은지, 그른지에 대한 내용이 이어질 것이다. (발상)

2nd 각 문단의 내용을 파악하고, 글의 논리적인 순서를 추론한다.

> (A): 우리가 '무언가를' 할 수 있을 때, 우리는 동물계 전체의 수면의 양과 질 사이의 관계를 이해하고, 수면 시간의 차이를 설명할 것이다.

➡ **(A) 앞:** **1** When we can 뒤에 생략된 어구가 (A) 앞에 있어야 한다.
　▶ 주어진 글에는 대동사 can으로 대신할 내용이 없음
　2 의미상 (A) 문단 앞은 ⟨아직은 우리가 '무언가를' 할 수 없다. 그래서 동물들의 수면의 양과 질 사이의 관계를 이해할 수 없고, 수면 시간의 차이를 설명할 수 없다.⟩는 내용일 것이다.
　(A) 뒤: 주어진 글은 과거의 일을 이야기하는데, (A)는 미래의 일을 이야기한다.
　▶ 주어진 글과 (A) 사이에 현재의 일이 등장하고, (A)는 글의 결론일 것이다.

> (B): 사실, (수면의) 질이 일반적으로 평가되는 방법은 수면의 질을 보여주는 실제 생물학적 척도에 대한 부족한 지표이다. 우리는 아직 수면의 질을 보여주는 실제 생물학적 척도를 얻을 수 없다.

➡ **(B) 앞:** **1** In truth는 앞에서 설명한 내용을 부연할 때 쓰인다.
　2 '부족한' 지표라고 했다. 따라서 (B) 앞에는 수면의 질로 종에 따라 수면이 다른 이유를 밝히려는 과학자의 생각이 틀렸다는 내용이 필요하다.
　▶ 주어진 글, (A)는 올 수 없음
　(B) 뒤: we cannot yet obtain ~과 (A)의 When we can이 연결된다.
　⟨(B) 아직은 수면의 질에 대한 실제 생물학적 척도를 얻을 수 없다. → (A) 얻을 수 있을 때 동물계 전체의 수면의 양과 질 사이의 관계를 이해하고, 수면 시간의 차이를 설명할 것이다.⟩라는 흐름이다.
　▶ 순서: (B) → (A)

> (C): 즉, 수면의 질이 우수한 종들은 수면 시간이 짧을 것이고, 그 반대의 경우도 마찬가지일 것이다. 이는 좋은 아이디어였지만, 수면 시간이 긴 종들이 더 질 좋은 수면을 취한다는, 정반대의 관계가 밝혀졌다.

➡ **(C) 앞:** That is(즉)는 앞에서 설명한 내용을 같은 맥락으로 부연할 때 쓰인다. 따라서 (C) 앞에는 수면의 질이 수면 시간에 영향을 미친다는 내용이 필요하다.
　▶ 주어진 글이 그런 내용임 (순서: 주어진 글 → (C))
　(C) 뒤: 수면의 질을 통해 수면 시간의 차이를 설명할 수 있다는 가설이 틀렸음을 뒷받침하는 부연 설명이 필요하다.
　▶ (B)가 수면의 질을 보여주는 실제 생물학적 척도를 얻을 수 없다는 내용이다.
　(순서: (C) → (B))

3rd 글이 한눈에 들어오도록 정리하여 정답을 확인한다.

주어진 글: 과학자들은 수면의 질을 평가하는 것이 수면 시간의 비밀을 밝힐 것이라고 생각했다.

→ **(C):** 즉, 수면의 질이 우수하면 수면 시간은 짧을 것이다. 그러나 수면 시간이 긴 종이 더 좋은 질의 수면을 취했다.

→ **(B):** 사실, 우리는 아직 수면의 질을 보여주는 실제 생물학적 척도를 얻을 수 없다.

→ **(A):** 그러한 척도를 얻을 수 있을 때, 우리는 동물계 전체의 수면의 양과 질 사이의 관계를 이해하고, 수면 시간의 차이를 설명할 수 있을 것이다.

▶ 주어진 글 다음에 이어질 글의 순서는 (C) → (B) → (A)이므로 정답은 ⑤임

어법 특강

> **＊ 관계부사의 생략**
>
> ─ 관계부사와 선행사 중 하나는 생략이 가능하지만, 관계부사 how와 선행사 the way는 함께 쓰지 못하므로 둘 중 하나는 반드시 생략해야 한다.
> • I remember the place where David wants to go.
> 　　　　　　　선행사　　관계부사
> 　(난 David가 가고 싶어 하는 장소를 기억한다.)
> • I won't forget the day when I met you.
> 　　　　　　　선행사　　관계부사
> 　(난 내가 널 만난 날을 잊지 않을 것이다.)
> • We know how Paul escaped from prison.
> 　　　앞에 선행사 the way가 생략됨
> 　(우리는 Paul이 탈옥한 방법을 안다.)
> • I like the way he spoke to me.
> 　　　뒤에 관계부사 how가 생략됨
> 　(나는 그가 내게 말하던 방식을 좋아한다.)

M 어휘 Review 정답 ━━━━━━━ 문제편 p. 278

01 거부[거절]하다	11 in (a) line with	21 ownership
02 축적하다	12 tend to	22 Imperializing
03 기본적인	13 call for	23 elaborate
04 (~보다) 열등한	14 in one's tracks	24 suspected
05 부여하다	15 bring on	25 dispersal
06 faithfully	16 modify	26 spatial
07 skeleton	17 conditions	27 naive
08 prediction	18 manipulation	28 inaccuracy
09 unfortunately	19 evidence	29 justify
10 economics	20 fallacy	30 evidential

N 01 정답 ④ *살충제 외의 방법이 떠오르게 된 계기

글의 흐름으로 보아, 주어진 문장이 들어가기에 가장 적절한 곳을 고르시오.

단서1 해충을 관리하는 살충제 외의 방법들이 더 고려되고 있는 또 다른 이유가 앞에 있어야 함

Also, / it has become difficult / for companies to develop new
　　　　가주어　　　　　　　　　　　　　　　진주어
　　　　　to develop의 의미상 주어
pesticides, / even those / that can have major beneficial effects
　　　　　　　　　부정대명사
and few negative effects. //

또한 / ~이 어려워졌다 / 기업들이 새로운 살충제를 개발하는 것이 / (~한) 것들조차 /
주요한 이로운 효과는 있지만 부정적인 효과는 거의 없을 수 있는 //

　　　동명사구 주어
Simply maintaining yields / at current levels / often requires /
　　　　　　　　　　　　　　　　　　　　　　단수 동사
new cultivars and management methods, /

단지 수확량을 유지하는 것도 / 현재의 수준으로 / 보통 필요로 한다 / 새로운 품종과 관리
기법을 /
〈이유〉의 부사절 접속사　　　　　　　　　　　　　　　주어
since pests and diseases continue to evolve, / and aspects / of the
chemical, physical, and social environment / can change / over
　　　　　　　　　　　　　　　　　　　　　　동사
several decades. //

해충과 질병이 계속 진화하므로 / 그리고 양상이 / 화학적, 물리적, 사회적 환경의 / 변할 수
있으므로 / 수십 년에 걸쳐 //
　　　　　　주어　　　　　동사　　　　목적어　　목적격 보어
(①) In the 1960s, / many people considered pesticides / to be
mainly beneficial / to mankind. //

1960년대에 / 많은 사람은 살충제를 여겼다 / 대체로 유익한 것으로 / 사람들에게 //

　　　　　　　　　　　주어
(②) Developing / new, broadly effective, and persistent
pesticides / often was considered / to be the best way / to control
　　　　　　　　동사　　　　　　　　　형용사적 용법(way 수식) *
pests on crop plants. //

개발하는 것은 / 새롭고 널리 효과를 거두고 지속하는 살충제를 / 흔히 여겨졌다 / 최고의
방법으로 / 농작물에의 해충을 통제하는 //
　　　　　　　　　　　　　가주어　　　　　　　　진주어절 접속사 ①
(③) Since that time, / it has become apparent / that broadly
effective pesticides / can have harmful effects / on beneficial
insects, / 단서2 살충제가 유익한 곤충에 해로운 영향을 미칠 수 있음이 분명해졌음

그때 이래로 / ~이 분명해졌다 / 널리 효과를 거두는 살충제가 / 해로운 영향을 미칠 수
있어서 / 유익한 곤충에 /
　　　　　　　　　　　　　　　　　진주어절 접속사 ②
which can negate their effects / in controlling pests, / and that
persistent pesticides can damage / non-target organisms in the
ecosystem, / such as birds and people. //

그것이 살충제의 효과를 무효화할 수 있으며 / 해충을 통제하는 것에서 / 지속하는 살충제는
해를 끼칠 수 있다는 것이 / 생태계의 목표 외 생물에게 / 새와 사람 같은 //

(④) Very high costs are involved / in following all of the
　　　　　　　　　　　　　　앞에 주격 관계대명사와 be동사가 생략됨
procedures / needed to gain government approval / for new
pesticides. // 단서3 기업이 새로운 살충제를 개발하는 것이 어려워진 이유를 부연함

매우 높은 비용이 수반된다 / 모든 절차를 따르는 것에 / 정부의 승인을 얻는 데 필요한 /
새로운 살충제에 대한 //
　　　　　　　　　　　　　　　　　　　　　　　　진행형 수동태
(⑤) Consequently, / more consideration is being given / to
other ways / to manage pests, /

결과적으로 / 더 많은 고려가 주어지고 있다 / 다른 방법들에 / 해충을 관리하는 /

such as incorporating greater resistance to pests / into cultivars
/ by breeding and using / other biological control methods. //

더 강한 해충 저항력을 포함하는 것 같은 / 품종에 / 개량하여 사용함으로써 / 다른 생물학적
통제 기법을 //

- beneficial ⓐ 유익한, 이로운　· yield ⓝ (농작물의) 수확량, 총수익
- pest ⓝ 해충　· aspect ⓝ (측)면, 양상　· mankind ⓝ 인류, 인간
- broadly ⓐⓓ 대략적으로, 넓게　· persistent ⓐ 지속하는, 끈질긴
- apparent ⓐ 분명한, 표면상의　· negate ⓥ 무효화하다
- procedure ⓝ 절차, 방법　· approval ⓝ 승인, 찬성

- consequently ⓐⓓ 그 결과, 따라서　· consideration ⓝ 숙고, 고려 사항
- incorporate ⓥ 포함하다　· resistance ⓝ 저항, 반대
- breed ⓥ (번식을 위해) 사육하다, 품종 개량을 하다
- biological ⓐ 생물학적인

단지 현재의 수준으로 수확량을 유지하는 것만도 해충과 질병이 계속 진화하고
화학적, 물리적, 사회적 환경의 양상이 수십 년에 걸쳐 변할 수 있으므로,
보통 새로운 품종과 관리 기법이 필요하다. (①) 1960년대에 많은 사람은
살충제가 사람들에게 대체로 유익한 것으로 여겼다. (②) 새롭고 널리 효과를
거두고 지속하는 살충제를 개발하는 것은 흔히 농작물 해충을 통제하는 최고의
방법으로 여겨졌다. (③) 그때 이래로, 널리 효과를 거두는 살충제가 유익한
곤충에 해로운 영향을 미칠 수 있어서 그것이 해충 통제 효과를 무효화할 수
있으며, 지속하는 살충제는 새와 사람 같은, 생태계의 목표 외 생물에게 해를
끼칠 수 있다는 것이 분명해졌다. (④ 또한, 기업들이 새로운 살충제를, 주요한
이로운 효과는 있지만 부정적인 효과는 거의 없을 수 있는 것들조차, 개발하는
것이 어려워졌다.) 매우 높은 비용이 새로운 살충제에 대한 정부의 승인을 얻는
데 필요한 모든 절차를 따르는 것에 수반된다. (⑤) 결과적으로, 다른 생물학적
통제 기법을 개량하여 사용함으로써 품종에 더 강한 해충 저항력을 포함하는 것
같은, 해충을 관리하는 다른 방법들이 더 많이 고려되고 있다.

| 문제 풀이 순서 | [정답률 53%]

1st 주어진 문장을 해석하고, 연결어, 지시어 등을 확인한다.

Also, it has become difficult for companies to develop
new pesticides, even those that can have major beneficial
effects and few negative effects. 단서1

또한, 기업들이 새로운 살충제를, 주요한 이로운 효과는 있지만 부정적인 효과는 거의
없을 수 있는 것들조차, 개발하는 것이 어려워졌다.

→ also는 앞에서 언급한 것과 같은 맥락의 설명을 추가할 때 쓰는 연결어이다. 단서1
주어진 문장은 살충제가 예전만큼 많이 사용되지 않는 이유를 설명하는 것이라고
예상할 수 있다. 발상
▶ 주어진 문장 앞에 살충제가 예전만큼 많이 사용되지 않는 또 다른 이유가 있어야
함

2nd 각 선택지의 앞뒤 흐름이 매끄러운지 확인한다.

- ①의 앞 문장과 뒤 문장

앞 문장: 단지 현재의 수준으로 수확량을 유지하는 것만도 해충과 질병이
계속 진화하고 화학적, 물리적, 사회적 환경의 양상이 수십 년에 걸쳐
변할 수 있으므로, 보통 새로운 품종과 관리 기법이 필요하다.
뒤 문장: 1960년대에 많은 사람은 살충제가 사람들에게 대체로 유익한
것으로 여겼다.

→ 앞 문장: 새로운 관리 기법이 필요하다고 했다.
뒤 문장: 1960년대에 새로운 관리 기법이었던 살충제에 대해 설명하기 시작한다.
앞 문장에서 새로운 관리 기법을 언급하고 살충제에 대한 내용이 이어진다.
▶ 주어진 문장이 ①에 들어갈 수 없음

- ②의 앞 문장과 뒤 문장

앞 문장: ①의 뒤 문장과 같음
뒤 문장: 새롭고 널리 효과를 거두고 지속하는 살충제를 개발하는 것은
흔히 농작물 해충을 통제하는 최고의 방법으로 여겨졌다.

→ 살충제를 긍정적으로 여겼던 과거의 내용이 앞뒤로 이어진다.
주어진 문장은 살충제가 어떤 부작용 때문에 예전만큼 많이 사용되지 않는 이유를
설명한다.
▶ 주어진 문장이 ②에 들어갈 수 없음

- ③의 앞 문장과 뒤 문장

> **앞 문장:** ②의 뒤 문장과 같음
> **뒤 문장:** 그때 이래로, 널리 효과를 거두는 살충제가 유익한 곤충에 해로운 영향을 미칠 수 있어서 그것이 해충 통제 효과를 무효화할 수 있으며, 지속하는 살충제는 새와 사람 같은, 생태계의 목표 외 생물에게 해를 끼칠 수 있다는 것이 분명해졌다.

➡ 살충제에 대한 긍정적인 평가에서 살충제의 부작용이 분명해졌다는 내용으로 자연스럽게 전환된다.
▶ 주어진 문장에 Also가 포함되어 있으므로, 긍정적인 평가 뒤인 ③에 주어진 문장이 들어갈 수는 없음

④의 앞 문장과 뒤 문장

> **앞 문장:** ③의 뒤 문장과 같음
> **뒤 문장:** 매우 높은 비용이 새로운 살충제에 대한 정부의 승인을 얻는 데 필요한 모든 절차를 따르는 것에 수반된다.

➡ 살충제가 예전만큼 많이 사용되지 않는 첫 번째 이유가 앞 문장에 등장한다.
〈살충제가 유익한 곤충에 해로운 영향을 미쳐서 해충 통제 효과를 무효화하고, 목표 외 생물에 해를 끼칠 수 있다. → 또한, 기업이 새로운 살충제를 개발하는 것이 어려워졌다.〉의 흐름이 자연스럽다.
▶ 주어진 문장이 ④에 들어가야 함

- ⑤의 앞 문장과 뒤 문장

> **앞 문장:** ④의 뒤 문장과 같음
> **뒤 문장:** 결과적으로, 다른 생물학적 통제 기법을 개량하여 사용함으로써 품종에 더 강한 해충 저항력을 포함하는 것 같은, 해충을 관리하는 다른 방법들이 더 많이 고려되고 있다.

➡ 기업이 새로운 살충제를 개발하는 것이 어려워졌다는 것에 대해 부연한 후, 해충을 관리하는 데 살충제 외의 방법이 더 많이 고려되고 있다는 결론을 내리는 흐름이다.
▶ 주어진 문장이 ⑤에 들어갈 수 없음

3rd 글이 한눈에 들어오도록 정리하여 정답을 확인한다.

새로운 품종과 관리 기법이 필요하다.
(①) 1960년대에는 살충제가 유익한 것으로 여겨졌고,
(②) 새로운 살충제를 개발하는 것이 해충을 통제하는 최고의 방법으로 여겨졌다.
(③) 이후로 살충제가 유익한 곤충에 해로운 영향을 미치고, 목표 외 생물에게 해를 끼칠 수 있다는 것이 분명해졌다.
(④ 또한 기업이 새로운 살충제를 개발하는 것이 어려워졌다.)
새로운 살충제에 대한 정부의 승인을 얻는 절차에 매우 높은 비용이 든다.
(⑤) 결과적으로 해충을 관리하는 살충제 외의 다른 방법이 더 많이 고려되고 있다.

── 어법 특강

> **✻ 형용사적 용법의 to부정사**
> – 형용사적 용법의 to부정사는 명사나 대명사를 뒤에서 수식할 수 있다.
> - I need someone to help me.
>   (나는 나를 도와줄 누군가가 필요하다.)
> - Please give me something to sit on.
>   (제게 앉을 만한 것을 좀 주세요.)
> - Eric has a lot of things to do.
>   (Eric은 해야 할 많은 일들이 있다.)
> - Don't make a promise to buy me a computer.
>   (내게 컴퓨터를 사주겠다는 약속을 하지 마세요.)

N 02 정답 ⑤ ✻로봇의 자신과 주변의 다른 실재물을 구별하는 능력 ─

> 글의 흐름으로 보아, 주어진 문장이 들어가기에 가장 적절한 곳을 고르시오.

재귀대명사(주어와 목적어가 동일)
If not, / the robot might endlessly chase itself / rather than the blocks. // **단서1** 그렇지 않으면 로봇이 블록이 아닌 자기 자신을 쫓아가게 될 수 있음
그렇지 않으면 / 로봇이 자기 자신을 끝없이 쫓아갈 수도 있다 / 블록이 아닌 //

people을 수식하는 분사
People involved in the conception and engineering of robots / designed to perceive and act / know how fundamental is / 문장의 동사
the ability to discriminate oneself / from other entities in the environment. // 형용사적 용법
로봇의 구상과 엔지니어링에 관여하는 사람들은 / 인지하고 행동하도록 설계된 / 얼마나 핵심적인지 알고 있다 / 자신을 구별하는 능력이 / 주위의 다른 실재물과 //

Without such an ability, / no goal-oriented action would be possible. //
그러한 능력이 없으면 / 목표 지향적인 행동은 불가능할 것이다 //

목적어절을 이끄는 접속사   robot을 수식하는 형용사
(①) Imagine / that you have to build a robot / able to search for blocks / scattered in a room / in order to pile them. //
상상해 보라 / 여러분이 로봇을 만들어야 한다고 / 블록을 찾을 수 있는 / 방에 흩어져 있는 / 블록을 쌓기 위해 //

require that 주어 (should) 동사원형: ~해야 한다고 요구하다
(②) Even this simple task would require / that your machine be able to discriminate /
이 간단한 작업조차 요구할 것이다 / 기계는 구별할 수 있어야 한다고 /
주격 관계대명사
between stimulation that originates from its own machinery / and stimulation that originates from the blocks in the environment. //
기계는 자신의 시스템에서 발생하는 자극과 / 주위의 블록에서 발생하는 자극을 //

목적어절을 이끄는 접속사
(③) Suppose / that you equip your robot with an artificial eye and an artificial arm / to detect, grab, and pile the blocks. // 부사적 용법(목적)
가정해 보라 / 로봇에 인공 눈과 인공 팔을 갖추게 하는 것을 / 블록을 감지하고, 잡고, 쌓도록 하기 위해 //
부사적 용법(목적)   **단서2** 로봇에게는 블록 감지와 자신의 팔 감지를 구별할 수 있는 시스템이 내장되어 있어야 함
(④) To be successful, / your machine will have to have / some built-in system / enabling it to discriminate / between the detection of a block / and the detection of its own arm. //
(이 작업을) 성공적으로 수행하려면 / 여러분의 기계에는 있어야 할 것이다 / 어떤 내장된 시스템이 / 구별할 수 있게 해주는 / 블록 감지와 / 자신의 팔 감지를 //
주격 관계대명사
(⑤) Your robot would engage in / circular, self-centered acts / that would drive it away / from the target or external goal. //
로봇은 하게 될 것이다 / 순환적이고 자기중심적인 행동을 / 자신을 멀어지게 하는 / 목표물이나 외부 목표에서 // **단서3** 로봇은 목표에서 멀어져 자기중심적인 행동을 하게 될 것임

- endlessly (ad) 끝없이 • chase (v) 쫓아가다, 추적하다
- conception (n) 구상, 고안 • fundamental (a) 핵심적인, 근본적인
- discriminate (v) 구별하다, 차별하다 • scatter (v) 흩어지게 하다
- pile (v) 쌓다 • stimulation (n) 자극
- originate from ~에서 발생하다 • machinery (n) 기계
- equip ~ with ... ~에게 …을 갖추게 하다 • artificial (a) 인공의, 인위적인
- detect (v) 감지하다, 발견하다 • enable (v) 가능하게 하다
- self-centered (a) 자기 중심[본위]의 • external (a) 외부의, 외적인

인지하고 행동하도록 설계된 로봇의 구상과 엔지니어링에 관여하는 사람들은 주위의 다른 실재물과 자신을 구별하는 능력이 얼마나 핵심적인지 알고 있다. 그러한 능력이 없으면 목표 지향적인 행동은 불가능할 것이다. (①) 여러분이 블록을 쌓기 위해 방에 흩어져 있는 블록을 찾을 수 있는 로봇을 만들어야 한다고 상상해 보라. (②) 이 간단한 작업을 하기 위해서도 기계는 자신의 시스템에서 발생하는 자극과 주위의 블록에서 발생하는 자극을 구별할 수 있어야 할 것이다. (③) 로봇에 인공 눈과 인공 팔을 갖추게 하여 블록을 감지하고, 잡고, 쌓도록 한다고 가정해 보라. (④) (이 작업을) 성공적으로 수행하려면 여러분의 기계에는 그것이 블록 감지와 자신의 팔 감지를 구별할

수 있게 해주는 어떤 시스템이 내장되어 있어야 할 것이다. (⑤ 그렇지 않으면 로봇이 블록이 아닌 자기 자신을 끝없이 쫓아갈 수도 있다.) 로봇은 자신을 목표물이나 외부 목표에서 멀어지게 하는 순환적이고 자기중심적인 행동을 하게 될 것이다.

| 문제 풀이 순서 | [정답률 58%]

1st 주어진 문장을 해석하고, 연결어, 지시어 등을 확인한다.

⌈ If not, / the robot might endlessly chase itself / rather than the
⌊ blocks. //
그렇지 않으면 / 로봇이 자기 자신을 끝없이 쫓아갈 수도 있다 / 블록이 아닌 //

➡ '그렇지 않으면(if not)' 로봇이 블록이 아니라 자신을 끝임없이 쫓아갈 수도 있다고 했다. 단서

▶ 주어진 문장 앞: 로봇이 블록을 쫓아가게 할 필요가 있는 조건이 제시될 것임
▶ 주어진 문장 뒤: 주어진 문장의 결과를 설명하는 내용이 제시될 것임 발상

2nd 각 선택지의 앞뒤 흐름이 매끄러운지 확인한다.

- ①의 앞 문장과 뒤 문장

⌈ 앞 문장: 인지하고 행동하도록 설계된 로봇의 구상과 엔지니어링에
관여하는 사람들은 주위의 다른 실재물과 자신을 구별하는 능력이 얼마나
핵심적인지 알고 있다. 그러한 능력이 없으면 목표 지향적인 행동은
불가능할 것이다.
⌊ 뒤 문장: 여러분이 블록을 쌓기 위해 방에 흩어져 있는 블록을 찾을 수 있는
로봇을 만들어야 한다고 상상해 보라.

➡ 앞 문장은 로봇을 설계할 때 주위의 다른 실재물과 자신을 구별하는 능력이 핵심이며, 이러한 능력이 없으면 목표 지향적 행동이 불가능하다고 했다.
뒤 문장에서는 예시로 블록을 쌓기 위해 방에 흩어진 블록을 찾는 로봇을 만드는 것을 상상해 보라고 한다. 따라서 두 문장은 자연스럽게 연결된다.

▶ 주어진 문장이 ①에 들어갈 수 없음

- ②의 앞 문장과 뒤 문장

⌈ 앞 문장: ①의 뒤 문장과 같음
뒤 문장: 이 간단한 작업(this simple task)을 하기 위해서도 기계는
자신의 시스템에서 발생하는 자극과 주위의 블록에서 발생하는 자극을
⌊ 구별할 수 있어야 할 것이다.

➡ 앞 문장에서는 블록을 쌓기 위해 방에 흩어져 있는 블록을 쌓는 로봇을 상상하라고 했다. 그리고 뒤에 이어지는 문장에서는 이 간단한 작업(블록 찾기)을 하기 위해 기계(로봇)가 자신의 시스템에서 발생하는 자극과 블록에서 발생하는 자극을 구별할 수 있어야 한다고 했으므로 자연스럽게 연결된다.

▶ 주어진 문장이 ②에 들어갈 수 없음

- ③의 앞 문장과 뒤 문장

⌈ 앞 문장: ②의 뒤 문장과 같음
뒤 문장: 로봇에 인공 눈과 인공 팔을 갖추게 하여 블록을 감지하고, 잡고,
⌊ 쌓도록 한다고 가정해 보라.

➡ 앞에서 블록 찾기를 위해 로봇이 자신의 자극과 블록의 구별할 수 있어야 한다고 했으며, 뒤에서는 로봇에 인공 눈과 팔을 갖추게 하여 블록을 감지하고 쌓을 수 있게 하는 상황을 가정하라고 했다.
로봇의 블록 찾기를 위한 설계에 대한 설명이 자연스럽게 이어지고 있다.

▶ 주어진 문장이 ③에 들어갈 수 없음

- ④의 앞 문장과 뒤 문장

⌈ 앞 문장: ③의 뒤 문장과 같음
뒤 문장: 성공적으로 수행하려면 여러분의 기계에는 그것이 블록 감지와
자신의 팔 감지를 구별할 수 있게 해주는 어떤 시스템이 내장되어 있어야
⌊ 할 것이다.

➡ 로봇이 인공 팔과 눈을 가지고 블록을 감지할 수 있게 한다고 한 뒤에, 이를 성공적으로 수행하기 위해 로봇 안에 블록 감지와 팔 감지를 구별할 수 있게 해주는 시스템이 내장되어야 함을 설명하고 있다.
인공 팔을 사용한 블록 쌓기에 대한 내용이 서술되고 있으므로 두 문장의 연결이 자연스럽다.

▶ 주어진 문장이 ④에 들어갈 수 없음

- ⑤의 앞 문장과 뒤 문장

⌈ 앞 문장: ④의 뒤 문장과 같음
뒤 문장: 로봇은 자신을 목표물이나 외부 목표에서 멀어지게 하는
⌊ 순환적이고 자기중심적인 행동을 하게 될 것이다.

➡ 앞에서 로봇이 인공 팔로 블록을 감지할 수 있게 하려면 로봇 안에 블록 감지와 팔 감지를 구별하게 해주는 시스템이 내장되어 있어야 할 것이라고 했다.
뒤에서는 로봇이 자신의 목표물이나 외부 목표에서 멀어지는 자기중심적인 행동을 하게 될 것이라고 했다.
주어진 문장은 '그렇지 않으면' 로봇이 블록이 아니라 자신을 끝임없이 쫓아갈 수도 있다고 했으므로, 주어진 문장을 이 문장 전에 넣어 로봇이 블록 감지와 팔 감지를 구분하지 못하면 블록이 아니라 자신을 끝임없이 쫓아감으로써 자신의 목표물에서 멀어지는 자기 중심적인 행동을 한다는 내용으로 글을 전개해야 한다.

▶ 주어진 문장이 ⑤에 들어가야 함

3rd 글이 한눈에 들어오도록 정리하여 정답을 확인한다.

인지하고 행동하도록 설계된 로봇의 구상에서 주위의 다른 실재물과 자신을 구별하는 능력은 핵심이다. 그러한 능력이 없으면 목표 지향적인 행동은 불가능할 것이다.
(①) 블록을 쌓기 위해 방에 흩어져 있는 블록을 찾을 수 있는 로봇을 만드는 것을 상상해라.
(②) 이 간단한 작업을 하기 위해서도 기계는 자신의 자극과 주위 블록에서 발생하는 자극을 구별할 수 있어야 한다.
(③) 로봇에 인공 눈과 인공 팔을 갖추게 하여 블록을 감지하고, 잡고, 쌓도록 한다고 가정하자.
(④) 성공적으로 수행하려면 로봇은 블록 감지와 자신의 팔 감지를 구별하는 시스템이 있어야 한다.
(⑤ 그렇지 않으면 로봇이 블록이 아닌 자기 자신을 끝없이 쫓아갈 수도 있다.)
로봇은 자신의 목표에서 멀어지는 자기중심적인 행동을 하게 될 것이다.

N 03 정답 ④ *영업 상의 비밀 보호법이 필요한 이유 ────

글의 흐름으로 보아, 주어진 문장이 들어가기에 가장 적절한 곳을 고르시오.
[3점]

┌───┐
│ 단서 1 however로 이어지므로 앞에는 법적 보호가 없다면 비밀이 노출될 위험이 있다는 것과 │
│ 반대 내용이 와야 함   │
│ Without any special legal protection / for trade secrets, /   │
│   목적어절을 이끄는 접속사   │
│ however, / the secretive inventor risks / that an employee or │
│ contractor will disclose the proprietary information. //   │
│ 어떤 특별한 법적 보호가 없다면 / 영업상의 비밀에 대한 / 그러나 / 비밀주의의 발명가는 │
│ 위험을 감수하게 된다 / 직원이나 계약자가 독점 정보를 드러낼 //   │
└───┘

Trade secret law aims / to promote innovation, / although it
accomplishes this objective / in a very different manner / than
patent protection. //
영업상의 비밀 법은 목표로 한다 / 혁신을 촉진하는 것을 / 비록 그것이 이 목표를
성취하더라도 / 매우 다른 방식으로 / 특허 보호와는 //
~에도 불구하고(전치사)
(①) Notwithstanding the advantages of obtaining a patent, /
many innovators prefer / to protect their innovation / through
secrecy. //
특허 취득의 장점에도 불구하고 / 많은 혁신가는 선호한다 / 자신의 혁신을 보호하는 것을 /
비밀 유지를 통해 //
목적어절을 이끄는 접속사
(②) They may believe / that the cost and delay of seeking a
목적어절을 이끄는 접속사
patent / are too great / or that secrecy better protects their
investment / and increases their profit. //
그들은 믿을 수도 있다 / 특허를 따는 데 있어서의 비용과 지연이 / 너무 크다고 / 또는 비밀
유지가 투자를 더 잘 보호한다고 / 그리고 이익을 증가시킨다고 //

(③) They might also believe / that the invention can best be utilized / over a longer period of time / than a patent would allow. //

그들은 또한 믿을 수도 있다 / 그 발명품이 최고로 활용될 수 있다고 / 더 오랜 기간 동안 / 특허가 허용할 것보다 //

단서 2 일단 아이디어가 공개되면, 공기처럼 자유롭게(걷잡을 수 없게) 유출됨

(④) Once the idea is released, / it will be "free as the air" / under the background norms / of a free market economy. //

일단 그 아이디어가 공개되면 / 그것은 '공기처럼 자유롭게' 유출될 것이다 / 이면 규범에 따라 / 자유 시장 경제의 //

lead+사람+to-v: ~가 …하도록 이끌다   inventor를 수식하는 분사

(⑤) Such a predicament would lead / any inventor seeking to rely upon secrecy / to spend an inordinate amount of resources / building high and impassable fences around their research facilities / 병렬 구조

spend+자원+-ing(~하는 데 자원을 쓰다)의 병렬 구조

이러한 곤경은 이끌 것이다 / 비밀 유지에 의존하려는 모든 발명가를 / 과도한 양의 자원을 소비하도록 / 자신의 연구 시설 주변에 높고 통과할 수 없는 울타리를 칠 /

and greatly limiting the number of people / with access to the proprietary information. //

그리고 사람의 수를 크게 제한할 / 독점 정보에 접근할 권리를 가진 //

- trade secret 영업상 비밀   • secretive ⓐ 비밀스러운
- disclose ⓥ 드러내다, 폭로하다   • proprietary ⓐ 독점의, 독점적인
- aim to ~하는 것을 목표로 하다   • innovation ⓝ 혁신
- accomplish ⓥ 이루다, 성취하다   • utilize ⓥ 활용하다
- inordinate ⓐ 과도한   • impassable ⓐ 통과할 수 없는

영업상의 비밀 법은 혁신을 촉진하는 것이 목표이지만, 특허 보호와는 매우 다른 방식으로 이 목표를 이룬다. (①) 특허 취득의 장점에도 불구하고 많은 혁신가는 비밀 유지를 통해 자신의 혁신을 보호하는 것을 선호한다. (②) 그들은 특허를 따는 데 있어서의 비용과 지연이 너무 크거나 비밀 유지가 투자를 더 잘 보호하고 수익을 증가시킨다고 믿을 수도 있다. (③) 그들은 또한 그 발명품이 특허가 허용할 것보다 더 오랜 기간 최고로 활용될 수 있다고 믿을 수도 있다. (④ 그러나 영업상의 비밀에 대한 어떤 특별한 법적 보호가 없다면, 비밀주의 발명가는 직원이나 계약자가 독점 정보를 드러낼 위험을 감수하게 된다.) 일단 그 아이디어가 공개되면, 그것은 자유 시장 경제의 이면 규범에 따라 '공기처럼 자유롭게' 유출될 것이다. (⑤) 이러한 곤경으로 인해 비밀 유지에 의존하려는 모든 발명가는 자신의 연구 시설 주변에 높고 통과할 수 없는 울타리를 치고 독점 정보에 접근할 권리를 가진 사람의 수를 크게 제한하는 데 과도한 양의 자원을 소비하게 될 것이다.

| 문제 풀이 순서 | [정답률 49%]

1st 주어진 문장을 해석하고, 연결어, 지시어 등을 확인한다.

Without any special legal protection / for trade secrets, / however, / the secretive inventor risks / that an employee or contractor will disclose the proprietary information. //

어떤 특별한 법적 보호가 없다면 / 영업상의 비밀에 대한 / 그러나 / 비밀주의 발명가는 위험을 감수하게 된다 / 직원이나 계약자가 독점 정보를 드러낼 //

➡ '그러나(however)'라고 하면서 법적 보호가 없는 상황에서 영업상의 비밀을 유지하려는 발명가가 직면할 위험을 언급하고 있으므로 앞에는 이와 대조적인 내용이 제시될 것이다. **단서**

▶ **주어진 문장 앞:** 비밀 유지가 법적으로 보호받을 때 발명가가 누릴 수 있는 이점이 제시될 것임 **발상**

▶ **주어진 문장 뒤:** 아이디어가 공개되었을 경우 발명가가 직면하는 위험을 언급하는 내용이 이어질 것임

2nd 각 선택지의 앞뒤 흐름이 매끄러운지 확인한다.

- **①의 앞 문장과 뒤 문장**

앞 문장: 영업상의 비밀 법은 혁신을 촉진하는 것이 목표이지만, 특허 보호와는 매우 다른 방식으로 이 목표를 이룬다.

뒤 문장: 특허 취득의 장점에도 불구하고 많은 혁신가는 비밀 유지를 통해 자신의 혁신을 보호하는 것을 선호한다.

➡ 앞 문장은 영업상의 비밀 법이 혁신을 촉진하지만 특허 보호와는 다르다고 했으며, 뒤 문장에서는 특허 취득의 장점에도 불구하고 많은 혁신가들이 비밀 유지를 선호한다고 했다.
비밀 유지와 특허 보호의 차이점을 앞에서 제시하고 뒤에서 특허보다는 비밀 유지를 선호한다고 했으므로 두 문장은 자연스럽게 연결된다.

▶ 주어진 문장이 ①에 들어갈 수 없음

- **②의 앞 문장과 뒤 문장**

앞 문장: ①의 뒤 문장과 같음

뒤 문장: 그들은(they) 특허를 따는 데 있어서의 비용과 지연이 너무 크거나 비밀 유지가 투자를 더 잘 보호하고 수익을 증가시킨다고 믿을 수도 있다.

➡ 앞 문장에서는 많은 혁신가들이 특허 취득보다 비밀 유지를 선호한다고 했고, 이어지는 문장에서는 그들(혁신가들)이 왜 특허 취득보다 비밀 유지를 더 선호하는지 그 이유(특허 취득의 비용 및 지연, 비밀 유지의 보호 및 수익 증가)를 설명하고 있으므로 두 문장의 연결은 자연스럽다.

▶ 주어진 문장이 ②에 들어갈 수 없음

- **③의 앞 문장과 뒤 문장**

앞 문장: ②의 뒤 문장과 같음

뒤 문장: 그들은 또한(also) 그 발명품이 특허가 허용할 것보다 더 오랜 기간 최고로 활용될 수 있다고 믿을 수도 있다.

➡ 앞부분에서 그들이 특허보다 비밀 유지를 선호하는 이유를 제시했으며 이어지는 문장에서 그들은 '또한(also)' 그 발명품(비밀 유지가 된 발명품)이 특허보다 더 오랜 기간 최고로 활용될 수 있다고 믿을 수도 있다는 내용을 언급하고 있으므로 두 문장의 연결은 자연스럽다.

▶ 주어진 문장이 ③에 들어갈 수 없음

④의 앞 문장과 뒤 문장

앞 문장: ③의 뒤 문장과 같음

뒤 문장: 일단 그 아이디어가 공개되면, 그것은 자유 시장 경제의 이면 규범에 따라 '공기처럼 자유롭게' 유출될 것이다.

➡ 앞 문장에서 그들이 비밀 유지가 된 발명품이 특허보다 더 오랜 기간 최고로 활용될 수 있다고 믿는다고 했다. 뒤 문장에서는 일단 그 아이디어가 공개되면(비밀이 유지되지 않으면), 그것이 걷잡을 수 없게 유출될 것이라고 말하고 있다.
주어진 문장은 '그러나(however)' 영업상의 비밀에 대한 어떤 특별한 법적 보호가 없다면 비밀이 드러날 위험을 감수하게 될 것이라고 했으므로, 주어진 문장을 이 사이에 넣어 비밀 유지가 많은 장점이 있으나 법으로 보호되지 않으면 유출될 수 있고 이것이 일단 유출되면 걷잡을 수 없게 된다는 내용으로 전개되어야 한다.

▶ 주어진 문장이 ④에 들어가야 함

- **⑤의 앞 문장과 뒤 문장**

앞 문장: ④의 뒤 문장과 같음

뒤 문장: 이러한 곤경(such a predicament)으로 인해 비밀 유지에 의존하려는 모든 발명가는 자신의 연구 시설 주변에 높고 통과할 수 없는 울타리를 치고 독점 정보에 접근할 권리를 가진 사람의 수를 크게 제한하는 데 과도한 양의 자원을 소비하게 될 것이다.

➡ 앞에서 일단 아이디어가 공개되면 그것이 공기처럼 자유롭게 유출될 것이라고 했으며, 뒤에 이어지는 문장에서는 '이러한 곤경'으로 인해 비밀 유지를 원하는 발명가가 자신의 연구 시설에 울타리를 치고 독점 정보에 접근할 권리를 가진 사람의 수를 제한하게 된다고 했다.
앞 문장이 원인, 뒤 문장이 결과를 언급하고 있으므로 두 문장이 자연스럽게 연결된다.

▶ 주어진 문장이 ⑤에 들어갈 수 없음

3rd 글이 한눈에 들어오도록 정리하여 정답을 확인한다.

영업상의 비밀 법은 혁신을 촉진하는 것이 목표이지만, 특허 보호와는 매우 다른 방식으로 이 목표를 이룬다.
(①) 특허 취득의 장점에도 불구하고 많은 혁신가는 비밀 유지를 선호한다.
(②) 그들은 특허 비용과 지연이 너무 크거나 비밀 유지가 투자를 더 잘 보호하고 수익을 증가시킨다고 믿는다.
(③) 그들은 또한 그 발명품이 특허가 허용할 것보다 더 오랜 기간 최고로 활용될 수 있다고 믿는다.

(④ 그러나 영업상의 비밀에 대한 어떤 특별한 법적 보호가 없다면, 비밀이 드러날 위험을 감수하게 된다.)

일단 그 아이디어가 공개되면, 그것은 공기처럼 자유롭게 유출될 것이다.

(⑤) 이러한 곤경으로 인해 비밀 유지에 의존하려는 모든 발명가는 자신의 연구 시설 주변에 울타리를 치고 독점 정보에 접근할 권리를 가진 사람의 수를 크게 제한한다.

한규진 | 2025 수능 응시 · 대구 계성고 졸

지문을 먼저 읽기 전에 반드시 주어진 문장을 먼저 읽어야 해. 주어진 문장에 힌트가 될 만한 연결어나 포인트들을 체크하고, 특히 문장에서 언급된 대상들을 파악해야 해. 그리고 지문에서 단절이 느껴지거나 생략된 부분이 있다고 느껴지는 부분을 위주로 보는 것도 방법이야. 이 문제에서는 주어진 문장에 however가 등장하고, ④ 앞뒤로 단절을 느낄 수 있어! ④ 앞에서는 비밀 유지의 베네핏을, 뒤에서는 아이디어의 공개 상황에서 문제를 이야기하므로 그 사이의 단절에 주어진 문장을 삽입해주자.

N 04 정답 ④ *물건의 다양하고 역동적인 생애(수명) 주기

글의 흐름으로 보아, 주어진 문장이 들어가기에 가장 가장 적절한 곳을 고르시오.

단서1 실제로 물건은 선형적 주기 모형을 따르지 않고 다양한 용도나 운명을 겪음

In reality, / objects do not conform / to a linear lifecycle model; /
실제로 / 물건은 따르지 않는다 / 선형적인 수명 주기 모형을 /
instead, / they undergo breakdowns, / await repairs, / are
병렬 구조
대신에 / 그것들은 고장을 겪는다 / 수리를 기다리거나 /
stored away, / or find themselves relegated to the basement, /
결과를 의미함
only to be rediscovered and repurposed later. //
사용되지 않고 보관되거나 / 지하실로 추방되거나 했다가 / 결국 나중에 다시 발견되어 용도가 변경되기도 하면서 //

By their very nature, / the concepts of maintenance and repair / are predominantly examined / from a process-oriented perspective. //
그야말로 본질적으로 / 정비와 수리의 개념은 / 주로 검토된다 / 과정 지향적인 관점에서 //

(①) The focus / in related scholarly discourse / often revolves / around the lifespan or lifecycle / of objects and technologies. //
초점은 / 관련된 학문적 담론의 / 주로 이루어진다 / 수명 또는 생애 주기를 중심으로 / 물건과 기술의 //

(②) In this context, / maintenance and repair are considered
주격 관계대명사   형용사적 용법
practices / that have the potential / to prolong the existence of
분사구문을 이룸
objects, / ensuring their sustained utilization / over an extended period. //
이러한 맥락에서 / 정비와 수리는 행위로 여겨진다 / 잠재력을 가진 / 물건의 존재를 연장하는 / 지속적인 활용을 보장하면서 / 장기간에 걸친 //

단서2 Krebs와 Weber는 기술의 선형적 수명 주기가 불완전한 정의를 제공한다고 함
(③) Krebs and Weber critically engage / with anthropomorphic
주격 관계대명사
metaphors / that imply a biography of things, /
Krebs와 Weber는 비판적으로 사용한다 / 의인화된 은유를 / 물건의 일대기를 암시하는 /
appropriately highlighting / that conventional understanding of
분사구문을 이룸   목적어절을 이끄는 접속사
the lifecycle of a technology, / from its acquisition to its disposal
from the household, / provides an incomplete definition. //
적절히 강조하면서 / 기술의 수명 주기에 대한 관례적인 이해가 / 기술의 획득부터 가정에서의 그것의 폐기에 이르기까지 / 불완전한 정의를 제공한다는 것을 //

(④) Additionally, / objects may enter recycling or second-hand
분사구문을 이룸   afterlife를 수식하는 분사
cycles, / leading to a dynamic afterlife / marked by diverse
applications. //   **단서3** 게다가 물건은 재활용 또는 중고품 순환 과정으로 들어가
게다가 / 물건은 재활용 또는 중고품 순환 과정으로 들어갈 수도 있다 / 역동적인 사후 생애로 이어지는 / 다양한 용도를 특징으로 하는 //
다양한 용도로 쓰임

(⑤) As such, / the life of an object exhibits / a far more
비교급 강조
complicated and adaptive path / than a simplistic linear progression. //
그와 같이 / 물건의 생애는 보여준다 / 훨씬 더 복잡하고 적응적인 경로를 / 단순한 선형적 진행보다는 //

- conform ⓥ 따르다   · linear ⓐ 선형적인
- maintenance ⓝ 정비   · predominantly ⓐⓓ 대부분, 주로
- scholarly ⓐ 학문적인   · discourse ⓝ 담론   · revolve ⓥ 돌다
- prolong ⓥ 연장하다   · metaphor ⓝ 은유, 비유
- biography ⓝ 전기, 일대기   · disposal ⓝ 폐기
- afterlife ⓝ 사후 생애   · application ⓝ 용도
- adaptive ⓐ 적응적인   · progression ⓝ 진행

그야말로 본질적으로, 정비와 수리의 개념은 과정 지향적인 관점에서 주로 검토된다. (①) 관련된 학문적 담론의 초점은 흔히 물건과 기술의 수명 또는 생애 주기를 중심으로 이루어진다. (②) 이러한 맥락에서 정비와 수리는 물건의 존재를 연장하여 장기간에 걸쳐 지속적인 활용을 보장할 수 있는 잠재력을 가진 행위로 여겨진다. (③) Krebs와 Weber는 물건의 일대기를 암시하는 의인화된 은유를 비판적으로 사용하여, 기술의 수명 주기에 대한 관례적인 이해가, 기술의 획득부터 가정에서의 그것의 폐기에 이르기까지, 불완전한 정의를 제공한다는 점을 적절히 강조한다. (④ 실제로 물건은 선형적인 수명 주기 모형을 따르지 않고, 대신에 고장을 겪거나, 수리를 기다리거나, 사용되지 않고 보관되거나, 지하실로 추방되거나 했다가, 결국 나중에 다시 발견되어 용도가 변경되기도 한다.) 게다가, 물건은 재활용 또는 중고품 순환 과정으로 들어갈 수도 있어서 다양한 용도가 특징인 역동적인 사후 생애를 맞이하기도 한다. (⑤) 그와 같이 물건의 생애는 단순한 선형적 진행보다는 훨씬 더 복잡하고 적응적인 경로를 보인다.

| 문제 풀이 순서 | [정답률 59%]

1st 주어진 문장을 해석하고, 연결어, 지시어 등을 확인한다.

In reality, / objects do not conform / to a linear lifecycle model; / instead, / they undergo breakdowns, / await repairs, / are stored away, / or find themselves relegated to the basement, / only to be rediscovered and repurposed later. //
실제로 / 물건은 따르지 않는다 / 선형적인 수명 주기 모형을 / 대신에 / 그것들은 고장을 겪는다 / 수리를 기다리거나 / 사용되지 않고 보관되거나 / 지하실로 추방되거나 했다가 / 결국 나중에 다시 발견되어 용도가 변경되기도 하면서 //

⇒ 현실에서는 물건이 단순한 선형적 생애 주기를 따르지 않고 다양한 방식으로 변화하며 유지된다는 내용이 제시되었으므로 앞에는 물건의 수명 주기를 단순히 선형적으로 보는 이론이 있다는 내용이 언급될 것이다. **단서**

▶ **주어진 문장 앞:** 물건의 단순한 선형적 수명 주기에 대한 이론이 제시될 것임 **발상**

▶ **주어진 문장 뒤:** 물건이 재활용과 용도 변경을 통해 어떻게 생명이 연장되고 있는지에 대한 설명이 이어질 것임

2nd 각 선택지의 앞뒤 흐름이 매끄러운지 확인한다.

- ①의 앞 문장과 뒤 문장

앞 문장: 그야말로 본질적으로, 정비와 수리의 개념은 과정 지향적인 관점에서 주로 검토된다.

뒤 문장: 관련된(related) 학문적 담론의 초점은 흔히 물건과 기술의 수명 또는 생애 주기를 중심으로 이루어진다.

⇒ 앞 문장은 정비와 수리의 개념이 과정 지향적 관점에서 검토된다고 했으며 뒤에서는 이와 관련된 학문적 담론이 흔히 물건과 기술의 수명 주기를 중심으로 이루어진다고 했으므로 두 문장의 연결은 자연스럽다.

▶ 주어진 문장이 ①에 들어갈 수 없음

- ②의 앞 문장과 뒤 문장

앞 문장: ①의 뒤 문장과 같음

뒤 문장: 이러한 맥락에서 정비와 수리는 물건의 존재를 연장하여 장기간에 걸쳐 지속적인 활용을 보장할 수 있는 잠재력을 가진 행위로 여겨진다.

앞 문장에서 정비와 수리에 관한 학문적 이론이 물건의 수명 주기를 중심으로 이루어짐을 밝힌 뒤, 이러한 맥락에서 정비와 수리가 물건의 존재를 연장하여 장기간에 걸친 활용을 보장하는 것임을 뒤 문장에서 설명하고 있으므로 두 문장은 자연스럽게 연결된다.

▶ 주어진 문장이 ②에 들어갈 수 없음

- **③의 앞 문장과 뒤 문장**

┌ 앞 문장: ②의 뒤 문장과 같음

│ 뒤 문장: Krebs와 Weber는 물건의 일대기를 암시하는 의인화된 은유를 비판적으로 사용하여, 기술의 수명 주기에 대한 관례적인 이해가, 기술의 획득부터 가정에서의 그것의 폐기에 이르기까지, 불완전한 정의를

└ 제공한다는 점을 적절히 강조한다.

➡ 앞 부분에서 정비와 수리는 물건의 존재를 연장하여 오래 활용하도록 하는 것임을 제시한 뒤, 이어지는 뒤 문장에서 이러한 기술의 수명 주기에 대한 관례적 이해가 기술의 획득부터 폐기에 이르는 전 과정을 불완전하게 제공하고 있다는 설명이 자연스럽게 이어지고 있다.

▶ 주어진 문장이 ③에 들어갈 수 없음

- **④의 앞 문장과 뒤 문장**

┌ 앞 문장: ③의 뒤 문장과 같음

│ 뒤 문장: 게다가(additionally), 물건은 재활용 또는 중고품 순환 과정으로 들어갈 수도 있어서 다양한 용도가 특징인 역동적인 사후 생애를

└ 맞이하기도 한다.

➡ 앞 문장에서 기술의 선형적 수명 주기에 대한 관례적 이해가 불완전함을 제시하고 있다.

뒤 문장에서는 '게다가(additionally)' 물건이 재활용 또는 중고품 순환 과정으로 들어가 역동적 사후 생애를 맞이한다고 했다.

주어진 문장은 현실에서 물건이 단순한 선형적 생애 주기를 따르지 않고 다양한 방식으로 변화하며 유지된다는 내용으로, 정비와 수리에 대한 학문적 담론이 불완전하다는 앞 문장과 '게다가' 물건이 재활용과 용도 변경의 역동적 상태를 겪는다는 뒤 문장 사이에 들어가야 자연스러운 글이 전개된다.

▶ 주어진 문장이 ④에 들어가야 함

- **⑤의 앞 문장과 뒤 문장**

┌ 앞 문장: ④의 뒤 문장과 같음

│ 뒤 문장: 그와 같이(as such) 물건의 생애는 단순한 선형적 진행보다는

└ 훨씬 더 복잡하고 적응적인 경로를 보인다.

➡ 앞에서 물건이 재활용과 중고품 순환 과정을 통해 역동적 생애를 맞이한다고 했으며, 이어지는 뒤 문장에서는 그와 같이 물건의 생애가 선형적이라기 보다는 훨씬 더 복잡한 경로를 보인다고 했으므로 두 문장은 자연스럽게 이어진다.

▶ 주어진 문장이 ⑤에 들어갈 수 없음

3rd 글이 한눈에 들어오도록 정리하여 정답을 확인한다.

정비와 수리의 개념은 과정 지향적인 관점에서 주로 검토된다.
(①) 관련된 학문적 담론은 물건과 기술의 수명 또는 생애 주기를 중심으로 이루어진다.
(②) 정비와 수리는 물건의 존재를 연장하여 장기간에 걸쳐 지속적인 활용을 보장하는 행위로 여겨진다.
(③) Krebs와 Weber는 기술의 수명 주기에 대한 관례적인 이해가 불완전한 정의를 제공한다고 강조한다.
(④ 실제로 물건은 선형적인 수명 주기 모형을 따르지 않고 나중에 다시 발견되거나 용도가 변경되는 등 다양한 과정을 겪는다.)
게다가 물건은 재활용 또는 중고품 순환 과정으로 들어갈 수도 있어서 역동적인 사후 생애를 맞이하기도 한다.
(⑤) 그와 같이 물건의 생애는 단순한 선형적 진행보다는 훨씬 더 복잡하고 적응적인 경로를 보인다.

배지오 | 2025 수능 응시·성남 낙생고 졸

문장 삽입 문제에서는 처음부터 주어진 문장에 집중하는 말고, 먼저 글을 일단 읽어서 주제를 파악하려고 했어. 이 글은 정비와 수리의 역할을 설명하는 글이고, 때문에 정비와 수리가 어떠한 기능을 하는지를 중점적으로 봤어. 이 글에서 수리와 정비는 the potential to prolong the existence of objects를 지니고 따라서 물건들은 선형적인 수명 주기를 갖는다고 말해. 하지만 Additinoally 이후로는 물건의 수명과 생애가 역동적임을 명시해. 따라서 In reality이라고 시작하며 수리와 정비를 통해 선형적인 생애 주기가 아닌 역동적인 생애 주기를 살아간다는 내용이 ④에 들어가는 것이 맞겠지!

N 05 정답 ④ *생태계 관리를 위한 미래 생태계 모습 예측하기

글의 흐름으로 보아, 주어진 문장이 들어가기에 가장 가장 적절한 곳을 고르시오. [3점]

Unfortunately, / at the scales, accuracy, and precision / most useful to protected area management, /
안타깝게도 / 규모, 정확성, 정밀도를 고려할 때 / 보호 지역 관리에 가장 유용한 /
┌─ not only A but also B: A뿐만 아니라 B도 ─┐
the future not only promises to be unprecedented, / but it also promises to be unpredictable. //　**단서 1** 불행히도 미래는 전례도 없고 예측할 수도 없는 것이 될 것임
미래는 전례가 없을 뿐만 아니라 / 예측할 수 없는 것이 될 것이다 //

부사적 용법(목적)
To decide whether and how to intervene in ecosystems, / protected area managers normally need / a reasonably clear idea / of what future ecosystems would be like / if they did not intervene. //
생태계에 개입할지 여부와 방법을 결정하기 위해 / 보호 지역 관리자는 일반적으로 필요로 한다 / 상당히 명확한 아이디어를 / 미래의 생태계가 어떨지 / 자신이 개입하지 않을 경우 //

(①) Management practices usually involve / defining a more desirable future condition / and implementing management
┌─ 병렬 구조 ─┐
actions를 수식하는 분사
actions / designed to push or guide ecosystems toward that condition. //
관리 관행에는 대체로 포함된다 / 더 바람직한 미래 상태를 규정하는 것이 / 그리고 관리 조치를 실행하는 것이 / 생태계를 그 상태 쪽으로 밀고 가거나 이끌도록 설계된 //

(②) Managers need confidence / in the likely outcomes of their interventions. //
관리자는 확신이 필요하다 / 개입의 가능한 결과에 대한 //

(③) This traditional and inherently logical approach / requires a high degree of predictive ability, / **단서 2** (관리자의 확신을 위해) 높은 수준의 예측 능력이 필요함
이러한 전통적이고 본질적으로 논리적인 접근 방식은 / 높은 수준의 예측 능력을 필요로 한다 /

and predictions must be developed / at appropriate spatial and
분사구문
temporal scales, / often localized and near-term. //
그리고 예측은 이루어져야 한다 / 적절한 공간적, 시간적 규모에서 / 종종 국지적이고 단기적으로 //

부사적 용법(목적)　　　　　　　　　　uncertainties를 수식하는 분사
(④) To illustrate this, / consider / the uncertainties involved in predicting climatic changes, / how ecosystems are likely to respond / to climatic changes, / **단서 3** 이를 설명하기 위해 기후 변화 예측의 불확실성을 고려해 보라고 함
이를 설명하기 위해 / 고려해 보라 / 기후 변화 예측과 관련된 불확실성을 / 생태계가 어떻게 반응할 것인지를 / 기후 변화에 /

주격 관계대명사
and the likely efficacy of actions / that might be taken / to counter adverse effects of climatic changes. //
그리고 조치의 가능한 효율을 / 취할 수도 있는 / 기후 변화의 해로운 영향에 대응하기 위해 //

(⑤) Comparable uncertainties surround / the nature and magnitude of future changes / in other ecosystem stressors. //
비슷한 불확실성이 존재한다 / 미래 변화의 성격과 규모에서도 / 다른 생태계 스트레스 요인의 //

- scale ⓝ 규모　　• accuracy ⓝ 정확성　　• precision ⓝ 정밀함
- unprecedented ⓐ 전례가 없는
- unpredictable ⓐ 예측할 수 없는, 예측이 불가능한
- intervene ⓥ 개입하다　　• define ⓥ 규정하다, 정의하다
- implement ⓥ 시행하다　　• confidence ⓝ 확신, 자신감
- inherently 젪 본질적으로, 내재적으로　　• appropriate ⓐ 적절한
- spatial ⓐ 공간의　　• temporal ⓐ 시간의, 시간의 제약을 받는
- localized ⓐ 국지적인, 국부적인　　• climatic change 기후 변화
- efficacy ⓝ 효율　　• counter ⓥ (무엇의 악영향에) 대응하다
- adverse ⓐ 부정적인, 불리한　　• comparable ⓐ 비슷한, 비교할 만한
- surround ⓥ 둘러싸다　　• magnitude ⓝ (엄청난) 규모

생태계에 개입할지 여부와 방법을 결정하기 위해 보호 지역 관리자는 자신이 개입하지 않을 경우 미래의 생태계가 어떨지 일반적으로 상당히 명확하게 알고 있을 필요가 있다. (①) 관리 관행에는 대체로 더 바람직한 미래 상태를 규정하고 생태계를 그 상태 쪽으로 밀고 가거나 이끌도록 설계된 관리 조치를 실행하는 것이 포함된다. (②) 관리자는 개입의 가능한 결과에 대한 확신이 필요하다. (③) 이러한 전통적이고 본질적으로 논리적인 접근 방식은 높은 수준의 예측 능력을 필요로 하며, 예측은 적절한 공간적, 시간적 규모에서, 종종 국지적이고 단기적인 규모로 이루어져야 한다. (④ 안타깝게도 보호 지역 관리에 가장 유용한 규모, 정확성, 정밀도를 고려할 때 미래는 전례가 없을 뿐만 아니라 예측할 수 없는 것이 될 것이다.) 이를 설명하기 위해 기후 변화 예측과 관련된 불확실성, 생태계가 기후 변화에 어떻게 반응할 것인지, 그리고 기후 변화의 해로운 영향에 대응하기 위해 취할 수도 있을 조치의 가능한 효율을 고려해 보라. (⑤) 다른 생태계 스트레스 요인의 미래 변화의 성격과 규모에서도 비슷한 불확실성이 존재한다.

| 문제 풀이 순서 | [정답률 73%]

1st 주어진 문장을 해석하고, 연결어, 지시어 등을 확인한다.

Unfortunately, / at the scales, accuracy, and precision / most useful to protected area management, / the future not only promises to be unprecedented, / but it also promises to be unpredictable. //
안타깝게도 / 규모, 정확성, 정밀도를 고려할 때 / 보호 지역 관리에 가장 유용한 / 미래는 전례가 없을 뿐만 아니라 / 예측할 수 없는 것이 될 것이다 //

➡ '불행히도(unfortunately)' 규모, 정확성, 정밀도를 고려할 때 미래는 전례도 없을 것이고 예측할 수 없는 것이 될 것이라고 했다. 단서

　▶ **주어진 문장 앞**: 규모, 정확성, 정밀도를 고려한 방식이 제시되어야 함
　▶ **주어진 문장 뒤**: 미래가 예측할 수 없는 것이 될 것이므로 이에 대한 대처나 결과가 이어질 것임 발상

2nd 각 선택지의 앞뒤 흐름이 매끄러운지 확인한다.

- **①의 앞 문장과 뒤 문장**

앞 문장: 생태계에 개입할지 여부와 방법을 결정하기 위해 보호 지역 관리자는 자신이 개입하지 않을 경우 미래의 생태계가 어떨지 일반적으로 상당히 명확하게 알고 있을 필요가 있다.
뒤 문장: 관리 관행에는 대체로 더 바람직한 미래 상태를 규정하고 생태계를 그 상태 쪽으로 밀고 가거나 이끌도록 설계된 관리 조치를 실행하는 것이 포함된다.

➡ 앞 문장에서 생태계에 개입할지 여부와 방법을 결정하기 위해 보호 지역 관리자는 미래 생태계가 어떻게 될지 명확히 알고 있을 필요가 있다고 했고, 뒤 문장에서는 따라서 더 바람직한 미래 상태를 규정하고 생태계를 그 상태 쪽으로 밀고 나가는 것이 필요하다고 했다. 따라서 두 문장은 자연스럽게 연결된다.

　▶ 주어진 문장이 ①에 들어갈 수 없음

- **②의 앞 문장과 뒤 문장**

앞 문장: ①의 뒤 문장과 같음
뒤 문장: 관리자는 개입의 가능한 결과에 대한 확신이 필요하다.

➡ 바람직한 미래 상태를 규정하고 생태계를 그 상태 쪽으로 밀고 가는 관리 조치가 필요하다고 한 앞 문장의 내용과, 관리자가 개입 가능한 결과에 대해 확신할 필요가 있다고 한 뒤 문장의 내용은 자연스럽게 연결된다.

　▶ 주어진 문장이 ②에 들어갈 수 없음

- **③의 앞 문장과 뒤 문장**

앞 문장: ②의 뒤 문장과 같음
뒤 문장: 이러한 전통적이고 본질적으로 논리적인 접근 방식(this traditional and inherently logical approach)은 높은 수준의 예측 능력을 필요로 하며, 예측은 적절한 공간적, 시간적 규모에서, 종종 국지적이고 단기적인 규모로 이루어져야 한다.

➡ '이러한 전통적이고 본질적으로 논리적인 접근 방식'은 앞 문장에서 언급한 관리자의 개입 가능한 결과에 대한 확신의 방법을 가리킨다. 그리고 이 방식은 공간적, 시간적 규모에서, 국지적이고 단기적인 규모로 이루어지는 높은 수준의 예측 능력을 필요로 한다는 내용이 자연스럽게 전개된다.

　▶ 주어진 문장이 ③에 들어갈 수 없음

- **④의 앞 문장과 뒤 문장**

앞 문장: ③의 뒤 문장과 같음
뒤 문장: 이(this)를 설명하기 위해 기후 변화 예측과 관련된 불확실성, 생태계가 기후 변화에 어떻게 반응할 것인지, 그리고 기후 변화의 해로운 영향에 대응하기 위해 취할 수도 있을 조치의 가능한 효율을 고려해 보라.

➡ 앞에서 전통적이고 본질적으로 논리적인 접근 방식이 높은 수준의 예측 능력을 필요로 한다고 했는데, 뒤에서는 이를 설명하기 위해 기후 변화 예측과 관련된 불확실성에 대응할 수 있는 조치의 효율을 고려해 보자고 했으므로 앞 문장과 뒤 문장의 전개가 대조적으로 이루어지고 있다.
주어진 문장은 '불행히도' 규모, 정확성, 정밀도를 고려할 때 미래는 전례도 없을 것이고 예측할 수 없는 것이 될 것이라고 했다.
따라서 주어진 문장이 뒤 문장으로 방향이 전환되기 전에 들어가 예측이 필요하지만 미래는 예측할 수 없는 것이 될 것이기 때문에 이러한 불확실성에 대응할 수 있는 조치를 고려해야 한다는 내용이 되어야 한다.

　▶ 주어진 문장이 ④에 들어가야 함

- **⑤의 앞 문장과 뒤 문장**

앞 문장: ④의 뒤 문장과 같음
뒤 문장: 다른 생태계 스트레스 요인의 미래 변화의 성격과 규모에서도 비슷한 불확실성이 존재한다.

➡ 앞에서 기후 변화 예측과 관련된 불확실성에 대응할 수 있는 조치의 효율을 고려해 보자고 했고, 뒤에서는 다른 생태계 스트레스 요인의 미래에도 비슷한 불확실성이 존재한다고 했으므로 두 문장이 자연스럽게 연결된다.

　▶ 주어진 문장이 ⑤에 들어갈 수 없음

3rd 글이 한눈에 들어오도록 정리하여 정답을 확인한다.

생태계에 개입할지 여부와 방법을 결정하기 위해 보호 지역 관리자는 미래의 생태계가 어떨지 명확히 알 필요가 있다.
(①) 더 바람직한 미래 상태를 규정하고 생태계를 그 상태 쪽으로 밀고 가려는 관리 조치가 필요하다.
(②) 관리자는 개입의 가능한 결과에 대한 확신이 필요하다.
(③) 이러한 방식은 적절한 공간적, 시간적 규모에서, 종종 국지적이고 단기적인 규모로 이루어지는 높은 수준의 예측을 필요로 한다.
(④ 안타깝게도 규모, 정확성, 정밀도를 고려할 때 미래는 전례도 없고 예측할 수도 없다.)
이를 설명하기 위해 기후 변화 예측과 관련된 불확실성 등에 대응할 수 있는 조치의 효율을 고려해 보라.
(⑤) 다른 생태계 스트레스 요인의 미래에도 비슷한 불확실성이 존재한다.

> 글의 흐름으로 보아, 주어진 문장이 들어가기에 가장 적절한 곳을 고르시오.

단서 1 지속적인 배출물 측정은 비용이 많이 들어서, 배출물에 직접 과세하는 것을 어렵게 할 수 있음
(단점 제시)

Continuous emissions measurement can be costly, / particularly where there are many separate sources of
관계부사(뒤에 완전한 절이 옴)
emissions, /
지속적인 배출물 측정은 비용이 많이 들 수 있으며 / 특히 개별 배출원이 많은 경우 /

and for many pollution problems / this may be a major

disincentive to direct taxation of emissions. //
그리고 많은 오염 문제에 있어 / 이는 배출물에 직접적으로 과세하는 것에 주요한 저해
요소가 될 수 있다 //

Environmental taxes / based directly on measured emissions
주어   앞에 which is 생략   과거분사
/ can, in principle, be very precisely targeted to the policy's
동사   삽입어구
environmental objectives. //
환경세는 / 측정된 배출물에 직접적으로 기반한 / 원칙적으로 그 정책의 환경적 목표를 매우
정확하게 겨냥할 수 있다 //

(①) If a firm pollutes more, / it pays additional tax / directly in

proportion to the rise in emissions. //
어떤 기업이 더 많이 오염시키면 / 그 기업은 추가 세금을 낸다 / 배출물 증가에 직접적으로
비례한 //

(②) The polluter thus has an incentive / to reduce emissions in
주격 관계대명사
any manner / that is less costly per unit of abatement / than the
비교급
tax on each unit of residual emissions. //
따라서 공해 기업은 동기를 갖게 된다 / 어떤 방식으로든 배출량을 줄이려는 / 감소 단위당
비용이 덜 드는 / 잔여 배출물의 단위당 세금보다 //
주절의 주어
(③) The great attraction of basing the tax directly on measured
주절의 동사   종속절 주어(복수)
emissions / is that the actions the polluter can take to reduce tax
보어절을 이끄는 접속사
liability / are actions that also reduce emissions. //
복수 동사   주격 관계대명사
세금을 측정된 배출물에 직접 기반하는 것의 매우 큰 매력은 / 공해 기업이 세금 부담액을
줄이기 위해 취할 수 있는 조치가 ~이다 / 배출물을 줄이는 조치이기도 하다는 점 //
복수 주어
(④) Nevertheless, the technologies / available for monitoring

the concentrations and flows of particular substances in waste
복수 동사(현재완료진행)
discharges / have been developing rapidly. //
그럼에도 불구하고, 기술은 / 폐기물 방출에서 특정 물질의 농도와 흐름을 관찰하는 데 이용할
수 있는 / 빠르게 발전해 오고 있다 // **단서 2** '그럼에도 불구하고' 측정 기술이 빠르게 발전하였다고
하였으므로, 앞에는 측정 기술의 단점이나 한계가 서술되어야 함
(⑤) In the future, it may be possible / to think of taxing
가주어   진주어
measured emissions / in a wider range of applications. //
앞으로는 가능할 수도 있다 / 측정된 배출물에 대한 세금 부과를 생각하는 것이 / 더 광범위한
적용으로 //

- continuous ⓐ 지속적인 · emission ⓝ 배출(물)
- measurement ⓝ 측정 · costly ⓐ 많은 비용이 드는
- disincentive ⓝ 저해 요소 · taxation ⓝ 과세
- in principle 원칙적으로 · in proportion to ~에 비례하여
- incentive ⓝ 동기, 유인, 장려책 · residual ⓐ 잔여의, 나머지의
- base ~ on … ~을 …에 기반하다 · concentration ⓝ 농도
- substance ⓝ 물질 · discharge ⓝ 방출, 배출

측정된 배출물에 직접적으로 기반한 환경세는 원칙적으로 그 정책의 환경적
목표를 매우 정확하게 겨냥할 수 있다. (①) 어떤 기업이 더 많이 오염시키면
그 기업은 배출물 증가에 직접적으로 비례한 추가 세금을 낸다. (②) 따라서
공해 기업은 잔여 배출물의 단위당 세금보다 감소 단위당 비용이 덜 드는
어떤 방식으로든 배출량을 줄이려는 동기를 갖게 된다. (③) 세금을 측정된
배출물에 직접 기반하는 것의 매우 큰 매력은 공해 기업이 세금 부담액을
줄이기 위해 취할 수 있는 조치가 배출물을 줄이는 조치이기도 하다는 점이다.

(④ 지속적인 배출물 측정은 특히 개별 배출원이 많은 경우 비용이 많이들
수 있으며, 많은 오염 문제에 있어 이는 배출물에 직접적으로 과세하는 것에
주요한 저해 요소가 될 수 있다.) 그럼에도 불구하고, 폐기물 방출에서 특정
물질의 농도와 흐름을 관찰하는 데 이용할 수 있는 기술은 빠르게 발전해 오고
있다. (⑤) 앞으로는 더 광범위한 적용으로 측정된 배출물에 대한 세금 부과를
생각하는 것이 가능할 수도 있다.

| 문제 풀이 순서 | [정답률 51%]

1st 주어진 문장을 해석하고, 연결어, 지시어 등을 확인한다.

Continuous emissions measurement can be costly, particularly
where there are many separate sources of emissions, and for
many pollution problems this may be a major [disincentive] to
direct taxation of emissions.
지속적인 배출물 측정은 특히 개별 배출원이 많은 경우 비용이 많이들 수 있으며, 많은 오염
문제에 있어 이는 배출물에 직접적으로 과세하는 것에 주요한 저해 요소가 될 수 있다.

➡ 주어진 문장은 지속적인 배출물 측정은 비용이 많이 들어서, 배출물에 직접
과세하는 것을 어렵게 할 수 있다는 단점이 '저해 요소'라는 말로 제시되고 있다.
▶ 주어진 문장 앞에는 지속적인 배출물 측정의 단점과 관련된 내용이 나올 것임

2nd 각 선택지의 앞뒤 흐름이 매끄러운지 확인한다.

- **①의 앞 문장과 뒤 문장**

앞 문장: 측정된 배출물에 직접적으로 기반한 환경세는 원칙적으로 그
정책의 환경적 목표를 매우 정확하게 겨냥할 수 있다.

뒤 문장: 어떤 기업이 더 많이 오염시키면 그 기업은 배출물 증가에
직접적으로 비례한 추가 세금을 낸다.

➡ 측정된 배출물에 직접 기반하는 환경세가 어떤 개념인지를 설명하고 있으며, 그
예시로 어떤 기업이 더 많이 오염시킬수록 더 많은 세금을 낸다는 부연 설명이
나오므로 두 문장은 자연스럽게 연결된다.
▶ 주어진 문장이 ①에 들어갈 수 없음

- **②의 앞 문장과 뒤 문장**

앞 문장: ①의 뒤 문장과 같음

뒤 문장: 따라서(thus) 공해 기업은 잔여 배출물의 단위당 세금보다
감소 단위당 비용이 덜 드는 어떤 방식으로든 배출량을 줄이려는
동기(incentive)를 갖게 된다.

➡ 기업에 대한 서술을 연결하고 있다. 오염물을 많이 배출할수록. 기업은 비례하여
세금이 부과되므로, 세금을 줄이려는 동기를 갖게 된다는 설명의 인과 관계가
성립한다.
▶ 주어진 문장이 ②에 들어갈 수 없음

- **③의 앞 문장과 뒤 문장**

앞 문장: ②의 뒤 문장과 같음

뒤 문장: 세금을 측정된 배출물에 직접 기반하는 것의 매우 큰 매력(great
attraction)은 공해 기업이 세금 부담액을 줄이기 위해 취할 수 있는
조치가 배출물을 줄이는 조치이기도 하다는 점이다.

➡ 앞 문장에서는 기업이 세금을 줄이기 위하여 배출량을 줄이려는 동기를 갖게
된다는 내용이 제시되었고, 뒤 문장은 세금을 배출물에 기반하는 것의 큰 장점에
대해 언급하고 있으므로 자연스럽게 연결된다.
▶ 주어진 문장이 ③에 들어갈 수 없음

- **④의 앞 문장과 뒤 문장**

앞 문장: ③의 뒤 문장과 같음

뒤 문장: 그럼에도 불구하고(Nevertheless), 폐기물 방출에서 특정 물질의
농도와 흐름을 관찰하는 데 이용할 수 있는 기술은 빠르게 발전해 오고
있다.

➡ 바로 앞 문장까지 글의 전체적인 흐름이 측정된 배출물에 기반하여 세금을
부과하는 것의 장점을 서술하였는데, '그럼에도 불구하고(Neverthelss)'라는 말
뒤에 이 측정 기술이 발전해오고 있다는 내용이 나오는 것은 어색하다.
배출물 측정의 단점을 서술하고 있는 내용이 들어가야 흐름이 자연스럽다.
▶ 주어진 문장이 ④에 들어가야 함

- ⑤의 앞 문장과 뒤 문장

┌ 앞 문장: ④의 뒤 문장과 같음

│ 뒤 문장: 앞으로는 더 광범위한 적용으로 측정된 배출물에 대한 세금 부과를
└ 생각하는 것이 가능할 수도 있다.

➡ 앞 문장에서 배출물 측정 기술이 발전해오고 있다고 하였고, 이는 앞으로 더욱
광범위한 적용을 가능하게 하는 것으로 연결된다.

▶ 주어진 문장이 ⑤에 들어갈 수 없음

3rd 글이 한눈에 들어오도록 정리하여 정답을 확인한다.

측정된 배출물에 직접적으로 기반한 환경세는 원칙적으로 그 정책의 환경적 목표를
매우 정확하게 겨냥할 수 있다.
(①) 어떤 기업이 더 많이 오염시키면 그 기업은 배출물 증가에 직접적으로 비례한
추가 세금을 낸다.
(②) 따라서 공해 기업은 어떤 방식으로든 배출량을 줄이려는 동기를 갖게 된다.
(③) 세금을 측정된 배출물에 직접 기반하는 것의 매우 큰 매력은 공해 기업이 취할 수
있는 조치가 배출물을 줄이는 조치이기도 하다는 점이다.
(④ 지속적인 배출물 측정은 비용이 많이 들 수 있으며, 배출물에 직접적으로 과세하는
것에 주요한 저해 요소가 될 수 있다.)
그럼에도 불구하고, 폐기물 방출에서 특정 물질의 농도와 흐름을 관찰하는 데 이용할
수 있는 기술은 빠르게 발전해 오고 있다.
(⑤) 앞으로는 더 광범위한 적용으로 측정된 배출물에 대한 세금 부과를 생각하는
것이 가능할 수도 있다.

N 07 정답 ⑤ ＊예술에서 주제(형상)와 스타일(배경) 간의 균형 ——

글의 흐름으로 보아, 주어진 문장이 들어가기에 가장 적절한 곳을
고르시오. [3점]

This active involvement provides a basis / for depth of
aesthetic processing and reflection on the meaning of the
work. // **단서1** '이러한 적극적인 관여'에 해당하는 것이 바로 앞에 제시되어야 함
이러한 적극적인 관여는 기반을 제공한다 / 미학적 처리의 과정 그리고 작품 의미 성찰의
깊이에 대한 //

There are interesting trade-offs / in the relative importance of
복수 동사   복수 주어
subject matter (i.e., figure) and style (i.e., background). //
흥미로운 균형이 있다 / 주제(즉, 형상)와 스타일(즉, 배경)의 상대적 중요성에는 //
단서2 구상주의적인 예술작품에 대한 설명이 먼저 제시됨
(①) In highly representational paintings, plays, or stories,
the focus is on subject matter that resembles everyday life / and
주격 관계대명사
the role of background style / is to facilitate the construction of
명사적 용법(보어)
mental models. //
고도로 구상주의적인 그림, 연극 또는 이야기에서는 / 초점이 일상생활과 유사한 주제에 있고
/ 배경 스타일의 역할은 / 심성 모형의 구성을 용이하게 하는 것이다 //

(②) Feelings of pleasure and uncertainty / carry the viewer /
복수 주어   복수 동사
along to the conclusion of the piece. //
즐거움과 불확실성의 감정은 / 관객을 이끌고 간다 / 작품의 결말까지 함께 //

(③) In highly expressionist works, / novel stylistic devices
work / in an inharmonious manner against the subject matter /
분사구문을 이끎
thereby creating a disquieting atmosphere. //
고도로 표현주의적인 작품에서는 / 새로운 스타일 장치가 작용하여 / 주제와 조화롭지 않은
방식으로 / 그럼으로써 불안한 분위기를 조성한다 //

(④) Thus, when the work is less "readable" (or easily
interpreted), / **단서3** 다소 난해한 표현주의 작품을 볼 때, 감상자는 미학적 태도가 필요하다는
것을 생각하게 됨(주어진 글에서 언급한 '이러한 적극적인 관여'임)
따라서 작품이 덜 '읽기 쉬운'(혹은 쉽게 해석되는) 상태일 때 /
its departure from conventional forms / reminds the viewer or
동사
reader / that an "aesthetic attitude" is needed / to appreciate the
whole episode. //
그것이 전통적인 방식에서 벗어났다는 것은 / 보는 사람이나 독자에게 상기시킨다 / '미학적
태도'가 필요하다는 것을 / 작품의 전체 내용을 제대로 감상하기 위해 //

(⑤) An ability to switch / between the "pragmatic attitude" of
주어   between A and B: A와 B 사이
everyday life and an "aesthetic attitude" / is fundamental to a
동사
balanced life. //
전환하는 능력은 / 일상생활의 '실용주의적 태도'와 '미학적 태도' 사이를 / 균형 잡힌 삶에
핵심적이다 //

- involvement ⓝ 관여, 참여   • a basis for ~의 기반
- reflection ⓝ 성찰   • trade-off ⓝ 균형, 교환
- subject matter 주제   • representational ⓐ 구상주의적인
- resemble ⓥ ~와 유사하다   • facilitate ⓥ ~을 용이하게 하다
- uncertainty ⓝ 불확실성   • expressionist ⓝ 표현주의자
- novel ⓐ 새로운, 참신한   • a stylistic device 문체(文體)상의 기교 장치
- inharmonious ⓐ 조화롭지 않은   • thereby ⓐⓓ 그렇게 함으로써
- disquieting ⓐ 불안한, 불안하게 하는   • departure ⓝ 벗어남
- conventional ⓐ 전통적인, 관습적인
- appreciate ⓥ 제대로 인식하다, 감상하다
- fundamental ⓐ 핵심적인, 근본적인

주제(즉, 형상)와 스타일(즉, 배경)의 상대적 중요성에는 흥미로운 균형이
있다. (①) 고도로 구상주의적인 그림, 연극 또는 이야기에서는 초점이
일상생활과 유사한 주제에 있고, 배경 스타일의 역할은 심성 모형의 구성을
용이하게 하는 것이다. (②) 즐거움과 불확실성의 감정은 관객을 작품의
결말까지 함께 이끌고 간다. (③) 고도로 표현주의적인 작품에서는 새로운
스타일 장치가 주제와 조화롭지 않은 방식으로 작용하여, 그럼으로써 불안한
분위기를 조성한다. (④) 따라서 작품이 덜 '읽기 쉬운'(혹은 쉽게 해석되는)
상태일 때, 그것이 전통적인 방식에서 벗어났다는 것은 보는 사람이나 독자에게
작품의 전체 내용을 제대로 감상하기 위해 '미학적 태도'가 필요하다는 것을
상기시킨다. (⑤ 이러한 적극적인 관여는 미학적 처리와 작품 의미 성찰의
깊이에 대한 기반을 제공한다.) 일상생활의 '실용주의적 태도'와 '미학적 태도'
사이를 전환하는 능력은 균형 잡힌 삶에 핵심적이다.

| 문제 풀이 순서 | [정답률 23%]

1st 주어진 문장을 해석하고, 연결어, 지시어 등을 확인한다.

┌This active involvement┐provides a basis for depth of aesthetic
processing and reflection on the meaning of the work.
└이러한 적극적인 관여는 미학적 처리와 작품 의미 성찰의 깊이에 대한 기반을 제공한다.

➡ This active involvement(이러한 적극적 관여)가 언급됐다. **단서**
▶ 주어진 문장 앞: '적극적 관여'라고 할 만한 상태나 행위가 제시될 것임 **발상**

2nd 각 선택지의 앞뒤 흐름이 매끄러운지 확인한다.

- ①의 앞 문장과 뒤 문장

┌ 앞 문장: 주제(즉, 형상)와 스타일(즉, 배경)의 상대적 중요성에는 흥미로운
│ 균형이 있다.
│ 뒤 문장: 고도로 구상주의적인 그림, 연극 또는 이야기에서는 초점이
│ 일상생활과 유사한 주제에 있고, 배경 스타일의 역할은 심성 모형의 구성을
└ 용이하게 하는 것이다.

➡ 앞 문장에서는 글의 핵심적인 내용이 되는 예술작품에서의 주제(형상)와
스타일(배경)의 중요성에 균형이 있다고 했다. 즉 이 글을 관통하는 두 가지
핵심어는 주제와 스타일이다.
뒤 문장에서는 구상주의적인 예술에서 주제와 스타일이 각각 어떠한지 설명하므로
자연스럽게 연결된다.
▶ 주어진 문장이 ①에 들어갈 수 없음

- ②의 앞 문장과 뒤 문장

┌ 앞 문장: ①의 뒤 문장과 같음

│ 뒤 문장: 즐거움과 불확실성의 감정은 관객을 작품의 결말까지 함께 이끌고
└ 간다.

➡ 앞의 내용에서 구상주의적 예술작품에서는 일상생활과 유사한 주제와 심성 모형이
구성을 용이하게 한다는 말이 언급되었고, 그래서 이런 주제와 배경이 관객들에게
어떤 영향을 주는지를 설명하고 있다.
▶ 주어진 문장이 ②에 들어갈 수 없음

- ③의 앞 문장과 뒤 문장

앞 문장: ②의 뒤 문장과 같음

뒤 문장: 고도로 표현주의적인 작품에서는 새로운 스타일 장치가 주제와 조화롭지 않은 방식으로 작용하여, 그럼으로써 불안한 분위기를 조성한다.

➡ 앞 문장까지는 구성주의적 예술작품에서의 주제와 배경, 그리고 관객에게 주는 영향을 언급하였다. 뒤에 나오는 문장부터는 다른 예시를 들기 위해 구성주의의 대립 개념으로 사용된 표현주의 작품의 언급을 시작한다.

▶ 주어진 문장이 ③에 들어갈 수 없음

- ④의 앞 문장과 뒤 문장

앞 문장: ③의 뒤 문장과 같음

뒤 문장: 따라서(Thus) 작품이 덜 '읽기 쉬운(쉽게 해석되는)' 상태일 때, 그것이 전통적인 방식에서 벗어났다는 것은 보는 사람이나 독자에게 작품의 전체 내용을 제대로 감상하기 위해 '미학적 태도'가 필요하다는 것을 상기시킨다.

➡ 글의 서술 패턴을 일관적으로 유지하려면, 앞서 나온 구성주의의 서술 패턴이 그랬던 것처럼, 표현주의의 특징과 그 특징이 감상자에게 미치는 영향이 나와야 한다.

예술작품이 읽기가 쉽지 않고 쉽게 해석되지 않는 상태일 때, 즉 표현주의 작품의 주제와 배경에 대한 언급이 ④의 앞 문장에서 먼저 제시되었다. 그렇다면 뒤 문장은 감상자에 대한 서술이 나와야 한다.

④ 뒤 문장에서 '따라서(Thus)'라고 하면서 관객이나 독자는 '미학적 태도'의 필요성을 상기시키게 된다는 내용이 제시되었다. 따라서 ④의 앞 문장과 뒤 문장은 먼저 제시된 서술 패턴을 일관성 있게 따르고 있다.

▶ 주어진 문장이 ④에 들어갈 수 없음

- ⑤의 앞 문장과 뒤 문장

앞 문장: ④의 뒤 문장과 같음

뒤 문장: 일상생활의 '실용주의적 태도'와 '미학적 태도' 사이를 전환하는 능력은 균형 잡힌 삶에 핵심적이다.

➡ 상대적으로 난해한 예술을 접할 때 미학적 태도가 필요하다는 말이 앞에서 나온 이후에, 미학적 태도에 구체적인 설명이 없이 실용주의적 태도와 미학적 태도 사이의 전환 능력이 균형잡힌 삶에 필요한 능력이라고 언급되어 있다.

주어진 문장의 '이러한 적극적인 관여'는 ⑤ 앞에서 나온 '미학적 태도를 상기시키는 것'을 지칭한다.

▶ 주어진 문장이 ⑤에 들어가야 함

3rd 글이 한눈에 들어오도록 정리하여 정답을 확인한다.

예술에서 주제(즉, 형상)와 스타일(즉, 배경)의 상대적 중요성에는 흥미로운 균형이 있다.

(①) 구상주의적(= 사실 표현) 작품에서는 초점이 일상생활과 유사한 주제에 있고, 배경 스타일의 역할은 심성 모형(감정)의 구성을 용이하게 하는 것이다.

(②) 즐거움과 불확실성의 감정은 관객을 작품의 결말까지 함께 이끌고 간다.

(③) 표현주의적인 작품에서는 새로운 스타일 장치가 주제와 조화롭지 않은 방식으로 작용하여, 그럼으로써 불안한 분위기를 조성한다.

(④) 따라서 작품이 덜 '읽기 쉬운' 상태일 때(= 즉, 표현주의 예술처럼 난해할 때), 작품이 전통적인 방식에서 벗어났다는 것은 감상자에게 '미학적 태도'가 필요하다는 것을 상기시킨다.

(⑤ 이러한 (감상자의) 적극적인 관여는 미학적 처리와 작품 의미 성찰의 깊이에 대한 기반을 제공한다.)

일상생활의 '실용주의적 태도'와 '미학적 태도' 사이를 전환하는 능력은 균형 잡힌 삶에 핵심적이다.

N 08 정답 ⑤ *높이 친 공을 잡는 데에 쓰이는 소뇌의 기능

글의 흐름으로 보아, 주어진 문장이 들어가기에 가장 가장 적절한 곳을 고르시오.

단서 1 소뇌를 사용할 수 있는 다른 방법을 '또한(also)'으로 언급했기에 앞에서 소뇌를 사용하는 방법이 나왔을 것임

We are also able to use the cerebellum / to anticipate what our actions would be / even if we don't actually take them. //

우리는 또한 소뇌를 사용할 수 있는데 / 우리의 행동들이 무엇일지 예측하는 데에 / 설령 우리가 그것들을 실제로 하지 않아도 그러하다 //

One way to catch a fly ball / is to solve all the differential equations / governing the ball's trajectory as well as your own movements / and at the same time reposition your body based on those solutions. // (병렬 구조)

높이 친 공을 잡는 한 가지 방법은 / 모든 미분 방정식을 풀고 / 여러분 자신의 움직임뿐만 아니라 그 공의 궤적을 지배하는 / 동시에 그 해법에 따라 여러분의 몸의 위치를 움직이는 것이다 //

(①) Unfortunately, you don't have a differential equation-solving device in your brain, / so instead you solve a simpler problem: / how to place the glove most effectively between the ball and your body. //

불행히도, 여러분은 여러분의 뇌에 미분 방정식을 푸는 장치가 없어서 / 대신 여러분은 더 간단한 문제를 푼다 / (어떻게 그 공과 여러분의 몸 사이에 글러브를 가장 효과적으로 위치시킬지) //

(②) The cerebellum assumes / that your hand and the ball should appear / in similar relative positions for each catch. // (목적어절을 이끄는 접속사)

소뇌는 가정한다 / 여러분의 손과 그 공이 나타나야 한다고 / 각 포구(捕球)마다 비슷한 상대적 위치에 //

(③) So, if the ball is dropping too fast / and your hand appears to be going too slowly, / it will direct your hand to move more quickly / to match the familiar relative position. // ((= the cerebellum))

그래서, 공이 너무 빠르게 떨어지고 있고 / 여러분의 손이 너무 느리게 움직이고 있는 것처럼 보이면 / 그것은 여러분의 손을 더 빠르게 움직이도록 지시할 것이다 / 익숙한 상대적 위치에 맞추기 위해 //

단서 2 소뇌를 사용하는 간단한 행동들에 대한 내용

(④) These simple actions by the cerebellum / to map sensory inputs onto muscle movements / enable us to catch the ball / without solving any differential equations. // (형용사적 용법; 5형식 동사+목적어+목적격 보어(to부정사))

소뇌에 의한 이러한 간단한 행동들은 / 감각 입력을 근육 움직임에 연결시키는 / 우리가 공을 잡을 수 있게 한다 / 그 어떤 미분 방정식도 풀지 않고 //

(⑤) Your cerebellum might tell you / that you could catch the ball but you're likely to crash into another player, / so maybe you should not take this action. // (목적어절을 이끄는 접속사)

단서 3 소뇌가 일어나지 않은 일에 대해서 행동과 그 결과를 예측할 수 있다는 예시임

여러분의 소뇌는 알려줄 수도 있고 / 여러분이 공을 잡을 수는 있지만 또 다른 선수와 충돌할 가능성이 있다는 것을 / 그러면 여러분은 이 행동을 하지 않는 편이 좋을지도 모른다 //

- anticipate ⓥ 기대하다, 예상하다
- govern ⓥ 지배하다
- reposition ⓥ ~의 위치를 바꾸다
- device ⓝ 장치
- place ⓥ 두다
- assume ⓥ 가정하다
- relative ⓐ 상대적인
- direct ⓥ 지시하다
- sensory ⓐ 감각의
- muscle ⓝ 근육

높이 친 공을 잡는 한 가지 방법은 여러분 자신의 움직임뿐만 아니라 그 공의 궤적을 지배하는 모든 미분 방정식을 풀고, 동시에 그 해법에 따라 여러분의 몸의 위치를 움직이는 것이다. (①) 불행히도, 여러분은 여러분의 뇌에 미분 방정식을 푸는 장치가 없어서, 대신 여러분은 더 간단한 문제(어떻게 그 공과 여러분의 몸 사이에 글러브를 가장 효과적으로 위치시킬지)를 푼다. (②) 소뇌는 여러분의 손과 그 공이 각 포구(捕球)마다 비슷한 상대적 위치에 나타나야 한다고 가정한다. (③) 그래서, 공이 너무 빠르게 떨어지고 있고 여러분의 손이 너무 느리게 움직이고 있는 것처럼 보이면, 그것은 여러분의 손을 더 빠르게 움직여 익숙한 상대적 위치에 맞추도록 지시할 것이다. (④)

감각 입력을 근육 움직임에 연결시키는 소뇌에 의한 이러한 간단한 행동들은 우리가 그 어떤 미분 방정식도 풀지 않고 공을 잡을 수 있게 한다. (⑤ 우리는 또한 우리의 행동들이 무엇일지 예측하는 데에 소뇌를 사용할 수 있는데 설령 우리가 그것들을 실제로 하지 않아도 그러하다.) 여러분의 소뇌는 여러분이 공을 잡을 수는 있지만 또 다른 선수와 충돌할 가능성이 있다는 것을 알려줄 수도 있고, 그러면 여러분은 이 행동을 하지 않는 편이 좋을지도 모른다.

| 문제 풀이 순서 | [정답률 53%]

1st 주어진 문장을 해석하고, 연결어, 지시어 등을 확인한다.

We are also able to use the cerebellum / to anticipate what our actions would be / even if we don't actually take them. //
우리는 <u>또한</u> 소뇌를 사용할 수 있는데 / 우리의 행동들이 무엇일지 예측하는 데에 / 설령 우리가 그것들을 실제로 하지 않아도 그러하다 //

➡ 소뇌를 사용하는 다른 방법을 '또한(also)'으로 언급하고 있기 때문에, 주어진 문장 앞에서는 소뇌를 사용하는 어떠한 방법이 소개되었을 것이다. (단서)
▶ 주어진 문장 앞: 소뇌를 사용하는 어떤 방법이 소개되었을 것임
▶ 주어진 문장 뒤: 실제로 행동을 하지 않아도 행동이 무엇일지 예측하는 것의 예시가 나올 것임 (발상)

2nd 각 선택지의 앞뒤 흐름이 매끄러운지 확인한다.

- ①의 앞 문장과 뒤 문장
앞 문장: 높이 친 공을 잡는 한 가지 방법은 복잡한 모든 미분 방정식을 풀고 몸을 움직이는 것이다.
뒤 문장: 뇌에는 미분 방정식을 푸는 장치는 없지만 글러브를 공과 몸사이에 가장 효과적으로 위치시키는 방법을 생각할 수는 있다.

➡ 앞 문장에서는 높이 공을 잡는 한가지 방법으로 복잡한 수학적 계산을 하는 방법을 소개하면서, 뒤 문장에서는 이러한 방법이 불가능하지만 우리 뇌로 글러브를 공과 몸 사이에 가장 효과적으로 위치시키는 방법은 생각해낼 수 있다고 하며 자연스럽게 연결된다.
▶ 주어진 문장이 ①에 들어갈 수 없음

- ②의 앞 문장과 뒤 문장
앞 문장: ①의 뒤 문장과 같음
뒤 문장: 소뇌는 여러분의 손과 그 공이 각 포구(捕球)마다 비슷한 상대적 위치에 나타나야 한다고 가정한다.

➡ 앞의 내용에서 뇌는 글러브를 공과 몸 사이에 가장 효과적으로 위치시키는 문제는 해결할 수 있다고 했으며, 뒤 문장에서는 어떤 식으로 위치시키는지에 대한 설명이 이어지고 있다.
▶ 주어진 문장이 ②에 들어갈 수 없음

- ③의 앞 문장과 뒤 문장
앞 문장: ②의 뒤 문장과 같음
뒤 문장: 그래서(So), 공이 너무 빠르게 떨어지고 있고 여러분의 손이 너무 느리게 움직이고 있는 것처럼 보이면, 그것은 여러분의 손을 더 빠르게 움직여 익숙한 상대적 위치에 맞추도록 지시할 것이다.

➡ 앞에서는 소뇌가 손과 공이 각 포구마다 비슷한 상대적 위치에 있어야 한다고 가정한다고 했고, 뒤에서는 공과 손의 상대적 위치에 따라 손의 움직임 속도를 변화시킨다는 내용이 온다.
따라서 상반되는 내용의 두 문장은 '그래서(So)'로 자연스럽게 연결된다.
▶ 주어진 문장이 ③에 들어갈 수 없음

- ④의 앞 문장과 뒤 문장
앞 문장: ③의 뒤 문장과 같음
뒤 문장: 감각 입력을 근육 움직임에 연결시키는 소뇌에 의한 이러한 간단한 행동들은 우리가 그 어떤 미분 방정식도 풀지 않고 공을 잡을 수 있게 한다.

➡ 앞 문장에서 소뇌는 공과 손의 상대적 위치를 맞추도록 한다고 했고, 뒤 문장에서는 이에 대한 설명을 하고 있다. (감각을 근육 움직임에 연결시켜서 미분 방정식을 풀지 않고도 공을 잡을 수 있게 해줌) 따라서 두 문장은 자연스럽게 연결된다.
▶ 주어진 문장이 ④에 들어갈 수 없음

- ⑤의 앞 문장과 뒤 문장
앞 문장: ④의 뒤 문장과 같음
뒤 문장: 여러분의 소뇌는 여러분이 공을 잡을 수는 있지만 또 다른 선수와 충돌할 가능성이 있다는 것을 알려줄 수도 있고, 그러면 여러분은 이 행동을 하지 않는 편이 좋을지도 모른다.

➡ 앞 문장까지는 감각 입력과 근육 움직임에 연결하는 소뇌가 공과 손의 상대적 위치가 맞도록 손의 움직임을 조정할 수 있다는 내용이 나온다. 하지만 뒤에서는 상대적 위치를 맞추는 것과는 다른 내용의 사례가 나온다.
주어진 문장에서 소뇌로 실제 행동을 하지 않더라도 우리 행동을 예측할 수 있다는 또 다른 기능을 소개하고 있으므로 주어진 문장은 ⑤에 들어가야 한다.
▶ 주어진 문장이 ⑤에 들어가야 함

3rd 글이 한눈에 들어오도록 정리하여 정답을 확인한다.

공을 잡는 하나의 방법은 궤적에 대한 방정식을 푼 후 몸을 움직이는 것이다.
(①) 뇌는 이런 방정식을 못 푸는 대신 공과 몸 사이에 글러브를 어떻게 놓을지 생각한다.
(②) 소뇌는 손과 공이 비슷한 상대적 위치에 있어야 한다고 가정한다.
(③) 공이 너무 빠르고 손이 느리면 손을 더 빠르게 움직여 상대적 위치를 맞추려고 한다.
(④) 감각 입력을 근육 움직임에 연결시키는 소뇌는 이런 방식으로 공을 잡을 수 있게 한다.
(⑤ 또한, 소뇌는 행동을 실제로 하지 않더라도 우리 몸이 어떤 행동을 할지 예측할 수 있다.)
공을 잡을 수 있지만 충돌한다는 가능성이 있음을 알려줄 수 있고, 그럼 우리는 그 행동을 안하는 것이 낫다.

N 09 정답 ⑤ *친사회적 행동을 일으킬 수 있는 요소

> 글의 흐름으로 보아, 주어진 문장이 들어가기에 가장 적절한 곳을 고르시오.

Following this pathway, / we act altruistically / when we feel empathy for a person / and can truly imagine a situation from their perspective. // 단서1 타인에 공감할 수 있고, 그들의 관점에서 상황을 볼 수 있을 때 이타적으로 행동함
이 경로를 따라서 / 우리는 이타적으로 행동한다 / 어떤 사람에 대한 공감을 느끼고 / 진정으로 그 관점에서부터 상황을 상상할 수 있을 때 //

Prosocial behavior / — that is, behavior that is intended to help another person — / can be motivated by two different pathways, / according to Daniel Batson at the University of Kansas. //
친사회적 행동 / 다시 말해, 다른 사람을 돕기 위해 의도된 행동은 / 두 가지 다른 경로로 동기 부여될 수 있다 / University of Kansas의 Daniel Batson에 따르면 //

(①) One pathway, the egoistic pathway, is largely self-focused: / we provide help / if the rewards to us outweigh the costs. //
첫 번째 경로인 자기중심적 경로는 주로 자신에게 초점이 맞추어져 있다 / 우리는 도움을 제공한다 / 우리에 대한 보상이 비용보다 더 중요하다면 //

동명사 주어   4형식 동사+간접목적어+직접목적어
(②) This pathway is the one that is operating / if we hand a homeless person a dollar / to make ourselves feel better. //
주격 관계대명사   부사적 용법(목적)
이 경로는 작동하는 것이다 / 만일 우리가 노숙자에게 1달러를 건넬 때 / 우리 자신들을 더 기분 좋게 만들기 위해서 //

(③) Doing so costs us very little / — only a dollar — / and the reward of doing so / — avoiding the guilt / we'd feel from simply walking by — / is greater. //
관계대명사가 생략된 관계절(guilt 수식)
그렇게 하는 것은 우리에게 거의 비용이 들게 하지 않으며 / 오로지 1달러만 / 그렇게 하는 것의 보상 / 죄책감을 피하는 것은 / 단지 그저 지나쳐가는 것에서부터 우리가 느끼게 될 / 더 크다 //

(④) But according to Bat-son's hypothesis, / there is another pathway, / which is other-focused / — it's motivated by a genuine desire / to help the other person, / even if we incur a cost for doing so. // **단서 2** 타자에게 초점이 맞춰져 있는 다른 경로가 있음

계속적 용법의 관계대명사

하지만 Batson의 가설에 따르면 / 또 다른 경로가 있으며 / 그것은 타자에게 초점이 맞추어져 있다 / 그것은 진실된 욕구에 의해서 동기 부여된다 / 다른 사람을 도와주려는 / 비록 그렇게 하는 것 때문에 우리가 비용을 치를지라도 //

(⑤) This ability to see the world from someone else's perspective / can lead us to help, / even if there are considerable costs. //

형용사적 용법(this ability 수식)
5형식 동사+목적어+목적격 보어

그 밖의 다른 누군가의 관점으로부터 세상을 볼 수 있는 이 능력은 / 우리로 하여금 돕도록 이끌 수 있다 / 비록 상당한 비용이 있을지라도 //

- altruistically [ad] 이타적으로   • empathy [n] 공감
- prosocial [a] 친사회적인   • egoistic [a] 자기 중심적인
- outweigh [v] ~보다 더 크다   • genuine [a] 진실된
- incur [v] 초래하다, 발생시키다   • considerable [a] 상당한

University of Kansas의 Daniel Batson에 따르면, 친사회적 행동 — 다시 말해, 다른 사람을 돕기 위해 의도된 행동 — 은 두 가지 다른 경로로 동기 부여될 수 있다. (①) 첫 번째 경로인 자기중심적 경로는 주로 자신에게 초점이 맞추어져 있다. 우리에 대한 보상이 비용보다 더 중요하다면 우리는 도움을 제공한다. (②) 이 경로는 만일 우리가 우리 자신들을 더 기분 좋게 만들기 위해서 노숙자에게 1달러를 건넬 때 작동하는 것이다. (③) 그렇게 하는 것은 우리에게 거의 비용이 들게 하지 않으며 — 오직 1달러만 — 그렇게 하는 것의 보상 — 단지 그저 지나쳐가는 것에서부터 우리가 느끼게 될 죄책감을 피하는 것 — 은 더 크다. (④) 하지만 Batson의 가설에 따르면, 또 다른 경로가 있으며, 그것은 타자에게 초점이 맞추어져 있다 — 그것은 비록 그렇게 하는 것 때문에 우리가 비용을 치를지라도, 다른 사람을 도와주려는 진실된 욕구에 의해서 동기 부여된다. (⑤ 이 경로를 따라서, 우리는 어떤 사람에 대한 공감을 느끼고 진정으로 그 관점에서부터 상황을 상상할 수 있을 때 이타적으로 행동한다.) 그 밖의 다른 누군가의 관점으로부터 세상을 볼 수 있는 이 능력은 비록 상당한 비용이 있을지라도 우리로 하여금 돕도록 이끌 수 있다.

| 문제 풀이 순서 | [정답률 58%]

1st 주어진 문장을 해석하고, 연결어, 지시어 등을 확인한다.

Following this pathway, / we act altruistically / when we feel empathy for a person / and can truly imagine a situation / from their perspective. //

이 경로를 따라서 / 우리는 이타적으로 행동한다 / 어떤 사람에 대한 공감을 느끼고 / 진정으로 상황을 상상할 수 있을 때 / 그 관점에서부터 //

⇒ '이 경로를 따라서(Following this pathway)' 타인에 공감을 느끼고 그들의 관점에서 상황을 상상할 수 있을 때 이타적으로 행동한다고 했다. **단서**
   ▶ **주어진 문장 앞**: 이타적으로 행동하게 되는 '이 경로'가 소개될 것임
   ▶ **주어진 문장 뒤**: 이타적인 행동을 하는 내용이 이어지게 될 것임 **발상**

2nd 각 선택지의 앞뒤 흐름이 매끄러운지 확인한다.

- ①의 앞 문장과 뒤 문장

앞 문장: University of Kansas의 Daniel Batson에 따르면, 친사회적 행동 — 다시 말해, 다른 사람을 돕기 위해 의도된 행동 — 은 두 가지 다른 경로로 동기 부여될 수 있다.
뒤 문장: 첫 번째 경로인 자기중심적 경로는 주로 자신에게 초점이 맞추어져 있다. 우리에 대한 보상이 비용보다 더 중요하다면 우리는 도움을 제공한다.

⇒ 친사회적 행동은 두 가지 경로로 동기부여 될 수 있음을 앞 문장에 소개하고, 뒤 문장에 바로 자신에게 주어질 보상 때문에 도움을 제공한다는 첫 번째 경로를 소개하고 있다. 따라서 두 문장은 자연스럽게 이어진다.
   ▶ 주어진 문장이 ①에 들어갈 수 없음

- ②의 앞 문장과 뒤 문장

앞 문장: ①의 뒤 문장과 같음
뒤 문장: 이 경로(This pathway)는 만일 우리가 우리 자신들을 더 기분 좋게 만들기 위해서 노숙자에게 1달러를 건넬 때 작동하는 것이다.

⇒ 자기 자신의 이익을 위해 타인을 돕는 행동을 한다는 앞 문장에 이어 '이 경로(This pathway)'라고 하며, 자기 기분을 좋게 하기 위해 노숙자에게 돈을 건넨다는 예시가 담긴 뒤 문장은 자연스럽게 연결된다.
   ▶ 주어진 문장이 ②에 들어갈 수 없음

- ③의 앞 문장과 뒤 문장

앞 문장: ②의 뒤 문장과 같음
뒤 문장: 그렇게 하는 것(Doing so)은 우리에게 거의 비용이 들게 하지 않으며 — 오로지 1달러만 — 그렇게 하는 것의 보상 — 단지 그저 지나쳐가는 것에서부터 우리가 느끼게 될 죄책감을 피하는 것 — 은 더 크다.

⇒ 앞 문장에서는 자기 기분을 위해 노숙자에게 돈을 건네는 예시가 소개되었고, 뒤 문장에는 앞 문장의 예시가 '그렇게 하는 것'으로 지칭되어 노숙자를 돕는 것의 자기중심적인 동기에 대한 설명이 있다. 따라서 두 문장은 자연스럽게 연결된다.
   ▶ 주어진 문장이 ③에 들어갈 수 없음

- ④의 앞 문장과 뒤 문장

앞 문장: ③의 뒤 문장과 같음
뒤 문장: 하지만(But) Batson의 가설에 따르면, 또 다른 경로가 있으며, 그것은 타자에게 초점이 맞추어져 있다 — 그것은 비록 그렇게 하는 것 때문에 우리가 비용을 치를지라도, 다른 사람을 도와주려는 진실된 욕구에 의해서 동기 부여된다.

⇒ 앞 문장까지는 자기중심적인 동기로 친사회적인 행동을 하게 된다는 첫 번째 경로가 소개되고 있다. 뒤 문장에서는 반대로 타자에게 초점이 맞춰진 동기가 작용되는 또 다른 경로가 소개되었으며 But으로 대조를 이루고 있다.
   ▶ 주어진 문장이 ④에 들어갈 수 없음

⑤의 앞 문장과 뒤 문장

앞 문장: ④의 뒤 문장과 같음
뒤 문장: 그 밖의 다른 누군가의 관점으로부터 세상을 볼 수 있는 이 능력(This ability)은 비록 상당한 비용이 있을지라도 우리로 하여금 돕도록 이끌 수 있다.

⇒ 앞 문장에서는 타자에게 초점이 맞춰진 동기로 친사회적인 행동을 하는 또 다른 경로가 소개되어 있으며, 뒤 문장에는 타인의 관점으로부터 세상을 바라보는 '이 능력'이 타인을 돕는 행동으로 이어질 수 있다는 내용이다.
주어진 문장은 타인에게 공감하고 그들의 입장에서 상황을 상상할 수 있을 때 이타적으로 행동한다는 내용이고, 뒤 문장의 '이 능력(This ability)'이 '그들의 입장에서 상황을 상상할 수 있는 능력'이 되므로 그 전에 들어가야 한다.
   ▶ 주어진 문장이 ⑤에 들어가야 함

3rd 글이 한눈에 들어오도록 정리하여 정답을 확인한다.

친사회적인 행동은 두가지 방식으로 일어날 수 있다.
(①) 첫 번째 방식은 보상이 비용보다 더 중요할 때 도움을 제공하는 자기중심적 방식이다.
(②) 이 방식은 기분을 더 좋게 만들기 위해 노숙자에게 돈을 줄 때 작동한다.
(③) 이렇게 하는 것은 비용(1달러)은 적으면서 보상(죄책감을 피함)은 더 크다.
(④) 타인을 돕고자 하는 진정한 욕구에 의해서 동기부여되는 다른 방식이 있다.
(⑤ 이 방식을 따라 우리는 타인에게 공감을 할 수 있고 그의 관점에서 상황을 볼 수 있을 때 이타적으로 행동한다.)
다른 누군가의 관점으로부터 세상을 볼 수 있는 이 능력은 비록 상당한 비용이 있을지라도 우리로 하여금 돕도록 이끌 수 있다.

N 10 정답 ⑤ *외재적 동기의 한계 및 내재적 동기의 필요성

글의 흐름으로 보아, 주어진 문장이 들어가기에 가장 적절한 곳을 고르시오.

Without the anchor of intrinsic motivation however, / even a small bump in the road may reset you back; / we may go back to eating meat in February / when the social support has disappeared. // **단서 1** 내재적 동기 없이는 친구들의 지지가 사라지면 작은 걸림돌에도 금세 채식주의를 포기하게 될 수도 있음
하지만 내재적 동기부여라는 닻이 없는 상태에서는 / 심지어 도로에 솟아오른 작은 턱조차도 당신을 다시 원래대로 돌아가게 할지 모르고 / 우리는 2월에는 고기를 먹는 것으로 되돌아갈지도 모른다 / 사회적 지지가 사라진 //

Our behaviour can be modified externally / without there being <동명사> strong personal motivation. //
우리의 행동은 외부적으로 수정될 수 있다 / 강력한 개인적 동기가 없는 상태에서 //

Everything from our supermarket shopping and online browsing choices / are examples of how our actions are shaped <의문사+주어+동사> / without our conscious choice or motivation. //
우리의 슈퍼마켓 쇼핑에서의 모든 것과 온라인에서의 훑어보기 선택지는 / 우리의 행동이 어떻게 형성되는지에 대한 예시이다 / 우리의 의식적인 선택이나 동기 없이도 //

(①) However, / when processes police us / but fail to truly <동사> influence us, / we do not continue with the behaviours / after the processes are removed. //
그러나 / 과정들이 우리를 통제하지만 / 진정으로 우리에게 영향을 미치지 못할 때 / 우리는 그 행동을 계속하지 않는다 / 그 과정들이 제거된 후에 //

(②) This is passive engagement rather than ownership. //
이는 소유라기보다는 수동적 참여이다 //
<전치사+관계대명사>
(③) A better way / in which we can be externally supported to take action / is by having friends who encourage us. //
더 좋은 방법은 / 우리가 행동을 하도록 외부적으로 지지받을 수 있는 / 우리를 격려해주는 친구를 갖는 것이다 //

(④) You may not be sold on going vegan, / but yet give veganism a try at the start of the year / because some of your friends suggest / you do it together. // **단서 2** 해의 시작에 친구들의 권유로 채식주의를 시도해볼 수 있음
당신은 완전한 채식 생활을 하는 것에 대해 설득되지 않을지도 모르지만 / 그 해의 시작에 완전한 채식 생활을 시도해 볼 것이다 / 당신의 친구들 중 몇 명이 제안하기 때문에 / 당신이 그것을 함께 해야 한다고 //
<5형식 동사+목적어+목적격 보어(동사원형)>
(⑤) Resonance helps us connect to / our internal motivation to change / rather than being 'pushed' from the outside, /
울림은 연결되도록 도와주며 / 변화하려는 우리의 내적 동기와 / 우리가 외부에서 '강요받는' 것보다는 //
<5형식 동사+목적어+목적격 보어(동사원형)>
and in turn helps us form a habit, / where our self-concept makes a shift / from 'someone who does not like cycling' to 'someone who cycles'. //
결과적으로 습관을 형성하도록 도와주며 / 그것에서 우리의 자아 개념은 이동하게 된다 / '자전거 타기를 좋아하지 않는 누군가'에서부터 '자전거를 타는 누군가'로 //

• intrinsic ⓐ 내재적인   • modify ⓥ 수정하다
• externally ⓐⓓ 외부적으로   • browse ⓥ 훑어보다
• police ⓥ 통제하다   • influence ⓥ 영향을 미치다
• remove ⓥ 지우다   • passive ⓐ 수동적인
• engagement ⓝ 참여   • self-concept ⓝ 자아 개념

우리의 행동은 강력한 개인적 동기가 없는 상태에서 외부적으로 수정될 수 있다. 우리의 슈퍼마켓 쇼핑에서의 모든 것과 온라인에서의 훑어보기 선택지는 우리의 의식적인 선택이나 동기 없이도 우리의 행동이 어떻게 형성되는지에 대한 예시이다. (①) 그러나 과정들이 우리를 통제하지만 진정으로 우리에게 영향을 미치지 못할 때, 그 과정들이 제거된 후에 우리는 그 행동을 계속하지 않는다. (②) 이는 소유라기보다는 수동적 참여이다. (③) 우리가 행동을

하도록 외부적으로 지지받을 수 있는 더 좋은 방법은 우리를 격려해주는 친구를 갖는 것이다. (④) 당신은 완전한 채식 생활을 하는 것에 대해 설득되지 않을지도 모르지만, 당신의 친구들 중 몇 명이 당신이 그것을 함께 해야 한다고 제안하기 때문에 그 해의 시작에 완전한 채식 생활을 시도해 볼 것이다. (⑤ 하지만 내재적 동기부여라는 닻이 없는 상태에서는 심지어 도로에 솟아오른 작은 턱조차도 당신을 다시 원래대로 돌아가게 할지 모르고, 우리는 사회적 지지가 사라진 2월에는 고기를 먹는 것으로 되돌아갈지도 모른다.) 울림은 우리가 외부에서 '강요받는' 것보다는 변화하려는 우리의 내적 동기와 연결되도록 도와주며, 결과적으로 습관을 형성하도록 도와주며, 그것에서 우리의 자아 개념은 '자전거 타기를 좋아하지 않는 누군가'에서부터 '자전거를 타는 누군가'로 이동하게 된다.

| **문제 풀이 순서** | [정답률 37%]

1st 주어진 문장을 해석하고, 연결어, 지시어 등을 확인한다.

Without the anchor of intrinsic motivation [however], / even a small bump in the road may reset you back; / we may go back to eating meat in February / when the social support has disappeared. //
[하지만] 내재적 동기부여라는 닻이 없는 상태에서는 / 심지어 도로에 솟아오른 작은 턱조차도 당신을 다시 원래대로 돌아가게 할지 모르고 / 우리는 2월에는 고기를 먹는 것으로 되돌아갈지도 모른다 / 사회적 지지가 사라진 //

➡ '하지만(however)'이라고 했으므로 주어진 문장 앞에서 2월 전에 고기를 먹지 않는다고 다짐했다는 내용이 나와야 할 것이다. **단서**
▶ **주어진 문장 앞:** 내재적 동기가 없는 상태와 2월 전에 고기를 먹지 않는다고 다짐했다는 내용이 나와야 할 것임
▶ **주어진 문장 뒤:** 닻으로 작용할 수 있는 내재적 동기에 대한 내용이 나올 것임 **발상**

2nd 각 선택지의 앞뒤 흐름이 매끄러운지 확인한다.

- ①의 앞 문장과 뒤 문장
앞 문장: 우리의 행동은 강력한 개인적 동기가 없는 상태에서 외부적으로 수정될 수 있다. 우리의 슈퍼마켓 쇼핑에서의 모든 것과 온라인에서의 훑어보기 선택지는 우리의 의식적인 선택이나 동기 없이도 우리의 행동이 어떻게 형성되는지에 대한 예시이다.
뒤 문장: [그러나(However)] 과정들이 우리를 통제하지만 진정으로 우리에게 영향을 미치지 못할 때, 그 과정들이 제거된 후에 우리는 그 행동을 계속하지 않는다.

➡ 앞 문장은 개인적 동기가 없는 상태에서 외부적으로 행동이 수정될 수 있다는 내용과 예시이다. 뒤 문장에서는 외부적인 과정이 우리에게 진정한 영향을 미치지 못할 때(내재화되지 못할 때) 과정이 없어지면 행동도 멈춘다는 내용이다. 따라서 두 문장은 However로 자연스럽게 연결된다.
▶ 주어진 문장이 ①에 들어갈 수 없음

- ②의 앞 문장과 뒤 문장
앞 문장: ①의 뒤 문장과 같음
뒤 문장: [이는(This)] 소유라기보다는 수동적 참여이다.

➡ 앞의 내용은 내재화되지 못한 외부적인 과정이 없어지면 그에 따른 행동도 멈춘다는 내용이고, 이는 뒤 문장에서 소유라기보다 수동적 참여라는 내용과 일맥상통한다.
▶ 주어진 문장이 ②에 들어갈 수 없음

- ③의 앞 문장과 뒤 문장
앞 문장: ②의 뒤 문장과 같음
뒤 문장: 우리가 행동을 하도록 외부적으로 지지받을 수 있는 더 좋은 방법은 우리를 격려해주는 친구를 갖는 것이다.

➡ 앞 부분에서는 외부적인 과정이 진정한 영향을 미치지 않았다면 행동에 지속적으로 영향을 미칠 수 없다는 내용이고, 뒤 문장은 외부적으로 지지받을 수 있는 더 좋은 방법을 설명하고 있다. 따라서 두 문장은 자연스럽게 연결된다.
▶ 주어진 문장이 ③에 들어갈 수 없음

- **④의 앞 문장과 뒤 문장**

앞 문장: ③의 뒤 문장과 같음

뒤 문장: 당신은 완전한 채식 생활을 하는 것에 대해 설득되지 않을지도 모르지만, 당신의 친구들 중 몇 명이 당신이 그것을 함께 해야 한다고 제안하기 때문에 그 해의 시작에 완전한 채식 생활을 시도해 볼 것이다.

⇒ 앞 문장에서는 친구를 갖는 것이 외부적으로 지지받을 수 있는 더 좋은 방법으로 소개되었다. 뒤 문장은 채식 생활에 설득되지 않더라도 친구들의 제안으로 해의 시작에 채식 생활을 시도해볼 것이라는 내용이다. 친구의 설득이 행동에 영향을 미치는 방식의 예시가 뒤에 나와 있으므로 두 문장은 자연스럽게 연결된다.

▶ 주어진 문장이 ④에 들어갈 수 없음

- **⑤의 앞 문장과 뒤 문장**

앞 문장: ④의 뒤 문장과 같음

뒤 문장: 울림은 우리가 외부에서 '강요받는' 것보다는 변화하려는 우리의 내적 동기와 연결되도록 도와주며, 결과적으로 습관을 형성하도록 도와주며, 그것에서 우리의 자아 개념이 '자전거 타기를 좋아하지 않는 누군가'에서부터 '자전거를 타는 누군가'로 이동하게 된다.

⇒ 앞 부분은 채식주의에 대해 완전히 설득되지는 않더라도 친구들의 제안으로 시작했다는 예시이다. 뒤 문장에서는 울림이 내적 동기와 연결되고 습관을 형성할 수 있도록 도와준다는 내용이다.
주어진 문장은 내재적 동기 없이 친구들의 사회적 지원이 사라지면 채식주의를 포기하고 고기를 다시 먹게 될 것이라는 내용이므로 ⑤에 들어가야 한다.

▶ 주어진 문장이 ⑤에 들어가야 함

3rd 글이 한눈에 들어오도록 정리하여 정답을 확인한다.

우리 행동은 강한 개인적 동기 없이 외재적으로 수정될 수도 있다.
(①) 하지만, 과정이 우리에게 진정으로 영향을 미치지 않는 경우, 과정이 멈추면 행동도 멈춘다.
(②) 이것은 소유라기보다 수동적 참여이다.
(③) 외재적 지지의 더 좋은 방식은 친구를 갖는 것이다.
(④) 채식주의에 완전히 설득되지 않더라도 친구의 권유로 시작하게 될 수 있다.
(⑤ 하지만 내재적 동기 없이 사회적 지지가 멈추면 채식주 역시 지속되지 못한다.)
울림은 우리가 외부에서 '강요받는' 것보다는 변화하려는 우리의 내적 동기와 연결되도록 도와주며, 결과적으로 습관을 형성하도록 도와준다.

N 11 정답 ④ ＊윤리와 객관성: 편견과 공정성의 역할

글의 흐름으로 보아, 주어진 문장이 들어가기에 가장 적절한 곳을 고르시오.

단서 1 객관성의 규범은 편견이 '없을' 수 있다고 생각했기 때문에 만들어진 것이 아님

The norms of objectivity were constructed / not because their
앞에 목적어절 접속사 that 생략
creators thought / most humans could be 'empty' of bias. //
객관성의 규범은 만들어졌다 / 그것을 만든 사람들이 생각했기 때문이 아니라 / 대부분의 인간은 편견이 '없을' 수 있다고 //

Emotional response to the world / is an inherent part of ethics. //
세상에 대한 감정적 반응은 / 윤리학의 내재적인 부분이다 //

In ethics, / appeals to compassion and empathy / can and should
be part of rational arguments / about ethical decisions. //
윤리학에서 / 연민과 공감에 대한 호소는 / 합리적인 주장의 일부가 될 수 있고 또 그래야 한다 / 윤리적 결정에 대한 //

Moreover, / the best practices of objectivity often combine /
partiality and impartiality. //
더욱이 / 객관성의 가장 좋은 실천들은 종종 결합한다 / 편파성과 공정성을 //

(①) In a trial, / the partiality of the prosecutor and the defense
attorney (and the parties they represent) occurs / within a larger
앞에 목적격 관계대명사 생략
impartial context. //
재판에서 / 검사와 변호인(및 그들이 대리하는 당사자들)의 편파성은 발생한다 / 더 공정한 맥락 안에서 //

(②) A judge or jury puts partial arguments / to the test of
병렬 구조
objective evidence / and to the impartial rules of law. //
판사나 배심원은 편파적인 주장들을 맡긴다 / 객관적인 증거의 시험대와 / 공정한 법 원칙에 //

(③) Ideally, / what is fair and objective emerges / during a trial
문장의 주어   동사
/ where partialities make their case / and are judged by objective
관계부사
norms. //
이상적으로 / 공정하고 객관적인 것은 드러난다 / 재판 동안 / 편파성이 자신의 주장을 하고 / 객관적인 규범에 의해 판단되는 //
단서 2 편견을 갖고 있어서 이를 보완하기 위해 규범을 만든 것임
((④)) The reverse is true: / the norms were constructed / because
of an acute awareness of human bias, / because it is evident. //
그 반대가 사실인데 / 그 규범은 만들어졌다 / 인간의 편견에 대한 예리한 인식 때문에 / 즉 그것이 명백하게 나타나기 때문에 //

(⑤) Rather than conclude that objectivity is impossible /
because bias is universal, / scientists, journalists, and others
concluded the opposite: /
객관성이 불가능하다고 결론을 내리기보다는 / 편견이 보편적이기 때문에 / 과학자, 언론인 그리고 다른 이들은 반대의 결론을 내렸다 /

we biased humans need the discipline of objectivity / to reduce
부사적 용법(목적)
the ineliminable presence of bias. //
즉 우리 편향된 인간은 객관성의 규율을 필요로 한다는 것이다 / 제거할 수 없는 편견의 존재를 줄이기 위해 //

- -
- norm ⓝ 규범   - bias ⓝ 편견   - inherent ⓐ 내재하는
- ethics ⓝ 윤리학   - empathy ⓝ 공감   - partiality ⓝ 편애
- impartiality ⓝ 불편부당, 공명정대   - trial ⓝ 재판
- defense attorney 피고측 변호사   - jury ⓝ 배심원단
- ideally ⓐⓓ 이상적으로   - acute ⓐ 예민한, 예리한
- discipline ⓝ 규율   - ineliminable ⓐ 제거할 수 없는

세상에 대한 감정적 반응은 윤리학의 내재적인 부분이다. 윤리학에서 연민과 공감에 대한 호소는 윤리적 결정에 대한 합리적인 주장의 일부가 될 수 있고 또 그래야 한다. 더욱이 객관성의 가장 좋은 실천들은 종종 편파성과 공정성을 결합한다. (①) 재판에서 검사와 변호인(및 그들이 대리하는 당사자들)의 편파성은 더 큰 공정한 맥락 안에서 발생한다. (②) 판사나 배심원은 편파적인 주장들을 객관적인 증거의 시험대와 공정한 법 원칙에 맡긴다. (③) 이상적으로, 공정하고 객관적인 것은 편파성이 자신의 주장을 하고 객관적인 규범에 의해 판단되는 재판 동안 드러난다. (④ 객관적인 규범은 그것을 만든 사람들이 대부분의 인간은 편견이 '없을' 수 있다고 생각했기 때문에 만들어진 것이 아니다.) 그 반대가 사실인데, 그 규범은 인간의 편견에 대한 예리한 인식 때문에, 즉 그것이 명백하게 나타나기 때문에 만들어졌다. (⑤) 편견이 보편적이기 때문에 객관성이 불가능하다고 결론을 내리기보다는 과학자, 언론인 그리고 다른 이들은 반대의 결론을 내렸다. 즉 우리 편향된 인간은 제거할 수 없는 편견의 존재를 줄이기 위해 객관성의 규율을 필요로 한다는 것이다.

| 문제 풀이 순서 | [정답률 40%]

1st 주어진 문장을 해석하고, 연결어, 지시어 등을 확인한다.

The norms of objectivity were constructed not because their
creators thought most humans could be 'empty' of bias. //
객관성의 규범은 그것을 만든 사람들이 대부분의 인간은 편견이 '없을' 수 있다고 생각했기 때문에 만들어진 것이 아니다.

⇒ 객관성의 규범은 편견이 '없을' 수 있다고 생각했기 때문에 만들어진 것이 아니다. **단서 1**
▶ 주어진 문장 뒤: 객관성의 규범이 만들어진 실제 이유에 대한 설명이 이어질 것이다.

2nd 각 선택지의 앞뒤 흐름이 매끄러운지 확인한다.

- **①의 앞 문장과 뒤 문장**

앞 문장: 더욱이 객관성의 가장 좋은 실천들은 종종 편파성과 공정성을 결합한다.

뒤 문장: 재판에서 검사와 변호인(및 그들이 대리하는 당사자들)의 편파성은 더 큰 공정한 맥락 안에서 발생한다.

⇒ 객관성은 편파성과 공정성을 결합할 때 가장 좋고, 실제로 재판에서도 이런 점이 반영된다는 내용이므로 두 문장은 자연스럽게 연결된다.
▶ 주어진 문장이 ①에 들어갈 수 없음

- ②의 앞 문장과 뒤 문장

┌ **앞 문장**: ①의 뒤 문장과 같음
│ **뒤 문장**: 판사나 배심원은 편파적인 주장들을 객관적인 증거의 시험대와
└ 공정한 법 원칙에 맡긴다.

➡ 객관성의 실천은 편파성과 공정성의 결합에 기반하므로 편파적인 주장을 공정한 법
원칙에 맡긴다는 내용은 흐름상 자연스럽다.

▶ 주어진 문장이 ②에 들어갈 수 없음

- ③의 앞 문장과 뒤 문장

┌ **앞 문장**: ②의 뒤 문장과 같음
│ **뒤 문장**: 이상적으로, 공정하고 객관적인 것은 편파성이 자신의 주장을 하고
└ 객관적인 규범에 의해 판단되는 재판 동안 드러난다.

➡ 객관적 증거와 법에 맡기면 결국 공정하고 객관적인 것은 재판 과정에서
드러난다고 설명하고 있으므로 두 문장은 자연스럽게 연결된다.

▶ 주어진 문장이 ③에 들어갈 수 없음

- **④의 앞 문장과 뒤 문장**

┌ **앞 문장**: ③의 뒤 문장과 같음
│ **뒤 문장**: 그 반대(The reverse)가 사실인데, 그 규범은 인간의 편견에 대한
└ 예리한 인식 때문에, 즉 그것이 명백하게 나타나기 때문에 만들어졌다.

➡ 재판을 통해서 공정성과 객관성이 드러난다고 설명하는 내용인데, '그 반대가
사실인데(The reverse is true)'라고 하면서 인간의 편견에 대해 설명하며 전혀
맞지 않는 흐름의 문장이 이어진다.
인간이 편견이 없을 수 있기 때문에 규범을 만든 것이 아니라는 내용이 들어가야 '그
반대가 사실인데(The reverse is true)'를 통해 규범이 만들어진 진정한 이유가
소개될 수 있다.

▶ 주어진 문장이 ④에 들어가야 함

- ⑤의 앞 문장과 뒤 문장

┌ **앞 문장**: ④의 뒤 문장과 같음
│ **뒤 문장**: 편견이 보편적이기 때문에 객관성이 불가능하다고 결론을
└ 내리기보다는 과학자, 언론인 그리고 다른 이들은 반대의 결론을 내렸다.

➡ 인간들에겐 편견이 존재하지만, 객관성 확보가 불가능한 것이 아니라 규범을
만듦으로써 이를 극복할 수 있다는 내용이므로 두 문장이 자연스럽게 연결된다.

▶ 주어진 문장이 ⑤에 들어갈 수 없음

3rd 글이 한눈에 들어오도록 정리하여 정답을 확인한다.

객관성의 가장 좋은 실천들은 종종 편파성과 공정성을 결합한다.
(①) 재판에서 편파성은 더 큰 공정한 맥락 안에서 발생한다.
(②) 편파적인 주장들을 객관적인 증거의 시험대와 공정한 법 원칙에 맡긴다.
(③) 공정하고 객관적인 것은 편파성이 자신의 주장을 하고 객관적인 규범에 의해
판단되는 재판 동안 드러난다.
(④ 객관성의 규범은 그것을 만든 사람들이 대부분의 인간은 편견이 '없을' 수 있다고
생각했기 때문에 만들어진 것이 아니다.)
반대로, 인간의 편견에 대한 인식 때문에 만들어졌다.
(⑤) 과학자, 언론인 그리고 다른 이들은 반대의 결론을 내렸다.
즉 제거할 수 없는 편견의 존재를 줄이기 위해 객관성의 규율을 필요로 한다.

N 12 정답 ③ ＊고양이의 야간 시력과 그 대가

글의 흐름으로 보아, 주어진 문장이 들어가기에 가장 적절한 곳을
고르시오. [3점]

단서 1 고양이가 어둠 속에서 잘 볼 수 있다는 내용과, 밝을 때와 가까운 물체는 잘 볼 수 없다는
내용 사이에 들어가야 함

┌ Cats 'pay' for this nighttime accuracy / with less accurate
│ daytime vision / and an inability to focus on close objects. //
│ 고양이는 이러한 야간의 정확성에 대한 '대가를 지불한다' / 덜 정확한 주간 시력과 /
└ 가까운 물체에 초점을 못 맞추는 것으로 //

단수 주어　동격절 접속사　　　　　　　　　　　단수 동사
The fact that cats' eyes glow in the dark / is part of their
enhanced light-gathering efficiency; /
고양이의 눈이 어둠 속에서 빛난다는 사실은 / 그것의 강화된 집광 효율성의 일부인데 /

there is a reflective layer behind the retina, / so light can hit the
retina / when it enters the eye, / or when it is reflected from
（it = light）
behind the retina. //
망막 뒤에는 반사 층이 있어서 / 그것이 망막에 닿을 수 있다 / 빛이 눈에 들어올 때나 / 망막
뒤에서 반사될 때 //

단수 주어　　　　　　관계대명사절　　　　　단수 동사①
(①) Light that manages to miss the retina / exits the eye / and
단수 동사②
creates that ghostly glow. //
망막을 어떤 식으로든 벗어난 빛은 / 눈을 빠져나와 / 그 유령 같은 빛을 만들어 낸다 //

(②) When cats' light-gathering ability is combined / with
the very large population of rods in their eyes, / the result is a
주격 관계대명사
predator / that can see exceptionally well in the dark. //
고양이의 집광 능력이 결합할 때 / 고양이의 눈 속 매우 많은 간상체의 개체 수와 / 그 결과는
포식자이다 / 어둠 속에서 유난히 잘 볼 수 있는 //

단서 2 밤에 잘 보고 낮과 가까운 물체는 잘 볼 수 없는 것을 가리킴
(③) This may seem counterproductive; / what is the point of
seeing a mouse in the dark / if, in that final, close moment, / the
cat can't focus on it? //
이것은 비생산적으로 보일 수 있는데 / 어둠 속에서 쥐를 보는 것이 무슨 의미가 있을까 / 만약
그 마지막, 아슬아슬한 순간에 / 고양이가 그것(쥐)에 초점을 맞출 수 없다면 //

(④) Tactile information comes into play at this time; / cats can
（them = their whiskers）
move their whiskers forward / and use them to get information
about objects / within the grasp of their jaws. //
이때 촉각 정보가 작용하기 시작하는데 / 고양이들은 콧수염을 앞으로 움직여서 / 그들의
턱으로 물체들에 대한 정보를 얻는 데 사용할 수 있다 / 물 수 있는 범위 내의 //

현재분사구(a cat 수식)
(⑤) So the next time you see a cat / seeming to nap in the bright
sunlight, / eyes half-closed, / remember that it may simply be
shielding its retina / from a surplus of light. //
그러므로 다음번에 여러분이 고양이를 보면 / 밝은 햇빛 속에서 낮잠을 자고 있는 것처럼
보이는 / 눈이 반쯤 감긴 채로 / 그것이 단순히 망막을 보호하고 있을 뿐일 수도 있다는 것을
기억하라 / 과도한 빛으로부터 //

- accuracy ⓝ 정확도　　　• enhanced ⓐ 높인, 강화된
- reflective ⓐ 빛을 반사하는　　• retina ⓝ 망막
- manage ⓥ (힘든 일을) 간신히[용케] 해내다　• ghostly ⓐ 귀신같은
- exceptionally ⓐⓓ 특별히
- counterproductive ⓐ 비생산적인, 역효과를 낳는
- come into play 작동[활동]하기 시작하다　• grasp ⓝ 통제, 범위
- surplus ⓝ 과잉

고양이의 눈이 어둠 속에서 빛난다는 사실은 그것의 강화된 집광 효율성의
일부인데, 망막 뒤에는 반사 층이 있어서 빛이 눈에 들어올 때나 망막 뒤에서
반사될 때 그것이 망막에 닿을 수 있다. (①) 망막을 어떤 식으로든 벗어난
빛은 눈을 빠져나와 그 유령 같은 빛을 만들어 낸다. (②) 고양이의 집광
능력이 고양이의 눈 속 매우 많은 간상체의 개체 수와 결합될 때, 그 결과는
어둠 속에서 유난히 잘 볼 수 있는 포식자이다. (③ 고양이는 덜 정확한 주간
시력과 가까운 물체에 초점을 못 맞추는 것으로 이러한 야간의 정확성에 대한
'대가를 지불한다.') 이것은 비생산적으로 보일 수 있는데, 만약 고양이가 그
마지막, 아슬아슬한 순간에 그것(쥐)에 초점을 맞출 수 없다면 어둠 속에서
쥐를 보는 것이 무슨 의미가 있을까? (④) 이때 촉각 정보가 작용하기
시작하는데, 고양이들은 콧수염을 앞으로 움직여서 그들의 턱으로 물 수 있는
범위 내의 물체들에 대한 정보를 얻는 데 사용할 수 있다. (⑤) 그러므로
다음번에 여러분이 밝은 햇빛 속에서, 눈이 반쯤 감긴 채로, 낮잠을 자고
있는 것처럼 보이는 고양이를 보면, 그것이 단순히 과도한 빛으로부터 망막을
보호하고 있을 뿐일 수도 있다는 것을 기억하라.

1st 주어진 문장을 해석하고, 연결어, 지시어 등을 확인한다.

Cats 'pay' for this nighttime accuracy with less accurate daytime vision and an inability to focus on close objects.
고양이는 덜 정확한 주간 시력과 가까운 물체에 초점을 못 맞추는 것으로 이러한 야간의 정확성에 대한 '대가를 지불한다.'

→ '이러한 야간의 정확성(this nighttime accuracy)'으로 미루어볼 때, 앞부분에 '이러한'으로 가리킬 만한 내용이 앞에 언급되어야 한다. **단서1**
  ▶ 주어진 문장 앞: 고양이가 야간에 정확하게 볼 수 있다는 내용
  ▶ 주어진 문장 뒤: 고양이가 밝을 때와 가까운 물체는 잘 볼 수 없다는 내용

2nd 각 선택지의 앞뒤 흐름이 매끄러운지 확인한다.

- ①의 앞 문장과 뒤 문장

앞 문장: 고양이의 눈이 어둠 속에서 빛난다는 사실은 그것의 강화된 집광 효율성의 일부인데, 망막 뒤에는 반사 층이 있어서 빛이 눈에 들어올 때나 망막 뒤에서 반사될 때 그것이 망막에 닿을 수 있다.

뒤 문장: 망막을 어떤 식으로든 벗어난 빛은 눈을 빠져나와 그 유령 같은 빛을 만들어 낸다.

→ 고양이의 눈이 어둠 속에서 빛나는 구조상의 이유를 앞뒤 문장에서 설명하고 있다.
  ▶ 주어진 문장이 ①에 들어갈 수 없음

- ②의 앞 문장과 뒤 문장

앞 문장: ①의 뒤 문장과 같음

뒤 문장: 고양이의 집광 능력이 고양이의 눈 속 매우 많은 간상체의 개체 수와 결합될 때, 그 결과는 어둠 속에서 유난히 잘 볼 수 있는 포식자이다.

→ 고양이가 가진 집광 능력에 대해 소개했고, 이로 인해 어둠 속에서 잘 볼 수 있는 포식자로서 사냥할 수 있다고 설명하므로 내용이 자연스럽게 연결된다.
  ▶ 주어진 문장이 ②에 들어갈 수 없음

- ③의 앞 문장과 뒤 문장

앞 문장: ②의 뒤 문장과 같음

뒤 문장: 이것(This)은 비생산적으로 보일 수 있는데, 만약 고양이가 그 마지막, 아슬아슬한 순간에 그것(쥐)에 초점을 맞출 수 없다면 어둠 속에서 쥐를 보는 것이 무슨 의미가 있을까?

→ '이것'으로 지칭하는 내용은 비생산적인 내용을 담고 있어야 하는데 앞 문장에는 집광 능력이 좋아서 어둠 속에서도 사냥을 잘할 수 있다는 내용이 나오므로 흐름상 어색하다.
  밤에 잘 볼 수 있지만 주간과 가까운 물체에는 초점을 못 맞춘다는 단점이 나와야 흐름이 자연스럽다.
  ▶ 주어진 문장이 ③에 들어가야 함

- ④의 앞 문장과 뒤 문장

앞 문장: ③의 뒤 문장과 같음

뒤 문장: 이때 촉각 정보가 작용하기 시작하는데, 고양이들은 콧수염을 앞으로 움직여서 그들의 턱으로 물 수 있는 범위 내의 물체들에 대한 정보를 얻는 데 사용할 수 있다.

→ 앞 문장에서 고양이가 사냥할 때 시각적인 제약이 있다는 내용이 나왔으므로 이를 보완할 수 있는 내용이 나와야 하고 촉각 정보를 활용하는 내용이 이어지는 것은 자연스럽다.
  ▶ 주어진 문장이 ④에 들어갈 수 없음

- ⑤의 앞 문장과 뒤 문장

앞 문장: ④의 뒤 문장과 같음

뒤 문장: 그러므로 다음번에 여러분이 밝은 햇빛 속에서, 눈이 반쯤 감긴 채로, 낮잠을 자고 있는 것처럼 보이는 고양이를 보면, 그것이 단순히 과도한 빛으로부터 망막을 보호하고 있을 뿐일 수도 있다는 것을 기억하라.

→ 집광 능력이 좋아서 낮에는 눈부심으로 인해서 눈을 반쯤 감고 있을 수도 있지만, 시각적 부족함을 촉각으로 보완해서 주변에 대한 정보를 얻을 수 있으니 자연스러운 상황이다.
  ▶ 주어진 문장이 ⑤에 들어갈 수 없음

3rd 글이 한눈에 들어오도록 정리하여 정답을 확인한다.

강화된 집광 효율성으로 인해 고양이의 눈이 어둠 속에서 빛난다.
(①) 망막을 벗어난 빛은 유령 같은 빛을 만들어 낸다.
(②) 고양이의 집광 능력은 어둠속에서 잘 볼 수 있게 한다.
(③ 반면 주간에는 덜 정확한 시력과 초점 맞추기에 어려움을 겪는다.)
초점 맞추기에 어려움이 있다면 단지 어둠속에서 잘 보는 것은 비생산적일 수 있다.
(④) 시각적 제약이 있을 경우 콧수염을 통해 촉각 정보를 활용한다.
(⑤) 낮에 고양이는 과도한 빛으로부터 눈을 보호하고자 눈을 반쯤 감고 있다.

N 13 정답 ④ *높은 보험료 부과 대상의 변화

글의 흐름으로 보아, 주어진 문장이 들어가기에 가장 적절한 곳을 고르시오.

But in the future, / real-time data collection will enable insurance companies / to charge pay-as-you-drive rates / depending on people's actual behavior on the road, /
~에 따라
그러나 미래에는 / 실시간 데이터 수집이 보험사로 하여금 할 수 있게 할 것이다 / '운전하는 대로 내는' 요금을 부과하는 것을 / 도로에서 사람들의 실제 행동에 따라 /
~와는 대조적으로
as opposed to generalized stereotypes / of certain "at-risk" groups. // **단서1** 위험군에 대한 고정관념에서 벗어나 실시간 데이터 수집으로 '운전하는 대로 내는 요금을 부과하는 미래와 반대되는 내용이 앞에 있어야 함
일반화된 고정 관념과는 대조적으로 / 특정 '위험군' 집단에 대한 //

Insurance companies are expected / to err on the safe side. //
보험 회사들은 예상된다 / 너무 만전을 기할 것으로 //

They calculate risks thoroughly, / carefully picking and choosing / the customers they insure. //
└ 분사구문의 병렬 구조 ┘
그들은 위험성을 매우 철저하게 계산한다 / 그리고 신중하게 고르고 선택한다 / 그들이 보험을 맡을 고객을 //

They are boring / because their role in the economy / is to shield everyone and everything / from disastrous loss. //
명사적 용법
그들은 따분하다 / 왜냐하면 경제에서 그들의 역할이 / 모든 사람과 모든 것을 보호하는 것이기 때문이다 / 막심한 손실로부터 //

(①) Unlike manufacturing, / nothing truly revolutionary ever happens / in the insurance industry. // **단서2** 오랫동안 보험사들은 '고위험군'을 분류해 그들에게 높은 보험료 부과
제조업과는 달리 / 진정으로 획기적인 일이 절대 일어나지 않는다 / 보험 산업에서는 //

(②) For centuries, / insurers have charged higher premiums / to people in "high-risk categories" / such as smokers, male drivers under the age of thirty, and extreme-sports enthusiasts. //
수 세기 동안 / 보험사들은 더 높은 보험표를 부과해 왔다 / '고위험군'에 속하는 사람들에게 / 흡연자, 30세 미만의 남성 운전자, 그리고 익스트림 스포츠에 열성적인 사람과 같은 //

단서3 이런 종류의 분류가 편견과 차별을 초래함
(③) This type of classification / frequently results in biases and outright discrimination / against disadvantaged groups. //
이런 종류의 분류는 / 편견과 노골적인 차별을 자주 초래한다 / 불이익을 받는 집단에 대한 //

(④) Bad or high-risk individual drivers / will end up paying more for insurance, / regardless of whether they are men or women, young or old. // **단서4** 성별이나 연령에 관계없이 운전 습관이 나쁘면 보험표를 더 내게 될 것임
접속사(=~이든 아니든)
악질의 혹은 고위험 개인 운전자들은 / 결국 보험료를 더 내게 될 것이다 / 그들이 남자든 여자든, 어리든지 나이가 많든지에 관계없이 //

(⑤) The Big Brother connotations are threatening, / but many people might agree / to the real-time monitoring of their driving behavior / if it means lower rates. //
= the real-time monitoring of their driving behavior
Big Brother(빅브라더)의 함축된 의미는 위협적이다 / 그러나 많은 사람들이 동의할 수도 있다 / 그들의 운전 행동을 실시간 감시하는 것에 / 그것이 더 낮은 요금을 의미한다면 //

· **real-time** ⓝ 실시간   · **rate** ⓝ 요금, 비율
· **generalize** ⓥ 일반화하다   · **stereotype** ⓝ 고정 관념
· **calculate** ⓥ 계산하다   · **insure** ⓥ (보험업자가) ~의 보험을 맡다

- shield ⓥ 보호하다　　• disastrous ⓐ 처참한, 형편없는
- manufacturing ⓝ 제조업　　• revolutionary ⓐ 혁명의
- premium ⓝ 보험료, 할증금　　• enthusiast ⓝ 열광적인 팬
- classification ⓝ 분류　　• bias ⓝ 편견　　• outright ⓐ 노골적인
- discrimination ⓝ 차별
- disadvantaged ⓐ 불이익을 받는, 불리한 조건에 놓인
- Big Brother 정보의 독점을 통해 사회를 통제하는 권력 또는 그러한 사회 체계를 일컫는 말　　• connotation ⓝ 함축(된 의미)　　• threaten ⓥ 협박하다

보험 회사들은 너무 만전을 기할 것으로 예상된다. 그들은 위험성을 매우 철저하게 계산하고, 그들이 보험을 맡을 고객을 신중하게 고르고 선택한다. 그들은 따분한데, 경제에서 그들의 역할이 모든 사람과 모든 것을 막심한 손실로부터 보호하는 것이기 때문이다. (①) 제조업과는 달리, 보험 산업에서는 진정으로 획기적인 일이 절대 일어나지 않는다. (②) 수 세기 동안 보험사들은 흡연자, 30세 미만의 남성 운전자, 그리고 익스트림 스포츠에 열성적인 사람과 같은 '고위험군'에 속한 사람들에게 더 높은 보험료를 부과해 왔다. (③) 이런 종류의 분류는 불이익을 받는 집단에 대한 편견과 노골적인 차별을 자주 초래한다. (④ 그러나 미래에는 실시간 데이터 수집이 보험사로 하여금 특정 '위험군' 집단의 일반화된 고정 관념과는 대조적으로 도로에서 사람들의 실제 행동에 따라 '운전하는 대로 내는' 요금을 부과할 수 있게 할 것이다.) 악질의 혹은 고위험 개인 운전자들은 그들이 남자든 여자든, 어리든지 나이가 많든지에 관계없이 결국 보험료를 더 내게 될 것이다. (⑤) Big Brother(빅브라더)의 함축된 의미는 위협적이지만, 그것이 더 낮은 요금을 의미한다면 많은 사람이 그들의 운전 행동을 실시간 감시하는 것에 동의할 수도 있다.

| 문제 풀이 순서 |　[정답률 47%]

1st 주어진 문장을 해석하고, 연결어, 지시어 등을 확인한다.

┌ But in the future, / real-time data collection will enable
│ insurance companies / to charge pay-as-you-drive rates /
│ depending on people's actual behavior on the road, / as
│ opposed to generalized stereotypes / of certain "at-risk"
└ groups. // 단서1
그러나 미래에는 / 실시간 데이터 수집이 보험사로 하여금 할 수 있게 할 것이다 / '운전하는 대로 내는' 요금을 부과하는 것을 / 도로에서 사람들의 실제 행동에 따라 / 일반화된 고정 관념과는 대조적으로 / 특정 '위험군' 집단에 대한 //

➡ 미래에는 특정 위험군 집단에 대한 고정 관념과는 대조적으로 실시간 데이터 수집을 통해 운전하는 대로 내는 요금을 부과하게 될 것이라고 했다. 단서
▶ 주어진 문장 앞: 특정 위험군 집단에 대한 일반적인 고정 관념이 제시되어야 함
▶ 주어진 문장 뒤: 운전하는 대로 내는 요금을 부과하는 것에 대한 추가 설명이 제시될 것임 발상

2nd 각 선택지의 앞뒤 흐름이 매끄러운지 확인한다.

- ①의 앞 문장과 뒤 문장

┌ 앞 문장: 그들은 따분한데, 경제에서 그들의 역할이 모든 사람과 모든 것을 막심한 손실로부터 보호하는 것이기 때문이다.
│ 뒤 문장: 제조업과는 달리, 보험 산업에서는 진정으로 획기적인 일이 절대
└ 일어나지 않는다.

➡ 그들(보험 회사들)이 따분하다고 했고, 보험 산업에서는 획기적인 일이 절대 일어나지 않는다고 했으므로 두 문장은 자연스럽게 연결된다.
▶ 주어진 문장이 ①에 들어갈 수 없음

- ②의 앞 문장과 뒤 문장

┌ 앞 문장: ①의 뒤 문장과 같음
│ 뒤 문장: 수 세기 동안 보험사들은 흡연자, 30세 미만의 남성 운전자, 그리고 익스트림 스포츠에 열성적인 사람과 같은 '고위험군'에 속한 사람들에게 더
└ 높은 보험료를 부과해 왔다.

➡ 보험 산업에서는 획기적인 일이 절대 일어나지 않는다고 한 앞 문장의 내용과, 보험사들이 '고위험군'에 속하는 사람들에게 더 높은 보험료를 부과해 왔다는 뒤 문장의 내용은 자연스럽게 연결된다.
▶ 주어진 문장이 ②에 들어갈 수 없음

- ③의 앞 문장과 뒤 문장

┌ 앞 문장: ②의 뒤 문장과 같음
│ 뒤 문장: 이런 종류의 분류는 불이익을 받는 집단에 대한 편견과 노골적인
└ 차별을 자주 초래한다.

➡ 앞 문장에서 고위험군에 속하는 사람들에게 높은 보험료를 부과하고 있다고 했고, 뒤 문장에서는 이런 종류의 분류가 불이익을 받는 집단에 대한 차별을 초래한다고 했다.
뒤 문장에서 언급한 '이런 종류의 분류'가 바로 고위험군에 속하는 사람들을 분류한 것을 일컫기 때문에 두 문장은 자연스럽게 연결된다.
▶ 주어진 문장이 ③에 들어갈 수 없음

- ④의 앞 문장과 뒤 문장

┌ 앞 문장: ③의 뒤 문장과 같음
│ 뒤 문장: 악질의 혹은 고위험 개인 운전자들은 그들이 남자든 여자든,
└ 어리든지 나이가 많든지에 관계없이 결국 보험료를 더 내게 될 것이다.

➡ 이런 종류의 분류가 불이익을 받는 집단에게 차별을 초래한다고 한 뒤에, 성별과 연령에 관계없이 악질 운전자들이 보험료를 더 내게 될 것이라고 했다.
주어진 문장은, 미래에는 특정 위험군 집단에 대한 고정 관념과는 대조적으로 '운전하는 대로 내는' 요금을 부과하게 될 것이라고 했다. 따라서 성별과 연령에 관계없이 악질 운전자들이 보험료를 더 내게 될 것이라고 한 뒤 문장으로 방향이 전환되기 전에 들어가야 한다.
▶ 주어진 문장이 ④에 들어가야 함

- ⑤의 앞 문장과 뒤 문장

┌ 앞 문장: ④의 뒤 문장과 같음
│ 뒤 문장: Big Brother(빅브라더)의 함축된 의미는 위협적이지만, 그것이 더
│ 낮은 요금을 의미한다면 많은 사람이 그들의 운전 행동을 실시간 감시하는
└ 것에 동의할 수도 있다.

➡ 앞 문장에서 (실시간 감시의 결과로) 성별과 연령에 관계없이 악질 운전자들이 보험료를 더 내게 될 것이라고 했고, 뒤 문장에서는 사람들이 더 낮은 요금을 의미한다면 운전 행동을 실시간 감시하는 것에 동의할 것이라고 했으므로 두 문장이 자연스럽게 연결된다.
▶ 주어진 문장이 ⑤에 들어갈 수 없음

3rd 글이 한눈에 들어오도록 정리하여 정답을 확인한다.

보험 회사는 고객을 신중하게 고르고, 모든 사람과 모든 것을 막심한 손실로부터 보호하기 때문에 따분하다.
(①) 제조업과 달리 보험 산업에서는 획기적인 일이 일어나지 않는다.
(②) 보험사들은 '고위험군'에 속하는 사람들에게 더 높은 보험료를 부과해 왔다.
(③) 이런 종류의 분류가 불이익을 받는 집단에 대한 차별을 초래한다.
(④ 미래에는 실시간 감시를 통해 운전하는 대로 내는 요금을 부과할 것이다.)
성별과 연령에 관계없이 악질 운전자가 더 높은 보험료를 내게 될 것이다.
(⑤) 보험료가 낮아진다면 사람들이 실시간 운전 행동 감시에 동의할 것이다.

N 14 정답 ② ＊원근법이 가져온 구상화의 특징과 변화 ────

글의 흐름으로 보아, 주어진 문장이 들어가기에 가장 적절한 곳을 고르시오. [3점]

단서1 '이것'이 알고 있던 것을 그렸던 초기 구상화와 대조적이라고 함

┌ This stands in contrast to earlier figurative art, / which had
│ 　　　　　　　　　　　　　　　　　　　관계대명사의 계속적 용법
│ been as focused on /
│ 이것은 초기 구상화와 대조적이다 / 초점이 맞추어져 있었던 /
│ 　　　— as ~ as ... : ~만큼 ~한
│ representing what the artist *knew* / about the objects and the
│ 사이에 목적격 관계대명사 that 생략
│ space / he or she was painting / as on how they *looked*. //
└ 그들이 '알고 있던' 것을 나타내는 데 / 사물과 공간에 대해 / 화가들이 그리고 있던 / 그것들이 어떻게 '보였는지'만큼이나 //

Almost all the figurative paintings / we are familiar with now /
are in perspective. //
　　　　　사이에 목적격 관계대명사 that 생략
거의 모든 구상화는 / 지금 우리에게 익숙한 / 원근법으로 그린 것이다 //

They present foreshortened figures and objects / that diminish /
접속사 　　　　　　　　　　　　주격 관계대명사(figures and objects) 수식
as they move away / from the focal point of the painting. //
그것들은 축소된 인물들과 사물들을 나타낸다 / 작아지는 / 멀어짐에 따라 / 그림의 초점에서 //

(①) A painting in perspective represents / how the world *looks*
to a person / seeing the scene / from a particular position in
　　　　　　　person을 수식하는 분사
space. //
원근법으로 그린 그림은 나타낸다 / 사람에게 세상에 어떻게 '보이는지'를 / 그 장면을 보는 /
공간의 특정 위치에서 //

(②) These pictures are beautiful / in their own right, / but they
do not represent scenes / as we might see them / if we were
　　　　　　　　　　　　접속사
looking at them. // 단서2 이런 그림들은 우리가 보고 있을 것 같은
　　　　　　　　　　　　　　장면들을 그리지 않는다고 함
이러한 그림들은 아름답다 / 그 자체로 / 그러나 그것들은 장면들을 나타내지는 않는다 /
우리가 보고 있을 것 같은 / 만약 우리가 그것들을 보고 있다면 //

(③) They are also less informative / as to the layout of the
사이에 목적격 관계대명사 that 생략
space / they represent. //
그것들은 또한 정보를 덜 준다 / 공간의 배치에 대해서도 / 그것들이 나타내는 //

(④) The fact / that perspective and information about spatial
　　　　　　동격의 접속사
layout / go together / reveals something important / about
seeing. //
사실은 / 시점과 공간 배치에 대한 정보가 / 함께 어우러진다는 / 중요한 무언가를 드러낸다 /
'보는 것'에 대한 //

(⑤) Not only do we see the world / through an egocentric
　　　　└─────┬─────┘ 부정어구(not only)로 인한 주어와 동사 도치
frame / but we also see it in a way /
not only A but also B: A뿐만 아니라 B도
우리는 세상을 볼 뿐만 아니라 / 자기중심적인 틀을 통해 / 방식으로 그것을 본다 /
　　　　　　　　　　　　　주격 관계대명사(way 수식)
that allows us to extract information / about distances to, and
　　　　　　　　　└─ objects를 수식하는 형용사 ─┘
sizes of, / objects relative to us, and relative to one another. //
우리로 하여금 정보를 추출하도록 하는 / 거리와 크기에 대한 / 우리에게 상대적인, 그리고
서로 상대적인 물체와의 //

- figurative art 구상화　　　• diminish ⓥ 작아지다, 줄어들다
- focal point (관심·활동의) 초점[중심]　　• informative ⓐ 정보를 주는
- layout ⓝ 배치　　• spatial ⓐ 공간의　　• reveal ⓥ 드러내다
- egocentric ⓐ 자기중심적인　　• extract ⓥ 추출하다
- relative ⓐ 상대적인

지금 우리에게 익숙한 거의 모든 구상화는 원근법으로 그린 것이다. 그것들은
그림의 초점에서 멀어짐에 따라 작아지는 축소된 인물들과 사물들을 나타낸다.
(①) 원근법으로 그린 그림은 공간의 특정 위치에서 그 장면을 보는
사람에게 세상이 어떻게 '보이는지'를 나타낸다. (② 이것은 그것들이 어떻게
'보였는지'만큼이나 화가들이 그리고 있던 사물과 공간에 대해 그들이 '알고
있던' 것을 나타내는 데 초점이 맞추어져 있었던 초기 구상화와는 대조적이다.)
이러한 그림들은 그 자체로 아름답지만, 그것들은 만약 우리가 그것들을 보고
있다면 우리가 보고 있을 것 같은 장면들을 나타내지는 않는다. (③) 그것들은
또한 그것들이 나타내는 공간의 배치에 대해서도 정보를 덜 준다. (④) 시점과
공간 배치에 대한 정보가 함께 어우러진다는 사실은 '보는 것'에 대한 중요한
무언가를 드러낸다. (⑤) 우리는 자기중심적인 틀을 통해 세상을 볼 뿐만
아니라, 우리로 하여금 우리에게 상대적인, 그리고 서로 상대적인 물체와의
거리와 (물체의) 크기에 대한 정보를 추출하도록 하는 방식으로 그것을 본다.

| 문제 풀이 순서 | [정답률 26%]

1st 주어진 문장을 해석하고, 연결어, 지시어 등을 확인한다.

This stands in contrast to earlier figurative art, / which had
been as focused on / representing what the artist *knew* / about
the objects and the space / he or she was painting / as on how
they *looked*. // 단서1
이것은 초기 구상화와 대조적이다 / 초점이 맞추어져 있었던 / 그들이 '알고 있던' 것을
나타내는 데 / 사물과 공간에 대해 / 화가들이 그리고 있던 / 그것들이 어떻게 '보였는지'
만큼이나 //

➡ '이것(this)'이 사물과 공간에 대해 알고 있던 것을 그리던 초기 구상화와
대조적이라고 하고 있으므로 단서 앞에는 이러한 this의 특징이 언급될 것이다.

▶ **주어진 문장 앞**: '알고 있던 것'을 그리는 초기 구상화와 대조적인 this의 특징이
제시될 것임 발상

▶ **주어진 문장 뒤**: 이것의 특징이 추가적으로 제시될 것임

2nd 각 선택지의 앞뒤 흐름이 매끄러운지 확인한다.

- **①의 앞 문장과 뒤 문장**

앞 문장: 그것들은 그림의 초점에서 멀어짐에 따라 작아지는 축소된
인물들과 사물들을 나타낸다.

뒤 문장: 원근법으로 그린 그림은 공간의 특정 위치에서 그 장면을 보는
사람에게 세상이 어떻게 '보이는지'를 나타낸다.

➡ 앞 문장은 원근법에 대한 설명이고, 뒤 문장에서 추가적으로 원근법으로 그린
그림은 세상이 어떻게 '보이는지'를 나타낸다고 했다. 따라서 두 문장은 자연스럽게
연결된다.

▶ 주어진 문장이 ①에 들어갈 수 없음

- **②의 앞 문장과 뒤 문장**

앞 문장: ①의 뒤 문장과 같음

뒤 문장: 이러한 그림들은 그 자체로 아름답지만, 그것들은 만약 우리가
그것들을 보고 있다면 우리가 보고 있을 것 같은 장면들을 나타내지는
않는다.

➡ 앞 문장에서는 원근법으로 그린 그림은 그 장면을 보는 사람에게 세상이 어떻게
'보이는지'를 나타낸다고 했다. 하지만 뒤에 이어지는 내용은 이러한 그림들이
우리가 '보고 있을 것 같은' 장면들을 나타내지는 않는다고 했다.
주어진 문장은 원근법으로 그린 그림이 '알고 있던 것'을 그리는 초기 구상화와
대조적이라는 내용이다. 따라서 '보고 있는 것'을 그리는 원근법으로 그린 그림에서
'보고 있을 것 같은' 장면들을 그리지 않는 초기 구상화로 화제가 전환되는 부분에
들어가야 하므로 ②에 들어가야 한다.

▶ 주어진 문장이 ②에 들어가야 함

- **③의 앞 문장과 뒤 문장**

앞 문장: ②의 뒤 문장과 같음

뒤 문장: 그것들은 또한(also) 그것들이 나타내는 공간의 배치에 대해서도
정보를 덜 준다.

➡ 앞부분에서 원근법으로 그린 그림과는 다르게 초기 구상화는 '알고 있던 것'을
그리기 때문에 우리가 보고 있을 것 같은 장면들을 나타내지 않는다고 했다. 뒤
문장에서는 그것들이 또한 공간의 배치에 대한 정보를 덜 준다고 했다. 따라서 초기
구상화의 특징을 설명하는 두 문장은 also로 자연스럽게 연결된다.

▶ 주어진 문장이 ③에 들어갈 수 없음

- **④의 앞 문장과 뒤 문장**

앞 문장: ③의 뒤 문장과 같음

뒤 문장: 시점과 공간 배치에 대한 정보가 함께 어우러진다는 사실은 '보는
것'에 대한 중요한 무언가를 드러낸다.

➡ 초기 구상화가 공간의 배치에 대한 정보를 덜 준다고 했고, 뒤에 이어지는 내용은
시점과 공간 배치에 대한 정보가 함께 어우러지는 것이 '보는 것'에 대한 중요한
무언가를 드러낸다고 했다. 두 문장은 공간 배치에 대한 이야기를 이어서 서술하고
있으므로 연결이 자연스럽다.

▶ 주어진 문장이 ④에 들어갈 수 없음

- **⑤의 앞 문장과 뒤 문장**

앞 문장: ④의 뒤 문장과 같음

뒤 문장: 우리는 자기중심적인 틀을 통해 세상을 볼 뿐만 아니라, 우리로
하여금 우리에게 상대적인, 그리고 서로 상대적인 물체와의 거리와
(물체의) 크기에 대한 정보를 추출하도록 하는 방식으로 그것을 본다.

➡ 시점과 공간 배치에 대한 정보가 '보는 것'에 중요하다고 했고, 뒤에서 물체와의
거리와 크기에 대한 정보를 추출하는 방식으로 세상을 본다고 했다.
뒤 문장이 앞 문장의 내용에 대한 구체적인 설명을 제시하고 있으므로 두 문장은
자연스럽게 연결된다.

▶ 주어진 문장이 ⑤에 들어갈 수 없음

3rd 글이 한눈에 들어오도록 정리하여 정답을 확인한다.

지금 우리에게 익숙한 거의 모든 구상화는 원근법으로 그린 것으로, 그림의 초점에서 멀어짐에 따라 작아지는 축소된 인물들과 사물들을 나타낸다.
(①) 원근법으로 그린 그림은 세상이 어떻게 '보이는지'를 나타낸다.
(② 이것은 사물과 공간에 대해 그들이 '알고 있던' 것을 그렸던 초기 구상화와는 대조적이다.)
이러한 그림들은 우리가 보고 있을 것 같은 장면들을 나타내지는 않는다.
(③) 그것들은 또한 공간의 배치에 대해서도 정보를 덜 준다.
(④) 시점과 공간 배치에 대한 정보가 함께 어우러진다는 사실은 '보는 것'에 중요하다.
(⑤) 우리는 물체와의 거리와 (물체의) 크기에 대한 정보를 추출하도록 하는 방식으로 세상을 본다.

자이쌤's Follow Me! —홈페이지에서 제공

N 15 정답 ② ＊다면 평가

글의 흐름으로 보아, 주어진 문장이 들어가기에 가장 적절한 곳을 고르시오. [3점]

A problem, however, is / that supervisors often work / in locations / apart from their employees / and therefore are not able to observe / their subordinates' performance. //
하지만 문제는 ~이다 / 관리자가 흔히 일하고 / 장소에서 / 자신의 직원들과 떨어진 / 따라서 관찰할 수 없다는 것 / 자신의 부하 직원들의 성과를 // **단서 1** 관리자가 부하 직원의 성과를 관찰할 수 없다는 문제가 있음

In most organizations, / the employee's immediate supervisor evaluates / the employee's performance. //
대부분의 조직에서 / 직원의 직속 상관은 평가한다 / 직원의 성과를 //
(①) This is because the supervisor is responsible / for the employee's performance, / providing supervision, / handing out assignments, / and developing the employee. // 분사구문의 병렬 구조
이것은 관리자가 책임지기 때문이다 / 직원의 성과를 / 감독을 제공하고 / 과업을 배정하며 / 그 직원을 계발하면서 // **단서 2** 관리자가 직원의 성과를 관찰할 수 없다는 내용이 먼저 나와야 함
(②) Should supervisors rate employees / on performance dimensions / they cannot observe? // 앞에 목적격 관계대명사가 생략됨
관리자는 직원들을 평가해야 하는가 / 성과 영역에 대해 / 자신이 관찰할 수 없는 //
(③) To eliminate this dilemma, / more and more organizations are implementing assessments / referred to as 360-degree evaluations. // '비교급 and 비교급': 점점 더 ~한/하게 선행사(주격 관계대명사와 be동사는 생략됨)
이러한 딜레마를 없애기 위해 / 점점 더 많은 조직이 평가를 시행하고 있다 / '다면 평가'라고 불리는 //
(④) Employees are rated / not only by their supervisors / but by coworkers, clients or citizens, professionals in other agencies with whom they work, / and subordinates. // 「전치사+목적격 관계대명사」 선행사
직원들은 평가를 받는다 / 자신의 관리자에 의해서만이 아니라 / 동료, 고객이나 시민, 다른 기관의 전문가들에 의해서도 / 자신이 함께 일하는 / 그리고 부하 직원들에 의해서도 //
(⑤) The reason for this approach is / that often coworkers and clients or citizens have / a greater opportunity / to observe an employee's performance / 형용사적 용법(a greater opportunity 수식)
이 방법을 시행하는 이유는 ~이다 / 동료와 고객이나 시민들이 흔히 가지며 / 더 좋은 기회를 / 어떤 직원의 성과를 관찰할 / 형용사적 용법(a better position 수식)
and are in a better position / to evaluate many performance dimensions. //
더 나은 위치에 있다는 것 / 많은 성과 영역을 평가할 //

- supervisor ⓝ 관리자, 감독 · apart ⓐⅾ (거리·공간상으로) 떨어져
- therefore ⓐⅾ 그러므로 · observe ⓥ 관찰하다
- performance ⓝ 성과, 수행 · organization ⓝ 조직, 단체
- immediate ⓐ 직속[직계]의 · evaluate ⓥ 평가하다
- responsible for ~에 책임이 있는 · supervision ⓝ 관리, 감독

- hand out ~을 나눠주다 · assignment ⓝ 과제, 임무
- rate ⓥ 평가하다 · dimension ⓝ 차원, 관점 · eliminate ⓥ 없애다
- implement ⓥ 시행하다 · assessment ⓝ 평가
- refer to as ~라고 언급하다 · degree ⓝ (각도의 단위인) 도
- evaluation ⓝ 평가 · coworker ⓝ 동료 · client ⓝ 고객
- citizen ⓝ 시민 · professional ⓝ 전문가
- agency ⓝ 대행사, (특정 서비스를 제공하는) 단체 · approach ⓝ 접근법
- opportunity ⓝ 기회

대부분의 조직에서, 직원의 직속 상관은 직원의 성과를 평가한다. (①) 이것은 그 관리자가 감독을 제공하고, 과업을 배정하며, 직원을 계발하면서, 직원의 성과를 책임지기 때문이다. (② 하지만, 문제는 관리자가 흔히 자신의 직원과 떨어진 장소에서 일하기 때문에, 자신의 부하 직원들의 성과를 관찰할 수 없다는 것이다.) 관리자는 자신이 관찰할 수 없는 성과 영역에 대해 직원들을 평가해야 하는가? (③) 이 딜레마를 없애기 위해, 점점 더 많은 조직이 '다면 평가'라고 불리는 평가를 시행하고 있다. (④) 직원들은 자신의 관리자에 의해서만이 아니라, 동료, 고객이나 시민, 자신이 함께 일하는 다른 기관의 전문가들, 그리고 부하 직원들에 의해서도 평가를 받는다. (⑤) 이 방법을 시행하는 이유는 동료와 고객이나 시민들이 흔히 어떤 직원의 성과를 관찰할 더 좋은 기회를 가지며, 많은 성과 영역을 평가할 더 나은 위치에 있다는 것이다.

| 문제 풀이 순서 | [정답률 77%]

1st 주어진 문장을 해석하고, 연결어, 지시어 등을 확인한다.

A problem, |however|, is that supervisors often work in locations apart from their employees and therefore are not able to observe their subordinates' performance. **단서 1**
|하지만|, 문제는 관리자가 흔히 자신의 직원과 떨어진 장소에서 일하기 때문에, 자신의 부하 직원들의 성과를 관찰할 수 없다는 것이다.

➡ however라고 했으므로 앞에 반대되는 내용이 나오고, 그 뒤에 주어진 문장을 넣어야 한다.
➡ 관리자가 자신의 부하 직원들의 성과를 관찰할 수 없다는 것이 문제라고 했으므로 주어진 문장의 앞 문장은 성과를 관찰해야 할 필요가 있다는 내용일 것이다.

2nd 각 선택지의 앞뒤 흐름이 매끄러운지 확인한다.

- ①의 앞 문장과 뒤 문장

> **앞 문장:** 대부분의 조직에서, 직원의 직속 상관은 직원의 성과를 평가한다.
> **뒤 문장:** 이것은 그 관리자가 감독을 제공하고, 과업을 배정하며, 직원을 계발하면서, 직원의 성과를 책임지기 때문이다.

➡ **앞 문장:** 조직에서 직속 상관은 직원의 성과를 평가한다.
 뒤 문장: 성과 평가의 이유에 대한 부연
'직원의 성과를 평가하는 것'을 뒤 문장에서 '이것'으로 표현하면서 연결된다.
▶ 주어진 문장이 ①에 들어갈 수 없음

- ②의 앞 문장과 뒤 문장

> **앞 문장:** ①의 뒤 문장과 같음
> **뒤 문장:** 관리자는 자신이 관찰할 수 없는 성과 영역에 대해 직원들을 평가해야 하는가? **단서 2**

➡ **뒤 문장:** 관찰할 수 없는 성과 영역에 대한 평가가 필요한지 의문 제기
관찰할 수 없는 성과 영역에 대한 언급이 앞에 있어야 한다.
➡ 주어진 문장에서 관리자가 부하 직원들의 성과를 관찰할 수 없다는 문제를 제기하고 있다.
▶ 주어진 문장이 ②에 들어가야 함

- ③의 앞 문장과 뒤 문장

> **앞 문장:** ②의 뒤 문장과 같음
> **뒤 문장:** 이 딜레마를 없애기 위해, 점점 더 많은 조직이 '다면 평가'라고 불리는 평가를 시행하고 있다.

➡ 앞 문장의 '관찰할 수 없는 성과 영역에 대한 평가'를, 뒤 문장에서 '이 딜레마'라고 표현했다.
평가에 관한 딜레마와 이를 해결하기 위한 '다면 평가'를 제시하면서 앞뒤 문장이 자연스럽게 연결된다.
▶ 주어진 문장이 ③에 들어갈 수 없음

- ④의 앞 문장과 뒤 문장

> **앞 문장:** ③의 뒤 문장과 같음
> **뒤 문장:** 직원들은 자신의 관리자에 의해서만이 아니라, 동료, 고객이나 시민, 자신이 함께 일하는 다른 기관의 전문가들, 그리고 부하 직원들에 의해서도 평가를 받는다.

➡ 앞 문장의 '다면 평가'에 관한 부연으로 앞뒤 문장이 자연스럽게 연결된다.
▶ 주어진 문장이 ④에 들어갈 수 없음

- ⑤의 앞 문장과 뒤 문장

> **앞 문장:** ④의 뒤 문장과 같음
> **뒤 문장:** 이 방법을 시행하는 이유는 동료와 고객이나 시민들이 흔히 어떤 직원의 성과를 관찰할 더 좋은 기회를 가지며, 많은 성과 영역을 평가할 더 나은 위치에 있다는 것이다.

➡ 앞 문장에 등장한 '다면 평가'를 뒤 문장에서 '이 방법'으로 지칭하며 이를 시행하는 이유를 부연하는 흐름이다.
▶ 주어진 문장이 ⑤에 들어갈 수 없음

3rd 글이 한눈에 들어오도록 정리하여 정답을 확인한다.

대부분의 조직에서 직속 상관은 직원의 성과를 평가한다.
(①) 이것은 관리자가 직원의 성과를 책임지기 때문이다.
(② 하지만, 문제는 관리자가 흔히 부하 직원들의 성과를 관찰할 수 없다는 것이다.)
관리자는 관찰할 수 없는 성과 영역에 대해 직원들을 평가해야 하는가?
(③) 이 딜레마를 없애기 위해 점점 많은 조직이 '다면 평가'를 시행하고 있다.
(④) 직원들은 관리자 외에도 여러 사람에 의해 평가받는다.
(⑤) 이를 시행하는 이유는 동료, 고객, 시민 등이 어떤 직원의 성과를 더 잘 관찰하고 많이 평가할 수 있기 때문이다.

N 16 정답 ⑤ * 과학자가 도덕적 가치를 배우는 방법

> **글의 흐름으로 보아, 주어진 문장이 들어가기에 가장 적절한 곳을 고르시오.**

단서 1 과학자라는 역할에 내재한 도덕적 가치에 대해 배우는 것과 반대되는 내용이 앞에 있어야 함

Instead, / much like the young child / learning how to play 'nicely', / the apprentice scientist gains his or her understanding / of the moral values / inherent in the role / by absorption from their colleagues / — socialization. //
대신 / 마치 어린아이처럼 / '착하게' 노는 법을 배우는 / 도제 과학자는 이해를 얻는다 / 도덕적 가치에 대한 / 그 역할에 내재한 / 동료들로부터의 흡수를 통해 / 사회화 //

As particular practices are repeated over time / and become more widely shared, / the values / that they embody / are reinforced and reproduced / and we speak of them / as becoming 'institutionalized'. //
특정 관행이 오랜 기간 반복됨에 따라 / 그리고 더 널리 공유됨에 (따라) / 가치는 / 그 관행이 구현하는 / 강화되고 재생산되며 / 우리는 그것들을 말한다 / '제도화'된다고 //

(①) In some cases, / this institutionalization has a formal face to it, /
어떤 경우에는 / 이러한 제도화는 그것에 공식적인 면모를 갖춘다 /
with+(대)명사+과거분사
with rules and protocols written down, / and specialized roles created / 부사적 용법(목적) to ensure / that procedures are followed correctly. //
규칙과 프로토콜이 문서화되는 채 / 전문화된 역할이 만들어지는 채 / 확실히 하고자 / 절차가 올바르게 지켜지도록 //

(②) The main institutions of state / — parliament, courts, police and so on — / 복수 주어 along with certain of the professions, / exhibit this formal character. // 복수 동사
국가의 주요 기관이 / 의회, 법원, 경찰 등 / 일부 전문직과 더불어 / 이러한 공식적인 성격을 보여준다 //

(③) Other social institutions, / perhaps the majority, / are not like this; / science is an example. //
다른 사회 기관들은 / 아마도 대다수 / 이와 같지 않을 것이다 / 과학이 그 예이다 //

(④) Although scientists are trained / 부사절 접속사(양보) in the substantive content of their discipline, / they are not formally instructed / in 'how to be a good scientist'. // **단서 2** 좋은 과학자가 되는 방법(도덕적 가치)에 대해 공식적으로 배우지 않음
과학자들은 훈련받겠지만 / 자기 학문의 실질적인 내용에 대해서는 / 그들은 공식적으로 교육받지 않는다 / '좋은 과학자가 되는 방법'에 대해서는 //

(⑤) We think / that these values, / along with the values / that 복수 주어 inform many of the professions, / are under threat, / just as the value of the professions themselves is under threat. // 복수 동사
우리는 생각한다 / 이러한 가치가 / 가치와 더불어 / 그 전문직에 관한 많은 것을 알려주는 / 위협받고 있다고 / 그 전문직 자체의 가치가 위협받고 있는 것과 꼭 마찬가지로 //

- absorption ⓝ 흡수 · colleague ⓝ 동료
- socialization ⓝ 사회화 · embody ⓥ 상징하다, 포함하다
- reinforce ⓥ 강화하다 · reproduce ⓥ 재생산하다
- institutionalize ⓥ 제도화하다 · parliament ⓝ 의회
- court ⓝ 법원 · exhibit ⓥ 보여주다 · substantive ⓐ 실질적인
- discipline ⓝ 학문 · instruct ⓥ 지시하다, 가르치다
- profession ⓝ 전문직, 직업 · threat ⓝ 위협

특정 관행이 오랜 기간 반복되고 더 널리 공유됨에 따라, 그 관행이 구현하는 가치는 강화되고 재생산되며 우리는 그것들이 '제도화'된다고 말한다. (①) 어떤 경우에는 이러한 제도화는 공식적인 면모를 갖추기도 하는데, 규칙과 프로토콜이 문서화되고 절차가 올바르게 지켜지도록 확실히 하고자 전문화된 역할이 만들어진다. (②) 의회, 법원, 경찰 등 국가의 주요 기관이 일부 전문직과 더불어 이러한 공식적인 성격을 보여준다. (③) 다른 사회 기관들, 아마도 대다수는 이와 같지 않을 것인데 과학이 그 예이다. (④) 과학자들은 자기 학문의 실질적인 내용에 대해서는 훈련받겠지만, '좋은 과학자가 되는 방법'에 대해서는 공식적으로 교육받지 않는다. (⑤ 대신, 마치 '착하게' 노는 법을 배우는 어린아이처럼 도제 과학자는 동료들로부터의 흡수, 즉 사회화를 통해 그 역할에 내재한 도덕적 가치에 대한 이해를 얻는다.) 우리는 이러한 가치가 그 전문직에 관한 많은 것을 알려주는 가치와 더불어, 그 전문직 자체의 가치가 위협받고 있는 것과 꼭 마찬가지로 위협받고 있다고 생각한다.

| 문제 풀이 순서 | [정답률 55%]

1st 주어진 문장을 해석하고, 연결어, 지시어 등을 확인한다.

> Instead, much like the young child learning how to play 'nicely', the apprentice scientist gains his or her understanding of the moral values inherent in the role by absorption from their colleagues — socialization.
> **대신,** 마치 '착하게' 노는 법을 배우는 어린아이처럼 도제 과학자는 동료들로부터의 흡수, 즉 사회화를 통해 그 역할에 내재한 도덕적 가치에 대한 이해를 얻는다.

➡ instead는 앞 문장과 반대되는 내용을 이을 때 쓰이는 부사이다.
과학자는 사회화(동료로부터의 흡수)를 통해 과학자의 역할에 내재한 도덕적 가치에 대해 이해한다. **단서**
→ instead를 통해 주어진 문장의 앞에 올 내용을 예상할 수 있음 **발상**
▶ **주어진 문장 앞:** 사회화를 통해 도덕적 가치에 대해 이해하는 것과 반대되는 내용

2nd 각 선택지의 앞뒤 흐름이 매끄러운지 확인한다.

- ①의 앞 문장과 뒤 문장

> **앞 문장:** 특정 관행이 오랜 기간 반복되고 더 널리 공유됨에 따라, 그 관행이 구현하는 가치는 강화되고 재생산되며 우리는 그것들이 '제도화' 된다고 말한다.
> **뒤 문장:** 어떤 경우에는 이러한 제도화(this institutionalization) 는 공식적인 면모를 갖추기도 하는데, 규칙과 프로토콜이 문서화되고 절차가 올바르게 지켜지도록 확실히 하고자 전문화된 역할이 만들어진다.

→ 앞 문장에서 특정 관행이 제도화되는 과정을 설명한 후, 뒤 문장에서 이러한 제도화(this institutionalization)에 대해 부연 설명했다.
▶ 주어진 문장이 ①에 들어갈 수 없음

- ②의 앞 문장과 뒤 문장

> **앞 문장:** ①의 뒤 문장과 같음
> **뒤 문장:** 의회, 법원, 경찰 등 국가의 주요 기관이 일부 전문직과 더불어 이러한 공식적인 성격(this formal character)을 보여준다.

→ 앞 문장에서 설명한 '공식적인 면모'를 '이러한 공식적인 성격(this formal character)'으로 표현하여 구체적인 경우를 설명한다. this formal character가 가리키는 것은 ②의 앞 문장에 등장하지, 주어진 문장에는 없다.
▶ 주어진 문장이 ②에 들어갈 수 없음

- ③의 앞 문장과 뒤 문장

> **앞 문장:** ②의 뒤 문장과 같음
> **뒤 문장:** 아마도 대다수의 다른 사회 기관들은 이(this)와 같지 않을 것인데 과학이 그 예이다.

→ 다른 사회 기관은 앞에서 설명한 바와 다르다면서, 앞에서 설명한 것을 지시대명사 this로 가리켰다. 지시대명사 this로 앞뒤 문장이 자연스럽게 연결된다.
▶ 주어진 문장이 ③에 들어갈 수 없음

- ④의 앞 문장과 뒤 문장

> **앞 문장:** ③의 뒤 문장과 같음
> **뒤 문장:** 과학자들은 자기 학문의 실질적인 내용에 대해서는 훈련받겠지만, '좋은 과학자가 되는 방법'에 대해서는 공식적으로 교육받지 않는다.

→ 글의 앞부분에서 설명한 바와는 다른 경우의 예시로 과학을 든 후, 뒤 문장에서 과학자에 대한 설명을 시작하는 자연스러운 흐름이다. 주어진 문장은 과학자에 대한 다른 한 가지 설명이 제시된 뒤에 들어가야 한다.
▶ 주어진 문장이 ④에 들어갈 수 없음

- ⑤의 앞 문장과 뒤 문장

> **앞 문장:** ④의 뒤 문장과 같음
> **뒤 문장:** 우리는 이러한 가치(these values)가 그 전문직에 관한 많은 것을 알려주는 가치와 더불어, 그 전문직 자체의 가치가 위협받고 있는 것과 꼭 마찬가지로 위협받고 있다고 생각한다.

→ 과학자는 '좋은 과학자가 되는 방법'에 대해서 공식적으로 교육받지 않는다.
↔ 대신 사회화를 통해 과학자라는 역할에 내재한 도덕적 가치에 대한 이해를 얻는다.
⑤의 앞 문장과 주어진 문장이 과학자가 도덕적 가치에 대해 이해하는 서로 다른 방법에 대해 이야기한다. ⑤의 뒤 문장에서 설명하는 '이러한 가치'가 바로 주어진 문장에 등장한 the moral values!
▶ 주어진 문장이 ⑤에 들어가야 함

3rd 글이 한눈에 들어오도록 정리하여 정답을 확인한다.

특정 관행이 오랜 기간 반복됨에 따라, 그 관행이 구현하는 가치는 강화되고 재생산되며 우리는 그것들이 '제도화'된다고 말한다.
(①) 이러한 제도화는 공식적인 면모를 갖추기도 하는데, 규칙과 프로토콜이 문서화되고 절차가 올바르게 지켜지도록 확실히 하고자 전문화된 역할이 만들어진다.
(②) 국가의 주요 기관이 일부 전문직과 더불어 이러한 공식적인 성격을 보여준다.
(③) 다른 사회 기관들, 아마도 대다수는 이와 같지 않을 것인데 과학이 그 예이다.
(④) 과학자들은 자기 학문의 실질적인 내용에 대해서는 훈련받겠지만, '좋은 과학자가 되는 방법'에 대해서는 공식적으로 교육받지 않는다.
(⑤ 대신, 도제 과학자는 동료들로부터의 흡수, 즉 사회화를 통해 그 역할에 내재한 도덕적 가치에 대한 이해를 얻는다.)
우리는 이러한 가치가, 그 전문직 자체의 가치가 위협받고 있는 것과 꼭 마찬가지로 위협받고 있다고 생각한다.

N 17 정답 ④ ＊bad과 wicked

글의 흐름으로 보아, 주어진 문장이 들어가기에 가장 적절한 곳은?

> I have still not exactly pinpointed / Maddy's character / since
> 주어 동사 간접목적어 직접목적어 이유의 부사절 접속사
> wickedness takes many forms. //
> 나는 여전히 정확하게 지적하지 않았다 / Maddy의 성격을 / 사악함은 여러 형태를 띠기 때문에 //

Imagine / I tell you / that Maddy is bad. //
생각해 보라 / 내가 여러분에게 말한다고 / Maddy가 나쁘다고 //
Perhaps you infer / from my intonation, or the context / in which
주어 동사 목적어 선행사 관계부사 where로 바꾸어 쓸 수 있음
we are talking, / that I mean morally bad. //
아마 여러분은 추론할 것이다 / 나의 억양이나 상황으로부터 / 우리가 말하고 있는 / 내가 도덕상 나쁘다는 것을 의미한다고 //
Additionally, / you will probably infer / that I am disapproving
병렬 구조
of Maddy, / or saying / that I think / you should disapprove of her, or similar, /
게다가 / 여러분은 아마 추론할 것이다 / 내가 Maddy를 못마땅해 하고 있다고 / 또는 말하고 있다고 / 내가 생각한다고 / 여러분이 그녀를 못마땅해하거나 그와 비슷해야 한다고 /
given typical linguistic conventions / and assuming / I am
분사구문의 병렬 구조
sincere. //
일반적인 언어 관행을 고려하고 / 상정하여 / 내가 진심이라고 //
(①) However, / you might not get a more detailed sense / of the particular sorts of way / in which Maddy is bad, / her typical
= etc. 관계부사 how를 대신하는 「전치사＋관계대명사」 ※
character traits, and the like, /
하지만 / 여러분은 더 자세한 인식을 얻지 못할 수도 있는데 / 특정 유형의 방식에 대해 / Maddy가 나쁜 / 그녀의 일반적인 성격 특성 등에 대해 /
이유의 부사절 접속사
since people can be bad / in many ways. //
사람들은 나쁠 수 있기 때문이다 / 여러 방면에서 //
(②) In contrast, / if I say / that Maddy is wicked, / then you get
조건의 부사절 접속사
more of a sense / of her typical actions and attitudes / to others. //
그에 반해서 / 만일 내가 말한다면 / Maddy는 사악하다고 / 그러면 여러분은 더 인식하게 된다 / 그녀의 일반적인 행동과 태도를 / 다른 사람들에 대한 //
단서 1 '사악한'이라는 낱말이 더 구체적이라고 했음
(③) The word 'wicked' is more specific / than 'bad'. //
'사악한'이라는 낱말은 더 구체적이다 / '나쁜'보다 //
(④) But there is more detail nevertheless, / perhaps a stronger connotation / of the sort of person Maddy is. //
그러나 그럼에도 불구하고 / 더 많은 세부 사항이 있다 / 아마도 더 두드러진 함축 / Maddy의 사람 유형에 대한 //
단서 2 '사악한'이라는 낱말에 더 많은 세부 사항이 있다는 내용이 역접으로 연결됨
(⑤) In addition, / and again assuming typical linguistic conventions, / you should also get a sense / that I am
동격절 접속사
disapproving of Maddy, /
게다가 / 그리고 다시 일반적인 언어 관행을 상정하면 / 여러분은 또한 인식할 것이다 / 내가 Maddy를 못마땅해 하고 있다고 /
병렬 구조 목적절 접속사
or saying / that you should disapprove of her, or similar, /
목적어절 접속사
assuming / that we are still discussing / her moral character. //
또는 말하고 있다고 / 여러분이 그녀를 못마땅해하거나 그와 비슷해야 한다고 / 상정하면서 / 우리가 여전히 논하고 있다고 / 그녀의 도덕적 성격을 //

- pinpoint ⓥ 정확히 기술[묘사]하다, 정확히 집어내다
- character ⓝ 성격, 특징 ・ infer ⓥ 추론하다, 암시하다
- intonation ⓝ 억양 ・ context ⓝ 맥락, 문맥, 전후 사정
- morally ⓐⓓ 도덕[도의]적으로
- disapprove ⓥ 못마땅하다, 좋지 않게 생각하다
- typical ⓐ 전형적인, 대표적인 ・ linguistic ⓐ 언어(학)의
- convention ⓝ 관습, 관례 ・ sincere ⓐ 진실된, 진정한
- trait ⓝ 특성 ・ wicked ⓐ 사악한, 못된
- attitude ⓝ 태도, 자세, 사고방식
- nevertheless ⓐⓓ 그렇기는 하지만, 그럼에도 불구하고

내가 여러분에게 Maddy가 나쁘다고 말한다고 생각해 보라. 아마 여러분은 나의 억양이나 우리가 말하고 있는 상황으로부터 내 뜻이 도덕상 나쁘다는 것이라고 추론할 것이다. 게다가 여러분은 아마, 일반적인 언어 관행을 고려하고 내가 진심이라고 상정한다면, 내가 Maddy를 못마땅하고 있다고, 또는 내 생각에 여러분이 그녀를 못마땅해하거나 그와 비슷해야 한다고 내가 말하고 있다고, 추론할 것이다. (①) 하지만 여러분은 Maddy가 나쁜 특정 유형의 방식, 그녀의 일반적인 성격 특성 등에 대해서는 더 자세하게 인식하지 못할 수도 있는데, 사람들은 여러 방면에서 나쁠 수 있기 때문이다. (②) 그에 반해서, 만일 내가 Maddy는 사악하다고 말한다면, 그러면 여러분은 다른 사람들에 대한 그녀의 일반적인 행동과 태도를 더 인식하게 된다. (③) '사악한'이라는 낱말은 '나쁜'보다 더 구체적이다. (④ 사악함은 여러 형태를 띠기 때문에 나는 여전히 Maddy의 성격을 정확하게 지적하지 않았다.) 그러나 그럼에도 불구하고 더 많은 세부 사항, 아마도 Maddy의 사람 유형에 대한 더 두드러진 함축이 있다. (⑤) 게다가, 그리고 다시 일반적인 언어 관행을 상정하면, 여러분은 또한, 우리가 여전히 그녀의 도덕적 성격을 논하고 있다고 상정하면서, 내가 Maddy를 못마땅해하고 있다고, 또는 여러분이 그녀를 못마땅해하거나 그와 비슷해야 한다고 내가 말하고 있다고 인식할 것이다.

| 문제 풀이 순서 | [정답률 53%]

1st 주어진 문장을 해석하고, 연결어, 지시어 등을 확인한다.

> I have still not exactly pinpointed Maddy's character since wickedness takes many forms.
> 사악함은 여러 형태를 띠기 때문에 나는 여전히 Maddy의 성격을 정확하게 지적하지 않았다.

➡ 사악함이 여러 형태를 띠므로 Maddy의 성격을 지적하지 않았다고 했다. 단서
➡ **주어진 문장 앞**: 사악함이 여러 형태를 띤다는 것과 관련된 내용이 와야 할 것이다. 발상

2nd 각 선택지의 앞뒤 흐름이 매끄러운지 확인한다.

- ①의 앞 문장과 뒤 문장

앞 문장: 내가 여러분에게 Maddy가 나쁘다고 말한다고 생각해 보라. 아마 여러분은 나의 억양이나 우리가 말하고 있는 상황으로부터 내 뜻이 도덕상 나쁘다는 것이라고 추론할 것이다. 게다가 여러분은 아마, 일반적인 언어 관행을 고려하고 내가 진심이라고 상정한다면, 내가 Maddy를 못마땅해하고 있다고, 또는 내 생각에 여러분이 그녀를 못마땅해하거나 그와 비슷해야 한다고 내가 말하고 있다고, 추론할 것이다.
뒤 문장: 하지만 여러분은 Maddy가 나쁜 특정 유형의 방식, 그녀의 일반적인 성격 특성 등에 대해서는 더 자세하게 인식하지 못할 수도 있는데, 사람들은 여러 방면에서 나쁠 수 있기 때문이다.

➡ **앞 문장**: '나쁘다'라는 말의 일반적 의미
   뒤 문장: '나쁘다'라는 말이 갖는 이면
   '나쁘다'라는 말의 일반적인 의미를 언급한 뒤 However로 반대의 내용, 즉 그 이면을 소개하면서 두 문장이 연결된다.
   ▶ 주어진 문장이 ①에 들어갈 수 없음

- ②의 앞 문장과 뒤 문장

앞 문장: ①의 뒤 문장과 같음
뒤 문장: 그에 반해서, 만일 내가 Maddy는 사악하다고 말한다면, 그러면 여러분은 다른 사람들에 대한 그녀의 일반적인 행동과 태도를 더 인식하게 된다.

➡ 앞 문장에서 '나쁘다'라는 말은 여러 방면에서 의미가 달라진다고 했다. In contrast를 사용하여 앞의 내용과 반대되는, 즉 '사악하다'라는 것은 일반적인 행동과 태도를 더 인식하게 한다는 흐름이다.
   ▶ 주어진 문장이 ②에 들어갈 수 없음

- ③의 앞 문장과 뒤 문장

앞 문장: ②의 뒤 문장과 같음
뒤 문장: '사악한'이라는 낱말은 '나쁜'보다 더 구체적이다. 단서1

➡ 앞 문장의 '사악하다'라는 말의 의미를 뒤 문장에서 부연한다.
   ▶ 주어진 문장이 ③에 들어갈 수 없음

- ④의 앞 문장과 뒤 문장

앞 문장: ③의 뒤 문장과 같음
뒤 문장: 그러나 그럼에도 불구하고(nevertheless) 더 많은 세부 사항, 아마도 Maddy의 사람 유형에 대한 더 두드러진 함축이 있다. 단서2

➡ **뒤 문장**: '사악하다'라는 말에 더 많은 세부 사항이 있다.
   표현의 차이와 여러 종에 걸친 그 표현의 확산
   nevertheless는 양보의 의미를 나타내는 연결어로써, '사악하다'라는 말이 충분히 정확하고 구체적이지 않다는 내용이 앞에 있어야 한다.
➡ 주어진 문장에서 사악함이 여러 형태를 띠기 때문에 여전히 Maddy의 성격을 정확히 지적하지 않았다고 했다.
   ▶ 주어진 문장이 ④에 들어가야 함

- ⑤의 앞 문장과 뒤 문장

앞 문장: ④의 뒤 문장과 같음
뒤 문장: 게다가, 그리고 다시 일반적인 언어 관행을 상정하면, 여러분은 또한, 우리가 여전히 그녀의 도덕적 성격을 논하고 있다고 상정하면서, 내가 Maddy를 못마땅해하고 있다고, 또는 여러분이 그녀를 못마땅해하거나 그와 비슷해야 한다고 내가 말하고 있다고 인식할 것이다.

➡ 앞 문장에 등장한 'Maddy의 사람 유형에 대한 더 두드러진 함축'을 뒤 문장에서 부연하는 흐름이다.
   ▶ 주어진 문장이 ⑤에 들어갈 수 없음

3rd 글이 한눈에 들어오도록 정리하여 정답을 확인한다.

'Maddy가 나쁘다'라고 하면 도덕상 나쁘다는 것으로 추론되며 화자가 Maddy를 못마땅해하고 있다고 추론할 것이다.
(①) 사람들은 여러 방면에서 나쁠 수 있다.
(②) 'Maddy가 사악하다'라고 하면 ('나쁘다'라는 말보다) 그녀의 일반적인 행동과 태도를 더 인식하게 된다.
(③) '사악한'은 '나쁜'보다 더 구체적이다.
(④ 사악함은 여러 형태이기 때문에 여전히 Maddy의 성격을 정확히 지적하지 않았다.)
Maddy의 사람 유형에 대해 더 두드러진 함축이 있다.
(⑤) 일반적인 언어 관행을 상정하면, 여전히 Maddy를 못마땅해하고 있다고 인식할 것이다.

✱「전치사+관계대명사」와 관계부사

– 관계대명사가 전치사의 목적어로 쓰인 경우 「전치사+관계대명사」의 형태로 쓰거나, 전치사는 원래 있는 자리에 그대로 있을 수 있다. 선행사가 시간, 장소, 이유, 방법을 나타낼 때 「전치사+관계대명사」는 관계부사 when, where, why, how로 쓸 수 있다.

- I want to visit the town. + The movie was filmed in the town.
  (나는 그 마을에 가보고 싶다.)　　　　(그 영화는 그 마을에서 촬영되었다.)
- I want to visit the town <u>in which</u> the movie was filmed.
  　　　　　　　　　　　　　전치사+관계대명사
- I want to visit the town <u>where</u> the movie was filmed.
  　　　　　　　　　　　　　관계부사(관계부사 앞에 전치사를 쓰면 안 된다.)
  (나는 그 영화가 촬영되었던 그 마을에 가보고 싶다.)

N 18 정답 ⑤ ✱반딧불이가 빛을 내는 또 다른 이유

글의 흐름으로 보아, 주어진 문장이 들어가기에 가장 적절한 곳은?

단서 1 반딧불이의 빛을 소용없게 만들자 박쥐가 반딧불이를 피하는 것을 배우는 데 두 배의 시간이 걸림

When the team painted fireflies' light organs dark, / a new set of bats / took twice as long / to learn / to avoid them. //
그 팀이 반딧불이의 빛이 나는 기관을 어둡게 칠했을 때 / 새로운 한 무리의 박쥐는 / 두 배 더 길게 걸렸다 / 배우는 데 / 그것들을 피하는 것을 //

Fireflies don't just light up their behinds / to attract mates, / they
　　　　　　　　　　　　　　　　부사적 용법(목적)
also glow / to tell bats / not to eat them. //
　　　　　　　　　명사적 용법(목적격 보어)
반딧불이는 꽁무니에 불을 밝히는 것만이 아니라 / 짝의 주의를 끌기 위해서 / 그들은 빛을 내기도 한다 / 박쥐에게 말하기 위해 / 자신들을 먹지 말라고 //

This twist in the tale of the trait / that gives fireflies their name /
주어　　　　　　　　　　　　목적격 관계대명사　　선행사
was discovered / by Jesse Barber and his colleagues. //
동사
특성에 대한 이야기의 이 반전은 / 반딧불이에게 그들의 이름을 지어주는 / 발견되었다 / Jesse Barber와 그의 동료들에 의해 //

The glow's warning role benefits / both fireflies and bats, /
주어　　　　감각 동사 주격 보어(형용사)
because these insects taste disgusting / to the mammals. //
빛의 경고 역할은 유익한데 / 반딧불이와 박쥐 모두에게 / 이 곤충이 역겨운 맛이 나기 때문이다 / 그 포유동물에게는 //

(①) When swallowed, / chemicals / released by fireflies /
　　　　　동사　　목적어　　목적격 보어　　　　　　주어
cause bats to throw them back up. //
삼켜지면 / 화학 물질이 / 반딧불이에 의해 배출되는 / 박쥐로 하여금 그것을 다시 토해내게 한다 //

(②) The team placed eight bats / in a dark room / with three or four fireflies / plus three times as many tasty insects, / including beetles and moths, / for four days. //
연구팀은 여덟 마리의 박쥐를 두었다 / 어두운 방에 / 서너 마리의 반딧불이와 / 세 배 더 많은 맛이 좋은 곤충들과 함께 / 딱정벌레와 나방을 포함한 / 나흘 동안 //

(③) During the first night, / all the bats captured at least
　　　　　　전치사　　　　　명사구
one firefly. //
첫날 밤 동안에 / 모든 박쥐는 적어도 한 마리의 반딧불이를 잡았다 //

(④) But by the fourth night, / most bats had learned / to avoid fireflies / and catch all the other prey instead. //
그러나 네 번째 밤에 이르러서는 / 대부분의 박쥐는 배웠다 / 반딧불이를 피하는 것을 / 그리고 대신 다른 모든 먹이를 잡는 것을 //
단서 2 반딧불이가 빛을 낼 때는 네 번째 밤에 이르러 대부분의 박쥐가 반딧불이를 피하는 것을 배움

(⑤) It had long been thought / that firefly bioluminescence
　　　　　　가주어　　　　　　　진주어절 접속사
mainly acted / as a mating signal, /
~한다고 오랫동안 생각되었다 / 반딧불이의 생물 발광(發光)은 주로 역할을 한다고 / 짝짓기 신호로서 /
but the new finding explains / why firefly larvae also glow /
　　　　　　　　　　　　목적어절을 이끄는 의문사 ✱
despite being immature for mating. //
　　동명사구
하지만 새로운 연구 결과는 설명한다 / 반딧불이 애벌레 역시 빛을 내는 이유를 / 짝짓기를 하기에 미숙함에도 불구하고 //

- firefly ⓝ 반딧불이　　• organ ⓝ (신체의) 기관, 장기　　• bat ⓝ 박쥐
- twist ⓝ 반전　　• trait ⓝ 특성, 특징　　• disgusting ⓐ 역겨운

- swallow ⓥ 삼키다　　• chemical ⓝ 화학 물질
- release ⓥ (가스·열 등을) 발산[방출]하다　　• throw up ~을 토하다
- beetle ⓝ 딱정벌레　　• moth ⓝ 나방　　• capture ⓥ 붙잡다, 포획하다
- prey ⓝ 먹이　　• finding ⓝ 연구 결과　　• immature ⓐ 미숙한

반딧불이는 짝의 주의를 끌기 위해서 꽁무니에 불을 밝히는 것만이 아니라, 박쥐에게 자기들을 먹지 말라고 말하기 위해 빛을 내기도 한다. 반딧불이의 이름을 지어주는 특성에 대한 이야기의 이 반전은 Jesse Barber와 그의 동료들에 의해 발견되었다. 빛이 하는 경고 역할은 반딧불이와 박쥐 모두에게 유익한데, 왜냐하면 이 곤충이 그 포유동물에게는 역겨운 맛이 나기 때문이다. (①) 반딧불이를 삼키면, 반딧불이가 배출하는 화학 물질 때문에 박쥐가 그것을 다시 토해내게 낸다. (②) 연구팀은 여덟 마리의 박쥐를 서너 마리의 반딧불이와, 그보다 세 배 더 많은 딱정벌레와 나방을 포함한 맛이 좋은 곤충들과 함께 어두운 방에 나흘 동안 두었다. (③) 첫날 밤 동안에, 모든 박쥐는 적어도 한 마리의 반딧불이를 잡았다. (④) 그러나 네 번째 밤에 이르러서는, 대부분의 박쥐는 반딧불이를 피하고 대신 다른 모든 먹이를 잡는 것을 배웠다. (⑤ 그 팀이 반딧불이에서 빛이 나는 기관을 어둡게 칠했을 때, 새로운 한 무리의 박쥐는 그것들을 피하는 것을 배우는 데 두 배의 시간이 걸렸다.) 오랫동안 반딧불이의 생물 발광(發光)은 주로 짝짓기 신호의 역할을 한다고 생각되었지만, 새로운 연구 결과는 짝짓기를 하기에 미숙함에도 불구하고 반딧불이 애벌레 역시 빛을 내는 이유를 설명한다.

| 문제 풀이 순서 | [정답률 50%]

1st 주어진 문장을 해석하고, 연결어, 지시어 등을 확인한다.

> When the team painted fireflies' light organs dark, a new set of bats took twice as long to learn to avoid them. **단서 1**
> 그 팀이 반딧불이에서 빛이 나는 기관을 어둡게 칠했을 때, 새로운 한 무리의 박쥐는 그것들을 피하는 것을 배우는 데 두 배의 시간이 걸렸다.

➡ 어떤 팀이 무슨 실험을 하는지 앞에 나오고, 그 뒤에 주어진 문장을 넣어야 한다.
➡ 새로운 한 무리의 박쥐가 나오므로 **단서** 다른 무리의 박쥐에 관한 내용이 앞에 나올 것이다. **발상**

2nd 각 선택지의 앞뒤 흐름이 매끄러운지 확인한다.

- ①의 앞 문장과 뒤 문장

> **앞 문장:** 반딧불이는 짝의 주의를 끌기 위해서 꽁무니에 불을 밝히는 것만이 아니라, 박쥐에게 자기들을 먹지 말라고 말하기 위해 빛을 내기도 한다. 반딧불이의 이름을 지어주는 특성에 대한 이야기의 이 반전은 Jesse Barber와 그의 동료들에 의해 발견되었다. 빛이 하는 경고 역할은 반딧불이와 박쥐 모두에게 유익한데, 왜냐하면 이 곤충이 그 포유동물에게는 역겨운 맛이 나기 때문이다.
>
> **뒤 문장:** 반딧불이를 삼키면, 반딧불이가 배출하는 화학 물질 때문에 박쥐가 그것을 다시 토해내게 낸다.

➡ **앞 문장:** 반딧불이는 박쥐에게 경고하기 위해서도 빛을 내는데, 이는 반딧불이가 역겨운 맛이 나기 때문에 양쪽 모두에게 유익하다.
뒤 문장: 박쥐가 반딧불이를 삼키면 반딧불이의 화학 물질 때문에 다시 토해낸다.
반딧불이가 역겨운 맛이 나기 때문에, 박쥐가 반딧불이를 삼키면 다시 토해낸다는 흐름이다.
▶ 주어진 문장이 ①에 들어갈 수 없음

- ②의 앞 문장과 뒤 문장

> **앞 문장:** ①의 뒤 문장과 같음
> **뒤 문장:** 연구팀은 여덟 마리의 박쥐를 서너 마리의 반딧불이와, 그보다 세 배 더 많은 딱정벌레와 나방을 포함한 맛이 좋은 곤충들과 함께 어두운 방에 나흘 동안 두었다.

➡ 앞 문장에서 박쥐가 반딧불이를 삼키면 토해낸다고 했으므로, 뒤 문장에서 반딧불이를 다른 곤충들과 섞어 박쥐와 함께 두는 실험이 나오는 흐름이다.
▶ 주어진 문장이 ②에 들어갈 수 없음

- ③의 앞 문장과 뒤 문장

> **앞 문장:** ②의 뒤 문장과 같음
> **뒤 문장:** 첫날 밤 동안에, 모든 박쥐는 적어도 한 마리의 반딧불이를 잡았다.

→ 앞 문장에 나타난 실험의 첫 번째 결과를 뒤 문장에서 설명한다.
  ▶ 주어진 문장이 ③에 들어갈 수 없음

- ④의 앞 문장과 뒤 문장

> **앞 문장:** ③의 뒤 문장과 같음
> **뒤 문장:** 그러나 네 번째 밤에 이르러서는, 대부분의 박쥐는 반딧불이를 피하고 대신 다른 모든 먹이를 잡는 것을 배웠다. 단서 2

→ 앞 문장에 나타난 첫 번째 결과에 이어서 두 번째 결과를 뒤 문장에서 설명한다.
  ▶ 주어진 문장이 ④에 들어갈 수 없음

- ⑤의 앞 문장과 뒤 문장

> **앞 문장:** ④의 뒤 문장과 같음
> **뒤 문장:** 오랫동안 반딧불이의 생물 발광(發光)은 주로 짝짓기 신호의 역할을 한다고 생각되었지만, 새로운 연구 결과는 짝짓기를 하기에 미숙함에도 불구하고 반딧불이 애벌레 역시 빛을 내는 이유를 설명한다.

→ **뒤 문장:** 반딧불이의 생물 발광의 또 다른 역할
반딧불이 발광 실험에서 다른 박쥐 무리를 비교하는 내용이 앞에 나와야 한다.
→ 주어진 문장에서 반딧불이의 빛이 나는 기관을 어둡게 칠하여 새로운 무리의 박쥐에게 실험한 내용이 나온다.
  ▶ 주어진 문장이 ⑤에 들어가야 함

3rd 글이 한눈에 들어오도록 정리하여 정답을 확인한다.

반딧불이는 박쥐에게 역겨운 맛이 나기 때문에, 자기들을 먹지 말라고 경고하기 위해서도 빛을 낸다.
(①) 반딧불이가 배출하는 화학 물질 때문에 박쥐가 그들을 삼키면 다시 토해내게 된다.
(②) 연구팀은 박쥐와 반딧불이와 맛이 좋은 곤충들을 함께 어두운 방에 두는 실험을 했다.
(③) 첫날 밤 동안에 모든 박쥐는 적어도 한 마리의 반딧불이를 잡았다.
(④) 네 번째 밤에는 대부분의 박쥐가 반딧불이를 피하고 다른 먹이를 잡는 것을 배웠다.
(⑤ 반딧불이의 빛이 나는 기관을 어둡게 칠하면 박쥐가 반딧불이를 피하는 것을 배우는 데 두 배의 시간이 걸렸다.)
반딧불이의 생물 발광은 짝짓기 신호의 역할 외에도 포식자에 대한 경고의 역할도 한다.

— 어법 특강

※ 명사절을 이끄는 의문사

〈의문사는 간접의문문〈의문사+주어+동사〉의 형태로 문장에서 주어, 목적어, 보어 역할을 하는 명사절을 이끈다.〉

- 주어 역할을 하는 간접의문문
  - Why he died is a mystery.
    (그가 왜 죽었는지는 미스터리이다.)

- 목적어 역할을 하는 간접의문문
  - Do you know when these houses were built?
    (이 건물들이 언제 지어졌는지 아십니까?)

- 보어 역할을 하는 간접의문문
  - The question is how he did this.
    (문제는 그가 어떻게 이것을 했느냐이다.)

> 글의 흐름으로 보아, 주어진 문장이 들어가기에 가장 적절한 곳을 고르시오. [3점]

> Personal stories connect / with larger narratives / to generate new identities. // 단서1 '개인의 이야기'가 '더 큰 이야기'와 연결됨 부사적 용법(결과)
> 개인의 이야기는 연결되어 / 더 큰 이야기와 / 새로운 정체성을 생성한다 //

The growing complexity / of the social dynamics / determining food choices / makes the job of marketers and advertisers / increasingly more difficult. //
커지는 복잡성이 / 사회적 역학의 / 식품 선택을 결정하는 / 마케팅 담당자와 광고주의 업무를 만든다 / 점점 더 어렵게 //
(①) In the past, / mass production allowed / for accessibility and affordability / of products, / as well as their wide distribution, / and was accepted / as a sign of progress. //
과거에 / 대량 생산은 허용했다 / 입수 가능성과 감당할 수 있는 비용을 / 제품의 / 그것의 광범위한 유통뿐 아니라 / 그리고 받아들여졌다 / 발전의 신호로 //
(②) Nowadays it is increasingly replaced / by the fragmentation of consumers / among smaller and smaller segments / that are supposed to reflect / personal preferences. //
요즘 그것은 점점 더 대체되고 있다 / 소비자 단편화에 의해 / 점점 더 작은 부문에서 / 반영해야 하는 / 개인의 선호를 //
(③) Everybody feels different and special / and expects products / serving his or her inclinations. //
모든 사람은 각기 다르고 특별하다고 느끼고 / 제품을 기대한다 / 자신의 기호를 만족시키는 //
(④) In reality, / these supposedly individual preferences / end up overlapping / with emerging, temporary, always changing, almost tribal formations /
현실에서 / 아마도 개인적인 이러한 선호는 / 겹치게 된다 / 최근에 생겨나고, 일시적이며, 항상 바뀌고, 거의 부족적인 형성물과 / 단서2 '개인적 선호'가 문화적 감성, 사회 정체성, 정치적 감성, 식생활과 건강에 관한 관심으로 '더 큰 이야기'와 겹치게 됨
solidifying / around cultural sensibilities, social identifications, political sensibilities, and dietary and health concerns. //
확고해지는 / 결국 문화적 감성, 사회 정체성, 정치적 감성, 식생활과 건강에 관한 관심을 중심으로 //
(⑤) These consumer communities / go beyond national boundaries, / feeding on global and widely shared repositories / of ideas, images, and practices. // = and then they feed
이들 소비자 집단은 / 국경을 넘어 / 전 세계의 널리 공유된 저장소로 인해 더 강화된다 / 개념, 이미지, 관습의 //

- narrative ⓝ 이야기
- complexity ⓝ 복잡성
- determine ⓥ 결정하다
- accessibility ⓝ 접근하기 쉬움
- distribution ⓝ 유통, 분배
- inclination ⓝ 기호, 성향
- overlap ⓥ 겹치다
- tribal ⓐ 부족의, 종족의
- sensibility ⓝ 감성, 감수성
- boundary ⓝ 경계[한계](선)
- identity ⓝ 정체성, 신원
- dynamics ⓝ 역학
- mass ⓐ 대량의
- affordability ⓝ 감당할 수 있는 비용
- progress ⓝ 발전
- segment ⓝ 부분
- supposedly ⓐⓓ 아마
- temporary ⓐ 일시적인
- solidify ⓥ 확고해지다
- dietary ⓝ 식생활

식품 선택을 결정하는 사회적 역학이 점점 복잡해지면서 마케팅 담당자와 광고주의 업무가 점점 더 어려워지고 있다. (①) 과거에 대량 생산은 제품을 광범위하게 유통하게 할 뿐만 아니라 제품을 입수하고 구매 비용을 감당할 수 있게 했으며, 발전의 신호로 받아들여졌다. (②) 요즘 그것은 개인의 선호를 반영해야 하는 점점 더 작은 부문에서 소비자 단편화에 의해 점점 더 대체되고 있다. (③) 모든 사람은 각기 다르고 특별하다고 느끼고, 자신의 기호를 만족시키는 제품을 기대한다. (④) 현실에서, 아마도 개인적인 이러한 선호는 결국 문화적 감성, 사회 정체성, 정치적 감성, 식생활과 건강에 관한 관심을 중심으로 확고해지는, 최근에 생겨나고, 일시적이며, 항상 바뀌고, 거의 부족적인 형성물과 겹치게 된다. (⑤ 개인의 이야기는 더 큰 이야기와 연결되어 새로운 정체성을 생성한다.) 이들 소비자 집단은 국경을 넘어 개념, 이미지, 관습의 전 세계의 널리 공유된 저장소로 인해 더 강화된다.

1st 주어진 문장을 해석하고, 연결어, 지시어 등을 확인한다.

> Personal stories connect with larger narratives to generate new identities. 단서1
> 개인의 이야기는 더 큰 이야기와 연결되어 새로운 정체성을 생성한다.

⇒ 개인의 이야기와 더 큰 이야기가 각각 무엇을 비유하는지 앞에 나오고, 그 뒤에 주어진 문장을 넣어야 한다.

2nd 각 선택지의 앞뒤 흐름이 매끄러운지 확인한다.

- ①의 앞 문장과 뒤 문장

> **앞 문장**: 식품 선택을 결정하는 사회적 역학이 점점 복잡해지면서 마케팅 담당자와 광고주의 업무가 점점 더 어려워지고 있다.
> **뒤 문장**: 과거에 대량 생산은 제품을 광범위하게 유통하게 할 뿐만 아니라 제품을 입수하고 구매 비용을 감당할 수 있게 했으며, 발전의 신호로 받아들여졌다.

⇒ **앞 문장**: 식품 선택을 결정하는 데 있어서 사회적 역학이 점점 복잡해지고 있다.
뒤 문장: 과거에 대량 생산은 발전의 신호였다.
앞 문장에서 식품 선택을 결정하는 사회적 역학의 변화 과정을 설명하며, 뒤 문장에서 과거의 대량 생산부터 차례대로 언급하므로 앞뒤 문장이 자연스럽게 연결된다.
▶ 주어진 문장이 ①에 들어갈 수 없음

- ②의 앞 문장과 뒤 문장

> **앞 문장**: ①의 뒤 문장과 같음
> **뒤 문장**: 요즘 그것은 개인의 선호를 반영해야 하는 점점 더 작은 부문에서 소비자 단편화에 의해 점점 더 대체되고 있다.

⇒ 앞 문장에서 과거의 대량 생산을 설명했으므로, 뒤 문장에서 오늘날의 소비자 단편화를 설명해야 앞뒤 문장이 자연스럽게 연결된다.
▶ 주어진 문장이 ②에 들어갈 수 없음

- ③의 앞 문장과 뒤 문장

> **앞 문장**: ②의 뒤 문장과 같음
> **뒤 문장**: 모든 사람은 각기 다르고 특별하다고 느끼고, 자신의 기호를 만족시키는 제품을 기대한다.

⇒ 앞 문장에 나타난 소비자 단편화를 뒤 문장에서 부연한다.
▶ 주어진 문장이 ③에 들어갈 수 없음

- ④의 앞 문장과 뒤 문장

> **앞 문장**: ③의 뒤 문장과 같음
> **뒤 문장**: 현실에서, 아마도 개인적인 이러한 선호는 결국 문화적 감성, 사회 정체성, 정치적 감성, 식생활과 건강에 관한 관심을 중심으로 확고해지는, 최근에 생겨나고, 일시적이며, 항상 바뀌고, 거의 부족적인 형성물과 겹치게 된다. 단서2

⇒ 앞 문장에 나타난 소비자의 각기 다른 기호를 부연한다.
▶ 주어진 문장이 ④에 들어갈 수 없음

- ⑤의 앞 문장과 뒤 문장

> **앞 문장**: ④의 뒤 문장과 같음
> **뒤 문장**: 이들 소비자 집단은 국경을 넘어 개념, 이미지, 관습의 전 세계의 널리 공유된 저장소로 인해 더 강화된다.

⇒ **뒤 문장**: 소비자 집단은 개념, 이미지, 관습의 전 세계의 널리 공유된 저장소로 강화된다.
개인적 선호가 광범위한 문제와 겹친다는 내용이 앞에 나와야 한다.
⇒ 주어진 문장에서 개인의 이야기는 더 큰 이야기와 연결된다는 비유가 나온다.
▶ 주어진 문장이 ⑤에 들어가야 함

3rd 글이 한눈에 들어오도록 정리하여 정답을 확인한다.

식품 선택을 결정하는 사회적 역학이 점점 복잡해진다.
(①) 과거에 대량 생산은 발전의 신호로 받아들여졌다.
(②) 오늘날 대량 생산은 소비자 단편화에 의해 대체되고 있다.
(③) 모든 사람은 자신의 기호를 만족시키는 제품을 기대한다.
(④) 개인적 선호는 부족적인 형성물, 즉 광범위한 문제와 겹친다.
(⑤ 개인의 이야기는 더 큰 이야기와 연결되어 새로운 정체성을 형성한다.)
이들 소비자 집단은 전 세계의 널리 공유된 저장소로 인해 더 강화된다.

N 20 정답 ⑤ * 로봇의 도입으로 인한 두려움 완화 방법

글의 흐름으로 보아, 주어진 문장이 들어가기에 가장 적절한 곳을 고르시오.

> Retraining current employees / for new positions / within the company / will also greatly reduce / their fear of being laid off. // 단서1 앞에 직원들의 두려움을 줄이는 또다른 방법이 제시되어 있어야 함
> 동명사구 주어 / 동사 / 목적어
> 현재 직원을 재교육하는 것은 / 새로운 직책을 위해 / 회사 내의 / 또한 크게 줄일 것이다 / 해고되는 것에 대한 그들의 두려움을 //

Introduction of robots into factories, / while employment of human workers is being reduced, / creates worry and fear. //
단수 주어 / 단수 동사 / 목적어
공장으로의 로봇의 도입은 / 인간 노동자의 고용이 줄어들고 있는 동안 / 걱정과 두려움을 불러일으킨다 //

(①) It is the responsibility of management / to prevent or, at least, to ease / these fears. //
가주어 / 진주어의 병렬 구조 *
~은 경영진의 책임이다 / 예방하거나 최소한 완화하는 것은 / 이러한 두려움을 //

(②) For example, / robots could be introduced / only in new plants / rather than replacing humans / in existing assembly lines. //
예를 들어 / 로봇은 도입될 수 있다 / 새로운 공장에만 / 인간을 대체하는 대신 / 기존 조립 라인에서 //

(③) Workers should be included / in the planning / for new factories / or the introduction of robots / into existing plants, / so they can participate / in the process. //
병렬 구조
노동자는 포함되어야 하고 / 계획하는 데 / 새로운 공장을 / 또는 로봇의 도입을 / 기존의 공장에 / 그 결과 그들은 참여할 수 있다 / 그 과정에 //

(④) It may be / that robots are needed / to reduce manufacturing costs / so that the company remains competitive, /
부사절 접속사(목적) / 부사적 용법(목적)
~일 수도 있다 / 로봇이 필요한 것일 / 제조원가를 낮추기 위해 / 회사가 경쟁력을 유지하도록 /
but planning / for such cost reductions / should be done jointly / by labor and management. //
하지만 계획은 / 그러한 원가절감을 위한 / 함께 행해져야 한다 / 노사에 의해 //

(⑤) Since robots are particularly good / at highly repetitive simple motions, /
부사절 접속사(이유)
로봇은 특히 잘하기 때문에 / 매우 반복적인 단순 동작을 /
the replaced human workers / should be moved to positions / where judgment and decisions / beyond the abilities of robots / are required. // 단서2 인간 노동자가 회사 내의 다른 직책으로 옮겨져야
관계부사 / 선행사
교체된 인간 노동자는 / 위치로 옮겨져야 한다 / 판단과 결정이 / 로봇의 능력을 넘어서는 / 요구되는 // 한다는 것에 대한 구체적인 설명이 이어짐

- current ⓐ 현재의   - lay off 해고하다, 휴직시키다
- introduction ⓝ 도입, 전래   - responsibility ⓝ 책임, 의무
- management ⓝ (사업체·조직의) 경영[관리](진)

- ease ⓥ (고통·괴로움 등을) 완화시키다[덜다]　• plant ⓝ 공장
- replace ⓥ 교체하다, 대신[대체]하다
- assembly ⓝ (차량·가구 등의) 조립
- manufacture ⓥ (기계를 이용하여 대량으로 상품을) 제조[생산]하다
- competitive ⓐ 경쟁력 있는　• reduction ⓝ 축소, 삭감
- jointly ⓐⓓ 함께, 공동으로　• repetitive ⓐ 반복적인
- motion ⓝ 동작, 몸짓　• judgment ⓝ 판단, 판결
- beyond (prep) (능력·한계 등을) 넘어서는

인간 노동자의 고용은 줄어들면서 공장에 로봇을 도입하는 것은 걱정과 두려움을 불러일으킨다. (①) 이러한 두려움을 예방하거나 최소한 완화하는 것은 경영진의 책임이다. (②) 예를 들어 로봇은 기존 조립 라인에서 인간을 대체하는 대신 새로운 공장에만 도입될 수 있다. (③) 노동자는 새로운 공장이나 기존 공장에 로봇을 도입하는 것을 계획하는 데 포함되어야 하는데, 그렇게 함으로써 그들은 그 과정에 참여할 수 있다. (④) 회사가 경쟁력을 유지하도록 제조원가를 낮추기 위해 로봇이 필요한 것일 수도 있지만, 그러한 원가절감을 위한 계획은 노사가 함께 해야 한다. (⑤ 회사 내의 새로운 직책을 위해 현재 직원을 재교육하는 것은 해고되는 것에 대한 그들의 두려움도 또한 크게 줄일 것이다.) 로봇은 특히 매우 반복적인 단순 동작을 잘하기 때문에 교체된 인간 노동자는 로봇의 능력을 넘어서는 판단과 결정이 필요한 위치로 옮겨져야 한다.

| 문제 풀이 순서 | [정답률 49%]

1st 주어진 문장을 해석하고, 연결어, 지시어 등을 확인한다.

> Retraining current employees for new positions within the company will [also] greatly reduce their fear of being laid off. 단서1
> 회사 내의 새로운 직책을 위해 현재 직원을 재교육하는 것은 해고되는 것에 대한 그들의 두려움도 또한 크게 줄일 것이다.

➡ also가 나오므로, 단서 새로운 직책을 위해 현재 직원을 재교육하는 것 외에도 직원들의 두려움을 줄이는 것이 앞에 나오고, 그 뒤에 주어진 문장을 넣어야 한다. 발상
➡ 무엇이 현재 직원들의 해고에 대한 걱정을 낮게 되는지 앞에 나올 것이다.

2nd 각 선택지의 앞뒤 흐름이 매끄러운지 확인한다.

- ①의 앞 문장과 뒤 문장

> 앞 문장: 인간 노동자의 고용은 줄어들면서 공장에 로봇을 도입하는 것은 걱정과 두려움을 불러일으킨다.
> 뒤 문장: 이러한 두려움을 예방하거나 최소한 완화하는 것은 경영진의 책임이다.

➡ 앞 문장: 인간 노동자의 고용을 로봇이 대체하는 데서 오는 걱정과 두려움
뒤 문장: 이러한 두려움을 예방하거나 완화할 경영진의 책임
앞 문장에서 로봇이 인간 노동자의 고용을 대체하는 데서 오는 두려움을 언급하며, 뒤 문장에서 이러한 두려움을 예방하는 책임을 언급하므로 앞뒤 문장이 자연스럽게 연결된다.
▶ 주어진 문장이 ①에 들어갈 수 없음
- ②의 앞 문장과 뒤 문장

> 앞 문장: ①의 뒤 문장과 같음
> 뒤 문장: 예를 들어 로봇은 기존 조립 라인에서 인간을 대체하는 대신 새로운 공장에만 도입될 수 있다.

➡ 앞 문장에서 로봇이 인간 노동력을 대체한다는 두려움을 예방할 책임을 언급하고 뒤 문장에서 그 예시로서 새로운 공장에만 로봇을 도입하는 것을 소개하는 흐름이다.
▶ 주어진 문장이 ②에 들어갈 수 없음

- ③의 앞 문장과 뒤 문장

> 앞 문장: ②의 뒤 문장과 같음
> 뒤 문장: 노동자는 새로운 공장이나 기존 공장에 로봇을 도입하는 것을 계획하는 데 포함되어야 하는데, 그렇게 함으로써 그들은 그 과정에 참여할 수 있다.

➡ 앞 문장과 더불어 로봇 도입 계획에 노동자가 참여할 수도 있다는 추가적인 예시를 제시한다.
▶ 주어진 문장이 ③에 들어갈 수 없음
- ④의 앞 문장과 뒤 문장

> 앞 문장: ③의 뒤 문장과 같음
> 뒤 문장: 회사가 경쟁력을 유지하도록 제조원가를 낮추기 위해 로봇이 필요한 것일 수도 있지만, 그러한 원가절감을 위한 계획은 노사가 함께 해야 한다.

➡ 앞 문장에 나타난 예시를 부연한다.
▶ 주어진 문장이 ④에 들어갈 수 없음
- ⑤의 앞 문장과 뒤 문장

> 앞 문장: ④의 뒤 문장과 같음
> 뒤 문장: 로봇은 특히 매우 반복적인 단순 동작을 잘하기 때문에 교체된 인간 노동자는 로봇의 능력을 넘어서는 판단과 결정이 필요한 위치로 옮겨져야 한다. 단서2

➡ 뒤 문장: 로봇으로 일자리가 대체된 인간 노동자는 단순노동을 넘어 판단과 결정이 필요한 위치로 옮겨져야 한다.
인간 노동자의 위치를 옮기는 것에 관한 내용이 앞에 나와야 한다.
➡ 주어진 문장에서 회사 내의 새로운 직책을 위해 현재 직원을 재교육하는 것이 나온다.
▶ 주어진 문장이 ⑤에 들어가야 함

3rd 글이 한눈에 들어오도록 정리하여 정답을 확인한다.

인간 노동자의 고용이 줄면서 공장에 로봇을 도입하는 것은 두려움을 불러일으킨다.
(①) 이러한 두려움을 예방하는 것은 경영진의 책임이다.
(②) 예를 들어 로봇은 기존 노동자를 대체하지 않고 새로운 공장에만 도입될 수 있다.
(③) 노동자는 로봇 도입 계획 과정에 참여할 수도 있다.
(④) 회사의 원가절감을 위한 계획은 노사가 함께 해야 한다.
(⑤ 새로운 직책을 위해 현재 직원을 재교육하는 것은 해고의 두려움을 줄일 것이다.)
로봇으로 교체된 인간 노동자는 판단과 결정이 필요한 위치로 옮겨져야 한다.

┌─ 어법 특강 ─

＊ **병렬 구조를 이루는 등위접속사**
- 등위접속사 and, but, or, so 등은 두 개 이상의 단어, 구, 절을 연결한다. 이때 동일한 품사와 문법적으로 같은 성분을 연결해야 한다.
- Don't forget to prepare a cutting board <u>and</u> a knife.
　(도마와 칼을 준비할 것을 잊지 마세요.)　　단어와 단어를 연결
- You can squeeze oranges by hand, <u>but</u> it's easier if you use a squeezer.　　문장과 문장을 연결
　(당신은 손으로 오렌지를 짤 수 있지만, 압착기를 사용하면 더 쉬워요.)
- Anyone caught faces a huge fine, <u>but</u> this has not discouraged selling their seats.　　문장과 문장을 연결
　(잡히면 누구나 엄청난 벌금에 처해지지만, 이것은 입장권을 파는 것을 막지는 못한다.)

글의 흐름으로 보아, 주어진 문장이 들어가기에 가장 적절한 곳은? [3점]

Note / that copyright covers the expression of an idea / and not the idea itself. // 단서1 모두 유사한 기능을 가진 많은 스마트폰이 저작권 침해가 아닌 이유
유의하라 / 저작권은 아이디어의 표현을 다룬다는 것을 / 아이디어 그 자체가 아니라 //

Designers draw on their experience of design / when approaching a new project. //
디자이너는 자신의 디자인 경험을 이용한다 / 새로운 프로젝트에 접근할 때 삽입절

This includes the use of previous designs / that they know work / — both designs / that they have created themselves / and those / that others have created. //
주격 관계대명사   생략 가능한 목적격 관계대명사
이것은 이전 디자인의 사용을 포함한다 / 효과가 있다고 그들이 알고 있는 / 디자인 둘 다 / 그들이 직접 만들었던 / 그리고 디자인 / 다른 사람들이 만들었던 //

(①) Others' creations often spark inspiration / that also leads / to new ideas and innovation. //
선행사   주격 관계대명사
다른 사람들의 창작물은 흔히 영감을 불러일으킨다 / 또한 이어지는 / 새로운 아이디어와 혁신으로 //

(②) This is well known and understood. //
이는 잘 알려져 있고 이해되는 일이다 //

(③) However, / the expression of an idea is protected / by copyright, / and people / who infringe on that copyright / can be taken to court and prosecuted. //
주어   동사
그러나 / 한 아이디어의 표현은 보호된다 / 저작권에 의해 / 그리고 사람들은 / 그 저작권을 침해하는 / 법정에 끌려가고 기소될 수 있다 // 단서2 This가 가리키는 것이 주어진 문장의 내용임

(④) This means, / for example, / that while there are numerous smartphones / all with similar functionality, / this does not represent / an infringement of copyright /
명사절 접속사   대조의 부사절 접속사
이것은 의미한다 / 예를 들어 / 많은 스마트폰이 있지만 / 모두 유사한 기능을 가진 / 이것이 나타내지 않는다는 것을 / 저작권 침해를 //

as the idea has been expressed / in different ways / and it is the expression / that has been copyrighted. //
이유의 부사절 접속사   it is ~ that 강조 구문
그 아이디어가 표현되었기 때문에 / 서로 다른 방식으로 / 그리고 바로 그 표현이 / 저작권 보호를 받기 (때문에) //

(⑤) Copyright is free / and is automatically invested in the author, / for instance, / the writer of a book or a programmer / who develops a program, /
주격 관계대명사   선행사
저작권은 무료이며 / 그 저작자에게 자동으로 부여된다 / 예를 들어 / 어떤 책의 저자나 프로그래머 / 프로그램을 개발하는 /
부사절 접속사(= if not)
unless they sign the copyright over / to someone else. //
그들이 저작권을 양도하지 않는 한 / 다른 누군가에게 //

- copyright ⓝ 저작권, 판권 ⓥ 저작권을 보호하다
- cover ⓥ 다루다, 포함하다   • draw on ~에 의지하다, ~을 이용하다
- previous ⓐ 이전의, 먼젓번의   • spark ⓥ 촉발시키다, 유발하다
- inspiration ⓝ (특히 예술적 창조를 가능하게 하는) 영감
- innovation ⓝ 혁신, 쇄신   • court ⓝ 법정, 법원
- numerous ⓐ 많은   • functionality ⓝ (상품 등의) 목적[기능], 기능성
- represent ⓥ 대표[대신]하다, (~에) 해당[상당]하다
- infringement ⓝ 위배, 위반
- automatically ⓐⓓ 자동적으로, 무의식적으로   • invest ⓥ 부여하다
- author ⓝ 작가, 저자, 입안자   • sign over (권리·재산 등을) 양도하다

디자이너는 새로운 프로젝트에 접근할 때 자신의 디자인 경험을 이용한다. 이것에는 효과가 있다고 그들이 알고 있는 이전의 디자인, 즉 그들이 직접 만들었던 디자인과 다른 사람들이 만들었던 디자인을 둘 다 활용하는 것이 포함된다. (①) 다른 사람들의 창작물은 흔히 새로운 아이디어와 혁신으로도 이어지는 영감을 불러일으킨다. (②) 이는 잘 알려져 있고 이해되는 일이다. (③) 그러나 한 아이디어의 표현은 저작권에 의해 보호되며, 그 저작권을 침해하는 사람들은 법정에 끌려가고 기소될 수 있다. (④ 저작권은 아이디어 그 자체가 아니라 아이디어의 표현을 다룬다는 점에 유의하라.) 이

것은 예를 들어, 모두 유사한 기능을 가진 많은 스마트폰이 있지만, 그 아이디어가 서로 다른 방식으로 표현되었고 저작권 보호를 받은 것은 그 표현이기 때문에 이것이 저작권 침해를 나타내지 않는다는 것을 의미한다. (⑤) 저작권은 무료이며, 저작자에게, 예를 들어 어떤 책의 저자나 프로그램을 개발하는 프로그래머, 그들이 저작권을 다른 누군가에게 양도하지 않는 한, 자동으로 부여된다.

| 문제 풀이 순서 | [정답률 50%]

1st 주어진 문장을 해석하고, 연결어, 지시어 등을 확인한다.

Note that copyright covers the expression of an idea and not the idea itself. 단서1
저작권은 아이디어 그 자체가 아니라 아이디어의 표현을 다룬다는 점에 유의하라.

➡ 저작권이 아이디어 자체를 다룬다는 내용이 앞에 나오고 그 뒤에 주어진 문장을 넣어야 한다.

2nd 각 선택지의 앞뒤 흐름이 매끄러운지 확인한다.

- **①의 앞 문장과 뒤 문장**

앞 문장: 디자이너는 새로운 프로젝트에 접근할 때 자신의 디자인 경험을 이용한다. 이것에는 효과가 있다고 그들이 알고 있는 이전의 디자인, 즉 그들이 직접 만들었던 디자인과 다른 사람들이 만들었던 디자인을 둘 다 활용하는 것이 포함된다.
뒤 문장: 다른 사람들의 창작물은 흔히 새로운 아이디어와 혁신으로도 이어지는 영감을 불러일으킨다.

➡ 앞 문장: 디자이너는 그들이 직접 만들었던 디자인과 다른 사람들이 만들었던 디자인을 활용하여 새로운 프로젝트에 접근한다.
뒤 문장: 다른 사람들의 창작물이 새로운 아이디어로 이어지는 영감을 불러일으킨다.
'다른 사람들이 만들었던 디자인'을 뒤 문장에서 '다른 사람들의 창작물'로 표현하면서 연결된다.
▶ 주어진 문장이 ①에 들어갈 수 없음

- **②의 앞 문장과 뒤 문장**

앞 문장: ①의 뒤 문장과 같음
뒤 문장: 이는 잘 알려져 있고 이해되는 일이다.

➡ 앞 문장에서 다른 사람들의 창작물이 새로운 아이디어의 영감을 불러일으킨다는 것을 뒤 문장에서 This로 언급하며 자연스럽게 연결된다.
▶ 주어진 문장이 ②에 들어갈 수 없음

- **③의 앞 문장과 뒤 문장**

앞 문장: ②의 뒤 문장과 같음
뒤 문장: 그러나 한 아이디어의 표현은 저작권에 의해 보호되며, 그 저작권을 침해하는 사람들은 법정에 끌려가고 기소될 수 있다.

➡ 앞 문장에서 다른 사람들의 창작물이 새로운 아이디어로 이어지는 것이 잘 알려져 있고 이해된다고 했지만, 뒤 문장에서 반대되는 내용을 나타내는 However를 사용하여 아이디어의 표현이 보호된다는 점을 언급하는 흐름이다.
▶ 주어진 문장이 ③에 들어갈 수 없음

- **④의 앞 문장과 뒤 문장**

앞 문장: ③의 뒤 문장과 같음
뒤 문장: 이것(This)은 예를 들어, 모두 유사한 기능을 가진 많은 스마트폰이 있지만, 그 아이디어가 서로 다른 방식으로 표현되었고 저작권 보호를 받은 것은 그 표현이기 때문에 이것이 저작권 침해를 나타내지 않는다는 것을 의미한다. 단서2

➡ **뒤 문장**: 저작권의 보호를 받는 것은 아이디어의 표현이기 때문에 유사한 기능을 가진 많은 스마트폰은 저작권 침해가 아니다.
This가 나타내는 내용은 아이디어의 표현과 관련된 것이며, 앞에 있어야 한다.
➡ 주어진 문장에서 저작권은 아이디어 자체가 아니라 아이디어의 표현을 다룬다고 했다.
▶ 주어진 문장이 ④에 들어가야 함
- **⑤의 앞 문장과 뒤 문장**

> **앞 문장**: ④의 뒤 문장과 같음
> **뒤 문장**: 저작권은 무료이며, 저작자에게, 예를 들어 어떤 책의 저자나 프로그램을 개발하는 프로그래머, 그들이 저작권을 다른 누군가에게 양도하지 않는 한, 자동으로 부여된다.

➡ 앞 문장에 등장한 저작권을 뒤 문장에서 부연하는 흐름이다.
▶ 주어진 문장이 ⑤에 들어갈 수 없음

3rd 글이 한눈에 들어오도록 정리하여 정답을 확인한다.

디자이너는 다른 사람들이 만들었던 디자인도 활용하여 새로운 프로젝트에 접근한다.
(①) 다른 사람들의 창작물은 새로운 아이디어로 이어지는 영감을 불러일으킨다.
(②) 다른 사람들의 창작물을 활용하는 것은 잘 알려져 있고 이해되는 일이다.
(③) 한 아이디어의 표현은 저작권에 의해 보호된다.
(④ 저작권은 아이디어 자체가 아니라 아이디어의 표현을 다룬다.)
유사한 기능을 가진 많은 스마트폰은 서로 다른 방식으로 표현되었다면 저작권 침해를 나타내지 않는다.
(⑤) 저작권은 무료이며 누군가에게 양도하지 않는 한 자동으로 부여된다.

N 22 정답 ② ＊개별 나무를 돕는 것이 미치는 영향 ————

> 글의 흐름으로 보아, 주어진 문장이 들어가기에 가장 적절한 곳을 고르시오. [3점]

단서 1 그것들이 건강하고 더 잘 자라지만 오래 살지는 못하는 이유가 앞에 있어야 함

> As a result, / they are fit and grow better, / but they aren't particularly long-lived. //
> 그 결과 / 그것들은 건강하고 더 잘 자라지만 / 그것들은 특별히 오래 살지는 못한다 //

When trees grow together, / nutrients and water can be optimally divided / among them all / so that each tree can grow / into the best tree / it can be. //
　　　　　　　　　　　　　부사절 접속사(목적)
나무가 함께 자랄 때는 / 영양분과 물이 최적으로 분배된다 / 그것들 모두 사이에서 / 각 나무가 성장할 수 있도록 / 최고의 나무로 / 그것이 될 수 있는 //

If you "help" individual trees / by getting rid of their supposed
부사절 접속사(조건)
competition, / the remaining trees are bereft. //
　　　　　　　주어
만약 여러분이 개별 나무를 '도와주면' / 그것의 경쟁자로 여겨지는 나무를 제거하여 / 나머지 나무를 잃게 된다 //

They send messages out to their neighbors unsuccessfully, / because nothing remains but stumps. //
그것들은 이웃 나무들에 성공적이지 못하게 메시지를 보낸다 / 그루터기 외에는 무엇도 남아있지 않기 때문에 //

Every tree now grows on its own, / giving rise / to great
　　　　　　　　　　　　　　　　= and it gives
differences in productivity. //
이제 모든 나무가 그것 나름대로 자라 / 생기게 한다 / 생산성에 큰 차이가 //

(①) Some individuals photosynthesize / like mad / until sugar
　　　　　주어
positively bubbles / along their trunk. //
　　　　　동사(완전자동사)
어떤 개체들은 광합성을 한다 / 미친 듯이 / 당분이 확연히 흘러넘칠 때까지 / 그것들의 줄기를 따라 //

(②) This is because a tree can be only as strong / as the forest /
주격관계대명사　　　　　　　　　　　　　　　　　　선행사
that surrounds it. //　　**단서 2** This가 가리키는 것이 주어진 글의 내용
　　　　　　　　　　　　　(나무가 특별히 오래 살지는 못하는 것)임
이는 나무는 ~만큼만 강할 수 있기 때문이다 / 숲만큼만 / 그것을 둘러싼 //

(③) And there are now a lot of losers / in the forest. //
그리고 지금 많은 패자가 있다 / 숲에는 //

(④) Weaker members, / who would once have been supported
　　　　　　　　　　　　복수 주어　　　　　　　　복수 동사
/ by the stronger ones, / suddenly fall behind. //
약한 구성원들이 / 한때는 지원을 받았을 / 강한 구성원들의 / 갑자기 뒤처진다 //

(⑤) Whether the reason for their decline / is their location and
　　　　　　　└── 부사절 접속사(~이든 …이든) ──┘
lack of nutrients, a passing sickness, or genetic makeup, / they now fall prey / to insects and fungi. //
그것들의 쇠락 원인이 / 위치와 영양분 부족이든, 일시적인 질병이든, 혹은 유전적 구성이든 / 이제 그것들은 먹이가 된다 / 곤충과 균류의 //

··

- nutrient ⓝ 영양분　　· optimally ⓐⓓ 최선으로, 최적으로
- get rid of 제거하다　　· suppose ⓥ 추측하다, 여기다
- competition ⓝ 경쟁자, 경쟁　· positively ⓐⓓ 분명히
- bubble ⓥ 흘러넘치다, 거품이 일다　· surround ⓥ 둘러싸다
- decline ⓝ 감소　　· genetic ⓐ 유전의
- fall prey to ~의 희생물이 되다　· fungi ⓝ 균류

나무가 함께 자랄 때는 각 나무가 가능한 최고의 나무로 성장할 수 있도록 영양분과 물이 그것들 모두 사이에서 최적으로 분배된다. 만약 여러분이 경쟁자로 여겨지는 나무를 제거하여 개별 나무를 '도와주면' 나머지 나무를 잃게 된다. 그것들은 그루터기 외에는 무엇도 남아있지 않기 때문에 이웃 나무들에 메시지를 보내지만, 소용이 없다. 이제 모든 나무가 그것 나름대로 자라 생산성에 큰 차이가 생긴다. (①) 어떤 개체들은 당분이 줄기를 따라 확연히 흘러넘칠 때까지 미친 듯이 광합성을 한다. (② 그 결과, 그것들은 건강하고 더 잘 자라지만 특별히 오래 살지는 못한다.) 이는 나무는 자신을 둘러싸고 있는 숲만큼만 강할 수 있기 때문이다. (③) 그리고 지금 숲에는 많은 패자가 있다. (④) 한때는 강한 구성원들의 지원을 받았을 약한 구성원들이 갑자기 뒤처진다. (⑤) 그것들의 쇠락 원인이 위치와 영양분 부족이든, 일시적인 질병이든, 혹은 유전적 구성이든, 이제 그것들은 곤충과 균류의 먹이가 된다.

| 문제 풀이 순서 |　[정답률 40%]

1st 주어진 문장을 해석하고, 연결어, 지시어 등을 확인한다.

> As a result, they are fit and grow better, but they aren't particularly long-lived.
> 그 결과, 그것들은 건강하고 더 잘 자라지만 특별히 오래 살지는 못한다.

➡ as a result는 앞에서 설명한 원인 때문에 일어나는 결과를 제시할 때 쓰이는 연결어이다.
▶ **주어진 문장 앞**: 어떤 나무가 건강하고 더 잘 자라지만 특별히 오래 살지는 못하는 현상의 원인이 될 만한 내용이 필요하고, they가 가리키는 것이 제시되어 있어야 함

2nd 각 선택지의 앞뒤 흐름이 매끄러운지 확인한다.

- **①의 앞 문장과 뒤 문장**

> **앞 문장**: 나무가 함께 자랄 때는 각 나무가 가능한 최고의 나무로 성장할 수 있도록 영양분과 물이 그것들 모두 사이에서 최적으로 분배된다. 만약 여러분이 경쟁자로 여겨지는 나무를 제거하여 개별 나무를 '도와주면' 나머지 나무를 잃게 된다. 그것들은 그루터기 외에는 무엇도 남아있지 않기 때문에 이웃 나무들에 메시지를 보내지만, 소용이 없다. 이제 모든 나무가 그것 나름대로 자라 생산성에 큰 차이가 생긴다.
> **뒤 문장**: 어떤 개체들은 당분이 줄기를 따라 확연히 흘러넘칠 때까지 미친 듯이 광합성을 한다.

➡ **앞 문장**: 나무가 함께 자랄 때는 영양분과 물이 최적으로 모든 나무에 분배되어 각 나무가 가능한 최고의 나무로 성장한다.
↔ 경쟁자 나무를 제거하여 개별 나무를 도와주면 나머지 나무를 잃게 되고, 모든 나무가 생산성에 큰 차이를 보인다.

뒤 문장: '어떤' 개체는 미친 듯이 광합성을 한다는 내용으로, 생산성에 큰 차이를 보인다는 앞 문장을 부연한다.
▶ 주어진 문장이 ①에 들어갈 수 없음
- ②의 앞 문장과 뒤 문장

앞 문장: ①의 뒤 문장과 같음
뒤 문장: 이는(This) 나무는 자신을 둘러싸고 있는 숲만큼만 강할 수 있기 때문이다.

→ 광합성을 넘칠 정도로 하기 때문에 건강하고 더 잘 자라는 것이다. ②의 앞 문장이 원인, 주어진 문장이 결과이다.
당분이 줄기를 따라 흘러넘칠 때까지 미친 듯이 광합성을 하는 '어떤 개체들': 건강하고 더 잘 자라지만 특별히 오래 살지는 못하는 '그것들(they)'
→ 나무는 자신을 둘러싼 숲만큼 강할 수 있기 때문에 주변에 아무 나무도 없는, 혼자서 미친 듯이 광합성을 하는 나무가 특별히 오래 살지는 못하는 것임
▶ 주어진 문장이 ②에 들어가야 함
- ③의 앞 문장과 뒤 문장

앞 문장: ②의 뒤 문장과 같음
뒤 문장: 그리고(And) 지금 숲에는 많은 패자가 있다.

→ 혼자서 미친 듯이 광합성을 하는 나무가 특별히 오래 살지는 못하는 이유가 이어진다.
나무는 그것을 둘러싼 숲만큼만 강할 수 있는데, 지금 숲에는 많은 패자가 있기 때문으로, 등위접속사 and로 앞뒤 문장이 매끄럽게 연결된다.
▶ 주어진 문장이 ③에 들어갈 수 없음
- ④의 앞 문장과 뒤 문장

앞 문장: ③의 뒤 문장과 같음
뒤 문장: 한때는 강한 구성원들의 지원을 받았을 약한 구성원들(Weaker members)이 갑자기 뒤처진다.

→ 앞 문장에서 제시한 losers를 Weaker members로 표현하여 설명을 자연스럽게 이어간다.
▶ 주어진 문장이 ④에 들어갈 수 없음
- ⑤의 앞 문장과 뒤 문장

앞 문장: ④의 뒤 문장과 같음
뒤 문장: 그것들의 쇠락 원인이 위치와 영양분 부족이든, 일시적인 질병이든, 혹은 유전적 구성이든, 이제 그것들은 곤충과 균류의 먹이가 된다.

→ 뒤 문장의 their, they가 가리키는 것이 앞 문장에 등장한다.
▶ 주어진 문장이 ⑤에 들어갈 수 없음

3rd 글이 한눈에 들어오도록 정리하여 정답을 확인한다.

나무가 함께 자랄 때는 각 나무가 가능한 최고의 나무로 성장할 수 있도록 영양분과 물이 그것들 모두 사이에서 최적으로 분배된다. 만약 여러분이 경쟁자로 여겨지는 나무를 제거하여 개별 나무를 '도와주면' 나머지 나무를 잃게 된다.
(①) 어떤 개체들은 당분이 줄기를 따라 확연히 흘러넘칠 때까지 광합성을 한다.
(② 그 결과, 그것들은 건강하고 더 잘 자라지만 특별히 오래 살지는 못한다.)
이는 나무는 자신을 둘러싸고 있는 숲만큼만 강할 수 있기 때문이다.
(③) 그리고 지금 숲에는 많은 패자가 있다.
(④) 한때는 강한 구성원들의 지원을 받았을 약한 구성원들이 갑자기 뒤처진다.
(⑤) 그것들의 쇠락 원인이 위치와 영양분 부족이든, 일시적인 질병이든, 혹은 유전적 구성이든, 이제 그것들은 곤충과 균류의 먹이가 된다.

글의 흐름으로 보아, 주어진 문장이 들어가기에 가장 적절한 곳을 고르시오.

In particular, / they define a group / as two or more people / who interact with, / and exert mutual influences on, / each other. //
단서 1 they가 가리키는 것이 social psychologists로, 그들이 전치사 with와 on의 목적어 group이라는 용어를 어떻게 더 정확하게 사용하는지 자세히 설명함
특히 / 그들은 집단을 정의한다 / 둘 이상의 사람들로 / 상호 작용을 하고 / 상호 영향력을 발휘하는 / 서로에게 //

In everyday life, / we tend to see any collection of people / as a group. //
일상생활에서 / 우리는 어떤 사람들의 무리라도 보는 경향이 있다 / 하나의 집단으로 //

(①) However, / social psychologists use this term / more precisely. //
단서 2 주어진 문장에서 설명한, 집단을 상호 작용하고, 상호 영향력을 발휘하는 둘 이상의 사람들로 정의한다는 내용을 this로 가리킴
그러나 / 사회 심리학자들은 이 용어를 사용한다 / 더 정확하게 //

(②) It is this sense of mutual interaction or inter-dependence /
it is ~ which 구문으로 주어가 강조됨
for a common purpose / which distinguishes the members of a group / from a mere aggregation of individuals. //
바로 이러한 서로의 상호 작용 또는 상호 의존감이 / 공동의 목적을 위한 / 집단의 구성원들을 구별한다 / 단순한 개인들의 집합으로부터 //

(③) For example, / as Kenneth Hodge observed, / a collection 단수 주어
of people / who happen to go for a swim / after work / on the same day each week /
예를 들어 / Kenneth Hodge가 진술한 바와 같이 / 사람들의 무리는 / 우연히 수영을 하러 가는 / 일을 마치고 / 매주 같은 날에 /

does not, strictly speaking, constitute a group / because these 단수동사
swimmers do not interact / with each other / in a structured manner. //
엄밀히 말하면 집단을 구성하지 않는다 / 이러한 수영하는 사람들은 상호 작용하지 않기 때문에 / 서로와 / 구조적인 방식으로 //

(④) By contrast, / a squad of young competitive swimmers / 단수 주어
who train every morning / before going to school / is a group / 단수 동사
대조적으로 / 경쟁을 하는 어린 수영 선수들의 팀은 / 매일 아침 훈련을 하는 / 학교에 가기 전에 / 집단'이다' /

because they not only share / a common objective (training for
not only A but also B로 동사구가 연결됨
competition) / but also interact with each other / in formal ways / (e.g., by warming up together beforehand). //
그들이 공유할 뿐만 아니라 / 공동의 목표(경기를 위한 훈련)를 / 또한 서로와 상호 작용하기 때문에 / 공식적인 방식으로 / (예를 들면, 미리 함께 준비운동을 함으로써) //

(⑤) It is this sense / of people coming together / to achieve a
it is ~ that 구문으로 주어가 강조됨
common objective / that defines a "team". // 부사적 용법(목적)
바로 이러한 생각이 / 사람들이 함께 모인다는 / 공동의 목표를 달성하기 위해 / '팀'을 정의한다 //

· interact ⓥ 소통하다, 상호 작용을 하다 · mutual ⓐ 상호 간의, 공통의
· term ⓝ 용어, 학기 · precisely ⓐⓓ 바로, 정확하게
· distinguish ⓥ 구별하다, 차이를 보이다 · mere ⓐ ~에 불과한
· observe ⓥ (논평·의견 등을) 말하다 · strictly ⓐⓓ 엄밀히, 정확히
· constitute ⓥ 구성하다, (단체를) 설립하다 · squad ⓝ 팀, (경찰의) 수사반
· objective ⓝ 목적, 목표 · formal ⓐ 공식적인, 격식을 차린
· beforehand ⓐⓓ 사전에 · define ⓥ 정의하다, 규정하다

일상생활에서 우리는 어떤 사람들의 무리라도 하나의 집단으로 보는 경향이 있다. (①) 그러나 사회 심리학자들은 이 용어를 더 정확하게 사용한다. (② 특히, 그들은 서로에게 상호 작용을 하고, 상호 영향력을 발휘하는 둘 이상의 사람들로 집단을 정의한다.) 집단의 구성원들을 단순한 개인들의 집합으로부터 구별하는 것은 바로 이러한 공동의 목적을 위한 서로의 상호 작용 또는 상호 의존감이다. (③) 예를 들어, Kenneth Hodge가 진술한 바와 같이, 매주 같은 날에 일을 마치고 우연히 수영을 하러 가는 사람들의 무리는 엄밀히 말하면 집단을 구성하지 않는데, 이러한 수영하는 사람들은 서로와 구조적인 방식으로 상호 작용하지 않기 때문이다. (④) 대조적으로, 매일 아침 학교에

가기 전에 훈련을 하는, 경쟁을 하는 어린 수영 선수들로 이루어진 팀은 공동의 목표(경기를 위한 훈련)를 공유할 뿐만 아니라 공식적인 방식(예를 들면, 미리 함께 준비운동을 함)으로 서로와 상호 작용하기 때문에 집단'이다'. (⑤) '팀'을 정의하는 것은 바로 공동의 목표를 달성하기 위해 사람들이 함께 모인다는 이러한 생각이다.

| 문제 풀이 순서 | [정답률 39%]

1st 주어진 문장을 해석하고, 연결어, 지시어 등을 확인한다.

> In particular, they define a group as two or more people who interact with, and exert mutual influences on, each other. 단서 1
>
> 특히, 그들은 서로에게 상호 작용을 하고, 상호 영향력을 발휘하는 둘 이상의 사람들로 집단을 정의한다.

➡ 집단을 정의하는 they(그들)가 누구인지 앞에 나온 후 그 뒤에 주어진 문장이 나와야 한다.
➡ 집단의 정의와 관련된 내용이 앞에 나올 것이다.

2nd 각 선택지의 앞뒤 흐름이 매끄러운지 확인한다.

- ①의 앞 문장과 뒤 문장

> 앞 문장: 일상생활에서 우리는 어떤 사람들의 무리라도 하나의 집단으로 보는 경향이 있다.
> 뒤 문장: 그러나 사회 심리학자들은 이 용어를 더 정확하게 사용한다.

➡ 앞 문장: 일상생활에서 집단의 정의
뒤 문장: 사회 심리학자들에게는 집단에 관한 더 정확한 정의가 있음
앞 문장의 '집단'을 뒤 문장에서 '이 용어'라고 표현하면서 연결된다.
▶ 주어진 문장이 ①에 들어갈 수 없음

- ②의 앞 문장과 뒤 문장

> 앞 문장: ①의 뒤 문장과 같음
> 뒤 문장: 집단의 구성원들을 단순한 개인들의 집합으로부터 구별하는 것은 바로 이러한 공동의 목적을 위한 서로의 상호 작용 또는 상호 의존감이다. 단서 2

➡ 뒤 문장: 집단이 단순한 개인들의 집합으로부터 구별되는 것은 공동의 목적을 위한 상호 작용 또는 상호 의존감이다.
앞 문장에서 사회 심리학자들이 사용하는 집단의 정의를 간략하게 언급했으므로 구체적인 내용이 뒤에 이어져야 한다. 하지만 뒤 문장에는 집단이 단순한 개인들의 집합으로부터 구별되는 특징을 설명한다.
➡ 주어진 문장에서 그들(사회 심리학자들)은 집단을 공동의 목적을 위해 상호 작용하고 상호 영향력을 발휘하는 둘 이상의 사람들로 정의한다고 했다.
▶ 주어진 문장이 ②에 들어가야 함

- ③의 앞 문장과 뒤 문장

> 앞 문장: ②의 뒤 문장과 같음
> 뒤 문장: 예를 들어, Kenneth Hodge가 진술한 바와 같이, 매주 같은 날에 일을 마치고 우연히 수영을 하러 가는 사람들의 무리는 엄밀히 말하면 집단을 구성하지 않는데, 이러한 수영하는 사람들은 서로와 구조적인 방식으로 상호 작용하지 않기 때문이다.

➡ 앞 문장에 등장한 집단의 특징 중 상호 작용을 뒤 문장에서 수영을 예로 들어 부연한다. 우연히 수영을 하러 가는 사람들의 무리, 즉 단순한 개인들의 집합은 상호 작용이 없다고 했다.
▶ 주어진 문장이 ③에 들어갈 수 없음

- ④의 앞 문장과 뒤 문장

> 앞 문장: ③의 뒤 문장과 같음
> 뒤 문장: 대조적으로(By contrast), 매일 아침 학교에 가기 전에 훈련을 하는, 경쟁을 하는 어린 수영 선수들로 이루어진 팀은 공동의 목표 (경기를 위한 훈련)를 공유할 뿐만 아니라 공식적인 방식(예를 들면, 미리 함께 준비운동을 함)으로 서로와 상호 작용하기 때문에 집단'이다'.

➡ By contrast는 앞의 내용과 반대되는 내용을 언급할 때 사용되므로, 앞 문장에서 나타난 단순한 개인들의 집합과는 반대로, '집단'의 정의에 부합하는 것으로서 '어린 수영 선수들로 이루어진 팀'을 예로 들었다.
▶ 주어진 문장이 ④에 들어갈 수 없음

- ⑤의 앞 문장과 뒤 문장

> 앞 문장: ④의 뒤 문장과 같음
> 뒤 문장: '팀'을 정의하는 것은 바로 공동의 목표를 달성하기 위해 사람들이 함께 모인다는 이러한 생각이다.

➡ 앞 문장에 등장한 어린 수영 선수들로 이루어진 팀, 즉 '집단'이 공동의 목표를 공유한다는 내용을 부연한다.
▶ 주어진 문장이 ⑤에 들어갈 수 없음

3rd 글이 한눈에 들어오도록 정리하여 정답을 확인한다.

일상생활에서 우리는 단순히 사람의 무리를 집단으로 보는 경향이 있다.
(①) 그러나 사회 심리학자들은 이 용어(집단)를 더 정확히 사용한다.
(② 그들은 '집단'을 상호 작용하고 상호 영향력을 발휘하는 둘 이상의 사람들로 정의한다.)
집단이 단순한 개인들의 집합과 다른 점은 공동의 목적을 위한 상호 작용 또는 상호 의존감이다.
(③) 우연히 수영을 하러 가는 사람들의 무리는 상호 작용이 없기 때문에 집단이 아니다.
(④) 대조적으로, 어린 수영 선수들로 이루어진 팀은 공동의 목표를 공유하고 공식적인 방식으로 상호 작용하기 때문에 집단이다.
(⑤) '팀'은 공동의 목표를 달성하기 위해 사람들이 모이는 것이다.

N 24 정답 ③ * 인간과 인공 지능의 협업

> 글의 흐름으로 보아, 주어진 문장이 들어가기에 가장 적절한 곳을 고르시오. [3점]

단서 1 인간이 인공 지능보다 더 큰 이점을 갖는다는 내용이 앞에 있어야 함

> However, / human reasoning is still notoriously prone / to confusion and error / when causal questions become sufficiently complex, / such as when it comes to assessing / the impact of policy interventions / across society. //
> 하지만 / 인간의 추론은 여전히 악명 높게 ~을 하기 쉽다 / 혼동과 실수를 / 인과 관계의 문제가 충분히 복잡해질 때 / 평가하는 경우처럼 / 정책 개입이 미치는 영향을 / 사회 전반에 //

Going beyond very simple algorithms, / some AI-based tools / hold out the promise / of supporting better causal and probabilistic reasoning / in complex domains. //
매우 간단한 알고리즘을 넘어서면서 / 일부 인공 지능 기반 도구들은 / 가능성을 보인다 / 더 나은 인과적 추론과 확률적 추론을 지원할 / 복잡한 영역에서 //

(①) Humans have a natural ability / to build / causal models of the world / — that is, to explain / why things happen / — that AI systems still largely lack. //
인간에게는 타고난 능력이 있다 / 만드는 / 세상의 인과적 모형을 / 즉 설명하는 / 어떤 일이 '왜' 일어나는지를 / 인공 지능 시스템에 여전히 많이 부족한 //

(②) For example, / while a doctor can explain / to a patient /
why a treatment works, / referring to the changes / it causes / in
the body, / 간접의문문(can explain의 목적어)
예를 들어 / 의사는 설명할 수 있는 반면 / 환자에게 / 어떤 치료가 왜 효과가 있는지 / 변화를
언급하면서 / 그것이 가져오는 / 몸에 /

a modern machine-learning system / could only tell you / that
복수 주어   복수 동사
patients / who are given this treatment / tend, on average, to get
better. // 단서2 인간이 기계 학습 시스템보다 더 나은 사례
현대의 기계 학습 시스템은 / 여러분에게 말할 수 있을 뿐이다 / 환자들이 / 이 치료를 받는 /
평균적으로 더 나아지는 경향이 있다고 / 단서3 주어진 문장의 경우를 가리킴

(③) In these cases, / supporting human reasoning / with more
                                               동사
structured AI-based tools / may be helpful. // 동명사구 주어
이런 경우에는 / 인간의 추론을 지원하는 것이 / 더 체계화된 인공 지능 기반 도구로 / 도움이
될 수 있다 //

(④) Researchers have been exploring / the use of Bayesian
Networks / — an AI technology / that can be used / to map out
the causal relationships / between events, /   병렬 구조
연구원들은 탐구해 오고 있다 / Bayesian Networks 사용을 / 인공 지능 기술 / 사용될 수
있는 / 인과 관계를 정리하는 데 / 사건 간의 /

and to represent degrees of uncertainty / around different areas
— / for decision support, / such as to enable / more accurate risk
assessment. //
그리고 불확실성의 정도를 나타내는 데 / 서로 다른 영역 주변의 / 의사 결정 지원을 위해 /
가능케 하는 것과 같은 / 더 정확한 위험 평가를 //

(⑤) These may be particularly useful / for assessing / the threat
                                 준부정어(거의 ~ 않는)
of novel or rare threats, / where little historical data is available,
/ such as the risk / of terrorist attacks and new ecological
disasters. //
이것들은 특히 유용할 수 있다 / 평가하는 데 / 새롭거나 드문 위협들의 위험을 / 이용할 수
있는 역사적 데이터가 거의 없는 / 위험과 같은 / 테러리스트 공격과 새로운 생태 재난의 //

- reasoning ⓝ 추론   · prone to ~의 경향이 있는
- confusion ⓝ 혼란, 혼동   · causal ⓐ 인과 관계의
- sufficiently ⓐⓓ 충분히   · complex ⓐ 복잡한
- assess ⓥ 평가하다   · impact ⓝ 영향, 충격   · policy ⓝ 정책, 방침
- intervention ⓝ 개입   · hold out ~을 보이다[드러내다]
- promise ⓝ 가능성, 징조   · probabilistic ⓐ 확률적인
- domain ⓝ 영역   · treatment ⓝ 치료   · work ⓥ 효과가 있다
- refer to ~을 언급하다   · on average 평균적으로
- structured ⓐ 체계화된   · map out ~을 세밀히 나타내다
- represent ⓥ 나타내다   · assessment ⓝ 평가
- threat ⓝ 협박, 위협   · ecological ⓐ 생태계[학]의

매우 간단한 알고리즘을 넘어서면서 일부 인공 지능 기반 도구들은 복잡한
영역에서 더 나은 인과적 추론과 확률적 추론을 지원할 가능성을 보인다.
(①) 인간에게는 인공 지능 시스템에 여전히 많이 부족한, 세상의 인과적
모형을 만드는, 즉 어떤 일이 '왜' 일어나는지를 설명하는 타고난 능력이 있다.
(②) 예를 들어, 의사는 환자에게 어떤 치료가 왜 효과가 있는지, 그것이 몸에
가져오는 변화를 언급하면서 설명할 수 있는 반면, 현대의 기계 학습 시스템은
이 치료를 받는 환자들이 평균적으로 더 나아지는 경향이 있다고 여러분에게
말할 수 있을 뿐이다. (③ 하지만 정책 개입이 사회 전반에 미치는 영향을
평가하는 경우처럼, 인과 관계의 문제가 충분히 복잡해지면 인간의 추론은
혼동하고 실수하기 쉽기로 여전히 악명 높다.) 이런 경우에는 더 체계화된 인공
지능 기반 도구로 인간의 추론을 지원하는 것이 도움이 될 수 있다.
(④) 연구원들은 더 정확한 위험 평가를 가능케 하는 것과 같은 의사
결정 지원을 위해 사건 간의 인과 관계를 정리하고 서로 다른 영역 주변의
불확실성의 정도를 나타내기 위해 사용될 수 있는 인공 지능 기술인 Bayesian
Networks 사용을 탐구해 오고 있다. (⑤) 이것들은 테러리스트 공격과
새로운 생태 재난의 위험과 같은, 이용할 수 있는 역사적 데이터가 거의 없는
새롭거나 드문 위협들의 위험을 평가하는 데 특히 유용할 수 있다.

| 문제 풀이 순서 | [정답률 43%]

1st 주어진 문장을 해석하고, 연결어, 지시어 등을 확인한다.

However, human reasoning is still notoriously prone
to confusion and error when causal questions become
sufficiently complex, such as when it comes to assessing
the impact of policy interventions across society. 단서1
하지만 정책 개입이 사회 전반에 미치는 영향을 평가하는 경우처럼, 인과 관계의
문제가 충분히 복잡해지면 인간의 추론은 혼동하고 실수하기 쉽기로 여전히 악명 높다.

→ 어떤 경우에는 인간의 추론이 혼동하고 실수하기 쉽기로 악명 높다는 내용이
역접의 연결어(However)로 이어진다.
▶ 주어진 문장의 앞부분: 인간의 추론이 이점을 갖는 경우를 설명하는 내용이어야 함

2nd 각 선택지의 앞뒤 흐름이 매끄러운지 확인한다.

- ①의 앞 문장과 뒤 문장

앞 문장: 매우 간단한 알고리즘을 넘어서면서 일부 인공 지능 기반
도구들은 복잡한 영역에서 더 나은 인과적 추론과 확률적 추론을
지원할 가능성을 보인다.
뒤 문장: 인간에게는 인공 지능 시스템에 여전히 많이 부족한, 세상의
인과적 모형을 만드는, 즉 어떤 일이 '왜' 일어나는지를 설명하는 타고난
능력이 있다.

→ 앞 문장: 일부 인공 지능 기반 도구들은 복잡한 영역에서 더 나은 능력을 보일
가능성이 있다.
뒤 문장: 인간이 인공 지능 시스템보다 더 뛰어난 능력이 있다.
→ 앞에서 말한 인공 지능 시스템보다 인간이 더 뛰어난 능력이 있다는 내용이 뒤
문장에 자연스럽게 이어진다.
▶ 주어진 문장이 ①에 들어갈 수 없음

- ②의 앞 문장과 뒤 문장

앞 문장: ①의 뒤 문장과 같음
뒤 문장: 예를 들어(For example), 의사는 환자에게 어떤 치료가
왜 효과가 있는지, 그것이 몸에 가져오는 변화를 언급하면서 설명할
수 있는 반면, 현대의 기계 학습 시스템은 이 치료를 받는 환자들이
평균적으로 더 나아지는 경향이 있다고 여러분에게 말할 수 있을
뿐이다.

→ For example(예를 들어)이라고 하며 인공 지능 시스템에는 없는 능력이
인간에게는 있는 사례를 제시한다.
▶ 주어진 문장이 ②에 들어갈 수 없음

- ③의 앞 문장과 뒤 문장

앞 문장: ②의 뒤 문장과 같음
뒤 문장: 이런 경우에는(In these cases) 더 체계화된 인공 지능 기반
도구로 인간의 추론을 지원하는 것이 도움이 될 수 있다.

→ **1** 앞 문장에서 인간이 인공 지능보다 더 뛰어난 경우에 대해 말했다.
2 these cases(이런 경우)로 가리킬 수 있는 것이 앞에 나와야 한다.
그 이유: 인간의 추론이 혼동하고 실수하기 쉽기로 악명 높을 수 있는 경우에 대한
내용이 필요함 (주어진 문장의 내용)
▶ 주어진 문장이 ③에 들어가야 함

- ④의 앞 문장과 뒤 문장

> **앞 문장:** ③의 뒤 문장과 같음
>
> **뒤 문장:** 연구원들은 더 정확한 위험 평가를 가능케 하는 것과 같은 의사 결정 지원을 위해 사건 간의 인과 관계를 정리하고 서로 다른 영역 주변의 불확실성의 정도를 나타내기 위해 사용될 수 있는 인공 지능 기술인 Bayesian Networks 사용을 탐구해 오고 있다.

➡ 앞에서 인공 지능 기반 도구로 인간의 추론을 지원하는 것이 유용하다는 내용이 나왔고, 뒤에서 인간의 추론을 지원하는 인공 지능 기술 Bayesian Networks를 소개하는 내용으로 자연스럽게 이어진다.

▶ 주어진 문장이 ④에 들어갈 수 없음

- ⑤의 앞 문장과 뒤 문장

> **앞 문장:** ④의 뒤 문장과 같음
>
> **뒤 문장:** 이것들은(These) 테러리스트 공격과 새로운 생태 재난의 위험과 같은, 이용할 수 있는 역사적 데이터가 거의 없는 새롭거나 드문 위협들의 위험을 평가하는 데 특히 유용할 수 있다.

➡ 앞 문장에서 Bayesian Networks를 소개하고, 뒤 문장에서 These로 가리키며 그것이 유용하게 이용될 수 있는 구체적 분야를 설명했다.

▶ 주어진 문장이 ⑤에 들어갈 수 없음

3rd 글이 한눈에 들어오도록 정리하여 정답을 확인한다.

일부 인공 지능 기반 도구들은 복잡한 영역에서 더 나은 인과적 추론과 확률적 추론을 지원할 가능성을 보인다.
(①) 인간에게는 인공 지능 시스템에 여전히 많이 부족한 특정한 타고난 능력이 있다.
(②) 예를 들어, 의사는 환자에게 어떤 치료가 왜 효과가 있는지, 그것이 몸에 가져오는 변화를 언급하면서 설명할 수 있는 반면, 현대의 기계 학습 시스템은 이 치료를 받는 환자들이 평균적으로 더 나아지는 경향이 있다고 말할 수 있을 뿐이다.
((③) 하지만 정책 개입이 사회 전반에 미치는 영향을 평가하는 경우처럼, 인과 관계의 문제가 충분히 복잡해지면 인간의 추론은 혼동하고 실수하기 쉽다.)
이런 경우에는 더 체계화된 인공 지능 기반 도구로 인간의 추론을 지원하는 것이 도움이 될 수 있다.
(④) 연구원들은 더 정확한 위험 평가를 가능케 하는 것과 같은 의사 결정 지원을 위해 사건 간의 인과 관계를 정리하고 서로 다른 영역 주변의 불확실성의 정도를 나타내기 위해 사용될 수 있는 인공 지능 기술인 Bayesian Networks 사용을 탐구해 오고 있다.
(⑤) 이것들은 테러리스트 공격과 새로운 생태 재난의 위험과 같은, 이용할 수 있는 역사적 데이터가 거의 없는 새롭거나 드문 위협들의 위험을 평가하는 데 특히 유용할 수 있다.

N 25 정답 ⑤ ＊도시와 대조되는 공간으로서의 공원

> 글의 흐름으로 보아, 주어진 문장이 들어가기에 가장 적절한 곳을 고르시오.

There's a reason for that: / traditionally, park designers attempted / to create such a feeling / **단서 1** 거리, 자동차, 건물과 뚜렷하게 분리된 느낌을 가리킴
거기에는 이유가 있다 / 전통적으로 공원 설계자들은 시도했다 / 그런 느낌을 만들어 내려고 /
by planting tall trees at park boundaries, / building stone walls, / and constructing other means of partition. //
병렬 구조(전치사 by의 목적어 역할을 하는 동명사)
공원 경계에 키 큰 나무를 심어서 / 돌담을 쌓아서 / 다른 칸막이 수단을 세워서 //

Parks take the shape / demanded by the cultural concerns / of their time. //
선행사(주격 관계대명사와 be동사는 생략됨)
공원은 형태를 취한다 / 문화적 관심사에 의해 요구되는 / 그것이 속한 시대의 //

Once parks are in place, / they are no inert stage / — their
부사절 접속사(조건)
purposes and meanings / are made and remade / by planners and by park users. //
일단 공원이 마련되면 / 그것은 비활성화된 단계가 아니다 / 그것의 목적과 의미는 / 만들어지고 다시 만들어진다 / 계획자와 공원 이용자에 의해 //

Moments of park creation are particularly telling, / however,
접속사(이유)
/ for they reveal and actualize ideas / about nature and its relationship to urban society. //
공원을 조성하는 순간들은 특히 효과적이다 / 그러나 / 그것이 생각을 드러내고 실현하기 때문에 / 자연과 그것이 도시 사회가 갖는 관계에 대한 //

명사절 주어
(①) Indeed, / what distinguishes a park / from the broader category of public space / is the representation of nature / that
단수 동사   목적격 관계대명사
parks are meant to embody. //
실제로 / 공원을 구별하는 것은 / 더 넓은 범주의 공공 공간과 / 자연의 표현이다 / 공원이 구현하도록 의도된 // └mean to-v: ~을 의도하다(작정하다)

(②) Public spaces include / parks, concrete plazas, sidewalks, even indoor atriums. //
공공 공간은 포함한다 / 공원, 콘크리트 광장, 보도, 심지어 실내 아트리움을 //

(③) Parks typically have / trees, grass, and other plants / as
접속사가 생략되지 않은 분사구문
their central features. //
일반적으로 공원은 갖고 있다 / 나무, 풀, 그리고 다른 식물들을 / 그들의 중심적인 특색으로 //

(④) When entering a city park, / people often imagine a sharp separation / from streets, cars, and buildings. //
도시 공원에 들어갈 때 / 사람들은 흔히 뚜렷한 분리를 상상한다 / 거리, 자동차, 그리고 건물과의 //
단서 2 거리, 자동차, 건물과 분리된 느낌을 위해 공원 경계에 키 큰 나무를 심고, 돌담을 쌓는 등의 칸막이를 세움

((⑤) What's behind this idea / is not only landscape architects'
명사절 주어   단수 동사
desire / to design aesthetically suggestive park spaces, /
이 생각의 배후에는 있는 것은 / 조경가의 욕망뿐만 아니라 / 미적으로 연상시키는 공원 공간을 설계하려는 / not only A but (also) B로 주격 보어가 연결됨
but a much longer history of Western thought / that envisions
선행사   주격 관계대명사
cities and nature / as antithetical spaces and oppositional forces. //
서구 사상의 훨씬 더 오래된 역사이기도 하다 / 도시와 자연을 상상하는 / 대조적인 공간과 반대 세력으로 //

- partition ⓝ 칸막이　　・inert ⓐ 비활성의, 기력이 없는
- telling ⓐ 효과적인, 강력한　　・actualize ⓥ 실현하다
- representation ⓝ 표현, 묘사　　・embody ⓥ 구현하다, 상징하다
- separation ⓝ 분리　　・landscape architect 조경사
- suggestive ⓐ 연상시키는　　・envision ⓥ 상상하다, 마음속에 그리다
- oppositional ⓐ 대립적인, 반대의

공원은 그것이 속한 시대의 문화적 관심사가 요구하는 형태를 취한다. 일단 공원이 마련되면, 그것은 비활성화된 단계가 아닌데 그것의 목적과 의미는 계획자와 공원 이용자에 의해 만들어지고 다시 만들어진다. 그러나 공원을 조성하는 순간들은 특히 효과적인데, 자연과 그것이 도시 사회와 갖는 관계에 대한 생각을 드러내고 실현하기 때문이다. (①) 실제로 공원을 더 넓은 범주의 공공 공간과 구별하는 것은 공원이 구현하려는 자연의 표현이다. (②) 공공 공간에는 공원, 콘크리트 광장, 보도, 심지어 실내 아트리움도 포함된다. (③) 일반적으로 공원에는 그들의 중심적인 특색으로 나무, 풀, 그리고 다른 식물들이 있다. (④) 도시 공원에 들어갈 때, 사람들은 흔히 거리, 자동차, 그리고 건물과의 뚜렷한 분리를 상상한다. (⑤ 거기에는 이유가 있는데, 전통적으로 공원 설계자들은 공원 경계에 키 큰 나무를 심고, 돌담을 쌓고, 다른 칸막이 수단을 세워 그런 느낌을 만들어 내려고 했다.) 이 생각의 배후에는 미적인 암시가 있는 공원 공간을 설계하려는 조경가의 욕망뿐만 아니라 도시와 자연을 대조적인 공간과 반대 세력으로 상상하는 훨씬 더 오래된 서구 사상의 역사가 있다.

1st 주어진 문장을 해석하고, 연결어, 지시어 등을 확인한다.

> There's a reason for that: traditionally, park designers attempted to create such a feeling by planting tall trees at park boundaries, building stone walls, and constructing other means of partition. **단서1**
> 거기에는 이유가 있는데, 전통적으로 공원 설계자들은 공원 경계에 키 큰 나무를 심고, 돌담을 쌓고, 다른 칸막이 수단을 세워 그런 느낌을 만들어 내려고 했다.

➡ such a feeling이 무엇을 가리키는지 앞에 나오고, 그 뒤에 주어진 문장을 넣어야 한다.

➡ 전통적으로 공원 설계자들이 공원 경계에 칸막이 수단을 세웠던 원인이 앞에 나올 것이다.

2nd 각 선택지의 앞뒤 흐름이 매끄러운지 확인한다.

- ①의 앞 문장과 뒤 문장

> **앞 문장:** 공원은 그것이 속한 시대의 문화적 관심사가 요구하는 형태를 취한다. 일단 공원이 마련되면, 그것은 비활성화된 단계가 아닌데 그것의 목적과 의미는 계획자와 공원 이용자에 의해 만들어지고 다시 만들어진다. 그러나 공원을 조성하는 순간들은 특히 효과적인데, 자연과 그것이 도시 사회와 갖는 관계에 대한 생각을 드러내고 실현하기 때문이다.
> **뒤 문장:** 실제로 공원을 더 넓은 범주의 공공 공간과 구별하는 것은 공원이 구현하려는 자연의 표현이다.

➡ **앞 문장:** 공원은 시대의 문화적 관심사를 반영한다.
뒤 문장: 공원은 그것이 구현하려는 자연의 표현으로 인해 공공 공간과 구별된다. 앞 문장의 '시대의 문화적 관심사'가 뒤 문장에서 '공원이 구현하려는 자연의 표현'으로 나타난다.
▶ 주어진 문장이 ①에 들어갈 수 없음

- ②의 앞 문장과 뒤 문장

> **앞 문장:** ①의 뒤 문장과 같음
> **뒤 문장:** 공공 공간에는 공원, 콘크리트 광장, 보도, 심지어 실내 아트리움도 포함된다.

➡ 앞 문장에 나타난 '공공 공간'을 부연하는 흐름이다.
▶ 주어진 문장이 ②에 들어갈 수 없음

- ③의 앞 문장과 뒤 문장

> **앞 문장:** ②의 뒤 문장과 같음
> **뒤 문장:** 일반적으로 공원에는 그들의 중심적인 특색으로 나무, 풀, 그리고 다른 식물들이 있다.

➡ 앞 문장의 공공 공간과 대조하여, 뒤 문장에서 공원의 구성을 부연하는 흐름이다.
▶ 주어진 문장이 ③에 들어갈 수 없음

- ④의 앞 문장과 뒤 문장

> **앞 문장:** ③의 뒤 문장과 같음
> **뒤 문장:** 도시 공원에 들어갈 때, 사람들은 흔히 거리, 자동차, 그리고 건물과의 뚜렷한 분리를 상상한다. **단서2**

➡ 앞 문장에서 공원의 자연적인 특징이 나오는데, 뒤 문장에서 도시 공원을 새롭게 언급하며 그것이 도시의 인공적인 특징과 분리될 것이라고 상상하는 흐름이다.
▶ 주어진 문장이 ④에 들어갈 수 없음

- ⑤의 앞 문장과 뒤 문장

> **앞 문장:** ④의 뒤 문장과 같음
> **뒤 문장:** 이 생각(this idea)의 배후에는 미적인 암시가 있는 공원 공간을 설계하려는 조경가의 욕망뿐만 아니라 도시와 자연을 대조적인 공간과 반대 세력으로 상상하는 훨씬 더 오래된 서구 사상의 역사가 있다.

➡ **뒤 문장:** 이 생각의 배후에는 조경가의 욕망과 서구 사상의 역사가 있다. 조경가의 욕망과 서구 사상의 역사와 관련된 this idea가 무엇인지 앞에 나타나야 한다. 주어진 문장의 '그런 느낌'은 앞 문장의 '자연과 인공물의 뚜렷한 분리'이다.

➡ 주어진 문장에서 전통적으로 공원 설계자들이 공원 경계에 자연적인 칸막이 수단을 세워 그런 느낌을 만들어 내려고 했다고 하므로, 이는 뒤 문장에 나타나는 '도시와 자연을 대조적인 공간으로 상상하는 오래된 서구 사상의 역사'와 부합한다.
▶ 주어진 문장이 ⑤에 들어가야 함

3rd 글이 한눈에 들어오도록 정리하여 정답을 확인한다.

공원은 시대의 문화적 관심사를 반영한다.
(①) 공원이 공공 공간과 다른 점은 공원이 구현하려는 자연의 표현이다.
(②) 공공 공간에는 공원, 콘크리트 광장, 보도, 실내 아트리움 등이 있다.
(③) 일반적으로 공원에는 중심적인 특색으로 자연이 있다.
(④) 사람들은 도시 공원이 인공물과 뚜렷하게 분리되어 있다고 상상한다.
(⑤ 이는 전통적으로 공원 설계자들이 공원에 자연적 경계를 세워 그런 느낌을 만들어 내려고 했기 때문이다.)
이 생각의 배후에는 조경가의 욕망뿐만 아니라 도시와 자연을 대조하는 오래된 서구 사상의 역사가 있다.

장성욱 | 동아대 의예과 2023년 입학·부산 대연고 졸

주어진 문장을 보면 우선 that과 such가 눈에 띄어. such a feeling을 느끼게 하기 위해 공원 설계자들이 시도했다는 내용이 나오니까 당연히 그 앞에 어떤 '느낌'이 있어야 하는데, ⑤ 앞에 등장한 people often imagine이 이와 연관된다는 것을 알 수 있어. 그리고 that도 앞 문장의 내용을 가리키며 자연스러운 문맥이 되지.

N 26 정답 ④ ＊자연스럽게 발전한 영화의 문법

글의 흐름으로 보아, 주어진 문장이 들어가기에 가장 적절한 곳은? [3점]

단서1 자연스럽게 발전했다는 내용이 Rather로 연결됨
> Rather, it evolved naturally / as certain devices were found / in practice / to be both workable and useful. //
> 오히려 그것은 자연스럽게 발전했다 / 특정 방법이 밝혀지면서 / 실제로 / 운용할 수 있고 유용한 것으로 //

Film has no grammar. //
영화에는 문법이 없다 //
(①) There are, however, some vaguely defined rules / of usage / in cinematic language, /
그러나 어렴풋이 정의된 몇 가지 규칙이 있다 / 사용에 관한 / 영화 언어에서 /
and the syntax of film / — its systematic arrangement — / orders these rules / and indicates relationships among them. // (병렬 구조)
그리고 영화의 문법은 / 그것의 체계적인 (처리) 방식 / 이러한 규칙들을 정리하고 / 그것들 사이의 관계를 보여준다 //
(②) As with written and spoken languages, / it is important (가주어)
to remember / that the syntax of film is a result / of its usage, / (진주어)
not a determinant of it. //
문어와 구어에서와 마찬가지로 / 기억하는 것이 중요하다 / 영화의 문법은 결과물이라는 것을 / 그것의 사용의 / 그것의 결정 요인이 아니라 //

(③) There is nothing preordained / about film syntax. //
단서 2 영화 문법은 미리 정해진 것이 아님
미리 정해진 것은 아무것도 없다 / 영화 문법에 관해 //

(④) Like the syntax of written and spoken language, / the
syntax of film is an organic development, / **단서 3** 영화 문법이 자연스럽게 발전했음
문어와 구어의 문법처럼 / 영화의 문법은 자연스러운 발전이고 /

descriptive rather than prescriptive, / and it has changed
considerably / over the years. //
규범적이기보다 기술적이고 / 그것은 상당히 변화했다 / 여러 해에 걸쳐 //

(⑤) "Hollywood Grammar" may sound laughable now, /
주어　　동사　　주격 보어
but during the thirties, forties, and early fifties / it was an accurate
선행사(관계부사는 생략됨)
model of the way / Hollywood films were constructed. //
'할리우드 문법'은 지금은 웃기는 것처럼 들릴지 모르지만 / 30년대, 40년대, 50년대 초반에는
/ 그것이 방식의 정확한 모델이었다 / 할리우드 영화가 제작되는 //

- -

- evolve ⓥ 발전하다　・device ⓝ 방법, 장치　・in practice 실제로는
- vaguely ⓪ 어렴풋이　・cinematic ⓐ 영화의
- syntax ⓝ 문법, 통사론　・systematic ⓐ 체계적인, 조직적인
- arrangement ⓝ (처리) 방식, 준비, 마련　・order ⓥ 정리하다
- indicate ⓥ 나타내다, 보여주다　・determinant ⓝ 결정 요인
- workable ⓐ 운용할 수 있는　・organic ⓐ 자연스러운, 서서히 생기는
- descriptive ⓐ 기술적인　・prescriptive ⓐ 규범적인
- laughable ⓐ 웃기는, 터무니없는　・accurate ⓐ 정확한

영화에는 문법이 없다. (①) 그러나 영화 언어 사용에 관한 어렴풋이 정의된
몇 가지 규칙이 있고, 영화의 문법, 즉 그것의 체계적인 (처리) 방식은 이러한
규칙들을 정리하고 그것들 사이의 관계를 보여준다. (②) 문어와 구어에서와
마찬가지로, 영화의 문법은 그것의 사용의 결과물이지, 그것의 결정 요인은 아
니라는 것을 기억하는 것이 중요하다. (③) 영화 문법에 관해 미리 정해진 것
은 아무것도 없다. (④ 오히려, 그것은 특정 방법이 실제로 운용할 수 있고 유용
한 것으로 밝혀지면서 자연스럽게 발전했다.) 문어와 구어의 문법처럼, 영화의
문법은 자연스럽게 발전한 것으로 규범적이기보다 기술적이고, 여러 해에 걸쳐
상당히 변화했다. (⑤) '할리우드 문법'은 지금은 웃기는 것처럼 들릴지 모르지
만, 30년대, 40년대, 50년대 초반에는 그것이 할리우드 영화가 제작되는 방식
의 정확한 모델이었다.

| 문제 풀이 순서 | [정답률 44%]

1st 주어진 문장을 해석하고, 연결어, 지시어 등을 확인한다.

> Rather, it evolved naturally as certain devices were found
> in practice to be both workable and useful. **단서 1**
> 오히려, 그것은 특정 방법이 실제로 운용할 수 있고 유용한 것으로 밝혀지면서
> 자연스럽게 발전했다.

➡ Rather가 나오므로, **단서** it이 자연스럽게 발전되었다는 것과 대조되는 내용이
앞에 나오고 그 뒤에 주어진 문장을 넣어야 한다. **발상**
➡ 실제로 운용할 수 있고 유용한 it이 무엇인지 앞에 나와야 한다.

2nd 각 선택지의 앞뒤 흐름이 매끄러운지 확인한다.

- ①의 앞 문장과 뒤 문장

> **앞 문장:** 영화에는 문법이 없다.
> **뒤 문장:** 그러나 영화 언어 사용에 관한 어렴풋이 정의된 몇 가지 규칙이
> 있고, 영화의 문법, 즉 그것의 체계적인 (처리) 방식은 이러한 규칙들을
> 정리하고 그것들 사이의 관계를 보여준다.

➡ **앞 문장:** 영화에는 문법이 없다.
뒤 문장: 그러나 영화 언어 사용에 관한 몇 가지 규칙이 있으며 영화의 문법은
이러한 규칙들을 정리하고 그것들 사이의 관계를 보여준다.
앞 문장에서 영화에는 문법이 없다고 했지만, 뒤 문장에서 however를 통해 영화
언어 사용에 관한 몇 가지 규칙이 있으며 영화 문법의 역할을 언급하는 흐름이다.
▶ 주어진 문장이 ①에 들어갈 수 없음

- ②의 앞 문장과 뒤 문장

> **앞 문장:** ①의 뒤 문장과 같음
> **뒤 문장:** 문어와 구어에서와 마찬가지로, 영화의 문법은 그것의 사용의
> 결과물이지, 그것의 결정 요인은 아니라는 것을 기억하는 것이
> 중요하다.

➡ 앞 문장에서 나타난 '영화 문법'을 뒤 문장에서 부연하는 흐름이다.
▶ 주어진 문장이 ②에 들어갈 수 없음

- ③의 앞 문장과 뒤 문장

> **앞 문장:** ②의 뒤 문장과 같음
> **뒤 문장:** 영화 문법에 관해 미리 정해진 것은 아무것도 없다. **단서 2**

➡ 앞 문장에서 나타난 '영화 문법'을 뒤 문장에서 부연하는 흐름이다.
▶ 주어진 문장이 ③에 들어갈 수 없음

④의 앞 문장과 뒤 문장

> **앞 문장:** ③의 뒤 문장과 같음
> **뒤 문장:** 문어와 구어의 문법처럼, 영화의 문법은 자연스럽게 발전한
> 것으로 규범적이기보다 기술적이고, 여러 해에 걸쳐 상당히 변화했다.
> **단서 3**

➡ **뒤 문장:** 영화 문법은 자연스럽게 발전한 것으로 기술적이고 상당히 변화했다.
영화 문법이 자연스럽게 발전했다는 내용이 앞에 있어야 한다.
➡ 주어진 문장에서 it이 자연스럽게 발전했다고 했는데, 이는 앞 문장의 '영화 문법'을
지칭한다.
▶ 주어진 문장이 ④에 들어가야 함

- ⑤의 앞 문장과 뒤 문장

> **앞 문장:** ④의 뒤 문장과 같음
> **뒤 문장:** '할리우드 문법'은 지금은 웃기는 것처럼 들릴지 모르지만,
> 30년대, 40년대, 50년대 초반에는 그것이 할리우드 영화가 제작되는
> 방식의 정확한 모델이었다.

➡ 앞 문장에 등장한 '영화 문법의 자연스러운 발전'을 부연하기 위해 '할리우드 문법'을
예로 들었다.
▶ 주어진 문장이 ⑤에 들어갈 수 없음

3rd 글이 한눈에 들어오도록 정리하여 정답을 확인한다.

영화에는 문법이 없다.
(①) 그러나 영화 언어 사용에 관한 몇 가지 규칙이 있고 영화 문법은 이러한 규칙들을
정리하고 그것들 사이의 관계를 보여준다.
(②) 영화의 문법은 그것의 사용의 결과물이지, 그것의 결정 요인은 아니다.
(③) 영화 문법에 미리 정해진 것은 없다.
(④ 오히려, 그것은 자연스럽게 발전했다.)
영화 문법은 자연스럽게 발전한 것으로 기술적이고 여러 해에 걸쳐 상당히 변화했다.
(⑤) '할리우드 문법'은 과거에 할리우드 영화가 제작되는 방식의 정확한 모델이었다.

글의 흐름으로 보아, 주어진 문장이 들어가기에 가장 적절한 곳은?

As long as you do not run out of copies / before completing this process, / you will know / that you have a sufficient number / to go around. //
여러분이 사본을 다 써버리지 않는 한 / 이 과정을 완료하기 전에 / 여러분은 알 것이다 / 여러분에게 충분한 수가 있다는 것을 / 사람들에게 돌아갈 //

We sometimes solve number problems / almost without realizing it. //
우리는 가끔 숫자 문제를 푼다 / 그것을 거의 깨닫지도 못한 채 //

(①) For example, / suppose / you are conducting a meeting / and you want to ensure / that everyone there has a copy of the agenda. //
예를 들어 / 가정해 보라 / 여러분이 회의를 진행하고 있고 / 여러분이 확실히 하기를 원한다고 / 그곳에 있는 모든 사람이 의제의 사본을 갖는 것을 // **단서** 주어진 문장의 this process가 가리키는 과정

(②) You can deal with this / by labelling each copy of the handout / in turn / with the initials of each of those present. //
여러분은 이것을 처리할 수 있다 / 그 유인물의 각 사본에 적음으로써 / 차례대로 / 참석한 사람들 각각의 이름의 첫 글자들을 // those를 수식하는 형용사

(③) You have then solved this problem / without resorting to arithmetic / and without explicit counting. //
그렇다면 여러분은 이 문제를 해결했다 / 산수에 의존하지 않고 / 명시적인 계산 없이 //

(④) There are numbers / at work for us / here / all the same / and they allow precise comparison of one collection / with another, /
숫자들이 있고 / 우리를 위해 일하고 있는 / 여기에는 / 그래도 / 그것들이 한 집합의 정확한 비교를 가능하게 한다 / 다른 집합과의 /

even though the members / that make up the collections / could have entirely different characters, / as is the case here, /
비록 그 구성원이 / 그 집합을 구성하는 / 완전히 다른 특징을 가질 수 있음에도 / 여기의 경우가 그런 것처럼 /

where one set is a collection of people, / while the other consists / of pieces of paper. //
한 세트는 사람들의 집합인 / 다른 세트는 구성된 반면에 / 종이로 //

(⑤) What numbers allow us to do / is to compare / the relative size of one set / with another. //
숫자가 우리로 하여금 하게 하는 것은 / 비교하는 것이다 / 한 세트의 상대적인 크기를 / 다른 세트와 //

- run out of ~을 다 써버리다[바닥내다]　• sufficient ⓐ 충분한
- go around (사람들에게 몫이) 돌아가다
- conduct a meeting 회의를 진행[주관]하다　• ensure ⓥ 확실하게 하다
- agenda ⓝ 의제, 안건　• handout ⓝ 유인물
- label ⓥ (표 등에 필요한 정보를) 적다
- initial ⓝ 이름의 첫 글자[머리글자]　• present ⓐ 참석한
- resort to ~에 의지하다　• explicit ⓐ 명시적인, 명백한
- all the same 그래도, 여전히　• comparison ⓝ 비교
- make up ~을 구성하다　• character ⓝ 특징, 특성, 인격, 성격
- collection ⓝ (물건·사람들의) 무리, 더미　• consist of ~으로 구성되다
- relative ⓐ 상대적인

우리는 가끔 거의 깨닫지도 못한 채 숫자 문제를 푼다. (①) 예를 들어, 여러분이 회의를 진행하고 있고 그곳에 있는 모든 사람이 의제의 사본을 확실히 갖게 하고 싶어 한다고 가정해 보라. (②) 여러분은 그 유인물의 각 사본에 참석한 사람들 각각의 이름 첫 글자들을 차례대로 적음으로써 이것을 처리할 수 있다. (③ 이 과정을 완료하기 전에 사본이 떨어지지 않는 한, 여러분은 사람들에게 돌아갈 충분한 수의 사본이 있다는 것을 알 것이다.) 그렇다면 여러분은 산수에 의존하지 않고, 명시적인 계산 없이 이 문제를 해결한 것이다. (④) 그래도 여기

에는 우리에게 영향을 미치고 있는 숫자들이 있고 그것들이 하나의 집합과 다른 집합을 정확히 비교할 수 있게 하는데, 그 집합을 구성하는 것들이 한 세트는 사람들의 집합이고 다른 세트는 종이로 구성된 여기의 경우가 그런 것처럼 완전히 다른 특징을 가질 수 있음에도 그러하다. (⑤) 숫자가 우리로 하여금 할 수 있게 하는 것은 한 세트의 상대적인 크기를 다른 세트와 비교하는 것이다.

| 문제 풀이 순서 |　[정답률 40%]

1st　주어진 문장을 해석하고, 연결어, 지시어 등을 확인한다.

As long as you do not run out of copies before completing this process, you will know that you have a sufficient number to go around.
이 과정을 완료하기 전에 사본이 떨어지지 않는 한, 여러분은 사람들에게 돌아갈 충분한 수의 사본이 있다는 것을 알 것이다.

➡ 사본을 떨어지게 하는 this process가 무엇인지 앞에 나오고 그 뒤에 주어진 문장을 넣어야 한다.

2nd　각 선택지의 앞뒤 흐름이 매끄러운지 확인한다.

- ①의 앞 문장과 뒤 문장

앞 문장: 우리는 가끔 거의 깨닫지도 못한 채 숫자 문제를 푼다.
뒤 문장: 예를 들어, 여러분이 회의를 진행하고 있고 그곳에 있는 모든 사람이 의제의 사본을 확실히 갖게 하고 싶어 한다고 가정해 보라.

➡ 앞 문장: 우리는 가끔 무의식중에 숫자 문제를 푼다.
뒤 문장: 예를 들어, 회의를 진행하는 중에 모든 사람이 의제의 사본을 확실히 갖게 하는 경우를 가정해 보라.
앞 문장의 '우리는 무의식중에 숫자 문제를 푼다.'라는 내용을 뒤 문장에서 회의 중 의제의 사본을 나누어주는 경우를 예로 들며 부연하고 있다.
▶ 주어진 문장이 ①에 들어갈 수 없음

- ②의 앞 문장과 뒤 문장

앞 문장: ①의 뒤 문장과 같음
뒤 문장: 여러분은 그 유인물의 각 사본에 참석한 사람들 각각의 이름 첫 글자들을 차례대로 적음으로써 이것을 처리할 수 있다. **단서**

➡ 앞 문장의 예시를 뒤 문장에서 구체적으로 설명하는 흐름이며, 각 사본에 참석자의 이름 첫 글자들을 차례대로 적는 경우를 언급했다.
▶ 주어진 문장이 ②에 들어갈 수 없음

- ③의 앞 문장과 뒤 문장

앞 문장: ②의 뒤 문장과 같음
뒤 문장: 그렇다면 여러분은 산수에 의존하지 않고, 명시적인 계산 없이 이 문제를 해결한 것이다.

➡ 뒤 문장: 산수와 명시적 계산 없이 문제를 해결하는 것
③의 앞 문장에서 유인물의 각 사본에 이름 첫 글자들을 차례대로 적는다는 과정이 나오는데, 과정만으로는 문제를 해결한 것이라고 할 수 없다.
➡ 주어진 문장은 이름 첫 글자들을 다 적기 전에 사본이 떨어지지 않는 한, 각 사람을 위한 충분한 사본이 있다는 내용이다. 따라서, 주어진 문장의 내용이 ③의 뒤에 이어져야 명시적인 계산 없이 이름 첫 글자를 적는 것만으로도 문제를 해결했음을 알 수 있다.
▶ 주어진 문장이 ③에 들어가야 함

- ④의 앞 문장과 뒤 문장

> **앞 문장:** ③의 뒤 문장과 같음
> **뒤 문장:** 그래도 여기에는 우리에게 영향을 미치고 있는 숫자들이 있고 그것들이 하나의 집합과 다른 집합을 정확히 비교할 수 있게 하는데, 그 집합을 구성하는 것들이 한 세트는 사람들의 집합이고 다른 세트는 종이로 구성된 여기의 경우가 그런 것처럼 완전히 다른 특징을 가질 수 있음에도 그러하다.

➡ 앞 문장의 사례를 집합 간 비교라는 내용으로 일반화하는 흐름이다.
▶ 주어진 문장이 ④에 들어갈 수 없음

- ⑤의 앞 문장과 뒤 문장

> **앞 문장:** ④의 뒤 문장과 같음
> **뒤 문장:** 숫자가 우리로 하여금 할 수 있게 하는 것은 한 세트의 상대적인 크기를 다른 세트와 비교하는 것이다.

➡ 앞 문장으로부터 원리를 도출하는 흐름이다.
▶ 주어진 문장이 ⑤에 들어갈 수 없음

3rd 글이 한눈에 들어오도록 정리하여 정답을 확인한다.

우리는 가끔 무의식적으로 숫자 문제를 푼다.
(①) 예를 들어, 회의 중에 모든 사람이 의제의 사본을 확실히 갖도록 한다고 가정해 보라.
(②) 각 사본에 참석자 각각의 이름 첫 글자들을 차례대로 적음으로써 이를 처리할 수 있다.
(③ 이 과정을 완료하기 전에 사본이 떨어지지 않는 한, 각 사람을 위한 충분한 사본이 있다는 것을 알 것이다.)
그렇다면 명시적 계산 없이 이 문제를 해결한 것이다.
(④) 이 과정에서도 영향을 미치는 숫자들이 있고 그것들이 집합 간 정확한 비교를 가능하게 한다.
(⑤) 숫자는 우리로 하여금 세트 간 상대적 크기를 비교할 수 있게 한다.

N 28 정답 ③ *손과 눈으로 하는 측정에 대한 의심

글의 흐름으로 보아, 주어진 문장이 들어가기에 가장 적절한 곳을 고르시오. [3점]

단서 1 손과 눈으로 측정하는 것은 추상적인 사고의 그것보다 열등한 지식, 다소 터무니없는 지식을 만들어 낸다고 여겨졌음

> Indeed, in the Middle Ages in Europe, / calculating by hand
> 단수 동사   동명사구 주어
> and eye / was sometimes seen / as producing a rather shabby
> sort of knowledge, / inferior to that of abstract thought. //
> 사실, 유럽의 중세 시대에는 / 손과 눈으로 측정하는 것은 / 때때로 여겨졌다 / 다소 터무니없는 종류의 지식을 만들어 낸다고 / 추상적인 사고의 그것보다 열등한 지식을 //

Babylonian astronomers created / detailed records of celestial
= and they use
movements / in the heavens, / using the resulting tables / to sieve
out irregularities / and, with them, / the favour of the gods. //
바빌로니아의 천문학자들은 만들었고 / 천체 운동에 대한 자세한 기록을 / 하늘에서의 / 그 결과표를 사용하여 / 불규칙성을 가려냈다 / 그리고 그것들로 / 신의 은총을 //

(①) This was the seed / of what we now call the scientific
전치사   명사절
method / — a demonstration / that accurate observations of the
동격절 접속사
world / could be used / to forecast its future. //
이것이 씨앗이었다 / 우리가 현재 과학적인 방법이라고 부르는 것의 / 보여 주는 것 / 세상에 대한 정확한 관찰이 / 사용될 수 있다는 것을 / 그것의 미래를 예측하기 위해 //

단서 2 손과 눈으로 하는 측정의 발전이 원활하지는 않음
(②) The importance of measurement / in this sort of cosmic
comprehension / did not develop smoothly / over the centuries. //
측정의 중요성은 / 이러한 종류의 우주의 이해에 있어서의 / 원활하게 발전하지는 않았다 / 수 세기 동안 //

단서 3 주어진 문장에 등장한, 손과 눈으로 하는 측정이 만들어 내는 지식에 대한 의심을 가리킴
(③) The suspicion was due to the influence / of ancient Greeks
/ in the era's scholasticism, /
그 의심은 영향 때문이었다 / 고대 그리스인들의 / 그 당시의 스콜라 철학의 /
particularly Plato and Aristotle, / who stressed / that the material
world was one / of unceasing change and instability. //
특히 플라톤과 아리스토텔레스의 / 강조했던 / 물질 세계는 하나라고 / 끊임없는 변화와 불안정의 //
(④) They emphasized / that reality was best understood / by
reference to immaterial qualities, / be they Platonic forms or
Aristotelian causes. //
양보의 부사절 접속사 whether가 생략되고 주어와 동사(원형)가 도치됨
그들은 강조했다 / 현실이 가장 잘 이해된다고 / 비물질적인 자질을 참조하여 / 플라톤적인 형태이든 아리스토텔레스적인 원인이든 //
(⑤) It would take the revelations / of the scientific revolution /
to fully displace these instincts, / with observations of the night
with 분사구문: with+(대)명사+현재분사/과거분사
sky / once again / proving decisive. //
뜻밖의 새로운 발견이 필요했을 것이고 / 과학적인 혁명이라는 / 이러한 직관을 완전히 대체하기 위해서는 / 밤하늘의 관찰이 / 다시 한 번 / 결정적임이 입증되었다 //

- shabby ⓐ 터무니없는, 부당한 • inferior to ~보다 열등한
- abstract ⓐ 추상적인 • irregularity ⓝ 변칙, 불규칙한 것
- favour ⓝ 호의, 친절, 은총 • demonstration ⓝ 입증, 설명
- forecast ⓥ 예측하다 • measurement ⓝ 측정
- cosmic ⓐ 우주의 • comprehension ⓝ 이해
- suspicion ⓝ 혐의, 의심 • revelation ⓝ 폭로, 발견, 드러냄
- revolution ⓝ 혁명 • displace ⓥ 대체하다 • instinct ⓝ 직관
- observation ⓝ 관찰 • decisive ⓐ 결정적인, 결단력 있는

바빌로니아의 천문학자들은 하늘에서의 천체 운동에 대한 자세한 기록을 만들었고, 그 결과표를 사용하여 불규칙성을, 그리고 그것들로 신의 은총을 가려냈다. (①) 이것이 우리가 현재 과학적인 방법이라고 부르는 것, 즉 세상에 대한 정확한 관찰이 미래를 예측하기 위해 사용될 수 있다는 것을 보여 주는 씨앗이었다. (②) 이러한 종류의 우주의 이해에 관한 측정의 중요성은 수 세기 동안 원활하게 발전하지는 않았다. (③ 사실, 유럽의 중세 시대에는 손과 눈으로 측정하는 것은 다소 터무니없는 종류의 지식, 즉 추상적인 사고의 그것보다 열등한 지식을 만들어 낸다고 때때로 여겨졌다.) 그 의심은 그 당시의 스콜라 철학의 고대 그리스인들, 특히 물질 세계는 끊임없는 변화와 불안정의 하나라고 강조했던 플라톤과 아리스토텔레스의 영향 때문이었다. (④) 그들은 현실이 플라톤적인 형태이든 아리스토텔레스적인 원인이든 비물질적인 자질을 참조하여 가장 잘 이해된다고 강조했다. (⑤) 이러한 직관을 완전히 대체하기 위해서는 과학적인 혁명이라는 뜻밖의 새로운 발견이 필요했을 것이고 밤하늘의 관찰이 결정적임이 다시 한 번 입증되었다.

| 문제 풀이 순서 | [정답률 45%]

1st 주어진 문장을 해석하고, 연결어, 지시어 등을 확인한다.

> Indeed, in the Middle Ages in Europe, calculating by hand
> and eye was sometimes seen as producing a rather
> shabby sort of knowledge, inferior to that of abstract
> thought.
> 사실, 유럽의 중세 시대에는 손과 눈으로 측정하는 것은 다소 터무니없는 종류의 지식, 즉 추상적인 사고의 그것보다 열등한 지식을 만들어 낸다고 때때로 여겨졌다.

➡ indeed는 앞에서 말한 내용을 반박하거나 부연할 때 주로 쓰이지만, 구체적으로 부연할 때도 쓰인다. ▶ indeed로 예상한 주어진 문장 앞에 올 내용
1 손과 눈으로 측정하는 것이 정확하다고 여겨졌음
2 손과 눈으로 측정하는 것이 늘 정확하다고 여겨졌던 것은 아님

2nd 각 선택지의 앞뒤 흐름이 매끄러운지 확인한다.

- **①**의 앞 문장과 뒤 문장

> **앞 문장:** 바빌로니아의 천문학자들은 하늘에서의 천체 운동에 대한 자세한 기록을 만들었고, 그 결과표를 사용하여 불규칙성을 가려냈다.
> **뒤 문장:** 이것(This)이 우리가 현재 과학적인 방법이라고 부르는 것의 씨앗이었다.

→ 바빌로니아의 천문학자들이 눈으로 측정하여 불규칙성을 가려낸 것이 우리가 현재 과학적인 방법이라고 부르는 것의 씨앗이라는 내용이 앞뒤로 이어진다. 뒤 문장의 주어인 This가 앞 문장을 가리킨다.
▶ 주어진 문장이 ①에 들어갈 수 없음

- **②**의 앞 문장과 뒤 문장

> **앞 문장:** ①의 뒤 문장과 같음
> **뒤 문장:** 이러한 종류의 우주의 이해(this sort of cosmic comprehension)에 있어서의 측정의 중요성은 수 세기 동안 원활하게 발전하지는 않았다.

→ 이러한 종류의 우주의 이해: 천체 운동을 눈으로 측정하여 우주를 이해하는 것 주어진 문장은 눈으로 측정하는 것이 원활하게 발전하지 않았다는 것에 대한 구체적인 부연이다.
▶ 주어진 문장이 ②에 들어갈 수 없음

- **③**의 앞 문장과 뒤 문장

> **앞 문장:** ②의 뒤 문장과 같음
> **뒤 문장:** 그 의심(The suspicion)은 물질 세계는 끊임없는 변화와 불안정의 하나라고 강조했던 플라톤과 아리스토텔레스의 영향 때문이었다.

→ The suspicion이 가리키는 것이 앞 문장에 등장하지 않는다.
The suspicion은, 주어진 문장에서 설명한, 손과 눈으로 측정하는 것이 추상적인 사고보다 열등한 지식을 만들어 낸다는 중세 유럽의 의심을 가리킨다.
▶ 주어진 문장이 ③에 들어가야 함

- **④**의 앞 문장과 뒤 문장

> **앞 문장:** ③의 뒤 문장과 같음
> **뒤 문장:** 그들(They)은 현실이 플라톤적인 형태이든 아리스토텔레스적인 원인이든 비물질적인 자질을 참조하여 가장 잘 이해된다고 강조했다.

→ 현실은 비물질적인 자질을 참조하여 가장 잘 이해된다고 강조한 They는 앞 문장에 등장한 '고대 그리스인들'을 가리킨다.
▶ 주어진 문장이 ④에 들어갈 수 없음

- **⑤**의 앞 문장과 뒤 문장

> **앞 문장:** ④의 뒤 문장과 같음
> **뒤 문장:** 이러한 직관(these instincts)을 완전히 대체하기 위해서는 과학적인 혁명이라는 뜻밖의 새로운 발견이 필요했을 것이고 밤하늘의 관찰이 결정적임이 다시 한 번 입증되었다.

→ these instincts: 밤하늘의 관찰, 즉 눈으로 하는 측정이 결정적이라는 것이 입증되어 대체된 것, 즉 현실은 비물질적인 자질을 참조하여 가장 잘 이해된다는 생각을 가리킨다.
▶ 주어진 문장이 ⑤에 들어갈 수 없음

3rd 글이 한눈에 들어오도록 정리하여 정답을 확인한다.

바빌로니아의 천문학자들은 천체 운동에 대한 자세한 기록을 만들었고, 그 결과표를 사용하여 불규칙성을, 그리고 그것들로 신의 은총을 가려냈다.
(①) 이것이 우리가 현재 과학적인 방법이라고 부르는 것, 즉 세상에 대한 정확한 관찰이 미래를 예측하기 위해 사용될 수 있다는 것을 보여 주는 씨앗이었다.
(②) 이러한 종류의 우주의 이해에 관한 측정의 중요성은 수 세기 동안 원활하게 발전하지는 않았다.
(③ 사실, 유럽의 중세 시대에는 손과 눈으로 측정하는 것은 다소 터무니없는 종류의 지식, 즉 추상적인 사고의 그것보다 열등한 지식을 만들어 낸다고 때때로 여겨졌다.) 그 의심은 특히 물질 세계는 끊임없는 변화와 불안정의 하나라고 강조했던 플라톤과 아리스토텔레스의 영향 때문이었다.
(④) 그들은 현실이 플라톤적인 형태이든 아리스토텔레스적인 원인이든 비물질적인 자질을 참조하여 가장 잘 이해된다고 강조했다.
(⑤) 이러한 직관을 완전히 대체하기 위해서는 과학적인 혁명이라는 뜻밖의 새로운 발견이 필요했을 것이고 밤하늘의 관찰이 결정적임이 다시 한 번 입증되었다.

N 29 정답 ④ ＊우리가 바쁠 때 선택의 변화 ——————

> 글의 흐름으로 보아, 주어진 문장이 들어가기에 가장 적절한 곳을 고르시오.

단서 1 실험의 결과를 제시하는 문장임

> The result was / that we don't always buy / what we like best,
> 　　　　　　주격 보어절 접속사　　부분 부정(항상 ~은 아님)
> / but when things have to happen quickly, / we tend to go for
> 　선행사　　　　주격 관계대명사
> the product / that catches our eye the most. //
> 결과는 ~이었다 / 우리가 항상 사지는 않지만 / 우리가 가장 좋아하는 것을 / 일이 빨리 일어나야 할 때 / 우리는 제품을 선택하는 경향이 있다는 것 / 우리의 눈에 가장 띄는

Often / time, or lack of time, / plays an important role / in the purchase of everyday products. //
종종 / 시간 또는 시간의 부족은 / 중요한 역할을 한다 / 일상 제품 구매에 //

Milica Milosavljevic and his coworkers / conducted an experiment / looking at the relationship / between visual salience and the decision / to purchase. //
　　　　　　　　　　　　　　형용사적 용법(the decision 수식)
Milica Milosavljevic과 그의 동료들은 / 실험을 수행했다 / 관계를 보는 / 시각적 두드러짐과 결정 간의 / 구매하려는 //

　　주어　　동사　　간접목적어　　　직접목적어
(①) They showed subjects 15 different food items / on fMRI, /
그들은 피실험자들에게 열다섯 가지의 다른 음식 품목들을 보여주었다 / 기능적 자기 공명 영상으로
선행사(목적격 관계대명사는 생략됨)
such as those / we find in a candy vending machine / at the train station, / that is, bars, chips, fruity items, etc. //
~한 것들과 같은 / 우리가 사탕 과자 자판기에서 발견하는 / 기차역에서 / 즉, 막대 모양의 과자, 감자칩, 과일 맛이 나는 품목 등 //

(②) These were rated / by the subjects / on a scale of 1–15 / according to "favorite snack" to "don't like at all." //
이것들은 등급이 매겨졌다 / 피실험자들에 의해 / 1 ~ 15의 척도로 / '가장 좋아하는 간식'에서 '전혀 좋아하지 않음'에 따라 //

(③) They were then presented / in varying brightness and time, / with subjects always having to make a choice / between two products. //
그러고 나서 그것들은 제시되었으며 / 달라지는 밝기와 시간에서 / 피실험자들은 항상 선택해야 했다 / 두 제품 중에서 // **단서 2** 주의가 산만할 때는 실제 선호는 뒤쪽으로 떨어지고
　　　　　　　　　　　　　　　　　눈에 잘 띄는 것이 두드러진다는 내용이 also로 이어짐
(④) If we are also distracted / because we are talking to someone,
　부사절 접속사(조건)　　　　　부사절 접속사(이유)
/ on the phone, / or our thoughts are elsewhere / at the moment, /
또한 우리가 주의가 산만해진다면 / 우리가 누군가와 이야기하고 있거나 / 통화 중이거나 / 또는 우리의 생각이 다른 곳에 있어서 / 그 순간에 /
our actual preference for a product / falls further into the background / and visual conspicuousness comes to the fore. //
어떤 제품에 대한 우리의 실제 선호는 / 뒤쪽으로 더 떨어지고 / 시각적으로 눈에 잘 띔이 두드러진다 //

(⑤) Colors play an important role / in this. //
색깔은 중요한 역할을 한다 / 여기에서 //

- visual ⓐ 시각적인 • purchase ⓥ 구매하다
- vending machine 자판기 • fruity ⓐ 과일 맛이 나는
- scale ⓝ 척도 • brightness ⓝ 밝기
- be distracted 주의가 산만해지다 • preference ⓝ 선호
- come to the fore 두드러지다

종종 시간 또는 시간의 부족은 일상 제품 구매에 중요한 역할을 한다. Milica Milosavljevic과 그의 동료들은 시각적 두드러짐과 구매 결정 간의 관계를 보는 실험을 수행했다. (①) 그들은 피실험자들에게 기능적 자기 공명 영상으로 우리가 기차역의 사탕 과자 자판기에서 발견하는 것들, 즉, 막대 모양의 과자, 감자칩, 과일 맛이 나는 품목 등과 같은 열다섯 가지의 다른 음식 품목들을 보여주었다. (②) 이것들은 피실험자들에 의해 '가장 좋아하는 간식'에서 '전혀 좋아하지 않음'에 따라 1~15의 척도로 등급이 매겨졌다. (③) 그리고 나서 그것들은 밝기와 시간을 달리하여 제시되었으며, 피실험자들은 항상 두 제품 중 선택해야 했다. (④ 결과는 우리가 항상 우리가 가장 좋아하는 것을 사지는 않지만, 일이 빨리 일어나야 할 때, 우리는 우리의 눈에 가장 띄는 제품을 선택하는 경향이 있다는 것이었다.) 또한 우리가 누군가와 이야기하고 있거나, 통화 중이거나, 그 순간에 우리의 생각이 다른 곳에 있어서 주의가 산만해질 때, 어떤 제품에 대한 우리의 실제 선호는 뒤쪽으로 더 떨어지고 시각적으로 눈에 잘 띔이 두드러진다. (⑤) 색깔은 여기에서 중요한 역할을 한다.

| 문제 풀이 순서 | [정답률 67%]

1st 주어진 문장을 해석하고, 연결어, 지시어 등을 확인한다.

> The result was that we don't always buy what we like best, but when things have to happen quickly, we tend to go for the product that catches our eye the most.
> 결과는 우리가 항상 우리가 가장 좋아하는 것을 사지는 않지만, 일이 빨리 일어나야 할 때, 우리는 우리의 눈에 가장 띄는 제품을 선택하는 경향이 있다는 것이었다.

→ 어떤 실험의 결과: 우리는 항상 우리가 가장 좋아하는 것을 사는 것은 아니다. 일이 빨리 일어나야 할 때 우리는 우리 눈에 가장 띄는 제품을 선택하는 경향이 있다.
주어진 문장 앞: 실험 과정에 대한 설명이 모두 제시된 이후에 결과를 제시하는 주어진 문장이 들어가야 함
주어진 문장 뒤: 제시된 실험 결과를 이용하여 일반적인 사실을 도출하는 내용이 주어진 문장 이후에 이어질 것임

2nd 각 선택지의 앞뒤 흐름이 매끄러운지 확인한다.

- ①의 앞 문장과 뒤 문장

> **앞 문장**: Milica Milosavljevic과 그의 동료들은 시각적 두드러짐과 구매 결정 간의 관계를 보는 실험을 수행했다.
> **뒤 문장**: 그들은 피실험자들에게 기능적 자기 공명 영상으로 우리가 기차역의 사탕 과자 자판기에서 발견하는 것들, 즉, 막대 모양의 과자, 감자칩, 과일 맛이 나는 품목 등과 같은 열다섯 가지의 다른 음식 품목들을 보여주었다.

⇒ 실험을 소개하는 문장과 실험 과정을 설명하기 시작하는 문장이 앞뒤로 이어진다. 따라서 그 사이에 실험의 결과를 설명하는 문장을 넣을 수 없다.
▶ 주어진 문장이 ①에 들어갈 수 없음

- ②의 앞 문장과 뒤 문장

> **앞 문장**: ①의 뒤 문장과 같음
> **뒤 문장**: 이것들은 피실험자들에 의해 '가장 좋아하는 간식'에서 '전혀 좋아하지 않음'에 따라 1~15의 척도로 등급이 매겨졌다.

⇒ 뒤 문장까지 실험 과정에 대해 설명하는 문장이 이어진다. 주어진 문장은 실험 과정에 대한 설명이 모두 끝난 이후에 들어가야 한다.
▶ 주어진 문장이 ②에 들어갈 수 없음

- ③의 앞 문장과 뒤 문장

> **앞 문장**: ②의 뒤 문장과 같음
> **뒤 문장**: 그리고 나서 그것들은 밝기와 시간을 달리하여 제시되었으며, 피실험자들은 항상 두 제품 중 선택해야 했다.

⇒ 여전히 실험 과정에 대해 설명하는 문장이 이어진다. 주어진 문장은 실험 과정에 대한 설명이 모두 끝난 이후에 들어가야 한다.
▶ 주어진 문장이 ③에 들어갈 수 없음

- ④의 앞 문장과 뒤 문장

> **앞 문장**: ③의 뒤 문장과 같음
> **뒤 문장**: 또한(also) 우리가 누군가와 이야기하고 있거나, 통화 중이거나, 그 순간에 우리의 생각이 다른 곳에 있어서 주의가 산만해질 때, 어떤 제품에 대한 우리의 실제 선호는 뒤쪽으로 더 떨어지고 시각적으로 눈에 잘 띔이 두드러진다.

⇒ 부사 also가 사용됨: 주의가 산만할 때는 실제 선호는 뒤로 물러나고 눈에 잘 띄는 것이 앞에 등장한다는 것과 비슷한 내용이 앞에 있어야 한다.
주어진 문장이 설명하는 실험의 결과가 이와 비슷한 현상을 이야기한다.
▶ 주어진 문장이 ④에 들어가야 함

- ⑤의 앞 문장과 뒤 문장

> **앞 문장**: ④의 뒤 문장과 같음
> **뒤 문장**: 색깔은 여기에서 중요한 역할을 한다.

⇒ 주의가 산만할 때는 실제로 선호하는 것보다 시각적으로 눈에 잘 띄는 것을 선택하게 되는데, 이때 색깔이 중요한 역할을 한다는 흐름이다. 또한, 주어진 문장이 also가 포함된 문장보다 앞에 들어갈 수 없다.
▶ 주어진 문장이 ⑤에 들어갈 수 없음

3rd 글이 한눈에 들어오도록 정리하여 정답을 확인한다.

시간 또는 시간의 부족은 일상 제품 구매에 중요한 역할을 한다. Milica Milosavljevic과 그의 동료들은 시각적 두드러짐과 구매 결정 간의 관계를 보는 실험을 수행했다.
(①) 피실험자들에게 기능적 자기 공명 영상으로 우리가 기차역의 사탕 과자 자판기에서 발견하는 것들 중 열다섯 가지의 다른 음식 품목들을 보여주었다.
(②) 이것들은 피실험자들에 의해 '가장 좋아하는 간식'에서 '전혀 좋아하지 않음'에 따라 1~15의 척도로 등급이 매겨졌다.
(③) 그리고 나서 그것들은 밝기와 시간을 달리하여 제시되었으며, 피실험자들은 항상 두 제품 중 선택해야 했다.
(④ 결과는 우리가 항상 우리가 가장 좋아하는 것을 사지는 않지만, 일이 빨리 일어나야 할 때, 우리는 우리의 눈에 가장 띄는 제품을 선택하는 경향이 있다는 것이었다.)
또한 우리가 누군가와 이야기하고 있거나, 통화 중이거나할 때, 어떤 제품에 대한 우리의 실제 선호는 뒤쪽으로 더 떨어지고 시각적으로 눈에 잘 띔이 두드러진다.
(⑤) 색깔은 여기에서 중요한 역할을 한다.

글의 흐름으로 보아, 주어진 문장이 들어가기에 가장 적절한 곳을 고르시오.

단서 1 영국에서 많은 사람들이 축구를 자신들의 경기로 본다는 내용이 앞에 있어야 함

However, / within British society / not everybody would see football / as 'their' game. //
부분 부정: 모두 ~한 것은 아닌
그러나 / 영국 사회 안에서 / 모든 사람이 축구를 보는 것은 아닐 것이다 / '자신들의' 경기로 //

If we look at contemporary British 'culture' / we will probably quickly conclude / that sport is an important part of the culture. //
생략 가능한 명사절 접속사
만약 우리가 현대 영국의 '문화'를 본다면 / 우리는 아마도 빠르게 결론지을 것이다 / 스포츠가 그 문화의 중요한 한 부분이라고 //

In other words, / it is something / that many people in the society / share and value. //
선행사   목적격 관계대명사
다시 말해서 / 그것은 ~한 것이다 / 사회의 많은 사람이 / 공유하고 가치 있게 여기는 //

(①) In addition, / we would also probably conclude / that the most 'important' sport / within British culture / is football. //
단수 주어   단수 동사
게다가 / 우리는 또한 아마도 결론을 내릴 것이다 / 가장 '중요한' 스포츠는 / 영국 문화에서 / 축구라고 //

(②) We would 'know' this / from the evidence / that on a daily basis / there is a significant amount of 'cultural' activity / all focused on football /
동격절 접속사
단서 2 축구에 초점이 맞춰진 상당량의 문화적 활동이 매일 있다는 증거로부터 영국 문화에서 가장 중요한 스포츠는 축구라고 결론 내림
우리는 이것을 '알' 것이다 / 증거로부터 / 매일 / 상당한 양의 '문화적' 활동이 있다는 / 모두 축구에 초점이 맞춰진 /

in terms of the amount of people / who play it, watch it, read about it and talk about it. //
병렬 구조
사람의 양의 관점에서 / 그것을 하고, 그것을 보고, 그것에 대해 읽고 그것에 대해 이야기하는 //

(③) It could be argued / from looking at their 'cultural' activities and habits, /
가주어
~라고 주장될 수 있다 / 그들의 '문화적' 활동과 습관을 보는 것으로부터 /
진주어절 접속사

that people / from a middle-class background / seem to prefer rugby / over football, / or that more women play netball / than football. //
단서 3 영국 문화에서 축구가 가장 중요한 스포츠라는 결론에 반하는 내용임
사람들은 / 중산층 배경을 가진 / 럭비를 선호하는 것처럼 보인다고 / 축구보다 / 또는 더 많은 여성들이 네트볼을 한다고 / 축구보다 //

(④) Equally, / if you went to the USA / and were talking about 'football', / most people would assume / you were talking about American football / rather than soccer. //
would assume의 목적어절을 이끄는 명사절 접속사가 생략됨
그와 동시에 / 만약 여러분이 미국에 가서 / '축구'에 대해 이야기하고 있다면 / 대부분의 사람은 가정할 것이다 / 여러분이 미식축구에 관해 이야기하고 있다고 / 축구보다는 //

(⑤) From this / we can conclude / that different cultures produce different ways / of understanding, or evaluating, / human activities such as sport. //
이로부터 / 우리는 결론지을 수 있다 / 서로 다른 문화들이 서로 다른 방식들을 만들어낸다고 / 이해하거나 평가하는 / 스포츠와 같은 인간 활동을 //

• contemporary ⓐ 현대의   • conclude ⓥ 결론을 짓다
• in other words 다시 말해서   • value ⓥ 가치 있게 여기다
• on a daily basis 매일   • significant ⓐ 상당한   • amount ⓝ 양
• in terms of ~의 관점에서   • argue ⓥ 주장하다
• assume ⓥ 추정하다   • evaluate ⓥ 평가하다

만약 우리가 현대 영국의 '문화'를 본다면 우리는 아마도 스포츠가 그 문화의 중요한 한 부분이라고 빠르게 결론지을 것이다. 다시 말해서, 그것은 사회의 많은 사람이 공유하고 가치 있게 여기는 것이다. (①) 게다가, 우리는 또한 영국 문화에서 가장 '중요한' 스포츠는 축구라고 아마도 결론을 내릴 것이다. (②) 축구를 하고, 축구를 보고, 축구에 대해 읽고 축구에 대해 이야기하는 사람의 양의 관점에서 그것에 모두 초점이 맞춰진 상당한 양의 '문화적' 활동이 매일 있다는 증거로부터 우리는 이것을 '알' 것이다. (③ 그러나 영국 사회 안에서 모든 사람이 축구를 '자신들의' 경기로 보는 것은 아닐 것이다.)

그들의 '문화적' 활동과 습관을 보는 것으로부터, 중산층 배경을 가진 사람들은 축구보다 럭비를 선호하는 것처럼 보이거나 더 많은 여성들이 축구보다 네트볼을 한다고 주장될 수 있다. (④) 그와 동시에, 만약 여러분이 미국에 가서 '축구'에 대해 이야기하고 있다면, 대부분의 사람은 여러분이 축구보다는 미식축구에 관해 이야기하고 있다고 가정할 것이다. (⑤) 이로부터 서로 다른 문화들이 스포츠와 같은 인간 활동을 이해하거나 평가하는 서로 다른 방식들을 만들어낸다고 우리는 결론지을 수 있다.

| 문제 풀이 순서 | [정답률 64%]

1st 주어진 문장을 해석하고, 연결어, 지시어 등을 확인한다.

However, within British society not everybody would see football as 'their' game.
그러나 영국 사회 안에서 모든 사람이 축구를 '자신들의' 경기로 보는 것은 아닐 것이다.

➡ 역접의 연결어 However가 문장을 앞 문장에 잇고 있다.
주어진 문장 앞: 영국 사회 안에서 많은 사람들이 축구를 자신들의 경기로 본다는 내용
주어진 문장 뒤: 영국 사회 안에서 모든 사람들이 축구를 자신들의 경기로 보지는 않는다는 것에 대한 부연

2nd 각 선택지의 앞뒤 흐름이 매끄러운지 확인한다.

- ①의 앞 문장과 뒤 문장

앞 문장: 다시 말해서, 그것은(it)은 사회의 많은 사람이 공유하고 가치 있게 여기는 것이다.
뒤 문장: 게다가(In addition), 우리는 또한 영국 문화에서 가장 '중요한' 스포츠는 축구라고 아마도 결론을 내릴 것이다.

➡ 앞 문장의 it은 그 앞 문장에 등장한 sport를 가리킨다.
스포츠가 영국 문화의 중요한 한 부분이라는 결론에 덧붙여(In addtion) 영국 문화에서 가장 중요한 스포츠는 축구라는 결론도 내릴 것이라는 내용이 앞뒤로 이어진다. 영국 문화에서 가장 중요한 스포츠가 축구라는 설명 앞에 주어진 문장이 들어갈 수는 없다.
▶ 주어진 문장이 ①에 들어갈 수 없음

- ②의 앞 문장과 뒤 문장

앞 문장: ①의 뒤 문장과 같음
뒤 문장: 축구를 하고, 축구를 보고, 축구에 대해 읽고 축구에 대해 이야기하는 사람의 양의 관점에서 그것에 모두 초점이 맞춰진 상당한 양의 '문화적' 활동이 매일 있다는 증거로부터 우리는 이것(this)을 '알' 것이다.

➡ this가 가리키는 것이 앞 문장의 내용, 즉 '영국 문화에서 가장 중요한 스포츠가 축구라는 것'이다.
▶ 주어진 문장이 ②에 들어갈 수 없음

- ③의 앞 문장과 뒤 문장

앞 문장: ②의 뒤 문장과 같음
뒤 문장: 그들의 '문화적' 활동과 습관을 보는 것으로부터, 중산층 배경을 가진 사람들은 축구보다 럭비를 선호하는 것처럼 보이거나 더 많은 여성들이 축구보다 네트볼을 한다고 주장될 수 있다.

➡ **앞 문장**: 모두 축구에 초점이 맞춰진 상당한 양의 문화적 활동이 매일 있다.
뒤 문장: 중산층은 축구보다 럭비를 선호한다. 더 많은 여성들이 축구보다 네트볼을 한다. 바로 이 내용이, 영국 사람들이 모두 축구를 자신의 경기로 보지는 않는다는 것에 대한 부연이다.
▶ 주어진 문장이 ③에 들어가야 함

- ④의 앞 문장과 뒤 문장

> **앞 문장**: ③의 뒤 문장과 같음
> **뒤 문장**: 그와 동시에, 만약 여러분이 미국에 가서 '축구'에 대해 이야기하고 있다면, 대부분의 사람은 여러분이 축구보다는 미식축구에 관해 이야기하고 있다고 가정할 것이다.

➡ 뒤 문장은 문화적 활동과 습관 때문에 미국에서의 축구 이야기는 축구가 아니라 미식축구에 관한 이야기라고 가정된다는 내용이다. Equally로 앞뒤 문장이 자연스럽게 이어진다. ▶ 주어진 문장이 ④에 들어갈 수 없다

- ⑤의 앞 문장과 뒤 문장

> **앞 문장**: ④의 뒤 문장과 같음
> **뒤 문장**: 이로부터 서로 다른 문화들이 스포츠와 같은 인간 활동을 이해하거나 평가하는 서로 다른 방식들을 만들어낸다고 우리는 결론지을 수 있다.

➡ 앞에서 설명한 것을 통해 내릴 수 있는 결론이 이어진다. 앞 문장보다 전에 영국에 관한 이야기가 끝났다. ▶ 주어진 문장이 ⑤에 들어갈 수 없다

3rd 글이 한눈에 들어오도록 정리하여 정답을 확인한다.

우리가 현대 영국의 '문화'를 본다면 우리는 아마도 스포츠가 그 문화의 중요한 한 부분이라고 빠르게 결론지을 것이다. 다시 말해서, 그것은 사회의 많은 사람이 공유하고 가치 있게 여기는 것이다. (①) 우리는 또한 영국 문화에서 가장 '중요한' 스포츠는 축구라고 아마도 결론을 내릴 것이다. (②) 축구에 모두 초점이 맞춰진 상당한 양의 '문화적' 활동이 매일 있다는 증거로부터 우리는 이것을 '알' 것이다. (③ 그러나 영국 사회 안에서 모든 사람이 축구를 '자신들의' 경기로 보는 것은 아닐 것이다.) 그들의 '문화적' 활동과 습관을 보는 것으로부터, 중산층 배경을 가진 사람들은 축구보다 럭비를 선호하는 것처럼 보이거나 더 많은 여성들이 축구보다 네트볼을 한다고 주장될 수 있다. (④) 만약 여러분이 미국에 가서 '축구'에 대해 이야기하고 있다면, 대부분의 사람은 여러분이 축구보다는 미식축구에 관해 이야기하고 있다고 가정할 것이다. (⑤) 서로 다른 문화들이 스포츠와 같은 인간 활동을 이해하거나 평가하는 서로 다른 방식들을 만들어낸다고 우리는 결론지을 수 있다.

N 31 정답 ⑤ *음악 제작 방식의 변화

> 글의 흐름으로 보아, 주어진 문장이 들어가기에 가장 적절한 곳을 고르시오.

Because the manipulation of digitally converted sounds meant / the reprogramming of binary information, / editing
단서 1 편집 작업이 매우 작은 수준으로 수행될 수 있었음
operations could be performed / with millisecond precision. //
디지털로 변환된 소리의 조작은 의미했으므로 / 2진법의 정보를 재프로그래밍하는 것을 / 편집 작업은 수행될 수 있었다 / 1,000분의 1초의 정밀도로 //

주어
The shift from analog to digital technology / significantly
동사   목적어절
influenced / how music was produced. //
아날로그 기술에서 디지털 기술로의 전환은 / 크게 영향을 미쳤다 / 음악이 제작되는 방식에 //
주어
First and foremost, / the digitization of sounds / — that is, their conversion into numbers — / enabled music makers to undo /
동사   목적어   목적격 보어
what was done. //
무엇보다도 / 소리의 디지털화 / 즉 그것의 숫자로의 변환은 / 음악 제작자들이 되돌릴 수 있게 해 주었다 / 기존의 작업을 //

(①) One could, in other words, twist and bend sounds / toward
전치사   동명사구
something new / without sacrificing the original version. //
다시 말해 소리를 비틀고 구부릴 수 있었다 / 어떤 새로운 것으로 / 원본을 희생하지 않으면서 //

(②) This "undo" ability made mistakes / considerably less momentous, / sparking the creative process / and encouraging a generally more experimental mindset. //
이러한 '되돌리기' 기능은 실수를 만들어 / 훨씬 덜 중대하게 / 창작 과정을 촉발하고 / 일반적으로 더 실험적인 사고방식을 장려했다 //

(③) In addition, / digitally converted sounds could be manipulated / simply by programming digital messages / rather
┌─ rather than으로 연결된 by의 목적어 ─┐
than using physical tools, / simplifying the editing process significantly. //
또한 / 디지털로 변환된 소리는 조작될 수 있어서 / 단순히 디지털 메시지를 프로그래밍함으로써 / 물리적인 도구를 사용하기보다는 / 편집 과정을 크게 간소화했다 //

(④) For example, / while editing once involved razor blades /
부사절 접속사(대조)
to physically cut and splice audiotapes, /
예를 들어 / 예전에 편집 과정은 면도기 칼날의 사용을 수반했지만 / 음성 녹음테이프를 물리적으로 자르고 합쳐 잇기 위해 /

it now involved / the cursor and mouse-click of the computer-based sequencer program, / which was obviously less time consuming. //
이제 그것은 수반했고 / 컴퓨터에 기반한 순서기 프로그램의 커서와 마우스 클릭을 / 그것은 분명 시간을 덜 소모했다 // **단서 2** 주어진 문장에서 말한 1,000분의 1초의 정밀도를 가리킴

(⑤) This microlevel access / at once / made it easier to conceal
가목적어   진목적어
/ any traces of manipulations / (such as joining tracks / in silent
└─ 병렬 구조 ─┘
spots) /
이러한 매우 작은 수준의 접근은 / 동시에 / 숨기는 것을 더 쉽게 만들었다 / 조작의 흔적을 / (트랙을 결합하는 것과 같은 / 무음 지점에서) /

and introduced new possibilities / for manipulating sounds / in audible and experimental ways. //
그리고 새로운 가능성을 내놓았다 / 소리를 조작하는 / 들릴 수 있고 실험적인 방식으로 //

- **manipulation** ⓝ 조작   - **convert** ⓥ 변환하다
- **millisecond** ⓝ 1,000분의 1초, 밀리초   - **precision** ⓝ 정밀도
- **significantly** ⓪ 크게   - **influence** ⓥ 영향을 미치다
- **first and foremost** 무엇보다도, 가장 중요하게
- **digitization** ⓝ 디지털화   - **conversion** ⓝ 변환
- **enable** ⓥ 가능하게 하다   - **in other words** 다시 말해서
- **bend** ⓥ 구부리다   - **undo** ⓥ 되돌리다
- **considerably** ⓪ 상당히, 훨씬   - **momentous** ⓐ 중대한
- **experimental** ⓐ 실험적인   - **razor blade** 면도기 칼날
- **sequencer** ⓝ 순서기(전자 녹음 장비의 하나)   - **obviously** ⓪ 분명히
- **microlevel** 매우 작은 수준의   - **conceal** ⓥ 숨기다
- **trace** ⓝ 흔적   - **track** ⓝ 트랙(테이프나 디스크의 데이터 구획 단위)
- **audible** ⓐ 들릴 수 있는

아날로그 기술에서 디지털 기술로의 전환은 음악이 제작되는 방식에 크게 영향을 미쳤다. 무엇보다도, 소리의 디지털화, 즉 그것의 숫자로의 변환은 음악 제작자들이 기존의 작업을 되돌릴 수 있게 해 주었다. (①) 다시 말해, 원본을 희생하지 않으면서 소리를 비틀고 구부려서 어떤 새로운 것으로 만들 수 있었다. (②) 이러한 '되돌리기' 기능은 실수를 훨씬 덜 중대하게 만들어, 창작 과정을 촉발하고 일반적으로 더 실험적인 사고방식을 장려했다. (③) 또한, 디지털로 변환된 소리는 물리적인 도구를 사용하기보다는 단순히 디지털 메시지를 프로그래밍함으로써 조작될 수 있어서, 편집 과정을 크게 간소화했다. (④) 예를 들어, 예전에 편집 과정은 음성 녹음테이프를 물리적으로 자르고 합쳐 잇기 위해 면도기 칼날의 사용을 수반했지만, 이제 그것은 컴퓨터에 기반한 순서기 프로그램의 커서와 마우스 클릭을 수반했고, 그것은 분명 시간을 덜 소모했다. (⑤ 디지털로 변환된 소리의 조작은 2진법의 정보를 재프로그래밍하는 것을 의미했으므로, 편집 작업은 1,000분의 1초의 정밀도로 수행될 수 있었다.) 이러한 매우 작은 수준의 접근은 (무음 지점에서 트랙을 결합하는 것과 같은) 조작의 흔적을 숨기는 것을 더 쉽게 만든 동시에, 들릴 수 있고 실험적인 방식으로 소리를 조작할 새로운 가능성을 내놓았다.

1st 주어진 문장을 해석하고, 연결어, 지시어 등을 확인한다.

Because the manipulation of digitally converted sounds meant the reprogramming of binary information, editing operations could be performed with milliseconds precision.
디지털로 변환된 소리의 조작은 2진법의 정보를 재프로그래밍하는 것을 의미했으므로, 편집 작업은 1,000분의 1초의 정밀도로 수행될 수 있었다.

➡ 편집 작업이 1,000분의 1초의 정밀도로 수행될 수 있었다. (단서)
▶ 주어진 문장 뒤: 편집 작업이 매우 정밀하게 수행될 수 있다는 사실이 미친 영향을 설명하는 내용이 이어질 것임 (발상)

2nd 각 선택지의 앞뒤 흐름이 매끄러운지 확인한다.

- ①의 앞 문장과 뒤 문장

앞 문장: 무엇보다도, 소리의 디지털화, 즉 그것의 숫자로의 변환은 음악 제작자들이 기존의 작업을 되돌릴 수 있게 해 주었다.
뒤 문장: 다시 말해(in other words), 원본을 희생하지 않으면서 소리를 비틀고 구부려서 어떤 새로운 것으로 만들 수 있었다.

➡ 소리의 디지털화가 가져온 변화 중 하나로 기존의 작업을 되돌릴 수 있게 된 것을 설명한다.
기존의 작업을 되돌릴 수 있다는 것은 곧 원본을 희생하지 않으면서 소리를 변형시켜 새로운 것을 만들 수 있었음을 의미한다는 흐름이다. in other words로 앞뒤 문장이 자연스럽게 연결된다.
▶ 주어진 문장이 ①에 들어갈 수 없음

- ②의 앞 문장과 뒤 문장

앞 문장: ①의 뒤 문장과 같음
뒤 문장: 이러한 '되돌리기' 기능(This "undo" ability)은 실수를 훨씬 덜 중대하게 만들어, 창작 과정을 촉발하고 일반적으로 더 실험적인 사고방식을 장려했다.

➡ 앞에서 설명한, 기존의 작업을 되돌릴 수 있는 기능을 '이러한 되돌리기 기능'으로 가리키며, 그것이 미친 영향을 설명한다. 앞 문장의 내용을 가리키는 지시형용사 This가 앞뒤 문장을 적절하게 연결한다.
▶ 주어진 문장이 ②에 들어갈 수 없음

- ③의 앞 문장과 뒤 문장

앞 문장: ②의 뒤 문장과 같음
뒤 문장: 또한(In addition), 디지털로 변환된 소리는 물리적인 도구를 사용하기보다는 단순히 디지털 메시지를 프로그래밍함으로써 조작될 수 있어서, 편집 과정을 크게 간소화했다.

➡ 아날로그 기술에서 디지털 기술로 전환된 것이 음악 제작 방식에 미친 또 다른 영향이 이어진다. 소리의 디지털화로 인한 두 가지 영향이 In addition을 통해 자연스럽게 연결된다. ▶ 주어진 문장이 ③에 들어갈 수 없음

- ④의 앞 문장과 뒤 문장

앞 문장: ③의 뒤 문장과 같음
뒤 문장: 예를 들어(For example), 예전에 편집 과정은 음성 녹음테이프를 물리적으로 자르고 합쳐 잇기 위해 면도기 칼날의 사용을 수반했지만, 이제 그것은 컴퓨터에 기반한 순서기 프로그램의 커서와 마우스 클릭을 수반했고, 그것은 분명 시간을 덜 소모했다.

➡ 물리적인 도구를 사용한 편집과 디지털 메시지를 프로그래밍함으로써 이루어지는 편집을 예시를 들어 구체적으로 설명한 문장이 이어진다. 면도기 칼날이 물리적인 도구의 예시인 것으로, 앞에서 설명한 것에 대한 구체적인 예시가 For example을 통해 자연스럽게 제시된다.
▶ 주어진 문장이 ④에 들어갈 수 없음

- ⑤의 앞 문장과 뒤 문장

앞 문장: ④의 뒤 문장과 같음
뒤 문장: 이러한 매우 작은 수준의 접근(This microlevel access)은 (무음 지점에서 트랙을 결합하는 것과 같은) 조작의 흔적을 숨기는 것을 더 쉽게 만든 동시에, 들릴 수 있고 실험적인 방식으로 소리를 조작할 새로운 가능성을 내놓았다.

➡ 앞 문장에 '매우 작은 수준의 접근'과 관련된 설명이 없다. 뒤 문장의 지시형용사 This가 자연스럽게 위해서는 1,000분의 1초의 정밀도로 편집 작업이 수행될 수 있었다는 내용의 주어진 문장이 ⑤에 들어가야 한다.
▶ 주어진 문장이 ⑤에 들어가야 함

3rd 글이 한눈에 들어오도록 정리하여 정답을 확인한다.

아날로그 기술에서 디지털 기술로의 전환은 음악이 제작되는 방식에 크게 영향을 미쳤다. 소리의 디지털화는 음악 제작자들이 기존의 작업을 되돌릴 수 있게 해 주었다. (①) 원본을 희생하지 않으면서 어떤 새로운 것으로 만들 수 있었다. (②) 이러한 '되돌리기' 기능은 실수를 훨씬 덜 중대하게 만들어, 창작 과정을 촉발하고 더 실험적인 사고방식을 장려했다. (③) 디지털로 변환된 소리는 단순히 디지털 메시지를 프로그래밍함으로써 조작될 수 있어서, 편집 과정을 크게 간소화했다. (④) 예를 들어, 예전에 편집 과정은 면도기 칼날의 사용을 수반했지만, 이제 그것은 순서기 프로그램의 커서와 마우스 클릭을 수반했고, 시간을 덜 소모했다. 이러한 매우 작은 수준의 접근은 조작의 흔적을 숨기는 것을 더 쉽게 만든 동시에, 들릴 수 있고 실험적인 방식으로 소리를 조작할 새로운 가능성을 내놓았다. (⑤ 디지털로 변환된 소리의 조작은 2진법의 정보를 재프로그래밍하는 것을 의미했으므로, 편집 작업은 1,000분의 1초의 정밀도로 수행될 수 있었다.) 이러한 매우 작은 수준의 접근은 조작의 흔적을 숨기는 것을 더 쉽게 만든 동시에, 들릴 수 있고 실험적인 방식으로 소리를 조작할 새로운 가능성을 내놓았다.

N 32 정답 ④ * 쾌락의 양과 질

글의 흐름으로 보아, 주어진 문장이 들어가기에 가장 적절한 곳을 고르시오.

단서 1 쾌락에 있어 보다 질적인 방식에 찬성하는 주장을 한 사람이 In contrast로 설명됨

In contrast, / the other major advocate of utilitarianism, John Stuart Mill, / argued for a more qualitative approach, /
둘 중 하나를 제외한 나머지 하나
그와 대조적으로 / 공리주의의 다른 주요 옹호자인 John Stuart Mill은 / 보다 질적인 접근 방식을 찬성하는 주장을 했다 /

assuming / that there can be different subjective levels of pleasure. //
가정하고 / 여러 주관적인 차원의 쾌락이 있을 수 있다고 //

Utilitarian ethics argues / that all action should be directed /
목적어절을 이끄는 접속사
toward achieving the greatest total amount of happiness / for the largest number of people. //
공리주의 윤리는 주장한다 / 모든 행동은 지향해야 한다고 / 최대 행복을 달성하는 것을 / 최대 다수의 //

(①) Utilitarian ethics assumes / that all actions can be evaluated / in terms of their moral worth, /
목적어절을 이끄는 접속사
공리주의 윤리는 가정한다 / 모든 행동이 평가될 수 있으며 / 도덕적 가치의 관점에서 /

and so the desirability of an action is determined / by its resulting hedonistic consequences. //

따라서 어떤 행동의 바람직함은 결정된다고 / 그 행동이 초래하는 쾌락적인 결과에 의해 //

(②) This is a consequentialist creed, / assuming / that the moral
= and it assumes
value and desirability of an action / can be determined / from its likely outcomes. //

이것은 결과주의의 신조인데 / 가정한다 / 어떤 행동의 도덕적 가치와 바람직함은 / 결정될 수 있다고 / 그것이 가져올 결과로부터 //

(③) Jeremy Bentham suggested / that the value of hedonistic outcomes / can be quantitatively assessed, /

Jeremy Bentham은 말했다 / 쾌락적인 결과의 가치는 / 정량적으로 평가될 수 있으며 /

so that the value of consequent pleasure can be derived / by multiplying its intensity and its duration. // **단서2** 쾌락을 정량적으로 평가할 수 있다고 주장한 사람이 등장함

따라서 결과적 쾌락의 가치가 도출될 수 있다고 / 그것의 강도와 지속성을 곱하여 //

(④) Higher-quality pleasures are more desirable / than lower-quality pleasures. // **단서3** 쾌락의 질에 관한 부연 설명이 이어짐

질 높은 수준의 쾌락이 더 바람직하다 / 질 낮은 수준의 쾌락보다 //

(⑤) Less sophisticated creatures / (like pigs!) / have an easier
전치사   명사구
access / to the simpler pleasures, /

덜 고상한 생명체에게는 / (돼지처럼!) / 더 쉬운 접근이 있지만 / 더 단순한 쾌락에 대한 /

but more sophisticated creatures like humans / have the capacity / to access higher pleasures / and should be motivated / to seek
병렬 구조
형용사적 용법(the capacity 수식)
those. //

인간처럼 더 고상한 생명체에게는 / 능력이 있으며 / 더 질 높은 쾌락에 접근할 수 있는 / 동기가 주어져야 한다 / 그것을 추구하도록 //

- advocate ⓝ 옹호자   - qualitative ⓐ 질적인   - ethics ⓝ 윤리
- direct ⓥ 지향하다   - evaluate ⓥ 평가하다   - moral ⓐ 도덕적인
- desirability ⓝ 바람직함   - consequentialist ⓝ 결과주의자
- assess ⓥ 평가하다   - derive ⓥ 도출하다   - multiply ⓥ 곱하다
- intensity ⓝ 강도   - duration ⓝ 지속성
- sophisticated ⓐ 고상한   - capacity ⓝ 능력
- motivate ⓥ 동기부여하다

공리주의 윤리는 모든 행동은 최대 다수의 최대 행복을 달성하는 것을 지향해야 한다고 주장한다. (①) 공리주의 윤리는 모든 행동이 도덕적 가치의 관점에서 평가될 수 있으며, 따라서 어떤 행동의 바람직함은 그 행동이 초래하는 쾌락적인 결과에 의해 결정된다고 가정한다. (②) 이것은 결과주의의 신조인데, 어떤 행동의 도덕적 가치와 바람직함은 그것이 가져올 결과로부터 결정될 수 있다고 가정한다. (③) Jeremy Bentham은 쾌락적인 결과의 가치는 정량적으로 평가될 수 있으며, 따라서 결과적 쾌락의 가치가 그것의 강도와 지속성을 곱하여 도출될 수 있다고 말했다. (④ 그와 대조적으로 공리주의의 다른 주요 옹호자인 John Stuart Mill은 여러 주관적인 차원의 쾌락이 있을 수 있다고 가정하고 보다 질적인 접근 방식을 찬성하는 주장을 했다.) 질 높은 수준의 쾌락이 질 낮은 수준의 쾌락보다 더 바람직하다. (⑤) 덜 고상한 생명체(돼지처럼!)에게는 더 단순한 쾌락에 대한 더 쉬운 접근이 있지만, 인간처럼 더 고상한 생명체에게는 더 질 높은 쾌락에 접근할 수 있는 능력이 있으며 그것을 추구하도록 동기가 주어져야 한다.

| 문제 풀이 순서 | [정답률 67%]

1st 주어진 문장을 해석하고, 연결어, 지시어 등을 확인한다.

> In contrast, the other major advocate of utilitarianism, John Stuart Mill, argued for a more qualitative approach, assuming that there can be different subjective levels of pleasure.
>
> 그와 대조적으로 공리주의의 다른 주요 옹호자인 John Stuart Mill은 여러 주관적인 차원의 쾌락이 있을 수 있다고 가정하고 보다 질적인 접근 방식을 찬성하는 주장을 했다.

→ 보다 질적인 접근 방식에 찬성하는 주장을 한 John Stuart Mill에 대한 내용이 In contrast, the other가 포함된 문장으로 설명된다. **단서**
  ▶ **주어진 문장 앞:** John Stuart Mill과 반대의 주장을 한 사람에 대한 내용이 있어야 한다. **발상**

2nd 각 선택지의 앞뒤 흐름이 매끄러운지 확인한다.

- ①의 앞 문장과 뒤 문장

> **앞 문장:** 공리주의 윤리는 모든 행동은 최대 다수의 최대 행복을 달성하는 것을 지향해야 한다고 주장한다.
> **뒤 문장:** 공리주의 윤리는 모든 행동이 도덕적 가치의 관점에서 평가될 수 있으며, 따라서 어떤 행동의 바람직함은 그 행동이 초래하는 쾌락적인 결과에 의해 결정된다고 가정한다.

→ 공리주의가 무엇인지에 대한 설명이 앞으로 이어진다. John Stuart Mill과 대조되는 주장을 펼친 사람에 대한 내용은 없으므로 주어진 문장의 자리가 아니다.
  ▶ 주어진 문장이 ①에 들어갈 수 없음

- ②의 앞 문장과 뒤 문장

> **앞 문장:** ①의 뒤 문장과 같음
> **뒤 문장:** 이것은(This) 결과주의의 신조인데, 어떤 행동의 도덕적 가치와 바람직함은 그것이 가져올 결과로부터 결정될 수 있다고 가정한다.

→ 뒤 문장의 This가 가리키는 것이 앞 문장(공리주의 윤리: 어떤 행동의 바람직함은 그 행동이 초래하는 쾌락적인 결과에 의해 결정된다고 가정함)에 등장한다. 앞뒤 문장이 지시대명사로 자연스럽게 이어진다.
  ▶ 주어진 문장이 ②에 들어갈 수 없음

- ③의 앞 문장과 뒤 문장

> **앞 문장:** ②의 뒤 문장과 같음
> **뒤 문장:** Jeremy Bentham은 쾌락적인 결과의 가치는 정량적으로 평가될 수 있으며, 따라서 결과적 쾌락의 가치가 그것의 강도와 지속성을 곱하여 도출될 수 있다고 말했다.

→ 쾌락적인 결과의 가치를 어떻게 평가할 것인가에 대해 Jeremy Bentham은 정량적으로 평가될 수 있다고 주장했다는 내용이 이어진다. John Stuart Mill의 주장과 대조되는 주장을 펼친 사람이 등장하는 문장보다 앞에 주어진 문장이 들어갈 수 없다.
  ▶ 주어진 문장이 ③에 들어갈 수 없음

- ④의 앞 문장과 뒤 문장

> **앞 문장:** ③의 뒤 문장과 같음
> **뒤 문장:** 질 높은 수준의 쾌락이 질 낮은 수준의 쾌락보다 더 바람직하다.

→ 앞 문장에서는 정량적 평가에 대해 이야기했는데, 뒤 문장에서는 쾌락의 질에 대해 이야기하는 상황이다. 쾌락에 대한 질적인 접근을 주장한 John Stuart Mill에 대해 설명한 주어진 문장이 중간에 들어가야 자연스러운 흐름이 된다.
  ▶ 주어진 문장이 ④에 들어가야 함

- ⑤의 앞 문장과 뒤 문장

> **앞 문장:** ④의 뒤 문장과 같음
> **뒤 문장:** 덜 고상한 생명체(돼지처럼!)에게는 더 단순한 쾌락에 대한 더 쉬운 접근이 있지만, 인간처럼 더 고상한 생명체에게는 더 질 높은 쾌락에 접근할 수 있는 능력이 있으며 그것을 추구하도록 동기가 주어져야 한다.

→ 질 높은 수준의 쾌락과 질 낮은 수준의 쾌락을 구체적인 예시를 들어 설명하는 문장이 이어진다. For example과 같은 연결어는 없지만, 앞뒤 문장이 내용상 자연스럽게 이어진다.
  ▶ 주어진 문장이 ⑤에 들어갈 수 없음

공리주의 윤리는 모든 행동은 최대 다수의 최대 행복을 달성하는 것을 지향해야 한다고 주장한다.
(①) 공리주의 윤리는 모든 행동이 도덕적 가치의 관점에서 평가될 수 있으며, 따라서 어떤 행동의 바람직함은 그 행동이 초래하는 쾌락적인 결과에 의해 결정된다고 가정한다.
(②) 어떤 행동의 도덕적 가치와 바람직함은 그것이 가져올 결과로부터 결정될 수 있다고 가정한다.
(③) Jeremy Bentham은 결과적 쾌락의 가치가 그것의 강도와 지속성을 곱하여 도출될 수 있다고 말했다.
(④ John Stuart Mill은 여러 주관적인 차원의 쾌락이 있을 수 있다고 가정하고 보다 질적인 접근 방식을 찬성하는 주장을 했다.)
질 높은 수준의 쾌락이 질 낮은 수준의 쾌락보다 더 바람직하다.
(⑤) 인간처럼 더 고상한 생명체에게는 더 질 높은 쾌락에 접근할 수 있는 능력이 있으며 그것을 추구하도록 동기가 주어져야 한다.

N 33 정답 ③ *예술 작품의 제작을 인정하는 데 필요한 것 —

글의 흐름으로 보아, 주어진 문장이 들어가기에 가장 적절한 곳을 고르시오. [3점]

단서 1 전문가의 경우에는 재료와 기법에 대한 더 깊은 친숙함이 흔히 유용함

In the case of specialists / such as art critics, / a deeper
familiarity with materials and techniques / is often useful / in
reaching an informed judgement / about a work. //
전문가의 경우 / 예술 비평가와 같은 / 재료와 기법에 대한 더 깊은 친숙함이 / 흔히
유용하다 / 충분한 정보에 기반한 판단에 도달하는 데 / 작품에 대한 //

Acknowledging the making of artworks / does not require / a
detailed, technical knowledge /
예술 작품의 제작을 인정하는 데는 / 필요하지 않다 / 자세하고 기술적인 지식이 /

of, say, how painters mix / different kinds of paint, / or how an
image editing tool works. //
예를 들어 화가가 섞는 방법에 관한 / 다양한 종류의 물감을 / 또는 이미지 편집 도구가
작동하는 방식과 같은 것에 관한 //

(①) All that is required / is a general sense / of a significant
difference / between working with paints / and working with
an imaging application. //
필요한 전부는 / 일반적인 감각이다 / 중요한 차이점에 대한 / 물감으로 작업하는 것과 /
이미징 앱을 사용하는 것의 //

(②) This sense might involve / a basic familiarity / with paints
and paintbrushes /
이러한 감각은 포함할 수도 있다 / 기본적인 친숙함을 / 물감과 붓에 대한 /

as well as a basic familiarity / with how we use computers, /
perhaps including / how we use consumer imaging apps. //
기본적인 친숙함뿐 아니라 / 우리가 컴퓨터를 사용하는 방법에 대한 / 아마도 포함하여 /
우리가 소비자 이미징 앱을 사용하는 방법을 //

(③) This is / because every kind of artistic material or tool
comes / with its own challenges and affordances / for artistic
creation. // 단서 2 모든 예술 재료나 도구가 예술 창작을 위한 고유한 도전과 행위 유발성을
동반하므로 재료와 기법에 대한 친숙함이 유용할 것임
이것은 ~이다 / 모든 종류의 예술 재료나 도구가 오기 때문(이다) / 그것의 고유한 도전과 행위
유발성을 / 예술 창작을 위한 //

(④) Critics are often interested / in the ways / artists exploit
/ different kinds of materials and tools / for particular artistic
effect. //
비평가들은 흔히 관심이 있다 / 방식에 / 예술가들이 활용하는 / 다양한 종류의 재료와 도구를
/ 특정한 예술적 효과를 위해 //

(⑤) They are also interested / in the success of an artist's
attempt / — embodied in the artwork itself — / to push the limits
/ of what can be achieved / with certain materials and tools. //
그들은 또한 관심이 있다 / 예술가의 시도 성공에 / 예술 작품 그 자체로 구현된 / 한계를
뛰어넘으려는 / 달성될 수 있는 것의 / 특정 재료와 도구로 //

- specialist ⓝ 전문가 • critic ⓝ 비평가 • familiarity ⓝ 친숙함
- informed ⓐ 충분한 정보에 기반한 • judgement ⓝ 판단
- acknowledge ⓥ 인정하다 • significant ⓐ 중요한
- imaging ⓝ 이미징(도형 이미지의 취득, 저장, 표시, 인쇄 등의 처리)
- involve ⓥ 포함하다 • familiarity ⓝ 친숙함
- embody ⓥ 구현하다 • attempt ⓝ 시도
- push the limit 한계를 뛰어넘다

예술 작품의 제작을 인정하는 데는, 예를 들어 화가가 다양한 종류의 물감을 섞는 방법이나 이미지 편집 도구가 작동하는 방식과 같은 것에 관한 자세하고 기술적인 지식이 필요하지 않다. (①) 필요한 전부는 물감으로 작업하는 것과 이미징 앱을 사용하는 것의 중요한 차이점에 대한 일반적인 감각일 뿐이다. (②) 이러한 감각은 우리가 소비자 이미징 앱을 사용하는 방법을 아마도 포함하여, 컴퓨터를 사용하는 방법에 대한 기본적인 친숙함뿐 아니라 물감과 붓에 대한 기본적인 친숙함을 포함할 수도 있다. (③ 예술 비평가와 같은 전문가의 경우, 재료와 기법에 대한 더 깊은 친숙함이 작품에 대한 충분한 정보에 기반한 판단에 도달하는 데 흔히 유용하다.) 이것은 모든 종류의 예술 재료나 도구가 예술 창작을 위한 그것의 고유한 도전과 행위 유발성을 동반하기 때문이다. (④) 비평가들은 흔히 예술가들이 특정한 예술적 효과를 위해 다양한 종류의 재료와 도구를 활용하는 방식에 관심이 있다. (⑤) 그들은 또한 예술 작품 그 자체로 구현된, 특정 재료와 도구로 달성할 수 있는 것의 한계를 뛰어넘으려는 예술가의 시도 성공에 관심이 있다.

| 문제 풀이 순서 | [정답률 43%]

1st 주어진 문장을 해석하고, 연결어, 지시어 등을 확인한다.

In the case of specialists such as art critics, a deeper
familiarity with materials and techniques is often useful
in reaching an informed judgement about a work.
예술 비평가와 같은 전문가의 경우, 재료와 기법에 대한 더 깊은 친숙함이 작품에 대한
충분한 정보에 기반한 판단에 도달하는 데 흔히 유용하다.

➡ 전문가의 경우에는 재료와 기법에 대한 친숙함이 작품을 판단하는 데 유용하다는 내용이다. 단서
▶ **주어진 문장 앞:** 전문가의 경우와 비교되는 다른 경우에 대한 설명이 있을 것임
주어진 문장 뒤: 재료와 기법에 대한 친숙함이 작품을 판단하는 데 유용하다는 것에 대한 부연이 이어질 것임 발상

2nd 각 선택지의 앞뒤 흐름이 매끄러운지 확인한다.

- ①의 앞 문장과 뒤 문장

앞 문장: 예술 작품의 제작을 인정하는 데는, 예를 들어 화가가 다양한 종류의 물감을 섞는 방법이나 이미지 편집 도구가 작동하는 방식과 같은 것에 관한 자세하고 기술적인 지식이 필요하지 않다.
뒤 문장: 필요한 전부는 물감으로 작업하는 것과 이미징 앱을 사용하는 것의 중요한 차이점에 대한 일반적인 감각일 뿐이다.

➡ 앞 문장에서 필요하지 않은 것, 뒤 문장에서 필요한 것을 설명한다. 뒤 문장의 주어인 All that is required로 앞뒤 문장이 자연스럽게 이어진다.
▶ 주어진 문장이 ①에 들어갈 수 없음

- ②의 앞 문장과 뒤 문장

앞 문장: ①의 뒤 문장과 같음
뒤 문장: 이러한 감각(This sense)은 우리가 소비자 이미징 앱을 사용하는 방법을 아마도 포함하여, 컴퓨터를 사용하는 방법에 대한 기본적인 친숙함뿐 아니라 물감과 붓에 대한 기본적인 친숙함을 포함할 수도 있다.

➡ 앞 문장에 등장한 a general sense를 뒤 문장에서 This sense로 가리키며 구체적으로 설명한다.
▶ 주어진 문장이 ②에 들어갈 수 없음

③의 앞 문장과 뒤 문장

> 앞 문장: ②의 뒤 문장과 같음
> 뒤 문장: 이것(This)은 모든 종류의 예술 재료나 도구가 예술 창작을 위한 그것의 고유한 도전과 행위 유발성을 동반하기 때문이다.

→ 예술 재료나 도구가 예술 창작을 위한 도전과 행위 유발성을 동반하기 때문에 재료와 기법에 대한 더 깊은 친숙함이 작품을 판단하는 데 유용한 것이다. This가 가리키는 것이 바로 주어진 문장의 내용이다.
▶ 주어진 문장이 ③에 들어가야 함

④의 앞 문장과 뒤 문장

> 앞 문장: ③의 뒤 문장과 같음
> 뒤 문장: 비평가들은 흔히 예술가들이 특정한 예술적 효과를 위해 다양한 종류의 재료와 도구를 활용하는 방식에 관심이 있다.

→ 비평가의 경우에 재료와 기법, 도구에 대한 친숙함이 유용하다고 한 이후 그 이유와 구체적인 부연이 이어진다. 주어진 문장은 비평가와 같은 전문가의 경우를 설명하기 시작하는 문장이므로, 비평가에 대한 설명이 시작된 이후에 들어갈 수 없다.
▶ 주어진 문장이 ④에 들어갈 수 없음

⑤의 앞 문장과 뒤 문장

> 앞 문장: ④의 뒤 문장과 같음
> 뒤 문장: 그들은 또한(They also) 예술 작품 그 자체로 구현된, 특정 재료와 도구로 달성할 수 있는 것의 한계를 뛰어넘으려는 예술가의 시도 성공에 관심이 있다.

→ 비평가들이 관심을 갖는 또 다른 것에 대한 설명이 이어진다. Critics를 가리키는 지시대명사 They, 앞에서 설명한 것 외의 관심사를 추가하는 부사 also가 앞뒤 문장을 자연스럽게 연결한다.
▶ 주어진 문장이 ⑤에 들어갈 수 없음

3rd 글이 한눈에 들어오도록 정리하여 정답을 확인한다.

예술 작품의 제작을 인정하는 데는, 화가가 다양한 종류의 물감을 섞는 방법 등과 같은 것에 관한 자세하고 기술적인 지식이 필요하지 않다.
(①) 필요한 것은 물감으로 작업하는 것과 이미징 앱을 사용하는 것의 중요한 차이점에 대한 일반적인 감각일 뿐이다.
(②) 이러한 감각은 소비자 이미징 앱을 사용하는 방법을 포함하여, 컴퓨터를 사용하는 방법에 대한 기본적인 친숙함뿐 아니라 물감과 붓에 대한 기본적인 친숙함을 포함할 수도 있다.
(③ 예술 비평가와 같은 전문가의 경우, 재료와 기법에 대한 더 깊은 친숙함이 작품에 대한 충분한 정보에 기반한 판단에 도달하는 데 흔히 유용하다.)
이것은 모든 종류의 예술 재료나 도구가 예술 창작을 위한 고유한 도전과 행위 유발성을 동반하기 때문이다.
(④) 비평가들은 예술가들이 특정한 예술적 효과를 위해 다양한 종류의 재료와 도구를 활용하는 방식에 관심이 있다.
(⑤) 그들은 예술 작품 그 자체로 구현된, 특정 재료와 도구로 달성할 수 있는 것의 한계를 뛰어넘으려는 예술가의 시도 성공에 관심이 있다.

380 자이스토리 영어 독해 실전

N 34 정답 ④ ＊학생을 돕는 방법

글의 흐름으로 보아, 주어진 문장이 들어가기에 가장 적절한 곳을 고르시오. [3점]

단서 1 학생들이 인지적 자원을 이용할 수 있었다는 내용이 역접의 연결어로 이어짐

But when students were given "worked-examples" / (such as pre-solved problems) / placed between problems to solve, /
선행사(주격 관계대명사와 be동사는 생략됨)
형용사적 용법(problems 수식)
하지만 학생들에게 '풀어진 예제들'이 주어지면 / (미리 풀어진 문제들과 같은) / 풀어야 할 문제들 사이에 위치된 /

studying the worked-examples / freed up cognitive resources / that allowed students / to see the key features of the problem / and to analyze the steps and reasons / behind problem-solving moves. //
동명사구 주어
병렬 구조(allowed의 목적격 보어)
풀어진 예제들을 공부하는 것은 / 인지적 자원을 이용 가능하게 했다 / 학생들이 ~하게 한 / 문제의 주요 특징을 보고 / 단계들과 이유들을 분석하게 / 문제 해결 조치의 이면에 있는 //

How can we help students / manage cognitive load / as they learn / to perform complex tasks? //
목적어로 to부정사를 취하는 learn
우리는 어떻게 학생을 도울 수 있을까 / 인지 부하를 관리하도록 / 그들이 배울 때 / 복잡한 과제를 수행하는 것을 //

One method / that has proved effective / in research studies / is to support / some aspects of a complex task / while students perform the entire task. //
주어
동사 명사적 용법(주격 보어)
한 가지 방법은 / 효과적이라고 입증된 / 조사 연구에서 / 지원하는 것이다 / 복잡한 과제의 일부 측면 / 학생이 전체 과제를 수행할 때 //

(①) For example, / Swelter and Cooper demonstrated this / with students / learning to solve problems / in a variety of quantitative fields / from statistics to physics. //
예를 들어 / Swelter와 Cooper는 이것을 보여 주었다 / 학생들을 통해 / 문제를 푸는 것을 배우는 / 다양한 정량적 분야에서 / 통계학에서 물리학까지 //

(②) They found / that when students were given typical word problems, / it was possible for them to solve the problems / without actually learning much. //
to solve의 의미상 주어
가주어
진주어
그들은 알아냈다 / 학생들에게 전형적인 문장제가 주어졌을 때 / 그들은 문제를 푸는 것이 가능했다는 것을 / 실제로 많이 배우는 것 없이 //

(③) This is / because the problems themselves were sufficiently demanding / that students had no cognitive resources available / to learn from what they did. //
이것은 ~이다 / 문제 자체가 충분히 어려워서 / 학생들이 이용할 수 있는 인지적 자원을 갖고 있지 않았기 때문(이다) / 자신이 한 일로부터 배우기 위해 //

(④) The researchers found / this improved students' performance / on subsequent problem solving. //
연구자들이 알아냈다 / 이것은 학생들의 수행 능력을 향상시켰다는 것을 / 차후 문제 풀이에서 //
단서 2 풀어진 예제들을 제시했을 때 차후 문제 풀이에서 학생들의 수행 능력이 향상됨

(⑤) This result, / called the *worked-example effect*, / is one example of a process / called *scaffolding*, /
단수 주어
단수 동사
이런 결과는 / '풀어진 예제 효과'라는 / 과정의 한 사례이며 / '발판 놓기'라는 /

by which instructors temporarily relieve / some of the cognitive load / so that students can focus / on particular dimensions of learning. //
부사절 접속사(목적)
그것에 의해 교사는 일시적으로 덜어 준다 / 인지 부하의 일부를 / 학생이 집중할 수 있도록 / 학습의 특정 측면에 //

- worked-example ⓝ 해결된 예제 • pre-solved ⓐ 미리 풀린
- free up ~을 이용 가능하게 하다 • cognitive ⓐ 인지의
- load ⓝ 부하 • demonstrate ⓥ 보여주다
- quantitative ⓐ 정량적인 • statistics ⓝ 통계학
- physics ⓝ 물리학 • sufficiently ⓐⅾ 충분히
- demanding ⓐ 어려운 • subsequent ⓐ 차후의
- temporarily ⓐⅾ 일시적으로 • relieve ⓥ 덜다
- dimension ⓝ 측면

학생이 복잡한 과제를 수행하는 것을 배울 때 그들이 인지 부하를 관리하는 것을 우리는 어떻게 도울 수 있을까? 조사 연구에서 효과적이라고 입증된 한 가지 방법은 학생이 전체 과제를 수행할 때 복잡한 과제의 일부 측면을 지원하는 것이다. (①) 예를 들어, Swelter와 Cooper는 통계학에서 물리학까지 다양한 정량적 분야에서 문제를 푸는 것을 배우는 학생들을 통해 이것을 보여 주었다. (②) 그들이 알아낸 바에 따르면, 학생들에게 전형적인 문장제가 주어졌을 때, 그들은 실제로 많이 배우는 것 없이 문제를 푸는 것이 가능했다. (③) 이것은 문제 자체가 충분히 어려워서 학생들이 자신이 한 일로부터 배우기 위해 이용할 수 있는 인지적 자원을 갖고 있지 않았기 때문이다. (④ 하지만 학생들에게 풀어야 할 문제들 사이에 있는 '풀어진 예제들'(미리 풀어진 문제들과 같은)이 주어지면, 풀어진 예제들을 공부하는 것은 학생들이 문제의 주요 특징을 보고 문제 해결 조처의 이면에 있는 단계들과 이유들을 분석하게 해준 인지적 자원을 이용 가능하게 했다.) 연구자들이 알아낸 바에 따르면, 이것은 차후 문제 풀이에서 학생들의 수행 능력을 향상시켰다. (⑤) '풀어진 예제 효과'라는 이런 결과는 '발판 놓기'라는 과정의 한 사례이며, 그것에 의해 교사는 학생이 학습의 특정 측면에 집중할 수 있도록 인지 부하의 일부를 일시적으로 덜어 준다.

| 문제 풀이 순서 | [정답률 56%]

1st 주어진 문장을 해석하고, 연결어, 지시어 등을 확인한다.

But when students were given "worked-examples" (such as pre-solved problems) placed between problems to solve, studying the worked-examples freed up cognitive resources that allowed students to see the key features of the problem and to analyze the steps and reasons behind problem-solving moves.

하지만 학생들에게 풀어야 할 문제들 사이에 있는 '풀어진 예제들'(미리 풀어진 문제들과 같은)이 주어지면, 풀어진 예제들을 공부하는 것은 학생들이 문제의 주요 특징을 보고 문제 해결 조처의 이면에 있는 단계들과 이유들을 분석하게 해준 인지적 자원을 이용 가능하게 했다.

➡ 풀어진 예제가 주어졌을 때: 인지적 자원을 이용하여 문제의 주요 특징을 보고 문제 해결 조처의 이면에 있는 단계와 이유를 분석했다.
　▶ **주어진 문장 앞:** 학생들이 인지 부하를 겪지 않고 제대로 배울 수 있었다는 내용이 But으로 이어지므로 [단서] 그 앞에는 인지 부하 때문에 배우지 못했다는 내용이 있어야 함 [발상]

2nd 각 선택지의 앞뒤 흐름이 매끄러운지 확인한다.

- **①의 앞 문장과 뒤 문장**

> **앞 문장:** 조사 연구에서 효과적이라고 입증된 한 가지 방법은 학생이 전체 과제를 수행할 때 복잡한 과제의 일부 측면을 지원하는 것이다.
> **뒤 문장:** 예를 들어(For example), Swelter와 Cooper는 통계학에서 물리학까지 다양한 정량적 분야에서 문제를 푸는 것을 배우는 학생들을 통해 이것(this)을 보여 주었다.

➡ 학생이 전체 과제를 수행할 때 복잡한 과제의 일부 측면을 지원하는 것이 효과적이라고 한 후 구체적인 예시로 설명하기 시작하는 흐름이다. For example과 this로 앞뒤 문장이 자연스럽게 이어진다.
　▶ 주어진 문장이 ①에 들어갈 수 없음

- **②의 앞 문장과 뒤 문장**

> **앞 문장:** ①의 뒤 문장과 같음
> **뒤 문장:** 그들이 알아낸 바에 따르면, 학생들에게 전형적인 문장제가 주어졌을 때, 그들은 실제로 많이 배우는 것 없이 문제를 푸는 것이 가능했다.

➡ 주어진 문장과 함께 생각해 보면, 전형적인 문장제가 주어졌을 때와 풀어진 예제들이 주어졌을 때가 대조된다는 것을 알 수 있다. 풀어진 예제들이 주어졌을 경우에 But이 포함되었으므로, 그보다 앞에 전형적인 문장제가 주어졌을 때에 대한 설명이 완료되어야 한다.
　▶ 주어진 문장이 ②에 들어갈 수 없음

- **③의 앞 문장과 뒤 문장**

> **앞 문장:** ②의 뒤 문장과 같음
> **뒤 문장:** 이것(This)은 문제 자체가 충분히 어려워서 학생들이 자신이 한 일로부터 배우기 위해 이용할 수 있는 인지적 자원을 갖고 있지 않았기 때문이다.

➡ 실제로 많이 배우는 것 없이 문제를 푸는 것이 가능한 이유에 대해서 설명하는 문장이 이어진다. This is because로 시작한 뒤 문장이 앞 문장에서 설명한 현상의 원인을 설명하는 자연스러운 흐름이다.
　▶ 주어진 문장이 ③에 들어갈 수 없음

- **④의 앞 문장과 뒤 문장**

> **앞 문장:** ③의 뒤 문장과 같음
> **뒤 문장:** 연구자들이 알아낸 바에 따르면, 이것은 차후 문제 풀이에서 학생들의 수행 능력을 향상시켰다.

➡ 학생들이 배우는 것 없이 문제를 풀었는데, 이것이 차후 문제 풀이에서 학생들의 수행 능력을 향상시켰다는 것은 앞뒤가 맞지 않는다. 주어진 문장이 ④에 들어가서, 풀어진 예제를 제시하는 것이 학생들로 하여금 문제의 주요 특징을 보고 문제 해결의 단계와 이유를 분석하게 했고, 이것이 차후 문제 풀이에서 학생들의 수행 능력을 향상시켰다는 흐름이 되어야 한다.
　▶ 주어진 문장이 ④에 들어가야 함

- **⑤의 앞 문장과 뒤 문장**

> **앞 문장:** ④의 뒤 문장과 같음
> **뒤 문장:** '풀어진 예제 효과'라는 이런 결과(This result)는 '발판 놓기'라는 과정의 한 사례이며, 그것에 의해 교사는 학생이 학습의 특정 측면에 집중할 수 있도록 인지 부하의 일부를 일시적으로 덜어 준다.

➡ This result가 가리키는 것이, 풀어진 예제를 제시함으로써 차후 문제 풀이에서 학생들의 수행 능력을 향상시켰다는 앞 문장의 내용이다. 앞뒤 문장이 자연스럽게 이어지므로 그 사이에 주어진 문장이 들어갈 수 없다.
　▶ 주어진 문장이 ⑤에 들어갈 수 없음

3rd 글이 한눈에 들어오도록 정리하여 정답을 확인한다.

학생이 복잡한 과제를 수행하는 것을 배울 때 그들이 인지 부하를 관리하는 것을 우리는 어떻게 도울 수 있을까? 효과적이라고 입증된 한 가지 방법은 복잡한 과제의 일부 측면을 지원하는 것이다.
(①) 예를 들어, Swelter와 Cooper는 다양한 정량적 분야에서 문제를 푸는 것을 배우는 학생들을 통해 이것을 보여 주었다.
(②) 학생들에게 전형적인 문장제가 주어졌을 때, 그들은 실제로 많이 배우는 것 없이 문제를 푸는 것이 가능했다.
(③) 이것은 문제 자체가 충분히 어려워서 학생들이 자신이 한 일로부터 배우기 위해 이용할 수 있는 인지적 자원을 갖고 있지 않았기 때문이다.
(④ 풀어진 예제들을 공부하는 것은 학생들이 문제의 주요 특징을 보고 문제 해결 조처의 이면에 있는 단계들과 이유들을 분석하게 해준 인지적 자원을 이용 가능하게 했다.)
연구자들이 알아낸 바에 따르면, 이것은 차후 문제 풀이에서 학생들의 수행 능력을 향상시켰다.
(⑤) '풀어진 예제 효과'라는 이런 결과는 '발판 놓기'라는 과정의 한 사례이며, 그것에 의해 교사는 학생이 학습의 특정 측면에 집중할 수 있도록 인지 부하의 일부를 일시적으로 덜어 준다.

글의 흐름으로 보아, 주어진 문장이 들어가기에 가장 적절한 곳을 고르시오. [3점]

On top of the hurdles / introduced / in accessing his or her
선행사(주격 관계대명사+be동사는 생략됨)
money, / if a suspected fraud is detected, /
난관에 더해 / 도입된 / 자신의 돈에 접근하는 데 / 만약 의심스러운 사기가 감지되면 /
the account holder has to deal / with the phone call / asking /
명사절 접속사
if he or she made the suspicious transactions. //
예금주는 응대해야만 한다 / 전화 통화를 / 묻는 / 본인이 그 의심스러운 거래를 했는지를 //
단서1 어떤 거래를 예금주 본인이 한 게 맞는지 묻는 전화 통화를 해야 함

Each new wave of technology / is intended / to enhance user
as well as로 연결된 to부정사(improve 앞에 to가 생략됨)
convenience, / as well as improve security, / but sometimes /
부분 부정(반드시 ~인 것은 아닌)
these do not necessarily go hand-in-hand. //
각각의 새로운 기술의 물결은 / 의도된다 / 사용자 편의성을 향상하도록 / 보안을 향상할 뿐만 아니라 / 하지만 때때로 / 이것들이 반드시 함께 진행되지는 않는다 //

For example, / the transition / from magnetic stripe to embedded
주어
chip / slightly slowed down transactions, / sometimes frustrating
동사
customers / in a hurry. //
예를 들어 / 전환은 / 마그네틱 띠에서 내장형 칩으로의 / 거래를 약간 늦췄는데 / 때로 고객을 좌절시켰다 / 바쁜 //

(①) Make a service too burdensome, / and the potential
customer / will go elsewhere. //
명령문에 이어지는 and: '~해라, 그러면 …'
서비스를 너무 부담스럽게 만들어라 / 그러면 잠재 고객은 / 다른 곳으로 갈 것이다 //

(②) This obstacle applies / at several levels. //
이런 장벽은 적용된다 / 여러 수준에서 //

(③) Passwords, double-key identification, and biometrics /
such as fingerprint-, iris-, and voice recognition / are all ways /
비밀번호, 이중 키 확인, 그리고 생체 인식은 / 지문, 홍채 및 음성 인식과 같은 / 모두 방법이다 /
keeping의 목적어와 목적격 보어
of keeping the account details hidden / from potential
keeping의 목적어와 목적격 보어
fraudsters, / of keeping your data dark. //
계정 세부 정보를 숨기는 / 잠재적인 사기꾼으로부터 / 여러분의 데이터를 비밀로 유지하는 //

(④) But they all inevitably add a burden / to the use of the
전치사 명사구
account. //
하지만 그것들은 모두 불가피하게 부담을 가중한다 / 계좌 사용에 //

(⑤) This is all useful / at some level / — indeed, it can be
가주어
reassuring / knowing / that your bank is keeping alert / to
protect you — /
진주어(동명사)
이것은 모두 도움이 되며 / 어느 정도 / 실제로 ~은 안심이 될 수 있다 / 아는 것은 / 여러분의 은행이 경계를 늦추지 않고 있다는 것을 / 여러분을 보호하기 위해 /

but it becomes tiresome / if too many such calls are received. //
하지만 그것은 귀찮아진다 / 그러한 전화를 너무 많이 받게 되면 //
단서2 주어진 문장에서 설명한, 거래를 한 것이 예금주 본인이 맞는지 묻는 전화를 가리킴

- suspect ⓥ 의심하다   • suspicious ⓐ 의심스러운, 수상쩍은
- transaction ⓝ 거래, 매매   • enhance ⓥ 강화하다, 증진하다
- convenience ⓝ 편의, 편리
- hand-in-hand ⓐ 손에 손을 잡은, 밀접히 연관된
- transition ⓝ 변이, 변화   • magnetic ⓐ 자석 같은, 자성의
- embed ⓥ (단단히) 끼워 넣다   • burdensome ⓐ 부담스러운, 힘든
- elsewhere ⓐⓓ 다른 곳에서[으로]   • obstacle ⓝ 장애(물)
- identification ⓝ 신원 확인   • biometrics ⓝ 생체 인식
- iris ⓝ (안구의) 홍채   • recognition ⓝ 인식, 승인
- fraudster ⓝ 사기꾼   • inevitably ⓐⓓ 필연적으로
- burden ⓝ 부담, 짐   • reassure ⓥ 안심시키다
- alert ⓐ (위험을) 경계하는, 기민한   • tiresome ⓐ 성가신

각각의 새로운 기술의 물결은 보안을 향상할 뿐만 아니라, 사용자 편의성을 향상하려는 의도이지만, 때때로 이것들이 반드시 함께 진행되지는 않는다. 예를 들어 마그네틱 띠에서 내장형 칩으로의 전환은 거래(의 속도)를 약간

늦췄는데, 때로 바쁜 고객을 좌절시켰다. (①) 서비스를 너무 부담스럽게 만들면, 잠재 고객은 다른 곳으로 갈 것이다. (②) 이런 장벽은 여러 수준에서 적용된다. (③) 비밀번호, 이중 키 확인, 지문, 홍채 및 음성 인식과 같은 생체 인식은 모두 잠재적인 사기꾼으로부터 계정 세부 정보를 숨기는, 즉 여러분의 데이터를 비밀로 유지하는 방법이다. (④) 하지만 그것들은 모두 불가피하게 계좌 사용에 부담을 가중한다. (⑤ 자신의 돈에 접근하는 데 도입된 난관에 더해, 만약 의심스러운 사기가 감지되면, 예금주는 본인이 그 의심스러운 거래를 했는지 묻는 전화 통화를 응대해야만 한다.) 이것은 모두 어느 정도 도움이 되며, 실제로, 여러분의 은행이 여러분을 보호하기 위해 경계를 늦추지 않고 있다는 것을 알게 되어 안심이 될 수 있지만, 그러한 전화를 너무 많이 받게 되면 귀찮아진다.

| 문제 풀이 순서 | [정답률 40%]

1st 주어진 문장을 해석하고, 연결어, 지시어 등을 확인한다.

On top of the hurdles introduced in accessing his or her money, if a suspected fraud is detected, the account holder has to deal with the phone call asking if he or she made the suspicious transactions. **단서1**
자신의 돈에 접근하는 데 도입된 난관에 더해, 만약 의심스러운 사기가 감지되면, 예금주는 본인이 그 의심스러운 거래를 했는지 묻는 전화 통화를 응대해야만 한다.

➡ 여러 난관들에 대한 내용이 앞에 나오고, 그 뒤에 주어진 문장을 넣어야 한다.

2nd 각 선택지의 앞뒤 흐름이 매끄러운지 확인한다.

- ①의 앞 문장과 뒤 문장

> **앞 문장:** 각각의 새로운 기술의 물결은 보안을 향상할 뿐만 아니라, 사용자 편의성을 향상하려는 의도이지만, 때때로 이것들이 반드시 함께 진행되지는 않는다. 예를 들어 마그네틱 띠에서 내장형 칩으로의 전환은 거래(의 속도)를 약간 늦췄는데, 때로 바쁜 고객을 좌절시켰다.
> **뒤 문장:** 서비스를 너무 부담스럽게 만들면, 잠재 고객은 다른 곳으로 갈 것이다.

➡ **앞 문장:** 기술의 물결로 인한 보안과 편의성의 향상이 반드시 함께 진행되지는 않는다.
뒤 문장: 서비스를 너무 부담스럽게 만들면, 잠재 고객은 다른 곳으로 갈 것이다.
앞 문장의 '보안 향상'이 뒤 문장에서 '서비스를 너무 부담스럽게 만드는 것'으로 나타났으며, 편의성 향상이 늦춰져 잠재 고객이 다른 곳으로 갈 것이라는 흐름이다.
▶ 주어진 문장이 ①에 들어갈 수 없음

- ②의 앞 문장과 뒤 문장

> **앞 문장:** ①의 뒤 문장과 같음
> **뒤 문장:** 이런 장벽은 여러 수준에서 적용된다.

➡ 앞 문장의 '서비스를 너무 부담스럽게 만드는 것'을 뒤 문장에서 '이런 장벽'으로 지칭한다.
▶ 주어진 문장이 ②에 들어갈 수 없음

- ③의 앞 문장과 뒤 문장

> **앞 문장:** ②의 뒤 문장과 같음
> **뒤 문장:** 비밀번호, 이중 키 확인, 지문, 홍채 및 음성 인식과 같은 생체 인식은 모두 잠재적인 사기꾼으로부터 계정 세부 정보를 숨기는, 즉 여러분의 데이터를 비밀로 유지하는 방법이다.

➡ 앞 문장의 '이런 장벽'의 예시로서 비밀번호, 이중 키 확인, 생체 인식 등을 들며 데이터를 비밀로 유지하는 방법을 소개하는 흐름이다.
▶ 주어진 문장이 ③에 들어갈 수 없음

- ④의 앞 문장과 뒤 문장

> **앞 문장:** ③의 뒤 문장과 같음
> **뒤 문장:** 하지만 그것들은 모두 불가피하게 계좌 사용에 부담을 가중한다.

➡ 앞 문장의 '데이터를 비밀로 유지하는 방법들'을 뒤 문장에서 they로 지칭하며 계좌 사용에 부담을 가중한다는 흐름이다.
▶ 주어진 문장이 ④에 들어갈 수 없음

- ⑤의 앞 문장과 뒤 문장

> **앞 문장:** ④의 뒤 문장과 같음
> **뒤 문장:** 이것은 모두 어느 정도 도움이 되며, 실제로, 여러분의 은행이 여러분을 보호하기 위해 경계를 늦추지 않고 있다는 것을 알게 되어 안심이 될 수 있지만, 그러한 전화(such calls)를 너무 많이 받게 되면 귀찮아진다. 단서2

➡ **뒤 문장:** 이것은 모두 어느 정도 도움이 되며 여러분을 안심시킬 수 있지만, 그러한 전화를 너무 많이 받으면 귀찮아진다.
such calls가 무엇인지 앞에 나타나야 한다.
➡ 주어진 문장에서 의심스러운 사기가 감지되면, '예금주 본인이 그 의심스러운 거래를 했는지 묻는 전화 통화'에 응대해야 한다고 했다. 이러한 전화는 은행이 경계를 늦추지 않고 있다는 것을 알게 하여 고객을 안심시킬 수 있지만, 너무 많이 받게 되면 부담스럽다는 흐름이다.
▶ 주어진 문장이 ⑤에 들어가야 함

3rd 글이 한눈에 들어오도록 정리하여 정답을 확인한다.

기술의 물결로 인한 보안과 편의성의 향상이 반드시 함께 진행되지는 않는다. (①) 서비스를 너무 부담스럽게 만들면, 잠재 고객은 다른 곳으로 갈 것이다. (②) 이런 장벽은 여러 수준에서 적용된다. (③) 비밀번호, 이중 키 확인, 생체 인식 등은 잠재적인 사기꾼으로부터 여러분의 데이터를 비밀로 유지하는 방법이다. (④) 하지만 그것들은 모두 불가피하게 계좌 사용에 부담을 가중한다. (⑤ 이러한 난관에 더해, 의심스러운 사기가 감지되면, 예금주는 본인 확인을 위한 전화 통화를 응대해야 한다.) 이것은 모두 도움이 되며 은행에 대해 안심할 수 있지만, 그러한 전화를 너무 많이 받으면 귀찮아진다.

N 36 정답 ③ ＊과학이 승자독식 대회라는 견해에 대한 반대 입장

> **글의 흐름으로 보아, 주어진 문장이 들어가기에 가장 적절한 곳을 고르시오.**

단서1 어떤 과학 대회들은 세계적인 수준으로 여겨짐

> Yes, / some contests are seen as world class, / such as identification of the Higgs particle / or the development of high temperature superconductors. //
> 물론 / 몇몇 대회는 세계적인 수준으로 여겨진다 / 힉스 입자의 확인 / 또는 고온 초전도체 개발과 같은 //

Science is sometimes described / as a winner-take-all contest, /
분사구문을 이끎
meaning that there are no rewards for being second or third. //
과학은 때때로 묘사되는데 / 승자독식 대회로 / 이는 2등이나 3등인 것에 대한 보상이 없다는 뜻이다 //

This is an extreme view / of the nature of scientific contests. //
이는 극단적인 견해이다 / 과학 대회의 본질에 대한 //

those who ~: ~한 사람들
(①) Even those who describe scientific contests in such a way / note that it is a somewhat inaccurate description, /
과학 대회를 그렇게 설명하는 사람들조차도 / 그것이 다소 부정확한 설명이라고 말하는데 /

given that replication and verification have social value / and are common in science. //
반복과 입증이 사회적 가치를 지니고 있으며 / 과학에서는 일반적이라는 점에서 //

관계부사(선행사: to the extent)   명사절 접속사
(②) It is also inaccurate / to the extent that it suggests / that 단서2 주어진 문장에서 말한 '소수의 세계적인 대회'와
상반되는 '다수의 다양한 분야의 과학 대회'를 설명함
only a handful of contests exist. //
또한 그것은 부정확하다 / 보여 줄 정도로 / 단지 소수의 대회만 존재한다는 것을 //

the number of: ~의 수 / a number of: 많은
(③) But many other contests / have multiple parts, / and the number of such contests / may be increasing. //
하지만 다른 많은 대회에는 / 다양한 부분이 있고 / 그런 대회의 수는 / 증가하고 있을 것이다 //

가주어①   진주어①
(④) By way of example, / for many years it was thought / that there would be "one" cure for cancer, /
예를 들어 / 여러 해 동안 생각되었다 / 암에 대해 '하나'의 치료법만 있다고 /

가주어②   진주어②
but it is now realized / that cancer takes multiple forms / and
진주어③
that multiple approaches are needed to provide a cure. //
하지만 이제 인식된다 / 암은 여러 가지 형태를 띠고 / 치료를 제공하기 위해 다양한 접근 방식이 필요하다고 //

(⑤) There won't be one winner / — there will be many. //
승자는 한 명이 아니라 / 여러 명이 있을 것이다 //

- identification ⓝ 확인　　· particle ⓝ 입자
- superconductor ⓝ 초전도체　　· winner-take-all ⓐ 승자독식의
- extreme ⓐ 극단적인　　· inaccurate ⓐ 부정확한
- a handful of 소수의　　· multiple ⓐ 다양한, 복합적인
- approach ⓝ 접근 방식　　· cure ⓝ 치료제

과학은 때로는 승자독식 대회로 묘사되는데, 이는 2등이나 3등인 것에 대한 보상이 없다는 뜻이다. 이는 과학 대회의 본질에 대한 극단적인 견해이다. (①) 과학 대회를 그렇게 설명하는 사람들조차도 그것이 다소 부정확한 설명이라고 말하는데, 반복과 입증이 사회적 가치를 지니고 있으며 과학에서는 일반적이라는 점에서 그렇다. (②) 또한 그것은 단지 소수의 대회만 존재한다는 것을 보여 줄 정도로 부정확하다. (③ 물론, 힉스 입자의 확인 또는 고온 초전도체 개발과 같은 몇몇 대회는 세계적인 수준으로 여겨진다.) 하지만 다른 많은 대회에는 다양한 부분이 있고, 그런 대회의 수는 증가하고 있을 것이다. (④) 예를 들어, 여러 해 동안 암에 대해 '하나'의 치료법만 있다고 생각되었지만, 암은 여러 가지 형태를 띠고 치료를 제공하기 위해 다양한 접근 방식이 필요하다고 이제 인식된다. (⑤) 승자는 한 명이 아니라 여러 명이 있을 것이다.

| 문제 풀이 순서 | [정답률 45%]

1st 주어진 문장을 해석하고, 연결어, 지시어 등을 확인한다.

> Yes, / some contests are seen as world class, / such as identification of the Higgs particle / or the development of high temperature superconductors. //
> 물론 / 몇몇 대회는 세계적인 수준으로 여겨진다 / 힉스 입자의 확인 / 또는 고온 초전도체 개발과 같은 //

➡ 특정 분야를 다루는 몇몇 과학 대회는 세계적인 수준으로 여겨진다고 했다. 단서
▶ 주어진 문장 앞: '특정 분야에 관한 소수의 대회'의 개념이 소개되고, 이 문장에서 구체적인 예시가 제시됨
▶ 주어진 문장 뒤: '특정 분야에 관한 소수의 대회'와 상반되는 개념이 등장할 것임 발상

2nd 각 선택지의 앞뒤 흐름이 매끄러운지 확인한다.

- ①의 앞 문장과 뒤 문장

> **앞 문장:** 이는 과학 대회의 본질에 대한 극단적인 견해이다.
> **뒤 문장:** 과학 대회를 그렇게 설명하는 사람들조차도 그것이 다소 부정확한 설명이라고 말하는데, 반복과 입증이 사회적 가치를 지니고 있으며 과학에서는 일반적이라는 점에서 그렇다.

→ 과학이 승자독식 대회로 묘사되는 것에 부정적인 입장을 드러내고 있다. 이러한 묘사는 과학 대회의 본질에 대한 극단적인 견해라고 말하고 있으며, 이 묘사를 일부 인정하는 사람들조차도 그 견해가 다소 부정확하다고 설명하고 있다. 따라서 두 문장은 자연스럽게 연결된다.

▶ 주어진 문장이 ①에 들어갈 수 없음

- **②의 앞 문장과 뒤 문장**

> 앞 문장: ①의 뒤 문장과 같음
> 뒤 문장: 또한(also) 그것은 단지 소수의 대회만 존재한다는 것을 보여 줄 정도로 부정확하다.

→ 과학 대회가 승자독식이라는 견해를 부정적으로 바라본 앞 문장의 내용과, 과학 대회가 소수만 존재한다는 것을 보여줄 정도로 부정확하다는 뒤 문장의 내용은 일맥상통한다. 따라서 두 문장은 also로 자연스럽게 연결된다.

▶ 주어진 문장이 ②에 들어갈 수 없음

- **③의 앞 문장과 뒤 문장**

> 앞 문장: ②의 뒤 문장과 같음
> 뒤 문장: 하지만(But) 다른 많은 대회에는 다양한 부분이 있고, 그런 대회의 수는 증가하고 있을 것이다.

→ 앞 문장에서는 '소수의 대회'를 설명하고 있고, 뒤 문장에서는 '다양한 분야의 많은 대회'를 설명하고 있어 but으로 대조를 이루고 있다.
주어진 문장은 앞 문장에서 설명한 '소수의 대회'에 관한 구체적인 예시이므로, '다양한 분야의 많은 대회'를 설명하고 있는 뒤 문장으로 소재가 전환되기 전에 들어가야 한다.

▶ 주어진 문장이 ③에 들어가야 함

- **④의 앞 문장과 뒤 문장**

> 앞 문장: ③의 뒤 문장과 같음
> 뒤 문장: 예를 들어(by way of example), 여러 해 동안 암에 대해 '하나'의 치료법만 있다고 생각되었지만, 암은 여러 가지 형태를 띠고 치료를 제공하기 위해 다양한 접근 방식이 필요하다고 이제 인식된다.

→ 앞 문장에서 '다양한 분야의 많은 부문'을 소개했고, 이에 대한 구체적인 예시로 뒤 문장에서 암에 대한 다양한 치료법과 접근법을 소개하고 있다. 따라서 by way of example로 자연스럽게 연결된다.

▶ 주어진 문장이 ④에 들어갈 수 없음

- **⑤의 앞 문장과 뒤 문장**

> 앞 문장: ④의 뒤 문장과 같음
> 뒤 문장: 승자는 한 명이 아니라 여러 명이 있을 것이다.

→ 앞 문장에서 암에 대한 다양한 치료법과 접근법을 소개했고, 이는 과학이 승자독식이 아닌 다양한 접근과 성과를 인정한다는 뜻이므로, 뒤 문장과 자연스럽게 연결된다.

▶ 주어진 문장이 ⑤에 들어갈 수 없음

3rd 글이 한눈에 들어오도록 정리하여 정답을 확인한다.

과학은 때로 승자독식 대회로 묘사되지만, 이는 극단적인 견해이다.
(①) 이 견해를 일부 인정하는 사람들도 부정확한 설명이라고 말한다.
(②) 이 견해는 또한 소수의 대회만 존재한다는 점에서도 부정확하다.
(③ 물론, 어떤 과학 대회들은 세계적인 수준으로 여겨지는 소수의 대회가 존재한다.)
하지만 다른 많은 대회에는 다양한 부분이 있고, 그런 대회의 수는 증가하고 있다.
(④) 예를 들어, 암에 대한 다양한 치료법과 접근 방식이 필요하다고 인식되고 있다.
(⑤) 승자는 하나가 아니라 여러 명일 것이다.

김아린 | 충남대 의예과 2024년 입학·대전한빛고 졸

일단 주어진 문장에 some contests라는 표현이 있어. 여기에 표시를 해놓고 글을 쭉 읽는 거야. 순조롭게 글이 읽히다가 갑자기 3번 문장에서 But many other contests가 나오는데, other라고 말하려면 그 앞에 some 등의 표현으로 일부 대회들에 대한 설명이 나와야 글이 매끄럽게 이어져.
이때 어색함을 느낀 그 지점에 주어진 문장을 넣어보는 거야. 어때, 이제 some contests와 many other contests가 잘 연결되지? 문장 삽입 문제를 풀 때는 내가 글 쓰는 사람이라고 생각하고 내가 작가라면 어떻게 썼을지 생각해보는 것도 추천해!

N 37 정답 ② * 지도자가 얻기 어려운 명료함

글의 흐름으로 보아, 주어진 문장이 들어가기에 가장 적절한 곳은? [3점]

주격 보어가 문두로 오면서 주어와 동사가 도치됨
Compounding the difficulty, / now more than ever, / is what ergonomists call information overload, / **단서1** 정보가 너무 많은 상황 (정보 과부하)에 대해 이야기함
어려움을 가중시키는 것은 / 이제 그 어느 때보다도 더 많이 / 인간 공학자들이 정보 과부하라고 부르는 것으로 /
선행사(복수 명사)
where a leader is overrun with inputs / — via e-mails,
추상적 의미의 장소에도 쓰이는 관계부사
meetings, and phone calls — / that only distract and confuse her thinking. //
주격 관계대명사절의 복수 동사
그 경우 지도자는 조언에 압도당한다 / 이메일, 회의, 통화를 통한 / 그 사람의 생각을 흐트러뜨리고 혼란스럽게 할 뿐인 //

Clarity is often a difficult thing / for a leader to obtain. //
명료함은 흔히 어려운 것이다 / 지도자가 얻기에 // to obtain의 의미상의 주어 / 형용사적 용법(thing 수식)
Concerns of the present tend to seem larger / than potentially greater concerns / that lie farther away. //
현재의 우려는 더 커 보이는 경향이 있다 / 잠재적으로 더 큰 우려보다 / 더 멀리 떨어져 있는 //
(①) Some decisions / by their nature / present great
복수 주어   복수 동사
complexity, / whose many variables must come together / a
to succeed의 의미상의 주어
certain way / for the leader to succeed. //
몇몇 결정은 / 그 본질상 / 엄청난 복잡성을 제시하는데 / 그것의 많은 변수들이 합쳐져야 한다 / 특정한 방식으로 / 지도자가 성공하기 위해서는 // **단서2** 지도자의 정보가 단편적인 경우가 Alternatively로 연결됨
(②) Alternatively, / the leader's information might be only fragmentary, / which might cause her to fill in the gaps / with
계속적 용법의 주격 관계대명사
assumptions — sometimes without recognizing them as such. //
그게 아니면 / 지도자의 정보는 그저 단편적인 것일 수도 있으며 / 이는 그 사람이 공백을 채우게 한다 / 추정들로 / 때로는 그것들을 그렇게 인식하지 못하면서 //
복수 주어
(③) And the merits / of a leader's most important decisions,
복수 동사
/ by their nature, / typically are not clear-cut. //
그리고 가치는 / 지도자의 가장 중요한 결정의 / 그 본질상 / 보통 명확하지 않다 //
(④) Instead / those decisions involve a process / of assigning
병렬 구조
weights / to competing interests, / and then determining, / based
determining의 목적어절
upon some criterion, / which one predominates. //
대신 / 그러한 결정에는 과정이 포함된다 / 중요성을 배정하는 / 상충되는 이익에 / 그리고 그 다음 결정하는 / 어떤 기준에 따라 / 어떤 것이 우위를 차지하는지 //
전치사
(⑤) The result / is one of judgment, of shades of gray; / like
동명사 saying의 목적어절 접속사
saying / that Beethoven is a better composer / than Brahms. //
그 결과는 / 판단에 따른 것, 회색의 미묘한 차이를 띤 것이다 / 말하는 것처럼 / 베토벤이 더 훌륭한 작곡가라고 / 브람스보다 //

- compound ⓥ 가중시키다   · information overload 정보 과부하
- overrun ⓥ 압도하다   · input ⓝ 조언, 입력
- distract ⓥ 흐트러뜨리다   · confuse ⓥ 혼란스럽게 하다
- clarity ⓝ 명료성   · present ⓝ 현재 ⓥ 제시[제공]하다
- potentially [ad] 잠재적으로   · variable ⓝ 변수

- alternatively 〔ad〕 그게 아니면　• assumption 〔n〕 추정, 가정
- merit 〔n〕 가치, 장점　• clear-cut 〔a〕 명확한
- assign 〔v〕 배정하다, 할당하다　• competing 〔a〕 상충되는
- criterion 〔n〕 기준(pl. criteria)　• predominate 〔v〕 우위를 차지하다
- shade 〔n〕 미묘한 차이　• composer 〔n〕 작곡가

명료함은 지도자가 흔히 얻기 어려운 것이다. 현재의 우려는 더 멀리 떨어져 있는 잠재적으로 더 큰 우려보다 더 커 보이는 경향이 있다. (①) 몇몇 결정은 그 본질상 엄청난 복잡성을 제시하는데, 지도자가 성공하기 위해서는 그것의 많은 변수들이 특정한 방식으로 합쳐져야 한다. (② 이제 그 어느 때보다도 어려움을 가중시키는 것은 인간 공학자들이 정보 과부하라고 부르는 것으로, 그 경우 지도자는 자신의 생각을 흐트러뜨리고 혼란스럽게 할 뿐인 이메일, 회의, 통화를 통한 조언에 압도당한다.) 그게 아니면, 지도자의 정보는 그저 단편적인 것일 수도 있으며, 이는 지도자가 공백을 추정으로 채우게 하는데, 때로는 그것을 추정으로 인식하지 못하면서 그렇게 할 수도 있다. (③) 그리고 지도자의 가장 중요한 결정의 가치는 그 본질상 보통 명확하지 않다. (④) 대신 그러한 결정에는 상충되는 이익에 중요성을 배정한 다음, 어떤 기준에 따라 어떤 것이 우위를 차지하는지 결정하는 과정이 포함된다. (⑤) 그 결과는 판단에 따른 것, 회색의 미묘한 차이를 띤 것으로, 그것은 베토벤이 브람스보다 더 훌륭한 작곡가라고 말하는 것과 같다.

| 문제 풀이 순서 | [정답률 36%]

1st 주어진 문장을 해석하고, 연결어, 지시어 등을 확인한다.

> Compounding the difficulty, now more than ever, is what ergonomists call |information overload|, where a leader is overrun with inputs — via e-mails, meetings, and phone calls — that only distract and confuse her thinking. 〔단서 1〕
>
> 이제 그 어느 때보다도 어려움을 가중시키는 것은 인간 공학자들이 |정보 과부하|라고 부르는 것으로, 그 경우 지도자는 자신의 생각을 흐트러뜨리고 혼란스럽게 할 뿐인 이메일, 회의, 통화를 통한 조언에 압도당한다.

➡ '정보 과부하'가 어떤 어려움을 가중시키는지 앞에 나온 후 그 뒤에 주어진 문장이 나와야 한다.

2nd 각 선택지의 앞뒤 흐름이 매끄러운지 확인한다.

- **①의 앞 문장과 뒤 문장**

> **앞 문장:** 명료함은 지도자가 흔히 얻기 어려운 것이다. 현재의 우려는 더 멀리 떨어져 있는 잠재적으로 더 큰 우려보다 더 커 보이는 경향이 있다.
>
> **뒤 문장:** 몇몇 결정은 그 본질상 엄청난 복잡성을 제시하는데, 지도자가 성공하기 위해서는 그것의 많은 변수들이 특정한 방식으로 합쳐져야 한다.

➡ **앞 문장:** 지도자가 명료함을 얻기 어렵고 현재의 우려가 미래의 우려보다 더 커 보이는 경향이 있다.
　　뒤 문장: 지도자가 성공하려면 복잡한 결정의 많은 변수들이 특정한 방식으로 합쳐져야 한다.
　　앞 문장에서 '지도자가 명료함을 얻기 어렵다'는 내용을 뒤 문장에서 '복잡한 결정의 변수를 특정 방식으로 합쳐야 한다'라고 부연하면서 연결된다.
　　▶ 주어진 문장이 ①에 들어갈 수 없음

- **②의 앞 문장과 뒤 문장**

> **앞 문장:** ①의 뒤 문장과 같음
> **뒤 문장:** |그게 아니면(Alternatively)|, 지도자의 정보는 그저 단편적인 것일 수도 있으며, 이는 지도자가 공백을 추정으로 채우게 하는데, 때로는 그것을 추정으로 인식하지 못하면서 그렇게 할 수도 있다. 〔단서 2〕

➡ **뒤 문장:** 그게 아니면, 지도자의 정보는 단편적일 수 있으며, 공백을 추정으로 채우게 한다.
　　앞 문장에서 지도자의 복잡한 결정과 그것의 많은 변수들을 언급했는데, 뒤 문장은 Alternatively로 시작하며 지도자의 정보가 단편적인 것일 수도 있다고 언급했다.

➡ 주어진 문장은 너무 많은 정보(정보 과부하) 때문에 지도자가 명료함을 얻기 어렵다는 내용이다. 이와 반대로 ②의 뒤 문장은 부사 Alternatively로 시작하며 '지도자의 정보가 너무 단편적인 경우'라는 대조적인 원인을 제시했다. 즉, '정보 과부하'에 이어 '정보가 너무 단편적인 경우'의 순서로 대조되는 원인을 제시하는 흐름이다.
　　▶ 주어진 문장이 ②에 들어가야 함

- **③의 앞 문장과 뒤 문장**

> **앞 문장:** ②의 뒤 문장과 같음
> **뒤 문장:** 그리고 지도자의 가장 중요한 결정의 가치는 그 본질상 보통 명확하지 않다.

➡ 지도자의 가장 중요한 결정의 가치가 명확하지 않다는 내용으로, 주제를 부연하는 흐름이다.
　　▶ 주어진 문장이 ③에 들어갈 수 없음

- **④의 앞 문장과 뒤 문장**

> **앞 문장:** ③의 뒤 문장과 같음
> **뒤 문장:** 대신 그러한 결정에는 상충되는 이익에 중요성을 배정한 다음, 어떤 기준에 따라 어떤 것이 우위를 차지하는지 결정하는 과정이 포함된다.

➡ 앞 문장의 '가장 중요한 결정'을 뒤 문장에서 those decisions로 지칭한다.
　　▶ 주어진 문장이 ④에 들어갈 수 없음

- **⑤의 앞 문장과 뒤 문장**

> **앞 문장:** ④의 뒤 문장과 같음
> **뒤 문장:** 그 결과는 판단에 따른 것, 회색의 미묘한 차이를 띤 것으로, 그것은 베토벤이 브람스보다 더 훌륭한 작곡가라고 말하는 것과 같다.

➡ 앞 문장에 등장한 결정의 결과를 뒤 문장에서 판단에 따른 것이라고 부연하는 흐름이다.
　　▶ 주어진 문장이 ⑤에 들어갈 수 없음

3rd 글이 한눈에 들어오도록 정리하여 정답을 확인한다.

명료함은 지도자가 흔히 얻기 어려운 것이다.
(①) 지도자가 성공하려면 몇몇 복잡한 결정의 많은 변수들을 특정 방식으로 합쳐야 한다.
(② 정보 과부하는 이 결정의 어려움을 가중시킨다.)
그게 아니면, 지도자의 정보가 단편적일 수도 있으며 이는 공백을 추정으로 채우게 한다.
(③) 지도자의 가장 중요한 결정의 가치는 본질상 보통 명확하지 않다.
(④) 그러한 결정에는 상충되는 이익 간 우위를 결정하는 과정이 포함된다.
(⑤) 그 결과는 판단에 따른 것, 미묘한 차이를 띠는 것이다.

글의 흐름으로 보아, 주어진 문장이 들어가기에 가장 적절한 곳을
고르시오. [3점]

단서1 주어진 문장은 앞의 내용과 역접을 이루며 이후 유사성이 깨지는 사례가 나올 것임

At the next step in the argument, however, / the analogy
breaks down. //
그러나 논거의 다음 단계에서는 / 그 유사성은 깨진다 //

Misprints in a book or in any written message / usually have a
negative impact on the content, / sometimes (literally) fatally. //
책이나 어떤 서면 메시지에서 오타가 발생하면 / 일반적으로 내용에 부정적인 영향을 미친다 /
때로는 (문자 그대로) 치명적이게 //

(①) The displacement of a comma, for instance, / may be a
matter of life and death. //
예를 들어, 쉼표의 위치가 잘못 찍히는 것은 / 생사가 걸린 문제일 수 있다 //

(②) Similarly most mutations / have harmful consequences
／ for the organism in which they occur, / meaning that they
reduce its reproductive fitness. //
전치사+관계대명사: organism)　분사구문을 이끎
마찬가지로 대부분의 돌연변이는 / 해로운 결과를 가져오는데 / 그것이 발생하는 유기체에 /
이는 그것들이 생식 적합성을 감소시킨다는 것을 뜻한다 //
주격 관계대명사(선행사: a mutation)
(③) Occasionally, however, / a mutation may occur / that
increases the fitness of the organism, /
그러나 때때로 / 돌연변이가 발생할 수 있는데 / 유기체의 적합성을 상승시키는 /

just as an accidental failure to reproduce the text of the
first edition / might provide more accurate or updated
information. //
이는 우연히 초판의 텍스트를 복사하지 못한 것이 / 더 정확하거나 최신의 정보를 제공할 수도
있는 것과 꼭 마찬가지이다 //

(④) A favorable mutation / is going to be more heavily
represented in the next generation, /
유리한 돌연변이는 / 다음 세대에 더 많이 나타날 것인데 /
전치사+관계대명사　　**단서2** 돌연변이와 글의 오류 간의
차이점을 설명하기 시작함
since the organism in which it occurred / will have more
offspring / and mutations are transmitted to the offspring. //
그 돌연변이가 발생한 유기체는 / 더 많은 자손을 낳을 것이고 / 돌연변이가 자손에게
전달되기 때문이다 //
전치사+관계대명사
(⑤) By contrast, / there is no mechanism / by which a book that
accidentally corrects the mistakes of the first edition / will tend
to sell better. //
대조적으로 / 메커니즘은 없다 / 우연히 초판의 오류를 바로잡은 책이 / 더 잘 팔리는 경향이
있을 //

- **misprint** ⓝ 오타　　• **impact** ⓝ 영향　　• **fatally** ⓐ 치명적으로
- **displacement** ⓝ (제자리에서 쫓겨난) 이동　　• **consequence** ⓝ 결과
- **organism** ⓝ 유기체　　• **reproductive** ⓐ 번식의, 생식의
- **fitness** ⓝ 적합성　　• **accidental** ⓐ 우연한　　• **offspring** ⓝ 자손
- **transmit** ⓥ 전달하다

책이나 어떤 서면 메시지에서 오타가 발생하면 일반적으로 내용에 부정적인
영향을, 때로는 (문자 그대로) 치명적이게, 미친다. (①) 예를 들어, 쉼표의
위치가 잘못 찍히는 것은 생사가 걸린 문제일 수 있다. (②) 마찬가지로
대부분의 돌연변이는 그것이 발생하는 유기체에 해로운 결과를 가져오는데
이는 그것들이 생식 적합성을 감소시킨다는 것을 뜻한다. (③) 그러나 때때로
유기체의 적합성을 상승시키는 돌연변이가 발생할 수 있는데, 이는 우연히
초판의 텍스트를 복사하지 못한 것이 더 정확하거나 최신의 정보를 제공할 수도
있는 것과 꼭 마찬가지이다. (④ 그러나 논거의 다음 단계에서는 그 유사성은
깨진다.) 유리한 돌연변이는 다음 세대에 더 많이 나타날 것인데 그 돌연변이가
발생한 유기체는 더 많은 자손을 낳을 것이고 돌연변이가 자손에게 전달되기
때문이다. (⑤) 대조적으로, 우연히 초판의 오류를 바로잡은 책이 더 잘
팔리는 경향이 있을 메커니즘은 없다.

| 문제 풀이 순서 |　[정답률 53%]

1st 주어진 문장을 해석하고, 연결어, 지시어 등을 확인한다.

At the next step in the argument, however, / the analogy
breaks down. //
그러나 논거의 다음 단계에서는 / 그 유사성은 깨진다 //

➡ however로 역접을 이루고 있으며, 이어질 주장에서는 앞에서 설명한 유사성이
깨질 것이다. **단서**
▶ **주어진 문장 앞**: 두 개념의 유사성을 주장한 내용이 제시됨
▶ **주어진 문장 뒤**: 두 개념의 유사성이 적용되지 않는 내용이 제시될 것임 **발상**

2nd 각 선택지의 앞뒤 흐름이 매끄러운지 확인한다.

- ①의 앞 문장과 뒤 문장

앞 문장: 책이나 어떤 서면 메시지에서 오타가 발생하면 일반적으로
내용에 부정적인 영향을, 때로는 (문자 그대로) 치명적이게, 미친다.
뒤 문장: 예를 들어(for instance), 쉼표의 위치가 잘못 찍히는 것은
생사가 걸린 문제일 수 있다.

➡ 앞 문장은 글에 오류가 발생하면 내용에 부정적인 영향을 미친다는 내용이다. 뒤
문장에서 구체적인 예시로 글에서 쉼표의 위치가 잘못 찍힌 것이 생사를 가르는
문제가 될 수 있다고 설명한다. 따라서 두 문장은 for instance로 자연스럽게
연결된다.
▶ 주어진 문장이 ①에 들어갈 수 없음

- ②의 앞 문장과 뒤 문장

앞 문장: ①의 뒤 문장과 같음
뒤 문장: 마찬가지로(Similarly) 대부분의 돌연변이는 그것이 발생하는
유기체에 해로운 결과를 가져오는데 이는 그것들이 생식 적합성을
감소시킨다는 것을 뜻한다.

➡ 앞의 내용에서 글의 오류가 치명적인 문제를 일으킬 수 있는 것처럼, 뒤 문장에서는
유기체의 돌연변이가 유기체에 생식 적합성 감소라는 치명적인 문제를 일으킬 수
있다고 설명하고 있다.
글의 오류와 돌연변이가 각각 부정적인 영향을 미칠 수 있다는 내용이므로
Similarly로 자연스럽게 연결된다.
▶ 주어진 문장이 ②에 들어갈 수 없음

- ③의 앞 문장과 뒤 문장

앞 문장: ②의 뒤 문장과 같음
뒤 문장: 그러나(however) 때때로 유기체의 적합성을 상승시키는
돌연변이가 발생할 수 있는데, 이는 우연히 초판의 텍스트를 복사하지
못한 것이 더 정확하거나 최신의 정보를 제공할 수도 있는 것과 꼭
마찬가지이다.

➡ 앞부분에서 글의 오류나 돌연변이 모두 부정적인 영향을 미칠 수 있다고 설명했다.
뒤 문장에서는 이러한 글이나 유기체의 오류가 반드시 부정적인 영향만을 미치는
것은 아니며, 긍정적인 오류도 있을 수 있다고 설명하고 있다.
따라서 상반되는 내용의 두 문장은 however로 자연스럽게 연결된다.
▶ 주어진 문장이 ③에 들어갈 수 없음

④의 앞 문장과 뒤 문장

앞 문장: ③의 뒤 문장과 같음
뒤 문장: 유리한 돌연변이는 다음 세대에 더 많이 나타날 것인데 그
돌연변이가 발생한 유기체는 더 많은 자손을 낳을 것이고 돌연변이가
자손에게 전달되기 때문이다.

앞 문장에서는 글의 오류와 돌연변이가 긍정적인 영향을 미칠 수 있다는 공통점을 소개했다. 하지만 뒤에 이어지는 내용은 돌연변이와 글의 오류가 무엇이 다른지 소개하고 있다.
주어진 문장은 두 개념의 공통점을 소개하다가 차이점을 제시하는 부분에 들어가야 하므로 ④에 들어가야 한다.
▶ 주어진 문장이 ④에 들어가야 함

- ⑤의 앞 문장과 뒤 문장

> 앞 문장: ④의 뒤 문장과 같음
> 뒤 문장: 대조적으로(By contrast), 우연히 초판의 오류를 바로잡은 책이 더 잘 팔리는 경향이 있을 메커니즘은 없다.

> 앞 문장에서 유리한 돌연변이는 다음 세대에 더 많이 나타날 수 있다고 설명한다. 뒤 문장에서는 이와는 대조적으로 글의 오류를 바로잡은 책이 더 잘 팔리게 될 메커니즘은 없다고 설명한다.
따라서 돌연변이와 글의 오류 간의 차이점을 설명하고 있으므로, 두 문장은 By contrast로 자연스럽게 연결된다.
▶ 주어진 문장이 ⑤에 들어갈 수 없음

3rd 글이 한눈에 들어오도록 정리하여 정답을 확인한다.

글에 오류가 발생하면 내용에 부정적인 영향을 미친다.
(①) 예를 들어, 쉼표의 위치가 잘못 찍힌 것이 생사의 문제가 되기도 한다.
(②) 마찬가지로, 유기체의 돌연변이도 생식 적합성이 감소하는 문제가 생긴다.
(③) 그러나 때로는 글의 오류나 돌연변이가 긍정적인 영향을 미치기도 한다.
(④ 다음 논거에서는 이 유사성이 깨진다.)
유리한 돌연변이는 다음 세대에 오히려 많이 나타날 것이다.
(⑤) 대조적으로, 글의 오류가 바로잡힌 글이 더 많이 팔릴 것이라는 메커니즘은 없다.

조수근 | 순천향대 의예과 2024년 입학·성남 태원고 졸

주어진 문장을 먼저 읽어보면, 유사성이 깨진다는 주어진 문장 앞부분에는 두 대상 간 유사성이, 뒷부분에는 두 대상 간 차이점이 서술될 것이라는 걸 예상할 수 있어. 그리고 지문을 읽을 때는, 주어진 문장은 일단 잊고 지문 자체를 확실하게 이해하는 걸 추천해. 지문을 다 읽고 나면 '유사성'을 다룬 부분과 '차이점'을 다룬 부분으로 넘어가는 지점을 쉽게 찾을 수 있을 거야!

N 39 정답 ⑤ * 잠의 역할

글의 흐름으로 보아, 주어진 문장이 들어가기에 가장 적절한 곳을 고르시오. [3점]

This is particularly true / since one aspect of sleep / is decreased responsiveness / to the environment. //
부사절 접속사(이유)
이것은 특히 사실이다 / 왜냐하면 잠의 한 가지 측면은 / 감소된 반응성이기 때문에 / 환경에 대한 **단서1** 잠을 잘 때는 환경에 대한 반응성이 감소함

The role / that sleep plays / in evolution / is still under study. //
단수 주어   단수 동사
역할은 / 잠이 하는 / 진화에 있어서 / 여전히 연구 중이다 //

(①) One possibility is / that it is an advantageous adaptive
주어   동사 주격 보어절 접속사
state / of decreased metabolism / for an animal / when there are no more pressing activities. //
한 가지 가능성은 ~이다 / 그것이 유리한 적응적 상태라는 것 / 줄어든 신진대사의 / 동물에게 / 더이상 긴급한 활동이 없을 때 //

(②) This seems true / for deeper states of inactivity / such as
선행사
hibernation / during the winter /
이것은 해당하는 것처럼 보인다 / 더 깊은 무활동 상태의 경우에 / 겨울잠과 같은 / 겨울 동안의 /

when there are few food supplies, / and a high metabolic cost /
관계부사
to maintaining adequate temperature. //
먹을 것이 거의 없고 / 높은 신진대사 비용이 드는 / 적절한 체온을 유지하는 데 //

(③) It may be true / in daily situations as well, / for instance /
to avoid의 의미상의 주어
for a prey species / to avoid predators / after dark. //
그것은 해당할지도 모른다 / 일상 상황에도 / 예를 들어 / 먹잇감이 되는 동물이 / 포식자를 피하는 / 어두워진 이후에 //

(④) On the other hand, / the apparent universality of sleep, / and the observation / that mammals / such as cetaceans / have developed /
동격절 접속사
다른 한 편으로는 / 잠의 분명한 보편성은 / 그리고 관찰 결과는 / 포유동물들이 / 고래목의 동물들과 같은 / 발전시켰다는 /

such highly complex mechanisms / to preserve sleep / on at least one side of the brain / at a time, / suggests / that sleep additionally provides / some vital service(s) / for the organism. //
목적어절 접속사
매우 고도로 복잡한 기제를 / 잠을 유지하는 / 적어도 뇌의 한 쪽에서는 / 한 번에 / 보여준다 / 잠이 추가로 제공한다는 것을 / 생명 유지와 관련된 어떤 도움(들)을 / 생명체에게 //

(⑤) If sleep is universal / even when this potential price must be paid, / **단서2** 환경에 대한 반응성의 감소라는 대가를 치러야 하는 때에도 잠을 자는 경우를 가리킴
잠이 보편적이라면 / 이러한 잠재적인 대가가 치러져야 할 때조차도 /

the implication may be / that it has important functions / that
선행사   주격 관계대명사
cannot be obtained / just by quiet, wakeful resting. //
함의는 ~일 수도 있다 / 그것이 중요한 기능을 갖고 있다는 것 / 얻어질 수 없는 / 조용한, 깨어 있는 상태의 휴식만으로는 //

- particularly ⓐⓓ 특히   · aspect ⓝ 측면, 양상
- responsiveness ⓝ 반응성   · evolution ⓝ 진화
- advantageous ⓐ 유리한   · adaptive ⓐ 적응할 수 있는
- state ⓝ 상태   · pressing ⓐ 긴급한
- true ⓐ (~에) 적용되는[해당하는]   · inactivity ⓝ 무활동
- hibernation ⓝ 겨울잠   · supply ⓝ 공급(량)
- metabolic ⓐ 신진대사의   · maintain ⓥ 유지하다
- adequate ⓐ 적절한   · temperature ⓝ 온도, 체온
- daily ⓐ 매일 일어나는   · prey ⓝ 먹이, 사냥감
- species ⓝ 종(생물 분류의 기초 단위)
- avoid ⓥ 피하다   · predator ⓝ 포식자   · apparent ⓐ 분명한
- universality ⓝ 보편성   · observation ⓝ 관찰
- cetacean ⓝ 고래목의 동물   · complex ⓐ 복잡한
- mechanism ⓝ (생물체 내에서 특정한 기능을 수행하는) 기제
- preserve ⓥ 보존하다   · suggest ⓥ 시사[암시]하다
- additionally ⓐⓓ 추가적으로   · vital ⓐ 생명 유지와 관련된
- organism ⓝ 생물(체)   · universal ⓐ 보편적인
- potential ⓐ 잠재적인   · implication ⓝ 함축, 암시
- function ⓝ 기능   · obtain ⓥ 얻다   · wakeful ⓐ 잠이 안 든

진화에 있어서 잠이 하는 역할은 여전히 연구 중이다. (①) 한 가지 가능성은 그것이 더이상 긴급한 활동이 없을 때 신진대사를 줄이는, 동물에게 유리한 적응적 상태라는 것이다. (②) 이것은 먹을 것이 거의 없고 적정한 체온을 유지하는 데 높은 신진대사 비용이 드는 겨울 동안의 겨울잠과 같은, 더 깊은 무활동 상태의 경우에 해당하는 것처럼 보인다. (③) 그것은, 예를 들어, 먹잇감이 되는 동물이 어두워진 이후에 포식자를 피하는 것처럼, 일상 상황에도 해당할지도 모른다. (④) 다른 한 편으로는, 잠의 분명한 보편성, 그리고 고래목의 동물들과 같은 포유동물들이 한 번에 적어도 뇌의 한 쪽에서는 잠을 유지하는 매우 고도로 복잡한 기제를 발전시켰다는 관찰 결과는 잠이 생명체에게 생명 유지와 관련된 어떤 도움(들)을 추가로 제공한다는 것을 보여준다. (⑤ 잠의 한 가지 측면은 환경에 대한 감소된 반응성이기 때문에 이것은 특히 사실이다.) 이러한 잠재적인 대가가 치러져야 할 때조차도 잠이 보편적이라면, 그것이 갖는 함의는 조용한, 깨어 있는 상태의 휴식만으로는 얻을 수 없는 중요한 기능을 그것이 갖고 있다는 것일 수도 있다.

1st 주어진 문장을 해석하고, 연결어, 지시어 등을 확인한다.

> [This] is particularly true since one aspect of sleep is decreased responsiveness to the environment. **단서 1**
> 잠의 한 가지 측면은 환경에 대한 감소된 반응성이기 때문에 [이것]은 특히 사실이다.

➡ 잠을 잘 때는 환경에 대한 반응성이 감소한다는 내용이 This(이것)로 이어진다. **단서**
▶ 주어진 문장의 앞부분: 환경에 대한 반응성이 감소하는 것과 관련된 내용이어야 함 **발상**

2nd 각 선택지의 앞뒤 흐름이 매끄러운지 확인한다.

- ①의 앞 문장과 뒤 문장

> **앞 문장:** 진화에 있어서 잠이 하는 역할은 여전히 연구 중이다.
> **뒤 문장:** 한 가지 가능성은 그것이 더이상 긴급한 활동이 없을 때 신진대사를 줄이는, 동물에게 유리한 적응적 상태라는 것이다.

➡ **앞 문장:** 잠이 진화에 대해 하는 역할을 언급했다.
뒤 문장: 잠은 신진대사를 줄이는 동물에게 유리한 적응적 상태라고 했다. 잠에 대한 내용이 이어지고 있으므로 앞 문장과 연결된다.
▶ 주어진 문장이 ①에 들어갈 수 없음

- ②의 앞 문장과 뒤 문장

> **앞 문장:** ①의 뒤 문장과 같음
> **뒤 문장:** 이것은 먹을 것이 거의 없고 적정한 체온을 유지하는 데 높은 신진대사 비용이 드는 겨울 동안의 겨울잠과 같은, 더 깊은 무활동 상태의 경우에 해당하는 것처럼 보인다.

➡ 앞에서 잠을 자면서 신진대사를 줄인다고 했고, 무활동 상태의 경우에 해당하는 것처럼 보인다는 문장으로 이어진다.
▶ 주어진 문장이 ②에 들어갈 수 없음

- ③의 앞 문장과 뒤 문장

> **앞 문장:** ②의 뒤 문장과 같음
> **뒤 문장:** 그것은, 예를 들어(for instance), 먹잇감이 되는 동물이 어두워진 이후에 포식자를 피하는 것처럼, 일상 상황에도 해당할지도 모른다.

➡ 앞 문장에 for instance로 이어지면서 어두워진 후에 포식자를 피한다는 예시가 이어지고 있으므로 자연스러운 흐름이다.
▶ 주어진 문장이 ③에 들어갈 수 없음

- ④의 앞 문장과 뒤 문장

> **앞 문장:** ③의 뒤 문장과 같음
> **뒤 문장:** 다른 한편으로는(On the other hand), 잠의 분명한 보편성, 그리고 고래목의 동물들과 같은 포유동물들이 한 번에 적어도 뇌의 한 쪽에서는 잠을 유지하는 매우 고도로 복잡한 기제를 발전시켰다는 관찰 결과는 잠이 생명체에게 생명 유지와 관련된 어떤 도움(들)을 추가로 제공한다는 것을 보여준다.

➡ 앞 문장에 이어서 잠의 역할에 대한 다른 설명이 나오는데, 생명 유지와 관련된 도움을 제공한다는 내용이 이어진다.
▶ 주어진 문장이 ④에 들어갈 수 없음

- ⑤의 앞 문장과 뒤 문장

> **앞 문장:** ④의 뒤 문장과 같음
> **뒤 문장:** 이러한 잠재적인 대가(this potential price)가 치러져야 할 때조차도 잠이 보편적이라면, 그것이 갖는 함의는 조용한, 깨어 있는 상태의 휴식만으로는 얻을 수 없는 중요한 기능을 그것이 갖고 있다는 것일 수도 있다.

➡ this potential price가 주어진 문장의 '환경에 대한 반응성의 감소'를 가리킨다. 주어진 문장은 잠을 자는 동안 환경에 대한 반응성이 감소한다는 내용으로, 앞부분에서 설명한 것과는 다른, 잠의 역할에 대한 두 번째 설명의 일부이므로 잠의 역할에 대한 첫 번째 설명이 모두 끝난 이후에 들어가야 한다.
▶ 주어진 문장이 ⑤에 들어가야 함

3rd 글이 한눈에 들어오도록 정리하여 정답을 확인한다.

진화에 있어서 잠이 하는 역할은 여전히 연구 중이다.
(①) 한 가지 가능성은 더이상 긴급한 활동이 없을 때 신진대사를 줄이는, 동물에게 유리한 적응적 상태라는 것이다.
(②) 이것은 겨울 동안의 겨울잠과 같은, 더 깊은 무활동 상태의 경우에 해당하는 것처럼 보인다.
(③) 예를 들어, 먹잇감이 되는 동물이 어두워진 이후에 포식자를 피하는 것처럼, 일상 상황에도 해당할지도 모른다.
(④) 다른 한 편으로는, 잠이 생명체에게 생명 유지와 관련된 어떤 도움(들)을 추가로 제공한다는 것을 보여준다.
(⑤ 잠의 한 가지 측 면은 환경에 대한 감소된 반응성이기 때문에 이것은 특히 사실이다.)
이러한 잠재적인 대가가 치러져야 할 때조차도 잠이 보편적이라면, 그것이 갖는 함의는 조용한, 깨어 있는 상태의 휴식만으로는 얻을 수 없는 중요한 기능을 그것이 갖고 있다는 것일 수도 있다.

N 40 정답 ③ ━━━━━━ ⭐ 2등급 대비 [정답률 57%]

＊흥미로운 집단적 탐지의 역학

> **글의 흐름으로 보아, 주어진 문장이 들어가기에 가장 적절한 곳을 고르시오. [3점]**

> This makes sense / from the perspective of information reliability. // **단서 1** This가 가리키는 것이 여러 개체의 이탈이 더 큰 도망 반응을 일으킨다는 것임
> 이것은 이치에 맞는다 / 정보 신뢰성의 관점에서 //

The dynamics of collective detection / have an interesting feature. //
집단적 탐지의 역학은 / 흥미로운 특징이 있다 //
Which cue(s) do individuals use / as evidence of predator attack? //
개체들은 어떤 단서를 사용하는가 / 포식자 공격의 증거로 //
In some cases, / when an individual detects a predator, / its best response / is to seek shelter. //
어떤 경우에는 / 개체가 포식자를 탐지할 때 / 그것의 최선의 반응은 / 피난처를 찾는 것이다 //
(①) Departure from the group / may signal danger to nonvigilant animals / and cause / what appears to be a coordinated flushing of prey / from the area. //
무리로부터의 이탈은 / 경계하지 않는 동물들에게 위험 신호를 보내서 / 야기할 수도 있다 /
먹잇감 동물의 조직화된 날아오르기로 보이는 것을 / 그 구역에서 //

(②) Studies / on dark-eyed juncos (a type of bird) / support
the view / that nonvigilant animals attend / to departures of
individual group mates /
연구는 / (새의 한 종류인) 검은 눈 검은방울새에 관한 / 견해를 뒷받침한다 / 경계하지 않는
동물들이 주목하지만 / 무리 친구들의 개별적 이탈에 /
but that the departure of multiple individuals / causes a greater
escape response / in the nonvigilant individuals. //
여러 개체의 이탈은 / 더 큰 도망 반응을 일으킨다는 / 경계하지 않는 동물에게 //
(③) If one group member departs, / it might have done so /
for a number of reasons / that have little to do with predation
threat. //
무리 구성원 하나가 이탈하는 경우 / 그것은 그렇게 했을 수 있다 / 여러 이유로 / 포식 위험과
관계가 거의 없는 //
(④) If nonvigilant animals escaped / each time a single member
left the group, / they would frequently respond / when there
was no predator (a false alarm). //
경계하지 않는 동물들이 도망한다면 / 단 하나의 구성원이 무리를 떠날 때마다 / 그것들은
자주 반응할 것이다 / 포식자가 전혀 없는 (가짜 경보인) 때에도 //
(⑤) On the other hand, / when several individuals depart the
group / at the same time, / a true threat is much more likely to
be present. //
반면에 / 여러 개체가 무리를 이탈할 때 / 동시에 / 진짜 위험이 존재할 가능성이 훨씬 더 크다 //

- reliability ⓝ 신뢰성, 신뢰도 · dynamic ⓝ ((pl.)) 역학, 원동력
- collective ⓐ 집단의, 공동의 · detection ⓝ 발견, 탐지
- cue ⓝ (무엇을 하라는) 신호 · detect ⓥ 감지하다, 발견하다
- shelter ⓝ (위험으로부터의) 대피처, 주거지 · departure ⓝ 떠남, 출발
- coordinate ⓥ (몸의 움직임을) 조정하다, 조직화하다
- prey ⓝ 먹이, 사냥감 · predation ⓝ (동물의) 포식

집단적 탐지의 역학은 흥미로운 특징이 있다. 개체들은 어떤 단서를 포식자
공격의 증거로 사용하는가? 어떤 경우에는 개체가 포식자를 탐지할 때 그것의
최선의 반응은 피난처를 찾는 것이다. (①) 무리로부터의 이탈은 경계하지
않는 동물들에게 위험 신호를 보내서 먹잇감 동물이 그 구역에서 조직화되어
날아오르는 것으로 보이는 것을 야기할 수도 있다. (②) (새의 한 종류인) 검은
눈 검은방울새에 관한 연구는 경계하지 않는 동물들이 무리 친구들의 개별적
이탈에 주목하지만 여러 개체의 이탈은 경계하지 않는 동물에게 더 큰 도망
반응을 일으킨다는 견해를 뒷받침한다. (③ 이것은 정보 신뢰성의 관점에서
이치에 맞는다.) 무리 구성원 하나가 이탈하는 경우, 그것은 포식 위험과 관계가
거의 없는 여러 이유로 그렇게 했을 수 있다. (④) 경계하지 않는 동물들이 단
하나의 구성원이 무리를 떠날 때마다 도망한다면, 그것들은 포식자가 전혀 없는
(가짜 경보인) 때에도 자주 반응할 것이다. (⑤) 반면에 여러 개체가 동시에
무리를 이탈할 때, 진짜 위험이 존재할 가능성이 훨씬 더 크다.

🏷 2등급❓ 글에 나타난 예시를 읽으면서 정보 신뢰성의 관점에 해당하는 부분을
찾아 주어진 문장을 넣어야 하는 2등급 대비 문제이다. 개별적 이탈과 여러 개체의
이탈로 대조되는 두 경우를 잘 살피면서 어떤 선택이 정보 신뢰성의 관점에서
이치에 맞는지 따져본다면 정답을 찾을 수 있을 것이다. 발상

| 문제 풀이 순서 |

1st 주어진 문장을 해석하고, 연결어, 지시어 등을 확인한다.

> This makes sense from the perspective of information
> reliability. 단서1
> 이것은 정보 신뢰성의 관점에서 이치에 맞는다.

➡ 정보 신뢰성에 관한 내용이 앞에 나오고, 그 뒤에 주어진 문장을 넣어야 한다.
➡ 정보 신뢰성의 관점에서 이치에 맞는 This가 무엇을 가리키는지 앞에 나올 것이다.

2nd 각 선택지의 앞뒤 흐름이 매끄러운지 확인한다.

- ①의 앞 문장과 뒤 문장

> **앞 문장:** 집단적 탐지의 역학은 흥미로운 특징이 있다. 개체들은 어떤
> 단서를 포식자 공격의 증거로 사용하는가? 어떤 경우에는 개체가
> 포식자를 탐지할 때 그것의 최선의 반응은 피난처를 찾는 것이다.
> **뒤 문장:** 무리로부터의 이탈은 경계하지 않는 동물들에게 위험 신호를
> 보내서 먹잇감 동물이 그 구역에서 조직화되어 날아오르는 것으로
> 보이는 것을 야기할 수도 있다.

➡ **앞 문장:** 집단적 탐지 역학이 가진 흥미로운 특징
  뒤 문장: 무리로부터의 이탈은 경계하지 않는 동물들에게 위험 신호를 보내서
  먹잇감 동물이 날아오르는 것처럼 보이게 할 수도 있다.
  앞 문장의 '포식자 공격의 증거'가 뒤 문장에서 '무리로부터의 이탈'로 나타났다.
  ▶ 주어진 문장이 ①에 들어갈 수 없음

- ②의 앞 문장과 뒤 문장

> **앞 문장:** ①의 뒤 문장과 같음
> **뒤 문장:** (새의 한 종류인) 검은눈 검은방울새에 관한 연구는 경계하지
> 않는 동물들이 무리 친구들의 개별적 이탈에 주목하지만 여러 개체의
> 이탈은 경계하지 않는 동물에게 더 큰 도망 반응을 일으킨다는 견해를
> 뒷받침한다. 단서2

➡ 앞 문장의 내용에 대해 검은눈 검은방울새라는 사례를 제시하여 부연하는
  흐름이다. 경계하지 않는 동물들이 무리 중 여러 개체의 이탈에 더 큰 도망 반응을
  일으킨다는 결과를 언급했다.
  ▶ 주어진 문장이 ②에 들어갈 수 없음

- ③의 앞 문장과 뒤 문장

> **앞 문장:** ②의 뒤 문장과 같음
> **뒤 문장:** 무리 구성원 하나가 이탈하는 경우, 그것은 포식 위험과 관계가
> 거의 없는 여러 이유로 그렇게 했을 수 있다.

➡ **뒤 문장:** 무리 구성원의 개별적 이탈은 포식 위험이 아닌 여러 이유로 그랬을 수도
  있다.
  주어진 문장의 this가 지칭하는 것은 ②의 뒤 문장의 '경계하지 않는 동물에게는
  여러 개체의 이탈이 더 큰 도망 반응을 일으킨다는 견해'이다.
➡ 정보 신뢰성, 즉 '믿을 만한 정보인지 아닌지'라는 관점에서 보면, 무리 구성원이
  개별적으로 이탈할 때보다는 여러 개체가 이탈하는 경우가 더 믿을 만한 정보이다.
  경계하지 않는 동물들에게는 이때 도망가는 것이 이치에 맞는다는 흐름으로 주어진
  문장과 ③의 뒤 문장이 자연스럽게 연결된다.
  ▶ 주어진 문장이 ③에 들어가야 함

- ④의 앞 문장과 뒤 문장

> **앞 문장:** ③의 뒤 문장과 같음
> **뒤 문장:** 경계하지 않는 동물들이 단 하나의 구성원이 무리를 떠날
> 때마다 도망한다면, 그것들은 포식자가 전혀 없는 (가짜 경보인) 때에도
> 자주 반응할 것이다.

➡ 앞 문장에서 나타난 '무리 구성원 하나의 이탈'에 관하여, 경계하지 않는 동물들이
  일일이 반응하는 경우를 뒤 문장에서 부연하는 흐름이다.
  ▶ 주어진 문장이 ④에 들어갈 수 없음

> **앞 문장:** ④의 뒤 문장과 같음
> **뒤 문장:** 반면에 여러 개체가 동시에 무리를 이탈할 때, 진짜 위험이 존재할 가능성이 훨씬 더 크다.

➡ On the other hand가 나오므로, 앞 문장의 경우와 반대되는 경우, 즉, 여러 개체가 동시에 무리를 이탈하는 경우를 설명한다.
　▶ 주어진 문장이 ⑤에 들어갈 수 없음

3rd 글이 한눈에 들어오도록 정리하여 정답을 확인한다.

집단적 탐지의 역학은 흥미로운 특징이 있다.
(①) 무리로부터의 이탈은 경계하지 않는 동물들에게 위험 신호를 보내서 먹잇감 동물이 그 구역에서 조직화되어 날아오르는 것으로 보이게 할 수 있다.
(②) 여러 개체의 이탈은 경계하지 않는 동물들로 하여금 더 큰 도망 반응을 일으키게 한다.
(③ 이것은 정보 신뢰성의 관점에서 이치에 맞는다.)
무리 구성원의 개별적 이탈은 포식 위험 외 여러 이유로 그렇게 했을 수도 있다.
(④) 경계하지 않는 동물들이 무리의 개별적 이탈 때마다 도망한다면, 가짜 경보일 때에도 자주 반응할 것이다.
(⑤) 반면 여러 개체의 이탈에 진짜 위험이 존재할 가능성이 더 크다.

N 41 정답 ④ ⟶ 　　　　　　⚫ 2등급 대비 [정답률 59%]

✱ 영화의 본질을 파괴한 기술 혁신

> **글의 흐름으로 보아, 주어진 문장이 들어가기에 가장 적절한 곳을 고르시오.** [3점]

> As long as the irrealism of the silent black and white film
> 　부사절 접속사(조건)　　　부사절의 주어
> predominated, / one could not take filmic fantasies / for
> 　　부사절의 동사
> representations of reality. //
> 무성 흑백 영화의 비현실주의가 지배하는 한 / 사람은 영화적 환상을 착각할 수 없었다 / 현실에 대한 묘사로 //

Cinema is valuable / not for its ability / to make visible / the
　　　　　　　not A but B로 연결된 전치사구
　　　　　　　　　　　to make의 목적격 보어와 목적어
hidden outlines of our reality, / but for its ability / to reveal /
what reality itself veils / — the dimension of fantasy. //
영화는 가치가 있다 / 그것의 능력 때문이 아니라 / 보이게 만드는 / 우리 현실의 숨겨진 윤곽을 / 그것의 능력 때문에 / 드러내는 / 현실 자체가 가리고 있는 것을 / 환상의 차원 //
　　　　　　　　　　　주격 보어를 이끄는 의문사
(①) This is / why, to a person, the first great theorists of
film decried / the introduction / of sound and other technical
innovations /
이것이 ~이다 / 왜 최초의 위대한 영화 이론가들이 이구동성으로 비난했는지 / 도입을 / 소리와 다른 기술 혁신의 //
　　　　　　　　　　주격 관계대명사
(such as color) / that pushed film / in the direction of realism. //
(색채와 같은) / 영화를 밀어붙였던 / 사실주의 쪽으로 //
(②) Since cinema was an entirely fantasmatic art, / these
　　　　부사절 접속사(이유)
innovations were completely unnecessary. //
영화는 전적으로 환상적인 예술이었기 때문에 / 이러한 혁신은 완전히 불필요했다 //
　　　　　　　　　　　　　　　　= only
(③) And what's worse, / they could do nothing but turn
filmmakers and audiences away / from the fantasmatic
dimension of cinema, /
그리고 설상가상으로 / 그것들은 영화제작자와 관객을 멀어지게 할 수 있을 뿐이었다 / 영화의 환상적인 차원으로부터 //
　　　　　　　　　　　　　= as they transformed
potentially transforming film / into a mere delivery device / for
representations of reality. //
잠재적으로 영화를 변형시키면서 / 단순한 전달 장치로 / 현실의 묘사를 위한 //

단서 기술 혁신이 도입되지 않았다면 지켜졌을 영화적 '환상'이 (주어진 문장) 소리와 색채(기술 혁신)로 파괴되었음

(④) But sound and color threatened / to create just such an
illusion, / thereby destroying / the very essence of film art. //
그러나 소리와 색채는 위협하여 / 바로 그러한 착각을 만들겠다고 / 파괴했다 / 영화 예술의 바로 그 본질을 //
　　　　　　　　　└ = and they destroyed
　　　　　　　　　　　　'(특정한 방식으로) 표현[말]하다, (말ㆍ글로) 옮기다'
(⑤) As Rudolf Arnheim puts it, / "The creative power of the
　　　'작동하기 시작하다'　　부사절 접속사(장소)
artist / can only come into play / where reality and the medium
of representation / do not coincide." //
Rudolf Arnheim이 표현한 것처럼 / "예술가의 창의적 힘은 / 오직 발휘될 수 있다 / 현실과 묘사의 매체가 / 일치하지 않는 곳에서만" //

- irrealism ⓝ 비현실주의　　· predominate ⓥ 지배적이다, 두드러지다
- filmic ⓐ 영화의, 영화적인　· representation ⓝ 묘사, 표현
- outline ⓝ 윤곽, 개요　　· reveal ⓥ (보이지 않던 것을) 드러내 보이다
- veil ⓥ 가리다　· dimension ⓝ 차원, 관점　· theorist ⓝ 이론가
- introduction ⓝ 도입, 전래　· innovation ⓝ 혁신, 획기적인 것
- realism ⓝ 사실주의　· entirely ⓐⓓ 완전히, 전적으로
- completely ⓐⓓ 완전히　· potentially ⓐⓓ 잠재적으로
- transform ⓥ (외양ㆍ모양을) 변형하다
- mere ⓐ 단지 ~의, (한낱) ~에 불과한　· threaten ⓥ 위협하다
- illusion ⓝ 착각, 환상　· destroy ⓥ 파괴하다, 말살하다
- essence ⓝ 본질, 진수　· medium ⓝ 매체　· coincide ⓥ 일치하다

영화는 우리 현실의 숨겨진 윤곽을 보이게 만드는 능력 때문이 아니라 현실 자체가 가리고 있는 것, 즉 환상의 차원을 드러내는 능력 때문에 가치가 있다. (①) 이것이 최초의 위대한 영화 이론가들이 영화를 사실주의 쪽으로 밀어붙였던 소리와 (색채와 같은) 다른 기술 혁신의 도입을 이구동성으로 비난한 이유이다. (②) 영화는 전적으로 환상적인 예술이었기 때문에 이러한 혁신은 완전히 불필요했다. (③) 그리고 설상가상으로 그것들은 잠재적으로 영화를 현실의 묘사를 위한 단순한 전달 장치로 변형시키면서, 영화제작자와 관객을 영화의 환상적인 차원으로부터 멀어지게 할 수 있을 뿐이었다. (④ 무성 흑백 영화의 비현실주의가 지배하는 한 영화적 환상을 현실에 대한 묘사로 착각할 수 없었다.) 그러나 소리와 색채는 바로 그러한 착각을 만들겠다고 위협하여 영화 예술의 바로 그 본질을 파괴했다. (⑤) Rudolf Arnheim이 표현한 것처럼 "예술가의 창의적 힘은 현실과 묘사의 매체가 일치하지 않는 곳에서만 발휘될 수 있다."

2등급 ? 영화적 환상과 이를 파괴하는 기술 혁신을 대조하는 내용으로, 정답 주변의 표현이 주어진 문장의 표현과 직접적으로 연결되지 않는다. **단서** 주어진 문장에서 'could not take ~ for'이라는 표현이 결국 illusion과 대응된다는 점을 찾아야 문제를 해결할 수 있다. **발상**

| 문제 풀이 순서 |

1st 주어진 문장을 해석하고, 연결어, 지시어 등을 확인한다.

> As long as the irrealism of the silent black and white film
> predominated, one could not take filmic fantasies for
> representations of reality.
> 무성 흑백 영화의 비현실주의가 지배하는 한 영화적 환상을 현실에 대한 묘사로 착각할 수 없었다.

➡ 무성 흑백 영화와 영화적 환상과 관련된 내용이 앞에 나오고 그 뒤에 주어진 문장을 넣어야 한다.

2nd 각 선택지의 앞뒤 흐름이 매끄러운지 확인한다.

- ①의 앞 문장과 뒤 문장

> **앞 문장:** 영화는 우리 현실의 숨겨진 윤곽을 보이게 만드는 능력 때문이 아니라 현실 자체가 가리고 있는 것, 즉 환상의 차원을 드러내는 능력 때문에 가치가 있다.
> **뒤 문장:** 이것이 최초의 위대한 영화 이론가들이 영화를 사실주의 쪽으로 밀어붙였던 소리와 (색채와 같은) 다른 기술 혁신의 도입을 이구동성으로 비난한 이유이다.

앞 문장: 환상의 차원을 드러내는 능력이라는 영화의 가치
뒤 문장: 최초의 영화 이론가들은 영화에 다른 기술 혁신의 도입을 비난했다.
앞 문장의 '환상의 차원'과 뒤 문장의 '사실주의'가 대조된다. 영화는 환상의 차원을 드러내기에 가치가 있지만 최초 영화 이론가들은 기술 혁신의 도입이 영화를 사실주의 쪽으로 밀어붙였기 때문에 이를 비난했다는 흐름이다.
▶ 주어진 문장이 ①에 들어갈 수 없음

- ②의 앞 문장과 뒤 문장

> **앞 문장:** ①의 뒤 문장과 같음
> **뒤 문장:** 영화는 전적으로 환상적인 예술이었기 때문에 이러한 혁신은 완전히 불필요했다.

➡ 앞 문장의 '기술 혁신'을 뒤 문장에서 '이러한 혁신'으로 지칭했다. 앞 문장에 나타난 최초의 영화 이론가들의 입장을 이어서 뒷받침한다.
▶ 주어진 문장이 ②에 들어갈 수 없음

- ③의 앞 문장과 뒤 문장

> **앞 문장:** ②의 뒤 문장과 같음
> **뒤 문장:** 그리고 설상가상으로 그것들은 잠재적으로 영화를 현실의 묘사를 위한 단순한 전달 장치로 변형시키면서, 영화제작자와 관객을 영화의 환상적인 차원으로부터 멀어지게 할 수 있을 뿐이었다.

➡ 앞 문장에 나타난 주장을 이어서 뒷받침한다.
▶ 주어진 문장이 ③에 들어갈 수 없음

- ④의 앞 문장과 뒤 문장

> **앞 문장:** ③의 뒤 문장과 같음
> **뒤 문장:** 그러나(But) 소리와 색채는 바로 그러한 착각(such an illusion)을 만들겠다고 위협하여 영화 예술의 바로 그 본질을 파괴했다. **단서**

➡ **뒤 문장:** 소리와 색채(기술 혁신)는 영화 예술의 그 본질(환상의 차원)을 파괴했다. such an illusion이 무엇인지 앞에 나와야 한다.
➡ 주어진 문장에 영화적 환상을 현실에 대한 묘사로 착각할 수 없었다는 내용이 나온다. 기술 혁신이 '그러한 착각'을 만들겠다고 위협하여 영화 예술의 본질인 환상의 차원을 파괴했다는 흐름이다.
▶ 주어진 문장이 ④에 들어가야 함

- ⑤의 앞 문장과 뒤 문장

> **앞 문장:** ④의 뒤 문장과 같음
> **뒤 문장:** Rudolf Arnheim이 표현한 것처럼 "예술가의 창의적 힘은 현실과 묘사의 매체가 일치하지 않는 곳에서만 발휘될 수 있다."

➡ 앞 문장의 내용을 부연하며, 현실(사실주의)과 묘사(환상의 차원)가 공존할 수 없다는 흐름이다.
▶ 주어진 문장이 ⑤에 들어갈 수 없음

3rd 글이 한눈에 들어오도록 정리하여 정답을 확인한다.

영화는 환상의 차원을 드러내는 능력 때문에 가치가 있다.
(①) 최초의 영화 이론가들은 영화를 사실주의 쪽으로 밀어붙였던 기술 혁신 도입을 비난했다.
(②) 영화는 전적으로 환상의 차원이기 때문에 이러한 혁신은 불필요했다.
(③) 기술 혁신은 잠재적으로 영화를 현실 묘사를 위한 수단으로 변형시키면서 영화제작자와 관객을 환상의 차원으로부터 멀어지게 할 뿐이었다.

(④ 비현실주의가 지배하는 한 영화적 환상을 현실에 대한 묘사로 착각할 수 없었다.)
소리와 색채(기술 혁신)는 그러한 착각을 만들겠다고 위협하여 영화 예술의 본질(환상의 차원)을 파괴했다.
(⑤) 예술가의 창의적 힘은 현실과 묘사의 매체가 일치하지 않는 곳에서만 발휘될 수 있다.

N 42 정답 ④ ——————— ☆ 2등급 대비 [정답률 61%]

＊물질의 특성에 대한 과거와 최근의 이해

> 글의 흐름으로 보아, 주어진 문장이 들어가기에 가장 적절한 곳을 고르시오.

It was not until relatively recent times / that scientists came
〜에 이르러서야 비로소 …했다
to understand the relationships / between the structural elements of materials / and their properties. //
비교적 최근에 이르러서야 / 비로소 과학자들이 관계를 이해하게 되었다 / 물질의 구조적 요소와 / 그것들의 특성 사이의 //

The earliest humans had access / to only a very limited number
                        선행사
of materials, / those that occur naturally: / stone, wood, clay,
                    주격 관계대명사절
skins, and so on. //
초기 인류는 접근할 수 있었다 / 매우 제한된 수의 물질에만 / 자연적으로 존재하는 물질 / 돌, 나무, 찰흙, 가죽 등 //
(①) With time, / they discovered techniques / for producing
              선행사
materials / that had properties / superior to those / of the natural
= properties   주격 관계대명사   = materials
ones; /
시간이 흐르면서 / 그들은 기술을 발견했는데 / 물질을 만들어내는 / 특성을 가진 / 물질보다 더 우수한 / 자연적인 특성의 /
these new materials included / pottery and various metals. //
이 새로운 물질은 포함했다 / 도자기와 다양한 금속을 //
(②) Furthermore, it was discovered / that the properties of
                   가주어   진주어절 접속사
a material could be altered / by heat treatments / and by the
                        전치사구의 병렬 구조
addition of other substances. //
게다가 〜이 발견되었다 / 물질의 특성이 바뀔 수 있다는 것이 / 열처리에 의해 / 그리고 여타 다른 물질의 첨가에 의해 **단서1** 초기 인류가 열처리와 다른 물질의 첨가를 통해
                                        물질의 특성이 바뀔 수 있음을 발견한 시기
(③) At this point, / materials utilization was totally a selection 선행사
process / that involved deciding / from a given, rather limited
          주격 관계대명사
set of materials, /
이 시기에 / 물질 이용은 전적으로 선택의 과정이었다 / 결정하는 것을 수반하는 / 주어진 상당히 제한된 물질 집합 중에서 /
the one / best suited for an application / based on its
= material
characteristics. //
물질을 / 용도에 가장 적합한 / 그것의 특성에 근거하여 **단서2** 초기 인류가 얻은 지식이 아니라
                                    비교적 최근에 얻어진 지식을 가리킴
(④) This knowledge, / acquired / over approximately the past
            주어
100 years, / has empowered them to fashion, / to a large degree,
            동사   목적어   목적격 보어
/ the characteristics of materials. //
이 지식은 / 획득된 / 대략 지난 100년 동안 / 그들이 형성할 수 있게 했다 / 상당한 정도로 / 물질의 특성을 //
(⑤) Thus, / tens of thousands of different materials have
evolved / with rather specialized characteristics / that meet the
                              선행사   주격 관계대명사
needs /
따라서 / 수만 가지의 다양한 물질이 발전했다 / 상당히 특화된 특성을 가진 / 요구를 충족하는 /
of our modern and complex society, / including metals, plastics, glasses, and fibers. //
현대적이고 복잡한 우리 사회의 / 금속, 플라스틱, 유리, 섬유를 포함하여 //

- structural ⓐ 구조적인　　• element ⓝ 요소　　• property ⓝ 특성
- clay ⓝ 찰흙　　• superior ⓐ (〜보다) 우수한　　• pottery ⓝ 도자기
- alter ⓥ 바꾸다　　• heat treatment 열처리　　• substance ⓝ 물질
- utilization ⓝ 이용, 활용　　• selection ⓝ 선택　　• rather ⓐⓓ 상당히

- suited ⓐ 적합한　　• application ⓝ 이용　　• acquired ⓐ 획득한
- approximately ⓐⓓ 대략　　• empower ⓥ ~할 수 있게 하다
- fashion ⓥ 형성하다, 만들다　　• degree ⓝ 정도
- evolve ⓥ 발달하다　　• fiber ⓝ 섬유

초기 인류는 매우 제한된 수의 물질, 즉 돌, 나무, 찰흙, 가죽 등 자연적으로 존재하는 물질에만 접근할 수 있었다. (①) 시간이 흐르면서 그들은 자연적인 특성의 물질보다 더 우수한 특성을 가진 물질을 만들어내는 기술을 발견했는데, 이 새로운 물질에는 도자기와 다양한 금속이 포함되었다. (②) 게다가, 물질의 특성이 열처리와 여타 다른 물질의 첨가로 바뀔 수 있다는 것이 발견되었다. (③) 이 시기에, 물질 이용은 주어진 상당히 제한된 물질 집합 중에서 물질의 특성에 근거하여 용도에 가장 적합한 물질을 결정하는 것을 수반하는 전적으로 선택의 과정이었다. (④ 비로소 과학자들이 물질의 구조적 요소와 물질 특성의 관계를 이해하게 된 것은 비교적 최근에 이르러서였다.) 대략 지난 100년 동안 획득된 이 지식으로 그들은 상당한 정도로 물질의 특성을 형성할 수 있게 되었다. (⑤) 따라서 금속, 플라스틱, 유리, 섬유를 포함하여, 현대적이고 복잡한 우리 사회의 요구를 충족하는 상당히 특화된 특성을 가진 수만 가지의 다양한 물질이 발전했다.

────────────────────

왜 2등급? 어려운 어휘가 다수 사용되었고, 시간의 흐름에 따라 물질에 관한 지식이 발전해왔다는 점을 파악해야 하는 문제이다. **단서** 정답 주변의 지시어를 잘 파악하여 과거에서 현재로 넘어가는 시점을 발견한다면 어렵지 않게 정답을 찾을 수 있을 것이다. **발상**

| 문제 풀이 순서 |

1st 주어진 문장을 해석하고, 연결어, 지시어 등을 확인한다.

> It was not until relatively recent times that scientists came to understand the relationships between the structural elements of materials and their properties.
> 비로소 과학자들이 물질의 구조적 요소와 물질 특성의 관계를 이해하게 된 것은 비교적 최근에 이르러서였다.

➡ 물질의 구조적 요소와 물질 특성의 관계를 이해하기 이전의 단계가 앞에 나오고 그 뒤에 주어진 문장을 넣어야 한다.
➡ 물질의 구조와 특성과 관련된 내용이 이어질 것이다.

2nd 각 선택지의 앞뒤 흐름이 매끄러운지 확인한다.

- **①의 앞 문장과 뒤 문장**

> **앞 문장:** 초기 인류는 매우 제한된 수의 물질, 즉 돌, 나무, 찰흙, 가죽 등 자연적으로 존재하는 물질에만 접근할 수 있었다.
> **뒤 문장:** 시간이 흐르면서 그들은 자연적인 특성의 물질보다 더 우수한 특성을 가진 물질을 만들어내는 기술을 발견했는데, 이 새로운 물질에는 도자기와 다양한 금속이 포함되었다.

➡ **앞 문장:** 초기 인류는 자연 물질에만 접근할 수 있었다.
　뒤 문장: 시간이 흐르면서 더 우수한 특성을 가진 물질을 만들어내는 기술을 발견했다.
　물질에 대한 접근에 있어서 앞 문장과 뒤 문장이 시간의 흐름에 따라 연결되어 있다. 인류가 초기에는 자연 물질에만 접근할 수 있었으나 시간이 흐르면서 더 우수한 특성을 가진 물질을 만들어냈다는 흐름이다.
　▶ 주어진 문장이 ①에 들어갈 수 없음

- **②의 앞 문장과 뒤 문장**

> **앞 문장:** ①의 뒤 문장과 같음
> **뒤 문장:** 게다가, 물질의 특성이 열처리와 여타 다른 물질의 첨가로 바뀔 수 있다는 것이 발견되었다.

➡ 앞 문장의 '기술 발견'에 이어서 뒤 문장에서 '물질의 특성이 바뀔 수 있다'라는 추가적인 발견을 언급하는 흐름이다.
　▶ 주어진 문장이 ②에 들어갈 수 없음

- **③의 앞 문장과 뒤 문장**

> **앞 문장:** ②의 뒤 문장과 같음
> **뒤 문장:** 이 시기에(At this point), 물질 이용은 주어진 상당히 제한된 물질 집합 중에서 물질의 특성에 근거하여 용도에 가장 적합한 물질을 결정하는 것을 수반하는 전적으로 선택의 과정이었다. **단서1**

➡ 앞 문장에 나타난 '물질의 특성이 바뀔 수 있음을 발견한' 시기를 뒤 문장에서 At this point로 지칭하고 있다. 이 시기에 물질의 이용이 가장 적합한 물질을 결정하는 '선택의 과정'이었다고 했다.
　▶ 주어진 문장이 ③에 들어갈 수 없음

- **④의 앞 문장과 뒤 문장**

> **앞 문장:** ③의 뒤 문장과 같음
> **뒤 문장:** 대략 지난 100년 동안 획득된 이 지식(This knowledge)으로 그들은 상당한 정도로 물질의 특성을 형성할 수 있게 되었다. **단서2**

➡ **뒤 문장:** 이 지식으로 물질의 특성을 형성할 수 있게 되었다.
　this knowledge가 무엇인지 앞에 나와야 한다.
➡ 주어진 문장에서 비교적 최근에 이르러서야 과학자들이 물질의 구조적 요소와 특성의 관계를 이해하게 되었다고 했으므로, 그러한 이해가 this knowledge와 대응한다. 따라서, 과학자들이 지난 100년 동안 획득된 물질 구조 및 특성의 관계에 대한 지식으로 물질의 특성을 형성할 수 있게 되었다는 흐름으로 앞뒤 문장이 연결된다.
　▶ 주어진 문장이 ④에 들어가야 함

- **⑤의 앞 문장과 뒤 문장**

> **앞 문장:** ④의 뒤 문장과 같음
> **뒤 문장:** 따라서 금속, 플라스틱, 유리, 섬유를 포함하여, 현대적이고 복잡한 우리 사회의 요구를 충족하는 상당히 특화된 특성을 가진 수만 가지의 다양한 물질이 발전했다.

➡ 앞 내용을 종합하며 뒤 문장에서 '현대에는 다양한 물질이 발전했다'라는 결론을 제시했다.
　▶ 주어진 문장이 ⑤에 들어갈 수 없음

3rd 글이 한눈에 들어오도록 정리하여 정답을 확인한다.

초기 인류는 자연 물질에만 접근할 수 있었다.
(①) 시간이 흐르면서 더 우수한 특성을 가진 물질을 만들어내는 기술을 발견했다.
(②) 게다가 물질의 특성이 바뀔 수 있다는 것이 발견되었다.
(③) 이 시기에 물질 이용은 가장 적합한 물질을 결정하는 선택의 과정이었다.
(④ 최근에 이르러서야 과학자들이 물질의 구조적 요소와 특성 사이의 관계를 이해하게 되었다.)
대략 지난 100년 동안 획득된 이 지식으로 그들은 물질의 특성을 형성할 수 있게 되었다.
(⑤) 따라서 우리 사회의 요구를 충족하는 특화된 특성을 가진 여러 물질이 발전했다.

* 기억의 편향 및 왜곡이 뉴스에 대한 반응에 미치는 영향

글의 흐름으로 보아, 주어진 문장이 들어가기에 가장 적절한 곳을 고르시오.
[3점]

> **단서 1** 뉴스 기사에 대한 기억들이 불완전하고 왜곡되었을 경우를 가정함
> But what if memories about news stories are faulty / and distort, forget, or invent what was actually reported? //
> 하지만 만약 뉴스 기사에 대한 기억들이 불완전하고 / 실제로 보도되었던 것을 왜곡하거나, 빠뜨리거나, (사실이 아닌 것으로) 지어낸다면 어떠한가 //

Memory often plays tricks. // 기억은 흔히 속임수를 쓴다 //

(①) According to Mlodinow, we give "unwarranted importance to memories / **that** are the most vivid and hence most available for retrieval /
　　　　　　주격 관계대명사
Mlodinow에 따르면, 우리는 '기억들에 부당한 중요성을 부여한다 / 가장 생생하고, 따라서 불러오기에 가장 용이한 /
　　　　사역동사+목적어+목적격 보어(형용사)
— our memory makes **it** easy to remember / the events that are unusual and striking / not the many events that are normal and dull." //
우리의 기억은 기억하는 것을 쉽게 만든다 / 색다르고 인상적인 사건들을 / 평범하고 지루한 많은 사건들이 아니라' //

(②) The self-serving bias works / because, as Trivers observes, "There are also many processes of memory / that can be biased to produce welcome results. / Memories are continually distorting in self-serving ways." //
자기 잇속만 차리는 편향이 작용하는데 / Trivers가 논평하듯이, '많은 기억의 과정들이 또한 있으며 / 기꺼이 받아들여지는 결과를 산출하도록 편향될 수 있는 / 기억들은 계속해서 자기 잇속만 차리는 방식으로 왜곡되고 있기' 때문이다 //
　　　　　목적어절을 이끄는 접속사
(③) A recent study argues / **that** several forms of cognitive bias cause distortions / in storing and retrieving memories. //
최근 한 연구는 주장한다 / 인지적인 편향의 몇몇 형태가 왜곡을 일으킨다고 / 기억들을 저장하고 불러오는 데 // **단서 2** 인지적 편향의 몇몇 형태가 기억을 저장하고 불러오는 데 왜곡을 일으킴

(④) This, in turn, has a bearing / on theories of agenda setting, priming, and framing, /
이것은, 결국, 영향을 미치는데 / 의제를 정하고, 준비하고, 구성하는 이론들에 /
　주격 관계대명사
which argue that how people respond to the news / is strongly influenced by what is most easily and readily accessible from their memories. //
이것들은 어떻게 사람들이 뉴스에 반응하는가가 / 그들의 기억들로부터 가장 쉽게 그리고 즉시 접근 가능한 것에 의해 강력하게 영향을 받는다고 주장한다 //
단서 3 그런 경우(뉴스 자체가 왜곡된 것이 아니라 기억이 왜곡된 경우, 즉 주어진 문장) 원래 뉴스 기사가 아니라 개인의 머릿속 기억의 조작일 수도 있음
(⑤) In such cases, / it may be the manipulation of memories in individual minds / **that** primes, frames, and sets the agenda, /
　　　　　　　　　주격 관계대명사
not the original news stories. //
그러한 경우에는 / 개인의 머릿속 기억들의 조작일 수도 있다 / 의제를 준비하고, 구성하고, 정하는 것은 / 원래의 뉴스 기사가 아니라 //

- faulty ⓐ 불완전한　　· distort ⓥ 왜곡하다
- unwarranted ⓐ 부당한　　· vivid ⓐ 생생한　　· unusual ⓐ 특이한
- bias ⓝ 편견 ⓥ 편견을 갖게 하다　　· self-serving ⓐ 자기 잇속만 차리는
- cognitive ⓐ 인지적인　　· agenda ⓝ 의제　　· prime ⓥ 준비하다
- readily 〔ad〕 손쉽게　　· manipulation ⓝ 조작

기억은 흔히 속임수를 쓴다. (①) Mlodinow에 따르면, 우리는 '가장 생생하고, 따라서 불러오기에 가장 용이한 기억들에 부당한 중요성'을 부여한다. '우리의 기억은 평범하고 지루한 많은 사건들이 아니라, 색다르고 인상적인 사건들을 기억하는 것을 쉽게 만든다.' (②) 자기 잇속만 차리는

편향이 작용하는데, Trivers가 논평하듯이, '기꺼이 받아들여지는 결과를 산출하도록 편향될 수 있는 많은 기억의 과정들이 또한 있으며, 기억들은 계속해서 자기 잇속만 차리는 방식으로 왜곡되고 있기' 때문이다. (③) 최근 한 연구는 인지적인 편향의 몇몇 형태가 기억들을 저장하고 불러오는 데 왜곡을 일으킨다고 주장한다. (④) 이것은, 결국, 의제를 정하고, 준비하고, 구성하는 이론들에 영향을 미치는데, 이것들은 어떻게 사람들이 뉴스에 반응하는가가 그들의 기억들로부터 가장 쉽게 그리고 즉시 접근 가능한 것에 의해 강력하게 영향을 받는다고 주장한다. (⑤) 하지만 만약 뉴스 기사에 대한 기억들이 불완전하고, 실제로 보도되었던 것을 왜곡하거나, 빠뜨리거나, (사실이 아닌 것으로) 지어낸다면 어떠한가? 그러한 경우에는, 의제를 준비하고, 구성하고, 정하는 것은 원래의 뉴스 기사가 아니라 개인의 머릿속 기억들의 조작일 수도 있다.

왜 1등급 **?** '인지적 편향'이라는 다소 어려운 용어가 등장하므로 글의 전체적인 내용을 잘 이해해야 한다. **단서** But, This, In such cases와 같은 연결어나 지시어를 이용해 문장들의 순서를 유기적으로 파악해야 정답을 찾을 수 있을 것이다. **발상**

| 문제 풀이 순서 |

1st 주어진 문장을 해석하고, 연결어, 지시어 등을 확인한다.

> **But** what if memories about news stories are faulty and distort, forget, or invent what was actually reported? **단서 1**
> 하지만 만약 뉴스 기사에 대한 기억들이 불완전하고, 실제로 보도되었던 것을 왜곡하거나, 빠뜨리거나, (사실이 아닌 것으로) 지어낸다면 어떠한가?

➡ 뉴스 기사가 아닌, 뉴스 기사에 대한 기억들이 불완전하다면 어떠한지 의문을 던지고 있다. **단서**
　▶ **주어진 문장 앞**: 뉴스 기사에 대한 언급이 있어야 함
　▶ **주어진 문장 뒤**: 뉴스 기사가 아닌, 이에 대한 기억이 왜곡된 경우 어떠한지에 대한 답이 나와야 함 **발상**

2nd 각 선택지의 앞뒤 흐름이 매끄러운지 확인한다.

- **①의 앞 문장과 뒤 문장**
　앞 문장: 기억은 흔히 속임수를 쓴다.
　뒤 문장: Mlodinow에 따르면, 우리는 '가장 생생하고, 따라서 불러오기에 가장 용이한 기억들에 부당한 중요성'을 부여한다. '우리의 기억은 평범하고 지루한 많은 사건들이 아니라, 색다르고 인상적인 사건들을 기억하는 것을 쉽게 만든다.'
➡ 앞 문장에서 기억은 속임수를 쓴다고 했으며, 뒤 문장에서는 어떤 식으로 속임수를 쓰는지(평범한 많은 사건들이 아닌, 색다르고 인상적인 사건을 더 쉽게 기억하며, 이런 기억에 부당한 중요성을 부여함) 설명하고 있기에 두 문장은 자연스럽게 연결된다.
　▶ 주어진 문장이 ①에 들어갈 수 없음

- **②의 앞 문장과 뒤 문장**
　앞 문장: ①의 뒤 문장과 같음
　뒤 문장: 자기 잇속만 차리는 편향(the self-serving bias)이 작용하는데, Trivers가 논평하듯이, '기꺼이 받아들여지는 결과를 산출하도록 편향될 수 있는 많은 기억의 과정들이 또한 있으며, 기억들은 계속해서 자기 잇속만 차리는 방식으로 왜곡되고 있기' 때문이다.
➡ 앞 문장의 내용은 인상깊은 기억만 쉽게 기억하는 왜곡 현상을 설명하고 있고, 뒤 문장에서는 이를 '자기 잇속만 차리는 편향(the self-serving bias)'이라고 부르며 기억은 편향되며 왜곡되고 있다는 추가 설명을 하고 있다. 따라서 두 문장은 자연스럽게 연결된다.
　▶ 주어진 문장이 ②에 들어갈 수 없음

┌ **앞 문장:** ②의 뒤 문장과 같음

│ **뒤 문장:** 최근 한 연구는 인지적인 편향의 몇몇 형태가 기억들을 저장하고
└ 불러오는 데 왜곡을 일으킨다고 주장한다.

⇒ 앞에서는 기억의 편향과 왜곡에 대한 설명을 하고 있고, 뒤에서는 인지적 편향이
기억의 왜곡을 일으킨다는 최근 연구를 소개하고 있기에 두 문장은 자연스럽게
이어진다.

　▶ 주어진 문장이 ③에 들어갈 수 없음

- ④의 앞 문장과 뒤 문장

┌ **앞 문장:** ③의 뒤 문장과 같음

│ **뒤 문장:** 이것은(This), 결국, 의제를 정하고, 준비하고, 구성하는 이론들에
│ 영향을 미치는데, 이것들은 어떻게 사람들이 뉴스에 반응하는가가 그들의
│ 기억들로부터 가장 쉽게 그리고 즉시 접근 가능한 것에 의해 강력하게
└ 영향을 받는다고 주장한다.

⇒ 앞 문장에서는 인지적 편향의 몇몇 형태가 기억의 왜곡을 일으킨다는 최근 연구를
소개했고, 뒤 문장에서는 이것이 의제를 정하고 준비하고 구성하는 이론에 영향을
미치며, 이런 이론들은 사람들의 뉴스에 대한 반응이 기억 중 쉽고 즉시 접근 가능한
것에 의해 강하게 영향을 받는다고 주장한다.
　반응이 여러 기억 중 쉽고 접근 가능한 것에 의해서 강하게 영향을 받는다는 것은 앞
문장의 인지적 편향이 기억의 왜곡을 일으킨다는 내용과 자연스럽게 이어진다.

　▶ 주어진 문장이 ④에 들어갈 수 없음

- ⑤의 앞 문장과 뒤 문장

┌ **앞 문장:** ④의 뒤 문장과 같음

│ **뒤 문장:** 그러한 경우에는(In such cases), 의제를 준비하고, 구성하고,
│ 정하는 것은 원래의 뉴스 기사가 아니라 개인의 머릿속 기억들의 조작일
└ 수도 있다.

⇒ 앞에서는 사람들이 뉴스에 반응하는 방식이 여러 기억들 중 가장 쉽고 즉시 접근
가능한 것에 의해 강력하게 영향을 받는다는 현상을 언급했다. 뒤에서는 '그런 경우'
뉴스 기사가 아니라 개인 기억의 조작이라고 했으나, 앞 문장에서 '그런 경우'에
해당하는 내용은 없다.
　주어진 문장은 뉴스 기사에 대한 기억이 불완전하고, 실제 보도된 것을 (기억에서)
왜곡하거나 지어낸다는 상황에 대한 내용이므로 ⑤에 들어가야 한다.

　▶ 주어진 문장이 ⑤에 들어가야 함

3rd 글이 한눈에 들어오도록 정리하여 정답을 확인한다.

기억은 속임수를 쓴다.
(①) 여러 사건 중 인상적인 사건들을 위주로 기억하게 된다.
(②) 기억에는 편향이 작용하며, 왜곡되고 있다.
(③) 최근 한 연구는 인지적 편향 중 일부가 기억의 왜곡을 일으킨다고 주장한다.
(④) 이것은 의제를 정하고 구성하는 이론에 영향을 미치며, 이런 이론들은 사람들이
뉴스에 반응하는 방식이 일부의 기억에만 강한 영향을 받는다고 주장한다.
(⑤ 하지만 만약 뉴스 기사에 대한 기억이 불완전하다면 어떠한가?)
그런 경우는 뉴스 기사가 아닌 개인 기억의 왜곡일 수 있다.

---

* 살라미 전술

> 글의 흐름으로 보아, 주어진 문장이 들어가기에 가장 적절한 곳을
> 고르시오. [3점]

It may be easier / to reach an agreement / when settlement
terms don't have to be implemented / until months in the
future. // not have to는 〈불필요〉 **단서 1** 당사자들이 시간 지평을 사용하는 사례임
must not은 〈금지〉
~이 더 쉬울 수 있다 / 합의에 도달하는 것이 / 합의 조건이 이행될 필요가 없을 때 / 향후
몇 개월까지 //

형용사적 용법(ways 수식)
Negotiators should try to find ways / to slice a large issue / into
smaller pieces, / known as using *salami tactics*. //
협상가들은 방법을 찾으려고 노력해야 한다 / 큰 문제를 나누는 / 더 작은 조각으로 / '살라미
전술'을 사용하는 것으로 알려진 //
복수 주어
(①) Issues / that can be expressed / in quantitative, measurable
복수 동사
units / are easy to slice. //
문제는 / 표현될 수 있는 / 양적이고 측정 가능한 단위로 / 나누기 쉽다 //
(②) For example, / compensation demands can be divided /
into cents-per-hour increments / or lease rates can be quoted / as
두 개의 절을 연결하는 등위접속사
dollars per square foot. //
예를 들어 / 보상 요구는 나뉠 수 있다 / 시간당 센트 증가로 / 또는 임대료는 시세가 매겨질
수 있다 / 평방 피트당 달러로 //
(③) When working / to fractionate issues of principle or
precedent, / ★분사구문에서 접속사가 생략되지 않음
작업을 할 때 / 원칙이나 관례의 쟁점을 세분화하기 위해 /
parties may use the time horizon /
당사자들은 시간 지평을 사용할 수 있다 /
go into effect: 효력이 발생하다
(when the principle goes into effect /
(원칙이 효력을 발휘하는 때 / **단서 2** '원칙이 효력을
or how long it will last） / 발휘하는 때'의 예시가
또는 그것이 얼마나 오래 지속될지) / '합의 조건이 이행되어야
형용사적 용법(a way 수식) 하는 시기'임
as a way / to fractionate the issue. //
방법으로 / 그 쟁점을 세분화하는 //
선행사 관계부사
(④) Another approach / is to vary the number of ways / that the
명사적 용법(주격 보어) ★
principle may be applied. //
또 다른 접근법은 / 방법의 수를 다양화하는 것이다 / 원칙이 적용될 수 있는 //
(⑤) For example, / a company may devise / a family emergency
leave plan / that allows employees the opportunity / to be away
from the company / allows의 간접목적어와 직접목적어 형용사적 용법
(the opportunity 수식)
예를 들어 / 회사는 고안할 수 있다 / 가족 비상 휴가 계획을 / 직원에게 기회를 제공하는 /
회사를 떠나있을 /
for a period / of no longer than three hours, / and no more
than once a month, / for illness / in the employee's immediate
family. //
기간 동안 / 세 시간 이내의 / 그리고 한 달에 한 번 이내의 / 질병에 대해 / 직원의 직계
가족의 //

- settlement ⓝ 합의 · implement ⓥ 이행하다
- negotiator ⓝ 협상가 · slice ⓥ 나누다, 자르다
- quantitative ⓐ 양적인 · measurable ⓐ 측정 가능한
- compensation ⓝ 보상 · lease ⓝ 임대차 계약 · rate ⓝ 요금, -료
- quote ⓥ 시세를 매기다, 인용하다 · precedent ⓝ 관례, 전례
- party ⓝ (계약 등의) 당사자 · vary ⓥ 달리 하다, 변화를 주다
- devise ⓥ 고안하다 · immediate ⓐ 가장 가까운, 직계의

　협상가들은 '살라미 전술'을 사용하는 것으로 알려진, 큰 문제를 더 작은
조각으로 나누는 방법을 찾으려고 노력해야 한다. (①) 양적이고 측정 가능한
단위로 표현될 수 있는 문제는 나누기 쉽다. (②) 예를 들어, 보상 요구는
시간당 센트 증가로 나누거나 임대료는 평방 피트당 달러로 시세를 매길 수
있다.

(③) 원칙이나 관례의 쟁점을 세분화하는 작업을 할 때, 당사자들은 그 쟁점을 세분화하는 방법으로 시간 지평(원칙이 효력을 발휘할 때 또는 그것이 얼마나 오래 지속되는지)을 사용할 수 있다. (④ 합의 조건이 향후 몇 개월까지 이행될 필요가 없을 때 합의에 도달하는 것이 더 쉬울 수 있다.) 또 다른 접근법은 원칙이 적용될 수 있는 방법의 수를 다양화하는 것이다. (⑤) 예를 들어, 회사는 직원의 직계 가족의 질병에 대해 직원에게 세 시간 이내, 한 달에 한 번 이내의 기간 동안 회사를 떠나있을 기회를 제공하는 가족 비상 휴가 계획을 고안할 수 있다.

오왜 **1등급 ?** '살라미 전술'이라는 생소한 소재를 다루고, 전반적으로 어휘 수준이 높다. **단서** 살라미 전술의 여러 방법 중에서 주어진 문장이 어떤 방법에 해당하는 예시인지 파악해야 정답을 찾을 수 있을 것이다. **발상**

| 문제 풀이 순서 |

1st 주어진 문장을 해석하고, 연결어, 지시어 등을 확인한다.

> It may be easier to reach an agreement when settlement terms don't have to be implemented until months in the future. **단서1**
> 합의 조건이 향후 몇 개월까지 이행될 필요가 없을 때 합의에 도달하는 것이 더 쉬울 수 있다.

➡ 합의 조건에 관한 내용이 앞에 나오고 그 뒤에 주어진 문장을 넣어야 한다.
➡ 합의에 도달하는 과정에 관한 내용이 이어질 것이다.

2nd 각 선택지의 앞뒤 흐름이 매끄러운지 확인한다.

- ①의 앞 문장과 뒤 문장

> **앞 문장:** 협상가들은 '살라미 전술'을 사용하는 것으로 알려진, 큰 문제를 더 작은 조각으로 나누는 방법을 찾으려고 노력해야 한다.
> **뒤 문장:** 양적이고 측정 가능한 단위로 표현될 수 있는 문제는 나누기 쉽다.

➡ **앞 문장:** 협상가들은 살라미 전술의 방법을 찾으려고 노력해야 한다.
뒤 문장: 양적인 문제는 나누기 쉽다.
앞 문장에서 '살라미 전술'을 소개하며 뒤 문장에서는 살라미 전술 중 하나의 경우로서 양적인 문제를 나누는 경우를 언급하는 흐름이다.
▶ 주어진 문장이 ①에 들어갈 수 없음

- ②의 앞 문장과 뒤 문장

> **앞 문장:** ①의 뒤 문장과 같음
> **뒤 문장:** 예를 들어, 보상 요구는 시간당 센트 증가로 나누거나 임대료는 평방 피트당 달러로 시세를 매길 수 있다.

➡ 앞 문장의 '양적인 문제를 나누는 것'에 대해 뒤 문장에서 예를 들어 설명하는 흐름이다.
▶ 주어진 문장이 ②에 들어갈 수 없음

- ③의 앞 문장과 뒤 문장

> **앞 문장:** ②의 뒤 문장과 같음
> **뒤 문장:** 원칙이나 관례의 쟁점을 세분화하는 작업을 할 때, 당사자들은 그 쟁점을 세분화하는 방법으로 시간 지평(원칙이 효력을 발휘할 때 또는 그것이 얼마나 오래 지속되는지)을 사용할 수 있다. **단서2**

➡ 앞 문장의 예시에 이어서 뒤 문장에서는 '시간 지평'을 사용한다는 새로운 방법을 언급하는 흐름이다.
▶ 주어진 문장이 ③에 들어갈 수 없음

- ④의 앞 문장과 뒤 문장

> **앞 문장:** ③의 뒤 문장과 같음
> **뒤 문장:** 또 다른 접근법은 원칙이 적용될 수 있는 방법의 수를 다양화하는 것이다.

➡ **뒤 문장:** 또 다른 접근법인 원칙 적용 방법의 다양화
Another approach가 나오므로 양적인 문제를 나누는 경우, 시간 지평을 사용하는 경우와 더불어 또 다른 접근법을 제시하는 것이다.
➡ 주어진 문장은 합의 조건의 이행 기간에 관한 내용이다. 이는 시간 지평의 예시이므로 ③의 뒤 문장에 이어지는 것이 자연스럽다.
▶ 주어진 문장이 ④에 들어가야 함

- ⑤의 앞 문장과 뒤 문장

> **앞 문장:** ④의 뒤 문장과 같음
> **뒤 문장:** 예를 들어, 회사는 직원의 직계 가족의 질병에 대해 직원에게 세 시간 이내, 한 달에 한 번 이내의 기간 동안 회사를 떠나있을 기회를 제공하는 가족 비상 휴가 계획을 고안할 수 있다.

➡ 앞 문장의 '원칙이 적용될 수 있는 방법의 다양화'에 관하여 뒤 문장에서 예시로 부연하는 흐름이다. ▶ 주어진 문장이 ⑤에 들어갈 수 없음

3rd 글이 한눈에 들어오도록 정리하여 정답을 확인한다.

협상가들은 살라미 전술의 방법을 찾으려고 노력해야 한다.
(①) 양적인 문제는 나누기 쉽다.
(②) 양적 문제의 예시로서 예를 들어 보상 요구나 임대료가 있다.
(③) 원칙이나 관례의 쟁점을 세분화하는 작업에는 시간 지평을 사용할 수 있다.
(④ 합의 조건이 향후 몇 개월까지 이행될 필요가 없을 때 합의 도달이 더 쉬울 수 있다.)
또 다른 접근법은 원칙이 적용될 수 있는 방법을 다양화하는 것이다.
(⑤) 그 예시로서 회사가 직원의 직계 가족의 질병에 대해 가족 비상 휴가 계획을 고안하는 것이 있다.

권주원 | 서울대 정치외교학부 2023년 입학·서울 배재고 졸
문장 넣기 유형에서 가장 중요한 것은 문장이 들어갈 자리에 대한 단서가 되는 단어들을 찾는 거야. 먼저 주어진 문장에 시간과 관련된 months라는 단어, 지문에는 time horizon이라는 표현이 등장해. 그래서 나는 time horizon이 등장하는 문장과 그 앞뒤에 주목했어.
그런데 ④의 뒤 문장을 보니 Another approach로 시작해서 시간과는 다른 이야기를 하고 있더라고. 그래서 ④에 주어진 문장이 들어가야 흐름이 적절하겠다는 생각을 했고, 주어진 문장을 넣고 글을 빠르게 읽어 보니까 흐름이 자연스러웠어.

━━━━━━━━━ 어법 특강
＊ 명사적 용법의 to부정사

－ 명사적 용법의 to부정사 : ～하기, ～하는 것
① 주어
• To talk is easier than to act. (말하는 것은 행동하는 것보다 쉽다.)
② 목적어
• She likes to eat junk food. (그녀는 정크푸드를 먹는 것을 좋아한다.)
③ 보어
• His only weak point is to talk too much.
(그의 유일한 단점은 말을 너무 많이 한다는 것이다.)
• I didn't expect you to understand.
(난 네가 이해할 거라고 예상하지 않았다.)

N 어휘 Review 정답

01 옹호자	11 in turn	21 optimally
02 정량적인	12 a basis for	22 implementing
03 현대의	13 run out of	23 inevitably
04 함축, 암시	14 in other words	24 shelter
05 상대적인	15 in principle	25 suspicious
06 demonstrate	16 voluntary	26 immature
07 compound	17 reliability	27 constitute
08 pest	18 comprehension	28 pad
09 approval	19 biological	29 empowered
10 inclination	20 beforehand	

O 요약문 완성하기

O 01 정답 ② ＊기근 예방을 위한 공적 개입의 역할과 필요성

단서 1 비상사태가 진정되면, 주로 경제 성장의 관점에서 기근 문제를 해결하고자 하는 경향이 있음(통념)
There is a tendency, / once the dust of an emergency has settled down, /
~하는 경향이 있다 / 일단 비상사태의 소요가 진정되고 나면 /
to seek the reduction of famine vulnerability / primarily in enhanced economic growth, / or the revival of the rural economy, / or the diversification of economic activities. //
기근 취약성 감소를 모색하는 / 주로 강화된 경제 성장이나 / 지방 경제의 회복 / 혹은 경제 활동의 다각화에서 //

단서 2 경제적 성공의 효과도 부인할 수는 없음
The potential contribution of greater economic success, / if it involves vulnerable groups, / cannot be denied. //
더 큰 경제적 성공의 잠재적 기여는 / 만약 그것이 취약 계층에 영향을 미친다면 / 부인할 수 없다 //

At the same time, / it is important to recognize that, / no matter how fast they grow, / countries where a large part of the population derive their livelihood from uncertain sources /
그와 동시에 / 인식하는 것이 중요하다 / 아무리 빠르게 성장하더라도 / 인구의 상당수가 그들의 생계를 불확실한 원천으로부터 마련하는 국가는 /
cannot hope to prevent famines / without specialized entitlement protection mechanisms / involving direct public intervention. //
기근 예방을 기대할 수 없다는 점을 / 특화된 재정 지원 혜택의 보호 방법 없이는 / 직접적인 공적 개입을 포함하는 //

단서 3 아무리 경제가 빨리 성장하더라도, 기근 예방을 위해서는 직접적인 공적 개입을 포함하는 기근에 특화된 재정 지원 혜택이 있어야 함
Rapid growth of the economy in Botswana, / or of the agricultural sector in Kenya, / or of food production in Zimbabwe, / explains at best only a small part of their success / in preventing recurrent threats of famine. //
부츠와나의 경제 / 케냐의 농업 부문 / 혹은 짐바브웨의 식량 생산의 급속한 성장은 / 기껏해야 그들이 성공한 작은 일부분만을 설명할 뿐이다 / 기근의 반복되는 위험을 방지하는 데 있어 /

The real achievements of these countries / lie in having provided direct public support / to their populations in times of crisis. //
이들 국가의 진정한 성과는 / 직접적인 공적 지원을 제공했었다는 것에 있다 / 위기 상황에서 국민들에게 //

단서 4 기근의 위기 상황에서 국민들에게 직접적인 공적 지원을 제공했던 것이 진정한 성과임을 보여준 국가들이 있음 (예시를 통한 부연 설명)

→ Although economic growth can be somewhat (A) **fruitful** / in diminishing a country's risk of famine, / direct approaches to helping the affected people / play a(n) (B) **critical** role in this process. //
비록 경제 성장이 어느 정도 효과적일 수 있지만 / 한 국가의 기근 위험을 줄이는 데 / 피해를 입은 사람들을 돕는 것에 대한 직접적인 접근이 / 이 과정에서 중요한 역할을 한다 //

- tendency ⓝ 경향
- dust ⓝ 소란, 소동
- emergency ⓝ 비상사태
- settle down 진정되다
- vulnerability ⓝ 취약성
- primarily ⓐⓓ 주로
- enhanced ⓐ 강화된
- revival ⓝ 회복, 부흥
- rural ⓐ 지방의, 시골의
- diversification ⓝ 다각화, 다양화
- potential ⓐ 잠재적인
- derive ~ from … ~을 …로부터 끌어내다, 얻다
- livelihood ⓝ 생계
- entitlement ⓝ 재정 지원 혜택
- mechanism ⓝ 방법, 메커니즘
- intervention ⓝ 개입
- sector ⓝ 부분, 분야
- at best 기껏해야
- recurrent ⓐ 반복되는
- crisis ⓝ 위기
- complicated ⓐ 복잡한
- fruitful ⓐ 생산적인, 효과적인
- dominant ⓐ 우세한
- restrictive ⓐ 제한적인

주어진 문장에 있는 결정적인 단서를 찾자!

일단 비상사태의 소요가 진정되고 나면, 주로 강화된 경제 성장이나 지방 경제의 회복, 혹은 경제 활동의 다각화에서 기근 취약성 감소를 모색하는 경향이 있다. 더 큰 경제적 성공의 잠재적 기여는, 만약 그것이 취약 계층에 영향을 미친다면, 부인할 수 없다. 그와 동시에, 아무리 빠르게 성장하더라도, 인구의 상당수가 그들의 생계를 불확실한 원천으로부터 마련하는 국가는 직접적인 공적 개입을 포함하는 특화된 재정 지원 혜택의 보호 방법 없이는 기근 예방을 기대할 수 없다는 점을 인식하는 것이 중요하다. 보츠와나의 경제, 케냐의 농업 부문, 혹은 짐바브웨의 식량 생산의 급속한 성장은 기껏해야 기근의 반복되는 위협을 방지하는 데 있어 그들이 성공한 작은 일부분을 설명할 뿐이다. 이들 국가의 진정한 성과는 위기 상황에서 국민들에게 직접적인 공적 지원을 제공했다는 데 있다.

→ 비록 경제 성장이 한 국가의 기근 위험을 줄이는 데 어느 정도 (A) **효과적일** 수 있지만, 피해를 입은 사람들을 돕는 것에 대한 직접적인 접근이 이 과정에서 (B) **중요한** 역할을 한다.

다음 글의 내용을 한 문장으로 요약하고자 한다. 빈칸 (A), (B)에 들어갈 말로 가장 적절한 것은?

	(A)		(B)	
①	productive 생산적인	—	complicated 복잡한	피해를 입은 사람을 직접 돕는 것이 복잡하다는 내용은 없음
②	fruitful 효과적인	—	critical 중요한	경제 성장도 일부 효과적일 수 있지만, 피해를 입은 사람들을 직접적으로 돕는 것이 중요하다는 내용
③	dominant 우세한	—	comprehensive 포괄적인	기근으로 피해를 입은 사람을 직접 공적으로 돕는 것은 포괄적이기보다는 세부적인 정책임
④	restrictive 제한적인	—	appropriate 적절한	경제 성장이 기근 위험을 줄이는 데 도움이 되지 않는다는 것은 글의 내용과 반대임
⑤	desirable 바람직한	—	cost-effective 비용 효율이 높은	기근 피해자를 직접 돕는 것이 비용 대비 효율이 높은지는 언급되어 있지 않음

왜 정답? [정답률 43%]

(A):
- 더 큰 경제 성장이 기근 취약계층에게도 도움을 줄 수 있다면 기근 위험을 줄이는 데 효과는 일부 인정할 수 있음

➡ 경제 성장의 관점에서 기근 문제를 해결하는 것은 '효과적'일 수 있다.

(B):
- 경제 성장이 아무리 빠르더라도, 기근을 겪는 사람들에게 특화된 국가의 직접적 지원은 필수임
- 보츠와나, 케냐, 짐바브웨등의 사례: 이 국가들은 국민들에게 직접적인 공적 지원을 제공했던 것이 진정한 성과임

➡ 국가가 직접적인 개입으로 기근 피해자에 특화된 지원을 하는 것은 예시로 든 국가들에서 알 수 있듯이, '중요한' 역할을 한다.
  ▶ 요약문의 빈칸에는 각각 '효과적인'과 '중요한'이 들어가야 하므로 정답은 ②임

왜 오답?
① 피해를 입은 사람을 직접 돕는 것이 복잡하다는 언급은 없다.
③ 기근으로 피해를 입은 사람을 직접 공적으로 돕는 것은 포괄적이기보다는 세부적인 정책이다.
④ 제한적이라는 말은 부정적 의미를 포함하므로, 경제 성장이 기근 위험을 줄이는 데 도움이 되지 않는다는 것은 글의 내용과 반대이다.
⑤ 기근 피해자를 직접 돕는 것이 비용 대비 효율이 높은지는 언급되어 있지 않다.

＊ 글의 흐름

통념	일단 비상사태가 진정되면, 주로 경제 성장의 관점에서 기근 문제를 해결하고자 하는 경향이 있고, 물론 경제적 성공의 효과도 부인할 수는 없음
주제	아무리 경제가 빨리 성장하더라도, 기근 예방을 위해서는 직접적인 공적 개입을 포함하는 기근에 특화된 재정 지원 혜택이 있어야 함
예시	기근의 위기 상황에서 예시로 든 국가들이 국민들에게 직접적인 공적 지원을 제공했던 것이 진정한 성과임

◎ 02 정답 ② ＊생존 특성의 두 가지 측면

The evolutionary process works / on the genetic variation / that is available. //
진화 과정은 작용한다 / 유전적 변이에 / 이용 가능한 //

It follows / that natural selection is unlikely to lead / to the evolution / of perfect, 'maximally fit' individuals. //
가주어 / 진주어절 접속사
~이 이어진다 / 자연 선택이 이어질 가능성은 작다는 것이 / 진화로 / 완벽하고 '최대로 적합한' 개체의 //

Rather, / organisms come to match their environments / by being 'the fittest available' or 'the fittest yet': / they are not 'the best imaginable'. //
단서 1 생물체의 특성이 현재의 환경과 모든 면에서 유사한 환경에서 유래하지 않기 때문에 적합성 결여가 발생함
그보다 / 생물체는 그것의 환경에 맞춰지게 된다 / '가능한 가장 적합한' 또는 '아직은 가장 적합한' 상태임으로써 / 그들이 '상상할 수 있는 가장 좋은 것'은 아니다 //
단수 주어 / 단수 동사 / 복수 주어

Part of the lack of fit arises / because the present properties of an organism / have not all originated / in an environment / similar in every respect / to the one / in which it now lives. //
복수 동사 / = environment 관계부사 where로 바꾸어 쓸 수 있음
적합성 결여의 일부는 발생한다 / 생물체가 가진 현재의 특성이 / 모두 유래한 것이 아니기 때문에 / 환경에서 / 모든 면에서 유사한 / 환경과 / 그 생물체가 현재 살고 있는 //

Over the course of its evolutionary history, / an organism's remote ancestors / may have evolved a set of characteristics / — evolutionary 'baggage' — / that subsequently constrain future evolution. //
과거 사실에 대한 불확실한 추측: may have p.p.
진화 역사의 과정에서 / 생물체의 먼 조상들은 / 일련의 특성들을 진화시켰을 수도 있다 / 진화적 '짐' / 후속적으로 미래의 진화를 제약하는 //
단서 2 생물체의 과거 조상은 현재 생물체에게 짐이 될 수도 있는 특성을 진화시켰을 수도 있음

For many millions of years, / the evolution of vertebrates has been limited / to what can be achieved / by organisms with a vertebral column. //
단수 주어 / 단수 동사
수백만 년 동안 / 척추동물의 진화는 제한되어 왔다 / 달성될 수 있는 것으로 / 척추를 가진 생물체에 의해 //

Moreover, / much of what we now see / as precise matches / between an organism and its environment / may equally be seen / as constraints: /
주어 / 동사
게다가 / 현재 우리가 보는 것의 대부분은 / 정확한 일치로 / 생물체와 그 환경 간의 / 똑같이 보일 수 있다 / 제약으로도 /

koala bears live successfully / on *Eucalyptus* foliage, / but, from another perspective, / koala bears cannot live / without *Eucalyptus* foliage. //
코알라는 성공적으로 생활하지만 / 유칼립투스 잎으로 / 다른 관점에서는 / 코알라는 살 수 없다 / 유칼립투스 잎 없이는 //

→ The survival characteristics / that an organism currently carries / may act as a(n) (A) **obstacle** / to its adaptability / when the organism finds itself / coping with changes / that arise in its (B) **surroundings**. //
주어 / 동사 / 주격 관계대명사절의 복수 동사 / 복수 선행사
생존 특성은 / 한 생물체가 현재 가지고 있는 / 장애물이 될 수 있다 / 그것의 적응성에 / 그 생물체가 스스로를 발견할 때 / 변화에 대처하는 / 그것의 환경에서 발생하는 //

- **evolutionary** ⓐ 진화의, 점진적인   • **variation** ⓝ 변이
- **arise** ⓥ 발생하다   • **property** ⓝ 특성
- **originate** ⓥ 비롯되다, 발생하다   • **respect** ⓝ 측면
- **remote** ⓐ 외진, 먼   • **evolve** ⓥ 진화하다
- **subsequently** ⓐⓓ 그 뒤에, 나중에   • **constrain** ⓥ ~하게 만들다
- **precise** ⓐ 정확한, 엄밀한   • **constraint** ⓝ 제약, 제한
- **foliage** ⓝ 나뭇잎   • **diet** ⓝ 먹거리   • **trait** ⓝ 특성

진화 과정은 이용 가능한 유전적 변이에 작용한다. 따라서 자연 선택이 완벽하고 '최대로 적합한' 개체의 진화로 이어질 가능성은 작다. 그보다, 생물체는 '가능한 가장 적합한' 또는 '아직은 가장 적합한' 상태로 환경에

맞춰지게 되는데, 즉 그들이 '상상할 수 있는 가장 좋은 것'은 아니다. 적합성 결여의 일부는 생물체가 가진 현재의 특성 모두가 그 생물체가 현재 살고 있는 환경과 모든 면에서 유사한 환경에서 유래한 것이 아니기 때문에 발생한다. 진화 역사의 과정에서, 생물체의 먼 조상들은 후속적으로 미래의 진화를 제약하는 일련의 특성들, 즉 진화적 '짐'을 진화시켰을 수도 있다. 수백만 년 동안 척추동물의 진화는 척추를 가진 생물체에 의해 달성될 수 있는 것으로 제한되어 왔다. 게다가, 현재 생물체와 그 환경 간의 정확한 일치로 보이는 것의 대부분은 제약으로도 볼 수 있는데, 코알라는 유칼립투스 잎으로 성공적으로 생활하지만, 다른 관점에서는 코알라는 유칼립투스 잎 없이는 살 수 없다.

→ 한 생물체가 현재 가지고 있는 생존 특성은 그 생물체가 (B) 환경에서 발생하는 변화에 대처하는 상황에 있을 때 적응성에 (A) 장애물이 될 수 있다.

다음 글의 내용을 한 문장으로 요약하고자 한다. 빈칸 (A), (B)에 들어갈 말로 가장 적절한 것은?

	(A)		(B)	
①	improvement 개선	—	diet 먹거리	'짐'과 같이 부정적인 의미여야 함
②	obstacle 장애물	—	surroundings 환경	생물체가 가진 생존 특성은 '환경'의 변화에 대처할 때 '장애물'이 될 수 있다는 내용
③	advantage 이점	—	genes 유전자	유전자가 달라진다는 내용은 없음
④	regulator 조절 장치	—	mechanisms 매커니즘	생존 특성이 조절 장치로서 역할을 한다는 내용이 아님
⑤	guide 길잡이	—	traits 특성	'짐'과 같이 부정적인 의미여야 함

왜 정답? [정답률 53%]

- **적합성의 결여가 발생하는 이유:** 생물체의 현재 특성이 그 생물체가 현재 살고 있는 환경과 모든 면에서 유사한 환경에서 유래한 것이 아니기 때문이다. 단서1
- 진화 과정에서 생물체의 과거 조상은 현재 생물체의 진화에 짐이 되는 특성을 진화시켰을 수도 있다. 단서2

➡ 한 생물체가 과거에 환경에 적응하면서 발달시킨 생존 특성이 과거와 달라진 환경에서는 짐이 될 수 있다는 내용이다.
　　→ **(A):** '짐'과 같은 의미를 나타내는 단어는 '장애물(obstacle)'이다.
　　(B): 생존할 수 있었던 특성이 장애물이 되는 것은 그 생물체가 처한 '환경(surroundings)'이 과거와 달라진 경우이다.
　▶ 요약문의 빈칸에는 각각 '장애물'과 '환경'이 들어가야 하므로 정답은 ②임

왜 오답?
① '짐'과 같이 부정적인 의미가 들어가야 하므로 '개선'이 될 수 있다는 것은 어색하다.
③ '유전자'의 변화에 대처한다는 내용은 나오지 않았으므로 적절하지 않다.
④ 생존 특성이 '조절 장치'로서 역할을 한다는 내용이 아니므로 내용과 맞지 않는다.
⑤ '짐'과 같이 부정적인 의미가 들어가야 하므로 '길잡이'가 될 수 있다는 것은 문맥에 맞지 않는다.

＊글의 흐름

도입	진화 과정은 이용 가능한 유전적 변이에 작용함
설명	적합성 결여의 일부는 생물체가 가진 현재의 특성이 현재 살고 있는 환경과 모든 면에서 유사한 환경에서 유래한 것이 아니기 때문에 발생함
부연	생물체의 먼 조상들은 후속적으로 미래의 진화를 제약하는 일련의 특성들, 즉 진화적 '짐'을 진화시켰을 수도 있음
예시	코알라는 유칼립투스 잎으로 성공적으로 생활하지만, 다른 관점에서는 코알라는 유칼립투스 잎 없이는 살 수 없음

O 03 정답 ① ＊합성 식품 성분 및 천연 식품 성분 ────

목적어절을 이끄는 접속사
People often assume / that synthetic food ingredients are more
= ingredients
harmful / than natural ones, / but this is not always the case. //
사람들은 흔히 가정한다 / 합성 식품 성분이 더 해롭다고 / 천연 성분보다 / 그러나 이것이 항상 그런 것은 아니다 // 단서1 사람들은 흔히 합성 성분이 천연 성분보다 더 해롭다고 가정하지만 항상 그런 것은 아님

Typically, / synthetic ingredients can be made / in a precisely
controlled fashion / and have well-defined compositions and
properties, / 분사구문을 이끎 allowing careful evaluation of their potential
toxicity. // 단서2 합성 성분은 정밀하게 통제된 방식으로 만들어질 수 있음
일반적으로 / 합성 성분은 만들어질 수 있다 / 정밀하게 통제된 방식으로 / 그리고 잘 정의된 성분의 조합과 특성을 가진다 / 잠재적인 독성의 주의 깊은 평가를 허락하면서 //

On the other hand, / natural ingredients often vary appreciably
/ in their composition and properties /
반면에 / 천연 성분은 상당히 차이를 보이는 경우가 많다 / 성분의 조합과 특성에서 /
분사구문을 이끎　　　　　　　　　　　사이에 time of year를 수식하는 관계부사 생략
depending on their origin, / the time of year they were harvested,
사이에 climate를 수식하는 목적격 관계대명사 생략
/ the climate they experienced throughout their lifetime, / the
soil quality, / and how they were isolated and stored. //
원산지에 따라 / 수확된 시기 / 살아 있을 때 경험한 기후 / 토양의 질 / 그리고 분리되고 저장된 방식 //

These variations can make / testing their safety / extremely
동사 make의 목적격 보어
difficult / — one is never sure / about the potential toxicity of
주격 관계대명사
minor components / that may vary / from time to time. //
이러한 변동성은 만들 수 있다 / 안전성을 테스트하는 것을 / 매우 어렵게 / 우리는 결코 확신할 수 없다 / 미세 성분들의 잠재적인 독성에 대해 / 달라질 수 있는 / 그때그때 //

In some cases, / a natural food component has been consumed
/ for hundreds or thousands of years / without causing any
obvious health problems / and can, therefore, be assumed / to
be safe. //
어떤 경우에는 / 천연 식품 성분이 소비되어 왔다 / 수백 년 또는 수천 년 동안 / 명백한 건강 문제를 일으키지 않고 / 그리고 따라서 가정될 수 있다 / 안전하다고 //

However, / one must still be very careful. //
하지만 / 여전히 매우 주의해야 한다 //

> → The (A) **controllability** of the production process for
> synthetic food ingredients / and the variability of natural food
> ingredients / may (B) **challenge** people's commonly held
> assumption / that the natural ingredients are more secure. //
> 합성 식품 성분 생산 과정의 통제 가능성과 / 천연 식품 성분의 변동성은 / 사람들의 일반적인 가정에 이의를 제기할 수 있다 / 천연 성분이 더 안전하다는 //

- ingredient ⓝ 성분, 재료　　・fashion ⓝ 방식
- composition ⓝ 조합　　・property ⓝ 특성　　・toxicity ⓝ 독성
- isolated ⓐ 고립된　　・variation ⓝ 변동성
- predictability ⓝ 예측 가능성　　・intensify ⓥ 강화하다
- affordability ⓝ 구입 가능성

사람들은 흔히 합성 식품 성분이 천연 성분보다 더 해롭다고 가정하지만, 이것이 항상 그런 것은 아니다. 일반적으로 합성 성분은 정밀하게 통제된 방식으로 만들어질 수 있으며, 성분의 조합과 특성이 잘 정의되어 있어 잠재적인 독성을 주의 깊게 평가할 수 있다. 반면에 천연 성분은 원산지, 수확된 시기, 살아 있을 때 경험한 기후, 토양의 질, 분리되고 저장된 방식에 따라 성분의 조합과 특성이 상당히 차이를 보이는 경우가 많다. 이러한 변동성으로 인해 안전성을 테스트하기가 매우 어려울 수 있는데, 그때그때 달라질 수 있는 미세 성분들의 잠재적인 독성에 대해 결코 확신할 수 없다. 어떤 경우에는 천연 식품 성분이 수백 년 또는 수천 년 동안 명백한 건강 문제를 일으키지 않고 소비되어 왔기에 안전하다고 가정될 수 있다. 하지만 여전히 매우 주의해야 한다.
→ 합성 식품 성분 생산 과정의 (A) **통제 가능성**과 천연 식품 성분의 변동성은 천연 성분이 더 안전하다는 사람들의 일반적인 가정에 (B) **이의를 제기할** 수 있다.

다음 글의 내용을 한 문장으로 요약하고자 한다. 빈칸 (A), (B)에 들어갈 말로 가장 적절한 것은?

합성 식품 성분의 관리 가능성은 가능할 수도 있으나, 이것이 천연 식품이 더 안전하다는 가정을 강화하는 것이 아니라 오히려 그 반대임

	(A)		(B)
①	controllability 통제 가능성	—	challenge 이의를 제기하다
②	predictability 예측 가능성	—	support 지지하다
③	manageability 관리 가능성	—	intensify 강화하다
④	affordability 구입 가능성	—	reverse 뒤바꾸다
⑤	accessibility 접근 가능성	—	question 의문을 제기하다

- 합성 식품 성분은 정밀하게 통제되기 때문에 그 통제 가능성이 사람들의 일반적 가정(천연 식품이 더 안전하다)에 이의를 제기함
- 합성 식품 성분의 예측 가능성이 천연 식품이 더 안전하다는 사람들의 가정을 지지한다는 내용의 글이 아님
- 합성 식품 성분의 구입 가능성이 천연 식품이 더 안전하다는 사람들의 생각을 뒤바꾸는 것이 아님
- 합성 식품에 대한 접근 가능성이 천연 식품이 더 안전하다는 것에 의문을 제기하는 것이 아님

✍ 왜 정답? [정답률 68%]

사람들의 일반적 생각	합성 식품 성분이 천연 성분보다 더 해로움
합성 성분의 특징	합성 성분은 정밀하게 통제된 방식으로 만들어지며 잠재적인 독성을 주의 깊게 평가 가능함
천연 성분의 특징	원산지, 수확된 시기, 기후, 토양의 질 등에 따라 성분의 조합과 특성에 변동성이 크고 안전성을 테스트하기가 매우 어려움

(A):
- 합성 성분은 정밀하게 통제된 방식으로 만들어진다고 했다.
- ➡ 즉, 합성 식품 성분의 생산 과정은 '통제 가능성(controllability)'을 갖는다.

(B):
- 합성 성분 생산 과정의 통제 가능성과 천연 성분의 변동성이 사람들이 일반적으로 천연 성분이 더 안전하다고 하는 가정을 반박한다는 내용이다.
- ➡ 즉, 사람들의 생각에 '이의를 제기(challenge)'하는 것이다.
- ▶ 요약문의 빈칸에는 각각 '통제 가능성'과 '이의를 제기하다'가 들어가야 하므로 정답은 ①임

✍ 왜 오답?

② 합성 식품 성분의 예측 가능성이 천연 식품이 더 안전하다는 사람들의 가정을 지지한다는 내용의 글이 아니다.

③ 합성 식품 성분의 관리 가능성은 자연스러우나, 이것이 천연 식품이 더 안전하다는 가정을 강화하는 것이 아니라 오히려 그 반대이다.

④ 합성 식품의 구입 가능성이 천연 식품이 더 안전하다는 사람들의 생각을 뒤바꾸는 것에 대한 글이 아니다.

⑤ 합성 식품에 대한 접근 가능성이 천연 식품이 더 안전하다는 것에 의문을 제기하는 것이 아니다.

* 글의 흐름

주제문	사람들은 합성 식품 성분이 더 해롭다고 생각하지만 항상 그런 것은 아님
근거 ①	합성 식품 성분은 정밀한 통제를 통해 생산, 잠재적 독성을 잘 평가할 수 있음
근거 ②	천연 성분은 변동성이 크고 잠재적 독성을 평가하기 어려울 수 있음
주제 재언급	천연 성분이 안전하다고 생각할 수 있으나 주의해야 함

백승준 | 2025 수능 응시 · 광주 광주숭원고 졸

이 문제의 경우 (A)는 production process for synthetic food ingredients의 특징을, (B)는 주어가 assumption에 미치는 영향이 들어가야 한다는 것을 알 수 있지. 이를 의식하고 글의 주제를 파악하면 쉽게 답을 찾을 수 있을 거야. precisely controlled fashion과 well-defined compositions and properties를 보면 (A)에 들어가야 할 단어의 의미를 확인할 수 있지. 또, 첫 문장의 but this is not always the case를 통해 사람들의 통념과는 반대되는 내용을 주장하는 글임을 파악하여 (B)에 들어갈 단어를 찾을 수 있어.

⭕ 04 정답 ① * 인간 언어가 다른 동물의 울음소리와 다르게 갖고 있는 특성

Human speech differs / from the cries of other species / in many ways. //
인간의 말은 다르다 / 다른 종의 울음소리와 / 여러 가지 면에서 //

보어절을 이끄는 접속사

One very important distinction is / that all other animals use / one call for one message / as the general principle of communication. // **단서 1** 동물은 하나의 메시지에 하나의 울음소리를 사용함
매우 중요한 한 가지 차이는 ~이다 / 다른 모든 동물은 사용한다는 것 / 하나의 메시지에 하나의 울음소리를 / 의사소통의 일반적인 원칙으로 //

목적어절을 이끄는 접속사

This means / that the number of possible messages is very restricted. // 핵심 주어
이는 의미한다 / 가능한 메시지의 수가 매우 제한적임을 //

If a new message is to be included in the system, / a new sound has to be introduced, too. //
시스템에 새로운 메시지가 포함되려면 / 새로운 소리도 도입되어야 한다 //

가주어 진주어 ①

After the first few tens of sounds / it becomes difficult / to invent 진주어 ②
new distinctive sounds, / and also to remember them / for the 사이에 관계부사 when 생략
next time / they are needed. //
처음 몇십 개의 소리가 있고 난 후에는 / 어려워진다 / 새로운 독특한 소리를 만들어 내는 것이 / 또한 그것을 기억하는 것이 / 다음을 위해 / 그것들이 필요할 //

Human speech builds / on the principle of combining a restricted number of sounds / into an unlimited number of messages. //
인간의 말은 기반으로 한다 / 제한된 수의 소리를 결합하는 원리를 / 무한한 수의 메시지를 만들어 내는 // **단서 2** 인간의 말은 제한된 수의 소리를 결합해 무한한 수의 메시지를 만들어 냄

In a typical human language / there are something like thirty or forty distinctive speech sounds. //
일반적인 인간의 언어에는 / 대략 30개 또는 40개의 독특한 말소리가 있다 //

부사적 용법(목적)

These sounds can be combined into chains / to form a literally unlimited number of words. //
이 소리들은 연쇄적으로 결합될 수 있다 / 말 그대로 무제한적인 수의 단어를 만들기 위해 //

주격 관계대명사

Even a small child, / who can communicate by only one word 주격 관계대명사
at a time, / uses a system for communication / that is infinitely system을 수식하는 분사
superior to any system / utilized by any other animal. //
심지어 어린아이도 / 한 번에 한 단어로만 의사소통을 할 수 있는 / 의사소통 시스템을 사용한다 / 어떤 시스템보다 엄청 더 뛰어난 / 다른 어느 동물에 의해 활용되는 //

> → In animal cries, / each call (A) **represents** a different message, / which limits the number of possible messages, / whereas human language creates an unlimited number of messages / using a (B) **finite** set of distinctive sounds. //
> 동물의 울음소리에서 / 각각의 울음소리는 서로 다른 메시지를 나타내므로 / 가능한 메시지의 수가 제한되는 / 반면, 인간의 언어는 무한한 수의 메시지를 만들어 낸다 / 한정된 수의 독특한 소리 집합을 사용하여 //

- species ⓝ 종(種: 생물 분류의 기초 단위)　· distinction ⓝ 차이, 구별
- principle ⓝ 원칙, 원리　· restricted ⓐ 제한된, 한정된
- introduce ⓥ 도입하다　· combine ⓥ 결합하다
- unlimited ⓐ 무제한의　· literally ⓐd 말 그대로
- infinitely ⓐd 엄청, 대단히, 무한히　· superior ⓐ 뛰어난, 우수한, 우월한
- utilize ⓥ 활용하다　· represent ⓥ 나타내다
- symbolize ⓥ 상징하다　· distort ⓥ 왜곡하다　· finite ⓐ 한정된
- novel ⓐ 새로운

인간의 말은 다른 종의 울음소리와 여러 가지 면에서 다르다. 매우 중요한 한 가지 차이는 다른 모든 동물은 의사소통의 일반적인 원칙으로 하나의 메시지에 하나의 울음소리를 사용한다는 것이다. 이는 가능한 메시지의 수가 매우 제한적임을 의미한다. 새로운 메시지가 시스템에 포함되려면, 새로운 소리도 도입되어야 한다. 처음 몇십 개의 소리가 있고 난 후에는 새로운 독특한 소리를 만들어 내는 것뿐만 아니라 다음에 필요할 때를 위해 그것을 기억하는 것

또한 어려워진다. 인간의 말은 제한된 수의 소리를 결합하여 무제한적인 수의 메시지를 만들어 내는 원리를 기반으로 한다. 일반적인 인간의 언어에는 대략 30개 또는 40개의 독특한 말소리가 있다. 이 소리들을 연쇄적으로 결합하여 말 그대로 무제한적인 수의 단어를 만들 수 있다. 심지어 한 번에 한 단어로만 의사소통을 할 수 있는 어린아이도 다른 어느 동물이 활용하는 어떤 시스템보다 엄청 더 뛰어난 의사소통 시스템을 사용한다.

→ 동물의 울음소리에서 각각의 울음소리는 서로 다른 메시지를 (A) **나타내므로** 가능한 메시지의 수가 제한되는 반면, 인간의 언어는 (B) **한정된** 수의 독특한 소리 집합을 사용하여 무한한 수의 메시지를 만들어 낸다.

다음 글의 내용을 한 문장으로 요약하고자 한다. 빈칸 (A), (B)에 들어갈 말로 가장 적절한 것은?
┌─ 동물이 울음소리로 서로 다른 메시지를 상징하는 것은 맞지만 인간의 언어가 보편적인 수의 소리
│ (A)   (B) 집합을 사용하는 것은 아님
① represents   —   finite   동물은 각각의 울음소리로 서로 다른 메시지를 나타내지만, 인간이
  나타내다   한정된   한정된 소리 집합을 사용하여 무한한 수의 메시지를 만들어 냄
② symbolizes   —   universal
  상징하다   보편적인
③ distorts   —   fixed   동물은 각 울음소리로 서로 다른 메시지를 왜곡하는 것이 아님
  왜곡하다   고정된
④ expresses   —   novel   동물이 각 울음소리로 서로 다른 메시지를 표현하는 것은 맞지만,
  표현하다   새로운   인간이 새로운 소리 집합을 사용하는 것이 아님
⑤ records   —   complex 동물이 각 울음소리로 서로 다른 메시지를 기록하는 것도,
  기록하다   복잡한   인간이 복잡한 소리 집합을 사용하는 것도 아님

왜 정답? [정답률 59%]

인간의 말	다른 종의 울음소리와 여러 면에서 다름
다른 동물들	하나의 메시지를 전달할 때 하나의 울음소리를 사용 → 가능한 메시지의 수가 매우 제한적 **단서 1**
인간의 언어	• 제한된 수의 소리를 결합하여 무제한적인 수의 메시지를 만들어 냄 **단서 2** • 30개 또는 40개의 말소리들을 연쇄적으로 결합하여 무제한적인 수의 단어를 만듦

(A):
• 동물은 하나의 메시지를 전달할 때 하나의 울음소리를 사용한다고 했다.
➡ 즉, 각각의 울음소리가 서로 다른 메시지를 '나타낸다(represents)'는 것이다.
(B):
• 하지만 인간은 30 또는 40개의 제한된 소리를 결합하여 무제한적인 수의 메시지를 만들어 낸다고 한다.
➡ 즉, 인간은 '한정된(finite)' 소리 집합을 사용하여 무한한 수의 메시지를 만들어 내는 것이다.
▶ 요약문의 빈칸에는 각각 '나타낸다'와 '한정된'이 들어가야 하므로 정답은 ①임

왜 오답?

② 동물이 각각의 울음소리로 서로 다른 메시지를 상징하는 것은 맞지만, 인간이 보편적인 수의 소리 집합을 사용한다는 언급은 없다.
③ 동물이 각 울음소리로 서로 다른 메시지를 왜곡하는 것이 아니다.
④ 동물이 각 울음소리로 서로 다른 메시지를 표현하는 것은 맞지만, 인간이 새로운 수의 소리 집합을 사용하는 것은 아니다.
⑤ 동물이 서로 다른 메시지를 기록하는 것도 아니고, 인간이 복잡한 수의 소리 집합을 사용한다고도 하지 않았다.

* 글의 흐름

주제문	인간의 말은 다른 동물들의 울음소리와 중요한 차이점이 있음
설명 ①	동물은 하나의 메시지를 위해 하나의 울음소리를 냄 → 가능한 메시지가 제한적
설명 ②	인간은 제한된 수의 소리를 결합하여 무제한적인 수의 메시지를 만들어 냄
주제 재언급	한 번에 한 단어로만 의사소통을 할 수 있는 어린아이도 다른 어느 동물이 활용하는 어떤 시스템보다 뛰어난 의사소통 시스템을 사용함

O 05 정답 ③ *시를 통해 철학을 할 수 있는가에 대한 논의

                                          현재완료 수동태
Philosophical interest in poetry has been dominated by the
         명사절 접속사
question / of whether poetry can aid philosophical thought and
promote philosophical inquiry. //
시에 대한 철학적 관심은 질문에 의해 지배되어 왔다 / 시가 철학적 사고를 돕고 철학적
탐구를 촉진할 수 있는지에 대한 //   **단서 1** 몇몇 철학자들은 자신의 작품을 운문으로 나타내는
                                    전통이 있음(시가 철학적 사고를 촉진함)
This focus reflects a tradition / of philosophers like Pope and
                            현재분사
Rumi presenting their philosophical work in verse. //
이 초점은 전통을 반영한다 / Pope와 Rumi와 같은 철학자들이 자신의 철학적 작품을
운문으로 나타내는 //   **단서 2** 몇몇 시인들의 작품은 철학의 산물로 평가받음
                                (시가 철학적 사고를 촉진함)
In addition, poets like William Wordsworth and T. S. Eliot /
                     현재완료 수동태
have been celebrated as poet-philosophers, / with their work
                                        과거분사
valued as the product of philosophy through poetry. //
게다가, William Wordsworth와 T.S.Eliot과 같은 시인들은 / 시인철학자로서 찬사를 받아
왔다 / 그들의 작품이 시를 통한 철학의 산물로 높이 평가받으며 //
                                      동명사의 의미상 주어   동명사
However, arguments against poetry having a role to play
in philosophical inquiry / have tended to focus on poetry's
(negative) relationship to truth /
그러나 시가 철학적 탐구에서 맡은 역할을 가지고 있다는 것에 반하는 주장들은 / 시와 진실
간의(부정적) 관계에 집중해 온 경향이 있다 /
단서 3 시가 철학적 탐구에서 어떤 역할을 맡고 있다는 것에 반하는 주장은 시와 진실 간의 부정적 관계에
집중함(시를 통해 철학할 수 없음)
(or, as John Koethe puts it, poetry's indifference to truth). //
(즉, John Koethe가 표현하듯, 진실에 대한 시의 무관심) //
Although we may accept works of poetry / as having
philosophical themes, / this does not amount to doing
                                    '~에 이르다'   동명사
philosophy through poetry. /
우리는 시 작품들을 받아들일 수도 있지만 / 철학적 주제를 갖는 것으로 / 이것은 철학을 시를
통해 하는 것과 마찬가지는 아니다 //
One such argument hinges on / the non-paraphrasability of
                    ┌── 명사구의 병렬 구조 ──┐
poetry and form-content unity. //
그러한 하나의 주장은 ~에 달려 있다 / 시의 다른 말로 바꾸어 표현할 수 없음과 형식내용의
통일성 여부에 //
The thought goes, if poetry is to play a role in philosophy, /
then it needs to be paraphrasable / (that is, its content must be
separable from its form). //
그 생각은 만약 시가 철학에서 역할을 하려면 / 그것은 다른 말로 바꾸어 표현할 수 있어야
한다는 것으로 이어진다 / (즉, 그것의 내용은 그것의 형식으로부터 반드시 분리될 수 있어야
한다) //
The assumption is that paraphrase is a mark of understanding /
and indicates / that some proposition has a fixed meaning and /
이 가정은 다른 말로 바꾸어 표현하는 것이 이해의 표시이며 / 보여준다 / 어떤 명제가 고정된
의미를 지닌다는 것과 /
        ┌── that절의 병렬 구조 ──┐
that only a proposition with a fixed meaning can be evaluated /
in terms of truth or falsity. //
고정된 의미를 지닌 명제만이 평가될 수 있다는 것을 / 진실 혹은 거짓이라는 면에서 //
Poetry resists paraphrase: / to change the words is to change
the poem. //
시는 다른 말로 바꾸어 표현하는 것에 저항한다 / 단어를 바꾸는 것은 시를 바꾸는 것이다 //

> → Some believe in the ability of poetry / to (A) **convey**
> philosophy, / but for others, its resistance to paraphrasing /
> (B) **restricts** its philosophical role. //
> 일부 사람들은 시의 능력을 믿는데 / 철학을 전달하는 / 다른 사람들에게는, 그것의 다른
> 말로 바꾸어 표현하는 것에 대한 저항이 / 그것의 철학적 역할을 제한한다 //

• **philosophical** ⓐ 철학적인   • **dominate** ⓥ 지배하다
• **promote** ⓥ 촉진하다   • **inquiry** ⓝ 질문
• **celebrate** ⓥ 찬사를 보내다   • **argument** ⓝ 논쟁
• **indifference** ⓝ 무관심   • **separable** ⓐ 분리될 수 있는
• **paraphrase** ⓝ 다른 말로 바꾸어 표현하는 것   • **evaluate** ⓥ 평가하다

- **misinterpret** ⓥ 잘못 해석하다 　• **restrict** ⓥ 제한하다
- **reinforce** ⓥ 강화하다 　• **broaden** ⓥ 넓히다

시에 대한 철학적 관심은 시가 철학적 사고를 돕고 철학적 탐구를 촉진할 수 있는지에 대한 질문에 의해 지배되어 왔다. 이 초점은 Pope와 Rumi와 같은 철학자들이 자신의 철학적 작품을 운문으로 나타내는 전통을 반영한다. 게다가, William Wordsworth와 T. S.Eliot과 같은 시인들은 그들의 작품이 시를 통한 철학의 산물로 높이 평가받으며 시인철학자로서 찬사를 받아 왔다. 그러나 시가 철학적 탐구에서 맡은 역할을 가지고 있다는 것에 반하는 주장들은 시와 진실 간의(부정적) 관계(즉, John Koethe가 표현하듯, 진실에 대한 시의 무관심)에 집중해 온 경향이 있다. 우리는 시 작품들이 철학적 주제를 갖는 것으로 받아들일 수도 있지만, 이것은 철학을 시를 통해 하는 것과 마찬가지는 아니다. 그러한 하나의 주장은 시의 다른 말로 바꾸어 표현할 수 없음과 형식내용의 통일성 여하에 달려 있다. 그 생각은 만약 시가 철학에서 역할을 하려면, 그것은 다른 말로 바꾸어 표현할 수 있어야 한다는 것(즉, 그것의 내용은 그것의 형식으로부터 반드시 분리될 수 있어야 한다)으로 이어진다. 이 가정은 다른 말로 바꾸어 표현하는 것이 이해의 표시이며 어떤 명제가 고정된 의미를 지닌다는 것과 고정된 의미를 지닌 명제만이 진실 혹은 거짓이라는 면에서 평가될 수 있다는 것을 보여 준다. 시는 다른 말로 바꾸어 표현하는 것에 저항한다. 단어를 바꾸는 것은 시를 바꾸는 것이다.

→ 일부 사람들은 철학을 (A) **전달하는** 시의 능력을 믿는데, 다른 사람들에게는, 그것의 다른 말로 바꾸어 표현하는 것에 대한 저항이 그것의 철학적 역할을 (B) **제한한다**.

다음 글의 내용을 한 문장으로 요약하고자 한다. 빈칸 (A), (B)에 들어갈 말로 가장 적절한 것은?

글의 초반 내용은 시가 철학을 전달할 수 있다는 내용이고, 후반 내용은 이와 반대되는 시로 철학을 할 수 없다는 내용이므로 적절함

	(A)		(B)
①	misinterpret 잘못 해석하다	—	limits 제한하다
②	deliver 전달하다	—	expands 확장하다
③	convey 전달하다	—	restricts 제한하다
④	reexamine 재검토하다	—	reinforces 강화하다
⑤	seek 찾다	—	broadens 넓히다

초반 내용은 철학을 전달하는 시의 능력을 믿는 사람들에 대한 내용이므로 (A)에서 철학을 '잘못 해석하다'는 것은 아님
글의 후반 내용은 시의 철학적 역할은 제한된다는 내용이므로 이를 '확장한다'는 것은 아님
후반부는 시의 철학적 역할이 제한된다는 내용이므로 이를 '강화한다'는 것은 아님
후반부는 시의 철학적 역할이 제한된다는 내용이므로 이를 '넓힌다'는 것은 아님

왜 정답? [정답률 58%]

시로 철학을 할 수 '있다'	철학자들 중 자신의 작품을 운문으로 나타낸 경우도 있고, 시인들의 작품 중 철학의 산물로 높이 평가받는 경우도 있다.
시로 철학을 할 수 '없다'	• 시가 철학적 주제는 가질 수 있어도, 철학을 시를 통해 하는 것과 같지는 않다. • 시가 철학에서 역할을 하려면, 내용을 다른 말로 바꿔 표현할 수 있어야 하는데 시는 그렇게 하지 못한다.

(A):
┌ 어떤 사람들은 철학을 (A)하는 시의 능력을 믿는다고 했고, 글의 전반부에서는 시로
└ 철학을 할 수 있다는 내용이 나온다.

➡ 즉, 일부 사람들은 철학을 '전달하는(convey)' 시의 능력을 믿을 것이다.

(B):
┌ 반면 다른 사람들에게는 시의 다른 말로 바꿔 표현하는 것에 대한 저항이 그것의
└ 철학적 역할을 (B)한다고 했다.

➡ 즉, 철학적 역할을 '제한한다(restricts)'고 해야 할 것이다.

▶ 요약문의 빈칸에는 각각 '전달하는'과 '제한한다'가 들어가야 하므로 정답은 ③임

왜 오답?
① 초반에는 어떤 사람들은 철학을 전하는 시의 능력을 믿는다는 내용이므로 철학을 '잘못 해석한다'는 것은 아니다.
② 후반부에 나온 내용은 시가 다른 말로 바꾸어 표현하지 못하기 때문에 시의 철학적 역할은 제한된다라는 내용이 나와야 하므로 철학적 역할을 '확장한다'는 것은 아니다.
④ 마찬가지로 후반부에는 시의 철학적 역할이 제한된다는 내용이므로 이를 '강화한다'는 것은 아니다.
⑤ 글의 후반에는 시의 철학적 역할이 제한된다고 했으므로 철학적 역할을 '넓힌다'는 것은 올 수 없다.

✱ 글의 흐름

주제문	시가 철학적 사고를 돕고 철학적 탐구를 촉진할 수 있는가?
찬성	• 철학자들 중 몇몇은 자신의 철학적 작품을 운문으로 나타내기도 함 • 시인들 중 몇몇의 작품은 시를 통한 철학의 산물로 높이 평가받음
반대	• 시가 철학 주제를 가질 수는 있지만 이는 시를 통해 철학을 하는 것과는 다름 • 시가 철학에서 역할을 하려면 내용을 다른 말로 바꿔 표현할 수 있어야 하지만 시는 그렇게 하지 못함

○ 06 정답 ① ✱당사자들의 관계에 따라 달라지는 의사소통 방식

단서 1 의사소통은 당사자들이 서로의 관계를 어떻게 판단하는가에 영향을 크게 받음
Communication is decisively influenced / by how the partners define their relationship with each other / at every moment of the communication process. //
의사소통은 결정적으로 영향을 받는다 / 당사자들이 서로에 대한 그들의 관계를 어떻게 정의하는가에 의해 / 의사소통 과정의 모든 순간에 //

If the communication is *symmetrical*, / this means that / both communication partners strive for equality / and interact accordingly. // **단서 2** 대칭적인 의사소통에서는 당사자들이 평등하게 상호작용하려고 함
만일 의사소통이 대칭적이라면 / 이것은 의미한다 / 의사소통의 양 당사자들이 평등을 추구하며 / 그에 따라 상호작용을 한다는 것을 //

They behave as mirror images of each other, / so to speak. // 　　　　말하자면
그들은 서로의 거울 이미지처럼 행동한다 / 말하자면 //

Strength is mirrored with strength, / weakness is mirrored with weakness, / or hardness is mirrored with hardness, etc. //
강함은 강함으로 반영되고 / 약함은 약함으로 반영되고 / 딱딱함은 딱딱함 등으로 반영된다 //

Complementary communication shows / a matching difference in behaviour. //
보완적 의사소통은 보여준다 / 행동에 있어서 짝을 이루는 차이를 //

It is not a matter of up and down, strong and weak, or good and
not A but B: A가 아니라 B
bad, / but of matching and expected difference. //
그것은 위와 아래, 강함과 약함, 또는 좋고 나쁨의 문제가 아니라 / 짝을 이루고 기대되는 차이의 문제이다 //

Such complementary relationships occur / between teachers and students, mother and child, or managers and employees, etc. //
그러한 보완적 관계는 일어난다 / 교사와 학생, 어머니와 자녀 또는 관리자와 직원 등과 같은 사이에서 //
간접의문문 구조(의문사+주어+동사)
What the expectations are in such relationships / depends, among other things, on the cultural background. //
그러한 관계에서의 기대가 무엇인가 하는 것은 / 다른 것들 중에서도, 문화적 배경에 달려 있다 //

If the expectations of complementarity are not met, / communication breakdowns occur. //
만일 보완성에 대한 기대가 충족되지 않는다면 / 의사소통의 중단이 일어난다 //

For example, / if an older person in Japan / is not treated with a certain respect by a younger person, / this circumstance can significantly impair communication / or even make it
　　　　　　　　　　　　　　　　　　　　　　5형식 동사+목적어+목적격 보어(형용사)
impossible. //
예를 들면 / 만일 일본에서 더 나이가 많은 사람이 / 더 젊은 사람에 의해 어떠한 존경심으로 대우받지 못한다면 / 이러한 상황은 심각하게 의사소통을 해치거나 / 심지어 그것을 불가능하게 만들 수 있다 //

→ The way the communication partners (A) **perceive** their relationship / determines the types of communication; / 의사소통 당사자들이 그들의 관계를 인식하는 방식이 / 의사소통의 유형을 결정한다 /

symmetrical communication revolves around / the pursuit of equality and the (B) **corresponding** interaction between them, / 대칭적 의사소통은 중심으로 하는 반면 / 평등 추구와 그들 사이의 상응하는 상호 작용을 /

whereas complementary communication involves / aligning with matching and expected differences / based on cultural background. // 보완적 의사소통은 포함한다 / 짝을 이루고 기대되는 차이들과 궤를 같이하는 것을 / 문화적 배경에 근거한 //

단수 주어 (The way the communication partners (A) perceive their)
단수 동사 (determines)

- define ⓥ 정의하다
- symmetrical ⓐ 대칭적인
- strive for ~를 얻으려 노력하다, 추구하다
- equality ⓝ 평등
- mirror ⓥ 반영하다
- complementary ⓐ 상호 보완적인
- occur ⓥ 일어나다, 발생하다
- significantly ⓐⓓ 심각하게, 상당히
- impair ⓥ 해치다
- align with ~에 맞추어 조정하다
- perceive ⓥ 인식하다
- describe ⓥ 설명하다
- manipulate ⓥ 조종하다
- regulate ⓥ 규제하다
- postponed ⓐ 지연된, 연기된
- transactional ⓐ 업무적인
- intimate ⓐ 친밀한

의사소통은 당사자들이 의사소통 과정의 모든 순간에 서로에 대한 그들의 관계를 어떻게 정의하는가에 의해 결정적으로 영향을 받는다. 만일 의사소통이 대칭적이라면, 이것은 의사소통의 양 당사자들이 평등을 추구하며 그에 따라 상호작용을 한다는 것을 의미한다. 말하자면, 그들은 서로의 거울 이미지처럼 행동한다. 강함은 강함으로 반영되고, 약함은 약함으로 반영되고, 딱딱함은 딱딱함 등으로 반영된다. 보완적 의사소통은 행동에 있어서 짝을 이루는 차이를 보여준다. 그것은 위와 아래, 강함과 약함, 또는 좋고 나쁨의 문제가 아니라, 짝을 이루고 기대되는 차이의 문제이다. 그러한 보완적 관계는 교사와 학생, 어머니와 자녀 또는 관리자와 직원등과 같은 사이에서 일어난다. 그러한 관계에서의 기대가 무엇인가 하는 것은, 다른 것들 중에서도, 문화적 배경에 달려있다. 만일 보완성에 대한 기대가 충족되지 않는다면, 의사소통의 중단이 일어난다. 예를 들면, 만일 일본에서 더 나이가 많은 사람이 더 젊은 사람에 의해 어떠한 존경심으로 대우받지 못한다면, 이러한 상황은 심각하게 의사소통을 해치거나 심지어 그것을 불가능하게 만들 수 있다.

→ 의사소통 당사자들이 그들의 관계를 (A) **인식하는** 방식이 의사소통의 유형을 결정한다; 대칭적 의사소통은 평등 추구와 그들 사이의 (B) **상응하는** 상호 작용을 중심으로 하는 반면, 보완적 의사소통은 문화적 배경에 근거한 짝을 이루고 기대되는 차이들과 궤를 같이하는 것을 포함한다.

다음 글의 내용을 한 문장으로 요약하고자 한다. 빈칸 (A), (B)에 들어갈 말로 가장 적절한 것은? [3점]

의사소통은 당사자들이 서로의 관계를 어떻게 판단하는가에 영향을 받으며, 대칭적 의사소통은 평등함을 추구하고 상호 작용 역시 평등하게 하려고

(A)		(B)
① perceive 인식하다	—	corresponding 상응하는 노력함
② describe 설명하다	—	postponed 연기되는
③ manipulate 조종하다	—	transactional 업무적인
④ regulate 규제하다	—	intimate 친밀한
⑤ develop 발전하다	—	lasting 지속하는

당사자들이 서로의 관계를 설명하는 내용이 아니며, 대칭적 의사소통이 당사자간 상호 작용을 연기하지도 않음
당사자들이 서로를 조종하는 것이 아니며, 업무적인 상호 작용은 이 글에서 언급되지 않음
당사자들 간 규제에 대한 내용은 없으며, 대칭적 의사소통은 친밀한 상호 작용보다는 공평한 상호 작용을 한다는 것이 중심이 됨
의사소통 방식을 결정 짓는 것은 당사자들 간 관계가 발전하는 방식이 아니며, 대칭적 의사소통은 지속적인 상호 작용에 초점을 둔 것이 아님

왜 정답? [정답률 72%]

소재 소개	의사소통은 당사자들이 서로의 관계를 어떻게 정의하는지에 결정적으로 영향을 받음 단서①
대칭적 의사소통	• 당사자 양쪽 다 평등함을 위해 노력하며 이에 맞게 상호 작용함 단서② • 강함은 강함으로, 약함은 약함으로, 딱딱함은 딱딱함으로, 서로의 거울 이미지처럼 행동함

(A):

의사소통 당사자들이 그들의 관계를 (A)하는 방식이 의사소통의 종류를 결정한다고 했다. 의사소통은 당사자들이 서로의 관계를 어떻게 판단하고 보는지에 따라 그 종류가 달라진다.

➡ 즉, (A)에는 판단하거나 인지하거나 '인식한다(perceive)'는 말이 와야 한다.

(B):

대칭적 의사소통은 평등함의 추구와 그들 사이의 (B) 상호 작용을 중심으로 한다. 대칭적 의사소통은 평등함을 추구하기에 상호 작용도 이에 따라 평등해야한다.

➡ 따라서 (B)에는 '그에 따른'의 의미와 같은 '상응하는(corresponding)'이라는 단어가 들어가야 한다.

▶ 요약문의 빈칸에는 각각 '인식하다'와 '상응하는'이 들어가야 하므로 정답은 ①임

왜 오답?

② 당사자들이 서로의 관계를 설명하는 것이 아니며, 대칭적 의사소통이 당사자 간의 상호 작용을 연기하지도 않는다.

③ 의사소통에서 당사자들이 서로를 조종하는 것이 아니며, 업무적 상호 작용은 이 글에서 다뤄지지 않았다.

④ 당사자들 간의 규제에 대한 내용은 없으며, 대칭적 의사소통은 친밀한 상호 작용보다는 공평한 상호 작용에 중점을 둔다.

⑤ 당사자들간의 관계를 발전시키는 것이 아닌 관계를 판단하거나 인지하는 것이 핵심이며 상호 작용이 지속되는 것은 대칭적 의사소통의 핵심이 아니다.

＊ 글의 흐름

발단	의사소통은 상호 작용 당사자들 간 관계에 영향을 받음
전개 ①	의사소통 유형 ① – 대칭적 의사소통: 공평함을 추구함
전개 ②	의사소통 유형 ② – 보완적 의사소통: 문화적 배경에 따른 상호 보완적 관계를 고려한 상호 작용을 함

O 07 정답 ① ＊혼자만의 시간이 예술과 성장에 중요한 이유

In one study, / researchers gave / more than five hundred visitors to an art museum / a special glove / that reported their movement patterns / along with physiological data such as their heart rates. //
간접목적어 (more than five hundred visitors to an art museum)
직접목적어 (a special glove)
한 연구에서 / 연구자들은 주었다 / 500명 이상의 한 미술관 방문객들에게 / 특별한 장갑을 / 그들의 움직임 패턴을 보고하는 / 심박수와 같은 생리학적인 데이터와 함께 //

The data showed / that when people were not distracted by chatting with companions, / they actually had a stronger emotional response to the art. // 단서① 타인과의 수다에 집중력을 잃지 않으면 예술품에 대해 더 강한 감정을 느끼게 됨
그 데이터는 보여 주었다 / 사람들이 동행자들과 수다를 떠는 것에 의해 주의를 빼앗기지 않을 때 / 그들이 실제로 예술품에 더 강한 감정적인 반응을 가진다는 것을 //

Of course, there's nothing wrong with chatting and letting the art slide past, / but think of the inspiration those museum visitors missed out on. // 단서② 대화하다가 작품에 집중하지 않을 경우 놓치는 것들이 있음
앞에 목적격 관계대명사 생략
물론 수다를 떨고 예술품을 지나치는 것은 잘못된 것이 아니지만 / 그 미술관 방문객들이 놓친 영감을 생각해 보라 //

Then apply that / to life in general. //
그 다음에 그것을 적용하라 / 일반적인 삶에 //

When we surround ourselves with other people, / we're not just missing out on / the finer details of an art exhibition. //
우리가 다른 사람들과 함께 있을 때 / 우리는 단지 놓치고 있는 것만이 아니다 / 미술 전시회의 더 세부적인 사항 //

We're missing out on / the chance to reflect and understand ourselves better. //
형용사적 용법(the chance 수식)
우리는 놓치고 있는 것이다 / 자신을 더 잘 성찰하고 이해할 수 있는 기회를 //

In fact, studies show / that if we never allow ourselves to be
alone, / it's just plain harder for us to learn. //
실제로 연구들은 보여 준다 / 만약 우리가 혼자 있는 것을 결코 허용하지 않는다면 / 우리가
배우는 것이 분명히 더 어렵다는 것을 // **단서 3** 마찬가지로 혼자만의 시간을 가지지 않으면
배우는 것이 더 어려움

Other research found / that young people who cannot stand
being alone / were less likely to develop creative skills / like
playing an instrument or writing /
다른 연구는 발견했다 / 혼자 있는 것을 견디지 못하는 젊은이들이 / 창의적인 기술을 개발할
가능성이 적었는데 / 악기 연주나 글쓰기와 같은 /

because the most effective practice of these abilities is often
done / while alone. //
왜냐하면 이러한 능력들의 가장 효과적인 연습이 대체로 행해지기 때문이다 / 혼자 있을 때 //

→ The study above shows / (A) **avoiding** conversation with
companions / while exploring an art museum / intensifies
emotional response to art, /
위의 연구는 보여 주며 / 동행자와의 대화를 피하는 것이 / 미술관을 관람하면서 /
예술품에 대한 정서적 반응을 강화한다는 것을 /
suggesting that absence of alone time may (B) **inhibit** /
personal growth and learning. //
혼자만의 시간의 부재가 저해할 수 있음을 시사한다 / 개인의 성장과 배움을 //

- heart rate 심장박동수 · distract ⓥ 집중이 안 되게 하다
- companion ⓝ 친구, 동지 · past ⓐⓓ (한 쪽에서 다른 쪽으로) 지나서
- inspiration ⓝ 영감 · miss out on ~을 놓치다 · plain ⓐⓓ 분명히
- intensify ⓥ 심화시키다 · inhibit ⓥ 저해하다
- restrain ⓥ 제지하다 · facilitate ⓥ 촉진하다, 가능하게 하다
- nurture ⓥ 육성하다 · dominate ⓥ 지배하다

한 연구에서 연구자들은 500명 이상의 한 미술관 방문객들에게 심박수와 같은
생리학적인 데이터와 함께 그들의 움직임 패턴을 보고하는 특별한 장갑을
주었다. 그 데이터는 사람들이 동행자들과 수다를 떠는 것에 의해 주의를
빼앗기지 않을 때 그들이 실제로 예술품에 더 강한 감정적인 반응을 가진다는
것을 보여 주었다. 물론 수다를 떨고 예술품을 지나치는 것은 잘못된 것이
아니지만 그 미술관 방문객들이 놓친 영감을 생각해 보라. 그다음에 그것을
일반적인 삶에 적용하라. 우리가 다른 사람들과 함께 있을 때 우리는 단지 미술
전시회의 더 세부적인 사항을 놓치고 있는 것만이 아니다. 우리는 자신을 더 잘
성찰하고 이해할 수 있는 기회를 놓치고 있는 것이다. 실제로 연구들은 만약
우리가 혼자 있는 것을 결코 허용하지 않는다면, 우리가 배우는 것이 분명히
더 어렵다는 것을 보여 준다. 다른 연구는 혼자 있는 것을 견디지 못하는
젊은이들이 악기 연주나 글쓰기와 같은 창의적인 기술을 개발할 가능성이
적었는데 왜냐하면 이러한 능력들의 가장 효과적인 연습이 대체로 혼자 있을 때
행해지기 때문이라는 것을 발견했다.
→ 위의 연구는 미술관을 관람하면서 동행자와의 대화를 (A) 피하는 것이
예술품에 대한 정서적 반응을 강화한다는 것을 보여 주며, 혼자만의 시간의
부재가 개인의 성장과 배움을 (B) 저해할 수 있음을 시사한다.

다음 글의 내용을 한 문장으로 요약하고자 한다. 빈칸 (A), (B)에 들어갈 말로
가장 적절한 것은?

	(A)	(B)
①	avoiding 피하는 것	inhibit 저해하다	(A) 미술관에서 대화하지 않을 때 강한 감정을 느끼고, (B) 일상에서 혼자 있을 때 더 자아를 성찰함
②	recalling 기억하는 것	restrain 제지하다	대화를 기억하는 것은 중요하지 않음
③	preventing 방지하는 것	enhance 강화하다	혼자만의 시간이 필요함
④	facilitating 촉진하는 것	nurture 육성하다	대화를 하지 않는 것이 중요
⑤	dominating 지배하는 것	minimize 최소화하다	대화하지 않는 것이 도움이 됨

왜 정답? [정답률 50%]

(A):
┌ 미술관 방문객들은 동행자들과 수다를 떠는 것에 의해 주의를 빼앗기지 않을 때
└ 그들이 실제로 예술품에 더 강한 감정적인 반응을 가짐 **단서 1**
➡ 동행자와의 대화를 '피하는 것'이 예술품에 대한 정서적 반응을 강화할 수 있다.

(B):
┌ 우리가 혼자 있는 것을 결코 허용하지 않는다면, 우리가 배우는 것이 분명히 더
└ 어려움 **단서 3**
➡ 혼자만의 시간의 부재가 개인의 성장과 배움을 '저해할' 수 있다.
▶ 요약문의 빈칸에는 각각 '피하는 것'과 '저해하다'가 들어가야 하므로 정답은 ①임

왜 오답?
② 대화하지 않는 것이 더 도움이 된다고 했다.
③ 혼자만의 시간이 필요하다고 했으므로 그 시간의 부재가 성장과 배움을 '강화하는'
것이 아니다.
④ 혼자만의 시간이 필요하다고 했으므로 그 시간의 부재가 성장과 배움을 '육성하는'
것이 아니다.
⑤ 대화하지 않는 것이 더 도움이 되므로 지배하는 것이 정서적 반응을 강화하는 것은
아니다.

* 글의 흐름

연구	미술관 방문객은 동행자들과 수다를 떠는 것에 의해 주의를 빼앗기지 않을 때 그들이 실제로 예술품에 더 강한 감정적인 반응을 가짐
적용	우리가 다른 사람들과 함께 있을 때 자신을 더 잘 성찰하고 이해할 수 있는 기회를 놓치고 있음
부연	혼자 있는 것을 견디지 못하는 젊은이들이 악기 연주나 글쓰기와 같은 창의적인 기술을 개발할 가능성이 적음

Ｏ 08 정답 ① ＊뇌 '가소성'의 의미

"Brain plasticity" is a term / we use / in neuroscience. //
'뇌 가소성'은 용어이다 / 우리가 사용하는 / 신경 과학에서 //
Whether intentionally or not, / "plasticity" suggests / that the
key idea is / to mold something once and keep it that way
forever: / to shape the plastic toy and never change it again. //
의도적이든 아니든 / '가소성'은 시사한다 / 핵심 개념이 ~이라고 / 무언가를 한 번 성형하고
그것을 그대로 영원히 유지하는 것 / 즉, 플라스틱 장난감의 모양을 만들고 다시는 그것을
바꾸지 않는 것 // **단서 1** '뇌 가소성'은 형태를 영원히 유지하는 것임을 시사함

But that's not what the brain does. //
하지만 그것은 뇌가 하는 것이 아니다 //

It carries on remolding itself / throughout your life. //
뇌는 그 자신을 계속 재성형한다 / 여러분의 생애 내내 // **단서 2** 뇌는 그 자신을 계속 재성형함

Think of a developing city, / and note the way / it grows,
improves, and responds to the world around it. //
개발 중인 도시를 생각해 보라 / 그리고 방식에 주목하라 / 그것이 성장하고, 진보하고, 주변
세상에 반응하는 //

Observe / where the city builds its truck stops, / how it crafts its
immigration policies, / and how it modifies its education and
legal systems. //
관찰하라 / 그 도시가 어디에 그것의 트럭 정류장을 짓는지 / 어떻게 그것의 이민 정책을
공들여 만드는지 / 그리고 어떻게 그것의 교육과 법률 체계를 수정하는지 //

A city is always changing. // 도시는 항상 변화하고 있다 //
A city is not designed by urban planners / and then immobilized
/ like a plastic object. //
도시는 도시 계획자들에 의해 설계되지 않는다 / 그리고 나서 고정되지 않는다 / 플라스틱
물건처럼 //

It continually develops. // 그것은 끊임없이 발전한다 //

Just like cities, / brains never reach an end point. //
도시와 마찬가지로 / 뇌는 결코 종점에 도달하지 않는다 //

We spend our lives / blossoming toward something, / even as
the target moves. //
우리는 삶을 보낸다 / 무언가를 향해 번성하면서 / 심지어 우리는 목표물이 움직이더라도 //

Consider the feeling of encountering a diary / that you wrote
many years ago. //
목적격 관계대명사(diary 수식)
일기를 우연히 발견했을 때의 감정을 생각해 보라 / 여러분이 수년 전에 쓴 //

It represents / the thinking, opinions, and viewpoint of someone
/ who was a bit different / from who you are now, / and that
주격 관계대명사(someone 수식)
previous person can sometimes border on the unrecognizable. //
그것은 나타낸다 / 누군가의 생각, 의견, 그리고 관점을 / 약간 다른 / 지금의 여러분과는 /
그리고 그 이전의 사람은 때때로 거의 몰라볼 정도의 사람이라고 말할 수 있다 //

Despite having the same name and the same early history, / in
전치사(~에도 불구하고)
the years between inscription and interpretation / the narrator
has altered. //
같은 이름과 같은 초기 역사를 가지고 있음에도 불구하고 / 새겨진 글과 해석 사이의 세월
동안 / 화자가 달라졌다 //

부사적 용법(목적)
The word "plastic" can be stretched / to fit this notion of ongoing
change. // 단서3 '플라스틱'이라는 단어는 변화를 의미할 수 있음
'플라스틱'이라는 단어는 확장될 수 있다 / 이러한 진행 중인 변화의 개념에 맞도록 //

→ While some understand / "brain plasticity" to mean
(A) permanence upon molding, / the brain is actually capable
of (B) transformation. //
어떤 사람들은 이해하는 반면 / 성형되자마자 '뇌 가소성'이 영속성을 의미한다고 / 뇌는
실제로 변화할 수 있다 //

- plasticity ⓝ 적응성, 가소성 · neuroscience ⓝ 신경 과학
- intentionally ⓐⓓ 의도적으로 · carry on 계속 가다[움직이다]
- craft ⓥ 공들여 만들다 · immigration policy 이민 정책
- modify ⓥ 수정하다 · immobilize ⓥ 고정시키다
- blossom ⓥ 번성하다 · interpretation ⓝ 해석
- narrator ⓝ 화자, 내레이터 · stretch ⓥ 늘이다
- notion ⓝ 개념, 생각 · ongoing ⓐ 진행 중인

'뇌 가소성'은 우리가 신경 과학에서 사용하는 용어이다. 의도적이든 아니든,
'가소성'은 핵심 개념이 무언가를 한 번 성형하고 그것을 그대로 영원히
유지하는 것이라고 시사한다. 즉, 플라스틱 장난감의 모양을 만들고 다시는
그것을 바꾸지 않는 것이다. 하지만 그것은 뇌가 하는 것이 아니다. 뇌는
여러분의 생애 내내 그 자신을 재성형하는 것을 계속한다. 개발 중인 도시를
생각해 보라, 그리고 그것이 성장하고, 진보하고, 주변 세상에 반응하는
방식에 주목하라. 그 도시가 어디에 그것의 트럭 정류장을 짓고, 어떻게 그것의
이민 정책을 공들여 만들고, 어떻게 그것의 교육과 법률 체계를 수정하는지
관찰하라. 도시는 항상 변화하고 있다. 도시는 도시 계획자들에 의해 설계되고
나서 플라스틱 물건처럼 고정되지 않는다. 그것은 끊임없이 발전한다. 도시와
마찬가지로, 뇌는 결코 종점에 도달하지 않는다. 심지어 우리가 목표물이
움직이더라도, 무언가를 향해 번성하며 삶을 보낸다. 여러분이 수년 전에 쓴
일기를 우연히 발견했을 때의 감정을 생각해 보라. 그것은 지금의 여러분과는
약간 다른 누군가의 생각, 의견, 그리고 관점을 나타내며, 그 이전의 사람은
때때로 거의 몰라볼 정도의 사람이라고 말할 수 있다. 같은 이름과 같은 초기
역사를 가지고 있음에도 불구하고, 새겨진 글과 해석 사이의 세월 동안 화자가
달라졌다. '플라스틱'이라는 단어는 이러한 진행 중인 변화의 개념에 맞도록
확장될 수 있다.
→ 어떤 사람들은 성형되자마자 '뇌 가소성'이 (A) 영속성을 의미한다고 이해하는
반면, 뇌는 실제로 (B) 변화할 수 있다.

**다음 글의 내용을 한 문장으로 요약하고자 한다. 빈칸 (A), (B)에 들어갈 말로
가장 적절한 것은?**

	(A)	(B)
①	permanence 영속성	transformation 변화
②	flexibility 유연성	sympathizing 동정
③	adaptability 적응성	restoration 회복
④	firmness 견고함	sympathizing 동정
⑤	mobility 이동성	transformation 변화

① 뇌가 한번 성형되면 영속성을 가진 것처럼
이해하는 사람들이 있지만, 실제로 뇌는 변화함
② 뇌가 유연성을 갖는다고 이해하는 사람들이
있다는 내용은 없음
③ 뇌의 적응성이나 회복에 대한 내용이 아님
④ 뇌가 동정한다고 할 수는 없음
⑤ 실제로 뇌가 변화하는 것은 맞지만
뇌가 이동성을 갖는 것은 아님

> 오H 정답 ? [정답률 67%]

뇌 가소성	한 번 성형되면 그대로 영원히 유지하는 것이 아니라 생애 내내 그 자신을 재성형하는 것을 계속하는 것 단서1, 단서2
도시와의 비유	도시는 플라스틱 물건처럼 고정되지 않고 끊임없이 발전함
일기와의 비유	새겨진 글과 해석 사이의 세월 동안 화자가 달라짐
'플라스틱'의 의미	진행 중인 변화의 개념에 맞도록 확장 가능 단서3

(A):
┌ '가소성'이라는 말을 뇌는 한 번 성형되면 그대로 영원히 형태를 유지하는 영속성을
└ 가진 것으로 생각하는 경향이 있다고 말하고 있다.
⇒ 즉, 어떤 사람들은 성형되자마자 '뇌 가소성'이 '영속성(permanence)'이나
'견고함(firmness)'을 의미한다고 이해한다.

(B):
┌ 하지만 도시나 일기와의 비유를 통해 뇌는 한 번 성형되면 영원히 형태를 유지하는
└ 것이 아니라 생애 내내 자신을 재성형하는 것을 계속한다고 했다.
⇒ 즉, 뇌는 실제로 '변화(transformation)'하는 것이다.
▶ 요약문의 빈칸에는 각각 '영속성'과 '변화'가 들어가야 하므로 정답은 ①임

> 오H 오답 ?
② 뇌가 유연성을 갖는다고 이해하는 사람들이 있는 반면, 실제로 뇌는 동정한다는
내용이 아니다.
③ 뇌의 적응성이나 회복에 대한 내용이 아니다.
④ 뇌가 동정한다고 할 수는 없는 내용이다.
⑤ 실제로 뇌가 변화하는 것은 맞지만 뇌가 이동성을 갖는다고 할 수 없다.

＊ 글의 흐름

주제	'가소성'이라는 단어는 뇌는 한 번 성형되면 영원히 유지되는 것을 시사하지만 실제로 뇌는 계속 재성형됨
예시 ①	도시는 한 번 설계된 후 끊임없이 발전함
예시 ②	오래 전에 쓴 일기를 발견하면 새겨진 글과 해석 사이의 세월 동안 화자가 달라짐
부연	'플라스틱'이라는 단어는 변화의 개념에 맞도록 확장될 수 있음

자이 쌤's Follow Me! – 홈페이지에서 제공

O 09 정답 ③ ＊그들이 나무를 심은 이유

주어 동격절 접속사
The idea / that *planting* trees / could have a social or political
동사
significance / appears to have been invented / by the English, /
though it has since spread widely. // to부정사의 완료형 수동태
생각은 / 나무를 '심는 것'이 / 사회적이거나 정치적인 의미를 가질 수 있다는 / 고안된 것처럼
보인다 / 영국인들에 의해 / 비록 그것이 이후에 널리 퍼져나가기는 했지만 //

According to Keith Thomas's history *Man and the Natural
World*, / seventeenth- and eighteenth-century aristocrats / began
planting hardwood trees, / usually in lines, /
Keith Thomas의 역사서, 〈Man and the Natural World〉에 따르면 / 17세기와 18세기의
귀족들은 / 활엽수를 심기 시작했다 / 보통은 줄을 지어 /

to declare / the extent of their property / and the permanence of
their claim / to it. // 단서1 자신의 재산에 대한 권리의 영속성을 선언하기 위해 나무를 심었음
선언하기 위해 / 자신의 재산 정도와 / 자신의 권리의 영속성을 / 그것에 대한 //

"What can be more pleasant," / the editor of a magazine for
gentlemen / asked his readers, /
"무엇이 더 즐거울 수 있겠는가" / 신사들을 위한 잡지의 편집자는 / 자신의 독자들에게 물었
다 /

to have의 목적어와 목적격 보어
"than to have the bounds and limits / of your own property /
preserved and continued / from age to age / by the testimony /
of such living and growing witnesses?" //
"경계와 한계가 ~하게 하는 것보다 / 여러분 자신의 재산의 / 보존되고 지속되게 / 대대로 /
증언에 의해 / 그런 살아 있고 성장하는 증인들의" //

Planting trees had the additional advantage / of being regarded
동명사구 주어   동격의 전치사
/ as a patriotic act, / 단서2 나무를 심는 것이 애국적인 행동으로 여겨졌음
나무를 심는 것은 추가적인 이점을 가졌다 / 여겨지는 / 애국적인 행동으로 /

for the Crown had declared / a severe shortage of the hardwood
전치사+관계대명사   선행사
/ on which the Royal Navy depended. //
군주가 선포했기 때문에 / 경재의 심각한 부족을 / 영국 해군이 의존하는 //

→ For English aristocrats, / planting trees served / as
형용사적 용법(statements 수식)
statements / to mark the (A) **lasting** ownership / of their land, /
영국의 귀족들에게 / 나무를 심는 것은 역할을 했고 / 표현의 / 지속적인 소유권을 표시하는
/ 자신의 땅에 대한 /

and it was also considered / to be a(n) (B) **exhibition** / of their
loyalty to the nation. //
그것은 또한 여겨졌다 / 표현으로 / 국가에 대한 그들의 충성심의 //

- political ⓐ 정치적인   · significance ⓝ 의미, 중요성
- appear to-v ~인 것 같다   · spread ⓥ 퍼지다, 확산되다
- according to ~에 의하면   · hardwood tree 활엽수
- declare ⓥ 선언하다   · extent ⓝ 정도, 규모   · property ⓝ 재산
- permanence ⓝ 영속성   · claim ⓝ (재산 등에 대한) 권리
- pleasant ⓐ 즐거운   · editor ⓝ 편집자   · bound ⓝ 경계(선)
- limit ⓝ 한계(점)   · preserve ⓥ 보존하다   · testimony ⓝ 증언
- witness ⓝ 증인, 목격자   · additional ⓐ 추가의
- advantage ⓝ 유리한 점   · regard as ~으로 여기다
- the Crown (군주 국가의) 정부   · severe ⓐ 심각한
- shortage ⓝ 부족   · depend ⓥ 의존하다   · ownership ⓝ 소유(권)

나무를 '심는 것'이 사회적이거나 정치적인 의미를 가질 수 있다는 생각은, 비록 이후에 널리 퍼져나가기는 했지만, 영국인들에 의해 고안된 것처럼 보인다. Keith Thomas의 역사서, 〈Man and the Natural World〉에 따르면, 17세기와 18세기의 귀족들은 자신의 재산 정도와 그것에 대한 자신의 권리의 영속성을 선언하기 위해 보통은 줄을 지어 활엽수를 심기 시작했다. 신사들을 위한 잡지의 편집자는 자신의 독자들에게 "그런 살아 있고 성장하는 증인들의 증언에 의해 여러분 자신의 재산 경계와 한계가 대대로 보존되고 지속되게 하는 것보다 무엇이 더 즐거울 수 있겠는가?"라고 물었다. 나무를 심는 것은 애국적인 행동으로 여겨지는 추가적인 이점을 가졌는데, 군주가 영국 해군이 의존하는 경재의 심각한 부족을 선포했기 때문이었다.

→ 영국의 귀족들에게, 나무를 심는 것은 자신의 땅에 대한 (A) **지속적인** 소유권을 표시하는 표현의 역할을 했고, 그것은 또한 국가에 대한 그들의 충성심의 (B) **표현**으로 여겨졌다.

다음 글의 내용을 한 문장으로 요약하고자 한다. 빈칸 (A), (B)에 들어갈 말로 가장 적절한 것은?

(A)	(B)	
① unstable 불안정한	confirmation 확인	살아 있고 성장하는 나무가 재산에 대한 대대로 이어지는 소유권을 표현함
② unstable 불안정한	exaggeration 과장	재산에 대한 권리의 영속성을 선언하기 위해 활엽수를 심었고,
③ lasting 지속적인	exhibition 표현	이는 애국적인 행동으로 여겨지기도 했음
④ lasting 지속적인	manipulation 조작	활엽수를 심는 것이 애국적인 행동으로 여겨졌음
⑤ official 공식적인	justification 정당화	나무를 긋는 토지의 경계가 공식적인지에 대한 언급은 없음

> **왜 정답?** [정답률 68%]

나무를 심어 자기 소유의 토지에 경계를 그음으로써 그 재산이 대대로 보존되고 지속되게 함 꿀팁

17세기와 18세기의 영국의 귀족들은 자신의 재산에 대한 자신의 권리의 영속성을 선언하기 위해 활엽수를 심었고, 영국 해군이 의존하는 경재가 심각하게 부족한 상황에서 활엽수를 심는 이러한 행위는 또한 애국적인 행동으로 여겨졌다고 했으므로 요약문의 빈칸에는 각각 ③ '지속적인'과 '표현'이 들어가야 한다.

> **왜 오답?** 활엽수에서 얻은 단단한 목재 꿀팁

①, ② 재산에 대한 '영속적인', '대대로 이어지는' 소유권을 선언하는 것이라고 했으므로 '불안정한' 소유권을 표시하는 것이 아니다.

④ 활엽수를 심는 것이 애국적인 행동으로 여겨졌다는 것이지, 나라에 대한 충성심을 '조작'하는 것으로 여겨졌다는 것이 아니다.

⑤ 나무를 심어서 토지의 경계를 표시하는 것이 '공식적인' 소유권으로 받아들여졌는지에 대한 언급은 없다.

＊ 글의 흐름

도입	영국인들에 의해 나무를 심는 것이 사회적 또는 정치적인 의미를 가질 수 있다고 고안됨
사회적 의미	Keith Thomas의 역사서 *Man and the Natural World*에 따르면 17세기, 18세기 귀족들은 재산과 권리의 영속성 선언을 위해 활엽수를 줄지어 심음
부연	살아 있고 성장하는 증인인 나무가 재산의 경계와 한계를 대대로 보존하고 지속하게 함
정치적 의미	영국 해군이 의존하는 경재가 부족했기 때문에 나무를 심는 것은 애국적인 행동으로 여겨지기도 했음

＊ 옥상 녹화사업 ⌐배경 지식

현대의 도시들이 부딪히고 있는 열섬현상을 해결하기 위한 한 가지 방법으로 옥상 녹화사업이 진행되고 있다.

옥상녹화는 건물 표면에 그늘을 만들고, 식물이 자라는 토양이 태양 빛이 건물 표면에 바로 닿는 것을 막는다. 그늘이 형성되면 표면의 온도는 낮아져 건물 내에 전달되는 열이 감소한다. 이에 따라 대기 중으로 다시 방출되는 열도 감소하여 건물 주변의 온도 역시 낮아진다. 옥상과 벽면이 녹화된 건물의 표면온도는 최대 11~25℃ 정도 감소한 것으로 나타났으며, 벽면녹화에 의해 최대 20℃까지 표면온도가 감소한 연구 결과가 있다.

⃝10 정답 ① ＊컴퓨터의 장점과 단점

The computer has, to a considerable extent, solved the problem
                  전치사구의 삽입
/ of acquiring, preserving, and retrieving information. //
컴퓨터는 문제를 상당한 정도로 해결했다 / 정보를 획득하고, 보존하고, 추출하는 //

Data can be stored / in effectively unlimited quantities / and in
manageable form. //   └ 전치사구의 병렬 구조 ┘
데이터는 저장될 수 있다 / 사실상 무한량으로 / 그리고 다루기 쉬운 형태로 //

The computer makes available a range of data / unattainable in
주어   동사   목적격 보어   목적어
the age of books. //
컴퓨터는 다양한 데이터를 이용할 수 있게 한다 / 책의 시대에는 얻을 수 없는 //
= The computer = data
It packages it effectively; / style is no longer needed / to make it
                                            뒤에 needed가 생략됨
accessible, / nor is memorization. //
그것은 그것을 효과적으로 짜임새 있게 담는다 / 방식은 더는 필요하지 않으며 / 그것을 이용할 수 있게 만드는 / 암기도 또한 필요하지 않다 //
                                              a single decision을 수식하는 과거분사구
In dealing with a single decision / separated from its context,
/ the computer supplies tools / unimaginable even a decade
ago. // 단서1 맥락과 분리된 한 가지 결정을 처리할 때 컴퓨터는 과거에는
                              상상할 수도 없었던 도구를 제공함
단 한 가지 결정을 처리할 때 / 맥락과 분리된 / 컴퓨터는 도구를 제공한다 / 10년 전만 해도
상상할 수 없었던 단서2 컴퓨터는 관점을 감소시킴
But it also diminishes perspective. //
하지만 그것은 또한 관점을 감소시킨다 //   반복되는 동사와 부사인 is so가 생략됨
Because information is so accessible / and communication
instantaneous, / there is a diminution of focus / on its significance,
                                      └ 전치사구의 병렬 구조 ┘
/ or even on the definition / of what is significant. //
정보가 매우 접근 가능하고 / 의사소통이 순간적이기 때문에 / 관심 집중의 감소가 있다 / 그것의 중요성에 대한 / 또는 심지어 정의에 대한 / 중요한 것의 //
                                          목적어   목적격 보어 ①
This dynamic may encourage policymakers / to wait for an
                          주어   동사
issue to arise / rather than anticipate it, /
이런 역학은 정책 입안자들을 부추길 수 있다 / 쟁점이 발생하기를 기다리도록 / 그것을 예상하기보다는 단서3 탈맥락화된 방식의 정보 처리는 결정의 순간을 연속적인
            목적격 보어 ②   상황의 일부가 아니라 고립되어 일어나는 일로 간주하게 함
and to regard moments of decision / as a series of isolated events
/ rather than part of a historical continuum. //
그리고 결정의 순간을 간주하도록 / 일련의 고립되어 일어나는 일로 / 역사적인 연속의 일부라기보다는 //

When this happens, / manipulation of information replaces reflection / as the principal policy tool. //
이런 일이 일어나면 / 정보 조작이 숙고를 대체한다 / 주요한 정책 도구로서의 //

> → Although the computer is clearly (A) **competent** / at handling information / in a decontextualized way, /
> 컴퓨터는 분명히 유능하지만 / 정보를 처리하는 데 있어서 / 탈맥락화된 방식으로 /
> it interferes / with our making (B) **comprehensive** judgments / related to the broader context, / as can be seen / in policymaking processes. //
> 그것은 방해한다 / 우리의 종합적인 판단 내리기를 / 더 광범위한 맥락과 관련된 / 보일 수 있는 것처럼 / 정책 결정 과정에서 //

· considerable ⓐ 상당한 · extent ⓝ (크기·중요성·심각성 등의) 정도
· acquire ⓥ 획득하다 · preserve ⓥ 보존하다
· effectively ⓐⓓ 사실상 · quantity ⓝ 양
· manageable ⓐ 조작[관리]할 수 있는, 처리하기[다루기] 쉬운
· a range of 다양한 · unattainable ⓐ 얻기 어려운 · age ⓝ 시대
· memorization ⓝ 암기 · diminish ⓥ 감소시키다
· perspective ⓝ 관점 · instantaneous ⓐ 순간적인
· significance ⓝ 중요성 · dynamic ⓝ 역학
· policymaker ⓝ 정책 입안자 · anticipate ⓥ 예상하다
· isolated ⓐ 고립된, 외딴 · continuum ⓝ 연속체
· manipulation ⓝ 조작 · reflection ⓝ 심사숙고
· principal ⓐ 주요한
· decontextualize ⓥ 탈맥락화하다, 문맥에서 떼어 놓고 고찰하다
· broad ⓐ 폭넓은, 넓은 · context ⓝ 맥락, 전후 사정
· process ⓝ 과정, 절차

컴퓨터는 정보를 획득하고, 보존하고, 추출하는 문제를 상당한 정도로 해결했다. 데이터는 사실상 무한량으로, 그리고 다루기 쉬운 형태로 저장될 수 있다. 컴퓨터는 책의 시대에는 얻을 수 없는 다양한 데이터를 이용할 수 있게 한다. 그것(컴퓨터)은 그것(데이터)을 효과적으로 짜임새 있게 담고, 그것을 이용할 수 있게 만드는 (특수한) 방식은 더는 필요하지 않으며 암기도 또한 필요하지 않다. 맥락과 분리된 단 한 가지 결정을 처리할 때 컴퓨터는 10년 전만 해도 상상할 수 없었던 도구들을 제공한다. 하지만 그것은 또한 관점을 감소시킨다. 정보에 매우 쉽게 접근할 수 있고 의사소통이 순간적이기 때문에, 그것의 중요성이나 심지어 중요한 것의 정의에 관한 관심 집중이 감소한다. 이런 역학은 정책 입안자들이 쟁점을 예상하기보다는 발생하기를 기다리게 하고, 결정의 순간을 역사적인 연속의 일부기보다는 일련의 고립되어 일어나는 일로 간주하게 한다. 이런 일이 일어나면, 정보 조작이 주요한 정책 도구로서의 숙고를 대체한다.
→ 컴퓨터는 탈맥락화된 방식으로 정보를 처리하는 데 있어서 (A) **유능한** 것이 분명하지만, 그것은 정책 결정 과정에서 볼 수 있는 것처럼 더 광범위한 맥락과 관련된 우리의 (B) **종합적인** 판단 내리기를 방해한다.

다음 글의 내용을 한 문장으로 요약하고자 한다. 빈칸 (A), (B)에 들어갈 말로 가장 적절한 것은?

	(A)	(B)
①	competent 유능한	comprehensive 종합적인
②	dominant 지배적인	biased 편향된
③	imperfect 완벽하지 않은	informed 잘 아는
④	impressive 인상적인	legal 합법적인
⑤	inefficient 비효율적인	timely 시기적절한

맥락과 분리된 결정을 내리는 데 유능하다면 더 광범위한 맥락과 관련된 종합적인 판단에는 도움이 안 될 것임
편향된 판단을 내리지 않는 것은 장점임
판단의 법적인 적절성 여부가 달라지는 것은 아님
맥락과 분리된 결정을 내리는 것은 잘함

<왜 정답? [정답률 61%] 전에는 상상할 수 없었던 도구를 제공함 = 유능함 꿀팁

역접의 연결어인 But을 기준으로 앞부분은 컴퓨터의 장점을, 뒷부분은 컴퓨터가 가져온 단점을 설명하는 글이다. 컴퓨터의 장점은 그것이 맥락과 분리된 한 가지 결정을 처리할 때 '유능하다'는 것이고, 단점은 그것이 관점을 감소시킨다는 것인데, 단점에 대해서는 정책 입안자의 행동을 통해 구체적으로 설명했다. 정책 입안자는 결정의 순간을 역사적인 연속의 일부가 아니라 고립되어 일어나는 일로 간주하게 되는데, 이는 앞뒤 맥락, 더 광범위한 맥락에 대한 '종합적인' 판단을 방해하는 것이므로 요약문의 빈칸에는 각각 ① '유능한', '종합적인'이 적절하다.

>왜 오답?

② 컴퓨터가 맥락에서 분리된 한 가지 결정을 내리는 데 유능하다는 것은 반대로 광범위한 맥락을 고려한 판단을 내리는 데는 컴퓨터가 도움이 되지 않는다는 것을 의미한다. '맥락 안에서'와 '맥락에서 분리된'이 이 글의 핵심이다.
③, ⑤ Although가 이끄는 부사절은 탈맥락화된 정보 처리 방식에 있어 컴퓨터가 갖는 장점을 이야기하는 것이므로 (A)에는 imperfect나 inefficient와 같은 부정적인 단어는 적절하지 않다.
④ 맥락에서 분리하여 결정을 내리는 것이 불법적인 판단이나 합법적인 판단으로 이어진다는 내용이 아니다.

* 글의 흐름

장점	컴퓨터는 데이터를 다루기 쉬운 형태로 무한량 저장하고 책의 시대에서는 얻을 수 없는 다양한 데이터를 이용할 수 있게 함
	맥락과 분리된 하나의 결정을 처리할 때 컴퓨터는 과거에는 상상도 할 수 없던 도구를 제공함
단점	컴퓨터의 의사소통이 순간적이기 때문에 각 결정은 연속된 일부라기보다는 고립되어 일어나는 일로 간주됨
	정책 입안자들은 쟁점을 예상하기보다는 발생하기를 기다리고, 이는 정보 조작이 주요한 정책 도구인 숙고를 대체하게 함

011 정답 ④ * 도시화가 가져온 것

The rise / of large, industrial cities / has had social consequences / that are often known / as urbanism. //
출현은 / 거대한 산업 도시의 / 사회적 결과를 가져왔다 / 흔히 알려진 / 도시화로 //

The city dissolves the informal controls / of the village or small town. // 단서 1 도시는 마을이나 작은 소도시의 비공식적인 통제를 해체함
도시는 비공식적인 통제를 해체한다 / 마을이나 작은 소도시의 //

Most urban residents are unknown / to one another, / and most social interactions in cities occur /
대부분의 도시 거주자는 알지 못하고 / 서로 / 도시에서의 대부분의 사회적 상호 작용은 일어난다 /

between people / who know each other / only in specific roles, / such as parking attendant, store clerk, or customer. //
사람들 사이에서 / 서로 아는 / 특정한 역할로만 / 주차 안내원, 가게 점원, 혹은 고객 같은 //

Individuals became more free to live / as they wished, / and in ways / that break away from social norms. //
개인들은 더 자유롭게 살 수 있게 되었다 / 자기가 원하는 대로 / 그리고 방식으로 / 사회 규범에서 벗어나는 //

In response, / and because the high density of city living requires / the pliant coordination / of many thousands of people, /
이에 대응하여 / 그리고 도시 생활의 높은 밀도가 필요로 하기 때문에 / 유순한 조정 / 수천 명의 /

urban societies have developed / a wide range of methods / to control urban behavior. // 단서 2 도시 사회는 도시 행동을 통제하는 다양한 방식을 개발함
도시 사회는 개발했다 / 매우 다양한 방식을 / 도시 행동을 통제하기 위한 //

These include regulations / that control / private land use, / building construction and maintenance (to minimize fire risk), / and the production / of pollution and noise. //
이것에는 규제가 포함된다 / 통제하는 / 토지의 사적 사용 / (화재 위험의 최소화를 위한) 건물 건설과 관리 / 발생을 / 오염과 소음의 // 단서 3 위에서 말한 방식으로 토지의 사적 사용 등을 통제하는 규제가 포함됨

> → The social conditions / in large, industrial cities / made urban societies (A) **remove** / the informal controls / of the village or small town, /
> 사회적 환경은 / 거대 산업 도시의 / 도시 사회가 없애게 만들었고 / 비공식적인 통제를 / 마을이나 작은 소도시의 /
> introducing (B) **restrictive** measures / to effectively induce / coordinated urban behaviors. //
> 규제 조치를 도입했다 / 효과적으로 유도하기 위해 / 조정된 도시 행동을 //

- rise ⓝ 출현, 발생 · consequence ⓝ 결과 · urbanism ⓝ 도시화
- dissolve ⓥ 해체하다 · informal ⓐ 비공식적인
- resident ⓝ 거주자, 주민 · interaction ⓝ 상호 작용
- occur ⓥ 일어나다, 발생하다 · attendant ⓝ 안내원, 수행원, 종업원
- norm ((pl.)) 규범 · density ⓝ 밀도 · coordination ⓝ 조정
- a wide range of 광범위한, 다양한 · regulation ⓝ 규제
- maintenance ⓝ (건물·기계 등을 정기적으로 점검·보수하는) 유지
- minimize ⓥ 최소화하다 · pollution ⓝ 오염
- condition ⓝ ((pl.)) (생활·작업 등의) 환경[상황]
- introduce ⓥ 도입하다, 들여오다 · measure ⓝ 조치, 정책
- induce ⓥ 설득하다, 유도하다

거대한 산업 도시의 출현은 흔히 도시화로 알려진 사회적 결과를 가져왔다. 도시는 마을이나 작은 소도시의 비공식적인 통제를 해체한다. 대부분의 도시 거주자는 서로 알지 못하고, 도시에서의 대부분의 사회적 상호 작용은 주차 안내원, 가게 점원, 혹은 고객 같은 특정한 역할로만 서로 아는 사람들 사이에서 일어난다. 개인들은 자기가 원하는 대로, 그리고 사회 규범에서 벗어나는 방식으로 더 자유롭게 살 수 있게 되었다. 이에 대응하여, 도시 생활의 높은 밀도가 수천 명의 유순한 조정을 필요로 하기 때문에, 도시 사회는 도시 행동을 통제하기 위한 매우 다양한 방식을 개발했다. 이것에는 토지의 사적 사용, (화재 위험의 최소화를 위한) 건물 건설과 관리, 오염과 소음 발생을 통제하는 규제가 포함된다.
→ 거대 산업 도시의 사회적 환경은 도시 사회가 마을이나 작은 소도시의 비공식적인 통제를 (A) 없애고 조정된 도시 행동을 효과적으로 유도하기 위해 (B) 규제 조치를 도입하게 했다.

다음 글의 내용을 한 문장으로 요약하고자 한다. 빈칸 (A), (B)에 들어갈 말로 가장 적절한 것은?

	(A)		(B)
①	limit 제한하다	—	permissive 관대한
②	maintain 유지하다	—	restrictive 규제하는
③	evaluate 평가하다	—	indirect 간접적인
④	remove 제거하다	—	restrictive
⑤	reinforce 강화하다	—	permissive

도시 사회는 '규제'를 개발했음
도시가 마을, 작은 소도시의 비공식적 통제를 해체했음
도시화가 진행되면서 마을, 작은 소도시의 비공식적인 통제가 해체되고 도시 행동을 통제하는 방식이 개발됨

왜 정답? [정답률 38%]

(A):

> 도시는 마을이나 작은 소도시의 비공식적인 통제를 해체한다. 단서1

→ 마을이나 작은 소도시의 비공식적인 통제를
'해체한다(dissolves) = 없앤다(remove)'

(B):

> · 도시 생활의 높은 밀도가 수천 명의 유순한 조정을 필요로 하기 때문에 도시 사회는 도시 행동을 통제하기 위한 매우 다양한 방식을 개발했다. 단서2
> · 이것에는 토지의 사적 사용, (화재 위험의 최소화를 위한) 건물 건설과 관리, 오염과 소음 발생을 통제하는 규제가 포함된다. 단서3

→ 도시 사회는 도시 행동을 통제하기 위해 토지의 사적 사용 등을 통제하는 규제를 포함하는 다양한 방식을 개발했다. = 도시 사회는 조정된 도시 행동을 효과적으로 유도하기 위해 규제(restrictive) 조치를 '도입했다'.
▶ 요약문의 빈칸에는 각각 ④ '제거하다'와 '규제하는'이 들어가야 함

왜 오답?

① 행동을 통제하기 위해 규제를 개발한 것이므로 비공식적인 통제를 '제한'하거나 '관대한' 조치라는 것은 맞지 않다.
② 도시화로 인해 마을이나 작은 소도시의 비공식적인 통제가 해체되었다. 그러므로 마을이나 작은 소도시의 비공식적인 통제를 '유지한다'는 것은 글과 맞지 않다.
③ 도시 사회가 기존의 마을이나 작은 소도시의 비공식적인 통제를 '평가한다'는 등의 언급은 없다.
⑤ '규제'는 구성원의 행동을 제한하거나 규제하는 조치이지, '관대한' 조치가 아니다.

도입	거대한 산업 도시의 출현은 도시화라는 사회적 결과를 가져왔음
부연 (도시화의 영향)	· 도시는 마을이나 작은 소도시의 비공식적인 통제를 해체함 · 도시는 도시 행동을 통제하기 위해 토지의 사적 사용 등을 통제하는 규제를 포함하여 다양한 방식을 개발했음

O12 정답 ① * 소멸한 원래의 동기

명령문에 이어지는 and: ~해라, 그러면 …
Put a hamster on a wheel, / and it will start running. //
햄스터를 쳇바퀴에 올려놓아라 / 그러면 그것은 달리기 시작할 것이다 //
Give the hamster a treat, / and it will run even longer. //
햄스터에게 먹을 것을 주어라 / 그러면 그것은 훨씬 더 오래 달릴 것이다 //
Stop dispensing the treats, / and the hamster will stop running / — completely. // 단서1 보상 없이도 달리던 햄스터에 보상을 주다가
주지 않으면 햄스터는 달리기를 완전히 멈출 것임
먹을 것을 주는 것을 그만두어라 / 그러면 햄스터는 달리기를 멈출 것이다 / 완전히 //
The original motivation / has thereby become extinguished. //
원래의 동기는 / 그것으로 소멸했다 //
The school system /
학교 시스템은 /
has been taking advantage of this psychological feature /
현재완료 진행형
이러한 심리적 특징을 이용해 왔다 /
by replacing / young children's natural curiosity and joy of discovery / with praise, grades, and other short-term performance boosters. //
대체함으로써 / 어린 아이들의 자연스러운 호기심과 발견의 기쁨을 / 칭찬, 성적, 그리고 다른 단기적인 성취 촉진책으로 //
As the story goes, / there once was an old man / who enjoyed watching sunsets / from his porch. //
이야기에 따르면 / 옛날에 한 노인이 있었다 / 해가 지는 것을 보는 것을 즐긴 / 자기 집 현관에서 //
One day, / a bunch of kids came over / and started playing loudly / in front of his house. // 단서2 아이들이 시끄럽게 놀기 시작함
어느 날 / 한 무리의 아이들이 와서 / 시끄럽게 놀기 시작했다 / 그의 집 앞에서 //
주어 동사 목적어 목적격 보어
The man asked the kids / to move over, / but they ignored him. //
그 남자는 아이들에게 요청했지만 / 비켜 달라고 / 그들은 그를 무시했다 //
Next day, / the children came again. //
다음날 / 아이들이 다시 왔다 //
병렬 구조
The man called them over, / gave each one a nickel, / and asked them / to make as much noise as they possibly could / — to which they happily obliged. // 단서3 아이들에게 시끄럽게 하는 것에 대해 보상을 줌
전치사+관계대명사
그 남자는 그들을 불러서 / 각각의 아이에게 5센트씩 주고 / 그들에게 요청했는데 / 그들이 할 수 있는 만큼 최대한 시끄러운 소리를 내어 달라고 / 그들은 그것에 즐겁게 따랐다 //
The man kept regularly handing out coins, / until one day he told the kids / that he was no longer paying them. //
told의 간접목적어와 직접목적어
그 남자는 계속해서 규칙적으로 동전을 나누어 주었다 / 어느 날 그가 아이들에게 말했던 때까지 / 그가 그들에게 더이상 돈을 주지 않겠다고 단서4 아이들에게 보상을 주는 것을 멈춤
"Then we aren't going to make noise for you," / the children announced / — and left. // 단서5 그러자 아이들이 시끄럽게 하는 것을 멈춤
"그렇다면 우리는 할아버지를 위해 시끄러운 소리를 내지 않을 거예요"라고 / 아이들은 알렸다 / 그리고 가 버렸다 //

★ 현재완료 진행 시제
have[has] been v-ing의 형태로, 과거에 시작된 일이 현재까지 계속되고 있음을 나타내는 현재완료의 (계속) 용법과 비슷하지만, 진행 중임을 좀 더 강조한다.

→ It is possible to (A) remove / an individual's willingness to do something / by consistently providing (B) rewards / for the action / for some time / and then withholding them. /
가주어 진주어
병렬 구조(by의 목적어)
없애는 것이 가능하다 / 무언가를 기꺼이 하고자 하는 개인의 마음을 / 보상을 일관되게 제공함으로써 / 그 행동에 대한 / 일정 기간 / 그런 다음 그것을 주지 않으므로써 //

- treat ⓝ 선물, 먹을 것 · dispense ⓥ 나누어 주다, 제공하다
- thereby ⓐⓓ 그렇게 함으로써 · extinguish ⓥ 끝내다, 없애다

- psychological ⓐ 정신의, 심리적인 · curiosity ⓝ 호기심
- praise ⓝ 칭찬, 찬사 · booster ⓝ 촉진제, (사기를) 높이는 것
- porch ⓝ 현관 · nickel ⓝ (미국·캐나다의) 5센트 동전
- oblige ⓥ 돕다, (도움 등을) 베풀다 · willingness ⓝ 기꺼이 하는 마음
- consistently ⓐⓓ 지속적으로 · withhold ⓥ 보류하다, 숨기다

햄스터를 쳇바퀴에 올려놓으면 그것은 달리기 시작할 것이다. 햄스터에게 먹을 것을 주면 그것은 훨씬 더 오래 달릴 것이다. 먹을 것을 주는 것을 그만두면 햄스터는 달리기를 완전히 멈출 것이다. 그것으로 원래의 동기는 소멸했다. 학교 시스템은 어린 아이들의 자연스러운 호기심과 발견의 기쁨을 칭찬, 성적, 그리고 다른 단기적인 성취 촉진책으로 대체함으로써 이러한 심리적 특징을 이용해 왔다.

이야기에 따르면, 옛날에 자기 집 현관에서 해가 지는 것을 보는 것을 즐긴 한 노인이 있었다. 어느 날, 한 무리의 아이들이 와서 그의 집 앞에서 시끄럽게 놀기 시작했다. 그 남자는 아이들에게 비켜 달라고 요청했지만, 그들은 그의 말을 무시했다. 다음날, 아이들이 다시 왔다. 그 남자는 그들을 불러서, 각각의 아이에게 5센트씩 주고, 그들이 할 수 있는 만큼 최대한 시끄러운 소리를 내어 달라고 요청했는데, 그들은 그것에 즐겁게 따랐다. 그 남자는 계속해서 규칙적으로 동전을 나누어 주다가, 어느 날 그들에게 돈을 더이상 주지 않겠다고 말했다. "그렇다면 우리는 할아버지를 위해 시끄러운 소리를 내지 않을 거예요."라고 알리고 아이들은 가 버렸다.
→ 행동에 대한 (B) 보상을 일정 기간 일관되게 제공하고, 그런 다음 그것을 주지 않음으로써 무언가를 기꺼이 하고자 하는 개인의 마음을 (A) 없애는 것이 가능하다.

다음 글의 내용을 한 문장으로 요약하고자 한다. 빈칸 (A), (B)에 들어갈 말로 가장 적절한 것은?

(A)	(B)	
① remove 없애다	rewards 보상	보상을 주다가 안 주면 보상 없이도 하던 것을 안 함
② remove	punishments 처벌	
③ boost 늘리다	explanations 설명	'먹을 것', '5센트'를 주는 것임
④ evaluate 평가하다	punishments	
⑤ boost	rewards	보상 없이도 하던 것을 하지 않게 됨

왜 정답? [정답률 60%]

첫 세 문장은, 보상 없이도 달리던 햄스터에게 달리는 것에 대해 보상을 주다가 주지 않으면 햄스터는 달리는 것을 완전히 멈춘다는 내용이다.

이어지는 두 번째 예시는, 집 앞에서 시끄럽게 놀던 아이들에게 시끄럽게 하는 것에 대해 보상을 주다가 멈추자 아이들이 시끄럽게 하는 것을 멈췄다는 내용이다. 두 가지 모두 '보상'을 제공하다가 제공하지 않음으로써 무언가를 하고자 하는 마음을 '없애는' 것이 가능하다는 것을 이야기하는 사례이므로 정답은 ①이다.

왜 오답?

②, ④ 햄스터에게 먹을 것을 주는 것과 아이들에게 5센트를 주는 것이 '처벌'을 주는 것은 아니다.

③, ⑤ 보상 없이도 달리던 햄스터가 달리는 것을 완전히 멈추고, 시끄럽게 놀던 아이들이 더이상 시끄러운 소리를 내지 않은 것으로, 원래의 동기가 '늘어난' 것이 아니라 소멸한 것이다.

＊ 글의 흐름

사례	보상 없이도 달리던 햄스터에게 달리는 것에 대해 보상을 주다가 주지 않으면 햄스터는 달리는 것을 완전히 멈춤
	집 앞에서 시끄럽게 놀던 아이들에게 시끄럽게 하는 것에 대해 보상을 주다가 멈추자 아이들이 시끄럽게 하는 것을 멈췄음
결론	보상을 제공하다가 제공하지 않음으로써 무언가를 하고자 하는 마음을 없애는 것이 가능함

O13 정답 ② ＊지나치지 않는 대자연

As a social species, / should we not all be synchronized / and therefore awake / at the same time / to promote maximal human interactions? //
사회적 종으로서 / 우리는 모두 동시성을 갖게 되어 / 깨어 있어야 하지 않을까 / 동시에 / 최대한의 인간 상호 작용을 촉진하기 위해 //

Perhaps not. //
아마도 아닐 것이다 //

Humans likely evolved to co-sleep / as families or even whole tribes, / not alone or as couples. //
인간은 함께 잠을 자도록 아마도 진화했을 것이다 / 가족이나 심지어 부족 전체로서 / 혼자나 짝으로 지어서가 아니라 //

Appreciating this evolutionary context, / the benefits / of such genetically programmed variation / in sleep/wake timing preferences / can be understood. //
이러한 진화적 맥락을 이해하면 / 이점이 / 그렇게 유전적으로 설계된 차이의 / 수면/기상 시간 선호도에서 / 이해될 수 있다 //

The night people in the group / would not be going to sleep / until one or two a.m., / and not waking / until nine or ten a.m. //
집단 중 저녁형 인간은 / 잠이 들지 않을 것이고 / 오전 한두 시까지 / 깨어나지 않을 것이다 / 오전 9~10시까지 //

The morning people, on the other hand, / would have retired for the night / at nine p.m. / and woken / at five a.m. //
반면에 아침형 인간은 / 잠자리에 들었을 것이고 / 오후 9시에 / 깨어났을 것이다 / 오전 5시에 //

Consequently, / the group as a whole / is only collectively vulnerable / (i.e., every person asleep) / for just four / rather than eight hours, /
결과적으로 / 집단 전체는 / 오직 집단적으로 취약하다 / (예를 들어, 모든 사람이 잠든 상태) / 단지 4시간 동안만 / 8시간이 아닌 /

despite everyone still getting the chance / for eight hours of sleep. //
모든 사람이 여전히 기회를 얻었음에도 불구하고 / 8시간의 수면을 위한 //

That's potentially a 50 percent increase / in survival fitness. //
그것은 잠재적으로 50퍼센트 증가이다 / 생존 적합도에 있어 //

Mother Nature would never pass / on a biological trait — here, the useful variability / in when individuals within a collective tribe / go to sleep and wake up — /
대자연은 절대로 지나치지 않을 것이다 / 생물학적 특성을 / 여기서는 유용한 변이성 / 집단 부족 내의 사람들이 / 잠들고 일어날 때에 있어 /

that could enhance / the survival safety / and thus fitness of a species / by this amount. //
높일 수 있는 / 생존 안전성과 / 그로 인한 종의 적합도를 / 그만큼 //

And so she hasn't. //
그래서 대자연은 지나치지 않았다 //

→ Individuals have (A) **differences** / in the time of the day / when they prefer to sleep and wake up, / which could promote their (B) **survivability** / as a group. //
사람들이 다름을 가지고 있고 / 하루의 시간대에서 / 그들이 자고 일어나기를 선호하는 / 이는 자신들의 생존 가능성을 높일 수 있다 / 집단으로서 //

- at the same time 동시에 · promote ⓥ 증진하다
- maximal ⓐ 최대한의 · evolve ⓥ 진화하다 · tribe ⓝ 부족
- appreciate ⓥ 이해하다, 감상하다 · evolutionary ⓐ 진화의
- context ⓝ 맥락 · genetically ⓐⓓ 유전적으로
- variation ⓝ 차이 · collectively ⓐⓓ 집합적으로
- potentially ⓐⓓ 잠재적으로 · survival fitness 생존 적합도
- trait ⓝ 특성 · variability ⓝ 변동성 · enhance ⓥ 높이다

사회적 종으로서, 우리는 모두 동시성을 갖게 되어 최대한의 인간 상호
작용을 촉진하기 위해 동시에 깨어 있어야 하지 않을까? 아마도 아닐 것이다.
인간은 혼자나 짝을 지어서가 아니라, 가족이나 심지어 부족 전체로서 함께
잠을 자도록 아마도 진화했을 것이다. 이러한 진화적 맥락을 이해하면,
수면/기상 시간 선호도에서 그렇게 유전적으로 설계된 차이의 이점이 이해될
수 있다. 집단 중 저녁형 인간은 오전 한두 시가 되어서야 잠이 들 것이고,
오전 9~10시가 되어서야 깨어날 것이다. 반면에 아침형 인간은 오후 9시에
잠자리에 들었을 것이고 오전 5시에 깨어났을 것이다. 결과적으로, 모든 사람이
여전히 8시간의 수면 기회를 얻었음에도 불구하고, 집단 전체는 8시간이 아닌
단지 4시간 동안만 오직 집단적으로 취약하다(예를 들어, 모든 사람이 잠든
상태). 그것은 잠재적으로 생존 적합도가 50퍼센트 증가하는 것이다. 대자연은
종의 생존 안전성과 그로 인한 적합도를 그만큼 높일 수 있는 생물학적 특성,
즉 여기서는, 집단 부족 내의 사람들이 잠들고 일어날 때의 유용한 변이성을
절대로 지나치지 않을 것이다. 그래서 대자연은 지나치지 않았다.
→ 사람들이 하루에 자고 일어나기를 선호하는 시간대에서 (A) 다름을 가지고
있고, 이는 집단으로서 자신들의 (B) 생존 가능성을 높일 수 있다.

다음 글의 내용을 한 문장으로 요약하고자 한다. 빈칸 (A), (B)에 들어갈 말로
가장 적절한 것은?

	(A)		(B)	
①	differences	—	originality	생존 적합도를 늘림
	다름		독창성	
②	differences	—	survivability	잠들고 일어나는 시간이 달라서
	다름		생존 가능성	생존 안전성이 높아짐
③	similarities	—	cooperation	저녁형 인간과 아침형 인간이 대조됨
	유사성		협력	
④	similarities	—	adaptation	
	유사성		적응	
⑤	regularities	—	mobility	규칙적인 수면 시간에 대한 내용이 아님
	규칙성		이동성	

⟩왜 정답? [정답률 67%]

- 집단 중 저녁형 인간: 오전 한두 시에 잠자리에 들어서 오전
  9~10시까지 잠 [단서 1]
- 아침형 인간: 오후 9시에 잠자리에 들어서 오전 5시에 일어남 [단서 2]
- 그것은 잠재적으로 생존 적합도가 50퍼센트 증가하는 것임 [단서 3]

➡ **(A)**: 사람마다 잠자리에 들고 일어나는 시간이 다르다는 내용이므로
differences(다름)가 적절하다.
　(B): 이러한 다름으로 인해 생존 적합도가 잠재적으로 50퍼센트 증가하고, 생존
안전성과 그로 인한 종의 적합도가 높아진다고 했으므로 survivability(생존
가능성)가 정답이다.
　▶ 요약문의 빈칸에는 각각 '다름'과 '생존 가능성'이 들어가야 하므로 정답은 ②임

⟩왜 오답?
① 사람들이 잠자리에 들고 일어나는 시간이 다르다는 사실이 '독창성'을 높이는 것은
아니다.
③ 저녁형 인간과 아침형 인간이 대조됐으므로 사람들이 자고 일어나는 시간대가
'유사성'을 가진 것이 아니라 정반대이다.
④ 사람들이 자고 일어나는 시간대가 다르고, 그것이 '적응'을 높이는 것도 아니다.
⑤ 규칙적인 수면 시간에 대한 내용이 아니고, 그것이 '이동성'을 높이는 내용도
아니다.

＊ 글의 흐름

도입	인간은 가족이나 심지어 부족 전체로서 함께 잠을 자도록 아마도 진화했을 것임
설명 ①	저녁형 인간과 아침형 인간이 잠자리에 들고 일어나는 시간이 다름
설명 ②	모든 사람이 같은 시간 동안의 수면 기회가 있어도, 집단 전체는 일부 시간 동안만 오직 집단적으로 취약함
예시	대자연은 집단 부족 내의 사람들이 잠들고 일어날 때의 유용한 변이성을 절대로 지나치지 않을 것임

suggest의 목적어절 접속사①
Experiments suggest / that animals, / just like humans, / tend to
prefer exaggerated, supernormal stimuli, /
실험들은 보여 준다 / 동물이 / 인간과 마찬가지로 / 과장되고 비범한 자극을 선호하는 경향이
있으며 / suggest의 목적어절 접속사②
and that a preference can rapidly propel itself / to extreme levels
/ (*peak shift effect*). //
선호는 빠르게 그 자체를 나아가게 할 수 있다는 것을 / 극단적인 수준으로 / ('정점 변경 효과') //
In one experiment, / through food rewards / rats were
conditioned / to prefer squares / to other geometric forms. //
한 실험에서 / 음식 보상을 통해 / 쥐는 조건화되었다 / 정사각형을 선호하도록 / 다른 기하학
형태보다 // [단서 1] 실험 단계 ①: 음식 보상을 통해 정사각형을 선호하도록 조건화됨
In the next step, / a non-square rectangle was introduced / and
associated / with an even larger reward / than the square. //
다음 단계에서 / 정사각형이 아닌 직사각형이 내놓아졌고 / 연관되었다 / 훨씬 더 큰 보상과 /
정사각형보다 // [단서 2] 실험 단계 ②: 훨씬 더 큰 보상과 연관되는 직사각형을 선호하는 것을 학습함
As expected, / the rats learned / to reliably prefer the rectangle. //
예상했듯이 / 쥐는 학습했다 / 직사각형을 확실히 선호하는 것을
주격 보어가 문두로 가면서 주어와 동사가 도치됨
Less predictable was the third part / of the experiment. //
세 번째 부분이 덜 예측 가능했다 / 그 실험의 // 형용사적 용법(the opportunity 수식)
The rats were offered the opportunity / to choose /
쥐는 기회를 제공받았다 / 선택할 /
선행사(목적격 관계대명사는 생략됨)
between the rectangle / they already knew / and associated
between A and B: A와 B 사이에서　　　　　　선행사
with large rewards / and another rectangle, / the proportions of
목적격 관계대명사
which were even more different / from those of a square. //
직사각형과 / 그들이 이미 알고 있고 / 큰 보상과 연관되었던 / 또 다른 직사각형 사이에서 /
그것의 비율이 훨씬 더 차이가 나는 / 정사각형의 그것과 //

Interestingly, rats picked / this novel variant, / without
undergoing / any reward-based conditioning / in favor of it. //
흥미롭게도 쥐는 골랐다 / 이 새로운 변형을 / 경험하지 않고도 / 어떠한 보상에 기반한
조건화도 / 그것을 위한 // [단서 3] 실험 단계 ③: 보상에 기반한 조건화를 경험하지 않고도 두 직사각형
주어　　　 사이에서 정사각형의 비율과 훨씬 더 차이가 나는 것을 고름
A possible explanation is / thus / that they chose the larger
동사　　　　　　 주격 보어절 접속사
difference / from the original square / (i.e., the exaggeration of
non-squareness). //
가능한 설명은 ~이다 / 따라서 / 그들이 더 큰 차이를 선택했다는 것 / 원래의 정사각형보다 /
('정사각형이 아닌 것'의 과장을) //

→In an experiment, / after first establishing an (A) **inclination**
/ to squares, / and then to non-square rectangles, /
한 실험에서 / 처음에는 기호를 확립한 후에 / 정사각형에 대한 / 그리고서 정사각형이 아닌
직사각형에 대한 /
rats were seen / to pursue (B) **severe** rectangularity / even
without any additional reward. //
쥐는 보였다 / 극단적인 직사각형의 성질을 추구하는 것으로 / 어떤 추가적 보상 없이도 //

- exaggerated ⓐ 과장된　　 - supernormal ⓐ 비범한
- stimuli ⓝ 자극　 - preference ⓝ 선호　 - propel ⓥ 나아가게 하다
- conditioned ⓐ 조건부의　 - geometric ⓐ 기하학의
- rectangle ⓝ 직사각형　 - associated with ~와 연관된
- reliably ⓐ 확실히　　 - predictable ⓐ 예측할 수 있는
- opportunity ⓝ 기회　　 - proportion ⓝ 비율
- inclination ⓝ 기호, 성향　 - severe ⓐ 극단적인
- vague ⓐ 희미한　　 - unexpected ⓐ 예상치 못한
- subtle ⓐ 미묘한

실험들은 동물이 인간과 마찬가지로 과장되고 비범한 자극을 선호하는
경향이 있으며 선호는 빠르게 그 자체를 극단적인 수준으로 나아가게 할 수
있다는 것('정점 변경 효과')을 보여 준다. 한 실험에서 음식 보상을 통해 쥐는
정사각형을 다른 기하학 형태보다 선호하도록 조건화되었다. 다음 단계에서
정사각형이 아닌 직사각형이 내놓아졌고 정사각형보다 훨씬 더 큰 보상과

연관되었다. 예상했듯이 쥐는 직사각형을 확실히 선호하는 것을 학습했다. 덜 예측 가능했던 것은 그 실험의 세 번째 부분이었다. 쥐는 그들이 이미 알고 있고 큰 보상과 연관되었던 직사각형과 그것의 비율이 정사각형의 그것과 훨씬 더 차이가 나는 또 다른 직사각형 사이에서 선택을 할 기회를 제공받았다. 흥미롭게도 쥐는 그것을 위한 보상에 기반한 조건화를 조금도 경험하지 않고도 이 새로운 변형을 골랐다. 따라서 가능한 설명은 그들이 원래의 정사각형보다 더 큰 차이, 즉 '정사각형이 아닌 것'의 과장을 선택했다는 것이다.

→ 한 실험에서 처음에는 정사각형, 그러고 나서 정사각형이 아닌 직사각형에 대한 (A) 기호를 확립한 후에 쥐는 어떤 추가적 보상 없이도 (B) 극단적인 직사각형의 성질을 추구하는 것으로 보였다.

다음 글의 내용을 한 문장으로 요약하고자 한다. 빈칸 (A), (B)에 들어갈 말로 가장 적절한 것은? [3점]

— even more different라고 설명했음

	(A)		(B)	
①	inclination 기호	—	severe 극단적인	어떤 사각형을 선호하는지에 대한 실험, 정사각형과의 비율 차이가 훨씬 더 큰 것을 선택함
②	opposition 반대	—	familiar 익숙한	
③	inclination 기호	—	vague 희미한	음식 보상을 통해 조건화됨
④	opposition 반대	—	unexpected 예상치 못한	
⑤	attachment 애착	—	subtle 미묘한	

왜 정답? [정답률 40%]

> ❶ 음식 보상을 통해 쥐가 정사각형을 선호하도록 조건화됨 **단서1**
> ❷ 훨씬 더 큰 보상과 연관된 직사각형이 제시되자 쥐가 직사각형을 확실히 선호하는 것을 학습함 **단서2**
> ❸ 조건화 없이도, 두 개의 직사각형 사이에서 정사각형의 비율과 훨씬 더 차이가 나는 비율의 직사각형을 고름 **단서3**

➡ **(A)**: 제시된 실험에서 확립한 것은 정사각형, 직사각형에 대한 선호, 즉 '기호(inclination)'이다.

(B): 쥐가 더 큰 보상을 통해 학습하지 않고도 선택한 것은 정사각형의 비율과 훨씬 더 차이가 나는 비율의 직사각형이었다. 직사각형의 특징이 더욱 명확한 것을 고른 것이므로, 이는 쥐가 '극단적인(severe)' 직사각형의 성질을 추구하는 것이라고 할 수 있다.

▶ 요약문의 빈칸에는 각각 ① '기호'와 '극단적인'이 들어가야 함

왜 오답?

② 직사각형에 대한 '반대'를 확립하거나 '익숙한' 직사각형의 성질을 선호하는 것이 아니다.
③ '희미한' 직사각형의 성질을 선호하는 것이라는 문장은 문맥에 맞지 않다.
④ 직사각형에 대한 '반대'를 확립하거나 '예상치 못한' 직사각형의 성질을 선호하는 것이 아니다.
⑤ 직사각형에 대한 '애착'을 확립하거나 '미묘한' 직사각형의 성질을 선호한다는 내용은 나오지 않았다.

* 글의 흐름

도입	실험들은 동물이 인간과 마찬가지로 과장되고 선호 자체를 극단적인 수준으로 나아가게 할 수 있다는 것을 보여 줌
실험 내용	음식 보상을 통해 쥐가 정사각형을 다른 기하학 형태보다 선호하도록 조건화되었고, 다음 단계에서 직사각형이 내놓아졌고 정사각형보다 훨씬 더 큰 보상과 연관되었음
실험 결과	쥐는 직사각형을 확실히 선호하는 것을 학습했고, 그것을 위한 보상에 기반한 조건화를 조금도 경험하지 않고도 이 새로운 변형을 골랐음
결론	그들이 원래의 정사각형보다 더 큰 차이, 즉 '정사각형이 아닌 것'의 과장을 선택했다는 것임

○15 정답 ② * 나만 그렇게 생각하는 것이 아니었어

주어
Research / from the Harwood Institute for Public Innovation in the USA / 동사 **shows** /
연구는 / 미국 Harwood Institute for Public Innovation으로부터의 / 보여준다 /
feel의 목적어절 접속사
that people feel / **that 'materialism' somehow comes** / **between** shows의 목적어절 접속사 **them and the satisfaction of their social needs.** //
사람들이 느낀다는 것을 / '물질주의'가 어떤 일인지 끼어든다 / 사람들은 물질주의가 그들의 사회적 욕구 의 만족 사이에 // **단서1** 충족을 방해한다고 느낌

주어
A report / **entitled** *Yearning for Balance*, / **based on a nationwide survey of Americans,** / 동사 **concluded** / 목적어절 접속사 **that they were 'deeply ambivalent** / **about wealth and material gain'.** //
보고서는 / 〈Yearning for Balance〉라는 제목의 / 미국인에 대한 전국적인 조사를 토대로 한 / 결론지었다 / 그들이 '대단히 양면 가치적'이라고 / '부와 물질적 이익에 관해' //

주어
A large majority of people wanted / 동사 **society** 목적어 **to 'move away** 목적격 보어 / **from greed and excess** / **toward a way of life** / **more centred on values, community, and family'.** //
대다수의 사람들은 원했다 / 사회가 '벗어나기를 / 탐욕과 과잉으로부터 / 삶의 방식으로 향하 여 / 가치, 공동체, 가족에 좀 더 초점을 맞춘' //

But they also felt / **that these priorities were not shared** / **by most of their fellow Americans,** / **who, they believed, had become** / 삽입절 **'increasingly atomized, selfish, and irresponsible'.** //
그러나 그들은 느끼기도 했다 / 이러한 우선순위가 공유되지 않는다고 / 그들의 대다수의 동료 미국인에 의해 / 그들이 믿기에 ~해진 / '점차 개별화되고, 이기적이며, 무책임해진' //

As a result / **they often felt isolated.** // **단서2** 자신의 우선순위가 공유되지
그 결과 / 그들은 종종 소외된 기분이 들었다 // 않는다고 느껴져 소외감을 느낌

However, the report says, / **that when brought together in focus groups** / **to discuss these issues,** / 초점집단: 시장 조사나 여론 조사를 위해 각 계층을
하지만 보고서는 말한다 / 초점집단으로 모였을 때 / 이러한 문제를 논의하기 위해 / 대표하도록 뽑은 소수의 사람들로 이뤄진 집단
부사적 용법(감정의 원인)
people were 'surprised and excited / **to find** / **that others share[d]** **their views'.** // **단서3** 사실 다른 사람들도 그들의 견해를 공유함
사람들은 '놀라고 흥분했다고 / 알게 되어 / 다른 사람들이 그들의 견해를 공유한[했다는'] 것을 // 주어, 선행사(목적격 관계대명사는 생략됨)
Rather than uniting us / **with others** / **in a common cause,** / **the unease** / **we feel** / **about the loss of social values** / **and the way** /
우리를 결속하기보다는 / 다른 사람들과 / 공동의 대의로 / 불안감은 / 우리가 느끼는 / 사회적 선행사(관계부사는 생략됨)
가치의 상실에 대해 / 그리고 방식에 대해 //

we are drawn / **into the pursuit of material gain** / 수동태 **is often** 동사 **experienced** / **as if it were a purely private ambivalence** / **which cuts us off from others.** //
우리가 끌려 들어가는 / 물질적 이익의 추구로 / 흔히 경험된다 / 마치 그것이 순전히 개인의 양면 가치인 것처럼 / 우리를 다른 사람들과 단절시키는 //

> → **Many Americans,** / **believing** / **that materialism keeps them** 주어 **from (A) pursuing social values,** /
> 많은 미국인은 / 믿는 / 물질주의가 그들이 사회적 가치를 추구하는 것을 막는다고 /
> **feel detached** / **from most others,** / **but this is actually a fairly** 동사 주격 보어 **(B) common concern.** //
> 소외되었다고 느낀다 / 대다수의 다른 사람들로부터 / 하지만 이것은 실제로 상당히 공통 적인 우려이다 //

- **materialism** ⓝ 물질주의
- **somehow** ⓐ𝒹 어떻게든, 왜 그런지 (모르겠지만), 왠지
- **entitled** ⓐ (~라는) 제목의   • **nationwide** ⓐ 전국적인
- **deeply** ⓐ𝒹 대단히, 깊이   • **gain** ⓝ 이익   • **greed** ⓝ 탐욕
- **excess** ⓝ 지나침, 과잉   • **center on** ~에 초점을 맞추다
- **priority** ⓝ 우선순위   • **fellow** ⓐ 같은 처지에 있는, 동료의
- **increasingly** ⓐ𝒹 점점 더, 갈수록 더
- **atomize** ⓥ 개별화하다, 세분화하다   • **selfish** ⓐ 이기적인
- **irresponsible** ⓐ 무책임한   • **isolate** ⓥ 소외시키다, 고립시키다
- **unite** ⓥ 결속하다   • **cause** ⓝ 대의

- pursuit ⓝ 추구, (원하는 것을) 좇음[찾음]　　• purely ⓐⓓ 순전히, 전적으로
- cut off from ~에서 고립시키다　　• detach ⓥ 떼다, 분리하다
- fairly ⓐⓓ 상당히, 꽤　　• concern ⓝ 우려, 걱정

미국 Harwood Institute for Public Innovation의 연구는 사람들이 '물질주의'가 어떤 일인지 그들과 그들의 사회적 욕구의 만족 사이에 끼어든다고 느낀다는 것을 보여준다. 미국인에 대한 전국적인 조사를 토대로 한, 〈Yearning for Balance〉라는 제목의 보고서는 그들이 '부와 물질적 이익에 관해 대단히 양면 가치적'이라고 결론지었다. 대다수의 사람은 사회가 '탐욕과 과잉에서 벗어나 좀 더 가치, 공동체, 가족 중심의 삶의 방식으로 향하기'를 원했다. 그러나 그들은 이러한 우선순위가 그들이 믿기에 '점차 개별화되고, 이기적이며, 무책임해진' 대다수의 동료 미국인에 의해 공유되지 않는다고 느끼기도 했다. 그 결과, 그들은 종종 소외된 기분이 들었다. 하지만, 보고서에 따르면, 이러한 문제를 논의하기 위해 초점집단으로 모였을 때, 사람들은 '다른 사람들이 그들의 견해를 공유한다[했다]는 것을 알게 되어 놀라고 흥분'했다. 사회적 가치의 상실과 물질적 이익의 추구로 끌려 들어가는 방식에 대해 우리가 느끼는 불안감은, 다른 사람들과 우리를 공동의 대의로 결속하기보다는 마치 우리를 다른 사람들과 단절시키는 순전히 개인의 양면 가치인 것처럼 경험되는 경우가 흔하다.

→ 물질주의가 그들이 사회적 가치를 (A) 추구하는 것을 막는다고 믿는 많은 미국인은 대다수의 다른 사람들로부터 소외되었다고 느끼지만, 이것은 실제로 상당히 (B) 공통적인 우려이다.

다음 글의 내용을 한 문장으로 요약하고자 한다. 빈칸 (A), (B)에 들어갈 말로 가장 적절한 것은?

(A) 사람들은 물질주의가 그들과 그들의 사회적 욕구의 충족 사이를 가로막는다고 느낌 (B) 사실 그들은 다른 사람들과 그들의 견해를 공유함

	(A)	(B)
①	pursuing 추구하는	unnecessary 물질주의에 대한 오해를 벗기는 글이 아님 불필요한
②	pursuing	common 공통적인
③	holding 지니는	personal 다른 사람들과 견해를 공유하므로 개인적인 우려가 아님 개인적인
④	denying 부정하는	ethical 물질주의는 사회적 가치의 추구에 부정적이라고 느끼는 사람들임 윤리적인
⑤	denying	primary 주된

〉왜 정답? [정답률 57%]

물질주의가 사람들과 사람들의 사회적 욕구의 만족 사이에 끼어든다는 것의 의미 꿀팁

사람들은 물질주의가 사회적 욕구의 충족을 방해한다고 느끼고, 사회가 탐욕과 과잉(물질주의)에서 벗어나 가치, 공동체, 가족(사회적 가치)에 좀 더 초점을 맞춘 삶의 방식으로 향하기를 원하지만, 이러한 생각이 다른 사람들과 공유되지 않는다고 느껴서 종종 소외된 기분이 든다고 했다. However 이후로는 이러한 사람들의 견해가 사실은 다른 사람들과 공유된다는 내용이 등장하므로 요약문의 빈칸에는 각각 ② '추구하는'과 '공통적인'이 적절하다.

〉왜 오답?

① 물질주의가 사회적 가치의 추구를 방해한다는 것이 '불필요한' 우려라는 요약문이 되려면 물질주의가 사실은 사회적 가치의 추구를 방해하지 않는다는 내용의 글이어야 한다.

③ 자신의 견해가 다른 사람들과 공유되지 않는다고 느끼지만 사실은 공유된다는 내용이므로 '개인적인' 우려라는 요약문은 글과 정반대가 된다. ─주의─

④, ⑤ 물질주의가 사회적 가치의 추구를 방해한다는 견해가 사실은 많은 사람들에 의해 공유된다는 내용이다. 물질주의가 사회적 가치를 부정하는 것을 막는다는 것은 물질주의가 사회적 가치 추구에 긍정적인 요소라는 의미가 되므로 글에 맞지 않는다.

＊ 글의 흐름

연구 결과 ①	사람들은 물질주의가 사회적 욕구를 충족시키는 것을 방해한다고 생각함
연구 결과 ②	사람들은 자신의 그러한 생각이 다른 사람들과 공유되지 않는다고 느껴서 종종 소외감을 느낌
반전	하지만 이 문제에 대해 논의하면서 사람들은 다른 사람들이 그들의 견해를 공유한다는 것을 알게 되어 놀라고 흥분했음

○ 16 정답 ①　＊관리자로서 기능하는 디자이너

형용사적 용법(A striving 수식)
A striving / to demonstrate individual personality / through designs / should not be surprising. //
　　　(추측)을 나타내는 조동사
노력은 / 개인의 개성을 보여주기 위한 / 디자인을 통해 / 놀랍지 않을 것이다 /

Most designers are educated / to work as individuals, / and design literature contains / countless references to 'the designer'. //
대부분의 디자이너는 교육받고 / 개인으로 일하도록 / 디자인 문헌은 담고 있다 /
'그 디자이너'에 대한 무수히 많은 언급을
　　　　　　동사와 주격 보어 사이에 삽입된 부사구
Personal flair / is without doubt an absolute necessity / in some product categories, / particularly relatively small objects, /
개인적인 재능이 / 의심할 여지가 없이 절대적으로 필요한 것이다 / 일부 상품 범주에서는 /
특히 상대적으로 작은 물건들

with a low degree of technological complexity, / such as furniture, lighting, small appliances, and housewares. //
낮은 단계의 기술적 복잡성을 가진 / 가구, 조명, 소형 가전, 그리고 가정용품들과 같은 //

In larger-scale projects, / however, / even where a strong personality exercises / powerful influence, / 단서 1 프로젝트의 '규모'가 변수임
더 큰 규모의 프로젝트에서 / 그러나 / 심지어 강한 개성이 발휘하는 곳에서도 / 강력한 힘을
　　　　동격절 접속사
the fact / that substantial numbers of designers / are employed / in implementing a concept / can easily be overlooked. //
사실이 / 상당한 수의 디자이너가 / 참여한다는 / 계획을 실행하는 데 / 쉽게 간과될 수 있다 //

The emphasis on individuality / is therefore problematic / — rather than actually designing, / many successful designer 'personalities' / function more / as creative managers. //
개성에 대한 강조는 / 그러므로 문제가 있다 / 실제로 디자인을 하기보다는 / 많은 성공한
디자이너 '유명인사들'이 / 더 많이 기능하는 / 창의적인 관리자로서 단서 2 많은 성공한 디자이너가
　　　　　　　　　　　　　　　　　　　to부정사의 수동태　　　관리자로서 더 많이 기능함
A distinction needs to be made / between designers working truly alone / and those / working in a group. //
　　　　　　　　　　　　　　　　　　　　　＝ designers
구분이 되어야 한다 / 진정으로 혼자 일하는 디자이너와 / 디자이너 사이에 / 집단을 이루어
일하는 단서 3 집단을 이루어 일하는 디자이너의 경우 창의성 못지않게 관리 조직과 과정이 중요할 수 있음
In the latter case, / management organization and processes / can be equally as relevant / as designers' creativity. //
　　　　　　　　　　　원급 비교
후자의 경우 / 관리 조직과 과정들이 / 똑같이 의미 있을 수 있다 / 디자이너들의 창의성만큼 //

→ Depending on the (A) **size** of a project, / the capacity
　　　　　　　　　　　　　　　　　　　　　　　　주어
of designers / to (B) **coordinate** team-based working environments /
프로젝트의 크기에 따라 / 디자이너의 능력이 / 팀 기반 작업 환경을 조정하는 /
동사
can be just as important / as their personal qualities. //
꼭 (~만큼) 중요할 수 있다 / 그들의 개인적 특성만큼 //

- demonstrate ⓥ 보여주다, 설명하다　　• contain ⓥ 포함하다, 억제하다
- countless ⓐ 셀 수 없이 많은　　• reference ⓝ 언급, 참조
- doubt ⓝ 의심, 의혹　　• absolute ⓐ 철저한, 완전한
- necessity ⓝ 필요(성), 불가피한 일
- degree ⓝ 정도, (각도 · 온도 단위의) 도　　• complexity ⓝ 복잡성, 복잡함
- appliance ⓝ (가정용) 기기　　• houseware ⓝ 가정용품
- substantial ⓐ (양 · 중요성 등이) 상당한　　• implement ⓥ 시행하다
- overlook ⓥ 간과하다, 내려다보다　　• emphasis ⓝ 강조(법)
- individuality ⓝ 개성, 특성　　• problematic ⓐ 문제가 있는[많은]
- personality ⓝ 성격, 유명인　　• distinction ⓝ 차이, 특별함
- relevant ⓐ 관련 있는, 유의미한　　• coordinate ⓥ 조직화하다, 조정하다

디자인을 통해 개인의 개성을 보여주기 위한 노력은 놀랍지 않을 것이다. 대부분의 디자이너는 개인으로 일하도록 교육받고, 디자인 문헌은 '그 디자이너'에 대한 무수히 많은 언급을 담고 있다. 개인적인 재능이 일부 상품 범주에서는 절대적으로 필요한 것임에는 의심할 여지가 없는데, 가구, 조명, 소형 가전, 그리고 가정용품들과 같은, 낮은 단계의 기술적 복잡성을 가진 상대적으로 작은 물건들에서 특히 그렇다. 그러나, 더 큰 규모의

프로젝트에서, 심지어 강한 개성이 강력한 힘을 발휘하는 곳에서도, 상당한 수의 디자이너가 계획을 실행하는 데 참여한다는 사실이 쉽게 간과될 수 있다. 그러므로 개성에 대한 강조는 문제가 있는데, 많은 성공한 디자이너 '유명인사들'이 실제로 디자인을 하기보다는 창의적인 관리자로서 더 많이 기능한다. 진정으로 혼자 일하는 디자이너와 집단을 이루어 일하는 디자이너는 구분되어야 한다. 후자의 경우, 관리 조직과 과정들이 디자이너들의 창의성 못지않게 똑같이 의미 있을 수 있다.

→ 프로젝트의 (A) 크기에 따라 팀 기반 작업 환경을 (B) 조정하는 디자이너의 능력이 그들의 개인적 특성 못지않게 똑같이 중요할 수 있다.

다음 글의 내용을 한 문장으로 요약하고자 한다. 빈칸 (A), (B)에 들어갈 말로 가장 적절한 것은?

(A)	(B)
프로젝트의 비용이 변수인 것은 아님	
① size 크기	coordinate 조정하는 _더 큰 규모의 프로젝트에서는 디자이너가 관리자로서 기능함_
② cost 비용	systematize 체계화하는
③ size 크기	identify 확인하는 _팀 기반 작업 환경을 확인한다는 내용은 없음_
④ cost	innovate 혁신하는
⑤ goal 목표	investigate 조사하는 _관리자로서 팀의 계획을 실행하는 역할을 하는 것임_

왜 정답? [정답률 71%]

상대적으로 작은 물건들에서는 디자이너의 개인적인 재능이 절대적으로 필요하지만, _관리자로서 기능한다는 것이 팀의 작업 환경을 조정한다는 것을 의미함_ (꿀팁) 디자이너들이 집단을 이루어 일하는 '더 큰 규모'의 프로젝트에서는 많은 성공한 디자이너들이 (창의적) 관리자로서 더 많이 기능하고, 이 경우에는 관리 조직과 과정이 창의성만큼 의미 있다는 내용이다.

따라서 요약문은 프로젝트의 '크기'에 따라 팀 기반 작업 환경을 '조정하는' 디자이너의 능력이 그들의 개인적 특성만큼 중요할 수 있다는 의미가 되어야 하므로 정답은 ①이다.

왜 오답?

②, ④, ⑤ 프로젝트의 규모가 크면 디자이너의 관리자로서의 능력이 창의성만큼 중요할 수도 있다는 내용으로, 프로젝트의 비용이나 목표가 변수인 것은 아니다. (주의)

③ 더 큰 규모의 프로젝트에서는 상당수의 디자이너가 (팀의) 계획을 실행하는 데 참여한다고 했지, 팀의 작업 환경을 확인하는 역할을 한다는 것이 아니다.

＊ 글의 흐름

대조	가구, 조명, 소형 가전, 가정용품과 같은 낮은 단계의 기술적 복잡성을 가진 상대적으로 작은 물건들에서는 디자이너의 개인적 재능이 절대적으로 필요함
	더 큰 규모의 프로젝트에서는 개성을 강조하는 것이 문제가 있는데, 많은 성공한 디자이너들은 실제로 관리자로서 더 많이 기능함
결론	혼자 일하는 디자이너와 집단을 이루어 일하는 디자이너는 구분되어야 하며, 후자의 경우에는 관리 조직과 과정이 창의성 못지않게 중요할 수 있음

O 17 정답 ② ＊역사 소설의 역할

Research for historical fiction may focus / on under-documented ordinary people, events, or sites. //
역사 소설을 위한 연구는 초점을 맞출 수 있다 / 문서로 덜 기록된 일반적인 사람, 사건, 또는 장소에 /
목적어로 to부정사나 원형부정사를 취하는 help
Fiction helps portray / everyday situations, feelings, and atmosphere / that recreate the historical context. //
주격 관계대명사
소설은 묘사하는 데 도움이 된다 / 일상적인 상황, 감정, 분위기를 / 역사적인 맥락을 재창조하는 //

Historical fiction adds "flesh / to the bare bones / that historians are able to uncover /
선행사   목적격 관계대명사   병렬 구조
역사 소설은 살을 붙이고 / 뼈대에 / 역사가들이 밝혀낼 수 있는 / **단서1** 역사 소설의 설명이 반드시 사실인 것은 아님
and by doing so / provides an account / that while not
부분 부정: 반드시 ~인 것은 아님   주격 관계대명사
necessarily true provides / a clearer indication / of past events,
주격 관계대명사절의 동사
circumstances and cultures." //
그렇게 함으로써 / 설명을 제공한다 / 반드시 사실이 아니더라도 제공하는 / 더 명확한 표현을 / 과거의 사건, 상황, 문화에 대한 //

Fiction adds color, sound, drama / to the past, / as much as it invents / parts of the past. // **단서2** 역사 소설은 과거의 일부를 지어내기까지 함
소설은 색채, 소리, 드라마를 더하여 / 과거에 / 지어내기까지 한다 / 과거의 부분들을 //

And Robert Rosenstone argues / that invention is not the weakness of films, / it is their strength. //
그리고 Robert Rosenstone은 주장한다 / 지어내는 것이 (역사) 영화의 약점이 아니고 / 강점이라고 //
can allow의 목적어와 목적격 보어
Fiction can allow users / to see parts of the past / that have never
〈이유〉의 전치사
— for lack of archives — been represented. //
소설은 사용자들이 / ~하도록 한다 / 과거의 일부를 보도록 / 역사 자료가 없어서 전혀 표현되지 않았던 // **단서3** 역사 소설은 사용자로 하여금 자료가 없어서 표현되지 않은 부분을 보게 함

In fact, Gilden Seavey explains / that if producers of historical fiction / had strongly held the strict academic standards, /
실제로 Gilden Seavey는 설명한다 / 역사 소설 제작자들이 / 엄격한 학술적 기준을 고수했다면 /
혼합가정법
many historical subjects would remain unexplored / for lack of appropriate evidence. //
많은 역사적 주제가 탐구되지 않은 채 남아있을 것이라고 / 적절한 증거가 없어서 //

Historical fiction should, therefore, not be seen / as the opposite of professional history, /
따라서 역사 소설은 여겨져서는 안 되며 / 전문적인 역사의 정반대의 것으로 /
선행사
but rather as a challenging representation of the past / from
전치사+관계대명사
which both public historians and popular audiences / may learn. // **단서4** 역사 소설로부터 대중 역사학자와 대중 관객이 모두 배울 수도 있음
오히려 과거에 대한 도전적인 표현으로 (여겨져야 한다) / 그것으로부터 대중 역사학자와 대중 관객이 모두 / 배울 수도 있는 //

> → While historical fiction reconstructs the past / using
> 부사절 접속사(대보)
> (A) insufficient evidence, /
> 역사 소설은 과거를 재구성하지만 / 불충분한 증거를 사용하여 /
> 선행사   계속적용법의 주격 관계대명사
> it provides an inviting description, / which may (B) enrich /
> people's understanding of historical events. //
> 그것은 매력적인 설명을 제공하는데 / 그것이 풍부하게 할 수도 있다 / 역사적 사건에 대한 사람들의 이해를 //

- fiction ⓝ 소설, 허구의 창작물
- under-documented ⓐ 문서로 덜 기록된   · ordinary ⓐ 평범한
- portray ⓥ 묘사하다   · atmosphere ⓝ 분위기   · context ⓝ 맥락
- flesh ⓝ 살   · uncover ⓥ 밝히다   · account ⓝ 설명
- indication ⓝ 표현   · circumstances ⓝ 상황
- archive ⓝ 역사 자료, 기록 보관소   · unexplored ⓐ 탐구되지 않은
- reconstruct ⓥ 재구성하다   · inviting ⓐ 매력적인

역사 소설을 위한 연구는 문서로 덜 기록된 일반적인 사람, 사건, 또는 장소에 초점을 맞출 수 있다. 소설은 역사적인 맥락을 재창조하는 일상적인 상황, 감정, 분위기를 묘사하는 데 도움이 된다. 역사 소설은 '역사가들이 밝혀낼 수 있는 뼈대에 살을 붙이고, 그렇게 함으로써 반드시 사실이 아니더라도 과거의 사건, 상황, 문화에 대한 더 명확한 표현을 제공하는 설명을 제공한다'. 소설은 과거에 색채, 소리, 드라마를 더하여 과거의 부분들을 지어내기까지 한다. 그리고 Robert Rosenstone은 지어내는 것이 (역사) 영화의 약점이 아니고 강점이라고 주장한다. 소설은 역사 자료가 없어서 전혀 표현되지 않았던 과거의 일부를 사용자들이 보도록 해 준다. 실제로 Gilden Seavey는 역사 소설 제작자들이 엄격한 학술적 기준을 고수했다면, 많은 역사적 주제가

적절한 증거가 없어서 탐구되지 않은 채 남아있을 것이라고 설명한다. 따라서 역사 소설은 전문적인 역사의 정반대의 것으로 여겨져서는 안 되며, 오히려 대중 역사학자와 대중 관객이 모두 그것으로부터 배울 수도 있는 과거에 대한 도전적인 표현으로 여겨져야 한다.

→ 역사 소설은 (A) **불충분한** 증거를 사용하여 과거를 재구성하지만, 그것은 매력적인 설명을 제공하는데, 그것이 역사적 사건에 대한 사람들의 이해를 (B) **풍부하게** 할 수도 있다.

다음 글의 내용을 한 문장으로 요약하고자 한다. 빈칸 (A), (B)에 들어갈 말로 가장 적절한 것은?

	(A)		(B)
①	insignificant 중요하지 않은	—	delay 사람들의 이해에 도움이 된다는 내용임 미룰
②	insufficient 불충분한	—	enrich 역사 소설은 불충분한 증거로 과거를 재구성하지만 풍부하게 할 사람들의 이해를 풍부하게 할 수 있다는 내용
③	concrete 구체적인	—	enhance 사실이 아닌 설명을 제공하기도 함 향상할
④	outdated 시대에 뒤떨어진	—	improve 시대에 뒤떨어진 증거를 이용한다는 언급은 없음 개선할
⑤	limited 제한된	—	disturb 제한된 증거를 사용하거나 이해를 방해하는 것이 아님 방해할

왜 정답? [정답률 55%]

역사 소설의 특징	• 사실이 아닌 설명을 제공하기도 함 • 과거의 일부를 지어내기까지 함
역사 소설의 역할	• 사용자로 하여금 역사 자료(증거)가 없어서 전혀 표현되지 않았던 과거의 일부를 보게 함 • 역사 소설로부터 대중 역사학자와 대중 관객이 모두 배울 수도 있음

→ **(A)**: 제시된 특징에 의하면 역사 소설은 명확한 증거에 기반하여 이야기를 만들어내는 것이 아니다. 역사 소설은 '불충분한(insufficient)' 증거를 사용하여 과거를 재구성한다는 의미를 나타낸다.

(B): 역사 소설은 과거에 대한 도전적인 표현으로서, 그것으로부터 역사학자와 관객이 모두 배울 수도 있다. 역사 소설이 역사적 사건에 대한 사람들의 이해를 '풍부하게 할(enrich)' 수도 있는 것이다.

▶ 요약문의 빈칸에는 각각 '불충분한'과 '풍부하게 할'이 들어가야 하므로 정답은 ②임

왜 오답?

① 역사 소설로부터 배울 수도 있다고 했으므로, 사람들의 이해에 긍정적인 영향을 미치는 것이므로 이해를 '미루는' 것이 아니다.

③ 사실이 아닌 설명을 제공하기도 한다고 했으므로, '구체적인' 증거를 사용하는 것은 아니다.

④ 역사 소설이 사용하는 증거가 시대에 '뒤떨어진다'는 언급은 없다.

⑤ '제한된' 증거를 사용하거나 이해를 '방해하는' 것이 아니다.

＊글의 흐름

도입	역사 소설을 위한 연구는 문서로 덜 기록된 일반적인 사람, 사건 등에 초점을 맞출 수 있고, 소설은 역사적인 맥락을 재창조하는 일상적인 상황, 감정 등을 묘사하는 데 도움이 됨
설명 ①	역사 소설은 사실이 아니더라도 과거의 사건, 상황, 문화에 대한 더 명확한 표현을 제공하는 설명을 제공하고, 소설은 과거의 부분들을 지어내기까지 함
설명 ②	Robert Rosenstone은 지어내는 것이 (역사) 영화의 강점이라고 주장하고, 실제로 Gilden Seavey는 역사 소설 제작자들이 엄격한 학술적 기준을 고수했다면, 많은 역사적 주제가 탐구되지 않은 채 남아있을 것이라고 설명함
결론	역사 소설은 역사의 정반대의 것으로 여겨져서는 안 되며, 대중 역사학자와 대중 관객이 그것으로부터 배울 수도 있는 과거에 대한 도전적인 표현으로 여겨져야 함

O 18 정답 ② ＊비밀 누설에 엄격한 마술사들

<u>prep</u> ~을 고려해볼 때
Perhaps not surprisingly, / given / how long magicians have
been developing / their craft, / a lot of creativity / in magic / is
= about   가산 명사와 불가산 명사 모두 수식할 수 있음
of the tweaking variety /
아마도 당연히 / ~을 생각해 보면 / 마술사들이 얼마나 오랫동안 발전시켜 왔는지를 / 자신들의 기술을 / 많은 창의성은 / 마술에서의 / 살짝 변화를 준 다양성에 관한 것이다 /

— some / of the most skilled and inventive magicians / gained
fame / by refining the execution of tricks / that have been known
/ for decades, or sometimes centuries. //   현재완료 수동태(계속)
일부는 / 가장 숙련되고 창의적인 마술사 중의 / 명성을 얻었다 / 마술 기법의 실행을 정교하게 함으로써 / 알려져 온 / 수십 년 혹은 때로는 수 세기 동안 //

Nevil Maskelyne, / one of magic's old masters, / claimed /
Nevil Maskelyne은 / 마술의 옛 거장 중 한 명인 / 주장했다 /
주어   동사
that "the difficulty / of producing a new magical effect / is
about equivalent / to that of inventing / a new proposition / in
Euclid." //   = the difficulty
'어려움은 / 새로운 마술적 효과를 내는 / 거의 같은 것이다 / 만들어 내는 어려움과 / 새로운 명제를 / 유클리드 기하학에서'라고 //
whether A or B: A이든 아니면 B이든   준부정어(거의 없는)   단서1 마술사는 모방에 대해서는 걱정을 덜 하는 것으로 보임
Whether it's because there's little / that's completely new, / or
for some other reason, / magicians seem to worry less / about
imitation. //
~한 것이 거의 없기 때문이든 / 완전히 새로운 / 아니면 어떤 다른 이유 때문이든 / 마술사는 덜 걱정하는 것으로 보인다 / 모방에 대해 // 단서2 대중에게 마술 기법의 비밀을 누설하는
강조 용법   마술사들에 대해서는 정말로 걱정함
They do, however, worry a lot / about *traitors* / — those magicians
/ who expose the secrets / behind a trick / to the public. //
하지만 그들은 정말로 많이 걱정한다 / '배신자들'에 대해 / 그러한 마술사들 / 비밀을 누설하는 / 마술 기법 뒤에 숨겨진 / 대중에게 // 단서3 마술 기법이 누설되면 마술 업계
접속사(일단 ~하면)   종사자 모두에게 피해를 줌
Once a trick is exposed / in this way, / its value as "magic" / is
destroyed, / and this harms everyone / in the industry. //
하나의 마술 기법이 누설되면 / 이런 식으로 / '마술'로서 그것의 가치가 / 없어지고 / 이것은 모든 사람에게 피해를 준다 / 그 업계에 종사하는 //

For this reason, / magicians' norms are focused / mostly on
punishing magicians / who expose tricks / to the public /
이런 이유로 / 마술사들의 규범은 / 초점이 맞춰진다 / 주로 마술사를 처벌하는 데 / 마술 기법을 누설하는 / 대중에게 / 단서4 마술사들의 규범은 주로 마술 기법을 대중에게
부사절 접속사(양보)   누설한 마술사를 처벌하는 데 초점이 맞춰져 있음
— even if the trick is / the exposer's own invention. //
비록 그 마술 기법이 ~이라고 하더라도 / 그 누설자 자신이 발명한 것 //

→ Magicians, / having long refined existing tricks, / are not
주어   동사
much worried / about (A) **copying** tricks, /
마술사들은 / 오랫동안 기존의 마술 기법을 정교하게 다듬어 온 / 그다지 걱정하지 않는다 / 마술 기법을 모방하는 것에 대해 /

but they are very strict / about (B) **disclosing** / the methods of
tricks / as it damages their industry. //
하지만 그들은 매우 엄격하다 / 누설하는 것에 대해 / 마술 기법의 방법을 / 그것이 자신들의 업계에 피해를 주기 때문에 //

• craft ⓝ 기술　　• inventive ⓐ 창의성이 풍부한　　• fame ⓝ 명성
• refine ⓥ 세련되게 하다　　• execution ⓝ 실행, 수행
• decade ⓝ 10년　　• claim ⓥ 주장하다　　• equivalent ⓐ 동등한
• proposition ⓝ 명제　　• imitation ⓝ 모방　　• traitor ⓝ 배신자
• expose ⓥ 폭로하다, 노출하다　　• norm ⓝ 기준, 규범
• strict ⓐ 엄격한　　• criticize ⓥ 비난하다
• modify ⓥ 변형하다, 수정하다　　• blend ⓥ 섞다, 혼합하다
• disclose ⓥ 공개하다, 드러내다　　• distort ⓥ 왜곡하다, 뒤틀다
• evaluate ⓥ 평가하다　　• underestimate ⓥ 과소평가하다

아마도 당연히, 마술사들이 자신들의 기술을 얼마나 오랫동안 발전시켜 왔는지를 생각해 보면, 마술에 존재하는 많은 창의성은 살짝 변화를 준 다양성에 관한 것인데, 가장 숙련되고 창의적인 마술사 중의 일부는 수십 년 혹은 때로는 수 세기 동안 알려져 온 마술 기법의 실행을 정교하게 함으로써 명성을 얻었다. 마술의 옛 거장 중 한 명인 Nevil Maskelyne은 '새로운 마술적 효과를 내는 어려움

은 유클리드 기하학에서 새로운 명제를 만들어 내는 어려움과 거의 같은 것이다.'라고 주장했다. 완전히 새로운 것이 거의 없기 때문이든, 아니면 어떤 다른 이유 때문이든, 마술사는 모방에 대해 덜 걱정하는 것으로 보인다. 하지만 그들은 '배신자', 즉 마술 기법 뒤에 숨겨진 비밀을 대중에게 누설하는 마술사들에 대해 정말로 많이 걱정한다. 이런 식으로 하나의 마술 기법이 누설되면 '마술'로서 그것의 가치가 없어지고, 이것은 그 업계에 종사하는 모든 사람에게 피해를 준다. 이런 이유로, 마술사들의 규범은, 비록 그 마술 기법이 그 누설자 자신이 발명한 것이라고 하더라도, 마술 기법을 대중에게 누설하는 마술사를 처벌하는 데 주로 초점이 맞춰져 있다.

→ 오랫동안 기존의 마술 기법을 정교하게 다듬어 온 마술사들은 마술 기법을 (A) **모방하는 것**에 대해 그다지 걱정하지 않지만, 그들은 자신들의 업계에 피해를 주기 때문에 마술 기법의 방법을 (B) **누설하는 것**에 대해 매우 엄격하다.

다음 글의 내용을 한 문장으로 요약하고자 한다. 빈칸 (A), (B)에 들어갈 말로 가장 적절한 것은?

	(A)		(B)	
①	copying 모방하는 것	—	blending 섞는 것	마술 기법을 섞는 것에 엄격한 것이 아님
②	copying	—	disclosing 누설하는 것	모방에 대해서는 덜 걱정하고 누설에 대해서는 정말로 걱정함
③	criticizing 비판하는 것	—	distorting 왜곡하는 것	마술 기법의 방법을 왜곡한다는 언급은 없음
④	modifying 수정하는 것	—	evaluating 평가하는 것	마술 기법을 평가하는 것에 대해 정말로 걱정한다는 것이 아님
⑤	modifying	—	underestimating 과소평가하는 것	

왜 정답? [정답률 58%]

마술에 존재하는 많은 창의성은 기존의 마술에 살짝 변화를 준 다양성에 관한 것으로, 마술사는 모방에 대해서는 걱정을 덜 하는 것처럼 보인다고 했다. 하지만 마술 기법의 비밀을 대중에게 누설하는 마술사들에 대해서는 정말로 걱정하는데, 그러한 누설이 마술 업계에 종사하는 모든 사람에게 피해를 주기 때문이라고 했으므로 요약문의 빈칸에는 각각 ② '모방하는 것'과 '누설하는 것'이 적절하다.

왜 오답?

> 어차피 마술사의 기술은 아주 오랫동안 발전시켜 온 기존의 마술에 살짝 변화를 준 것이니까 꿀팁

①, ④ 기존의 마술을 모방하거나 수정하는 것에 대해서는 별로 걱정하지 않지만, 마술 기법을 대중에게 누설하는 것에 대해서는 정말로 걱정한다는 것이지, 그것을 섞거나 평가하는 것에 엄격한 것이 아니다.

③, ⑤ 마술 기법을 비판하거나 그 방법을 과소평가한다는 내용은 언급되지 않았다.

* 글의 흐름

도입	마술에서의 창의성은 기존의 마술을 살짝 변형하는 것이고, 마술사들은 이미 오래된 기존의 마술을 더 정교하게 바꾸면서 명성을 얻음
인용	마술의 옛 거장인 Nevil Maskelyne은 새로운 마술을 만드는 것은 유클리드 기하학에서 새로운 명제를 만들어 내기만큼 어렵다고 주장함
부연 ①	완전히 새로운 마술이 거의 없으므로 마술사는 모방은 걱정하지 않지만, 마술 기법의 비밀을 누설하는 배신자는 걱정함
부연 ②	마술 기법 하나가 누설되면 업계에 종사하는 모든 사람이 피해를 보기 때문에 자신이 발명한 마술일지라도 비밀을 누설하는 마술사는 처벌함

O 19 정답 ① * 과학자들이 다양한 연구를 할 수 있는 이유

뒤에 who are(주격 관계대명사+be동사) 생략
Even those with average talent / can produce notable work in the various sciences, / so long as they do not try to embrace all ~하는 한: 부사절 접속사
of them at once. //
단서 1 다양한 과학 분야에서 성과를 내기 위해서는 한 주제 다음에 다른 주제로, 즉 다른 기간에 다른 분야를 연구해야 함
평균적인 재능을 가진 사람이라도 / 다양한 과학 분야에서 주목할 만한 성과를 낼 수 있는데 / 한 번에 그것들 모두를 수용하려고 하지 않는 한 그렇다 //

Instead, they should concentrate attention / on one subject after another / (that is, in different periods of time), / although later work will weaken / earlier attainments in the other spheres. //
대신에 그들은 집중해야 하는데 / 한 주제 다음에 다른 주제로 / (즉, 다른 기간에) / 비록 나중의 작업은 약화시킬 수 있지만 말이다 / 다른 영역에서의 더 이전의 성취를 //

This amounts to saying / that the brain adapts to universal 명사절 접속사
science in *time* / but not in *space*. //
이것은 말하는 것과 마찬가지이다 / 뇌가 보편적인 과학에 '시간' 속에서 적응하는 것이지 / '공간' 속에서 적응하는 것이 아니라고 // 단서 2 뇌는 보편적인 과학에 '시간'의 차원에 적응하므로, 시간을 달리하면 다른 과학에 적응할 수 있음
뒤에 who are(주격 관계대명사+be동사) 생략
In fact, even those with great abilities / proceed in this way. //
사실, 뛰어난 능력을 가진 사람들도 / 이런 식으로 나아간다 //

Thus, when we are astonished / by someone with publications in different scientific fields, / realize that each topic was explored 명사절 접속사
/ during a specific period of time. // each+단수 명사+단수 동사 명령문
따라서, 우리가 놀랄 때 / 서로 다른 과학 분야에 출판물을 가진 사람에게 / 각 주제가 탐구되었다는 것을 인식하라 / 특정 기간 동안 //

Knowledge gained earlier certainly will not have disappeared / 과거분사(knowledge 수식) 미래완료 시제
from the mind of the author, / but it will have become simplified 미래완료 시제의 수동태
/ by condensing into formulas or greatly abbreviated symbols. // by -ing: ~함으로써
더 이전에 얻은 지식은 확실히 사라지지 않았을 것이지만 / 저자의 마음에서 / 그것은 단순화되었을 것이다 / 공식이나 크게 축약된 기호로 응축됨 // 단서 3 이전에 얻은 지식은 공식이나 축약된 기호로 응축되어 남아 있음

Thus, sufficient space remains / for the perception and learning of new images / on the cerebral blackboard. // 자동사(수동태 불가)
따라서 충분한 공간이 남아 있다 / 새로운 이미지를 인식하고 학습할 수 있는 / 대뇌 칠판에 // 단서 4 이를 통해 대뇌에서는 새로운 학습을 할 수 있는 공간을 확보함

→ Exploring one scientific subject after another / (A) **enables** remarkable work across the sciences, /
하나의 과학 주제를 탐구한 다음에 다른 주제를 탐구하는 것은 / 과학 전반에 걸친 주목할 만한 작업을 가능하게 하는데 /

as the previously gained knowledge / is retained in simplified forms within the brain, / which (B) **leaves** room for new learning. //
이전에 습득된 지식은 / 뇌 안에서 단순화된 형태로 유지되며 / 이는 새로운 학습을 위한 공간을 남겨두기 때문이다 //

- notable ⓐ 주목할 만한
- embrace ⓥ 수용하다, 포괄하다
- concentrate ⓥ 집중하다
- attainment ⓝ 성취, 성과
- sphere ⓝ 영역
- amount to ~와 마찬가지이다
- universal ⓐ 보편적인
- proceed ⓥ 나아가다, 진행하다
- simplified ⓐ 단순화된
- formula ⓝ 공식
- abbreviate ⓥ 축약하다
- sufficient ⓐ 충분한
- perception ⓝ 인식

평균적인 재능을 가진 사람이라도 다양한 과학 분야에서 주목할 만한 성과를 낼 수 있는데, 한 번에 그것들 모두를 수용하려고 하지 않는 한 그렇다. 대신에 그들은 한 주제 다음에 다른 주제로 (즉, 다른 기간에) 집중해야 하는데, 비록 나중의 작업은 다른 영역에서의 더 이전의 성취를 약화시킬 수 있지만 말이다. 이것은 뇌가 보편적인 과학에 '시간' 속에서 적응하는 것이지 '공간' 속에서 적응하는 것이 아니라고 말하는 것과 마찬가지이다. 사실, 뛰어난 능력을 가진 사람들도 이런 식으로 나아간다. 따라서, 우리가 서로 다른 과학 분야에 출판물을 가진 사람에게 놀랄 때, 각 주제가 특정 기간 동안 탐구되었다는 것을 인식하라. 더 이전에 얻은 지식은 확실히 저자의 마음에서 사라지지 않았을 것이지만 그것은 공식이나 크게 축약된 기호로 응축됨으로써 단순화되었을 것이다. 따라서 대뇌 칠판에 새로운 이미지를 인식하고 학습할 수 있는 충분한 공간이 남아 있다.

→ 하나의 과학 주제를 탐구한 다음에 다른 주제를 탐구하는 것은 과학 전반에 걸친 주목할 만한 작업을 (A) **가능하게 하는데**, 이전에 습득된 지식은 뇌 안에서 단순화된 형태로 유지되며 이는 새로운 학습을 위한 공간을 (B) **남겨두기** 때문이다.

다음 글의 내용을 한 문장으로 요약하고자 한다. 빈칸 (A), (B)에 들어갈 말로 가장 적절한 것은?

(A)	(B)	
① enables 가능하게 하다	leaves 남겨두다	시간의 차이를 두고 연구를 진행하면 다양한 분야에서의 성과가 가능한데, 이는 뇌가 새로운 학습을 위한 공간을 남겨두기 때문임
② challenges 어렵게 하다	spares 남겨놓다	시간의 차이를 두고 연구를 진행하면 다양한 분야에서의 성과가 '어려워' 지거나 '지연되는' 것이 아님
③ delays 지연시키다	creates 만들다	
④ requires 필요로 하다	removes 없애다	뇌가 과거의 지식을 응축함으로써 새로운 학습을 위한 공간을 '없애거나' '줄이는' 것이 아님
⑤ invites 가져오다	diminishes 줄이다	

왜 정답? [정답률 58%]

한 과학자가 다양한 과학 분야에서 성과를 낼 수 있는 이유	한 주제 다음에 다른 주제로 (즉, 다른 시간대로) 연구하기 때문에 가능함
뇌의 특징	• 보편적인 과학에 '시간' 속에서 적용하는 것이지 '공간' 속에서 적용하는 것이 아님 • 이전에 얻은 지식은 공식이나 축약된 기호로 응축됨 • 이 과정을 통해 새로운 학습을 위한 공간을 남겨둠

(A): 뇌는 보편적인 과학에 '시간' 속에서 적용하는 것이지 '공간' 속에서 적용하는 것이 아니라고 하고 있다. 따라서 과학의 여러 분야에서 성과를 거두는 과학자들은 같은 시간에 여러 일을 동시에 처리하지 않는다. 즉, 시간 차이를 두고 새로운 학습을 하는 것은 과학의 여러 분야에 걸친 업적을 '가능하게 하거나(enables)' '가져오는(invites)' 것이다.

(B): 뇌는 시간이 지나면 이전에 습득한 지식을 없애지 않고 단순한 형태로 저장한다. 이를 통해 대뇌에서는 새로운 학습을 위한 공간이 확보된다고 한다. 즉, 뇌는 시간이 지나면 이전의 학습을 단순화된 형태로 저장하여 새로운 학습을 위한 공간을 '남겨두거나(leaves)' '남겨놓거나(spares)' 만드는(creates)' 것이다.

▶ 요약문의 빈칸에는 각각 '가능하게 하다'와 '남겨두다'가 들어가야 하므로 정답은 ①임.

왜 오답?

② 한 주제 다음에 다른 주제를 연구하는 것은 다양한 연구를 가능하게 한다고 했으므로, 이를 '어렵게 한다'는 것은 아니다.

③ 마찬가지로 다양한 연구를 가능하게 한다고 했으므로 이를 '지연시킨다'는 것은 아니다.

④ 앞서 배운 지식은 단순한 형태로 응축하여 새로운 학습을 위한 공간을 남겨둔다고 했으므로, 이를 '없앤다'는 것은 아니다.

⑤ 마찬가지로 새로운 학습을 위한 공간을 남겨둔다고 했으므로 이를 '줄인다'는 것은 아니다.

＊ 글의 흐름

주제문	과학자들은 다양한 분야에 걸쳐 눈에 띄는 성과를 거둘 수 있음
근거	이는 뇌가 '시간' 차원에서 보편적인 과학에 적용하기 때문임
주제문 구체화	다양한 과학 분야의 책을 출판한 과학자들은 각 주제를 서로 다른 시기에 연구함
근거 구체화	이는 뇌가 더 이전에 배운 지식은 단순한 기호와 공식으로 응축하고, 새로운 학습을 위한 공간을 대뇌에 남겨두기 때문임

류이레 | 연세대 의예과 2024년 입학·광주대동고 졸
요약문 문제는 긴 문장들이 많아도 요약문의 단어와 매칭되는 지문의 단어 위주로 읽는다면 쉽게 답을 고를 수 있어! 이 문제에서는 첫 번째 문장의 can produce notable work, 두 번째 문장의 one subject after another, 그리고 Thus로 시작하는 마지막 문장의 sufficient space ramains 등이 직접적으로 요약문과 연결되는 단서들이었지.

O 20 정답 ① ＊음악 교육의 현실

[단서 1] 음악은 현재에만 존재함 선행사 관계부사
Music has no past; / it exists / only at the moment / when it happens, / and no two performances are identical. //
음악에는 과거가 없다 / 그것은 존재하며 / 그것이 일어나는 순간에만 / 어떤 두 연주도 동일하지 않다 //

This is music's greatest asset / because it brings out the essential 'now' / without implications / of a past and a potential future. //
이것은 음악의 가장 큰 자산이다 / 그것이 가장 중요한 '지금'을 불러일으키기 때문에 / 암시하지 않고 / 과거와 잠재적 미래를 //

준부정어가 문두로 가면서 주어와 동사가 도치됨
Thus, Stravinsky pointed out / that only through music / are we able to 'realize the present.' //
따라서 Stravinsky는 지적했다 / 음악을 통해서만 / 우리는 '현재를 실현할' 수 있다고 //

Musical 'meaning' cannot be separated / from the act of presentation. //
음악의 '의미'는 분리될 수 없다 / 연주 행위와 //

[단서 2] 음악을 현재화할 필요성은 교육 개념과 잘 어울리지 않음
단수 주어
However, / the necessity of *present*-ing music / — making it present here and now, / without which it will not be music at all — / does not sit easily / with a concept of education / 선행사
그러나 / 음악을 '현재화'할 필요성은 / 음악을 여기 지금 존재하게 하는 것인데 / 그것 없이는 그것은 전혀 음악이 아닐 것이다 / 잘 어울리지 않는다 / 교육 개념과 /

관계대명사의 병렬 구조
that rests mainly upon received factual knowledge / and which, by tradition, uses the past / to make sense of the present. //
주로 일반적으로 인정되는 사실적 지식에 의존하고 / 전통적으로 과거를 이용하는 / 현재를 이해하기 위해 //

[단서 3] 교육 개념은 일반적으로 인정되는 사실적 지식에 의존함

If we want music to have a role / in general education, /
음악이 어떤 역할을 하기를 우리가 원한다면 / 일반 교육에서 /

가주어
it would seem logical / to acknowledge this difference / and give prominence to activities / that will involve all pupils working directly with music. // 진주어
~이 타당해 보일 것이다 / 이러한 차이를 인정하고 / 활동에 중점을 두는 것이 / 모든 학생이 음악을 직접 다루는 것을 포함하는 //

형용사적 용법(attempts 수식)
Yet, / in spite of numerous attempts / to develop a more *musical* music curriculum / for the majority of school pupils, /
그러나 / 수많은 시도에도 불구하고 / 더 '음악적인' 음악 교육 과정을 개발하려는 / 대다수 학생을 위해 /

the emphasis is / still on pupils absorbing factual information about music. // **[단서 4]** 음악 교육의 강조점은 여전히 학생이 음악에 대한 사실적 정보를 흡수하는 데 있음
강조점은 있다 / 여전히 학생이 음악에 대한 사실적 정보를 흡수하는 데 //

→ Music's quality of being in the present / is (A) **overlooked** / in formal music education, / where delivering factual knowledge / is (B) **prioritized**. //
선행사(추상적 의미의 장소) 관계부사
현재에 존재한다는 음악의 특성은 / 간과되는데 / 정규 음악 교육에서 / 거기에서는 사실적 지식 전달이 / 우선시된다 //

- identical ⓐ 동질적인 • asset ⓝ 자산 • implication ⓝ 암시
- presentation ⓝ 공연 • necessity ⓝ 필요성
- rest (up)on 의존하다 • received ⓐ 인정받는 • tradition ⓝ 전통
- make sense of 이해하다 • acknowledge ⓥ 인정하다
- prominence ⓝ 중점 • pupil ⓝ 학생 • numerous ⓐ 수많은
- attempt ⓝ 시도 • absorb ⓥ 흡수하다 • overlook ⓥ 간과하다
- prioritize ⓥ 우선시하다

음악에는 과거가 없는데, 즉, 음악은 그것이 일어나는 순간에만 존재하며 어떤 두 연주도 동일하지 않다. 이것은 음악이 과거와 잠재적 미래를 암시하지 않고 가장 중요한 '지금'을 불러일으키기 때문에 음악의 가장 큰 자산이다. 따라서 Stravinsky는 음악을 통해서만 우리는 '현재를 실현할' 수 있다고 지적했다. 음악의 '의미'는 연주 행위와 분리될 수 없다. 그러나 음악을 '현재화'할 필요성은, 음악을 여기 지금 존재하게 하는 것인데, 그것 없이는 음악은 전혀

음악이 아닐 것이다. 주로 일반적으로 인정되는 사실적 지식에 의존하고 전통적으로 현재를 이해하기 위해 과거를 이용하는 교육 개념과 잘 어울리지 않는다. 음악이 일반 교육에서 어떤 역할을 하기를 원한다면 이러한 차이를 인정하고 모든 학생이 음악을 직접 다루는 것을 포함하는 활동에 중점을 두는 것이 타당해 보일 것이다. 그러나 대다수 학생을 위해 더 '음악적인' 음악 교육 과정을 개발하려는 수많은 시도에도 불구하고, 강조점은 여전히 학생이 음악에 대한 사실적 정보를 흡수하는 데 있다.

→ 현재에 존재한다는 음악의 특성은 정규 음악 교육에서 (A) **간과되고** 있는데, 거기에서는 사실적 지식 전달이 (B) **우선시된다**.

다음 글의 내용을 한 문장으로 요약하고자 한다. 빈칸 (A), (B)에 들어갈 말로 가장 적절한 것은?

	(A)		(B)	
①	overlooked 간과하다	—	prioritized 우선시된다	음악의 현재성이 간과되고, 사실적 지식 전달이 강조됨
②	overlooked	—	restricted 제한된다	사실적 지식 전달을 강조함
③	dismissed 일축하다	—	disregarded 무시된다	사실적 지식 전달을 '무시하는' 것과 반대임
④	achieved 달성하다	—	treasured 귀하게 여겨지다	음악의 현재성은 교육 개념과 잘 안 어울림
⑤	achieved	—	challenged 도전하다	

왜 정답? [정답률 64%]

(A):

> 음악의 가장 큰 자산: 음악은 현재(그것이 일어나는 순간)에만 존재한다.
> 그러나(However) 음악을 현재화할 필요성은 교육 개념과 잘 어울리지 않는다.

(B):

> 교육 개념은 일반적으로 인정되는 사실적 지식에 의존하고, 여전히 학생이 음악에 대한 사실적 정보를 흡수하는 것을 강조한다.

→ 정규 음악 교육에서 일어나는 일, 즉 현재에 존재한다는 음악의 특성은
  ① '간과되고', 사실적 지식 전달이 '우선시된다'.
  ▶ 요약문의 빈칸에는 '간과되고'와 '우선시된다'가 들어가야 하므로 정답은 ①임

왜 오답?

② 사실적 지식 전달을 강조한다고 했으므로 '제한되는' 것이 아니다.
③ 사실적 지식 전달을 '무시하는' 것과 반대이므로 적절하지 않다.
④ 현재에 존재한다는 음악의 특성이 음악 교육을 통해 달성되는 것은 아니다.
⑤ 사실적 지식 전달이 '도전받는다'는 것은 적절하지 않다.

＊ 글의 흐름

도입	음악은 그것이 일어나는 순간에만 존재하며 어떤 두 연주도 동일하지 않고, 이것은 음악이 가장 중요한 '지금'을 불러일으키기 때문에 음악의 가장 큰 자산임
설명 ①	Stravinsky는 음악을 통해서만 우리는 '현재를 실현할' 수 있다고 지적했고, 음악을 '현재화'할 필요성은, 음악을 여기 지금 존재하게 하는 것인데, 그것 없이는 음악은 전혀 음악이 아닐 것임
설명 ②	주로 일반적으로 인정되는 사실적 지식에 의존하고 전통적으로 현재를 이해하기 위해 과거를 이용하는 교육 개념과 잘 어울리지 않음
결론	대다수 학생을 위해 더 '음악적인' 음악 교육 과정을 개발하려는 수많은 시도에도 불구하고, 강조점은 여전히 학생이 음악에 대한 사실적 정보를 흡수하는 데 있음

O 21 정답 ③ ＊화석 증거의 한계

단서1 화석화와 이후의 발견에 환경이 영향을 미침
Some environments are more likely to lead / to fossilization and subsequent discovery / than others. //
어떤 환경은 이어질 가능성이 더 높다 / 화석화와 이후의 발견으로 / 다른 환경보다 //
단수 주어
Thus, we cannot assume / that more fossil evidence / from a
단수 동사 목적어절 접속사
particular period or place / means / that more individuals were present / at that time, / or in that place. // 단서2 화석 증거가 많음을 근거로
따라서 우리는 추정할 수 없다 / 더 많은 화석 증거가 / 특정 기간이나 장소로부터의 / 의미한 개체군의 크기를 추정할 수 없음
다고 / 더 많은 개체가 있었다는 것을 / 그 당시에 / 또는 그 장소에 //
It may just be / that the circumstances / at one period of time, /
주격 보어절 접속사
or at one location, / were more favourable for fossilization / than they were at other times, or in other places. //
그것은 그저 ~일 수 있다 / 상황이 / 어느 시기의 / 또는 어느 장소의 / 화석화에 더 유리했던 것 / 다른 시기나 다른 장소에서 그랬던 것보다 //
단수 주어
Likewise, / the absence of hominin fossil evidence / at a
단수 동사
particular time or place / does not have the same implication / as its presence. //
마찬가지로 / 인류 화석 증거가 없다는 것은 / 특정 시기나 장소에 / 같은 암시를 나타내지는 않는다 / 그것이 있을 때와 //
As the saying goes, / 'absence of evidence is not evidence / of
'말하다'라는 의미로 쓰인 go
absence'. //
속담이 말하듯이 / '증거가 없다는 것이 증거는 아니다 / 부재의' //
Similar logic suggests / that taxa are likely to have arisen /
to부정사의 완료형
before they first appear / in the fossil record, /
비슷한 논리는 암시한다 / 분류군(群)들은 생겼을 가능성이 있다는 것을 / 그것들이 처음 나타나기 전에 / 화석 기록에 //
to부정사의 완료형 prep (특정한 시간을) 지나[이후]
and they are likely to have survived / beyond the time of their most recent appearance / in the fossil record. //
그리고 그것들은 살아남았을 가능성이 있다는 것을 / 그것들의 가장 최근의 등장 시기 이후에도 / 화석 기록에서 //
Thus, / the first appearance datum, / and the last appearance datum / of taxa / in the hominin fossil record /
따라서 / 첫 번째 등장 자료와 / 마지막 등장 자료는 / 분류군의 / 인류 화석 기록에 있어서 /
are likely to be conservative statements / about the times / of origin and extinction of a taxon. // 단서3 화석 증거가 진술한 한 분류군의 기원과
멸종의 시기는 정확하지 않음
적게 잡아 말한 진술일 가능성이 있다 / 시기에 대해 / 한 분류군의 기원과 멸종의 //

> → Since fossilization and fossil discovery are affected / by
> 이유의 부사절 접속사
> (A) **environmental** conditions, /
> 화석화와 화석의 발견은 영향을 받기 때문에 / 환경적인 조건에 의해 /
> the fossil evidence of a taxon / cannot definitely (B) **clarify** / its population size or the times / of its appearance and extinction. //
> 한 분류군의 화석 증거는 / 확실하게 규명할 수는 없다 / 그 개체군의 크기나 시기를 / 그것의 등장과 멸종의 //

- fossilization ⓝ 화석화   • fossil ⓝ 화석   • evidence ⓝ 증거
- particular ⓐ 특정한, 특별한   • circumstance ⓝ 환경, 상황
- favourable ⓐ 유리한   • absence ⓝ 부재, 없음
- implication ⓝ 암시, 함축   • presence ⓝ 존재함, 있음
- saying ⓝ 속담   • logic ⓝ 논리, 타당성   • arise ⓥ 생기다
- appear ⓥ 나타나다, ~인 것 같다   • datum ⓝ 자료(pl. data)
- conservative ⓐ (실제 수나 양보다) 적게 잡은, 보수적인
- statement ⓝ 진술   • extinction ⓝ 멸종, 소멸
- definitely ⓐⓓ 분명히, 확실히   • population ⓝ 인구, (모든) 주민, 개체군

어떤 환경은 다른 환경보다 화석화가 이루어지고 이후에 발견으로 이어질 가능성이 더 높다. 따라서 특정 기간이나 장소에서 더 많은 화석 증거가 나온다는 것이 그 당시나 그 장소에 더 많은 개체가 있었다는 것을 의미한다고 추정할 수는 없다. 그것은 어느 시기나 어느 장소의 상황이 다른 시기나 다른 장소에서보다

화석화에 더 유리했던 것일 수 있다. 마찬가지로, 특정 시기나 장소에 인류 화석 증거가 없다는 것은 그것이 있을 때와 같은 암시를 나타내지는 않는다. 속담에도 있듯이, '증거가 없다는 것이 없다는 증거는 아니다.' 비슷한 논리에 따르면, 분류군(群)은 화석 기록에 처음 나타나기 전에 생겼을 가능성이 있고, 그것은 가장 최근의 화석 기록에 등장했던 시기 이후에도 살아남았을 가능성이 있다. 따라서 인류 화석 기록에 있어서 분류군의 첫 번째 등장 자료와 마지막 등장 자료는 한 분류군의 기원과 멸종 시기에 대해 적게 잡아 말한 진술일 가능성이 있다.
→ 화석화와 화석의 발견은 (A) 환경적인 조건에 의해 영향을 받기 때문에, 한 분류군의 화석 증거는 그 개체군의 크기나 등장 시기와 멸종 시기를 확실하게 (B) 규명할 수는 없다.

다음 글의 내용을 한 문장으로 요약하고자 한다. 빈칸 (A), (B)에 들어갈 말로 가장 적절한 것은?

	(A)		(B)	
①	experimental 실험적인		confirm 확인함	화석화와 이후의 발견 가능성이 환경마다 다름
②	experimental 실험적인		reveal 드러냄	
③	environmental 환경적인		clarify 규명함	화석화와 화석의 발견이 환경의 영향을 받으므로 화석 증거를 통해 어떤 개체군에 대해 규명할 수 없음
④	environmental		conceal 감춤	화석 증거가 드러내는 암시에 한계가 있다는 내용임
⑤	accidental 우연한		mask 가림	화석화에 영향을 미치는 '특정한' 환경적 요인이 있다는 내용임

왜 정답? [정답률 67%]

첫 문장에서 화석화와 이후의 발견이 환경의 영향을 받는다고 했고, 이어지는 문장에서 화석화와 이후의 발견이 환경의 영향을 받기 때문에 화석 증거가 더 많다고 해서 어느 시기, 어느 장소에 더 많은 개체가 있었다고 추정할 수 없다고 했다. 마지막 문장은 화석 증거가 한 분류군의 기원과 멸종의 시기를 정확히 알려주지 않는다는 내용이므로 요약문의 빈칸에는 각각 ③ '환경적인'과 '규명할'이 들어가야 한다.

왜 오답?

①, ② 어떤 환경은 다른 환경보다 화석화와 이후의 발견으로 이어질 가능성이 더 높다고 했으므로 이는 화석화에 영향을 미치는 요소가 환경적인 조건이라는 의미이다. 화석화가 실험적인 요소의 영향을 받는다는 언급은 없다.

④, ⑤ 화석 증거가 드러내는 암시가 갖는 한계에 대한 내용이다. 화석화와 화석의 발견이 어떤 개체군에 대한 정보를 감춘다거나 가린다는 것은 글의 내용에 맞지 않는다.

> 개체군의 크기나 기원/멸종의 시기를 명확히 알려주지 않는다는 것이 한계 **꿀팁**

＊ 글의 흐름

도입	화석화와 이후의 발견에 환경적 요인이 영향을 미침
부연 ①	따라서 화석 증거가 더 많다고 해서 더 많은 개체가 있었던 것이 아님
부연 ②	또한 화석 증거가 말하는 한 개체군의 기원과 멸종의 시기가 정확한 것이 아님
요약	화석화와 화석의 발견은 환경적 조건에 영향을 받으므로 한 분류군의 화석 증거는 그 개체군의 크기나 등장/멸종의 시기를 확실하게 규명할 수 없음

───── **배경 지식** ─────

＊ 화석화작용(fossilization)

화석(fossil)이란 단어는 '땅을 파다'를 의미하는 라틴어 fossilium에서 유래되었다. 중세 시대에는 지하에서 나오는 암석, 광물 및 보석 등 '땅속에서 파낸 모든 것'들을 지칭했지만, 1700년대부터 현재 통용되는 화석의 의미가 사용되기 시작했다. 실제 초기의 광물학책들은 화석의 책으로 불리기도 했다.

화석화작용은 생존하던 생물이 죽어서 그 사체가 화석이 되어가는 전 과정을 말한다. 크게 두 단계의 과정으로 볼 수 있으며, 첫 번째 단계는 유해가 퇴적물에 매몰될 때까지이고, 두 번째 단계는 매몰 후 매몰된 사체가 화석이 될 때까지의 과정이다.

＊장인정신이 마주치는 장애물

"Craftsmanship" may suggest a way of life / that declined / with the arrival of industrial society / — but this is misleading. //
　　　　　　　　　　　　　　　선행사　　주격 관계대명사
'장인정신'은 삶의 방식을 나타낼지도 모른다 / 쇠퇴한 / 산업 사회의 도래와 함께 / 하지만 이것은 오해의 소지가 있다 //

Craftsmanship names / an enduring, basic human impulse, / the desire / to do a job well for its own sake. //
　주어　　　　동사　　　　　　목적어
단서 1 장인정신은 '지속적이고' 기본적인 인간의 충동을 말함
장인정신은 말한다 / 지속적이고 기본적인 인간의 충동을 / 욕망 / 일 자체를 위해 그것을 잘하고 싶은 //
형용사적 용법(the desire 수식)

Craftsmanship cuts a far wider swath / than skilled manual labor; /
　　　　　　　　비교급 강조 부사
장인정신은 훨씬 더 넓은 구획을 가른다 / 숙련된 육체노동보다 /

it serves / the computer programmer, the doctor, and the artist; / parenting improves / when it is practiced / as a skilled craft, / as does citizenship. //
　　주어　　　　동사(완전자동사)　　　　　주어와 동사가 도치됨
그것은 도움이 된다 / 컴퓨터 프로그래머, 의사, 예술가에게 / 양육은 향상된다 / 그것이 실행될 때 / 숙련된 기술로서 / 시민정신이 그런 것처럼 //

In all these domains, / craftsmanship focuses / on objective standards, / on the thing in itself. //
단서 2 사회적, 경제적 조건이 장인정신을 방해함
이 모든 영역에서 / 장인정신은 초점을 맞춘다 / 객관적인 기준에 / 그 자체의 것 //

Social and economic conditions, / however, / often stand in the way / of the craftsman's discipline and commitment: /
　주어　　　　　　　　　　　　　　동사
사회적, 경제적 조건은 / 그러나 / 흔히 방해한다 / 장인의 수련과 전념을 /

schools may fail to provide the tools / to do good work, / and workplaces may not truly value / the aspiration for quality. //
학교는 도구를 제공하지 못할 수 있고 / 일을 잘하기 위한 / 직장은 진정으로 가치 있게 여기지 않을 수 있다 / 품질에 대한 열망을 //

And though craftsmanship can reward an individual / with a sense of pride in work, / this reward is not simple. //
부사절 접속사(양보)
그리고 비록 장인정신이 개인에게 보상을 줄 수 있지만 / 일에 대한 자부심으로 / 이 보상은 간단하지 않다 //

The craftsman often faces / conflicting objective standards of excellence; /
분사가 단독으로 명사를 수식할 때는 명사 앞에 옴
장인은 흔히 직면한다 / 뛰어남에 대한 상충하는 객관적 기준에 /

the desire / to do something well for its own sake / can be weakened / by competitive pressure, / by frustration, / or by obsession. //
　주어　　형용사적 용법(the desire 수식)　　　　　동사
욕망은 / 어떤 일 그 자체를 위해 그것을 잘하려는 / 약화될 수 있다 / 경쟁적 압력에 의해 / 좌절에 의해 / 또는 집착에 의해 //

> → Craftsmanship, / a human desire / that has (A) **persisted**
> 　주어　　　선행사　　주격 관계대명사
> over time / in diverse contexts, / often encounters factors / that
> (B) **limit** its full development. //
> 　　　　　　　　　　　　동사　　　선행사　　주격 관계대명사
> 장인정신은 / 인간의 욕망인 / 시간이 지남에 따라 존속해 온 / 다양한 상황에서 / 흔히 요소들과 마주친다 / 그것의 완전한 발전을 제한하는 //

───────────────

- craftsmanship ⓝ 장인정신　　　• misleading ⓐ 오해의 소지가 있는
- name ⓥ 말하다, 명명하다　　　• enduring ⓐ 지속적인
- impulse ⓝ 충동　　　• manual ⓐ 육체노동의, 손으로 하는
- serve ⓥ 도움이 되다, 기여하다　　　• parenting ⓝ 양육, 육아
- craft ⓝ 기술, (수)공예　　　• citizenship ⓝ 시민정신
- domain ⓝ 영역　　　• stand in the way of ~을 방해하다
- discipline ⓝ 수련, 규율　　　• commitment ⓝ 전념, 헌신
- aspiration ⓝ 열망, 염원　　　• conflicting ⓐ 상충하는
- weaken ⓥ 약화시키다　　　• competitive ⓐ 경쟁적인
- frustration ⓝ 좌절　　　• obsession ⓝ 집착　　　• cultivate ⓥ 양성하다
- accelerate ⓥ 가속화하다　　　• diminish ⓥ 줄어들다

'장인정신'은 산업 사회의 도래와 함께 쇠퇴한 삶의 방식을 나타낼지도 모르지만, 이것은 오해의 소지가 있다. 장인정신은 지속적이고 기본적인 인간의 충동, 즉 일 자체를 위해 그것을 잘하고 싶은 욕망을 말한다. 장인정신은 숙련된 육체노동보다 훨씬 더 넓은 구획을 가르는데, 그것은 컴퓨터 프로그래머, 의사, 예술가에게 도움이 되고, 시민정신과 마찬가지로 그것이 숙련된 기술로서 실행될 때 양육은 향상된다. 이 모든 영역에서 장인정신은 객관적인 기준, 즉 그 자체의 것에 초점을 맞춘다.

그러나 사회적, 경제적 조건은 흔히 장인의 수련과 전념을 방해하는데, 즉 학교는 일을 잘하기 위한 도구를 제공하지 못할 수 있고, 직장은 품질에 대한 열망을 진정으로 가치 있게 여기지 않을 수 있다. 그리고 비록 장인정신이 일에 대한 자부심으로 개인에게 보상을 줄 수 있지만, 이 보상은 간단하지 않다. 장인은 흔히 뛰어남에 대한 상충하는 객관적 기준에 직면하며, 어떤 일 그 자체를 위해 그것을 잘하려는 욕망은 경쟁적 압력에 의해, 좌절에 의해 또는 집착에 의해 약화될 수 있다.
→ 다양한 상황에서 시간이 지남에 따라 (A) **존속해** 온 인간의 욕망인 장인정신은 흔히 그것의 완전한 발전을 (B) **제한하는** 요소들과 마주친다.

다음 글의 내용을 한 문장으로 요약하고자 한다. 빈칸 (A), (B)에 들어갈 말로 가장 적절한 것은?

	(A)		(B)	
①	persisted 존속했다	—	limit 제한하다	장인정신은 지속적인 인간의 충동을 말함, 사회적, 경제적 조건이 장인정신을 방해함
②	persisted 존속했다	—	cultivate 양식하다	장인의 수련과 전념을 방해한다고 했음
③	evolved 발달했다	—	accelerate 가속화하다	
④	diminished 줄어들었다	—	shape 형성하다	장인정신이 쇠퇴했다는 것은 오해의 소지가 있음
⑤	diminished 줄어들었다	—	restrict 제한하다	

와 2등급? 지문에 등장하는 어휘들은 그렇게 어렵다고 볼 수 없으나 장인정신이 마주치는 장애물이라는 글의 내용을 잘 파악하기 힘들 수 있다. 그러나 요약문을 먼저 살펴보고 글을 읽으면 훨씬 쉬워지는 문제이다.

| 문제 풀이 순서 |

1st 요약문을 통해 글에서 무엇을 찾아야 하는지 확인한다.

> 다양한 상황에서 시간이 지남에 따라 (A) _____ 해 온 인간의 욕망인 장인정신은 흔히 그것의 완전한 발전을 (B) _____ 하는 요소들과 마주친다.

→ **(A):** 장인정신이 시간이 지남에 따라 존속해 온, 발달해 온, 줄어들어 온 인간의 욕망인지
(B): 장인정신이 그것의 완전한 발전을 제한하는, 양성하는, 가속화하는, 형성하는 제한하는 요소를 마주치는지

2nd 글에서 장인정신에 대해 어떻게 설명하는지 확인한다.

(A):

> 장인정신은 지속적이고 기본적인 인간의 충동, 즉 일 자체를 위해 그것을 잘하고 싶은 욕망을 말한다. **단서1**

→ '지속적인 인간의 충동' = '시간이 지남에 따라 존속해 온 인간의 욕망'
▶ (A)에는 ①, ② persisted가 들어가야 함

(B):

> 그러나 사회적, 경제적 조건은 흔히 장인의 수련과 전념을 방해한다. **단서2**

→ '사회적 경제적 조건이 장인의 수련과 전념을 방해한다' = '장인정신은 그것의 완전한 발전을 제한하는 요소들을 마주친다'
▶ (B)에는 ① limit가 들어가야 함

3rd 전체 글의 내용을 정리하여 요약문이 적절한지 확인한다.

도입	장인정신이 산업 사회의 도래와 함께 쇠퇴한 삶의 방식을 나타낸다는 것은 오해임
부연 ①	장인정신은 지속적인 인간의 충동을 말함
부연 ②	사회적, 경제적 조건이 흔히 장인정신을 방해함
예시	학교는 일을 잘하기 위한 도구를 제공하지 못할 수 있고, 직장은 품질에 대한 열망을 진정으로 가치 있게 여기지 않을 수 있음

→ 다양한 상황에서 시간이 지남에 따라 (A) 존속해 온 인간의 욕망인 장인정신은 흔히 그것의 완전한 발전을 (B) 제한하는 요소들과 마주친다.

| 선택지 분석 |

① persisted — limit 존속했다 — 제한하다
장인정신은 쇠퇴하지 않았다고 했고, 장인정신에 대한 경제적, 사회적 요인을 방해하는 것에 대해 말했다.

② persisted — cultivate 존속했다 — 양성하다
장인의 수련과 전념을 방해하는 사회적, 경제적 요소를 마주친다는 것으로, 장인정신을 '양성하는' 요소라는 표현은 글과 반대된다.

③ evolved — accelerate 발달했다 — 가속하다
장인정신을 '가속화하는' 요소라는 표현은 글과 반대되는 내용이다.

④ diminished — shape 줄어들었다 — 형성하다
장인정신이 쇠퇴한 삶의 방식을 나타낼지도 모른다는 것은 오해의 소지가 있으며, 장인정신은 지속적인 인간의 충동을 말한다고 했으므로 장인정신이 시간이 지남에 따라 '줄어든' 인간의 욕망이라고 요약하는 것은 적절하지 않다.

⑤ diminished — restrict 줄어들었다 — 제한하다
장인정신은 지속적인 인간의 충동을 말한다고 했으므로 시간이 지남에 따라 '줄어든' 인간의 욕망이라고 하는 것은 어색하다.

조현준 | 전북대 의예과 2023년 입학·익산 이리고 졸
요약문을 먼저 읽는 것이 도움이 되는데, 보통 (A)는 지문의 앞부분에, (B)는 지문의 뒷부분에 관련 내용이 있어. 난 요약문으로 이 글이 craftsmanship에 관한 글임을 알았는데, 글의 앞부분을 보니까 craftsmanship이 오랜 기간 이어져 왔다고 하더라고! 그러니까 (A)에는 persisted! 그리고 글의 뒷부분은 craftsmanship은 그것을 가로막는 요인을 만난다는 내용이었어. 그래서 (B)에는 '방해한다'와 비슷한 의미인 limit가 적절하겠다고 생각했지.

O 23 정답 ① ☆ 2등급 대비 [정답률 62%]

＊신체적 움직임과 사회적 불평등

Mobilities in transit / offer a broad field / to be explored / _{to부정사의 수동태}
by different disciplines in all faculties, / in addition to the humanities. //
통행의 이동성은 / 광범위한 분야를 제공한다 / 탐구될 / 모든 학부의 여러 다른 학과에 의해 / 인문학뿐만 아니라 //

In spite of increasing acceleration, / for example / in travelling through geographical or virtual space, / our body becomes _{주어}
more and more / a passive non-moving container, / _{주격 보어} _{동사}
증가하는 속도에도 불구하고 / 예를 들어 / 지리적 공간이나 가상의 공간을 이동하는 데에서 / 우리의 몸은 점점 ~이 되는데 / 수동적이고 움직이지 않는 컨테이너가 /

which is transported by artefacts / or loaded up / with inner feelings of being mobile / in the so-called information society. //
그것은 인공물에 의해 운송되거나 / 가득 채워진다 / 이동한다는 내적 느낌으로 / 이른바 정보 사회에서 //

Technical mobilities turn human beings / into some kind of terminal creatures, / 단서1 정보 사회의 기술적 이동성은 인간이
신체를 움직이는 것을 덜·필요하게 만들었음
기술적 이동성은 인간을 바꾸는데 / 일종의 불치병에 걸린 존재로 /

who spend most of their time / at rest / and who need
계속적 용법의 주격 관계대명사의 병렬 구조
to participate in sports / in order to balance / their daily disproportion of motion and rest. //

그는 대부분의 시간을 보내고 / 휴식을 취하며 / 스포츠에 참여할 필요가 있다 / 균형을 맞추기
위해 / 그들의 일상적인 운동과 휴식의 불균형을 //

Have we come closer / to Aristotle's image of God / as the immobile mover, /

우리는 더 가까워졌는가 / 아리스토텔레스의 신의 이미지에 / 움직이지 않으면서도 움직이는
존재로서의 / 단서2 일부 인간(엘리트)은 자신을 움직일 필요가 없으면서도
돈, 사물, 사람을 움직이는 힘을 행사함   형용사적 용법(power 수식)
when elites exercise their power / to move money, things and people, / while they themselves do not need to move at all? //

엘리트가 그들의 힘을 행사할 때 / 돈, 사물, 사람을 움직이는 / 자신은 전혀 움직일 필요가
없으면서 //

단서3 엘리트가 아닌 다른 사람은 이동성으로 구조화된 사회적 배제의 희생자들임
Others, / at the bottom of this power, / are victims / of mobility-structured social exclusion. //

다른 사람들은 / 이 권력의 밑바닥에 있는 / 희생자들이다 / 이동성으로 구조화된 사회적
배제의 //

They cannot decide / how and where to move, / but are just moved around / or locked out or even locked in / without either
                     either A or B로 연결된 명사구
the right to move or the right to stay. //

그들은 결정할 수 없지만 / 어떻게 어디로 이동할지 / 그저 이리저리 옮겨지거나 / 내쳐지거나
심지어 갇히기도 한다 / 이동할 권리도 머무를 권리도 없이 //

→ In a technology and information society, / human beings,
                                              복수 주어
/ whose bodily movement is less (A) **necessary**, / appear
  to부정사의 완료형
to have gained / increased mobility and power, /   복수 동사

기술과 정보 사회에서 / 인간은 / 신체의 움직임이 덜 필요한 / 이룬 것처럼 보이는데 /
이동성과 권력의 증가를 /

and such a mobility-related human condition / raises the
                                              동격의 전치사
issue / of social (B) **inequality**. //

이동성과 관련된 그러한 인간의 상태는 / 문제를 제기한다 / 사회적 불평등이라는 //

- mobility ⓝ 이동성, 유동성
- broad ⓐ 폭넓은, 일반적인
- faculty ⓝ 능력, (대학의) 학부
- acceleration ⓝ 가속(도)
- virtual ⓐ (컴퓨터를 이용한) 가상의
- transport ⓥ 이동하다, 수송하다
- terminal ⓐ 불치병에 걸린, (질병이) 말기의
- immobile ⓐ 움직이지 않는
- bodily ⓐ 신체의
- transit ⓝ 수송, 교통 체계
- discipline ⓝ 규율, (대학의) 학과목
- humanity ⓝ 인류, ((pl.)) 인문학
- geographical ⓐ 지리(학)적인
- passive ⓐ 수동적인, 소극적인
- artefact ⓝ 인공물, 가공물
- disproportion ⓝ 불균형
- exclusion ⓝ 제외, 배제

통행의 이동성은 인문학뿐만 아니라 모든 학부의 여러 다른 학과에서 탐구할
수 있는 광범위한 분야를 제공한다. 예를 들어, 지리적 공간이나 가상의
공간을 이동하는 데에서 속도가 증가하고 있음에도 불구하고, 우리의 몸은
점점 수동적이고 움직이지 않는 컨테이너가 되는데, 그것은 인공물에 의해
운송되거나 이른바 정보 사회에서 이동한다는 내적 느낌으로 가득 채워진다.
기술적 이동성은 인간을 일종의 불치병에 걸린 존재로 바꾸는데, 그는 대부분의
시간을 휴식을 취하며 보내고 그들의 일상적인 운동과 휴식의 불균형을
균형 맞추기 위해 스포츠에 참여할 필요가 있다. 엘리트가 돈, 사물, 사람을
움직이는 힘을 행사하면서 자신은 전혀 움직일 필요가 없을 때, 우리는
아리스토텔레스의 움직이지 않으면서도 움직이는 존재로서의 신의 이미지에
더 가까워졌는가? 이 권력의 밑바닥에 있는 다른 사람들은 이동성으로
구조화된 사회적 배제의 희생자들이다. 그들은 어떻게 어디로 이동할지 결정할
수 없지만, 이동할 권리도 머무를 권리도 없이 그저 이리저리 옮겨지거나
내쳐지거나 심지어 갇히기도 한다.
→ 기술과 정보 사회에서, 신체의 움직임이 덜 (A) **필요한** 인간은 이동성과
권력의 증가를 이룬 것처럼 보이는데, 이동성과 관련된 그러한 인간의 상태는
사회적 (B) **불평등**이라는 문제를 제기한다.

다음 글의 내용을 한 문장으로 요약하고자 한다. 빈칸 (A), (B)에 들어갈 말로
가장 적절한 것은?

	(A)		(B)	
①	necessary 필요한	—	inequality 불평등	기술적 이동성을 통해 덜 움직일 수 있게 된 인간이 힘을 행사할 수 있게 되었지만 희생자도 있음
②	necessary 필요한	—	growth 성장	┐
③	limited 제한된	—	consciousness 의식	┘ 사회적 성장이나 의식이 문제라는 내용은 없음
④	desirable 바람직한	—	service 봉사	권력을 가진 엘리트와 권력의 밑바닥에 있는 희생자가 존재하는 상태임
⑤	desirable 바람직한	—	divide 분열	움직이는 것이 바람직한지, 덜 바람직한지로 구분한 것이 아님

왜 2등급 ? 긴 문장으로 이루어져 있어 해석에 어려움이 있고 선택지 중에서
매력적인 오답이 있다. 단서 사회적 불평등의 배경인 정보 사회와, 이동성의
측면에서 엘리트와 권력의 밑바닥에 있는 사람들이 대조되고 있음을 이해해야 할
것이다. 발상

| 문제 풀이 순서 |

1st 요약문을 통해 글에서 무엇을 찾아야 하는지 확인한다.

요약문	기술과 정보 사회에서, 신체의 움직임이 덜 '(A)한' 인간은 이동성과 권력의 증가를 이룬 것처럼 보이는데, 이동성과 관련된 그러한 인간의 상태는 사회적 '(B)라는' 문제를 제기한다.

→ 글에서 찾아야 하는 것
(A): 기술과 정보 사회에서 신체의 움직임이 덜 필요한, 제한되는, 바람직한
인간인지.
(B): 그러한 인간의 상태는 사회적 불평등, 성장, 의식, 봉사, 분열이라는 문제를
제기했는지.

2nd 글의 내용을 파악하여 요약문을 완성한다.

(A): 기술적 이동성은 인간을 일종의 불치병에 걸린 존재로 바꾸는데,
… 단서1 엘리트가 돈, 사물, 사람을 움직이는 힘을 행사하면서 자신은
전혀 움직일 필요가 없을 때 … 단서2

→ 기술적 이동성이 인간을 불치병에 걸리게 했는데, 이 불치병은 인간이 신체를
움직일 필요성을 더 작게 만드는 것이다. 한편 엘리트는 다른 것들을 움직이는 힘을
행사하면서 자신은 전혀 움직일 필요가 없다고 했으므로, 빈칸 (A)에는 ①, ②의
necessary가 들어가야 한다.

(B): 이 권력의 밑바닥에 있는 다른 사람들은 이동성으로 구조화된
사회적 배제의 희생자들이다. 단서3

→ 권력의 밑바닥에 있는 사람들은 이동성으로 구조화된 사회적 배제의 희생자라고
했다. 이러한 상태는 앞서 언급된 엘리트와 최하층을 대조하며 사회적
불평등이라는 문제를 제기한다. 따라서 빈칸 (B)에는 ① inequality가 적절하다.
▶ 기술과 정보 사회에서, 신체의 움직임이 덜 '필요한' 인간은 이동성과 권력의
증가를 이룬 것처럼 보이는데, 이동성과 관련된 그러한 인간의 상태는 사회적
'불평등'이라는 문제를 제기한다.

3rd 글의 흐름을 정리하면서 정답이 맞는지 다시 한번 확인한다.

	대부분의 시간을 휴식을 취하며 보내고 단지 운동과 휴식의 불균형을 맞추기 위해 스포츠에 참여해야 하는 존재 꿀팁
도입	지리적 공간이나 가상의 공간을 이동하는 속도의 증가에도 불구하고 우리의 몸은 점점 수동적이고 움직이지 않는 상태가 됨
부연	기술적 이동성은 인간을 일종의 불치병에 걸린 존재로 바꿈
대조	이러한 사회에서 엘리트는 권력을 행사하는 반면 다른 사람들은 이동성으로 구조화된 사회적 배제의 희생자가 됨

① **necessary — inequality** 필요한 – 불평등
기술적 이동성이 신체의 움직임이 덜 필요한 엘리트와 그렇지 않은 사람들 사이의 사회적 불평등을 낳는다는 내용이다.

② **necessary — growth** 필요한 – 성장
누군가 권력을 갖지만 다른 사람은 사회적으로 배제되는 상태가 사회적 성장이라는 문제를 제기한다는 것은 어색하다.

③ **limited — consciousness** 제한된 – 의식
신체의 움직임이 덜 제한된 인간이 아니라 움직일 필요가 없는 인간이 기술과 정보 사회에서 이동성과 권력의 증가를 이룬 것처럼 보이는 것이다.

④ **desirable — service** 바람직한 – 봉사
운동과 휴식의 균형을 맞추기 위해 스포츠에 참여해야 한다고 했지, 신체의 움직임이 덜 바람직한 인간이 이동성과 권력의 증가를 이룬다는 것은 자연스럽지 않다.

⑤ **desirable — divide** 바람직한 – 분열
운동과 휴식의 균형을 맞추기 위해 스포츠에 참여해야 한다고 했지, 신체의 움직임이 덜 바람직한 인간이 이동성과 권력의 증가를 이룬다는 것은 자연스럽지 않다.

O 24 정답 ①　　　　　　　　　　⚙ 1등급 대비 [정답률 60%]

＊설명에 대한 철학적 이론 두 가지

Philip Kitcher and Wesley Salmon have suggested / that there are two possible alternatives / among philosophical theories of explanation. //
Philip Kitcher와 Wesley Salmon은 제안했다 / 두 가지 가능한 대안이 있다고 / 설명에 대한 철학적 이론들 중
　둘 중 한 가지 관점　　　동격절 접속사
One is the view / that scientific explanation consists / in the *unification* / of broad bodies of phenomena / under a minimal number of generalizations. // 단서 1 광범위한 현상들을 최소한으로 적은 수의 일반화 아래로 통합하는 것
하나는 견해이다 / 과학적 설명이 있다는 / '통합'에 / 현상들의 광범위한 모음의 / 최소한으로 적은 수의 일반화 아래에

According to this view, / the (or perhaps, a) goal of science is / to construct / an economical framework / of laws or generalizations /
　　　　　　 명사적 용법(주격 보어)　선행사
이 견해에 따르면 / 과학의 목표(혹은 어쩌면 한 가지 목표)는 ~이다 / 구성하는 것 / 경제적인 틀을 / 법칙이나 일반화의 /
　　　주격 관계대명사
that are capable of subsuming / all observable phenomena. //
포섭할 수 있는 / 모든 관찰할 수 있는 현상들을 //

Scientific explanations / organize and systematize our knowledge / of the empirical world; /
과학적 설명은 / 우리의 지식을 조직하고 체계화한다 / 경험적 세계에 대한 /
　　　　　　 the 비교급, the 비교급: ~할수록 더 …한/하게
the more economical the systematization, / the deeper our understanding / of what is explained. // 단서 2 체계화가 더 경제적일수록 설명되는 것에 대한 우리의 이해가 더 깊음
체계화가 더 경제적일수록 / 우리의 이해는 더 깊다 / 설명되는 것에 대한 //
　둘 중 나머지 한 관점
The other view / is the *causal/mechanical* approach. //
다른 관점은 / '인과 관계적/기계적' 접근이다 //

According to it, / a scientific explanation of a phenomenon / consists of uncovering the mechanisms / that produced the phenomenon of interest. //
　　　　　　　　　　　　　　선행사　　주격 관계대명사
그것에 따르면 / 어떤 현상에 대한 과학적인 설명은 / 메커니즘을 밝히는 것으로 이루어진다 / 관심 있는 그 현상을 만들어 낸 //
　　　　　 see A as B: A를 B로 여기다[보다]
This view sees / the explanation of individual events / as primary, / with the explanation of generalizations / flowing from them. // 단서 3 일차적으로 개별 사건으로부터 일반화가 도출됨
　　　　　　　　　　　　　　　　with+(대)명사+분사:
이 관점은 본다 / 개별 사건들에 대한 설명을 / 일차적으로 / 일반화에 대한 설명이 / 그것들로부터 흘러나오는 채로　~가 …한[된] 채로
　　　　　　 단서 4 과학적 일반화는 '규칙성'을 만들어 내는 인과적 메커니즘에서 비롯됨
That is, / the explanation of scientific generalizations comes /
　　선행사　　　　　　　　　주격 관계대명사
from the causal mechanisms / that produce the regularities. //
즉 / 과학적 일반화에 대한 설명은 비롯된다 / 인과적 메커니즘에서 / 규칙성을 만들어 내는 //

→ Scientific explanations can be made / either by seeking / the (A) **least** number of principles / covering all observations /
과학적 설명은 만들어질 수 있다 / 찾음으로써 / 최소한의 수의 원리를 / 모든 관찰을 포함하는 /
　　　　　either A or B로 연결된 수단의 전치사구
or by finding general (B) **patterns** / drawn from individual phenomena. //
또는 일반적인 패턴을 발견함으로써 / 개별 현상으로부터 도출된 //

- **alternative** ⓝ 대안, 대체 가능한 것　　· **philosophical** ⓐ 철학의
- **theory** ⓝ 이론, 학설　　· **consist in** (주요 특징 등이) ~에 있다
- **unification** ⓝ 통합　　· **broad** ⓐ 광대한, 광범위한
- **body** ⓝ 많은 양, 많은 모음　　· **phenomenon** ⓝ 현상(pl. phenomena)
- **minimal** ⓐ 최소의, 아주 적은　　· **generalization** ⓝ 일반화
- **construct** ⓥ 구성하다, 건설하다　　· **economical** ⓐ 경제적인, 알뜰한
- **framework** ⓝ (판단·결정 등을 위한) 틀　　· **capable of** ~을 할 수 있는
- **observable** ⓐ 관찰할 수 있는　　· **systematize** ⓥ 체계화하다
- **causal** ⓐ 인과 관계의
- **mechanical** ⓐ (행동·반응 등이) 기계적인, 기계에 의한
- **approach** ⓝ 접근법　　· **consist of** ~로 구성되다
- **uncover** ⓥ 밝히다, 알아내다　　· **primary** ⓐ 일차적인, 주요한
- **regularity** ⓝ 규칙적임, 규칙성　　· **seek** ⓥ 찾다, 추구하다
- **observation** ⓝ 관찰, 감지　　· **general** ⓐ 일반적인, 보통의

Philip Kitcher와 Wesley Salmon은 설명에 대한 철학적 이론들 중 두 가지 가능한 대안이 있다고 제안했다. 하나는 과학적 설명이 최소한으로 적은 수의 일반화 아래에 현상들의 광범위한 모음을 '통합'하는 데 있다는 견해이다. 이 견해에 따르면 과학의 목표(혹은 어쩌면 한 가지 목표)는 모든 관찰할 수 있는 현상들을 포섭할 수 있는 법칙이나 일반화의 경제적인 틀을 구성하는 것이다. 과학적 설명은 경험적 세계에 대한 우리의 지식을 조직하고 체계화하는데, 체계화가 더 경제적일수록, 설명되는 것에 대한 우리의 이해는 더 깊다. 다른 관점은 '인과 관계적/기계적' 접근이다.

그것에 따르면, 어떤 현상에 대한 과학적인 설명은 관심 있는 그 현상을 만들어 낸 메커니즘을 밝히는 것으로 이루어진다. 이 관점은 개별 사건들에 대한 설명을 일차적으로 보고, 일반화에 대한 설명이 그것들로부터 흘러나온다고 본다. 즉, 과학적 일반화에 대한 설명은 규칙성을 만들어 내는 인과적 메커니즘에서 비롯된다.

→ 과학적 설명은 모든 관찰을 포함하는 (A) **최소한의** 수의 원리를 찾거나 개별 현상으로부터 도출된 일반적인 (B) **패턴**을 발견함으로써 만들어질 수 있다.

다음 글의 내용을 한 문장으로 요약하고자 한다. 빈칸 (A), (B)에 들어갈 말로 가장 적절한 것은?
첫 번째 견해는 일반화의 '수'가 적어야 한다는 것이 핵심임

(A)	(B)
① least 최소한의	— patterns 패턴
② fixed 고정된	— features 특징
③ limited 제한된	— functions 기능
④ fixed 고정된	— rules 규칙
⑤ least 최소한의	— assumptions 가정

최소한으로 적은 수의 일반화로 통합하는 것, 개별 사건들에서 일반화를 도출하는 것

두 번째 견해는 개별 사건들에서 규칙성을 만들어 내는 것(일반화)이 핵심임

왜 1등급❓ 과학적 설명이 만들어지는 두 가지 방식에 대한 내용의 글임을 이해했더라도 선택지에 있는 단어들을 요약문에 정확하게 대입하지 못하면 틀릴 수 있는 1등급 대비 문제이다.

| 문제 풀이 순서 |

1st 요약문을 통해 글에서 무엇을 찾아야 하는지 확인한다.

과학적 설명은 모든 관찰을 포함하는 (A) ＿＿＿＿한 수의 원리를 찾거나 개별 현상으로부터 도출된 일반적인 (B) ＿＿＿＿을 발견함으로써 만들어질 수 있다.

⇒ 과학적 설명이 만들어지는 두 가지 방식에 대해 설명하는 글일 것이다.

   (A) 방식 1: 모든 관찰을 포함하는 <u>최소한의, 고정된, 제한된</u> 수의 원리를 찾기
   (B) 방식 2: 개별 현상으로부터 도출된 일반적인 패턴, 특징, 기능, 규칙, 가정을 발견하기

2nd 글을 읽고, 과학적 설명이 만들어지는 방식을 확인한다.

(A):

> • 하나는 과학적 설명이 <u>최소한</u>으로 적은 수의 일반화 아래에 현상들의 광범위한 모음을 '통합'하는 데 있다는 견해이다. **단서 1**
> • 과학적 설명은 경험적 세계에 대한 우리의 지식을 조직하고 체계화하는데, 체계화가 더 <u>경제적</u>일수록, 설명되는 것에 대한 우리의 이해는 더 깊다. **단서 2**

⇒ 광범위한 현상들을 최소한으로 적은 수의 일반화로 통합한다.
   체계화가 경제적일수록, 즉 체계의 단계가 적을수록 우리의 이해가 더 깊다.
   ▶ **(A) 방식 1**: 모든 관찰을 포함하는 ① '<u>최소한의</u>' 수의 원리를 찾기

(B):

> • 이 관점은 개별 사건들에 대한 설명을 일차적으로 보고, 일반화에 대한 설명이 그것들로부터 흘러나온다고 본다. **단서 3**
> • 과학적 일반화에 대한 설명은 <u>규칙성</u>을 만들어 내는 인과적 메커니즘에서 비롯된다. **단서 4**

⇒ '개별 사건으로부터 흘러나오다' = '개별 현상으로부터 도출되다'
   '일반화', '규칙성' = '일반적인 패턴'
   ▶ **(B) 방식 2**: 개별 현상으로부터 도출된 일반적인 ① '<u>패턴</u>' 발견하기

3rd 전체 글의 내용을 정리하여 요약문이 적절한지 확인한다.

도입	Philip Kitcher와 Wesley Salmon은 설명에 대한 철학적 이론 중 두 가지 가능한 대안이 있다고 제안함
대안 ①	관찰할 수 있는 모든 현상을 최소한의 수의 일반화로 통합하는 것
부연	경험하는 세계에 대한 우리의 지식을 경제적으로 체계화할수록 우리의 이해는 더 깊어짐
대안 ②	인과 관계적/기계적 접근은 어떤 현상을 만들어낸 메커니즘(인과적 메커니즘)을 밝히는 것임
부연	개별 사건에서 일반화에 대한 설명이 흘러나오고, 규칙성을 만들어 내는 인과적 메커니즘에서 과학적 일반화가 비롯됨

⇒ 과학적 설명은 모든 관찰을 포함하는 (A) <u>최소한의</u> 수의 원리를 찾거나 개별현상으로부터 도출된 일반적인 (B) <u>패턴</u>을 발견함으로써 만들어질 수 있다.

| 선택지 분석 |

① least — patterns 최소한의 — 패턴
최소한으로 적은 수의 일반화로 통합하고, 개별 사건에서 일반화를 도출하고, 규칙성을 만들어 내야 한다고 했다.

② fixed — features 고정된 — 특징
첫 번째 견해의 핵심은 일반화의 수가 최소한이어야 한다는 것이다. 즉, 광범위한 현상들이 최소한으로 적은 수의 일반적인 원리로 설명되어야 한다는 의미로, '고정된' 원리와는 관련이 없다.

③ limited — functions 제한된 — 기능
두 번째 견해의 핵심은 과학적 일반화에 대한 설명이 개별 사건을 토대로 하여 규칙성을 만들어 내는 인과적 메커니즘에서 비롯된다는 것이다. 따라서 개별 사건으로부터 일반적인 '기능'이 도출된다고 하는 것은 어색하다.

④ fixed — rules 고정된 — 규칙
광범위한 현상들이 최소한으로 적은 수의 일반적인 원리로 설명되어야 하므로 '고정된' 원리와는 관련이 없다.

⑤ least — assumptions 최소한의 — 가정
두 번째 견해에 따르면 개별 사건으로부터 일반적인 '가정'이 도출된다고 하는 것은 어색하다.

O 25 정답 ③ ─── ☻ 1등급 대비 [정답률 57%]

＊보편적이지 않은 '정치 권력'이라는 개념

From a cross-cultural perspective / the equation / between public leadership and dominance / is questionable. //
비교 문화적 관점에서 / 등식은 / 대중적인 지도력과 지배력 사이의 / 의심스럽다 //

What does one mean / by 'dominance'? //
무엇을 의미하는가 / '지배력'으로 //

Does it indicate / coercion? //
그것은 나타내는가 / 강제를 //

Or control / over 'the most valued'? //
아니면 통제를 (나타내는가) / '가장 가치 있는 것'에 대한 //

'Political' systems may be / about both, either, or conceivably neither. //
'정치적' 시스템은 ～일 수 있다 / 둘 다에 관한 것일, 둘 중 하나에 관한 것일, 아니면 아마도 둘 다에 관한 것이 아닐 //

The idea of 'control' would be a bothersome one / for many peoples, / as for instance among many native peoples of Amazonia /
'통제'라는 생각은 성가신 것일 것이다 / 많은 부족에게는 / 예를 들어 아마존의 많은 원주민 부족 사이에서처럼 /

where all members of a community are fond / of their personal autonomy / and notably allergic / to any obvious expression / of control or coercion. //
공동체의 모든 구성원이 좋아하고 / 개인의 자율성을 / 몹시 싫어하는 / 어떤 명백한 표현이든 / 통제나 강제의 //

단서 1 서양의 고정관념인 '강제적인' 힘으로서의 정치 권력에 대한 개념은 보편적인 것이 아님

The conception of political power / as a *coercive* force, / while it may be a Western fixation, / is not a universal. //
정치 권력이라는 개념은 / '강제적인' 힘으로서 / 서양의 고정관념일지 모르겠지만 / 보편적인 것이 아니다 //

It is very unusual / for an Amazonian leader / to give an order. //
～은 매우 이례적이다 / 아마존의 지도자가 / 명령을 내리는 것은 //

If many peoples do not view political power / as a coercive force, / nor as the most valued domain, /
많은 부족이 정치 권력을 여기지 않는다면 / 강제적인 힘으로 / '또한 가장 가치 있는 영역으로' /

단서 2 많은 부족이 정치 권력을 강제적인 힘, 지배로 여기지 않으므로 '정치적인 것'을 '지배'로 비약하는 것은 불안정한 비약이라는 것임

then the leap / from 'the political' to 'domination' / (as coercion), / and from there to 'domination of women', / is a shaky one. //
비약은 / '정치적인 것'에서 '지배'로 / (강제로서의) / '그리고 거기에서' '여성에 대한 지배'로 / 불안정한 비약이다 //

As Marilyn Strathern has remarked, / the notions of 'the political' and 'political personhood' / are cultural obsessions of our own, / a bias long reflected / in anthropological constructs. //
Marilyn Strathern이 말한 것처럼 / '정치적인 것'과 '정치적 개성'이라는 개념은 / 우리 자신의 문화적 강박 관념이다 / 오랫동안 반영된 편견 / 인류학적 구성 개념에 //

> → It is (A) **misguided** / to understand political power / in other cultures / through our own notion of it /
> ～은 잘못 이해된 것인데 / 정치 권력을 이해하는 것은 / 다른 문화에서의 / 그것에 대한 우리 자신의 개념을 통해 /
>
> because ideas of political power are not (B) **uniform** / across cultures. //
> 왜냐하면 정치 권력에 관한 생각은 일률적이지 않기 때문이다 / 여러 문화에 걸쳐 //

- - - - - - - - - -

• cross-cultural ⓐ 다양한 문화들이 섞인   • perspective ⓝ 시각, 관점
• equation ⓝ 등식, 동일시, 방정식   • dominance ⓝ 권세, 지배, 우세
• questionable ⓐ 의심스러운, 미심쩍은   • indicate ⓥ 나타내다, 시사하다
• conceivably ⓐd 생각할 수 있는 바로는, 상상컨대
• bothersome ⓐ 성가신   • be fond of ～을 좋아하다
• notably ⓐd 현저히, 뚜렷이

- allergic ⓐ 몹시 싫어하는, (~에 대해) 알레르기가 있는
- obvious ⓐ 분명한, 명백한
- coercive ⓐ 강압적인 · force ⓝ 물리력, 힘
- fixation ⓝ 집착, 고정 · universal ⓐ 일반적인, 보편적인
- leap ⓝ (상상·논리의) 비약, 도약, 급증
- shaky ⓐ 떨리는, 휘청거리는, 불안정한 · remark ⓥ 언급[발언]하다
- notion ⓝ 개념, 관념 · personhood ⓝ 개인적 특질, 개성
- obsession ⓝ 강박, 집착 · bias ⓝ 편견, 편향

비교 문화적 관점에서 대중적인 지도력과 지배력 사이의 등식은 의심스럽다. '지배력'이 의미하는 바는 무엇인가? 그것은 강제를 나타내는가? 아니면 '가장 가치 있는 것'에 대한 통제인가? '정치적' 시스템은 둘 다에 관한 것일 수도, 둘 중 하나에 관한 것일 수도, 아니면 아마도 둘 다에 관한 것이 아닐 수도 있다. '통제'라는 생각은 많은 부족에게는 성가신 것일 텐데, 예를 들어 공동체의 모든 구성원이 개인의 자율성을 좋아하고 통제나 강제가 명백하게 표현되는 어떤 것이든 몹시 싫어하는 아마존의 많은 원주민 부족 사이에서처럼 말이다. 서양의 고정관념일지 모르겠지만, '강제적인' 힘으로서 정치 권력이라는 개념은 보편적인 것이 아니다. 아마존의 지도자가 명령을 내리는 것은 매우 이례적이다. 많은 부족이 정치 권력을 강제적인 힘으로, '또한 가장 가치 있는 영역으로' 여기지 않는다면, '정치적인 것'에서 (강제로서의) '지배'로, '그리고 거기에서' '여성에 대한 지배'로 비약하는 것은 불안정한 비약이다. Marilyn Strathern이 말한 것처럼, '정치적인 것'과 '정치적 개성'이라는 개념은 우리 자신의 문화적 강박 관념으로, 인류학적 구성 개념에 오랫동안 반영된 편견이다.
→ 정치 권력에 대한 우리 자신의 개념을 통해 다른 문화에서의 정치 권력을 이해하는 것은 (A) 잘못 이해된 것인데, 왜냐하면 정치 권력에 관한 생각은 여러 문화에 걸쳐 (B) 일률적이지 않기 때문이다.

다음 글의 내용을 한 문장으로 요약하고자 한다. 빈칸 (A), (B)에 들어갈 말로 가장 적절한 것은?

서양의 고정관념으로 생각하는 것은 적절하거나 효과적이지 않음

(A)	(B)
① rational 합리적인	— flexible 유연하지 (B)에는 '유연한, 융통성 있는'의 반의어가 필요함
② appropriate 적절한	— commonplace 흔하지
③ misguided 잘못 이해된	— uniform 일률적이지 정치 권력에 관한 생각은 보편적이지 않으므로 서양의 고정관념으로 이해하는 것은 잘못된 것임
④ unreasonable 불합리한	— varied 다양하지 (B)에는 '다양한'의 반의어가 필요함
⑤ effective 효과적인	— objective 객관적이지

─────────────────────

ⓦ 1등급? 어휘 수준이 높고, 선택지가 전부 다른 단어로 이루어져 있어 하나하나 확인하며 정답을 골라야 하는 1등급 대비 문제이다. 요약문으로부터 간략하게 주제를 파악한 뒤에, ⓒ universal과 shaky라는 형용사를 발견하여 연관시킨다면 어렵지 않게 정답을 찾을 수 있을 것이다. ⓦ

| 문제 풀이 순서 |

1st 요약문을 통해 글에서 무엇을 찾아야 하는지 확인한다.

요약문	정치 권력에 대한 우리 자신의 개념을 통해 다른 문화에서의 정치 권력을 이해하는 것은 '(A)한' 것인데, 왜냐하면 정치 권력에 관한 생각은 여러 문화에 걸쳐 '(B)하지' 않기 때문이다.

⇒ 글에서 찾아야 하는 것
  (A): 정치 권력에 대한 우리 자신의 개념을 통해 다른 문화에서의 정치 권력을 이해하는 것은 합리적인, 적절한, 잘못 이해된, 불합리한, 효과적인 것인지.
  (B): 정치 권력에 관한 생각은 여러 문화에 걸쳐 유연하지, 흔하지, 일률적이지, 다양하지, 객관적이지 않는지.

2nd 글의 내용을 파악하여 요약문을 완성한다.

> (A), (B): 서양의 고정관념일지 모르겠지만, '강제적인' 힘으로서 정치 권력이라는 개념은 보편적인 것이 아니다. **단서1**
> '정치적인 것'에서 (강제로서의) '지배'로, '그리고 거기에서' '여성에 대한 지배'로 비약하는 것은 불안정한 비약이다. **단서2**

─────────────────────

⇒ '강제적인' 힘으로서의 정치 권력이라는 개념은 서양의 고정관념일 수는 있지만 보편적인 것이 아니라고 했다. 정치 권력에 대한 서양의 개념을 통해 다른 문화에서의 정치 권력을 이해하려 한다면 잘못 이해한 것이며, 이는 정치 권력에 대한 개념이 보편적이지(일률적이지) 않기 때문이다. 따라서 빈칸 (A)에는 ③의 misguided, 빈칸 (B)에는 ③의 uniform이 들어가야 한다.
  ▶ 정치 권력에 대한 우리 자신의 개념을 통해 다른 문화에서의 정치 권력을 이해하는 것은 '잘못 이해된' 것인데, 왜냐하면 정치 권력에 관한 생각은 여러 문화에 걸쳐 '일률적이지' 않기 때문이다.

3rd 글의 흐름을 정리하면서 정답이 맞는지 다시 한번 확인한다.

도입	정치적 시스템은 통제와 강제에 관련된 것일 수도 있고, 아닐 수도 있음
전개	'강제적인' 힘으로서 정치 권력이라는 개념은 서양의 고정관념일지도 모르고 보편적이지 않음
부연	많은 부족이 정치 권력을 강제적인 힘으로 여기지 않으면 '정치적인 것'에서 '지배'로 비약하는 것은 불안정한 비약임
인용	Marilyn Strathern은 '정치적인 것'과 '정치적 개성'은 우리 자신의 문화적 강박 관념이라고 했음

| 선택지 분석 |

① **rational — flexible** 합리적인 — 유연하지
강제적인 힘으로서 정치 권력을 이해하는 것이 보편적이지 않다고 했으므로 (B)에는 flexible이나 varied의 반의어가 들어가야 한다.

② **appropriate — commonplace** 적절한 — 흔하지
서양의 고정관념으로 다른 문화의 정치 권력을 이해하는 것이 적절하다거나 효과적이라고 하는 것은 글의 내용에 맞지 않는다.

③ **misguided — uniform** 잘못 이해된 — 일률적이지
한 국가의 입장에서 정치 권력을 이해한다면 잘못 이해한 것이며 그 개념은 여러 문화에 걸쳐 보편적이지 않다는 내용이다.

④ **unreasonable — varied** 불합리한 — 다양하지
강제적인 힘으로서 정치 권력을 이해하는 것이 보편적이지 않다고 했으므로 (B)에는 flexible이나 varied의 반의어가 들어가야 한다.

⑤ **effective — objective** 효과적인 — 객관적이지
서양의 고정관념으로 다른 문화의 정치 권력을 이해하는 것이 적절하다거나 효과적이라고 하는 것은 글의 내용에 맞지 않는다.

─────────────── 어법 특강

✳ to부정사의 의미상 주어

– 대부분 문장에서 행위자를 알 수 있는 경우를 제외하고, 「for+명사/목적격 대명사」를 to부정사 앞에 표시해 준다. (예외적으로, 사람의 성격이나 태도와 같은 형용사가 보어로 올 때 「of+명사/목적격 대명사」로 표시한다.)

- Here are some tips for you to remember.
  (여기 네가 기억할 몇 가지 팁이 있다.)
- It is important for everyone to take part equally in discussions.
  (모든 사람이 공평하게 논의에 참여하는 것이 중요하다.)
- This is big enough for my dog to wear.
  (이것은 우리 강아지가 입기에 충분히 크다.)
- It was stupid of you to make such a mistake.
  (네가 그런 실수를 한 것은 어리석었다.)

O 어휘 Review 정답

01 지나침, 과잉	11 in contrast	21 isolated
02 이해하다, 감상하다	12 settle down	22 dissolves
03 설명	13 at best	23 instantaneous
04 조정	14 rest (up)on	24 portray
05 기호, 성향	15 differ from	25 industries
06 prioritize	16 norms	26 Substantial
07 testimony	17 associated	27 broad
08 fellow	18 properties	28 restricted
09 disclose	19 doubt	29 acknowledge
10 passive	20 insecure	

요약문을 먼저 읽고 주제를 파악하자!

P 장문의 이해 (문제편 p. 323~349)

P 01~02 ＊고정된 파이가 협상에 미치는 영향

Many negotiators assume / that all negotiations involve a fixed
　　　　　　　　　　　　생략 가능한 목적격 관계대명사
pie. //

많은 협상가는 가정한다 / 모든 협상이 고정된 파이를 수반한다고 //

Negotiators often approach integrative negotiation
opportunities / as zero-sum situations / or win-lose exchanges. //

협상가들은 자주 통합 협상 기회를 접근한다 / 제로섬 상황이나 / 승패 교환으로 //

1번 단서 1: 고정된 파이를 믿는 사람들은 통합적인 합의와 상호 이익이 되는 절충안이 없다고 생각함

Those / who believe in the mythical fixed pie / assume / that
복수 주어　　　　　　　　　　　　　　　　　　　　　복수 동사
parties' interests / stand in opposition, / with no possibility /

for integrative settlements and mutually beneficial trade-offs, /

사람들은 / 허구의 고정된 파이를 믿는 / 가정한다 / 당사자들의 이해관계가 / 반대 입장에
있다고 / 가능성이 없는 / 통합적인 합의와 상호 이익이 되는 절충안의 /
　　　　　　　　　　　　　　　　　　형용사적 용법(efforts 수식)
so they (a) suppress efforts / to search for them. //

그래서 그들은 노력을 억누른다 / 그것들을 찾으려는 //
　　　　　　　　　　　　주어
In a hiring negotiation, / a job applicant / who assumes / that
　　　　　　　　　　　　　　　　　　　　　　　　동사
salary is the only issue / may insist on $75,000 / when the

employer is offering $70,000. // **2번** 단서 1: 급여만 협상의 대상이라고 생각할 때는
통합적인 합의와 상호 이익이 되는 절충안이 없다고 생각함
고용 협상에서 / 구직자는 / 생각하는 / 급여가 유일한 문제라고 / 7만 5천 달러를 요구할 수
있다 / 고용주가 7만 달러를 제시할 때 //
　　　　　　　　　　　　only가 이끄는 부사절이 강조되어 문두로 나가면서 주어와 동사가 도치됨
Only when the two parties discuss the possibilities further / do

they discover / that moving expenses and starting date / can

also be negotiated, / **2번** 단서 2: 급여 외에 다른 요소도 협상의 대상이 될 수 있음을
발견하면 상호 이익이 되는 절충안을 찾을 수도 있음
두 당사자가 가능성에 대해 더 자세히 논의할 때만 / 그들은 사실을 발견하는데 / 이사 비용과
시작 날짜가 / 또한 협상될 수 있다는 /

which may (b) block(→ facilitate) / resolution of the salary

issue. //

이는 방해할(→ 촉진할) 수 있을 것이다 / 급여 문제의 해결을 //
　　　　　　　　　　　　　　　　　　　　　　　　　　　　　단수 동사
The tendency / to see negotiation / in fixed-pie terms / (c) varies
단수 주어　　　형용사적 용법(The tendency 수식)
/ depending on how people view / the nature of a given conflict

situation. //

경향은 / 협상을 보는 / 고정된 파이 관점에서 / 달라진다 / 사람들이 어떻게 보느냐에 따라 /
주어진 갈등 상황의 본질을 //

This was shown / in a clever experiment by Harinck, de Dreu,

and Van Vianen / involving a simulated negotiation / between

prosecutors and defense lawyers / over jail sentences. //

이는 밝혀졌다 / Harinck, de Dreu와 Van Vianen에 의한 기발한 실험에서 / 모의 협상을
포함하는 / 검사와 피고측 변호인 간의 / 징역형에 대한 //

Some participants were told / to view their goals / in terms of
　　　　　　　　　　　　　　　능동태 문장의 목적격 보어
personal gain / (e.g., arranging a particular jail sentence / will

help your career), /

어떤 참가자들은 들었고 / 그들의 목표를 보라고 / 개인적 이득의 관점에서 / (예를 들어, 특정
징역형을 정하는 것이 / 당신의 경력에 도움이 될 것이다) /

others were told / to view their goals / in terms of effectiveness
　　　　　　　　　　　능동태 문장의 목적격 보어
/ (a particular sentence / is most likely to prevent recidivism), /

다른 참가자들은 들었으며 / 그들의 목표를 보라고 / 효과성의 관점에서 / (특정 형은 / 상습적
범행을 방지할 가능성이 가장 크다) /

and still others were told / to focus on values / (a particular jail
　　　　　　　　　　　　　　능동태 문장의 목적격 보어
sentence / is fair and just). //

그리고 또 다른 참가자들은 들었다 / 가치에 초점을 맞추라고 / (특정 징역형은 공정하고
정당하다) //

Negotiators / focusing on personal gain / were most likely
_{복수 주어}   _{복수 동사}
to come under the influence / of fixed-pie beliefs / and approach
                                        _{병렬 구조}
the situation (d) competitively. //

협상가들은 / 개인적 이득에 초점을 맞춘 / 영향을 받을 가능성이 가장 컸다 / 고정된 파이에 대한 믿음의 / 그리고 상황에 경쟁적으로 접근할 (가능성이 가장 컸다) //

Negotiators / focusing on values / were least likely to see the
_{복수 주어}   _{복수 동사}
problem / in fixed-pie terms / and more inclined / to approach
the situation cooperatively. //
협상가들은 / 가치에 초점을 맞춘 / 문제를 볼 가능성이 가장 낮았고 / 고정된 파이 관점에서 / 경향이 더 컸다 / 상황에 협력적으로 접근하려는 //

Stressful conditions / such as time constraints / contribute to this
_{복수 주어}   _{복수 동사}
common misperception, / which in turn may lead / to (e) less
                        _{계속적 용법의 주격 관계대명사}
integrative agreements. //

스트레스가 많은 조건은 / 시간 제약과 같은 / 이러한 흔한 오해의 원인이 되며 / 이는 결국 이어질 수 있다 / 덜 통합적인 합의로 //

- negotiator ⓝ 협상가   • integrative ⓐ 통합하는
- negotiation ⓝ 협상   • mythical ⓐ 허구의, 가상의
- settlement ⓝ 합의, 해결   • suppress ⓥ 억누르다
- insist ⓥ 고집하다, 주장하다   • expense ⓝ 돈, 비용
- resolution ⓝ 해결   • tendency ⓝ 경향   • given ⓐ 정해진
- jail sentence 징역형   • in terms of ~면에서는
- be inclined to ~하는 경향이 있다
- cooperatively ⓐⅾ 협력하여, 협조적으로   • constraint ⓝ 제약
- alternative ⓝ 대안

많은 협상가는 모든 협상이 고정된 파이를 수반한다고 가정한다. 협상가들은 자주 통합 협상 기회를 제로섬 상황이나 승패 교환으로 접근한다. 허구의 고정된 파이를 믿는 사람들은 당사자들의 이해관계가 통합적인 합의와 상호 이익이 되는 절충안의 가능성이 없는 반대 입장에 있다고 가정하기 때문에 이를 찾으려는 노력을 (a) 억누른다. 고용 협상에서 급여가 유일한 문제라고 생각하는 구직자는 고용주가 7만 달러를 제시할 때 7만 5천 달러를 요구할 수 있다. 두 당사자가 가능성에 대해 더 자세히 논의할 때만 이사 비용과 시작 날짜 또한 협상할 수 있다는 사실을 발견하게 되는데, 이는 급여 문제의 해결을 (b) 방해할(→ 촉진할) 수 있다. 협상을 고정된 파이 관점에서 보는 경향은 사람들이 주어진 갈등 상황의 본질을 어떻게 보느냐에 따라 (c) 달라진다. 이는 Harinck, de Dreu와 Van Vianen의, 징역형에 대한 검사와 피고측 변호인 간의 모의 협상을 포함하는 기발한 실험에서 밝혀졌다. 어떤 참가자들은 개인적 이득의 관점에서 그들의 목표를 보라는 말을 들었고(예를 들어, 특정 징역형을 정하는 것이 당신의 경력에 도움이 될 것이다), 다른 참가자들은 그들의 목표를 효과성의 관점에서 보라는 말을 들었으며(특정 형은 상습적 범행을 방지할 가능성이 가장 크다), 그리고 또 다른 참가자들은 가치에 초점을 맞추라는 말을 들었다(특정 징역형은 공정하고 정당하다). 개인적 이득에 초점을 맞춘 협상가들은 고정된 파이에 대한 믿음의 영향을 받아 상황에 (d) 경쟁적으로 접근할 가능성이 가장 컸다. 가치에 초점을 맞춘 협상가들은 문제를 고정된 파이 관점에서 볼 가능성이 가장 낮았고 상황에 협력적으로 접근하려는 경향이 더 컸다. 시간 제약과 같은 스트레스가 많은 조건은 이러한 흔한 오해의 원인이 되며, 이는 결국 (e) 덜 통합적인 합의로 이어질 수 있다.

P 01 정답 ③

윗글의 제목으로 가장 적절한 것은?

① Fixed Pie: A Key to Success in a Zero-sum Game
고정된 파이: 제로섬 게임에서 성공의 열쇠   협상을 제로섬 상황으로 보게 함
② Fixed Pie Tells You How to Get the Biggest Salary
고정된 파이는 여러분에게 가장 큰 급여를 받는 방법을 알려 준다   예시로 든 상황으로 만든 오답
③ Negotiators, Wake Up from the Myth of the Fixed Pie!
협상가들이여, 고정된 파이라는 미몽에서 깨어나라!   고정된 파이 관점에서 벗어나라는 조언의 글
④ Want a Fairer Jail Sentence? Stick to the Fixed Pie
더 공정한 징역형을 원하는가? 고정된 파이를 고수하라   글의 일부분으로 만든 오답
⑤ What Alternatives Maximize Fixed-pie Effects?
어떤 대안이 고정된 파이 효과를 극대화하는가?   고정된 파이 효과를 최소화하라는 내용임

왜 정답? [정답률 57%]

- 허구의 고정된 파이를 믿는 협상가는 협상을 제로섬 상황이나 승패 교환으로 생각하여 통합적인 합의와 상호 이익이 되는 절충안의 가능성이 없다고 가정한다. **1번 단서 1**
- 개인적 이득에 초점을 맞추는 협상가는 고정된 파이에 대한 믿음에 영향을 받아 상황에 경쟁적으로 접근한다.
  ↔ 가치에 초점을 맞추는 협상가는 고정된 파이 관점에서 문제를 보지 않고, 상황에 협력적으로 접근한다. **1번 단서 2**

➡ 협상할 때 고정된 파이 관점에서 벗어나라는 내용이므로, 제목으로 적절한 것은 ③ '협상가들이여, 고정된 파이라는 미몽에서 깨어나라!'이다.

왜 오답?

① 고정된 파이 관점에서 접근하면 협상을 제로섬 게임으로 보게 된다는 내용이다.
② 급여가 문제되는 고용 협상이 예시로 등장한 것으로 만든 오답이다.
④ 징역형에 대한 모의 협상이 구체적 부연으로 등장한 것으로 만든 오답이다.
⑤ 고정된 파이 효과를 극대화하는 방법을 설명한 글이 아니다.

P 02 정답 ②

밑줄 친 (a)~(e) 중에서 문맥상 낱말의 쓰임이 적절하지 않은 것은?

① (a) 고정된 파이를 믿는 사람들의 특징   ② (b) 고정된 파이에서 벗어나는 경우
억누르다   방해하다
③ (c) 갈등 상황의 본질을 어떻게 보느냐에 따라   ④ (d) 고정된 파이에 대한 믿음의 영향을
다르게 달라지는 예시가 등장함   경쟁적으로 많이 받음
⑤ (e) 오해가 낳는 결과
덜

왜 정답? [정답률 37%]

② (b) block 방해하다

고용 협상에서 급여가 유일한 문제라고 생각하는 구직자는 고용주가 7만 달러를 제시할 때 7만 5천 달러를 요구할 수 있다. 두 당사자가 가능성에 대해 더 자세히 논의할 때만 이사 비용과 시작 날짜 또한 협상할 수 있다는 사실을 발견하게 되는데, 이는 급여 문제의 해결을 (b) 방해할 수 있다.
촉진할

➡ '고용 협상에서 급여가 유일한 문제라고 생각하는 경우'와 '이사 비용과 시작 날짜 또한 협상할 수 있음을 발견하는 경우'가 대조된다. 이사 비용과 시작 날짜를 논의함으로써 급여 문제에 대한 절충안에 합의할 수 있다는 내용이다.
▶ block을 반의어인 facilitate(촉진하다) 등의 단어로 바꿔야 함

왜 오답?

① (a) suppress 억누르다

허구의 고정된 파이를 믿는 사람들은 당사자들의 이해관계가 통합적인 합의와 상호 이익이 되는 절충안의 가능성이 없는 반대 입장에 있다고 가정한다. 그래서(so) 이를 찾으려는 노력을 (a) 억누른다.

➡ 통합적인 합의와 상호 이익이 되는 절충안의 가능성이 없다고 가정한다면, 그것들을(통합적인 합의와 상호 이익이 되는 절충안을) 찾으려고 하지 않을 것이다.
▶ suppress는 문맥에 맞음

③ (c) varies 다르다

- 협상을 고정된 파이 관점에서 보는 경향은 사람들이 주어진 갈등 상황의 본질을 어떻게 보느냐에 따라 (c) 달라진다.
- 개인적 이득에 초점을 맞춘 협상가들은 고정된 파이에 대한 믿음의 영향을 받아 상황에 경쟁적으로 접근할 가능성이 가장 컸다.
- 가치에 초점을 맞춘 협상가들은 문제를 고정된 파이 관점에서 볼 가능성이 가장 낮았고 상황에 협력적으로 접근하려는 경향이 더 컸다.

→ 이어지는 예시: 모의 협상에서 개인적 이득에 초점을 맞출 때, 효과성의 관점에서 목표를 볼 때, 가치에 초점을 맞출 때 고정된 파이 관점에서 문제를 보는 정도가 달라진다는 것을 보여줌
협상을 고정된 파이 관점에서 보는 경향이 문제를 어떻게 보느냐에 따라 달라지는 예시이다.
▶ varies는 문맥에 적절함

④ (d) competitively 경쟁적으로

- 허구의 고정된 파이를 믿는 사람들은 당사자들의 이해관계가 통합적인 합의와 상호 이익이 되는 절충안의 가능성이 없는 반대 입장에 있다고 가정하기 때문에 이를 찾으려는 노력을 억누른다.
- 개인적 이득에 초점을 맞춘 협상가들은 고정된 파이에 대한 믿음의 영향을 받아 상황에 (d) 경쟁적으로 접근할 가능성이 가장 컸다.

→ 개인적 이득에 초점을 맞춘 협상가: 고정된 파이에 대한 믿음의 영향을 받을 가능성이 가장 큼
이들은 당사자의 이해관계가 절충될 수 없는 반대 입장에 있다고 생각하므로, 상황에 '경쟁적으로(competitively)' 접근한다는 설명은 적절하다.
▶ competitively는 문맥에 적절함

⑤ (e) less 덜

시간 제약과 같은 스트레스가 많은 조건은 이러한 흔한 오해의 원인이 되며, 이는 결국 (e) 덜 통합적인 합의로 이어질 수 있다.

→ 스트레스가 많은 조건이 오해의 원인이 되고, 오해로 인해 통합적인 합의에 도달하지 못한다는 흐름이다. '덜 통합적인(less integrative)'이라는 의미가 되어야 한다.
▶ less는 문맥에 적절함

P 03~04 ＊인간 진화와 발전의 도구인 인간의 손

Imagine / grabbing a piece of paper / between your thumb and index finger. //
상상해 보라 / 한 장의 종이를 쥐는 것을 / 여러분의 엄지손가락과 집게손가락 사이에 //
= are grabbing a piece of paper ~ index finger
Maybe you already are, / as you turn this page. //
어쩌면 여러분은 이미 하고 있을지도 모른다 / 이 페이지를 넘기면서 //

We use / this type of forceful, pad-to-pad precision gripping / without thinking about it, / and literally in a snap. //
우리는 사용한다 / 이러한 유형의 힘을 써서 손가락 끝 살이 맞닿는 정밀하게 쥐는 법을 / 그것에 대하여 아무 생각 없이 / 말 그대로 순식간에 //

Yet / it was a breakthrough / in human evolution. //
그러나 / 그것은 획기적 발전이었다 / 인류 진화의 // 【3번】 단서 1: 이것(앞에서 언급한 손으로 집기)가 인류 진화의 획기적 발전이었음

Other primates exhibit / some kinds of precision grips / in the handling and use of objects, / but not with the kind of
목적 관계대명사
(a) efficient opposition / that our hand anatomy allows. //
다른 영장류도 보인다 / 일종의 정밀한 쥐기를 / 물체를 다루고 사용할 때 / 그러나 효율적인 마주 닿음의 종류는 아니다 / 우리 손의 해부학적 구조가 허용하는 //

In a single hand, / humans can easily hold / and manipulate objects, / even small and delicate ones, /
= objects
한 손에서 / 인간은 쉽게 잡을 수 있다 / 그리고 물체를 조작할 수 있다 / 작고 깨지기 쉬운 것들조차도
————— 분사구문의 병렬 구조 —————
while adjusting our fingers to their shape / and reorienting them / with (b) displacements of our fingertip pads. //
모양에 맞게 우리의 손가락을 조정하면서 / 그리고 그것의 방향을 바꾸면서 / 우리의 손가락 끝 살 부분을 이동시켜 //

Our relatively long, powerful thumb / and other anatomical
분사구문   주격 관계대명사
attributes, / including our flat nails / (which nearly all primates
make의 목적격 보어
possess), / make this (c) possible. //
우리의 비교적 길고 강력한 엄지손가락이 / 그리고 다른 해부학적 속성들이 / 평평한 손톱을 포함하여 / (거의 모든 영장류가 소유한) / 이것을 가능하게 한다 //

Just picture / trying — and failing — to dog-ear this page / with pointy, curved claws. //
한번 상상해 보라 / 이 페이지의 모서리를 집으려고 시도하다가 실패하는 것을 / 끝이 뾰족하고 굽은 발톱으로 //

With a unique combination of traits, / the human hand shaped our history. // 【3번】 단서 2: 인간의 손이 인류 역사를 이룸
고유한 특성의 조합으로 / 인간의 손은 인류의 역사를 이루었다 //

No question, / stone tools couldn't have become / a keystone of
주격 관계대명사
human technology and subsistence / (d) without hands / that could do the job, / 【4번】 단서 1: 인간의 손이 없었다면 석기가 인간 기술과 생계의 핵심이 될 수 없었을 것임
의심할 여지 없이 / 석기는 될 수 없었을 것이다 / 인간 기술과 생계의 핵심이 / 손이 없었다면 / 그 일을 할 수 있는 /
주격 관계대명사
along with a nervous system / that could regulate and coordinate the necessary signals. //
신경계와 함께 / 필요한 신호를 조절하고 조정할 수 있는 //

Anybody who's ever attempted to make / a spear tip or arrowhead / from a rock /
만들어 보려 한 사람이라면 누구라도 / 창 촉이나 화살촉을 / 돌로 /
【4번】 단서 2: 석기를 만들 때는 손으로 강하게 쥐는 것, 지속적인 회전과 재배치, 강하고 주의 깊게 두드리는 것 등이 배제되는 것이 아니라 필요함(요구됨)
knows that it (e) excludes(→ requires) strong grips, / constant
목적어절을 이끄는 접속사
rotation and repositioning, / and forceful, careful strikes / with another hard object. //
그것이 강하게 쥐는 것을 배제한다(→ 요구한다)는 것을 안다 / 지속적인 회전과 재배치 / 그리고 강하고 주의 깊게 두드리는 것을 / 또 다른 단단한 물체로 //

And even with a fair amount of know-how, / it can be a bloody business. //
그리고 상당한 정도의 요령을 가지고서도 / 이것은 피투성이가 되는 작업일 수 있다 //

- index finger 집게손가락   • forceful ⓐ 강력한
- precision ⓝ 정확성, 정밀성   • in a snap 순식간에
- breakthrough ⓝ 돌파구, 획기적인 발전   • evolution ⓝ 진화
- manipulate ⓥ 조작하다   • delicate ⓐ 깨지기 쉬운
- reorient ⓥ 방향을 바꾸다   • displacement ⓝ 이동
- attribute ⓝ 속성   • dog-ear ⓥ 모서리를 접다
- pointy ⓐ 끝이 뾰족한   • combination ⓝ 조합   • trait ⓝ 특성
- coordinate ⓥ 조정하다   • exclude ⓥ 배제하다   • leap ⓝ 도약

여러분의 엄지손가락과 집게손가락 사이에 한 장의 종이를 쥐는 것을 상상해 보라. 어쩌면 여러분은 이 페이지를 넘기면서 이미 하고 있을지도 모른다. 우리는 이러한 유형의 힘을 써서 손가락 끝 살이 맞닿는 정밀하게 쥐는 법을 그것에 대하여 아무 생각 없이, 말 그대로 순식간에 사용한다. 그러나 그것은 인류 진화의 획기적 발전이었다. 다른 영장류도 물체를 다루고 사용할 때 일종의 정밀한 쥐기를 보이지만, 우리 손의 해부학적 구조가 허용하는 종류의 (a) 효율적인 (엄지와 다른 손가락의) 마주 닿음은 아니다. 한 손에서, 인간은 작고 깨지기 쉬운 물체조차도 쉽게 잡고 조작할 수 있으며, 한편 모양에 맞게 우리의 손가락을 조정하고 우리의 손가락 끝 살 부분을 (b) 이동시켜 그것의 방향을 바꿀 수 있다. 우리의 비교적 길고 강력한 엄지손가락과 (거의 모든 영장류가 소유한) 평평한 손톱을 포함하여 다른 해부학적 속성들이 이것을

(c) 가능하게 한다. 끝이 뾰족하고 굽은 발톱으로 이 페이지의 모서리를 접으려다가 실패하는 모습을 한번 상상해 보라. 고유한 특성의 조합으로, 인간의 손은 인류의 역사를 이루었다. 의심할 여지 없이, 필요한 신호를 조절하고 조정할 수 있는 신경계와 함께 그 일을 할 수 있는 손이 (d) 없었다면 석기는 인간 기술과 생계의 핵심이 될 수 없었을 것이다. 돌로 창 촉이나 화살촉을 만들어 보려 한 사람이라면 누구라도 그것이 강하게 쥐는, 지속적인 회전과 재배치, 그리고 또 다른 단단한 물체로 강하고 주의 깊게 두드리는 것을 (e) 배제한다는(→ 요구한다는) 것을 안다. 그리고 상당한 정도의 요령을 가지고서도, 이것은 피투성이가 되는 작업일 수 있다.

P 03 정답 ②

윗글의 제목으로 가장 적절한 것은?

① Anatomical Distance Between Humans and Other Primates
인간과 다른 영장류 사이의 해부학적 거리   인간과 다른 영장류 사이의 해부학적 거리에 관한 글이 아님
②Human Hands: A Decisive Leap in the Evolutionary Path
인간의 손: 진화 경로의 결정적 도약   인간의 손이 인간 진화와 발전을 이끌었다는 내용임
③ Our Hands: An Unexpected Outcome of Evolution 우리의 손이 예상치
우리의 손: 예상치 못한 진화의 결과   못한 진화의 결과라는 내용이 아니라 손을 통해 진화를 이끌었다는 내용임
④ Human Grip: The Dilemma of Human Survival
인간의 쥐기: 인간 생존의 딜레마   인간의 쥐기가 인간 생존의 딜레마라는 언급은 없음
⑤ Hidden Power of the Daily Use of Tools
도구의 일상적 사용의 숨겨진 힘   도구의 일상적 사용의 숨겨진 힘을 다룬 글이 아님

> **왜** 정답 ? [정답률 69%]

요지	• 인간이 손가락 끝 살을 맞닿아 정밀한 방식으로 물건을 쥐는 것은 인류 진화의 획기적 발전이었음
부연 ①	• 다른 영장류도 손을 사용해 쥐기를 할 수 있음 • 인간 고유의 해부학적 특성으로 인해 다른 영장류는 할 수 없는 효율적인 손 동작이 가능함
부연 ②	• 인간의 손은 인류의 역사를 이룸 • 신경계와 더불어 손을 통해 석기가 인간 기술과 생계의 핵심이 됨

▶ 인간이 손가락 끝 살을 맞닿아 정밀한 방식으로 물건을 쥐는 것은 인류 진화의 획기적 발전이었다는 내용의 글이므로 ② '인간의 손: 진화 경로의 결정적 도약'이 제목으로 적절하다.

> **왜** 오답 ?

① 인간과 다른 영장류 사이의 해부학적 거리에 관한 글이 아니다.
③ 우리의 손이 예상치 못한 진화의 결과라는 내용이 아니라 손을 통해 진화를 이끌었다는 내용이다. 함정
④ 인간의 쥐기가 인간 생존의 딜레마라는 언급은 없다.
⑤ 도구의 일상적 사용의 숨겨진 힘을 다룬 글이 아니다.

P 04 정답 ⑤

밑줄 친 (a)~(e) 중에서 문맥상 낱말의 쓰임이 적절하지 않은 것은? [3점]

다른 영장류도 일종의 쥐기를 할 수 있지만 인간   인간은 해부학적 구조상 손가락을 조정하고
① (a) 손의 해부학적 구조가 허용하는 '효율적인'   ② (b) 손가락 끝 살 부분을 '이동'시켜 그것의
효율적인 쥐기는 아님   이동 방향을 바꿀 수 있음
③ (c)   ④ (d) 인간의 손이 '없었다면' 석기는 인간 기술의
가능한   없었다면 생계와 핵심이 될 수 있었을 것임
⑤ (e) 돌로 창 촉이나 화살촉을 만들기 위해서는 손을 사용한 강한 쥐기, 지속적인 회전과 재배치,
배제하다 강하고 신중하게 두드리기가 배제되는 것이 아니라 '요구됨'
우리의 엄지손가락과 해부학적 속성들이 손가락을 조정하고 손가락 끝을 이동시키는 것을 '가능하게' 함

> **왜** 정답 ? [정답률 70%]

⑤ (e) excludes 배제하다

돌로 창 촉이나 화살촉을 만들어 보려 한 사람이라면 누구라도 그것이 강하게 쥐는, 지속적인 회전과 재배치, 그리고 또 다른 단단한 물체로
                                                                     요구한다는
강하고 주의 깊게 두드리는 것을 (e) ~~배제한다는~~ 것을 안다.

➡ 인간의 손이 없었다면 석기는 인간 기술과 생계의 핵심이 될 수 없었을 것이라고 했다. 그러므로 돌로 창 촉이나 화살촉을 만들기 위해서는 손을 사용한 강한 쥐기, 지속적인 회전과 재배치, 그리고 또 다른 단단한 물체로 강하고 신중하게 두드리기가 배제되는 것이 아니라 '요구된다'는 맥락이 되어야 한다.

▶ excludes를 반의어인 requires(요구하다) 등의 단어로 바꿔야 함

> **왜** 오답 ?

① (a) efficient 효율적인

다른 영장류도 물체를 다루고 사용할 때 일종의 정밀한 쥐기를 보이지만, 우리 손의 해부학적 구조가 허용하는 종류의 (a) 효율적인 (엄지와 다른 손가락의) 마주 닿음은 아니다.

➡ 다른 영장류도 일종의 쥐기를 할 수 있지만 인간 손의 해부학적 구조가 허용하는 '효율적인' 쥐기는 아니라고 하는 것은 적절하다.

▶ efficient는 문맥에 맞음

② (b) displacements 이동

한 손에서, 인간은 작고 깨지기 쉬운 물체조차도 쉽게 잡고 조작할 수 있으며, 한편 모양에 맞게 우리의 손가락을 조정하고 우리의 손가락 끝 살 부분을 (b) 이동시켜 그것의 방향을 바꿀 수 있다.

➡ 인간은 해부학적 구조의 특성상 손가락을 조정하고 손가락 끝 살 부분을 '이동'시켜 그것의 방향을 바꿀 수 있을 것이다.

▶ displacements는 문맥에 맞음

③ (c) possible 가능한

우리의 비교적 길고 강력한 엄지손가락과 (거의 모든 영장류가 소유한) 평평한 손톱을 포함하여 다른 해부학적 속성들이 이것을 (c) 가능하게 한다.

➡ 우리의 비교적 길고 강력한 엄지손가락과 평평한 손톱 등의 해부학적 속성들이, 이전 문장에서 언급한 손가락을 조정하고 손가락 끝 살 부분을 이동시켜 그것의 방향을 바꾸는 것을 '가능하게' 한다고 표현하는 것은 적절하다.

▶ possible은 문맥에 맞음

④ (d) without 없었다면

의심할 여지 없이, 필요한 신호를 조절하고 조정할 수 있는 신경계와 함께 그 일을 할 수 있는 손이 (d) 없었다면 석기는 인간 기술과 생계의 핵심이 될 수 없었을 것이다.

➡ 인간의 손이 인류 역사를 이루었으며 신경계와 함께 그 일을 할 수 있는 인간의 손이 '없었다면' 석기가 인간 기술의 생계와 핵심이 될 수 없었을 것이라고 표현한 것은 자연스럽다.

▶ without은 문맥에 맞음

People are correct / when they feel / that the written poetry of
literate societies / and the oral poetry of non-literate ones /
사람들은 옳다 / 그들이 느낄 때 / 문자 기반 사회에서 문자로 쓰인 시와 / 그리고 문자에
의존하지 않는 사회에서 말로 전달되는 시가 /

differ considerably from the everyday language / spoken in the
community. //
일상의 언어와 상당히 다르다고 / 공동체에서 사용되는 //

Listeners not only accept / the (a) strange use of words,
rearrangement of word order, assonance, alliteration, rhythm,
rhyme, compression of thought, and so on — /
감상자는 받아들일 뿐만 아니다 / 단어의 낯선 사용, 어순의 재배열, 유운, 두운, 운율, 운,
사고의 압축 등을 /

they actually expect / to find these things in poetry / and they
are disappointed / when poetry does not sound "poetic." //
그들은 실제로 기대한다 / 시에서 이러한 요소들을 발견하기를 / 그리고 실망한다 / 시가
'시적으로' 들리지 않을 때는 //

But those who regard poetry / as a (b) different category of
language altogether / are deaf / to the true achievements of the
poet. //
그러나 시를 간주하는 사람들은 / 완전히 다른 범주의 언어로 / 귀를 기울이지 않는다 / 시인의
진정한 업적에 //

Rather, / the poet artfully manipulates / the same raw materials
of his language / as are used in everyday speech; /
오히려 / 시인은 교묘히 조작한다 / 동일한 언어의 원료를 / 일상의 언어에서 사용되는 것과 /

his skill is / to find new possibilities / in the resources already in
the language. // **5번** 단서 1: 시인이 일상의 언어를 조작하여 새로운 가능성을 찾아낸다고 함
그의 솜씨는 ~이다 / 새로운 가능성을 찾아내는 것 / 이미 언어에 있는 자원에서 /

In much the same way / that people living at the seashore /
become so accustomed to the sound of waves / that they no
longer hear it, / **6번** 단서: 바닷가 사람들이 파도 소리에 익숙해져 그것을 듣지 못하는 것과 마찬가지라고 함
아주 마찬가지로 / 바닷가에 사는 사람들이 / 파도 소리에 너무 익숙해져서 / 더 이상 그것을
듣지 못하는 것과 //

most of us have become (c) sensitive(→ insensitive) / to the
flood tide of words, / millions of them every day, / that hit our
eardrums. //
우리 대부분은 민감하게(→ 무감각하게) 된다 / 홍수처럼 쏟아지는 말에 / 매일 수백만 개의 /
우리의 고막을 때리는 //

One function of poetry is / to depict the world with a (d) fresh
perception / — to make it strange — / so that we will listen to
language once again. // **5번** 단서 2: 시는 신선한 인식으로 세상을 묘사하는 기능이 있음
시의 한 가지 기능은 ~이다 / 신선한 인식으로 세상을 묘사하는 것 / 즉 그것을 낯설게 만드는
것 / 그래서 우리가 다시 한번 언어에 귀를 기울이게 하는 것이다 //

But the successful poet / never departs so far / into the strange
world of language / that none of his listeners can (e) follow
him. //
그러나 성공을 이룬 시인은 / 결코 멀리 떠나지는 않는다 / 낯선 언어의 세계로 / 결코 자신의
청취자 중 누구도 자신을 따라가지 못할 만큼 //

He still remains the communicator, / the man of speech. //
그는 여전히 전달자로 남아 있다 / 즉 언어의 능숙한 사용자로 //

- considerably ⓐⓓ 상당히   · rearrangement ⓝ 재배열
- rhyme ⓝ 운(음조가 비슷한 글자)   · poetic ⓐ 시적인
- compression ⓝ 압축   · category ⓝ 범주
- altogether ⓐⓓ 완전히   · deaf ⓐ 귀를 기울이지 않는
- achievement ⓝ 업적   · artfully ⓐⓓ 교묘하게
- manipulate ⓥ 능숙하게 조작하다   · seashore ⓝ 해안
- be accustomed to ~에 익숙해지다   · eardrum ⓝ 고막
- depart ⓥ 떠나다   · refresh ⓥ 새롭게 하다
- inspiration ⓝ 영감   · cite ⓥ 인용하다

사람들이 문자 기반 사회에서 문자로 쓰인 시와 문자에 의존하지 않는 사회에서
말로 전달되는 시가 공동체에서 사용되는 일상의 언어와 상당히 다르다고 느낄
때 그들은 옳은 것이다. 감상자는 단어의 (a) 낯선 사용, 어순의 재배열, 유운,
두운, 운율, 운, 사고의 압축 등을 받아들일 뿐만 아니라 실제로 시에서 이러한
요소들을 발견하기를 기대하며, 시가 '시적으로' 들리지 않을 때는 실망한다.
그러나 시를 완전히 (b) 다른 범주의 언어로 간주하는 사람들은 시인의 진정한
업적에 귀를 기울이지 않는다. 오히려 시인은 일상의 언어에서 사용되는 것과
동일한 언어의 원료를 교묘히 조작하는데, 그의 솜씨는 이미 언어에 있는
자원에서 새로운 가능성을 찾아내는 것이다. 바닷가에 사는 사람들이 파도
소리에 너무 익숙해져서 더 이상 그것을 듣지 못하는 것과 아주 마찬가지로,
우리 대부분은 고막을 때리는 매일 수백만 단어로 홍수처럼 쏟아지는 말에
(c) 민감하게(→ 무감각하게) 된다. 시의 한 가지 기능은 (d) 신선한 인식으로
세상을 묘사하여, 즉 그것을 낯설게 만들어서, 우리가 다시 한번 언어에 귀를
기울이게 하는 것이다. 그러나 성공을 이룬 시인은 낯선 언어의 세계로 결코
자신의 청취자 중 누구도 자신을 (e) 따라가지 못할 만큼 멀리 떠나지는 않는다.
그는 여전히 (효과적인) 전달자, 즉 언어의 능숙한 사용자로 남아 있다.

P 05 정답 ①

윗글의 제목으로 가장 적절한 것은?
시인이 일상 언어를 조작하여 익숙한 언어에 대해 새로운 인식을 제공한다고 함
① Make It New: How Poetry Refreshes Everyday Language
새롭게 만들기: 시가 일상의 언어를 새롭게 하는 방법
② Why Do Poets No Longer Seek Inspiration from Nature? 시인이
시인은 왜 더 이상 자연에서 영감을 구하지 않는가?   자연에서 영감을 구하지 않는다는 내용이 아님
③ The Influence of Natural Sounds on Poetic Expression 자연에서의
자연에서의 소리가 시적 표현에 끼치는 영향   소리가 시적 표현에 끼치는 영향에 대한 글이 아님
④ Ways to Cite Poetic Expressions in Everyday Speech 일상적인
일상적인 연설에서 시적 표현을 인용하는 방법   연설이 아니라 일상의 언어와 시의 언어에 대해 말했음
⑤ Beauty Rediscovered: The Return of Oral Poetry
재발견된 아름다움: 구전 시의 귀환   단순히 시와 관련된 것으로 만든 오답

▶왜 **정답**? [정답률 65%]

도입	· 시가 공동체에서 사용되는 일상의 언어와 상당히 다르다고 느낌 · 단어의 낯선 사용, 어순의 재배열, 유운, 두운, 운율, 운, 사고의 압축 등을 기대하고, 시가 '시적으로' 들리지 않을 때는 실망함
요지	· 시인은 일상의 언어에서 사용되는 것과 동일한 언어를 조작해 이미 언어에 있는 자원에서 새로운 가능성을 찾음 **5번 단서1**
부연	· 우리는 너무 일상적인 것에 무감각해짐 · 그러나 시가 신선한 인식으로 세상을 묘사하여 우리가 다시 한번 언어에 귀를 기울이게 함 **5번 단서2**

▶ 시인이 일상의 언어를 조작하여 그에 대한 새로운 인식을 불러일으킨다는 내용의
글이므로 ① '새롭게 만들기: 시가 일상의 언어를 새롭게 하는 방법'이 제목으로
적절하다.

▶왜 **오답**?
② 시인이 자연에서 영감을 구하지 않는다는 내용의 글이 아니다.
③ 자연에서의 소리가 시적 표현에 끼치는 영향에 대한 글이 아니다.
④ 일상적인 연설이 아니라 일상의 언어에 대해 언급했다.
⑤ 단순히 시와 관련된 오답일 뿐, 구전 시의 귀환이나 재발견에 대해 다루지 않았다.

P 06 정답 ③

밑줄 친 (a)~(e) 중에서 문맥상 낱말의 쓰임이 적절하지 않은 것은? [3점]
① (a) 시에서 쓰이는 언어가 단어의 '낯선' 사용을   ② (b) 시를 완전히 '다른' 범주의 언어로 간주하는
낯선 포함할 것이라고 사람들이 기대   다른 사람들에 대해 앞에서 언급함
③ (c) 매일 듣는 수백만 개의 단어는 사람들의 귀에   ④ (d) 시인이 일상의 언어를 조작하여 새로운 인식을
민감한 익숙해져 민감한 것이 아니고 '무감각해짐'   신선한 불러일으킨다고 했으므로 '신선한'
⑤ (e) 청취자가 '따라가지' 못할 만큼 먼 낯선   인식으로 묘사하는 것임
따라가다 언어의 세계로 떠나지는 않음

왜 정답? [정답률 56%]

③ (c) sensitive 민감한

바닷가에 사는 사람들이 파도 소리에 너무 익숙해져서 더 이상 그것을 듣지 못하는 것과 아주 마찬가지로(In much the same way), 우리 대부분은 고막을 때리는 매일 수백만 단어로 홍수처럼 쏟아지는 말에 (c) 민감하게 된다.
무감각하게

➡ 바닷가에 사는 사람들이 파도 소리에 너무 익숙해져 그것을 듣지 못하는 것과 마찬가지라고 했으므로 우리는 매일 수백만 개의 단어를 듣기 때문에 말에 '민감하게' 되는 것이 아니라 '무감각해지게' 된다고 해야 함

▶ sensitive(민감한)의 반대 의미를 갖는 insensitive(무감각한)로 바꿔야 함

왜 오답?

① (a) strange 낯선

감상자는 단어의 (a) 낯선 사용, 어순의 재배열, 유운, 두운, 운율, 운, 사고의 압축 등을 받아들일 뿐만 아니라 실제로 시에서 이러한 요소들을 발견하기를 기대하며, 시가 '시적으로' 들리지 않을 때는 실망한다.

➡ 시에서 발견되는 일상적이지 않은 언어의 요소들을 나열하고 있으므로 단어의 '낯선' 사용이라고 하는 것은 적절하다.

▶ strange는 문맥에 맞음

② (b) different 다른

그러나 시를 완전히 (b) 다른 범주의 언어로 간주하는 사람들은 시인의 진정한 업적에 귀를 기울이지 않는다.

➡ 앞에서 계속 시적 언어가 일상 언어와 다른 것을 기대하는 사람들에 대해 서술했으므로 시를 완전히 '다른' 범주의 언어로 간주하는 사람들이라고 표현하는 것은 자연스럽다.

▶ different는 문맥에 맞음

④ (d) fresh 신선한

시의 한 가지 기능은 (d) 신선한 인식으로 세상을 묘사하여, 즉 그것을 낯설게 만들어서, 우리가 다시 한번 언어에 귀를 기울이게 하는 것이다.

➡ 이전 문장에서 시인이 일상의 언어를 교묘히 조작하고 이미 언어에 있는 자원에서 새로운 가능성을 찾아낸다고 했으므로 시가 '신선한' 인식으로 세상을 묘사, 즉 그것을 낯설게 만들어서, 언어에 귀를 기울이게 한다고 표현하는 것은 적절하다.

▶ fresh는 문맥에 맞음

⑤ (e) follow 따라가다

그러나 성공을 이룬 시인은 낯선 언어의 세계로 결코 자신의 청취자 중 누구도 자신을 (e) 따라가지 못할 만큼 멀리 떠나지는 않는다.

➡ 시인은 일상적 언어를 사용해 그에 대한 새로운 인식을 불러일으키는 것이지 낯선 언어를 사용하는 것이 아니므로 청취자가 '따라가지' 못할 만큼 먼 낯선 언어의 세계로 떠나지 않는다고 표현한 것은 자연스럽다.

▶ follow는 문맥에 맞음

P 07~08 ✱의사결정에서 윤리적 사고의 중요성

조건절을 이끄는 접속사
If we understand critical thinking / as: 'the identification and evaluation of evidence to guide decision-making', /
우리가 비판적 사고를 이해한다면 / '의사결정을 안내하기 위한 증거의 검증 및 평가'로서 /
주어   동사
then ethical thinking is / about identifying ethical issues and
동명사의 병렬 구조
evaluating these issues from different perspectives / to guide
의문사+to부정사
how to respond. // **7번** 단서 1: 윤리적 사고는, 윤리적 사안을 식별하고 다양한 관점에서 평가해
어떻게 대응할지 안내하는 것
윤리적 사고는 ~이다 / 윤리적 사안을 식별하고 이러한 사안을 다양한 관점에서 평가하여 /
어떻게 대응할지를 안내하는 것 //

This form of ethics / is distinct from / higher levels of conceptual
ethics or theory. //
이러한 형태의 윤리는 / ~과는 구별된다 / 더 높은 수준의 개념적 윤리나 이론 //

7번 단서 2: 윤리적 문제에는 명백하게 옳고 그른 대응이 없음
The nature of an ethical issue or problem from this perspective /
보어절 접속사
is that there is no clear right or wrong response. //
이러한 관점에서 윤리적 사안이나 문제의 본질은 / 명백하게 옳거나 그른 대응이 없다는
것이다 //
가주어   진주어절을 이끄는 접속사
It is therefore (a) essential / that students learn to think through
ethical issues / rather than follow a prescribed set of ethical
codes or rules. //
따라서 필수적이다 / 학생들은 윤리적 문제를 충분히 생각하는 법을 배우는 것이 / 규정된
일련의 윤리 규범이나 규칙을 따르는 것보다는 //
7번 단서 3: 윤리적인 행동은 '각기 다른 개인들이 각자 옳다고 생각하는 원칙에 따라 행동하는 것'임
There is a need to (b) encourage recognition / that, although
동격절을 이끄는 접속사
being ethical is defined / as acting 'in accordance with the
주격 관계대명사
principles of conduct that are considered correct', /
인식을 장려할 필요가 있다 / 비록 윤리적인 행동이 정의된다고 하더라도 / '옳다고 생각되는
행동 원칙에 따라' 행동하는 것으로 /
맨 앞의 that과 연결되는 부분
these principles vary both between and within individuals. //
이러한 원칙은 개인 간 그리고 개인 내에서도 다를 수 있다(는 인식을) //
선행사를 포함하는 관계대명사   동사
What a person (c) values / relates to their social, religious, or
civic beliefs / influenced by their formal and informal learning
과거분사
experiences. //
개인이 가치 있게 여기는 것은 / 사회적, 종교적, 혹은 시민으로서의 신념과 관련이 있다 /
그들의 공식적이고 또 비공식적인 학습 경험에 의해 영향받은 //

Individual perspectives may also be context (d) dependent, /
분사구문(= and it means)
meaning that / under different ircumstances, / at a different
목적어절 접속사
time, /
개인의 관점은 또한 상황에 따라 달라질 수도 있는데 / 이는 의미한다 / 다른 환경에서 / 다른
시간에 /

when they are feeling a different way, / the same individual
may make different choices. //
그들이 다른 감정을 느끼고 있을 때 / 동일한 개인이 다른 선택을 할 수도 있음 //

Therefore, in order to analyse ethical issues and think ethically /
가주어   진주어   주격 관계대명사
it is necessary to understand the personal factors / that influence
your own 'code of behaviour' /
따라서 윤리적 사안을 분석하고 윤리적으로 사고하기 위해서는 / 개인적 요인들을 이해하는
것이 필요하다 / 자신의 '행동 규범'에 영향을 미치는 /
= the personal factors ~ behaviour
and how these may (e) coincide(→ vary), / alongside recognizing
목적어절 접속사   주격 관계대명사
and accepting / that the factors that drive other people's codes
and decision making / may be different. //
그리고 이것들이 어떻게 일치할(→ 달라질) 수 있는지 / 그와 동시에 인식하고 받아들이는 것 /
다른 사람들의 행동 규범과 의사결정에 영향을 미치는 요소들이 / 다를 수 있다는 점을 //
8번 단서: 윤리적 사고에는 행동 규범에 영향을 주는 개인적
요인이 각자 다르다는 것을 인식하는 것이 필요함

- identification ⓝ 검증, 식별
- evaluation ⓝ 평가
- ethical ⓐ 윤리적인
- perspective ⓝ 관점
- distinct ⓐ 구별되는[뚜렷이 다른]
- think through 충분히 생각하다
- prescribe ⓥ 규정[지시]하다, 처방하다
- recognition ⓝ 인식, 인정
- in accordance with ~에 따라, ~에 부합되게
- civic ⓐ (도)시의, 시민의
- coincide ⓥ 일치하다, 동시에 일어나다
- alongside prep ~옆에, 나란히
- priority ⓝ 우선(권)

우리가 비판적 사고를 '의사결정을 안내하기 위한 증거의 검증 및 평가'로 이해한다면, 윤리적 사고는 윤리적 사안을 식별하고 이러한 사안을 다양한 관점에서 평가하여 어떻게 대응할지를 안내하는 것이다. 이러한 형태의 윤리는 더 높은 수준의 개념적 윤리나 이론과는 구별된다. 이러한 관점에서 윤리적 사안이나 문제의 본질은 명백하게 옳거나 그른 대응이 없다는 것이다. 따라서 학생들은 규정된 일련의 윤리 규범이나 규칙을 따르는 것보다는 윤리적 문제를 충분히 생각하는 법을 배우는 것이 (a) 필수적이다. 비록 윤리적인 행동이 '옳다고 여겨지는 행동 원칙에 따라' 행동하는 것으로 정의된다고 하더라도, 이러한 원칙은 개인 간 그리고 개인 내에서도 다를 수 있다는 인식을 (b) 장려할 필요가 있다. 개인이 (C) 가치 있게 여기는 것은 그들의 공식적이고 또 비공식적인 학습 경험에 의해 영향받은 사회적, 종교적, 혹은 시민으로서의

신념과 관련이 있다. 개인의 관점은 또한 상황에 따라 (d) 달라질 수도 있는데, 이는 다른 환경에서, 다른 시간에, 그들이 다른 감정을 느끼고 있을 때, 동일한 개인이 다른 선택을 할 수도 있음을 의미한다. 따라서 윤리적 사안을 분석하고 윤리적으로 사고하기 위해서는 자신의 '행동 규범'에 영향을 미치는 개인적 요인들과, 이것들이 어떻게 (e) 일치할(→ 달라질) 수 있는지 이해하며, 그와 동시에 다른 사람들의 행동 규범과 의사결정에 영향을 미치는 요소들이 다를 수 있다는 점을 인식하고 받아들이는 것이 필요하다.

P 07 정답 ③

윗글의 제목으로 가장 적절한 것은?
비판적 추론은 윤리적 사고가 아니라 비판적 사고의 과정으로 서두에 제시되어 있음
① Critical Reasoning: A Road to Ethical Decision-making
비판적 추론: 윤리적 의사결정으로 가는 길
② Far-reaching Impacts of Ethics on Behavioural Codes 개인마다 각기
윤리가 행동 규범에 미치는 광범위한 영향 다른 요인들이 개인의 행동 규범에 미치는 영향에 대한 글임
③ Ethical Thinking: A Walk Through Individual Minds 윤리적 사고의
윤리적 사고: 개인의 마음을 거니는 여정 행동 규범과 의사결정은 개인마다 다를 수 있다는 글임
④ Exploring Ethical Theory in the Eyes of the Others
타인의 눈에 비친 윤리 이론 탐구 타인과 윤리 이론 탐구는 이 글의 중심 내용이 아님
⑤ Do Ethical Choices Always Take Priority?
윤리적 선택이 항상 우선인가? 윤리적 선택은 사람마다 다를 수 있다고 했음

왜 정답? [정답률 52%]

도입	• 윤리적 사고는, 윤리적 사안을 식별하고 다양한 관점에서 평가해 어떻게 대응할지 안내하는 것임 • 명백하게 옳고 그른 대응이 없음
부연	• 윤리적인 행동은 '각기 다른 개인들이 각자 옳다고 생각하는 원칙에 따라 행동하는 것'임
결론	• 개인적 행동 규범에 영향을 주는 개인 요인이 달라질 수 있음

▶ 따라서 ③ '윤리적 사고: 개인의 마음을 거니는 여정'이 제목으로 적절하다.

왜 오답?
① 비판적 추론은 윤리적 사고가 아니라 비판적 사고의 과정으로 서두에 제시되어 있다.
② 윤리가 행동 규범에 미치는 영향이 아니라, 개인마다 각기 다른 요인들이 개인의 행동 규범에 미치는 영향에 대한 글이다.
④ 타인과 윤리 이론 탐구는 이 글의 중심 내용이 아니다.
⑤ 윤리적 선택은 사람마다 다를 수 있다고 하였으며, 우선순위에 대한 글이 아니다.

P 08 정답 ⑤

밑줄 친 (a)~(e) 중에서 문맥상 낱말의 쓰임이 적절하지 않은 것은? [3점]
① (a) 옳고 그름을 나눌 수 없으므로 윤리적 문제에 ② (b) 개인 간의 인식이 다를 수 있다는 인식을
필수적인 대해 충분히 생각하는 것은 '필수적'임 장려하다 '장려해야' 할 것임
③ (c) ④ (d) 개인의 관점은 상황에 따라서도 '달라질 수'
가치 있게 여기다 (상황에 따라) 다른 있다는 말은 적절함
⑤ (e) 행동 규범에 영향을 미치는 요인들이 다를 수 있으므로 어떻게
일치하다 '일치하는지'가 아니라 달라질 수 있는지를 이해해야 함
└ 개인이 윤리적이라고 생각하는 것들, 즉 '가치 있게 여기는' 것들은 경험에 따라 다를 수 있음

왜 정답? [정답률 47%]

⑤ (e) coincide 일치하다

따라서 윤리적 사안을 분석하고 윤리적으로 사고하기 위해서는 자신의 '행동 규범'에 영향을 미치는 개인적 요인들과, 이것들이 어떻게 (e) 일치할 달라질 수 있는지 이해하며, 그와 동시에 다른 사람들의 행동 규범과 의사결정에 영향을 미치는 요소들이 다를 수 있다는 점을 인식하고 받아들이는 것이 필요하다.

➡ 윤리적 사고와 행동이 개인마다 다르며, 상황에 따라 달라질 수 있다는 점을 설명하고 있고, 이는 윤리적 사안에 대한 개인의 대응이 상황에 따라 변할 수 있다는 것을 의미한다.
　▶ coincide(일치하다)를 반의어인 vary(달라지다)로 바꿔야 함

왜 오답?

① (a) essential 필수적인

따라서 학생들은 규정된 일련의 윤리 규범이나 규칙을 따르는 것보다는 윤리적 문제를 충분히 생각하는 법을 배우는 것이 (a) 필수적이다.

➡ 앞에 나온 문장에서 '윤리적 사안이나 문제의 본질은 명백하게 옳거나 그른 대응이 없다는 것'이라고 하였으므로, 정해진 규칙을 따르는 것보다 윤리적 사고를 배우는 것이 '필수적'이다.
　▶ essential은 문맥에 맞음

② (b) encourage 장려하다

비록 윤리적인 행동이 '옳다고 여겨지는 행동 원칙에 따라' 행동하는 것으로 정의된다고 하더라도, 이러한 원칙은 개인 간 그리고 개인 내에서도 다를 수 있다는 인식을 (b) 장려할 필요가 있다.

➡ 원칙이 있더라도, 개인마다 다를 수 있다는 내용이 이어지고, 이러한 인식을 윤리적 사고를 통해 '장려한다'는 내용이다.
　▶ encourage는 문맥에 맞음

③ (c) values 가치 있게 여기다

개인이 (c) 가치 있게 여기는 것은 그들의 공식적이고 또 비공식적인 학습 경험에 의해 영향받은 사회적, 종교적, 혹은 시민으로서의 신념과 관련이 있다.

➡ 개인이 윤리적이라고 생각하는 것, 즉 '가치 있게 여기는' 것들은 경험에 따라 다를 수 있다.
　▶ values는 문맥에 맞음

④ (d) dependent (상황에 따라) 다른

개인의 관점은 또한 상황에 따라 (d) 달라질 수도 있는데, 이는 다른 환경에서, 다른 시간에, 그들이 다른 감정을 느끼고 있을 때, 동일한 개인이 다른 선택을 할 수도 있음을 의미한다.

➡ 개인의 가치가 경험에 따라 다르다는 내용이 앞 문장에 제시되었으며, 따라서 개인의 관점은 상황에 따라서도 '달라질' 수 있다는 말은 적절하다.
　▶ dependent는 문맥에 맞음

P 09~10 * 말, 사진, 그림이 되는 것의 조건

핵심 주어(복수)　　　　　　　　　　　　　동격의 that
Vocal sounds produced by parrots, / regardless of the fact that they may be audibly indistinguishable from spoken words /
앵무새가 내는 목소리는 / 그것이 들리기에는 소리내어진 말과 구별되지 않을 수도 있다는 사실에도 불구하고 /
　　　　　　┌ 병렬 구조　　　동격의 that
and regardless of the fact that someone or some group of people may take them to be words, / are not words. //
　　　　　　　　　　　　　복수 동사
그리고 누군가 또는 어떤 사람들의 집단이 그것들을 말이라고 여길 수도 있다는 사실에도 불구하고 / 말이 아니다 //

They are not given a semantic dimension / by physical (a) similitude to spoken words. //
그것들은 의미론적 차원이 주어지지 않는다 / 소리내어진 말과의 물리적 유사성으로 //
부정어(구)(not, never, hardly, scarcely 등)로 인한 도치
Nor can the "talk" of a parrot be given a semantic dimension / by being taken to be a set of (b) linguistic acts. //
앵무새의 '말'도 의미론적 차원이 주어질 수 없다 / 일련의 언어적 행위로 여겨지는 것으로도 //

In like manner, / weather etchings on a stone or shapes in the clouds, / regardless of how physically similar they may be / to written words or drawings of objects /
마찬가지로 / 돌에 있는 날씨 식각(날씨로 인해 새겨진 형상) 혹은 구름의 모양들은 / 그들이 물리적으로 얼마나 비슷한지와 관계없이 / 쓰여진 말이나 사물의 그림들과 /

and regardless of what they are taken to be by observers, / are
　　　　　　　　　　　　　　　　수동태
not words or pictures. //
그리고 그들이 관찰자들에 의해 무엇으로 여겨질지와 관계없이 / 말이나 그림이 아니다 //

They do not have the appropriate etiology / and they have no inherent semantic content or object. //

그것들에는 적절한 원인의 추구가 없고 / 그것들은 내재된 의미론적 내용이나 대상도 없다 //

They are simply (c) physical objects / that resemble certain other things. //
주격 관계대명사

그것들은 단순히 물리적 사물일 뿐이다 / 특정한 다른 것들을 닮은 //

For observers, / they may call to mind the things they (d) resemble. //

관찰자들에게 / 그것들은 그들이 닮은 사물들을 상기시킬 수도 있다 //

In this regard, they may function / as natural signs by virtue of the physical resemblance, / but they have no semantic content / about which one could be right or wrong. //
~의 힘으로

이런 점에서, 그것들은 기능할 수도 있지만 / 물리적 유사성 덕분에 자연적 기호로 / 그것들은 의미론적 내용을 가지지 않는다 / 어떤 것이 옳거나 그를 수 있다는 것에 대한 //

If people take A to be a sign of B / by virtue of some nonsemantic relation that holds, or is believed to hold, between A and B, / A is a sign of B. //
주격 관계대명사

만약 사람들이 'A'를 'B'의 기호로 받아들인다면 / 'A'와 'B' 사이에 있는, 혹은 있다고 여겨지는, 어떤 비의미론적 연관성 덕분에 / 'A'는 'B'의 기호이다 //

But words, pictures, and images are not that way. //

하지만, 말, 사진, 그림은 그런 식이 아니다 //

They (e) exclude(→ have) a semantic content / to be understood. //

그것들은 의미론적 내용을 배제한다(→ 가진다) / 이해되어야 할 //

- vocal ⓐ 목소리의, 발성의 · audibly ⓐⓓ 들리도록
- indistinguishable ⓐ 구분이 안 되는 · dimension ⓝ 차원
- similitude ⓝ 유사함 · linguistic ⓐ 언어의
- appropriate ⓐ 적절한 · inherent ⓐ 내재하는
- resemble ⓥ 닮다 · exclude ⓥ 제외하다, 배제하다
- subtext ⓝ 언외의 의미, 숨은 의미

앵무새가 내는 목소리는, 그것이 들리기에는 소리내어진 말과 구별되지 않을 수도 있다는, 그리고 누군가 또는 어떤 사람들의 집단이 그것들을 말이라고 여길 수도 있다는 사실에도 불구하고, 말이 아니다. 그것들은 소리내어진 말과의 물리적 (a) 유사성으로 의미론적 차원이 주어지지 않는다. 앵무새의 '말'도 일련의 (b) 언어적 행위로 여겨지는 것으로도 의미론적 차원이 주어질 수 없다. 마찬가지로, 돌에 있는 날씨 식각(날씨로 인해 새겨진 형상) 혹은 구름의 모양들은, 그들이 쓰여진 말이나 사물의 그림들과 물리적으로 얼마나 비슷한지와 관계없이 그리고 그들이 관찰자들에 의해 무엇으로 여겨질지와 관계없이, 말이나 그림이 아니다. 그것들에는 적절한 원인의 추구가 없고, 그것들은 내재된 의미론적 내용이나 대상도 없다. 그것들은 단순히 특정한 다른 것들을 닮은 (c) 물리적 사물일 뿐이다. 관찰자들에게, 그것들은 그들이 (d) 닮은 사물들을 상기시킬 수도 있다. 이런 점에서, 그것들은 물리적 유사성 덕분에 자연적 기호로 기능할 수도 있지만, 그것들은 어떤 것이 옳거나 그를 수 있다는 것에 대한 의미론적 내용을 가지지 않는다. 만약 사람들이 'A'와 'B' 사이에 있는, 혹은 있다고 여겨지는, 어떤 비의미론적 연관성 덕분에 'A'를 'B'의 기호로 받아들인다면, 'A'는 'B'의 기호이다. 하지만, 말, 사진, 그림은 그런 식이 아니다. 그것들은 이해되어야 할 의미론적 내용을 (e) 배제한다(→ 가진다).

P 09 정답 ①

윗글의 제목으로 가장 적절한 것은? 인간의 말, 글, 그림 등과 유사한 동물의 소리와 자연물이 있을 수 있지만 의미론적으로 의미가 없다는 내용의 글임
① Why Not All Physical Resemblances Are Semantically Meaningful
모든 물리적 유사성이 의미론적으로 유의미하지 않은 이유
② Uncovering Similarities in Human and Animal Vocal Sounds 인간과 동물
인간과 동물의 발성 소리에서의 유사성 발견   소리에서 비슷한 점을 찾는 것이 이 글의 핵심은 아님
③ Physical Objects: An Effective Medium to Deliver Subtext
물리적 객체: 숨은 의미를 전달하는 효과적인 매체   숨은 의미를 전달하는 것에 대한 내용은 없음
④ Using Semantic Relation Makes Language Learning Easy
의미적 관계를 이용하는 것은 언어 학습을 용이하게 한다   언어 학습에 대한 글이 아님
⑤ How Vocally Produced Words Shape Our Perception
발음된 단어가 우리의 인식을 형성하는 방법   단어가 우리의 인식을 만든다는 내용의 글이 아님

왜 정답? [정답률 71%]

- 앵무새가 내는 목소리, 돌에 있는 날씨 각각과 구름의 모양은 말, 글, 그림과 비슷하더라도 내재된 의미론적 내용이 없기 때문에 말, 글, 그림은 아니다. 9번 단서 1
- 물리적 유사성 때문에 자연적 기호로 기능할 수는 있지만, 말, 사진, 그림이 되기 위해서는 의미론적 내용이 있어야 한다. 9번 단서 2

▶ 인간의 말, 글, 그림 등과 유사한 동물의 소리와 자연물이 있을 수 있지만 의미론적으로 의미가 없다는 내용의 글이므로 ① '모든 물리적 유사성이 의미론적으로 유의미하지 않은 이유'가 제목으로 적절하다.

왜 오답?

② 앵무새가 내는 소리가 인간의 말소리와 비슷하다는 예시가 초반에 나오긴 하지만, 유사성 발견이 이 글의 핵심은 아니다.
③ 물리적 객체가 숨은 의미를 전달한다는 언급은 없다.
④ 의미적 관계와 언어 학습에 대한 글이 아니다.
⑤ 단어가 우리의 인식을 형성한다는 내용은 아니다.

P 10 정답 ⑤

밑줄 친 (a)~(e) 중에서 문맥상 낱말의 쓰임이 적절하지 않은 것은? [3점]
그것들(앵무새가 내는 목소리)은 사람의 말과   앵무새가 내는 목소리가 '언어적' 행위로 유사하게
① (a) '유사성'이 있어서 구별되지 않을 수도 있음   ② (b) 들려도 의미론적 차원이 주어질 수 없음
유사성 그것들(돌에 있는 날씨 식각이나 구름의   언어적 그것들(돌에 있는 날씨 식각이나 구름의
③ (c) 모양)은 글이나 그림과 비슷하지만, 단순히   ④ (d) 모양)은 그들이 '닮은' 사물을 떠올리게 할
물리적 닮은 '물리적' 사물일 뿐임   닮다 수 있음
⑤ (e) 그것들(특정 다른 것들(말, 사진, 그림)을 닮은 사물)은
배제하다 의미론적 내용을 배제하는 것이 아니라 '가짐'

왜 정답? [정답률 58%]

⑤ (e) exclude 배제하다

하지만, 말, 사진, 그림은 그런 식이 아니다. 그것들은 이해되어야 할 의미론적 내용을 (e) 배제한다.
가진다

→ 인간의 말, 사진이나 그림과 유사한 모습을 띄는 동물의 소리나 자연물이 있고, 이런 것들은 비의미론적 연관성으로 기호가 될 수는 있지만, 말, 사진, 그림은 그렇지 않다고 했다.
위에서도 의미적 내용이 없기에 말이나 글이 될 수 없다는 내용이 반복해서 나오고 있으므로 말, 사진, 그림은 이해되어야 할 의미론적 내용을 '배제한다'고 하는 것이 아니라 '가진다'고 해야 함

▶ exclude(배제하다)의 반대 의미를 갖는 have(가진다)로 바꿔야 함

왜 오답?

① (a) similitude 유사성

그것들(They)은 소리내어진 말과의 물리적 (a) 유사성으로 의미론적 차원이 주어지지 않는다.

→ '그것들(They)'은 앵무새가 내는 목소리이며, 사람이 소리내서 하는 말과 구별되지 못한다고 앞 문장에서 말했으므로, 소리내어진 말과의 물리적 '유사성'은 문맥상 적절하다.

▶ similitude는 문맥에 맞음

② (b) linguistic 언어적

앵무새의 '말'도 일련의 (b) 언어적 행위로 여겨지는 것으로도 의미론적 차원이 주어질 수 없다.

→ 앞 문장에서 인간의 말과 물리적으로 유사하다고 의미론적 차원이 주어지지는 않는다는 내용이 나왔기에 앵무새의 '말'을 일련의 '언어적' 행위로 여겨도 의미론적 차원이 주어질 수 없다는 것은 문맥상 적절하다.

▶ linguistic은 문맥에 맞음

③ (c) physical 물리적

그것들(They)은 단순히 특정한 다른 것들을 닮은 (c) 물리적 사물일 뿐이다.

→ 이 문장에서 '그것들(They)'은 돌에 있는 날씨 식각 혹은 구름 모양이고, (앞의 앵무새 목소리와 비슷하게) 말이나 그림과 물리적으로 유사할 수 있다는 특징을 갖고 있기에 이것들이 닮은 '물리적' 사물일 뿐이라고 하는 것은 적절하다.

▶ physical은 문맥에 맞음

④ (d) resemble 닮다

┌ 관찰자들에게, 그것들(they)은 그들이 (d) 닮은 사물들을 상기시킬 수도
└ 있다.

➡ 문장에서 '그것들(they)'은 돌에 있는 날씨 식각 또는 구름 모양이고, 관찰자는 이를
보고 쓰여진 말이나 그림으로 여길 수 있다는 내용이므로 '닮은' 것은 적절하다.

▶ resemble은 문맥에 맞음

P 11~12 *shrinkflation의 정의와 예시

We have seen a clear rise / in something called 'shrinkflation'. //
우리는 뚜렷한 증가를 보아왔다 / 'shrinkflation'이라고 불리는 것의 //

A basket of products is measured / for inflation by price, / not by
volume or weight. //
한 바구니의 제품은 측정된다 / 가격에 의해 인플레이션이 / 부피나 무게가 아니라 //
11번 단서 1: 크기가 줄었어도 가격이 같으면 기술적으로 가격 상승은 일어나지 않은 것임
If the products shrink in size but the price stays the same, /
technically no price (a) increase has occurred. //
만일 제품의 크기가 줄어들지만 가격은 그대로 유지된다면 / 기술적으로 어떤 가격 상승도
일어나지 않는다 //

But people aren't stupid, / they know what that means. //
그러나 사람들은 바보가 아니고 / 그들은 그것이 무엇을 의미하는지 알고 있다 //
11번 단서 2: 이런 현상은 시리얼이나 초콜릿 바까지 모든 것에 볼 수 있음
You can see this in everything / from the reduced amount of
(= products shrink in size but the price stays the same)
cereal in a box to smaller-sized chocolate bars. //
여러분은 이것을 모든 것에서 볼 수 있다 / 상자에 든 시리얼의 감소된 양부터 더 작은 크기의
초콜릿 바에 이르기까지 //

You can see it / in the form of ever-larger apertures / in toothpaste
tubes and powders of various sorts. //
여러분은 이것을 볼 수 있다 / 그 어느 때보다 더 큰 입구의 형태에서 / 치약 튜브와 다양한
종류의 가루 제품의 //
                                    명사적 용법(보어)
The purpose of these changes / is to make the consumer use up
the product (b) faster / and to pay more per weight. //
이러한 변화의 목적은 / 소비자가 제품을 더 빨리 다 써버리고 / 무게 당 더 많은 돈을
지불하도록 만드는 것이다 //

Toilet paper and paper towel rolls / have ever-larger tube centres
and ever-fewer sheets, / while the price remains the same. //
화장지와 종이 타월 롤은 / 그 어느 때보다 더 큰 튜브 중심과 그 어느 때보다 더 적은 면수를
가지고 있다 / 가격은 그대로인 반면에 //

There are (c) fewer potato crisps in the bag / and cookies in the
box. //
봉지에는 더 적은 수의 감자칩이 있고 상자에는 더 적은 수의 쿠키가 있다 //
12번 단서: 액체 통 아래의 움푹 들어간 곳이 크면 실제보다 안의 내용물이 더 많다는 착시를 불러일으킬 것임
Bottles of liquids such as perfumes have ever-larger dimples on
                 주격 관계대명사(dimples 수식)
the bottom / that displace the product and (d) prevent(→ make)
the illusion / of more inside than there is. //
향수와 같은 액체 병의 바닥에는 그 어느 때보다 더 큰 움푹 들어간 곳이 있다 / 제품을
대체하고 착각을 방지하는(→ 만드는) / 내부에 있는 것보다 더 많이 있다는 //

Shrinkflation is not restricted to retail products. //
shrinkflation은 소매 제품에만 국한되지 않는다 //

Apartments are shrinking, too. // 아파트도 줄어들고 있다 //
11번 단서 3: 아파트는 더 작아졌지만 평방 피트당 비용이 더 들게 됨
Micro apartments are smaller / than anything we lived in before
/ but cost more per square foot. //
초소형 아파트는 더 작지만 / 우리가 전에 살았던 그 어떤 것보다 / 평방 피트당 비용이 더
든다 //
            주격 관계대명사   수여동사+간접목적어+직접목적어(that절)
Shrinkflation is a signal that tells us / that companies are facing
higher costs. //
shrinkflation은 알려주는 신호이다 / 회사들이 더 높은 비용에 직면하고 있다는 것을 //
                        동격의 that
It is a signal / that price pressures are starting to (e) build. //
그것은 신호이다 / 가격 압박이 심해지기 시작했다는 //

• measure ⓥ (치수·양 등을 표준 단위로) 측정하다
• inflation ⓝ 인플레이션 (물가 상승률) • shrink ⓥ 줄어들다

• amount ⓝ 양   • various ⓐ 다양한   • sort ⓝ 종류
• liquid ⓐ 액체의   • prevent ⓥ 방지하다   • pressure ⓝ 압박
• era ⓝ 시대   • strategy ⓝ 전략   • innovative ⓐ 획기적인
• attract ⓥ 마음을 끌다

우리는 'shrinkflation'이라고 불리는 것의 뚜렷한 증가를 보아왔다. 한
바구니의 제품은 부피나 무게가 아니라 가격에 의해 인플레이션이 측정된다.
만일 제품의 크기가 줄어들지만 가격은 그대로 유지된다면, 기술적으로 어떤
가격 (a) 상승도 일어나지 않는다. 그러나 사람들은 바보가 아니고, 그들은
그것이 무엇을 의미하는지 알고 있다. 여러분은 이것을 상자에 든 시리얼의
감소된 양부터 더 작은 크기의 초콜릿 바에 이르기까지 모든 것에서 볼 수
있다. 여러분은 이것을 치약 튜브와 다양한 종류의 가루 제품의 그 어느때보다
더 큰 입구의 형태에서 볼 수 있다. 이러한 변화의 목적은 소비자가 제품을
(b) 더 빨리 다 써버리고 무게 당 더 많은 돈을 지불하도록 만드는 것이다.
가격은 그대로인 반면에, 화장지와 종이 타월 롤은 그 어느 때보다 더 큰
튜브 중심과 그 어느 때보다 더 적은 면수를 가지고 있다. 봉지에는 (c) 더
적은 수의 감자칩이 있고 상자에는 더 적은 수의 쿠키가 있다. 향수와 같은
액체 병의 바닥에는 제품을 대체하고 내부에 있는 것보다 더 많이 있다는
착각을 (d) 방지하는(→ 만드는) 그 어느 때보다 더 큰 움푹 들어간 곳이
있다. shrinkflation은 소매 제품에만 국한되지 않는다. 아파트도 줄어들고
있다. 초소형 아파트는 우리가 전에 살았던 그 어떤 것보다 더 작지만 평방
피트당 비용이 더 든다. shrinkflation은 회사들이 더 높은 비용에 직면하고
있다는 것을 알려주는 신호이다. 그것은 가격 압박이 (e) 심해지기 시작했다는
신호이다.

P 11 정답 ②

윗글의 제목으로 가장 적절한 것은?
① Small Sizes Win Consumers Over in the Era of Shrinkflation 작은 크기가 소비자들에게 인기가 많아졌다는 내용이 아님
   Shrinkflation 시대에 소형 제품이 소비자를 사로잡는다
②Hidden Inflation: Paying the Same for Shrunken Goods
   숨겨진 인플레이션: 축소된 제품에 동일한 가격 지불하기
③ Business Marketing Strategy: Stand Out, Don't Shrink
   비즈니스 마케팅 전략: 축소되지 않고 돋보이기   마케팅 전략으로 눈에 띄게 해야 한다는 언급은 없음
④ Innovative Changes in Smaller-Sized Daily Products 제품의 크기가 줄긴
   소형 일상 제품의 혁신적인 변화 했으나, 이는 shrinkflation 때문에 일어난 현상이지 혁신적 변화는 아님
⑤ Buy One, Get One Free: How Companies Attract You 하나를 사면
   하나를 사면 하나가 무료: 기업이 소비자를 유인하는 방법   하나를 무료로 주는 것에 대한 언급은 없음
─ 가격은 같지만 크기나 더 작아진 현상을 shrinkflation이라고 하며, 이는 인플레이션은 아니지만
   비슷한 의미를 가짐

왜 정답? [정답률 72%]

shrinkflation의 증가	• 인플레이션은 가격만 고려함 • shirnkflation은 제품의 크기는 줄어들지만 가격이 같은 경우임 **11번 단서 1**
소매 제품의 예시	크기와 양이 줄어든 과자, 입구가 커진 용기, 더 큰 튜브 중심과 더 적은 면수를 가진 화장지나 종이 타월 롤, 바닥의 움푹 들어간 곳이 더 커진 액체 통 **11번 단서 2**
아파트 예시	• 초소형 아파트의 크기 축소 • shrinkflation은 기업이 더 높은 비용에 직면하고 있고 가격 압박이 더 커지고 있다는 것을 의미함 **11번 단서 3**

▶ 소매 제품과 아파트의 예시를 들며 Shrinkflation의 증가에 대해 말하는 내용의
글이므로 ② '숨겨진 인플레이션: 축소된 제품에 동일한 가격 지불하기'가 제목으로
적절하다.

왜 오답?
① 작은 크기가 소비자들에게 인기가 많아졌다는 내용이 아니다.
③ 기업들이 더 높은 비용 때문에 크기를 줄인다는 내용이지, 마케팅 전략으로 제품을
   눈에 띄게 해야 한다는 언급은 없다.
④ 일상 제품의 크기가 줄었다는 내용은 나오지만, 이것은 혁신적인 변화가 아니라
   shrinkflation 때문에 일어난 현상이다.
⑤ 하나를 사면 하나를 공짜로 주는 전략에 대한 내용은 없다.

P 12 정답 ④

✎왜 정답? [정답률 72%]

④ (d) prevent 방지하는

향수와 같은 액체 병의 바닥에는 제품을 대체하고 내부에 있는 것보다 더 많이 있다는 착각을 (d) ~~방지하는~~ 그 어느 때보다 더 큰 움푹 들어간 곳이 있다.
만드는

➡ shrinkflation의 본질은 가격은 같으나 소비자가 제품을 더 빨리 쓰고 무게당 더 많은 돈을 지불하도록 제품을 줄이거나 수정하는 것임. 액체 병 바닥에 움푹 들어간 곳이 더 커졌다는 것은 제품을 대체하고 내부에 있는 것보다 제품이 더 많이 있다는 착각을 방지하는 것이 아니라 착각을 불러일으키거나 '만드는' 것임

▶ prevent(방지하는)의 반대 의미를 갖는 make(만드는)로 바꿔야 함

✎왜 오답?

① (a) increase 상승

만일 제품의 크기가 줄어들지만 가격은 그대로 유지된다면, 기술적으로 어떤 가격 (a) 상승도 일어나지 않는다.

➡ 크기가 줄어들어도 가격이 같으면 가격 상승은 일어나지 않을 것이므로 적절하다.

▶ increase는 문맥에 맞음

② (b) faster 더 빨리

이러한 변화의 목적은 소비자가 제품을 (b) 더 빨리 다 써버리고 무게 당 더 많은 돈을 지불하도록 만드는 것이다.

➡ 치약과 파우더의 입구를 크게 하는 것은 제품을 빠르게 쓰도록 하는 목적일 것이므로 적절한 표현이다.

▶ faster은 문맥에 맞음

③ (c) fewer 더 적은

봉지에는 (c) 더 적은 수의 감자칩이 있고 상자에는 더 적은 수의 쿠키가 있다.

➡ 앞에서는 전부 가격은 같아도 양을 줄인다는 예시가 나온다. 따라서 과자 봉지나 상자에 과자가 '더 적게' 들어가는 것이 적절하다.

▶ fewer는 문맥에 맞음

⑤ (e) build 심해지다

그것은 가격 압박이 (e) 심해지기 시작했다는 신호이다.

➡ shrinkflation은 회사가 더 높은 비용을 마주하고 있다는 신호라고 했으므로 가격 압박이 '심해지기' 시작했다는 것은 적절하다.

▶ build는 문맥에 맞음

P 13~14 ＊색맹의 진화적 이유와 생존

There are a number of human characteristics / that would seem
주격 관계대명사
to be disadvantageous / yet continue to survive, generation
병렬 구조(would 뒤)
after generation. // **13번** 단서: 불리한 유전적 특징이 있어도 생존에 큰 문제가 없을 수 있음
많은 인간의 특징들이 있다 / 불리해 보일지 모르지만 / 대대로 계속해서 살아남는 //

One example is color blindness. // 한 가지 예가 색맹이다 //

Most color blindness is associated with genes / on the X
chromosome. //
대부분의 색맹은 유전자와 관련이 있다 / X염색체의 //

Women have two X chromosomes, / so if this problem occurs on
'하나'   '나머지 하나'
one of them, / the other can (a) compensate. //
여성은 2개의 X염색체를 가지고 있어서 / 만약 이 문제가 그중 한 개에서 발생하면 / 다른
하나가 상쇄할 수 있다 //

But men have only one X chromosome. //
하지만 남성은 단 하나의 X염색체를 가지고 있다 //

If the mutation occurs there, / that male is color blind. //
                              지시형용사
만약 돌연변이가 거기서 일어난다면 / 그 남자는 색맹이다 //

We might ask / why such a (b) deficiency would survive / and
                목적어절을 이끄는 의문사
not die out. //
우리는 질문할지 모른다 / 왜 그런 결점이 살아남아서 / 사라지지 않는지 //

To understand this, / we can consider ancient hunter-gatherers,
/ with the men doing most of the hunting for meat / and the
women doing most of the gathering of fruits and nuts. //
이것을 이해하기 위해 / 고대의 수렵 채집인들을 살펴볼 수 있는데 / 남성은 고기를 위한
사냥의 대부분을 / 여성은 과일과 견과류 채집의 대부분을 한다 //

Gathering fruits, especially berries, and nuts is much more
                                         가주어
productive / if it is easy to distinguish the red or purple fruit /
          진주어
from the green leaves of the plant. //
과일, 특히 베리류와 견과류를 채집하는 것은 훨씬 더 생산적이다 / 만약 빨간색이나 보라색
과일을 구별하는 것이 쉽다면 / 식물의 녹색 잎으로부터 //

If red-green color blindness were common among women, / the
resulting (c) lack of productivity would likely cause / this trait
                                            cause의 목적어와 목적격 보어(to부정사)
to die out relatively quickly. //
만약 여성들 사이에 적록 색맹이 흔하다면 / 그로 인한 생산성의 부족은 만들 가능성이 있다 /
이 특성이 비교적 빨리 소멸하도록 //

On the other hand, the men out hunting / don't much rely on
being able to contrast red from green. //
반면 사냥에 나간 남성들은 / 초록색으로부터 빨간색을 대조시킬 수 있는 것에 크게 의존하지
않는다 //

Most of the animals they are hunting have fur or feathers / that
help의 목적어와 목적격 보어(원형부정사)   앞에 목적격 관계대명사 생략
help them hide. //
그들이 사냥하는 대부분의 동물들은 털이나 깃털을 가지고 있다 / 그것들이 숨는 것을
도와주는 //

Rather than relying on color, / the hunter relies on an acute
형용사적 용법(ability 수식)   **14번** 단서: 불리하게 여겨질 유전적 요인이
ability to detect motion. //   오히려 순기능을 가질 수도 있음
색에 의존하기보다는 / 사냥꾼은 움직임을 감지하는 예리한 능력에 의존한다 //

It is conceivable / that a (d) reduction in color contrast in these
가주어   진주어절 접속사
circumstances / might actually enhance one's ability / to detect
형용사적 용법(ability 수식)
subtle motions. //
생각할 만하다 / 이러한 상황에서 색 대비의 감소는 / 사람의 능력을 실제로 향상시킬지
모른다고 / 미묘한 움직임을 감지하는 //

Given that a hunted animal blends into its surroundings, / less
background color variation / would be (e) more(→ less) of a
visual distraction. //
사냥당하는 동물이 주변 환경에 섞여 들어가 있다는 것을 고려할 때 / 배경색의 더 적은
변동은 / 더 많은(→ 더 적은) 시각적인 방해가 될 것이다 //

- disadvantageous ⓐ 불리한
- generation after generation 자손 대대로 · color blindness 색맹
- compensate ⓥ 보상하다 · deficiency ⓝ 결점
- distinguish ⓥ 구별하다 · die out 멸종되다, 소멸하다
- contrast ⓥ 대조하다 · detect ⓥ 발견하다, 감지하다
- conceivable ⓐ 상상할 수 있는, 가능한 · circumstance ⓝ 환경, 상황
- given that ~을 고려하면 · surroundings ⓝ 환경
- variation ⓝ 변화, 변동 · genetic ⓐ 유전의
- destine ⓥ (운명으로) 정해지다 · vanish ⓥ 사라지다, 소멸하다

불리해 보일지 모르지만 대대로 계속해서 살아남는 많은 인간의 특징들이 있다. 한 가지 예가 색맹이다. 대부분의 색맹은 X염색체의 유전자와 관련이 있다. 여성은 2개의 X염색체를 가지고 있어서 만약 이 문제가 그중 한 개에서 발생하면 다른 하나가 (a) 상쇄할 수 있다. 하지만 남성은 단 하나의 X염색체를 가지고 있다. 만약 돌연변이가 거기서 일어난다면, 그 남자는 색맹이다. 우리는 왜 그런 (b) 결점이 살아남아서 사라지지 않는지 질문할지 모른다. 이것을 이해하기 위해 고대의 수렵 채집인들을 살펴볼 수 있는데, 남성은 고기를 위한

사냥의 대부분을 여성은 과일과 견과류 채집의 대부분을 한다. 만약 식물의 녹색 잎으로부터 빨간색이나 보라색 과일을 구별하는 것이 쉽다면 과일, 특히 베리류와 견과류를 채집하는 것은 훨씬 더 생산적이다. 만약 여성들 사이에 적록 색맹이 흔하다면, 그로 인한 생산성의 (c) 부족은 이 특성이 비교적 빨리 소멸하도록 만들 가능성이 있다. 반면 사냥에 나간 남성들은 초록색으로부터 빨간색을 대조시킬 수 있는 것에 크게 의존하지 않는다. 그들이 사냥하는 대부분의 동물들은 그것들이 숨는 것을 도와주는 털이나 깃털을 가지고 있다. 색에 의존하기보다는 사냥꾼은 움직임을 감지하는 예리한 능력에 의존한다. 이러한 상황에서 색 대비의 (d) 감소는 미묘한 움직임을 감지하는 사람의 능력을 실제로 향상시킬지 모른다고 생각할 만하다. 사냥당하는 동물이 주변 환경에 섞여 들어가 있다는 것을 고려할 때, 배경색의 더 적은 변동은 (e) 더 많은(→ 더 적은) 시각적인 방해가 될 것이다.

P 13 정답 ④

윗글의 제목으로 가장 적절한 것은?

① Genetic Code: The Key to Conquering Disorders
유전자 암호: 장애 정복의 열쇠 　　　　　　　　유전자 분석을 통해 장애를 해결하는 내용이 아님
② Ancient People's Challenges from Genetic Weaknesses
유전적 약점으로 인한 고대인들의 도전 　　　　　　　　　　　관련 없음
③ What Makes a Great Hunter: An Ability to Move Quickly
위대한 사냥꾼이 되기 위한 조건: 빠르게 움직이는 능력 　　　　　　　언급되지 않음
④ In Evolution, Disadvantageous Doesn't Mean Destined to Vanish
진화에서의 불리함이 곧 소멸은 아니다 　　　생존에 불리해 보이는 색맹이 오히려 도움이 되었음
⑤ Various Biological Factors Causing Red-Green Color Blindness
적록 색맹을 유발하는 다양한 생물학적 요인들 　　　　　다양한 유발 요인을 알 수 없음

왜 정답? [정답률 58%]

불리한 유전적 특징을 가졌지만 소멸하지 않고 생존하는 경우가 있다며 색맹을 예로 들어 설명하고 있다.
▶ 따라서 ④ '진화에서의 불리함이 곧 소멸은 아니다'가 제목으로 적절하다.

왜 오답?

① 장애 극복을 위해서 유전자를 분석하는 내용은 언급되어 있지 않다.
② 오히려 색맹이 도움이 되었다는 내용이다.
③ 빠른 움직임을 인식하는 내용은 관련이 있으나 사냥꾼의 자질로 빠른 움직임을 꼽고 있지는 않다.
⑤ 적록 색맹은 언급되었으나 다양한 생물학적 유발 요인에 대해서는 언급하지 않았다.

P 14 정답 ⑤

밑줄 친 (a)~(e) 중에서 문맥상 낱말의 쓰임이 적절하지 않은 것은? [3점]

① (a) 두 개가 있다면 하나에 문제가 생겨도 　　② (b) 돌연변이로 인해 문제가 발생하는 것은
상쇄하다 　상쇄시킬 수 있음 　　　　　　　결점 '결점'에 해당함
③ (c) 채집이 어려운 것은 생산성의 '부족'을 　　④ (d) 적록색맹은 색 대비가 '감소'하는 것임
부족 야기할 수 있음 　　　　　　　　　　　감소
⑤ (e) 배경색의 더 적은 변동은 '더 적은'
더 많은 　시각적인 방해를 의미함

왜 정답? [정답률 61%]

⑤ (e) more 더 많은

사냥당하는 동물이 주변 환경에 섞여 들어가 있다는 것을 고려할 때, 배경색의 더 적은 변동은 (e) 더 많은 시각적인 방해가 될 것이다.
➡ 색맹은 배경색의 더 적은 변동을 가질 것이고, 이는 움직임을 감지하는 능력이 중요한 사냥에 있어서 '더 적은' 시각적인 방해를 할 것이다.
▶ more(더 많은)는 반의어인 less(더 적은)로 바꿔야 함

왜 오답?

① (a) compensate 상쇄하다

여성은 2개의 X염색체를 가지고 있어서 만약 이 문제가 그중 한 개에서 발생하면 다른 하나가 (a) 상쇄할 수 있다.
➡ 동일한 염색체가 두 개 있으면 하나에 문제가 생겨도 다른 하나가 '상쇄해서' 문제점을 야기하지 않을 수 있다.
▶ compensate는 문맥에 맞음

---

② (b) deficiency 결점

- 우리는 왜 그런 (b) 결점이 살아남아서 사라지지 않는지 질문할지 모른다.
➡ 생존에 있어 불리한 유전적 요인들을 '결점'으로 볼 수 있다.
▶ deficiency는 문맥에 맞음

③ (c) lack 부족

만약 여성들 사이에 적록 색맹이 흔하다면, 그로 인한 생산성의 (c) 부족은 이 특성이 비교적 빨리 소멸하도록 만들 가능성이 있다.
➡ 유전적 결함으로 인해서 능력이 저하되고 생산성이 '부족'한 경우 생존에 문제가 생긴다.
▶ lack은 문맥에 맞음

④ (d) reduction 감소

이러한 상황에서 색 대비의 (d) 감소는 미묘한 움직임을 감지하는 사람의 능력을 실제로 향상시킬지 모른다고 생각할 만하다.
➡ 색맹은 색 대비가 '감소'된 상태로 세상을 바라보는 것이고, 이는 움직임을 감지하는 능력을 향상시킬 수 있다.
▶ reduction은 문맥에 맞음

P 15~16 ＊자기 대화 관리를 통한 생각 재구성 ——

You are the narrator / of your own life. //
여러분은 내레이터이다 / 자기 자신의 삶의 //
　　　　　　　　　　전치사+관계대명사
The tone and perspective / with which you describe each experience / generates feelings / associated with that narration. //
어조와 관점이 / 각 경험을 묘사하는 / 감정을 만들어 낸다 / 그 내레이션과 관련된 //
　　　　　　　　　find+목적어+목적격 보어
For example, / if you find yourself constantly assuming, /
예를 들어 / 계속해서 가정하는 자신의 모습을 알게 된다면 /
"This is hard," / "I wonder whether I'm going to survive," / or "It looks like this is going to turn out badly," / you'll generate (a) anxious feelings. //
"이건 어려워." / "내가 살아남을 수 있을지 모르겠어." / 또 "일이 안 좋게 되어갈 것 같아."라고 / 여러분은 불안 감정을 만들어 낼 것이다 //
15번 단서 1: 생각을 재구성하라고 함 　　　　way를 수식하는 절
It's time to restructure the way / you think. //
이제는 방식을 재구성할 때다 / 여러분이 생각하는 //
　　　　　　　　　주어-동사 도치 　　동격의 접속사
Underlying this narration / are the beliefs / that (b) frame your experience / and give it meaning. // 15번 단서 2: 내레이션(말)의 기저에는 경험에 영향을 미치는
이러한 내레이션의 기저에는 / 신념이 존재한다 / 여러분의 경험에 틀을 씌우고 / 그것에 의미를 부여하는 // 틀을 씌우는(경험에 영향을 미치는) 신념이 존재함
　　　　　　　　think of A as B: A를 B라고 생각하다
Think of your beliefs / as having many layers. //
여러분의 신념을 생각해 보자 / 여러 층이 있다고 //
　　　　　　　　　주어-동사 도치
On the surface / are your *automatic thoughts*. //
그 표면에 / 바로 '자동적 사고'가 존재한다 //
These are like short tapes / that momentarily flash through your mind. //
　　　　　　　　　　　주격 관계대명사(tapes 수식)
이것은 짧은 테이프와 같다 / 순간적으로 여러분의 머릿속을 스쳐 가는 //
　　　　　　　　　　　　　　　　목적격 관계대명사(self-talk 수식)
Call these automatic thoughts / a form of "self-talk" / that you use as you navigate through the day. // 15번 단서 3: 자동적 사고는
이 자동적 사고를 부르자 / "자기 대화"의 한 종류로 / 여러분이 하루를 항해해 나가며 　자기 대화의 한 종류임
사용하는 //
You (c) produce / a wide variety of these automatic thoughts, / some consciously and some unconsciously. //
여러분은 만들어 낸다 / 매우 다양한 자동적 사고를 / 일부는 의식적으로, 일부는 무의식적으로 //
　　　　　　　　　　　　주격 관계대명사(thoughts 수식)
For example, / automatic thoughts that (d) relieve(→ fuel) anxiety / go something like this: /
예를 들어 / 불안감을 완화하는(→ 불안감에 기름을 붓는) 자동적 사고는 / 이런 식으로 흘러간다 /

You walk into a room, / see a few new people, / and say to yourself, / "Oh no, I don't like this. This is not good." //

여러분이 방에 들어가서 / 처음 보는 사람 몇 명을 보고 / 자신에게 말한다 / "이런, 나는 이거 싫어. 이건 좋지 않아." // ─ **16번** 단서 1: 싫고 좋지 않다는 말 = 부정적인 말

Or, / "These people will soon find out / that I am full of anxiety / and will reject me." // **16번** 단서 2: 불안감이 가득하다는 것을 알고 자신을 거부할 거라는 말

또는 / "이 사람들은 곧 알아챌 거야 / 내가 불안감이 가득하다는 것을 / 그리고 날 거부할 거야." //

주격 관계대명사(habits 수식)
Automatic thoughts are bad habits / that (e) cloud fresh and positive experiences. //

자동적 사고는 나쁜 습관이다 / 새롭고 긍정적인 경험을 우울하게 만드는 //

They can turn a potentially good experience / into one fraught with anxiety. // **16번** 단서 3: 자동적 사고는 좋은 경험을 불안감으로 가득찬 것으로 바꿈

그것들은 잠재적으로 좋은 경험을 바꿀 수 있다 / 불안감으로 가득찬 것으로 //

목적어절을 이끄는 접속사
If you tell yourself / that you are always stressed or full of
사이에 주어와 동사 생략
anxiety / before doing something new, / that new experience will be tainted / by that anxiety. //

만약 여러분이 스스로에게 말한다면 / 항상 스트레스를 받고 불안감으로 가득하다고 / 새로운 무언가를 하기 전에 / 그 새로운 경험은 오염될 것이다 / 그 불안에 의해 //

- tone ⓝ 어조 • perspective ⓝ 관점 • generate ⓥ 만들어 내다
- associate ⓥ 연관 짓다, 연상하다 • assume ⓥ 가정하다
- restructure ⓥ 재구성하다 • underlying ⓐ 기저의
- layer ⓝ 층, 막 • surface ⓝ 표면
- momentarily ⓐⓓ 순간적으로 • automatic ⓐ 무의식의, 반사적인
- navigate ⓥ 항해하다 • anxiety ⓝ 불안감 • reject ⓥ 거부하다
- potentially ⓐⓓ 잠재적으로 • heighten ⓥ 고조되다

여러분은 자기 자신의 삶의 내레이터이다. 각 경험을 묘사하는 어조와 관점이 그 내레이션과 관련된 감정을 만들어 낸다. 예를 들어, "이건 어려워.", "내가 살아남을 수 있을지 모르겠어.", 또 "일이 안 좋게 되어갈 것 같아."라고 계속해서 가정하는 자신의 모습을 알게 된다면, 여러분은 (a) 불안 감정을 만들어 낼 것이다. 이제는 여러분의 사고 방식을 재구성할 때다. 이러한 내레이션의 기저에는 여러분의 경험에 (b) 틀을 씌우고 그것에 의미를 부여하는 신념이 존재한다. 여러분의 신념에 여러 층이 있다고 생각해 보자. 그 표면에 바로 '자동적 사고'가 존재한다. 이것은 순간적으로 여러분의 머릿속을 스쳐가는 짧은 테이프와 같다. 이 자동적 사고를 여러분이 하루를 항해해 나가며 사용하는 "자기 대화"의 한 종류로 부르자. 여러분은 매우 다양한 자동적 사고를 일부는 의식적으로, 일부는 무의식적으로 (c) 만들어 낸다. 예를 들어, 불안감을 (d) 완화하는(→ 불안감에 기름을 붓는) 자동적 사고는 이런 식으로 흘러간다: 여러분이 방에 들어가서 처음 보는 사람 몇 명을 보고, 자신에게 말한다. "이런, 나는 이거 싫어. 이건 좋지 않아." 또는 "이 사람들은 곧 내가 불안감이 가득하다는 것을 알아채고 날 거부할 거야." 자동적 사고는 새롭고 긍정적인 경험을 (e) 우울하게 만드는 나쁜 습관이다. 그것들은 잠재적으로 좋은 경험을 불안감으로 가득찬 것으로 바꿀 수 있다. 만약 여러분이 새로운 무언가를 하기 전에 항상 스트레스를 받고 불안감으로 가득하다고 스스로에게 말한다면, 그 새로운 경험은 그 불안에 의해 오염될 것이다.

P 15 정답 ③

윗글의 제목으로 가장 적절한 것은?

① The Role of Automatic Thoughts in Language Learning
언어 학습에서 자동적 사고의 역할   언어 학습에서 자동적 사고가 하는 역할에 대한 글이 아님
② Self-talk: The Best Way to Improve Your Speech 자기 대화가 말하기
자기 대화: 말하기 능력을 향상시키는 최고의 방법   능력을 향상시키는 방법이라고 하지 않았음
③ Reshaping Thoughts: Manage Your Self-talk 자기 대화를 관리하고 생각을
생각 재구성하기: 당신의 자기 대화를 관리하라   바꾸어야 불안감이나 스트레스가 줄어든다는 내용임
④ Heightened Anxiety Leads to Productivity
높은 불안은 생산성으로 이어진다   높은 불안이 생산성으로 이어진다는 내용의 글이 아님
⑤ Ways to Read Others' Inner Thoughts
다른 사람의 내면 생각을 읽는 방법   다른 사람의 내면 생각을 읽는 방법을 제시하지 않았음

왜 정답? [정답률 71%]

도입	• 여러분은 자기 삶의 내레이터 • 각 경험을 묘사하는 어조와 관점이 그 내레이션과 관련된 감정을 만들어 냄(부정적인 말 → 불안 감정)
요지	• 사고 방식을 재구성할 때임 • '자기 대화'의 한 종류인 자동적 사고가 존재하고, 이를 의식적 또는 무의식적으로 만들어 냄
부연	불안감을 만드는 자동적 사고(부정적이거나 싫다고 스스로에게 하는 말)는 새롭고 긍정적인 경험을 우울하게 만드는 나쁜 습관

▶ 불안감을 만드는 자동적 사고를 재구성하고 자기 대화를 관리하라는 내용의 글이므로 ③ '생각 재구성하기: 당신의 자기 대화를 관리하라'가 제목으로 적절하다.

왜 오답?

① 언어 학습에서 자동적 사고가 하는 역할에 대한 글이 아니다.
② 자기 대화가 말하기 능력을 향상시키는 방법이라고 하지 않았다.
④ 높은 불안이 생산성으로 이어진다는 내용의 글이 아니다.
⑤ 다른 사람의 내면 생각을 읽는 방법을 제시하지 않았다.

P 16 정답 ④

밑줄 친 (a)~(e) 중에서 문맥상 낱말의 쓰임이 적절하지 않은 것은? [3점]

① (a) 부정적인 말들이 '불안' 감정을 만들어 냄   ② (b) 부정적인 내레이션이 경험에 '틀을 씌우는'
불안한   틀을 씌우다 신념을 부여함
③ (c) 자동적 사고는 스스로 '만들어 내는' 것이   ④ (d) 부정적 말들은 불안감을 완화하는 것이
만들어 내다 맞음   완화하다 아니라 불안감을 '증폭시킴'
⑤ (e) 자동적 사고가 긍정적 경험을 '우울하게 만드는' 것임
우울하게 만들다

왜 정답? [정답률 51%]

④ (d) relieve 완화하다

불안감에 기름을 붓는
예를 들어(For example), 불안감을 (d) ~~완화하는~~ 자동적 사고는 이런 식으로 흘러간다: 여러분이 방에 들어가서 처음 보는 사람 몇 명을 보고, 자신에게 말한다. "이런, 나는 이거 싫어. 이건 좋지 않아." 또는 "이 사람들은 곧 내가 불안감이 가득하다는 것을 알아채고 날 거부할 거야."

➡ 싫다거나 좋지 않다거나 불안감이 가득하다는 것을 알고 자신을 거부할 거라는 생각은 불안감을 완화하는 것이 아니라 불안감을 자극하거나 '증가시키는' 것임

▶ relieve(완화하다)의 반대 의미를 갖는 fuel(기름을 붓다)로 바꿔야 함

왜 오답?

① (a) anxious 불안한

예를 들어(For example), "이건 어려워.", "내가 살아남을 수 있을지 모르겠어.", 또 "일이 안 좋게 되어갈 것 같아."라고 계속해서 가정하는 자신의 모습을 알게 된다면, 여러분은 (a) 불안 감정을 만들어 낼 것이다.

➡ 어렵다거나 살아남을 수 있을지 모르겠다거나 일이 안 좋게 되어갈 것 같다는 것은 '불안' 감정을 만들어 내는 것이다.

▶ anxious는 문맥에 맞음

② (b) frame 틀을 씌우다

이러한 내레이션(this narration)의 기저에는 여러분의 경험에 (b) 틀을 씌우고 그것에 의미를 부여하는 신념이 존재한다.

➡ '이러한 내레이션(this narration)'은 앞에서 언급한 부정적인 말을 의미하고, 이 말이 불안 감정을 만들어 낸다고 했으므로 이러한 내레이션의 기저에 여러분의 경험에 '틀을 씌우고' 의미를 부여하는 신념이 있다고 하는 것은 적절하다.

▶ frame은 문맥에 맞음

③ (c) produce 만들어 내다

여러분은 매우 다양한 자동적 사고를 일부는 의식적으로, 일부는 무의식적으로 (c) 만들어 낸다.

➡ 자동적 사고는 '자기 대화'의 한 종류로 스스로 '만들어 내는' 것이 맞다.

▶ produce는 문맥에 맞음

⑤ (e) cloud 우울하게 하다

─ 자동적 사고는 새롭고 긍정적인 경험을 (e) 우울하게 만드는 나쁜
└ 습관이다.

➡ 앞에서 자동적 사고의 결과인 부정적인 말들을 나열하고 이것이 불안감에 기름을
붓는다고 했으므로 문맥상 자동적 사고가 긍정적인 경험을 '우울하게 만든다'고
하는 것은 적절하다.

▶ cloud는 문맥에 맞음

P 17~18 ＊고정 관념적 추정의 장단점

Douglas Hofstadter is a scholar / who writes / about
　　　　　　　　　선행사　　　주격 관계대명사
stereotypical thinking. //
Douglas Hofstadter는 학자이다 / 글을 쓰는 / 고정 관념적 사고에 대해 //
주어　　　동사
He discusses / what he calls *default assumptions*. //
　　　　　　　　　　　　　목적어절
그는 논의한다 / 자신이 '기본 가정'이라고 일컫는 것에 대해 //

Default assumptions are (a) preconceived notions / about the
likely state of affairs / — what we assume to be true / in the
absence of specific information. //
기본 가정은 선입관이다 / 상황의 있음 직한 상태에 대한 / 우리가 사실이라고 가정하는 것 /
구체적인 정보의 부재 속에서 //

17번 단서 1: 비서는 여성이라는 고정 관념 때문에 '비서'를 언급하면 그 비서가 여성이라고 가정함
Given no other information, / when I mention "secretary," /
　　　　　　　　　　　　　　　앞에 목적어절 접속사 that이 생략됨
you are likely to assume / the secretary is a woman, / because
"woman" and "secretary" are associated stereotypically. //
다른 정보가 전혀 없다면 / 내가 '비서'를 언급할 때 / 여러분은 아마도 가정할 것이다 / 그
비서가 여성이라고 / '여성'과 '비서'는 고정 관념으로 연관되어 있기 때문에 //

In the absence of specific details, / people rely on the stereotype
/ as a default assumption / for filling in the (b) blanks. //
구체적인 세부 사항이 없으면 / 사람들은 고정 관념에 의존한다 / 기본 가정으로서의 / 그
공백을 채우기 위한 //

Default assumptions have a tendency, / in Hofstadter's words,
/ to "permeate / our mental representations / and channel our
　　　　　　　　　형용사적 용법(a tendency 수식)
thoughts." //
기본 가정은 경향이 있다 / Hofstadter의 말에 따르면 / '스며드는 / 우리의 정신적 표현에 /
그리고 우리의 생각을 (특정 방향으로) 돌리는' //

For instance, / given the words "cat," "dog," and "chases," / you
are likely to think first / of a dog chasing a cat. //
예를 들어 / '고양이', '개', '쫓다'라는 단어가 주어지면 / 여러분은 아마도 맨 먼저 생각할
것이다 / 고양이를 쫓는 개를 //

This line of thought (c) reflects / a default assumption / that, all
　　　　　　　　　　　　　　　　동격절 접속사
else being equal, / the dog is more likely to chase the cat / than
the other way around. //
이런 사고방식은 반영한다 / 기본 가정을 / 다른 모든 것이 똑같다면 / 개가 고양이를 쫓을
가능성이 더 크다는 / 그 반대보다 //

Default assumptions are rooted / in our socially learned
associative clusters and linguistic categories. //
기본 가정은 뿌리박고 있다 / 우리의 사회적으로 학습된 연상 (사고) 무리와 언어 범주에 //

They are (d) useless(→ useful) / in that people cannot always
afford the time / it would take / to consider every theoretical
possibility / that confronts them. //
18번 단서 1: 기본 가정이 유용하게 쓰일 수 있는 상황임
그것들은 쓸모없다(→ 유용하다) / 사람들이 시간을 항상 감당할 수는 없다는 점에서 / 걸릴 /
모든 이론적 가능성을 고려하는 데 / 자신에게 닥친 //
18번 단서 2: 기본 가정이 틀리는 경우가 많다는 내용이 Nonetheless로 이어짐
Nonetheless, / default assumptions are often wrong. //
그렇기는 하지만 / 기본 가정이 틀리는 경우가 많다 //

Default assumptions are only one type / of language-based
categorization. //
기본 가정은 한 가지 유형일 뿐이다 / 언어 기반 분류의 //

Hofstadter is particularly interested / in race-based and gender-
based categorization and default assumptions. //
Hofstadter는 특히 관심이 있다 / 인종 기반 및 성별 기반 분류와 기본 가정에 //

　　　　　　　　　　　　　　　　　　　　　　　　미래시제를
　　　　　　　　　　　　　　　생략 가능한 명사절 접속사　나타내는
　　　　　　　　　　　　　　　　　　　　　　　　현재진행형
For instance, / if you hear / that your school basketball team is
playing tonight, / do you assume / it's the men's team? //
예를 들어 / 만약 여러분이 듣는다면 / 여러분의 학교 농구팀이 오늘 밤에 경기를 한다고 /
여러분은 가정하는가 / 그것이 남자팀이라고 **17번** 단서 2: '운동-남자'라는 고정 관념 때문에
　　　　　　　　　　　　　　　　　　　　　　학교 농구팀이 남자팀이라고 가정함
Most people would assume so / unless a *qualifier* is (e) added / to
　　　　　　　　　　　　　　　= if not
provide specific information. //
대부분의 사람은 그렇게 가정할 것이다 / '수식어'가 추가되지 않으면 / 구체적인 정보를
제공하기 위해 //

In this case, / the qualifier would be / "the *women's* basketball
team is playing tonight." //
이 경우에 / 그 수식어는 ~일 것이다 / "'여자' 농구팀이 오늘 밤에 경기를 할 것이다" //

- -

- scholar ⓝ 장학생, 학자　　· stereotypical ⓐ 고정관념의
- discuss ⓥ 논의하다　　· notion ⓝ 개념　　· state ⓝ 상태
- affair ⓝ (현재 얘기되거나 다뤄지는) 일[사건]　　· assume ⓥ 추정하다
- absence ⓝ 부재, 없음　　· mention ⓥ 언급하다
- associate ⓥ 결부[연관] 짓다
- stereotype ⓝ 고정 관념, 정형화된 생각[이미지]
- tendency ⓝ 성향, 기질, 경향　　· representation ⓝ 표현
- channel ⓥ 특정한 방향으로 돌리다　　· chase ⓥ 쫓다
- root ⓥ 뿌리박다　　· associative ⓐ 연상의
- linguistic ⓐ 언어(학)의
- afford ⓥ (~을 살·할 금전적·시간적) 여유[형편]가 되다
- theoretical ⓐ 이론적인　　· confront ⓥ 직면하다
- nonetheless ⓐⓓ 그렇기는 하지만, 그렇더라도
- categorization ⓝ 범주화

Douglas Hofstadter는 고정 관념적 사고에 대해 글을 쓰는 학자이다. 그는
자신이 '기본 가정'이라고 일컫는 것에 대해 논의한다. 기본 가정은 상황의 있음
직한 상태에 대한 (a) 선입관인데, 구체적인 정보가 없을 때 우리가 사실이라고
가정하는 것이다. 다른 정보가 전혀 없다면, 내가 '비서'를 언급할 때, 여러분은
아마도 그 비서가 여성이라고 가정할 것인데, '여성'과 '비서'는 고정 관념으로
연관되어 있기 때문이다. 구체적인 세부 사항이 없으면, 사람들은 그
(b) 공백을 채우기 위한 기본 가정으로서의 고정 관념에 의존한다.
Hofstadter의 말에 따르면, 기본 가정은 '우리의 정신적 표현에 스며들고
우리의 생각을 (특정 방향으로) 돌리는' 경향이 있다. 예를 들어, '고양이', '개',
'쫓다'라는 단어가 주어지면, 여러분은 아마도 개가 고양이를 쫓는 것을 맨 먼저
생각할 것이다. 이런 사고방식은 다른 모든 것이 똑같다면 개가 고양이를 쫓을
가능성이 그 반대보다 더 크다는 기본 가정을 (c) 반영한다.
기본 가정은 사회적으로 학습된 연상 (사고) 무리와 언어 범주에 뿌리박고
있다. 그것들은 사람들이 자신이 직면한 모든 이론적 가능성을 고려하는 데
걸릴 시간을 항상 감당할 수는 없다는 점에서 (d) 쓸모없다(→ 유용하다).
그렇기는 하지만, 기본 가정이 틀리는 경우가 많다. 기본 가정은 언어 기반
분류의 한 가지 유형일 뿐이다. Hofstadter는 인종 기반 및 성별 기반 분류와
기본 가정에 특히 관심이 있다. 예를 들어, 만약 여러분의 학교 농구팀이 오늘
밤에 경기를 한다고 듣는다면, 여러분은 그것이 남자팀이라고 가정하는가?
구체적인 정보를 제공하기 위해 '수식어'가 (e) 추가되지 않으면 대부분의
사람은 그렇게 가정할 것이다. 이 경우에 그 수식어는 "'여자' 농구팀이 오늘
밤에 경기를 할 것이다."일 것이다.

P 17 정답 ③

윗글의 제목으로 가장 적절한 것은?

① Quest for Novelty: Our Survival Instinct 고정 관념, 기본 가정에 대한 내용임
　새로움에 대한 추구: 우리의 생존 본능
② Gossip as a Source of Social Information 소문에 영향을 받는다는 것이 아님
　사회적 정보의 원천으로서의 소문
③ The Bias Behind Stereotypical Assumptions 고정 관념에 따라 추정함
　고정 관념적 추정 이면의 편견
④ The More Information, The More Confusion Given no other
　더 많은 정보, 더 많은 혼란　　　　　　　　information 등으로 만든 오답
⑤ Creativity: Free from the Prison of Our Assumptions 창의성에 대한
　창의성: 우리의 추정이라는 감옥으로부터 자유로운　　　　　내용이 아님

'고양이', '개', '쫓다'라는 단어가 주어지면, 여러분은 아마도 고양이를 쫓는 개를 맨 먼저 생각할 것이다. 이런 사고방식은 다른 모든 것이 똑같다면 개가 고양이를 쫓을 가능성이 그 반대보다 더 크다는 기본 가정을 (c) 반영한다.

➡ '고양이', '개', '쫓다'라는 단어가 주어질 때 맨 먼저 고양이를 쫓는 개를 떠올리는 이유: 다른 모든 것이 똑같다면 개가 고양이를 쫓을 가능성이 그 반대보다 더 크다는 기본 가정을 '반영하기' 때문임
  ▶ reflects는 문맥에 맞음

⑤ (e) added 추가된

만약 여러분의 학교 농구팀이 오늘 밤에 경기를 한다고 듣는다면, 여러분은 그것이 남자팀이라고 가정하는가? 구체적인 정보를 제공하기 위해 '수식어'가 (e) 추가되지 않으면 대부분의 사람은 그렇게 가정할 것이다. 이 경우에 그 수식어는 "'여자' 농구팀이 오늘 밤에 경기를 할 것이다."일 것이다.

➡ your school basketball team is playing tonight을 the women's basketball team is playing tonight으로 바꿨다.
  → women's라는 수식어가 '추가되었음'
  ▶ added는 문맥에 맞음

🅿 19~20 ＊실험에서 주의해야 할 점

> studies를 수식하는 현재분사구

In studies / examining the effectiveness of vitamin C, / researchers typically divide the subjects / into two groups. //
연구에서 / 비타민 C의 효과를 조사하는 / 연구원들은 일반적으로 실험 대상자들을 나눈다 / 두 집단으로 //

One group (the experimental group) / receives a vitamin C supplement, / and the other (the control group) does not. //
> 둘 중 하나   둘 중 나머지 하나
한 집단(실험집단)은 / 비타민 C 보충제를 받고 / 다른 집단(통제 집단)은 받지 않는다 //

Researchers observe both groups / to determine / whether one group has fewer or shorter colds / than the other. //
> 의문시되는 사실을 이야기할 때 쓰는 명사절 접속사
연구원들은 두 집단 모두를 관찰한다 / 알아내기 위해 / 한 집단이 감기에 더 적게 또는 더 짧게 걸리는지를 / 다른 집단보다 //

The following discussion describes / some of the pitfalls / inherent in an experiment of this kind / and ways / to (a) avoid them. //
> 형용사적 용법(ways 수식)
이어지는 논의는 설명한다 / 함정 중 일부와 / 이러한 종류의 실험에 내재한 / 방법을 / 그것들을 피하는 //

In sorting subjects into two groups, / researchers must ensure / that each person has an (b) equal chance / of being assigned / to either the experimental group or the control group. //
> either A or B: A 또는 B
실험 대상자를 두 집단으로 분류할 때 / 연구원들은 반드시 확실히 해야 한다 / 각 개인이 동일한 확률을 갖는다는 것을 / 배정될 / 실험집단 또는 통제 집단 둘 중 한 곳에 //

This is accomplished / by randomization; / that is, the subjects are chosen randomly / from the same population / by flipping a coin / or some other method / involving chance. //
이는 달성된다 / 임의 추출에 의해 / 즉 실험 대상자는 임의로 선정된다 / 동일 모집단에서 / 동전 던지기에 의해 / 또는 어떤 다른 방법에 의해 / 우연이 포함된 //

Randomization helps to ensure / that results reflect the treatment / and not factors / that might influence / the grouping of subjects. //
> = that results do not reflect factors
임의 추출은 확실히 하는 데 도움이 된다 / 결과가 처리를 반영하는 것을 / 그리고 요인은 반영하지 않는 것을 / 영향을 줄지도 모르는 / 실험 대상자의 분류에 //

- '여성'과 '비서'는 고정 관념으로 연관되어 있기 때문에, 다른 정보가 전혀 없다면, 비서가 여성이라고 가정한다. **17번 단서 1**
- 여러분의 학교 농구팀이 오늘 밤에 경기를 한다고 들으면, 다른 수식어가 추가되지 않는 한, 그것이 남자팀이라고 가정할 것이다. **17번 단서 2**

➡ 우리는 '비서-여성', '운동-남자'라는 기본 가정, 즉 고정 관념을 반영한 추정을 한다. '편견'이라는 표현이 글에 직접적으로 드러나지는 않지만, '고정 관념에 의한 추정'에서 '편견'을 추론할 수 있다.
  ▶ 제목으로 적절한 것은 ③ '고정 관념적 추정 이면의 편견'이다.

➤오답?

① 우리가 생존을 위해 본능적으로 새로운 것을 추구한다는 내용이 아니다.
② 소문에 영향을 받는다는 것이 아니라, 고정 관념, 선입관에 영향을 받아 추정한다는 것이다.
④ 아무런 정보가 주어지지 않을 때 고정 관념이 크게 작용한다는 것이지, 정보가 많을수록 더 혼란해진다는 것이 아니다.
⑤ 창의성과 관련된 내용이 전혀 아니다.

🅿 18 정답 ④

밑줄 친 (a)~(e) 중에서 문맥상 낱말의 쓰임이 적절하지 않은 것은?

① (a) 선입관 = '사전에 형성된' 관념
  사전에 형성된
② (b) 구체적인 세부 사항이 '없는' 경우
  공백
③ (c) 개가 고양이를 쫓을 확률이 더 크다는 기본 가정을 반영한 결과가 고양이를 쫓는
  반영하다
④ (d) 기본 가정의 단점이 Nonetheless로 이어짐
  쓸모없는
⑤ (e) 추가되는 수식어 women's가 추가됨
  개를 맨 먼저 생각하는 것임

➤오탭 정답? [정답률 72%]

④ (d) useless 쓸모없는

기본 가정은 사람들이 자신이 직면한 모든 이론적 가능성을 고려하는 데 걸릴 시간을 항상 감당할 수는 없다는 점에서 (d) ~~쓸모없다~~.
유용하다
<u>그렇기는 하지만(Nonetheless)</u>, 기본 가정이 틀리는 경우가 많다.

➡ 기본 가정이 틀리는 경우가 많다는 내용이 Nonetheless로 이어진다.
  → 앞 문장은 기본 가정의 장점을 설명해야 한다.
➡ 사람들이 자신이 직면한 모든 이론적 가능성을 고려할 시간이 항상 있는 것은 아니다.
  → 기본 가정(선입관)을 이용하는 것이 유용한 이유임
  ▶ useless를 반의어인 useful(유용한)로 바꿔야 함

➤오답?

① (a) preconceived 사전에 형성된

기본 가정은 상황의 있음 직한 상태에 대한 (a) 선입관인데, 구체적인 정보가 없을 때 우리가 사실이라고 가정하는 것이다.

➡ **선입관:** 어떤 대상에 대하여 이미 마음속에 가지고 있는 고정적인 관념이나 관점 '이미' 마음속에 가지고 있는 생각을 '사전에 형성된(preconceived) 관념(notion)'이라고 표현했다.
  ▶ preconceived는 문맥에 맞음

② (b) blanks 공백, 여백

구체적인 세부 사항이 없으면, 사람들은 그 (b) 공백을 채우기 위한 기본 가정으로서의 고정 관념에 의존한다.

➡ 구체적인 세부 사항이 '없다'는 것을 '공백'이라고 표현했다.
  ▶ blanks는 문맥에 맞음

Importantly, / the two groups of people / must be similar / and must have the same track record / with respect to colds /

중요한 것으로는 / 두 집단의 사람들이 / 비슷해야 하고 / 동일한 기록을 가지고 있어야 한다 / 감기와 관련하여 /　**19번** 단서: 비타민 C 보충제 외에 다른 요인은 두 집단이 비슷해야 함

to (c) rule out the possibility / that observed differences / in the rate, severity, or duration of colds / might have occurred anyway. //
　　　　　　동격절 접속사　　　　　　　　　　　　　　　과거 사실에 대한 추측을 나타내는 might have p.p.

가능성을 배제하기 위해 / 관찰한 차이가 / 감기의 비율, 심각성, 또는 지속 기간에서 / 어떤 식으로든 일어났을지도 모른다는 //

If, for example, the control group would normally catch / twice as many colds / as the experimental group, / then the findings prove (d) nothing. //
　　　　　　　　　　　　　　　　　　　experiments를 수식하는 현재분사구

예를 들어, 통제 집단이 보통 걸린다면 / 두 배 많은 감기를 / 실험집단보다 / 연구 결과는 아무것도 입증하지 못한다 //

In experiments / involving a nutrient, / the diets of both groups / must also be (e) different(→ similar), / especially with respect to the nutrient / being studied. //
　　　　the nutrient를 수식하는 현재분사구

실험에서 / 영양분을 포함하는 / 두 집단의 식단은 / 또한 달라야(→ 비슷해야) 한다 / 특히 영양분에 관련해 / 연구 중인 //　**20번** 단서: 평소 식단이 다르면 비타민 C 보충제의 어떤 효과도 불분명해짐

If those in the experimental group were receiving / less vitamin C / from their usual diet, / then any effects of the supplement / may not be apparent. //
부사절 접속사(조건)

실험집단에 속한 사람들이 섭취하고 있다면 / 더 적은 비타민 C를 / 그들의 평소 식단에서 / 보충제의 어떤 효과도 / 분명하지 않을 수 있다 //

- typically ⓐ 일반적으로 ・subject ⓝ 실험[연구] 대상, 피험자
- supplement ⓝ 보충(제) ・observe ⓥ 관찰하다
- determine ⓥ 알아내다, 밝히다 ・inherent ⓐ 내재하는, 고유한
- sort ⓥ 분류하다 ・assign ⓥ 배정하다, 맡기다
- accomplish ⓥ 달성하다 ・randomization ⓝ 임의 추출
- flip ⓥ 톡 던지다 ・factor ⓝ 요인 ・rule out ~을 배제하다
- rate ⓝ 비율 ・severity ⓝ 심함, 격렬[맹렬]함
- duration ⓝ 지속 (기간) ・nutrient ⓝ 영양분
- with respect to ~에 관하여 ・apparent ⓐ 분명한
- irrelevant ⓐ 무관한 ・in-depth ⓐ 면밀한, 철저하고 상세한
- analysis ⓝ 분석

비타민 C의 효과를 조사하는 연구에서, 연구원들은 일반적으로 실험 대상자들을 두 집단으로 나눈다. 한 집단(실험집단)은 비타민 C 보충제를 받고 다른 집단(통제 집단)은 받지 않는다. 연구원들은 한 집단이 다른 집단보다 감기에 더 적게 또는 더 짧게 걸리는지를 알아내기 위해 두 집단 모두를 관찰한다. 이어지는 논의는 이러한 종류의 실험에 내재한 함정 중 일부와 이를 (a) 피하는 방법을 설명한다. 실험 대상자를 두 집단으로 분류할 때, 연구원들은 반드시 각 개인이 실험집단 또는 통제 집단 둘 중 한 곳에 배정될 확률이 (b) 동일하도록 해야 한다. 이는 임의 추출에 의해 달성되는데 즉 실험 대상자는 동전 던지기나 우연이 포함된 어떤 다른 방법에 의해 동일 모집단에서 임의로 선정된다. 임의 추출은 반드시 결과에 처리가 반영되도록, 실험 대상자의 분류에 영향을 줄지도 모르는 요인은 반영되지 않도록 하는 데 도움이 된다. 중요한 것은, 감기의 비율, 심각성, 또는 지속 기간에서 관찰된 차이가 어떤 식으로든 일어났을지도 모른다는 가능성을 (c) 배제하기 위해 감기와 관련하여 두 집단의 사람들이 비슷하고 동일한 기록을 가지고 있어야 한다는 것이다. 예를 들어, 통제 집단이 보통 실험집단보다 감기에 두 배 많이 걸린다면 연구 결과는 (d) 아무것도 입증하지 못한다. 영양분을 포함하는 실험에서, 두 집단의 식단 또한 (e) 달라야(→ 비슷해야) 하며, 연구 중인 영양분에 관련해서 특히 그래야 한다. 실험집단에 속한 사람들이 평소 식단에서 비타민 C를 적게 섭취하고 있다면, 보충제의 어떤 효과도 분명하지 않을 수 있다.

P 19 정답 ②

윗글의 제목으로 가장 적절한 것은?

① Perfect Planning and Faulty Results: A Sad Reality in Research
　완벽한 계획과 불완전한 결과: 연구의 슬픈 현실　　　완전한 결과를 위한 실험 계획을 설명함
② Don't Let Irrelevant Factors Influence the Results!
　상관없는 요인이 결과에 영향을 미치지 않도록 하라!　비타민 C 보충제 외의 요소는 똑같아야 함
③ Protect Human Subjects Involved in Experimental Research!
　실험 연구에 참여하는 인간 실험 대상자들을 보호하라!　실험 대상이 되는 인간을 보호하라는 것이 아님
④ What Nutrients Could Better Defend Against Colds?
　어떤 영양분이 감기를 더 잘 막을 수 있을까?　　　실험 결과를 설명하는 글이 아님
⑤ In-depth Analysis of Nutrition: A Key Player for Human Health
　영양에 대한 심층 분석: 인간의 건강을 위한 핵심 요소　　실험을 할 때 주의할 점을 설명한 글임

〉왜 정답 ? [정답률 67%]

비타민 C가 감기에 미치는 영향을 알아보기 위해 한 집단은 비타민 C 보충제를 받고, 다른 집단은 받지 않는 실험에서 주의해야 하는 사항을 설명하는 글이다. 임의 추출에 의해 실험 대상자를 두 집단으로 나누는데, 두 집단이 비슷하고 감기에 있어 동일한 기록을 갖는 것이 중요하다고 했다. 이는 비타민 C 보충제 이외의 요소가 실험 결과에 영향을 미치면 연구 결과는 아무것도 입증하지 못하기 때문으로, 마지막 문장에서는 평소 식단에서 섭취하는 비타민 C의 양이 다르면 비타민 C 보충제의 효과가 분명하지 않을 수 있다고 했다. 비타민 C 보충제 이외의 평소 식단과 같은 요인이 실험 결과에 영향을 미치지 않게 하라는 내용의 글에는 ② '상관없는 요인이 결과에 영향을 미치지 않도록 하라!'가 제목으로 적절하다.

〉왜 오답 ?

① 계획을 완벽하게 세워도 불완전한 결과가 나온다는 내용이 아니다. 완전한 결과를 위한 실험 설계 방법에 대해 알려주는 글이다.

③ 인간을 대상으로 실험할 때 실험 대상자들을 보호해야 한다고 주장하는 글이 아니다.

④, ⑤ 비타민 C 보충제가 감기에 미치는 영향을 알아보는 실험을 통해 실험을 어떻게 진행해야 유효한 결과를 얻는지 설명한 것이다. 감기나 영양소 자체에 대한 실험 결과를 알려주는 것이 아니다.

P 20 정답 ⑤

밑줄 친 (a)~(e) 중에서 문맥상 낱말의 쓰임이 적절하지 않은 것은?

① (a) 완전한 연구를 하는 방법에 대한 설명이 피하다 이어짐
② (b) '임의로' 선정되므로, 실험집단으로 배정될 동일한 확률과 통제 집단으로 배정될 확률이 같음
③ (c) 변수의 영향(비타민 C 보충제) 외에 어떤 배제하다 식으로든 감기에 걸렸을 가능성을 배제해야 함
④ (d) 통제 집단이 '보통' 감기에 더 많이 걸린다면 아무것도 이 연구의 결과는 아무것도 입증하지 못함
⑤ (e) 식단도 비슷해야 비타민 C 보충제의 효과를 다른 알 수 있음

〉왜 정답 ? [정답률 60%]

비타민 C가 감기에 미치는 영향을 알아보기 위한 실험에서 한 집단은 비타민 C 보충제를 받고 다른 집단은 받지 않는다고 했다. 비타민 C 보충제 이외의 요소는 같아야 한다는 내용으로, 평소 식단에서 섭취하는 비타민 C의 양이 다르면 비타민 C 보충제의 어떠한 효과도 불분명하다는 문장이 이어지므로 ⑤ (e) different를 similar 또는 same 등의 단어로 바꾸어야 한다.

〉왜 오답 ?

① 비타민 C의 효과를 조사하기 위해 비타민 C 보충제를 이용하는 연구에서 주의할 점을 설명하는 글이므로, 함정을 '피하는' 방법을 설명한다는 것은 자연스럽다. [다시 말해, 비타민 C 보충제 이외의 요소 때문에] 〔꿀팁〕

② 임의 추출에 의해 달성되는 것은 실험 대상자가 실험집단이나 통제 집단 중 한 곳에 배정될 '동일한' 확률을 갖는다는 것이다.

③ 두 집단의 사람들이 비슷해야 하고 감기와 관련된 동일한 기록을 가져야 하는 이유는 감기와 관련된 두 집단의 차이가 어떤 식으로든 일어났을지도 모른다는 가능성을 '배제하기' 위해서이다.

④ 원래(보통) 통제 집단이 실험집단보다 감기에 두 배 더 걸린다면 비타민 C 보충제를 받지 않은 통제 집단이 감기에 더 많이 걸린다는 연구 결과는 '아무것도' 입증하지 못하는 것이다.

Generalization promotes cognitive economy, / so that we don't
_{등위접속사(결과)}
focus on particulars / that don't matter. //
일반화는 인지 경제성을 촉진하여 / 우리는 세부 사항에 집중하지 않는다 / 중요하지 않은 /

The great Russian neuropsychologist Alexander Luria / studied
a patient, Solomon Shereshevsky, / with a memory impairment
_{주격 관계대명사}　_{전치사}　_{명사절}
/ that was the (a) opposite / of what we usually hear about /
러시아의 위대한 신경심리학자인 Alexander Luria는 / Solomon Shereshevsky라는
환자를 연구했다 / 기억 장애를 가진 / 반대인 / 우리가 일반적으로 듣는 것의 /

— Solomon didn't have amnesia, the loss of memories; / he had
_{동사 had의 목적어절}
/ what Luria called hypermnesia /
Solomon은 기억상실증, 기억을 잃는 것을 가진 것이 아니다 / 그는 가지고 있었다 / Luria
가 기억과잉증이라고 부른 것을 /
_{생략 가능한 명사절 접속사}
(we might say / that his superpower was superior memory). //
(우리는 말할 수 있다 / 그의 엄청난 힘이 우월한 기억력이었다고) //
_{주어　　　　　　　　동사　　목적어　　목적격 보어}
His supercharged memory / allowed him to perform amazing
feats, /
_{to perform의 목적어}
그의 과한 기억력은 / 그가 놀라운 재주를 수행하게 했다 /
_{선행사}
such as repeating speeches / word for word / that he had heard
_{목적격 관계대명사}
only once, / or complex mathematical formulas, / long sequences
_{선행사(목적격 관계대명사는 생략됨)}
of numbers, / and poems in foreign languages / he didn't even
speak. //
연설을 반복하는 것과 같은 / 한 마디 한 마디 / 그가 단 한 번 들었던 / 또는 복잡한 수학
공식을 / 숫자의 긴 배열을 / 그리고 외국어로 된 시를 / 그가 심지어 말할 줄도 모르는 //
_{동명사구 주어}
Before you think / that having such a fantastic memory / would
be great, / it came with a (b) cost: / _{21번 단서 1: 환상적인 기억력을 갖는 것은}
_{대가를 수반했음}
여러분이 생각하기 전에 / 그러한 환상적인 기억력을 갖는 것이 / 좋을 것이라고 / 그것은
대가를 수반했다 /

Solomon wasn't able to form abstractions / because he
remembered every detail / as distinct. //
Solomon은 추상화를 할 수 없었다 / 그가 모든 세부 사항을 기억했기 때문에 / 별개의
것으로 //
_{21번 단서 2: 대가: 사람들을 알아보는 데 특별한 어려움을 겪는 것}
He had particular trouble / identifying people. //
그는 특별한 어려움을 겪었다 / 사람들을 알아보는 데 //
_{앞에 관계부사가 생략됨}
From a neurocognitive standpoint, / every time you see a face, /
it is (c) unlikely(→ likely) / that it looks at least slightly different
/ from the last time /
신경인지적 관점에서 볼 때 / 여러분이 어떤 얼굴을 볼 때마다 / ~할 가능성이 없다
(→ 가능성이 있다) / 그것이 적어도 약간 다르게 보일 / 지난번과는 /

— you're viewing it / at a different angle and distance /
than before, / and you might be encountering / a different
expression. // _{22번 단서: 이전과는 다른 각도와 거리에서 보고 있고,}
_{(이전과는) 다른 표정을 마주치고 있을 수 있다는 내용이 이어짐}
여러분은 그것을 보고 있다 / 다른 각도와 거리에서 / 이전과는 / 그리고 여러분은 마주치고
있을지도 모른다 / 다른 표정을 //
_{부사절 접속사(때)}
While you're interacting with a person, / their face goes through
a parade of expressions. //
여러분이 어떤 사람과 상호 작용하는 동안 / 그들의 얼굴은 일련의 표정을 겪는다 //

Because your brain can (d) generalize, / you see / all of these
different manifestations of the face / as belonging to the same
person. //
여러분의 뇌가 일반화할 수 있기 때문에 / 여러분은 본다 / 얼굴의 이러한 모든 다른 표현들을
/ 같은 사람에게 속한 것으로 //

Solomon couldn't do that. // Solomon은 그렇게 할 수 없었다 //
_{동명사구 주어}
As he explained to Luria, / (e) recognizing his friends and
_{단수 동사}
colleagues / was nearly impossible / because "everyone has so
many faces." //
그가 Luria에게 설명했듯이 / 그의 친구들과 동료들을 알아보는 것은 / 거의 불가능했다 /
"모든 사람들이 너무 많은 얼굴을 가지고 있기" 때문에 //

- generalization ⓝ 일반화　　· promote ⓥ 촉진하다
- amnesia ⓝ 기억상실증　　· supercharged ⓐ 과급된, 과한
- perform ⓥ 수행하다　　· feat ⓝ 솜씨, 재주
- mathematical ⓐ 수학의　　· complex ⓐ 복잡한
- formula ⓝ 공식　　· sequence ⓝ 배열　　· abstraction ⓝ 추상화
- distinct ⓐ 별개의　　· identify ⓥ 알아보다
- neurocognitive ⓐ 신경인지적인　　· standpoint ⓝ 관점
- angle ⓝ 각도　　· interact ⓥ 상호작용하다
- manifestation ⓝ 징후, 표명　　· belong to ~에 속하다

일반화는 인지 경제성을 촉진하여, 우리는 중요하지 않은 세부 사항에 집중하지
않는다. 러시아의 위대한 신경심리학자인 Alexander Luria는 Solomon
Shereshevsky라는 환자를 연구했는데, 그는 우리가 일반적으로 듣는 것의
(a) 반대인 기억 장애를 가지고 있었다. 즉 Solomon은 기억상실증, 기억을
잃는 것을 가진 것이 아니다. Luria가 기억과잉증이라고 부른 것을 가지고
있었다(우리는 그의 엄청난 힘이 우월한 기억력이었다고 말할 수 있다). 그의
과한 기억력은 그가 단 한 번 들었던 연설의 한 마디, 한 마디, 또는 복잡한
수학 공식, 숫자의 긴 배열, 그리고 그가 심지어 말할 줄도 모르는 외국어로 된
시를 반복하는 것과 같이, 놀라운 재주를 수행할 수 있게 해주었다. 여러분이
그러한 환상적인 기억력을 갖는 것이 좋을 것이라고 생각하기 전에, 그것은
(b) 대가를 수반했다. Solomon은 모든 세부 사항을 별개의 것으로 기억했기
때문에 추상화를 할 수 없었다. 그는 사람들을 알아보는 데 특별한 어려움을
겪었다. 신경인지적 관점에서 볼 때, 여러분이 어떤 얼굴을 볼 때마다,
지난번과는 적어도 약간 다르게 보일 (c) 가능성이 없다(→ 가능성이 있다).
즉 여러분은 이전과는 다른 각도와 거리에서 그것을 보고 있으며, 여러분은
다른 표정을 마주치고 있을지도 모른다. 여러분이 어떤 사람과 상호 작용하는
동안, 그들의 얼굴에 일련의 표정이 지나간다. 여러분의 뇌가 (d) 일반화할 수
있기 때문에, 여러분은 얼굴의 이러한 모든 다른 표현들을 같은 사람에게 속한
것으로 본다. Solomon은 그렇게 할 수 없었다. 그가 Luria에게 설명했듯이,
그의 친구들과 동료들을 (e) 알아보는 것은 "모든 사람들이 너무 많은 얼굴을
가지고 있기" 때문에 거의 불가능했다.

P 21 정답 ④

윗글의 제목으로 가장 적절한 것은?
① Face Recognition Technologies: Blessing or Not?
　얼굴 인식 기술: 축복인가 아닌가?　　　　　　얼굴 인식 '기술'에 대한 내용이 아님
② The Faster You Memorize, the Faster You Forget
　당신이 더 빨리 기억할수록, 당신은 더 빨리 잊는다　　　기억의 속도에 대한 언급은 없음
③ Generalization Can Be Both a Shortcut and a Trap!
　일반화는 지름길일 수도 있고 함정일 수도 있다!　　　일반화에 대한 설명이 아님
④ The Flaw in Cognition Caused by Flawless Memory
　결함 없는 기억력으로 야기된 인지에서의 결함　　기억과잉증 환자가 얼굴을 알아보지 못함
⑤ Why It Gets Difficult to Remember Details As You Age
　당신이 나이 들수록 세부 사항을 기억하는 게 어려워지는 이유　　노화와 관련된 내용이 아님

> **왜** 정답 ? [정답률 54%]

- Solomon은 우월한 기억력을 가졌다. 그는 한 번 들은 연설과 그가 말할 줄도
  모르는 외국어로 된 시를 반복하는 것과 같은 놀라운 재주가 있었다.
- 이러한 그의 환상적인 기억력은 대가를 수반했다. 그는 사람들을 알아보는
  데 특별한 어려움을 겪었다. 그는 자신의 친구와 동료를 알아보는 것이 거의
  불가능했다.

➡ 우월한 기억력 때문에 사람을 알아보지 못했다는 것이므로 제목으로 ④ '결함 없는
기억력으로 야기된 인지에서의 결함'이 적절하다.

> **왜** 오답 ?

① 얼굴을 인식하는 기술의 장단점을 설명한 글이 아니다.
② 기억의 속도가 망각의 속도와 관련이 있다는 것이 아니다.
③ 일반화를 하지 못해서 얼굴을 알아보지 못한다고 했다.
⑤ 노화와 기억력의 관계에 대한 글이 아니다.

P 22 정답 ③

밑줄 친 (a)~(e) 중에서 문맥상 낱말의 쓰임이 적절하지 <u>않은</u> 것은? [3점]

① (a) 기억상실증과 반대인 기억과잉증
　　정반대
② (b) 추상화를 할 수 없었음
　　대가
③ (c) 이전과는 다른 각도와 거리에서 보고 있음
　　~할 가능성이 없는
④ (d) 다른 표현을 일반화하기 때문에 같은
　　일반화하다 사람에게 속한 것으로 봄
⑤ (e) Solomon은 그렇게 할 수 없었음
　　알아보다

왜 정답? [정답률 70%]

③ (c) unlikely ~할 가능성이 없는

> 여러분이 어떤 얼굴을 볼 때마다, 지난번과는 적어도 약간 다르게 보일 (c) ~~가능성이 없다~~. 여러분은 이전과는 다른 각도와 거리에서 그것을 보고 있으며, 여러분은 다른 표정을 마주치고 있을지도 모른다.
> ※ (c 밑) 가능성이 있다

→ 이전과는 다른 각도와 거리에서 어떤 얼굴을 보고 있으며, 다른 표정을 마주치고 있을 수 있다. 즉, 그 어떤 얼굴이 지난번과는 적어도 약간은 다르게 보일 '가능성이 있는' 것이다.
　▶ unlikely를 반의어인 likely(가능성이 있는)로 바꿔야 함

왜 오답?

① (a) opposite 정반대

> Solomon은 우리가 일반적으로 듣는 것의 (a) 반대인 기억 장애를 가지고 있었다. 그는 기억을 잃는 기억상실증을 가진 것이 아니라, Luria가 기억과잉증이라고 부른 것을 가지고 있었다. 우리는 그의 엄청난 힘이 우월한 기억력이었다고 말할 수 있다.

→ 우리가 일반적으로 듣는 것: 기억을 잃는 기억상실증
Solomon이 가진 것: 기억과잉증, 우월한 기억력
Solomon은 우리가 일반적으로 듣는 것과 '반대'인 기억 장애를 앓았다.
　▶ opposite은 문맥에 맞음

② (b) cost 대가

> 그것은 (b) 대가를 수반했다. Solomon은 모든 세부 사항을 별개의 것으로 기억했기 때문에 추상화를 할 수 없었다.

→ 기억과잉증으로 인해 Solomon은 추상화를 할 수 없었다. 우월한 기억력을 가져온 기억과잉증의 '대가'로 그는 추상화를 할 수 없었다.
　▶ cost는 문맥에 맞음

④ (d) generalize 일반화하다

> 여러분의 뇌가 (d) 일반화할 수 있기 때문에, 여러분은 얼굴의 이러한 모든 다른 표현들을 같은 사람에게 속한 것으로 본다.

→ 얼굴의 모든 다른 표현을 같은 사람에게 속한 것으로 보는 이유는 그 모든 다른 표현을 '일반화할 수 있기' 때문이다.
　▶ generalize는 문맥에 맞음

⑤ (e) recognizing 알아보다

> 그는 사람들을 알아보는 데 특별한 어려움을 겪었다. 그가 Luria에게 설명했듯이, 그의 친구들과 동료들을 (e) 알아보는 것은 "모든 사람들이 너무 많은 얼굴을 가지고 있기" 때문에 거의 불가능했다.

→ 앞에서 Solomon이 사람들을 알아보는 데 특별한 어려움을 겪었다고 한 후 그 이유를 설명했다. 그 후에 다시 한번 Solomon은 친구와 동료를 '알아보는 것'이 불가능했다고 이야기했다.
　▶ recognizing은 문맥에 맞음

P 23~24 ＊livewired와 hardwired

부사절 접속사(양보)
Although we humans are equipped / with reflexive responses / for survival, / at birth / we are (a) helpless. //
비록 우리 인간이 갖추고 있을지라도 / 반사 반응을 / 생존을 위해 / 태어날 때 / 우리는 무력하다 //

병렬 구조(spend의 목적어)
We spend about a year / unable to walk, / about two more / before we can articulate full thoughts, /
우리는 대략 1년을 보내고 / 걸을 수 없는 상태로 / 대략 2년을 더 (보내며) / 우리가 완전한 생각을 분명히 말할 수 있기까지 /

and many more years / unable to provide for ourselves. //
더 많은 시간을 (보낸다) / 우리 스스로를 부양할 수 없는 상태로 //

We are totally dependent / on those around us / for our survival. //
우리는 완전히 의존적이다 / 우리 주변의 사람들에게 / 우리의 생존을 위해 //

Now compare this / to many other mammals. //
이제 이것을 비교해 보아라 / 많은 다른 포유동물과 //

Dolphins, for instance, are born / swimming; / giraffes learn to stand / within hours; / a baby zebra can run / within forty-five minutes of birth. //
예를 들어 돌고래는 태어난다 / 헤엄치면서 / 기린은 서는 법을 배운다 / 몇 시간 내에 / 새끼 얼룩말은 달릴 수 있다 / 태어난 지 45분 내에 //

Across the animal kingdom, / our cousins are strikingly (b) independent / soon after they're born. //
전체 동물의 왕국에서 / 우리의 사촌들은 놀라울 정도로 독립적이다 / 그들이 태어난 직후 //

On the face of it, / that seems like a great advantage / for other species / — but in fact / it signifies a limitation. //
겉보기에는 / 그것이 엄청난 이점처럼 보인다 / 다른 종들에게는 / 하지만 사실 / 그것은 한계를 의미한다 //

부사절 접속사(원인)
Baby animals develop quickly / because their brains are wiring up / according to a largely preprogrammed routine. //
새끼 동물은 빠르게 성장한다 / 그것들의 뇌가 연결되어 있기 때문에 / 대부분 미리 프로그램된 루틴에 따라 //

But that (c) preparedness / trades off with flexibility. //
하지만 그러한 준비됨은 / 유연성과 서로 교환된다 //

명사절 접속사(Imagine의 목적어절)
Imagine / if some unfortunate rhinoceros found itself / on the Arctic tundra, / or on top of a mountain in the Himalayas, / or in the middle of a metropolis. //
상상해 보아라 / 만약 어떤 운 나쁜 코뿔소가 자신을 발견했다고 / 북극 툰드라에서 / 또는 히말라야 산맥의 산꼭대기에서 / 또는 대도시의 한가운데에서 //

형용사적 용법(capacity 수식)
It would have no capacity / to adapt / (which is why we don't find rhinos / in those areas). //
그것은 능력이 없을 것이다 / 적응할 / (이것이 우리가 코뿔소를 발견하지 않는 이유이다 / 그러한 지역에서) //

단수 주어　　　　　　　　　　　　　　　　단수 동사(완전자동사)
This strategy / of arriving with a pre-arranged brain / works / inside a particular niche / in the ecosystem /
이러한 전략은 / 미리 배열된 뇌와 함께 오는 / 잘 작동한다 / 특정한 적합한 장소 안에서는 / 생태계 안의 /

명령문에 이어지는 and: ~하라. 그러면 …할 것이다
— but put an animal / outside of that niche, / and its chances of thriving / are (d) low. //
하지만 어떤 동물을 두어라 / 그 적합한 장소 밖에 / 그러면 그것의 번성할 가능성은 / 낮다 //

In contrast, / humans are able to thrive / in many different environments, / from the frozen tundra / to the high mountains / to crowded urban centers. // 23번 단서 1: 인간은 다양한 환경에 적응하고 번성할 수 있음
대조적으로 / 인간은 번성할 수 있다 / 많은 다른 환경에서 / 얼어붙은 툰드라에서 / 높은 산맥까지 / 북적거리는 도시 중심지까지 //

This is possible / because the human brain is born / remarkably incomplete. // 23번 단서 2, 24번 단서 1: 인간의 뇌는 불완전한 채로 태어남
이는 가능하다 / 인간의 뇌가 태어나기 때문에 / 놀라울 정도로 불완전한 채로 //

Instead of arriving / with everything wired up / — let's call it "hardwired" — / a human brain (e) forbids(→ enables) itself / to be shaped / by the details of life experience. //
주어 / 동사 / 목적어(재귀대명사) / 목적격 보어 (to부정사의 수동태)
오는 대신에 / 모든 것이 연결된 채로 / 소위 '타고난' 채로 / 인간의 뇌는 그것 자체가 ~하는 것을 막는다(→ 가능하게 한다) / 형성되는 것을 삶의 경험의 세세한 것에 의해 //
전치사 / 명사구

This leads to long periods of helplessness / as the young brain slowly molds / to its environment. //
24번 단서 2: 인간의 뇌는 그것의 환경에 맞게 형성되어 감
이것은 오랜 기간의 무력함으로 이어진다 / 미숙한 뇌가 천천히 형성되어 가면서 / 그것의 환경에 맞게 //

It's "livewired." //
그것은 '살아가면서 연결된다' //

- be equipped with ~을 갖추고 있다
- reflexive response 반사 반응
- helpless ⓐ 무력한
- articulate ⓥ 분명히 표현하다
- dependent ⓐ 의존적인
- strikingly ⓐⓓ 눈에 띄는, 현저한
- signify ⓥ 의미하다
- limitation ⓝ 한계
- flexibility ⓝ 유연성
- unfortunate ⓐ 운이 없는
- capacity ⓝ 능력
- niche ⓝ 적합한 장소, 틈새
- thrive ⓥ 번성하다
- remarkably ⓐⓓ 놀라울 정도로
- wired up 연결된 채로
- forbid ⓥ 금지하다, 막다
- mold ⓥ 형성되다, 만들다
- evolutionary ⓐ 진화의
- tragedy ⓝ 비극

비록 우리 인간이 생존을 위해 반사 반응을 갖추고 있을지라도 태어날 때 우리는 (a) 무력하다. 우리는 대략 1년을 걸을 수 없는 상태로 보내고, 우리가 완전한 생각을 분명히 말할 수 있기까지 대략 2년을 더 보내며, 더 많은 시간을 우리 스스로를 부양할 수 없는 상태로 보낸다. 우리는 우리의 생존을 위해 우리 주변의 사람들에게 완전히 의존적이다. 이제 이것을 많은 다른 포유동물과 비교해 보아라. 예를 들어 돌고래는 헤엄치면서 태어난다. 기린은 몇 시간 내에 서는 법을 배운다. 새끼 얼룩말은 태어난 지 45분 내에 달릴 수 있다. 전체 동물의 왕국에서 우리의 사촌들은 그들이 태어난 직후 놀라울 정도로 (b) 독립적이다. 겉보기에는 그것이 다른 종들에게는 엄청난 이점처럼 보이지만 사실은 그것은 한계를 의미한다. 새끼 동물은 대부분 미리 프로그램된 루틴에 따라 그것들의 뇌가 연결되어 있기 때문에 빠르게 성장한다. 하지만 그러한 (c) 준비됨은 유연성과 서로 교환된다. 만약 어떤 운 나쁜 코뿔소가 북극 툰드라에서 또는 히말라야 산맥의 산꼭대기에서 또는 대도시의 한가운데에서 자신을 발견했다고 상상해 보아라. 그것은 적응할 능력이 없을 것이다(이것이 우리가 코뿔소를 그러한 지역에서 발견하지 않는 이유이다). 이러한 미리 배열된 뇌와 함께 오는 전략은 생태계 안의 특정한 적합한 장소 안에서는 잘 작동하지만 어떤 동물을 그 적합한 장소 밖에 두면 그것의 번성할 가능성은 (d) 낮다. 대조적으로 인간은 얼어붙은 툰드라에서 높은 산맥, 북적거리는 도시 중심지까지 많은 다른 환경에서 번성할 수 있다. 이는 인간의 뇌가 놀라울 정도로 불완전한 채로 태어나기 때문에 가능하다. 모든 것이 연결된 채로, 즉 소위 '타고난' 채로 오는 대신에 인간의 뇌는 그것 자체가 삶의 경험의 세세한 것에 의해 형성되는 것을 (e) 막는다(→ 가능하게 한다). 이것은 미숙한 뇌가 그것의 환경에 맞게 천천히 형성되어 가면서 오랜 기간의 무력함으로 이어진다. 그것은 '살아가면서 연결된다'.

P 23 정답 ②

윗글의 제목으로 가장 적절한 것은?

① Rewire Your Brain to Enhance Your Courage! 용기와 관련된 내용이 아님
당신의 용기를 북돋기 위해 당신의 뇌를 다시 배선하라!
②Born Unfinished: A Gift of Adaptability to Humans 불완전한 채로
완료되지 않은 채 태어난: 인간에게 주어진 적응성이라는 선물 태어났기 때문에 적응할 수 있음
③ Evolutionary Rivalry Between Humans and Animals
인간과 동물 사이의 진화적인 경쟁 인간과 동물의 경쟁을 다룬 것이 아님
④ How Does Human-Centered Thinking Bring Tragedy?
어떻게 인간 중심적인 사고가 비극을 야기하는가? 인간이 동물을 해친다는 것이 아님
⑤ Human Brains Develop Through Interaction with Other Species
인간의 두뇌는 다른 종과의 상호 작용을 통해 발달한다 환경과의 상호 작용을 통해 발달함

왜 정답? [정답률 72%]

인간	동물
주변 사람들에게 완전히 의존해야 하는 무력한 상태로 태어남	태어난 직후부터 헤엄치고, 서고, 달릴 수 있는 준비된 상태로 태어남
환경에 맞게 천천히 형성되어 가기 때문에 많은 다른 환경에서 적응하고 번성할 수 있음	특정한 적합한 장소 안에서는 잘 작동하지만, 그 외의 장소에서는 번성할 가능성이 낮음

➡ 인간은 불완전한 채로 태어나기 때문에 많은 다른 환경에 적응하고 번성할 수 있다는 내용이다.
▶ 따라서 제목은 ② '완료되지 않은 채 태어난: 인간에게 주어진 적응성이라는 선물'이 적절하다.

왜 오답?

① '용기'에 대해 이야기하는 글이 아니다.
③ 인간과 동물이 대조되는 것은 맞지만, 진화적으로 경쟁한다는 것은 아니다.
④ 인간 중심적인 사고가 동물에게 비극적인 영향을 미친다는 언급은 없다.
⑤ 인간의 두뇌는 환경과의 상호 작용을 통해 발달한다는 내용이다.

P 24 정답 ⑤

밑줄 친 (a)~(e) 중에서 문맥상 낱말의 쓰임이 적절하지 않은 것은?

① (a) 걷지도 못하고 말도 못하며 스스로를 무력한 부양하지도 못함
② (b) 의존적인 인간과 대조됨 독립적인
③ (c) 준비된 상태로 태어나는 동물을 설명함 준비됨
④ (d) 잘 작동하는 특정 장소 외에서 일어나는 일 낮은
⑤(e) 삶의 경험에 의해 형성되는 것임 막다

왜 정답? [정답률 57%]

⑤ (e) forbids 막다

> 인간의 뇌는 놀라울 정도로 불완전한 채로 태어난다. 인간의 뇌는 그것 자체가 삶의 경험의 세세한 것에 의해 형성되는 것을 (e) ~~막다~~. 미숙한 뇌는 그것의 환경에 맞게 천천히 형성되어 간다.
> 가능하게 한다

➡ 인간의 뇌는 놀라울 정도로 불완전한 채로 태어난 후에 환경에 맞게 천천히 형성된다는 내용이다. 이는 인간의 뇌가 그것이 겪는 경험에 의해 형성된다는 의미이다.
▶ forbids(막다)를 enables(가능하게 하다) 등으로 바꿔야 함

왜 오답?

① (a) helpless 무력한

> 태어날 때 우리는 (a) 무력하다. 우리는 대략 1년을 걸을 수 없는 상태로 보내고, 우리가 완전한 생각을 분명히 말할 수 있기까지 대략 2년을 더 보내며, 더 많은 시간을 우리 스스로를 부양할 수 없는 상태로 보낸다.

➡ 걸을 수 없고, 완전한 생각을 분명히 말할 수 없으며, 스스로를 부양할 수 없는 상태라는 부연이 이어진다.
▶ 인간은 '무력하다'는 설명은 적절하므로 helpless는 문맥에 맞음

② (b) independent 독립적인

> 예를 들어 돌고래는 헤엄치면서 태어난다. 기린은 몇 시간 내에 서는 법을 배운다. 새끼 얼룩말은 태어난 지 45분 내에 달릴 수 있다. 전체 동물의 왕국에서 우리의 사촌들은 그들이 태어난 직후 놀라울 정도로 (b) 독립적이다.

➡ 생존을 위해 주변의 사람들에게 완전히 의존해야(dependent) 하는 인간 ↔ 태어나서 얼마 지나지 않아 헤엄치고, 일어서며, 달릴 수 있는 동물
▶ dependent의 반의어인 independent는 문맥에 맞음

③ (c) preparedness 준비됨

> 하지만 그러한 (c) 준비됨은 유연성과 서로 교환된다. 만약 어떤 운 나쁜 코뿔소가 북극 툰드라에서 또는 히말라야 산맥의 산꼭대기에서 또는 대도시의 한가운데에서 자신을 발견했다고 상상해 보아라. 그것은 적응할 능력이 없을 것이다.

➡ **코뿔소에게 없는 것**: 새로운 환경에 적응하는 능력(유연성)
코뿔소에게 있는 것: 특정한 장소에서 빠르게 성장하도록 준비된 채로 태어나는 것
▶ 코뿔소에게 있는 것을 '그러한 '준비됨'이라고 표현하는 것은 적절하므로 preparedness는 문맥에 맞음

④ (d) low 낮은

> 이러한 미리 배열된 뇌와 함께 오는 전략은 생태계 안의 특정한 적합한 장소 안에서는 잘 작동하지만 어떤 동물을 그 적합한 장소 밖에 두면 그것의 번성할 가능성은 (d) 낮다.

➡ 특정한 적합한 장소에서는 잘 작동한다는 내용과 역접의 연결어 but으로 이어진다. 그 적합한 장소 밖에서는 잘 작동할 가능성, 즉 번성할 가능성은 '낮다'고 하는 것이 자연스럽다.
▶ low는 문맥에 맞음

P 25~26 ＊학교에서 배운 것을 기억하지 못하는 이유

_{단수 주어} _{앞에 관계부사가 생략됨} _{앞에 목적어절 접속사가 생략됨}
One reason / we think / we forget most of what we learned in school _{단수 동사} is that we underestimate / what we actually remember. // _{25번 단서 1: 학교에서 배운 것의 대부분을 잊어버린다고 생각하는 것은 실제로 기억하는 것을 과소평가하기 때문임}
한 가지 이유는 / 우리가 생각하는 / 우리가 학교에서 배운 것 대부분을 잊어버린다고 / 우리가 과소평가한다는 것이다 / 실제로 기억하는 것을 //

_{앞에 목적어절 접속사가 생략됨}
Other times, / we know / we remember something, / but we _{생략되지 않은 목적어절 접속사} don't recognize / that we learned it in school. //
다른 때에 / 우리는 알지만 / 우리가 어떤 것을 기억한다는 것은 / 우리는 인식하지 못한다 / 그것을 학교에서 배웠다는 것을 // _{25번 단서 2: 어떤 것을 기억한다는 것은 알지만 그것을 학교에서 배웠다는 것을 인식하지 못하는 것임}

_{동명사 주어}
Knowing / where and when you learned something / is usually _{단수 동사} called *context information*, / and context is handled / by (a) different memory processes / than memory for the content. //
아는 것은 / 여러분이 무언가를 어디에서 언제 배웠는지를 / 보통 '맥락 정보'라고 불리는데 / 맥락은 다루어진다 / 다른 기억 절차로 / 그 내용에 대한 기억과는 //

_{가주어} _{진주어}
Thus, it's quite possible / to retain content / without remembering the context. //
따라서 ~은 지극히 가능하다 / 내용을 기억해 두는 것은 / 맥락을 기억하지 않고 //

For example, / if someone mentions a movie / and you think to yourself / that you heard / it was terrible / but can't remember / _{목적어 역할을 하는 의문사절} (b) where you heard that, /
예를 들어 / 만약 누군가가 한 영화에 대해 언급하고 / 여러분은 마음속으로 생각한다면 / 여러분이 들었지만 / 그것이 끔찍하다고 / 기억할 수 없다고 / 그것을 어디에서 들었는지 /

you're recalling the content, / but you've lost the context. //
여러분은 그 내용을 기억하고 있지만 / 맥락을 잃어버린 것이다 //

_{부사적 용법(easier 수식)}
Context information is frequently (c) easier / to forget / than content, / and it's the source / of a variety of memory illusions. //
맥락 정보는 흔히 더 쉬우며 / 잊어버리기에 / 내용보다 / 그것은 근원이다 / 다양한 기억 착각의 //

For instance, / people are (d) unconvinced / by a persuasive _{부사절 접속사(조건)} argument / if it's written by someone / who is not very credible /
예를 들어 / 사람들은 확신하지 못한다 / 설득력 있는 주장에 대해 / 그것이 누군가에 의해 쓰였다면 / 별로 신뢰할 수 없는 /

(e.g., / someone with a clear financial interest / in the topic). //
(예를 들면 / 확실한 금전상의 이익을 지닌 사람 / 그 주제에 대한) //

_{주어} _{완전자동사}
But in time, / readers' attitudes, on average, change / in the direction of the persuasive argument. //
하지만 결국에 / 독자의 태도는 대체로 변화한다 / 그 설득력 있는 주장의 방향으로 //

Why? //
왜일까 //

Because readers are likely to remember / the content of the argument / but forget the source / — someone who is not credible. // _{병렬 구조(to forget의 to는 생략됨)}
독자는 기억할 가능성이 크지만 / 그 주장의 내용을 / 그 출처를 잊어버릴 가능성이 크기 때문이다 / 그 신뢰할 수 없는 사람 // _{26번 단서: 지식의 출처를 기억하는 게 어렵기 때문에 학교에서 배운 것을 대부분 잊어버리고 쉽게 결론 내리는 것임}

If remembering the source of knowledge is difficult, / you can _{가주어} see / how it would be (e) challenging(→ easy) / to conclude _{진주어} / you don't remember much from school. //
만약 지식의 출처를 기억하는 게 어렵다면 / 여러분은 알 수 있다 / ~이 어려울(→ 쉬울) 것임을 / 결론 내리는 것이 / 여러분이 학교에서 배운 것을 많이 기억하지 못한다고 //

- -

- underestimate ⓥ 과소평가하다 · recognize ⓥ 인식하다
- context ⓝ 맥락 · retain ⓥ 기억해 두다, 잊지 않다
- frequently ⓐⒹ 자주, 빈번히 · unconvinced ⓐ 확신하지 못하는
- persuasive ⓐ 설득력 있는 · argument ⓝ 주장
- credible ⓐ 신뢰할 수 있는 · financial interest 금전적 이익
- conclude ⓥ 결론을 내리다

우리가 학교에서 배운 것 대부분을 잊어버린다고 생각하는 한 가지 이유는 우리가 실제로 기억하는 것을 과소평가하기 때문이다. 다른 때에, 우리는 우리가 어떤 것을 기억한다는 것은 알지만, 우리는 그것을 학교에서 배웠다는 것을 인식하지 못한다. 여러분이 무언가를 어디에서 언제 배웠는지를 아는 것을 보통 '맥락 정보'라고 하는데, 맥락은 그 내용에 대한 기억과는 (a) 다른 기억 절차로 다루어진다. 따라서, 맥락을 기억하지 않고 내용을 기억해 두는 것은 지극히 가능하다. 예를 들어, 만약 누군가가 한 영화에 대해 언급하고 여러분은 그것이 끔찍하다고 들었지만, 그것을 (b) 어디에서 들었는지 기억할 수 없다고 마음속으로 생각한다면, 그 내용은 기억하고 있지만 맥락은 잃어버린 것이다. 맥락 정보는 흔히 내용보다 잊어버리기 (c) 더 쉬우며, 그것은 다양한 기억 착각의 근원이다. 예를 들어, 별로 신뢰할 수 없는 사람(예를 들면, 그 주제에 대한 확실한 금전상의 이익을 지닌 사람)이 쓴 설득력 있는 주장에 대해 사람들은 (d) 확신하지 못한다. 하지만 결국에 독자의 태도는 대체로 그 설득력 있는 주장의 방향으로 변화한다. 왜일까? 독자는 그 주장의 내용은 기억하겠지만 그 출처, 즉 그 신뢰할 수 없는 사람은 잊어버릴 가능성이 크기 때문이다. 만약 지식의 출처를 기억하는 게 어렵다면, 여러분이 학교에서 배운 것을 많이 기억하지 못한다고 결론 내리기가 (e) 어려울(→ 쉬울) 것임을 알 수 있다.

P 25 정답 ①

윗글의 제목으로 가장 적절한 것은? _{어디에서 배웠는지를 기억하지 못해서 하는 오해임}
①Learned Nothing in School?: How Memory Tricks You
_{학교에서 배운 것이 없는가?: 기억이 어떻게 여러분을 속이는가}
②Why We Forget Selectively: Credibility of Content _{내용의 신뢰성에 따라 선택적으로 잊어버린다는 것이 아님}
_{우리가 선택적으로 잊어버리는 이유: 내용의 신뢰성}
③The Constant Battle Between Content and Context
_{내용과 맥락 사이의 끊임없는 싸움} _{내용과 맥락이 충돌한다는 언급은 없음}
④How Students Can Learn More and Better in School
_{학생들이 학교에서 더 많이 그리고 더 잘 배울 수 있는 방법} _{기억에 관한 내용임}
⑤Shift Your Focus from Who to What for Memory Building
_{기억 형성을 위해 여러분의 초점을 누구에서 무엇으로 전환하라} _{무엇을 기억하기가 더 쉽다는 내용임}

？왜 정답 ？ [정답률 51%]

현상	학교에서 배운 대부분을 잊어버린다고 생각함
이유	어떤 것을 기억한다는 것은 알지만, 그것을 학교에서 배웠다는 것은 인식하지 못하기 때문임
부연	내용에 대한 기억과 그것을 어디에서 언제 배웠는지(맥락 정보)에 대한 기억은 다른 기억 절차로 처리됨 → 내용은 기억하지만 맥락 정보는 기억하지 못하는 것이 지극히 가능함

➡ '내용'은 기억하지만, 그것을 언제, 어디에서 배웠는지는 기억하지 못하기 때문에 학교에서 배운 것이 없다고 생각한다는 것이다.

▶ ① '학교에서 배운 것이 없는가: 기억이 어떻게 여러분을 속이는가'가 제목으로 적절함

왜 오답?

② 믿을 만한 정보는 기억하고, 믿을 만하지 못한 정보는 잊어버린다는 내용이 아니다.
③ 내용과 맥락이 충돌한다는 내용이 아니다.
④ 학교에서 배운 것을 대부분 잊어버린다고 생각하는 이유를 설명하는 글이다.
⑤ 맥락 정보는 흔히 내용보다 잊어버리기가 더 쉽다고 했다.

P 26 정답 ⑤

밑줄 친 (a)~(e) 중에서 문맥상 낱말의 쓰임이 적절하지 않은 것은?

① (a) 내용은 기억하지만 맥락은 기억하지 않는 게 다름
② (b) 맥락 정보: 무언가를 '어디에서' 배웠는지 어디에서
③ (c) 맥락 정보를 잊어버린 경우가 예시로 제시됨 더 쉬운
④ (d) '하지만' '결국' 그 설득력 있는 주장의 방향으로 변화함 확신하지 못하는
⑤ (e) 출처를 기억하는 게 어려운 경우에 일어나는 일 어려운

왜 정답? [정답률 50%]

⑤ (e) challenging 어려운

> 만약 지식의 출처를 기억하는 게 어렵다면, 여러분이 학교에서 배운 것을 많이 기억하지 못한다고 결론 내리기가 (e) 어려울 것임을 알 수 있다.
> 쉬울

➡ 지식의 출처를 기억하는 것이 어려움 → 학교에서 배웠다는 것을 기억하지 못함 → 학교에서 배운 것을 많이 기억하지 못한다고 결론 내림

▶ challenging을 반의어인 easy(쉬운)로 바꿔야 함

왜 오답?

① (a) different 다른

> 여러분이 무언가를 어디에서 언제 배웠는지를 아는 것을 보통 '맥락 정보'라고 하는데, 맥락은 그 내용에 대한 기억과는 (a) 다른 기억 절차로 다루어진다. 따라서(Thus), 맥락을 기억하지 않고 내용을 기억해 두는 것은 지극히 가능하다.

➡ 맥락은 기억하지 않고, 내용을 기억하는 것이 지극히 가능한 이유는 맥락이 그 내용을 기억하는 절차와 '다른' 기억 절차로 다루어지기 때문이다.

▶ different는 문맥에 맞음

② (b) where 어디에서

> 예를 들어, 만약 누군가가 한 영화에 대해 언급하고 여러분은 그것이 끔찍하다고 들었지만, 그것을 (b) 어디에서 들었는지 기억할 수 없다고 마음속으로 생각한다면, 그 내용은 기억하고 있지만 맥락은 잊어버린 것이다.

➡ **맥락 정보**: 무언가를 '어디에서' '언제' 배웠는지에 대한 정보
맥락을 잊어버린 상황: 영화에 대한 평가를 '어디에서' 들었는지 기억할 수 없는 것
→ 어떤 내용을 들은 '장소'를 맥락 정보라고 한다.

▶ where는 문맥에 맞음

③ (c) easier 더 쉬운

> 맥락 정보는 흔히 내용보다 잊어버리기 (c) 더 쉬우며, 그것은 다양한 기억 착각의 근원이다. 예를 들어(For example), ~ 독자는 그 주장의 내용은 기억하겠지만 그 출처, 즉 그 신뢰할 수 없는 사람은 잊어버릴 가능성이 크기 때문이다.

➡ 어떤 주장의 내용은 기억하지만, 그 주장의 출처, 즉 맥락 정보는 잊어버릴 가능성이 크다는 예시가 이어진다. 맥락 정보가 내용보다 잊어버리기에 '더 쉽다'는 것이다.

▶ easier는 문맥에 맞음

④ (d) unconvinced 확신하지 못하는

> 예를 들어, 별로 신뢰할 수 없는 사람(예를 들면, 그 주제에 대한 확실한 금전상의 이익을 지닌 사람)이 쓴 설득력 있는 주장에 대해 사람들은 (d) 확신하지 못한다. 하지만 결국에(But in time) 독자의 태도는 대체로 그 설득력 있는 주장의 방향으로 변화한다.

➡ 결국에는(But in time) 그 설득력 있는 주장의 방향으로 변화한다고 했으므로, 처음에는 그 주장에 대해 '확신하지 못하는' 것이다.

▶ unconvinced는 문맥에 맞음

P 27~28 * 슬립 베이스 방식과 그 이점

복수 주어 복수 동사
Posts / that hold up signs, street lights, and utility lines / need to be strong and durable enough / to withstand winds, storms, tsunamis, and earthquakes. //

기둥들은 / 표지판, 가로등, 송전선을 지탱하는 / 충분히 튼튼하고 내구성이 있어야 한다 / 바람, 폭풍, 쓰나미, 지진을 견디기에 // **27번** 단서 1: 기둥은 충격에 쉽게 부서져야 함   2(구)동사의 수동태는 동사만 be p.p.로 바꾸고 부사나 전치사는 그대로 씀

Every so often, / though, / these same posts are called upon / to do something crucial but fundamentally at odds / with their everyday function: / they need to break (a) easily / on impact. //

종종 / 그러나 / 이 동일한 기둥들은 요청받는다 / 중요하지만 근본적으로 상충하는 일을 하도록 / 그것들의 일상적 기능과 / 그것들은 쉽게 부서질 필요가 있다 / 충격에 //

If hit / by a fast-moving vehicle, / posts need to come apart / in just the right way / in order to reduce damage and save lives. //
부사절 접속사가 생략되지 않음

치였을 경우 / 빠르게 달리는 차량에 / 기둥이 분리되어야 한다 / 올바른 방식으로 / 피해를 줄이고 생명을 구하기 위해서 //   to부정사의 〈목적〉의 의미를 강조함   **27번** 단서 2: 생명을 구하기 위해 기둥이 올바르게 분리되어야 함

Engineers have spent a lot of time / attempting to resolve / this apparent paradox. //   spend+시간/돈+(in)+동명사: ~하는 데 시간/돈을 쓰다

엔지니어들은 많은 시간을 보내 왔다 / 해결하려고 시도하는 데 / 이 명백한 역설을 //

One of the ways / to get robust posts to break properly / is called / a "slip base" system.   to get의 목적어와 목적격 보어   단수 동사
단수 주어

방법들 중 하나는 / 튼튼한 기둥이 제대로 부서지도록 하는 / 불린다 / '슬립 베이스' 시스템이라고 //

Instead of using / a single continuous post, / a slip base approach (b) joins / two separate posts / close to ground level / using a connector plate. //

사용하는 대신 / 하나의 단일한 연속 기둥을 / 슬립 베이스 접근 방식은 결합한다 / 두 개의 분리된 기둥을 / 지면 높이에서 가까이에 / 연결 판을 사용하여 //

This joint allows the pair to break apart / at an (c) intended juncture. //
주어   동사   목적어   목적격 보어

이 연결 부위는 그 기둥 쌍이 분리되도록 한다 / 의도된 접합점에서 //   **28번** 단서 1: 하부 기둥은 땅에 박힘

It works basically like this: / a lower post is put in the ground, / then an upper post is attached to it / using breakaway bolts. //

그것은 기본적으로 다음과 같이 작동한다 / 하부 기둥은 땅에 박히고 / 상부 기둥은 그 위에 붙여진다 / 분리되는 볼트를 사용해서 //

These bolts are made / to fracture or dislodge / when the post gets hit hard enough, /

이 볼트들은 만들어진다 / 분리되거나 이탈되도록 / 기둥이 충분히 세게 부딪힐 때 /

so the upper post gets knocked over / while the lower post passes safely / under the moving vehicle. //   **28번** 단서 2: 하부 기둥은 안전하게 지나쳐짐

그래서 상부 기둥은 치여 넘어진다 / 하부 기둥은 안전하게 지나쳐지는 반면에 / 움직이는 차량 아래로 //

When everything works / as designed, / such posts can also help / slow down a vehicle / and (d) minimize damage. //
can help의 목적격 보어 ①   can help의 목적격 보어 ②

모든 것이 작동하면 / 설계된 대로 / 그러한 기둥은 또한 도움이 될 수 있다 / 차량 속도를 늦추고 / 손상을 최소화하는 데 //

주어 / 동사 / 주격 보어

Subsequent infrastructure repair / becomes easier / as well /
이후의 기반 시설 수리도 / 더 쉬워진다 / 또한 /

— in many cases, / a new upper post can simply be bolted / onto the (e) damaged(→ undamaged) base post / below it, / which requires less material and work. // **28판** 단서 3: 부서진 상부 기둥만 교체하는 것이 비용이 더 적게 듦
많은 경우 / 새 상부 기둥은 쉽게 볼트로 고정될 수 있고 / 손상된(→ 손상되지 않은) 베이스 기둥에 / 그 밑의 / 이것은 더 적은 재료와 작업을 필요로 한다 //

The critical plate-to-plate connections / underpinning slip systems / can be obvious / to the naked eye / or tucked away / under plate covers. //
중요한 판과 판의 연결부는 / 슬립 시스템의 기초가 되는 / 분명히 보일 수 있다 / 육안으로 / 또는 숨겨질 수 있다 / 판의 덮개 아래에 //

- post ⓝ 기둥, 말뚝 · hold up (쓰러지지 않도록) ~을 떠받치다
- sign ⓝ 표지판, 간판 · utility ⓝ (수도 · 가스 · 전기 등의) 공익 사업
- durable ⓐ 내구성이 있는, 오래가는 · withstand ⓥ 견뎌[이겨] 내다
- every so often 가끔, 종종 · call upon (~에게 …을) 요구하다
- crucial ⓐ 중대한, 결정적인
- fundamentally ⓐⓓ 근본[본질]적으로, 완전히
- at odds 상충하는, 조화를 이루지 못하는 · impact ⓝ 충돌, 충격
- come apart 부서지다, 흩어지다 · attempt ⓥ 시도하다, 애써 보다
- resolve ⓥ 해결하다, 다짐하다 · apparent ⓐ 분명한, 명백한
- paradox ⓝ 역설(적인 상황) · robust ⓐ 튼튼한, 강력한
- properly ⓐⓓ 제대로, 적절히 · separate ⓐ 분리된, 따로 떨어진
- plate ⓝ (금속으로 된) 판 · joint ⓝ 연결 부위, 관절
- apart ⓐⓓ 조각조각, 산산이, 따로 · basically ⓐⓓ 근본[기본]적으로
- attach ⓥ 붙이다, 첨부하다 · breakaway ⓐ 분리[이탈]한
- fracture ⓥ 파열[균열]되다 · knock over ~을 때려눕히다
- subsequent ⓐ 그[이] 다음의, 차후의
- infrastructure ⓝ 사회[공공] 기반 시설 · material ⓝ (물건의) 재료
- critical ⓐ 비판적인, 대단히 중요한 · underpin ⓥ 뒷받침하다, 보강하다
- obvious ⓐ 분명한, 확실한 · naked ⓐ 벌거벗은, 아무것도 걸치지 않은
- tuck away ~을 숨기다[(안전한 곳에) 보관하다] · ruin ⓥ 망치다
- sustainable ⓐ (환경 파괴 없이) 지속 가능한

표지판, 가로등, 송전선을 지탱하는 기둥들은 바람, 폭풍, 쓰나미, 지진을 견디기에 충분히 튼튼하고 내구성이 있어야 한다. 그러나 종종, 이 동일한 기둥들은 그것들의 일상적 기능과 근본적으로 상충하는 중요한 일을 하도록 요청받는다. 즉 그것들은 충격에 (a) 쉽게 부서질 필요가 있다. 빠르게 달리는 차량에 치였을 경우, 피해를 줄이고 생명을 구하기 위해서 기둥이 올바른 방식으로 분리되어야 한다. 엔지니어들은 이 명백한 역설을 해결하려고 시도하는 데 많은 시간을 보내 왔다. 튼튼한 기둥이 제대로 부서지도록 하는 방법들 중 하나는 '슬립 베이스' 시스템이라고 불린다. 하나의 단일한 연속 기둥을 사용하는 대신, 슬립 베이스 접근 방식은 연결 판을 사용하여 지면 높이에서 가까운 곳에 두 개의 분리된 기둥을 (b) 결합한다. 이 연결 부위는 그 기둥 쌍이 (c) 의도된 접합점에서 분리되도록 한다. 그것은 기본적으로 다음과 같이 작동한다. 하부 기둥은 땅에 박히고, 상부 기둥은 분리되는 볼트를 사용해서 그 위에 붙여진다. 기둥이 충분히 세게 부딪칠 때 이 볼트들은 분리되거나 이탈되도록 만들어지기 때문에, 하부 기둥은 움직이는 차량 아래로 안전하게 지나쳐지는 반면에 상부 기둥은 치어 넘겨진다. 모든 것이 설계된 대로 작동하면 그러한 기둥은 또한 차량 속도를 늦추고 손상을 (d) 최소화하는 데 도움이 될 수 있다. 또한 이후의 기반 시설 수리도 더 쉬워진다. 즉, 많은 경우, 새 상부 기둥은 그 밑의 (e) 손상된(→ 손상되지 않은) 베이스 기둥에 쉽게 볼트로 고정될 수 있고, 이것은 더 적은 재료와 작업을 필요로 한다. 슬립 시스템의 기초가 되는 중요한 판과 판의 연결부는 육안으로 분명히 보이거나 판의 덮개 아래에 숨겨질 수 있다.

P 27 정답 ②

윗글의 제목으로 가장 적절한 것은?

① How Street Posts Ruin the City View 기둥이 도시 경관을 망친다는 것이 아님
  거리의 기둥이 도시 경관을 망치는 방식
② Breakaway Posts Save Lives and Cost
  부서지는 기둥이 생명과 비용을 구한다   올바르게 부서지면 생명을 구하고 수리에 더 적은 비용이 듦
③ Fewer Road Signs, Fewer Traffic Accidents
  더 적은 도로 표지판, 더 적은 교통사고   도로 표지판을 줄여야 한다는 것이 아님
④ Recycled Materials Lead to Sustainable Cities
  재활용된 재료가 지속 가능한 도시로 이어진다   재료를 재활용하라는 것이 아님
⑤ Dilemma Between Safety and Cost-efficiency
  안전과 비용 효율성 사이의 딜레마   안전과 비용 효율성 둘 다 충족시킴

> **왜 정답?** [정답률 73%]

[꿀팁] 상충하는 두 요건을 this apparent paradox로 표현함

표지판, 가로등, 송전선 등을 지탱하는 기둥은 튼튼해야 하지만 동시에 충격에 쉽게 부서질 필요가 있다면서, 기둥이 차에 치였을 경우 올바른 방식으로 부서져야 생명을 구할 수 있다고 했다.
이후 기둥이 올바르게 부서지도록 고안한 슬립 베이스 시스템에 대해 설명하면서, 기둥이 올바르게 부서지면 수리에 드는 재료와 작업, 즉 비용도 더 적게 든다고 했으므로 정답은 ② '부서지는 기둥이 생명과 비용을 구한다'이다.

> **왜 오답?**

① 거리의 기둥들이 도시 경관을 해친다는 내용이 아니다.
③ 도로 표지판을 줄이는 것이 교통사고 감소에 도움이 된다는 언급은 없다.
④ less material이 언급되긴 했지만, 재료를 재활용해야 한다는 내용은 아니다.
⑤ 소개한 슬립 베이스 시스템은 안전과 비용 효율성의 두 마리 토끼를 모두 잡을 수 있는 방식이다. [주의]

P 28 정답 ⑤

밑줄 친 (a)~(e) 중에서 문맥상 낱말의 쓰임이 적절하지 않은 것은? [3점]

① (a) 튼튼해야 한다는 것과 상충하는 일임   ② (b) 연결 판을 사용하면 두 개의 분리된
  쉽게   결합하다 기둥을 결합하는 것임
③ (c) 상부 기둥은 넘어지지만 하부 기둥은   ④ (d) 손상을 최소화하기 위한 설계임
  의도된 안전하게 지나쳐질 수 있는 접합점   최소화하다
⑤ (e) 하부 기둥은 땅에 박혀 있음
  손상된

> **왜 정답?** [정답률 55%]

슬립 베이스 방식은 하부 기둥을 땅에 박고 그 위에 분리되는 볼트를 이용해서 상부 기둥을 붙이는데, 이렇게 함으로써 상부 기둥은 충격에 넘어지지만 하부 기둥은 안전하게 차량 아래로 지나쳐진다.
이후의 수리가 더 쉽다는 것 역시 넘어진 상부 기둥만 새것으로 교체하여 손상되지 않은 원래의 하부 기둥에 연결하면 되기 때문으로, 베이스 기둥을 설명하는 ⑤은 damaged가 아니라 '손상되지 않은'을 의미하는 반의어 undamaged로 바꿔야 한다.

> **왜 오답?**

① 충분히 튼튼하고 내구성이 있어야 한다는 것과 근본적으로 상충하는 일이므로 '쉽게' 부서져야 한다는 것은 자연스럽다.
② 연결 판을 이용한다는 것으로 보아 하나의 단일한 연속 기둥을 사용하는 대신 두 개의 분리된 기둥을 '결합한다'는 것은 문맥에 맞다.
③ 상부 기둥은 넘어지지만 하부 기둥은 안전하게 지나쳐질 수 있는 지점을 찾아 그곳에서 두 기둥을 연결하는 것이므로 '의도된' 접합점이라는 표현은 적절하다.
④ 손상을 최소화하도록 설계된 방식이므로 모든 것이 설계된 대로 작동한다면 손상을 '최소화하는' 데 도움이 될 것이다.

✱ 내진구조

큰 지진이 발생했을 때 건물이 피해를 입지 않도록 고려한 건축구조를 말한다. 목조, 철근, 콘크리트 등은 서로 다른 구조체로 이루어져 있으므로 그 특성에 맞는 내진설계를 해야 하는데, 지진의 힘을 각 구조부재에 어떻게 분담시키는가가 중요하다.

건물 내부 가로축을 튼튼하게 만들어 건축물을 강화하거나, 제진 장치를 이용한 구조물을 제작해 부착하거나, 지반과 건물을 분리하여 땅의 흔들림을 감소시키는 등의 설계를 할 수 있다. 우리나라의 건축법 시행령 제10조 1항에서 "건축물은 자중(自重)·적재하중·적석·풍압·토압·수압·지진 기타 진동 및 충격에 대하여 안전한 구조를 가져야 한다."라고 포괄적으로 규정되어 있을 뿐, 별도의 내진구조에 관한 규정은 없으므로 적절한 내진 대책이 필요하다.

P 29~30 ✱텍스트 이해에 있어 문맥의 중요성

To the extent / that sufficient context has been provided, / the reader can come / to a well-crafted text /
경우에 / 충분한 문맥이 제공된 / 독자는 다가올 수 있다 / 잘 만들어진 텍스트에 /

with no expert knowledge / and come away with a good approximation / of what has been intended / by the author. //
전문적 지식 없이도 / 그리고 아주 근접한 것을 가지고 떠날 수 있다 / 의도된 것과 / 작가에 의해 //
29번 단서 1: 충분한 문맥이 제공되면 텍스트를 잘 이해할 수 있음
30번① 전문적인 지식 없이도 작가의 의도에 매우 근접할 수 있음

The text has become a public document / and the reader can read it / with a (a) minimum of effort and struggle; /
텍스트는 공문서와 같은 것이 되어서 / 독자는 그것을 읽을 수 있다 / 최소한의 노력과 분투로 /

his experience comes close / to what Freud has described / as the deployment of "evenly-hovering attention." //
전치사 명사절을 이끄는 관계대명사
그의 경험이 가까워진다 / 프로이트가 설명한 것에 / '고르게 주의를 기울이는 것'의 (전략적인) 배치로 //
30번② 스스로를 작가의 손에 맡긴다는 것과 and로 이어짐

He puts himself in the author's hands / (some have had this experience / with great novelists / such as Dickens or Tolstoy) / and he (b) follows / where the author leads. //
의문사가 이끄는 follows의 목적어절
그는 작가의 손에 자신을 맡기고 / (어떤 사람들이 이런 경험을 가졌다 / 위대한 소설가와 / 디킨스나 톨스토이와 같은) / 그는 따라간다 / 작가가 이끄는 곳으로 //

The real world has vanished / and the fictive world has taken its place. //
현실 세계는 사라지고 / 허구의 세계가 그것의 자리를 차지했다 //

Now consider / the other extreme. //
30번③ 앞에 제시된 것과 정반대의 경우를 설명함
이제 생각해 보자 / 다른 극단을 //
선행사 관계부사 where로 바꾸어 쓸 수 있음

When we come to a badly crafted text / in which context and content are not happily joined, /
29번 단서 2: 문맥과 내용이 적절하게 결합되지 않으면 텍스트를 이해하기 어려움
우리가 제대로 만들어지지 않은 텍스트를 맞닥뜨리면 / 문맥과 내용이 적절하게 결합되지 않은 /

we must struggle to understand, / and our sense / of what the author intended / probably bears (c) close(→ little) correspondence / to his original intention. //
동사
우리는 이해하려고 애써야 하고 / 우리의 이해는 / 작가가 의도한 바에 대한 / 아마도 밀접한 (→ 거의 없는) 관련성을 지닐 것이다 / 그의 본래 의도와 //
주어 동사 간접목적어 직접목적어

An out-of-date translation / will give us this experience; /
시대에 뒤떨어진 번역은 / 우리에게 이런 경험을 줄 것이다 //

as we read, / we must bring the language up to date, / and understanding comes only / at the price of a fairly intense struggle / with the text. //
동명사 주어는 단수로 취급함
우리가 읽을 때 / 우리는 언어를 최신의 것으로 해야 하고 / 이해는 오직 온다 / 꽤 격렬한 분투의 대가로만 / 텍스트와의 //

30번④ '시대에 뒤떨어진 번역'과 같은 맥락으로 사용됨
Badly presented content / with no frame of reference / can provide (d) the same experience; / we see the words / but have no sense / of how they are to be taken. //
잘못 제시된 내용도 / 참조의 틀이 없는 / 같은 경험을 제공할 수 있다 / 우리는 단어를 보지만 / 이해하지 못한다 / 그것들이 어떻게 받아들여져야 하는지를 //
동사(has assumed)

The author / who fails to provide the context / has (e) mistakenly assumed / that his picture of the world is shared / by all his readers /
주어(선행사) 주격 관계대명사
30번⑤ 잘못된 가정임
작가는 / 문맥을 제공하지 못한 / 잘못 가정하고 / 세상에 대한 자신의 그림이 공유된다고 / 그의 모든 독자들에 의해 / has assumed와 병렬 구조
동명사구 주어

and fails to realize / that supplying the right frame of reference / is a critical part / of the task of writing. //
단수 동사 주격 보어
29번 단서 3: 적절한 문맥을 제공하는 것이 글쓰기의 중대한 부분임
깨닫지 못한다 / 적절한 참조의 틀을 제공하는 것이 / 중대한 부분임을 / 글을 쓰는 일의 //

- to the extent that ~한 경우에, ~하는 한
- sufficient ⓐ 충분한
- context ⓝ 맥락, 전후 사정, 문맥
- come away with ~을 가지고 떠나다
- approximation ⓝ 근접한 것, 비슷한 것
- struggle ⓝ 투쟁, 분투 ⓥ 투쟁[고투]하다
- vanish ⓥ 사라지다
- fictive ⓐ 허구의
- extreme ⓝ 극단
- happily ⓐⓓ 적절하게
- correspondence ⓝ 관련성
- original ⓐ 원래의
- out-of-date 시대에 뒤떨어진, 구식의
- translation ⓝ 번역
- up to date 최신의
- at the price of ~을 대가로[희생하여]
- fairly ⓐⓓ 꽤, 상당히
- intense ⓐ 격렬한, 강렬한
- reference ⓝ 참조
- mistakenly ⓐⓓ 잘못(하여)
- critical ⓐ 중대한
- lighthouse ⓝ 등대
- narrow ⓐ 좁은
- outlook ⓝ 관점, 세계관

충분한 문맥이 제공된 경우, 독자는 전문적 지식 없이도 잘 만들어진 텍스트에 다가와 작가가 의도한 바와 아주 근접한 것을 가지고 떠날 수 있다. 텍스트는 공문서와 같은 것이 되어서 독자는 (a) 최소한의 노력과 분투로 그것을 읽을 수 있는데, 그의 경험이 프로이트가 '고르게 주의를 기울이는 것'의 (전략적인) 배치로 설명한 것과 가까워진다. 그는 작가의 손에 자신을 맡기고(어떤 사람들이 디킨스나 톨스토이와 같은 위대한 소설가와 이런 경험을 가졌던 것처럼) 작가가 이끄는 곳으로 (b) 따라간다. 현실 세계는 사라지고 허구의 세계가 그것을 대신했다. 이제 다른 극단의 경우를 생각해 보자. 문맥과 내용이 적절하게 결합하지 않은, 제대로 만들어지지 않은 텍스트의 경우, 우리는 이해하려고 애써야 하고, 작가가 의도한 바에 대한 우리의 이해는 아마도 그의 본래 의도와 (c) 밀접한(→ 거의 없는) 관련성을 지닐 것이다. 시대에 뒤떨어진 번역은 우리에게 이런 경험을 줄 것인데, 우리가 읽을 때, 우리는 언어를 최신의 것으로 해야 하고 이해는 텍스트와의 꽤 격렬한 분투의 대가로만 온다. 참조의 틀이 없는 잘못 제시된 내용도 (d) 같은 경험을 제공할 수 있는데, 우리는 단어를 보지만 그것들이 어떻게 받아들여져야 하는지를 이해하지 못한다. 문맥을 제공하지 못한 작가는 세상에 대한 자신의 그림을 모든 독자가 공유한다고 (e) 잘못 가정하고, 적절한 참조의 틀을 제공하는 것이 글을 쓰는 일의 중대한 부분임을 깨닫지 못한다.

P 29 정답 ④

윗글의 제목으로 가장 적절한 것은?

① Building a Wall Between Reality and the Fictive World
현실과 허구의 세계 사이에 벽 세우기 / 현실 세계에서 허구의 세계로 이동함
② Creative Reading: Going Beyond the Writer's Intentions
창의적 독서: 작가의 의도를 넘어서는 것 / 작가의 의도를 이해하기 위한 올바른 문맥에 대한 내용임
③ Usefulness of Readers' Experiences for Effective Writing
효과적인 글쓰기를 위한 독자 경험의 유용성 / 글쓰기에 있어 독자의 경험이 유용하다는 내용이 아님
④ Context in Writing: A Lighthouse for Understanding Texts
글쓰기에서의 문맥: 텍스트 이해를 위한 등대 / 충분한 문맥이 제공되면 텍스트를 잘 이해함
⑤ Trapped in Their Own Words: The Narrow Outlook of Authors
자기 자신의 말에 갇히다: 작가들의 좁은 견해 / 작가들의 견해가 좁다는 내용이 아님

왜 정답? [정답률 57%]

충분한 문맥이 제공된 경우에는 독자가 전문적인 지식 없이도 작가의 의도와 아주 근접할 수 있다는 첫 문장의 내용과, 문맥과 내용이 적절하게 결합되지 않은 텍스트를 맞닥뜨리면 그것을 이해하기 위해 고군분투해야 한다는 내용을 통해 이 글이 텍스트의 이해에 있어서의 문맥의 중요성을 이야기하고 있음을 알 수 있다. 마지막 문장에서는 글쓰기에 있어 적절한 참조의 틀, 즉 적절한 문맥을 제공하는 것이 중대한 부분이라고 했으므로 이 글의 제목은 ④ '글쓰기에서의 문맥: 텍스트 이해를 위한 등대'가 적절하다.

'등대', '벽' 등의 비유적인 표현이 의미하는 바를 제대로 이해해야 함 ⟨꿀팁⟩

왜 오답?

① 충분한 문맥이 제공되면 독자는 자신을 작가의 손에 맡기고 현실의 세계에서 허구의 세계로 작가를 따라간다고 했다.

② 작가의 의도를 이해하는 데 있어서의 문맥의 중요성을 이야기하는 글이다.

③ 효과적인 글쓰기에 영향을 미치는 독자의 경험에 대한 글이 아니다.

⑤ 작가들의 좁은 견해가 아니라 작가들이 적절한 문맥을 제공하지 않는 것에 대해 문제를 제기하는 글이다.

P 30 정답 ③

밑줄 친 (a)~(e) 중에서 문맥상 낱말의 쓰임이 적절하지 않은 것은? [3점]

① (a) 전문적인 지식 없이도 텍스트를 이해할 수 있음   최소한도 있음
② (b) 스스로를 작가의 손에 맡김   따라가다
③ (c) 앞부분과 반대의 경우를 설명함   밀접한
④ (d) '시대에 뒤떨어진 번역'과 같은   똑같은 맥락임
⑤ (e) 잘못된 가정이 이어짐   잘못하여

왜 정답? [정답률 54%]

Now consider the other extreme.(이제 다른 극단을 생각해 보자.) 이후로 앞부분과 반대되는 내용이 제시되는데, 충분한 문맥이 제공되면 독자는 전문적 지식 없이도 작가가 의도한 것을 이해할 수 있다는 것이 앞부분의 내용이다. 그렇다면, 문맥과 내용이 적절하게 결합되지 않은, 제대로 만들어지지 않은 텍스트를 맞닥뜨리면 독자는 텍스트를 이해하기 위해 분투해야 할 것이고, 작가의 의도를 제대로 이해하지 못할 것이므로 ③ '밀접한'은 반의어인 little(거의 없는) 등의 어휘로 바꾸어야 한다.

왜 오답?

① 전문적 지식 없이도 텍스트를 이해할 수 있다는 것은 큰 노력 없이, 최소한의 노력으로 이해할 수 있다는 의미이다.

② 스스로를 작가의 손에 맡긴다고 했으므로 작가가 이끄는 곳으로 따라간다는 것은 적절하다.

④ '시대에 뒤떨어진 번역'과 '참조의 틀 없이 잘못 제시된 내용'은 둘 다 문맥이 잘못된 텍스트를 의미하므로 두 가지가 같은 경험을 제공한다는 것은 적절하다. [주의]

⑤ 충분한 문맥을 제공하지 않고 세상에 대한 자신의 그림이 모든 독자들에 의해 공유될 것이라는 가정은 잘못된 것이므로 mistakenly(잘못하여)는 적절하다.

P 31~32 * '자연에 대한 지배'라는 표현의 변화

The domination of nature / is a familiar trope / in environmental ethics and environmental political theory. //
자연에 대한 지배는 / 익숙한 수사적 표현이다 / 환경 윤리와 환경 정치 이론에서 //

Its history is tied more broadly / to the rise of modern science, philosophy, and politics. //
그것의 역사는 더 광범위하게 결부되어 있다 / 근대 과학, 철학, 정치학의 등장과 //

주어 / 형용사적 용법(The effort 수식) / 선행사 / 주격 관계대명사
The effort / to understand the causal relations / that govern the physical world / so as to intervene in these relations /
so as to-v: ~하기 위해
노력은 / 인과 관계를 이해하고자 하는 / 물리적 세계를 지배하는 / 이러한 관계에 개입하기 위해 /

선행사 / 주격 관계대명사
in ways / that could, as Francis Bacon put it, "ameliorate the human condition," / marked the beginning of modernity / in the West. //
동사
방법으로 / Francis Bacon이 말한 것처럼 '인간의 조건을 개선할' 수 있는 / 근대성의 시작을 알렸다 / 서구에서 //

[32번] 단서 1: '자연에 대한 지배'가 명백히 좋은 것으로 여겨졌음
For a long time, / the "domination of nature" referred to this effort / to understand and (a) control the nonhuman environment, /
형용사적 용법(effort 수식)
and it was seen / as a clearly good thing. //
오랫동안 / '자연에 대한 지배'는 이러한 노력을 가리켰고 / 인간 이외의 환경을 이해하고 통제하려는 / 그것은 여겨졌다 / 명백히 좋은 것으로 //

목적격 보어
This effort made (b) possible / new technologies and rising economic prosperity, / promised an end / to many forms of human suffering, / and demonstrated the triumph of reason / over ignorance and superstition. //
주어 / 동사① / 목적어 / 동사② / 동사③
이러한 노력은 가능하게 했고 / 새로운 기술과 증가하는 경제적 번영을 / 종식을 약속했으며 / 여러 형태의 인간 고통의 / 이성의 승리를 보여 주었다 / 무지와 미신에 대한 //

Its costs began to be (c) invisible(→ visible) / with industrialization / in the nineteenth century, /
그것의 대가는 보이지 않기(→ 보이기) 시작했는데 / 산업화와 함께 / 19세기에 /

[31번] 단서: '명백한' 환경 파괴를 야기했다는 것은 그것(자연에 대한 지배)의 대가가 보였다는 것을 의미함
which generated obvious environmental damage / and caused /
계속적 용법의 주격 관계대명사
among many people / a sense of alienation / from the land / and the more-than-human communities / composing it. //
그것은 명백한 환경 파괴를 야기했고 / 초래했다 / 많은 사람에게 / 소외감을 / 땅으로부터 / 그리고 인간 너머의 공동체로부터 / 그것을 구성하는 //

One sees a growing (d) unease / about these costs / in novels of the era / such as Mary Shelley's *Frankenstein* (1818), /
사람들은 불안감이 커지는 것을 본다 / 이러한 대가에 대한 / 그 시대의 소설들에서 / Mary Shelley의 *Frankenstein*(1818)과 같은 /

in poems / like Wordsworth's "Michael" (1800) and later Whitman's *Leaves of Grass* (1855), / and in the early nature writing of Thoreau's *Walden* (1854). //
시들에서 / Wordsworth의 'Michael'(1800)와 이후 Whitman의 *Leaves of Grass*(1855)와 같은 / 그리고 자연을 다룬 초기 작품인 Thoreau의 *Walden*(1854)에서 //

Yet / systematic, critical analysis / of the domination of nature / as a problem / came into its own / only with the environmental studies movement / in the 1970s. //
주어 / 동사
그러나 / 체계적이고 비판적인 분석은 / 자연에 대한 지배의 / 문제로서 / 진가를 발휘했다 / 환경 연구 운동이 등장하고서야 / 1970년대에 //

[32번] 단서 2: 1970년대 이후로 '자연에 대한 지배'라는 표현은 부정적인 의미를 갖게 됨
Since then, / the trope has come to have a broadly (e) negative meaning, / with the domination of nature being viewed / as harmful and illegitimate, / as well as dangerous to human interests. //
「with+명사+현재분사(수동태)」분사구문
그 이후로 / 그 수사적 표현은 대체로 부정적 의미를 갖게 되었다 / 자연에 대한 지배는 여겨지면서 / 해롭고 부당한 것으로 / 인간의 이익에 위험할 뿐만 아니라 //

- domination ⓝ 지배
- philosophy ⓝ 철학
- govern ⓥ 지배하다
- prosperity ⓝ 번영
- superstition ⓝ 미신
- generate ⓥ 야기하다
- compose ⓥ 구성하다
- systematic ⓐ 체계적인

- ethics ⓝ 윤리
- politics ⓝ 정치학
- intervene ⓥ 개입하다
- triumph ⓝ 승리
- industrialization ⓝ 산업화
- alienation ⓝ 소외
- unease ⓝ 불안감
- come into its own 진가를 발휘하다

- tie ⓥ 결부하다
- causal ⓐ 인과의
- mark ⓥ 알리다
- ignorance ⓝ 무지

- era ⓝ 시대

자연에 대한 지배는 환경 윤리와 환경 정치 이론에서 익숙한 수사적 표현이다. 그것의 역사는 근대 과학, 철학, 정치학의 등장과 더 광범위하게 결부되어 있다. Francis Bacon이 말한 것처럼 '인간의 조건을 개선할' 수 있는 방법으로 물리적 세계를 지배하는 인과 관계에 개입하기 위해 이러한 관계를 이해하고자 하는 노력은 서구에서 근대성의 시작을 알렸다. 오랫동안 '자연에 대한 지배'는 인간 이외의 환경을 이해하고 (a) 통제하려는 이러한 노력을 가리켰고, 그것은 명백히 좋은 것으로 여겨졌다. 이러한 노력은 새로운 기술과 증가하는 경제적 번영을 (b) 가능하게 했고, 여러 형태의 인간 고통의 종식을 약속했으며, 무지와 미신에 대한 이성의 승리를 보여 주었다. 그것의 대가는 19세기 산업화와 함께 (c) 보이지 않기(→ 보이기) 시작했는데, 그것은 명백한 환경 파괴를 야기했고 많은 사람에게 땅과 땅을 구성하는 인간 너머의 공동체로부터 소외감을 초래했다. 사람들은 Mary Shelley의 Frankenstein(1818)과 같은 그 시대의 소설들, Wordsworth의 'Michael'(1800)과 이후 Whitman의 Leaves of Grass(1855)와 같은 시들, 그리고 자연을 다룬 초기 작품인 Thoreau의 Walden(1854)에서 이러한 대가에 대한 (d) 불안감이 커지는 것을 본다. 그러나 자연에 대한 지배를 문제로 삼는 체계적이고 비판적인 분석은 1970년대

환경 연구 운동이 등장하고서야 진가를 발휘했다. 그 이후로 자연에 대한 지배는 인간의 이익에 위험할 뿐만 아니라 해롭고 부당한 것으로 여겨지면서 그 수사적 표현은 대체로 (e) 부정적 의미를 갖게 되었다.

P 31 정답 ①

윗글의 제목으로 가장 적절한 것은?

① Changing Perspectives on the Domination of Nature
자연에 대한 지배에 있어서의 변화하는 관점들　명백히 좋은 것은 부정적 의미를 갖게 됨
② Science Starts from a Desire for Knowledge
과학은 지식에 대한 욕구에서 시작된다　과학의 밑바탕을 설명한 것이 아님
③ Ethics Is Central to Every Discipline
윤리가 모든 학문의 중심이다　윤리의 중요성이 주제가 아님
④ Nature in Literature Is Not Real
문학에서의 자연은 진짜가 아니다　여러 문학 작품이 등장한 것으로 만든 오답
⑤ Is Going Green Really Green?
친환경으로 가는 것이 정말 친환경인가?　'자연에 대한 지배'라는 표현에 대한 설명임

왜 정답? [정답률 84%]

- '자연에 대한 지배'라는 익숙한 수사적 표현은 오랫동안 명백히 좋은 것으로 여겨졌음
- 19세기 산업화와 함께 그것(자연에 대한 지배)의 대가가 드러났고, 1970년대 이후로 그 수사적 표현은 대체로 부정적인 의미를 갖게 되었음

⇒ 자연에 대한 지배를 보는 관점이 달라졌다는 내용이므로 정답은 ① '자연에 대한 지배에 있어서의 변화하는 관점들'이 적절함

왜 오답?

② '자연에 대한 지배'라는 표현이 근대 과학의 등장과 결부된다는 언급으로 만든 오답이다.
③ 윤리가 모든 학문의 기초라는 내용이 아니다.
④ 소설, 시 등의 문학 작품이 언급된 것으로 만든 오답이다.
⑤ 친환경의 실체를 이야기하는 글이 아니다.

P 32 정답 ③

밑줄 친 (a)~(e) 중에서 문맥상 낱말의 쓰임이 적절하지 않은 것은?

① (a) 자연에 대한 '지배'와 일맥상통함　　② (b) 명백히 좋은 것으로 여겨졌음
통제하다　　　　　　　　　　　　　　　　가능한
③ (c) 명백한 환경 파괴를 야기했음　　　④ (d) 부정적인 영향을 설명함
보이지 않는　　　　　　　　　　　　　　불안감
⑤ (e) 해롭고 부당한 것으로 여겨짐
부정적인

왜 정답? [정답률 68%]

③ (c) invisible 보이지 않는

보이기
그것의 대가는 19세기 산업화와 함께 (c) ~~보이지 않기~~ 시작했는데, 그것은 명백한 환경 파괴를 야기했고 많은 사람에게 땅과 땅을 구성하는 인간 너머의 공동체로부터 소외감을 초래했다.

⇒ '명백한' 환경 파괴를 야기했다는 것은 그것의 대가가 보이기 시작했다는 의미이다.
▶ invisible을 반의어인 visible(보이는)로 바꿔야 함

왜 오답?

① (a) control 통제하다

오랫동안 '자연에 대한 지배'는 인간 이외의 환경을 이해하고 (a) 통제하려는 이러한 노력을 가리켰고, 그것은 명백히 좋은 것으로 여겨졌다.

⇒ '자연에 대한 지배'란 자연을 '통제한다'는 것을 의미한다. domination과 control이 일맥상통한다.
▶ control은 문맥에 맞음

② (b) possible 가능한

오랫동안 '자연에 대한 지배'는 인간 이외의 환경을 이해하고 통제하려는 이러한 노력을 가리켰고, 그것은 명백히 좋은 것으로 여겨졌다. 이러한 노력은 새로운 기술과 증가하는 경제적 번영을 (b) 가능하게 했고, 여러 형태의 인간 고통의 종식을 약속했으며, 무지와 미신에 대한 이성의 승리를 보여 주었다.

⇒ 인간 이외의 환경을 통제하려는 노력이 명백히 좋은 것으로 여겨졌던 이유는 그러한 노력이 새로운 기술과 증가하는 번영을 '가능하게' 했기 때문이다. 자연에 대한 지배의 긍정적인 면을 설명하는 문장이다.
▶ possible은 문맥에 맞음

④ (d) unease 불안감

그것은 명백한 환경 파괴를 야기했고 많은 사람에게 땅과 땅을 구성하는 인간 너머의 공동체로부터 소외감을 초래했다. 사람들은 Mary Shelley의 *Frankenstein*(1818)과 같은 그 시대의 소설들, Wordsworth의 'Michael'(1800)과 이후 Whitman의 *Leaves of Grass*(1855)와 같은 시들, 그리고 자연을 다룬 초기 작품인 Thoreau의 *Walden*(1854)에서 이러한 대가에 대한 (d) 불안감이 커지는 것을 본다.

⇒ 자연에 대한 지배가 명백한 환경 파괴를 야기하는 등의 대가를 초래한다면 사람들의 '불안감'은 커질 것이다.
▶ unease는 문맥에 맞음

⑤ (e) negative 부정적인

그 이후로 자연에 대한 지배는 인간의 이익에 위험할 뿐만 아니라 해롭고 부당한 것으로 여겨지면서 그 수사적 표현은 대체로 (e) 부정적인 의미를 갖게 되었다.

⇒ 해롭고 부당한 것으로 여겨졌다는 것은 대체로 '부정적인' 의미를 갖게 되었음을 의미한다.
▶ negative는 문맥에 맞음

자이 쌤's Follow Me! —홈페이지에서 제공

P 33~34 ＊더 이상 토지에 얽매이지 않는 물 권리

34번 (a)의 단서: 물의 이용 권리가 토지 소유와 연관되어 있었음

In many mountain regions, / rights of access to water are associated / with the possession of land /
많은 산악 지역에서 / 물을 이용할 권리가 연관되어 있다 / 토지의 소유와 /

— until recently in the Andes, for example, / land and water
전치사 until 뒤에는 명사나 부사(구)가 올 수 있음
rights were (a) combined / so water rights were transferred / with the land. //
예를 들어 최근까지 안데스 산맥에서는 / 토지와 물 권리가 결합되어 / 물 권리가 이전되었다 / 토지와 함께 //

However, / through state land reforms and the development / of additional sources of supply, / water rights have become separated / from land, / and may be sold at auction. //
그러나 / 주(州) 토지 개혁과 개발을 통해 / 추가 공급원의 / 물 권리가 분리되어 / 토지로부터 / 경매에 부쳐질 수도 있다 //　**34번** (b)의 단서: 물 권리가 경매에 부쳐질 수 있음

This therefore (b) favours those / who can pay, / rather than
선행사　주격 관계대명사
ensuring access / to all in the community. //
그러므로 이것은 사람에게 유리하다 / 비용을 지불할 수 있는 / 이용할 권리를 보장하기보다는 / 지역 사회의 모든 사람에게 //

선행사　　　　　　　　　　　　　관계부사
The situation arises, therefore, / where individuals may hold land / with no water. // **33번** 단서 1: 토지 소유와 물에 대한 권리가 분리되는 상황이 생김
따라서 상황이 생긴다 / 땅을 개인이 보유할 수도 있는 / 물이 없는 //

In Peru, / the government grants water to communities / separately from land, / and it is up to the community / to allocate it. //
_{가주어} _{진주어}

페루에서는 / 정부가 지역 사회에 물을 주고 / 토지와는 별도로 / ~은 공동체의 몫이다 / 그것을 분배하는 것은 //

Likewise in Yemen, / the traditional allocation was one measure (*tasah*) of water / to one hundred '*libnah*' of land. //

예멘에서도 마찬가지로, / 전통적인 분배는 한 단위(타사)의 물이었다 / 100 '립나'의 토지에 //

This applied / only to traditional irrigation supplies / — from runoff, wells, etc., / where a supply was (c) guaranteed. //
_{관계부사}

이것은 적용되었다 / 전통적인 관개(灌漑) 공급에만 / 유수(流水), 우물 등으로부터의 / 공급이 보장된 // 이유의 부사절 접속사 **34번** (c)의 단서: 불확실한 수원이 되는 갑작스럽게 불어난 물과 대조됨

Water / derived from the capture of flash floods / is not subject to Islamic law / as this constitutes an uncertain source, /

물은 / 갑작스럽게 불어난 물의 억류로부터 얻어진 / 이슬람 율법의 영향을 받지 않고 / 이것이 불확실한 수원(水源)이 되는 것으로 여겨지기 때문에 / 앞에 주격 관계대명사와 be동사가 생략됨

and is therefore free for those / able to collect and use it. //

따라서 사람들에게는 무료이다 / 그것을 모아서 사용할 수 있는 // **33번** 단서 2: 토지 단위에 따라 물 권리를 분배하는 것이 회피됨

However, / this traditional allocation / per unit of land / has been bypassed, / partly by the development of new supplies, /

그러나, / 이 전통적인 분배는 / 토지 단위에 따른 / 회피되었다 / 부분적으로는 새로운 공급의 개발에 의해서 /

but also by the (d) decrease(→ increase) / in cultivation of a crop / of substantial economic importance. //
34번 (e)의 단서: 경제적으로 중요함

감소(→ 증가)에 의해서도 / 작물의 재배에서의 / 경제적으로 상당히 중요한 //작물이 물을 더 많이 필요로 함

This crop is harvested / throughout the year / and thus requires more / than its fair share of water. //
34번 (d)의 단서: 일 년 내내 수확됨

이 작물은 수확되고 / 일 년 내내 / 따라서 더 많이 필요로 한다 / 그것의 적정한 몫의 물보다 //

The economic status of the crop (e) ensures / that water rights can be bought or bribed away / from subsistence crops. //
_{목적어절을 이끄는 명사절 접속사}

그 작물의 경제적 지위는 보장한다 / 물 권리가 구입되거나 매수될 수 있음을 / 생계형 작물로부터 //

- region ⓝ 지방, 지역   · be associated with ~와 관련되다
- possession ⓝ 소유   · transfer ⓥ 이전하다   · reform ⓝ 개혁
- auction ⓝ 경매   · favour ⓥ ~에 유리하다, ~에 편들다
- ensure ⓥ 반드시 ~하게[이게] 하다, 보장하다
- arise ⓥ 생기다, 발생하다   · grant ⓥ (인정하여 정식으로) 주다, 수여하다
- separately ⓐⓓ 별도로, 각기   · allocate ⓥ 분배하다, 할당하다
- measure ⓝ (치수 · 양 등을 나타내는) 단위
- runoff ⓝ (땅속으로 흡수되지 않고 흐르는) 유수(流水)   · well ⓝ 우물
- guarantee ⓥ 보장하다   · derived from ~에서 얻은
- capture ⓝ 포획, 억류   · flash flood 갑작스럽게 불어난 물
- be subject to ~의 영향을 받다
- constitute ⓥ ~이 되는 것으로 여겨지다, 구성하다
- per ⓟⓡⓔⓟ 각[매] ~에 대하여, ~당[마다]   · unit ⓝ 구성 단위
- bypass ⓥ 회피하다, 무시하다, 우회하다   · cultivation ⓝ 재배
- crop ⓝ 작물   · substantial ⓐ 상당한
- harvest ⓥ 수확하다, 거둬들이다   · fair ⓐ 타당한, 공정한
- share ⓝ (여러 사람이 나눠 가지는 것의) 몫, 지분
- status ⓝ 신분, 자격, 지위

많은 산악 지역에서, 물을 이용할 권리가 토지의 소유와 연관되어 있는데, 예를 들어, 최근까지 안데스 산맥에서는 토지와 물 권리가 (a) 결합되어 토지와 함께 물 권리가 이전되었다. 그러나 주(州) 토지 개혁과 추가 공급원의 개발을 통해 물 권리가 토지와 분리되어 경매에 부쳐질 수도 있다. 그러므로 이것은 지역 사회의 모든 사람에게 이용할 권리를 보장하기보다는, 비용을 지불할 수 있는 사람에게 (b) 유리하다. 따라서 물이 없는 땅을 개인이 보유할 수도 있는 상황이 생긴다. 페루에서는, 정부가 토지와는 별도로 지역 사회에 물을 주고, 그것을 분배하는 것은 공동체의 몫이다. 예멘에서도 마찬가지로, 전통적인 분배는 100 '립나'의 토지에 한 단위(타사)의 물이었다. 이것은 공급이 (c) 보장된 유수(流水), 우물 등의 전통적인 관개(灌漑) 공급에만 적용되었다. 갑작스럽게 불어난 물을

억류해서 얻어진 물은 불확실한 수원(水源)이 되는 것으로 여겨지기 때문에 이슬람 율법의 영향을 받지 않고, 따라서 그 물을 모아서 사용할 수 있는 사람들에게는 무료이다. 그러나 토지 단위에 따른 이 전통적인 분배는 부분적으로는 새로운 공급의 개발에 의해서뿐만 아니라, 경제적으로 상당히 중요한 작물의 재배 (d) 감소(→ 증가)에 의해서도 회피되었다. 이 작물은 일 년 내내 수확되고, 따라서 적정한 몫의 물 그 이상을 필요로 한다. 그 작물의 경제적 지위는 생계형 작물로부터 물 권리를 사거나 매수할 수 있도록 (e) 보장한다.

ⓟ 33 정답 ①

윗글의 제목으로 가장 적절한 것은?

① Water Rights No Longer Tied to Land
   더는 토지에 얽매이지 않는 물 권리   물 권리가 토지와 분리되어 경매에 부쳐질 수도 있음
② Strategies for Trading Water Rights
   물 권리 매매 전략   물 권리를 어떻게 매매하는지를 설명한 것이 아님
③ Water Storage Methods: Mountain vs. Desert
   물 저장 방법: 산 대(對) 사막   물을 어떻게 저장하는지 설명하지 않았음
④ Water Supplies Not Stable in Mountain Regions
   산악 지역에서 안정적이지 않은 물 공급   불안정한 물 공급에 대해서만 이야기한 것이 아님
⑤ Unending Debates: Which Crop We Should Grow
   끝없는 논쟁: 우리는 어떤 작물을 재배해야 하는가   어떤 작물을 재배할지에 대한 내용이 아님

왜 정답? [정답률 76%]

물 권리가 토지와 연관되어 있다는 내용의 첫 문장 이후에 토지 개혁과 추가 공급원의 개발을 통해 물 권리가 토지와 분리되었다는 내용이 However로 이어진다. 이후로 계속해서 토지와 별도로 움직이는 물 권리에 대해 이야기하고 있으므로 제목으로 ① '더는 토지에 얽매이지 않는 물 권리'가 적절하다.

왜 오답?

② 물 권리를 어떻게 매매해야 하는지 그 전략에 대해 조언한 글이 아니다.
③ 산과 사막에서 물을 어떻게 저장하는지 설명한 것이 아니다.
④ 첫 문장에 mountain regions가 언급된 것으로 만든 오답이다. _{함정}
⑤ 어떤 작물을 재배해야 하는가에 대한 논쟁을 소개한 글이 아니다.

ⓟ 34 정답 ④

밑줄 친 (a)~(e) 중에서 문맥상 낱말의 쓰임이 적절하지 않은 것은? [3점]

① (a) 물 권리가 토지의 소유와 연관됨   ② (b) 물 권리가 경매에 부쳐질 수 있음
   결합된   유리하다
③ (c) 갑자기 불어난 물과 대조됨   ④ (d) 일 년 내내 수확되는 작물을 설명함
   보장된   감소
⑤ (e) 일 년 내내 수확되는 작물이 많은 물을 필요로 함
   보장하다

왜 정답? [정답률 77%]

물 권리가 토지 소유와 분리된 이유로서 경제적으로 상당히 중요한 작물의 재배에 대해 언급했다. 이러한 작물이 일 년 내내 수확된다고 했으므로 재배의 감소가 아니라 증가라고 해야 흐름에 맞다. 따라서 ④ '감소'는 반의어인 '증가(increase)'로 바꾸어야 한다.

왜 오답?

① 첫 문장에서 말한, 물 권리가 토지 소유와 연관된다는 내용에 대한 예시이므로 combined(결합된)는 적절하다.
② 물 권리가 경매에 부쳐질 수도 있다고 했으므로 이는 비용을 지불할 수 있는 사람에게 유리한(favours) 것이다.
③ 뒤에 이어지는 '불확실한 수원이 되는 갑작스럽게 불어난 물'과 대조되는 공급으로서 제시된 것이므로 공급이 보장되었다고(guaranteed) 하는 것은 적절하다.
⑤ 경제적으로 상당히 중요한 작물이 많은 양의 물을 필요로 한다면, 이 작물의 경제적 지위가 생계형 작물로부터 물 권리를 사거나 매수할 수 있음을 보장할 (ensures) 것이다.

avoid+동명사 목적어
One way to avoid / contributing to overhyping a story / would
명사적 용법(보어)
be to say nothing. //
피하는 한 가지 방법은 / 이야기를 과대광고하는 것에 대한 기여를 / 아무 말도 하지 않는
것이다 //

주격 관계대명사(선행사: scientists)
However, that is not a realistic option / for scientists who feel
형용사적 용법(responsibility 수식)
a strong sense of responsibility / to inform the public and
to inform과 to offer 병렬 연결
policymakers / and/or to offer suggestions. //
그러나 그것은 현실적인 선택지가 아니다 / 강한 책임감을 느끼는 과학자들에게는 / 대중과
정책 입안자에게 정보를 전해야 한다는 / 그리고/또는 제안을 제공해야 한다는 //
동명사 주어(단수 취급)　　　　　　　단수 동사
Speaking with members of the media / has (a) advantages /
in getting a message out / and perhaps receiving favorable
　　　　　　　　　병렬 구조
recognition, /
언론 구성원들과의 대화는 / 장점이 있다 / 메시지를 알려지게 하고 / 아마 호의적인 인정을
받을 수 있다는 /
of의 목적어의 병렬 구조
but it runs the risk / of misinterpretations, the need for repeated
clarifications, and entanglement in never-ending controversy. //
그러나 위험을 감수한다 / 오해를 일으키고 반복적인 해명이 필요하며 끝없는 논란에 얽힐 /
whether+to부정사: ~할지 안 할지
Hence, the decision of whether to speak with the media / tends
to be highly individualized. // **35번** 단서: 과학자들이 언론과 대화할지 말지를
결정하는 것은 매우 개인적인 경향이 있음
따라서 언론과 대화할 여부는 / 아주 개인적으로 결정되는 경향이 있다 //
가주어　　　　　　　　의미상 주어　　　　진주어
Decades ago, / it was (b) unusual / for Earth scientists to have
주격 관계대명사
results / that were of interest to the media, / and consequently
거의 ~없는(부정어)　　= interesting (of+명사 = 형용사)
few media contacts were expected or encouraged. //
수십 년 전에 / 일반적이지 않았다 / 지구과학자들이 연구 결과를 발표하는 것은 / 언론의
흥미를 끄는 / 따라서 결과적으로 언론과의 접촉이 기대되거나 권장되는 것은 거의 없었다 //
a(the) few 소수의　　　　주격 관계대명사
In the 1970s, / the few scientists who spoke frequently with the
media / were often (c) criticized / by their fellow scientists / for
동명사의 완료형 (이전 시점)
having done so. //
1970년대에는 / 언론과 자주 대화하는 소수의 과학자들은 / 흔히 비난을 받았다 / 동료
과학자들로부터 / 그렇게 한 것에 대해 //

The situation now is quite different, / as many scientists feel a
responsibility to speak out / because of the importance of global
warming and related issues, /
지금은 상황이 아주 다른데 / 많은 과학자가 공개적으로 말해야 한다는 책임감을 느끼고
있으며 / 지구 온난화와 관련 문제의 중요성 때문에 /

and many reporters share these feelings. //
많은 기자도 이런 감정들을 공유하고 있기 때문이다 //
명사절 접속사
In addition, / many scientists are finding / that they (d) enjoy
/ the media attention / and the public recognition that comes
주격 관계대명사
with it. //
게다가 / 많은 과학자는 알아 가고 있다 / 자신이 즐기고 있다는 사실을 / 언론의 주목과 / 그에
따른 대중의 인정을 //

At the same time, / other scientists continue to resist speaking
with reporters, / **36번** 단서: 과학자가 언론과의 접촉을 피하는 이유는 언론 보도로 자신의
연구 결과가 잘못 인용되거나 불쾌해질 수 있는 위험을 감수하려는 것이 아니라
동시에 / 다른 과학자들은 기자들과의 대화를 계속 물리치며 / 피하려는 것임

thereby preserving more time for their science / and (e) running
분사구문의 병렬 구조
(→ avoiding) the risk / of being misquoted / and the other
unpleasantries associated with media coverage. //
그렇게 함으로써 자신의 과학을 위해 더 많은 시간을 지켜 내고 / 위험을 감수한다(→ 피한다)
/ 잘못 인용되는 / 그리고 언론 보도와 관련된 다른 불쾌한 일들의 //

- contribute to ~에 기여하다　　・ responsibility ⓝ 책임
- recognition ⓝ 인정　　・ run a risk of ~의 위험이 있다
- misinterpretation ⓝ 오해　　・ clarification ⓝ 해명
- controversy ⓝ 논란　　・ resist ⓥ 저항하다, 물리치다
- preserve ⓥ 보존하다　　・ misquote ⓥ (말이나 글을) 잘못 인용하다
- unpleasantry ⓝ 불쾌한 상황　　・ coverage ⓝ (언론의) 보도

이야기를 과대광고하는 것에 대한 기여를 피하는 한 가지 방법은 아무 말도 하지 않는 것이다. 그러나 그것은 대중과 정책 입안자에게 정보를 전하고/전하거나 제안을 제공해야 한다는 강한 책임감을 느끼는 과학자들에게는 현실적인 선택지가 아니다. 언론 구성원들과의 대화는 메시지를 알려지게 하고 아마 호의적인 인정을 받을 수 있다는 (a) 장점이 있지만, 오해를 일으키고 반복적인 해명이 필요하며 끝없는 논란에 얽힐 위험을 감수한다. 따라서 언론과 대화할지 여부는 아주 개인적으로 결정되는 경향이 있다. 수십 년 전에 지구과학자들이 언론의 흥미를 끄는 연구 결과를 발표하는 것은 (b) 일반적이지 않았고, 따라서 결과적으로 언론과의 접촉이 기대되거나 권장되는 것은 거의 없었다. 1970년대에는, 언론과 자주 대화하는 소수의 과학자들은 흔히 그렇게 한 것에 대해 동료 과학자들로부터 (c) 비난을 받았다. 지금은 상황이 아주 다른데, 많은 과학자가 지구 온난화와 관련 문제의 중요성 때문에 공개적으로 말해야 한다는 책임감을 느끼고 있으며 많은 기자도 이런 감정들을 공유하고 있기 때문이다. 게다가, 많은 과학자는 자신이 언론의 주목과 그에 따른 대중의 인정을 (d) 즐기고 있다는 사실을 알아 가고 있다. 동시에, 다른 과학자들은 기자들과의 대화를 계속 물리치며, 그렇게 함으로써 자신의 과학을 위해 더 많은 시간을 지켜 내고, 잘못 인용되거나 언론 보도와 관련된 다른 불쾌한 일들의 위험을 (e) 감수한다(→ 피한다).

P 35　정답 ②

윗글의 제목으로 가장 적절한 것은?
① The Troubling Relationship Between Scientists and the Media
　과학자와 언론 간의 문제가 있는 관계　과학자와 언론 간의 관계가 성가시거나 문제가 있다는 내용이 아님
② A Scientist's Choice: To Be Exposed to the Media or Not?
　과학자의 선택: 언론에 노출될 것인가, 말 것인가?
　　　　　　　　　　　과학자들이 언론과 접촉할 것인지에 대한 결정은 매우 개인적임
③ Scientists! Be Cautious When Talking to the Media　언론이 과학자에게
　과학자들이여! 언론에 말할 때 조심하시오　　미치는 부정적인 영향만을 다루는 글이 아님
④ The Dilemma over Scientific Truth and Media Attention
　과학적 진실과 언론의 주목에 대한 딜레마　　과학적 진실과 언론의 딜레마에 관한 내용이 아님
⑤ Who Are Responsible for Climate Issues, Scientists or the Media?
　누가 기후 문제에 책임이 있나, 과학자인가, 언론인가?　　기후 문제의 책임에 관한 내용이 아님

왜 정답? [정답률 58%]

과학자가 언론에 노출되는 것은 장단점이 있음
- **장점**: 자신의 메시지를 전달하고 인정받을 수 있음
- **단점**: 오해, 해명할 필요, 논란 등의 위험이 있음
　따라서 과학자가 언론과 접촉할지의 여부는 개인적으로 결정되는 경향이 있음
- **과거에는**: 언론과 접촉했던 소수의 과학자들이 비난을 받았음
- **오늘날에는**: 언론에서 공개적으로 자신의 의견을 말할 책임을 느끼는
　과학자들이 많음
　이와 동시에 기자들과의 대화를 물리치는 과학자도 있음

▶ ② '과학자의 선택: 언론에 노출될 것인가, 말 것인가?'가 제목으로 적절함

왜 오답?
① 과학자와 언론 간의 관계가 성가시거나 문제가 있다는 내용이 아니다.
③ 과학자들이 언론과 대화할 때 발생하는 부정적인 영향만을 다루는 글이 아니다.
④ 과학적 진실과 언론의 딜레마에 관한 내용이 아니다.
⑤ 기후 문제의 책임에 관한 내용이 아니다.

김아린 | 충남대 의예과 2024년 입학·대전한빛고 졸
난 시험장에서 글을 쭉 읽다가 Hence라는 표현을 보고 일단 표시해놓았어. 마지막까지 읽으니 글의 후반부에서도 다시 그 내용이 나오더라고. 41~42번 문제는 장문이라 조금 어려울 수 있지만, 나처럼 부사나 접속사 표현에서 힌트를 얻으면서 푸는 것도 좋을 거 같아. 또, many scientists, other scientists처럼 서로 다른 그룹을 대조하는 부분도 유심히 살펴보자!

P **36** 정답 ⑤

밑줄 친 (a)~(e) 중에서 문맥상 낱말의 쓰임이 적절하지 않은 것은?

① (a) '장점'이 있음
과학자들이 언론과 대화하는 것은 일부

② (b) 결과를 발표하는 경우는 '일반적이지 않았음'
과거에는 과학자들이 언론의 주목을 끌 만한 연구 일반적이지 않은

③ (c) 과거에 언론과 접촉했던 소수의 과학자는 자신의 행동으로 '비난을 받았음'
비난을 받았다

④ (d) 오늘날에는 과학자들이 언론의 주목과 대중의 인정을 '즐기고 있음'
즐기고 있다

⑤ (e) 오늘날 언론과의 접촉을 계속 물리치는 과학자들은 감수한다 언론 보도로 인한 불쾌한 일들을 '피하고자' 하는 것임

조수근 | 순천향대 의예과 2024년 입학·성남 태원고 졸

나는 지문을 읽기 전에 밑줄이 있는 어휘의 반의어를 미리 밑줄 아래에 써놓고 지문을 읽거든. 이 문제에서도 ⑤의 running 아래에 avoiding을 써놓고, 지문을 읽을 때 무엇이 더 적합한지 판단하는 거야. 이런 식으로 문제를 풀면 적절하지 않은 어휘를 더 명확하게 찾을 수 있고, 반의어로 대체되는 것이 더 자연스럽다는 것을 확인함으로써 내가 고른 답에 대한 확신을 얻을 수 있어.

◦왜 정답? [정답률 58%]

⑤ (e) running (위험을) 감수한다

> 동시에(at the same time) 다른 과학자들은 기자들과의 대화를 계속 물리치며, 그렇게 함으로써 자신의 과학을 위해 더 많은 시간을 지켜 내고, 잘못 인용되거나 언론 보도와 관련된 다른 불쾌한 일들의 위험을 (e) 감수한다. 피한다

➡ 오늘날에는 과학자들이 언론에서 자신의 의견을 책임감 있게 말하는 경향이 많아지고, 많은 과학자가 언론의 관심과 대중의 인정을 즐기고 있다. 동시에(at the same time) 언론과의 접촉을 계속 물리치는 과학자들도 있다. 그 이유는 과학자들이 더 많은 시간을 아낄 수 있고, 자신의 의견이 언론에 잘못 인용되는 등 불쾌한 일을 겪을 위험을 '감수하는' 것이 아니라 '피하고자' 하는 것이다. ▶ running(감수하다)의 반의어인 avoiding(피하다)으로 바꿔야 함

◦왜 오답?

① (a) advantages 장점

> 언론 구성원들과의 대화는 메시지를 알려지게 하고 아마 호의적인 인정을 받을 수 있다는 (a) 장점이 있지만, 오해를 일으키고 반복적인 해명이 필요하며 끝없는 논란에 얽힐 위험을 감수한다.

➡ 과학자들이 언론과 대화하는 것은 자신의 메시지를 대중에게 알리고 인정을 받을 수 있다는 '장점'이 있는 것이다. ▶ advantages는 문맥에 맞음

② (b) unusual 일반적이지 않은

> 수십 년 전에(Decades ago) 지구과학자들이 언론의 흥미를 끄는 연구 결과를 발표하는 것은 (b) 일반적이지 않았고, 따라서 결과적으로 언론과의 접촉이 기대되거나 권장되는 것은 거의 없었다.

➡ '수십 년 전에(Decades ago)' 과학자들이 언론의 주목을 끌 만한 연구 결과를 발표하는 경우가 '일반적이지 않아서' 언론과의 접촉이 그다지 장려되지 않았다고 하는 것은 적절하다. ▶ unusual은 문맥에 맞음

③ (c) criticized 비난을 받았다

> 1970년대에는(In the 1970s), 언론과 자주 대화하는 소수의 과학자들은 흔히 그렇게 한 것에 대해 동료 과학자들로부터 (c) 비난을 받았다.

➡ 과거에는 과학자들이 언론과 접촉하는 것이 권장되지 않았기 때문에, 언론과 접촉했던 소수의 과학자는 자신의 행동으로 비난을 받았다고 하는 것은 적절하다. ▶ criticized는 문맥에 맞음

④ (d) enjoy 즐기다

> 게다가, 많은 과학자는 자신이 언론의 주목과 그에 따른 대중의 인정을 (d) 즐기고 있다는 사실을 알아 가고 있다.

➡ 오늘날 과학자들은 언론과 접촉하여 자신의 목소리를 내야 할 책임감을 느끼고, 언론의 주목과 대중의 인정을 즐기고 있다고 하는 것은 자연스럽다. ▶ enjoy는 문맥에 맞음

P **37~38** * 개미 우화가 보여 주는 것

Our irresistible tendency / to see things / in human terms / — 주어　형용사적 용법(tendency 수식)*
that we are often mistaken / in attributing complex human motives and processing abilities / to other species — /
우리의 억누를 수 없는 경향은 / 사물을 보는 / 인간의 견지에서 / 우리가 흔히 잘못 생각하는 것 / 복잡한 인간의 동기와 처리 능력이 있다고 / 다른 종들에게 /

does not mean / that an animal's behavior is not, in fact, complex. // 동사　목적어절 접속사
의미하지 않는다 / 동물의 행동이 사실 복잡하지 않다는 것을 //

Rather, it means / that the complexity of the animal's behavior / is not purely a (a) product / of its internal complexity. // 동사　　주어
오히려 그것은 의미한다 / 동물 행동의 복잡성이 / 순전히 산물이 아니라는 것을 / 그것의 내적 복잡성의 //

Herbert Simon's "parable of the ant" / makes this point very clearly. //
Herbert Simon의 '개미 우화'는 / 이 점을 매우 분명하게 말해 준다 //

Imagine an ant / walking along a beach, / and (b) visualize / tracking the trajectory of the ant / as it moves. // Imagine의 목적어와 목적격 보어
개미 한 마리를 상상해 보라 / 해변을 따라 걷는 / 그리고 머릿속에 그려보라 / 그 개미의 이동 경로를 추적하는 것을 / 그것이 이동함에 따라 //

The trajectory would show / a lot of twists and turns, / and would be very irregular and complicated. // 병렬 구조
그 이동 경로는 보여 줄 것이고 / 많은 급커브와 회전을 / 매우 불규칙하고 복잡할 것이다 //

One could then suppose / that the ant had / equally complicated (c) internal navigational abilities, /
그렇다면 가정할 수 있다 / 그 개미가 가졌다고 / 동등하게 복잡한 내적 항행 능력을 / 병렬 구조

and work out / what these were likely to be / by analyzing the trajectory / to infer the rules and mechanisms / that could produce / such a complex navigational path. // 선행사　주격 관계대명사
그리고 알아낼 수 있다 / 이것이 무엇일 수 있는지를 / 그 이동 경로를 분석함으로써 / 규칙과 기제를 추론하기 위해 / 만들어 낼 수 있는 / 그런 복잡한 항행 경로를 //

The complexity of the trajectory, / however, / "is really a complexity / in the surface of the beach, / not a complexity in the ant." // 38번 단서: 개미의 이동 경로의 복잡성은 개미의 내적 복잡성이 아니라 해변 지면의 복잡성임
그 이동 경로의 복잡성은 / 하지만 / '실제로 복잡성이다 / 해변 지면에서의 / 그 개미 내면의 복잡성이 아니라 //

In reality, / the ant may be using / a set of very (d) complex(→ simple) rules: /
사실 / 그 개미는 사용하고 있을지도 모른다 / 일련의 매우 복잡한(→ 단순한) 규칙들을 /

it is the interaction of these rules / with the environment / that actually produces the complex trajectory, / not the ant alone. // it is ~ that 강조 구문
바로 이 규칙들의 상호 작용이 / 환경과의 / 그 복잡한 이동 경로를 실제로 만들어 낸다 / 그 개미 단독으로가 아니라 // 37번 단서: 개미의 복잡한 행동을 만들어 내는 것은 개미가 사용하고 있을지 모르는 규칙들과 환경의 상호 작용임

Put more generally, / the parable of the ant illustrates / that there is no necessary correlation /
더 일반적으로 말하자면 / 개미 우화는 보여 준다 / 필연적인 상관관계가 없다는 것을 /
between the complexity of an (e) <u>observed</u> behavior / and the complexity of the mechanism / that produces it. //
관찰된 행동의 복잡성과 / 기제의 복잡성 사이의 / 그것을 만들어 내는 //

- irresistible ⓐ 억누를[저항할] 수 없는, 거부할 수 없는
- term ⓝ 용어, 말　• attribute to ~의 덕분[탓]으로 돌리다
- complex ⓐ 복잡한　• motive ⓝ 동기, 이유
- purely ⓐd 순전히, 전적으로, 오직　• internal ⓐ 내부의, 체내의
- track ⓥ 추적하다, 뒤쫓다　• twist ⓝ (도로 · 강 등의) 굽이[급커브]
- turn ⓝ 돌기, 방향 전환, 회전　• irregular ⓐ 불규칙적인, 고르지 못한
- equally ⓐd 똑같이, 동일[동등]하게　• work out ~을 알아내다[해결하다]
- infer ⓥ 추론하다, 암시하다　• path ⓝ 길, 방향
- put ⓥ 표현[말]하다, (말 · 글로) 옮기다　• illustrate ⓥ 분명히 보여주다
- correlation ⓝ 연관성, 상관관계

인간의 견지에서 사물을 보는 우리의 억누를 수 없는 경향, 즉 다른 종들에게 복잡한 인간의 동기와 처리 능력이 있다고 우리가 흔히 잘못 생각하는 것은 동물의 행동이 사실 복잡하지 않다는 것을 의미하는 것은 아니다. 오히려 그것은 동물 행동의 복잡성이 순전히 그것의 내적 복잡성의 (a) 산물이 아니라는 의미이다. Herbert Simon의 '개미 우화'는 이 점을 매우 분명하게 말해 준다. 개미 한 마리가 해변을 따라 걷는 것을 상상하고, 그 개미가 이동함에 따라 그 이동 경로를 추적하는 것을 (b) 머릿속에 그려보라. 그 이동 경로는 많은 급커브와 회전을 보여 줄 것이고, 매우 불규칙하고 복잡할 것이다. 그렇다면 그 개미에게 동등하게 복잡한 (c) 내적 항행 능력이 있다고 가정하고, 그런 복잡한 항행 경로를 만들어 낼 수 있는 규칙과 기제를 추론하기 위해 그 이동 경로를 분석함으로써 이것이 무엇일 수 있는지를 알아낼 수 있을 것이다. 하지만 그 이동 경로의 복잡성은 '실제로 해변 지면에서의 복잡성이지 그 개미의 내적 복잡성이 아니다.' 사실 그 개미는 일련의 매우 (d) 복잡한(→ 단순한) 규칙들을 사용하고 있을 지도 모르는데, 그 복잡한 이동 경로를 실제로 만들어 내는 것은 바로 이 규칙들과 환경의 상호 작용이지, 그 개미 단독으로는 아니다. 더 일반적으로 말하자면, 개미 우화는 (e) 관찰된 행동의 복잡성과 그것을 만들어 내는 기제의 복잡성 사이의 필연적인 상관관계가 없음을 보여 준다.

Ⓟ 37 정답 ③

윗글의 제목으로 가장 적절한 것은?
① Open the Mysterious Door to Environmental Complexity!
　환경의 복잡성에 이르는 신비의 문을 열래！　　　　　　동물 행동의 복잡성의 원인을 설명함
② Peaceful Coexistence of Human Beings and Animals
　인간과 동물의 평화로운 공존　　　　　　인간과 동물의 공존을 설명한 것이 아님
③ What Makes the Complexity of Animal Behavior?
　무엇이 동물 행동의 복잡성을 만드는가?　　　　질문에 대한 답을 글에서 제시함
④ Animals' Dilemma: Finding Their Way in a Human World
　동물의 딜레마: 인간 세계에서 자신의 길을 찾아가기　　동물이 겪는 딜레마에 대한 내용이 아님
⑤ Environmental Influences on Human Behavior Complexity
　인간 행동 복잡성에 미치는 환경의 영향　　　　인간 행동이 아니라 동물 행동을 설명함

왜 정답? [정답률 55%]
개미의 이동 경로가 복잡한 것은 개미의 내적 복잡성 때문이 아니라 개미가 사용하고 있을지도 모르는 규칙들과 환경의 상호 작용 때문이라는 내용으로, ③ '무엇이 동물 행동의 복잡성을 만드는가?'라는 제목에 대한 대답을 제시하는 글이다.

왜 오답?
① 해변의 지면이 복잡하기 때문에 개미의 이동 경로가 복잡하다는 언급은 있지만, 환경의 복잡성에 대해 설명하는 글이 아니다.
② 인간과 동물의 공존에 대한 내용이 아니다.
④ 인간 세계에서 동물이 딜레마를 겪는다는 것이 아니다.
⑤ 인간 행동이 아니라 동물 행동의 복잡성에 대해 설명하는 글이다.

Ⓟ 38 정답 ④

밑줄 친 (a)~(e) 중에서 문맥상 낱말의 쓰임이 적절하지 않은 것은? [3점]
① (a) 동물 행동의 복잡성이 동물의 내적 복합성으로 인한 것이 아님　산물
② (b) 이동 경로를 추적하는 상황을 머릿속에 그리다　가정함
③ (c) 내적 복잡성을 가정함　내부의
④ (d) 개미의 내적 복잡성이 아니라 복잡한 해변 지면의 복잡성임
⑤ (e) 개미의 이동 경로를 관찰함　관찰된

왜 정답? [정답률 54%]
개미가 보이는 행동의 복잡성이 개미의 내적 복잡성이 아니라 실제로는 해변 지면의 복잡성이라고 한 것으로 보아 개미가 매우 '복잡한' 규칙들을 사용할지도 모른다는 설명이 In reality(사실)로 이어지는 것은 적절하지 않다. 따라서 ④ complex(복잡한)을 그 반의어인 simple(단순한) 등의 낱말로 바꾸어야 한다.

> 앞에서 설명한 '겉으로 드러난 내용'과 다른 '실제 일어난 내용'을 뒤에서 말할 때 쓰임 🍯

왜 오답?
① 동물(개미)이 보이는 행동의 복잡성이 내적 복잡성의 산물이 아니라는 점을 설명하는 글이다.
② 개미의 이동 경로를 추적하는 상황을 가정하는 것이므로 머릿속에 그려보라고 하는 것은 적절하다.
③ 개미의 복잡한 이동 경로를 보고 개미가 내적 복잡성을 지녔다고 가정할 수 있지만 사실 그렇지 않다는 내용이다.
⑤ 머릿속으로 가정하는 상황이지만 어쨌든 개미의 행동을 관찰하는 것이므로 observed(관찰된)는 적절하다.

─── 어법 특강

＊ to부정사의 명사, 형용사, 부사적 용법
－ to부정사는 문장에 따라 명사, 형용사, 부사의 역할을 한다.

1. 명사적 용법 : '～ 하는 것'의 의미로 주어, 목적어, 보어 역할을 한다.
- He could not afford to buy a new bag.
　(그는 새 가방을 살 여유가 없었다.)
- It is wrong to fight with your brother.
　(너의 남동생과 싸우는 것은 옳지 않다.)

2. 형용사적 용법: 명사를 수식하며 '～할'이라는 의미로 해석하면 된다.
- I have a lot of homework to do today.
　(나는 오늘 해야 할 숙제가 많다.)

3. 부사적 용법: 문맥에 따라 다양한 의미를 가지는데, 보통 '～하기 위해서, ～하려고'라는 의미의 목적으로 많이 쓰인다. 그 외에 (감정의) 원인, 결과, 조건 등의 의미를 가진다.
- What can we do to save energy?
　(에너지를 절약하기 위해 우리는 무엇을 할 수 있을까?)

Ⓟ 39~40 ＊주변 사람들의 반응으로 판단하는 것 ────

Once an event is noticed, / an onlooker must decide / if it is
　부사절 접속사　　　　　　　　　　　명사절 접속사(불확실하거나 의문시되는 사실)
truly an emergency. //
일단 어떤 사건이 목격되면 / 구경하는 사람은 결정해야 한다 / 그것이 정말로 비상 상황인지 //
Emergencies are not always clearly (a) labeled / as such; /
　　　　　　　　부분 부정: 항상 ~인 것은 아님
비상 상황은 항상 명확하게 꼬리표가 붙어 있는 것은 아니다 / 그와 같은 것으로 /
"smoke" / pouring into a waiting room / may be caused by fire,
　주어
/ or it may merely indicate a leak / in a steam pipe. //
　　　　　　　　　동사
'연기'는 / 대기실로 쏟아져 들어오는 / 화재에 의해 발생될 수도 있고 / 또는 그것은 단순히 누출을 나타낼 수도 있다 / 증기 파이프의 //
Screams in the street may signal / an attack or a family quarrel. //
거리에서의 비명은 나타낼 수도 있다 / 공격이나 가족 간의 다툼을 //

A man / lying in a doorway / may be having a coronary / — or he may simply be sleeping off a drunk. //

한 남자는 / 출입구에 누워 있는 / 관상동맥증을 앓고 있을 수도 있고 / 또는 그가 그저 술을 깨려고 잠을 자고 있을 수도 있다 // **39번** 단서 1: 어떻게 반응해야 하는지 판단하기 위해 자기 주변 사람들을 살펴봄

A person / trying to interpret a situation / often looks at those around him / to see / how he should react. //
*to see*의 목적어로 쓰인 간접의문문   동사

사람은 / 어떤 상황을 해석하려고 하는 / 흔히 자기 주변 사람들을 본다 / 알기 위해 / 자신이 어떻게 반응해야 하는지 //

If everyone else is calm and indifferent, / he will tend to remain so; / if everyone else is reacting strongly, / he is likely to become alert. //

만약 다른 모든 사람이 침착하고 무관심하다면 / 그는 그런 상태를 유지하려는 경향이 있을 것이다 / 다른 모든 사람이 강하게 반응하고 있다면 / 그는 아마 경계하게 될 것이다 //

This tendency is not merely blind conformity; / ordinarily we derive much valuable information / about new situations / from how others around us behave. //
셀 수 없는 명사 information 수식 / 전치사의 목적어로 쓰인 간접의문문 **39번** 단서 2: 우리는 주변 사람들의 행동으로부터 많은 정보를 얻음

이러한 경향은 단순히 맹목적인 순응이 아니다 / 보통 우리는 많은 귀중한 정보를 얻는다 / 새로운 상황에 관한 / 우리 주변의 다른 사람들이 어떻게 행동하는지로부터 //

It's ~ who로 강조되는 주어
It's a (b) rare traveler / who, in picking a roadside restaurant, chooses / to stop at one / where no other cars appear / in the parking lot. //
동사   선행사 / 명사적 용법(*chooses*의 목적어) / 관계부사

드문 여행객이 / 길가의 식당을 고를 때 선택한다 / 식당에서 멈추기로 / 다른 차가 없는 / 주차장에 // **40번** 단서 1: 주변 사람들의 행동으로부터 귀중한 정보를 얻는다는 내용에 역접으로 연결됨

But occasionally the reactions of others provide / (c) accurate(→ false) information. //

그러나 때때로 다른 사람들의 반응은 제공한다 / 정확한(→ 틀린) 정보를 //

The studied nonchalance of patients / in a dentist's waiting room / is a poor indication / of their inner anxiety. //

연구된 환자의 무관심은 / 치과병원 대기실에서 / 형편없는 암시이다 / 그들의 내면의 불안에 대한 / **40번** 단서 2: 주변 사람들의 반응이 형편없는 암시인 예시가 이어짐

가주어
It is considered embarrassing / to "lose your cool" in public. //
진주어

~은 창피한 일로 여겨진다 / 사람들 앞에서 '냉정함을 잃는' 것은 //

In a potentially acute situation, / then, / everyone present will appear more (d) unconcerned / than he is in fact. //

잠재적으로 심각한 상황에서 / 그렇다면 / 그곳에 있는 모든 사람은 더 무관심한 것처럼 보일 것이다 / 실제로 그가 그런 것보다 //

A crowd can thus force (e) inaction / on its members / by implying, / through its passivity, / that an event is not an emergency. //
부사구가 동명사와 목적어절 사이에 삽입됨

따라서 군중은 가만히 있는 것을 강제할 수 있다 / 그것의 구성원들에게 / 넌지시 비춤으로써 / 그것의 수동성을 통해 / 사건이 비상 상황이 아님을 //

명사절 접속사
Any individual / in such a crowd / fears / that he may appear a fool / if he behaves / as though it were. //
부사절 접속사   뒤에 *an emergency*가 생략됨

누구라도 / 그런 군중 속에 있는 / 두려워한다 / 자신이 바보처럼 보일까 봐 / 자신이 행동하면 / 그 사건이 비상 상황인 것처럼 //

- onlooker ⓝ 구경꾼 • merely ⓐⓓ 그저, 단지 • leak ⓝ 누출, 누설
- quarrel ⓝ 말다툼, 불만 • alert ⓐ 경계하는, 기민한
- tendency ⓝ 경향, 성향 • blind ⓐ 눈이 먼, 맹목적인
- conformity ⓝ (규칙에) 따름 • derive ⓥ 끌어내다, 얻다
- valuable ⓐ 귀중한, 값비싼 • anxiety ⓝ 불안(감), 염려
- embarrassing ⓐ 난처한, 당혹스러운 • cool ⓝ 냉정, 침착
- potentially ⓐⓓ 잠재적으로, 어쩌면 • acute ⓐ 극심한, 예민한
- passivity ⓝ 수동성, 소극성

일단 어떤 사건이 목격되면, 구경하는 사람은 그것이 정말로 비상 상황인지 결정해야 한다. 비상 상황은 항상 명확하게 그와 같은 것으로 (a) 꼬리표가 붙어 있는 것은 아닌데, 대기실로 쏟아져 들어오는 '연기'는 화재에 의해 발생할 수도 있고 단순히 증기 파이프의 누출을 나타낼 수도 있다. 거리에서의 비명은 공격이나 가족 간의 다툼을 나타낼 수도 있다. 출입구에 누워 있는 한 남자는 관상동맥증을 앓고 있을 수도 있고 그저 술을 깨려고 잠을 자고 있을 수도 있다. 어떤 한 상황을 해석하려고 하는 사람은 자신이 어떻게 반응해야 하는지 알기 위해 흔히 자기 주변 사람들을 본다. 만약 다른 모든 사람이 침착하고 무관심하다면, 그는 그런 상태를 유지하려는 경향이 있을 것이고, 다른 모든 사람이 강하게 반응하고 있다면, 그는 아마 경계하게 될 것이다. 이러한 경향은

단순히 맹목적인 순응이 아닌데, 보통 우리는 우리 주변의 다른 사람들이 어떻게 행동하는지로부터 새로운 상황에 관한 많은 귀중한 정보를 얻는다. 길가의 식당을 고를 때 주차장에 다른 차가 없는 식당에서 멈추는 여행객은 (b) 드물다. 그러나 때때로 다른 사람들의 반응은 (c) 정확한(→ 틀린) 정보를 제공한다. 연구된 치과병원 대기실 환자의 무관심은 그들의 내면의 불안을 제대로 보여주지 않는다. 사람들 앞에서 '냉정함을 잃는' 것은 창피한 일로 여겨진다. 그렇다면, 잠재적으로 심각한 상황에서, 그곳에 있는 모든 사람은 실제보다 더 (d) 무관심한 것처럼 보일 것이다. 따라서 군중은 수동성을 통해 사건이 비상 상황이 아님을 넌지시 비춤으로써 구성원들이 (e) 가만히 있도록 강제할 수 있다. 그런 군중 속에 있는 사람은 누구라도 그 사건이 비상 상황인 것처럼 행동하면 자신이 바보처럼 보일까 봐 두려워한다.

P 39 정답 ①

윗글의 제목으로 가장 적절한 것은?

① Do We Judge Independently? The Effect of Crowds
우리는 독립적으로 판단을 하는가? 군중의 영향   주변 사람들의 반응을 보고 판단함
② Winning Strategy: How Not to Be Fooled by Others
승리 전략: 다른 사람에 속지 않는 방법   속지 않는 방법을 설명한 것이 아님
③ Do Emergencies Affect the Way of Our Thinking?
비상 상황이 우리의 사고방식에 영향을 끼치는가?   비상 상황인지 판단하는 근거에 대한 내용임
④ Stepping Towards Harmony with Your Neighbors
이웃과의 조화를 향해 발걸음을 내딛다   '주변 사람들'로 만든 오답
⑤ Ways of Helping Others in Emergent Situations
비상의 상황에서 다른 사람을 돕는 방법

⟲오 정답? [정답률 66%]

어떤 사건을 목격했을 때 그것이 정말 비상 상황인지 판단하는 데 있어 주변 사람들의 반응을 살피면서, 그러한 판단 근거가 정확한 경우도 있고 그렇지 않은 경우도 있다는 내용이다.
정확하든 아니든 판단에 있어 주변 사람들의 반응을 근거로 삼는다는 내용이므로 제목으로 ① '우리는 독립적으로 판단을 하는가? 군중의 영향'이 적절하다.

⟲오 오답?

② 마지막 문장에서 바보처럼 보일까 봐 주변 사람들과 비슷하게 행동한다고 하면서 a fool이 언급된 것으로 만든 오답이다. 함정

③, ⑤ 비상 상황인지 아닌지를 판단하는 데 있어 주변 사람들의 반응을 살핀다는 내용으로, 비상 상황이 우리의 사고방식에 영향을 미친다거나 비상 상황에서 어떻게 다른 사람을 돕는지 설명한 것이 아니다.

④ '주변 사람들'이 핵심 소재인 것으로 만든 오답이다.

P 40 정답 ③

밑줄 친 (a)~(e) 중에서 문맥상 낱말의 쓰임이 적절하지 않은 것은?

① (a) 비상 상황일 수도 있고 아닐 수도 있는 꼬리표를 붙이다   ② (b) 주변 사람들로부터 얻는 정보가 귀중한 드문 경우가 귀중함
③ (c) 주변 사람들로부터 얻는 정보가 귀중한 정확한 경우의 예시에 역접으로 연결됨   ④ (d) 사람들 앞에서 냉정을 잃는 것이 창피한 무관심한 일로 여겨지는 상황임
⑤ (e) 군중이 비상 상황이 아니라고 암시하는 상황임 행동하지 않음

⟲오 정답? [정답률 56%]

주변 사람들로부터 판단의 근거를 얻는 것이 바람직한 경우와 그렇지 않은 경우를 나누어 설명한 글이다.
주변 사람들로부터 '귀중한' 정보를 얻는 예시에 역접의 연결어로 이어졌으므로 (c)가 포함된 문장은 주변 사람들의 반응이 ③ '정확한' 정보를 제공한다는 것이 아니라 '귀중하지 않은', 즉 틀린(false) 정보를 제공한다는 등의 내용이 되어야 한다.

⟲오 오답?

① 연기, 거리에서의 비명, 출입구에 누워 있는 남자가 비상 상황임을 나타낼 수도 있고 아닐 수도 있다는 예시가 이어지는 것으로 비상 상황이 항상 명확하게 꼬리표가 붙는 것은 아니라는 표현은 적절하다.

② 다른 사람들이 이용하지 않는 음식점을 선택하는 여행객은 드물다는 예시를 들어 우리가 주변의 다른 사람들로부터 귀중한 정보를 얻는다는 앞 문장을 부연했다.

④ 사람들 앞에서 냉정함을 잃는 것이 창피한 일로 여겨지는 상황에서는 사람들이 실제보다 더 무관심한 것처럼 보일 것이다.

⑤ 주변 사람들의 반응을 보고 비상 상황인지를 판단한다고 했으므로, 군중은 일어난 일이 비상 상황이 아니라고 넌지시 암시함으로써 개인에게 어떤 행동을 하지 않도록 강제할 수 있을 것이다.

P 41~42　　　　　　　　　　　　　 ⊙ 2등급 대비

＊사생활에 대한 권리

The right to privacy may extend / only to the point / where it does not restrict / someone else's right / to freedom of expression / or right to information. //
사생활에 대한 권리는 확대될 수 있다 / 정도까지만 / 그것이 제한하지 않는 / 다른 사람의 권리를 / 표현의 자유에 대한 / 또는 정보에 대한 권리를 //

The scope of the right to privacy / is (a) similarly restricted / by the general interest / in preventing crime / or in promoting public health. //
사생활에 대한 권리의 범위는 / 비슷하게 제한된다 / 공공이익에 의해 / 범죄 예방이나 / 공중 보건 증진에서의 // 42번 단서 1: 사생활에 대한 권리의 한계를 설명한 내용에 역접으로 연결됨

However, / when we move away / from the property-based notion of a right / (where the right to privacy would protect, / for example, / images and personality), /
하지만 / 우리가 옮겨갈 때 / 속성에 기반을 둔 권리 개념에서 / (사생활에 대한 권리가 보호하는 / 예를 들어 / 이미지와 인격을) //

to modern notions / of private and family life, / we find it (b) easier(→ harder) / to establish the limits of the right. //
현대적 개념으로 / 사생활과 가족의 생활이라는 / 우리는 ～이 더 쉽다는(→ 더 어렵다는) 것을 알게 된다 / 그 권리의 한계를 설정하기가 //

This is, of course, the strength / of the notion of privacy, / in that it can adapt / to meet / changing expectations and technological advances. // 41번 단서 1, 42번 단서 2: 사생활 개념이 변화하는 기대와 기술 진보에 맞게 변한다면, 즉 진화한다면 사생활에 대한 권리의 한계를 설정하는 것이 어려울 것임
이것은 물론 강점이다 / 사생활 개념의 / 그것이 적응할 수 있다는 점에서 / 대처하기 위해 / 변화하는 기대와 기술 진보에 //

In sum, / what is privacy today? //
요컨대 / 오늘날 사생활이란 '무엇'인가 //

The concept includes a claim / that we should be unobserved, / and that certain information and images / about us / should not be (c) circulated / without our permission. //
그 개념은 주장을 포함한다 / 우리가 주시당하지 않아야 한다는 / 그리고 특정 정보와 이미지가 / 우리에 관한 / 유포되어서는 안 된다는 / 우리의 허락 없이 //

Why did these privacy claims arise? //
'왜' 이러한 사생활 주장들이 생겼는가 //

They arose / because powerful people took offence / at such observation. //
그것은 생겼다 / 영향력 있는 사람들이 불쾌감을 느꼈기 때문에 / 그렇게 주시당하는 것에 //

Furthermore, / privacy incorporated the need / to protect the family, home, and correspondence / from arbitrary (d) interference /
게다가 / 사생활은 필요성을 포함했고 / 가족, 가정, 그리고 서신을 보호할 / 임의의 간섭으로부터 //

and, in addition, / there has been a determination / to protect honour and reputation. //
또한 / 확고한 의지가 있었다 / 명예와 평판을 보호하려는 //

How is privacy protected? //
사생활은 '어떻게' 보호되는가 //

Historically, privacy was protected / by restricting circulation / of the damaging material. //
역사적으로 사생활은 보호되었다 / 유포를 제한함으로써 / 피해를 주는 자료의 //

But if the concept of privacy / first became interesting legally / as a response / to reproductions of images / through photography and newspapers, /
그러나 사생활 개념이 / 처음 법적으로 관심을 끌게 되었다면 / 대응으로 / 이미지의 재생산에 대한 / 사진과 신문을 통한 //

more recent technological advances, / such as data storage, digital images, and the Internet, / (e) pose new threats to privacy. //
더 근래의 기술 발전은 / 자료 저장, 디지털 이미지, 그리고 인터넷과 같은 / 사생활에 새로운 위협을 제기한다 //

The right to privacy / is now being reinterpreted / to meet those challenges. // 41번 단서 2: 사생활에 대한 권리가 최근에 제기된 문제들에 대처하기 위해 재해석되고 있음
사생활에 대한 권리는 / 이제 재해석되고 있다 / 그러한 문제들에 대처하기 위해 //

- right ⓝ 권리, 권한　　・privacy ⓝ 사생활　　・extend ⓥ 확대하다
- restrict ⓥ 제한하다　　・expression ⓝ 표현　　・scope ⓝ 범위
- similarly ⓐⓓ 비슷하게　　・general ⓐ 보편적인, 일반적인
- prevent ⓥ 예방하다　　・crime ⓝ 범죄　　・promote ⓥ 촉진하다
- public ⓐ 공공의　　・property-based 속성에 기반을 둔
- notion ⓝ 개념, 생각　　・personality ⓝ 인격, 성격
- modern ⓐ 현대적인　　・private ⓐ 사적인　　・establish ⓥ 설정하다
- limit ⓝ 한계　　・strength ⓝ 강점, 장점　　・in that ～라는 관점에서
- adapt ⓥ 적응하다　　・meet ⓥ 잘 대처하다
- expectation ⓝ 기대, 예상　　・technological ⓐ 기술상의
- advance ⓝ 발전, 진보　　・in sum 요컨대　　・concept ⓝ 개념
- include ⓥ 포함하다　　・claim ⓝ 주장, 권리
- unobserved ⓐ 주시당하지 않는　　・certain ⓐ 특정한, 어떤
- circulate ⓥ 유포하다　　・permission ⓝ 허락, 허가
- arise ⓥ 생기다, 발생하다　　・offence ⓝ 모욕　　・observation ⓝ 관찰
- furthermore ⓐⓓ 게다가　　・incorporate ⓥ 포함하다
- correspondence ⓝ 서신, 편지　　・interference ⓝ 간섭, 참견
- determination ⓝ 결심, 결정　　・honour ⓝ 명예
- reputation ⓝ 평판　　・material ⓝ 자료, 재료, 소재
- legally ⓐⓓ 법률적으로　　・response ⓝ 대응, 대답
- reproduction ⓝ 재생산　　・recent ⓐ 최근의
- storage ⓝ 저장, 보관　　・pose ⓥ (문제 등을) 제기하다
- threat ⓝ 위협　　・reinterpret ⓥ 재해석하다　　・challenge ⓝ 도전

사생활에 대한 권리는 다른 사람의 표현의 자유에 대한 권리나 정보에 대한 권리를 제한하지 않는 정도까지만 확대될 수 있다. 사생활에 대한 권리의 범위는 범죄 예방이나 공중 보건 증진에서의 공공이익에 의해 (a) 비슷하게 제한된다. 하지만 우리가 속성에 기반을 둔 권리 개념(예를 들어, 사생활에 대한 권리가 이미지와 인격을 보호하는)에서 사생활과 가족의 생활이라는 현대적 개념으로 옮겨갈 때, 우리는 그 권리의 한계를 설정하기가 (b) 더 쉽다(→ 더 어렵다는) 것을 알게 된다. 이것은 물론 변화하는 기대와 기술 진보에 대처하기 위해 적응할 수 있다는 점에서, 사생활 개념의 강점이다.
요컨대, 오늘날 사생활이란 '무엇'인가? 그 개념은 우리가 주시당하지 않아야 한다는 주장과 우리에 관한 특정 정보와 이미지가 우리의 허락 없이 (c) 유포되어서는 안 된다는 주장을 포함한다. '왜' 이러한 사생활 주장들이 생겼는가? 그것은 영향력 있는 사람들이 그렇게 주시당하는 것에 불쾌감을 느꼈기 때문에 생겼다. 게다가 사생활은 가족, 가정, 그리고 서신을 임의의 (d) 간섭으로부터 보호할 필요성을 포함했고, 또한 명예와 평판을 보호하려는 확고한 의지가 있었다. 사생활은 '어떻게' 보호되는가? 역사적으로 사생활은 피해를 주는 자료의 유포를 제한함으로써 보호되었다. 그러나 사생활 개념이 사진과 신문을 통한 이미지의 재생산에 대한 대응으로 처음 법적으로 관심을 끌게 되었다면, 자료 저장, 디지털 이미지, 그리고 인터넷과 같은 더 근래의 기술 발전은 사생활에 새로운 위협을 (e) 제기한다. 사생활에 대한 권리는 이제 그러한 문제들에 대처하기 위해 재해석되고 있다.

P 41 정답 ③

윗글의 제목으로 가장 적절한 것은?

① Side Effects of Privacy Protection Technologies
사생활 보호 기술의 부작용　　　　　　　　　사생활을 보호하는 기술에 대한 내용이 아님
② The Legal Domain of Privacy Claims and Conflicts
사생활 주장과 갈등의 법률적 영역　　　　　　legally가 언급된 것으로 만든 오답
③ The Right to Privacy: Evolving Concepts and Practices
사생활에 대한 권리: 진화하는 개념과 실제　사생활 개념이 변화함에 따라 사생활에 대한 권리도 진화함
④ Who Really Benefits from Looser Privacy Regulations?
더 느슨한 사생활 규정으로부터 누가 정말 득을 보는가? 사생활 규정의 엄격함의 정도에 대한 언급은 없음
⑤ Less Is More: Reduce State Intervention in Privacy!
적을수록 좋다: 사생활에 대한 국가의 개입을 줄여라! 현상을 설명하는 것이지, 어떤 주장을 드러내는 것이 아님

2등급? 모든 선택지에 '사생활'이라는 공통된 단어가 들어가 있어서 단서 글을 유심히 읽지 않으면 헷갈리기 쉬운 문제였다. 발상

| 문제 풀이 순서 | [정답률 71%]

1st 선택지와 앞부분을 통해 핵심 소재를 확인하고 글의 내용을 예상한다.

선택지	모든 선택지에 '사생활'이라는 어휘가 등장한다.
앞부분	사생활에 대한 권리는 다른 사람의 표현의 자유에 대한 권리나 정보에 대한 권리를 제한하지 않는 정도까지만 확대될 수 있다.

➡ 사생활에 대한 권리가 다른 사람의 권리를 제한하지 않는 정도까지만 확대될 수 있다고 했으므로 사생활 권리의 범위를 다루는 내용이 이어질 것이다.

2nd **1st** 에서 발상한 것을 토대로 글을 읽고, 내용을 파악하여 제목을 고른다.

- 이것은 물론 변화하는 기대와 기술 진보에 대처하기 위해 적응할 수 있다는 점에서 사생활 개념의 강점이다. **41번** 단서 1
- 사생활에 대한 권리는 이제 그러한 문제들에 대처하기 위해 재해석되고 있다. **41번** 단서 2

➡ 사생활 개념은 변화하는 기대와 기술 진보에 적응할 수 있다는 강점이 있고, 최근의 기술 발전이 제기하는 새로운 위협에 대처하기 위해 사생활에 대한 권리가 재해석되고 있다는 내용이다. 즉, 사생활 개념은 시대에 따라 변화하고 그에 따라 사생활에 대한 권리 역시 진화한다는 것이다. 따라서 이 글의 제목으로 가장 적절한 것은 ③ '사생활에 대한 권리: 진화하는 개념과 실제'이다.

| 선택지 분석 |

① Side Effects of Privacy Protection Technologies
사생활 보호 기술의 부작용
자료 저장, 디지털 이미지, 인터넷과 같은 최근의 기술 발전은 사생활을 보호하는 기술의 예시로서 언급된 것이 아니라 최근의 기술 발전에 발맞추어 사생활에 대한 권리가 재해석되고 있다는 설명을 하기 위해 언급되었다.

② The Legal Domain of Privacy Claims and Conflicts
사생활 주장과 갈등의 법률적 영역
사생활 개념이 처음에는 사진과 신문을 통한 이미지의 재생산에 대한 대응으로 법적인 관심을 끌었다는 내용으로 만든 오답이다.

③ The Right to Privacy: Evolving Concepts and Practices
사생활에 대한 권리: 진화하는 개념과 실제
사생활 개념이 시대에 따라 변화하고 사생활에 대한 권리 역시 진화한다는 내용이다.

④ Who Really Benefits from Looser Privacy Regulations?
더 느슨한 사생활 규정으로부터 누가 정말 득을 보는가?
사생활 개념을 더 엄격하게 규정하는지, 느슨하게 규정하는지를 설명한 것이 아니라 상황에 따라 변화하는 사생활 개념에 대한 내용이다.

⑤ Less Is More: Reduce State Intervention in Privacy!
적을수록 좋다: 사생활에 대한 국가의 개입을 줄여라!
개인의 사생활에 대해 국가가 개입하지 말라는 주장을 펴는 글이 아니다.

P 42 정답 ②

밑줄 친 (a)~(e) 중에서 문맥상 낱말의 쓰임이 적절하지 않은 것은? [3점]

① (a) 사생활에 대한 권리가 제한되는 경우가 비슷하게 앞뒤로 이어짐
② (b) 사생활 개념이 변화하면 사생활에 대한 더 쉬운 권리의 한계를 설정하는 것이 더 어려움
③ (c) '사진과 신문을 통한 이미지의 재생산'과 유포되는 같은 맥락임
④ (d) 사생활은 자신의 가족, 가정, 서신을 간섭 외부로부터 보호할 필요성을 포함함
⑤ (e) 최근의 기술 발전이 제기하는 새로운 위협에 대처하기 위해 재해석됨 제기하다

2등급? 주제와 일관되지 않는 표현을 찾기 위해, 단서 정답이 포함된 문장에 나타난 연결어로 어조를 파악해야 할 것이다. 발상

정답? [정답률 70%]
② (b) easier 더 쉬운

하지만(However) 우리가 속성에 기반을 둔 권리 개념(예를 들어, 사생활에 대한 권리가 이미지와 인격을 보호하는)에서 사생활과 가족의 생활이라는 현대적 개념으로 옮겨갈 때, 우리는 그 권리의 한계를 설정하기가 (b) 더 쉽다는 (더 어렵다는) 것을 알게 된다.

➡ 사생활의 권리의 한계를 설명한 첫 두 문장에 역접의 연결어 However로 이어진 것으로 보아, (b)가 포함된 문장은 사생활에 대한 권리의 한계를 설정하는 것이 더 '어렵다'는 의미가 되어야 한다.
▶ easier를 반의어인 harder(더 어려운)로 바꿔야 함

오답?
① (a) similarly 비슷하게

사생활에 대한 권리의 범위는 범죄 예방이나 공중 보건 증진에서의 공공이익에 의해 (a) 비슷하게 제한된다.

➡ 앞 문장에서 사생활에 대한 권리가 확대될 수 있는 정도, 즉 사생활에 대한 권리의 한계를 설명했고, (a)가 포함된 문장에서도 사생활에 대한 권리가 제한되는 경우를 설명했으므로 사생활에 대한 권리의 범위는 '비슷하게' 제한된다.
▶ similarly는 문맥에 맞음

③ (c) circulated 유포되는

그 개념은 우리가 주시당하지 않아야 한다는 주장과 우리에 관한 특정 정보와 이미지가 우리의 허락 없이 (c) 유포되어서는 안 된다는 주장을 포함한다.

➡ 사진과 신문을 통한 이미지의 재생산에 대한 대응으로 사생활 개념이 법적인 관심을 끌었다는 후반부의 내용을 통해 우리에 관한 특정 정보와 이미지가 우리의 허락 없이 '유포되어서는' 안 된다는 주장이 사생활 개념에 포함됨을 알 수 있다.
▶ circulated는 문맥에 맞음

④ (d) interference 간섭

게다가 사생활은 가족, 가정, 그리고 서신을 임의의 (d) 간섭으로부터 보호할 필요성을 포함했고, 또한 명예와 평판을 보호하려는 확고한 의지가 있었다.

➡ 외부로부터 주시당하는 것에 불쾌감을 느꼈기 때문에 사생활에 대한 주장들이 생겨났다는 것으로 보아 사생활이 가족, 가정, 서신을 임의의 '간섭'으로부터 보호할 필요성을 포함한다는 것은 적절하다.
▶ interference는 문맥에 맞음

⑤ (e) pose 제기하다

> 그러나 사생활 개념이 사진과 신문을 통한 이미지의 재생산에 대한 대응으로 처음 법적으로 관심을 끌게 되었다면, 자료 저장, 디지털 이미지, 그리고 인터넷과 같은 더 근래의 기술 발전은 사생활에 새로운 위협을 (e) 제기한다.

⇒ 최근의 기술 발전이 '제기한' 사생활에 대한 새로운 위협들에 대처하기 위해 사생활에 대한 권리가 재해석되고 있다는 흐름이다.

▶ pose는 문맥에 맞음

────── 배 경 지 식

✻ 사생활(privacy)

개인에게 관계되는 개념으로, 당사자의 허락 없이 보거나 공개할 수 없는 개인의 비밀에 속하는 사항을 말한다. 사생활은 특히 19세기 이후의 미국에서 발전한 개념이지만, 사상적으로는 개인주의와 자유주의의 발전 속에 계보를 갖는다.

오늘날 사생활의 법적 보호나 개인정보 수집의 규제에 대한 필요성이 강하게 요구되고 있는데, 이는 복지 국가화와 함께 진행되어 온 관리사회화, 고도 정보기술의 산업화와 보급, 대중 매체나 인터넷의 발달 등이 사생활에 큰 위협이 되고 있기 때문이다.
사생활은 개인의 자율성 및 고유성의 존중과 자유롭게 열린 민주주의의 형성이라는 두 가지 관념을 지닌다.

P 43~44 ────────────────── ★ 2등급 대비

✻ 전문가를 능가하는 간단한 공식

There is evidence / that even very simple algorithms /
　　　　　　　　동격절 접속사
can outperform expert judgement / on simple prediction problems. // 43번 단서 1: 간단한 예측 문제에 있어 간단한 공식이 전문가의 판단을 능가할 수 있음
증거가 있다 / 매우 간단한 알고리즘조차도 / 전문가의 판단을 능가할 수 있다는 / 간단한 예측 문제에 대한 //

For example, / algorithms have proved more (a) accurate / than humans /
　　　　　　　　ㄴ비교의 두 대상ㅡ
예를 들어 / 알고리즘이 더 정확하다고 입증되었다 / 인간보다 /
　　　　　　　　　　　　　　　　　앞에 주격 관계대명사와 be동사가 생략됨
in predicting / whether a prisoner / released on parole / will go on to commit another crime, / or in predicting / whether a
　　동명사 predicting의 목적어절 접속사
potential candidate will perform well / in a job in future. //
예측하는 데 / 죄수가 / 가석방으로 풀려난 / 계속해서 다른 범죄를 저지를 것인지 / 또는 예측하는 데 / 잠재적인 지원자가 일을 잘할 것인지를 / 장차 직장에서 //

In over 100 studies / across many different domains, / half of all cases show /
　　　　　　　주어부에 부분을 나타내는 표현이 쓰이면 of 뒤의 명사의 수에 동사의 수를 일치시킴
100개가 넘는 연구에서 / 많은 다른 영역에 걸친 / 모든 사례의 절반은 보여준다 /

simple formulas make (b) better significant predictions / than human experts, / and the remainder / (except a very small handful), / show a tie / between the two. // 43번 단서 2: 간단한 공식이
　　　　　　　　　　　　　　　　　　　　　　　　　　　　　인간 전문가보다 더 나은 예측을 함
간단한 공식이 더 나은 중요한 예측을 하고 / 인간 전문가보다 / 그 나머지는 / (아주 적은 소수를 제외하고) / 무승부를 보여준다 / 둘 사이의 //
　　　　　　　　　　　　　　　　　　　　　　　　　앞에 주격 관계대명사와 be동사가 생략됨
When there are a lot of different factors involved / and a
부사절 접속사(시간)
situation is very uncertain, / simple formulas can win out / by
　　　　　　　　　　　　　　　　　　　　병렬 구조(by의 목적어)
focusing / on the most important factors / and being consistent, /
관련된 많은 다른 요인이 있을 때 / 그리고 상황이 매우 불확실할 (때) / 간단한 공식이 승리할 수 있다 / 초점을 맞춤으로써 / 가장 중요한 요소에 / 그리고 일관적임으로써 /

while human judgement is too easily influenced / by particularly salient and perhaps (c) irrelevant considerations. //
인간의 판단은 너무 쉽게 영향을 받는 반면에 / 특히 두드러지고 아마도 관련이 없는 고려 사항에 의해 //

A similar idea is supported / by further evidence / that
　　　　　　　　　　　　　　　　　　　동격절 접속사
'checklists' can improve / the quality of expert decisions / in a range of domains /
유사한 생각이 뒷받침된다 / 추가적인 증거에 의해 / '점검표'가 향상될 수 있다는 / 전문가의 결정의 질을 / 다양한 영역에서 /

by ensuring / that important steps or considerations aren't missed / when people are feeling (d) relaxed(→ overloaded). //
　동명사 ensuring의 목적어절 접속사
확실히 함으로써 / 중요한 조치나 고려 사항이 놓쳐지지 않는다는 것을 / 사람들이 편안하다고 (→ 일이 너무 많다고) 느낄 때 //

For example, / treating patients in intensive care / can require
　　　　　　　　　동명사구 주어　　　　　　　　　　　　동사
hundreds of small actions / per day, / and one small error could cost a life. // 44번 단서: 집중 치료 중인 환자를 치료하는 것은 편안하게 느껴지는 일이 아님
　　　　　　　　　　　　　　　주어　　　　　　　　　　　　동사
예를 들어 / 집중 치료 중인 환자를 치료하는 것은 / 수백 가지의 작은 조치를 필요로 할 수 있으며 / 하루에 / 작은 실수 하나가 목숨을 잃게 할 수 있다 //

Using checklists / to ensure / that no crucial steps are missed /
　동명사구 주어　　부사적 용법(목적) to ensure의 목적어절 접속사
has proved to be remarkably (e) effective /
단수 동사
점검표를 사용하는 것은 / 확실히 하기 위해 / 어떠한 중요한 조치도 놓쳐지지 않는 것을 / 현저하게 효과적이라는 것이 입증되었다 /

in a range of medical contexts, / from preventing live infections / to reducing pneumonia. //
　　　　　　　　　　　　　　from A to B로 연결된 동명사구
다양한 의학적 상황에서 / 당면한 감염을 예방하는 것에서부터 / 폐렴을 줄이는 것에 이르기까지 //

────────────────────────────

• evidence ⓝ 증거　　• outperform ⓥ 능가하다
• judgement ⓝ 판단　　• prediction ⓝ 예측　　• accurate ⓐ 정확한
• release ⓥ 풀어 주다, 석방[해방]하다
• commit ⓥ (그릇된 일 · 범죄를) 저지르다[범하다]
• potential ⓐ 잠재적인　　• candidate ⓝ 지원자, 응시자
• domain ⓝ (지식 · 활동의) 영역[분야]　　• formula ⓝ 공식
• significant ⓐ 중요한　　• remainder ⓝ 나머지
• handful ⓝ 줌, 움큼　　• tie ⓝ 동점, 무승부　　• factor ⓝ 요소
• uncertain ⓐ 불확실한　　• win out 승리하다, 성취하다
• consistent ⓐ 일관된, 변함없는　　• consideration ⓝ 숙고, 고려 사항
• a range of 다양한　　• ensure ⓥ 보장하다
• intensive ⓐ 집중적인, 많은 주의를 기울여야 하는
• crucial ⓐ 중대한, 결정적인　　• remarkably ⓐⓓ 놀랍게도
• live ⓐ 당면한, 현재 관심을 모으는　　• infection ⓝ 감염
• prioritise ⓥ 우선순위를 매기다　　• myth ⓝ 신화, 근거 없는 믿음
• simplicity ⓝ 간단함, 평이함　　• beat ⓥ 이기다

매우 간단한 알고리즘조차도 간단한 예측 문제에 대한 전문가의 판단을 능가할 수 있다는 증거가 있다. 예를 들어, 가석방으로 풀려난 죄수가 계속해서 다른 범죄를 저지를 것인지 예측하거나, 잠재적인 지원자가 장차 직장에서 일을 잘할 것인지를 예측하는 데 알고리즘이 인간보다 더 (a) 정확하다고 입증되었다. 많은 다른 영역에 걸친 100개가 넘는 연구에서, 모든 사례의 절반은 간단한 공식이 인간 전문가보다 (b) 더 나은 중요한 예측을 하고, 그 나머지(아주 적은 소수를 제외하고)는 둘 사이의 무승부를 보여준다.

관련된 많은 다른 요인이 있고 상황이 매우 불확실할 때, 가장 중요한 요소에 초점을 맞추고 일관성을 유지함으로써 간단한 공식이 승리할 수 있는 반면, 인간의 판단은 특히 두드러지고 아마도 (c) 관련이 없는 고려 사항에 의해 너무 쉽게 영향을 받는다. 사람들이 (d) 편안하다고(→ 일이 너무 많다고) 느낄 때 중요한 조치나 고려 사항을 놓치지 않도록 함으로써 '점검표'가 다양한 영역에서 전문가의 결정의 질을 향상할 수 있다는 추가적인 증거가 유사한 생각을 뒷받침한다. 예를 들어, 집중 치료 중인 환자를 치료하려면 하루에 수백 가지의 작은 조치가 필요할 수 있으며, 작은 실수 하나로 목숨을 잃게 할 수 있다. 어떠한 중요한 조치라도 놓치지 않기 위해 점검표를 사용하는 것은 당면한 감염을 예방하는 것에서부터 폐렴을 줄이는 것에 이르기까지 다양한 의학적 상황에서 현저하게 (e) 효과적이라는 것이 입증되었다.

P 43 정답 ①

윗글의 제목으로 가장 적절한 것은?

① The Power of Simple Formulas in Decision Making
의사 결정을 할 때의 간단한 공식의 힘   인간 전문가보다 더 나음
② Always Prioritise: Tips for Managing Big Data
항상 우선순위를 결정하라: 빅 데이터 관리 요령   우선순위의 중요성에 대한 내용이 아님
③ Algorithms' Mistakes: The Myth of Simplicity
알고리즘의 실수: 단순함에 대한 근거 없는 믿음   알고리즘이 인간의
④ Be Prepared! Make a Checklist Just in Case   판단을 이긴다는 글임
준비하라! 만일의 경우를 대비해 점검표를 만들어라   지엽적인 내용으로 만든 오답
⑤ How Human Judgement Beats Algorithms
인간의 판단이 알고리즘을 이기는 방법

2등급? 글 전체의 핵심 단어인 알고리즘이 오히려 정답인 선택지에 직접적으로 언급되지 않았다. **단서** 지문에 나타난 알고리즘의 특징을 정리하여 그것이 어느 상황에서 유용하게 쓰이는지 파악해야 문제를 해결할 수 있을 것이다. **발상**

| 문제 풀이 순서 | [정답률 57%]

1st 선택지와 앞부분을 통해 핵심 소재를 확인하고 글의 내용을 예상한다.

선택지	거의 모든 선택지에 '의사 결정', '우선 순위', '빅 데이터', '알고리즘', '판단'과 같은 표현들이 등장한다.
앞부분	매우 간단한 알고리즘조차도 간단한 예측 문제에 대한 전문가의 판단을 능가할 수 있다는 증거가 있다. **43번** 단서 1

➡ 알고리즘이 간단한 예측 문제에 대한 전문가의 판단을 능가할 수 있다는 증거가 있다고 했으므로 알고리즘의 예측 능력을 다루는 내용이 이어질 것이다.

2nd **1st** 에서 발상한 것을 토대로 글을 읽고, 내용을 파악하여 제목을 고른다.

- 간단한 공식이 인간 전문가보다 더 나은 중요한 예측을 하고, … **43번** 단서 2

➡ 간단한 예측 문제에 있어 매우 간단한 알고리즘조차도 전문가의 판단을 능가할 수 있다는 문장으로 글을 시작했다. 이후로 간단한 공식이 인간 전문가보다 더 나은 중요 예측을 한다는 설명과 이성적이지 않은 인간의 판단과 대조되는 간단한 공식의 장점에 대한 부연이 이어진다. 따라서 이 글의 제목으로 가장 적절한 것은 ① '의사 결정을 할 때의 간단한 공식의 힘'이다.

| 선택지 분석 |

① **The Power of Simple Formulas in Decision Making**
의사 결정을 할 때의 간단한 공식의 힘
간단한 공식(알고리즘)이 전문가의 판단을 능가할 정도로 더 나은 예측을 한다는 내용이다.

② **Always Prioritise: Tips for Managing Big Data**
항상 우선순위를 결정하라: 빅 데이터 관리 요령
우선순위 결정의 중요성이나 빅 데이터에 관련된 내용이 아니다.

③ **Algorithms' Mistakes: The Myth of Simplicity**
알고리즘의 실수: 단순함에 대한 근거 없는 믿음
알고리즘이 인간의 판단을 능가하는 경우를 설명하는 글이므로 제목으로 적절하지 않다.

④ **Be Prepared! Make a Checklist Just in Case**
준비하라! 만일의 경우를 대비해 점검표를 만들어라
간단한 공식이 승리할 수 있다는 생각을 뒷받침하는 증거로 점검표에 의해 향상되는 전문가의 결정의 질을 든 것이다. 점검표 자체에 대해 이야기하는 글이 아니다.

⑤ **How Human Judgement Beats Algorithms**
인간의 판단이 알고리즘을 이기는 방법
알고리즘이 인간의 판단을 능가하는 경우를 설명하는 글이므로 제목으로 적절하지 않다.

장성욱 | 동아대 의예과 2023년 입학·부산 대연고 졸

장문 유형의 제목 문제는 글에서 주제문 찾고 키워드 두 개를 뽑아야 해. 두 개의 키워드가 주제문과 같은 의미로 제시된 선택지가 바로 정답이거든.

이 글은 두 번째 문장에 For example이 포함되어 첫 문장이 주제문이라는 것을 쉽게 알 수 있었어. 주제를 뒷받침하는 사례가 이어지는 거라고 생각했거든. 첫 문장에서 찾은 키워드는 simple algorithms와 expert judgement이고, 주제는 '간단한 알고리즘이 전문가의 판단을 능가할 수 있다.'였어. 두 단어를 포함하면서 주제문과 같은 방향을 가진 선택지를 찾으면 정답은 ①이야. 물론 단어를 그대로 쓰지는 않았고, algorithms는 formulas로, judgement는 decision making으로 바뀌었지만 말이야!

P 44 정답 ④

밑줄 친 (a)~(e) 중에서 문맥상 낱말의 쓰임이 적절하지 않은 것은?

① (a) 알고리즘이 전문가의 판단을 능가하는 사례   ② (b)
정확한   더 나은
③ (c) 간단한 공식과 대조되는 인간의 판단   ④ (d) 집중 치료 중인 환자를 치료하는 것이
관련이 없는   편안한 사례임
⑤ (e) 전문가의 결정의 질을 향상함
효과적인

2등급? 글의 주제에서 단서를 파악하는 문제가 아니었다. **단서** 정답이 포함된 문장 뒤에 제시된 상황으로부터 단서를 파악해야 할 것이다. **발상**

정답? [정답률 62%]

④ (d) relaxed 편안한

> 사람들이 (d) 편안하다고_{일이 너무 많다고} 느낄 때 중요한 조치나 고려 사항을 놓치지 않도록 함으로써 '점검표'가 다양한 영역에서 전문가의 결정의 질을 향상할 수 있다는 추가적인 증거가 유사한 생각을 뒷받침한다.

➡ 이어지는 사례의 내용은 하루에 수백 가지의 작은 조치를 필요로 하는 집중 치료 중인 환자를 치료하는 데 있어 어떠한 중요한 조치도 놓치지 않기 위해 점검표를 사용한다는 것이다.
이는 취해져야 하는 조치가 너무 많을 때 점검표가 도움이 되는 상황에 대한 사례이므로 ④ (d) relaxed를 overloaded(일이 너무 많은 등)의 단어로 바꿔야 한다. ▶ relaxed를 반의어인 overloaded(일이 너무 많은)로 바꿔 볼 것

오답?

① (a) accurate 정확한

> 예를 들어, 가석방으로 풀려난 죄수가 계속해서 다른 범죄를 저지를 것인지 예측하거나, 잠재적인 지원자가 장차 직장에서 일을 잘할 것인지를 예측하는 데 알고리즘이 인간보다 더 (a) 정확하다고 입증되었다.

➡ 매우 간단한 알고리즘조차 전문가의 판단을 능가할 수 있다는 앞 문장에 대한 예시로 알고리즘이 인간보다 더 '정확하다고' 입증된 예측의 사례를 설명한다.
▶ accurate는 문맥에 맞음

② (b) better 더 나은

> 많은 다른 영역에 걸친 100개가 넘는 연구에서, 모든 사례의 절반은 간단한 공식이 인간 전문가보다 (b) 더 나은 중요한 예측을 하고, 그 나머지(아주 적은 소수를 제외하고)는 둘 사이의 무승부를 보여준다.

➡ 글의 흐름이 전환되지 않았으므로, 절반의 연구 사례가 간단한 공식(알고리즘)이 인간 전문가보다 '더 나은' 중요한 예측을 한다는 것을 보여준다는 설명은 흐름에 적절하다. ▶ better는 문맥에 맞음

③ (c) irrelevant 관련이 없는

> 관련된 많은 다른 요인이 있고 상황이 매우 불확실할 때, 가장 중요한 요소에 초점을 맞추고 일관성을 유지함으로써 간단한 공식이 승리할 수 있는 반면, 인간의 판단은 특히 두드러지고 아마도 (c) 관련이 없는 고려 사항에 의해 너무 쉽게 영향을 받는다.

➡ 가장 중요한 요소에 초점을 맞추고 일관성을 유지하는 간단한 공식과, '관련 없는' 고려 사항에 너무 쉽게 영향을 받는 인간의 판단이 대조된다.

▶ irrelevant는 문맥에 맞음

⑤ (e) effective 효과적인

> 어떠한 중요한 조치라도 놓치지 않기 위해 점검표를 사용하는 것은 당면한 감염을 예방하는 것에서부터 폐렴을 줄이는 것에 이르기까지 다양한 의학적 상황에서 현저하게 (e) 효과적이라는 것이 입증되었다.

➡ 점검표가 전문가의 결정의 질을 향상할 수 있음을 보여주는 추가적인 증거에 대해 이야기하는 문장으로, 어떠한 중요한 조치도 놓치지 않기 위해 점검표를 사용하는 것이 '효과적이라는' 것이 입증되었다는 설명은 적절하다.

▶ effective는 문맥에 맞음

권주원 | 서울대 정치외교학부 2023년 입학·서울 배재고 졸

정답인 (d)를 찾기 위해서는 글 전체의 내용보다는 바로 뒤 문장에 나오는 예시를 분석해야 해서 생각보다 까다로웠던 문제야. 처음 (d)가 포함된 문장을 읽었을 때는 '어? 당연히 편안하다고 느낄 때도 점검표가 있으면 실수가 없지 않을까?'라고 생각해서 정답을 찾기가 어려웠어.
하지만 뒤에 이어지는 예시를 읽으면 (d)가 정답임을 알 수 있는데, treating patients in intensive라는 상황은 편안하다고 느끼는 상황이 아니라 긴장되고 급박한 상황이잖아. 그래서 뒤의 예시와 자연스럽게 연결되려면 (d) relaxed가 들어가는 것은 부적절하다는 결론을 내릴 수 있었어.

P 45~46 ⭐ 1등급 대비

* 상상력이 따라잡기 어려운 기후 변화

Climate change experts and environmental humanists alike
　　　　　　　　　　주어
agree /
동사
기후 변화 전문가들과 환경 인문주의자들은 똑같이 동의한다 /
　　목적어절 접속사
that the climate crisis / is, at its core, a crisis of the imagination
/ and much of the popular imagination / is shaped by fiction. //
기후 위기가 / 근원적으로 상상력의 위기이며 / 대중적 상상력의 많은 부분이 / 소설에 의해
형성된다는 데 // **45번** 단서 1: 기후 위기는 근원적으로 상상력의 위기인데,
　　　　　　　　대중적 상상력의 많은 부분이 소설에 의해 형성됨
In his 2016 book *The Great Derangement*, / anthropologist and
novelist Amitav Ghosh / takes on this relationship / between
imagination and environmental management, /
자신의 2016년도 책 〈The Great Derangement〉에서 / 인류학자이자 소설가인 Amitav
Ghosh는 / 이러한 관계를 다루면서 / 상상과 환경 관리 사이의 /
arguing / that humans have failed to respond / to climate change
　　　　현재분사 arguing의 목적어절 접속사
/ at least in part / because fiction (a) fails to believably represent
it. // **45번** 단서 2: 대중적 상상력의 많은 부분을 형성하는 소설이 기후 변화를 믿을 만하게 표현하지 못함
주장한다 / 인간이 대응하는 데 실패했다고 / 기후 변화에 / 최소한 부분적으로는 / 소설이
그것을 믿을 수 있게 표현하지 못하기 때문에 //

Ghosh explains / that climate change is largely absent / from
　　　　　동사 explains의 목적어절 접속사
contemporary fiction /
Ghosh는 설명한다 / 기후 변화는 대체로 존재하지 않는다고 / 현대 소설에 /　앞에 목적격
　　　　　　　　　　　　　　　　　　　　　　　　　　　　관계대명사가 생략됨
because the cyclones, floods, and other catastrophes / it brings
to mind / simply seem too "improbable" / to belong in stories /
about everyday life. // **45번** 단서 3: 기후 변화가 상상력을 벗어나기 때문에
　　　　　　　　　　현대 소설이 기후 변화를 다루지 못함
사이클론, 홍수, 그리고 다른 큰 재해들이 / 그것이 상기시키는 / 그야말로 너무 '있을 것 같지
않은' 처럼 보이기 때문에 / 이야기에 속하기에는 / 일상생활에 관한 //
But climate change does not only reveal itself / as a series of
(b) extraordinary events. //
그러나 기후 변화는 자신을 드러내지 않는다 / 일련의 놀라운 사건들로만 //
In fact, / as environmentalists and ecocritics / from Rachel
Carson to Rob Nixon / have pointed out, /
사실 / 환경론자들과 생태 비평가들이 / Rachel Carson에서 Rob Nixon에 이르는 /
지적했듯이 / **46번** 단서 1: 환경 변화가 빠르게 진행된다면 감지할 수 있을 것임
environmental change can be "imperceptible"; / it proceeds
(c) rapidly(→ gradually), / only occasionally producing /
"explosive and spectacular" events. //
환경 변화는 '감지할 수 없을' 수 있다 / 그것은 빠르게(→ 점진적으로) 진행되며 / 단지 이따금
만들어 낸다 / '폭발적이고 극적인' 사건들을 //
Most climate change impacts / cannot be observed day-to-day,
/ but they become (d) visible / when we are confronted / with
　　　　　　　　　　　　　　　　　〈시간〉의 부사절 접속사
their accumulated impacts. //
대부분의 기후 변화의 영향은 / 매일 관찰될 수는 없지만 / 그것들은 눈에 보이게 된다 /
우리가 직면할 때 / 그것들의 축적된 영향에 //
Climate change evades our imagination / because it poses /
significant representational challenges. //
기후 변화는 우리의 상상을 벗어난다 / 그것이 제기하기 때문에 / 커다란 표현상의 도전을 //
It cannot be observed / in "human time," / which is / why
documentary filmmaker Jeff Orlowski, / who tracks climate
　　　　　　주어　　　　　　　　　　　　　　주격 관계대명사
change effects / on glaciers and coral reefs, /
그것은 관찰될 수 없는데 / '인간의 시간' 동안에는 / 그것이 ~이다 / 왜 다큐멘터리 영화
제작자 Jeff Orlowski가 / 기후 변화의 영향을 추적하는 / 빙하와 산호초에 미치는 /
동사
uses "before and after" photographs / taken several months
apart / in the same place / to (e) highlight changes / that occurred
gradually. // **46번** 단서 2: 점진적으로 일어난 환경 변화를 강조하기 위해
　　　　　　　　　　같은 장소에서 수개월 간격으로 찍은 전후 사진을 이용함
'전과 후' 사진을 이용하는 (이유이다) / 수개월 간격으로 찍힌 / 같은 장소에서 / 변화를
강조하기 위해 / 점진적으로 일어난 //

- humanist ⓝ 인문주의자, 인도주의자 · crisis ⓝ 위기
- core ⓝ 중심부 · derangement ⓝ 혼란 (상태)
- contemporary ⓐ 동시대의, 현대의 · flood ⓝ 홍수, 쇄도
- improbable ⓐ 있을 것 같지 않은, 별난
- extraordinary ⓐ 기이한, 비범한 · environmentalist ⓝ 환경론자
- imperceptible ⓐ (너무 작아서) 감지할 수 없는 · occasionally ⓐd 가끔
- explosive ⓐ 폭발성의, (분노를) 촉발하는
- spectacular ⓐ 장관을 이루는, 극적인 · impact ⓝ 영향, 충격
- day-to-day ⓐ 그날그날의, 매일 행해지는
- accumulate ⓥ 축적하다 · pose ⓥ (위협·문제 등을) 제기하다
- significant ⓐ 중요한, 커다란
- representational ⓐ 표현적인, 대표(제)의
- track ⓥ 추적하다, 뒤쫓다 · glacier ⓝ 빙하 · coral reef 산호초
- highlight ⓥ 강조하다 · gradually ⓐd 서서히

기후 변화 전문가들과 환경 인문주의자들은 기후 위기가 근원적으로 상상력의 위기이며 대중적 상상력의 많은 부분이 소설에 의해 형성된다는 데 똑같이 동의한다. 인류학자이자 소설가인 Amitav Ghosh는 자신의 2016년도 책 〈The Great Derangement〉에서 상상과 환경 관리 사이의 이러한 관계를 다루면서, 인간이 기후 변화에 대응하는 데 실패한 것은 최소한 부분적으로는 소설이 그것을 믿을 수 있게 표현하지 (a) 못하기 때문이라고 주장한다. Ghosh는 기후 변화는 그것이 상기시키는 사이클론, 홍수, 그리고 다른 큰 재해들이 그야말로

일상생활에 관한 이야기에 속하기에는 너무 '있을 것 같지 않은' 것처럼 보이기 때문에 현대 소설에 대체로 존재하지 않는다고 설명한다. 그러나 기후 변화는 일련의 (b) 놀라운 사건들로만 자신을 드러내는 것은 아니다. 사실, Rachel Carson에서 Rob Nixon에 이르는 환경론자들과 생태 비평가들이 지적했듯이, 환경 변화는 '감지할 수 없을' 수 있는데, 즉 그것은 (c) 빠르게(→ 점진적으로) 진행되며, 단지 이따금 '폭발적이고 극적인' 사건들을 만들어 낼 뿐이다. 대부분의 기후 변화의 영향은 매일 관찰될 수는 없지만, 우리가 그것들의 축적된 영향에 직면할 때 그것들은 (d) 눈에 보이게 된다. 기후 변화는 그것이 커다란 표현상의 도전을 제기하기 때문에 우리의 상상을 벗어난다. 그것은 '인간의 시간' 동안에는 관찰될 수 없는데, 그것이 빙하와 산호초에 미치는 기후 변화의 영향을 추적하는 다큐멘터리 영화 제작자 Jeff Orlowski가 점진적으로 일어난 변화를 (e) 강조하기 위해 수개월 간격으로 같은 장소에서 찍은 '전과 후' 사진을 이용하는 이유이다.

P 45 정답 ③

윗글의 제목으로 가장 적절한 것은?

① Differing Attitudes Towards Current Climate Issues
   현재의 기후 문제에 대한 다양한 태도   기후 문제를 대하는 여러 태도를 나열한 것이 아님
② Slow but Significant: The History of Ecological Movements
   느리지만 중요한: 생태 운동의 역사   생태 운동의 역사를 설명하는 글이 아님
③ The Silence of Imagination in Representing Climate Change
   기후 변화를 표현하는 데 있어서의 상상력의 침묵   소설(상상력)에 기후 변화가 존재하지 않음
④ Vivid Threats: Climate Disasters Spreading in Local Areas
   뚜렷한 위협: 지역에서 퍼져나가는 기후 재앙들   기후 변화로 인한 구체적인 재해를 설명한 것이 아님
⑤ The Rise and Fall of Environmentalism and Ecocriticism
   환경주의와 생태 비평의 흥망성쇠   환경주의나 생태 비평이 소재가 아님

1등급? 기후 변화와 상상력이라는, 무관해 보이는 두 소재를 다룸으로써 주제를 파악하기 어렵고 전반적으로 어휘 수준이 높았다. **단서** '소설에 등장하지 않는다'라는 것이 '상상력을 넘어선다'라는 표현으로 연결되어야 문제를 해결할 수 있을 것이다. **발상**

| 문제 풀이 순서 | [정답률 62%]

1st 선택지와 앞부분을 통해 핵심 소재를 확인하고 글의 내용을 예상한다.

선택지	거의 모든 선택지에 '기후 문제', '생태', '환경'과 같은 표현들이 등장한다.
앞부분	기후 변화 전문가들과 환경 인문주의자들은 기후 위기가 근원적으로 상상력의 위기이며 대중적 상상력의 많은 부분이 소설에 의해 형성된다는 데 똑같이 동의한다. **45번** 단서1

➡ 이 글은 기후 변화와 환경과 관련된 내용일 것이다.
➡ 앞부분에서 기후 위기가 상상력의 위기이며 상상력의 많은 부분이 소설에 의해 형성된다고 했으므로 기후 위기와 상상력의 관계에 관한 설명이 나올 것이다.

2nd **1st** 에서 발상한 것을 토대로 글을 읽고, 내용을 파악한다.

- ··· 인간이 기후 변화에 대응하는 데 실패한 것은 최소한 부분적으로는 소설이 그것을 믿을 수 있게 표현하지 (a) 못하기 때문이라고 주장한다. **45번** 단서2
- Ghosh는 기후 변화는 그것이 상기시키는 사이클론, 홍수, 그리고 다른 큰 재해들이 그야말로 일상생활에 관한 이야기에 속하기에는 너무 '있을 것 같지 않은' 것처럼 보이기 때문에 현대 소설에 대체로 존재하지 않는다고 설명한다. **45번** 단서3

➡ 소설이 기후 변화를 믿을 만하게 표현하지 못하며, 기부 변화로 인한 재해는 그야말로 너무 있을 것 같지 않아서 소설에 등장하지 않는다고 했다.

3rd 글의 주제에 알맞은 제목을 고른다.

➡ 결국 '기후 변화가 우리의 상상력을 넘어서기 때문에 표현되지 않는다'라는 것이 이 글의 주제이다. 따라서 ③ '기후 변화를 표현하는 데 있어서의 상상력의 침묵'이 이 글의 제목으로 가장 적절하다.

| 선택지 분석 |

① **Differing Attitudes Towards Current Climate Issues**
현재의 기후 문제에 대한 다양한 태도
기후 문제에 대해 기후 변화 전문가, 환경 인문주의자, 환경론자, 생태 비평가 등이 서로 다른 태도를 보인다는 등의 글이 아니다.

② **Slow but Significant: The History of Ecological Movements**
느리지만 중요한: 생태 운동의 역사
생태 운동의 역사가 느리게 진행되었지만 중요하다는 내용은 아니다.

③ **The Silence of Imagination in Representing Climate Change**
기후 변화를 표현하는 데 있어서의 상상력의 침묵
기후 변화가 우리의 상상력을 넘어서기 때문에 표현되지 않는다는 내용이다.

④ **Vivid Threats: Climate Disasters Spreading in Local Areas**
뚜렷한 위협: 지역에서 퍼져나가는 기후 재앙들
the cyclones, floods, and other catastrophes가 언급된 것으로 만든 오답이다.
기후 변화로 인한 이러한 기후 재앙들을 구체적으로 설명하는 것이 아니다.

⑤ **The Rise and Fall of Environmentalism and Ecocriticism**
환경주의와 생태 비평의 흥망성쇠
environmentalists and ecocritics로 만든 오답이다. 이 글은 상상력을 넘어서는 기후 변화에 대해 이야기하는 글이다.

P 46 정답 ③

밑줄 친 (a)~(e) 중에서 문맥상 낱말의 쓰임이 적절하지 않은 것은? [3점]

① (a) 기후 위기 인식에 소설이 영향을 미침   ② (b) 환경 변화는 감지할 수 없을 수 있음
   실패하다   놀라운
③ (c) 마지막 문장에서 기후 변화로 인한 변화가   ④ (d) cannot be observed와 but으로 연결됨
   빠르게 점진적으로 일어난다고 했음   눈에 보이는
⑤ (e) 같은 장소에서 수개월 간격으로 찍은
   강조하다 전후 사진을 이용하는 이유임

1등급? 정답을 고르기 위해 정답인 선택지가 포함된 문장뿐만 아니라 마지막 문장도 살펴야 하는 1등급 대비 문제이다.

| 문제 풀이 순서 | [정답률 60%]

1st 각 낱말의 의미를 먼저 확인하고, 반의어를 미리 생각해 놓는다.

(a) fails: 실패하다 ↔ succeeds: 성공하다
(b) extraordinary: 놀라운 ↔ ordinary: 평범한
(c) rapidly: 빠르게 ↔ gradually: 점진적으로
(d) visible: 눈에 보이는 ↔ invisible: 눈에 보이지 않는
(e) highlight: 강조하다 ↔ overlook: 간과하다

➡ 선택지에 제시된 낱말과 반대 의미를 나타내는 낱말을 넣었을 때 문맥이 성립되는 경우에 정답인 경우가 많다. 그런데 모든 선택지가 반의어를 떠올릴 수 있으므로 정답이 될 가능성이 있어서 앞뒤 내용을 잘 파악해야 한다.

2nd 선택지의 앞뒤 내용을 파악해서 문맥이 자연스러운지 확인한다.

① (a) fails 못하다

··· 인간이 기후 변화에 대응하는 데 실패한 것은 최소한 부분적으로는 소설이 그것을 믿을 수 있게 표현하지 (a) 못하기 때문이라고 주장한다.

➡ 앞 문장에서 기후 위기 대처에 소설이 영향을 미친다고 했으므로, 인간이 기후 변화에 대응하는 데 실패한 부분적인 이유는 소설이 기후 변화를 믿을 수 있게 표현하지 '못하기' 때문이다.
▶ fails는 문맥에 맞음

② (b) extraordinary 놀라운

그러나 기후 변화는 일련의 (b) 놀라운 사건들로만 자신을 드러내는 것은 아니다.

➡ 앞 문장에서 기후 변화는 그것이 상기시키는 사이클론, 홍수, 그리고 다른 큰 재해들이 너무 '있을 것 같지 않은' 것처럼 보인다고 했으므로, 기후 변화는 일련의 '놀라운' 사건들로만 자신을 드러내는 것은 아니라는 표현은 적절하다.
▶ extraordinary는 문맥에 맞음

③ (c) rapidly 빠르게

> … 환경 변화는 '감지할 수 없을' 수 있는데, 즉 그것은 (c) 빠르게
> 진행되며, 단지 이따금 '폭발적이고 극적인' 사건들을 만들어 낼 뿐이다.

→ (c)가 포함된 절 앞뒤로, 환경 변화는 감지할 수 없을 수 있다는 내용과 폭발적이고
극적인 사건들은 단지 이따금 일어날 뿐이라는 내용이 이어진다. 이는 환경 변화가
빠르고 폭발적이며 극적으로 진행되는 것이 아니라는 것을 의미한다.
▶ rapidly는 문맥에 맞지 않음 → 반의어로 바꿔 볼 것

> … 환경 변화는 '감지할 수 없을' 수 있는데, 즉 그것은 점진적으로
> 진행되며, 단지 이따금 '폭발적이고 극적인' 사건들을 만들어 낼 뿐이다.

→ 마지막 문장에서 한 다큐멘터리 영화 제작자는 '점진적으로' 일어난 기후
변화의 영향을 추적하기 위해 같은 장소에서 수개월 간격으로 찍은 전후 사진을
이용한다고 했다. rapidly를 반의어인 gradually로 바꿔야 앞뒤 문맥이
자연스러워지므로 정답은 ③이다.

④ (d) visible 눈에 보이는

> 대부분의 기후 변화의 영향은 매일 관찰될 수는 없지만, 우리가
> 그것들의 축적된 영향에 직면할 때 그것들은 (d) 눈에 보이게 된다.

→ 역접의 연결어 but을 사이에 두고 cannot be observed와 visible이 자연스럽게
이어진다.
▶ visible은 문맥에 맞음

⑤ (e) highlight 강조하다

> 그것은 '인간의 시간' 동안에는 관찰될 수 없는데, 그것이 빙하와
> 산호초에 미치는 기후 변화의 영향을 추적하는 다큐멘터리 영화 제작자
> Jeff Orlowski가 점진적으로 일어난 변화를 (e) 강조하기 위해 수개월
> 간격으로 같은 장소에서 찍은 '전과 후' 사진을 이용하는 이유이다.
> **40번** 단서 2

→ 기후 변화의 영향을 추적하는 다큐멘터리에 같은 장소에서 수개월 간격으로 찍은
사진을 이용하는 것은 점진적으로 일어난 변화를 '강조하기' 위해서일 것이다.
▶ highlight는 문맥에 맞음

───── 배경 지식

＊ 기후(climate)와 날씨(weather)

사전적으로 기후는 일정한 지역에 장기간에 걸쳐 나타나는 대기 현상의
평균적인 상태를 말한다. 즉 날씨가 시시각각 변화하는 순간적인 대기 현상이라면,
기후는 장기간의 대기 현상을 종합한 것이다.

기후는 서양적인 의미로는 지후(地候), 동양적인 의미로는 24절기, 72후(候) 등
시후(時候)의 뜻이 강하다. 현재 우리가 사용하는 기후라는 말속에는 양자가 모두
포함되어 있다. 따라서 기후는 지구상의 특정한 장소에서 해마다 반복되는 가장
뚜렷한 대기 상태의 종합이라고 할 수 있다. 날씨는 길지 않은 시간대의 종합적인
기상 상태를 말한다. 다시 말해 기압, 기온, 습도, 바람, 구름의 양과 형태, 강수량,
일조, 대기의 혼탁한 정도 등의 기상요소를 종합한 대기의 상태인 것이다.

＊언어의 본질적 특성인 분류

명사구 주어 / 단수 동사
Classifying things together into groups / is something we do /
가주어 / 진주어 / 앞에 목적격 관계대명사가 생략됨
all the time, / and it isn't hard / to see why. //
사물들을 묶어서 그룹으로 분류하는 것은 / 우리가 하는 일이며 / 항상 / ~은 어렵지 않다 /
그 이유를 이해하는 것은 //

Imagine / trying to shop in a supermarket / where the food was
관계부사
arranged / in random order / on the shelves: /
상상해보라 / 슈퍼마켓에서 쇼핑하려고 하는 것을 / 음식이 배열된 / 마구잡이로 / 진열대에 //

tomato soup / next to the white bread / in one aisle, / chicken
soup / in the back / next to the 60-watt light bulbs, /
토마토 수프 / 흰 빵 옆에 / 한 통로에서는 / 치킨 수프 / 뒤쪽에 있는 / 60와트 백열전구 옆에 /

one brand of cream cheese / in front / and another / in aisle 8 /
near the cookies. //
한 크림치즈 브랜드 / 앞쪽에 / 또다른 하나 / 8번 통로에 / 쿠키 근처에 //

The task / of finding what you want / would be (a) time-
동격의 전치사 / finding의 목적어절
consuming and extremely difficult, / if not impossible. //
일은 / 여러분이 원하는 것을 찾는 / 시간이 많이 걸리고 매우 어려울 것이다 / 불가능하지는
않더라도 //

In the case of a supermarket, / someone had to (b) design / the
system of classification. //
슈퍼마켓의 경우 / 누군가는 설계해야 했다 / 분류 체계를 //

But there is also a ready-made system of classification /
앞에 주격 관계대명사와 be동사가 생략됨
embodied in our language. //
하지만 기성의 분류 체계도 있다 / 우리 언어에 포함되어 있는 // **48번** 단서: 단어 '개'는 특정 부류의
동물들을(개를 다른 동물들과 구별함
The word "dog," / for example, / groups together a certain class
병렬 구조
of animals / and distinguishes them / from other animals. //
'개'라는 단어는 / 예를 들어 / 특정 부류의 동물들을 함께 분류하여 / 그것들을 구별한다 / 다
른 동물들로부터 //

too ~ to-v: …하기에는 너무 ~한
Such a grouping may seem too (c) abstract(→ obvious) / to be
called a classification, / but this is only because you have already
mastered / the word. //
그러한 분류가 너무 추상적으로(→ 분명해) 보일 수 있지만 / 분류라고 불리기에는 / 이것은 단
지 여러분이 이미 숙달했기 때문이다 / 그 단어를 //

a child를 수식하는 현재분사구
As a child / learning to speak, / you had to work hard / to (d)
learn the system of classification / your parents were trying / to
선행사(to teach의 직접목적어) / 앞에 목적격 관계대명사가 생략됨
teach you. //
아이로서 / 말하기를 배우는 / 여러분은 열심히 노력해야 했다 / 분류 체계를 배우기 위해 / 여
러분의 부모님이 애썼던 / 여러분에게 가르치려고 //

get the hang of: ~을 할[쓸] 줄 알게 되다
Before you got the hang of it, / you probably made mistakes, /
calling의 목적어와 목적격 보어
like calling the cat a dog. //
여러분이 그것을 이해하기 전에 / 여러분은 아마 실수를 했을 것이다 / 고양이를 개라고 부르
는 것과 같은 //
──── 혼합가정법＊
If you hadn't learned to speak, / the whole world would seem /
like the (e) unorganized supermarket; /
만약 여러분이 말하기를 배우지 않았다면 / 온 세상이 보일 것이다 / 정돈되지 않은 슈퍼마켓
처럼 /

you would be in the position of an infant, / for whom every
선행사 / 전치사+관계대명사
object is new and unfamiliar. //
여러분은 유아의 처지에 있을 것이다 / 모든 물건이 새롭고 낯선 //

In learning / the principles of classification, / therefore, / we'll
선행사 / 주격 관계대명사
be learning / about the structure / that lies at the core of our
language. // **47번** 단서: 분류의 원리를 배우는 것은 언어의 핵심에 있는 구조를 배우는 것임
배울 때 / 분류의 원리를 / 그러므로 / 우리는 배우고 있을 것이다 / 구조에 대해 / 우리 언어
의 핵심에 있는 //

- -

• classify A into B A를 B로 분류하다   • arrange ⓥ 배열하다, 정리하다
• random ⓐ 마구잡이의, 임의의   • order ⓝ 순서, 명령, 주문
• aisle ⓝ 통로, 복도   • time-consuming (많은) 시간이 걸리는

- extremely **ad** 매우, 극도로 · classification **n** 분류(법)
- ready-made 이미 만들어진, 기성의
- embody **v** 포함하다, 상징[구현]하다
- distinguish A from B A를 B와 구별하다
- abstract **a** 추상적인, 관념적인 · master **v** 숙달하다, 통달하다
- unorganized **a** 조직화되어 있지 않은, 정돈되지 않은
- infant **n** 유아, 아기 · core **n** 핵심, 중심부

사물들을 묶어서 그룹으로 분류하는 것은 우리가 항상 하는 일이며, 그 이유를 이해하는 것은 어렵지 않다. 음식이 진열대에 마구잡이로 배열된 슈퍼마켓에서 쇼핑하려고 한다고 상상해보라. 한 통로에서는 흰 빵 옆에 토마토 수프가 있고, 치킨 수프는 뒤쪽에 있는 60와트 백열전구 옆에 있고, 한 크림치즈 브랜드는 앞쪽에, 또다른 하나는 쿠키 근처의 8번 통로에 있다. 여러분이 원하는 것을 찾는 일은, 불가능하지는 않더라도, (a) 시간이 많이 걸리고 매우 어려울 것이다. 슈퍼마켓의 경우, 누군가는 분류 체계를 (b) 설계해야 했다. 하지만 또한 우리 언어에 포함되어 있는 기성의 분류 체계도 있다. 예를 들어, '개'라는 단어는 특정 부류의 동물들을 함께 분류하여 다른 동물들과 구별한다. 분류라고 하기에는 그러한 분류가 너무 (c) 추상적으로(→ 분명해) 보일 수 있지만, 이것은 단지 여러분이 이미 그 단어를 숙달했기 때문이다. 말하기를 배우는 아이로서, 여러분은 부모님이 가르치려고 애썼던 분류 체계를 (d) 배우기 위해 열심히 노력해야 했다. 여러분이 그것을 이해하기 전에, 아마 고양이를 개라고 부르는 것과 같은 실수를 했을 것이다. 만약 여러분이 말하기를 배우지 않았다면, 온 세상이 (e) 정돈되지 않은 슈퍼마켓처럼 보일 것이다. 여러분은 모든 물건이 새롭고 낯선 유아의 처지에 있을 것이다. 그러므로 분류의 원리를 배울 때, 우리는 우리 언어의 핵심에 있는 구조에 대해 배우고 있을 것이다.

P 47 정답 ②

윗글의 제목으로 가장 적절한 것은?
① Similarities of Strategies in Sales and Language Learning
영업과 언어 학습 전략의 유사성　　　　　영업 전략이나 언어 학습 전략은 언급되지 않음
②Classification: An Inherent Characteristic of Language
분류: 언어의 본질적 특성　　　분류의 원리를 배우는 것은 언어의 핵심에 있는 구조를 배우는 것임
③ Exploring Linguistic Issues Through Categorization
범주화를 통한 언어학적 문제 탐색　　　언어학적 문제를 탐색하는 방법에 대한 글이 아님
④ Is a Ready-Made Classification System Truly Better?
기성의 분류 시스템이 정말 더 나은가?　　a ready-made system of classification으로 만든 오답
⑤ Dilemmas of Using Classification in Language Education
언어 교육에서 분류 활용의 딜레마　　　딜레마가 있다는 내용이 아님

왜 1등급 **?** 마지막 문장을 제외한 대부분이 예시로 채워져 있어서 주제를 단번에 파악하기 쉽지 않다. **단서** 하지만 글의 마지막 문장에 therefore와 함께 핵심 주제가 있으므로 이 문장을 잘 찾는다면 글의 제목을 정하는 것은 어렵지 않을 것이다. **발상**

| 문제 풀이 순서 | [정답률 60%]

1st 선택지와 앞부분을 통해 핵심 소재를 확인하고 글의 내용을 예상한다.

선택지	거의 모든 선택지에 '언어', '분류'와 같은 표현들이 등장한다.
앞부분	사물들을 묶어서 그룹으로 분류하는 것은 우리가 항상 하는 일이며, 그 이유를 이해하는 것은 어렵지 않다.

→ 이 글은 언어의 분류와 관련된 내용일 것이다.

→ 앞부분에서 사물들을 분류하는 것은 일상적이며, 그 이유를 이해하는 것은 어렵지 않다고 했으므로 분류의 이유에 관한 설명이 나올 것이다.

2nd **1st** 에서 발상한 것을 토대로 글을 읽고, 내용을 파악한다.

- 그러므로 분류의 원리를 배울 때, 우리는 우리 언어의 핵심에 있는 구조에 대해 배우고 있을 것이다. **47번** 단서 1

→ 언어의 핵심에 있는 구조는 분류의 원리라는 내용으로, therefore를 통해 이 글의 결론을 제시했다.

3rd 글의 주제에 알맞은 제목을 고른다.

→ 결국 '분류는 언어의 핵심 구조이다'라는 것이 이 글의 주제이다. 따라서 ③ '분류: 언어의 본질적 특성'이 이 글의 제목으로 가장 적절하다.

| 선택지 분석 |

① **Similarities of Strategies in Sales and Language Learning**
영업과 언어 학습 전략의 유사성
슈퍼마켓의 영업 전략이 언어를 학습하는 전략과 유사하다는 내용이 아니다.

②**Classification: An Inherent Characteristic of Language**
분류: 언어의 본질적 특성
분류가 언어의 핵심 구조라는 내용이다.

③ **Exploring Linguistic Issues Through Categorization**
범주화를 통한 언어학적 문제 탐색
분류 체계를 이해하기 전에는 고양이를 개라고 부르는 것과 같은 실수를 했을 것이라는 내용으로 '언어학적 문제'라는 함정을 만들었다. 언어학적 문제를 탐색하는 데 있어 범주화를 사용하는 것을 설명하는 것이 아니다.

④ **Is a Ready-Made Classification System Truly Better?**
기성의 분류 시스템이 정말 더 나은가?
기성의 분류 시스템과 새로운 분류 시스템을 대조하는 것이 아니다.

⑤ **Dilemmas of Using Classification in Language Education**
언어 교육에서 분류 활용의 딜레마
언어를 교육하는 데 분류를 활용하는 것에 딜레마가 있다는 언급은 없다.

P 48 정답 ③

밑줄 친 (a)~(e) 중에서 문맥상 낱말의 쓰임이 적절하지 않은 것은?
① (a) 제품이 마구잡이로 배열된 슈퍼마켓에서　② (b) 이미 만들어진 분류 체계가 있는 언어와
　시간이 많이 걸리는 원하는 것을 찾는 일　　　　설계하다 다른 점
③ (c) 우리가 이미 '개'라는 단어를 숙달한 경우에　④ (d) 말하기를 배우는 것은 분류 체계를
　추상적인 대한 설명임　　　　　　　　　　　　　배우다 배우는 것임
⑤ (e) 분류 체계가 없는 슈퍼마켓을 가리킴
　정돈되지 않은

왜 1등급 **?** 정답을 고르기 위해 정답인 선택지가 포함된 문장뿐만 아니라 중간 부분의 예시를 같이 살펴야 하는 1등급 대비 문제이다.

| 문제 풀이 순서 | [정답률 54%]

1st 각 낱말의 의미를 먼저 확인하고, 반의어를 미리 생각해 놓는다.

- (a) time-consuming: 시간이 많이 걸리는 ↔ time-saving: 시간을 절약해 주는
- (b) design: 설계하다 ↔ ?
- (c) abstract: 추상적인 ↔ obvious: 분명한
- (d) learn: 배우다 ↔ teach: 가르치다
- (e) unorganized: 정돈되지 않은 ↔ organized: 정돈된

→ 선택지에 제시된 낱말과 반대 의미를 나타내는 낱말을 넣었을 때 문맥이 성립되는 경우에 정답인 경우가 많다. (b)를 제외한 모든 선택지의 반의어를 떠올릴 수 있으므로 각 선택지의 앞뒤 내용을 잘 파악해야 한다.

2nd 선택지의 앞뒤 내용을 파악해서 문맥이 자연스러운지 확인한다.
① (a) time-consuming 시간이 많이 걸리는

여러분이 원하는 것을 찾는 일은, 불가능하지는 않더라도, (a) 시간이 많이 걸리고 매우 어려울 것이다.

→ 제품이 분류 체계 없이 진열대에 마구잡이로 배열된 슈퍼마켓에서 원하는 것을 찾는 일은 '시간이 많이 걸릴' 것이다.
▶ time-consuming은 문맥에 맞음
② (b) design 설계하다

슈퍼마켓의 경우, 누군가는 분류 체계를 (b) 설계해야 했다.

→ 슈퍼마켓의 경우에는 누군가가 분류 체계를 '설계해야' 했다는 것과 우리 언어에는 이미 만들어진 분류 체계가 있다는 내용이 역접의 연결어 But으로 자연스럽게 이어진다.
▶ design은 문맥에 맞음

③ (c) abstract 추상적인

분류라고 하기에는 그러한 분류가 너무 (c) 추상적으로 보일 수 있지만,
이것은 단지 여러분이 이미 그 단어를 숙달했기 때문이다.

➡ 우리가 어떤 단어를 숙달했다면, 그 단어를 다른 단어와 구분하는 것을 분류라고
부르기에 '추상적으로' 보일 수 있다는 설명은 자연스럽지 않다.
▶ abstract는 문맥에 맞지 않음 → 반의어로 바꿔 볼 것

분류라고 하기에는 그러한 분류가 너무 분명해 보일 수 있지만, 이것은
단지 여러분이 이미 그 단어를 숙달했기 때문이다.

➡ abstract를 반의어인 obvious로 바꿔야 앞뒤 문맥이 자연스러워지므로 정답은
③이다.

④ (d) learn 배우다

말하기를 배우는 아이로서, 여러분은 부모님이 가르치려고 애썼던 분류
체계를 (d) 배우기 위해 열심히 노력해야 했다.

➡ 분류의 원리를 배우는 것은 언어의 핵심에 있는 구조를 배우는 것이라는 내용의
글이므로 말을 배우는 아이는 분류 체계를 '배우려고' 노력하는 것이라는 설명은
적절하다.
▶ learn은 문맥에 맞음

⑤ (e) unorganized 정돈되지 않은

만약 여러분이 말하기를 배우지 않았다면, 온 세상이 (e) 정돈되지 않은
슈퍼마켓처럼 보일 것이다.

➡ 말을 배우지 않은 것은 분류 체계를 배우지 않은 것이고, 이는 세상이 앞에서 설명한
'정돈되지 않은' 슈퍼마켓과 같다는 의미이다.
▶ unorganized는 문맥에 맞음

━━━━━ 어법 특강 ━━━━━

＊ 혼합가정법

조건절	주절
if+주어+had p.p. (가정법 과거완료) (과거에) ~했더라면	주어+조동사의 과거형+동사원형 (가정법 과거) (지금) …할 텐데
if+주어+동사의 과거형/were (가정법 과거) (지금) ~하다면	주어+조동사의 과거형+have p.p. (가정법 과거완료) (과거에) …했을 텐데

• If he had taken my advice, he might still be alive.
(그가 만약 내 충고를 받아들였다면 그는 아직 살아 있을지도 모를 텐데.)

• If he were not a very rich man, he could not have donated that
much money.
(그가 무척 부유한 사람이 아니라면 그가 그렇게 많은 돈을 기부하지는 못했을 텐데.)

01 경향, 성향
02 틈새
03 투쟁, 분투
04 서서히
05 신뢰할 수 있는
06 prescribed
07 underestimate
08 superstition
09 interference
10 era
11 engage in
12 belong to
13 rule out
14 come away with
15 be inclined to
16 reputation
17 intense
18 duration
19 absence
20 subjects
21 ends
22 dependent
23 perspectives
24 negotiations
25 improbable
26 artfully
27 distinct
28 circulated
29 mistakenly

글의 주제를 먼저 파악하고
'제목'을 고르자!

Q 복합 문단의 이해

문제편 p. 351~374

Q 01~03 *Sophia가 래프팅을 제안한 이유

동명사 주어   단수 동사
(A) Fighting / against the force of the water / was a thrilling challenge. //

맞서 싸우는 것은 / 물의 힘에 / 짜릿한 도전이었다 //

= as she paid
Sophia tried to keep herself planted firmly / in the boat, / paying attention to the waves / crashing against the rocks. //

Sophia는 단단히 버티어 자리 잡고 있으려고 애썼다 / 배에 / 물결에 주목하면서 / 바위에 세게 부딪치는 //

keep A from -ing: A가 ~하지 못하게 하다   부사적 용법(목적)
As the water got rougher, / she was forced to paddle harder / to keep the waves / from tossing her into the water. //

물이 더 거칠어지자 / 그녀는 더 열심히 노를 저을 수밖에 없었다 / 물결이 ~하지 못하게 / 자기를 물속으로 내동댕이치지 // **3번** Mia와 Rebecca는 보트의 균형을 유지하려고 열심히 노를 저었음

Her friends Mia and Rebecca / were paddling eagerly / behind her / to balance the boat. //

그녀의 친구들인 Mia와 Rebecca는 / 열심히 노를 젓고 있었다 / 그녀의 뒤에서 / 보트의 균형을 유지하려고 //

They were soaked / from all of the spray. //

그들은 흠뻑 젖었다 / 모든 물보라로 // **1번** 단서 1: Mia가 Sophia에게 괜찮은지 물었음

Mia shouted to Sophia, / "Are you OK? // Aren't (a) you scared?" //
= Sophia

Mia는 Sophia에게 소리쳤다 / "너 괜찮니 // 너 무섭지 않니"라고 //

*(A) 문단 요약: Sophia와 Mia, Rebecca는 보트 위에서 균형을 유지하며 열심히 노를 젓고 있음

(B) "You've got a good point. //

"네 말은 정말 일리가 있어 //

가주어   **1번** 단서 2: 대학을 졸업하기 전에 모험적인 일을 진주어   해보고 싶었다는 Sophia의 말이 일리 있다고 말함
It's a real advantage / to graduate from college / with the mindset / of a daring adventurer," / Mia said. //

~은 정말 유리한 점이야 / 대학을 졸업하는 것은 / 마음가짐으로 / 위험을 마다하지 않는 모험가의"라고 / Mia가 말했다 // **3번 ②** Rebecca는 몽골에 가서 그곳에서 영어를 가르친 경험이 있음

Rebecca quickly added, / "That's why I went to Mongolia / before I started my first job / out of college. //

Rebecca가 재빨리 덧붙였다 / "그게 내가 몽골에 간 이유야 / 내가 내 첫 직장 생활을 시작하기 전에 / 대학을 나와서 //

동명사구 주어   단수 동사
Teaching English there / for two months / was a big challenge / for me. //

그곳에서 영어를 가르친 것은 / 두 달 동안 / 큰 도전이었어 / 내게 //

= Rebecca
But (b) I learned a lot / from the experience. //

그런데 나는 많은 것을 배웠어 / 그 경험에서 //

주어   동사   간접목적어 직접목적어   형용사적 용법(the courage 수식)
It really gave me the courage / to try anything / in life." //

그것은 정말 내게 용기를 주었어 / 무슨 일이든 시도할 / 인생에서" //

= Sophia's
Listening to her friends, / Sophia looked / at (c) her own
= As she listened
reflection in the water / and saw a confident young woman / smiling back at her. //

자기 친구들의 말을 들으면서 / Sophia는 보았고 / 물에 비친 그녀 자신의 모습을 / 자신만만한 젊은 여자를 보았다 / 자신에게 미소를 되돌려주는 //

*(B) 문단 요약: 몽골에서 영어를 가르쳤던 경험을 이야기하며 Rebecca는 친구의 말에 동의함

1번 단서 3: Sophia가 괜찮다고 대답함

(C) "I'm great!" / Sophia shouted back excitedly. //

"나는 아주 좋아"라고 / Sophia는 신이 나서 되받아 소리쳤다 //

Even though the boat was getting thrown around, / the girls managed to avoid / hitting any rocks. // **3번 ③** Sophia와 두 친구는 보트가 바위에 부딪치는 것을 피했음

보트가 이리저리 내던져지고 있었지만 / 그 여자들은 용케 피했다 / 어느 바위에도 부딪치는 것을 //

seemed, felt보다 더 이전 시점을 나타내는 대과거
Suddenly, / almost as quickly as the water had got rougher, / the river seemed to calm down, / and they all felt relaxed. //

갑자기 / 거의 물이 더 거칠어졌던 것만큼 빠르게 / 강이 잔잔해지는 것처럼 보였고 / 그들은 모두 긴장을 풀었다 //

With a sigh of relief, / Sophia looked around. //

안도의 한숨을 쉬면서 / Sophia는 주변을 둘러보았다 //

What+a/an+형용사+명사(+주어+동사), 감탄문
"Wow! // What a wonderful view!" / (d) she shouted. //
= Sophia

"우아 // 정말 멋진 풍경이다"라고 / 그녀는 소리쳤다 //

The scenery around them / was breathtaking. //

그들 주변의 경치는 / 숨이 멎을 정도로 멋졌다 //

Everyone was speechless. //

모두가 말문이 막혔다 //

형용사적 용법(the best thing 수식)
As they enjoyed / the emerald green Rocky Mountains, / Mia said, / "No wonder rafting is the best thing / to do / in Colorado!" // **1번** 단서 4: Mia가 래프팅이 Colorado에서 할 수 있는 최고의 일이라고 말함

그들이 즐길 때 / 에메랄드빛 녹색의 Rocky 산맥을 / Mia가 말했다 / "래프팅이 최고의 일이라는 것은 당연해 / 할 수 있는 / Colorado에서" //

*(C) 문단 요약: 강이 잔잔해지고 세 친구들은 멋진 주변 경치를 감상함

= As she agreed
(D) Agreeing with her friend, / Rebecca gave a thumbs-up. //

자기 친구에게 동의하면서 / Rebecca는 엄지를 들어 올렸다 //

"Sophia, your choice was excellent!" / she said / with a delighted smile. // **1번** 단서 5: 래프팅이 Colorado에서 할 수 있는 최고의 일이라는 Mia의 말에 동의함

"Sophia, 네 선택은 탁월했어"라고 / 그녀는 말했다 / 기쁜 미소를 띠면서 //

"I thought you were afraid of water, though, Sophia," / Mia said. //

"근데, Sophia, 나는 네가 물을 무서워 한다고 생각했어"라고 / Mia가 말했다 //

뒤에 afraid of water가 생략됨
Sophia explained, / "Well, I was / before I started rafting. // But I graduate from college / in a few months. // **3번 ④** 래프팅을 시작하기 전에는 물을 무서워 했음

Sophia가 설명했다 / "음, 나는 그랬지 / 내가 래프팅을 시작하기 전에는 // 하지만 나는 대학을 졸업해 / 몇 달 후에 // **1번** 단서 6, **3번 ⑤** Sophia는 대학을 졸업하기 전에 모험적인 것을 하기를 원했음

And, before I do, / I wanted to do something really adventurous / to test my bravery. //

그리고 내가 그러기 전에 / 나는 진짜 모험적인 것을 해보고 싶었어 / 내 용기를 시험할 //

명사절(목적어절) 접속사
I thought / that if I did something completely crazy, / it might
부사절 접속사(조건)
give (e) me / more confidence / when I'm interviewing for jobs." //
= Sophia

나는 생각했어 / 내가 완전히 미친 짓을 하면 / 그것이 나에게 줄 거라고 / 더 많은 자신감을 / 내가 취업 면접을 할 때" //

Now they could see / why she had suggested / going rafting. //

이제 그들은 알 수 있었다 / 왜 그녀가 제안했는지 / 래프팅을 하러 가는 것을 //

*(D) 문단 요약: 대학 졸업을 앞둔 Sophia는 취업 면접에 자신감을 줄 것이라고 생각해 친구들에게 래프팅을 하러 가자고 제안했음

- force ⓝ 힘, 물리력 · thrilling ⓐ 아주 신나는 · challenge ⓝ 도전
- plant ⓥ 자리를 잡다, 심다 · firmly ⓐd 확고히
- crash ⓥ (세게) 부딪치다 · rough ⓐ 거친
- toss ⓥ (가볍게 아무렇게나) 던지다 · eagerly ⓐd 열심히
- balance ⓥ 균형을 유지하다 · soaked ⓐ 물에 흠뻑 젖은
- spray ⓝ 물보라 · advantage ⓝ 유리한 점
- mindset ⓝ 사고방식, 태도 · daring ⓐ 대담한
- adventurer ⓝ 모험가 · courage ⓝ 용기
- reflection ⓝ (물·거울 등에 비친) 모습 · confident ⓐ 자신감 있는
- excitedly ⓐd 흥분하여 · manage to-v 용케 ~을 해내다
- avoid ⓥ 피하다, 모면하다 · suddenly ⓐd 갑자기
- calm down 진정하다 · sigh ⓝ 한숨 · relief ⓝ 안도, 안심
- view ⓝ 풍경 · scenery ⓝ 경치
- breathtaking ⓐ (너무 아름답거나 놀라워서) 숨이 막히는
- speechless ⓐ 말문이 막힌 · thumbs-up 찬성, 격려
- delighted ⓐ 아주 기뻐하는 · explain ⓥ 설명하다
- adventurous ⓐ 모험적인 · bravery ⓝ 용기
- completely ⓐd 완전히 · confidence ⓝ 자신감
- suggest ⓥ 제안하다

(A) 물의 힘에 맞서 싸우는 것은 짜릿한 도전이었다. Sophia는 바위에 세게 부딪히는 물결에 주목하면서 배에 단단히 버티어 자리 잡고 있으려고 애썼다. 물이 더 거칠어지자, 그녀는 물결이 자기를 물속으로 내동댕이치지 못하게 더 열

심히 노를 저을 수밖에 없었다. 그녀의 친구들인 Mia와 Rebecca는 보트의 균형을 유지하려고 그녀의 뒤에서 열심히 노를 젓고 있었다. 그들은 모든 물보라로 흠뻑 젖었다. Mia는 Sophia에게 "너 괜찮니? (a) 너 무섭지 않니?"라고 소리쳤다.

(C) "나는 아주 좋아!"라고 Sophia는 신이 나서 되받아 소리쳤다. 보트가 이리저리 내던져지고 있었지만 그 여자들은 용케 어느 바위에도 부딪치는 것을 피했다. 갑자기, 거의 물이 더 거칠어졌던 것만큼 빠르게 강이 잔잔해지는 것처럼 보였고, 그들은 모두 긴장을 풀었다. 안도의 한숨을 쉬면서, Sophia는 주변을 둘러보았다. "우와! 정말 멋진 풍경이다!"라고 (d) 그녀는 소리쳤다. 그들 주변의 경치는 숨이 멎을 정도로 멋졌다. 모두가 말문이 막혔다. 그들이 에메랄드빛 녹색의 Rocky 산맥을 즐길 때, Mia가 말했다. "래프팅이 Colorado에서 할 수 있는 최고의 일이라는 것은 당연해!"

(D) 자기 친구에게 동의하면서 Rebecca는 엄지를 들어 올렸다. "Sophia, 네 선택은 탁월했어!"라고 그녀는 기쁜 미소를 띠면서 말했다. "근데, Sophia, 나는 네가 물을 무서워 한다고 생각했어."라고 Mia가 말했다. Sophia가 설명하기를, "음, 내가 래프팅을 시작하기 전에는 그랬지. 하지만 나는 몇 달 후에 대학을 졸업해. 그리고, 그러기 전에, 나는 내 용기를 시험할 진짜 모험적인 것을 해보고 싶었어. 나는 완전히 미친 짓을 하면 그것이 (e) 나에게 취업 면접할 때 더 많은 자신감을 줄 거라고 생각했어." 이제 그들은 왜 그녀가 래프팅을 하러 가자고 제안했는지 알 수 있었다.

(B) "네 말은 정말 일리가 있어. 위험을 마다하지 않는 모험가의 마음가짐으로 대학을 졸업하는 것은 정말 유리한 점이야."라고 Mia가 말했다. Rebecca가 재빨리 덧붙여 말하기를, "그게 내가 대학을 나와서 첫 직장 생활을 시작하기 전에 몽골에 간 이유야. 그곳에서 두 달 동안 영어를 가르친 것은 내게 큰 도전이었어. 그런데 (b) 나는 그 경험에서 많은 것을 배웠어. 그것은 정말 내게 인생에서 무슨 일이든 시도할 용기를 주었어." 자기 친구들의 말을 들으면서, Sophia는 물에 비친 (c) 그녀 자신의 모습을 보았고 자신에게 미소를 되돌려주는 자신만만한 젊은 여자를 보았다.

Q 01 정답 ③

주어진 글 (A)에 이어질 내용을 순서에 맞게 배열한 것으로 가장 적절한 것은?

① (B) − (D) − (C) ─── (B)의 '일리가 있는 말'은 Sophia가 (D)에서 한 말임
② (C) − (B) − (D) ─── Mia가 Sophia에게 괜찮은지 물음 − Sophia가 괜찮다고 대답하고, Mia는 래프팅이 최고의 일이라고 말함 − Rebecca가 Mia의 말에 동의하고, Sophia는 래프팅을 원했던 이유를 말함 − Rebecca가 Sophia의 말이 일리가 있다며 자신의 비슷한 경험을 이야기함
③ (C) − (D) − (B)
④ (D) − (B) − (C) ─── (D)에서 Rebecca가 동의한 말은 (C)에서 Mia가 한 말임
⑤ (D) − (C) − (B)

왜 정답? [정답률 90%]

(A)에서 거친 파도와 싸우면서 Mia가 Sophia에게 괜찮은지 물었고, (C)에서 Sophia가 아주 좋다고 대답했다. 파도가 잦아지고 숨 막히게 멋진 경치를 보며 Mia가 래프팅이 Colorado에서 할 수 있는 최고의 일이라고 말했고, (D)에서 Rebecca가 Mia의 말에 동의하며 엄지를 들어 올렸다. 대학을 졸업하기 전에 정말 모험적인 것을 해보고 싶었다는 Sophia의 말이 (D)의 후반부에 등장하는데, (B)에서는 Rebecca가 이런 Sophia의 말이 일리가 있다면서 자신의 비슷한 경험을 이야기하므로 전체 글의 흐름은 ③ (C) − (D) − (B)가 적절하다.

왜 오답?

①, ② (B)에서 Rebecca가 일리가 있다고 한 것은 Sophia가 (D)에서 한 말, 즉 대학을 졸업하기 전에 모험적인 일을 해보고 싶었다는 말이므로 (B) 앞에 (D)가 있어야 한다. **주의**

④, ⑤ (A)는 거친 파도에 맞서 싸우면서 Mia가 Sophia에게 괜찮은지 묻는 내용으로 끝났다. 따라서 Rebecca가 친구의 말에 동의하면서 엄지를 들어 올렸다는 문장으로 시작한 (D)가 (A) 바로 뒤에 이어지는 것은 어색하다.

Q 02 정답 ②

밑줄 친 (a)~(e) 중에서 가리키는 대상이 나머지 넷과 다른 것은?

① (a) Sophia ② (b) Rebecca ③ (c) Sophia's ④ (d) Sophia ⑤ (e) Sophia

왜 정답? [정답률 92%]

Mia, Rebecca, Sophia 중에서 (a), (c), (d), (e)는 모두 Sophia를 가리키는데, 몽골에서 두 달 동안 영어를 가르친 경험에서 많은 것을 배웠다는 (b)는 Rebecca를 가리키므로 정답은 ②이다.

왜 오답?

① Mia가 Sophia에게 묻는 것이므로 you는 Sophia를 가리킨다.
③ Sophia가 본 것은 물에 비친 자신의 모습이므로 her는 Sophia를 가리킨다.
④ 안도의 한숨을 쉬면서 주변을 둘러본 Sophia가 소리친 것이다.
⑤ Sophia가 말하는 것이므로 me는 Sophia를 가리킨다.

Q 03 정답 ⑤

윗글에 관한 내용으로 적절하지 않은 것은?

① Mia와 Rebecca는 보트의 균형을 유지하려고 애썼다.
　Her friends Mia and Rebecca were paddling eagerly behind her to balance the boat.
② Rebecca는 몽골에서 영어를 가르친 경험이 있다.
　Rebecca quickly added, "That's why I went to Mongolia / Teaching English there
③ Sophia와 친구들이 함께 탄 보트는 바위에 부딪치지 않았다.
　the girls managed to avoid hitting any rocks
④ Sophia는 래프팅을 하기 전에는 물을 두려워했다.
　Sophia explained, "Well, I was before I started rafting.
⑤ Sophia는 용기를 시험할 모험을 대학 졸업 후에 하길 원했다.
　And, before I do, I wanted to do something really adventurous to test my bravery.

왜 정답? [정답률 91%]

(D)에서 Sophia는 자신이 몇 달 후에 대학을 졸업하는데, 그러기 전에 자신의 용기를 시험할 정말 모험적인 것을 해보고 싶었다고(And, before I do, I wanted to do something really adventurous to test my bravery.) 말했다. 졸업 후에 하기를 원한 것이 아니므로 ⑤은 글과 일치하지 않는다.

왜 오답?

① Sophia의 친구들인 Mia와 Rebecca가 보트의 균형을 유지하려고 열심히 노를 젓고 있었다. (Her friends Mia and Rebecca were paddling eagerly ~ to balance the boat.)
② Rebecca는 첫 직장 생활을 시작하기 전에 몽골에 가서 두 달 동안 영어를 가르쳤다. (Rebecca quickly added, "That's why I went to Mongolia / Teaching English there)
③ 거친 파도에 보트가 이리저리 내던져졌지만 Mia, Rebecca, Sophia의 보트는 어느 바위에도 부딪치지 않았다. (the girls managed to avoid hitting any rocks)
④ Sophia가 물을 무서워 한다고 생각했다는 Mia의 말에 Sophia는 래프팅을 시작하기 전에는 그랬다고 대답했다. (Sophia explained, "Well, I was before I started rafting.)

Q 04~06 ＊하이킹을 통해 서로의 진심을 알게 된 부자 ─────

used to-v: (과거에) ~하곤 했다
(A) "Do you remember / when Sean used to tell me / that I was the best dad in the world?" //
　　　　　　　　　　　　　목적어절을 이끄는 접속사

"기억나요 / Sean이 말하곤 했던 때가 / 나에게 내가 세상에서 최고의 아빠라고" //

Ethan asked his wife, Grace. // Ethan이 아내 Grace에게 물었다 //

"Yes, I do. / I always envied / your relationship with Sean," / she replied. // **6번 ①** Grace는 항상 Ethan과 Sean의 관계가 부러웠다고 함

"네, 기억해요 / 항상 나는 부러워했어요 / 당신과 Sean의 관계를" / 그녀가 대답했다 //
　　　　　　　　　　　　　　　　　　　　　　　　　　　　　　　= Ethan's
Ethan then shared / how things had changed / since (a) his son started middle school. //

그런 다음 Ethan은 이야기했다 / 상황이 어떻게 변했는지 / 자신의 아들 Sean이 중학교에 다니기 시작한 이후로 //

　　　　　　　　　　　　　　　noticed의 목적격 보어
Grace had noticed / Ethan often pushing Sean / to study harder. //

Grace는 알아챘었다 / Ethan이 자주 Sean에게 밀어붙이는 것을 / 공부를 더 열심히 하라고 //

"Maybe he isn't that into school right now. //
"아마도 지금 그 애는 학교에 그다지 관심이 없을 거예요 //

How about going hiking, / just the two of you?" / she suggested. // 6번 ② Grace가 Ethan에게 Sean과 둘이서 하이킹할 것을 권했음
하이킹하러 가는 건 어때요 / 당신과 Sean 단둘이서 / 그녀가 제안했다 //
분사구문을 이끎   목적어절을 이끄는 접속사
He agreed, / and realizing / that both his and Sean's hiking jackets / were still at the laundry, / he asked his wife / to go and pick them up with him. // 4번 단서 1, 6번 ④ : Ethan이 Grace에게 함께 세탁소에 가서 세탁물 찾아오자고 함
그는 동의했다 / 그리고 깨닫고서 / 자신과 Sean의 하이킹 재킷이 / 여전히 세탁소에 있다는 것을 / 아내에게 부탁했다 / 자신과 함께 가서 그것을 찾아오자고 //

*(A) 문단 요약: 아들 Sean과의 관계가 예전 같지 않다는 Ethan에게 Grace는 함께 하이킹을 갈 것을 권유했고, Ethan은 Grace에게 함께 세탁 맡긴 재킷을 찾으러 가자고 함

4번 단서 2: Ethan과 Grace가 세탁소에서 재킷을 찾아 집으로 옴
명사절을 이끄는 접속사   앞에 목적격 관계대명사 생략
(B) Ethan and Grace came back home / with the jackets / and checked / if Sean had everything else / he needed for hiking. //
Ethan과 Grace는 집으로 돌아왔다 / 재킷을 들고 / 그리고 확인했다 / Sean이 그 외 모든 것을 갖고 있는지 / 하이킹에 필요한 //

Luckily, / in his drawers / they found / his hat, shoes, sunglasses, and hiking sticks. // 6번 ③ Sean의 서랍에서 선글라스를 발견함
다행히 / 서랍에서 / 그들은 발견했다 / 그의 모자, 신발, 선글라스, 등산지팡이를 //

When Sean returned from school, / Ethan softly said, / "Sean, let's go hiking this Saturday, / just the two of us." //
Sean이 학교에서 돌아오자 / Ethan은 부드럽게 말했다 / "Sean, 이번 주 토요일에 하이킹하러 가자 / 우리 단 둘이서" //
= Ethan
Though Sean thanked (b) him / for the suggestion, / he said / he had to go to the library. //
뒤에 목적어절을 이끄는 접속사 생략
Sean은 그에게 고맙다고 했지만 / 제안해줘서 / 그는 말했다 / 도서관에 가야 한다고 //

Grace stepped in, / "You know, / the weather this weekend / will be the best of the year. // Why not enjoy it?" //
Grace가 끼어들었다 / "있잖아, / 이번 주말 날씨가 / 올해 최고일 거야 // 즐기지 않을래?" //
= Sean
After a moment's hesitation, / (c) he agreed. // 4번 단서 3: Sean이 하이킹 제안을 수락함
잠시 망설인 후 / 그는 동의했다 //

*(B) 문단 요약: 세탁물을 찾아온 Ethan과 Grace는 Sean의 하이킹 용품을 서랍에서 찾아내고, Sean이 집에 돌아온 후 하이킹 계획에 대해 이야기함. Sean은 처음에는 거절하나 Grace의 설득으로 수락하게 됨

(C) "When did you bring the jackets in?" / the clerk at the laundry asked. // 4번 단서 4: 세탁소 직원이 재킷을 언제 맡겼는지 물음
"언제 재킷을 맡기셨나요" / 세탁소 점원이 물었다 //

"Maybe two weeks ago," / Ethan replied. //
"아마 2주 쯤이에요" / Ethan은 대답했다 //
= Ethan
Then, / Grace quickly reminded (d) him, / "Honey, we actually left them here a month ago." //
그러자 / Grace가 재빨리 그에게 상기시켰다 / "여보, 사실은 그것을 한 달 전에 여기에 두고 갔어요" //
부사적 용법(목적)
The clerk went into the storage area / to look for the clothes. //
점원은 보관 구역으로 들어갔다 / 그 옷들을 찾아보기 위해 //

Finally, / he returned with the jackets / and handed them to Ethan. //
마침내 / 그는 재킷을 들고 돌아왔다 / 그리고 Ethan에게 그것들을 건네주었다 //

The clerk politely said / "I am sorry, / but please collect your items earlier / next time. // Our storage is too full." //
점원이 공손하게 말했다 / "죄송합니다만 / 물건을 더 일찍 찾아가 주세요 / 다음에는 // 저희 보관 공간이 너무 꽉 찼습니다" //

Ethan felt embarrassed / for the late collection / and apologized. //
Ethan은 민망함을 느꼈다 / 늦은 수거에 대해 / 그리고 사과했다 //

*(C) 문단 요약: 세탁물을 찾으러 간 Ethan에게 아내가 한 달 전에 맡겼음을 상기시켜 주고, 직원은 세탁물을 빨리 찾아갈 것을 당부했고, Ethan은 이를 부끄러워하며 사과함

(D) The weather was perfect. //
날씨는 완벽했다 //

Ethan and Sean set off hiking / along the valley by Aicken Mountain. // 4번 단서 5: Ethan과 Sean이 하이킹을 하러 감
Ethan과 Sean은 하이킹을 시작했다 / Aicken Mountain 계곡을 따라 //

They walked in silence / until Sean fell over a rock / and twisted his ankle. // 6번 ⑤ Sean이 돌에 걸려 넘어짐
그들은 말없이 걸었다 / Sean이 돌에 걸려 넘어졌을 때까지 / 그리고 발목을 삐끗했을 때까지 //
분사구문
Realizing he couldn't walk, / Ethan carried his son down on his back. //
그가 걸을 수 없다는 것을 깨닫고는 / Ethan은 아들을 등에 업고 내려갔다 //
동격
He felt Sean's heartbeat, / something he hadn't felt / since Sean was a baby. // 사이에 something을 수식하는 목적격 관계대명사 생략
그는 Sean의 심장 박동을 느꼈다 / 느껴보지 못했던 무언가였다 / Sean이 아기였을 때 이후로 //

Suddenly, / Sean said, / "Dad, I'm sorry. //
갑자기 / Sean이 말했다 / "아빠, 미안해요 //
= Ethan
At some point, / I started to become afraid / of disappointing (e) you. //
어느 순간부터 / 두려워지기 시작했어요 / 아빠를 실망하게 하는 것이 //

But you are still the best dad." //
하지만 아빠는 여전히 최고의 아빠예요 //
분사구문
Energized, / he felt no weight on his back / and replied, /
힘이 솟아나 / Ethan은 등에 아무런 무게도 느껴지지 않았다 / 그리고 대답했다 /

"You are the best son, / no matter what." //
"넌 최고의 아들이야 / 무슨 일이 있어도" //

*(D) 문단 요약: 하이킹을 하던 중 Sean은 돌에 걸려 넘어져 발목을 삐게 되고, Ethan은 아들을 업은 채 이동했고, Sean이 건넨 진심에 힘을 얻고 Sean에게도 최고의 아들이라고 말함

• envy ⓥ 부러워하다   • hesitation ⓝ 망설임
• remind ⓥ 상기시키다   • politely ⓐⅾ 정중하게
• embarrassed ⓐ 당황스러운, 민망한   • apologize ⓥ 사과하다
• in silence 조용히, 말없이   • twist ⓥ 삐끗하다
• energize ⓥ 열기[열정]를 돋우다

(A) "Sean이 나에게 내가 세상에서 최고의 아빠라고 말하곤 했던 거 기억나요?" Ethan이 아내 Grace에게 물었다. "네, 기억해요. 항상 나는 당신과 Sean의 관계를 부러워했어요."라고 그녀가 대답했다. 그런 다음 Ethan은 (a) 자신의 아들 Sean이 중학교에 다니기 시작한 이후로 상황이 어떻게 변했는지 이야기했다. Grace는 Ethan이 자주 Sean에게 공부를 더 열심히 하라고 밀어붙이는 것을 알아챘다. "아마도 지금 그 애는 학교에 그다지 관심이 없을 거예요. 당신과 Sean 단둘이서 하이킹하러 가는 건 어때요?"라고 그녀가 제안했다. 그는 동의했고, 자신과 Sean의 하이킹 재킷이 여전히 세탁소에 있다는 것을 깨닫고는 아내에게 자신과 함께 가서 그것을 찾아오자고 부탁했다.

(C) "언제 재킷을 맡기셨나요?"라고 세탁소 점원이 물었다. "아마 2주 전쯤이에요."라고 Ethan은 대답했다. 그러자 "여보, 사실은 그것을 한 달 전에 여기에 두고 갔어요."라고 Grace가 재빨리 (d) 그에게 상기시켰다. 점원은 보관 구역으로 들어가 그 옷들을 찾아보았다. 마침내 그는 재킷을 들고 돌아와 Ethan에게 건네주었다. "죄송합니다만, 다음에는 물건을 더 일찍 찾아가 주세요. 저희 보관 공간이 너무 꽉 찼습니다."라고 점원이 공손하게 말했다. Ethan은 늦은 수거에 대해 민망함을 느끼며 사과했다.

(B) Ethan과 Grace는 재킷을 들고 집으로 돌아와 Sean이 하이킹에 필요한 그 외의 모든 것을 갖고 있는지 확인했다. 다행히 그들은 서랍에서 그의 모자, 신발, 선글라스, 등산지팡이를 발견했다. Sean이 학교에서 돌아오자 Ethan은 부드럽게 말했다. "Sean, 이번 주 토요일에 우리 단둘이서 하이킹하러 가자." Sean은 (b) 그에게 제안해줘서 고맙다고 했지만, 도서관에 가야 한다고 말했다. Grace가 끼어들었다. "있잖아, 이번 주말 날씨가 올해 최고일 거야. 즐기지 않을래?" 잠시 망설인 후 (c) 그는 동의했다.

(D) 날씨는 완벽했다. Ethan과 Sean은 Aicken Mountain 계곡을 따라 하이킹을 시작했다. 그들은 말없이 걷다가 Sean이 돌에 걸려 넘어져 발목을 삐끗했다. 그가 걸을 수 없다는 것을 깨닫고는 Ethan은 아들을 등에 업고

내려갔다. 그는 Sean의 심장 박동을 느꼈는데, 이는 Sean이 아기였을 때 이후로 처음 느끼는 것이었다. 갑자기 Sean이 말했다. "아빠, 미안해요. 어느 순간부터 (e) 아빠를 실망하게 할까 봐 두려워지기 시작했어요. 하지만 아빠는 여전히 최고의 아빠예요." 힘이 솟아나 Ethan은 등에 아무런 무게도 느껴지지 않았으며 "넌 무슨 일이 있어도 최고의 아들이야."라고 말했다.

Q 04 정답 ②

주어진 글 (A)에 이어질 내용을 순서에 맞게 배열한 것으로 가장 적절한 것은?
세탁소에 갔다가 집으로 돌아온 내용인 (B) 앞에 세탁소에 가는 (C)가 와야 함

① (B) — (D) — (C) ┐ 아들 Sean과의 관계가 예전 같지 않다는 Ethan에게 Grace는 함께
②(C) — (B) — (D) │ 하이킹을 갈 것을 권유했음 - Ethan과 Grace가 세탁소에 가서 맡긴
③ (C) — (D) — (B) │ 재킷을 찾음 - 집으로 돌아와 아들 Sean에게 하이킹 계획을 전하고
④ (D) — (B) — (C) │ Sean은 잠시 주저하다 이를 수락함 - 함께 하이킹을 간 Ethan과
⑤ (D) — (C) — (B) │ Sean이 서로에게 진심을 전하며 관계가 개선됨
                    │ (D)는 하이킹을 하다가 서로의 진심을 확인하는 결말임
                    └ 하이킹 제안을 하고 이를 수락하는 내용인 (B)가 함께 하이킹을 하는 내용인 (D)보다 앞에 나와야 함

왜 정답·오답? [정답률 93%]

(A): 아들과의 관계가 예전 같지 않다는 Ethan에게 Grace는 함께 하이킹을 갈 것을 권유하고, Ethan은 Grace에게 함께 세탁 맡긴 재킷을 찾으러 가자고 했다.

→ Ethan과 Grace가 세탁소에 가서 세탁물을 찾는 장면이 이어질 것이다.

(B): 세탁물을 찾아온 Ethan과 Grace는 Sean에게 하이킹 계획에 대해 이야기하고, Sean은 처음에는 거절하나 Grace의 설득으로 이를 수락하게 되었다.

→ 세탁소에서 집으로 돌아와 Sean에게 하이킹 제안을 하는 내용이므로 (B) 앞에는 세탁소에 가서 세탁물을 찾는 장면이, (B) 뒤에는 하이킹을 수락했으므로 하이킹을 가는 장면이 나올 것이다.

(C): Grace와 함께 세탁물을 찾으러 간 Ethan은 한 달 전에 맡긴 세탁물을 이제야 찾아가는 것임을 인지하고, 세탁물을 빨리 찾아가 줄 것을 당부하는 직원의 부탁에 사과했다.

→ Ethan이 Grace와 함께 세탁소에 가서 세탁물을 찾는 내용이므로 (C) 앞에는 세탁소에 가서 세탁물을 찾자는 제안이나 관련 내용이 나와야 한다. 또한 (C) 뒤에는 세탁물을 찾고 난 이후의 상황이 전개되어야 한다.

(D): 함께 하이킹을 하던 중 Sean은 돌에 걸려 넘어져 발목을 삐게 되고, Ethan은 아들을 업은 채 이동했고, 서로 진심을 전할 기회를 갖게 되었다.

→ 함께 하이킹을 하는 내용이므로 (D) 앞에는 하이킹 제안을 하고 이를 수락하는 내용이 나와야 한다. 또한 Ethan과 Sean이 하이킹을 하며 서로의 진심을 전하고 관계가 개선되는 내용이 제시되므로 (D)가 글의 결말 부분일 확률이 높다.
▶ (A): 아들과의 관계가 예전 같지 않다는 Ethan에게 Grace는 함께 하이킹을 갈 것을 권유하고, Ethan은 Grace에게 세탁 맡긴 재킷을 찾으러 가자고 했음 → (C): Ethan은 한 달 전에 맡긴 세탁물을 이제야 찾아가는 것임을 인지하고, 세탁물을 빨리 찾아가 줄 것을 당부하는 직원의 부탁에 사과했음 → (B): Ethan과 Grace는 Sean에게 하이킹 계획에 대해 이야기하고, Sean은 처음에는 거절하나 Grace의 설득으로 수락하게 되었음 → (D): 하이킹을 하던 중 Sean은 돌에 걸려 넘어져 발목을 삐게 되고, Ethan은 아들을 업고 이동했고, 서로 진심을 전할 기회를 갖게 되었음
▶ 사건이 진행되는 순서는 ② (C) – (B) – (D)임

백승준 | 2025 수능 응시 · 광주 광주숭원고 졸
빠르게 각각의 문단의 첫 부분과 마지막 부분을 보며 이어지는 연결고리를 찾아내는 것이 중요해. (A)의 마지막 부분에서 세탁소에 있는 재킷을 찾으러 간다는 내용이 있으니 세탁소에서 점원과 나누는 대화가 제시된 (C)가 처음으로 이어지겠지. 또, 다음으로 (B)의 첫 부분에서 재킷을 가지고 집에 돌아왔다는 내용이 있으니 (B)가 다음으로 이어질 거야. (B)의 나머지 부분에선 Sean이 하이킹 가는 것에 동의하는 내용이 나오니 하이킹하며 일어나는 일이 제시된 (D)가 마지막으로 이어질 거야.

Q 05 정답 ③

밑줄 친 (a)~(e) 중에서 가리키는 대상이 나머지 넷과 다른 것은?
① (a)   ② (b)   ③(c)   ④ (d)   ⑤ (e)
= Ethan's = Ethan   = Sean   = Ethan   = Ethan

왜 정답? [정답률 92%]

③ (c) he: 하이킹을 가자는 아버지 Ethan의 제안에 Sean이 잠시 주저하다가 동의한 것이다. ▶ Sean

왜 오답?

① (a) his: 아내 Grace에게 Ethan이 그의 아들이 중학생이 되고 난 이후 아들과 자신과의 관계가 변하게 되었다고 했다. ▶ Ethan

② (b) him: 하이킹을 가자는 Ethan의 제안에 대해 Sean이 고맙다고 한 것이다. ▶ Ethan

④ (d) him: Grace가 남편 Ethan에게 한 달 전에 세탁물을 맡기고 갔음을 상기시켜 주고 있다. ▶ Ethan

⑤ (e) you: Sean이 아버지 Ethan에게 아버지를 실망시키는 것이 두려워지기 시작했다고 했다. ▶ Ethan

한규진 | 2025 수능 응시 · 대구 계성고 졸
이 문제를 잘 풀 수 있는 꿀팁은 읽으면서 지문 안에 있는 선택지 위에 등장인물의 이름을 덧쓰는 거야. 시간이 아까우니 이름을 다 쓰지는 말고, 이름의 첫 글자 정도를 써줘! 이렇게 하면 중간에 멈추지 않을 수 있어서 글을 읽어내려가는 속도를 줄이지 않을 수 있고 흐름도 끊기지 않아. 글을 다 읽고 나중에 답을 체크할 때는 글자만 확인해주면 되니까 다시 글을 읽을 필요도 없어! 시간을 많이 벌 수 있는 방법이니까 꼭 해보길 바라!

Q 06 정답 ④

윗글에 관한 내용으로 적절하지 않은 것은?
① Grace는 Ethan과 Sean의 관계를 부러워했다고 말했다.
"I always envied your relationship with Sean," she replied.
② Grace는 Ethan에게 Sean과 둘이서 하이킹할 것을 권했다.
How about going hiking, just the two of you?" she suggested.
③ Sean의 선글라스가 서랍장 안에 있었다.
Luckily, in his drawers they found his hat, shoes, sunglasses, and hiking sticks.
④Ethan은 혼자서 세탁소에 하이킹 재킷을 찾으러 갔다.
he asked his wife to go and pick them up with him
⑤ Sean은 하이킹하는 도중 돌에 걸려 넘어졌다.
Sean fell over a rock and twisted his ankle.

왜 정답? [정답률 92%]

④ Ethan은 혼자서 세탁소에 하이킹 재킷을 찾으러 간 것이 아니라 아내에게 함께 가자고 했다. (he asked his wife to go and pick them up with him)

왜 오답?

① Grace는 Ethan과 Sean의 관계를 부러워했다고 말했다. ("I always envied your relationship with Sean," she replied.)

② Grace는 Ethan에게 Sean과 둘이서 하이킹할 것을 권했다. (How about going hiking, just the two of you?" she suggested.)

③ Sean의 선글라스가 서랍장 안에 있었다. (Luckily, in his drawers they found his hat, shoes, sunglasses, and hiking sticks.)

⑤ Sean은 하이킹하는 도중 돌에 걸려 넘어졌다. (Sean fell over a rock and twisted his ankle.)

배지오 | 2025 수능 응시 · 성남 낙생고 졸
여러 등장인물이 어떤 일을 혼자 하는지, 아니면 둘이 하는지도 잘 파악해야 해. 여기서는 (A) 문단과 (C) 문단을 보면 답을 알 수 있어. (A) 문단의 끝 문장에서 분명히 Ethan은 Grace와 '함께(with)' Sean의 등산복을 가지러 가자고 했거든. (C) 문단에서도 Grace와 Ethan이 세탁소에서 대화하고 있음을 알 수 있지. 그러면 Ethan이 혼자서 세탁소에 갔다는 ④이 정답이겠지? 이렇게 한 문단을 읽고도 정답이라는 확신이 들지 않으면 분명히 이어지는 다른 문단에서도 힌트가 나올 가능성이 높으니까 불안해하지 말자고!

9번① Helen이 중고 거래 앱에서 알림을 받음

seller를 수식하는 분사

(A) Helen was thrilled / when she received a notification / on a second-hand shopping app from a seller / named Anna. //

Helen은 매우 기뻤다 / 알림을 받았을 때 / 중고 쇼핑 앱에서 Anna라는 판매자로부터 //

leaves를 수식하는 분사

For months, / she had been looking for a *Philodendron gloriosum*, / a Colombian plant / with dark, velvety leaves shaped like hearts. //

몇 달 동안 / 그녀는 Philodendron gloriosum을 찾고 있었다 / 콜롬비아 식물 / 하트 모양의 짙은 벨벳 같은 잎을 가진 //

She had almost given up on / getting one. //

그녀는 거의 포기할 뻔했다 / 이 식물을 구하는 것을 //

Anna, though, had put one up for sale. //

하지만 Anna가 매물로 한 그루를 내놓았다 //

= Anna

The posting read, / "(a) I'm selling my favorite plant, / because I'm moving abroad. //

게시글은 적혀 있었다 / "제가 제일 좋아하는 식물을 팔려고 합니다 / 해외로 이사하게 되었기 때문에요. //

7번 단서 1: 오늘 식물을 가져가면 시세의 절반 가격에 팔고자 한다는 메시지를 받음

계속적 용법의 관계대명사

If you pick it up today from Edincester Heights, / you can have it for the current price, / which is half the market rate." //

만약 이 식물을 오늘 Edincester Heights에서 가져가시면 / 현재 가격으로 가져가실 수 있습니다 / 시장 시세의 절반 가격인 //

* (A) 문단 요약: 식물을 구하고 싶었던 Helen은 중고 거래 앱을 통해 Anna에게서 해외로 나가게 되어 식물을 시세의 절반 가격에 팔고자 한다는 메시지를 받음

분사구문

(B) Arriving at the building, / Helen could identify Julia / by the large paper bag she was holding. //

사이에 목적격 관계대명사 that 생략

건물에 도착했을 때 / Helen은 Julia를 알아볼 수 있었다 / 그녀가 들고 있는 커다란 종이봉투로 //

leaves를 수식하는 분사

The bag had leaves / sticking out of the top. //

그 봉투는 나뭇잎을 가지고 있었다 / 윗부분에 삐져나와 있는 // **7번** 단서 2: 건물에 도착해서 Helen은 Julia를 바로 알아봄.

= Helen

(b) She said, "You must be Julia!" //

9번② Julia가 종이 가방을 들고 있었음

그녀는 "당신이 Julia가 틀림없겠군요!"라고 말했다 //

분사구문

Laughing, / the woman said, / "Yes! Please take good care of this plant. //

웃으면서 / 그 여자는 말했다 / "네! 이 식물을 잘 돌봐주세요 //

Anna had it for six years, / so she considers it family." //

Anna가 이 식물을 6년 동안 키웠어요 / 그래서 그녀는 이것을 가족이라고 생각해요." //

From the bag, / she pulled out another plant, / a tiny one with thick, glossy leaves. //

봉투에서 / 그녀는 식물 하나를 더 꺼냈다 / 두껍고 윤기 나는 잎을 가진 작은 식물을 //

"Are you familiar with this? // "이것을 잘 아세요? //

It's called a Dragon's Tail. // 용의 꼬리라고 해요.

사이에 목적어절을 이끄는 접속사 that 생략

(c) My housemate said you could take it too, / if you'd like." //

제 룸메이트가 당신이 이것도 가져가도 된다고 말했어요 / 만약 원한다면" //

* (B) 문단 요약: Helen은 Julia를 만나 구매하기로 한 식물을 건네받고, 다른 식물까지 추가로 구매 제안을 받음

7번 단서 3, **9번③** Helen이 판매자에게 메시지를 보냄

(C) Helen immediately messaged the seller. //

Helen은 즉시 판매자에게 메시지를 보냈다 //

= Anna's

"Hello! I'm interested in purchasing (d) your plant. //

"안녕하세요! 제가 당신의 식물을 구매하는 데에 관심이 있어요. //

If it works for your schedule, I can be there / in 10 minutes!" //

일정이 맞으신다면, 제가 거기로 갈 수 있어요 / 10분 안에 //

9번③ 판매자(Anna)가 Helen에게 답함

Anna replied, "Hi, there! // Anna는 답했다 / "안녕하세요! //

I am at work right now, / but my housemate, Julia, can meet you in front of the building." //

저는 지금 일하는 중이지만 / 제 룸메이트 Julia가 당신을 건물 앞에서 만날 수 있어요." //

분사구문을 이끎(Being 생략)

Unable to believe her good luck, / Helen typed back in excitement, / "Great! I can leave now. //

자신의 행운을 믿지 못한 채 / Helen은 흥분하여 답장했다 / "좋아요! 저는 지금 출발할 수 있어요. //

9번④ Helen이 검정색 야구 모자를 쓰겠다고 함

I'll wear a black baseball cap." // 검은 야구 모자를 쓰고 있을게요." //

* (C) 문단 요약: Helen은 판매자에게 메시지를 보내 식물을 사겠다고 하고, 판매자인 Anna는 룸메이트인 Julia가 대신 거래 현장에 나갈 것이라고 메시지를 보냄

7번 단서 4: 다른 식물까지 추가로 구매 제안을 받은 것에 대해 Helen이 좋다고 함

(D) Helen exclaimed, / "Yes, I'd love to! //

Helen이 말했다 / "네, 그러고 싶어요! //

Please thank Anna for me. // Anna에게 저를 대신해서 고맙다고 전해주세요 //

Both are in such wonderful condition. // 둘 다 정말 멋진 상태네요 //

Do you have any tips for keeping them in good shape?" //

그것들을 상태가 좋게 유지하기 위한 어떤 팁이 있으세요?" //

분사구문 **9번⑤** Julia가 자신은 식물 전문가는 아니라고 함

Handing over the bag, Julia replied, / "I'm not a plant expert,

목적어절을 이끄는 접속사

but I know / that Anna kept them away from windows /

부사적 용법(목적)

to avoid direct sunlight. //

봉투를 건네며 Julia는 답했다 / "제가 식물 전문가는 아닙니다, 그러나 저는 알아요 / Anna가 그것들을 창문에서 멀리 두었다는 것을 / 직사광선을 피하고자 //

= Anna

Why don't you message (e) her? //

그녀에게 메시지를 보내보는 건 어떠세요? //

She would be happy to offer advice." //

그녀가 기꺼이 조언을 해줄 거예요." //

"I'll be sure to do that," / Helen said, as she handed over the cash. //

7번 단서 5: 돈을 건넴(거래가 마무리됨)

"꼭 그렇게 할게요." / Helen은 현금을 건네주며 말했다 //

* (D) 문단 요약: Helen은 두 가지 식물을 키우는 것에 대한 조언을 구하고 Julia는 자신은 전문가가 아니므로 Anna에게 메시지를 보내 물어보라고 하며, Helen은 그러겠다고 하고 돈을 건넴

- thrilled ⓐ 황홀해 하는   · notification ⓝ 알림, 통지
- second-hand ⓐ 중고의   · market rate 시장 시세
- stick out of ~ 밖으로 삐져나오다   · identify ⓥ 알아보다
- glossy ⓐ 윤이 나는   · immediately ⓐⓓ 즉시
- type ⓥ 타자 치다[입력하다]   · in excitement 흥분하여
- exclaim ⓥ 외치다, 소리치다   · condition ⓝ 상태
- in good shape 상태가 좋은   · expert ⓝ 전문가

(A) Helen은 중고 쇼핑 앱에서 Anna라는 판매자로부터 알림을 받았을 때 매우 기뻤다. 그녀는 몇 달 동안 하트 모양의 짙은 벨벳 같은 잎을 가진 콜롬비아 식물인 Philodendron gloriosum을 찾고 있었다. 그녀는 이 식물을 구하는 것을 거의 포기할 뻔했다. 하지만 Anna가 한 그루를 매물로 내놓았다. 게시글에는 "(a) 제가 해외로 이사하게 되어 제일 좋아하는 식물을 팔려고 합니다. 오늘 Edincester Heights에서 이 식물을 가져가시면 시장 시세의 절반 가격인 현재 가격으로 가져가실 수 있습니다."라고 적혀 있었다.

(C) Helen은 즉시 판매자에게 메시지를 보냈다. "안녕하세요! 제가 (d) 당신의 식물을 구매하고 싶어요. 일정이 맞으신다면, 10분 안에 거기로 갈 수 있을 것 같아요!" Anna는 "안녕하세요! 저는 지금 일하는 중이지만, 제 룸메이트 Julia가 당신을 건물 앞에서 만날 수 있어요."라고 답했다. Helen은 자신의 행운을 믿지 못한 채 흥분하여 "좋아요! 저는 지금 출발할 수 있어요. 검은 야구 모자를 쓰고 있을게요."라고 답장했다.

(B) 건물에 도착했을 때 Helen은 Julia가 들고 있는 커다란 종이봉투로 그녀를 알아볼 수 있었다. 그 봉투의 윗부분에는 나뭇잎이 삐져나와 있었다. (b) 그녀는 "당신이 Julia가 틀림없겠군요!"라고 말했다. 그 여자는 웃으며 "네! 이 식물을 잘 돌봐주세요. 6년 동안 키워서 Anna는 이 식물이 가족이라고 생각해요."라고 말했다. 그녀는 봉투에서 두껍고 윤기 나는 잎을 가진 작은 식물 하나를 더 꺼냈다. "이것을 잘 아세요? 용의 꼬리라고 해요. (c) 제 룸메이트가 당신이 원한다면 이것도 가져가도 된다고 했어요."

(D) Helen이 "네, 그러고 싶어요! Anna에게 저를 대신해서 고맙다고 전해주세요. 둘 다 정말 멋진 상태네요. 그것들을 상태가 좋게 유지하기 위한 어떤 팁이 있나요?"라고 외쳤다. Julia는 봉투를 건네며 "제가 식물 전문가는 아니지만 Anna가 직사광선을 피하고자 그것들을 창문에서 멀리 두었다는 건 알아요. (e) 그녀에게 메시지를 보내보는 건 어떠세요? 그녀가 기꺼이 조언을 해줄 거예요." Helen은 현금을 건네주며 "꼭 그렇게 할게요."라고 말했다.

주어진 글 (A)에 이어질 내용을 순서에 맞게 배열한 것으로 가장 적절한 것은?

① (B) — (D) — (C) 주어진 글 뒤에 Julia를 만나는 (B)가 바로 올 수는 없음

② (C) — (B) — (D)

③ (C) — (D) — (B) (C)에서 식물 거래 약속을 잡았으므로 뒤에는 Helen과 Julia가 처음 만나 식물을 거래하는 (B)가 이어져야 함

④ (D) — (B) — (C) (A)에서 식물 판매 글을 본 Helen이 판매자와 연락을 주고받아 거래 약속을 정하는 내용이 이어져야 하므로 (A) 다음에는 (C)가 나와야 함

⑤ (D) — (C) — (B)

식물을 구하고 싶었던 Helen은 중고 거래 앱을 통해 Anna에게서 식물을 시세의 절반 가격에 팔고자 한다는 메시지를 받음 - Helen이 판매자인 Anna에게 연락해 거래 약속을 잡음 - Anna 대신 룸메이트 Julia가 거래 장소에 나와 식물을 건네주고 다른 식물까지 추가로 구매 의사가 있으냐 물음 - Helen은 이를 승낙하고 식물 키우는 것에 대한 조언을 구한 뒤, 돈을 건넴

왜 정답 · 오답? [정답률 95%]

(A): 식물을 구하고 싶었던 Helen은 중고 거래 앱을 통해 Anna에게서 해외로 나가게 되어 식물을 시세의 절반 가격에 팔고자 한다는 메시지를 받았다.

→ Helen이 Anna의 메시지에 대해 대응하는 내용이 이어질 것이다.

(B): Helen은 Julia를 만나 구매하기로 한 식물을 건네 받고, 다른 식물까지 추가로 구매 제안을 받았다.

→ Helen이 Julia를 만나 식물을 거래하는 내용이므로 (B) 앞에는 식물 거래에 대해 약속을 정하는 내용이 나와야 한다. 또한 (B) 뒤에는 추가로 구매 제안을 받은 식물에 대한 Helen의 반응이 나올 것이다.

(C): Helen은 판매자에게 메시지를 보내 식물을 사겠다고 하고, 판매자인 Anna는 룸메이트인 Julia가 대신 거래 현장에 나갈 것이라고 메시지를 보냈다.

→ Helen이 판매자에게 메시지를 보내 식물 거래에 대한 약속을 정하는 내용이므로 (C) 앞에는 Helen이 식물 거래에 대한 정보를 얻는 내용이 나와야 한다. 또한 (C) 뒤에는 Julia와 만나 식물을 거래하는 내용이 이어질 것이다.

(D): Helen은 두 가지 식물을 키우는 것에 대한 조언을 구하고 Julia는 자신이 전문가가 아니므로 Anna에게 메시지를 보내 물어보라고 하며, Helen은 그러겠다고 하고 돈을 건넸다.

→ Helen이 두 가지 식물을 가지게 되었으므로 (D) 앞에는 식물을 두 개나 구매하게 된 과정이 나와야 한다. Helen이 돈을 건네는 것으로 글이 끝나기 때문에 식물 거래가 마무리된 결말 부분으로 볼 수 있다.

▶ (A) 식물을 구하고 싶었던 Helen은 중고 거래 앱을 통해 Anna에게서 해외로 나가게 되어 식물을 시세의 절반 가격에 팔고자 한다는 메시지를 받았음 →

(C): Helen은 판매자에게 메시지를 보내 식물을 사겠다고 하고, 판매자인 Anna는 룸메이트인 Julia가 대신 거래 현장에 나갈 것이라고 메시지를 보냈음 →

(B): Helen은 Julia를 만나 구매하기로 한 식물을 건네 받고, 다른 식물까지 추가로 구매 제안을 받았음 → (D): Helen은 두 가지 식물을 키우는 것에 대한 조언을 구하고 Julia는 자신은 전문가가 아니므로 Anna에게 메시지를 보내 물어보라고 하며, Helen은 그러겠다고 하고 돈을 건넸음

▶ 사건이 진행되는 순서는 ② (C) – (B) – (D)임

Q 08 정답 ②

밑줄 친 (a)~(e) 중에서 가리키는 대상이 나머지 넷과 다른 것은?

① (a)　② (b)　③ (c)　④ (d)　⑤ (e)
= Anna　= Helen　= Anna　= Anna's　= Anna

왜 정답? [정답률 91%]

② (b) she: Helen이 쇼핑백을 들고 있는 Julia를 알아보고 당신이 Julia가 틀림 없다고 말을 걸 것이다. ▶ Helen

왜 오답?

① (a) I: 중고 거래 앱에 식물을 파는 메시지를 올린 사람은 Anna이다. ▶ Anna

③ (c) My housemate: Anna 대신 거래 현장에 나온 Julia가 내 룸메이트(Anna)가 다른 식물도 원하면 가져가도 좋다는 말을 했음을 전하고 있다. ▶ Anna

④ (d) your: Helen이 Anna의 메시지를 보고 당신의 식물을 구매하고 싶다고 했다. ▶ Anna

⑤ (e) her: 식물에 대해 더 자세히 알고 싶으면 Anna에게 메시지를 해보라고 Julia가 말한 것이다. ▶ Anna

Q 09 정답 ⑤

윗글에 관한 내용으로 적절하지 않은 것은?

① Helen은 중고 거래 앱에서 알림을 받았다. Helen was thrilled when she received a notification on a second-hand shopping app from a seller named Anna.

② Julia는 큰 종이 가방을 들고 있었다. Helen could identify Julia by the large paper bag she was holding.

③ Helen은 판매자와 메시지를 주고받았다. Helen immediately messaged the seller. Anna replied.

④ Helen은 야구 모자를 쓰겠다고 답했다. I'll wear a black baseball cap.

⑤ Julia는 자신이 식물 전문가라고 말했다. Julia replied, "I'm not a plant expert

왜 정답? [정답률 96%]

⑤ Julia는 자신이 식물 전문가는 아니라고 했다. (Julia replied, "I'm not a plant expert)

왜 오답?

① Helen은 중고 거래 앱에서 알림을 받았다. (Helen was thrilled when she received a notification on a second-hand shopping app from a seller named Anna.)

② Julia는 큰 종이 가방을 들고 있었다. (Helen could identify Julia by the large paper bag she was holding.)

③ Helen은 판매자와 메시지를 주고받았다. (Helen immediately messaged the seller. Anna replied.)

④ Helen은 야구 모자를 쓰겠다고 답했다. (I'll wear a black baseball cap.)

Q 10~12 ＊긴장을 극복한 성공적인 공연

분사구문
(A) Garcia stood outside Frontcountry Mall, / waiting for his brother, Jeff. //

Garcia는 Frontcountry Mall 밖에 서서 / 동생 Jeff를 기다리고 있었다 //

과거완료 수동태
Garcia's band had been chosen to perform / at the welcoming ceremony for a large group of students / from their sister university in Singapore. //

Garcia의 밴드는 공연하도록 선택되었다 / 대규모 학생단을 위한 환영식에서 / 싱가포르에 있는 자매 대학교에서 온 //

Garcia was hoping / to find the perfect clothing for the performance. //

Garcia는 소망하고 있었다 / 그 공연을 위한 완벽한 의상을 찾기를 //

= Garcia 과거완료　help+목적어+(to) 동사원형
That was why (a) he had asked Jeff / to help him pick out new clothes. //

그것이 그가 Jeff에게 요청한 이유였다 / 자신이 새로운 옷을 고르는 것을 도와달라고 //

"I'm sorry. I'm late because traffic was terrible," / Jeff apologized as he arrived. // **12번①** Jeff는 교통 체증 때문에 늦었음

"미안해. 교통상황이 끔찍해서 늦었어." / Jeff는 도착하며 사과했다 //

현재완료
"Don't worry. I haven't waited long," / Garcia replied as they entered the lively shopping center. // **10번** 단서 1: 공연 의상을 사기 위해 쇼핑센터로 감

"걱정하지 마. 그렇게 오래 기다리지 않았어." / Garcia는 그들이 활기가 넘치는 쇼핑센터로 들어가면서 답했다 //

＊(A) 문단 요약: Garcia가 공연 의상 준비를 위해 쇼핑센터에서 동생인 Jeff를 만남

(B) The band performance was the first event of the ceremony. //

밴드 공연은 그 환영식의 첫 번째 행사였다 //

each+단수 / each of+복수
The host introduced the band, / and each member took their place on stage. //

진행자가 밴드를 소개했고 / 각 멤버가 무대 위에서 자리를 잡았다 //

Garcia stood at the center of the stage. //
Garcia가 무대 한가운데에 섰다 // **12번②** Garcia는 환영식 공연 무대의 중앙에 섰음

As he started playing, / everyone fell silent, / fascinated by the
music. // (분사구문)
그가 연주를 시작하자 / 모든 이가 숨죽였다 / 그 음악에 매료되어 //

Garcia's trumpet playing was flawless. //
Garcia의 트럼펫 연주는 나무랄 데 없었다 //

When the band was finished, / the audience loudly cheered. //
밴드가 공연을 마쳤을 때 / 관객은 큰소리로 환호했다 // **12번③** 밴드가 환영식 공연에서
연주를 마치자 관객은 환호했음

After the show, / Jeff approached Garcia. //
공연이 끝난 후에 / Jeff가 Garcia에게 다가왔다 //

"It was fantastic. / I think that was the best performance
(현재완료) I've ever seen," (b) he said. // **10번** 단서 2: 공연이 성공적으로 마무리 됨
= Jeff
"환상적이었어. / 내가 여태껏 본 것 중 최고의 공연이었어."라고 그가 말했다 //

Garcia beamed with joy at his brother's praise. //
Garcia는 동생의 칭찬에 기뻐서 활짝 웃었다 //

　*(B) 문단 요약: Garcia는 성공적으로 무대에 올라 공연을 마치고, 동생 Jeff가 이를
　칭찬함

(C) Garcia felt good / as he arrived at the concert hall for the
rehearsal / wearing his new clothes. // **10번** 단서 3: 새로 산 옷을 입고 리허설을
(분사구문)   위해 콘서트홀에 도착함
Garcia는 기분이 좋았다 / 예행연습을 위해 콘서트홀에 도착했을 때 / 그 새로운 옷들을 입고 //

His confidence was, however, quickly changed to nervousness /
when he thought of how many people would be there. // (간접의문문: 의문사+주어+동사)
하지만, 그의 자신감은 금방 초조함으로 변했다 / 얼마나 많은 사람들이 그곳에 있을 것인가를
생각했을 때 // **12번④** Garcia는 리허설을 앞두고 긴장감을 느꼈음

As the rehearsal began, / (c) he struggled with the rhythm,
making several mistakes. // (분사구문)　= Garcia
예행연습이 시작되자 / 그는 여러 차례 실수를 저지르면서 리듬과 씨름했다 //

Tom, Garcia's band mate, came over and put a hand on Garcia's
back, / saying, "Don't worry, I'll be right behind (d) you." // = Garcia
Garcia의 밴드 동료인 Tom이 다가와 Garcia의 등에 손을 얹었다 / "걱정하지 마. 내가 바로
네 뒤에 있을게."라고 말하면서 //

He looked at his friend, took a deep breath / and started to feel
much better. //
그는 자신의 친구를 바라보고, 심호흡을 하니 / 훨씬 더 나은 기분이 들기 시작했다 //

　*(C) 문단 요약: 리허설이 시작되자, Garcia는 긴장을 하여 실수를 연발하고, 밴드
　동료인 Tom이 긴장을 풀어주며 격려함

(D) "Aren't these cool?" Garcia asked, / pointing at a patterned
red shirt and yellow pants he had found in the store. // (분사구문)
Garcia가 "이것들 근사하지 않니?"라고 물었다 / 상점에서 발견한 무늬가 있는 붉은색 셔츠와
노란색 바지를 가리키며 //

"Um, I think they're a bit too colorful," Jeff objected. //
"음, 내 생각엔 그것들이 살짝 지나치게 화려한 것 같아." Jeff가 반대했다 //

Instead, / Jeff picked out a white shirt and black jeans. //
그 대신 / Jeff는 흰색 셔츠와 검은색 청바지를 골랐다 // **12번⑤** Garcia는 Jeff가
고른 색상의 옷을 입음

He asked the store clerk, / "Don't you think these would look
= Garcia
great on (e) my brother?" //
그는 상점 직원에게 물었다 / "이것들이 제 형에게 잘 어울릴 것으로 생각하지 않으세요?"
라고 //

The clerk stopped her work and looked at the clothes, / quickly
agreeing with Jeff's choice. // (분사구문)
그 직원은 일을 멈추고 그 옷들을 보았다 / 얼른 Jeff의 선택에 동의하며 //

Garcia bought the recommended clothes, / saying, "Maybe I'll
wear these for tonight's rehearsal, too." // **10번** 단서 4: 옷을 산 이후
오늘 밤 리허설이 있음
Garcia는 추천받은 옷들을 샀다 / "아마도 나는 이것들을 오늘 밤 예행연습에도 입어야겠어."
라고 말하며 //

　*(D) 문단 요약: Garcia가 동생과 점원의 추천을 받아 무대에서 입을 옷을 삼

- welcoming ceremony 환영식　　・ sister ⓝ 자매(기관)
- pick out ~을 고르다　　・ apologize ⓥ 사과하다

- lively ⓐ 활기 넘치는　　・ introduce ⓥ 소개하다
- take one's place 있어야 할 곳에 가다, 자리를 잡다
- fascinate ⓥ 매료시키다　　・ flawless ⓐ 나무랄 데 없는
- cheer ⓥ 환호하다　　・ beam ⓥ 활짝 웃다
- rehearsal ⓝ 예행연습, 리허설　　・ confidence ⓝ 자신감
- struggle with ~와 씨름하다　　・ patterned ⓐ 무늬가 있는
- object ⓥ 반대하다　　・ clerk ⓝ 점원, 직원

(A) Garcia는 Frontcountry Mall 밖에 서서 동생 Jeff를 기다리고 있었다. Garcia의 밴드는 싱가포르에 있는 자매 대학교에서 온 대규모 학생단을 위한 환영식에서 공연하도록 선택되었다. Garcia는 그 공연을 위한 완벽한 의상을 찾기를 소망하고 있었다. 그것이 (a) 그가 Jeff에게 자신이 새로운 옷을 고르는 것을 도와달라고 요청한 이유였다. "미안해. 교통상황이 끔찍해서 늦었어." Jeff는 도착하며 사과했다. Garcia는 그들이 활기 넘치는 쇼핑센터로 들어가면서 "걱정하지 마. 그렇게 오래 기다리지 않았어."라고 답했다.
(D) Garcia가 상점에서 발견한 무늬가 있는 붉은색 셔츠와 노란색 바지를 가리키며 "이것을 근사하지 않니?"라고 물었다. "음, 내 생각엔 그것들이 살짝 지나치게 화려한 것 같아." Jeff가 반대했다. 그 대신, Jeff는 흰색 셔츠와 검은색 청바지를 골랐다. 그는 상점 직원에게 "이것들이 (e) 제 형에게 잘 어울릴 것으로 생각하지 않으세요?"라고 물었다. 그 직원은 일을 멈추고 그 옷들을 보며 얼른 Jeff의 선택에 동의했다. Garcia는 "아마도 나는 이것들을 오늘 밤 예행연습에도 입어야겠어."라고 말하며 추천받은 옷들을 샀다.
(C) Garcia는 예행연습을 위해 그 새로운 옷들을 입고 콘서트홀에 도착했을 때 기분이 좋았다. 하지만, 그의 자신감은, 얼마나 많은 사람들이 그곳에 있을 것인가를 생각했을 때, 금방 초조함으로 변했다. 예행연습이 시작되자, (c) 그는 여러 차례 실수를 저지르면서 리듬과 씨름했다. Garcia의 밴드 동료인 Tom이 다가와 Garcia의 등에 손을 얹고 "걱정하지 마. 내가 바로 (d) 네 바로 뒤에 있을게."라고 말했다. 그는 자신의 친구를 바라보고, 심호흡을 하니, 훨씬 더 나은 기분이 들기 시작했다.
(B) 밴드 공연은 그 환영식의 첫 번째 행사였다. 진행자가 밴드를 소개했고, 각 멤버가 무대 위에서 자리를 잡았다. Garcia가 무대 한가운데에 섰다. 그가 연주를 시작하자, 모든 이가 그 음악에 매료되어 숨죽였다. Garcia의 트럼펫 연주는 나무랄 데 없었다. 밴드가 공연을 마쳤을 때, 관객은 큰소리로 환호했다. 공연이 끝난 후에 Jeff가 Garcia에게 다가왔다. "환상적이었어. 내가 여태껏 본 것 중 최고의 공연이었어."라고 (b) 그가 말했다. Garcia는 동생의 칭찬에 기뻐서 활짝 웃었다.

Q 10　정답 ⑤

주어진 글 (A)에 이어질 내용을 순서에 맞게 배열한 것으로 가장 적절한 것은?

① (B) — (D) — (C) 성공적으로 공연을 마친 (B)는 결말임
② (C) — (B) — (D) ┐ 리허설 장면인 (C)가 쇼핑센터에서 옷을 고르면서 리허설에
　　　　　　　　　┘ 입고 간다고 하는 (D)보다 먼저 올 수 없음
③ (C) — (D) — (B)
④ (D) — (B) — (C) 리허설 연습을 하는 (C)가 결말인 (B)보다 먼저 와야 함
⑤ (D) — (C) — (B) Garcia가 공연 의상 준비를 위해 쇼핑센터에서 동생인 Jeff를 만남 -
Garcia가 동생과 점원의 추천을 받아 무대에서 입을 옷을 삼 - 리허설이 시작되자, Garcia는
긴장을 하여 실수를 연발하고, Tom이 긴장을 풀며 격려함 - Garcia는 성공적으로 공연을
마치고, 동생 Jeff가 이를 칭찬함

왜 정답・오답? [정답률 83%]

(A): Garcia가 공연 의상 준비를 위해 쇼핑센터에서 동생인 Jeff를
만났다.
➡ 쇼핑센터에 들어가는 것으로 글이 시작되므로 쇼핑센터에서 옷을 고르는 내용이
이어질 것이다.

(B): Garcia는 성공적으로 무대에 올라 공연을 마치고, 동생 Jeff가 이를
칭찬했다.
➡ 성공적으로 공연을 마치고 관객들의 환호와 동생의 칭찬을 받은 Garcia의
모습이므로 글의 결말일 것이다.

```
(C): 리허설이 시작되자, Garcia는 긴장을 하여 실수를 연발하고, 밴드
동료인 Tom이 긴장을 풀라며 격려했다.
```

→ 리허설에서의 긴장한 모습을 보여주고 Tom이 격려해주는 내용이 나오므로 뒤에는
이를 극복하고 공연에서 어떻게 하는지 결말에 해당하는 내용인 (B)가 이어져야
한다.

– (D): Garcia가 동생과 점원의 추천을 받아 무대에서 입을 옷을 샀다.

→ 쇼핑센터에서 동생과 점원의 추천을 받아 무대에서 입을 옷을 사고, 그날 밤
리허설에도 입고 가겠다고 했으므로 뒤에 리허설에 대한 내용인 (C)가 이어져야
한다.

▶ (A) Garcia가 공연 의상 준비를 위해 쇼핑센터에서 동생인 Jeff를 만남 → (D)
Garcia가 동생과 점원의 추천을 받아 무대에서 입을 옷을 삼 → (C) 리허설이
시작되자, Garcia는 긴장을 하여 실수를 연발하고, Tom이 긴장을 풀라며 격려함
→ (B) Garcia는 성공적으로 공연을 마치고, 동생 Jeff가 이를 칭찬함

▶ 사건이 진행되는 순서는 ⑤ (D) – (C) – (B)임

Q 11 정답 ②

밑줄 친 (a)~(e) 중에서 가리키는 대상이 나머지 넷과 다른 것은?

① (a)　　② (b)　　③ (c)　　④ (d)　　⑤ (e)
= Garcia　　= Jeff　　= Garcia　　= Garcia　　= Garcia

〉왜 정답 ? [정답률 88%]

② (b) he: 공연이 끝난 후 '내가 본 공연 중에 최고였어'라고 말하였고, 바로 다음
문장에서 '동생'의 칭찬에 기분이 좋았다는 말이 나왔으므로 Jeff이다. ▶ Jeff

〉왜 오답 ?

① (a) he: Jeff에게 무대에서 입을 새로운 옷을 골라 달라고 부탁한 것은
Garcia이다. ▶ Garcia

③ (c) he: 초조함으로 인해 리허설에서 실수를 한 사람은 Garcia이다. ▶ Garcia

④ (d) you: 실수를 한 Garcia에게 Tom이 다가와서 해주는 말이므로, Garcia이다.
▶ Garcia

⑤ (e) my brother: Jeff가 형을 위해 옷을 골라서 '형'에게 잘 어울리지 않겠냐고
물었으므로 여기서 형은 Garcia이다. ▶ Garcia

Q 12 정답 ⑤

윗글에 관한 내용으로 적절하지 않은 것은?

① Jeff는 교통 체증 때문에 늦었다.
　"I'm sorry. I'm late because traffic was terrible," Jeff apologized as he arrived.
② Garcia는 환영식 공연 무대의 중앙에 섰다.
　Garcia stood at the center of the stage.
③ 밴드가 환영식 공연에서 연주를 마치자 관객은 환호했다.
　When the band was finished, the audience loudly cheered.
④ Garcia는 리허설을 앞두고 긴장감을 느꼈다. His confidence was, however,
　quickly changed to nervousness when he thought of how many people would be there.
⑤ Garcia는 본인이 가리킨 색상의 옷을 구매했다.
　Instead, Jeff picked out a white shirt and black jeans

〉왜 정답 ? [정답률 94%]

⑤ Garcia가 고른 붉은색 셔츠와 노란색 바지는 너무 화려하다며 Jeff가 반대했으며,
대신 Jeff가 흰색 셔츠와 검은색 청바지를 골랐다. (Instead, Jeff picked out a
white shirt and black jeans)

〉왜 오답 ?

① Jeff는 교통 체증 때문에 늦었다. ("I'm sorry. I'm late because traffic was
terrible," Jeff apologized as he arrived.)
② Garcia는 환영식 공연 무대의 중앙에 섰다. (Garcia stood at the center of
the stage.)
③ 밴드가 환영식 공연에서 연주를 마치자 관객은 환호했다. (When the band was
finished, the audience loudly cheered.)
④ Garcia는 리허설을 앞두고 긴장감을 느꼈다. (His confidence was, however,
quickly changed to nervousness when he thought of how many
people would be there.)

Q 13~15 ＊토끼와 거래한 눈사람

(A) One frosty morning, / a rabbit was jumping about on a hill. //
　　　　　　　　　　　　　　　　　　　　　　　　'뛰어 돌아다니다'
어느 서리가 내린 아침 / 토끼 한 마리가 언덕에서 뛰어 돌아다니고 있었다 //
　　　　　　　　　　　　주격 관계대명사　　과거완료 수동태
There stood a snowman / which had been made by some
children. // 그곳에는 눈사람이 서 있었다 / 어떤 아이들이 만든 //

He had a broom in his hand and a carrot nose. //
그는 그의 손에 빗자루, 그리고 당근 코를 가지고 있었다 //

The rabbit saw the carrot / and swallowed hard. //
토끼는 당근을 보고 / 침을 삼켰다 // **15번 ①** 토끼는 당근을 보고 침을 삼킴

"I will have a delicious breakfast," / (a) he thought and jumped
　　　　　　　　　　　　　　분사구문　　　　= the rabbit
up, / reaching out for the snowman's nose. //
그는 '나는 맛있는 아침을 먹을 거야' / 라고 생각하고 뛰어올라 / 눈사람의 코로 손을 뻗었다 //
13번 단서 1: 토끼가 무언가에 맞음
But before the rabbit even touched him, / something hit him
　　　　　　　　　　　　　　　　부사
hard. // 그러나 토끼가 심지어 그에게 닿기도 전에 / 무언가가 그를 강하게 때렸다 //

　＊(A) 문단 요약: 눈사람의 당근 코를 보고 먹으려고 손을 뻗은 토끼는 무언가에 의해
　　맞음
　　13번 단서 2, **15번 ②** '제안'에 신이 난 토끼는 눈사람에게 기다리라고 하고 사라짐
(B) Excited by the offer, / the rabbit told the snowman to wait
　　　분사구문
and disappeared. //
그 제안에 신이 나서 / 토끼는 눈사람에게 기다리라고 말하고 사라졌다 //

　　　　　　　　　　　　　　　　　　　　분사구문
(b) He returned shortly, dragging a sled / and said to the
　= the rabbit
snowman, / "Let's go!" //
그는 썰매를 끌며 곧 돌아왔다 / 눈사람에게 말했다 / '갑시다!' //

The sled ran smoothly over the snow. // 썰매는 눈 위를 부드럽게 달렸다 //

The snowman with joy waved his broom. //
눈사람은 기쁨에 자신의 빗자루를 흔들었다 // **15번 ③** 눈사람은 기쁨에 자신의 빗자루를 흔들었음

After a while, / they arrived in the middle of the village. //
얼마 후에 / 그들은 마을 가운데에 도착했다 //

"Here we are," said the rabbit. // "다왔어요,"라고 토끼가 말했다 //
　　　　　　　　　　　　　　　　　　　　　　　분사구문을 이끎
"Thank you. Here's the carrot," said the snowman, / giving
　　　　　　　　　　　　　　　　　　　　　　= the rabbit.
(c) him his carrot. **13번** 단서 3: 눈사람은 토끼에게 당근을 줌
"고마워. 자, 당근이야," 눈사람은 말했다 / 그에게 자신의 당근을 주면서 //

　＊(B) 문단 요약: 토끼는 썰매로 눈사람을 마을까지 데려다줬고, 눈사람은 토끼에게
　　자기 당근을 줌

(C) The rabbit hesitated for a moment. // 토끼는 잠시 망설였다 //
　　　　　　　　　　　　　　　　　동격의 that　　　　　　(= carrot)
"Come on, take it. // I have a feeling that I'll get a new one,"
urged the snowman. //
"자, 가져가 / 나는 새로운 것을 얻을 거라는 느낌이 들어,"라고 눈사람이 재촉했다 //
13번 단서 4: 토끼는 당근을 받음
(d) He finally accepted the carrot / and leapt back into the
　= the rabbit
woods. // 그는 마침내 당근을 받았고 / 숲속으로 껑충 뛰어들어갔다 //

Not long after, / the children gathered around the snowman. //
얼마 지나지 않아서 / 아이들은 눈사람 주변으로 모였다 // **15번 ④** 아이들은 눈사람에게
　　　　　　　　　　　　　분사구문　　　　　　　　　　　　　　　　싱싱한 당근을 줬음
Noticing that he had no nose, / they gave him a fresh carrot. //
그에게 코가 없다는 것을 알아차리자 / 그들은 그에게 싱싱한 당근을 주었다 //

From that time on, / the snowman stood in the middle of the
village, / with a broom in his hand and a marvelous new carrot
nose. //
그때부터 / 눈사람은 마을 가운데에서, 서 있었다 / 그의 손에 빗자루, 그리고 멋진 새 당근
코를 가지고 //

　＊(C) 문단 요약: 토끼는 당근을 받고 숲 속으로 갔고, 아이들은 눈사람에게 새로운
　　당근을 줌
　　13번 단서 5, **15번 ⑤** 커다란 빗자루로 그(토끼)를 위협함
(D) "Go Away!" / the snowman threatened him with his great
broom. // "저리 가!" / 눈사람이 그의 커다란 빗자루로 그를 위협했다 //

"Sorry, Mr. Snowman, I just..." / murmured the rabbit. //
"미안해요, 눈사람 씨, 나는 그냥…." / 토끼가 웅얼거렸다 //
　　　　　　　　　　　　　　　= the snowman
"You wanted to eat my nose!," (e) he shouted. //
"너는 내 코를 먹고 싶어 했어!"라고 그가 소리쳤다 //

"I was so hungry and it looked so tasty," apologized the rabbit. // (= the snowman's nose = carrot) "난 너무 배가 고팠고 그것은 너무 맛있어 보였어요," 라고 토끼가 사과했다 //

The snowman thought for a moment. // 눈사람은 잠시 생각해 보았다 //

"Hmm... Here, I am bored by myself. //
"흠…, 여기에서, 나는 혼자서 지루해 //

I would like to go to the village / where the children are. // 관계부사
나는 마을에 가고 싶어 / 아이들이 있는 //

If you take me there, / I'll give you my carrot,"/ said the snowman. // **13번** 단서 6: 눈사람이 당근을 주는 대신 마을로 데려다 달라는 제안을 함
만약 나를 거기로 데려가 준다면 / 나는 너에게 내 당근을 줄게," 라고 눈사람이 말했다 //

*(D) 문단 요약: 배가 고파서 당근을 먹으려 했다는 토끼의 말을 듣고 눈사람은 마을로 데려다 주면 당근을 주겠다는 제안을 함

- frosty ⓐ 서리가 내리는, 몹시 추운 • swallow ⓥ 삼키다
- reach out (손 등을) 뻗다 • offer ⓝ 제안
- disappear ⓥ 사라지다 • hesitate ⓥ 망설이다
- urge ⓥ 재촉하다 • gathered around ~의 주위에 모이다
- marvelous ⓐ 놀라운

(A) 어느 서리가 내린 아침, 토끼 한 마리가 언덕에서 뛰어 돌아다니고 있었다. 그곳에는 어떤 아이들이 만든 눈사람이 서 있었다. 그는 그의 손에 빗자루, 그리고 당근 코를 가지고 있었다. 토끼는 당근을 보고 침을 삼켰다. (a) 그는 '나는 맛있는 아침을 먹을 거야,'라고 생각하고 뛰어올라, 눈사람의 코로 손을 뻗었다. 그러나 토끼가 심지어 그에게 닿기도 전에, 무언가가 그를 강하게 때렸다. (D) "저리 가!" 눈사람이 그의 커다란 빗자루로 그를 위협했다. "미안해요, 눈사람 씨, 나는 그냥….," 토끼가 웅얼거렸다. "너는 내 코를 먹고 싶어 했어!"라고 (e) 그가 소리쳤다. "난 너무 배가 고팠고 그것은 너무 맛있어 보였어요,"라고 토끼가 사과했다. 눈사람은 잠시 생각해 보았다. "흠…, 여기에서, 나는 혼자서 지루해. 나는 아이들이 있는 마을에 가고 싶어. 만약 나를 거기로 데려가 준다면, 나는 너에게 내 당근을 줄게,"라고 눈사람이 말했다. (B) 그 제안에 신이 나서, 토끼는 눈사람에게 기다리라고 말하고 사라졌다. (b) 그는 썰매를 끌며 곧 돌아왔고 눈사람에게 말했다. "갑시다!" 썰매는 눈 위를 부드럽게 달렸다. 눈사람은 기쁨에 자신의 빗자루를 흔들었다. 얼마 후에, 그들은 마을 가운데에 도착했다. "다왔어요,"라고 토끼가 말했다. "고마워. 자, 당근이야," 눈사람은 (c) 그에게 자신의 당근을 주면서 말했다. (C) 토끼는 잠시 망설였다. "자, 가져가. 나는 새로운 것을 얻을 거라는 느낌이 들어,"라고 눈사람이 재촉했다. (d) 그는 마침내 당근을 받았고 숲속으로 껑충 뛰어 들어갔다. 얼마 지나지 않아서, 아이들은 눈사람 주변으로 모였다. 그에게 코가 없다는 것을 알아차리자, 그들은 그에게 싱싱한 당근을 주었다. 그때부터, 눈사람은 마을 가운데에서, 그의 손에 빗자루, 그리고 멋진 새 당근 코를 가지고 서 있었다.

Q 13 정답 ④

주어진 글 (A)에 이어질 내용을 순서에 맞게 배열한 것으로 가장 적절한 것은?

① (B) — (D) — (C) (B)에서 토끼가 받은 '제안'이 주어진 글에 없음
② (C) — (B) — (D) (C)는 눈사람이 아이들에게 새로운 당근을 받게 되는 결말임
③ (C) — (D) — (B) ┐ 언덕에 서 있는 눈사람의 당근 코를 보고 먹으려고 손을 뻗은 토끼는 무언가에 의해 맞았음 - 눈사람이 빗자루로 토끼를 위협했고,
④ (D) — (B) — (C) │ 토끼가 사과하자 눈사람은 마을로 데려다주면 당근을 주겠다고 제안했음 - 토끼는 썰매를 가져와 마을에 눈사람을 데려다주었으며,
⑤ (D) — (C) — (B) │ 눈사람은 자기 당근을 토끼에게 줬음 - 토끼는 당근을 받고 숲속으로 들어갔고, 아이들은 눈사람에게 새로운 당근을 주었음
└ (B)에서 눈사람이 토끼에게 당근을 주고 나서 (C)에서 아이들에게 새로운 당근을 받는 내용이 이어져야 함

왜 정답·오답? [정답률 91%]

┌ (A): 눈사람의 당근 코를 보고 먹으려고 손을 뻗은 토끼는 무언가에 의해
└ 맞았다.
➡ 토끼가 무엇에 맞았는지를 알려주는 내용이 이어질 것이다.

┌ (B): 토끼는 썰매로 눈사람을 마을까지 데려다줬고, 답례로 눈사람은
└ 토끼에게 자기 당근을 줬다.
➡ 토끼가 눈사람을 마을로 데려다주고, 눈사람은 토끼에게 당근을 줬다는 내용이므로 (B) 앞에는 토끼가 눈사람을 마을까지 데려다준 계기가 나와야 한다.

┌ (C): 토끼는 당근을 받고 숲 속으로 갔고, 아이들은 눈사람에게 새로운
└ 당근을 줬다.
➡ 토끼가 당근을 받고, 눈사람은 이때부터 마을 가운데에 있었다는 내용이므로, 눈사람이 토끼에게 당근을 준 (B)가 (C)의 앞에 와야 하고, (C)는 이 글의 결말에 해당할 것이다.

┌ (D): 배가 고파서 당근을 먹으려 했다는 토끼의 말을 듣고 눈사람은 마을로
└ 데려다 주면 당근을 주겠다는 제안을 했다.
➡ 배가 고파서 그랬다는 토끼의 말에 눈사람은 마을로 데려다주면 당근을 주겠다는 제안을 한다는 내용이므로, 토끼가 눈사람의 당근에 손을 뻗었다가 맞은 (A)가 (D) 앞에 와야 하고, 제안을 받아들여서 눈사람을 마을로 데려갔다는 내용인 (B)가 (D) 뒤에 와야 한다.

▶ (A) 언덕에 서 있는 눈사람의 당근 코를 보고 먹으려고 손을 뻗은 토끼는 무언가에 의해 맞았다. → (D) 눈사람이 빗자루로 토끼를 위협했고, 토끼는 배가 고파서 그랬다고 사과하자 눈사람은 마을로 자기를 데려다주면 당근을 주겠다고 제안했다. → (B) 제안에 신이 난 토끼는 썰매를 가져와 마을에 눈사람을 데려다 주었으며, 눈사람은 자기 당근을 토끼에게 줬다. → (C) 토끼는 당근을 받고 숲속으로 들어갔고, 아이들은 눈사람에게 새로운 당근을 주었다.

▶ 사건이 진행되는 순서는 ④ (D) – (B) – (C)임

Q 14 정답 ⑤

밑줄 친 (a)~(e) 중에서 가리키는 대상이 나머지 넷과 다른 것은?

① (a) | ② (b) | ③ (c) | ④ (d) | ⑤(e)
= the rabbit | = the rabbit | = the rabbit | = the rabbit | = the snowman

왜 정답? [정답률 91%]

⑤ (e) he: 내 코를 먹고 싶어 했다고 소리를 친 대상은 눈사람이다. ▶the snowman

왜 오답?

① (a) he : 맛있는 아침을 먹을거라고 생각하고 뛰어오른 대상은 토끼이다. ▶ the rabbit
② (b) He : 썰매를 끌며 돌아온 대상은 토끼이다. ▶ the rabbit
③ (c) him : 눈사람이 자기 당근을 준 대상은 토끼이다. ▶ the rabbit
④ (d) He : 당근을 받아들이고 숲속으로 뛰어들어간 대상은 토끼이다. ▶ the rabbit

Q 15 정답 ⑤

윗글에 관한 내용으로 적절하지 않은 것은?

① 토끼는 당근을 보고 침을 삼켰다.
The rabbit saw the carrot and swallowed hard.
② 토끼는 눈사람에게 기다리라고 말하고 사라졌다.
the rabbit told the snowman to wait and disappeared
③ 눈사람은 기쁨에 빗자루를 흔들었다.
The snowman with joy waved his broom.
④ 아이들은 눈사람에게 싱싱한 당근을 주었다.
they gave him a fresh carrot
⑤ 토끼가 빗자루로 눈사람을 위협했다.
the snowman threatened him with his great broom

왜 정답? [정답률 91%]

⑤ 토끼가 위협한 것이 아니라, 눈사람이 빗자루로 토끼를 위협했다. (the snowman threatened him with his great broom)

왜 오답?

① 토끼는 당근을 보고 침을 삼켰다. (The rabbit saw the carrot and swallowed hard.)
② 토끼는 눈사람에게 기다리라고 말하고 사라졌다. (the rabbit told the snowman to wait and disappeared)
③ 눈사람은 기쁨에 빗자루를 흔들었다. (The snowman with joy waved his broom.)
④ 아이들은 눈사람에게 싱싱한 당근을 주었다. (they gave him a fresh carrot)

(A) On the northwestern coastline of Lake Superior / is the city of Duluth, / the westernmost port for transatlantic cargo ships. //
Lake Superior의 북서쪽 해안에 / Duluth시가 있는데 / 대서양을 가로지르는 화물선들을 위한 최서단 항구이다 //

18번 ① 몽구스 한 마리가 인도에서 배를 타고 Duluth로 왔음
A lot of cargo comes into Duluth: / coal, iron ore, grain, clothing and, / in November 1962, a mongoose from India. //
A lot of 뒤의 명사와 동사가 수 일치 되어야 함
많은 화물이 Duluth로 들어온다 / 석탄, 철 광석, 곡물, 의류, 그리고 / 1962년 11월에는 인도로부터 온 몽구스 //

The merchant seamen had enjoyed his company on the long journey / and had sat drinking tea with him, /
상선원들은 오랜 여행 기간 동안 그의 동행을 즐겼고 / 그와 차를 마시며 앉았으나 /

= a mongoose(= Mr. Magoo)
but they decided he deserved a life on dry land / so they presented (a) him as a gift / to the city's Lake Superior Zoo. //
그들은 그가 육지에서 살 가치가 있다고 결정했고 / 그래서 그들은 그를 선물로서 제공했다 / 그 도시의 Lake Superior 동물원에 //

= Lloyd Hackl's
Lloyd Hackl, the director of the zoo, was delighted / and named (b) his new mongoose Mr. Magoo. //
그 동물원의 원장인 Lloyd Hackl은 기뻐했고 / 그의 새로운 몽구스를 Mr. Magoo라고 이름 지었다 //

16번 단서 1, **18번 ②** : Mr. Magoo는 침략종으로 명명되어 사형 선고를 받음
His fate took an unexpected turn / when, labeled an invasive species, / federal agents sentenced him to death. //
분사구문을 이룸
그의 운명은 예상하지 못한 전환점을 맞았다 / 침략종이라고 명명되어 / 연방 요원들이 그에게 사형 선고를 했을 때 //

＊(A) 문단 요약: Duluth의 Lake Superior Zoo에 선물된 Mr. Magoo라는 몽구스가 침략종으로 분류되어 사형 선고를 받음

분사구문
(B) Living out his days in the zoo, / Mr. Magoo became a beloved figure. // **16번** 단서 2: Mr. Magoo는 동물원에서 여생을 보냄
동물원에서 그의 여생을 보내면서 / Mr. Magoo는 사랑받는 인물이 되었다 //

His daily routine included / enjoying an egg, sipping tea, / and charming zoo workers with his friendly nature. //
그의 매일의 일과는 포함했다 / 달걀을 먹고, 차를 마시며 / 동물원 직원들을 그의 다정한 성품으로 매혹시키는 것을 //

Popular among visitors, especially children, / he received numerous letters and Christmas cards. // **18번 ③** 인기가 있었기에 수많은 편지와 크리스마스 카드를 받음
방문객들, 특별히 아이들 사이에서 인기가 있어서 / 그는 수많은 편지와 크리스마스 카드를 받았다 //

When Mr. Magoo died peacefully in January 1968, / his obituary in the *Duluth Herald* read: "OUR MR. MAGOO OF ZOO IS DEAD."//
Mr. Magoo가 1968년 1월에 평화롭게 죽었을 때 / Duluth Herald의 그의 사망 기사 '동물원의 우리 Mr. Magoo가 죽었다'라고 쓰였다 //

= Mr. Magoo
The new zoo director, Basil Norton, / vowed not to replace (c) him: / "Another mongoose could never take his place / in the hearts and affections of Duluth people,"/ he said. //
새로운 동물원장인 Basil Norton은 / 그를 대체하지 않겠다고 맹세했다 / '또 다른 몽구스는 그의 자리를 차지할 수 없다 / 결코 Duluth 사람들의 마음과 애정에서'라고 / 그가 말했다 //

＊(B) 문단 요약: 인기와 사랑을 한 몸에 받으며 동물원에서 여생을 보낸 Mr. Magoo는 평화롭게 죽었음

(C) The citizens of Duluth / were not taking the death sentence lying down // **16번** 단서 3: Duluth의 시민들은 사형 선고를 참지 않음
Duluth의 시민들은 / 그 사형 선고를 순순히 참고 있지 않았다 //

It was pointed out that, / as the only mongoose in the country, / Mr. Magoo was never going to be able to reproduce, / so the country was unlikely to be overrun by the species. //
지적되었다 / 그 나라의 유일한 몽구스로서 / Mr. Magoo는 결코 번식을 할 수 없을 것이고 / 그래서 그 나라는 그 생물 종에 의해서 우글거리게 되지 않을 것이라는 점이 //

demand (that) 주어 (should) 동사원형: ~해야 한다고 요구하다
They demanded / he be allowed to live out his days in peace. //
그들은 요구했다 / 그가 평화롭게 여생을 살도록 허락되어야 한다고 //

Petitions were signed and sent to powerful figures / like the U.S. Secretary of the Interior Stewart Udall, U.S. Senator Hubert Humphrey, / and Duluth Mayor George Johnson. //
청원들이 서명되고 영향력이 큰 인물들에게 보내졌다 / 미국 내무부 장관인 Stewart Udall, 미국 상원의원인 Hubert Humphrey / 그리고 Duluth 시장인 George Johnson같은 //

A campaign, brilliantly nicknamed *No Noose for the Mongoose*, / was backed by more than 10,000 citizens. // **18번 ④** 10,000명이 넘는 시민들이 캠페인을 지지함
'몽구스에게 올가미를 씌우지 말라'라고 훌륭하게 별명이 지어진 캠페인이 / 10,000명이 넘는 시민들에 의해 지지를 받았다 //

동격의 that
There were even suggestions / that the zoo director should take (d) him into hiding. //
= Mr. Magoo
제안조차 있었다 / 심지어 동물원장이 그를 숨겨야 한다는 //

＊(C) 문단 요약: 유일한 몽구스라 번식을 할 수 없을 것이라는 점을 지적하며 Duluth 시민들은 사형 선고를 반대하는 캠페인을 벌임

(D) Thanks to the efforts of the citizens of Duluth, / Mr. Magoo was pardoned. // **16번** 단서 4: 시민들의 캠페인 노력 덕분에 Mr. Magoo는 사면을 받음
Duluth의 시민들의 노력 덕분에 / Mr. Magoo는 사면을 받았다 //

주격 관계대명사
A statement from Udall read, / "Acting on the authority / that permits importation of prohibited mammals — including mongooses — / for zoological, education, medical and scientific purposes, /
Udall의 성명서는 쓰여 있었다 / '권한에 따라서 / 금지된 포유류들의 수입을 허용하는 — 몽구스들을 포함해서 / 동물학적, 교육적, 의학적 그리고 과학적 목적을 위해 /

목적어절 접속사
I recommend / that Mr. Magoo be granted non-political asylum in the United States." // **18번 ⑤** Mr. Magoo의 미국 망명이 허가됨
나는 권고한다 / Mr. Magoo가 미국에서 비정치적인 망명이 허가되어야 한다'라고 //

목적어절 접속사   동명사의 의미상 주어   동명사
He added / that it was dependent upon / Mr. Magoo maintaining (e) his "bachelor existence." //
= Mr. Magoo's
그는 덧붙였다 / 그것은 달려 있다고 / Mr. Magoo가 그의 '미혼의 삶'을 유지하는 것에 //

The *News Tribune* joyfully proclaimed, / "MAGOO TO STAY. U.S. Asylum Granted."//
News Tribune은 기뻐하며 공표했다 / 'MAGOO 머무르게 됨. 미국 망명 허가됨'이라고 //

President Kennedy declared: / "Let the story of the saving of Magoo stand / as a classic example of government by the people."//
Kennedy 대통령은 선언했다 / 'Magoo의 구출 이야기가 남아있게 하자'라고 / 시민들에 의한 정부의 모범적인 사례로 //

＊(D) 문단 요약: Duluth 시민들의 노력 덕분에 Mr. Magoo는 사면을 받았으며, 미국에서의 망명도 허가됨

- **transatlantic** ⓐ 대서양 횡단의   • **deserve** ⓥ ~받을만 하다
- **delight** ⓥ 기뻐하다   • **name** ⓥ 이름을 지어주다
- **fate** ⓝ 운명, 숙명   • **invasive** ⓐ 침습성의
- **sentence** ⓥ 사형 선고하다   • **charm** ⓥ 매혹시키다
- **nature** ⓝ 성품   • **numerous** ⓐ 수많은   • **obituary** ⓝ 사망기사
- **vow** ⓥ 맹세하다   • **affection** ⓝ 애정   • **reproduce** ⓥ 번식하다
- **overrun** ⓥ 급속히 퍼지다, 들끓다   • **authority** ⓝ 권한
- **permit** ⓥ 허락하다   • **importation** ⓝ 수입
- **prohibit** ⓥ 금지하다

(A) Lake Superior의 북서쪽 해안에 Duluth시가 있는데, 대서양을 가로지르는 화물선들을 위한 최서단 항구이다. 많은 화물이 Duluth로 들어온다: 석탄, 철광석, 곡물, 의류, 그리고 1962년 11월에는 인도로부터 온 몽구스. 상선원들은 오랜 여행 기간 동안 그의 동행을 즐겼고, 그와 차를 마시며 앉았으나, 그들은 그가 육지에서 살 가치가 있다고 결정했고 그래서 그들은 (a) 그를 그 도시의 Lake Superior 동물원에 선물로서 제공했다. 그 동물원의 원장인 Lloyd Hackl은 기뻐했고 (b) 그의 새로운 몽구스를 Mr. Magoo라고 이름 지었다. 침략종이라고 명명되어 연방 요원들이 그에게 사형 선고를 했을 때 그의 운명은 예상하지 못한 전환점을 맞았다.

(C) Duluth의 시민들은 그 사형 선고를 순순히 참고 있지 않았다. 그 나라의 유일한 몽구스로서 Mr. Magoo는 결코 번식을 할 수 없을 것이고, 그래서 그

나라는 그 생물종에 의해서 우글거리게 되지 않을 것이라는 점이 지적되었다. 그들은 그가 평화롭게 여생을 살도록 허락되어야 한다고 요구했다. 청원들이 서명되고 미국 내무부 장관인 Stewart Udall, 미국 상원의원인 Hubert Humphrey, 그리고 Duluth 시장인 George Johnson같은 영향력이 큰 인물들에게 보내졌다. '몽구스에게 올가미를 씌우지 말라'라고 훌륭하게 별명이 지어진 캠페인이 10,000명이 넘는 시민들에 의해 지지를 받았다. 심지어 동물원장이 (d) 그를 숨겨야 한다는 제안조차 있었다.

(D) Duluth의 시민들의 노력 덕분에, Mr. Magoo는 사면을 받았다. Udall의 성명서는 '금지된 포유류들—몽구스들을 포함해서—의 수입을 동물학적, 교육적, 의학적 그리고 과학적 목적을 위해 허용하는 권한에 따라서, 나는 Mr. Magoo가 미국에서 비정치적인 망명이 허가되어야 한다고 권고한다'라고 쓰여 있었다. 그는 그것은 Mr. Magoo가 (e) 그의 '미혼의 삶'을 유지하는 것에 달려 있다고 덧붙였다. News Tribune은 'MAGOO 머무르게 됨, 미국 망명 허가됨'이라고 기뻐하며 공표했다. Kennedy 대통령은 'Magoo의 구출 이야기가 시민들에 의한 정부의 모범적인 사례로 남아있게 하자'라고 선언했다.

(B) 동물원에서 그의 여생을 보내면서, Mr. Magoo는 사랑받는 인물이 되었다. 그의 매일의 일과는 달걀을 먹고, 차를 마시며, 동물원 직원들을 그의 다정한 성품으로 매혹시키는 것을 포함했다. 방문객들, 특별히 아이들 사이에서 인기가 있어서, 그는 수많은 편지와 크리스마스 카드를 받았다. Mr. Magoo가 1968년 1월에 평화롭게 죽었을 때, Duluth Herald의 그의 사망 기사는 '동물원의 우리 Mr. Magoo가 죽었다'라고 쓰였다. 새로운 동물원장인 Basil Norton은 (c) 그를 대체하지 않겠다고 맹세했다: '또 다른 몽구스는 결코 Duluth 사람들의 마음과 애정에서 그의 자리를 차지할 수 없다'라고 그가 말했다.

Q 16 정답 ③

주어진 글 (A)에 이어질 내용을 순서에 맞게 배열한 것으로 가장 적절한 것은?

① (B) — (D) — (C) └ (B)에서는 Mr. Magoo의 여생과 죽음에 대한 내용이 나와 있기에 그 이후에 (C)에 Mr. Magoo의 사형 반대 캠페인과 (D)의 사형 면제가 나오는 것은 적절하지 않음

② (C) — (B) — (D) └ (B)에서 Mr. Magoo의 죽음에 대한 내용까지 소개되었는데 이후

③ (C) — (D) — (B) (D)에서 망명이 허가되었다는 흐름은 어색함

④ (D) — (B) — (C) └ Duluth 시민들의 노력에 대한 내용이 주어진 글 (A)에 나오지

⑤ (D) — (C) — (B) 않으므로 (D)가 바로 올 수 없음

└ Duluth의 Lake Superior Zoo에 선물된 Mongoose는 침략종이라 판단되어 사형 선고가 내려짐 - 시민들이 이에 반대하는 캠페인을 벌임 - 결국 사형이 면제되었고 망명이 허가됨 - 남은 여생을 동물원에서 평화롭게 보낸 후 죽음

왜 정답·오답? [정답률 70%]

┌ (A): 한 상인으로부터 Duluth의 Lake Superior Zoo에 선물된 Mr.
└ Magoo라는 몽구스가 침략종으로 분류되어 사형 선고를 받았다.

→ 사형 선고에 대한 사람들의 반응이 나올 것이다.

┌ (B) 인기와 사랑을 한 몸에 받으며 동물원에서 여생을 보낸 Mr. Magoo는 평화롭게 죽었고, Mr. Magoo를 대체할 몽구스는 없을 것이라
└ 동물원장은 밝혔다.

→ Mr. Magoo는 동물원에서 남은 생을 보내고 평화롭게 죽었다고 나와 있으므로 (B)가 글의 결말에 해당할 것이다.

┌ (C): 유일한 몽구스라 번식을 할 수 없을 것이라는 이유를 들며 Duluth
└ 시민들은 사형 선고를 반대하는 캠페인을 벌였다.

→ 시민들이 Mr. Magoo의 사형 선고를 반대하는 캠페인을 벌인 부분으로, (C)의 앞에는 사형 선고에 대한 내용이 필요하다. 또한, 이후에는 캠페인을 벌인 결과가 나올 것이다.

┌ (D): Duluth 시민들의 노력 덕분에 Mr. Magoo는 사면을 받았으며,
└ 미국에서의 망명도 허가되었다.

→ Duluth 시민들이 힘을 모아 반대한 덕분에 Mr. Magoo는 사면을 받았으며 계속 미국에 있어도 된다는 허가를 받았으므로, (D)의 앞에는 Duluth 시민들의 노력에 대한 내용이 필요하다. 그리고 이후에 Mr. Magoo가 어떻게 살았는지에 관한 내용이 이어질 것이다.

▶ (A): 한 상인으로부터 Duluth의 Lake Superior Zoo에 선물된 Mr. Magoo라는 몽구스가 침략종으로 분류되어 사형 선고를 받았음 → (C): 유일한 몽구스라 번식을 할 수 없을 것이라는 이유를 들며 Duluth 시민들은 사형 선고를 반대하는 캠페인을 벌였음 → (D): Duluth 시민들의 노력 덕분에 Mr. Magoo는 사면을 받았으며, 미국에서의 망명도 허가되었음 → (B): 인기와 사랑을 한 몸에 받으며 동물원에서 여생을 보낸 Mr. Magoo는 평화롭게 죽었고, Mr. Magoo를 대체할 몽구스는 없을 것이라 동물원장은 밝혔음

▶ 사건이 진행되는 순서는 ③ (C) – (D) – (B)임

Q 17 정답 ②

밑줄 친 (a)~(e) 중에서 가리키는 대상이 나머지 넷과 다른 것은?

= Mongoose (Mr. Magoo)

① (a)   ② (b)   ③ (c)   ④ (d)   ⑤ (e)
         = Lloyd Hackl's   = Mr. Magoo   = Mr. Magoo   = Mr. Magoo's

왜 정답? [정답률 62%]

② (b) his: 기뻐하며 새로운 몽구스에게 Mr. Magoo라고 이름을 지어준 사람은 동물원장 Lloyd Hackl이다. ▶ Lloyd Hackl's

왜 오답?

① (a) him : 도시의 Lake Superior Zoo에 선물된 대상은 (이후에 Mr. Magoo 라고 이름 붙여질) 몽구스이다. ▶ Mongoose (Mr. Magoo)

③ (c) him : 동물원장이 대체하지 않겠다고 맹세한 대상은 Mr. Magoo이다.
▶ Mr. Magoo

④ (d) him : 동물원장이 숨겨야 한다고 사람들이 제안한 대상은 Mr. Magoo이다.
▶ Mr. Magoo

⑤ (e) his : 미혼의 삶을 유지해야 하는 대상은 Mr. Magoo이다. ▶ Mr. Magoo's

Q 18 정답 ⑤

윗글에 관한 내용으로 적절하지 않은 것은?

① 몽구스 한 마리가 배를 타고 Duluth로 왔다. A lot of cargo comes into Duluth: coal, iron ore, grain, clothing and, in November 1962, a mongoose from India.

② Mr. Magoo는 사형을 선고받았다. labeled an invasive species, federal agents sentenced him to death

③ Mr. Magoo는 수많은 편지와 카드를 받았다. he received numerous letters and Christmas cards

④ 10,000명이 넘는 시민들이 No Noose for the Mongoose 캠페인을 지지했다. A campaign, brilliantly nicknamed No Noose for the Mongoose, was backed by more than 10,000 citizens.

⑤ Mr. Magoo의 미국 망명이 허가되지 않았다. I recommend that Mr. Magoo be granted non-political asylum in the United States.

왜 정답? [정답률 84%]

⑤ Mr. Magoo는 미국에서 비정치적인 망명이 허가되었다 (I recommend that Mr. Magoo be granted non-political asylum in the United States.)

왜 오답?

① 몽구스 한 마리가 배를 타고 Duluth로 왔다.
(A lot of cargo comes into Duluth: coal, iron ore, grain, clothing and, in November 1962, a mongoose from India.)

② Mr. Magoo는 사형을 선고받았다.
(labeled an invasive species, federal agents sentenced him to death)

③ Mr. Magoo는 수많은 편지와 카드를 받았다.
(he received numerous letters and Christmas cards)

④ 10,000명이 넘는 시민들이 No Noose for the Mongoose 캠페인을 지지했다.
(A campaign, brilliantly nicknamed No Noose for the Mongoose, was backed by more than 10,000 citizens.)

Q 19~21 ＊관점의 차이를 이해한 쌍둥이

(A) Pamela and Maggie were identical twins. //
Pamela와 Maggie는 일란성 쌍둥이였다. //

Even their parents found it hard / to tell them apart. //
가목적어   진목적어(to부정사)
심지어 그들의 부모도 어려워했다 / 그들을 구별하는 것을 //

But although they looked identical, / they were different in every other way. // **21번①** 자매는 외모를 제외한 모든 면에서 서로 달랐음
비록 그들이 똑같아 보였지만 / 그들은 다른 모든 부분에서 달랐다 //

They didn't have anything in common, / so they fought all the time. //
그들은 공통점이 없었고 / 그래서 그들은 항상 싸웠다 //

Pamela thought / that (a) <u>her sister</u> was weird and = Maggie
incomprehensible, / and of course Maggie felt the same way. //
Pamela는 생각했다 / 그녀의 자매가 이상하며 이해할 수 없다고 / 물론 Maggie도 똑같이느꼈다 //

＊(A) 문단 요약: Pamela와 Maggie는 항상 싸웠고 서로를 이해할 수 없었음

(B) Tired of the endless arguments, / their mother Rachel
앞에 Being 생략
decided to put an end to them. // **19번** 단서 1, **21번②**: Rachel은 두 딸의 언쟁을 끝내기로 결심함
끝없는 언쟁에 지친 / 그들의 어머니 Rachel은 그것을 끝내기로 결심했다 //

She would make them understand / that each of their points of
make의 목적어와 목적격 보어(원형부정사)
view could be correct. //
그녀는 그들이 이해하게 만들려 했다 / 그들의 관점 각각이 옳을 수 있다는 것을 //

One day, the twins were brought to the dining table / where a big board stood in the middle. //
관계부사
하루는 쌍둥이들이 식탁으로 불려 왔다 / 큰 판자가 가운데 세워져 있는 //

Pamela sat on one side of the board / and (b) <u>her twin</u> on the = Maggie
= other side of the board
other. //
Pamela는 판자의 한쪽에 앉았다 / 그녀의 쌍둥이는 다른 한쪽에 //

Rachel asked Pamela / what the color of the board was. //
명사절을 이끄는 관계대명사
Rachel은 Pamela에게 물었다 / 판자의 색깔이 무엇이냐고 //
21번③ Pamela는 판자가 검은색이라고 대답함

"Black," she said. // "검은색이요"라고 그녀가 대답했다 //

＊(B) 문단 요약: Rachel은 쌍둥이를 화해시키려 큰 판자를 세워 양쪽에 앉게 하고 Pamela에게 판자의 색을 물었음

(C) For example, / Pamela was always upset / at her sister
동명사의 의미상 주어
waking up early in the morning. // **19번** 단서 2: 서로를 이해하지 못하는 예시가 제시됨
예를 들어 / Pamela는 항상 기분이 언짢았다 / 그녀의 자매가 이른 아침에 일어나는 것에 대해 //

(c) <u>She</u> didn't understand / why her sister couldn't finish
= Pamela
what she needed to do at night / and sleep peacefully the next morning. //
그녀는 이해하지 못했다 / 그녀의 자매가 왜 해야 할 일을 밤에 끝내고 다음 날 아침에 편히 잘 수 없는지 //

To Maggie, / staying up past the time (d) <u>she</u> began to feel sleepy
동명사 주어(단수 취급)   = Maggie
/ was exhausting. //
단수 동사
Maggie에게는 / 그녀가 졸린 것을 느끼기 시작한 시간이 지나고도 깨어 있는 것이 / 매우 피곤한 일이었다 //

Besides, / she loved the fresh morning air. //
게다가 / 그녀는 상쾌한 아침 공기를 좋아했다 // **21번④** Maggie는 상쾌한 아침 공기를 좋아함

They had fights / about simple things like this / every day. //
그들은 싸웠다 / 이와 같은 단순한 일들로 / 매일 //

＊(C) 문단 요약: 서로 다른 생활 패턴을 가지고 있어서 서로를 이해하지 못함

접속사가 생략되지 않은 분사구문
(D) After hearing Pamela's answer, / Rachel asked the same
= Maggie
question to (e) <u>the other daughter</u>. // **19번** 단서 3: Pamela의 답변이
앞에 와야 함
Pamela의 대답을 들은 후에 / Rachel은 다른 딸에게 똑같은 질문을 했다 //

She replied / it was white. // 그녀는 대답했다 / 그것이 하얀색이라고 //

Predictably, / they began arguing. // 예상대로 / 그들은 언쟁을 시작했다 //

Rachel then asked them / to switch seats. //
asked의 목적어와 목적격 보어(to부정사)
그러자 Rachel은 그들에게 요청했다 / 자리를 바꾸도록 // **21번⑤** 두 딸이 자리를 바꾸도록 요청했음

Each sitting on a new chair, / they were surprised to realize / the board was black on one side / and white on the other. //
각자 새로운 의자에 앉자 / 그들은 깨닫고 놀랐다 / 그 판자의 한쪽이 검은색이고 / 다른 한쪽이 하얀색이라는 것을 //

분사구문
Understanding what their mother wanted to say, / they promised / they would never insist the other was wrong again. //
그들의 어머니가 하고자 했던 말을 이해하고 / 그들은 약속했다 / 다시는 서로가 틀렸다고 주장하지 않겠다고 //

＊(D) 문단 요약: 쌍둥이는 어머니의 가르침을 이해하고 서로가 틀렸다고 주장하지 않기로 함

- **identical twins** 일란성 쌍둥이   - **tell apart** 구별하다, 분간하다
- **in common** 공통적으로   - **incomprehensible** ⓐ 이해할 수 없는
- **put an end to** ~을 끝내다, 그만두게 하다
- **stay up** (평상시보다 더 늦게까지) 안 자다[깨어 있다]
- **exhausting** ⓐ 진을 빼는, 기진맥진하게 만드는
- **insist** ⓥ 고집하다, 주장하다

(A) Pamela와 Maggie는 일란성 쌍둥이였다. 심지어 그들의 부모도 그들을 구별하는 것을 어려워했다. 비록 그들이 똑같아 보였지만 그들은 다른 모든 부분에서 달랐다. 그들은 공통점이 없었고, 그래서 그들은 항상 싸웠다. Pamela는 (a) 그녀의 자매가 이상하며 이해할 수 없다고 생각했고 물론 Maggie도 똑같이 느꼈다.

(C) 예를 들어 Pamela는 그녀의 자매가 이른 아침에 일어나는 것에 대해 항상 기분이 언짢았다. (c) 그녀는 그녀의 자매가 왜 해야 할 일을 밤에 끝내고 다음 날 아침에 편히 잘 수 없는지 이해하지 못했다. Maggie에게는 (d) 그녀가 졸린 것을 느끼기 시작한 시간이 지나고도 깨어 있는 것은 매우 피곤한 일이었다. 게다가 그녀는 상쾌한 아침 공기를 좋아했다. 그들은 이와 같은 단순한 일들로 매일 싸웠다.

(B) 끝없는 언쟁에 지친 그들의 어머니 Rachel은 그것을 끝내기로 결심했다. 그녀는 그들의 관점 각각이 옳을 수 있다는 것을 그들이 이해하게 만들려 했다. 하루는 쌍둥이들이 큰 판자가 가운데 세워져 있는 식탁으로 불려 왔다. Pamela는 판자의 한쪽에, (b) 그녀의 쌍둥이는 다른 한쪽에 앉았다. Rachel은 Pamela에게 판자의 색깔이 무엇이냐고 물었다. "검은색이요."라고 그녀가 대답했다.

(D) Pamela의 대답을 들은 후에 Rachel은 (e) 다른 딸에게 똑같은 질문을 했다. 그녀는 그것이 하얀색이라고 대답했다. 예상대로 그들은 언쟁을 시작했다. 그러자 Rachel은 그들에게 자리를 바꾸도록 요청했다. 각자 새로운 의자에 앉자 그들은 그 판자의 한쪽이 검은색이고 다른 한쪽이 하얀색이라는 것을 깨닫고 놀랐다. 그들의 어머니가 하고자 했던 말을 이해하고, 그들은 다시는 서로가 틀렸다고 주장하지 않겠다고 약속했다.

Q 19 정답 ②

주어진 글 (A)에 이어질 내용을 순서에 맞게 배열한 것으로 가장 적절한 것은?
(A)의 예시가 (C)에 나오므로 바로 뒤에 와야 함
① (B) — (D) — (C) ┌ Pamela와 Maggie는 일란성 쌍둥이지만 외모를 제외한 모든 면에서
② (C) — (B) — (D) │ 달랐음 - Pamela와 Maggie는 매우 다른 생활 패턴을 가지고 있었고
③ (C) — (D) — (B) │ 자주 싸웠음 - Rachel은 두 딸이 서로를 이해할 수 있도록 기회를
④ (D) — (B) — (C) │ 만들었음 - 두 자매는 서로의 입장을 이해하게 되었음
⑤ (D) — (C) — (B) └ (D)에는 결론이 나오고 있기 때문에 가장 뒤에 위치해야 자연스러움
③ (C) — (D) — (B) Pamela의 대답이 (B)에 나옴

왜 정답·오답? [정답률 92%]

┌ (A): Pamela와 Maggie는 일란성 쌍둥이지만 외모를 제외한 모든
└ 면에서 달라서 그들은 항상 싸웠다.
➡ 그들이 싸운 구체적인 예시가 이어질 것이다.

┌ (B): Rachel은 두 딸이 서로의 관점을 이해할 수 있는 기회를 만들었다.
│ 큰 판자를 가져와 양쪽에 두 자매를 앉혔고 Pamela에게 판자의 색깔을
└ 묻자 그녀는 검은색이라고 답했다.
➡ Rachel이 두 딸의 싸움을 해결하기 위해 노력하는 내용이다. 불화에 대한 내용이 모두 끝나고 (B)가 와야 한다.

└ (C): Pamela와 Maggie는 매우 다른 생활 패턴을 가지고 있었고 자주 싸웠다.

➡ 쌍둥이가 구체적으로 어떻게 다른지 소개하면서 싸운 예시를 제공하고 있으므로 (A)와 (B)의 사이에 와야 한다.

┌ (D): 서로 자리를 바꿔서 앉도록 했고 두 자매는 서로의 입장을 이해하게
└ 되었다. 어머니의 의도를 깨달은 두 자매는 서로가 틀렸다고 주장하지 않기로 다짐했다.

➡ 서로의 입장을 이해하며 다시는 서로가 틀렸다고 주장하지 않기로 다짐했다는 내용이므로 가장 마지막에 오는 것이 자연스럽다.

▶ (A) Pamela와 Maggie는 일란성 쌍둥이지만 외모를 제외한 모든 면에서 달랐음 → (C) 예를 들어, Pamela와 Maggie는 매우 다른 생활 패턴을 가지고 있었고 자주 싸웠음 → (B) 이에 지친 Rachel은 두 딸이 서로를 이해할 수 있도록 기회를 만들었음 → (D) 두 자매는 서로의 입장을 이해하게 되었고, 다시는 서로가 틀렸다고 주장하지 않기로 다짐함

▶ 사건이 진행되는 순서는 ② (C) – (B) – (D)임

Q 20 정답 ③

밑줄 친 (a)~(e) 중에서 가리키는 대상이 나머지 넷과 다른 것은?

① (a)   ② (b)   ③(c)   ④ (d)   ⑤ (e)
= Maggie   = Maggie   = Pamela   = Maggie   = Maggie

왜 정답? [정답률 86%]

③ (c) She: 전날 할 일을 끝내고 다음 날 아침에 편히 자지 못하는 것에 대해 Maggie가 이해할 수 없었던 사람 ▶ Pamela

왜 오답?

① (a) her sister: Pamela가 이상하고 이해할 수 없다고 여긴 사람 ▶ Maggie
② (b) her twin : Pamela의 쌍둥이 ▶ Maggie
④ (d) she: 졸릴 때 깨어 있는 것을 피곤하게 여긴 사람 ▶ Maggie
⑤ (e) the other daughter: Rachel의 Pamela 외의 다른 딸 ▶ Maggie

Q 21 정답 ③

윗글에 관한 내용으로 적절하지 않은 것은?

① 자매는 외모를 제외한 모든 면에서 서로 달랐다.
   although they looked identical, they were different in every other way
② Rachel은 두 딸의 언쟁을 끝내기로 결심했다.
   their mother Rachel decided to put an end to them
③Pamela는 판자가 흰색이라고 대답했다.
   "Black," she said.
④ Maggie는 상쾌한 아침 공기를 좋아했다.
   she loved the fresh morning air
⑤ Rachel은 두 딸이 자리를 바꾸도록 요청했다.
   Rachel then asked them to switch seats.

왜 정답? [정답률 92%]

Pamela는 판자가 검은색이라고 대답했으므로 ("Black," she said.) 흰색이라고 한 ③이 적절하지 않다.

왜 오답?

① 자매는 외모를 제외한 모든 면에서 서로 달랐다. (although they looked identical, they were different in every other way)
② Rachel은 두 딸의 언쟁을 끝내기로 결심했다. (their mother Rachel decided to put an end to them)
④ Maggie는 상쾌한 아침 공기를 좋아했다. (she loved the fresh morning air)
⑤ Rachel은 두 딸이 자리를 바꾸도록 요청했다. (Rachel then asked them to switch seats.)

Q 22~24 ✱젊은 시절 야구 선수였던 Tommy 할아버지의 추억

(A) Once upon a time / in the small town of Meadowville, / there
<small>boy를 수식하는 분사</small>
lived a curious boy / named Tommy. //
옛날 옛적 / Meadowville의 작은 마을에 / 호기심 많은 소년이 살고 있었다 / Tommy라는 이름의 //

<small>Tommy's grandfather를 설명하는 분사</small>
Tommy's grandfather, / affectionately known as Grandpa Joe, /
had always been a mysterious figure to (a) him. //
<small>= Tommy</small>
Tommy의 할아버지는 / 애정 어린 표현으로 Grandpa Joe로 알려진 / 항상 그에게 신비로운 인물이었다 //

Grandpa Joe was a man of few words, / but his eyes lit up from
<small>stories를 수식하는 분사</small>
stories / untold. //
Grandpa Joe는 말수가 적은 사람이었지만 / 그의 눈은 이야기들로 빛이 났다 / 말하지 않은 //
<small>접속사가 생략되지 않은 분사구문</small>
One lazy summer afternoon, / while searching the garage, /
Tommy found an old, forgotten box. // <small>24번①</small> Tommy가 오래되고 잊혀진 상자를 발견함
어느 나른한 여름 오후 / 차고를 탐색하던 중 / Tommy는 오래되고 잊혀진 상자를 발견했다 //
<small>= Tommy</small>
As (b) he opened it, / the treasure of memories spilled out, /
<small>card를 수식하는 분사</small>
including an old baseball card / featuring a young Grandpa
Joe. // <small>22번</small> 단서 1: 할아버지가 등장하는 카드가 쏟아짐
그가 그것을 열었을 때 / 추억의 보물이 쏟아졌다 / 오래된 야구 카드를 포함한 / 젊은 Grandpa Joe가 등장하는 //

✱(A) 문단 요약: Tommy의 할아버지인 Grandpa Joe는 항상 신비로운 인물이었으며, 어느 날 Tommy는 차고에서 할아버지가 등장하는 오래된 야구 카드 등이 든 상자를 발견함

(B) A spark of nostalgia lit up Grandpa Joe's eyes / as he took the card. //
노스탤지어의 반짝임이 Grandpa Joe의 눈을 밝혔다 / 그가 카드를 가져가면서 //

Memories flooded back, / and he told stories of his youthful
days / on the baseball field. // <small>22번 단서 2, 24번②</small>: 할아버지가 야구장에서 보낸 젊은 시절 이야기를 함
기억들이 다시 밀려들어 왔고 / 그는 그의 젊은 시절 이야기를 했다 / 야구장에서 보낸 //

Grandpa Joe spoke of the thrill of the game / and the joy of
hitting a home run. //
Grandpa Joe는 경기의 전율에 관해 이야기했다 / 그리고 홈런을 치는 기쁨 //
<small>Tommy를 설명하는 분사</small>
Tommy, / fascinated by these stories, / felt more connected to
his grandfather. //
Tommy는 / 이러한 이야기들에 매료된 / 할아버지와 더 연결되었다고 느꼈다 //
<small>= Tommy</small>
Eager to learn more, / (c) he asked Grandpa Joe / to teach him
about baseball. // <small>22번</small> 단서 3: Tommy가 할아버지에게 야구를 가르쳐 달라고 함
더 배우기를 열망하여 / 그는 Grandpa Joe에게 부탁했다 / 야구를 가르쳐 달라고 //

✱(B) 문단 요약: Grandpa Joe는 야구장에서 보낸 자신의 젊은 시절 이야기를 들려주었고, Tommy는 이에 매료되어 야구를 가르쳐 달라고 부탁함
<small>= Grandpa Joe</small>
(C) They spent afternoons in the backyard / as (d) he shared the
wisdom of the game / with his grandson. //
그들은 뒷마당에서 오후를 보냈다 / 그가 경기의 지혜를 나누어 주면서 / 그의 손자에게 //
<small>동사의 병렬 구조</small>
Together, / they practiced hitting, catching, / and even laughed
over the mistakes. // <small>22번</small> 단서 4, <small>24번③</small>: 그들은 함께 공 치기, 잡기를 연습함
함께 / 그들은 공 치기, 잡기를 연습하였고 / 심지어 실수들을 웃어 넘겼다 //

As they bonded over baseball, / the gap between generations
closed. //
그들이 야구를 통해 유대감을 형성하면서 / 세대 간의 격차가 줄어들었다 //

Grandpa Joe's eyes no longer held / just the twinkle of untold
stories; / they now radiated warmth / and shared memories. //
Grandpa Joe의 눈은 더 이상 지니지 않았다 / 말하지 않은 이야기들의 반짝임만을 / 이제는 따뜻함으로 반짝였다 / 그리고 함께 나눈 기억으로 //

✱(C) 문단 요약: Grandpa Joe는 Tommy와 함께 야구 연습을 하였고 그들은 야구를 통해 유대감을 형성하며 세대 간 격차를 줄임

(D) Tommy's eyes widened with excitement / as he examined
the card. //
Tommy의 눈이 흥분으로 커졌다 / 그가 카드를 살펴보면서 //

In the card, / Grandpa Joe stood proudly / in a baseball
uniform. // **22번** 단서 5, **24번 ④** 카드 속에서 할아버지는 야구 유니폼을 입고 있음
카드 속에서 / Grandpa Joe는 당당하게 서 있었다 / 야구 유니폼을 입고 //
<u>사이에 목적격 관계대명사 생략</u>
He was not the quiet person / Tommy knew. //
그는 조용한 사람이 아니었다 / Tommy가 알던 //

Intrigued by this discovery, / Tommy rushed inside the house /
부사적 용법(목적)
to find Grandpa Joe. // **24번 ⑤** Tommy는 할아버지를 찾아 집 밖이 아닌 집 안으로 들어감
이 발견으로 호기심이 불러 일으켜져서 / Tommy는 집 안으로 서둘러 들어갔다 / Grandpa
Joe를 찾아 //

"Hey, Grandpa! / I found this cool baseball card of you. /
Were you a baseball player?" / (e) <u>he</u> asked, / eyes filled with
= Tommy 의미상 주어가 생략되지 않은 분사구문
curiosity. // **22번** 단서 6: Tommy가 할아버지에게 야구 선수였는지 물음
"할아버지! / 제가 할아버지의 이 멋진 야구 카드를 찾았어요 / 야구 선수셨어요?" / 그는
물었다 / 호기심으로 가득찬 눈으로 //

  *(D) 문단 요약: Tommy는 카드 속에서 할아버지가 유니폼을 입고 서 있는 모습을
  보고 호기심이 생겨 할아버지에게 야구 선수였는지를 물었음

- curious ⓐ 호기심 많은
- affectionately ⓐd 애정 어린 표현으로, 다정하게
- mysterious ⓐ 이해하기 힘든, 신비로운
- a man of few words 과묵한 사람, 말수가 적은 사람
- garage ⓝ 차고   · spill ⓥ 쏟아져 나오다   · nostalgia ⓝ 향수(鄕愁)
- youthful ⓐ 젊은   · fascinated ⓐ 매료된   · eager ⓐ 열망하는
- wisdom ⓝ 지혜   · radiate ⓥ 반짝이다, 빛나다
- proudly ⓐd 당당하게   · intrigue ⓥ 호기심을 불러일으키다, 흥미를 끌다
- discovery ⓝ 발견

(A) 옛날 옛적 Meadowville의 작은 마을에 Tommy라는 이름의 호기심 많은
소년이 살고 있었다. 애정 어린 표현으로 Grandpa Joe로 알려진 Tommy의
할아버지는 항상 (a) <u>그에게</u> 신비로운 인물이었다. Grandpa Joe는 말수가
적은 사람이었지만, 그의 눈은 말하지 않은 이야기들로 빛이 났다. 어느 나른한
여름 오후, 차고를 탐색하던 중, Tommy는 오래되고 잊혀진 상자를 발견했다.
(b) <u>그가</u> 그것을 열었을 때, 젊은 Grandpa Joe가 등장하는 오래된 야구 카드를
포함한 추억의 보물이 쏟아졌다.
(D) 그가 카드를 살펴보면서 Tommy의 눈이 흥분으로 커졌다. 카드 속에서,
Grandpa Joe는 야구 유니폼을 입고 당당하게 서 있었다. 그는 Tommy가 알던
조용한 사람이 아니었다. 이 발견으로 호기심이 불러 일으켜져서, Tommy는
Grandpa Joe를 찾아 집 안으로 서둘러 들어갔다. "할아버지! 제가 할아버지의
이 멋진 야구 카드를 찾았어요. 야구 선수셨어요?" (e) <u>그는</u> 호기심으로 가득찬
눈으로 물어보았다.
(B) 그가 카드를 가져가면서 노스탤지어의 반짝임이 Grandpa Joe의 눈을
밝혔다. 기억들이 다시 밀려 들어 왔고, 그는 야구장에서 보낸 그의 젊은
시절 이야기를 했다. Grandpa Joe는 경기의 전율과 홈런을 치는 기쁨에
관해 이야기했다. Tommy는 이러한 이야기들에 매료되어 할아버지와 더
연결되었다고 느꼈다. 더 배우기를 열망하여, (c) <u>그는</u> Grandpa Joe에게
야구를 가르쳐 달라고 부탁했다.
(C) 그들은 뒷마당에서 오후를 보내며, (d) <u>그는</u> 그의 손자에게 경기의 지혜를
나누어 주었다. 함께, 그들은 공 치기, 잡기를 연습하였고 심지어 실수들을
웃어 넘겼다. 그들이 야구를 통해 유대감을 형성하며, 세대 간의 격차가
줄어들었다. Grandpa Joe의 눈은 더 이상 말하지 않은 이야기들의 반짝임을
지니지 않았고, 이제는 따뜻함과 함께 나눈 기억으로 반짝였다.

Q 22 정답 ④

주어진 글 (A)에 이어질 내용을 순서에 맞게 배열한 것으로 가장 적절한 것은?

① (B) — (D) — (C)   (B)에서 야구를 가르쳐 달라고 했으므로 야구를 연습했다는 내용이
                      나오는 (C)가 바로 뒤에 이어져야 함
② (C) — (B) — (D)   야구를 연습해서 유대감을 형성했다는 (C)는 주어진 글에
                      이어질 수 없음
③ (C) — (D) — (B)   Tommy는 할아버지인 Grandpa Joe의 차고에서 할아버지가
④ (D) — (B) — (C)   등장하는 오래된 야구 카드를 찾음 - 유니폼을 입은 할아버지의
                      모습으로 호기심이 생겨 야구 선수였던 자신의 젊은 시절 이야기를 들려 주었고 Tommy는
⑤ (D) — (C) — (B)   야구를 가르쳐 달라고 함 - 할아버지와 Tommy는 같이 야구를
                      연습하여 유대감을 형성함
  야구를 통해 유대감을 형성한 (C)는 글의 결말임

474 자이스토리 영어 독해 실전

> **왜** 정답 · 오답? [정답률 80%]

(A): Tommy의 할아버지인 Grandpa Joe는 항상 신비로운
    인물이었으며, 어느 날 Tommy는 차고에서 할아버지가 등장하는 오래된
    야구 카드 등이 든 상자를 발견했다.

→ Tommy가 할아버지가 등장하는 야구 카드를 발견했으므로 야구 카드에 대한
    내용이 더 이어질 것이다.

(B): Grandpa Joe는 야구장에서 보낸 자신의 젊은 시절 이야기와 경기의
    전율, 홈런의 기쁨 등을 들려 주었고, Tommy는 이에 매료되어 야구를
    가르쳐 달라고 부탁했다.

→ 할아버지가 야구장에서 보낸 자신의 젊은 시절에 대해 이야기를 들려주는
    내용이므로 (B) 앞에는 이야기를 들려주게 된 계기가 나와야 한다. 또한 Tommy가
    야구를 가르쳐 달라고 부탁했으므로 (B) 뒤에는 야구를 가르쳐 주는 것에 대한
    내용이 나올 것이다.

(C): Grandpa Joe는 Tommy와 함께 야구 연습을 하였고 그들은
    야구를 통해 유대감을 형성하며 세대 간 격차를 줄였다.

→ 할아버지와 Tommy가 야구 연습을 하는 것에 대한 내용이므로 (C) 앞에 야구를
    연습하게 된 계기가 나와야 한다. 또한 야구를 통해 할아버지와 관계가 좋아졌다는
    결과가 서술되므로 글의 결말 부분이다.

(D): Tommy는 카드 속에서 할아버지가 유니폼을 입고 서 있는 모습을
    보고 호기심이 생겨 할아버지에게 야구 선수였는지를 물었다.

→ Tommy가 카드 속에서 유니폼을 입은 할아버지를 보았다고 했으므로 (D) 앞에는
    카드를 발견한 과정이 나와야 한다. 또한 (D)의 뒤에는 Tommy의 질문에 대한
    할아버지의 답이 이어질 것이다.

  ▶ (A) Tommy는 차고에서 할아버지인 Grandpa Joe가 등장하는 오래된
    야구 카드 등이 든 상자를 발견했음 → (D) Tommy는 카드 속에서 할아버지가
    유니폼을 입고 서 있는 모습을 보고 할아버지에게 야구 선수였는지를 물었음 →
    (B) Grandpa Joe는 야구장에서 보낸 자신의 젊은 시절 이야기를 들려주었고,
    Tommy는 야구를 가르쳐 달라고 부탁했음 → (C) Grandpa Joe는 Tommy와
    함께 야구 연습을 하였고 그들은 유대감을 형성하며 세대 간 격차를 줄였음
  ▶ 사건이 진행되는 순서는 ④ (D) – (B) – (C)임

Q 23 정답 ④

밑줄 친 (a)~(e) 중에서 가리키는 대상이 나머지 넷과 <u>다른</u> 것은?

① (a)   ② (b)   ③ (c)   ④(d)   ⑤ (e)
= Tommy   = Tommy   = Tommy   = Grandpa Joe   = Tommy

> **왜** 정답? [정답률 71%]

④ (d) he: 손자에게 경기의 지혜를 나누어준 사람은 Tommy의 할아버지를
    가리킨다. ▶ Grandpa Joe

> **왜** 오답?

① (a) him : 할아버지를 신비롭게 여긴 사람은 Tommy이다. ▶ Tommy
② (b) he : 상자를 연 사람은 Tommy이다. ▶ Tommy
③ (c) he : 야구를 좀 더 가르쳐달라고 한 사람은 Tommy이다. ▶ Tommy
⑤ (e) he : 야구 선수였냐고 물은 사람은 Tommy이다. ▶ Tommy

Q 24 정답 ⑤

윗글에 관한 내용으로 적절하지 <u>않은</u> 것은?

① Tommy는 차고에서 오래되고 잊혀진 상자를 발견했다.
  Tommy found an old, forgotten box.
② Grandpa Joe는 야구장에서 보낸 그의 젊은 시절 이야기를 했다.
  he told stories of his youthful days on the baseball field
③ 그들은 함께 공 치기, 잡기를 연습했다.
  Together, they practiced hitting, catching
④ 야구 카드 속에서 Grandpa Joe는 야구 유니폼을 입고 있었다.
  In the card, Grandpa Joe stood proudly in a baseball uniform.
⑤ Tommy는 Grandpa Joe를 찾기 위해 집 밖으로 서둘러 나왔다.
  Tommy rushed inside the house to find Grandpa Joe.

왜 정답? [정답률 91%]

⑤ Tommy는 Grandpa Joe를 찾기 위해 집 안으로 서둘러 들어갔다.
(Tommy rushed inside the house to find Grandpa Joe.)

왜 오답?

① Tommy는 차고에서 오래되고 잊혀진 상자를 발견했다.
(Tommy found an old, forgotten box.)

② Grandpa Joe는 야구장에서 보낸 그의 젊은 시절 이야기를 했다.
(he told stories of his youthful days on the baseball field)

③ 그들은 함께 공 치기, 잡기를 연습했다.
(Together, they practiced hitting, catching)

④ 야구 카드 속에서 Grandpa Joe는 야구 유니폼을 입고 있었다.
(In the card, Grandpa Joe stood proudly in a baseball uniform.)

Q 25~27 ★옳은 일을 한 Steven

(A) "Congratulations!" //
"축하합니다" //

That was the first word / that Steven saw / when he opened the envelope / that his dad handed to him. //
그것이 첫 단어였다 / Steven이 본 / 그가 봉투를 열었을 때 / 그의 아빠가 그에게 건네준 //

He knew / that he would win the essay contest. //
그는 알고 있었다 / 자신이 에세이 대회에서 우승할 것을 //

Overly excited, / he shouted, "Hooray!" //
매우 신이 나서 / 그는 "만세"라고 소리쳤다 //

At that moment, / two tickets to Ace Amusement Park, the prize, / slipped out of the envelope. //
그 순간 / 상품인 Ace 놀이공원 입장권 두 장이 / 봉투 밖으로 미끄러져 나왔다 //

He picked them up / and read the letter thoroughly / while sitting on the stairs / in front of his house. // 27번 ① 집 앞 계단에 앉아 편지를 자세히 읽었음
그는 그것을 집어 들고는 / 편지를 자세히 읽었다 / 계단에 앉아 / 자신의 집 앞에 있는 //

"Wait a minute! // That's not my name!" / (a) he said, puzzled. //
"잠깐만 // 내 이름이 아니네"라고 / 그는 당황하며 말했다 //

The letter was addressed / to his classmate Stephanie, / who had also participated in the contest. //
그 편지는 주소가 적혀 있었고 / 그의 반 친구인 Stephanie에게 / 또한 대회에 참가한 //

*(A) 문단 요약: Steven은 에세이 대회의 우승자에게 보내지는 편지를 받고 기뻐하다가 다른 사람의 이름을 발견하고 당황함

(B) Once Steven had heard his dad's words, / tears started to fill up / in his eyes. // 25번 단서 1: 옳은 일을 하라고 아빠가 조언한 것을 가리킴
Steven은 아빠의 말을 듣고 나자 / 눈물이 차오르기 시작했다 / 그의 눈에 //

"I was foolish," / Steven said regretfully. //
"제가 바보 같았어요"라고 / Steven은 후회하며 말했다 //

He took the letter and the prize to school / and handed them to Stephanie. //
그는 편지와 상품을 학교로 가져가 / Stephanie에게 그것들을 건네주었다 //

He congratulated her wholeheartedly / and she was thrilled. //
그는 그녀를 진심으로 축하해 주었고 / 그녀는 몹시 기뻐했다 //

On the way home after school, / his steps were light and full of joy. // 27번 ② 방과 후에 집으로 오는 길에 발걸음이 가벼웠음
방과 후에 집으로 오는 길에 / 그의 발걸음은 가벼웠고 기쁨으로 가득 찼다 //

That night, / his dad was very pleased to hear / what he had done at school. //
그날 밤 / 그의 아빠는 듣고 매우 흡족했다 / 그가 학교에서 한 행동을 //

"(b) I am so proud of you, Steven," / he said. //
"나는 네가 매우 자랑스럽단다, Steven"이라고 / 그는 말했다 //

Then, without a word, / he handed Steven two Ace Amusement Park tickets / and winked. //
그런 다음 아무 말 없이 / 그는 Steven에게 Ace 놀이공원 입장권 두 장을 건네주며 / 윙크를 했다 //

*(B) 문단 요약: 옳은 일을 한 Steven과 그를 칭찬하는 그의 아빠

(C) "If I don't tell Stephanie, / perhaps she will never know," / Steven thought for a moment. // 25번 단서 2: 진짜 우승자는 Stephanie이고, 편지가 잘못 배달된 것을 깨달은 다음에 한 생각
'내가 Stephanie에게 말하지 않으면 / 아마 그녀는 결코 알지 못할 거야'라고 / Steven은 잠시 생각했다 //

He remembered / that the winner would only be notified by mail. //
그는 기억했다 / 우승자는 우편으로만 통보된다는 것을 //

As long as he kept quiet, / nobody would know. //
그가 조용히 있기만 한다면 / 아무도 알지 못할 것이다 //

So he decided / to sleep on it. //
그래서 그는 결심했다 / 그것에 대해 자면서 생각해 보기로 //

The next morning, / he felt miserable / and his dad recognized it right away. //
다음 날 아침 / 그는 비참한 기분이었고 / 그의 아빠는 즉시 그것을 알아차렸다 //

"What's wrong, (c) Son?" / asked his dad. //
"아들, 무슨 일이야" / 그의 아빠가 물었다 //

Steven was hesitant at first / but soon disclosed his secret. //
Steven은 처음에는 주저했지만 / 곧 자신의 비밀을 털어놓았다 //

After listening attentively to the end, / his dad advised him / to do the right thing. // 27번 ③ 아빠는 아들에게 옳은 일을 하라고 조언했음
주의 깊게 끝까지 다 들은 후 / 그의 아빠는 그에게 조언했다 / 옳은 일을 하라고 //

*(C) 문단 요약: Steven의 아빠는 Steven에게 옳은 일을 하라고 조언함

(D) Reading on, / Steven realized / the letter had been delivered mistakenly. // 25번 단서 3: 편지를 계속 읽고 편지가 잘못 배달된 것을 깨달음
계속 읽었을 때 / Steven은 깨달았다 / 편지가 잘못 배달된 것을 //

"Unfortunately," it should have gone to Stephanie, / who was the real winner. // should have p.p.: ~했어야 했다 27번 ④ 실제 우승자는 Stephanie였음
'불행히도' 그것은 Stephanie에게 갔어야 했다 / 실제 우승자인 //

(d) He looked at the tickets / and then the letter. //
그는 입장권을 쳐다보고 / 그다음 편지를 //

He had really wanted those tickets. //
그는 그 입장권을 정말 갖고 싶었다 //

He had planned to go there / with his younger sister. // 27번 ⑤ 놀이공원에 여동생과 갈 계획이었음
그는 그곳에 갈 계획이었다 / 그의 여동생과 //

Steven was his sister's hero, / and he had bragged to her / that he would win the contest. //
Steven은 여동생의 우상이었고 / 그는 그녀에게 자랑했었다 / 자신이 대회에서 우승할 것이라고 //

However, / if she found out / that her hero hadn't won, / she would be terribly disappointed, / and (e) he would feel ashamed. //
그러나 / 그녀가 알게 되면 / 자신의 우상이 우승하지 못한 것을 / 그녀는 매우 실망할 것이고 / 그는 수치스러움을 느낄 것이었다 //

*(D) 문단 요약: 편지를 계속 읽고 편지가 잘못 배달되었음을 알게 됨

- envelope ⓝ 봉투   • hand ⓥ 건네다, 넘겨주다
- thoroughly ⓐⓓ 자세히, 철저히   • overly ⓐⓓ 너무, 몹시
- puzzled ⓐ 어리둥절해 하는, 얼떨떨한
- address ⓥ (편지 봉투에) 주소를 쓰다, (~ 앞으로 우편물을) 보내다
- regretfully ⓐⓓ 유감스러운 듯, 유감스럽게도
- wholeheartedly ⓐⓓ 진심으로
- thrilled ⓐ (너무 좋아서) 황홀해 하는, 아주 신이 난
- notify ⓥ 통보하다, 알리다
- sleep on ~에 대해 하룻밤 자며 생각하다   • miserable ⓐ 비참한
- hesitant ⓐ 주저하는   • disclose ⓥ 털어놓다, 누설하다
- attentively ⓐⓓ 조심스럽게, 정중히   • mistakenly ⓐⓓ 잘못하여, 실수로
- terribly ⓐⓓ 대단히, 몹시   • ashamed ⓐ 수치스러운, 창피한

(A) "축하합니다!" 그것이 아빠가 자신에게 건네준 봉투를 열었을 때 Steven이 본 첫 단어였다. 그는 자신이 에세이 대회에서 우승할 것을 알고 있었다. 매우 신이 나서, 그는 "만세!"라고 소리쳤다. 그 순간 상품인 Ace 놀이공원 입장권 두 장이 봉투 밖으로 미끄러져 나왔다. 그는 그것을 집어 들고는 자신의 집 앞

계단에 앉아 편지를 자세히 읽었다. "잠깐만! 내 이름이 아니네!"라고 (a) 그는 당황하며 말했다. 그 편지는 그의 반 친구인 Stephanie에게로 주소가 적혀 있었고, 그녀 또한 대회에 참가했었다.

(D) 계속 읽었을 때, Steven은 편지가 잘못 배달된 것을 깨달았다. '불행히도', 그것은 Stephanie에게 갔어야 했고, 그녀가 실제 우승자였다. (d) 그는 입장권을 쳐다본 다음 편지를 쳐다보았다. 그는 그 입장권이 정말 갖고 싶었다. 그는 여동생과 그곳에 갈 계획이었다. Steven은 여동생의 우상이었고, 그는 자신이 대회에서 우승할 것이라고 그녀에게 자랑했었다. 그러나 그녀가 자신의 우상이 우승하지 못한 것을 알게 되면, 그녀는 매우 실망할 것이고, (e) 그는 수치스러움을 느낄 것이었다.

(C) '내가 Stephanie에게 말하지 않으면, 아마 그녀는 결코 알지 못할 거야.'라고 Steven은 잠시 생각했다. 그는 우승자는 우편으로만 통보된다는 것을 기억했다. 그가 조용히 있기만 한다면, 아무도 알지 못할 것이다. 그래서 그는 그것에 대해 자면서 생각해 보기로 했다. 다음 날 아침 그는 비참한 기분이었고, 그의 아빠는 즉시 그것을 알아차렸다. "(c) 아들, 무슨 일이야?" 그의 아빠가 물었다. 처음에는 주저했지만, Steven은 곧 자신의 비밀을 털어놓았다. 주의 깊게 끝까지 다 들은 후, 그의 아빠는 그에게 옳은 일을 하라고 조언했다.

(B) 아빠의 말을 듣고 나자, Steven의 눈에 눈물이 차오르기 시작했다. "제가 바보 같았어요."라고 Steven은 후회하며 말했다. 그는 편지와 상품을 학교로 가져가 Stephanie에게 건네주었다. 그는 그녀를 진심으로 축하해 주었고, 그녀는 몹시 기뻐했다. 방과 후에 집으로 오는 길에 그의 발걸음은 가벼웠고 기쁨으로 가득 찼다. 그날 밤, 그의 아빠는 그가 학교에서 한 행동에 관해 듣고 매우 흡족했다. "(b) 나는 네가 매우 자랑스럽단다, Steven."이라고 그는 말했다. 그런 다음 그는 아무 말 없이 Steven에게 Ace 놀이공원 입장권 두 장을 건네주며 윙크를 했다.

Q 25 정답 ⑤

주어진 글 (A)에 이어질 내용을 순서에 맞게 배열한 것으로 가장 적절한 것은?

① (B) — (D) — (C) 〔(B)는 글의 결말임〕

② (C) — (B) — (D) ┐
③ (C) — (D) — (B) ┘ (C) 전에 진짜 우승자가 Stephanie임을 알게 되어야 함

④ (D) — (B) — (C) 〔Stephanie에게 축하 인사를 한 후 Stephanie에게 사실대로 말하지 않는 것에 대해 생각하는 것은 어색함〕

⑤ (D) — (C) — (B) 〔(D) 진짜 우승자가 Stephanie임을 깨달음 – (C) 아빠가 옳은 일을 하라고 조언함 – (B) 아빠의 조언을 듣고 Stephanie에게 사실대로 이야기함〕

> **왜 정답?** [정답률 87%]

집 앞 계단에 앉아 편지를 읽다가 편지에 Stephanie의 이름과 주소가 쓰여 있음을 발견했다는 내용의 (A) 뒤에는 계속 편지를 읽다가 편지가 잘못 배달되었음을 깨닫는 (D)가 와야 한다. 그 사실을 깨달은 뒤에 자신이 Stephanie에게 말하지 않으면 그녀는 결코 알지 못할 것이라고 생각하는 (C)가 이어지고, 아빠의 조언대로 옳은 일을 하는 (B)가 마지막에 오는 것이 자연스러우므로 정답은 ⑤ (D) – (C) – (B) 이다.

> **왜 오답?**

〔꿀팁: (A)에서는 Stephanie의 이름과 주소를 보고 당황하기만 했지, 그녀가 우승자임을 알지는 못했음〕

① Stephanie에게 사실대로 말한 후 축하 인사까지 하고 가벼운 발걸음으로 집으로 돌아오는 (B)는 글의 결말에 해당한다.

②, ③ Stephanie가 진짜 우승자라는 것을 알게 된 후에 든 생각이 (C)에 제시되므로 (C) 앞에 (D)가 있어야 한다.

④ Stephanie에게 축하 인사까지 한 이후에 '내가 Stephanie에게 말하지 않으면 아마 그녀는 결코 알지 못할 거야.'라고 생각하는 것은 어색하다.

Q 26 정답 ②

밑줄 친 (a)~(e) 중에서 가리키는 대상이 나머지 넷과 다른 것은?

① (a) Steven ② (b) Steven's dad ③ (c) Steven ④ (d) Steven ⑤ (e) Steven

> **왜 정답?** [정답률 91%]

Steven과 그의 아빠 중에서 Steven을 자랑스러워 한 ② (b)는 Steven의 아빠를 가리키고 나머지는 모두 Steven을 가리킨다.

> **왜 오답?**

① 편지에 쓰인 이름이 자신의 이름이 아님을 발견하고 당황하며 말한 것은 Steven이다.

③ Steven의 아빠가 Son이라고 부르는 대상은 Steven이다.

④ 입장권과 편지를 쳐다본 사람은 Steven이다.

⑤ Steven이 우승하지 못한 것에 대해 실망할 사람은 Steven의 여동생이고, 그에 대해 수치스러움을 느낄 사람은 Steven이다.

Q 27 정답 ②

윗글에 관한 내용으로 적절하지 않은 것은?

① Steven은 집 앞 계단에 앉아 편지를 자세히 읽었다.
   read the letter thoroughly while sitting on the stairs in front of his house

② 방과 후에 집으로 돌아오는 Steven의 발걸음은 무거웠다.
   On the way home after school, his steps were light and full of joy.

③ 아버지는 Steven에게 옳은 일을 하라고 조언했다.
   his dad advised him to do the right thing

④ 에세이 대회에서 우승한 사람은 Stephanie였다.
   it should have gone to Stephanie, who was the real winner

⑤ Steven은 여동생과 놀이공원에 갈 계획이었다.
   He had planned to go there with his younger sister.

> **왜 정답?** [정답률 88%]

Stephanie에게 사실대로 말하고 편지와 상품을 건네며 진심으로 축하한 뒤, 집으로 돌아오는 Steven의 발걸음이 가볍고 기쁨으로 가득 찼다고(On the way home after school, his steps were light and full of joy.) 했으므로 ②은 글의 내용에 적절하지 않다.

> **왜 오답?**

① 집 앞 계단에 앉아 편지를 자세히 읽었다. (read the letter thoroughly while sitting on the stairs in front of his house)

③ 그의 아빠는 그에게 옳은 일을 할 것을 조언했다. (his dad advised him to do the right thing)

④ 편지는 진짜 우승자인 Stephanie에게 갔어야 했다. (it should have gone to Stephanie, who was the real winner)

⑤ 그는 자신의 여동생과 Ace 놀이공원에 갈 계획이었다. (He had planned to go there with his younger sister.)

Q 28~30 ＊Katie를 도운 Sally

〔30번 ① Sally는 사진 수업을 마치고 집으로 돌아옴〕

(A) When Sally came back home / from her photography class, / she could hear Katie / moving around, / chopping things / on a wooden cutting board. //

Sally가 집에 돌아왔을 때 / 그녀의 사진 수업에서 / 그녀는 Katie의 소리를 들을 수 있었다 / 이리저리 다니며 / 재료를 썰고 있는 / 나무 도마 위에서 //

Wondering / what her roommate was doing, / (a) she ran to the kitchen. //
   〔현재분사 Wondering의 목적어로 쓰인 간접의문문   = Sally〕

궁금해서 / 룸메이트가 무엇을 하는지 / 그녀는 부엌으로 달려갔다 //

Sally watched Katie cooking something / that looked delicious. //
   〔선행사   주격 관계대명사〕

Sally는 Katie가 무언가를 요리하고 있는 것을 보았다 / 맛있어 보이는 //

But Katie didn't notice her / because she was too focused / on preparing for her cooking test / the next day. //

하지만 Katie는 그녀를 알아차리지 못했다 / 그녀가 너무 집중한 나머지 / 요리 시험을 준비하는 것에 / 그 다음 날 //

She was trying to remember / what her professor had said in class / that day. //
was trying보다 앞선 시점을 나타내는 대과거
그녀는 기억하려고 애쓰고 있었다 / 수업 시간에 그녀의 교수님이 말했던 것을 / 그날 //

*(A) 문단 요약: 집에 돌아온 Sally는 요리 시험 준비에 한창인 룸메이트 Katie를 봄

(B) Katie, / surprised by her roommate's words, / turned her head to Sally / and sighed, / "I don't know. // This is really hard." //
28번 단서 2: (D)에서 Sally가 도울 수 있는 일이 있을지 물은 것을 말함
Katie는 / 룸메이트의 말에 깜짝 놀라 / Sally에게 고개를 돌리며 / 한숨을 쉬었다 / "모르겠어 // 이건 정말 어렵네" //

30번 ② Brown 교수님은 시각적인 면이 음식의 핵심 부분을 구성한다고 말했음
Stirring her sauce for pasta, / Katie continued, / "Professor Brown said / that visual aspects make up / a key part of a meal. //
그녀의 파스타 소스를 저으면서 / Katie는 이어 말했다 / "Brown 교수님은 말씀하셨어 / 시각적인 면이 구성한다고 / 음식의 핵심 부분을 //

My recipe seems good, / but I can't think of any ways / to alter the feeling of the final dish." //
주어 동사   주격 보어   형용사적 용법(ways 수식)
내 요리법은 좋은 것 같지만, / 나는 어떤 방법도 떠오르지 않아 / 최종 요리의 느낌을 바꿀" //

Visibly frustrated, / (b) she was just about to throw away / all of her hard work / and start again, / when Sally suddenly stopped her. //
=Katie   병렬 구조
눈에 띄게 실망하여 / 그녀는 막 던져버리려던 참이었다 / 그녀의 힘들인 노력을 / 그리고 다시 시작하려던 / Sally가 갑자기 그녀를 멈춰 세웠을 때 //

*(B) 문단 요약: Katie는 교수님이 말한 요리의 시각적인 면을 바꿀 만한 방법이 떠오르지 않음

(C) "Wait! // You don't have to start over. // You just need to add some color / to the plate." //
28번 단서 3: 음식을 막 던져버리려던 Katie를 멈춰 세움
"잠깐만 // 넌 다시 시작할 필요 없어 / 넌 그저 약간의 색을 더하기만 하면 돼 / 요리에" //

Being curious, / Katie asked, / "How can (c) I do that?" //
=Katie
호기심을 느껴서 / Katie가 물었다 / "내가 어떻게 그걸 할 수 있어" //

Sally took out a container of vegetables / from the refrigerator / and replied, / "How about making colored pasta / to go with (d) your sauce?" //
=Katie's
30번 ③ Sally는 냉장고에서 채소가 든 그릇을 꺼냈음
Sally는 채소가 든 그릇을 꺼내 / 냉장고에서 / 대답했다 / "색깔이 있는 파스타를 만드는 건 어때 / 네 소스와 어울리는" //

30번 ④ Sally는 색깔 있는 파스타를 만드는 것이 어렵지 않다고 했음
Smiling, she added, / "It's not that hard, / and all you need / are brightly colored vegetables / to make your pasta green, orange, or even purple." //
to make의 목적어와 목적격 보어
웃으면서 그녀는 덧붙였다 / "그렇게 어렵지 않아 / 그리고 네게 필요한 건 / 밝은 색깔의 채소뿐이야 / 네 파스타를 초록색, 오렌지색, 심지어 보라색으로 만들" //

Katie smiled, / knowing / that now she could make her pasta / with beautiful colors / like a photographer. //
=as she knew
Katie는 미소 지었다 / 알고 / 이제 그녀가 자신의 파스타를 만들 수 있다는 것을 / 아름다운 색으로 / 사진작가처럼 //

*(C) 문단 요약: Sally는 Katie에게 어렵지 않다면서 소스와 어울리는 색깔이 있는 파스타를 만드는 건 어떤지 제안함

28번 단서 4: Katie의 교수님이 수업 시간에 말한 것
(D) In that class, / Professor Brown said, / "You have to present your food properly, / considering every stage / of the dining experience. // Imagine / you are a photographer." //
그 수업에서 / Brown 교수는 말했다 / "여러분은 여러분의 음식을 적절하게 선보여야 합니다 / 모든 단계를 고려하여 / 식사 경험의 / 상상하세요 / 여러분이 사진작가라고" //

=As she recalled
Recalling / what the professor had mentioned, / Katie said to herself, / "We need to see our ingredients as colors / that make up a picture." //
떠올리며 / 교수님이 말한 것을 / Katie는 혼잣말을 했다 / "우리는 재료를 색으로 봐야 해 / 그림을 구성하는" //

30번 ⑤ Katie는 요리 시험 준비에 어려움을 겪고 있었음
Sally could clearly see / that Katie was having a hard time / preparing for her cooking test. //
Sally는 분명히 알 수 있었다 / Katie가 어려움을 겪고 있다는 것을 / 그녀의 요리 시험을 준비하는 데 //

Trying to make (e) her feel better, / Sally kindly asked, / "Is there anything I can do to help?" //
=Katie
그녀의 기분을 더 좋게 해주고자 / Sally는 친절하게 물었다 / "내가 도울 수 있는 일이 있을까" //
앞에 목적격 관계대명사 생략됨

*(D) 문단 요약: 어려움을 겪고 있는 Katie에게 Sally는 자신이 도울 수 있는 일이 있을지 물어봄

- chop ⓥ (음식 재료를 토막으로) 썰다   · sigh ⓥ 한숨을 쉬다
- stir ⓥ (휘)젓다   · aspect ⓝ 측면   · make up ~을 구성하다[이루다]
- alter ⓥ 바꾸다   · visibly ⓐⓓ 눈에 띄게
- frustrated ⓐ 좌절감을 느끼는   · plate ⓝ 접시, 요리
- curious ⓐ 궁금한   · container ⓝ 그릇   · reply ⓥ 대답하다
- go with 잘 어울리다   · brightly ⓐⓓ 밝게, 환하게
- present ⓥ 제시[제출]하다   · properly ⓐⓓ 적절히   · dining ⓝ 식사
- recall ⓥ 상기하다   · mention ⓥ 말하다, 언급하다
- ingredient ⓝ 재료

(A) Sally가 사진 수업을 마치고 집에 돌아왔을 때, 그녀는 Katie가 이리저리 다니며 나무 도마 위에서 재료를 썰고 있는 소리를 들을 수 있었다. 룸메이트가 무엇을 하는지 궁금해서 (a) 그녀는 부엌으로 달려갔다. Sally는 Katie가 맛있어 보이는 무언가를 요리하고 있는 것을 보았다. 하지만 Katie는 그다음 날 요리 시험을 준비하는 것에 너무 집중한 나머지 그녀를 알아차리지 못했다. 그녀는 그날 수업 시간에 그녀의 교수님이 말했던 것을 기억하려고 애쓰고 있었다.

(D) 그 수업에서 Brown 교수는 "식사 경험의 모든 단계를 고려하여 음식을 적절하게 선보여야 합니다. 여러분이 사진작가라고 상상하세요."라고 말했다. 교수님의 말씀을 떠올리며 Katie는 "우리는 재료를 그림을 구성하는 색으로 봐야 해."라고 혼잣말을 했다. Sally는 Katie가 요리 시험 준비에 어려움을 겪고 있다는 것을 분명히 알 수 있었다. Sally는 (e) 그녀의 기분을 더 좋게 해주고자, "내가 도울 수 있는 일이 있을까?"라고 친절하게 물었다.

(B) 룸메이트의 말에 깜짝 놀란 Katie는 Sally에게 고개를 돌리며 "모르겠어. 이건 정말 어렵네."하며 한숨을 쉬었다. Katie는 파스타 소스를 저으면서 이어 말했다. "Brown 교수님은 시각적인 면이 음식의 핵심 부분을 구성한다고 말씀하셨어. 내 요리법은 좋은 것 같지만, 최종 요리의 느낌을 바꿀 어떤 방법도 떠오르지 않아." Sally가 갑자기 그녀를 멈춰 세웠을 때, 눈에 띄게 실망한 (b) 그녀는 힘들인 노력을 막 던져버리고 다시 시작하려던 참이었다.

(C) "잠깐만! 다시 시작할 필요 없어. 요리에 약간의 색을 더하기만 하면 돼." 호기심을 느낀 Katie가 (c) 내가 어떻게 그걸 할 수 있어?"라고 물었다. Sally는 냉장고에서 채소가 든 그릇을 꺼내 (d) 네 소스와 어울리는 색깔이 있는 파스타를 만드는 건 어때?"라고 대답했다. 웃으면서 그녀는 "그렇게 어렵지 않아, 그리고 넌 네 파스타를 초록색, 오렌지색, 심지어 보라색으로 만들 밝은 색깔의 채소만 있으면 돼."라고 덧붙였다. Katie는 이제 자신이 사진작가처럼 아름다운 색으로 파스타를 만들 수 있다는 것을 알고 미소 지었다.

Q 28 정답 ④

주어진 글 (A)에 이어질 내용을 순서에 맞게 배열한 것으로 가장 적절한 것은?

① (B) — (D) — (C) (A)에서 Sally는 Katie에게 말하지 않음
② (C) — (B) — (D) (A)에는 Katie가 요리를 다시 시작하려고 한다는 언급이 없음
③ (C) — (D) — (B)
④ (D) — (B) — (C) Katie는 요리 시험을 준비하면서 어려움을 겪음 – Sally가 Katie에게 도움이 필요한지 물어봄 – 자신의 요리에 실망한 Katie가 요리를 다시 시작하려고 함 – Sally가 다시 시작할 필요 없이 약간의 색만 더하면 된다고 조언하며 도와줌
⑤ (D) — (C) — (B) (B)에서 요리를 버리려던 Katie를 (C)에서 Sally가 말리는 것임

왜 정답? [정답률 84%]

Katie가 수업 시간에 교수님이 말했던 것을 기억하려고 애쓰고 있었다는 내용으로 끝난 (A)에는 수업에서 Brown 교수가 말한 내용이 등장하는 (D)가 이어지는 것이 적절하다. (D)에서 Sally는 Katie에게 자신이 도울 것이 있는지 물었는데, (B)에서 Sally의 이 말에 Katie가 깜짝 놀랐고, 자신의 요리에 실망하여 요리를 버리려던 Katie를 (C)에서 Sally가 멈춰 세우고 조언을 하는 흐름이 자연스러우므로 정답은 ④ (D) – (B) – (C)이다.

왜 오답? '내가 도울 수 있는 일이 있을까?' 꿀팁

① Katie를 깜짝 놀라게 한 Sally의 말은 (D)에 등장한다.
②, ③ (C)는 Sally가 요리를 다시 시작하려는 Katie를 말리는 내용으로 시작하므로, 그 앞에 Katie가 자신의 요리를 버리려고 했다는 (B)가 있어야 한다.
⑤ 자신의 파스타를 아름다운 색으로 만들 수 있다는 것을 알게 되었는데 눈에 띄게 실망하여 요리를 버리려고 하는 것은 앞뒤가 맞지 않는다.

Q 29 정답 ①

밑줄 친 (a)~(e) 중에서 가리키는 대상이 나머지 넷과 다른 것은?

① (a) Sally　② (b) Katie　③ (c) Katie　④ (d) Katie's　⑤ (e) Katie

왜 정답? [정답률 87%]

Sally와 Katie 중에서 룸메이트가 무엇을 하는지 궁금해서 부엌으로 달려간 (a)는 Sally를 가리키고 나머지는 모두 Katie를 가리키므로 정답은 ①이다.

왜 오답?

② 자신의 요리를 던져버리려던 것은 Katie이다.
③ Katie가 한 말이므로 I는 Katie를 가리킨다.
④ Sally가 한 말이므로 your sauce는 Katie의 소스를 가리킨다.
⑤ Sally가 Katie를 기분 좋게 해주려고 자신이 도울 수 있는 것이 있는지 물었다.

Q 30 정답 ④

윗글에 관한 내용으로 적절하지 않은 것은?

① Sally는 사진 수업 후 집으로 돌아왔다.
　When Sally came back home from her photography class
② Brown 교수님은 음식에서 시각적인 면이 중요하다고 말했다.
　Professor Brown said that visual aspects make up a key part of a meal.
③ Sally는 냉장고에서 채소가 든 그릇을 꺼냈다.
　Sally took out a container of vegetables from the refrigerator
④ Sally는 색깔 있는 파스타를 만드는 것이 어렵다고 말했다.
　It's not that hard
⑤ Katie는 요리 시험 준비에 어려움을 겪고 있었다.
　Katie was having a hard time preparing for her cooking test

왜 정답? [정답률 90%]

Sally는 소스와 어울리는 색깔이 있는 파스타를 만드는 게 어떤지 제안한 후 그것은 그렇게 어렵지 않다고(It's not that hard) 했으므로 ④이 정답이다.

왜 오답?

① Sally는 사진 수업 후 집으로 돌아왔다. (When Sally came back home from her photography class)
② Brown 교수님은 시각적인 면이 음식의 핵심 부분을 구성한다고 말했다. (Professor Brown said that visual aspects make up a key part of a meal.)
③ Sally는 냉장고에서 채소가 든 그릇을 꺼냈다. (Sally took out a container of vegetables from the refrigerator)
⑤ Sally는 Katie가 요리 시험을 준비하는 데 어려움을 겪고 있다는 것을 알 수 있었다. (Katie was having a hard time preparing for her cooking test)

Q 31~33 ✳Emilia와 Layla의 영국 여행

(A) Walking out of Charing Cross Station in London, / Emilia and her traveling companion, Layla, / already felt their hearts pounding. //
　　　　　　　　　　　　　　　　　felt의 목적어와 목적격 보어
London의 Charing Cross 역에서 걸어 나오면서 / Emilia와 그녀의 여행 동반자인 Layla는 / 벌써 가슴이 두근거리는 것을 느꼈다 //

비인칭 주어
It was the second day / of their European summer trip. //
둘째 날이었다 / 그들의 유럽 여름 여행의 //　31번 단서 1: Emilia와 Layla의 유럽 여행 둘째 날이었음

They were about to visit / one of the world's most famous art galleries. //　31번 단서 1: National Gallery를 막 방문할 참이었음
그들은 방문할 참이었다 / 세계에서 가장 유명한 미술관 중 하나를 //
　　　　　　　　　목적으로 to부정사를 취하는 start
The two of them started hurrying / with excitement. //
그들 두 사람은 서두르기 시작했다 / 흥분하여 //

Suddenly, Emilia shouted, / "Look! // There it is! // We're finally at the National Gallery!" //
갑자기 Emilia가 소리쳤다 / "봐 // 저기 있어 // 우리는 드디어 National Gallery에 도착했어"라고 //
　　　　　　　　　　　　　　　= Emilia's
Layla laughed and responded, / "(a) Your dream's finally come true!" //
Layla는 웃으며 대답했다 / "너의 꿈이 드디어 이루어졌구나"라고 //

  *(A) 문단 요약: National Gallery에 방문할 참인 Emilia와 Layla

(B) "Don't lose hope yet! // Which gallery is the special exhibition at?" / Layla asked. //　31번 단서 2: 〈Sunflowers〉는 특별 전시회를 위해 다른 미술관에 대여되었다는 Emilia의 말에 연결됨
"아직 희망을 잃지 마 // 특별 전시회는 어느 미술관에서 하는 거야"라고 / Layla는 물었다 //

Emilia responded, / "Well, his *Sunflowers* is still in England, / but it's at a gallery in Liverpool. // That's a long way, isn't it?" //
Emilia는 대답했다 / "음, 그의 〈Sunflowers〉는 여전히 영국에 있지만 / 그것은 Liverpool의 미술관에 있어 / 그곳은 거리가 멀지, 그렇지 않아"라고 //
　　　　　　　　　　　　　　　　　　　　　비인칭 주어
After a quick search on her phone, / Layla stated, / "No! // It's 동사완전자동사 only two hours to Liverpool / by train. // The next train leaves / 〈시간〉의 부사구 in an hour. // Why don't we take it?" //　33번 ② Liverpool로 가는 기차를 타자고 제안함
전화로 빠르게 검색해 본 다음 / Layla는 말했다 / "아냐 // Liverpool까지 겨우 두 시간 거리야 / 기차로 // 다음 기차는 떠나 / 한 시간 후에 // 우리 그걸 타는 게 어때?"라고 //

After considering the idea, / Emilia, now relieved, responded, /
그 생각을 고려해 본 다음 / 이제 마음이 놓인 Emilia는 대답했다 /
　　　　　　　= Layla
"Yeah, / but (b) you always wanted / to see Rembrandt's paintings. // Let's do that first, Layla! // Then, after lunch, / we can catch the next train." //　33번 ③ 점심 식사 후에 기차를 타자고 했음
"응 / 하지만 너는 항상 원했잖아 / Rembrandt의 그림들을 보기를 // 그걸 먼저 하자, Layla // 그런 다음 점심 식사 후에 / 그다음 기차를 탈 수 있어"라고 //

Layla smiled brightly. //
Layla가 밝게 미소를 지었다 //

  *(B) 문단 요약: Layla가 보기를 원한 그림들을 먼저 본 후 Emilia가 좋아하는 그림을 보러 가기로 함

(C) However, / after searching all the exhibition rooms, / Emilia and Layla couldn't find van Gogh's masterpiece / anywhere. //
그러나 / 모든 전시실을 찾아본 후에도 / Emilia와 Layla는 van Gogh의 걸작을 찾을 수가 없었다 / 어디에서도 //　31번 단서 3: van Gogh의 〈Sunflowers〉를 보기를 고대했지만, 어디서도 찾을 수 없었음

"That's weird. // Van Gogh's *Sunflowers* should be here. // Where is it?" //
"그거 이상하네 // van Gogh의 〈Sunflowers〉는 여기 있어야 하는데 // 그게 어디에 있지" //
　주어　　　동사　주격 보어　　　주어　　　동사　주격 보어
Emilia looked upset, / but Layla kept calm and said, / "Maybe
　　　　　　　　　= Emilia
(c) you've missed / a notice about it. // Check / the National Gallery app." //
Emilia는 속상해 보였지만 / Layla는 침착함을 유지하며 말했다 / "아마 네가 놓쳤을 거야 / 그것에 대한 공지를 // 확인해 봐 / National Gallery의 앱을"이라고 //

Emilia checked it quickly. //
Emilia는 빠르게 그것을 확인했다 //　33번 ④ National Gallery의 앱을 확인한 후 이곳에 〈Sunflowers〉가 없다고 말함

Then, she sighed, / "*Sunflowers* isn't here! // It's been lent to a different gallery / for a special exhibition. // (d) I can't believe / 　　　　　　　　　　　　　　　　　　　　　= Emilia I didn't check!" //
그런 다음 그녀는 한숨을 쉬었다 / "〈Sunflowers〉는 여기에 없어 // 그것은 다른 미술관에 대여되었어 / 특별 전시회를 위해 // 나는 믿을 수가 없어 / 내가 확인을 안 했다는 걸" //

  *(C) 문단 요약: Emilia가 보려고 했던 그림이 다른 미술관에 대여되었음을 알게 됨

(D) Upon entering the National Gallery, / Emilia knew exactly / where to go first. //　31번 단서 4: National Gallery를 방문할 참이었다는 (A)에 이어짐
National Gallery에 들어가자마자 / Emilia는 정확하게 알았다 / 먼저 어디로 가야 할지를 //
　　　　　= Emilia
(e) She grabbed Layla's hand / and dragged her hurriedly / to find van Gogh's *Sunflowers*. //
그녀는 Layla의 손을 꼭 잡고 / 서둘러 그녀를 끌고 갔다 / van Gogh의 〈Sunflowers〉를 찾으러 //
33번 ⑤ van Gogh의 〈Sunflowers〉는 Emilia가 가장 좋아하는 그림임
It was Emilia's favorite painting / and had inspired her / to become a painter. //　　　　　　　　　　had inspired의 목적어와 목적격 보어
그것은 Emilia가 가장 좋아하는 그림이며 / 그녀에게 영감을 주었다 / 화가가 되도록 //

Emilia loved / his use of bright colors and light. //
Emilia는 아주 좋아했다 / 그의 밝은 색상과 빛의 사용을 //

She couldn't wait / to finally see his masterpiece / in person. //
그녀는 기다릴 수 없었다 / 그의 걸작을 드디어 보는 것을 / 직접 //

"It'll be amazing / to see how he communicated / the feelings of isolation and loneliness / in his work," / she said eagerly. //
*가주어 *진주어
"~은 놀라울 거야 / 그가 전달한 방식을 보는 것은 / 고립과 고독의 느낌을 / 자기 작품에서" 라고 / 그녀는 잔뜩 기대하며 말했다 //

*(D) 문단 요약: 자신이 좋아하는 그림을 볼 생각에 잔뜩 기대에 부푼 Emilia

- companion ⓝ 친구, 동행
- pound ⓥ (가슴이) 마구 뛰다, 두드리다
- exhibition ⓝ 전시(회)
- relieved ⓐ 안도하는
- brightly 쥬 밝게, 환하게
- masterpiece ⓝ 걸작, 명작
- weird ⓐ 기묘한, 이상한
- calm ⓐ 침착한, 잔잔한
- sigh ⓥ 한숨을 쉬다
- grab ⓥ (단단히) 쥐다
- drag ⓥ 끌다, 끌고 가다
- hurriedly 쥬 급히, 서둘러
- isolation ⓝ 고립, 분리
- eagerly 쥬 갈망하여, 몹시

(A) London의 Charing Cross 역에서 걸어 나오면서, Emilia와 그녀의 여행 동반자인 Layla는 벌써 가슴이 두근거리는 것을 느꼈다. 그들의 유럽 여름 여행 둘째 날이었다. 그들은 세계에서 가장 유명한 미술관 중 하나를 방문할 참이었다. 그들 두 사람은 흥분하여 서두르기 시작했다. 갑자기 Emilia가 "봐! 저기 있어! 우리는 드디어 National Gallery에 도착했어!"라고 소리쳤다. Layla는 웃으며, "(a) 너의 꿈이 드디어 이루어졌구나!"라고 대답했다.
(D) National Gallery에 들어가자마자, Emilia는 먼저 어디로 가야 할지를 정확하게 알았다. (e) 그녀는 van Gogh의 〈Sunflowers〉를 찾으러 Layla의 손을 꼭 잡고 서둘러 그녀를 끌고 갔다. 그것은 Emilia가 가장 좋아하는 그림이며 그녀가 화가가 되도록 영감을 주었다. Emilia는 그의 밝은 색상과 빛의 사용을 아주 좋아했다. 그녀는 그의 걸작을 드디어 직접 보기를 열망했다. 그녀는 "그가 자기 작품에서 고립과 고독의 느낌을 전달한 방식을 보면 놀라울 거야."라고 잔뜩 기대하며 말했다.
(C) 그러나, 모든 전시실을 찾아본 후에도, Emilia와 Layla는 van Gogh의 걸작을 어디에서도 찾을 수가 없었다. "그거 이상하네. van Gogh의 〈Sunflowers〉는 여기 있어야 하는데. 그게 어디에 있지?" Emilia는 속상해 보였지만, Layla는 침착함을 유지하며 "아마 (c) 네가 그것에 대한 공지를 놓쳤을 거야. National Gallery의 앱을 확인해 봐."라고 말했다. Emilia는 빠르게 그것을 확인했다. 그런 다음, 그녀는 한숨을 쉬며, 〈Sunflowers〉는 여기에 없어! 그것은 특별 전시회를 위해 다른 미술관에 대여되었어. 내가 확인을 안 했다는 걸 (d) 나는 믿을 수가 없어!"라고 말했다. (B) Layla는 "아직 희망을 잃지 마! 특별 전시회는 어느 미술관에서 하는 거야?"라고 물었다. Emilia는 "음, 그의 〈Sunflowers〉는 여전히 영국에 있지만, 그것은 Liverpool의 미술관에 있어. 그곳은 거리가 멀지, 그렇지 않아?"라고 대답했다. 전화로 빠르게 검색해 본 다음, Layla는 "아냐! Liverpool까지 기차로 겨우 두 시간 거리야. 다음 기차는 한 시간 후에 떠나. 우리 그걸 타는 게 어때?"라고 말했다. 그 생각을 고려해 본 다음, 이제 마음이 놓인 Emilia는 "응, 하지만 (b) 너는 항상 Rembrandt의 그림들을 보고 싶어 했잖아. 그걸 먼저 하자, Layla! 그런 다음, 점심 식사 후에, 그다음 기차를 탈 수 있어."라고 대답했다. Layla가 밝게 미소를 지었다.

Q 31 정답 ⑤

주어진 글 (A)에 이어질 내용을 순서에 맞게 배열한 것으로 가장 적절한 것은?
① (B) — (D) — (C) the special exhibition에 대한 언급이 (A)에는 없음
② (C) — (B) — (D) ┐
③ (C) — (D) — (B) ┘ (A)와 (C)는 However로 연결될 만한 내용이 아님
④ (D) — (B) — (C) 두 사람이 일정 조율을 마친 (B)가 맨 마지막에 와야 함
⑤ (D) — (C) — (B) National Gallery를 막 방문할 참임 – 미술관에 들어가자마자 van Gogh의 〈Sunflowers〉를 찾으러 감 – 〈Sunflowers〉가 Liverpool의 다른 미술관에 대여되었음을 알게 됨 – 점심 식사를 하고 Liverpool로 가는 기차를 타기로 함

> 왜 정답 ? [정답률 89%]
(A)에서 두 사람은 National Gallery를 방문할 참이었으므로 'National Gallery에 들어가자마자'라는 뜻인 Upon entering the National Gallery로 시작하는 (D)가 (A)에 이어진다.
(D)에서 National Gallery에 들어가자마자 두 사람은 가장 먼저 van Gogh의 〈Sunflowers〉를 찾으러 갔으므로, '그러나' van Gogh의 걸작을 어디에서도 찾을 수 없었다는 문장으로 시작한 (C)가 (D)에 이어진다.
(C)에서 Emilia는 National Gallery의 앱을 확인한 후 van Gogh의 〈Sunflowers〉가 특별 전시회를 위해 다른 미술관에 대여되었다고 말했으므로, 그 특별 전시회가 어느 미술관에서 하는지 묻는 Layla의 말로 시작한 (B)가 (C) 뒤에 이어진다.
따라서 세 문단의 적절한 순서는 ⑤ (D) – (C) – (B)이다.

> 왜 오답 ?
①, ④ (B)에서 Layla는 특별 전시회에 대해 묻는데, (A)나 (D)에는 특별 전시회에 대한 언급이 없다.
②, ③ van Gogh의 걸작을 어디에서도 찾을 수가 없었다는 문장과 However로 연결되기에 적절한 것은 van Gogh의 그 작품을 찾으러 갔다는 등의 내용이다.

Q 32 정답 ②

밑줄 친 (a)~(e) 중에서 가리키는 대상이 나머지 넷과 다른 것은?
① (a) Emilia's ② (b) Layla ③ (c) Emilia ④ (d) Emilia ⑤ (e) Emilia

> 왜 정답 ? [정답률 92%]   Emilia가 you로 가리킨 사람 꿀팁
Emilia와 Layla 중에서 Rembrandt의 그림을 보기를 항상 원했던 (b)는 Layla를 가리키고 나머지는 모두 Emilia를 가리키므로 정답은 ②이다.

> 왜 오답 ?
① Layla가 한 말이므로 your는 Emilia를 가리키는 소유격 대명사이다.
③ Layla가 한 말이므로 you는 Emilia를 가리키는 주격 대명사이다.
④ Emilia가 한숨을 쉬며 한 말이므로 I는 Emilia를 가리킨다.
⑤ Layla의 손을 꼭 잡은 사람은 Emilia이다.

Q 33 정답 ③

윗글에 관한 내용으로 적절하지 않은 것은?
① Emilia와 Layla는 유럽 여행 중이었다. It was the second day of their European summer trip.
② Layla는 Emilia에게 Liverpool로 가자고 제안했다. Why don't we take it?
③ Emilia는 기차를 점심 식사 전에 타자고 말했다. Then, after lunch, we can catch the next train.
④ National Gallery에는 van Gogh의 Sunflowers가 없었다. Sunflowers isn't here!
⑤ Emilia는 van Gogh의 Sunflowers를 좋아했다. It was Emilia's favorite painting

> 왜 정답 ? [정답률 93%]
점심 식사 후에 그다음 기차를 타자고(Then, after lunch, we can catch the next train.) 했으므로 ③은 글과 일치하지 않는다.

> 왜 오답 ?
① Emilia와 Layla의 유럽 여행 둘째 날에 일어난 일이다. (It was the second day of their European summer trip.)
② Layla는 Emilia에게 Liverpool로 가는 기차를 타자고 제안했다. (Why don't we take it?)
④ National Gallery 앱을 확인한 후 van Gogh의 〈Sunflowers〉가 그곳에 없다고 말했다. (Sunflowers isn't here!)
⑤ van Gogh의 〈Sunflowers〉는 Emilia가 가장 좋아하는 그림이었다. (It was Emilia's favorite painting)

(A) In the gym, / members of the taekwondo club / were busy practicing. //
be busy (in) -ing: ~하느라 바쁘다
체육관에서 / 태권도 동아리 회원들이 / 연습하느라 바빴다 //

Some were trying to kick / as high as they could, / and some were striking the sparring pad. //
몇 명은 발차기를 하려고 애쓰고 있었고 / 가능한 한 높이 / 몇 명은 겨루기 패드를 치고 있었다 //

Anna, / the head of the club, / was teaching the new members / basic moves. // 36번① Anna는 신입 회원에게 기본 동작을 가르쳤음
Anna는 / 동아리 회장인 / 신입 회원들에게 가르치고 있었다 / 기본 동작을 //

Close by, / her friend Jane was assisting Anna. //
바로 옆에서 / 그녀의 친구인 Jane이 Anna를 보조하고 있었다 //

Jane noticed / that Anna was glancing / at the entrance door of the gym. //
Jane은 알아차렸다 / Anna가 힐끗 보고 있다는 것을 / 체육관의 출입문을 //

She seemed / to be expecting someone. // 34번 단서 1: Jane이 Anna에게 Cora를 기다리고 있는지 물어봄
그녀는 보였다 / 누군가를 기다리고 있는 것처럼 //

At last, / when Anna took a break, / Jane came over to (a) her
부사절 접속사(시간)   = Anna
and asked, / "Hey, are you waiting for Cora?" //
드디어 / Anna가 휴식을 취할 때 / Jane이 그녀에게 다가와서 물었다 / "야, 너 Cora를 기다리고 있니"라고 //

*(A) 문단 요약: Jane이 태권도 동아리 회장인 Anna에게 Cora를 기다리고 있냐고 물어봄 34번 단서 2: (D)에서 등장한 Cora가 걸어 들어옴

(B) Cora walked in / like a wounded soldier / with bandages / on her face and arms. //
Cora는 걸어 들어왔다 / 부상당한 군인처럼 / 붕대를 하고서 / 그녀의 얼굴과 두 팔에 //

Surprised, / Anna and Jane simply looked at her / with their eyes wide open. // 36번② Cora가 들어오자 Anna와 Jane은 「with+(대)명사+분사」 구문으로
                                         놀라고 휘둥그레진 눈으로 그녀를 쳐다봤음 wide open 앞에 being이 생략됨
놀라서 / Anna와 Jane은 그녀를 바라볼 뿐이었다 / 두 눈을 크게 뜨고서 //

Cora explained, / "I'm sorry I've been absent. //
Cora는 설명했다 / "계속 오지 못해서 미안해 //

I got into a bicycle accident, / and I was in the hospital / for two days. //
           주어   동사 간접목적어   직접목적어
난 자전거 사고가 나서 / 입원해 있었어 / 이틀 동안 //

Finally, / the doctor gave me the okay / to practice." //
마침내 / 의사 선생님이 나에게 동의를 하셨어 / 연습해도 좋다"이라고 //

Anna said excitedly, / "No problem! // We're thrilled / to have you back!" //
                                   부사적 용법(감정의 원인)
Anna가 흥분하여 말했다 / "괜찮아 // 우리는 신난다 / 네가 돌아오게 되어"라고 //

Then, Jane gave Anna an apologetic look, / and (b) she
        주어   동사 간접목적어   직접목적어   = Anna
responded / with a friendly pat on Jane's shoulder. //
그때 Jane이 Anna에게 사과하는 표정을 보였고 / 그녀는 대답했다 / Jane의 어깨를 토닥이는 것으로 //

*(B) 문단 요약: Cora는 자전거 사고로 입원하느라 못 왔다고 말했고, Jane은 Anna에게 사과하는 표정을 지음 34번 단서 3: (A)에서 Jane이 Anna에게 물어본 것에 Anna가 고개를 끄덕여 대답함

(C) Anna answered the question / by nodding uneasily. //
Anna는 그 질문에 대답했다 / 걱정스럽게 고개를 끄덕여서 //

In fact, / Jane knew / what her friend was thinking. //
          주어 동사   목적어절
사실 Jane은 알고 있었다 / 자기 친구가 무엇을 생각하고 있는지 //

Cora was a new member, / whom Anna had personally invited
선행사   목적격 관계대명사
/ to join the club. //
Cora는 신입 회원인데 / 그녀에게 Anna가 직접 청했었다 / 동아리에 가입할 것을 //

Anna really liked (c) her. //
                       = Cora
Anna는 그녀를 진정으로 좋아했다 //

Although her budget was tight, / Anna bought Cora / a
                                주어   동사   간접목적어
taekwondo uniform. // 36번③ Anna가 Cora에게 태권도 도복을 사 주었음
                                      직접목적어
자신의 예산이 빠듯했지만 / Anna는 Cora에게 사주었다 / 태권도 도복을 //

When she received it, / Cora thanked her and promised, / "I'll come to practice and work hard / every day." //
그것을 받았을 때 / Cora는 그녀에게 고마움을 표시하면서 약속했다 / "나는 연습하러 와서 열심히 할 거야 / 매일"이라고 //

However, unexpectedly, / she came to practice only once / and then never showed up again. //
하지만 예상과 달리 / 그녀는 연습하러 딱 한 번 왔고 / 그러고 나서 다시는 나타나지 않았다 //

*(C) 문단 요약: Anna가 직접 데려온 신입 회원 Cora는 연습하러 한 번만 오고 다시 나오지 않았음
부사절 접속사(이유)   36번④ Cora는 여러 연습을 빠졌음
(D) Since Cora had missed several practices, / Anna wondered /
과거의 일에 대한 추측을 나타내는 could have p.p
what could have happened. // 34번 단서 4: Cora가 딱 한 번 오고 난 이후로 나타나지 않자 Anna가 무슨 일이 있는지 궁금해함
Cora가 여러 번의 연습에 빠졌기 때문에 / Anna는 궁금했다 / 무슨 일이 있었을지 //

Jane, on the other hand, was disappointed / and said judgingly, / "Still waiting for her, huh? //
반면 Jane은 실망하여 / 재단하듯이 말했다 / "아직도 그녀를 기다리는 거야. 응 //

I can't believe / (d) you don't feel disappointed or angry. //
                    = Anna
나는 믿을 수가 없어 / 네가 실망감이나 분노를 느끼지 않는 것을 //

Why don't you forget / about her?" //
잊어버리는 것이 어때 / 그녀에 대해"라고 //

앞에 명사절(목적어절) 접속사가 생략됨
Anna replied, / "Well, I know / most newcomers don't keep
                               생략되지 않은 명사절(목적어절) 접속사
their commitment / to the club, / but I thought / that Cora would
be different. // 36번⑤ Anna는 Cora가 대부분의 신입 회원과 다를 거라고 생각했음
Anna는 대답했다 / "글쎄, 난 알지만 / 대다수의 새로 온 사람들이 약속을 지키지 않는다는 것은 / 동아리에 대한 / 난 생각했어 / Cora는 다를 것이라고 //

She said / she would come every day and practice." //
그녀는 말했거든 / 매일 와서 연습할 거라고"라고 //
                            = Anna   swing open: 활짝 열리다
Just as Jane was about to respond / to (e) her, / the door swung open. //
Jane이 바로 막 대답하려 했을 때 / 그녀에게 / 문이 활짝 열렸다 //

There she was! //
거기 그녀가 있었다 //

*(D) 문단 요약: Jane과 달리 Anna는 Cora가 다른 새로 온 사람들과 다를 것으로 생각했고, Cora가 태권도장에 나타남

• strike ⓥ (손이나 무기로) 때리다[치다]
• sparring ⓝ ((태권도)) 겨루기, ((권투)) 스파링(시합에 대비한 연습)
• assist ⓥ 돕다, 보조하다   • glance ⓥ 힐끗 보다
• expect ⓥ (오기로 되어 있는 대상을) 기다리다
• wounded ⓐ 부상을 입은, 다친   • absent ⓐ 없는, 결석한
• thrilled ⓐ 아주 흥분한, 신이 난 • apologetic ⓐ 미안해하는, 사과하는
• pat ⓝ 쓰다듬기, 토닥거리기   • nod ⓥ (고개를) 끄덕이다
• uneasily ⓐ 걱정스럽게, 불안 속에 • personally ⓐ 직접, 개인적으로
• budget ⓝ 예산   • tight ⓐ (금전적으로) 빠듯한
• unexpectedly ⓐ 예상외로, 예상과 다르게
• show up (예정된 곳에) 나타나다   • wonder ⓥ 궁금해하다
• judgingly ⓐ 재단하듯이   • commitment ⓝ 약속, 책임

(A) 체육관에서, 태권도 동아리 회원들이 부지런히 연습하고 있었다. 몇 명은 가능한 한 높이 발차기를 하려고 애쓰고 있었고, 몇 명은 겨루기 패드를 치고 있었다. 동아리 회장인 Anna는 신입 회원들에게 기본 동작을 가르치고 있었다. 바로 옆에서 그녀의 친구인 Jane이 Anna를 보조하고 있었다. Jane은 Anna가 체육관의 출입문을 힐끗 보고 있다는 것을 알아차렸다. 그녀는 누군가를 기다리고 있는 것처럼 보였다. 드디어 Anna가 휴식을 취할 때 Jane이 (a) 그녀에게 다가와서 "야, Cora를 기다리고 있니?"라고 물었다.

(C) Anna는 걱정스럽게 고개를 끄덕여 그 질문에 대답했다. 사실, Jane은 자기 친구가 무엇을 생각하고 있는지 알고 있었다. Cora는 신입 회원인데, 그녀에게 Anna가 동아리에 가입하라고 직접 청했었다. Anna는 (c) 그녀를 진정으로 좋아했다. 자신의 예산이 빠듯했지만, Anna는 Cora에게 태권도 도복을 사주었다. 그것을 받았을 때, Cora는 그녀에게 고마움을 표시하면서 "매일 연습하러 와서 열심히 할 거야."라고 약속했다. 하지만, 예상과 달리, 그녀는 연습하러 딱 한 번 왔고 그러고 나서 다시는 나타나지 않았다.

(D) Cora가 여러 번의 연습에 빠졌기 때문에 Anna는 무슨 일이 있었을지 궁금했다. 반면 Jane은 실망하여 "아직도 그녀를 기다리는 거야, 응? 나는 (d) 네가 실망감이나 분노를 느끼지 않는 것을 믿을 수가 없어. 그녀에 대해 잊어버리는 것이 어때?"라고 재단하듯이 말했다. Anna는 "글쎄, 난 대다수의 새로 온 사람들이 동아리에 대한 약속을 지키지 않는 것은 알지만, Cora는 다를 것이라고 생각했어. 그녀는 매일 와서 연습할 거라고 말했거든."이라고 대답했다. Jane이 바로 막 (e) 그녀에게 대답하려 했을 때, 문이 활짝 열렸다. 거기 그녀가 있었다! (B) Cora는 얼굴과 두 팔에 붕대를 하고서 부상당한 군인처럼 걸어 들어왔다. 놀란 Anna와 Jane은 두 눈을 크게 뜨고서 그녀를 바라볼 뿐이었다. Cora는 "계속 오지 못해서 미안해. 난 자전거 사고가 나서 이틀 동안 입원해 있었어. 마침내 의사 선생님이 나에게 연습해도 좋다는 동의를 하셨어."라고 설명했다. Anna가 "괜찮아! 우리는 네가 돌아오게 되어 신난다."라고 흥분하여 말했다. 그때, Jane이 Anna에게 사과하는 표정을 보였고, (b) 그녀는 Jane의 어깨를 토닥이는 것으로 대답했다.

Q 34 정답 ③

주어진 글 (A)에 이어질 내용을 순서에 맞게 배열한 것으로 가장 적절한 것은?

① (B) — (D) — (C) — Cora가 등장해 그동안 빠진 이유를 설명하는 (B)는 맨 마지막에 와야 함
② (C) — (B) — (D) — Jane이 Anna에게 Cora를 기다리고 있는지 물어봄 – Anna가 고개를 끄덕여 대답했음 – Cora는 연습하러 딱 한 번 이후로 나타나지 않음 – Anna는 Cora에게 무슨 일이 있는지 궁금했지만 Jane은 그녀를 잊으라고 말함 –
③ (C) — (D) — (B) — Cora가 나타나서 자신이 빠졌던 이유를 설명함
④ (D) — (B) — (C) — Jane이 Anna에게 Cora를 기다리고 있는지 물은 것에 대한 대답이
⑤ (D) — (C) — (B) — (D)보다 먼저 나와야 함

> **왜 정답?** [정답률 85%]

Jane이 Anna에게 Cora를 기다리고 있는지 묻는 것으로 끝난 (A)에는 Anna가 걱정스럽게 고개를 끄덕여 그 질문에 대답했다는 문장으로 시작한 (C)가 이어진다. (C)는 Cora가 딱 한 번 연습하러 나온 후에 다시는 나타나지 않았다는 문장으로 끝났으므로, 그녀에게 무슨 일이 있는지 Anna가 궁금해했다는 문장으로 시작한 (D)가 이어져야 하고, 활짝 열린 문에 Cora가 있었다는 문장으로 끝난 (D)에는 얼굴과 두 팔에 붕대를 하고서 걸어 들어온 Cora가 그동안 자신이 나오지 못한 이유를 설명하는 (B)가 이어지는 것이 적절하다. 따라서 정답은 ③ (C) – (D) – (B)이다.

> **왜 오답?**

①, ② Cora가 걸어 들어왔다는 (B) 앞에 문이 활짝 열리고 그곳에 Cora가 있었다는 (D)가 있어야 한다. [주의]

④, ⑤ (A)가 Jane이 Anna에게 Cora를 기다리고 있는지 묻는 문장으로 끝났으므로, Anna가 Jane의 질문에 고개를 끄덕여 대답했다는 (C)가 (D)보다 먼저 (A)에 이어져야 한다.

Q 35 정답 ③

밑줄 친 (a)~(e) 중에서 가리키는 대상이 나머지 넷과 다른 것은?

① (a) Anna ② (b) Anna ③ (c) Cora ④ (d) Anna ⑤ (e) Anna

> **왜 정답?** [정답률 93%]

Anna와 Jane, Cora 중에서 (a), (b), (d), (e)는 모두 Anna를 가리키는 반면에 Anna가 진정으로 좋아한 (c)는 Cora를 가리키므로 정답은 ③이다.

> **왜 오답?**

① Anna가 휴식을 취할 때 Jane이 Anna에게 다가와 물은 것이다.
② Jane이 Anna에게 표정으로 사과했고, Anna가 Jane의 어깨를 토닥이는 것으로 대답한 것이다.
④ Jane이 Anna에게 하는 말이므로 you는 Anna를 가리킨다.
⑤ Jane이 Anna에게 대답하려고 할 때 문이 활짝 열린 것이다.

Q 36 정답 ②

윗글에 관한 내용으로 적절하지 않은 것은?

① Anna는 신입 회원에게 태권도를 가르쳤다.
   Anna, the head of the club, was teaching the new members basic moves.
② Anna와 Jane은 Cora를 보고 놀라지 않았다.
   Surprised, Anna and Jane simply looked at her with their eyes wide open.
③ Anna는 Cora에게 태권도 도복을 사 주었다.
   Anna bought Cora a taekwondo uniform
④ Cora는 여러 차례 연습에 참여하지 않았다.
   Cora had missed several practices
⑤ Anna는 Cora를 대다수의 신입 회원과 다를 것이라 생각했다.
   I thought that Cora would be different

> **왜 정답?** [정답률 82%]

Cora가 들어오자 Anna와 Jane은 놀라고 휘둥그레진 눈으로 그녀를 쳐다봤다고(Surprised, Anna and Jane simply looked at her with their eyes wide open.) 했으므로 ②은 글과 일치하지 않는다.

> **왜 오답?**

① 태권도 클럽의 회장인 Anna가 신입 회원들에게 기본 동작을 가르치고 있었다. (Anna, the head of the club, was teaching the new members basic moves.)
③ Anna는 Cora에게 태권도 도복을 사 주었다. (Anna bought Cora a taekwondo uniform)
④ Cora는 여러 차례 연습에 참여하지 않았다. (Cora had missed several practices)
⑤ Anna는 Cora가 대다수의 새로 온 사람들과 다르리라고 생각했다. (I thought that Cora would be different)

Q 37~39 * 기숙사 방 꾸미기

(A) It was the first day of the semester. //
그날은 학기 첫날이었다 // **39번 ①** Noah는 학기 첫날 자신의 기숙사 방을 둘러보고 실망했음
Looking around his shared dorm room, / Noah thought / that it looked exactly like every other dorm room / at the university, / and he became disappointed. //
자신의 공용 기숙사 방을 둘러보면서 / Noah는 생각했다 / 그것이 다른 모든 기숙사 방과 완전히 똑같이 생겼다고 / 대학교의 / 그리고 그는 실망했다 //

asked의 목적어절
His roommate Steve noticed it / and asked what was wrong. //
그의 룸메이트 Steve는 그것을 알아차리고 / 무슨 일이 있는지 물었다 //

Noah answered quietly / that he thought / their room was totally boring. //
Noah는 조용히 대답했다 / 그가 생각한다고 / 그들의 방이 완전히 지루하다고 //
= Noah / the space가 느끼는 것이 아니라 느껴지는 것임
(a) He wished the space felt / a bit more like *their* space. //
그는 그 공간이 느껴지길 원했다 / 약간 더 '자신들의' 공간처럼 // **37번** 단서 1: 다음날 방을 개인화하자고 제안함

Steve agreed and suggested / that they could start personalizing the room / like Noah wanted, / the next day. //
Steve는 동의했고 제안했다 / 그들이 방을 개인화하는 것을 시작할 수 있다고 / Noah가 원하는 것처럼 / 다음날 //

*(A) 문단 요약: 학기 첫날 기숙사 방을 보고 실망하여 다음날 방을 꾸미기로 함

(B) As they walked through a furniture store, / Steve found a pretty yellow table. // **37번** 단서 2: 탁자를 사러 가기로 결정한 후 나가서 예쁜 노란색 탁자를 발견함
그들이 걸어서 가구점을 지나갈 때 / Steve는 예쁜 노란색 탁자를 발견했다 //
(이유)의 부사절 접속사
Since he knew / that yellow was Noah's favorite color, / Steve = Noah   asked의 직접목적어절
asked (b) him / what he thought about buying that table. //
그가 알았기 때문에 / 노란색이 Noah가 가장 좋아하는 색깔이라는 것을 / Steve는 그에게 물었다 / 그 탁자를 사는 것에 대해 그가 어떻게 생각하느냐고 //

Noah was happy about the yellow table / and said / it would make their room more unique. // **39번 ②** Noah는 노란색 탁자가 자신들의 방을 더 독특하게 만들 것이라고 말했음
Noah는 노란색 탁자에 대해 만족했고 / 말했다 / 그것이 자신들의 방을 더 독특하게 만들 것이라고 //

Delighted, Noah added, / "Well, yesterday our room was just like any other place / at this school. // But after today, / (c)I really feel / like it'll be *our* place." //
= Noah

기뻐하며 Noah는 덧붙였다 / "자, 어제 우리 방은 다른 장소와 그저 똑같았어 / 이 학교의 / 하지만 오늘 이후로 / 나는 정말로 느껴져 / 이곳이 '우리의' 장소가 되리라고"라고 //

Now, they both knew / that the place would provide them / with energy and refreshment. //
provide A with B: A에게 B를 제공하다

이제 그들 둘 다 알았다 / 그 장소가 그들에게 제공하리라는 것을 / 에너지와 상쾌함을 //

*(B) 문단 요약: 노란색 탁자를 구입함으로써 기숙사 방을 자신들의 장소로 만듦

(C) Noah hardly slept that night / making plans for the room. //
Noah는 그날 밤 거의 잠을 자지 못했다 / 방을 위한 계획을 짜느라 //

After Steve woke up, / they started to rearrange the furniture. //
Steve가 일어난 후 / 그들은 가구를 다시 배치하기 시작했다 //

All of the chairs and the sofa / in their room / were facing the TV. //
37번 단서 3, 39번 ③ 다음날 Steve가 일어난 후 함께 가구 재배치를 시작함
모든 의자와 소파는 / 그들의 방에 있는 / TV를 향하고 있었다 //

Noah mentioned to Steve / that most of their visitors / usually just sat and watched TV / instead of chatting. //
Noah는 Steve에게 말했다 / 그들의 방문객 대부분이 / 보통 그저 앉아서 TV를 본다고 / 담소를 나누는 대신 //

In response to (d) his idea, / Steve suggested, / "How about we
= Noah's
put the sofa / over there by the wall / so it will be easier to have conversations?" //
가주어   진주어
그의 생각에 응하여 / Steve는 제안했다 / "소파를 놓는 게 어때 / 저쪽 벽 옆에 / 대화를 나누는 것을 더 쉽도록"이라고 //
37번 단서 4: 소파를 벽 옆으로 옮겼음

Noah agreed, / and they moved it / by the wall. //
Noah는 동의했고 / 그들은 그것을 옮겼다 / 벽 옆으로 //
37번 단서 5: 소파의 위치를 옮기고 난 후 일어난 일이 이어짐

*(C) 문단 요약: 다음날 가구를 재배치하며 방을 개인화하기 시작함

(D) After changing the place of the sofa, / they could see / that they now had a lot of space / in the middle of their room. //
소파의 위치를 바꾼 후 / 그들은 볼 수 있었다 / 그들에게 이제 넓은 공간이 생겨난 것을 / 그들의 방 한가운데에 //

Then, Noah remembered / that his brother Sammy had a big table / in his living room / for playing board games / and told Steve about it. // 39번 ④ Noah는 Sammy의 거실에 커다란 탁자가 있던 것을 떠올렸음
그때 Noah는 기억했고 / 자신의 동생 Sammy가 커다란 탁자를 가지고 있다는 것을 / 그의 거실에 / 보드게임을 하기 위해 / Steve에게 그것에 대해 말했다 //

Steve and Noah both really enjoyed / playing board games. //
Steve와 Noah 둘 다 정말 즐겼다 / 보드게임 하는 것을 // 39번 ⑤ Noah와 Steve 둘 다 보드게임 하는 것을 즐겼음

So, Steve replied to Noah, / "(e)I think / putting a table / in the
= Steve   동명사구 주어
middle of our room / would be great for drinking tea / as well as
동사
playing board games!" //
그래서 Steve는 Noah에게 대답했다 / "나는 생각해 / 탁자를 놓는 것은 / 우리 방 한가운데에 / 차를 마시기에도 아주 좋을 것 같다고 / 보드게임을 하는데 뿐만 아니라"라고 //

Both Noah and Steve agreed / and decided to go shopping for a table. // 37번 단서 6: 탁자를 사러 가기로 함
Noah와 Steve는 모두 동의했고 / 탁자를 사러 가기로 결정했다 //

*(D) 문단 요약: 차를 마시고 보드게임을 할 탁자를 사러 가기로 결정함

- semester ⓝ 학기   · dorm ⓝ 기숙사, 공동 침실
- totally ⓐⓓ 완전히, 전적으로   · personalize ⓥ 개인화하다
- delighted ⓐ 아주 기뻐하는, 즐거워하는
- refreshment ⓝ 원기 회복, (행사에 제공되는) 다과
- rearrange ⓥ 재배열하다, 재조정하다

(A) 그날은 학기 첫날이었다. 자신의 공용 기숙사 방을 둘러보면서, Noah는 그것이 대학교의 다른 모든 기숙사 방과 완전히 똑같이 생겼다는 생각이 들어서 실망했다. 그의 룸메이트 Steve는 그것을 알아차리고 무슨 일이 있는지 물었다. Noah는 그들의 방이 완전히 지루하다는 생각이 든다고 조용히 대답했다. (a) 그는 그 공간이 약간 더 '자신들의' 공간처럼 느껴지길 원했다. Steve는 동의했고, 다음날 Noah가 원하는 것처럼 방을 개인화하는 것을 시작할 수 있다고 제안했다.

(C) Noah는 방을 위한 계획을 짜느라 그날 밤 거의 잠을 자지 못했다. Steve가 일어난 후, 그들은 가구를 다시 배치하기 시작했다. 그들의 방에 있는 모든 의자와 소파는 TV를 향하고 있었다. Noah는 Steve에게 방문객 대부분이 담소를 나누는 대신 보통 그저 앉아서 TV를 본다고 말했다. (d) 그의 생각에 응하여 Steve는 "소파를 저쪽 벽 옆에 놓아서 대화를 나누는 것을 더 쉽게 하는 것이 어때?"라고 제안했다. Noah는 동의했고, 그들은 그것을 벽 옆으로 옮겼다.

(D) 소파의 위치를 바꾼 후, 그들은 이제 방 한가운데에 넓은 공간이 생겨난 것을 볼 수 있었다. 그때, Noah는 자신의 동생 Sammy가 보드게임을 하기 위해 그의 거실에 커다란 탁자를 가지고 있다는 것을 기억했고 Steve에게 그것에 대해 말했다. Steve와 Noah 둘 다 보드게임 하는 것을 정말 즐겼다. 그래서 Steve는 Noah에게 "우리 방 한가운데에 탁자를 놓는 것은 보드게임을 하는데 뿐만 아니라 차를 마시기에도 아주 좋을 것 같다고 (e) 나는 생각해!"라고 대답했다. Noah와 Steve는 모두 동의했고 탁자를 사러 가기로 결정했다.

(B) 그들이 걸어서 가구점을 지나갈 때, Steve는 예쁜 노란색 탁자를 발견했다. 노란색이 Noah가 가장 좋아하는 색깔이라는 것을 알았기 때문에, Steve는 (b) 그에게 그 탁자를 사는 것에 대해 어떻게 생각하느냐고 물었다. Noah는 노란색 탁자에 대해 만족했고 그것이 자신들의 방을 더 독특하게 만들 것이라고 말했다. 기뻐하며 Noah는 "자, 어제 우리 방은 이 학교의 다른 장소와 그저 똑같았어. 하지만 오늘 이후로, (c) 나는 정말로 이곳이 '우리의' 장소가 되리라고 느껴져."라고 덧붙였다. 이제, 그들 둘 다 그 장소가 그들에게 에너지와 상쾌함을 제공하리라는 것을 알았다.

Q 37 정답 ③

주어진 글 (A)에 이어질 내용을 순서에 맞게 배열한 것으로 가장 적절한 것은?

① (B) — (D) — (C) (A)에는 탁자를 사러 가자는 언급이 없음
② (C) — (B) — (D) 탁자를 사러 가기로 결정한 후 나가서 노란색 탁자를 발견하는 흐름이어야 함
③ (C) — (D) — (B) 다음날 방을 개인화하기로 함 – 다음날 가구를 재배치하며 소파의 위치를 옮김 – 소파의 위치를 바꾼 후 탁자를 사러 가기로 결정함 – 예쁜 노란색 탁자를 발견해서 구입하기로 함
④ (D) — (B) — (C)
⑤ (D) — (C) — (B)
(A)에서 소파의 위치를 바꿨다는 언급은 없음

⟩**왜** 정답 ? [정답률 90%]

다음날 방을 개인화하자는 Steve의 제안으로 끝난 (A)에는 그날 밤 Noah가 잠을 못 잤고, 다음날 Steve가 일어난 후 가구 재배치를 시작했다는 (C)가 이어진다. (C)에서 두 사람은 소파의 위치를 옮겼고, (D)에서는 소파의 위치를 바꾼 후 탁자를 사러 가기로 결정했다. 마지막으로 (B)에서 탁자를 사러 갔다가 예쁜 노란색 탁자를 발견했으므로 정답은 ③ (C)-(D)-(B)이다.

⟩**왜** 오답 ?

① (A)의 일이 일어난 날 밤이 (C)의 that night이고, (B)는 그 다음 날이므로 (C)가 (B)보다 앞에 있어야 한다.
② 탁자를 사러 가기로 결정한 후에 나가서 노란색 탁자를 발견하여 구입하기로 했다는 흐름이 적절하다.
④, ⑤ (D)는 소파의 위치를 바꾼 후의 일이므로 그 앞에 소파를 벽 옆으로 옮겼다는 내용이 나오는 (C)가 있어야 한다.

Q 38 정답 ⑤

밑줄 친 (a)~(e) 중에서 가리키는 대상이 나머지 넷과 다른 것은?

① (a) Noah   ② (b) Noah   ③ (c) Noah   ④ (d) Noah's   ⑤ (e) Steve

⟩**왜** 정답 ? [정답률 91%]

기숙사 룸메이트인 Steve와 Noah 중에서 나머지는 모두 Noah를 가리키는 반면 ⑤은 Steve가 Noah에게 한 말이므로 Steve를 가리킨다.

> **왜 오답?**
① 기숙사 방에 실망하며 그것이 약간 더 '자신들의' 공간처럼 느껴지길 원한 것은 Noah이다.
② Steve가 질문한 대상은 Noah이다.
③ Noah가 기뻐하며 덧붙인 말이므로 Noah를 가리킨다.
④ 모든 의자와 소파가 TV를 향하고 있어서 방문객들이 그저 앉아서 TV를 본다는 Noah의 생각에 응하여 Steve가 제안한 것이다.

Q 39 정답 ③

윗글에 관한 내용으로 적절하지 않은 것은?
① Noah는 학기 첫날 자신의 기숙사 방을 둘러보고 실망했다.
It was the first day ~ and he became disappointed
② Noah는 노란색 탁자가 자신들의 방을 더 독특하게 만들 것이라고 말했다.
Noah ~ said it would make their room more unique.
③ Noah는 Steve가 잠든 사이에 가구를 다시 배치했다.
After Steve woke up, they started to rearrange the furniture.
④ Noah는 Sammy의 거실에 커다란 탁자가 있던 것을 떠올렸다.
Noah remembered that his brother Sammy had a big table in his living room
⑤ Noah와 Steve 둘 다 보드게임 하는 것을 즐겼다.
Steve and Noah both really enjoyed playing board games.

> **왜 정답?** [정답률 93%]

Steve가 일어난 후에 함께 가구를 다시 배치하기 시작했으므로(After Steve woke up, they started to rearrange the furniture.) ③은 글과 일치하지 않는다.

> **왜 오답?**
① 학기 첫날에 Noah는 자신의 기숙사 방을 둘러보고 다른 모든 기숙사 방과 똑같다고 생각해 실망했다. (It was the first day ~ and he became disappointed)
② Noah는 노란색 탁자에 대해 만족했고 그것이 자신들의 방을 더 독특하게 만들 것이라고 말했다. (Noah ~ said it would make their room more unique.)
④ Noah는 자신의 동생 Sammy가 보드게임을 하기 위해 그의 거실에 커다란 탁자를 가지고 있었다는 것을 기억했다. (Noah remembered that his brother ~ in his living room)
⑤ Steve와 Noah 둘 다 보드게임 하는 것을 정말 즐겼다. (Steve and Noah both really enjoyed playing board games.)

Q 40~42 *아빠의 생신 선물

(A) "Hailey, be careful!" //
"Hailey, 조심해" //
Camila yelled uneasily, / watching her sister carrying a huge cake / to the table. //
= as she watched   진행 중인 동작에 초점을 맞춘 현재분사 목적격 보어
Camila는 걱정되어 소리쳤다 / 자신의 여동생이 커다란 케이크를 옮기는 것을 보며 / 테이블로 //
"Don't worry, Camila," / Hailey responded, / smiling. //
"걱정 마, Camila" / Hailey는 대답했다 / 미소 지으며 //
부사절 접속사(시간)
Camila relaxed / only when Hailey had safely placed the cake / on the party table. // 42번 ① Hailey는 생일 케이크를 테이블로 무사히 옮겨 놓았음
Camila는 안심했다 / Hailey가 케이크를 무사히 올려 두었을 때에야 / 파티 테이블에 //
"Dad will be here shortly. // What gift did (a) you buy / for his birthday?" / Camila asked / out of interest. //
= Hailey
"아빠가 곧 오실 거야 // 너는 무슨 선물을 샀어 / 아빠 생일을 위해" // Camila는 물었다 / 호기심에서 //
"Dad will be surprised / to find out what it is!" / Hailey answered / with a wink. //
to find out의 목적어로 쓰인 간접의문문
"아빠가 깜짝 놀라실 거야 / 그게 뭔지 알면" / Hailey는 대답했다 / 윙크를 하며 //
  *(A) 문단 요약: 아빠의 생일 파티를 준비하는 Hailey와 Camila
can help의 목적어(원형부정사)
(B) "Dad, these glasses can help correct / your red-green color blindness," / said Hailey. // 40번 단서 1: (C)에 등장한 a pair of glasses를 가리킴
"아빠, 이 안경은 교정하는 / 데 도움이 될 수 있어요 / 아빠의 적록색맹을"이라고 / Hailey가 말했다 //
└인용문 뒤에서 주어와 동사가 도치됨
He slowly put them on, / and stared at the birthday presents / on the table. // 42번 ② 아버지는 생일 선물로 받은 안경을 직접 써 보았음
그는 천천히 그것을 쓰고 / 생일 선물을 바라보았다 / 테이블 위에 있는 //

Seeing vivid red and green colors / for the first time ever, / he started to cry. //
= When he saw
선명한 빨강색과 초록색을 보고 / 지금껏 처음으로 / 그는 울기 시작했다 //
"Incredible! // Look at those wonderful colors!" / He shouted / in amazement. //
"믿을 수가 없구나 // 저 경이로운 색깔들을 보렴" / 그는 소리쳤다 / 깜짝 놀라 //
Hailey told him in tears, / "Dad, I'm glad / you can now finally enjoy / the true beauty of rainbows and roses. //
Hailey는 눈물을 흘리며 그에게 말했다 / "아빠, 난 기뻐요 / 아빠가 이제 마침내 즐길 수 있어서 / 무지개와 장미의 진정한 아름다움을 //
Red represents love / and green represents health. // You deserve both." //
빨강색은 사랑을 나타내고 / 초록색은 건강을 나타내요 // 아빠는 둘 다 누릴 자격이 있으세요" //
= Hailey's
Camila nodded, / seeing / how happy / (b) her gift of the glasses had made / their dad. //
Camila는 고개를 끄덕였다 / 보면서 / 얼마나 행복하게 / 그녀의 안경 선물이 만들었는지 / 그들의 아빠를 //
  *(B) 문단 요약: Hailey가 선물한 안경 덕분에 아빠가 빨강색과 초록색을 구분할 수 있게 됨
42번 ⑤ 50세 생일임
(C) "Happy birthday! // You're fifty today, Dad. // We love you!" // Camila said / before (c) her sister handed him / a small parcel. //
= Hailey
"생일 축하드려요 // 오늘 쉰 살이세요, 아빠 // 저희는 아빠를 사랑해요" // Camila가 말했다 / 그녀의 동생이 그에게 건네기 전에 / 작은 꾸러미를 // 40번 단서 2: Hailey가 준 꾸러미 안에서 안경을 발견함
분사구문 Opening it으로 바꿀 수 있음
When he opened it, / he discovered a pair of glasses inside. //
그가 그것을 열었을 때 / 그는 안에서 안경을 발견했다 //
"Hailey, Dad doesn't have eyesight problems," / Camila said, puzzled. // 42번 ③ Hailey는 아버지가 색맹이라는 사실을 최근에 알게 되었음
"Hailey, 아빠에게 시력 문제는 없어"라고 / Camila가 어리둥절해하며 말했다 //
"Actually Camila, I recently found out / he has long been suffering from color blindness. // He's kept it a secret / so as not to worry us," / Hailey explained. //
so as to-v: ~하기 위해서
"사실은 Camila, 난 최근에 알게 되었어 / 아빠가 오랫동안 색맹을 앓고 있다는 것을 // 아빠는 그것을 비밀로 해왔어 / 우리를 걱정시키지 않으려고"라고 / Hailey가 설명했다 //
  *(C) 문단 요약: 아빠에게 안경을 선물한 것을 보고 어리둥절해하는 Camila에게 사실 아빠가 색맹이라는 것을 알림
(D) "I bet / (d) you bought a wallet or a watch for him," / Camila said. //
= Hailey
"난 확신해 / 너는 아빠를 위해 지갑이나 시계를 샀을 거라고"라고 / Camila가 말했다 //
비교급 강조 부사
In reply, Hailey answered, / "No. // I bought something much more personal. // By the way, there's something / (e) you should know about Dad..." //
= Camila
대구하면서 Hailey는 대답했다 / "아니 / 난 훨씬 더 개인적인 것을 샀어 // 그건 그렇고 / ~한 것이 있어 / 언니가 아빠에 대해 알아야 하는"이라고 //
They were suddenly interrupted / by the doorbell ringing. //
그들의 대화는 갑자기 중단되었다 / 초인종이 울리는 것에 의해 //
It was their dad / and they were overjoyed / to see him. //
그들의 아빠였고 / 그들은 매우 기뻐했다 / 그를 보고 //
부사적 용법(감정의 원인)
"My lovely ladies, thank you for inviting me / to your place / for my birthday." // 42번 ④ 아버지가 Hailey와 Camila의 집을 방문했음
"사랑하는 우리 아가씨들, 나를 초대해줘서 고맙구나 / 너희들 집에 / 내 생일에" //
He walked in joyfully, / hugging his daughters. //
그는 기쁨에 차서 걸어 들어와 / 그의 딸들을 껴안았다 // 40번 단서 3: 아빠가 Camila와 Hailey의 집에 도착함
관계부사
They all walked into the dining room, / where he was greeted / with a rainbow-colored birthday cake and fifty red roses. //
그들은 모두 식당으로 들어갔고 / 그곳에서 그는 환영받았다 / 무지개색 생일 케이크와 50송이의 빨간 장미로 // 42번 ⑤ 아버지는 장미 50송이를 받았음
  *(D) 문단 요약: 아빠가 생일 파티를 위해 Hailey와 Camila의 집에 도착함

- uneasily ⓐⓓ 걱정되어
- color blindness 색맹
- represent ⓥ 나타내다, 의미하다
- parcel ⓝ 꾸러미, 소포
- puzzle ⓥ 어리둥절하게 만들다
- personal ⓐ 개인적인
- overjoyed ⓐ 매우 기쁜
- shortly ⓐⓓ 곧, 얼마 안 되어
- amazement ⓝ (대단한) 놀라움
- nod ⓥ 고개를 끄덕이다
- eyesight ⓝ 시력
- suffer from ~을 앓다
- interrupt ⓥ 중단시키다, 가로막다
- greet ⓥ 맞이하다

(A) "Hailey, 조심해!" Camila는 동생이 테이블로 커다란 케이크를 옮기는 것을 보며 걱정되어 소리쳤다. "걱정 마, Camila." Hailey는 미소 지으며 답했다. Camila는 Hailey가 파티 테이블에 케이크를 무사히 올려 두었을 때 비로소 안심했다. "아빠가 곧 오실 거야. (a) 너는 아빠 생일을 위해 무슨 선물을 샀어?" Camila는 호기심에서 물었다. "그게 뭔지 알면 아빠가 깜짝 놀라실 거야!" Hailey는 윙크를 하며 답했다.

(D) "틀림없이 (d) 너는 아빠를 위해 지갑이나 시계를 샀을 거야."라고 Camila가 말했다. 대꾸하면서 Hailey는 "아니, 난 훨씬 더 개인적인 것을 샀어. 그건 그렇고 (e) 언니가 아빠에 대해 알아야 할 게 있어…"라고 대답했다. 초인종이 울리면서 그들의 대화는 갑자기 중단되었다. 그들의 아빠가 왔고 그들은 그를 보고 매우 기뻐했다. "사랑하는 우리 아가씨들, 내 생일에 너희들 집에 초대해줘서 고맙구나." 그는 기쁨에 차서 걸어 들어와 딸들을 껴안았다. 그들은 모두 식당으로 들어갔고, 그곳에서 그는 무지개색 생일 케이크와 50송이의 빨간 장미로 환영받았다.

(C) "생일 축하드려요! 오늘 쉰 살이세요, 아빠. 사랑해요!"라고 Camila가 말하고 나서 (c) 그녀의 동생이 그에게 작은 꾸러미를 드렸다. 그것을 열었을 때 그는 안에서 안경을 발견했다. "Hailey, 아빠에게 시력 문제는 없어."라고 Camila가 어리둥절해하며 말했다. "사실은 Camila, 난 아빠가 오랫동안 색맹을 앓고 있다는 것을 최근에 알게 되었어. 아빠는 우리를 걱정시키지 않으려고 그것을 비밀로 해왔어."라고 Hailey가 설명했다.

(B) "아빠, 이 안경은 적록색맹을 교정하는 데 도움이 될 수 있어요."라고 Hailey가 말했다. 그는 천천히 그것을 쓰고, 테이블 위에 있는 생일 선물을 바라보았다. 지금껏 처음으로 선명한 빨강색과 초록색을 보고 그는 울기 시작했다. "믿을 수가 없구나! 저 경이로운 색깔들을 보렴!" 그는 깜짝 놀라 소리쳤다. Hailey는 눈물을 흘리며 그에게 말했다. "아빠, 난 아빠가 이제 마침내 무지개와 장미의 진정한 아름다움을 즐길 수 있어서 기뻐요. 빨강색은 사랑을 나타내고 초록색은 건강을 나타내요. 아빠는 둘 다 누릴 자격이 있으세요." Camila는 (b) 그녀의 안경 선물이 그들의 아빠를 얼마나 행복하게 했는지를 보며 고개를 끄덕였다.

Q 40 정답 ⑤

주어진 글 (A)에 이어질 내용을 순서에 맞게 배열한 것으로 가장 적절한 것은?

① (B) ― (D) ― (C) ← (B)의 these glasses보다 (C)의 a pair of glasses가 먼저 나와야 함
② (C) ― (B) ― (D) ┐
③ (C) ― (D) ― (B) ┘ 아빠가 딸들의 집에 도착했다는 내용의 (D)가 (C)보다 앞에 있어야 함
④ (D) ― (B) ― (C)
⑤ (D) ― (C) ― (B) 아빠가 도착함 - Hailey가 선물로 안경을 준비했음이 밝혀짐 - 아빠가 안경을 직접 써 보고 울기 시작함
　Camila와 Hailey가 아빠의 생신 파티를 준비함 -

왜 정답? [정답률 91%]

Camila와 Hailey가 아버지의 생신 파티를 준비하는 내용으로 끝난 (A)에는 아버지가 두 딸의 집에 도착한 (D)가 가장 먼저 이어진다.

그다음 Hailey가 선물로 준비한 것이 안경임이 밝혀지는 (C)가 이어진 후, 안경을 these glasses로 가리키며 안경에 대해 설명하는 (B)가 (C) 뒤에 오는 것이 적절하므로 정답은 ⑤ (D) ― (C) ― (B)이다.

왜 오답?

① (B)의 these glasses가 가리키는 것이 (A)에 없다.
②, ③ "Happy birthday!"라고 말하기 전에 아버지가 딸들의 집에 도착했다는 내용이 먼저 나와야 한다.
④ (C)의 a pair of glasses가 먼저 나온 후에 (B)의 these glasses가 나와야 한다.

조현준 | 전북대 의예과 2023년 입학·익산 이리고 졸

(A)에서는 아직 아버지가 오지 않았으니까 갑자기 아버지가 사건을 이끌어 나가는 것은 개연성이 없어. 그러니까 (A) 다음은 (D)이지. 마찬가지로 (B)의 첫 문장에 등장하는 these glasses가 갑자기 나오면 연결이 안 되니까 (C)가 (B)보다 먼저 나와야 해!

Q 41 정답 ⑤

밑줄 친 (a)~(e) 중에서 가리키는 대상이 나머지 넷과 다른 것은?

① (a) Hailey　② (b) Hailey's　③ (c) Hailey　④ (d) Hailey　⑤ (e) Camila

왜 정답? [정답률 85%]

Hailey와 Camila 중에서 Hailey가 아빠에 대해 이야기하면서 you로 가리키는 ⑤ (e)는 Camila이다. 나머지는 모두 Hailey를 가리킨다.

왜 오답?

① Camila가 Hailey에게 물어보는 것이므로 you는 Hailey이다.
② Hailey의 안경 선물이 아빠를 얼마나 행복하게 만들었는지를 보면서 Camila가 고개를 끄덕인 것이다.
③ Camila의 동생이므로 Hailey를 말한다.
④ Camila가 Hailey를 you로 가리키며 Hailey가 아빠를 위해 지갑이나 시계를 샀을 거라고 말하는 것이다.

장성욱 | 동아대 의예과 2023년 입학·부산 대연고 졸

이 문제는 무엇보다도 등장인물이 누구이고, 그들이 서로 어떤 관계인지 파악하는 것이 가장 중요하다고 볼 수 있어. 누가 누구에게 하는 말인지를 정확하게 파악하고 앞뒤 내용을 확인하면 (a), (b), (c), (d)는 모두 Camila의 자매인 Hailey이고, (e)만 Camila라는 것을 쉽게 알 수 있어.

Q 42 정답 ④

윗글에 관한 내용으로 적절하지 않은 것은?

① Hailey는 생일 케이크를 테이블로 무사히 옮겨 놓았다.
　Hailey had safely placed the cake on the party table
② 아버지는 생일 선물로 받은 안경을 직접 써 보았다.
　He slowly put them on
③ Hailey는 아버지가 색맹이라는 사실을 최근에 알게 되었다.
　I recently found out he has long been suffering from color blindness
④ Hailey와 Camila는 아버지의 집을 방문하였다.
　My lovely ladies, thank you for inviting me to your place
⑤ 아버지는 자신의 나이와 똑같은 수의 장미를 받았다.
　You're fifty today, Dad., he was greeted with ~ fifty red roses

왜 정답? [정답률 87%]

아버지가 집에 들어오면서 딸들에게 자신을 그들의 집에 초대한 것에 대해 고맙다고 인사를 했으므로(My lovely ladies, thank you for inviting me to your place) ④은 글과 일치하지 않는다.

왜 오답?

① Hailey는 생일 케이크를 테이블로 무사히 옮겨 놓았다. (Hailey had safely placed the cake on the party table)
② 아버지는 생일 선물로 받은 안경을 직접 써 보았다. (He slowly put them on)
③ Hailey는 아버지가 색맹이라는 사실을 최근에 알게 되었다. (I recently found out he has long been suffering from color blindness)
⑤ 아버지의 50세 생일이었고, 아버지는 50송이 장미로 환영받았다. (You're fifty today, Dad., he was greeted with ~ fifty red roses)

Q 43~45 *Paderewski의 공연에서 있었던 일

(A) Ignace Jan Paderewski, the famous composer-pianist, / was
scheduled to perform / at a great concert hall in America. //
유명한 작곡가이자 피아니스트인 Ignace Jan Paderewski가 / 공연할 예정이었다 / 미국의
한 큰 연주회장에서 //

It was an evening / to remember / — black tuxedos and long
evening dresses, a high-society event. //
저녁이었다 / 기억할 / 검은 턱시도와 긴 이브닝드레스, 상류사회의 행사 //

Present in the audience / that evening / was a mother / with her
nine-year-old son. //
청중석에 참석했다 / 그날 저녁 / 한 어머니가 / 그녀의 9살짜리 아들과 함께 //

Tired of waiting, / (a) he squirmed constantly / in his seat. //
기다리는 것이 지겨워서 / 그는 계속해서 꼼지락댔다 / 자신의 자리에서 //

His mother was in hopes / that her son would be encouraged /
to practice the piano / if he could just hear the great Paderewski
at the keyboard. //
그의 어머니는 기대했다 / 자신의 아들이 동기부여 될 것이라고 / 피아노 연습을 하도록 / 만약
그가 위대한 Paderewski가 연주하는 것을 들을 수 있다면 //

So, / against his wishes, / he had come. //
그래서 / 그의 바람과 달리 / 그는 왔다 //

*(A) 문단 요약: 유명한 작곡가이자 피아니스트인 Ignace Jan Paderewski
연주회에 온 소년이 지루해하면서 계속해서 꼼지락댐

(B) The roar of the crowd became quiet / as hundreds of frowning
faces pointed / in (b) his direction. //
군중의 와자지껄한 소리가 조용해졌다 / 수백 명의 찌푸린 얼굴들이 향하면서 / 그의 방향으로 //

Irritated and embarrassed, / they began to shout: /
짜증이 나고 당황한 채로 / 그들은 크게 소리치기 시작했다 /

"Get that boy away from there!" // "Who'd bring a kid that
young in here?" // "Where's his mother?" // "Stop (c) him!" //
"저 소년을 저기서 나오게 해!" // "누가 저렇게 어린아이를 여기에 데려왔어" // "그의 엄마는
어디 있지" // "그를 멈춰!" //

Backstage, / Paderewski overheard the sounds out front / and
quickly put together / in his mind / what was happening. //
무대 뒤에서 / Paderewski는 객석에서 나는 소리를 우연히 들었고 / 재빨리 정리했다 / 그의
마음속에 / 무슨 일이 일어나고 있는지 //

Hurriedly, / he grabbed his coat / and rushed toward the stage. //
서둘러 / 그는 자신의 정장 상의를 들고 / 무대 쪽으로 달려갔다 //

*(B) 문단 요약: 얼굴을 찌푸린 군중이 소년을 보며 소리쳤고, 이를 들은
Paderewski가 무대 쪽으로 달려갔음

(C) As she turned / to talk with friends, / her son could stay
seated no longer. //
그녀가 몸을 돌렸을 때 / 친구들과 이야기하기 위해 / 그녀의 아들은 더 이상 앉아 있을 수가
없었다 //

(d) He slipped away from her side, / strangely drawn / to the
black concert grand piano / and its leather stool / on the huge
stage / flooded with blinding lights. //
그는 그녀의 옆에서 빠져나갔다 / 이상하게 이끌려 / 검은색 연주회용 그랜드 피아노와 /
그것의 가죽 의자에 / 큰 무대 위의 / 눈부신 빛으로 가득 찬 //

Without much notice / from the sophisticated audience, / the
boy sat down at the piano stool, / staring wide-eyed at the black
and white keys. //
별다른 주목을 받지 않고 / 세련된 청중들로부터 / 소년은 피아노 의자에 앉아 / 눈을 크게
뜨고 흑백의 건반을 응시했다 //

He placed his small, shaky fingers / in the right location / and
began to play "Chopsticks." //
그는 작고 떨리는 손가락들을 놓고 / 정확한 위치에 / 'Chopsticks(젓가락 행진곡)'를
연주하기 시작했다 //

*(C) 문단 요약: 자리에서 빠져나온 소년이 피아노로 젓가락 행진곡을 연주하기
시작했음

(D) Without one word of announcement / Paderewski bent
over behind the boy, / reached around both sides, / began to
improvise a countermelody / to harmonize with and enhance
"Chopsticks." //
한 마디 공지도 없이 / Paderewski는 그 소년의 뒤에서 몸을 구부리며 / 양쪽으로 손을 뻗었고
/ 카운터멜로디를 즉흥 연주하기 시작했다 / 'Chopsticks'와 조화를 이루고 향상하는 //

As the two of them played together, / (e) he kept whispering / in
the boy's ear: / "Keep going. // Don't quit. // Keep on playing...
don't stop... don't quit." //
그들 두 사람이 함께 연주하면서 / 그는 계속 속삭였다 / 그 소년의 귀에 / "계속하렴"
그만두지 마 // 계속 연주하렴… 멈추지 마… 그만두지 마" //

Together, / the old master and the little boy / transformed
an embarrassing situation / into a wonderfully creative
experience. //
함께 / 그 나이 많은 거장과 그 어린 소년은 / 난처한 상황을 바꾸었다 / 놀랍도록 창의적인
경험으로 //

The audience was mesmerized. //
청중은 매혹되었다 //

*(D) 문단 요약: Paderewski가 소년과 함께 연주를 하며 난처한 상황을 창의적인
경험으로 바꾸었음

- be scheduled to ~할 예정이다
- constantly ad 계속
- roar n 함성
- frowning a 찌푸린
- irritated a 짜증난
- embarrassed a 당황한
- hurriedly ad 서둘러
- backstage ad 무대 뒤에서
- overhear v 우연히 듣다
- slip away 빠져나가다
- leather stool 가죽의자
- flooded with ~로 가득찬
- sophisticated a 세련된
- stare v 응시하다
- shaky a 떨리는
- location n 위치
- harmonize v 조화를 이루다
- enhance v 높이다
- transform v 변형시키다
- whisper v 속삭이다
- creative a 창의적인

(A) 유명한 작곡가이자 피아니스트인 Ignace Jan Paderewski가 미국의
한 큰 연주회장에서 공연할 예정이었다. 검은 턱시도와 긴 이브닝드레스,
즉 상류사회의 행사로 기억할 저녁이었다. 그날 저녁 청중석에 한 어머니가
9살짜리 아들과 함께 참석했다. 기다리는 것이 지겨워서, (a) 그는
자신의 자리에서 계속해서 꼼지락댔다. 그의 어머니는 만약 그가 위대한
Paderewski가 연주하는 것을 들을 수만 있다면 자신의 아들이 피아노 연습을
하도록 동기부여 될 것이라고 기대했다. 그래서, 비록 그가 원치 않았지만,
그는 오게 되었다.

(C) 그녀가 친구들과 이야기하기 위해 몸을 돌렸을 때, 그녀의 아들은 더 이상
앉아 있을 수가 없었다. (d) 그는 눈부신 빛으로 가득 찬 큰 무대 위 검은색
연주회용 그랜드 피아노와 그것의 가죽 의자에 이상하게 이끌려, 그녀의
옆에서 빠져나갔다. 세련된 청중들로부터 별다른 주목을 받지 않고, 소년은
피아노 의자에 앉아 눈을 크게 뜨고 흑백의 건반을 응시했다. 그는 작고 떨리는
손가락들을 정확한 위치에 놓고 'Chopsticks(젓가락 행진곡)'를 연주하기
시작했다.

(B) 수백 명의 찌푸린 얼굴들이 (b) 그의 방향으로 향하면서 군중의 와자지껄한
소리가 조용해졌다. 짜증이 나고 당황한 채로, 그들은 크게 소리치기 시작했다.
"저 소년을 저기서 나오게 해!" "누가 저렇게 어린아이를 여기에 데려왔어?"

"그의 엄마는 어디 있지?" "(c) 그를 멈춰!" 무대 뒤에서, Paderewski는 객석에서 나는 소리를 우연히 들었고 무슨 일이 일어나고 있는지 재빨리 마음속에 정리했다. 서둘러, 그는 자신의 정장 상의를 들고 무대 쪽으로 달려갔다.

(D) 한 마디 공지도 없이 Paderewski는 그 소년의 뒤에서 몸을 구부리며, 양쪽으로 손을 뻗었고, 'Chopsticks'와 조화를 이루고 향상하는 카운터멜로디를 즉흥 연주하기 시작했다. 그들 두 사람이 함께 연주하면서, (e) 그는 그 소년의 귀에 계속 속삭였다. "계속하렴. 그만두지 마. 계속 연주하렴… 멈추지 마… 그만두지 마." 그 나이 많은 거장과 그 어린 소년은 함께 난처한 상황을 놀랍도록 창의적인 경험으로 바꾸었다. 청중은 매혹되었다.

Q 43 정답 ②

주어진 글 (A)에 이어질 내용을 순서에 맞게 배열한 것으로 가장 적절한 것은?

① (B) ― (D) ― (C) 군중의 얼굴을 찌푸리게 한 일이 (B) 앞에 있어야 함
② (C) ― (B) ― (D)
③ (C) ― (D) ― (B) (D)에서 두 사람이 함께 젓가락 행진곡을 연주하기 전에 청중이 소리치는 내용이 나와야 함
④ (D) ― (B) ― (C)
⑤ (D) ― (C) ― (B) (D)는 일화의 결론임

엄마를 따라 연주회에 온 소년이 지겨워서 자리에서 계속 꼼지락댐 - 결국 엄마 옆에서 빠져나와 무대의 피아노에서 젓가락 행진곡을 연주 - 청중이 크게 소리치자 Paderewski가 서둘러 무대로 나옴 - 두 사람이 함께 젓가락 행진곡을 연주함

왜 정답·오답? [정답률 88%]

(A): 원치 않은 연주회에 온 9살짜리 소년이 공연 시작을 기다리기 지루해하면서 자기 자리에서 계속해서 꼼지락댔다.

➡ 지루함을 못 견딘 소년이 결국 말썽을 부렸다는 내용이 이어질 것이라고 예상할 수 있다.

(B): 얼굴을 찌푸린 군중이 소년을 보며 "저 소년을 저기서 나오게 해!" "누가 저렇게 어린아이를 여기에 데려왔어?" "그의 엄마는 어디 있지?" "그를 멈춰!"라고 소리쳤고, 이를 들은 Paderewski가 서둘러 무대 쪽으로 달려갔다.

➡ 소년의 어떤 행동이 군중으로 하여금 얼굴을 찌푸리게 했는지가 (B) 앞에 있어야 한다. (B) 뒤에는 무대로 나온 Paderewski가 어떤 행동을 했는지가 이어져야 한다.

(C): 자리에서 빠져나온 소년이 무대 위의 피아노로 젓가락 행진곡을 연주하기 시작했다.

➡ 자리에서 계속해서 꼼지락대던 소년이 결국 자리에서 빠져나왔다고 했으므로 (A)가 (C) 앞에 와야 한다. 또한, (B) 앞에 군중으로 하여금 얼굴을 찌푸리게 한 소년의 행동이 나와야 한다고 했으므로 (C)가 (B) 앞에 와야 한다.

(D): Paderewski가 소년과 함께 연주를 하며 난처한 상황을 놀랍도록 창의적인 경험으로 바꾸었다.

➡ Paderewski가 무대로 나와 한 행동이 등장하므로 이야기의 결론이다.
▶ (A) 원치 않은 연주회에 온 소년이 지루해하면서 자기 자리에서 계속해서 꼼지락댔다. → (C) 자리에서 빠져나온 소년이 피아노로 젓가락 행진곡을 연주하기 시작했다. → (B) 얼굴을 찌푸린 군중이 소년을 보며 소리쳤고, 이를 들은 Paderewski가 서둘러 무대 쪽으로 달려갔다. → (D) Paderewski가 소년과 함께 연주를 하며 난처한 상황을 창의적인 경험으로 바꾸었다.
▶ 사건이 진행되는 순서는 ② (C) ― (B) ― (D)임

Q 44 정답 ⑤

밑줄 친 (a)~(e) 중에서 가리키는 대상이 나머지 넷과 다른 것은?

① (a) = the boy ② (b) = the boy's ③ (c) = the boy ④ (d) = the boy ⑤ (e) = Paderewski

왜 정답? [정답률 87%]

⑤ (e) he: 소년의 귀에 계속 속삭였던 것은 Paderewski이다. ▶ Paderewski

왜 오답?

① (a) he: 기다리는 것이 지겨워서 자신의 자리에서 계속해서 꼼지락댔던 것은 9살짜리 소년이다. ▶ the boy
② (b) his: 군중의 찌푸린 얼굴이 소년이 있는 방향을 향한 것이다. ▶ the boy
③ (c) him: 군중이 소년을 멈추라고 말한 것이다. ▶ the boy
④ (d) He: 소년이 엄마의 옆에서 빠져나간 것이다. ▶ the boy

Q 45 정답 ⑤

윗글에 관한 내용으로 적절하지 않은 것은?

① 소년은 연주회에 오고 싶지 않았으나 오게 되었다.
  against his wishes, he had come
② 짜증이 나고 당황한 관중은 크게 소리치기 시작했다.
  Irritated and embarrassed, they began to shout
③ Paderewski는 서둘러 무대로 달려갔다.
  Hurriedly, he grabbed his coat and rushed toward the stage.
④ 소년은 무대 위 피아노 의자에 앉아 건반을 응시했다.
  the boy sat down at the piano stool, staring wide-eyed at the black and white keys
⑤ Paderewski는 짧은 공지 후 소년과 함께 연주했다.
  Without one word of announcement ~ began to improvise a countermelody

왜 정답? [정답률 79%]

⑤ Paderewski는 한 마디 공지도 없이 즉흥 연주를 시작했다. (Without one word of announcement ~ began to improvise a countermelody)

왜 오답?

① 소년은 연주회에 오고 싶지 않았으나 오게 되었다.
  (against his wishes, he had come)
② 짜증이 나고 당황한 관중은 크게 소리치기 시작했다.
  (Irritated and embarrassed, they began to shout)
③ Paderewski는 서둘러 무대로 달려갔다.
  (Hurriedly, he grabbed his coat and rushed toward the stage.)
④ 소년은 무대 위 피아노 의자에 앉아 건반을 응시했다.
  (the boy sat down at the piano stool, staring wide-eyed at the black and white keys)

Q 46~48 ＊오지랖 넓은 Emily

(A) In a peaceful town / surrounded by rolling hills, / there lived a kind-hearted young woman / named Emily. //
앞에 주격 관계대명사와 be동사가 생략됨
평화로운 마을에 / 완만한 구릉이 많은 언덕으로 에워싸인 / 마음씨 좋은 젊은 여자가 살고 있었다 / Emily라는 //

형용사적 용법(desire 수식)
She had a strong desire / to make a difference in the world, / yet often felt / that her efforts were insignificant. //
병렬 구조
그녀에게는 강한 열망이 있었으나 / 세상을 바꾸고자 하는 / 자주 느꼈다 / 자신의 노력이 보잘것없다고 //

One day, / Emily crossed paths with Martha, / an elderly lady / known / for (a) her sour mood and tendency / to keep to herself. //
= Martha's   형용사적 용법(tendency 수식)
어느 날 / Emily는 Martha와 마주쳤는데 / 나이 든 여자인 / 알려진 / 그녀의 시큰둥한 분위기와 경향으로 / 남들과 어울리지 않고 혼자 지내려는 //

prompting의 목적어와 목적격 보어
Curiosity sparked within Emily, / prompting her to initiate a conversation with Martha. // 48번① Emily는 호기심이 생겨 Martha와 대화를 시작하게 되었음
Emily 안에서 생긴 호기심이 / 그녀로 하여금 Martha와 대화를 시작하게 했다 //

＊(A) 문단 요약: 세상을 바꾸고자 하는 Emily가 시큰둥하고 남들과 어울리지 않고 혼자 지내려는 Martha와 대화를 시작했음

(B) The event showcased / the great works of many local artists, / with a special surprise awaiting Martha. // 48번② 많은 지역 예술가의 작품을 전시함

`with+명사+현재분사(수동태) 분사구문`

그 행사에서는 전시했는데 / 많은 지역 예술가들의 훌륭한 작품들을 / 특별 깜짝 이벤트가 Martha를 기다리고 있었다 //

Emily had carefully prepared a section / dedicated to Martha's paintings, / hoping to unveil it / to her and the community. //

Emily는 신중하게 구역을 준비하고 / Martha의 그림에 헌정된 / 그것을 공개하기를 희망했다 / 그녀와 지역 사회에 //

The day of the exhibition arrived, / and the townspeople eagerly gathered, / excited to witness / the artistic wonders of their community. //

전시회 날이 다가왔고 / 마을 사람들은 열렬히 모여들었다 / 보게 되어 신이 나서 / 자기가 사는 지역 사회의 뛰어난 예술 작품들을 //

Emily anxiously awaited Martha's arrival, / wondering how Martha would react / to the surprise / (b) she had planned. //

`=Emily`

Emily는 Martha의 도착을 애타게 기다렸다 / Martha가 어떻게 반응할지 궁금해하며 / 깜짝 이벤트에 / 자신이 계획한 //

Martha finally entered the exhibition hall, / and her eyes filled with tears / as she stood / in front of her own artworks. //

Martha는 마침내 전시장에 들어섰고 / 그녀의 눈에는 눈물이 가득 고였다 / 그녀가 섰을 때 / 자신의 예술 작품 앞에 // 46번 단서 1: Martha가 마침내 전시회장에 와서 자신의 예술 작품 앞에 섰음

*(B) 문단 요약: Martha가 전시회장에 도착해서 자신의 예술 작품 앞에 섰을 때 그녀의 눈에 눈물이 가득 고였음 46번 단서 2: 자신의 작품들을 살펴봄

(C) Martha slowly made her way through the section / dedicated to (c) her paintings, / examining each piece / with a mix of nostalgia and longing. //

`=Martha's`

Martha는 구역을 돌아보며 / 천천히 자신의 그림에 헌정된 / 각 작품을 살펴보았다 / 향수와 동경이 섞인 감정으로 // 48번③ 마을 사람들은 Martha의 반응을 보고 마음이 뭉클했음

The crowd watched in silence, / their hearts touched by Martha's emotional response. //

사람들은 말없이 지켜보았다 / Martha의 감동적인 반응에 마음이 뭉클하여 // 48번④ Martha는 마지막에 이르러 Emily를 향해 미소를 지었음

As Martha reached the last painting, / she turned to Emily / with a bright smile, / tears still shining in her eyes. //

Martha가 마지막 그림에 이르렀을 때 / 그녀는 Emily를 향해 돌아섰다 / 환한 미소를 지으며 / 여전히 자신의 두 눈에 눈물이 반짝인 채로 //

생략 가능한 목적격 관계대명사

"Emily, you've given me back / a part of myself / that I thought was lost forever," / Martha whispered, / (d) her voice shaking with gratitude. //

`=Martha's`

"Emily, 당신은 나에게 되돌려 줬어요 / 나 자신의 일부를 / 내가 영원히 잃어버렸다고 생각했던"이라고 / Martha는 속삭였다 / 고마움에 떨리는 그녀의 목소리로 //

"I had forgotten the joy / that art once brought me, / but you've reminded me of its power." //

"나는 즐거움을 잊고 있었는데 / 미술이 예전에 내게 가져다주던 / 당신은 그것의 힘을 나에게 상기시켜 주었어요" //

*(C) 문단 요약: Martha는 자신의 그림에 헌정된 구역을 돌아봤고, Emily에게 감사 인사를 했음

전치사   명사구

(D) Despite Martha's initial resistance, / Emily persistently reached out to her, / sharing stories / and expressing genuine interest in (e) her life. // 46번 단서 3: Emily와의 대화를 처음에는 거절했음

`=Martha's`

Martha가 처음에는 거절했음에도 불구하고 / Emily는 지속적으로 그녀에게 다가가서 / 이야기를 나누고 / 그녀의 삶에 대한 진정한 관심을 표현했다 //

Through their conversations, / Emily discovered / that Martha had once been a famous painter. //

대화를 통해 / Emily는 알게 되었다 / Martha가 한때 유명한 화가였다는 것을 //

However, she had lost her passion for art / due to personal hardships. // 48번⑤ Martha는 개인적인 역경 때문에 미술에 대한 열정을 잃었음

하지만, 그녀는 미술에 대한 열정을 잃었다 / 개인적인 역경 때문에 //

`to help의 목적어`

Deeply moved by her sorrow, / Emily resolved / to help revive Martha's creative spirit. //

`resolved의 목적어`

그녀의 슬픔에 크게 마음이 움직여 / Emily는 결심했다 / Martha의 창조적인 영혼을 되살리는 것을 돕기로 //

So, she organized an art exhibition / in the town's community center. //

그래서 그녀는 미술 전시회를 준비했다 / 마을의 주민 센터에서 //

*(D) 문단 요약: Emily는 Martha가 유명한 화가였지만, 역경 때문에 열정을 잃었다는 사실을 알게 되었고, Martha를 돕기 위해 미술 전시회를 준비했음

• rolling hill 완만한 구릉이 많은 언덕 • desire ⓝ 열망
• insignificant ⓐ 보잘 것 없는 • tendency ⓝ 경향
• keep to oneself 남들과 어울리지 않다 • spark ⓥ 유발하다
• prompt ⓥ ~하게 하다 • initiate ⓥ 시작하다
• await ⓥ 기다리다 • be dedicated to ~에 헌신하다
• unveil ⓥ 공개하다 • exhibition ⓝ 전시회
• artistic wonder 뛰어난 예술작품 • anxiously ⓐⓓ 애타게
• examine ⓥ 꼼꼼히 살펴보다 • nostalgia ⓝ 향수
• longing ⓝ 동경 • initial ⓐ 처음의 • resistance ⓝ 거절
• persistently ⓐⓓ 지속적으로 • genuine ⓐ 진정한
• hardship ⓝ 역경 • resolve ⓥ 결심하다 • revive ⓥ 되살리다

(A) 완만한 구릉이 많은 언덕으로 에워싸인 평화로운 마을에 Emily라는 마음씨 좋은 젊은 여자가 살고 있었다. 그녀에게는 세상을 바꾸고자 하는 강한 열망이 있었으나, 자주 자신의 노력이 보잘것없다고 느꼈다. 어느 날, Emily는 Martha와 마주쳤는데, 그녀는 (a) 그녀의 시큰둥한 분위기와 남들과 어울리지 않고 혼자 지내려는 경향이 있는 것으로 알려진 나이 든 여자였다. Emily는 호기심이 생겨 Martha와 대화를 시작하게 되었다.

(D) Martha가 처음에는 거절했음에도 불구하고, Emily는 지속적으로 그녀에게 다가가서, 이야기를 나누고 (e) 그녀의 삶에 대한 진정한 관심을 표현했다. 대화를 통해, Emily는 Martha가 한때 유명한 화가였다는 것을 알게 되었다. 하지만, 그녀는 개인적인 역경 때문에 미술에 대한 열정을 잃었다. 그녀의 슬픔에 크게 마음이 움직여 Emily는 Martha의 창조적인 영혼을 되살리는 것을 돕기로 결심했다. 그래서 그녀는 마을의 주민 센터에서 미술 전시회를 준비했다.

(B) 그 행사에서는 많은 지역 예술가들의 훌륭한 작품들을 전시했는데, 특별 깜짝 이벤트가 Martha를 기다리고 있었다. Emily는 신중하게 Martha의 그림에 헌정된 구역을 준비하고 그것을 그녀와 지역 사회에 공개하기를 희망했다. 전시회 날이 다가왔고, 마을 사람들은 자기가 사는 지역 사회의 뛰어난 예술 작품들을 보게 되어 신이 나서 열렬히 모여들었다. Emily는 (b) 자신이 계획한 깜짝 이벤트에 Martha가 어떻게 반응할지 궁금해하며 그녀의 도착을 애타게 기다렸다. Martha는 마침내 전시회장에 들어섰고, 자신의 예술 작품 앞에 섰을 때 그녀의 눈에는 눈물이 가득 고였다.

(C) 그녀는 천천히 (c) 자신의 그림에 헌정된 구역을 돌아보며, 향수와 동경이 섞인 감정으로 각 작품을 살펴보았다. 사람들은 Martha의 감동적인 반응에 마음이 뭉클하여 말없이 지켜보았다. 마지막 그림에 이르렀을 때, Martha는 여전히 자신의 두 눈에 눈물이 반짝인 채로 환한 미소를 지으며 Emily를 향해 돌아섰다. "Emily, 당신은 내가 영원히 잃어버렸다고 생각했던 나 자신의 일부를 나에게 되돌려 줬어요."라고 Martha는 고마움에 떨리는 (d) 자신의 목소리로 속삭였다. "미술이 예전에 내게 가져다주던 즐거움을 잊고 있었는데, 당신은 그것의 힘을 나에게 상기시켜 주었어요."

Q 46 정답 ④

주어진 글 (A)에 이어질 내용을 순서에 맞게 배열한 것으로 가장 적절한 것은?

① (B) — (D) — (C) The event가 가리키는 것이 (A)에 없음
② (C) — (B) — (D) (C)는 Martha가 전시회장에 도착한 이후의 일임
③ (C) — (D) — (B) Emily가 시큰둥하고 남들과 어울리지 않고 혼자 지내려는 Martha와 대화를 시작했음 - Emily는 Martha가 유명한 화가였지만, 역경 때문에 열정을 잃었다는 사실을 알게 되었고, Martha를 돕기 위해 미술 전시회를 준비했음 - Emily는 Martha의 그림에 헌정된 구역을 준비하고, Martha가 자신의 예술 작품 앞에 섰을 때 그녀의 눈에 눈물이 가득 고였음 - Martha는 자신의 그림에 헌정된 구역을 돌아봤고, Emily에게 감사 인사를 했음
④ (D) — (B) — (C)
⑤ (D) — (C) — (B) Martha가 Emily에게 감사 인사를 하는 (C)는 결말임

> (A): 세상을 바꾸고자 하는 Emily가 어느 날 시큰둥하고 남들과 어울리지 않고 혼자 지내려는 Martha와 대화를 시작했다.

→ Martha와의 대화의 시작이 어땠는지, 어떤 대화를 나누었는지가 이어질 것이다.

> (B): 많은 지역 예술가들의 작품을 전시한 행사에서 Emily는 Martha의 그림에 헌정된 구역을 준비하고, 마침내 Martha가 전시회장에 도착해서 자신의 예술 작품 앞에 섰을 때 그녀의 눈에 눈물이 가득 고였다.

→ 앞에는 Emily가 Martha의 작품을 전시하게 된 계기가 필요하고, 뒤에는 자신에게 헌정된 전시 구역을 준비한 Emily에게 Martha가 감사를 표할 것이다.

> (C): Martha는 자신의 그림에 헌정된 구역을 돌아봤고, Emily에게 "미술이 예전에 내게 가져다주던 즐거움을 잊고 있었는데, 당신은 그것의 힘을 나에게 상기시켜 주었어요."라고 감사 인사를 했다.

→ 앞에는 Emily가 Martha를 위해 그녀의 작품을 전시했다는 내용이 필요하다. 그리고 뒤에는 마지막 작품을 본 후 Martha가 Emily에게 감사 인사를 하는 것으로 글이 마무리될 것이다.

> (D): Martha는 처음에는 Emily와의 대화를 거절했지만, 마침내 대화하게 되었다. Emily는 Martha가 유명한 화가였지만, 역경 때문에 열정을 잃었다는 사실을 알게 되었고, Martha를 돕기 위해 미술 전시회를 준비했다.

→ 앞에는 Emily가 Martha와의 대화를 시도했다는 내용이 필요하고, 뒤에는 Emily가 Martha의 작품을 전시한 전시회가 열렸다는 흐름이 되어야 한다.
▶ (A): 세상을 바꾸고자 하는 Emily가 시큰둥하고 남들과 어울리지 않고 혼자 지내려는 Martha와 대화를 시작했다. → (D): Martha는 처음에는 대화를 거절했지만, 마침내 대화하게 되었다. Emily는 Martha가 유명한 화가였지만, 역경 때문에 열정을 잃었다는 사실을 알게 되었고, Martha를 돕기 위해 미술 전시회를 준비했다. → (B): Emily는 Martha의 그림에 헌정된 구역을 준비하고, 마침내 Martha가 전시회장에 도착해서 자신의 예술 작품 앞에 섰을 때 그녀의 눈에 눈물이 가득 고였다. → (C): Martha는 자신의 그림에 헌정된 구역을 돌아봤고, Emily에게 "미술이 예전에 내게 가져다주던 즐거움을 잊고 있었는데, 당신은 그것의 힘을 나에게 상기시켜 주었어요."라고 감사 인사를 했다.
▶ 사건이 진행되는 순서는 ④ (D) – (B) – (C)임

Q 47 정답 ②

밑줄 친 (a)~(e) 중에서 가리키는 대상이 나머지 넷과 다른 것은?

① (a) = Martha's ② (b) = Emily ③ (c) = Martha's ④ (d) = Martha's ⑤ (e) = Martha's

> 왜 정답? [정답률 76%]

② (b) she: 깜짝 이벤트를 계획한 것은 Emily이다. ▶ Emily

> 왜 오답?

① (a) her: 시큰둥한 분위기로 알려진 것은 Martha이다. ▶ Martha
③ (c) her: Martha가 자신의 그림에 헌정된 구역을 돌아본 것이다. ▶ Martha
④ (d) her: Emily에게 감사 인사를 하면서 목소리가 떨린 것은 Martha이다. ▶ Martha
⑤ (e) her: Emily가 관심을 표현한 것은 Martha의 삶이다. ▶ Martha

Q 48 정답 ②

윗글에 관한 내용으로 적절하지 않은 것은?

① Emily는 호기심이 생겨 Martha와 대화를 시작하게 되었다.
Curiosity sparked within Emily, prompting her to initiate a conversation with Martha.
② 미술 전시회에서는 Martha의 작품만 전시했다.
The event showcased the great works of many local artists
③ 마을 사람들은 Martha의 반응을 보고 마음이 뭉클했다.
The crowd watched in silence, their hearts touched by Martha's emotional response.
④ Martha는 마지막 그림에 이르러 Emily를 향해 미소를 지었다.
As Martha reached the last painting, she turned to Emily with a bright smile
⑤ Martha는 개인적인 역경 때문에 미술에 대한 열정을 잃었다.
she had lost her passion for art due to personal hardships

> 왜 정답? [정답률 90%]

② 미술 전시회에서는 많은 지역 예술가들의 작품들을 전시했다. (The event showcased the great works of many local artists)

> 왜 오답?

① Emily는 호기심이 생겨 Martha와 대화를 시작하게 되었다.
(Curiosity sparked within Emily, prompting her to initiate a conversation with Martha.)
③ 마을 사람들은 Martha의 반응을 보고 마음이 뭉클했다.
(The crowd watched in silence, their hearts touched by Martha's emotional response.)
④ Martha는 마지막 그림에 이르러 Emily를 향해 미소를 지었다.
(As Martha reached the last painting, she turned to Emily with a bright smile)
⑤ Martha는 개인적인 역경 때문에 미술에 대한 열정을 잃었다.
(she had lost her passion for art due to personal hardships)

Q 49~51 ✱꾀를 부린 Sally가 집으로 가져간 것

(A) The children arrived / at sunrise / at their grandmother's house. //
아이들은 도착했다 / 동틀 녘에 / 그들의 할머니 댁에 //
They always gathered / at this time of year / to assist with her corn harvest. // 51번 ① 할머니의 옥수수 수확을 돕기 위해 모였음
그들은 항상 모였다 / 한 해의 이맘때 / 그녀의 옥수수 수확을 돕기 위해 //
In return, / their grandmother would reward them / with a present / and by cooking a delicious feast. //
그에 대한 보답으로 / 그들의 할머니는 그들에게 보답하곤 했다 / 선물로 / 그리고 맛있는 진수성찬을 요리해줌으로써 //
The children were all in great spirits. //
아이들은 모두 아주 활기 넘쳤다 //
But not Sally. //
하지만 Sally는 아니었다 //
She disliked working / in the corn field / as she hated the heat and the dust. //
그녀는 일하는 것을 싫어했다 / 옥수수 밭에서 / 그녀가 더위와 먼지를 몹시 싫어했기 때문에 //
(a) She sat silently / as the others took a sack each / and then sang their way to the field. // 49번 단서 1: 아이들이 밭을 향해 감
그녀는 아무 말 없이 앉아 있었다 / 다른 아이들이 각자 자루를 들고 / 노래를 부르며 밭으로 향할 때 //
*(A) 문단 요약: 할머니의 옥수수 수확을 돕기 위해 모인 아이들과 옥수수 밭에서 일하는 것을 무척 싫어하는 Sally 51번 ② Sally는 덥고 짜증이 나서 옥수수 밭을 떠나기를 원했음
(B) Sally just wanted / to get her present and leave the field / because she was starting / to get hot and feel irritated. //
Sally는 그저 원했다 / 그녀의 선물을 받고 밭을 떠나기를 / 그녀가 시작하고 있었기 때문에 / 덥고 짜증이 나기 //
(b) She had only filled her sack twice, / but the others were now taking their third sacks / to the granary. //
그녀는 자루를 두 번만 채웠지만 / 다른 아이들은 이제 세 번째 자루를 나르고 있었다 / 곡물 창고로 //

주어 동사(완전자동사)
Sally sighed heavily. //
Sally는 무겁게 한숨을 쉬었다 //

Then an idea struck her. //
그때 한 가지 묘안이 그녀에게 떠올랐다 // 병렬 구조(목적의 to부정사)

To make the sack lighter / and speed things up, / she quickly filled her last sack / with corn stalks. //
자루를 더 가볍게 만들기 위해 / 그리고 일의 속도를 내기 위해 / 그녀는 자신의 마지막 자루를 재빨리 채웠다 / 옥수수 줄기로 //

49번 단서 2: 할머니가 가장 먼저 도착한 Sally에게 세 번째 자루에 이름을 쓰라고 요청함

Sally reached the granary first, / and her grandmother asked (c) her / to put aside the final load / and write her name on it. //
　　　= Sally
Sally는 곡물창고에 가장 먼저 도착했고 / 할머니는 그녀에게 요청했다 / 마지막에 가져온 짐을 한쪽에 놓고 / 그 위에 그녀의 이름을 쓰라고 // 병렬 구조(asked의 목적격 보어) *

*(B) 문단 요약: 마지막 세 번째 자루를 옥수수 줄기로 채워 곡물창고에 가져온 Sally

(C) They reached the field / and started to work happily. //
그들은 들판에 도착해서 / 즐겁게 일하기 시작했다 // **49번** 단서 3: 밭에 도착해 일하기 시작함

Soon after, / Sally joined them with her sack. //
곧이어 / Sally는 자신의 자루를 가지고 그들과 합류했다 //

Around mid-morning, / their grandmother came / with ice-cold lemonade and peach pie. //
오전 중반쯤 / 할머니는 왔다 / 얼음처럼 차가운 레모네이드와 복숭아 파이를 가지고 //

After finishing, / the children continued working / until the sun was high / and their sacks were bursting. //
　　　　　　　　　　　until의 목적어로 쓰인 명사절의 병렬 구조
다 먹은 뒤에 / 아이들은 계속 일을 했다 / 해가 높이 뜰 때까지 / 그리고 자신들의 자루가 터질 때까지 // **51번 ③** 아이들은 각자 옥수수 자루를 들고 세 번씩 곡물창고로 이동해야 했음

Each child had to make three trips / to the granary. //
아이들은 각자 세 번 이동해야 했다 / 곡물창고로 //

Grandmother was impressed / by their efforts / and (d) she wanted to give them presents accordingly. //
　　　　　　　　　　　　　　　= grandmother
할머니는 감동하였고 / 그들의 노력에 / 그녀는 그에 맞춰 그들에게 선물을 주고 싶어 했다 //

*(C) 문단 요약: 밭에 도착하여 일하기 시작하는 아이들과 그들에게 선물을 주고자 하는 할머니

주어 동사 목적어 목적격 보어 *
(D) Grandmother asked the other children / to do the same thing. //
할머니는 다른 아이들에게도 요청했다 / 똑같은 일을 하도록 // **49번** 단서 4: 다른 아이들에게도 세 번째 자루에 이름을 쓰라고 요청함

Then, / all of the children enjoyed / their grandmother's delicious lunch. // **51번 ④** 아이들은 할머니의 점심을 즐겼음
그러고 나서 / 아이들은 모두 즐겼다 / 할머니의 맛있는 점심을 //

"I am so pleased with your work," / she told them / after lunch. //
"난 너희가 한 일에 너무도 기쁘단다"라고 / 할머니가 그들에게 말했다 / 점심 식사 후에 //

"This year, / you can all take home / your final load / as a present!" //
"올해엔 / 너희들 모두 집에 가져가도 된단다 / 너희의 마지막 짐을 / 선물로" //

The children cheered for joy, / gladly thanked her, / and lifted their sacks / to take home. //
　　　　　　　　　　병렬 구조
아이들은 기뻐서 환호했고 / 기꺼이 그녀에게 감사하며 / 자신들의 자루를 들어 올려 / 집으로 가져갔다 //

Sally was terribly disappointed. //
Sally는 몹시 실망했다 // = only **51번 ⑤** Sally의 자루에는 옥수수 줄기만 있었음

There was nothing but useless corn stalks / in (e) her sack. //
쓸모없는 옥수수 줄기 외에는 아무것도 없었다 / 그녀의 자루에는 // = Sally's

She then made the long walk home, / pretending that she was carrying / a heavy load. //
　　　　　　　　　　　　준동사인 현재분사 pretending의 목적어절
곧이어 그녀는 먼 길을 걸어 집으로 갔다 / 자신이 운반하는 체하면서 / 무거운 짐을 //

*(D) 문단 요약: 쓸모없는 옥수수 줄기만 있는 자루를 선물로 받게 된 Sally

- at sunrise 동틀 녘에　　• assist with ~을 돕다　　• harvest ⓝ 수확
- in return (~에 대한) 보답으로　　• feast ⓝ 진수성찬
- in spirits 활기 넘치는　　• dust ⓝ 먼지, 티끌　　• sack ⓝ 자루
- irritated ⓐ 짜증이 난　　• sigh ⓥ 한숨 쉬다
- strike ⓥ (생각·아이디어가) 갑자기 떠오르다[들다]
- put aside ~을 한쪽에 두다　　• load ⓝ 짐, 화물　　• soon after 곧이어

- burst ⓥ 터지다　　• accordingly ⓐⓓ 그에 맞춰
- be pleased with ~에 기뻐하다　　• cheer ⓥ 환호성을 지르다, 환호하다
- terribly ⓐⓓ 몹시　　• pretend ⓥ ~인 체하다

(A) 아이들은 동틀 녘에 할머니 댁에 도착했다. 그들은 항상 한 해의 이맘때 그녀의 옥수수 수확을 돕기 위해 모였다. 그에 대한 보답으로, 할머니는 선물로 그리고 맛있는 진수성찬을 요리해줌으로써 그들에게 보답하곤 했다. 아이들은 모두 아주 활기 넘쳤다. 하지만 Sally는 아니었다. 그녀는 더위와 먼지를 몹시 싫어했기 때문에 옥수수 밭에서 일하는 것을 싫어했다. 다른 아이들이 각자 자루를 들고 노래를 부르며 밭으로 향할 때 (a) 그녀는 아무 말 없이 앉아 있었다. (C) 그들은 들판에 도착해서 즐겁게 일하기 시작했다. 곧이어 Sally는 자신의 자루를 가지고 그들과 합류했다. 오전 중반쯤 할머니는 얼음처럼 차가운 레모네이드와 복숭아 파이를 가지고 왔다. 다 먹은 뒤에, 아이들은 해가 높이 뜨고 자신들의 자루가 터질 때까지 계속 일을 했다. 아이들은 각자 곡물창고로 세 번 이동해야 했다. 할머니는 그들의 노력에 감동하였고, (d) 그녀는 그에 맞춰 그들에게 선물을 주고 싶어 했다.

(B) Sally는 덥고 짜증이 나기 시작해서 그저 그녀의 선물을 받고 밭을 떠나고 싶었다. (b) 그녀는 자루를 두 번만 채웠지만, 다른 아이들은 이제 세 번째 자루를 곡물창고로 나르고 있었다. Sally는 무겁게 한숨을 쉬었다. 그때 한 가지 묘안이 떠올랐다. 자루를 더 가볍게 만들고 일의 속도를 내기 위해, 그녀는 마지막 자루를 옥수수 줄기로 재빨리 채웠다. Sally는 곡물창고에 가장 먼저 도착했고, 할머니는 (c) 그녀에게 마지막에 가져온 짐을 한쪽에 놓고 그 위에 그녀의 이름을 쓰라고 했다.

(D) 할머니는 다른 아이들에게도 똑같이 하도록 했다. 그러고 나서 아이들은 모두 할머니의 맛있는 점심을 즐겼다. "난 너희들이 한 일에 너무도 기쁘단다. 올해엔 너희들 모두 마지막에 가져온 짐을 선물로 집에 가져가도 된단다."라고 점심 식사 후에 할머니가 그들에게 말했다. 아이들은 기뻐서 환호했고, 기꺼이 그녀에게 감사했으며, 자신들의 자루를 들어 올려 집으로 가져갔다. Sally는 몹시 실망했다. (e) 그녀의 자루에는 쓸모없는 옥수수 줄기 외에는 아무것도 없었다. 곧이어 그녀는 자신이 무거운 짐이라도 가지고 가는 체하면서 먼 길을 걸어 집으로 갔다.

Q 49 정답 ②

주어진 글 (A)에 이어질 내용을 순서에 맞게 배열한 것으로 가장 적절한 것은?

① (B) — (D) — (C) 일을 시작하기도 전에 세 번째 자루를 나른다는 것은 어색함
② (C) — (B) — (D) (C) 밭에 도착해서 일하기 시작함 - (B) 할머니가 Sally에게 마지막 자루에 이름을 쓸 것을 요청함 - (D) 다른 아이들에게도 자루에 이름을 쓸 것을 요청함
③ (C) — (D) — (B) (D)의 the same thing이 가리키는 것이 (B)에 등장함
④ (D) — (B) — (C)
⑤ (D) — (C) — (B) 마지막 자루를 옮기고 난 이후의 일이 (D)에 등장함

> **왜 정답?** [정답률 85%]

아이들이 각자 자루를 들고 밭으로 향하는 (A) 뒤에는 밭(들판)에 도착해서 일하기 시작하는 (C)가 이어지는 것이 적절하다. (D)는 할머니가 다른 아이들에게도 똑같은 일을 하도록 요청했다는 내용으로 시작하는데, 그 똑같은 일이란 (B)에서 할머니가 Sally에게 요청한 것인 세 번째 자루에 자신의 이름을 쓰는 것을 의미한다. 따라서 (B)가 (D) 앞에 와야 하므로 (A)에 이어지는 올바른 순서는 ② (C)-(B)-(D)이다.

> **왜 오답?**

① (B)에서 아이들은 세 번째 자루를 나르고 있으므로 밭에 도착해서 일하기 시작 했다는 (C)가 (B)보다 앞에 와야 한다. **주의**

③ (D)에서 할머니가 다른 아이들에게 하도록 요청한 the same thing이 의미하는 바가 (B)에 등장하므로 (B)가 (D)보다 먼저 와야 한다.

④, ⑤ (D)는 마지막 자루를 나르고 난 이후의 일이므로 맨 마지막에 오는 것이 적절하다.

Q 50 정답 ④

밑줄 친 (a)~(e) 중에서 가리키는 대상이 나머지 넷과 다른 것은?

① (a) Sally ② (b) Sally ③ (c) Sally ④ (d) grandmother ⑤ (e) Sally's

> **왜 정답?** [정답률 93%]

(a), (b), (c), (e)는 옥수수 밭에서 일하기 싫어한 Sally를 가리키는 반면 아이들에게 선물을 주고 싶어 했던 (d)는 할머니를 가리킨다. 따라서 ④은 가리키는 대상이 나머지와 다르다.

> **왜 오답?**

① 다른 아이들이 자루를 들고 노래를 부르며 밭으로 향할 때 아무 말 없이 앉아 있었던 것은 Sally이다.

② 다른 아이들이 세 번째 자루를 나르고 있을 때 자루를 두 번만 채웠던 것은 Sally이다.

③ 마지막에 가져온 짐에 이름을 쓰라고 요청한 사람은 할머니이고, 그녀는 Sally에게 요청을 한 것이다.

⑤ 쓸모없는 옥수수 줄기만 들어 있었던 것은 Sally의 자루이다.

Q 51 정답 ⑤

윗글에 관한 내용으로 적절하지 않은 것은?

① 아이들은 할머니의 옥수수 수확을 돕기 위해 모였다.
They always gathered ~ with her corn harvest.

② Sally는 덥고 짜증나서 옥수수 밭을 떠나고 싶었다.
Sally just wanted ~ to get hot and feel irritated.

③ 아이들은 각자 세 번씩 옥수수가 담긴 자루를 곡물창고로 날라야 했다.
Each child had to make three trips to the granary.

④ 할머니는 아이들에게 맛있는 점심을 제공했다.
Then, all of the children enjoyed their grandmother's delicious lunch.

⑤ Sally는 옥수수가 담긴 무거운 자루를 가지고 집으로 갔다.
There was nothing but useless corn stalks in her sack.

> **왜 정답?** [정답률 82%]

Sally의 자루에는 쓸모없는 옥수수 줄기밖에 없었다고(There was nothing but useless corn stalks in her sack.) 했으므로 ⑤은 글과 일치하지 않는다.

> **왜 오답?**

① 아이들은 항상 한 해의 이맘때 할머니의 옥수수 수확을 돕기 위해 모였다. (They always gathered at this time of year to assist with her corn harvest.)

② (B)에서 Sally는 덥고 짜증이 나기 시작해서 밭을 떠나고 싶었다고 했다. (Sally just wanted ~ to get hot and feel irritated.)

③ 아이들은 각자 곡물창고로 세 번 이동해야 했다는(Each child had to make three trips to the granary.) 것은 옥수수가 담긴 자루를 세 번 곡물창고로 날라야 했다는 의미이다. **주의**

④ 모든 아이들이 할머니의 맛있는 점심을 즐겼다. (Then, all of the children enjoyed their grandmother's delicious lunch.)

─── 어법 특강 ───

＊ 동명사 vs. 명사적 용법의 to부정사

– 동명사 : ~하기, ~하는 것

① 주어
• Working out every day is good for your health.
(매일 운동하는 것은 너의 건강에 좋다.)

② 목적어
• Stop watching so much TV.
(TV를 너무 많이 보는 것을 멈춰라.)

③ 보어
• Her hobby is reading books about history.
(그녀의 취미는 역사에 관한 책을 읽는 것이다.)

④ 전치사의 목적어
• There are lots of myths about taking care of bad breath.
(입 냄새를 없애는 것에 대한 많은 속설이 있다.)

– 명사적 용법의 to부정사 : ~하기, ~하는 것

① 주어
• To talk is easier than to act.
(말하는 것은 행동하는 것보다 쉽다.)

② 목적어
• She likes to eat junk food.
(그녀는 정크푸드를 먹는 것을 좋아한다.)

③ 보어
• His only weak point is to talk too much.
(그의 유일한 단점은 말을 너무 많이 한다는 것이다.)

Q 52~54 ＊가정 경찰관 Sean ─────

(A) In this area, / heavy snow in winter / was not uncommon. //
이 지역에서는 / 겨울에 폭설이 내리는 것이 / 드물지 않았다 //

Sometimes it poured down / for hours and hours / and piled up very high. // ──병렬 구조──
때로는 쏟아져 내려 / 몇 시간 동안 / 아주 높이 쌓였다 //

Then, / no one could go out. //
그러면 / 아무도 나갈 수 없었다 //

54번 ① 폭설 때문에 엄마는 사무실 업무를 식탁에서 하고 있었음

Today too, / because of the heavy snow, / Mom was doing her office work / at the kitchen table. //
전치사   명사구
오늘도 / 폭설로 인해 / 엄마는 그녀의 사무실 업무를 보고 있었다 / 주방 식탁에서 //

Felix, the high schooler, / had to take online classes / in his room. //
고등학생 Felix는 / 온라인 수업을 들어야 했다 / 자기 방에서 //

Five-year-old Sean, / who normally went to kindergarten, / was sneaking around in the house / playing home policeman. //
주어(선행사)   관계대명사   동사
다섯 살짜리 Sean은 / 평소에는 유치원에 가던 / 집안 이곳저곳을 몰래 돌아다니고 있었다 / 가정 경찰관 놀이를 하며 // = Sean

(a) The kindergartener wanted to know / what his family members were up to, / and was checking up on everyone. //
병렬 구조
그 유치원생은 알고 싶었다 / 그의 가족들이 무엇을 하는지 / 그리고 모두를 확인하고 있었다 //
*(A) 문단 요약: Sean은 엄마와 형 Felix가 무엇을 하는지 확인하고 있었음

(B) "All right. // I'm sure / you're doing your work." //
"그래 // 난 확신해 / 네가 네 일을 하고 있을 거라고" //
52번 단서 1: (D)에서 Felix가 과학 수업의 강의 영상을 보고 있다고 한 것에 대한 대답

Mom replied, / and then sharply added a question. //
엄마가 대답하고 / 그리고서 재빨리 질문을 덧붙였다 //

"Sean, what are you doing?" //
"Sean, '넌' 뭐 하고 있니" //

Sean's face immediately became blank, / and he said, "Nothing." //
Sean은 즉시 얼빠진 표정이 되었고 / 그는 "아무것도 안 해요"라고 말했다 //

"Come here, Honey, / and you can help me." //
"얘야, 이리 오렴 / 그러면 날 도와줄 수 있어" //

Sean ran to the kitchen right away. //
Sean은 곧바로 주방으로 달려갔다 // **54번 ②** Sean은 엄마가 오라고 하자 주방으로 달려갔음

"What can I do for you, Mom?" //
"엄마, 내가 뭘 도와줄까요" //

생략 가능한 명사절 접속사＊
His voice was high, / and Felix could sense / that his brother was excited. //
그의 목청은 높았고 / Felix는 느낄 수 있었다 / 동생이 신이 났다는 것을 //
부사적 용법(감정의 원인)   = Sean

Felix was pleased / to get rid of (b) the policeman, / and now he could concentrate on the lesson, / at least till Sean came back. //
Felix는 기뻤고 / 경찰관에게서 벗어나서 / 이제 그는 수업에 집중할 수 있었다 / 적어도 Sean이 돌아올 때까지 //
*(B) 문단 요약: 엄마가 Sean을 주방으로 부르자 Felix는 그에게서 벗어나 수업에 집중할 수 있어서 기뻤음

490 자이스토리 영어 독해 실전

(C) While checking on his family, / Sean interfered in their
business / as if it was his own. //

그의 가족을 확인하는 동안 / Sean은 그들의 일에 간섭했다 / 그것이 자기 일인 것처럼 //

This time, / (c) the playful and curious boy was interested / in
his brother Felix, / who committed himself to studying / no
matter where he was. //
선행사   주격 관계대명사(계속적 용법)   = wherever

이번에는 / 그 장난기 많고 호기심 많은 아이가 관심을 보였는데 / 그의 형 Felix에게 / 그는
공부에 전념했다 / 그가 어디에 있든지 //

54번 ③ Sean은 몰래 형의 방을 들여다보았음

Sean secretly looked inside his brother's room / from the door,
/ and shouted toward the kitchen / where Mom was working, /
선행사   관계부사
"Mom, Felix isn't studying. //

Sean은 형의 방을 몰래 들여다보고는 / 문에서 / 주방을 향해 소리쳤다 / 엄마가 일하고 있는
/ '엄마, Felix가 공부를 안 하고 있어요 //

He's just watching a funny video." //

그는 재미있는 영상을 보고 있을 뿐이에요" //

Sean was naughtily smiling / at his brother. //

Sean은 짓궂게 웃고 있었다 / 형을 바라보며 //

*(C) 문단 요약: Sean은 형의 방을 몰래 들여다보고 주방에 있는 엄마에게 형이 공부
를 안 하고 있다고 말함

(D) Felix was mad / because (d) his little brother was bothering
him. // **52번** 단서 3: (C)에서 Sean이 Felix를 성가시게 한 것과 연결됨

Felix는 화가 났다 / 동생이 자신을 성가시게 하고 있었기 때문에 //

Felix was studying science / using a video / posted on the school
web site. // **54번 ④** Felix는 동영상을 이용해서 과학을 공부하고 있었음   a video를 수식하는 과거분사구

Felix는 과학을 공부하고 있었다 / 영상을 이용해서 / 학교 웹 사이트에 올라온 //

He made an angry face / at the naughty boy. //

그는 화난 표정을 지었다 / 그 개구쟁이 아이를 향해 //

Right then, / Mom asked loudly from the kitchen, / "What are
you doing, Felix?" //

바로 그때 / 엄마가 주방에서 큰소리로 물었다 / "Felix, 무얼 하고 있니"라고 //

Felix's room was located next to the kitchen, / and he could hear
Mom clearly. // **54번 ⑤** Felix의 방은 주방 옆에 있었음

Felix의 방은 주방 옆에 있었고 / 그는 엄마의 말을 똑똑히 들을 수 있었다 //

"I'm watching a lecture video / for my science class." //

"저는 강의 영상을 보고 있어요 / 과학 수업의" //

Felix argued against Sean's accusation / and mischievously
┌병렬 구조┐   =Felix's
stuck (e) his tongue out / at his little brother. //

Felix는 Sean의 비난을 반박하고 / 장난기 있게 자신의 혀를 내밀었다 / 자신의 동생에게 //

*(D) 문단 요약: Felix는 Sean이 성가시게 해서 화가 났고, 엄마가 Felix에게 무엇을
하고 있냐고 묻자 과학을 공부하고 있다고 대답함

- heavy ⓐ (양·정도 등이 보통보다) 많은[심한]
- pour ⓥ (눈·비가) 마구 쏟아지다
- pile up (양이) 많아지다[쌓이다]   • normally ⓐⅾ 보통(은), 보통 때는
- kindergarten ⓝ 유치원   • sharply ⓐⅾ 날카롭게, 재빨리, 급격히
- immediately ⓐⅾ 즉시, 즉각   • blank ⓐ 멍한, 무표정한, 빈
- sense ⓥ 감지하다, 느끼다   • playful ⓐ 장난기 많은, 놀기 좋아하는
- bother ⓥ 신경 쓰이게 하다, 괴롭히다
- post ⓥ (안내문 등을) 게시[공고]하다   • naughty ⓐ 짓궂은, 버릇없는
- argue ⓥ 주장하다, 다투다   • accusation ⓝ 혐의 (제기), 비난

(A) 이 지역에서는 겨울에 폭설이 내리는 것이 드문 일이 아니었다. 때로는
몇 시간이고 쏟아져 내려 아주 높이 쌓였다. 그러면 아무도 나갈 수 없었다.
오늘 또한 폭설로 인해 엄마는 주방 식탁에서 사무실 업무를 보고 있었다. 고
등학생 Felix는 자기 방에서 온라인 수업을 들어야 했다. 평소에는 유치원에
가던 다섯 살짜리 Sean은 가정 경찰관 놀이를 하며 집안 이곳저곳을 몰래 돌
아다니고 있었다. (a) 그 유치원생은 가족들이 무엇을 하는지 알고 싶었고,
모두를 확인하고 있었다.
(C) Sean은 가족을 확인하는 동안 그들의 일이 자기 일인 것처럼 그 일에 간섭
했다. 이번에는 (c) 그 장난기 많고 호기심 많은 아이가 형 Felix에게 관심을 보
였는데, 그는 어디에 있든지 공부에 전념했다. Sean은 문에서 형의 방을 몰래
들여다보고는, 엄마가 일하고 있는 주방을 향해 "엄마, Felix가 공부를 안 하고
있어요. 재미있는 영상을 보고 있을 뿐이에요."라고 소리쳤다. Sean은 형을 바
라보며 짓궂게 웃고 있었다.

(D) Felix는 (d) 동생이 자신을 성가시게 하고 있었기 때문에 화가 났다. Felix
는 학교 웹 사이트에 올라온 영상을 이용해서 과학을 공부하고 있었다. 그
는 그 개구쟁이 아이를 향해 화난 표정을 지었다. 바로 그때 엄마가 주방에
서 큰소리로 "Felix, 무얼 하고 있니?"라고 물었다. Felix의 방은 주방 옆에
있었고, 그는 엄마의 말을 똑똑히 들을 수 있었다. "과학 수업의 강의 영상
을 보고 있어요." Felix는 Sean의 비난을 반박하고는 장난기 있게 동생에게
(e) 자신의 혀를 내밀었다.
(B) "그래. 넌 틀림없이 네 일을 하고 있을 거야."라고 엄마가 대답하고 나서 재
빨리 질문을 덧붙였다. "Sean, '넌' 뭐 하고 있니?" Sean은 즉시 얼빠진 표정
이 되었고, 그는 "아무것도 안 해요."라고 말했다. "애야, 이리 오렴. 그러면 날
도와줄 수 있어." Sean은 곧바로 주방으로 달려갔다. "엄마, 내가 뭘 도와줄까
요?" 그의 목청은 높았고, Felix는 동생이 신이 났다는 것을 느낄 수 있었다.
Felix는 (b) 경찰관에게서 벗어나서 기뻤고, 적어도 Sean이 돌아올 때까지 이제
그는 수업에 집중할 수 있었다.

Q 52 정답 ③

주어진 글 (A)에 이어질 내용을 순서에 맞게 배열한 것으로 가장 적절한 것은?

① (B) — (D) — (C)   (B)에 등장하는 엄마의 말은 (D)에 등장한 Felix의 대답에 대한 것임
② (C) — (B) — (D)
③ (C) — (D) — (B)   (C) Sean이 엄마에게 Felix가 공부하고 있지 않다고 말함 – (D) 엄마가 Felix에게 무엇을 하고 있는지 묻고 Felix가 공부 중이라고 대답함 – (B) 엄마가 Felix의 대답에 대해 답하고 나서 Sean을 부름
④ (D) — (B) — (C)
⑤ (D) — (C) — (B)   (D) 앞에 Sean이 Felix를 성가시게 하는 내용이 와야 함

＞오ㅐ 정답? [정답률 89%]

유치원생, 즉 Sean이 그의 가족들이 모두 무엇을 하는지 확인하고 있었다는 내
용으로 끝난 (A)에는 Sean이 가족을 확인하면서 그들의 일에 간섭했다는 내용으
로 시작한 (C)가 이어진다. (C)에서 Sean이 엄마에게 Felix가 공부를 안 하고 있다
고 말했는데, 이를 듣고 엄마가 Felix에게 무엇을 하고 있는지 물은 것이므로 (D)가
(C) 뒤에 이어진다. 강의 영상을 보고 있다는 Felix의 말에 엄마가 "그래. 넌 틀림없
이 네 일을 하고 있을 거야."라고 Felix에게 대답하는 것이므로 (D) 뒤에는 (B)가 와
서 전체 글의 흐름은 ③ (C)-(D)-(B)가 된다.

＞오ㅐ 오답?

①, ② (B)에서 엄마가 "그래. 넌 틀림없이 네 일을 하고 있을 거야."라고 한 것은
과학 공부를 하고 있다는 Felix의 말에 대한 대답이다.

④, ⑤ Sean이 Felix를 성가시게 하는 내용이 (C)에 등장하므로 (D) 앞에 (C)가 와
야 한다.   (A)에서는 단순히 Sean이 가족들이 무엇을   꿀팁
하는지 확인하고 있었다고만 했음

Q 53 정답 ⑤

밑줄 친 (a)~(e) 중에서 가리키는 대상이 나머지 넷과 다른 것은?

① (a) Sean   ② (b) Sean   ③ (c) Sean   ④ (d) Sean   ⑤ (e) Felix's

＞오ㅐ 정답? [정답률 87%]

유치원에 다니는 다섯 살짜리 Sean과 그의 고등학생 형 Felix 중에서 자신의 동생
에게 혀를 내민 (e)는 Felix를 가리키고 나머지는 모두 Sean을 가리키므로 정답은
⑤이다.

＞오ㅐ 오답?

① 유치원생은 평소 유치원에 가는 다섯 살짜리 Sean을 가리킨다.
② 가정 경찰관 놀이를 하던 동생 Sean을 가리킨다.
③ 장난을 좋아하고 호기심이 많은 소년은 형에게 관심이 있었던 Sean이다. 주의
④ Felix의 동생을 의미하므로 Sean을 가리킨다. his가 가리키는 것이 Felix이다.

Q 54 정답 ④

윗글에 관한 내용으로 적절하지 않은 것은?

① 엄마는 폭설로 인해 집에서 업무를 보고 있었다.
　　because of the heavy snow, Mom was doing her office work at the kitchen table
② Sean은 엄마가 불러서 주방으로 달려갔다.
　　Sean ran to the kitchen right away.
③ Sean은 몰래 형의 방을 들여다보았다.
　　Sean secretly looked inside his brother's room
④ Felix는 자신의 방에서 게임을 하고 있었다.
　　Felix was studying science using a video
⑤ Felix의 방은 주방 옆에 있었다.
　　Felix's room was located next to the kitchen

❯ 왜 정답 ? [정답률 90%]

Felix는 동영상을 이용해서 과학을 공부하고 있었다고(Felix was studying science using a video) 했으므로 ④은 글과 일치하지 않는다.

❯ 왜 오답 ?

① 폭설 때문에 엄마는 사무실 업무를 식탁에서 하고 있었다. (because of the heavy snow, Mom was doing her office work at the kitchen table)
② 주방에서 일하고 있던 엄마가 부르자(Come here, Honey) Sean은 주방으로 달려갔다. (Sean ran to the kitchen right away.)
③ Sean은 형의 방을 몰래 들여다보았다. (Sean secretly looked inside his brother's room)
⑤ Felix의 방은 주방 옆에 있었다. (Felix's room was located next to the kitchen)

─ 어법 특강

✻ 명사절 접속사 that vs. 관계대명사 that

– 접속사 that은 명사절을 이끌고, 관계대명사 that은 형용사절을 이끈다.

- 목적어절을 이끄는 접속사 that
- I didn't know **that** she was married.
 (그녀가 결혼을 했다는 것을 나는 몰랐다.)
- Accepting a job means **that** you accept the responsibility.
 (어떤 일을 맡는다는 것은 당신이 책임을 지는 것을 의미한다.)
- The police realized **that** they had made a terrible mistake.
 (경찰은 그들이 끔찍한 실수를 저질렀다는 것을 알게 되었다.)
- Researchers say **that** heart disease can be caused by high stress.
 (연구자들은 심장병이 높은 스트레스에 의해 초래될 수 있다고 말한다.)
- They learned **that** they are not alone.
 (그들은 그들이 혼자가 아니라는 것을 알게 되었다.)

- 형용사절을 이끄는 목적격 관계대명사 that
- It's a song **that** my mother taught me.
 (그것은 나의 어머니가 내게 가르쳐주신 노래이다.)
- We were talking about the film **that** we saw last night.
 (우리는 어젯밤에 본 영화에 관해서 이야기하고 있었다.)
- In the store, I saw a jacket **that** I wanted to buy.
 (상점에서 나는 내가 사고 싶어 했던 재킷을 봤다.)
- Joe lost his watch **that** his father had given to him.
 (Joe는 그의 아버지가 그에게 준 시계를 잃어버렸다.)
- There are many things in life **that** we do not know.
 (인생에는 우리가 모르는 많은 것들이 있다.)

Q 55~57 ✻고통스러운 과거를 자전거 타기로 극복한 Clara

(A) Emma and Clara stood side by side on the beach road, /
with+목적어+분사: 목적어가 ~한 채로
with their eyes fixed on the boundless ocean. //
Emma와 Clara는 해변 도로에 나란히 서 있었다 / 끝없이 펼쳐진 바다에 시선을 고정하고 //

The breathtaking scene that surrounded them / was beyond
　　　　　　　　　주격 관계대명사(선행사:scene)
description. //
그들을 둘러싸고 있는 숨 막히는 풍경은 / 말로 표현할 수 없을 정도였다 //

Just after sunrise, / they finished their preparations / for the
bicycle ride along the beach road. // 57번① Emma와 Clara는 자전거 탈 준비를
일출 직후에 / 그들은 준비를 마쳤다 / 해변 도로를 따라 자전거를 탈 // 일출 직후에 마침

Emma turned to Clara with a question, / "Do you think this will
be your favorite ride ever?" //
Emma는 Clara를 보며 물었다 / "이것이 네 인생 최고의 라이딩이 될 것 같니?"라고 //

Clara's face lit up with a bright smile / as she nodded. //
Clara의 얼굴이 환한 미소로 밝아졌다 / 그녀가 고개를 끄덕일 때 //

　　　　　　　= Clara
"Definitely! / (a) I can't wait to ride / while watching those
　　　　　　　　　　　　　　　　　부사절에서 주어와 be동사 생략
beautiful waves!" //
"물론이지! / 나는 어서 자전거를 타고 싶어 / 저 아름다운 파도를 보면서" //

 ✻(A) 문단 요약: Emma와 Clara는 해변 도로를 따라 바다를 보면서 자전거를 탈 준비를 마침

(B) When they reached their destination, / Emma and Clara
stopped their bikes. // 55번 단서 1: 목적지에 도착함
그들의 목적지에 도착했을 때 / Emma와 Clara는 자전거를 멈췄다 //

　　　　　　　　　　　　　　　　분사구문
Emma approached Clara, / saying "Bicycle riding is unlike
swimming, isn't it?" // ┌57번② Clara는 자전거 타기와 수영이 꽤 비슷하다고 말함
Emma는 Clara에게 다가가 / "자전거 타기는 수영과는 다르지, 그렇지 않니?"라고 물었다 //

Clara answered with a smile, / "Quite similar, actually. / Just like
　　　　　　　　　　　　사역동사+목적어+원형부정사
swimming, / riding makes me feel truly alive." //
Clara는 미소를 지으며 대답했다 / "사실은, 상당히 비슷해 / 수영과 꼭 마찬가지로 / 자전거 타기는 나에게 정말 살아있다는 느낌이 들게 해 줘."라고 //

　　　　　　　　　　　 = Clara　　 가주어　　　　　　진주어
She added, / "It shows (b) me / what it means to live /
부사절에서 주어와 be동사 생략
while facing life's tough challenges." //
그녀는 덧붙였다 / "그것은 나에게 보여줘."라고 / 산다는 것이 어떤 의미인지 / 인생의 힘든 도전에 직면하면서 //

Emma nodded in agreement and suggested, / "Your first beach
bike ride was a great success. / How about coming back next
　　　　　　　　　　　　　　　　　　　how about -ing ~?: ~하는 것이 어때?
summer?" //
Emma는 동의하면서 고개를 끄덕이고 제안했다 / "너의 첫 번째 해변 자전거 타기는 정말 대성공이었어 / 내년 여름에 다시 오는 건 어때?"라고 //
　　　　　　　　　　　　　　　　　　 = Emma
Clara replied with delight, / "With (c) you, absolutely!" //
Clara는 기뻐하면서 대답했다 / "너와 함께라면, 물론이지!"라고 //

 ✻(B) 문단 요약: Clara는 자전거 타기와 수영이 인생의 힘든 도전에서도 삶의 의미를 보여준다는 점에서 비슷하다고 말하며, 내년 여름에 Emma와 다시 올 것을 약속함

(C) Clara used to be a talented swimmer, / but she had to give
　　　　　　used to-v: ~하곤 했다
up her dream / of becoming an Olympic medalist in swimming
/ because of shoulder injuries. // 57번③ Clara는 올림픽 수영 경기에서 메달을 따고
Clara는 재능 있는 수영 선수였지만 / 그녀는 자신의 꿈을 포기해야만 했다 / 올림픽 수영 메달리스트가 되겠다는 / 어깨 부상으로 인해 // 싶다는 꿈을 포기해야 함

Yet she responded to the hardship / in a constructive way. //
하지만 그녀는 그 고난에 대응했다 / 건설적인 방식으로 //

After years of hard training, / she made an incredible recovery /
　　　　　　　　　　　　　　　　병렬 구조
and found a new passion for bike riding. //
수년간의 고된 훈련 끝에 / 그녀는 믿기 어려운 회복을 이뤄냈고 / 자전거 타기에 대한 새로운 열정을 발견했다 //

　　　　　　　　　　　　　　　　　　　　make+목적어+목적격 보어
Emma saw / how the painful past made her maturer / and how
　　 = Clara　make+목적어+목적격 보어
it made (d) her stronger in the end. //
Emma는 보았다 / 고통스러운 과거가 그녀를 어떻게 더 성숙하게 만들어 주었고 / 그리고 그것이 결국에는 그녀를 어떻게 더 강하게 만들어 주었는지를 //

분사구문을 이끎
One hour later, / Clara, riding ahead of Emma, turned back and shouted, / "Look at the white cliff!" // **55번** 단서 2: 1시간 동안 자전거를 탄 후에 목적지를 발견함
한 시간 후에 / Emma보다 앞장서 가던 Clara가 뒤를 돌아보며 외쳤다 / "저 하얀 절벽을 봐!"라고 //

*(C) 문단 요약: Clara는 부상으로 수영의 꿈을 포기해야 했지만, 고된 훈련과 회복 끝에 자전거 타기에 대한 열정을 발견하는 등 더 성숙하고 강해짐

(D) Emma and Clara jumped on their bikes / and started to pedal / toward the white cliff / where the beach road ended. // 관계부사(선행사: at the white cliff)
Emma와 Clara는 자전거에 올라타서 / 페달을 밟기 시작했다 / 하얀 절벽을 향해 / 해변 도로가 끝나는 // **55번** 단서 3, **57번** ④ Emma와 Clara는 자전거를 타고 하얀 절벽 쪽으로 갔음

Speeding up and enjoying the wide blue sea, / Emma couldn't hide her excitement and exclaimed, / "Clara, the view is amazing!" // 분사구문
속도를 내고 넓고 푸른 바다를 즐기면서 / Emma는 자신의 흥분을 감추지 못하고 외쳤다 / "Clara, 경치가 정말 멋져!"라고 //

Clara's silence, however, seemed to say / that she was lost in her thoughts. // 명사절 접속사
하지만, Clara의 침묵은 말하는 것 같았다 / 그녀가 자기 생각에 빠져 있다는 것을 //

Emma understood the meaning of her silence. //
Emma는 그녀가 침묵하는 의미를 이해했다 // **57번** ⑤ Emma는 Clara의 침묵의 의미를 이해했음
분사구문을 이끎
Watching Clara riding beside her, / Emma thought about Clara's past tragedy, / which (e) she now seemed to have overcome. // = Clara   to부정사의 완료형
자기 옆에서 자전거를 타고 있는 Clara를 지켜보며 / Emma는 Clara의 과거 비극에 대해 생각했다 / 지금은 그녀가 극복한 것처럼 보이는 //

*(D) 문단 요약: Emma는 Clara에게 말을 걸었지만, Clara는 자기 생각에 빠져서 답을 하지 않았고, Emma는 Clara의 과거를 떠올리며 침묵을 이해함

· breathtaking ⓐ 숨 막히게 하는
· beyond description 말로 표현할 수 없을 정도의
· destination ⓝ 목적지   · injury ⓝ 부상   · hardship ⓝ 고난
· constructive ⓐ 건설적인   · mature ⓐ 성숙한   · cliff ⓝ 절벽
· exclaim ⓥ 외치다   · tragedy ⓝ 비극   · overcome ⓥ 극복하다

(A) Emma와 Clara는 끝없이 펼쳐진 바다에 시선을 고정하고, 해변 도로에 나란히 서 있었다. 그들을 둘러싸고 있는 숨 막히는 풍경은 말로 표현할 수 없을 정도였다. 일출 직후에, 그들은 해변 도로를 따라 자전거를 탈 준비를 마쳤다. Emma는 Clara를 보며, "이것이 네 인생 최고의 라이딩이 될 것 같니?"라고 물었다. Clara가 고개를 끄덕일 때 그녀의 얼굴이 환한 미소로 밝아졌다. "물론이지! (a) 나는 저 아름다운 파도를 보면서 어서 자전거를 타고 싶어!"

(D) Emma와 Clara는 자전거에 올라타서 해변 도로가 끝나는 하얀 절벽을 향해 페달을 밟기 시작했다. 속도를 내고 넓고 푸른 바다를 즐기면서, Emma는 자신의 흥분을 감추지 못하고 "Clara, 경치가 정말 멋져!"라고 외쳤다. 하지만, Clara의 침묵은 그녀가 자기 생각에 빠져 있다는 것을 말하는 것 같았다. Emma는 그녀가 침묵하는 의미를 이해했다. 자기 옆에서 자전거를 타고 있는 Clara를 지켜보며, Emma는 지금은 (e) 그녀가 극복한 것처럼 보이는, Clara의 과거 비극에 대해 생각했다.

(C) Clara는 재능 있는 수영 선수였지만, 어깨 부상으로 인해 올림픽 수영 메달리스트가 되겠다는 자신의 꿈을 포기해야만 했다. 하지만 그녀는 그 고난에 건설적인 방식으로 대응했다. 수년간의 고된 훈련 끝에, 그녀는 믿기 어려운 회복을 이뤄냈고 자전거 타기에 대한 새로운 열정을 발견했다. Emma는 고통스러운 과거가 그녀를 어떻게 더 성숙하게 만들어 주었고, 그리고 그것이 결국에는 (d) 그녀를 어떻게 더 강하게 만들어 주었는지를 보았다. 한 시간 후에, Emma보다 앞장서 가던 Clara가 뒤를 돌아보며 "저 하얀 절벽을 봐!"라고 외쳤다.

(B) 그들의 목적지에 도착했을 때, Emma와 Clara는 자전거를 멈췄다. Emma는 Clara에게 다가가 "자전거 타기는 수영과는 다르지, 그렇지 않니?"라고 물었다. Clara는 미소를 지으며 "사실은, 상당히 비슷해. 수영과 꼭 마찬가지로 자전거 타기는 나에게 정말 살아있다는 느낌이 들게 해 줘."라고 대답했다. "그것은 (b) 나에게 인생의 힘든 도전에 직면하면서 산다는 것이 어떤 의미인지 보여줘."라고 그녀는 덧붙였다. Emma는 동의하면서 고개를

끄덕이고, "너의 첫 번째 해변 자전거 타기는 정말 대성공이었어. 내년 여름에 다시 오는 건 어때?"라고 제안했다. Clara는 "(c) 너와 함께라면, 물론이지!"라고 기뻐하면서 대답했다.

Q 55 정답 ⑤

주어진 글 (A)에 이어질 내용을 순서에 맞게 배열한 것으로 가장 적절한 것은?

① (B) — (D) — (C) (C)에서 한 시간 동안 자전거 타기를 마친 후에 (B)에서 목적지에 도착했다는 내용이 나와야 함

② (C) — (B) — (D) (D)에서 Clara의 침묵을 언급한 후에 (C)에서 그 이유로 Clara의 과거를 설명해야 함

③ (C) — (D) — (B)

④ (D) — (B) — (C) 다시 오기로 약속하는 (B)는 결말임

⑤ (D) — (C) — (B)
Emma와 Clara는 해변 도로를 따라 바다를 보면서 자전거를 탈 준비를 마침 - Emma는 Clara의 과거를 떠올리며 Clara의 침묵을 이해함 - Clara는 부상으로 수영의 꿈을 포기해야 했지만 더 성숙하고 강해짐 - Clara는 자전거 타기와 수영이 비슷하다고 말하며, 내년 여름에 Emma와 다시 올 것을 약속함

▶ **왜** 정답·오답? [정답률 70%]

(A): Emma와 Clara는 해변 도로를 따라 바다를 보면서 자전거를 탈 준비를 마쳤다.

⇒ Emma와 Clara가 자전거를 탈 준비를 마쳤으므로, 이후에는 목적지를 정하고 자전거 타기를 시작하는 내용이 이어질 것이다.

(B): Emma와 Clara는 목적지에 도착했다. Clara는 자전거 타기와 수영이 인생의 힘든 도전에서도 삶의 의미를 보여준다는 점에서 비슷하다고 말하며, 내년 여름에 Emma와 다시 올 것을 약속했다.

⇒ Emma와 Clara가 목적지에 도착했다는 내용이므로 (B)의 앞에는 자전거를 타는 과정이 필요하다. 그리고 둘은 내년 여름에 다시 자전거를 탈 것을 약속하고 있으므로 (B)가 글의 결말에 해당할 것이다.

(C): Clara는 과거에 부상으로 수영의 꿈을 포기해야 했지만, 고된 훈련과 회복 끝에 자전거 타기에 대한 열정을 발견하는 등 더 성숙하고 강해졌다.

⇒ Clara의 과거의 고난을 회상하는 부분으로, (C)의 앞에는 Clara의 과거를 떠올릴 만한 계기가 필요하다. 그리고 한 시간 동안 자전거를 탄 뒤 목적지를 발견하는 내용에서 끝나므로, 목적지에 도착한 내용이 이어질 것이다.

(D): Emma는 자전거를 타면서 멋진 경치에 흥분하여 Clara에게 말을 걸었지만, Clara는 자기 생각에 빠져서 답을 하지 않았고, Emma는 Clara의 과거를 떠올리며 그 침묵을 이해했다.

⇒ Emma와 Clara는 자전거를 타기 시작했으므로, (D)의 앞에는 자전거를 탈 준비를 하는 과정이 필요하다. 그리고 Emma는 Clara의 침묵의 의미를 이해한다는 내용에서 끝나므로, Clara가 극복한 고난에 관한 내용이 이어질 것이다.
▶ (A): Emma와 Clara는 해변 도로를 따라 바다를 보면서 자전거를 탈 준비를 마쳤다. → (D): Emma는 자전거를 타면서 멋진 경치에 흥분하여 Clara에게 말을 걸었지만, Clara는 자기 생각에 빠져서 답을 하지 않았고, Emma는 Clara의 과거를 떠올리며 그 침묵을 이해했다. → (C): Clara는 과거에 부상으로 수영의 꿈을 포기해야 했지만, 고된 훈련과 회복 끝에 자전거 타기에 대한 열정을 발견하는 등 더 성숙하고 강해졌다. → (B): Emma와 Clara는 목적지에 도착했다. Clara는 자전거 타기와 수영이 인생의 힘든 도전에서도 삶의 의미를 보여준다는 점에서 비슷하다고 말하며, 내년 여름에 Emma와 다시 올 것을 약속했다.
▶ 사건이 진행되는 순서는 ⑤ (D) – (C) – (B)임

류이레 | 연세대 의예과 2024년 입학·광주대동고 졸

43번은 내용만 따라가도 간단하게 답을 고를 수 있고 36, 37번 문제처럼 명시적 근거까지 체크해서 답의 쐐기를 박을 수도 있어. 이 문제에서는 (D)에 Emma, Clara가 자전거를 타고, 페달을 밟기 '시작'했다는 내용, (C)에 Clara의 수영선수로서의 과거, (B)에 Clara의 수영선수 시절에 대한 간략한 언급과 함께 도달지에 도달했다는 내용이 있잖아.

나는 시험장에서 이런 간단한 단서도 체크하면서 내가 고른 선택지에 확신을 갖고 남은 시간 동안 헷갈리는 문제를 고민해서 100점을 맞을 수 있었어!

Q 56 정답 ③

밑줄 친 (a)~(e) 중에서 가리키는 대상이 나머지 넷과 다른 것은?

① (a) I
= Clara
② (b) me
= Clara
③ (c) you
= Emma
④ (d) her
= Clara
⑤ (e) she
= Clara

왜 정답? [정답률 91%]

③ (c) you: Clara가 내년에도 함께 자전거를 타러 오겠다고 한 사람은 Emma를 가리킨다. ▶ Emma

왜 오답?

① (a) I : 고개를 끄덕이며 어서 자전거를 타고 싶다고 대답한 사람은 Clara이다.
▶ Clara

② (b) me : 수영과 자전거 타기에서 삶의 의미를 찾았다고 대답한 사람은 Clara이다.
▶ Clara

④ (d) her : 고통스러운 과거를 극복하며 더 성숙하고 강해진 사람은 Clara이다.
▶ Clara

⑤ (e) she : 과거의 비극을 이미 극복한 것으로 보이는 사람은 Clara이다.
▶ Clara

김아린 | 충남대 의예과 2024년 입학·대전한빛고 졸

43~45번 문제는 소재가 쉽고 글이 편하게 읽혀서 난 듣기 평가 도중에 푸는 것도 추천해. 이 문제를 풀 때는 글을 읽으면서 밑줄 친 (a)~(e) 밑에 가리키는 대상의 이름을 한 글자 정도만 적으면서 본인이 가장 알아보기 쉬운 방법으로 구분하면 금방 답을 찾을 수 있어! Emma는 E, Clara는 C라고 적으면 되겠지? 그리고 말하는 사람이 누구인지에 따라서 헷갈릴 수 있으니까, 큰따옴표가 있을 때는 말하는 사람이 누구인지도 꼼꼼하게 확인해보자!

Q 57 정답 ③

윗글에 관한 내용으로 적절하지 않은 것은?

① Emma와 Clara는 자전거 탈 준비를 일출 직후에 마쳤다.
Just after sunrise, they finished their preparations for the bicycle ride

② Clara는 자전거 타기와 수영이 꽤 비슷하다고 말했다.
Clara answered with a smile, "Quite similar, actually."

③ Clara는 올림픽 수영 경기에서 메달을 땄다.
she had to give up her dream of becoming an Olympic medalist in swimming

④ Emma와 Clara는 자전거를 타고 하얀 절벽 쪽으로 갔다.
Emma and Clara jumped on their bikes ~ where the beach road ended.

⑤ Emma는 Clara의 침묵의 의미를 이해했다.
Emma understood the meaning of her silence.

왜 정답? [정답률 91%]

③ Clara는 올림픽 수영 경기에서 메달을 따고 싶다는 꿈을 포기해야 했다. (she had to give up her dream of becoming an Olympic medalist in swimming)

왜 오답?

① Emma와 Clara는 자전거 탈 준비를 일출 직후에 마쳤다.
(Just after sunrise, they finished their preparations for the bicycle ride)

② Clara는 자전거 타기와 수영이 꽤 비슷하다고 말했다.
(Clara answered with a smile, "Quite similar, actually.")

④ Emma와 Clara는 자전거를 타고 하얀 절벽 쪽으로 갔다.
(Emma and Clara jumped on their bikes and started to pedal toward the white cliff where the beach road ended.)

⑤ Emma는 Clara의 침묵의 의미를 이해했다.
(Emma understood the meaning of her silence.)

조수근 | 순천향대 의예과 2024년 입학·성남 태원고 졸

많은 친구들이 장문을 급하게 읽다가 세부사항을 놓쳐서 실수를 하더라고. 가장 확실하고 안전한 방법은 43, 44번 문제와 동시에 45번 문제를 푸는 거야. 전체적인 흐름을 파악하는 동시에 세부사항도 같이 챙기는 거지. 만약 앞 문제들을 풀면서 지문을 다 읽었는데도 45번 문제를 풀 때 내용이 기억 안 나서 지문을 다시 읽으면 시간을 많이 낭비할 수밖에 없어.

Q 58~60 ⭐ 2등급 대비

＊선물을 되찾은 Ellen

(A) **When invited by her mother** / to go shopping after lunch, / 생략되지 않은 부사절 접속사 Ellen hesitantly replied, / "Sorry, Mom. // **I have an English essay assignment** / I need to finish." // 60번① Ellen은 끝내야 할 영어 과제가 있었음

어머니에게 초대되었을 때 / 점심 식사 후 쇼핑하러 가자고 / Ellen은 주저하며 대답했다 / "죄송해요, 엄마 // 영어 에세이 과제가 있어요 / 끝내야 할"이라고 //

Her mother persisted, / "Come on! // Your father's birthday is just around the corner, / and you wanted to buy his birthday present by yourself." //

그녀의 어머니는 고집했다 / "어서 가자 // 네 아빠 생일이 얼마 남지 않았는데 / 네가 직접 생일 선물을 사고 싶어 했잖아"라고 //

Ellen suddenly realized / that her father's birthday was just two days away. //

Ellen은 갑자기 깨달았다 / 아버지의 생일이 이틀밖에 남지 않았다는 것을 //

= Ellen
So (a) **she** altered her original plan / to do the assignment in 형용사적 용법(plan 수식) the library / and decided to go to the shopping mall / with her 명사적 용법(decided의 목적어) mother. // 58번 단서 1: 어머니와 쇼핑몰에 가기로 결정함

그래서 그녀는 원래 계획을 변경하고 / 도서관에서 과제를 하려던 / 쇼핑몰에 가기로 마음먹었다 / 어머니와 함께 //

＊(A) 문단 요약: Ellen이 어머니와 함께 아버지의 생일 선물을 사러 쇼핑몰에 가기로 했음

(B) Ellen wanted to get a strawberry smoothie in the cafe, / but it was sold out. // 58번 단서 2: Ellen이 카페에 도착함

Ellen은 카페에서 딸기 스무디를 마시고 싶었지만 / 그것은 매진된 상태였다 //

So she bought a yogurt smoothie / instead. //
60번② 카페에서 요거트 스무디를 샀음

그래서 요거트 스무디를 샀다 / 대신 //

The cafe was not very busy / for a Saturday afternoon, / and Ellen settled at a large table / to work on her assignment. //

카페는 그다지 붐비지 않았고 / 토요일 오후치고는 / Ellen은 큰 테이블에 자리를 잡았다 / 과제를 하기 위해 //

However, after a while, / a group of students came in, / and there weren't any large tables left. // 60번③ 한 무리의 학생이 카페에 들어왔음

하지만 잠시 후 / 한 무리의 학생들이 들어왔고 / 남아있는 큰 테이블이 더는 없었다 //

= Ellen
One of them came over to Ellen's table / and politely asked, / "Could (b) **you** possibly move / to that smaller table?" //

학생 중 한 명이 Ellen의 테이블로 와서 / 정중하게 물었다 / "당신이 옮겨 주실 수 있나요 / 저 작은 테이블로"라고 //

Ellen replied, / "It's okay. // I was just leaving anyway." //

Ellen은 대답했다 / "괜찮아요 // 어차피 나가려던 참이었거든요"라고 //

She hurriedly gathered her assignment / leaving the shoe bag behind / under the table. //

Ellen은 서둘러 과제를 챙겼다 / 신발 가방을 두고 / 테이블 밑에 //

*(B) 문단 요약: 카페에서 과제를 하다가 작은 테이블로 옮겨달라는 부탁을 받고 서둘러 나오면서 테이블 밑에 신발 가방을 두고 나옴　**58번** 단서 3: 어머니와 Ellen이 쇼핑몰에 도착함

(C) Upon arrival at the shopping center, / her mother inquired, / "Ellen, have you decided / what to buy / for his birthday present?" //

쇼핑 센터에 도착하자마자 / 어머니가 물었다 / "Ellen, 결정했니 / 무엇을 살지 / 아빠의 생일 선물로"라고 //

She quickly replied, / "(c) I would like to buy him / a pair of soccer shoes." //
　　　　　　　　　= Ellen　　　　　**60번 ④** Ellen의 아버지는 최근에 아침 축구 클럽에 가입했음

Ellen은 재빨리 대답했다 / "저는 그에게 사드리고 싶어요 / 축구화 한 켤레를"이라고 //

Ellen knew / that her father had joined the morning soccer club recently / and needed some new soccer shoes. //
　　　　　　　　　병렬 구조

Ellen은 알고 있었다 / 아버지가 최근에 아침 축구 클럽에 가입하여 / 새 축구화가 필요하다는 것을 //

She entered a shoe store / and selected a pair of red soccer shoes. //

그녀는 신발 가게에 들어가 / 빨간색 축구화 한 켤레를 골랐다 //

After buying the present, / she told her mother, / "Mom, now, I'm going to do my assignment in the cafe / while you are shopping." //

선물을 산 후 / 그녀는 어머니에게 말했다 / "엄마, 이제 저는 카페에서 과제를 할 거예요 / 엄마가 쇼핑하는 동안"이라고 //

*(C) 문단 요약: 쇼핑 센터에서 생일 선물로 축구화를 산 후 카페에 가서 과제를 하겠다고 말했음

(D) "It must be in the cafe," / Ellen suddenly exclaimed / when
　　　　　확신을 나타내는 조동사
(d) she realized / the gift for her father was missing / upon
　= Ellen　　　　　　　　**58번** 단서 4: 카페에서 나와 집에 돌아옴
returning home. //

"그게 분명 카페에 있을 거예요"라고 / Ellen은 갑자기 소리쳤다 / 그녀가 깨달았을 때 / 아버지를 위한 선물이 없어졌다는 것을 / 집에 돌아와 //

She felt so disheartened, / worrying it would be impossible /
　진주어　　　　　　　　　　　가주어
to find it. //

그녀는 너무 낙담하면서 / ~이 불가능할 것이라고 걱정했다 / 그것을 찾는 것이 //

"Why don't you call the cafe?" / suggested her mother. //

"카페에 전화해 보는 건 어떠니"라고 / 그녀의 어머니는 제안했다 //

When she phoned the cafe / and asked about the shoe bag, / the manager said / that she would check and let her know. //

그녀가 카페에 전화를 걸어 / 신발 가방에 관해 묻자 / 매니저는 말했다 / 확인해 보고 알려주겠다고 //　**60번 ⑤** Ellen은 카페에 전화를 걸었음

After a few minutes, / she called back and told Ellen / that
　　　　　　　　　　　told의 간접목적어와 직접목적어절
(e) she had just discovered it. //
　　　　　　　　　접속사
= the manager

몇 분 후 / 그녀는 다시 전화를 걸어 Ellen에게 말했다 / 자신이 방금 그것을 찾았다고 //

Ellen was so pleased / that the birthday gift had been found. //

Ellen은 매우 기뻐했다 / 생일 선물이 발견되어서 //

*(D) 문단 요약: 집에 돌아와서 생일 선물이 없어진 것을 발견하고 카페에 전화했고 나중에 그것을 찾았다고 하자 매우 기뻐했음

- hesitantly 머뭇거리며, 주저하며 · assignment ⓝ 과제
- persist ⓥ 집요하게 계속하다, 고집하다 · alter ⓥ 변경하다, 고치다
- settle ⓥ 자리를 잡다 · gather ⓥ 모으다 · inquire ⓥ 묻다
- exclaim ⓥ 소리치다, 외치다 · disheartened ⓐ 실망한
- discover ⓥ 찾다, 발견하다

(A) 점심 식사 후 쇼핑하러 가자는 어머니의 요청에 Ellen은 주저하며 "죄송해요, 엄마. 끝내야 할 영어 에세이 과제가 있어요."라고 대답했다. 그녀의 어머니는 "어서 가자! 네 아빠 생일이 얼마 남지 않았는데 네가 직접 생일 선물을 사고 싶어 했잖아!"라고 고집했다. Ellen은 갑자기 아버지의 생일이

이틀밖에 남지 않았다는 사실을 깨달았다. 그래서 그녀는 도서관에서 과제를 하려던 원래 계획을 변경하고 어머니와 함께 쇼핑몰에 가기로 마음먹었다. (C) 쇼핑 센터에 도착하자마자 어머니가 "Ellen, 아빠의 생일 선물로 무엇을 살지 결정했니?"라고 물었다. Ellen은 재빨리 "저는 축구화 한 켤레를 사드리고 싶어요."라고 대답했다. Ellen은 아버지가 최근에 아침 축구 클럽에 가입하여 새 축구화가 필요하다는 것을 알고 있었다. 그녀는 신발 가게에 들어가 빨간색 축구화 한 켤레를 골랐다. 선물을 산 후 어머니에게 "엄마, 이제 엄마가 쇼핑하는 동안 저는 카페에서 과제를 할 거예요."라고 말했다. (B) Ellen은 카페에서 딸기 스무디를 마시고 싶었지만 그것은 매진된 상태였다. 그래서 대신 요거트 스무디를 샀다. 카페는 토요일 오후치고는 그다지 붐비지 않았고, Ellen은 과제를 하기 위해 큰 테이블에 자리를 잡았다. 하지만 잠시 후 한 무리의 학생들이 들어왔고, 남아있는 큰 테이블이 더는 없었다. 학생 중 한 명이 Ellen의 테이블로 와서 정중하게 "당신이 저 작은 테이블로 옮겨 주실 수 있나요?"라고 물었다. Ellen은 "괜찮아요. 어차피 나가려던 참이었거든요."라고 대답했다. Ellen은 신발 가방을 테이블 밑에 두고 서둘러 과제를 챙겼다. (D) 그녀가 집에 돌아와 아버지를 위한 선물이 없어졌다는 사실을 깨닫자 Ellen은 갑자기 "그게 분명 카페에 있을 거예요."라고 소리쳤다. 그녀는 너무 낙담하면서 선물을 찾는 것이 불가능할 것이라고 걱정했다. 그녀의 어머니는 "카페에 전화해 보는 건 어떠니?"라고 제안했다. 그녀가 카페에 전화를 걸어 신발 가방에 관해 묻자, 매니저는 확인해 보고 알려주겠다고 말했다. 몇 분 후 그녀는 다시 전화를 걸어 Ellen에게 자신이 방금 신발 가방을 찾았다고 말했다. Ellen은 생일 선물을 찾았다는 사실에 매우 기뻐했다.

왜 2등급? 가리키는 대상을 찾는 문제에서 여성이 세 명(Ellen, Ellen의 어머니, 카페 매니저) 등장하여 헷갈릴 수 있고, 글을 전체적으로 읽으면서 사건을 구성하는 요소를 꼼꼼히 확인해야 하는 2등급 대비 문제이다.

Q 58 정답 ②

주어진 글 (A)에 이어질 내용을 순서에 맞게 배열한 것으로 가장 적절한 것은?

① (B) — (D) — (C) 카페에 가기 전에 축구화를 구입했으므로 (B)보다 (C)가 먼저 와야 함
② (C) — (B) — (D)
③ (C) — (D) — (B) (D)에서 집에 돌아오기 전에 카페에서 과제를 한 내용인 (B)가 와야 함
④ (D) — (B) — (C) 쇼핑 센터에서 선물을 사고, 카페에서 과제를 한 후 집에 돌아왔으므로
⑤ (D) — (C) — (B) (D)는 결말임

Ellen이 어머니와 함께 아버지의 생일 선물을 사러 쇼핑몰에 가기로 했다 – 생일 선물로 축구화를 산 후 카페에 가서 과제를 하겠다고 말했다 – 카페에서 요거트 스무디를 사서 과제를 했다 – 집에 돌아와 생일 선물이 없어진 것을 발견하고 카페에 전화했다

왜 정답·오답? [정답률 93%]

(A): Ellen은 영어 에세이 숙제가 있지만 원래 도서관에서 하려던 계획을 변경해서 어머니와 함께 아버지의 생일 선물을 사러 쇼핑몰에 가기로 했다.

➡ 쇼핑몰에 간 후에 어떤 일이 일어나는지에 대한 내용이 이어질 것이다.

(B): 카페에서 요거트 스무디를 사서 자리를 잡고 과제를 하다가 작은 테이블로 옮겨달라는 부탁을 받고 서둘러 나오면서 테이블 밑에 신발 가방을 두고 나왔다.

➡ 카페에 있다고 했으므로 이 앞에 카페에 들어간 내용이 먼저 나와야 한다.

(C): 쇼핑 센터에서 Ellen은 아버지의 생일 선물로 축구화 한 켤레를 산 후, 엄마가 쇼핑하는 동안 카페에서 과제를 하겠다고 말했다.

➡ 쇼핑몰에서 축구화를 산 뒤에 Ellen은 카페에서 과제를 하겠다고 말했으므로 카페에 가겠다고 처음 언급한 내용인 (C)가 (B) 앞에 와야 한다.

(D): 집에 돌아와서 생일 선물이 없어진 것을 발견하고 카페에 전화했고 매니저가 그것을 찾았다고 하자 매우 기뻐했다.

➡ 집에 와서 아버지의 생일 선물이 없어진 것을 발견했는데 카페에 전화했다고 했으므로 (B)에 이어지는 내용이다.
▶ (A) Ellen이 어머니와 함께 아버지의 생일 선물을 사러 쇼핑몰에 가기로 했다.
→ (C) 쇼핑 센터에서 생일 선물로 축구화를 산 후 카페에 가서 과제를 하겠다고 말했다. → (B) 카페에서 요거트 스무디를 사서 과제를 했다. → (D) 집에 돌아와서 생일 선물이 없어진 것을 발견하고 카페에 전화했다.
▶ 사건이 진행되는 순서는 ② (C) – (B) – (D)임

Q 59 정답 ⑤

밑줄 친 (a)~(e) 중에서 가리키는 대상이 나머지 넷과 다른 것은?
① (a) = Ellen   ② (b) = Ellen   ③ (c) = Ellen   ④ (d) = Ellen   ⑤ (e) = the manager

> 오H 정답 ?   [정답률 92%]
⑤ (e) she: Ellen에게 전화를 걸어 자신이 신발 가방을 찾았다고 말한 사람은 매니저이다. ▶ the manager

> 오H 오답 ?
① (a) she: 도서관에서 과제를 하려고 계획했던 사람은 Ellen이다. ▶ Ellen
② (b) you: 학생 중 한 명이 Ellen에게 다가와서 한 말이므로, 학생이 한 말에서 you는 Ellen이다. ▶ Ellen
③ (c) I: Ellen이 대답한 것이므로 I는 Ellen이다. ▶ Ellen
④ (d) she: Ellen이 아버지를 위한 선물이 없어졌다는 것을 깨닫고 소리를 지른 것이므로 she는 Ellen이다. ▶ Ellen

Q 60 정답 ②

윗글에 관한 내용으로 적절하지 <u>않은</u> 것은?
① Ellen은 끝내야 할 영어 과제가 있었다.
   I have an English essay assignment I need to finish.
② 카페에서는 요거트 스무디를 팔지 않았다.
   So she bought a yogurt smoothie instead.
③ 한 무리의 학생들이 카페에 들어왔다.
   a group of students came in
④ Ellen의 아버지는 최근에 아침 축구 클럽에 가입했다.
   her father had joined the morning soccer club recently
⑤ Ellen은 카페에 전화를 걸었다.
   she phoned the cafe

> 오H 정답 ?   [정답률 92%]
② 딸기 스무디가 매진되어 요거트 스무디를 대신 샀다. (So she bought a yogurt smoothie instead.)

> 오H 오답 ?
① Ellen은 끝내야 할 영어 과제가 있었다.
   (I have an English essay assignment I need to finish.)
③ 한 무리의 학생들이 카페에 들어왔다.
   (a group of students came in)
④ Ellen의 아버지는 최근에 아침 축구 클럽에 가입했다.
   (her father had joined the morning soccer club recently)
⑤ Ellen은 카페에 전화를 걸었다.
   (she phoned the cafe)

Q 61~63 ——————— ⭐ 2등급 대비

＊산에서의 하룻밤

(A) In July, / people in the city often escaped / to relax in the mountains. // 7월에 / 도시 사람들은 흔히 벗어났다 / 산에서 휴식하고자 //

Sean didn't yet know it, / but he was about to have the
                                      be about to-v: 막 ~하려는 참이다
experience of a lifetime. //
Sean은 아직 그것을 몰랐지만 / 막 일생의 경험을 하려는 참이었다 //

"When I look around, / all I see is the work / I haven't finished / and the bills / I haven't paid," / he complained over the phone /
                         앞에 목적격 관계대명사가 생략됨   63번 ① 친구 Alex에게 전화로 투덜거림
to his friend and doctor, Alex. //
"내가 주위를 둘러보니 / 보이는 것이라고는 온통 일과 / 내가 마치지 못한 / 납부 고지서뿐이야 / 내가 내지 않은"이라고 / 그는 전화로 투덜거렸다 / 친구이자 의사인 Alex에게 //

                                                                = Sean
Concerned about Sean, / he said, / "(a) You've been stressed / for weeks. // Come see me for medical treatment / if things don't improve." //
Sean이 걱정되어 / 그는 말했다 / "자네는 스트레스를 받았어 / 여러 주 동안 // 의학 치료를 받으러 내게 오게 / 상태가 나아지지 않으면"이라고 //

＊(A) 문단 요약: 스트레스를 받은 Sean이 의사이자 친구인 Alex에게 투덜거리자 Alex는 의학 치료를 받으러 자신에게 오라고 제안했음

        주절보다 앞선 시제를 나타내는 완료형 분사구문 ＊   부사적 용법(감정의 원인)
(B) Having hiked for several hours, / Sean was thrilled / to reach the top of Vincent Mountain. // 61번 단서 1: 정상에 도착함
몇 시간을 등산한 후에 / Sean은 짜릿함을 느꼈다 / Vincent 산 정상에 이르러 //

As Toby started to bark, / Sean turned around and found / him
                                          63번 ② Toby가 커다란 연못 쪽으로
running toward a large pond. //   뛰어가는 것을 봤음
Toby가 짖기 시작하자 / Sean은 돌아서서 보았다 / 녀석이 커다란 연못 쪽으로 뛰어가는 것을 //

"What a nice, quiet place," / Sean whispered to himself. //
"정말 멋지고 고요한 곳이군"이라고 / Sean은 머릿속으로 속삭였다 //

Among the trees, / he could ease the stress / of recent weeks. //
나무 사이에서 / 그는 스트레스를 덜 수 있었다 / 최근 몇 주간의 //

As night approached, / however, / the wind blew fiercely. //
밤이 다가오자 / 하지만 / 바람이 세차게 불었다 // 63번 ③ 밤이 되자 바람이 세차게 불었음

Sean became nervous. // Sean은 불안해졌다 //
                                        = Sean
Unable to sleep, / (b) he called to his companion, / "Come here, Boy!" //
앞에 being이 생략됨
잠을 이룰 수 없어 / 그는 자신의 동반자에게 소리쳤다 / "녀석아, 이리로 오렴!"하고 //

He held the dog close / in an effort / to ignore the fear / rushing
                                       형용사적 용법(an effort 수식)
in. // 그는 그 개를 꼭 안았다 / 노력에서 / 두려움을 무시하려는 / 밀려드는 //

＊(B) 문단 요약: 몇 시간의 등산 끝에 Sean과 Toby는 Vincent 산 정상에 이르렀고, 밤이 다가오자 두려움이 밀려들었음

(C) After what felt like the longest night / of Sean's life, / the sky finally turned a beautiful shade of pink, / and the warm sun shone around him. // 61번 단서 2: 정상에서 하룻밤을 보내고 다음 날이 됨
가장 긴 듯 느껴진 밤이 지나고 / Sean의 삶에서 / 하늘은 마침내 아름다운 분홍 색조로 변해 / 따뜻한 햇볕이 그의 주위에 비쳤다 //

He packed up his equipment, / enjoying his last moments / in the mountain air. // 그는 장비를 꾸렸다 / 마지막 순간을 즐기면서 / 산 공기 속에서 //

Finding Toby energetically running / next to the campsite, /
                        = Toby
Sean said, / "(c) You must be as excited as I am / after surviving
                                    확신의 조동사
a night like that!" //
Toby가 활기차게 뛰어다니는 모습을 보면서 / 야영지 옆에서 / Sean은 말했다 / "네 녀석도 나만큼 신이 나는 모양이구나 / 그런 밤을 버티고 나서"라고 //
                                      63번 ④ 기쁨을 안고 산에서 내려옴
Sean went down the mountain / with a renewed sense of joy, / and he exclaimed, / "My treatment worked like a charm!" //
Sean은 산에서 내려갔고 / 새로워진 기쁨의 느낌을 안고 / 탄성을 질렀다 / "내 치료가 계획대로 잘 진행되었어!"라고 //

＊(C) 문단 요약: 아름다운 아침이 찾아오자 Sean은 산에서 내려가며 자신의 치료가 계획대로 잘 진행되었다고 탄성을 질렀음

61번 단서 3: 의학 치료를 받으러 오라는 친구이자 의사의 제안에 대답함 = Sean

(D) Upon hearing this offer, / Sean replied, / "Thanks, / but (d) I know just the treatment / I need." //

이 제안을 듣자 / Sean은 답했다 / "고맙네만 / 나는 꼭 맞는 치료를 알고 있네 / 내게 필요한"이라고 //

63번 ⑥ 자신이 읽은 Vincent 산 등산에 관해 이야기했음

He told his friend / about the Vincent Mountain hike / he had read about. //

앞에 목적격 관계대명사가 생략됨

그는 친구에게 말했다 / Vincent 산 등산에 관해 / 자신이 읽었던 //

Alex anxiously warned, / "Even in the summer, / hiking can be dangerous. // Don't forget your safety checklist." //

Alex는 걱정스럽게 주의를 주었다 / "여름에조차 / 등산은 위험할 수 있네 // 안전 점검표를 잊지 말게"라고 //

= Sean
Following his friend's words, / (e) he added protective gear / to his camping equipment. //

친구의 말에 따라 / 그는 보호 장구를 추가했다 / 야영 장비에 //

Sean put on his hiking clothes / and tied up his boots. //

Sean은 등산복을 입고 / 등산화의 끈을 묶었다 //

He almost forgot his new hiking sticks / as he walked out the door / with his dog, Toby. //

61번 단서 4: Toby와 함께 산에 가려고 문을 나섰음

그는 새 등산용 지팡이를 거의 잊을 뻔했다 / 문을 나설 때 / 자기 개, Toby와 함께 //

★(D) 문단 요약: Sean은 거절한 후 등산복을 입고, 등산화를 신고 Toby와 함께 문을 나섰음

- be about to V 막 ~하려는 참이다
- bill ⓝ 계산서, 납부 고지서
- concerned ⓐ 걱정하는
- medical treatment 의학 치료
- bark ⓥ (개가) 짖다
- ease ⓥ 덜다, 완화하다
- fiercely ⓐⓓ 거세게, 사납게
- companion ⓝ 동반자, 동료
- pack up ~을 꾸리다
- equipment ⓝ 장비
- energetically ⓐⓓ 활기차게
- exclaim ⓥ 탄성을 지르다
- work like a charm (계획대로) 잘 진행되다
- upon V-ing ~하자마자
- anxiously ⓐⓓ 걱정스럽게
- gear ⓝ 장구, 장비

(A) 7월에 도시 사람들은 흔히 산에서 휴식하고자 벗어났다. Sean은 아직 그것을 몰랐지만, 막 일생의 경험을 하려는 참이었다. "내가 주위를 둘러보니, 보이는 것이라고는 온통 내가 마치지 못한 일과 내가 내지 않은 납부 고지서뿐이야."라고 Sean은 친구이자 의사인 Alex에게 전화로 투덜거렸다. Sean이 걱정되어, 그는 "자네는 여러 주 동안 스트레스를 받았어. 상태가 나아지지 않으면 의학 치료를 받으러 내게 오게."라고 말했다. (D) 이 제안을 듣자, Sean은 "고맙네만, 나는 내게 필요한 꼭 맞는 치료를 알고 있네."라고 답했다. 그는 친구에게 자신이 읽었던 Vincent 산 등산에 관해 말했다. Alex는 "여름에조차 등산은 위험할 수 있네. 안전 점검표를 잊지 말게."라고 걱정스럽게 주의를 주었다. 친구의 말에 따라, 그는 야영 장비에 보호 장구를 추가했다. Sean은 등산복을 입고 등산화의 끈을 묶었다. 그는 자기 개, Toby와 함께 문을 나설 때 새 등산용 지팡이를 거의 잊을 뻔했다. (B) 몇 시간을 등산한 후에, Sean은 Vincent 산 정상에 이르러 짜릿함을 느꼈다. Toby가 짖기 시작하자, Sean은 돌아서서 녀석이 커다란 연못 쪽으로 뛰어가는 것을 보았다. "정말 멋지고 고요한 곳이군."이라고 Sean은 머릿속으로 속삭였다. 나무 사이에서, 그는 최근 몇 주간의 스트레스를 덜 수 있었다. 하지만 밤이 다가오자, 바람이 세차게 불었다. Sean은 불안해졌다. 잠을 이룰 수 없어 그는 "녀석아, 이리로 오렴!"하고 자신의 동반자에게 소리쳤다. 그는 밀려드는 두려움을 무시하려는 노력에서 그 개를 꼭 안았다. (C) Sean의 삶에서 가장 긴 듯 느껴진 밤이 지나고, 하늘은 마침내 아름다운 분홍 색조로 변해, 따뜻한 햇볕이 그의 주위에 비쳤다. 그는 산 공기 속에서 마지막 순간을 즐기면서 장비를 꾸렸다. Toby가 활기차게 야영지 옆에서 뛰어다니는 모습을 보면서, Sean은 "그런 밤을 버티고 나서 네 녀석도 나만큼 신이 나는 모양이구나!"라고 말했다. Sean은 새로워진 기쁨의 느낌을 안고 산에서 내려갔고, "내 치료가 계획대로 잘 진행되었어!"라고 탄성을 질렀다.

왜? 2등급? 가리키는 대상을 찾는 문제에서 선택지가 모두 다른 단어로 이루어져 있어 문맥을 정확히 파악해야 하고, 상황이 어떻게 변화하는지 꼼꼼히 확인해야 하는 2등급 대비 문제이다.

Q 61 정답 ④

주어진 글 (A)에 이어질 내용을 순서에 맞게 배열한 것으로 가장 적절한 것은?

① (B) — (D) — (C) 등산을 하러 집을 나서는 (D)가 (B)보다 앞에 나와야 함
② (C) — (B) — (D) ─ (D)의 this offer가 가리키는 것이 (A)에 등장함
③ (C) — (D) — (B) ─ Sean이 의사이자 친구인 Alex에게 투덜거리자 Alex는 치료를 받으러 자신에게 오라고 제안했음 - Sean은 거절한 후 등산복을 입고 Toby와 함께 문을 나섰음 - Sean과 Toby는 산 정상에 이르렀고, 밤이 다가오자 두려움이 밀려들었음 - 아침이 찾아오자 Sean은 산에서 내려가며 치료가 계획대로 잘 진행되었다고 탄성을 질렀음
④ (D) — (B) — (C)
⑤ (D) — (C) — (B) ─ (B)에서 밤이 다가왔고, (C)에서 밤이 지나갔음

왜 정답·오답? [정답률 94%]

(A): 여러 주 동안 스트레스를 받은 Sean이 의사이자 친구인 Alex에게 전화를 걸어 투덜거리자 Alex는 의학 치료를 받으러 자신에게 오라고 제안했다.

➡ Alex의 제안에 대한 Sean의 대답이 이어질 텐데, 의학 치료가 일생의 경험은 아닐 거라고 예상할 수 있으므로, Sean은 아마도 Alex의 제안을 거절할 것이다.

(B): 몇 시간의 등산 끝에 Sean과 Toby는 Vincent 산 정상에 이르렀고, 밤이 다가오고 바람이 세차게 불자 두려움이 밀려들었다.

➡ (B)의 앞에는 등산을 시작한다거나 등산을 하겠다는 Vincent의 대답이 필요하고, 밤이 다가와 두려움이 밀려들었다고 했으므로 뒤에는 정상에서 어떤 사건이 벌어졌다거나 무사히 밤을 보내고 아침이 되었다는 내용이 이어질 것이다.

(C): 밤이 지나고 아름다운 아침이 찾아왔다. Sean은 새로워진 기쁨의 느낌을 안고 산에서 내려가며 자신의 치료가 계획대로 잘 진행되었다고 탄성을 질렀다.

➡ 밤이 지났다고 했으므로 앞에는 밤이 되어 바람이 세차게 불었다는 (B)가 필요하다. 그리고 Sean이 계획한 치료가 계획대로 잘 진행되었다는 내용이므로 (C)가 글의 결말에 해당할 것이다.

(D): Sean은 이 제안(this offer)을 거절한 후 등산복을 입고, 등산화를 신고 Toby와 함께 문을 나섰다.

➡ this offer가 가리키는 것이, (A)에서 Alex가 말한, 자신에게 와서 의학 치료를 받으라는 제안이므로 (A) 뒤에 (D)가 와야 한다. 뒤에는 등산을 하러 문을 나선 후 정상에 이르렀다는 흐름이 적절하므로 (B)가 와야 한다.

▶ (A) 스트레스를 받은 Sean이 의사이자 친구인 Alex에게 전화를 걸어 투덜거리자 Alex는 의학 치료를 받으러 자신에게 오라고 제안했다.
→ (D): Sean은 거절한 후 등산복을 입고, 등산화를 신고 Toby와 함께 문을 나섰다.
→ (B): 몇 시간의 등산 끝에 Sean과 Toby는 Vincent 산 정상에 이르렀고, 밤이 다가오고 바람이 세차게 불자 두려움이 밀려들었다.
→ (C): 밤이 지나고 아름다운 아침이 찾아오자 Sean은 새로워진 기쁨의 느낌을 안고 산에서 내려가며 자신의 치료가 계획대로 잘 진행되었다고 탄성을 질렀다.
▶ 사건이 진행되는 순서는 ④ (D) – (B) – (C)임

Q 62 정답 ③

밑줄 친 (a)~(e) 중에서 가리키는 대상이 나머지 넷과 다른 것은?

① (a)= Sean   ② (b)= Sean   ③(c) = Toby   ④ (d)= Sean   ⑤ (e)= Sean

오배 정답? [정답률 91%]

③ (c) You: Sean이 Toby에게 하는 말이므로 You는 Toby를 가리킨다. ▶ Toby

오배 오답?

① (a) You: Alex가 Sean에게 한 말이므로 You는 Sean을 가리킨다. ▶ Sean

② (b) he: Toby에게 이리로 오라고 소리친 사람은 Sean이다. ▶ Sean

④ (d) I: Sean이 자신에게 필요한 꼭 맞는 치료를 안다고 말하는 것이므로 I는
   Sean을 가리킨다. ▶ Sean

⑤ (e) he: Alex의 말에 따라 야영 장비에 보호 장구를 추가한 사람은 Sean이다.
   ▶ Sean

Q 어휘 Review 정답 ——— 문제편 p. 375

01 수확	11 pick out	21 pounding
02 비참한	12 manage to-v	22 spray
03 친구, 동행	13 put aside	23 terribly
04 급히, 서둘러	14 in return	24 gathered
05 침착한, 잔잔한	15 be scheduled to	25 isolation
06 dorm	16 semester	26 aspects
07 initiate	17 daring	27 rearrange
08 stir	18 grab	28 ease
09 puzzled	19 alter	29 disclosed
10 prompt	20 notification	30 accordingly

Q 63 정답 ③

윗글에 관한 내용으로 적절하지 않은 것은?

① Sean은 친구 Alex에게 어려움을 토로했다.
   he complained over the phone to his friend and doctor, Alex
② Toby가 큰 연못으로 달려갔다.
   found him running toward a large pond
③ 밤이 되자 바람이 잦아들었다.
   As night approached, however, the wind blew fiercely.
④ Sean은 산을 내려오며 기쁨을 느꼈다.
   Sean went down the mountain with a renewed sense of joy
⑤ Sean은 Vincent Mountain 하이킹에 대해 읽은 적이 있다.
   about the Vincent Mountain hike he had read about

오배 정답? [정답률 82%]

③ 밤이 다가오자 바람이 세차게 불었다. (As night approached, however, the
   wind blew fiercely.)

오배 오답?

① Sean은 친구 Alex에게 어려움을 토로했다.
   (he complained over the phone to his friend and doctor, Alex)
② Toby가 큰 연못으로 달려가는 것을 봤다.
   (found him running toward a large pond)
④ Sean은 새로워진 기쁨의 느낌을 안고 산에서 내려갔다.
   (Sean went down the mountain with a renewed sense of joy)
⑤ Sean은 자신이 읽은 Vincent Mountain 하이킹에 대해 이야기했다.
   (about the Vincent Mountain hike he had read about)

——— 어법 특강 ———

* **주의해야 할 분사구문**

– 분사구문의 주어와 주절의 주어가 다른 경우, 분사구문에 의미상 주어를 표시해
   준다.

• It being very cold, we made a fire.
   (날씨가 추워서 우리는 불을 지폈다.)

– 「with+목적어+분사」는 '~한[된] 채'라는 뜻으로, 목적어와 분사의 관계가 능동
   이면 현재분사를, 수동이면 과거분사를 쓴다.

• She sat there, with tears running down her cheeks.
   (그녀는 뺨에 눈물을 흘리면서 그곳에 앉아 있었다.)

• He sat in the chair with his legs crossed.
   (그는 다리를 꼬고 의자에 앉아 있었다.)

– 수동태가 분사구문이 될 때 앞에 being이나 having been이 생략되어 형용사나
   과거분사로 시작한다.

• (Being) Tired with hard work, he fell asleep with TV on.
   (과로로 피곤해서 그는 TV를 켜놓은 채 잠이 들었다.)

선택지의 일부분이 틀리는
경우에 유의하자!

1회 01 정답 ④ *곤충의 사회성과 인간의 사회성 간의 차이

Compared to other primates, / we are freakishly social and cooperative; /
다른 영장류들과 비교해서 / 우리는 이상할 정도로 사회적이고 협력적이다 /

not only 부정어가 문두로 오면서 주어와 동사가 도치됨
not only do we sit obediently on airplanes, / we labor collectively
병렬 구조 (동사)
to build houses, / specialize in different skills, / and live lives /
that are driven by our specific role in the group. //
우리는 비행기에 순종적으로 앉아있을 뿐만 아니라 / 우리는 집을 짓기 위해 집단으로
노동하고 / 다른 기술에 전문화되고 / 삶을 산다 / 집단 내에서의 특정한 역할로 이끌린
to pull off의 의미상 주어
This is quite a trick for a primate to pull off, / considering our
most recent evolutionary history. // 단서1 인간은 다른 영장류와 달리 매우 사회적이고
협력적임
이는 영장류가 해내기에는 꽤 어려운 것이다 / 우리의 가장 최근 진화 역사를 고려한다면 //

Hive life is (literally) a no-brainer for ants: /
군집 생활은 (말 그대로) 개미들에게는 쉽게 할 수 있는 일이다 /
동명사구 주어
They share the same genes, / so sacrificing for the common good
단수동사
/ is not really a sacrifice / — if I'm an ant, / the common good
simply is my good. // 단서2 사회적 곤충인 개미에게는 공익이 곧 사익임
그들은 같은 유전자를 공유한다 / 그래서 공익을 위해 희생하는 것은 / 그다지 희생이 아니다 /
내가 만약 개미라면 / 공익은 그저 내 이익이다 //
과거분사구 (apes 수식)
Humans, though, are apes, / evolved to cooperate / only in a
limited way / with close relatives and perhaps fellow tribe
members, / 단서3 하지만 인간은 긴밀한 관계를 맺은 주변과만 협력하도록 진화됨
하지만 인간은 유인원이다 / 협력하도록 진화된 / 한정된 방식으로만 / 가까운 친척이나 아마
동료 부족 구성원들과 /
앞에 being이 생략된 분사구문
acutely alert to the dangers / of being manipulated, misled, or
exploited by others. //
위험에 예민하게 경각심을 느끼는 / 타인에 의해 조종되고 오도되고 착취될 //
병렬 구조   분사구문
And yet we march in parades, / sit in obedient rows reciting lessons,
/ conform to social norms, /
하지만 우리는 보조를 맞춰 걷고 / 수업을 낭독하며 순종적으로 줄을 맞춰 앉고 / 사회적
규범에 순응하고 /
주격 관계대명사
and sometimes sacrifice our lives / for the common good / with
an enthusiasm that would put a soldier ant to shame. //
때로는 우리의 삶을 희생한다 / 공익을 위해 / 병정개미들을 부끄럽게 만들 열정으로 //
동명사구 주어
Trying to hammer a square primate peg / into a circular social
insect hole / is bound to be difficult. //
사각형의 영장류 말뚝을 망치질하는 것을 시도하는 것은 / 둥근 사회적 곤충 구멍에 / 어려울
수밖에 없다 //
단수 동사

• primate ⑪ 영장류   • cooperative ⓐ 협력적인
• obediently ⓐⓓ 순종적으로   • pull off ~을 해내다
• common good 공익   • ape ⑪ 유인원   • fellow ⑪ 동료
• acutely ⓐⓓ 예민하게   • alert ⓐ 경각심을 느끼는
• manipulate ⓥ 조종하다   • mislead ⓥ 오도하다
• exploit ⓥ 착취하다   • march ⓥ 행진하다   • row ⑪ 줄, 열
• recite ⓥ 낭독하다   • conform to ~을 따르다
• hammer ⓥ 망치로 두드리다   • peg ⑪ 말뚝
• downgrade ⓥ 훼손시키다   • communal ⓐ 공동의, 공용의

다른 영장류들과 비교해서, 우리는 이상할 정도로 사회적이고 협력적이다.
우리는 비행기에 순종적으로 앉아있을 뿐만 아니라, 우리는 집을 짓기 위
해 집단으로 노동하고, 다른 기술에 전문화되고, 집단 내에서의 특정한 역
할로 이끌린 삶을 산다. 이는 우리의 가장 최근 진화 역사를 고려한다면,
영장류가 해내기에는 꽤 어려운 것이다. 군집 생활은 (말 그대로) 개미들에
게는 쉽게 할 수 있는 일이다. 그들은 같은 유전자를 공유하기 때문에, 공
익을 위해 희생하는 것은 그다지 희생이 아니다. 내가 만약 개미라면, 공익

은 그저 내 이익이다. 하지만 인간은 가까운 친척이나 아마 동료 부족 구성
원들과 한정된 방식으로만 협력하도록 진화된 유인원이며, 타인에 의해 조
종되고 오도되고 착취될 위험에 예민하게 경각심을 느낀다. 하지만 우리는
보조를 맞춰 걷고, 수업을 낭독하며 순종적으로 줄을 맞춰 앉고, 사회적 규
범에 순응하고, 때로는 공익을 위해 병정개미들을 부끄럽게 만들 열정으로
우리의 삶을 희생한다. 둥근 사회적 곤충 구멍에 사각형의 영장류 말뚝을
망치질하는 것을 시도하는 것은 어려울 수밖에 없다.

다음 글에서 밑줄 친 부분이 의미하는 바로 가장 적절한 것은? [4점]

① downgrade humans' superiority over apes and ants 유인원과
유인원과 개미에 대한 인간의 우월함을 훼손시키는 것   개미 간의 사회성 차이를 설명했을 뿐임
② enforce the collaboration between apes and social insects
유인원과 사회적 곤충들 간의 협력을 강화하는 것   두 종 사이의 협력을 강화하는 내용은 아님
③ manipulate hive insects into adopting ape-like
characteristics 반대되는 내용임
유인원과 같은 특징을 채택하도록 군집 곤충을 조종하는 것
④ suppress our traits as apes in order to pursue communal
benefits 인간이 곤충처럼 사회성을 발휘하는 것이 어렵다는 내용임
공익을 추구하기 위해 우리의 유인원으로서의 특징을 억누르는 것
⑤ maximize apes' physical capabilities in contributing to the
common good 신체적 능력에 관한 언급은 없음
공익에 기여하는 유인원의 신체적 능력을 최대화하는 것

│ 문제 풀이 순서 │   [정답률 55%]

1st 첫 문장과 밑줄 친 부분이 포함된 문장을 읽고, 글의 내용을 예상한다.

첫 문장	다른 영장류들과 비교해서, 우리는 이상할 정도로 사회적이고 협력적이다.
밑줄 친 부분이 포함된 문장	둥근 사회적 곤충 구멍에 사각형의 영장류 말뚝을 망치질하는 것을 시도하는 것은 어려울 수밖에 없다.

➡ 일반적인 영장류들과 다른 사회적인 인간의 특성을 설명하는 글이다. 이를
사회적이지 않은 영장류(사각형의 말뚝)가 사회적인 곤충(둥근 구멍)의 특성에
맞게 행동하는 것으로 묘사하고 있다. 따라서 밑줄 친 부분은 곤충의 특징을 따르는
인간의 특징에 해당할 것이다.

2nd 글의 나머지 부분을 읽고, 밑줄 친 부분의 의미를 파악한다.

인간의 협력적인 측면은 가까운 관계에만 국한되도록 진화했기 때문에 공익보다는
사익 추구를 강조한 반면, 개미의 협력적인 측면은 공익을 위해 사익을 희생할
정도이다. 즉, 영장류가 추구하는 사회성과 개미가 추구하는 사회성이 서로 다르다는
것이 중심 내용이다.

➡ 이를 바탕으로 밑줄 친 부분의 의미를 파악하면 ④ '공익을 추구하기 위해 우리의
유인원으로서의 특징을 억누르는 것'이다.

│ 선택지 분석 │

① **downgrade humans' superiority over apes and ants**
유인원과 개미에 대한 인간의 우월함을 훼손시키는 것
유인원과 개미 간의 사회성 차이를 설명했을 뿐, 우월함을 설명한 내용은 아니다.

② **enforce the collaboration between apes and social insects**
유인원과 사회적 곤충들 간의 협력을 강화하는 것
유인원과 곤충 각각을 설명했을 뿐, 두 종 사이의 협력을 강화한다는 내용은 아니다.

③ **manipulate hive insects into adopting ape-like characteristics**
유인원과 같은 특징을 채택하도록 군집 곤충을 조종하는 것
글과 반대의 내용이다.

④ **suppress our traits as apes in order to pursue communal
benefits** 공익을 추구하기 위해 우리의 유인원으로서의 특징을 억누르는 것
인간이 곤충처럼 공익을 더 추구하며 사회성을 발휘하는 것이 어렵다는 내용이다.

⑤ **maximize apes' physical capabilities in contributing to the
common good** 공익에 기여하는 유인원의 신체적 능력을 최대화하는 것
유인원은 공익보다는 한정된 관계를 추구하는 종이라고 설명하고 있으며, 신체적
능력에 관한 언급은 없다.

모의고사 **1회**

1회 02 정답 ① *바로크 미술의 특징

By the start of the 16th century, / the Renaissance movement
had given birth / to the Protestant Reformation / and an era of
profound religious change. //
16세기 시작 무렵에 / 르네상스 운동은 일으켰다 / 종교 개혁과 / 심오한 종교적 변화의 시대를 //
The art of this period / reflected the disruption / caused by this
shift. // **단서1** 종교적 변화에 의해 야기된 혼란을 반영한 이 시기의 예술이 바로크 미술
이 시기의 예술은 / 혼란을 반영했다 / 이러한 변화에 의해 야기된 //

Appropriately named the Baroque, / meaning irregular or
distorted, /
바로크라고 적절하게 이름 붙여진 / 불규칙적인 혹은 왜곡된 의미하는 / **단서2** 바로크 미술의 특징을 설명하기 시작함
European painting in the 16th century / largely focused on
capturing / motion, drama, action, and powerful emotion. //
16세기 유럽의 화법은 / 포착하는 데 주로 초점을 두었다 / 움직임, 극적임, 행동, 그리고
강력한 감정을 //

Painters employed the strong visual tools / of dramatic
composition, intense contrast of light and dark, and emotionally
provocative subject matter / to stir up feelings of disruption. //
화가들은 강력한 시각적 도구들을 사용했다 / 극적인 구도, 강렬한 명암 대비, 그리고
감정적으로 자극하는 소재라는 / 혼란의 감정을 불러일으키기 위해 //

Religious subjects were often portrayed / in this era / through
new dramatic visual language, / a contrast / to the reverential
portrayal / of religious figures / in earlier traditions. //
종교적인 주제들은 종종 묘사되었다 / 이 시대에서 / 새로운 극적인 시각적 언어를 통해 / 차이
/ 경건한 묘사와 / 종교적 인물들에 대한 / 이전의 전통에서의 //

In order to capture the social disruption / surrounding
Christianity and the Roman Catholic Church, /
사회적 혼란을 포착하기 위해 / 기독교와 로마 가톨릭 교회를 둘러싼 /

many artists abandoned / old standards of visual perfection /
from the Classical and Renaissance periods / in their portrayal
of religious figures. //
많은 예술가들이 버렸다 / 시각적인 완벽이라는 오래된 기준을 / 고전주의와 르네상스
시대로부터의 / 종교적 인물들에 대한 자신들의 묘사에 있어 //

- era ⓝ 시대, 시기 • profound ⓐ 심각한, 심오한
- reflect ⓥ 반영하다 • disruption ⓝ 혼란, 분열 • shift ⓝ 변화
- irregular ⓐ 불규칙한, 고르지 못한 • distort ⓥ 왜곡하다
- capture ⓥ 사로잡다, 포착하다 • composition ⓝ 구도, 구성 요소
- intense ⓐ 강렬한, 극심한 • contrast ⓝ 대조, 차이
- provocative ⓐ 도발적인 • subject ⓝ 대상, 주제
- matter ⓝ 문제, 사안 • stir up ~을 일으키다
- portray ⓥ 묘사하다, 그리다 • figure ⓝ 인물, 사람
- abandon ⓥ 버리다, 유기하다 • standard ⓝ 기준, 표준
- portrayal ⓝ 묘사

16세기 시작 무렵에 르네상스 운동은 종교 개혁과 심오한 종교적 변화의
시대를 일으켰다. 이 시기의 예술은 이러한 변화에 의해 야기된 혼란을
반영했다. 불규칙적인 혹은 왜곡된을 의미하는, 바로크라고 적절하게 이름
붙여진, 16세기 유럽의 화법은 움직임, 극적임, 행동, 그리고 강력한 감정을
포착하는 데 주로 초점을 두었다. 화가들은 혼란의 감정을 불러일으키기 위해
극적인 구도, 강력한 명암 대비, 그리고 감정적으로 자극하는 소재라는 강력한
시각적 도구들을 사용했다. 종교적인 주제들은 새로운 극적인 시각적 언어를
통해 이 시대에서 종종 묘사되었는데, 이는 이전의 전통에서의 종교적 인물들에
대한 경건한 묘사와 대조를 이루었다. 기독교와 로마 가톨릭 교회를 둘러싼
사회적 혼란을 포착하기 위해 많은 예술가들이 종교적 인물들에 대한 자신들의
묘사에 있어 고전주의와 르네상스 시대로부터의 시각적인 완벽이라는 오래된
기준을 버렸다.

다음 글의 주제로 가장 적절한 것은?

① characteristics of Baroque paintings caused by religious disruption
   종교적 혼란에 의해 야기된 바로크 미술의 특징 ← 종교적 변화에 의한 혼란을 반영했음
② impacts of the Baroque on the development of visual perfectionism
   바로크가 시각적 완벽주의의 발달에 미친 영향 ← 시각적 완벽이라는 오래된 기준을 버렸음
③ efforts of Baroque painters to imitate the Renaissance style
   르네상스 스타일을 모방하려는 바로크 화가들의 노력 ← 르네상스 시대의 기준을 버렸음
④ roles of Baroque artists in stabilizing the disrupted society
   혼란에 빠진 사회를 안정화하는 데 있어, 바로크 예술가들의 역할 ← 혼란을 안정시켰다는 언급은 없음
⑤ reasons of idealizing religious figures in Baroque paintings
   바로크 미술에서 종교적 인물을 이상화한 이유 ← 종교적 인물들을 경건하게 묘사한 것은 이전의 전통임

왜 정답? [정답률 67%]

16세기 초에 르네상스 운동은 종교 개혁과 심오한 종교적 변화의 시대를
일으켰는데, 이러한 변화에 의해 야기된 혼란을 바로크 미술이 반영했다고 하면서,
바로크 미술의 특징을 구체적으로 설명하는 글이므로 정답은 ① '종교적 혼란에
의해 야기된 바로크 미술의 특징'이다.

[꿀팁] 강력한 시각적 도구를 사용했다는 것 등이 특징임

왜 오답?

②, ③ 바로크 예술가들은 바로크 미술 이전의 고전주의와 르네상스 시대에
추구되었던 시각적인 완벽이라는 오래된 기준을 버렸다.
④ 종교적 변화로 인한 혼란을 반영한 16세기 초의 예술은 '불규칙적인',
'왜곡된'을 의미하는 '바로크'라고 적절하게 이름 붙여졌다고 했으므로
안정화와는 거리가 멀다.
⑤ 바로크 예술가들은 종교적 인물들을 묘사함에 있어 경건함이나 시각적인
완벽이라는 기준을 버렸다.

1회 03 정답 ② *사업 윤리가 본질적으로 직면한 어려움

Business ethics was born in scandal. //
사업 윤리는 스캔들 속에서 태어났다 //

It seems to regenerate itself / with each succeeding wave of
scandal. //
그것은 다시 태어나는 것처럼 보인다 / 매번 새로운 스캔들이 발생할 때마다 //

And, there are two problems here. // **단서1** 사업 윤리에 두 가지 문제가 있음
그리고, 여기에는 두 가지 문제가 있다 //

단서2 사업 윤리의 첫 번째 문제(사업을 사회의 독립된 기관으로 볼 여유가 없음)
The first is / that our world is so interconnected / that we can
no longer afford / to see business as a separate institution in
society, / subject to its own moral code. //
첫 번째 문제는 ~이다 / 우리의 세계가 너무 상호 연결되어 있어서 / 우리에게 더 이상 여유가
없다는 것 / 사업을 사회의 독립된 기관으로 볼 / 그 자체의 도덕적 기준에 따르는 //

Business must be thoroughly situated in society. //
사업은 철저히 사회에 위치해야 한다 //

This means / that we can no longer accept / the now rather
commonplace narrative about businesspeople / being economic
profit-maximizers and little else. //
이는 의미한다 / 우리가 더 이상 받아들일 수 없다는 것을 / 이제는 꽤 흔한 사업가들에 대한
서사를 / 경제적 이익을 극대화하는 존재라는 //

Business is a deeply human institution set in our societies / and
interconnected all over the world. //
사업은 우리의 사회에 깊게 뿌리를 두고 있는 인간적 제도이다 / 그리고 전 세계적으로 상호
연결된 //

단서3 사업 윤리의 두 번째 문제(사업 윤리가 사업이 도덕적으로 의심스러운 존재로서 시작된다는 전제를 벗어나지 못함)
The second problem is / that business ethics, / by being reborn in
scandal, / never escapes the presumption / that business starts
off / by being morally questionable. //
두 번째 문제는 ~이다 / 사업 윤리가 / 스캔들 속에서 다시 태어남으로써 / 전제를 벗어나지
못한다는 것 / 사업이 시작된다는 / 도덕적으로 의심스러운 존재로서 //

It never seems to get any credit / for the good / it brings into the
world, / only questions about the bad. //
사업은 신뢰를 얻지 못하는 것처럼 보인다 / 선한 면에 대한 / 그것이 세상에 가져오는 / 오직
나쁜 점에 대한 질문만 //

In fact, / capitalism may well be the greatest system / of social
cooperation / that we have ever invented. //
목적격 관계대명사
사실 / 자본주의는 가장 위대한 시스템일 수 있다 / 사회 협력의 / 우리가 지금까지 발명한 //
= if it is the greatest system ~ invented
But, if it is, / then it must stand the critical test / of our best
thinkers, / if for no other reason than / to make it better. //
하지만, 만약 그렇다면 / 자본주의는 반드시 비판적 검증을 거쳐야 한다 / 우리 최고의
사상가들의 / 어떤 이유라도 / 그것을 더 좋게 만들기 위해서는 //
핵심 주어   목적어절을 이끄는 접속사
Simply assuming / that capitalism is either unquestionably
morally good / or unquestionably morally problematic / violates
both scholarly and practical norms. //
단순히 가정하는 것은 / 자본주의가 의심의 여지 없이 도덕적으로 선하거나 / 의심의 여지
없이 도덕적으로 문제가 있다고 / 학문적 및 실용적 기준을 모두 위반한다 //

- ethics ⓝ 윤리   · regenerate ⓥ 재생되다, 다시 태어나다
- succeeding ⓐ 계속되는, 다음의
- interconnected ⓐ 상호 연락[연결]된   · separate ⓐ 분리된
- thoroughly ⓐ 철저히   · situated ⓐ 위치해 있는
- profit ⓝ 이익   · presumption ⓝ 전제
- questionable ⓐ 의심스러운   · cooperation ⓝ 협력
- scholarly ⓐ 학문적인   · practical ⓐ 실용적인   · obstacle ⓝ 장애물

사업 윤리는 스캔들 속에서 태어났다. 그것은 매번 새로운 스캔들이 발생할
때마다 다시 태어나는 것처럼 보인다. 여기에는 두 가지 문제가 있다. 첫
번째 문제는 우리의 세계가 너무 상호 연결되어 있어서 사업을 사회의 독립된
기관으로 보고, 그 자체의 도덕적 기준에 따라 다룰 여유가 더 이상 없다는
것이다. 사업은 사회에 철저히 위치해야 한다. 이는 우리가 더 이상 사업가들이
경제적 이익을 극대화하는 존재라는 이제는 꽤 흔한 서사를 받아들일 수 없음을
의미한다. 사업은 우리의 사회에 뿌리를 두고 있으며, 전 세계적으로 상호
연결된 깊은 인간적 제도이다. 두 번째 문제는 사업 윤리가 스캔들 속에서 다시
태어남으로써 사업이 본래 도덕적으로 의심스러운 존재라는 전제를 벗어나지
못한다는 것이다. 사업은 세상에 가져오는 선한 면에 대한 신뢰를 얻지 못하고
오직 나쁜 점에 대한 질문만 받는 것처럼 보인다. 사실, 자본주의는 우리가
지금까지 발명한 사회 협력의 가장 위대한 시스템일 수 있다. 하지만 그렇다면,
자본주의는 반드시 우리 최고의 사상가들의 비판적 검증을 거쳐야 하며, 그
이유가 무엇이든 간에 그것을 더 좋게 만들기 위해서이다. 자본주의가 의심의
여지없이 도덕적으로 선하거나 의심의 여지없이 도덕적으로 문제가 있다고
단순히 가정하는 것은 학문적 및 실용적 기준을 모두 위반하는 것이다.

다음 글의 제목으로 가장 적절한 것을 고르시오. [3점]

① Forget Scandals, Let's Innovate!
  스캔들은 잊어라. 혁신하자!   스캔들을 잊고 혁신하는 내용이 아니라 관련 문제를 다룬 글임
② Innate Challenges of Business Ethics
  사업 윤리의 고유한 도전   사업 윤리가 스캔들과 관련하여 직면하는 두 가지 주요 문제를 다루고 있음
③ Unavoidable Obstacles of Human Institutions   인간 제도의 피할 수 없는
  인간 제도의 피할 수 없는 장애물 문제점이나 장애에 대해 다룬 것이 아니라 사업 윤리의 문제점을 다룬 글임
④ Business Ethics: An Emerging Scholarly Norm
  사업 윤리: 새로운 학문적 규범의 출현   사업 윤리를 새로운 학문적 규범의 출현으로 설명하는 글이 아님
⑤ Business Ethics as A Magic Bullet for Success
  성공을 위한 만능 해결책으로서의 사업 윤리   성공을 위한 만능 해결책으로서의 사업 윤리를 다룬 글이 아님

〉왜 정답? [정답률 57%]

전반부	· 사업 윤리의 첫 번째 문제: 우리의 세계가 너무 상호 연결되어 있어서 사업을 사회의 독립된 기관으로 보고, 그 자체의 도덕적 기준에 따라 다룰 수가 없음 [단서1]
후반부	· 사업 윤리의 두 번째 문제: 사업이 본래 도덕적으로 의심스러운 존재라는 전제를 벗어나지 못하고 오직 나쁜 점에 대한 질문만 받는 것 [단서2]

▶ 사업 윤리가 스캔들과 관련하여 직면한 두 가지 문제점에 대해 다루고 있는
글이므로 ② '사업 윤리의 고유한 도전'이 글의 제목으로 가장 적절하다.

〉왜 오답?

① 스캔들을 잊고 혁신하자는 내용이 아니라 관련 문제를 다룬 글이다.
③ 인간 제도의 피할 수 없는 문제점이나 장애에 대해 다룬 것이 아니라 사업 윤리의
  문제점을 다룬 글이다.   주의
④ 사업 윤리를 새로운 학문적 규범의 출현으로 설명하는 글이 아니다.
⑤ 성공을 위한 만능 해결책으로서의 사업 윤리를 다룬 글이 아니다.

1회 04 정답 ④ ＊유아의 새로운 이미지에 대한 끌림 ──
[단서1] 새로운 것을 보는 것에 대한 유아의 선호가 무척 강함
Infants' preference / for looking at new things / is so strong / that
                                          so+형용사/부사+that S V: 너무 ~해서 …하다
psychologists began to realize /
유아의 선호는 / 새로운 것을 보는 것에 대한 / 너무 강해서 / 심리학자들은 깨닫기 시작했다 /
that they could use it / as a test / of infants' visual discrimination,
/ and even their *memory*. //   = infants' preference for looking at new things
그들이 그것을 사용할 수 있다는 것을 / 테스트로 / 유아들의 시각적 식별과 심지어 그들의
'기억'에 관한 //
Could an infant tell the difference / between two similar
images? //
유아가 차이를 알 수 있을까 / 두 개의 비슷한 이미지 간의 //
Between two similar shades / of the same color? //
비슷한 두 색조 간의 / 같은 색의 // 주절의 시제보다 앞선 때를 나타내는 동명사의 완료형
Could an infant recall / having seen something / an hour, a day,
a week ago? //
유아가 떠올릴 수 있을까 / 무언가를 봤다는 것을 / 한 시간 전, 하루 전, 일주일 전에 //
The inbuilt attraction to novel images / held the answer. //
새로운 이미지로의 내재된 끌림이 / 해답을 쥐었다 //
If the infant's gaze lingered, / it suggested / that the infant could
tell / that a similar image was nonetheless different / in some
way. // [단서2] 새로운 것을 보려는 선호가 강한 유아가 계속 쳐다봤다는 것은,
                비슷하지만 그래도 다르다는 것을 유아가 안다는 것을 암시함(시각적 식별 테스트)
만약 유아의 시선이 계속 머물렀다면 / 그것은 암시했다 / 그 유아가 알 수 있다는 것을 /
비슷한 이미지가 그래도 다르다는 것을 / 어떤 식으로든 //
If the infant, / after a week / without seeing an image, / didn't
look at it much / when it was shown again, /
만일 그 유아가 / 일주일 후에 / 이미지를 보지 않고 / 그것을 별로 보지 않았다면 / 그것이
다시 보였을 때 / 《확신》의 조동사   주절의 시제보다 앞선 때를 나타내는
the infant must be able at some level to *remember* / having seen 동명사의 완료형
it / the week before. // [단서3] 새로운 것을 보려는 선호가 강한 유아가 별로 보지 않는 것은
                              이전에 그것을 본 것을 유아가 기억한다는 것을 의미함(기억 테스트)
그 유아는 어느 정도 '기억'할 수 있음에 틀림없다 / 그것을 보았던 것을 / 일주일 전에 //
In most cases, / the results revealed / that infants were more
cognitively capable / earlier / than had been previously
assumed. //
대부분 경우에 / 그 결과는 드러냈다 / 유아가 더 인지적으로 유능했다는 것을 / 더 일찍 /
이전에 추정되었던 것보다 // 주어   동사   주격 보어
The visual novelty drive became, / indeed, / one of the most
powerful tools / in psychologists' toolkit, / unlocking a host of
deeper insights / into the capacities of the infant mind. // '다수의, 많은'
시각적으로 새로운 것에 대한 욕구는 되었다 / 실로 / 가장 강력한 도구 중 하나가 /
심리학자의 도구 모음 중 / 많은 더 깊은 통찰력을 드러내며 / 유아의 정신 능력에 대한 //

- infant ⓝ 유아, 아기   · psychologist ⓝ 심리학자
- realize ⓥ 깨닫다, 알아차리다, (목표 등을) 실현[달성]하다
- visual ⓐ 시각의   · discrimination ⓝ 차별, 식별력
- shade ⓝ 색조, 미묘한 차이   · gaze ⓝ 응시
- linger ⓥ 오래 머물다, 오랜 시간을 보내다
- nonetheless ⓐ 그렇기는 하지만, 그럼에도
- reveal ⓥ 드러내다, 밝히다   · cognitively ⓐ 인식적으로
- capable ⓐ (능력·특질상) ~을 할 수 있는, 유능한
- previously ⓐ 이전에, 과거에   · assume ⓥ 추정하다
- novelty ⓝ 새로움, 참신함   · drive ⓝ 충동, 욕구
- toolkit ⓝ 연장 세트, 도구[수단]들   · unlock ⓥ 열다, (비밀 등을) 드러내다
- insight ⓝ 통찰력, 이해, 간파
- capacity ⓝ (~을 이해하거나 할 수 있는) 능력, 용량
- distortion ⓝ 왜곡, 찌그러짐   · infancy ⓝ 유아기

유아는 새로운 것을 보려는 선호가 너무 강해서 심리학자들은 그것을 유아들의
시각적 식별과 심지어 그들의 '기억'에 관한 테스트로 사용할 수 있다는 것을
깨닫기 시작했다. 유아가 두 개의 비슷한 이미지 간의 차이를 알 수 있을까? 같은
색의 비슷한 두 색조 간의 차이는? 한 시간 전, 하루 전, 일주일 전에 무언가를
봤다는 것을 유아가 떠올릴 수 있을까? **새로운 이미지로의 내재된 끌림**이 해답을

쥐었다. 만약 유아의 시선이 계속 머물렀다면, 그것은 그 유아가 비슷한 이미지가 그래도 어떤 식으로든 다르다는 것을 알 수 있다는 것을 암시했다. 만일 그 유아가, 이미지를 보지 않고 일주일 후에, 그 이미지가 다시 보였을 때 그것을 별로 보지 않았다면, 그 유아는 일주일 전에 그것을 보았던 것을 어느 정도 '기억할' 수 있음에 틀림없다. 대부분 경우에 그 결과는 이전에 추정되었던 것보다 유아가 더 일찍 인지적으로 더 유능했다는 것을 드러냈다. 실로, 시각적으로 새로운 것에 대한 욕구는, 유아의 정신 능력에 대한 많은 더 깊은 통찰력을 드러내며, 심리학자의 도구 모음 중 가장 강력한 도구 중 하나가 되었다.

다음 빈칸에 들어갈 말로 가장 적절한 것을 고르시오.

① Memory distortion in infancy 자신이 봤던 것을 기억하는 유아의 기억력을 이야기함
유아기의 기억 왜곡
② Undeveloped vision of newborns 비슷하지만 다른 것을 찾아냄
신생아의 발달되지 않은 시력
③ The preference for social interaction 유아가 사회적 상호 작용을 선호한다는
사회적 상호 작용에 대한 선호 언급은 없음
④ The inbuilt attraction to novel images 새로운 것을 보려는 강한 선호
새로운 이미지로의 내재된 끌림
⑤ Infants' communication skills with parents 부모와의 의사소통에 대한
유아의 부모와의 의사소통 기술 내용이 아님

왜 정답? [정답률 50%]

새로운 것을 보려는 유아의 강한 선호가 유아의 시각적 식별과 기억에 관한 테스트에 이용된다는 첫 문장 이후로, 새로운 것을 보려는 유아의 선호를 통해 어떻게 유아의 시각적 식별과 기억을 테스트하는지에 대한 구체적인 예시가 이어지므로 해답을 쥔 것은 ④ '새로운 이미지로의 내재된 끌림'이라고 하는 것이 적절하다.

> ① 새로운 것을 보려는 선호가 강한 유아가 계속 본다면 비슷하지만 다르다는 것을 유아가 안다는 것을 의미함 **꿀팁**
> ② 유아가 별로 보지 않는다면 전에 봤음을 기억한다는 의미임

왜 오답?

① 유아가 일주일 전에 봤던 이미지를 정확히 기억한다는 것을 보여주는 예시이다.
② 유아가 비슷하지만 그래도 차이가 있는 이미지를 구별한다는 것을 보여주는 예시이다.
③, ⑤ 유아가 사회적 상호 작용을 선호한다거나 부모와의 의사소통 기술을 갖고 있다는 언급은 없다.

1회 05 정답 ⑤ *무지함을 아는 것에서 시작하는 배움*

단수 주어 / 단수 동사
The quest for knowledge / in the material world / is a never-ending pursuit, /
지식 탐구는 / 물질적인 세계에서 / 끝없는 추구이지만 /

but the quest does not mean / that a thoroughly schooled person
목적어절 접속사의 병렬 구조
is an educated person / or that an educated person is a wise person. //
그 탐구가 의미하지는 않는다 / 온전하게 학교 교육을 받은 사람이 배운 사람이라거나 / 배운 사람이 현명한 사람임을 //

단서 1 우리가 무지하다는 것을 모르는 것에 의해 자주 눈이 멀

We are too often blinded / by our ignorance of our ignorance, / and our pursuit of knowledge / is no guarantee of wisdom. //
우리는 너무 자주 눈이 멀고 / 우리의 무지함에 대한 우리의 무지에 의해 / 우리의 지식 추구가 / 현명함을 보장하는 것은 아니다 //

the+형용사: 복수 보통명사
Hence, / we are prone to becoming the blind / leading the blind /
그래서 / 우리는 앞 못 보는 사람들이 되기 쉽다 / 앞 못 보는 사람들을 이끄는 /
주어
because our overemphasis on competition / in nearly everything
동사 목적어 목적격 보어
/ makes looking good more important / than being good. //
경쟁에 대한 우리의 과도한 강조는 / 거의 모든 것에서 / 훌륭해 보이는 것을 더 중요하게 만들기 때문에 / 훌륭한 것보다 //

주어
The resultant fear / of being thought a fool and criticized /
동사
therefore is one of greatest enemies / of true learning. //
그 결과로 생기는 두려움은 / 바보라고 여겨져 비판받는 것에 대한 / 그래서 가장 큰 적 중 하나이다 / 진정한 배움의 //

Although our ignorance is undeniably vast, / it is from the
it is ~ that 강조구문
vastness of this selfsame ignorance / that our sense of wonder
grows. // **단서 2** 광대한 무지함으로부터 경이감이 발전함
우리의 무지함이 부인할 수 없을 정도로 크지만 / 이 똑같은 무지함의 광대함으로부터 / 우리의 경이감이 자란다 //

But, / when we do not know / we are ignorant, / we do not
부사적 용법(enough 수식)
know enough / to even question, / let alone investigate, / our
ignorance. // **단서 3** 우리가 무지하다는 것을 모르면 우리의 무지함에 대해 의문을 제기하지도 못함
그런데 / 우리가 모를 때 / 우리가 무지하다는 것을 / 우리는 충분히 알지 못한다 / 의문을 제기할 만큼 / 조사하는 것은 말할 것도 없이 / 우리의 무지함에 대해 //

No one can teach another person / anything. //
아무도 다른 사람에게 가르칠 수 없다 / 그 어떤 것도 //
주어
동사 주격 보어
All / one can do / with and for someone else / is to facilitate
learning / by helping the person / to discover the wonder of
helping의 목적어와 목적격 보어
their ignorance. //
전부는 / 한 사람이 할 수 있는 / 다른 누군가와 함께 그리고 그 사람을 위해서 / 배움을 촉진하는 것이다 / 그 사람을 도움으로써 / 자신의 무지함의 경이로움을 발견하도록 //

- quest ⓝ 탐구, 탐색　　• pursuit ⓝ 추구, (원하는 것을) 좇음
- thoroughly ⓐⓓ 온전하게　　• school ⓥ 교육하다
- blind ⓥ 눈이 멀게 만들다　　• ignorance ⓝ 무지, 무식
- guarantee ⓝ 보장　　• hence ⓐⓓ 이런 이유로
- overemphasis ⓝ 과도한 강조　　• competition ⓝ 경쟁
- resultant ⓐ 그 결과로 생기는　　• criticize ⓥ 비판[비난]하다
- undeniably ⓐⓓ 부인할 수 없을 정도로　　• vast ⓐ 광대한
- wonder ⓝ 경탄, 경이(감)　　• let alone ~은 고사하고
- investigate ⓥ 조사하다　　• facilitate ⓥ 촉진하다

물질적인 세계에서 지식 탐구는 끝없는 추구이지만 그 탐구가 온전하게 학교 교육을 받은 사람이 배운 사람이라거나 배운 사람이 현명한 사람임을 의미하지는 않는다. 우리의 무지함에 대한 우리의 무지에 의해 우리는 너무 자주 눈이 멀고 우리의 지식 추구가 현명함을 보장하는 것은 아니다. 그래서 거의 모든 것에서 경쟁에 대한 우리의 과도한 강조는 훌륭해 보이는 것을 훌륭한 것보다 더 중요하게 만들기 때문에 우리는 앞 못 보는 사람들을 이끄는 앞 못 보는 사람들이 되기 쉽다. 그 결과로 생기는, 바보라고 여겨져 비판받는 것에 대한 두려움은, 그래서 진정한 배움의 가장 큰 적 중 하나이다. 우리의 무지함이 부인할 수 없을 정도로 크지만, 우리의 경이감이 자라는 것은 다름 아닌 이 똑같은 무지함의 광대함으로부터이다. 그런데, 우리가 무지하다는 것을 우리가 모를 때 우리의 무지함에 대해 조사하는 것은 말할 것도 없이 의문을 제기할 만큼 충분히 알지 못한다. 아무도 다른 사람에게 그 어떤 것도 가르칠 수 없다. 우리가 다른 누군가와 함께 그리고 그 사람을 위해서 할 수 있는 전부는 그 사람이 **자신의 무지함의 경이로움을 발견하도록** 도움으로써 배움을 촉진하는 것이다.

다음 빈칸에 들어갈 말로 가장 적절한 것을 고르시오.

① find their role in teamwork 협동 작업에서의 각자의 역할에 대한 내용이 아님
협동 작업에서 자신의 역할을 찾도록
② learn from others' successes and failures another person, someone
다른 사람들의 성공과 실패에서 배우도록 else로 만든 오답
③ make the most of technology for learning '무지함'이 핵심 소재임
학습을 위해 기술을 최대한 이용하도록
④ obtain knowledge from wonderful experts 남에게서 배울 수는 없음
훌륭한 전문가들로부터 지식을 얻도록
⑤ discover the wonder of their ignorance 무지하다는 것조차 알지 못하는 게
자신의 무지함의 경이로움을 발견하도록 문제임

| 문제 풀이 순서 | [정답률 66%]

1st 먼저 빈칸 문장의 앞뒤 내용을 확인한다.

> 아무도 다른 사람에게 어떤 것도 가르칠 수 없다. 한 사람이 다른 누군가와 함께 그리고 그 사람을 위해 할 수 있는 전부는 그 사람이 _____ 도움으로써 배움을 촉진하는 것이다.

→ 배움은 다른 사람의 가르침으로부터 얻는 것이 아니다. → '온전하게 학교 교육을
첫 문장의 내용
받은 사람이 배운 사람인 것은 아니다.'와 연결됨 **단서**
빈칸을 채우려면, 다른 사람의 배움을 촉진하기 위해 우리가 할 수 있는 것이 무엇인지 글에서 찾아야 한다. **발상**

2nd 글의 나머지 부분을 읽고, 타인의 배움을 촉진하기 위해 우리가 할 수 있는 것을 찾는다.

> - 우리는 우리가 무지하다는 것을 모르는 것에 의해 너무 자주 눈이 먼다. **단서 1**
> - 우리의 무지함은 광대하지만, 이 광대한 무지함으로부터 우리의 경이감이 자란다. **단서 2**
> - 우리가 무지하다는 것을 우리가 모르면, 우리는 우리의 무지함에 대해 조사는커녕 의문을 제기하지도 못한다. **단서 3**

➡ 우리의 무지함으로부터 우리의 경이감이 자라지만, 우리는 우리가 무지하다는 것조차 모른다. ➡ 우리가 무지하다는 것을 알게 해야 함
  ▶ 다른 사람의 배움을 촉진하려면 그 사람이 ⑤ '자신의 무지함의 경이로움을 발견하도록' 도와야 한다.

| 선택지 분석 |

① **find their role in teamwork** 협동 작업에서 자신의 역할을 찾도록
다른 사람을 돕는 방법에 대해 이야기하는 것은 맞지만, 협동 작업에서 역할을 제대로 수행하도록 돕는 것은 아니다.

② **learn from others' successes and failures** 다른 사람들의 성공과 실패에서 배우도록
자신이 무지하다는 것을 깨닫는 것으로부터 배움이 시작된다는 내용이라고 할 수 있다.

③ **make the most of technology for learning** 학습을 위해 기술을 최대한 이용하도록
기술, technology에 대한 언급은 없다.

④ **obtain knowledge from wonderful experts** 훌륭한 전문가들로부터 지식을 얻도록
학교 교육을 받았다고 해서 배운 사람인 것은 아니고, 아무도 다른 사람에게 그 어떤 것도 가르칠 수 없다고 했다.

⑤ **discover the wonder of their ignorance** 자신의 무지함의 경이로움을 발견하도록
자신이 무지하다는 것을 모르면 그 무지함에 대해 조사는커녕 의문을 제기할 수도 없다. 그러므로 무지하다는 것을 발견하도록 도와야 한다.

1회 06 정답 ④ ＊사람의 유형이 관계에 미치는 영향 ──────

단서 1 파트너 사이의 균형과 조화는 파트너에 대한 초기 매력과 관심의 요인임
Although a balance or harmony between partners clearly develops / over time / in a relationship, / it is also a factor / in initial attraction and interest / in a partner. //
파트너 사이의 균형이나 조화는 분명히 발전하지만 / 시간이 지남에 따라 / 관계에서 / 그것은 요인이기도 하다 / 초기 매력과 관심의 / 파트너에 대한 //

That is, / to the extent / that two people share / similar verbal and nonverbal habits / in a first meeting, / they will be more comfortable with one another. //
즉 / 정도까지 / 두 사람이 공유하는 / 비슷한 언어적 그리고 비언어적 습관을 / 첫 만남에서 / 그들은 서로 더 편안할 것이다 //

For example, / fast-paced individuals / talk and move quickly and are more expressive, / whereas slow-paced individuals have a different tempo / and are less expressive. //
예를 들어 / 속도가 빠른 사람들은 / 빠르게 말을 하고 움직이며 더 표현력이 있다 / 속도가 느린 사람들은 다른 속도를 갖고 / 표현력이 덜한 반면 //

Initial interactions / between people / at opposite ends of such a continuum / may be more difficult / than those between similar types. //   = initial interactions
초기 상호 작용은 / 사람들 간의 / 이러한 연속체의 반대쪽 끝에 있는 / 더 어려울 수 있다 / 유사한 유형 간의 그것들보다 //

In the case of contrasting styles, / individuals may be less interested / in pursuing a relationship / than if they were similar / in interaction styles. // **단서 2** 대조적인 유형의 사람들은, 유형이 유사한 경우보다, 관계를 발전시키는 데 관심이 적을 수 있음
대조적인 유형의 경우 / 사람들은 관심이 적을 수 있다 / 관계를 추구하는 것에 / 그들이 유사한 경우보다 / 상호 작용 유형에 있어서 //

복수 주어
Individuals with similar styles, / however, / are more comfortable **복수 동사①**
/ and find / that they just seem to "click" with one another. // **복수 동사②**
비슷한 유형의 사람들은 / 그러나 / 더 편안하고 / 느낀다 / 그들이 딱 서로 '즉시 마음이 통하는' 것 같다는 것을 //

Thus, / **behavioral coordination** may provide a selection filter / for the initiation of a relationship. //
따라서 / 행동의 조화는 선택 필터를 제공할 수 있다 / 관계의 시작을 위한 //

- **initial** ⓐ 처음의 · **attraction** ⓝ 매력 · **extent** ⓝ 정도, 크기
- **verbal** ⓐ 언어의 · **nonverbal** ⓐ 비언어의
- **expressive** ⓐ 나타내는 · **continuum** ⓝ 연속체
- **contrasting** ⓐ 대조적인 · **pursue** ⓥ 추구하다, 계속하다
- **interaction** ⓝ 상호 작용 · **coordination** ⓝ 조화, 합동
- **selection** ⓝ 선발, 선택 · **deficit** ⓝ 부족
- **adaptability** ⓝ 적응성, 순응성 · **negotiation** ⓝ 협상
- **unconditional** ⓐ 무조건적인 · **acceptance** ⓝ 수용

파트너 사이의 균형이나 조화는 관계에서 시간이 지남에 따라 분명히 발전하지만, 그것은 파트너에 대한 초기 매력과 관심의 요인이기도 하다. 즉, 두 사람이 첫 만남에서 비슷한 언어적 그리고 비언어적 습관을 공유하는 정도까지 그들은 서로 더 편안할 것이다. 예를 들어, 속도가 빠른 사람들은 빠르게 말을 하고 움직이며 더 표현력이 있는 반면, 속도가 느린 사람들은 다른 속도를 갖고 표현력이 덜하다. 이러한 연속체의 반대쪽 끝에 있는 사람들 간의 초기 상호 작용은 유사한 유형 간의 그것들보다 더 어려울 수 있다. 대조적인 유형의 경우 사람들은 그들이 상호 작용 유형에 있어서 유사한 경우보다 관계를 추구하는 것에 관심이 적을 수 있다. 그러나 비슷한 유형의 사람들은 더 편안하고 그들이 딱 서로 '즉시 마음이 통하는' 것 같다는 것을 느낀다. 따라서 **행동의 조화**는 관계의 시작을 위한 선택 필터를 제공할 수 있다.

다음 빈칸에 들어갈 말로 가장 적절한 것을 고르시오.
① information deficit 정보가 충분한지 부족한지가 변수인 것이 아님
  정보 부족
② cultural adaptability 문화적으로 적응할 수 있는지 여부에 대한 내용이 아님
  문화적 적응성
③ meaning negotiation '협상'과 관련된 언급은 없음
  의미 협상
④ behavioral coordination 습관이 비슷한지 여부가 영향을 미침
  행동의 조화
⑤ unconditional acceptance 대조적인 유형인 경우를 설명했음
  무조건적인 수용

모의고사 1회

왜 정답? [정답률 61%]

> - 파트너 사이의 균형이나 조화는 파트너에 대한 초기 매력과 관심의 요인이다. **단서 1**
> - 대조적인 유형인 경우에는, 유사한 유형인 경우보다, 관계를 추구하는 데 관심이 더 적을 수 있다. **단서 2**

➡ 파트너 사이의 균형이나 조화, 즉 사람들의 유형이 대조적인지 혹은 유사한지가 관계의 추구, 관계의 시작에 영향을 미칠 수 있다는 내용이다.
  ▶ '파트너 사이의 균형이나 조화'를 의미하는 가장 적절한 말은 ④ '행동의 조화'이다.

왜 오답?
① '첫 만남'이라는 상황에서 연상되는 오답이다. **주의**
② 서로 다른 문화의 사람들이 서로의 문화에 적응할 수 있는지 여부가 관계에 영향을 미친다는 내용이 아니다.
③ verbal, nonverbal 등의 어휘로 '의미'를 연상할 수는 있지만, 의미 협상과 관련된 내용은 없다.
⑤ 대조적인 유형의 경우에는 사람들이 관계를 추구하는 데 관심이 더 적을 수 있다고 했으므로, '무조건적인 수용'은 글의 내용에 맞지 않는다.

1회 07 정답 ④ *주장과 설득

"National forests need more roads / like farmers need more drought." //
"국립 숲에는 도로가 더 필요하다 / 농부가 가뭄을 더 필요로 하는 것처럼" //

지각동사+목적어+목적격 보어(동사원형)　　주격 관계대명사
We heard somebody say this / who was trying to persuade
목적어절을 이끄는 접속사
an audience / that more roads would be bad / for our national
forests. // 단서 1 더 많은 도로가 국립 숲에 해로울 수 있다는 것을 설득하려고 했던 누군가가
국립 숲에는 도로가 더 필요하다는 말을 한 것을 들었음
우리는 누군가 이 말을 한 것을 들었다 / 청중에게 설득하려고 했던 / 더 많은 도로가
해로울 수 있다는 것을 / 우리 국립 숲에 //

(A) An argument attempts / to prove or support a conclusion. //
주장은 시도한다 / 결론을 증명하거나 지지하려고 // 단서 2 (C)의 마지막에 언급한 주장에 대한
내용이 이어짐

문장의 주어로 복수 취급
When you attempt to persuade someone, / you attempt to win
him or her / to your point of view; / trying to persuade and
trying to argue / are logically distinct enterprises. //
누군가를 설득하려고 할 때 / 당신은 그 사람을 이기려고 시도한다 / 당신의 관점으로 /
설득하려는 것과 주장을 하려는 것은 / 논리적으로 다른 활동이다 //

True, / when you want to persuade somebody of something, /
you might use an argument. //
물론 / 누군가에게 무언가를 설득하고 싶을 때 / 주장을 사용할 수도 있다 //
단서 3 (A)의 마지막에 설득하고 싶을 때 주장을 사용한다는 것과 연결되는 반대 내용

부분 부정
(B) But not all arguments attempt to persuade, / and many
attempts to persuade / do not involve arguments. //
그러나 모든 주장이 설득을 시도하는 것은 아니다 / 그리고 많은 설득 시도가 / 주장을
포함하지 않는다 //

앞 문장(giving ~ people)을 부연 설명하는 절을 이끄는 관계대명사
In fact, / giving an argument / is often one of the least effective
methods / of persuading people / — which, of course, is / why
so few advertisers bother with arguments. //
사실 / 주장을 제시하는 것은 / 가장 효과적이지 않은 방법 중 하나인 경우가 많다 / 사람들을
설득하는 / 물론 이는 / 광고주들이 주장을 잘 하지 않는 이유이다 //

People notoriously are persuaded / by the weakest of
arguments / and sometimes are undisturbed / by even quite
good arguments. //
사람들은 잘 알려져 있듯이 설득된다 / 가장 약한 주장에 의해 / 때로는 개의치 않는다 / 꽤
좋은 주장에 대해서도 //

주격 관계대명사
(C) The remark, / however, / is not an argument; / it's just a
statement / that portrays road building in the forests in a bad
light. // 단서 4 '그 발언(주어진 글에서 언급한 내용)'은 숲 속 도로 건설을 나쁘게 묘사한 진술일 뿐
주장이 아님
그 발언은 / 그러나 / 주장이 아니다 / 단지 진술일 뿐이다 / 숲 속 도로 건설을 나쁘게 묘사한 //

Now, / some writers define an argument / as an attempt / to
persuade somebody of something. //
지금 / 어떤 작가들은 주장을 정의한다 / 시도로 / 누군가에게 무언가를 설득하려는 //

This is not correct. // 이는 올바르지 않다 //

- persuade ⓥ 설득하다　　• argument ⓝ 주장
- logically ⓐⓓ 논리적으로　　• distinct ⓐ 뚜렷이 다른
- involve ⓥ 포함하다
- undisturbed ⓐ (마음이) 흔들리지 않는, 개의치 않는
- remark ⓝ 발언　　• portray ⓥ 묘사하다　　• define ⓥ 정의하다

"국립 숲에는 농부가 가뭄을 더 필요로 하는 것처럼 도로가 더 필요하다. (국립 숲에는 농부가 가뭄을 필요로 하지 않는 것처럼 도로가 필요 없다)" 우리는 더 많은 도로가 국립 숲에 해로울 수 있다는 것을 청중에게 설득하려고 했던 누군가가 이 말을 한 것을 들었다. (C) 그러나 그 발언은 주장도 아니고, 단지 숲 속 도로 건설을 나쁘게 묘사한 진술일 뿐이다. 지금, 어떤 작가들은 주장을 누군가에게 무언가를 설득하려는 시도로 정의한다. 이는 올바르지 않다. (A) 주장은 결론을 증명하거나 지지하려는 시도이다. 누군가를 설득하려고 할 때, 그 사람을 자신의 관점으로 이끌려는 것이고, 설득하려는 것과 주장을 하려는 것은 논리적으로 다른 활동이다. 물론 누군가에게 무언가를 설득하고 싶을 때 주장을 사용할 수도 있다. (B) 모든 주장이 설득을 시도하는 것은 아니며, 많은

설득 시도가 주장을 포함하지 않는다. 사실, 주장을 제시하는 것은 사람들을 설득하는 가장 효과적이지 않은 방법 중 하나인 경우가 많고, 이는 물론 광고주들이 주장을 잘 하지 않는 이유이기도 하다. 사람들은 잘 알려져 있듯이 가장 약한 주장에도 설득당하고, 때로는 꽤 좋은 주장에 대해서도 전혀 개의치 않는 경우가 많다.

주어진 글 다음에 이어질 글의 순서로 가장 적절한 것을 고르시오. [3점]

① (A) — (C) — (B) (A)는 주장에 대한 문장으로 시작하는데 주어진 글에 관련 내용이 없음

② (B) — (A) — (C) 주어진 글 바로 뒤에는 (C), 즉 숲 속 도로 건설을 나쁘게 묘사한 진술이 '그 발언'이라고 지칭하는 내용이 이어져야 함

③ (B) — (C) — (A) 더 많은 도로가 국립 숲에 해로울 수 있다는 것을 설득하려고 했던 누군가가 국립 숲에는 도로가 더 필요하다는 말을 한 것을 들었음 -

④ (C) — (A) — (B) 주장을 누군가를 설득하는 시도로 정의하는 것으로 정의함 - 설득과 주장은 다른 활동인데, 물론 설득할 때 주장을 제시할 수도 있음

⑤ (C) — (B) — (A) - 주장을 제시하는 게 설득하는 가장 효과적이지 않은 방법 중 하나임
(A)에서 설득할 때 주장을 사용할 수도 있다고 한 뒤, 반대 내용을 But으로 (B)에 이어져야 함

| 문제 풀이 순서 |　[정답률 59%]

1st　각 문단의 내용을 파악하고, 글의 논리적인 순서를 추론한다.

주어진 글: "국립 숲에는 농부가 가뭄을 필요로 하지 않는 것처럼 도로가 필요 없다." 우리는 더 많은 도로가 국립 숲에 해로울 수 있다는 것을 청중에게 설득하려고 했던 누군가가 이 말을 한 것을 들었다.

⇒ 더 많은 도로가 숲에 해로울 수 있다는 것을 청중에게 설득하려는 말을 들었다고 했다. 단서

주어진 글 뒤: 들은 말에 대한 감상이나 반응 등 그에 대한 부연 설명이 이어질 것이다. 발상

(A) 주장은 결론을 증명하거나 지지하려는 시도이다. 누군가를 설득하려고 할 때, 그 사람을 자신의 관점으로 이끌려는 것이고, 설득하려는 것과 주장을 하려는 것은 논리적으로 다른 활동이다. 물론 누군가에게 무언가를 설득하고 싶을 때 주장을 사용할 수도 있다.

⇒ **(A) 앞:** 주장은 결론을 증명하거나 지지하려는 시도로, 설득과 주장은 다른 활동이라고 하면서 주장에 대한 내용이 나왔으므로, 주장이라는 단어가 언급되기 전의 배경 설명이나 관련된 내용이 제시되어야 한다.

▶ 주어진 글이 (A) 앞에 올 수 없음

(A) 뒤: 물론 누군가를 설득하려고 할 때 주장을 사용할 수도 있다고 한 것으로 보아 그것이 가지는 한계나 문제점이 이어질 것이다.

(B) 모든 주장이 설득을 시도하는 것은 아니며, 많은 설득 시도가 주장을 포함하지 않는다. 사실, 주장을 제시하는 것은 사람들을 설득하는 가장 효과적이지 않은 방법 중 하나인 경우가 많고, 이는 물론 광고주들이 주장을 잘 하지 않는 이유이기도 하다. 사람들은 잘 알려져 있듯이 가장 약한 주장에도 설득당하고, 때로는 꽤 좋은 주장에 대해서도 전혀 개의치 않는 경우가 많다.

⇒ **(B) 앞:** 주장을 제시하는 것은 사람들을 설득하는 가장 효과적이지 않은 방법들 중 하나라고 했으므로, 설득할 때 주장을 제시할 수 있음이 언급되어야 한다.

▶ 순서: (A) → (B)

(B) 뒤: 주장을 제시하는 것이 설득에 영향을 미치지 않는다는 내용에 대한 예시를 들었으므로 관련 예시가 더 이어지거나 마무리 내용일 가능성이 크다.

▶ (B)가 글의 마지막일 확률이 큼

(C) 그러나 그 발언(The remark)은 주장도 아니고, 단지 숲 속 도로 건설을 나쁘게 묘사한 진술일 뿐이다. 지금, 어떤 작가들은 주장을 누군가에게 무언가를 설득하려는 시도로 정의한다. 이는 올바르지 않다.

⇒ **(C) 앞:** '그 발언(The remark)'이라고 하면서 숲 속 도로 건설을 나쁘게 묘사한 진술이라는 것이 언급되었으므로 앞에는 숲 속 도로 건설을 나쁘게 묘사한 발언이 나와야 한다. ▶ 순서: 주어진 글 → (C)

(C) 뒤: 주장을 누군가를 설득하려는 시도로 정의하는 것이 올바르지 않다고 한 진술에 대한 부연 설명이나 관련 내용이 나와야 한다. 이 내용이 (A)에 있다.

▶ 순서: 주어진 글 → (C) → (A) → (B)

주어진 글: 더 많은 도로가 숲에 해로울 수 있다는 것을 청중에게 설득하려는 말을 들었다.

→ **(C):** 이는 숲 속 도로 건설을 나쁘게 묘사한 진술일 뿐이며, 주장을 설득하려는 시도로 정의하는 것은 올바르지 않다.

→ **(A):** 설득과 주장은 다른 활동인데, 물론 설득할 때 주장을 제시할 수도 있다.

→ **(B):** 주장은 설득에 가장 효과적이지 않은 방법 중 하나로, 주장이 사람들을 설득하는 데 유의미한 영향을 미치지 못한다.

▶ 주어진 글 다음에 이어질 글의 순서는 (C) → (A) → (B)이므로 정답은 ④임

1회 08 정답 ③ *마케팅 기회도 되는 위험한 동물

The desire / to see and interact with animals, / shaped as it is
주어 형용사적 용법(The desire 수식)
/ by popular culture, / can be a motivating factor for travel, /
동사
욕구는 / 동물들을 보고 상호 작용하려는 / 지금과 같이 형성된 / 대중문화에 의해 / 여행의 동기부여 요인이 될 수 있다 /

but negative perceptions of certain animals / can perform an
entirely opposite role / in discouraging people / from visiting
some destinations. //
하지만 특정 동물들에 대한 부정적인 인식은 / 완전히 정반대의 역할을 할 수 있다 / 사람들을 만류하는 / 어떤 목적지들을 방문하는 것으로부터 //

단서1 위험한 동물에 대한 두려움이 마케팅 기회로 전환된 예시가 이어짐
선행사
(A) For example, / there are a variety of t-shirt and tea towel
designs / which celebrate the dangerous animals / that can be
주격 관계대명사 선행사 주격 관계대명사
encountered in Australia. //
예를 들어 / 다양한 티셔츠와 행주 디자인들이 있다 / 위험한 동물들을 기념하는 / 호주에서 마주칠 수 있는 //

선행사
This is a whimsical reconfiguration / of the perceived threat /
목적격 관계대명사
that these animals pose / to some tourists / considering travel
to this country. //
이것은 기발한 재구성이다 / 인식된 위험의 / 이 동물들이 제기하는 / 일부 관광객들에게 / 이 나라로의 여행을 고려하는 //

(B) The harmful effects of animals / on tourism experiences /
has been the subject of analysis / in a small number of studies, /
동물의 해로운 영향이 / 관광 체험에 미치는 / 분석 주제가 되어 왔다 / 소수 연구에서 /

but deaths or injuries / caused by animals / to tourists / are tiny /
in comparison to other causes / such as drowning and vehicular
accidents. // 단서2 위험한 동물에 대한 부정적인 인식이 사람들의 관광을 막는다는
주어진 문장에 역접으로 연결되는 내용이 이어짐
하지만 사망이나 부상은 / 동물에 의해 초래된 / 관광객들에게 / 미미하다 / 다른 원인에 비해 / 익사와 교통사고와 같은 //

(C) Nevertheless, / the possibility / that they might encounter a
단수 주어 동격절 접속사
dangerous animal / such as shark or snake / or catch a disease /
such as malaria 단서3 동물에 의한 사고가 미미함에도 불구하고 일어나는 일이 이어짐
그럼에도 불구하고 / 가능성은 / 그들이 위험한 동물과 마주칠지도 모르는 / 상어나 뱀과 같은 / 또는 걸릴지도 모르는 / 말라리아와 같은 질병에 /

단수 동사
is sufficient to stop / at least some tourists / from visiting
선행사 관계부사
destinations / where such threats exist. //
단념시키기에 충분하다 / 적어도 일부 관광객들을 / 목적지들을 방문하는 것으로부터 / 그러한 위협이 존재하는 //

Sometimes this fear is turned / into a marketing opportunity. //
때때로 이 두려움은 전환된다 / 마케팅 기회로 //

- interact ⓥ 상호작용하다   • motivating ⓐ 동기를 부여하는
- factor ⓝ 요인   • perception ⓝ 인식   • entirely ⓪ 완전히
- discourage ⓥ 낙담시키다, 만류하다   • destination ⓝ 목적지
- tea towel 행주   • threat ⓝ 위협   • pose ⓥ 제기하다
- analysis ⓝ 분석   • in comparison to ~에 비해
- drown ⓥ 익사하다   • vehicular ⓐ 차량의
- nevertheless ⓪ 그럼에도 불구하고

대중문화에 의해 지금과 같이 형성된, 동물들을 보고 상호 작용하려는 욕구는 여행의 동기부여 요인이 될 수 있지만, 특정 동물들에 대한 부정적인 인식은 사람들이 어떤 목적지들을 방문하는 것을 만류하는 완전히 정반대의 역할을 할 수 있다. (B) 소수 연구에서 분석 주제가 동물이 관광 체험에 미치는 해로운 영향이 되어 왔는데, 동물에 의해 관광객들에게 초래된 사망이나 부상은 익사와 교통사고와 같은 다른 원인에 비해 미미하다. (C) 그럼에도 불구하고, 그들이 상어나 뱀과 같은 위험한 동물과 마주칠지 모르거나 말라리아와 같은 질병에 걸릴지도 모르는 가능성은 적어도 일부 관광객들이 그러한 위험이 존재하는 목적지들을 방문하는 것을 단념시키기에 충분하다. 때때로 이 두려움은 마케팅 기회로 전환된다. (A) 예를 들어, 호주에서 마주칠 수 있는 위험한 동물들을 기념하는 다양한 티셔츠와 행주 디자인들이 있다. 이것은 이 나라로의 여행을 고려하는 일부 관광객들에게 이 동물들이 제기하는 인식된 위험의 기발한 재구성이다.

주어진 글 다음에 이어질 글의 순서로 가장 적절한 것을 고르시오.

(C)에 대한 예시가 (A)에 이어짐
① (A) — (C) — (B) (A)는 마케팅 기회와 관련된 예시를 설명하므로 앞에 올 수 없음

② (B) — (A) — (C) 특정 동물에 대한 부정적 인식이 어떤 곳을 방문하는 것을 만류할 수
있음 - 하지만 동물에 의한 사고는 다른 원인에 비해 미미함 - 그럼에도
③ (B) — (C) — (A) 불구하고 그런 사고의 가능성은 일부 관광객을 단념시킴 - 이러한
두려움은 티셔츠나 행주 디자인 등의 마케팅 기회로 전환되기도 함

④ (C) — (A) — (B) 주어진 문장의 뒷부분과 (C)의 앞부분은 Nevertheless로
⑤ (C) — (B) — (A) 연결되기에 적절하지 않음

| 문제 풀이 순서 | [정답률 70%]

1st 각 문단의 내용을 파악하고, 글의 논리적인 순서를 추론한다.

> **주어진 글:** 대중문화에 의해 지금과 같이 형성된, 동물들을 보고 상호 작용하려는 욕구는 여행의 동기부여 요인이 될 수 있지만, 특정 동물들에 대한 부정적인 인식은 사람들이 어떤 목적지들을 방문하는 것을 만류하는 완전히 정반대의 역할을 할 수 있다.

→ 동물을 보고 상호 작용하려는 욕구가 여행의 동기부여 요인이 되기도 하지만, 특정 동물에 대한 부정적인 인식 때문에 어떤 목적지를 방문하지 않기도 한다는 내용이다. **주어진 글 뒤:** but 이하의 내용이 핵심이므로, 단서 이후로는 특정 동물에 대한 부정적인 인식에 대한 내용이 이어질 것이다. 발상

> **(A):** 예를 들어(For example), 호주에서 마주칠 수 있는 위험한 동물들을 기념하는 다양한 티셔츠와 행주 디자인들이 있다. 이것은 이 나라로의 여행을 고려하는 일부 관광객들에게 이 동물들이 제기하는 인식된 위험의 기발한 재구성이다.

→ 주어진 글에서 말한 특정 동물이 위험한 동물을 가리킨다는 것을 알 수 있다.
(A) 앞: For example로 보아 (A) 앞에 위험한 동물을 이용하여 상품을 만든다는 언급이 있어야 하는데, 주어진 글에는 그러한 내용이 없다.
▶ 주어진 글이 (A) 앞에 올 수 없음

(A) 뒤: 여행을 단념시키기도 하는 위험한 동물이 티셔츠 등의 상품에 이용되는 예시를 제시하며, 이는 위험한 동물이 제기하는 위협을 기발하게 재구성하는 것이라는 결론을 내린다. ▶ (A)가 글의 결론이라고 예상할 수 있음

> **(B):** 소수 연구에서 분석 주제가 동물이 관광 체험에 미치는 해로운 영향이 되어 왔는데, 동물에 의해 관광객들에게 초래된 사망이나 부상은 익사와 교통사고와 같은 다른 원인에 비해 미미하다.

→ 관광객이 동물 때문에 사망하거나 부상을 입는 경우는 교통사고나 익사와 같은 다른 원인에 비해 미미하다는 내용이 역접의 연결어 but으로 이어진다.
(B) 앞: 관광객이 동물 때문에 관광을 단념한다는 내용이 필요하다.
▶ 주어진 글이 그러한 내용임 (순서: 주어진 글 → (B))
(B) 뒤: 동물에 의한 사고 확률이 미미하기 때문에 동물이 여행에 미치는 영향이 작다거나 또는 그러한 확률이 미미함에도 불구하고 동물 때문에 여행을 하지 않는다는 내용이 이어질 것이다. ▶ (A)는 그런 내용이 아님

모의고사
1회

(C): 그럼에도 불구하고(Nevertheless), 그들이 상어나 뱀과 같은 위험한 동물과 마주칠지 모르거나 말라리아와 같은 질병에 걸릴지도 모르는 가능성은 적어도 일부 관광객들이 그러한 위험이 존재하는 목적지들을 방문하는 것을 단념시키기에 충분하다. 때때로 이 두려움은 마케팅 기회로 전환된다.

→ **(C) 앞:** Nevertheless로 연결되는 것으로 보아, (C) 앞에는 상어나 뱀 등의 위험한 동물로 인한 사고의 가능성이 낮다는 내용이 필요하다.
  ▶ (B)가 그런 내용임 (순서: 주어진 글 → (B) → (C))
  (C) 뒤: 위험한 동물에 대한 두려움이 마케팅 기회로 전환되는 것을 보여주는 예시가 이어지는 것이 적절하다.
  ▶ (A)가 위험한 동물이 마케팅에 사용되는 예시를 설명함 (순서: 주어진 글 → (B) → (C) → (A))

2nd 글이 한눈에 들어오도록 정리하여 정답을 확인한다.

주어진 글: 동물을 보고 동물과 상호 작용하려는 욕구는 여행의 동기부여 요인이 될 수 있지만, 특정 동물에 대한 부정적인 인식은 어떤 목적지를 여행하지 않게 하는 역할을 하기도 한다.
→ **(B):** 하지만 동물에 의해 초래된 사고는 다른 원인에 비해 미미하다.
→ **(C):** 그럼에도 불구하고 위험한 동물로 인한 사고의 가능성은 일부 관광객이 특정 목적지를 방문하는 것을 단념하게 한다. 이러한 두려움은 마케팅 기회로 전환되기도 한다.
→ **(A):** 예를 들어, 호주에서 마주칠 수 있는 위험한 동물을 기념하는 다양한 티셔츠와 행주 디자인이 있다.
  ▶ 주어진 글 다음에 이어질 글의 순서는 (B) → (C) → (A)이므로 정답은 ③임

1회 09 정답 ⑤ *프랑스의 교육 개혁 및 새로운 대학 시스템 구축

글의 흐름으로 보아, 주어진 문장이 들어가기에 가장 적절한 곳을 고르시오. [3점]

> **단서 1** '이 사업'의 주요 수단이 교육 개혁, 특히 대학 시스템의 구축이라고 함
> A principal vehicle of this enterprise / was educational reform / and specifically the building of a university system
> 과거분사(university system 수식)
> / dedicated to the ideals of science, reason, and humanism. //
> 이 사업의 주요 수단은 / 교육 개혁이었다 / 특히 대학 시스템의 구축이었다 / 과학, 이성, 인본주의의 이상에 헌신하는 //

분사구문을 이끎
Writing just after the end of World War I, / an acute observer of the French philosophical scene judged /
제1차 세계대전 직후 글에서 / 프랑스 철학계에 대한 예리한 관찰자는 평가했다 /
목적어절을 이끄는 접속사
that "philosophical research had never been more abundant, / more serious, and more intense / among us / than in the last thirty years." //
"철학적 연구는 더 풍부했던 적이 없었다 / 더 진지하고, 더 강렬했던 / 우리 사이에서 / 지난 30년보다" //

~ 때문에[덕분에]: 뒤에 명사구가 옴
(①) This flowering was / due to the place of philosophy / in the
과거분사(system 수식)
new educational system / set up by the Third Republic / in the wake of the demoralizing defeat in the Franco-Prussian War. //
이러한 철학의 발전은 / 철학이 차지한 위치 덕분이었다 / 새로운 교육 시스템에서 / 제3공화국에 의해 설정된 / 프로이센 프랑스 전쟁에서의 비참한 패배의 여파로 //

(②) The French had been humiliated / by the capture of
had been에 연결되는 동사
Napoleon III at Sedan / and wasted by the long siege of Paris. //
프랑스는 굴욕감을 느꼈다 / 세단에서 나폴레옹 3세가 포로로 잡힌 것에 의해 / 그리고 파리에서의 긴 포위로 인해 황폐해졌다 //

선행사를 포함하는 관계대명사
(③) They had also been terrified / by what most of the bourgeoisie saw / as seventy-three days of anarchy / under the radical socialism of the Commune. //
그들은 또한 두려움을 느꼈다 / 대부분의 부르주아가 경험한 것에 의해 / 73일 간의 무정부 상태로서 / 공산당의 급진적 사회주의 하에서 //

(④) Much of the new Republic's effort at spiritual restoration / was driven / by a rejection of the traditional values of
계속적 용법의 목적격 관계대명사 = the new Republic
institutional religion, / which it aimed to replace / with an enlightened worldview. // **단서 2** 새로운 공화국은 기존의 전통적 가치를 거부하고 이를 계몽된 세계관으로 대체하고자 함
영적 회복에 대한 새로운 공화국의 노력 대부분은 / 비롯되었다 / 제도 종교의 전통적 가치에 대한 거부에 의해 / 그것(새로운 공화국)이 대체하려고 목표로 한 것 / 계몽된 세계관으로 //

(⑤) Albert Thibaudet highlighted / the importance of this reform / when he labeled the Third Republic / "the republic of professors." // **단서 3** '이 개혁'의 중요성에 대해 강조하면서 '교수들의 공화국으로 지칭함
Albert Thibaudet는 강조했다 / 이 개혁의 중요성을 / 제3공화국을 지칭하면서 / "교수들의 공화국"이라고 //

- vehicle ⓝ 수단 - enterprise ⓝ 사업 - reform ⓝ 개혁
- dedicate to ~에 헌신하다 - humanism ⓝ 인본주의
- acute ⓐ 예리한 - philosophical ⓐ 철학적인
- demoralize ⓥ 사기를 꺾다 - humiliate ⓥ 굴욕감을 주다
- terrified ⓐ 겁이 난 - bourgeoisie ⓝ 중산층, 부르주아
- radical ⓐ 급진적인 - restoration ⓝ 복원
- enlightened ⓐ 계몽된 - label ⓥ 지칭하다

제1차 세계대전 직후 글에서, 프랑스 철학계에 대한 예리한 관찰자는 "철학적 연구는 지난 30년간 우리 사이에서 그 어느 때보다도 풍부하고, 진지하며, 강렬했다"고 평가했다. (①) 이러한 철학의 발전은 프로이센 프랑스 전쟁에서의 패배로 인해 설정된 제3공화국의 새로운 교육 시스템에서 철학이 차지한 위치 덕분이었다. (②) 프랑스는 세단에서 나폴레옹 3세가 포로로 잡힌 것에 굴욕감을 느꼈으며 파리에서의 긴 포위로 인해 황폐해졌다. (③) 또한 그들은 대부분의 부르주아가 공산당의 급진적 사회주의 하에서 73일 간의 무정부 상태로서 경험한 것에 대해 두려움을 느꼈다. (④) 새로운 공화국의 영적 회복 노력은 제도 종교의 전통적인 가치를 거부하고, 이를 계몽된 세계관으로 대체하는 것을 목표로 하는 데서 비롯되었다. (⑤ 이 사업의 주요 수단은 교육 개혁, 특히 과학, 이성, 인본주의의 이상에 헌신하는 대학 시스템의 구축이었다.) Albert Thibaudet는 제3공화국을 "교수들의 공화국"이라고 칭하면서 이 개혁의 중요성을 강조했다.

| 문제 풀이 순서 | [정답률 52%]

1st 주어진 문장을 해석하고, 연결어, 지시어 등을 확인한다.

A principal vehicle of this enterprise / was educational reform / and specifically the building of a university system / dedicated to the ideals of science, reason, and humanism. //
'이 사업'의 주요 수단은 / 교육 개혁이었다 / 특히 대학 시스템의 구축이었다 / 과학, 이성, 인본주의의 이상에 헌신하는 //

→ '이 사업(this enterprise)'의 주요 수단이 교육 개혁, 특히 대학 시스템의 구축이었다고 했으므로 앞에는 교육 개혁을 필요로 하는 '이 사업'이 무엇인지에 대한 설명이 제시되어야 한다. **단서**
  ▶ **주어진 문장 앞:** 교육 개혁을 필요로 하는 이 사업이 무엇인지 제시될 것임 **발상**
  ▶ **주어진 문장 뒤:** 교육 개혁이나 대학 시스템의 구축에 대한 부연 설명이 이어질 것임

2nd 각 선택지의 앞뒤 흐름이 매끄러운지 확인한다.

- ①의 앞 문장과 뒤 문장

앞 문장: 제1차 세계대전 직후 글에서, 프랑스 철학계에 대한 예리한 관찰자는 "철학적 연구는 지난 30년간 우리 사이에서 그 어느 때보다도 풍부하고, 진지하며, 강렬했다"고 평가했다.
뒤 문장: 이러한 철학의 발전(This flowering)은 프로이센 프랑스 전쟁에서의 패배로 인해 설정된 제3공화국의 새로운 교육 시스템에서 철학이 차지한 위치 덕분이었다.

→ 앞 문장은 프랑스 철학계가 지난 30년간 그 어느 때보다도 풍부하고 진지하며 강렬하게 발전했다고 했다. 뒤 문장에서는 '이러한 철학의 발전(This flowering)'이 전쟁에서의 패배로 인해 설정된 새로운 교육 시스템에서 철학이 차지한 위치 덕분이라고 했다. 따라서 두 문장은 자연스럽게 연결된다.
  ▶ 주어진 문장이 ①에 들어갈 수 없음

- ②의 앞 문장과 뒤 문장

앞 문장: ①의 뒤 문장과 같음

뒤 문장: 프랑스는 세단에서 나폴레옹 3세가 포로로 잡힌 것에 굴욕감을 느꼈으며 파리에서의 긴 포위로 인해 황폐해졌다.

➡ 앞 문장에서는 전쟁에서의 패배가 새로운 교육 시스템에서의 철학의 위치에 영향을 미쳤음이 언급되었으며, 뒤에 이어지는 문장에서는 전쟁 패배에서 느낀 프랑스의 굴욕에 대해 설명하고 있으므로 자연스럽게 연결되고 있다.

▶ 주어진 문장이 ②에 들어갈 수 없음

- ③의 앞 문장과 뒤 문장

앞 문장: ②의 뒤 문장과 같음

뒤 문장: 또한(also) 그들은 대부분의 부르주아가 공산당의 급진적 사회주의 하에서 73일 간의 무정부 상태로서 경험한 것에 대해 두려움을 느꼈다.

➡ 앞부분에서 프랑스가 전쟁 패배로 인해 느낀 굴욕감 등에 대해 언급한 뒤, 뒤 문장에서는 '또한(also)' 그들이 무정부 상태를 경험한 것에 대해 두려움을 느꼈다고 했으므로 두 문장의 연결이 자연스럽다.

▶ 주어진 문장이 ③에 들어갈 수 없음

- ④의 앞 문장과 뒤 문장

앞 문장: ③의 뒤 문장과 같음

뒤 문장: 새로운 공화국의 영적 회복 노력은 제도 종교의 전통적인 가치를 거부하고, 이를 계몽된 세계관으로 대체하는 것을 목표로 하는 데서 비롯되었다.

➡ 앞의 두 문장에서 프랑스가 전쟁 패배로 인해 겪은 굴욕감, 무정부 상태를 경험한 두려움 등 영적 상처를 받았음을 제시했으며, 뒤에서는 영적 회복을 위해 전통적 가치를 계몽된 세계관으로 대체할 목표를 세웠음을 언급했으므로 두 문장이 자연스럽게 연결된다.

▶ 주어진 문장이 ④에 들어갈 수 없음

- ⑤의 앞 문장과 뒤 문장

앞 문장: ④의 뒤 문장과 같음

뒤 문장: Albert Thibaudet는 제3공화국을 "교수들의 공화국"이라고 칭하면서 이 개혁(this reform)의 중요성을 강조했다.

➡ 앞 문장에서 영적 회복을 위해 전통적 가치를 계몽된 세계관으로 대체할 목표를 세웠다고 했다. 뒤 문장에서는 제3공화국이 교수들의 공화국이라고 불리며 '이 개혁(this reform)'의 중요성이 강조된다고 했다.
주어진 문장은 '이 사업'의 주요 수단이 교육 개혁, 특히 대학 시스템의 구축이라고 했으므로, 주어진 문장을 ⑤에 넣어야 영적 회복이라는 사업의 수단으로 교육 개혁, 즉 대학 시스템의 구축이 제시되었으며 이 개혁, 즉 교육 개혁의 중요성이 강조되면서 제3공화국이 교수들의 공화국이라고 지칭된다는 내용이 전개될 수 있다.

▶ 주어진 문장이 ⑤에 들어가야 함

3rd 글이 한눈에 들어오도록 정리하여 정답을 확인한다.

제1차 세계대전 직후, 프랑스의 철학적 연구는 지난 30년간 그 어느 때보다도 풍부하고, 진지하며, 강렬했다는 평가가 나왔다.
(①) 이러한 철학의 발전은 전쟁에서의 패배로 인해 설정된 제3공화국의 새로운 교육 시스템에서 철학이 차지한 위치 덕분이다.
(②) 프랑스는 나폴레옹 3세가 포로로 잡힌 것에 굴욕감을 느꼈으며 파리에서의 긴 포위로 인해 황폐해졌다.
(③) 또한 그들은 73일간의 무정부 상태를 경험한 것에 대해 두려움을 느꼈다.
(④) 새로운 공화국의 영적 회복 노력은 전통적인 가치를 계몽된 세계관으로 대체하는 것을 목표로 했다.
(⑤ 이 사업의 주요 수단은 교육 개혁, 특히 과학, 이성, 인본주의의 이상에 헌신하는 대학 시스템의 구축이었다.)
제3공화국을 "교수들의 공화국"이라고 칭하면서 이 개혁의 중요성을 강조했다.

1회 10 정답 ① *살을 빼기 어려운 이유

There is no question / that losing weight is hard. //
의심의 여지가 없다 / 체중을 줄이는 것이 힘들다는 것은 //

According to one calculation, / you must walk 35 miles / or jog for seven hours / to lose just one pound. //
_{부사적 용법(목적)}
한 계산법에 따르면 / 여러분은 35마일을 걷거나 / 일곱 시간 동안 조깅을 해야 한다 / 단지 1파운드를 빼기 위해서 //

One big problem with exercise is / that we don't track it / very scrupulously. //
_{주격 보어절 접속사}
운동과 관련한 한 가지 큰 문제는 ~이다 / 우리가 그것을 추적하지 않는다는 것 / 매우 용의주도하게 //

단서1 사람들은 자신이 운동에서 소모한 칼로리를 과대평가함
A study in America found / that people overestimated the number of calories / they burned in a workout / by a factor of four. //
_{앞에 목적격 관계대명사가 생략됨}
미국의 한 연구는 발견했다 / 사람들이 칼로리의 숫자를 과대평가한다는 것을 / 그들이 운동에서 소모한 / 네 배만큼 //

단서2 운동으로 소모한 칼로리의 약 두 배를 섭취함
They also then consumed, / on average, / about twice as many calories / as they had just burned off. //
_{원급 비교를 이용한 배수 표현}
그리고서 그들은 또한 섭취했다 / 평균적으로 / 칼로리의 약 두 배를 / 자신이 방금 태운 //

As Daniel Lieberman noted / in *The Story of the Human Body*, /
Daniel Lieberman이 언급했듯이 / 《The Story of the Human Body》에서 /
_{부사구가 조동사와 본동사 사이에 삽입됨}
a worker on a factory floor / will in a year expend about 175,000 more calories / than a desk worker / — equivalent / to more than sixty marathons. //
작업 현장에 있는 근로자는 / 한 해에 약 175,000칼로리를 더 소비할 것이다 / 사무직 근로자보다 / 해당하는 것 / 60번이 넘는 마라톤에 //

That's pretty impressive, / but here's a reasonable question: / how many factory workers look / as if they run a marathon / every six days? //
그것은 꽤 인상적이긴 하지만 / 여기에 타당한 질문이 있다 / 얼마나 많은 공장 근로자들이 보이는가 / 그들이 마라톤을 뛰는 것처럼 / 6일마다 //

To be cruelly blunt, / not many. //
가혹하게 단도직입적으로 말해서 / 많지는 않다 //

That's / because most of them, / like most of the rest of us, / replace all those burnt calories, / and then some, / when they are not working. //
_{전치사구가 because절의 주어와 동사 사이에 삽입됨}
그것은 ~이다 / 그들 중 대부분은 / 나머지 우리 대부분처럼 / 모든 연소된 칼로리를 다시 돌려놓기 때문 / 그런 다음 얼마간을 / 그들이 일하고 있지 않을 때 //

> → Losing weight is hard / because people usually think / they burned a (A) **larger** number of calories / than they actually did /
> _{동명사구 주어 / 단수 동사}
> 체중을 줄이는 것은 어렵다 / 사람들은 대개 생각하기 때문에 / 자신이 더 많은 칼로리를 소모했다고 / 자신이 실제로 그런 것보다 /
>
> and (B) **undo** exercise / by eating a lot of food. //
> 그리고 운동을 원상태로 돌리기 때문에 / 다량의 음식을 섭취함으로써 //

- calculation ⑪ 계산, 산출
- jog ⓥ 조깅하다
- track ⓥ 추적하다, 뒤쫓다
- overestimate ⓥ 과대평가하다
- workout ⑪ 운동
- by a factor of (증감 규모가) ~(배) 만큼
- consume ⓥ 소모하다, 먹다
- on average 평균적으로
- burn off ~을 태워서 제거하다, (운동으로 칼로리 등을) 태우다
- expend ⓥ (돈·시간·에너지를) 쏟다[들이다]
- equivalent ⓐ 동등한, 맞먹는
- impressive ⓐ 인상적인, 인상[감명] 깊은
- reasonable ⓐ 타당한, 사리에 맞는
- cruelly ⓐⓓ 잔인하게, 지독하게
- blunt ⓐ 직설적인, 무딘
- replace ⓥ 대신[대체]하다, (제자리에) 다시 놓다

체중을 줄이는 것이 힘들다는 것은 의심의 여지가 없다. 한 계산법에 따르면, 단지 1파운드를 빼기 위해서 여러분은 35마일을 걷거나 일곱 시간 동안 조깅을 해야 한다. 운동과 관련한 한 가지 큰 문제는 우리가 그것을 매우 용의주도하게 추적하지 않는다는 것이다. 미국의 한 연구는 사람들이 운동에서 소모한

칼로리의 숫자를 네 배만큼 과대평가한다는 것을 발견했다. 그리고서 그들은 또한 자신이 방금 태운 칼로리의 약 두 배를 평균적으로 섭취했다. Daniel Lieberman이 〈The Story of the Human Body〉에서 언급했듯이, 작업 현장에 있는 근로자는 한 해에 사무직 근로자보다 약 175,000칼로리를 더 소비할 것이다. 이는 60번이 넘는 마라톤에 해당한다. 그것은 꽤 인상적이긴 하지만, 여기에 타당한 질문이 있다. 얼마나 많은 공장 근로자들이 6일마다 마라톤을 뛰는 것처럼 보이는가? 가혹하게 단도직입적으로 말해서, 많지는 않다. 왜냐하면 그들 중 대부분은, 나머지 우리 대부분처럼, 그들이 일하고 있지 않을 때, 모든 연소된 칼로리와 그런 다음 얼마간의 칼로리를 다시 돌려놓기 때문이다.

→ 사람들은 주로 자신이 실제보다 (A) <u>더 많은</u> 칼로리를 소모했다고 생각하고 다량의 음식을 섭취함으로써 운동을 (B) <u>원상태로 돌리기</u> 때문에, 체중을 줄이는 것은 어렵다.

다음 글의 내용을 한 문장으로 요약하고자 한다. 빈칸 (A), (B)에 들어갈 말로 가장 적절한 것은?

	(A)		(B)	
①	larger 더 많은	—	undo 원상태로 돌리다	실제보다 더 많은 칼로리를 소모했다고 생각하고, 운동으로 소모한 칼로리보다 더 많은 칼로리를 먹음
②	larger 더 많은	—	intensify 강화하다	운동한 것이 소용 없게 만든다는 것임
③	higher 더 높은	—	supplement 보충하다	운동 외의 다른 체중 감량 노력을 한다는 언급은 없음
④	smaller 더 작은	—	continue 계속하다	실제보다 더 많은 칼로리를 소모했다고 생각함
⑤	smaller 더 작은	—	delay 미루다	

왜 정답? [정답률 67%]

체중을 줄이는 것이 힘든 이유에 대해 설명하는 글로, 사람들은 그들이 운동으로 소모한 칼로리를 과대평가하고, 운동으로 소모한 칼로리의 약 두 배를 섭취한다고 했다.

즉, 사람들은 자신이 실제로 소모한 것보다 ① '더 많은' 칼로리를 소모했다고 생각하고, 운동으로 소모한 칼로리보다 더 많은 칼로리를 섭취함으로써 운동한 것을 ① '원상태로 돌리기' 때문에 체중을 줄이기가 어려운 것이다.

왜 오답?

[because가 이끄는 이유의 부사절에 빈칸이 있음] 꿀팁

②, ③ 운동으로 소모한 칼로리보다 두 배 더 많은 칼로리를 섭취한다고 했으므로 운동을 강화하거나 보충하는 것이 아니다.

④, ⑤ 사람들은 그들이 운동으로 소모한 칼로리를 네 배만큼 과대평가한다고 했으므로 자신이 실제로 소모한 것보다 '더 적은' 칼로리를 소모했다고 생각한다는 것은 글과 맞지 않다.

* 글의 흐름

도입	체중을 줄이는 것은 의심의 여지 없이 힘듦
이유 ①	사람들은 그들이 운동으로 소모한 칼로리를 네 배만큼 과대평가함
이유 ②	평균적으로 소모한 칼로리의 약 두 배를 더 섭취함

─ 배경 지식 ─

* 칼로리(calorie)

'열'을 뜻하는 라틴어 'calor'에서 유래한 칼로리는 물체가 주고받는 에너지를 나타내는 단위이다. 물리학에서 칼로리(cal)는 물 1g의 온도를 1℃ 올리는 데 드는 열량을 이야기한다. 에너지의 다른 단위인 '줄(J)'로 환산하면 1칼로리는 약 4.2줄인데, 물리학자는 에너지의 기본 단위로 칼로리 대신 줄을 쓴다.

칼로리 단위가 많이 쓰이는 분야는 영양학으로, 음식이 가진 열량을 표현할 때 주로 사용된다. 이때는 물리학의 칼로리와 다르게 물 1kg의 온도를 1℃ 올리는 데 드는 열량이 기준이라서, 단위를 'kcal(킬로칼로리)'로 표기한다. 우리가 섭취하는 탄수화물과 단백질은 1g당 약 4kcal, 지방은 1g당 약 9kcal의 에너지를 낼 수 있다.

1회 11~12 * 문화유산의 종잡을 수 없는 본질

Cultural heritage can be understood / in the narrow sense / as the reservoir of cultural elements / that are recognized as being significant and worthy / of preservation and transfer to succeeding generations. //
수동태 동사 / be worthy of ~: ~할 가치가 있다
문화유산은 이해될 수 있다 / 좁은 의미에서 / 문화적 요소의 저장소라고 / 중요하고 가치 있다고 인정되는 / 보존하고 다음 세대에 전수할 //

Cultural heritage in the wide sense, however, / is understood / as a dynamic discursive area / 11번 단서 1: 문화유산은 역동적이고 종잡을 수 없는 영역임
수동태 동사 / 「전치사+관계대명사」
그러나 문화유산은 넓은 의미에서 / 이해된다 / 역동적이고 종잡을 수 없는 영역으로 /

within which the cultural resources of the past, and their significance, / are constructed through social interaction. //
과거의 문화 자원들과 그들의 중요성이 / 사회적 상호작용을 통해 구축되는 //

Once (a) extracted from this discursive area, / the reservoir becomes just an empty and meaningless collection of artefacts and ideas / embedded in various forms. //
부사절의 「주어+be동사」 생략 / 과거분사구 (artefacts and ideas 수식)
이 종잡을 수 없는 영역에서 그 추출된다면 / 저장소는 그저 텅 빈, 의미 없는 공예품들과 아이디어들의 모음이 된다 / 다양한 형태에 내포된 //

Such an understanding of cultural heritage / is rooted / in the idea of (b) collective memory / introduced by Maurice Halbwachs. //
과거분사구 (idea 수식)
문화유산에 대한 이러한 이해는 / 뿌리를 둔다 / 집단 기억이라는 개념에 / Maurice Halbwachs에 의해 도입된 //

He argues / that our memory about the past / is socially constructed. //
목적어절 접속사
그는 주장한다 / 우리의 과거에 관한 기억은 / 사회적으로 구축된다고 //

To some extent, / social conditions determine / what and how we remember. // 11번 단서 2: 사회적 조건은 우리가 어떻게 기억할지를 결정함
의문사가 이끄는 명사절
어느 정도 / 사회적 조건은 결정한다 / 우리가 무엇을 어떻게 기억할지를 //

The phenomenon of tradition and cultural heritage being socially determined / is emphasized by Eric Hobsbawn and Terence Ranger, /
being socially determined의 의미상 주어
전통과 문화유산이 사회적으로 결정되는 현상은 / Eric Hobsbawn과 Terence Ranger에 의해 강조되다 /

who consider that tradition is not reproduced / but rather (c) invented. //
계속적 용법의 주격 관계대명사
그들은 그 전통이 재현되는 것이 아니라 / 오히려 발명되는 것이라고 여긴다 //

Belief in the discursive nature of cultural heritage / is based on the conviction / 12번 단서: 문화유산의 본질은 종잡을 수 없음
문화유산의 종잡을 수 없는 본질에 대한 믿음은 / 확신에 기반하고 있다 /

that the criteria for determining / which artefacts and behavioural patterns should be transmitted to posterity / are (d) stable(→ unstable). //
동격절 접속사 / 복수 주어 / 복수 동사
결정하는 기준이 / 어떤 공예품들과 행동 양식이 후대에 전수되어야 하는지를 / 안정적이라는 (→ 안정적이지 않다는) //

On the one hand, / a reservoir of cultural heritage is subject to selection / and is determined / by global flows, new technology, economics, cultural policy, or the sentiments of decision-makers. //
~의 대상이 되다
한편으로는 / 문화유산의 저장소는 선택의 대상이고 / 결정된다 / 세계적 흐름, 새로운 기술, 경제, 문화 정책, 또는 의사결정자들의 감정에 의해 //

On the other hand, such a reservoir / is the object of continual reinterpretation, /
반면, 그러한 저장소는 / 지속적인 재해석의 대상이다 /

which is influenced / by the social position, background, biography, and cultural competences / of the individuals who participate in a culture. //
주격 관계대명사 / 주격 관계대명사
영향을 받는 / 사회적 지위, 배경, 전기, 문화적 역량에 의해 / 한 문화에 참여하는 개인들의 //

Social interaction / is the (e) essence of transition in cultural heritage. // 11번 단서 3: 사회적 상호작용은 문화유산에서 전승의 본질임
사회적 상호작용은 / 문화유산에서 전승의 본질이다 //

- cultural heritage 문화유산
- reservoir ⓝ 저장소
- preservation ⓝ 보존
- succeeding ⓐ 이어지는
- discursive ⓐ 종잡을 수 없는, 산만한
- artefact ⓝ 공예품, 인공물
- embed ⓥ 내포하다
- root ⓥ 뿌리를 두다
- reproduce ⓥ 재현하다, 재생산하다
- sentiment ⓝ 감정
- continual ⓐ 계속적인
- reinterpretation ⓝ 재해석
- biography ⓝ 전기, 일대기
- competence ⓝ 역량

문화유산은 좁은 의미에서 중요하고 보존하고 다음 세대에 전수할 가치 있다고 인정되는 문화적 요소의 저장소라고 이해될 수 있다. 그러나 문화유산은 넓은 의미에서 과거의 문화 자원들과 그들의 중요성이 사회적 상호작용을 통해 구축되는 역동적이고 종잡을 수 없는 영역으로 이해된다. 이 종잡을 수 없는 영역에서 (a) 추출된다면 저장소는 다양한 형태에 내포된 공예품들과 아이디어들의 그저 텅 빈, 의미 없는 모음이 된다. 문화유산에 대한 이러한 이해는 Maurice Halbwachs에 의해 도입된 (b) 집단 기억이라는 개념에 뿌리를 둔다. 그는 우리의 과거에 관한 기억은 사회적으로 구축된다고 주장한다. 어느 정도, 사회적 조건은 우리가 무엇을 어떻게 기억할지를 결정한다. 전통과 문화유산이 사회적으로 결정되는 현상은 Eric Hobsbawn과 Terence Ranger에 의해 강조되는데, 그들은 그 전통이 재현되는 것이 아니라 오히려 (c) 발명되는 것이라고 여긴다.

문화유산의 종잡을 수 없는 본질에 대한 믿음은 어떤 공예품들과 행동 양식이 후대에 전수되어야 하는지를 결정하는 기준이 (d) 안정적이라는(→ 안정적이지 않다는) 확신에 기반하고 있다. 한편으로는, 문화유산의 저장소는 선택의 대상이고, 세계적 흐름, 새로운 기술, 경제, 문화 정책, 또는 의사결정자들의 감정에 의해 결정된다. 반면, 그러한 저장소는 한 문화에 참여하는 개인들의 사회적 지위, 배경, 전기, 문화적 역량에 의해 영향을 받는 지속적인 재해석의 대상이다. 사회적 상호작용은 문화유산에서 전승의 (e) 본질이다.

₁회 11 정답 ③

윗글의 주제로 가장 적절한 것은? [3점]

① the significance of cultural heritage preservation
문화유산 보존의 중요성　　　　　　　　　문화유산의 본질을 설명한 글임
② procedures to build a reservoir for cultural heritage artefacts
문화유산 공예품을 위한 저장소를 설립하는 절차　　저장소를 설립하는 절차에 관한 글은 아님
③ cultural heritage's discursive characteristic as a social construct
문화유산의 사회적 구성물로서의 종잡을 수 없는 특성 Cultural heritage ~ through social interaction.
④ discursive efforts by social organizations to designate world heritages 사회단체들에 관한 언급은 없음
세계유산을 지정하기 위한 사회단체들의 종잡을 수 없는 노력
⑤ established criteria for categorizing artefacts based on historical values 어떤 공예품이 역사적으로 가치 있다고 선택될지에 관한 기준은 정해지지 않았다고 함
역사적 가치에 기반한 공예품 범주화를 위한 확립된 기준

⟩왜 정답? [정답률 0%]

⌐ • 그러나 문화유산은 넓은 의미에서 과거의 문화 자원들과 그들의 중요성이 사회적 상호작용을 통해 구축되는 역동적이고 종잡을 수 없는 영역으로 이해된다. 단서1
⊢ • 어느 정도, 사회적 조건은 우리가 무엇을 어떻게 기억할지를 결정한다. 단서2
∟ • 사회적 상호작용은 문화유산에서 전승의 본질이다. 단서3

⇒ 문화유산이 선택되고 전수되는 것이 사회적으로 구축되며, 그 기준이 명확하지 않기 때문에 종잡을 수 없는 특징을 지닌다는 글이다. 어떤 문화 자원들이 중요한지는 사회적 상호작용을 통해 결정되며, 사회적 조건과 의사결정자들의 선택이 문화유산의 전승의 본질이라는 점을 설명하고 있다.

▶ 따라서 글의 주제로 적절한 것은 ③ '문화유산의 사회적 구성물로서의 종잡을 수 없는 특성'이다.

⟩왜 오답?

① 문화유산을 보존해야 하는 중요성이 아니라, 문화유산의 본질을 설명한 글이다.
② 문화유산을 저장소로 설명한 글이지, 저장소를 설립하는 절차에 관한 글은 아니다.
④ 세계유산이나 사회단체들에 관한 언급은 없었다.
⑤ 글의 내용과 반대되는 내용이다. (◀▶ 이유: 어떤 공예품이 역사적으로 가치 있다고 선택될지에 관한 기준은 확립되지 않아서 종잡을 수 없는 특징을 보인다고 설명했다.)

₁회 12 정답 ④

밑줄 친 (a)~(e) 중에서 문맥상 낱말의 쓰임이 적절하지 않은 것은? [3점]

① (a) 종잡을 수 없는 영역에서 '추출되면' 추출되다 의미없는 모음이 됨
② (b) 문화유산은 사회적 상호작용을 통해 집단의 구축되는 것임
③ (c) 사회적 담론을 거쳐 선택되고 만들어짐 발명되다
④ (d) 명확한 기준이 없음 안정적인
⑤ (e) 문화유산은 사회적 상호작용으로 구축됨 본질

⟩왜 정답? [정답률 45%]

④ (d) stable 안정적인

⌐ 문화유산의 종잡을 수 없는 본질에 대한 믿음은 어떤 공예품들과 행동 양식이 후대에 전수되어야 하는지를 결정하는 기준이 (d) 안정적이라는 확신에 기반하고 있다. 안정적이지 않다는
∟

⇒ 문화유산의 종잡을 수 없는 본질은 어떤 유물이 문화유산으로서의 가치가 있는지에 관한 명확한 기준이 있는 것이 아니라, 오히려 사회적 상호작용과 의사결정권자들에 의해 선택되기 때문에 그 기준이 '안정적이지 않다'.

▶ stable을 unstable(안정적이지 않은)과 같은 어휘로 바꾸어야 함

⟩왜 오답?

① (a) extracted 추출되다

⌐ 이 종잡을 수 없는 영역에서 (a) 추출된다면 저장소는 다양한 형태에 내포된 공예품들과 아이디어들의 그저 텅 빈, 의미 없는 모음이 된다.
∟

⇒ 종잡을 수 없는 영역은 사회적 상호작용을 통해 구축된 것이기 때문에 그곳에서 '추출된다면', 그 저장소는 과거의 공예품이나 아이디어들을 아무 의미 없이 모아놓은 것이 된다. ▶ extracted는 문맥에 맞음

② (b) collective 집단의

⌐ 문화유산에 대한 이러한 이해는 Maurice Halbwachs에 의해 도입된 ∟ (b) 집단 기억이라는 개념에 뿌리를 둔다.

⇒ 문화유산을 사회적 상호작용으로 구축된 종잡을 수 없는 것이라 이해하는 것은 '집단의' 기억이라는 것을 바탕으로 한다. ▶ collective는 문맥에 맞음

③ (c) invented 발명되다

⌐ 전통과 문화유산이 사회적으로 결정되는 현상은 Eric Hobsbawn과 Terence Ranger에 의해 강조되는데, 그들은 그 전통이 재현되는 것이 아니라 오히려 (c) 발명되는 것이라고 여긴다.
∟

⇒ 전통과 문화유산은 사회적으로 결정되기 때문에, 문화유산은 과거의 모든 유물을 보존함으로써 그 전통을 재현하는 것이 아니라, 사회적 담론을 거쳐 선택되고 만들어진, 즉 '발명된' 것이다. ▶ invented는 문맥에 맞음

⑤ (e) essence 본질

⌐ 사회적 상호작용은 문화유산에서 전승의 (e) 본질이다.

⇒ 어떤 문화유산을 선택하고 후대에 전수할지는 사회적 상호작용으로 구축되는 것이라 했으므로, 사회적 상호작용은 문화유산 전승의 '본질'이다.

▶ essence는 문맥에 맞음

2회 01 정답 ④ * 권위자들 앞에서 자기 행동을 정당화하기

분사구문 / 부사적 용법 (목적)
Serving in the military, / I relied heavily on this saying / to guide my actions. //
군대에 복무하면서 / 나는 이 속담에 매우 의지했다 / 내 행동을 안내하기 위해 //

복합관계부사 / 형용사적 용법 (decision 수식)
Whenever I had a difficult decision to make, / I would ask
재귀 용법의 재귀대명사
myself, / "Can you stand before the long green table?" //
내가 내리기 어려운 결정이 있을 때마다 / 나는 자신에게 묻곤 했다 / "당신은 긴 초록색 탁자 앞에 설 수 있나요"라고 //

과거분사구 (tables 수식)
Since WWII, / the conference tables used in military boardrooms
과거완료 수동태
/ had been constructed / of long, narrow pieces of furniture /
과거분사구 (furniture 수식)
covered in green felt. //
제2차 세계대전 이래로 / 군대 이사회실에서 사용된 회의 탁자는 / 만들어졌다 / 길고 좁은 가구 조각들로 / 초록색 펠트로 덮인 //

복합관계부사 / 주격 관계대명사
Whenever a formal proceeding took place / that required multiple officers to adjudicate an issue, / the officers would gather around the table. // [단서 1] 긴 초록색 탁자는 군대 장교들이 사안을 판결하기 위한 공식 회의 장소임
공식 회의가 있을 때마다 / 여러 장교들이 사안을 판결할 필요가 있는 / 장교들은 탁자 주위로 모이곤 했다 //

The point of the saying was simple. // [단서 2] 장교들 앞에서 주장의 정당성을 입증할 수 없다면 자기 행동을 돌아봐야 함
속담의 요점은 단순하다 //

make a case: 주장의 정당함을 입증함 / 현재분사구 (the officers 수식)
If you *couldn't* make a good case / to the officers sitting around the long green table, / then you should reconsider your actions. //
당신이 주장이 정당함을 잘 입증'할 수 없다면' / 긴 초록색 탁자에 둘러 앉아있는 장교들에게 / 그러면 당신은 당신의 행동을 재고해야 한다 //

be about to-v: 막 ~하려고 하다
Every time I was about to make an important decision, / I asked
재귀 용법의 재귀대명사
myself, /
내가 중요한 결정을 내리려고 할 때마다 / 나는 자신에게 물었다 /

병렬 구조
"Can I stand before the long green table / and be satisfied / that I took all the right actions?" // [단서 3] 긴 초록색 탁자 앞에 선다는 것은 자신이 올바른 행동을 취했다고 만족할 수 있는지를 묻는 것임
"나는 긴 초록색 탁자 앞에 설 수 있는가 / 그리고 만족할 수 있는가 / 내가 모든 올바른 행동을 취했다고"라고 //

앞에 목적격 관계대명사 생략
It is one of the most fundamental questions / a leader must ask
helped의 목적어와 목적격 보어 (원형부정사)
themselves / — and the old saying helped me remember / what steps to take. //
그것은 가장 근본적인 질문 중 하나 / 지도자가 자신들에게 물어봐야 할 / 그리고 오래된 속담은 나를 기억하도록 도왔다 / 무슨 절차를 취해야 하는지를 //

- conference ⓝ 회의
- boardroom ⓝ 중역 회의실
- proceeding ⓝ 행사
- require ⓥ 필요로 하다
- reconsider ⓥ 재고하다
- fundamental ⓐ 근본적인
- assistance ⓝ 도움
- knowledgeable ⓐ 지식이 많은
- courageously [ad] 대담하게
- convincingly [ad] 설득력 있게, 납득이 가도록
- authority figure 권위자
- persuade ⓥ 설득하다

군대에 복무하면서 나는 내 행동을 안내하기 위해 이 속담에 매우 의지했다. 내가 내리기 어려운 결정이 있을 때마다, 나는 자신에게 "당신은 긴 초록색 탁자 앞에 설 수 있나요?"라고 묻곤 했다. 제2차 세계대전 이래로, 군대 이사회실에서 사용된 회의 식탁은 초록색 펠트로 덮인 길고 좁은 가구 조각들로 만들어졌다. 여러 장교들이 사안을 판결할 필요가 있는 공식 회의가 있을 때마다, 장교들은 탁자 주위로 모이곤 했다. 속담의 요점은 단순하다. 당신이 긴 초록색 탁자에 둘러 앉아있는 장교들에게 주장이 정당함을 잘 입증할 수 없다면, 당신은 당신의 행동을 재고해야 한다. 내가 중요한 결정을 내리려고 할 때마다, 나는 자신에게 "나는 긴 초록색 탁자 앞에 서서 내가 모든 올바른 행동을 취했다고 만족할 수 있는가?"라고 물었다. 그것은 지도자가 자신들에게 물어봐야 할 가장 근본적인 질문 중 하나다. 그리고 오래된 속담은 무슨 절차를 취해야 하는지를 기억하도록 나를 도왔다.

밑줄 친 stand before the long green table이 다음 글에서 의미하는 바로 가장 적절한 것은? [4점]

If you *couldn't* make ~ you should reconsider your actions.

① adapt your strategy to constantly changing field conditions
당신의 전략을 끊임없이 변화하는 현장 상황에 맞춰 조정한다 / 상황에 맞게 바꾸는 것이 중요한 것이 아님
② request assistance in your task from those more knowledgeable
더 지식이 많은 사람에게 당신의 업무에 대한 도움을 요청한다 / 권위자들에게 도움을 요청하는 내용이 아님
③ courageously carry out your plan without the approval of peers
동료들의 승인 없이 당신의 계획을 대담하게 수행한다 / 관련 없음
④ convincingly justify your actions to a group of authority figures
당신의 행동을 권위자 집단에 설득력 있게 정당화한다
⑤ persuade your peers that their campaign strategy is not realistic
캠페인 전략이 현실적이지 않다고 당신의 동료를 설득한다 / 캠페인 전략에 대해 설득한다는 내용은 언급되지 않았음

→ 왜 정답? [정답률 65%]

- 군대에서는 초록색 펠트로 덮인 길고 좁은 가구 조각들로 만들어진 회의 탁자를 사용함 → '긴 초록색 탁자'는 군대 장교들이 사안을 판결하는 공식 회의 장소임 [단서 1]
- 공식 회의 중 장교들 앞에서 자기 주장의 정당성을 입증할 수 없다면 자기 행동을 돌아봐야 함 → 긴 초록색 탁자 앞에 선다는 것은 자신이 올바른 행동을 취했다고 만족할 수 있는지를 묻는 것임 [단서 2, 3]

→ 자신의 행동을 안내하기 위해 '긴 초록색 탁자 앞에 선다'라는 행동 지침을 떠올린다고 했으며, 이는 권위자들 앞에서 자기 주장을 정당화할 수 있는지를 고민해 본다는 의미이다.
▶ 따라서 정답은 ④ '당신의 행동을 권위자 집단에 설득력 있게 정당화한다'이다.

→ 왜 오답?
① 전략을 상황에 맞게 바꾼다는 내용은 언급되지 않았다.
② 권위자들에게 자신의 주장을 정당화한다는 내용이지, 그들에게 도움을 요청하는 내용이 아니다.
③ 동료들의 승인 없이 계획을 수행한다는 내용은 언급되지 않았다.
⑤ 캠페인 전략에 대해 설득한다는 내용은 언급되지 않았다.

2회 02 정답 ① * 연주자의 개성을 반영하는 재즈 음악

No clear-cut category can encompass all jazz. //
모든 재즈를 포괄할 수 있는 명확한 범주는 없다 //

[단서 1] 각 연주자의 표현 방식은 고유한 스타일이며, 그렇지 않으면 재즈가 아님
Each performer's idiom / is a style unto itself; / if it were not so,
가정법 과거
/ the music would hardly be jazz. //
각 연주자의 표현 방식은 / 고유한 스타일이다 / 그렇지 않다면 / 그 음악은 재즈라고 할 수 없다 //

Jazz, / like almost all other music, / comprises three artistic activities: / creating, performing, and listening. //
재즈는 / 거의 모든 다른 음악과 마찬가지로 / 세 가지 예술 활동으로 구성된다 / 창작, 연주, 그리고 감상 //

In traditional Western European music, / these three activities are not always performed / by the same individual, / although
= are performed
they quite often are. //
전통적인 서양 음악에서는 / 이 세 가지 활동이 항상 수행되지 않는다 / 같은 개인에 의해 / 하지만 종종 같은 사람이 수행하기도 한다 //

가주어 / 의미상 주어 / 진주어
In jazz, / however, / it is necessary / for the performer / to combine all three at the same time. //
재즈에서는 / 그러나 / 필요하다 / 연주자가 / 이 세 가지를 동시에 결합하는 것이 //

문장의 동사 ①
Musical creation is an active part / of any jazz performance / and
문장의 동사 ②
depends on the performers' understanding / of the developing
동격 / 과거분사
creation, / an understanding gained only by their ability to
형용사적 용법
listen well. //
음악적 창작은 적극적인 부분이다 / 모든 재즈 공연의 / 그리고 연주자의 이해에 달려 있다 / 진행 중인 창작에 대한 / 즉 그들의 잘 듣는 능력으로만 얻어지는 이해 //

They must react instantaneously / to what they hear from their fellow performers, / and their own contribution must be consistent / with the unfolding themes and moods. //
연주자들은 즉석으로 반응해야 한다 / 동료 연주자들로부터 듣는 것에 / 그리고 자신의 기여는 일관되어야 한다 / 펼쳐지는 주제와 분위기에 //

Every act of musical creation in jazz is, / therefore, / as individual as the performer / creating it. // 현재분사(performer 수식) 단서2 재즈에서의 모든 음악적 창작 행위가 연주자만큼이나 개별적이라고 함
재즈에서의 모든 음악적 창작 행위는 ~이다 / 따라서 / 연주자만큼이나 개별적 / 그것을 창조하는 //

- encompass ⓥ 포함하다, 포괄하다 ・ idiom ⓝ 표현 양식
- comprise ⓥ 구성되다[이뤄지다] ・ instantaneously ⓐ 즉석으로
- contribution ⓝ 기여 ・ be consistent with ~와 일관되다
- individuality ⓝ 개성 ・ compose ⓥ 작곡하다

모든 재즈를 포괄할 수 있는 명확한 범주는 없다. 각 연주자의 표현 방식은 고유한 스타일이며, 그렇지 않다면 그 음악은 재즈라고 할 수 없다. 재즈는 거의 모든 다른 음악과 마찬가지로 세 가지 예술 활동으로 구성된다: 창작, 연주, 그리고 감상. 전통적인 서양 음악에서는 이 세 가지 활동이 항상 같은 개인에 의해 수행되지 않지만, 종종 같은 사람이 수행하기도 한다. 그러나 재즈에서는 연주자가 이 세 가지를 동시에 결합해야 한다. 음악적 창작은 모든 재즈 공연의 적극적인 부분이며, 이는 연주자들이 진행 중인 창작을 이해하는 데 달려 있다. 이 이해는 그들이 잘 듣는 능력으로만 얻을 수 있다. 연주자들은 동료 연주자들로부터 듣는 것에 즉각적으로 반응해야 하고, 자신의 기여는 펼쳐지는 주제와 분위기에 일관되어야 한다. 따라서 재즈에서의 모든 음악적 창작 행위는 그것을 창조하는 연주자만큼이나 개별적이다.

다음 글의 주제로 가장 적절한 것은?
재즈가 연주자만큼이나 개별적이며 연주자의 고유한 스타일이 없으면 재즈가 아니라고 함
① traits of jazz reflecting performers' individuality
연주자의 개성을 반영하는 재즈의 특성
② how to compose jazz for a great performance
좋은 연주를 위한 재즈 작곡 방법   좋은 연주를 위한 재즈 작곡 방법에 대한 글이 아님
③ similarities between jazz and Western music
재즈와 서양 음악 간 공통점   재즈와 서양 음악 간 공통점에 대한 내용이 아님
④ celebrated figures in the modern jazz scene
현대 재즈 분야의 유명 인사들   현대 재즈 분야의 유명 인사들이 언급되지 않음
⑤ influences of traditional music on jazz
전통 음악이 재즈에 미친 영향   전통 음악의 특성이 언급되었으나 재즈에 미친 영향에 대한 글이 아님

왜 정답? [정답률 68%]

전반부	각 연주자의 표현 방식은 고유한 스타일이며, 그렇지 않으면 재즈라고 할 수 없음 단서1
중반부	・음악을 구성하는 세 가지 예술 활동: 창작, 연주, 감상 ・재즈에서는 연주자가 이 세 가지를 동시에 결합하고, 연주자의 능력에 달려 있음
후반부	재즈에서의 모든 음악적 창작 행위는 그것을 창조하는 연주자만큼이나 개별적임 단서2

▶ 따라서 이 글의 주제는 ① '연주자의 개성을 반영하는 재즈의 특성'이다.

왜 오답?
② 좋은 연주를 위한 재즈 작곡 방법에 대한 글이 아니다.
③ 재즈와 서양 음악 간 공통점이 언급되지 않았다.
④ 현대 재즈 분야의 유명 인사들이 언급된 글이 아니다.
⑤ 전통 음악의 특성이 언급은 되었으나 재즈에 미친 영향에 대한 글이 아니다.

2회 03 정답 ② *자신이 만든 문제를 스스로 해결한 F. Yates

There is a story / about F. Yates, a prominent UK statistician. // 동격
한 이야기가 있다 / 저명한 영국의 통계학자인 F. Yates에 대한 //

During his student years / at St. John's College, Cambridge, / Yates had been keen / on a form of sport. //
그의 학생 시절에 / Cambridge에 있는 St. John's College에서의 / Yates는 매우 관심이 많았다 / 스포츠의 한 형태에 //

It consisted of climbing / about the roofs and towers / of the college buildings / at night. //
그것은 올라 다니는 것으로 구성되었다 / 지붕과 탑들을 / 대학 건물들의 / 밤에 //

In particular, / the chapel of St. John's College / has a massive neo-Gothic tower / adorned with statues of saints, / 앞에 주격 관계대명사와 be동사가 생략됨
특히 / St. John's College 예배당은 / 거대한 신고딕 양식의 탑이 있는데 / 성인들의 동상으로 장식된 /   단서1 Yates는 성인들의 동상에 흰 가운을 입히면 더 품위 있어 보일 것이라고 생각함
and to Yates / it appeared obvious / that it would be more decorous / if these saints were properly attired / in surplices. //
Yates에게는 / ~이 분명해 보였다 / 그것이 더 품위 있어 보일 것이 / 이 성인들이 적절하게 입혀지면 / 흰 가운으로 //   단서2 어느 날 밤에 그 일을 함

One night / he climbed up and did the job; / next morning / the result was generally much admired. //
어느 날 밤 / 그는 기어올라서 그 일을 했다 / 다음날 아침 / 그 결과는 대체로 많은 칭찬을 받았다 //

But / the College authorities were unappreciative / and began to consider means / of divesting the saints / of their newly acquired garments. // 병렬 구조
하지만 / 대학 당국은 인정해 주지 않았으며 / 방안을 고려하기 시작했다 / 그 성인들에게서 벗기는 / 그들의 새롭게 획득된 의복을 //

This was not easy, / since they were well out of reach / of any ordinary ladder. // 부사절 접속사(원인)
이것은 쉽지 않았다 / 그것들은 도무지 닿을 수 없는 곳에 있었기 때문에 / 일반 사다리로는 //

An attempt / to lift the surplices off / from above, / using ropes / with hooks attached, / was unsuccessful. // 형용사적 용법(An attempt 수식)
시도는 / 흰 가운을 들어 올리려는 / 위에서 / 밧줄을 사용하여 / 갈고리가 달린 / 성공하지 못했다 //

No progress was being made / and eventually Yates came forward and volunteered / to climb up / in the daylight / and bring them down. // 단서3 흰 가운을 벗기는 것이 실패하자 Yates가 자신이 그 문제를 해결했다고 함
아무런 진전도 이루어지지 않았으며 / 결국 Yates가 나서서 자원했다 / 기어올라 / 대낮에 / 그것들을 갖고 내려오겠다고 //   단서4 Yates는 그 일을 해냄

This he did / to the admiration of the crowd / that assembled. //
그는 이 일을 하여 / 군중을 감탄하게 했다 / 모인 //
부정어 없이 목적어가 문두에 오면 도치가 일어나지 않음

- prominent ⓐ 저명한, 유명한 ・ statistician ⓝ 통계학자
- keen ⓐ 매우 관심이 많은, 열중하는 ・ consist of ~로 구성되다
- chapel ⓝ 예배당 ・ massive ⓐ 거대한
- neo-Gothic 신고딕 양식의 ・ adorn ⓥ 장식하다, 꾸미다
- statue ⓝ 동상, 조각상 ・ saint ⓝ 성인(聖人), 성-
- attire ⓥ (옷을) 차려 입히다 ・ admire ⓥ 칭찬하다, 감탄하다
- authority ⓝ ((pl.)) 당국, 관계자 ・ unappreciative ⓐ 인정하지 않는
- garment ⓝ 의복 ・ attempt ⓝ 시도 ・ hook ⓝ 갈고리
- progress ⓝ 진전, 진척, 발전 ・ eventually ⓐ 결국
- assemble ⓥ 모이다, 조립하다

영국의 저명한 통계학자, F. Yates에 대한 이야기가 있다. Cambridge에 있는 St. John's College에 다니던 학생 시절에, Yates는 스포츠의 한 형태에 매우 관심이 많았다. 그것은 밤에 대학 건물들의 지붕과 탑들을 올라 다니는 것으로 구성되었다. 특히, St. John's College 예배당에는 성인들의 동상으로 장식된 거대한 신고딕 양식의 탑이 있는데, Yates에게는 이 성인들에게 적절하게 흰 가운을 입혀 주면 더 품위 있어 보일 것이 분명해 보였다. 어느 날 밤 그는 기어올라서 그 일을 했으며, 다음날 아침 그 결과는 대체로 많은 칭찬을 받았다. 하지만 대학 당국은 인정해 주지 않았으며 그 성인들에게서 새롭게 획득한 그들의

의복을 벗기는 방안을 고려하기 시작했다. 그것들은 일반 사다리로는 도무지 닿을 수 없는 곳에 있었기 때문에, 이것은 쉽지 않았다. 갈고리가 달린 밧줄을 사용하여 위에서 흰 가운을 들어 올리려는 시도는 성공하지 못했다. 아무런 진전도 이루어지지 않았으며 결국 Yates가 나서서 대낮에 기어올라 그것들을 갖고 내려오겠다고 자원했다. 그는 이 일을 하여 모인 군중을 감탄하게 했다.

다음 글의 제목으로 가장 적절한 것은?

① A Scary Legend About the Statues at St. John's College
St. John's College에 있는 동상들에 대한 으스스한 전설　　동상 자체에 대한 글이 아님
② A Student Who Solved a Problem of His Own Making
그 자신이 만든 문제를 해결한 학생　　자신이 입힌 흰 가운을 자신이 벗김
③ Standards of Beauty Varying from Person to Person
사람마다 다른 미의 기준　　대체로 칭찬을 받았음
④ A Smart Professor Who Identified a Criminal
범죄자를 알아본 똑똑한 교수　　특정한 교수에 대한 언급은 없음
⑤ A Success Story of a Mysterious Architect
불가사의한 건축가의 성공담　　F. Yates가 건축가인 것은 아님

왜 정답? [정답률 74%]

대학 건물들의 지붕과 탑을 올라 다니는 스포츠에 매우 관심이 많았던 F. Yates가 어느 날 밤에 St. John's College 예배당 탑에 장식된 성인들의 동상에 흰 가운을 입혔다. 대학 당국이 이 흰 가운을 벗기는 것에 실패하자 F. Yates가 나서서 그 일을 했다고 했으므로 제목은 ② '그 자신이 만든 문제를 해결한 학생'이 적절하다.

왜 오답?

① St. John's College 예배당의 동상들에 흰 가운을 입혔다가 벗긴 일화에 대한 글이다. 그 동상들에 전해지는 전설에 대한 언급은 없다.
③ 흰 가운을 입힌 것은 대체로 칭찬 받았다고 했다. 따라서 사람마다 미의 기준이 다르다는 것은 제목으로 적절하지 않다.
④ F. Yates가 범죄자라거나 그가 범죄자라는 것을 어느 똑똑한 교수가 알아차렸다는 내용이 아니다.
⑤ 등장인물인 F. Yates는 영국의 저명한 통계학자이지, 건축가가 아니다.

배경 지식

＊ 통계학

통계학은 수학적 지식을 바탕으로 자연 현상이나 사회 현상, 경제 현상의 다양한 특성 및 정보를 과학적으로 분석하고 결과를 끌어내는 이론과 방법에 관한 학문으로, 수리 통계학과 추측 통계학으로 나뉜다.

수리 통계학은 집단 현상에 관한 숫자 데이터를 확률론 등의 수학 이론을 사용하여 처리하는 통계학이고, 추측 통계학은 한 표본의 조사로부터 전체 집단의 현상을 추리하는 통계학이다.

2회 04 정답 ② ＊Osborne이 가진 역사 기록의 신뢰성에 대한 회의

In terms of education, / history has not always received a good press. //
교육 측면에서 / 역사학은 항상 좋은 평가를 받지 못했다 //
분사구문
Advising his son / in 1656, / Francis Osborne was far from enthusiastic / about the subject. //
그의 아들에게 조언하면서 / 1656년에 / Francis Osborne은 결코 열정적이지 않았다 / 이 주제에 대해 //
단서1 모순된 보고를 들은 경험이 있음
His experience / of hearing contradictory reports / about the Civil Wars of his own time (contemporary history), / led him to be doubtful / about the **reliability** of records / of less recent events. //
그의 경험은 / 모순된 보고들을 들은 / 그의 시대에 벌어진 내전(현대사)에 대한 / 그를 회의적으로 이끌었다 / 기록의 신뢰성에 대한 / 덜 최근의(더 오래된) 사건들의 //
단서2 역사의 기록이 거짓이거나 우연한 믿음을 나타낸다고 결론 지음
삽입절
Such historical records, / he concluded, / were likely to present / a 'false, or at best but a contingent beliefe'; / and as such they
따라서
hardly warranted serious study. //
= historical records
그러한 역사의 기록이 / 그는 결론지었다 / 나타낼 가능성이 컸다 / '거짓이거나, 기껏해야 우연적인 믿음' / 따라서 그것들은 진지한 연구의 가치가 거의 없었다 //

단서3 Osborne은 신뢰할 수 없는 역사를 공부함으로써 아들이 시간 낭비하는 것을 걱정함
Osborne's anxiety about his son / potentially wasting his time /
주격 관계대명사
by studying history that is unreliable, / implies an understanding of history / as being ideally of a certain kind /
Osborne의 아들에 대한 걱정 / 그의 시간을 낭비할까 하는 / 신뢰할 수 없는 역사 공부를 함으로써 / 역사에 대한 이해를 암시한다 / 특정한 형태에 대한 이상적인 것임을 /
— the kind that yields certain, 'factual' knowledge about the past. //
즉 확실하고 과거에 대한 '사실적인' 지식을 제공하는 형태 //
양보의 부사절 접속사
Now, / although that model was already under challenge / in Osborne's day, / it has persisted / to some extent up to our own time. //
오늘날 / 비록 그 모델은 이미 도전을 받고 있었지만 / Osborne의 시대에 / 그것은 여전히 지속되고 있다 / 오늘날까지도 어느 정도 //

• press ⓝ 평가　　• enthusiastic ⓐ 열정적인
• contradictory ⓐ 모순된　　• persist ⓥ 계속[지속]되다
• extent ⓝ 정도　　• reliability ⓝ 신뢰성
• conciseness ⓝ 간결함　　• predictability ⓝ 예측 가능성

교육 측면에서 역사학은 항상 좋은 평가를 받지 못했다. 1656년, Francis Osborne은 아들에게 조언하면서 이 주제에 대해 결코 열정적이지 않았다. 그의 시대에 벌어진 내전(현대사)에 대한 모순된 보고들을 들은 그의 경험은 그가 더 오래된 사건들에 대한 기록의 **신뢰성**에 회의감을 느끼도록 했다. 그래서 그는 역사 기록이 '거짓이거나, 기껏해야 우연적인 믿음'일 가능성이 크다고 결론지었고, 따라서 그것들을 진지하게 연구할 가치가 없다고 판단했다. Osborne이 아들이 신뢰할 수 없는 역사 공부로 시간을 낭비할까 걱정하는 것은 역사에 대한 이상적인 이해가 특정한 형태 — 즉 과거에 대한 확실하고 '사실적인' 지식을 제공하는 형태 — 임을 암시한다. 비록 그 모델은 Osborne의 시대에 이미 도전을 받고 있었지만, 오늘날까지도 어느 정도 지속되고 있다.

다음 빈칸에 들어갈 말로 가장 적절한 것을 고르시오.

① continuity 최근이 아닌 사건 기록의 지속성에 회의감을 느낀다는 내용이 아님
지속성
② reliability 과거의 사건 기록의 신뢰성에 대해 회의감을 느낀다고 했음
신뢰성
③ rediscovery 과거의 사건 기록의 재발견에 대해 회의감을 느낀다는 언급은 없음
재발견
④ conciseness 역사 기록의 간결함에 대해 회의감을 느꼈다는 내용이 아님
간결함
⑤ predictability 과거 사건 기록의 예측 가능성에 대해 회의감을 느낀 것은 아님
예측 가능성

왜 정답? [정답률 67%]

빈칸 문장	그의 시대에 벌어진 내전(현대사)에 대한 모순된 보고들을 들은 그의 경험은 그가 더 오래된 사건들에 대한 기록의 _____에 회의감을 느끼도록 했다.

➡ 빈칸에는 그(Osborne)가 덜 최근의(더 오래된) 사건들에 대한 기록, 즉 역사의 무엇에 대해 회의감을 느꼈는지가 나와야 한다.

• 그의 시대에 벌어진 내전(현대사)에 대한 모순된 보고들을 들은 그의 경험 단서1
• 그는 역사 기록이 '거짓이거나, 기껏해야 우연적인 믿음'일 가능성이 크다고 결론 지음 단서2
• Osborne이 아들이 신뢰할 수 없는 역사 공부로 시간을 낭비할까 걱정함 단서3

➡ Osborne이 역사에 대한 모순된 보고를 들으며 역사를 거짓이거나 기껏해야 우연적인 믿음일 가능성이 큰 것으로 여기고, 아들이 신뢰할 수 없는 역사를 공부하면서 시간 낭비하는 것을 걱정했다는 내용의 글이다.
▶ 그러므로 Osborne이 더 오래된 사건들에 대한 기록의 '신뢰성'에 회의감을 느꼈다고 할 수 있으므로 ②이 정답이다.

왜 오답?

① 최근이 아닌 사건 기록의 지속성에 회의감을 느낀다는 내용이 아니다.
③ 과거의 사건 기록의 재발견에 대해 회의감을 느낀다는 언급은 없다.
④ 역사 기록의 간결함에 대해 회의감을 느꼈다는 내용의 글이 아니다.
⑤ 과거 사건 기록의 예측 가능성에 대해 회의감을 느낀 것은 아니다.

2회 05 정답 ① *교육을 받아야 하는 모든 지능

Every intelligence has to **be taught**. //
모든 지능은 교육을 받아야 한다 //
단서 1 인간의 뇌(지능의 예시)는 고양이와 개를 구별하기 전에 여러 가지 예를 보아야 한다고 함

A human brain, / which is genetically primed to categorize
　　　　　　　　　　주격 관계대명사
things, / still needs to see a dozen examples / as a child / before
＝human brain
it can distinguish between cats and dogs. //
인간의 뇌는 / 유전적으로 사물을 분류하도록 준비되어 있는 / 여전히 여러 가지 예를 볼
필요가 있다 / 어린 시절에 / 고양이와 개를 구별할 수 있기 전에 //
　　　비교급 강조
That's even more true for artificial minds. //
그것은 인공지능의 경우 훨씬 더 사실이다 //
단서 2 컴퓨터(지능의 예시)도 실력이 늘기 전에 게임을 많이 해봐야 한다고 함

Even the best-programmed computer / has to play / at least a
thousand games of chess / before it gets good. //
가장 잘 프로그래밍된 컴퓨터도 / 해야 한다 / 체스 게임을 최소한 천 번은 / 실력이 늘어나기
전에 //

Part of the AI breakthrough / lies in the incredible amount of
collected data / about our world, / which provides the schooling
　　　　　　　　　　　계속적 용법의 주격 관계대명사
　목적격 관계대명사
/ that AIs need. // **단서 3** 인공지능은 학습을 필요로 한다고 함
인공지능의 혁신 부분은 / 방대한 양의 수집된 데이터에 있다 / 우리 세계에 대한 / 이
데이터는 학습을 제공한다 / 인공지능이 필요로 하는 //

Massive databases, self-tracking, web cookies, online footprints,
terabytes of storage, decades of search results, / and the entire
　　　　　　　　　　　　　현재분사
digital universe became the teachers / making AI smart. //
대량의 데이터베이스, 자기 추적, 웹 쿠키, 온라인 발자국, 테라바이트의 저장 용량, 수십 년의
검색 결과 / 그리고 전체 디지털 우주가 교사가 되었다 / 인공지능을 똑똑하게 만드는 //

Andrew Ng explains it this way: / "AI is akin / to building a
rocket ship. //
Andrew Ng은 그것을 이렇게 설명한다 / "인공지능은 비슷하다 / 로켓을 만드는 것과 //

You need a huge engine / and a lot of fuel. //
거대한 엔진이 필요하다 / 그리고 많은 연료가 //

The rocket engine is the learning algorithms / but the fuel is the
huge amounts of data / we can feed / to these algorithms." //
　　　　　　　　사이에 목적격 관계대명사 생략
로켓 엔진은 학습 알고리즘이다 / 그러나 연료는 방대한 양의 데이터이다 / 우리가 공급할 수
있는 / 이러한 알고리즘에" //

- **genetically** [ad] 유전적으로　　・ **categorize** ⓥ 분류하다
- **dozen** ⓐ 십 여개의, 다수의　　・ **distinguish** ⓥ 구별하다
- **breakthrough** ⓝ 돌파구, 혁신 부분　　・ **schooling** ⓝ 학습
- **self-tracking** ⓝ 자기 추적　　・ **akin** ⓐ ~와 유사한　　・ **fuel** ⓝ 연료
- **exceed** ⓥ 초과하다, 초월하다　　・ **govern** ⓥ 통치하다, 통제하다
- **calculate** ⓥ 계산하다　　・ **possibility** ⓝ 가능성

모든 지능은 **교육을 받아야** 한다. 인간의 뇌는 유전적으로 사물을 분류하도록
준비되어 있지만, 고양이와 개를 구별하기 위해서는 어린 시절에 여러 가지
예를 보아야 한다. 인공지능의 경우는 더더욱 그렇다. 가장 잘 프로그래밍된
컴퓨터도 체스 게임을 최소한 천 번은 해야 실력이 늘어난다. 인공지능의 혁신
부분은 우리 세계에 대한 방대한 양의 수집된 데이터에 있다. 이 데이터는
인공지능이 필요로 하는 학습을 제공한다. 대량의 데이터베이스, 자기 추적, 웹
쿠키, 온라인 발자국, 테라바이트의 저장 용량, 수십 년의 검색 결과, 그리고
전체 디지털 우주가 인공지능을 똑똑하게 만드는 교사가 되었다. Andrew
Ng은 그것을 이렇게 설명한다: "인공지능은 로켓을 만드는 것과 비슷하다.
거대한 엔진과 많은 연료가 필요하다. 로켓 엔진은 학습 알고리즘이지만,
연료는 이러한 알고리즘에 공급할 수 있는 방대한 양의 데이터이다."

다음 빈칸에 들어갈 말로 가장 적절한 것을 고르시오.

① **be taught** 인간의 뇌, 컴퓨터, 인공지능은 모두 능력을 발휘하기 전에 같은 것을 여러 번 보는 등의
　교육을 받아야 학습이 필요하다는 내용의 글임
② **exceed itself** 모든 지능(뇌, 컴퓨터 등)이 그 자체의 능력을 초월해야 한다고 하지 않았음
　그 자체를 초월해야
③ **think by itself** 모든 지능이 스스로 생각해야 한다는 내용이 아님
　스스로 생각해야
④ **be governed by rules** 모든 지능이 규칙에 의해 통제되어야 한다고 하지 않았음
　규칙에 의해 통제되어야
⑤ **calculate all possibilities** 모든 지능이 모든 가능성을 계산해야만 한다는 내용이 아님
　모든 가능성을 계산해야

왜 정답? [정답률 69%]

| 빈칸 문장 | 모든 지능은 _____ 한다. |

→ 빈칸에는 모든 지능이 '어떠한' 특성을 가져야 하는지가 언급되어야 한다.

- 인간의 뇌는 고양이와 개를 구별하기 위해서 어린 시절에 여러 가지 예를 보아야
　한다. **단서 1**
- 가장 잘 프로그래밍된 컴퓨터도 체스 게임을 최소한 천 번은 해야 실력이
　늘어난다. **단서 2**
- 인공지능이 필요로 하는 학습을 제공해야 한다. **단서 3**

→ 인간의 뇌나 컴퓨터 등을 지능의 예로 들면서 능력을 발휘하기 전에 여러 번 비슷한
　예를 보거나 같은 게임을 많이 해봐야 한다고 언급했으며, 인공지능은 학습을
　필요로 한다고 명시적으로 언급하고 있는 내용의 글이다.
　여러 번 비슷한 예를 보거나 같은 게임을 해보는 것 또한 무언가를 배우는 학습이나
　교육에 대한 예시로 볼 수 있다.

▶ 그러므로 모든 지능에게 필요한 것은 ① '교육을 받아야' 하는 것이다.

왜 오답?

② 모든 지능(뇌, 컴퓨터 등)이 그 자체의 능력을 초월해야 한다고 하지 않았다.
③ 모든 지능이 스스로 생각해야 한다는 내용이 아니다.
④ 모든 지능이 규칙에 의해 통제되어야 한다고 하지 않았다.
⑤ 모든 지능이 모든 가능성을 계산해야만 한다는 내용의 글이 아니다.

2회 06 정답 ① *사냥 집단의 종교관

　　　　　　　　　　　　　단수 주어
Lewis-Williams believes / that the religious view of hunter
　　　　　　　　단수 동사
groups / was a contract / between the hunter and the hunted. //
Lewis-Williams는 믿는다 / 사냥 집단의 종교관은 / 계약이었다고 / 사냥꾼과 사냥감 간의 //
　　주어　　　　　　　　　　　　　동사　　　목적어　　목적격 보어
'The powers of the underworld / allowed people to kill animals,
conj. ~라면, ~라는 조건에서
/ provided people responded / in certain ritual ways, /
'지하 세계의 신들이 / 사람들에게 동물을 살생하도록 허용했다 / 사람들이 반응하는 조건에서
/ 특정한 의식의 방식으로 /

such as taking fragments of animals / into the caves / and
　　　　　병렬 구조
inserting them / into the "membrane".' //
동물의 작은 일부를 가져가서 / 동굴로 / 그것을 넣는 것과 같은 / '지하 세계로 통하는 바위
표면에'' //

This is borne out / in the San. //
이것은 유지된다 / San 족에서 //　　**단서 1** San 족(사냥 집단)에게는 존중하는 관습이 있음

Like other shamanistic societies, / they have admiring practices
/ between human hunters and their prey, / suffused with taboos
/ derived from extensive natural knowledge. //
다른 무속 사회처럼 / 그들에게는 존중하는 관습이 있는데 / 사냥하는 인간과 그들의 먹이
간의 / 금기로 가득 차 있다 / 광범위한 자연 지식에서 유래한 / **단서 2** 경의를 표하는 것이 살생의
　　　　　　　　　　　　　　　　　　　　　　　　　　　불안을 줄이는 한 가지 수단임
These practices suggest / that honouring may be one method /
of softening the disquiet of killing. //
이런 관습들은 보여 준다 / 경의를 표하는 것이 한 가지 수단일 수도 있다는 것을 / 살생의
불안을 경감하는 //
　　　　　　　　　　　　　　　　　　　　　　조동사로 쓰인 need
It should be said / that this disquiet needn't arise / because
there is something fundamentally wrong / with a human killing
another animal, /
~라고 말해질 수 있다 / 이런 불안은 일어날 필요는 없다 / 근본적으로 잘못된 무언가가
있기 때문에 / 인간이 다른 동물을 죽이는 것에 /

but simply because we are aware / of doing the killing. //
그저 우리가 의식하고 있어서라고 / 살생한다는 것을 //
　　　　　　　　　　　　　　　　　　　주어　　　동사　　　목적어
And perhaps, too, / because in some sense / we 'know' / what
we are killing. //
그리고 또한 어쩌면 / 어떤 의미에서는 / 우리가 '알기' 때문일 수도 있다 / 우리가 무엇을
살생하고 있는지 //

We make sound guesses / that the pain and desire for life / we

_{동격절 접속사}　　　_{앞에 목적격 관계대명사가 생략됨}

feel / — our worlds of experience — / have a counterpart in the

animal / we kill. // **단서3** 우리가 살생하는 동물에게도 우리와 같은 고통과 살고자 하는

욕망이 있다는 타당한 추측에서 문제가 생김

우리는 타당한 추측을 한다 / 고통과 살고자 하는 욕망은 / 우리가 느끼는 / 우리의 경험의

세계 / 동물에게 상응하는 것이 있다고 / 우리가 살생하는 //

As predators, / this can create problems for us. //

포식자로서 / 이것은 우리에게 문제를 만들어 낼 수 있다 //

_{형용사적 용법(One way 수식)}　　　_{명사적 용법(주격 보어)}

One way / to smooth those edges, / then, / is to **view that prey**

/ **with respect**. //

한 가지 방법은 / 그런 문제를 완화하는 / 그렇다면 / 그 먹이를 바라보는 것이다 / 존중하면서 //

- religious ⓐ 종교의, 독실한　　• contract ⓝ 계약
- provided [conj] (만약) ~라면　　• ritual ⓐ 의식상의, 의식을 위한
- fragment ⓝ 작은 일부, 파편　　• bear out ~을 유지하다, ~을 지지하다
- admire ⓥ 존경하다　　• practice ⓝ 관습　　• taboo ⓝ 금기
- derive from ~에서 유래하다　　• extensive ⓐ 광범위한, 폭넓은
- honour ⓥ 존경하다, 경의를 표하다　　• method ⓝ 방법
- soften ⓥ 부드럽게 하다, 누그러뜨리다　　• disquiet ⓝ 불안
- arise ⓥ 생기다, 일어나다　　• fundamentally [ad] 근본[본질]적으로
- aware of ~을 알고 있는　　• sound ⓐ 타당한
- counterpart ⓝ 상응하는 것　　• predator ⓝ 포식자
- smooth ⓥ 완화하다　　• edge ⓝ 문제, 위기
- domesticate ⓥ (동물을) 길들이다[사육하다], (작물을) 재배하다
- supernatural ⓐ 초자연적인　　• worship ⓥ 예배하다, 숭배하다

Lewis-Williams는 사냥 집단이 가진 종교관은 사냥꾼과 사냥감 간의
계약이었다고 믿는다. '지하 세계의 신들이 사람들에게 동물을 살생하도록
허용했는데, 사람들이 동물의 작은 일부를 동굴로 가지고 들어가서 그것을
'지하 세계로 통하는 바위 표면' 속에 넣는 것과 같은 특정한 의식의 방식으로
반응하는 조건에서였다.' 이것은 San족에서 유지된다. 다른 무속 사회처럼,
그들에게는 사냥하는 인간과 그들의 먹이 간의 존중하는 관습이 있는데, (그
관습은) 광범위한 자연 지식에서 유래한 금기로 가득 차 있다. 이런 관습들은
경의를 표하는 것이 살생의 불안을 경감하는 한 가지 수단일 수도 있다는
것을 보여 준다. 이런 불안은 인간이 다른 동물을 죽이는 것에 근본적으로
잘못된 무언가가 있기 때문에 일어날 필요는 없고, 그저 우리가 살생한다는
것을 의식하고 있어서라고 말할 수 있다. 그리고 또한 어쩌면 어떤 의미에서는
우리가 무엇을 살생하고 있는지 '알기' 때문일 수도 있다. 우리가 느끼는
고통과 살고자 하는 욕망은, 우리의 경험의 세계는, 우리가 살생하는 동물에게
상응하는 것이 있다고 우리는 타당한 추측을 한다. 포식자로서, 이것은
우리에게 문제를 만들어 낼 수 있다. 그렇다면, 그런 문제를 완화하는 한 가지
방법은 그 먹이를 존중하면서 바라보는 것이다.

다음 빈칸에 들어갈 말로 가장 적절한 것을 고르시오.

① view that prey with respect 경의를 표하는 것이 살생의 불안을 줄이는 방법임
　그 먹이를 존중하면서 바라보는
② domesticate those animals 동물 사냥에 대한 내용임
　그 동물들을 길들이는
③ develop tools for hunting 사냥 도구에 대한 언급은 없음
　사냥을 위한 도구를 개발하는
④ avoid supernatural beliefs The powers of the underworld, membrane
　초자연적인 믿음을 피하는 　　등으로 만든 오답
⑤ worship our ancestors' spirits 조상을 숭배하기 위해 제물을 바치는 것이 아님
　우리 조상의 정신을 숭배하는

왜 정답? [정답률 55%]

San 족(사냥 집단)의 관습: 사냥하는 인간과 그들의 먹이 사이에 존중하는 관습이
있음

→ 존중하는 것, 즉 경의를 표하는 것은 살생의 불안을 줄이는 수단임

→ 살생의 불안: 우리가 살생하는 동물도 우리와 마찬가지로 고통과 살고자 하는
욕망이 있다는 타당한 추측으로 만들어지는 문제

▶ 그러한 문제를 완화하는 한 가지 방법이 ① '그 먹이를 존중하면서 바라보는'
것이다.

왜 오답?

② 동물을 사냥하는 것에 대한 내용이지, 동물을 길들이는 것은 아니다.

③ '사냥'이라는 소재로 만든 오답이다.

④ '지하 세계의 신', '지하 세계로 통하는 바위 표면' 등이 언급된 것으로 만든 오답이다.
　초자연적인 믿음을 통해 살생의 불안을 경감하는 것이다.

⑤ 조상을 숭배하기 위해 동물을 사냥하여 바치는 것이 아니다.

2회 07 정답 ③ ＊감정이 의사 결정에 미치는 영향

A large body of research / in decision science / has indicated /

많은 연구는 / 의사 결정 과학에 대한 / 보여주었다 **단서1** 당면한 가능성에 대한 감정적 평가가
_{주어}　　　명시적인 평가를 대신하여 자주 쓰임

that one attribute / that is regularly substituted / for an explicit

assessment / of decision costs and benefits / is an affective

valuation / of the prospect at hand. // _{동사}

하나의 속성이 / 대신하여 자주 쓰이는 / 명시적인 평가를 / 의사 결정 비용과 편익에 대한 /
감정적 평가라고 / 당면한 가능성에 대한 //

단서2 감전될 확률에 둔감해진 사람들의 평가를 구체적으로 설명함

(A) People were willing to pay / almost as much / to avoid a 1
_{원급 비교}

percent probability / of receiving a shock / as they were to pay /

to avoid a 99 percent probability / of receiving a shock. //

사람들은 기꺼이 지불하고자 했다 / 거의 ~만큼 많이 / 1퍼센트의 확률을 피하기 위해서 /
감전될 / 그들이 지불하려는 만큼 / 99퍼센트의 확률을 피하기 위해 / 감전될 //

_{주어}

Clearly / the affective reaction / to the thought of receiving a

shock / was overwhelming the subjects' ability / to evaluate the
_{동사}　　　_{형용사적 용법(ability 수식)}

probabilities associated. //

분명히 / 감정적 반응이 / 감전된다는 생각에 대한 / 피실험자들의 능력을 압도하고 있었다 /
관련된 확률을 평가하는 // **단서3** This가 가리키는 것은 주어진 글의 '감정적 평가'이며,
감정적 평가의 장점을 설명함

(B) This is often a very rational attribute / to substitute / — affect

does convey useful signals / as to the costs and benefits / of

outcomes. //

이것은 흔히 매우 합리적인 속성이다 / 대신하여 쓰이는 / 감정은 정말로 유용한 신호를
전달하기 / 비용과 편익에 대한 / 결과의 //

_{주어}　　　_{동사(완전자동사)}

A problem sometimes arises, / however, / when affective

valuation is not supplemented / by any analytic processing and

adjustment / at all. //

때로 문제가 발생한다 / 그러나 / 감정적 평가가 보완되지 않을 때 / 그 어떤 분석적 처리와
조정으로도 / 전혀 / **단서4** 분석적 처리와 조정으로 보완되지 않은 감정적 평가로 인해
문제가 발생하는 사례가 이어짐

(C) For example, / sole reliance / on affective valuation / can
_{can make의 목적어와 목적보어}

make people insensitive / to probabilities and to quantitative
_{선행사}　　　_{주격 관계대명사}

features / of the outcome / that should effect decisions. //

예를 들어 / 오로지 의존하는 것은 / 감정적 평가에만 / 사람들을 둔감하게 만들 수 있다 /
확률과 양적 특징에 / 결과의 / 의사 결정을 초래할 //

_{선행사}

One study demonstrated / that people's evaluation of a
_{관계부사}

situation / where they might receive a shock / is insensitive / to

the probability of receiving the shock / **단서5** 사람들의 평가가 감전될 확률에
둔감하다는 것을 보여 주는 연구를 예로 듦

한 연구는 보여 주었다 / 상황에 대한 사람들의 평가가 / 그들이 감전될지도 모르는 /
둔감하다는 것을 / 감전될 확률에 /

because their thinking is swamped / by affective evaluation of

the situation. //

그들의 사고가 압도되기 때문에 / 그 상황에 대한 감정적 평가에 의해 //

- body ⓝ 많은 양[모음]　　• indicate ⓥ 나타내다, 시사하다
- attribute ⓝ 자질, 속성　　• regularly [ad] 정기적으로, 자주
- substitute ⓥ 대신하다, 대체하다　　• explicit ⓐ 분명한, 명시적인
- assessment ⓝ 평가　　• affective ⓐ 감정적인
- valuation ⓝ 평가　　• prospect ⓝ 가능성, 전망　　• at hand 당면한
- willing ⓐ 기꺼이 하는　　• probability ⓝ 확률
- overwhelm ⓥ 압도하다, 어쩔 줄 모르게 만들다　　• subject ⓝ 피실험자
- evaluate ⓥ 평가하다　　• convey ⓥ 전달하다
- supplement ⓥ 보완하다　　• analytic ⓐ 분석적인
- processing ⓝ 처리　　• adjustment ⓝ 수정, 조정
- sole ⓐ 유일한, 단독의　　• reliance ⓝ 의존, 의지
- insensitive ⓐ 둔감한　　• quantitative ⓐ 양적인
- feature ⓝ 특징　　• effect ⓥ 초래하다
- demonstrate ⓥ 입증[실증]하다

의사 결정 과학에 대한 많은 연구는 의사 결정 비용과 편익에 대한 명시적인 평가를 대신하여 자주 쓰이는 하나의 속성이 당면한 가능성에 대한 감정적 평가라고 보여주었다. (B) 이것은 대신하여 쓰이는 매우 합리적인 속성인 경우가 흔한데, 감정은 정말로 결과의 비용과 편익에 대한 유용한 신호를 전달한다. 그러나 감정적 평가가 그 어떤 분석적 처리와 조정으로도 전혀 보완되지 않으면, 때로 문제가 발생하기도 한다. (C) 예를 들어, 오로지 감정적 평가에만 의존하는 것은 의사 결정을 초래할, 결과의 확률과 양적 특징에 사람들이 둔감해지게 할 수 있다. 한 연구는 감전될지도 모르는 상황에 대한 사람들의 평가가, 그 상황에 대한 감정적 평가에 의해 그들의 사고가 압도되기 때문에, 감전될 확률에 둔감하다는 것을 보여 주었다. (A) 사람들은 1퍼센트의 감전될 확률을 피하기 위해서, 99퍼센트의 감전될 확률을 피하기 위해 그들이 지불하려는 것과 거의 맞먹을 만큼을 기꺼이 지불하고자 했다. 분명히, 감전된다는 생각에 대한 감정적 반응이 (감전과) 관련된 확률을 평가하는 피실험자들의 능력을 압도하고 있었다.

주어진 글 다음에 이어질 글의 순서로 가장 적절한 것을 고르시오.

① (A) — (C) — (B) (C)에서 소개한 연구를 구체적으로 설명하는 것이 (A)임
② (B) — (A) — (C) 당면한 가능성에 대한 감정적 평가는 명시적 평가를 대신하여 자주 쓰이는 속성임 - 이것은 흔히 매우 합리적인 속성이지만, 때로 문제를 일으킴
③ (B) — (C) — (A) - 한 연구는 감전될지도 모르는 상황에 대한 감정적 평가에 압도되어 상황에 대한 사람들의 평가가 감전될 확률에 둔감해진다는 것을 보여 줌 - 사람들은 1퍼센트의 감전될 확률을 피하는 데, 99퍼센트의 감전될 확률을 피하는 것과 거의 비슷한 금액을 기꺼이 지불하고자 했음
④ (C) — (A) — (B)
⑤ (C) — (B) — (A) (C)는 (B)에서 소개한 문제의 사례를 보여 주는 문단임

| 문제 풀이 순서 | [정답률 50%]

1st 각 문단의 내용을 파악하고, 글의 논리적인 순서를 추론한다.

주어진 글: 의사 결정 비용과 편익에 대한 명시적인 평가를 대신하여 자주 쓰이는 하나의 속성이 당면한 가능성에 대한 감정적 평가이다.

➡ **주어진 글 뒤:** 감정적 평가를 기반으로 의사 결정을 하는 것을 구체적으로 설명하면서 그것의 장단점에 대한 내용이 이어질 것이다. (발상)

(A): 사람들은 1퍼센트의 감전될 확률을 피하는 데, 99퍼센트의 감전될 확률을 피하는 것과 거의 비슷한 금액을 기꺼이 지불하고자 했다. 분명히, 감전된다는 생각에 대한 감정적 반응이 감전과 관련된 확률을 평가하는 피실험자들의 능력을 압도하고 있었다.

➡ **(A) 앞:** (A)는 감정적 반응으로 인해 합리적인 결정을 내리지 못하는 사례이다.
▶ 감정적 평가를 기반으로 한 의사 결정의 단점부터 제시되는 글이라면 (A) 앞에 주어진 글이 올 수도 있음
(A) 뒤: 마찬가지로, 감정적 평가를 기반으로 한 의사 결정의 단점부터 제시되는 글이라면 (A) 뒤에는 그것의 장점이 이어져야 한다.

(B): 이것(This)은 대신하여 쓰이는 흔히 매우 합리적인 속성인데, 감정은 정말로 결과의 비용과 편익에 대한 유용한 신호를 전달한다. 그러나(however) 감정적 평가가 그 어떤 분석적 처리와 조정으로도 전혀 보완되지 않으면, 때로 문제가 발생하기도 한다.

➡ **(B) 앞:** (B)의 앞부분은 장점, 뒷부분은 단점이다.
단점을 설명하는 문장에 역접의 연결어(however)가 포함되었으므로, 이 글은 장점을 설명한 후에 단점을 이야기하는 흐름이다.
This가 가리키는 것이 주어진 글에 등장한 '감정적 평가'이다.
▶ (B) 앞에 주어진 문장이 있어야 함 (순서: 주어진 문장 → (B))
(B) 뒤: 감정적 평가로 인해 문제가 발생하기도 한다는 설명을 부연하는 내용이 필요하다.
▶ (A)가 감정적 평가의 단점에 대한 내용이므로 (B) 뒤에 (A)가 올 수도 있음

(C): 예를 들어(For example), 오로지 감정적 평가에만 의존하는 것은 의사 결정을 초래할, 결과의 확률과 양적 특징에 사람들이 둔감해지게 할 수 있다. 한 연구는 감전될지도 모르는 상황에 대한 사람들의 평가가, 그 상황에 대한 감정적 평가에 의해 그들의 사고가 압도되기 때문에, 감전될 확률에 둔감하다는 것을 보여 주었다.

➡ **(C) 앞:** For example은 앞서 설명한 것에 대한 구체적인 사례를 제시할 때 쓰인다.
(C)는 분석적 처리와 조정으로 보완되지 않은 감정적 평가가 문제를 일으키는 사례(한 연구)를 설명하기 시작한다.
▶ (C) 앞에 (B)가 있어야 함 (순서: 주어진 글 → (B) → (C))
(C) 뒤: (C)의 '감전될 확률'을 (A)에서 1퍼센트, 99퍼센트라는 구체적인 수치를 들어 설명하는 흐름이다.
▶ (C) 뒤에 (A)가 이어져야 함 (순서: 주어진 글 → (B) → (C) → (A))

2nd 글이 한눈에 들어오도록 정리하여 정답을 확인한다.

주어진 글: 의사 결정 비용과 편익에 대한 명시적인 평가를 대신하여 자주 쓰이는 하나의 속성이 당면한 가능성에 대한 감정적 평가이다.

➡ **(B):** 이것(감정적 평가)은 정말로 결과의 비용과 편익에 대한 유용한 신호를 전달하는 매우 합리적인 속성인 경우가 흔하다. 하지만 정적 평가가 분석적 처리와 조정으로 보완되지 않으면, 문제가 발생하기도 한다.

➡ **(C):** 예를 들어, 한 연구는 감전될지도 모르는 상황에 대한 사람들의 평가가, 그 상황에 대한 감정적 평가에 의해 그들의 사고가 압도되기 때문에, 감전될 확률에 둔감하다는 것을 보여 주었다.

➡ **(A):** 사람들은 1퍼센트의 감전될 확률을 피하는 데, 99퍼센트의 감전될 확률을 피하는 것과 거의 비슷한 금액을 기꺼이 지불하고자 했다. 분명히 감전된다는 생각에 대한 감정적 반응이 감전과 관련된 확률을 평가하는 피실험자들의 능력을 압도하고 있었다.

▶ 주어진 글 다음에 이어질 글의 순서는 (B) → (C) → (A)이므로 정답은 ③임

2회 08 정답 ④ *언어 사용의 창조적인 측면

In the course of acquiring a language, / children are exposed / to only a finite set of utterances. //
언어를 습득하는 과정에서 / 아이들은 노출된다 / 유한한 발화에만 //

Yet they come to use and understand / an infinite set of sentences. //
하지만 그들은 사용하고 이해하게 된다 / 무한한 문장들을 //

단서 1 그들이 동일한 문법에 도달하리라고 예상되지 않는 상황이 앞에 있어야 함
(A) Yet, they all arrive / at pretty much the same grammar. //
하지만 그들은 모두 도달한다 / 거의 동일한 문법에 //

목적격 관계대명사   부사적 용법(목적)
The input / that children get / is haphazard / in the sense / that caretakers do not talk to their children / to illustrate / a particular point of grammar. //
동격절 접속사
입력은 / 아이들이 받는 / 무작위적이다 / ~라는 점에서 / 돌봐주는 사람들이 자신의 아이들에게 말하지는 않는다는 / 예를 들어 보여주기 위해 / 문법의 특정한 점을 //

Yet, all children develop / systematic knowledge of a language. //
하지만 모든 아이들은 발달시킨다 / 언어에 대한 체계적인 지식을 //

전치사   명사구
(B) Thus, / despite the severe limitations and variation / in the input / children receive, / and also in their personal circumstances, /
앞에 목적격 관계대명사가 생략됨
단서 2 모든 아이가 언어에 대한 체계적인 지식을 발달시키기 때문에 일어나는 일이 이어짐
따라서 / 극심한 한계와 변동에도 불구하고 / 입력에서의 / 아이들이 받는 / 그리고 또한 그들의 개인적인 상황에서의 //

they all develop / a rich and uniform system / of linguistic knowledge. //
그들 모두는 발달시킨다 / 풍부하고 동일한 체계를 / 언어 지식의 //

단수 주어   단수 동사
The knowledge / attained / goes beyond the input / in various ways. //
지식은 / 습득된 / 그 입력을 넘어선다 / 다양한 방식으로 //

정답 및 해설 **515**

(C) This has been referred to / as the creative aspect / of language use. // **단서 3** 유한한 발화에만 노출됨에도 불구하고 무한한 문장을 사용하고 이해하게 되는 현상을 가리킴
이것은 일컬어져 왔다 / 창조적인 측면으로 / 언어 사용의 //

This 'creativity' does not refer to the ability / to write poetry or novels /
형용사적 용법(the ability 수식)
이 '창조성'은 능력을 말하지 않는다 / 시나 소설을 쓰는 /

but rather the ability / to produce and understand / an unlimited
형용사적 용법(the ability 수식)
set of new sentences / never spoken or heard previously. //
오히려 능력을 (말한다) / 만들어내고 이해할 수 있는 / 무한한 새로운 문장을 / 이전에 결코 말하거나 듣지 못한 //

단수 주어, 선행사   단수 동사
The precise linguistic input / children receive / differs from child
앞에 목적격 관계대명사가 생략됨
to child; / no two children are exposed / to exactly the same set of utterances. //
정확한 언어적 입력은 / 아이들이 받는 / 아이들마다 다르다 / 어떤 두 아이도 노출되지 않는다 / 정확히 똑같은 발화에 //

- -

- be exposed to ~에 노출되다   • finite ⓐ 유한한
- utterance ⓝ 발화   • grammar ⓝ 문법   • input ⓝ 투입, 입력
- illustrate ⓥ 보여주다   • systematic ⓐ 체계적인
- despite prep ~에도 불구하고   • limitation ⓝ 제한
- variation ⓝ 변동   • circumstance ⓝ 환경
- linguistic ⓐ 언어의   • attain ⓥ 습득하다, 이르다
- refer to ~을 언급하다   • poetry ⓝ 시   • creativity ⓝ 창의성
- precise ⓐ 정확한   • differ ⓥ 다르다

언어를 습득하는 과정에서 아이들은 유한한 발화에만 노출된다. 하지만 그들은 무한한 문장들을 사용하고 이해하게 된다. (C) 이것은 언어 사용의 창조적인 측면으로 일컬어져 왔다. 이 '창조성'은 시나 소설을 쓰는 능력이라기보다는 이전에 결코 말하거나 듣지 못한 새로운 문장을 무한히 만들어내고 이해하는 능력을 말한다. 아이들이 받는 정확한 언어적 입력은 아이들마다 다르며, 두 아이가 정확히 똑같은 발화에 노출되는 경우는 없다. (A) 하지만 그들은 모두 거의 동일한 문법에 도달한다. 돌봐주는 사람들이 문법의 특정한 점을 예를 들어 보여주기 위해 자신의 아이들에게 말하지는 않는다는 점에서 아이들이 받는 입력은 무작위적이다. 하지만 모든 아이들은 언어에 대한 체계적인 지식을 발달시킨다. (B) 따라서, 아이들이 받는 입력에서의, 그리고 또한 그들의 개인적인 상황에서의 극심한 한계와 변동에도 불구하고, 그들 모두는 언어 지식의 풍부하고 동일한 체계를 발달시킨다. 습득된 지식은 다양한 방식으로 그 입력을 넘어선다.

주어진 글 다음에 이어질 글의 순서로 가장 적절한 것을 고르시오. [3점]
① (A) — (C) — (B) 주어진 문장은 아이들의 공통점을 이야기하므로 (A)와 역접이 아님
② (B) — (A) — (C) 아이들 모두가 언어 지식의 풍부하고 동일한 체계를 발달시키는 원인이 (A)에 등장하지 않으므로 (C) 앞에 올 수 없음
③ (B) — (C) — (A) (C)의 this가 가리키는 것은 주어진 문장에 나옴
④ (C) — (A) — (B)
⑤ (C) — (B) — (A) (B)의 원인 내용인 (A)가 앞에 와야 함
└ 아이들은 유한한 발화에만 노출되지만 무한한 문장을 사용하고 이해하게 됨 - 이는 언어 사용의 창조적 측면으로 일컬어지고, 아이들이 노출되는 발화는 모두 다름 - 아이들은 모두 언어에 대한 체계적인 지식을 발달시킴 - 아이들 모두 언어 지식의 풍부하고 동일한 체계를 발달시킴

| 문제 풀이 순서 | [정답률 58%]

1st 각 문단의 내용을 파악하고, 글의 논리적인 순서를 추론한다.

주어진 글: 언어를 습득하는 과정에서 아이들은 유한한 발화에만 노출된다. 하지만 그들은 무한한 문장들을 사용하고 이해하게 된다.

➡ 유한한 발화에만 노출되지만 무한한 문장을 사용하고 이해하게 되는 아이들의 언어 습득 과정을 설명하는 글이다.
  주어진 글 뒤: 이러한 언어 습득에 대한 구체적인 설명이 이어질 것이다.

(A): 하지만(Yet) 그들은 모두 거의 동일한 문법에 도달한다. 돌봐주는 사람들이 문법의 특정한 점을 예를 들어 보여주기 위해 자신의 아이들에게 말하지는 않는다는 점에서 아이들이 받는 입력은 무작위적이다. 하지만 모든 아이들은 언어에 대한 체계적인 지식을 발달시킨다.

➡ **(A) 앞:** 아이들이 모두 거의 동일한 문법에 도달하리라고 예상되지 않는 상황이 등장해야 Yet이 자연스럽다.
  ▶ 주어진 글은 아이들의 공통점을 이야기하므로 (A) 앞에 오기에 적절하지 않음
  (A) 뒤: 모든 아이가 언어에 대한 체계적인 지식을 발달시킨다는 것에 대한 부연이 이어질 것이다.
  ▶ 아이들의 공통점을 이야기하는 문단이 필요함

(B): 따라서(Thus), 아이들이 받는 입력에서의, 그리고 또한 그들의 개인적인 상황에서의 극심한 한계와 변동에도 불구하고, 그들 모두는 언어 지식의 풍부하고 동일한 체계를 발달시킨다. 습득된 지식은 다양한 방식으로 그 입력을 넘어선다.

➡ **(B) 앞:** 아이들이 모두 언어 지식의 풍부하고 동일한 체계를 발달시키는 원인이 필요하다. (A)에서 설명한, 모든 아이가 거의 동일한 문법에 도달하고, 언어에 대한 체계적 지식을 발달시킨다는 사실이 그 원인이 될 수 있다.
  ▶ (A)가 (B) 앞에 와야 함 (순서: (A) → (B))
  (B) 뒤: 무작위적인 입력을 받지만, 언어에 대한 체계적인 지식을 발달시킨다는 (A)의 내용을 '습득된 지식은 다양한 방식으로 그 입력을 넘어선다.'고 표현했다.
  ▶ 글의 결론이라고 예상할 수 있음

(C): 이것은(This) 언어 사용의 창조적인 측면으로 일컬어져 왔다. 이 '창조성'은 시나 소설을 쓰는 능력이라기보다는 이전에 결코 말하거나 듣지 못한 새로운 문장을 무한히 만들어내고 이해하는 능력을 말한다. 아이들이 받는 정확한 언어적 입력은 아이들마다 다르며, 두 아이가 정확히 똑같은 발화에 노출되는 경우는 없다.

➡ **(C) 앞:** This는 이전에 말하거나 듣지 못한 새로운 문장을 무한히 만들어내고 이해하는 능력을 말한다. 주어진 문장에서 아이들의 이러한 능력에 대해 이야기했다.
  ▶ This가 가리키는 것이 주어진 문장에 등장함 (순서: 주어진 글 → (C))
  (C) 뒤: 아이들이 받는 언어적 입력은 서로 다르며, 어떤 아이도 정확히 똑같은 발화에 노출되는 경우는 없다. 즉, 아이들이 모두 거의 동일한 문법에 도달하리라고 예상되지 않는 상황이다.
  ▶ (A) 앞에 필요한 상황이 (C)에 등장함 (순서: 주어진 글 → (C) → (A) → (B))

2nd 글이 한눈에 들어오도록 정리하여 정답을 확인한다.

주어진 글: 언어 습득 과정에서 아이들은 유한한 발화에만 노출되지만, 무한한 문장들을 사용하고 이해하게 된다.
→ **(C):** 이것은 언어 사용의 창조적인 측면으로 일컬어져 왔다. 아이들이 받는 언어적 입력은 아이들마다 다르다.
→ **(A):** 하지만 아이들은 모두 거의 동일한 문법에 도달하고, 모든 아이들은 언어에 대한 체계적 지식을 발달시킨다.
→ **(B):** 따라서 입력에서의 극심한 한계와 변동에도 불구하고 아이들은 모두 언어 지식의 풍부하고 동일한 체계를 발달시킨다.
▶ 주어진 글 다음에 이어질 글의 순서는 (C) → (A) → (B)이므로 정답은 ④임

정답 ④ ＊변화를 겪거나 겪지 않는 신호

글의 흐름으로 보아, 주어진 문장이 들어가기에 가장 적절한 곳을 고르시오.

단서1 많은 신호가 변화를 겪는다는 내용이 But으로 연결됨

But many signals, / as they are passed from generation to generation / by whatever means, / go through changes / that make them / either more elaborate or simply different. //
복수 주어 / 복수 동사
그러나 많은 신호가 / 그것이 대대로 전달될 때 / 어떤 방법에 의해서든 / 변화를 겪는다 / 그것을 만드는 / 더욱 정교하게 또는 단순히 다르게 //

so ~ that S V: 너무 ~해서 …하다
Many of the ritualized displays / performed by animals / look so bizarre to us / that we wonder / how they came about. //
의례화된 표현 중에 많은 것이 / 동물들에 의해 행해지는 / 우리에게 너무 기이하게 보여서 / 우리는 궁금해 한다 / 그것이 어떻게 생겨났는지 //

생략 가능한 「주격 관계대명사+be동사」
(①) Most / of the various forms of signaling / that are used / by different species of animals / have not arisen afresh / in each separate species. //
복수 명사 / 주어부 부분을 나타내는 표현이 쓰이면 of 뒤의 명사의 수에 동사의 수를 일치시킴
대부분은 / 다양한 신호 보내기 형식의 / 사용되는 / 여러 종의 동물들에 의해 / 새로 생겨나지 않았다 / 각 개별 종에서 //

(②) As one species evolves into another, / particular forms of signaling / may be passed on, / owing to the effects / of both genes and learning or experience. //
both A and B로 연결됨
하나의 종이 다른 종으로 진화하면서 / 특정한 신호 보내기 형식이 / 전달될 수도 있다 / 영향 때문에 / 유전자 및 학습이나 경험의 //

(③) Some signals have significance / across many species, / and so remain much the same / over generations / and in a number of species. // **단서2** 몇몇 신호는 거의 똑같이 남아 있다는 내용임
병렬 구조
몇몇 신호들은 중요성을 지니며 / 여러 종에 걸쳐서 / 그래서 거의 똑같이 남아 있다 / 세대를 넘어 / 그리고 많은 종에 //
단서3 하나의 특정 표현을 하는 신호에 약간의 변화, 차이가 있는 것을 볼 수 있음

(④) If we examine / closely related species, / we can often see slight variations / in a particular display /
우리가 조사하면 / 밀접하게 관련된 종을 / 우리는 약간의 차이를 자주 볼 수 있고 / 하나의 특정한 표현에서 /

and we can piece together an explanation / for the spread of the display / across species. //
우리는 설명을 종합할 수 있다 / 그 표현의 확산에 대한 / 여러 종에 걸친 //

과거의 일에 대한 추측을 나타내는 may have p.p.
(⑤) Some very elaborate displays / may have begun / as simpler versions / of the same behavioral pattern / that became more elaborate /
선행사 / 주격 관계대명사
매우 정교한 몇몇 표현은 / 시작했을지도 모른다 / 더 단순한 형태로 / 똑같은 행동 양식의 / 더 정교해졌던 /

as they developed and were passed on / from generation to generation. //
그것이 발전하고 전달될 때 / 대대로 //

- generation ⓝ 세대 · means ⓝ 방법, 수단 · elaborate ⓐ 정교한
- ritualize ⓥ 의례화하다 · display ⓝ 표현, 전시
- perform ⓥ 수행[시행]하다 · wonder ⓥ 궁금해 하다
- come about 생기다, 일어나다 · arise ⓥ 발생하다 · afresh ⓐⓓ 새로
- pass on ~에게 전하다 · owing to ~ 때문에 · gene ⓝ 유전자
- variation ⓝ 변화, 변형 · piece together ~을 종합하다
- spread ⓝ 확산, 전파 · behavioral ⓐ 행동의

동물들이 행하는 의례화된 표현 중에 많은 것이 우리에게 너무 기이하게 보여서 우리는 그런 표현이 어떻게 생겨났는지 궁금해 한다. (①) 여러 종의 동물들에 의해 사용되는 다양한 신호 보내기 형식의 대부분은 각 개별 종에서 새로 생겨나지 않았다. (②) 하나의 종이 다른 종으로 진화하면서, 유전자 및 학습이나 경험의 영향 때문에 특정한 신호 보내기 형식이 전달될 수도 있다. (③) 몇몇 신호들은 여러 종에 걸쳐서 중요성을 지니며, 그래서 세대를 넘어, 그리고 많은 종에 거의 똑같이 남아 있다. (④ 그러나 많은 신호가 어떤 방법에 의해서든 대대로 전달될 때 그것을 더욱 정교하게 또는 단순히 다르게 만드는 변화를 겪는다.) 밀접하게 관련된 종을 조사하면, 우리는 하나의 특정한

표현에서 약간의 차이를 자주 볼 수 있고, 여러 종에 걸친 그 표현의 확산에 대한 설명을 종합할 수 있다. (⑤) 매우 정교한 몇몇 표현은 그것이 발전하고 대대로 전달될 때 더 정교해졌던, 똑같은 행동 양식의 더 단순한 형태로 시작했을지도 모른다.

| 문제 풀이 순서 | [정답률 59%]

1st 주어진 문장을 해석하고, 연결어, 지시어 등을 확인한다.

But many signals, as they are passed from generation to generation by whatever means, go through changes that make them either more elaborate or simply different. **단서1**
그러나 많은 신호가 어떤 방법에 의해서든 대대로 전달될 때 그것을 더욱 정교하게 또는 단순히 다르게 만드는 변화를 겪는다.

➡ But이라고 했으므로 앞에 반대되는 내용이 나오고, 그 뒤에 주어진 문장을 넣어야 한다.

➡ 많은 신호가 전달될 때 변화를 겪는다고 했으므로 **단서** 주어진 문장의 앞 문장은 신호가 변화를 겪지 않는다는 내용일 것이다. **발상**

2nd 각 선택지의 앞뒤 흐름이 매끄러운지 확인한다.

- ①의 앞 문장과 뒤 문장

앞 문장: 동물들이 행하는 의례화된 표현 중에 많은 것이 우리에게 너무 기이하게 보여서 우리는 그런 표현이 어떻게 생겨났는지 궁금해 한다.
뒤 문장: 여러 종의 동물들에 의해 사용되는 다양한 신호 보내기 형식의 대부분은 각 개별 종에서 새로 생겨나지 않았다.

➡ 앞 문장: 동물들이 행하는 의례화된 표현의 기원에 대한 호기심
뒤 문장: 신호 보내기 형식의 대부분은 개별 종에서 새로 생겨나지 않았음(변화되지 않았음)
'의례화된 표현'을 뒤 문장에서 '신호 보내기 형식'으로 표현하면서 연결된다.
▶ 주어진 문장이 ①에 들어갈 수 없음

- ②의 앞 문장과 뒤 문장

앞 문장: ①의 뒤 문장과 같음
뒤 문장: 하나의 종이 다른 종으로 진화하면서, 유전자 및 학습이나 경험의 영향 때문에 특정한 신호 보내기 형식이 전달될 수도 있다.

➡ 앞 문장의 신호 보내기 형식이 개별 종에서 새로 생겨나지 않았다는 내용에 이어서, 유전자, 학습, 경험 등에 의해 그것이 전달될 가능성이 자연스럽게 연결된다.
▶ 주어진 문장이 ②에 들어갈 수 없음

- ③의 앞 문장과 뒤 문장

앞 문장: ②의 뒤 문장과 같음
뒤 문장: 몇몇 신호들은 여러 종에 걸쳐서 중요성을 지니며, 그래서 세대를 넘어, 그리고 많은 종에 거의 똑같이 남아 있다. **단서2**

➡ 신호 보내기 형식이 전달되는 이유, 즉 여러 종에 걸쳐서 중요성을 지닌다는 이유가 나오면서 많은 종에 똑같이 남아 있다는 흐름으로 앞뒤 문장이 자연스럽게 연결된다.
▶ 주어진 문장이 ③에 들어갈 수 없음

- ④의 앞 문장과 뒤 문장

앞 문장: ③의 뒤 문장과 같음
뒤 문장: 밀접하게 관련된 종을 조사하면, 우리는 하나의 특정한 표현에서 약간의 차이를 자주 볼 수 있고, 여러 종에 걸친 그 표현의 확산에 대한 설명을 종합할 수 있다. **단서3**

→ 뒤 문장: 표현의 차이와 여러 종에 걸친 그 표현의 확산

표현의 변화와 관련된 내용이 앞에 있어야 한다. 주어진 문장에서 표현이 대대로 전달될 때 변화를 겪는다고 했다.

▶ 주어진 문장이 ④에 들어가야 함

- ⑤의 앞 문장과 뒤 문장

> **앞 문장**: ④의 뒤 문장과 같음
>
> **뒤 문장**: 매우 정교한 몇몇 표현은 그것이 발전하고 대대로 전달될 때 더 정교해졌던, 똑같은 행동 양식의 더 단순한 형태로 시작했을지도 모른다.

→ 앞 문장에 등장한 '표현에서 약간의 차이'를 뒤 문장에서 부연하는 흐름이다.

▶ 주어진 문장이 ⑤에 들어갈 수 없음

3rd 글이 한눈에 들어오도록 정리하여 정답을 확인한다.

우리는 동물들이 행하는 의례화된 표현 중 많은 것이 어떻게 생겨났는지 궁금해 한다. (①) 여러 종의 다양한 신호 보내기 형식 대부분은 개별 종에서 새로 생겨나지 않았다. (②) 하나의 종이 진화하면서 특정 신호 보내기 형식이 전달될 수도 있다. (③) 몇몇 신호들은 여러 종에 걸쳐서 중요하기 때문에 많은 종에 거의 똑같이 남아 있다. (④ 많은 신호가 대대로 전달될 때 변화를 겪는다.) 밀접한 종에서 하나의 특정 표현이 약간 차이가 있음을 볼 수 있다. (⑤) 매우 정교한 몇몇 표현은 단순한 형태로 시작하여 대대로 전달될 때 더 정교해졌을지도 모른다.

2회 10 정답 ① ＊얼굴 만지기의 역할

<u>Martin Grunwald,</u> / leader of the Haptic Research Laboratory
주어
at the University of Leipzig, / <u>feels</u> / psychologists do not pay
동사
nearly enough attention / to our sense of touch. //

Martin Grunwald는 / Leipzig 대학의 Haptic Research Laboratory의 대표인 / 느낀다 / 심리학자들이 결코 충분한 주의를 기울이지 않는다고 / 우리의 촉각에 //

With this in mind, / he researched the way / people
(앞에 being이 생략됨)   (앞에 관계부사가 생략됨)
spontaneously touch their faces. //

이를 염두에 두고 / 그는 방식을 연구했다 / 사람들이 자신들의 얼굴을 자연스럽게 만지는 //

We all do it. //

우리 모두 그것을 한다 //

You might be doing it right now / while reading this. //
= while you read this

여러분은 그것을 바로 지금 하고 있을지도 모른다 / 이것을 읽는 동안 //

These movements are not for communication / and, in most cases, / we are not even aware of them. //

이러한 동작들은 의사소통을 위해서가 아니며 / 대개의 경우 / 우리는 심지어 그것들을 의식하지 않는다 //

But that does not mean / they serve no purpose, / as Grunwald
(앞에 접속사 that이 생략됨)
discovered. //

하지만 그것은 의미하지 않는다 / 그것들이 아무런 목적에 기여하지 않는다는 것을 / Grunwald가 발견했던 것처럼 //

He measured / the brain activity of test subjects / while they tried
〈시간〉의 부사절 접속사
to remember / a sequence of haptic stimuli / for five minutes. //

그는 측정했다 / 피실험자들의 뇌 활동을 / 그들이 기억하려고 노력하는 동안 / 일련의 촉각 자극을 / 5분 동안 //

단서 1 불쾌한 소음으로 피실험자를 방해하자 그들이 자신의 얼굴을 만지는 비율이 급격히 증가했음

When he disturbed them / with unpleasant noises, / the subjects
〈시간〉의 부사절 접속사
dramatically increased the rate / at which they touched their
선행사   전치사+관계대명사
faces. //

그가 그들을 방해했을 때 / 불쾌한 소음으로 / 피실험자들은 비율을 급격히 늘렸다 / 그들이 자신들의 얼굴을 만지는 //

When the noises upset / the rhythm of their brains / and
병렬 구조
threatened to disrupt / the subjects' concentration, /

그 소음이 엉망으로 만들고 / 그들의 뇌의 리듬을 / 방해하겠다고 위협할 때 / 피실험자들의 집중력을 /
주어   동사   목적어   목적격 보어(원형부정사)

단서 2 스스로를 만지는 것은 집중력을 되찾도록 도왔음

self-touch helped them / get their concentration back on track. //

스스로를 만지기는 그들을 도왔다 / 자신들의 집중력을 다시 정상 궤도에 들어서게 하도록 //

To put it another way: / self-touch grounded their minds. //

달리 말하면 / 스스로를 만지기가 그들의 정신을 붙들어 맸다 //

> → Even though touching our own faces seems / to serve no
> 동명사구 주어   단수 동사
> special purpose, / the research showed /
>
> 비록 우리 자신의 얼굴을 만지는 것이 보이지만 / 특별한 목적에 기여하지 않는 것처럼 / 연구는 보여주었다 /
>
> that the rate of subjects' self-touch (A) **escalated** / in
> 주어   동사
> accordance with the exposure / to unpleasant noises, / and
> this behavior helped their minds / stay (B) **focused**. //
> 주어   동사   목적어   목적격 보어(원형부정사)
>
> 피실험자들의 스스로를 만지기의 비율이 상승했으며 / 노출에 따라 / 불쾌한 소음에의 / 이러한 행동은 그들의 정신을 도와주었다는 것을 / 집중된 상태를 유지하도록 //

- laboratory ⓝ 실험실 · sense ⓝ 감각
- spontaneously ⓐ𝒹 자발적으로, 자연스럽게
- serve ⓥ 도움이 되다, 기여하다 · measure ⓥ 측정하다, 재다
- subject ⓝ 실험[연구] 대상, 피험자 · a sequence of 일련의
- stimulus ⓝ 자극((pl. stimuli)) · disturb ⓥ 방해하다
- dramatically ⓐ𝒹 극적으로 · rate ⓝ 비율, -율
- upset ⓥ 잘못되게[틀어지게] 만들다 · threaten ⓥ 위협하다
- concentration ⓝ 집중, 농도 · on track 궤도에 올라, 순조롭게

Leipzig 대학의 Haptic Research Laboratory의 대표인 Martin Grunwald는 심리학자들이 우리의 촉각에 결코 충분한 주의를 기울이지 않는다고 느낀다. 이를 염두에 두고, 그는 사람들이 자신들의 얼굴을 자연스럽게 만지는 방식을 연구했다. 우리 모두 그것(얼굴을 자연스럽게 만지는 것)을 한다. 여러분은 이것을 읽는 동안 그것을 지금 하고 있을지도 모른다. 이러한 동작들은 의사소통을 위해서가 아니며, 대개의 경우 우리는 심지어 그것들을 의식하지 않는다. 하지만 그것은 Grunwald가 발견했던 것처럼, 그것들이 아무런 목적에 기여하지 않는다는 것을 의미하지 않는다. 그는 피실험자들이 5분 동안 일련의 촉각 자극을 기억하려고 노력하는 동안 그들의 뇌 활동을 측정했다. 그가 불쾌한 소음으로 그들을 방해했을 때 피실험자들은 자신들의 얼굴을 만지는 비율을 급격하게 늘렸다. 그 소음이 그들의 뇌의 리듬을 엉망으로 만들고 피실험자들의 집중력을 방해하려 들었을 때, 스스로를 만지기는 그들이 자신들의 집중력을 다시 정상 궤도에 들어서게 하도록 도와주었다. 달리 말하면, 스스로를 만지기가 그들의 정신을 붙들어 맸다.
→ 비록 우리 자신의 얼굴을 만지는 것이 특별한 목적에 기여하지 않는 것처럼 보이지만, 연구는 피실험자들의 스스로를 만지기의 비율이 불쾌한 소음에의 노출에 따라 (A) 상승했으며, 이러한 행동은 그들의 정신이 (B) 집중된 상태를 유지하도록 도와주었다는 것을 보여주었다.

다음 글의 내용을 한 문장으로 요약하고자 한다. 빈칸 (A), (B)에 들어갈 말로 가장 적절한 것은?

(A)	(B)	
① escalated 상승한	— focused 집중된	불쾌한 소음으로 방해 받으면 얼굴을 만지는 비율을 높였고, 얼굴을 만지는 것은 집중력이 돌아오도록 도왔음
② escalated 상승한	— creative 창의적인	'집중력'과 관련된 것이지, '창의력'은 언급되지 않았음
③ varied 달라졌다	— hopeful 희망에 찬	얼굴 만지기를 통해 희망이 생기는 것이 아님
④ normalized 정상화됐다	— keen 열렬한	소음의 방해를 받아 달라졌던 얼굴 만지기 비율이 정상으로 돌아오는 것이 아님
⑤ normalized 정상화됐다	— calm 침착한	돌아오는 것이 아님

왜 정답? [정답률 70%]

Martin Grunwald는 사람들이 자신의 얼굴을 무의식적으로 만지는 것에 대해 연구했는데, 그가 불쾌한 소음으로 피실험자의 집중을 방해했을 때 피실험자는 자신의 얼굴을 만지는 비율을 급격하게 '늘렸고', 스스로를 만지는 것이 피실험자의 '집중력이 돌아오도록' 도왔다는 것을 발견했다고 했으므로 요약문의 빈칸에는 각각 ① '상승했다'와 '집중된'이 들어가야 한다.

>왜 오답?

② 스스로를 만지는 비율이 상승한 것은 맞지만, 그것이 창의적인 상태를 유지하는 것에 도움을 준 것은 아니다.

③ 얼굴을 만지는 것을 통해 희망에 찬 상태로 유지되었다는 것은 글에서 전혀 언급되지 않았다.

④, ⑤ 스스로를 만지는 비율이 정상화된다는 것은 증가했거나 감소했던 비율이 되돌아온다는 의미인데, 이는 글에서 설명한 실험 결과와 맞지 않는다.

* 글의 흐름

도입	Martin Grunwald는 사람들이 무의식적으로 자신의 얼굴을 만지는 것에 대해 연구했음
실험 과정	피실험자가 일련의 촉각 자극을 기억하려고 노력하는 동안 그들의 뇌 활동을 측정했음
	실험자가 불쾌한 소음으로 피실험자를 방해했을 때 피실험자는 자신의 얼굴을 만지는 비율을 급격히 늘렸음
실험 결과	스스로를 만지는 것은 피실험자가 자신의 집중력을 다시 정상 궤도에 들어서게 하도록 도왔음

②회 11~12 * 화산폭발과 지진으로 멸망한 폼페이

Pompeii was destroyed / by the catastrophic eruption of Mount Vesuvius in 79 A.D., / entombing residents under layers of volcanic ash. //
폼페이는 무너졌다 / 기원후 79년 베수비오산의 재앙과 같은 분출로 / 주민들을 화산재층 아래에 파묻으며 //

But there is more to this story / of an ancient Roman city's doom. // **11번** 단서 1: 고대 로마 도시의 파멸에 관한 이야기는 많은 것이 있음
하지만 이 이야기에는 더 많은 것이 있다 / 고대 로마 도시의 파멸에 관한 //

Research published in the journal *Frontiers in Earth Science* / offers proof / that Pompeii was simultaneously wrecked / by a massive earthquake. // **11번** 단서 2: 연구는 폼페이가 지진으로 파괴되었다는 증거를 제공함
학술지 *Frontiers in Earth Science*에서 출판된 연구는 / 증거를 제공한다 / 폼페이가 동시에 파괴되었다는 / 거대한 지진으로 //

The discovery establishes / a new timeline for the city's collapse / and shows / that fresh approaches to research / can (a) reveal additional secrets / from well-studied archaeological sites. //
이 발견은 수립한다 / 그 도시의 붕괴에 대한 새로운 연대표를 / 그리고 보여준다 / 연구에 대한 신선한 접근이 / 추가적인 비밀을 밝힐 수 있다는 것을 / 깊이 연구된 고고학적 현장에서 //

Researchers have always had an idea / that seismic activity contributed to the city's destruction. //
연구원들은 생각을 항상 가져왔다 / 지진 활동이 도시의 파괴에 이바지했다는 //

The ancient writer Pliny the Younger reported / that the eruption of Vesuvius had been accompanied / by violent shaking. //
고대 작가 Pliny the Younger는 보고했다 / 베수비오의 분출은 수반되었다는 것을 / 격렬한 흔들림과 함께 //

But, until now, no evidence had been discovered / to (b) support this historical account. //
하지만 지금까지 어떠한 증거도 밝혀지지 않았다 / 이 역사적인 이야기를 지지할 //

A team of researchers led by Domenico Sparice from Italy / decided to investigate this (c) gap in the record. //
이탈리아의 Domenico Sparice가 이끈 연구팀이 / 기록에서의 이 차이를 조사하기로 결정했다 //

Dr. Sparice said / that excavations of Pompeii to date / had not included experts in the field of archaeoseismology, / which deals with the effects of earthquakes on ancient buildings. //
Sparice 박사는 말했다 / 지금까지 폼페이 발굴은 / 고고 지진학 분야의 전문가들을 포함하지 않았다는 것 / 고대 건축물들에 지진이 미친 영향을 다루는 //

Contributions from (d) specialists in this area / were key to the discovery, / he said. //
이 분야의 전문가들로부터의 의견이 / 발견의 열쇠였다고 / 그는 말했다 //

"The effects of seismicity have been speculated by past scholars, / but no factual evidence has been reported before our study," / Dr. Sparice said, / adding that the finding was "very exciting." //
지진 활동도의 영향은 과거의 학자들에 의해 추측되어 왔다 / 하지만 어떠한 사실적 증거도 우리의 연구 이전에 보고된 적이 없었다 / Sparice 박사가 말했다 / 연구 결과가 "매우 흥미로웠다"라고 덧붙이며 //

The team focused / on the Insula of the Chaste Lovers. // **12번** 단서: 폼페이에서는 화산 분출로 인해 화가들의 작업이 중단됨
연구팀은 집중했다 / 순결한 연인들의 공동 주택에 //

This area encompasses several buildings, / including a bakery and a house / where painters were evidently interrupted by the eruption, / leaving their paintings (e) colored(→ uncolored). //
이 지역은 몇몇 건축물들을 망라한다 / 빵집과 가옥을 포함한 / 화가들이 분명히 분출로 인해 중단된 / 그들의 그림을 색칠된(→ 색칠되지 않은) 채로 남겨둔 채 //

After excavation and careful analysis, / the researchers concluded / that walls in the insula had collapsed / because of an earthquake. // **11번** 단서 3: 공동 주택의 벽들이 지진으로 무너졌다고 결론지음
발굴과 면밀한 분석 후에 / 연구원들은 결론지었다 / 공동 주택의 벽들이 무너졌다고 / 지진 때문에 //

- catastrophic ⓐ 재앙의, 처참한 · eruption ⓝ 분출
- entomb ⓥ 파묻다, 뒤덮다 · volcanic ⓐ 화산의 · ash ⓝ 재, 잿더미
- doom ⓝ 파멸, 죽음 · frontier ⓝ 선구자 · earth science 지구과학
- simultaneously ⓐⓓ 동시에 · wreck ⓥ 파괴하다
- timeline ⓝ 연대표 · collapse ⓝ 붕괴
- archaeological ⓐ 고고학의 · violent ⓐ 격렬한
- account ⓝ 이야기 · archaeoseismology ⓝ 고고 지진학
- seismicity ⓝ 지진 활동도 · speculate ⓥ 추측하다
- factual ⓐ 사실적인 · insula ⓝ (고대 로마의) 집단 주택
- chaste ⓐ 순결한 · encompass ⓥ 망라하다, 포함하다
- interrupt ⓥ 중단시키다, 방해하다

폼페이는 기원후 79년 베수비오산의 재앙과 같은 분출로 주민들을 화산재 층 아래에 파묻으며 무너졌다. 하지만 고대 로마 도시의 파멸에 관한 이 이야기에는 더 많은 것이 있다. 학술지 *Frontiers in Earth Science*에서 출판된 연구는 폼페이가 동시에 거대한 지진으로 파괴되었다는 증거를 제공한다. 이 발견은 그 도시의 붕괴에 대한 새로운 연대표를 수립하고, 연구에 대한 신선한 접근이 깊이 연구된 고고학적 현장에서 추가적인 비밀을 (a) 밝힐 수 있다는 것을 보여준다. 연구원들은 지진 활동이 도시의 파괴에 이바지했다는 생각을 항상 가져왔다. 고대 작가 Pliny the Younger는 베수비오의 분출은 격렬한 흔들림과 함께 수반되었다는 것을 보고했다. 하지만 지금까지 이 역사적인 이야기를 (b) 지지할 어떠한 증거도 밝혀지지 않았다. 이탈리아의 Domenico Sparice가 이끈 한 연구팀이 기록에서의 이 (c) 차이를 조사하기로 결정했다. Sparice 박사는 지금까지 폼페이 발굴은 고대 건축물들에 지진이 미친 영향을 다루는 고고 지진학 분야의 전문가들을 포함하지 않았다는 것을 말했다. 이 분야의 (d) 전문가들로부터의 의견이 발견의 열쇠였다고 그는 말했다. 지진 활동도의 영향은 과거의 학자들에 의해 추측되어 왔지만, 우리의 연구 이전에 어떠한 사실적 증거도 보고된 적이 없었다고 Sparice 박사가 말했으며, 연구 결과가 "매우 흥미로웠다"라고 덧붙였다. 연구팀은 순결한 연인들의 공동 주택에 집중했다. 이 지역은 몇몇 건축물들을 망라하는데, 화가들이 분명히 분출로 인해 그들의 그림을 (e) 색칠된(→ 색칠되지 않은) 채로 남겨둔 채 중단된 빵집과 가옥을 포함한다. 발굴과 면밀한 분석 후에, 연구원들은 공동 주택의 벽들이 지진 때문에 무너졌다고 결론지었다.

2회 11 정답 ⑤

윗글의 제목으로 가장 적절한 것은?

① Who Found Pompeii Covered with Volcanic Ashes
누가 화산재로 뒤덮인 폼페이를 발견했는가   화산재로 뒤덮인 폼페이를 발견한 사람에 관한 내용이 아님

② Mt. Vesuvius's Influence on the Scenery of Pompeii
베수비오산이 폼페이의 경치에 미친 영향   베수비오산과 폼페이의 경치에 관한 내용은 언급되지 않음

③ The Eruption of Mt. Vesuvius Triggered by Earthquake
지진으로 촉발된 베수비오산의 분출   지진 때문에 화산이 분출했다는 내용은 아님

④ Seismic Timeline by Archaeological Discovery in Pompeii
폼페이에서의 고고학적 발견에 의한 지진의 연대표   연대표 자체가 전체 글의 제목이 될 수는 없음

⑤ The Eruption of Mt. Vesuvius Wasn't Pompeii's Only Killer
베수비오산의 분출이 폼페이의 유일한 학살자는 아니었다
But there is more to this story of an ancient Roman city's doom.

왜 정답? [정답률 0%]

- 하지만 고대 로마 도시의 파멸에 관한 이 이야기에는 더 많은 것이 있다. **단서 1**
- Frontiers in Earth Science(지구과학의 선구자들)라는 학술지에 출판된 연구는 폼페이가 동시에 거대한 지진으로 파괴되었다는 증거를 제공한다. **단서 2**
- 발굴과 면밀한 분석 후에, 연구원들은 공동 주택의 벽들이 지진 때문에 무너졌다고 결론지었다. **단서 3**

→ 폼페이 멸망의 원인은 단순히 화산폭발만이 아니라, 이와 수반된 지진도 큰 영향을 미쳤다는 점을 설명하고 있다.
▶ 따라서 글의 제목으로 가장 적절한 것은 ⑤ '베수비오산의 분출이 폼페이의 유일한 학살자는 아니었다'이다.

왜 오답?

① 화산재로 뒤덮인 폼페이를 발견한 사람에 관한 내용이 아니다. (▶◀ 이유: 글에 언급된 Pliny the Younger는 폼페이 멸망 당시 격렬한 흔들림이 있었다고 보고했던 사람이고, Domenico Sparice는 지진이 폼페이에 미친 영향을 밝혀낸 사람이다.)

② 베수비오산과 폼페이의 경치에 관한 내용은 언급되지 않았다.

③ 폼페이 멸망 당시 화산 분출과 지진이 동시에 발생했다는 내용이지, 지진 때문에 화산이 분출했다는 인과 관계에 관한 설명은 없다.

④ 폼페이에서 진행된 고고학적 연구가 지진의 연대표에 새로운 시각을 제공했다는 내용은 언급되었으나, 글의 전체 내용은 지진도 폼페이 멸망에 영향을 주었다는 내용이다. 따라서 지진의 연대표 자체가 전체 글의 제목이 될 수는 없다.

2회 12 정답 ⑤

밑줄 친 (a)~(e) 중, 문맥상 낱말의 쓰임이 적절하지 않은 것은? [3점]

① (a) 고고학에서 추가적인 비밀을 밝히다 '밝힐' 수 있게 해줌
② (b) 앞의 내용에 '하지만'으로 연결되므로 지지하다 '지지할' 증거를 찾지 못한 것임
③ (c) '증언'과 '증거'를 '차이'로 받음 차이
④ (d) 그전까지 전문가들을 포함하지 않았음 전문가들
⑤ (e) 화가들의 작업은 중단되었으므로 색칠된 색칠되지 않은 채로 남겨뒀을 것임

왜 정답? [정답률 70%]

⑤ (e) colored 색칠된

┌ 이 지역은 몇몇 건축물들을 망라하는데, 화가들이 분명히 분출로 인해
│   색칠되지 않은
└ 그들의 그림을 (e) 색칠된 채로 남겨둔 채 중단된 빵집과 가옥을 포함한다.

→ 폼페이에서는 화산 분출로 인해 화가들의 작업이 중단되었음 → 따라서 당시 화가들의 작업은 '색칠된 채' 남겨져 있었다는 표현은 적절하지 않음
▶ 화가들의 작품은 화산 분출로 중단되었으므로 colored를 uncolored(색칠되지 않은)와 같은 단어로 바꾸어야 함

왜 오답?

① (a) reveal 밝히다

┌ 이 발견은 그 도시의 붕괴에 대한 새로운 연대표를 수립하고, 연구에 대한
│ 신선한 접근이 깊이 연구된 고고학적 현장에서 추가적인 비밀을 (a) 밝힐
└ 수 있다는 것을 보여준다.

→ 학술지의 연구에 따르면, 폼페이는 거대한 지진으로도 파괴되었다는 증거가 있음
→ 이 발견은 폼페이의 붕괴에 대한 새로운 시선을 제공하고, 고고학 현장에서도 추가적인 비밀을 '밝힐' 수 있게 해줌 ▶ reveal은 문맥에 맞음

---

② (b) support 지지하다

┌ 하지만(But) 지금까지 이 역사적인 이야기를 (b) 지지할 어떠한 증거도
│ 밝혀지지 않았다.   But은 '고대 작가가 화산과 지진이 동시에 발생했다고 보고했다'라는
└   앞의 내용에 증거가 없는 상황임을 소개함

→ 앞 문장에서 고대 작가가 베수비오 화산 분출은 지진을 수반했다고 보고함 → 지금까지 그 작가의 역사적인 이야기를 '지지할' 증거가 발견되지 않았다는 내용이 '하지만'으로 연결되는 것은 적절함 ▶ support는 문맥에 맞음

③ (c) gap 차이

┌ 이탈리아의 Domenico Sparice가 이끈 한 연구팀이 기록에서의 이 (c)
└ 차이를 조사하기로 결정했다.

→ 고대 작가는 베수비오 화산의 분출이 격렬한 흔들림(지진)을 수반했다고 보고함 → 하지만, 이 이야기를 지지할 어떠한 증거도 밝혀지지 않았음
따라서 이탈리아의 연구팀은 지진이 수반되었다는 '증언'은 있지만, 이를 뒷받침할 '증거'가 없는 '차이'를 조사하고자 했다는 표현은 문맥상 적절함
▶ gap은 문맥에 맞음

④ (d) specialists 전문가들

┌ 이 분야의 (d) 전문가들로부터의 의견이 발견의 열쇠였다고 그는 말했다.

→ 이탈리아의 연구팀은 지금까지의 폼페이 발굴이 지진 전문가를 포함하지 않았다고 지적함 → 이탈리아 연구팀은 지진 활동의 영향으로 인한 건축물들을 발견했으므로, 지진 분야의 '전문가들'로부터 받은 의견이 새로운 발견의 열쇠였다는 표현은 문맥상 적절함 ▶ specialists는 문맥에 맞음

3회 01 정답 ① ＊인터넷을 검색한 사람들이 갖는 오해

Two independent research groups / have discovered / that we
부사절 접속사(시간)
have "confusion / at the frontier" / when we search the Internet. //
두 개의 독립적인 연구 집단은 / 발견했다 / 우리가 '혼란'을 느낀다는 것을 / '경계에 있어서의'
/ 우리가 인터넷을 검색할 때 //

Adrian Ward, a psychologist at the University of Texas, found
/ that engaging in Internet searches / increased / people's
핵심 문장   동명사구 주어   동사   목적어
cognitive self-esteem, /
Texas 대학의 심리학자 Adrian Ward는 알아냈다 / 인터넷 검색을 하는 것이 / 강화했다는
것을 / 사람들의 인지적 자존감을 /
형용사적 용법(ability 수식)
their sense of their own ability / to remember and process
information. //
자신의 능력에 대한 그들의 느낌 / 정보를 기억하고 처리하는
선행사(목적격 관계대명사는 생략됨)
Moreover, / people / who searched the Internet / for facts / they
주어
didn't know / and were later asked / where they found the
information /
또한 / 사람들은 / 인터넷을 검색한 / 사실을 찾아 / 자신이 몰랐던 / 그리고 나중에 질문받은
/ 어디에서 그 정보를 찾았는지를 /
동사
often misremembered and reported / that they had known it all
along. // 단서1 자신이 몰랐던 사실을 인터넷으로 검색한 사람들은
자신이 그것을 내내 알고 있었다고 잘못 기억함
자주 잘못 기억하면서 말했다 / 자신이 그것을 내내 알고 있었다고 //

Many of them completely forgot / ever having conducted the
search. // forget -ing: ~한 것을 잊다 / forget to-v: ~할 것을 잊다
그들 중 다수는 완전히 잊어버렸다 / 검색을 했다는 것조차 //

They gave themselves the credit / instead of the Internet. //
그들은 스스로에게 공을 돌렸다 / 인터넷 대신 //

In a different set of studies, / researchers found / 단서2 특정 질문에
다른 일련의 연구에서 / 연구원들은 알아냈다 /   답하기 위해 인터넷을
                        검색한 사람은 그렇지 않은 사람보다 관련 없는
                        질문에 답하는 자신의 능력을 더 높이 평가함
that those / who had searched the Internet / to answer specific
주어
동사
questions / rated their ability / to answer unrelated questions /
as higher / than those / who had not. // 형용사적 용법(ability 수식)
사람들이 / 인터넷을 검색한 / 특정한 질문에 답하기 위해 / 자신들의 능력을 평가했다는 것을
/ 관련이 없는 질문에 답하는 / 더 높게 / 사람들보다 / 그렇게 하지 않았던 //

The act / of searching the Internet / and finding answers / to one
동사   목적어   목적격 보어
set of questions / caused the participants to increase their sense
/ that they knew the answers / to all questions, /
행위는 / 인터넷을 검색하여 / 답을 찾는 / 일련의 질문에 대한 / 참가자로 하여금 그들의 느
낌을 강화했다 / 자신이 답을 알고 있다는 / 모든 질문에 대한 /
선행사   소유격 관계대명사
including those / whose answers they had not researched. //
질문을 포함한 / 자신이 그 답을 조사하지 않은 //
단서3 인터넷을 검색하여 답을 찾는 행위는 자신이 답을 알고 있다는 느낌을 강화함

- independent ⓐ 독립적인   · confusion ⓝ 혼란
- frontier ⓝ 경계, 국경   · psychologist ⓝ 심리학자
- engage in ~에 관여[참여]하다   · cognitive ⓐ 인지[인식]의
- self-esteem ⓝ 자존감, 자부심   · misremember ⓥ 부정확하게 기억하다
- all along 그동안 내내   · conduct ⓥ (특정한 활동을) 하다
- credit ⓝ 공적, 칭찬   · rate ⓥ 평가하다
- overestimate ⓥ 과대평가하다   · prone to-v ~하기 쉬운
- put off ~을 미루다   · overwhelmed ⓐ 압도된   · vast ⓐ 방대한
- strive ⓥ 분투하다   · distinguish ⓥ 구별하다

두 개의 독립적인 연구 집단은 인터넷을 검색할 때 우리가 '경계에 있어서의 혼
란'을 느낀다는 것을 발견했다. Texas 대학의 심리학자 Adrian Ward는 인터넷
검색을 하는 것이 사람들의 인지적 자존감, 즉 정보를 기억하고 처리하는 능력에
대한 그들의 느낌을 강화했다는 것을 알아냈다. 또한 자신이 몰랐던 사실을 인터
넷에서 검색한 다음 나중에 어디에서 그 정보를 찾았는지를 질문받은 사람들은
자주 자신이 그 정보를 내내 알고 있었다고 잘못 기억하면서 말했다. 그들 중 다
수는 검색을 했다는 것조차 완전히 잊어버렸다.

그들은 인터넷 대신 스스로에게 공을 돌렸다. 다른 일련의 연구에서, 연구원들
은 특정한 질문에 답하기 위해 인터넷을 검색한 사람들이 그렇게 하지 않았던 사
람들보다 관련이 없는 질문에 답하는 자신의 능력을 더 높게 평가했다는 것을
알아냈다. 인터넷을 검색하여 일련의 질문에 대한 답을 찾는 행위는 자신이 답을
조사하지 않은 질문을 포함한 모든 질문에 대한 답을 자신이 알고 있다는 참가자
들의 느낌을 강화했다.

**밑줄 친 we have "confusion at the frontier"가 다음 글에서 의미하는 바
로 가장 적절한 것은? [3점]**

① we tend to overestimate our knowledge and ability
   우리는 우리의 지식과 능력을 과대평가하는 경향이 있다   몰랐던 것을 내내 알고 있었다고 생각함
② we are prone to putting off making final decisions
   우리는 최종 결정을 하는 것을 미루는 경향이 있다 인터넷 검색과 결정의 연기의 상관관계를 설명한 것이 아님
③ we often forget how easily we lose our self-esteem
   우리는 종종 우리가 얼마나 쉽게 우리의 자존감을 잃는지 잊는다 인터넷 검색으로 자존감을 잃는다는 것이 아님
④ we are overwhelmed by a vast amount of information
   우리는 막대한 양의 정보에 의해 압도당한다
⑤ we strive to distinguish false information from the truth
   우리는 진실로부터 잘못된 정보를 구별하기 위해 노력한다 '인터넷 검색', '정보'가 언급된 것으로 만든 오답

왜 정답? [정답률 52%]   인터넷에서 검색하기 전부터 꿀팁

두 번째 문장에서, 연구를 통해 인터넷을 검색하는 것이 사람들의 '인지적' 자존감
을 강화한다는 것을 알아냈다고 한 후 그에 대한 자세한 설명이 이어지는 글이다.
'자신이 몰랐던 사실을 인터넷에서 검색한 사람은 자신이 그 사실을 내내 알고 있
었던 것으로 잘못 기억한다', '특정 질문에 답하기 위해 인터넷을 검색한 사람들은
그렇지 않은 사람들보다 관련 없는 질문에 답하는 자신의 능력을 더 높게 평가한
다', '인터넷을 검색하여 답을 찾는 행위는 자신이 모든 질문에 대한 답을 안다는 사
람들의 느낌을 강화한다'는 부연 설명을 통해 인터넷을 검색할 때 우리가 혼란을
느낀다는 것의 의미가 ① '우리는 우리의 지식과 능력을 과대평가하는 경향이 있
다'임을 알 수 있다.

왜 오답?

② 인터넷을 검색하면 최종 결정을 미루게 된다는 것을 보여 주는 연구 결과가 아
니다.
③ self-esteem이 언급된 것으로 만든 오답이다. 이 글의 핵심은 단순한
self-esteem이 아니라 cognitive self-esteem이고, 자존감을 잃는 것이 아니
라 강화하는 것이다.
④, ⑤ 인터넷에서 어떤 정보를 검색하는 것에 대한 글이 보통 '인터넷에 있는 막
대한 양의 정보', '그러한 막대한 정보에는 잘못된 정보도 포함되어 있다'는
등의 주제를 갖는다는 점으로 만든 오답이다. 주의

3회 02 정답 ③ ＊이른 직업 결정이 잘못될 수 있는 이유

〈시간의 부사절 접속사〉
Most of us make our career choices / when we are about
eighteen. // 단서1 대부분의 사람들은 18세쯤에 진로를 선택하는데,
          이때 사람들은 제한된 경험과 기술을 지님
우리 대부분은 우리의 진로를 선택한다 / 우리가 열여덟 살일 때에 //

At eighteen, / you have limited experience, very limited skills /
열여덟 살에 / 여러분은 제한된 경험과 매우 제한적인 기술을 지니고 있고 /
주어부에 most of가 쓰이면 of 뒤의 명사에 수를 일치시킴
and most of what you know comes /
여러분이 알고 있는 것의 대부분은 온다 /
주어와 동사의 수 일치
from your parents, your environment   부분을 나타내는 most of
and the structured school system /   뒤에 명사절 what you
                                             know가 쓰였다.
여러분의 부모, 여러분의 환경, 그리고 구조화된 학교 체계로부터 /   명사구나 명사절은 단수
you have gone through. //   취급하므로 동사 역시 단수
여러분이 경험한 // 앞에 목적격 관계대명사가 생략됨   동사인 comes가 왔다.

You are usually slightly better at some skills / because you have
spent a bit more time / on them. //
여러분은 보통 몇 가지 기술에 약간 더 능숙하다 / 여러분이 조금 더 많은 시간을 투자했기
때문에 / 그것에 //
병렬 구조
Maybe someone in your environment / was good at something
/ and passionate enough / to get you interested / in spending
                                     to get의 목적어와 목적격 보어의 관계가
more time / in that area. //   수동이므로 목적격 보어로 과거분사가 옴
아마도 여러분 주변에 있는 누군가가 / 어떤 것에 능숙하고 / 충분히 열정적이었을 수도 있다 /
여러분이 흥미를 느끼게 하기에 / 더 많은 시간을 보내는 데 / 그 분야에 //

It is also possible / that you might have a specific physical
feature / — such as being tall — / that might make you better at
certain activities, / such as playing basketball. //
가주어   진주어절 접속사   might make의
                                                            목적어와 목적격 보어
~은 또한 가능하다 / 여러분이 특정한 신체적 특징을 갖고 있을 수도 있는 것은 / 키가 큰
것과 같은 / 여러분이 특정 활동을 더 잘하게 할 수도 있는 / 농구를 하는 것과 같은 //

In any case, / most people make a decision / regarding their
career and direction in life / based on their limited experiences
and biases / in their childhood and teenage years. //
어쨌든 / 대부분의 사람들이 결정을 내린다 / 그들의 삶의 진로와 방향에 대한 / 그들의 제한된
경험과 편견을 바탕으로 / 그들의 유년기와 청소년기의 //
                                      대부분의 사람들은 유년기, 청소년기의
                                      제한된 경험과 편견을 바탕으로 진로를 결정함

This decision will come to dominate their life / for many years
형용사적 용법(many years 수식)
/ to come. //
이 결정은 그들의 삶을 지배하게 될 것이다 / 많은 세월 동안 / 다가올 //

No wonder / so many get it wrong! //
당연하다 / 매우 많은 사람이 그것을 잘못하는 것이 //

It is easier to get it wrong / than to get it right, / because
가주어   진주어
statistically, there are more wrong ways / than right ways. //
그것을 잘못하는 것이 더 쉽다 / 그것을 올바르게 하는 것보다 / 통계적으로 잘못된 방법이 더
많기 때문에 / 올바른 방법보다 //

- slightly [ad] 약간, 조금   - passionate [a] 열정을 느끼는, 열렬한
- physical [a] 신체의, 물리적인   - feature [n] 특징, 특성
- regarding [prep] ~에 관하여   - bias [n] 편견, 성향
- dominate [v] 지배하다, (두드러지는) 특징이 되다
- statistically [ad] 통계(학)상으로   - factor [n] 요인, 인자
- aptitude [n] 소질, 적성

우리 대부분은 열여덟 살쯤에 진로를 선택한다. 열여덟 살에 여러분은
제한된 경험과 매우 제한적인 기술을 지니고 있고, 여러분이 알고 있는 것의
대부분은 여러분의 부모, 여러분의 환경, 그리고 여러분이 경험한 구조화된
학교 시스템으로부터 온다. 여러분은 보통 몇 가지 기술에 약간 더 능숙한데,
그것에 조금 더 많은 시간을 투자했기 때문이다. 아마도 여러분 주변에 있는
누군가가 어떤 것에 능숙하고 여러분이 그 분야에 더 많은 시간을 보내는 데
흥미를 느끼게 할 만큼 열정적이었을 수도 있다. 또한 여러분은 농구를 하는
것과 같은 특정 활동을 더 잘하게 할 수도 있는 큰 키와 같은 특정한 신체적
특징을 갖고 있을 수도 있다.

어쨌든 대부분의 사람들이 유년기와 청소년기의 제한된 경험과 편견을
바탕으로 삶의 진로와 방향에 대한 결정을 내린다. 이 결정은 다가올 많은 세월
동안 그들의 삶을 지배하게 될 것이다. 매우 많은 사람이 잘못된 결정을 내리는
것이 당연하다! 올바른 결정을 내리기보다 잘못된 결정을 내리기가 더 쉬운데,
이는 통계적으로, 올바른 방법보다 잘못된 방법이 더 많기 때문이다.

다음 글의 주제로 가장 적절한 것은?

① social factors that make employment unstable
고용을 불안정하게 만드는 사회적 요인들   고용 불안정에 대한 내용이 아님
② useful statistics for making a right career choice
올바른 직업 선택을 하는 데 유용한 통계   직업 선택을 돕는 글이 아님
③ reasons that an early career choice can go wrong
이른 직업 결정이 잘못될 수 있는 이유
                              제한된 경험을 바탕으로 하기 때문임
④ necessity to find one's aptitude as early as possible
자신의 적성을 가능한 빨리 찾을 필요성   이른 직업 결정은 잘못될 확률이 높음
⑤ how to overcome biases in making one's career choices
자신의 직업 선택을 하는 데 있어 편견을 극복하는 방법
                                      biases로 만든 오답

왜 정답? [정답률 82%]   get it wrong의 it이 의미하는 것이 '진로 결정'임   꿀팁

우리 대부분은 제한된 경험과 기술을 지닌 열여덟 살쯤에 유년기와 청소년기의
제한된 경험과 편견을 바탕으로 삶의 진로와 방향을 결정한다면서,
매우 많은 사람들이 잘못된 결정을 내리는 것이 당연하다고 하는 것으로 보아
이 글의 주제는 ③ '이른 직업 결정이 잘못될 수 있는 이유'이다.

제한된 경험과 기술을 지닌 나이에 제한된
경험과 편견을 바탕으로 결정하기 때문임   꿀팁

왜 오답?

① 고용 불안정 또는 그 원인이 되는 사회적 요인에 대한 글이 아니다.
② 이른 직업 선택이 잘못되는 이유를 설명하는 것이지, 올바른 직업을 선택하는
  데 도움이 되는 통계를 알려주는 것이 아니다.
④ 직업 선택을 너무 이른 시기에 하면 안 된다고 말하는 글로 볼 수 있다.
⑤ biases가 언급된 것으로 만든 오답이다. 직업에 대한 편견 등에 대해서는
  언급되지 않았다.

 자이 쌤's Follow Me! – 홈페이지에서 제공

3회 03 정답 ② *시간에 기반을 둔 촉각

think of A as B: A를 B로 여기다[생각하다]
People don't usually think of touch / as a temporal phenomenon,
/ but it is every bit as time-based / as it is spatial. //
사람들은 보통 촉각을 생각하지 않는다 / 시간의 현상으로 / 그러나 그것은 전적으로 시간에
기반을 둔다 / 그것이 공간적인 만큼 //   단서1 촉각은 전적으로 시간에 기반을 둠

You can carry out an experiment / to see for yourself. //
여러분은 실험을 할 수 있다 / 직접 알아보기 위해 //
                                              병렬 구조(Ask의 목적격 보어)
Ask a friend / to cup his hand, / palm face up, / and close his
                              생략된 분사 being의 의미상의
eyes. //   주어(palm)가 생략되지 않은 분사구문
친구에게 요청해 보라 / 손을 컵 모양으로 동그랗게 모아 쥐고 / 손바닥이 위로 향하게 하여 /
눈을 감으라고 //

Place a small ordinary object / in his palm / — a ring, an eraser,
                            병렬 구조
anything will do — / and ask him to identify it / without moving
                                          ask의 목적격 보어
any part of his hand. //
작은 평범한 물건을 올려놓고 / 그의 손바닥에 / 반지, 지우개, 무엇이든 괜찮다 / 그것이 무엇
인지 알아보라고 그에게 요청해 보라 / 손의 어떤 부분도 움직이지 말고 //

He won't have a clue / other than weight and maybe overall
size. //
그는 어떤 단서도 갖지 못할 것이다 / 무게와 아마 전체적인 크기 외에 //

Then tell him / to keep his eyes closed / and move his fingers /
                          tell의 목적격 보어(to부정사)의 병렬 구조
over the object. //
그런 다음 그에게 말하라 / 눈을 감은 채로 / 손가락을 움직여 보라고 / 그 물건 위로 //

He'll most likely identify it / at once. //
그는 거의 틀림없이 그것이 무엇인지 알아낼 것이다 / 즉시 //

By allowing the fingers to move, / you've added time / to the
sensory perception of touch. //   단서2 촉각에 시간을 더하면 물체가 무엇인지
손가락을 움직이게 함으로써 / 여러분은 시간을 더했다 / 촉각이라는 감각적 지각에 //   즉시 알아낼 수 있음

There's a direct analogy / between the fovea / at the center of
your retina / and your fingertips, / both of which have high
acuity. //
직접적인 유사함이 있는데 / 중심와(窩)와 (~의) 사이에 / 망막의 중심에 있는 / 여러분의 손가
락 끝 (사이에) / 둘 다 높은 예민함을 가진다 //
주어   형용사적 용법(Your ability 수식)
Your ability / to make complex use of touch, / such as buttoning
your shirt / or unlocking your front door / in the dark, /
여러분의 능력은 / 촉각을 복잡하게 사용하는 / 셔츠 단추를 잠그거나 / 현관문을 여는 것과 같
이 / 어둠 속에서 /   단서3 촉각을 복잡하게 사용하는 능력은 촉각의 지속적이고 시간에 따라
동사   달라지는 패턴에 의존함
depends / on continuous time-varying patterns / of touch
sensation. //
의존한다 / 지속적이고 시간에 따라 달라지는 패턴에 / 촉각이라는 감각의 //

- temporal [a] 시간의, 시간의 제약을 받는   - phenomenon [n] 현상
- every bit 어느 모로 보나, 전적으로   - spatial [a] 공간의, 공간적인
- carry out ~을 수행하다   - cup [v] 두 손을 (컵 모양으로) 동그랗게 모아 쥐다
- palm [n] 손바닥   - ordinary [a] 평범한, 일상적인
- object [n] 물건, 물체   - identify [v] 확인하다, 알아보다
- clue [n] 단서, 실마리   - at once 동시에, 즉시
- overall [a] 종합[전반]적인, 전체의   - sensory [a] 감각의
- perception [n] 지각, 자각   - direct [a] 직접적인
- fingertip [n] 손가락 끝   - acuity [n] (지각의) 예민함
- button [v] 단추를 잠그다   - continuous [a] 지속적인, 계속되는
- sensation [n] 느낌, 감각   - major [a] 주요한, 중대한
- humanity [n] 인류, 인간성   - matter [v] 중요하다, 문제되다
- essence [n] 본질, 진수   - timely [a] 시기적절한, 때맞춘
- booster [n] 촉진제

사람들은 보통 촉각을 시간의 현상으로 생각하지 않지만, 그것은 그것이 공간적
인 만큼 전적으로 시간에 기반을 둔다. 여러분은 직접 알아보기 위해 실험을 할
수 있다. 친구에게 손바닥이 위로 향하게 하여 손을 컵 모양으로 동그랗게 모아
쥐고, 눈을 감으라고 요청해 보라. 그의 손바닥에 작은 평범한 물건을 올려놓

고, 반지, 지우개, 무엇이든 괜찮다, 손의 어떤 부분도 움직이지 말고 그것이 무엇인지 알아보라고 요청해 보라. 그는 무게와 아마 전체적인 크기 외에 다른 어떤 단서도 갖지 못할 것이다. 그런 다음 그에게 눈을 감은 채로 그 물건 위로 손가락을 움직여 보라고 말하라. 그는 거의 틀림없이 그것이 무엇인지 즉시 알아낼 것이다. 여러분은 손가락을 움직이게 함으로써 촉각이라는 감각적 지각에 시간을 더했다. 망막의 중심에 있는 중심와(窩)와 여러분의 손가락 끝 사이에 직접적인 유사함이 있는데, 둘 다 예민함이 높다는 것이다. 어둠 속에서 셔츠 단추를 잠그거나 현관문을 여는 것과 같이 촉각을 복잡하게 사용하는 여러분의 능력은 촉각의 지속적이고 시간에 따라 달라지는 패턴에 의존한다.

다음 글의 제목으로 가장 적절한 것은?

① Touch and Movement: Two Major Elements of Humanity
촉각과 움직임: 인간의 두 가지 주요 요소　　　　손가락을 움직이게 했다는 것으로 만든 오답
②Time Does Matter: A Hidden Essence of Touch
시간은 정말 중요하다: 촉각의 숨겨진 본질　　촉각은 사실 시간에 기반을 둠
③ How to Use the Five Senses in a Timely Manner
오감을 적시에 사용하는 방법　　　　　　촉각에 대해서만 이야기함
④ The Role of Touch in Forming the Concept of Time
시간 개념 형성에서 촉각의 역할　　　　촉각에 시간을 더하는 것임
⑤ The Surprising Function of Touch as a Booster of Knowledge
지식의 촉진제로서 촉각의 놀라운 기능　　　　지식 습득을 촉진한다는 내용은 없음

>왜 정답? [정답률 75%]

첫 문장에서부터 촉각이 전적으로 시간에 기반을 둔다고 이야기했다. 이후로 손가락을 움직이게 함으로써 촉각에 시간을 더하면 손 위에 있는 물체가 무엇인지 즉시 알아낼 수 있다고 했고, 촉각을 복잡하게 사용하는 능력은 촉각의 지속적이고 시간에 따라 달라지는 패턴에 의존한다고 한 것으로 보아 제목이 ② '시간은 정말 중요하다: 촉각의 숨겨진 본질'임을 알 수 있다.

>왜 오답?

> 우리가 보통 촉각을 시간의 현상으로 생각하지 않기 때문에 '숨겨진'이라고 표현함 [꿀팁]

① 친구의 손가락을 움직이게 하면 물체가 무엇인지 즉시 알아낼 것이라는 내용으로 만든 오답이다. 손가락을 움직이게 함으로써 시간을 더했다는 것이지, 손가락의 움직임 그 자체가 중요한 것은 아니다.
③ 촉각에 대해서 이야기한 글로, 다섯 가지 감각을 제때 사용하는 방법을 설명한 것이 아니다.
④ 촉각에 시간이 더해져서 어둠 속에서 셔츠 단추를 잠그거나 현관문을 여는 것처럼 촉각을 복잡하게 사용할 수 있다는 것이지, 시간 개념 형성에 촉각이 어떤 역할을 한다는 것이 아니다.
⑤ 촉각을 통해 지식 습득이 촉진된다는 등의 내용이 아니다.

> 시간 개념 형성에 촉각이 더해지는 것이 아니라 촉각에 시간이 더해지는 것 [꿀팁]

[3회] 04 정답 ① ★불확실성의 불안을 줄이기 위한 사회의 노력

In several ways, / uncertainty can be understood as pervasive / and written into the very script of life. //
여러 면에서 / 불확실성은 만연한 것으로 이해될 수 있다 / 그리고 삶의 본질 속에 쓰여 있는 것으로 //

Due to this, / the craving for certainty has only become / a means of stemming a perceived tide of phenomena / that cannot yet be grasped / and, to an even lesser extent, controlled. //
（주격 관계대명사 / be에 연결된 동사）
이로 인해 / 확실성에 대한 갈망은 되어 버렸다 / 인식된 현상의 흐름을 막기 위한 수단이 / 아직 파악할 수 없는 / 그리고 더욱이 통제할 수 없는 //

Consequently, / the interplay / between the desire to overcome uncertainty / and instead strive towards certainty /
따라서 / 상호 작용은 / 불확실성을 극복하는 것과 / 확실성을 추구하려는 욕망 사이의 /

became inscribed into humans and society / as a way of influencing the present and the future. // [단서 1] 인간은 불확실성을 극복하고 확실성을 추구하려 함
인간과 사회에 각인되었다 / 현재와 미래에 영향을 미치는 방법으로서 //

This interplay is as old as the hills / and is rooted / in the human hope for security /
이 상호 작용은 언덕만큼 아주 오래되었다 / 그리고 뿌리를 두고 있다 / 인간의 안전에 대한 희망에 / [단서 2] 불확실성을 극복하고 확실성을 추구하려는 상호 작용은 인간의 안전, 생존, 편안함, 안녕을 위해 필요하다고 여겨짐

and the material, technological and social protection / regarded as necessary for survival, comfort, and wellbeing. //
（과거분사(protection 수식)）
그리고 물질적, 기술적, 사회적 보호에 / 인간의 생존, 편안함, 안녕을 위해 필요하다고 여겨지는 //

Mokyr shows / how Western capitalist societies are indebted / to all the systematic attempts / to **reduce insecurity in terms of uncertainty**. //
Mokyr는 보여준다 / 서구 자본주의 사회가 얼마나 빚을 지고 있는지를 / 체계적인 시도에 / 불확실성의 맥락에서 불안을 줄이기 위한 //

According to Mokyr, / the strong belief in technical progress / and the continuous improvement of various aspects of life / are rooted in the reasoning /
（복수 주어 / 복수 동사）
Mokyr에 따르면 / 기술 발전에 대한 강한 신념 / 그리고 삶의 여러 측면의 지속적인 개선은 / 이성에 뿌리를 두고 있다 /
（주격 관계대명사）
that emerged and developed in the philosophical movement of the Enlightenment / and which created a "space" / for humans' "desire to know" / and practically experiment with a wide range of activities. //
（주격 관계대명사）
계몽주의 철학 운동에서 발생하고 발전한 / 그리고 '공간'을 만들어 준 / 인간의 '알고자 하는 욕망'에 / 그리고 다양한 활동을 실제로 실험할 수 있는 //

- pervasive ⓐ 만연한　　• craving ⓝ 갈망, 열망
- grasp ⓥ 이해하다, 파악하다　　• overcome ⓥ 극복하다
- interplay ⓝ 상호 작용　　• inscribe ⓥ (이름 등을) 쓰다[새기다]
- root ⓥ 뿌리를 내리다　　• indebt ⓥ ~에게 빚을 지게 하다
- insecurity ⓝ 불안감　　• outdo ⓥ 능가하다
- forerunner ⓝ 선구자　　• negate ⓥ 부정하다
- interpretation ⓝ 해석　　• minimize ⓥ 최소화하다
- overloaded ⓐ 과부하된

여러 면에서 불확실성은 만연하며 삶의 본질 속에 쓰여 있다고 이해될 수 있다. 이로 인해 확실성에 대한 갈망은 아직 파악할 수 없고, 더욱이 통제할 수 없는 인식된 현상의 흐름을 막기 위한 수단이 되어버렸다. 따라서 불확실성을 극복하고 확실성을 추구하려는 욕망 간의 상호 작용은 현재와 미래에 영향을 미치는 방법으로서 인간과 사회에 각인되었다. 이 상호 작용은 언덕만큼 아주 오래된 것으로, 인간의 안전에 대한 희망과 생존, 편안함, 안녕을 위해 필요하다고 여겨지는 물질적, 기술적, 사회적 보호에 뿌리를 두고 있다. Mokyr는 서구 자본주의 사회가 **불확실성의 맥락에서 불안을 줄이기 위한** 체계적인 시도에 빚을 지고 있음을 보여준다. Mokyr에 따르면, 기술 발전에 대한 강한 신념과 삶의 여러 측면의 지속적인 개선은 계몽주의 철학 운동에서 발생하고 발전한 이성에 뿌리를 두고 있으며, 이는 인간의 '알고자 하는 욕망'과 다양한 활동을 실제로 실험할 수 있는 '공간'을 만들어주었다.

다음 빈칸에 들어갈 말로 가장 적절한 것을 고르시오. [4점]
불확실성을 극복하고 확실성을 추구하는 것이 인간의 안전이나 생존 등을 위해 필요한 보호라고 여긴다고
①reduce insecurity in terms of uncertainty 했으므로 불확실성의 측면에서
불확실성의 맥락에서 불안을 줄이기 위한　　　　불안을 줄이려고 한 것이 맞음
② outdo their forerunners in scientific areas 과학 영역에서 선구자들을
과학적 영역에서 선구자를 능가하기 위한　　　능가하기 위한 시도를 한 것이 아님
③ negate errors in interpretation of certainty 확실성에 대한 해석에서 오류를
확실성에 대한 해석에서 오류를 부정하기 위한　　부정하기 위한 체계적인 시도를 했다는 내용은 없음
④ minimize the potential of human reasoning
인간 이성의 잠재력을 최소화하기 위한　　인간 이성의 잠재력을 최소화하기 위한 시도를 했다고 하지 않았음
⑤ survive the overloaded world of information 과부하된 정보 세계에서
과부하된 정보 세계에서 살아남기 위한　　　살아남기 위한 체계적인 시도를 했다는 내용이 아님

>왜 정답? [정답률 35%]

빈칸 문장	Mokyr는 서구 자본주의 사회가 ＿＿＿＿＿＿＿ 체계적인 시도에 빚을 지고 있음을 보여준다.

➡ 빈칸에는 서구 사회에 '어떤' 체계적인 시도에 빚을 지고 있는지, 다시 말해 무엇을 위해 노력하고 있는지가 나와야 한다.

- 불확실성을 극복하고 확실성을 추구하려는 욕망 간의 상호 작용은 현재와 미래에 영향을 미치는 방법으로서 인간과 사회에 각인됨 [단서 1]
- 이 상호 작용은 아주 오래된 것으로, 인간의 안전에 대한 희망과 생존, 편안함, 안녕을 위해 필요하다고 여겨지는 물질적, 기술적, 사회적 보호에 뿌리를 둠 [단서 2]

➡ 불확실성을 극복하고 확실성을 추구하려는 욕망 간 상호 작용이 인간과 사회에 각인되어 있으며, 이것이 인간의 안전 및 생존, 편안함, 안녕을 위한 보호에서 비롯된 것임을 언급하고 있는 내용의 글이다.

▶ 그러므로 서구 사회가 무엇을 위해 노력하고 있는지에 대한 빈칸 문장에는 서구 사회가 '불확실성 속에서 불안을 줄이기 위한' 노력을 하고 있다는 ①이 들어가야 한다.

왜 오답?

② 과학 영역에서 선구자들을 능가하기 위한 시도를 한 것이 아니다.

③ 확실성에 대한 해석에서 오류를 부정하기 위한 체계적인 시도를 했다는 내용은 없다.

④ 인간 이성의 잠재력을 최소화하기 위한 시도를 했다고 하지 않았다.

⑤ 과부하된 정보 세계에서 살아남기 위한 체계적인 시도를 했다는 내용이 아니다.

3회 05 정답 ② * 민주주의를 정의하는 의사소통 문화

So many accounts of democracy / emphasize legislative processes or policy outcomes, / but these often miss the depth of connection / between communication and political culture. //
많은 민주주의에 대한 설명은 / 입법 과정이나 정책 결과를 강조한다 / 그러나 이는 깊은 연관성을 종종 놓치게 된다 / 의사소통과 정치 문화 간의 //

When culture is discussed, / it's often in the context / of liberal-democratic values. //
문화에 대해 논의할 때 / 그것은 주로 맥락 안에 놓인다 / 자유민주주의 가치의 //
사이에 목적격 관계대명사 생략

But the question we're asking is: / What determines the valence of those values? //
하지만 우리가 묻고자 하는 질문은 이렇다 / 무엇이 이러한 가치의 의미를 결정하는가 //
단서 1 민주주의가 문화에 의해 좌우된다면 우리는 어떤 조건에서 이러한 가치가 긍정 또는 부정되는지 알아야 함
If a democracy stands or falls / on the quality of the culture /
현재분사(culture 수식)
propping it up, / then we ought to know / under what conditions / those values are affirmed and rejected. //
만약 민주주의가 좌우된다면 / 문화의 질에 의해 / 그것을 지탱하는 / 그러면 우리는 알아야 한다 / 어떤 조건에서 / 이러한 가치가 긍정되거나 부정되는지를 //
사이에 목적어절 접속사 that 생략
We believe / those conditions are determined / by a society's tools of communication, / facilitated through media, / to persuade. // **단서 2** 그러한 조건(민주주의를 좌우하는)이 의사소통 도구, 즉 미디어를 통해 결정되거나 촉진됨
우리는 믿는다 / 그러한 조건이 결정된다고 / 사회의 의사소통 도구에 의해 / 미디어를 통해 촉진된다고 / 설득하도록 //

Indeed, / **democracies are defined / by their cultures of communication**. //
실제로 / 민주주의는 정의된다 / 의사소통 문화에 의해 //

If a democracy consists of citizens / deciding, collectively, / 현재분사(citizens 수식)
what ought to be done, / then the manner / through which they persuade one another / determines nearly everything else / that follows. //
주격 관계대명사
만약 민주주의가 시민들로 구성된다면 / 집단적으로 무엇을 해야 할지를 결정하는 / 그러면 방식이 / 그들이 서로를 설득하는 / 거의 모든 것을 결정하게 된다 / 이후에 일어나는 //

And that privileges media ecology / as the master political science. //
그리고 그것은 미디어 생태계를 우대한다 / 주요 정치 과학으로 //

Some of its foremost practitioners, / like Marshall McLuhan and Neil Postman, / sensed, / far better than political scientists or sociologists, /
비교급 강조 부사
주요 실천자들 중 몇 명은 / Marshall McLuhan이나 Neil Postman과 같은 / 인식했다 / 정치 과학자나 사회학자보다 훨씬 더 잘 /
목적어절을 이끄는 접속사   not just(only) A but also B: A 뿐만 아니라 B도
that our media environment decides / not just what we pay attention to / but also how we think and orient ourselves in the world. // **단서 3** 우리의 미디어 환경이 우리가 주목하는 것, 사고하고 방향을 정하는 것을 결정함
우리의 미디어 환경이 결정한다는 것을 / 우리가 주목하는 것뿐만 아니라 / 세상에서 사고하고 방향을 정하는 방식까지 //

- democracy ⓝ 민주주의   · emphasize ⓥ 강조하다
- legislative ⓐ 입법의   · context ⓝ 맥락
- facilitate ⓥ 용이하게 하다, 촉진하다
- privilege ⓥ 특권을 주다, 우대하다
- orient ⓥ 지향하게 하다, 방향을 정하다   · inevitable ⓐ 피할 수 없는
- thrive ⓥ 번창하다   · sustain ⓥ 살아가게 하다, 유지하다
- dynamics ⓝ 역학

많은 민주주의에 대한 설명은 입법 과정이나 정책 결과를 강조하지만, 이는 종종 의사소통과 정치 문화 간의 깊은 연관성을 놓치게 된다. 문화에 대해 논의할 때, 그것은 주로 자유민주주의 가치를 맥락으로 삼는 경우가 많다. 하지만 우리가 묻고자 하는 질문은 이렇다: 이러한 가치의 의미를 결정하는 것은 무엇인가? 만약 민주주의가 그것을 지탱하는 문화의 질에 의해 좌우된다면, 우리는 이러한 가치가 어떤 조건에서 긍정되거나 부정되는지를 알아야 한다. 우리는 그러한 조건이 사회의 의사소통 도구에 의해 결정되며, 이는 미디어를 통해 설득을 가능하게 한다고 믿는다. 실제로 민주주의는 **의사소통 문화에 의해 정의된다**. 만약 민주주의가 집단적으로 무엇을 해야 할지를 결정하는 시민들로 구성된다면, 그들이 서로를 설득하는 방식이 이후에 일어나는 거의 모든 것을 결정하게 된다. 이는 미디어 생태계를 주요 정치 과학으로 우대한다. Marshall McLuhan이나 Neil Postman과 같은 주요 실천자들은 정치 과학자나 사회학자보다 훨씬 더 잘 인식했는데, 우리의 미디어 환경이 우리가 주목하는 것뿐만 아니라 세상에서 사고하고 방향을 정하는 방식까지 결정한다는 것이다.

다음 빈칸에 들어갈 말로 가장 적절한 것을 고르시오. [4점]

① media will soon solve communication issues in democracy
미디어가 곧 민주주의의 의사소통 문제를 해결할 것이다 ─ 미디어가 민주주의의 의사소통 문제를 해결할 것이라는 내용이 아님

② democracies are defined by their cultures of communication
민주주의는 의사소통 문화에 의해 정의된다 ─ 민주주의의 가치를 결정하는 조건이 의사소통 도구와 미디어에 영향을 받는다고 했으므로 민주주의가 의사소통 문화에 의해 정의됨

③ conflicts between individuality and collectivity are inevitable
개별성과 집합성 간의 갈등은 피할 수 없다 ─ 개별성과 집합성의 갈등에 대한 글이 아님

④ democracy thrives on order rather than endless public discourse
민주주의는 무질서한 토론보다는 질서 있는 환경에서 번성한다 ─ 민주주의가 무질서한 토론보다 질서 있는 환경에서 번성한다는 내용이 아님

⑤ democracies can be sustained by valuing socioeconomic dynamics
민주주의는 사회경제적 역동성을 중시함으로써 유지될 수 있다 ─ 민주주의가 사회경제적 역동성을 중시함으로써 유지될 수 있다는 글이 아님

왜 정답? [정답률 33%]

빈칸 문장	실제로 _____.

→ 뒤 문장을 통해 민주주의의 특성에 대해 서술하고 있는 부분임을 알 수 있으므로 빈칸에는 민주주의가 이 글에서 어떤 특성이 있다고 이야기하고 있는지를 제시해야 한다.

- 만약 민주주의가 문화에 의해 좌우된다면, 이러한 가치가 어떤 조건에서 긍정되거나 부정되는지를 알아야 함 **단서 1**
- 그러한 조건은 사회의 의사소통 도구에 의해 결정되며, 미디어를 통해 설득 가능함 **단서 2**
- 우리의 미디어 환경이 우리가 주목하는 것뿐만 아니라 세상에서 사고하고 방향을 정하는 방식까지 결정함 **단서 3**

→ 민주주의를 좌우하는(결정하는) 조건은 의사소통 도구와 미디어를 통해 결정되며 우리의 미디어 환경이 우리가 주목하는 것뿐만 아니라 세상에서 사고하고 방향을 정하는 방식까지 결정한다는 내용의 글이다.

▶ 그러므로 빈칸에는 '민주주의는 의사소통 문화에 의해 정의된다'는 ②이 들어가야 한다.

왜 오답?

① 미디어가 민주주의의 의사소통 문제를 해결할 것이라는 내용이 아니다.

③ 개별성과 집합성의 갈등에 대한 글이 아니다.

④ 민주주의가 무질서한 토론보다 질서 있는 환경에서 번성한다는 내용이 아니다. (함정)

⑤ 민주주의가 사회경제적 역동성을 중시함으로써 유지될 수 있다는 글이 아니다.

3회 06 정답 ③ * John Locke의 이론이 한 역할

명사절 접속사
The empiricist philosopher John Locke argued / that when the human being was first born, / the mind was simply a blank slate
부사절 접속사(시간)
— a tabula rasa — / waiting to be written on / by experience. //
경험주의 철학자 John Locke는 주장했다 / 인간이 처음 태어났을 때 / 그 마음은 그저 빈 석판인 tabula rasa였다고 / 기록되기를 기다리는 / 경험에 의해 //

Locke believed / that our experience shapes / who we are / and who we become /
shapes의 목적어절의 병렬 구조
Locke는 믿었다 / 우리의 경험이 형성한다고 / 우리가 누구인지를 / 그리고 우리가 어떤 사람이 되는지를 /

— and therefore he also believed / that, given different experiences, / human beings would have different characters. //
그래서 그는 또한 믿었다 / 다른 경험이 주어지면 / 인간은 다른 성격을 가질 것이라고 //

The influence of these ideas was profound, / particularly for the new colonies in America, / for example, /
이런 생각의 영향은 컸다 / 특히 미국의 새로운 식민지에서 / 예를 들어 /

because these were conscious attempts / to make a new start /
형용사적 용법(attempts 수식)

and to form a new society. //
단서 2 Locke의 생각은 새로운 사회를 형성하려는 시도였던 미국의 새로운 식민지에서 큰 영향을 미쳤음
이들은 의식적인 시도였기 때문에 / 새로운 시작을 하고 / 새로운 사회를 형성하려는 //

The new society was to operate / on a different basis / from that
〈예정〉을 나타내는 be to-v 용법   = the basis

of European culture, / which was based / on the feudal system /
선행사
새로운 사회는 작동될 것이었는데 / 다른 기반에서 / 유럽 문화의 그것과는 / 그것은 기반을 두었고 / 봉건 제도에 /
관계부사 where로 바꿀 수 있음

in which people's place in society / was almost entirely determined / by birth, / and which therefore tended to emphasize / innate characteristics. //
사람들의 사회적 지위가 / 거의 전적으로 결정되는 / 출생에 의해 / 따라서 그것은 강조하는 경향이 있었던 / 선천적인 특성을 //

Locke's emphasis / on the importance of experience / in forming the human being / provided **an optimistic framework** / for **those** / **trying to form a different society**. //
Locke의 강조는 / 경험의 중요성에 대한 / 인간을 형성하는 것에서 / 낙관적인 틀을 제공했다 / 사람들을 위한 / 다른 사회를 형성하려는 //

- **philosopher** ⓝ 철학자 · **blank** ⓐ 빈 · **character** ⓝ 성격, 특징
- **influence** ⓝ 영향 · **profound** ⓐ 엄청난, 심오한
- **colony** ⓝ 식민지 · **conscious** ⓐ 의식하는, 자각하는
- **attempt** ⓝ 시도 · **form** ⓥ 형성하다
- **operate** ⓥ 운용하다, 작동하다 · **basis** ⓝ 근거, 기준, 기반
- **entirely** ⓐⓓ 전적으로, 완전히 · **innate** ⓐ 선천적인
- **characteristic** ⓝ 특징, 특질 · **emphasis** ⓝ 강조, 역점
- **foundation** ⓝ 토대, 기초 · **reinforce** ⓥ 강화하다, 보강하다
- **tie** ⓥ 묶다, 결부시키다 · **colonial** ⓐ 식민(지)의
- **value** ⓥ 소중하게[가치 있게] 생각하다[여기다] · **optimistic** ⓐ 낙관적인
- **framework** ⓝ 뼈대, 틀, 체계 · **access** ⓝ 접근권, 접촉 기회
- **expertise** ⓝ 전문 지식[기술]

경험주의 철학자 John Locke는 인간이 처음 태어났을 때, 그 마음은 경험에 의해 기록되기를 기다리는 그저 빈 석판인 tabula rasa였다고 주장했다. Locke는 우리의 경험이 우리가 누구인지, 우리가 어떤 사람이 되는지를 형성한다고 믿었고, 그래서 그는 또한 다른 경험이 주어지면, 인간은 다른 성격을 가질 것이라고 믿었다. 이런 생각의 영향은 특히 예를 들어 미국의 새로운 식민지에서 컸는데, 왜냐하면 이들 식민지는 새로운 시작을 하고 새로운 사회를 형성하려는 의식적인 시도였기 때문이었다. 새로운 사회는 유럽 문화의 기반과는 다른 기반에서 작동될 것이었는데, 유럽 문화는 사람들의 사회적 지위가 거의 전적으로 출생에 의해 결정되는 봉건 제도에 기반을 두었고, 따라서 그것은 선천적인 특성을 강조하는 경향이 있었다. 인간의 형성에서 경험이 갖는 중요성에 대한 Locke의 강조는 **다른 사회를 형성하려는 사람들을 위한 낙관적인 틀**을 제공했다.

다음 빈칸에 들어갈 말로 가장 적절한 것을 고르시오. [3점]

① foundations for reinforcing ties between European and colonial societies
유럽과 다른 새로운 사회 건설에 큰 영향을 미침
유럽 사회와 식민 사회 사이의 유대감을 강화하기 위한 토대

② new opportunities for European societies to value their tradition
유럽 사회가 자신의 전통을 소중히 생각하는 새로운 기회   새로운 사회를 형성하는 것임

③ an optimistic framework for those trying to form a different society
새로운 사회=기존의 유럽과는 다른 사회
다른 사회를 형성하려는 사람들을 위한 낙관적인 틀

④ an example of the role that nature plays in building character
성격을 형성하는 데 있어 천성이 하는 역할의 예시   성격 형성에 미치는 경험의 역할을 강조함

⑤ an access to expertise in the areas of philosophy and science
철학과 과학 영역에서 전문지식으로의 접근권   philosopher로 만든 오답

왜 정답? [정답률 44%]

Locke의 믿음: 다른 경험이 주어지면 인간은 다른 성격을 가질 것이다. 단서 1
Locke의 믿음이 큰 영향을 미친 경우: 새로운 사회를 형성하려는 의식적인 시도였던 미국의 새로운 식민지에서 그 영향이 컸다. 단서 2 유럽과는 다른 기반에서 작동할 사회
▶ Locke의 생각은 ③ '다른 사회를 형성하려는 사람들에게 낙관적인 틀'을 제공했다.

왜 오답?

① 유럽 사회와는 다른 새로운 사회를 형성하는 데 큰 영향을 미친 것이다.
② 유럽 사회를 변화시키는 데 Locke의 주장이 긍정적인 역할을 했다는 것이 아니다.
④ 인간의 성격은 경험에 의해 형성된다는 것이 Locke의 생각이다.
⑤ Locke가 철학자였다는 언급으로 만든 오답이다.

3회 07 정답 ② * Timbuktu의 도서관에 보관된 수집물이 과거와 현재 처한 상황 ─

On January 26, 2013, / a band of al-Qaeda militants / entered the ancient city of Timbuktu / on the southern edge of the Sahara Desert. // 단서 1 알카에다 무장단체가 고대 도시 Timbuktu에 침입했음
2013년 1월 26일 / 알카에다 무장단체가 / 고대 도시 Timbuktu에 침입했다 / 사하라 사막의 남쪽에 위치한 //

(A) The mayor of Bamako, / who witnessed the event, / called
주격 관계대명사
the burning of the manuscripts / "a crime against world cultural heritage." // 단서 2 (B)에서 언급한 '이 사건'을 목격한 시장이 원고의 불태움을 세계 문화 유산에 대한 범죄라고 말했음
Bamako 시장은 / 이 사건을 목격한 / 원고의 불태움을 언급했다 / "세계 문화 유산에 대한 범죄"라고 //

And he was right / — or he would have been, / if it weren't for
= would have been right   가정법 과거
the fact / that he was also lying. //
동격절을 이끄는 접속사
그리고 그는 옳았다 / 혹은 옳았을 것이다 / 만약 그것이 사실이 아니었다면 / 그가 또한 거짓말을 한 것이 //
단서 3 '그들(주어진 글에서 언급한 알카에다 무장단체)'은 중세 도서관에 불을 질렀음

(B) There, / they set fire to a medieval library / of 30,000 manuscripts / written in Arabic and several African languages / and ranging in subject / from astronomy to geography, history to medicine. //
분사(manuscript 수식)의 병렬 구조
그곳에서 / 그들은 중세 도서관에 불을 질렀다 / 30,000개의 원고가 있는 / 아랍어와 여러 아프리카 언어로 쓰인 / 그리고 다양한 주제를 다루고 있는 / 천문학에서 지리학까지, 그리고 역사에서 의학까지 //

Unknown in the West, / this was the collected wisdom / of an entire continent, / the voice of Africa / at a time when Africa was
분사구문   관계부사
thought / not to have a voice at all. //
서구에서는 잘 알려지지 않았던 / 이 자료는 집합된 지혜였다 / 아프리카 대륙 전체의 / 그리고 아프리카의 목소리였다 / 아프리카가 여겨지던 시기에 / 전혀 목소리를 가지지 않은 것으로 //

(C) In fact, just before, / African scholars had collected / a random assortment of old books / and left them out / for the terrorists to burn. // 단서 4 그 직전에 아프리카 학자들은 책을 무작위로 모아 태우도록 내버려 두었음
사실, 그 직전 / 아프리카 학자들은 수집했다 / 무작위의 오래된 책들의 모음을 / 그리고 내버려 두었다 / 테러리스트들이 불태우도록 //

Today, / the collection lies hidden in Bamako, / the capital of Mali, / moldering in the high humidity. //
분사구문
오늘날 / 그 수집물은 Bamako에 숨겨져 있다 / Mali의 수도인 / 높은 습기 속에서 썩어가면서 //

What was rescued by ruse / is now once again in jeopardy, / this
단수 주어   단수 동사
time by climate. //
속임수로 구출된 것이 / 이제 다시 위험에 처하게 되었다 / 이번에는 기후로 인해 //

- **witness** ⓥ 목격하다 · **manuscript** ⓝ 원고 · **heritage** ⓝ 유산
- **medieval** ⓐ 중세의 · **astronomy** ⓝ 천문학
- **geography** ⓝ 지리학 · **assortment** ⓝ 모음 · **molder** ⓥ 썩다
- **humidity** ⓝ 습도 · **in jeopardy** 위기에 처한

2013년 1월 26일, 알카에다 무장단체가 사하라 사막의 남쪽에 위치한 고대 도시 Timbuktu에 침입했다. (B) 그들은 아랍어와 여러 아프리카 언어로 쓰인

30,000개의 원고가 담긴 중세 도서관에 불을 질렀고, 이 원고들은 천문학에서 지리학, 역사에서 의학에 이르는 다양한 주제를 다루고 있었다. 서구에서는 잘 알려지지 않았던 이 자료는 아프리카 대륙 전체의 집합된 지혜였으며, 아프리카가 전혀 목소리를 가지지 못한 것으로 여겨졌던 시기의 아프리카의 목소리였다. (A) 이 사건을 목격한 Bamako 시장은 원고의 불태움을 "세계 문화 유산에 대한 범죄"라고 언급했다. 그리고 그는 옳았다 — 혹은 만약 그가 거짓말을 한 것이 아니었다면 그는 맞는 말을 했던 것이었다. (C) 사실, 그 직전 아프리카 학자들은 무작위로 오래된 책들을 수집해 테러리스트들이 불태우도록 내버려 두었다. 오늘날, 그 수집물은 Mali의 수도 Bamako에 숨겨져 있으며, 높은 습기 속에서 썩어가고 있다. 속임수로 구출된 것이 이제 다시 기후로 인해 위험에 처하게 되었다.

주어진 글 다음에 이어질 글의 순서로 가장 적절한 것을 고르시오. [3점]

① (A) — (C) — (B) 주어진 글에서 알카에다 무장단체가 침입했다는 사실만 제시할 뿐 원고의 불태움에 대해서는 언급하지 않았으므로 (A)가 주어진 글 다음에 올 수 없음

②(B) — (A) — (C) 알카에다 무장단체가 고대 도시 Timbuktu에 침입했음 - 알카에다 무장단체가 원고로 가득한 도서관에 불을 지름 - 이 사건을 목격한 시장이 이를 세계 문화 유산에 대한 범죄라고 했지만 이는 사실이 아님 - 테러리스트들이 태운 것은 무작위로 모은 책이었고, 그 원고들은 잘 숨겨져 있음

③ (B) — (C) — (A) '그 직전에'라고 시작하는 (C)와 연결될 수 있는 내용이 주어진 글에 없음

④ (C) — (A) — (B)

⑤ (C) — (B) — (A)

—(C)는 원고들이 태워지지 않고 오늘날까지 잘 남아 있음을 언급하고 있으므로 제일 마지막에 와야 함

| 문제 풀이 순서 | [정답률 45%]

1st 각 문단의 내용을 파악하고, 글의 논리적인 순서를 추론한다.

┌ **주어진 글:** 2013년 1월 26일, 알카에다 무장단체가 사하라 사막의 남쪽에
└ 위치한 고대 도시 Timbuktu에 침입했다.

⇒ 알카에다 무장단체가 고대 도시에 침입했다. **단서**
  주어진 글 뒤: 무장단체가 그 도시에서 한 일이나 그 도시에 침입한 이유에 대해
  제시될 것이다. **발상**

┌ **(A)** 이 사건(the event)을 목격한 Bamako 시장은 원고의 불태움을
  "세계 문화 유산에 대한 범죄"라고 언급했다. 그리고 그는 옳았다 — 혹은
└ 만약 그가 거짓말을 한 것이 아니었다면 그는 맞는 말을 했던 것이었다.

⇒ **(A) 앞:** '이 사건(the event)'을 목격한 뒤 원고의 불태움을 세계 문화 유산에 대한
  범죄라고 언급했으므로 '이 사건'과 원고의 불태움에 대해 제시되어야 한다.
  ▶ 주어진 글이 (A) 앞에 올 수 없음
  (A) 뒤: 그가 거짓말을 했고, 그의 말이 옳지 않다고 했으므로 진실에 대해
  언급되어야 한다.

┌ **(B)** 그들(They)은 아랍어와 여러 아프리카 언어로 쓰인 30,000개의
  원고가 담긴 중세 도서관에 불을 질렀고, 이 원고들은 천문학에서 지리학,
  역사에서 의학에 이르는 다양한 주제를 다루고 있었다. 서구에서는 잘
  알려지지 않았던 이 자료는 아프리카 대륙 전체의 집합된 지혜였으며,
  아프리카가 전혀 목소리를 가지지 못한 것으로 여겨졌던 시기의
└ 아프리카의 목소리였다.

⇒ **(B) 앞:** '그들(They)'이 아랍어와 아프리카 언어로 쓰인 다양한 주제를 다룬 원고가
  가득한 도서관에 불을 질렀다고 했으므로, 그들이 누구이며 무엇을 했는지에 대해
  언급되어야 한다. 이 내용이 주어진 글에 나와 있다. ▶ 순서: 주어진 글 → (B)
  (B) 뒤: 이 자료가 '아프리카 대륙의 지혜이자 목소리'라는 가치에 대한 부연
  설명이나 화제로 인해 이 가치 있는 자료가 어떤 결과에 직면하게 되었는지 나와야
  한다. ▶ 순서: (B) → (A)

┌ **(C)** 사실(In fact), 그 직전 아프리카 학자들은 무작위로 오래된 책들을
  수집해 테러리스트들이 불태우도록 내버려 두었다. 오늘날, 그 수집물은
  Mali의 수도 Bamako에 숨겨져 있으며, 높은 습기 속에서 썩어가고
└ 있다. 속임수로 구출된 것이 이제 다시 기후로 인해 위험에 처하게 되었다.

⇒ **(C) 앞:** '사실(In fact)'이라는 표현을 통해 앞에는 아프리카 학자들이 무작위로
  모은 책을 태우도록 내버려 두었으며 수집품이 훼손되지 않고 숨겨져 있는
  현실과는 반대되는 내용(책이 불태워졌다)이 제시되어야 한다. ▶ 순서: (A) → (C)
  (C) 뒤: 과거 불에 태워질 위기를 극복하고 보관 중인 수집물이 현재 처한 상황에
  대해 서술하고 있으므로 (C)가 글의 마지막에 와야 할 것이다.
  ▶ 순서: 주어진 글 → (B) → (A) → (C)

2nd 글이 한눈에 들어오도록 정리하여 정답을 확인한다.

주어진 글: 알카에다 무장단체가 고대 도시에 침입했다.

→ **(B):** 원고로 가득한 중세 도서관을 불태웠는데, 그 원고는 아프리카의 지혜이자
  목소리였다.

→ **(A):** 이 원고 불태움 사건을 세계 문화 유산에 대한 범죄라고 언급했으나 사실 이
  말은 옳지 않다.

→ **(C):** 무작위로 모은 책이 태워진 것으로 실제 수집물은 잘 숨겨져 현재 습기에
  영향을 받는 중이다.

▶ 주어진 글 다음에 이어질 글의 순서는 (B) → (A) → (C)이므로 정답은 ②임

3회 08 정답 ④ ＊언어 자원의 두 가지 특징

글의 흐름으로 보아, 주어진 문장이 들어가기에 가장 적절한 곳을 고르시오.

단서 1 우리의 언어 자원이 역사적으로 정해진 의미를 지닌 채 온다는 내용이 앞에 있어야 함

However, / while our resources come / with histories
 of meanings, / *how they come to mean* / at a particular
communicative moment / is always open / to negotiation. //
하지만 / 우리의 자원들이 오지만 / 의미의 역사를 지닌 채 / '그것들이 어떻게 의미하게
되는가'는 / 특정한 의사소통의 순간에 / 항상 열려 있다 / 협상에 //

The linguistic resources / we choose to use / do not come to
us / as empty forms / ready to be filled / with our personal
intentions; /
언어 자원들은 / 우리가 사용하기로 선택하는 / 우리에게 오지 않는다 / 텅 빈 형태로 / 채워질
준비가 된 / 우리의 개인적인 의도로 /

rather, they come to us / with meanings / already embedded
within them. //
오히려 그것들은 우리에게 온다 / 의미들과 함께 / 그것들 안에 이미 뿌리 박힌 //

(①) These meanings, / however, / are not derived / from some
universal, logical set of principles; /
이런 의미들은 / 그런데 / 유래하지 않는다 / 어떤 보편적이고 논리적인 일련의 원리들에서 /
rather, as with their shapes, / they are built up / over time / from
their past uses / in particular contexts /
오히려 그것들의 형태에서처럼 / 그것들은 만들어진다 / 오랜 시간에 걸쳐 / 그것들의 이전의
사용에서 / 특정한 상황들에서 /

by particular groups of participants / in the accomplishment of
particular goals / that, in turn, are shaped / by myriad cultural,
historical and institutional forces. //
특정한 참가자 집단에 의해 / 특정한 목적의 달성에의 / 결국 형성되는 / 무수히 많은 문화적,
역사적, 그리고 제도적인 힘들에 의해 //

(②) The linguistic resources / we choose to use / at particular
communicative moments / come to these moments / with their
conventionalized histories of meaning. //
언어 자원들은 / 우리가 사용하기로 선택하는 / 특정한 의사소통의 순간들에 / 이런 순간들에
온다 / 관습화된 의미의 역사를 지니고 //
단서 2 언어 자원의 관습성: 역사적으로 결정된 의미를 지님

(③) It is their conventionality / that binds us / to some degree /
to particular ways / of realizing our collective history. //
그것들의 관습성이 / 우리를 묶는다 / 어느 정도 / 특정한 방식에 / 우리의 집단적인 역사를
실현하는 //
단서 3 언어 자원을 사용할 때 두 가지 행위가 일어나는 근거가 앞에 있어야 함

(④) Thus, / in our individual uses / of our linguistic resources /
we accomplish two actions simultaneously. //
그래서 / 우리의 개별적인 사용에서 / 우리의 언어 자원의 / 우리는 두 가지 행위를 동시에
이룬다 //

(⑤) We create / their typical — historical — contexts of use
/ and at the same time / we position ourselves / in relation to
these contexts. //
우리는 만든다 / 그것들의 전형적인, 역사적인, 사용의 맥락을 / 그리고 동시에 / 우리는 우리
자신의 입장을 취한다 / 이런 맥락과 관련하여 //

- negotiation ⓝ 협상, 교섭, 절충 · linguistic ⓐ 언어(학)의
- be filled with ~으로 가득 차다 · intention ⓝ 의도
- rather ⓐⅾ 오히려, 차라리 · embedded ⓐ 뿌리 박힌
- be derived from ~에서 유래하다 · universal ⓐ 보편적인
- logical ⓐ 논리적인 · over time 오랜 시간에 걸쳐
- context ⓝ 상황, 맥락 · accomplishment ⓝ 달성, 성취
- in turn 결국 · institutional ⓐ 제도적인 · force ⓝ 물리력, 힘
- conventionalized ⓐ 관습화된 · bind ⓥ 묶다
- to some degree 어느 정도 · collective ⓐ 집단적인
- accomplish ⓥ 완수하다, 성취하다 · simultaneously ⓐⅾ 동시에
- typical ⓐ 전형적인 · position ⓥ (특정한 위치에) 두다[배치하다]
- in relation to ~와 관련하여

우리가 사용하기로 선택하는 언어 자원들은 우리의 개인적인 의도로 채워질 준비가 된 텅 빈 형태로 우리에게 온다기보다는, 그것들 안에 이미 뿌리 박힌 의미들과 함께 우리에게 온다. (①) 그런데 이런 의미들이 어떤 보편적이고 논리적인 일련의 원리들에서 유래한다기보다는, 그것들의 형태에서처럼, 그것들은 결국 무수히 많은 문화적, 역사적, 그리고 제도적인 힘들에 의해 형성되는, 특정한 목적의 달성에 참가하는 특정한 집단에 의해 특정한 상황들에서 그것들의 이전의 사용에서 오랜 시간에 걸쳐 만들어진다. (②) 특정한 의사소통의 순간들에 우리가 사용하기로 선택하는 언어 자원들은 관습화된 의미의 역사를 지니고 이런 순간들에 온다. (③) 우리의 집단적인 역사를 실현하는 특정한 방식에 우리를 어느 정도 묶는 것은 바로 그것들의 관습성이다. (④ 하지만, 우리의 자원들이 의미의 역사를 지닌 채 오지만 특정한 의사소통의 순간에 '그것들이 어떻게 의미하게 되는가'는 항상 협상의 여지가 있다.) 그래서, 우리의 언어 자원을 우리가 개별적으로 사용할 때 우리는 두 가지 행위를 동시에 이룬다. (⑤) 우리는 그것들의 전형적인, 즉 역사적인 사용의 맥락을 만들면서 동시에 우리는 이런 맥락과 관련하여 우리 자신의 입장을 취한다.

| 문제 풀이 순서 | [정답률 41%]

1st 주어진 문장을 해석하고, 연결어, 지시어 등을 확인한다.

> [However,] while our resources come with histories of meanings, how they come to mean at a particular communicative moment is always open to negotiation. 단서1
> [하지만] 우리의 자원들이 의미의 역사를 지닌 채 오지만, 특정한 의사소통의 순간에 '그것들이 어떻게 의미하게 되는가'는 항상 협상의 여지가 있다.

➡ 자원이 의미의 역사를 지닌 채 온다는 것이 역접의 연결어(However, while)로 이어진다. 단서
  ▶ 주어진 문장이 들어갈 곳: 자원이 역사적으로 정해진 의미를 지닌 채 우리에게 온다는 내용이 완료되고 새로운 것을 설명하기 시작하는 자리

2nd 각 선택지의 앞뒤 흐름이 매끄러운지 확인한다.

- **①의 앞 문장과 뒤 문장**

> **앞 문장:** 우리가 사용하기로 선택하는 언어 자원들은 우리의 개인적인 의도로 채워질 준비가 된 텅 빈 형태로 우리에게 오지 않고, 그것들 안에 이미 뿌리 박힌 의미들과 함께 온다.
>
> **뒤 문장:** 그런데 이런 의미들이 어떤 보편적이고 논리적인 일련의 원리들에서 유래한다기보다는, 그것들의 형태에서처럼, 그것들은 결국 무수히 많은 문화적, 역사적, 그리고 제도적인 힘들에 의해 형성되는, 특정한 목적의 달성에 참가하는 특정한 집단에 의해 특정한 상황들에서 그것들의 이전의 사용에서 오랜 시간에 걸쳐 만들어진다.

➡ 앞 문장: 언어 자원은 그 의미가 이미 만들어진 채 우리에게 온다.
  뒤 문장: 의미가 어떻게 만들어지는지에 대한 구체적인 부연
  → 언어 자원은 역사적으로 정해진 의미를 지닌다는 내용이 뒤 문장에도 이어진다.
  ▶ 주어진 문장이 ①에 들어갈 수 없음

- **②의 앞 문장과 뒤 문장**

> **앞 문장:** ①의 뒤 문장과 같음
>
> **뒤 문장:** 특정한 의사소통의 순간들에 우리가 사용하기로 선택하는 언어 자원들은 관습화된 의미의 역사를 지니고 이런 순간들에 온다.

➡ 언어 자원은 관습화된 의미의 역사를 지니고 온다는 내용이 뒤 문장까지 이어짐
  ▶ 주어진 문장이 ②에 들어갈 수 없음

- **③의 앞 문장과 뒤 문장**

> **앞 문장:** ②의 뒤 문장과 같음
>
> **뒤 문장:** 우리의 집단적인 역사를 실현하는 특정한 방식에 우리를 어느 정도 묶는 것은 바로 그것들의 관습성이다.

➡ 앞 문장에서 '언어 자원들은 관습화된 의미의 역사를 지닌다'고 한 것을, 뒤 문장에서 '그것들(언어 자원들)의 관습성'이라고 표현했다.
  ▶ 앞뒤 문장이 자연스럽게 연결되고, 언어 자원은 역사적으로 형성된 의미를 지닌다는 것에 대한 부연이 뒤 문장까지 이어지므로 ③에 주어진 문장이 들어갈 수는 없음

- **④의 앞 문장과 뒤 문장**

> **앞 문장:** ③의 뒤 문장과 같음
>
> **뒤 문장:** [그래서(Thus)] 우리의 언어 자원을 우리가 개별적으로 사용할 때 우리는 두 가지 행위를 동시에 이룬다.

➡ 1 언어 자원의 의미가 역사적으로 결정된 채 우리에게 온다는 내용이 앞 문장에서 끝난다.
  2 Thus는 인과 관계의 연결어로, 결과를 설명하는 문장에 쓰인다.
  우리가 언어 자원을 사용할 때 두 가지 행위를 동시에 이루는 이유가 앞에 있어야 한다.
  그 이유: 언어 자원은 역사적으로 결정된 의미를 지닌 채 오지만, 특정 순간에 어떻게 의미하게 되는지는 협상의 여지가 있음(주어진 문장의 내용)
  ▶ 주어진 문장이 ④에 들어가야 함

- **⑤의 앞 문장과 뒤 문장**

> **앞 문장:** ④의 뒤 문장과 같음
>
> **뒤 문장:** 우리는 언어 자원의 역사적인 사용의 맥락을 만들면서 동시에 우리는 이런 맥락과 관련하여 우리 자신의 입장을 취한다.

➡ 앞 문장에 등장한 '두 가지 행위'가 무엇인지 뒤 문장에서 구체적으로 부연하는 흐름이다.
  ▶ 주어진 문장이 ⑤에 들어갈 수 없음

3rd 글이 한눈에 들어오도록 정리하여 정답을 확인한다.

우리가 사용하는 언어 자원은 텅 빈 형태로 오는 것이 아니라 이미 뿌리 박힌 의미와 함께 온다.
(①) 이런 의미는 보편적이고 논리적인 일련의 원리로 만들어지는 것이 아니라 오랜 시간에 걸쳐 그것을 사용하는 집단에 의해 만들어진다.
(②) 우리가 사용하는 언어 자원은 관습화된 의미의 역사를 지니고 오며,
(③) 언어 자원의 관습성이 우리의 집단적인 역사를 실현하는 방식에 우리를 묶는다.
(④ 하지만, 언어 자원은 의미의 역사를 지닌 채 오긴 하지만, 특정 순간에 어떻게 의미하게 될지는 협상의 여지가 있다.)
그래서 언어 자원을 개별적으로 사용할 때 두 가지 행위를 이룬다.
(⑤) 첫 번째 행위는 언어 자원의 역사적인 사용의 맥락을 만드는 것, 두 번째 행위는 이런 맥락과 관련하여 우리 자신의 입장을 취하는 것이다.

모의고사 3회

＊「it is ~ that」강조 구문

- 강조하고자 하는 어구를 it is와 that 사이에 둔다. 강조되는 말이 사람이면 that
  대신 who를, 강조되는 말이 장소면 that 대신 where를 쓸 수 있다.

- It is saying "no" that is really hard.
  saying "no"를 강조함
  ('아니요'라고 말하는 것은 정말로 힘든 것이다.)

- It was Antonio that[who] drew the pictures.
  사람 Antonio를 강조함
  (그림들을 그린 것은 바로 Antonio다.)

- It was in Spain that[where] Joel met his wife.
  장소 in Spain을 강조함
  (Joel이 그의 아내를 만난 것은 바로 스페인에서이다.)

---

③회 09 정답 ② ＊'동물'이라는 단어

**글의 흐름으로 보아, 주어진 문장이 들어가기에 가장 적절한 곳을
고르시오.**

단서 1 인간과 동물 사이에는 하나의 경계가 있는 것이 아니라 복합적이고 이질적인 경계가 있음

Jacques Derrida argues / that instead of one line / between
　　　　　　　　　　목적격절 접속사　　　　부사구
Man on the one side / and Animal on the other, / there is a

multiple and heterogeneous border;
Jacques Derrida는 주장한다 / 하나의 선 대신에 / 한쪽에 있는 '인간'과 / 다른 한쪽에
있는 '동물' 사이의 / 복합적이고 이질적인 경계가 있다고 /

beyond the edge of the "so-called human," / we find a
heterogeneous plurality / of the living. // **단서 2** 인간 이외의 살아 있는
　　　　　　　　　　　　　　　　　　　　　　　것들에게는 다양한 특성이 있음
'소위 인간'의 가장자리 너머에서 / 우리는 이질적 복수성을 발견한다 / 살아 있는 것들의 //

Language, / and the word "animal," / deceives us. //
언어는 / 그리고 '동물'이라는 단어는 / 우리를 속인다 //

The word "animal" categorizes / all non-human animals / and
　　　　　　　　　　병렬 구조
distances humans / from other animals. //
'동물'이라는 단어는 분류하고 / 인간이 아닌 모든 동물을 / 인간을 떼어 놓는다 / 다른
동물로부터 //

　　　　　　　　　동명사구 주어
(①) Seeing all other animals / as one group / in contrast to
　　　　　　　　　　　　　　　　　　　단수 동사
humans / reinforces anthropocentrism, /
모든 다른 동물을 보는 것은 / 하나의 그룹으로 / 인간과 대조되는 / 인간 중심주의를
강화하는데 /
계속적 용법의 주격 관계대명사(선행사: 앞 절)　　　　선행사
which contributes / to the legitimization of practices / in which
other animals are used / for human benefit. // 관계부사 where를 대신하는
　　　　　　　　　　　　　　　　　　　　　　　　「전치사+관계대명사」
이는 기여한다 / 관행의 정당화에 / 다른 동물이 이용되는 / 인간의 이득을 위해 //

(②) To account for this multitude, / using the word "animot" /
has been proposed. // **단서 3** 주어진 글에 등장한 이질적인 복수성을 의미함
이 다양성을 설명하기 위해 / 'animot'이라는 단어를 사용하는 것이 / 제안되어 왔다 //

(③) In speech / it refers to the plural, / the multiplicity of
animals, / which is necessary / because there is no one
　　　　　　계속적 용법의 주격 관계대명사(선행사: 앞 절)
"animal." //
언어에서 / 그것은 복수를 가리키는데 / 동물의 다양성 / 이는 필요하다 / 하나의 '동물'만
있지는 않기 때문에 //

(④) The "mot" in "animot" refers / to the act of naming / and
the risks / involved in drawing a distinction / between human
선행사(주격 관계대명사와 be동사는 생략됨)
and animal / by the human. //
'animot'의 'mot'은 나타낸다 / 명명하는 행위와 / 위험을 / 구분을 짓는 데 수반되는 / 인간과
동물 사이의 / 인간에 의한 //

　　　　　　　　　　　　　　동격절 접속사
(⑤) It reminds us of the fact / that it is a word for animals, / not
a reference / to an existing group of animals. //
그것은 우리로 하여금 사실을 상기시킨다 / 그것이 동물들을 위한 단어라는 / 가리키는 것이
아니라 / 기존의 동물 집단을 //

- multiple ⓐ 많은, 다수의　　・heterogeneous ⓐ 이질적인
- plurality ⓝ 복수성　　・deceive ⓥ 속이다
- categorize ⓥ 분류하다　　・distance ⓥ 떨어지게 하다, 떼어 놓다
- in contrast to 대조적으로　　・reinforce ⓥ 강화하다
- anthropocentrism ⓝ 인간 중심주의　　・contribute ⓥ 기여하다
- legitimate ⓥ 정당화하다　　・account for 설명하다
- multitude ⓝ 다양성　　・distinction ⓝ 구분, 구별
- reference ⓝ 언급, 참조

언어, 그중에서도 '동물'이라는 단어는 우리를 속인다. '동물'이라는 단어는
인간이 아닌 모든 동물을 분류하고 인간을 다른 동물로부터 떼어 놓는다. (①)
모든 다른 동물을 인간과 대조되는 하나의 그룹으로 보는 것은 인간 중심주의를
강화하는데, 이는 다른 동물이 인간의 이득을 위해 이용되는 관행의 정당화에
기여한다. (② Jacques Derrida는 한쪽에 있는 '인간'과 다른 한쪽에 있는 '동물'
사이의 하나의 선 대신에 복합적이고 이질적인 경계가 있다고 주장하는데,
'소위 인간'의 가장자리 너머에서 우리는 살아 있는 것들의 이질적인 복수성을
발견한다.) 이 다양성을 설명하기 위해 'animot'이라는 단어를 사용하는 것이
제안되어 왔다. (③) 언어에서 그것은 복수, 즉 동물의 다양성을 가리키는데,
이는 하나의 '동물'만 있지는 않기 때문에 필요하다. (④) 'animot'의 'mot'은
명명하는 행위와 인간에 의한 인간과 동물 사이의 구분을 짓는 데 수반되는
위험을 나타낸다. (⑤) 그것은 우리로 하여금 그것이 기존의 동물 집단을
가리키는 것이 아니라 동물들을 위한 단어라는 사실을 상기시킨다.

| 문제 풀이 순서 |　[정답률 45%]

1st 주어진 문장을 해석하고, 연결어, 지시어 등을 확인한다.

Jacques Derrida argues that instead of one line between
Man on the one side and Animal on the other, there is a
multiple and heterogeneous border; beyond the edge of
the "so-called human," we find a heterogeneous plurality
of the living.
Jacques Derrida는 한쪽에 있는 '인간'과 다른 한쪽에 있는 '동물' 사이의 하나의
선 대신에 복합적이고 이질적인 경계가 있다고 주장하는데, '소위 인간'의 가장자리
너머에서 우리는 살아 있는 것들의 이질적인 복수성을 발견한다.

➡ Jacques Derrida의 주장: 인간과 동물 사이에는 하나의 경계가 있는 것이 아니라
복합적이고 이질적인 경계가 있다. 인간 이외의 살아 있는 것들에게서 이질적인
복수성(다양성)이 발견된다.
　▶ 주어진 문장을 통해 그 앞뒤에 올 내용을 예상할 수 있음
　주어진 문장 앞: 인간과 동물을 하나의 기준으로 구분하는 것의 부적절함
　주어진 문장 뒤: 동물의 다양성을 반영하는 기준에 대한 부연

2nd 각 선택지의 앞뒤 흐름이 매끄러운지 확인한다.

- ①의 앞 문장과 뒤 문장

앞 문장: '동물'이라는 단어는 인간이 아닌 모든 동물로부터 인간을 떼어
놓는다.
뒤 문장: 모든 다른 동물을 인간과 대조되는 하나의 그룹으로 보는 것은
인간 중심주의를 강화하는데, 이는 인간의 이득을 위해 다른 동물들이
이용되는 관행의 정당화에 기여한다.

➡ 하나의 기준으로 모든 동물을 인간과 구분하는 것의 부당함이 뒤 문장까지
이어진다.
　▶ 주어진 문장이 ①에 들어갈 수 없음

- ②의 앞 문장과 뒤 문장

앞 문장: ①의 뒤 문장과 같음
뒤 문장: 이 다양성(this multitude)을 설명하기 위해, 'animot'이라는
단어를 사용하는 것이 제안되어 왔다.

→ ②의 앞 문장(①의 뒤 문장)은 '단 하나의 기준'의 부당함을 나타내는 내용으로, 뒤 문장의 this multitude가 가리키는 것이 앞 문장에 등장하지 않는다.
그 이유: 주어진 문장에서 설명한 '복합적이고 이질적인 경계', '이질적인 복수성'이 this multitude가 의미하는 바이다. (주어진 문장의 내용)
▶ 주어진 문장이 ②에 들어가야 함

- ③의 앞 문장과 뒤 문장

> **앞 문장:** ②의 뒤 문장과 같음
> **뒤 문장:** 언어에서 그것(it)은 복수, 즉 동물의 다양성을 가리킨다.

→ 뒤 문장의 주어인 it이 가리키는 것이 앞 문장에 등장한 animot이다.
▶ 주어진 문장이 ③에 들어갈 수 없음

- ④의 앞 문장과 뒤 문장

> **앞 문장:** ③의 뒤 문장과 같음
> **뒤 문장:** 'animot'의 'mot'은 명명하는 행위와 인간에 의한 인간과 동물 사이의 구분을 짓는 데 수반되는 위험을 나타낸다.

→ ②의 뒤 문장에서 animot이라는 단어를 소개한 후, 그것에 대한 설명이 계속 이어진다.
▶ 주어진 문장은 단어 animot에 대한 내용이 아니므로 ④에 들어갈 수 없음

- ⑤의 앞 문장과 뒤 문장

> **앞 문장:** ④의 뒤 문장과 같음
> **뒤 문장:** 그것(It)은 우리로 하여금 그것이 기존의 동물 집단을 가리키는 것이 아니라 동물들을 위한 단어라는 사실을 상기시킨다.

→ 주어인 It이 가리키는 것: 인간에 의한 인간과 동물 사이의 구분을 짓는 데 수반되는 위험을 나타내는 mot
▶ 주어진 문장이 ⑤에 들어갈 수 없음

3rd 글이 한눈에 들어오도록 정리하여 정답을 확인한다.

'동물'이라는 단어는 인간이 아닌 모든 동물을 분류하고 인간을 다른 동물로부터 떼어 놓는다.
(①) 다른 동물을 인간과 대조되는 하나의 그룹으로 보는 것은 인간 중심주의를 강화하는데, 이는 다른 동물이 인간의 이득을 위해 이용되는 관행의 정당화에 기여한다.
(②) Jacques Derrida는 한쪽에 있는 '인간'과 다른 한쪽에 있는 '동물' 사이의 하나의 선 대신에 복합적이고 이질적인 경계가 있다고 주장하는데, '소위 인간'의 가장자리 너머에서 우리는 살아 있는 것들의 이질적인 복수성을 발견한다.)
이 다양성을 설명하기 위해 'animot'이라는 단어를 사용하는 것이 제안되어 왔다.
(③) 언어에서 그것은 복수, 즉 동물의 다양성을 가리킨다.
(④) 'animot'의 'mot'은 명명하는 행위와 인간에 의한 인간과 동물 사이의 구분을 짓는 데 수반되는 위험을 나타낸다.
(⑤) 우리에게 그것이 기존의 동물 집단을 가리키는 것이 아니라 동물들을 위한 단어라는 사실을 상기시킨다.

3회 10 정답 ① * 효과적인 브레인스토밍 기법: 독립적으로 작업하기

부사적 용법(목적)
To be really smart, / an online group needs to obey one final rule / — and a rather counterintuitive one. // (= rule)
진정으로 똑똑해지기 위해서 / 온라인 그룹은 하나의 마지막 규칙을 따라야 한다 / 그리고 다소 반직관적인 규칙을 //

The members can't have too much contact / with one another. //
구성원들은 너무 많이 접촉할 수 없다 / 서로 서로

단서 1 최상의 결과를 위해 구성원들은 독립적으로 생각하고 작업할 수 있어야 함
To work best, / the members of a collective group / ought to be able / to think and work independently. //
부사적 용법(목적)
최상의 결과를 내기 위해서 / 집단의 구성원들은 / 할 수 있어야 한다 / 독립적으로 생각하고 작업하는 것을 //

관계부사
This rule came to light / in 1958, / when social scientists tested different techniques of brainstorming. //
이 규칙은 드러났다 / 1958년에 / 사회 과학자들이 다양한 브레인스토밍 기법을 시험해 보면서 //

They posed a thought-provoking question: / If humans had an extra thumb on each hand, / what benefits and problems would emerge? //
그들은 생각을 자극하는 질문을 던졌다 / 만약 인간이 각 손에 추가 엄지손가락을 가진다면 / 어떤 이점과 문제가 생길까 //

have의 목적격 보어(동사원형)
Then they had / two different types of groups / brainstorm answers. //
그런 다음 그들은 시켰다 / 두 가지 유형의 그룹에게 / 답을 브레인스토밍하도록 //

In one group, the members worked face-to-face; / in the other group, the members each worked independently, / then pooled their answers at the end. //
한 그룹은, 구성원들이 직접 만나 작업했다 / 다른 그룹은, 각자가 독립적으로 작업했다 / 그리고 나서 마지막에 답을 모았다 //

단서 2 직접 만나는 사람들이 더 생산적일 것으로 예상했지만 사실은 그렇지 않았다고 함
You might expect / the people working face-to-face to be more productive, / but that wasn't the case. //
현재분사(people 수식)
너는 예상했을 것이다 / 직접 만나는 사람들이 더 생산적일 것이라고 / 사실은 그렇지 않았다 //

The team with independently working members / produced almost twice as many ideas. // **단서 3** 독립적으로 작업한 팀이 거의 두 배에 가까운 아이디어를 만들어 냄
독립적으로 작업한 팀이 / 거의 두 배에 가까운 아이디어를 만들어 냈다 //

병렬 구조
Traditional brainstorming simply doesn't work / as well as thinking alone, / then pooling results. //
전통적인 브레인스토밍은 효과적이지 않다 / 혼자 생각하는 것만큼 / 그리고 나서 결과를 모으는 것만큼 //

> → In brainstorming, / group members who have direct contact / produce (A) **fewer** ideas / than those who work physically separately from one another, / which is against our (B) **intuition**.
> 주격 관계대명사 / 주격 관계대명사 / 계속적 용법의 관계대명사
> 브레인스토밍에서 / 직접 접촉을 가진 그룹 구성원들은 / 더 적은 아이디어를 생산하며 / 서로 물리적으로 분리되어 작업하는 사람들보다 / 이는 우리의 직관과 반대이다 //

- obey ⓥ 따르다 • counterintuitive ⓐ 직관에 반하는
- contact ⓥ 접촉하다 • thought-provoking ⓐ 생각을 자극하는
- benefit ⓝ 혜택, 이점 • emerge ⓥ 출현하다
- face-to-face ⓐ 대면하는 • pool ⓥ 모으다
- expect ⓥ 예상하다 • productive ⓐ 생산적인
- separately 예 분리되어 • intuition ⓝ 직관

진정으로 똑똑해지기 위해서 온라인 그룹은 하나의 마지막 규칙, 그리고 다소 반직관적인 규칙을 따라야 한다. 구성원들 간의 접촉이 너무 많아서는 안 된다. 최상의 결과를 내기 위해서 집단의 구성원들은 독립적으로 생각하고 작업할 수 있어야 한다. 이 규칙은 1958년에 사회 과학자들이 다양한 브레인스토밍 기법을 테스트하면서 드러났다. 그들은 생각을 자극하는 질문을 던졌다: 만약 인간이 각 손에 추가 엄지손가락을 가진다면 어떤 이점과 문제가 생길까? 그런 다음 두 가지 유형의 그룹이 답을 브레인스토밍하도록 했다. 한 그룹은

구성원들이 직접 만나 작업했으며, 다른 그룹은 각자가 독립적으로 작업한 후 마지막에 답을 모았다. 직접 만나는 사람들이 더 생산적일 것이라고 예상할 수 있지만, 사실은 그렇지 않았다. 독립적으로 작업한 팀이 거의 두 배에 가까운 아이디어를 만들어냈다. 전통적인 브레인스토밍은 혼자 생각한 후 결과를 모으는 것만큼 효과적이지 않다.

→ 브레인스토밍에서 직접 접촉을 가진 그룹 구성원들은 서로 물리적으로 분리되어 작업하는 사람들보다 (A) 더 적은 아이디어를 생산하며, 이는 우리의 (B) 직관과 반대이다.

다음 글의 내용을 한 문장으로 요약하고자 한다. 빈칸 (A), (B)에 들어갈 말로 가장 적절한 것은?

	(A)	(B)	
①	fewer 더 적은	intuition 직관	직접 접촉을 가진 집단이 분리되어 작업한 사람들보다 '더 적은' 아이디어를 생산했으며 이것이 우리의 예상(직관)과는 반대라고 했음
②	fewer 더 적은	benefit 이익	직접 접촉을 가진 집단이 더 적은 아이디어를 생산한 것은 맞지만 이것이 우리의 이익과 반대라는 내용은 아님
③	more 더 많은	conclusion 결론	직접 접촉을 가진 집단이 분리되어 작업한 사람들보다 더 많은 아이디어를 생산한 것이 아니라 오히려 반대임
④	more 더 많은	intuition 직관	직접 접촉을 가진 집단이 독립적으로 작업한 사람들보다 더 많은 아이디어를 생산한 것이 아니며 이것이 우리의 직관과 반대라고 할 수 없음
⑤	smarter 더 현명한	benefit 이익	직접 접촉을 가진 집단이 독립적으로 작업한 사람들보다 더 현명하다거나 이것이 우리의 이익과 반대라는 내용의 글이 아님

왜 정답? [정답률 62%]

똑똑한 온라인 집단의 규칙	구성원들이 접촉 없이 독립적으로 생각하고 작업해야 함 **단서1**
규칙의 등장과 입증	1958년 시행된 브레인스토밍 기법 테스트 → 직접 만나 작업 vs. 독립적으로 작업 → 예상과는 다르게 독립적인 작업이 더 많은 아이디어를 생산함 **단서2**
결론	전통적인 브레인스토밍(대면)은 혼자 생각한 후 결과를 모으는 것만큼 생산적이지 않음

(A):
- 브레인스토밍을 할 때 독립적으로 생각하고 결과물을 모은 집단이 직접 만난 집단보다 두 배 가까이 많은 아이디어를 생산했다고 했다.
➡ 즉, 직접 만난 집단이 물리적으로 분리되어 작업하는 사람들보다 '더 적은(fewer)' 아이디어를 생산했다는 것이다.

(B):
- 독립적으로 생각한 집단이 더 많은 아이디어를 만들어 낸 것이 우리의 예상과 달랐다고 했다.
➡ 다시 말해, 우리의 '직관(intuition)'과 달랐다는 것이다.
▶ 요약문의 빈칸에는 각각 '더 적은'과 '직관'이 들어가야 하므로 정답은 ①임

왜 오답?

② 직접 접촉을 가진 집단이 분리되어 작업한 사람들보다 더 적은 아이디어를 생산한 것은 맞지만 이것이 우리의 이익과 반대라는 내용은 아니다.

③ 직접 접촉을 가진 집단이 분리되어 작업한 사람들보다 더 많은 아이디어를 생산한 것도 아니고, 이것이 우리의 결론과 반대라고 할 수도 없다.

④ 직접 접촉을 가진 집단이 독립적으로 작업한 사람들보다 더 많은 아이디어를 생산한 것이 아니며 이것이 우리의 직관과 반대라고 할 수 없다.

⑤ 직접 접촉을 가진 집단이 독립적으로 작업한 사람들보다 더 현명하다거나 이것이 우리의 이익과 반대라는 내용의 글이 아니다.

＊ 글의 흐름

주제문	진정으로 똑똑한 온라인 그룹은 구성원들이 접촉하지 않고 독립적으로 작업해야 한다는 규칙이 있음
구체화	1958년 브레인스토밍 기법 테스트 → 직접 만나 작업 vs. 혼자 작업 → 직접 만났을 때 더 생산적일 것이라는 예상과는 다르게 혼자 작업했을 때 더 많은 아이디어를 생산함
주제 재언급	전통적 브레인스토밍 기법이 혼자 생각한 후 결과를 모으는 것만큼 효과적이지 않음

3회 11~12 ＊사회공동체에서 도덕의 역할

Morality is changeable and culture-dependent / and expresses socially desirable behavior. //
도덕성은 바뀔 수 있고 문화 의존적이다 / 그리고 사회적으로 바람직한 행동을 나타낸다 //

But even if morality is changeable, / it is by no means arbitrary, / (= never)
그러나 도덕성이 바뀔 수 있다 하더라도 / 그것은 결코 임의적이지는 않다 /
부사절 접속사 (이유) · 강조 용법의 재귀대명사

especially since the change process itself takes a relatively (a) long time / (measured in years rather than weeks). //
과거분사구 (time 수식)
특히 변화 과정 자체가 비교적 긴 시간이 소요되기 때문에 / (주 단위보다는 연 단위로 측정되는) //

This is also because a social value framework / — and thus morality — / provides an important orientation function: /
이것은 또한 사회적 가치의 틀이 / 즉 도덕성이 / 중요한 길잡이의 기능을 제공하기 때문이다 /

Since time immemorial, / people have been thinking about moral issues / and dealing with them. //
현재완료 진행시제
아득한 예로부터 / 사람들은 도덕적 이슈에 관해 생각해 왔다 / 그리고 그것들을 다뤄 왔다 //
가목적어 · 진목적어절 접속사

This makes it clear / that (b) consistent values, norms, and moral concepts always play a major role / when people organize themselves in social communities. // **11번** 단서 1: 사람들이 공동체에서 도덕은 중요한 역할을 한다는 것을 분명하게 함
재귀 용법의 재귀대명사
이것은 분명하게 만든다 / 일관된 가치, 규범, 도덕적 개념은 항상 중요한 역할을 한다는 것을 / 사람들이 스스로를 사회공동체에 조직할 때 //
result in + 결과 / result from + 원인

Ultimately, this also results in answers to questions / of justice, solidarity, and care / as well as the distribution of goods and resources. //
B as well as A: A뿐만 아니라 B도
결국, 이것은 또한 질문의 답을 낳는다 / 정의, 연대, 돌봄에 대한 / 재화와 자원의 분배뿐만 아니라 //

Morality acts here / as the (c) common lowest denominator / for a given society. // **11번** 단서 2, **12번** 단서 1: 인간은 공동체에 수용되기 위해 공동체의 도덕을 따를 것으로 예측할 수 있음
도덕성은 여기에 작용한다 / 최소한의 공통 분모로 / 주어진 사회에서 //
동격절 접속사 · 현재분사구 (the values 수식)

The (d) advantage is based on the fact / that the values underlying morality / convey a socially accepted basic understanding / and provide orientation / in concrete decision-making situations. //
장점은 사실에 기반한다 / 도덕성의 기저를 이루는 가치들이 / 사회적으로 수용되는 기본 이해를 전달하고 / 방향성을 제공한다는 / 구체적인 의사결정 상황에서 //
makes의 목적어와 목적격 보어 (형용사)

This makes morality functional and efficient / for social groups: /
이것은 도덕성을 실용적이고 효율적으로 만든다 / 사회 집단에 /
부사적 용법 (목적)

In order to be accepted in a community, / the individual will strive / not to act against this community. //
공동체에 수용되기 위해서 / 개인은 노력할 것이다 / 이 공동체에 반하는 행동을 하지 않도록 //

Conversely, this means / that the behavior of the individual and the social group / is ultimately (e) unpredictable(→ predictable). //
반대로 이것은 의미한다 / 개인과 사회 집단의 행동이 / 궁극적으로 예측 불가능하다 (→ 예측 가능하다는) 것을 //

As a result, / uncertainty about behavior is reduced / and trust is built up. // **11번** 단서 3, **12번** 단서 2: 행동에 관한 불확실성은 감소됨
결과적으로 / 행동에 관한 불확실성은 감소된다 / 그리고 신뢰는 쌓인다 //

- morality ⓝ 도덕성
- changeable ⓐ 바뀔 수 있는
- dependent ⓐ 의존적인
- desirable ⓐ 바람직한
- relatively ⓐⓓ 비교적으로
- framework ⓝ 틀, 체계
- orientation ⓝ 길잡이, 방향성
- immemorial ⓐ 아주 오래전의
- consistent ⓐ 일관된, 불변한
- organize ⓥ 조직하다, 편성하다
- solidarity ⓝ 결속, 연대
- distribution ⓝ 분배
- advantage ⓝ 장점
- underlie ⓥ 기저를 이루다
- uncertainty ⓝ 불확실성

도덕성은 바뀔 수 있고 문화 의존적이며, 사회적으로 바람직한 행동을 나타낸다. 그러나 도덕성이 바뀔 수 있다 하더라도, 그것은 특히 변화 과정 자체가 (주 단위보다는 연 단위로 측정되는) 비교적 (a) 긴 시간이 소요되기 때문에 결코 임의적이지는 않다. 이것은 또한 사회적 가치의 틀, 즉 도덕성이 중요한 길잡이의 기능을 제공하기 때문이다. 아득한 예로부터, 사람들은 도덕적 문제에 관해 생각해 왔고 다뤄 왔다. 이것은 사람들이 스스로를 사회공동체에 조직할 때 (b) 일관된 가치, 규범, 도덕적 개념은 항상 중요한 역할을 한다는 것을 분명하게 한다. 결국, 이것은 또한 재화와 자원의 분배뿐만 아니라 정의, 연대, 돌봄에 관한 질문의 답을 낳는다.

도덕성은 여기에 주어진 사회에서 최소한의 (c) 공통 분모로 작용한다. (d) 장점은 도덕성의 기저를 이루는 가치들이 사회적으로 수용되는 기본 이해를 전달하고 구체적인 의사결정 상황에서 방향성을 제공한다는 사실에 기반한다. 이것은 도덕성을 사회 집단에 실용적이고 효율적으로 만든다. 즉, 공동체에 수용되기 위해서 이 공동체에 반하는 행동을 하지 않도록 개인은 노력할 것이다. 반대로, 이것은 개인과 사회 집단의 행동이 궁극적으로 (e) 예측 불가능하다는(→ 예측 가능하다는) 것을 의미한다. 결과적으로, 행동에 관한 불확실성은 감소되고 신뢰는 쌓인다.

③회 11 정답 ③

윗글의 주제로 가장 적절한 것은? [4점]

① disregard of morality found in extreme conditions
극단적인 조건에서 발견되는 도덕성 무시   단순히 도덕성이 언급된 것으로 만든 오답
② justice and solidarity as basic elements of morality
도덕의 기본 요소로서의 정의와 연대   도덕의 기본 요소가 핵심 내용은 아님
③ fundamental role of morality in human communities
인간 커뮤니티에서 도덕의 근본적인 역할   사회공동체로 도덕이 중요한 역할을 한다는 내용
④ development of morality through cultural exchanges
문화 교류를 통한 도덕성 개발   문화 교류를 통한 도덕성 개발과 관련되는 내용은 없음
⑤ punishment of moral code violations across societies
사회 전반의 도덕률 위반 처벌   도덕률 위반 처벌에 대한 내용은 없음

왜 정답? [정답률 51%]

중반부	사람들이 공동체에서 도덕은 중요한 역할을 한다는 것을 분명하게 함
후반부	• 공동체에 수용되기 위해 공동체에 반하는 행동을 하지 않도록 노력함 • 행동에 관한 불확실성은 감소됨

➡ 이 글은 사회공동체에서 도덕의 역할에 대한 내용이므로 주제로 ③ '인간 커뮤니티에서 도덕의 근본적인 역할'이 가장 적절하다.

왜 오답?

① 단순히 도덕성이 언급된 것으로 만든 오답일 뿐이다. 함정
② 도덕의 기본 요소가 핵심 내용은 아니다.
④ 문화 교류를 통한 도덕성 개발과 관련되는 내용은 없다.
⑤ 도덕률 위반 처벌에 대한 언급은 나오지 않았다.

③회 12 정답 ⑤

밑줄 친 (a)~(e) 중에서 문맥상 낱말의 쓰임이 적절하지 않은 것은? [3점]

① (a) 도덕성은 그 변화 과정 자체도 비교적 길 긴
② (b) 일관된 도덕 개념이 사회공동체의 일관된 조직에 중요함
③ (c) 사회 집단을 이루는 최소한의 공통 분모가 됨 공통의
④ (d) 공동체의 방향성을 안내해준다는 장점 장점을 지님
⑤ (e) 도덕 규범을 따를 것으로 예측할 수 있음 예측 불가능한

왜 정답? [정답률 60%]

⑤ (e) unpredictable 예측 불가능한

반대로, 이것은 개인과 사회 집단의 행동이 궁극적으로

(e) 예측 불가능하다는 것을 의미한다. 결과적으로, 행동에 관한
      예측 가능하다는
불확실성은 감소되고 신뢰는 쌓인다.

➡ 도덕성은 공동체를 유지하기 위한 기준을 마련해주고, 구성원들은 공동체에 수용되기 위해 공동체의 도덕 규범을 따를 것으로 예측할 수 있다는 내용이다. 이는 개인과 사회 집단의 행동은 도덕적일 것으로 '예측 불가능한' 것이 아니라 '예측 가능하다'는 것을 뜻한다.

▶ 행동에 관한 불확실성 또한 감소되므로 unpredictable을 predictable과 같은 어휘로 바꿔야 함

왜 오답?

① (a) long 긴

그러나 도덕성이 바뀔 수 있다 하더라도, 그것은 특히 변화 과정 자체가 (주 단위보다는 연 단위로 측정되는) 비교적 (a) 긴 시간이 소요되기 때문에 결코 임의적이지는 않다.

➡ 주 단위가 아닌 연 단위로 측정된다는 것은 '긴' 시간에 일어나는 것임을 알 수 있다.

▶ long은 문맥에 맞음

② (b) consistent 일관된

이것은 사람들이 스스로를 사회공동체에 조직할 때 (b) 일관된 가치, 규범, 도덕적 개념은 항상 중요한 역할을 한다는 것을 분명하게 한다.

➡ 도덕성은 임의적이지 않고 최소한의 기준을 제시하므로, '일관된' 도덕 개념이 사회공동체 조직에 중요하다는 것을 알 수 있다.

▶ '일관된' 도덕성이 중요하므로 consistent는 문맥에 맞음

③ (c) common 공통의

결국, 이것은 또한 재화와 자원의 분배뿐만 아니라 정의, 연대, 돌봄에 관한 질문의 답을 낳는다. 도덕성은 여기에 주어진 사회에서 최소한의 (c) 공통 분모로 작용한다.

➡ 도덕성은 사회공동체를 형성하는 데 도움을 주고, 사회의 모든 구성원이 '공통으로' 지키는 최소한의 규칙으로 작용한다는 내용이다.

▶ 도덕성은 최소한의 '공통' 분모이므로 common은 문맥에 맞음

④ (d) advantage 장점

(d) 장점은 도덕성의 기저를 이루는 가치들이 사회적으로 수용되는 기본 이해를 전달하고 구체적인 의사결정 상황에서 방향성을 제공한다는 사실에 기반한다.

➡ 도덕성의 기반이 되는 가치들이 사회적으로 수용되는 기준을 마련하고 의사결정 상황에서 방향성을 제공한다는 '장점'을 지닌다는 내용이다.

▶ 도덕성의 '장점'을 설명하고 있으므로 advantage는 문맥에 맞음

모의고사
③회

memo

memo

memo

memo

🍀 차 례

고난도 유형 독해 모의고사

단어장 전체 pdf

A 목적 찾기

A01
□ comment ⓝ 댓글
□ inappropriate ⓐ 부적절한
□ relevant ⓐ 관련이 있는
□ keep ~ in mind ~을 염두에
　두다

A02
□ occasion ⓝ 행사, 때
□ admission ⓝ 입장
□ food stand 음식 노점
□ valued ⓐ 귀중한, 소중한
□ celebrate ⓥ 축하하다
□ feature ⓝ 특색
□ scenery ⓝ 경치
□ confident ⓐ 자신감 있는, 확
　신하는

A03
□ sign up for ~에 등록하다
□ scheduled ⓐ 예정된
□ downpour ⓝ 폭우
□ slippery ⓐ 미끄러운

A04
□ loyalty ⓝ 충심, 충성
□ thrilled ⓐ 매우 기쁜
□ exclusive ⓐ 독점적인
□ reservation ⓝ 예약
□ depart ⓥ 출발하다
□ specialty ⓝ 특별 (사항)
□ onboard ⓐ 선내의, 기내의
□ advantage ⓝ 편의, 제의
□ aboard ⓐⓓ 승선하여, 탑승하여
□ unforgettable ⓐ 잊을 수 없
　는
□ journey ⓝ 여행

A05
□ appreciate ⓥ 감사하다
□ invitation ⓝ 초대
□ thoughtfulness ⓝ 사려 깊음
□ overseas ⓐ 해외의
□ work out (일이) 잘 풀리다
□ attend ⓥ 참석하다
□ opportunity ⓝ 기회

A06
□ flextime ⓝ 유연 근무제
□ eligible ⓐ ~할[가질] 수 있는
□ staffer ⓝ 직원
□ submit ⓥ 제출하다
□ supervisor ⓝ 감독관
□ approve ⓥ 승인하다, 찬성하다
□ adversely ⓐⓓ 불리하게, 반대로

A07
□ concerning ⓟⓡⓔⓟ ~에 관한
　[관련된]
□ shooting ⓝ (영화) 촬영
□ disruption ⓝ 혼란
□ grant ⓥ 승인하다, 허락하다
□ permission ⓝ 허락, 승인

A08
□ privilege ⓝ 영광, 특권
□ insight ⓝ 통찰력
□ invaluable ⓐ 귀중한

A09
□ current ⓐ 현재의
□ sign up for ~을 신청하다
□ discount ⓝ 할인
□ state ⓥ 명시하다, 진술하다
□ newsletter ⓝ 소식지
□ celebrate ⓥ 기념하다, 축하
　하다
□ anniversary ⓝ 기념일
□ offer ⓥ 제공하다

□ further ⓐ 추가의
□ benefit ⓝ 혜택
□ include ⓥ 포함하다
□ admission ⓝ 입장, 입장료
□ up to ~까지
□ merchandise ⓝ 상품
□ exhibition ⓝ 전시회
□ opening ⓝ 개막식
□ contact ⓥ 연락하다

A10
□ popularity ⓝ 인기
□ additional ⓐ 추가의
□ rental ⓝ 대여, 임대
□ in advance 미리, 사전에

A11
□ director ⓝ 책임자
□ charity ⓝ 자선
□ raise ⓥ (자금을) 모으다
□ reputation ⓝ 명성
□ positive ⓐ 긍정적인
□ reply ⓝ 답변

A12
□ currently ⓐⓓ 현재, 지금
□ exhibition ⓝ 전시(회)
□ artwork ⓝ 예술 작품
□ submit ⓥ 출품하다, 제출하다
□ local ⓐ 지역의
□ theme ⓝ 주제, 테마
□ explore ⓥ 탐험하다
□ throughout ⓟⓡⓔⓟ ~ 동안
　쭉, 내내
□ rent ⓥ 빌리다, 임차하다
□ response ⓝ 답변, 대답

A13
□ impress ⓥ 감명[감동]을 주다,
　(마음 · 기억 등에) 강하게 남다
□ deliver ⓥ (연설 · 강연 등을)
　하다

□lecture ⓝ 강의, 강연

□manage ⓥ 운영하다, (힘든 일을) 해내다

□insight ⓝ 통찰력, 식견, 이해

A14
□mayor ⓝ 시장, 구청장

□championship ⓝ 선수권 대회

□on behalf of ~을 대표[대신]하여

□national ⓐ 전국적인, 국가의

□move ⓥ 감동시키다

□impress ⓥ 감명을 주다

□entire ⓐ 전체의

A15
□thanks to ~ 덕분에

□further ⓐ 더 멀리에[로]

□lifeguard ⓝ 구조원

□sign up for ~에 등록하다[신청하다]

□registration ⓝ 등록

□additional ⓐ 추가적인

□appreciate ⓥ 감사하다

□consideration ⓝ 고려

A16
□launch ⓥ 시작하다, 개시하다

□a variety of 다양한

□production ⓝ 제작

□consist of ~로 구성되다

□advanced ⓐ 고급의

□talented ⓐ 재능이 있는

A17
□greeting ⓝ 인사, 인사말

□drive ⓝ (조직적인) 운동

□participate ⓥ 참가[참여]하다

□donation ⓝ 기부, 기증

□usual ⓐ 평상시의, 보통의

□perishable ⓐ 잘 상하는 [썩는]

□canned ⓐ 통조림으로 된

□distribute ⓥ 분배[배부]하다, 유통시키다

□truly ⓐ 정말로, 진심으로

□appreciate ⓥ 고마워하다

□blessing ⓝ 축복

A18
□identify ⓥ (신원 등을) 식별하다[확인하다]

□sight ⓝ 보기, 봄, 시력

□community ⓝ 공동체, 지역 사회

□passionate ⓐ 열정적인

□under (prep) ~ 중인

□construction ⓝ 건설, 공사

A19
□road construction 도로 공사

□take place 발생하다

□raise concerns 염려를 불러 일으키다

□volunteer ⓝ 자원 봉사

□direct traffic 교통정리를 하다

□take part 참여하다

□participation ⓝ 참여

□in advance 미리

□contribution ⓝ 기여

A20
□notice ⓝ 통지

□address ⓥ 주소를 적다

□unclaimed ⓐ 찾아가지 않은

□for an extended period 오랫동안

□responsibility ⓝ 책임

□ensure ⓥ 보장하다

□resident ⓝ 입주민

□claim ⓥ 찾아가다

□genuinely ⓐ 진심으로

B 심경의 이해

B01
□sigh ⓥ 한숨을 쉬다

□passenger ⓝ 승객

□glow ⓝ (은은한) 불빛

B02
□desperately ⓐ 필사적으로

□due ⓐ 마감일이 된

□draw ⓥ 이끌다, 당기다

□immediately ⓐ 즉시

□fantastic ⓐ 환상적인

B03
□absolutely ⓐ 전적으로, 틀림없이

□five-star 최고급의

□downtown ⓐ 시내에, 시내로

□reservation ⓝ 예약

□indifferent ⓐ 무관심한

□jealous ⓐ 질투하는

□embarrassed ⓐ 당황스러운

B04
□chaotic ⓐ 혼란 상태의

□intense ⓐ 격심한

□security ⓝ 보안 (검색)

□glance ⓥ 힐끗힐끗 보다

□boarding gate 탑승구

□announcement ⓝ (안내) 방송

□unexpected ⓐ 예기치 못한

□ browse ⓥ 둘러보다
□ joyful ⓐ 즐거운
□ indifferent ⓐ 무관심한
□ satisfied ⓐ 만족스러워 하는

B05
□ threatening ⓐ 위협적인
□ freeze ⓥ 얼다
□ retreat ⓥ 물러가다
□ completely ⓐ𝖽 완전히
□ immense ⓐ 거대한, 엄청난
□ relief ⓝ 안도

B06
□ craft ⓥ 공들여 만들다
□ polish ⓥ 다듬다
□ impressive ⓐ 인상적인
□ rift ⓝ 균열
□ in vain 헛된

B07
□ stare ⓥ 응시하다
□ flip ⓥ 휙 젖히다
□ palm ⓝ 손바닥
□ sweaty ⓐ 땀투성이의
□ melt away 차츰 사라지다
□ sympathetic ⓐ 동정 어린

B08
□ wreckage ⓝ 잔해, 난파
□ life preserver (물에 빠진 사람들이 물에 떠 있게 하는) 구명구
□ spy ⓥ 보다
□ drain away 빠져나가다, 배출하다
□ hang on 꽉 붙잡다
□ glance ⓥ 흘깃 보다
□ relief ⓝ 안도, 안심

B09
□ log in to ~에 접속하다
□ counseling ⓝ 상담, 조언

□ session ⓝ (특정한 활동을 위한) 시간[기간]
□ counselor ⓝ 상담사
□ through prep ~을 통해
□ in person 직접
□ concern ⓝ 우려
□ go away 없어지다
□ actually ⓐ𝖽 실제로
□ convenient ⓐ 편리한
□ expect ⓥ 예상하다
□ as if 마치 ~인 것처럼
□ definitely ⓐ𝖽 분명히

B10
□ mechanic ⓝ 정비공
□ back and forth 왔다갔다
□ deeply ⓐ𝖽 매우, 깊이
□ replace ⓥ 교체하다
□ wipe ⓥ 닦다
□ overall ⓐ 종합적인, 전체의
□ at ease 걱정 없이, 편안한
□ afford ⓥ 감당하다

B11
□ injure ⓥ 부상을 입다
□ freeze ⓥ 얼어붙다
□ serious ⓐ 심각한
□ wrist ⓝ 손목
□ surgery ⓝ 수술
□ completely ⓐ𝖽 완전히
□ cheer ⓝ 환호(성)
□ attempt ⓥ 시도하다

B12
□ explore ⓥ 탐험[탐사]하다, 연구하다
□ numerous ⓐ 매우 많은, 다수로 이루어진
□ fossil ⓝ 화석
□ overflow ⓥ (마음이 ~으로) 넘치다, 범람하다

□ anticipation ⓝ 예상, 예측, 기대
□ common ⓐ 흔한, 공동의, 보통의
□ species ⓝ 종(種)
□ life-long ⓐ 평생의, 긴 세월의
□ rare ⓐ 보기 드문, 희귀한
□ eagerly ⓐ𝖽 열심히, 간절히
□ wander ⓥ 돌아다니다, 헤매다
□ throughout prep 도처에, ~ 동안 내내
□ deserted ⓐ 버림받은, 황폐한
□ set ⓥ (해·달이) 지다
□ reach ⓝ (닿을 수 있는) 거리[범위]
□ darken ⓥ 어두워지다, 어둡게[우울하게] 만들다
□ sigh ⓥ 한숨을 쉬다, 탄식하듯 말하다

B13
□ competition ⓝ 경쟁, 대회, 시합
□ firm ⓐ 확고한
□ dominate ⓥ 장악하다
□ national ⓐ 국가의, 전국적인
□ compete ⓥ 경쟁하다, (시합 등에) 참가하다
□ rank ⓥ (등급·등위·순위를) 매기다[평가하다]
□ fall short of ~이 부족하다, ~에 못 미치다
□ bronze ⓝ 청동
□ heartbroken ⓐ 상심한

B14
□ special needs kid 특수 아동
□ therapist ⓝ 치료사

□out of the blue 느닷없이, 갑자기

□concerned ⓐ 걱정하는

□grin ⓥ 활짝 웃다

□swell ⓥ (감정이) 부풀다, 벅차다

□grown-up ⓝ 어른

B15

□upcoming ⓐ 다가오는, 곧 있을

□surf ⓥ 인터넷을 검색하다

□come across ~을 우연히 발견하다

□harsh ⓐ 혹독한, 가혹한

□worthwhile ⓐ ~할 가치가 있는

□reluctantly ⓐⓓ 마지못해

□ancient ⓐ 아주 오래된

□run-down ⓐ 황폐한

□harmony ⓝ 조화, 화합, 화음

□energetic ⓐ 활기찬

□sensational ⓐ 선풍적인

□far ⓐⓓ 훨씬, 아주

B16

□back and forth 왔다갔다

□direction ⓝ 방향

□feel at ease 마음을 놓다, 안도하다

□lean back 상체를 뒤로 젖히다

□unoccupied ⓐ 빈, 비어 있는

B17

□beat ⓥ 능가하다, (시합 등에서) 이기다

□dramatically ⓐⓓ 극적으로

□progress ⓥ 진전을 보이다, 진행하다

□definitely ⓐⓓ 분명히, 틀림없이

□confident ⓐ 자신감 있는

□motivate ⓥ 동기를 부여하다

B18

□pull away 출발하다

□disappointment ⓝ 실망감

□wash ⓥ 밀려오다

□ferry terminal 여객선 터미널

□head out 나가다

□complete ⓐ 완전한

B19

□approach ⓥ 다가가다[오다]

□toddler ⓝ 아장아장 걷는 아이

□reply ⓝ 대답, 답장

□artwork ⓝ 그림, (박물관의) 미술품

□recognize ⓥ 알아보다, 인정하다

□beard ⓝ 턱수염

B20

□deeply ⓐⓓ (대단히 · 몹시의 뜻으로) 깊이[크게]

□troubled ⓐ 걱정하는, 불안한, 괴로운

□uneasiness ⓝ 불안, 근심, 릴깨

□reddish ⓐ 발그레한, 불그스름한

□beat ⓥ (심장이) 고동치다

□settle down 진정되다, ~을 진정시키다

□recall ⓥ 상기하다, 기억해 내다

□figure out (생각한 끝에) ~을 이해하다[알아내다], (양 · 비용 등을) 계산[산출]하다

□absolutely ⓐⓓ 전적으로, 틀림없이

□oppose ⓥ 겨루다, 반대하다

□steady ⓐ 흔들림 없는, 안정된

B21

□day trip 당일치기 여행

□scheduled ⓐ 예정된

□sightseeing ⓝ 관광

□sign up 신청하다

□sigh ⓝ 한숨

□all of a sudden 갑자기

□spring off ~에서 벌떡 일어나다

B22

□arrive ⓥ (어떤 순간이) 도래하다

□registration ⓝ 등록

□point ⓝ (특정한) 지점[장소]

□sign ⓝ 징후, 조짐, 기색, 흔적

□concerned ⓐ 걱정[염려]하는

□traffic ⓝ 차량들, 교통(량)

□terrible ⓐ 끔찍한

□relax ⓥ 긴장이 풀리다, 안심하다

□register ⓥ 등록하다

□head ⓥ (특정 방향으로) 가다[향하다]

C 주장 찾기

C01

□anticipation ⓝ 기대

□assistant ⓝ 비서, 조수, 보조원

□saving grace 장점, 미덕

□termination ⓝ 결단력

□infallibility ⓝ 무오류성

□crucial ⓐ 중대한, 결정적인

□utilize ⓥ 활용하다

□overseer ⓝ 감독관

□foreseeable future 가까운 미래

C

C02
- certain ⓐ 어떤, 무슨
- hindrance ⓝ 방해요인, 장애물
- multifaceted ⓐ 다면적인
- premature ⓐ 이른
- specialization ⓝ 전문화
- direction ⓝ 방향
- domain ⓝ 영역
- enhance ⓥ 높이다
- generality ⓝ 일반성
- specificity ⓝ 특수성
- productivity ⓝ 생산성
- excessive ⓐ 지나친
- underestimate ⓥ 과소평가하다
- unavailable ⓐ 손에 넣을 수 없는, 활용할 수 없는
- fixedness ⓝ 고정성
- chaos ⓝ 혼돈
- vagueness ⓝ 모호함
- shallowness ⓝ 얕음
- transfer ⓥ 이전하다
- optimal ⓐ 최선의
- couple ⓥ 연결하다
- discipline ⓝ 분야

C03
- universally ⓐⓓ 보편적으로
- accomplish ⓥ 이루다
- hold attention 주의를 유지하다
- enhance ⓥ 향상시키다
- productivity ⓝ 생산성
- derail ⓥ 탈선시키다, 망치다
- desirable ⓐ 바람직한
- connect to ~와 관련시키다 [연결하다]
- outcome ⓝ 결과, 성과

- educator ⓝ 교육자
- take advantage of ~을 활용하다
- command ⓥ 지배하다, 지휘하다

C04
- essential ⓐ 필수적인
- progress ⓝ 진보
- foundation ⓝ 토대, 기반
- reliable ⓐ 신뢰할 수 있는
- accurate ⓐ 정확한
- accumulation ⓝ 축적
- unregulated ⓐ 규제받지 않는
- unknowingly ⓐⓓ 자신도 모르게
- participate in ~에 참여하다
- circulate ⓥ 유포하다
- violence ⓝ 폭력
- take on ~을 (떠)맡다
- enhancement ⓝ 강화
- safeguard ⓥ 보호하다
- informed ⓐ 사실 이해에 입각한, 정보에 근거한
- rational ⓐ 합리적인

C05
- channel ⓥ 전하다, 보내다
- instinctively ⓐⓓ 본능적으로
- ancestor ⓝ 조상, 선조
- ally ⓝ 협력자
- child-rearing ⓝ 자녀 양육
- nurture ⓥ 양육하다, 길러주다
- quality ⓝ 질
- curiosity ⓝ 호기심
- empathy ⓝ 감정이입
- entrepreneurship ⓝ 기업가 정신
- childhood ⓝ 어린시절
- develop ⓥ 발달시키다

- beneficial ⓐ 유익한
- integral ⓐ 필수적인
- competent ⓐ 유능한
- conversation ⓝ 대화

C06
- author ⓝ 필자, 작가
- career ⓝ 경력
- obsess ⓥ (생각이나 마음을) 사로잡다
- income ⓝ 수입
- discover ⓥ 발견하다

C07
- middle-aged ⓐ 중년의
- connective tissue 결합 조직
- peak ⓥ 절정에 달하다
- load tolerance 내하중(견딜 수 있는 무게)
- typical ⓐ 전형적인
- dysfunction ⓝ 기능 장애
- superficial ⓐ 피상적인
- weight room 체력 단련실
- restore ⓥ 회복시키다

C08
- by definition 당연히, 말 그대로
- self-concept ⓝ 자아 개념
- responsibility ⓝ 책임
- as such 이처럼, 이와 같이
- assume ⓥ (권력·책임을) 맡다
- proactive ⓐ 주도적인
- contribute to ~에 기여하다
- facilitator ⓝ 촉진자
- alongside (prep) ~와 함께, ~와 동시에
- promote ⓥ 촉진하다
- achievement ⓝ 성취
- extend ⓥ 확장하다

□course ⓝ 강의
□growth ⓝ 성장
□foster ⓥ 촉진하다, 기르다
□engagement ⓝ 참여
□assign ⓥ 부여하다
□relevant ⓐ 관련 있는, 적절한

C09

□inspire ⓥ 영감을 주다
□development ⓝ 발달
□air ⓥ 방송하다
□critique ⓥ 비평하다
□popular culture 대중문화
□healthy ⓐ 건전한, 건강한
□process ⓝ 과정, 절차
□public ⓐ 공개적인
□debate ⓝ 토론
□deserve ⓥ (보수·도움·벌 등을) 받아야 마땅하다
□criticism ⓝ 비판
□popularization ⓝ 대중화
□greatly ⓐ 크게
□enhance ⓥ 향상시키다
□improve ⓥ 개선하다
□widespread ⓐ 널리 퍼진
□majority ⓝ (특정 집단 내의) 대다수
□novel ⓝ 소설
□play ⓝ 희곡, 연극
□script ⓝ 대본
□humanities ⓝ 인문학
□furthermore ⓐ 뿐만 아니라
□few ⓐ (수가) 많지 않은
□source material 원자료
□further ⓐ 더, 게다가
□screenplay ⓝ 영화 대본
□present ⓥ 보여주다, 제시하다
□contemporary ⓐ 동시대의, 현대의

□particularly ⓐ 특히
□influential ⓐ 영향력 있는
□introduction ⓝ 도입, 전래
□attractive ⓐ 매력적인

C10

□solution ⓝ 해결책
□replace ⓥ 대신[대체]하다
□seriously ⓐ 진지하게, 심(각)하게
□branch ⓝ (지식의) 분야, 나뭇가지, 분점
□moral ⓐ 도덕과 관련된
□suppose ⓥ 가정하다
□batch ⓝ 묶음, 무리
□method ⓝ 방법
□configuration ⓝ 배치, 배열
□accomplish ⓥ 성취하다
□end ⓝ 목적
□company ⓝ 함께 있음
□appreciatively ⓐ 고마워하며
□nonviolently ⓐ 비폭력적으로

C11

□common ⓐ 흔한, 공동의, 보통의
□consider ⓥ 고려하다, 생각하다
□experiment ⓥ 실험하다, 시험 삼아 해 보다
□objective ⓝ 목적, 목표
□reality ⓝ 현실, 사실, 실체
□insight ⓝ 통찰력, 식견, 이해
□latest ⓐ 최신(식)의, 최근의
□thorough ⓐ 철저한, 완전한
□merely ⓐ 그저, 단지
□fulfillment ⓝ (의무·직무 등의) 이행, 실천

□vague ⓐ (기억 등이) 희미한, 모호한
□presence ⓝ (특정한 곳에) 있음, 존재(함)
□serve ⓥ 도움이 되다, (상품·서비스를) 제공하다
□improvement ⓝ 향상, 개선
□sort ⓝ 종류, 유형, 분류
□preferably ⓐ 되도록이면, 가급적이면
□measurable ⓐ 측정할 수 있는
□drive ⓥ (특정한 행동을 하도록) 만들다, 추진하다

C12

□expertise ⓝ 전문 지식[기술]
□domain ⓝ (지식·활동 등의) 영역[분야]
□considerable ⓐ 많은, 상당한
□effort ⓝ 수고, 애
□specific ⓐ 특정한, 구체적인
□acquire ⓥ 습득하다, 얻다
□imperfectly ⓐ 불완전하게, 불충분하게
□worth ⓐ ~의 가치가 있는, ~할 가치가 있는
□clear ⓐ 분명한, 확실한
□concentrate ⓥ 집중하다, 전념하다, 집중시키다
□actively ⓐ 활발히, 적극적으로

C13

□deny ⓥ 부인[부정]하다
□engage in ~에 관여[참여]하다
□argument ⓝ 논쟁
□carry ⓥ (어떤 결과를) 수반하다
□significant ⓐ 중대한, 중요한

□argue ⓥ 언쟁을 하다, 다투다

□examine ⓥ 조사[검토]하다

□with a view toward ~하려고, ~할 목적으로

□fall short 부족하다, 모자라다

□dismiss ⓥ 묵살[일축]하다

□obviously ⓐⓓ 확실히, 분명히

□compelling ⓐ 설득력 있는

□measure up with ~과 겨루다

□toe-to-toe 정면으로 맞붙어

□adjustment ⓝ 조정

□call for ~을 요구하다

□revise ⓥ 변경[수정]하다

□suspend ⓥ 유예[중단]하다

□altogether ⓐⓓ 완전히, 전적으로

C 14

□technology ⓝ 기술

□intentional ⓐ 의도적인

□essential ⓐ 필수적인

□neurological ⓐ 신경학적인

□repair ⓝ 회복

□spiritual ⓐ 정신적인

□clarity ⓝ 명료성

□solitude ⓝ 고독

□anxiety ⓝ 불안

□markedly ⓐⓓ 두드러지게

□physically ⓐⓓ 물리적으로

□access ⓥ 접근하다

□impulse ⓝ 충동

□free ⓥ 자유롭게 하다

□constant ⓐ 지속적인

□connectivity ⓝ 연결성

□normalize ⓥ 정상화하다

□deactivation ⓝ 비활성화

□reassemble ⓥ 다시 모으다

C 15

□condition ⓝ 상태, 환경, 상황

□weave ⓥ 짜다, 엮다

□fabric ⓝ 구조, 직물

□expand ⓥ 확장하다, 넓히다

□reach ⓝ 거리, 범위

□peer ⓝ 동료, 또래

□spot ⓥ 발견하다, 찾다, 알아채다

□colleague ⓝ (같은 직장이나 직종에 종사하는) 동료

□catch the bug 병에 걸리다

□varied ⓐ 다양한

□concentrate ⓥ 집중하다

□cultivate ⓥ 함양하다, 경작하다

□exposure ⓝ 접근, 노출

□uniquely ⓐⓓ 독특하게, 유일하게

□residential ⓐ 주거의

C 16

□anthropology ⓝ 인류학

□relevant ⓐ 적절한

□address ⓥ 다루다

□vital ⓐ 중요한

□resolve ⓥ 해결하다

□statistics ⓝ 통계

□crucial ⓐ 중대한, 결정적인

□discipline ⓝ 학문

□profession ⓝ 전문 직업

□enable ⓥ ~을 할 수 있게 하다

□interpretation ⓝ 해석

□comprehensively ⓐⓓ 완전히, 철저히

□quantitative data 양적 데이터

□qualitative ⓐ 질적인

□approach ⓝ 접근법

□nuance ⓝ 미묘한 차이, 뉘앙스

C 17

□athlete ⓝ (운동)선수

□on track 제대로 진행되고 있는

□specific ⓐ 구체적인, 특정한

□lack ⓥ 부족하다

□frustrating ⓐ 좌절감을 주는

□progress ⓝ 진전, 진행

□drive ⓝ 추진력, 투지

□utilize ⓥ 활용[이용]하다

□gear ⓝ (특정 목적용) 장치

□maximize ⓥ 극대화하다

□physical ⓐ 육체의, 물질의

□sustain ⓥ 지속하다, 존재하게 하다

□motivation ⓝ 동기 부여, 자극

□mindset ⓝ 사고방식, 태도

□strengthen ⓥ 강화하다

□polish ⓥ (좋아지도록) 다듬다

□desire ⓝ 욕구, 갈망

□spin ⓥ 돌다, 질주하다

C 18

□occasionally ⓐⓓ 가끔, 때때로

□merely ⓐⓓ 단지, 그저

□come out 알려지다, 드러나다

□state ⓥ 말하다

□indirect ⓐ 간접적인

□means ⓝ 수단

□annoyance ⓝ 불쾌감

□companion ⓝ 동료

□indicate ⓥ 나타내다

□hostility ⓝ 적개심

□numerous ⓐ 수많은

□frown ⓥ 얼굴을 찡그리다

□genuinely ⓐⓓ 진정으로

□swiftly ⓐⓓ 신속히, 빨리

□switch over ~을 바꾸다

□turn up 등장하다, 나타나다

□incredibly ⓐⓓ 믿을 수 없을 정도로

□vague ⓐ 모호한

□temper ⓝ 짜증, 성질

□irritated ⓐ 짜증이 난

□absence ⓝ 없음, 부재

□regarding (prep) ~에 관하여

C19

□contribute ⓥ 기여하다

□creation ⓝ 창작품

□maintenance ⓝ 유지

□concise ⓐ 간결한

□description ⓝ 설명, 기술

□critical ⓐ 중요한

□representation ⓝ 표현, 묘사

□playbook ⓝ 플레이 북(팀의 공격과 수비의 작전을 그림과 함께 기록한 책)

□shift ⓝ 변화

□transform ⓥ 바꾸다

C20

□competent ⓐ 능숙한, 만족할 만한

□motivate ⓥ 동기를 부여하다

□observe ⓥ 관찰하다, 목격하다

□custom ⓝ 관습, 풍습

□short-sighted ⓐ 근시안의

□intercultural ⓐ 다른 문화 간의

□iceberg ⓝ 빙산

□surface ⓝ 표면, 지면

□attempt ⓥ 시도하다

□dimension ⓝ 차원, 관점

□foundation ⓝ 토대, 기초

□norm ⓝ 규범, 표준

□violate ⓥ (법·합의 등을) 위반하다

□judgment ⓝ 판단, 심판

C21

□encounter ⓥ 만나다, 경험하다

□uncertainty ⓝ 불확실성

□destination ⓝ 목적지

□intuition ⓝ 직관

□potent ⓐ 강력한

□shortcut ⓝ 지름길

□mathematical ⓐ 수학적인

□eliminate ⓥ 없애다, 제거하다

□proportion ⓝ 비율

C22

□confident ⓐ 자신감 있는

□misconception ⓝ 오해

□fearlessly (ad) 두려움 없이

□hold on to ~을 고수하다

□matter to ~에게 중요하다

□expand ⓥ 확장하다

□tend to ~하는 경향이 있다

□inevitably (ad) 불가피하게

C23

□chemist ⓝ 화학자

□extensive ⓐ 광범위한

□discipline ⓝ 학문

□overlook ⓥ 간과하다

□oblige ⓥ 의무를 다하다

□competent ⓐ 능숙한

□contribute ⓥ 기여하다

□perspective ⓝ 관점

□readability ⓝ 가독성

□reader-centered ⓐ 독자 중심의

□mentality ⓝ 사고방식

□mindful ⓐ 유의하는

□beneficial ⓐ 유익한

D 밑줄 친 부분의 의미 찾기

D

D01

□conclude ⓥ 결론을 내리다, 끝나다

□stuck ⓐ 움직일 수 없는, 갇힌

□suit ⓥ 어울리다, 맞다

□lack ⓥ 부족하다, 없다

□convergence ⓝ 집합점, 수렴

□nonlinear ⓐ 직선이 아닌

□chaotic ⓐ 혼돈 상태인

D02

□pure ⓐ 순수한, 완전한

□objective ⓐ 객관적인

□perspective ⓝ 관점, 시각

□reality ⓝ 현실

□precisely (ad) 바로, 정확하게

□universal ⓐ 보편적인, 일반적인

□authoritative ⓐ 권위적인

□theoretical ⓐ 이론의, 이론적인

□construct ⓝ 생각, 건축물

□philosopher ⓝ 철학자

□intelligible ⓐ (쉽게) 이해할 수 있는

D03

□architect ⓝ 건축가

□empire ⓝ 제국

□architecture ⓝ 건축

□symbolically (ad) 상징적으로

□statement ⓝ 성명

□class ⓥ 분류하다

□physician ⓝ 의사

□profession ⓝ 직업

□practice ⓥ 활동하다
□practical ⓐ 실용적인
□theoretical ⓐ 이론적인
□aspire ⓥ 열망하다
□draftsmanship ⓝ 제도
□astronomy ⓝ 천문학
□manual ⓐ 손의
□scholarship ⓝ 학문
□authority ⓝ 권위
□correspond ⓥ 상응하다
□substance ⓝ 실체

D04

□anthropologist ⓝ 인류학자
□go about ~을 시작하다
□insist ⓥ 주장하다
□significant ⓐ 상당한, 중요한
□ethnographer ⓝ 민족지학자
□remote ⓐ 외딴
□in question 연구[논의]되고 있는
□seek out ~을 찾아내다
□colonial ⓐ 식민지의
□missionary ⓝ 선교사
□accommodation ⓝ 숙박 시설
□venture into ~을 탐험하다
□primarily ⓐⓓ 주로
□conduct ⓥ (특정한 활동을) 하다
□collaborative ⓐ 공동의
□struggle to ~하려고 애쓰다
□examine ⓥ 조사하다

D05

□conversation ⓝ 대화
□nonverbal ⓐ 비언어적인
□apply to 적용하다
□pick up on 알아차리다
□specific ⓐ 구체적인

□unprompted ⓐ 자발적인
□roundabout ⓐ 둘러가는, 우회적인
□reveal ⓥ 밝히다, 드러내다
□intention ⓝ 의도
□distract ⓥ 방해하다
□unexpected ⓐ 예상치 못한

D06

□breadth ⓝ 폭, 너비
□burn out 에너지를 소진하다
□spectrum ⓝ 범위, 스펙트럼
□account for 설명하다
□categorize ⓥ 분류하다
□manage to 힘든 일을 겨우(간신히) 하다
□competently ⓐⓓ 유능하게
□partial ⓐ 부분적인
□have[give, say] the last word 결정적 발언을 하다, 마지막 진술을 하다
□exhaustion ⓝ 탈진
□all-or-nothing ⓐ 양자택일의, 이것 아니면 저것인
□criterion ⓝ 기준 (복수형: criteria)
□applicable ⓐ 해당되는
□severity ⓝ 심각성

D07

□beam ⓝ 빛줄기
□catch a glimpse 얼핏 보다
□delicate ⓐ 연약한
□blood vessel 혈관
□cast ⓥ (그림자를) 드리우다
□cease ⓥ 중단되다
□momentarily ⓐⓓ 잠깐, 곧
□stabilization ⓝ 안정화
□fixate ⓥ 정착[고정]시키다

□approximate ⓐ 거의 정확한, 근사치인
□blurry ⓐ 흐릿한
□sensitively ⓐⓓ 민감하게
□distortion ⓝ 왜곡
□shaky ⓐ 떨리는, 불안한

D08

□perception ⓝ 인식, 지각
□input ⓝ 투입, 입력
□auditory ⓐ 청각의
□correlation ⓝ 상관 관계
□significant ⓐ 유의미한
□label ⓥ 라벨[표]을 붙이다
□subject ⓝ 피험자
□revise ⓥ 수정하다
□placebo effect 위약 효과(가짜 약이지만 약을 복용하고 있다는 데 대한 심리효과 따위로 실제 환자의 상태가 좋아지는 것)
□psychological ⓐ 정신적인
□dismiss ⓥ 묵살하다

D09

□ownership ⓝ 소유권
□metaphor ⓝ 비유
□dramatically ⓐⓓ 극적으로
□transform ⓥ 변화시키다
□interpersonal ⓐ 대인관계에 관련된
□reference ⓝ 언급
□license ⓥ 허가하다
□give away 증여하다
□split up 분리하다
□lease ⓝ 임대차 계약
□plumber ⓝ 배관공
□party ⓝ 당사자
□obligation ⓝ 의무
□priority ⓝ 우선권

□aspect ⓝ 측면

D10

□reputation ⓝ 평판

□immediate ⓐ 즉각적인, 당면한

□intrigue ⓝ 관심, 흥미

□charitable ⓐ 관대한, 자선의

□boost ⓥ 북돋우다, 높이다

□chance ⓝ 가능성

□converse ⓝ 정반대

□favor ⓝ 호의

□indirect ⓐ 간접적인

□reciprocity ⓝ 호혜(互惠)

□encourage ⓥ 권장[장려]하다, 용기를 북돋우다

□by the same token 마찬가지로

□shape ⓥ 형성하다

□possibility ⓝ 가능성

□trouble ⓥ 괴롭히다, 애 먹이다

□deed ⓝ 행동

□consequence ⓝ 결과

□charity ⓝ 너그러움, 관용

□mean-spirited ⓐ 비열한

□cast ⓥ (빛을) 발하다, (그림자를) 드리우다

□conflict ⓝ 갈등, 충돌

□regardless of ~에 상관없이

□ultimately ⓐⓓ 궁극적으로, 근본적으로

□reap ⓥ 거두다, 수확하다

□sow ⓥ (씨를) 뿌리다[심다]

D11

□habit ⓝ 습관

□switch ⓥ 전환하다, 바꾸다

□reactive ⓐ 반응을 보이는

□block off ~을 막다[차단하다]

□chunk ⓝ 덩어리, 많은 양

□priority ⓝ 우선 사항, 우선권

□frustrated ⓐ 좌절감을 느끼는

□productive ⓐ 생산적인

□article ⓝ (신문 · 잡지의) 글, 기사

□a string of 여러 개의, 일련의

□particularly ⓐⓓ 특별히

□by definition 당연히, 분명히

□approach ⓝ 접근법, 처리 방법

□go against the grain 천성을 거스르다

□expectation ⓝ 예상, 기대

□pressure ⓝ 압박, 압력

□willpower ⓝ 의지력

□upset ⓥ 속상하게 만들다

□disappoint ⓥ 실망시키다

□abandon ⓥ 버리다, 포기하다

□inbox ⓝ 받은 편지함

□otherwise ⓐⓓ 그렇지 않으면

□sacrifice ⓥ 희생하다

□potential ⓝ 잠재력

□illusion ⓝ 환상

□professionalism ⓝ 전문성

D12

□physician ⓝ 의사

□macroeconomist ⓝ 거시 경제학자

□economy-wide ⓐ 경제 전반에 걸친

□granted ⓐⓓ 물론

□tricky ⓐ 까다로운

□penicillin ⓝ 페니실린

□alternative ⓐ (기존의 것과) 다른

□squeeze ⓥ 쥐어짜다

□complicated ⓐ 복잡한

□particle ⓝ 입자

D13

□gold plating 금도금

□needlessly ⓐⓓ 불필요하게

□enhance ⓥ 향상시키다

□added value 부가 가치

□with respect to ~에 관하여

□in other words 다시 말해

□justification ⓝ 명분, 정당화

□other than ~외에

□demonstrate ⓥ 입증하다, 나타내다

□component ⓝ 요소

□enrich ⓥ 강화하다

□temptation ⓝ 유혹

□in all good faith 선의로

D14

□play a critical role 중요한 역할을 수행하다

□scatter ⓥ 분산시키다, 흩뜨리다

□let go of ~을 해소하다 [놓아주다]

□fixate on ~에 집착하다

□perspective ⓝ 관점

□tie down to ~에 옭아매다

□superficial ⓐ 피상적인

□anxiety-provoking ⓐ 불안을 유발하는

□heighten ⓥ 높이다

□widened ⓐ 확장된

□turn down 약화하다

□nonstick ⓐ 들러붙지 않는

D15

□existence ⓝ 존재, 실재

□inherently ⓐⓓ 본질적으로, 선천적으로

□innovation ⓝ 혁신

□startup ⓝ 신생 기업

□disrupt ⓥ 무너뜨리다, 방해하다

□status quo 현재 상태

□long-term 장기적인

□exceptionally ⓐⓓ 대단히

□rare ⓐ 드문

□alter ⓥ 바꾸다

□persuade ⓥ 설득하다

□necessitate ⓥ 필요로 하다

□ideally ⓐⓓ 이상적으로

□be associated with ~와 관련되다

□game-changing 판도를 바꾸는, 획기적인

□wildly ⓐⓓ 크게, 몹시

□discipline ⓝ 분야, 훈련

□half-life 반감기

□habituate ⓥ 익숙하게 만들다

□term ⓝ 용어, 기간

□accounting ⓝ 회계 (업무)

D 16

□light up 환해지다

□predict ⓥ 예상하다

□threaten ⓥ 협박하다

□stereotype ⓝ 고정관념

□psychologist ⓝ 심리학자

□portray ⓥ 묘사하다

□socioeconomically ⓐⓓ 사회 경제적으로

□unemployed ⓐ 실직한

□appear ⓥ ~인 것 같다

□physiologically ⓐⓓ 생리학 적으로

□blood vessel 혈관

□constrict ⓥ 수축하다

□violate ⓥ 위반하다, 침해하다

□descriptive ⓐ 서술하는, 기술적인

□prescriptive ⓐ 지시하는, 규범적인

□phenomenon ⓝ 현상

□neuroscientific ⓐ 신경과 학의

□protest ⓝ 항의

□conditioned to ~에 적응된

D 17

□synonymous ⓐ 동의어의

□flash ⓝ 반짝임, 섬광

□inspired ⓐ (능력이) 탁월한, 영감을 받은

□associated ⓐ 관련된

□inventive ⓐ 창의[독창]적인

□exemplar ⓝ 대표적인 예, 본보기

□worthy ⓐ (~을 받을) 자격이 있는, 받을 만한

□surround ⓥ 둘러싸다

□match ⓥ 일치하다, 맞먹다

□introduction ⓝ 도입, 전래

□spread ⓝ 확산, 전파

□key ⓐ 핵심적인, 가장 중요한

□transformation ⓝ 전환, (완전한) 변화

□industrial ⓐ 산업[공업]의

□characterize ⓥ 특징이 되다, 특징짓다

□iron ⓝ 철, 쇠

□coal ⓝ 석탄

□steam ⓝ 증기

□post-industrial ⓐ 후기 산업의

□petroleum ⓝ 석유

□combustion ⓝ (물질의 화학적) 연소

□distinctive ⓐ 독특한, 뚜렷이 구별되는

□stamp ⓝ 흔적, 우표

□dazzle ⓥ 눈이 부시게 하다, 황홀하게 하다

D 18

□proverb ⓝ 속담

□historian ⓝ 사학자

□tale ⓝ 이야기, 소설

□glorify ⓥ 미화하다

□role ⓝ 역할

□put across ~을 이해시키다

□rate ⓝ 속도, 비율

□consumption ⓝ 소비[소모] (량)

□completely ⓐⓓ 완전히, 전적으로

□unsustainable ⓐ 지속 불가능한

□wetland ⓝ 습지(대)

□wasteland ⓝ 황무지, 불모지

□coastal ⓐ 해안의

□sensitive ⓐ 세심한, 민감한

□disposable ⓐ 사용 후 버리게 되어 있는, 자유롭게 사용할 수 있는

□accelerate ⓥ 가속화하다

□cut down on ~을 줄이다

□alter ⓥ 바꾸다, 고치다

□violation ⓝ 위반, 위배, 침입

□right ⓝ 권리, 권한

□uncover ⓥ 알아내다

□urge ⓥ 강력히 권고[촉구]하다

□shift ⓝ 변화

□underrepresent ⓥ 실제의 수량·정도보다 적게[낮게] 표시하다

□restrict ⓥ 제한[한정]하다

D19

□ far from 전혀 ~이 아닌
□ synonym ⓝ 동의어
□ capitalism ⓝ 자본주의
□ consumerism ⓝ 소비지상주의
□ term ⓝ (지속되는 · 정해진) 기간
□ capital ⓝ 자본금, 자산
□ formation ⓝ 형성
□ all but 사실상, 거의
□ thrift ⓝ 절약
□ elementary ⓐ 기본적인, 초보의
□ sustainable ⓐ 지속 가능한
□ saving ⓝ ((pl.)) 저축한 돈, 저금
□ confusion ⓝ 혼란, 혼돈
□ policy ⓝ 정책, 방침
□ reinforce ⓥ 강화하다, 증원하다
□ interest ⓝ 이자, 이익
□ deny ⓥ 부정하다, 거부하다
□ material ⓐ 물질[물리]적인
□ consumption ⓝ 소비[소모](량)

D20

□ expect ⓥ 예상하다, 기대하다
□ figure out ~을 알아내다
□ fluid ⓝ 액체
□ consider ⓥ 고려하다, 숙고하다
□ familiar ⓐ 익숙한, 친숙한
□ object ⓝ 물건, 물체
□ interact ⓥ 상호 작용을 하다
□ pound ⓥ (특히 요란한 소리를 내며 여러 차례) 치다[두드리다]
□ nail ⓝ 못

□ functional ⓐ 기능적인, 기능상의
□ fixedness ⓝ 정착, 고착, 고정
□ relief ⓝ 안도(감)
□ curse ⓝ 저주
□ ironically ⓐⓓ 얄궂게도, 반어적으로

D21

□ initial ⓐ 초기의, 처음의
□ claim ⓥ 주장하다, 요구하다 ⓝ 주장
□ newsworthiness ⓝ 보도[뉴스] 가치가 있음
□ novelty ⓝ 신기함, 새로움
□ vulnerable ⓐ 취약한, 상처받기 쉬운
□ undermine ⓥ 손상[약화]시키다
□ subsequent ⓐ 그[이]다음의, 차후의
□ assume ⓥ 추정[상정]하다
□ quote ⓥ 인용하다, 전달하다
□ majority ⓝ 다수, 대부분
□ blameworthy ⓐ 탓할 만한, 책임이 있는
□ cite ⓥ 인용하다
□ abstract ⓝ (책 · 연설 · 서류의) 개요
□ overstate ⓥ 과장하다, 허풍을 떨다
□ draw ⓥ (마음을) 끌다
□ prestigious ⓐ 명망 있는[높은], 일류의
□ uncritically ⓐⓓ 무비판적으로
□ bait ⓝ 미끼
□ piece ⓝ (글 · 음악 · 미술 등의 작품) 한 점

□ stress ⓥ 강조하다
□ incompatibility ⓝ 불일치, 양립할 수 없음

D22

□ immaturity ⓝ 미성숙
□ species ⓝ 종
□ be correlated with ~와 상호 관련이 있다
□ evolutionary ⓐ 진화의
□ strategy ⓝ 전략
□ flexibility ⓝ 유연성
□ intelligence ⓝ 지능
□ developmental ⓐ 발달의
□ division of labor 분업
□ succeed ⓥ 성공하다
□ dependent ⓐ 의존적인
□ efficient ⓐ 효율적인
□ effective ⓐ 효과적인
□ agent ⓝ 행위자
□ executive ⓝ 경영진, 이사
□ characteristic ⓝ 성격

D23

□ modify ⓥ 수정[변경]하다
□ oblige ⓥ 강요하다, 의무 지우다
□ adjust ⓥ 적응하다, 조정하다
□ in exchange 그 대신
□ grant ⓥ 주다, 부여[수여]하다, 승인[허락]하다
□ relief ⓝ 경감, 완화, 안심
□ burden ⓝ 부담, 짐
□ above all 무엇보다도, 특히
□ pursue ⓥ 추구하다, 계속하다
□ sacrifice ⓝ 희생(물)
□ worth ⓐ ~할 가치가 있는
□ apparent ⓐ 분명한, 누가 봐도 알 수 있는

□civilization ⓝ 문명, 문명화

□swell ⓥ 붓다, 부풀다

□imposition ⓝ (새로운 법률·세금 등의) 시행[도입], 부담

□enslavement ⓝ 노예화, 노예 상태

□autonomous ⓐ 자율[자주]적인

□glue ⓥ (접착제로) 붙이다

□monopolize ⓥ 독점하다

□accelerate ⓥ 가속화되다[하다]

□overwhelm ⓥ 어쩔 줄 모르게 만들다, 압도하다

□costly ⓐ 많은 돈이 드는, 대가[희생]가 큰

□incorporate ⓥ 포함하다

□hierarchical ⓐ 계급[계층]에 따른

D24

□core ⓐ 핵심적인, 가장 중요한

□retailer ⓝ 소매업자

□boost ⓥ 북돋우다

□accompanying ⓐ 동반하는

□assembly ⓝ (기계 부품의) 조립

□installation ⓝ 설치

□home goods 가정용품

□incomplete ⓐ 미완성의

□contract ⓝ 계약(서)

□layer ⓥ 층층이 쌓다

□on top of ~뿐 아니라, ~ 외에도

□explore ⓥ 탐구하다

□component ⓝ 구성 요소, 부품

□breakthrough ⓝ 획기적 발전, 돌파구

□primary ⓐ 주된, 주요한, 기본적인

D25

□centerpiece ⓝ 중심물, 주목할 존재

□construction ⓝ 건설, 구성

□subjectivity ⓝ 주관성

□application ⓝ 적용

□reason ⓝ 이성, 사리(事理)

□critique ⓝ 비평한 글, 평론

□enlighten ⓥ (설명하여) 이해시키다[깨우치다]

□whereabout ⓝ 소재, 행방

□entry ⓝ (사전·장부 등의 개별) 항목

□happenstance ⓝ (특히 좋은 결과로 이어지는) 우연

□insight ⓝ 통찰력

□narrative ⓝ 이야기, 묘사

□formation ⓝ 형성

□explore ⓥ 탐험하다

□emerge ⓥ 드러나다, 알려지다

□formulation ⓝ 정확한 표현[어구], 공식화

□sphere ⓝ (활동·영향·관심) 영역

□self-inspection ⓝ 자체 검사

□self-critique ⓝ 자기 비판

□means ⓝ 수단, 방법

□reflect on ~을 반성하다[되돌아보다]

□process ⓝ 과정

□alternate ⓐ 대신인, 번갈아 나오는

□ego ⓝ 자아

□selfhood ⓝ 자아, 개성

D26

□flick ⓥ (버튼·스위치를) 휙 누르다

□collaboration ⓝ 협력, 협업

□obstacle ⓝ 장애물

□voluntarily ⓐⓓ 자발적으로

□out of the loop (상황을) 잘 알지 못하는

□enterprise ⓝ 기업, 회사

□individual ⓝ 개인

□isolate ⓥ 고립시키다

□security ⓝ 안전, 보안

□adjust ⓥ 조정하다

□risky ⓐ 위험한

□right ⓐⓓ 곧바로, 정확히, 꼭

□reassure ⓥ 안심시키다

□hyperconnected ⓐ 과잉 연결된

□periodically ⓐⓓ 주기적으로

□generate ⓥ 만들어 내다, 발생시키다

□diverse ⓐ 다양한

□mature ⓐ 성숙한

□enforce ⓥ 시행[집행]하다

□interaction ⓝ 상호 작용

□punishment ⓝ 처벌

□physical ⓐ 물리적인

□barrier ⓝ 장벽, 장애물

□norm ⓝ 규범, 표준

□prohibit ⓥ 금지하다, 방해하다

□cooperation ⓝ 협력

□devote ⓥ 전념하다, 헌신하다

□productivity ⓝ 생산성

D27

□purchase ⓝ 유리한 입장, 강점

□moral ⓐ 도덕적인
□ethical ⓐ 윤리적인
□climate ⓝ 기후
□qualify ⓥ 자격이 있다
□comment on ~을 판단하다
□reform ⓝ (사회·제도 등의)
개혁[개정]
□colony ⓝ (동일 지역에 서식하
는 동·식물의) 군집
□collapse ⓝ 붕괴, 와해
□very ⓐ (다름 아닌) 바로 그[이]
□expertise ⓝ 전문 지식
□specialized ⓐ 전문적인, 전
문화된
□domain ⓝ (지식·활동의) 영역
[분야]
□ignorance ⓝ 무지, 무식
□relevant ⓐ 관련 있는
□observation ⓝ 관찰, 주시
□assessment ⓝ 평가
□gather ⓥ 모으다, 수집하다
□blind ⓐ 맹목적인, 비논리적인
□designate ⓥ (특정한 자리나
직책에) 지정하다
□devote ⓥ (노력·시간·돈 등
을) 바치다[쏟다]
□sort out ~을 처리하다[해결하
다]

D28
□describe ⓥ 기술하다
□possession ⓝ 소유
□simultaneously ⓐⓓ 동시에
□sidetrack ⓥ 곁길로 새게 하다
□scatterbrained ⓐ 침착하지
못한
□abandon ⓥ 버리다, 포기하다
□constant ⓐ 끊임없는
□stimulation ⓝ 자극

□convenience ⓝ 편의
□restrain ⓥ 저지하다
□analyze ⓥ 분석하다
□comprehend ⓥ 이해하다
□thoroughly ⓐⓓ 철저하게

E 요지 찾기

E01
□intimate ⓐ 친밀한
□speech community 언어
공동체
□accommodate ⓥ 수용하다
□ethically ⓐⓓ 윤리적으로
□code ⓝ 관례
□at will 마음대로
□promote ⓥ 촉진하다, 장려하
다
□property ⓝ 재산, 소유물
□hunter-gatherer 수렵·채
집인
□circle ⓝ (관심·직업 등으로 연
결된 사람들의) …계[사회]
□mutual aid 상호 협력

E02
□reside ⓥ 살다, 거주하다
□sensible ⓐ 분별있는,
합리적인
□validity ⓝ 유효함, 타당성
□instinct ⓝ 본능
□protective ⓐ 방어적인
□challenge ⓝ 도전, 과제
□validate ⓥ 입증하다, 인증하다
□present ⓥ 제시하다

□acquaintance ⓝ 지인
□evidence ⓝ 증거
□cognitive ⓐ 인식의, 인지의
□trustworthy ⓐ 신뢰할 수
있는
□mechanism ⓝ 기제, 방법
□perform ⓥ 수행하다
□virtual ⓐ 가상의
□tendency ⓝ 경향, 성향

E03
□consequence ⓝ 결과
□relevant ⓐ 중요한, 의미 있는
□mood ⓝ 기분
□facilitate ⓥ 촉진하다
□accomodate ⓥ 수용하다
□perspective ⓝ 관점
□appreciation ⓝ 이해
□arena ⓝ 장, 터
□promote ⓥ 촉진하다
□constructive ⓐ 건설적인

E04
□be capable of ~할 수 있다
□suppose ⓥ 추정하다
□conceive ⓥ 상상하다
□wicked ⓐ 사악한
□agency ⓝ 주체성
□moral ⓐ 도덕적(인); ⓝ 도덕성
□cultivate ⓥ 함양[배양]하다, 기
르다
□desirable ⓐ 바람직한
□discourage ⓥ (못하게) 막다
□harmful ⓐ 해로운
□predisposition ⓝ 성향
□cooperate ⓥ 협력하다

E05
□consists of ~로 구성되다
□formulate ⓥ 표현[진술]하다

E

□ deliberately @d 의도[계획]적으로

□ practical @ 실용적인

□ transmit ⓥ 전송하다

□ metaphor ⓝ 비유

□ extend ⓥ 연장하다

□ conscious @ 의식적인

E06

□ organizational @ 구조적인

□ forster ⓥ 강화하다, 조성하다

□ condition ⓝ 조건

□ inspire ⓥ 영감을 주다

□ cohesion ⓝ 결속력

□ ethical @ 윤리적인

□ validate ⓥ 입증하다, 인증하다

□ absence ⓝ 부재

□ misinterpret ⓥ 잘못 해석하다, 오해하다

□ account for 설명하다, 차지하다

E07

□ opposition ⓝ 반대

□ wilderness ⓝ 황야, 황무지

□ environmentalist ⓝ 환경 운동가

□ corporate @ 기업의

□ interest ⓝ 이익

□ designate ⓥ 지정하다

□ residential @ 거주지의

□ infrastructure ⓝ 사회 기반 시설

□ clash ⓥ (의견 차이 등에 의해) 충돌하다

□ prevail ⓥ 만연하다

□ exclude ⓥ 배제하다

□ outweigh ⓥ …보다 더 크다, 능가하다

□ inconsistent @ 부합하지 않는

□ biocentric @ 생명을 중심으로 하는

□ underlying @ 근본적인

E08

□ multilingual @ 여러 언어를 하는

□ likelihood ⓝ 가능성

□ curse ⓝ 저주

□ taboo ⓝ 금기

□ physiological @ 생리적인

□ vary ⓥ 다르다

□ financial @ 재정의

□ well-being ⓝ 풍요

□ poverty ⓝ 빈곤

□ hardship ⓝ 고난, 어려움

□ discrimination ⓝ 차별

□ parental @ 부모의

E09

□ contractor ⓝ 계약자, 도급업자

□ construct ⓥ 건설하다

□ project ⓝ 주택 계획, 주택 단지

□ weight ⓝ 중요성, 무게

□ process ⓝ 과정, 절차

□ proper @ 적절한

□ force ⓥ 강요하다, ~하게 하다

□ detailed @ 상세한, 면밀한

□ allow ⓥ 허락하다, 가능하게 하다

□ methodology ⓝ 방법론

□ thereby @d 그렇게 함으로써

□ discover ⓥ 발견하다

□ restriction ⓝ 제약, 제한

□ risk ⓝ 위험 (요소)

□ address ⓥ (어려운 문제 등을) 다루다

□ estimate ⓥ 추정하다

□ far @d 훨씬

□ phase ⓝ 단계, 국면

□ particular @ 특정한

□ material ⓝ 재료

□ execution ⓝ 실행, 수행

□ goal ⓝ 목표

□ workable @ 실행 가능한

□ scheme ⓝ 계획

□ resource ⓝ 자원

□ efficiently @d 능률적으로

□ allowable @ 허용되는

□ given @ (이미) 정해진, 주어진

□ budget ⓝ 예산

□ guarantee ⓥ 보장하다

□ proceed ⓥ 진행하다

□ flawlessly @d 흠 없이

□ meet ⓥ 충족시키다

□ objective ⓝ 목표

□ improve ⓥ 개선하다

□ chance ⓝ 가능성

E10

□ profession ⓝ 전문직

□ engage in ~에 관예[참여]하다

□ negotiate ⓥ 협상하다

□ intend ⓥ 의도하다

□ define ⓥ 규정하다

□ terms ⓝ (합의 · 계약 등의) 조건

□ tension ⓝ 긴장

□ pursuit ⓝ 추구

□ demand ⓝ 요구

□ accountability ⓝ 책임, 의무

□ grant ⓥ 부여하다, 승인하다

□ willingness ⓝ 기꺼이 하는 마음

□ contribute ⓥ 기여하다

□ conduct ⓥ 수행하다

□ affair ⓝ 일, 문제

□ consistent ⓐ 일치하는, 일관된

□ broad ⓐ 폭넓은, 넓은

□ expertise ⓝ 전문 지식

□ confer ⓥ 부여[수여]하다

□ authority ⓝ 권한, 권위

□ readily ⓐd 손쉽게

□ at the expense of ~을 희생하면서

□ observe ⓥ 말하다, 관찰하다

□ qualify ⓥ 자격을 주다

□ civil ⓐ 시민의

□ liberty ⓝ 자유

□ proportion ⓝ 비율

□ disposition ⓝ 성향, 기질

□ moral ⓐ 도덕적인

□ appetite ⓝ 욕구, 식욕

□ irreversibly ⓐd 돌이킬 수 없게

E11

□ hazard ⓝ 위험 (요인)

□ biological ⓐ 생물학적인

□ physical ⓐ 물리적인

□ chemical ⓐ 화학적인

□ promote ⓥ 조장[촉진]하다

□ exposure ⓝ (유해한 환경 등에의) 노출[접함]

□ contaminant ⓝ 오염 물질

□ breathing ⓝ 호흡

□ polluted ⓐ 오염된, 더럽혀진

□ chemically ⓐd 화학적으로

□ circumstance ⓝ 상황, 환경

□ involuntary ⓐ 자기도 모르게 하는

□ reduction ⓝ 감소

□ elimination ⓝ 제거

□ societal ⓐ 사회의

□ public ⓐ 대중의, 공공의

□ awareness ⓝ (중요성에 대한) 의식, 인식

□ measure ⓝ 조치, 정책

□ morally ⓐd 도덕적으로

□ arsenic ⓝ ((화학)) 비소(砒素)

□ passively ⓐd 수동적으로

□ outrage ⓥ 격분[격노]하게 만들다

E12

□ definition ⓝ 정의

□ implication ⓝ 함의, 내포된 뜻

□ emphasize ⓥ 강조하다

□ exclude ⓥ 배제하다

□ exclusive ⓐ 상위의, 상류의, 고급의

□ inactive ⓐ 활동적이지 않은

□ relatively ⓐd 상대적으로

□ negatively ⓐd 부정적으로

□ integrate ⓥ 융합하다, 통합하다

□ overall ⓐ 전반적인

□ benefit ⓝ 이점

□ likely ⓐ 가능성이 있는

E13

□ inseparable ⓐ 분리할 수 없는

□ weave ⓥ (옷감 · 바구니 등을) 짜다[엮다], 짜서[엮어서] 만들다

□ fabric ⓝ 직물, 천

□ skilled ⓐ 숙련된, 노련한

□ sensitivity ⓝ 감수성

□ extremely ⓐd 극도로, 극히

□ aspect ⓝ 측면, 양상

□ transmit ⓥ 전달하다

□ characterize ⓥ 특징짓다

□ expose ⓥ 접하게[경험하게] 하다, (유해한 환경 등에) 노출시키다

□ artistically ⓐd 예술[미술]적으로

□ meaningful ⓐ 의미 있는, 중요한

□ engaging ⓐ 호감이 가는, 매력적인

□ prior to ~에 앞서, ~보다 먼저

□ bias ⓝ 편향, 치우친 생각

□ preference ⓝ 선호, 애호

□ prejudice ⓝ 편견

E14

□ drafter ⓝ (계획 · 문서 등의) 입안자

□ attentive ⓐ 주의를 기울이는, 신경을 쓰는

□ moral ⓐ 도덕상의, 도의적인

□ morality ⓝ 도덕(성)

□ legislative ⓐ 입법의, 입법부의

□ debate ⓝ 토론, 논쟁

□ controversial ⓐ 논란이 많은

□ irrelevant ⓐ 무관심한, 상관없는

□ taxation ⓝ 조세, 과세 제도

□ fundamental ⓐ 근본적인, 핵심적인

□ application ⓝ 적용, 응용, 신청(서)

□ distributive ⓐ 분배의, 유통의

□ justice ⓝ 정의, 공정성

□ legislature ⓝ 입법 기관, 입법부

□ identify ⓥ 확인하다, 발견하다

□ policy ⓝ 정책, 방침

□ ethics ⓝ 윤리학

□ analysis ⓝ 분석

E15

□ ecosystem ⓝ 생태계

□ management ⓝ 관리

□ be linked to ~와 연결되다

□ infrastructure ⓝ 사회 기반 시설

□ address ⓥ 다루다

□ trade-off ⓝ 교환, 균형

□ conservation ⓝ 보존

□ livelihood ⓝ 생계

□ distribution ⓝ 분배

□ implement ⓥ 실행하다

□ at the expense of ~의 희생으로

□ marginalized ⓐ 소외된

□ obstacle ⓝ 장애물

□ sustainable ⓐ 지속 가능한

□ identify ⓥ 확인하다

□ negotiate ⓥ 협상하다

□ flexibility ⓝ 유연성

□ cope with ~에 대처하다

□ unexpected ⓐ 예상치 못한

E16

□ notion ⓝ 개념, 생각

□ privacy ⓝ 사생활, 비밀

□ paradox ⓝ 역설

□ engagement ⓝ 참여

□ manner ⓝ 방식, 태도

□ explode ⓥ 폭발하다

□ awareness ⓝ (중요성에 대한) 의식[관심]

□ rich ⓐ 풍부한

□ conflicted ⓐ 갈등을 겪는

□ current ⓐ 현재의

□ armed ⓐ 무장한

□ passive ⓐ 수동적인, 소극적인

□ bystander ⓝ 구경꾼, 행인

E17

□ overcome ⓥ 극복하다

□ obstacle ⓝ 장애(물)

□ hinder ⓥ 방해하다

□ evolution ⓝ 진화, 발전

□ propel ⓥ 몰다, 밀다

□ valuable ⓐ 귀중한

□ preserve ⓥ 보존하다

□ generation ⓝ 세대

□ remarkable ⓐ 놀라운, 주목할 만한

□ relativity ⓝ 상대성

□ absence ⓝ 없음, 부재

□ discover ⓥ 발견하다

□ leap ⓝ 도약, 급증

E18

□ adapt ⓥ 개조하다

□ density ⓝ 밀도, 농도

□ distribution ⓝ 분포, 배치

□ potential ⓝ 잠재력, 가능성

□ congested ⓐ 붐비는, 혼잡한

□ cargo ⓝ 짐, 화물

□ acquisition ⓝ 매입, 취득

□ maintenance ⓝ 유지

□ convey ⓥ 운반하다, 전달하다

□ tricycle ⓝ 세발자전거

□ implement ⓥ 시행하다

□ parcel ⓝ 소포

□ catering ⓝ 음식 공급

□ district ⓝ 지역, 구역

□ extension ⓝ 확장, 확대

□ dedicated ⓐ 전용의

E19

□ prior to ~에 앞서, ~보다 먼저

□ exclusively ⓐⅾ 배타적으로, 독점적으로

□ critic ⓝ 비평가, 평론가

□ release ⓝ (대중들에게) 발표 [공개]

□ well ⓐⅾ 아주, 상당히

□ preview ⓥ 시사평을 쓰다, 사전 검토[조사]하다

□ accessible ⓐ 접근[이용] 가능한

□ advanced ⓐ 선진의, 고급[상급]의, 후기의

□ spread ⓥ 퍼뜨리다, 확산시키다

□ availability ⓝ 이용[입수] 가능성

□ democratize ⓥ 민주화하다

□ obtain ⓥ 얻다, 입수하다

□ simultaneously ⓐⅾ 동시에, 일제히

□ publicize ⓥ 광고하다, 알리다

□ endlessly ⓐⅾ 끝없이, 무한히

□ mass ⓝ ((pl.)) (일반) 대중

□ particular ⓐ 특정한, 특별한

□ consciously ⓐⅾ 의식[자각] 하여, 의식적으로

□ subconsciously ⓐⅾ 잠재 의식적으로

E20

□ prioritize ⓥ 우선순위를 매기다, 우선시하다

□ one-off ⓐ 일회성의

□ upsetting ⓐ 속상하게 하는

□ significantly ⓐⅾ 상당히

□ influential ⓐ 영향력 있는

□ customer base 고객층

□ favorable ⓐ 호의적인

□ acknowledge ⓥ 감사하다, 인정하다

□ appreciation ⓝ 감사

□ unanswered ⓐ 답을 못한

E21

□ assimilate ⓥ 동화하다

□ host culture 주류 문화

□ conflict ⓝ 갈등

□ multiculturalist ⓝ 다문화
주의자

□ partial ⓐ 부분적인

□ immigrant ⓝ 이민자

□ retain ⓥ 유지하다

□ conform ⓥ 순응하다

□ be determined by ~에 의
해 결정되다

□ migrate ⓥ 이주하다

□ exclusion ⓝ 배제

□ poverty ⓝ 빈곤

□ transform ⓥ 변화시키다

□ enlightenment ⓝ 계몽

□ diversity ⓝ 다양성

□ people of color 유색 인종

E22

□ work out 잘 되어가다

□ resolve ⓥ 해결하다

□ sufficiently ⓐⓓ 충분히

□ worthwhile ⓐ 가치있는

□ filmmaker ⓝ 영화감독

□ engage ⓥ 몰입하다

F 주제 찾기

F01

□ considerable ⓐ 상당한, 주
목할 만한

□ psychologist ⓝ 심리학자

□ indeed ⓐⓓ 정말, 사실

□ circumstance ⓝ (주변)
상황, 환경

□ draw out ~을 끌어내다
[뽑아내다]

□ neurally ⓐⓓ 신경(계)으로

□ implement ⓥ 실행하다

□ architecture ⓝ 건축, 구조

□ categorize ⓥ 분류하다

□ context ⓝ 맥락, 전후 사정

□ invariant ⓐ 변함없는, 변치
않는

□ evolution ⓝ 진화, 발전

□ plastic ⓐ 형태를 바꾸기 쉬운,
가짜의

□ modify ⓥ 수정하다, 조정하다

F02

□ emphasise ⓥ 강조하다

□ era ⓝ 시대

□ be forced to ~하도록 강요당
하다

□ earning ⓝ 획득, 소득

□ modernise ⓥ 현대화하다

□ mount ⓥ 시작하다

□ competitive ⓐ 경쟁을 하는,
경쟁력 있는

□ budget ⓝ 예산

□ prioritise ⓥ 우선시하다

□ consumable ⓐ 소비할 수
있는, 소비재의

□ unlit ⓐ 불을 켜지 않은

□ unglamorous ⓐ 매력적이지
못한, 따분한

□ storage ⓝ 저장 공간

□ conservation ⓝ 보호, 보존

□ need ⓝ 욕구, 요구

□ commitment ⓝ 헌신

F03

□ Industrial Age 산업 시대

□ capital ⓝ 자본

□ around the clock 24시간
내내

□ shift ⓝ 교대 근무

□ hum ⓥ 웅웅거리다, 활기가 넘치
다

□ industrialization ⓝ 산업화

□ potential ⓐ 잠재적인

□ wage ⓝ 임금

□ reorganize ⓥ 재조직하다

F04

□ phenomena ⓝ 현상

□ ordinary ⓐ 평범한

□ succession ⓝ 연속

□ frightened ⓐ 겁먹은

□ accustomed ⓐ 익숙한

□ physicist ⓝ 물리학자

□ account for 설명하다

□ notice ⓥ 알아차리다

□ singular ⓐ 기묘한

□ widespread ⓐ 광범위한

□ mythical ⓐ 신화적인

□ influence ⓝ 영향

□ perception ⓝ 인식

□ pose ⓥ (위협·문제 등을)
제기하다

F05

□ desire ⓝ 욕구

□ rooted ⓐ ~에 뿌리[근원]를 둔

□ abstract ⓐ 추상적인

□ multitude ⓝ 다수

□ visualize ⓥ 시각화하다

□ conceptualize ⓥ 개념화하다

□ fundamental ⓐ 근본적인

□ preserve ⓥ 보존하다

□ document ⓥ 기록하다

□ persist ⓥ 계속[지속]되다

□ satisfactory ⓐ 만족스러운,
충분한

□ essential ⓐ 필수적인

□ evaluation ⓝ 평가

F06

□ plot ⓥ 표시하다
□ slope ⓝ 기울기, 경사면
□ emphasize ⓥ 강조하다
□ facilitate ⓥ 용이하게 하다, 가능하게 하다
□ anticipatory ⓐ 기대한, 예측한
□ multivariate ⓐ 다변량의
□ reactionary ⓐ 반응적인
□ endeavor ⓝ 노력, 시도
□ hasty ⓐ 급한, 서두르는
□ comprehensive ⓐ 포괄적인, 종합적인

F07

□ attachment ⓝ 부속물, 부착
□ decline ⓝ 감소, 하락
□ referential ⓝ 지시성
□ tendency ⓝ 경향
□ capitalism ⓝ 자본주의
□ association ⓝ 연관, 연상
□ accustomed ⓐ 익숙한
□ definition ⓝ 정의
□ emerging ⓐ 신흥의, 새로 만들어진
□ customary ⓐ 관례적인, 관습상의
□ pretense ⓝ 겉치레, 가식
□ reliability ⓝ 신뢰성

F08

□ molecule ⓝ 분자
□ bind with ~와 결합하다
□ receptor ⓝ (인체의) 수용기 [감각기]
□ nerve cell 신경 세포
□ fire ⓥ (열의 · 관심 등이) 불타게 하다

□ alert ⓐ 경계하는
□ hormone ⓝ 호르몬
□ adrenal ⓐ 신장 부근의
□ intake ⓝ 섭취
□ consistent ⓐ 거듭되는, 일정한
□ counteract ⓥ 대응하다
□ consequence ⓝ 결과
□ deprivation ⓝ 박탈, 부족
□ temptation ⓝ 유혹

F09

□ sociologist ⓝ 사회학자
□ tribe ⓝ 부족
□ reputation ⓝ 평판
□ trustworthy ⓐ 신뢰할 수 있는
□ override ⓥ ~보다 더 중요하다
□ mortality ⓝ 죽음
□ irrational ⓐ 비이성적인
□ death sentence 사형 선고
□ drive ⓝ 욕구
□ oppose ⓥ 반대하다
□ favor ⓥ 편들다, 유리하게 하다
□ objective ⓐ 객관적인

F10

□ induce ⓥ 유발[초래]하다
□ insofar as ~하는 한
□ underlying ⓐ 근본적인
□ possess ⓥ 보유하다
□ precision ⓝ 정확성
□ seek ⓥ 추구하다 《sought-sought》
□ celebrate ⓥ 찬양하다, 축하하다
□ grasp ⓥ 이해하다, 파악하다, 움켜잡다
□ phenomenon ⓝ 현상 《pl. phenomena》
□ immeasurability ⓝ 헤아릴 수 없음

□ constrain ⓥ 제한[제약]하다
□ stimulate ⓥ 자극하다
□ hence ⓐ 그러므로, 이런 이유로
□ associated ⓐ 관련된
□ indefinable ⓐ 규정할 수 없는
□ formless ⓐ 형태가 없는
□ namely ⓐ 다시 말해
□ consist of ~으로 이루어지다 [구성되다]
□ struggle ⓥ 열심히 노력하다
□ decode ⓥ 해독하다, 이해하다
□ momentarily ⓐ 잠깐, 일시적으로
□ violate ⓥ 어기다, 위반하다
□ diversity ⓝ 다양성
□ inherent ⓐ 내재하는, 선천적인
□ imperfection ⓝ 불완전 (상태)
□ inclination ⓝ 경향, 성향

F11

□ measure ⓝ 조치, 정책
□ continual ⓐ 거듭[반복]되는
□ carry on ~을 계속하다
□ internalized ⓐ 내면화된
□ likewise ⓐ 똑같이, 또한
□ encounter ⓥ 마주치다 ⓝ 만남, 접촉
□ evaluation ⓝ 평가
□ profile ⓝ 개요(서)
□ argument ⓝ 논쟁, 언쟁
□ exchange ⓝ 교환, 교류 ⓥ (이야기를) 주고받다
□ address ⓥ 건네다, 보내다
□ advantage ⓝ 유리한 점, 이점

□demonstrate ⓥ 입증[실증]하다

□effectively ⓐⓓ 효과적으로, 실질적으로

□imitate ⓥ 모방하다, 본뜨다

□debate ⓥ 논쟁하다

□synchronize ⓥ 동시에 발생하다[움직이다]

□cooperate ⓥ 협력[협조]하다

□inherently ⓐⓓ 본래

□via ⓟ ~을 통해, ~을 경유하여[거쳐]

□cognitive ⓐ 인식[인지]의

□trait ⓝ 특성

F12

□conventional wisdom 통념

□philosopher ⓝ 철학자

□credit A with B A에게 B가 있다고 믿다

□minimize ⓥ 최소화하다

□eliminate ⓥ 배제하다

□be identified with ~와 동일시되다

□trace ⓥ (기원·원인을) 추적하다[추적하여 밝혀내다]

□construction ⓝ 구성물

□embody ⓥ 구현하다, 구체화하다

□reflect ⓥ 반영하다, 나타내다

□individuality ⓝ 개인성

□structurally ⓐⓓ 구조적으로

□connectivity ⓝ 연결(성)

□fiction ⓝ 허구

□grammatical ⓐ 문법적인

□illusion ⓝ 환상, 착각

□inherent ⓐ 내재하는

□collectivity ⓝ 집단성

□separate ⓥ 구별하다

□acknowledgment ⓝ 인정, 시인

□interdependence ⓝ 상호의존

F13

□effortlessly ⓐⓓ 쉽게, 노력하지 않고

□absorption ⓝ 몰두, 몰입

□role ⓝ 역할

□narratively ⓐⓓ 이야기식으로

□structure ⓥ 조직하다, 구조화하다

□identify with ~와 동일시하다

□towards ⓟ ~ 쪽으로, ~을 향하여

□adolescence ⓝ 청소년기

□give up ~을 포기하다

□instead ⓐⓓ 대신에

□base ⓝ 기반, 기초

□develop ⓥ 발전하다

□fiction ⓝ 허구, 소설

□play ⓝ 연극, 희곡

□novel ⓝ 소설

□nowadays ⓐⓓ 요즘에는

□regress ⓥ 퇴행[퇴보]하다

□derive from ~에서 유래하다

□metaphorical ⓐ 은유[비유]의

□transformation ⓝ 변화, 변신

□self ⓝ 자아, 자신, 본모습

F14

□disclosure ⓝ (기업의) 정보 공개

□as opposed to ~와는 대조적으로

□aggressive ⓐ 공격적인, 공세적인

□regulation ⓝ 규제, 단속

□flexibility ⓝ 유연성, 융통성

□operation ⓝ 작용, 운용, 수술

□regulatory ⓐ 규제력을 지닌

□blunt ⓐ 무딘

□unintended ⓐ 의도하지 않은

□appliance ⓝ (가정용) 기기, 가전제품

□provision ⓝ 제공, 공급

□potential ⓐ 잠재적인

□attribute ⓝ 속성, 자질

□interfere ⓥ 방해하다, 간섭하다

F15

□address ⓥ (문제·상황 등에 대해) 고심하다[다루다]

□employ ⓥ (기술·방법 등을) 쓰다[이용하다]

□symbolic ⓐ 상징적인

□mathematical ⓐ 수학적인

□procedure ⓝ (특히 어떤 일을 늘·제대로 하는) 절차[방법]

□theoretical ⓐ 이론적인

□statement ⓝ 진술

□element ⓝ 요소

□presuppose ⓥ 전제로 하다

□comparable ⓐ 비슷한

□unity ⓝ 통일성

□account ⓝ 설명, 기술

□identification ⓝ 식별, 확인

□attempt ⓥ 시도하다

□interpretation ⓝ 해석, 이해

□rationalization ⓝ 이론적 설명

□lack ⓝ 부족, 결핍

F

□standard ⓐ 표준적인, 기준이 되는

F16

□overwhelming ⓐ 압도적인, 저항하기 힘든

□contagion ⓝ 전염

□intervention ⓝ 개입

□abstract ⓐ 추상적인

□conceptual ⓐ 개념의, 구상의

□concrete ⓐ 사실에 의거한, 구체적인

□flee ⓥ 도망가다

□mounting ⓐ 증가하는

□evoke ⓥ 떠올려주다

□guilt ⓝ 죄책감

□climate change 기후 변화

□proactive ⓐ 예방적인

□denial ⓝ 부정

□despair ⓝ 절망

□remote ⓐ 외딴, 동떨어진

□impact ⓝ 영향

□contribution ⓝ 기여

F17

□base ⓥ (~에) 근거[기초]를 두다

□observation ⓝ 관찰, 감시, 의견

□payoff ⓝ 이득, 보상, 분배

□assess ⓥ 평가하다

□factor ⓝ 요인, 인자

□advantage ⓝ 이점, 장점

□resource ⓝ 자원, 재료

□trialability ⓝ 시험 (사용) 가능성

□flaw ⓥ 망가뜨리다, 파기하다

□laboratory ⓝ 실험실

□plot ⓝ (소설 · 영화 등의) 구성, 줄거리

□facility ⓝ ((pl.)) (생활의 편리를 위한) 시설[기관]

□confront ⓥ 정면으로 부딪치다, 맞서다

□phenomenon ⓝ 현상 (pl. phenomena)

□acquire ⓥ 습득하다, 취득하다

F18

□arise ⓥ 생기다, 발생하다

□collaborative ⓐ 공동의

□assign ⓥ (일 · 책임 등을) 맡기다[배정하다], 할당하다

□automate ⓥ 자동화하다

□fashion ⓝ (행동 · 문화 등의) 방식

□capability ⓝ 역량, 능력

□monitor ⓥ 감시하다

□alert ⓐ 기민한, 주의를 게을리하지 않는

□extreme ⓐ 극도의, 극심한

□precision ⓝ 정확(성), 정밀(성)

□accuracy ⓝ 정확(성)

□divide up ~을 분배하다

□component ⓝ (구성) 요소, 부품

□take advantage of ~을 이용하다

□strength ⓝ 힘, 기운, 강점, 장점

□rely upon ~에 의존[의지]하다

□genetically ⓐⓓ 유전적으로, 유전자 상으로

□biologically ⓐⓓ 생물학적으로

□unsuited ⓐ 부적합한, 어울리지 않는

□overcome ⓥ 극복하다

□allocate ⓥ 할당하다

□unfit ⓐ 부적합한

□pursue ⓥ 추구하다

F19

□market incentive 시장 인센티브

□carbon capture 탄소 포집

□habitat ⓝ 서식지

□ecosystem ⓝ 생태계

□exceed ⓥ 초과하다

□initiative ⓝ 계획

□estimate ⓥ 추정하다

□tropical ⓐ 열대의

□regulation ⓝ 규제

□purification ⓝ 정화

□erosion ⓝ 침식

□hectare ⓝ 헥타르(땅 면적의 단위)

□favor ~ over … ~를 …보다 선호하다

□extractive ⓐ 채취의, 채광의

F20

□blossoming ⓐ 번창하는

□appearance ⓝ 출현

□resource ⓝ 자원

□agriculture ⓝ 농업

□burial ⓝ 매장지

□bury ⓥ 매장하다

□protein ⓝ 단백질

□mineral ⓝ 무기질

□pronounce ⓥ 뚜렷하게 하다

F21

□three-dimensional ⓐ 3차원의

□extension ⓝ 연장선

□along with ~와 함께

G

□take-away ⓝ 핵심, 요점

□progress ⓝ 발전

□contemporary ⓐ 현대의

□partition ⓝ 칸막이벽

□cubicle ⓝ 작은 개인 방

□alike ⓐ 비슷한

□cost-efficient ⓐ 비용 효율적인

□incorporate ⓥ 통합하다

□retro ⓐ 복고풍의

G05

□cooperation ⓝ 협력

□equality ⓝ 평등

□perception ⓝ 인식

□core ⓐ 핵심적인

□self-worth ⓝ 자아 존중감, 자부심

□confirm ⓥ 견고하게 하다

□hormonal ⓐ 호르몬의

□crave ⓥ 갈망[열망]하다

□characteristic ⓝ 특성

□belong to ⓥ ~에 속하다

□activate ⓥ 활성화시키다

□breed ⓥ 새끼를 낳다, 초대하다

□mutual ⓐ 상호간의

□sympathy ⓝ 동정

□resolve ⓥ 해결하다

G06

□benevolently ⓐⓓ 호의적으로

□illiteracy ⓝ 문맹

□attain ⓥ 얻다

□inflict on ~에 영향을 주다, 타격을 주다

□sustain ⓥ 살아가게 하다, 지속시키다

□civility ⓝ 시민성

□privileged ⓐ 특권을 가진

□backfire ⓥ 부작용을 낳다

□diversity ⓝ 다양성

G07

□commanding ⓐ 인상적인

□vast ⓐ 방대한

□indicate ⓥ 나타내다

□examine ⓥ 조사하다

□apparently ⓐⓓ 겉보기에는, 외관상으로는

□absorption ⓝ 흡수

□scattering ⓝ 분산

□absorb ⓥ 흡수하다

□scatter ⓥ 흩뿌리다

□wavelength ⓝ 파장

□depth ⓝ 깊이

□intensity ⓝ 강도

□inhabitant ⓝ 서식 동물

□deceptive ⓐ 기만적인

□microorganism ⓝ 미생물

G08

□matter ⓥ 중요하다

□hence ⓐⓓ 이런 이유로

□doorstep ⓝ 문간

□proverb ⓝ 속담

□shade ⓝ 그늘

□dispose of ~을 버리다

□solely ⓐⓓ 단지, 오로지

□for the sake of ~을 위해서

□preserve ⓥ 보존하다, 유지하다

□in play 작용하여, 영향을 끼치는

□management ⓝ 관리

□infrastructure ⓝ 사회 기반 시설

G09

□joint ⓐ 공동의, 합동의

□intelligence ⓝ 지능

□synergistic ⓐ (반응·효과 등이) 상승[상조]적인

□contribution ⓝ 기여, 이바지

□agent ⓝ 행위자, 대리인

□telecommute ⓥ (컴퓨터 등의) 통신 시설을 이용하여 재택근무하다

□concentrate ⓥ 집중하다, 모으다

□coordinate ⓥ 조정하다, 조직화하다

□accomplish ⓥ 완수하다, 성취하다

□peer ⓝ (나이 등이 비슷한) 또래

□independent ⓐ 독립적인

□agenda ⓝ 의제, 안건

□artificial ⓐ 인공의

□intelligent ⓐ 지능적인, 지능이 있는

G10

□restructure ⓥ 재구성하다, 개혁하다

□shift ⓝ 변화

□spontaneously ⓐⓓ 자발적으로

□like-minded ⓐ 생각[뜻]이 비슷한

□emerge ⓥ 생겨나다

□improvisational ⓐ 즉흥적인

□collaboration ⓝ 공동 작업, 협력

□translate ⓥ 바꾸다

□emergence ⓝ 출현

□outcome ⓝ 결과

□agenda ⓝ 의사 일정, 의제

□predictable ⓐ 예측할 수 있는

□executive ⓝ 경영진, 간부
□improvised ⓐ 즉흥의
□efficient ⓐ 효율적인
□conflicting ⓐ 모순되는, 상충되는

G11

□enormous ⓐ 막대한, 거대한
□immediate ⓐ 인접한
□surroundings ⓝ 환경
□dispersed ⓐ 분산된
□virtually ⓐⓓ 사실상, 거의
□odd ⓐ 이상한
□give off ~을 방출하다
□stationary ⓐ 움직이지 않는, 정지된
□nature ⓝ 천성, 본성
□broad ⓐ (폭이) 넓은, 일반[개괄]적인
□generate ⓥ 생성하다
□put ~ to use ~을 이용하다
□store ⓥ 저장하다
□portable ⓐ 휴대[이동]가 쉬운, 휴대용의
□fulfill ⓥ (약속 · 요구 등을) 이행하다[충족시키다]

G12

□obviously ⓐⓓ 분명히
□bond ⓝ 결합 관계
□perspective ⓝ 관점
□evolution ⓝ 진화
□chemistry ⓝ 화학
□by definition 본질적으로
□atomic bonding 원자 결합
□potential ⓝ 가능성
□come apart 분리되다
□retain ⓥ 보유하다
□afresh ⓐⓓ 새롭게

G13

□domain ⓝ 영역
□journalism ⓝ 저널리즘 (기사거리를 모으고 기사를 쓰는 일)
□by definition 당연히
□accessibility ⓝ 접근성
□extend ⓥ 연장하다
□shelf life 유통기한
□cite ⓥ 인용하다
□readiness ⓝ 준비
□engage ⓥ 참여하다
□underlying ⓐ 기저의
□apparent ⓐ 분명한
□emergent ⓐ 명백한, 뚜렷한
□manifest ⓐ 분명한
□short-lived ⓐ 수명이 짧은
□spectacle ⓝ 구경거리

G14

□ultimately ⓐⓓ 궁극적으로, 결국
□element ⓝ 요소, 성분
□inanimate ⓐ 무생물의
□coal ⓝ 석탄
□oxygen ⓝ 산소
□globe ⓝ 지구, 세계
□band together (무엇을 달성하기 위해) 함께 뭉치다
□greenhouse ⓝ 온실
□emission ⓝ 배출
□shrink ⓥ 줄어들다, 오그라들다
□availability ⓝ 이용할 수 있음, 가능성
□species ⓝ 종(種)
□extinct ⓐ 멸종된
□renowned ⓐ 유명한
□biologist ⓝ 생물학자
□present ⓥ 제시하다, 보여 주다

□face ⓥ 직면하다
□biodiversity ⓝ 생물 다양성
□automatically ⓐⓓ 자동적으로
□physical ⓐ 물리적인, 신체의

G15

□assumption ⓝ 가정, 가설
□prime mover 원동력
□evolution ⓝ 진화
□absence ⓝ 없음, 부재
□resist ⓥ 저항하다
□genetic ⓐ 유전의
□emergence ⓝ 출현
□evolve ⓥ 진화하다
□point out ~을 지적하다[가리키다]
□organ ⓝ (신체 내의) 장기[기관]
□adaptation ⓝ 적응
□immediate ⓐ 즉각적인
□vastly ⓐⓓ 대단히, 엄청나게
□response ⓝ 대응, 응답
□gradually ⓐⓓ 점진적으로, 서서히
□superior ⓐ 우월한

G16

□anthropologist ⓝ 인류학자
□region ⓝ 지역, 지방
□fascinate ⓥ 마음을 사로잡다
□inference ⓝ 추론(한 것)
□spill over into ~로 번지다
□ritual ⓝ 의식, 의례
□rhythmic ⓐ 리듬의, 주기적인
□altered ⓐ 바뀐
□consciousness ⓝ 의식, 자각
□shamanistic ⓐ 샤머니즘적인, 주술적인

G

□undergo ⓥ 겪다, 받다

□transformation ⓝ 변화, 탈바꿈

□identify ⓥ 알아보다, 확인하다

□observe ⓥ 관찰하다, 목격하다

□merge ⓥ 합치다, 합병하다

□humanlike ⓐ 인간 같은, 인간적인

□intention ⓝ 의도, 목적

□dawn ⓝ 새벽, (어떤 일의) 시작

G17

□primary ⓐ 주요한

□expectation ⓝ 기대

□composer ⓝ 작곡가

□identify ⓥ 밝혀내다

□a sequence of 일련의

□leap ⓝ 도약

□note ⓝ 음정

□typical ⓐ 전형적인

□stepwise ⓐ 단계적인

□tone ⓝ 음조

□scale ⓝ 음계

□theorist ⓝ 이론가

□tendency ⓝ 경향

□temporary ⓐ 일시적인

□harmonic ⓐ 화성의

□octave ⓝ 옥타브

□schematic ⓐ 도식적인

□violation ⓝ 위반

□soothe ⓥ 달래다

□tension ⓝ 긴장

G18

□initiate ⓥ 개시하다, 착수시키다

□individually ⓐⓓ 개별적으로

□adopt ⓥ 취하다, 채택하다

□flush from ~에서 쫓아내다

□block ⓥ 방해하다, 막다

□route ⓝ 길, 경로

□deadly ⓐ 치명적인, 죽음의

□interpretation ⓝ 해석

□collective ⓐ 집단적인

□appearance ⓝ 출현, 나타남

□specialized ⓐ 전문화된, 전문적인

□illusion ⓝ 환상, 착각

□collaboration ⓝ 협력, 합작

□emerge ⓥ 나오다, 생겨나다

□mentality ⓝ (개인·집단의) 사고방식

G19

□overtourism ⓝ 과잉 관광(지역 규모에 비해 너무 많은 관광객이 오는 현상)

□rest on ~에 기초하다

□assumption ⓝ 가정

□frame as ~로 규정하다

□bounded ⓐ 경계가 확실한

□boundary ⓝ 경계

□attraction ⓝ 관광 명소

□capacity ⓝ 수용력

□destination ⓝ 목적지

□victim ⓝ 피해자

□out of proportion 균형이 안 맞는

□degradation ⓝ (질적) 저하

□leakage ⓝ 유출

□dynamics ⓝ 역학

G20

□accurate ⓐ 정확한

□humble ⓥ 겸허하게 하다

□observe ⓥ 보다, 목격하다

□absolutely ⓐⓓ 완전히, 전적으로

□adjust ⓥ 조정하다

□satisfy ⓥ (필요·욕구 등을) 충족하다[채우다]

□curiously ⓐⓓ 호기심에서, 이상하게도, 기묘하게도

□attainable ⓐ 달성 가능한

□absolute ⓐ 완전한, 완벽한

□precision ⓝ 정확, 정밀

□inherently ⓐⓓ 본질적으로

□summit ⓝ 정상, 꼭대기

□integrate ⓥ 통합하다

□yet to-v 아직 ~하지 않은

□onward ⓐ 앞으로[계속 이어서] 나아가는

□integrate ⓥ 통합하다

G21

□neuropsychological ⓐ 신경심리학적인

□approach ⓝ 접근법, 처리 방법

□emphasize ⓥ 강조하다

□loss ⓝ 상실, 분실

□perception ⓝ 인식, 지각

□motivational ⓐ 동기의, 동기를 주는

□theory ⓝ 이론

□indicate ⓥ 나타내다, 보이다

□gain ⓝ 이득, 이점

□qualitative ⓐ 질적인

□considerable ⓐ 상당한

□body ⓝ 많은 양[모음]

□evidence ⓝ 증거

□prioritize ⓥ 우선순위를 매기다

□close ⓐ 친(밀)한, 가까운

□focus on ~에 주력하다

□achieve ⓥ 성취하다

□emotional ⓐ 감정의

□attend ⓥ 주의를 기울이다

□ignore ⓥ 무시하다

□goal ⓝ 목표

□implication ⓝ 영향, 결과, 암시

□process ⓥ 처리하다

□cue ⓝ 신호

□environment ⓝ 환경

□particular ⓐ 특별한

□presence ⓝ 존재(함)

□bias ⓝ 편향, 편견

□tendency ⓝ 경향, 성향

□notice ⓥ 의식하다, 주목하다

□compared to ~와 비교하여

□role ⓝ 역할

□aspect ⓝ 측면, 양상

G22

□remark ⓝ 주목

□satellite ⓝ 위성

□particularly ⓐⓓ 특히, 특별히

□average ⓐ 평균의, 일반적인, 보통의

□gravitational ⓐ 중력의

□illusion ⓝ 환영

□obstacle ⓝ 장애물

□technology ⓝ 기술

G23

□basis ⓝ 근거, 기반

□extremely ⓐⓓ 극도로, 극히

□sensitive ⓐ 세심한, 민감한

□detect ⓥ 감지하다

□perceive ⓥ 감지[인지]하다

□betray ⓥ 배신하다, 등지다

□exemplify ⓥ 전형적인 예가 되다

□perception ⓝ 인식

G24

□mend ⓥ 고치다, 수리하다

□restore ⓥ 복원하다, 복구하다

□creativity ⓝ 창의력, 독창성

□original ⓐ 원래의, 최초의

□preindustrial ⓐ 산업화 이전의, 산업 혁명 전의

□blacksmith ⓝ 대장장이

□immediate ⓐ (시간적·공간적으로) 아주 가까운, 직속[직계]의

□customize ⓥ 주문 제작하다

□modify ⓥ (더 알맞도록) 수정[변경]하다

□transform ⓥ (외양·모양을) 변형하다

□routine ⓐ 일상적인, 보통의

□extension ⓝ 연장(선)

□fabrication ⓝ 제작, 제조

□industrialization ⓝ 산업화

□mass ⓐ 대량의, 대규모의

□province ⓝ 영역, 분야

□tender ⓝ 관리자, 감시인

□grasp ⓝ (~에 대한) 이해[파악]

□comprehension ⓝ 이해

□intention ⓝ 의도, 계획

□manufacturer ⓝ (대규모의) 제조업자[회사]

□subdivision ⓝ 세분, 다시 나눔

□labour ⓝ (육체적인) 노동[작업]

□pistol ⓝ 권총, 회전 탄창이 없는 소형의 총

G25

□governance ⓝ 통치

□administration ⓝ 행정 (업무)

□administrative ⓐ 행정[관리]상의

□urban ⓐ 도시의

□institution ⓝ 기관, 단체

□evolve ⓥ 진화하다

□citizenry ⓝ 시민들

□taxation ⓝ 과세

□maintenance ⓝ 보수, 유지

□utility ⓝ (수도·전기·가스 등의) 공익사업

□frequently ⓐⓓ 자주

□displace ⓥ 대체하다

□involvement ⓝ 관여, 참여

□replacement ⓝ 대체, 교체

□responsibility ⓝ 책임

□substitute ⓝ 대체재[물]

□consequentially ⓐⓓ 결과적으로

□philosophical ⓐ 철학의

□associated ⓐ 관련된

□diminish ⓥ 줄어들다

□substitution ⓝ 대체, 대리

□duty ⓝ 의무

□implication ⓝ 영향, 결과

□responsive ⓐ 반응하는

□sound ⓐ 건전한

□contemporary ⓐ 현대의, 당대의

G26

□psychologist ⓝ 심리학자

□commit ⓥ 전념하다, (그릇된 일을) 저지르다

□enthusiast ⓝ 열렬한 지지자

□expressive ⓐ (생각·감정을) 나타내는

□score ⓝ 악보, 점수

□metric ⓐ 미터법의

□potential ⓐ 잠재적인, 가능성이 있는

G

□variation ⓝ 변화, 변형

□tempo ⓝ (음악의) 박자, 속도

□tonal ⓐ 음색의, 음조의

□composition ⓝ 구성 요소, (음악·미술) 작품

□diverge ⓥ 갈라지다, 나뉘다

□individually ⓐⓓ 개별적으로

□expressivity ⓝ 표현성, 표현의 풍부함

□worthwhile ⓐ 가치[보람] 있는

□repertoire ⓝ 연주[노래] 목록

□interpretation ⓝ 해석, 이해, 설명

□enrich ⓥ 풍요롭게 하다, 강화하다

□animate ⓥ 생기를 불어넣다

H 도표의 이해

H01
□renewable ⓐ 재생할 수 있는

□generation ⓝ (전기·열 등의) 발생

□capacity ⓝ 능력, 용량

□respective ⓐ 각각의

H02
□resident ⓝ 거주자, 주민

□patent ⓝ 특허(권)

□application ⓝ 신청(서)

□population ⓝ 인구

□origin ⓝ (사람의) 출신, 기원

□maintain ⓥ 유지하다

H03
□employ ⓥ 고용하다

□director ⓝ 감독

□writer ⓝ 작가

□editor ⓝ 편집자

□producer ⓝ 제작자

H04
□respondent ⓝ 응답자

□familiar with ~에 친숙한

□concept ⓝ 개념

□respectively ⓐⓓ 각각

H05
□awareness ⓝ 인식

□feature ⓥ 포함하다

□demonstrate ⓥ 입증하다

□predictive ⓐ 예측의

□classification ⓝ 분류

H06
□greenhouse gas 온실가스

□emission ⓝ 배출

□freshwater ⓝ 담수

H07
□conduct ⓥ 수행하다

□share ⓝ 지분, 비율

□respondent ⓝ 응답자

□respectively ⓐⓓ 각각

H08
□preferable ⓐ 선호되는

□respondent ⓝ 응답자

□sink ⓥ 가라앉다

H09
□population ⓝ 개체 수, 인구

□except for ~을 제외하고는

□decrease ⓥ 감소하다

□exceed ⓥ 초과하다

H10
□respondent ⓝ 응답자

□actively ⓐⓓ 적극적으로

□exceed ⓥ 넘다

H11
□destination ⓝ 행선지, 목적지

□overnight ⓐ 숙박의, 일박의

□arrival ⓝ 도착(한 사람[것])

□region ⓝ 지역, 지방

□additional ⓐ 추가의

□immediately ⓐⓓ 바로, 즉시

H12
□above ⓐ 위의, 앞서 말한

□based on ~에 근거하여

□survey ⓝ (설문) 조사

□conduct ⓥ (특정한 활동을) 하다

□previous ⓐ 이전의

□among prep ~ 중에

□consumption ⓝ 소비(량)

□format ⓝ (전반적인) 구성 방식, 형식

H13
□suburb ⓝ 교외, 근교

□exceed ⓥ 넘어서다

H14
□solar ⓐ 태양열을 이용한

□corresponding ⓐ 상응하는

□with regard to ~에 관해서

□exhibit ⓥ 보여주다

□regarding prep ~에 관해

□display ⓥ 나타내다

H15
□share ⓝ 점유율, 지분

□middle class 중산층

□region ⓝ 지역

□project ⓥ 예상하다, 추정하다

□ basis ⓝ 기반, 기초
□ capture ⓥ 포착하다
□ previously ⓐⓓ 이전에
□ establish ⓥ 설립하다

I05
□ public figure 공인, 유명 인사
□ mature ⓐ 어른스러운
□ drop out of ~을 중퇴하다
□ trick ⓝ 묘기, 마술
□ outstanding ⓐ 뛰어난
□ columnist ⓝ 정기 기고가, 칼럼니스트
□ wit ⓝ 재치
□ at the height of ~이 한창일 때에
□ install ⓥ 설치하다

I06
□ prehistorian ⓝ 선사학자
□ spark ⓥ 촉발시키다
□ archaeology ⓝ 고고학
□ serve as ~의 역할을 하다, 일하다

I07
□ complete ⓥ 끝내다, 완성하다
□ assistant ⓝ 조수
□ publish ⓥ 출판하다
□ conjointly ⓐⓓ 결합하여, 공동으로
□ dedicate oneself to ~ ~에 전념하다

I08
□ abandon ⓥ 그만두다
□ mechanic ⓝ 정비공
□ frequent ⓥ 자주 다니다
□ civil service (정부의) 공무원 [행정] 조직[업무]
□ recognition ⓝ 인정

□ humorous ⓐ 재미있는, 해학적인

I09
□ settle ⓥ 정착하다
□ behavioral ⓐ 행동에 관한
□ in turn 결국
□ drop out of ~에서 중퇴하다
□ obtain ⓥ 얻다
□ founder ⓝ 창시자, 설립자
□ complexity science 복잡계 과학

I10
□ film director ⓝ 영화 감독
□ outbreak ⓝ 발생
□ serve ⓥ 복무하다, 제공하다
□ army ⓝ 군대
□ wound ⓥ 상처를 입히다
□ enormously ⓐⓓ 엄청나게, 대단히
□ successful ⓐ 성공한, 출세한
□ award ⓥ 수여하다
□ throughout ⓟⓡⓔⓟ ~동안, 도처에
□ lifetime ⓝ 일생, 생애
□ achievement ⓝ 업적
□ influence ⓝ 영향력
□ endure ⓥ 오래가다, 지속되다

I11
□ former ⓐ 과거의, 이전의, 전자의
□ Czech ⓐ 체코의
□ athlete ⓝ (운동) 선수
□ consider A B A를 B로 여기다
□ long-distance ⓐ 장거리의
□ distinctive ⓐ 독특한, 특유의
□ factory ⓝ 공장

□ participate in ~에 참가하다
□ race ⓝ 달리기 (시합), 경주
□ win ⓥ (경기 등에서 이겨) 따다 [타다]
□ serious ⓐ 진지한, 심각한
□ devote ⓥ (노력 · 시간을) 바치다
□ break ⓥ (기록을) 깨다
□ record ⓝ 기록
□ noted for ~로 유명한
□ personality ⓝ 성격
□ athletic ⓐ 육상(경기)의

I12
□ encourage ⓥ 격려하다, 권장하다
□ assistant ⓝ 조수, 보조원
□ architecture ⓝ 건축 (양식)
□ renewal ⓝ 재개발
□ ambitious ⓐ 어마어마한, 야심 찬
□ architect ⓝ 건축

I13
□ construction ⓝ 건설
□ escape ⓥ 달아나다, 탈출하다
□ at one's height ~가 한창일 때
□ supply ⓥ 공급하다
□ troop ⓝ 군대
□ go out of business 파산하다
□ imprison ⓥ 감옥에 수감하다
□ debt ⓝ 빚, 부채
□ goods ⓝ 상품, 제품
□ officially ⓐⓓ 공식적으로
□ opening ceremony 개통식

I14

- □ risk-taker ⓝ 모험을 좋아하는 사람
- □ struggle ⓥ 어려움을 겪다
- □ learning disability 학습 장애
- □ resign ⓥ 그만두다
- □ expedition ⓝ 원정
- □ North Pole 북극
- □ sled ⓝ 썰매
- □ on foot 도보로
- □ Antarctica ⓝ 남극

I15

- □ virtuoso ⓝ 거장, 명장
- □ distinguished ⓐ 저명한, 성공한
- □ doctoral degree 박사 학위
- □ recital ⓝ 독주회
- □ landmark ⓝ 획기적인 것
- □ extensively ⓐⓓ 폭넓게

I16

- □ immigrant ⓝ 이민자, 이주민
- □ leading ⓐ 선두의, 가장 중요한
- □ comparison ⓝ 비교, 비유
- □ earn ⓥ (돈을) 벌다, (자격이 되어서) 얻다
- □ actively ⓐⓓ 활발하게, 적극적으로
- □ scholarly ⓐ 학자의, 전문적인
- □ cooperation ⓝ 협력, 협조
- □ theory ⓝ 학설, 이론

I17

- □ drop out 탈퇴하다, 중퇴하다
- □ pursue a career 경력을 추구하다
- □ leading role 주연
- □ reviewer ⓝ 평론가

- □ praise ⓥ 칭찬하다
- □ extraordinary ⓐ 놀라운, 비범한
- □ ethnicity ⓝ 인종
- □ prevent A from B A를 B로부터 막다
- □ cast ⓥ 배역을 맡기다
- □ frustrated ⓐ 좌절한
- □ talent ⓝ 인재
- □ prestige ⓝ 명성
- □ notable ⓐ 주목할 만한, 저명한
- □ advocate ⓥ 지지하다
- □ donate ⓥ 기부하다
- □ refugee ⓝ 난민
- □ currency ⓝ 화폐

I18

- □ physicist ⓝ 물리학자
- □ institute ⓝ 기관
- □ associate professor 부교수
- □ acceptance ⓝ 인정
- □ contribution ⓝ 공헌, 기여
- □ priceless ⓐ 대단히 귀중한
- □ unimaginable ⓐ 상상할 수 없는

I19

- □ renowned ⓐ 유명한
- □ sociologist ⓝ 사회학자
- □ theorist ⓝ 이론가
- □ translate ⓥ 번역[통역]하다

I20

- □ influential ⓐ 영향력 있는, 영향력이 큰
- □ economist ⓝ 경제학자, 경제 전문가
- □ economic ⓐ 경제의, 경제성이 있는

- □ brief ⓐ 짧은, 간단한
- □ introduction ⓝ 입문서, 도입, 소개
- □ economics ⓝ 경제학
- □ entitle ⓥ 제목을 붙이다
- □ classic ⓝ 고전, 명작
- □ microeconomic ⓐ 미시(微視) 경제학의
- □ philosopher ⓝ 철학자
- □ democracy ⓝ 민주주의
- □ ethics ⓝ 윤리학, 도덕
- □ retire ⓥ 은퇴[퇴직]하다
- □ active ⓐ 활동적인, 적극적인

I21

- □ heritage ⓝ 유산, 혈통
- □ architecture ⓝ 건축학
- □ found ⓥ 설립하다, 세우다
- □ firm ⓝ 회사
- □ figure ⓝ 인물
- □ pragmatism ⓝ 실용주의
- □ appreciation ⓝ 감탄, 공감
- □ standardize ⓥ 표준화하다
- □ uniform ⓐ 획일적인
- □ discrimination ⓝ 차별
- □ citizenship ⓝ 시민권
- □ prestigious ⓐ 명망 있는, 일류의
- □ fabric ⓝ 직물

I22

- □ leave one's mark on ~에 발자취를 남기다
- □ physiological ⓐ 생리적인
- □ degree ⓝ 학위
- □ intellect ⓝ 지적 능력, 지력
- □ will ⓝ 의지
- □ hardworking ⓐ 근면한, 부지런히 일하는
- □ scholar ⓝ 학자

□ academic position 교수직
□ oppose ⓥ 반대하다
□ mechanistic ⓐ 기계론적인
□ interpretation ⓝ 해석
□ poorly ⓐd 좋지 못하게, 저조하게

□ somewhat ⓐd 다소, 약간
□ department ⓝ 학과, 부서
□ celebrate ⓥ 찬양하다, 기리다
□ intellectual ⓐ 지능의, 지적인
□ achievement ⓝ 업적

J 실용문의 이해

J01
□ rare ⓐ 드문, 희귀한
□ spot ⓝ (특정한) 곳, 장소
□ vivid ⓐ 선명한, 생생한
□ limit ⓥ 제한[한정]하다
□ rooftop ⓝ (건물의) 옥상
□ observe ⓥ 관측하다, 관찰하다
□ notice ⓝ 안내문, 공지 사항
□ via ⓟrep ~을 통하여

J02
□ tuition ⓝ 수업, 교습, 수업료
□ fee ⓝ 요금, 수수료
□ full ⓐ 완전한, 모든
□ payment ⓝ 지불, 납입
□ refund ⓥ 환불하다
□ policy ⓝ 방침
□ contact ⓥ 연락하다

J03
□ additional ⓐ 추가적인
□ admission ⓝ 입장료

□ refundable ⓐ 환불할 수 있는
□ physical ⓐ 물리적인, 실물의

J04
□ annual ⓐ 연례의
□ sculpture ⓝ 조각
□ slide ⓝ 미끄럼틀
□ transportation ⓝ 교통

J05
□ fit ⓝ 알맞은 것, 적합한 것
□ annual ⓐ 연례의
□ prospective student 입학 희망 학생
□ admission ⓝ 입학
□ registration ⓝ 등록

J06
□ showcase ⓥ 뽐내다
□ capture ⓥ 포착하다
□ renewable ⓐ 재생 가능한
□ submission ⓝ 출품, 출품작
□ submit ⓥ 제출하다
□ selection committee 선정 위원회

J07
□ wildlife ⓝ 야생 동물
□ previous ⓐ 이전의
□ feed ⓥ 먹이를 주다
□ caretaker ⓝ 사육사, 돌보는 사람

J08
□ field trip 현장 학습
□ fine ⓐ 좋은, 질 높은
□ coastal ⓐ 해안의
□ feature ⓝ 특징, 특색
□ include ⓥ 포함하다
□ department ⓝ 부서

J09
□ track ⓥ 기록하다
□ log ⓥ (일지에) 기록하다
□ deadline ⓝ 마감일
□ submit ⓥ 제출하다
□ record ⓥ 기록하다
□ announce ⓥ 발표하다

J10
□ following ⓐ 다음에 나오는
□ ensure ⓥ 반드시 …하게[이게] 하다
□ available ⓐ 이용할 수 있는
□ parking lot 주차장

J11
□ enchanting ⓐ 매력적인, 황홀케 하는
□ accompany ⓥ 동행하다
□ guardian ⓝ 후견인
□ refund ⓝ 환불

J12
□ aisle ⓝ 통로
□ consist of ~로 구성되다
□ calculator ⓝ 계산기
□ sign up for 신청하다

J13
□ Scottish ⓐ 스코틀랜드의
□ soak up ~을 흡수하다
□ hold back 기다리다

J14
□ hands-on ⓐ 직접 해 보는
□ apron ⓝ 앞치마
□ guardian ⓝ 보호자
□ public transportation 대중교통 수단

J15
□ safe ⓝ 금고
□ insert ⓥ 넣다

J

□ suspect ⓝ 용의자
□ right ⓐ 적절한, 적당한

J26
□ encourage ⓥ 권장하다, 고무하다
□ reduce ⓥ 줄이다
□ participate ⓥ 참가하다, 참여하다
□ participant ⓝ 참가자
□ additional ⓐ 추가의

J27
□ eager ⓥ 열망하다
□ awaken ⓥ 깨우다
□ charity bazaar 자선 바자회

J28
□ renovation ⓝ 보수, 개조
□ minimize ⓥ 최소화하다
□ inconvenience ⓝ 불편(함)
□ sincerely ⓐⓓ 진심으로
□ appreciate ⓥ 고마워하다

J29
□ poetry ⓝ (집합적으로) 시
□ poet ⓝ 시인
□ introduction ⓝ 소개, 도입
□ poem ⓝ (한 편의) 시
□ aloud ⓐⓓ 큰 소리로
□ participant ⓝ 참가자, 참여자
□ receive ⓥ 받다, 받아들이다
□ expert ⓐ 전문가의, 전문적인
□ registration fee 등록비
□ inquiry ⓝ 문의
□ via ⓟⓡⓔⓟ ~을 통해, ~을 거쳐

J30
□ benefit ⓝ (모금을 위한) 자선 행사
□ charity ⓝ 자선
□ profit ⓝ (금전적) 이익, 수익

□ donate ⓥ 기부하다, 기증하다
□ local ⓐ 지역의, 현지의
□ performance ⓝ 공연, 연주
□ attraction ⓝ 흥미를 끄는 것 [장소], 매력
□ display ⓝ 전시, 진열
□ purchase ⓝ 구입, 구매

J31
□ appreciate ⓥ 감상하다
□ accompany ⓥ 동행하다
□ participant ⓝ 참가자
□ registration ⓝ 등록

J32
□ no later than 늦어도 ~까지 는
□ refund ⓝ 환불
□ feed ⓥ 먹이를 주다

J33
□ oyster ⓝ 굴
□ toddler ⓝ (아장아장 걷는) 유아
□ sign up for ~을 신청[가입] 하다
□ take place 개최되다, 일어나다
□ resident ⓝ 주민

J34
□ encourage ⓥ 격려하다, 북돋 우다
□ talent ⓝ 재능
□ monthly fee 월 수강료
□ include ⓥ 포함하다
□ discount ⓝ 할인
□ allow ⓥ 허락하다, 용납하다
□ mind ⓥ 언짢아하다, 신경쓰다

J35
□ geography ⓝ 지리
□ annual ⓐ 매년의, 연례의
□ submission ⓝ 제출

□ voting ⓝ 투표
□ exhibition ⓝ 전시

J36
□ explore ⓥ 탐색[탐험]하다, 탐구하다
□ register ⓥ 등록하다, 기록하다
□ via ⓟⓡⓔⓟ ~을 통해, (어떤 장소 를) 경유하여[거쳐]
□ payment ⓝ 지급, 지불
□ additional ⓐ 추가의
□ complete ⓥ 완료하다, 끝마치 다

J37
□ orchard ⓝ 과수원
□ unfortunately ⓐⓓ 불행하 게도
□ constraint ⓝ 제약
□ pre-registration ⓝ 사전 예약
□ accompany ⓥ 동반하다

J38
□ analyst ⓝ 분석가
□ author ⓝ 작가, 저자
□ lecture ⓝ 강의, 강연
□ participation ⓝ 참가, 참여
□ registration ⓝ 등록, 신고
□ application ⓝ 신청(서)
□ beverage ⓝ (물 외의) 음료
□ permit ⓥ 허용[허락]하다
□ participant ⓝ 참가자

J39
□ international ⓐ 국제적인
□ appreciate ⓥ 감상하다
□ admission price 입장료
□ exhibition ⓝ 전시회
□ souvenir ⓝ 기념품
□ inquiry ⓝ 질문, 문의

J40

- □ professional ⓐ 직업[직종]의, 전문적인
- □ tuition ⓝ 수업, 교습
- □ cover ⓥ 다루다, 포함하다
- □ equipment ⓝ 장비, 용품
- □ lighting ⓝ 조명 (시설)
- □ delay ⓥ 미루다, 연기하다

J41

- □ celebrate ⓥ 기념하다
- □ opening ⓝ 개장
- □ parking lot 주차장
- □ participation fee 참가비
- □ registration ⓝ 등록

J42

- □ show off ~을 자랑하다, 뽐내다
- □ talent ⓝ 재주, 재능
- □ submission ⓝ 제출
- □ format ⓝ 방식
- □ maximum ⓐ 최대[최고]의
- □ criterion ⓝ 기준
  (pl. criteria)

J43

- □ shoot ⓥ 촬영하다
- □ memorable ⓐ 기억할 만한
- □ theme ⓝ 주제
- □ submission ⓝ 출품(작)
- □ entry ⓝ 출품(작), 응모

K 빈칸 완성하기

K01

- □ prior to ~ 이전에
- □ lift ~ out of ~을 들어서 벗어나게 하다

- □ dwelling ⓝ 거주지
- □ transport ⓥ 이동시키다
- □ time-consuming ⓐ 시간이 많이 걸리는
- □ one-of-a-kind 단 하나뿐인 것
- □ multiplication ⓝ 증가, 증식
- □ take place 이루어지다
- □ periodical ⓝ 정기 간행물
- □ capitalism ⓝ 자본주의
- □ globe ⓝ 세계
- □ limitless ⓐ 무제한의
- □ circulation ⓝ 순환
- □ virtually ⓐⓓ 사실상
- □ democratise ⓥ 민주화하다
- □ spatiotemporal ⓐ 시공간적인

K02

- □ literature ⓝ 문학
- □ foster ⓥ 촉진하다, 강화하다
- □ concentrate on ~에 중점을 두다
- □ piecemeal ⓐ 단편적인
- □ superficial ⓐ 피상적인
- □ inhabit ⓥ ~에 깃들다, ~에 거주하다
- □ pinpoint ⓥ 정확히 찾아내다
- □ unfold ⓥ 전개되다
- □ insight ⓝ 통찰력
- □ sensibility ⓝ 감성[감수성]
- □ alternative ⓐ 대안적인
- □ involvement ⓝ 몰입

K03

- □ centralize ⓥ 중앙집권화하다
- □ constitute ⓥ 구성하다
- □ impose ⓥ 부과하다
- □ will ⓝ 유언장
- □ trust ⓝ 신탁금

- □ negotiable ⓐ 절충 가능한
- □ trustee ⓝ 신탁 관리자
- □ guardian ⓝ 후견인
- □ occupy ⓥ 차지하다
- □ reinforce ⓥ 강화하다

K04

- □ consensus ⓝ 합의
- □ sensory ⓐ 감각의
- □ overload ⓝ 과부하
- □ disorient ⓥ 방향을 잃게 하다
- □ send ~ into a holding pattern ~가 제자리를 맴돌게 하다
- □ hypothesis ⓝ 가설
- □ escape ⓥ 달아나다, 탈출하다
- □ perceive ⓥ 인식하다
- □ diffuse ⓐ 널리 퍼진, 분산된
- □ halo ⓝ 광륜(光輪), 후광
- □ portal ⓝ 입구, 정문
- □ reference point 기준점, 참조점
- □ porch ⓝ 현관
- □ trap ⓥ 가두다
- □ target ⓥ 겨냥하다
- □ reject ⓥ 거부하다

K05

- □ defect ⓝ 결함
- □ static ⓝ 잡음
- □ ignore ⓥ 무시하다
- □ endure ⓥ 참다, 견디다
- □ via (prep) 경유하여
- □ determine ⓥ 결정하다
- □ seasoned ⓐ 노련한
- □ instinctual ⓐ 본능적인
- □ forgive ⓥ 용서하다
- □ forgetful ⓐ 잘 잊는
- □ desirous ⓐ 바라는

K06
- sumptuary law 사치 금지법
- pass ⓥ (투표로 법안 등을) 통과시키다
- touch on ~에 관해 언급하다, 관여하다
- furnishing ⓝ 가구
- enforce ⓥ (법률 등을) 시행하다
- boundary ⓝ 경계
- encode ⓥ 부호화하다
- peasant ⓝ 소작농
- craftsman ⓝ 공예가
- signifier ⓝ 기표
- earthy ⓐ 흙의
- russet ⓝ 적갈색
- explicitly ⓐⓓ 명백하게
- confine ⓥ 국한시키다
- scarlet ⓝ 진홍색
- preserve ⓝ 전유물

K07
- be bound to 의무가 있다
- favorably ⓐⓓ 호의적으로
- regard ⓥ 여기다, 생각하다
- vendor ⓝ 판매자
- inquire ⓥ 문의하다
- acquire ⓥ 얻다
- satisfaction ⓝ 만족
- exceed ⓥ 넘다, 넘어서다
- retailer ⓝ 소매업자
- generate ⓥ 발생시키다, 만들어내다
- livestream selling 실시간 스트리밍 판매
- demonstrate ⓥ 보여주다, 입증하다
- immediately ⓐⓓ 즉시
- convenient ⓐ 편리한, 간편한

- rare ⓐ 드문, 희귀한
- examine ⓥ 조사하다
- convince ⓥ 설득하다
- must-have 꼭 필요한

K08
- point up ~을 강조하다
- vehicle ⓝ 매개체, 매개물
- strictly speaking 엄밀히 말해서
- framework ⓝ 틀
- convention ⓝ 관습
- mediation ⓝ 매개, 중개, 조정
- collectively ⓐⓓ 집합적으로
- have little bearing on ~과 거의 관계가 없다
- aesthetic ⓐ 미(학)적인
- face ⓝ 측면
- present ⓥ 제시하다, 나타내다
- quality ⓝ 특성, 특징
- correctly ⓐⓓ 올바르게
- perceive ⓥ 인지[인식]하다
- other than ~을 제외하고, ~과 다른
- might (very) well 아마 ~일 것이다
- distinct ⓐ 별개의

K09
- unconvinced ⓐ 확신하지 못하는
- depiction ⓝ 묘사, 서술
- prehistoric ⓐ 선사 시대의
- typically ⓐⓓ 일반적으로, 보통
- hind ⓐ 뒤의
- hook ⓥ 갈고리로 걸다
- airborne ⓐ 하늘에 떠 있는
- suspension ⓝ 공중에 떠 있기, (일시적) 정지

- adhere to ~을 고수하다
- intuition ⓝ 직감, 직관

K10
- constructive ⓐ 건설적인
- destructive ⓐ 파괴적인
- mental ⓐ 정신적인
- expand ⓥ 확장하다
- think back 회상하다
- prediction ⓝ 예측
- account for 설명하다
- embrace ⓥ 안다, 받아들이다
- belief ⓝ 믿음
- in other words 다시 말해
- build upon ~을 기반으로 하다
- maintain ⓥ 유지하다
- tie ⓝ 연결
- foster ⓥ 양육하다
- ever-evolving ⓐ 계속 진화하는

K11
- challenge ⓥ 이의를 제기하다
- conventional wisdom 사회적[일반적] 통념
- ground-reaction force 지면 반발력
- transmit ⓥ 전달하다
- impact ⓝ 부딪힘, 충돌, 충격
- extremely ⓐⓓ 극도로, 극히
- gradually ⓐⓓ 점진적으로, 서서히
- subconsciously ⓐⓓ 잠재의식적으로
- adjust ⓥ 조정하다
- stiffness ⓝ 경직도, 뻣뻣한 정도
- prior to ~에 앞서, 먼저
- strike ⓝ 치기, 때리기, 차기

□perception ⓝ 인식, 지각

□hardness ⓝ 경도(硬度), 단단함

□soak up ~을 흡수하다

□yielding ⓐ 물렁한, 유연한

□strikingly ⓐ𝖽 놀랄 만큼

□a wide range of 아주 다양한

□contrary to ~와 반대로

K12

□apparently ⓐ𝖽 겉으로 보기에

□screwdriver ⓝ 나사돌리개, 드라이버

□automatically ⓐ𝖽 자동적으로, 무의식적으로

□adjust ⓥ 조정하다

□literally ⓐ𝖽 말 그대로

□extend ⓥ (팔·다리 등을) 뻗다, 확장하다

□take ~ into account ~을 계산에 넣다

□comprehend ⓥ 이해하다

□instantly ⓐ𝖽 즉시, 즉각

□possessive ⓐ 소유욕이 강한

□pilot ⓥ 조종하다

□instantaneously ⓐ𝖽 순간적으로

□fist ⓝ 주먹

□hood ⓝ 모자, (자동차 등의) 덮개

□irritate ⓥ 짜증나게 하다

□personally ⓐ𝖽 인신공격적으로, (개인적인) 모욕감을 주도록

□reasonable ⓐ 합리적인

□nonetheless ⓐ𝖽 그렇기는 하지만, 그렇더라도

□utility ⓝ 유용, 효용

K13

□commonality ⓝ 공통점

□conceptual ⓐ 개념의

□decouple ⓥ 분리시키다

□object ⓝ 물체

□detach ⓥ 떼다

□invention ⓝ 발명, 창작

□personalized ⓐ 개인화된

□draftsmanship ⓝ 제도공의 기술

□install ⓥ 설치하다

□predetermined ⓐ 미리 정해진

□instruction ⓝ 지침

□state ⓥ 말하다

□dependence ⓝ 의존

□effectively ⓐ𝖽 효율적으로

□carry out 수행하다

□algorithm ⓝ 알고리즘

□automaton ⓝ 자동 장치

□agent ⓝ 행위자

□initiate ⓥ 시작하다

□artwork ⓝ 예술품

□trace ⓥ 추적하다

□spontaneity ⓝ 자발성

□authenticity ⓝ 진정성

K14

□transit card 교통 카드

□transportation ⓝ 교통, 운송

□well-intentioned ⓐ 선의의

□civic-minded ⓐ 시민 의식이 있는

□auditorium ⓝ 강당

□across the nation 전국의

□discussion ⓝ 토론

□intensely ⓐ𝖽 자극히, 몹시

□objection ⓝ 반대

□engineering ⓝ 공학

□be rooted in ~에 뿌리를 두다

□assumption ⓝ 추정, 가정

□bottom line 순익

K15

□experimenter ⓝ 실험자

□exclaim ⓥ 소리치다, 외치다

□supposedly ⓐ𝖽 아마, 추정하건대

□conclude ⓥ 결론을 내리다

□distraction ⓝ 주의를 딴 데로 돌리기

□relieve ⓥ 완화하다

□discomfort ⓝ 불편

□mismatch ⓝ 불일치

□peer ⓝ 동료

□escape ⓥ 벗어나다, 탈출하다

□self-awareness ⓝ 자기 인식

□constructive ⓐ 건설적인

□intense ⓐ 강렬한, 극심한

□self-reflection ⓝ 자기반성

K16

□universal ⓐ 보편적인, 일반적인

□avoid ⓥ (회)피하다, 모면하다

□object ⓝ 물건, 물체

□previously ⓐ𝖽 이전에, 사전에

□encounter ⓥ 마주치다, 맞닥뜨리다

□treat ⓥ 다루다, 대하다

□caution ⓝ 조심

□persist ⓥ 집요하게[끈질기게] 계속하다

□interfere ⓥ 방해하다, 간섭하다

K

□feed ⓥ 먹을 것을 먹다

□necessary ⓐ 필요한, 필연적인

□activity ⓝ 활동

□extent ⓝ 정도

□benefit ⓝ 이득, 혜택

□withdraw ⓥ (뒤로) 물러나다

□shell ⓝ 껍데기, 껍질

□puff ⓝ (훅 날아오는 작은 양의) 공기[연기]

□cast ⓥ (빛을) 발하다, (그림자를) 드리우다

□overcome ⓥ 극복하다

□habituate ⓥ 습관이 되다, 길들이다

□occur ⓥ 일어나다, 발생하다

□confront ⓥ 마주치다, 직면하게 만들다

□strange ⓐ 낯선, 이상한

□inexperienced ⓐ 경험이 부족한, 미숙한

□freeze ⓥ 얼다, 얼어붙다

□attempt ⓥ 시도하다

□hide ⓥ 숨다, 감추다

□sooner or later 조만간, 머지않아

□possibility ⓝ 가능성, 가능함

□exist ⓥ 존재하다, 있다

□pose ⓥ (위협 · 문제 등을) 제기하다

□immediate ⓐ 즉각적인, 당면한

□threat ⓝ 위협

□close ⓐ 철저한, 면밀한

□inspection ⓝ 검사

□worthwhile ⓐ ~할 가치가 있는

□weigh ⓥ 따져 보다, 저울질하다

□predict ⓥ 예측하다

□operate ⓥ 움직이다, 작동하다

□stimulus ⓝ 자극 ((pl. stimuli))

□surrounding ⓐ 주위의

K 17

□philosophy ⓝ 철학

□interaction ⓝ 상호 작용

□interrelation ⓝ 상호 관계

□priority ⓝ 우위

□distinguish ⓥ 구별하다

□in terms of ~의 면에서, ~에 관하여

□stress ⓥ 강조하다

□particularity ⓝ 특수성

□universality ⓝ 보편성

□highway ⓝ 고속도로

□differentiate ⓥ 구별하다

□with respect to ~에 관하여

□subtle ⓐ 미묘한

□fundamental ⓐ 근본적인, 필수적인

□substance ⓝ 물질, 실체

□emphasize ⓥ 강조하다

□subordinate ⓐ 종속된

□in contrast to ~와 반대로, 대조적으로

□deduce ⓥ 추론하다

K 18

□televised ⓐ 텔레비전으로 방송되는

□constitute ⓥ 구성하다, 이루다

□be subject to ~의 영향을 받다

□tension ⓝ (필요 · 이해의 차이로 인한) 긴장[갈등] 상태

□informational ⓐ 지식을 주는, 정보를 제공하는

□engage ⓥ 끌어들이다, 참여시키다

□entertainingly ⓐⓓ 재미있게

□current affairs (현재의 정치적 · 사회적 사건들인) 시사(時事)

□stick to ~을 고수하다[지키다]

□adopt ⓥ (특정한 방식이나 자세를) 채택하다[취하다]

□idiom ⓝ 어법, 표현 양식

□impact ⓝ 영향

□perspective ⓝ 관점, 시각

□contemporary ⓐ 현대의, 당대의

□construction ⓝ 구성

□rely ⓥ 의존하다, 믿다

□edit ⓥ 편집하다, 수정하다

□flashy ⓐ 현란한, 호화스러운

□enhance ⓥ 높이다, 증진하다

□unwilling ⓐ 꺼리는, 마지못해 하는

□endure ⓥ 견디다, 참다

□verbal ⓐ 언어의, 구두의

□orientation ⓝ 지향

□arguably ⓐⓓ 아마 틀림없이, 주장하건대

□structural ⓐ 구조적인, 구조상의

K 19

□examine ⓥ 조사[검토]하다

□consider ⓥ 고려하다, 여기다

□vastly ⓐⓓ 엄청나게

□aspect ⓝ 측면

□visibility ⓝ 가시성, 눈에 잘 보임

□identify ⓥ 확인하다, 알아보다

□tangible ⓐ 유형의, 만질 수 있는

□reconstruct ⓥ 재구성하다

□intangible ⓐ 무형의, 만질 수 없는

□draw ⓥ (결론·생각 등을) 도출하다

□inference ⓝ 추론

□relatively ⓐⓓ 상대적으로, 비교적

□diet ⓝ 식습관

□remains ⓝ 유물, 유적

□necessarily ⓐⓓ 어쩔 수 없이, 필연적으로

□interpretation ⓝ 해석

K20

□risk ⓝ 위험, 위험 요소

□regarding ⓟⓡⓔⓟ ~에 관하여 [대하여]

□wording ⓝ (글·연설에서, 특히 신중히 골라 쓴) 단어 선택

□offend ⓥ 불쾌하게 하다

□prejudice ⓥ 편견을 갖게 하다

□unfair ⓐ 부당한

□forbid ⓥ 금지하다

□split ⓥ 분리하다, 나누다

□composition ⓝ 작문, 작품, 작곡

□acknowledge ⓥ 인정하다

□crime ⓝ 끔찍한 일, 범죄

□position paper 의견서, 성명서

□convince ⓥ 납득시키다

□council ⓝ 의회

□security personnel 보안 요원

□compel ⓥ 강요[강제]하다

□accompany ⓥ 동반하다, 동행하다

□rare ⓐ 희귀한, 드문

□automatic ⓐ 자동의, 무의식적인

□recollection ⓝ 회상, 기억

□notion ⓝ 생각, 개념

□competence ⓝ 능력

□reveal ⓥ 드러내다, 밝히다

□distort ⓥ 왜곡하다

□comprehension ⓝ 이해력

□fierce ⓐ 격렬한, 맹렬한

K21

□significant ⓐ 중요한

□aid ⓥ 돕다

□internal ⓐ 내적인, 내부의

□subjective ⓐ 주관적인

□couple ⓥ 결합하다

□cognitive ⓐ 인지의

□extend ⓥ 확장하다

□external ⓐ 외부의, 외적인

□disciplinary ⓐ 규율의

□institutional ⓐ 제도적인, 제도상의

□attain ⓥ 얻다

□status ⓝ 지위, 중요도

□hard-nosed ⓐ 엄격한, 냉철한

□no-nonsense ⓐ 현실적인

□data-driven ⓐ 데이터 기반의

□procedure ⓝ 절차

□architectural ⓐ 건축학의

□allowable ⓐ 허용되는

□courtroom ⓝ 법정

□trial ⓝ 재판

□spatial ⓐ 공간의

□arrangement ⓝ 배치

□convention ⓝ 관습

□manipulate ⓥ 다루다, 조작하다

□advocate ⓝ 지지자, 옹호자

□comprise ⓥ ~으로 구성되다

K22

□reverse ⓝ 정반대

□liberation ⓝ 해방

□possession ⓝ 소유

□stimulus-driven ⓐ 자극 유발의

□heuristic ⓐ 체험적인

□instinct ⓝ 본능

□reliance ⓝ 의존

□intensify ⓥ 심화시키다

□burden ⓝ 부담, 짐

□inevitability ⓝ 필연성

K23

□profitable ⓐ 수익성이 있는

□conscious ⓐ 의식하는, 자각하는

□conventional wisdom 일반 통념

□mediate ⓥ 영향을 주다, 중재하다

□trap ⓥ 가두다, 붙잡다

□violate ⓥ 침해하다

□sponsor ⓥ 후원하다

K24

□investment ⓝ 투자

□equipment ⓝ 장비

□personnel ⓝ 인력, 직원

□return ⓝ 수익

□guarantee ⓝ 보장

□appropriate ⓐ 적합한

□majority ⓝ 대다수

□ownership ⓝ 소유권

□organisation ⓝ 조직

□modernisation ⓝ 현대화

□infrastructure ⓝ 기간 시설

K

□profitability ⓝ 수익성
□installation ⓝ 설치
□continent ⓝ 대륙
□oriented to ~을 우선하는
□in line with ~와 일치하다
□current ⓐ 현재의
□advanced ⓐ 진보된

K25

□extend ⓥ (~에) 이르다, 미치다
□companionship ⓝ 동료 관계
□involvement ⓝ 관여
□self-development ⓝ 자기계발
□self-sufficiency ⓝ 자족
□passionately ⓐⓓ 열렬하게
□yearn ⓥ 갈망하다, 동경하다
□uncertainty ⓝ 불확실성
□document ⓥ 기록하다
□extraordinary ⓐ 보기 드문, 뛰어난
□clarity ⓝ 명료함
□attachment ⓝ 유대, 애착
□existence ⓝ 존재
□relative ⓐ 상대적인
□collective ⓐ 집단적인
□entirely ⓐⓓ 아주, 완전히
□rubric ⓝ 항목
□sympathy ⓝ 공감, 동정
□philosophical ⓐ 철학적인
□self-reliant ⓐ 자립적인
□wholeheartedly ⓐⓓ 진정으로, 전적으로

K26

□preservation ⓝ 보존
□address ⓥ 다루다, 해결하다
□analog ⓐ 아날로그의

□medium ⓝ 매체, 수단 (복수형: media)
□bit stream 비트 스트림(비트 단위로 전송하는 데이터)
□regardless of ~와 관계없이
□device ⓝ 장치, 기기
□carrier ⓝ 운반 용기
□delicate ⓐ 취약한
□migrate ⓥ 옮기다, 이동하다

K27

□progress ⓝ 발전, 진전
□predominate ⓥ 지배적이다
□qualitatively ⓐⓓ 질적으로
□physics ⓝ 물리학
□revolutionize ⓥ 대변혁[혁신]을 일으키다
□photoelectric ⓐ 광전자를 이용한
□theory ⓝ 이론
□relativity ⓝ 상대성 이론, 상대성
□equation ⓝ 방정식
□scatter ⓥ (흩)뿌리다
□vary ⓥ 다르다
□vanish ⓥ 없어지다
□fade ⓥ 바래다, 희미해지다

K28

□insect-eating plant 식충식물
□stand out 눈에 띄다
□rigid ⓐ 뻣뻣한, 단단한
□horizontal ⓐ 수평의
□lure ⓥ 꾀다, 유혹하다
□unsuspecting ⓐ 의심하지 않는
□digestive juice 소화액
□cross section 횡단면, 단면도

□neutral ⓐ 중립의(위치에 있는)
□structural ⓐ 구조상의
□diving board 다이빙 도약대
□chaotic ⓐ 혼돈 상태의
□vibration ⓝ 진동
□exploit ⓥ 이용하다
□modify ⓥ 수정하다, 바꾸다

K29

□continually ⓐⓓ 지속적으로
□coordination ⓝ 협응, 협조
□handwriting ⓝ 필기
□mastery ⓝ 숙달, 통달
□eliminate ⓥ 제거하다
□logical ⓐ 타당한, 논리적인
□characteristic ⓝ 특징
□earlier ⓐ 초기의
□intense ⓐ 강렬한
□preoccupation ⓝ 집착
□whole ⓐ 전체의, 온전한
□give way to ~로 바뀌다
□correctness ⓝ 정확성
□conventional ⓐ 상투적인, 관습적인
□literal ⓐ 사실에 충실한, 글자 그대로의
□accompanying ⓐ 수반하는
□originality ⓝ 독창성
□characterize ⓥ 특징짓다
□firmly ⓐⓓ 단호히, 확고히
□grounded ⓐ 현실에 기반을 둔
□metaphor ⓝ 은유(법)
□by now 이제
□gaseous ⓐ 기체의
□mass ⓝ 덩어리
□float ⓥ 떠다니다

□in contrast with[to] ~와 대조를 이루어

□innocent ⓐ 순진한

□stem ⓝ 줄기

K30

□commonsense ⓐ 상식적인

□moral status 도덕적 지위

□conform ⓥ 따르다

□responsibility ⓝ 책임

□offend ⓥ 기분 상하게 하다, 불쾌하게 여겨지다

□determine ⓥ 결정하다

□sacrifice ⓝ 희생

□benefit ⓝ 이익

□recipient ⓝ 수혜자

□assert ⓥ 주장하다

□organ donor 장기 기증자

□mortal ⓐ 치명적인

□remarkably ⓐd 놀랍게도

□explicit ⓐ 명백한

□denial ⓝ 부인, 부정

□deserving ⓐ (도움 · 보답 · 칭찬 등을) 받을 만한[자격이 있는]

□assurance ⓝ 확신

□in one's shoes ~의 입장에서

□obligation ⓝ 의무

□humanity ⓝ 인류

□appreciation ⓝ 감탄, 찬사

□in return 대신에, 답례로

□inapplicable ⓐ 적용되지 않는, 사용할 수 없는

K31

□satisfy ⓥ 만족시키다

□desire ⓝ 욕구

□take charge of ~을 책임지다

□accomplish ⓥ 완수하다, 성취하다

□circumstance ⓝ 상황

□judgment ⓝ 판단

□spoil ⓥ 망치다

□mistreat ⓥ 학대하다

□equally ⓐd 마찬가지로

□pointless ⓐ 무의미한

□well-being ⓝ 안녕, (건강과) 행복

□alter ⓥ 바꾸다, 변경하다

□concern ⓥ 영향을 미치다

□argument ⓝ 논쟁

□react ⓥ 반응하다

□comprehend ⓥ 이해하다

□rationalize ⓥ 합리화하다

K32

□insightful ⓐ 통찰력 있는

□seek ⓥ 찾다, 추구하다

□emphasize ⓥ 강조하다

□strategic ⓐ 전략적인

□self-ignorance 자기 무지

□excuse ⓝ 핑계, 변명

□engage in ~에 참여[관여]하다

□excessively ⓐd 지나치게, 과도하게

□pleasurable ⓐ 즐거운

□harmful ⓐ 해로운

□present-biased 현재에 편향되어 있는

□avoid ⓥ 피하다, 모면하다

□guilt ⓝ 죄책감

□shame ⓝ 수치심, 창피

□trade-off 절충, 균형

□counsel ⓥ 조언[충고]하다, 상담하다

□agent ⓝ 행위자, (일정 권한을 가진) 대리인[점]

□risk ⓝ 위험

□benefit ⓝ 혜택

□prefer ⓥ 선호하다

□delay ⓥ 미루다

□receipt ⓝ 수령, 받기, 인수

□mad ⓐ 몹시 화가 난

K33

□emphasis ⓝ 강조

□value ⓥ 소중하게 생각하다

□orientation ⓝ 방향성

□reshape ⓥ 모양을 고치다, 재형성하다

□salary ⓝ 급료

□stimulating ⓐ 자극이 되는

□consumption ⓝ 소비

□progressively ⓐd 계속해서, 점진적으로

□determine ⓥ 결정하다

□sustenance ⓝ 자양물, 지속, 생존

□practical ⓐ 현실적인, 실용적인

□component ⓝ 구성요소

□nonmaterial ⓐ 비물질적인

□aspect ⓝ 측면

□exotic ⓐ 이국적인

□symbolize ⓥ 상징하다

□distinctive ⓐ 독특한

□postindustrial ⓐ 탈공업화의

□boycott ⓥ 구매를 거부하다

□violate ⓥ 위반하다

□ecological ⓐ 생태적인

□ethical ⓐ 윤리적인

K

K34

□newsworthy ⓐ 뉴스 가치가 있는, 뉴스거리가 되는

□define ⓥ 정의하다, 규정하다

□regardless of ~에 상관없이 [구애받지 않고]

□transmission ⓝ 방송, 전송, 전염

□struggle ⓥ 분투하다, 애쓰다

□ignore ⓥ 무시하다

□major ⓐ 주요한, 중대한

K35

□contribute ⓥ 제공하다, 기여하다

□labor ⓝ 노동력

□on a regular basis 정기적으로

□agricultural ⓐ 농업의

□harvest ⓥ 수확하다

□crisis ⓝ 위기 상황

□rebuild ⓥ 다시 세우다, 다시 조립하다

□barn ⓝ 헛간

□accounting ⓝ 회계

□regulate ⓥ 규제하다

□repair ⓥ 수리하다

□manual ⓐ 육체노동의, 수동의

□call on 요청하다

□legally ⓐd 법적으로

K36

□arguably ⓐd 거의 틀림없이

□dedicate ⓥ 바치다, 전념하다

□fraction ⓝ 부분, 분수

□elaborate ⓐ 정교한, 정성을 들인

□twig ⓝ 나뭇가지

□backdrop ⓝ 배경

□acrobatic ⓐ 곡예의

□imitation ⓝ 모방

□beehive ⓝ 벌집

□hummingbird ⓝ 벌새

□gauge ⓥ 측정하다

□cognitive ⓐ 인식의

□appreciate ⓥ 감상하다

□for one's own sake 자신을 위해

□straightforward ⓐ 간단한, 솔직한

□indicator ⓝ 지표

□reproduction ⓝ 번식

□aggressiveness ⓝ 공격성

K37

□innate ⓐ 내재된

□graze ⓥ 풀을 뜯다

□dependent on ~에 의존하는

□consume ⓥ 섭취하다

□mating ⓝ 짝짓기

□nest ⓥ 둥지를 틀다

□prey ⓝ 먹이

□tend to ~하는 경향이 있다

□governed ⓐ 지배되는

□instinct ⓝ 본능

□flexible ⓐ 유연한

□behavioral ⓐ 행동의

□neurobiologist ⓝ 신경 생물학자

□evolutionary ⓐ 진화의

□vary ⓥ 서로 다르다

□combination ⓝ 결합

□nervous system ⓝ 신경계

□adequate ⓐ 적합한

□infinite ⓐ 무한한

□requirement ⓝ 요건

K38

□temple ⓝ 신전, 사원

□function ⓥ 기능하다, 작용하다

□administrative ⓐ 관리 [행정]상의

□authority ⓝ 당국, 권한

□govern ⓥ 통치하다, 다스리다, 지배하다

□commodity ⓝ 상품, 물품

□redistribution ⓝ 재분배, 재배급

□discovery ⓝ 발견, 발견된 것 [사람]

□complex ⓝ (건물) 단지, (관련 있는 것들의) 덩어리[집합체]

□token ⓝ 표시, 징표

□consequently ⓐd 그 결과, 따라서

□evolve ⓥ (점진적으로) 발달[진전]하다

□centralize ⓥ 중앙 집권화하다

□governance ⓝ 지배, 관리

□domestic ⓐ 국내의, 가정(용)의

□literacy ⓝ 글을 읽고 쓸 줄 아는 능력

□identifiable ⓐ 인식 가능한, 알아볼 수 있는

□pictogram ⓝ 그림 문자

□consistent ⓐ 일치하는, 한결 같은

□mutually ⓐd 서로, 상호 간에

□literate ⓐ 글을 읽고 쓸 줄 아는

□party ⓝ 정당, 단체, (소송·계약 등의) 당사자

□abstract ⓐ 관념적인, 추상적인

□ensure ⓥ 반드시 ~하게 하다, 보장하다

□religious ⓐ 종교의
□communal ⓐ 공동의, 공용의

K39
□revolution ⓝ 혁명
□victorious ⓐ 승리한
□claim ⓥ 주장하다
□resolve ⓥ 해결하다
□fundamental ⓐ 근본적인
□prospect ⓝ 전망
□paradigm ⓝ 패러다임
□assumption ⓝ 가정
□point of view 관점
□standpoint ⓝ 관점
□impartially ⓐⓓ 공정하게
□genuine ⓐ 진정한
□progress ⓝ 진보
□neutral ⓐ 중립의
□assess ⓥ 평가하다
□cumulative ⓐ 누적되는
□exclude ⓥ 배제하다
□conclusively ⓐⓓ 결론적으로
□justification ⓝ 정당화
□inevitably ⓐⓓ 불가피하게

K40
□fuel ⓥ 기름을 끼얹다; 부추기다
□massive ⓐ 대규모의
□central city 중심 도시
□suburban area 교외 지역
□suburb ⓝ 교외
□dependent on ~에 의존하는
□automobile ⓝ 자동차
□signal ⓥ 신호를 주다, 알리다
□shift ⓝ 전환
□public transportation 대중 교통
□freeway ⓝ 초고속도로

□decline ⓝ 감소
□loss ⓝ 쇠퇴
□leisure ⓝ 여가

K41
□state ⓝ 상태
□becoming ⓝ ((철학)) 생성
□destination ⓝ 목적지
□mode ⓝ 방식
□mild ⓐ (정도가) 심하지 않은, 가벼운
□stem from ~에서 비롯되다
□notion ⓝ 개념
□progress ⓝ 진전, 진척
□subtle ⓐ 미묘한
□dramatic ⓐ 극적인
□generate ⓥ 발생시키다
□technological ⓐ 기술적인
□circular ⓐ 순환적인
□expansion ⓝ 팽창, 확장
□Enlightenment ⓝ ((the)) 계몽주의
□civilization ⓝ 문명
□star ⓥ 주연을 맡아 돋보이다
□accumulation ⓝ 축적
□conceal ⓥ 감추다, 숨기다

K42
□recognise ⓥ 인식하다, 알아보다
□interdependence ⓝ 상호 의존
□individual ⓝ 개인
□integration ⓝ 통합
□internalise ⓥ (사상·태도 등을) 내면화하다
□contradictory ⓐ 모순되는
□logical ⓐ 논리적인, 타당한
□implication ⓝ 영향, 결과, 함축

□consequence ⓝ 결과
□discovery ⓝ 발견
□reasoning ⓝ 추론, 추리
□inherent ⓐ 내재하는
□integral ⓐ 내장된, 일부로서 포함되어 있는, 필수적인
□conceptual ⓐ 개념의
□premise ⓝ 전제
□prime number 소수(素數)
□cumulative ⓐ 누적되는
□ripe ⓐ 익은, 숙성한
□outgrowth ⓝ 결과물, 파생물
□abstract ⓐ 추상적인
□basis ⓝ 근거, 기반
□universalism ⓝ 보편성

K43
□typically ⓐⓓ 일반적으로
□attach ⓥ 첨부하다
□relevant ⓐ 관련 있는
□underlying ⓐ 기본적인
□machinery ⓝ 시스템
□straightforward ⓐ 간단한
□classification ⓝ 분류
□object ⓝ 개체
□detection ⓝ 감지
□method ⓝ 방법
□output ⓝ 출력
□capture ⓥ 포착하다

K44
□eyes-on-the-prize ⓐ 자기 목표에 몰두하는
□mentality ⓝ 사고방식
□over-confident ⓐ 과신하는
□self-disciplined ⓐ 자기 훈련이 되는
□optimistically ⓐⓓ 낙관적으로

□per-visit fee 방문 당 이용료

□trim ⓥ 줄이다

□in a single sitting 앉은 자리에서

□give in to ~에 굴복하다

□temptation ⓝ 유혹

□remarkable ⓐ 놀라운

□manage to ~하기 위해 애쓰다

□rosy ⓐ 장밋빛의

□optimism ⓝ 낙관주의

K45

□ecological ⓐ 생태계의

□surface ⓝ 표면, 수면

□foundation ⓝ 토대, 기초

□disrupt ⓥ 방해하다, 지장을 주다

□raw ⓐ 날것의, 가공되지 않은

□quantity ⓝ 양, 수량

□contaminant ⓝ 오염 물질

□drag out ~을 끄집어내다

□compound ⓝ 화합물, 혼합물

□mine ⓥ 채굴하다, 캐다

□lead ⓝ ((화학)) 납

□petroleum ⓝ 석유

□substance ⓝ 물질, 본질

□bowel ⓝ 창자, 가장 깊은 곳

□introduce ⓥ (처음으로) 들여오다, 시작하다

□ecology ⓝ 생태계, 생태학

□matter ⓝ 물질, 성분

□carbon ⓝ 탄소

□toxic ⓐ 유독성의

K46

□dynamo ⓝ ((pl.)) 발전기

□slang ⓝ 속어, 은어

□outgrowth ⓝ 결과물

□expose ⓥ 노출하다, 접하게 하다

□spread ⓥ 퍼지다, 퍼뜨리다

□outward ⓐd 외부로

□transmissible ⓐ 전염성의

□noted ⓐ 저명한, 잘 알려진

□linguist ⓝ 언어학자

□composite ⓐ 합성의, 복합의

□drive ⓥ 추진하다, 몰아붙이다

□far-reaching ⓐ 멀리까지 미치는

K47

□remote ⓐ 먼

□wide-angled ⓐ 폭넓은

□philosophical ⓐ 철학적인

□immediate ⓐ 직접적인

□notably ⓐd 특히

□rush around 서두르다

□blow out of proportion 과장하다

□contribute to ~의 원인이 되다

□anxiety ⓝ 불안

□ancestral ⓐ 선조의

□perspective ⓝ 시야

□calm ⓥ 진정시키다

□disquieted ⓐ 불안한

□when it comes to ~에 관한 한

□trivial ⓐ 사소한

□appreciate ⓥ 이해하다

□unfortunate ⓐ 불운한

□turn out 판명되다

□keep one's head 평정심을 유지하다

□lose one's head 평정심을 잃다

K48

□at once 동시에

□treat ⓥ (특정한 태도로) 대하다

□ground A in B A의 기초를 B에 두다

□uniformity ⓝ 획일성

□interplay ⓝ 상호 작용

□build A into B A를 B에 포함시키다

□concept ⓝ 개념

□equation ⓝ 동일시

□immune ⓐ (질병이나 공격 등을) 면한

□distortion ⓝ 왜곡

□content ⓝ 내용

□take ~ into account ~을 고려하다

□the latter 후자

□relevant ⓐ 관련이 있는

□identical ⓐ 동일한, 똑같은

□differential ⓐ 차이를 나타내는

□in respect of ~에 관해서

□rejection ⓝ 거부

□legitimate ⓐ 합법적인, 합당한

□abandon ⓥ 버리다, 포기하다

K49

□territory ⓝ 영역, 영토

□partition ⓥ 분할하다, 나누다

□insight ⓝ 통찰력, 이해

□arrangement ⓝ 배치, 배열

□assign ⓥ (일·책임 등을) 맡기다, (가치·기능 등을) 부여하다

□separate ⓐ 분리된, 관련 없는

□specialization ⓝ 특수[전문]화

□ cabin ⓝ 오두막집, 객실

□ weave ⓥ (옷감을) 짜다[엮다]

□ neat ⓐ 정돈된, 깔끔한

□ functional ⓐ 기능적인, 가동되는

□ varying ⓐ 가지각색의, 바뀌는

□ extent ⓝ 정도, 규모

□ wallow ⓥ (물·진흙 등의 속에서) 뒹굴다

□ set aside 따로 떼어 두다

K50

□ on offer 제공되는, 이용할[살] 수 있는

□ identity ⓝ 정체성, 신원

□ idealize ⓥ 이상화하다

□ nostalgia ⓝ 향수(鄕愁)

□ context ⓝ 맥락, 문맥

□ attachment ⓝ 애착, 믿음

□ socialize ⓥ (사람들과) 어울리다, 사회화하다

□ affection ⓝ 애착, 보살핌

□ attendance ⓝ 출석, 참석

□ argument ⓝ 논쟁, 주장

□ differentiation ⓝ 차별, 구별

□ afford ⓥ 제공하다

K51

□ literature ⓝ (특정 분야의) 문헌, 문학

□ formalist ⓝ 형식주의자, 이론주의자

□ autonomy ⓝ 자율성, 자주성

□ biography ⓝ 전기(傳記)

□ literary ⓐ 문학적인, 문학의

□ assumption ⓝ 가정, 추정

□ self-contained ⓐ 자족적인, 자립하는

□ entity ⓝ 독립체

□ correspondence ⓝ 관련성, 서신, 편지

□ relevant ⓐ 관련 있는, 적절한

□ contain ⓥ 포함하다, 함유하다

K52

□ hinge ⓝ (문·뚜껑 등의) 경첩

□ countless ⓐ 무수한, 셀 수 없이 많은

□ overall ⓐ 전반적인

□ structure ⓝ 구조, 구성 ⓥ 구조화하다, 조직하다

□ random ⓐ 임의의, 무작위의

□ determine ⓥ 결정하다

□ gene ⓝ 유전자

□ complicated ⓐ 복잡한

K53

□ mark ⓥ 표시하다

□ quarter-hour ⓝ 15분(간)

□ acquire ⓥ 얻다, 습득하다

□ hand ⓝ (시계) 바늘

□ unprecedented ⓐ 전례 없는

□ measure ⓥ 측정하다, 재다

□ precisely ⓐ 정확하게

□ find expression in ~의 모습으로 나타나다

□ prime ⓐ 주된, 중요한

□ argue ⓥ 주장하다, 논증하다

□ clock in 출근 시간을 기록하다

□ timesheet ⓝ 출퇴근 시간 기록 용지

□ slice ⓥ 얇게 베다[썰다]

□ pace ⓝ 속도

□ reject ⓥ 거절[거부]하다

□ swiftly ⓐ 신속히, 빨리

□ fire ⓥ 해고하다

□ cruel ⓐ 잔혹한, 잔인한

□ feed ⓥ (필요·욕구 등을) 충족시키다

□ brilliantly ⓐ 훌륭하게

□ depict ⓥ 묘사하다

□ contain ⓥ 포함하다

□ deadly ⓐ 치명적인

□ statistical ⓐ 통계의, 통계(학)상의

K54

□ argue ⓥ 주장하다, 다투다

□ content ⓐ (가진 것에) 만족하는

□ existence ⓝ 실재, 존재

□ lack ⓝ 부족, 결핍

□ psychic ⓐ 마음의, 초자연적인

□ tension ⓝ 긴장 (상태)

□ minimal ⓐ 최소의, 아주 적은

□ awaken ⓥ (감정을) 불러일으키다, 깨우다

□ drive ⓝ 욕구, 추진력 ⓥ (특정한 행동을 하도록) 만들다

□ alter ⓥ 바꾸다, 변하다

□ possess ⓥ 지니다, 소유하다

□ motive ⓝ 동기, 이유

□ consume ⓥ (연료·에너지·시간을) 소모하다

□ propose ⓥ 제안하다

□ passive ⓐ 수동적인

□ accidental ⓐ 우연한, 돌발적인

□ merely ⓐ 단지, 그저

□ seek ⓥ 추구하다, 찾다

□ active ⓐ 적극적인

□ shaper ⓝ 만드는 사람

□ generate ⓥ 만들어 내다, 발생하다

□ thereby ⓐ 그렇게 함으로써

□ basis ⓝ 기반, 이유

K55

□ rationale ⓝ 근본적 이유, 논리적 근거

□ assess ⓥ 평가하다, 가늠하다

□ survivability ⓝ 생존 가능성

□ risky ⓐ 위험한

□ deadly ⓐ 생명을 앗아가는, 치명적인

□ associate ⓥ 연상하다, 결부[연관] 짓다

□ exact ⓐ 정확한, 정밀한

□ short ⓐ 부족한, ~이 없는

□ live on ~을 먹고 살다

□ solely ⓐ 오로지, 단독으로

□ diverse ⓐ 다양한

□ means ⓝ 수단, 방법

□ suitable ⓐ 적합한, 적절한

□ tie ⓝ 유대 (관계), 결속

K56

□ futuristic ⓐ 미래의

□ composer ⓝ 작곡가

□ shy away from ~을 피하다

□ piece ⓝ 작품, 곡

□ possess ⓥ 가지다, 보유하다

□ structure ⓝ 구조

□ interfere with ~을 저해[방해]하다

□ recognizable ⓐ 알아볼 수 있는

□ galaxy ⓝ 은하계

□ familiarity ⓝ 친숙함

□ acceptable ⓐ 받아들일 수 있는

K57

□ psychological ⓐ 심리학의

□ subject ⓝ 피실험자

□ identify ⓥ 확인하다, 파악하다

□ state of mind 마음 상태

□ invariably ⓐ 언제나, 변함없이

□ theorist ⓝ 이론가

□ illustrate ⓥ 분명히 보여주다, 그려넣다

□ call upon to-v ~하도록 요청하다

□ striking ⓐ 놀라운

□ determinate ⓐ 확정적인

□ at stake 관건이 되는

□ encounter ⓥ 마주치다

□ isolated ⓐ 고립된, 괴리된

K58

□ consciousness ⓝ 의식

□ oddly ⓐ 이상하게

□ framework ⓝ 틀, 골조

□ structure ⓥ 구조화하다

□ conventional ⓐ 전통적인

□ manner ⓝ 방식

□ division ⓝ 구분

□ desperately ⓐ 심하게, 극도로

□ mislead ⓥ (사실을) 오도[호도]하다

□ extent ⓝ 범위

□ smooth ⓥ 매끄럽게[반반하게] 하다

□ divorce ⓥ 단절시키다, 분리하다

□ partition ⓥ 나누다, 분할하다

□ arise ⓥ 생겨나다

K59

□ critical ⓐ 중요한, 중대한

□ bring about ~을 불러일으키다[유발하다]

□ stable ⓐ 안정적인

□ institutional ⓐ 제도적인

□ point out ~을 지적하다

□ resource ⓝ 자원

□ monitor ⓥ 감시하다, 관리하다

□ significant ⓐ 중요한, 의미 있는

□ insight ⓝ 통찰(력), 안식(眼識)

□ prospect ⓝ (성공할) 전망

□ centrally ⓐ 중심에, 중앙에

□ state power 공권력, 국가 권력

□ in comparison with ~에 비해서

□ assume ⓥ (권력·책임을) 지다[맡다]

□ responsibility ⓝ 책임, 책무

□ emphasize ⓥ 강조하다

□ democratic ⓐ 민주적인

□ conflict ⓝ 갈등, 충돌

□ institution ⓝ (대학·은행 등과 같은) 기관[단체], 협회

□ devise ⓥ (계획·방법 등을) 고안하다

□ ensure ⓥ 보장하다, 반드시 ~하게[이게] 하다

□ observance ⓝ 준수, 엄수

K60

□ fanciful ⓐ 별난, 기발한

□ illustrate ⓥ 분명히 보여주다, 실증하다

□ melodic ⓐ 운율의

□ a handful of 소수의, 한 줌의

□ composer ⓝ 작곡가

□ brilliant ⓐ 훌륭한, 눈부신

□ symphony ⓝ 교향곡

□ exceptional ⓐ 특출한, 예외적인

□ mileage ⓝ (특정 상황에서 얻을 수 있는) 이득, 사용(량)

□ tap ⓥ (가볍게) 톡톡 두드리다

□ movement ⓝ (큰 음악 작품의) 한 부분, 움직임

□ motto ⓝ 좌우명, ((음악)) 주제구

□ thread ⓝ 실, (이야기의) 맥락

□ brushwork ⓝ (화가의) 화법[붓놀림]

□ cohesive ⓐ 화합[결합]하는

□ statement ⓝ 표현, 서술

□ mighty ⓐ 웅장한, 힘센

□ stem ⓥ 유래하다, 생기다

□ inventiveness ⓝ 독창적임

K61

□ manufacturer ⓝ 제조재[사]

□ innovation ⓝ 혁신, 쇄신

□ vast ⓐ (범위·크기 등이) 방대한

□ majority ⓝ (특정 집단 내에서) 다수

□ commercialize ⓥ 상업화하다

□ accordingly ⓐⓓ 그런 이유로, 그에 맞춰

□ department ⓝ (조직의) 부서

□ explore ⓥ 탐험하다, 탐구하다

□ suitable ⓐ 적합한, 적절한

□ address ⓥ (어려운 문제 등을) 다루다, 처리하다

□ and so forth ~ 등등

□ prototype ⓝ 원형, 시제품

□ encounter ⓥ 맞닥뜨리다

□ reject ⓥ 거부[거절]하다

□ outlier ⓝ 영외 거주자, 분리물

□ firm ⓝ 회사

□ unsystematic ⓐ 비체계적인

□ route ⓝ 길, 노선

K62

□ colony ⓝ 군집, 집단

□ hive ⓝ 벌집

□ illustrative ⓐ 예증이 되는, 분명히 보여주는

□ regulate ⓥ 규제[조절]하다

□ unload ⓥ 넘겨주다

□ workforce ⓝ 노동력

□ respective ⓐ 각각의

K63

□ client ⓝ 의뢰인, 고객

□ primary ⓐ 주된, 기본적인, 초기의

□ tailor ⓝ 재단사

□ craftsman ⓝ (수)공예가, 장인(匠人)

□ talented ⓐ (타고난) 재능이 있는

□ suggestion ⓝ 제안, 암시

□ rise ⓝ 성공, 출세

□ elevate ⓥ (정도를) 높이다, (들어)올리다

□ climate ⓝ 기후, 분위기

□ admiration ⓝ 감탄, 존경

□ flourish ⓥ 번창하다

K64

□ crucial ⓐ 중요한

□ optional ⓐ 선택의

□ extent ⓝ 정도

□ pedestrian ⓝ 보행자

□ indication ⓝ 지표, 표시

□ insufficient ⓐ 부족한, 불충분한

□ transit ⓝ 운송

□ function ⓝ 기능

□ conversely ⓐⓓ 반대로

□ conspicuous ⓐ 눈에 띄는

□ inviting ⓐ 매력적인, 유혹적인

□ temptation ⓝ 유혹

□ quarter ⓝ 구역, 지구

□ complex ⓝ (건물) 단지

□ occupy ⓥ 차지하다

□ public transportation 대중 교통

□ administrative ⓐ 행정의

□ concentrate ⓥ 집중하다, 모으다

K65

□ commonly ⓐⓓ 흔히

□ novel ⓐ 참신한

□ original ⓐ 독창적인

□ appropriate ⓐ 적절한

□ feasible ⓐ 실현 가능한

□ irrelevant ⓐ 무의미한

□ unremarkable ⓐ 특별한 것이 없는, 평범한

□ ignore ⓥ 간과하다

□ innovate ⓥ 혁신하다

□ evaluate ⓥ 평가하다

□ abandon ⓥ 포기하다, 버리다

□ essentially ⓐⓓ 본질적으로, 근본적으로

□ subsequently ⓐⓓ 나중에

□ practical ⓐ 실용적인, 현실적인

□ frequently ⓐⓓ 자주

□ give way to ~에 굴히다

□ tension ⓝ 긴장 상태

K66

□ behavior ⓝ 행동

□ elegant ⓐ 우아한

□ influence ⓥ 영향을 미치다

□ analogy ⓝ 비유, 유사점

□ illustrate ⓥ 설명하다

□ adequately ⓐⓓ 적절히

□ intricate ⓐ 복잡한
□ architecture ⓝ 구조, 건축
□ assemble ⓥ 조립하다
□ reactive ⓐ 반응을 하는
□ inject ⓥ 주입하다
□ accelerate ⓥ 가속화하다
□ malfunction ⓥ 제대로 작동하지 않다
□ periodically ⓐⓓ 주기적으로

K67
□ imitatively ⓐⓓ 모방하여
□ symbol ⓝ 상징
□ awkward ⓐ 어색한
□ interpretation ⓝ 해석
□ illuminate ⓥ 밝히다
□ mean ⓝ 수단
□ complex ⓐ 복잡한
□ sequence ⓝ 순서[차례]
□ intentional ⓐ 의도적인
□ accidental ⓐ 우연한, 뜻하지 않은
□ reproduce ⓥ 재현하다
□ unprecedented ⓐ 전례 없는
□ coincide ⓥ 일치하다

K68
□ strategy ⓝ 전략
□ advancement ⓝ 발전
□ monument ⓝ 기념비
□ utility ⓝ 유용성
□ prove ⓥ 입증하다
□ extent ⓝ 정도[규모]
□ bother ⓥ 신경 쓰다, 애를 쓰다
□ investigate ⓥ 조사하다
□ validity ⓝ 유효함, 타당성
□ falsification ⓝ 반증
□ hypothesis ⓝ 가설

□ expert ⓝ 전문가
□ mark ⓥ 나타내다
□ crucial ⓐ 중대한, 결정적인
□ collapse ⓥ 붕괴하다
□ temporal ⓐ 시간의

K69
□ motivation ⓝ 동기
□ accidental ⓐ 우연한, 돌발적인
□ label ⓥ 이름을 붙이다
□ consciously ⓐⓓ 의식적으로
□ isolate ⓥ 고립시키다, 격리하다
□ deny ⓥ 부정하다
□ silence ⓥ 침묵을 지키다

K70
□ operate ⓥ 운영하다
□ linear ⓐ 일직선의
□ perspective ⓝ 시각
□ minimize ⓥ 최소화하다
□ maximize ⓥ 극대화하다
□ eliminate ⓥ 지우다
□ prolong ⓥ 연장하다
□ ownership ⓝ 소유권
□ profit ⓝ 이익, 수익
□ frequently ⓐⓓ 자주

K71
□ offspring ⓝ 자식
□ identify ⓥ 식별하다, 구분하다
□ seedling ⓝ 묘목
□ delicate ⓐ 연약한
□ curb ⓥ 억제하다
□ expand ⓥ 확장하다
□ trunk ⓝ (나무의) 몸통
□ exhausted ⓐ 기진맥진한
□ considerably ⓐⓓ 상당히
□ instructive ⓐ 교육적인, 유익한

K72
□ psychology ⓝ 심리학
□ external ⓐ 외부의
□ separate ⓐ 분리된
□ realm ⓝ 영역
□ in the mood for ~가 마음에 내켜서
□ bin ⓝ (흔히 뚜껑이 달린 저장용) 통

K73
□ biological ⓐ 생물학적인
□ bioluminescence ⓝ 생물 발광
□ sweep ⓥ 쓸다
□ victim ⓝ 피해자
□ threat ⓝ 위협
□ rod-like ⓐ 막대 형태의
□ fierce ⓐ 사나운
□ jaw ⓝ 턱
□ predator ⓝ 포식자
□ a bellyful of 배에 가득한
□ bomber aircraft 폭격기
□ spotlight ⓝ 환한 조명
□ conceal ⓥ 숨기다
□ silhouette ⓝ 외형[윤곽], 실루엣
□ subtle ⓐ 미묘한
□ illumination ⓝ 빛, 발광

K74
□ span ⓥ 걸치다
□ restrict ⓥ 제한하다
□ traffic light 신호등
□ import ⓥ 수입하다
□ install ⓥ 설치하다
□ traditionally ⓐⓓ 전통적으로
□ out of the ordinary 특이한, 색다른
□ dominant ⓐ 주된

□ awkward ⓐ 어색한, 불편한
□ assertive ⓐ 단호한
□ opt ⓥ 택하다
□ henceforth ⓐ ~ 이후로
□ correspond ⓥ 부합하다
□ ban ⓥ 금하다

K75
□ growth ⓝ 성장
□ academic ⓐ 학업의, 학과의
□ discipline ⓝ 지식[학문] 분야, 학과
□ sub- pref 「아래」, 「하위」
□ particular ⓐ 특정한
□ figure ⓝ 인물, 사람
□ critic ⓝ 평론가
□ principle ⓝ 원칙, 원리
□ practice ⓝ 관행, 관례
□ select ⓥ 선발[선택]하다
□ organize ⓥ 정리하다, 체계화하다
□ worthy ⓐ (~을 받을) 자격이 있는, 받을 만한
□ remain ⓥ 계속 ~이다
□ struggle ⓝ 힘든 일, 투쟁
□ moreover ⓐ 게다가
□ draw apart (~으로부터) 떨어져[사라져] 가다
□ further ⓐ 더 멀리에[로]
□ toward prep 무렵, ~쯤
□ object ⓝ 물건, 대상
□ valued ⓐ 귀중한, 평가된
□ route ⓝ 길, 경로
□ decline ⓝ 감소
□ status ⓝ 지위, 신분
□ intellectual ⓐ 지적인
□ pursuit ⓝ 추구, (시간과 에너지를 들여서 하는) 일[활동]

□ aspect ⓝ 측면
□ increasingly ⓐ 점점 더
□ invisible ⓐ 보이지 않는
□ naked ⓐ 아무것도 걸치지 않은, 벌거벗은
□ classification ⓝ 분류
□ promise ⓥ ~의 조짐을 보이다
□ cutting-edge ⓐ 최첨단의
□ knowledge ⓝ 지식
□ mere ⓐ ~에 불과한
□ indicate ⓥ 나타내다

K76
□ feature ⓝ 특색, 특징
□ strip of ~을 빼앗다
□ subjectivity ⓝ 주관성
□ aspect ⓝ 측면
□ quantify ⓥ 양을 나타내다, 수량화하다
□ observer ⓝ 관찰자
□ artistry ⓝ 예술가적 기교
□ envision ⓥ 마음속에 그리다
□ seek ⓥ 추구하다
□ participate ⓥ 참여하다
□ maintain ⓥ 유지하다
□ harmonize ⓥ 조화를 이루다
□ disengage ⓥ 분리하다, 풀다

K77
□ tradition ⓝ 전통
□ distinction ⓝ 구별
□ perception ⓝ 지각
□ sensual ⓐ 감각의
□ supremacy ⓝ 패권, 우위
□ assertion ⓝ 주장
□ inherent ⓐ 내재하는, 본질적으로
□ unreliable ⓐ 믿을 수 없는
□ illusion ⓝ 오해, 환상
□ figure ⓝ 형체

□ application ⓝ 적용
□ perspective ⓝ 관점
□ conclude ⓥ 결론을 내리다
□ representation ⓝ 묘사, 나타낸 것

K78
□ disengagement ⓝ 이탈, 자유, 해방
□ be concerned with ~에 관심을 두다
□ fictional ⓐ 허구적인
□ considerable ⓐ 상당한, 많은
□ exaggerate ⓥ 과장하다, 지나치게 강조하다
□ silliness ⓝ 어리석음, 우둔한 짓
□ make up ~을 꾸며내다[지어내다]
□ grant ⓥ 부여하다, 허락하다
□ licence ⓝ (창작상의) 파격, 허용
□ poetic ⓐ 시적인
□ correct ⓥ (남의 실수를) 바로잡다[지적하다]
□ spill ⓥ 쏟다, 흘리다
□ interrupt ⓥ 방해하다, 중단하다

K79
□ genetic engineering 유전 공학
□ cloning ⓝ 복제
□ distribute ⓥ 퍼뜨리다
□ identical ⓐ 똑같은
□ threat ⓝ 위협
□ diversity ⓝ 다양성
□ habitat ⓝ 서식지
□ artificial ⓐ 인위적인, 인공적인

K

□ millennium ⓝ 천년
(pl. millennia)

□ mass ⓐ 대량의, 대규모의

□ biodiversity ⓝ 생물의
다양성

□ convert ⓥ 전환하다

□ transgenic ⓐ 이식 유전자에
의한

□ alteration ⓝ 변형

□ conversely ⓐⓓ 정반대로,
역으로

□ renewed ⓐ 재개된, 새로워진

□ property ⓝ 특성

□ harbor ⓥ (계획 · 생각 등을)
품다

□ obesity ⓝ 비만

K80

□ newly ⓐⓓ 최근에, 새로

□ access ⓝ 입장, 접근

□ specific ⓐ 특정한, 구체적인

□ fingerprint ⓝ 지문

□ neuroscience ⓝ 신경 과학

□ throughout ⓟⓡⓔⓟ 도처에,
~ 동안 내내

□ previously ⓐⓓ 미리, 사전에

□ assume ⓥ 추정하다, 가정하
다

□ in response to ~에 응하여
[답하여]

□ immediate ⓐ 즉각적인,
당면한

□ distant ⓐ 먼, 떨어져 있는

□ establish ⓥ 설립하다, 확립
하다

□ refine ⓥ 정제하다, 개선하다

□ neural ⓐ 신경의

□ result in ~을 낳다[야기하다]

□ impulse ⓝ 자극, 충격

□ efficiently ⓐⓓ 효율적으로,
유효하게

□ stabilize ⓥ 안정시키다

□ strengthen ⓥ 강화하다,
더 튼튼하게 하다

□ relatively ⓐⓓ 비교적, 상대적
으로

□ weaken ⓥ 약화시키다

□ eventually ⓐⓓ 결국

□ sculpt ⓥ 조각하다, 형상[형태]
을 만들다

□ initial ⓐ 처음의, 초기의

□ gear ⓥ 적응시키다, 맞게 조정
하다

□ twin ⓥ 결부시키다, 밀접하게
연결시키다

□ organ ⓝ (인체 내의) 장기

□ portray ⓥ 그리다, 묘사하다

K81

□ ahead of ~보다 앞선

□ worthless ⓐ 가치가 없는

□ ideally ⓐⓓ 이상적으로

□ open up ~을 가능하게 하다

□ futuristic ⓐ 미래지향적인

□ unconventional ⓐ 관습에
얽매이지 않는

□ visionary ⓐ 비현실적인

□ initially ⓐⓓ 처음에는

□ critical ⓐ 중요한

□ catch up 따라잡다

□ genetic ⓐ 유전의

□ insight ⓝ 통찰력

□ early adopter 얼리 어답터
(신제품을 먼저 사서 써 보는 사람)

□ urgent ⓐ 긴급한

□ independently ⓐⓓ 독립적
으로

K82

□ foreground ⓥ 특히 중시하다

□ textuality ⓝ 텍스트성

□ interrelated ⓐ 상호 연관된

□ representational ⓐ 표현
의, 나타내는

□ predominate ⓥ 두드러지다,
지배적이다

□ illustration ⓝ 삽화

□ complement ⓥ 보완하다

□ enhance ⓥ 높이다, 향상하다

K83

□ criticism ⓝ 비판

□ repetition ⓝ 반복

□ dismiss ⓥ 무시하다

□ borrowing ⓝ 차용

□ overlap ⓝ 중복

□ philosopher ⓝ 철학자

□ authorship ⓝ 원저자

□ matter ⓥ 문제가 되다

□ feel free to 마음대로 ~하다

□ adjustment ⓝ 수정

□ improvement ⓝ 개선

□ adapt ⓥ 적용하다

□ put ... into practice ~을
실행에 옮기다

K84

□ perceive ⓥ 인식하다

□ perception ⓝ 인식

□ apply ⓥ 적용하다

□ countless ⓐ 수많은

□ fullness ⓥ 풍부함

□ in turn 결국

□ subtle ⓐ 미묘한

□ perfumer ⓝ 조향사

□ at one's disposal 마음대로

□ differentiate ⓥ 구별하다

□variation ⓝ 차이
□regardless of ~에 관계없이
□linguistic ⓐ 언어적인

K85

□figure ⓝ 형상, 인물
□motif ⓝ 모티프, 주제
□stare at ~을 응시하다
□patch ⓝ (특히 주변과는 다른 조그만) 부분
□constant ⓐ 끊임없는, 거듭되는
□integrate ⓥ 통합되다
□solid ⓐ 확실한, 단단한
□thereby ⓐⓓ 그렇게 함으로써
□engage in ~에 참여하다
□hypothesis ⓝ 가설
□in the way of (의문문이나 부정문에서) ~라고 할 만한 것이
□desperately ⓐⓓ 절망적으로, 필사적으로
□confirmation ⓝ 확인
□crack ⓝ (무엇이 갈라져 생긴) 금
□profile ⓝ 옆모습, 옆얼굴
□leap ⓥ 뛰다, 뛰어오르다[넘다]
□strategy ⓝ 전략
□distract ⓥ (정신이) 집중이 안 되게[산만하게] 하다
□project ⓥ (빛·영상 등을) 비추다[투영하다]
□strengthen ⓥ 강화하다

K86

□integration ⓝ 통합
□facilitator ⓝ 일을 용이하게 하는 것[사람], 촉진자
□vary ⓥ 서로[각기] 다르다
□twist ⓝ 돌리기, 비틀기

□variation ⓝ 변화, 변형
□familiarity ⓝ 익숙함, 친근함
□certainly ⓐⓓ 틀림없이, 분명히
□emerging ⓐ 신흥의, 떠오르는
□introduce ⓥ (모르던 것을) 소개하다[접하게 하다]
□fascination ⓝ 매력, 매혹
□frustration ⓝ 불만, 좌절감
□outdated ⓐ 구식인
□involuntarily ⓐⓓ 모르는 사이에, 본의 아니게
□misuse ⓝ 남용, 오용
□persist ⓥ 계속[지속]되다

K87

□contemporary ⓐ 현대의, 동시대의
□employ ⓥ (기술·방법 등을) 쓰다[이용하다]
□practice ⓝ (의사·변호사 등 전문직 종사자의) 업무
□reference ⓝ 언급, 참조
□abstractionist ⓝ 추상파 화가
□critic ⓝ 비평가, 평론가
□admire ⓥ 칭찬하다, 감탄하다
□marked ⓐ 뚜렷한
□contrast ⓝ 차이, 대조
□label ⓥ 꼬리표를 붙이다, (~라고) 분류하다
□disapprovingly ⓐⓓ 못마땅하여, 비난하여
□appropriately ⓐⓓ 적당하게, 알맞게
□integrate ⓥ 통합하다
□portable ⓐ 휴대가 쉬운, 휴대용의
□surpass ⓥ 능가하다, 뛰어넘다

□resemble ⓥ 닮다, 비슷하다
□bulky ⓐ 부피가 큰

K88

□concept ⓝ 개념
□cultural ⓐ 문화와 관련된
□statement ⓝ 진술
□strike A as B A에게 B라는 인상을 주다
□insight ⓝ 통찰력
□landscape ⓝ 풍경
□blend ⓝ 혼합(물)
□distinction ⓝ 차이, 구분
□settler ⓝ 정착민
□descendant ⓝ 후손, 자손
□fond ⓐ 허황된, 좋아하는
□uncontrolled ⓐ 통제되지 않은
□association ⓝ 연관(성), 협회
□expression ⓝ 표현, 표정
□admiration ⓝ 감탄, 존경
□wilderness ⓝ 황야, 황무지
□ecological ⓐ 생태계[학]의
□certainly ⓐⓓ 분명히, 틀림없이
□logic ⓝ 논리
□self-regulating ⓐ 자체적으로 규제하는
□not necessarily 반드시 ~은 아닌
□stable ⓐ 안정된
□dynamic ⓝ 역동성
□independent of ~와는 관계없이
□intervention ⓝ 개입, 중재, 조정
□context ⓝ 맥락, 전후 사정
□interaction ⓝ 상호 작용
□determine ⓥ 결정하다, 알아내다
□regulate ⓥ 규제[통제]하다

K89

□ investigate ⓥ 조사[연구]하다

□ response ⓝ 반응, 대답

□ despite (prep) ~에도 불구하고

□ complex ⓐ 복잡한

□ repertoire ⓝ (할 수 있는) 모든 것[목록]

□ discriminate ⓥ 식별하다, 차별하다

□ recording ⓝ 녹음(된 것)

□ overlap ⓥ 겹치게 하다, 포개지다

□ playback ⓝ 재생(된 내용)

□ suggest ⓥ 말하다, (뜻을) 비치다

□ aggressive ⓐ 공격적인

□ versus (prep) ~에 비해

□ occur ⓥ 발생하다, 일어나다

□ loudspeaker ⓝ 확성기

□ boundary ⓝ 경계(선)

□ separate ⓥ 분리하다, 나누다

□ subject ⓝ 연구[실험] 대상

□ treat ⓥ 대하다, 취급하다

□ demonstrate ⓥ 입증하다

□ highly (ad) 매우

K90

□ discipline ⓝ 지식 분야, 학과목

□ autobiographical ⓐ 자서전적인

□ literary ⓐ 문학의, 문학적인

□ wilderness ⓝ 황야, 버려진 땅

□ regularity ⓝ 규칙적임, 정기적임

□ impose ⓥ 도입하다, 부과하다

□ untamed ⓐ 길들지 않은

□ depth ⓝ 깊이

□ orderly ⓐ 정돈된, 질서 있는

□ essential ⓐ 필수적인, 본질적인

□ imaginative ⓐ 창의적인, 상상력이 풍부한

□ scholar ⓝ 학자, 장학생

□ somewhat (ad) 어느 정도, 다소

□ venture ⓥ (위험을 무릅쓰고) 가다

K91

□ paradoxical ⓐ 역설적인

□ description ⓝ 설명, 서술

□ commentary ⓝ 해설, 논평

□ account ⓝ 말, 설명

□ eagerly (ad) 열렬히, 열심히

□ consult ⓥ 찾아보다

□ cover ⓥ 다루다, 취재하다

□ contemporary ⓐ 동시대의

□ discipline ⓝ 분야, 부문

□ standing ⓝ 지위

□ correspond ⓥ 상응하다

□ readership ⓝ (특정 신문 등의) 독자 수[층]

□ pay packet 급여 봉투

□ dismissal ⓝ 묵살, 일축

□ reluctance ⓝ 꺼림, 내키지 않음

□ admire ⓥ 존경하다, 선망하다

□ censor ⓥ 검열하다

K92

□ precision ⓝ 정확성

□ determinacy ⓝ 확정성, 결정된 상태

□ necessary requirement 필요조건

□ meaningful ⓐ 의미 있는, 중요한

□ progress ⓝ 발전, 진보

□ to a large extent 상당 부분

□ ongoing ⓐ 진행 중인

□ achieve ⓥ 달성하다, 성취하다

□ representation ⓝ 진술, 설명, 묘사

□ refinement ⓝ 정제, 정련

□ varied ⓐ 다양한

□ insight ⓝ 통찰(력), 안식(眼識)

□ continuous ⓐ 계속되는, 지속적인

□ narrow down 좁히다, 줄이다

□ approximation ⓝ 근접, 근사

□ explosion ⓝ 폭발적인 증가

□ unmask ⓥ 정체를 밝히다, 가면을 벗기다

□ illusion ⓝ 환상, 착각

□ alternative ⓐ 대안적인, 대체의

□ analysis ⓝ 분석, 해석

□ regard ⓥ 여기다, 평가하다

□ confusion ⓝ 혼란, 혼동

K93

□ perception ⓝ 인식, 지각

□ arise ⓥ 생기다, 일어나다

□ confine ⓥ 국한하다

□ be devoted to ~에 할애되다

□ enrich ⓥ 풍부하게 하다

□ meter ⓝ 박자

□ key ⓝ (장·단조의) 조성

□ relatively (ad) 비교적, 상대적으로

□ consistent ⓐ 일관성이 있는

□ typical ⓐ 전형적인

□uniformity ⓝ 일치, 통일성
□occasional ⓐ 이따금의
□tonality ⓝ 조성
□emerge ⓥ 드러나다
□narrow ⓥ 좁히다
□fundamental ⓐ 근본적인
□diversity ⓝ 다양성

L 흐름에 맞지 않는 문장 찾기

L01

□conflict ⓝ 갈등
□flee ⓥ 달아나다
□initially ⓐⓓ 처음에
□sufficient ⓐ 충분한
□straight away 즉시, 지체 없이
□optimal ⓐ 최고[최적]의
□considerable ⓐ 상당한, 많은
□obtain ⓥ 얻다, 구하다
□territory ⓝ 영토, 지역
□at stake 위태로운, 성패가 달려 있는
□circumstance ⓝ 환경, 상황
□constant ⓐ 끊임없는, 변함 없는
□interval ⓝ 간격, 사이
□opponent ⓝ 상대, 반대자
□maximize ⓥ 극대화하다, 최대한 활용하다
□assessment ⓝ 평가
□vital ⓐ 필수적인
□likely ⓐ 예상되는, 그럴듯한
□outcome ⓝ 결과

L02

□kinship ⓝ 친족
□tie ⓝ ((pl.)) 유대 관계
□modern ⓐ 현대의
□frequently ⓐⓓ 자주
□get-together (비격식적인) 모임
□relative ⓝ 친척
□regularly ⓐⓓ 자주, 규칙적으로
□refer to ~을 언급[표현]하다
□behaviour ⓝ 행동
□modified ⓐ 수정된
□extend ⓥ 확대하다
□structure ⓝ 구조
□multigenerational ⓐ 다세대의
□maintain ⓥ 유지하다
□rest on ~에 기초하다
□co-residence 공동 거주
□corporate ⓐ 공동의
□close ⓐⓓ 가까이
□require ⓥ 필요로 하다
□geographical ⓐ 지리(학)적인
□separate ⓥ 분리하다
□considerable ⓐ 상당한, 많은
□distance ⓝ 거리
□decision ⓝ 결정
□in contrast ~와 대조적으로
□traditional ⓐ 전통적인
□away from ~에서 떠나서
□seek ⓥ 찾다, 추구하다
□opportunity ⓝ 기회
□occupational ⓐ 직업의
□advancement ⓝ 발전

L03

□expansion ⓝ 확장
□revolutionize ⓥ 혁신을 일으키다
□significance ⓝ 중요성
□considerable ⓐ 상당한
□apart from ~외에도
□flexibility ⓝ 유연성, 신축성
□equipment ⓝ 장비
□reasonably ⓐⓓ 합리적으로
□invaluable ⓐ 매우 유용한, 귀중한

L04

□stock ⓝ 재고
□specific ⓐ 특정한
□collection ⓝ 소장품
□devote ⓥ (~에) 바치다, 기울이다
□full-time ⓐ 전업의, 전시간(근무, 노동)의
□inevitably ⓐⓓ 필연적으로
□as a matter of course 당연히
□enquire ⓥ 문의하다
□availability ⓝ 구매 가능 여부, 이용 가능성
□crucially ⓐⓓ 중요하게
□routinely ⓐⓓ 정례적으로, 일상적으로
□occasionally ⓐⓓ 가끔
□purchase ⓝ 구매
□circulate ⓥ 배포하다, 돌리다
□multiply ⓥ 배가하다, 늘리다
□expand ⓥ 확장하다

L05

□memorize ⓥ 암기하다
□overlap ⓥ 겹치다

□storage ⓝ 저장, 보관
□reproduce ⓥ 재현하다
□uneven ⓐ 고르지 않은
□pitch ⓝ 음정
□irregular ⓐ 불규칙적인
□tempo ⓝ 박자
□note ⓝ 음, 음표
□fine-tune ⓐ 미세 조정을 하다
□accurate ⓐ 정확한
□template ⓝ 본보기
□emerge ⓥ 드러나다, 판명되다
□deafen ⓥ 귀를 먹게 만들다

L06
□achieve ⓥ 성취하다, 달성하다
□policy ⓝ 정책
□warn ⓥ 경고하다
□exceed ⓥ 넘다
□adaptation ⓝ 적응
□relevant ⓐ 관련 있는
□measure ⓝ 조치
□innovative ⓐ 혁신적인

L07
□obligation ⓝ 의무
□distinctive ⓐ 독특한
□authentic ⓐ 진짜의
□fulfill ⓥ 충족하다, 이행하다
□personalization ⓝ 개인화
□refined ⓐ 정제된
□construction ⓝ 구조
□essential ⓐ 필수적인
□consent ⓝ 합의, 동의
□individuality ⓝ 특성, 개성
□reflexive ⓐ 성찰적인

L08
□human race 인류
□trace back to …의 기원
[유래]이 …까지 거슬러 올라가다

□roughly ⓐⓓ 대략
□wipe out 몰살하다, ~을 완전히
파괴하다
□ruler ⓝ 통치자
□conqueror ⓝ 정복자
□expressively ⓐⓓ 표현적으로
□symbolize ⓥ 상징하다
□thrive ⓥ 번성하다

L09
□collaborate ⓥ 협력하다
□encounter ⓥ 마주치다
□variance ⓝ 차이, 불일치
□interfere ⓥ 방해하다
□intentionality ⓝ 의도성
□address ⓥ (문제·상황 등에
대해) 고심하다[다루다]
□translingual ⓐ 초언어적인
□barrier ⓝ 장벽
□avenue ⓝ 수단; 큰 길
□exposure ⓝ 노출
□normalize ⓥ 표준화하다,
정상화하다
□examine ⓥ 조사하다
□constantly ⓐⓓ 끊임없이
□considered ⓐ 중히 여겨지는,
깊이 생각한
□community ⓝ 주민, 공동체

L10
□principle ⓝ 원리
□proof ⓝ 증거
□determine ⓥ 알아내다, 결정
하다
□appropriate ⓐ 적합한
□examine ⓥ 조사[검토]하다
□comparison ⓝ 비교
□validate ⓥ 확인하다
□consequently ⓐⓓ 그 결과,
결과적으로

□peer ⓝ 동료, 또래
□critical ⓐ 중요한
□compliance ⓝ 순응
□employ ⓥ 이용하다
□oriented ⓐ ~을 지향하는
□behavioral ⓐ 행동의, 행동에
관한
□weight ⓝ 비중을 더하다
□subsequent ⓐ 그[이] 다음의,
차후의
□evidence ⓝ 증거, 증언
□in this regard 이와 관련하여
□promote ⓥ 홍보하다
□persuasive ⓐ 설득력이 있는
□collectivistic ⓐ 집단주의의
□individualistic ⓐ 개인주의
의

L11
□theoretical ⓐ 이론적인
□perspective ⓝ 관점
□insight ⓝ 통찰
□immigration ⓝ 이주, 이민
□assume ⓥ 추정[상정]하다
□utility ⓝ 효용
□maximization ⓝ 극대화
□represent ⓥ 제시하다
□rational ⓐ 합리적인
□migration ⓝ (사람·동물의
대규모) 이주, 이동
□assessment ⓝ 평가
□versus ⓟⓡⓔⓟ ~ 대(對)
□monetary ⓐ 금전(상)의
□show off ~을 과시하다
□status ⓝ 지위
□luxurious ⓐ 사치스러운
□expense ⓝ 비용
□uncertainty ⓝ 불확실성

□adapt ⓥ 적응하다
□associated ⓐ 관련된
□separation ⓝ 헤어짐
□take ~ into account ~을 고려하다

L12

□introduction ⓝ 도입, 전래
□substantially ⓐⓓ 상당히, 많이
□conduct ⓥ (업무 등을) 수행하다[처리하다]
□cooperation ⓝ 협력, 협동
□firm ⓝ 기업, 회사
□involve ⓥ 수반하다
□integration ⓝ 통합
□multiple ⓐ 다수의, 다양한
□resulting ⓐ 결과로 초래된[나타난]
□cover ⓥ 포함하다
□ensure ⓥ 보장하다, 확실하게 하다
□sustainable ⓐ (오랫동안) 지속[유지] 가능한
□entire ⓐ 전체의, 온
□surround ⓥ 둘러싸다, 에워싸다
□fundamentally ⓐⓓ 근본적으로, 완전히
□profitable ⓐ 수익성이 있는, 이득이 되는
□cut off ~을 잘라내다
□cooperate ⓥ 협력하다, 협조하다
□existence ⓝ 존재

L13

□branch ⓝ 분파, 분점
□examine ⓥ 조사하다, 검토하다

□structure ⓝ 구조
□assumption ⓝ 가정
□precisely ⓐⓓ 정확히
□ambiguous ⓐ 애매모호한
□signify ⓥ 의미하다, 중요하다
□correspondence ⓝ 상응, 관련성
□signifier ⓝ 기표
□signified ⓝ 기의
□vary ⓥ 각기 다르다
□deconstruct ⓥ 해체하다
□underlying ⓐ 근본적인, 기저에 있는
□inconsistency ⓝ 불일치성, 모순되는 부분
□perceive ⓥ 인식하다
□alternative ⓐ 대안적인, 대체의
□overlay ⓥ 덮어씌우다, 더하다
□reference ⓝ 외연, 언급
□distinguish ⓥ 구별하다

L14

□grain ⓝ 곡물
□perishable ⓐ 잘 상하는
□deteriorate ⓥ 악화되다
□spoil ⓥ 상하다, 못쓰게 만들다
□surplus ⓐ 잉여의, 과잉의
□crop ⓝ 농작물
□harvest ⓝ 수확, 추수
□preserve ⓥ 보존하다, 지키다
□restrict ⓥ 제한하다, 통제하다
□microbe ⓝ 미생물
□toxin ⓝ 독소
□inactivate ⓥ 비활성화하다
□static ⓐ 고정된, 정지 상태의
□in regard to ~에 대한
□airtight ⓐ 밀폐된

L15

□obvious ⓐ 분명한
□written ⓐ 쓰여진
□variable ⓐ 가변적인
□mention ⓥ 언급하다
□prominent ⓐ 중요한, 눈에 띄는
□locality ⓝ 지역
□in question 연구 중인
□personality ⓝ 성격, 인물
□significant ⓐ 중요한
□occur ⓥ 발생하다
□twist ⓝ 비틀기
□extremely ⓐⓓ 극도로
□district ⓝ 지역
□priority ⓝ 우선 순위
□preferably ⓐⓓ 되도록

L16

□highly ⓐⓓ 크게, 대단히
□setting ⓝ 환경, 장소
□commercialized ⓐ 상업화된
□commodity ⓝ 상품, 일용품
□value ⓥ 소중하게[가치 있게] 여기다
□potential ⓝ 가능성, 잠재력
□resident ⓝ 거주자, 주민
□identity ⓝ 정체성
□generate ⓥ 창출하다, 만들어 내다
□conversion ⓝ 전환, 변환
□element ⓝ 요소, 성분
□take on (성질·기운 등을) 띠다
□wilderness ⓝ 황무지
□typically ⓐⓓ 보통, 일반적으로
□mountainous ⓐ 산이 많은, 산악의

□region ⓝ 지방, 지역
□evolve ⓥ 발전하다, 진화하다
□a sort of 일종의
□perceive ⓥ 인식하다
□associated with ~와 관련된

L17
□accord ⓥ 부합하게 하다
□a great deal of 많은
□on one's own 스스로
□intensely ⓐⓓ 심하게
□relative to ~에 비하여
□punishment ⓝ 처벌
□bond ⓝ 유대감
□sort ⓝ 분류
□independence ⓝ 독립성
□competition ⓝ 경쟁
□parental ⓐ 부모의
□nuclear family 핵가족
□extended family 대가족
□on balance 모든 것을 감안하여
□relatively ⓐⓓ 상대적으로
□intimate ⓐ 친밀한

L18
□proposition ⓝ 일, 문제
□maintain ⓥ 유지하다
□persuasive ⓐ 설득력이 있는
□sharp ⓐ 예리한
□efficiency ⓝ 효율성
□intersection ⓝ 교차하는 지점
□idle ⓥ 빈둥거리다
□come up with ~을 생각해 내다
□navigational ⓐ 항해의
□instruction ⓝ 지시

□fender bender 가벼운 접촉 사고

L19
□widespread ⓐ 널리 퍼진
□sadly ⓐⓓ 애석하게도, 불행히
□mistaken ⓐ 틀린, 잘못된
□myth ⓝ 근거 없는 통념, 잘못된 믿음
□leafy ⓐ 잎이 무성한, 녹음이 우거진
□suburb ⓝ 교외
□ecological ⓐ 생태계[학]의, 생태상의
□destruction ⓝ 파괴, 파멸
□artificial ⓐ 인공[인조]의
□suck up ~을 빨아먹다[빨아들이다]
□precious ⓐ 귀한, 소중한
□exhaust ⓝ 배기가스
□dweller ⓝ 거주자
□transit ⓝ 대중교통
□in terms of ~의 측면에서
□illustrate ⓥ 보여주다
□tendency ⓝ 성향, 경향
□get tired of ~에 싫증이 나다
□urban ⓐ 도시의, 도회지의
□settle ⓥ 정착하다

L20
□essential ⓐ 필수적인, 근본적인
□preferential ⓐ 우선권[특혜]을 주는, 특혜인
□organ ⓝ (인체 내의) 장기[기관]
□tissue ⓝ ((생물)) 조직
□shoot ⓝ (새로 돋아난) 순[싹]
□barren ⓐ 척박한, 열매가 안 열리는

□scale ⓝ 규모, 범위
□scar ⓝ 흉터, 상처
□composition ⓝ 구성 (요소)
□atmosphere ⓝ (지구의) 대기, 분위기
□regeneration ⓝ ((생물)) 재생, 부흥
□resprout ⓥ 재발아하다
□disturb ⓥ 방해하다, 불안하게 만들다
□reseed ⓥ 다시 씨를 뿌리다, 자생하다

L21
□unite ⓥ 통합[결속]시키다
□initially ⓐⓓ 처음에
□conflict ⓝ 갈등, 충돌
□reframe ⓥ 다시 구성하다
□potentially ⓐⓓ 가능성 있게, 잠재적으로
□divisive ⓐ 분열을 초래하는
□merely ⓐⓓ 그저, 한낱
□in perspective 진상을 올바르게, 올바른 균형으로
□unify ⓥ 통합[통일]하다
□recount ⓥ 이야기하다, 말하다
□reinforce ⓥ 강화하다, 보강하다
□unity ⓝ 통합, 통일
□key ⓐ 가장 중요한, 핵심적인
□dumpster fire 재앙, 극도로 혼란스러운 상황
□preserve ⓥ 지키다, 보호하다
□spark ⓥ 촉발시키다, 유발하다
□multiple ⓐ 많은, 다수[복수]의
□party ⓝ 정당, 단체, (소송·계약 등의) 당사자
□indicate ⓥ 나타내다, 보여주다

□capture ⓥ 사로잡다, 포착하다

□commercial ⓝ (텔레비전·라디오의) 광고 (방송)

□enact ⓥ (법을) 제정하다, 일으키다

□bond ⓝ 유대, 결속

□informal ⓐ 격식에 얽매이지 않는, 비공식의

L22

□countless ⓐ 무수한, 셀 수 없이 많은

□recognise ⓥ 인정하다

□decode ⓥ (암호를) 해독하다

□instruction ⓝ 지시, 설명

□address ⓥ 대처하다

□incredibly ⓐ 놀랍도록

□sparingly ⓐ 드물게, 인색하게

□authoritative ⓐ 권위가 있는

□measured ⓐ 침착한

□tone ⓝ 어조

□panicked ⓐ 당황한

L23

□expert ⓝ 전문가

□extensive ⓐ 광범위한

□domain ⓝ 영역, 범위

□component ⓝ 요소, 부품

□automate ⓥ 자동화하다

□cognitive ⓐ 인식의, 인지의

□load ⓝ 부하, 짐

□process ⓥ 처리하다, 가공하다

□isolate ⓥ 격리하다, 분리하다

□necessarily ⓐ 어쩔 수 없이, 필연적으로

□fluency ⓝ 유창성, 능숙도

□struggle ⓥ 애쓰다, 고군분투하다

□relative ⓐ 비교상의, 상대적인

L24

□acceptance ⓝ 수용

□factor ⓝ 요인

□reliance ⓝ 의존

□face-to-face 대면의

□misperception ⓝ 오해, 오인

□discomfort ⓝ 불편함

□flexible ⓐ 유연한

□bottom line 최종 결산 결과

□limitation ⓝ 한계

□emerge ⓥ 등장하다

□be suited for ~에 적합하다

□advance ⓝ 진보

□expansion ⓝ 확대

□workforce ⓝ 노동력

□balance ⓥ 균형을 맞추다

□barrier ⓝ 장벽

□dominant ⓐ 지배적인

□implications ⓝ 영향

□with regard to ~에 관련하여

M 글의 순서 정하기

M01

□intentional ⓐ 의도적인

□aboriginal ⓐ 호주 원주민의

□millennia ⓝ (millennium의 복수형) 천년

□stockman ⓝ 목축업자

□woody ⓐ 숲이 우거진

□vegetation ⓝ 초목

□stimulate ⓥ 자극하다

□recolonize ⓥ 다시 대량 서식하다

□woody plant 목본성 식물(木本性 植物)

□shrub ⓝ 관목(灌木)

□shoot ⓝ 새싹, 순

□reinforce ⓥ 강화하다

M02

□complexity ⓝ 복잡성

□implication ⓝ 영향, 함축

□implantable ⓐ 체내에 삽입되는

□transform ⓥ 변화시키다

□commercial ⓐ 상업의

□intend ⓥ 의도하다

□elaborate ⓐ 정교한

□flourish ⓥ 번성하다, 창궐하다

□consequence ⓝ 결과

M03

□enforcement ⓝ 집행

□party ⓝ 당사자

□reputational capital 평판 자본

□devalue ⓥ 평가 절하하다

□undermaintain ⓥ 제대로 관리하지 않다

□assessment ⓝ 평가

□expense ⓝ 비용

□extreme ⓐ 극적인

□reputation ⓝ 평판

□overuse ⓥ 남용하다

□underreport ⓥ (소득·수입 등을) 적게 신고하다

□yield ⓝ 수확량

□demonstrate ⓥ 입증하다

□close-knit ⓐ 긴밀히 맺어진

M04

□startle ⓥ 놀래다

□infect ⓥ 감염시키다

□contagion ⓝ 전염

□linear ⓐ (직)선의

□antipredatory ⓐ 포식자 회피의

□scan ⓥ 살피다, 훑어보다

□coordination ⓝ (신체) 조정력

□significantly ⓐⓓ 상당히

M05

□accumulate ⓥ 축적하다, 쌓다

□adjustment ⓝ 조정

□unit ⓝ 단위

□strength ⓝ 힘

□slightly ⓐⓓ 약간

□compatible ⓐ 양립될 수 있는

□accommodate ⓥ 수용하다

□store ⓥ 저장하다

□separately ⓐⓓ 개별적으로

□organize ⓥ 조직하다

□modify ⓥ 수정하다

□material ⓝ 자료, 재료

M06

□obtain ⓥ 얻다

□pre-emptive ⓐ 선제의

□evolve ⓥ 발달[진전]하다[시키다]

□maintain ⓥ 유지하다

□survival ⓝ 생존

□regain ⓥ 되찾다

□damage ⓥ 손상을 주다

□heal ⓥ 치유하다

□wound ⓝ 상처

□complex ⓐ 복잡한

□immune system 면역 체계

□ward off 피하다, 물리치다

□infection ⓝ 감염

□anticipate ⓥ 예측하다

M07

□human resource(s) management 인적 자원 관리((구성원의 잠재적 능력을 육성, 개발하여 조직의 전략적 목표를 달성하는 데 기여하는 활동))

□practice ⓝ 관행

□organizational learning 조직 학습(組織 學習)

□assist ⓥ 지원하다, 돕다

□mechanism ⓝ 기법

□cross-train ⓥ 두 가지 이상의 일이 가능하도록 훈련시키다

□peer ⓝ 동료

□systemically ⓐⓓ 조직적으로

□function ⓝ 기능

□dramatically ⓐⓓ 극적으로, 획기적으로

□emphasis ⓝ 중점, 강조

□transfer ⓥ 전수하다

□preset ⓐ 미리 조절한

□insufficient ⓐ 충분하지 않은

□address ⓥ 대응[대처]하다

□shifting ⓐ 변화하는

□timely ⓐ 시기적절한

□facilitator ⓝ 촉진자

M08

□infancy ⓝ 유아기

□absorb ⓥ 흡수하다

□infer ⓥ 추론하다

□detect ⓥ 감지하다

□capacity ⓝ 능력

□ignore ⓥ 무시하다

□observant ⓐ 관찰력 있는

□sensitive ⓐ 예민한, 세심한

□identify ⓥ 알아보다

□nonverbal ⓐ 비언어적인

M09

□include ⓥ 포함하다

□correctness ⓝ 정확함

□alert ⓥ 주의를 환기시키다

□awe ⓝ 경외감

□wonder ⓝ 놀라움

□prompt ⓥ 유도하다, 촉발하다

□point to 가리키다

M10

□constraint ⓝ 제약

□element ⓝ 요소

□idealized ⓐ 이상화된

□organize ⓥ 조직하다

□democratic ⓐ 민주적인

□institutionalize ⓥ 제도화하다

□labour ⓝ 노동

□wield ⓥ 행사하다, 휘두르다

□significant ⓐ 중요한

M11

□photosynthesis ⓝ 광합성

□convert ⓥ 전환하다

□carbon dioxide 이산화탄소

□carbohydrate ⓝ 탄수화물

□microorganism ⓝ 미생물

□consume ⓥ 소비하다

□respire ⓥ 호흡하다, (나무가 공기를) 내뿜다

□atmosphere ⓝ 대기, 공기

□biomass ⓝ 바이오매스 연료 (메탄 · 수소로 만든 합성 연료)

□fungi ⓝ 균류

□compound ⓝ 화합물

□deforestation ⓝ 산림파괴
□plowing ⓝ 경작
□severely ⓐd 심각하게
□disturb ⓥ 교란하다, 방해하다

M12
□philosopher ⓝ 철학자
□go back in time 시간을 거스르다
□sort ⓝ 분류
□notion ⓝ 개념, 생각
□construct ⓥ 구성하다
□presupposition ⓝ 예상
□interfere ⓥ 간섭하다

M13
□universal ⓐ 보편적인
□indicator ⓝ 지표
□awareness ⓝ 의식
□grant permission 허가하다
□impose ⓥ 부과하다
□blackout ⓝ 일시적인 의식 [시력/기억] 상실
□onward ⓐ 앞으로[계속 이어서] 나아가는
□outer ⓐ 바깥의
□sense organ 감각 기관
□perceptual ⓐ 지각의
□barricade ⓝ 장애물, 바리케이드

M14
□pursuit ⓝ 일, 연구
□varying ⓐ 다양한
□flexible ⓐ 유연한
□combination ⓝ 조합
□adjust ⓥ 적응하다, 조절하다
□analytical ⓐ 분석적인
□spectrum ⓝ 범위, 스펙트럼
□concerto ⓝ 협주곡

□exacting ⓐ 고된
□spontaneously ⓐd 자발적으로
□consciousness ⓝ 의식
□myth ⓝ 전설
□portray ⓥ 그리다, 묘사하다
□inhibition ⓝ 억제
□fundamental ⓝ 원리, 기초
□theory ⓝ 이론
□germ ⓝ 기원, 싹틈
□reflect ⓥ 깊이 생각하다, 심사숙고하다

M15
□integrate ⓥ 통합시키다
□suburban ⓐ 교외의
□interpretation ⓝ 해석
□sustainable ⓐ 지속 가능한
□Landscape Urbanist 경관 도시론자
□prioritize ⓥ 우선시하다
□disrupt ⓥ 방해하다
□wetland ⓝ 습지
□advocate ⓥ 주장하다, 옹호하다
□overly ⓐd 지나치게
□idealistic ⓐ 이상주의적인
□dynamics ⓝ 역학 관계
□inequality ⓝ 불평등
□aesthetic ⓐ 미적인
□popularize ⓥ 대중화시키다
□controversial ⓐ 논란의 소지가 있는
□relatively ⓐd 비교적
□habitat ⓝ 서식지
□diverse ⓐ 다양한

M16
□spatial ⓐ 공간의

□reference point 기준(점)
□paradox ⓝ 역설
□landmark ⓝ 주요 지형지물
□define ⓥ 규정하다
□paradigm ⓝ 전형적인 예
□repeated ⓐ 반복되는
□researcher ⓝ 연구원
□estimate ⓥ 추정하다 ⓝ 추정
□distance ⓝ 거리
□ordinary ⓐ 평범한, 보통의
□violate ⓥ 위반하다
□elementary ⓐ 기본적인
□principle ⓝ 원칙
□judgement ⓝ 추정, 판단
□not necessarily 반드시 ~은 아닌
□coherent ⓐ 일관성이 있는
□remarkable ⓐ 주목할 만한
□finding ⓝ 결과

M17
□firm ⓝ 회사
□invest ⓥ 투자하다
□shipbuilding ⓝ 조선(업)
□sufficiently ⓐd 충분히
□scale ⓝ 규모
□venture ⓝ (사업상의) 모험
□profitable ⓐ 수익성이 있는
□outcome ⓝ 결과
□investment ⓝ 투자
□shipyard ⓝ 조선소
□steelmaker ⓝ 제강업자
□end up 결국 ~이 되다
□equilibrium ⓝ 균형, 평형 ((pl. equilibria))
□reach ⓥ ~에 이르다
□reinforce ⓥ 강화하다
□assume ⓥ 가정하다

M

□potential ⓐ 잠재적인

□steel ⓝ 강철

□figure ⓥ (~일 거라고) 생각하다

□otherwise ⓐⓓ 그렇지 않으면

□economist ⓝ 경제학자

□key ⓐ 핵심적인

□input ⓝ 투입

□boil down to 결국 ~이 되다

□factory ⓝ 공장

□close ⓐⓓ 가까이

□investor ⓝ 투자자

□region ⓝ 지역

M18

□ingredient ⓝ 성분

□mainstream ⓐ 주류의

□profitable ⓐ 수익성이 있는

□volume ⓝ (~의) 양

□populous ⓐ 다수의

□given that ~을 고려하면

□niche ⓝ (시장의) 틈새

□offering ⓝ 제품

□downside ⓝ 부정적인 면

□obvious ⓐ 뻔한

□restrictive ⓐ 제한하는

□criterion ⓝ 기준
((pl. criteria))

□typical ⓐ 일반적인

□inferior ⓐ (~보다) 열등한

□core ⓐ 핵심적인

□dimension ⓝ 차원

□economies of scale 규모의 경제

□distribution ⓝ 유통

M19

□evidence ⓝ 증거, 흔적

□creature ⓝ 생물, 생명이 있는 존재

□sequential ⓐ 순차적인, 잇따라 일어나는

□feature ⓝ 특색, 특징

□ancestor ⓝ 조상, 선조

□organism ⓝ 유기체, 생물(체)

□evolve ⓥ 진화하다, 발달하다

□reject ⓥ 거부[거절]하다

□countless ⓐ 셀 수 없이 많은

□examination ⓝ 조사, 검토

□evolutionary ⓐ 진화의

□prediction ⓝ 예측, 예견

□layer ⓝ 층, 겹

□appearance ⓝ 출현, 나타남

□opposite ⓝ 반대(되는 것)

□demonstrate ⓥ 입증하다, 보여주다

M20

□commercial ⓐ 상업적인

□launch ⓥ 시작하다, 출시하다

□assistant ⓝ 조수, 도우미

□eventually ⓐⓓ 결국

□motorize ⓥ 동력화하다

□device ⓝ 장치

□manipulation ⓝ 조작, 조종

□capability ⓝ 능력

□distinct ⓐ 뚜렷한

□suggestive of ~을 암시하는

□engagement ⓝ 참여, 교감

□intermediate ⓝ 매개[중재]자

□rich ⓐ 다채로운

□encouragement ⓝ 격려

□incentive ⓝ 동기, 장려[우대]책

M21

□drive ⓥ (사람을 특정한 방식의 행동을 하도록) 만들다

□innovator ⓝ 혁신가, 도입자

□substitute ⓥ 대용하다, 대체하다

□conserve ⓥ 아껴 쓰다, 보존하다

□alternative ⓝ 대안, 대안이 되는 것

□emerge ⓥ 생겨나다, 모습을 드러내다

□green tax 환경세(환경을 오염시키거나 파괴하는 행위자에게 부과하는 세금)

□landfill ⓝ 쓰레기 매립

□labor expense 인건비

□provision ⓝ 제공, 공급

□disposal ⓝ (무엇을 없애기 위한) 처리, 처분

□household ⓝ (한 집에 사는 사람들을 일컫는) 가정

□innovation ⓝ 혁신, 쇄신

□internalize ⓥ (문화·사상 등을) 자신의 것으로 만들다[내면화하다]

□flow ⓝ 흐름

M22

□consist in ~에 있다

□worldly ⓐ 세속적인, 속세의

□existence ⓝ 존재

□disclose ⓥ 밝히다, 드러내다

□relevant ⓐ 적절한, 타당한

□notion ⓝ 개념

□enjoyment ⓝ 즐거움, 기쁨

□eternal ⓐ 영원한

□naturalistic ⓐ 자연주의적인

□metaphysical ⓐ 형이상학의

□universal ⓐ 보편적인

□ norm ⓝ 규범
□ point out ~을 지적하다 [말하다]
□ conclusion ⓝ 결론, (최종적인) 판단
□ somewhat ⓐⓓ 어느 정도, 약간

M23

□ likeness ⓝ 유사성, 닮음
□ fictional ⓐ 허구의, 가상의
□ respect ⓝ (측)면, 점, 사항
□ content ⓝ (책·프로그램 등의) 내용
□ worldview ⓝ 세계관
□ conception ⓝ 개념, 생각
□ relevance ⓝ 적절성, 타당성
□ neutral ⓐ 중립적인
□ objective ⓐ 객관적인
□ convey ⓥ (생각·감정 등을) 전달하다[전하다]
□ subjective ⓐ 주관적인
□ motive ⓝ 동기, 이유
□ stand ⓥ (어떤 상태·관계·입장에) 있다
□ untouched ⓐ 손을 대지 않은, 본래 그대로의
□ inner ⓐ 내적인, 내면의
□ quality ⓝ 특성, 특징
□ function ⓥ 역할을 하다, 기능하다
□ impression ⓝ (사람·사물로부터 받는) 인상[느낌]
□ interpret ⓥ (의미를) 설명[해석]하다
□ encounter ⓥ 접하다, 마주하다
□ literature ⓝ 문학 (작품)

□ process ⓥ 처리하다, 가공하다
□ consciousness ⓝ 의식
□ existing ⓐ 기존의, 현재 존재하는
□ infinite ⓐ 한계가 없는, 무한한
□ chaos ⓝ 혼돈, 혼란
□ modify ⓥ (더 알맞도록) 수정[변경]하다
□ perceive ⓥ 인식하다, 인지하다

M24

□ classify ⓥ 분류하다
□ generalize ⓥ 일반화하다
□ undoubtedly ⓐⓓ 의심할 여지 없이
□ feature ⓝ 특징
□ tendency ⓝ 경향
□ stereotype ⓝ 고정 관념 ⓥ 고정 관념화하다
□ mentally ⓐⓓ 정신적으로
□ sort ⓥ 분류하다
□ based on ~에 기초하여
□ perceive ⓥ 인식하다
□ afterwards ⓐⓓ 그 후에
□ differentiate ⓥ 차별화하다
□ significance ⓝ 중요성
□ variation ⓝ 변화
□ perform ⓥ 수행하다
□ awareness ⓝ 인식
□ inaccuracy ⓝ 부정확성
□ flexibility ⓝ 유연성
□ arouse ⓥ 불러일으키다
□ imply ⓥ 암시하다
□ bias ⓝ 편견
□ differ in ~에 대해 다르다

M25

□ feminine ⓐ 여성의

□ masculine ⓐ 남성의
□ sturdy ⓐ 튼튼한
□ towering ⓐ 우뚝 솟은
□ gender ⓝ 성
□ indicate ⓥ 나타내다
□ assign ⓥ 부여하다
□ subconsciously ⓐⓓ 무의식적으로
□ characteristics ⓝ 특성

M26

□ blush ⓥ 얼굴을 붉히다
□ involuntary ⓐ 원치 않는, 자기도 모르게 하는
□ embarrassment ⓝ 어색함, 쑥쓰러움
□ self-consciousness ⓝ 자의식
□ brief ⓐ 짧은
□ cohesion ⓝ 화합, 응집력
□ favourable ⓐ 좋은, 호의적인
□ awkward ⓐ 어색한, 곤란한
□ bring on ~을 야기하다
□ psychologist ⓝ 심리학자
□ recognize ⓥ 인정하다
□ norm ⓝ 규범

M27

□ fine art 미술
□ oil painting 유화
□ watercolour ⓝ 수채화
□ sculpture ⓝ 조각(품)
□ institution ⓝ 기관
□ territoriality ⓝ 영토권
□ monetary ⓐ 금전적인
□ standing ⓝ 지위
□ evidential ⓐ 증거의
□ aesthetic ⓐ 미적인
□ elevate ⓥ 격상시키다, 높이다

M

□evaluation ⓝ 감정, 평가

□notion ⓝ 개념, 관념, 생각

□consideration ⓝ 사려, 숙고, 고려 사항

□motivate ⓥ 이유[원인]가 되다, 동기를 부여하다

□preservation ⓝ 보존

□serve ⓥ 도움이 되다, 기여하다

□documentary ⓐ 기록의

□portrait ⓝ 초상화, 인물 사진

□townspeople ⓝ 시민

M28

□perception ⓝ 인식

□imagination ⓝ 상상

□confirmation effect 확증 효과

□blindly 쪬 맹목적으로

□construct ⓥ 구축하다

□ignorant ⓐ 무지한

□puzzling ⓐ 이해하기 어려운

□extraordinary ⓐ 놀라운

□disregard ⓥ 무시하다

□ignorance ⓝ 무지

□portray ⓥ 묘사하다

□faithfully 쪬 충실하게

□striking ⓐ 눈에 띄는

□element ⓝ 요소

□beard ⓝ 턱수염

M29

□finely 쪬 미세하게

□tune ⓥ 조정하다

□adaptive response 적응 반응

□gardener ⓝ 정원사

□poor nutrition 영양 실조

□in contrast 반대로

□abundance ⓝ 풍부

□risk averse 위험을 회피하는

□developmental ⓐ 발달의

□unevenness ⓝ 불균형

□so as to-v ~하기 위하여

□reproduction ⓝ 번식

□nonproductive ⓐ 비생산적인

□constantly 쪬 지속적으로

□availability ⓝ 가용성

□risk-taking ⓐ 위험을 감수하는

□lengthen ⓥ 연장하다

□supplemental ⓐ 보충의

□proliferate ⓥ 증식시키다

□patch ⓝ 작은 땅, 지대

□temporal ⓐ 시간의

□spatial ⓐ 공간의

M30

□identify ⓥ (신원 등을) 확인하다[알아보다]

□measure ⓝ 조치, 정책

□promote ⓥ 촉진하다, 홍보하다

□efficiency ⓝ 효율(성), 능률

□fundamental ⓐ 근본[본질]적인, 핵심적인

□investment ⓝ 투자(액)

□perspective ⓝ 관점, 시각

□competitiveness ⓝ 경쟁력, 경쟁적인 것

□productivity ⓝ 생산성

□externality ⓝ 외부 효과

□take ~ into account ~을 고려하다[계산에 넣다]

□macroeconomic ⓐ 거시 경제의

□dependence ⓝ 의존, 의지

□calculation ⓝ 계산, 산출

□reduction ⓝ 감소, 할인

M31

□representation ⓝ 표현

□merge ⓥ 합병하다

□imperialize ⓥ 제국주의화하다

□intellectually 쪬 지적으로

□depend upon ~에 의존하다

□contemporary ⓐ 현대의

□accompany ⓥ 동반하다

□coincidence ⓝ 우연의 일치, 우연

□colonization ⓝ 식민지화

M32

□negotiation ⓝ 협상

□explore ⓥ 탐색하다

□conflicting ⓐ 상충하는

□acceptable ⓐ 수용할 수 있는

□outcome ⓝ 결과

□irreconsilable ⓐ 화해할 수 없는

□party ⓝ 당사자

□polarise ⓥ 양극화를 초래하다

□dominate ⓥ 지배하다

□publicity ⓝ 홍보

□divert ⓥ 방향을 바꾸게 하다

□intelligence ⓝ 정보, 기밀

□identification ⓝ (실체를) 밝힘, 확인

□intention ⓝ 의도

□clarify ⓥ 명확하게 하다

□refine ⓥ 정제하다

□substance ⓝ 실체

M33

□objective ⓝ 목적, 목표

□defenseless ⓐ 무방비의, 방어할 수 없는

□ temporarily (ad) 일시적으로, 임시로

□ blind (v) 눈이 멀게 만들다, 앞이 안 보이게 만들다, 맹목적이 되게 만들다

□ commander (n) 지휘관, 사령관

□ strategist (n) 전략가

□ representative (n) 대표(자), 대리인

□ constitutional (a) 헌법(상)의, 구조상의

□ intention (n) 의사, 의도

□ will (n) 의지(력)

□ clearly (ad) 분명히, 또렷하게

□ force (n) 물리력, 힘

□ insight (n) 통찰력

□ capture (v) 사로잡다, 포착하다

□ phrase (n) 구절, 관용구

□ continuation (n) 계속, 지속, 연속

□ means (n) 수단, 방법

□ transmit (v) 전달하다, 알리다

□ confrontation (n) 대립, 대치

□ publicly (ad) 공공연하게, 공개적으로

□ attribute to ~의 덕분[탓]으로 돌리다

□ eventual (a) 궁극[최종]적인

M34

□ raise (v) 불러일으키다, 자아내다

□ advocate (v) 지지하다, 옹호하다

□ compliance (n) (법·명령 등의) 준수, (명령 등에) 따름

□ prohibit (v) 금지하다

□ prescription (n) 처방(전), 지시

□ implementation (n) 이행, 수행

□ deception (n) 속임, 기만

□ omission (n) 생략, 누락

□ commit (v) (그릇된 일을) 저지르다, (~할 것을) 의무 지우다

□ silence (n) 침묵, 고요

□ potential (a) 가능성이 있는, 잠재적인

□ false (a) 틀린, 사실이 아닌

□ delightful (a) 정말 기분 좋은

□ at work 작용하고 있는

□ fragile (a) 부서지기[손상되기] 쉬운

□ acrylic (a) 아크릴로 만든

□ sculpture (n) 조각(품), 조소

□ command (n) 명령

M35

□ common (a) 흔한, 공동의

□ strategy (n) 계획, 전략

□ passive (a) 수동적인, 소극적인

□ misdirection (n) 잘못된 지시[지도], 엉뚱한 곳으로 보내기

□ repetition (n) 반복

□ over and over 반복해서, 여러 번 되풀이하여

□ navigate (v) 길을 찾다, 조종하다

□ immediate (a) 즉각적인, 당면한

□ reflexive (a) 반사적인, 반응하는

□ malicious (a) 악의적인, 적의 있는

□ take advantage of ~을 이용하다

□ distract (v) (주의를) 딴 데로 돌리게 하다, 집중이 안 되게 하다

□ examine (v) 조사[검토]하다, 검사[진찰]하다

□ tip off ~에게 제보하다[귀띔하다]

□ amiss (a) 잘못된

□ draw away from (주의 등을) ~로부터 돌리다

□ surface (n) 표면, 지면, 수면

□ utilize (v) 활용[이용]하다

□ ubiquitous (a) 어디에나 있는, 아주 흔한

□ navigational (a) 항해(술)의

M36

□ realm (n) 영역, 범위

□ outcome (n) 결과

□ extent (n) 정도, 규모

□ excessively (ad) 지나치게, 매우

□ predict (v) 예측하다

□ uncertain (a) 불확실한, 불분명한

□ instinct (n) 본능, 직감

□ imply (v) 암시하다, 의미하다

□ repress (v) 참다, 억누르다

□ awareness (n) 의식, 관심

□ distort (v) (형체를) 비틀다, (사실을) 왜곡하다

M37

□ pronounce (v) 선언하다

□ measure (n) 척도

□ entitled to-v ~할 자격이 있는

□ empathy (n) 감정이입, 공감

□ grief (n) 슬픔

□ backbone (n) 척추, 등뼈

□ amphibian (n) 양서류

□ reptile (n) 파충류

□ mammal (n) 포유류

□ skeleton (n) 골격

M

□ organ ⓝ (인체 내의) 장기[기관]
□ nervous system 신경계
□ standard ⓝ 기준, 표준
□ overlook ⓥ 간과하다
□ drive train 동력 전달 체계
□ internal ⓐ 내부의
□ naive ⓐ 순진한
□ exterior ⓝ 겉모습

M38
□ ripening ⓝ 숙성
□ bring about ~을 야기하다 [초래하다]
□ softening ⓝ 연화
□ chemical ⓝ 화학 물질
□ flavour ⓝ 맛, 풍미
□ induce ⓥ 유도하다
□ interfere with ~을 방해하다
□ spray ⓥ 살포하다
□ biotechnologist ⓝ 생명공학자
□ delay ⓥ 지연하다
□ decay ⓝ 부패
□ worthless ⓐ 가치가 없는
□ transport ⓥ 운송하다

M39
□ body ⓝ 많은 양[모음]
□ stand ⓥ (특정 조건 · 상황에) 있다
□ canal ⓝ 운하, 수로
□ downstream ⓐ (강) 하류의
□ passage ⓝ 뱃길, 통행, 통로
□ opposite ⓐ 반대의, 다른 편의
□ in (a) line with ~와 일직선을 이루는
□ vessel ⓝ (대형) 선박
□ upstream ⓐⓓ 상류로
□ basin ⓝ 물웅덩이, 대야

□ artificial ⓐ 인공의, 인위적인
□ concrete ⓐ 콘크리트로 된

M40
□ struggle with ~으로 고투하다, ~을 해결하려고 노력하다
□ major ⓐ 주된, 주요한
□ respondent ⓝ 응답자
□ derive A from B A를 B에서 얻다
□ adversity ⓝ 역경
□ reevaluate ⓥ 재평가하다
□ priority ⓝ 우선순위
□ insight ⓝ 통찰
□ acquire ⓥ 얻다
□ strength ⓝ 강점, 장점, 힘
□ intermediate ⓐ 중간의
□ moderate ⓐ 적당한
□ foster ⓥ 촉진하다, 키우다
□ follow-up 후속의, 뒤따르는
□ laboratory ⓝ 실험실 ⓐ 실험(실)의
□ intermediate ⓐ 중간의, 중급의
□ predictive ⓐ 예측[예견]의
□ deal with ~을 처리하다[다루다]
□ in the face of ~에 직면하여
□ adaptation ⓝ 적응
□ initiate ⓥ 개시되게 하다, 착수시키다
□ measure ⓥ 측정하다, 재다
□ exposure ⓝ (유해한 환경 등에의) 노출, (직접) 경험[체험]함, 접함
□ curvilinear ⓐ 곡선으로 이루어진

M41
□ norm ⓝ 규범
□ conform to ~에 순응하다

□ prescribe ⓥ 지시하다, 규정하다
□ utter ⓥ 말하다
□ prescriptive ⓐ 지시하는
□ alternately ⓐⓓ 다른 방식으로
□ conformity ⓝ 순응
□ regularity ⓝ 규칙성
□ rational ⓐ 이성적인
□ moral ⓐ 도덕적인

M42
□ economics ⓝ 경제학
□ principle ⓝ 원칙, 원리
□ sink ⓥ 가라앉다
□ fallacy ⓝ 오류, 틀린 생각
□ ownership ⓝ 소유(권)
□ overvalue ⓥ 지나치게 가치를 두다
□ played-out ⓐ 영향력[효력]이 다 된
□ argument ⓝ 논쟁, 언쟁
□ pursuit ⓝ 추구, 추적
□ abandon ⓥ 버리다, 포기하다
□ tendency ⓝ 경향, 추세
□ commitment ⓝ 전념, 약속

M43
□ exhibit ⓥ (특징 등을) 보이다
□ flexibility ⓝ 유연성
□ trick ⓝ 묘책, 속임수
□ in terms of ~라는 면에서
□ conserve ⓥ 보존하다
□ organism ⓝ 유기체
□ reproduce ⓥ 생식하다, 재생산하다
□ signature ⓝ (고유성을 잘 나타내는) 특징
□ prey on ~을 먹이로 하다
□ predator ⓝ 포식자

□protective ⓐ 방어하는

□adaptation ⓝ 적응

□trait ⓝ 특성, 특징

□reproductive ⓐ 생식의, 번식의

□fitness ⓝ 적합성

□variation ⓝ 차이, 변화

M44

□price ⓥ 값을 매기다[정하다]

□compensate ⓥ 보수[급여]를 지불하다

□make sense 타당하다

□settle ⓥ 해결하다, 합의를 보다

□ensure ⓥ 보장하다

□settlement ⓝ 합의(금)

□bill ⓥ 비용을 청구하다

□payment ⓝ 지불금

M45

□consciously ⓐⓓ 의식적으로

□claim ⓝ 주장, 권리

□worldview ⓝ 세계관

□necessarily ⓐⓓ 어쩔 수 없이, 필연적으로

□account ⓝ 설명, 해석

□excuse ⓝ 변명, 이유

□prove ⓥ 증명하다

□acceptable ⓐ 용인되는, 허용할 수 있는

□circumstance ⓝ 환경, 상황

□notion ⓝ 개념, 생각

□call for ~을 요구하다

□insert ⓥ 끼워 넣다, 삽입하다

□justify ⓥ 정당화하다, 해명하다

□motive ⓝ 동기, 이유

M46

□measure ⓝ 척도

□vary ⓥ 서로 다르다

□considerably ⓐⓓ 상당히

□species ⓝ 종(생물 분류의 기초 단위)

□suspect ⓥ 추측하다

□assess ⓥ 평가하다

□quantity ⓝ 양, 수량

□shed ⓥ (빛·소리·냄새 등을) 발산하다

□currently ⓐⓓ 현재

□incomprehensible ⓐ 이해할 수 없는

□investigation ⓝ 연구, 조사

□degree ⓝ 정도

□unresponsiveness ⓝ 무반응

□continuity ⓝ 연속성

□index ⓝ 지표

□biological ⓐ 생물학의

□obtain ⓥ 얻다

□superior ⓐ 우수한

□accomplish ⓥ 성취하다

□vice versa 반대의 경우도 마찬가지

□exception ⓝ 제외, 예외

□opposite ⓐ 정반대의

N 주어진 문장 넣기

N01

□beneficial ⓐ 유익한, 이로운

□yield ⓝ (농작물의) 수확량, 총수익

□pest ⓝ 해충

□aspect ⓝ (측)면, 양상

□mankind ⓝ 인류, 인간

□broadly ⓐⓓ 대략적으로, 넓게

□persistent ⓐ 지속하는, 끈질긴

□apparent ⓐ 분명한, 표면상의

□negate ⓥ 무효화하다

□procedure ⓝ 절차, 방법

□approval ⓝ 승인, 찬성

□consequently ⓐⓓ 그 결과, 따라서

□consideration ⓝ 숙고, 고려 사항

□incorporate ⓥ 포함하다

□resistance ⓝ 저항, 반대

□breed ⓥ (번식을 위해) 사육하다, 품종 개량을 하다

□biological ⓐ 생물학적인

N02

□endlessly ⓐⓓ 끝없이

□chase ⓥ 쫓아가다, 추적하다

□conception ⓝ 구상, 고안

□fundamental ⓐ 핵심적인, 근본적인

□discriminate ⓥ 구별하다, 차별하다

□scatter ⓥ 흩어지게 하다

□pile ⓥ 쌓다

□stimulation ⓝ 자극

□originate from ~에서 발생하다

□machinery ⓝ 기계

□equip ~ with ... ~에게 ...을 갖추게 하다

□artificial ⓐ 인공의, 인위적인

□detect ⓥ 감지하다, 발견하다

□enable ⓥ 가능하게 하다

□self-centered ⓐ 자기 중심[본위]의

□external ⓐ 외부의, 외적인

N03

- trade secret 영업상 비밀
- secretive ⓐ 비밀스러운
- disclose ⓥ 드러내다, 폭로하다
- proprietary ⓐ 독점의, 독점적인
- aim to ~하는 것을 목표로 하다
- innovation ⓝ 혁신
- accomplish ⓥ 이루다, 성취하다
- utilize ⓥ 활용하다
- inordinate ⓐ 과도한
- impassable ⓐ 통과할 수 없는

N04

- conform ⓥ 따르다
- linear ⓐ 선형적인
- maintenance ⓝ 정비
- predominantly ⓐⓓ 대부분, 주로
- scholarly ⓐ 학문적인
- discourse ⓝ 담론
- revolve ⓥ 돌다
- prolong ⓥ 연장하다
- metaphor ⓝ 은유, 비유
- biography ⓝ 전기, 일대기
- disposal ⓝ 폐기
- afterlife ⓝ 사후 생애
- application ⓝ 용도
- adaptive ⓐ 적응적인
- progression ⓝ 진행

N05

- scale ⓝ 규모
- accuracy ⓝ 정확성
- precision ⓝ 정밀함
- unprecedented ⓐ 전례가 없는

- unpredictable ⓐ 예측할 수 없는, 예측이 불가능한
- intervene ⓥ 개입하다
- define ⓥ 규정하다, 정의하다
- implement ⓥ 시행하다
- confidence ⓝ 확신, 자신감
- inherently ⓐⓓ 본질적으로, 내재적으로
- appropriate ⓐ 적절한
- spatial ⓐ 공간의
- temporal ⓐ 시간의, 시간의 제약을 받는
- localized ⓐ 국지적인, 국부적인
- climatic change 기후 변화
- efficacy ⓝ 효율
- counter ⓥ (무엇의 악영향에) 대응하다
- adverse ⓐ 부정적인, 불리한
- comparable ⓐ 비슷한, 비교할 만한
- surround ⓥ 둘러싸다
- magnitude ⓝ (엄청난) 규모

N06

- continuous ⓐ 지속적인
- emission ⓝ 배출(물)
- measurement ⓝ 측정
- costly ⓐ 많은 비용이 드는
- disincentive ⓝ 저해 요소
- taxation ⓝ 과세
- in principle 원칙적으로
- in proportion to ~에 비례하여
- incentive ⓝ 동기, 유인, 장려책
- residual ⓐ 잔여의, 나머지의
- base ~ on ... ~을 …에 기반하다

- concentration ⓝ 농도
- substance ⓝ 물질
- discharge ⓝ 방출, 배출

N07

- involvement ⓝ 관여, 참여
- a basis for ~의 기반
- reflection ⓝ 성찰
- trade-off ⓝ 균형, 교환
- subject matter 주제
- representational ⓐ 구상주의적인
- resemble ⓥ ~와 유사하다
- facilitate ⓥ ~을 용이하게 하다
- uncertainty ⓝ 불확실성
- expressionist ⓝ 표현주의자
- novel ⓐ 새로운, 참신한
- a stylistic device 문체(文體)상의 기교 장치
- inharmonious ⓐ 조화롭지 않은
- thereby ⓐⓓ 그렇게 함으로써
- disquieting ⓐ 불안한, 불안하게 하는
- departure ⓝ 벗어남
- conventional ⓐ 전통적인, 관습적인
- appreciate ⓥ 제대로 인식하다, 감상하다
- fundamental ⓐ 핵심적인, 근본적인

N08

- anticipate ⓥ 기대하다, 예상하다
- govern ⓥ 지배하다
- reposition ⓥ ~의 위치를 바꾸다
- device ⓝ 장치

□place ⓥ 두다
□assume ⓥ 가정하다
□relative ⓐ 상대적인
□direct ⓥ 지시하다
□sensory ⓐ 감각의
□muscle ⓝ 근육

N09
□altruistically ⓐⓓ 이타적으로
□empathy ⓝ 공감
□prosocial ⓐ 친사회적인
□egoistic ⓐ 자기 중심적인
□outweigh ⓥ ~보다 더 크다
□genuine ⓐ 진실된
□incur ⓥ 초래하다, 발생시키다
□considerable ⓐ 상당한

N10
□intrinsic ⓐ 내재적인
□modify ⓥ 수정하다
□externally ⓐⓓ 외부적으로
□browse ⓥ 훑어보다
□police ⓥ 통제하다
□influence ⓥ 영향을 미치다
□remove ⓥ 지우다
□passive ⓐ 수동적인
□engagement ⓝ 참여
□self-concept ⓝ 자아 개념

N11
□norm ⓝ 규범
□bias ⓝ 편견
□inherent ⓐ 내재하는
□ethics ⓝ 윤리학
□empathy ⓝ 공감
□partiality ⓝ 편애
□impartiality ⓝ 불편부당, 공명정대
□trial ⓝ 재판
□defense attorney 피고측 변호사

□jury ⓝ 배심원단
□ideally ⓐⓓ 이상적으로
□acute ⓐ 예민한, 예리한
□discipline ⓝ 규율
□ineliminable ⓐ 제거할 수 없는

N12
□accuracy ⓝ 정확도
□enhanced ⓐ 높인, 강화된
□reflective ⓐ 빛을 반사하는
□retina ⓝ 망막
□manage ⓥ (힘든 일을) 간신히 [용케] 해내다
□ghostly ⓐ 귀신같은
□exceptionally ⓐⓓ 특별히
□counterproductive ⓐ 비생산적인, 역효과를 낳는
□come into play 작동[활동]하기 시작하다
□grasp ⓝ 통제, 범위
□surplus ⓝ 과잉

N13
□real-time ⓝ 실시간
□rate ⓝ 요금, 비율
□generalize ⓥ 일반화하다
□stereotype ⓝ 고정 관념
□calculate ⓥ 계산하다
□insure ⓥ (보험업자가) ~의 보험을 맡다
□shield ⓥ 보호하다
□disastrous ⓐ 처참한, 형편없는
□manufacturing ⓝ 제조업
□revolutionary ⓐ 혁명의
□premium ⓝ 보험료, 할증금
□enthusiast ⓝ 열광적인 팬
□classification ⓝ 분류

□bias ⓝ 편견
□outright ⓐ 노골적인
□discrimination ⓝ 차별
□disadvantaged ⓐ 불이익을 받는, 불리한 조건에 놓인
□Big Brother 정보의 독점을 통해 사회를 통제하는 권력 또는 그러한 사회 체계를 일컫는 말
□connotation ⓝ 함축(된 의미)
□threaten ⓥ 협박하다

N14
□figurative art 구상화
□diminish ⓥ 작아지다, 줄어들다
□focal point (관심·활동의) 초점 [중심]
□informative ⓐ 정보를 주는
□layout ⓝ 배치
□spatial ⓐ 공간의
□reveal ⓥ 드러내다
□egocentric ⓐ 자기중심적인
□extract ⓥ 추출하다
□relative ⓐ 상대적인

N15
□supervisor ⓝ 관리자, 감독
□apart ⓐⓓ (거리·공간상으로) 떨어져
□therefore ⓐⓓ 그러므로
□observe ⓥ 관찰하다
□performance ⓝ 성과, 수행
□organization ⓝ 조직, 단체
□immediate ⓐ 직속[직계]의
□evaluate ⓥ 평가하다
□responsible for ~에 책임이 있는
□supervision ⓝ 관리, 감독
□hand out ~을 나눠주다
□assignment ⓝ 과제, 임무

N

□rate ⓥ 평가하다
□dimension ⓝ 차원, 관점
□eliminate ⓥ 없애다
□implement ⓥ 시행하다
□assessment ⓝ 평가
□refer to as ~라고 언급하다
□degree ⓝ (각도의 단위인) 도
□evaluation ⓝ 평가
□coworker ⓝ 동료
□client ⓝ 고객
□citizen ⓝ 시민
□professional ⓝ 전문가
□agency ⓝ 대행사, (특정 서비스를 제공하는) 단체
□approach ⓝ 접근법
□opportunity ⓝ 기회

N16

□absorption ⓝ 흡수
□colleague ⓝ 동료
□socialization ⓝ 사회화
□embody ⓥ 상징하다, 포함하다
□reinforce ⓥ 강화하다
□reproduce ⓥ 재생산하다
□institutionalize ⓥ 제도화하다
□parliament ⓝ 의회
□court ⓝ 법원
□exhibit ⓥ 보여주다
□substantive ⓐ 실질적인
□discipline ⓝ 학문
□instruct ⓥ 지시하다, 가르치다
□profession ⓝ 전문직, 직업
□threat ⓝ 위협

N17

□pinpoint ⓥ 정확히 기술[묘사]하다, 정확히 집어내다

□character ⓝ 성격, 특징
□infer ⓥ 추론하다, 암시하다
□intonation ⓝ 억양
□context ⓝ 맥락, 문맥, 전후 사정
□morally ⓐⓓ 도덕[도의]적으로
□disapprove ⓥ 못마땅하다, 좋지 않게 생각하다
□typical ⓐ 전형적인, 대표적인
□linguistic ⓐ 언어(학)의
□convention ⓝ 관습, 관례
□sincere ⓐ 진실된, 진정한
□trait ⓝ 특성
□wicked ⓐ 사악한, 못된
□attitude ⓝ 태도, 자세, 사고 방식
□nevertheless ⓐⓓ 그렇기는 하지만, 그럼에도 불구하고

N18

□firefly ⓝ 반딧불이
□organ ⓝ (신체의) 기관, 장기
□bat ⓝ 박쥐
□twist ⓝ 반전
□trait ⓝ 특성, 특징
□disgusting ⓐ 역겨운
□swallow ⓥ 삼키다
□chemical ⓝ 화학 물질
□release ⓥ (가스 · 열 등을) 발산[방출]하다
□throw up ~을 토하다
□beetle ⓝ 딱정벌레
□moth ⓝ 나방
□capture ⓥ 붙잡다, 포획하다
□prey ⓝ 먹이
□finding ⓝ 연구 결과
□immature ⓐ 미숙한

N19

□narrative ⓝ 이야기
□identity ⓝ 정체성, 신원
□complexity ⓝ 복잡성
□dynamics ⓝ 역학
□determine ⓥ 결정하다
□mass ⓐ 대량의
□accessibility ⓝ 접근하기 쉬움
□affordability ⓝ 감당할 수 있는 비용
□distribution ⓝ 유통, 분배
□progress ⓝ 발전
□segment ⓝ 부분
□inclination ⓝ 기호, 성향
□supposedly ⓐⓓ 아마
□overlap ⓥ 겹치다
□temporary ⓐ 일시적인
□tribal ⓐ 부족의, 종족의
□solidify ⓥ 확고해지다
□sensibility ⓝ 감성, 감수성
□dietary ⓝ 식생활
□boundary ⓝ 경계[한계](선)

N20

□current ⓐ 현재의
□lay off 해고하다, 휴직시키다
□introduction ⓝ 도입, 전래
□responsibility ⓝ 책임, 의무
□management ⓝ (사업체 · 조직의) 경영[관리](진)
□ease ⓥ (고통 · 괴로움 등을) 완화시키다[덜다]
□plant ⓝ 공장
□replace ⓥ 교체하다, 대신[대체]하다
□assembly ⓝ (차량 · 가구 등의) 조립

□manufacture ⓥ (기계를 이용하여 대량으로 상품을) 제조[생산]하다

□competitive ⓐ 경쟁력 있는

□reduction ⓝ 축소, 삭감

□jointly ⓐ 함께, 공동으로

□repetitive ⓐ 반복적인

□motion ⓝ 동작, 몸짓

□judgment ⓝ 판단, 판결

□beyond (prep) (능력·한계 등을) 넘어서는

N21

□copyright ⓝ 저작권, 판권 ⓥ 저작권을 보호하다

□cover ⓥ 다루다, 포함하다

□draw on ~에 의지하다, ~을 이용하다

□previous ⓐ 이전의, 먼젓번의

□spark ⓥ 촉발시키다, 유발하다

□inspiration ⓝ (특히 예술적 창조를 가능하게 하는) 영감

□innovation ⓝ 혁신, 쇄신

□court ⓝ 법정, 법원

□numerous ⓐ 많은

□functionality ⓝ (상품 등의) 목적[기능], 기능성

□represent ⓥ 대표[대신]하다, (~에) 해당[상당]하다

□infringement ⓝ 위배, 위반

□automatically ⓐ 자동적으로, 무의식적으로

□invest ⓥ 부여하다

□author ⓝ 작가, 저자, 입안자

□sign over (권리·재산 등을) 양도하다

N22

□nutrient ⓝ 영양분

□optimally ⓐ 최선으로, 최적으로

□get rid of 제거하다

□suppose ⓥ 추측하다, 여기다

□competition ⓝ 경쟁자, 경쟁

□positively ⓐ 분명히

□bubble ⓥ 흘러넘치다, 거품이 일다

□surround ⓥ 둘러싸다

□decline ⓝ 감소

□genetic ⓐ 유전의

□fall prey to ~의 희생물이 되다

□fungi ⓝ 균류

N23

□interact ⓥ 소통하다, 상호 작용을 하다

□mutual ⓐ 상호 간의, 공통의

□term ⓝ 용어, 학기

□precisely ⓐ 바로, 정확하게

□distinguish ⓥ 구별하다, 차이를 보이다

□mere ⓐ ~에 불과한

□observe ⓥ (논평·의견 등을) 말하다

□strictly ⓐ 엄밀히, 정확히

□constitute ⓥ 구성하다, (단체를) 설립하다

□squad ⓝ 팀, (경찰의) 수사반

□objective ⓝ 목적, 목표

□formal ⓐ 공식적인, 격식을 차린

□beforehand ⓐ 사전에

□define ⓥ 정의하다, 규정하다

N24

□reasoning ⓝ 추론

□prone to ~의 경향이 있는

□confusion ⓝ 혼란, 혼동

□causal ⓐ 인과 관계의

□sufficiently ⓐ 충분히

□complex ⓐ 복잡한

□assess ⓥ 평가하다

□impact ⓝ 영향, 충격

□policy ⓝ 정책, 방침

□intervention ⓝ 개입

□hold out ~을 보이다[드러내다]

□promise ⓝ 가능성, 징조

□probabilistic ⓐ 확률적인

□domain ⓝ 영역

□treatment ⓝ 치료

□work ⓥ 효과가 있다

□refer to ~을 언급하다

□on average 평균적으로

□structured ⓐ 체계화된

□map out ~을 세밀히 나타내다

□represent ⓥ 나타내다

□assessment ⓝ 평가

□threat ⓝ 협박, 위협

□ecological ⓐ 생태계[학]의

N25

□partition ⓝ 칸막이

□inert ⓐ 비활성의, 기력이 없는

□telling ⓐ 효과적인, 강력한

□actualize ⓥ 실현하다

□representation ⓝ 표현, 묘사

□embody ⓥ 구현하다, 상징하다

□separation ⓝ 분리

□landscape architect 조경사

□suggestive ⓐ 연상시키는

□envision ⓥ 상상하다, 마음속에 그리다

□oppositional ⓐ 대립적인, 반대의

N

N26

- □ evolve ⓥ 발전하다
- □ device ⓝ 방법, 장치
- □ in practice 실제로는
- □ vaguely ⓐ𝖽 어렴풋이
- □ cinematic ⓐ 영화의
- □ syntax ⓝ 문법, 통사론
- □ systematic ⓐ 체계적인, 조직적인
- □ arrangement ⓝ (처리) 방식, 준비, 마련
- □ order ⓥ 정리하다
- □ indicate ⓥ 나타내다, 보여주다
- □ determinant ⓝ 결정 요인
- □ workable ⓐ 운용할 수 있는
- □ organic ⓐ 자연스러운, 서서히 생기는
- □ descriptive ⓐ 기술적인
- □ prescriptive ⓐ 규범적인
- □ laughable ⓐ 웃기는, 터무니 없는
- □ accurate ⓐ 정확한

N27

- □ run out of ~을 다 써버리다 [바닥내다]
- □ sufficient ⓐ 충분한
- □ go around (사람들에게 몫이) 돌아가다
- □ conduct a meeting 회의 를 진행[주관]하다
- □ ensure ⓥ 확실하게 하다
- □ agenda ⓝ 의제, 안건
- □ handout ⓝ 유인물
- □ label ⓥ (표 등에 필요한 정보를) 적다
- □ initial ⓝ 이름의 첫 글자[머리글 자]

- □ present ⓐ 참석한
- □ resort to ~에 의지하다
- □ explicit ⓐ 명시적인, 명백한
- □ all the same 그래도, 여전히
- □ comparison ⓝ 비교
- □ make up ~을 구성하다
- □ character ⓝ 특징, 특성, 인격, 성격
- □ collection ⓝ (물건·사람들 의) 무리, 더미
- □ consist of ~으로 구성되다
- □ relative ⓐ 상대적인

N28

- □ shabby ⓐ 터무니없는, 부당한
- □ inferior to ~보다 열등한
- □ abstract ⓐ 추상적인
- □ irregularity ⓝ 변칙, 불규칙 한 것
- □ favour ⓝ 호의, 친절, 은총
- □ demonstration ⓝ 입증, 설명
- □ forecast ⓥ 예측하다
- □ measurement ⓝ 측정
- □ cosmic ⓐ 우주의
- □ comprehension ⓝ 이해
- □ suspicion ⓝ 혐의, 의심
- □ revelation ⓝ 폭로, 발견, 드러냄
- □ revolution ⓝ 혁명
- □ displace ⓥ 대체하다
- □ instinct ⓝ 직관
- □ observation ⓝ 관찰
- □ decisive ⓐ 결정적인, 결단력 있는

N29

- □ visual ⓐ 시각적인
- □ purchase ⓥ 구매하다

- □ vending machine 자판기
- □ fruity ⓐ 과일 맛이 나는
- □ scale ⓝ 척도
- □ brightness ⓝ 밝기
- □ be distracted 주의가 산만해 지다
- □ preference ⓝ 선호
- □ come to the fore 두드러지 다

N30

- □ contemporary ⓐ 현대의
- □ conclude ⓥ 결론을 짓다
- □ in other words 다시 말해서
- □ value ⓥ 가치 있게 여기다
- □ on a daily basis 매일
- □ significant ⓐ 상당한
- □ amount ⓝ 양
- □ in terms of ~의 관점에서
- □ argue ⓥ 주장하다
- □ assume ⓥ 추정하다
- □ evaluate ⓥ 평가하다

N31

- □ manipulation ⓝ 조작
- □ convert ⓥ 변환하다
- □ millisecond ⓝ 1,000분의 1초, 밀리초
- □ precision ⓝ 정밀도
- □ significantly ⓐ𝖽 크게
- □ influence ⓥ 영향을 미치다
- □ first and foremost 무엇보 다도, 가장 중요하게
- □ digitization ⓝ 디지털화
- □ conversion ⓝ 변환
- □ enable ⓥ 가능하게 하다
- □ in other words 다시 말해서
- □ bend ⓥ 구부리다
- □ undo ⓥ 되돌리다

□considerably @d 상당히, 훨씬

□momentous @ 중대한

□experimental @ 실험적인

□razor blade 면도기 칼날

□sequencer ⓝ 순서기(전자 녹음 장비의 하나)

□obviously @d 분명히

□microlevel @ 매우 작은 수준의

□conceal ⓥ 숨기다

□trace ⓝ 흔적

□track ⓝ 트랙(테이프나 디스크의 데이터 구획 단위)

□audible @ 들릴 수 있는

N32

□advocate ⓝ 옹호자

□qualitative @ 질적인

□ethics ⓝ 윤리

□direct ⓥ 지향하다

□evaluate ⓥ 평가하다

□moral @ 도덕적인

□desirability ⓝ 바람직함

□consequentialist ⓝ 결과주의자

□assess ⓥ 평가하다

□derive ⓥ 도출하다

□multiply ⓥ 곱하다

□intensity ⓝ 강도

□duration ⓝ 지속성

□sophisticated @ 고상한

□capacity ⓝ 능력

□motivate ⓥ 동기부여하다

N33

□specialist ⓝ 전문가

□critic ⓝ 비평가

□familiarity ⓝ 친숙함

□informed @ 충분한 정보에 기반한

□judgement ⓝ 판단

□acknowledge ⓥ 인정하다

□significant @ 중요한

□imaging ⓝ 이미징(도형 이미지의 취득, 저장, 표시, 인쇄 등의 처리)

□involve ⓥ 포함하다

□familiarity ⓝ 친숙함

□embody ⓥ 구현하다

□attempt ⓝ 시도

□push the limit 한계를 뛰어넘다

N34

□worked-example ⓝ 해결된 예제

□pre-solved @ 미리 풀린

□free up ~을 이용 가능하게 하다

□cognitive @ 인지의

□load ⓝ 부하

□demonstrate ⓥ 보여주다

□quantitative @ 정량적인

□statistics ⓝ 통계학

□physics ⓝ 물리학

□sufficiently @d 충분히

□demanding @ 어려운

□subsequent @ 차후의

□temporarily @d 일시적으로

□relieve ⓥ 덜다

□dimension ⓝ 측면

N35

□suspect ⓥ 의심하다

□suspicious @ 의심스러운, 수상쩍은

□transaction ⓝ 거래, 매매

□enhance ⓥ 강화하다, 증진하다

□convenience ⓝ 편의, 편리

□hand-in-hand @ 손에 손을 잡은, 밀접히 연관된

□transition ⓝ 변이, 변화

□magnetic @ 자석 같은, 자성의

□embed ⓥ (단단히) 끼워 넣다

□burdensome @ 부담스러운, 힘든

□elsewhere @d 다른 곳에서[으로]

□obstacle ⓝ 장애(물)

□identification ⓝ 신원 확인

□biometrics ⓝ 생체 인식

□iris ⓝ (안구의) 홍채

□recognition ⓝ 인식, 승인

□fraudster ⓝ 사기꾼

□inevitably @d 필연적으로

□burden ⓝ 부담, 짐

□reassure ⓥ 안심시키다

□alert @ (위험을) 경계하는, 기민한

□tiresome @ 성가신

N36

□identification ⓝ 확인

□particle ⓝ 입자

□superconductor ⓝ 초전도체

□winner-take-all @ 승자독식의

□extreme @ 극단적인

□inaccurate @ 부정확한

□a handful of 소수의

□multiple @ 다양한, 복합적인

□approach ⓝ 접근 방식

□cure ⓝ 치료제

N37

- □compound ⓥ 가중시키다
- □information overload 정보 과부하
- □overrun ⓥ 압도하다
- □input ⓝ 조언, 입력
- □distract ⓥ 흐트러뜨리다
- □confuse ⓥ 혼란스럽게 하다
- □clarity ⓝ 명료성
- □present ⓝ 현재 ⓥ 제시[제공]하다
- □potentially ⓪d 잠재적으로
- □variable ⓝ 변수
- □alternatively ⓪d 그게 아니면
- □assumption ⓝ 추정, 가정
- □merit ⓝ 가치, 장점
- □clear-cut ⓐ 명확한
- □assign ⓥ 배정하다, 할당하다
- □competing ⓐ 상충되는
- □criterion ⓝ 기준 (pl. criteria)
- □predominate ⓥ 우위를 차지하다
- □shade ⓝ 미묘한 차이
- □composer ⓝ 작곡가

N38

- □misprint ⓝ 오타
- □impact ⓝ 영향
- □fatally ⓪d 치명적으로
- □displacement ⓝ (제자리에서 쫓겨난) 이동
- □consequence ⓝ 결과
- □organism ⓝ 유기체
- □reproductive ⓐ 번식의, 생식의
- □fitness ⓝ 적합성
- □accidental ⓐ 우연한

- □offspring ⓝ 자손
- □transmit ⓥ 전달하다

N39

- □particularly ⓪d 특히
- □aspect ⓝ 측면, 양상
- □responsiveness ⓝ 반응성
- □evolution ⓝ 진화
- □advantageous ⓐ 유리한
- □adaptive ⓐ 적응할 수 있는
- □state ⓝ 상태
- □pressing ⓐ 긴급한
- □true ⓐ (~에) 적용되는[해당하는]
- □inactivity ⓝ 무활동
- □hibernation ⓝ 겨울잠
- □supply ⓝ 공급(량)
- □metabolic ⓐ 신진대사의
- □maintain ⓥ 유지하다
- □adequate ⓐ 적절한
- □temperature ⓝ 온도, 체온
- □daily ⓐ 매일 일어나는
- □prey ⓝ 먹이, 사냥감
- □species ⓝ 종(생물 분류의 기초 단위)
- □avoid ⓥ 피하다
- □predator ⓝ 포식자
- □apparent ⓐ 분명한
- □universality ⓝ 보편성
- □observation ⓝ 관찰
- □cetacean ⓝ 고래목의 동물
- □complex ⓐ 복잡한
- □mechanism ⓝ (생물체 내에서 특정한 기능을 수행하는) 기제
- □preserve ⓥ 보존하다
- □suggest ⓥ 시사[암시]하다
- □additionally ⓪d 추가적으로

- □vital ⓐ 생명 유지와 관련된
- □organism ⓝ 생물(체)
- □universal ⓐ 보편적인
- □potential ⓐ 잠재적인
- □implication ⓝ 함축, 암시
- □function ⓝ 기능
- □obtain ⓥ 얻다
- □wakeful ⓐ 잠이 안 든

N40

- □reliability ⓝ 신뢰성, 신뢰도
- □dynamic ⓝ ((pl.)) 역학, 원동력
- □collective ⓐ 집단의, 공동의
- □detection ⓝ 발견, 탐지
- □cue ⓝ (무엇을 하라는) 신호
- □detect ⓥ 감지하다, 발견하다
- □shelter ⓝ (위험으로부터의) 대피처, 주거지
- □departure ⓝ 떠남, 출발
- □coordinate ⓥ (몸의 움직임을) 조정하다, 조직화하다
- □prey ⓝ 먹이, 사냥감
- □predation ⓝ (동물의) 포식

N41

- □irrealism ⓝ 비현실주의
- □predominate ⓥ 지배적이다, 두드러지다
- □filmic ⓐ 영화의, 영화적인
- □representation ⓝ 묘사, 표현
- □outline ⓝ 윤곽, 개요
- □reveal ⓥ (보이지 않던 것을) 드러내 보이다
- □veil ⓥ 가리다
- □dimension ⓝ 차원, 관점
- □theorist ⓝ 이론가
- □introduction ⓝ 도입, 전래

□innovation ⓝ 혁신, 획기적
   인 것

□realism ⓝ 사실주의

□entirely ⓐⓓ 완전히, 전적으로

□completely ⓐⓓ 완전히

□potentially ⓐⓓ 잠재적으로

□transform ⓥ (외양·모양을)
   변형하다

□mere ⓐ 단지 ~의, (한낱) ~에
   불과한

□threaten ⓥ 위협하다

□illusion ⓝ 착각, 환상

□destroy ⓥ 파괴하다, 말살하다

□essence ⓝ 본질, 진수

□medium ⓝ 매체

□coincide ⓥ 일치하다

N42

□structural ⓐ 구조적인

□element ⓝ 요소

□property ⓝ 특성

□clay ⓝ 찰흙

□superior ⓐ (~보다) 우수한

□pottery ⓝ 도자기

□alter ⓥ 바꾸다

□heat treatment 열처리

□substance ⓝ 물질

□utilization ⓝ 이용, 활용

□selection ⓝ 선택

□rather ⓐⓓ 상당히

□suited ⓐ 적합한

□application ⓝ 이용

□acquired ⓐ 획득한

□approximately ⓐⓓ 대략

□empower ⓥ ~할 수 있게
   하다

□fashion ⓥ 형성하다, 만들다

□degree ⓝ 정도

□evolve ⓥ 발달하다

□fiber ⓝ 섬유

N43

□faulty ⓐ 불완전한

□distort ⓥ 왜곡하다

□unwarranted ⓐ 부당한

□vivid ⓐ 생생한

□unusual ⓐ 특이한

□bias ⓝ 편견 ⓥ 편견을 갖게 하다

□self-serving ⓐ 자기 잇속만
   차리는

□cognitive ⓐ 인지적인

□agenda ⓝ 의제

□prime ⓥ 준비하다

□readily ⓐⓓ 손쉽게

□manipulation ⓝ 조작

N44

□settlement ⓝ 합의

□implement ⓥ 이행하다

□negotiator ⓝ 협상가

□slice ⓥ 나누다, 자르다

□quantitative ⓐ 양적인

□measurable ⓐ 측정 가능한

□compensation ⓝ 보상

□lease ⓝ 임대차 계약

□rate ⓝ 요금, -료

□quote ⓥ 시세를 매기다, 인용
   하다

□precedent ⓝ 관례, 전례

□party ⓝ (계약 등의) 당사자

□vary ⓥ 달리 하다, 변화를 주다

□devise ⓥ 고안하다

□immediate ⓐ 가장 가까운,
   직계의

O 요약문 완성하기

O01

□tendency ⓝ 경향

□dust ⓝ 소란, 소동

□emergency ⓝ 비상사태

□settle down 진정되다

□vulnerability ⓝ 취약성

□primarily ⓐⓓ 주로

□enhanced ⓐ 강화된

□revival ⓝ 회복, 부흥

□rural ⓐ 지방의, 시골의

□diversification ⓝ 다각화,
   다양화

□potential ⓐ 잠재적인

□derive ~ from ... ~을 …로
   부터 끌어내다, 얻다

□livelihood ⓝ 생계

□entitlement ⓝ 재정 지원 혜택

□mechanism ⓝ 방법, 메커니
   즘

□intervention ⓝ 개입

□sector ⓝ 부분, 분야

□at best 기껏해야

□recurrent ⓐ 반복되는

□crisis ⓝ 위기

□complicated ⓐ 복잡한

□fruitful ⓐ 생산적인, 효과적인

□dominant ⓐ 우세한

□restrictive ⓐ 제한적인

O02

□evolutionary ⓐ 진화의,
   점진적인

□variation ⓝ 변이

□arise ⓥ 발생하다

□property ⓝ 특성

O

□originate ⓥ 비롯되다, 발생하다

□respect ⓝ 측면

□remote ⓐ 외진, 먼

□evolve ⓥ 진화하다

□subsequently ⓐⓓ 그 뒤에, 나중에

□constrain ⓥ ~하게 만들다

□precise ⓐ 정확한, 엄밀한

□constraint ⓝ 제약, 제한

□foliage ⓝ 나뭇잎

□diet ⓝ 먹거리

□trait ⓝ 특성

○03

□ingredient ⓝ 성분, 재료

□fashion ⓝ 방식

□composition ⓝ 조합

□property ⓝ 특성

□toxicity ⓝ 독성

□isolated ⓐ 고립된

□variation ⓝ 변동성

□predictability ⓝ 예측 가능성

□intensify ⓥ 강화하다

□affordability ⓝ 구입 가능성

○04

□species ⓝ 종(種: 생물 분류의 기초 단위)

□distinction ⓝ 차이, 구별

□principle ⓝ 원칙, 원리

□restricted ⓐ 제한된, 한정된

□introduce ⓥ 도입하다

□combine ⓥ 결합하다

□unlimited ⓐ 무제한의

□literally ⓐⓓ 말 그대로

□infinitely ⓐⓓ 엄청, 대단히, 무한히

□superior ⓐ 뛰어난, 우수한, 우월한

□utilize ⓥ 활용하다

□represent ⓥ 나타내다

□symbolize ⓥ 상징하다

□distort ⓥ 왜곡하다

□finite ⓐ 한정된

□novel ⓐ 새로운

○05

□philosophical ⓐ 철학적인

□dominate ⓥ 지배하다

□promote ⓥ 촉진하다

□inquiry ⓝ 질문

□celebrate ⓥ 찬사를 보내다

□argument ⓝ 논쟁

□indifference ⓝ 무관심

□separable ⓐ 분리될 수 있는

□paraphrase ⓝ 다른 말로 바꾸어 표현하는 것

□evaluate ⓥ 평가하다

□misinterpret ⓥ 잘못 해석하다

□restrict ⓥ 제한하다

□reinforce ⓥ 강화하다

□broaden ⓥ 넓히다

○06

□define ⓥ 정의하다

□symmetrical ⓐ 대칭적인

□strive for ~를 얻으려 노력하다, 추구하다

□equality ⓝ 평등

□mirror ⓥ 반영하다

□complementary ⓐ 상호 보완적인

□occur ⓥ 일어나다, 발생하다

□significantly ⓐⓓ 심각하게, 상당히

□impair ⓥ 해치다

□align with ~에 맞추어 조정하다

□perceive ⓥ 인식하다

□describe ⓥ 설명하다

□manipulate ⓥ 조종하다

□regulate ⓥ 규제하다

□postponed ⓐ 지연된, 연기된

□transactional ⓐ 업무적인

□intimate ⓐ 친밀한

○07

□heart rate 심장박동수

□distract ⓥ 집중이 안 되게 하다

□companion ⓝ 친구, 동지

□past ⓐⓓ (한 쪽에서 다른 쪽으로) 지나서

□inspiration ⓝ 영감

□miss out on ~을 놓치다

□plain ⓐⓓ 분명히

□intensify ⓥ 심화시키다

□inhibit ⓥ 저해하다

□restrain ⓥ 제지하다

□facilitate ⓥ 촉진하다, 가능하게 하다

□nurture ⓥ 육성하다

□dominate ⓥ 지배하다

○08

□plasticity ⓝ 적응성, 가소성

□neuroscience ⓝ 신경 과학

□intentionally ⓐⓓ 의도적으로

□carry on 계속 가다[움직이다]

□craft ⓥ 공들여 만들다

□immigration policy 이민 정책

□modify ⓥ 수정하다

□immobilize ⓥ 고정시키다

□blossom ⓥ 번성하다

□interpretation ⓝ 해석

□narrator ⓝ 화자, 내레이터

□stretch ⓥ 늘이다

□notion ⓝ 개념, 생각
□ongoing ⓐ 진행 중인

O 09
□political ⓐ 정치적인
□significance ⓝ 의미, 중요성
□appear to-v ~인 것 같다
□spread ⓥ 퍼지다, 확산되다
□according to ~에 의하면
□hardwood tree 활엽수
□declare ⓥ 선언하다
□extent ⓝ 정도, 규모
□property ⓝ 재산
□permanence ⓝ 영속성
□claim ⓝ (재산 등에 대한) 권리
□pleasant ⓐ 즐거운
□editor ⓝ 편집자
□bound ⓝ 경계(선)
□limit ⓝ 한계(점)
□preserve ⓥ 보존하다
□testimony ⓝ 증언
□witness ⓝ 증인, 목격자
□additional ⓐ 추가의
□advantage ⓝ 유리한 점
□regard as ~으로 여기다
□the Crown (군주 국가의) 정부
□severe ⓐ 심각한
□shortage ⓝ 부족
□depend ⓥ 의존하다
□ownership ⓝ 소유(권)

O 10
□considerable ⓐ 상당한
□extent ⓝ (크기·중요성·심각성 등의) 정도
□acquire ⓥ 획득하다
□preserve ⓥ 보존하다
□effectively ⓐ 사실상
□quantity ⓝ 양

□manageable ⓐ 조작[관리]할 수 있는, 처리하기[다루기] 쉬운
□a range of 다양한
□unattainable ⓐ 얻기 어려운
□age ⓝ 시대
□memorization ⓝ 암기
□diminish ⓥ 감소시키다
□perspective ⓝ 관점
□instantaneous ⓐ 순간적인
□significance ⓝ 중요성
□dynamic ⓝ 역학
□policymaker ⓝ 정책 입안자
□anticipate ⓥ 예상하다
□isolated ⓐ 고립된, 외딴
□continuum ⓝ 연속체
□manipulation ⓝ 조작
□reflection ⓝ 심사숙고
□principal ⓐ 주요한
□decontextualize ⓥ 탈맥락화하다, 문맥에서 떼어 놓고 고찰하다
□broad ⓐ 폭넓은, 넓은
□context ⓝ 맥락, 전후 사정
□process ⓝ 과정, 절차

O 11
□rise ⓝ 출현, 발생
□consequence ⓝ 결과
□urbanism ⓝ 도시화
□dissolve ⓥ 해체하다
□informal ⓐ 비공식적인
□resident ⓝ 거주자, 주민
□interaction ⓝ 상호 작용
□occur ⓥ 일어나다, 발생하다
□attendant ⓝ 안내원, 수행원, 종업원
□norm ⓝ ((pl.)) 규범
□density ⓝ 밀도

□coordination ⓝ 조정
□a wide range of 광범위한, 다양한
□regulation ⓝ 규제
□maintenance ⓝ (건물·기계 등을 정기적으로 점검·보수하는) 유지
□minimize ⓥ 최소화하다
□pollution ⓝ 오염
□condition ⓝ ((pl.)) (생활·작업 등의) 환경[상황]
□introduce ⓥ 도입하다, 들여오다
□measure ⓝ 조치, 정책
□induce ⓥ 설득하다, 유도하다

O 12
□treat ⓝ 선물, 먹을 것
□dispense ⓥ 나누어 주다, 제공하다
□thereby ⓐ 그렇게 함으로써
□extinguish ⓥ 끝내다, 없애다
□psychological ⓐ 정신의, 심리적인
□curiosity ⓝ 호기심
□praise ⓝ 칭찬, 찬사
□booster ⓝ 촉진제, (사기를) 높이는 것
□porch ⓝ 현관
□nickel ⓝ (미국·캐나다의) 5센트 동전
□oblige ⓥ 돕다, (도움 등을) 베풀다
□willingness ⓝ 기꺼이 하는 마음
□consistently ⓐ 지속적으로
□withhold ⓥ 보류하다, 숨기다

O

O13

□at the same time 동시에
□promote ⓥ 증진하다
□maximal ⓐ 최대한의
□evolve ⓥ 진화하다
□tribe ⓝ 부족
□appreciate ⓥ 이해하다, 감상하다
□evolutionary ⓐ 진화의
□context ⓝ 맥락
□genetically ⓐⓓ 유전적으로
□variation ⓝ 차이
□collectively ⓐⓓ 집합적으로
□potentially ⓐⓓ 잠재적으로
□survival fitness 생존 적합도
□trait ⓝ 특성
□variability ⓝ 변동성
□enhance ⓥ 높이다

O14

□exaggerated ⓐ 과장된
□supernormal ⓐ 비범한
□stimuli ⓝ 자극
□preference ⓝ 선호
□propel ⓥ 나아가게 하다
□conditioned ⓐ 조건부의
□geometric ⓐ 기하학의
□rectangle ⓝ 직사각형
□associated with ~와 연관된
□reliably ⓐⓓ 확실히
□predictable ⓐ 예측할 수 있는
□opportunity ⓝ 기회
□proportion ⓝ 비율
□inclination ⓝ 기호, 성향
□severe ⓐ 극단적인
□vague ⓐ 희미한

□unexpected ⓐ 예상치 못한
□subtle ⓐ 미묘한

O15

□materialism ⓝ 물질주의
□somehow ⓐⓓ 어떻게든, 왜 그런지 (모르겠지만), 왠지
□entitled ⓐ (~라는) 제목의
□nationwide ⓐ 전국적인
□deeply ⓐⓓ 대단히, 깊이
□gain ⓝ 이익
□greed ⓝ 탐욕
□excess ⓝ 지나침, 과잉
□center on ~에 초점을 맞추다
□priority ⓝ 우선순위
□fellow ⓐ 같은 처지에 있는, 동료의
□increasingly ⓐⓓ 점점 더, 갈수록 더
□atomize ⓥ 개별화하다, 세분화하다
□selfish ⓐ 이기적인
□irresponsible ⓐ 무책임한
□isolate ⓥ 소외시키다, 고립시키다
□unite ⓥ 결속하다
□cause ⓝ 대의
□pursuit ⓝ 추구, (원하는 것을) 좇음[찾음]
□purely ⓐⓓ 순전히, 전적으로
□cut off from ~에서 고립시키다
□detach ⓥ 떼다, 분리하다
□fairly ⓐⓓ 상당히, 꽤
□concern ⓝ 우려, 걱정

O16

□demonstrate ⓥ 보여주다, 설명하다

□contain ⓥ 포함하다, 억제하다
□countless ⓐ 셀 수 없이 많은
□reference ⓝ 언급, 참조
□doubt ⓝ 의심, 의혹
□absolute ⓐ 철저한, 완전한
□necessity ⓝ 필요(성), 불가피한 일
□degree ⓝ 정도, (각도·온도 단위의) 도
□complexity ⓝ 복잡성, 복잡함
□appliance ⓝ (가정용) 기기
□houseware ⓝ 가정용품
□substantial ⓐ (양·중요성 등이) 상당한
□implement ⓥ 시행하다
□overlook ⓥ 간과하다, 내려다보다
□emphasis ⓝ 강조(법)
□individuality ⓝ 개성, 특성
□problematic ⓐ 문제가 있는[많은]
□personality ⓝ 성격, 유명인
□distinction ⓝ 차이, 특별함
□relevant ⓐ 관련 있는, 유의미한
□coordinate ⓥ 조직화하다, 조정하다

O17

□fiction ⓝ 소설, 허구의 창작물
□under-documented ⓐ 문서로 덜 기록된
□ordinary ⓐ 평범한
□portray ⓥ 묘사하다
□atmosphere ⓝ 분위기
□context ⓝ 맥락
□flesh ⓝ 살
□uncover ⓥ 밝히다

□account ⓝ 설명
□indication ⓝ 표현
□circumstances ⓝ 상황
□archive ⓝ 역사 자료, 기록 보관소
□unexplored ⓐ 탐구되지 않은
□reconstruct ⓥ 재구성하다
□inviting ⓐ 매력적인

O18
□craft ⓝ 기술
□inventive ⓐ 창의성이 풍부한
□fame ⓝ 명성
□refine ⓥ 세련되게 하다
□execution ⓝ 실행, 수행
□decade ⓝ 10년
□claim ⓥ 주장하다
□equivalent ⓐ 동등한
□proposition ⓝ 명제
□imitation ⓝ 모방
□traitor ⓝ 배신자
□expose ⓥ 폭로하다, 노출하다
□norm ⓝ 기준, 규범
□strict ⓐ 엄격한
□criticize ⓥ 비난하다
□modify ⓥ 변형하다, 수정하다
□blend ⓥ 섞다, 혼합하다
□disclose ⓥ 공개하다, 드러내다
□distort ⓥ 왜곡하다, 뒤틀다
□evaluate ⓥ 평가하다
□underestimate ⓥ 과소평가하다

O19
□notable ⓐ 주목할 만한
□embrace ⓥ 수용하다, 포괄하다

□concentrate ⓥ 집중하다
□attainment ⓝ 성취, 성과
□sphere ⓝ 영역
□amount to ~와 마찬가지이다
□universal ⓐ 보편적인
□proceed ⓥ 나아가다, 진행하다
□simplified ⓐ 단순화된
□formula ⓝ 공식
□abbreviate ⓥ 축약하다
□sufficient ⓐ 충분한
□perception ⓝ 인식

O20
□identical ⓐ 동질적인
□asset ⓝ 자산
□implication ⓝ 암시
□presentation ⓝ 공연
□necessity ⓝ 필요성
□rest (up)on 의존하다
□received ⓐ 인정받는
□tradition ⓝ 전통
□make sense of 이해하다
□acknowledge ⓥ 인정하다
□prominence ⓝ 중점
□pupil ⓝ 학생
□numerous ⓐ 수많은
□attempt ⓝ 시도
□absorb ⓥ 흡수하다
□overlook ⓥ 간과하다
□prioritize ⓥ 우선시하다

O21
□fossilization ⓝ 화석화
□fossil ⓝ 화석
□evidence ⓝ 증거
□particular ⓐ 특정한, 특별한
□circumstance ⓝ 환경, 상황
□favourable ⓐ 유리한

□absence ⓝ 부재, 없음
□implication ⓝ 암시, 함축
□presence ⓝ 존재함, 있음
□saying ⓝ 속담
□logic ⓝ 논리, 타당성
□arise ⓥ 생기다
□appear ⓥ 나타나다, ~인 것 같다
□datum ⓝ 자료(pl. data)
□conservative ⓐ (실제 수나 양보다) 적게 잡은, 보수적인
□statement ⓝ 진술
□extinction ⓝ 멸종, 소멸
□definitely ⓐⓓ 분명히, 확실히
□population ⓝ 인구, (모든) 주민, 개체군

O22
□craftsmanship ⓝ 장인정신
□misleading ⓐ 오해의 소지가 있는
□name ⓥ 말하다, 명명하다
□enduring ⓐ 지속적인
□impulse ⓝ 충동
□manual ⓐ 육체노동의, 손으로 하는
□serve ⓥ 도움이 되다, 기여하다
□parenting ⓝ 양육, 육아
□craft ⓝ 기술, (수)공예
□citizenship ⓝ 시민정신
□domain ⓝ 영역
□stand in the way of ~을 방해하다
□discipline ⓝ 수련, 규율
□commitment ⓝ 전념, 헌신
□aspiration ⓝ 열망, 염원
□conflicting ⓐ 상충하는
□weaken ⓥ 약화시키다

□ competitive ⓐ 경쟁적인

□ frustration ⓝ 좌절

□ obsession ⓝ 집착

□ cultivate ⓥ 양성하다

□ accelerate ⓥ 가속화하다

□ diminish ⓥ 줄어들다

O23

□ mobility ⓝ 이동성, 유동성

□ transit ⓝ 수송, 교통 체계

□ broad ⓐ 폭넓은, 일반적인

□ discipline ⓝ 규율, (대학의) 학과목

□ faculty ⓝ 능력, (대학의) 학부

□ humanity ⓝ 인류, ((pl.)) 인문학

□ acceleration ⓝ 가속(도)

□ geographical ⓐ 지리(학)적인

□ virtual ⓐ (컴퓨터를 이용한) 가상의

□ passive ⓐ 수동적인, 소극적인

□ transport ⓥ 이동하다, 수송하다

□ artefact ⓝ 인공물, 가공물

□ terminal ⓐ 불치병에 걸린, (질병이) 말기의

□ disproportion ⓝ 불균형

□ immobile ⓐ 움직이지 않는

□ exclusion ⓝ 제외, 배제

□ bodily ⓐ 신체의

O24

□ alternative ⓝ 대안, 대체 가능한 것

□ philosophical ⓐ 철학의

□ theory ⓝ 이론, 학설

□ consist in (주요 특징 등이) ~에 있다

□ unification ⓝ 통합

□ broad ⓐ 광대한, 광범위한

□ body ⓝ 많은 양, 많은 모음

□ phenomenon ⓝ 현상 (pl. phenomena)

□ minimal ⓐ 최소의, 아주 적은

□ generalization ⓝ 일반화

□ construct ⓥ 구성하다, 건설하다

□ economical ⓐ 경제적인, 알뜰한

□ framework ⓝ (판단 · 결정 등을 위한) 틀

□ capable of ~을 할 수 있는

□ observable ⓐ 관찰할 수 있는

□ systematize ⓥ 체계화하다

□ causal ⓐ 인과 관계의

□ mechanical ⓐ (행동 · 반응 등이) 기계적인, 기계에 의한

□ approach ⓝ 접근법

□ consist of ~로 구성되다

□ uncover ⓥ 밝히다, 알아내다

□ primary ⓐ 일차적인, 주요한

□ regularity ⓝ 규칙적임, 규칙성

□ seek ⓥ 찾다, 추구하다

□ observation ⓝ 관찰, 감지

□ general ⓐ 일반적인, 보통의

O25

□ cross-cultural ⓐ 다양한 문화들이 섞인

□ perspective ⓝ 시각, 관점

□ equation ⓝ 등식, 동일시, 방정식

□ dominance ⓝ 권세, 지배, 우세

□ questionable ⓐ 의심스러운, 미심쩍은

□ indicate ⓥ 나타내다, 시사하다

□ conceivably ⓐⓓ 생각할 수 있는 바로는, 상상컨대

□ bothersome ⓐ 성가신

□ be fond of ~을 좋아하다

□ notably ⓐⓓ 현저히, 뚜렷이

□ allergic ⓐ 몹시 싫어하는, (~에 대해) 알레르기가 있는

□ obvious ⓐ 분명한, 명백한

□ coercive ⓐ 강압적인

□ force ⓝ 물리력, 힘

□ fixation ⓝ 집착, 고정

□ universal ⓐ 일반적인, 보편적인

□ leap ⓝ (상상 · 논리의) 비약, 도약, 급증

□ shaky ⓐ 떨리는, 휘청거리는, 불안정한

□ remark ⓥ 언급[발언]하다

□ notion ⓝ 개념, 관념

□ personhood ⓝ 개인적 특질, 개성

□ obsession ⓝ 강박, 집착

□ bias ⓝ 편견, 편향

P 장문의 이해

P01~02

□ negotiator ⓝ 협상가

□ integrative ⓐ 통합하는

□ negotiation ⓝ 협상

□ mythical ⓐ 허구의, 가상의

□ settlement ⓝ 합의, 해결

□ suppress ⓥ 억누르다

□ insist ⓥ 고집하다, 주장하다

□ expense ⓝ 돈, 비용

□ resolution ⓝ 해결

□ tendency ⓝ 경향

□ given ⓐ 정해진

□ jail sentence 징역형

□ in terms of ~면에서는

□ be inclined to ~하는 경향이 있다

□ cooperatively ⓐⓓ 협력하여, 협조적으로

□ constraint ⓝ 제약

□ alternative ⓝ 대안

P03~04

□ index finger 집게손가락

□ forceful ⓐ 강력한

□ precision ⓝ 정확성, 정밀성

□ in a snap 순식간에

□ breakthrough ⓝ 돌파구, 획기적인 발전

□ evolution ⓝ 진화

□ manipulate ⓥ 조작하다

□ delicate ⓐ 깨지기 쉬운

□ reorient ⓥ 방향을 바꾸다

□ displacement ⓝ 이동

□ attribute ⓝ 속성

□ dog-ear ⓥ 모서리를 접다

□ pointy ⓐ 끝이 뾰족한

□ combination ⓝ 조합

□ trait ⓝ 특성

□ coordinate ⓥ 조정하다

□ exclude ⓥ 배제하다

□ leap ⓝ 도약

P05~06

□ considerably ⓐⓓ 상당히

□ rearrangement ⓝ 재배열

□ rhyme ⓝ 운(음조가 비슷한 글자)

□ poetic ⓐ 시적인

□ compression ⓝ 압축

□ category ⓝ 범주

□ altogether ⓐⓓ 완전히

□ deaf ⓐ 귀를 기울이지 않는

□ achievement ⓝ 업적

□ artfully ⓐⓓ 교묘하게

□ manipulate ⓥ 능숙하게 조작하다

□ seashore ⓝ 해안

□ be accustomed to ~에 익숙해지다

□ eardrum ⓝ 고막

□ depart ⓥ 떠나다

□ refresh ⓥ 새롭게 하다

□ inspiration ⓝ 영감

□ cite ⓥ 인용하다

P07~08

□ identification ⓝ 검증, 식별

□ evaluation ⓝ 평가

□ ethical ⓐ 윤리적인

□ perspective ⓝ 관점

□ distinct ⓐ 구별되는[뚜렷이 다른]

□ think through 충분히 생각하다

□ prescribe ⓥ 규정[지시]하다, 처방하다

□ recognition ⓝ 인식, 인정

□ in accordance with ~에 따라, ~에 부합되게

□ civic ⓐ (도시의, 시민의

□ coincide ⓥ 일치하다, 동시에 일어나다

□ alongside (prep) ~옆에, 나란히

□ priority ⓝ 우선(권)

P09~10

□ vocal ⓐ 목소리의, 발성의

□ audibly ⓐⓓ 들리도록

□ indistinguishable ⓐ 구분이 안 되는

□ dimension ⓝ 차원

□ similitude ⓝ 유사함

□ linguistic ⓐ 언어의

□ appropriate ⓐ 적절한

□ inherent ⓐ 내재하는

□ resemble ⓥ 닮다

□ exclude ⓥ 제외하다, 배제하다

□ subtext ⓝ 언외의 의미, 숨은 의미

P11~12

□ measure ⓥ (치수·양 등을 표준 단위로) 측정하다

□ inflation ⓝ 인플레이션 (물가 상승률)

□ shrink ⓥ 줄어들다

□ amount ⓝ 양

□ various ⓐ 다양한

□ sort ⓝ 종류

□ liquid ⓐ 액체의

□ prevent ⓥ 방지하다

□ pressure ⓝ 압박

□ era ⓝ 시대

□ strategy ⓝ 전략

□ innovative ⓐ 획기적인

□ attract ⓥ 마음을 끌다

P13~14

□ disadvantageous ⓐ 불리한

□ generation after generation 자손 대대로

□ color blindness 색맹

□ compensate ⓥ 보상하다

□ deficiency ⓝ 결점

□distinguish ⓥ 구별하다

□die out 멸종되다, 소멸하다

□contrast ⓥ 대조하다

□detect ⓥ 발견하다, 감지하다

□conceivable ⓐ 상상할 수 있는, 가능한

□circumstance ⓝ 환경, 상황

□given that ~을 고려하면

□surroundings ⓝ 환경

□variation ⓝ 변화, 변동

□genetic ⓐ 유전의

□destine ⓥ (운명으로) 정해지다

□vanish ⓥ 사라지다, 소멸하다

P15~16

□tone ⓝ 어조

□perspective ⓝ 관점

□generate ⓥ 만들어 내다

□associate ⓥ 연관 짓다, 연상하다

□assume ⓥ 가정하다

□restructure ⓥ 재구성하다

□underlying ⓐ 기저의

□layer ⓝ 층, 막

□surface ⓝ 표면

□momentarily ⓐⓓ 순간적으로

□automatic ⓐ 무의식의, 반사적인

□navigate ⓥ 항해하다

□anxiety ⓝ 불안감

□reject ⓥ 거부하다

□potentially ⓐⓓ 잠재적으로

□heighten ⓥ 고조되다

P17~18

□scholar ⓝ 장학생, 학자

□stereotypical ⓐ 고정관념의

□discuss ⓥ 논의하다

□notion ⓝ 개념

□state ⓝ 상태

□affair ⓝ (현재 얘기되거나 다뤄지는) 일[사건]

□assume ⓥ 추정하다

□absence ⓝ 부재, 없음

□mention ⓥ 언급하다

□associate ⓥ 결부[연관] 짓다

□stereotype ⓝ 고정 관념, 정형화된 생각[이미지]

□tendency ⓝ 성향, 기질, 경향

□representation ⓝ 표현

□channel ⓥ 특정한 방향으로 돌리다

□chase ⓥ 쫓다

□root ⓥ 뿌리박다

□associative ⓐ 연상의

□linguistic ⓐ 언어(학)의

□afford ⓥ (~을 살·할 금전적·시간적) 여유[형편]가 되다

□theoretical ⓐ 이론적인

□confront ⓥ 직면하다

□nonetheless ⓐⓓ 그렇기는 하지만, 그럴더라도

□categorization ⓝ 범주화

P19~20

□typically ⓐⓓ 일반적으로

□subject ⓝ 실험[연구] 대상, 피험자

□supplement ⓝ 보충(제)

□observe ⓥ 관찰하다

□determine ⓥ 알아내다, 밝히다

□inherent ⓐ 내재하는, 고유한

□sort ⓥ 분류하다

□assign ⓥ 배정하다, 맡기다

□accomplish ⓥ 달성하다

□randomization ⓝ 임의추출

□flip ⓥ 톡 던지다

□factor ⓝ 요인

□rule out ~을 배제하다

□rate ⓝ 비율

□severity ⓝ 심함, 격렬[맹렬]함

□duration ⓝ 지속 (기간)

□nutrient ⓝ 영양분

□with respect to ~에 관하여

□apparent ⓐ 분명한

□irrelevant ⓐ 무관한

□in-depth ⓐ 면밀한, 철저하고 상세한

□analysis ⓝ 분석

P21~22

□generalization ⓝ 일반화

□promote ⓥ 촉진하다

□amnesia ⓝ 기억상실증

□supercharged ⓐ 과급된, 과한

□perform ⓥ 수행하다

□feat ⓝ 솜씨, 재주

□mathematical ⓐ 수학의

□complex ⓐ 복잡한

□formula ⓝ 공식

□sequence ⓝ 배열

□abstraction ⓝ 추상화

□distinct ⓐ 별개의

□identify ⓥ 알아보다

□neurocognitive ⓐ 신경인지적인

□standpoint ⓝ 관점

□angle ⓝ 각도

□interact ⓥ 상호작용하다

□manifestation ⓝ 징후, 표명

□belong to ~에 속하다

P23~24

□be equipped with ~을 갖추고 있다

□ reflexive response 반사 반응

□ helpless ⓐ 무력한

□ articulate ⓥ 분명히 표현하다

□ dependent ⓐ 의존적인

□ strikingly ⓐⓓ 눈에 띄는, 현저한

□ signify ⓥ 의미하다

□ limitation ⓝ 한계

□ flexibility ⓝ 유연성

□ unfortunate ⓐ 운이 없는

□ capacity ⓝ 능력

□ niche ⓝ 적합한 장소, 틈새

□ thrive ⓥ 번성하다

□ remarkably ⓐⓓ 놀라울 정도로

□ wired up 연결된 채로

□ forbid ⓥ 금지하다, 막다

□ mold ⓥ 형성되다, 만들다

□ evolutionary ⓐ 진화의

□ tragedy ⓝ 비극

P25~26

□ underestimate ⓥ 과소평 가하다

□ recognize ⓥ 인식하다

□ context ⓝ 맥락

□ retain ⓥ 기억해 두다, 잊지 않다

□ frequently ⓐⓓ 자주, 빈번히

□ unconvinced ⓐ 확신하지 못하는

□ persuasive ⓐ 설득력 있는

□ argument ⓝ 주장

□ credible ⓐ 신뢰할 수 있는

□ financial interest 금전적 이익

□ conclude ⓥ 결론을 내리다

P27~28

□ post ⓝ 기둥, 말뚝

□ hold up (쓰러지지 않도록) ~을 떠받치다

□ sign ⓝ 표지판, 간판

□ utility ⓝ (수도·가스·전기 등의) 공익 사업

□ durable ⓐ 내구성이 있는, 오래가는

□ withstand ⓥ 견뎌[이겨] 내다

□ every so often 가끔, 종종

□ call upon (~에게 …을) 요구하 다

□ crucial ⓐ 중대한, 결정적인

□ fundamentally ⓐⓓ 근본[본 질]적으로, 완전히

□ at odds 상충하는, 조화를 이루 지 못하는

□ impact ⓝ 충돌, 충격

□ come apart 부서지다, 흩어 지다

□ attempt ⓥ 시도하다, 애써 해 보다

□ resolve ⓥ 해결하다, 다짐하다

□ apparent ⓐ 분명한, 명백한

□ paradox ⓝ 역설(적인 상황)

□ robust ⓐ 튼튼한, 강력한

□ properly ⓐⓓ 제대로, 적절히

□ separate ⓐ 분리된, 따로 떨어 진

□ plate ⓝ (금속으로 된) 판

□ joint ⓝ 연결 부위, 관절

□ apart ⓐⓓ 조각조각, 산산이, 따로

□ basically ⓐⓓ 근본[기본]적으로

□ attach ⓥ 붙이다, 첨부하다

□ breakaway ⓐ 분리[이탈]한

□ fracture ⓥ 파열[균열]되다

□ knock over ~을 때려눕히다

□ subsequent ⓐ 그[이] 다음 의, 차후의

□ infrastructure ⓝ 사회[공공] 기반 시설

□ material ⓝ (물건의) 재료

□ critical ⓐ 비판적인, 대단히 중 요한

□ underpin ⓥ 뒷받침하다, 보강 하다

□ obvious ⓐ 분명한, 확실한

□ naked ⓐ 벌거벗은, 아무것도 걸치지 않은

□ tuck away ~을 숨기다[(안전 한 곳에) 보관하다]

□ ruin ⓥ 망치다

□ sustainable ⓐ (환경 파괴 없 이) 지속 가능한

P29~30

□ to the extent that ~한 경 우에, ~하는 한

□ sufficient ⓐ 충분한

□ context ⓝ 맥락, 전후 사정, 문맥

□ come away with ~을 가지 고 떠나다

□ approximation ⓝ 근접한 것, 비슷한 것

□ struggle ⓝ 투쟁, 분투 ⓥ 투쟁[고투]하다

□ vanish ⓥ 사라지다

□ fictive ⓐ 허구의

□ extreme ⓝ 극단

□ happily ⓐⓓ 적절하게

□ correspondence ⓝ 관련 성

□ original ⓐ 원래의

□ out-of-date 시대에 뒤떨어진, 구식의

□ translation ⓝ 번역
□ up to date 최신의
□ at the price of ~을 대가로 [희생하여]
□ fairly ⓐⓓ 꽤, 상당히
□ intense ⓐ 격렬한, 강렬한
□ reference ⓝ 참조
□ mistakenly ⓐⓓ 잘못(하여)
□ critical ⓐ 중대한
□ lighthouse ⓝ 등대
□ narrow ⓐ 좁은
□ outlook ⓝ 관점, 세계관

P31~32
□ domination ⓝ 지배
□ ethics ⓝ 윤리
□ tie ⓥ 결부하다
□ philosophy ⓝ 철학
□ politics ⓝ 정치학
□ causal ⓐ 인과의
□ govern ⓥ 지배하다
□ intervene ⓥ 개입하다
□ mark ⓥ 알리다
□ prosperity ⓝ 번영
□ triumph ⓝ 승리
□ ignorance ⓝ 무지
□ superstition ⓝ 미신
□ industrialization ⓝ 산업화
□ generate ⓥ 야기하다
□ alienation ⓝ 소외
□ compose ⓥ 구성하다
□ unease ⓝ 불안감
□ era ⓝ 시대
□ systematic ⓐ 체계적인
□ come into its own 진가를 발휘하다

P33~34
□ region ⓝ 지방, 지역

□ be associated with ~와 관련되다
□ possession ⓝ 소유
□ transfer ⓥ 이전하다
□ reform ⓝ 개혁
□ auction ⓝ 경매
□ favour ⓥ ~에 유리하다, ~에 편들다
□ ensure ⓥ 반드시 ~하게[이게] 하다, 보장하다
□ arise ⓥ 생기다, 발생하다
□ grant ⓥ (인정하여 정식으로) 주다, 수여하다
□ separately ⓐⓓ 별개로, 각기
□ allocate ⓥ 분배하다, 할당하다
□ measure ⓝ (치수·양 등을 나타내는) 단위
□ runoff ⓝ (땅속으로 흡수되지 않고 흐르는) 유수(流水)
□ well ⓝ 우물
□ guarantee ⓥ 보장하다
□ derived from ~에서 얻은
□ capture ⓥ 포획, 억류
□ flash flood 갑작스럽게 불어난 물
□ be subject to ~의 영향을 받다
□ constitute ⓥ ~이 되는 것으로 여겨지다, 구성하다
□ per ⓟⓡⓔⓟ 각[매] ~에 대하여, ~당[마다]
□ unit ⓝ 구성 단위
□ bypass ⓥ 회피하다, 무시하다, 우회하다
□ cultivation ⓝ 재배
□ crop ⓝ 작물
□ substantial ⓐ 상당한
□ harvest ⓥ 수확하다, 거둬들이다
□ fair ⓐ 타당한, 공정한

□ share ⓝ (여러 사람이 나눠 가지는 것의) 몫, 지분
□ status ⓝ 신분, 자격, 지위

P35~36
□ contribute to ~에 기여하다
□ responsibility ⓝ 책임
□ recognition ⓝ 인정
□ run a risk of ~의 위험이 있다
□ misinterpretation ⓝ 오해
□ clarification ⓝ 해명
□ controversy ⓝ 논란
□ resist ⓥ 저항하다, 물리치다
□ preserve ⓥ 보존하다
□ misquote ⓥ (말이나 글을) 잘못 인용하다
□ unpleasantry ⓝ 불쾌한 상황
□ coverage ⓝ (언론의) 보도

P37~38
□ irresistible ⓐ 억누를[저항할] 수 없는, 거부할 수 없는
□ term ⓝ 용어, 말
□ attribute to ~의 덕분[탓]으로 돌리다
□ complex ⓐ 복잡한
□ motive ⓝ 동기, 이유
□ purely ⓐⓓ 순전히, 전적으로, 오직
□ internal ⓐ 내부의, 체내의
□ track ⓥ 추적하다, 뒤쫓다
□ twist ⓝ (도로·강 등의) 굽이 [급커브]
□ turn ⓝ 돌기, 방향 전환, 회전
□ irregular ⓐ 불규칙적인, 고르지 못한
□ equally ⓐⓓ 똑같이, 동일[동등]하게

□work out ~을 알아내다 [해결하다]

□infer ⓥ 추론하다, 암시하다

□path ⓝ 길, 방향

□put ⓥ 표현[말]하다, (말·글로) 옮기다

□illustrate ⓥ 분명히 보여주다

□correlation ⓝ 연관성, 상관 관계

P39~40

□onlooker ⓝ 구경꾼

□merely ⓐⒹ 그저, 단지

□leak ⓝ 누출, 누설

□quarrel ⓝ 말다툼, 불만

□alert ⓐ 경계하는, 기민한

□tendency ⓝ 경향, 성향

□blind ⓐ 눈이 먼, 맹목적인

□conformity ⓝ (규칙에) 따름

□derive ⓥ 끌어내다, 얻다

□valuable ⓐ 귀중한, 값비싼

□anxiety ⓝ 불안(감), 염려

□embarrassing ⓐ 난처한, 당혹스러운

□cool ⓝ 냉정, 침착

□potentially ⓐⒹ 잠재적으로, 어쩌면

□acute ⓐ 극심한, 예민한

□passivity ⓝ 수동성, 소극성

P41~42

□right ⓝ 권리, 권한

□privacy ⓝ 사생활

□extend ⓥ 확대하다

□restrict ⓥ 제한하다

□expression ⓝ 표현

□scope ⓝ 범위

□similarly ⓐⒹ 비슷하게

□general ⓐ 보편적인, 일반적인

□prevent ⓥ 예방하다

□crime ⓝ 범죄

□promote ⓥ 촉진하다

□public ⓐ 공공의

□property-based 속성에 기반을 둔

□notion ⓝ 개념, 생각

□personality ⓝ 인격, 성격

□modern ⓐ 현대적인

□private ⓐ 사적인

□establish ⓥ 설정하다

□limit ⓝ 한계

□strength ⓝ 강점, 장점

□in that ~라는 관점에서

□adapt ⓥ 적용하다

□meet ⓥ 잘 대처하다

□expectation ⓝ 기대, 예상

□technological ⓐ 기술상의

□advance ⓝ 발전, 진보

□in sum 요컨대

□concept ⓝ 개념

□include ⓥ 포함하나

□claim ⓝ 주장, 권리

□unobserved ⓐ 주시당하지 않는

□certain ⓐ 특정한, 어떤

□circulate ⓥ 유포하다

□permission ⓝ 허락, 허가

□arise ⓥ 생기다, 발생하다

□offence ⓝ 모욕

□observation ⓝ 관찰

□furthermore ⓐⒹ 게다가

□incorporate ⓥ 포함하다

□correspondence ⓝ 서신, 편지

□interference ⓝ 간섭, 참견

□determination ⓝ 결심, 결정

□honour ⓝ 명예

□reputation ⓝ 평판

□material ⓝ 자료, 재료, 소재

□legally ⓐⒹ 법률적으로

□response ⓝ 대응, 대답

□reproduction ⓝ 재생산

□recent ⓐ 최근의

□storage ⓝ 저장, 보관

□pose ⓥ (문제 등을) 제기하다

□threat ⓝ 위협

□reinterpret ⓥ 재해석하다

□challenge ⓝ 도전

P43~44

□evidence ⓝ 증거

□outperform ⓥ 능가하다

□judgement ⓝ 판단

□prediction ⓝ 예측

□accurate ⓐ 정확한

□release ⓥ 풀어 주다, 석방 [해방]하다

□commit ⓥ (그릇된 일·범죄를) 저지르다[범하다]

□potential ⓐ 잠재적인

□candidate ⓝ 지원자, 응시자

□domain ⓝ (지식·활동의) 영역 [분야]

□formula ⓝ 공식

□significant ⓐ 중요한

□remainder ⓝ 나머지

□handful ⓝ 줌, 움큼

□tie ⓝ 동점, 무승부

□factor ⓝ 요소

□uncertain ⓐ 불확실한

□win out 승리하다, 성취하다

□consistent ⓐ 일관된, 변함없는

□consideration ⓝ 숙고, 고려 사항

□ a range of 다양한
□ ensure ⓥ 보장하다
□ intensive ⓐ 집중적인, 많은 주의를 기울여야 하는
□ crucial ⓐ 중대한, 결정적인
□ remarkably ⓐⓓ 놀랍게도
□ live ⓐ 당면한, 현재 관심을 모으는
□ infection ⓝ 감염
□ prioritise ⓥ 우선순위를 매기다
□ myth ⓝ 신화, 근거 없는 믿음
□ simplicity ⓝ 간단함, 평이함
□ beat ⓥ 이기다

P45~46
□ humanist ⓝ 인문주의자, 인도주의자
□ crisis ⓝ 위기
□ core ⓝ 중심부
□ derangement ⓝ 혼란 (상태)
□ contemporary ⓐ 동시대의, 현대의
□ flood ⓝ 홍수, 쇄도
□ improbable ⓐ 있을 것 같지 않은, 별난
□ extraordinary ⓐ 기이한, 비범한
□ environmentalist ⓝ 환경론자
□ imperceptible ⓐ (너무 작아서) 감지할 수 없는
□ occasionally ⓐⓓ 가끔
□ explosive ⓐ 폭발성의, (분노를) 촉발하는
□ spectacular ⓐ 장관을 이루는, 극적인
□ impact ⓝ 영향, 충격

□ day-to-day ⓐ 그날그날의, 매일 행해지는
□ accumulate ⓥ 축적하다
□ pose ⓥ (위협·문제 등을) 제기하다
□ significant ⓐ 중요한, 커다란
□ representational ⓐ 표현적인, 대표(제)의
□ track ⓥ 추적하다, 뒤쫓다
□ glacier ⓝ 빙하
□ coral reef 산호초
□ highlight ⓥ 강조하다
□ gradually ⓐⓓ 서서히

P47~48
□ classify A into B A를 B로 분류하다
□ arrange ⓥ 배열하다, 정리하다
□ random ⓐ 마구잡이의, 임의의
□ order ⓝ 순서, 명령, 주문
□ aisle ⓝ 통로, 복도
□ time-consuming (많은) 시간이 걸리는
□ extremely ⓐⓓ 매우, 극도로
□ classification ⓝ 분류(법)
□ ready-made 이미 만들어진, 기성의
□ embody ⓥ 포함하다, 상징[구현]하다
□ distinguish A from B A를 B와 구별하다
□ abstract ⓐ 추상적인, 관념적인
□ master ⓥ 숙달하다, 통달하다
□ unorganized ⓐ 조직화되어 있지 않은, 정돈되지 않은
□ infant ⓝ 유아, 아기
□ core ⓝ 핵심, 중심부

Q 복합 문단의 이해

Q01~03
□ force ⓝ 힘, 물리력
□ thrilling ⓐ 아주 신나는
□ challenge ⓝ 도전
□ plant ⓥ 자리를 잡다, 심다
□ firmly ⓐⓓ 확고히
□ crash ⓥ (세게) 부딪치다
□ rough ⓐ 거친
□ toss ⓥ (가볍게 아무렇게나) 던지다
□ eagerly ⓐⓓ 열심히
□ balance ⓥ 균형을 유지하다
□ soaked ⓐ 물에 흠뻑 젖은
□ spray ⓝ 물보라
□ advantage ⓝ 유리한 점
□ mindset ⓝ 사고방식, 태도
□ daring ⓐ 대담한
□ adventurer ⓝ 모험가
□ courage ⓝ 용기
□ reflection ⓝ (물·거울 등에 비친) 모습
□ confident ⓐ 자신감 있는
□ excitedly ⓐⓓ 흥분하여
□ manage to-v 용케 ~을 해내다
□ avoid ⓥ 피하다, 모면하다
□ suddenly ⓐⓓ 갑자기
□ calm down 진정하다
□ sigh ⓝ 한숨
□ relief ⓝ 안도, 안심
□ view ⓝ 풍경
□ scenery ⓝ 경치
□ breathtaking ⓐ (너무 아름답거나 놀라워서) 숨이 막히는

□speechless ⓐ 말문이 막힌

□thumbs-up 찬성, 격려

□delighted ⓐ 아주 기뻐하는

□explain ⓥ 설명하다

□adventurous ⓐ 모험적인

□bravery ⓝ 용기

□completely ⓐd 완전히

□confidence ⓝ 자신감

□suggest ⓥ 제안하다

Q04~06

□envy ⓥ 부러워하다

□hesitation ⓝ 망설임

□remind ⓥ 상기시키다

□politely ⓐd 정중하게

□embarrassed ⓐ 당황스러운, 민망한

□apologize ⓥ 사과하다

□in silence 조용히, 말없이

□twist ⓥ 삐끗하다

□energize ⓥ 열기[열정]를 돋우다

Q07~09

□thrilled ⓐ 황홀해 하는

□notification ⓝ 알림, 통지

□second-hand ⓐ 중고의

□market rate 시장 시세

□stick out of ~ 밖으로 삐져나오다

□identify ⓥ 알아보다

□glossy ⓐ 윤이 나는

□immediately ⓐd 즉시

□type ⓥ 타자 치다[입력하다]

□in excitement 흥분하여

□exclaim ⓥ 외치다, 소리치다

□condition ⓝ 상태

□in good shape 상태가 좋은

□expert ⓝ 전문가

Q10~12

□welcoming ceremony 환영식

□sister ⓝ 자매(기관)

□pick out ~을 고르다

□apologize ⓥ 사과하다

□lively ⓐ 활기 넘치는

□introduce ⓥ 소개하다

□take one's place 있어야 할 곳에 가다, 자리를 잡다

□fascinate ⓥ 매료시키다

□flawless ⓐ 나무랄 데 없는

□cheer ⓥ 환호하다

□beam ⓥ 활짝 웃다

□rehearsal ⓝ 예행연습, 리허설

□confidence ⓝ 자신감

□struggle with ~와 씨름하다

□patterned ⓐ 무늬가 있는

□object ⓥ 반대하다

□clerk ⓝ 점원, 직원

Q13~15

□frosty ⓐ 서리가 내리는, 몹시 추운

□swallow ⓥ 삼키다

□reach out (손 등을) 뻗다

□offer ⓝ 제안

□disappear ⓥ 사라지다

□hesitate ⓥ 망설이다

□urge ⓥ 재촉하다

□gathered around ~의 주위에 모이다

□marvelous ⓐ 놀라운

Q16~18

□transatlantic ⓐ 대서양 횡단의

□deserve ⓥ ~받을만 하다

□delight ⓥ 기뻐하다

□name ⓥ 이름을 지어주다

□fate ⓝ 운명, 숙명

□invasive ⓐ 침습성의

□sentence ⓥ 사형 선고하다

□charm ⓥ 매혹시키다

□nature ⓝ 성품

□numerous ⓐ 수많은

□obituary ⓝ 사망기사

□vow ⓥ 맹세하다

□affection ⓝ 애정

□reproduce ⓥ 번식하다

□overrun ⓥ 급속히 퍼지다, 들끓다

□authority ⓝ 권한

□permit ⓥ 허락하다

□importation ⓝ 수입

□prohibit ⓥ 금지하다

Q19~21

□identical twins 일란성 쌍둥이

□tell apart 구별하다, 분간하다

□in common 공통적으로

□incomprehensible ⓐ 이해할 수 없는

□put an end to ~을 끝내다, 그만두게 하다

□stay up (평상시보다 더 늦게까지) 안 자다[깨어 있다]

□exhausting ⓐ 진을 빼는, 기진맥진하게 만드는

□insist ⓥ 고집하다, 주장하다

Q22~24

□curious ⓐ 호기심 많은

□affectionately ⓐd 애정 어린 표현으로, 다정하게

□mysterious ⓐ 이해하기 힘든, 신비로운

□a man of few words 과묵한 사람, 말수가 적은 사람

□garage ⑪ 차고

□spill ⓥ 쏟아져 나오다

□nostalgia ⑪ 향수(鄕愁)

□youthful ⓐ 젊은

□fascinated ⓐ 매료된

□eager ⓐ 열망하는

□wisdom ⑪ 지혜

□radiate ⓥ 반짝이다, 빛나다

□proudly ⓐ 당당하게

□intrigue ⓥ 호기심을 불러일으키다, 흥미를 끌다

□discovery ⑪ 발견

Q25~27

□envelope ⑪ 봉투

□hand ⓥ 건네다, 넘겨주다

□thoroughly ⓐ 자세히, 철저히

□overly ⓐ 너무, 몹시

□puzzled ⓐ 어리둥절해 하는, 얼떨떨한

□address ⓥ (편지 봉투에) 주소를 쓰다, (~ 앞으로 우편물을) 보내다

□regretfully ⓐ 유감스러운 듯, 유감스럽게도

□wholeheartedly ⓐ 진심으로

□thrilled ⓐ (너무 좋아서) 황홀해 하는, 아주 신이 난

□notify ⓥ 통보하다, 알리다

□sleep on ~에 대해 하룻밤 자며 생각하다

□miserable ⓐ 비참한

□hesitant ⓐ 주저하는

□disclose ⓥ 털어놓다, 누설하다

□attentively ⓐ 조심스럽게, 정중히

□mistakenly ⓐ 잘못하여, 실수로

□terribly ⓐ 대단히, 몹시

□ashamed ⓐ 수치스러운, 창피한

Q28~30

□chop ⓥ (음식 재료를 토막으로) 썰다

□sigh ⓥ 한숨을 쉬다

□stir ⓥ (휘)젓다

□aspect ⑪ 측면

□make up ~을 구성하다[이루다]

□alter ⓥ 바꾸다

□visibly ⓐ 눈에 띄게

□frustrated ⓐ 좌절감을 느끼는

□plate ⑪ 접시, 요리

□curious ⓐ 궁금한

□container ⑪ 그릇

□reply ⓥ 대답하다

□go with 잘 어울리다

□brightly ⓐ 밝게, 환하게

□present ⓥ 제시[제출]하다

□properly ⓐ 적절히

□dining ⑪ 식사

□recall ⓥ 상기하다

□mention ⓥ 말하다, 언급하다

□ingredient ⑪ 재료

Q31~33

□companion ⑪ 친구, 동행

□pound ⓥ (가슴이) 마구 뛰다, 두드리다

□exhibition ⑪ 전시(회)

□relieved ⓐ 안도하는

□brightly ⓐ 밝게, 환하게

□masterpiece ⑪ 걸작, 명작

□weird ⓐ 기묘한, 이상한

□calm ⓐ 침착한, 잔잔한

□sigh ⓥ 한숨을 쉬다

□grab ⓥ (단단히) 쥐다

□drag ⓥ 끌다, 끌고 가다

□hurriedly ⓐ 급히, 서둘러

□isolation ⑪ 고립, 분리

□eagerly ⓐ 갈망하여, 몹시

Q34~36

□strike ⓥ (손이나 무기로) 때리다 [치다]

□sparring ⑪ ((태권도)) 겨루기, ((권투)) 스파링(시합에 대비한 연습)

□assist ⓥ 돕다, 보조하다

□glance ⓥ 힐끗 보다

□expect ⓥ (오기로 되어 있는 대상을) 기다리다

□wounded ⓐ 부상을 입은, 다친

□absent ⓐ 없는, 결석한

□thrilled ⓐ 아주 흥분한, 신이 난

□apologetic ⓐ 미안해하는, 사과하는

□pat ⑪ 쓰다듬기, 토닥거리기

□nod ⓥ (고개를) 끄덕이다

□uneasily ⓐ 걱정스럽게, 불안 속에

□personally ⓐ 직접, 개인적으로

□budget ⑪ 예산

□tight ⓐ (금전적으로) 빠듯한

□unexpectedly ⓐ 예상외로, 예상과 다르게

□show up (예정된 곳에) 나타나다

□wonder ⓥ 궁금해하다

□judgingly ⓐⓓ 재단하듯이
□commitment ⓝ 약속, 책임

Q37~39
□semester ⓝ 학기
□dorm ⓝ 기숙사, 공동 침실
□totally ⓐⓓ 완전히, 전적으로
□personalize ⓥ 개인화하다
□delighted ⓐ 아주 기뻐하는, 즐거워하는
□refreshment ⓝ 원기 회복, (행사에 제공되는) 다과
□rearrange ⓥ 재배열하다, 재조정하다

Q40~42
□uneasily ⓐⓓ 걱정되어
□shortly ⓐⓓ 곧, 얼마 안 되어
□color blindness 색맹
□amazement ⓝ (대단한) 놀라움
□represent ⓥ 나타내다, 의미하다
□nod ⓥ 고개를 끄덕이다
□parcel ⓝ 꾸러미, 소포
□eyesight ⓝ 시력
□puzzle ⓥ 어리둥절하게 만들다
□suffer from ~을 앓다
□personal ⓐ 개인적인
□interrupt ⓥ 중단시키다, 가로막다
□overjoyed ⓐ 매우 기쁜
□greet ⓥ 맞이하다

Q43~45
□be scheduled to ~할 예정이다
□constantly ⓐⓓ 계속
□roar ⓝ 함성
□frowning ⓐ 찌푸린

□irritated ⓐ 짜증난
□embarrassed ⓐ 당황한
□hurriedly ⓐⓓ 서둘러
□backstage ⓐⓓ 무대 뒤에서
□overhear ⓥ 우연히 듣다
□slip away 빠져나가다
□leather stool 가죽의자
□flooded with ~로 가득찬
□sophisticated ⓐ 세련된
□stare ⓥ 응시하다
□shaky ⓐ 떨리는
□location ⓝ 위치
□harmonize ⓥ 조화를 이루다
□enhance ⓥ 높이다
□transform ⓥ 변형시키다
□whisper ⓥ 속삭이다
□creative ⓐ 창의적인

Q46~48
□rolling hill 완만한 구릉이 많은 언덕
□desire ⓝ 열망
□insignificant ⓐ 보잘 것 없는
□tendency ⓝ 경향
□keep to oneself 남들과 어울리지 않다
□spark ⓥ 유발하다
□prompt ⓥ ~하게 하다
□initiate ⓥ 시작하다
□await ⓥ 기다리다
□be dedicated to ~에 헌신하다
□unveil ⓥ 공개하다
□exhibition ⓝ 전시회
□artistic wonder 뛰어난 예술작품
□anxiously ⓐⓓ 애타게
□examine ⓥ 꼼꼼히 살펴보다
□nostalgia ⓝ 향수

□longing ⓝ 동경
□initial ⓐ 처음의
□resistance ⓝ 거절
□persistently ⓐⓓ 지속적으로
□genuine ⓐ 진정한
□hardship ⓝ 역경
□resolve ⓥ 결심하다
□revive ⓥ 되살리다

Q49~51
□at sunrise 동틀 녘에
□assist with ~을 돕다
□harvest ⓝ 수확
□in return (~에 대한) 보답으로
□feast ⓝ 진수성찬
□in spirits 활기 넘치는
□dust ⓝ 먼지, 티끌
□sack ⓝ 자루
□irritated ⓐ 짜증이 난
□sigh ⓥ 한숨 쉬다
□strike ⓥ (생각·아이디어가) 갑자기 떠오르대[들다]
□put aside ~을 한쪽에 두다
□load ⓝ 짐, 화물
□soon after 곧이어
□burst ⓥ 터지다
□accordingly ⓐⓓ 그에 맞춰
□be pleased with ~에 기뻐하다
□cheer ⓥ 환호성을 지르다, 환호하다
□terribly ⓐⓓ 몹시
□pretend ⓥ ~인 체하다

Q52~54
□heavy ⓐ (양·정도 등이 보통보다) 많은[심한]
□pour ⓥ (눈·비가) 마구 쏟아지다

□pile up (양이) 많아지다[쌓이다]

□normally ⓐ 보통(은), 보통 때는

□kindergarten ⓝ 유치원

□sharply ⓐ 날카롭게, 재빨리, 급격히

□immediately ⓐ 즉시, 즉각

□blank ⓐ 멍한, 무표정한, 빈

□sense ⓥ 감지하다, 느끼다

□playful ⓐ 장난기 많은, 놀기 좋아하는

□bother ⓥ 신경 쓰이게 하다, 괴롭히다

□post ⓥ (안내문 등을) 게시[공고]하다

□naughty ⓐ 짓궂은, 버릇없는

□argue ⓥ 주장하다, 다투다

□accusation ⓝ 혐의 (제기), 비난

Q55~57

□breathtaking ⓐ 숨 막히게 하는

□beyond description 말로 표현할 수 없을 정도의

□destination ⓝ 목적지

□injury ⓝ 부상

□hardship ⓝ 고난

□constructive ⓐ 건설적인

□mature ⓐ 성숙한

□cliff ⓝ 절벽

□exclaim ⓥ 외치다

□tragedy ⓝ 비극

□overcome 극복하다

Q58~60

□hesitantly ⓐ 머뭇거리며, 주저하며

□assignment ⓝ 과제

□persist ⓥ 집요하게 계속하다, 고집하다

□alter ⓥ 변경하다, 고치다

□settle ⓥ 자리를 잡다

□gather ⓥ 모으다

□inquire ⓥ 묻다

□exclaim ⓥ 소리치다, 외치다

□disheartened ⓐ 실망한

□discover ⓥ 찾다, 발견하다

Q61~63

□be about to V 막 ~하려는 참이다

□bill ⓝ 계산서, 납부 고지서

□concerned ⓐ 걱정하는

□medical treatment 의학 치료

□bark ⓥ (개가) 짖다

□ease ⓥ 덜다, 완화하다

□fiercely ⓐ 거세게, 사납게

□companion ⓝ 동반자, 동료

□pack up ~을 꾸리다

□equipment ⓝ 장비

□energetically ⓐ 활기차게

□exclaim ⓥ 탄성을 지르다

□work like a charm (계획대로) 잘 진행되다

□upon V-ing ~하자마자

□anxiously ⓐ 걱정스럽게

□gear ⓝ 장구, 장비

1회 모의고사

01

□primate ⓝ 영장류

□cooperative ⓐ 협력적인

□obediently ⓐ 순종적으로

□pull off ~을 해내다

□common good 공익

□ape ⓝ 유인원

□fellow ⓝ 동료

□acutely ⓐ 예민하게

□alert ⓐ 경각심을 느끼는

□manipulate ⓥ 조종하다

□mislead ⓥ 오도하다

□exploit ⓥ 착취하다

□march ⓥ 행진하다

□row ⓝ 줄, 열

□recite ⓥ 낭독하다

□conform to ~을 따르다

□hammer ⓥ 망치로 두드리다

□peg ⓝ 말뚝

□downgrade ⓥ 훼손시키다

□communal ⓐ 공동의, 공용의

02

□era ⓝ 시대, 시기

□profound ⓐ 심각한, 심오한

□reflect ⓥ 반영하다

□disruption ⓝ 혼란, 분열

□shift ⓝ 변화

□irregular ⓐ 불규칙한, 고르지 못한

□distort ⓥ 왜곡하다

□capture ⓥ 사로잡다, 포착하다

□composition ⓝ 구도, 구성 요소

□intense ⓐ 강렬한, 극심한

□contrast ⓝ 대조, 차이

□provocative ⓐ 도발적인

□subject ⓝ 대상, 주제

□matter ⓝ 문제, 사안

□stir up ~을 일으키다

□portray ⓥ 묘사하다, 그리다

□figure ⓝ 인물, 사람
□abandon ⓥ 버리다, 유기하다
□standard ⓝ 기준, 표준
□portrayal ⓝ 묘사

03
□ethics ⓝ 윤리
□regenerate ⓥ 재생되다, 다시 태어나다
□succeeding ⓐ 계속되는, 다음의
□interconnected ⓐ 상호 연락[연결]된
□separate ⓐ 분리된
□thoroughly ⓐⓓ 철저히
□situated ⓐ 위치해 있는
□profit ⓝ 이익
□presumption ⓝ 전제
□questionable ⓐ 의심스러운
□cooperation ⓝ 협력
□scholarly ⓐ 학문적인
□practical ⓐ 실용적인
□obstacle ⓝ 장애물

04
□infant ⓝ 유아, 아기
□psychologist ⓝ 심리학자
□realize ⓥ 깨닫다, 알아차리다, (목표 등을) 실현[달성]하다
□visual ⓐ 시각의
□discrimination ⓝ 차별, 식별력
□shade ⓝ 색조, 미묘한 차이
□gaze ⓝ 응시
□linger ⓥ 오래 머물다, 오랜 시간을 보내다
□nonetheless ⓐⓓ 그렇기는 하지만, 그럴더라도
□reveal ⓥ 드러내다, 밝히다

□cognitively ⓐⓓ 인식적으로
□capable ⓐ (능력·특질상) ~을 할 수 있는, 유능한
□previously ⓐⓓ 이전에, 과거에
□assume ⓥ 추정하다
□novelty ⓝ 새로움, 참신함
□drive ⓝ 충동, 욕구
□toolkit ⓝ 연장 세트, 도구[수단]들
□unlock ⓥ 열다, (비밀 등을) 드러내다
□insight ⓝ 통찰력, 이해, 간파
□capacity ⓝ (~을 이해하거나 할 수 있는) 능력, 용량
□distortion ⓝ 왜곡, 찌그러짐
□infancy ⓝ 유아기

05
□quest ⓝ 탐구, 탐색
□pursuit ⓝ 추구, (원하는 것을) 좇음
□thoroughly ⓐⓓ 온전하게
□school ⓥ 교육하다
□blind ⓥ 눈이 멀게 만들다
□ignorance ⓝ 무지, 무식
□guarantee ⓝ 보장
□hence ⓐⓓ 이런 이유로
□overemphasis ⓝ 과도한 강조
□competition ⓝ 경쟁
□resultant ⓐ 그 결과로 생기는
□criticize ⓥ 비판[비난]하다
□undeniably ⓐⓓ 부인할 수 없을 정도로
□vast ⓐ 광대한
□wonder ⓝ 경탄, 경이(감)
□let alone ~은 고사하고
□investigate ⓥ 조사하다
□facilitate ⓥ 촉진하다

06
□initial ⓐ 처음의
□attraction ⓝ 매력
□extent ⓝ 정도, 크기
□verbal ⓐ 언어의
□nonverbal ⓐ 비언어의
□expressive ⓐ 나타내는
□continuum ⓝ 연속체
□contrasting ⓐ 대조적인
□pursue ⓥ 추구하다, 계속하다
□interaction ⓝ 상호 작용
□coordination ⓝ 조화, 합동
□selection ⓝ 선발, 선택
□deficit ⓝ 부족
□adaptability ⓝ 적응성, 순응성
□negotiation ⓝ 협상
□unconditional ⓐ 무조건적인
□acceptance ⓝ 수용

07
□persuade ⓥ 설득하다
□argument ⓝ 주장
□logically ⓐⓓ 논리적으로
□distinct ⓐ 뚜렷이 다른
□involve ⓥ 포함하다
□undisturbed ⓐ (마음이) 흔들리지 않는, 개의치 않는
□remark ⓝ 발언
□portray ⓥ 묘사하다
□define ⓥ 정의하다

08
□interact ⓥ 상호작용하다
□motivating ⓐ 동기를 부여하는
□factor ⓝ 요인
□perception ⓝ 인식

□entirely @ad 완전히

□discourage ⓥ 낙담시키다, 만류하다

□destination ⓝ 목적지

□tea towel 행주

□threat ⓝ 위협

□pose ⓥ 제기하다

□analysis ⓝ 분석

□in comparison to ~에 비해

□drown ⓥ 익사하다

□vehicular @ 차량의

□nevertheless @ad 그럼에도 불구하고

09

□vehicle ⓝ 수단

□enterprise ⓝ 사업

□reform ⓝ 개혁

□dedicate to ~에 헌신하다

□humanism ⓝ 인본주의

□acute @ 예리한

□philosophical @ 철학적인

□demoralize ⓥ 사기를 꺾다

□humiliate ⓥ 굴욕감을 주다

□terrified @ 겁이 난

□bourgeoisie ⓝ 중산층, 부르주아

□radical @ 급진적인

□restoration ⓝ 복원

□enlightened @ 계몽된

□label ⓥ 지칭하다

10

□calculation ⓝ 계산, 산출

□jog ⓥ 조깅하다

□track ⓥ 추적하다, 뒤쫓다

□overestimate ⓥ 과대평가하다

□workout ⓝ 운동

□by a factor of (증감 규모가) ~(배) 만큼

□consume ⓥ 소모하다, 먹다

□on average 평균적으로

□burn off ~을 태워서 제거하다, (운동으로 칼로리 등을) 태우다

□expend ⓥ (돈·시간·에너지를) 쏟다[들이다]

□equivalent @ 동등한, 맞먹는

□impressive @ 인상적인, 인상[감명] 깊은

□reasonable @ 타당한, 사리에 맞는

□cruelly @ad 잔인하게, 지독하게

□blunt @ 직설적인, 무딘

□replace ⓥ 대신[대체]하다, (제자리에) 다시 놓다

11~12

□cultural heritage 문화유산

□reservoir ⓝ 저장소

□preservation ⓝ 보존

□succeeding @ 이어지는

□discursive @ 종잡을 수 없는, 산만한

□artefact ⓝ 공예품, 인공물

□embed ⓥ 내포하다

□root ⓥ 뿌리를 두다

□reproduce ⓥ 재현하다, 재생산하다

□sentiment ⓝ 감정

□continual @ 계속적인

□reinterpretation ⓝ 재해석

□biography ⓝ 전기, 일대기

□competence ⓝ 역량

2회 모의고사

01

□conference ⓝ 회의

□boardroom ⓝ 중역 회의실

□proceeding ⓝ 행사

□require ⓥ 필요로 하다

□reconsider ⓥ 재고하다

□fundamental @ 근본적인

□assistance ⓝ 도움

□knowledgeable @ 지식이 많은

□courageously @ad 대담하게

□convincingly @ad 설득력 있게, 납득이 가도록

□authority figure 권위자

□persuade ⓥ 설득하다

02

□encompass ⓥ 포함하다, 포괄하다

□idiom ⓝ 표현 양식

□comprise ⓥ 구성되다[이뤄지다]

□instantaneously @ad 즉석으로

□contribution ⓝ 기여

□be consistent with ~와 일관되다

□individuality ⓝ 개성

□compose ⓥ 작곡하다

03

□prominent @ 저명한, 유명한

□statistician ⓝ 통계학자

□keen @ 매우 관심이 많은, 열중하는

□consist of ~로 구성되다

□chapel ⓝ 예배당

□massive ⓐ 거대한

□neo-Gothic 신고딕 양식의

□adorn ⓥ 장식하다, 꾸미다

□statue ⓝ 동상, 조각상

□saint ⓝ 성인(聖人), 성–

□attire ⓥ (옷을) 차려 입히다

□admire ⓥ 칭찬하다, 감탄하다

□authority ⓝ ((pl.)) 당국,
　관계자

□unappreciative ⓐ 인정하
　지 않는

□garment ⓝ 의복

□attempt ⓝ 시도

□hook ⓝ 갈고리

□progress ⓝ 진전, 진척, 발전

□eventually ⓐⓓ 결국

□assemble ⓥ 모이다,
　조립하다

04

□press ⓝ 평가

□enthusiastic ⓐ 열정적인

□contradictory ⓐ 모순된

□persist ⓥ 계속[지속]되다

□extent ⓝ 정도

□reliability ⓝ 신뢰성

□conciseness ⓐ 간결함

□predictability ⓝ 예측 가능성

05

□genetically ⓐⓓ 유전적으로

□categorize ⓥ 분류하다

□dozen ⓐ 십 여개의, 다수의

□distinguish ⓥ 구별하다

□breakthrough ⓝ 돌파구,
　혁신 부분

□schooling ⓝ 학습

□self-tracking ⓝ 자기 추적

□akin ⓐ ~와 유사한

□fuel ⓝ 연료

□exceed ⓥ 초과하다, 초월하다

□govern ⓥ 통치하다, 통제하다

□calculate ⓥ 계산하다

□possibility ⓝ 가능성

06

□religious ⓐ 종교의, 독실한

□contract ⓝ 계약

□provided ⓒⓞⓝⓙ (만약) ~라면

□ritual ⓐ 의식상의, 의식을 위한

□fragment ⓝ 작은 일부, 파편

□bear out ~을 유지하다, ~을
　지지하다

□admire ⓥ 존경하다

□practice ⓝ 관습

□taboo ⓝ 금기

□derive from ~에서 유래하다

□extensive ⓐ 광범위한,
　폭넓은

□honour ⓥ 존경하다, 경의를
　표하다

□method ⓝ 방법

□soften ⓥ 부드럽게 하다,
　누그러뜨리다

□disquiet ⓝ 불안

□arise ⓥ 생기다, 일어나다

□fundamentally ⓐⓓ 근본
　[본질]적으로

□aware of ~을 알고 있는

□sound ⓐ 타당한

□counterpart ⓝ 상응하는 것

□predator ⓝ 포식자

□smooth ⓥ 완화하다

□edge ⓝ 문제, 위기

□domesticate ⓥ (동물을) 길
　들이다[사육하다], (작물을) 재배하다

□supernatural ⓐ 초자연적인

□worship ⓥ 예배하다, 숭배하다

07

□body ⓝ 많은 양[모음]

□indicate ⓥ 나타내다, 시사하다

□attribute ⓝ 자질, 속성

□regularly ⓐⓓ 정기적으로, 자주

□substitute ⓥ 대신하다, 대체
　하다

□explicit ⓐ 분명한, 명시적인

□assessment ⓝ 평가

□affective ⓐ 감정적인

□valuation ⓝ 평가

□prospect ⓝ 가능성, 전망

□at hand 당면한

□willing ⓐ 기꺼이 하는

□probability ⓝ 확률

□overwhelm ⓥ 압도하다,
　어쩔 줄 모르게 만들다

□subject ⓝ 피실험자

□evaluate ⓥ 평가하다

□convey ⓥ 전달하다

□supplement ⓥ 보완하다

□analytic ⓐ 분석적인

□processing ⓝ 처리

□adjustment ⓝ 수정, 조정

□sole ⓐ 유일한, 단독의

□reliance ⓝ 의존, 의지

□insensitive ⓐ 둔감한

□quantitative ⓐ 양적인

□feature ⓝ 특징

□effect ⓥ 초래하다

□demonstrate ⓥ 입증[실증]
　하다

08

□be exposed to ~에 노출되
　다

□finite ⓐ 유한한
□utterance ⓝ 발화
□grammar ⓝ 문법
□input ⓝ 투입, 입력
□illustrate ⓥ 보여주다
□systematic ⓐ 체계적인
□despite ⓟⓡⓔⓟ ~에도 불구하고
□limitation ⓝ 제한
□variation ⓝ 변동
□circumstance ⓝ 환경
□linguistic ⓐ 언어의
□attain ⓥ 습득하다, 이르다
□refer to ~을 언급하다
□poetry ⓝ 시
□creativity ⓝ 창의성
□precise ⓐ 정확한
□differ ⓥ 다르다

09
□generation ⓝ 세대
□means ⓝ 방법, 수단
□elaborate ⓐ 정교한
□ritualize ⓥ 의례화하다
□display ⓝ 표현, 전시
□perform ⓥ 수행[시행]하다
□wonder ⓥ 궁금해 하다
□come about 생기다, 일어
   나다
□arise ⓥ 발생하다
□afresh ⓐⓓ 새로
□pass on ~에게 전하다
□owing to ~ 때문에
□gene ⓝ 유전자
□variation ⓝ 변화, 변형
□piece together ~을 종합
   하다
□spread ⓝ 확산, 전파
□behavioral ⓐ 행동의

10
□laboratory ⓝ 실험실
□sense ⓝ 감각
□spontaneously ⓐⓓ 자발적
   으로, 자연스럽게
□serve ⓥ 도움이 되다, 기여하다
□measure ⓥ 측정하다, 재다
□subject ⓝ 실험[연구] 대상, 피
   험자
□a sequence of 일련의
□stimulus ⓝ 자극
   ((pl. stimuli))
□disturb ⓥ 방해하다
□dramatically ⓐⓓ 극적으로
□rate ⓝ 비율, -율
□upset ⓥ 잘못되게[틀어지게] 만
   들다
□threaten ⓥ 위협하다
□concentration ⓝ 집중,
   농도
□on track 궤도에 올라, 순조롭게

11~12
□catastrophic ⓐ 재앙의, 처
   참한
□eruption ⓝ 분출
□entomb ⓥ 파묻다, 뒤덮다
□volcanic ⓐ 화산의
□ash ⓝ 재, 잿더미
□doom ⓝ 파멸, 죽음
□frontier ⓝ 선구자
□earth science 지구과학
□simultaneously ⓐⓓ 동시에
□wreck ⓥ 파괴하다
□timeline ⓝ 연대표
□collapse ⓝ 붕괴
□archaeological ⓐ 고고학의
□violent ⓐ 격렬한

□account ⓝ 이야기
□archaeoseismology
   ⓝ 고고 지진학
□seismicity ⓝ 지진 활동도
□speculate ⓥ 추측하다
□factual ⓐ 사실적인
□insula ⓝ (고대 로마의) 집단 주택
□chaste ⓐ 순결한
□encompass ⓥ 망라하다,
   포함하다
□interrupt ⓥ 중단시키다, 방해
   하다

3회 모의고사

01
□independent ⓐ 독립적인
□confusion ⓝ 혼란
□frontier ⓝ 경계, 국경
□psychologist ⓝ 심리학자
□engage in ~에 관여[참여]
   하다
□cognitive ⓐ 인지[인식]의
□self-esteem ⓝ 자존감,
   자부심
□misremember ⓥ 부정확하
   게 기억하다
□all along 그동안 내내
□conduct ⓥ (특정한 활동을)
   하다
□credit ⓝ 공적, 칭찬
□rate ⓥ 평가하다
□overestimate ⓥ 과대평가
   하다
□prone to-v ~하기 쉬운

□ put off ~을 미루다
□ overwhelmed ⓐ 압도된
□ vast ⓐ 방대한
□ strive ⓥ 분투하다
□ distinguish ⓥ 구별하다

02
□ slightly ⓐ 약간, 조금
□ passionate ⓐ 열정을 느끼는, 열렬한
□ physical ⓐ 신체의, 물리적인
□ feature ⓝ 특징, 특성
□ regarding (prep) ~에 관하여
□ bias ⓝ 편견, 성향
□ dominate ⓥ 지배하다, (두드러지는) 특징이 되다
□ statistically ⓐ 통계(학)상으로
□ factor ⓝ 요인, 인자
□ aptitude ⓝ 소질, 적성

03
□ temporal ⓐ 시간의, 시간의 제약을 받는
□ phenomenon ⓝ 현상
□ every bit 어느 모로 보나, 전적으로
□ spatial ⓐ 공간의, 공간적인
□ carry out ~을 수행하다
□ cup ⓥ 두 손을 (컵 모양으로) 동그랗게 모아 쥐다
□ palm ⓝ 손바닥
□ ordinary ⓐ 평범한, 일상적인
□ object ⓝ 물건, 물체
□ identify ⓥ 확인하다, 알아보다
□ clue ⓝ 단서, 실마리
□ at once 동시에, 즉시
□ overall ⓐ 종합[전반]적인, 전체의

□ sensory ⓐ 감각의
□ perception ⓝ 지각, 자각
□ direct ⓐ 직접적인
□ fingertip ⓝ 손가락 끝
□ acuity ⓝ (지각의) 예민함
□ button ⓥ 단추를 잠그다
□ continuous ⓐ 지속적인, 계속되는
□ sensation ⓝ 느낌, 감각
□ major ⓐ 주요한, 중대한
□ humanity ⓝ 인류, 인간성
□ matter ⓥ 중요하다, 문제되다
□ essence ⓝ 본질, 진수
□ timely ⓐ 시기적절한, 때맞춘
□ booster ⓝ 촉진제

04
□ pervasive ⓐ 만연한
□ craving ⓝ 갈망, 열망
□ grasp ⓥ 이해하다, 파악하다
□ overcome ⓥ 극복하다
□ interplay ⓝ 상호 작용
□ inscribe ⓥ (이름 등을) 쓰다 [새기다]
□ root ⓥ 뿌리를 내리다
□ indebt ⓥ ~에게 빚을 지게 하다
□ insecurity ⓝ 불안감
□ outdo ⓥ 능가하다
□ forerunner ⓝ 선구자
□ negate ⓥ 부정하다
□ interpretation ⓝ 해석
□ minimize ⓥ 최소화하다
□ overloaded ⓐ 과부하된

05
□ democracy ⓝ 민주주의
□ emphasize ⓥ 강조하다
□ legislative ⓐ 입법의
□ context ⓝ 맥락

□ facilitate ⓥ 용이하게 하다, 촉진하다
□ privilege ⓥ 특권을 주다, 우대하다
□ orient ⓥ 지향하게 하다, 방향을 정하다
□ inevitable ⓐ 피할 수 없는
□ thrive ⓥ 번창하다
□ sustain ⓥ 살아가게 하다, 유지하다
□ dynamics ⓝ 역학

06
□ philosopher ⓝ 철학자
□ blank ⓐ 빈
□ character ⓝ 성격, 특징
□ influence ⓝ 영향
□ profound ⓐ 엄청난, 심오한
□ colony ⓝ 식민지
□ conscious ⓐ 의식하는, 자각하는
□ attempt ⓝ 시도
□ form ⓥ 형성하다
□ operate ⓥ 운용하다, 작동하다
□ basis ⓝ 근거, 기준, 기반
□ entirely ⓐ 전적으로, 완전히
□ innate ⓐ 선천적인
□ characteristic ⓝ 특징, 특질
□ emphasis ⓝ 강조, 역점
□ foundation ⓝ 토대, 기초
□ reinforce ⓥ 강화하다, 보강하다
□ tie ⓥ 묶다, 결부시키다
□ colonial ⓐ 식민(지)의
□ value ⓥ 소중하게[가치 있게] 생각하다[여기다]
□ optimistic ⓐ 낙관적인
□ framework ⓝ 뼈대, 틀, 체계

모의고사
3회

MEMO